THE NUTTALL
DICTIONARY

OF

QUOTATIONS

THE NUTTALL
DICTIONARY

OF

QUOTATIONS

From Ancient and Modern, English and Foreign Sources

INCLUDING

PHRASES, MOTTOES, MAXIMS, PROVERBS, DEFINITIONS, APHORISMS,
AND SAYINGS OF WISE MEN, IN THEIR BEARING ON LIFE,
LITERATURE, SPECULATION, SCIENCE, ART,
RELIGION, AND MORALS

ESPECIALLY IN THE MODERN ASPECTS OF THEM

SELECTED AND COMPILED BY THE

REV. JAMES WOOD

EDITOR OF "NUTTALL'S STANDARD DICTIONARY"

NEW EDITION

*With Supplement of over 1000 Quotations,
including many from Modern Authors*

Compiled by A. L. HAYDON

FREDERICK WARNE AND CO. LTD.
LONDON AND NEW YORK

ISBN 0 7232 0159 5

PRINTED IN GREAT BRITAIN BY
COMPTON PRINTING LTD
LONDON & AYLESBURY
1499.470

PREFACE

THE present "Book of Quotations" was undertaken in the belief that, notwithstanding the compilations in existence, there was room for another that should glean its materials from a wider area, and that should have more respect to the requirements, both speculative and practical, of the times we live in. The widespread materials at command had never yet been collected into a single volume, and certain modern writings, fraught with a wisdom that supremely deserves our regard, had hardly been quarried in at all.

The Editor has therefore studied to compile a more comprehensive collection; embracing something of this wisdom, which naturally bears more directly on the interests of the present day. To these interests the Editor has all along had an eye, and he has been careful to collect, from ancient sources as well as modern, sayings that seem to reveal an insight into them, and bear pertinently upon them; they are such as are specified on the title-page, and they are one and all more than passing ones. The aphorisms which wise men have uttered on these vital topics can never fail to deserve our regard, and they will prove edifying to us, even should we, led by a higher wisdom, be inclined to say nay to them. For, as it has been said, "The errors of a wise man are more instructive than the truths of a fool. The wise man travels in lofty, far-seeing regions; the fool in low-lying, high-fenced lanes; retracing the footsteps of the former, to discover where he deviated, whole provinces of the universe are laid open to us; in the path of the latter, granting even that he has not deviated at all, little is laid open to us but two wheel-ruts and two hedges."

The quotations collected in this book (particularly those bearing on the vital interests referred to) are, it will be generally admitted, the words of wise men; therefore the Editor has endeavoured to ascertain and give the names of their authors, when not known. For, though the truth and worth of the sayings are nowise dependent on their authorship, it is well to know who those were that felt the burden they express, and found relief in uttering them. What was of moment to them, may well be of moment to others, and must be worthy of all regard and well deserving of being laid to heart.

The quotations given are for most part independent of the context, and are perfectly intelligible in their own light. They are all more or less of an aphoristic quality, and the meaning and application are evident

v

to any one who understands the subject of which they treat. Except in the case of quotations from Shakespeare, the reader will observe that the Editor has quoted only the names of the authors or the books from which they are taken.

As for the other qualities of these quotations, they will be found to be in general brief in expression and pointed in application, and not a few of them winged as well as barbed. A great many are pregnant in meaning; suggest more than they express; and are the coinage of minds of no ordinary penetration and grasp of thought. While some of them are so simple that a child might understand them, there are others that border on regions in which the clearest-headed and surest-footed might stumble and come to grief.

The Editor's task was to produce a work that should embrace gleanings from different fields of literature, and he hopes the reader will allow that his selection has not been made in the dark, and that what he has given is of the true quality, as well as enough in quantity for most readers to digest. If the quality be good, the quantity is of little account, for what has been said of Reason may be said of Wisdom which is its highest expression: "Whoso hath any, hath access to the whole."

The Arrangement adopted is alphabetical, and follows the order of the initial letters of the initial word or words, and should at once commend itself, as a topical one would have been too cumbersome, for, in that case, it would have been frequently necessary to introduce the same quotation under several different heads.

The Index is topical, and a copious one, referring to subjects of which there is anything of significance said. It does not include mottoes, and rarely proverbs; for, apart from the difficulty of indexing the latter, the attempt would almost have doubled the size of the book, and rendered it altogether unwieldy. The Index, too, is limited to subjects that are not in the alphabetical order in the body of the book. Thus there was no need to index what is said on "Art," on p. 18, on "Beauty," on p. 26, or on "Christianity," on pp. 42, 43, as the reader will expect to find something concerning them where they occur in the order adopted.

With these preliminary explanations the Editor leaves his book— the pleasant labour of more than three years—in the hands of the public, assured that they will judge of it by its own merits, and that they will be generous enough to acquit him of having compiled either a superfluous or an unserviceable work.

NOTE

*The INDEX extends from page 571 to page 659
and Index to Supplement, page 21 to page 28*

THE INDEX should be referred to whenever the quotation does not begin with the essential word.

The work is a dictionary of full quotations in alphabetical order; and the INDEXES are a guide to it in which the references are classified under subjects, giving not only the page but the paragraph where the quotation appears.

For example: The exact words are required concerning the rift in the lute; and under the word "lute" in the INDEX the reference is to page 206, paragraph 24, where the full quotation is given from Tennyson:

> "It is the little rift within the lute
> That by and by will make the music mute,
> And, ever widening, slowly silence all."

As another example we will verify the saying as to the relative power of the sword and the pen. Here the reference under "sword" is page 27, paragraph 51, and we find the full quotation from Lytton's "Richelieu," in which the Cardinal says:

> " Beneath the rule of men entirely great
> The pen is mightier than the sword."—

thus giving the qualification that is so little regarded.

LIST OF ABBREVIATIONS

USED IN THIS DICTIONARY.

Amer.	American.	*Luc.*	Lucan.
Apul.	Apuleius.	*Lucr.*, *Lucret.*	Lucretius.
Arist.	Aristotle.	*M.*	Motto.
Aul. Gell.	Aulus Gellius.	*Macrob.*	Macrobius.
Bret.	Breton.	*Mart.*	Martial.
Cæs.	Cæsar.	*Mol.*	Molière.
Catull.	Catullus.	*Per.*	Persius.
Cic.	Cicero.	*Petron.*	Petronius.
Claud.	Claudius, Claudian.	*Phæd.*, *Phædr.*	Phædrus.
Corn.	Corneille.	*Plaut.*	Plautus.
Curt.	Curtius.	*Port.*	Portuguese.
Dan.	Danish.	*Pr.*	Proverb.
Dut.	Dutch.	*Pub. Syr.*	Publius Syrus.
Ecclus.	Ecclesiasticus.	*Quinct.*	Quinctilian.
Eurip.	Euripides.	*Russ.*	Russian.
Fr.	French.	*Sall.*	Sallust.
Fris.	Frisian.	*Sc.*	Scotch.
Gael.	Gaelic.	*Schill.*	Schiller.
Ger.	German.	*Sen.*	Seneca.
Gr.	Greek.	*Sh.*	Shakespeare.
Heb.	Hebrew.	*Soph.*	Sophocles.
Hom.	Homer.	*Sp.*	Spanish.
Hor.	Horace.	*Stat.*	Statius.
It.	Italian.	*St. Aug.*	St. Augustine.
Jul.	Julius.	*Sueton.*	Suetonius.
Just.	Justinian.	*Swed.*	Swedish.
Juv.	Juvenal.	*Tac.*	Tacitus.
L.	Law.	*Ter.*	Terence.
Laber.	Labertius.	*Tert.*	Tertullian.
La Font.	La Fontaine.	*Tibull.*	Tibullus.
La Roche.	La Rochefoucauld.	*Turk.*	Turkish.
Lat.	Latin.	*Virg.*	Virgil.
Liv.	Livy.		

DICTIONARY OF QUOTATIONS.

A.

A' are guid lasses, but where do a' the ill wives come frae ? *Sc. Pr.*

A are no freens that speak us fair. *Sc. Pr.*

A aucun biens viennent en dormant—Good things come to some while asleep. *Fr. Pr.*

Ab abusu ad usum non valet consequentia—The abuse of a thing is no argument against its use. *L. Max.*

5 Ab actu ad posse valet illatio—From what has happened we may infer what may happen.

A bad beginning has a bad, or makes a worse, ending. *Pr.*

A bad dog never sees the wolf. *Pr.*

A bad thing is dear at any price. *Pr.*

Ab alio expectes, alteri quod feceris—As you do to others, you may expect another to do to you. *Laber.*

10 A barren sow was never good to pigs. *Pr.*

A bas—Down ! down with ! *Fr.*

A beast that wants discourse of reason. *Ham., i. 2.*

A beau is everything of a woman but the sex, and nothing of a man beside it. *Fielding.*

A beau jeu beau retour—One good turn deserves another. *Fr. Pr.*

15 A beautiful form is better than a beautiful face, and a beautiful behaviour than a beautiful form. *Emerson.*

A beautiful object doth so much attract the sight of all men, that it is in no man's power not to be pleased with it. *Clarendon.*

A beautiful woman is the "hell" of the soul, the "purgatory' of the purse, and the "paradise" of the eyes. *Fontenelle.*

A beggarly account of empty boxes. *Rom. and Jul., v. 1.*

A beggar's purse is always empty. *Pr.*

20 A belief in the Bible, the fruit of deep meditation, has served me as the guide of my moral and literary life. I have found it a capital safely invested, and richly productive of interest. *Goethe.*

Abends wird der Faule fleissig—Towards evening the lazy man begins to be busy. *Ger. Pr.*

A beneficent person is like a fountain watering the earth and spreading fertility. *Epicurus.*

Aberrare a scopo—To miss the mark.

Abeunt studia in mores—Pursuits assiduously prosecuted become habits.

Ab extra—From without. **25**

Abgründe liegen im Gemüthe, die tiefer als die Hölle sind—There are abysses in the mind that are deeper than hell. *Platen.*

Ab honesto virum bonum nihil deterret — Nothing deters a good man from what honour requires of him. *Sen.*

A big head and little wit. *Pr.*

Ab igne ignem—Fire from fire.

Abiit, excessit, evasit, erupit—He has left, gone **30·** off, escaped, broken away. *Cic. of Catiline's flight.*

Ability to discern that what is true is true, and that what is false is false, is the characteristic of intelligence. *Swedenborg.*

Ab incunabilis—From the cradle.

Ab initio—From the beginning.

Ab inopia ad virtutem obsepta est via—The way from poverty to virtue is an obstructed one. *Pr.*

Ab intra—From within. **35**

Ab irato—In a fit of passion.

A bird in the hand is worth two in the bush. *Pr.*

A bis et à blanc—By fits and starts. *Fr.*

A bitter and perplex'd "What shall I do?" is worse to man than worst necessity. *Schiller.*

A black hen will lay a white egg. *Pr.* **40**

A blind man should not judge of colours. *Pr.*

A blockhead can find more faults than a wise man can mend. *Gael. Pr.*

A blue-stocking despises her duties as a woman, and always begins by making herself a man. *Rousseau.*

Abnormis sapiens—Wise without learning. *Hor.*

A bon chat bon rat—A good rat to match a good **45** cat. Tit for tat. *Pr.*

A bon chien il ne vient jamais un bon os—A good bone never falls to a good dog. *Fr. Pr.*

A bon droit—Justly ; according to reason. *Fr.*

A bon marché—Cheap. *Fr.*

A book may be as great a thing as a battle. *Disraeli.*

A book should be luminous, but not volumi- **50** nous. *Bovee.*

Ab origine—From the beginning.

About Jesus we must believe no one but himself. *Amiel.*

Above all Greek, above all Roman fame. *Pope.*

Above all things reverence thyself. *Pythagoras.*

Above the cloud with its shadow is the star with its light. *Victor Hugo.*

Ab ovo—From the beginning (*lit.* from the egg).

5 Ab ovo usque ad mala—From the beginning to the end (*lit.* from the egg to the apples).

A bras ouverts—With open arms. *Fr.*

A brave man is clear in his discourse, and keeps close to truth. *Arist.*

A brave spirit struggling with adversity is a spectacle for the gods. *Sen.*

A breath can make them, as a breath has made. *Goldsmith.*

10 Abrégé—Abridgment. *Fr.*

Absence lessens weak, and intensifies violent, passions, as wind extinguishes a taper and lights up a fire. *La Roche.*

Absence makes the heart grow fonder. *Bayly.*

Absence of occupation is not rest; / A mind quite vacant is a mind distress'd. *Cowper.*

Absens hæres non erit—The absent one will not be the heir. *Pr.*

15 Absent in body, but present in spirit. *St. Paul.*

Absit invidia—Envy apart.

Absit omen—May the omen augur no evil.

Absolute fiends are as rare as angels, perhaps rarer. *J. S. Mill.*

Absolute freedom is inhuman. *Rahel.*

20 Absolute individualism is an absurdity. *Amiel.*

Absolute nothing is the aggregate of all the contradictions of the world. *Jonathan Edwards.*

Absque argento omnia vana—Without money all is vain.

Abstineto a fabis—Having nothing to do with elections (*lit.* Abstain from beans, the ballot at Athens having been by beans).

Absurdum est ut alios regat, qui seipsum regere nescit—It is absurd that he should govern others, who knows not how to govern himself. *L. Max.*

25 Abundat dulcibus vitiis—He abounds in charming faults of style. *Quint.*

Ab uno ad omnes—From one to all. *M.*

Ab uno disce omnes—From a single instance you may infer the whole.

Ab urbe condita (A.U.C.)—From the building of the city, *i.e.*, of Rome.

A bureaucracy always tends to become a pedantocracy. *J. S. Mill.*

30 A burnt child dreads the fire. *Pr.*

Abusus non tollit usum—Abuse is no argument against use. *Pr.*

Academical years ought by rights to give occupation to the whole mind. It is this time which, well or ill employed, affects a man's whole after-life. *Goethe.*

A cader va chi troppo in alto sale—He who climbs too high is near a fall. *It.*

A capite ad calcem—From head to heel.

35 A careless master makes a negligent servant. *Pr.*

A carper will cavil at anything. *Pr.*

A carrion kite will never make a good hawk. *Pr.*

"A cat may look at a king," but can it *see* a king when it looks at him? *Ruskin.*

A causa perduta parole assai—Plenty of words when the cause is lost. *It. Pr.*

Accasca in un punto quel che non accasca in 40 cento anni—That may happen in a moment which may not occur again in a hundred years. *It. Pr.*

Accedas ad curiam—You may go to the court. A writ to remove a case to a higher court. *L. Term.*

Accensa domo proximi, tua quoque periclitatur—When the house of your neighbour is on fire, your own is in danger. *Pr.*

Accent is the soul of speech; it gives it feeling and truth. *Rousseau.*

Acceptissima semper / Munera sunt, auctor quæ pretiosa facit—Those presents are always the most acceptable which owe their value to the giver. *Ovid.*

Accident ever varies; substance can never 45 suffer change or decay. *Wm. Blake.*

Accidents rule men, not men accidents. *Herodotus.*

Accipe nunc, victus tenuis quid quantaque secum afferat. In primis valeas bene—Now learn what and how great benefits a moderate diet brings with it. Before all, you will enjoy good health. *Hor.*

Accipere quam facere præstat injuriam—It is better to receive than to do an injury. *Cic.*

Acclinis falsis animus meliora recusat—The mind attracted by what is false has no relish for better things. *Hor.*

Accusare nemo se debet nisi coram Deo—No 50 man is bound to accuse himself unless it be before God. *L. Max.*

Accuse not Nature; she hath done her part; / Do thou thine. *Milton.*

Acer et vehemens bonus orator—A good orator is pointed and impassioned. *Cic.*

Acerrima proximorum odia—The hatred of those most closely connected with us is the bitterest. *Tac.*

Acerrimus ex omnibus nostris sensibus est sensus videndi—The keenest of all our senses is the sense of sight. *Cic.*

A certain degree of soul is indispensable to 55 save us the expense of salt. *Ben Jonson.*

A certain tendency to insanity has always attended the opening of the religious sense in men, as if they had been "blasted with excess of light." *Emerson.*

A chacun selon sa capacité, à chaque capacité selon ses œuvres—Every one according to his talent, and every talent according to its works. *Fr. Pr.*

A chacun son fardeau pèse—Every one thinks his own burden heavy. *Fr. Pr.*

A change came o'er the spirit of my dream. *Byron.*

A chaque fou plaît sa marotte—Every fool is 60 pleased with his own hobby. *Fr. Pr.*

A character is a completely-fashioned will. *Novalis.*

Ach! aus dem Glück entwickelt sich Schmerz —Alas! that from happiness there so often springs pain. *Goethe.*

A cheerful life is what the Muses love; / A soaring spirit is their prime delight. *Wordsworth.*

Acheruntis pabulum—Food for Acheron. *Plaut.*

Ach ! es geschehen keine Wunder mehr—Alas! there are no more any miracles. *Schiller.*

A child is a Cupid become visible. *Novalis.*

A child may have too much of its mother's blessing. *Pr.*

5 A chill air surrounds those who are down in the world. *George Eliot.*

A chip of the old block.

A Christian is God Almighty's gentleman. *Hare.*

Ach ! unsre Thaten selbst, so gut als unsre Leiden / Sie hemmen unsers Lebens Gang —We are hampered, alas ! in our course of life quite as much by what we do as by what we suffer. *Goethe.*

Ach ! vielleicht indem wir hoffen / Hat uns Unheil getroffen—Ah ! perhaps while we are hoping, mischief has already overtaken us. *Schiller.*

10 Ach wie glücklich sind die Todten !—Ah ! how happy the dead are ! *Schiller.*

Ach ! zu des Geistes Flügeln, wird so leicht kein körperlicher Flügel sich gesellen—Alas ! no fleshly pinion will so easily keep pace with the wings of the spirit. *Goethe.*

A circulating library in a town is an ever-green tree of diabolical knowledge. *Sheridan.*

A circumnavigator of the globe is less influenced by all the nations he has seen than by his nurse. *Jean Paul.*

A clear conscience is a sure card. *Pr.*

15 A cock aye craws crousest (boldest) on his ain midden-head. *Sc. Pr.*

A cœur ouvert—With open heart ; with candour. *Fr.*

A cœur vaillant rien d'impossible—To a valiant heart nothing is impossible. *Fr. Pr.*

A cold hand, a warm heart. *Pr.*

A combination, and a form, indeed / Where every god did seem to set his seal / To give the world assurance of a man. *Ham.,* iii. 4.

20 A' complain o' want o' siller ; nane o' want o' sense. *Sc. Pr.*

A compte—In part payment (*lit.* on account). *Fr.*

A confesseurs, médecins, avocats, la vérité ne cèle de ton cas—Do not conceal the truth from confessors, doctors, and lawyers. *Fr. Pr.*

A conscience without God is a tribunal without a judge. *Lamartine.*

A consistent man believes in destiny, a capricious man in chance. *Disraeli.*

25 A constant fidelity in small things is a great and heroic virtue. *Bonaventura.*

A constant friend is a thing hard and rare to find. *Plutarch.*

A contre cœur—Against the grain. *Fr.*

A corps perdu—With might and main. *Fr.*

A countenance more in sorrow than in anger. *Ham.,* i. 2.

30 A courage to endure and to obey. *Tennyson.*

A couvert—Under cover. *Fr.*

Acqua lontana non spegne fuoco vicino—Water afar won't quench a fire at hand. *It. Pr.*

A crafty knave needs no broker. *Pr. quoted in Hen. VI.*

A craw's nae whiter for being washed. *Sc. Pr.*

A creation of importance can be produced only 35 when its author isolates himself ; it is ever a child of solitude. *Goethe.*

Acribus initiis, incurioso fine—Full of ardour at the beginning, careless at the end. *Tac.*

A critic should be a pair of snuffers. He is often an extinguisher, and not seldom a thief. *Hare.*

A crowd is not company. *Bacon.*

A crown / Golden in show, is but a wreath of thorns. *Milton.*

A crown is no cure for the headache. *Pr.* 40

A cruce salus—Salvation from the cross. *M.*

A cruel story runs on wheels, and every hand oils the wheels as they run. *Ouida.*

A crust of bread and liberty. *Pope.*

Acta exteriora indicant interiora secreta—Outward acts betray the secret intention. *L. Max.*

Act always so that the immediate motive of 45 thy will may become a universal rule for all intelligent beings. *Kant.*

Acti labores jucundi—The remembrance of past labours is pleasant.

Action can be understood and again represented by the spirit alone. *Goethe.*

Action is but coarsened thought. *Amiel.*

Action is the right outlet of emotion. *Ward Beecher.*

Actions speak louder than words. *Pr.* 50

Actis ævum implet, non segnibus annis—His lifetime is full of deeds, not of indolent years. *Ovid.*

Activity is the presence, and character the record, of function. *Greenough.*

Actum est de republicâ—It is all over with the republic.

Actum ne agas—What has been done don't do over again. *Cic.*

Actus Dei nemini facit injuriam—The act of 55 God does wrong to no man. *L. Max.*

Actus legis nulli facit injuriam—The act of the law does wrong to no man. *L. Max.*

Actus me invito factus, non est meus actus— An act I do against my will is not my act. *L. Max.*

Actus non facit reum, nisi mens sit rea—The act does not make a man guilty, unless the mind be guilty. *L. Max.*

Act well your part ; there all the honour lies. *Pope.*

A cuspide corona—From the spear a crown, *i.e.,* 60 honour for military exploits. *M.*

A custom / More honoured in the breach than the observance. *Ham.,* i. 4.

Adam muss eine Eve haben, die er zeiht was er gethan—Adam must have an Eve, to blame for what he has done. *Ger. Pr.*

Ad amussim—Made exactly by rule.

A danger foreseen is half avoided. *Pr.*

Adaptiveness is the peculiarity of human 65 nature. *Emerson.*

Ad aperturam—Wherever a book may be opened.

Ad arbitrium—At pleasure.

Ad astra per ardua—To the stars by steep paths. *M.*

A Daniel come to judgment. *Mer. of Ven.,* iv. 1.

Ad avizandum—Into consideration. *Scots Law.* 70

A day may sink or save a realm. *Tennyson.*

A day of grace (*Gunst*) is as a day in harvest; one must be diligent as soon as it is ripe. *Goethe.*

A day wasted on others is not wasted on one's self. *Dickens.*

Ad calamitatem quilibet rumor valet—When a disaster happens, every report confirming it obtains ready credence.

Ad captandum vulgus—To catch the rabble.

5 Addere legi justitiam decus—It is to one's honour to combine justice with law. *M.*

A death-bed repentance seldom reaches to restitution. *Junius.*

A deep meaning resides in old customs. *Schiller.*

A democracy is a state in which the government rests directly with the majority of the citizens. *Ruskin.*

10 Adeo in teneris consuescere multum est—So much depends on habit in the tender years of youth. *Virg.*

Ad eundem—To the same degree. Said of a graduate passing from one university to another.

Ad extremum—At last.

Ad finem—To the end.

Ad Græcas kalendas—At the Greek calends, *i.e.*, never.

15 Ad gustum—To one's taste.

Adhibenda est in jocando moderatio—Moderation should be used in joking. *Cic.*

Ad hoc—For this purpose.

Ad hominem—Personal (*lit.* to the man).

Adhuc sub judice lis est—The affair is not yet decided.

20 Adhuc tua messis in herba est—Your crop is still in grass. *Ovid.*

A die—From that day.

Adieu la voiture, adieu la boutique—Adieu to the carriage, adieu to the shop, *i.e.*, to the business. *Fr. Pr.*

Adieu, paniers! vendanges sont faites—Farewell, baskets! vintage is over. *Fr.*

Ad infinitum—To infinity.

25 Ad interim—Meanwhile.

Ad internecionem—To extermination.

A Dio spiacente ed a' nemici sui—Hateful to God and the enemies of God. *Dante.*

A Dios rogando y con el mazo dando—Praying to God and smiting with the hammer. *Sp. Pr.*

A discrétion—Without any restriction (*lit.* at discretion). *Fr.*

30 Ad libitum—At pleasure.

Ad majorem Dei gloriam—To the greater glory of God (*M. of the Jesuits*).

Ad mala quisque animum referat sua—Let each recall his own woes. *Ovid.*

Admiration praises; love is dumb. *Börne.*

Ad modum—In the manner.

35 Ad nauseam—To disgust; sickening.

Ad ogni santo la sua torcia—To every saint his own torch, *i.e.*, his place of honour. *It. Pr.*

Ad ogni uocello suo nido è bello—Every bird thinks its own nest beautiful. *It. Pr.*

Ad ognuno par più grave la croce sua—Every one thinks his own cross the hardest to bear. *It. Pr.*

A dog's life—hunger and ease.

A dog winna yowl if you fell him wi' a bane. 40 *Sc. Pr.*

Adolescentem verecundum esse decet—A young man ought to be modest. *Plaut.*

Ad omnem libidinem projectus homo—A man addicted to every lust.

Adó sacan y non pon, presto llegan al hondon—By ever taking out and never putting in, one soon reaches the bottom. *Sp. Pr.*

Ad patres—Dead; to death (*lit.* to the fathers).

A downright contradiction is equally mys- 45 terious to wise men as to fools. *Goethe.*

Ad perditam securim manubrium adjicere—To throw the helve after the hatchet, *i.e.*, to give up in despair.

Ad perniciem solet agi sinceritas—Honesty is often goaded to ruin. *Phædr.*

Ad pœnitendum properat, cito qui judicat—He who decides in haste repents in haste. *Pub. Syr.*

Ad populum phaleras, ego te intus et in cute novi—To the vulgar herd with your trappings; for me, I know you both inside and out. *Pers.*

Ad quæstionem legis respondent judices, ad 50 quæstionem facti respondent juratores—It is the judge's business to answer to the question of law, the jury's to answer to the question of fact. *L.*

Ad quod damnum—To what damage. *L.*

Ad referendum—For further consideration.

Ad rem—To the point (*lit.* to the thing).

A droit—To the right. *Fr.*

A drop of honey catches more flies than a 55 hogshead of vinegar. *Pr.*

A drop of water has all the properties of water, but it cannot exhibit a storm. *Emerson.*

A drowning man will catch at a straw. *Pr.*

Adscriptus glebæ—Attached to the soil.

Adsit regula, peccatis quæ pœnas irroget æquas—Have a rule apportioning to each offence its appropriate penalty. *Hor.*

Adstrictus necessitate—Bound by necessity. *Cic.* 60

Ad summum—To the highest point.

Ad tristem partem strenua est suspicio—One is quick to suspect where one has suffered harm before. *Pub. Syr.*

Ad unguem—To a nicety (*lit.* to the nail).

Ad unum omnes—All to a (*lit.* one) man.

A dur âne dur aiguillon—A hard goad for a stub- 65 born ass. *Fr. Pr.*

Ad utrumque paratus—Prepared for either case.

Ad valorem—According to the value.

Advantage is a better soldier than rashness. *Hen. V.*, iii. 6.

Adversa virtute repello—I repel adversity by valour. *M.*

Adversity is a great schoolmistress, as many 70 a poor fellow knows that has whimpered over his lesson before her awful chair. *Thackeray.*

Adversity's sweet milk—philosophy. *Rom. and Jul.*, iii. 3.

Adversus solem ne loquitor—Speak not against the sun, *i.e.*, don't argue against what is sun-clear. *Pr.*

Ad vitam aut culpam—Till some misconduct be proved (*lit.* for life or fault).

Ad vivum—To the life.

A dwarf sees farther than the giant when he 75 has the giant's shoulders to mount on. *Coleridge.*

Ægis fortissima virtus—Virtue is the strongest shield. *M.*

Ægrescit medendo—The remedy is worse than the disease (*lit.* the disorder increases with the remedy).

Ægri somnia vana—The delusive dreams of a sick man. *Hor.*

Ægroto, dum anima est, spes est—While a sick man has life, there is hope. *Pr.*

5 Ae half o' the world doesna ken how the ither half lives. *Sc. Pr.*

Ae man may tak' a horse to the water, but twenty winna gar (make) him drink. *Sc. Pr.*

Ae man's meat is anither man's poison. *Sc. Pr.*

Æmulatio æmulationem parit—Emulation begets emulation. *Pr.*

Æmulus atque imitator studiorum ac laborum—A rival and imitator of his studies and labours. *Cic.*

10 Aendern und bessern sind zwei—To change, and to change for the better, are two different things. *Ger. Pr.*

Æquabiliter et diligenter—By equity and diligence. *M.*

Æquâ lege necessitas / Sortitur insignes et imos—Necessity apportions impartially to high and low alike. *Hor.*

Æquam memento rebus in arduis / Servare mentem, non secus in bonis / Ab insolenti temperatam / Lætitiâ—Be sure to preserve an unruffled mind in adversity, as well as one restrained from immoderate joy in prosperity. *Hor.*

Æquam servare mentem—To preserve an even temper. *M.*

15 Æquanimiter—With equanimity. *M.*

Æqua tellus / Pauperi recluditur / Regumque pueris—The impartial earth opens alike for the child of the pauper and of the king. *Hor.*

Æquo animo—With an even or equable mind. *M.*

Æquum est / Peccatis veniam poscentem reddere rursus—It is fair that he who begs to be forgiven should in turn forgive. *Hor.*

Ære perennius—More enduring than brass. *Hor.*

20 Ærugo animi, rubigo ingenii—Rust, *viz.*, idleness, of mind is the blight of genius, *i.e.*, natural capability of every kind.

Æs debitorem leve, gravius inimicum facit—A slight debt makes a man your debtor ; a heavier one, your enemy. *Laber.*

Ætatem non tegunt tempora—Our temples do not conceal our age.

Æternum inter se discordant—They are eternally at variance with each other. *Ter.*

Ævo rarissima nostro simplicitas—Simplicity a very rare thing now-a-days. *Ovid.*

25 A fact is a great thing : a sentence printed, if not by God, then at least by the Devil. *Carlyle.*

A fact in our lives is valuable, not so far as it is true, but as it is significant. *Goethe.*

A facto ad jus non datur consequentia—Inference from the fact to the law is not legitimate. *L. Max.*

"A fair day's wages for a fair day's work," is as just a demand as governed men ever made of governing ; yet in what corner of this planet was that ever realised ? *Carlyle.*

A fair face may hide a foul heart. *Pr.*

30 A faithful friend is a true image of the Deity. *Napoleon.*

A fault confessed is half redressed. *Pr.*

A favour does not consist in the service done, but in the spirit of the man who confers it. *Sen.*

A fellow-feeling makes one wondrous kind. *Garrick.*

A fellow who speculates is like an animal on a barren heath, driven round and round by an evil spirit, while there extends on all sides of him a beautiful green meadow-pasture. *Goethe.*

35 "A few strong instincts and a few plain rules" suffice us. *Emerson, from Wordsworth.*

Affaire d'amour—A love affair. *Fr.*

Affaire d'honneur—An affair of honour ; a duel. *Fr.*

Affaire du cœur—An affair of the heart. *Fr.*

Affairs that depend on many rarely succeed. *Guicciardini.*

40 Affection lights a brighter flame / Than ever blazed by art. *Cowper.*

Affirmatim—In the affirmative.

Afflavit Deus et dissipantur—God sent forth his breath, and they are scattered. *Inscription on medal struck to commemorate the destruction of the Spanish Armada.*

Afflictions are blessings in disguise. *Pr.*

A fiery soul, which, working out its way / Fretted the pigmy body to decay. *Dryden.*

45 A fin—To the end.

A fine quotation is a diamond on the finger of a man of wit, and a pebble in the hand of a fool. *J. Roux.*

A fixed idea ends in madness or heroism. *Victor Hugo.*

A flute lay side by side with Frederick the Great's baton of command. *Jean Paul.*

A fly is as untamable as a hyena. *Emerson.*

50 A fog cannot be dispelled with a fan. *Japan. Pr.*

A fond—Thoroughly (*lit.* to the bottom).

A fonte puro pura defluit aqua—From a pure spring pure water flows. *Pr.*

A fortiori—With stronger reason.

A fool always accuses other people ; a partially wise man, himself ; a wholly wise man, neither himself nor others. *Herder.*

55 A fool always finds a greater fool to admire him. *Boileau.*

A fool and his money are soon parted. *Pr.*

A fool flatters himself, a wise man flatters the fool. *Bulwer.*

A fool is often as dangerous to deal with as a knave, and always more incorrigible. *Colton.*

A fool is wise in his own conceit. *Pr.*

60 A fool knows more in his own house than a wise man in another's. *Pr.*

A fool may give a wise man counsel. *Pr.*

A fool may make money, but it takes a wise man to spend it. *Pr.*

A fool may sometimes have talent, but he never has judgment. *La Roche.*

A fool may speer (ask) mair questions than a wise man can answer. *Sc. Pr.*

65 A fool resents good counsel, but a wise man lays it to heart. *Confucius.*

A fool's bolt is soon shot. *Hen. V.,* iii. 7.

A fool's bolt may sometimes hit the mark. *Pr.*

A fool when he is silent is counted wise. *Pr.*

A fool who has a flash of wit creates astonishment and scandal, like a hack-horse setting out to gallop. *Chamfort.*

A fop is the mercer's friend, the tailor's fool, and his own foe. *Lavater.*

A force de mal aller tout ira bien—By dint of going wrong all will go right. *Fr. Pr.*

A force de peindre le diable sur les murs, il finit par apparaître en personne—If you keep painting the devil on the walls, he will by and by appear to you in person. *Fr. Pr.*

5 A friend in court makes the process short. *Pr.*

A friend is a person with whom I may be sincere. *Emerson.*

A friend is never known till needed. *Pr.*

A friend loveth at all times. *Bible.*

A friend may well be reckoned the masterpiece of Nature. *Emerson.*

10 A friend's eye is a good looking-glass. *Gael. Pr.*

A friendship will be young at the end of a century, a passion old at the end of three months. *Nigu.*

A friend to everybody is a friend to nobody. *Pr.*

A fronte præcipitium, a tergo lupus—A precipice before, a wolf behind. *Pr.*

After dinner rest awhile; after supper walk a mile. *Pr.*

15 After life's fitful fever he sleeps well. *Macb.,* iii. 2.

After meat mustard, *i.e.,* too late.

After the spirit of discernment, the next rarest things in the world are diamonds and pearls. *La Bruyère.*

After-wit is everybody's wit. *Pr.*

A full cup is hard to carry. *Pr.*

20 A ganging fit (foot) is aye getting. *Sc. Pr.*

A gauche—To the left. *Fr.*

Age does not make us childish, as people say ; it only finds us still true children. *Goethe.*

Age is a matter of feeling, not of years. *G. W. Curtis.*

Age without cheerfulness is a Lapland winter without a sun. *Colton.*

25 A genius is one who is endowed with an excess of nervous energy and sensibility. *Schopenhauer.*

Agent de change—A stockbroker. *Fr.*

A gentleman makes no noise ; a lady is serene. *Emerson.*

A gentleman's first characteristic is fineness of nature. *Ruskin.*

A gentleman that will speak more in a minute than he will stand to in a month. *Rom. and Jul.,* ii. 4.

30 Age quod agis—Attend to (*lit.* do) what you are doing.

Agere considerate pluris est quam cogitare prudenter—It is of more consequence to act considerately than to think sagely. *Cic.*

Agiotage—Stockbroking. *Fr.*

A giving hand, though foul, shall have fair praise. *Love's L. Lost,* iv. 1.

Agnosco veteris vestigia flammæ—I own I feel traces of an old passion. *Virg.*

35 A God all mercy is a God unjust. *Young.*

A God speaks softly in our breast ; softly, yet distinctly, shows us what to hold by and what to shun. *Goethe.*

A gold key opens every door. *Pr.*

A good bargain is a pick-purse. *Pr.*

A good beginning makes a good ending. *Pr.*

40 A good book is the precious life-blood of a master-spirit, embalmed and treasured up on purpose to a life beyond life. *Milton.*

A good friend is my nearest relation. *Pr.*

A good horse should be seldom spurred. *Pr.*

A good inclination is only the first rude draught of virtue, but the finishing strokes are from the will. *South.*

A good king is a public servant. *Ben Jonson.*

45 A good laugh is sunshine in a house. *Thackeray.*

A good law is one that holds, whether you recognise it or not; a bad law is one that cannot, however much you ordain it. *Ruskin.*

A good man in his dark striving is, I should say, conscious of the right way. *Goethe.*

A good man shall be satisfied from himself. *Bible.*

A good marksman may miss. *Pr.*

50 A good name is sooner lost than won. *Pr.*

A good presence is a letter of recommendation. *Pr.*

A good reader is nearly as rare as a good writer. *Willmott.*

A good rider on a good horse is as much above himself and others as the world can make him. *Lord Herbert of Cherbury.*

A good road and a wise traveller are two different things. *Pr.*

55 A good solid bit of work lasts. *George Eliot.*

A good surgeon must have an eagle's eye, a lion's heart, and a lady's hand. *Pr.*

A good thought is a great boon. *Bovee.*

A good wife and health are a man's best wealth. *Pr.*

A gorge déployée—With full throat. *Fr.*

60 A government for protecting business and bread only is but a carcase, and soon falls by its own corruption to decay. *A. B. Alcott.*

A government may not waver; once it has chosen its course, it must, without looking to right or left, thenceforth go forward. *Bismarck.*

A grands frais—At great expense. *Fr.*

A grave and a majestic exterior is the palace of the soul. *Chinese Pr.*

A great anguish may do the work of years, and we may come out from that baptism of fire with a soul full of new awe and new pity. *George Eliot.*

65 A great deal may and must be done which we dare not acknowledge in words. *Goethe.*

A great genius takes shape by contact with another great genius, but less by assimilation than by friction. *Heine.*

A great licentiousness treads on the heels of a reformation. *Emerson.*

A great man is he who can call together the most select company when it pleases him. *Landor.*

A great man is one who affects the mind of his generation. *Disraeli.*

70 A great man living for high ends is the divinest thing that can be seen on earth. *G. S. Hillard.*

A great man quotes bravely, and will not draw on his invention when his memory serves him with a word as good. *Emerson.*

A great master always appropriates what is good in his predecessors, and it is this which makes him great. *Goethe.*

A great observer, and he looks / Quite through the deeds of men. *Jul. Cæs.*, i. 2.

A great reputation is a great noise ; the more there is made, the farther off it is heard. *Napoleon.*

5 A great revolution is never the fault of the people, but of the government. *Goethe.*

A great scholar is seldom a great philosopher. *Goethe.*

A great spirit errs as well as a little one, the former because it knows no bounds, the latter because it confounds its own horizon with that of the universe. *Goethe.*

A great thing can only be done by a great man, and he does it without effort. *Ruskin.*

A great thing is a great book, but greater than all is the talk of a great man. *Disraeli.*

10 A great writer does not reveal himself here and there, but everywhere. *Lowell.*

Agree, for the law is costly. *Pr.*

A green winter makes a fat churchyard. *Pr.*

A grey eye is a sly eye ; a brown one indicates a roguish humour ; a blue eye expresses fidelity ; while the sparkling of a dark eye is, like the ways of Providence, always a riddle. *Bodenstedt.*

A growing youth has a wolf in his belly. *Pr.*

15 Agues come on horseback and go away on foot. *Pr.*

A guilty conscience needs no accuser. *Pr.*

A hair of the dog that bit him. *Pr.*

A haute voix—Loudly ; audibly. *Fr.*

A heart to resolve, a head to contrive, and a hand to execute. *Gibbon.*

20 A hedge between, keeps friendship green. *Pr.*

Ah ! il n'y a plus d'enfants—Ah ! there are no children now-a-days ! *Mol.*

Ah me ! for aught that ever I could read . . . / The course of true love never did run smooth. *Mid. N.'s Dream*, i. 1.

Ah me ! how sweet this world is to the dying ! *Schiller.*

A hook's well lost to catch a salmon. *Pr.*

25 A horse ! a horse ! my kingdom for a horse. *Rich. III.*, v. 4.

Ah ! pour être dévot, je n'en suis pas moins homme—Though I am a religious man, I am not therefore the less a man. *Mol.*

Ah ! quam dulce est meminisse—Ah ! how sweet it is to remember ! *M.*

Ah ! that deceit should steal such gentle shapes / And with a virtuous visor hide deep vice. *Rich. III.*, ii. 2.

A hundred years cannot repair a moment's loss of honour. *Pr.*

30 A hungry belly has no ears. *Pr.*

Ah ! vitam perdidi operose nihil agendo—I have lost my life, alas ! in laboriously doing nothing. *Grotius.*

Aide-toi, et le ciel t'aidera—Help yourself and Heaven will help you. *Fr.*

Αἱ συμφοραὶ ποιοῦσι μακρολόγους—Misfortunes make men talk loquaciously. *Appian.*

Αἰδὼς ὄλωλεν—Modesty has died out. *Theognis.*

Ainsi que son esprit, tout peuple a son langage—Every nation has its own language as 35 well as its own temperament. *Voltaire.*

Air de fête—Looking festive. *Fr.*

Air distingué—Distinguished looking. *Fr.*

Airs of importance are the credentials of impotence. *Lavater.*

Aisé à dire est difficile à faire—Easy to say is hard to do. *Fr. Pr.*

A jest loses its point when he who makes it 40 is the first to laugh. *Schiller.*

A jest's prosperity lies in the ear / Of him that hears it, never in the tongue / Of him that makes it. *Love's L. Lost*, v. 2.

A Jove principium—Beginning with Jove.

A judge who cannot punish, associates himself in the end with the criminal. *Goethe.*

A judicious (verständiger) man is of much value for himself, of little for the whole. *Goethe.*

A king of shreds and patches. *Ham.*, iii. 4. 45

A king's son is no nobler than his company. *Gael. Pr.*

A knavish speech sleeps in a foolish ear. *Ham.*, iv. 2.

A l'abandon—At random ; little cared for. *Fr.*

A la belle étoile—In the open air. *Fr.*

A la bonne heure—Well-timed ; very well. *Fr.* 50

A l'abri—Under shelter. *Fr.*

A la chandelle la chèvre semble demoiselle—By candlelight a goat looks like a young lady. *Fr. Pr.*

A la dérobée—By stealth. *Fr.*

A la fin saura-t-on qui a mangé le lard—We shall know in the end who ate the bacon. *Fr. Pr.*

A la française—In the French fashion. *Fr.* 55

A la lettre—Literally. *Fr.*

A la mode—According to the fashion. *Fr.*

A l'amour satisfait tout son charme est ôté—When love is satisfied all the charm of it is gone. *Corneille.*

A la portée de tout le monde—Within reach of every one. *Fr.*

A la presse vont les fous—Fools go in crowds. 60 *Fr. Pr.*

Alas ! the devil's sooner raised than laid. *Sheridan.*

A last judgment is necessary, because fools flourish. *Wm. Blake.*

A last judgment is not for making bad men better, but for hindering them from oppressing the good. *Wm. Blake.*

A latere—From the side of (sc. the Pope).

A lazy man is necessarily a bad man ; an 65 idle, is necessarily a demoralised population. *Draper.*

Albæ gallinæ filius—The son of a white hen.

Album calculum addere—To give a white stone, i.e., to vote for, by putting a white stone into an urn, a black one indicating rejection.

Al corral con allo—Out of the window with it. *Sp.*

Alea belli—The hazard of war.

Alea jacta est—The die is cast. 70

Alea judiciorum—The hazard or uncertainty of law.

A leaden sword in an ivory scabbard. *Pr.*

A learned man is a tank; a wise man is a spring. *W. R. Alger.*

Al enemigo, si vuelve la espalda, la puente de plata—Make a bridge of silver for the flying enemy. *Sp. Pr.*

Alere flammam—To feed the flame.

Ales volat propriis—A bird flies to its own.

5 Al fin se canta la Gloria—Not till the end is the Gloria chanted. *Sp. Pr.*

Al fresco—In the open air. *It.*

Aliam excute quercum—Go, shake some other oak (of its fruit). *Pr.*

Alia res sceptrum, alia plectrum—Ruling men is one thing, fiddling to them another. *Pr.*

A liar is always lavish of oaths. *Corneille.*

10 A liar should have a good memory. *Pr.*

Alias—Otherwise.

Alia tentanda via est—We must try another way.

Alibi—Elsewhere.

A lie is like a snowball; the farther you roll it, the bigger it becomes. *Luther.*

15 A lie has no legs, but scandal has wings. *Pr.*

A lie which is half a truth is ever the blackest of lies. *Tennyson.*

Aliena negotia centum / Per caput, et circa saliunt latus—A hundred affairs of other people leap through my head and at my side. *Hor.*

Aliena negotia curo / Excussus propriis—I attend to other people's affairs, baffled with my own. *Hor.*

Aliena nobis, nostra plus aliis placent—That which belongs to others pleases us most; that which belongs to us pleases others more. *Pub. Syr.*

20 Aliena opprobria sæpe / Absterrent vitiis—We are often deterred from crime by the disgrace of others. *Hor.*

Aliena optimum frui insania—It is best to profit by the madness of other people. *Pr.*

Aliena vitia in oculis habemus; a tergo nostra sunt—We keep the faults of others before our eyes; our own behind our backs. *Sen.*

Alieni appetens, sui profusus—Covetous of other men's property, prodigal of his own. *Sall.*

Alieni temporis flores—Flowers of other days.

25 Alieno in loco haud stabile regnum est—Sovereignty over a foreign land is insecure. *Sen.*

Alieno more vivendum est mihi—I must live according to another's humour. *Ter.*

Alienos agros irrigas tuis sitientibus—You water the fields of others, while your own are parched. *Pr.*

A lie should be trampled on and extinguished wherever found. *Carlyle.*

A lie which is all a lie may be met and fought with outright / But a lie which is part a truth is a harder matter to fight. *Tennyson.*

30 A life that is worth writing at all is worth writing minutely. *Longfellow.*

A light heart lives long. *Pr.*

Alii sementem faciunt, alii metentem—Some do the sowing, others the reaping.

Aliis lætus, sapiens sibi—Cheerful for others, wise for himself. *Pr.*

A l'impossible nul n'est tenu—No one can be held bound to do what is impossible. *Fr. Pr.*

35 A l'improviste—Unawares. *Fr.*

Aliorum medicus, ipse ulceribus scates—A physician to others, while you yourself are full of ulcers.

Alio sub sole—Under another sky (*lit.* sun).

Aliquando bonus dormitat Homerus—Sometimes even the good Homer nods. *Hor.*

Aliquis non debet esse judex in propria causa —No one may sit as judge in his own case. *L.*

Alis volat propriis—He flies with his own wings. 40 *M.*

A little body often harbours a great soul. *Pr.*

A little fire is quickly trodden out ; / Which being suffered, rivers cannot quench. 3 *Hen. VI.,* iv. 8.

A little is better than none. *Pr.*

A little learning is a dangerous thing / Drink deep, or taste not the Pierian spring. *Pope.*

A little leaven leaveneth the whole lump. 45 *Pr.*

A little more than kin, and less than kind. *Ham.,* i. 2.

A little neglect may breed great mischief. *Franklin.*

A little philosophy inclineth a man's mind to atheism, but depth in philosophy bringeth men's minds about to religion. *Bacon.*

A little spark maks muckle wark. *Sc. Pr.*

Alitur vitium vivitque tegendo—Evil is nour- 50 ished and grows by concealment. *Virg.*

Aliud est celare, aliud tacere—To conceal is one thing, to say nothing is another. *L. Max.*

Aliud et idem—Another and the same.

Aliud legunt pueri, aliud viri, aliud senes—Boys read books one way, men another, old men another. *Ter.*

A living dog is better than a dead lion. *Pr.*

Alle anderen Dinge müssen; der Mensch ist 55 das Wesen, welches will—All other things must; man is the only creature who wills. *Schiller.*

Alle Frachten lichten, sagte der Schiffer, da warf er seine Frau über Bord—All freights lighten, said the skipper, as he threw his wife into the sea. *Ger. Pr.*

Allegans contraria non est audiendus—No one is to be heard whose evidence is contradictory. *L. Max.*

Allen gehört, was du denkest; dein eigen ist nur, was du fühlest — What you think belongs to all; only what you feel is your own. *Schiller.*

Aller Anfang ist heiter; die Schwelle ist der Platz der Erwartung—Every beginning is cheerful ; the threshold is the place of expectation. *Goethe.*

Aller Anfang ist schwer, sprach der Dieb, und 60 stahl zuerst einen Amboss—Every beginning is difficult, said the thief, when he began by stealing an anvil. *Ger. Pr.*

Alle Schuld rächt sich auf Erden—Every offence is avenged on earth. *Goethe.*

Alles Gescheidte ist schon gedacht worden : man muss nur versuchen, es noch einmal zu denken—Everything wise has already been thought ; one can only try and think it once more. *Goethe.*

Alles Vergängliche ist nur ein Gleichniss—Everything transitory is only an allegory. *Goethe.*

Alles wanket, wo der Glaube fehlt — All is unsteady (*lit.* wavers) where faith fails. *Ger. Pr.*

Alles wäre gut, wär kein Aber dabei—Everything would be right if it were not for the " Buts." *Ger. Pr.*

Alles, was ist, ist vernünftig—Everything which is, is agreeable to reason. *Hegel.*

Alles zu retten, muss alles gewagt werden—To save all, we must risk all. *Schiller.*

5 All advantages are attended with disadvantages. *Hume.*

All are but parts of one stupendous whole / Whose body Nature is, and God the soul. *Pope.*

All argument will vanish before one touch of Nature. *Colman.*

All are not hunters that blow the horn. *Pr.*

All are not saints that go to church. *Pr.*

10 All are not soldiers that go to the wars. *Pr.*

All are not thieves that dogs bark at. *Pr.*

All art is great, and good, and true, only so far as it is distinctively the work of manhood in its entire and highest sense. *Ruskin.*

All balloons give up their gas in the pressure of things, and collapse in a sufficiently wretched manner erelong. *Carlyle.*

All battle is misunderstanding. *Goethe.*

15 All beginnings are easy; it is the ulterior steps that are of most difficult ascent and most rarely taken. *Goethe.*

All cats are grey in the dark. *Pr.*

All censure of a man's self is oblique praise; it is in order to show how much he can spare. *Johnson.*

All cruelty springs from weakness. *Sen.*

All death in nature is birth. *Fichte.*

20 All deep joy has something of awful in it. *Carlyle.*

All delights are vain; but that most vain / Which, with pain purchas'd, doth inherit pain. *Love's L. Lost,* i. 1.

All destruction, by violent revolution or howsoever it be, is but new creation on a wider scale. *Carlyle.*

All disputation makes the mind deaf, and when people are deaf I am dumb. *Joubert.*

Ἀλλ' ἔστιν, ἔνθα χὴ δίκη βλάβην φέρει—Sometimes justice does harm. *Sophocles.*

25 All evil is as a nightmare; the instant you begin to *stir* under it, the evil is gone. *Carlyle.*

All evils, when extreme, are the same. *Corneille.*

All faults are properly shortcomings. *Goethe.*

All faiths are to their own believers just / For none believe because they will, but must. *Dryden.*

All feet tread not in one shoe. *Pr.*

30 All flesh consorteth according to its kind, and a man will cleave to his like. *Ecclus.*

All forms of government are good, so far as the wise and kind in them govern the unwise and unkind. *Ruskin.*

All good colour is in some degree pensive, and the purest and most thoughtful minds are those which love colour the most. *Ruskin.*

All good government must begin at home. *H. R. Haweis.*

All good has an end but the goodness of God. *Gael. Pr.*

All good things / Are ours, nor soul helps 35 flesh more now / Than flesh helps soul. *Browning.*

All good things go in threes. *Ger. and Fr. Pr.*

All governments are to some extent a treaty with the Devil. *Jacobi.*

All great art is the expression of man's delight in God's work, not in his own. *Ruskin.*

All great discoveries are made by men whose feelings run ahead of their thinkings. *C. H. Parkhurst.*

All great peoples are conservative. *Car-* 40 *lyle.*

All great song has been sincere song. *Ruskin.*

All healthy things are sweet-tempered. *Emerson.*

All his geese are swans. *Pr.*

All history is an inarticulate Bible. *Carlyle.*

All immortal writers speak out of their hearts. 45 *Ruskin.*

All imposture weakens confidence and chills benevolence. *Johnson.*

All inmost things are melodious, naturally utter themselves in song. *Carlyle.*

All is but toys. *Macb.,* ii. 3.

All is good that God sends us. *Pr.*

All is influence except ourselves. *Goethe.* 50

All is not gold that glitters. *Pr.*

All is not lost that's in peril. *Pr.*

All live by seeming. *Old Play.*

All living objects do by necessity form to themselves a skin. *Carlyle.*

Allmächtig ist doch das Gold; auch Mohren 55 kann's bleichen—Gold is omnipotent; it can make even the Moor white. *Schiller.*

All mankind love a lover. *Emerson.*

All man's miseries go to prove his greatness. *Pascal.*

All martyrdoms looked mean when they were suffered. *Emerson.*

All measures of reformation are effective in proportion to their timeliness. *Ruskin.*

All men are bores except when we want them. 60 *Holmes.*

All men are born sincere and die deceivers. *Vauvenargues.*

All men are fools, and with every effort they differ only in the degree. *Boileau.*

All men commend patience, though few be willing to practise it. *Thomas à Kempis.*

All men have their price. *Anon.*

All men honour love, because it looks up, and 65 not down. *Emerson.*

All men, if they work not as in the great task-master's eye, will work wrong. *Carlyle.*

All men live by truth, and stand in need of expression. *Emerson.*

All men may dare what has by man been done. *Young.*

All men that are ruined are ruined on the side of their natural propensities. *Burke.*

All men think all men mortal but themselves. 70 *Young.*

All men would be masters of others, and no man is lord of himself. *Goethe.*

All men who know not where to look for truth, save in the narrow well of self, will find their own image at the bottom and mistake it for what they are seeking. *Lowell.*

All minds quote. Old and new make up the warp and woof of every moment. *Emerson.*

All mischief comes from our inability to be alone. *La Bruyère.*

5 All money is but a divisible title-deed. *Ruskin.*

All my possessions for a moment of time! *Queen Elizabeth's last words.*

All nature is but art unknown to thee. / All chance, direction which thou canst not see. / All discord, harmony not understood; / All partial evil, universal good. *Pope.*

All nobility in its beginnings was somebody's natural superiority. *Emerson.*

All objects are as windows through which the philosophic eye looks into infinitude. *Carlyle.*

10 All orators are dumb when beauty pleadeth. *Sh.*

ἀλλ' οὐ Ζεὺς ἄνδρεσσι νοήματα πάντα τελευτᾶ —Zeus, however, does not give effect to all the schemes of man. *Hom.*

Ἄλλος ἐγώ—Alter ego. *Zeno's definition of a friend.*

All our evils are imaginary, except pain of body and remorse of conscience. *Rousseau.*

All our most honest striving prospers only in unconscious moments. *Goethe.*

15 All passions exaggerate; and they are passions only because they do exaggerate. *Chamfort.*

All pleasure must be bought at the price of pain. *John Foster.*

All power appears only in transition. *Novalis.*

All power, even the most despotic, rests ultimately on opinion. *Hume.*

All power of fancy over reason is a degree of insanity. *Johnson.*

20 All promise outruns performance. *Emerson.*

All public disorder proceeds from want of work. *Courier.*

All speech, even the commonest, has something of song in it. *Carlyle.*

All strength lies within, not without. *Jean Paul.*

All strong men love life. *Heine.*

25 All strong souls are related. *Schiller.*

All's well that ends well. *Pr.*

All talent, all intellect, is in the first place moral. *Carlyle.*

All that a man has he will give for right relations with his mates. *Emerson.*

All that glisters is not gold: / Gilded tombs do worms infold. *Mer. of Ven.*, ii. 7.

30 All that is best in the great poets of all countries is not what is national in them, but what is universal. *Longfellow.*

All that is human must retrograde, if it do not advance. *Gibbon.*

All that is noble is in itself of a quiet nature, and appears to sleep until it is aroused and summoned forth by contrast. *Goethe.*

All that lives must die, / Passing through nature to eternity. *Ham.*, i. 2.

All that man does and brings to pass is the vesture of a thought. *Sartor Resartus.*

All that mankind has done, thought, gained, 35 or been, it is all lying in magic preservation in the pages of books. *Carlyle.*

All that tread the globe are but a handful to the tribes that slumber in its bosom. *Bryant.*

All the armed prophets have conquered, all the unarmed have perished. *Machiavelli.*

All the arts affecting culture (*i.e.*, the fine arts) have a certain common bond, and are connected by a certain blood relationship with each other. *Cic.*

All the difference between the wise man and the fool is, that the wise man keeps his counsel, and the fool reveals it. *Gael. Pr.*

All the diseases of mind, leading to fatalest 40 ruin, are due to the concentration of man upon himself, whether his heavenly interests or his worldly interests, matters not. *Ruskin.*

All the faults of the man I can pardon in the player; no fault of the player can I pardon in the man. *Goethe.*

All the good of which humanity is capable is comprised in obedience. *J. S. Mill.*

All the great ages have been ages of belief. *Emerson.*

All the keys don't hang at one man's girdle. *Pr.*

All the makers of dictionaries, all the com-45 pilers of opinions already printed, we may term plagiarists, but honest plagiarists, who arrogate not the merit of invention. *Voltaire.*

All the perfumes of Arabia will not sweeten this little hand. *Macb.*, v. 1.

All the pursuits of men are the pursuits of women also, and in all of them a woman is only a weaker man. *Plato.*

All the thinking in the world does not bring us to thought; we must be right by nature, so that good thoughts may come. *Goethe.*

All the wit in the world is not in one head. *Pr.*

All the wit in the world is thrown away upon 50 the man who has none. *Bruyère.*

All the world's a stage / And all the men and women merely players. *As You Like It*, ii. 7.

All things are double, one against another. Good is set against evil, and life against death. *Ecclus.*

All things are for the sake of the good, and it is the cause of everything beautiful. *Plato.*

All things are in perpetual flux and fleeting. *Pr.*

All things are symbolical, and what we call 55 results are beginnings. *Plato.*

All things happen by necessity; in Nature there is neither good nor bad. *Spinoza.*

All things that are / Are with more spirit chased than enjoyed. *Mer. of Ven.*, ii. 6.

All things that love the sun are out of doors. *Wordsworth.*

All this (in the daily press) does not concern one in the least; one is neither the wiser nor the better for knowing what the day brings forth. *Goethe.*

All true men are soldiers in the same army, 60 to do battle against the same enemy—the empire of darkness and wrong. *Carlyle.*

All truth is not to be told at all times. *Pr.*

All virtue is most rewarded, and all wickedness most punished, in itself. *Bacon.*

All went as merry as a marriage-bell. *Byron.*

All, were it only a withered leaf, works together with all. *Carlyle.*

All will be as God wills. *Gael. Pr.*

5 All wise men are of the same religion, and keep it to themselves. *Lord Shaftesbury.*

All women are good, *viz.*, for something or nothing. *Pr.*

All work and no play makes Jack a dull boy. *Pr.*

Allzugrosse Zartheit der Gefühle ist ein wahres Unglück—It is a real misfortune to have too great delicacy of feeling. *C. J. Weber.*

Allzustraff gespannt, zerspringt der Bogen—If the bow is overstrained, it breaks. *Schiller.*

10 Allzuviel ist nicht genug — Too much is not enough. *Ger. Pr.*

Alma mater—A benign mother; applied to one's university, also to the "all-nourishing" earth.

Al molino, ed alla sposa / Sempre manca qualche cosa—A mill and a woman are always in want of something. *It. Pr.*

Almost all our sorrows spring out of our relations with other people. *Schopenhauer.*

Almsgiving never made any man poor. *Pr.*

15 A loan should come laughing home. *Pr.*

A l'œuvre on connait l'artisan—By the work one knows the workman. *La Font.*

A loisir—At leisure. *Fr.*

Alomban és szerelemben nincs lehetetlenséej—In dreams and in love there are no impossibilities. *J. Arany.*

Along the cool sequester'd vale of life / They kept the noiseless tenor of their way. *Gray.*

20 A los bobos se les aperece la Madre de Dios—The mother of God appears to fools. *Sp. Pr.*

A lover's eyes will gaze an eagle blind. *Love's L. Lost,* iv. 3.

Alte fert aquila—The eagle bears me on high. *M.*

Altera manu fert lapidem, altera panem ostentat—He carries a stone in one hand, and shows bread in the other. *Pr*

Altera manu scabunt, altera feriunt—They tickle with one hand and smite with the other. *Pr.*

25 Alter ego—Another or second self.

Alter idem—Another exactly the same.

Alter ipse amicus—A friend is a second self. *Pr.*

Alterius non sit qui suus esse potest—Let no man be slave of another who can be his own master. *M. of Paracelsus.*

Alter remus aquas, alter mihi radat arenas—Let me skim the water with one oar, and with the other touch the sands, *i.e.*, so as not to go out of my depth.

30 Alterum tantum—As much more.

Although men are accused of not knowing their weakness, yet perhaps as few know their strength. *Swift.*

Although the last, not least. *King Lear,* i. 1.

Altissima quæque flumina minimo sono labuntur—The deepest rivers flow with the least noise. *Curt.*

Alt ist das Wort, doch bleibet hoch und wahr der Sinn—Old is the Word, yet does the meaning abide as high and true as ever. *Faust.*

Altro diletto che' mparar, non provo—Learning is my sole delight. *Petrarch.* 35

Always filling, never full. *Cowper.*

Always have two strings to your bow. *Pr.*

Always strive for the whole; and if thou canst not become a whole thyself, connect thyself with a whole as a ministering member. *Schiller.*

Always there is a black spot in our sunshine, the shadow of ourselves. *Carlyle.*

Always to distrust is an error, as well as always 40 to trust. *Goethe.*

Always win fools first; they talk much, and what they have once uttered they will stick to. *Helps.*

Amabilis insania—A fine frenzy. *Hor.*

A machine is not a man or a work of art; it is destructive of humanity and art. *Wm. Blake.*

A madness most discreet, / A choking gall and a preserving sweet, *i.e.*, Love is. *Rom. and Jul.,* i. 1.

A mad world, my masters. *Middleton.* 45

A main armée—By force of arms. *Fr.*

Ama l'amico tuo con il diffetto suo—Love your friend with all his faults. *It. Pr.*

A man at sixteen will prove a child at sixty. *Pr.*

A man belongs to his age and race, even when he acts against them. *Renan.*

A man, be the heavens praised, is sufficient 50 for himself; yet were ten men, united in love, capable of being and doing what ten thousand singly would fail in. *Carlyle.*

A man can be so changed by love as to be unrecognisable as the same person. *Ter.*

A man *can* do no more than he can. *Pr.*

A man can keep another's secret better than his own; a woman, her own better than another's. *La Bruyère.*

A man canna wive and thrive the same year. *Sc. Pr.*

A man can never be too much on his guard 55 when he writes to the public, and never too easy towards those with whom he converses. *D'Alembert.*

A man can receive nothing except it be given him from heaven. *John Baptist.*

A man cannot be in the seventeenth century and the nineteenth at one and the same moment. *Carlyle's experience while editing Cromwell's Letters.*

A man cannot spin and reel at the same time. *Pr.*

A man cannot whistle and drink at the same time. *Pr.*

A man dishonoured is worse than dead. *Cer-* 60 *vantes.*

A man does not represent a fraction, but a whole number; he is complete in himself. *Schopenhauer.*

A man hears only what he understands. *Goethe.*

A man he was to all the country dear, / And passing rich with forty pounds a year. *Goldsmith.*

A man in a farm and his thoughts away, is better out of it than in it. *Gael. Pr.*

A man in debt is so far a slave. *Emerson.* 65

A man in the right, with God on his side, is in the majority, though he be alone. *Amer. Pr.*

A man is a fool or his own physician at forty. *Pr.*

A man is a golden impossibility. *Emerson.*

A man is always nearest to his good when at home, and farthest from it when away. *J. G. Holland.*

5 A man is king in his own house. *Gael. Pr.*

A man is never happy till his vague striving has itself marked out its proper limitation. *Goethe.*

A man is not born the second time, any more than the first, without travail. *Carlyle.*

A man is not as God, / But then most godlike being most a man. *Tennyson.*

A man is not strong who takes convulsion fits, though six men cannot hold him; only he that can walk under the heaviest weight without staggering. *Carlyle.*

10 A man is only a relative and a representative nature. *Emerson.*

A man is the façade of a temple wherein all wisdom and all good abide. *Emerson.*

A man is the prisoner of his power. *Emerson.*

A man lives by believing something; not by debating and arguing about many things. *Carlyle.*

A man may be proud of his house, and not ride on the rigging (ridge) of it. *Sc. Pr.*

15 A man may do what he likes with his own. *Pr*

A man may smile, and smile, and be a villain. *Ham.*, i. 5.

A man may spit in his nieve and do little. *Sc. Pr.*

A man may survive distress, but not disgrace. *Gael. Pr.*

A man / More sinn'd against than sinning. *King Lear*, iii. 2.

20 A man must ask his wife's leave to thrive. *Pr.*

A man must become wise at his own expense. *Montaigne.*

A man must be healthy before he can be holy. *Mme. Swetchine.*

A man must be well off who is irritated by trifles, for in misfortune trifles are not felt. *Schopenhauer.*

A man must carry knowledge with him if he would bring home knowledge. *Johnson.*

25 A man must seek his happiness and inward peace from objects which cannot be taken away from him. *W. von Humboldt.*

A man must take himself for better, for worse, as his portion. *Emerson.*

A man must thank his defects, and stand in some terror of his talents. *Emerson.*

A man must verify or expel his doubts, and convert them into certainty of Yes *or* No. *Carlyle.*

A man must wait for the right moment. *Schopenhauer.*

30 A man never feels the want of what it never occurs to him to ask for. *Schopenhauer.*

A man never rises so high as when he knows not whither he is going. *Oliver Cromwell.*

A man of intellect without energy added to it is a failure. *Chamfort.*

A man of maxims only is like a Cyclops with one eye, and that eye in the back of his head. *Coleridge.*

A man of pleasure is a man of pains. *Young.*

A man often pays dear for a small frugality. 35 *Emerson.*

A man of the world must seem to be what he wishes to be. *La Bruyère.*

A man of wit would often be much embarrassed without the company of fools. *La Roche.*

A man only understands what is akin to some things already in his mind. *Amiel.*

A man places himself on a level with him whom he praises. *Goethe.*

A man protesting against error is on the way 40 towards uniting himself with all men that believe in truth. *Carlyle.*

A man so various, that he seem'd to be, / Not one, but all mankind's epitome. *Dryden.*

A man that is young in years may be old in hours, if he have lost no time. *Bacon.*

A man used to vicissitudes is not easily dejected. *Johnson.*

A man who cannot gird himself into harness will take no weight along these highways. *Carlyle.*

A man who claps his Pegasus into a harness, 45 and urges on his muse with the whip, will have to pay to Nature the penalty of this trespass. *Schopenhauer.*

A man who does not know rigour cannot pity either. *Carlyle.*

A man who feels that his religion is a slavery has not began to comprehend the real nature of it. *J. G. Holland.*

A man who has nothing to do is the devil's playfellow. *J. G. Holland.*

A man who is ignorant of foreign languages is ignorant of his own. *Goethe.*

A man who reads much becomes arrogant and 50 pedantic; one who sees much becomes wise, sociable, and helpful. *Lichtenberg.*

A man will love or hate solitude—that is, his own society—according as he is himself worthy or worthless. *Schopenhauer.*

A man will not be observed in doing that which he can do best. *Emerson.*

A man with half a volition goes backwards and forwards, and makes no way on the smoothest road. *Carlyle.*

A man with knowledge but without energy, is a house furnished but not inhabited; a man with energy but no knowledge, a house dwelt in but unfurnished. *John Sterling.*

A man's a man for a' that. *Burns.* 55

A man's aye crousest in his ain cause. *Sc. Pr.*

A man's best fortune or his worst is his wife. *Pr.*

A man's best things are nearest him, / Lie close about his feet. *Monckton Milnes.*

A man's fate is his own temper. *Disraeli.*

A man's friends belong no more to him than 60 he to them. *Schopenhauer.*

A man's gift makes room for him. *Pr.*

A man's happiness consists infinitely more in admiration of the faculties of others than in confidence in his own. *Ruskin.*

A man's house is his castle. *Pr.*

A man's power is hooped in by a necessity, which, by many experiments, he touches on every side until he learns its arc. *Emerson.*

A man's task is always light if his heart is 65 light. *Lew Wallace.*

A man's virtue is to be measured not by his extraordinary efforts, but his everyday conduct. *Pascal.*

A man's walking is a succession of falls. *Pr.*

A man's wife is his blessing or his bane. *Gael. Pr.*

Amantes, amentes—In love, in delirium. *Ter.*

5 Amantium iræ amoris redintegratio est—The quarrels of lovers bring about a renewal of love. *Ter.*

A man who cannot mind his own business is not to be trusted with the king's. *Saville.*

A ma puissance—To my power. *M.*

Amare et sapere vix deo conceditur—To be in love and act wisely is scarcely in the power of a god. *Faber.*

Ἁμαρτωλαὶ . . . ἐν ἀνθρώποισιν ἕπονται θνητοῖς—Proneness to sin cleaves fast to mortal men. *Theognis.*

10 Ambigendi locus — Reason for questioning or doubt.

Ambiguas in vulgum spargere voces—To scatter ambiguous reports among the people. *Virg.*

Ambition is not a vice of little people. *Montaigne.*

Ambition is the germ from which all growth in nobleness proceeds. *T. D. English.*

Ambos oder Hammer—One must be either anvil or hammer. *Ger. Pr.*

15 Ame damnée—Mere tool, underling. *Fr.*

Ame de boue—Base, mean soul. *Fr.*

Amende honorable—Satisfactory apology; reparation. *Fr.*

A mensâ et thoro—From bed and board ; divorced.

A menteur, menteur à demi—To a liar, a liar and a half, *i.e.*, one be a match for him. *Fr.*

20 Amentium, haud amantium—Of lunatics, not lovers.

A merchant shall hardly keep himself from doing wrong. *Ecclus.*

A merciful man is merciful to his beast. *Bible.*

A mere madness to live like a wretch and die rich. *Burton.*

A merry heart doeth good like a medicine ; but a broken spirit drieth the bones. *Bible.*

25 A merveille—To a wonder. *Fr.*

Am Golde hängt doch Alles—On gold, after all, hangs everything. *Margaret in "Faust."*

Amici, diem perdidi—Friends, I have lost a day. *Titus* (at the close of a day on which he had done good to no one).

Amici probantur rebus adversis—Friends are proved by adversity. *Cic.*

Amici vitium ni feras, prodis tuum—Unless you bear with the faults of a friend, you betray your own. *Pub. Syr.*

30 Amico d'ognuno, amico di nessuno—Everybody's friend is nobody's friend. *It. Pr.*

Amicorum esse communia omnia — Friends' goods are all common property. *Pr.*

Amicum ita habeas posse ut fieri hunc inimicum scias—Be on such terms with your friend as if you knew he may one day become your enemy. *Laber.*

Amicum perdere est damnorum maximum—To lose a friend is the greatest of losses. *Syr.*

Amicus animæ dimidium—A friend the half of life.

35 Amicus certus in re incerta cernitur—A true friend is seen when fortune wavers. *Ennius.*

Amicus curiæ—A friend to the court, *i.e.*, an uninterested adviser in a case.

Amicus est unus animus in duobus corporibus —A friend is one soul in two bodies. *Arist.*

Amicus humani generis—A friend of the human race.

Amicus Plato, sed magis amica veritas—Plato is my friend, but truth is my divinity (*lit.* more a friend).

Amicus usque ad aras—A friend to the very 40 altar, *i.e.*, to the death.

A mighty maze ! but not without a plan. *Pope.*

A millstone and a man's heart are kept constantly revolving ; where they have nothing to grind, they grind and fray away their own substance. *Logan.*

A mirror is better than a whole gallery of ancestral portraits. *Menzel.*

A miser is as furious about a halfpenny as the man of ambition about the conquest of a kingdom. *Adam Smith.*

A miss is as good as a mile. *Pr.* 45

"Am I to be saved ? or am I to be lost ? " Certain to be lost, so long as you put that question. *Carlyle.*

Amittit famam qui se indignis comparat—He loses repute who compares himself with unworthy people. *Phædr.*

Amittit merito proprium, qui alienum appetit —He who covets what is another's, deservedly loses what is his own. (Moral of the fable of the dog and the shadow.) *Phædr.*

Am meisten Unkraut trägt der fettste Boden —The fattest soil brings forth the most weeds. *Ger. Pr.*

A mob is a body voluntarily bereaving itself 50 of reason and traversing its work. *Emerson.*

A modest confession of ignorance is the ripest and last attainment of philosophy. *R. D. Hitchcock.*

A moment's insight is sometimes worth a life's experience. *Holmes.*

A monarchy is apt to fall by tyranny ; an aristocracy, by ambition ; a democracy, by tumults. *Quarles.*

Among nations the head has alway preceded the heart by centuries. *Jean Paul.*

Among the blind the one-eyed is a king. *Pr.* 55

Amor al cor gentil ratto s' apprende.—Love is quickly learned by a noble heart. *Dante.*

Amor a nullo amato amar perdona—Love spares no loved one from loving. *Dante.*

Amor bleibt ein Schalk, und wer ihm vertraut, ist betrogen—Cupid is ever a rogue, and whoever trusts him is deceived. *Goethe.*

Amore è di sospetti fabro—Love is a forger of suspicions. *It. Pr.*

Amore sitis uniti—Be ye united in love. 60

Amor et melle et felle est fecundissimus—Love is most fruitful both of honey and gall. *Plaut.*

Amor et obœdientia—Love and obedience. *M.*

Amor gignit amorem—Love begets love.

Amor omnibus idem—Love is the same in all. *Virg.*

Amor patriæ—Love of one's country. 65

Amor proximi—Love for one's neighbour.

Amor tutti eguaglia—Love makes all equal. *It. Pr.*

Amoto quæramus seria ludo—Jesting aside, let us give attention to serious business. *Hor.*

Amour avec loyaulté—Love with loyalty. *M.*

Amour fait moult, argent fait tout—Love can do much, but money can do everything. *Fr. Pr.*

Amour propre—Vanity; self-love. *Fr.*

5 A mouse never trusts its life to one hole only. *Plaut.*

Amphora cœpit / Institui: currente rota cur urceus exit?—A vase was begun; why from the revolving wheel does it turn out a worthless pitcher? *Hor.*

Ampliat ætatis spatium sibi vir bonus; hoc est / Vivere bis vitâ posse priore frui—The good man extends the term of his life; it is to live twice, to be able to enjoy one's former life. *Mar.*

Am Rhein, am Rhein, da wachsen uns're Reben—On the Rhine, on the Rhine, there grow our vines! *Claudius.*

Am sausenden Webstuhl der Zeit—On the noisy loom of Time. *Goethe.*

10 Amt ohne Geld macht Diebe—Office without pay makes thieves. *Ger. Pr.*

A mucho hablar, mucho errar—Talk much, err much. *Sp. Pr.*

A multitude of sparks yields but a sorry light. *Amiel.*

Anacharsis among the Scythians—A wise man among unwise.

An acre in Middlesex is better than a principality in Utopia. *Macaulay.*

15 An acre of performance is worth a whole world of promise. *Howell.*

Analysis is not the business of the poet. His office is to portray, not to dissect. *Macaulay.*

Analysis kills spontaneity, just as grain, once it is ground into flour, no longer springs and germinates. *Amiel.*

An ambassador is an honest man sent to lie abroad for the commonwealth. *Sir H Wotten.*

An ambitious man is slave to everybody. *Feijoó.*

20 A name is no despicable matter. Napoleon, for the sake of a great name, broke in pieces almost half a world. *Goethe.*

An appeal to fear never finds an echo in German hearts. *Bismarck.*

An archer is known by his aim, not by his arrows. *Pr.*

An arc in the movement of a large intellect does not differ sensibly from a straight line. *Holmes.*

An Argus at home, a mole abroad. *Pr.*

25 An army, like a serpent, goes on its belly. *Frederick the Great (?).*

A narrow faith has much more energy than an enlightened one *Amiel.*

An artist is a person who has submitted to a law which it is painful to obey, that he may bestow a delight which it is gracious to bestow. *Ruskin.*

An artist is only then truly praised by us when we forget him in his work. *Lessing.*

An artist must have his measuring tools, not in the hand, but in the eye. *Michael Angelo.*

30 An artist should be fit for the best society, and should keep out of it. *Ruskin.*

An ass may bray a good while before he shakes the stars down. *George Eliot.*

A nation which labours, and takes care of the fruits of labour, would be rich and happy, though there were no gold in the universe. *Ruskin.*

Ἀνάγκᾳ δ'οὐδὲ θεοὶ μάχονται—The gods themselves do not fight against necessity. *Gr. Pr.*

Anche il mar, che è si grande, si pacifica—Even the sea, great though it be, grows calm. *It. Pr.*

Anch' io sono pittore—I too am a painter. *Cor-* 35 *reggio before a picture of Raphael's.*

Anche la rana morderebbe se avesse denti—Even the frog would bite if it had teeth. *It. Pr.*

Ancient art corporealises the spiritual; modern spiritualises the corporeal. *Börne.*

Ancient art is plastic; modern, pictorial. *Schlegel.*

And better had they ne'er been born / Who read to doubt, or read to scorn. *Scott.*

And can eternity belong to me, / Poor pensioner 40 on the bounties of an hour? *Young.*

And earthly power doth then show likest God's, / When mercy seasons justice. *Mer. of Ven.*, iv. 1.

And e'en his failings lean'd to virtue's side. *Goldsmith.*

And found no end, in wand'ring mazes lost. *Milton.*

And he is oft the wisest man / Who is not wise at all. *Wordsworth.*

"And is this all?" cried Cæsar at his height, 45 disgusted. *Young.*

An dives sit omnes quærunt, nemo an bonus—Every one inquires if he is rich; no one asks if he is good.

And Mammon wins his way where seraphs might despair. *Byron.*

And much it grieved my heart to think / What man has made of man. *Wordsworth.*

And, often times, excusing of a fault / Doth make the fault worse by the excuse. *King John*, iv. 2.

And so, from hour to hour, we ripe and ripe, / 50 And then, from hour to hour, we rot and rot, / And thereby hangs a tale. *As You Like It*, ii. 7.

And still they gazed, and still the wonder grew, / That one small head could carry all he knew. *Goldsmith.*

And this our life, exempt from public haunt, finds tongues in trees, books in the running brooks, sermons in stones, and good in everything. *As You Like It*, ii. 1.

A needle's eye is wide enough for two friends; the whole world is too narrow for two foes. *Pers. Pr.*

Ἀνέχου καὶ ἀπέχου—Bear and forbear. *Epictetus.*

A nemico che fugge, fa un ponte d'oro—Make 55 a bridge of gold for an enemy who is flying from you. *It. Pr.*

An empty purse fills the face with wrinkles. *Pr*

An epigram often flashes light into regions where reason shines but dimly. *Whipple.*

Ἀνὴρ ὁ φεύγων καὶ πάλιν μαχήσεται—The man who runs away will fight again.

An error is the more dangerous in proportion to the degree of truth which it contains. *Amiel.*

An evening red and morning grey, is a sure sign of a fair day. *Pr.*

A new broom sweeps clean. *Pr.*

A new life begins when a man once secs with his own eyes all that before he has but partially read or heard of. *Goethe.*

A new principle is an inexhaustible source of new views. *Vauvenargues.*

5 An eye like Mars, to threaten or command. *Ham.*, iii. 4.

Anfang heiss, Mittel lau, Ende kalt—The beginning hot, the middle lukewarm, the end cold. *Ger. Pr.*

Angels are bright still, though the brightest fell. *Macb.*, iv. 3.

Angels come to visit us, and we only know them when they are gone. *George Eliot.*

Anger is like / A full-hot horse; who, being allow'd his way, / Self-mettle tires him. *Hen. VIII.*, i. 2.

10 Anger is one of the sinews of the soul. *Fuller.*

Anger resteth in the bosom of fools. *Bible.*

Anger, when it is long in coming, is the stronger when it comes, and the longer kept. *Quarles.*

Anglicè—In English.

Angling is somewhat like poetry; men are to be born so. *Isaak Walton.*

15 Anguis in herbâ—A snake in the grass.

An honest citizen who maintains himself industriously has everywhere as much freedom as he wants. *Goethe.*

An honest man's the noblest work of God. *Pope.*

An honest tale speeds best, being plainly told. *Rich. III.*, iv. 4.

An idle brain is the devil's workshop. *Pr.*

20 An idler is a watch that wants both hands; / As useless if it goes as if it stands. *Cowper.*

An ill-willie (ill-natured) cow should have short horns. *Sc. Pr.*

An ill wind that blows nobody good. *Pr.*

An ill workman quarrels with his tools. *Pr.*

Animal implume bipes—A two-legged animal without feathers. *Plato's definition of man.*

25 Animals can enjoy, but only men can be cheerful. *Jean Paul.*

Anima mundi—The soul of the world.

Animo ægrotanti medicus est oratio—Kind words are as a physician to an afflicted spirit. *Pr.*

Animo et fide—By courage and faith. *M.*

Animo, non astutia—By courage, not by craft. *M.*

30 Animum pictura pascit inani—He feeds his soul on the unreal picture. *Virg.*

Animum rege, qui nisi paret imperat—Rule your spirit well, for if it is not subject to you, it will lord it over you. *Hor.*

Animus æquus optimum est ærumnæ condimentum—A patient mind is the best remedy for trouble. *Plaut.*

Animus furandi—The intention of stealing. *L.*

Animus homini, quicquid sibi imperat, obtinet—The mind of man can accomplish whatever it resolves on.

35 Animus hominis semper appetit agere aliquid—The mind of man is always longing to do something. *Cic.*

Animus non deficit æquus—Equanimity does not fail us. *M.*

Animus quod perdidit optat / Atque in præteritâ se totus imagine versat—The mind yearns after what is gone, and loses itself in dreaming of the past. *Petron.*

An indifferent agreement is better than a good verdict. *Pr.*

An individual helps not; only he who unites with many at the proper time. *Goethe.*

An individual man is a fruit which it cost all 40 the foregoing ages to form and ripen. *Emerson.*

An infant crying in the night, / An infant crying for the light; / And with no language but a cry. *Tennyson.*

An infinitude of tenderness is the chief gift and inheritance of all truly great men. *Ruskin.*

An innocent man needs no eloquence; his innocence is instead of it. *Ben Jonson.*

An iron hand in a velvet glove. *Charles V., said of a gentle compulsion.*

An irreverent knowledge is no knowledge; 45 it may be a development of the logical or other handicraft faculty, but is no culture of the soul of a man. *Carlyle.*

An nescis longas regibus esse manus?—Do you not know that kings have long, *i.e.*, far-grasping, hands? *Ovid.*

An nescis, quantilla prudentia mundus regatur (*or* regatur orbis)?—Do you not know with how very little wisdom the world is governed? *Axel Oxenstjerna to his son.*

An nichts Geliebtes muszt du dein Gemüt / Also verpfänden, dass dich sein Verlust / Untröstbar machte—Never so set your heart on what you love that its loss may render you inconsolable. *Herder.*

Anno domini—In the year of our Lord.

Anno mundi—In the year of the world. 50

Annus mirabilis—The year of wonders.

A noble heart will frankly capitulate to reason. *Schiller.*

A noble man cannot be indebted for his culture to a narrow circle. The world and his native land must act on him. *Goethe.*

An obstinate man does not hold opinions, but they hold him. *Pope.*

A nod for a wise man, and a rod for a fool. 55 *Heb. Pr.*

An old bird is not to be caught with chaff. *Pr.*

An old knave is no babe. *Pr.*

An old man in a house is a good sign in a house. *Heb. Pr.*

An old warrior is never in haste to strike the blow. *Metastasio.*

An open confession is good for the soul. *Pr.* 60

An open door may tempt a saint. *Pr.*

Another such victory and we are done. *Pyrrhus after his second victory over the Romans.*

An ounce of a man's own wit is worth a pound of other peoples'. *Sterne.*

An ounce of cheerfulness is worth a pound of sadness to serve God with. *Fuller.*

An ounce of discretion is worth a pound of 65 wit. *Pr.*

An ounce o' mother-wit is worth a pound o' clergy. *Sc. Pr.*

An ounce of practice is worth a pound of preaching. *Pr.*

An quidquid stultius, quam quos singulos contemnas, eos aliquid putare esse universos?—Can there be any greater folly than the respect you pay to men collectively when you despise them individually? *Cic.*

Ἄνθρωπος ὢν τοῦτ' ἴσθι καὶ μέμνησ' ἀει—Being a man, know and remember always that thou art one. *Philemon Comicus.*

Ἄνθρωπος φύσει ζῷον πολιτικόν—Man is by nature an animal meant for civic life. *Arist.*

Ante lucem—Before daybreak.

5 Ante meridiem—Before noon.

Ante omnia—Before everything else.

Antequam incipias, consulto; et ubi consulueris, facto opus est—Before you begin, consider well; and when you have considered, act. *Sall.*

Ante senectutem curavi, ut bene viverem; in senectute, ut bene moriar—Before old age, it was my chief care to live well; in old age, it is to die well. *Sen.*

Ante tubam tremor occupat artus—We tremble all over before the bugle sounds. *Virg.*

10 Ante victoriam ne canas triumphum—Don't celebrate your triumph before you have conquered.

Anticipation forward points the view. *Burns.*

Antiquâ homo virtute ac fide—A man of antique valour and fidelity. *M.*

Antiquitas sæculi juventus mundi—The ancient time of the world was the youth of the world. *Bacon.*

An unimaginative person can neither be reverent nor kind. *Ruskin.*

15 Anxiety is the poison of human life. *Blair.*

Any nobleness begins at once to refine a man's features; any meanness or sensuality to imbrute them. *Thoreau.*

Any port in a storm. *Sc. Pr.*

Any road will lead you to the end of the world. *Schiller.*

Anything for a quiet life. *Pr.*

20 "A pack of kinless loons;" *said of Cromwell's judges by the Scotch.*

Apage, Satana—Begone, Satan!

A patron is one who looks with unconcern on a man struggling for life in the water, and when he has reached the land encumbers him with help. *Johnson.*

Ἅπαξ λεγόμενον—A word that occurs only once in an author or book.

A peck of March dust is worth a king's ransom. *Pr.*

25 A pedant is a precocious old man. *De Bouffiers.*

A penny hained (saved) is a penny gained. *Sc. Pr.*

Aperçu—A sketch. *Fr.*

A perfect woman, nobly planned, / To warn, to comfort, and command. *Wordsworth.*

Aperit præcordia liber—Wine opens the seals of the heart. *Hor.*

30 A perte de vue—Beyond the range of vision. *Fr.*

Aperto mala cum est mulier, tum demum est bona—A woman when she is openly bad, is at least honest.

Aperto vivere voto—To live with every wish avowed. *Pers.*

A pet lamb makes a cross ram. *Pr.*

Aphorisms are portable wisdom. *W. R. Alger.*

Apio opus est—There is need of parsley, *i.e.*, 35 to strew on the grave, meaning that one is dying.

A pity that the eagle should be mew'd, / While kites and buzzards prey at liberty. *Rich. III.*, i. 1.

A place for everything, and everything in its place. *Pr.*

A plague of sighing and grief; it blows a man up like a bladder. *1 Hen. IV.*, i. 4.

A plant often removed cannot thrive. *Pr.*

A pleasing figure is a perpetual letter of re- 40 commendation. *Bacon.*

Ἄπληστος πίθος—A cask that cannot be filled (being pierced at the bottom with holes.) *Pr.*

A plomb—Perpendicularly; firmly. *Fr.*

A poem is the very image of life expressed in its eternal truth. *Schelling.*

A poet is a nightingale, who sits in the darkness and sings to cheer its own solitude with sweet sounds. *Shelley.*

A poet must be before his age, to be even with 45 posterity. *Lowell.*

A poet must sing for his own people. *Stedman.*

A poet on canvas is exactly the same species of creature as a poet in song. *Ruskin.*

A poison which acts not at once is not therefore a less dangerous poison. *Lessing.*

A position of eminence makes a great man greater and a little man less. *La Bruyère.*

Apothegms are, in history, the same as the 50 pearls in the sand or the gold in the mine. *Erasmus.*

Ἀπ' ἐχθρῶν πολλὰ μανθάνουσιν οἱ σοφοί—Wise men learn many things from their enemies. *Aristoph.*

A point—To a point exactly. *Fr.*

Apollo himself confessed it was ecstasy to be a man among men. *Schiller.*

A posse ad esse—From possibility to actuality.

A posteriori—From the effect to the cause; by 55 induction.

Apothecaries would not sugar their pills unless they were bitter. *Pr.*

A pound of care won't pay an ounce of debt. *Pr.*

Apparent rari nantes in gurgite vasto—A few are seen swimming here and there in the vast abyss. *Virg.*

Appetitus rationi pareat—Let reason govern desire. *Cic.*

Applause is the spur of noble minds, the aim 60 and end of weak ones. *Colton.*

Après la mort le médecin—After death the doctor. *Fr. Pr.*

Après la pluie, le beau temps—After the rain, fair weather. *Fr. Pr.*

Après nous le déluge—After us the deluge! *Mme. de Pompadour.*

A primrose by a river's brim / A yellow primrose was to him, / And it was nothing more. *Wordsworth.*

A prince can mak' a belted knight, / A mar- 65 quis, duke, and a' that; / But an honest man's aboon his might, / Gude faith, he maunna fa' that. *Burns.*

A priori—From the cause to the effect ; by deduction.

A progress of society on the one hand, a decline of souls on the other. *Amiel.*

A promise is a debt. *Gael. Pr.*

A propensity to hope and joy is real riches ; one to fear and sorrow, real poverty. *Hume.*

5 A prophet is not without honour, save in his own country, and in his own house. *Jesus.*

A propos—To the point ; seasonably ; in due time. *Fr.*

A propos de bottes—By-the-bye. *Fr.*

A proverb is good sense brought to a point. *John Morley.*

A proverb is much matter decocted into few words. *Fuller.*

10 Apt alliteration's artful aid. *Churchill.*

Apt to revolt, and willing to rebel, / And never are contented when they're well. *Defoe.*

A puñadas entran las buenas hadas—Good luck pushes its way (*lit.* gets on) by elbowing. *Sp. Pr.*

A purpose you impart is no longer your own. *Goethe.*

A quatre épingles—With four pins, *i.e.*, done up like a dandy. *Fr.*

15 Aquel pierde venta que no tiene que venda—He who has nothing to sell loses his market. *Sp. Pr.*

A quien tiene buena muger, ningun mal le puede venir, que no sea de sufrir—To him who has a good wife no evil can come which he cannot bear. *Sp., Pr.*

Aquilæ senectus—The old age of the eagle. *Ter.*

Aquila non capit muscas—An eagle does not catch flies. *M.*

A qui veut rien n'est impossible—Nothing is impossible to one with a will. *Fr. Pr.*

20 A raconter ses maux, souvent on les soulage—Our misfortunes are often lightened by relating them. *Corneille.*

A ragged colt may make a good horse. *Pr.*

Aranearum telas texere—To weave spiders' webs, *i.e.*, a tissue of sophistry.

Arbeit ist des Blutes Balsam : / Arbeit ist der Tugend Quell—Labour is balm to the blood : labour is the source of virtue. *Herder.*

Arbiter bibendi—The master of the feast (*lit.* the judge of the drinking).

25 Arbiter elegantiarum—The arbitrator of elegances ; the master of the ceremonies.

Arbiter formæ—Judge of beauty.

Arbitrary power is most easily established on the ruins of liberty abused to licentiousness. *Washington.*

Arbore dejecta qui vult ligna colligit—When the tree is thrown down, any one that likes may gather the wood. *Pr.*

Arbores serit diligens agricola, quarum aspiciet baccam ipse nunquam—The industrious husbandman plants trees, not one berry of which he will ever see. *Cic.*

30 "Arcades ambo," *id est*, blackguards both. *Byron.*

Arcana imperii—State, or government, secrets.

Ἀρχὴ ἄνδρα δείξει—Office will prove the man.

Architecture is petrified music. *Schelling, De Staël, Goethe.*

Architecture is the work of nations. *Ruskin.*

Ἄρχων οὐδεὶς ἁμαρτάνει τότε ὅταν ἄρχων ᾖ— 35 No ruler can sin so long as he is a ruler.

Ardeat ipsa licet, tormentis gaudet amantis—Though she is aflame herself, she delights in the torments of her lover. *Juv.*

Ardentia verba—Glowing words.

Arde verde por seco, y pagan justos por pecadores—Green burns for dry, and just men smart (*lit.* pay) for transgressors. *Sp. Pr.*

Ardua molimur : sed nulla nisi ardua virtus—I attempt an arduous task ; but there is no worth that is not of difficult achievement.

A really great talent finds its happiness in 40 execution. *Goethe.*

A reasoning mule will neither lead nor drive. *Mallett.*

A rebours—Reversed. *Fr.*

A reconciled friend is a double enemy. *Pr.*

A reculons—Backwards. *Fr.*

A re decedunt—They wander from the point. 45

A refusal is less than nothing. *Platen.*

Arena sine calce—Sand without cement, *i.e.*, speech unconnected. *Suet.*

Arenæ mandas semina—You are sowing grain in the sand. *Pr.*

A republic is properly a polity in which the state, with its all, is at every man's service ; and every man, with his all, is at the state's service. *Ruskin.*

Ares, no ares, renta me pagues—Plough or not 50 plough, you must pay rent all the same. *Sp. Pr.*

A rez de chaussée—Even with the ground. *Fr.*

Argent comptant—Ready money. *Fr.*

Argent comptant porte medicine—Ready money works great cures. *Fr. Pr.*

Argentum accepi, dote imperium vendidi—I have received money, and sold my authority for her dowry. *Plaut.*

Argilla quidvis imitaberis uda—You may model 55 any form you please out of damp clay. *Hor.*

Argument, as usually managed, is the worst sort of conversation ; as it is generally in books the worst sort of reading. *Swift.*

Argument is like an arrow from a cross-bow, which has great force though shot by a child. *Bacon.*

Argumentum ad crumenam—An appeal to self-interest.

Argumentum ad hominem—An argument in refutation drawn from an opponent's own principles (*lit.* an argument to the man).

Argumentum ad ignorantiam—An argument 60 founded on the ignorance of an adversary.

Argumentum ad invidiam—An argument which appeals to low passions.

Argumentum ad judicium—An appeal to common sense.

Argumentum ad misericordiam—An appeal to the mercy of your adversary.

Argumentum ad populum—An appeal to popular prejudice.

Argumentum ad verecundiam—An appeal to 65 respect for some authority.

Argumentum baculinum—Club argument, *i.e.*, by physical force.

Argus at home, a mole abroad. *It. Pr.*

Argus-eyes—Eyes ever wakeful and watchful

A righteous man regardeth the life of his beast, but the tender mercies of the wicked are cruel. *Bible.*

Ἄριστον μέτρον—A mean or middle course is best. *Cleobulus.*

Ἄριστον μὲν ὕδωρ—Water is best. *Pindar.*

Aristocracy has three successive ages — of superiorities, of privileges, and of vanities; having passed out of the first, it degenerates in the second, and dies away in the third. *Chateaubriand.*

5 Arma amens capio; nec sat rationis in armis— I madly take to arms; but have not wit enough to use them to any purpose. *Virg.*

Arma cerealia—The arms of Ceres, *i.e.*, implements connected with the preparation of corn and bread.

Arm am Beutel, krank am Herzen—Poor in purse, sick at heart. *Goethe.*

Arma pacis fulcra — Arms are the props of peace. *M.*

Arma tenenti omnia dat, qui justa negat—He who refuses what is just, gives up everything to an enemy in arms. *Luc.*

10 Arma, viri, ferte arma; vocat lux ultima victos,/ Nunquam omnes hodie moriemur inulti — Arms, ye men, bring me arms! their last day summons the vanquished. We shall never all die unavenged this day. *Virg.*

Armé de foi hardi—Bold from being armed with faith. *M.*

Armes blanches—Side arms. *Fr.*

Arm in Arm mit dir, / So fordr' ich mein Jahrhundert in die Schranken—Arm in arm with thee, I defy the century to gainsay me. *Schiller.*

Arms and the man I sing. *Virg.*

15 Armuth des Geistes Gott erfreut, / Armuth, und nicht Armseligkeit—It is poverty of spirit that God delights in—poverty, and not beggarliness. *Claudius.*

Armuth ist der sechste Sinn—Poverty is the sixth sense. *Ger. Pr.*

Armuth ist die grösste Plage, / Reichtum ist das höchste Gut — Poverty is the greatest calamity, riches the highest good. *Goethe.*

Armuth ist listig, sie fängt auch einen Fuchs —Poverty is crafty; it outwits (*lit.* catches) even a fox. *Ger. Pr.*

Armuth und Hunger haben viel gelehrte Jünger—Poverty and hunger have many learned disciples. *Ger. Pr.*

20 A rogue is a roundabout fool. *Coleridge.*

A rolling stone gathers no moss. *Pr.*

A Rome comment à Rome — At Rome do as Rome does. *Fr. Pr.*

A royal heart is often hid under a tattered coat. *Dan. Pr.*

Arrectis auribus adsto—I wait with listening ears. *Virg.*

25 Arrière pensée—A mental reservation. *Fr.*

Arrogance is the obstruction of wisdom. *Bion.*

Ars artium omnium conservatrix—The art preservative of all others, *viz.*, printing.

Ars est celare artem—It is the perfection of art to conceal art. *Ovid.*

Ars est sine arte, cujus principium est mentiri, medium laborare, et finis mendicare—It is an art without art, which has its beginning in falsehood, its middle in toil, and its end in poverty. *Applied originally to the pursuits of the Alchemists.*

Ars longa, vita brevis—Art is long, life is short. 30

Ars varia vulpis, ast una echino maxima—The fox has many tricks; the hedgehog only one, and that greatest of all. *Pr.*

Art does not represent things falsely, but truly as they appear to mankind. *Ruskin.*

Arte magistra—By the aid of art. *Virg.*

Art is a jealous mistress. *Emerson.*

Art is long and time is fleeting, / And our 35 hearts, though stout and brave, / Still, like muffled drums, are beating / Funeral marches to the grave. *Longfellow.*

Art is noble, but the sanctuary of the human soul is nobler still. *W. Winter.*

Art is not the bread indeed, but it is the wine of life. *Jean Paul.*

Art is simply a bringing into relief of the obscure thought of Nature. *Amiel.*

Art is the mediatrix of the unspeakable. *Goethe.*

Art is the path of the creator to his work. 40 *Emerson.*

Art is the work of man under the guidance and inspiration of a mightier power. *Hare.*

Artists are of three classes: those who perceive and pursue the good, and leave the evil; those who perceive and pursue the good and evil together, the whole thing as it verily is; and those who perceive and pursue the evil, and leave the good. *Ruskin.*

Artium magister—Master of arts.

Art may err, but Nature cannot miss. *Dryden.*

Art may make a suit of clothes, but Nature 45 must produce a man. *Hume.*

Art must anchor in nature, or it is the sport of every breath of folly. *Hazlitt.*

Art must not be a superficial talent, but must begin further back in man. *Emerson.*

Art, not less eloquently than literature, teaches her children to venerate the single eye. *Willmott.*

Art not thou a man? *Bible.*

Art rests on a kind of religious sense, on a 50 deep, steadfast earnestness; and on this account it unites so readily with religion. *Goethe.*

Art thou afraid of death, and dost thou wish to live for ever? Live in the whole that remains when thou hast long been gone (wenn du lange dahin bist). *Schiller.*

A rude âne rude ânier—A stubborn driver to a stubborn ass. *Fr. Pr.*

A rusty nail, placed near the faithful compass, / Will sway it from the truth, and wreck the argosy. *Scott.*

A sage is the instructor of a hundred ages. *Emerson.*

A saint abroad, a devil at home. *Pr.* 55

A saint in crape is twice a saint in lawn. *Pope.*

As all men have some access to primary truth, so all have some art or power of communication in the head, but only in the artist does it descend into the hand. *Emerson.*

As a man makes his bed, so must he lie. *Gael. Pr.*

As a priest, or interpreter of the holy, is the noblest and highest of all men; so is a sham priest the falsest and basest. *Carlyle.*

A satirical poet is the check of the layman on 60 bad priests. *Dryden.*

As a tree falls, so shall it lie. *Pr.*

ἄσβεστος γέλως—Unquenchable, or Homeric, laughter. *Hom.*

A scalded cat dreads cauld water. *Sc. Pr.*

As dear to me as are the ruddy drops / That visit my sad heart. *Jul. Cæs.,* ii. 1.

A second Daniel. *Mer. of Ven.,* iv. 1.

5 A secret is in my custody if I keep it; but if I blab it, it is I that am prisoner. *Arab Pr.*

A self-denial no less austere than the saint's is demanded of the scholar. *Emerson.*

As ever in my great taskmaster's eye. *Milton.*

As every great evil, so every excessive power wears itself out at last. *Herder.*

As falls the dew on quenchless sands, / Blood only serves to wash ambition's hands. *Byron.*

10 As for discontentments, they are in the politic body like humours in the natural, which are apt to gather a preternatural heat and inflame. *Bacon.*

As formerly we suffered from wickedness, so now we suffer from the laws. *Tac.*

As for murmurs, mother, we grumble a little now and then, to be sure. But there's no love lost between us. *Goldsmith.*

As for talkers and futile persons, they are commonly vain and credulous withal. *Bacon.*

As from the wing no scar the sky retains, / The parted wave no furrow from the keel ; So dies in human hearts the thought of death. *Young.*

15 As good be out of the world as out of the fashion. *Pr.*

As good almost kill a man as kill a good book ; who kills a man kills a reasonable creature, God's image ; but he who destroys a good book kills reason itself. *Milton.*

As guid fish i' the sea as e'er came oot o't. *Sc. Pr.*

As guid may haud (hold) the stirrup as he that loups on. *Sc. Pr.*

A's guid that God sends. *Sc. Pr.*

20 As he alone is a good father who at table serves his children first, so is he alone a good citizen who, before all other outlays, discharges what he owes to the state. *Goethe.*

As he who has health is young, so he who owes nothing is rich. *Pr.*

A short cut is often a wrong cut. *Dan. Pr.*

A sicht (sight) o' you is guid for sair een. *Sc. Pr.*

A sick man's sacrifice is but a lame oblation. *Sir Thomas Browne.*

25 As idle as a painted ship / Upon a painted ocean. *Coleridge.*

A sight to dream of, not to tell. *Coleridge.*

A silent man's words are not brought into court. *Dan. Pr.*

A sillerless (moneyless) man gangs fast through the market. *Sc. Pr.*

A silver key can open an iron lock. *Pr.*

30 A simple child, / That lightly draws its breath, / And feels its life in every limb, / What should it know of death? *Wordsworth.*

A simple maiden in her flower, / Is worth a hundred coats of arms. *Tennyson.*

A simple, manly character need never make an apology. *Emerson.*

As in a theatre, the eyes of men, / After a well-graced actor leaves the stage, / Are idly bent on him that enters next, / Thinking his prattle to be tedious. *Rich. II.,* v. 2.

A single grateful thought turned heavenwards is the most perfect prayer. *Lessing.*

A single moment may transform everything. 35 *Wieland.*

A single word is often a concentrated poem, a little grain of pure gold, capable of being beaten out into a broad extent of gold-leaf. *Trench.*

Asinum sub fræno currere docere—To teach an ass to obey the rein, *i.e.,* to labour in vain. *Pr.*

Asinus ad lyram—An ass at the lyre, *i.e.,* one unsusceptible of music.

Asinus asino, et sus sui pulcher—An ass is beautiful to an ass, and a pig to a pig. *Pr.*

Asinus in tegulis—An ass on the house-tiles. 40

Asinus inter simias—An ass among apes, *i.e.,* a fool among people who make a fool of him. *Pr.*

Asinus in unguento—An ass among perfumes, *i.e.,* things he cannot appreciate.

As is the garden, such is the gardener. *Heb. Pr.*

As is the man, so is his God. *Rückert, Goethe.*

A sip is the most that mortals are permitted 45 from any goblet of delight. *A. B. Alcott.*

Ask, and it shall be given you ; seek, and ye shall find ; knock, and it shall be opened to you. *Jesus.*

Ask for the old paths, where is the good way, and walk therein. *Bible.*

Ask me no questions, and I'll tell you no fibs. *Goldsmith.*

Ask why God made the gem so small, / And why so huge the granite? / Because God meant mankind should set / The higher value on it. *Burns.*

As long as any man exists, there is some need 50 of him. *Emerson.*

As long lives a merry heart as a sad. *Pr.*

As love without esteem is capricious and volatile, esteem without love is languid and cold. *Swift.*

A slow fire makes sweet malt. *Pr.*

A small man, if he stands too near a great, may see single portions well, and, if he will survey the whole, must stand too far off, where his eyes do not reach the details. *Goethe.*

A small sorrow distracts us, a great one makes 55 us collected. *Jean Paul.*

A small unkindness is a great offence. *Hannah More.*

As man, perhaps, the moment of his breath, / Receives the lurking principle of death ; / The young disease, that must subdue at length, / Grows with his growth, and strengthens with his strength. *Pope.*

As many suffer from too much as too little. *Bovee.*

A smart coat is a good letter of introduction. *Dut. Pr.*

As merry as the day is long. *Much Ado,* ii. 1. 60

A smile abroad is oft a scowl at home. *Tennyson.*

A smile re-cures the wounding of a frown. *Shakespeare.*

As much love, so much mind, or heart. *Lat. Pr.*

As much virtue as there is, so much appears ; as much goodness as there is, so much reverence it commands. *Emerson.*

A snapper up of unconsidered trifles. *Winter's Tale*, iv. 2.

A society of people will cursorily represent a certain culture, though there is not a gentleman or a lady in the group. *Emerson.*

A soldier, / Seeking the bubble reputation / Even in the cannon's mouth. *As You Like It*, ii. 7.

A solis ortu usque ad occasum—From where the sun rises to where it sets.

5 A song will outlive all sermons in the memory. *Henry Giles.*

A sorrow's crown of sorrow is remembering happier things. *Tennyson.*

A sorrow shared is but half a trouble, / But a joy that's shared is a joy made double. *Pr.*

A' sottili cascano le brache—The cloak sometimes falls off a cunning man. *It. Pr.*

A soul without reflection, like a pile / Without inhabitant, to ruin runs. *Young.*

10 A spark neglected makes a mighty fire. *Herrick.*

A species is a succession of individuals which perpetuates itself. *Cuvier.*

Asperæ facetiæ ubi multum ex vero traxere, acrem sui memoriam relinquunt—Satire, when it comes near the truth, leaves a sharp sting behind it. *Tac.*

Asperius nihil est humili, cum surgit in altum —Nothing is more offensive than a low-bred man in a high station. *Claud.*

Aspettare e non venire, Stare in letto e non dormire, / Ben servire e non gradire, / Son tre cose da morire—To wait for what never comes, to lie abed and not sleep, to serve and not be advanced, are three things to die of. *It. Pr.*

15 A spirit may be known from only a single thought. *Swedenborg.*

As poor as Job. *Merry Wives*, v. 5.

A spot is most seen on the finest cloth. *Pr.*

As proud go behind as before. *Pr.*

A spur in the head is worth two in the heels. *Pr.*

20 As reason is a rebel unto faith, so is passion unto reason. *Sir T. Browne.*

Assai acqua passa per il molino, che il molinaio non se n'accorge—A good deal of water passes by the mill which the miller takes no note of. *It. Pr.*

Assai basta, e troppo guasta—Enough is enough, and too much spoils. *It. Pr.*

Assai ben balla, à chi fortuna suona—He dances well to whom fortune pipes. *It. Pr.*

Assai è ricco à chi non manca—He is rich enough who has no wants. *It. Pr.*

25 Assai guadagna chi vano sperar perde—He gains a great deal who loses a vain hope. *It. Pr.*

Assai sa, chi non sa, se tacer sa—He who knows not, knows a good deal if he knows how to hold his tongue. *It. Fr.*

Assez a qui se contente—He has enough who is content. *Fr. Pr.*

Assez dort qui rien ne fait—He sleeps enough who does nothing. *Fr. Pr.*

Assez gagne qui malheur perd — He gains enough who gets rid of a sorrow. *Fr. Pr.*

30 Assez sait qui sait vivre et se taire—He knows enough who knows how to live and how to keep his own counsel. *Fr. Pr.*

Assez tôt si assez bien—Soon enough if well enough. *Fr. Pr.*

Assez y a, si trop n'y a—There is enough where there is not too much. *Fr. Pr.*

Associate with the good, and you will be esteemed one of them. *Sp. Pr.*

As some tall cliff, that lifts its awful form, / Swells from the vale, and midway leaves the storm, / Though round its breast the rolling clouds are spread, / Eternal sunshine settles on its head. *Goldsmith.*

As soon as a man is born he begins to die. 35 *Ger. Pr.*

As soon as beauty is sought, not from religion and love, but for pleasure, it degrades the seeker. *Emerson.*

As soon as the soul sees any object, it stops before that object. *Emerson.*

Assume a virtue, if you have it not. *Ham.*, iii. 4.

Assumpsit—An action on a verbal promise. *L.*

Assurance is two-thirds of success. *Gael. Pr.* 40

A state is never greater than when all its superfluous hands are employed in the service of the public. *Hume.*

A state of violence cannot be perpetual, or disaster and ruin would be universal. *Bp. Burnet.*

A statesman requires rather a large converse with men, and much intercourse in life, than deep study of books. *Burke.*

A stern discipline pervades all Nature, which is a little cruel that it may be very kind. *Spenser.*

As the births of living creatures at first are 45 ill-shapen, so are all innovations, which are the births of time. *Bacon.*

As the first order of wisdom is to know thyself, so the first order of charity is to be sufficient for thyself. *Ruskin.*

As the fool thinks, the bell clinks. *Pr.*

As the good man saith, so say we : / As the good woman saith, so it must be. *Pr.*

As the husband is, the wife is : / Thou art mated with a clown, / And the grossness of his nature / Will have weight to drag thee down. *Tennyson.*

As the man is, so is his strength. *Bible.* 50

As the old cock crows, the young one learns. *Pr.*

As there is no worldly gain without some loss, so there is no worldly loss without some gain. *Quarles.*

As the sun breaks through the darkest clouds, / So honour peereth in the meanest habit. *Tam. of Shrew*, iv. 3.

As the youth lives in the future, so the man lives with the past ; no one knows rightly how to live in the present. *Grillparzer.*

As thy days, so shall thy strength be. *Bible.* 55

A still, small voice. *Bible.*

A stitch in time saves nine. *Pr.*

As to the value of conversions, God alone can judge. *Goethe.*

Astra castra, numen lumen—The stars my camp, the deity my light. *M.*

Astræa redux—Return of the goddess of justice. 60

A straight line is the shortest in morals as well as in geometry. *Rahel.*

A strange fish. *Tempest*, ii. 2.

Astra regunt homines, sed regit astra Deus—
The stars govern men, but God governs the stars.

A strenuous soul hates cheap success. *Emerson.*

A strong memory is generally joined to a weak judgment. *Montaigne.*

A strong soil that has produced weeds may be made to produce wheat with far less difficulty than it would cost to make it produce nothing. *Colton.*

5 Astronomy has revealed the great truth that the whole universe is bound together by one all-pervading influence. *Leitch.*

A' Stuarts are no sib (related) to the king (the family name of the Scotch kings being Stuart). *Sc. Pr.*

Astutior coccyge—More crafty than the cuckoo (who deposits her eggs in another bird's nest). *Pr.*

A subject's faults a subject may proclaim, / A monarch's errors are forbidden game. *Cowper.*

A substitute shines brightly as a king, until a king be by. *Mer. of Ven.*, v. 1.

10 A sudden thought strikes me, / Let us swear an eternal friendship. *Canning.*

A sunbeam passes through pollution unpolluted. *Eusebius.*

A surfeit of sweetest things. *Mid. N.'s Dream*, ii. 3.

As water spilt upon the ground, which cannot be gathered up again. *Bible.*

As we advance in life, we learn the limits of our abilities. *Froude.*

15 As we are born to watch, so others are born to watch over us while working. *Goldsmith.*

As weel be oot o' the world as oot o' the fashion. *Sc. Pr.*

As wholesome meat corrupteth to little worms, so good forms and orders corrupt into a number of petty observances. *Bacon.*

As yet a child, not yet a fool to fame, / I lisp'd in numbers, for the numbers came. *Pope.*

As you do to others, expect others to do to you. *Pr.*

20 As you make your bed you must lie on it. *Pr.*

As you sow you shall reap. *Pr.*

A tale never loses in the telling. *Pr.*

A talisman that shall turn base metal into precious, Nature acknowledges not; but a talisman to turn base souls into noble, Nature has given us; and that is a "philosopher's stone," but it is a stone which the builders refuse. *Ruskin.*

A tâtons—Groping. *Fr.*

25 A tattler is worse than a thief. *Pr.*

A (man of) teachable mind will hang about a wise man's neck. *Bp. Patrick.*

At every trifle scorn to take offence ; / That always shows great pride or little sense. *Pope.*

At first one omits writing for a little while ; and then one stays a little while to consider of excuses ; and at last it grows desperate, and one does not write at all. *Swift.*

Ἀθάνατους μὲν πρῶτα θεούς, νόμῳ ὡς διάκειται
Τίμα—Reverence, first of all, the immortal gods, as prescribed by law. *Pythagoras.*

30 At the gates of the forest the surprised man of the world is forced to leave his city estimates of great and small, wise and foolish. *Emerson.*

Atheism is rather in the life than in the heart of man. *Bacon.*

Atheism leaves a man to sense, to philosophy, to natural piety, to laws, to reputation, all which may be guides to an outward moral virtue, though religion were not ; but superstition dismounts all these, and erecteth an absolute monarchy in the minds of men. *Bacon.*

A thief knows a thief, as a wolf knows a wolf. *Pr.*

A thing is the bigger of being shared. *Gael. Pr.*

A thing is what it is, only in and by means of 35 its limit. *Hegel.*

A thing is worth what it *can* do for you, not what you choose to pay for it. *Ruskin.*

A thing of beauty is a joy for ever ; / Its loveliness increases ; it will never / Pass into nothingness. *Keats.*

A thing you don't want is dear at any price. *Pr.*

A thinking man is the worst enemy the Prince of Darkness can have. *Carlyle.*

A third interprets motion, looks, and eyes, / 40 At every word a reputation dies. *Pope.*

A thorn is a changed bud. *T. Lynch.*

A thorough-paced antiquary not only remembers what others have thought proper to forget, but he also forgets what others think proper to remember. *Colton.*

A thousand years scarce serve to form a state ; / An hour may lay it in the dust. *Byron.*

A thread will tie an honest man better than a rope will do a rogue. *Sc. Pr.*

A threatened blow is seldom given. *Pr.* 45

A threefold cord is not quickly broken. *Bible.*

A thrill passes through all men at the reception of a new truth, or at the performance of a great action, which comes out of the heart of nature. . . . By the necessity of our constitution, a certain enthusiasm attends the individual's consciousness of that Divine presence. *Emerson.*

At ingenium ingens / Inculto latet hoc sub corpore—Yet under this rude exterior lies concealed a mighty genius. *Hor.*

At no age should a woman be allowed to govern herself as she pleases. *H. Mann.*

A tocherless dame sits lang at hame. *Sc. Pr.* 50

A toom (empty) pantry maks a thriftless guidwife. *Sc. Pr.*

A tort et à travers—Without consideration ; at random. *Fr.*

A toute force—With all one's force. *Fr.*

A toute seigneur tout honneur—Let every one have his due honour. *Fr. Pr.*

At pulchrum est digito monstrari et dicier hic 55 est—Yet it is a fine thing to be pointed at with the finger and have it said, This is he ! *Persius.*

Atque in rege tamen pater est—And yet in the king there is the father. *Ovid.*

Atqui vultus erat multa et præclara minantis —And yet you had the look of one that promised (*lit.* threatened) many fine things. *Hor.*

A trade of barbarians. *Napoleon on war.*

A tragic farce. *Lille.*

A travelled man has leave to lie. *Pr.* 60

A traveller of taste at once perceives that the wise are polite all the world over, but that fools are only polite at home. *Goldsmith.*

A tree is known by its fruit. *Pr.*

Atria regum hominibus plena sunt, amicis vacua—The courts of kings are full of men, empty of friends. *Sen.*

Atrocitatis mansuetudo est remedium—Gentleness is the antidote for cruelty. *Phædr.*

A true-bred merchant is the best gentleman in the nation. *Defoe.*

A true genius may be known by this sign, that the dunces are all in confederacy against him. *Swift.*

5 A true man hates no one. *Napoleon.*

A truly great genius will be the first to prescribe limits for its own exertions. *Brougham.*

A truth / Looks freshest in the fashion of the day. *Tennyson.*

A truth to an age that has rejected and trampled on it, is not a word of peace, but a sword. *Henry George.*

At spes non fracta—Yet hope is not broken. *M.*

10 Attempts at reform, when they fail, strengthen despotism; as he that struggles tightens those cords he does not succeed in breaking. *Colton.*

Attempt the end, and never stand to doubt; / Nothing's so hard, but search will find it out. *Herrick.*

Attendez à la nuit pour dire que le jour a été beau—Wait till night before saying that the day has been fine. *Fr. Pr.*

Attention makes the genius; all learning, fancy, and science depend on it. *Willmott.*

At the sight of a *man* we too say to ourselves, Let us be *men. Amiel.*

15 At thirty, man suspects himself a fool, / Knows it at forty, and reforms his plan. / At fifty, chides his infamous delay. / Pushes his prudent purpose to resolve. / Resolves—and re-resolves; then dies the same. *Young.*

At twenty years of age, the will reigns; at thirty, the wit; and at forty, the judgment. *Grattan.*

A tu hijo, buen nombre y oficio—To your son a good name and a trade. *Sp. Pr.*

A tutti non si adatta una sola scarpa—One shoe does not fit every foot. *It. Pr.*

At vindictum bonum vita jucundius ipsa. Nempe hoc indocti—But revenge is a blessing sweeter than life itself; so rude men feel. *Juv.*

20 At whose sight all the stars / Hide their diminished heads. *Milton.*

Au bon droit—By good right. *Fr.*

Au bout de son Latin—At his wit's end (*lit.* at the end of his Latin). *Fr.*

Au bout du compte—After the close of the account; after all. *Fr.*

Auch aus entwölkter Höhe / Kann der zündende Donner schlagen; / Darum in deinen fröhlichen Tagen / Fürchte des Unglücks tückische Nähe—Even out of a cloudless heaven the flaming thunderbolt may strike; therefore in thy days of joy have a fear of the spiteful neighbourhood of misfortune. *Schiller.*

25 Auch Bücher haben ihr Erlebtes, das ihnen nicht entzogen werden kann—Even books have their lifetime, of which no one can deprive them. *Goethe.*

Auch das Schöne muss sterben—Even what is beautiful must die. *Schiller.*

Auch der Löwe muss sich vor der Mücke wehren—Even the lion has to defend itself against flies. *Ger. Pr.*

Auch die Gerechtigkeit trägt eine Binde, / Und schliesst die Augen jedem Blendwerk zu—Even Justice wears a bandage, and shuts her eyes on everything deceptive. *Goethe.*

Auch die Kultur, die alle Welt beleckt, / Hat auf den Teufel sich erstreckt—Culture, which has licked all the world into shape, has reached even the devil. *Goethe.*

Auch die Kunst ist Himmelsgabe, / Borgt sie 30 gleich von ird'scher Glut—Art is a gift of Heaven, yet does it borrow its fire from earthly passion. *Schiller.*

Auch ein Haar hat seinen Schatten—Even a hair casts its shadow. *Ger. Pr.*

Auch für die rauhe Brust giebt's Augenblicke / Wo dunkle Mächte Melodien wecken—Even the rude breast has moments in which dark powers awaken melodies. *Körner.*

Auch ich war ein Jüngling mit lockigem Haar, / An Mut und an Hoffnungen reich—I too was once a youth with curly locks, rich in courage and in hopes. *Lortzing.*

Auch ich war in Arkadien geboren, / Und ward daraus entführt vom neidischen Glücke. / Ist hier der Rückweg? fragt' ich jede Brücke, / Der Eingang hier? fragt' ich an allen Thoren—I too was born in Arcadia, and was lured away by envious Fortune. "Is this the way back?" asked I at every bridge-way; "This the entrance?" asked I at every portal. *Rückert.*

Auch in der That ist Raum für Ueberlegung— 35 Even in the moment of action there is room for consideration. *Goethe.*

Auch was Geschriebenes forderst du, Pedant? / Hast du noch keinen Mann, nicht Mannes-Wort gekannt?—Dost thou, O pedant, require something written too? Hast thou never yet known a man, not word of man? *Faust.*

Au courant—Perfectly acquainted with. *Fr.*

Auctor pretiosa facit—The giver makes the gift valuable. *M.*

Aucto splendore resurgo—I rise again with access of splendour. *M.*

Aucun chemin de fleurs ne conduit à la gloire 40 —No path of flowers conducts to glory. *La Font.*

Audacia pro muro habetur—Daring is regarded as a wall. *Sallust.*

Audacter calumniare, semper aliquid hæret—Calumniate boldly, always some of it sticks. *Bacon.*

Audacter et sincere—Boldly and heartily. *M.*

Audax ad omnia fœmina, quæ vel amat vel odit—A woman, when she either loves or hates, will dare anything. *Pr.*

Audax omnia perpeti / Gens humana ruit per 45 vetitum et nefas—Daring to face all hardships, the human race dashes through every human and divine restraint. *Hor.*

Aude aliquid brevibus Gyaris et carcere dignum, / Si vis esse aliquis—Dare to do something worthy of transportation and imprisonment, if you wish to be somebody. *Juv.*

Audendo magnus tegitur timor—Great fear is concealed under daring. *Lucan.*

Audentes Fortuna juvat—Fortune favours the brave. *Virg.*

Au dernier les os—For the last the bones. *Fr. Pr.*

Aude sapere—Dare to be wise. 50

Au désespoir—In despair. *Fr.*

Audi alteram partem—Hear the other party; hear both sides. *L. Max.*

Audiatur et altera pars—Let the other side also have a hearing. *Sen.*

Audio sed taceo—I hear, but say nothing. *M.*

Audita querela—The complaint having been investigated. *L.*

5 Auditque vocatus Apollo—And Apollo hears when invoked. *Virg.*

Audi, vide, tace, si vis vivere in pace—Use your ears and eyes, but hold your tongue, if you would live in peace.

Au fait—Expert; skilful. *Fr.*

Auf dem Grund des Glaubenmeeres / Liegt die Perle der Erkenntniss ; / Heil dem Taucher, der sie findet—At the bottom of the faith-sea lies the pearl of knowledge ; happy the diver that finds it. *Bodenstedt.*

Auf den Bergen ist Freiheit—On the mountains is freedom. *Schiller.*

10 Auf die warnenden Symptome sieht kein Mensch, auf die Schmeichelnden und Versprechenden allein ist die Aufmerksamkeit gerichtet—To the warning word no man has respect, only to the flattering and promising is his attention directed. *Goethe.*

Auf Dinge, / die nicht mehr zu ändern sind, / Muss auch kein Blick zurück mehr fallen ! Was / Gethan ist, ist gethan und bleibt's—On things which are no more to be changed a backward glance must be no longer cast ! What is done is done, and so remains. *Schiller.*

Auf ebnem Boden straucheln ist ein Scherz, / Ein Fehltritt stürzt vom Gipfel dich herab—To stumble on a level surface is matter of jest ; by a false step on a height you are hurled to the ground. *Goethe.*

Auferimur cultu : gemmis auroque teguntur / Omnia ; pars minima est ipsa puella sui—Dress deceives us : jewels and gold hide everything : the girl herself is the least part of herself. *Ovid.*

Aufgeschoben ist nicht aufgehoben—Postponed is not abandoned. *Ger. Pr.*

15 Aufklärung—Illuminism. *Ger.*

Au fond—To the bottom. *Fr.*

Aufrichtig zu sein kann ich versprechen ; unparteiisch zu sein aber nicht—I can promise to be candid, but not to be impartial. *Goethe.*

Auf Teufel reimt der Zweifel nur ; / Da bin ich recht am Platze—Only Zweifel (doubt) rhymes to Teufel (devil) ; here am I quite at home. *The Sceptic in " Faust."*

Auf Wind und Meer gebautes Glück ist schwankend—The fortune is insecure that is at the mercy of wind and wave. *Gutzkow.*

20 Augiæ cloacas purgare—To cleanse the Augean stables, *i.e.*, achieve an arduous and disagreeable work. *Sen.*

Augusto felicior, Trajano melior—A more fortunate man than Augustus, and a more excellent than Trajan. *Eutrop.*

Aujourd'hui marié, demain marri—To-day married, to-morrow marred. *Fr. Pr.*

Aula regis—The court of the king.

Auld folk are twice bairns. *Sc. Pr.*

25 Auld Nature swears the lovely dears, / Her noblest work she classes, O ; / Her 'prentice han' she tried on man, / An' then she made the lasses, O. *Burns.*

Au nouveau tout est beau—Everything is fine that is new. *Fr. Pr.*

Au pis aller—At the worst. *Fr.*

Au plaisir fort de Dieu—By the all-powerful will of God. *M.*

Aura popularis—Popular favour (*lit.* breeze).

Aurea mediocritas—The golden mean. 30

Aurea nunc vere sunt sæcula ; plurimus auro / Venit honos : auro conciliatur amor—The age we live in is the true age of gold ; by gold men attain to the highest honour, and win even love itself. *Ovid.*

Aureo piscari hamo—To fish with a golden hook.

Au reste—For the rest. *Fr.*

Au revoir—Farewell till we meet again. *Fr.*

Auri sacra fames—The accursed lust of gold. 35 *Virg.*

Auro loquente nihil pollet quævis ratio—When gold speaks, no reason the least avails. *Pr.*

Aurora musis amica—Aurora is friendly to the Muses. *Pr.*

Aus dem Gebet erwächst des Geistes Sieg—It is from prayer that the spirit's victory springs. *Schillerbuch.*

Aus dem Kleinsten setzt / Sich Grosses zusammen zuletzt, / Und keins darf fehlen von allen, / Wenn nicht das Ganze soll fallen—Out of the smallest a great is at length composed, and none of all can fail, unless the whole is fated to break up. *Rückert.*

Aus dem Leben heraus sind der Wege drei 40 dir geöffnet, / Zum Ideale führt einer, der andre zum Tod—Two ways are open for thee out of life ; one conducts to the ideal, the other to death. *Schiller.*

Aus der Jugendzeit, aus der Jugendzeit / Klingt ein Lied mir immerdar, / O wie liegt so weit, O wie liegt so weit, / Was mein einst war—Out of youth-time, out of youth-time sounds a lay of mine ever ; O how so far off lies, how so far off lies, what once was mine ! *Rückert.*

Aus der schlechtesten Hand kann Wahrheit noch mächtig wirken ; / Bei dem Schönen allein macht das Gefäss den Gehalt—Truth may work mightily though in the hand of the sorriest instrument ; in the case of the beautiful alone the casket constitutes the jewel (*lit.* the vessel makes the content). *Schiller.*

Aus derselben Ackerkrume / Wächst das Unkraut wie die Blume / Und das Unkraut macht sich breit—Out of the same gardenmould grows the weed as the flower, and the weed flaunts itself abroad. *Bodenstedt.*

A useful trade is a mine of gold. *Pr.*

A useless life is an early death. *Goethe.* 45

Aus grauser Tiefe tritt das Höhe kühn hervor; / Aus harter Hülle kämpft die Tugend sich hervor ; / Der Schmerz ist die Geburt der höhern Naturen—Out of a horrible depth the height steps boldly forth ; out of a hard shell virtue fights its way to the light ; pain is the birth (medium) of the higher natures. *Tiedge.*

Aus jedem Punkt im Kreis zur Mitte geht ein Steg. / Vom fernsten Irrtum selbst zu Gott zurück ein Weg—There is a way from every point in a circle to the centre ; from the farthest error there is a way back to God Himself. *Rückert.*

Aus Mässigkeit entspringt ein reines Glück—Out of moderation a pure happiness springs. *Goethe.*

Auspicium melioris ævi—The pledge of happier times. *M.*

Aussitôt dit, aussitôt fait—No sooner said than done. *Fr.*

Aus ungelegten Eiern werden spät junge Hühner—Chickens are long in coming out of unlaid eggs. *Ger. Pr.*

Ausus est vana contemnere—He dared to scorn vain fears.

5 Aut amat, aut odit mulier; nil est tertium—A woman either loves or hates; there is no alternative. *Pub. Syr.*

Autant chemine un homme en un jour qu'un limaçon en cent ans—A man travels as far in a day as a snail in a hundred years. *Fr. Pr.*

Autant dépend chiche que large, et à la fin plus davantage—Niggard spends as much as generous, and in the end a good deal more. *Fr. Pr.*

Autant en emporte le vent—All idle talk (*lit.* so much the wind carries away). *Fr. Pr.*

Autant pèche celui que tient le sac que celui qui met dedans—He is as guilty who holds the bag as he who puts in. *Fr. Pr.*

10 Autant vaut l'homme comme il s'estime—A man is rated by others as he rates himself. *Fr. Pr.*

Aut bibat, aut abeat—Either drink or go.

Aut Cæsar aut nihil—Either Cæsar or nobody. *M. of Cæsar Borgia.*

Authority, not majority. *Stahl.*

Authors alone, with more than savage rage, / Unnatural war with brother authors wage. *Churchill.*

15 Authors are martyrs, witnesses to the truth, or else nothing. *Carlyle.*

Authors may be divided into falling stars, planets, and fixed stars: the first have a momentary effect; the second, a much longer duration; and the third are unchangeable, possess their own light, and shine for all time. *Schopenhauer.*

Aut insanit homo, aut versus facit—The man is either mad, or he is making verses. *Hor.*

Aut non tentaris, aut perfice — Either don't attempt it, or go through with it. *Ovid.*

Auto-da-fé—An act of faith; a name applied to certain proceedings of the Inquisition connected with the burning of heretics.

20 'Αυτὸς ἔφα—He himself said it; *ipse dixit.*

Aut prodesse volunt aut delectare poetæ—Poets wish either to profit or to please. *Hor.*

Autrefois acquis—Acquitted before. *Fr.*

Aut regem aut fatuum nasci oportere—A man ought to be born either a king or a fool. *Pr. in Sen.*

Autre temps, autres mœurs—Other times, other fashions. *Fr.*

25 Aut vincere aut mori—Either to conquer or die.

Aut virtus nomen inane est, / Aut decus et pretium recte petit experiens vir — Either virtue is an empty name, or the man of enterprise justly aims at honour and reward. *Hor.*

Aux armes—To arms. *Fr.*

Aux grands maux les grands remèdes—Desperate maladies require desperate remedies. *Fr. Pr.*

Auxilium ab alto—Help from above. *M.*

30 Auxilium meum a Domino—My help cometh from the Lord. *M.*

Avant propos—Prefatory matter. *Fr.*

Avaler des couleuvres—To put up with abuse (*lit.* swallow snakes). *Fr.*

A valiant and brave soldier seeks rather to preserve one citizen than to destroy a thousand enemies. *Scipio.*

Avancez—Advance. *Fr.*

Avarice has ruined more men than prodigality. 35 *Colton.*

Avarus, nisi cum moritur, nil recte facit—A miser does nothing right except when he dies. *Pr.*

Avec un Si on mettrait Paris dans une bouteille—With an "if" one might put Paris in a bottle. *Fr. Pr.*

A verbis ad verbera—From words to blows.

A verse may find him who a sermon flies, / And turn delight into a sacrifice. *George Herbert.*

A very excellent piece of villany. *Tit. Andron.,* 40 ii. 3.

A very good woman may make but a paltry man. *Pope.*

A veste logorata poco fede vien prestata—A shabby coat finds small credit. *It. Pr.*

A vinculo matrimonii—From the bond or tie of marriage.

A virtuous name is the sole precious good for which queens and peasants' wives must contest together. *Schiller.*

Avise la fin—Consider the end. *Fr.* 45

Avito viret honore—He flourishes with inherited honours. *M.*

Avoid the evil, and it will avoid thee. *Gael. Pr.*

A volonté—At will. *Fr.*

A votre santé—To your health. *Fr.*

A wee bush is better than nae bield (shelter). 50 *Sc. Pr.*

A weel-bred dog gaes oot when he sees them preparing to kick him oot. *Sc. Pr.*

A well-bred man is always sociable and complaisant. *Montaigne.*

A well-cultivated mind is, so to say, made up of all the minds of the centuries preceding. *Fontenelle.*

A well-governed appetite is a great part of liberty. *Sen.*

A well-written life is almost as rare as a well- 55 spent one. *Carlyle.*

A wicked fellow is the most pious when he takes to it. He'll beat you all in piety. *Johnson.*

A wilful man must have his way. *Pr.*

A willing mind makes a light foot. *Pr.*

A wise man gets learning frae them that hae nane. *Sc. Pr.*

A wise man is never less alone than when 60 alone. *Pr.*

A wise man is strong; yea, a man of knowledge increaseth strength. *Bible.*

A wise man neither suffers himself to be governed, nor attempts to govern others. *La Bruyère.*

A wise man should have money in his head, but not in his heart. *Swift.*

A wise man will make more opportunities than he finds. *Bacon.*

A wise physician, skill'd our wounds to heal, / Is more than armies to the public weal. *Pope.*

A wise scepticism is the first attribute of a good critic. *Lowell.*

A wise writer does not reveal himself here and there, but everywhere. *Lowell.*

A witless heed (head) mak's weary feet. *Sc. Pr.*

5 A wit with dunces, and a dunce with wits. *Pope.*

A wolf in sheep's clothing. *Pr.*

A woman conceals what she does not know. *Pr.*

A woman has two smiles that an angel might envy : the smile that accepts the lover before the words are uttered, and the smile that lights on the first-born baby, and assures it of a mother's love. *Haliburton.*

A woman in love is a very poor judge of character. *J. G. Holland.*

10 A woman moved is like a fountain troubled, / Muddy, ill-seeming, thick, bereft of beauty. *Tam. of Sh.*, v. 2.

A woman's friendship borders more closely on love than a man's. *Coleridge.*

A woman's head is always influenced by her heart ; but a man's heart is always influenced by his head. *Lady Blessington.*

A woman sometimes scorns what best contents her. *Two Gent. of Ver.*, iii. 1.

A woman's whole life is a history of the affections. *W. Irving.*

15 A word and a stone let go cannot be recalled. *Pr.*

A word from a friend is doubly enjoyable in dark days. *Goethe.*

A word once vulgarised can never be rehabilitated. *Lowell.*

A word sooner wounds than heals. *Goethe.*

A word spoken in season, at the right moment, is the mother of ages. *Carlyle.*

20 A word spoken in due season, how good is it? *Bible.*

A work of real merit finds favour at last. *A. B. Alcott.*

A world all sincere, a believing world ; the like has been ; the like will again be—cannot help being. *Carlyle.*

A world in the hand is worth two in the bush. *Emerson.*

A world this in which much is to be done, and little to be known. *Goethe.*

25 A worn-out sinner is sometimes found to make the best declaimer against sin. *Lamb.*

A worthless man will always remain worthless, and a little mind will not, by daily intercourse with great minds, become an inch greater. *Goethe.*

A wounded spirit who can bear ? *Bible.*

A wound never heals so well that the scar cannot be seen. *Dan. Pr.*

A wreck on shore is a beacon at sea. *Dut. Pr.*

30 A wretched soul, bruised with adversity, / We bid be quiet when we hear it cry ; / But were we burdened with like weight of pain, / As much, or more, we should ourselves complain. *Com. of Errors*, ii. 1.

Ay, but to die, and go we know not where ; / To lie in cold obstruction and to rot. *Meas. for Meas.*, iii. 1.

Aye free, aff-han' your story tell, when wi' a bosom crony ; / But still keep something to yoursel' / Ye scarcely tell to ony. *Burns.*

Aye in a hurry, and aye ahint. *Sc. Pr.*

Ay, every inch a king. *King Lear*, iv. 6.

Ay me! for aught that ever I could read, / 35 Could ever hear by tale or history, / The course of true love never did run smooth. *Mid. N.'s Dream*, i. 1.

Aymez loyauté—Love loyalty. *M.*

A young man idle, an old man needy. *It. Pr.*

Ay, sir, to be honest as this world goes, is to be one man picked out of two thousand. *Ham.*, ii. 2.

B.

Bachelor, a peacock ; betrothed, a lion ; wedded, an ass. *Sp. Pr.*

"Bad company," muttered the thief, as he 40 stepped to the gallows between the hangman and a monk. *Dut. Pr.*

Bad is by its very nature negative, and can do nothing ; whatsoever enables us to do anything, is by its very nature good. *Carlyle.*

Bad laws are the worst sort of tyranny. *Burke.*

Bad men excuse their faults ; good men will leave them. *Ben Jonson.*

Bal abonné—A subscription ball. *Fr.*

Bal champêtre—A country ball. *Fr.* 45

Ballon d'essai—A balloon sent up to ascertain the direction of the wind ; any test of public feeling. *Fr.*

Banish the canker of ambitious thoughts. 2 *Hen. VI.*, i. 2.

Bankrupt of life, yet prodigal of ease. *Dryden.*

Barba bagnata è mezza rasa. A beard well lathered is half shaved. *It. Pr.*

Barbæ tenus sapientes—Wise as far as the beard 50 goes. *Pr.*

Barbarism is no longer at our frontiers ; it lives side by side with us. *Amiel.*

Barbarism is the non-appreciation of what is excellent. *Goethe.*

Barbarus hic ego sum, quia non intelligor ulli —I am a barbarian here, for no one understands what I say. *Ovid.*

Barbouillage—Scribbling. *Fr.*

Barking dogs seldom bite. *Pr.* 55

Bas bleu—A blue-stocking. *Fr.*

Base envy withers at another's joy, / And hates that excellence it cannot reach. *Thomson.*

Base in kind, and born to be a slave. *Cowper.*

Base men, being in love, have then a nobility in their natures more than is native to them. *Othello*, ii. 1.

Base souls have no faith in great men. *Rous-* 60 *seau.*

Bashfulness is an ornament to youth, but a reproach to old age. *Arist.*

Bashfulness is but the passage from one season of life to another. *Bp. Hurd.*

Basis virtutum constantia — Constancy is the basis of all the virtues. *M.*

Battering the gates of heaven with storms of prayer. *Tennyson.*

Battle's magnificently stern array. *Byron.*

Be a philosopher; but, amidst all your philosophy, be still a man. *Hume.*

Beard was never the true standard of brains. *Fuller.*

Bear one another's burdens. *St. Paul.*

5 Bear wealth, poverty will bear itself. *Pr.*

Be a sinner and sin manfully (fortiter), but believe and rejoice in Christ more manfully still. *Luther to Melanchthon.*

Be as you would seem to be. *Pr.*

Beatæ memoriæ—Of blessed memory.

Beati monoculi in regione cæcorum—Blessed are the one-eyed among those who are blind. *Pr.*

10 Beatus ille qui procul negotiis, / Ut prisca gens mortalium, / Paterna rura bobus exercet suis, / Solutus omni fœnore—Happy the man who, remote from busy life, is content, like the primitive race of mortals, to plough his paternal lands with his own oxen, freed from all borrowing and lending. *Hor.*

Beaucoup de mémoire et peu de jugement—A retentive memory and little judgment. *Fr. Pr.*

Beau idéal—Ideal excellence, or one's conception of perfection in anything. *Fr.*

Beau monde—The fashionable world. *Fr.*

Beauté et folie sont souvent en compagnie—Beauty and folly go often together. *Fr. Pr.*

15 Beauties in vain their pretty eyes may roll; / Charms strike the sight, but merit wins the soul. *Pope.*

Beautiful it is to understand and know that a thought did never yet die; that as thou, the originator thereof, hast gathered it and created it from the whole past, so thou wilt transmit to the whole future. *Carlyle.*

Beauty blemished once, for ever's lost. *Shakespeare.*

Beauty can afford to laugh at distinctions; it is itself the greatest distinction. *Bovee.*

Beauty carries its dower in its face. *Dan. Pr.*

20 Beauty depends more on the movement of the face than the form of the features. *Mrs. Hall.*

Beauty doth varnish age, as if new-born, / And gives the crutch the cradle's infancy. / O, 'tis the sun that maketh all things shine. *Love's L's. Lost, iv. 3.*

Beauty draws us with a single hair. *Pope.*

Beauty is a good letter of introduction. *Ger. Pr.*

Beauty is a hovering, shining, shadowy form, the outline of which no definition holds. *Goethe.*

25 Beauty is an all-pervading presence. *Channing.*

Beauty is a patent of nobility. *G. Schwab.*

Beauty is as summer fruits, which are easy to corrupt and cannot last. *Bacon.*

Beauty is a witch, / Against whose charms faith melteth into blood. *Much Ado, ii. 1.*

Beauty is bought by judgment of the eye, / Not utter'd by base sale of chapmen's tongues. *Love's L's. Lost, ii. 1.*

30 Beauty is but a vain and doubtful good. *Shakespeare.*

Beauty is everywhere a right welcome guest. *Goethe.*

Beauty is never a delusion. *Hawthorne.*

Beauty is the flowering of virtue. *Gr. Pr.*

Beauty is the highest principle and the highest aim of art. *Goethe.*

Beauty is the pilot of the young soul. *Emerson.* 35

Beauty is the purgation of superfluities. *Michael Angelo.*

Beauty is truth, truth beauty—that is all / Ye know on earth, and all ye need to know. *Keats.*

Beauty is worse than wine; it intoxicates both holder and the beholder. *Zimmermann.*

Beauty, like wit, to judges should be shown; / Both most are valued where they best are known. *Lyttelton.*

Beauty lives with kindness. *Two Gen. of* 40 *Ver., iv. 2.*

Beauty provoketh thieves sooner than gold. *As You Like It, i. 3.*

Beauty should be the dowry of every man and woman. *Emerson.*

Beauty stands / In the admiration only of weak minds, / Led captive. *Milton.*

Beauty's tears are lovelier than her smile. *Campbell.*

Beauty too rich for use; for earth too dear. 45 *Rom. and Jul., i. 5.*

Beauty, when unadorned, adorned the most. *Thomson.*

Beauty without expression tires. *Emerson.*

Beauty without grace is a violet without smell. *Pr.*

Beaux esprits—Men of wit. *Fr.*

Be bold, be bold, and everywhere be bold. 50 *Spenser.*

Be checked for silence, / But never tax'd for speech. *All's Well, i. 1.*

Be commonplace and cringing, and everything is within your reach. *Beaumarchais.*

Bedenkt, der Teufel der ist alt, / So werdet alt ihn zu verstehen—Consider, the devil is old; therefore grow old to understand him. *Goethe.*

Be discreet in all things, and so render it unnecessary to be mysterious about any. *Wellington.*

Be England what she will, / With all her faults 55 she is my country still. *Churchill.*

Bees will not work except in darkness; thought will not work except in silence; neither will virtue work except in secrecy. *Carlyle.*

Before a leaf-bud has burst, its whole life acts; in the full-blown flower there is no more; in the leafless root there is no less. *Emerson.*

Before every one stands an image (Bild) of what he ought to be; so long as he is not that, his peace is not complete. *Rückert.*

Before honour is humility. *Bible.*

Before man made us citizens, great Nature 60 made us men. *Lowell.*

Before the curing of a strong disease, / Even in the instant of repair and health, / The fit is strongest; evils that take leave, / On their departure most of all show evil. *King John, iii. 4.*

Before the immense possibilities of man, all mere experience, all past biography, however spotless and sainted, shrinks away. *Emerson.*

Before the revelations of the soul, Time, Space, and Nature shrink away. *Emerson.*

Before you trust a man, eat a peck of salt with him. *Pr.*

Beggars, mounted, run their horse to death. *3 Hen. VI.,* i. 4.

Beggars must not be choosers. *Pr.*

Beggar that I am, I am even poor in thanks. *Ham.* ii. 2.

Begnügt euch doch ein Mensch zu sein—Let it content thee that thou art a man. *Lessing.*

5 Begun is half done. *Pr.*

Behaupten ist nicht beweisen—Assertion is no proof. *Ger. Pr.*

Behaviour is a mirror in which each one shows his image. *Goethe.*

Behind a frowning providence / God hides a shining face. *Cowper.*

Behind us, as we go, all things assume pleasing forms, as clouds do afar off. *Emerson.*

10 Behind every individual closes organisation ; before him opens liberty. *Emerson.*

Behind every mountain lies a vale. *Dut. Pr.*

Behold how great a matter a little fire kindleth. *St. James.*

Beholding heaven and feeling hell. *Moore.*

Behold now is the accepted time. *St. Paul.*

15 Behold the child, by Nature's kindly law, / Pleased with a rattle, tickled with a straw. *Pope.*

Bei den meisten Menschen gründet sich der Unglaube in einer Sache auf blinden Glauben in einer andern—With most men unbelief in one thing is founded on blind belief in another. *Lichtenberg.*

Bei Geldsachen hört die Gemütlichkeit auf— When money is in question, good day to friendly feeling. *D. Hansemann.*

Beinahe bringt keine Mücke um—Almost never killed a fly. *Ger. Pr.*

Being alone when one's belief is firm, is not to be alone. *Auerbach.*

20 Being done, / There is no pause. *Othello,* v. 2.

Being without well-being is a curse ; and the greater being, the greater curse. *Bacon.*

Be in possession, and thou hast the right, and sacred will the many guard it for thee. *Schiller.*

Be it never so humble, there's no place like home. *J. H. Payne.*

Bei wahrer Liebe ist Vertrauen—With true love there is trust. *Ph. Reger.*

25 Be just and fear not; / Let all the ends thou aim'st at be thy country's, / Thy God's, and truth's. *Henry VIII.,* iii. 2.

Be just before you be generous. *Pr.*

Beleidigst du einen Mönch, so knappen alle Kuttenzipfel bis nach Rom—Offend but one monk, and the lappets of all cowls will flutter as far as Rome. *Ger. Pr.*

Bel esprit—A person of genius ; a brilliant mind. *Fr.*

Belief and love,—a believing love, will relieve us of a vast load of care. *Emerson.*

30 Belief consists in accepting the affirmations of the soul; unbelief, in denying them. *Emerson.*

Believe not each accusing tongue, / As most weak persons do; / But still believe that story wrong / Which ought not to be true. *Sheridan.*

Believe not every spirit. *St. John.*

Bella ! horrida bella !—War ! horrid war ! *Virg.*

Bella femmina che ride, vuol dire borsa che piange—The smiles of a pretty woman are the tears of the purse. *It. Pr.*

Bella matronis detestata—Wars detested by 35 mothers. *Hor.*

Belle, bonne, riche, et sage, est une femme en quatre étages—A woman who is beautiful, good, rich, and wise, is four stories high. *Fr. Pr.*

Belle chose est tôt ravie—A fine thing is soon snapt up. *Fr. Pr.*

Bellet ein alter Hund, so soll man aufschauen —When an old dog barks, one must look out. *Ger. Pr.*

Bellicæ virtutis præmium—The reward of valour in war. *M.*

Bellua multorum capitum—The many-headed 40 monster, *i.e.,* the mob.

Bellum internecinum—A war of extermination.

Bellum ita suscipiatur, ut nihil aliud nisi pax quæsita videatur—War should be so undertaken that nothing but peace may seem to be aimed at. *Cic.*

Bellum nec timendum nec provocandum—War ought neither to be dreaded nor provoked. *Plin. the Younger.*

Bellum omnium in omnes—A war of all against all.

Bellum, pax rursus—A war, and again a peace. 45 *Ter.*

βέλτιον θανεῖν ἅπαξ ἢ διὰ βίον τρέμειν— Better die outright than be all one's life long in terror. *Æsop.*

Bemerke, höre, schweige. Urteile wenig, frage viel—Take note of what you see, give heed to what you hear, and be silent. Judge little, inquire much. *Platen.*

Be modest without diffidence, proud without presumption. *Goethe.*

Benchè la bugia sia veloce, la verità l'arriva— Though a lie may be swift, truth overtakes it. *It. Pr.*

Beneath the loveliest dream there coils a fear. 50 *T. Watts.*

Beneath the rule of men entirely great, the pen is mightier than the sword. *Bulwer Lytton.*

Beneath those rugged elms, that yew-tree's shade, / Where heaves the turf in many a mouldering heap, / Each in his narrow cell for ever laid, / The rude forefathers of the hamlet sleep. *Gray.*

Ben è cieco chi non vede il sole—He is very blind who does not see the sun. *It. Pr.*

Benedetto è quel male che vien solo—Blessed is the misfortune that comes alone. *It. Pr.*

Bene est cui Deus obtulit / Parca quod satis 55 est manu—Well for him to whom God has given enough with a sparing hand. *Hor.*

Benefacta male locata, malefacta arbitror— Favours injudiciously conferred I reckon evils. *Cic.*

Benefacta sua verbis adornant—They enhance their favours by their words. *Plin.*

Beneficia dare qui nescit injuste petit—He who knows not how to bestow a benefit is unreasonable if he expects one. *Pub. Syr.*

Beneficia plura recipit qui scit reddere—He receives most favours who knows how to return them. *Pub. Syr.*

Beneficium accipere libertatem vendere est— 60 To accept a favour is to forfeit liberty. *Laber.*

Beneficium dignis ubi des, omnes obliges—Where you confer a benefit on those worthy of it, you confer a favour on all. *Pub. Syr.*

Beneficium invito non datur—There is no conferring a favour (involving obligation) on a man against his will. *L. Max.*

Beneficus est qui non sua, sed alterius causa benigne facit — He is beneficent who acts kindly, not for his own benefit, but for another's. *Cic.*

Bene merenti bene profuerit, male merenti par erit—To a well-deserving man God will show favour, to an ill-deserving He will be simply just. *Plaut.*

5 **Bene merentibus**—To the well-deserving. *M.*

Bene nummatum decorat Suedela Venusque—The goddesses of persuasion and of love adorn the train of the well-moneyed man. *Hor.*

Bene orasse est bene studuisse—To have prayed well is to have striven well.

Bene qui latuit, bene vixit—Well has he lived who has lived well in obscurity. *Ovid.*

Benevolence is the distinguishing characteristic of man. *Mencues.*

10 **Benigno numine**—By the favour of Providence. *M.*

Benignus etiam dandi causam cogitat—The benevolent man even weighs the grounds of his liberality. *Pr.*

Be no one like another, yet every one like the Highest; to this end let each one be perfect in himself. *Goethe.*

Be not angry that you cannot make others what you wish them to be, since you cannot make yourself what you wish to be. *Thomas à Kempis.*

Be not overcome of evil, but overcome evil with good. *St. Paul.*

15 **Be not righteous overmuch.** *Bible.*

Be not the first by whom the new is tried, / Nor yet the last to lay the old aside. *Pope.*

Ben trovato—Well invented. *It.*

Be our joy three-parts pain! Strive, and hold cheap the strain; / Learn, nor account the pang; dare, never grudge the throe! *Browning.*

Berretta in mano non fece mai danno—Cap in hand never harmed any one. *It. Pr.*

20 **Bescheiden freue dich des Ruhms, / So bist du wert des Heiligthums**—If thou modestly enjoy thy fame, thou ᵣᵣt not unworthy to rank with the holy. *Goethe.*

Bescheidenheit ist eine Zier, / Doch weiter kommt man ohne ihr—Modesty is an ornament, yet people get on better without it. *Ger. Pr.*

Beseht die Gönner in der Nähe! Halb sind sie kalt, halb sind sie roh—Look closely at those who patronise you. Half are unfeeling, half untaught. *Goethe.*

Besiegt von einem, ist besiegt von allen—Overpowered by one is overpowered by all. *Schiller.*

Be silent, or say something better than silence. *Sp. Pr.*

25 **Be slow in choosing a friend, but slower in changing him.** *Sc. Pr.*

Be sober, be vigilant. *St. Peter.*

Besser ein Flick als ein Loch—Better a patch than a hole. *Ger. Pr.*

Besser ein magrer Vergleich als ein fetter Prozess—Better is a lean agreement than a fat lawsuit. *Ger. Pr.*

Besser frei in der Fremde als Knecht daheim—Better free in a strange land than a slave at home. *Ger. Pr.*

30 **Besser freundlich versagen als unwillig gewähren**—Better a friendly refusal than an unwilling consent (*lit.* pledge). *Ger. Pr.*

Besser Rat kommt über Nacht—Better counsel comes over-night. *Lessing.*

Besser was als gar nichts—Better something than nothing at all. *Ger. Pr.*

Besser zweimal fragen dann einmal irre gehn—Better ask twice than go wrong once. *Ger. Pr.*

Be still and have thy will. *Tyndal.*

35 **Be stirring as the time; be fire with fire; / Threaten the threatner, and outface the brow / Of bragging horror; so shall inferior eyes, / That borrow their behaviours from the great, / Grow great by your example, and put on / The dauntless spirit of resolution.** *King John, v. 1.*

Best men are moulded out of faults. *Meas. for Meas., v. 1.*

Be strong, and quit yourselves like men. *Bible.*

Best time is present time. *Pr.*

Be substantially great in thyself, and more than thou appearest unto others. *Sir Thomas Browne.*

40 **Be sure you can obey good laws before you seek to alter bad ones.** *Ruskin.*

Be sure your sin will find you out. *Bible.*

Be swift to hear, slow to speak. *Pr.*

Bête noir—An eyesore; a bugbear (*lit.* a black beast). *Fr.*

Beter eens in den hemel dan tienmaal aan de deur—Better once in heaven than ten times at the door. *Dut. Pr.*

45 **Be thankful for your ennui; it is your last mark of manhood.** *Carlyle.*

Be thou as chaste as ice, as pure as snow, thou shalt not escape calumny. *Ham., iii. 1.*

Be thou assured, if words be made of breath, / And breath of life, I have no life to breathe / What thou hast said to me. *Ham., iii. 4.*

Be thou faithful unto death. *St. John.*

Bêtise—Folly; piece of folly. *Fr.*

50 **Be to her virtues very kind; / Be to her faults a little blind.** *Prior.*

Betrogene Betrüger—The deceiver deceived. *Lessing.*

Betrügen und betrogen werden, / Nichts ist gewöhnlicher auf Erden—Nothing is more common on earth than to deceive and be deceived. *Seume.*

Betrug war Alles, Lug, und Schein—All was deception, a lie, and illusion. *Goethe.*

Bettelsack ist bodenlos—The beggar's bag has no bottom. *Ger. Pr.*

55 **Better a blush in the face than a blot in the heart.** *Cervantes.*

Better a child should be ignorant of a thousand truths than have consecrated in its heart a single lie. *Ruskin.*

Better a diamond with a flaw than a pebble without one. *Chinese Pr.*

Better a fortune in a wife than with a wife. *Pr.*

Better a fremit freend than a freend fremit, *i.e.*, a stranger for a friend than a friend turned stranger. *Sc. Pr.*

Better a living dog than a dead lion. *Pr.*

Better an egg to-day than a hen to-morrow. *Pr.*

5 Better an end with terror than a terror without end. *Schill.*

Better a toom (empty) house than an ill tenant. *Sc. Pr.*

Better a witty fool than a foolish wit. *Twelfth Night,* i. 5.

Better bairns greet (weep) than bearded men. *Sc. Pr.*

Better be at the end o' a feast than the beginning o' a fray. *Sc. Pr.*

10 Better be a nettle in the side of your friend than his echo. *Emerson.*

Better be a poor fisherman than have to do with the governing of men. *Danton.*

Better be disagreeable in a sort than altogether insipid. *Goethe.*

Better be idle than ill employed. *Sc. Pr.*

Better bend than break. *Pr.*

15 Better be persecuted than shunned. *Ebers.*

Better be poor than wicked. *Pr.*

Better be unborn than untaught. *Gael. Pr.*

Better buy than borrow. *Pr.*

Better deny at once than promise long. *Pr.*

20 Better far off, than—near, be ne'er the near'. *Rich. II.,* v. 1.

Better far to die in the old harness than to try to put on another. *J. G. Holland.*

Better fifty years of Europe than a cycle of Cathay. *Tennyson.*

Better go back than go wrong. *Pr.*

Better go to bed supperless than rise in debt. *Sc. Pr.*

25 Better haud (hold on) wi' the hound than rin wi' the hare. *Sc. Pr.*

Better is an ass that carries us than a horse that throws us. *J. G. Holland.*

Better it is to be envied than pitied. *Pr.*

Better keep the deil oot than hae to turn him oot. *Sc. Pr.*

Better keep weel than mak' weel. *Sc. Pr.*

30 Better knot straws than do nothing. *Gael. Pr.*

Better lose a jest than a friend. *Pr.*

Better mad with all the world than wise all alone. *Fr. Pr.*

Better my freen's think me fremit as fasheous, *i.e.*, strange rather than troublesome. *Sc. Pr.*

Better never begin than never make an end. *Pr.*

35 Better not be at all / Than not be noble. *Tennyson.*

Better not read books in which you make the acquaintance of the devil. *Niebuhr.*

Better one-eyed than stone-blind. *Pr.*

Better one living word than a hundred dead ones. *Ger. Pr.*

Better rue sit than rue flit, *i.e.*, regret remaining than regret removing. *Sc. Pr.*

40 Better say nothing than nothing to the purpose. *Pr.*

Better sit still than rise and fa'. *Sc. Pr.*

Better sma' fish than nane. *Sc. Pr.*

Better suffer for truth than prosper by falsehood. *Dan. Pr.*

Better ten guilty escape than one innocent man suffer. *Pr.*

Better that people should laugh at one while 45 they instruct, than that they should praise without benefiting. *Goethe.*

Better the ill ken'd than the ill unken'd, *i.e.*, the ill we know than the ill we don't know. *Sc. Pr.*

Better the world know you as a sinner than God as a hypocrite. *Dan. Pr.*

Better to ask than go astray. *Pr.*

Better to get wisdom than gold. *Bible.*

Better to hunt in fields for health unbought, / 50 Than fee the doctor for a nauseous draught. / The wise for cure on exercise depend; / God never made his work for man to mend. *Dryden.*

Better to reign in hell than serve in heaven. *Milton.*

Better to say "Here it is" than "Here it was.' *Pr.*

Better understand the world than condemn it. *Gael. Pr.*

Better untaught than ill taught. *Pr.*

Better wear out than rust out. *Bishop Cum-* 55 *berland.*

Better wear shoon (shoes) than sheets. *Sc. Pr.*

Better wrong with the many than right with the few. *Port. Pr.*

Between a woman's "Yes" and "No" you may insert the point of a needle. *Ger. Pr.*

Between saying and doing there's a long road. *Pr.*

Between the acting of a dreadful thing / And 60 the first motion, all the interim is / Like a phantasma or a hideous dream. *Jul. Cæs.,* ii. 1.

Between the deil and the deep sea. *Sc. Pr.*

Between us and hell or heaven there is nothing but life, which of all things is the frailest. *Pascal.*

Beware, my lord, of jealousy ; / It is the green-eyed monster that doth mock / The meat it feeds on. *Othello,* iii. 3.

Beware of a silent dog and still water. *Pr.*

Beware of a silent man and a dog that does 65 not bark. *Pr.*

Beware of a talent which you cannot hope to cultivate to perfection. *Goethe.*

Beware / Of entrance to a quarrel; but, being in, / Bear 't that the opposed may beware of thee. *Ham.,* i. 3.

Beware of false prophets. *Jesus.*

Beware of " Had I wist." *Pr.*

Beware of one who has nothing to lose. *It.* 70 *Pr.*

Beware of too much good staying in your hand. *Emerson.*

Beware the fury of a patient man. *Dryden.*

Beware when the great God lets loose a thinker on this planet. *Emerson.*

Be warned by thy good angel and not ensnared by thy bad one. *Bürger.*

Be wisely worldly ; be not worldly wise. 75 *Quarles.*

Be wise to-day; 'tis madness to defer. *Young.*

Be wise with speed; / A fool at forty is a fool indeed. *Young.*

Bewunderung verdient ein Wunder wohl, / Doch scheint ein Weib kein echtes Weib zu sein, / So bald es nur Bewunderung verdient—What is admirable justly calls forth our admiration, yet a woman seems to be no true woman who calls forth nothing else. *Platen.*

Be ye therefore wise as serpents, and harmless as doves. *Jesus.*

5 Bezwingt des Herzens Bitterkeit. Es bringt / Nicht gute Frucht, wenn Hass dem Hass begegnet—Control the heart's bitterness. Nothing good comes of returning hatred for hatred. *Schiller.*

Bibula charta—Blotting-paper.

Bien dire fait rire; bien faire fait taire—Saying well makes us laugh; doing well makes us silent. *Fr. Pr.*

Bien est larron qui larron dérobe—He is a thief with a witness who robs another. *Fr. Pr.*

Bien nourri et mal appris—Well fed but ill taught. *Fr. Pr.*

10 Bien perdu bien connu—We know the worth of a thing when we have lost it. *Fr.*

Bien predica quien bien vive—He preaches well who lives well. *Sp. Pr.*

Bien sabe el asno en cuya cara rabozna—The ass knows well in whose face he brays. *Sp. Pr.*

Bien sabe el sabio que no sabe, el nescio piensa que sabe—The wise man knows well that he does not know; the ignorant man thinks he knows. *Sp. Pr.*

Bien sabe la vulpeja con quien trebeja—The fox knows well with whom he plays tricks. *Sp. Pr.*

15 Bien vengas, mal, si vienes solo—Welcome, misfortune, if thou comest alone. *Sp. Pr.*

Bien vient à mieux, et mieux à mal—Good comes to better and better to bad. *Fr. Pr.*

Big destinies of nations or of persons are not founded *gratis* in this world. *Carlyle.*

Bigotry murders religion, to frighten fools with her ghost. *Colton.*

Big words seldom accompany good deeds. *Dan. Pr.*

20 Billet-doux—A love-letter. *Fr.*

Biography is the most universally pleasant, the most universally profitable, of all reading. *Carlyle.*

Biography is the only true history. *Carlyle.*

Birds of a feather flock together. *Pr.*

Birds of prey do not flock together. *Port. Pr.*

25 Birth is much, but breeding is more. *Pr.*

Bis dat qui cito dat—He gives twice who gives quickly. *L. Pr.*

Bis est gratum quod opus est, si ultro offeras—That help is doubly acceptable which you offer spontaneously when we stand in need. *Pub. Syr.*

Bis interimitur qui suis armis perit—He dies twice who perishes by his own weapons or devices. *Pub. Syr.*

Bisogna amar l'amico con i suoi difetti—We must love our friend with all his defects. *It. Pr.*

30 Bis peccare in bello non licet—It is not permitted to blunder in war a second time. *Pr.*

Bist du Amboss, sei geduldig; bist du Hammer, schlage hart—Art thou anvil, be patient; art thou hammer, strike hard. *Ger. Pr.*

Bist du ein Mensch? so fühle meine Noth—Art thou a man? then feel for my wretchedness. *Margaret in "Faust."*

Bist du mit dem Teufel du und du, / Und willst dich vor der Flamme scheuen?—Art thou on familiar terms with the devil, and wilt thou shy at the flame? *Goethe's "Faust."*

Bis vincit qui se vincit in victoria—He conquers twice who, at the moment of victory, conquers (*i.e.*, restrains) himself. *Pub. Syr.*

35 Bitin' and scartin' 's Scotch folk's wooing. *Sc. Pr.*

Black detraction will find faults where they are not. *Massinger.*

Blame is the lazy man's wages. *Dan. Pr.*

Blame where you must, be candid where you can, / And be each critic the good-natured man. *Goldsmith.*

Blanc-bec—A greenhorn. *Fr.*

40 Blasen ist nicht flöten; ihr musst die Finger bewegen—To blow on the flute is not to play on it; you must move the fingers as well. *Goethe.*

Blasphemy is wishing ill to anything, and its outcome wishing ill to God; while Euphemy is wishing well to everything, and its outcome wishing well to—"Ah, wad ye tak' a thocht, and men'." *Ruskin.*

Blasted with excess of light. *Gray.*

Bleib nicht allein, denn in der Wüste trat / Der Satansengel selbst dem Herrn des Himmels—Remain not alone, for it was in the desert that Satan came to the Lord of Heaven himself. *Schiller.*

Bless, and curse not. *St. Paul.*

45 Blessed are they that have not seen, and yet have believed. *Jesus.*

Blessed are they that hear the Word of God, and keep it. *Bible.*

Blessed be he who first invented sleep; it covers a man all over like a cloak. *Cervantes.*

Blessed be nothing. *Pr.*

Blessed is he that considereth the poor. *Bible.*

50 Blessed is he that continueth where he is; here let us rest and lay out our seed-fields; here let us learn to dwell. *Carlyle.*

Blessed is he who expects nothing, for he shall never be disappointed. *Swift.*

Blessed is he who is made happy by the sound of a rat-tat. *Thackeray.*

Blessed is the man that endureth temptation. *St. James.*

Blessed is the voice that, amid dispiritment, stupidity, and contradiction, proclaims to us, Euge! (*i.e.*, Excellent! Bravo!). *Carlyle.*

55 Blessedness is a whole eternity older than damnation. *Jean Paul.*

Blessings are upon the head of the just. *Bible.*

Blinder Eifer schadet nur—Blind zeal only does harm. *M. G. Lichtwer.*

Blinder Gaul geht geradezu—A blind horse goes right on. *Ger. Pr.*

Blindfold zeal can do nothing but harm—harm everywhere, and harm always. *Lichtner.*

60 Bloemen zijn geen vruchten—Blossoms are not fruits. *Dut. Pr.*

Blood is thicker than water. *Pr.*

Blosse Intelligenz ohne correspondirende Energie des Wollens ist ein blankes Schwert in der Scheide, verächtlich, wenn es nie und nimmer gezückt wird—Mere intelligence without corresponding energy of the will is a polished sword in its scabbard, contemptible, if it is never drawn forth. *Lindner.*

Blow, blow, thou winter wind, / Thou art not so unkind / As man's ingratitude. *As You Like It, ii. 7.*

Blow, wind! come, wrack! / At least we'll die with harness on our back. *Macb., v. 5.*

Blue are the hills that are far from us. *Gael. Pr.*

5 Blunt edges rive hard knots. *Troil. and Cress., i. 3.*

Blushes are badges of imperfection. *Wycherley.*

Blut ist ein ganz besondrer Saft—Blood is a quite peculiar fluid. *Mephisto. in Faust.*

Boca de mel, coração de fel—A tongue of honey, a heart of gall. *Port. Pr.*

Boca que diz sim, diz naõ—The mouth that can say "Yea," can say "Nay." *Port. Pr.*

10 Bodily exercise profiteth little. *St. Paul.*

Bœotum in crasso jurares aëre natum—You would swear he was born in the foggy atmosphere of the Bœotians. *Hor.*

Bois ont oreilles et champs œillets—Woods have ears and fields eyes. *Fr. Pr.*

Bole com o rabo o caõ, naõ por ti, senaõ pelo paõ—The dog wags his tail, not for you, but for your bread. *Port. Pr.*

Bon accord—Good harmony. *M.*

15 Bonæ leges malis ex moribus procreantur—Good laws grow out of evil acts. *Macrob.*

Bona fide—In good faith ; in reality.

Bona malis paria non sunt, etiam pari numero ; nec lætitia ulla minimo mœrore pensanda—The blessings of life do not equal its ills, even when of equal number ; nor can any pleasure, however intense, compensate for even the slightest pain. *Pliny.*

Bona nemini hora est, ut non alicui sit mala—There is no hour good for one man that is not bad for another. *Pub. Syr.*

Bonarum rerum consuetudo est pessima—Nothing can be worse than being accustomed to good things. *Pub. Syr.*

20 Bona vacantia—Goods that have no owner. *L.*

Bon avocat, mauvais voisin—A good lawyer is a bad neighbour. *Fr. Pr.*

Bon bourgeois—A substantial citizen. *Fr.*

Bon chien chasse de race—A good dog hunts from pure instinct. *Fr. Pr.*

Bon diable—A good-natured fellow. *Fr.*

25 Bon droit a besoin d'aide—A good cause needs help. *Fr. Pr.*

Bon gré, mal gré—Whether willing or not. *Fr.*

Bon guet chasse maladventure—A good lookout drives ill-luck away. *Fr. Pr.*

Bonne épée point querelleur—A good swordsman is not given to quarrel. *Fr. Pr.*

Bonne est la maille que sauve le denier—Good is the farthing that saves the penny. *Fr. Pr.*

30 Bonhomie—Good nature. *Fr.*

Boni pastoris est tondere pecus, non deglubere—It is the duty of a good shepherd to shear his sheep, not to flay them. *Tiberius Cæsar, in reference to taxation.*

Bonis avibus—Under favourable auspices.

Bonis nocet quisquis pepercerit malis—He does injury to the good who spares the bad. *Pub. Syr.*

Bonis omnia bona—All things are good to the good. *M.*

35 Bonis quod benefit haud perit—A kindness done to good men is never thrown away. *Plaut.*

Bonis vel malis avibus—Under good, or evil, omens.

Bon jour—Good day. *Fr.*

Bon jour, bonne œuvre—The better the day, the better the deed. *Fr. Pr.*

Bon marché tire l'argent hors de la bourse—A good bargain is a pick-purse. *Fr. Pr.*

40 Bon mot—A witticism or jest. *Fr.*

Bon naturel—Good nature or disposition. *Fr.*

Bonne—A nurse. *Fr.*

Bonne bouche—A delicate morsel. *Fr.*

Bonne et belle assez—Good and handsome enough. *Fr. M.*

45 Bonne journée fait qui de fol se délivre—He who rids himself of a fool does a good day's work. *Fr. Pr.*

Bonne renommée vaut mieux que ceinture dorée—A good name is worth more than a girdle of gold. *Fr. Pr.*

Bonnet rouge—The cap of liberty. *Fr.*

Bonnie feathers mak' bonnie fowls. *Sc. Pr.*

Bon poète, mauvais homme—Good as a poet, bad as a man. *Fr.*

50 Bon sang ne peut mentir—Good blood disdains to lie. *Fr. Pr.*

Bons et máos mantem cidade—Good men and bad make a city. *Port. Pr.*

Bons mots n'épargnent nuls—Witticisms spare nobody. *Fr. Pr.*

Bon soir—Good evening. *Fr.*

Bon ton—The height of fashion. *Fr.*

55 Bonum ego quam beatum me esse nimio dici mavolo—I would much rather be called good than well off. *Plaut.*

Bonum est fugienda aspicere in alieno malo—Well if we see in the misfortune of another what we should shun ourselves. *Pub. Syr.*

Bonum est, pauxillum amare sane, insane non bonum est—It is good to be moderately sane in love ; to be madly in love is not good. *Plaut.*

Bonum summum quo tendimus omnes—That supreme good at which we all aim. *Lucret.*

Bonus animus in mala re dimidium est mali—Good courage in a bad affair is half of the evil overcome. *Plaut.*

60 Bonus atque fidus / Judex honestum prætulit utili—A good and faithful judge ever prefers the honourable to the expedient. *Hor.*

Bonus dux bonum reddit militem—The good general makes good soldiers. *L. Pr.*

Bonus vir semper tiro—A good man is always a learner.

Bon vivant—A good liver. *Fr.*

Bon voyage—A pleasant journey or voyage. *Fr.*

65 Books are divisible into two classes, the books of the hour and the books of all time. *Ruskin.*

Books are embalmed minds. *Bovee.*

Books are made from books. *Voltaire.*

Books cannot always please, however good ; / Minds are not ever craving for their food. *Crabbe.*

Books generally do little else than give our errors names. *Goethe.*

Books, like friends, should be few and well chosen. *Joineriana.*

Books still accomplish miracles; they persuade men. *Carlyle.*

Books, we know, / Are a substantial world, pure and good. *Wordsworth.*

5 Boomen die men veel verplant gedijen zelden —Trees you transplant often, seldom thrive. *Dut. Pr.*

Borgen thut nur einmal wohl—Borrowing does well only once. *Ger. Pr.*

Born to excel and to command! *Congreve.*

Borrowing from Peter to pay Paul. *Cic.*

Borrowing is not much better than begging; just as lending on interest is not much better than stealing. *Lessing.*

10 Bos alienus subinde prospectat foras—A strange ox every now and then turns its eyes wistfully to the door. *Pr.*

Böser Brunnen, da man Wasser muss eintragen—It is a bad well into which you must pour water. *Ger. Pr.*

Böser Pfennig kommt immer wieder—A bad penny always comes back again. *Ger. Pr.*

Bos in lingua—He has an ox on his tongue, *i.e.*, a bribe to keep silent, certain coins in Athens being stamped with an ox. *Pr.*

Bos lassus fortius figit pedem—The tired ox plants his foot more firmly. *Pr.*

15 Botschaft hör' ich wohl, allein mir fehlt der Glaube—I hear the message indeed, but I want the faith. *Goethe's "Faust."*

βουλεύου πρὸ ἔργων, ὅπως μὴ μωρὰ πέληται —Before the act consider, so that nothing foolish may arise out of it. *Gr. Pr.*

Bought wit is best, *i.e.*, bought by experience. *Pr.*

Boutez en avant—Push forward. *Fr.*

Bowels of compassion. *St. John.*

20 Brag is a good dog, but Holdfast is better. *Pr.*

Brain is always to be bought, but passion never comes to market. *Lowell.*

Brave men are brave from the very first. *Corneille.*

Bread at pleasure, / Drink by measure. *Pr.*

Bread is the staff of life. *Swift.*

25 Breathes there the man with soul so dead, / Who never to himself hath said, / "This is my own, my native land?" *Scott.*

Breathe his faults so quaintly, / That they may seem the taints of liberty; / The flash and outbreak of a fiery mind. *Ham.* ii. 1.

Breed is stronger than pasture. *George Eliot.*

Brevet d'invention—A patent. *Fr.*

Breveté—Patented. *Fr.*

30 Breve tempus ætatis satis est longum ad bene honesteque vivendum—A short term on earth is long enough for a good and honourable life. *Cic.*

Brevi manu—Offhand; summarily (*lit.* with a short hand).

Brevis a natura nobis vita data est: at memoria bene redditæ vitæ est sempiterna—A short life has been given us by Nature, but the memory of a well-spent one is eternal. *Cic.*

Brevis esse laboro, obscurus fio—When labouring to be concise, I become obscure. *Hor.*

Brevis ipsa vita est, sed longior malis—Life itself is short, but lasts longer than misfortunes. *Pub. Syr.*

Brevis voluptas mox doloris est parens—Short- 35 lived pleasure is the parent of pain. *Pr.*

Brevity is the body and soul of wit. *Jean Paul.*

Brevity is the soul of wit. *Ham.*, iii. 2.

Bric-à-brac—Articles of vertu or curiosity. *Fr.*

Bricht ein Ring, so bricht die ganze Katte— A link broken, the whole chain broken. *Ger. Pr.*

Brief as the lightning in the collied night, / 40 That, in a spleen, unfolds both heaven and earth, / And ere a man hath power to say, "Behold!" / The jaws of darkness do devour it up. *Mid. N.s' Dream*, i. 1.

Briefe gehören unter die wichtigsten Denkmäler die der einzelne Mensch hinterlassen kann—Letters are among the most significant memorials a man can leave behind him. *Goethe.*

Briller par son absence—To be conspicuous by its absence. *Fr.*

Bring down my grey hairs with sorrow to the grave. *Bible.*

Bring forth men-children only! / For thy undaunted mettle should compose / Nothing but males. *Macb.*, i. 7.

Broad thongs may be cut from other people's 45 leather. *It. Pr.*

Broken friendships may be sowthered (soldered), but never sound. *Sc. Pr.*

Brouille sera à la maison si la quenouille est maîtresse—There will be disagreement in the house if the distaff holds the reins. *Fr. Pr.*

Brûler la chandelle par les deux bouts—To burn the candle at both ends. *Fr.*

Brute force holds communities together as an iron nail, if a little rusted with age, binds pieces of wood; but intelligence binds like a screw, which must be gently turned, not driven. *Draper.*

Brutum fulmen—A harmless thunderbolt. *L.* 50

Brutus, thou sleep'st; awake, and see thyself. *Jul. Cæs.*, ii. 1.

Brutus will start a spirit as soon as Cæsar. *Jul. Cæs.*, i. 2.

Bûche tortue fait bon feu—A crooked log makes a good fire. *Fr. Pr.*

Buen siglo haya quien dijó bolta—Blessings on him that said, Right about face! *Sp. Pr.*

Buey viejo sulco derecho—An old ox makes a 55 straight furrow. *Sp. Pr.*

Buffoonery is often want of wit. *Bruyère.*

Bullies are generally cowards. *Pr.*

Buon cavallo non ha bisogno di sproni—Don't spur a willing horse. *It. Pr.*

Burlaos con el loco en casa, burlará con vos en la plaza—Play with the fool in the house and he will play with you in the street. *Sp. Pr.*

Burnt bairns dread the fire. *Sc. Pr.* 60

Business dispatched is business well done, but business hurried is business ill done. *Bulwer Lytton.*

Busy readers are seldom good readers. *Wieland.*

But a bold peasantry, their country's pride, / When once destroyed, can never be supplied. *Goldsmith.*

But all was false and hollow; though his tongue / Dropp'd manna, and could make the worse appear / The better reason, to perplex and dash / Maturest counsels. *Milton.*

But by bad courses may be understood, / That their events can never fall out good. *Rich. II.*, ii. 1.

But Cristes lore, and his apostles twelve, / He taught, but first he folwed it himselve. *Chaucer.*

5 But earthlier happy is the rose distilled, / Than that which, withering on the virgin thorn, / Grows, lives, and dies in single blessedness. *Mid. N's. Dream*, i. 1.

But evil is wrought by want of thought / As well as want of heart. *Hood.*

But facts are chiels that winna ding, / An' douna be disputed. *Burns.*

But far more numerous was the herd of such / Who think too little and who talk too much. *Dryden.*

But for women, our life would be without help at the outset, without pleasure in its course, and without consolation at the end. *Jouy.*

10 But from the heart of Nature rolled / The burdens of the Bible old. *Emerson.*

But human bodies are sic fools, / For a' their colleges and schools, / That, when nae real ills perplex them, / They make enow themsels to vex them. *Burns.*

But hushed be every thought that springs / From out the bitterness of things. *Wordsworth.*

But I am constant as the northern star, / Of whose true-fixed and resting quality, / There is no fellow in the firmament. *Jul. Cæs.*, iii. 1.

But I will wear my heart upon my sleeve / For daws to peck at. *Othello*, i. 1.

15 But man, proud man, / Drest in a little brief authority, / Most ignorant of what he's most assured, / His glassy essence,—like an angry ape, / Plays such fantastic tricks before high Heaven / As make the angels weep. *Meas. for Meas.*, ii. 2.

But men may construe things after their fashion, clean from the purpose of the things themselves. *Jul. Cæs.*, i. 3.

But men must work, and women must weep, / Though storms be sudden and waters deep, / And the harbour bar be moaning. *C. Kingsley.*

But mercy is above this sceptred sway; / It is enthroned in the hearts of kings, / It is an attribute to God Himself, / And earthly power doth then show likest God's / When mercy seasons justice. *Mer. of Ven.*, iv. 1.

But now our fates from unmomentous things / May rise like rivers out of little springs. *Campbell.*

20 But O for the touch of a vanish'd hand, / And the sound of a voice that is still. *Tennyson.*

But O what damned minutes tells he o'er, / Who dotes, yet doubts; suspects, yet strongly loves? *Othello*, iii. 3.

But pleasures are like poppies spread, / You seize the flower, its bloom is shed; / Or, like the snowfall on the river, / A moment white— then melts for ever. *Burns.*

But Shakespeare's magic could not copied be; / Within that circle none durst walk but he. *Dryden.*

But shapes that come not at an earthly call, / Will not depart when mortal voices bid. *Wordsworth.*

But souls that of His own good life partake, / 25 He loves as His own self; dear as His eye / They are to Him; He'll never them forsake; / When they shall die, then God Himself shall die: / They live, they live in blest eternity. *H. More.*

But spite of all the criticising elves, / Those that would make us feel, must feel themselves. *Churchill.*

But there are wanderers o'er eternity, / Whose bark drives on and on, and anchor'd ne'er shall be. *Byron.*

But there 's nothing half so sweet in life / As love's young dream. *Moore.*

But thought 's the slave of life, and life time's fool; / And time, that takes survey of all the world, / Must have a stop. *1 Henry IV.*, v. 4.

But to see her was to love her—love but her, 30 and love for ever. *Burns.*

But truths on which depend our main concern, / That 'tis our shame and misery not to learn, / Shine by the side of every path we tread, / With such a lustre, he that runs may read. *Cowper.*

But war's a game which, were their subjects wise, / Kings would not play at. *Cowper.*

But were I Brutus, / And Brutus Antony, there were an Antony / Would ruffle up your spirits, and put a tongue / In every wound of Cæsar, that should move / The stones of Rome to rise and mutiny. *Jul. Cæs.*, iii. 2.

But what fate does, let fate answer for. *Sheridan.*

But whether on the scaffold high, / Or in the 35 battle's van, / The fittest place where man can die / Is where he dies for man. *M. J. Barry.*

But who would force the soul, tilts with a straw / Against a champion cased in adamant. *Wordsworth.*

But winter lingering chills the lap of May. *Goldsmith.*

But words are things, and a small drop of ink, / Falling, like dew, upon a thought, produces / That which makes thousands, perhaps millions, think. *Byron.*

But wouldst thou know what's heaven? I'll tell thee what: / Think what thou canst not think, and heaven is that. *Quarles.*

But yesterday the word of Cæsar might / 40 Have stood against the world; now lies he there, / And none so poor to do him reverence. *Jul. Cæs.*, iii. 2.

Buying is cheaper than asking. *Ger. Pr.*

Buy the truth, and sell it not. *Bible.*

Buy what ye dinna want, an' ye'll sell what ye canna spare. *Sc. Pr.*

By-and-by is easily said. *Ham.*, iii. 2.

By any ballot-box, Jesus Christ goes just as 45 far as Judas Iscariot. *Carlyle.*

By blood a king, in heart a clown. *Tennyson.*

By bravely enduring it, an evil which cannot be avoided is overcome. *Pr.*

By desiring little, a poor man makes himself rich. *Democritus.*

By dint of dining out, I run the risk of dying by starvation at home. *Rousseau.*

By doing nothing we learn to do ill. *Pr.*

By education most have been misled. *Dryden.*

5 By experience we find out a short way by a long wandering. *Roger Ascham.*

By nature man hates change; seldom will he quit his old home till it has actually fallen about his ears. *Carlyle.*

By night an atheist half believes a God. *Young.*

By nothing do men more show what they are than by their appreciation of what is and what is not ridiculous. *Goethe.*

By others' faults wise men correct their own. *Pr.*

10 By persisting in your path, though you forfeit the little, you gain the great. *Emerson.*

By pious heroic climbing of our own, not by arguing with our poor neighbours, wandering to right and left, do we at length reach the sanctuary—the victorious summit, and see with our own eyes. *Carlyle.*

By pride cometh contention. *Bible.*

By robbing Peter he paid Paul . . . and hoped to catch larks if ever the heavens should fall. *Rabelais.*

By seeking and blundering we learn. *Goethe.*

15 By shallow rivers to whose falls / Melodious birds sing madrigals. *Marlowe.*

By sports like these are all their cares beguil'd, / The sports of children satisfy the child. *Goldsmith.*

By strength of heart the sailor fights with roaring seas. *Wordsworth.*

By the long practice of caricature I have lost the enjoyment of beauty: I never see a face but distorted. *Hogarth to a lady who wished to learn caricature.*

By three methods we may learn wisdom: first, by reflection, which is the noblest; second, by imitation, which is the easiest; and third, by experience, which is the bitterest. *Confucius.*

20 By time and counsel do the best we can: / Th' event is never in the power of man. *Herrick.*

C.

Ca' (drive) a cow to the ha' (hall), and she'll rin to the byre. *Sc. Pr.*

Cabin'd, cribb'd, confin'd. *Macb.,* iii. 4.

25 Cacoëthes carpendi—An itch for fault-finding.

Cacoëthes scribendi—An itch for scribbling.

Cacoëthes loquendi—An itch for talking.

Cada cousa a seu tempo—Everything has its time. *Port. Pr.*

Cada qual en seu officio—Every one to his trade. *Port. Pr.*

Cada qual hablé en lo que sabe—Let every one talk of what he understands. *Sp. Pr.*

Cada uno es hijo de sus obras—Every one is the son of his own works; *i.e.*, is responsible for his own acts. *Sp. Pr.*

30 Cadenti porrigo dextram—I extend my right hand to a falling man. *M.*

Cadit quæstio—The question drops, *i.e.*, the point at issue needs no further discussion. *L.*

Cæca invidia est, nec quidquam aliud scit quam detrectare virtutes—Envy is blind, and can only disparage the virtues of others. *Livy.*

Cæca regens vestigia filo—Guiding blind steps by a thread.

Cæsarem vehis, Cæsarisque fortunam—You carry Cæsar and his fortunes; fear not, therefore. *Cæsar to a pilot in a storm.*

Cæsar non supra grammaticos—Cæsar has no 35 authority over the grammarians. *Pr.*

Cæsar's wife should be above suspicion. *Plut.*

Cæteris major qui melior—He who is better than others is greater. *M.*

Cahier des charges—Conditions of a contract. *Fr.*

Ça ira—It shall go on (a French Revolution song). *Ben. Franklin.*

Caisse d'amortissement—Sinking fund. *Fr.* 40

Calamitosus est animus futuri anxius—The mind that is anxious about the future is miserable. *Sen.*

Calamity is man's true touchstone—*Beaumont and Fletcher.*

Calf love, half love; old love, cold love. *Fris. Pr.*

Call a spade a spade.

Call him wise whose actions, words, and steps 45 are all a clear Because to a clear Why. *Lavater.*

Callida junctura—Skilful arrangement. *Hor.*

Call me what instrument you will, though you fret me, you cannot play on me. *Ham.,* iii. 2.

Call not that man wretched who, whatever ills he suffers, has a child he loves. *Southey, Coleridge.*

Call not the devil; he will come fast enough without. *Dan. Pr.*

Call your opinions your creed, and you will 50 change it every week. Make your creed simply and broadly out of the revelation of God, and you may keep it to the end. *P. Brooks.*

Calmness of will is a sign of grandeur. The vulgar, far from hiding their will, blab their wishes. A single spark of occasion discharges the child of passions into a thousand crackers of desire. *Lavater.*

Calumnies are sparks which, if you do not blow them, will go out of themselves. *Boerhaave.*

Calumny is like the wasp which worries you; which it were best not to try to get rid of, unless you are sure of slaying it, for otherwise it will return to the charge more furious than ever. *Chamfort.*

Calumny will sear / Virtue itself: these shrugs, these hums and ha's. *Winter's Tale,* ii. 1.

Camelus desiderans cornua etiam aures per- 55 didit—The camel begging for horns was deprived of his ears as well. *Pr.*

Campos ubi Troja fuit—The fields where Troy once stood. *Lucan.*

Campus Martius—A place of military exercise (*lit.* field of Mars).

Canaille—The rabble. *Fr.*

Canam mihi et Musis—I will sing to myself and the Muses, *i.e.*, if no one else will listen. *Anon.*

"Can" and "shall," well understood, mean the same thing under this sun of ours. *Carlyle*.

Can anybody remember when the times were not hard and money not scarce? or when sensible men, and the right sort of men, and the right sort of women, were plentiful? *Emerson*.

Can ch' abbaia non morde—A dog that barks does not bite. *It. Pr.*

Can che morde non abbaia in vano—A dog that bites does not bark in vain. *It. Pr.*

5 Can despots compass aught that hails their sway? / Or call with truth one span of earth their own, / Save that wherein at last they crumble bone by bone? *Byron*.

Candida pax homines, trux decet ira feras—Wide-robed peace becomes men, ferocious anger only wild beasts. *Ovid*.

Candide et caute—With candour and caution. *M.*

Candide et constanter—With candour and constancy. *M.*

Candide secure—Honesty is the best policy. *M.*

10 Candidus in nauta turpis color : æquoris unda / Debet et a radiis sideris esse niger—A fair complexion is a disgrace in a sailor ; he ought to be tanned, from the spray of the sea and the rays of the sun. *Ovid*.

"Can do" is easy (easily) carried aboot. *Sc. Pr.*

Candor dat viribus alas—Candour gives wings to strength. *M.*

Candour is the brightest gem of criticism. *Disraeli*.

Canes timidi vehementius latrant quam mordent—Cowardly dogs bark more violently than they bite. *Q. Curt.*

15 Cane vecchio non abbaia indarno—An old dog does not bark for nothing. *It. Pr.*

Can I choose my king? I can choose my King Popinjay, and play what farce or tragedy I may with him ; but he who is to be my ruler, whose will is higher than my will, was chosen for me in heaven. *Carlyle*.

Canina facundia—Dog (*i.e.*, snarling) eloquence. *Appius*.

Canis a non canedo—Dog is called " canis," from " non cano," not to sing. *Varro*.

Canis in præsepi—The dog in the manger (that would not let the ox eat the hay which he could not eat himself).

20 Cannon and firearms are cruel and damnable machines. I believe them to have been the direct suggestion of the devil. *Luther*.

Can storied urn or animated bust / Back to its mansion call the fleeting breath? / Can honour's voice provoke the silent dust, / Or flattery soothe the dull cold ear of death? *Gray*.

Canst thou not minister to a mind diseas'd, / Pluck from the memory a rooted sorrow, / Raze out the written troubles of the brain? / And with some sweet oblivious antidote, / Cleanse the stuff'd bosom of that perilous stuff / Which weighs upon the heart? *Macb.*, v. 3.

Can such things be, / And overcome us like a summer's cloud, / Without our special wonder? *Macb.*, iii. 4.

Cantabit vacuus coram latrone viator — The penniless traveller will sing in presence of the robber. *Juv.*

Can that which is the greatest virtue in philo- 25 sophy, doubt, be in religion, what we priests term it, the greatest of sins? *Bovee*.

Can the Ethiopian change his skin, or the leopard his spots? *Bible*.

Can there any good thing come out of Nazareth? *Nathanael*.

Cantilenam eandem canis—You are always singing the same tune, *i.e.*, harping on one theme. *Ter.*

Cant is properly a double-distilled lie, the second power of a lie. *Carlyle*.

Cant is the voluntary overcharging or pro- 30 longing of a real sentiment. *Hazlitt*.

Can wealth give happiness? look around and see, / What gay distress! what splendid misery! / Whatever fortunes lavishly can pour, / The mind annihilates and calls for more. *Young*.

Can we wonder that men perish and are forgotten, when their noblest and most enduring works decay? *Ausonius*.

"Can you tell a plain man the plain road to heaven?"—"Surely. Turn at once to the right, then go straight forward." *Bp. Wilberforce*.

Caõ que muito ladra, nunca bom para a caça —A dog that barks much is never a good hunter. *Port. Pr.*

Capable of all kinds of devotion, and of all 35 kinds of treason, raised to the second power, woman is at once the delight and the terror of man. *Amiel*.

Capacity without education is deplorable, and education without capacity is thrown away. *Saadi*.

Cap-à-pié—From head to foot. *Fr.*

Capias—A writ to order the seizure of a defendant's person. *L.*

Capias ad respondendum—You may take him to answer your complaint. *L.*

Capias ad satisfaciendum—You may take him 40 to satisfy your claim. *L.*

Capiat, qui capere possit—Let him take who can. *Pr.*

Capistrum maritale—The matrimonial halter. *Juv.*

Capitis nives—The snowy locks of the head. *Hor.*

Capo grasso, cervello magro—Fat head, lean brains. *It. Pr.*

Captivity is the greatest of all evils that can 45 befall man. *Cervantes*.

Captivity, / That comes with honour, is true liberty. *Massinger*.

Captum te nidore suæ putat ille culinæ—He thinks he has caught you with the savoury smell of his kitchen. *Juv.*

Caput artis est, decere quod facias—The chief thing in any art you may practise is that you do only the one you are fit for. *Pr.*

Caput inter nubila condit—(Fame) hides her head amid the clouds. *Virg.*

Caput mortuum—The worthless remains ; a ninny. 50

Caput mundi—The head of the world, *i.e.*, Rome, both ancient and modern.

Cara al mio cuor tu sei, / Ciò ch'è il sole agli occhi miei—Thou art as dear to my heart as the sun to my eyes. *It. Pr.*

Care, and not fine stables, makes a good horse. *Dan. Pr.*

Care is no cure, but rather a corrosive, / For things that are not to be remedied. *1 Hen. VI.*, iii. 3.

Care is taken that trees do not grow into the sky. *Goethe.*

Care keeps his watch in every old man's eye, / And where care lodges, sleep will never lie. *Rom. and Jul.*, ii. 2.

5 Care killed the cat. *Pr.*

Carelessness is worse than theft. *Gael. Pr.*

Careless their merits or their faults to scan, / His pity gave ere charity began. *Goldsmith.*

Care's an enemy to life. *Twelfth Night*, i. 3.

Cares are often more difficult to throw off than sorrows ; the latter die with time, the former grow with it. *Jean Paul.*

10 Care that has enter'd once into the breast, / Will have the whole possession ere it rest. *Ben Jonson.*

Caret—It is wanting.

Caret initio et fine—It has neither beginning nor end.

Caret periculo, qui etiam cum est tutus cavet —He is not exposed to danger who, even when in safety, is on his guard. *Pub. Syr.*

Care to our coffin adds a nail, no doubt, / And every grin, so merry, draws one out. *Wolcot.*

15 Care will kill a cat, but ye canna live without it. *Sc. Pr.*

Carica volontario non carica—A willing burden is no burden. *It. Pr.*

Car il n'est si béau jour qui n'amène sa nuit— There is no day, however glorious, but sets in night. *Fr.*

Carior est illis homo quam sibi—Man is dearer to them (*i.e.*, the gods) than to himself. *Juv.*

Cari sunt parentes, cari liberi, propinqui, familiares ; sed omnes omnium caritates, patria una complexa est—Dear are our parents, dear our children, our relatives, and our associates, but all our affections for all these are embraced in our affection for our native land. *Cic.*

20 Carmen perpetuum primaque origine mundi ad tempora nostra—A song for all ages, and from the first origin of the world to our own times. *Transposed from Ovid.*

Carmen triumphale—A song of triumph.

Carmina nil prosunt ; nocuerunt carmina quondam—My rhymes are of no use ; they once wrought me harm. *Ovid.*

Carmina spreta exolescunt ; si irascare, agnita videntur—Abuse, if you slight it, will gradually die away ; but if you show yourself irritated, you will be thought to have deserved it. *Tac.*

Carmine di superi placantur, carmine Manes —The gods above and the gods below are alike propitiated by song. *Hor.*

25 Carmine fit vivax virtus ; expersque sepulcri, notitiam seræ posteritatis habet—By verse virtue is made immortal ; and, exempt from burial, obtains the homage of remote posterity. *Ovid.*

Carpet knights. *Burton.*

Carpe diem—Make a good use of the present. *Hor.*

Carry on every enterprise as if all depended on the success of it. *Richelieu.*

Carte blanche—Unlimited power to act (*lit.* blank paper). *Fr.*

Car tel est votre plaisir—For such is our pleasure. 30 *Fr.*

Casa hospidada, comida y denostada—A house which is filled with guests is both eaten up and spoken ill of. *Sp. Pr.*

Casa mia, casa mia, per piccina che tu sia, tu mi sembri una badia—Home, dear home, small though thou be, thou art to me a palace. *It. Pr.*

Casar, casar, e que do governo ?—Marry, marry, and what of the management of the house? *Port. Pr.*

Casar, casar, soa bem, e sabe mal—Marrying sounds well, but tastes ill. *Port. Pr.*

Cassis tutissima virtus—Virtue is the safest 35 helmet. *M.*

Casta ad virum matrona parendo imperat—A chaste wife acquires an influence over her husband by obeying him. *Laber.*

Casta moribus et integra pudore—Of chaste morals and unblemished modesty. *Mart.*

Cast all your cares on God ; that anchor holds. *Tennyson.*

Cast forth thy act, thy word, into the ever-living, ever-working universe. It is a seed-grain that cannot die ; unnoticed to-day, it will be found flourishing as a banyan-grove, perhaps, alas ! as a hemlock forest, after a thousand years. *Carlyle.*

Cast him (a lucky fellow) into the Nile, and he 40 will come up with a fish in his mouth. *Arab. Pr.*

Castles in the air cost a vast deal to keep up. *Bulwer Lytton.*

Castor gaudet equis, ovo prognatus eodem / Pugnis—Castor delights in horses ; he that sprung from the same egg, in boxing. *Hor.*

Castrant alios, ut libros suos, per se graciles, alieno adipe suffarciant—They castrate the books of others, that they may stuff their own naturally lean ones with their fat. *Jovius.*

Cast thy bread upon the waters, for thou shalt find it after many days. *Bible.*

Cast thy bread upon the waters ; God will 45 know of it, if the fishes do not. *Eastern Pr.*

Casus belli—A cause for war ; originally, fortune of war.

Casus quem sæpe transit, aliquando invenit— Misfortune will some time or other overtake him whom it has often passed by. *Pub. Syr.*

Casus ubique valet ; semper tibi pendeat hamus. / Quo minimè credas gurgite, piscis erit— There is scope for chance everywhere ; let your hook be always hanging ready. In the eddies where you least expect it, there will be a fish. *Ovid.*

Catalogue raisonné—A catalogue topically arranged. *Fr.*

Catch as catch can. *Antiochus Epiphanes.* 50

Catching a Tartar, *i.e.*, an adversary too strong for one.

Catch not at the shadow and lose the substance. *Pr.*

Catch, then, O catch the transient hour ; / Improve each moment as it flies ; / Life's a short summer—man a flower— / He dies— alas ! how soon he dies ! *Johnson.*

Catholicism commonly softens, while Protestantism strengthens, the character; but the softness of the one often degenerates into weakness, and the strength of the other into hardness. *Lecky.*

Cato contra mundum—Cato against the world.

Cato esse, quam videri, bonus malebat—Cato would rather be good than seem good. *Sallust.*

Cattiva è quella lana, che non si può tingere—Bad is the cloth that won't dye. *It. Pr.*

5 Cattivo è quel sacco che non si puo rappezzare—Bad is the sack that won't patch. *It. Pr.*

Cattle go blindfold to the common to crop the wholesome herbs, but man learns to distinguish what is wholesome (Heil) and what is poisonous (Gift) only by experience. *Rückert.*

Catus amat pisces, sed non vult tingere plantas—Puss likes fish, but does not care to wet her feet. *Pr.*

Causa causans—The Cause of causes.

Causa latet, vis est notissima—The cause is hidden, but the effect is evident enough. *Ovid.*

10 Causa sine qua non—An indispensable condition.

Cause and effect are two sides of one fact. *Emerson.*

Cause and effect, means and end, seed and fruit, cannot be severed; for the effect already blooms in the cause, the end pre-exists in the means, the fruit in the seed. *Emerson.*

Cause célèbre—A celebrated trial or action at law. *Fr.*

Caute, non astute—Cautiously, not craftily. *M.*

15 Caution is the parent of safety. *Pr.*

Cautious age suspects the flattering form, and only credits what experience tells. *Johnson.*

Cautis pericla prodesse aliorum solent—Prudent people are ever ready to profit from the experiences of others. *Phædr.*

Cautus enim metuit foveam lupus, accipiterque / Suspectos laqueos, et opertum miluus hamum—For the wary wolf dreads the pitfall, the hawk the suspected snare, and the fish the concealed hook. *Hor.*

Cavallo ingrassato tira calci—A horse that is grown fat kicks. *It. Pr.*

20 Cave ab homine unius libri—Beware of a man of or a book. *Pr.*

Caveat actor—Let the doer be on his guard. *L.*

Caveat emptor—Let the buyer be on his guard. *L.*

Cave canem—Beware of the dog.

Cavendo tutus—Safe by caution. *M.*

25 Cave paratus—Be on guard while prepared. *M.*

Caviare to the general. *Ham.*, ii. 2.

Cease, every joy, to glimmer in my mind, / But leave,—oh I leave the light of hope behind I / What though my winged hours of bliss have been, / Like angel-visits, few and far between? *Campbell.*

Cease to lament for that thou canst not help, / And study help for that which thou lament'st. *Two Gent. of Ver.*, iii. 1.

Cedant arma togæ—Let the military yield to the civil power (*lit.* to the gown). *Cic.*

30 Cedant carminibus reges, regumque triumphi—Kings, and the triumphs of kings, must yield to the power of song. *Ovid.*

Cedat amor rebus; res age, tutus eris—Let love give way to business; give attention to business, and you will be safe. *Ovid.*

Cede Deo—Yield to God. *Virg.*

Cede nullis—Yield to none. *M.*

Cede repugnanti; cedendo victor abibis—Yield to your opponent; by so doing you will come off victor in the end. *Ovid.*

Cedite, Romani scriptores; cedite, Graii—Give 35 place, ye Roman writers; give place, ye Greeks (ironically applied to a pretentious author). *Prop.*

Cedunt grammatici; vincuntur rhetores / Turba tacet—The grammarians give way; the rhetoricians are beaten off; all the assemblage is silent. *Juv.*

Cela fera comme un coup d'épée dans l'eau—It will be all lost labour (*lit.* like a sword-stroke in the water). *Fr. Pr.*

Cela m'échauffe la bile—That stirs up my bile. *Fr.*

Cela n'est pas de mon ressort—That is not in my department, or line of things. *Fr.*

Cela saute aux yeux—That is quite evident 40 (*lit.* leaps to the eyes). *Fr. Pr.*

Cela va sans dire—That is a matter of course. *Fr.*

Cela viendra—That will come some day. *Fr.*

Celebrity is but the candle-light which will show *what* man, not in the least make him a better or other man. *Carlyle.*

Celebrity is the advantage of being known to people whom we don't know, and who don't know us. *Chamfort.*

Celebrity is the chastisement of merit and the 45 punishment of talent. *Chamfort.*

Celer et audax—Swift and daring. *M.*

Celer et fidelis—Swift and faithful. *M.*

Celerity is never more admired / Than by the negligent. *Ant. & Cleop.*, iii. 7.

Celsæ graviore casu / Decidunt turres—Lofty towers fall with no ordinary crash. *Hor.*

Celui est homme de bien qui est homme de 50 biens—He is a good man who is a man of goods. *Fr. Pr.*

Celui-là est le mieux servi, qui n'a pas besoin de mettre les mains des autres au bout de ses bras—He is best served who has no need to put other people's hands at the end of his arms. *Rousseau.*

Celui qui a grand sens sait beaucoup—A man of large intelligence knows a great deal. *Vauvenargues.*

Celui qui aime mieux ses trésors que ses amis, mérite de n'être aimé de personne—He who loves his wealth better than his friends does not deserve to be loved by any one. *Fr. Pr.*

Celui qui dévore la substance du pauvre, y trouve à la fin un os qui l'étrangle—He who devours the substance of the poor will in the end find a bone in it to choke him. *Fr. Pr.*

Celui qui est sur épaules d'un géant voit plus 55 loin que celui qui le porte—He who is on the shoulders of a giant sees farther than he does who carries him. *Fr. Pr.*

Celui qui veut, celui-là peut—The man who wills is the man who can. *Fr.*

Ce ne sont pas les plus belles qui font les grandes passions—It is not the most beautiful women that inspire the greatest passion. *Fr. Pr.*

Ce n'est pas être bien aisé que de rire—Laughing is not always an index of a mind at ease. *Fr.*

Ce n'est que le premier pas qui coûte—It is only the first step that is difficult (*lit.* costs). *Fr.*

Censor morum—Censor of morals and public conduct.

Censure is the tax a man pays to the public for being eminent. *Swift.*

5 Cent ans n'est guère, mais jamais c'est beaucoup—A hundred years is not much, but "never" is a long while. *Fr. Pr.*

Cento carri di pensieri, non pagaranno un' oncia di debito—A hundred cartloads of care will not pay an ounce of debt. *It. Pr.*

Cent 'ore di malinconia non pagano' un quattrino di' debito—A hundred hours of vexation will not pay one farthing of debt. *It. Pr.*

Centum doctûm hominum consilia sola hæc devincit dea / Fortuna—This goddess, Fortune, single-handed, frustrates the plans of a hundred learned men. *Plaut.*

Ce que femme veut, Dieu le veut—What woman wills, God wills. *Fr. Pr.*

10 Ce qui fait qu'on n'est pas content de sa condition, c'est l'idée chimérique qu'on forme du bonheur d'autrui—What makes us discontented with our condition is the absurdly exaggerated idea we have of the happiness of others. *Fr. Pr.*

Ce qu'il nous faut pour vaincre, c'est de l'audace, encore de l'audace, toujours de l'audace !—In order to conquer, what we need is to dare, still to dare, and always to dare. *Danton.*

Ce qui manque aux orateurs en profondeur, / Ils vous le donnent en longueur—What orators want in depth, they make up to you in length. *Montesquieu.*

Ce qui ne vaut pas la peine d'être dit, on le chante—What is not worth the trouble of being said, may pass off very fairly when it is sung. *Beaumarchais.*

Ce qui suffit ne fut jamais peu—What is enough was never a small quantity. *Fr. Pr.*

15 Ce qui vient de la flûte, s'en retourne au tambour—What is earned by the fife goes back to the drum ; easily gotten, easily gone. *Fr. Pr.*

Ce qu'on apprend au berceau dure jusqu'au tombeau—What is learned in the cradle lasts till the grave. *Fr. Pr.*

Ce qu'on fait maintenant, on le dit ; et la cause en est bien excusable : on fait si peu de chose—Whatever we do now-a-days, we speak of ; and the reason is this : it is so very little we do. *Fr.*

Cercato ho sempre solitaria vita / (Le rive il sanno, e le campagne e i boschi)—I have always sought a solitary life. (The river-banks and the open fields and the groves know it.)

Ceremonies are different in every country ; but true politeness is everywhere the same. *Goldsmith.*

20 Ceremony is necessary as the outwork and defence of manners. *Chesterfield.*

Ceremony is the invention of wise men to keep fools at a distance. *Steele.*

Ceremony keeps up all things ; 'tis like a penny glass to a rich spirit or some excellent water ; without it the water were spilt, the spirit lost. *Selden.*

Ceremony leads her bigots forth, / Prepared to fight for shadows of no worth ; / While truths, on which eternal things depend, / Find not, or hardly find, a single friend. *Cowper.*

Ceremony was but devised at first / To set a gloss on faint deeds . . . / But where there is true friendship, there needs none. *Timon of Athens,* i. 2.

Cereus in vitium flecti, monitoribus asper—25 (Youth), pliable as wax to vice, obstinate under reproof. *Hor.*

Cernit omnia Deus vindex—God as avenger sees all things. *M.*

Certa amittimus dum incerta petimus—We lose things certain in pursuing things uncertain. *Plaut.*

Certain defects are necessary to the existence of the individual. It would be painful to us if our old friends laid aside certain peculiarities. *Goethe.*

Certain it is that there is no kind of affection so purely angelic as that of a father to a daughter. In love to our wives there is desire ; to our sons, ambition ; but to our daughters there is something which there are no words to express. *Addison.*

Certe ignoratio futurorum malorum utilius est 30 quam scientia—It is more advantageous not to know than to know the evils that are coming upon us. *Cic.*

Certiorari—To order the record from an inferior to a superior court. *L.*

Certum est quia impossibile est—I am sure of it because it is impossible. *Tert.*

Certum pete finem—Aim at a definite end. *M.*

Cervantes smiled Spain's chivalry away. *Byron.*

Ces discours sont fort beaux dans un livre—All 35 that would be very fine in a book, *i.e.*, in theory, but not in practice. *Boileau.*

Ces malheureux rois / Dont on dit tant de mal, ont du bon quelquefois—Those unhappy kings, of whom so much evil is said, have their good qualities at times. *Andrieux.*

Ce sont les passions qui font et qui défont tout —It is the passions that do and that undo everything. *Fontenelle.*

Ce sont toujours les aventuriers qui font de grandes choses, et non pas les souverains des grandes empires—It is always adventurers who do great things, not the sovereigns of great empires. *Montesquieu.*

Cessante causa, cessat et effectus—When the cause is removed, the effect must cease also. *Coke.*

Cessio bonorum—A surrender of all one's pro- 40 perty to creditors. *Scots Law.*

C'est-à-dire—That is to say. *Fr.*

C'est dans les grands dangers qu'on voit les grands courages—It is amid great perils we see brave hearts. *Regnard.*

C'est double plaisir de tromper le trompeur—It is a double pleasure to deceive the deceiver. *La Font.*

C'est fait de lui—It is all over with him. *Fr.*

C'est la grande formule moderne : Du travail, 45 toujours du travail, et encore du travail—The grand maxim now-a-days is : To work, always to work, and still to work. *Gambetta.*

C'est là le diable—There's the devil of it, *i.e.*, there lies the difficulty. *Fr.*

C'est la prospérité qui donne des amis, c'est l'adversité qui les éprouve—It is prosperity that gives us friends, adversity that proves them. *Fr.*

C'est le chemin des passions qui m'a conduit à la philosophie—It is by my passions I have been led to philosophy. *Rousseau.*

C'est le commencement de la fin—It is the beginning of the end. *Talleyrand on the Hundred Days.*

C'est le crime qui fait honte, et non pas l'échafaud—It is the crime, not the scaffold, which is the disgrace. *Corneille.*

5 C'est le geai paré des plumes du paon—He is the jay decked with the peacock's feathers. *Fr.*

C'est le ton qui fait la musique—In music everything depends on the tone. *Fr. Pr.*

C'est le valet du diable, il fait plus qu'on ne lui ordonne—He who does more than he is bid is the devil's valet. *Fr. Pr.*

C'est l'imagination qui gouverne le genre humain—The human race is governed by its imagination. *Napoleon.*

C'est partout comme chez nous—It is everywhere the same as among ourselves. *Fr. Pr.*

10 C'est peu que de courir; il faut partir à point—It is not enough to run, one must set out in time. *Fr. Pr.*

C'est plus qu'un crime, c'est une faute—It is worse than a crime; it is a blunder. *Fouché.*

C'est posséder les biens que de savoir s'en passer—To know how to dispense with things is to possess them. *Regnard.*

C'est son cheval de bataille—That is his forte (*lit.* war-horse). *Fr.*

C'est trop aimer quand on en meurt—It is loving too much to die of loving. *Fr. Pr.*

15 C'est une autre chose—That's another matter. *Fr.*

C'est une grande folie de vouloir être sage tout seul—It is a great folly to wish to be wise all alone. *La Roche.*

C'est une grande misère que de n'avoir pas assez d'esprit pour bien parler, ni assez de jugement pour se taire—It is a great misfortune not to have enough of ability to speak well, nor sense enough to hold one's tongue. *La Bruyère.*

C'est un zéro en chiffres—He is a mere cipher. *Fr.*

Cet animal est très méchant : / Quand on l'attaque, il se défend—That animal is very vicious; it defends itself if you attack it. *Fr.*

20 Ceteris paribus—Other things being equal.

Ceterum censeo—But my decided opinion is. *Cato.*

Cet homme va à bride abattue—That man goes at full speed (*lit.* with loose reins). *Fr. Pr.*

Ceux qui parlent beaucoup, ne disent jamais rien—Those who talk much never say anything worth listening to. *Boileau.*

Ceux qui s'appliquent trop aux petites choses deviennent ordinairement incapables des grandes—Those who occupy their minds too much with small matters generally become incapable of great. *La Roche.*

25 Chacun à sa marotte—Every one to his hobby. *Fr. Pr.*

Chacun à son goût—Every one to his taste. *Fr.*

Chacun à son métier, et les vaches seront bien gardées—Let every one mind his own business, and the cows will be well cared for. *Fr. Pr.*

Chacun cherche son semblable—Like seeks like. *Fr. Pr.*

Chacun dit du bien de son cœur et personne n'en ose dire de son esprit—Every one speaks well of his heart, but no one dares boast of his wit. *La Roche.*

Chacun doit balayer devant sa propre porte— 30 Everybody ought to sweep before his own door. *Fr. Pr.*

Chacun en particulier peut tromper et être trompé ; personne n'a trompé tout le monde, et tout le monde n'a trompé personne—Individuals may deceive and be deceived ; no one has deceived every one, and every one has deceived no one. *Bonhours.*

Chacun n'est pas aise qui danse—Not every one who dances is happy. *Fr. Pr.*

Chacun porte sa croix—Every one bears his cross. *Fr.*

Chacun pour soi et Dieu pour tous—Every one for himself and God for all. *Fr. Pr.*

Chacun tire l'eau à son moulin—Every one 35 draws the water to his own mill. *Fr. Pr.*

Chacun vaut son prix—Every man has his value. *Fr.*

Χαλεπὰ τὰ καλά—What is excellent is difficult.

Chance corrects us of many faults that reason would not know how to correct. *La Roche.*

Chance generally favours the prudent. *Joubert.*

Chance is but the pseudonym of God for those 40 particular cases which He does not choose to subscribe openly with His own sign-manual. *Coleridge.*

Chance is the providence of adventurers. *Napoleon.*

Chance will not do the work : / Chance sends the breeze, / But if the pilot slumber at the helm, / The very wind that wafts us towards the port / May dash us on the shelves. *Scott.*

Chances, as they are now called, I regard as guidances, and even, if rightly understood, commands, which, as far as I have read history, the best and sincerest men think providential. *Ruskin.*

Change is inevitable in a progressive country —is constant. *Disraeli.*

Change of fashions is the tax which industry 45 imposes on the vanity of the rich. *Chamfort.*

Changes are lightsome, an' fules are fond o' them. *Sc. Pr.*

Change yourself, and your fortune will change too. *Port. Pr.*

Chansons-à-boire—Drinking-songs. *Fr.*

Chapeau bas—Hats off. *Fr.*

Chapelle ardente—Place where a dead body lies 50 in state. *Fr.*

Chapter of accidents. *Chesterfield.*

Chaque âge a ses plaisirs, son esprit, et ses mœurs—Every age has its pleasures, its style of wit, and its peculiar manners. *Boileau.*

Chaque branche de nos connaissances passe successivement par trois états théorétiques différents : l'état théologique, ou fictif ; l'état métaphysique, ou abstrait ; l'état scientifique, ou positif—Each department of knowledge passes in succession through three different theoretic stages : the theologic stage, or fictitious ; the metaphysical, or abstract ; the scientific, or positive. *A. Comte.*

Chaque demain apporte son pain—Every to-morrow supplies its own loaf. *Fr. Pr.*

Chaque instant de la vie est un pas vers la mort—Each moment of life is one step nearer death. *Corneille.*

Chaque médaille a son revers—Every medal has its reverse. *Fr. Pr.*

Chaque potier vante sa pot—Every potter cracks up his own vessel. *Fr. Pr.*

5 Char-à-bancs—A pleasure car. *Fr.*

Character gives splendour to youth, and awe to wrinkled skin and grey hairs. *Emerson.*

Character is a fact, and that is much in a world of pretence and concession. *A. B. Alcott.*

Character is a perfectly educated will. *Novalis.*

Character is a reserved force which acts directly by presence and without means. *Emerson.*

10 Character is a thing that will take care of itself. *J. G. Holland.*

Character is centrality, the impossibility of being displaced or overset. *Emerson.*

Character is higher than intellect. Thinking is the function; living is the functionary. *Emerson.*

Character is impulse reined down into steady continuance. *C. H. Parkhurst.*

Character is the result of a system of stereo-typed principles. *Hume.*

15 Character is the spiritual body of the person, and represents the individualisation of vital experience, the conversion of unconscious things into self-conscious men. *Whipple.*

Character is victory organised. *Napoleon.*

Character is what Nature has engraven on us ; can we then efface it ? *Voltaire.*

Characters are developed, and never change. *Disraeli.*

Character teaches over our head, above our wills. *Emerson.*

20 Character wants room ; must not be crowded on by persons, nor be judged of from glimpses got in the press of affairs or a few occasions. *Emerson.*

Charbonnier est maître chez soi—A coalheaver's house is his castle. *Fr.*

Charge, Chester, charge ! On, Stanley, on ! / Were the last words of Marmion. *Scott.*

Chargé d'affaires—A subordinate diplomatist. *Fr.*

Charity begins at hame, but shouldna end there. *Sc. Pr.*

25 Charity begins at home. *Pr.*

Charity draws down a blessing on the chari-table. *Le Sage.*

Charity gives itself rich ; covetousness hoards itself poor. *Ger. Pr.*

Charity is the scope of all God's commands. *St. Chrysostom.*

Charity is the temple of which justice is the foundation, but you can't have the top with-out the bottom. *Ruskin.*

30 Charity shall cover the multitude of sins. *St. Peter.*

Charm'd with the foolish whistling of a name. *Cowley.*

Charms strike the sight, but merit wins the soul. *Pope.*

Charms which, like flowers, lie on the surface and always glitter, easily produce vanity ; whereas other excellences, which lie deep like gold and are discovered with difficulty, leave their possessors modest and proud. *Jean Paul.*

Charta non erubescit — A document does not blush. *Pr.*

35 Chasse cousin—Bad wine, *i.e.*, such as was given to poor relations to drive them off. *Fr.*

Chassez le naturel, il revient au galop—Drive out Nature, she is back on you in a trice. *Fr. from Hor.*

Chaste as the icicle / That's curded by the frost from purest snow, / And hangs on Dian's temple. *Coriolanus*, v. 3.

Chastise the good, and he will grow better ; chastise the bad, and he will grow worse. *It. Pr.*

Chastity is like an icicle ; if it once melts, that's the last of it. *Pr.*

40 Chastity is the band that holds together the sheaf of all holy affections and duties. *Vinet.*

Chastity, lost once, cannot be recalled ; it goes only once. *Ovid.*

Châteaux en Espagne. Castles in the air (*lit.* castles in Spain). *Fr.*

Chat échaudé craint l'eau froide—A scalded cat dreads cold water. *Fr. Pr.*

Cheapest is the dearest. *Pr.*

45 Che dorme coi cani, si leva colle pulci—Those who sleep with dogs will rise up with fleas. *It. Pr.*

Cheerfulness is health ; the opposite, melan-choly, is disease. *Haliburton.*

Cheerfulness is just as natural to the heart of a man in strong health as colour to his cheek. *Ruskin.*

Cheerfulness is the best promoter of health, and is as friendly to the mind as to the body. *Addison.*

Cheerfulness is the daughter of employment. *Dr. Horne.*

50 Cheerfulness is the heaven under which every-thing but poison thrives. *Jean Paul.*

Cheerfulness is the very flower of health. *Schopenhauer.*

Cheerfulness opens, like spring, all the blossoms of the inward man. *Jean Paul.*

Cheese is gold in the morning, silver at mid-day, and lead at night. *Ger. Pr.*

Chef de cuisine—A head-cook. *Fr.*

55 Chef-d'œuvre—A masterpiece. *Fr.*

Chemin de fer—The iron way, the railway. *Fr.*

Che ne può la gatta se la massaia è matta—How can the cat help it if the maid is fool (enough to leave things in her way)? *It. Pr.*

Che quegli è tra gli stolti bene abbasso, / Che senza distinzion afferma o niega, / Così nell' un, come nell' altro passo—He who without discrimination affirms or denies, ranks lowest among the foolish ones, and this in either case, *i.e.*, in denying as well as affirming. *Dante.*

Chercher à connaître, c'est chercher à douter—To seek to know is to seek occasion to doubt. *Fr.*

60 Che sarà, sarà—What will be, will be. *M.*

Chevalier d'industrie—One who lives by persever-ing fraud (*lit.* a knight of industry). *Fr.*

Chevaux de frise—A defence of spikes against cavalry. *Fr.*

Chewing the food of sweet and bitter fancy. *As You Like It*, iv. 3.

Chew the cud of politics. *Swift.*

Chi altri giudica, sè condanna—Whoso judges others condemns himself. *It. Pr.*

5 Chi ama, crede—He who loves, believes. *It. Pr.*

Chi ama, qual chi muore / Non ha da gire al ciel dal mondo altr' ale—He who loves, as well as he who dies, needs no other wing by which to soar from earth to heaven. *Michael Angelo.*

Chi ama, teme—He who loves, fears. *It. Pr.*

Chi asino è, e cervo esser si crede, al saltar del fosso se n'avvede—He who is an ass and thinks he is a stag, will find his error when he has to leap a ditch. *It. Pr.*

Chi compra ciò pagar non può, vende ciò che non vuole—He who buys what he cannot pay for, sells what he fain would not. *It. Pr.*

10 Chi compra ha bisogno di cent occhi—He who buys requires an hundred eyes *It. Pr.*

Chi compra terra, compra guerra—Who buys land, buys war. *It. Pr.*

Chi con l'occhio vede, di cuor crede—Seeing is believing (*lit.* he who sees with the eye believes with the heart). *It. Pr.*

Chi da il suo inanzi morire s'apparecchia assai patire—He who gives of his wealth before dying, prepares himself to suffer much. *It. Pr.*

Chi dinanzi mi pinge, di dietro mi tinge—He who paints me before, blackens me behind. *It. Pr.*

15 Chi due padroni ha da servire, ad uno ha da mentire—Whoso serves two masters must lie to one of them. *It. Pr.*

Chi é causa del suo mal, pianga se stesso—He who is the cause of his own misfortunes may bewail them himself. *It. Pr.*

Chi edifica, sua borsa purifica—He who builds clears his purse. *It. Pr.*

Chien sur son fumier est hardi—A dog is bold on his own dunghill. *Fr. Pr.*

Chi erra nelle decine, erra nelle migliaja—He who errs in the tens, errs in the thousands. *It. Pr.*

20 Chiesa libera in libero stato—A free church in a free state. *Cavour.*

Chi fa il conto senza l'oste, gli convien farlo due volte—He who reckons without his host must reckon again. *It. Pr.*

Chi fa quel ch' e' può, non fa mai bene—He who does all he can do never does well. *It. Pr.*

Chi ha capo di cera non vada al sole—Let not him whose head is of wax walk in the sun. *It. Pr.*

Chi ha danari da buttar via, metta gli operaj, e non vi stia—He who has money to squander, let him employ workmen and not stand by them. *It. Pr.*

25 Chi ha denti, non ha pane ; e chi ha pane, non ha denti—He who has teeth is without bread, and he who has bread is without teeth. *It. Pr.*

Chi ha, è—He who has, is.

Chi ha l'amor nel petto, ha lo sprone a' fianchi —He who has love in his heart has spurs in his sides. *It. Pr.*

Chi ha lingua in bocca, può andar per tutto—He who has a tongue in his head can travel all the world over. *It. Pr.*

Chi ha paura del diavolo, non fa roba—He who has a dread of the devil does not grow rich. *It. Pr.*

Chi ha sanità è ricco, e non lo sa—He who has **30** good health is rich, and does not know it. *It. Pr.*

Chi ha sospetto, di rado è in difetto—He who suspects is seldom at fault. *It. Pr.*

Chi ha tempo, non aspetti tempo—He who has time, let him not wait for time.

Childhood and youth see all the world in persons. *Emerson.*

Childhood has no forebodings ; but then it is soothed by no memories of outlived sorrow. *George Eliot.*

Childhood is the sleep of reason. *Rousseau.* **35**

Childhood itself is scarcely more lovely than a cheerful, kindly, sunshiny old age. *Mrs. Child.*

Childhood often holds a truth in its feeble fingers which the grasp of manhood cannot retain, and which it is the pride of utmost age to recover. *Ruskin.*

Childhood shows the man, as morning shows the day. *Milton.*

Childhood, who like an April morn appears, / Sunshine and rain, hopes clouded o'er with fears. *Churchill.*

Children always turn toward the light. *Hare.* **40**

Children and chickens are always a-picking. *Pr.*

Children and drunk people speak the truth. *Pr.*

Children and fools speak the truth. *Pr.*

Children are certain sorrows, but uncertain joys. *Dan. Pr.*

Children are the poor man's wealth. *Dan. Pr.* **45**

Children are very nice observers, and they will often perceive your slightest defects. *Fénelon.*

Children blessings seem, but torments are, / When young, our folly, and when old, our fear. *Otway.*

Children generally hate to be idle ; all the care is then that their busy humour should be constantly employed in something of use to them. *Locke.*

Children have more need of models than of critics. *Joubert.*

Children have scarcely any other fear than **50** that produced by strangeness. *Jean Paul.*

Children, like dogs, have so sharp and fine a scent, that they detect and hunt out everything—the bad before all the rest. *Goethe.*

Children of night, of indigestion bred. *Churchill of dreams.*

Children of wealth or want, to each is given / One spot of green, and all the blue of heaven. *Holmes.*

Children see in their parents the past, they again in their children the future ; and if we find more love in parents for their children than in children for their parents, this is sad indeed, but natural. Who does not fondle his hopes more than his recollections ? *Cötvös.*

Children should have their times of being off **55** duty, like soldiers. *Ruskin.*

Children should laugh, but not mock ; and when they laugh, it should not be at the weaknesses and the faults of others. *Ruskin.*

Children suck the mother when they are young, and the father when they are old. *Pr.*

Children sweeten labours, but they make misfortunes more bitter. *Bacon.*

Children tell in the highway what they hear by the fireside. *Port. Pr.*

Children think not of what is past, nor what is to come, but enjoy the present time, which few of us do. *La Bruyère.*

5 Chi lingua ha, a Roma va—He who has a tongue may go to Rome, *i.e.*, may go anywhere. *It. Pr.*

Chi nasce bella, nasce maritata—She who is born a beauty is born married. *It. Pr.*

Chi niente sa, di niente dubita—He who knows nothing, doubts nothing. *It. Pr.*

Chi non dà fine al pensare, non dà principio al fare—He who is never done with thinking never gets the length of doing. *It. Pr.*

Chi non ha cuore, abbia gambe—He who has no courage should have legs (to run). *It. Pr.*

10 Chi non ha, non è—He who has not, is not. *It. Pr.*

Chi non ha piaghe, se ne fa—He who has no worries makes himself some. *It. Pr.*

Chi non ha testa, abbia gambe—He who has no brains should have legs. *It. Pr.*

Chi non istima vien stimato—To disregard is to win regard. *It. Pr.*

Chi non puo fare come voglia, faccia come puo—He who cannot do as he would, must do as he can. *It. Pr.*

15 Chi non sa fingere, non sa vivere—He that knows not how to dissemble knows not how to live. *It. Pr.*

Chi non vede il fondo, non passi l'acqua—Who sees not the bottom, let him not attempt to wade the water. *It. Pr.*

Chi non vuol servir ad un sol signor, a molto ha da servir—He who will not serve one master will have to serve many. *It. Pr.*

Chi offende, non perdona mai—He who offends you never forgives you. *It. Pr.*

Chi offende scrive nella rena, chi è offeso nel marmo—He who offends writes on sand; he who is offended, on marble. *It. Pr.*

20 Chi parla semina, chi tace raccoglie—Who speaks, sows; who keeps silence, reaps. *It. Pr.*

Chi piglia leone in assenza suol temer del topi in presenza—He who takes a lion far off will shudder at a mole close by. *It. Pr.*

Chi piu sa, meno crede—Who knows most, believes least. *It. Pr.*

Chi più sa, meno parla—Who knows most, says least. *It. Pr.*

Chi sa la strada, puo andar di trotto—He who knows the road can go at a trot. *It. Pr.*

25 Chi sa poco presto lo dice—He who knows little quickly tells it. *It. Pr.*

Chi serve al commune serve nessuno—He who serves the public serves no one. *It. Pr.*

Chi si affoga, s'attaccherebbe a' rasoj—A drowning man would catch at razors. *It. Pr.*

Chi si fa fango, il porco lo calpestra—He who makes himself dirt, the swine will tread on him. *It. Pr.*

Chi si trova senz' amici, è come un corpo senz' anima—He who is without friends is like a body without a soul. *It. Pr.*

Chi sta bene, non si muova—Let him who is 30 well off remain where he is. *It. Pr.*

Chi tace confessa—Silence is confession. *It. Pr.*

Chi t'ha offeso non ti perdonera mai—He who has offended you will never forgive you. *It. Pr.*

Chi troppo abbraccia nulla stringe—He who grasps at too much holds fast nothing. *It. Pr.*

Chi tutto vuole, tutto perde—Covet all, lose all. *It. Pr.*

Chivalry was founded invariably by knights 35 who were content all their lives with their horse and armour and daily bread. *Ruskin.*

Chi va piano, va sano, chi va sano va lontano—He who goes softly goes safely, and he who goes safely goes far. *It. Pr.*

Chi va, vuole; chi manda, non se ha cura—He who goes himself, means it; he who sends another does not care. *It. Pr.*

Chi vuol dell' acqua chiara, vada alla fonte—He who wants the water pure must go to the spring-head. *It. Pr.*

Chi vuol esser mal servito tenga assai famiglia—Let him who would be ill served keep plenty servants. *It. Pr.*

Chi vuol il lavoro mal fatto, paghi innanzi 40 tratto—If you wish your work ill done, pay beforehand. *It. Pr.*

Chi vuol presto e ben, faccia da se—He who wishes a thing done quickly and well, must do it himself. *It. Pr.*

Choose a good mother's daughter, though her father were the devil. *Gael. Pr.*

Choose always the way that seems the best, however rough it may be. Custom will render it easy and agreeable. *Pythagoras.*

Choose an author as you choose a friend. *Earl of Roscommon.*

Choose thy speech. *Gael. Pr.* 45

Choose your wife as you wish your children to be. *Gael. Pr.*

Chords that vibrate sweetest pleasure / Thrill the deepest notes of woe. *Burns.*

Chose perdue, chose connue—A thing lost is a thing known, *i.e.*, valued. *Fr. Pr.*

Χωρὶς τό τ' εἰπεῖν πολλά καὶ τὰ καίρια—Volubility of speech and pertinency are sometimes very different things. *Sophocles.*

Christen haben keine Nachbarn—Christians 50 have no neighbours. *Ger. Pr.*

Christianity has not yet penetrated into the whole heart of Jesus. *Amiel.*

Christianity appeals to the noblest feelings of the human heart, and these are emotion and imagination. *Shorthouse.*

Christianity has a might of its own; it is raised above all philosophy, and needs no support therefrom. *Goethe.*

Christianity has made martyrdom sublime and sorrow triumphant. *Chapin.*

Christianity is a religion that can make men 55 good, only if they are good already. *Hegel.*

Christianity is salvation by the conversion of the will; humanism by the enlightenment of the mind. *Amiel.*

Christianity is the apotheosis of grief, the marvellous transmutation of suffering into triumph, the death of death and the defeat of sin. *Amiel.*

Christianity is the practical demonstration that holiness and pity, justice and mercy, may meet together and become one in man and in God. *Amiel.*

Christianity is the root of all democracy, the highest fact in the rights of men. *Novalis.*

Christianity is the worship of sorrow. *Goethe.*

Christianity's husk and shell / Threaten its heart like a blight. (*J. B.*) *Selkirk.*

5 Christianity teaches us to love our neighbour. Modern society acknowledges no neighbour. *Disraeli.*

Christianity, which is always true to the heart, knows no abstract virtues, but virtues resulting from our wants, and useful to all. *Chateaubriand.*

Christianity without the cross is nothing. *W. H. Thomson.*

Christians have burnt each other, quite persuaded / That all the apostles would have done as they did. *Byron.*

Christ is not valued at all, unless He is valued above all. *St. Augustine.*

10 Christ left us not a system of logic, but a few simple truths. *B. R. Haydon.*

Christmas comes but once a year. *Pr.*

Christ never wrote a tract, but He went about doing good. *Horace Mann.*

Christ's truth itself may yet be taught / With something of the devil's spirit. (*J. B.*) *Selkirk.*

Churches are not built on Christ's principles, but on His tropes. *Emerson.*

15 Ci-devant—Former. *Fr.*

Cieco è l'occhio, se l'animo è distratto—The eye sees nothing if the mind is distracted. *It. Pr.*

Ciencia es locura si buen senso no la cura—Knowledge is of little use if it is not under the direction of good sense. *Sp. Pr.*

Ci-gît—Here lies. *Fr.*

Cineri gloria sera venit—Glory comes too late to one in the dust. *Mart.*

20 Ciò che Dio vuole, io voglio—What God wills, I will. *M.*

Ciò che si usa, non ha bisogno di scusa—That which is customary needs no excuse. *It. Pr.*

Circles are prais'd, not that abound / In largeness, but th' exactly round; / So life we praise, that does excel, / Not in much time, but acting well. *Waller.*

Circles in water as they wider flow, / The less conspicuous in their progress grow, / And when at last they trench upon the shore, / Distinction ceases, and they're view'd no more. *Crabbe.*

Circles to square, and cubes to double, / Would give a man excessive trouble. *Prior.*

25 Circuitus verborum—A roundabout story or expression.

Circulus in probando—Begging the question, or taking for granted the point at issue (*lit.* a circle in the proof).

Circumstances are beyond the control of man, but his conduct is in his own power. *Disraeli.*

Circumstances are things *round about;* we are *in* them, not *under* them. *Lander.*

Circumstances form the character, but, like petrifying matters, they harden while they form. *Lander.*

Circumstances? I make circumstances. 30 *Napoleon.*

Cita mors ruit—Death is a swift rider.

Citharœdus / Ridetur chorda qui semper oberrat eadem—The harper who is always at fault on the same string is derided. *Hor.*

Cities force growth, and make men talkative and entertaining, but they make them artificial. *Emerson.*

Cities give not the human senses room enough. *Emerson.*

Cities have always been the fire-places (*i.e.*, 35 *foci*) of civilisation, whence light and heat radiated out into the dark, cold world. *Theodore Parker.*

Citius venit periculum cum contemnitur—When danger is despised, it arrives the sooner. *Syr.*

Civil dissension is a viperous worm / That gnaws the bowels of the commonwealth. *1 Hen. VI.*, iii. 1.

Civilisation degrades the many to exalt the few. *A. B. Alcott.*

Civilisation depends on morality. *Emerson.*

Civilisation is the result of highly complex 40 organisation. *Emerson.*

Civilisation means the recession of passional and material life, and the development of social and moral life. *Ward Beecher.*

Civilisation tends to corrupt men, as large towns vitiate the air. *Amiel.*

Civility costs nothing, and buys everything. *M. Wortley Montagu.*

Clamorous labour knocks with its hundred hands at the golden gate of the morning. *Newman Hall.*

Claqueur—One hired to applaud. *Fr.* 45

Clarior e tenebris—The brighter from the obscurity. *M.*

Clarum et venerabile nomen—An illustrious and honoured name.

Classical quotation is the parole of literary men all over the world. *Johnson.*

Classisch ist das Gesunde, romantisch das Kranke—The healthy is classical, the unhealthy is romantic. *Goethe.*

Claude os, aperi oculos—Keep thy mouth shut, 50 but thy eyes open.

Claudite jam rivos, pueri; sat prata biberunt—Close up the sluices now, lads; the meadows have drunk enough. *Virg.*

Clausum fregit—He has broken through the enclosure, *i.e.*, committed a trespass. *L.*

Clay and clay differs in dignity, / Whose dust is both alike. *Cymbeline*, iv. 2.

Cleanliness is near of kin to godliness. *Pr.*

Clear and bright it should be ever, / Flowing 55 like a crystal river; / Bright as light, and clear as wind. *Tennyson on the Mind.*

Clear conception leads naturally to clear and correct expression. *Boileau.*

Clear writers, like clear fountains, do not seem so deep as they are; the turbid look the most profound. *Lander.*

Clear your mind of cant. *Johnson.*

Clemency alone makes us equal with the gods. *Claudianus.*

Clemency is one of the brightest diamonds in 60 the crown of majesty. *W. Secker.*

Cleverness is serviceable for everything, sufficient for nothing. *Amiel.*

Clever people will recognise and tolerate nothing but cleverness. *Amiel.*

Climbing is performed in the same posture as creeping. *Swift.*

Clocks will go as they are set; but man, irregular man, is never constant, never certain. *Otway.*

5 Close sits my shirt, but closer sits my skin. *Pr.*

Clothes are for necessity; warm clothes, for health; cleanly, for decency; lasting, for thrift; and rich, for magnificence. *Fuller.*

Clothes have made men of us; they are threatening to make clothes-screens of us. *Carlyle.*

Clothes make the man. *Dut. Pr.*

Clouds are the veil behind which the face of day coquettishly hides itself, to enhance its beauty. *Jean Paul.*

10 Coal is a portable climate. *Emerson.*

Cobblers go to mass and pray that the cows may die (*i.e.*, for the sake of their hides). *Port. Pr.*

Cobra buena fama, y échate á dormir—Get a good name, and go to sleep. *Sp. Pr.*

Cobre gana cobre que no huesos de hombre—Money (*lit.* copper) breeds money and not man's bones. *Sp. Pr.*

Coelitus mihi vires—My strength is from heaven. *M.*

15 Coelo tegitur qui non habet urnam—He who has no urn to hold his bones is covered by the vault of heaven. *Lucan.*

Coelum ipsum petimus stultitia — We assail heaven itself in our folly. *Hor.*

Coelum non animum mutant qui trans mare currunt—Those who cross the sea change only the climate, not their character. *Hor.*

Coerced innocence is like an imprisoned lark; open the door, and it is off for ever. *Haliburton.*

Cogenda mens est ut incipiat—The mind must be stimulated to make a beginning. *Sen.*

20 Cogi qui potest nescit mori—He who can be compelled knows not how to die. *Sen.*

Cogitatio nostra coeli munimenta perrumpit, nec contenta est, id, quod ostenditur, scire—Our thoughts break through the muniments of heaven, and are not satisfied with knowing what is offered to sense observation. *Sen.*

Cogito, ergo sum—I think, therefore I am. *Descartes.*

Cognovit actionem—He has admitted the action. *L.*

Coigne of vantage. *Macb.,* i. 6.

25 Coin heaven's image / In stamps that are forbid. *Meas. for Meas.,* ii. 4.

Cold hand, warm heart. *Pr.*

Cold pudding settles one's love. *Pr.*

Collision is as necessary to produce virtue in men, as it is to elicit fire in inanimate matter; and chivalry is the essence of virtue. *Lord John Russell.*

Colonies don't cease to be colonies because they are independent. *Disraeli.*

30 Colour answers to feeling in man; shape, to thought; motion, to will. *John Sterling.*

Colour blindness, which may mistake drab for scarlet, is better than total blindness, which sees no distinction of colour at all. *George Eliot.*

Colour is the type of love. Hence it is especially connected with the blossoming of the earth, and with its fruits; also with the spring and fall of the leaf, and with the morning and evening of the day, in order to show the waiting of love about the birth and death of man. *Ruskin.*

Colours are the smiles of Nature . . . her laughs, as in the flowers. *Leigh Hunt.*

Colubram in sinu fovere—To cherish a serpent in one's bosom.

Columbus discovered no isle or key so lonely 35 as himself. *Emerson.*

Combien de héros, glorieux, magnanimes, ont vécu trop d'un jour—How many famous and high-souled heroes have lived a day too long! *J. B. Rousseau.*

Combinations of wickedness would overwhelm the world, did not those who have long practised perfidy grow faithless to each other. *Johnson.*

Come, and trip it as you go, / On the light fantastic toe. *Milton.*

Come, civil night, / Thou sober-suited matron, all in black. *Rom. and Jul.,* iii. 2.

Come, cordial, not poison. *Rom. and Jul.,* v. 1. 40

Comedians are not actors; they are only imitators of actors. *Zimmermann.*

Come è duro calle—How hard is the path. *Dante.*

Come, fair Repentance, daughter of the skies! / Soft harbinger of soon returning virtue; / The weeping messenger of grace from heaven. *Browne.*

Come forth into the light of things, / Let Nature be your teacher. *Wordsworth.*

Come he slow or come he fast, / It is but 45 Death who comes at last. *Scott.*

Come like shadows, so depart. *Bowles.*

Come, my best friends, my books, and lead me on. *Cowley.*

Come one, come all! this rock shall fly / From its firm base as soon as I. *Scott.*

Comes jucundus in via pro vehiculo est—A pleasant companion on the road is as good as a carriage. *Pub. Syr.*

Come the three corners of the world in arms, / 50 And we shall shock them. Nought shall make us rue, / If England to itself do rest but true. *King John,* v. 7.

Come, we burn daylight. *Rom. and Jul.,* i. 4.

Come what come may, / Time and the hour runs through the roughest day. *Macb.,* i. 3.

Come what sorrow can, / It cannot countervail th' exchange of joy / That one short minute gives me in her sight. *Rom. and Jul.,* ii. 6.

Comfort is the god of this world, but comfort it will never obtain by making it an object. *Whipple.*

Comfort's in heaven; and we are on the earth, / 55 Where nothing lives but crosses, care, and grief. *Rich. II.,* ii. 2.

Coming events cast their shadows before. *Campbell.*

Comitas inter gentes—Courtesy between nations.

Command large fields, but cultivate small ones. *Virg.*

Comme il faut—As it should be. *Fr.*

Comme je fus—As I was. *M.* 60

Comme je trouve—As I find it. *M.*

Commend a fool for his wit or a knave for his honesty, and he will receive you into his bosom. *Fielding.*

Commend me rather to him who goes wrong in a way that is his own, than to him who walks correctly in a way that is not. *Goethe.*

Commerce changes the fate and genius of nations. *T. Gray.*

Commerce flourishes by circumstances, precarious, contingent, transitory, almost as liable to change as the winds and waves that waft it to our shores. *Colton.*

5 Commerce has set the mark of selfishness, the signet of all-enslaving power, upon a shining ore and called it gold. *Shelley.*

Commerce is a game of skill, which every one canno' play, which few men can play well. *Emerson.*

Commerce is one of the daughters of Fortune, inconstant and deceitful as her mother. She chooses her residence where she is least expected, and shifts her abode when her continuance is, in appearance, most firmly settled. *Johnson.*

Commit a crime, and the earth is made of glass. *Emerson.*

Committunt multi eadem diverso crimina fato, / Ille crucem sceleris pretium tulerit, hic diadema—How different the fate of men who commit the same crimes! For the same villany one man goes to the gallows, and another is raised to a throne.

10 Common as light is love, / And its familiar voice wearies not ever. *Shelley.*

Common chances common men can bear. *Coriolanus*, iv. 1.

Common distress is a great promoter both of friendship and speculation. *Swift.*

Common fame is seldom to blame. *Pr.*

Commonly they use their feet for defence whose tongue is their weapon. *Sir P. Sidney.*

15 Common men are apologies for men; they bow the head, excuse themselves with prolix reasons, and accumulate appearances, because the substance is not. *Emerson.*

Common-place people see no difference between one man and another. *Pascal.*

Common-sense is calculation applied to life. *Amiel.*

Common-sense is the average sensibility and intelligence of men undisturbed by individual peculiarities. *W. R. Alger.*

Common-sense is the genius of humanity. *Goethe.*

20 Common-sense is the measure of the possible; it is calculation applied to life. *Amiel.*

Common souls pay with what they do; nobler souls, with what they are. *Emerson.*

Communautés commencent par bâtir leur cuisine—Communities begin with building their kitchen. *Fr. Pr.*

Commune bonum—A common good.

Commune naufragium omnibus est consolatio—A shipwreck (disaster) that is common is a consolation to all. *Pr.*

25 Commune periculum concordiam parit—A common danger tends to concord. *L.*

Communia esse amicorum inter se omnia—All things are common among friends. *Ter.*

Communibus annis—One year with another.

Communi consensu—By common consent.

Communion is the law of growth, and homes only thrive when they sustain relations with each other. *J. G. Holland.*

Communism is the exploitation of the strong 30 by the weak. In communism, inequality springs from placing mediocrity on a level with excellence. *Proudhon.*

Como canta el abad, así responde el monacillo—As the abbot sings, the sacristan answers. *Sp. Pr.*

Compagnon de voyage—A fellow-traveller. *Pr.*

Company, villanous company, has been the spoil of me. 1 *Hen. IV.*, iii. 3.

Comparaison n'est pas raison—Comparison is no proof. *Fr. Pr.*

Compare her face with some that I shall 35 show, / And I will make thee think thy swan a crow. *Rom. and Jul.*, i. 2.

Comparisons are odious. *Burton.*

Comparisons are odorous. *Much Ado*, iii. 5.

Compassion to the offender who has grossly violated the laws is, in effect, a cruelty to the peaceable subject who has observed them. *Junius.*

Compassion will cure more sins than condemnation. *Ward Beecher.*

Compendia dispendia—Short cuts are round-40 about ways.

Compendiaria res improbitas, virtusque tarda—Vice is summary in its procedure, virtue is slow.

Compesce mentem—Restrain thy irritation. *Hor.*

Complaining never so loud, and with never so much reason, is of no use. *Emerson.*

Complaining profits little; stating of the truth may profit. *Carlyle.*

Complaint is the largest tribute heaven re-45 ceives, and the sincerest part of our devotion. *Swift.*

Compliments are only lies in court clothes. *J. Sterling.*

Componitur orbis / Regis ad exemplum; nec sic inflectere sensus / Humanos edicta valent, quam vita regentis—Manners are fashioned after the example of the king, and edicts have less effect on them than the life of the ruler. *Claud.*

Compose thy mind, and prepare thy soul calmly to obey; such offering will be more acceptable to God than every other sacrifice. *Metastasio.*

Compositum miraculi causa—A story trumped up to astonish. *Tac.*

Compos mentis—Of a sound mind. 50

Compound for sins they are inclined to / By damning those they have no mind to. *Butler.*

Comprendre c'est pardonner—To understand is to pardon. *Mad. de Staël.*

Compte rendu—Report, return. *Fr.*

Con agua pasada no muele molino—The mill grinds no corn with water that has passed. *Sp. Pr.*

Con amore—With love; earnestly. *It.* 55

Con arte e con inganno si vive mezzo l'anno; con inganno si vive l'altra parte—People live with art and deception one half the year, and with deception and art the other half. *It. Pr.*

Conceal not the meanness of thy family, nor think it disgraceful to be descended from peasants; for when it is seen thou art not thyself ashamed, no one will endeavour to make thee so. *Cervantes.*

Conceit in weakest bodies strongest works. *Ham.*, iii. 4.

Conceit may puff a man up, but never prop him up. *Ruskin.*

Concentration is the secret of strength in politics, in war, in trade, in short, in all the management of human affairs. *Emerson.*

5 Concio ad clerum—An address to the clergy.

Concordia discors—A jarring or discordant concord. *Ovid.*

Concordia res parvæ crescunt, discordia maximæ dilabuntur—With concord small things increase, with discord the greatest go to ruin. *Sall.*

Concours—A competition. *Fr.*

Condemnable idolatry is insincere idolatry—a human soul clinging spasmodically to an Ark of the Covenant, which it half feels is now a phantasm. *Carlyle.*

10 Condemn the fault, and not the actor of it ! / Why, every fault's condemned ere it be done. *Meas. for Meas.*, ii. 2.

Condense some daily experience into a glowing symbol, and an audience is electrified. *Emerson.*

Con dineros no te conocerás, sin dineros no te conocerán—With money you would not know yourself; without it, no one would know you. *Sp. Pr.*

Condition, circumstance, is not the thing, / Bliss is the same in subject or in king. *Pope.*

Conditions are pleasant or grievous to us according to our sensibilities. *Lew. Wallace.*

15 Con el Rey y con la Inquisicion, chitos—With the King and the Inquisition, hush ! *Sp. Pr.*

Confessed faults are half mended. *Sc. Pr.*

Confess yourself to Heaven ; / Repent what's past ; avoid what is to come ; / And do not spread the compost on the weeds, / To make them ranker. *Ham.*, iii. 4.

Confess you were wrong yesterday; it will show you are wise to-day. *Pr.*

Confidence imparts a wondrous inspiration to its possessor. It bears him on in security, either to meet no danger or to find matter of glorious trial. *Milton.*

20 Confidence in another man's virtue is no slight evidence of a man's own. *Montaigne.*

Confidence in one's self is the chief nurse of magnanimity. *Sir P. Sidney.*

Confidence is a plant of slow growth in an aged bosom. *Chatham.*

Confidence is a thing not to be produced by compulsion. Men cannot be forced into trust. *D. Webster.*

Confido, conquiesco—I trust, and am at rest. *M.*

25 Confine your tongue, lest it confine you. *Pr.*

Confrère—A brother monk or associate. *Fr.*

Confusion now hath made his masterpiece. / Most sacrilegious murder hath broke ope / The Lord's anointed temple, and stole thence / The life o' the building. *Macb.*, ii. 1.

Confusion worse confounded. *Milton.*

Congé d'élire—A leave to elect. *Fr.*

30 Con poco cervello si governa il mondo—The world is governed with small wit. *It. Pr.*

Conquer we shall, but we must first contend ; / 'Tis not the fight that crowns us, but the end. *Herrick.*

Conscia mens recti famæ mendacia risit—The mind conscious of integrity ever scorns the lies of rumour. *Ovid.*

Conscience does make cowards of us all ; / And thus the native hue of resolution / Is sicklied o'er with the pale cast of thought ; / And enterprises of great pith and moment, / With this regard, their currents turn awry, / And lose the name of action. *Ham.*, iii. 1.

Conscience is but a word that cowards use, / Devised at first to keep the strong in awe ; / Our strong arms be our conscience, swords our law. *Rich. III.*, v. 3.

Conscience is our magnetic needle ; / reason, 35 our chart. *Joseph Cook.*

Conscience is the chamber of justice. *Origen.*

Conscience is the compass of the unknown. *Joseph Cook.*

Conscience is the sentinel of virtue. *Johnson.*

Conscience is the voice of the soul; the passions, of the body. *Rousseau.*

Conscience is wiser than science. *Lavater.* 40

Conscientia mille testes—Conscience is equal to a thousand witnesses. *Pr.*

Con scienza—With a knowledge of the subject. *It.*

Consecrated is the spot which a good man has trodden. *Goethe.*

Consecration is going out into the world where God Almighty is, and using every power for His glory. *Ward Beecher.*

Conseil d'état—Council of state. 45

Consensus facit legem—Consent makes the law. *L.*

Consequitur quodcunque petit—He attains to whatever he aims at. *M.*

Conservatism is the pause on the last movement. *Emerson.*

Consideration, like an angel, came, / And whipp'd th' offending Adam out of him, / Leaving his body as a paradise, / To envelop and contain celestial spirits. *Henry V.*, i. 1

Consider the lilies of the field, how they grow; 50 they toil not, neither do they spin; and yet I say unto you, that even Solomon in all his glory was not arrayed like one of these. *Jesus.*

Consilio et animis—By counsel and courage. *M.*

Conspicuous by its absence. *Lord John Russell.*

Constans et fidelitate—Constant and with faithfulness. *M.*

Constant attention wears the active mind, / Blots out her powers, and leaves a blank behind. *Churchill.*

Constantia et virtute—By constancy and virtue. 55 *M.*

Constantly choose rather to want less than to have more. *Thomas à Kempis.*

Constant occupation prevents temptation. *It. Pr.*

Constant thought will overflow in words unconsciously. *Byron.*

Consuetudinis magna vis est—The force of habit is great. *Cic.*

Consuetudo est altera lex—Custom is a second 60 law. *L.*

Consuetudo est secunda natura—Custom is a second nature. *St. Aug.*

Consuetudo pro lege servatur—Custom is observed as law. *L.*

Consult duty, not events. *Landor.*

Contaminate our fingers with base bribes ? . . . I'd rather be a dog and bay the moon than such a Roman. *Jul. Cæs.*, iv. 3.

Contas na maõ, e o demonio no coraçaõ—Rosary in the hand, and the devil in the heart. *Port. Pr.*

Contemni est gravius stultitiæ quam percuti—To be despised is more galling to a foolish man than to be whipped.

Contemporaries appreciate the man rather than his merit; posterity will regard the merit rather than the man. *Colton.*

Contempt is a dangerous element to sport in ; a deadly one, if we habitually live in it. *Carlyle.*

Contempt is a kind of gangrene, which, if it seizes one part of a character, corrupts all the rest by degrees. *Johnson.*

10 Contempt is the only way to triumph over calumny. *Mde. de Maintenon.*

Contented wi' little, an' cantie (cheerily happy) wi' mair. *Burns.*

Content if hence th' unlearn'd their wants may view, / The learn'd reflect on what before they knew. *Pope.*

Contention is a hydra's head ; the more they strive, the more they may. *Burton.*

Contention, like a horse / Full of high feeding, madly hath broken loose, / And bears all down before him. *2 Hen.*, i. 1.

15 Contentions fierce, / Ardent, and dire, spring from no petty cause. *Scott.*

Contentions for trifles can get but a trifling victory. *Sir P. Sidney.*

Content is better than riches. *Pr.*

Content is the true philosopher's stone. *Pr.*

Contentment, as it is a short road and pleasant, has great delight and little trouble. *Epictetus.*

20 Contentment consisteth not in adding more fuel, but in taking away some fire. *Fuller.*

Contentment is natural wealth. *Socrates.*

Contentment will make a cottage look as fair as a palace. *W. Secker.*

Contentment without money is the philosopher's stone. *Lichtwer.*

Content's a kingdom, and I wear that crown. *Heywood.*

25 Content thyself to be obscurely good ; / When vice prevails, and impious men bear sway, / The post of honour is a private station. *Addison.*

Content with poverty, my soul I arm ; / And virtue, though in rags, will keep me warm. *Dryden after Hor.*

Contesa vecchia tosto si fa nuova—An old feud is easily renewed. *It. Pr.*

Conticuere omnes, intentique ora tenebant—All were at once silent and listened intent. *Virg.*

Continued eloquence wearies. *Pascal.*

30 Contra bonos mores—Against good morals.

Contra malum mortis, non est medicamen in hortis—Against the evil of death there is no remedy in the garden.

Contraria contrariis curantur—Contraries are cured by contraries.

Contrast increases the splendour of beauty, but it disturbs its influence ; it adds to its attractiveness, but diminishes its power. *Ruskin.*

Contrat social—The social compact, specially Rousseau's theory thereof.

Contra verbosos noli contendere verbis ; / 35 Sermo datur cunctis, animi sapientia paucis —Don't contend with words against wordy people ; speech is given to all, wisdom to few. *Cato.*

Contredire, c'est quelquefois frapper à une porte, pour savoir s'il y a quelqu'un dans la maison—To contradict sometimes means to knock at the door in order to know whether there is any one in the house. *Fr. Pr.*

Contre fortune bon cœur—Against change of fortune set a bold heart. *Fr. Pr.*

Contre les rebelles, c'est cruauté que d'estre humain et humanité d'estre cruel—Against rebels it is cruelty to be humane, and humanity to be cruel. *Corneille Muis.*

Contre-temps—A mischance. *Fr.*

Contrivances of the time / For sowing broad-40 cast the seeds of crime. *Longfellow.*

Contumeliam si dicis, audies—If you utter abuse, you must expect to receive it. *Plaut.*

Conversation enriches the understanding ; but solitude is the school of genius. *Gibbon.*

Conversation in society is found to be on a platform so low as to exclude science, the saint, and the poet. *Emerson.*

Conversation is an abandonment to ideas, a surrender to persons. *A. B. Alcott.*

Conversation is an art in which a man has all 45 mankind for competitors. *Emerson.*

Conversation is a traffic ; and if you enter into it without some stock of knowledge to balance the account perpetually, the trade drops at once. *Sterne.*

Conversation will not corrupt us if we come to the assembly in our own garb and speech, and with the energy of health to select what is ours and reject what is not. *Emerson.*

Converse with a mind that is grandly simple, and literature looks like word-catching. *Emerson.*

Conversion—a grand epoch for a man ; properly the one epoch ; the turning-point which guides upwards, or guides downwards, him and his activities for evermore. *Carlyle.*

Conversion is the awakening of a soul to see 50 into the awful *truth* of things ; to see that Time and its shows all rest on Eternity, and this poor earth of ours is the threshold either of heaven or hell. *Carlyle.*

Convey a libel in a frown, / And wink a reputation down. *Swift.*

Convey thy love to thy friend as an arrow to the mark ; not as a ball against the wall, to rebound back again. *Quarles.*

Conviction, never so excellent, is worthless till it convert itself into conduct. *Carlyle.*

Copia verborum—Superabundance of words.

Coraçaõ determinado, naõ soffre conselho—He 55 brooks no advice whose mind is made up. *Port. Pr.*

Coram domino rege—Before our lord the king.

Coram nobis—Before the court.

Coram non judice—Before one who is not a judge.

Corbies (crows) and clergy are kittle shot (hard to hit). *Sc. Pr.*

Corbies dinna pick oot corbies' een, *i.e.*, harm each other. *Sc. Pr.*

Cordon bleu—A skilful cook (*lit.* a blue ribbon). *Fr.*

Cordon sanitaire—A guard to prevent a disease spreading. *Fr.*

5 Corn is gleaned with wind, and the soul with chastening. *Geo. Herbert.*

Cor nobile, cor immobile—A noble heart is an immovable heart.

Coronat virtus cultores suos—Virtue crowns her votaries. *M.*

Corpo ben feito naõ ha mester capa—A body that is well made needs no cloak. *Port. Pr.*

Corpora lente augescunt, cito extinguuntur—All bodies are slow in growth, rapid in decay. *Tac.*

10 Corporations cannot commit treason, nor be outlawed nor excommunicated, for they have no souls. *Coke.*

Corporations have neither bodies to be punished nor souls to be damned. *Thurlow.*

Corporis et fortunæ bonorum, ut initium, finis est. Omnia orta occidunt, et aucta senescunt—The blessings of health and fortune, as they have a beginning, must also have an end. Everything rises but to fall, and grows but to decay. *Sall.*

Corpo satollo non crede all' affamato—A satisfied appetite does not believe in hunger. *It. Pr.*

Corps d'armée—A military force. *Fr.*

15 Corps diplomatique—The diplomatic body. *Fr.*

Corpus Christi—Festival in honour of the Eucharist or body of Christ.

Corpus delicti—The body of the offence. *L.*

Corpus sine pectore—A body without a soul. *Hor.*

Correct counting keeps good friends. *Gael. Pr.*

20 Correction does much, but encouragement does more. *Goethe.*

Correction is good, administered in time. *Dan. Pr.*

Corre lontano chi non torna mai—He runs a long way who never turns. *It. Pr.*

Corrigenda—Corrections to be made.

Corrupted freemen are the worst of slaves. *Garrick.*

25 Corruption is like a ball of snow, when once set a rolling it must increase. *Colton.*

Corruptions can only be expiated by the blood of the just ascending to heaven by the steps of the scaffold. *De Tocqueville.*

Corruptio optimi pessima—The corruption of the best is the worst. *Anon.*

Corruptissima in republica plurimæ leges—In a state in which corruption abounds laws are very numerous. *Tac.*

Cor unum, via una—One heart, one way. *M.*

30 Corvées—Forced labour, formerly exacted of the peasantry in France. *Fr.*

Cosa ben fatta è fatta due volte—A thing well done is twice done. *It. Pr.*

Cosa fatta, capo ha—A thing which is done has a head, *i.e.*, it is never done till completed. *It. Pr.*

Cosa mala nunca muere—A bad thing never dies. *Sp. Pr.*

Così fan tutti—So do they all. *It.*

Cos ingeniorum—A whetstone to their wit. 35

Costly thy habit as thy purse can buy, / But not expressed in fancy; rich, not gaudy; / For the apparel oft proclaims the man. *Ham.*, i. 3.

Costumbre hace ley—Custom becomes law. *Sp. Pr.*

Could everything be done twice, it would be done better. *Ger. Pr.*

Could great men thunder / As Jove himself does, Jove would ne'er be quiet; / For every pelting, petty officer / Would use his heaven for thunder; nothing but thunder. *Meas. for Meas.*, ii. 2.

Could we forbear dispute and practise love, / 40 We should agree as angels do above. *Waller.*

Could you see every man s career in life, you would find a woman clogging him . . . or cheering him and goading him. *Thackeray.*

Couleur de rose—A flattering representation. *Fr.*

Count art by gold, and it fetters the feet it once winged. *Ouida.*

Count the world not an inn, but an hospital; and a place not to live in, but to die in. *Colton.*

Countries are well cultivated, not as they 45 are fertile, but as they are free. *Montesquieu.*

Coup de grace—The finishing stroke. *Fr.*

Coup de main—A bold effort; a surprise.

Coup de pied—A kick. *Fr.*

Coup de soleil—Stroke of the sun. *Fr.*

Coup d'essai—First attempt. *Fr.* 50

Coup d'état—A sudden stroke of policy. *Fr.*

Coup de théâtre—Theatrical effect. *Fr.*

Coup d'œil—A glance of the eye; a prospect.

Courage against misfortune, and reason against passion. *Pr.*

Courage and modesty are the most unequivocal 55 of virtues, for they are of a kind that hypocrisy cannot imitate. *Goethe.*

Courage consists in equality to the problem before us. *Emerson.*

Courage consists not in blindly overlooking danger, but in meeting it with the eyes open. *Jean Paul.*

Courage consists not in hazarding without fear, but being resolutely minded in a just cause. *Plutarch.*

Courage! even sorrows, when once they are vanished, quicken the soul, as rain the valley. *Salis.*

Courage is generosity of the highest order, 60 for the brave are prodigal of the most precious things. *Colton.*

Courage is on all hands considered an essential of high character. *Froude.*

Courage is the wisdom of manhood; foolhardiness, the folly of youth. *Pr.*

Courage mounteth with occasion. *King John*, ii. 1.

Courage never to submit or yield. *Milton.*

Courage of soul is necessary for the triumphs 65 of genius. *Mme. de Staël.*

Courage of the soldier awakes the courage of woman. *Emerson.*

Courage, or the degree of life, is as the degree of circulation of the blood in the arteries. *Emerson.*

Courage sans peur—Courage without fear. *Fr.*

Courage, sir, / That makes man or woman look their goodliest. *Tennyson.*

Courage, so far as it is a sign of race, is peculiarly the mark of a gentleman or a lady; but it becomes vulgar if rude or insensitive. *Ruskin.*

5 Courtesy costs nothing. *Pr.*

Courtesy is cumbersome to him that kens it not. *Sc. Pr.*

Courtesy is often sooner found in lowly sheds with smoky rafters, than in tapestry halls and courts of princes, where it first was named. *Milton.*

Courtesy itself must convert to disdain, if you come in her presence. *Much Ado,* i. 1.

Courtesy never broke one's crown. *Gael. Pr.*

10 Courtesy of temper, when it is used to veil churlishness of deed, is but a knight's girdle around the breast of a base clown. *Scott.*

Courtship consists in a number of quiet attentions, not so pointed as to alarm, nor so vague as not to be understood. *Sterne.*

Coûte qu'il coûte—Let it cost what it may. *Fr.*

Cover yourself with honey and the flies will fasten on you. *Pr.*

Covetous men need money least, yet most affect it; and prodigals, who need it most, do least regard it. *Theod. Parker*

15 Covetousness bursts the bag. *Pr.*

Covetousness is a sort of mental gluttony, not confined to money, but greedy of honour and feeding on selfishness. *Chamfort.*

Covetousness is ever attended with solicitude and anxiety. *B. Franklin.*

Covetousness is rich, while modesty goes barefoot. *Phædrus.*

Covetousness, like jealousy, when it has once taken root, never leaves a man but with his life. *T. Hughes.*

20 Covetousness often starves other vices. *Sc. Pr.*

Covetousness swells the principal to no purpose, and lessens the use to all purposes. *Jeremy Taylor.*

Covetousness, which is idolatry. *St. Paul.*

Coward dogs / Most spend their mouths when what they seem to threaten / Runs far before them. *Henry V.,* ii. 4.

Cowardice is the dread of what will happen. *Epictetus.*

25 Cowards are cruel, but the brave / Love mercy, and delight to save. *Gay.*

Cowards die many times before their deaths; / The valiant never taste of death but once. / Of all the wonders that I yet have heard, / It seems to me most strange that men should fear; / Seeing that death, a necessary end, / Will come when it will come. *Jul. Cæsar,* ii. 2.

Cowards falter, but danger is often overcome by those who nobly dare. *Queen Elizabeth.*

Cowards father cowards, and base things sire base; / Nature hath meal and bran, contempt and grace. *Cymb.,* iv. 2.

Cowards tell lies, and those that fear the rod. *G. Herbert.*

Crabbed age and youth / Cannot live together. 30 *Shakespeare.*

Craftiness is a quality in the mind and a vice in the character. *Sanial Dubay.*

Craft maun hae claes (clothes), but truth gaes naked. *Sc. Pr.*

Crafty men contemn studies; simple men admire them; and wise men use them; for they teach not their own use; but that is wisdom without them, and above them won by observation. *Bacon.*

Craignez honte—Fear shame. *M.*

Craignez tout d'un auteur en courroux—Fear 35 the worst from an enraged author. *Fr.*

Crambe repetita—Cabbage repeated (kills). *Juv.*

Cras credemus, hodie nihil—To-morrow we will believe, but not to-day. *Pr.*

Crea el cuervo, y sacarte ha los ojos—Breed up a crow and he will peck out your eyes. *Sp. Pr.*

Creaking waggons are long in passing. *Fris. Pr.*

Created half to rise and half to fall, / Great 40 lord of all things, yet a prey to all; / Sole judge of truth, in endless error hurl'd; / The glory, jest, and riddle of the world. *Pope.*

Creation is great, and cannot be understood. *Carlyle.*

Creation lies before us like a glorious rainbow; but the sun that made it lies behind us, hidden from us. *Jean Paul.*

Creation's heir, the world, the world is mine. *Goldsmith.*

Creation sleeps! 'Tis as the general pulse / Of life stood still, and Nature made a pause, / An awful pause, prophetic of her end. *Young.*

Credat Judæus Apella—Apella, the Jew, may 45 believe that; I cannot. *Hor.*

Crede quod est quod vis—Believe that that is which you wish to be. *Ovid.*

Crede quod habes, et habes—Believe that you have it, and you have it.

Credit keeps the crown o' the causey, *i.e.,* is not afraid to show its face. *Sc. Pr.*

Creditors have better memories than debtors. *Pr.*

Credo, quia absurdum—I believe it because it is 50 absurd. *Tert.*

Credula res amor est—Love is a credulous affection. *Ovid.*

Credula vitam / Spes fovet, et fore cras semper ait melius—Credulous hope cherishes life, and ever whispers to us that to-morrow will be better. *Tibull.*

Credulity is perhaps a weakness almost inseparable from eminently truthful characters. *Tuckerman.*

Credulity is the common failing of inexperienced virtue. *Johnson.*

Creep before you gang (walk). *Sc. Pr.* 55

Crescentem sequitur cura pecuniam, / Majorumque fames — Care accompanies increasing wealth, and a craving for still greater riches. *Hor.*

Crescit amor nummi quantum ipsa pecunia crescit—The love of money increases as wealth increases. *Juv.*

Crescit occulto velut arbor ævo—It grows as a tree with a hidden life. *Hor.*

Crescit sub pondere virtus—Virtue thrives under oppression. *M.*

Cressa ne careat pulchra dies nota—Let not a day so fair be without its white mark. *Hor.*

Creta an carbone notandi?—Are they to be marked with chalk or charcoal? *Hor.*

5 Crime and punishment grow out of one stem. Punishment is a fruit that, unsuspected, ripens within the flower of the pleasure that concealed it. *Emerson.*

Crime cannot be hindered by punishment, but only by letting no man grow up a criminal. *Ruskin.*

Crime, like virtue, has its degrees. *Racine.*

Crimen læsæ majestatis—Crime of high treason.

Crimen quos inquinat, æquat—Crime puts those on an equal footing whom it defiles.

10 Crimes generally punish themselves. *Goldsmith.*

Crimes sometimes shock us too much; vices almost always too little. *Hare.*

Crimina qui cernunt aliorum, non sua cernunt, / Hi sapiunt aliis, desipiuntque sibi—Those who see the faults of others, but not their own, are wise for others and fools for themselves. *Pr.*

Crimine ab uno / Disce omnes—From the base character of one learn what they all are. *Virg.*

Cripples are aye better schemers than walkers. *Sc. Pr.*

15 Criticism is a disinterested endeavour to learn and propagate the best that is known and thought in the world. *Matthew Arnold.*

Criticism is as often a trade as a science, requiring, as it does, more health than wit, more labour than capacity, more practice than genius. *La Bruyère.*

Criticism is like champagne, nothing more execrable if bad, nothing more excellent if good. *Colton.*

Criticism is not construction; it is observation. *G. W. Curtis.*

Criticism must never be sharpened into anatomy. The life of the imagination, as of the body, disappears when we pursue it. *Willmott.*

20 Criticism often takes from the tree caterpillars and blossoms together. *Jean Paul.*

Criticism should be written for the public, not the artist. *Wm. Winter.*

Critics all are ready made. *Byron.*

Critics are men who have failed in literature and art. *Disraeli.*

Critics are sentinels in the grand army of letters, stationed at the corners of newspapers and reviews to challenge every new author. *Longfellow.*

25 Critics must excuse me if I compare them to certain animals called asses, who, by gnawing vines, originally taught the great advantage of pruning them. *Shenstone.*

Crosses are ladders that lead to heaven. *Pr.*

Crows do not pick out crows' eyes. *Pr.*

Cruci dum spiro fido—Whilst I breathe I trust in the cross. *M.*

Crudelem medicum intemperans æger facit—A disorderly patient makes a harsh physician. *Pub. Syr.*

Crudelis ubique / Luctus, ubique pavor, et 30 plurima mortis imago—Everywhere is heart-rending wail, everywhere consternation, and death in a thousand shapes. *Virg.*

Cruel as death, and hungry as the grave. *Thomson.*

Cruel men are the greatest lovers of mercy; avaricious, of generosity; proud, of humility, —in others. *Colton.*

Cruelty in war buyeth conquest at the dearest price. *Sir P. Sidney.*

Cruelty is no more the cure of crimes than it is the cure of sufferings. *Landor.*

Crux criticorum—The puzzle of critics. 35

Crux est si metuas quod vincere nequeas—It is torture to fear what you cannot overcome. *Ausonius.*

Crux medicorum—The puzzle of physicians.

Cry "Havock," and let slip the dogs of war. *Jul. Cæs.*, iii. 1.

Cucullus non facit monachum—The cowl does not make the monk. *Pr.*

Cudgel thy brains no more about it, for your 40 dull ass will not mend his pace with beating. *Ham.*, v. 1.

Cui bono?—Whom does it benefit?

Cuidar muitas cousas, fazer huma—Think of many things, do only one. *Port. Pr.*

Cuidar naõ he saber—Thinking is not knowing. *Port. Pr.*

Cui lecta potenter erit res / Nec facundia deseret hunc nec lucidus ordo—He who has chosen a theme suited to his powers will never be at a loss for felicitous language or lucid arrangement. *Hor.*

Cuilibet in arte sua perito credendum est— 45 Every man is to be trusted in his own art. *Pr.*

Cui licitus est finis, etiam licent media—Where the end is lawful the means are also lawful. *A Jesuit maxim.*

Cui malo?—Whom does it harm?

Cui mens divinior atque os / Magna sonaturum des nominis hujus honorem—To him whose soul is more than ordinarily divine, and who has the gift of uttering lofty thoughts, you may justly concede the honourable title of poet. *Hor.*

Cui non conveniat sua res, ut calceus olim, / Si pede major erit, subvertet, si minor, uret —As a shoe, when too large, is apt to trip one, and when too small, to pinch the feet; so is it with him whose fortune does not suit him. *Hor.*

Cui placet alterius, sua nimirum est odio sors 50 —When a man envies another's lot, it is natural he should be discontented with his own. *Hor.*

Cui placet, obliviscitur; cui dolet, meminit—Acts of kindness are soon forgotten, but the memory of an offence remains. *Pr.*

Cui prodest scelus, is fecit—He has committed the crime who profits by it. *Sen.*

Cuique suum—His own to every one. *Pr.*

Cui serpe mozzica, lucenta teme—Whom a serpent has bitten fears a lizard. *It. Pr.*

Cujus est solum, ejus est usque ad cœlum—He 55 who owns the soil owns everything above it to the very sky. *L.*

Cujus rei libet simulator atque dissimulator—A finished pretender and dissembler. *Sall.*

Cujusvis hominis est errare: nullius nisi insipientis in errore perseverare—Every one is liable to err; none but a fool will persevere in error. *Cic.*

Cujus vita fulgor, ejus verba tonitrua — His words are thunderbolts whose life is as lightning. *Mediæval Pr.*

Cujus vulturis hoc erit cadaver?—To what harpy's will shall this carcass fall? *Mart.*

Cul de sac—A street, a lane or passage, that has no outlet. *Fr.*

5 Culpam pœna premit comes—Punishment follows hard upon crime as an attendant. *Hor.*

Cultivated labour drives out brute labour. *Emerson.*

Cultivate not only the cornfields of your mind, but the pleasure-grounds also. *Whately.*

Cultivation is as necessary to the mind as food to the body. *Cic.*

Culture, aiming at the perfection of the man as the end, degrades everything else, as health and bodily life, into means. *Emerson.*

10 Culture enables us to express ourselves. *Hamerton.*

Culture implies all which gives the mind possession of its own powers. *Emerson.*

Culture inverts the vulgar views of nature, and brings the mind to call that apparent which it uses to call real, and that real which it uses to call visionary. *Emerson.*

Culture is a study of perfection. *Matthew Arnold.*

Culture is the passion for sweetness and light, and (what is more) the passion for making them prevail. *Matthew Arnold.*

15 Culture (is the process by which a man) becomes all that he was created capable of being, resisting all impediments, casting off all foreign, especially all noxious, adhesions, and showing himself at length in his own shape and stature, be these what they may. *Carlyle.*

Culture merely for culture's sake can never be anything but a sapless root, capable of producing at best a shrivelled branch. *J. W. Cross.*

Culture must not omit the arming of the man. *Emerson.*

Culture of the thinking, the dispositions (*Gesinnungen*), and the morals is the only education that deserves the name, not mere instruction. *Herder.*

Cum grano salis—With a grain of salt, *i.e.*, with some allowance.

20 Cum privilegio—With privilege.

Cunctando restituit rem—He restored the cause (of Rome) by delay. *Said of Fabius, surnamed therefore Cunctator.*

Cuncti adsint, meritæque expectent præmia palmæ—Let all attend, and expect the rewards due to well-earned laurels. *Virg.*

Cunctis servatorem liberatoremque acclamantibus—All hailing him as saviour and deliverer.

Cunning is the art of concealing our own defects, and discovering other people's weaknesses. *Hazlitt.*

25 Cunning is the dwarf of wisdom. *W. G. Alger.*

Cunning is the intensest rendering of vulgarity, absolute and utter. *Ruskin.*

Cunning is to wisdom as an ape to a man. *William Penn.*

Cunning leads to knavery; 'tis but a step, and that a very slippery, from the one to the other. Lying only makes the difference; add that to cunning, and it is knavery. *La Bruyère.*

Cunning signifies especially a habit or gift of over-reaching, accompanied with enjoyment and a sense of superiority. *Ruskin.*

30 Cunning surpasses strength. *Ger. Pr.*

Cupias non placuisse nimis—Do not aim at too much popularity. *Mart.*

Cupid is a knavish lad, / Thus to make poor females mad. *Mid. N. Dream,* iii. 2.

Cupid makes it his sport to pull the warrior's plumes. *Sir P. Sidney.*

Cupido dominandi cunctis affectibus flagrantior est—The desire of rule is the most ardent of all the affections of the mind. *Tac.*

35 Cupid's butt-shaft is too hard for Hercules' club. *Love's L. Lost,* i. 2.

Curæ leves loquuntur, ingentes stupent—Light troubles are loud-voiced, deeper ones are dumb. *Sen.*

Cura facit canos—Care brings grey hairs. *Pr.*

Cura pii dis sunt, et qui coluere, coluntur—The pious-hearted are cared for by the gods, and they who reverence them are reverenced. *Ovid.*

Cura ut valeas—Take care that you keep well. *Cic.*

40 Curiosa felicitas—Studied felicity of thought or of style.

Curiosis fabricavit inferos—He fashioned hell for the inquisitive. *St. Augustine.*

Curiosity is a desire to know why and how; such as is in no living creature but man. *Hobbes.*

Curiosity is lying in wait for every secret. *Emerson.*

Curiosity is one of the forms of feminine bravery. *Victor Hugo.*

45 Curiosity is the direct incontinency of the spirit. Knock, therefore, at the door before you enter on your neighbour's privacy; and remember that there is no difference between entering into his house and looking into it. *Jeremy Taylor.*

Curiosity is the kernel of the forbidden fruit. *Fuller.*

Curiosus nemo est, quin idem sit malevolus—Nobody is inquisitive about you who does not also bear you ill-will. *Plaut.*

Curious to think how, for every man, any the truest fact is modelled by the nature of the man. *Carlyle.*

Currente calamo—With a running pen.

50 Cursed be the social ties that warp us from the living truth. *Tennyson.*

Curse on all laws but those which love has made. *Pope.*

Curses always recoil on the head of him who imprecates them. If you put a chain around the neck of a slave, the other end fastens itself around your own. *Emerson.*

Curses are like chickens; they always return home. *Pr.*

Curses, not loud, but deep, mouth-honour, breath, / Which the poor heart would fain deny, but dare not. *Macb.,* v. 3.

Curst be the man, the poorest wretch in life, / The crouching vassal to the tyrant wife, / Who has no will but by her high permission; / Who has not sixpence but in her possession; / Who must to her his dear friend's secret tell; / Who dreads a curtain lecture worse than hell. / Were such the wife had fallen to my part, / I'd break her spirit or I'd break her heart. *Burns.*

Curst be the verse, how well soe'er it flow, / That tends to make one worthy man my foe, / Give virtue scandal, innocence a fear, / Or from the soft-ey'd virgin steal a tear. *Pope.*

Curs'd merchandise, where life is sold, / And avarice consents to starve for gold. *Rowe from Lucan.*

Custom does often reason overrule, / And only serves for reason to the fool. *Rochester.*

5 Custom doth make dotards of us all. *Carlyle.*

Custom forms us all; / Our thoughts, our morals, our most fixed belief, / Are consequences of our place of birth. *A. Hill.*

Custom is the law of one set of fools, and fashion of another; but the two often clash, for precedent is the legislator of the one and novelty of the other. *Colton.*

Custom is the plague of wise men and the idol of fools. *Pr.*

Custom may lead a man into many errors, but it justifies none. *Fielding.*

10 Custom reconciles to everything. *Burke.*

Custos morum—The guardian of morality.

Custos regni—The guardian of the realm.

Custos rotulorum—The keeper of the rolls.

Cutis vulpina consuenda est cum cute leonis—The fox's skin must be sewed to that of the lion. *L. Pr.*

15 Cut men's throats with whisperings. *Ben Jonson.*

Cut off even in the blossoms of my sin, / Unhousel'd, disappointed, unanel'd; / No reckoning made, but sent to my account / With all my imperfections on my head. *Ham.,* i. 5.

Cut out the love of self, like an autumn lotus, with thy hand. *Buddha.*

Cutting honest throats by whispers. *Scott.*

Cut your coat according to your cloth. *Pr.*

D.

20 Daar niets goeds in is, gaat niets goeds uit—Where no good is in, no good comes out. *Dut. Pr.*

Daar 't een mensch wee doet, daar heeft hij de hand—A man lays his hand where he feels the pain. *Dut. Pr.*

Daar twee kijven hebben ze beiden schuld—When two quarrel both are to blame. *Dut. Pr.*

Daar zijn meer dieven als er opgehangen worden—There are more thieves than are hanged. *Dut. Pr.*

Dabit Deus his quoque finem—God will put an end to these calamities also. *Virg.*

25 Da capo—From the beginning. *It.*

D'accord—Agreed; in tune. *Fr.*

Da chi mi fido, / Guardi mi Dio. / Da chi non mi fido, / Mi guarderò io—From him I trust may God keep me; from him I do not trust I will keep myself. *It. Pr.*

Dachtet ihr, der Löwe schliefe, weil er nicht brüllte?—Did you think the lion was sleeping because it did not roar? *Schiller.*

Da die Götter menschlicher noch waren, / Waren Menschen göttlicher—When the gods were more human, men were more divine. *Schiller.*

Dádivas quebrantan peñas—Gifts dissolve rocks. 30 *Sp. Pr.*

Da du Welt nicht kannst entsagen, / Erobre dir sie mit Gewalt—Where thou canst not renounce the world, subdue it under thee by force. *Platen.*

Dafür bin ich ein Mann dass sich aushalte in dem was ich begonnen, dass ich einstehe mit Leib und Leben für das Trachten meines Geistes—For this end am I a man, that I should persevere steadfastly in what I have began, and answer with my life for the aspiration of my spirit. *Laube.*

Daily life is more instructive than the most effective book. *Goethe.*

δαῖτος ἐΐσης—An equal diet. *Hom.*

Δάκρυ' ἀδάκρυα—Tearless tears. *Eurip.* 35

Dal detto al fatto v'è un gran tratto—From saying to doing is a long stride. *It. Pr.*

Da locum melioribus—Make way for your betters. *Ter.*

Dame donde me asiente, que yo me haré donde me acueste—Give where I may sit down, and I will make where I may lie down. *Sp. Pr.*

Dames quêteuses—Ladies who collect for the poor. *Fr.*

Dämmerung ist Menschenlos in jeder Be- 40 ziehung—Twilight (of dawn) is the lot of man in every relation. *Feuchtersleben.*

Damna minus consueta movent—Losses we are accustomed to, affect us little. *Juv.*

Damnant quod non intelligunt—They condemn what they do not understand. *Quinct.*

Damn'd neuters, in their middle way of steering, / Are neither fish, nor flesh, nor good red-herring. *Dryden.*

Damnosa hæreditas—An inheritance which entails loss. *L.*

Damnosa quid non imminuit dies?—What is 45 there that corroding time does not impair? *Hor.*

Damnum absque injuria—Loss without injustice. *L.*

Damnum appellandum est cum mala fama lucrum—Gain at the expense of credit must be set down as loss. *Pr.*

Damn with faint praise, assent with civil leer, / And, without sneering, teach the rest to sneer. / Willing to wound, and yet afraid to strike; / Just hint a fault, and hesitate dislike. *Pope.*

Danari fanno danari—Money breeds money. *It. Pr.*

Dance attendance on their lordships' pleasure. 50 *Hen. VIII.,* v. 2.

Dan Chaucer, well of English undefiled, / On Fame's eternal bead-roll worthy to be filed. *Spenser.*

Dandies, when first-rate, are generally very agreeable men. *Bulwer Lytton.*

Danger for danger's sake is senseless. *Victor Hugo.*

Danger is the very basis of superstition. It produces a searching after help supernaturally when human means are no longer supposed to be available. *B. R. Haydon.*

Danger levels man and brute, / And all are fellows in their need. *Byron.*

5 Danger past, God forgotten. *Pr.*

Dannosa è il dono che toglie la libertà—Injurious is the gift that takes away our liberty. *It. Pr.*

Dans l'adversité de nos meilleurs amis, nous trouvons toujours quelque chose qui ne nous déplait pas—In the misfortune of our best friends we find always something which does not displease us. *La Roche.*

Dans la morale, comme l'art, dire n'est rien, faire est tout—In morals as in art, talking is nothing, doing is all. *Renan.*

Dans l'art d'intéresser consiste l'art d'écrire—The art of writing consists in the art of interesting. *Fr.*

10 Dans le nombre de quarante ne fait-il pas un zéro?—In the number forty is there not bound to be a cipher? *Fr.*

Dans les conseils d'un état, il ne faut pas tant regarder ce qu'on doit faire, que ce qu'on peut faire—In the councils of a state, the question is not so much what ought to be done, as what can be done. *Fr.*

Dante was very bad company, and was never invited to dinner. *Emerson.*

Dante, who loved well because he hated, / Hated wickedness that hinders loving. *Browning.*

Dantur opes nulli nunc nisi divitibus—Wealth now-a-days goes all to the rich. *Mart.*

15 Dapes inemptæ—Dainties unbought, *i.e.,* home produce. *Hor.*

Dapibus supremi / Grata testudo Jovis—The shell (lyre) a welcome accompaniment at the banquets of sovereign Jove. *Hor.*

Dare pondus idonea fumo—Fit only to give importance to trifles (*lit.* give weight to smoke). *Pr.*

Dare to be true, nothing can need a lie; / A fault which needs it most, grows two thereby. *George Herbert.*

Daring nonsense seldom fails to hit, / Like scattered shot, and pass with some for wit. *Butler.*

20 Darkness visible. *Milton.*

Darkness which may be felt. *Bible.*

Dark night, that from the eye his function takes, / The ear more quick of apprehension makes. *Mid. N. Dream,* iii. 2.

Dark with excessive bright. *Milton.*

Das Alte stürzt, es ändert sich die Zeit, / Und neues Leben blüht aus den Ruinen—The old falls, the time changes, and new life blossoms out of the ruins. *Schiller.*

25 Das Alter der göttlichen Phantasie / Es ist verschwunden, es kehret nie—The age of divine fantasy is gone, never to return. *Schiller.*

Das Alter wägt, die Jugend wagt—Age considers, youth ventures. *Raupach.*

Das arme Herz, hienieden / Von manchem Sturm bewegt, / Erlangt den wahren Frieden, / Nur, wo es nicht mehr schlägt—The poor heart, agitated on earth by many a storm, attains true peace only when it ceases to beat. *Salis-Seewis.*

Das Auge des Herrn schafft mehr als seine beiden Hände—The master's eye does more than both his hands. *Ger. Pr.*

Das begreife ein andrer als ich!—Let another try to understand that; I cannot. *A. Lortzing.*

Das Beste, was wir von der Geschichte haben, 30 ist der Enthusiasmus, den sie erregt—The best benefit we derive from history is the enthusiasm which it excites. *Goethe.*

Das Edle zu erkennen ist Gewinnst / Der nimmer uns entrissen werden kann—The ability to appreciate what is noble is a gain which no one can ever take from us. *Goethe.*

Das einfach Schöne soll der Kenner schätzen ; / Verziertes aber spricht der Menge zu—The connoisseur of art must be able to appreciate what is simply beautiful, but the common run of people are satisfied with ornament. *Goethe.*

Das Erste und Letzte, was vom Genie gefordert wird, ist Wahrheitsliebe—The first and last thing which is required of genius is love of truth. *Goethe.*

Das Geeinte zu entzweien, das Entzweite zu einigen, ist das Leben der Natur—Dividing the united, uniting the divided, is the life of Nature. *Goethe.*

Das Geheimniss ist für die Glücklichen— 35 Mystery is for the favoured of fortune. *Schiller.*

Das Genie erfindet, der Witz findet bloss— Genius invents, wit merely finds. *Weber.*

Das Gesetz ist der Freund des Schwachen— Law is the protector of the weak. *Schiller.*

Das Gesetz nur kann uns Freiheit geben— Only law can give us freedom. *Goethe.*

Das Gewebe dieser Welt ist aus Nothwendigkeit und Zufall gebildet ; die Vernunft des Menschen stellt sich zwischen beide, und weiss sie zu beherrschen—The web of this world is woven out of necessity and contingency ; the reason of man places itself between the two, and knows how to control them. *Goethe.*

Das glaub' ich—That is exactly my opinion. 40 *Ger. Pr.*

Das Glück deiner Tage / Wäge nicht mit der Goldwage. / Wirst du die Krämerwage nehmen, / So wirst du dich schämen und dich bequemen—Weigh not the happiness of thy days with goldsmith's scales. Shouldst thou take the merchant's, thou shalt feel ashamed and adapt thyself. *Goethe.*

Das Glück giebt Vielen zu viel, aber Keinem genug—Fortune gives to many too much, but to no one enough. *Ger. Pr.*

Das glücklichste Wort es wird verhöhnt, / Wenn der Hörer ein Schiefohr ist—The happiest word is scorned, if the hearer has a twisted ear. *Goethe.*

Das grosse unzerstörbare Wunder ist der Menschenglaube an Wunder—The great indestructible miracle is man's faith in miracle. *Jean Paul.*

Das Grösste, was dem Menschen begegnen 45 kann, ist es wohl, in der eigenen Sache die allgemeine zu vertheidigen—The noblest function, I should say, that can fall to man is to vindicate all men's interests in vindicating his own. *Ranke.*

Das hat die Freude mit dem Schmerz gemein, / Dass sie die Menschen der Vernunft beraubt —Joy has this in common with pain, that it bereaves man of reason. *Platen.*

Das Heiligste, die Pflicht, ist leider das, was wir am öftersten in uns bekämpfen und meistens wider Willen thun — Duty, alas! which is the most sacred instinct in our nature, is that which we most frequently struggle with in ourselves, and generally do against our will. *R. Gutzkow.*

Das Herz gleicht dem Mühlsteine der Mehl gibt, wenn man Korn aufschüttet, aber sich selbst zerreibt, wenn man es unterlässt—The heart is like a millstone, which yields meal if you supply it with grain, but frets itself away if you neglect to do so. *Weber.*

Das Herz und nicht die Meinung ehrt den Mann—It is his heart, and not his opinion, that is an honour to a man. *Schiller.*

5 Das höchste Glück ist das, welches unsere Mängel verbessert und unsere Fehler ausgleicht—The best fortune that can fall to a man is that which corrects his defects and makes up for his failings. *Goethe.*

Das Hohngelächter der Hölle — The scoffing laughter of Hell. *Lessing.*

Das Ideal in der Kunst, Grösse in Ruhe darzustellen, sei das Ideal auf dem Throne— Let the ideal in art, the representation of majesty in repose, be the ideal on the throne. *Jean Paul.*

Das ist die wahre Liebe, die immer und immer sich gleich bleibt, / Wenn man ihr alles gewährt, wenn man ihr alles versagt—That is true love which is ever the same (*lit.* equal to itself), whether everything is conceded to it or everything denied. *Goethe.*

Das Jahrhundert / Ist meinem Ideal nicht reif. Ich lebe / Ein Bürge derer, welche kommen werden—The century is not ripe for my ideal; I live as an earnest of those that are to come. *Schiller.*

10 Das Kind mit dem Bade verschütten—To throw away the child with the bath, *i.e.,* the good with the bad. *Ger. Pr.*

Das Kleine in einen grossen Sinne behandeln, ist Hoheit des Geistes ; das Kleine für gross und wichtig halten, ist Pedantismus — To treat the little in a large sense is elevation of spirit ; to treat the little as great and important is pedantry. *Feuchersleben.*

Das Leben dünkt ein ew'ger Frühling mir— Life seems to me an eternal spring. *Lortzing.*

Das Leben eines Staates ist, wie ein Strom, in fortgehender Bewegung ; wenn der Strom steht, so wird er Eis oder Sumpf—The life of a state, like a stream, lies in its onward movement ; if the stream stagnates, it is because it is frozen or a marsh. *J. v. Müller.*

Das Leben gehört den Lebendigen an, und wer lebt, muss auf Wechsel gefasst sein—Life belongs to the living, and he who lives must be prepared for changes. *Goethe.*

15 Das Leben heisst Streben—Life is a striving. *Ger. Pr.*

Das Leben ist die Liebe / Und des Lebens Leben Geist—Life is love, and the life of life, spirit. *Goethe.*

Das Leben ist nur ein Moment, der Tod ist auch nur einer—Life is but a moment, death also is but another. *Schiller.*

Das Leben lehrt uns, weniger mit uns / Und andern strenge sein—Life teaches us to be less severe both with ourselves and others. *Goethe.*

Das Nächste das Liebste—The nearest is the dearest. *Ger. Pr.*

Das Nächste steht oft unergreifbar fern—What 20 is nearest is often unattainably far off. *Goethe.*

Da spatium tenuemque moram ; male cuncta ministrat / Impetus—Allow time and slight delay ; haste and violence ruin everything. *Stat.*

Das Publikum, das ist ein Mann / Der alles weiss und gar nichts kann—The public is a personage who knows everything and can do nothing. *L. Roberts.*

Das Recht hat eine wächserne Nase—Justice has a nose of wax. *Ger. Pr.*

Das Reich der Dichtung ist das Reich der Wahrheit / Schliesst auf das Heiligthum, es werde Licht—The kingdom of poetry is the kingdom of truth ; open the sanctuary and there is light. *A. v. Chamisso.*

Das Schicksal ist ein vornehmer aber theurer 25 Hofmeister—Fate is a distinguished but expensive pedagogue. *Goethe.*

Das schönste Glück des denkenden Menschen ist, das Erforschliche erforscht zu haben, und das Unerforschliche ruhig zu verehren—The fairest fortune that can fall to a thinking man is to have searched out the searchable, and restfully to adore the unsearchable. *Goethe.*

Das schwere Herz wird nicht durch Worte leicht—Words bring no relief to a saddened heart. *Schiller.*

Das Schwerste in allen Werken der Kunst ist dass dasjenige, was sehr ausgearbeitet worden, nicht ausgearbeitet scheine—The most difficult thing in all works of art is to make that which has been most highly elaborated appear as if it had not been elaborated at all. *Winkelmann.*

Das Siegel der Wahrheit ist Einfachheit— The seal of truth is simplicity. *Boerhave.*

Das sind die Weisen, / Die durch Irrtum zur 30 Wahrheit reisen ; / Die bei dem Irrtum verharren, / Das sind die Narren—Those are wise who through error press on to truth ; those are fools who hold fast by error. *Rückert.*

Das Sprichwort sagt : Ein eigner Herd, / Ein braves Weib sind Gold und Perlen wert— A proverb says : A hearth of one's own and a good wife are worth gold and pearls. *Goethe.*

Das Talent arbeitet, das Genie schafft—Talent works, genius creates. *Schumann.*

Das Unglück kann die Weisheit nicht, Doch Weisheit kann das Unglück tragen—Misfortune cannot endure wisdom, but wisdom can endure misfortune. *Bodenstedt.*

Das Universum ist ein Gedanke Gottes—The universe is a thought of God. *Schiller.*

Das Unvermeidliche mit Würde trage—Bear 35 the inevitable with dignity. *Streckfuss.*

Das Vaterland der Gedanken ist das Herz ; an dieser Quelle muss schöpfen, wer frisch trinken will—The native soil of our thoughts is the heart ; whoso will have his fresh must draw from this spring. *Börne.*

Das Verhängte muss geschehen, / Das Gefürchtete muss nahn—The fated must happen ; the feared must draw near. *Schiller.*

Das Volk ist frei ; seht an, wie wohl's ihm geht ! —The people are free, and see how well they enjoy it. *Mephisto. in "Faust."*

Das Volk schätzt Stärke vor allem—The people rate strength before everything. *Goethe.*

Das Vortreffliche it unergründlich, man mag damit anfangen was man will—What is excellent cannot be fathomed, probe it as and where we will. *Goethe.*

Das Wahre ist gottähnlich ; es erscheint nicht unmittelbar, wir müssen es aus seinen Manifestationen errathen—Truth is like God ; it reveals itself not directly ; we must divine it out of its manifestations. *Goethe.*

Das Warum wird offenbar, / Wann die Toten aufersteh'n—We shall know the wherefore when the dead rise again. *Müllner.*

5 Das was mir wichtig scheint, hältst du für Kleinigkeiten ; / Das was mich ärgert hat bei dir nichts zu bedeuten—What is to me important you regard as a trifle, and what puts me out has with you no significance. *Goethe.*

Das Weib sieht tief, der Mann sieht weit. Dem Manne ist die Welt das Herz, dem Weibe ist das Herz die Welt—The woman's vision is deep reaching, the man's far reaching. With the man the world is his heart, with the woman her heart is her world. *Grabbe.*

Das Wenige verschwindet leicht dem Blick, / Der vorwärts sieht, wie viel noch übrig bleibt —The little (achieved) is soon forgotten by him who looks before him and sees how much still remains to be done. *Goethe.*

Das Werk lobt den Meister—The work praises the artist. *Ger. Pr.*

Das Wort ist frei, die That ist stumm, der Gehorsam blind — The word is free, action dumb, obedience blind. *Schiller.*

10 Das Wunder ist des Glaubens liebstes Kind— Miracle is the pet child of faith. *Goethe.*

Data fata secutus—Following what is decreed by fate. *M.*

Dat Deus immiti cornua curta bovi—God gives the vicious ox short horns. *Pr.*

Dà tempo al tempo—Give time to time. *It. Pr.*

Date obolum Belisario—Give a mite to Belisarius !

15 Dat Galenus opes, dat Justinianus honores / Sed Moses sacco cogitur ire pedes—Galen gives wealth, Justinian honours, but Moses must go afoot with a beggar's wallet.

Dat inania verba, / Dat sine mente sonum— He utters empty words ; he utters sound without meaning. *Virg.*

Dat veniam corvis, vexat censura columbas— He pardons the ravens, but visits with censure the doves. *Juv.*

Daub yourself with honey, and you'll be covered with flies. *Pr.*

Dauer im Wechsel — Persistence in change. *Goethe.*

20 Da veniam lacrymis—Forgive these tears.

Da ventura a tu hijo, y echa lo en el mar— Give your son luck and then throw him into the sea. *Sp. Pr.*

Davus sum, non Œdipus—I am a plain man, and no Œdipus (who solved the riddle of the Sphinx). *Ter.*

Dawted dochters mak' dawly wives, *i.e.,* petted daughters make slovenly wives. *Sc. Pr.*

Day follows the murkiest night ; and when the time comes, the latest fruits also ripen. *Schiller.*

Day is driven on by day, and the new moons 25 hasten to their wane. *Smart, from Hor.*

Daylight will come, though the cock does not crow. *Dan. Pr.*

Days should speak, and multitude of years should teach wisdom. *Bible.*

De adel der ziel is meer waardig dan de adel des geslachts—Nobility of soul is more honourable than nobility by birth. *Dut. Pr.*

Dead men open living men's eyes. *Sp. Pr.*

Dead scandals form good subjects for dissec- 30 tion. *Byron.*

De alieno largitor, et sui restrictor—Lavish of what is another's, tenacious of his own. *Cic.*

Deal mildly with his youth ; / For young hot colts, being raged, do rage the more. *Rich. II.,* ii. 1.

Deal so plainly with man and woman as to constrain the utmost sincerity and destroy all hope of trifling with you. *Emerson.*

Dear is cheap, and cheap is dear. *Port. Pr.*

Dear son of memory, great heir of fame. 35 *Milton on Shakespeare.*

Death and life are in the power of the tongue. *Bible.*

Death-bed repentance is sowing seed at Martinmas. *Gael. Pr.*

Death borders upon our birth, and our cradle stands in the grave. *Bp. Hall.*

Death but supplies the oil for the inextinguishable lamp of life. *Coleridge.*

Death comes equally to us all, and makes us 40 all equal when it comes. *Donne.*

Death finds us 'mid our playthings—snatches us, / As a cross nurse might do a wayward child, / From all our toys and baubles. *Old Play.*

Death gives us sleep, eternal youth, and immortality. *Jean Paul.*

Death is a black camel that kneels at every man's door. *Turk. Pr.*

Death is a commingling of eternity with time ; in the death of a good man eternity is seen looking through time. *Goethe.*

Death is a fearful thing. *Meas. for Meas.,* 45 iii. 1.

Death is a friend of ours, and he who is not ready to entertain him is not at home. *Bacon.*

Death is but another phasis of life, which also is awful, fearful, and wonderful, reaching to heaven and hell. *Carlyle.*

Death is but a word to us. Our own experience alone can teach us the real meaning of the word. *W. v. Humboldt.*

Death is but what the haughty brave, / The weak must bear, the wretch must crave. *Byron.*

Death is sure / To those that stay and those 50 that roam. *Tennyson.*

Death is the only physician, the shadow of his valley the only journeying that will cure us of age and the gathering fatigue of years. *George Eliot.*

Death is the quiet haven of us all. *Wordsworth.*

Death is the tyrant of the imagination. *Barry Cornwall.*

Death is the wish of some, the relief of many, and the end of all. *Sen.*

Death joins us to the great majority ; / 'Tis to be borne to Platos and to Cæsars ; / 'Tis to be great for ever ; / 'Tis pleasure, 'tis ambition, then, to die. *Young.*

Death lays his icy hand on kings. *Shirley.*

Death levels all distinctions.

Death lies on her, like an untimely frost, / Upon the sweetest flower of all the field. *Rom. and Jul.*, iv. 5.

5 Death may expiate faults, but it does not repair them. *Napoleon.*

Death opens the gate of fame, and shuts the gate of envy after it. *Sterne, after Bacon.*

Death pays all debts. *Pr.*

Death puts an end to all rivalship and competition. The dead can boast no advantage over us, nor can we triumph over them. *Hazlitt.*

Death rides in every passing breeze, / He lurks in every flower. *Heber.*

10 Death's but a path that must be trod, / If man would ever pass to God. *Parnell.*

Death shuns the wretch who fain the blow would meet. *Byron.*

Death, so called, is a thing which makes men weep, / And yet a third of life is passed in sleep. *Byron.*

Death stands behind the young man's back, before the old man's face. *T. Adams.*

Death treads in pleasure's footsteps round the world. *Young.*

15 Death will have his day. *Rich. II.*, iii. 2.

De auditu—By hearsay.

Debate is masculine, conversation is feminine ; the former angular, the latter circular and radiant of the underlying unity. *A. B. Alcott.*

De beste zaak heeft nog een goed' advocaat noodig—The best cause has need of a good pleader. *Dut. Pr.*

Debetis velle quæ velimus—You ought to wish as we wish. *Plaut.*

20 De bonne grace—With good grace ; willingly. *Fr.*

De bonne lutte—By fair means. *Fr.*

De bon vouloir servir le roy—To serve the king with good-will. *M.*

Debt is the worst kind of poverty. *Pr.*

Debt is to a man what the serpent is to the bird ; its eye fascinates, its breath poisons, its coil crushes both sinew and bone ; its jaw is the pitiless grave. *Bulwer Lytton.*

25 Debts make the cheeks black. *Arab. Pr.*

De calceo sollicitus, at pedem nihil curans—Anxious about the shoe, but careless about the foot. *L. Pr.*

Deceit and falsehood, whatever conveniences they may for a time promise or produce, are, in the sum of life, obstacles to happiness. *Johnson.*

Deceit is a game played only by small minds. *Corneille.*

Decency is the least of all laws, yet it is the one which is the most strictly observed. *La Roche.*

30 Deceptio visus—Optical illusion.

Decet affectus animi neque se nimium erigere nec subjicere serviliter—We ought to allow the affections of the mind to be neither too much elated nor abjectly depressed. *Cic.*

Decet imperatorem stantem mori—An emperor ought to die at his post (*lit.* standing). *Vespasian.*

Decet patriam nobis cariorem esse quam nosmetipsos—Our country ought to be dearer to us than ourselves. *Cic.*

Decet verecundum esse adolescentem—It becomes a young man to be modest. *Plaut.*

Decies repetita placebit—Ten times repeated, it 35 will still please. *Hor.*

Decipimur specie recti—We are deceived by the semblance of rectitude. *Hor.*

Decipit / Frons prima multos—First appearances deceive many.

Decision and perseverance are the noblest qualities of man. *Goethe.*

Declaring the end from the beginning, and from the ancient times the things that are not yet done. *Bible.*

Decori decus addit avito—He adds honour to 40 the honour of his ancestors. *M.*

Decorum ab honesto non potest separari—Propriety cannot be sundered from what is honourable. *Cic.*

De court plaisir, long repentir—A short pleasure, a long penance. *Fr.*

Decrevi—I have decreed. *M.*

Decus et tutamen—An honour and defence. *M.*

Dedecet philosophum abjicere animum—It does 45 not beseem a philosopher to be dejected. *Cic.*

De die in diem—From day to day.

Dedimus potestatem—We have given power. *L.*

Dediscit animus sero quod didicit diu—The mind is slow in unlearning what it has been long learning. *Sen.*

Deeds survive the doers. *Horace Mann.*

Deep calleth unto deep. *Bible.*   50

Deep insight will always, like Nature, ultimate its thought in a thing. *Emerson.*

Deep in the frozen regions of the north, / A goddess violated brought thee forth, / Immortal liberty. *Smollett.*

Deep on his front engraven / Deliberation sat, and public care. *Milton.*

Deep subtle wits, / In truth, are master spirits in the world. *Joanna Baillie.*

Deep vengeance is the daughter of deep 55 silence. *Alfieri.*

Deep vers'd in books, and shallow in himself. *Milton.*

De ezels dragen de haver, en de paarden eten die—Asses fetch the oats and horses eat them. *Dut. Pr.*

De facto—In point of fact.

Defeat is a school in which truth always grows strong. *Ward Beecher.*

Defeat is nothing but education, nothing but 60 the first step to something better. *Wendell Phillips.*

Defect in manners is usually the defect of fine perception. *Emerson.*

Defectio virium adolescentiæ vitiis efficitur sæpius quam senectutis—Loss of strength is more frequently due to the faults of youth than of old age. *Cic.*

Defendit numerus junctæque umbone phalanges—Their numbers protect them and their compact array. *Juv.*

Defend me, common sense, say I, / From reveries so airy, from the toil / Of dropping buckets into empty wells, / And growing old with drawing nothing up. *Cowper.*

Defend me from my friends; I can defend myself from my enemies. *Maréchal Villars.*

Deference is the most complicate, the most indirect, and the most elegant of all compliments. *Shenstone.*

Defer no time; / Delays have dangerous ends. 1 *Henry VI.*, iii. 2.

5 Defer not the least virtue; life's poor span / Make not an ell, by trifling in thy woe. / If thou do ill, the joy fades, not the pains ; / If well, the pain doth fade, the joy remains. *George Herbert.*

Defer not till to-morrow to be wise, / To-morrow's sun to thee may never rise. *Congreve.*

Deficiunt vires—Ability is wanting.

Defienda me Dios de my—God defend me from myself. *Sp. Pr.*

Definition of words has been commonly called a mere exercise of grammarians; but when we come to consider the innumerable evils men have inflicted on each other from mistaking the meaning of words, the exercise of definition certainly begins to assume rather a more dignified aspect. *Sydney Smith.*

10 Deformed, unfinished, sent before my time / Into this breathing world, scarce half made up, / And that so lamely and unfashionable, / That dogs bark at me as I halt by them. *Rich. III.*, i. 1.

Deformity is daring; it is its essence to overtake mankind by heart and soul, and make itself the equal, ay, the superior of the rest. *Byron.*

De fumo in flammam—Out of the frying-pan into the fire. *Pr.*

Dégagé—Free and unrestrained. *Fr.*

De gaieté de cœur—In gaiety of heart ; sportively ; wantonly. *Fr.*

15 Degeneres animos timor arguit—Fear is proof of a low-born soul. *Virg.*

Degli uomini si può dire questo generalmente che sieno ingrate, volubili simulatori, fuggitori pericoli, cupidi di guadagno—Of mankind we may say in general that they are ungrateful, fickle, hypocritical, intent on a whole skin and greedy of gain. *Machiavelli.*

Degrees infinite of lustre there must always be, but the weakest among us has a gift, however seemingly trivial, which is peculiar to him, and which, worthily used, will be a gift also to his race for ever. *Ruskin.*

De gustibus non disputandum—There is no disputing about tastes.

De hambre a nadie vi morir, de mucho comer a cien mil—I never saw a man die of hunger, but thousands die of overfeeding. *Sp. Pr.*

20 De haute lutte—By main force. *Fr.*

De hoc multi multa, omnes aliquid, nemo satis —Of this many have said many things, all something, no one enough.

Dei gratia—By the grace of God.

Dei jussu non unquam credita Teneris—Fated she (*i.e.*, Cassandra) never to be believed by her Trojan countrymen. *Virg.*

Deil stick pride, for my dog deed o'd. *Sc. Pr.*

Deil tak' the hin'most! on they drive, / Till 25 a' their weel-swall'd kytes belyve / Are bent like drums, / And auld guid man maist like to rive / "Bethankit" hums. *Burns.*

Dein Auge kann die Welt trüb' oder hell dir machen ; / Wie du sie ansiehst, wird sie weinen oder lachen—Thy eye can make the world dark or bright for thee ; as thou look'st on it, it will weep or laugh. *Rückert.*

De industria—Purposely.

De integro—Over again ; anew.

Δεῖ φέρειν τὰ τῶν θέων—We must bear what the gods lay on us.

Dei plena sunt omnia—All things are full of God. 30 *Cic.*

Déjeûner à la fourchette—A meat breakfast. *Fr.*

De jure—By right.

De kleine dieven hangt men, de groote laat men loopen—We hang little thieves and let great ones off. *Dut. Pr.*

Del agua mansa me libre Dios ; que de la recia me guardaré yo—From smooth water God guard me ; from rough, I can guard myself. *Sp. Pr.*

De lana caprina—About goat's wool, *i.e.*, a worth- 35 less matter.

Delay has always been injurious to those who are ready. *Lucan.*

Delay in vengeance gives a heavier blow. *J. Ford.*

Delay of justice is injustice. *Landor.*

Delectando pariterque monendo—By pleasing as well as instructing. *Hor.*

Delenda est Carthago—Carthage must be de- 40 stroyed. *Cato Major.*

Del giudizio, ognun ne vende—Of judgment every one has some to sell. *It. Pr.*

Deliberando sæpe perit occasio—An opportunity is often lost through deliberation. *Pub. Syr.*

Deliberandum est diu quod statuendum est semel—We must take time for deliberation, where we have to determine once for all. *Pub. Syr.*

Deliberate treachery entails punishment upon the traitor. *Junius.*

Deliberate with caution, but act with decision ; 45 and yield with graciousness or oppose with firmness. *Colton.*

Deliberat Roma, perit Saguntum—While Rome deliberates, Saguntum perishes. *Pr.*

Delicacy is to the affections what grace is to the beauty. *Degerando.*

Delicacy of taste has the same effect as delicacy of passion ; it enlarges the sphere both of our happiness and misery, and makes us sensible to pain as well as pleasures, which escape the rest of mankind. *Hume.*

Deliciæ illepidæ atque inelegantes—Unmannerly and inelegant pleasures. *Catull.*

Deligas tantum quem diligas—Choose only him 50 whom you love.

Delightful task! to rear the tender thought, / To teach the young idea how to shoot. *Thomson.*

Deliramenta doctrinæ—The crazy absurdities of learned men. *L.*

Delirant reges, plectuntur Achivi—Whatsoever devilry kings do, the Greeks must pay the piper. *Hor.*

Deliriums are dreams not rounded with a sleep. *Jean Paul.*

Deliverer, God hath appointed thee to free the oppressed and crush the oppressor. *Bryant.*

Dell' albero non si giudica dalla scorza—You can't judge of a tree by its bark. *It. Pr.*

De loin c'est quelque chose, et de près ce n'est rien—At a distance it is something, at hand nothing. *La Fontaine.*

5 Delphinum sylvis appingit, fluctibus aprum—He paints a porpoise in the woods, a boar amidst the waves. *Hor.*

De lunatico inquirendo—To inquire into a man's state of mind.

Delusion and weakness produce not one mischief the less because they are universal. *Burke.*

Delusion may triumph, but the triumphs of delusion are but for a day. *Macaulay.*

Delusions are as necessary to our happiness as realities. *Bovee.*

10 Delusive ideas are the motives of the greatest part of mankind, and a heated imagination the power by which their actions are incited. The world in the eye of a philosopher may be said to be a large madhouse. *Mackenzie.*

Del vero s'adira l'uomo—It is the truth that irritates a man. *It. Pr.*

De mal en pis—From bad to worse. *Fr.*

De male quæsitis vix gaudet tertius hæres—A third heir seldom enjoys what is dishonestly acquired. *Juv.*

Demean thyself more warily in thy study than in the street. If thy public actions have a hundred witnesses, thy private have a thousand. *Quarles.*

15 De medietate linguæ—Of a moiety of languages, *i.e.*, foreign jurymen. *L.*

Dem Esel träumet von Disteln—When the ass dreams, it is of thistles. *Ger. Pr.*

Dem Glücklichen schlägt keine Stunde—When a man is happy he does not hear the clock strike. *Ger. Pr.*

Dem harten Muss bequemt sich Will' und Grille—To hard necessity one's will and fancy (must) conform. *Goethe.*

Dem Herrlichsten, was auch der Geist empfangen, drängt Stoff sich an—Matter presses heavily on the noblest efforts of the spirit. *Goethe, in "Faust."*

20 Dem Hunde, wenn er gut gezogen / Wird selbst ein weiser Mann gewogen—Even a wise man will attach himself to the dog when he is well bred. *Goethe.*

De minimis non curat lex—The law takes no notice of trifles. *L.*

Dem Menschen ist / Ein Mensch noch immer lieber als ein Engel—A man is ever dearer to man than an angel. *Lessing.*

Democracies are prone to war, and war consumes them. *W. H. Seward.*

Democracy has done a wrong to everything that is not first-rate. *Amiel.*

25 Democracy is always the work of kings. Ashes, which in themselves are sterile, fertilise the land they are cast upon. *Landor.*

Democracy is, by the nature of it, a self-cancelling business, and gives in the long-run a net result of zero. *Carlyle.*

Democracy is the healthful life-blood which circulates through the veins and arteries, which supports the system, but which ought never to appear externally, and as the mere blood itself. *Coleridge.*

Democracy is the most powerful solvent of military organisation. The latter is founded on discipline; the former on the negation of discipline. *Renan.*

De monte alto—From a lofty mountain. *M.*

De mortuis nil nisi bonum (or bene)—Let nothing 30 be said of the dead but what is favourable.

De motu proprio—From the suggestion of one's own mind; spontaneously.

Dem thätigen Menschen kommt es darauf an, dass er das Rechte thue; ob das Rechte geschehe, soll ihn nicht kümmern—With the man of action the chief concern is that he do the right thing; the success of that ought not to trouble him. *Goethe.*

Den Bösen sind sie los; die Bösen sind geblieben—They are rid of the Wicked One, (but) the wicked are still there. *Goethe.*

De nihilo nihil, in nihilum nil posse reverti—From nothing is nothing, and nothing can be reduced to nothing.

Denique non omnes eadem mirantur amantque 35 —All men do not admire and love the same things. *Hor.*

Den Irrthum zu bekennen, schändet nicht—It is no disgrace to acknowledge an error. *R. Gutzkov.*

Denken und Thun, Thun und Denken, das ist die Summe aller Weisheit von jeher anerkannt, von jeher geübt, nicht eingesehen von einem jeden—To think and act, to act and think, this is the sum of all the wisdom that has from the first been acknowledged and practised, though not understood by every one, *i.e.*, (as added) the one must continually act and react on the other, like exhaling and inhaling, must correspond as question and answer. *Goethe.*

Denke nur niemand, dass man auf ihn als den Heiland gewartet habe—Let no one imagine that he is the man the world has been waiting for as its deliverer. *Goethe.*

Den leeren Schlauch bläst der Wind auf, / Den leeren Kopf der Dünkel—The empty bag is blown up with wind, the empty head with self-conceit. *Claudius.*

Den Mantel nach dem Winde kehren—To trim 40 one's sails (*lit.* to turn one's cloak) to the wind. *Ger. Pr.*

Den Menschen Liebe, den Göttern Ehrfurcht —To men, affection; to gods, reverence. *Grillparzer.*

Denn geschwätzig sind die Zeiten, / Und sie sind auch wieder stumm—For the times are babbly, and then again the times are dumb. *Goethe.*

De non apparentibus, et non existentibus, eadem est ratio—Things which do not appear are to be treated as the same as those which do not exist. *Coke.*

De novo—Anew.

Den Profit som kom seent, er bedre end aldeles 45 ingen—The profit which comes late is better than none at all. *E. H. Vessel.*

Den rechten Weg wirst nie vermissen, / Handle nur nach Gefühl und Gewissen—Wilt thou never miss the right way, thou hast only to act according to thy feeling and conscience. *Goethe.*

Den schlecten Mann muss man verachten / Der nie bedacht was er vollbringt—We must spurn him as a worthless man who never applies his brains to what he is working at. *Schiller.*

Dens theonina—A calumniating disposition (*lit.* tooth).

Deo adjuvante non timendum—God assisting, there is nothing to be feared.

Deoch an doris—The parting cup. *Gael.*

5 Deo dante nil nocet invidia, et non dante, nil proficit labor—When God gives, envy injures us not; when He does not give, labour avails not.

Deo date—Give unto God. *M.*

Deo duce, ferro comitante—God my guide, my sword my companion. *M.*

Deo duce, fortuna comitante—God for guide, fortune for companion. *M.*

Deo ducente—God guiding. *M.*

10 Deo favente—With God's favour.

Deo fidelis et regi—Faithful to God and the king. *M.*

Deo gratias—Thanks to God.

Deo honor et gloria—To God the honour and glory. *M.*

Deo ignoto—To the unknown God.

15 Deo juvante—With God's help.

De omnibus rebus, et quibusdam aliis—About everything, and certain things else.

De omni re scibile et quibusdam aliis—On everything knowable and some other matters.

Deo, non fortuna—From God, not fortune. *M.*

Deo, optimo maximo—To God, the best and greatest. *M.*

20 Deo, patriæ, amicis — For God, country, and friends. *M.*

Deo, regi, patriæ—To God, king, and country. *M.*

Deo, regi, vicino—For God, king, and our neighbour. *M.*

Deo, reipublicæ, amicis—To God, the state, and friends. *M.*

Deorum cibus est—A feast fit for the gods.

25 De oui et non vient toute question—All disputation comes out of "Yes" and "No." *Fr. Pr.*

Deo volente—With God's will.

Depart from the highway and transplant thyself in some enclosed ground; for it is hard for a tree that stands by the wayside to keep her fruit till it be ripe. *St. Chrysostom.*

De paupertate tacentes / Plus poscente ferent—Those who say nothing of their poverty fare better than those who beg. *Hor.*

De' peccati de' signori fanno penitenza i poveri—The poor do penance for the sins of the rich. *It. Pr.*

30 Dependence goes somewhat against the grain of a generous mind; and it is no wonder, considering the unreasonable advantage which is often taken of the inequality of fortune. *Jeremy Collier.*

Dependence is a perpetual call upon humanity, and a greater incitement to tenderness and pity than any other motive whatsoever. *Addison.*

Depend upon it, if a man talks of his misfortunes, there is something in them that is not disagreeable to him. *Johnson.*

De pilo, *or* de filo, pendet—It hangs by a hair. *Pr.*

De pis en pis—From worse to worse. *Fr.*

De plano—With ease.

35 De præscientia Dei—Of the foreknowledge of God.

Deprendi miserum est — To be caught is a wretched experience.

Depressus extollor—Having been depressed, I am exalted. *M.*

De profundis—Out of the depths.

De propaganda fide—For propagating the Catholic faith.

40 De publico est elatus—He was buried at the public expense. *Livy.*

Der Ausgang giebt den Thaten ihre Titel—It is the issue that gives to deeds their title. *Goethe.*

Der beste Prediger ist die Zeit—Time is the best preacher. *Ger. Pr.*

Der Böse hat nicht nur die Guten, sonder nauch die Bösen gegen sich—The bad man has not only the good, but also the evil opposed to him. *Bischer.*

45 Der brave Mann denkt an sich selbst zuletzt—The brave man thinks of himself last of all. *Schiller.*

Der civilisierte Wilde ist der schlimmste aller Wilden—The civilised savage is the worst of all savages. *C. J. Weber.*

Der den Augenblick ergreift / Das ist der rechte Mann—He who seizes the moment is the right man. *Goethe.*

Der Dichter steht auf einer höhern Warte / Als auf den Zinnen der Partei—The poet stands on a higher watch-tower than the pinnacle of party. *Freiligrath.*

Der echte Geist schwingt sich empor / Und rafft die Zeit sich nach—The genuine spirit soars upward, and snatches the time away after it. *Uhland.*

50 Derelictio communis utilitatis contra naturam—The abandonment of what is for the common good is a crime against nature. *Cic.*

Der Erde Paradies und Hölle / Liegt in dem Worte "Weib"—Heaven and Hell on earth lie in the word "woman." *Seume.*

Der Fluss bleibt trüb, der nicht durch einen See gegangen, / Das Herz unsauber, das nicht durch ein Weh gegangen—The river remains troubled that has not passed through a lake, the heart unpurified that has not passed through a woe. *Rückert.*

Der Frauen Zungen ja nimmer ruhn—Women's tongues never rest. *A. v. Chamisso.*

Der Friede ist immer die letzte Absicht des Krieges—Peace is ever the final aim of war. *Wieland.*

55 Der Fuchs ändert den Pelz und behält den Schalk—The fox changes his skin but keeps his knavery. *Ger. Pr.*

Der Fürst ist nichts, als der erste Diener des Staates—The prince is nothing but the first servant of the state. *Frederick the Great.*

Der Geist, aus dem wir handeln, ist das Höchste—The spirit from which we act is the principal (*lit.* the highest) matter. *Goethe.*

Der Geist der Medicin ist leicht zu fassen / Ihr durchstudiert die gross' und kleine Welt ; / Um es am Ende gehn zu lassen, / Wie's Gott gefällt—The spirit of medicine is easy to master ; you study through the great and the little worlds, to let it go in the end as God pleases. *Mephisto. in "Faust."*

Der Geist, der stets verneint—The spirit that constantly denies, that says everlastingly " No." *Goethe's " Mephistopheles."*

Der Geist ist immer autochthone—Spirit is always indigenous, *i.e.*, always native to the soil out of which it springs. *Goethe.*

Der geringste Mensch kann complet sein, wenn er sich innerhalb der Gränzen seiner Fähigkeiten und Fertigkeiten bewegt—The humblest mortal may attain completeness if he confine his activities within the limits of his capability and skill. *Goethe.*

Der Glaube ist der rechte, der, dass er der rechte bleibt, nicht gezwungen ist einen andern irrgläubig zu finden—That faith is the orthodox which, that it may remain such, is under no necessity of finding another heterodox. *Börne.*

5 **Der Gott, der mir im Busen wohnt, / Kann tief mein Innerstes erregen ; der über allen meinen Kräften thront, er kann nach aussen nichts bewegen**—The God who dwells in my breast can stir my inmost soul to its depths ; he who sits as sovereign over all my powers has no control over things beyond. *Goethe.*

Der grösste Mensch bleibt stets ein Menschenkind—The greatest man remains always a manchild, or son of man. *Goethe.*

Der grösste Schritt ist der aus der Thür—The greatest step is that out of the door. *Ger. Pr.*

Der gute Mann braucht überall viel Boden—The good man needs always large room. *Lessing.*

Der gute Wille ist in der Moral alles ; aber in der Kunst ist nichts : da gilt, wie schon das Wort andeutet, allein Können—Goodwill is everything in morals, but in art it is nothing : in it, as the word indicates, only ability counts for aught. *Schopenhauer.*

10 **Der Hahn schliesst die Augen, wann er krähet, weil er es auswendig kann**—The cock shuts his eyes when he crows, because he has it by heart. *Ger. Pr.*

Der Handelnde ist immer gewissenlos, es hat niemand Gewissen, als der Betrachtende—The man who acts merely is always without conscience ; no one has conscience but the man who reflects. *Goethe.*

Der hat die Macht, an den die Menge glaubt—He has the power whom the majority believe in. *Raupach.*

Der hat nie das Glück gekostet, der's in Ruh geniessen will—He has never tasted happiness who will enjoy it in peace. *Th. Körner.*

Der Hauptfehler des Menschen bleibt, dass er so viele kleine hat—Man's chief fault is ever that he has so many small ones. *Jean Paul.*

15 **Der Himmel giebt die Gunst des Augenblicks / Wer schnell sie fasst, wird Meister des Geschicks**—Heaven gives the grace needed for the moment ; he who seizes it quickly becomes master of his fate. *Raupach.*

Der Himmel kann ersetzen / Was er entzogen hat—What Heaven has taken away, Heaven can make good. *Rückert.*

Der Historiker ist ein rückwärts gekehrter Prophet—The historian is a prophet with his face turned backwards. *F. v. Schlegel.*

Der höchste Stolz und der höchste Kleinmuth ist die höchste Unkenntniss seiner selbst—Extreme pride and extreme dejection are alike extreme ignorance of one's self. *Spinoza.*

Der höchste Vorwurf der Kunst für denkende Menschen ist der Mensch—The highest subject of art for thinking men is man. *Winkelmann.*

Deridet, sed non derideor—He laughs, but I am 20 not laughed at.

Der Irrthum ist recht gut, so lange wir jung sind ; man muss ihn nur nicht mit ins Alter schleppen—Error is very well so long as we are young, but we must not drag it with us into old age. *Goethe.*

Der ist edel, / Welcher edel fühlt und handelt—He is noble who feels and acts nobly. *Heine.*

Der Jugend Führer sei das Alter ; beiden sei / Nur wenn sie als Verbundne wandeln, Glück versichert—Be age the guide of youth ; both will be happy only if they go hand in hand (*lit.* as confederates) together. *Goethe.*

Der Jüngling kämpft, damit der Greis geniesse—The youth fights that the old man may enjoy. *Goethe.*

Der kann nicht klagen über harten Spruch, 25 den man zum Meister seines Schicksals macht—He cannot complain of a hard sentence who is made master of his own fate. *Schiller.*

Der kleine Gott der Welt bleibt stets von gleichem Schlag / Und ist so wunderlich, als wie am ersten Tag—The little god of the world (*i.e.*, man) continues ever of the same stamp, and is as odd as on the first day. *Goethe.*

Der Krieg ist die stärkende Eisenkur der Menschheit—War is the strengthening iron cure of humanity. *Jean Paul.*

Der Künstler muss mit Feuer entwerfen und mit Phlegma ausführen—The artist must invent (*lit.* sketch) with ardour and execute with coolness. *Winkelmann.*

Der Lebende hat Recht—The living has right on his side. *Schiller.*

Der Mann, der das Wenn und das Aber 30 erdacht / Hat sicher aus Häckerling Gold schon gemacht—The man who invented "if" and "but" must surely have converted chopt straw into gold. *G. A. Bürger.*

Der Mann muss hinaus ins feindliche Leben—A man must go forth to face life with its enmities. *Schiller.*

Der Mensch begreift niemals wie anthropmorphisch er ist—Man never comprehends how anthropomorphic his conceptions are. *Goethe.*

Der Mensch denkt, Gott lenkt—Man proposes, God disposes. *Ger. Pr.*

Der Menschenkenner steht überall an seinem Platze—He who knows man is everywhere in his place. *Klinger.*

Der Mensch erfährt, er sei auch wer er mag, / 35 Ein letztes Glück und einen letzten Tag—No man, be he who he may, but experiences a last happiness and a last day. *Goethe.*

Der Mensch hat nur allzusehr Ursache, sich vor dem Menschen zu schützen—Man has only too much reason to guard himself from man. *Goethe.*

Der Mensch ist ein nachahmendes Geschöpf und wer der vorderste ist, führt die Herde—Man is an imitative being, and the foremost leads the flock. *Schiller.*

Der Mensch ist entwickelt, nicht erschaffen—Man has been developed, not created. *Oken.*

Der Mensch ist frei geschaffen, ist frei, / Und würd' er in Ketten geboren!—Man has been created free, is free, even were he born in chains. *Schiller.*

Der Mensch ist frei wie der Vogel im Käfig; er kann sich innerhalb gewisser Grenzen bewegen—Man is free as the bird in the cage : he has powers of motion within certain limits. *Lavater.*

Der Mensch ist im Grunde ein wildes, entsetzliches Thier—Man is at bottom a savage animal and an object of dread, as we may see (it is added) he still is when emancipated from all control. *Schopenhauer.*

Der Mensch ist nicht bloss ein denkendes, er ist zugleich ein empfindendes Wesen. Er ist ein Ganzes, eine Einheit vielfacher, innig verbundner Kräfte, und zu diesem Ganzen muss das Kunstwerk reden—Man is not merely a thinking, he is at the same time a sentient, being. He is a whole, a unity of manifold, internally connected powers, and to this whole must the work of art speak. *Goethe.*

5 Der Mensch ist nicht geboren frei zu sein / Und für den Edeln ist kein schöner Glück / Als einem Fürst, den er ehrt, zu dienen —Man is not born to be free; and for the noble soul there is no fairer fortune than to serve a prince whom he regards with honour. *Goethe.*

Der Mensch ist selbst sein Gott, sein Beruf ist : Handeln—Man is a god to himself, and his calling is to act. *Tiedge.*

Der Mensch ist, was er isst—Man is what he eats. *L. Feuerbach.*

Der Mensch liebt nur einmal—Man loves only once. *Ger. Pr.*

Der Mensch muss bei dem Glauben verharren, dass das Unbegreifliche begreiflich sei; er würde sonst nicht forschen—Man must hold fast by the belief that the incomprehensible is comprehensible ; otherwise he would not search. *Goethe.*

10 Der Mensch muss ein Höheres, ein Göttliches anerkennen—ob in sich oder über sich, gleichviel—Man must acknowledge a higher, a divine —whether in himself or over himself, no matter. *Hamerling.*

Der Mensch versuche die Götter nicht—Let not man tempt the gods. *Schiller.*

Der Mensch war immer Mensch, voll Unvollkommenheit—Man has ever been man, full of imperfection. *J. P. Uz.*

Der Mensch, wo ist er her ? / Zu schlecht für einen Gott, zu gut für's Ungefähr-- Man, whence is he? Too bad to be the work of a god, too good for the work of chance. *Lessing.*

Der Muth der Wahrheit ist die erste Bedingung des philosophischen Studiums—The courage of truth is the first qualification for philosophic study. *Hegel.*

15 Dernier ressort—A last resource. *Fr.*

Der Pfaff liebt seine Herde, doch die Lämmlein mehr als die Widder—The priest loves his flock, but the lambs more than the rams. *Ger. Pr.*

Der preise glücklich sein, der von / Den Göttern dieser Welt entfernt lebt—Let him count himself happy who lives remote from the gods of this world. *Goethe.*

Der Rathgeber eines Höheren handelt klüglich, wenn er sein geistiges Uebergewicht verbirgt, wie das Weib seine Schönheit verhüllt um des Sieges desto gewisser zu sein—The adviser of a superior acts wisely if he conceals his spiritual superiority, as the woman veils her beauty in order to be the more certain of conquering. *Zachariae.*

Derrière la croix souvent se tient le diable— Behind the cross the devil often lurks. *Fr. Pr.*

Der Ring macht Ehen, / Und Ringe sind's, die 20 eine Kette machen—The ring makes marriage, and rings make a chain. *Schiller.*

Der Rose süsser Duft genügt, / Man braucht sie nicht zum stechen / Und wer sich mit dem Duft begnügt / Den wird ihr Dorn nicht stechen—The sweet scent of the rose suffices ; one needs not break it off, and he who is satisfied therewith will not be stung by the thorn. *Bodenstedt.*

Der Schein regiert die Welt, und die Gerechtigkeit ist nur auf der Bühne—Appearance rules the world, and we see justice only on the stage. *Schiller.*

Der Schein, was ist er, dem das Wesen fehlt ? / Das Wesen wär' es, wenn es nicht erschiene ? —The appearance, what is it without the reality? And what were the reality without the appearance? (the clothes, as "Sartor" has it, without the man, or the man without the clothes). *Goethe.*

Der Schmerz ist die Geburt der höheren Naturen—Pain is the birth of higher natures. *Tiedge.*

Der Sinn erweitert, aber lähmt; die That 25 belebt, aber beschränkt—Thought expands, but lames ; action animates, but narrows. *Goethe.*

Der Stärkste hat Recht—The right is with the strongest. *Ger. Pr.*

Der Stein im Sumpf / Macht keine Ringe—You can make no rings if you throw a stone into a marsh. *Goethe.*

Der Tod entbindet von erzwungnen Pflichten— Death releases from enforced duties. *Schiller.*

Der Umgang mit Frauen ist das Element guter Sitten—The society of women is the nursery of good manners. *Goethe.*

Der Verständige findet fast alles lächerlich, 30 der Vernünftige fast nichts—The man of analytic, or critical, intellect finds something ridiculous in almost everything ; the man of synthetic, or constructive, intellect, in almost nothing. *Goethe.*

Der Vortrag macht des Redners Glück—It is delivery that makes the orator's success. *Goethe.*

Der Wahn ist kurz, die Reu' ist lang—The illusion is brief, the remorse is long. *Schiller.*

Der Weg der Ordnung, ging er auch durch Krümmen, / Er ist kein Umweg—The path which good order prescribes is the direct one, even though it has windings. *Schiller.*

Der Weise hat die Ohren lang, die Zunge kurz—The wise man has long ears and a short tongue. *Ger. Pr.*

Der Weise kann des Mächtigen Gunst entbeh- 35 ren, / Doch nicht der Mächtige des Weisen Lehren—The wise man can dispense with the favour of the mighty, but not the mighty man with the wisdom of the wise. *Bodenstedt.*

Der Wille ist des Werkes Seele—What we will is the soul of what we do. *Ger. Pr.*

Der wird stets das Beste missen / Wer nicht borgt, was andre wissen—He will always lack what is best who does not give credit to what others know. *Rückert.*

Der Witz ist die Freiheit des Sklaven—The witty sally is the freedom of the slave. *Ruge.*

Der Zug des Herzens ist des Schicksals Stimme—In the drawing of the heart is the oracle of fate. *Schiller.*

Descend a step in choosing thy wife ; ascend a step in choosing thy friend. *The Talmud.*

5 Description is always a bore, both to the describer and the describee. *Disraeli.*

Deserted, at his utmost need, / By those his former bounty fed, / On the bare earth exposed he lies, / With not a friend to close his eyes. *Dryden.*

Desiderantem quod satis est, neque / Tumultuosum sollicitat mare, / Non verberatæ grandine vineæ / Fundusque mendax—A storm at sea, a vine-wasting hail tempest, a disappointing farm, cause no anxiety to him who is content with enough. *Hor.*

Desideratum—A thing desired, but regretfully wanting.

Desine fata Deum flecti sperare precando—Cease to hope that the decrees of the gods can bend to prayer. *Virg.*

10 Desinit in piscem mulier formosa superne—A beautiful woman in the upper parts terminating in a fish. *Hor.*

Désir de Dieu et désir de l'homme sont deux—What God wishes and man wishes are two different things. *Fr. Pr.*

Desires are the pulse of the soul. *Manton.*

Des Lebens Mühe / Lehrt uns allein des Lebens Güter schätzen—The labour of life alone teaches us to value the good things of life. *Goethe.*

Des Mannes Mutter ist der Frau Teufel. The husband's mother is the wife's devil. *Ger. Pr.*

15 Des Menschen Engel ist die Zeit—Time is man's angel. *Schiller.*

Des Menschens Leben ist / Ein kurzes Blühen und ein langes Welken—The life of man is a short blossoming and a long withering. *Uhland.*

Despair defies even despotism ; there is that in my heart would make its way through hosts with levelled spears. *Byron.*

Despair is like froward children, who, when you take away one of their playthings, throw the rest into the fire for madness. *Charron.*

Despair is the only genuine atheism. *Jean Paul.*

20 Despair takes heart when there's no hope to speed ; / The coward then takes arms and does the deed. *Herrick.*

Despair—the last dignity of the wretched. *H. Giles.*

Despatch is the soul of business. *Chesterfield.*

Desperate diseases need desperate remedies. *Pr.*

Despise anxiety and wishing, the past and the future. *Jean Paul.*

25 Despise not any man, and do not spurn anything ; for there is no man that has not his hour, nor is there anything that has not its place. *Rabbi Ben Azai.*

Despise not the discoveries of the wise, but acquaint thyself with their proverbs, for of them thou shalt learn instruction. *Ecclus.*

Despise your enemy and you will soon be beaten. *Port. Pr.*

Despite his titles, power, and pelf, / The wretch concentred all in self, / Living, shall forfeit fair renown, / And, doubly dying, shall go down / To the vile dust, from whence he sprung, / Unwept, unhonoured, and unsung. *Scott.*

Despondency comes readily enough to the most sanguine. *Emerson.*

Desponding fear, of feeble fancies full, / Weak 30 and unmanly, loosens every power. *Thomson.*

Despotism is a legitimate mode of government in dealing with barbarians, provided the end be their improvement, and the means justified by actually effecting that end. *J. S. Mill.*

Despotism is essential in most enterprises ; I am told they do not tolerate "freedom of debate" on board a seventy-four. *Carlyle.*

Despotism is often the effort of Nature to cure herself from a worse disease. *Robert, Lord Lytton.*

Despotism sits nowhere so secure as under the effigy and ensigns of freedom. *Landor.*

Despotismus ist der schwarze Punkt in aller 35 Menschen Herzen—Despotism is the black spot in the hearts of all men. *C. J. Weber.*

Desque nací lloré, y cada día nace porqué—I wept as soon as I was born, and every day explains why. *Sp. Pr.*

Des Rats bedarf die Seele nicht, die Rechtes will—The soul which wills what is right needs no counsel. *Platen.*

Destiny is our will, and will is nature. *Disraeli.*

Destitutus ventis remos adhibe—The wind failing, ply the oars.

Destroy his fib or sophistry—in vain ! / The 40 creature's at his dirty work again. *Pope.*

Des Uebels Quelle findest du nicht aus, und aufgefunden fliesst sie ewig fort—The well-spring of evil thou canst not discover, and even if discovered, it flows on continually. *Goethe.*

Desunt cætera—The remainder is wanting.

Desunt inopiæ multa, avaritiæ omnia—Poverty is in want of many things, avarice of everything. *L. Pr.*

Des Zornes Ende ist der Reue Anfang—The end of anger is the beginning of repentance. *Bodenstedt.*

Deteriores omnes sumus licentia—We are all 45 the worse for the license. *Ter.*

Determined, dared, and done. *Smart.*

Detested sport, that owes its pleasures to another's pain. *Cowper.*

De tijd is aan God en ons—Time is God's and ours. *Dut. Pr.*

Det ille veniam facile, cui venia est opus—He who needs pardon should readily grant it. *Sen.*

Detour—A circuitous march. *Fr.* 50

De tout s'avise à qui pain faut—A man in want of bread is ready for anything. *Fr. Pr.*

Detraction's a bold monster, and fears not / To wound the fame of princes, if it find / But any blemish in their lives to work on. *Massinger.*

De trop—Too much, or too many ; out of place. *Fr.*

Detur aliquando otium quiesque fessis—Leisure and repose should at times be given to the weary. *Sen.*

Detur digniori—Let it be given to the most worthy. *M.*

Detur pulchriori—Let it be given to the fairest. *The inscription on the golden apple of discord.*

Deum cole, regem serva—Worship God, preserve the king. *M.*

5 Deum colit, qui novit—He who knows God worships Him. *Sen.*

Deus avertat—God forbid.

Deus ex machina—A mechanical instead of a rational or spiritual explanation (*lit.* a god mechanically introduced).

Deus hæc fortasse benigna / Reducet in sedem vice—God will perhaps by a gracious change restore these things to a stable condition. *Hor.*

Deus id vult—God wills it. *War-cry of the Crusaders before Jerusalem.*

10 Deus major columna—God is the greater support. *M.*

Deus mihi providebit—God will provide for me. *M.*

Deus omnibus quod sat est suppeditat—God supplies enough to all. *M.*

Deus vult—It is God's will.

Deux hommes se rencontrent bien, mais jamais deux montagnes—Two men may meet, but never two mountains. *Fr.*

15 Deux yeux voient plus clair qu'un—A ghost was never seen by two pair of eyes (*lit.* two eyes see more clearly than one). *Fr.*

Devil take the hindmost. *Beaumont and Fletcher.*

Devine si tu peux, et choisis si tu l'oses—Solve the riddle if you can, and choose if you dare. *Corneille.*

Devise, wit; write, pen; for I am for whole volumes in folio. *Love's L. Lost,* i. 2.

De vive voix—Verbally. *Fr.*

20 Devote each day to the object then in time, and every evening will find something done. *Goethe.*

Devotion in distress is born, but vanishes in happiness. *Dryden.*

Devotion, when it does not lie under the check of reason, is apt to degenerate into enthusiasm (fanaticism). *Addison.*

De waarheid is eene dochter van den tijd—Truth is a daughter of Time. *Dut. Pr.*

Dewdrops are the gems of morning, but the tears of mournful eve. *Coleridge.*

25 De wereld wil betrogen zijn—The world likes to be deceived. *Dut. Pr.*

Dexterity or experience no master can communicate to his disciple. *Goethe.*

Dextras dare—To give right hands to each other.

Dextro tempore—At a lucky moment. *Hor.*

Diamonds cut diamonds. *Ford.*

30 Di bene fecerunt, inopis me quodque pusilli / Finxerunt animi, raro et perpauca loquentis —The gods be praised for having made me of a poor and humble mind, with a desire to speak but seldom and briefly. *Hor.*

Dicam insigne, recens, adhuc / Indictum ore alio—I will utter something striking, something fresh, something as yet unsung by another's lips. *Hor.*

Dicenda tacenda locutus—Saying things that should be, and things that should not be, said. *Hor.*

Dicere quæ puduit, scribere jussit amor—What I was ashamed to say, love has ordered me to write. *Ovid.*

Dicique beatus / Ante obitum nemo supremaque funera debet—No one should be called happy before he is dead and buried. *Ovid.*

Dicta fides sequitur—The promise is no sooner 35 given than fulfilled. *Ovid.*

Dicta tibi est lex—The conditions have been laid before you. *Hor.*

Dictum de dicto—A report founded on hearsay.

Dictum factum—No sooner said than done. *Ter.*

Dictum sapienti sat est—A word to a wise man is enough. *Plaut. and Ter.*

Did charity prevail, the press would prove / A 40 vehicle of virtue, truth, and love. *Cowper.*

Did I know that my heart was bound to temporal possessions, I would throw the flaming brand among them with my own hand. *Schiller.*

"Did I not tell you that after thunder rain would be sure to come on?" *Socrates to his friends when, after a volley of upbraidings, Xantippe threw a jugful of water at his head.*

Didst thou but know the inly touch of love, / Thou wouldst as soon go kindle fire with snow, / As seek to quench the fire of love with words. *Two Gen. of Ver.,* ii. 7.

Did you ever hear of Captain Wattle? / He was all for love and a little for the bottle. *C. Dibdin.*

Die Aemter sind Gottes; die Amtleute Teufels 45 —Places are God's; place-holders are the devil's. *Ger. Pr.*

Die alleinige Quelle des Rechts ist das gemeinsame Bewusstsein des ganzen Volks; der allgemeine Geist—The only fountain of justice is the common consciousness of the whole people; the spirit common to all of them. *Lasalle.*

Die Alten sind die einzigen Alten, die nie alt werden—The ancients (*i.e.,* the Greeks and Romans) are the only ancients that never grow old. *C. J. Weber.*

Die Anmut macht unwiderstehlich—Grace makes its possessor irresistible. *Goethe.*

Die ärgsten Studenten werden die frömmsten Prediger—The worst-behaved students turn out the most pious preachers. *Ger. Pr.*

Die Armen müssen tanzen wie die Reichen 50 pfeifen—The poor must dance as the rich pipe. *Ger. Pr.*

Die Augen glauben sich selbst, die Ohren andern Leuten—The eyes believe themselves, the ears other people. *Ger. Pr.*

Die Augen sind weiter als der Bauch—The eyes are larger than the belly. *Ger. Pr.*

Die besten Freunde stehen im Beutel—Our best friends are in our purse. *Ger. Pr.*

Die Bewunderung preist, die Liebe ist stumm —Admiration praises, love is dumb. *Börne.*

Die Blumen zu pflegen, / Das Unkraut zu 55 tilgen, / Ist Sache des Gärtners—The gardener's business is to root out the weeds and tend the flowers. *Bodenstedt.*

Die Botschaft hör' ich wohl, allein mir fehlt der Glaube—I hear the message, but I lack the faith. *Goethe.*

Die Damen geben sich und ihren Putz zum besten / Und spielen ohne Gage mit—The ladies by their presence and finery contribute to the treat and take part in the play without pay from us. *The Theatre Manager in Goethe's "Faust."*

Die Dämmerung ist das freundliche Licht der Liebenden—The gloaming is the light that befriends the wooer. *Seume.*

Die de wereld wel beziet, men zag nooit schoonder niet—Whoso considers the world well must allow he has never seen a better. *Dut. Pr.*

5 Die Dornen, die Disteln, sie stechen gar sehr, doch stechen die Altjungfernzungen noch mehr—Thorns and thistles prick very sore, but old maids' tongues sting much more. *C. Geibel.*

Die een ander jaagt zit zelfs niet stil—He who chases another does not sit still himself. *Dut. Pr.*

Die Ehe ist Himmel und Hölle—Marriage is heaven and hell. *Ger. Pr.*

Die eigentliche Religion bleibt ein Inneres, ja Individuelles, denn sie hat ganz allein mit dem Gewissen zu thun; dieses soll erregt, soll beschwichtigt werden—Religion, properly so called, is ever an inward, nay, an individual thing, for it has to do with nothing but the conscience, which has now to be stirred up, now to be soothed. *Goethe.*

Die Einsamkeit ist noth; doch sei nur nicht gemein, / So kannst du überall in einer Wüste sein—Solitude is painful; only be not vulgar, for then you may be in a desert everywhere. *Angelus Silesius.*

10 Die Eintracht nur macht stark und gross, / Die Zwietracht stürzet alles nieder—Only concord makes us strong and great; discord overthrows everything. *Gellert.*

Die Erde wird durch Liebe frei; / Durch Thaten wird sie gross—Through love the earth becomes free; through deeds, great. *Goethe.*

Die Erinnerung ist das einzige / Paradies, aus dem wir nicht vertrieben werden kann—Remembrance is the only paradise from which we cannot be driven. *Jean Paul.*

Die Fabel ist der Liebe Heimatwelt, / Gern wohnt sie unter Feen, Talismanen, / Glaubt gern an Götter, weil sie göttlich ist—Fable is love's native world, is fain to dwell among fairies and talismans, and to believe in gods, being herself divine. *Schiller.*

Die Frauen sind das einzige Gefäss, was uns Neuern noch geblieben ist, um unsere Idealität hineinzugiessen—Woman is the only vessel which still remains to us moderns into which we can pour our ideals. *Goethe.*

15 Die Frauen tragen ihre Beweise im Herzen, die Männer im Kopfe—Women carry their logic in their hearts; men, in their heads. *Kotzebue.*

Die Freiheit der Vernunft ist unser wahres Leben—The freedom of reason is our true life. *Tiedge.*

Die Freiheit kann nicht untergehn, / So lange Schmiede Eisen hämmern—The sun of freedom cannot set so long as smiths hammer iron. *E. M. Arndt.*

Die Freude kennst du nicht, wenn du nur Freuden kennest; / Dir fehlt das ganze Licht, wenn du's in Strahlen trennest—Joy knowest thou not if thou knowest only joys; the whole light is wanting to thee if thou breakest it up into rays. *Rückert.*

Die Freudigkeit ist die Mutter aller Tugenden—Joyousness is the mother of all virtues. *Goethe.*

Die Gegenwart ist eine mächtige Göttin; Lern' 20 ihren Einfluss kennen—The present is a potent divinity; learn to acquaint thyself with her power. *Goethe.*

Die Geheimnisse der Lebenspfade darf und kann man nicht offenbaren; es giebt Steine des Anstosses, über die ein jeder Wanderer stolpern muss. Der Poet aber deutet auf die Stelle hin—The secrets of the way of life may not and cannot be laid open; there are stones of offence along the path over which every wayfarer must stumble. The poet, or inspired teacher, however, points to the spot. *Goethe.*

Die Geisterwelt ist nicht verschlossen / Dein Sinn ist zu, dein Herz ist todt—The spirit-world is not shut; thy sense is shut, thy heart is dead. *Goethe.*

Die Geschichte der Wissenschaften ist eine grosse Fuge, in der die Stimmen der Völker nach und nach zum Vorschein kommen—The history of the sciences is a great fugue, in which the voices of the nations come one by one into notice. *Goethe.*

Die Geschichte des Menschen ist sein Charakter—The history of a man is in his character. *Goethe.*

Die Gesetze der Moral sind auch die der 25 Kunst—The laws of morals are also those of art. *Schumann.*

Die Glocken sind die Artillerie der Geistlichkeit—Bells are the artillery of the Church. *Joseph II.*

Die goldne Zeit, wohin ist sie geflohen? / Nach der sich jedes Herz vergebens sehnt—The golden age, whither has it fled? after which every heart sighs in vain. *Goethe.*

Die Götter brauchen manchen guten Mann / Zu ihrem Dienst auf dieser weiten Erde. Sie haben noch auf dich gezählt—The upper powers need many a good man for their service on this wide earth. They still reckon upon thee. *Goethe.*

Die Götter sprechen nur durch unser Herz zu uns—The gods speak to us only through our heart. *Goethe.*

Die grosse Moral—das Interesse, sagte Mira- 30 beau, tötet in der Regel die kleine—das Gewissen—The great moral teacher, interest, as Mirabeau said, ordinarily slays conscience, the less. *C. J. Weber.*

Die grössten Menschen hängen immer mit ihrem Jahrhundert durch eine Schwachheit zusammen—It is always through a weakness that the greatest men are connected with their generation. *Goethe.*

Die grössten Schwierigkeiten liegen da, wo wir sie nicht suchen—The greatest difficulties lie there where we are not seeking for them. *Goethe.*

Die het in het vuur verloren heeft, moet het in de asch zoeken—What is lost in the fire must be searched for in the ashes. *Dut. Pr.*

Die Hindus der Wüste geloben keine Fische zu essen—The Hindus of the desert take a vow to eat no fish. *Goethe.*

Die höchste Naturschönheit ist das gott-gleiche Wesen: der Mensch — The most beautiful object in Nature is the godlike creature man. *Oken.*

Die höchste Weisheit ist, nicht weise stets zu sein — It is the highest wisdom not to be always wise. *M. Opitz.*

Die Hölle selbst hat ihre Rechte? — Has Hell itself its rights? *Goethe.*

Die Ideale sind zerronnen, / Die einst das trunkne Herz geschwellt — The ideals are all melted into air which once swelled the intoxicated heart. *Schiller.*

5 **Die Idee ist ewig und einzig. . . . Alles was wir gewahr werden und wovon wir reden können, sind nur Manifestationen der Idee** — The idea is one and eternal. . . . Everything we perceive, and of which we can speak, is only a manifestation of the idea. *Goethe.*

Die Irrthümer des Menschen machen ihn eigentlich liebenswürdig — It is properly man's mistakes, or errors, that make him lovable. *Goethe.*

Diejenige Regierung ist die beste, die sich überflüssig macht — That government is best which makes itself unnecessary. *W. v. Humboldt.*

Die Kinder sind mein liebster Zeitvertreib — My dearest pastime is with children. *Chamisso.*

Die Kirche hat einen guten Magen, hat ganze Länder aufgefressen, und doch noch nie sich übergessen — The Church has a good stomach, has swallowed up whole countries, and yet has not overeaten herself. *Goethe, in " Faust."*

10 **Die Kirche ist's, die heilige, die hohe, / Die zu dem Himmel uns die Leiter baut** — The Church, the holy, the high, it is that rears for us the ladder to heaven. *Schiller.*

Die Kleinen reden gar so gern von dem was die Grossen thun — Small people are so fond of talking of what great people do. *Ger. Pr.*

Die Klugheit sich zur Führerin zu wählen / Das ist es, was den Weisen macht — It is the choice of prudence for his guide that makes the wise man. *Schiller.*

Die Kraft ist schwach, allein die Lust ist gross — The strength is weak, but the desire is great. *Goethe.*

Die kranke Seele muss sich selber helfen — The sick soul must work its own cure (*lit.* help itself). *Gutzkow.*

15 **Die Krankheit des Gemütes löset sich / In Klagen und Vertraun am leichtesten auf** — Mental sickness finds relief most readily in complaints and confidences. *Goethe.*

Die Kunst darf nie ein Kunststück werden — Art should never degenerate into artifice. *Ger.*

Die Kunst geht nach Brod — Art goes a-begging. *Ger. Pr.*

Die Kunst ist eine Vermittlerin des Unaussprechlichen — Art is a mediatrix of the unspeakable. *Goethe.*

Die Leidenschaften sind Mängel oder Tugenden, nur gesteigerte — The passions are vices or virtues, only exaggerated. *Goethe.*

20 **Die Leidenschaft flieht, / Die Liebe muss bleiben; / Die Blume verblüht, / Die Frucht muss treiben** — Passion takes flight, love must abide; the flower fades, the fruit must ripen. *Schiller.*

Die letzte Wahl steht auch dem Schwächsten offen; / Ein Sprung von dieser Brücke macht mich frei — The last choice of all is open even to the weakest; a leap from this bridge sets me free. *Schiller.*

Die Liebe hat kein Mass der Zeit; sie keimt / Und blüht und reift in einer schönen Stunde — Love follows no measure of time; it buds and blossoms and ripens in one happy hour. *Körner.*

Die Liebe ist der Liebe Preis — Love is the price of love. *Schiller.*

Die Liebe macht zum Goldpalast die Hütte — Love converts the cottage into a palace of gold. *Hölty.*

Die Lieb' umfasst des Weibes volles Leben, / 25 Sie ist ihr Kerker und ihr Himmelreich — Love embraces woman's whole life; it is her prison and her kingdom of heaven. *Chamisso.*

Die Lust ist mächtiger als alle Furcht der Strafe — Pleasure is more powerful than all fear of the penalty. *Goethe.*

Die Lust zu reden kommt zu rechter Stunde, / Und wahrhaft fliesst das Wort aus Herz und Munde — The inclination to speak comes at the right hour, and the word flows true from heart and lip. *Goethe.*

Die Manifestationen der Idee als des Schönen, ist eben so flüchtig, als die Manifestationen des Erhabenen, des Geistreichen, des Lustigen, des Lächerlichen. Dies ist die Ursache, warum so schwer darüber zu reden ist — The manifestation of the idea as the beautiful is just as fleeting as the manifestation of the sublime, the witty, the gay, and the ludicrous. This is the reason why it is so difficult to speak of it. *Goethe.*

Die Meisterhaft gilt oft für Egoismus — Mastery passes often for egoism. *Goethe.*

Die Menge macht den Künstler irr' und scheu 30 — The multitude is a distraction and scare to the artist. *Goethe.*

Die Menschen fürchtet nur, wer sie nicht kennt, / Und wer sie meidet, wird sie bald verkennen — Only he shrinks from men who does not know them, and he who shuns them will soon misknow them. *Goethe.*

Die Menschen kennen einander nicht leicht, selbst mit dem besten Willen und Vorsatz; nun tritt noch der böse Wille hinzu, der Alles entstellt — Men do not easily know one another, even with the best will and intention; presently ill-will comes forward, which disfigures all. *Goethe.*

Die Menschen sind im ganzen Leben blind — Men are blind all through life. *Goethe.*

Die Menschheit geben uns Vater und Mutter, die Menschlichkeit aber gibt uns nur die Erziehung — Human nature we owe to father and mother, but humanity to education alone. *Weber.*

Die Milde ziemt dem Weibe, / Dem Manne 35 ziemt die Rache, the man — Mercy becomes the woman; avengement, the man. *Bodenstedt.*

Die Mode ist weiblichen Geschlechts, hat folglich ihre Launen — Mode is of the female sex, and has consequently their whims. *C. J. Weber.*

Die monarchische Regierungsform ist die dem Menschen natürliche — Monarchy is the form of government that is natural to mankind. *Schopenhauer.*

Die Moral steckt in kurzen Sprüchen besser, als in langen Reden und Predigten — A moral lesson is better expressed in short sayings than in long discourse. *Immermann.*

Diem perdidi! — I have lost a day! *Titus, on finding that he had done no worthy action during the day.*

Die Mütter geben uns von Geiste Wärme, und die Väter Licht—Our mothers give to our spirit heat, our fathers light. *Jean Paul.*

Die Natur ist ein unendlich geteilter Gott—Nature is an infinitely divided God. *Schiller.*

Die Natur weiss allein, was sie will—Nature alone knows what she aims at. *Goethe.*

Die of a rose in aromatic pain. *Pope.*

5 Die Phantasie ward auserkoren / Zu öffnen uns die reiche Wunderwelt—Fantasy was appointed to open to us the rich realm of wonders. *Tiedge.*

Die Rachegötter schaffen im Stillen—The gods of vengeance act in silence. *Schiller.*

Dies adimit ægritudinem—Time cures our griefs. *L. Pr.*

Die Schönheit ist das höchste Princip und der höchste Zweck der Kunst—Beauty is the highest principle and the highest aim of art. *Goethe.*

Die Schönheit ist vergänglich, die ihr doch / Allein zu ehren scheint. Was übrig bleibt, / Das reizt nicht mehr, und was nicht reizt, ist tot—Beauty is transitory, which yet you seem alone to worship. What is left no longer attracts, and what does not attract is dead. *Goethe.*

10 Die Schönheit ruhrt, doch nur die Anmuth sieget, / Und Unschuld nur behält den Preis—Beauty moves us, though only grace conquers us, and innocence alone retains the prize. *Seume.*

Die Schulden sind der nächste Erbe—Debts fall to the next heir. *Ger. Pr.*

Die Schwierigkeiten wachsen, je näher man dem Ziele kommt—Difficulties increase the nearer we approach the goal. *Goethe.*

Dies datus—A day given for appearing in court. *L.*

Dies faustus—A lucky day.

15 Dies infaustus—An unlucky day.

Die Sinne trügen nicht, aber das Urteil trügt—The senses do not deceive, but the judgment does. *Goethe.*

Dies iræ, dies illa, / Sæclum solvet in favilla / Teste David cum Sibylla—The day of wrath, that day shall dissolve the world in ashes, as David and the Sibyl say.

Dies non—A day when there is no court.

Die Sorgen zu bannen, / (Das Unkraut des Geistes), den Kummer zu scheuchen, / Die Schmerzen zu lindern, / Ist Sache des Sängers—To banish cares (the wild crop of the spirit), to chase away sorrow, to soothe pain, is the business of the singer. *Bodenstedt.*

20 Die Sorg' um Künft'ges niemals frommt; Man fühlt kein Uebel, bis es kommt. / Und wenn man's fühlt, so hilft kein Rat; / Weisheit ist immer zu früh und zu spat—Concern for the future boots not; we feel no evil till it comes. And when we feel it, no counsel avails; wisdom is always too early and too late. *Rückert.*

Dies religiosi—Religious days; holidays.

Die süssesten Trauben hängen am höchsten—The sweetest grapes hang highest. *Ger. Pr.*

Diet cures more than doctors. *Pr.*

Die te veel onderneemt slaagt zelden—He who undertakes too much seldom succeeds. *Dut. Pr.*

25 Die That allein beweist der Liebe Kraft—The act alone shows the power of love. *Goethe.*

Die Thätigkeit ist was den Menschen glücklich macht; / Die, erst das Gute schaffend, bald ein Uebel selbst / Durch göttlich wirkende Gewalt in Gutes kehrt—It is activity which renders man happy, which, by simply producing what is good, soon by a divinely working power converts an evil itself into a good. *Goethe.*

Die Todten reiten schnell!—The dead ride fast! *Bürger.*

Die treue Brust des braven Manns allein ist ein sturmfester Dach in diesen Zeiten—The loyal heart of the good man is in these times the only storm-proof place of shelter. *Schiller.*

Die Tugend des Menschen, der nach dem Geboten der Vernunft lebt, zeigt sich gleich gross in Vermeidung, wie in Ueberwindung der Gefahren—The virtue of the man who lives according to the commands of reason manifests itself quite as much in avoiding as in overcoming danger. *Spinoza.*

Die Tugend grosser Seelen ist Gerechtigkeit 30—The virtue of great souls is justice. *Platen.*

Die Tugend ist das höchste Gut, / Das Laster Weh dem Menschen thut—Virtue is man's highest good, vice works him nought but woe. *Goethe.*

Die Tugend ist nicht ein Wissen, sondern ein Wollen—Virtue is not a knowing, but a willing. *Zachariae.*

Die Tugend ohne Lohn ist doppelt schön—Virtue unrewarded is doubly beautiful. *Seume.*

Dieu aide à trois sortes de personnes, aux fous, aux enfants, et aux ivrognes—God protects three sorts of people, fools, children, and drunkards. *Fr. Pr.*

Dieu avec nous—God with us. *M.* 35

Dieu ayde—God help me. *M.*

Dieu défend le droit—God defends the right. *M.*

Dieu donne le froid selon le drap—God gives the cold according to the cloth. *Fr. Pr.*

Dieu et mon droit—God and my right. *M.*

Dieu fit du repentir la vertu des mortels—God 40 has made repentance the virtue of mortals. *Voltaire.*

Dieu garde la lune des loups—God guards the moon from the wolves. *Fr. Pr.*

Dieu mésure le froid à la brebis tondue—God measures the cold to the shorn lamb. *Fr. Pr.*

Die unbegreiflich hohen Werke / Sind herrlich wie am ersten Tag—The incomprehensibly high works are as glorious as on the first day. *Goethe.*

Dieu nous garde d'un homme qui n'a qu'une affaire—God keep us from a man who knows only one subject. *Fr. Pr.*

Die Unschuld hat im Himmel einen Freund 45—Innocence has a friend in heaven. *Schiller.*

Die Unsterblichkeit ist nicht jedermann's Sache—Immortality is not every man's business or concern. *Goethe.*

Dieu pour la tranchée, qui contre?—If God is our defence, who is against us? *M.*

Dieu seul devine les sots—God only understands fools. *Fr. Pr.*

Die veel dienstboden heeft, die heeft veel dieven—He who has many servants has many thieves. *Dut. Pr.*

Die vernünftige Welt ist als ein grosses unsterbliches Individuum zu betrachten, das unaufhaltsam das Nothwendige bewirkt und dadurch sich sogar über das Zufällige zum Herrn macht—The rational world is to be regarded as a great immortal individuality, that is ever working out for us the necessary (*i.e.*, an order which all must submit to), and thereby makes itself lord and master of everything contingent (or accidental). *Goethe.*

Die Vernunft ist auf das Werdende, der Verstand auf das Gewordene angewiesen; jene bekümmert sich nicht: wozu? dieser fragt nicht: woher?—Reason is directed to what is a-doing or proceeding, understanding to what is done or past; the former is not concerned about the "whereto," the latter inquires not about the "whence." *Goethe.*

Die Wacht am Rhein—"The watch on the Rhine." *A German national song.*

Die Wahrheit richtet sich nicht nach uns, sondern wir müssen uns nach ihr richten—The truth adjusts itself not to us, but we must adjust ourselves to it. *Claudius.*

5 Die Wahrheit schwindet von der Erde / Auch mit der Treu' ist es vorbei. / Die Hunde wedeln noch und stinken / Wie sonst, doch sind sie nicht mehr treu—Truth is vanishing from the earth, and of fidelity is the day gone by. The dogs still wag the tail and smell the same as ever, but they are no longer faithful. *Heine.*

Die Wahrheit zu sagen ist nützlich dem, der höret, schädlich dem, der spricht—Telling the truth does good to him who hears, harm to him who speaks. *Ger. Pr.*

Die wankelmüt'ge Menge, / Die jeder Wind herumtreibt! Wehe dem, / Der auf dies Rohr sich lehnet—The fickle mob, how they are driven round by every wind that blows! Woe to him who leans on this reed! *Schiller.*

Die Weiber lieben die Stärke ohne sie nachzuahmen; die Männer die Zartheit, ohne sie zu erwiedern—Women admire strength without affecting it; men delicacy without returning it. *Jean Paul.*

Die Weiber meiden nichts so sehr als das Wörtchen Ja; wenigstens sagen sie es erst nach dem Nein—Women are shy of nothing so much as the little word "Yes;" at least they say it only after they have said "No." *Jean Paul.*

10 Die Weisen wägen ihre Worte mit der Goldwage—The wise weigh their words in the balance of the goldsmith. *Ecclus.*

Die Weiseste merken höchstens nur wie das Schicksal sie leitet, und sind es zufrieden—The wisest know at highest only how destiny is leading them, and are therewith content. *Forster.*

Die Welt der Freiheit trägt der Mensch in seinem Innern, / Und Tugend ist der Freiheit Götterkind—Man bears the world of freedom in his heart, and virtue is freedom's divine child. *Tiedge.*

Die Weltgeschichte ist das Weltgericht—The history of the world is the judgment of the world. *Schiller.*

Die Welt ist dumm, die Welt ist blind, / Wird täglich abgeschmackter—The world is stupid, the world is blind, becomes daily more absurd. *Heine.*

15 Die Welt ist ein Gefängniss—The world is a prison. *Goethe.*

Die Welt ist voller Widerspruch—The world is full of contradiction. *Goethe.*

Die Welt ist vollkommen überall, / Wo der Mensch nicht hinkommt mit seiner Qual—The world is all perfect except where man comes with his burden of woe. *Schiller.*

Die Worte sind gut, sie sind aber nicht das Beste. Das Beste wird nicht deutlich durch Worte—Words are good, but are not the best. The best is not to be understood by words. *Goethe.*

Die Zeiten der Vergangenheit / Sind uns ein Buch mit sieben Siegeln; / Was Ihr den Geist der Zeiten heisst / Das ist im Grund' der Herrn eigner Geist, / In dem die Zeiten sich bespiegeln—The times that are past are a book with seven seals. What ye call the spirit of the times is at bottom but the spirit of the gentry in which the times are mirrored. *Goethe, in "Faust."*

Die Zeit ist schlecht, doch giebt's noch grosse 20 Seelen!—The times are bad, yet there are still great souls. *Körner.*

Die Zukunft decket Schmerzen und Glücke—The future hides in it gladness and sorrow. *Goethe.*

Different good, by art or nature given, / To different nations, makes their blessings even. *Goldsmith.*

Different minds / Incline to different objects; one pursues / The vast alone, the wonderful, the wild; / Another sighs for harmony and grace, / And gentlest beauty. *Akenside.*

Different times different manners. *It. Pr.*

Difficile est crimen non prodere vultu—It is 25 difficult not to betray guilt by the countenance. *Ovid.*

Difficile est longum subito deponere amorem—It is difficult to relinquish at once a long-cherished passion. *Catull.*

Difficile est plurimum virtutem revereri, qui semper secunda fortuna sit usus—It is difficult for one who has enjoyed uninterrupted good fortune to have a due reverence for virtue. *Cic.*

Difficile est proprie communia dicere—It is difficult to handle a common theme with originality. *Hor.*

Difficile est satiram non scribere—It is difficult not to indulge in (*lit.* to write) satire. *Juv.*

Difficile est tristi fingere mente jocum—It is 30 difficult to feign mirth when one is in a gloomy mood. *Tibulle.*

Difficilem oportet aurem habere ad crimina—One should be slow in listening to criminal accusations. *Pub. Syr.*

Difficilia quæ pulchra—The really good is of difficult attainment. *L. Pr.*

Difficilis, facilis, jucundus, acerbus es idem; / Nec tecum possum vivere, nec sine te—Cross but easy-minded, pleasant and sour together, I can neither live with thee nor yet without thee. *Mart.*

Difficilis in otio quies—Tranquillity is difficult if one has nothing to do.

Difficilius est sarcire concordiam quam rum-35 pere—It is more difficult to restore harmony than sow dissension.

Difficult to sweep the intricate foul chimneys of law. *Carlyle.*

Difficulties are meant to rouse, not discourage. *Channing.*

Difficulties are things that show what men are. *Epictetus.*

Difficulties may surround our path, but if the difficulties be not in ourselves, they may generally be overcome. *Jowett.*

Difficulties strengthen the mind, as labour does the body. *Sen.*

Difficulty, abnegation, martyrdom, death, are the allurements that act on the heart of man. Kindle the inner genial life of him, you have a flame that burns up all lower considerations. *Carlyle.*

Diffugiunt, cadis / Cum fæce siccatis, amici, / Ferre jugum pariter dolosi—When the wine-casks are drained to the lees, our friends soon disperse, too faithless to bear as well the yoke of misfortune. *Hor.*

5 Diffused knowledge immortalises itself. *Sir J. Macintosh.*

Dignity and love do not blend well, nor do they continue long together. *Ovid.*

Dignity consists not in possessing honours, but in deserving them. *Arist.*

Dignity is often a veil between us and the real truth of things. *Whipple.*

Dignity of position adds to dignity of character, as well as dignity of carriage. *Bovee.*

10 Dignum laude virum Musa vetat mori—The Muse takes care that the man who is worthy of honour does not die. *Hor.*

Digressions in a book are like foreign troops in a state, which argue the nation to want a heart and hands of its own; and often either subdue the natives, or drive them into the most unfruitful corners. *Swift.*

Digressions incontestably are the sunshine; they are the life, the soul of reading. *Sterne.*

Dii laboribus omnia vendunt—The gods sell all things to hard labour. *Pr.*

Dii majores et minores—Gods of a higher and lower degree.

15 Dii majorum gentium—The twelve gods of the highest order.

Dii penates—Household gods.

Di irati laneos pedes habent—The gods when angry have their feet covered with wool. *Pr.*

Dii rexque secundent—May God and the king favour us. *M.*

Diis aliter visum—The gods have decreed otherwise. *Virg.*

20 Diis proximus ille est / Quem ratio, non ira movet—He is nearest to the gods whom reason, not passion, impels. *Claud.*

Dilationes in lege sunt odiosæ—Delays in the law are odious. *L.*

Dilettantism, hypothesis, speculation, a kind of amateur-search for truth, toying and coquetting with truth; this is the sorest sin, the root of all imaginable sins. *Carlyle.*

Dilexi justiciam et odi iniquitatem, propterea morior in exilio—I have loved justice and hated injustice, therefore die I an exile. *Gregory VII. on his death-bed.*

Diligence increases the fruits of labour. *Hesiod.*

25 Diligence is the mother of good fortune. *Cervantes.*

Diligentia, qua una virtute omnes virtutes reliquæ continentur—Diligence, the one virtue that embraces in it all the rest. *Cic.*

Diligent, that includes all virtues in it a student can have. *Carlyle, to the Students of Edinburgh University.*

Diligent working makes an expert workman. *Dan. Pr.*

Diligitur nemo, nisi cui fortuna secunda est—Only he is loved who is the favourite of fortune. *Ovid.*

Dimidium facti, qui cœpit, habet—He who has 30 begun has half done. *Hor.*

Ding (knock) down the nests, and the rooks will flee awa. *Sc. Pr., used to justify the demolition of the religious houses at the Reformation.*

Dinna curse him, sir; I have heard a good man say that a curse was like a stone flung up to the heavens, and maist like to return on his head that sent it. *Scott.*

Dinna gut your fish till you get them. *Sc. Pr.*

Dinna lift me before I fa'. *Sc. Pr.*

Dinna scald your ain mou' wi ither folk's kail 35 (broth). *Sc. Pr.*

Di nos quasi pilas homines habent—The gods treat us mortals like so many balls to play with. *Plaut.*

Diogenes has well said that the only way to preserve one's liberty was being always ready to die without pain. *Goethe.*

Dios es el que sana, y el médico lleva la plata —Though God cures the patient, the doctor pockets the fee. *Sp. Pr.*

Dios me dé contienda con quien me entienda—God grant me to argue with such as understand me. *Sp. Pr.*

Di picciol uomo spesso grand' ombra—A little 40 man often casts a long shadow. *It. Pr.*

Dira necessitas—Cruel necessity. *Hor.*

Dirigo—I direct. *M.*

Dirt is not dirt, but only something in the wrong place. *Palmerston.*

Diruit, ædificat, mutat quadrata rotundis—He pulls down, he builds up, he changes square into round. *Hor.*

Dir war das Unglück eine strenge Schule— 45 Misfortune was for thee a hard school. *Schiller.*

Disappointment is often the salt of life. *Theodore Parker.*

Disasters, do the best we can, / Will reach both great and small; / And he is oft the wisest man / Who is not wise at all. *Wordsworth.*

Disce aut discede—Learn or leave.

Disce pati—Learn to endure.

Disce, puer, virtutem ex me, verumque labo- 50 rem, / Fortunam ex aliis—Learn, my son, valour and patient toil from me, good fortune from others. *Virg.*

Disciplined inaction. *Sir J. Macintosh.*

Discipulus est prioris posterior dies — Each succeeding day is the scholar of the preceding. *Pub. Syr.*

Discite justitiam moniti, et non temnere divos —Warned by me, learn justice, and not to despise the gods. *Virg.*

Discit enim citius, meminitque libentius illud / Quod quis deridet quam quod probat et veneratur—Each learns more readily, and retains more willingly, what makes him laugh than what he approves of and respects. *Hor.*

Discontent is like ink poured into water, which 55 fills the whole fountain full of blackness. It casts a cloud over the mind, and renders it more occupied about the evil which disquiets it than about the means of removing it. *Feltham.*

Discontent is the want of self-reliance; it is infirmity of will. *Emerson.*

Discontent makes us to lose what we have; contentment gets us what we want. Fretting never removed a cross nor procured a comfort; quiet submission doth both. *Jacomb.*

Discontents are sometimes the better part of our life. *Feltham.*

Discord oft in music makes the sweeter lay. *Spenser.*

5 Discreet women have neither eyes nor ears. *Fr. Pr.*

Discrepant facta cum dictis—The facts don't agree with the statements. *Cic.*

Discretion / And hard valour are the twins of honour, / And, nursed together, make a conqueror; / Divided, but a talker. *Beaumont and Fletcher.*

Discretion is the perfection of reason, and a guide to us in all the duties of life. *La Bruyère.*

Discretion is the salt, and fancy the sugar, of life; the one preserves, the other sweetens it. *Bovee.*

10 Discretion of speech is more than eloquence, and to speak agreeably to him with whom we deal is more than to speak in good words or in good order. *Bacon.*

Discretion, the best part of valour. *Beaumont and Fletcher.*

Disdain and scorn ride sparkling in her eye, / Misprising what they look on. *Much Ado, iii. 1.*

Diseased nature oftentimes breaks forth / In strange eruptions, and the teeming earth / Is with a kind of cholic pinch'd and vex'd / By the imprisoning of unruly wind / Within her womb, which, for enlargement striving, / Shakes the old beldam earth, and topples down / Steeples and moss-grown towers. *Hen. IV., iii. 1.*

Diseases, desperate grown, / By desperate appliance are relieved, / Or not at all. *Ham., iv. 3.*

15 Diseur de bons mots—A sayer of good things; a would-be wit. *Fr.*

Diseuse de bonne aventure—A mere fortune-teller. *Fr.*

Disgrace consists infinitely more in the crime than in the punishment. *Bacon.*

Disguise our bondage as we will, / 'Tis woman, woman rules us still. *Moore.*

Disguise thyself as thou wilt, still, Slavery, thou art a bitter draught. *Sterne.*

20 Dishonesty is the forsaking of permanent for temporary advantages. *Bovee.*

Dishonest men conceal their faults from themselves as well as others; honest men know and confess them. *Bovee.*

Dishonesty will stare honesty out of countenance any day in the week, if there is anything to be got by it. *Dickens.*

Dishonour waits on perfidy. The villain / Should blush to think a falsehood; 'tis the crime / Of cowards. *C. Johnson.*

Disillusion is the chief characteristic of old age.

Disjecta membra—Scattered remains.

Disjecti membra poetæ—Limbs of the dismembered poet. *Hor.*

Disjice compositam pacem, sere crimina belli—Dash the patched-up peace, sow the seeds of wicked war. *Virg.*

Dismiss your vows, your feigned tears, your flattery; / For where a heart is hard, they make no battery. *Shakespeare.*

Disobedience is the beginning of evil and the broad way to ruin. *D. Davies.*

Disorder in a drawing-room is vulgar; in an 30 antiquary's study, not; the black stain on a soldier's face is not vulgar, but the dirty face of a housemaid is. *Ruskin.*

Disorder is dissolution, death. *Carlyle.*

Disorder makes nothing at all, but unmakes everything. *Prof. Blackie.*

Disponendo me, non mutando me—By displacing, not by changing me. *M.*

Disputandi pruritus ecclesiarum scabies—The itch for controversy is the scab of the Church. *Wotton.*

Dissensions, like small streams at first begun, / 35 Unseen they rise, but gather as they run. *Garth.*

Dissimulation in youth is the forerunner of perfidy in old age. *Blair.*

Dissimulation is but faint policy, for it asketh a strong wit and a strong heart to know when to tell the truth and to do it. *Bacon.*

Distance produces in idea the same effect as in real perspective. *Scott.*

Distance sometimes endears friendship, and absence sweeteneth it. *Howell.*

Distinction is an eminence that is attained but 40 too frequently at the expense of a fireside. *Simms.*

Distinction is the consequence, never the object, of a great mind. *W. Allston.*

Distinction, with a broad and powerful fan / Puffing at all, winnows the light away. *Troil. and Cress., i. 3.*

Distingué—Distinguished; eminent; gentleman-like. *Fr.*

Distinguished talents are not necessarily connected with discretion. *Junius.*

Distortion is the agony of weakness. It is the 45 dislocated mind whose movements are spasmodic. *Willmott.*

Distrahit animum librorum multitudo—A multitude of books distracts the mind. *Sen.*

Distrait—Absent in mind. *Fr.*

Distressed valour challenges great respect, even from enemies. *Plutarch.*

Distringas—You may distrain. *L.*

Distrust and darkness of a future state / 50 Make poor mankind so fearful of their fate, / Death in itself is nothing; but we fear / To be we know not what, we know not where. *Dryden.*

Dites-moi ce que tu manges, je te dirai ce que tu es—Tell me what you eat, and I will tell you what you are. *Brillat-Savarin.*

Ditissimus agris—An extensive landed proprietor.

Di tutte le arti maestro è amore—Love is master of all arts. *It. Pr.*

Diversité, c'est ma devise—Variety, that is my motto. *La Fontaine.*

Dives agris, dives positis in fœnore nummis— 55 Rich in lands, rich in money laid out at interest. *Hor.*

Dives aut iniquus est aut iniqui hæres—A rich man is an unjust man, or the heir of one. *Pr.*

Dives est, cui tanta possessio est, ut nihil optet amplius—He is rich who wishes no more than he has. *Cic.*

Dives qui fieri vult, / Et cito vult fieri—He who wishes to become rich, is desirous of becoming so at once. *Juv.*

Divide et impera—Divide and govern.

5 Divina natura dedit agros, ars humana ædificavit urbes—Divine nature gave the fields, man's invention built the cities. *Varro.*

Divination seems heightened to its highest power in woman. *A. B. Alcott.*

Divine love is a sacred flower, which in its early bud is happiness, and in its full bioom is heaven. *Hervey.*

Divine moment, when over the tempest-tossed soul, as over the wild-weltering chaos, it was spoken: Let there be light. Even to the greatest that has felt such a moment, is it not miraculous and God-announcing; even as, under simpler figures, to the humblest and least? *Carlyle.*

Divine Philosophy, by whose pure light / We first distinguish, then pursue the right; / Thy power the breast from every error frees, / And weeds out all its vices by degrees. *Juv.*

10 Divine *right*, take it on the great scale, is found to mean divine *might* withal. *Carlyle.*

Divines but peep on undiscovered worlds, / And draw the distant landscape as they please. *Dryden.*

Divinity should be empress, and philosophy and other arts merely her servants. *Luther.*

Divitiæ grandes homini sunt, vivere parce / Æquo animo—It is great wealth to a man to live frugally with a contented mind. *Lucr.*

Divitiæ virum faciunt—Riches make the man.

15 Divitiarum et formæ gloria fluxa atque fragilis; virtus clara æternaque habetur—The glory of wealth and of beauty is fleeting and frail; virtue is illustrious and everlasting. *Sall.*

Divitis servi maxime servi—Servants to the rich are the most abject.

Divorce from this world is marriage with the next. *Talmud.*

Dla przyjaciela nowego / Nie opuszczaj starego!—To keep a new friend, never break with the old. *Russ. Pr.*

Do as others do, and few will laugh at you. *Dan. Pr.*

20 Do as the bee does with the rose, take the honey and leave the thorn. *Amer. Pr.*

Do as the lassies do; say "No" and tak' it. *Sc. Pr.*

Dobrze to w kazdym znaleść przyjaciela!—How delightful to find a friend in every one. *Brodzinski.*

Docendo discimus—We learn by teaching.

Dochters zijn broze waren—Daughters are fragile ware. *Dut. Fr.*

25 Doch werdet ihr nie Herz zu Herzen schaffen / Wenn es auch nicht von Herzen geht—Yet will ye never bring heart to heart unless it goes out cf your own. *Goethe.*

Dociles imitandis / Turpibus ac pravis omnes sumus—We are all easily taught to imitate what is base and depraved. *Juv.*

Docti rationem artis intelligunt, indocti voluptatem—The learned understand the principles of art, the unlearned feel the pleasure only. *Quinct.*

Doctor Luther's shoes don't fit every village priest. *Ger. Pr.*

Doctor utriusque legis—Doctor of both civil and canon law.

Doctrina sed vim promovet insitam / Rectique 30 cultus pectora roborant—But instruction improves the innate powers, and good discipline strengthens the heart. *Hor.*

Doctrine is nothing but the skin of truth set up and stuffed. *Ward Beecher.*

Does Homer interest us now, because he wrote of what passed beyond his native Greece, and two centuries before he was born; or because he wrote what passed in God's world, which is the same after thirty centuries? *Carlyle.*

Do falta dicha, por demas es diligencia—Diligence is of no use where luck is wanting. *Sp. Pr.*

Dogmatic jargon, learn'd by heart, / Trite sentences, hard terms of art, / To vulgar ears seem so profound, / They fancy learning in the sound. *Gay.*

Do good and throw it into the sea; if the fish 35 know it not, the Lord will. *Turk. Pr.*

Do good by stealth, and blush to find it fame. *Pope.*

Do good to thy friend to keep him, to thy enemy to gain him. *Ben. Franklin.*

Dogs should not be taught to eat leather (so indispensable for leashes and muzzles). *Ger. Pr.*

Dogs that bark at a distance ne'er bite at hand. *Sc. Pr.*

Doing good is the only certainly happy action 40 of a man's life. *Sir P. Sidney.*

Doing is activity; and he will still be doing. *Hen. V.,* iii. 7.

Doing is the great thing; for if people resolutely do what is right, they come in time to like doing it. *Ruskin.*

Doing leads more surely to saying than saying to doing. *Vinet.*

Doing nothing is doing ill. *Pr.*

Dolce far niente—Sweet idleness. *It.*   45

Dolci cose a vedere, e dolci inganni—Things sweet to see, and sweet deceptions. *Ariosto.*

Dolendi modus, timendi non autem—There is a limit to grief, but not to fear. *Pliny.*

Doli non doli sunt, nisi astu colas—Fraud is not fraud, unless craftily planned. *Plaut.*

Dolium volvitur—An empty vessel rolls easily. *Pr.*

Dolori affici, sed resistere tamen—To be affected 50 with grief, but still to resist it. *Pliny.*

Dolus an virtus, quis in hoste requirat?—Who inquires in an enemy whether it be stratagem or valour? *Virg.*

Dolus versatur in generalibus—Fraud deals in generalities. *L.*

Domandar chi nacque prima, l'uovo o la gallina—Ask which was first produced, the egg or the hen. *It. Pr.*

Domestic happiness is the end of almost all our pursuits, and the common reward of all our pains. *Fielding.*

Domestic happiness! thou only bliss / Of hap- 55 piness that has survived the Fall. *Cowper.*

Domi manere convenit felicibus—Those who are happy at home should remain at home. *Pr.*

Domine, dirige nos—Lord, direct us!

Domini pudet, non servitutis—I am ashamed of my master, but not of my condition as a servant. *Sen.*

Dominus illuminatio mea—The Lord is my light. *M.*

5 Dominus providebit—The Lord will provide. *M.*

Dominus videt plurimum in rebus suis—The master sees best in his own affairs. *Phæd.*

Dominus vobiscum, et cum spiritu tuo—The Lord be with you, and with thy spirit.

Domitæ naturæ—Of a tame nature.

Domus amica domus optima—The house of a friend is the best house.

10 Domus et placens uxor—Thy house and pleasing wife.

Domus sua cuique tutissimum refugium—The safest place of refuge for every man is his own home. *Coke.*

Dona præsentis cape lætus horæ, et / Linque severa—Gladly enjoy the gifts of the present hour, and banish serious thoughts. *Hor.*

Donatio mortis causa—A gift made in prospect of death. ' *L.*

Don de plaire—The gift of pleasing. *Fr.*

15 Donec eris felix multos numerabis amicos; / Tempora si fuerint nubila, solus eris—So long as you are prosperous you will reckon many friends; if fortune frowns on you, you will be alone. *Ovid.*

Done to death by slanderous tongues. *Much Ado*, v. 3.

Donna di finestra, uva di strada—A woman at the window is a bunch of grapes by the wayside. *It. Pr.*

Donna è mobile come piume in vento—Woman is as changeable as a feather in the wind. *Verdi.*

Donner de si mauvaise grâce qu'on n'a pas d'obligation—To give so ungraciously as to do away with any obligation. *Fr.*

20 Donner une chandelle à Dieu et une au diable —To give one candle to God and another to the devil. *Fr. Pr.*

Donnez, mais, si vous pouvez, épargnez au pauvre, la honte de tendre la main—Give, but, if possible, spare the poor man the shame of holding out the hand. *Diderot.*

Dono dedit—Gave as a gift.

Do not allow your daughters to be taught letters by a man, though he be a St Paul or a St. Francis of Assisi. The saints are in heaven. *Bp. Liguori.*

Do not ask if a man has been through college. Ask if a college has been through him. *Chapin.*

25 Do not, as some ungracious pastors do, / Show me the steep and thorny way to heaven, / Whilst. like a puffed and reckless libertine, / Himself the primrose path of dalliance treads, / And recks not his own rede. *Ham.*, i. 3.

Do not flatter your benefactors. *Buddhist Pr.*

Do not, for one repulse, forego the purpose / That you resolv'd to effect. *Tempest*, iii. 2.

Do not give dalliance / Too much the rein; the strongest oaths are straw / To the fire i' the blood. Be more abstemious, / Or else good night your vow. *Tempest*, iv. 1.

Do not halloo till you are out of the wood. *Pr.*

Do not lose the present in vain perplexities 30 about the future. If fortune lours to-day, she may smile to-morrow. *Sir T. Martin.*

Do not refuse the employment which the hour brings you for one more ambitious. *Emerson.*

Do not talk Arabic in the house of a Moor. *Sp. Pr.*

Do not tell a friend anything that you would conceal from an enemy. *Ar. Pr.*

Do not think of one falsity as harmless, and one as slight, and another as unintended. Cast them all aside ; it is better our hearts should be swept clean of them. *Ruskin.*

Do not train boys to learning by force or harsh- 35 ness ; but direct them to it by what amuses their minds, so that you may be the better able to discover with accuracy the peculiar bent of the genius of each. *Plato.*

Do not trouble yourself too much about the light on your statue ; the light of the public square will test its value. *Michael Angelo to a young sculptor.*

Don't be a cynic and disconsolate preacher. Don't bewail and moan. Omit the negative propositions. Nerve us with incessant affirmatives. Don't waste yourself in rejection, nor bark against the bad, but chant the beauty of the good. *Emerson.*

Don't be "consistent," but be simply true. *Holmes.*

Don't budge, if you are at ease where you are. *Ger. Pr.*

Don't despise a slight wound or a poor relative. 40 *Dan. Pr.*

Don't dissipate your powers ; strive constantly to concentrate them. Genius thinks it can do whatever it sees others doing, but it is sure to repent of every ill-judged outlay. *Goethe.*

Don terrible de la familiarité—The terrible gift of familiarity. *Mirabeau.*

Don't fly till your wings are fledged. *Ger. Pr.*

Don't hate ; only pity and avoid those that follow lies. *Carlyle.*

Don't put too fine a point to your wit, for fear 45 it should get blunted. *Cervantes.*

Don't quit the highway for a short cut. *Port. Pr.*

Don't reckon your chickens before they are hatched. *Pr.*

Don't throw away the old shoes till you've got new ones. *Dut. Pr.*

Donum exitiale Minervæ — The fatal gift to Minerva, *i.e.*, the wooden horse, by means of which the Greeks took Troy. *Virg.*

Do on the hill as ye do in the ha'. *Sc. Pr.* 50

Do right ; though pain and anguish be thy lot, / Thy heart will cheer thee when the pain's forgot : / Do wrong for pleasure's sake, then count thy gains, / The pleasure soon departs, the sin remains. *Bp. Shuttleworth.*

Dormit aliquando jus, moritur nunquam—A right is sometimes in abeyance, but never abolished. *L.*

Dormiunt aliquando leges, nunquam moriuntur—The law sleeps sometimes, but never dies. *L.*

Dos d'âne—Saddleback (*lit.* ass's back). *Fr.*

Dos est magna parentum / Virtus—The virtue 55 of parents is a great dowry. *Hor.*

Dos est uxoria lites—Strife is the dowry of a wife. *Ovid.*

Δόσις δ'ὀλίγη τε, φίλη τε—Gift both dainty and dear. *Hom.*

Dos linajes solo hay en el mundo, el "tener" y el "no tener"—There are but two families in the world, those who have, and those who have not. *Cervantes.*

Δός μοι ποῦ στῶ καὶ τὴν γῆν κινήσω—Give me where to stand, and I will move the earth. *Archimedes.*

5 Dost thou love life ? Then do not squander time, for that is the stuff life is made of. *B. Franklin.*

Dost thou love me? I know thou wilt say aye; / And I will take thy word. Yet if thou swear'st, / Thou may'st prove false ; at lovers' perjuries / They say Jove laughs. *Rom. and Jul.,* ii. 2.

Dost thou love pictures? We will fetch thee straight / Adonis painted by a running brook ; / And Cytherea all in sedges hid ; / Which seem to move and wanton with her breath ; / Even as the waving sedges play with wind. *Tam. the Shrew,* Ind. 2.

Dost thou think, because thou art virtuous, there are to be no more cakes and ale ? *Twelfth Night,* ii. 3.

Do that which is assigned you, and you cannot hope too much or dare too much. *Emerson.*

10 Do the duty that lies nearest to you. Every duty which is bidden to wait returns with seven fresh duties at its back. *Kingsley.*

Do the duty which lies nearest to thee. Thy second duty will already have become clearer. *Carlyle.*

Do thine own task, and be therewith content. *Goethe.*

Doth not the appetite alter? A man loves the meat in his youth that he cannot endure in his age. *Much Ado,* ii. 3.

Doth the eagle know what is in the pit, / Or wilt thou go ask the mole? *William Blake.*

15 Do thy little well, and for thy comfort know, / Great men can do their greatest work no better than just so. *Goethe.*

Double, double, toil and trouble, / Fire burn, and caldron bubble. *Macb.,* iv. 1.

Double, double toil and trouble ; that is the life of all governors that really govern ; not the spoil of victory, only the glorious toil of battle can be theirs. *Carlyle.*

Double entendre—A double meaning. *Fr.*

Double entente—Double signification. *Fr.*

20 Doubting the reality of love leads to doubting everything. *Amiel.*

Doubting things go ill often hurts more / Than to be sure they do. *Cymbeline,* i. 7.

Doubt is an incentive to truth, and patient inquiry leadeth the way. *H. Ballou.*

Doubt is the abettor of tyranny. *Amiel.*

Doubt is the vestibule which all must pass before they can enter into the temple of wisdom. *Colton.*

25 Doubtless the pleasure is as great / Of being cheated as to cheat. *Butler.*

Doubt of any sort cannot be removed except by action. *Goethe.*

Doubt thou the stars are fire ; / Doubt that the sun doth move ; / Doubt truth to be a liar ; / But never doubt I love. *Ham.,* ii. 2.

Douceur—A bribe. *Fr.*

Do ut des—I give that you may give. *Maxim of Bismarck.*

Doux yeux—Tender glances. *Fr.* 30

Dove bisognan rimedj, il sospirar non vale—Where remedies are needed, sighing is of no use. *It. Pr.*

Dove è grand' amore, quivi è gran dolore—Where the love is great the pain is great. *It. Pr.*

Dove è il Papa, ivi è Roma—Where the Pope is, Rome is. *It. Pr.*

Dove è l'amore, là è l'occhio—Where love is, there the eye is. *It. Pr.*

Dove entra il vino, esce la vergogna—When 35 wine enters modesty goes. *It. Pr.*

Dove la voglia è pronta, le gambe son leggiere —When the will is prompt, the legs are light. *It. Pr.*

Do weel and doubt nae man ; do ill and doubt a' men. *Sc. Pr.*

Do we not all submit to death? The highest sentence of the law, sentence of death, is passed on all of us by the fact of birth ; yet we live patiently under it, patiently undergo it when the hour comes. *Carlyle.*

Dower'd with the hate of hate, the scorn of scorn, / The love of love. *Tennyson, of the poet.*

Do what he will, he cannot realise / Half he 40 conceives — the glorious vision flies ; / Go where he may, he cannot hope to find / The truth, the beauty pictured in the mind. *Rogers.*

Do what we can, summer will have its flies ; if we go a-fishing, we must expect a wet coat. *Emerson.*

Down, thou climbing sorrow ; / Thy element's below. *King Lear,* ii. 4.

Downward to climb and backward to advance. *Pope.*

Downy sleep, death's counterfeit. *Macb.,* iii. 2.

Do you think the porter and the cook have no 45 anecdotes, no experiences, no wonders for you ? *Emerson.*

Do you wish to find out the really sublime? Repeat the Lord's Prayer. *Napoleon.*

Dramatis personæ—Characters represented.

Draw thyself from thyself. *Goethe.*

Dream after dream ensues, / And still they dream that they shall still succeed / And still are disappointed. *Cowper.*

Dream delivers us to dream, and there is no 50 end to illusion. *Emerson.*

Dreams are but interludes which fancy makes. / When monarch reason sleeps, this mimic wakes ; / Compounds a medley of disjointed things, / A mob of cobblers and a court of kings ; / Light fumes are merry, grosser fumes are sad ; / Both are the reasonable soul run mad. *Dryden.*

Dreams are excursions into the limbo of things, a semi-deliverance from the human prison. *Amiel.*

Dreams are the bright creatures of poem and legend, who sport on the earth in the night season, and melt away with the first beams of the sun. *Dickens.*

Dreams are the children of an idle brain, / Begot of nothing but vain phantasy ; / Which are as thin of substance as the air, / And more inconstant than the wind. *Rom. and Jul.*, i. 4.

Dreams, books, are each a world ; and books, we know, / Are a substantial world, both pure and good ; / Round these, with tendrils strong as flesh and blood, / Our pastime and our happiness will grow. *Wordsworth.*

Dreams, indeed, are ambition ; for the substance of the ambitious is merely the shadow of a dream. *Ham.*, ii. 2.

Dreams, in general, take their rise from those incidents that have occurred during the day. *Herodotus.*

5 Dreams in their development have breath / And tears and torture and the touch of joy ; / They leave a weight upon our waking thoughts ; / They take a weight from off our waking toils ; / They do divide our being ; they become a portion of ourselves as of our time, / And look like heralds of eternity. *Byron.*

Dreigers vechten niet—Those who threaten don't fight. *Dut. Pr.*

Dress has a moral effect upon the conduct of mankind. *Sir J. Barrington.*

Drinking water neither makes a man sick nor in debt, nor his wife a widow. *John Neal.*

Drink nothing without seeing it, sign nothing without reading it. *Port. Pr.*

10 Drink not the third glass, which thou canst not tame / When once it is within thee ; but before, / May'st rule it as thou list ; and pour the shame, / Which it would pour on thee, upon the floor. *G. Herbert.*

Drink to me only with thine eyes, / And I will pledge with mine ; / Or leave a kiss but in the cup, / And I'll not look for wine. *Ben Jonson.*

Drink waters out of thine own cistern, and running waters out of thine own well. *Bible.*

Drive a coach and six through an act of parliament. *Baron S. Kice.*

Drive a cow to the ha' and she'll run to the byre. *Sc. Pr.*

15 Drive thy business, let not thy business drive thee. *Franklin.*

Droit d'aubaine—The right of escheat ; windfall.

Droit des gens—Law of nations. *Fr.*

Droit et avant—Right and forward. *Fr.*

Droit et loyal—Right and loyal. *Fr.*

20 Drones hive not with me. *Mer. of Ven.*, ii. 5.

Drowsiness shall clothe a man with rags. *Bible.*

Drudgery and knowledge are of kin, / And both descended from one parent sin. *S. Butler.*

Drunkenness is the vice of a good constitution or of a bad memory ;—of a constitution so treacherously good than it never bends till it breaks ; or of a memory that recollects the pleasures of getting intoxicated, but forgets the pains of getting sober. *Colton.*

Drunkenness is voluntary madness. *Sen.*

Δρυὸς πεσούσης πᾶς ἀνὴρ ξυλεύεται—When an oak falls, every one gathers wood. *Men.*

Dry light is ever the best, *i.e.*, from one who, as disinterested, can take a dispassionate view of a matter. *Heraclitus.*

Dry shoes won t catch fish. *Gael Pr.*

Duabus sedere sellis—To sit between two stools.

Du bist am Ende was du bist—Thou art in the end what thou art. *Goethe.*

Dubitando ad veritatem pervenimus—By way 30 of doubting we arrive at the truth. *Cic.*

Dubiam salutem qui dat afflictis, negat—He who offers to the wretched a dubious deliverance, denies all hope. *Sen.*

Ducats are clipped, pennies are not. *Ger. Pr.*

Duce et auspice — Under his guidance and auspices. *M.*

Duces tecum—You must bring with you (certain documents). *L.*

Duce tempus eget—The time calls for a leader. 35 *Lucan.*

Du choc des esprits jaillissent les étincelles— When great spirits clash, sparks fly about. *Fr. Pr.*

Ducis ingenium, res / Adversæ nudare solent, celare secundæ—Disasters are wont to reveal the abilities of a general, good fortune to conceal them. *Hor.*

Ducit amor patriæ—The love of country leads me. *M.*

Du côté de la barbe est la toute-puissance— The male alone has been appointed to bear rule. *Molière.*

Ductor dubitantium—A guide to those in doubt. 40

Ducunt volentem fata, nolentem trahunt—Fate leads the willing, and drags the unwilling. *Sen. from Cleanthes.*

Du fort au faible—On an average (*lit.* from the strong to the weak). *Fr.*

Du glaubst zu schieben und du wirst geschoben —Thou thinkest thou art shoving and thou art shoved. *Goethe.*

Du gleichst dem Geist, den du begreifst / Nicht mir—Thou art like to the spirit which thou comprehendest, not to me. *Goethe.*

Du hast das nicht, was andre haben, / 45 Und andern mangeln deine Gabe ; / Aus dieser Unvollkommenheit / Entspringt die Geselligkeit — Thou hast not what others have, and others want what has been given thee ; out of such defect springs good-fellowship. *Gellert.*

Du haut de ces pyramides quarante siècles nous contemplent—From the height of these pyramids forty centuries look down on us. *Napoleon to his troops in Egypt.*

Dulce domum—Sweet home. *A school song.*

Dulce est desipere in loco—It is pleasant to play the fool (*i.e.* relax) sometimes. *Hor.*

Dulce est miseris socios habuisse doloris—It is a comfort to the wretched to have companions in misfortune.

Dulce et decorum est pro patria mori—It is 50 sweet and glorious to die for one's country. *Hor.*

Dulce periculum— Sweet danger. *M.*

Dulce sodalitium — A pleasant association of friends.

Dulcibus est verbis alliciendus amor—Love is to be won by affectionate words. *Pr.*

Dulcique animos novitate tenebo—And I will hold your mind captive with sweet novelty. *Ovid.*

Dulcis amor patriæ, dulce videre suos—Sweet 55 is the love of country, sweet to see one s kindred. *Ovid.*

Dulcis inexpertis cultura potentis amici; / Expertus metuit—The cultivation of friendship with the great is pleasant to the inexperienced, but he who has experienced it dreads it. *Hor.*

Dull, conceited hashes, / Confuse their brains in college classes; / They gang in stirks, and come oot asses, / Plain truth to speak. *Burns.*

Dull not device by coldness and delay. *Othello,* ii. 3.

Dumb dogs and still waters are dangerous. *Ger. Pr.*

5 Dumbie winna lee. *Sc. Pr.*

Dumb jewels often, in their silent kind, / More than quick words do move a woman's mind. *Two Gent. of Ver.,* iii. 1.

Dum deliberamus quando incipiendum incipere jam serum est—While we are deliberating to begin, the time to begin is past. *Quinet.*

Dum fata fugimus, fata stulti incurrimus—While we flee from our fate, we like fools rush on it. *Buchanan.*

Dum in dubio est animus, paulo momento huc illuc impellitur—While the mind is in suspense, a very little sways it one way or other. *Ter.*

10 Dum lego, assentior—Whilst I read, I assent. *Cic.*

Dum loquor, hora fugit—While I am speaking, time flies. *Ovid.*

Dummodo morata recte veniat, dotata est satis—Provided she come with virtuous principles, a woman brings dowry enough. *Plaut.*

Dummodo sit dives, barbarus ipse placet—If he be only rich, a very barbarian pleases us. *Ovid.*

Dum ne ob malefacta peream, parvi æstimo—So be I do not die for evil-doing, I care little for dying. *Plaut.*

15 Du moment qu'on aime, on devient si doux—From the moment one falls in love, one becomes sweet in the temper. *Marmontel.*

Dum se bene gesserit—So long as his behaviour is good. *L.*

Dum singuli pugnant, universi vincuntur—While they fight separately, the whole are conquered. *Tacit.*

Dum spiro, spero—While I breathe, I hope. *M.*

Dum tacent, clamant—While silent, they cry aloud, *i.e.,* their silence bespeaks discontent. *Cic.*

20 Du musst steigen oder sinken, / Du musst herrschen und gewinnen, / Oder dienen und verlieren, / Leiden oder triumphiren, / Amboss oder Hammer sein—Thou must mount up or sink down, must rule and win or serve and lose, suffer or triumph, be anvil or hammer. *Goethe.*

Dum vires annique sinunt, tolerate labores: / Jam veniet tacito curva senecta pede—While your strength and years permit, you should endure labour; bowed old age will soon come on with silent foot. *Ovid.*

Dum vitant stulti vitia, in contraria currunt—While fools shun one set of faults, they run into the opposite one. *Hor.*

Dum vivimus, vivamus—While we live, let us live. *M.*

D'une vache perdue, c'est quelque chose de recouvrer la queue—When a cow is lost, it is something to recover the tail. *Fr. Pr.*

25 Duo quum faciunt idem non est idem—When two do the same thing, it is not the same. *Ter.*

Duos qui sequitur lepores neutrum capit—He who follows two hares is sure to catch neither. *Pr.*

Dupes indeed are many; but of all dupes there is none so fatally situated as he who lives in undue terror of being duped. *Carlyle.*

Durante beneplacito—During good pleasure.

Durante vita—During life.

Dura più incudine che il martello—The anvil 30 lasts longer than the hammer. *It. Pr.*

Durate, et vosmet rebus servate secundis—Be patient, and preserve yourself for better times. *Virg.*

Durch Vernünfteln wird Poesie vertrieben / Aber sie mag das Vernüftige lieben—Poetry loves what is true in reason, but is scared away (dispersed) by subtlety in reasoning. *Goethe.*

Durum et durum non faciunt murum—Hard and hard (*i.e.,* without mortar) do not make a wall.

Durum! Sed levius fit patientia / Quicquid corrigere est nefas—'Tis hard! But that which we are not permitted to correct is rendered lighter by patience. *Hor.*

Durum telum necessitas—Necessity is a hard 35 weapon. *Pr.*

Du sollst mit dem Tode zufrieden sein. / Warum machst du dir das Leben zur Pein?—Thou shouldst make peace (*lit.* be content) with death. Why then make thy life a torture to thee? *Goethe.*

Dusting, darning, drudging, nothing is great or small, / Nothing is mean or irksome: love will hallow it all. *Dr. Walter Smith.*

Dust long outlasts the storied stone. *Byron.*

Dust thou art, and unto dust thou shalt return. *Bible.*

Du sublime au ridicule il n'y a qu'un pas—There 40 is but one step from the sublime to the ridiculous. *Napoleon.*

Dutchmen must have wide breeches. *Fris. Pr.*

Duties are but coldly performed which are but philosophically fulfilled. *Mrs. Jameson.*

Duties are ours; events are God's. *Cecil.*

Duty by habit is to pleasure turn'd; / He is content who to obey has learn'd. *Sir E. Brydges.*

Duty demands the parent's voice / Should sanc- 45 tify the daughter's choice, / In that is due obedience shown; / To choose belongs to her alone. *Moore.*

Duty, especially out of the domain of love, is the veriest slavery in the world. *J. G. Holland.*

Duty has the virtue of making us feel the reality of a positive world, while at the same time it detaches us from it. *Amiel.*

Duty is a power which rises with us in the morning, and goes to bed with us in the evening. *Gladstone.*

Duty is the demand of the passing hour. *Goethe.*

Duty scorns prudence, and criticism has few 50 terrors for a man with a great purpose. *Disraeli.*

Duty—the command of Heaven, the eldest voice of God. *Kingsley.*

Dux fœmina facti—A woman the leader in the deed. *Virg.*

E.

Each animal out of its habitat would starve. *Emerson.*

Each change of many-colour'd life he drew, / Exhausted worlds, and then imagined new. *Johnson.*

Each creature is only a modification of the other ; the likeness in them is more than the difference, and their radical law is one and the same. *Emerson.*

Each creature seeks its perfection in another. *Luther.*

5 Each day still better other's happiness, / Until the heavens, envying earth's good hap, / Add an immortal title to your crown, *Rich. II.*, i. 1.

Each departed friend is a magnet that attracts us to the next world, and the old man lives among graves. *Jean Paul.*

Each good thought or action moves / The dark world nearer to the sun, *Whittier.*

Each heart is a world. You find all within yourself that you find without. The world that surrounds you is the magic glass of the world within you. *Lavater.*

Each human heart can properly exhibit but one love, if even one ; the "first love, which is infinite," can be followed by no second like unto it. *Carlyle.*

10 Each in his narrow cell for ever laid, / The rude forefathers of the hamlet sleep. *Gray.*

Each man begins the world afresh, and the last man repeats the blunders of the first. *Amiel.*

Each man can learn something from his neighbour ; at least he can learn to have patience with him—to live and let live. *Kingsley.*

Each man has his fortune in his own hands, as the artist has a piece of rude matter, which he is to fashion into a certain shape. *Goethe.*

Each man has his own vocation ; his talent is his call. There is one direction in which all space is open to him. *Emerson.*

15 Each man sees over his own experience a certain stain of error, whilst that of other men looks fair and ideal. *Emerson.*

Each man's chimney is his golden milestone, is the central point from which he measures every distance through the gateways of the world around him. *Longfellow.*

Each mind has its own method. A true man never acquires after college rules. *Emerson.*

Each must stand on his glass tripod, if he would keep his electricity. *Emerson.*

Each one of us here, let the world go how it will, and be victorious or not victorious, has he not a life of his own to lead ? *Carlyle.*

20 Each particle of matter is an immensity, each leaf a world, each insect an inexplicable compendium. *Lavater.*

Each plant has its parasite, and each created thing its lover and poet. *Emerson.*

Each present joy or sorrow seems the chief. *Sh.*

Each sin at heart is Deicide. *Aubrey de Vere (the younger).*

Each substance of a grief hath twenty shadows, / Which show like grief itself, but are not so ; / For sorrow's eye, glazed with blinding tears, / Divides one thing entire to many objects. *Rich. II.*, ii. 2.

Each thing is a half, and suggests another thing 25 to make it whole ; as spirit, matter ; man, woman ; odd, even ; subjective, objective ; in, out ; motion, rest ; yea, nay. *Emerson.*

Each thing lives according to its kind ; the heart by love, the intellect by truth, the higher nature of man by intimate communion with God. *Chapin.*

Each year one vicious habit rooted out, in time might make the worst man good. *Ben. Franklin.*

Ea fama vagatur—That report is in circulation.

Eagles fly alone ; they are but sheep that always herd together. *Sir P. Sidney.*

Eamus quo ducit gula—Let us go where our 30 appetite prompts us. *Virg.*

Early and provident fear is the mother of safety. *Burke.*

Early birds catch the worms. *Sc. Pr.*

Early, bright, transient, chaste, as morning dew, / She sparkled, was exhaled, and went to heaven. *Young.*

Early master soon knave (servant). *Sc. Pr.*

Early start makes easy stages. *Amer. Pr.* 35

Early to bed and early to rise, makes a man healthy, wealthy, and wise. *Pr.*

Earn well the thrifty months, nor wed / Raw Haste, half-sister to Delay. *Tennyson.*

Earnest and sport go well together. *Dan. Pr.*

Earnestness alone makes life eternity. *Goethe.*

Earnestness in life, even when carried to an 40 extreme, is something very noble and great. *W. v. Humboldt.*

Earnestness is a quality as old as the heart of man. *G. Gilfillan.*

Earnestness is enthusiasm tempered by reason. *Pascal.*

Earnestness is the cause of patience ; it gives endurance, overcomes pain, strengthens weakness, braves dangers, sustains hope, makes light of difficulties, and lessens the sense of weariness in overcoming them. *Bovee.*

Earnestness is the devotion of all the faculties. *Bovee.*

Earth changes, but thy soul and God stand 45 sure. *Browning.*

Earth felt the wound ; and Nature from her seat, / Sighing through all her work, gave sign of woe / That all was lost. *Milton.*

Earth has scarcely an acre that does not remind us of actions that have long preceded our own, and its clustering tombstones loom up like reefs of the eternal shore, to show us where so many human barks have struck and gone down. *Chapin.*

Earth hath no sorrow that heaven cannot heal. *Moore.*

Earth hath nothing more tender than a woman's heart when it is the abode of piety. *Luther.*

Earth is here (in Australia) so kind, just tickle 50 her with a hoe and she laughs with a harvest. *Douglas Jerrold.*

Earthly pride is like a passing flower, that springs to fall and blossoms but to die. *Kirke White.*

Earth, sea, man, are all in each. *Dante Gabriel Rossetti.*

Earth, that's Nature s mother, is her tomb. *Rom. and Jul.*, ii. 3.

Earth to earth, ashes to ashes, dust to dust, in sure and certain hope of the Resurrection. *Burial Service.*

Earth, turning from the sun, brings night to man. *Young.*

5 Earth with her thousand voices praises God. *Coleridge.*

Earth s crammed with heaven, / And every common bush afire with God. *Leigh.*

Earth's noblest thing, a woman perfected. *Lowell.*

Ease and honour are seldom bed-fellows. *Sc. Pr.*

Ea sola voluptas / Solamenque mali—That was his sole delight and solace in his woe. *Virg.*

10 East and west, home (hame) is best. *Eng. and Sc. Pr.*

Ea sub oculis posita negligimus; proximorum incuriosi, longinqua sectamur—We disregard the things which lie under our eyes; indifferent to what is close at hand, we inquire after things that are far away. *Pliny.*

Easy-crying widows take new husbands soonest; there's nothing like wet weather for transplanting. *Holmes.*

Easy writing's curst hard reading. *Sheridan.*

Eat at your own table as you would eat at the table of the king. *Confucius.*

15 Eat at your pleasure, drink in measure. *Pr.*

Eating little and speaking little can never do harm. *Pr.*

Eating the bitter bread of banishment. *Rich. II.,* iii. 1.

Eat in measure and defy the doctor. *Sc. Pr.*

Eat to please thyself, but dress to please others. *Ben. Franklin.*

20 Eat-weel's drink-weel's brither. *Sc. Pr.*

Eat what you like, but pocket nothing. *Pr.*

Eau bénite de cour—False promises (*lit.* holy water of the court). *Fr.*

Eau sucrée—Sugared water. *Fr.*

'Εαυτὸν τιμωρούμενος — The self-tormentor. *Menander.*

25 Ebbe il migliore / De' miei giorni la patria—The best of my days I devoted to my country. *It.*

E bello predicare il digiuno a corpo pieno—It is easy to preach fasting with a full belly. *It. Pr.*

Eben die ausgezeichnetsten Menschen bedürfen der Religion am meisten, weil sie die engen Grenzen unseres menschlichen Verstandes am liebhaftesten empfinden—It is just the most eminent men that need religion most, because they feel most keenly the narrow limits of our human understanding. *Cötvös.*

Eben wo Begriffe fehlen, / Da stellt ein Wort zur rechten Zeit sich ein—It is just where ideas fail that a word comes most opportunely to the rescue. *Goethe.*

E buon comprare quando un altro vuol vendere—It is well to buy when another wishes to sell. *It. Pr.*

30 Ecce homo—Behold the man! *Pontius Pilate.*

Ecce iterum Crispinus!—Another Crispinus, by Jove! (a profligate at the court of Domitian). *Juv.*

Eccentricity has always abounded when and where strength of character has abounded; and the amount of eccentricity in a society has been proportional to the amount of genius, mental vigour, and moral courage it contained. That so few now dare to be eccentric, marks the chief danger of the time. *J. S. Mill.*

Eccentricity is sometimes found connected with genius, but it does not coalesce with true wisdom. *Jay.*

Ecce signum—Here is the proof.

Eccovi l'uom ch' è stato all' Inferno—See, there's 35 the man that has been in hell. *It.* (*Said of Dante by the people of Verona.*)

Echoes we: listen! / We cannot stay, / As dewdrops glisten, / Then fade away. *Shelley.*

Echo is the voice of a reflection in a mirror. *Hawthorne.*

'Εχθρὸς γάρ μοι κεῖνος, ὁμῶς 'Αΐδαο πύλῃσιν, / ''Ος χ' ἕτερον μὲν κεύθει ἐνὶ φρέσιν, ἄλλο δε βάξει—Hateful to me as the gates of Hades is he who conceals one thing in his mind and utters another. *Hom.*

'Εχθρῶν ἄδωρα δῶρα—An enemy's gifts are no gifts. *Soph.*

Eclaircissement—The clearing up of a thing. *Fr.* 40

Eclat de rire—A burst of laughter. *Fr.*

E cœlo descendit γνῶθι σεαυτόν—From heaven came down the precept, "Know thyself." *Juv.*

Economy does not consist in the reckless reduction of estimates; on the contrary, such a course almost necessarily tends to increased expenditure. There can be no economy where there is no efficiency. *Disraeli.*

Economy is an excellent lure to betray people into expense. *Zimmermann.*

Economy is half the battle of life; it is not so 45 hard to earn money as to spend it. *Spurgeon.*

Economy is the parent of integrity, of liberty, and of ease, and the beauteous sister of temperance, of cheerfulness, and health. *Johnson.*

Economy no more means saving money than it means spending money. It means the administration of a house, its stewardship; spending or saving, that is, whether money or time, or anything else, to the best possible advantage. *Ruskin.*

E contra—On the other hand.

E contrario—On the contrary.

Ecorcher l'anguille par la queue—To begin at 50 the wrong end (*lit.* to skin an eel from the tail). *Fr.*

Ecrasez l'infâme—Crush to pieces the abomination, *i.e.,* superstition. *Voltaire.*

Edel ist, der eidel thut—Noble is that noble does. *Ger. Pr.*

Edel macht das Gemüth, nicht das Geblüt—It is the mind, not the blood, that ennobles. *Ger. Pr.*

Edel sei der Mensch / Hülfreich und gut / Denn das allein / Unterscheidet ihn / Von allen Wesen / Die wir kennen—Be man noble, helpful, and good; for that alone distinguishes him from all the beings we know. *Goethe.*

Edition de luxe—A splendid and expensive edi- 55 tion of a book. *Fr.*

Editiones expurgatæ—Editions with objectionable passages eliminated.

Editio princeps—The original edition.

Edo, ergo ego sum—I eat, therefore I am. *Monkish Pr.*

Educated persons should share their thoughts with the uneducated, and take also a certain part in their labours. *Ruskin.*

Educate men without religion, and you make them but clever devils. *Wellington.*

5 Education alone can conduct us to that enjoyment which is at once best in quality and infinite in quantity. *H. Mann.*

Education begins its work with the first breath of the child. *Jean Paul.*

Education begins the gentleman, but reading, good company, and reflection must finish him. *Locke.*

Education commences at the mother's knee, and every word spoken within the hearing of little children tends towards the formation of character. *H. Ballou.*

Education does not mean teaching people to know what they do not know; it means teaching them to behave as they do not behave. *Ruskin.*

10 Education gives fecundity of thought, copiousness of illustration, quickness, vigour, fancy, words, images, and illustrations; it decorates every common thing, and gives the power of trifling without being undignified and absurd. *Sydney Smith.*

Education, however indispensable in a cultivated age, produces nothing on the side of genius. Where education ends, genius often begins. *Isaac Disraeli.*

Education is a better safeguard of liberty than a standing army. *E. Everett.*

Education is generally the worse in proportion to the wealth and grandeur of the parents. *D. Swift.*

Education is only like good culture; it changes the size, but not the sort. *Ward Beecher.*

15 Education is only second to nature. *H. Bushnell.*

Education is our only political safety. Outside of this ark all is deluge. *H. Mann.*

Education is the apprenticeship of life. *Willmott.*

Education is the constraining and directing of youth towards that right reason which the law affirms, and which the experience of the best of our elders has sanctioned as truly great. *Plato.*

Education is the only interest worthy the deep, controlling anxiety of the thoughtful man. *Wendell Phillips.*

20 Education is the leading human souls to what is best, and making what is best of them. The training which makes men happiest in themselves also makes them most serviceable to others. *Ruskin.*

Education may work wonders as well as in warping the genius of individuals as in seconding it. *A. B. Alcott.*

Education of youth is not a bow for every man to shoot in that counts himself a teacher, but will require sinews almost equal to those which Homer gave Ulysses. *Milton.*

Education ought, as a first principle, to stimulate the will to activity. *Zachariae.*

Education should be as broad as man. *Emerson.*

Ἢ ἥκιστα ἢ ἥδιστα—Either the least or the 25 pleasantest.

Een diamant van eene dochter wordt een glas van eene vrouw—A diamond of a daughter becomes a glass of a wife. *Dut. Pr.*

Een dief maakt gelegenheid—A thief makes opportunity. *Dut. Pr.*

E'en from the tomb the voice of Nature cries, / E'en in our ashes live their wonted fires. *Gray.*

Een hond aan een been kent geene vrienden —A dog with a bone knows no friends. *Dut. Pr.*

Een kleine pot wordt haast heet—A little pot 30 becomes soon hot. *Dut. Pr.*

Eenmaal is geen gewoonte—Once is no custom. *Dut. Pr.*

Een once geduld is meer dan een pond verstand—One ounce of patience is worth more than a pound of brains. *Dut. Pr.*

E'en though vanquished he could argue still. *Goldsmith.*

ἡ εὐδαιμονία τῶν αὐτάρχων ἐστι—Happiness is theirs who are sufficient for themselves. *Arist.*

Effloresco—I flourish. *M.* 35

Effodiuntur opes, irritamenta malorum—Riches, the incentives to evil, are dug out of the earth. *Ovid.*

Efforts, to be permanently useful, must be uniformly joyous,—a spirit all sunshine,— graceful from very gladness,—beautiful because bright. *Carlyle.*

Effugit mortem, quisquis contempserit: timidissimum quemque consequitur—Whoso despises death escapes it, while it overtakes him who is afraid of it. *Curt.*

E flamma cibum petere—To live by desperate means (*lit.* to seek food from the flames). *Pr.*

Efter en god Avler kommer en god Oder— 40 After an earner comes a waster. *Dan. Pr.*

Eftsoons they heard a most melodious sound. *Spenser.*

E fungis nati homines—Upstarts (*lit.* men born of mushrooms).

Egad! I think the interpreter is the hardest to be understood of the two. *Sheridan.*

ἡ γὰρ φύσις βέβαιον, οὐ τὰ χρήματα—It is only the character of a man, not his wealth, that is stable. *Arist.*

Egen Arne er Guld værd—A hearth of one's own 45 is worth gold. *Dan. Pr.*

Eggs and oaths are easily broken. *Dan. Pr.*

Eggs of an hour, bread of a day, wine of a year, but a friend of thirty years is best. *It. Pr.*

Ἐγγύα· πάρα δ'ἄτη—Be security, and mischief is nigh. *Thales.*

Egli ha fatto il male, ed io mi porto la pena— He has done the mischief, and I pay the penalty. *It. Pr.*

Egli vende l'uccello in su la frasca—He sells the 50 bird on the branch. *It. Pr.*

Egli venderebbe sino alla sua parte del sole— He would sell even his share in the sun. *It. Pr.*

Ἡ γλῶσσ' ὀμώμοχ', ἡ δὲ φρὴν ἀνώμοτος—My tongue has sworn, but my mind is unsworn. *Eurip.*

Ego apros occido, alter fruitur pulpamento—I kill the boars, another enjoys their flesh. *Pr.*

Ego de caseo loquor, tu de creta respondes—While I talk to you of cheese, you talk to me of chalk. *Erasmus.*

Ego ero post principia—I will get out of harm's way (*lit.* I will keep behind the first rank). *Ter.*

Ego et rex meus—I and my king. *Cardinal Wolsey.*

Ego hoc feci—That was my doing.

5 Egoism is the source and summary of all faults and miseries whatsoever. *Carlyle.*

Ego meorum solus sum meus—I am myself the only friend I have. *Ter.*

Ego nec studium sine divite vena, / Nec rude quid prosit video ingenium—I see not what good can come from study without a rich vein of genius, or from genius untrained by art. *Hor.*

Ego primam tollo, nominor quoniam Leo—I carry off the first share because my name is Lion. *Phædr. in the fable of the lion a-hunting with weaker companions.*

Ego, si bonam famam mihi servasso, sat ero dives—If I keep my good character, I shall be rich enough. *Plaut.*

10 Ego spem pretio non emo—I do not purchase hope with money, *i.e.,* I do not spend my resources upon vain hopes. *Ter.*

Ego sum, ergo omnia sunt—I am, and therefore all things are.

Ego sum rex Romanus et supra grammaticam —I am king of the Romans, and above grammar. *The Emperor Sigismund at the Council of Constance.*

Egotism erects its centre in itself; love places it out of itself in the axis of the universal whole. *Schiller.*

Egotism is the tongue of vanity. *Chamfort.*

15 Egotists are the pest of society. *Emerson.*

Egotists cannot converse; they talk to themselves only. *A. B. Alcott.*

Egregii mortales, altique silenti—A being of extraordinary and profound silence. *Hor.*

Eher schätzet man das Gute / Nicht, als bis man es verlor—We do not learn to value our blessings till we have lost them. *Herder.*

Ehestand, Wehestand—State of wedlock, state of sorrow. *Ger. Pr.*

20 Eheu ! fugaces, Posthume, Posthume, / Labuntur anni, nec pietas moram / Rugis et instanti senectæ / Afferet, indomitæque morti—Alas ! Posthumus, our years glide fleetly away, nor can piety stay wrinkles and advancing age and unvanquished death. *Hor.*

Eheu ! quam brevibus pereunt ingentia causis ! — Alas ! what trifling causes often wreck the vastest enterprises. *Claud.*

Ehren und Leben / Kann Niemand zurück geben — No man can give back honour and life. *Ger. Pr.*

Ehret die Frauen ! Sie flechten und weben / Himmlische Rosen ins irdische Leben — Honour to the women ! they plait and weave roses of heaven for the life of earth. *Schiller.*

Ehret die Frauen ! Sie stricken und weben / Wollene Strümpfe fürs frostige Leben— Honour to the women ! they knit and weave worsted stockings for our frosty life. *Volkswitz.*

25 Ehrlich währt am längsten—Honesty lasts longest. *Ger. Pr.*

Εἰ δὲ θεὸν ἀνήρ τις ἔλπεται λαθέμεν / Ἑρδὼν, ἁμαρτάνει—If any man hopes that his deeds will pass unobserved by the Deity, he is mistaken. *Pindar.*

Eident (diligent) youth makes easy age. *Sc. Pr.*

Eifersucht ist eine Leidenschaft, die mit Eifer sucht was Leiden schafft—Jealousy is a passion which seeks with zeal what yields only misery. *Schleiermacher.*

Eigenliebe macht die Augen trübe—Self-love clouds the eyes. *Ger. Pr.*

30 "Ei ist Ei," sagte der Küster, aber er nahm das Gans Ei—"An egg is an egg," said the sexton, but he took the goose-egg. *Ger. Pr.*

Eild and poortith are ill to thole, *i.e.,* age and poverty are hard to bear. *Sc. Pr.*

Eild should hae honour, *i.e.,* old people should. *Sc. Pr.*

Eile mit Weile—Haste with leisure. *Ger. Pr.*

Ein alter Fuchs läuft nicht zum zweiten Mal in's Garn—An old fox does not run into the snare a second time. *Ger. Pr.*

35 Ein Arzt darf auch dem Feind sich nicht entziehen—A physician may not turn his back even on an enemy. *Gutzkow.*

Ein Augenblick, gelebt im Paradiese, / Wird nicht zu theuer mit dem Tod gebüsst—A moment lived in paradise is not purchased too dearly at the ransom of death. *Schiller.*

Einbildungskraft wird nur durch Kunst, besonders durch Poesie geregelt. Es ist nichts fürchterlicher als Einbildungskraft ohne Geschmack—Power of imagination is regulated only by art, especially by poetry. There is nothing more frightful than imaginative faculty without taste. *Goethe.*

Einbläsereien sind der Teufels Redekunst— Insinuations are the devil's rhetoric. *Goethe.*

Ein Diadem erkämpfen ist gross; es wegwerfen ist göttlich—To gain a crown by fighting for it is great; to reject it is divine. *Schiller.*

40 Ein Ding ist nicht bös, wenn man es gut versteht—A thing is not bad if we understand it well. *Ger. Pr.*

Eine Bresche ist jeder Tag, / Die viele Menschen erstürmen ; / Wer da auch fallen mag, / Die Todten sich niemals thürmen—Every day is a rampart breach which many men are storming ; fall in it who may, no pile is forming of the slain. *Goethe.*

Ein edler Mann wird durch ein gutes Wort / Der Frauen weit geführt—A noble man is led a long way by a good word from women. *Goethe.*

Ein edler Mensch zieht edle Menschen an / Und weiss sie fest zu halten—A noble man attracts noble men, and knows how to hold them fast. *Goethe.*

Ein edles Beispiel macht die schweren Thaten leicht—A noble example makes difficult enterprises easy. *Goethe.*

45 Eine grosse Epoche hat das Jahrhundert geboren ; / Aber der grosse Moment findet ein kleines Geschlecht—The century has given birth to a great epoch, but it is a small race the great moment appeals to. *Schiller.*

Eine Hälfte der Welt verlacht die andere— One half of the world laughs at the other half. *Ger. Pr.*

Eine Handvoll Gewalt ist besser als Sackvoll Recht—A handful of might is better than a sackful of right. *Ger. Pr.*

Ein eigen Herd, ein braves Weib, sind Gold und Perlen werth—A hearth of one's own and a good wife are as good as gold and pearls. *Ger. Pr.*

Einen Wahn verlieren macht weiser als eine Wahrheit finden—Getting rid of a delusion makes us wiser than getting hold of a truth. *Börne.*

Einer kann redet und Sieben können singen —One can speak and seven can sing. *Ger. Pr.*

Einer neuen Wahrheit nichts ist schädlicher als ein alter Irrtum—Nothing is more harmful to a new truth than an old error. *Goethe.*

Eine Rose gebrochen, ehe der Sturm sie entblättert—A rose broken ere the storm stripped its petals. *Lessing.*

5 Eine schöne Menschenseele finden / Ist Gewinn —It is a true gain to find a beautiful human soul. *Herder.*

Ein Esel schimpft den andern Langohr—One ass nicknames another Longears. *Ger. Pr.*

Eines schickt sich nicht für Alle ! / Sehe jeder wie er's treibe, / Sehe jeder wo er bleibe, / Und wer steht, dass er nicht falle—One thing does not suit every one ; let each man see how he gets on, where his limits are ; and let him that standeth take heed lest he fall. *Goethe.*

Ein Feind ist zu viel, und hundert Freunde sind zu wenig—One foe is too many, a hundred friends are too few. *Ger. Pr.*

Ein fester Blick, ein hoher Mut, / Die sind zu allen Zeiten gut—A steady eye and a lofty mind are at all times good. *Bechstein.*

10 Ein geistreich aufgeschlossenes Wort / Wirkt auf die Ewigkeit. The influence of a spiritually elucidated (or embodied) word is eternal. *Goethe.*

Eingestandene Uebereilung ist oft lehrreicher, als kalte überdachte Unfehlbarkeit—A confessed precipitancy is often more instructive than a coldly considered certainty. *Lessing.*

Ein Gift, welches nicht gleich wirkt, ist darum kein minder gefährliches Gift—A poison which does not take immediate effect is therefore none the less a dangerous poison. *Lessing.*

Ein Gott ist, ein heiliger Wille lebt, / Wie auch der menschliche wanke ; / Hoch über der Zeit und dem Raume webt / Lebendig der höchste Gedanke—A god is, a holy will lives, however man's will may waver ; high over all time and space the highest thought weaves itself everywhere into life's web. *Schiller.*

Ein grosser Fehler ; dass man sich mehr dünkt als man ist, und sich weniger schätzt, als man werth ist—It is a great mistake for people to think themselves more than they are, and to value themselves less than they are worth. *Goethe.*

15 Ein Herz das sich mit Sorgen quält / Hat selten frohe Stunden—A heart which tortures itself with care has seldom hours of gladness. *Old Ger. Song.*

Ein jeder ist sich selbst der grösste Feind— Every one is his own greatest enemy. *Schefer.*

Ein jeder lebt's, nicht vielen ist's bekannt— Though every one lives it (life), it is not to many that it is known. *Goethe.*

Ein jeder lernet nur, was er lerneu kann ; / Doch der den Augenblick ergreift, / Das ist der rechte Mann—Each one learns only what he can ; yet he who seizes the passing moment is the proper man. *Goethe.*

Ein jeder Wechsel schreckt den Glücklichen— Every change is a cause of uneasiness to the favoured of fortune. *Schiller.*

20 Ein Komödiant könnt' einen Pfarren lehren— A playactor might instruct a parson. *Goethe.*

Ein Kranz ist gar viel leichter binden / Als ihm ein würdig Haupt zu finden—It is very much easier to bind a wreath than to find a head worthy to wear it. *Goethe.*

Ein langes Hoffen ist süsser, als ein kurzes Ueberraschen—A long hope is sweeter than a short surprise. *Jean Paul.*

Ein leerer Sack steht nicht aufrecht—An empty sack does not stand upright. *Ger. Pr.*

Ein mächtiger Vermittler ist der Tod—Death is a powerful reconciler. *Schiller.*

Einmal gerettet, ist's für tausend Male—To 25 be saved once is to be saved a thousand times. *Goethe.*

Ein Mann der recht zu wirken denkt / Muss auf das beste Werkzeug halten—A man who intends to work rightly must select the most effective instrument. *Goethe.*

Ein Mann, ein Wort ; ein Wort, ein Mann—A man, a word ; a word, a man. *Ger. Pr.*

Ein Mensch ohne Verstand ist auch ein Mensch ohne Wille—A man without understanding is also a man without will or purpose. *Feuerbach.*

Ein Mühlstein wird nicht moosig—A millstone does not become covered with moss. *Ger. Pr.*

Ein niedrer Sinn ist stolz im Glück, im Leid 30 bescheiden ; / Bescheiden ist im Glück ein edler, stolz im Leiden—A vulgar mind is proud in prosperity and humble in adversity ; a noble mind is humble in prosperity and proud in adversity. *Rückert.*

Ein "Nimm hin" ist besser als zehn "Helf Gott"—One "Take this" is better than ten of "God help you." *Ger. Pr.*

Ein offenes Herz zeigt eine offene Stirn—An open brow shows an open heart. *Schiller.*

Ein Pfennig mit Recht ist besser denn tausend mit Unrecht—A penny by right is better than a thousand by wrong. *Ger. Pr.*

Ein Schauspiel für Götter, / Zwei Liebende zu sehn !—To witness two lovers is a spectacle for gods. *Goethe.*

Ein Theil bin ich von jener Kraft, / Die stets 35 das Böse will und stets das Gute schafft— I am a part of that power which continually wills the evil and continually creates the good. *Mephistopheles, in "Faust."*

Ein Titel muss sie erst vertraulich machen—A degree is the first thing necessary to bespeak confidence in your profession. *Goethe, in "Faust."*

Ein Tropfen Hass, der in dem Freudenbecher / Zurückbleibt, macht den Segensdrank zum Gifte—A drop of hate that is left in the cup of joy converts the blissful draught into poison. *Schiller.*

Ein unterrichtetes Volk lässt sich leicht regieren— An educated people can be easily governed. *Frederick the Great.*

Ein üppig lastervolles Leben büsst sich / In Mangel und Erniedrigung allem—Only in want and degradation can a life of sensual profligacy be atoned for. *Schiller.*

Ein Vater ernährt eher zehn Kinder, denn zehn 40 Kinder einen Vater—One father supports ten children sooner than ten children one father. *Ger. Pr.*

Ein Vergnügen erwarten ist auch ein Vergnügen—To look forward to a pleasure is also a pleasure. *Lessing.*

Ein Volk ohne Gesetze gleicht einem Menschen ohne Grundsätze—A people without laws is like a man without principles. *Zachariae.*

Ein vollkommener Widerspruch / Bleibt gleich geheimnissvoll für Kluge wie für Thoren—A flat contradiction is ever equally mysterious to wise folks as to fools. *Goethe.*

Ein Wahn der mich beglückt, / Ist eine Wahrheit wert die mich zu Boden drückt—An illusion which gladdens me is worth a truth which saddens me (*lit.* presses me to the ground). *Wieland.*

Ein wandernd Leben / Gefällt der freien Dichterbrust—A wandering life delights the free heart of the poet. *Arion.*

Ein wenig zu spät ist viel zu spät—A little too late is much too late. *Ger. Pr.*

5 Ein Wörtlein kann ihn fällen—A little word can slay him. *Luther, of the Pope.*

Ein Wort nimmt sich, ein Leben nie zurück—A word may be recalled, a life never. *Schiller.*

Εἰς ἀνὴρ οὐδεὶς ἀνήρ—One man is no man. *Gr. Pr.*

Either sex alone is half itself. *Tennyson.*

Eith (quickly) learned, soon forgotten. *Sc. Pr.*

10 Εἴ τι ἀγαθὸν θέλεις, παρὰ σεαυτοῦ λάβε—If you would have anything good, seek for it from yourself. *Arrian.*

Ejusdem farinæ—Of the same kidney (*lit.* meal).

Ejusdem generis—Of the same kind.

El agujero llama al ladron—The hole tempts the thief. *Sp. Pr.*

El amor verdadero no sufre cosa encubierta—True love suffers no concealment. *Sp. Pr.*

15 Elati animi comprimendi sunt—Minds which are too much elated ought to be kept in check.

El corazon manda les carnes—The heart bears up the body. *Sp. Pr.*

El corazon no es traidor—The heart is no traitor. *Sp. Pr.*

El dar es honor, y el pedir dolor—To give is honour; to lose, grief. *Sp. Pr.*

El diablo saba mucho, porque es viejo—The devil knows a great deal, for he is old. *Sp. Pr.*

20 El dia que te casas, ó te matas ó te sanas—The day you marry, it is either kill or cure. *Sp. Pr.*

El Dorado—A region of unimagined wealth fabled at one time to exist in S. America ; a dreamland of wealth. *Sp.*

Elegance is necessary to the fine gentleman, dignity is proper to noblemen, and majesty to kings. *Hazlitt.*

Elegit—He has chosen. A writ empowering a creditor to hold lands for payment of a debt. *L.*

Elephants endors'd with towers. *Milton.*

25 Elève le corbeau, il te crèvera les yeux—Bring up a raven, he will pick out your eyes. *Fr. Pr.*

Elige eum cujus tibi placuit et vita et oratio—Make choice of him who recommends himself to you by his life as well as address. *Sen.*

Elk het zijne is niet te veel—Every one his own is not too much. *Dut. Pr.*

Ell and tell is gude merchandise, *i.e.*, ready money is. *Sc. Pr.*

Elle a trop de vertus pour n'être pas chrétienne—She has too many virtues not to be a Christian. *Corn.*

30 Elle n'en fit point la petite bouche—She did not mince matters (*lit.* make a small mouth about it). *Fr. Pr.*

Elle riait du bout des dents—She gave a forced laugh (*lit.* laughed with the end of her teeth). *Fr. Pr.*

El malo siempre piensa engaño—The bad man always suspects some knavish intention. *Sp. Pr.*

El mal que de tu boca sale, en tu seno se cae—The evil which issues from thy mouth falls into thy bosom. *Sp. Pr.*

El mal que no tiene cura es locura—Folly is the one evil for which there is no remedy. *Sp. Pr.*

35 Elocution is the adjustment of apt words and sentiments to the subject in debate. *Cic.*

Eloignement—Estrangement. *Fr.*

Eloquence, at its highest pitch, leaves little room for reason or reflection, but addresses itself entirely to the fancy or the affections, captivates the willing hearers, and subdues their understanding. *Hume.*

Eloquence is a pictorial representation of thought. *Pascal.*

Eloquence is in the assembly, not in the speaker. *Wm. Pitt.*

40 Eloquence is like flame : it requires matter to feed on, motion to excite it, and it brightens as it burns. *Tac.*

Eloquence is the appropriate organ of the highest personal energy. *Emerson.*

Eloquence is the child of knowledge. When the mind is full, like a wholesome river, it is also clear. *Disraeli.*

Eloquence is the language of nature, and cannot be learned in the schools. *Colton.*

Eloquence is the painting of thought ; and thus those who, after having painted it, still add to it, make a picture instead of a portrait. *Pascal.*

45 Eloquence is the poetry of prose. *Bryant.*

Eloquence is the power to translate a truth into language perfectly intelligible to the person to whom you speak. *Emerson.*

Eloquence is to the sublime as a whole to its part. *La Bruyère.*

Eloquence must be grounded on the plainest narrative. *Emerson.*

Eloquence shows the power and possibility of man. *Emerson.*

50 Eloquence the soul, song charms the sense. *Milton*

Eloquence, to produce her full effect, should start from the head of the orator, as Pallas from the brain of Jove, completely armed and equipped. *Colton.*

El pan comido, la compañia deshecha—The bread eaten, the company dispersed. *Sp. Pr.*

El pie del dueño estierco para la heredad—The foot of the owner is manure for the farm. *Sp. Pr.*

El que trabaja, y madra, hila oro—He that labours and perseveres spins gold. *Sp. Pr.*

55 El rey va hasta do poede, y no hasta do quiere—The king goes as far as he may, not as far as he would. *Sp. Pr.*

El rey y la patria—For king and country. *Sp.*

El rio pasado, el santo olvidádo—The river (danger) past, the saint (delivery) forgotten. *Sp. Pr.*

El sabio muda consejo, el necio no—The wise man changes his mind, the fool never. *Sp. Pr.*

El secreto á voces—An open secret. *Calderon.*

El tiempo cura el enfermo, que ne el unguento—It is time and not medicine that cures the disease. *Sp. Pr.*

Elucet maxime animi excellentia magnitudoque in despiciendis opibus—Excellence and greatness of soul are most conspicuously displayed in contempt of riches.

El villano en su tierra, y el hidalgo donde quiera—The clown in his own country, the gentleman where he pleases. *Sp. Pr.*

Elysian beauty, melancholy grace, / Brought from a pensive through a happy place. *Wordsworth.*

5 E mala cosa esser cattivo, ma è peggiore esser conosciuto—It is a bad thing to be a knave, but worse to be found out. *It. Pr.*

Emas non quod opus est, sed quod necesse est : / Quod non opus est, asse carum est—Buy not what you want, but what you need ; what you don't want is dear at a cent. *Cato.*

Embarras de richesses—An encumbrance of wealth. *D'Allainval.*

Embonpoint — Plumpness or fulness of body. *Fr.*

E meglio aver oggi un uovo, che dimani una gallina—Better an egg to-day than a hen to-morrow. *It. Pr.*

10 E meglio cader dalla finestra che dal tetto—It is better to fall from the window than the roof. *It. Pr.*

E meglio dare che non aver a dare—Better give than not have to give. *It. Pr.*

E meglio domandar che errare—Better ask than lose your way. *It. Pr.*

E meglio esse fortunato che savio—'Tis better to be born fortunate than wise. *It. Pr.*

E meglio esser uccel di bosco che di gabbia—Better to be a bird in the wood than one in the cage. *It. Pr.*

15 E meglio il cuor felice che la borsa—Better the heart happy than the purse (full). *It. Pr.*

E meglio lasciare che mancare—Better leave than lack. *It. Pr.*

E meglio perder la sella che il cavallo—Better lose the saddle than the horse. *It. Pr.*

E meglio sdrucciolare col piè che con la lingua—Better slip with the foot than the tongue. *It. Pr.*

E meglio senza cibo restar che senz' onore—Better be without food than without honour. *It. Pr.*

20 E meglio una volta che mai—Better once than never. *It. Pr.*

E meglio un buon amico che cento parente—One true friend is better than a hundred relations. *It. Pr.*

ἡ μεν γὰρ σοφία οὐδέν θεωρεῖ ἐξ ὧν ἔσται εὐδαίμων ἄνθρωπος—Wisdom never contemplates what will make a happy man. *Arist.*

Emere malo quam rogare—I had rather buy than beg.

Emerge from unnatural solitude, look abroad for wholesome sympathy, bestow and receive. *Dickens.*

25 Emeritus—One retired from active official duties.

Emerson tells us to hitch our waggon to a star ; and the star is without doubt a good steed, when once fairly caught and harnessed, but it takes an astronomer to catch it. *J. Borroughs.*

Emerson wants Emersonian epigrams from Carlyle, and Carlyle wants Carlylean thunder from Emerson. The thing which a man's nature calls him to do, what else is so well worth his doing ? *John Borroughs.*

Eminent positions are like the summits of rocks ; only eagles and reptiles can get there. *Mme. Necker.*

Eminent stations make great men greater and little men less. *La Bruyère.*

Emori nolo, sed me esse mortuum nihil curo 30 —I would not die, but care not to be dead. *Cæs.*

Emotion is always new. *Victor Hugo.*

Emotion is the atmosphere in which thought is steeped, that which lends to thought its tone or temperature, that to which thought is often indebted for half its power. *H. R. Haweis.*

Emotion, not thought, is the sphere of music ; and emotion quite as often precedes as follows thought. *H. R. Haweis.*

Emotion turning back on itself, and not leading on to thought or action, is the element of madness. *John Sterling.*

'Εμοῦ θανόντος γαῖα μιχθήτω πυρί—When I 35 am dead the earth will be mingled with fire. *Anon.*

Empfindliche Ohren sind, bei Mädchen so gut als bei Pferden, gute Gesundheitszeichen—In maidens as well as in horses, sensitive ears are signs of good health. *Jean Paul.*

Empires and nations flourish and decay, / By turns command, and in their turns obey. *Ovid.*

Empires are only sandhills in the hour-glass of Time ; they crumble spontaneously by the process of their own growth. *Draper.*

Empires flourish till they become commercial, and then they are scattered abroad to the four winds. *Wm. Blake.*

Empirical sciences prosecuted simply for their 40 own sake, and without a philosophic tendency, resemble a face without eyes. *Schopenhauer.*

Employment and hardships prevent melancholy. *Johnson.*

Employment gives health, sobriety, and morals. *D. Webster.*

Employment is enjoyment. *Pr.*

Employment is Nature's physician, and is essential to human happiness. *Galen.*

Employ thy time well if thou meanest to gain 45 leisure, and, since you are not sure of a minute, throw not away an hour. *Ben. Franklin.*

'Εμποδίζει τὸν λόγον ὁ φόβος—Fear hampers speech. *Demades.*

Empressement—Ardour ; warmth. *Fr.*

Empta dolore docet experientia—Experience bought with pain teaches effectually. *Pr.*

Empty vessels make the most noise. *Pr.*

Emulation admires and strives to imitate great 50 actions ; envy is only moved to malice. *Balzac.*

Emulation, even in the brutes, is sensitively nervous ; see the tremor of the thoroughbred racer before he starts. *Bulwer Lytton.*

E multis paleis paulum fructus collegi—Out of much chaff I have gathered little grain. *Pr.*

Emunctæ naris—Of nice discernment (*lit.* scent). *Hor.*

Ἔνα . . . ἀλλὰ λέοντα—One, but a lion. *Æsop.*

En ami—As a friend. *Fr.*

En amour comme en amitié, un tiers souvent nous embarrasse—A third person is often an annoyance to us in love as in friendship. *Fr.*

5 En arrière—In the rear. *Fr.*

En attendant—In the meantime. *Fr.*

En avant—Forward ; on. *Fr.*

En badinant—In jest. *Fr.*

En beau—In a favourable light. *Fr.*

10 En bloc—In a lump. *Fr.*

En boca cerrada no entra mosca—Flies don't enter a shut mouth. *Sp. Pr.*

En bon train—In a fair way. *Fr.*

En buste—Half-length. *Fr.*

En cada tierra su uso—Every country has its own custom. *Sp. Pr.*

15 Encouragement after censure is as the sun after a shower. *Goethe.*

En cuéros—Naked. *Sp.*

Endeavouring, by logical argument, to prove the existence of God, were like taking out a candle to look for the sun. *Carlyle, after Kant.*

Endeavour not to settle too many habits at once, lest by variety you confound them, and so perfect none. *Locke.*

En dernier ressort—As a last resource. *Fr.*

20 En déshabille—In an undress. *Fr.*

En Dieu est ma fiance—In God is my trust. *M.*

En Dieu est tout—All depends on God. *M.*

Endurance is nobler than strength, and patience than beauty. *Ruskin.*

Endurance is the crowning quality, and patience all the passion, of great hearts. *Lowell.*

25 En échelon—Like steps. *Fr.*

En effet—In fact ; substantially. *Fr.*

Ene i Raad, ene i Sorg—Alone in counsel, alone in sorrow. *Dan. Pr.*

En el rio do no hay pezes por demas es echar redes—It is in vain to cast nets in a river where there are no fish. *Sp. Pr.*

En émoi—In a flutter or ferment. *Fr.*

30 Energy may be turned to bad uses; but more good may always be made of an energetic nature than of an indolent and impassive one. *J. S. Mill.*

Energy will do anything that can be done in this world ; no talents, no circumstances, no opportunities will make a two-legged animal a man without it. *Goethe.*

Ἐν ἔρμασι δε νικᾷ τύχη, οὐ σθένος—In great acts it is not our strength but our good fortune that has triumphed. *Pindar.*

En famille—In a domestic state. *Fr.*

Enfant gâté du monde qu'il gâtait—A child spoiled by the world which he spoiled. *Said of Voltaire.*

35 Enfants de famille—Children of the family. *Fr.*

Enfants perdus—The forlorn hope (*lit.* lost children). *Fr.*

Enfants terribles—Dreadful children ; precocious youths who say and do rash things to the annoyance of their more conservative seniors. *Fr.*

Enfant trouvé—A foundling. *Fr.*

Enfermer le loup dans la bergerie—To shut up the wolf in the sheepfold ; to patch up a wound or a disease. *Fr. Pr.*

En fin les renards se trouvent chez le pelletier 40 —Foxes come to the furrier's in the end. *Fr. Pr.*

Enflamed with the study of learning and the admiration of virtue: stirred up with high hopes of living to be brave men and worthy patriots, dear to God, and famous to all ages. *Milton.*

En foule—In a crowd. *Fr.*

England expects this day that every man shall do his duty. *Nelson, his signal at Trafalgar.*

England is a domestic country: here home is revered and the hearth sacred. *Disraeli.*

England is a paradise for women and a hell 45 for horses ; Italy a paradise for horses and a hell for women. *Burton.*

England is safe if true within itself. 3 *Hen. VI.,* iv. 1.

English speech, the sea that receives tributaries from every region under heaven. *Emerson.*

En grace affié—On grace depend. *Fr.*

En grande tenue—In full dress. *Fr.*

En habiles gens—Like able men. *Fr.* 50

Enjoying things which are pleasant, that is not the evil ; it is the reducing of our moral self to slavery by them that is. *Carlyle.*

Enjoyment soon wearies both itself and us ; effort, never. *Jean Paul.*

Enjoyment stops when indolence begins. *Pollock.*

Enjoy the blessings of this day, if God sends them, and the evils bear patiently and sweetly. For this day only is ours ; we are dead to yesterday and we are not born to to-morrow. *Jeremy Taylor.*

Enjoy what God has given thee, and willingly 55 dispense with what thou hast not. Every condition has its own joys and sorrows. *Gellert.*

Enjoy what thou hast inherited from thy sires if thou wouldst possess it ; what we employ not is an oppressive burden ; what the moment brings forth, that only can it profit by. *Goethe.*

Enjoy when you can, and endure when you must. *Goethe.*

Enjoy your little while the fool is seeking for more. *Sp. Pr.*

Enjoy your own life without comparing it with that of another. *Condorcet.*

En la cour du roi chacun y est pour soi—In the 60 court of the king it is every one for himself. *Fr. Pr.*

Enlarge not thy destiny ; endeavour not to do more than is given thee in charge. *Gr. Oracle.*

En la rose je fleuris—In the rose I flourish. *M.*

En mariage, comme ailleurs, contentement passe richesse—In marriage, as in other states, contentment is better than riches. *Molière.*

En masse—In a body. *Fr.*

En mauvaise odeur—In bad repute. *Fr.* 65

Ennemi ne s'endort—An enemy does not go to sleep. *Fr. Pr.*

Ennui has perhaps made more gamblers than avarice, more drunkards than thirst, and perhaps as many suicides as despair. *Colton.*

Ennui is a growth of English root, though nameless in our language. *Byron.*

Ennui is a word which the French invented, though of all nations in Europe they know the least of it. *Bancroft.*

Ennui is our greatest enemy. *Justus Möser.*

Ennui is the desire of activity without the fit means of gratifying the desire. *Bancroft.*

5 Ennui shortens life and bereaves the day of its light. *Emerson.*

Ennui, the parent of expensive and ruinous vices. *Ninon de l'Enclos.*

Enough is as good as a feast. *Pr.*

Enough is better than too much. *Pr.*

Enough is great riches. *Dan. Pr.*

10 Enough is the wild-goose-chase of most men's lives. *Brothers Mayhew.*

Enough—no foreign foe could quell / Thy soul, till from itself it fell; / Yes, self-abasement paved the way / To villain bonds and despot sway. *Byron.*

Enough requires too much; too much craves more. *Quarles.*

En papillote.—In curl-papers. *Fr.*

En parole je vis—I live by the word. *Fr.*

15 En passant—By the way. *Fr.*

En pension—Board at a pension. *Fr.*

En petit champ croît bien bon blé—Very good corn grows in a little field. *Fr. Pr.*

En peu d'heure Dieu labeure—God works in moments, *i.e.,* His work is soon done. *Fr.*

En plein jour—In open day. *Fr.*

20 En potence—In the form of a gallows. *Fr.*

En présence—In sight of each other. *Fr.*

En queue—Behind.

Enquire not what is in another man's pot. *Pr.*

En rapport—In relation ; in connection. *Fr.*

25 En règle—According to rules. *Fr.*

En resumé—Upon the whole. *Fr.*

En revanche—In revenge ; to return ; to make amends. *Fr.*

En route—On the way. *Fr.*

En salvo está el que repica—He is in safe quarters who sounds the alarm. *Sp. Pr.*

30 Ense et aratro—With sword and plough. *M.*

En suite—In company. *Fr.*

En suivant la vérité—In following the truth. *Fr.*

Entente cordiale—A good or cordial understanding. *Fr.*

Enthusiasm begets enthusiasm. *Longfellow.*

35 Enthusiasm flourishes in adversity, kindles in the hour of danger, and awakens to deeds of renown. *Dr. Chalmers.*

Enthusiasm gives life to what is invisible, and interest to what has no immediate action on our comfort in this world. *Mme. de Staël.*

Enthusiasm imparts itself magnetically, and fuses all into one happy and harmonious unity of feeling and sentiment. *A. B. Alcott.*

Enthusiasm is grave, inward, self-controlled ; mere excitement, outward, fantastical, hysterical, and passing in a moment from tears to laughter. *John Sterling.*

Enthusiasm is the genius of sincerity, and truth accomplishes no victories without it. *Bulwer Lytton.*

Enthusiasm is the height of man ; it is the 40 passing from the human to the divine. *Emerson.*

Enthusiasm is the leaping lightning, not to be measured by the horse-power of the understanding. *Emerson.*

Entienda primero, y habla postrero—Hear first and speak afterwards. *Sp. Pr.*

Entire affection hateth nicer hands. *Spenser.*

Entire love is a worship and cannot be angry. *Leigh Hunt.*

'Εν τῷ φρονεῖν γὰρ μηδὲν ἥδιστος βίος — The 45 happiest life consists in knowing nothing. *Soph.*

Entourage—Surroundings. *Fr.*

En toute chose il faut considérer la fin—In everything we must consider the end. *Fr.*

Entre chien et loup—In the dusk (*lit.* between dog and wolf). *Fr.*

Entre deux vins—To be half-seas over; to be mellow. *Fr.*

Entre esprit et talent il y a la proportion du 50 tout à sa partie—Wit is to talent as a whole to a part. *La Bruyère.*

Entre le bon sens et le bon goût il y a la différence de la cause à son effet—Between good sense and good taste, there is the same difference as that between cause and effect. *La Bruyère.*

Entre nos ennemis les plus à craindre sont souvent les plus petits—Of our enemies, the smallest are often the most to be dreaded. *La Fontaine.*

Entre nous—Between ourselves. *Fr.*

Entzwei und gebiete—Divide and rule. *Ger. Pr.*

Entzwei und gebiete ! Tüchtig Wort : Verein' 55 und leite, Bessrer Hort—Divide and rule, an excellent motto : unite and lead, a better.

En vérité—In truth.

En vérité l'amour ne saurait être profond, s'il n'est pas pur—Love, in fact, can never be deep unless it is pure.

En vieillissant on devient plus fou et plus sage —As men grow old they become both foolisher and wiser. *Fr. Pr.*

En villig Hielper töver ei til man beder—One who is willing to help does not wait till he is asked. *Dan. Pr.*

Envy, among other ingredients, has a mixture 60 of the love of justice in it. We are more angry at undeserved than at deserved good fortune. *Hazlitt.*

Envy does not enter an empty house. *Dan. Pr.*

Envy feels not its own happiness but by comparison with the misery of others. *Johnson.*

Envy, if surrounded on all sides by the brightness of another's prosperity, like the scorpion confined with a circle of fire, will sting itself to death. *Colton.*

Envy is a passion so full of cowardice and shame, that nobody ever had the confidence to own it. *Rochester.*

Envy is ignorance. *Emerson.* 65

Envy is littleness of soul. *Hazlitt.*

Envy is more irreconcilable than hatred. *La Roche.*

Envy is the antagonist of the fortunate. *Epictetus.*

Envy is the deformed and distorted offspring of egotism. *Hazlitt.*

Envy is the most acid fruit that grows on the stock of sin, a fluid so subtle that nothing but the fire of divine love can purge it from the soul. *H. Ballou.*

Envy, like the worm, never runs but to the fairest fruit; like a cunning bloodhound, it singles out the fattest deer in the flock. *J. Beaumont.*

Envy ne'er does a gude turn but when it means an ill ane. *Sc. Pr.*

Envy will merit as its shade pursue, / But, like a shadow, proves the substance true. *Pope.*

5 Eodem collyrio mederi omnibus—To cure all by the same ointment.

Eo instanti—At that instant.

Eo magis præfulgebat quod non videbatur—He shone the brighter that he was not seen. *Tac.*

Επεα πτερόεντα—Winged words. *Hom.*

Epicuri de grege porcus—A pig of the flock of Epicurus.

10 Ἐπὶ τὸ πολὺ ἀδικοῦσιν οἱ ἄνθρωποι, ὅταν δύνωνται—In general men do wrong whenever circumstances enable them. *Arist.*

E pluribus unum—One of many.

"Eppur si muove"—Yet it moves. *Galileo, after he had been forced to swear that the earth stood still.*

Equality (Gleichheit) is always the firmest bond of love. *Lessing.*

Equality (*i.e.*, in essential nature) is the sacred law of humanity. *Schiller.*

15 Eques ipso melior Bellerophonte—A better horseman than Bellerophon himself. *Hor.*

Equi et poetæ alendi, non saginandi—Horses and poets should be fed, not pampered. *Charles IX. of France.*

Equity is a roguish thing; for law we have a measure . . . (but) equity is according to the conscience of him who is chancellor, and, as that is larger or narrower, so is equity. *Selden.*

Equity judges with lenity, laws with severity. *Scott.*

Equivocation is half way to lying, and lying is the whole way to hell. *W. Penn.*

20 Equo frænato est auris in ore—The ear of the bridled horse is in the mouth. *Hor.*

Equo ne credite, Teucri—Trust not the horse, Trojans. *Virg.*

Erant in officio, sed tamen qui mallent imperantium mandata interpretari, quam exsequi—They attended to their regulations, but still as if they would rather debate about the commands of their superiors than obey them. *Tacit.*

Erase que se era—What has been has been. *Sp. Pr.*

Erasmus laid the egg (*i.e.*, of the Reformation), and Luther hatched it.

25 Er, der einzige Gerechte / Will für Jedermann das Rechte / Sei, von seinen hundert Namen, / Dieser hochgelobet!—Amen! He, the only Just, wills for each one what is right. Be of His hundred names this one the most exalted. Amen. *Goethe.*

Ere sin could blight or sorrow fade, / Death came with friendly care, / The opening bud to heaven conveyed, / And bade it blossom there. *Coleridge.*

Ere we censure a man for seeming what he is not, we should be sure that we know what he is. *Carlyle.*

Er geht herum, wie die Katze um den heissen Brei—He goes round it like a cat round hot broth. *Ger. Pr.*

Ἔργον δ'οὐδὲν ὄνειδος—Labour is no disgrace. *Hesiod.*

Erfahrung bleibt des Lebens Meisterin—Ex-30 perience is ever life's mistress. *Goethe.*

Erfüllte Pflicht empfindet sich immer noch als Schuld, weil man sich nie ganz genug gethan—Duty fulfilled ever entails a sense of further obligation, because one feels he has never done enough to satisfy himself. *Goethe.*

Er hat noch nie die Stimme der Natur gehört—He has not yet heard the voice of Nature. *Schiller.*

Eripe te moræ—Tear thyself from all that detains thee. *Hor.*

Eripe turpi / Colla jugo. Liber, liber sum, dic age—Tear away thy neck from the base yoke. Come, say, I am free; I am free. *Hor.*

Eripit interdum, modo dat medicina salutem—35 Medicine sometimes destroys health, sometimes restores it. *Ovid.*

"Eripuit cœlo fulmen sceptrumque tyrannis"—He snatched the lightning from heaven and the sceptre from tyrants. (*On the bust of Franklin.*)

Eris mihi magnus Apollo—You shall be my great Apollo. *Virg.*

Erlaubt ist was gefällt; erlaubt ist was sich ziemt—What pleases us is permitted us; what is seemly is permitted us. *Goethe.*

Ernste Thätigkeit söhnt zuletzt immer mit dem Leben aus—Earnest activity always reconciles us with life in the end. *Jean Paul.*

Ernst ist der Anblick der Nothwendigkeit. / 40 Nicht ohne Schauder greift des Menschen Hand / In des Geschicks geheimnissvolle Urne—Earnest is the aspect of necessity. Not without a shudder is the hand of man thrust into the mysterious urn of fate. *Schiller.*

Ernst ist das Leben; heiter ist die Kunst—Life is earnest; art is serene. *Schiller.*

Erquickung hast du nicht gewonnen, / Wenn sie dir nicht aus eigner Seele quillt—Thou hast gained no fresh life unless it flows to thee direct out of thine own soul. *Goethe.*

Errantem in viam reducito—Lead back the wanderer into the right way.

Errare humanum est—It is human to err.

Errare malo cum Platone, quam cum istis vera 45 sentire—I had rather be wrong with Plato than think right with these men. *Cic.*

Errata—Errors in print.

Erringen will der Mensch, er will nicht sicher sein—Man will ever wrestle; he will never trust. *Goethe.*

Erring is not cheating. *Ger. Pr.*

Error cannot be defended but by error. *Bp. Jewel.*

Error is always more busy than ignorance. 50 Ignorance is a blank sheet on which we may write, but error is a scribbled one from which we must first erase. *Colton.*

Error is always talkative. *Goldsmith.*

Error is but opinion in the making. *Milton.*

Error is but the shadow of truth. *Stillingfleet.*

Error is created; truth is eternal. *Wm. Blake.*

Error is on the surface; truth is hid in great depths. *Goethe.*

Error is sometimes so nearly allied to truth that it blends with it as imperceptibly as the colours of the rainbow fade into each other. *W. B. Clulow.*

Error is worse than ignorance. *Bailey.*

5 Error never leaves us, yet a higher need always draws the striving spirit gently on to truth. *Goethe.*

Error of opinion may be tolerated where reason is left free to combat it. *Jefferson.*

Errors like straws upon the surface flow; / He who would search for pearls must dive below. *Dryden.*

Error, sterile in itself, produces only by means of the portion of truth which it contains. *Mme. Swetchine.*

Errors, to be dangerous, must have a great deal of truth mingled with them; . . . from pure extravagance, and genuine, unmingled falsehood, the world never has sustained, and never can sustain, any mischief. *Sydney Smith.*

10 Error, when she retraces her steps, has farther to go before she can arrive at truth than ignorance. *Colton.*

Erröten macht die Hässlichen so schön : / Und sollte Schöne nicht noch schöner machen ?—Blushing makes even the ugly beautiful, and should it not make beauty still more beautiful? *Lessing.*

Ersparte Wahl ist auch ersparte Mühe—Selection saved is trouble saved. *Platin.*

Er steckt seine Nase in Alles—He thrusts his nose into everything. *Ger. Pr.*

Erst seit ich liebe ist das Leben schön, / Erst seit ich liebe, weiss ich, dass ich lebe—Only since I loved is life lovely ; only since I loved knew I that I lived. *Körner.*

15 Erst wägen, dann wagen—First weigh, then venture. *M. of Moltke.*

Ertragen muss was der Himmel sendet. / Unbilliges erträgt kein edles Herz—We must bear what Heaven sends. No noble heart will bear injustice. *Schiller.*

Erudition is not like a lark, which flies high and delights in nothing but singing ; 'tis rather like a hawk, which soars aloft indeed, but can stoop when she finds it convenient, and seize her prey. *Bacon.*

Er wünscht sich einen grossen Kreis / Um ihn gewisser zu erschüttern—He desires a large circle in order with greater certainty to move it deeply. *Goethe.*

Es bedarf nur einer Kleinigkeit, um zwei Liebende zu unterhalten—Any trifle is enough to entertain two lovers. *Goethe.*

20 Es bildet ein Talent sich in der Stille, / Sich ein Character in dem Strom der Welt—A talent is formed in retirement, a character in the current of the world. *Goethe.*

Es bildet / Nur das Leben den Mann, und wenig bedeuten die Worte—Only life forms the man, and words signify little. *Goethe.*

Eschew fine words as you would rouge ; love simple ones as you would native roses on your cheek. *Hare.*

Escuchas al agujero ; oirás de tú mal y del ageno—Listen at the keyhole ; you will hear evil of yourself as well as your neighbour. *Sp. Pr.*

E se finxit velut araneus—He spun from himself like a spider.

Esel singen schlecht, weil sie zu hoch anstim- 25 men—Asses sing abominably, because they pitch their notes at too high a key. *Ger. Pr.*

Es erben sich Gesetz' und Rechte / Wie eine ewige Krankheit fort—Laws and rights descend like an inveterate inherited disease. *Goethe.*

Es findet jeder seinen Meister—Every one finds his master. *Ger. Pr.*

Es geht an—It is a beginning. *Ger.*

Es giebt eine Höflichkeit des Herzens ; sie ist der Liebe verwandt—There is a courtesy of the heart which is allied to love ; out of it there springs the most obliging courtesy of external behaviour. *Goethe.*

Es giebt eine Schwelgerei des Geistes wie 30 es eine Schwelgerei der Sinne giebt—There is a debauchery of spirit, as there is of senses. *Börne.*

Es giebt gewisse Dinge, wo ein Frauenzimmer immer schärfer sieht, als hundert Augen der Mannspersonen—There are certain things in which a woman's vision is sharper than a hundred eyes of the male. *Lessing.*

Es giebt keine andre Offenbarung, als die Gedanken der Weisen—There is no other revelation than the thoughts of the wise among men. *Schopenhauer.*

Es giebt kein Gesetz was hat nicht ein Loch, wer's finden kann—There is no law but has in it a hole for him who can find it. *Ger. Pr.*

Es giebt Männer welche die Beredsamkeit weiblicher Zungen übertreffen, aber kein Mann besitzt die Beredsamkeit weiblicher Augen—There are men the eloquence of whose tongues surpasses that of women, but no man possesses the eloquence of women's eyes. *Weber.*

Es giebt mehr Diebe als Galgen—There are 35 more thieves than gallows. *Ger. Pr.*

Es giebt Menschen, die auf die Mängel ihrer Freunde sinnen ; dabei kommt nichts heraus. Ich habe immer auf die Verdienste meiner Widersacher Acht gehabt und davon Vortheil gezogen—There are men who brood on the failings of their friends, but nothing comes of it. I have always had respect to the merits of my adversaries, and derived profit from doing so. *Goethe.*

Es giebt Naturen, die gut sind durch das was sie erreichen, andere durch das was sie verschmähen—There are natures which are good by what they attain, and others that are so by what they disdain. *H. Grimm.*

Es giebt nur eine Religion, aber es kann vielerlei Arten der Glaubens geben—There is only one religion, but there may be divers forms of belief. *Kant.*

Es hört doch Jeder nur was er versteht—Every one hears only what he understands. *Goethe.*

Es irrt der Mensch, so lang er strebt—Man is 40 liable to err as long as he strives. *Goethe.*

Es ist besser, das geringste Ding von der Welt zu thun, als eine halbe Stunde für gering halten—It is better to do the smallest thing in the world than to regard half an hour as a small thing. *Goethe.*

Es ist bestimmt in Gottes Rath / Dass man vom Liebsten, was man hat, / Muss scheiden—It is ordained in the counsel of God that we must all part from the dearest we possess. *Feuchtersleben.*

Es ist das Wohl des Ganzen, wovon jedes patriotische, wovon selbst jedes eigennützige Gemüth das seinige hofft—It is the welfare of the whole from which every patriotic, and even every selfish, soul expects its own. *Gentz.*

Es ist der Geist, der sich den Körper baut—It is the spirit which builds for itself the body. *Schiller.*

Es ist freundlicher das menschliche Leben anzulachen, als es anzugrinzen—It is more kindly to laugh at human life than to grin at it. *Wieland.*

Es ist klug und kühn den unvermeidlichen Uebel entgegenzugehen—It shows sense and courage to be able to confront unavoidable evil. *Goethe.*

5 Es ist nicht gut, wenn derjenige der die Fackel trägt, zugleich auch den Weg sucht—It is not good when he who carries the torch has at the same time also the way to seek. *Cötvös.*

Es ist nicht nötig, dass ich lebe, wohl aber, dass ich meine Pflicht thue und für mein Vaterland kämpfe—It is not a necessity that I should live, but it is that I should do my duty and fight for my fatherland. *Frederick the Great.* (?)

Es ist öde, nichts ehren können, als sich selbst —It is dreary for a man to be able to worship nothing but himself. *Hebbel.*

Es ist schwer gegen den Augenblick gerecht sein; der gleichgültige macht uns Langeweile, am Guten hat man zu tragen und am Bösen zu schleppen—It is difficult to be square with the moment; the indifferent one is a bore to us (*lit.* causes us *ennui*); with the good we have to bear and with the bad to drag. *Goethe.*

Es ist so schwer, den falschen Weg zu meiden —It is so difficult to avoid the wrong way. *Goethe.*

10 Es ist unköniglich zu weinen—ach, / Und hier nicht weinen ist unväterlich—To weep is unworthy of a king—alas! and not to weep now is unworthy of a father. *Schiller.*

Es kämpft der Held am liebsten mit dem Held —Hero likes best to fight with hero. *Körner.*

Es kann der beste Herz in dunkeln Stunden fehlen—The best heart may go wrong in dark hours. *Goethe.*

Es kann ja nicht immer so bleiben / Hier unter dem wechselnden Mond—Sure it cannot always be so here under the changing moon. *Kotzebue.*

Es kann nichts helfen ein grosses Schicksal zu haben, wenn man nicht weiss, dass man eines hat—It is of no avail for a man to have a great destiny if he does not know that he has one. *Rahel.*

15 Es kommen Fälle vor im Menschenleben, / Wo's Weisheit ist, nicht allzu weise sein— There are situations in life when it is wisdom not to be too wise. *Schiller.*

Es leben Götter, die den Hochmut rächen— There live gods who take vengeance on pride. *Schiller.*

Es liebt die Welt das Strahlende zu schwärtzen, / Und das Erhabne in den Staub zu ziehn—The world is fain to obscure what is brilliant, and to drag down to the dust what is exalted. *Schiller.*

Es liesse sich Alles trefflich schlichten, Könnte man die Sachen zweimal verrichten—Everything could be beautifully adjusted if matters could be a second time arranged. *Goethe.*

Es muss auch solche Käuze geben — There must needs be such fellows in the world too. *Goethe.*

ἡ σοφίας πήγη διὰ βιβλίων ῥέει—The fountain 20 of wisdom flows through books. *Gr. Pr.*

Espérance en Dieu—Hope in God. *M.*

Espionage—The spy system. *Fr.*

Esprit borné—Narrow mind. *Fr.*

Esprit de corps—Spirit of brotherhood in a corporate body. *Fr.*

Esprit de parti—Party spirit. *Fr.* 25

Esprit fort—A free-thinker. *Fr.*

Esprit juste—Sound mind. *Fr.*

Esprit vif—Ready wit. *Fr.*

Es reift keine Seligkeit unter dem Monde—No happiness ever comes to maturity under the moon. *Schiller.*

Essayez—Try. *M.* 30

Esse bonum facile est, ubi quod vetet esse remotum est—It is easy to be good, when all that prevents it is far removed. *Ovid.*

Esse quam videri—To be rather than to seem.

Ἔσσεται ἦμαρ ὅτ' ἄν ποτ' ὀλώλη Ἴλιος ἱρή— A day will come when the sacred Ilium shall be no more. *Hom.*

Es schwinden jedes Kummers Falten / So lang des Liebes Zauber walten—The wrinkles of every sorrow disappear as long as the spell of love is unbroken. *Schiller.*

Es sind nicht alle frei, die ihrer Ketten spotten 35 —All are not free who mock their chains. *Ger. Pr.*

Es sind so gute Katzen die Mäuse verjagen, als die sie fangen—They are as good cats that chase away the mice as those that catch them. *Ger. Pr.*

Es steckt nicht in Spiegel was man im Spiegel sieht—That is not in the mirror which you see in the mirror. *Ger. Pr.*

Es steht ihm an der Stirn' geschrieben, / Das er nicht mag eine Seele lieben—It stands written on his forehead that he cannot love a single soul. *Goethe, of Mephistopheles.*

Establish thou the work of our hands upon us; yea, the work of our hands establish thou it. *Bible.*

Est aliquid fatale malum per verba levare— 40 It is some alleviation of an incurable disease to speak of it to others. *Ovid.*

Est animus tibi / Rerumque prudens, et secundis / Temporibus dubiisque rectus—You possess a mind both sagacious in the management of affairs, and steady at once in prosperous and perilous times. *Hor.*

Est animus tibi, sunt mores et lingua, fidesque—Thou hast a man's soul, cultured manners and power of expression, and fidelity. *Hor., of a gentleman.*

Est assez riche qui ne doit rien—He is rich enough who owes nothing. *Fr. Pr.*

Est aviditas dives, et pauper pudor—Covetousness is rich, while modesty is poor. *Phaedr.*

Est bonus, ut melior vir / Non alius quisquam 45 —He is so good that no man can be better. *Hor.*

Est brevitate opus, ut currat sententia—There is need of conciseness that the thought may run on. *Hor.*

Est demum vera felicitas, felicitate dignum videri—True happiness consists in being condered deserving of it. *Pliny.*

Est deus in nobis, agitante calescimus illo—There is a god in us, who, when he stirs, sets us all aglow. *Ovid.*

Est deus in nobis, et sunt commercia cœli—There is a god within us, and we hold commerce with the sky. *Ovid.*

5 Esteem a man of many words and many lies much alike. *Fuller.*

Esteem is the harvest of a whole life spent in usefulness; but reputation is often bestowed upon a chance action, and depends most on success. *G. A. Sala.*

Est enim lex nihil aliud nisi recta et a numine deorum tracta ratio, imperans honesta, prohibens contraria—For law is nothing else but right reason supported by the authority of the gods, commanding what is honourable and prohibiting the contrary. *Cic.*

Est egentissimus in sua re—He is in very straitened circumstances.

Est etiam miseris pietas, et in hoste probatur—Regard for the wretched is a duty, and deserving of praise even in an enemy. *Ovid.*

10 Est etiam, ubi profecto damnum præstet facere, quam lucrum—There are occasions when it is certainly better to lose than to gain. *Plaut.*

Est genus hominum qui esse primos se omnium rerum volunt, / Nec sunt—There is a class of men who wish to be first in everything, and are not. *Ter.*

Est hic, / Est ubivis, animus si te non deficit æquus—It (happiness) is here, it is everywhere, if only a well-regulated mind does not fail you. *Hor.*

Est miserorum, ut malevolentes sint atque invideant bonis—'Tis the tendency of the wretched to be ill-disposed towards and to envy the fortunate. *Plaut.*

Est modus in rebus; sunt certi denique fines, / Quos ultra citraque nequit consistere rectum —There is a mean in all things; there are, in fine, certain fixed limits, on either side of which what is right and true cannot exist. *Hor.*

15 Est multi fabula plena joci—It is a story full of fun. *Ovid.*

Est natura hominum novitatis avida—It is the nature of man to hunt after novelty. *Pliny.*

Estne Dei sedes nisi terra, et pontus, et aër, / Et cœlum, et virtus? Superos quid quærimus ultra? / Jupiter est, quodcunque vides, quodcunque moveris—Has God a dwelling other than earth and sea and air and heaven and virtue? Why seek we the gods beyond? Whatsoever you see, wheresoever you go, there is Jupiter. *Luc.*

Est nobis voluisse satis—To have willed suffices us. *Tibull.*

Esto perpetua—Let it be perpetual.

20 Esto quod es; quod sunt alii, sine quemlibet esse: / Quod non es, nolis; quod potes esse, velis—Be what you are; let whoso will be what others are. Don't be what you are not, but resolutely be what you can.

Esto quod esse videris—Be what you seem to be.

Esto, ut nunc multi, dives tibi, pauper amicis—Be, as many now are, rich to yourself, poor to your friends. *Juv.*

Est pater ille quem nuptiæ demonstrant—He is the father whom the marriage-rites point to as such. *L.*

Est profecto Deus, qui quæ nos gerimus auditque et videt—There is certainly a God who both hears and sees the things which we do. *Plaut.*

Est proprium stultitiæ aliorum cernere vitia, 25 oblivisci suorum—It is characteristic of folly to discern the faults of others and forget its own. *Cic.*

Est quadam prodire tenus, si non datur ultra—You may advance to a certain point, if it is not permitted you to go farther. *Hor.*

Est quædam flere voluptas, / Expletur lachrymis egeriturque dolor—There is a certain pleasure in weeping; grief is soothed and alleviated by tears. *Ovid.*

Est quoque cunctarum novitas carissima rerum —Novelty is the dearest to us of all things. *Ovid.*

Es trägt Verstand und rechter Sinn / Mit wenig Kunst sich selber vor; und wenn's euch Ernst ist was zu sagen / Ist's nötig Worten nachzujagen?—Understanding and good sense find utterance with little art; and when you have seriously anything to say, is it necessary to hunt for words? *Goethe.*

Es trinken tausend sich den Tod, ehe einer 30 stirbt vor Durstes Noth—A thousand will drink themselves to death ere one die under stress of thirst. *Ger. Pr.*

Est tempus quando nihil, est tempus quando aliquid, nullum tamen est tempus in quo dicenda sunt omnia—There is a time when nothing may be said, a time when something may, but no time when all things may. *A Monkish Adage.*

Esurienti ne occurras—Don't throw yourself in the way of a hungry man.

Es will einer was er soll, aber er kann's nicht machen; es kann einer was er soll, aber er will's nicht; es will und kann einer, aber er weiss nicht, was er soll—One would what he should, but he can't; one could what he should, but he won't; one would and could, but he knows not what he should. *Goethe.*

Es wird wohl auch drüben nicht anders seyn als hier—Even *over there* it will not be otherwise than it is *here*, I ween. *Goethe.*

Ή τὰν ἤ ἐπὶ τᾶν—Either this or upon this. (*The 35 Spartan mother to her son on handing him his shield.*)

E tardegradis asinis equus non prodiit—The horse is not the progeny of the slow-paced ass.

Et cætera—And the rest.

Et c'est être innocent que d'être malheureux—And misfortune is the badge of innocence. *La Font.*

Et credis cineres curare sepultos?—And do you think that the ashes of the dead concern themselves with our affairs? *Virg.*

Et daligt hufoud hade han, men hjertat det 40 var godt—He had a stupid head, but his heart was good. *Swed. Pr.*

Et decus et pretium recti—Both the ornament and the reward of virtue. *M.*

E tenui casa sæpe vir magnus exit—A great man often steps forth from a humble cottage. *Pr.*

Eternal love made me. *Dante.*

Eternal smiles his emptiness betray, / As shallow streams run dimpling all the way. *Pope.*

Eternity, depending on an hour. *Young.*

Eternity looks grander and kinder if Time grow meaner and more hostile. *Carlyle.*

5 Eternity of being and well-being simply for being and well-being's sake, is an ideal belonging to appetite alone, and which only the struggle of mere animalism (*Thierheit*), longing to be infinite gives rise to. *Schiller.*

Et facere et pati fortiter Romanum est—Bravery and endurance make a man a Roman. *Liv.*

Et genus et formam regina pecunia donat—Money, like a queen, confers both rank and beauty. *Hor.*

Et genus et proavos, et quæ non fecimus ipsi, / Vix ea nostra voco—We can scarcely call birth and ancestry and what we have not ourselves done, our own. *Ovid.*

Et genus et virtus, nisi cum re, vilior alga est—Without money both birth and virtue are as worthless as seaweed. *Hor.*

10 Ethics makes man's soul mannerly and wise, but logic is the armoury of reason, furnished with all offensive and defensive weapons. *Fuller.*

Et hoc genus omne—And everything of this kind.

Etiam celeritas in desiderio, mora est—When we long for a thing, even despatch is delay. *Pub. Syr.*

Etiam fera animalia, si clausa teneas, virtutis obliviscuntur—Even savage animals, if you keep them in confinement, forget their fierceness.

Etiam fortes viros subitis terreri—Even brave men may be alarmed by a sudden event. *Tac.*

15 Etiam innocentes cogit mentiri dolor—Pain makes even the innocent forswear themselves. *Pub. Syr.*

Etiam oblivisci quod scis, interdum expedit—It is sometimes expedient to forget what you know. *Pub. Syr.*

Etiam sanato vulnere cicatrix manet—Though the wound is healed, a scar remains.

Etiam sapientibus cupido gloriæ novissima exuitur—Even by the wise the desire of glory is the last of all passions to be laid aside. *Tac.*

Et jam summa procul villarum culmina fumant, / Majoresque cadunt altis de montibus umbræ —And now the cottage roofs yonder smoke, and the shadows fall longer from the mountain-tops. *Virg.*

20 Et je sais, sur ce fait, / Bon nombre d'hommes qui sont femmes—And I know a great many men who in this particular are women. *La Font.*

Et l'avare Achéron ne lâche pas sa proie—And greedy Acheron lets not go his prey. *Racine.*

Et le combat cessa faute de combattants—And the battle ceased for want of combatants. *Corneille.*

Et l'on revient toujours / A ses premiers amours —One returns always to his first love. *Fr. Pr.*

Et mala sunt vicina bonis—There are bad qualities near akin to good. *Ovid.*

25 Et male tornatos incudi reddere versus—And take back ill-polished stanzas to the anvil. *Hor.*

Et mea cymba semel vasta percussa procella / Illum, quo læsa est, horret adire locum—My bark, once shaken by the overpowering storm, shrinks from approaching the spot where it has been shattered. *Ovid.*

Et mihi res, non me rebus, subjungere conor—My aim ever is to subject circumstances to myself, not myself to them. *Hor.*

Et minimæ vires frangere quassa valent—A very small degree of force will suffice to break a vessel that is already cracked. *Ovid.*

Et monere, et moneri, proprium est veræ amicitiæ—To give counsel as well as take it, is a feature of true friendship. *Cic.*

Et nati natorum, et qui nascentur ab illis—The 30 children of our children, and those who shall be born of them, *i.e.*, our latest posterity.

Et nova fictaque nuper habebunt verba fidem, si / Græco fonte cadunt parce detorta—And new and lately invented terms will be well received, if they descend, with slight deviation, from a Grecian source. *Hor.*

Et pudet, et metuo, semperque eademque precari, / Ne subeant animo tædia justa tuo —I am ashamed to be always begging and begging the same things, and fear lest you should conceive for me the disgust I merit. *Ovid.*

Et quæ sibi quisque timebat, / Unius in miseri exitium conversa tulere—And what each man dreaded for himself, they bore lightly when diverted to the destruction of one poor wretch. *Virg.*

Et quiescenti agendum est, et agenti quiescendum est—He who is indolent should work, and he who works should take repose. *Sen.*

Et qui nolunt occidere quenquam / Posse 35 volunt—Even those who have no wish to kill another would like to have the power. *Juv.*

Et quorum pars magna fui—And in which I played a prominent part. *Virg.*

Etre capable de se laisser servir n'est pas une des moindres qualités que puisse avoir un grand roi—The ability to enlist the services of others in the conduct of affairs is one of the most distinguishing qualities of a great monarch. *Richelieu.*

Etre pauvre sans être libre, c'est le pire état où l'homme puisse tomber—To be poor without being free is the worst condition into which man can sink. *Rousseau.*

Etre sur le qui vive—To be on the alert. *Fr.*

Etre sur un grand pied dans le monde—To be in 40 high standing (*lit.* on a great foot) in the world. *Fr.*

Et rose elle a vécu ce que vivent les roses / L'espace d'un matin—As rose she lived the life of a rose for but the space of a morning. *Malherbe.*

Et sanguis et spiritus pecunia mortalibus—Money is both blood and life to men. *Pr.*

Et semel emissum volat irrevocabile verbum—And a word once uttered flies abroad never to be recalled. *Hor.*

Et sequentia, Et seq.—And what follows

Et sic de ceteris—And so of the rest. 45

Et sic de similibus—And so of the like.

" Et tu, Brute fili "—And thou, son Brutus. *Cæsar, at sight of Brutus among the conspirators.*

Et vaincre sans péril serait vaincre sans gloire —To conquer without peril would be to conquer without glory. *Corneille.*

Et vitam impendere vero—Stake even life for truth. *M.*

Et voilà justement comme on écrit l'histoire—And that is exactly how history is written. *Voltaire.*

Etwas ist besser als gar nichts—Something is better than nothing at all. *Ger. Pr.*

Euch zu gefallen war mein höchstes Wunsch ;/ Euch zu ergötzen war mein letzer Zweck—To please you was my highest wish ; to delight you was my last aim. *Goethe.*

5 Εὕδοντι κύρτος αἱρεῖ—While the fisher sleeps the net takes. *Gr. Pr.*

Euge, poeta !—Well done, poet ! *Pers.*

Eum ausculta, cui quatuor sunt aures—Listen to him who has four ears, *i.e.*, who is readier to hear than to speak. *Pr.*

Εὕρηκα—I have found it. *Archimedes when he found out the way to test the purity of Hiero's golden crown.*

Europe's eye is fixed on mighty things, / The fall of empires and the fate of kings. *Burns.*

10 Εὐτυχία πολύφιλος—Success is befriended by many people. *Gr. Pr.*

Εὐτυχῶν μὴ ἴσθι ὑπερήφανος, ἀπορήσας μὴ ταπεινοῦ—Be not uplifted in prosperity nor downcast in adversity. *Cleobulus.*

E' va più d'un asino al mercato—There is more than one ass goes to the market. *It. Pr.*

Evasion is unworthy of us, and is always the intimate of equivocation. *Balzac.*

Evasions are the common subterfuge of the hard-hearted, the false, and impotent, when called upon to assist. *Lavater.*

15 Even a fly has its spleen. *It. Pr.*

Even a fool, when he holdeth his peace, is counted wise. *Bible.*

Even a frog would bite if it had teeth. *It. Pr.*

Even a haggis could charge down-hill. *Scott.*

Even a hair casts a shadow. *Pr.*

20 Even a horse, though he has four feet, will stumble. *Pr.*

Even among the apostles there was a Judas. *It. Pr.*

Even beauty cannot palliate eccentricity. *Balzac.*

Even by means of our sorrows we belong to the eternal plan. *W. v. Humboldt.*

Even foxes are outwitted and caught. *It. Pr.*

25 Even in a righteous cause force is a fearful thing ; God only helps when men can help no more. *Schiller.*

Evening is the delight of virtuous age ; it seems an emblem of the tranquil close of busy life. *Bulwer Lytton.*

Even in social life, it is persistency which attracts confidence, more than talents and accomplishments. *Whipple.*

Even perfect examples lead astray by tempting us to overleap the necessary steps in their development, whereby we are for the most part led past the goal into boundless error. *Goethe.*

Even so my sun one early morn did shine, / With all triumphant splendour on my brow ;/ But out, alack! it was but one hour mine. *Sh.*

Even success needs its consolations. *George* 30 *Eliot.*

Even that fish may be caught which resists most stoutly against it. *Dan. Pr.*

Even the just man has need of help. *It. Pr.*

Even the lowest book of chronicles partakes of the spirit of the age in which it was written. *Goethe.*

Even then a wish (I mind its power), / A wish that to my latest hour / Shall strongly heave my breast, / That I, for puir auld Scotland's sake, / Some usefu' plan or beuk could make, / Or sing a sang at least. *Burns at the plough.*

Even though the cloud veils it, the sun is ever 35 in the canopy of heaven (*Himmelszelt*). A holy will rules there ; the world does not serve blind chance. *F. K. Weber.*

Even though vanquished, he could argue still. *Goldsmith.*

Even thou who mourn'st the daisy's fate, / That fate is thine—no distant date ; / Stern Ruin's ploughshare drives elate / Full on thy bloom, / Till crush'd beneath the farrow's weight / Shall be thy doom. *Burns.*

Events are only the shells of ideas; and often it is the fluent thought of ages that is crystallised in a moment by the stroke of a pen or the point of a bayonet. *Chapin.*

Events of all sorts creep or fly exactly as God pleases. *Cowper.*

Eventus stultorum magister est—Only the event 40 teaches fools. *Liv.*

Even weak men when united are powerful. *Schiller.*

Evêque d'or, crosse de bois ; crosse d'or, évêque de bois—Bishop of gold, staff of wood ; bishop of wood, staff of gold. *Fr. Pr.*

Ever, as of old, the thing a man will do is the thing he feels commanded to do. *Carlyle.*

Ever charming, ever new, / When will the landscape tire the view ? *John Dyer.*

Ever learning, and never able to come to the 45 knowledge of the truth. *St. Paul.*

Evermore thanks, the exchequer of the poor. *Rich. II.*, ii. 3.

Ever must pain urge us to labour, and only in free effort can any blessedness be imagined for us. *Carlyle.*

Ever must the sovereign of mankind be fitly entitled king, *i.e.*, the man who *kens* and *can*. *Carlyle.*

Ever since Adam's time fools have been in the majority. *Casimir Delavigne.*

Ever take it for granted that man collectively 50 wishes that which is right ; but take care never to think so of one ! *Schiller.*

Every absurdity has a champion to defend it ; for error is talkative. *Goldsmith.*

Every action is measured by the depth of the sentiment from which it proceeds. *Emerson.*

Every advantage has its tax, but there is none on the good of virtue : that is the incoming of God himself. or absolute existence. *Emerson.*

Every age regards the dawning of new light as the destroying fire of morality ; while that very age itself, with heart uninjured, finds itself raised one degree of light above the preceding. *Jean Paul.*

Every attempt to crush an insurrection with means inadequate to the end foments instead of suppressing it. *C. Fox.*

Every author, in some degree, portrays himself in his works, be it even against his will. *Goethe.*

Every base occupation makes one sharp in its practice and dull in every other. *Sir P. Sidney.*

Every bean has its black. *Pr.*

5 Every beginning is cheerful; the threshold is the place of expectation. *Goethe.*

Every beloved object is the centre of a paradise. *Novalis.*

Every being is a moving temple of the Infinite. *Jean Paul.*

Everybody is wise after the event. *Pr.*

Everybody knows that fanaticism is religion caricatured; yet with many, contempt of fanaticism is received as a sure sign of hostility to religion. *Whipple.*

10 Everybody knows that government never began anything. It is the whole world that thinks and governs. *W. Phillips.*

Everybody likes and respects self-made men. It is a great deal better to be made in that way than not to be made at all. *Holmes.*

Everybody says it, and what everybody says must be true. *J. F. Cooper.*

Everybody's business in the social system is to be agreeable. *Dickens.*

Everybody's business is nobody's. *Pr.*

15 Everybody's friend is nobody's. *Pr.*

Every book is good to read which sets the reader in a working mood. *Emerson.*

Every book is written with a constant secret reference to the few intelligent persons whom the writer believes to exist in the million. *Emerson.*

Every brave life out of the past does not appear to us so brave as it really was, for the forms of terror with which it wrestled are now overthrown. *Jean Paul.*

Every brave man is a man of his word. *Corneille.*

20 Every brave youth is in training to ride and rule his dragon. *Emerson.*

Every bullet has its billet. *Pr.*

Every Calvary has its Olivet. *H. Giles.*

Every capability, however slight, is born with us; there is no vague general capability in man. *Goethe.*

Every child is to a certain extent a genius, and every genius is to a certain extent a child. *Schopenhauer.*

25 Every cloud engenders not a storm. *3 Hen. VI., v. 3.*

Every cloud that spreads above / And veileth love, itself is love. *Tennyson.*

Every cock is proud on his own dunghill. *Pr.*

Every conceivable society may well be figured as properly and wholly a Church, in one or other of these three predicaments: an audibly preaching and prophesying Church, which is the best; a Church that struggles to preach and prophesy, but cannot as yet till its Pentecost come; a Church gone dumb with old age, or which only mumbles delirium prior to dissolution. *Carlyle.*

Every cottage should have its porch, its oven, and its tank. *Disraeli.*

Every couple is not a pair. *Pr.* 30

Every craw thinks her ain bird whitest. *Sc. Pr.*

Every creature can bear well-being except man. *Gael. Pr.*

Every crime has in the moment of its perpetration its own avenging angel. *Schiller.*

Every day hath its night, every weal its woe. *Pr.*

Every day in thy life is a leaf in thy history. 35 *Arab. Pr.*

Every day is the best day in the year. No man has learned anything rightly until he knows that every day is Doomsday. *Emerson.*

Every day should be spent by us as if it were to be our last. *Pub. Syr.*

Every department of knowledge passes successively through three stages: the theological, or fictitious; the metaphysical, or abstract; and the scientific, or positive. *Comte.*

Every desire bears its death in its very gratification. *W. Irving.*

Every desire is a viper in the bosom, who, 40 when he was chill, was harmless, but when warmth gave him strength, exerted it in poison. *Johnson.*

Every dog must have his day. *Swift.*

Every door may be shut but death's door. *Pr.*

Every established religion was once a heresy. *Buckle.*

Every event that a man would master must be mounted on the run, and no man ever caught the reins of a thought except as it galloped past him. *Holmes.*

Every evil to which we do not succumb is a 45 benefactor; we gain the strength of the temptation we resist. *Emerson.*

Every excess causes a defect; every deficit, an excess. Every sweet has its sour; every evil, its good. Every faculty which is a receiver of pleasure has an equal penalty put on its abuse. *Emerson.*

Every experiment, by multitudes or by individuals, that has a sensual and selfish aim, will fail. *Emerson.*

Every faculty is conserved and increased by its appropriate exercise. *Epictetus.*

Every fancy that we would substitute for a reality is, if we saw it aright and saw the whole, not only false, but every way less beautiful and excellent than that which we sacrifice to it. *J. Sterling.*

Every flood has its ebb. *Dut. Pr.* 50

Every fool thinks himself clever enough. *Dan. Pr.*

Every fool will be meddling. *Bible.*

Every foot will tread on him who is in the mud. *Gael. Pr.*

Every form of freedom is hurtful, except that which delivers us over to perfect command of ourselves. *Goethe.*

Every form of human life is romantic. *T. W. Higginson.*

Every fresh acquirement is another remedy 55 against affliction and time. *Willmott.*

Every friend is to the other a sun and a sunflower also: he attracts and follows. *Jean Paul.*

Every generation laughs at the old fashions, but follows religiously the herd. *Thoreau.*

Every generous action loves the public view, yet no theatre for virtue is equal to a consciousness of it. *Cic.*

Every genius has most power in his own language, and every heart in its own religion. *Jean Paul.*

Every genius is defended from approach by quantities of unavailableness. *Emerson.*

5 Every genuine work of art has as much reason for being as the earth and the sun. *Emerson.*

Every gift which is given, even though it be small, is in reality great if it be given with affection. *Pindar.*

Every good act is charity. A man's true wealth hereafter is the good that he does in this world to his fellows. *Mahomet.*

Every good gift and every perfect gift is from above. *St. James.*

Every good gift comes from God. *Pr.*

10 Every good picture is the best of sermons and lectures : the sense informs the soul. *Sydney Smith.*

Every good writer has much idiom ; it is the life and spirit of language. *Landor.*

Every great and commanding movement in the annals of the world is the triumph of enthusiasm. *Emerson.*

Every great and original writer, in proportion as he is great or original, must himself create the taste by which he is to be relished. *Wordsworth.*

Every great book is an action, and every great action is a book. *Luther.*

15 Every great genius has a special vocation, and when he has fulfilled it, he is no longer needed. *Goethe.*

Every great man is unique. *Emerson.*

Every great mind seeks to labour for eternity. All men are captivated by immediate advantages ; great minds alone are excited by the prospect of distant good. *Schiller.*

Every great poem is in itself limited by necessity, but in its suggestions unlimited and infinite. *Longfellow.*

Every great reform which has been effected has consisted, not in doing something new, but in undoing something old. *Buckle.*

20 Every great writer is a writer of history, let him treat on almost what subject he may He carries with him for thousands of years a portion of his times ; and, indeed, if only his own effigy were there, it would be greatly more than a fragment of his century. *Landor.*

Every healthy effort is directed from the inward to the outward world. *Goethe.*

Every heart knows its own bitterness. *Pr.*

Every hero becomes a bore at last. *Emerson.*

Every heroic act measures itself by its contempt of some external good ; but it finds its own success at last, and then the prudent also extol. *Emerson.*

25 Every honest miller has a golden thumb. *Pr.*

Every hour has its end. *Scott.*

Every house is builded by some man ; but he that built all things is God. *St. Paul.*

Every human being is intended to have a character of his own, to be what no other is, to do what no other can. *Channing.*

Every human feeling is greater and larger than the exciting cause—a proof, I think, that man is designed for a higher state of existence. *Coleridge.*

Every idea must have a visible unfolding. 30 *Victor Hugo.*

Every idle word that men shall speak, they shall give account thereof in the day of judgment. *Jesus.*

Every inch a king. *Lear,* iv. 6.

Every inch of joy has an ell of annoy. *Sc. Pr.*

Every individual colour makes on men an impression of its own, and thereby reveals its nature to the eye as well as the mind. *Goethe.*

Every individual nature has its own beauty. 35 *Emerson.*

Every inordinate cup is unbless'd, and the ingredient is a devil. *Othello,* ii. 3.

Every joy that comes to us is only to strengthen us for some greater labour that is to succeed. *Fichte.*

Every knave is a thorough knave, and a thorough knave is a knave thoughout. *Bp. Berkeley.*

Every light has its shadow. *Pr.*

Every little fish expects to become a whale. 40 *Dan. Pr.*

Every little helps. *Pr.*

Every little helps, as the sow said when she snapt at a gnat. *Dan. Pr.*

Every loving woman is a priestess of the past. *Amiel.*

Every man alone is sincere ; at the entrance of a second person, hypocrisy begins. *Emerson.*

Every man as an individual is secondary to 45 what he is as a worker for the progress of his kind and the glory of the gift allotted to him. *Stedman.*

Every man can build a chapel in his breast, himself the priest, his heart the sacrifice, and the earth he treads on the altar. *Jeremy Taylor.*

Every man can guide an ill wife but him that has her. *Sc. Pr.*

Every man carries an enemy in his own bosom. *Dan. Pr.*

Every man carries within him a potential madman. *Carlyle.*

Every man deems that he has precisely the 50 trials and temptations which are the hardest to bear ; but they are so because they are the very ones he needs. *Jean Paul.*

Every man desires to live long, but no man would be old. *Swift.*

Every man feels instinctively that all the beautiful sentiments in the world weigh less than a single lovely action. *Lowell.*

Every man has a bag hanging before him in which he puts his neighbour's faults, and another behind him in which he stows his own. *Coriolanus,* ii. 1.

Every man has a goose that lays golden eggs, if he only knew it. *Amer. Pr.*

Every man has at times in his mind the ideal 55 of what he should be, but is not. In all men that really seek to improve, it is better than the actual character. *Theo. Parker.*

Every man hath business and desire, / Such as it is. *Ham.*, i. 5.

Every man has his fault, and honesty is his. *Timon of Athens*, iii. 1.

Every man has his lot, and the wide world before him. *Dan. Pr.*

Every man has his own style, just as he has his own nose. *Lessing.*

5 Every man has his weak side. *Pr.*

Every man has in himself a continent of undiscovered character. Happy is he who acts the Columbus to his own soul. *Sir J. Stephens.*

Every man has just as much vanity as he wants understanding. *Pope.*

Every man hath a good and a bad angel attending on him in particular all his life long. *Burton.*

Every man, however good he may be, has a still better man dwelling in him which is properly himself, but to whom nevertheless he is often unfaithful. It is to this interior and less unstable being that we should attach ourselves, not to the changeable every-day man. *W. v. Humboldt.*

10 Every man in his lifetime needs to thank his faults. *Emerson.*

Every man is an impossibility until he is born ; everything impossible till we see it a success. *Emerson.*

Every man is a quotation from all his ancestors. *Emerson.*

Every man is a rascal as soon as he is sick. *Johnson.*

Every man is exceptional. *Emerson.*

15 Every man is his own greatest dupe. *A. B. Alcott.*

Every man is not so much a workman in the world as he is a suggestion of that he should be. Men walk as prophecies of the next age. *Emerson.*

Every man is the architect of his own fortune. *Sallust.*

Every man must carry his own sack to the mill. *Dan. Pr.*

Every man must in a measure be alone in the world. No heart was ever cast in the same mould as that which we bear within us. *Berne.*

20 Every man of sound brain whom you meet knows something worth knowing better than yourself. *Bulwer Lytton.*

Every man ought to have his opportunity to conquer the world for himself. *Emerson.*

Every man rejoices twice when he has a partner of his joy. *Jeremy Taylor.*

Every man seeks the truth, but God only knows who has found it. *Chesterfield.*

Every man shall bear his own burden. *St. Paul.*

25 Every man shall kiss his lips that giveth a right answer. *Bible.*

Every man should study conciseness in speaking ; it is a sign of ignorance not to know that long speeches, though they may please the speaker, are the torture of the hearer. *Feltham.*

Every man stamps his value on himself. The price we challenge for ourselves is given us. *Schiller.*

Every man takes care that his neighbour shall not cheat him. *Emerson.*

Every man acts truly so long as he acts his nature, or some way makes good the faculties in himself. *Sir T. Browne.*

Every man turns his dreams into realities as 30 far as he can. Man is cold as ice to the truth, but as fire to falsehood. *La Fontaine.*

Every man who observes vigilantly and resolves steadfastly grows unconsciously into a genius. *Bulwer Lytton.*

Every man who strikes blows for power, for influence, for institutions, for the right, must be just as good an anvil as he is a hammer. *J. G. Holland.*

Every man who would do anything well must come to us from a higher ground. *Emerson.*

Every man willingly gives value to the praise which he receives, and considers the sentence passed in his favour as the sentence of discernment. *Johnson.*

Every man, within that inconsiderable figure 35 of his, contains a whole spirit - kingdom and reflex of the All ; and, though to the eye but some six standard feet in size, reaches downwards and upwards, unsurveyable, fading into the regions of immensity and eternity. *Carlyle.*

Every man without passions has within him no principle of action nor motive to act. *Helvetius.*

Every man's blind in his ain cause. *Sc. Pr.*

Every man's destiny is in his own hands. *Sydney Smith.*

Every man's follies are the caricature resemblances of his wisdom. *J. Sterling.*

Every man's life lies within the present. *Marcus Antoninus.* 40

Every man's man has a man, and that gar'd the Tarve (a Douglas Castle) fa'. *Sc. Pr.*

Every man's own reason is his best Œdipus. *Sir Thomas Browne.*

Every man's powers have relation to some kind of work, and wherever he finds that kind of work which he can do best, he finds that by which he can best build up or make his manhood. *J. G. Holland.*

Every man's reason is every man's oracle. *Bolingbroke.*

Every moment, as it passes, is of infinite 45 value, for it is the representative of a whole eternity. *Goethe.*

Every moment instructs, and every object, for wisdom is infused into every form. It has been poured into us as blood ; it convulsed us as pain ; it slid into us as pleasure. *Emerson.*

Every morsel to a satisfied hunger is only a new labour to a tired digestion. *South.*

Every mortal longs for his parade-place ; would still wish, at banquets, to be master of some seat or other wherein to overtop this or that plucked goose of the neighbourhood. *Carlyle.*

Every movement in the skies or upon the earth proclaims to us that the universe is under government. *Draper.*

Every natural action is graceful. *Emerson.* 50

Every natural fact is a symbol of some spiritual fact. *Emerson.*

Every newly discovered truth judges the world, separates the good from the evil, and calls on faithful souls to make sure their election. *Julia W. Howe.*

Every new opinion, at its starting, is precisely in a minority of one. *Carlyle.*

Every noble crown is, and on earth will ever be, a crown of thorns. *Carlyle.*

Every noble life leaves the fibre of it interwoven for ever in the work of the world. *Ruskin.*

Every noble work is at first impossible. *Carlyle.*

5 Every novel is a debtor to Homer. *Emerson.*

Every offence is not a hate at first. *Mer. of Ven.*, iv. 1.

Every one believes in his youth that the world really began with him, and that all merely exists for his sake. *Goethe.*

Every one bows to the bush that bields (protects) him, *i.e.*, pays court to him that does so. *Sc. Pr.*

Every one can master a grief but he that has it. *Much Ado*, iii. 2.

10 Every one complains of his memory, no one of his judgment. *La Roche.*

Every one draws the water to his own mill. *Pr.*

Every one excels in something in which another fails. *Pub. Syr.*

Every one fault seeming monstrous till his fellow-fault came to match it. *As You Like It*, iii. 2.

Every one finds sin sweet and repentance bitter. *Dan. Pr.*

15 Every one for himself and God for us all. *Pr.*

Every one has a trial of his own : my wife is mine. Happy is he who has no other. *Saying of Pittacus.*

Every one is a preacher under the gallows. *Dut. Pr.*

Every one is as God made him, and often a great deal worse. *Cervantes.*

Every one is his own worst enemy. *Schefer.*

20 Every one is judge of what a man seems, no one of what a man is. *Schiller.*

Every one is poorer in proportion as he has more wants, and counts not what he has, but wishes only what he has not. *Manlius.*

Every one is well or ill at ease according as he finds himself. *Montaigne.*

Every one knows best where his shoe pinches him. *Pr.*

Every one knows better than he practises, and recognises a better law than he obeys. *Froude.*

25 Every one knows good counsel except him who needs it. *Ger. Pr.*

Every one of us believes in his heart, or would like to have others believe, that he is something which he is not. *Thackeray.*

Every one of us shall give account of himself to God. *Bible.*

Every one rakes the fire under his own pot. *Dan. Pr.*

Every one regards his duty as a troublesome master from whom he would like to be free. *La Roche.*

30 Every one should sweep before his own door. *Pr.*

Every one sings as he has the gift, and marries as he has the luck. *Port. Pr.*

Every one that asketh receiveth ; and he that seeketh findeth ; and to him that knocketh it shall be opened. *Jesus.*

Every one that doeth evil hateth the light. *St. John.*

Every one that is of the truth heareth my voice. *Jesus.*

Every one thinks his own burden the heaviest. 35 *Pr.*

Every one who is able to administer what he has, has enough. *Goethe.*

Every one would be wise ; no one will become so. *Feuchtersleben.*

Every one would rather believe than exercise his own judgment. *Sen.*

Every opinion reacts on him who utters it. *Emerson.*

Every other master is known by what he 40 utters ; the master of style commends himself to me by what he wisely passes over in silence. *Schiller.*

Every painter ought to paint what he himself loves. *Ruskin.*

Every passion gives a particular cast to the countenance, and is apt to discover itself in some feature or other. *Addison.*

Every people has its prophet. *Arab. Pr.*

Every period of life has its peculiar prejudices. Whoever saw old age that did not applaud the past and condemn the present? *Montaigne.*

Every period of life has its peculiar tempta- 45 tions and dangers. *J. Hawes.*

Every period of life is obliged to borrow its happiness from the time to come. *Johnson.*

Every person who manages another is a hypocrite. *Thackeray.*

Every petition to God is a precept to man. *Jeremy Taylor.*

Every place is safe to him who lives with justice. *Epictetus.*

Every pleasure pre-supposes some sort of 50 activity. *Schopenhauer.*

Every poet, be his outward lot what it may, finds himself born in the midst of prose ; he has to struggle from the littleness and obstruction of an actual world into the freedom and infinitude of an ideal. *Carlyle.*

Every power of both heaven and earth is friendly to a noble and courageous activity. *J. Burroughs.*

Every production of genius must be the production of enthusiasm. *Disraeli.*

Every race has its own habitat. *Knox.*

Every reader reads himself out of the book 55 that he reads. *Goethe.*

Every real master of speaking or writing uses his personality as he would any other serviceable material. *Holmes.*

Every real need is appeased and every vice stimulated by satisfaction. *Amiel.*

Every rightly constituted mind ought to rejoice, not so much in knowing anything clearly, as in feeling that there is infinitely more which it cannot know. *Ruskin.*

Every rose has its thorn. *Pr.*

Every scripture is to be interpreted by the 60 same spirit which gave it forth. *Quoted by Emerson.*

Every sect, as far as reason will help it, gladly uses it ; when it fails them, they cry out it is matter of faith, and above reason. *Locke.*

Every shadow points to the sun. *Emerson.*

Every ship is a romantic object except that we sail in. *Emerson.*

Every shoe fits not every foot. *Pr.*

Every shot does not bring down a bird. *Dut. Pr.*

Every soo (sow) to its ain trough. *Sc. Pr.*

5 Every species of activity is met by a negation. *Goethe.*

Every spirit builds itself a house, and beyond its house a world, and beyond its world a heaven. *Emerson.*

Every spirit makes its house, but afterwards the house confines the spirit. *Emerson.*

Every step of life shows how much caution is required. *Goethe.*

Every step of progress which the world has made has been from scaffold to scaffold and from stake to stake. *Wendell Phillips.*

10 Every Stoic was a Stoic, but in Christendom where is the Christian? *Emerson.*

Every style formed elaborately on any model must be affected and strait-laced. *Whipple.*

Every subject's duty is the king's, but every subject's soul is his own. *Hen. V.*, iv. 1.

Every tear of sorrow sown by the righteous springs up a pearl. *Matthew Henry.*

Everything a man parts with is the cost of something. Everything he receives is the compensation of something. *J. G. Holland.*

15 Everything calls for interest, only it must be an interest divested of self-interest and sincere. *Desjardins.*

Everything comes if a man will only wait. *Disraeli.*

Everything, even piety, is dangerous in a man without judgment. *Stanislaus.*

Everything good in a man thrives best when properly recognised. *J. G. Holland.*

Everything good in man leans on what is higher. *Emerson.*

20 Everything good is on the highway. *Emerson.*

Everything great is not always good, but all good things are great. *Demosthenes.*

Everything holy is before what is unholy; guilt presupposes innocence, not the reverse; angels, but not fallen ones, were created. *Jean Paul.*

Everything in life, to be of value, must have a sequence. *Goethe.*

Everything in nature contains all the powers of nature. Everything is made of one hidden stuff. *Emerson.*

25 Everything in nature goes by law, and not by luck. *Emerson.*

Everything in nature has a positive and a negative pole. *Emerson.*

Everything in nature is a puzzle until it finds its solution in man, who solves it in some way with God, and so completes the circle of creation. *T. T. Munger.*

Everything in the world can be borne except a long succession of beautiful days. *Goethe.*

Everything in this world depends upon will. *Disraeli.*

30 Everything in this world is a tangled yarn; we taste nothing in its purity; we do not remain two moments in the same state. *Rousseau.*

Everything is as you take it. *Pr.*

Everything is beautiful, seen from the point of the intellect; but all is sour if seen as experience. *Emerson.*

Everything is good as it comes from the hands of the Creator; everything degenerates in the hands of man. *Rousseau.*

Everything is mere opinion. *M. Aurelius*

Everything is sold to skill and labour. *Hume.* 35

Everything is sweetened by risk. *A. Smith.*

Everything is what it is, and not another thing. *Bishop Butler.*

Everything is worth the money that can be got for it. *Pub. Syr.*

Everything looks easy that is practised to perfection. *Goethe.*

Everything rises but to fall, and increases but 40 to decay. *Sall.*

Everything runs to excess; every good quality is noxious if unmixed; and to carry the danger to the edge of ruin, Nature causes each man's peculiarity to superabound. *Emerson.*

Everything springs into being and passes away according to law, yet how fluctuating is the lot that presides over the life which is to us so priceless. *Goethe.*

Everything that exceeds the bounds of moderation has an unstable foundation. *Sen.*

Everything that happens, happens of necessity. *Schopenhauer.*

Everything that happens in this world is part 45 of a great plan of God running through all time. *Ward Beecher.*

Everything that happens to us leaves some trace behind it, and everything insensibly contributes to make us what we are. *Goethe.*

Everything that is exquisite hides itself. *J. Roux.*

Everything that is popular deserves the attention of the philosopher; although it may not be of any worth in itself, yet it characterises the people. *Emerson.*

Everything that looks to the future elevates human nature; for never is life so low as when occupied with the present. *Landor.*

Everything that tends to emancipate us from 50 external restraint without adding to our own power of self-government is mischievous. *Goethe.*

Everything unnatural is imperfect. *Napoleon.*

Everything useful to the life of man arises from the ground, but few things arise in that condition which is requisite to render them useful. *Hume.*

Every thought that arises in the mind, in its rising aims to pass out of the mind into act; just as every plant, in the moment of generation, struggles up to the light. *Emerson.*

Every thought was once a poem. *Emerson.* (?)

Every thought which genius and piety throw 55 into the world alters the world. *Emerson.*

Every time a man smiles, much more when he laughs, it adds something to his fragment of life. *Sterne.*

Every time you forgive a man you weaken him and strengthen yourself. *Amer. Pr.*

Every transition is a crisis, and a crisis presupposes sickness. *Goethe.*

Every traveller has a home of his own, and he learns to appreciate it the more from his wandering. *Dickens.*

Every tree that bringeth not forth good fruit is hewn down and cast into the fire. *Jesus.*

Every true man's apparel fits your thief. *Meas. for Meas.*, iv. 2.

Every tub must stand on its own bottom. *Pr.*

5 Every unpleasant feeling is a sign that I have become untrue to my resolutions. *Jean Paul.*

Every unpunished murder takes away something from the security of every man's life. *Dan. Webster.*

Every vicious habit and chronic disease communicates itself by descent, and by purity of birth the entire system of the human body and soul may be gradually elevated, or by recklessness of birth degraded, until there shall be as much difference between the well-bred and ill-bred human creature (whatever pains be taken with their education) as between a wolf-hound and the vilest mongrel cur. *Ruskin.*

Every violation of truth is a stab at the health of society. *Emerson.*

Every wanton and causeless restraint of the will of the subject, whether practised by a monarch, a nobility, or a popular assembly, is a degree of tyranny. *Blackstone.*

10 Everywhere I am hindered of meeting God in my brother, because he has shut his own temple doors, and recites fables merely of his brother's or his brother's brother's God. *Emerson.*

Everywhere in life the true question is, not what we gain, but what we do; so also in intellectual matters it is not what we receive, but what we are made to give, that chiefly contents and profits us. *Carlyle.*

Everywhere the formed world is the only habitable one. *Carlyle.*

Everywhere the human soul stands between a hemisphere of light and another of darkness; on the confines of two everlasting, hostile empires, Necessity and Free Will. *Carlyle.*

Everywhere the individual seeks to show himself off to advantage, and nowhere honestly endeavours to make himself subservient to the whole. *Goethe.*

15 Every white will have its black, / And every sweet its sour. *T. Percy.*

Every why hath a wherefore. *Com. of Errors*, ii. 2.

Every wise woman buildeth her house, but the foolish plucketh it down with her hands. *Bible.*

Every word was once a poem. *Emerson.*

Every worm beneath the moon / Draws different threads, and late and soon / Spins, toiling out his own cocoon. *Tennyson.*

20 Every youth, from the king's son downwards, should learn to do something finely and thoroughly with his hand. *Ruskin.*

E vestigio—Instantly.

Evil and good are everywhere, like shadow and substance; (for men) inseparable, yet not hostile, only opposed. *Carlyle.*

Evil, be thou my good. *Milton.*

Evil comes to us by ells and goes away by inches. *Pr.*

Evil communications corrupt good manners. 25 *Pr.*

Evil events from evil causes spring. *Aristophanes.*

Evil is a far more cunning and persevering propagandist than good, for it has no inward strength, and is driven to seek countenance and sympathy. *Lowell.*

Evil is generally committed under the hope of some advantage the pursuit of virtue seldom obtains. *B. R. Haydon.*

Evil is merely privative, not absolute; it is like cold, which is the privation of heat. All evil is so much death or nonentity. *Emerson.*

Evil is wrought by want of thought / As well 30 as want of heart. *T. Hood.*

Evil, like a rolling stone upon a mountain-top, / A child may first impel, a giant cannot stop. *Trench.*

Evil men understand not judgment, but they that seek the Lord understand all things. *Bible.*

Evil news rides post, while good news bates. *Milton.*

Evil often triumphs, but never conquers. *J. Roux.*

Evil, what we call evil, must ever exist while 35 man exists; evil, in the widest sense we can give it, is precisely the dark, disordered material out of which man's freewill has to create an edifice of order and good. Ever must pain urge us to labour; and only in free effort can any blessedness be imagined for us. *Carlyle.*

Evils can never pass away; for there must always remain something which is antagonistic to good. *Plato.*

Evils that take leave, / On their departure most of all show evil. *King John*, iii. 4.

Evolare rus ex urbe tanquam ex vinculis—To fly from the town into the country, as though from bonds. *Cic.*

Ewig jung zu bleiben / Ist, wie Dichter schreiben / Hochstes Lebensgut; / Willst du es erwerben / Musst du frühe sterben—To continue eternally young is, as poets write, the highest bliss of life; wouldst thou attain to it, thou must die young. *Rückert.*

Ewig zu sein in jedem Momente—To be eternal 40 at every moment. *Schleiermacher.*

Ex abrupto—Without preparation.

Ex abundante cautela — From excessive precaution. *L.*

Ex abusu non arguitur ad usum—There is no arguing from the *abuse* of a thing against the *use* of it. *L.*

Ex abusu non argumentum ad desuetudinem —The abuse of a thing is no argument for its discontinuance. *L.*

Exact justice is commonly more merciful in 45 the long run than pity, for it tends to foster in men those stronger qualities which make them good citizens. *Lowell.*

Ex æquo—By right.

Ex æquo et bono—In justice and equity.

Exaggeration is a blood relation to falsehood. *H. Ballou.*

Exaggeration is to paint a snake and add legs. *Chinese Pr.*

Examine the religious principles which have, in fact, prevailed in the world. You will scarcely be persuaded that they are anything but sick men's dreams. *Hume.*

Examine your soul and its emotions, and thoughts will be to you so many glorious revelations of the Godhead. *Nourisson.*

Example acquires tenfold authority when it speaks from the grave. *W. Phillips.*

Example has more followers than reason. *Bovee.*

5 Example is a hazardous lure; where the wasp gets through, the gnat sticks. *La Fontaine.*

Example is more efficacious than precept. *Johnson.*

Example is more forcible than precept. People look at me six days in the week, to see what I mean on the seventh. *Cecil.*

Example is the school of mankind, and they will learn no other. *Burke.*

Examples of rare intelligence, yet more rarely cultivated, are not lights kindled for a moment; they live on here in their good deeds, and in their venerated memories. *Gladstone.*

10 Examples would indeed be excellent things, were not people so modest that none will set them, and so vain that none will follow them. *Hare.*

Ex animo---From the soul; heartily.

Ex aperto—Openly.

Ex auribus cognoscitur asinus—An ass is known by his ears. *Pr.*

Ex cathedra—From the chair; with authority.

15 Excellence is never granted to man but as the reward of labour. *Sir Jos. Reynolds.*

Excellent wretch! Perdition catch my soul, / But I do love thee! and when I love thee not, / Chaos is come again. *Othello,* iii. 3.

Excelsior—Still higher.

Except a corn of wheat fall into the ground and die, it abideth alone; but if it die, it bringeth forth much fruit. *Jesus.*

Except by mastership and servantship, there is no conceivable deliverance from tyranny and slavery. *Carlyle.*

20 Except I be by Silvia in the night, / There is no music in the nightingale. *Two Gent. of Ver.,* iii. 1.

Except in knowing what it has to do and how to do it, the soul cannot resolve the riddle of its destiny. *Ed.*

Except in obedience to the heaven-chosen is freedom not so much as conceivable. *Carlyle.*

Except pain of body and remorse of conscience, all our evils are imaginary. *Rousseau.*

Except the Lord build the house, they labour in vain that build it; except the Lord keep the city, the watchman waketh in vain. *Bible.*

25 Except ye be converted and become as little children, ye shall not enter into the kingdom of heaven. *Jesus.*

Exceptio probat regulam—The exception proves the rule.

Exceptis excipiendis—The requisite exceptions being made.

Excepto quod non simul esses, cætera lætus—Except that you were not with me, in other respects I was happy.

Excerpta—Extracts. *L.*

Excess generally causes reaction, and pro- 30 duces a change in the opposite direction, whether it be in the seasons, or in individuals, or in governments. *Plato.*

Excess in apparel is costly folly. The very trimming of the vain world would clothe all the naked ones. *Wm. Penn.*

Excess of wealth is cause of covetousness. *Marlowe.*

Excessit ex ephebis—He has come to the age of manhood. *Ter.*

Excessive distrust is not less hurtful than its opposite. Most men become useless to him who is unwilling to risk being deceived. *Vauvenargues.*

Excitari, non hebescere — To be spirited, not 35 sluggish. *M*

Exclusa opes omnes—All hope is gone. *Plaut.*

Ex commodo—Leisurely.

Ex concesso—Admittedly.

Ex confesso—Confessedly.

Ex curia—Out of court. 40

Excusing of a fault / Doth make the fault worse by the excuse. *King John,* iv. 2.

Ex debito justitiæ—From what is due to justice; from a regard to justice.

Ex delicto—From the crime.

Ex desuetudine amittuntur privilegia—Rights are forfeited by disuse. *L.*

Ex diuturnitate temporis omnia præsumuntur 45 esse solemniter acta—Everything established for a length of time is presumed to have been done in due form. *L.*

Exeat—Let him depart.

Exegi monumentum ære perennius — I have reared a memorial of myself more durable than brass. *Hor.*

Exempli gratia—By way of example.

Exemplo plus quam ratione vivimus—We live more by example than reason.

Exemplumque Dei quisque est in imagine 50 parva—Each man is the copy of his God in small. *Manil.*

Exercise is labour without weariness. *Johnson.*

Exercise the muscles well, but spare the nerves always. *Schopenhauer.*

Exercitatio optimus est magister—Practice is the best master. *Pr.*

Exercitatio potest omnia—Perseverance conquers all difficulties.

Exeunt omnes—All retire. 55

Ex facie—Evidently.

Ex factis non ex dictis amici pensandi—Friends are to be estimated from deeds, not words. *Liv.*

Ex facto jus oritur—The law arises out of the fact, *i.e.,* it cannot till then be put in force. *L.*

Ex fide fortis—Strong from faith. *M.*

Ex fumo dare lucem—To give light from smoke 60 *M.*

Ex humili magna ad fastigia rerum / Extollit, quoties voluit fortuna jocari—As oft as Fortune is in a freakish mood, she raises men from a humble station to the imposing summit of things. *Juv.*

Ex hypothesi—Hypothetically

Exigite ut mores teneros ceu pollice ducat, / Ut si quis cera vultum facit—Require him as with his thumb to mould their youthful morals, just as one fashions a face with plastic wax. *Juv.*

Exigui numero, sed bello vivida virtus—Few in number, yet their valour ardent for war. *Virg.*

Exiguum est ad legem bonum esse—It is but a small matter to be good in the eye of the law only. *Sen.*

Exile is terrible to those who have, as it were, a circumscribed habitation ; but not to those who look upon the whole globe as one city. *Cic.*

5 Exilioque domos et dulcia limina mutant / Atque alio patriam quærunt sub sole jacentem — They exchange their home and sweet thresholds for exile, and seek under another sun another home. *Virg.*

Ex improviso— Unexpectedly.

Ex industria—Purposely.

Ex inimico cogita posse fieri amicum—Think that you may make a friend of an enemy. *Sen.*

Ex integro—Anew ; afresh.

10 Ex intervallo—At some distance.

Existence is not to be measured by mere duration. *Caird.*

Exitio est avidium mare nautis— The greedy sea is destruction to the sailors. *Hor.*

Ex malis eligere minima—Of evils to choose the least. *Cic.*

Ex malis moribus bonæ leges natæ sunt— From bad manners good laws have sprung. *Coke.*

15 Ex mero motu—Of one's own free will.

Ex nihilo nihil fit—Nothing produces nothing.

Ex officio—By virtue of his office.

Ex opere operato—By the external act.

Exoriare aliquis nostris ex ossibus ultor—An avenger shall arise out of my bones. *Virg.*

20 Ex otio plus negotii quam ex negotio habemus —Our leisure gives us more to do than our business.

Ex parte—One-sided.

Ex pede Herculem—We judge of the size of the statue of Hercules by the foot.

Expect injuries ; for men are weak, and thou thyself doest such too often. *Jean Paul.*

Expediency is the science of exigencies. *Kossuth.*

25 Expense of time is the most costly of all expenses. *Theophrastus.*

Experience, a jewel that I have purchased at an infinite rate. *Merry Wives,* ii. 2.

Experience converts us to ourselves when books fail us. *A. B. Alcott.*

Experience is a text to which reflection and knowledge supply the commentary. *Schopenhauer.*

Experience is by industry achieved, / And perfected by swift course of time. *Two Gent. of Ver.,* i. 3.

30 "Experience is the best teacher," only the school-fees are heavy. *Hegel.* (?)

Experience is the grand spiritual doctor. *Carlyle.*

Experience is the mistress of fools. *Pr.*

Experience is the only genuine knowledge. *Goethe.*

Experience keeps a dear school, but fools will learn in no other, and scarce in that ; for it is true we may give advice, but we cannot give conduct. *Ben. Franklin.*

Experience makes even fools wise. *Pr.* 35

Experience makes us see a wonderful difference between devotion and goodness. *Pascal.*

Experience takes dreadfully high school-wages, but teaches as no other. *Carlyle.*

Experience teaches us again and again that there is nothing men have less command over than their tongues. *Spinoza.*

Experience teacheth that resolution is a sole help in need. (?)

Experience that is bought is good, if not too 40 dear. *Pr.*

Experience to most men is like the stern-lights of a ship, which illumine only the track it has passed. *Coleridge.*

Experientia docet—Experience teaches. *Pr.*

Experimentum crucis—A decisive experiment.

Expert men can execute, but learned men are more fit to judge and censure. *Bacon.*

Experto credite—Believe one who has had ex- 45 perience. *Virg.*

Expertus metuit—He who has had experience is afraid. *Hor.*

Expetuntur divitiæ ad perficiendas voluptates —Riches are coveted to minister to our pleasures.

Explorant adversa viros ; perque aspera duro / Nititur ad laudem virtus interrita clivo— Adversity tries men, and virtue struggles after fame, regardless of the adverse heights. *Sil. Ital.*

Ex post facto—After the event. *L.*

Expression alone can invest beauty with 50 supreme and lasting command over the eye. *Fuseli.*

Expressio unius est exclusio alterius — The naming of one man is the exclusion of another. *L.*

Ex professo—As one who knows ; professedly.

Ex quovis ligno non fit Mercurius—A Mercury is not to be made out of any log. *Pr.*

Ex scintilla incendium—From a spark a conflagration. *Pr.*

Ex tempore—Off-hand ; unpremeditated. 55

Extended empire, like expanded gold, ex-changes solid strength for feeble splendour. *Johnson.*

External manners of lament / Are merely shadows to the unseen grief / That swells with silence in the tortured soul. *Rich. II.,* iv. 1.

Extinctus amabilis idem — He will be beloved when he is dead (who was envied when he was living). *Hor.*

Extinguished theologians lie about the cradle of every science, as the strangled snakes beside that of Hercules. *Huxley.*

Extra ecclesiam nulla salus—Outside the Church 60 there is no safety.

Extra lutum pedes habes—You have got your feet out of the mud. *Pr.*

Extra muros—Beyond the walls.

Extra telorum jactum—Beyond bow-shot.

Extrema gaudii luctus occupat—Grief treads on the confines of gladness. *Pr.*

Extrema manus nondum operibus ejus imposita est—The finishing hand has not yet been put to his works.

Extreme justice is often extreme injustice.

Extremes beget extremes. *Pr.*

5 Extreme in all things! hadst thou been betwixt, / Thy throne had still been thine, or never been. *Byron.*

Extremes in nature equal ends produce; / In man they join to some mysterious use. *Pope.*

Extremes meet. *Pr.*

Extremes, though contrary, have the like effects; extreme heat mortifies, like extreme cold; extreme love breeds satiety as well as extreme hatred; and too violent rigour tempts chastity as much as too much license. *Chapman.*

Extremis malis extrema remedia — Extreme remedies for extreme evils. *Pr.*

10 Extremity is the trier of spirits. *Coriol.* iv. 1.

Exuerint sylvestrem animum, cultuque frequenti, / In quascunque voces artes, haud tarda sequentur—They lay aside their rustic ideas, and by repeated instruction will advance apace into whatever arts you may initiate them. *Virg.*

Ex umbra in solem—Out of the shade into the sunshine. *Pr.*

Ex ungue leonem—The lion may be known by his claw.

Ex uno disce omnes—From one judge of all.

15 **Ex vita discedo, tanquam ex hospitio, non tanquam ex domo**—I depart from life as from an inn, not as from a home. *Cic.*

Ex vitio alterius sapiens emendat suum—From the faults of another a wise man will correct his own. *Laber.*

Ex vitulo bos fit—From a calf an ox grows up.

Ex vultibus hominum mores colligere—To construe men's characters by their looks.

Eye hath not seen, nor ear heard, neither have entered into the heart of man, the things which God hath prepared for them that love him. *St. Paul.*

20 Eye Nature's walks, shoot folly as it flies, / And catch the manners living as they rise. *Pope.*

Eyes are better, on the whole, than telescopes or microscopes. *Emerson.*

Eyes bright, with many tears behind them. *Carlyle, on his Wife.*

Eyes not down-dropp'd nor over-bright, but fed with the clear-pointed flame of chastity. *Tennyson.*

Eyes / Of microscopic power, that could discern / The population of a dewdrop. *J. Montgomery.*

25 Eyes raised towards heaven are always beautiful, whatever they be. *Joubert.*

Eyes speak all languages; wait for no letter of introduction; they ask no leave of age or rank; they respect neither poverty nor riches, neither learning, nor power, nor virtue, nor sex, but intrude and come again, and go through and through you in a moment of time. *Emerson.*

Eyes will not see when the heart wishes them to be blind; desire conceals truth as darkness does the earth. *Sen.*

Ez for war, I call it murder; / There you hev it plain and flat; / I don't want to go no furder / Than my Testyment for that. *Lowell.*

F.

Fa bene, e non guardare a chi—Do good, no matter to whom. *It. Pr.*

Faber suæ fortunæ—The maker of his own fortune. *Sall.* 30

Fabricando fabri fimus—We become workmen by working. *Pr.*

Fabula, nec sentis, tota jactaris in urbe—You are the talk, though you don't know it, of the whole town. *Ovid.*

Faces are as legible as books, only they are read in much less time, and are much less likely to deceive us. *Lavater.*

Faces are as paper money, for which, on demand, there frequently proves to be no gold in the coffer. *F. G. Trafford.*

Faces are but a gallery of portraits. *Bacon.* 35

Faces which have charmed us the most escape us the soonest. *Scott.*

Fac et excusa—Do it and so justify yourself. *Pr.*

Facetiarum apud præpotentes in longum memoria est—It is long before men in power forget the jest they have been the subject of. *Tac.*

Fach—Department. *Ger.*

Facienda—Things to be done. 40

Facies non omnibus una, / Nec diversa tamen; qualem decet esse sororum—The features were not the same in them all, nor yet are they quite different, but such as we would expect in sisters. *Ovid.*

Facies tua computat annos—Your face records your age. *Juv.*

Facile est imperium in bonis—It is easy to rule over the good. *Plaut.*

Facile est inventis addere—It is easy to add to or improve on what has been already invented. *Pr.*

Facile largiri de alieno—It is easy to be generous 45 with what is another's. *Pr.*

Facile omnes cum valemus recta consilia / Ægrotis damus—We can all, when we are well, easily give good advice to the sick. *Ter.*

Facile princeps—The admitted chief; with ease at the top.

Facilis descensus Averno est, / Noctes atque dies patet atri janua Ditis; / Sed revocare gradum superasque evadere ad auras, / Hoc opus, hic labor est—The descent to hell is easy; night and day the gate of gloomy Dis stands open; but to retrace your steps and escape to the upper air, this is a work, this is a toil. *Virg.*

Facilius crescit quam inchoatur dignitas—It is more easy to obtain an accession of dignity than to acquire it in the first instance. *Laber.*

Facilius sit Nili caput invenire—It would be 50 easier to discover the source of the Nile. *Old Pr.*

Facinus audax incipit, / Qui cum opulento pauper homine cœpit rem habere aut negotium—The poor man who enters into partnership with a rich makes a risky venture. *Plaut.*

Facinus majoris abollæ—A crime of a very deep dye (*lit.* one committed by a man who wears the garb of a philosopher). *Juv.*

Facinus quos inquinat æquat—Those whom guilt stains it equals, *i.e.*, it puts on even terms. *Lucan.*

Facit indignatio versum—Indignation gives inspiration to verse.

5 **Facito aliquid operis, ut semper te diabolus inveniat occupatum**—Keep doing something, so that the devil may always find you occupied. *St. Jerome.*

Faciunt næ intelligendo, ut nihil intelligant—They are so knowing that they know nothing. *Ter.*

Façon de parler—A manner of speaking. *Fr.*

Facsimile—An engraved resemblance of a man's handwriting; an exact copy of anything (*lit.* do the like).

Facta canam; sed erunt qui me finxisse loquantur—I am about to sing of facts; but some will say I have invented them. *Ovid.*

10 **Facta ejus cum dictis discrepant**—His actions do not harmonise with his words. *Cic.*

Facta, non verba—Deeds, not words.

Fact is better than fiction, if only we could get it pure. *Emerson.*

Facts are apt to alarm us more than the most dangerous principles. *Junius.*

Facts are chiels that winna ding, / And downa be disputed. *Burns.*

15 **Facts are stubborn things.** *Le Sage.*

Facts are to the mind the same thing as food to the body. *Burke.*

Facts—historical facts, still more biographical —are sacred hierograms, for which the fewest have the key. *Carlyle.*

Factis ignoscite nostris / Si scelus ingenio scitis abesse meo—Forgive what I have done, since you know all evil intention was far from me. *Ovid.*

Factotum—A man of all work (*lit.* do everything).

20 **Factum abiit; monumenta manent**—The event is an affair of the past; the memorial of it is still with us. *Ovid.*

Factum est—It is done. *M.*

Factum est illud; fieri infectum non potest—It is done and cannot be undone. *Plaut.*

Fader og Moder ere gode, end er Gud bedre—Father and mother are kind, but God is kinder. *Dan. Pr.*

Fæx populi—The dregs of the people.

25 **Fagerhed uden Tugt, Rose uden Hugt**—Beauty without virtue is a rose without scent. *Dan. Pr.*

Fähigkeiten werden vorausgesetzt; sie sollen zu Fertigkeiten werden—Capacities are presupposed: they are meant to develop into capabilities, or skilled dexterities. *Goethe.*

Failures are with heroic minds the stepping-stones to success. *Haliburton.*

Fain would I, but I dare not; I dare, and yet I may not; / I may, although I care not, for pleasure when I play not. *Raleigh.*

"Fain would I climb, but that I fear a fall." *Raleigh on a pane of glass, to which Queen Elizabeth added,* "If thy heart fail thee, then why climb at all?"

Fainéant—Do nothing. *Fr.* 30

Faint heart never won fair lady. *Pr.*

Faint not; the miles to heaven are but few and short. *S. Rutherford.*

Fair and softly goes far in a day. *Pr.*

Fair enough, if good enough. *Pr.*

Fair fa' guid drink, for it gars (makes) folk 35 **speak as they think.** *Sc. Pr.*

Fair fa' your honest, sonsie face, / Great chieftain o' the puddin' race! / Abune them a' ye tak' your place, / Paunch, tripe, or thairm; / Weel are ye wordy o' a grace / As lang's my airm. *Burns to a Haggis.*

Fair flowers don't remain lying by the highway. *Ger. Pr.*

Fair folk are aye fusionless (pithless). *Sc. Pr.*

Fair is not fair, but that which pleaseth. *Pr.*

Fair maidens wear nae purses (the lads always 40 paying their share). *Sc. Pr.*

Fair play's a jewel. *Pr.*

Fair tresses man's imperial race ensnare, / And beauty draws us with a single hair. *Pope.*

Fair words butter no parsnips. *Pr.*

Faire bonne mine à mauvaise jeu—To put a good face on the matter. *Fr.*

Faire le chien couchant—To play the spaniel; to 45 cringe. *Fr.*

Faire le diable à quatre—To play the devil or deuce. *Fr.*

Faire le pendant—To be the fellow. *Fr.*

Faire mon devoir—To do my duty. *Fr.*

Faire patte de velours—To coax (*lit.* make a velvet paw). *Fr.*

Faire prose sans le savoir—To speak prose 50 without knowing it. *Molière.*

Faire sans dire—To act without talking. *Fr.*

Faire un trou pour en boucher un autre—To make one hole in order to stop another. *Fr. Pr.*

Fairest of stars, last in the train of night, / If better thou belong not to the dawn. *Milton.*

Fais ce que dois, advienne que pourra—Do your duty, come what may. *Fr. Pr.*

Fait accompli—A thing already done. *Fr.* 55

Faith affirms many things respecting which the senses are silent; but nothing that they deny. *Pascal.*

Faith always implies the disbelief of a lesser fact in favour of a greater. A little mind often sees the unbelief, without seeing the belief, of large ones. *Holmes.*

Faith and joy are the ascensive forces of song. *Stedman.*

Faith builds a bridge across the gulf of death, / To break the shock blind Nature cannot shun, / And lands thought smoothly on the farther shore. *Young.*

Faith builds a bridge from the old world to the 60 **next.** *Young.*

Faith doth not lie dead in the breast, but is lovely and fruitful in bringing forth good works. *Cranmer.*

Faith, fanatic faith, once wedded fast, / To save dear falsehood, hugs it to the last. *Moore.*

Faith has given man an inward willingness, a world of strength wherewith to front a world of difficulty. *Carlyle.*

Faith in a better than that which appears is no less required by art than religion. *John Sterling.*

Faith is generally strongest in those whose character may be called weakest. *Mme. de Staël.*

Faith is letting down our nets into the untransparent deeps at the Divine command, not knowing what we shall take. *Faber.*

Faith is like love; it does not admit of being forced. *Schopenhauer.*

5 Faith is love taking the form of aspiration. *Channing.*

Faith is loyalty to some inspired teacher, some spiritual hero. *Carlyle.*

Faith is necessary to victory. *Hazlitt.*

Faith is nothing but spiritualised imagination. *Ward Beecher.*

Faith is nothing more than obedience. *Voltaire.*

10 Faith is not reason's labour, but repose. *Young.*

Faith is not the beginning, but the end of all knowledge. *Goethe.*

Faith is our largest manufacturer of good works, and wherever her furnaces are blown out, morality suffers. *Birrell.*

Faith is required at thy hands, and a sincere life, not loftiness of intellect or inquiry into the deep mysteries of God. *Thomas à Kempis.*

Faith is taking God at His word. *Evans.*

15 Faith is that courage in the heart which trusts for all good to God. *Luther.*

Faith is the creator of the Godhead; not that it creates anything in the Divine Eternal Being, but that it creates that Being in us. *Luther.*

Faith is the heroism of intellect. *C. H. Parkhurst.*

Faith is the soul of religion, and works the body. *Colton.*

Faith loves to lean on Time's destroying arm. *Holmes.*

20 Faith makes us, and not we it; and faith makes its own forms. *Emerson.*

Faith, mighty faith, the promise sees, / And looks to that alone; / Laughs at impossibilities, / And cries—"It shall be done." *C. Wesley.*

Faith opens a way for the understanding; unbelief closes it. *St. Augustine.*

Faith without works is like a bird without wings. *J. Beaumont.*

Faith's abode / Is mystery for evermore, / Its life, to worship and adore, / And meekly bow beneath the rod, / When the day is dark and the burden sore. *Dr. Walter Smith.*

25 Faiths that are different in their roots, / Where the will is right and the heart is sound, / Are much the same in their fruits. *J. B. Selkirk.*

Faithful are the wounds of a friend. *Bible.*

Faithful found / Among the faithless; faithful only he. *Milton.*

Faithfulness and sincerity are the highest things. *Confucius.*

Falla pouco, e bem, ter-te-haô por alguem— Speak little and well, they will take you for somebody. *Port. Pr.*

Fallacia / Alia aliam trudit—One falsehood 90 begets another (*lit.* thrusts aside another). *Ter.*

Fallacies we are apt to put upon ourselves by taking words for things. *Locke.*

Fallentis semita vitæ—The pathway of deceptive or unnoticed life. *Hor.*

Fallit enim vitium, specie virtutis et umbra, / Cum sit triste habitu, vultuque et veste severum—For vice deceives under an appearance and shadow of virtue when it is subdued in manner and severe in countenance and dress. *Juv.*

Fallitur, egregio quisquis sub principe credit / Servitium. Nunquam libertas gratior extat / Quam sub rege pio—Whoso thinks it slavery to serve under an eminent prince is mistaken. Liberty is never sweeter than under a pious king. *Claud.*

Falls have their risings, wanings have their 35 primes, / And desperate sorrows wait for better times. *Quarles.*

Falsch ist das Geschlecht der Menschen— False is the race of men. *Schiller.*

False as dicers' oaths. *Ham.,* iii. 4.

False by degrees and exquisitely wrong. *Canning.*

False face must hide what the false heart doth know. *Macb.,* i. 7.

False folk should hae mony witnesses. *Sc.* 40 *Pr.*

False freends are waur than bitter enemies. *Sc. Pr.*

False friends are like our shadow, close to us while we walk in the sunshine, but leaving us the instant we cross into the shade. *Bovee.*

False glory is the rock of vanity. *La Bruyère.*

False modesty is the masterpiece of vanity. *La Bruyère.*

False modesty is the most decent of all false-45 hood. *Chamfort.*

False shame is the parent of many crimes. *Fox.*

Falsehood and death are synonymous. *Bancroft.*

Falsehood borders so closely upon truth, that a wise man should not trust himself too near the precipice. (?)

Falsehood is cowardice; truth is courage. *H. Ballou.*

Falsehood is easy, truth is difficult. *George* 50 *Eliot.*

Falsehood is folly. *Hom.*

Falsehood is never so successful as when she baits her hook with truth. *Colton.*

Falsehood is our one enemy in this world. *Carlyle.*

Falsehood is so much the more commendable, by how much more it resembles truth, and is the more pleasing the more it is doubtful and possible. *Cervantes.*

Falsehood is the devil's daughter, and speaks 55 her father's tongue. *Dan. Pr.*

Falsehood is the essence of all sin. *Carlyle.*

Falsehood, like poison, will generally be rejected when administered alone; but when blended with wholesome ingredients may be swallowed unperceived. *Whately.*

Falsehood, like the dry rot, flourishes the more in proportion as air and light are excluded. *Whately.*

Falso damnati crimine mortis—Condemned to die on a false charge. *Virg.*

Falsum in uno, falsum in omni—False in one thing, false in everything.

Falsus honor juvat, et mendax infamia terret / Quem nisi mendosum et medicandum—Undeserved honour delights, and lying calumny alarms no one but him who is full of falsehood and needs to be reformed. *Hor.*

Fama clamosa—A current scandal.

5 **Fama crescit eundo**—Rumour grows as it goes. *Virg.*

Fama nihil est celerius—Nothing circulates more swiftly than scandal. *Livy.*

Famæ damna majora sunt, quam quæ æstimari possint—The loss of reputation is greater than can be possibly estimated. *Livy.*

Famæ laboranti non facile succurritur—It is not easy to repair a damaged character. *Pr.*

Famam extendere factis. To extend one's fame by valiant feats. *Virg.*

10 **Fame and censure with a tether / By fate are always linked together.** *Swift.*

Fame at its best is but a poor compensation for all the ills of existence. *Mrs. Oliphant.*

Fame comes only when deserved, and then it is as inevitable as destiny, for it is destiny. *Longfellow.*

Fame is a fancied life in others' breath. *Pope.*

Fame is an undertaker that pays but little attention to the living, but bedizens the dead, furnishes out their funerals, and follows them to the grave. *Colton.*

15 **Fame is a revenue payable only to our ghosts.** *Mackenzie.*

Fame is a shuttlecock. If it be struck only at one end of a room, it will soon fall to the floor. To keep it up, it must be struck at both ends. *Johnson.*

Fame is but the breath of the people, and that often unwholesome. *Pr.*

Fame is no plant that grows on mortal soil. *Milton.*

Fame is not won on downy plumes nor under canopies. *Dante.*

20 **Fame is the advantage of being known by people of whom you yourself know nothing, and for whom you care as little.** *Stanislaus.*

Fame is the breath of popular applause. *Herrick.*

Fame is the perfume of noble deeds. *Socrates.*

Fame is the spur that the clear spirit doth raise, / (That last infirmity of noble minds,) / To scorn delights and live laborious days. *Milton.*

Fame may be compared to a scold ; the best way to silence her is to let her alone, and she will at last be out of breath in blowing her own trumpet. *Fuller.*

25 **Fame only reflects the estimate in which a man is held in comparison with others.** *Schopenhauer.*

Fame sometimes hath created something of nothing. *Fuller.*

Fame usually comes to those who are thinking about something else ; very rarely to those who say to themselves, "Go to now, let us be a celebrated individual." *Holmes.*

Fame, we may understand, is no sure test of merit, but only a probability of such : it is an accident, not a property, of a man ; like light, it can give little or nothing, but at most may show what is given ; often it is but a false glare, dazzling the eyes of the vulgar, lending, by casual extrinsic splendour, the brightness and manifold glance of the diamond to pebbles of no value. *Carlyle.*

Fame with men, / Being but ampler means to serve mankind, / Should have small rest or pleasure in herself, / But work as vassal to the larger love, / That dwarfs the petty love of one to one. *Tennyson.*

Fames et mora bilem in nasum conciunt—30 Hunger and delay stir up one's bile (*lit.* in the nostrils). *Pr.*

Fames, pestis, et bellum, populi sunt pernicies—Famine, pestilence, and war are the destruction of a people.

Familiare est hominibus omnia sibi ignoscere—It is common to man to pardon all his own faults.

Familiarity breeds contempt. *Pr.*

Familiarity is a suspension of almost all the laws of civility which libertinism has introduced into society under the notion of ease. *La Roche.*

Family likeness has often a deep sadness in it. 35 *George Eliot.*

Famine hath a sharp and meagre face. *Dryden.*

Fammi indovino, e ti farò ricco—Make me a prophet, and I will make you rich. *It. Pr.*

Fanaticism is a fire which heats the mind indeed, but heats without purifying. *Warburton.*

Fanaticism is such an overwhelming impression of the ideas relating to the future world as disqualifies for the duties of this. *R. Hall.*

Fanaticism is to superstition what delirium is 40 to fever and rage to anger. *Voltaire.*

Fanaticism obliterates the feelings of humanity. *Gibbon.*

Fanaticism, soberly defined, / Is the false fire of an o'erheated mind. *Cowper.*

Fancy is capricious ; wit must not be searched for, and pleasantry will not come in at a call. *Sterne.*

Fancy is imagination in her youth and adolescence. *Landor.*

Fancy kills and fancy cures. *Sc. Pr.* 45

Fancy requires much, necessity but little. *Ger. Pr.*

Fancy restrained may be compared to a fountain, which plays highest by diminishing the aperture. *Goldsmith.*

Fancy rules over two-thirds of the universe, the past and the future, while reality is confined to the present. *Jean Paul.*

Fancy runs most furiously when a guilty conscience drives it. *Fuller.*

Fancy surpasses beauty. *Pr.* 50

Fancy, when once brought into religion, knows not where to stop. *Whately.*

Fanfaronnade—Boasting. *Fr.*

Fanned fires and forced love ne'er did weel. *Sc. Pr.*

Fantastic tyrant of the amorous heart, / How hard thy yoke! how cruel is thy dart! / Those 'scape thy anger who refuse thy sway, / And those are punished most who most obey. *Prior.*

Fantasy is of royal blood; the senses, of noble descent; and reason, of civic (*bürgerlichen*) origin. *Feuerbach.*

Fantasy is the true heaven-gate and hell-gate of man. *Carlyle.*

Far ahint maun follow the faster. *Sc. Pr.*

5 Far-awa fowls hae aye fair feathers. *Sc. Pr.*

Far better it is to know everything of a little than a little of everything. *Pickering.*

Far frae court, far frae care. *Sc. Pr.*

Far from all resort of mirth / Save the cricket on the hearth. *Milton.*

Far from home is near to harm. *Fris. Pr.*

10 Far from the madding crowd's ignoble strife, / Their sober wishes never learned to stray; / Along the cool sequester'd vale of life / They kept the noiseless tenor of their way. *Gray.*

Far greater numbers have been lost by hopes / Than all the magazines of daggers, ropes, / And other ammunitions of despair, / Were ever able to despatch by fear. *Butler.*

Far niente—A do-nothing.

Far-off cows have long horns. *Gael. Pr.*

Far-off fowls hae feathers fair, / And aye until ye try them; / Though they seem fair, still have a care, / They may prove waur than I am. *Burns.*

15 Far or forgot to me is near; / Shadow and sunlight are the same; / The vanished gods to me appear; / And one to me are shame and fear. *Emerson.*

Fare, fac—Speak, do.

Fare thee well! and if for ever, / Still for ever fare thee well! / E'en though unforgiving, never / 'Gainst thee shall my heart rebel. *Byron.*

Fare you weel, auld Nickie-ben! / O wad ye tak' a thocht and men'! / Ye aiblins micht— I dinna ken— / Still hae a stake: / I'm wae to think upo' yon den, / E'en for your sake. *Burns.*

Farewell, a long farewell to all my greatness! / This is the state of man: to-day he puts forth / The tender leaves of hope, to-morrow blossoms, / And bears his blushing honours thick upon him: / The third day comes a frost, a killing frost: / And when he thinks, good easy man, full surely / His greatness is a-ripening, nips his root, / And then he falls, as I do. *Hen. VIII.*, iii. 2.

20 Farewell! God knows when we shall meet again. / I have a faint cold fear thrills through my veins, / That almost freezes up the heat of life. *Rom. and Jul.*, iv. 3.

Farewell, happy fields, / Where joy for ever dwells; hail, horror, hail! *Milton.*

Farewell the tranquil mind! farewell content! / Farewell the plumed troop and the big wars / That make ambition virtue! oh, farewell! / Farewell the neighing steed and the shrill trump, / The spirit-stirring drum, the ear-piercing fife, / The royal banner, and all quality, / Pride, pomp, and circumstance of glorious war! *Othello*, iii. 3.

Farewell to Lochaber, farewell to my Jean, / Where heartsome wi' thee I hae mony days been; / For Lochaber no more, Lochaber no more, / We'll maybe return to Lochaber no more. *Allan Ramsay.*

Farì quæ sentiat—To speak what he thinks. *M.*

Farmers are the founders of civilisation. 25 *Daniel Webster.*

Farrago libelli—The medley of that book of mine. *Juv.*

Fas est et ab hoste doceri—It is right to derive instruction even from an enemy. *Ovid.*

Fashionability is a kind of elevated vulgarity. *G. Darley.*

Fashion, a word which fools use, / Their knavery and folly to excuse. *Churchill.*

Fashion begins and ends in two things it 30 abhors most—singularity and vulgarity. *Hazlitt.*

Fashion is a potency in art, making it hard to judge between the temporary and the lasting. *Stedman.*

Fashion is aristocratic-autocratic. *J. G. Holland.*

Fashion is, for the most part, nothing but the ostentation of riches. *Locke.*

Fashion is gentility running away from vulgarity, and afraid to be overtaken by it. It is a sign that the two things are not far asunder. *Hazlitt.*

Fashion is the great governor of the world. 35 *Fielding.*

Fashion is the science of appearances, and it inspires one with the desire to seem rather than to be. *Locke.*

Fashion seldom interferes with Nature without diminishing her grace and efficiency. *Tuckerman.*

Fashion wears out more apparel than the man. *Much Ado*, iii. 3.

Fast and loose. *Love's L. Lost*, i. 1.

Fast bind, fast find. *Pr.* **40**

Faster than his tongue / Did make offence, his eye did heal it up. *As You Like It*, iii. 5.

Fastidientis est stomachi multa degustare— Tasting so many dishes shows a dainty stomach. *Sen.*

Fasti et nefasti dies—Lucky and unlucky days.

Fat hens are aye ill layers. *Sc. Pr.*

Fat paunches make lean pates, and dainty 45 bits / Make rich the ribs, but bankrupt quite the wits. *Love's L. Lost*, i. 1.

Fata obstant—The fates oppose it.

Fata volentem ducunt, nolentem trahunt—Fate leads the willing, and drags the unwilling.

Fate follows and limits power; power attends and antagonises fate; we must respect fate as natural history, but there is more than natural history. *Emerson.*

Fate hath no voice but the heart's impulses. *Schiller.*

Fate is a distinguished but an expensive tutor. 50 *Goethe.*

Fate is character. *W. Winter.*

Fate is ever better than design. *Thos. Doubleday.*

Fate is known to us as limitations. *Emerson.*

Fate is nothing but the deeds committed in a former state of existence. *Hindu saying.*

Fate is the friend of the good, the guide of the wise, the tyrant of the foolish, the enemy of the bad. *W. R. Alger.*

Fate is unpenetrated causes. *Emerson.*

Fate leads the willing, but drives the stubborn. *Pr.*

Fate made me what I am, may make me nothing ; / But either that or nothing must I be ; / I will not live degraded. *Byron.*

5 Fate steals along with silent tread, / Found oftenest in what least we dread ; / Frowns in the storm with angry brow, / But in the sunshine strikes the blow. *Cowper.*

Fatetur facinus is qui judicium fugit—He who shuns a trial confesses his guilt. *L.*

Father of all ! in every age, / In every clime adored, / By saint, by savage, and by sage, / Jehovah, Jove, or Lord. *Pope.*

Fathers alone a father's heart can know, / What secret tides of sweet enjoyment flow / When brothers love ! But if their hate succeeds, / They wage the war, but 'tis the father bleeds. *Young.*

Fathers first enter bonds to Nature's ends ; / And are her sureties ere they are a friend's. *George Herbert.*

10 Fathers that wear rags / Do make their children blind ; / But fathers that wear bags / Do make their children kind. *King Lear,* ii. 4.

Fathers their children and themselves abuse / That wealth a husband for their daughters choose. *Shirley.*

Fatigatis humus cubile est—To the weary the bare ground is a bed. *Curt.*

Fatta la legge, trovata la malizia—As soon as a law is made its evasion is found out. *It. Pr.*

Faulheit ist der Schlüssel zur Armuth—Sloth is the key to poverty. *Ger. Pr.*

15 Faulheit ist Dummheit des Körpers, und Dummheit Faulheit des Geistes—Sluggishness is stupidity of body, and stupidity sluggishness of spirit. *Seume.*

Faultily faultless, icily regular, splendidly null. *Tennyson.*

Faults are beauties in lover's eyes. *Theocritus.*

Faults are thick when love is thin. *Pr.*

Faute de grives le diable mange des merles— For want of thrushes the devil eats blackbirds. *Fr. Pr.*

20 Faux pas—A false step. *Fr.*

Favete linguis—Favour with words of good omen (*lit.* by your tongues). *Ovid.*

Favourable chance is the god of all men who follow their own devices instead of obeying a law they believe in. *George Eliot.*

Favour and gifts disturb justice. *Dan. Pr.*

Favour is deceitful, and beauty is vain : but a woman that feareth the Lord, she shall be praised. *Bible.*

25 Favours, and especially pecuniary ones, are generally fatal to friendship. *Hor. Smith.*

Favours unused are favours abused. *Sc. Pr.*

Fax mentis honestæ gloria—Glory is the torch of an honourable mind. *M.*

Fax mentis incendium gloriæ—The flame of glory is the torch of the mind. *M.*

Fay ce que voudras—Do as your please. *M.*

30 Fear always springs from ignorance. *Emerson.*

Fear and sorrow are the true characters and inseparable companions of most melancholy. *Burton.*

Fear can keep a man out of danger, but courage only can support him in it. *Pr.*

Fear God and keep his commandments ; for this is the whole duty of man. *Bible.*

Fear God ; honour the king. *St. Peter.*

Fear guards the vineyard. *It. Pr.*   35

Fear guides more to their duty than gratitude. *Goldsmith.*

Fear has many eyes. *Cervantes.*

Fear hath torment. *St. John.*

Fear is an instructor of great sagacity, and the herald of all revolutions. It has boded, and mowed, and gibbered for ages over government and property. *Emerson.*

Fear is described by Spenser to ride in armour, 40 at the clashing whereof he looks afeared of himself. *Peacham.*

Fear is far more painful to cowardice than death to true courage. *Sir P. Sidney.*

Fear is the underminer of all determinations ; and necessity, the victorious rebel of all laws. *Sir P. Sidney.*

Fear is the virtue of slaves ; but the heart that loveth is willing. *Longfellow.*

Fear is worse than fighting. *Gael. Pr.*

Fear not that tyrants shall rule for ever, / Or 45 the priests of the bloody faith ; / They stand on the brink of that mighty river / Whose waves they have tainted with death. *Shelley.*

Fear not the confusion (*Verwirrung*) outside of thee, but that within thee ; strive after unity, but seek it not in uniformity ; strive after repose, but through the equipoise, not through the stagnation (*Stillstand*), of thy activity. *Schiller.*

Fear not the future ; weep not for the past. *Shelley.*

Fear not, then, thou child infirm ; / There's no god dare wrong a worm. *Emerson.*

Fear not where Heaven bids come ; / Heaven's never deaf but when man's heart is dumb. *Quarles.*

Fear of change / Perplexes monarchs. *Milton.* 50

Fear oftentimes restraineth words, but makes not thought to cease. *Lord Vaux.*

Fear sometimes adds wings to the heels, and sometimes nails them to the ground and fetters them from moving. *Montaigne.*

Fear to do base, unworthy things is valour ; / If they be done to us, to suffer them / Is valour too. *Ben Jonson.*

Fear's a fine spur. *Samuel Lover.*

Fear's a large promiser ; who subject live / 55 To that base passion, know not what they give. *Dryden.*

Fears of the brave and follies of the wise. *Johnson.*

Fearfully and wonderfully made. *Bible.*

Fearless minds climb soonest into crowns. 3 *Hen. VI.*, iv. 7.

Feasting makes no friendship. *Pr.*

Feast-won, fast-lost. *Tim. of Athens*, ii. 2.   60

Feather by feather the goose is plucked. *Pr.*

Fecisti enim nos ad te, et cor inquietum donec requiescat in te—Thou hast made us for Thee, and the heart knows no rest until it rests in Thee. *St. Augustine.*

Fecit—He did it.

Fecundi calices quem non fecere disertum ?— Whom have not flowing cups made eloquent? *Hor.*

Fede ed innocenzia son reperte / Solo ne' par-goletti—Faith and innocence are only to be found in little children. *Dante.*

Feeble souls always set to work at the wrong time. *Cardinal de Retz.*

5 Feebleness is sometimes the best security. *Pr.*

Feed a cold and starve a fever. *Pr.*

Feed no man in his sins ; for adulation / Doth make thee parcel-devil in damnation. *George Herbert.*

Feeling comes before reflection. *H. R. Haweis.*

Feeling should be stirred only when it can be sent to labour for worthy ends. *Brooke.*

10 Feelings are always purest and most glowing in the hour of meeting and farewell ; like the glaciers, which are transparent and rose-hued only at sunrise and sunset, but throughout the day grey and cold. *Jean Paul.*

Feelings are like chemicals ; the more you analyse them, the worse they smell. *Kingsley.*

Feelings come and go like light troops follow-ing the victory of the present ; but principles, like troops of the line, are undisturbed, and stand fast. *Jean Paul.*

Feelings, like flowers and butterflies, last longer the later they are delayed. *Jean Paul.*

Fehlst du, lass dich's nicht betrüben ; Denn der Mangel führt zum Lieben ; / Kannst dich nicht vom Fehl befrein, / Wirst du Andern gern verzeihn—Shouldst thou fail, let it not trouble thee, for failure (*lit.* defect) leads to love. If thou canst not free thyself from failure, thou wilt never forgive others. *Goethe.*

15 Feindlich ist die Welt / Und falsch gesinnt ; Es liebt ein jeder nur / Sich selbst—Hostile is the world, and falsely disposed. In it each one loves himself alone. *Schiller.*

Felices errore suo — Happy in their error. *Lucan.*

Felices ter et amplius / Quos irrupta tenet copula, nec, malis / Divulsus quærimoniis, / Suprema citius solvet amor die—Thrice happy they, and more than thrice, whom an unbroken link binds together, and whom love, unimpaired by evil rancour, will not sunder before their last day. *Hor.*

Felicitas nutrix est iracundiæ—Prosperity is the nurse of hasty temper. *Pr.*

Feliciter is sapit, qui periculo alieno sapit— He is happily wise who is wise at the expense of another. *M.*

20 Felicity lies much in fancy. *Pr.*

Felicity, not fluency, of language is a merit. *Whipple.*

Felix, heu nimium felix—Happy, alas ! too happy ! *Virg.*

Felix qui nihil debet—Happy is he who owes nothing.

Felix qui potuit rerum cognoscere causas— Happy he who has succeeded in learning the causes of things. *Virg.*

25 Felix, qui quod amat, defendere fortiter andet —Happy he who dares courageously to defend what he loves. *Ovid.*

Fell luxury ! more perilous to youth than storms or quicksands, poverty or chains. *Hannah More.*

Fell sorrow's tooth doth never rankle more / Than when it bites but lanceth not the sore. *Rich. II.,* i. 3.

Fellowship in treason is a bad ground of con-fidence. *Burke.*

Felo de se—A suicide. *L.*

Female friendships are of rapid growth. 30 *Disraeli.*

Feme covert—A married woman. *L.*

Feme sole—An unmarried woman. *L.*

Femme, argent et vin ont leur bien et leur venin — Women, money, and wine have their blessing and their bane. *Fr. Pr.*

Femme de chambre—A chambermaid. *Fr.*

Femme de charge—A housekeeper. *Fr.* 35

Femme rit quand elle peut, et pleure quand elle veut—A woman laughs when she can, and weeps when she likes. *Fr. Pr.*

Feræ naturæ—Of a wild nature.

Fere libenter homines id quod volunt credunt —Men in general are fain to believe that which they wish to be true. *Cæs.*

Feriis caret necessitas — Necessity knows no holiday.

Ferme fugiendo in media fata ruitur— How 40 often it happens that men fall into the very evils they are striving to avoid. *Liv.*

Ferme modèle—A model farm. *Fr.*

Fern von Menschen wachsen Grundsätze ; unter ihnen Handlungen—Principles develop themselves far from men ; conduct develops among them. *Jean Paul.*

Ferreus assiduo consumitur annulus usu—By constant use an iron ring is consumed. *Ovid.*

Ferro, non gladio—By iron, not by my sword. *M.*

Fervet olla, vivit amicitia—As long as the pot 45 boils, friendship lasts. *Pr.*

Fervet opus—The work goes on with spirit. *Virg.*

Festina lente—Hasten slowly. *Pr.*

Festinare nocet, nocet et cunctatio sæpe ; / Tempore quæque suo qui facit, ille sapit— It is bad to hurry, and delay is often as bad ; he is wise who does everything in its proper time. *Ovid.*

Festinatione nil tutius in discordiis civilibus— Nothing is safer than despatch in civil quarrels. *Tac.*

Festinatio tarda est—Haste is tardy. *Pr.* 50

Fetch a spray from the wood and place it on your mantel-shelf, and your household ornaments will seem plebeian beside its nobler fashion and bearing. It will wave superior there, as if used to a more refined and polished circle. It has a salute and response to all your enthusiasm and heroism. *Thoreau.*

Fête champêtre—A rural feast. *Fr.*

Fêtes des mœurs—Feasts of morals. *Fr.*

Fette Küche, magere Erbschaft—A fat kitchen, a lean legacy. *Ger. Pr.*

Feu de joie—Firing of guns in token of joy. 55 *Fr.*

Few are fit to be entrusted with themselves. *Pr.*

Few are open to conviction, but the majority of men to persuasion. *Goethe.*

Few, few shall part where many meet; The snow shall be their winding-sheet, / And every turf beneath their feet / Shall be a soldier's sepulchre. *Campbell.*

Few have all they need, none all they wish. *R. Southwell.*

Few have borne unconsciously the spell of loveliness. *Whittier.*

Few have the gift of discerning when to have done. *Swift.*

5 Few have wealth, but all must have a home. *Emerson.*

Few love to hear the sins they love to act. *Pericles,* i. 1.

Few may play with the devil and win. *Pr.*

Few men are much worth loving in whom there is not something well worth laughing at. *Hair.*

Few men have been admired by their domestics. *Montaigne.*

10 Few men dare show their thoughts of worst or best. *Byron.*

Few men have any next; they live from hand to mouth without plan, and are ever at the end of their line. *Emerson.*

Few men have imagination enough for the truth of reality. *Goethe.*

Few men have virtue to withstand the highest bidder. *Washington.*

Few minds wear out; more rust out. *Bovee.*

15 Few mortals are so insensible that their affections cannot be gained by mildness, their confidence by sincerity, their hatred by scorn or neglect. *Zimmerman.*

Few of the many wise apothegms which have been uttered, from the time of the seven sages of Greece to that of Poor Richard, have prevented a single foolish action. *Macaulay.*

Few people know how to be old. *La Roche.*

Few persons have courage to appear as good as they really are. *Hair.*

Few spirits are made better by the pain and languor of sickness; as few great pilgrims become eminent saints. *Thomas à Kempis.*

20 Few take wives for God's sake, or for fair looks. *Pr.*

Few things are impossible to diligence and skill. *Johnson.*

Few things are impracticable in themselves; and it is from want of application rather than want of means that men fail of success. *La Roche.*

Few things are more unpleasant than the transaction of business with men who are above knowing or caring what they have to do. *Johnson.*

Fiandeira, fiai manso, que me estorvais, que estou rezando—Spinner, spin quietly, so as not to disturb me; I am praying. *Port. Pr.*

25 Fiar de Dios sobre buena prenda—Trust in God upon good security. *Sp. Pr.*

Fiat experimentum in corpore vili — Let the experiment be made on some worthless body.

Fiat justitiam, pereat mundus—Let justice be done, and the world perish. *Pr.*

Fiat justitia, ruat cœlum—Let justice be done, though the heavens should fall in. *Pr.*

Fiat lux—Let there be light.

Fickleness has its rise in the experience of the 30 deceptiveness of present pleasures, and in ignorance of the vanity of absent ones. *Pascal.*

Ficta voluptatis causa sit proxima veris— Fictions meant to please should have as much resemblance as possible to truth. *Hor.*

Fiction is a potent agent for good in the hands of the good. *Mme. Necker.*

Fiction lags after truth, invention is unfruitful, and imagination cold and barren. *Burke.*

Fiction, while the feigner of it knows that he is feigning, partakes, more than we suspect, of the nature of lying; and has ever an, in some degree, unsatisfactory character. *Carlyle.*

Fictis meminerit nos jocari fabulis—Be it re- 35 membered that we are amusing you with tales of fiction. *Phædr.*

Fidarsi è bene, ma non fidarsi è meglio—To trust one's self is good, but not to trust one's self is better. *It. Pr.*

Fidati era un buon uomo, Nontifidare era meglio—Trust was a good man, Trust not was a better. *It. Pr.*

Fide abrogata, omnis humana societas tollitur —If good faith be abolished, all human society is dissolved. *Livy.*

Fide et amore—By faith and love. *M.*

Fide et fiducia—By faith and confidence. *M.* 40

Fide et fortitudine — By faith and fortitude. *M.*

Fide et literis—By faith and learning. *M.*

Fide, non armis—By good faith, not by arms. *M.*

Fidei coticula crux—The cross is the touchstone of faith. *M.*

Fidei defensor—Defender of the faith. 45

Fideli certa merces—The faithful are certain of their reward. *M.*

Fidelis ad urnam—Faithful to death (*lit.* the ashes-urn). *M.*

Fidelis et audax—Faithful and intrepid. *M.*

Fidélité est de Dieu—Fidelity is of God. *M.*

Fideliter et constanter—Faithfully and firmly. 50 *M.*

Fidelity, diligence, decency, are good and indispensable; yet, without faculty, without light, they will not do the work. *Carlyle.*

Fidelity is the sister of justice. *Hor.*

Fidelity purchased with money, money can destroy. *Sen.*

Fidelius rident tiguria — The laughter of the cottage is more hearty and sincere than that of the court. *Pr.*

Fidem qui perdit perdere ultra nil potest—He 55 who loses his honour has nothing else he can lose. *Pub. Syr.*

Fidem qui perdit, quo se servet relicuo?—Who loses his good name, with what can he support himself in future? *Pub. Syr.*

Fides facit fidem—Confidence awakens confidence. *Pr.*

Fides probata coronat—Approved faith confers a crown. *M.*

Fides Punica—Punic faith; treachery.

Fides servanda est—Faith must be kept. *Plaut* 60

Fides sit penes auctorem—Credit this to the author.

Fides ut anima, unde abiit, eo nunquam redit
—Honour, like life, when once it is lost, is never
recovered. *Pub. Syr.*

Fidus Achates—A faithful companion (of Æneas).
Virg.

Fidus et audax—Faithful and intrepid. *M.*

Fie! fie! how wayward is this foolish love, /
That like a testy babe will scratch the
nurse, / And presently, all humbled, kiss
the rod. *Two Gent. of Verona*, i. 2.

5 Fiel pero desdichado—True though unfortunate.
Sp.

Fierce fiery warriors fought upon the clouds, /
In ranks and squadrons, and right form of
war, / Which drizzled blood upon the Capitol.
Jul. Cæs., ii. 2.

Fieri facias—See it be done. *A writ empowering a sheriff to levy the amount of a debt or
damages.*

Fight on, thou brave true heart, and falter not,
through dark fortune and through bright;
the cause thou fightest for, so far as it is
true, is very sure of victory. *Carlyle.*

Fight the good fight. *St. Paul.*

10 Filii non plus possessionum quam morborum
hæredes sumus—We sons are heirs no less to
diseases than to estates.

Filius nullius—The son of no one; a bastard.
L.

Filius terræ — A son of the earth; one low-
born.

Fille de chambre—A chambermaid. *Fr.*

Fille de joie—A woman of pleasure; a prostitute.
Fr.

15 Fin contre fin—Diamond cut diamond. *Fr.*

Fin de siècle—Up to date. *Fr.*

Find earth where grows no weed, and you
may find a heart where no error grows.
Knowles.

Find employment for the body, and the mind
will find enjoyment for itself. *Pr.*

Find fault, when you must find fault, in private,
if possible, and some time after the offence,
rather than at the time. *Sydney Smith.*

20 Find mankind where thou wilt, thou findest it
in living movement, in progress faster or
slower; the phœnix soars aloft, hovers with
outstretched wings, filling earth with her
music; or, as now, she sinks, and with
spheral swan-song immolates herself in flame,
that she may soar the higher and sing the
clearer. *Carlyle.*

Find out men's wants and will, / And meet
them there. All worldly joys go less / To
the one joy of doing kindnesses. *Herbert.*

Finding your able man, and getting him invested with the symbols of ability, is the
business, well or ill accomplished, of all
social procedure whatsoever in this world.
Carlyle.

Fine art is that in which the hand, the head,
and the heart of man go together; the head
inferior to the heart, and the hand inferior to
both heart and head. *Ruskin.*

Fine by defect and delicately weak. *Pope.*

25 Fine by degrees and beautifully less. *Prior.*

Fine feathers make fine birds. *Pr.*

Fine feelings, without vigour of reason, are
in the situation of the extreme feathers of a
peacock's tail—dragging in the mud. *John
Foster.*

Fine manners are the mantle of fair minds.
None are truly great without this ornament.
A. B. Alcott.

Fine manners need the support of fine manners
in others. *Emerson.*

Fine sense and exalted sense are not half so 30
useful as common sense. *Pope.*

Fine speeches are the instruments of knaves /
Or fools, that use them when they want
good sense; / Honesty needs no disguise or
ornament. *Otway.*

Fine words without deeds go not far. *Dan.
Pr.*

Finem respice—Have regard to the end.

Finge datos currus, quid agas?—Suppose the
chariot (of the sun) committed to you, what
would you do? *Apollo to Phaethon in Ovid.*

Fingers were made before forks, and hands 35
before knives. *Swift.*

Fingunt se medicos quivis idiota, sacerdos,
Judæus, monachus, histrio, rasor, anus—Any
untrained person, priest, Jew, monk, playactor,
barber, or old wife is ready to prescribe for you
in sickness. *Pr.*

Finis coronat opus—The end crowns the work,
i.e., first enables us to determine its merits.
Pr.

Fire and sword are but slow engines of destruction in comparison with the tongue of
the babbler. *Steele.*

Fire and water are good servants but bad
masters. *Pr.*

Fire in the heart sends smoke into the head. 40
Ger. Pr.

Fire is the best of servants; but what a
master! *Carlyle.*

Fire maks an auld wife nimble. *Sc. Pr.*

Fire that's closest kept burns most of all. *Two
Gent. of Verona*, i. 2.

Fire trieth iron, and temptation a just man.
Thomas à Kempis.

Firmior quo paratior—The stronger the better 45
prepared. *M.*

Firmness, both in sufferance and exertion,
is a character I would wish to possess. I
have always despised the whining yelp of
complaint and the cowardly feeble resolve.
Burns.

First assay / To stuff thy mind with solid
bravery; / Then march on gallant: get substantial worth: / Boldness gilds finely, and
will set it forth. *George Herbert.*

First cast the beam out of thine own eye, and
then thou shalt see clearly to cast out the
mote out of thy brother's eye. *Jesus.*

First catch your hare. *Mrs. Glass's advice to
the housewife.*

First come, first served. *Pr.* 50

First deserve and then desire. *Sc. Pr.*

First flower of the earth and first gem of the
sea. *Moore.*

First keep thyself in peace, and then thou
shalt be able to keep peace among others.
Thomas à Kempis.

First must the dead letter of religion own
itself dead, and drop piecemeal into dust, if
the living spirit of religion, freed from its
charnel-house, is to arise in us, new-born of
heaven, and with new healing under its
wings. *Carlyle.*

First resolutions are not always the wisest, but they are usually the most honest. *Lessing.*

First worship God ; he that forgets to pray / Bids not himself good-morrow nor good day. *T. Randolph.*

Fishes live in the sea, . . . as men do on land—the great ones eat up the little ones. *Pericles,* ii. 1.

Fit cito per multas præda petita manus—The spoil that is sought by many hands quickly accumulates. *Ovid.*

5 Fit erranti medicina confessio—Confession is as healing medicine to him who has erred.

Fit fabricando faber—A smith becomes a smith by working at the forge. *Pr.*

Fit in dominatu servitus, in servitute dominatus—In the master there is the servant, and in the servant the master (*lit.* in masterhood is servanthood, in servanthood masterhood). *Cic.*

Fit scelus indulgens per nubila sæcula virtus —In times of trouble leniency becomes crime.

Fit the foot to the shoe, not the shoe to the foot. *Port. Pr.*

10 Fit words are fine, but often fine words are not fit. *Pr.*

Five great intellectual professions have hitherto existed in every civilised nation : the soldier's, to defend it ; the pastor's, to teach it ; the physician's, to keep it in health ; the lawyer's, to enforce justice in it ; and the merchant's, to provide for it ; and the duty of all these men is, on due occasion, to die for it. *Ruskin.*

Five minutes of to-day are worth as much to me as five minutes in the next millennium. *Emerson.*

Fix'd to no spot is happiness sincere ; / 'Tis nowhere to be found, or everywhere. *Pope.*

Fixed like a plant on his peculiar spot, / To draw nutrition, propagate, and rot. *Pope.*

15 Flagrante bello—During the war.

Flagrante delicto—In the very act.

Flames rise and sink by fits ; at last they soar / In one bright flame, and then return no more. *Dryden.*

Flamma fumo est proxima—Where there is smoke there is fire (*lit.* flame is very close to smoke). *Plaut.*

Flatter not the rich ; neither do thou appear willingly before the great. *Thomas à Kempis.*

20 Flatterers are cats that lick before, and scratch behind. *Ger. Pr.*

Flatterers are the bosom enemies of princes. *South.*

Flatterers are the worst kind of traitors. *Raleigh.*

Flattery brings friends, but the truth begets enmity. *Pr.*

Flattery corrupts both the receiver and the giver, and adulation is not of more service to the people than to kings. *Burke.*

25 Flattery is a base coin, to which only our vanity gives currency. *La Roche.*

Flattery is the bellows blows up sin ; / The thing which is flattered, but a spark, / To which that blast gives heat and stronger glowing ; / Whereas reproof, obedient and in order, / Fits kings, as they are men, for they may err. *Pericles,* i. 2.

Flattery is the destruction of all good fellowship. *Disraeli.*

Flattery is the food of pride, and may be well assimilated to those cordials which hurt the constitution while they exhilarate the spirits. *Arliss' Lit. Col.*

Flattery labours under the odious charge of servility. *Tac.*

Flattery sits in the parlour when plain deal- 30 ing is kicked out of doors. *Pr.*

Flattery's the turnpike road to Fortune's door. *Walcot.*

Flebile ludibrium—A " tragic farce ; " a farce to weep at.

Flebit, et insignis tota cantabitur urbe— He shall rue it, and be a marked man and the talk of the whole town. *Hor.*

Flectere si nequeo superos, Acheronta movebo —If I cannot influence the gods, I will stir up Acheron. *Virg.*

Flecti, non frangi—To bend, not to break. *M.* 35

Flee sloth, for the indolence of the soul is the decay of the body. *Cato.*

Flee you ne'er so fast, your fortune will be at your tail. *Sc. Pr.*

Flesh will warm in a man to his kin against his will. *Gael. Pr.*

Flet victus, victor interiit—The conquered one weeps, the conqueror is ruined.

Fleur d'eau—Level with the water. *Fr.* 40

Fleur de terre—Level with the land. *Fr.*

Fleurs-de-lis—Lilies. *Fr.*

Fleying (frightening) a bird is no the way to catch it. *Sc. Pr.*

Flies are easier caught with honey than vinegar. *Fr. Pr.*

Fling away ambition ; / By that sin fell the 45 angels ; how can man, then, / The image of his Maker, hope to win by it ? *Hen. VIII.,* iii. 2.

Flints may be melted, but an ungrateful heart cannot ; no, not by the strongest and noblest flame. *South.*

Floriferis ut apes in saltibus omnia libant— As bees sip of everything in the flowery meads. *Lucret.*

Flour cannot be sown and seed-corn ought not to be ground. *Goethe.*

Flowers and fruits are always fit presents— flowers, because they are a proud assertion that a ray of beauty outvalues all the utilities of man. *Emerson.*

Flowers are the beautiful hieroglyphics of 50 Nature, by which she indicates how much she loves us. *Goethe.*

Flowers are the pledges of fruit. *Dan. Pr.*

Flowers are the sweetest things God ever made and forgot to put a soul into. *Ward Beecher.*

Flowers never emit so sweet and strong a fragrance as before a storm. *Jean Paul.*

Flowers of rhetoric in sermons and serious discourses are like the blue and red flowers in corn, pleasing to those who come only for amusement, but prejudicial to him who would reap profit from it. *Pope.*

Fluctus in simpulo exitare—To raise a tempest 55 in a teapot. *Cic.*

Fluvius cum mari certas—You but a river, and contending with the ocean. *Pr.*

Fly idleness, which yet thou canst not fly / By dressing, mistressing, and compliment. / If these take up thy day, the sun will cry / Against thee; for his light was only lent. *George Herbert.*

Fœdum inceptu, fœdum exitu—Bad in the beginning, bad in the end. *Livy.*

Fœnum habet in cornu, longe fuge, dummodo risum / Excutiat sibi, non hic cuiquam parcit amico— He has (like a wild bull) a wisp of hay on his horn: fly afar from him; if only he raise a laugh for himself, there is no friend he would spare. *Hor.*

Foliis tantum ne carmina manda; / Ne turbata volent rapidis ludibria ventis—Only commit not thy oracles to leaves, lest they fly about dispersed, the sport of rushing winds. *Virg.*

5 Folk canna help a' their kin (relatives). *Sc. Pr.*

Folk wi' lang noses aye tak' till themsels. *Sc. Pr.*

Folks as have no mind to be o' use have always the luck to be out o' the road when there's anything to be done. *George Eliot.*

Folks must put up with their own kin as they put up with their own noses. *George Eliot.*

Folle est la brébis qui au loup se confesse—It is a silly sheep that makes the wolf her confessor. *Fr. Pr.*

10 Follow love and it will flee, flee love and it will follow thee. *Pr.*

Follow the copy though it fly out of the window. *Printer's saying.*

Follow the customs or fly the country. *Dan. Pr.*

Follow the devil faithfully, you are sure to go to the devil. *Carlyle.*

Follow the river, and you will get to the sea. *Pr.*

15 Follow the road, and you will come to an inn. *Port. Pr.*

Follow the wise few rather than the vulgar many. *It. Pr.*

Folly, as it grows in years, / The more extravagant appears. *Butler.*

Folly ends where genuine hope begins. *Cowper.*

Folly is its own burden. *Sen.*

20 Folly is the most incurable of maladies. *Sp. Pr.*

Folly, letting down buckets into empty wells, and growing old with drawing nothing up. *Cowper.*

Folly loves the martyrdom of fame. *Byron.*

Fond fools / Promise themselves a name from building churches. *Randolph.*

Fond gaillard—A basis of joy or gaiety. *Fr.*

25 Fons et origo mali—The source and origin of the mischief.

Fons malorum—The origin of evil.

Fons omnium viventium—The fountain of all living things.

Fontes ipsi sitiunt—Even the fountains complain of thirst. *Pr.*

Food can only be got out of the ground, or the air, or the sea. *Ruskin.*

30 Food fills the wame and keeps us livin'; / Though life's a gift no worth receivin', / When heavy dragg'd wi' pine and grievin'; / But oil'd by thee, the wheels o' life gae doon-hill scrievin' / Wi' rattlin' glee. *Burns, on Scotch drink.*

Food for powder. *1 Hen. IV., iv. 2.*

Fool before all is he who does not instantly seize the right moment; who has what he loves before his eyes, and yet swerves (*schweift*) aside. *Platen.*

Fool not; for all may have, / If they dare try, a glorious life or grave. *George Herbert.*

Fool, not to know that love endures no tie, / And Jove but laughs at lovers' perjury. *Dryden.*

Fool of fortune. *King Lear, iv. 6.* 35

Fooled thou must be, though wisest of the wise; / Then be the fool of virtue, not of vice. *Persian saying.*

Foolish legislation is a rope of sand, which perishes in the twisting. *Emerson.*

Foolish people are a hundred times more averse to meet with wise people than wise people are to meet with foolish. *Saadi.*

Fools and bairns shouldna see things half done. *Sc. Pr.*

Fools and obstinate men make lawyers rich. 40 *Pr.*

Fools are apt to imitate only the defects of their betters. *Swift.*

Fools are aye fond o' flittin', and wise men o' sittin'. *Sc. Pr.*

Fools are aye seeing ferlies (wonderful things). *Sc. Pr.*

Fools are known by looking wise. *Butler.*

Fools are my theme; let satire be my song. 45 *Byron.*

Fools ask what's o'clock, but wise men know their time. *Pr.*

Fools build houses, and wise men buy them. *Ger. Pr.*

Fools can indeed find fault, but cannot act more wisely. *Langbern.*

Fools for arguments use wagers. *Butler.*

Fools grant whate'er ambition craves, / And 50 men, once ignorant, are slaves. *Pope.*

Fools grow of themselves without sowing or planting. *Rus. Pr.*

Fools grow without watering. *Pr.*

Fools invent fashions and wise men follow them. *Fr. Pr.*

Fools learn nothing from wise men, but wise men much from fools. *Dut. Pr.*

Fools make a mock at sin. *Bible.* 55

Fools mak' feasts, and wise men eat them. / Wise men mak' jests, and fools repeat them. *Sc. Pr.*

Fools may our scorn, not envy raise, / For envy is a kind of praise. *Gay.*

Fools measure actions after they are done by the event; wise men beforehand, by the rules of reason and right. *Bp. Hale.*

Fools need no passport. *Dan. Pr.*

Fools ravel and wise men redd (unravel). *Sc. Pr.* 60

Fools, to talking ever prone, / Are sure to make their follies known. *Gay.*

Fools with bookish knowledge are children with edged weapons; they hurt themselves and put others in pain. *Zimmermann.*

Footpaths give a private, human touch to the landscape that roads do not. They are sacred to the human foot. They have the sentiment of domesticity, and suggest the way to cottage doors and to simple, primitive times. *John Burroughs.*

Foppery is never cured; once a coxcomb, always a coxcomb. *Johnson.*

For age, long age! / Nought else divides us from the fresh young days / Which men call ancient. *Lewis Morris.*

For a genuine man it is no evil to be poor. *Carlyle.*

For a just man falleth seven times, and riseth up again. *Bible.*

5 For a large conscience is all one, / And signifies the same with none. *Hudibras.*

For all a rhetorician's rules / Teach nothing but to name his tools. *Butler.*

For all he did he had a reason, / For all he said, a word in season; / And ready ever was to quote / Authorities for what he wrote. *Butler.*

For all men live and judge amiss / Whose talents do not jump with his. *Butler.*

For all right judgment of any man or thing it is useful, nay, essential, to see his good qualities before pronouncing on his bad. *Carlyle.*

10 For all their luxury was doing good. *L. Garth.*

For an honest man half his wits are enough; for a knave, the whole are too little. *It Pr.*

For an orator delivery is everything. *Goethe.*

For a republic you must have men. *Amiel.*

For as a fly that goes to bed / Rests with his tail above his head, / So, in this mongrel state of ours, / The rabble are the supreme powers. *Butler.*

15 For as a ship without a helm is tossed to and fro by the waves, so the man who is careless and forsaketh his purpose is many ways tempted. *Thomas à Kempis.*

For a' that, and a' that, / Our toils obscure, and a' that; / The rank is but the guinea's stamp, / The man's the gowd for a' that. *Burns.*

For a tint (lost) thing carena. *Sc. Pr.*

For aught I see, they are as sick that surfeit with too much as they that starve with nothing. *Mer. of Ven.*, i. 2.

For aught that ever I could read, / Could ever hear by tale or history, / The course of true love never did run smooth. *Mid. N.'s Dream*, i. 1.

20 For a web begun God sends thread. *Fr. and It. Pr.*

For behaviour, men learn it, as they take diseases, one of another. *Bacon.*

For blessings ever wait on virtuous deeds, / And though a late, a sure reward succeeds. *Congreve.*

For Brutus is an honourable man, / So are they all, all honourable men. *Jul. Cæs.*, iii. 2.

For captivity, perhaps your poor watchdog is as sorrowful a type as you will easily find. *Ruskin.*

25 For contemplation he and valour form'd, / For softness she and sweet attractive grace; / He for God only, she for God in him, / His fair large front and eye sublime declared. *Milton.*

For cowards the road of desertion should be left open; they will carry over to the enemy nothing but their fears. *Bovee.*

For dear to gods and men is sacred song. *Pope.*

For ebbing resolution ne'er returns, / But falls still further from its former shore. *Home.*

For emulation hath a thousand sons, / That one by one pursue; if you give way, / Or hedge aside from the direct forthright, / Like to an enter'd tide, they all rush by, / And leave you hindmost. *Troil. and Cres.* iii. 3.

For ever and a day. *As You Like It*, iv. 1.   30

For ever is not a category that can establish itself in this world of time. *Carlyle.*

For every dawn that breaks brings a new world, / And every budding bosom a new life. *Lewis Morris.*

For every grain of wit there is a grain of folly. *Emerson.*

For every ten jokes thou hast got an hundred enemies. *Sterne.*

For everything you have missed, you have 35 gained something else; and for everything you gain, you lose something. *Emerson.*

For fate has wove the thread of life with pain, / And twins e'en from the birth are misery and man. *Pope.*

For faith, and peace, and mighty love / That from the Godhead flow, / Show'd them the life of heaven above / Springs from the earth below. *Emerson.*

For fault o' wise men fools sit on binks (seats, benches). *Sc. Pr.*

For fools rush in where angels fear to tread. *Pope.*

For forms of government let fools contest; / 40 Whate'er is best administered is best. *Pope.*

For Freedom's battle, once begun, / Bequeath'd by bleeding sire to son, / Though baffled oft, is ever won. *Byron.*

For glances beget ogles, ogles sighs, / Sighs wishes, wishes words, and words a letter; / And then God knows what mischief may arise / When love links two young people in one fetter. *Byron.*

For gold the merchant ploughs the main, / The farmer ploughs the manor; / But glory is the soldier's prize, / The soldier's wealth is honour. *Burns.*

For good and evil must in our actions meet; / Wicked is not much worse than indiscreet. *Donne.*

For greatest scandal waits on greatest state. 45 *Shakespeare.*

For grief indeed is love, and grief beside. *Mrs. Browning.*

For he being dead, with him is beauty slain, / And, beauty dead, black chaos comes again. *Shakespeare.*

For he, by geometric scale, / Could take the size of pots of ale. *Butler.*

For· he is but a bastard to the time / That doth not smack of observation. *King John*, i. 1.

For he lives twice who can at once employ / 50 The present well and e'en the past enjoy. *Pope.*

For he that fights and runs away / May live to fight another day; / But he who is in battle slain, / Can never rise and fight again. *Goldsmith.*

For he that worketh high and wise, / Nor pauses in his plan, / Will take the sun out of the skies / Ere freedom out of man. *Emerson.*

For his bounty, / There was no winter in't ; an autumn 'twas, / That grew the more by reaping. *Ant. and Cleop.*, v. 2.

For his chaste Muse employed her heaven-taught lyre / None but the noblest passions to inspire, / Not one immoral, one corrupted thought, / One line which, dying, he could wish to blot. *Littelton on Thomson.*

For hope is but the dream of those that wake. *Prior.*

5 For I am nothing if not critical. *Othello*, ii. 1.

For I am full of spirit, and resolved / To meet all perils very constantly. *Jul. Cæs.*, v. 1.

For I say this is death, and the sole death, / When a man's loss comes to him from his gain, / Darkness from light, from knowledge ignorance, / And lack of love from love made manifest. *Browning.*

For it so falls out, / That what we have we prize not to the worth / While we enjoy it, but being lack'd and lost, / Why, then we rack the value. *Much Ado*, iv. 1.

For it stirs the blood in an old man's heart, / And makes his pulses fly, / To catch the thrill of a happy voice / And the light of a pleasant eye. *N. P. Willis.*

10 For just experience tells, in every soil, / That those that think must govern those that toil. *Goldsmith.*

For knowledge is a barren tree and bare, / Bereft of God, and duty but a word, / And strength but tyranny, and love, desire, / And purity a folly. *Lewis Morris.*

For knowledge is a steep which few may climb, / While duty is a path which all may tread. *Lewis Morris.*

For let our finger ache, and it endues / Our other healthful members ev'n to that sense / Of pain. *Othello*, iii. 4.

For loan oft loses both itself and friend. *Ham.*, i. 3.

15 For love of grace, / Lay not the flattering unction to your soul / That not your trespass but my madness speaks. *Ham.*, iii. 4.

For lovers' eyes more sharply sighted be / Than other men's, and in dear love's delight / See more than any other eyes can see. *Spenser.*

For man's well-being faith is properly the one thing needful; with it, martyrs, without weak, can cheerfully endure the shame and the cross ; and without it, worldlings puke up their sick existence by suicide in the midst of luxury. *Carlyle.*

For man there is but one misfortune, when some idea lays hold of him which exerts no influence upon his active life, or still more, which withdraws him from it. *Goethe.*

For men are brought to worse diseases / By taking physic than diseases, / And therefore commonly recover / As soon as doctors give them over. *Butler.*

20 For men at most differ as heaven and earth, / But women, worst and best, as heaven and hell. *Tennyson.*

For men cherish love, for gods reverence. *Grillparzer.*

For men may come and men may go, / But I go on for ever. *Tennyson.*

For modes of faith let graceless zealots fight ; / His can't be wrong whose life is in the right. *Pope.*

For murder, though it hath no tongue, will speak / With most miraculous organ. *Ham.*, ii. 2.

For my means, I'll husband them so well, / 25 They shall go far with little. *Ham.*, iv. 5.

For my name and memory I leave to men's charitable speeches, to foreign nations, and to the next ages. *Bacon.*

For nought so vile that on the earth doth live, / But to the earth some special good doth give ; / Nor aught so good, but, strain'd from that fair use, / Revolts from true birth, stumbling on abuse. *Rom. and Jul.*, ii. 3.

For now we see through a glass darkly, but then face to face. *St. Paul.*

For oaths are straws, men's faith are wafer cakes, / And holdfast is the only dog, my duck. *Hen. V.*, ii. 3.

For of all sad words of tongue or pen, / The 30 saddest were these : " It might have been." *Whittier.*

For of fortunes sharpe adversite, / The worst kind of infortune is this, / A man that hath been in prosperite, / And it remember when it passéd is. *Chaucer.*

For of the soul the body form doth take, / For soul is form, and doth the body make. *Spenser.*

For one man who can stand prosperity, there are a hundred that will stand adversity. *Carlyle.*

For one person who can think, there are at least a hundred who can observe. An accurate observer is, no doubt, rare ; but an accurate thinker is far rarer. *Buckle.*

For one rich man that is content there are a 35 hundred who are not. *Pr.*

For one word a man is often deemed wise, and for one word he is often deemed foolish. *Confucius.*

For our pleasure, the lackeyed train, the slow parading pageant, with all the gravity of grandeur, moves in review ; a single coat, or a single footman, answers all the purposes of the most indolent refinement as well ; and those who have twenty, may be said to keep one for their own pleasure, and the other nineteen merely for ours. *Goldsmith.*

For pity is the virtue of the law, / And none but tyrants use it cruelly. *Timon of Athens*, iii. 5.

For pleasures past I do not grieve, / Nor perils gathering near ; / My greatest grief is that I leave / Nothing that claims a tear. *Byron.*

For poems to have beauty of style is not 40 enough ; they must have pathos also, and lead at will the hearer's soul. *Hor.*

For present grief there is always a remedy. However much thou sufferest, hope. The greatest happiness of man is hope. *Leopold Schefer.*

For rarely do we meet in one combined / A beauteous body and a virtuous mind. *Juv.*

For rhetoric, he could not ope / His mouth, but out there flew a trope. *Butler.*

For rhyme the rudder is of verses, / With which, like ships, they steer their courses. *Butler.*

For right is right, since God is God, / And right the day must win ; / To doubt would be disloyalty, / To falter would be sin. *F. W. Faber.*

For sacred even to gods is misery. *Pope.*

5 For Satan finds some mischief still / For idle hands to do. *Watts.*

For slander lives upon succession, / For ever housed where it gets possession. *Comedy of Errors, iii. 1.*

For solitude sometimes is best society, / And short retirement urges sweet return. *Milton.*

For sufferance is the badge of all our tribe. *Mer. of Ven., i. 3.*

For suffering and enduring there is no remedy but striving and doing. *Carlyle.*

10 For that fine madness still he did retain / Which rightly should possess a poet's brain. *Drayton.*

For the apotheosis of Reason we have substituted that of Instinct ; and we call everything instinct which we find in ourselves, and for which we cannot trace any rational foundation. *J. S. Mill.*

For the bow cannot possibly stand always bent, nor can human nature or human frailty subsist without some lawful recreation. *Cervantes.*

For the buyer a hundred eyes are too few, for the seller one is enough. *It. Pr.*

For thee the family of man has no use ; it rejects thee ; thou art wholly as a dissevered limb : so be it ; perhaps it is better so. *Carlyle, or Teufelsdröckh rather, arrived at the " Centre of Indifference, through which whoso travels from the Negative Pole to the Positive must necessarily pass."*

15 For the fashion of this world passeth away. *St. Paul.*

For the gay beams of lightsome day / Gild but to flout the ruins grey. *Scott.*

For the greatest crime of man is that he was born. *Calderon.*

For the narrow mind, whatever he attempts, is still a trade ; for the higher, an art ; and the highest, in doing one thing does all ; or, to speak less paradoxically, in the one thing which he does rightly, he sees the likeness of all that is done rightly. *Goethe.*

For the rain it raineth every day. *Lear, iii. 2.*

20 For there's nae luck aboot the hoose, / There's nae luck ava', / There's little pleesure in the hoose / When oor guidman's awa'. *W. J. Mickle.*

For there was never yet philosopher / That could endure the toothache patiently. *Much Ado, v. 1.*

For the sake of one good action a hundred evil actions should be condoned. *Chinese Pr.*

For the son of man there is no noble crown, well-worn or even ill-worn, but is a crown of thorns. *Carlyle.*

For the true the price is paid before you enjoy it ; for the false, after you enjoy it. *John Foster.*

For the world was built in order, / And the 25 atoms march in tune ; / Rhyme the pipe, and the Time the warder, / The sun obeys them and the moon. *Emerson.*

For they can conquer who believe they can. *Dryden.*

For 'tis a truth well known to most, / That whatsoever thing is lost, / We seek it, ere it comes to light, / In every cranny but the right. *Cowper.*

For 'tis the mind that makes the body rich : / And as the sun breaks through the darkest clouds, / So honour peereth in the meanest habit. *Tam. of Shrew, iv. 3.*

For to him that is joined to all the living there is hope : for a living dog is better than a dead lion. *Bible.*

For to see and eek for to be seye. *Chaucer.* 30

For truth has such a face and such a mien, / As to be loved needs only to be seen. *Dryden.*

For truth is precious and divine, / Too rich a pearl for carnal swine. *Butler.*

For use almost can change the stamp of Nature, / And either curb the devil or throw him out / With wondrous potency. *Ham., iii. 4.*

For us, the winds do blow, / The earth doth rest, heaven move, and fountains flow ; / Nothing we see but means our good, / As our delight, or as our treasure ; / The whole is either our cupboard of food, / Or cabinet of pleasure. *George Herbert.*

For virtue's sake I am here ; but if a man, 35 for his task, forgets and sacrifices all, why shouldst not thou ? *Jean Paul.*

For virtue's self may too much zeal be had ; / The worst of madmen is a saint run mad. *Pope.*

For want of a block a man will stumble at a straw. *Swift.*

For want of a nail the shoe was lost, for want of a shoe the horse was lost, and for want of a horse the rider was lost. *Ben. Franklin.*

For wealth is all things that conduce / To man's destruction or his use ; / A standard both to buy and sell / All things from heaven down to hell. *Butler.*

For what are men who grasp at praise sublime, / 40 But bubbles on the rapid stream of time, / That rise and fall, that swell and are no more, / Born and forgot, ten thousand in an hour. *Young.*

For what are they all in their high conceit, / When man in the bush with God may meet ? *Emerson.*

For what thou hast not, still thou striv'st to get, / And what thou hast, forgetst. *Meas. for Meas., iii. 1.*

For when disputes are wearied out, / 'Tis interest still resolves the doubt. *Butler.*

For where is any author in the world / Teaches such beauty as a woman's eye? *Love's L. Lost, iv. 3.*

For while a youth is lost in soaring thought, / 45 And while a mind grows sweet and beautiful, / And while a spring-tide coming lights the earth, / And while a child, and while a flower is born, / And while one wrong cries for redress and finds / A soul to answer, still the world is young. *Lewis Morris.*

For whom ill is fated, him it will strike. *Gael Pr.*

For whom the heart of man shuts out, / Straightway the heart of God takes in, / And fences them all round about / With silence 'mid the world's loud din. *Lowell.*

For who to dumb forgetfulness a prey, / This pleasing anxious being e'er resigned, / Left the warm precincts of the cheerful day, / Nor cast one longing lingering look behind? *Gray.*

For who would lose, / Though full of pain, this intellectual being, / Those thoughts that wander through eternity ; / To perish rather, swallowed up and lost, / In the wide womb of uncreated night? *Milton.*

For wisdom cries out in the streets, and no man regards it. 1 *Henry IV.*, i. 2.

5 For youth no less becomes / The light and careless livery that it wears, / Than settled age his sables and his weeds, / Importing health and graveness. *Ham.*, iv. 7.

Forbear to judge, for we are sinners all. 2 *Hen. VI.*, iii. 3.

Forbearance is not acquittance. *Ger. Pr.*

Forbid a fool do a thing, and that he will do. *Sc. Pr.*

Forbidden fruit is sweetest. *Pr.*

10 Force and right rule everything in this world ; force till right is ready. *Joubert.* (?)

Force can never annul right. *Berryer.*

Force is no argument. *John Bright.*

Forced love does not last. *Dut. Pr.*

Forced prayers are no gude for the soul. *Sc. Pr.*

15 Force n'a pas droit—Might knows no right. *Fr. Pr.*

Force rules the world, and not opinion, but opinion is that which makes use of force. *Pascal.*

Force without forecast is of little avail. *Pr.*

Foresight is indeed necessary in trusting, but still more necessary in distrusting. *Cötvös.*

Forewarned, forearmed. *Cervantes.*

20 Forget the hours of thy distress, but never forget what they taught thee. *Gessner.*

Forget thyself to marble. *Milton.*

Forgetting of a wrong is a mild revenge. *Pr.*

Forgetting one's self, or knowing one's self, around these everything turns. *Auerbach.*

Forgiveness is better than revenge ; for forgiveness is the sign of a gentle nature, but revenge the sign of a savage nature. *Epictetus.*

25 Forgiveness is commendable, but apply not ointment to the wound of an oppressor. *Saadi.*

Forgiveness is the divinest of victories. *Schiller.*

Forgiveness to the injured does belong, / But they ne'er pardon who have done the wrong. *Dryden.*

Forgiven is not forgotten. *Ger. Pr.*

Forgotten pains, when follow gains. *Sc. Pr.*

30 Forma bonum fragile est—Beauty is a fragile good. *Ovid.*

Forma viros neglecta decet—Neglect of appearance becomes men. *Ovid.*

Formerly it was the fashion to preach the natural ; now it is the ideal. *Schlegel.*

Formerly the richest countries were those in which Nature was most bountiful ; now the richest countries are those in which man is most active. *Buckle.*

Formerly when great fortunes were only made in war, war was business ; but now when great fortunes are only made by business, business is war. *Bovee.*

Formidabilior cervorum exercitus, duce leone, 35 quam leonum cervo—An army of stags would be more formidable commanded by a lion, than one of lions commanded by a stag. *Pr.*

Formosa facies muta commendatio est—A handsome face is a mute recommendation. *Pub. Syr.*

Formosos sæpe inveni pessimos, / Et turpi facie multos cognovi optimos—I have often found good-looking people to be very base, and I have known many ugly people most estimable. *Phæd.*

Forms which grow round a substance will be true, good ; forms which are consciously put round a substance, bad. *Carlyle.*

Formulas are the very skin and muscular tissue of a man's life ; and a most blessed indispensable thing, so long as they have vitality withal, and are a living skin and tissue to him. *Carlyle.*

Forsake not God till you find a better maister. 40 *Sc. Pr.*

Forsan et hæc olim meminisse juvabit ; Durate, et vosmet rebus servate secundis—Perhaps it will be a delight to us some day to recall these misfortunes. Bear them, therefore, and reserve yourselves for better times. *Virg.*

Forsan miseros meliora sequentur—Perhaps a better fortune awaits the unhappy. *Virg.*

Fors et virtus miscentur in unum—Fortune and valour are blended into one. *Virg.*

Forte è l'aceto di vin dolce—Strong is vinegar from sweet wine. *It. Pr.*

Forte et fidele—Strong and loyal. *M.* 45

Fortem facit vicina libertas senem — The approach of liberty makes even an old man brave. *Sen.*

Fortem posce animum mortis terrore carentem, / Qui spatium vitæ extremum inter munera ponat Naturæ—Pray for a strong soul free from the fear of death, which regards the final period of life among the gifts of Nature. *Juv.*

Fortes creantur fortibus et bonis ; / Est in juvencis, est in equis patrum / Virtus, nec imbellem feroces / Progenerant aquilæ columbam—Brave men are generated by brave and good : there is in steers and in horses the virtue of their sires, nor does the fierce eagle beget the unwarlike dove. *Hor.*

Forte scutum salus ducum—The safety of leaders is a strong shield. *M.*

Fortes fortuna adjuvat — Fortune assists the 50 brave. *Ter.*

Fortes in fine assequendo et suaves in modo assequendi simus—Let us be resolute in prosecuting our purpose and mild in the manner of attaining it. *Aquaviva.*

Forti et fideli nihil difficile—To the brave and true nothing is difficult. *M.*

Fortify courage with the true rampart of patience. *Sir P. Sidney.*

Fortify yourself with moderation ; for this is an impregnable fortress. *Epictetus.*

Fortior et potentior est dispositio legis quam hominis—The disposition of the law is stronger and more potent than that of man. *L.*

Fortis cadere, cedere non potest—A brave man may fall, but cannot yield. *M.*

Fortis et constantis animi est, non perturbari in rebus asperis—It shows a brave and resolute spirit not to be agitated in exciting circumstances. *Cic.*

Fortis sub forte fatiscet — A brave man will yield to a brave. *M.*

5 Fortiter et recte—Courageously and honourably. *M.*

Fortiter ferendo vincitur malum quod evitari non potest—By bravely enduring it, an evil which cannot be avoided is overcome. *Pr.*

Fortiter, fideliter, feliciter — Boldly, faithfully, successfully. *M.*

Fortiter geret crucem—He will bravely support the cross. *M.*

Fortiter in re, suaviter in modo—Vigorous and resolute in deed, gentle in manner.

10 Fortitude is the guard and support of the other virtues. *Locke.*

Fortitude is the marshal of thought, the armour of the will, and the fort of reason. *Bacon.*

Fortitude is to be seen in toils and dangers; temperance in the denial of sensual pleasures; prudence in the choice between good and evil; justice in awarding to every one his due. *Cic.*

Fortitude rises upon an opposition; and, like a river, swells the higher for having its course stopped. *Jeremy Collier.*

Fortitudini—For bravery. *M.*

15 Fortuito quodam concursu atomorum—Certain fortuitous concourse of atoms. *Cic.*

Fortunæ cætera mando—I commit the rest to fortune. *Ovid.*

Fortunæ filius—A child or favourite of fortune. *Hor.*

Fortunæ majoris honos, erectus et acer—An honour to his elevated station, upright and brave. *Claud.*

Fortuna favet fatuis — Fortune favours fools. *Pr.*

20 Fortuna favet fortibus—Fortune favours the brave. *Pr.*

Fortuna magna magna domino est servitus—A great fortune is a great slavery to its owner. *Pub. Syr.*

Fortunam debet quisque manere suam—Every one ought to live within his means. *Ovid.*

Fortuna meliores sequitur—Fortune befriends the better man. *Sall.*

Fortuna miserrima tuta est—A very poor fortune is safe. *Ovid.*

25 Fortuna multis dat nimium, nulli satis—To many fortune gives too much, to none enough. *Mart.*

Fortuna nimium quem fovet, stultum facit—Fortune makes a fool of him whom she favours too much. *Pub. Syr.*

Fortuna non mutat genus—Fortune does not change nature. *Hor.*

Fortuna obesse nulli contenta est semel—Fortune is not content to do one an ill turn only once. *Pub. Syr.*

Fortuna opes auferre, non animum potest—Fortune may bereave us of wealth, but not of courage. *Sen.*

30 Fortuna parvis momentis magnas rerum commutationes efficit—Fortune in brief moments works great changes in our affairs.

Fortuna sequatur—Let fortune follow. *M.*

Fortunato omne solum patria est—To a favourite of fortune every land is his country.

Fortunatus et ille deos qui novit agrestes—Happy the man who knows the rural gods. *Virg.*

Fortunatus' purse—A purse which supplies you with all you wish.

35 Fortuna vitrea est, tum cum splendet frangitur—Fortune is like glass; while she shines she is broken. *Pub. Syr.*

Fortune brings in some boats that are ill-steered. *Cymbeline, iv. 3.*

Fortune can take from us nothing but what she gave. *Pr.*

Fortune does not change men; it only unmasks them. *Mme. Riccoboni.*

Fortune favours the brave, as the old proverb says, but forethought much more. *Cic.*

40 Fortune has rarely condescended to be the companion of genius. *Isaac Disraeli.*

Fortune hath something of the nature of a woman, who, if she be too closely wooed, goes commonly the farther off. *Charles V.*

Fortune is like a mirror—it does not alter men it only shows men just as they are. *Billings.*

Fortune is like the market, where many times, if you can stay a little, the price will fall. *Bacon.*

Fortune is merry, and in this mood will give us anything. *Jul. Cæs., iii. 2.*

45 Fortune is not content to do a man one ill turn. *Bacon.*

Fortune is the rod of the weak, and the staff of the brave. *Lowell.*

Fortune makes folly her peculiar care. *Churchill.*

Fortune makes him a fool whom she makes her darling. *Bacon.*

Fortune often knocks at the door, but the fool does not invite her in. *Dan. Pr.*

50 Fortune reigns in the gifts of the world, not in the lineaments of nature. *As You Like It, i. 2.*

Fortune! There is no fortune; all is trial, or punishment, or recompense, or foresight. *Voltaire.*

Fortune turns round like a mill-wheel, and he that was yesterday at the top lies to-day at the bottom. *Sp. Pr.*

Forward, forward let us range, / Let the great world spin for ever down the ringing grooves of change. *Tennyson.*

Forwardness spoils manners. *Gael. Pr.*

55 Foster the beautiful, and every hour thou callest new flowers to birth. *Schiller.*

Foul cankering rust the hidden treasure frets; / But gold that's put to use, more gold begets. *Shakespeare.*

Foul deeds will rise, / Though all the earth o'erwhelm them, to men's eyes. *Ham., i. 2.*

Fou (full) o' courtesy, fou o' craft. *Sc. Pr.*

Four eyes see more than two. *Pr.*

Four hostile newspapers are more to be feared than a thousand bayonets. *Napoleon.*

Foxes have holes, and the birds of the air have nests; but the Son of Man hath not where to lay his head. *Jesus.*

Foy est tout—Faith is everything. *M.*

Foy pour devoir—Faith for duty. *Old Fr.*

5 Frae saving comes having. *Sc. Pr.*

Fragili quærens illidere dentem / Offendet solido—Trying to fix her tooth in some tender part, / Envy will strike against the solid. *Hor.*

Fraile que pide por Dios pide por dos—The friar who begs for God begs for two. *Sp. Pr.*

Frailty, thy name is woman. *Ham.*, i. 2.

Frame your mind to mirth and merriment, / Which bars a thousand harms and lengthens life. *Tam. of Sh.*, Ind. 2.

10 Frangas, non flectes—You may break, but you will not bend me.

Frappe fort--Strike hard. *M.*

Fraternité ou la Mort — Fraternity or death. *The watchword of the first French Revolution. Fr.*

Frauen, richtet nur nie des Mannes einzelne Thaten; / Aber über den Mann sprechet das richtende Wort—Women, judge ye not the individual acts of the man; the word that pronounces judgment is above the man. *Schiller.*

Frauen und Jungfrauen soll man loben, es sei wahr oder erlogen — Truly or falsely, women and maidens must be praised. *Ger. Pr.*

15 Fraus est celare fraudem—It is a fraud to conceal fraud. *L.*

Frau und Mond leuchten mit fremden Licht—Madame and the moon shine with borrowed light. *Ger. Pr.*

Freedom and slavery, the one is the name of virtue, the other of vice, and both are acts of the will. *Epictetus.*

Freedom and whisky gang thegither! / Tak' aff your dram. *Burns.*

Freedom consists not in refusing to recognise anything above us, but in respecting something which is above us. *Goethe.*

20 Freedom exists only with power. *Schiller.*

Freedom has a thousand charms to show, / That slaves, howe'er contented, never know. *Cowper.*

Freedom is a new religion—the religion of our time. *Heine.*

Freedom is not caprice, but room to enlarge. *C. A. Bartol.*

Freedom is only granted us that obedience may be more perfect. *Ruskin.*

25 Freedom is only in the land of dreams, and the beautiful only blooms in song. *Schiller.*

Freedom is the eternal youth of nations. *Gen. Foy.*

Freedom's sun cannot set so long as smiths hammer iron. *C. M. Arndt.*

Free governments have committed more flagrant acts of tyranny than the most perfect despotic governments which we have ever known. *Burke.*

Free-livers on a small scale, who are prodigal within the compass of a guinea. *W. Irving.*

30 Freends are like fiddle-strings; they maunna be screwed ower tight. *Sc. Pr.*

Freethinkers are generally those who never think at all. *Sterne.*

Free will I be in thought and in poetry; in action the world hampers us enough. *Goethe.*

Freie Kirche im freien Staat—A free Church in a free State. *Cavour.*

Freilich erfahren wir erst im Alter, was uns in der Tugend begegnete—Not till we are old is it that we learn to know (*lit.* experience) what we met with when young. *Goethe.*

35 Frei muss ich denken, sprechen und atmen Gottes Luft, / Und wer die drei mir raubet, der legt mich in die Gruft—Freely must I think, speak, and breathe what God inspires in me, and he who robs me of these three entombs me. *Chamisso.*

Freits (prognostications) follow those who look to them. *Sc. Pr.*

Frei von Tadel zu sein ist der niedrigste Grad und der höchste, / Denn nur die Ohnmacht führt oder die Grösse dazu—To be free from blame is to be of the lowest and highest grade, for only imbecility or greatness leads to it. *Schiller.*

Freiwillige Abhängigkeit ist der schönste Zustand, und wie wäre der möglich ohne Liebe?—Voluntary dependence is the noblest condition we can be in; and how were that possible without love? *Goethe.*

Fremde Kinder, wir lieben sie nie so sehr als die eignen; / Irrtum das eigne Kind, ist uns dem Herzen so nah—We never love the child of another so much as our own; for this reason error, which is our own child, is so near to our heart. *Goethe.*

40 Fremdes Pferd und eigene Sporen haben bald den Wind verloren—Another's horse and our own spurs soon outstrip the wind. *Ger. Pr.*

Freno indorato non megliora il cavallo—A golden bit, no better a horse. *It. Pr.*

Frequent and loud laughter is the characteristic of folly and ill-manners. *Chesterfield.*

Fresh as a bridegroom, and his chin, new reap'd, / Show'd like a stubble-field at harvest-home; / He was perfuméd like a milliner, / And 'twixt his finger and his thumb he held / A pouncet-box, which ever and anon / He gave his nose, and took 't away again. *Hen. IV.*, i. 3.

Fret not over the irretrievable, but ever act as if thy life were just begun. *Goethe.*

45 Fret not thyself because of evil men, neither be thou envious at the wicked; for there shall be no reward to the evil man; the candle of the wicked shall be put out. *Bible.*

Fretting cares make grey hairs. *Pr.*

Freude hat mir Gott gegeben—God has to me given joy. *Schiller.*

Freud' muss Leid, Leid muss Freude haben—Joy must have sorrow; sorrow, joy. *Goethe.*

Freundschaft ist ein Knotenstock auf Reisen, / Lieb' ein Stäbchen zum Spazierengehn—Friendship is a sturdy stick to travel with; love a slender cane to promenade with. *Chamisso.*

50 Friar Modest never was prior. *It. Pr.*

Friend after friend departs; / Who hath not lost a friend? / There is no union here of hearts / That finds not here an end. *J. Montgomery.*

Friend, hast thou considered the "rugged, all-nourishing earth," as Sophocles well names her; how she feeds the sparrow on the housetop, much more her darling, man? *Carlyle.*

Friend, however thou camest by this book, I will assure thee thou wert least in my thoughts when I writ it. *Bunyan.*

"Friend, I never gave thee any of my jewels!" "No, but you have let me look at them, and that is all the use you can make of them yourself; moreover, you have the trouble of watching them, and that is an employment I do not much desire." *Goldsmith.*

Friends and acquaintances are the surest passports to fortune. *Schopenhauer.*

Friends are lost by calling often and calling seldom. *Gael. Pr.*

5 Friends are ourselves. *Donne.*

Friends are rare, for the good reason that men are not common. *Joseph Roux.*

Friends are the leaders of the bosom, being more ourselves than we are, and we complement our affections in theirs. *A. B. Alcott.*

Friends, like mushrooms, spring up in out-of-the-way places. *Pr.*

Friends may meet, / But mountains never greet. *Pr.*

10 Friends reveal to each other most clearly exactly that upon which they are silent. *Goethe.*

Friends should associate friends in grief and woe. *Tit. Andron.*, v. 3.

Friends should be weighed, not told. *Coleridge.*

Friends show me what I can do; foes teach me what I should do. *Schiller.*

Friends, such as we desire, are dreams and fables. *Emerson.*

15 Friends will be much apart. They will respect more each other's privacy than their communion, for therein is the fulfilment of our high aims and the conclusion of our arguments. . . . The hours my friend devotes to me were snatched from a higher society. *Thoreau.*

Friendship can originate and acquire permanence only practically (*pracktisch*). Liking (*Neigung*), and even love, contribute nothing to friendship. True, active, productive friendship consists in this, that we keep the same pace (*gleichen Schritt*) in life, that my friend approves of my aims, as I of his, and that thus we go on steadfastly (*unverrückt*) together, whatever may be the difference otherwise between our ways of thinking and living. *Goethe.*

Friendship canna stand a' on ae side. *Sc. Pr.*

Friendship, in the old heroic sense of that term, no longer exists; except in the cases of kindred or other legal affinity, it is in reality no longer expected or recognised as a virtue among men. *Carlyle.*

Friendship is a plant which one must water often. *Ger. Pr.*

20 Friendship is a vase, which, when it is flawed by heat, or violence, or accident, may as well be broken at once; it never can be trusted after. *Landor.*

Friendship is but a name. *Napoleon.*

Friendship is communion. *Arist.*

Friendship is constant in all other things, / Save in the office and affairs of love; / Therefore, all hearts in love use their own tongues; / Let every eye negotiate for itself, / And trust no agent. *Much Ado,* ii. 1.

Friendship is infinitely better than kindness. *Cic.*

Friendship is like a debt of honour; the 25 moment it is talked of, it loses its real name, and assumes the more ungrateful form of obligation. *Arliss' Lit. Col.*

Friendship is love with understanding. *Ger. Pr.*

Friendship is love without its flowers or veil. *Hare.*

Friendship is love without its wings. *Byron.*

Friendship is no plant of hasty growth. *Joanna Baillie.*

Friendship is one soul in two bodies. *Por-* 30 *phyry.*

Friendship is stronger than kindred. *Pub. Syr.*

Friendship is the greatest bond in the world. *Jeremy Taylor.*

Friendship is the ideal; friends are the reality; the reality always remains far apart from the ideal. *Joseph Roux.*

Friendship is the marriage of the soul. *Voltaire.*

Friendship is the shadow of the evening, 35 which strengthens with the setting sun of life. *La Fontaine.*

Friendship is too pure a pleasure for a mind cankered with ambition or the lust of power and grandeur. *Junius.*

Friendship, like love, is but a name, / Unless to one you stint the flame. *Gay.*

Friendship, like love, is self-forgetful. *H. Giles.*

Friendship, like the immortality of the soul, is too good to be believed. *Emerson.*

Friendship made in a moment is of no moment. 40 *Pr.*

Friendship often ends in love; but love in friendship—never. *Colton.*

Friendship should be surrounded with ceremonies and respects, and not crushed into corners. *Emerson.*

Friendship, unlike love, which is weakened by fruition, grows up, thrives, and increases by enjoyment; and being of itself spiritual, the soul is reformed by the habit of it. *Montaigne.*

Friendships are discovered rather than made. *Mrs. Stowe.*

Friendship's as it's kept. *Gael. Pr.* 45

Friendship's full of dregs. *Timon of Athens,* i. 2.

Friendships that are disproportioned ever terminate in disgust. *Goldsmith.*

Friendship's the privilege / Of private men. *N. Tate.*

Friendship's the wine of life; but friendship new is neither strong nor pure. *Young.*

Friendships which are born in misfortune are 50 more firm and lasting than those which are formed in happiness. *D'Urfey.*

Frigidam aquam effundere—To throw cold water on a business.

Frisch gewagt ist halb gewonnen—Boldly ventured is half done (won). *Ger. Pr.*

From a bad paymaster get what you can. *Pr.*

From a closed door the devil turns away. *Port. Pr.*

From camp to camp, through the foul womb of night, / The hum of either army stilly sounds, / That the fix'd sentinels almost receive / The secret whispers of each other's watch ; / Fire answers fire, and through their paly flames / Each battle sees the other's umber'd face ; / Steed threatens steed in high and boastful neighs, / Piercing the night's dull ear, and from the tents / The armourers, accomplishing the knights, / With busy hammers closing rivets up, / Give dreadful note of preparation. *Hen. V.*, iv. (*chorus*).

From every moral death there is a new birth ; / in this wondrous course of his, man may indeed linger, but cannot retrograde or stand still. *Carlyle.*

From every spot on earth we are equally near heaven and the infinite. *Amiel.*

From grave to gay, from lively to severe. *Pope.*

5 From great folks great favours are to be expected. *Cervantes.*

From hand to mouth will never make a worthy man. *Gael. Pr.*

From hearing comes wisdom, from speaking repentance. *Pr.*

From Helicon's harmonious springs / A thousand rills their mazy progress take. *Gray.*

From his cradle / He was a scholar, and a ripe and good one ; / Exceeding wise, fair-spoken, and persuading ; / Lofty and sour to them that loved him not, / But to those men who sought him, sweet as summer ; / And to add greater honours to his age / Than man could give ; he died fearing God. *Hen. VIII.*, iv. 2.

10 From ignorance our comfort flows ; / The only wretched are the wise. *Prior.*

From kings and priests and statesmen war arose, / Whose safety is man's deep embittered woe, / Whose grandeur his debasement. *Shelley.*

From labour health, from health contentment springs. *Beattie.*

From lowest place where virtuous things proceed, / The place is dignified by the doer's deed. *As You Like It*, ii. 3.

From obedience and submission spring all other virtues, as all sin does from self-opinion. *Montaigne.*

15 From our ancestors come our names, from our virtues our honours. *Pr.*

From out the throng and stress of lies, / From out the painful noise of sighs, / One voice of comfort seems to rise, / It is the meaner part that dies. *Lewis Morris.*

From pillar to post—originally from whipping-post to pillory, *i.e.* from bad to worse. *Pr.*

From saying " No," however cleverly, no good can come. *Goethe.*

From seeming evil still educing good. *Thomson.*

20 From servants hasting to be gods. *Pollock.*

From small beginnings come great things. *Dut. Pr.*

From stratagem to stratagem we run, / And he knows most who latest is undone ; / An honest man will take a knave's advice, / But idiots only will be cozened twice. *Dryden.*

From the beginning and to the end of time, Love reads without letters and counts without arithmetic. *Ruskin.*

From the deepest desire oftentimes ensues the deadliest hate. *Socrates.*

From thee, great God, we spring, to thee we 25 tend, / Path, motive, guide, original and end. *Johnson.*

" From the height of these pyramids forty centuries look down on you." *Napoleon to his troops in Egypt.*

From the lowest depth there is a path to the loftiest height. *Carlyle.*

From the low prayer of want and plaint of woe / O never, never turn away thine ear ! / Forlorn is this bleak wilderness below, / Ah ! what were man should heaven refuse to hear ! *Beattie.*

From the same flower the bee extracts honey and the wasp gall. *It. Pr.*

From the summit of power men no longer turn 30 their eyes upward, but begin to look about them. *Lowell.*

From the sum / Of duty, blooms sweeter and more divine / The fair ideal of the race, than comes / From glittering gains of learning. *Lewis Morris.*

From time to time in history men are born a whole age too soon. *Emerson.*

From within or from behind, a light shines through us upon things, and makes us aware that we are nothing, but the light is all. *Emerson.*

From women's eyes this doctrine I derive : / They sparkle still the right Promethean fire ; / They are the books, the arts, the academes, / That show, contain, and nourish all the world ; / Else none at all in aught proves excellent. *Love's L. Lost*, iv. 3.

From yon blue heaven above us bent, / The 35 grand old gardener and his wife / Smile at the claims of long descent. *Tennyson.*

Fromm, Klug, Weis, und Mild, gehört in des Adels Schild—The words pious, prudent, wise, and gentle are appropriately suitable on the shield of a noble. *Ger. Pr.*

Fromme Leute wohnen weit auseinander— Good people dwell far apart. *Ger. Pr.*

Frömmigkeit ist kein Zweck, sondern ein Mittel, um durch die reinste Gemüthsruhe zur höchsten Cultur zu gelangen—Piety is not an end, but a means to attain the highest culture through the purest peace of mind. *Goethe.*

Fronti nulla fides—There is no trusting external appearances (*lit.* features). *Juv.*

Frost and fraud both end in foul. *Pr.* 40

Frost is God's plough. *Fuller.*

Fructu non foliis arborem æstima—Judge of a tree from its fruit, not from its leaves. *Phæd.*

Frugality, and even avarice, in the lower orders of mankind are true ambition. These afford the only ladder for the poor to rise to preferment. *Goldsmith.*

Frugality is an estate. *Pr.*

Frugality is founded on the principle that all 45 riches have limits. *Burke.*

Frugality is good, if liberality be joined with it. *Wm. Penn.*

Frugality may be termed the daughter of prudence, the sister of temperance, and the parent of liberty. *Johnson.*

Fruges consumere nati—Born merely to consume the fruits of the earth. *Hor.*

Frühe Hochzeit, lange Liebe—Early marriage, long love. *Ger. Pr.*

Fruit is seed. *Pr.*

Frustra fit per plura, quod fieri potest per paucora—It is vain to do by many agencies what may be done by few.

5 Frustra Herculi—In vain to speak against Hercules. *Pr.*

Frustra laborat qui omnibus placere studet—He labours in vain who studies to please everybody. *Pr.*

Frustra retinacula tendens / Ferter equis auriga, neque audit currus habenas—In vain as he tugs at the reins is the charioteer borne along by the steeds, and the chariot heeds not the curb. *Virg.*

Frustra vitium vitaveris illud, / Si te alio pravus detorseris—In vain do you avoid one fault if you perversely turn aside into another. *Hor.*

Fugam fecit—He has taken to flight. *L.*

10 Fuge magna ; licet sub paupere tecto / Reges et regum vita præcurrere amicos—Shun grandeur ; under a poor roof you may surpass even kings and the friends of kings in your life. *Hor.*

Fugere est triumphus—Flight (*i.e.*, from temptation) is a triumph. *Pr.*

Fugit improbus, ac me / Sub cultro linquit—The wag runs away and leaves me with the knife at my throat, *i.e.*, to be sacrificed. *Hor.*

Fugit irreparabile tempus—Time flies, never to be repaired. *Virg.*

Fühlst du dein Herz durch Hass von Menschen wegetrieben— / Thu' ihnen Gutes ! schnell wirst du sie wieder lieben—Shouldst thou feel thy heart repelled from men through hatred, do thou them good, soon shall thy love for them revive in thee. *B. Paoli.*

15 Fuimus—We have been. *M.*

Fuimus Troes, fuit Ilium, et ingens / Gloria Teucrorum—We Trojans are no more ; Ilium is no more, and the great renown of the Teucri. *Virg.*

Fuit hæc sapientia quondam, / Publica privatis secernere, sacra profanis, / Concubitu prohibere vago, dare jura maritis, / Oppida moliri, leges incidere ligno—This of old was accounted wisdom, to separate public from private property, things sacred from profane, to restrain from vagrant concubinage, to ordain laws for married people, to build cities, to engrave laws on tablets. *Hor.*

Fuit Ilium—Troy was.

Fules are aye fond o' flittin'. *Sc. Pr.*

20 Fulgente trahit constrictos gloria curru, / Non minus ignotos generosis—Glory draws all bound to her shining car, low-born and high-born alike. *Hor.*

Full little knowest thou that hast not tried / What hell it is in suing long to bide ; / To lose good days that might be better spent, / To waste long nights in pensive discontent. *Spenser.*

Full many a day for ever is lost / By delaying its work till to-morrow ; / The minutes of sloth have often cost / Long years of bootless sorrow. *Eliza Cook.*

Full many a gem of purest ray serene / The dark unfathom'd caves of ocean bear ; / Full many a flower is born to blush unseen, / And waste its sweetness on the desert air. *Gray.*

Full many a stoic eye and aspect stern / Masks hearts where grief has little left to learn ; / And many a withering thought lies hid, not lost, / In smiles that least befit who wears them most. *Byron.*

Full of sound and fury, / Signifying nothing. 25 *Macb.*, v. 5.

Full oft have letters caused the writers / To curse the day they were inditers. *Butler.*

Full of wise saws and modern instances. *As You Like It*, ii. 7.

Full seldom doth a man repent, or use / Both grace and will to pick the vicious quitch / Of blood and custom wholly out of him, / And make all clean, and plant himself afresh. *Tennyson.*

Full twenty times was Peter fear'd / For once that Peter was respected. *Wordsworth.*

Full vessels give the least sound. *Pr.* 30

Full wise is he that can himselven knowe. *Chaucer.*

Fully to possess and rule an object, one must first study it for its own sake. *Goethe.*

Fumos vendere—To sell smoke. *Mart.*

Fumum, et opes, strepitumque Romæ—The smoke, the wealth, and din of the town. *Juv.*

Functus officio—Having discharged his duties 35 and resigned.

Fundamentum est justitiæ fides—The foundation of justice is good faith. *Cic.*

Fungar vice cotis, acutum / Reddere quæ ferrum valet, exsors ipsa secandi—I will discharge the office of a whetstone, which can give an edge to iron, though it cannot cut itself. *Hor.*

Fürchterlich / Ist einer der nichts zu verlieren hat—Terrible is a man who has nothing to lose. *Goethe.*

Für den Dialektiker ist die Welt ein Begriff, für den Schöngeist ein Bild, für den Schwärmer ein Traum, für den Forscher Wahrheit—For the thinker the world is a thought ; for the wit, an image ; for the enthusiast, a dream ; for the inquirer, truth. *L. Büchner.*

Für eine Nation ist nur das gut was aus ihrem 40 eignen Kern und ihrem eignen allgemeinen Bedürfniss hervorgegangen, ohne Nachäffung einer andern—Only that is good for a nation which issues from its own heart's core and its own general wants, without apish imitation of another ; since (it is added) what may to one people, at a certain stage, be wholesome nutriment, may perhaps prove a poison for another. *Goethe.*

Für einen Leichnam bin ich nicht zu Haus ; / Mir geht es wie der Katze mit der Maus—For a dead one I am not at home ; I am like the cat with the mouse. *Goethe's Mephistopheles.*

Für ewig ist ja nicht gestorben, was man für diese Welt begräbt—What is buried for this world is not for ever dead. *K. v. Holtei.*

Für Gerechte giebt es keine Gesetze—There are no laws for just men. *Ger. Pr.*

Furiosus absentis loco est—A madman is treated as one absent. *Coke.*

Furiosus furore suo punitur—A madman is pun- 45 ished by his own madness. *L.*

Furor arma ministrat—Their rage finds them arms. *Virg.*

Furor fit læsa sæpius patientia—Patience, when outraged often, is converted into rage. *Pr.*

Furor iraque mentem præcipitant—Rage and anger hurry on the mind. *Virg.*

Furor loquendi—A rage for speaking.

Furor poëticus—The poet's frenzy.

Furor scribendi—A rage for writing.

5 Für seinen König muss das Volk sich opfern, / Das ist das Schicksal und das Gesetz der Welt—For its chief must the clan sacrifice itself; that is the destiny and law of the world. *Schiller.*

Fürst Bismarck glaubt uns zu haben, und wir haben ihn—Prince Bismarck thinks he has us, and we have him. *Socialist organ.*

Fürsten haben lange Hände und viele Ohren—Princes have long hands and many ears. *Ger. Pr.*

Further I will not flatter you, / That all I see in you is worthy love, / Than this; that nothing do I see in you / That should merit hate. *King John,* ii. 2.

Fury wasteth, as patience lasteth. *Pr.*

10 Futurity is impregnable to mortal kin; no prayer pierces through heaven's adamantine walls. *Schiller.*

Futurity is the great concern of mankind. *Burke.*

Futurity still shortens, and time present sucks in time to come. *Sir Thomas Browne.*

Fuyez les procès sur toutes les choses, la conscience s'y intéresse, la santé s'y altère, les biens s'y dissipent—Avoid lawsuits beyond all things; they pervert conscience, impair your health, and dissipate your property. *La Bruyère.*

G.

Gäb es keine Narren, so gäb es keine Weisen—Were there no fools, there would be no wise men. *Ger. Pr.*

15 Gaieté de cœur—Gaiety of heart. *Fr.*

Gaiety is often the reckless ripple over depths of despair. *Chapin.*

Gaiety is the soul's health; sadness is its poison. *Stanislaus.*

Gaiety overpowers weak spirits; good-humour recreates and revives them. *Johnson.*

Gaiety pleases more when we are assured that it does not cover carelessness. *Mme. de Staël.*

20 Gain at the expense of reputation should be called loss. *Pub. Syr.*

'Gainst the tooth of time / And rasure of oblivion. *Meas. for Meas ,* v. 1.

Galea spes salutis—Hope is the helmet of salvation. *M.*

Galeatum sero duelli pœnitet—After donning the helmet it is too late to repent of war, *i.e.,* after enlistment. *Juv.*

Gallantry thrives most in a court atmosphere. *Mme. Necker.*

25 Gallicè—In French.

Gallus in sterquilinio suo plurimum potest—The cock is proudest on his own dunghill. *Pr.*

Gambling is the child of avarice, but the parent of prodigality. *Colton.*

Gambling with cards, or dice, or stocks, is all one thing; it is getting money without giving an equivalent for it. *Ward Beecher.*

Game is a civil gunpowder, in peace / Blowing up houses with their whole increase. *Herbert.*

Γαμεῖν ὁ μέλλων εἰς μετάνοιαν ἔρχεται—He 30 who is about to marry is on the way to repentance. *Gr. Pr.*

Games of chance are traps to catch school-boy novices and gaping country squires, who begin with a guinea and end with a mortgage. *Cumberland.*

Gaming finds a man a cully and leaves him a knave. *T. Hughes.*

Gaming has been resorted to by the affluent as a refuge from *ennui;* it is a mental dram, and may succeed for a moment, but, like other stimuli, it produces indirect debility. *Colton.*

Gaming is the destruction of all decorum; the prince forgets at his dignity, and the lady her modesty. *Marchioness d'Alembert.*

Gammel Mands Sagn er sielden usand—An 35 old man's sayings are rarely untrue. *Dan. Pr.*

Γάμος γὰρ ἀνθρώποισιν εὐκταῖον κακόν—Marriage is an evil men are eager to embrace. *Men.*

Gang to bed wi' the lamb and rise wi' the laverock (lark). *Sc. Pr.*

Garçon—A boy; a waiter. *Fr.*

Garde à cheval—Horse-guards; mounted guard. *Fr.*

Garde à pied—Foot-guards. *Fr.* 40

Garde à vous—Attention. *Fr.*

Garde-chasse—Gamekeeper. *Fr.*

Garde du corps—A bodyguard. *Fr.*

Garde-feu—A fire-guard. *Fr.*

Garde-fou—A hand-rail. *Fr.* 45

Gardez—Keep it. *Fr.*

Gardez bien—Take care. *Fr.*

Gardez cela pour la bonne bouche—Keep that for a tit-bit. *Fr. Pr.*

Gardez la foi—Guard the faith. *M.*

Garments that have once a rent in them are 50 subject to be torn on every nail, and glasses that are once cracked are soon broken; such is a good man's name once tainted with just reproach. *Bp. Hall.*

Garrit aniles / Ex re fabellas—He relates old women's tales very apropos. *Hor.*

Gar Vieles lernt man, um es wieder zu vergessen ;/ Um an den Ziel zu stehen, muss man die Bahn durchmessen—Much we learn only to forget it again; to stand by the goal, we must traverse all the way to it. *Rückert.*

Gâteau et mauvaise coutume se doivent rompre—A cake and a bad custom are fated to be broken. *Fr. Pr.*

Gâter une chandelle pour trouver une épingle—To waste a candle to find a pin. *Fr. Pr.*

Gather gear by every wile that's justified by 55 honour; / Not for to hide it in a hedge, nor for a train attendant; / But for the glorious privilege of being independent. *Burns.*

Gather the rosebuds while ye may, / Old Time is still a-flying, / And this same flower that smiles to-day, / To-morrow will be dying. *Herrick.*

Gathering gear (wealth) is pleasant pain. *Sc. Pr.*

Gathering her brows like gathering storm, / Nursing her wrath to keep it warm. *Burns.*

Gato maullador nunca buen cazador—A mewing cat is never a good mouser. *Sp. Pr.*

Gaude, Maria Virgo—Rejoice, Virgin Mary.

Gaudeamus—Let us have a joyful time.

Gaudent prænomine molles / Auriculæ—His delicate ears are delighted with a title. *Hor.*

5 Gaudet equis, canibusque, et aprici gramine campi—He delights in horses, and dogs, and the grass of the sunny plain. *Hor.*

Gaudet tentamine virtus — Virtue rejoices in being put to the test.

Gaudetque viam fecisse ruina—He rejoices at having made his way by ruin. *Lucan, of Julius Cæsar.*

Gave / His body to that pleasant country's earth, / And his pure soul unto his captain Christ, / Under whose colours he had fought so long. *Rich. II.*, iv. 1.

Gay hope is theirs by fancy fed, / Less pleasing when possest ; / The tear forgot as soon as shed, / The sunshine of the breast. *Gray.*

10 Gear is easier gained than guided. *Pr.*

Geben ist Sache des Reichen—Giving is the business of the rich. *Goethe.*

Gebrade duijven vliegen niet door de lucht— Roasted pigeons don't fly through the air. *Dut. Pr.*

Gebratene Tauben, die einem im Maul fliegen ? —Do pigeons fly ready-roasted into one's mouth? *Ger. Pr.*

Gebraucht der Zeit, sie geht so schell von hinnen, / Doch Ordnung lehrt euch Zeit gewinnen—Make the most of time, it glides away so fast ; but order teaches you to gain time. *Goethe.*

15 Gebt ihr ein Stück, se gebt es gleich in Stücken —If your aim is to give a piece, be sure you give it in pieces. *Goethe.*

Gedanken sind zollfrei, aber nicht höllenfrei— Thoughts are toll-free, but not hell-free. *Ger. Pr.*

Gedenke zu leben—Think of living. *Goethe.*

Gedichte sind gemalde Fensterscheiben— Poems are painted window-panes, *i.e.*, when genuine, they transmit heaven's light through a contracted medium coloured by human feeling and fantasy. *Goethe.*

Gedult gaat boven geleerdheid—Patience excels learning. *Dut. Pr.*

20 Gedwongen liefde vergaat haast—Love that is forced does not last. *Dut. Pr.*

Geese are plucked as long as they have any feathers. *Dut. Pr.*

Gefährlich ist's, den Leu zu wecken, / Verderblich ist des Tigers Zahn ; / Jedoch der schrecklichste der Schrecken, / Das ist der Mensch in seinem Wahn—Dangerous it is to rouse the lion, fatal is the tiger's tooth, but the most frightful of terrors is man in his self-delusion. *Schiller.*

Gefährlich ist's ein Mordgewehr zu tragen / Und auf den Schützen springt der Pfeil zurück—It is dangerous to carry a murderous weapon, and the arrow rebounds on the archer. *Schiller.*

Gefährlich ist's mit Geistern sich gesellen— To fraternise with spirits is a dangerous game. *Goethe.*

25 Gefährte munter kürzt die Meilen — Lively companionship shortens the miles. *Ger. Pr.*

Gefühl ist alles ; / Name ist Schall und Rauch / Umnebelnd Himmelsglut — Feeling is all ; name is sound and smoke veiling heaven's splendour. *Goethe.*

Gegen grosse Vorzüge eines andern giebt es kein Rettungsmittel als die Liebe—To countervail the inequalities arising from the great superiority of one over another there is no specific but love. *Goethe.*

Gegner glauben uns widerlegen, wenn sie ihre Meinung wieder holen und auf die unsrige nicht achten—Our adversaries think they confute us by repeating their own opinion and paying no heed to ours. *Goethe.*

Geheimnissvoll am lichten Tag / Lässt sich Natur des Schleiers nicht berauben, / Und was sie deinem Geist nicht offenbaren mag, / Das zwingst du ihr nicht ab mit Hebeln und mit Schrauben—In broad daylight inscrutable, Nature does not suffer her veil to be taken from her, and what she does not choose to reveal to the spirit, thou wilt not wrest from her by levers and screws. *Goethe.*

30 Geld beheert de wereld. Money rules the world. *Dut. Pr.*

Geld est der Mann—Money makes (*lit.* is) the man. *Ger. Pr.*

Geld im Beutel vertreibt die Schwermuth— Money in the purse drives away melancholy. *Ger. Pr.*

Gelegenheit macht den Dieb — Opportunity makes the thief. *Ger. Pr.*

Gelehrte Dummkopf—A learned blockhead ; dryasdust.

35 Γέλως ἄκαιρος ἐν βροτοῖς δεινὸν κακόν—Ill-timed laughter in men is a grievous evil. *Men.*

Gemeen goed, geen goed—Common goods, no goods. *Dut. Pr.*

Gemsen steigen hoch und werden doch gefangen —The chamois climb high, and yet are caught. *Ger. Pr.*

General abstract truth is the most precious of all blessings ; without it man is blind ; it is the eye of reason. *Rousseau.*

General infidelity is the hardest soil which the propagators of a new religion can have to work upon. *Paley.*

40 General suffering is the fruit of general misbehaviour, general dishonesty. *Carlyle.*

General truths are seldom applied to particular occasions. *Johnson.*

Generally all warlike people are a little idle, and love danger better than travail. *Bacon.*

Generally speaking, an author's style is a faithful copy of his mind. If you would write a lucid style, let there first be light in your own mind ; and if you would write a grand style, you ought to have a grand character. *Goethe.*

Generations are as the days of toilsome mankind ; death and birth are the vesper and the matin bells that summon mankind to sleep, and to rise refreshed for new advancement. *Carlyle.*

45 Generosity during life is a very different thing from generosity in the hour of death ; one proceeds from genuine liberality and benevolence, the other from pride or fear. *Horace Mann.*

Generosity is catching : and if so many escape it, it is somewhat for the same reason that countrymen escape the small-pox—because they meet with no one to give it to them. *Lord Greville.*

Generosity is the flower of justice. *Hawthorne.*

Generosity is the part of the soul raised above the vulgar. *Goldsmith.*

Generosity should never exceed ability. *Cic.*

5 Generosity, wrong placed, becomes a vice. A princely mind will undo a private family. *Fuller.*

Generous souls are still most subject to credulity. *Sir W. Davenant.*

Geniesse, wenn du kannst, und leide, wenn du musst, / Vergiss den Schmerz, erfrische das Vergnügen—Enjoy if thou canst, endure if thou must ; / forget the pain and revive the pleasure. *Goethe.*

Genius and virtue, like diamonds, are best plain set. *Emerson.*

Genius always gives its best at first, prudence at last. *Lavater.*

10 Genius begins great works, labour alone finishes them. *Joubert.*

Genius believes its faintest presentiment against the testimony of all history, for it knows that facts are not ultimates, but that a state of mind is the ancestor of everything. *Emerson.*

Genius borrows nobly. *Emerson.*

Genius can never despise labour. *Abel Stevens.*

Genius cannot escape the taint of its time more than a child the influence of its begetting. *Ouida.*

15 Genius can only breathe freely in an atmosphere of freedom. *J. S. Mill.*

Genius counts all its miracles poor and short. *Emerson.*

Genius does not need a special language ; it newly uses whatever tongue it finds. *Stedman.*

Genius does what it must, and talent does what it can. *Owen Meredith.*

Genius easily hews out its figure from the block, but the sleepless chisel gives it life. *Willmott.*

20 Genius, even as it is the greatest good, is the greatest harm. *Emerson.*

Genius ever stands with nature in solemn union, and what the one foretells the other will fulfil. *Schiller.*

Genius finds its own road and carries its own lamp. *Willmott.*

Genius grafted on womanhood is like to overgrow it and break its stem. *Holmes.*

Genius has privileges of its own ; it selects an orbit for itself ; and be this never so eccentric, if it is indeed a celestial orbit, we mere star-gazers must at last compose ourselves, must cease to cavil at it, and begin to observe it and calculate its laws. *Carlyle.*

25 Genius in poverty is never feared, because Nature, though liberal in her gifts in one instance, is forgetful in another. *B. R. Haydon.*

Genius invents fine manners, which the baron and the baroness copy very fast, and, by the advantage of a palace, better the instruction. They stereotype the lesson they have learned into a mode. *Emerson.*

Genius is always ascetic, and piety and love. *Emerson.*

Genius is always a surprise, but it is born with great advantages when the stock from which it springs has been long under cultivation. *Holmes.*

Genius is always consistent when most audacious. *Stedman.*

Genius is always impatient of its harness ; its 30 wild blood makes it hard to train. *Holmes.*

Genius is always more suggestive than expressive. *Abel Stevens.*

Genius is always sufficiently the enemy of genius by over-influence. *Emerson.*

Genius is a nervous disease. *De Tours.*

Genius is ever a secret to itself. *Carlyle.*

Genius is ever the greatest mystery to itself. 35 *Schiller.*

Genius is inconsiderate, self-relying, and, like unconscious beauty, without any intention to please. *I. M. Wise.*

Genius is intensity of life ; an overflowing vitality which floods and fertilises a continent or a hemisphere of being ; which makes a nature many-sided and whole, while most men remain partial and fragmentary. *H. W. Mabie.*

Genius is lonely without the surrounding presence of a people to inspire it. *T. W. Higginson.*

Genius is mainly an affair of energy. *Matthew Arnold.*

Genius is not a single power, but a combination 40 of great powers. It reasons, but it is not reasoning ; it judges, but it is not judgment ; imagines, but it is not imagination ; it feels deeply and fiercely, but it is not passion. It is neither, because it is all. *Whipple.*

Genius is nothing but a great capacity for patience. *Buffon.*

Genius is nothing but labour and diligence. *Hogarth.*

Genius is nothing more than our common faculties refined to a greater intensity. *Haydon.*

Genius is nothing more than the effort of the idea to assume a definite form. *Fichte.*

Genius is nourished from within and without. 45 *Willmott.*

Genius is only as rich as it is generous. *Thoreau.*

Genius is religious. *Emerson.*

Genius is that in whose power a man is. *Lowell.*

Genius is that power of man which by its deeds and actions gives laws and rules ; and it does not, as used to be thought, manifest itself only by over-stepping existing laws, breaking established rules, and declaring itself above all restraint. *Goethe.*

Genius is the gold in the mine ; talent is the 50 miner who works and brings it out. *Lady Blessington.*

Genius is the power of carrying the feelings of childhood into the powers of manhood. *Coleridge.*

Genius is the transcendent capacity of taking trouble first of all. *Carlyle.*

Genius is the very eye of intellect and the wing of thought ; it is always in advance of its time, and is the pioneer for the generation which it precedes. *Simms.*

Genius is to other gifts what the carbuncle is to the precious stones. It sends forth its own light, whereas other stones only reflect borrowed light. *Schopenhauer.*

Genius loci—The presiding genius of the place.

Genius makes its observations in shorthand; talent writes them out at length. *Bovee.*

Genius may at times want the spur, but it stands as often in need of the curb. *Longinus.*

5 Genius melts many ages into one. . . . A work of genius is but the newspaper of a century, or perchance of a hundred centuries. *Hawthorne.*

Genius must be born, and never can be taught. *Dryden.*

Genius of a kind is necessary to make a fortune, and especially a large one. *La Bruyère.*

Genius only commands recognition when it has created the taste which is to appreciate it. *Froude.*

Genius only leaves behind it the monuments of its strength. *Hazlitt.*

10 Genius should be the child of genius, and every child should be inspired. *Emerson.*

Genius, the Pythian of the beautiful, leaves its large truths a riddle to the dull. *Bulwer Lytton.*

Genius unexerted is no more genius than a bushel of acorns is a forest of oaks. *Beecher.*

Genius will reconcile men to much. *Carlyle.*

Genius works in sport, and goodness smiles to the last. *Emerson.*

15 Gens d'armes—Armed police. *Fr.*

Gens de bureau—Officials in a government office. *Fr.*

Gens de condition—People of rank. *Fr.*

Gens d'église—Churchmen. *Fr.*

Gens de guerre—Soldiers. *Fr.*

20 Gens de langues—Linguists. *Fr.*

Gens de lettres—Literary people. *Fr.*

Gens de lois—Lawyers. *Fr.*

Gens de même famille—Birds of a feather. *Fr.*

Gens de peu—The lower classes. *Fr.*

25 Gens togata—The nation with the toga, *i.e.*, the Roman.

Gentility is nothing else but ancient riches. *Lord Burleigh.*

Gentility without ability is waur (worse) than plain begging. *Sc. Pr.*

Gentle passions brighten the horizon of our existence, move without wearing, warm without consuming, and are the badges of true strength. *Feuchtersleben.*

Gentle words, quiet words, are, after all, the most powerful words. They are more convincing, more compelling, more prevailing. *W. Gladden.*

30 Gentleman, in its primal, literal, and perpetual meaning, is a man of pure race. *Ruskin.*

Gentleman is a term which does not apply to any station, but to the mind and the feelings in every station. *Talfourd.*

Gentlemanliness is just another word for intense humanity. *Ruskin.*

Gentlemen have to learn that it is no part of their duty or privilege to live on other people's toil; that there is no degradation in the hardest manual or the humblest servile labour, when it is honest. *Ruskin.*

"Gentlemen of the jury, you will now consider your verdict." *Lord Tenterden's last words.*

Gentleness corrects whatever is offensive in 35 our manners. *Blair.*

Gentleness! more powerful than Hercules. *Ninon de l'Enclos.*

Gentleness, when it weds with manhood, makes a man. *Tennyson.*

Gently comes the world to those / That are cast in gentle mould. *Tennyson.*

Gently didst thou ramble round the little circle of thy pleasures, jostling no creature in thy way: for each one's sorrows thou hadst a tear; for each man's need thou hadst a shilling. *Sterne's Uncle Toby.*

Gently, gently touch a nettle, / And it stings 40 you for your pains; / Grasp it like a man of mettle, / And it soft as silk remains. *Aaron Hill.*

Genug ist über einer Sackvoll—Enough excels a sackful. *Ger. Pr.*

Genuine morality depends on no religion, though every one sanctions it and thereby guarantees to it its support. *Schopenhauer.*

Genuine religion is matter of feeling rather than matter of opinion. *Bovee.*

Genuine simplicity of heart is a healing and cementing principle. *Burke.*

Genus et proavos et quæ non fecimus ipsi, / 45 Vix ea nostra voco—Birth, ancestry, and what we have ourselves not done, I would hardly call our own. *Ovid.*

Genus humanum superavit—He surpassed the human race in natural ability. *Lucret.*

Genus immortale manet, multosque per annos / Stat fortuna domus, et avi numerantur avorum—The race continues immortal, and through many years the fortune of the house stands steadfast, and it numbers grandsires of grandsires. *Virg.*

Genus irritabile vatum—The sensitive tribe of poets.

Γηράσκω δ' ἀεὶ πολλὰ διδασκόμενος—Always learning many things the older I grow. *Solon.*

Gerechtigkeit ist mehr die männliche, Men- 50 schenliebe mehr die weibliche Tugend—Justice is properly the virtue of the man, charity of the woman. *Schopenhauer.*

Geredt ist geredt, man kann es mit einem Schwamme abwischen—What is said is said; there is no sponge that can wipe it out. *Ger. Pr.*

Germanicè—In German.

Gescheite Leute sind immer das beste Konversationslexikon—Clever people are always the best Conversations-lexicon. *Goethe.*

Geschichte ist eigentlich nichts anderes, als eine Satire auf die Menschheit—History is properly nothing else but a satire on humanity. *C. J. Weber.*

Geschrei macht den Wolf grösser als er ist— 55 Fear makes the wolf bigger than he is. *Ger. Pr.*

Gesellschaft ist die Grossmutter der Menschheit durch ihre Töchter, die Erfindungen— Society is the grandmother of humanity through her daughters, the inventions. *C. J. Weber.*

Gesetz ist mächtig, mächiger ist die Noth— Law is powerful; necessity is more so. *Goethe.*

Gesetzlose Gewalt ist die furchbarste Schwäche —Lawless power is the most frightful weakness. *Herder.*

Gespenster sind für solche Leute nur / Die sehn sie wollen—Ghosts visit only those who look for them. *Holtei.*

Get a good name and go to sleep. *Pr.*

Get money, honestly if you can, but get **money**. *Pr.*

Get once into the secret of any Christian act, and you get practically into the secret of Christianity itself. *Ed.*

5 Get on the crupper of a good stout hypothesis, and you may ride round the world. *Sterne.*

Get place and wealth, if possible, with grace ; / If not, by any means get wealth and place. *Pope.*

Get spindle and distaff ready, and God will send the flax. *Pr.*

Get thee to a nunnery ! *Ham.*, iii. 1.

Get to live ; / Then live and use it ; else it is not true / That thou hast gotten. *Herbert.*

10 Get what ye can and keep what ye hae. *Sc. Pr.*

Get your enemies to read your works in order to mend them, for your friend is so much your second self that he will judge too like you. *Pope.*

Geteilte Freud' ist doppelt Freude—Joy shared is joy doubled. *Goethe.*

Gewalt ist die beste Beredsamkeit—Power is the most persuasive rhetoric. *Schiller.*

Gewinnen ist leichter als Erhalten—Getting is easier than keeping. *Ger. Pr.*

15 Gewöhne dich, da stets der Tod dir dräut, / Dankbar zu nehmen, was das Leben beut— Accustom thyself, since death ever threatens thee, to accept with a thankful heart whatever life offers thee. *Bodenstedt.*

Gewöhnlich glaubt Mensch, wenn er nur Worte hört, / Es müsse sich dabei doch auch was denken lassen — Men generally believe, when they hear only words, that there must be something in it. *Goethe.*

Ghosts ! There are nigh a thousand million walking the earth openly at noontide ; some half-hundred have vanished from it, some half-hundred have arisen in it, ere thy watch ticks once. *Carlyle.*

Giant Antæus in the fable acquired new strength every time he touched the earth ; so some brave minds gain fresh energy from that which depresses and crushes others. *Murphy.*

Gibier de potence—A gallows-bird. *Fr.*

20 Gie a bairn his will and a whelp his fill, an' neither will do well. *Sc. Pr.*

Gie a beggar a bed, and he'll pay you with a louse. *Sc. Pr.*

Gie him tow enough and he'll hang himsel', *i.e.*, give him enough of his own way. *Sc. Pr.*

Gie me a canny hour at e'en, / My arms about my dearie, O, / An' warl'ly cares an' warl'ly men / May a' gang tapsalteerie, O. *Burns.*

Gie me ae spark o' Nature's fire ! / That's a' the learning I desire ; / Then though I drudge through dub and mire, / At pleugh or cart, / My Muse, though hamely in attire, / May touch the heart. *Burns.*

25 Gie me a peck o' oaten strae, / An' sell your wind for siller. *The cow to the piper who put her off with piping to her.*

Gie the deil his due, an' ye'll gang till him. *Sc. Pr.*

Gie the greedy dog a muckle bane. *Sc. Pr.*

Gie wealth to some be-ledger'd cit, / In cent. per cent. ; / But gie me real, sterling wit, / And I'm content. *Burns.*

Gie your heart to God and your awms (alms) to the poor. *Sc. Pr.*

Gie your tongue mair holidays than your head. 30 *Sc. Pr.*

Giebt es Krieg, so macht der Teufel die Hölle weiter—When war falls out, the devil enlarges hell. *Ger. Pr.*

Giebt's schönre Pflichten für ein edles Herz / Als ein Verteidiger der Unschuld sein, / Das Recht der unterdrückten zu beschirmen ?— What nobler task is there for a noble heart than to take up the defence of innocence and protect the rights of the oppressed? *Schiller.*

Gierigheid is niet verzadigd voor zij den mond vol aarde heeft—Greed is never satisfied till its mouth is filled with earth. *Dut. Pr.*

Giff-gaff maks gude friends, *i.e.*, mutual giving. *Sc. Pr.*

Gift of prophecy has been wisely denied to 35 man. Did a man foresee his life, and not merely hope it and grope it, and so by necessity and free-will make and fabricate it into a reality, he were no man, but some other kind of creature, superhuman or subterhuman. *Carlyle.*

Gifts are as gold that adorns the temple ; grace is like the temple that sanctifies the gold. *Burkett.*

Gifts are often losses. *It. Pr.*

Gifts come from on high in their own peculiar forms. *Goethe.*

Gifts from the hand are silver and gold, but the heart gives that which neither silver nor gold can buy. *Ward Beecher.*

Gifts make their way through stone walls. 40 *Pr.*

Gifts weigh like mountains on a sensitive heart. *Mme. Fée.*

Gigni pariter cum corpore, et una / Crescere sentimus pariterque senescere mentem—We see that the mind is born with the body, that it grows with it, and also ages with it. *Lucret.*

Gin (if) ye hadna been among the craws, ye wadna hae been shot. *Sc. Pr.*

Giovine santo, diavolo vecchio—A young saint, an old devil. *It. Pr.*

Gird your hearts with silent fortitude, / Suffer- 45 ing yet hoping all things. *Mrs. Hemans.*

Girls we love for what they are ; young men for what they promise to be. *Goethe.*

Give a boy address and accomplishments, and you give him the mastery of palaces and fortunes where he goes. *Emerson.*

Give a dog an ill name and hang him. *Pr.*

Give a hint to a man of sense and consider the thing done. *Pr.*

Give alms, that thy children may not ask 50 them. *Dan. Pr.*

Give a man luck and throw him into the sea. *Pr.*

Give ample room and verge enough. *Gray.*

Give an ass oats, and it runs after thistles. *Dut. Pr.*

Give, and it shall be given to you. *Jesus.*

Give and spend, / And God will send. *Pr.* 55

Give and take. *Pr.*

Give a rogue rope enough, and he will hang himself. *Pr.*

Give, but, if possible, spare the poor man the shame of begging. *Diderot.*

Give every flying minute / Something to keep in store. *Walker.*

Give every man his due. *Pr.*

5 Give every man thine ear, but few thy voice ; / Take each man's censure, but reserve thy judgment. *Ham.*, i. 3.

Give from below what ye get from above, / Light for the heaven-light, love for its love, / A holy soul for the Holy Dove. *Dr. Walter Smith.*

Give God the margin of eternity to justify Himself in. *Haweis.*

Give him an inch and he'll take an ell. *Pr.*

Give him a present ! give him a halter. *Mer. of Ven.*, ii. 2.

10 Give me again my hollow tree, / A crust of bread, and liberty. *Pope.*

Give me a look, give me a face, / That makes simplicity a grace, / Robes loosely flowing, hair as free ; / Such sweet neglect more taketh me, / Than all the adulteries of art ; / They strike mine eyes, but not my heart. *Ben Jonson.*

Give me but / Something whereunto I may bind my heart ; / Something to love, to rest upon, to clasp / Affection's tendrils round. *Mrs. Hemans.*

Give me health and a day, and I will make the pomp of emperors ridiculous. *Emerson.*

Give me insight into to-day, and you may have the antique and future worlds. . . . This idea has inspired the genius of Goldsmith, Burns, Cowper, and, in a newer time, of Goethe, Wordsworth, and Carlyle. Their writing is blood-warm. *Emerson.*

15 Give me my Romeo: and, when he shall die, / Take him and cut him out in little stars, / And he will make the face of heaven so fine / That all the world will be in love with night, / And pay no homage to the garish sun. *Rom. and Jul.*, iii. 2.

Give me that man / Who is not passion's slave, and I will wear him / In my heart's core, ay, in my heart of hearts. *Ham.*, iii. 2.

Give me the avow'd, th' erect, the manly foe, / Bold I can meet, perhaps may turn, his blow ; / But of all plagues, good Heaven, thy wrath can send, / Save, save, oh ! save me from the candid friend. *Canning.*

Give me the eloquent cheek, where blushes burn and die. *Mrs. Osgood.*

Give me the liberty to know, to think, to believe, and to utter freely, according to conscience, above all other liberties. *Milton.*

20 Give neither counsel nor salt till you are asked for it. *Pr.*

Give not that which is holy to the dogs, neither cast ye your pearls before swine. *Jesus.*

Give only so much to one that you may have to give to another. *Dan. Pr.*

Give orders, but no more, and nothing will be done. *Sp. and Port. Pr.*

Give pleasure to the few ; to please many is vain. *Schiller.*

25 Give ruffles to a man who wants a shirt. *Fr. Pr.* (?)

Give sorrow words; the grief that does not speak, / Whispers the o'erfraught heart, and bids it break. *Macbeth*, iv. 3.

Give the devil his due. 1 *Hen. IV.*, i. 2.

Give the devil rope enough and he will hang himself. *Pr.*

Give thy need, thine honour, and thy friend his due. *Herbert.*

30 Give thy thoughts no tongue, / Nor any unproportioned thought his act. / Be thou familiar, but by no means vulgar; / The friends thou hast, and their adoption tried, / Grapple them to thy soul with hoops of steel ; / But do not dull thy palm with entertainment / Of each new-hatch'd unfledged comrade. *Ham.*, i. 3.

Give to a gracious message / An host of tongues ; but let ill tidings tell / Themselves when they be felt. *Ant. and Cleo.*, ii. 5.

Give to him that asketh of thee, and from him that would borrow of thee turn not thou away. *Jesus.*

Give to the masses nothing to do, and they will topple down thrones and cut throats; give them the government here, and they will make pulpits useless, and colleges an impertinence. *Wendell Phillips.*

Give tribute, but not oblation, to human wisdom. *Sir P. Sidney.*

35 Give unto me, made lowly wise, / The spirit of self-sacrifice ; / The confidence of reason give ; / And in the light of truth thy bondman let me live. *Wordsworth.*

Give us the man who sings at his work ! Be his occupation what it may, he will be equal to any of those who follow the same pursuit in silent sullenness. He will do more in the same time ; he will do it better ; he will persevere longer. *Carlyle.*

Give way to your betters. *Pr.*

Give you a reason on compulsion ? If reasons were as plenty as blackberries, I would give no man a reason upon compulsion. 1 *Hen. IV.*, ii. 4.

Give your tongue more holiday than your hands or eyes. *Rabbi Ben Azai.*

40 Given a living man, there will be found clothes for him ; he will find himself clothes ; but the suit of clothes pretending that it is both clothes and man— *Carlyle.*

Given a world of knaves, to educe an Honesty from their united action, is a problem that is becoming to all men a palpably hopeless one. *Carlyle.*

Given the men a people choose, the people itself, in its exact worth and worthlessness, is given. *Carlyle.*

Gives not the hawthorn bush a sweeter shade / To shepherds, looking on their silly sheep, / Than doth a rich embroider'd canopy / To kings that fear their subjects' treachery. 3 *Hen. VI.*, ii. 5.

Giving alms never lessens the purse. *Sp. Pr.*

45 Giving away is the instrument for accumulated treasures ; it is like a bucket for the distribution of the waters deposited in the bowels of a well. *Hitopadesa.*

Giving to the poor increaseth a man's store. *Sc. Pr.*

Gladiator in arena consilium capit—The gladiator is taking advice when he is already in the lists. *Pr.*

Glänzendes Elend—Shining misery. *Goethe.*

Glasses and lasses are brittle ware. *Sc. Pr.*

Glaube nur, du hast viel gethan / Wenn dir Geduld gewöhnest an—Assure yourself you have accomplished no small feat if only you have learned patience. *Goethe.*

Γλαῦκ' Ἀθήναζε—Owls to Athens.

5 Glebæ ascriptus—Attached to the soil.

Gleiches Blut, gleiches Gut, und gleiche Jahre machen die besten Heirathspaare — Like blood, like estate, and like age make the happiest wedded pair. *Ger. Pr.*

Gleich sei keiner dem andern; doch gleich sei jeder dem Höchsten. Wie das zu machen? Es sei jeder vollendet in sich—Let no one be like another, yet every one like the Highest. How is this to be done? Be each one perfect in himself. *Goethe.*

Gleich und Gleich gesellt sich gern, sprach der Teufel zum Köhler—Like will to like, as the devil said to the charcoal-burner. *Ger. Pr.*

Gleichheit est immer das festeste Band der Liebe—Equality is the firmest bond of love. *Lessing.*

10 Gleichheit ist das heilige Gesetz der Menschheit—Equality is the holy law of humanity. *Schiller.*

Gli alberi grandi fanno più ombra che frutto—Large trees yield more shade than fruit. *It. Pr.*

Gli amici legano la borsa con un filo di ragnatelo—Friends tie their purses with a spider's thread. *It. Pr.*

Gli uomini alla moderna, e gli asini all' antica—After the modern stamp men, and after the ancient, asses. *It. Pr.*

Gli uomini fanno la roba, e le donne la conservano—Men make the wealth and women husband it. *It. Pr.*

15 Gli uomini hanno gli anni che sentono, e le donne quelli che mostrano—Men are as old as they feel, and women as they look. *It. Pr.*

Gli uomini hanno men rispetto di offendere uno che si facci amare che uno che si facci temere—Men shrink less from offending one who inspires love than one who inspires fear. *Machiavelli.*

Gloria in excelsis Deo—Glory to God in the highest.

Gloria vana florece, y no grana—Glory which is not real may flower, but will never fructify. *Sp. Pr.*

Gloria virtutis umbra — Glory is the shadow (*i.e.*, the attendant) of virtue.

Gloriæ et famæ jactura facienda est, publicæ utilitatis causa—A surrender of glory and fame must be made for the public advantage. *Cic.*

Gloriam qui spreverit, veram habet—He who despises glory will have true glory. *Livy.*

Glories, like glow-worms, afar-off shine bright, / But looked at near, have neither heat nor light. *Webster.*

Glorious men are the scorn of wise men, the admiration of fools, the idols of parasites, and the slaves of their own vaunts. *Bacon.*

Glory and gain the industrious tribe provoke ; / And gentle dulness ever loves a joke. *Pope.*

25 Glory fills the world with virtue, and, like a beneficent sun, covers the whole earth with flowers and fruits. *Vauvenargues.*

Glory grows guilty of detested crimes. *Love's L. Lost,* iv. 1

Glory is like a circle in the water, / Which never ceaseth to enlarge itself, / Till, by broad spreading, it disperse to naught. 1 *Hen. VI.,* i. 2.

Glory is safe when it is deserved ; not so popularity ; the one lasts like mosaic, the other is effaced like a crayon drawing. *Boufflers.*

Glory is so enchanting that we love whatever we associate with it, even though it be death. *Pascal.*

Glory is the fair child of peril. *Smollett.* 30

Glory is the unanimous praise of good men. *Cic.*

Glory long has made the sages smile, / 'Tis something, nothing, words, illusion, wind, / Depending more upon the historian's style / Than on the name a person leaves behind. *Byron.*

Glory relaxes often and debilitates the mind ; censure stimulates and contracts—both to an extreme. *Shenstone.*

Glück auf dem Weg—Good luck by the way. *Ger. Pr.*

Glück macht Mut—Luck inspires pluck. *Goethe.* 35

Glück und Weiber haben die Narren lieb—Fortune and women have a liking for fools. *Ger. Pr.*

Glücklich, glücklich nenn' ich den / Dem Daseins letzte Stunde / Schlägt in seiner Kinder Mitte—Happy ! happy call I him the last hour of whose life strikes in the midst of his children. *Grillparzer.*

Glücklich wer jung in jungen Tagen, / Glücklich wer mit Zeit gestählt, Gelernt des Lebens Ernst zu tragen—Happy he who is young in youth, happy who is hardened as steel with time, has learned to bear life's earnestness. *Puschkin.*

Gluttony and drunkenness have two evils attendant on them ; they make the carcass smart as well as the pocket. *Marcus Antoninus.*

Gluttony is the source of all our infirmities 40 and the fountain of all our diseases. As a lamp is choked by a superabundance of oil, a fire extinguished by an excess of fuel, so is the natural health of the body destroyed by intemperate diet. *Burton.*

Gluttony kills more than the sword. *Pr.*

Gluttony, where it prevails, is more violent, and certainly more despicable, than avarice itself. *Johnson.*

Gnarling sorrow hath less power to bite / The man that mocks at it and sets it light. *Rich. II.,* i. 3.

Gnats are unnoticed whereso'er they fly, / But eagles gazed upon by every eye. *Shakespeare.*

Γνῶθι σεαυτόν—Know thyself. 45

Go deep enough, there is music everywhere. *Carlyle.*

Go down the ladder when thou marriest a wife ; go up when thou choosest a friend. *Rabbi Ben Azai.*

Go, miser, go ; for lucre sell thy soul ; / Truck wares for wares, and trudge from pole to pole, / That men may say, when thou art dead and gone : / " See what a vast estate he left his son ! " *Dryden.*

Go, poor devil, get thee gone; why should I hurt thee? This world, surely, is wide enough to hold both thee and me. *Uncle Toby to the fly that had tormented him, as he let it out by the window.*

Go to Jericho and let your beards grow. *See 2 Sam. x. 5.*

Go to the ant, thou sluggard; consider her ways, and be wise. *Bible.*

Go to your bosom; / Knock there, and ask your heart what it doth know / That's like my brother's fault; if it confess / A natural guiltiness, such as his is, / Let it not sound a thought upon your tongue / Against my brother's life. *Meas. for Meas.,* ii. 2.

5 Go where you may, you still find yourself in a conditional world. *Goethe.*

Go whither thou wilt, thou shalt find no rest but in humble subjection to the government of a superior. *Thomas à Kempis.*

Go, wondrous creature, mount where science guides. / Go, measure earth, weigh air, and state the tides; / Instruct the planets in what orbs to run, / Correct old Time, and regulate the sun; / Go, teach Eternal Wisdom how to rule, / Then drop into thyself and be a fool. *Pope.*

Go you and try a democracy in your own house. *Lycurgus, to one who asked why he had not instituted a democracy.*

Go, you may call it madness, folly ; / You shall not chase my gloom away; / There's such a charm in melancholy, / I would not, if I could, be gay. *Rogers.*

10 Gobe-mouches—A fly-catcher ; one easily gulled. *Fr.*

God alone can properly bind up a bleeding heart. *J. Roux.*

God alone is true ; God alone is great ; alone is God. *Laboulaye.*

God answers sharp and sudden on some prayers, / And thrusts the thing we have prayed for in our face, / A gauntlet with a gift in it. *Mrs. Browning.*

God asks no man whether he will accept life. That is not the choice. You must take it ; the only choice is how. *Ward Beecher.*

15 God asks not what, but whence, thy work is : from the fruit / He turns His eye away, to prove the inmost root. *Trench.*

God assists those who rise early in the morning. *Sp. Pr.*

God blesses still the generous thought, / And still the fitting word He speeds, / And truth, at His requiring taught, / He quickens into deeds. *Whittier.*

God blesses the seeking, not the finding. *Ger. Pr.*

God builds His temple in the heart and on the ruins of churches and religions. *Emerson.*

20 God comes at last, when we think He is farthest off. *Pr.*

God comes in distress, and distress goes. *Gael. Pr.*

God comes to see us without bell. *Pr.*

God comes with leaden feet, but strikes with iron hands. *Pr.*

God created man in his own image. *Bible.*

25 God deals His wrath by weight, but His mercy without weight. *Pr.*

God deceiveth thee not. *Thomas à Kempis.*

God defend me from the man of one book. *Pr.*

God desireth to make your burden light to you, for man hath been created weak. *Koran.*

God does not measure men by inches. *Sc. Pr.*

God does not pay every week, but He pays at 30 the end. *Dut. Pr.*

God does not require us to live on credit ; He pays what we earn as we earn it, good or evil, heaven or hell, according to our choice. *C. Mildmay.*

God does not smite with both hands. *Sp. Pr.*

God does not weigh criminality in our scales. God's measure is the heart of the offender, a balance so delicate that a tear cast in the other side may make the weight of error kick the beam. *Lowell.*

God does with His children as a master does with his pupils ; the more hopeful they are, the more work He gives them to do. *Plato.*

God enters by a private door into every indi-35 vidual. *Emerson.*

God estimates us not by the position we are in, but by the way in which we fill it. *T. Edwards.*

God gave thy soul brave wings ; put not those feathers / Into a bed to sleep out all ill weathers. *Herbert.*

God gives all things to industry. *Pr.*

God gives birds their food, but they must fly for it. *Dut. Pr.*

God gives every bird its nest, but does not 40 throw it into the nest. *J. G. Holland.*

God gives his angels charge of those who sleep, / But He Himself watches with those who wake. *Harriet E. H. King.*

God gives sleep to the bad, in order that the good may be undisturbed. *Saadi.*

God gives strength to bear a great deal, if we only strive ourselves to endure. *Hans Andersen.*

God gives the will ; necessity gives the law. *Dan. Pr.*

God gives us love. Something to love / He 45 lends us ; but when love is grown / To ripeness, that on which it throve / Falls off, and love is left alone. *Tennyson.*

God giveth speech to all, song to the few. *Dr. Walter Smith.*

God grant you fortune, my son, for knowledge avails you little. *Sp. Pr.*

God hands gifts to some, whispers them to others. *W. R. Alger.*

God hangs the greatest weights on the smallest wires. *Bacon.*

God has been pleased to prescribe limits to His 50 own power, and to work out His ends within these limits. *Paley.*

God has commanded time to console the unhappy. *Joubert.*

God has connected the labour which is essential to the bodily sustenance with the pleasures which are healthiest for the heart ; and while He made the ground stubborn, He made its herbage fragrant and its blossoms fair. *Ruskin.*

God has delegated Himself to a million deputies. *Emerson.*

God has given a prophet to every people in its own tongue. *Arab Pr.*

God has given nuts to some who have no teeth. *Port. Pr.*

God has given us wit and flavour, and brightness and laughter, and perfumes to enliven the days of man's pilgrimage, and to charm his pained steps over the burning marl. *Sydney Smith.*

God has His little children out at nurse in many a home. *Dr. Walter Smith.*

God has lent us the earth for our life; it is a great entail. *Ruskin.*

5 God has made man to take pleasure in the use of his eyes, wits, and body; and the foolish creature is continually trying to live without looking at anything, without thinking about anything, and without doing anything. *Ruskin.*

God has made sunny spots in the heart; why should we exclude the light from them? *Haliburton.*

God has not said all that thou hast said. *Gael. Pr.*

God has sunk souls in dust, that by that means they may burst their way through errors to truth, through faults to virtue, and through sufferings to bliss. *Engel.*

God hath anointed thee to free the oppressed and crush the oppressor. *Bryant.*

10 God hath given to man a short time here upon earth, and yet upon this short time eternity depends. *Jeremy Taylor.*

God hath given you one face, and you make yourselves another: you jig, you amble, and you lisp, and you nickname God's creatures, and make your wantonness your ignorance. *Ham., iii. 1.*

God hath many sharp-cutting instruments and rough files for the polishing of His jewels. *Leighton.*

God hath yoked to Guilt her pale tormentor, Misery. *Bryant.*

God help the children of dependence! *Burns.*

15 God help the poor, for the rich can help themselves. *Sc. Pr.*

God help the rich folk, for the poor can beg. *Sc. Pr.*

God help the sheep when the wolf is judge. *Dan. Pr.*

God help the teacher, if a man of sensibility and genius, when a booby father presents him with his booby son, and insists on lighting up the rays of science in a fellow's head whose skull is impervious and inaccessible by any other way than a positive fracture with a cudgel. *Burns.*

God helps the strongest. *Ger. and Dut. Pr.*

20 God helps those who help themselves. *Pr.*

God Himself cannot do without wise men. *Luther.*

God Himself cannot procure good for the wicked. *Welsh Triad.*

God is able to do more than man can understand. *Thomas à Kempis.*

God is a circle whose centre is everywhere, and its circumference nowhere. *St. Augustine.*

25 God is a creditor who has no bad debts. *Ger. Pr.*

God is a good worker, but He loves to be helped. *Basque Pr.*

God is alpha and omega in the great world; endeavour to make Him so in the little world. *Quarles.*

God is always ready to strengthen those who strive lawfully. *Thomas à Kempis.*

God is a shower to the heart burnt up with grief, a sun to the face deluged with tears. *Joseph Roux.*

God is a sure paymaster. He may not pay 30 at the end of every week or month or year, but He pays in the end. *Anne of Austria.*

God is a *tabula rasa*, on which nothing more stands written than what thou thyself hast inscribed thereon. *Luther.*

God is at once the great original I and Thou. *Jean Paul.*

God is better served in resisting a temptation to evil than in many formal prayers. *W Penn.*

God is goodness itself, and whatsoever is good is of Him. *Sir P. Sidney.*

God is glorified, not by our groans, but by our 35 thanksgivings; and all good thought and good action claim a natural alliance with good cheer. *Willmott.*

God is great, and we know Him not; neither can the number of His years be searched out. *Bible.*

God is great in what is the greatest and the smallest. *Herder.*

God is greater than man. *Bible.*

God is His own interpreter. *Cowper.*

God is in heaven, and thou upon earth; there- 40 fore let thy words be few. *Bible.*

God is in the generation of the righteous. *Bible.*

God is in the word "ought," and therefore it outweighs all but God. *Joseph Cook.*

God is kind to fou (drunk) folk and bairns. *Sc. Pr.*

God is light. *St. John.*

God is love. *St. John.*   45

God is more delighted in adverbs than in nouns, *i.e.*, not in what is done so much as how it is done. *Heb. Pr.*

God is, nay, alone is; for with like emphasis we cannot say that anything else is. *Carlyle.*

God is not a man, that He should lie; neither the son of man, that he should repent: hath He said it, and shall He not do it? or hath He spoken, and shall He not make it good? *Bible.*

God is not found by the tests that detect you an acid or a salt. *Dr. Walter Smith.*

God is not so poor in felicities or so niggard in 50 His bounty that He has not wherewithal to furnish forth two worlds. *W. R. Greg.*

God is not to be known by marring His fair works and blotting out the evidence of His influences upon His creatures; not amidst the hurry of crowds and the crash of innovation, but in solitary places, and out of the glowing intelligences which He gave to men of old. *Ruskin.*

God is on the side of virtue; for whoever dreads punishment suffers it, and whoever deserves it dreads it. *Colton.*

God is patient, because eternal. *St. Augustine.*

God is spirit. *Jesus.*

God made all the creatures, and gave them our love and our fear, / To give sign we and they are His children, one family here. *Browning.*

God is the great composer; men are only the performers. Those grand pieces which are played on earth were composed in heaven. *Balzac.*

God is the light which, never seen itself, makes all things visible, and clothes itself in colours. Thine eye feels not its ray, but thine heart feels its warmth. *Jean Paul.*

God is the number, the weight, and the measure which makes the world harmonious and eternal. *Renan.*

5 God is the perfect poet, / Who in His person acts His own creations. *Browning.*

God is the reason of those who have no reason. *Renan.*

God is where He was. *Pr.*

God is with every great reform that is necessary, and it prospers. *Goethe.*

God keep me from my friends; from my enemies I will keep myself. *It. Pr.*

10 God knows I'm no the thing I should be, / Nor am I ev'n the thing I could be; / But twenty times I rather would be / An atheist clean, / Than under Gospel colours hid be, / Just for a screen. *Burns.*

God Konge er bedre end gammel Lov—A good king is better than an old law. *Dan. Pr.*

God loveth a cheerful giver. *St. Paul.*

God made him, and therefore let him pass for a man. *Mer. of Ven.*, i. 2.

God made man to go by motives, and he will not go without them, any more than a boat without steam or a balloon without gas. *Ward Beecher.*

15 God made man upright, but they have sought out many inventions. *Bible.*

God made me one man; love makes me no more / Till labour come, and make my weakness score. *Herbert.*

God made the country; man made the town. *Cowper.*

God made the flowers to beautify / The earth and cheer man's careful mood; / And he is happiest who hath power / To gather wisdom from a flower, / And wake his heart in every hour / To pleasant gratitude. *Wordsworth.*

God made us, and we admire ourselves. *Sp. Pr.*

20 God manifests Himself to men in all wise, good, humble, generous, great, and magnanimous souls. *Lavater.*

God may consent, but only for a time. *Emerson.*

God moves in a mysterious way / His wonders to perform; / He plants His footsteps in the sea, / And rides upon the storm. *Cowper.*

God must needs laugh outright, could such a thing be, to see His wondrous manikins here below. *Hugo von Trimberg, quoted by Carlyle.*

God narrows Himself to come near man, and man narrows himself to come near God. *Ed.*

25 God never forsakes His own. *Pr.*

God never imposes a duty without giving the time to do it. *Ruskin.*

God never made His work for man to mend. *Dryden.*

God never meant that man should scale the heavens / By strides of human wisdom . . . He commands us in His Word / To seek Him rather where His mercy shines. *Cowper.*

God never pardons; the laws of the universe are irrevocable. God always pardons; sense of condemnation is but another word for penitence, and penitence is already new life. *Wm. Smith.*

30 God never sends mouths but He sends meat. *Dan. Pr.*

God never shuts one door but He opens another. *Irish Pr.*

God offers to every man his choice between truth and repose. *Emerson.*

God often visits us, but most of the time we are not at home. *Joseph Roux.*

God only opened His hand to give flight to a thought that He had held imprisoned from eternity. *J. G. Holland.*

35 God pardons like a mother, who kisses the offence into everlasting forgetfulness. *Ward Beecher.*

God permits, but not for ever. *Pr.*

God said, Let there be light; and there was light. *Bible.*

God save the fools, and don't let them run out; for, without them, wise men couldn't get a living. *Amer. Pr.*

God save the mark. 1 *Hen. IV.*, i. 3.

40 God send us some siller, for they're little thought o' that want it. *Sc. Pr.*

God send you mair sense and me mair siller. *Sc. Pr.*

God sendeth and giveth both mouth and the meat. *Tusser.*

God sends meat and the devil sends cooks. *It. Pr.*

God sends nothing but what can be borne. *It. Pr.*

45 God should be the object of all our desires, the end of all our actions, the principle of all our affections, and the governing power of our whole souls. *Massillon.*

God, sir, he gart kings ken that there was a lith in their neck. *Boswell's father of Cromwell.*

God stays long, but strikes at last. *Pr.*

God taketh an account of all things. *Koran.*

God tempers the wind to the shorn lamb. *Sterne.*

50 God the first garden made, and the first city Cain. *Cowley.*

God, through the voice of Nature, calls the mass of men to be happy; He calls a few among them to the grander task of being severely but serenely sad. *W. R. Greg.*

God trusts every one with the care of his own soul. *Sc. Pr.*

God will accept your first attempt, not as a perfect work, but as a beginning. *Ward Beecher.*

God will not make Himself manifest to cowards. *Emerson.*

55 God will punish him who sees and him who is seen. *Eastern saying.*

God, when He makes the prophet, does not unmake the man. *Locke.*

God works in moments. *Fr. Pr.*

God writes the gospel not in the Bible alone, but on trees and flowers, and clouds and stars. *Luther.*

God's commandments are the iron door into Himself. To keep them is to have it opened, and His great heart of love revealed. *S. W. Duffield.*

God's creature is one. He makes man, not men. His true creature is unitary and infinite, revealing himself indeed in every finite form, but compromised by none. *Henry James.*

5 God's free mercy streameth / Over all the world, / And His banner gleameth, / Everywhere unfurled. *How.*

God's goodness is the measure of His providence. *More.*

God's help is nearer than the door. *Irish Pr.*

God's in His heaven: / All's right with the world! *Browning.*

God's justice, tardy though it prove perchance, / Rests never on the track till it reach / Delinquency. *Browning.*

10 God's men are better than the devil's men, and they ought to act as though they thought they were. *Ward Beecher.*

God's mill grinds slow but sure. *George Herbert.*

God's mills grind slow, but they grind woe. *Eastern saying.*

God's providence is on the side of clear heads. *Ward Beecher.*

God's sovereignty is not in His right hand or His intellect, but His love. *Ward Beecher.*

15 Gods water over Gods akker laten loopen— Let God's waters run over God's fields. *Dut. Pr.*

God's way of making worlds is to make them make themselves. *Prof. Drummond.*

Godfrey sent the thief that stole the cash away, / And punished him that put it in his way. *Pope.*

"Godlike men love lightning;" godless men love it not; shriek murder when they see it, shutting their eyes, and hastily putting on smoked spectacles. *Carlyle.*

Godliness is profitable unto all things, having promise of the life that now is, and of that which is to come. *St. Paul.*

20 Godliness with contentment is great gain. *St. Paul.*

Godly souls have often interdicted the gratifications of the flesh in order to help their spirits in the Godward direction. *John Pulsford.*

Godt Haandværk har en gylden Grund—A good handicraft rests on a golden foundation. *Dan. Pr.*

Goed verloren, niet verloren; moed verloren, veel verloren; eer verloren, meer verloren; ziel verloren, al verloren—Money lost, nothing lost; courage lost, much lost; honour lost, more lost; soul lost, all lost. *Dut. Pr.*

Goethe's devil is a cultivated personage and acquainted with the modern sciences; sneers at witchcraft and the black art even while employing them, and doubts most things, nay, half disbelieves even his own existence. *Carlyle.*

Going by railroad I do not consider as travel-25 ling at all; it is merely "being sent" to a place, and very little different from becoming a parcel. *Ruskin.*

Going to ruin is silent work. *Gael. Pr.*

Gold and diamonds are not riches. *Ruskin.*

Gold beheert de wereld—Gold rules the world *Dut. Pr.*

Gold does not satisfy love; it must be paid in its own coin. *Mme. Deluzy.*

Gold, father of flatterers, of pain and care 30 begot, / A fear it is to have thee, and a pain to have thee not. *Palladas.*

Gold glitters most when virtue shines no more. *Young.*

Gold has wings which carry everywhere except to heaven. *Rus. Pr.*

Gold is a wonderful clearer of the understanding; it dissipates every doubt and scruple in an instant, accommodates itself to the meanest capacities, silences the loud and clamorous, and brings over the most obstinate and inflexible. *Addison.*

Gold is Cæsar's treasure, man is God's; thy gold hath Cæsar's image, and thou hast God's. *Quarles.*

Gold is the fool's curtain, which hides all his 35 defects from the world. *Feltham.*

Gold is the sovereign of all sovereigns. *Pr.*

Gold is tried in the fire, friendship in need. *Dan. Pr.*

Gold liegt tief im Berge, aber Koth am Wege —Gold lies deep in the mountain, but dirt on the highway. *Ger. Pr.*

Gold, like the sun, which melts wax and hardens clay, expands great souls and contracts bad hearts. *Rivarol.*

Gold that is put to use more gold begets. 40 *Sh.*

Gold thou may'st safely touch; but if it stick / Unto thy hands, it woundeth to the quick. *Herbert.*

Gold, worse poison to men's souls, / Doing more murder in this loathsome world, / Than these poor compounds that thou may'st not sell. *Sh.*

Gold's worth is gold. *It. Pr.*

Golden chains are heavy, and love is best! *Dr. Walter Smith.*

Golden lads and girls all must, / As chimney-45 sweepers, come to dust. *Cymb.*, iv. 2.

Gone for ever is virtue, once so prevalent in the state, when men deem a mischievous citizen worse than its bitterest enemy, and punish him with severer penalties. *Cic.*

Gone is gone; no Jew will lend upon it. *Ger. Pr.*

Good actions done in secret are the most worthy of honour. *Pascal.*

Good actions give strength to ourselves and inspire good actions in others. *S. Smiles.*

Good advice can be given, a good name cannot 50 be given. *Turk. Pr.*

Good advice / Is beyond all price. *Pr.*

Good advice may be communicated, but not good manners. *Turk. Pr.*

Good ale needs no wisp (of hay for advertisement). *Sc. Pr.*

Good and bad men are less so than they seem. *Coleridge.*

Good and evil are names that signify our appetites and aversions. *Hobbes.*

Good and evil will grow up in this world together; and they who complain in peace of the insolence of the populace must remember that their insolence in peace is bravery in war. *Johnson.*

Good and quickly seldom meet. *Pr.*

Good as is discourse, silence is better, and shames it. *Emerson.*

5 Good bees never turn drones. *Pr.*

Good books, like good friends, are few and chosen, the more select the more enjoyable. *A. B. Alcott.*

Good bread needs baking. *Pr. in Goethe.*

Good-breeding carries along with it a dignity that is respected by the most petulant. *Chesterfield.*

Good-breeding differs, if at all, from high-breeding, only as it gracefully remembers the rights of others, rather than gracefully insists on its own. *Carlyle.*

10 Good-breeding is benevolence in trifles, or the preference of others to ourselves in the little daily occurrences of life. *Chatham.*

Good-breeding is surface Christianity. *Holmes.*

Good-breeding is the result of much good sense, some good nature, and a little self-denial for the sake of others. *Chesterfield.*

Good-breeding shows itself most where to an ordinary eye it appears least. *Addison.*

Good-bye, proud world! I'm going home; Thou art not my friend, and I'm not thine. *Emerson.*

15 Good company and good discourse are the very sinews of virtue. *Izaak Walton.*

Good company upon the road is the shortest cut. *Pr.*

Good counsel is no better than bad counsel, if it is not taken in time. *Dan. Pr.*

Good counsel rejected returns to enrich the giver's bosom. *Goldsmith.*

Good counsels observed are chains to grace. *Fuller.*

20 Good counsel tendered to fools rather provokes than satisfies them. A draught of milk to serpents only increases their venom. *Hitopadesa.*

Good counsel without good fortune is a windmill without wind. *Ger. Pr.*

Good counsellors lack no clients. *Meas. for Meas.*, i. 2.

Good courage breaks ill-luck. *Pr.*

Good deeds in this life are coals raked up in embers to make a fire next day. *Sir T. Overbury.*

25 Good discourse sinks differences and seeks agreements. *A. B. Alcott.*

Good digestion wait on appetite, / And health on both. *Macb.*, iii. 4.

Good example always brings forth good fruits. *S. Smiles.*

Good example is half a sermon. *Ger. Pr.*

Good fortune is the offspring of our endeavours, although there be nothing sweeter than ease. *Hitopadesa.*

30 Good gear goes in sma' book (bulk). *Sc. Pr.*

Good-humour and generosity carry the day with the popular heart all the world over. *Alex. Smith.*

Good-humour may be said to be one of the very best articles of dress one can wear in society. *Thackeray.*

Good hunters track closely. *Dut. Pr.*

Good husbandry is good divinity. *Pr.*

Good is a good doctor, but Bad is sometimes 35 better. *Emerson.*

Good is best when soonest wrought, / Lingering labours come to nought. *Southwell.*

Good is good, but better carrieth it. *Pr.*

Good is never a something into which a man can be borne, but always a something born of the man, which he himself carries, and which does not carry him. *Ed.*

Good is not got without grief. *Gael. Pr.*

Good is the delay that makes sure. *Port.* 40 *Pr.*

Good judges are as rare as good authors. *St. Evremond.*

Good laws often proceed from bad manners. *Pr.*

Good leading makes good following. *Dut. Pr.*

Good luck comes by cuffing. *Pr.*

Good luck is the willing handmaid of upright, 45 energetic character, and conscientious observance of duty. *Lowell.*

Good luck lies in odd numbers. *Merry Wives,* v. 1.

Good management is better than a good income. *Port. Pr.*

Good manners are made up of petty sacrifices. *Emerson.*

Good manners are part of good morals. *Whately.*

Good manners give integrity a bleeze, / When 50 native virtues join the arts to please. *Allan Ramsay.*

Good manners is the art of making those people easy with whom we converse. Whoever makes the fewest persons uneasy is the best bred in the company. *Swift.*

Good maxims are the germs of all excellence. *Joubert.*

Good men are the stars, the planets of the ages wherein they live, and illustrate the times. *Ben Jonson.*

Good mind, good find. *Pr.*

Good name in man and woman, dear my lord, / 55 Is the immediate jewel of their souls ; / Who steals my purse, steals trash ; 'tis something, nothing ; / 'Twas mine, 'tis his, and has been slave to thousands ; / But he that filches from me my good name, / Robs me of that which not enriches him, / And makes me poor indeed. *Othello,* iii. 2.

Good-nature and good sense are usually companions. *Pope.*

Good-nature and good sense must ever join ; / To err is human, to forgive divine. *Pope.*

Good-nature is more agreeable in conversation than wit, and gives a certain air to the countenance which is more aimiable than beauty. *Addison.*

Good-nature is stronger than tomahawks. *Emerson.*

Good-nature is the beauty of the mind, and, 60 like personal beauty, wins almost without anything else. *Hanway.*

Good-nature is the very air of a good mind, the sign of a large and generous soul, and the peculiar soil in which virtue flourishes. *Goodman.*

Good-night, good-night; parting is such sweet sorrow / That I will say good-night till it be to-morrow. *Rom. and Jul.*, ii. 2.

Good pastures make fat sheep. *As You Like It*, iii. 2.

Good people live far apart. *Ger. Pr.*

Good poetry is always personification, and heightens every species of force by giving it a human volition. *Emerson.*

Good poets are the inspired interpreters of the gods. *Plato.*

Good qualities are the substantial riches of the mind, but it is good-breeding that sets them off to advantage. *Locke.*

Good reasons must of force give place to better. *Jul. Cæs.*, iv. 3.

Good right needs good help. *Dut. Pr.*

10 Good-sense and good-nature are never separated, though the ignorant world has thought otherwise. *Dryden.*

Good-sense, which only is the gift of Heaven, / And though no science, fairly worth the seven. *Pope.*

Good shepherd, tell this youth what 'tis to love. . . . It is to be all made of sighs and tears. . . . It is to be all made of faith and service. . . . It is to be all made of fantasy, / All made of passion, and all made of wishes; / All adoration, duty, and observance; / All humbleness, all patience, and impatience; / All purity, all trial, all observance. *As You Like It*, v. 2.

Good sword has often been in poor scabbard. *Gael. Pr.*

Good take heed / Doth surely speed. *Pr.*

15 Good taste cannot supply the place of genius in literature, for the best proof of taste, when there is no genius, would be not to write at all. *Mme. de Staël.*

Good taste comes more from the judgment than from the mind. *La Roche.*

Good taste is the flower of good sense. *A. Poincelot.*

Good taste is the modesty of the mind; that is why it cannot be either imitated or acquired. *Mme. Girardin.*

Good the more / Communicated more abundant grows. *Milton.*

20 Good things take time. *Dut. Pr.*

Good thoughts are no better than good dreams unless they be executed. *Emerson.*

Good to begin well, but better to end well. *Pr.*

Good to the heels the well-worn slipper feels / When the tired player shuffles off the buskin; / A page of Hood may do a fellow good / After a scolding from Carlyle or Ruskin. *Lowell.*

Good unexpected, evil unforeseen, / Appear by turns, as fortune shifts the scene; / Some rais'd aloft, come tumbling down amain / And fall so hard, they bound and rise again. *Lord Lansdowne.*

25 Good ware makes a quick market. *Pr.*

Good-will is everything in morals, but nothing in art; in art, capability alone is anything. *Schopenhauer.*

Good-will, like a good name, is got by many actions and lost by one. *Jeffrey.*

Good wine is a good familiar creature, if it be well used. *Othello*, ii. 3.

Good wine is its own recommendation. *Dut. Pr.*

Good wine needs no brandy. *Amer. Pr.* 30

Good wine needs no bush, *i.e.*, advertisement. *Pr.*

Good women grudge each other nothing, save only clothes, husbands, and flax. *Jean Paul.*

Good words and no deeds. *Pr.*

Good words cool more than cold water. *Pr.*

Good words cost nothing and are worth much. 35 *Pr.*

Good words do more than hard speeches; as the sunbeams, without any noise, will make the traveller cast off his cloak, which all the blustering winds could not do, but only make him bind it closer to him. *Leighton.*

Good works will never save you, but you will never be saved without them. *Pr.*

Good writing and brilliant discourse are perpetual allegories. *Emerson.*

Goodman Fact is allowed by everybody to be a plain-spoken person, and a man of very few words; tropes and figures are his aversion. *Addison.*

Goodness and being in the gods are one; / He 40 who imputes ill to them makes them none. *Euripides.*

Goodness consists not in the outward things we do, but in the inward thing we are. *Chapin.*

Goodness is beauty in its best estate. *Marlowe.*

Goodness is everywhere, and is everywhere to be found, if we will only look for it. *P. Desjardins.*

Gorgons, and hydras, and chimæras dire. *Milton.*

Gossiping and lying go hand in hand. *Pr.* 45

Gossip is a sort of smoke that comes from the dirty tobacco-pipes of those who diffuse it; it proves nothing but the bad taste of the smoker. *George Eliot.*

Gott hilft nur dann, wenn Menschen nicht mehr helfen—God comes to our help only when there is no more help for us in man. *Schiller.*

Gott ist ein unaussprechlicher Seufzer, in Grunde der Seele gelegen—God is an unutterable sigh planted in the depth of the soul. *Jean Paul.*

Gott ist eine leere Tafel, auf der / Nichts weiter steht, als was du selbst / Darauf geschrieben—God is a blank tablet on which nothing further is inscribed than what thou hast thyself written thereupon. *Luther.*

Gott ist mächiger und weiser als wir; darum 50 macht er mit uns nach seinem Gefallen—God is mightier and wiser than we; therefore he does with us according to his good pleasure. *Goethe.*

Gott ist überall, ausser wo er seinem Statthalter hat—God is everywhere except where his vicar is. *Ger. Pr.*

Gottlob! wir haben das Original—God be praised, we have still the original. *Lessing.*

Gott macht gesund, und der Doktor kriegt das Geld—God cures us, and the doctor gets the fee. *Ger. Pr.*

Gott mit uns—God with us. *Ger.*

Gott müsst ihr im Herzen suchen und finden— Ye must seek and find God in the heart. *Jean Paul.*

Gott schuf ja aus Erden den Ritter und Knecht. / Ein hoher Sinn adelt auch niedres Geschlecht—God created out of the clay the knight and his squire. A higher sense ennobles even a humble race. *Bürger.*

Gott-trunkener Mensch—A god-intoxicated man. *Novalis, of Spinoza.*

5 Gott verlässt den Mutigen nimmer—God never forsakes the stout of heart. *Körner.*

Göttern kann man nicht vergelten; / Schön ist's, ihnen gleich zu sein—We cannot recompense the gods ; beautiful it is to be like them. *Schiller.*

Gottes Freund, der Pfaffen Feind—God's friend, priest's foe. *Ger. Pr.*

Gottes ist der Orient, / Gottes ist der Occident, / Nord- und Sudliches Gelände / Ruht im Friede seiner Hände—God's is the east, God's is the west ; north region and south rests in the peace of his hands. *Goethe.*

Gottes Mühle geht langsam, aber sie mahlt fein—God's mill goes slow, but it grinds fine. *Ger. Pr.*

10 Göttliche Apathie und thierische Indifferenz werden nur zu oft verwechselt—Divine indifference and brutish indifference are too often confounded. *Feuchtersleben.*

Goutte à goutte—Drop by drop. *Fr.*

Govern the lips as they were palace-doors, the king within ; / Tranquil and fair and courteous be all words which from that presence win. *Sir Edwin Arnold.*

Government and co-operation are in all things the laws of life ; anarchy and competition, the laws of death. *Ruskin.*

Government arrogates to itself that it alone forms men. . . . Everybody knows that Government never began anything. It is the whole world that thinks and governs. *Wendell Phillips.*

15 Government began in tyranny and force, in the feudalism of the soldier and the bigotry of the priest ; and the ideas of justice and humanity have been fighting their way like a thunderstorm against the organised selfishness of human nature. *Wendell Phillips.*

Government has been a fossil ; it should be a plant. *Emerson.*

Government is a contrivance of human wisdom to provide for human wants. *Burke.*

Government is a necessary evil, like other gocarts and crutches. Our need of it shows exactly how far we are still children. All governing over-much kills the self-help and energy of the governed. *Wendell Phillips.*

Government is a trust, and the officers of the government are trustees ; and both the trust and the trustees are created for the benefit of the people. *H. Clay.*

20 Government is the greatest combination of forces known to human society. It can command more men and raise more money than any and all other agencies combined. *D. D. Field.*

Government must always be a step ahead of the popular movement (*Bewegung*). *Count Arnim.*

Government of the people, by the people and for the people, shall not perish from the earth. *Abraham Lincoln.*

Government of the will is better than increase of knowledge. *Pr.*

Government should direct poor men what to do. *Emerson.*

Governments exist only for the good of the 25 people. *Macaulay.*

Governments exist to protect the rights of minorities. *Wendell Phillips.*

Governments have their origin in the moral identity of men. *Emerson.*

Gowd (gold) gets in at ilka (every) gate except heaven. *Sc. Pr.*

Gowd is gude only in the hand o' virtue. *Sc. Pr.*

Goza tû de tu poco, mientras busca mas el 30 loco— Enjoy your little while the fool is in search of more. *Sp. Pr.*

Grace abused brings forth the foulest deeds, / As richest soil the most luxuriant weeds. *Cowper.*

Grace has been defined the outward expression of the inward harmony of the soul. *Hazlitt.*

Grace in women has more effect than beauty. *Hazlitt.*

Grace is a light superior to Nature, which should direct and preside over it. *Thomas à Kempis.*

Grace is a plant, where'er it grows / Of pure 35 and heavenly root ; / But fairest in the youngest shows, / And yields the sweetest fruit. *Cowper.*

Grace in garments, in movements, and manners ; beauty in the nude and in forms. *Joubert.*

Grace is more beautiful than beauty. *Emerson.*

Grace is the beauty of form under the influence of freedom. *Schiller.*

Grace is the proper relation of the acting person to the action. *Winckelmann.*

Grace is to the body what good sense is to the 40 mind. *La Roche.*

Grace pays its respects to true intrinsic worth, not to the mere signs and trappings of it, which often only show where it ought to be, not where it really is. *Thomas à Kempis.*

Grace was in all her steps, heav'n in her eye, / In every gesture dignity and love. *Milton.*

Gracefulness cannot subsist without ease. *Rousseau.*

Gradatim—Step by step ; by degrees.

Gradu diverso, via una—By different steps but 45 the same way.

Gradus ad Parnassum—A help to the composition of classic poetry.

Græcia capta ferum victorem cepit, et artes / Intulit agresti Latio—Greece, conquered herself, in turn conquered her uncivilised conqueror, and imported her arts into rusticated Latium. *Hor.*

Gram. loquitur ; Dia. vera docet ; Rhe. verba colorat ; Mu. canit ; Ar. numerat ; Geo. ponderat ; As. docet astra—Grammar speaks ; dialectics teaches us truth ; rhetoric gives colouring to our speech ; music sings ; arithmetic reckons ; geometry measures ; astronomy teaches us the stars.

Grammar knows how to lord it over kings, and with high hand make them obey. *Molière.*

Grammaticus Rhetor Geometres Pictor Aliptes / Augur Schœnobates Medicus Magus—omnia novit—Grammarian, rhetorician, geometrician, painter, anointer, augur, tight-rope dancer, physician, magician—he knows everything. *Juv.*

Grain of glory mixt with humbleness / Cures both a fever and lethargicness. *Herbert.*

Grand besoin a de fol qui de soi-même le fait—He has great need of a fool who makes himself one. *Fr. Pr.*

5 Grand bien ne vient pas en peu d'heures—Great wealth is not gotten in a few hours. *Fr.*

Grande parure—Full dress. *Fr.*

Grandescunt aucta labore—They grow with increase of toil. *M.*

Grandeur and beauty are so very opposite, that you often diminish the one as you increase the other. *Shenstone.*

Grandeur has a heavy tax to pay. *Alex. Smith.*

10 Grand parleur, grand menteur—Great talker, great liar. *Fr. Pr.*

Grand venteur, petit faiseur—Great boaster, little doer. *Fr. Pr.*

Grant but memory to us, and we can lose nothing by death. *Whittier.*

Granted the ship comes into harbour with shrouds and tackle damaged; the pilot is blameworthy; he has not been all-wise and all-powerful; but to know how blameworthy, tell us first whether his voyage has been round the globe or only to Ramsgate and the Isle of Dogs. *Carlyle.*

Gran victoria es la que sin sangre se alcanza—Great is the victory that is gained without bloodshed. *Sp. Pr.*

15 Grasp all, lose all. *Pr.*

Grass grows not on the highway. *Pr.*

Grata naturam vincit—Grace overcomes Nature.

Grata superveniet quæ non sperabitur hora—The hour of happiness will come the more welcome when it is not expected. *Hor.*

Gratiæ expectativæ—Expected benefits.

20 Gratia gratiam parit—Kindness produces kindness. *Pr.*

Gratia, Musa, tibi. Nam tu solatia præbes; / Tu curæ requies, tu medicina mali—Thanks to thee, my Muse. For thou dost afford me comfort; thou art a rest from my cares, a cure for my woes. *Ovid.*

Gratia placendi—The satisfaction of pleasing.

Gratia pro rebus merito debetur inemtis—Thanks are justly due for things we have not to pay for. *Ovid.*

Gratior et pulchro veniens in corpore virtus—Even virtue appears more lovely when enshrined in a beautiful form. *Virg.*

25 Gratis—For nothing.

Gratis anhelans, multa agendo nihil agens—Out of breath for nothing, making much ado about nothing. *Phæd.*

Gratis asseritur—It is asserted but not proved.

Gratitude is a duty which ought to be paid, but which none have a right to expect. *Rousseau.*

Gratitude is a keen sense of favours to come. *Talleyrand.*

30 Gratitude is a species of justice. *Johnson.*

Gratitude is memory of the heart. (?)

Gratitude is never conferred but where there have been previous endeavours to excite it; we consider it as a debt, and our spirits wear a load till we have discharged the obligation. *Goldsmith.*

Gratitude is one of the rarest of virtues. *Theodore Parker.*

Gratitude is the fairest blossom which springs from the soul; and the heart of man knoweth none more fragrant. *H. Ballou.*

35 Gratitude is the least of virtues, ingratitude the worst of vices. *Pr.*

Gratitude is with most people only a strong desire for greater benefits to come. *La Roche.*

Gratitude once refused can never after be recovered. *Goldsmith.*

Gratitude which consists in good wishes may be said to be dead, as faith without good works is dead. *Cervantes.*

Gratis dictum—Said to no purpose; irrelevant to the question at issue.

40 Gratum hominem semper beneficium delectat; ingratum semel—A kindness is always delightful to a grateful man; to an ungrateful, only at the time of its receipt. *Sen.*

Grau' Haare sind Kirchhofsblumen—Gray hairs are churchyard flowers. *Ger. Pr.*

Grau, teurer Freund, ist alle Theorie, / Und grün des Lebens goldner Baum—Gray, dear friend, is all theory, and green life's golden tree. *Goethe.*

Grave nihil est homini quod fert necessitas—No burden is really heavy to a man which necessity lays on him.

Grave paupertas malum est, et intolerabile, quæ magnum domat populum—The poverty which oppresses a great people is a grievous and intolerable evil.

45 Grave pondus illum magna nobilitas premit—His exalted rank weighs heavy on him as a grievous burden. *Sen.*

Grave senectus est hominibus pondus—Old age is a heavy burden to man.

Graves, the dashes in the punctuation of our lives. *S. W. Duffield.*

Grave virus / Munditiæ pepulere—More elegant manners expelled this offensive style. *Hor.*

Graviora quædam sunt remedia periculis—Some remedies are worse than the disease. *Pub. Syr.*

50 Gravis ira regum semper—The anger of kings is always heavy. *Sen.*

Gravissimum est imperium consuetudinis—The empire of custom is most mighty. *Pub. Syr.*

Gravity is a mysterious carriage of the body, invented to cover the defects of the mind. *La Roche.*

Gravity is a taught trick to gain credit of the world for more sense and knowledge than a man is worth. *Sterne.*

Gravity is only the bark of wisdom, but it preserves it. *Confucius.*

55 Gravity is the ballast of the soul, which keeps the mind steady. *Fuller.*

Gravity is the best cloak for sin in all countries. *Fielding.*

Gravity is the inseparable companion of pride. *Goldsmith.*

Gravity is twin brother to stupidity. *Bovee.*

Gravity, with all its pretensions, was no better, but often worse, than what a French wit had long ago defined it, viz., a mysterious carriage of the body to cover the defects of the mind. *Sterne.*

Gray hairs seem to my fancy like the light of a soft moon, silvering over the evening of life. *Jean Paul.*

Gray is all theory, and green the while is the golden tree of life. *Goethe.*

5 Gratiano speaks an infinite deal of nothing. ... His reasons are as two grains of wheat hid in two bushels of chaff; you will seek all day ere you find them; and when you have them, they are not worth the search. *Mer. of Ven.*, i. 1.

Great actions crown themselves with lasting bays;/Who well deserves needs not another's praise. *Heath.*

Great acts grow out of great occasions, and great occasions spring from great principles, working changes in society and tearing it up by the roots. *Hazlitt.*

Great ambition is the passion of a great character. He who is endowed with it may perform very good or very bad actions; all depends upon the principles which direct him. *Napoleon.*

Great art dwells in all that is beautiful; but false art omits or changes all that is ugly. Great art accepts Nature as she is, but directs the eyes and thoughts to what is most perfect in her; false art saves itself the trouble of direction by removing or altering whatever is objectionable. *Ruskin.*

10 Great attention to what is said and sweetness of speech, a great degree of kindness and the appearance of awe, are always tokens of a man's attachment. *Hitopadesa.*

Great barkers are nae biters. *Sc. Pr.*

Great boast, small roast. *Pr.*

Great books are written for Christianity much oftener than great deeds are done for it. *H. Mann.*

Great causes are never tried on their merits; but the cause is reduced to particulars to suit the size of the partisans, and the contention is ever hottest on minor matters. *Emerson.*

15 Great countries are those that produce great men. *Disraeli.*

Great cowardice is hidden by a bluster of daring. *Lucan.*

Great cry but little wool, as the devil said when he shear'd his hogs. *Pr.*

Great deeds cannot die; / They with the sun and moon renew their light, / For ever blessing those that look on them. *Tennyson.*

Great deeds immortal are—they cannot die, / Unscathed by envious blight or withering frost, / They live, and bud, and bloom; and men partake / Still of their freshness, and are strong thereby. *Aytoun.*

20 Great dejection often follows great enthusiasm. *Joseph Roux.*

Great edifices, like great mountains, are the work of ages. *Victor Hugo.*

Great endowments often announce themselves in youth in the form of singularity and awkwardness. *Goethe.*

Great, ever fruitful; profitable for reproof, for encouragement, for building up in manful purposes and works, are the words of those that in their day were men. *Carlyle.*

Great evils one triumphs over bravely, but the little eat away one's heart. *Mrs. Carlyle.*

Great fleas have little fleas / Upon their backs 25 to bite 'em; / And little fleas have lesser fleas, / And so ad infinitum. *Lowell.*

Great folks have five hundred friends because they have no occasion for them. *Goldsmith.*

Great fools have great bells. *Dut. Pr.*

Great genial power consists in being altogether receptive. *Emerson.*

Great geniuses have always the shortest biographies. *Emerson.*

Great gifts are for great men. *Pr.*   30

Great God, I had rather be / A Pagan suckled in some creed outworn; / So might I, standing on this pleasant lea, / Have glimpses that would make me less forlorn. *Wordsworth.*

Great grief makes those sacred upon whom its hand is laid. Joy may elevate, ambition glorify, but sorrow alone can consecrate. *H. Greeley.*

Great griefs medicine the less. *Cymbeline*, iv. 2.

Great haste makes great waste. *Ben. Franklin.*

Great honours are great burdens; but on 35 whom / They're cast with envy, he doth bear two loads. *Ben Jonson.*

Great joy is only earned by great exertion. *Goethe.*

Great is he who enjoys his earthenware as if it were plate, and not less great the man to whom all his plate is no more than earthenware. *Sen.*

Great is not great to the greater. *Sir P. Sidney.*

Great is self-denial! Life goes all to ravels and tatters where that enters not. *Carlyle.*

Great is song used to great ends. *Tennyson.* 40

Great is the soul, and plain. It is no flatterer, it is no follower; it never appeals from itself. *Emerson.*

Great is the strength of an individual soul true to its high trust; mighty is it, even to the redemption of a world. *Mrs. Child.*

Great is truth, and mighty above all things. *Apocrypha.*

Great is wisdom; infinite is the value of wisdom. It cannot be exaggerated; it is the highest achievement of man. *Carlyle.*

Great joy, especially after a sudden change 45 and revolution of circumstances, is apt to be silent, and dwells rather in the heart than on the tongue. *Fielding.*

Great knowledge, if it be without vanity, is the most severe bridle of the tongue. *Jeremy Taylor.*

Great lies are as great as great truths, and prevail constantly and day after day. *Thackeray.*

Great lords have great hands, but they do not reach to heaven. *Dan. Pr.*

Great Mammon!—greatest god below the sky. *Spenser.*

Great men are always of a nature originally melancholy. *Arist.*

Great men are among the best gifts which God bestows upon a people. *G. S. Hillard.*

Great men are like eagles, and build their nest on some lofty solitude. *Schopenhauer.*

Great men are more distinguished by range and extent than by originality. *Emerson.*

5 Great men are never sufficiently known but in struggles. *Burke.*

Great men are not always wise. *Bible.*

Great men are rarely isolated mountain-peaks; they are the summits of ranges. *T. W. Higginson.*

Great men are sincere. *Emerson.*

Great men are the fire-pillars in this dark pilgrimage of mankind; they stand as heavenly signs, ever-living witnesses of what has been, prophetic tokens of what may still be, the revealed, embodied possibilities of human nature. *Carlyle.*

10 Great Men are the inspired (speaking and acting) Texts of that Divine Book of Revelations, whereof a Chapter is completed from epoch to epoch, and by some named History. *Carlyle.*

Great men are the modellers, patterns, and in a wide sense creators, of whatsoever the general mass of men contrived to do and attain. *Carlyle.*

Great men are the true men, the men in whom Nature has succeeded. *Amiel.*

Great men are they who see that spiritual is stronger than any material force, that thoughts rule the world. *Emerson.*

Great men do not content us. It is their solitude, not their force, that makes them conspicuous. *Emerson.*

15 Great men do not play stage tricks with the doctrines of life and death; only little men do that. *Ruskin.*

Great men essay enterprises because they think them great, and fools because they think them easy. *Vauvenargues.*

Great men get more by obliging inferiors than by disdaining them. *South.*

Great men, great nations have ever been perceivers of the terror of life, and have manned themselves to face it. *Emerson.*

Great men have their parasites. *Sydney Smith.*

20 Great men lose somewhat of their greatness by being near us; ordinary men gain much. *Landor.*

Great men may jest with saints; 'tis wit in them, / But in the less, foul profanation. *Meas. for Meas.,* ii. 2.

Great men need to be lifted upon the shoulders of the whole world, in order to conceive their great ideas or perform their great deeds; that is, there must be an atmosphere of greatness round about them. A hero cannot be a hero unless in a heroic world. *Hawthorne.*

Great men not only know their business, but they usually know that they know it, and are not only right in their main opinions, but they usually know that they are right in them. *Ruskin.*

Great men oft die by vile Bezonians. 2 *Hen. VI.,* iv. 1.

25 Great men often rejoice at crosses of fortune, just as brave soldiers do at wars. *Sen.*

Great men or men of great gifts you will easily find, but symmetrical men never. *Emerson.*

Great men, said Themistocles, are like the oaks, under the branches of which men are happy in finding a refuge in the time of storm and rain; but when they have to pass a sunny day under them, they take pleasure in cutting the bark and breaking the branches. *Goethe.*

Great men should drink with harness on their throats. *Tim. of Athens,* i. 2.

Great men should think of opportunity, and not of time. Time is the excuse of feeble and puzzled spirits. *Disraeli.*

Great men stand like solitary towers in the 30 city of God, and secret passages running deep beneath external Nature give their thoughts intercourse with higher intelligences, which strengthens and consoles them, and of which the labourers on the surface do not even dream. *Longfellow.*

Great men, though far above us, are felt to be our brothers; and their elevation shows us what vast possibilities are wrapped up in our common humanity. They beckon us up the gleaming heights to whose summits they have climbed. Their deeds are the woof of this world's history. *Moses Harvey.*

Great men too often have greater faults than little men can find room for. *Landor.*

Great men will always pay deference to greater. *Landor.*

Great minds erect their never-failing trophies on the firm base of mercy. *Massinger.*

Great minds had rather deserve contempor- 35 aneous applause without obtaining it, than obtain without deserving it. *Colton.*

Great minds, like Heaven, are pleased in doing good, / Though the ungrateful subjects of their favours / Are barren in return. *Rowe.*

Great minds seek to labour for eternity. All other men are captivated by immediate advantages; great minds are excited by the prospect of distant good. *Schiller.*

Great names stand not alone for great deeds; they stand also for great virtues, and, doing them worship, we elevate ourselves. *H. Giles.*

Great part of human suffering has its root in the nature of man, and not in that of his institutions. *Lowell.*

Great passions are incurable diseases; the 40 very remedies make them worse. *Goethe.*

Great patriots must be men of great excellence; this alone can secure to them lasting admiration. *H. Giles.*

Great people and champions are special gifts of God, whom He gives and preserves; they do their work and achieve great actions, not with vain imaginations or cold and sleepy cogitations, but by motion of God. *Luther.*

Great pleasures are much less frequent than great pains. *Hume.*

Great poets are no sudden prodigies, but slow results. *Lowell.*

Great poets try to describe what all men see 45 and to express what all men feel; if they cannot describe it, they let it alone. *Ruskin.*

Great profits, great risks. *Chinese Pr.*

Great results cannot be achieved at once; and we must be satisfied to advance in life as we walk, step by step. *S. Smiles.*

Great revolutions, whatever may be their causes, are not lightly commenced, and are not concluded with precipitation. *Disraeli.*

Great souls are always royally submissive, reverent to what is over them; only small, mean souls are otherwise. *Carlyle.*

Great souls are not cast down by adversity. *Pr.*

5 Great souls are not those which have less passion and more virtue than common souls, but only those which have greater designs. *La Roche.*

Great souls attract sorrows as mountains do storms. But the thunder-clouds break upon them, and they thus form a shelter for the plains around. *Jean Paul.*

Great souls care only for what is great. *Amiel.*

Great souls endure in silence. *Schiller.*

Great souls forgive not injuries till time has put their enemies within their power, that they may show forgiveness is their own. *Dryden.*

10 Great spirits and great business do keep out this weak passion (love). *Bacon.*

Great talents are rare, and they rarely recognise themselves. *Goethe.*

Great talents have some admirers, but few friends. *Niebuhr.*

Great talkers are like leaky pitchers, everything runs out of them. *Pr.*

Great talkers are little doers. *P*

15 Great thieves hang little ones. *Ge*

Great things are done when men and mountains meet; / These are not done by jostling in the street. *Wm. Blake.*

Great things through greatest hazards are achiev'd, / And then they shine. *Beaumont.*

Great thoughts and a pure heart are the things we should beg for ourselves from God. *Goethe.*

Great thoughts come from the heart. *Vauvenargues.*

20 Great thoughts, great feelings come to them, / Like instincts, unawares. *M. Milnes.*

Great thoughts reduced to practice become great acts. *Hazlitt.*

Great towns are but a large sort of prison to the soul, like cages to birds or pounds to beasts. *Charron.*

Great warmth at first is the certain ruin of every great achievement. Doth not water, although ever so cool, moisten the earth? *Hitopadesa.*

Great warriors, like great earthquakes, are principally remembered for the mischief they have done. *Bovee.*

25 Great wealth, great care. *Dut. Pr.*

Great wits are sure to madness near allied, / And thin partitions do their bounds divide. *Dryden.*

Great wits to madness nearly are allied; / Both serve to make our poverty our pride. *Emerson.*

Great women belong to history and to self-sacrifice. *Leigh Hunt.*

Great works are performed. not by strength, but by perseverance. *Johnson.*

Great writers and orators are commonly econo- 30 mists in the use of words. *Whipple.*

Greater love hath no man than this, that a man lay down his life for his friends. *Jesus.*

Greater than man, less than woman. *Essex, of Queen Elizabeth.*

Greatest scandal waits on greatest state. *Shakespeare.*

Greatly to find quarrel in a straw, / When honour's at the stake. *Ham., iv. 4.*

Greatness and goodness are not means, but 35 ends. *Coleridge.*

Greatness appeals to the future. *Emerson.*

Greatness, as we daily see it, is unsociable. *Landor.*

Greatness can only be rightly estimated when minuteness is justly reverenced. Greatness is the aggregation of minuteness; nor can its sublimity be felt truthfully by any mind unaccustomed to the affectionate watching of what is least. *Ruskin.*

Greatness doth not approach him who is for ever looking down. *Hitopadesa.*

Greatness envy not; for thou mak'st thereby / 40 Thyself the worse, and so the distance greater. *Herbert.*

Greatness, in any period and under any circumstances, has always been rare. It is of elemental birth, and is independent alike of its time and its circumstances. *W. Winter.*

Greatness is a spiritual condition worthy to excite love, interest, and admiration; and the outward proof of greatness is that we excite love, interest, and admiration. *Matthew Arnold.*

Greatness is its own torment. *Theodore Parker.*

Greatness is like a laced coat from Monmouth Street, which fortune lends us for a day to wear, to-morrow puts it on another's back. *Fielding.*

Greatness is not a teachable nor gainable 45 thing, but the expression of the mind of a God-made man: teach, or preach, or labour as you will, everlasting difference is set between one man's capacity and another's; and this God-given supremacy is the priceless thing, always just as rare in the world at one time as another. . . . And nearly the best thing that men can generally do is to set themselves, not to the attainment, but the discovery of this: learning to know gold, when we see it, from iron-glance, and diamond from flint-sand, being for most of us a more profitable employment than trying to make diamonds of our own charcoal. *Ruskin.*

Greatness is nothing unless it be lasting. *Napoleon.*

Greatness lies not in being strong, but in the right using of strength. He is greatest whose strength carries up the most hearts by the attraction of his own. *Ward Beecher.*

Greatness may be present in lives whose range is very small. *Phil. Brooks.*

Greatness of mind is not shown by admitting small things, but by making small things great under its influence. He who can take no interest in what is small will take false interest in what is great. *Ruskin.*

Greatness, once and for ever, has done with opinion. *Emerson.*

Greatness, once fallen out with fortune, / Must fall out with men too; what the declined is, / He shall as soon read in the eyes of others / As feel in his own fall. *Troil. and Cress.*, iii. 3.

Greatness stands upon a precipice; and if prosperity carry a man never so little beyond his poise, it overbears and dashes him to pieces. *Colton.*

Greatness, thou gaudy torment of our souls, / The wise man's fetter and the rage of fools. *Otway.*

5 Greatness, with private men / Esteem'd a blessing, is to me a curse; / And we, whom from our high births they conclude / The only free men, are the only slaves: / Happy the golden mean. *Massinger.*

Greediness bursts the bag. *Pr.*

Greedy folk hae lang airms. *Sc. Pr.*

Greedy misers rail at sordid misers. *Helvetius.*

Greek architecture is the flowering of geometry. *Emerson.*

10 Greek art, and all other art, is fine when it makes a man's face as like a man's face as it can. *Ruskin.*

Greif' nicht leicht in ein Wespennest, Doch wenn du greifst, so stehe fest — Attack not thoughtlessly a wasp's nest, but if you do, stand fast. *M. Claudius.*

Greife schnell zum Augenblicke, nur die Gegenwart ist dein—Quickly seize the moment: only the present is thine. *Körner.*

Grex totus in agris / Unius scabie cadit—The entire flock in the fields dies of the disease introduced by one. *Juv.*

Grex venalium—A venal pack. *Sueton.*

15 Grey hairs are wisdom—if you hold your tongue; / Speak—and they are but hairs, as in the young. *Philo.*

Grief best is pleased with grief's society. *Shakespeare.*

Grief boundeth where it falls, / Not with an empty hollowness, but weight. *Rich. II.*, i. 2.

Grief divided is made lighter. *Pr.*

Grief fills the room up of my absent child, / Lies in his bed, walks up and down with me; / Puts on his pretty look, repeats his words, / Remembers me of all his gracious parts, / Stuffs out his vacant garments with his form: Then have I reason to be fond of grief. *King John*, iii. 4.

20 Grief finds some ease by him that like doth bear. *Spenser.*

Grief hallows hearts, even while it ages heads. *Bailey.*

Grief has its time. *Johnson.*

Grief knits two hearts in closer bonds than happiness ever can, and common sufferings are far stronger links than common joys. *Lamartine.*

Grief is a species of idleness, and the necessity of attention to the present, preserves us from being lacerated and devoured by sorrow for the past. *Dr. Johnson.*

25 Grief is a stone that bears one down, but two bear it lightly. *W. Hauff.*

Grief is only the memory of widowed affection. *James Martineau.*

Grief is proud and makes his owner stout. *King John*, iii. 1.

Grief is so far from retrieving a loss that it makes it greater; but the way to lessen it is by a comparison with others' losses. *Wycherley.*

Grief is the agony of an instant; the indulgence of grief the blunder of a life. *Disraeli.*

Grief is the culture of the soul; it is the true 30 fertiliser. *Mme. de Girardin.*

Grief, like a tree, has tears for its fruit. *Philemon.*

Grief makes one hour ten. *Rich. II.*, i. 3.

Grief or misfortune seems to be indispensable to the development of intelligence, energy, and virtue. *Fearon.*

Grief sharpens the understanding and strengthens the soul, whereas joy seldom troubles itself about the former, and makes the latter either effeminate or frivolous. *F. Schubert.*

Grief should be / Like joy, majestic, equable, 35 sedate, / Conforming, cleansing, raising, making free. *Aubrey de Vere (the younger).*

Grief should be the instructor of the wise; / Sorrow is knowledge: they who know the most / Must mourn the deepest o'er the fatal truth, / The Tree of Knowledge is not that of Life. *Byron.*

Grief still treads upon the heels of Pleasure. *Congreve.*

Grief, which disposes gentle natures to retirement, to inaction, and to meditation, only makes restless spirits more restless. *Macaulay.*

Griefs assured are felt before they come. *Dryden.*

Grim-visaged war hath smooth'd his wrinkled 40 front. . . . He capers nimbly in a lady's chamber, / To the lascivious pleasing of a lute. *Rich. III.*, i. 1.

Grind the faces of the poor. *Bible.*

Gross and vulgar minds will always pay a higher respect to wealth than to talent; for wealth, although it is a far less efficient source of power than talent, happens to be far more intelligible. *Colton.*

Gross Diligenz und klein Conscienz macht reich—Great industry and little conscience make one rich. *Ger. Pr.*

Gross ist, wer Feinde tapfer überwand; / Doch grösser ist, wer sie gewonnen—Great is he who has bravely vanquished his enemies, but greater is he who has gained them. *Seume.*

Gross kann man sich im Glück, erhaben nur 45 im Unglück zeigen—One may show himself great in good fortune, but exalted only in bad. *Schiller.* (?)

Gross und leer, wie das Heidelberger Fass—Big and empty, like the Heidelberg tun. *Ger. Pr.*

Grosse Leidenschaften sind Krankheiten ohne Hoffnung; was sie heilen könnte, macht sie erst recht gefährlich—Great passions are incurable diseases; what might heal them is precisely that which makes them so dangerous. *Goethe.*

Grosse Seelen dulden still—Great souls endure in silence. *Schiller.*

Grosser Herren Leute lassen sich was bedünken—Great people's servants think themselves of no small consequence. *Ger. Pr.*

Grudge not another what you canna get your-sel'. *Sc. Pr.*

Grudge not one against another. *St. James.*

Guardalo ben, guardalo tutto / L'uom senza danar quanto è brutto—Watch him well, watch him closely ; the man without money, how worthless he is ! *It. Pr.*

Guardati da aceto di vin dolce—Beware of the vinegar of sweet wine. *It. Pr.*

5 Guardati da chi non ha che perdere—Beware of him who has nothing to lose. *It. Pr.*

Guardati dall' occasione, e ti guarderà / Dio da peccati—Keep yourself from opportunities, and God will keep you from sins. *It. Pr.*

Guards from outward harms are sent ; / Ills from within thy reason must prevent. *Dryden.*

Guard well thy thought ; / Our thoughts are heard in heaven. *Young.*

Gude advice is ne'er out o' season. *Sc. Pr.*

10 Gude bairns are eith to lear, *i.e.*, easy to teach. *Sc. Pr.*

Gude breeding and siller mak' our sons gentle-men. *Sc. Pr.*

Gude claes (clothes) open a' doors. *Sc. Pr.*

Gude folk are scarce, tak' care o' ane. *Sc. Pr.*

Gude foresight furthers the wark. *Sc. Pr.*

15 Gude wares mak' a quick market. *Sc. Pr.*

Guds Raadkammer har ingen Nögle — To God's council-chamber we have no key. *Dan. Pr.*

Guenille, si l'on veut ; ma guenille m'est chère —Call it a rag, if you please ; my rag is dear to me. *Molière.*

Guerra al cuchillo—War to the knife. *Sp.*

Guerra cominciata, inferno scatinato—War be-gun, hell let loose. *It. Pr.*

20 Guerre à mort—War to the death. *Fr.*

Guerre à outrance—War of extermination ; war to the uttermost. *Fr.*

Guerre aux châteaux, paix aux chaumières ! —War to the castles, peace to the cottages ! *Fr.*

Guessing is missing (the point). *Dut. Pr.*

Guilt is a spiritual Rubicon. *Jane Porter.*

25 Guilt is ever at a loss, and confusion waits upon it. *Congreve.*

Guilt is the source of sorrow ; 'tis the fiend, / Th' avenging fiend that follows us behind / With whips and stings. *Rowe.*

Guilt, though it may attain temporal splen-dour, can never confer real happiness. *Scott.*

Guiltiness will speak, though tongues were out of use. *Othello, v. 1.*

Guilty consciences make men cowards. *Van-brugh.*

30 Gunpowder is the emblem of politic revenge, for it biteth first and barketh afterwards ; the bullet being at the mark before the noise is heard, so that it maketh a noise not by way of warning, but of triumph. *Fuller.*

Gunpowder makes all men alike tall . . . Here-by at last is the Goliath powerless and the David resistless ; savage animalism is no-thing, inventive spiritualism is all. *Carlyle.*

Gustatus est sensus ex omnibus maxime voluptarius—The sense of taste is the most exquisite of all. *Cic.*

Gut Gewissen ist ein sanftes Ruhekissen—A good conscience is a soft pillow. *Ger. Pr.*

Gut verloren, etwas verloren ; / Ehre verloren, viel verloren ; / Mut verloren, alles verloren —Wealth lost, something lost ; honour lost, much lost ; courage lost, all lost. *Goethe.*

Güte bricht einem kein Bein—Kindness breaks 35 no one's bones. *Ger. Pr.*

Guter Rath kommt über Nacht—Good counsel comes over-night. *Ger. Pr.*

Guter Rath lässt sich geben, aber gute Sitte nicht—Good advice may be given, but manners not. *Turkish Pr.*

Gutes aus Gutem, das kann jedweder Ver-ständige bilden ; / Aber der Genius ruft Gutes aus Schlechtem hervor—Good out of good is what every man of intellect can fashion, but it takes genius to evoke good out of bad. *Schiller.*

Gutes und Böses kommt unerwartet dem Menschen ; / Auch verkündet, glauben wir's nicht—Good and evil come unexpected to man ; even if foretold, we believe it not. *Goethe.*

Gutta cavat lapidem, consumitur annulus 40 usu, / Et teritur pressa vomer aduncus humo — The drop hollows the stone, the ring is worn by use, and the crooked ploughshare is frayed away by the pressure of the earth. *Ovid.*

Gutta cavat lapidem non vi, sed sæpe cadendo —The drop hollows the stone not by force, but by continually falling. *Pr.*

Gutta fortunæ præ dolio sapientiæ—A drop of good fortune rather than a cask of wisdom. *Pr.*

H.

Ha ! lass dich den Teufel bei einem Haar fassen, und du bist sein auf ewig—Ha ! let the devil seize thee by a hair, and thou art his for ever. *Lessing.*

Ha ! welche Lust, Soldat zu sein—Ah ! what a pleasure it is to be a soldier. *Boieldieu.*

Hab' mich nie mit Kleinigkeiten abgegeben— 45 I have never occupied myself with trifles. *Schiller.*

"Habe gehabt," ist ein armer Mann—"I have had," is a poor man. *Ger. Pr.*

Habeas corpus—A writ to deliver one from prison, and show reason for his detention, with a view to judge of its justice, *lit.* you may have the body. *L.*

Habeas corpus ad prosequendum—You may bring up the body for the purpose of prosecution. *L. Writ.*

Habeas corpus ad respondendum—You may bring up the body to make answer. *L. Writ.*

Habeas corpus ad satisfaciendum—You may 50 bring up the body to satisfy. *L. Writ.*

Habemus confitentem reum—We have the con-fession of the accused. *L.*

Habemus luxuriam atque avaritiam, publice egestatem, privatim opulentiam—We have luxury and avarice, but as a people poverty, and in private opulence. *Cato in Sall.*

Habent insidias hominis blanditiæ mali—Under the fair words of a bad man there lurks some treachery. *Phaedr.*

Habent sua fata libelli—Books have their des-tinies. *Hor.*

Habeo senectuti magnam gratiam, quæ mihi sermonis aviditatem auxit—I owe it to old age, that my relish for conversation is so increased. *Cic.*

Habere derelictui rem suam—To neglect one's affairs. *Aul. Gell.*

Habere et dispertire—To have and to distribute.

Habere facias possessionem—You shall cause to take possession. *L. Writ.*

5 Habere, non haberi—To hold, not to be held.

Habet aliquid ex iniquo omne magnum exemplum, quod contra singulos, utilitate publica rependitur—Every great example of punishment has in it some tincture of injustice, but the wrong to individuals is compensated by the promotion of the public good. *Tac.*

Habet iracundia hoc mali, non vult regi—There is in anger this evil, that it will not be controlled. *Sen.*

Habet salem—He has wit; he is a wag.

Habit and imitation are the source of all working and all apprenticeship, of all practice and all learning, in this world. *Carlyle.*

10 Habit gives endurance, and fatigue is the best nightcap. *Kincaid.*

Habit, if not resisted, soon becomes necessity. *St. Augustine.*

Habit is a cable. We weave a thread of it every day, and at last we cannot break it. *Horace Mann.*

Habit is a second nature, which destroys the first. *Pascal.*

Habit is necessary to give power. *Hazlitt.*

15 Habit is ten times nature. *Wellington.*

Habit is the deepest law of human nature. *Carlyle.*

Habit is the purgatory in which we suffer for our past sins. *George Eliot.*

Habit is too arbitrary a master for my liking. *Lavater.*

Habit, with its iron sinews, clasps and leads us day by day. *Lamartine.*

20 Habits are at first cobwebs, at last cables. *Pr.*

Habits (of virtue) are formed by acts of reason in a persevering struggle through temptation. *Bernard Gilpin.*

Habits leave their impress upon the mind, even after they are given up. *Spurgeon.*

Habitual intoxication is the epitome of every crime. *Douglas Jerrold.*

Hablar sin pensar es tirar sin encarar—Speaking without thinking is shooting without taking aim. *Sp. Pr.*

25 Hac mercede placet—I accept the terms.

Hac sunt in fossa Bedæ venerabilis ossa—In this grave lie the bones of the Venerable Bede. *Inscription on Bede's tomb.*

Hac urget lupus, hac canis—On one side a wolf besets you, on the other a dog. *Hor.*

Hactenus—Thus far.

Had Cæsar or Cromwell changed countries, the one might have been a sergeant and the other an exciseman. *Goldsmith.*

30 Had God meant me to be different, He would have created me different. *Goethe.*

Had I but serv'd my God with half the zeal / I serv'd my king, He would not in mine age / Have left me naked to mine enemies. *Hen. VIII., iii. 2.*

Had I succeeded well, I had been reckoned amongst the wise; so ready are we to judge from the event. *Euripides.*

Had not God made this world, and death too, it were an insupportable place. *Carlyle.*

Had religion been a mere chimæra, it would long ago have been extinct; were it susceptible of a definite formula, that formula would long ago have been discovered. *Renan.*

Had sigh'd to many, though he loved but one. 35 *Byron.*

Had we never loved sae kindly, / Had we never loved sae blindly, / Never met or never parted, / We had ne'er been broken-hearted! *Burns.*

Hæ nugæ seria ducent / In mala—These trifles will lead to serious mischief. *Hor.*

Hæ tibi erunt artes, pacisque imponere morem, / Parcere subjectis et debellare superbos—These shall be thy arts, to lay down the law of peace, to spare the conquered, and to subdue the proud. *Virg.*

Hae you gear (goods), or hae you nane, / Tine (lose) heart, and a's gane. *Sc. Pr.*

Hæc a te non multum abludit imago—This 40 picture bears no small resemblance to yourself. *Hor.*

Hæc amat obscurum; volet hæc sub luce videri, / Judicis argutum quæ non formidat acumen; Hæc placuit semel; hæc decies repetita placebit—One (poem) courts the shade; another, not afraid of the critic's keen eye, chooses to be seen in a strong light; the one pleases but once, the other will still please if ten times repeated. *Hor.*

Hæc brevis est nostrorum summa malorum—Such is the short sum of our evils. *Ovid.*

Hæc ego mecum / Compressis agito labris; ubi quid datur oti, / Illudo chartis—These things I revolve by myself with compressed lips. When I have any leisure, I amuse myself with my writings. *Hor.*

Hæc est condicio vivendi, aiebat, eoque / Responsura tuo nunquam est par fama labori—"Such is the lot of life," he said, "and so your merits will never receive their due meed of praise." *Hor.*

Hæc generi incrementa fides—This fidelity will 45 bring new glory to our race. *M.*

Hæc olim meminisse juvabit—It will be a joy to us to recall this, some day. *Virg.*

Hæc omnia transeunt—All these things pass away. *M.*

Hæc perinde sunt, ut illius animus, qui ea possidet. / Qui uti scit, ei bona, illi qui non utitur recte, mala—These things are exactly according to the disposition of him who possesses them. To him who knows how to use them, they are blessings; to him who does not use them aright, they are evils. *Ter.*

Hæc prima lex in amicitia sanciatur, ut neque rogemus res turpes, nec faciamus rogati—Be this the first law established in friendship, that we neither ask of others what is dishonourable, nor ourselves do it when asked. *Cic.*

Hæc scripsi non otii abundantia, sed amoris 50 erga te—I have written this, not as having abundance of leisure, but out of love for you. *Cic.*

Hæc studia adolescentiam alunt, senectutem oblectant, secundas res ornant, adversis solatium ac perfugium præbent, delectant domi, non impediunt foris, pernoctant nobiscum, peregrinantur, rusticantur—These studies are the food of youth and the consolation of old age ; they adorn prosperity and are the comfort and refuge of adversity ; they are pleasant at home and are no encumbrance abroad ; they accompany us at night, in our travels, and in our rural retreats. *Cic.*

Hæc studia oblectant—These studies are our delight. *M.*

Hæc sunt jucundi causa cibusque mali—These things are at once the cause and food of this delicious malady. *Ovid.*

Hæc vivendi ratio mihi non convenit—This mode of living does not suit me. *Cic.*

5 Hæredis fletus sub persona risus est—The weeping of an heir is laughter under a mask. *Pr.*

Hæreditas nunquam ascendit—The right of inheritance never lineally ascends. *L*

Hæres jure repræsentationis—An heir by right of representation. *L.*

Hæres legitimus est quem nuptiæ demonstrant —He is the lawful heir whom marriage points out as such. *L.*

Hæret lateri lethalis arundo—The fatal shaft sticks deep in her side. *Virg.*

10 Halb sind sie kalt, Halb sind sie roh—Half of them are without heart, half without culture. *Goethe.*

Half a house is half a hell. *Ger. Pr.*

Half a loaf is better than no bread. *Pr.*

Half a man's wisdom goes with his courage. *Emerson.*

Half a word fixed upon, or near, the spot is worth a cartload of recollection. *Gray to Palgrave.*

15 Half the ease of life oozes away through the leaks of unpunctuality. *Anon.*

Half the gossip of society would perish if the books that are truly worth reading were but read. *George Dawson.*

Half the ills we hoard within our hearts are ills because we hoard them. *Barry Cornwall.*

Half the logic of misgovernment lies in this one sophistical dilemma : if the people are turbulent, they are unfit for liberty ; if they are quiet, they do not want liberty. *Macaulay.*

Half-wits greet each other. *Gael. Pr.*

20 Hältst du Natur getreu im Augenmerk, / Frommt jeder tüchtige Meister dir : / Doch klammerst du dich blos an Menschenwerk, / Wird alles, was du schaffst, Manier—If you keep Nature faithfully in view, the example of every thorough master will be of service to you ; but if you merely cling to human work, all that you do will be but mannerism. *Geibel.*

Hanc personam induisti, agenda est—You have assumed this part, and you must act it out. *Sen.*

Hanc veniam petimusque damusque vicissim— We both expect this privilege, and give it in return. *Hor.*

Hands that the rod of empire might have sway'd, / Or waked to ecstasy the living lyre. *Gray.*

Handsome is that handsome does. *Pr.*

Handsomeness is the more animal excellence, 25 beauty the more imaginative. *Hare.*

Häng' an die grosse Glocke nicht / Was jemand im Vertrauen spricht — Blaze not abroad to others what any one confides to you in secret. *Claudius.*

Hang a thief when he's young, and he'll no steal when he's auld. *Sc. Pr.*

Hang constancy ! you know too much of the world to be constant, sure. *Fielding.*

Hang sorrow ! care will kill a cat, / And therefore let's be merry. *G. Wither.*

Hänge nicht alles auf einen Nagel—Hang not 30 all on one nail. *Ger. Pr.*

Hanging and wiving goes by destiny. *Mer. of Ven.*, ii. 9.

Hannibal ad portas—Hannibal is at the gates. *Cic.*

Hap and mishap govern the world. *Pr.*

Happiest they of human race, / To whom God has granted grace / To read, to fear, to hope, to pray, / To lift the latch and force the way ;/ And better had they ne'er been born, / Who read to doubt, or read to scorn. *Scott.*

Happily to steer / From grave to gay, from 35 lively to severe. *Pope.*

Happiness consists in activity ; it is a running stream, and not a stagnant pool. *J. M. Good.*

Happiness depends not on the things, but on the taste. *La Roche.*

Happiness grows at our own firesides, and is not to be picked up in strangers' galleries. *Douglas Jerrold.*

Happiness is a ball after which we run wherever it rolls, and we push it with our feet when it stops. *Goethe.*

Happiness is a chimæra and suffering a reality. 40 *Schopenhauer.*

Happiness is "a tranquil acquiescence under an agreeable delusion." *Quoted by Sterne.*

Happiness is but a dream, and sorrow a reality. *Voltaire.*

Happiness is deceitful as the calm that precedes the hurricane, smooth as the water on the verge of the cataract, and beautiful as the rainbow, that smiling daughter of the storm. *Arliss' Lit. Col.*

Happiness is like the mirage in the desert ; she tantalises us with a delusion that distance creates and that contiguity destroys. *Arliss' Lit. Col.*

Happiness is like the statue of Isis, whose 45 veil no mortal ever raised. *Landor.*

Happiness is matter of opinion, of fancy, in fact, but it must amount to conviction, else it is nothing. *Chamfort.*

Happiness is neither within us nor without us ; it is the union of ourselves with God. *Pascal.*

Happiness is nothing but the conquest of God through love. *Amiel.*

Happiness is only evident to us by deliverance from evil. *Nicole.*

Happiness is the fine and gentle rain which 50 penetrates the soul, but which afterwards gushes forth in springs of tears. *M. de Guérin.*

Happiness is unrepented pleasure. *Socrates.*

Happiness lies first of all in health. *G. W. Curtis.*

Happiness, like Juno, is a goddess in pursuit, but a cloud in possession, deified by those who cannot enjoy her, and despised by those who can. *Arliss' Lit. Col.*

Happiness never lays its fingers on its pulse. *A. Smith.*

Happiness springs not from a large fortune, but temperate habits and simple wishes. Riches increase not by increase of the supply of want, but by decrease of the sense of it, —the minimum of it being the maximum of them. *Ed.*

Happiness, that grand mistress of ceremonies in the dance of life, impels us through all its mazes and meanderings, but leads none of us by the same route. *Arliss' Lit. Col.*

5 Happiness travels incognita to keep a private assignation with contentment, and to partake of a tête-à-tête and a dinner of herbs in a cottage. *Arliss' Lit. Col.*

Happiness, when unsought, is often found, and when unexpected, often obtained; while those who seek her the most diligently fail the most, because they seek her where she is not. *Arliss' Lit. Col.*

Happy are they that hear their detractions, and can put them to mending. *Much Ado,* ii. 3.

Happy child! the cradle is still to thee an infinite space; once grown into a man, and the boundless world will be too small to thee. *Schiller.*

Happy contractedness of youth, nay, of mankind in general, that they think neither of the high nor the deep, of the true nor the false, but only of what is suited to their own conceptions. *Goethe.*

10 Happy he for whom a kind heavenly sun brightens the ring of necessity into a ring of duty. *Carlyle.*

Happy he that can abandon everything by which his conscience is defiled or burdened. *Thomas à Kempis.*

Happy in that we are not over-happy; / On Fortune's cap we are not the very button. *Ham.,* ii. 2.

Happy is he who soon discovers the chasm that lies between his wishes and his powers. *Goethe.*

Happy is that house and blessed is that congregation where Martha still complains of Mary. *S. Bern.*

15 Happy he whose last hour strikes in the midst of his children. *Grillparzer.*

Happy is he that is happy in his children. *Pr.*

Happy is he to whom his business itself becomes a puppet, who at length can play with it, and amuse himself with what his situation makes his duty. *Goethe.*

Happy is the boy whose mother is tired of talking nonsense to him before he is old enough to know the sense of it. *Hare.*

Happy is the hearing man; unhappy the speaking man. *Emerson.*

20 Happy is the man who can endure the highest and the lowest fortune. He who has endured such vicissitudes with equanimity has deprived misfortune of its power. *Sen.*

Happy is the man whose father was to the devil. *Pr.*

Happy lowly clown! / Uneasy lies the head that wears a crown! 2 *Hen. IV.,* iii. 1.

Happy men are full of the present, for its bounty suffices them; and wise men also, for its duties engage them. Our grand business undoubtedly is not to see what lies dimly at a distance, but to do what lies clearly at hand. *Carlyle.*

Happy season of virtuous youth, when shame is still an impassable celestial barrier, and the sacred air-castles of hope have not shrunk into the mean clay hamlets of reality, and man by his nature is yet infinite and free. *Carlyle.*

Happy that I can / Be crossed and thwarted 25 as a man, / Not left in God's contempt apart, / With ghastly smooth life, dead at heart, / Tame in earth's paddock, as her prize. *Browning.*

Happy the man, and happy he alone, / He who can call to-day his own; / He who, secure within, can say, / To-morrow do thy worst, for I have lived to-day. *Dryden, after Horace.*

Happy the man to whom Heaven has given a morsel of bread without his being obliged to thank any other for it than Heaven itself. *Cervantes.*

Happy the people whose annals are blank in History's book. *Montesquieu.*

Happy thou art not; / For what thou hast not still thou striv'st to get, / And what thou hast, forgett'st. *Meas. for Meas.,* iii. 1.

Happy who in his verse can gently steer, / 30 From grave to light, from pleasant to severe. *Dryden.*

Hard is the factor's rule; no better is the minister's. *Gael. Pr.*

Hard pounding, gentlemen; but we shall see who can pound the longest. *Wellington at Waterloo.*

Hard with hard builds no houses; soft binds hard. *Pr.*

Hard work is still the road to prosperity, and there is no other. *Ben. Franklin.*

Hardness ever of hardiness is mother. *Cym-* 35 *beline,* iii. 6.

Hardship is the native soil of manhood and self-reliance. *John Neal.*

Harm watch, harm catch. *Pr.*

Hart kann die Tugend sein, doch grausam nie, / unmenschlich nie—Virtue may be stern, though never cruel, never inhuman. *Schiller.*

Harvests are Nature's bank dividends. *Haliburton.*

Has any man, or any society of men, a truth 40 to speak, a piece of spiritual work to do; they can nowise proceed at once and with the mere natural organs, but must first call a public meeting, appoint committees, issue prospectuses, eat a public dinner; in a word, construct or borrow machinery, wherewith to speak it and do it. Without machinery they were hopeless, helpless; a colony of Hindoo weavers squatting in the heart of Lancashire. *Carlyle.*

Has patitur pœnas peccandi sola voluntas. / Nam scelus intra se tacitum qui cogitat ullum, / Facti crimen habet—Such penalties does the mere intention to sin suffer; for he who meditates any secret wickedness within himself incurs the guilt of the deed. *Juv.*

Has pœnas garrula lingua dedit—This punishment a prating tongue brought on him. *Ovid.*

Has vaticinationes eventus comprobavit—The event has verified these predictions. *Cic.*

Hassen und Neiden / Muss der Biedre leiden. / Es erhöht des Mannes Wert, / Wenn der Hass sich auf ihn kehrt—The upright must suffer hatred and envy. It enhances the worth of a man if hatred pursues him. *Gottfried von Strassburg.*

Hast du im Thal ein sichres Haus, / Dann wolle nie zu hoch hinaus—Hast thou a secure house in the valley? Then set not thy heart on a higher beyond. *Förster.*

Haste and rashness are storms and tempests, breaking and wrecking business; but nimbleness is a full, fair wind, blowing it with speed to the haven. *Fuller.*

Haste is of the devil. *Koran.*

Haste makes waste, and waste makes want, and want makes strife between the gudeman and the gudewife. *Sc. Pr.*

Haste trips up its own heels, fetters and stops itself. *Sen.*

Haste turns usually on a matter of ten minutes too late. *Bovee.*

10 **Hasty resolutions seldom speed well.** *Pr.*

Hat man die Liebe durchgeliebt / Fängt man die Freundschaft an—After love friendship (*lit.* when we have lived through love we begin friendship). *Heine.*

Hate injures no one; it is contempt that casts men down. *Goethe.*

Hate makes us vehement partisans, but love still more so. *Goethe.*

Hâtez-vous lentement, et sans perdre courage—Leisurely, and don't lose heart. *Fr.*

15 **Hath fortune dealt thee ill cards? Let wisdom make thee a good gamester.** *Quarles.*

Hath not a Jew eyes? hath not a Jew hands, organs, dimensions, senses, affections, passions? fed with the same food, hurt with the same weapons, subject to the same diseases, healed by the same means, warmed and cooled by the same winter and summer, as a Christian is? If you prick us, do we not bleed? if you tickle us, do we not laugh? if you poison us, do we not die? and if you wrong us, shall not we revenge? *Mer. of Venice,* iii. 1.

Hatred does not cease by hatred at any time; hatred ceases by love. *Buddha.*

Hatred is a heavy burden. It sinks the heart deep in the breast, and lies like a tombstone on all joys. *Goethe.*

Hatred is active, and envy passive, disgust; there is but one step from envy to hate. *Goethe.*

20 **Hatred is but an inverse love.** *Carlyle.*

Hatred is keener than friendship, less keen than love. *Vauvenargues.*

Hatred is like fire; it makes even light rubbish deadly. *George Eliot.*

"Hätte ich gewusst," ist ein armer Mann—"If I had known," is a poor man. *Ger. Pr.*

Haud æquum facit, / Qui quod didicit, id dediscit—He does not do right who unlearns what he has learnt. *Plaut.*

25 **Haud facile emergunt quorum virtutibus obstat / Res angusta domi**—Not easily do those attain to distinction whose abilities are cramped by domestic poverty. *Juv.*

Haud ignara ac non incauta futuri—Neither ignorant nor inconsiderate of the future. *Hor.*

Haud ignara mali miseris succurrere disco—Not unfamiliar with misfortune myself, I have learned to succour the wretched. *Virg.*

Haud passibus æquis—With unequal steps. *Virg.*

Haut et bon—Great and good. *M.*

Haut goût—High flavour. *Fr.* 30

Have a care o' the main chance. *Butler.*

Have a spécialité, a work in which you are at home. *Spurgeon.*

Have any deepest scientific individuals yet dived down to the foundations of the universe and gauged everything there? Did the Maker take them into His counsel, that they read His ground-plan of the incomprehensible All, and can say, This stands marked therein, and no more than this? Alas! not in any wise. *Carlyle.*

Have I a religion, have I a country, have I a love, that I am ready to die for? are the first trial questions to itself of a true soul. *Ruskin.*

Have I in conquest stretched mine arm so far / 35 **To be afeard to tell gray-beards the truth?** *Jul. Cæs.,* ii. 2.

Have I not earn'd my cake in baking of it? *Tennyson.*

Have more than thou showest; / Speak less than thou knowest; / Lend less than thou owest; / Learn more than thou trowest; / Set less than thou throwest. *King Lear,* i. 4.

Have not all nations conceived their God as omnipresent and eternal, as existing in a universal Here, an everlasting Now? *Carlyle.*

Have not thy cloak to make when it begins to rain. *Pr.*

Have the French for friends, but not for neigh- 40 **bours.** *Pr.*

Have you found your life distasteful? / My life did, and does, smack sweet. / Was your youth of pleasure wasteful? / Mine I saved and hold complete. / Do your joys with age diminish? / When mine fail me, I'll complain. / Must in death your daylight finish? / My sun sets to rise again. *Browning.*

Have you known how to compose your manners, you have achieved a great deal more than he who has composed books. Have you known how to attain repose, you have achieved more than he who has taken cities and subdued empires. *Montaigne.*

Have you not heard it said full oft, / A woman's nay doth stand for nought? *Shakespeare.*

Have you prayed to-night, Desdemona? *Othello,* v. 2.

Having food and raiment, let us be therewith 45 **content.** *St. Paul.*

Having is having, come whence it may. *Ger. Pr.*

Having is in no case the fruit of lusting, but of living. *Ed.*

Having sown the seed of secrecy, it should be properly guarded and not in the least broken; for being broken, it will not prosper. *Hitopadesa.*

Having waste ground enough, / Shall we desire to raze the sanctuary / And pitch our evils there? *Meas. for Meas.,* ii. 2.

Hay buena cuenta, y no paresca blanca—The account is all right, but the money-bags are empty. *Sp. Pr.*

He alone has energy that cannot be deprived of it. *Lavater.*

He alone is happy, and he is truly so, who can say, "Welcome life, whatever it brings! welcome death, whatever it is!" *Bolingbroke.*

He alone is worthy of respect who knows what is of use to himself and others, and who labours to control his self-will. *Goethe.*

5 He also that is slothful in his work is brother to him that is a great waster. *Bible.*

He always wins who sides with God. *Faber.*

He becometh poor that dealeth with a slack hand; but the hand of the diligent maketh rich. *Bible.*

He behoves to have meat enou' that sal stop ilka man's mou'. *Sc. Pr.*

He best restrains anger who remembers God's eye is upon him. *Plato.*

10 He buys very dear who begs. *Port. Pr.*

He by whom the geese were formed white, parrots stained green, and peacocks painted of various hues—even He will provide for their support. *Hitopadesa.*

He can ill run that canna gang (walk). *Sc. Pr.*

He cannot lay eggs, but he can cackle. *Dut. Pr.*

He cannot see the wood for the trees. *Ger. Pr.*

15 He cast off his friends, as a huntsman his pack, / For he knew, when he pleased, he could whistle them back. *Goldsmith.*

He cometh unto you with a tale which holdeth children from play and old men from the chimney-corner. *Sir P. Sidney.*

He conquers grief who can take a firm resolution. *Goethe.*

He could distinguish and divide / A hair 'twixt south and south-west side. *Butler.*

He cries out before he is hurt. *It. Pr.*

20 He dances well to whom fortune pipes. *Pr.*

He doesna aye flee when he claps his wings. *Sc. Pr.*

He does not deserve wine who drinks it as water. *Bodenstedt.*

He does nothing who endeavours to do more than is allowed to humanity. *Johnson.*

He doeth much that doeth a thing well. *Thomas à Kempis.*

25 He doeth well that serveth the common good rather than his own will. *Thomas à Kempis.*

He doth bestride the narrow world / Like a Colossus; and we petty men / Walk under his huge legs, and peep about / To find ourselves dishonourable graves. *Jul. Cæs., i. 2.*

He doubts nothing who knows nothing. *Port. Pr.*

He draweth out the thread of his verbosity finer than the staple of his argument. *Love's L. Lost, v. 1.*

He draws nothing well who thirsts not to draw everything. *Ruskin.*

30 He either fears his fate too much, / Or his deserts are small, / Who dares not put it to the touch / To win or lose it all. *Marquis of Montrose.*

He frieth in his own grease. *Pr.*

He gave his honours to the world again, / His blessed part to heaven, and slept in peace. *Hen. VIII., iv. 2.*

He giveth His beloved sleep. *Bible.*

He goeth back that continueth not. *St. Augustine.*

He goeth better that creepeth in his way 35 than he that runneth out of his way. *St. Augustine.*

He had a face like a benediction. *Cervantes.*

He had been eight years upon a project for extracting sunbeams out of cucumbers, which were to be put in phials hermetically sealed, and let out to warm the air in raw inclement seasons. *Swift.*

He had never kindly heart, / Nor ever cared to better his own kind, / Who first wrote satire with no pity in it. *Tennyson.*

He has a bee in his bonnet, *i.e.*, is hare-brained. *Sc. Pr.*

He has a head, and so has a pin. *Port. 40 Pr.*

He has a killing tongue and a quiet sword, by the means whereof 'a breaks words and keeps whole weapons. *Hen. V., iii. 2.*

He has faut (need) o' a wife wha marries mam's pet. *Sc. Pr.*

He has hard work who has nothing to do. *Pr.*

He has no religion who has no humanity. *Arab. Pr.*

He has not learned the lesson of life who 45 does not every day surmount a fear. *Emerson.*

He has paid dear, very dear, for his whistle. *Ben. Franklin.*

He has seen a wolf. *Pr. of one who suddenly curbs his tongue.*

He has verily touched our hearts as with a live coal from the altar who in any way brings home to our heart the noble doings, feelings, darings, and endurances of a brother man. *Carlyle.*

He has wit at will that, when angry, can sit him still. *Sc. Pr.*

He hath a heart as sound as a bell, and his 50 tongue is the clapper; for what his heart thinks his tongue speaks. *Much Ado, iii. 2.*

He hath a tear for pity, and a hand / Open as day for melting charity. *2 Hen. IV., iv. 4.*

He hath ill repented whose sins are repeated. *St. Augustine.*

He hath never fed of the dainties that are bred in a book. *Love's L. Lost, iv. 2.*

He honours God that imitates Him. *Sir T. Browne.*

He in whom there is much to be developed will 55 be later than others in acquiring true perceptions of himself and the world. *Goethe.*

He is a fool who empties his purse, or store, to fill another's. *Sp. Pr.*

He is a fool who thinks by force or skill / To turn the current of a woman's will. *S. Tuke.*

He is a great and a good man from whom the needy, or those who come for protection, go not away with disappointed hopes and discontented countenances. *Hitopadesa.*

He is a great man who inhabits a higher sphere of thought, into which other men rise with labour and difficulty : he has but to open his eyes to see things in a true light and in large relations, while they must make painful corrections, and keep a vigilant eye on many sources of error. *Emerson.*

He is a happy man that hath a true friend at his need, but he is more truly happy that hath no need of his friend. *Arthur Warwick.*

He is a hard man who is only just, and he a sad man who is only wise. *Voltaire.*

He is a little chimney, and heated hot in a moment ! *Longfellow.*

5 He is a little man ; let him go and work with the women ! *Longfellow.*

He is a madman (*Rasender*) who does not embrace and hold fast the good fortune which a god (*ein Gott*) has given into his hand. *Schiller.*

He is a man who doth not suffer his members and faculties to cause him uneasiness. *Hitopadesa.*

He is a minister who doth not behave with insolence and pride. *Hitopadesa.*

He is a poor smith who cannot bear smoke. *Pr.*

10 He is a strong man who can hold down his opinion. *Emerson.*

He is a true sage who learns from all the world. *Eastern Pr.*

He is a very valiant trencherman ; he hath an excellent stomach. *Much Ado, i. 1.*

He is a wise child that knows his own father. *Pr.*

He is a wise man who does not grieve for the things which he has not, but rejoices for those which he has. *Epictetus.*

15 He is a wise man who knoweth that his words should be suited to the occasion, his love to the worthiness of the object, and his anger according to his strength. *Hitopadesa.*

He is a wise man who knows what is wise. *Xenophon.*

He is a worthy person who is much respected by good men. *Hitopadesa.*

He is all there when the bell rings. *Pr.*

He is an eloquent man who can speak of low things acutely, and of great things with dignity, and of moderate things with temper. *Cic.*

20 He is an unfortunate and on the way to ruin who will not do what he can, but is ambitious to do what he cannot. *Goethe.*

He is below himself who is not above an injury. *Quarles.*

He is best served who has no need to put the hands of others at the end of his arms. *Rousseau.*

He is but a bastard to the time / That doth not smack of observation. *King John, i. 1.*

He is but the counterfeit of a man who hath not the life of a man. *Shakespeare.*

25 He is gentil that doth gentil dedes. *Chaucer.*

He is great who is what he is from nature, and who never reminds us of others. *Emerson.*

He is happiest, be he king or peasant, who finds peace in his own home. *Goethe.*

He is happy who is forsaken by his passions. *Hitopadesa.*

He is happy whose circumstances suit his temper ; but he is more excellent who can suit his temper to any circumstances. *Hare.*

He is just as truly running counter to God's 30 will by being intentionally wretched as by intentionally doing wrong. *W. R. Greg.*

He is kind who guardeth another from misfortune. *Hitopadesa.*

He is lifeless that is faultless. *Pr.*

He is my friend that grinds at my mill. *Pr.*

He is my friend that helps me, and not he that pities me. *Pr.*

He is nearest to God who has the fewest wants. 35 *Dan. Pr.*

He is neither fish, nor flesh, nor good red herring. *Pr.*

He is no wise man that will quit a certainty for an uncertainty. *Johnson.*

He is noble who feels and acts nobly. *Heine.*

He is not a bad driver who knows how to turn. *Dan. Pr.*

He is not a true man of science who does not 40 bring some sympathy to his studies, and expect to learn something by behaviour as well as application. *Thoreau.*

He is not only idle who does nothing, but he is idle who might be better employed. *Socrates.*

He is not the best carpenter who makes the most chips. *Pr.*

He is not yet born who can please everybody. *Dan. Pr.*

He is oft the wisest man / Who is not wise at all. *Wordsworth.*

He is richest that has fewest wants. *Pr.* 45

He is the best dressed gentleman whose dress no one observes. *Trollope.*

He is the best gentleman that is the son of his own deserts, and not the degenerated heir of another's virtue. *Victor Hugo.*

He is the free man whom the truth makes free, / And all are slaves besides. *Cowper.*

He is the greatest artist who has embodied in the sum of his works the greatest number of the greatest ideas. *Ruskin.*

He is the greatest conqueror who has con- 50 quered himself. *Pr.*

He is the greatest whose strength carries up the most hearts by the attraction of his own. *Ward Beecher.*

He is the half part of a blessèd man, / Left to be finishèd by such as she ; / And she a fair divided excellence, / Whose fulness of perfection lies in him. *King John, ii. 2.*

He is the rich man in whom the people are rich, and he is the poor man in whom the people are poor ; and how to give access to the masterpieces of art and nature is the problem of civilisation. *Emerson.*

He is the rich man who can avail himself of all men's faculties. *Emerson.*

He is the world's master who despises it, its 55 slave who prizes it. *It. Pr.*

He is truly great who is great in charity. *Thomas à Kempis.*

He is ungrateful who denies a benefit ; he is ungrateful who hides it ; he is ungrateful who does not return it ; he, most of all, who has forgotten it. *Sen.*

He is well paid that is well satisfied. *Mer. of Ven.*, iv. 1.

He is wise that is wise to himself. *Euripides.*

He is wise who can instruct us and assist us in the business of daily virtuous living; he who trains us to see old truth under academic formularies may be wise or not, as it chances, but we love to see wisdom in unpretending forms, to recognise her royal features under a week-day vesture. *Carlyle.*

He is wit's pedlar, and retails his wares / At wakes and wassails, meetings, markets, fairs; / And we that sell by gross, the Lord doth know, / Have not the grace to grace it with such show. *Love's L. Lost*, v. 2.

5 He is wrong who thinks that authority based on force is more weighty and more lasting than that which rests on kindness. *Ter.*

He jests at scars that never felt a wound. *Rom. and Jul.*, ii. 2.

He judged the cause of the poor and needy; then it was well with him: was not this to know me? saith the Lord. *Bible.*

He kens muckle wha kens when to speak, but far mair wha kens when to haud (hold) his tongue. *Sc. Pr.*

He knew what's what, and that's as high / As metaphysic wit can fly. *Butler.*

10 He knocks boldly at the door who brings good news. *Pr.*

He knows best what good is that has endured evil. *Pr.*

He knows little who will tell his wife all he knows. *Fuller.*

He knows much who knows how to hold his tongue. *Pr.*

He knows not how to speak who cannot be silent, still less how to act with vigour and decision. *Lavater.*

15 He knows not what love is that has no children. *Pr.*

He knows the water the best who has waded through it. *Pr.*

He knows very little of mankind who expects, by facts or reasoning, to convince a determined party-man. *Lavater.*

He left a name at which the world grew pale, / To point a moral or adorn a tale. *Johnson.*

He lies there who never feared the face of man. *The Earl of Morton at John Knox's grave.*

20 He life's war knows / Whom all his passions follow as he goes. *George Herbert.*

He little merits bliss who others can annoy. *Thomson.*

He lives twice who can at once employ / The present well and e'en the past enjoy. *Pope.*

He lives who lives to God alone, / And all are dead beside; / For other source than God is none / Whence life can be supplied. *Cowper.*

He looks the whole world in the face, / For he owes not any man. *Longfellow.*

25 He loses his thanks who promises and delays. *Pr.*

He loves but lightly who his love can tell. *Petrarch.*

He makes no friend who never made a foe. *Tennyson.*

He (your Father) maketh His sun to rise on the evil and on the good, and sendeth rain on the just and on the unjust. *Jesus.*

He maun lout (stoop) that has a laigh (low) door. *Sc. Pr.*

He may rate himself a happy man who lives 30 remote from the gods of this world. *Goethe.*

Hé, mon ami, tire-moi du danger; tu feras après ta harangue—Hey! my friend, help me out of my danger first; you can make your speech afterwards. *La Fontaine.*

He most lives / Who thinks most, feels the noblest, acts the best. *P. J. Bailey.*

He must be a good shot who always hits the mark. *Dut. Pr.*

He must be a thorough fool who can learn nothing from his own folly. *Hare.*

He must cry loud who would frighten the devil. 35 *Dan. Pr.*

He must needs go that the devil drives. *Pr.*

He must stand high who would see his destiny to the end. *Dan. Pr.*

He must mingle with the world that desires to be useful. *Johnson.*

He needs a long spoon who eats out of the same dish with the devil. *Pr.*

He needs no foil, but shines by his own proper 40 light. *Dryden.*

He ne'er made a gude darg (day's work) wha gaed (went) grumbling about it. *Sc. Pr.*

He never is crowned / With immortality, who fears to follow / Where airy voices lead. *Keats.*

He never knew pain who never felt the pangs of love. *Platen.*

He never lees (lies) but when the holland's (holly's) green, *i.e.*, always. *Sc. Pr.*

He never yet stood sure that stands secure. 45 *Quarles.*

He on whom Heaven bestows a sceptre knows not the weight of it till he bears it. *Corneille.*

He only employs his passion who can make no use of his reason. *Cic.*

He only is advancing in life whose heart is getting softer, whose blood warmer, whose brain quicker, and whose spirit is entering into living peace. *Ruskin.*

He only is an acute observer who can observe minutely without being observed. *Lavater.*

He only is exempt from failures who makes 50 no efforts. *Whately.*

He only is great of heart who floods the world with a great affection. He only is great of mind who stirs the world with great thoughts. He only is great of will who does something to shape the world to a great career; and he is greatest who does the most of all these things, and does them best. *R. D. Hitchcock.*

He only is rich who owns the day. *Emerson.*

He only who forgets to hoard has learned to live. *Keble.*

He ought to remember benefits on whom they are conferred; he who confers them ought not to mention them. *Cic.*

He paidles a guid deal in the water, but he 55 tak's care no to wet his feet. *Sc. Pr.*

He prayeth best who loveth best / All things, both great and small; / For the dear Lord who loveth us, / He made and loveth all. *Coleridge.*

He preaches well who lives well. *Sp. Pr.*

He presents me with what is always an acceptable gift who brings me news of a great thought before unknown. *Bovee.*

He rais'd a mortal to the skies, / She drew an angel down. *Dryden.*

He raises not himself up whom God casts down. *Goethe.*

He reads much : / He is a great observer, and he looks / Quite through the deeds of men : he loves no plays, / As thou dost, Anthony ; he hears no music : / Seldom he smiles ; and smiles in such a sort / As if he mock'd himself, and scorn'd his spirit / That could be moved to smile at anything : / Such men as he be never at heart's ease / Whiles they behold a greater than themselves ; / And therefore are they very dangerous. *Jul. Cæs.*, i. 2.

5 He rideth easily enough whom the grace of God carrieth. *Thomas à Kempis.*

He runs far who never turns. *It. Pr.*

He scarce is knight, yea, but half-man, nor meet / To fight for gentle damsel, he who lets / His heart be stirr'd with any foolish heat / At any gentle damsel's waywardness. *Tennyson.*

He serves his party best who serves his country best. *R. B. Hayes.*

He shall be a god to me who can rightly divide and define. *Quoted by Emerson.*

10 He shone with the greater splendour because he was not seen. *Tac.*

He sins as much who holds the sack as he who puts into it. *Fr. Pr.*

He sleeps as dogs do when wives bake, *i.e.*, is wide awake, though pretending not to see. *Sc. Pr.*

He spends best that spares to spend again. *Pr.*

He submits himself to be seen through a microscope who suffers himself to be caught in a fit of passion. *Lavater.*

15 He swallows the egg and gives away the shell in alms. *Ger. Pr.*

He that answereth a matter before he heareth it, it is folly and shame unto him. *Bible.*

He that aspires to be the head of a party will find it more difficult to please his friends than to perplex his foes. He must often act from false reasons, which are weak, because he dares not avow the true reasons, which are strong. *Colton.*

He that at twenty is not, at thirty knows not, and at forty has not, will never either be, or know, or have. *It. Pr.*

He that believeth shall not make haste. *Bible.*

20 He that blows the coals in quarrels he has nothing to do with, has no right to complain if the sparks fly in his face. *Ben. Franklin.*

He that boasts of his ancestors confesses that he has no virtue of his own. *Charron.*

He that builds by the wayside has many masters. *Pr.*

He that buyeth magistracy must sell justice. *Pr.*

He that buys what he does not want, must often sell what he does want. *Pr.*

25 He that, by often arguing against his own sense, imposes falsehoods on others, is not far from believing them himself. *Locke.*

He that by the plough would thrive, / Himself must either hold or drive. *Pr.*

He that by usury and unjust gain increaseth his substance, he shall gather it for him that will pity the poor. *Bible.*

He that can be patient has his foe at his feet. *Dut. Pr.*

He that can be won with a feather will be lost with a straw. *Pr.*

He that can conceal his joys is greater than he 30 who can hide his griefs. *Lavater.*

He that can define, he that can answer a question so as to admit of no further answer, is the best man. *Emerson.*

He that can discriminate is the father of his father. *The Vedas.*

He that can endure / To follow with allegiance a fall'n lord, / Does conquer him that did his master conquer, / And earns a place i' the story. *Ant. and Cleop.*, iii. 11.

He that can heroically endure adversity will bear prosperity with equal greatness of soul; for the mind that cannot be dejected by the former is not likely to be transported by the latter. *Fielding.*

He that can write a true book to persuade 35 England, is not he the bishop and archbishop, the primate of England and of all England ? *Carlyle.*

He that cannot be the servant of many will never be master, true guide, and deliverer of many. *Carlyle.*

He that cannot keep his mind to himself cannot practise any considerable thing whatever. *Carlyle.*

He that cannot pay in purse must pay in person. *Pr.*

He that ceases to be a friend never was a good one. *Pr.*

He that claims, either in himself or for another, 40 the honours of perfection will surely injure the reputation which he designs to assist. *Johnson.*

He that climbs the tall tree has won a right to the fruit : / He that leaps the wide gulf should prevail in his suit. *Scott.*

He that comes unca'd (uninvited) sits unsair'd (unserved). *Sc. Pr.*

He that cometh to seek after knowledge with a mind to scorn and censure, shall be sure to find matter for his humour, but none for his instruction. *Bacon.*

He that complies against his will, / Is of the same opinion still. *Butler.*

He that conquers himself conquers an enemy. 45 *Gael. Pr.*

He that cuts himself wilfully deserves no salve. *Pr.*

He that defers his charity until he is dead is, if a man weighs it rightly, rather liberal of another man's goods than his own. *Bacon.*

He that descends not to word it with a shrew does worse than beat her. *L'Estrange.*

He that deserves nothing should be content with anything. *Pr.*

He that dies, pays all debts. *Tempest*, iii. 2. 50

He that does a base thing in zeal for his friend burns the golden thread that ties their hearts together. *Jeremy Taylor.*

He that does not knot his thread will lose his first stitch. *Gael.*

He that does not know those things which are of use and necessity for him to know, is but an ignorant man, whatever he may know besides. *Tillotson.*

He that does what he can, does what he ought. *Pr.*

He that does you a very ill turn will never forgive you. *Pr.*

5 He that doeth evil hateth the light. *Jesus.*

He that doeth truth cometh to the light. *St. John.*

He that doth not plough at home won't plough abroad. *Gael. Pr.*

He that doth the ravens feed, / Yea, providently caters for the sparrow, / Be comfort to my age. *As You Like It*, ii. 3.

He that eats longest lives longest. *Pr.*

10 He that endureth is not overcome. *Pr.*

He that, ever following her (Duty's) commands, / On with toil of heart and knees and hands, / Thro' the long gorge to the far light has won / His path upward, and prevail'd, / Shall find the toppling crags of Duty scaled, / Are close upon the shining tablelands / To which our God Himself is moon and sun. *Tennyson.*

He that falls into sin, is a man ; that grieves at it, is a saint ; that boasteth of it, is a devil ; yet some glory in that shame, counting the stains of sin the best complexion of their souls. *Fuller.*

He that feareth is not made perfect in love. *St. John.*

He that fights and runs away / May live to fight another day. *Goldsmith.*

He that filches from me my good name / Robs me of that which not enriches him, / And makes me poor indeed. *Othello*, iii. 3.

He that finds something before it is lost will die before he falls ill. *Dut. Pr.*

He that flees not will be fled from. *Gael. Pr.*

He that gallops his horse on Blackstone edge / May chance to catch a fall. *Old song.*

He that gets gear (wealth) before he gets wit, is but a short time master o' it. *Sc. Pr.*

20 He that gets patience, and the blessing which / Preachers conclude with, hath not lost his pains. *George Herbert.*

He that gives to the poor lends to the Lord. *Pr.*

He that goes a-borrowing goes a-sorrowing. *Pr.*

He that goes softly goes safely. *Pr.*

He that grasps at too much holds nothing fast. *Pr.*

25 He that has a head of wax should not walk in the sun. *Pr.*

He that has a head will not want a hat. *It. Pr.*

He that has a wife has a master. *Sc. Pr.*

He that has ae sheep in a flock will like a' the lave (rest) better for 't. *Sc. Pr.*

He that has an ill wife likes to eat butter (but her, *i.e.* without her). *Sc. Pr.*

30 He that has been taught only by himself has had a fool for a master. *Ben Jonson.*

He that has just enough can soundly sleep ; / The o'ercome only fashes fowk to keep. *Allan Ramsay.*

He that has light within his own clear breast may sit in the centre and enjoy bright day. *Milton.*

He that has lost his faith, what staff has he left ? *Bacon.*

He that has muckle would aye hae mair. *Sc. Pr.*

He that has no head needs no hat. *Sp. Pr.* 35

He that has no sense at thirty will never have any. *Pr.*

He that has no shame has no conscience. *Pr.*

He that has siller in his purse canna want (do without) a head on his shoulders. *Sc. Pr.*

He that has to choose has trouble. *Dut. Pr.*

He that hateth gifts shall live. *Bible.* 40

He that hath a beard is more than a youth, and he that hath no beard is less than a man. *Much Ado*, ii. 1.

He that hath a satirical vein, as he maketh others afraid of his wit, so he hath need to be afraid of others' memory. *Bacon.*

He that hath a trade hath an estate, and he that hath a calling hath an office of profit and honour. *Ben. Franklin.*

He that hath a wife and children hath given hostages to fortune ; for they are impediments to great enterprises, either of virtue or mischief. *Bacon.*

He that hath but gained the title of a jester, 45 let him assure himself the fool is not far off. *Quarles.*

He that hath care of keeping days of payment is lord of another man's purse. *Lord Burleigh.*

He that hath ears to hear, let him hear. *Jesus.*

He that hath gained an entire conquest over himself will find no mighty difficulties to subdue all other opposition. *Thomas à Kempis.*

He that hath knowledge spareth his words. *Bible.*

He that hath mercy on the poor, happy is he. 50 *Bible.*

He that hath no rule over his own spirit is like a city that is broken down and without walls. *Bible.*

He that hath pity upon the poor lendeth to the Lord. *Bible.*

He that hath sense hath strength. *Hitopadesa.*

He that hears much and speaks not at all, / Shall be welcome both in bower and hall. *Pr.*

He that high growth on cedars did bestow, / 55 Gave also lowly mushrooms leave to grow. *R. Southwell.*

He that hinders not a mischief is guilty of it. *Pr.*

He that humbles himself shall be exalted. *Pr.*

He that imposes an oath makes it, / Not he that for convenience takes it. *Butler.*

He that increaseth knowledge increaseth sorrow. *Bible.*

He that invented the Maiden, first hanselled it, 60 *i.e.*, first put it to the proof. (*The Maiden was a kind of guillotine.*) *Sc. Pr.*

He that is a friend to himself is a friend to all men. *Sen.*

He that is born of a hen must scrape for a living. *Pr.*

He that is courteous at all, will be courteous to all. *Gael. Pr.*

He that is discontented and troubled is tossed with divers suspicions; he is neither quiet himself, nor suffereth others to be quiet. *Thomas à Kempis.*

He that is doing nothing is seldom without helpers. *Pr.*

5 He that is down needs fear no fall; / He that is low no pride. *Bunyan.*

He that is down, the world cries " Down with him!" *Pr.*

He that is embarked with the devil must sail with him. *Dut. Pr.*

He that is faithful in that which is least is faithful also in much; and he that is unjust in the least, is unjust also in the much. *Jesus.*

He that is full of himself is very empty. *Pr.*

10 He that is ill to himself will be good to nobody. *Pr.*

He that is not against us is on our part. *Jesus.*

He that is not handsome at twenty, strong at thirty, rich at forty, nor wise at fifty, will never be handsome, strong, wise, or rich. *Pr.*

He that is not open to conviction is not qualified for discussion. *Whately.*

He that is not with me is against me. *Jesus.*

15 He that is of a merry heart hath a continual feast. *Bible.*

He that is proud eats up himself; pride is his own glass, his own trumpet, his own chronicle; and whatever praises itself but in the deed devours the deed in the praise. *Troil. and Cress.*, ii. 3.

He that is robb'd, not wanting what is stolen, / Let him not know 't, and he's not robb'd at all. *Othello*, iii. 3.

He that is ready to slip is as a lamp despised in the thought of him that is at ease. *Bible.*

He that is slow to anger is better than the mighty; and he that ruleth his spirit, than he that taketh a city. *Bible.*

20 He that is slow to wrath is of great understanding. *Bible.*

He that is spiritual judgeth all things, yet he himself is judged of no man. *St. Paul.*

He that is surety for another, is never sure himself. *Pr.*

He that is the inferior of nothing can be the superior of nothing, the equal of nothing. *Carlyle.*

He that is tied with one slender string, such as one resolute struggle would break, is prisoner only to his own sloth; and who would pity his thraldom? *Decay of Piety.*

25 He that is to-day a king, to-morrow shall die. *Ecclus.*

He that is violent in the pursuit of pleasure won't mind to turn villain for the purchase. *M. Aurelius.*

He that is well-ordered and disposed within himself careth not for the strange and perverse behaviour of men. *Thomas à Kempis.*

He that keeks (pries) through a keyhole may see what will vex him. *Sc. Pr.*

He that keepeth his way preserveth his soul. *Bible.*

He that kills a man when he is drunk must be 30 hanged for it when he is sober. *Pr.*

He that knoweth not that which he ought to know, is a brute beast among men; he that knoweth no more than he hath need of, is a man among brute beasts; and he that knoweth all that may be known, is a god amongst men. *Pythagoras.*

He that knows a little of the world will admire it enough to fall down and worship it; he that knows it most will most despise it. *Colton.*

He that knows, and knows not that he knows, is asleep. Arouse him. *Arabian Pr.*

He that knows, and knows that he knows, is wise. Follow him. *Arabian Pr.*

He that knows is strong. *Gael. Pr.* 35

He that knows not, and knows not that he knows not, is stupid. Shun him. *Arabian Pr.*

He that knows not, and knows that he knows not, is good. Teach him. *Arabian Pr.*

He that lacks time to mourn lacks time to mend. *Sir H. Taylor.*

He that lies down with dogs will rise up with fleas. *Pr.*

He that lives in perpetual suspicion lives the 40 life of a sentinel, of a sentinel never relieved. *Young.*

He that lives longest sees most. *Gael. Pr.*

He that lives must grow old; and he that would rather grow old than die, has God to thank for the infirmities of old age. *Johnson.*

He that lives upon hopes will die fasting. *Ben. Franklin.*

He that lives with cripples learns to limp. *Pr.*

He that lives with wolves will learn to howl. 45 *Pr.*

He that loses his conscience has nothing left that is worth keeping. *Izaak Walton.*

He that loves Christianity better than truth will soon love his own sect or party better than Christianity. *Coleridge.*

He that loves God aright must not desire that God should love him in return, *i.e.*, love to God, as to man, should be entirely unselfish. *Spinoza.*

He that loveth a book will never want a faithful friend, a wholesome counsellor, a cheerful companion, an effectual comforter. *Isaac Barrow.*

He that loveth danger shall perish therein. 50 *Ecclus.*

He that loveth father and mother more than me is not worthy of me. *Jesus.*

He that loveth not his brother, whom he hath seen, how can he love God, whom he hath not seen? *St. John.*

He that loveth pleasure shall be a poor man. *Bible.*

He that loveth silver shall not be satisfied with silver; nor he that loveth abundance with increase. *Bible.*

He that maketh haste to be rich shall not be 55 innocent. *Bible.*

He that marries before he is wise will die before he thrive. *Sc. Pr.*

He that marries for money sells his liberty. *Pr.*

He that meddleth with strife belonging not to him is like one that taketh a dog by the ears. *Bible.*

He that needs five thousand pound to live, / Is full as poor as he that needs but five. *George Herbert.*

He that never thinks can never be wise. *Johnson.*

5 He that observeth the wind shall not sow; and he that regardeth the clouds shall not reap. *Bible.*

He that on pilgrimages goeth ever, / Becometh holy late or never. *Pr.*

He that oppresseth the poor to increase his riches, and he that giveth to the rich, shall surely come to want. *Bible.*

He that pities another minds himsel'. *Sc. Pr.*

He that prieth in at her windows shall also hearken at her doors. *Ecclus.*

10 He that promises too much means nothing. *Pr.*

He that purposes to be happy by the affection or acquaintance of the best, the greatest man alive, will always find his mind unsettled and perplexed. *Thomas à Kempis.*

He that questioneth much will learn much. *Bacon.*

He that revels in a well-chosen library has innumerable dishes, and all of admirable flavour. *W. Godwin.*

He that ruleth among men must be just, ruling in the fear of God. *Bible.*

15 He that runs in the dark may well stumble. *Pr.*

He that runs may read. *Pr.*

He that seeks others to beguile, / Is oft o'ertaken in his own wile. *Pr.*

He that seeks to have many friends never has any. *It. Pr.*

He that serves the altar should live by the altar. *Pr.*

20 He that shuts his eyes against a small light would not be brought to see that which he had no mind to see, let it be placed in never so clear a light and never so near him. *Atterbury.*

He that sows in the highway loses his corn. *Pr.*

He that sows iniquity shall reap sorrow. *Pr.*

He that spares the bad injures the good. *Pr.*

He that spares the rod spoils the child. *Pr.*

25 He that speaks the thing he should not / Must often hear the thing he would not. *Pr.*

He that speaks the truth will find himself in sufficiently dramatic situations. *Prof. Wilson.*

He that spends his gear (property) before he gets it will hae little gude o't. *Sc. Pr.*

He that stands upon a slippery place / Makes nice of no vain hold to stay him up. *King John, iii. 4.*

He that steals a preen (pin) will steal a better thing. *Sc. Pr.*

30 He that steals for others will be hanged for himself. *Pr.*

He that strikes with the sword shall perish by the sword. *Pr.*

He that studieth revenge keepeth his own wounds green. *Bacon.*

He that takes away reason to make way for revelation puts out the light of both. *Locke.*

He that talks deceitfully for truth must hurt it more by his example than he promotes it by his arguments. *Atterbury.*

He that talks much errs much. *Pr.* 35

He that talks much lies much. *Pr.*

He that tholes (bears up) o ercomes. *Sc. Pr.*

He that tilleth his land shall have plenty of bread. *Bible.*

He that turns not from every sin, turns not aright from any one sin. *Brooks.*

He that undervalues himself will undervalue 40 others, and he that undervalues others will oppress them. *Johnson.*

He that voluntarily continues ignorant is guilty of all the crimes which ignorance produces. *Johnson.*

He that waits long at the ferry will get over some time. *Gael. Pr.*

He that walketh uprightly walks surely. *Bible.*

He that walketh with wise men shall be wise; but a companion of fools shall be destroyed. *Bible.*

He that wants good sense is unhappy in having 45 learning, for he has thereby only more ways of exposing himself; and he that has sense knows that learning is not knowledge, but rather the art of using it. *Steele.*

He that wants money, means, and content is without three good friends. *As You Like It, iii. 2.*

He that will be angry for anything will be angry for nothing. *Sallust.*

He that will believe only what he can fully comprehend must have a very long head or a very short creed. *Colton.*

He that will carry nothing about him but gold will be every day at a loss for readier change. *Pope.*

He that will have his son have a respect for 50 him must have a great reverence for his son. *Locke.*

He that will lose his friend for a jest, deserves to die a beggar by the bargain. *Fuller.*

He that will love life and see good days, let him refrain his tongue from evil, and his lips that they speak no guile. *St. Peter.*

He that will not reason is a bigot; he that cannot, is a fool; and he that dare not, is a slave. *Sir W. Drummond.*

He that will not when he may, / When he will he shall have nay. *Pr.*

He that will not work shall not eat. *Pr.* 55

He that will to Cupar, maun to Cupar, *i.e.*, he that will to jail, must to jail. *Sc. Pr.*

He that will watch Providence will never want a Providence to watch. *Flavel.*

He that winketh with the eye causeth sorrow. *Bible.*

He that winna be counselled canna be helped. *Sc. Pr.*

He that winna save a penny will ne'er hae 60 ony. *Sc. Pr.*

He that won't plough at home won't plough abroad. *Gael. Pr.*

He that would be rich in a year will be hanged in half a year. *Pr.*

He that would be singular in his apparel had need of something superlative to balance that affectation. *Feltham.*

He that would have eggs must endure the cackling of the hens. *Pr.*

He that would have his virtue published is not the servant of virtue, but of glory. *Johnson.*

He that would live in peace and rest / Must hear, and see, and say the best. *Pr.*

5 He that would reap well must sow well. *Pr.*

He that would reckon up all the accidents preferments depend upon, may as well undertake to count the sands or sum up infinity. *South.*

He that would relish success to purpose should keep his passion cool and his expectation low. *Collier.*

He that would reproach an author for obscurity should look into his own mind to see whether it is quite clear there. In the dusk the plainest writing is illegible. *Goethe.*

He that wrestles with us strengthens our nerves and sharpens our skill. *Burke.*

10 He that wrongs his friend / Wrongs himself more, and ever bears about / A silent court of justice in his breast, / Himself the judge and jury, and himself / The prisoner at the bar, ever condemned. *Tennyson.*

He the cross who longest bears / Finds his sorrow's bounds are set. *Winkworth.*

He thinks no evil who means no evil. *Gael. Pr.*

He thinks too much; such men are dangerous. *Jul. Cæs.*, i. 2.

He thought as a sage though he felt as a man. *J. Beattie.*

15 He thought he thought, and yet he did not think, / But only echoed still the common talk, / As might an empty room. *Walter C. Smith.*

He thought the World to him was known, / Whereas he only knew the Town; / In men this blunder still you find, / All think their little set—Mankind. *Hannah More.*

He travels safe and not unpleasantly who is guarded by poverty and guided by love. *Sir P. Sidney.*

He trudged along, unknowing what he sought, / And whistled as he went, for want of thought. *Dryden.*

He wants wit that wants resolved will. *Two Gent. of Ver.*, ii. 6.

20 He was a bold man that first ate an oyster. *Swift.*

He was a man, take him for all in all, / I shall not look upon his like again. *Ham.*, i. 2.

He was a scholar, and a ripe and good one; / Exceeding wise, fair spoken, and persuading; / Lofty and sour to them that loved him not; / But to those men that sought him, sweet as summer. *Hen. VIII.*, iv. 2.

He was exhaled; his great Creator drew / His spirit, as the sun the morning dew. *Dryden.*

He was my friend, faithful and just to me. *Jul. Cæs.*, iii. 2.

25 He was not of an age, but for all Time, / Sweet Swan of Avon. *Ben Jonson.*

He was perfumed like a milliner, / And 'twixt his finger and his thumb he held / A pouncetbox, which ever and anon / He gave his nose, and took 't away again. 1 *Hen. IV.*, i. 3.

He was scant o' news that told that his father was hanged. *Sc. Pr.*

He was the Word that spake it; / He took the bread and brake it; / And what that Word did make it, / I do believe and take it. *Dr. Donne.*

He wears his faith but as the fashion of his hat. *Much Ado*, i. 1.

He wha eats but (only) ae dish seldom needs 30 the doctor. *Sc. Pr.*

He who asks a favour for another has the confidence which a sense of justice inspires; while he who solicits for himself experiences all the embarrassment and shame of one appealing for mercy. *La Bruyère.*

He who avoids the temptation avoids the sin. *Pr.*

He who begins with trusting every one will end with estimating every one a knave. *Hebbel.*

He who breaks confidence has for ever forfeited it. *Schopenhauer.*

He who can at all times sacrifice pleasure to 35 duty approaches sublimity. *Lavater.*

He who can conceal his joys is greater than he who can conceal his griefs. *Lavater.*

He who can enjoy the intimacy of the great, and on no occasion disgust them by familiarity or disgrace them by servility, proves that he is as perfect a gentleman by nature as his companions are by rank. *Colton.*

He who cannot bear foes deserves no friend. *Schafer.*

He who cannot profit you as a friend may at any time injure you as an enemy. *Gellert.*

He who carries his heart on his tongue runs 40 the risk of expectorating it. *Saar.*

He who ceases to grow greater grows smaller. *Amiel.*

He who ceases to pray ceases to prosper. *Pr.*

He who coldly lives to himself and his own will may gratify many a wish, but he who strives to guide others well must be able to dispense with much. *Goethe.*

He who combines every defect will be more likely to find favour in the world than the man who is possessed of every virtue. *Fr. Pr.*

He who comes up to his own ideal of greatness 45 must always have had a very low standard of it in his mind. *Hazlitt.*

He who commits injustice is ever made more wretched than he who suffers it. *Plato.*

He who conforms to the rule which the genius of the human understanding whispers secretly in the ear of every new-born being, viz., to test action by thought and thought by action, cannot err; and if he errs, he will soon find himself again in the right way. *Goethe.*

He who considers too much will accomplish little. *Schiller.*

He who deals with honey will sometimes be licking his fingers. *Pr.*

He who despises mankind will never get the 50 best out of either others or himself. *Tocqueville.*

He who did well in war just earns the right /
To begin doing well in peace. *Browning.*

He who does a good deed is instantly ennobled ;
he who does a mean deed, is by the action
itself contracted. *Emerson.*

He who does evil that good may come, pays
a toll to the devil to let him into heaven.
Hare.

He who does me good teaches me to be good.
Pr.

5 He who does not advance falls backward.
Amiel.

He who does not expect a million of readers
should not write a line. *Goethe.*

He who does not help us at the needful moment
never helps ; he who does not counsel at the
needful moment never counsels. *Goethe.*

He who does not imagine in stronger and
better lineaments, and in stronger and better
light than his perishing mortal eye can see,
does not imagine at all. *Wm. Blake.*

He who does not know foreign languages
knows nothing of his own. *Goethe.*

10 He who does not lose his wits over certain
matters has none to lose. *Lessing.*

He who does not think too highly of himself
is more than he thinks. *Goethe.*

He who does nothing for others does nothing
for himself. *Goethe.*

He who doth not speak an unkind word to his
fellow-creatures is master of the whole world
to the extremities of the ocean. *Hitopadesa.*

He who dwells in temporary semblances and
does not penetrate into the eternal substance,
will not answer the sphinx-riddle of to-day
or of any day. *Carlyle.*

15 He who enquires into a matter has often
found more at a glance than he wished to
find. *Lessing.*

He who entereth uncalled for, unquestioned
speaketh much, and regardeth himself with
satisfaction, to his prince appeareth one of
a weak judgment. *Hitopadesa.*

He who esteems trifles for themselves is a
trifler ; he who esteems them for the conclusions he draws from them or the advantage to which they can be put, is a philosopher. *Bulwer.*

He who exercises wisdom exercises the knowledge which is about God. *Epictetus.*

He who fears not death fears not threats.
Corneille.

20 He who fears nothing is not less powerful than
he whom all fear. *Schiller.*

He who feeds the ravens / Will give His children bread. *Cowper.*

He who feels he is right is stronger than king's
hosts ; he who doubts he is not right has no
strength whatever. *Carlyle.*

He who finds a God in the physical world will
also find one in the moral, which is History.
Jean Paul.

He who formeth a connection with an honest
man from his love of truth, will not suffer
thereby. *Hitopadesa.*

25 He who gives up the smallest part of a secret
has the rest no longer in his power. *Jean
Paul.*

He who goes alone may start to-day ; but he
who travels with another must wait till that
other is ready. *Thoreau.*

He who has a bonnie wife needs mair than twa
een. *Sc. Pr.*

He who has a thousand friends has not a friend
to spare, / And he who has one enemy will
meet him everywhere. *Ali Ben Abu Saleb.*

" He who has been born has been a first man,"
has had lying before his young eyes, and as
yet unhardened into scientific shapes, a world
as plastic, infinite, divine, as lay before the
eyes of Adam himself. *Carlyle.*

He who has been once very foolish will never 30
be very wise. *Montaigne.*

He who has done enough for the welfare (*den
Besten*) of his own time has lived for all times.
Schiller.

He who has imagination without learning has
wings without feet. *Joubert.*

He who has less than he desires should know
that he has more than he deserves. *Lichtenberg.*

He who has lost confidence can lose nothing
more. *Boiste.*

He who has love in his heart has spurs in his 35
heels. *Pr.*

He who has made no mistakes in war has
never made war. *Turenne.*

He who has most of heart knows most of
sorrow. *P. J. Bailey.*

He who has no ear for poetry is a barbarian,
be he who he may. *Goethe.*

He who has no opinion of his own, but depends
upon the opinion and taste of others, is a
slave. *Klopstock.*

He who has no passions has no principle, nor 40
motive to act. *Helvetius.*

He who has no vision of Eternity will never
get a true hold of Time. *Carlyle.*

He who has no wish to be happier is the
happiest of men. *W. R. Alger.*

He who has not been a servant cannot become a praiseworthy master ; it is meet that
we should plume ourselves rather on acting
the part of a servant properly than that of
the master, first towards the laws, and next
towards our elders. *Plato.*

He who has not known poverty, sorrow, contradiction, and the rest, and learned from
them the priceless lessons they have to teach,
has missed a good opportunity of schooling.
Carlyle.

He who has not the weakness of friendship 45
has not the strength. *Joubert.*

He who has nothing to boast of but his ancestry is like a potato ; the only good belonging to him is underground. *Sir T.
Overbury.*

He who has published an injurious book sins
in his very grave, corrupts others while he
is rotting himself. *South.*

He who has reason and good sense at his
command needs few of the arts of the orator.
Goethe.

He who imitates what is evil always exceeds ;
he who imitates what is good always falls
short. *Guicciardini.*

He who in any way shows us better than we 50
knew before that a lily of the fields is beautiful, does he not show it us as an effluence of
the fountain of all beauty—as the handwriting, made visible there, of the great
Maker of the universe ? *Carlyle.*

He who indulges his senses in any excesses renders himself obnoxious to his own reason ; and, to gratify the brute in him, displeases the man, and sets his two natures at variance. *Scott.*

He who, in opposition to his own happiness, delighteth in the accumulation of riches, carrieth burdens for others and is the vehicle of trouble. *Hitopadesa.*

He who intends to be a great man ought to love neither himself nor his own things, but only what is just, whether it happens to be done by himself or by another. *Plato.*

He who is a fool and knows it is not very far from being a wise man. *J. B. (Selkirk).*

5 He who is conscious of guilt cannot bear the innocence of others : he tries to reduce other characters to his own level. *C. Fox.*

He who is deficient in the art of selection may, by showing nothing but the truth, produce all the effect of the grossest falsehood. It perpetually happens that one writer tells less truth than another, merely because he tells more truth. *Macaulay.*

He who is destitute of principles is governed, theoretically and practically, by whims. *Jacobi.*

He who is firm in his will moulds the world to himself. *Goethe.*

He who is good has no kind of envy. *Plato.*

10 He who is in disgrace with the sovereign is disrespected by all. *Hitopadesa.*

He who is lord of himself, and exists upon his own resources, is a noble but a rare being. *Sir E. Brydges.*

He who is most slow in making a promise is the most faithful in the performance of it. *Rousseau.*

He who is moved to tears by every word of a priest is generally a weakling and a rascal when the feeling evaporates. *Fr. v. Sallet.*

He who is not possessed of such a book as will dispel many doubts, point out hidden treasures, and is, as it were, a mirror of all things, is even an ignorant man. *Hitopadesa.*

15 He who is of no use to himself is of no use to any one. *Dan. Pr.*

He who is one with himself is everything. *Auerbach.*

He who is only half instructed speaks much, and is always wrong ; he who knows it wholly, is content with acting, and speaks seldom or late. *Goethe.*

He who is only just is stern ; he who is only wise lives in gloom. *Voltaire.*

He who is servant to (*dient*) the public is a poor animal (*Thier*) ; he torments himself, and nobody thanks him for it. *Goethe.*

20 He who is suave with all (*lieblich thun mit allen will*) gets on with none : he pleases no one who tries to please thousands. *Bodenstedt.*

He who is the master of all opinions never can be the bigot of any. *W. R. Alger.*

He who is too much afraid of being duped has lost the power of being magnanimous. *Amiel.*

He who is weighty is willing to be weighed. *Pr.*

He who is willing to work finds it hard to wait. *Pr.*

He who knows himself well will very soon 25 learn to know all other men : it is all reflection (*Zurückstrahlung*). *Lichtenberg.*

He who knows how to sunder jest and earnest is a wise man, and who by cheerful playfulness reinvigorates himself for strenuous diligence. *Rückert.*

He who knows not the world, knows not his own place in it. *Marcus Aurelius.*

He who knows right principles is not equal to him who loves them. *Confucius.*

He who laughs at crooked men should need walk very straight. *Pr.*

He who laughs can commit no deadly sin. 30 *Goethe's Mother.*

He who lays out for God lays up for himself. *Pr.*

He who learns and makes no use of his learning is a beast of burden with a load of books. *Saadi.*

He who learns the rules of wisdom without conforming to them in his life, is like a man who labours in his fields but does not sow. *Saadi.*

He who likes borrowing dislikes paying. *Pr.*

He who lives, and strives, and suffers for others 35 dear to him, is to be envied ; he who lives only for himself is poor. *H. Lingg.*

He who lives to no purpose lives to a bad purpose. *Nevius.*

He who lives wisely to himself and his own heart looks at the busy world through the loopholes of retreat, and does not want to mingle in the fray. *Hazlitt.*

He who loses wealth loses much, who loses a friend loses more, who loses his spirits loses all. *Sp. Pr.*

He who loves goodness harbours angels, reveres reverence, and lives with God. *Emerson.*

He who loves not books before he comes to 40 thirty years of age will hardly love them enough afterwards to understand them. *Clarendon.*

He who loves with purity considers not the gift of the lover, but the love of the giver. *Thomas à Kempis.*

He who makes claims (*Ansprüche*), shows by doing so that he has none to make. *Seume.*

He who makes constant complaint gets little compassion. *Pr.*

He who makes religion his first object makes it his whole object. *Ruskin.*

He who means to teach others may indeed 45 often suppress the best of what he knows, but he must not himself be half-instructed. *Goethe.*

He who mistrusts humanity is quite as often deceived as he who trusts men. *Jean Paul.*

He who mocks the infant's faith / Shall be mock'd in age and death. *Wm. Blake.*

He who never in his life was foolish was never a wise man. *Heine.*

He who obeys is almost always better than he who commands. *Renan.*

He who offers God a second place offers Him 50 no place. *Ruskin.*

He who ordained the Sabbath loves the poor. *Holmes*

He who overcomes his egoism rids himself of the most stubborn obstacle that blocks the way to all true greatness and all true happiness. *Cötvös.*

He who partakes in another's joys is more humane than he who partakes in his griefs. *Lavater.*

He who parts with his property before his death may prepare himself for bitter experiences. *Fr. Pr.*

He who pleased everybody died before he was born. *Pr.*

5 He who praises everybody praises nobody. *Johnson.*

He who promises runs in debt. *Talmud.*

He who reaches the goal receives the crown, and often he who deserves it goes without it. *Goethe.*

He who receives a sacrament does not perform a good work; he receives a benefit. *Luther.*

He who reforms himself has done more towards reforming the public than a crowd of noisy impotent patriots. *Lavater.*

10 He who says, "I sought, yet I found not," be sure he lies; he who says, 'I sought not and found," be sure he deceives; he who says, "I sought and found," him believe—he speaks true. *Rückert.*

He who says what he likes must hear what he does not like. *Dan. Pr.*

He who scrubs every pig he sees will not long be clean himself. *Pr.*

He who seeks only for applause from without has all his happiness in another's keeping. *Goldsmith.*

He who seeks the truth should be of no country. *Voltaire.*

15 He who seeth not the filthiness of evil wanteth a great foil to perceive the beauty of virtue. *Sir P. Sidney.*

He who sends mouths will send meat. *Pr.*

He who serves God serves a good Master. *Pr.*

He who serves the public serves a fickle master. *Dut. Pr.*

He who serves under reason anticipates necessity. *Herder.*

20 He who speaks sows; he who keeps silence reaps. *It. Pr.*

He who spends himself for all that is noble, and gains by nothing but what is just, will hardly be notably wealthy or distressfully poor. *Plato.*

He who stays in the valley will never cross the mountain. *Pr.*

He who steals an egg would steal an ox. *Pr.*

He who strikes terror into others is himself in continual fear. *Claudian.*

25 He who tastes every man's broth often burns his mouth. *Dan. Pr.*

He who tells a lie is not sensible how great a task he undertakes, for he must be forced to invent twenty more to maintain that one. *Pope.*

He who tells the failings of others to you will be ready to tell your failings to others. *Turk. Pr.*

He who the sword of Heaven will bear / Should be as holy as severe. *Meas. for Meas., iii. 2.*

He who thinks for himself, and imitates rarely, is a free man. *Klopstock.*

He who thinks his place below him will certainly be below his place. *Saville.*

He who thinks to save anything by his religion besides his soul will be loser in the end. *Bp. Barlow.*

He who thinks too much will accomplish little. *Schiller.*

He who traces nothing of God in his own soul will never find God in the world of matter— mere circlings of force there of iron regulation, of universal death and merciless indifference. *Carlyle.* 30

He who travels to be amused, or to get somewhat which he does not carry, travels away from himself, and grows old even in youth among old things. *Emerson.*

He who trusts a secret to his servant makes his own man his master. *Dryden.*

He who waits for dead men's shoes may go barefoot. *Pr.*

He who wants any help or prop, in addition to the internal evidences of its truth for his belief, never was and never will be a Christian. *B. R. Haydon.*

He who wants everything must know many things, do many things to procure even a few; different from him whose indispensable knowledge is this only, that a finger will pull the bell! *Carlyle.* 35

He who will be great must collect himself; only in restriction does the master show himself. *Goethe.*

He who will deaden one half of his nature to invigorate the other half will become at best a distorted prodigy. *Sir J. Stephen.* 40

He who will do faithfully needs to believe firmly. *Carlyle.*

He who will eat the nut must crack it. *Frisian Pr.*

He who will not be ruled by the rudder must be ruled by the rock. *Cornish Pr.*

He who will sell his fame will also sell the public interest. *Solon.*

He who will work aright must not trouble himself about what is ill done, but only do well himself. *Goethe.* 45

He who wills all, wills in effect nothing, and brings it to nothing. *Hegel.*

He who wishes to secure the good of others has already secured his own. *Confucius.*

He who works with symbols merely is a pedant, a hypocrite, and a bungler. *Goethe.*

He who would be everywhere will be nowhere. *Dan. Pr.*

He who would bring home the wealth of the Indies must carry the wealth of the Indies with him. *Sp. Pr.* 50

He who would climb the ladder must begin at the bottom. *Ger. Pr.*

He who would gather honey must brave the sting of the bees. *Dut. Pr.*

He who would gather roses must not fear thorns. *Dut. Pr.*

He who would not be frustrate of his hope to write well hereafter in laudable things ought himself to be a true poem. *Milton.*

He who would pry behind the scenes oft sees a counterfeit. *Dryden.* 55

He who would rule must hear and be deaf, must see and be blind. *Ger. Pr.*

He who would write heroic poems must make his whole life a heroic poem. *Milton, quoted by Carlyle.*

He whom God has gifted with a love of retirement possesses, as it were, an extra sense. *Bulwer Lytton.*

He whom God steers sails safely. *Pr.*

5 He whom the inevitable cannot overcome is unconquerable. *Epictetus.*

He whom toil has braced or manly play, / As light as air each limb, each thought as clear as day. *Thomson.*

He whose actions sink him even beneath the vulgar has no right to those distinctions which should be the reward only of merit. *Goldsmith.*

He whose days are passed away without giving or enjoying, puffing like the bellows of a blacksmith, liveth but by breathing. *Hitopadesa.*

He whose goodness is part of himself is what is called a real man. *Mencius.*

10 He whose sympathy goes lowest is the man from whom kings have the most to fear. *Emerson.*

He whose understanding can discern what is, and judge what should or should not be applied to prevent misfortune, never sinketh under difficulties. *Hitopadesa.*

He whose word and deed you cannot predict, who answers you without any supplication in his eye, who draws his determination from within, and draws it instantly,—that man rules. *Emerson.*

He whose work is on the highway will have many advisers. *Sp. Pr.*

He will never have true friends who is afraid of making enemies. *Hazlitt.*

15 He will never set the Thames on fire. *Pr.*

He would fain fly, but wants wings. *Pr.*

He works hard who has nothing to do. *Pr.*

He wrought all kind of service with a noble ease / That graced the lowliest act in doing it. *Tennyson.*

He's a blockhead who wants a proof of what he can't perceive, / And he's a fool who tries to make such a blockhead believe. *Wm. Blake.*

20 He's a man who dares to be / Firm for truth when others flee. *Pr.*

He's a silly body that's never missed. *Sc. Pr.*

He's a wise man wha can take care o' himsel'. *Sc. Pr.*

He's armed without that's innocent within. *Pope.*

He's idle that may be better employed. *Sc. Pr.*

25 He's looking for the blade o' corn in the stack o' chaff. *J. M. Barrie.*

He's most truly valiant / That can wisely suffer the worst that man / Can breathe ; and make his wrongs his outsides : / To wear them like his raiment, carelessly, / And ne'er prefer his injuries to his heart, / To bring it into danger. *Timon of Athens, iii. 5.*

He's only great who can himself command. *Lansdowne.*

He's well worth (deserving of) sorrow that buys it with his ain siller. *Sc. Pr.*

He's wise that's wise in time. *Sc. Pr.*

Headstrong liberty is lashed with woe. *Com* 30 *of Errors, ii. 1.*

Health and cheerfulness mutually beget each other. *Spectator.*

Health consists with temperance alone. *Pope.*

Health is better than wealth. *Pr.*

Health is the condition of wisdom, and the sign is cheerfulness—an open and noble temper. *Emerson.*

Health is the first of all liberties, and happi- 35 ness gives us the energy which is the basis of health. *Amiel.*

Health lies in labour, and there is no royal road to it but through toil. *Wendell Phillips.*

Health, longevity, beauty are other names for personal purity, and temperance is the regimen for all. *A. B. Alcott.*

Healthy action is always a balance of forces ; and all extremes are dangerous ; the excess of a good thing being often more dangerous in its social consequences than the excess of what is radically bad. *Prof. Blackie, to Young Men.*

Hear God, and God will hear you. *Pr.*

Hear it not, Duncan ; for it is a knell / That 40 summons thee to heaven or to hell. *Macb., ii. 1.*

Hear much and speak little ; for the tongue is the instrument of the greatest good and the greatest evil that is done in this world. *Raleigh.*

Hear one side, and you will be in the dark ; hear both, and all will be clear. *Haliburton.*

Hear ye not the hum / Of mighty workings? *Keats.*

Hearsay is half lies. *Pr.*

Hearts are flowers ; they remain open to the 45 softly falling dew, but shut up in the violent downpour of rain. *Jean Paul.*

Hearts are stronger than swords. *Wendell Phillips.*

Hearts grow warmer the farther you go / Up to the North with its hills and snow. *Walter C. Smith.*

Hearts may agree though heads differ. *Sc. Pr.*

Hearts philanthropic at times have the trick / Of the old hearts of stone. *Walter C. Smith.*

Heart's-ease is a flower which blooms from 50 the grave of desire. *W. R. Alger.*

Heat and darkness, and what these two may breed. *Carlyle.*

Heat cannot be separated from fire, or beauty from the eternal. *Dante.*

Heat not a furnace for your foe so hot / That it doth singe yourself. *Hen. VIII., i. 1.*

Heaven and God are best discerned through tears ; scarcely, perhaps, are discerned at all without them. *James Martineau.*

Heaven and yourself / Had part in this fair 55 maid (Juliet) ; now heaven hath all. *Rom. and Jul., iv. 5.*

Heaven bestows / At home all riches that wise Nature needs. *Cowley.*

Heaven doth with us as we with torches do, / Not light them for themselves ; for if our virtues / Did not go forth of us, 'twere all alike / As if we had them not. *Meas. for Meas., i. 1.*

Heaven finds means to kill your joys with love. *Rom. and Jul.*, v. 3.

Heaven from all creatures hides the book of fate, / All but the page prescribed—their present state. *Pope.*

Heaven has no rage like love to hatred turned, / Nor hell a fury like a woman scorned. *Congreve.*

Heaven hath many tongues to talk of it, more eyes to behold it, but few hearts that rightly affect it. *Bp. Hall.*

5 Heaven is above all yet; there sits a Judge / That no king can corrupt. *Hen. VIII.*, iii. 1.

Heaven is as near by sea as by land. *Pr.*

Heaven is in thy faith; happiness in thy heart. *Arndt.*

Heaven is never deaf but when man's heart is dumb. *Quarles.*

Heaven is not always angry when He strikes, / But most chastises those whom most He likes. *Pomfret.*

10 Heaven lies about us in our infancy. *Wordsworth.*

Heaven never helps the man that will not act. *Sophocles.*

Heaven often regulates effects by their causes, and pays the wicked what they have deserved. *Corneille.*

Heaven trims our lamps while we sleep. *A. B. Alcott.*

Heaven, which really in one sense is merciful to sinners, is in no sense merciful to fools, but even lays pitfalls for them and inevitable snares. *Ruskin.*

15 Heaven's above all; and there be souls that must be saved, and there be souls that must not be saved. *Othello*, ii. 3.

Heavens! can you then thus waste, in shameful wise, / Your few important days of trial here? / Heirs of eternity! yborn to rise / Through endless states of being, still more near / To bliss approaching, and perfection clear. *Thomson.*

Heaven's eternal wisdom hath decreed that man of man should ever stand in need. *Theocritus.*

Heaven's fire confounds when fann'd with folly's breath. *Quarles.*

Heaven's gates are not so highly arched as princes' palaces; they that enter there must go upon their knees. *Daniel Webster.*

20 Heavens! if privileged from trial, / How cheap a thing were virtue! *Thomson.*

Heaven's Sovereign saves all beings but Himself that hideous sight—a naked human heart. *Young.*

Heav'n finds an ear when sinners find a tongue. *Quarles.*

Heav'n is for thee too high; be lowly wise. *Milton.*

Heav'n is not always got by running. *Quarles.*

25 Heav'n is not day'd. Repentance is not dated. *Quarles.*

Hebt mich das Glück, so bin ich froh, Und sing in dulci jubilo; / Senkt sich das Rad und quetscht mich nieder, / So denk' ich: nun, es hebt sich wieder—When Fortune lifts me up, then am I glad and sing in sweet exultation; when she sinks down and lays me prostrate, then I begin to think, Now it will rise again. *Goethe.*

Hectora quis nosset, si felix Troja fuisset? / Publica virtuti per mala facta via est—Who would have known of Hector if Troy had been fortunate? A highway is open to virtue through the midst of misfortunes. *Ovid.*

Hectors Liebe stirbt im Lethe nicht—Hector's love does not perish in the floods of Lethe. *Schiller.*

Hedges between keep friendship green. *Pr.*

Hedgerows and Hercules-pillars, however per-30 fect, are to be reprobated as soon as they diminish the free world of a future man. *Jean Paul.*

Heilig sei dir der Tag; doch schätze das Leben nicht höher / Als ein anderes Gut, und alle Güter sind trüglich—Sacred be this day to thee, yet rate not life higher than another good, for all our good things are illusory. *Goethe.*

Hei mihi! difficile est imitari gaudia falsa! / Difficile est tristi fingere mente jocum—Ah me! it is hard to feign the joys one does not feel, hard to feign mirth when one's heart is sad. *Tib.*

Hei mihi! qualis erat! quantum mutatus ab illo / Hectore, qui redit, exuvias indutus Achilli—Ah me, how sad he looked! how changed from that Hector who returned in triumph arrayed in the spoils of Achilles. *Virg.*

Heitern Sinn und reine Zwecke / Nun, man kommt wohl eine Strecke—Serene sense and pure aims, that means a long stride, I should say. *Goethe.*

"Hélas! que j'en ai vu mourir de jeunes filles" 35 —"Alas, how many young girls have I seen die of that!" *Victor Hugo.*

Hell and destruction are never full, so the eyes of men are never satisfied. *Bible.*

Hell is on both sides of the tomb, and a devil may be respectable and wear good clothes. *C. H. Parkhurst.*

Hell is paved with good intentions. *Johnson.*

Hell is paved with the skulls of priests. *Modified from St. Chrysostom.*

Hell lies near, / Around us, as does heaven, 40 and in the world, / Which is our Hades, still the chequered souls, / Compact of good and ill—not all accurst, / Nor altogether blest—a few brief years / Travel the little journey of their lives, / They know not to what end. *Lewis Morris.*

Helluo librorum—A devourer of books.

Help others and seek to avenge no injury. *Fors.*

Help which is long on the road is no help. *Pr.*

Help yourself and your friends will help you. *Pr.*

Helpless mortal! Thine arm can destroy 45 thousands at once, but cannot enclose even two of thy fellow-creatures at once in the embrace of love and sympathy. *Jean Paul.*

Hence, babbling dreams; you threaten here in vain; / Conscience, avaunt, Richard's himself again. *Colley Cibber.*

Her angel's face, / As the great eye of heaven, shined bright, / And made a sunshine in the shady place. *Spenser.*

Her eyes are homes of silent prayer. *Tennyson.*

Her feet, beneath her petticoat / Like little mice stole in and out, / As if they fear'd the light; / But oh! she dances such a way, / No sun upon an Easter-day / is half so fine a sight. *Sir J. Suckling.*

Her own person, / It beggar'd all description. *Ant. and Cleop.*, ii. 2.

Her sun is gone down while it was yet day. *Bible.*

Her voice was ever soft, / Gentle, and low— an excellent thing in woman. *King Lear*, v. 3.

5 Hercules himself must yield to odds; / And many strokes, though with a little axe, / Hew down and fell the hardest-timber'd oak. *3 Hen. VI.*, ii. 1.

Here eyes do regard you / In Eternity's stillness; / Here is all fulness, / Ye brave, to reward you. / Work and despair not. *Goethe.*

Here have we no continuing city, but we seek one to come. *St. Paul.*

Here have we war for war, and blood for blood, / Controlment for controlment. *King John*, i. 1.

Here I and sorrows sit; / Here is my throne; bid kings come bow to it. *King John*, iii. 1.

10 Here I lay, and thus I bore my point. *1 Hen. IV.*, ii. 4.

Here in the body pent, / Absent from Him I roam, / Yet nightly pitch my moving tent / A day's march nearer home. *J. Montgomery.*

Here lies Johnny Pigeon! / What was his religion, / Wha e'er desires to ken / To some ither warl' / Maun follow the carl, / For here Johnny Pigeon had nane. *Burns.*

Here lies one whose name was writ in water. *Keat's epitaph.*

Here lies our sovereign lord the king, / Whose word no man relies on; / He never says a foolish thing, / Nor ever does a wise one. *Rochester on Charles II.'s chamber-door.*

15 Here lieth one, believe it if you can, / Who, though an attorney, was an honest man! *Epitaph.*

Here, on earth we are as soldiers fighting in a foreign land, that understand not the plan of the campaign, and have no need to understand it, seeing well what is at our hand to be done. *Carlyle.*

Here or nowhere is America. *Goethe.*

Here our souls / Though amply blest, / Can never find, although they seek, / A perfect rest. *Procter.*

Here was a Cæsar! when comes such another? *Jul. Cæs.*, iii. 2.

20 Here's a sigh for those who love me, / And a smile for those who hate, / And whatever sky's above me, / Here's a heart for every fate. *Byron.*

Hereditary bondsmen! know ye not, / Who would be free, themselves must strike the blow? *Byron.*

Hereditary honours are a noble and a splendid treasure to descendants. *Plato.*

Heroes are much the same, the point's agreed, / From Macedonia's madman to the Swede. *Pope.*

Heroism is an obedience to a secret impulse of an individual's character. *Emerson.*

Heroism is the brilliant triumph of the soul 25 over fear; fear of poverty, of suffering, of calumny, of sickness, of isolation and death. . . . It is the dazzling and glorious concentration of courage. *Amiel.*

Heroism is the self-devotion of genius manifesting itself in action. *Hare.*

Heroism, the Divine relation which, in all times, unites a great man to other men. *Carlyle.*

Hero-worship exists, has existed, and will for ever exist, universally among mankind. *Carlyle.*

Herradura que chacotea clavo le falta—A clattering hoof means a nail gone. *Sp. Pr.*

Herrenlos ist auch der Freiste nicht—Even 30 the most emancipated is not without a master. *Schiller.*

Herrschaft gewinn ich, Eigentum; / Die That ist alles, nichts der Ruhm—Lordship, aye ownership, is my conquest; the deed is everything, the fame of it nothing. *Goethe.*

Heu melior quanto sors tua sorte meâ!— Alas! how much better is your fate than mine!" *Ovid.*

Heu nihil invitis fas quenquam fidere divis— Alas! it is not permitted to any one to feel confident when the gods are adverse. *Virg.*

Heu pietas! Heu prisca fides—Alas! for piety! Alas! for ancient faith! *Virg.*

Heu! quam difficile est crimen non prodere 35 vultu!—Alas! how difficult it is not to betray guilt by our looks! *Ovid.*

Heu! quam difficilis gloriæ custodia est!— Alas! how difficult is the custody of glory. *Pub. Syr.*

Heu! quam miserum est ab eo lædi, de quo non ausis queri—Alas! how galling is it to be injured by one against whom you dare make no complaint. *Pub. Syr.*

Heu quantum fati parva tabella vehit!—Ah! with what a weight of destiny is this one slight plank freighted! *Ovid.*

Heu! totum triduum!—What! three whole days of waiting! *Ter.*

Heureka—I have found it out. *Gr.*   40

Heureux commencement est la moitié de l'œuvre—A work well begun is half done. *Fr. Pr.*

Heute muss dem Morgen nichts borgen—Today must borrow nothing of to-morrow. *Ger. Pr.*

Heute roth, Morgen todt—To-day red, tomorrow dead. *Ger. Pr.*

Hi motus animorum atque hæc certamina tanta / Pulveris exigui jactu compressa quiescent—These passions of soul, these conflicts so fierce, will cease, and be repressed by the casting of a little dust. *Virg.*

Hiatus maxime deflendus—A deficiency or blank 45 very much to be deplored.

Hibernicis ipsis hibernior—More Irish than the Irish themselves.

Hic dies, vere mihi festus, atras / Eximet curas —This day, for me a true holiday, shall banish gloomy cares. *Hor.*

Hic est aut nusquam quod quærimus—Here or else nowhere is what we are aiming at. *Hor.*

Hic est mucro defensionis tuæ—This is the point of your defence. *Cic.*

Hic et nunc—Here and now.   50

Hic et ubique—Here and everywhere.

Hic finis fandi—Here let the conversation end.

Hic funis nihil attraxit—This bait has taken no fish ; this scheme has not answered. *Pr.*

Hic gelidi fontes, hic mollia prata, Lycori, / Hic nemus, hic toto tecum consumerer ævo —Here are cool springs, Lycoris, here velvet meads, here a grove ; here with thee could I pass my whole life. *Virg.*

5 Hic hæret aqua !—This is the difficulty (*lit.* here the water (in the water-clock) stops.

Hic jacet—Here lies.

Hic locus est partes ubi se via findit in ambas —This is the spot where the way divides in two branches. *Virg.*

Hic murus aheneus esto, / Nil conscire sibi, nulla pallescere culpa—Be this our wall of brass, to be conscious of no guilt, to turn pale at no charge brought against us. *Hor.*

Hic niger est ; hunc tu, Romane, caveto—This fellow is black ; have a care of him, Roman. *Hor.*

10 Hic nigræ succus loliginis, hæc est / Ærugo mera—This is the very venom of dark detraction ; this is pure malignity. *Hor.*

Hic patet ingeniis campus, certusque merenti / Stat favor : ornatur propriis industria donis —Here is a field open for talent, and here merit will have certain favour, and industry be graced with its due reward. *Claud.*

Hic Rhodos, hic salta—Here is Rhodes ; here leap.

Hic rogo, non furor est ne moriare mori ?—I ask, is it not madness to die that you may not die? *Mart.*

Hic situs est Phaëton currus auriga paterni ; / Quem si non tenuit, magnis tamen excidit ausis—Here lies buried Phaëton, the driver of his father's car, which if he did not manage, still he perished in a great attempt. *Ovid.*

15 Hic transitus efficit magnum vitæ compendium —This change effects a great saving of time (*lit.* life).

Hic ubi nunc urbs est, tum locus urbis erat— Here, where the city now stands, was at that time nothing but its site. *Ovid.*

Hic ver assiduum, atque alienis mensibus æstas—Here (in Italy) is ceaseless spring, and summer in months in which summer is alien. *Virg.*

Hic victor cæstus artemque repono — Here victorious I lay aside my cestus and my net. *Virg.*

Hic vigilans somniat—He sleeps awake. *Plaut.*

20 Hic vivimus ambitiosa / Paupertate omnes— We all live here in a state of ostentatious poverty. *Juv.*

Hid jewels are but lost. *Quarles.*

Hier bin ich Mensch, hier darf ich's sein— Here am I a man, here may I be one. *Goethe.*

Hier ist die Zeit durch Thaten zu beweisen, / Dass Manneswürde nicht der Götterhöhe weicht—Now is the time to show by deeds that the dignity of a man does not yield to the sublimity of the gods. *Goethe.*

Hier ist keine Heimat—Jeder treibt / Sich an dem andern rasch und fremd vorüber, / Und fragt nicht nach seinem Schmerz—Here is no home for a man : every one drives past another hastily and unneighbourly, and inquires not after his pain. *Schiller.*

Hier sitz' ich auf Rasen mit Veilchen bekränzt 25 —Here sit I upon the sward wreathed with violets. *K. Schmidt.*

Hier stehe ich ! Ich kann nicht anders. Gott helfe mir ! Amen—Here stand I. I cannot act otherwise. So help me God ! *Luther at the Diet of Worms.*

Hier steht einer, der wird mich rächen—Here stands one who will avenge me. *Frederick William of Prussia, pointing to his son.*

High air-castles are cunningly built of words, the words well-bedded in good logic mortar ; wherein, however, no knowledge will come to lodge. *Carlyle.*

High birth is an accident, not a virtue. *Metastasio.*

High erected thoughts seated in the heart of 30 courtesy. *Sir P. Sidney.*

High houses are usually empty in the upper storey. *Ger. Pr.*

High is the head of the stag on the mountain crag. *Gael. Pr.*

High station has to be resigned in order to be appreciated. *Pascal.*

Hilarisque tamen cum pondere virtus—Virtue may be gay, yet with dignity. *Statius.*

Hilft Gott uns nicht, kein Kaiser kann uns 35 helfen — God helps us not ; no emperor can. *Schiller.*

Hills peep o'er hills ; and alps on alps arise. *Pope.*

Hilo y aguja, media vestidura — Needle and thread are half clothing. *Sp. Pr.*

Him only pleasure leads and peace attends, / Him, only him, the shield of Jove defends, / Whose means are fair and spotless as his ends. *Wordsworth.*

Him who makes chaff of himself the cows will eat. *Arab. Pr.*

Hin ist die Zeit, da Bertha spann—Gone is the 40 'time when Queen Bertha span. *Ger. Pr.*

Hin ist hin ! Verloren ist verloren—Gone is gone ! Lost is lost. *G. A. Bürger.*

Hinc illæ lachrymæ—Hence these tears. *Virg.*

Hinc lucem et pocula sacra—Hence light to us and sacred draughts. *M. of Cambridge University.*

Hinc omne principium, huc refer exitum—To them (the gods) ascribe every undertaking, to them the issue. *Hor.*

Hinc subitæ mortes atque intestata senectus 45 —Hence (from sensual indulgence) sudden deaths and intestate old age. *Juv.*

Hinc totam infelix vulgatur fama per urbem —Hence the unhappy news is spread abroad through the whole city. *Virg.*

Hinc usura vorax, avidumque in tempore fænus, / Et concussa fides, et multis utile bellum—Hence (from the ambition of Cæsar) arise devouring usury, grasping interest, shaken credit, and war of advantage to many. *Lucan.*

Hinc venti dociles resono se carcere solvunt, / Et cantum accepta pro libertate rependunt —Hence the obedient winds are loosed from their sounding prison, and repay the liberty they have received with a tune. *Of an organ.*

His bark is waur nor (worse than) his bite. *Sc. Pr.*

His Christianity was muscular. *Disraeli.* 50

His failings lean'd to virtue's side. *Goldsmith.*

His kissing is as full of sanctity as the touch of holy bread. *As You Like It,* iii. 4.

His imagination resembled the wings of an ostrich. It enabled him to run, though not to soar. *Macaulay.*

His lachrymis vitam damus, et miserescimus ultro—To these tears we grant him life, and pity him besides. *Virg.*

His legibus solutis respublica stare non potest —With these laws repealed, the republic cannot last. *Cic.*

5 His life was gentle, and the elements / So mix'd in him, that Nature might stand up, / And say to all the world : This was a man ! *Jul. Cæs.,* v. 5.

His nature is too noble for the world ; / He would not flatter Neptune for his trident, / or Jove for his power to thunder. *Coriolanus,* iii. 2.

His nunc præmium est, qui recta prava faciunt —Nowadays those are rewarded who make right appear wrong. *Ter.*

His opinion who does not see spiritual agency in history is not worth any man's reading. *Wm. Blake.*

His own character is the arbiter of every one's fortune. *Pub. Syr.*

10 His rash, fierce blaze of riot cannot last, / For violent fires soon outburn themselves. *Rich. II.,* ii. 1.

His saltem accumulem donis, et fungar inani munere—These offerings at least I would bestow upon him, and discharge a duty though it no longer avails. *Virg.*

His speech was like a tangled chain ; / Nothing impaired, but all disordered. *Mid. Night's Dream,* v. 1.

His thoughts look through his words. *Ben Jonson.*

His time is for ever, everywhere his place. *Cowley.*

15 His tongue could make the worse appear the better reason. *Milton.*

His tongue / Dropp'd manna, and could make the worse appear / The better reason, to perplex and dash / Maturest counsels. *Milton.*

His very foot has music in 't, / As he comes up the stair. *W. J. Mickle.*

His wit invites you by his looks to come, / But when you knock, it never is at home. *Cowper.*

His words are bonds, his oaths are oracles. *Two Gent. of Verona,* ii. 7.

20 Historia quo quomodo scripta delectat—History, however written, is always a pleasure to us. *Pliny.*

Histories are as perfect as the historian is wise, and is gifted with an eye and a soul. *Carlyle.*

Histories make men wise ; poets, witty ; the mathematics, subtle ; natural philosophy, deep ; morals, grave ; logic and rhetoric, able to contend. *Bacon.*

History and experience prove that the most passionate characters are the most fanatically rigid in their feelings of duty, when their passion has been trained to act in that direction. *J. S. Mill.*

History, as it lies at the root of all science, is also the first distinct product of man's spiritual nature, his earliest expression of what may be called thought. *Carlyle.*

History ensures for youth the understanding 25 of the ancients. *Diodorus.*

History has only to do with what is true, and what is only probable should be relegated to the imaginary domain of romance and poetical fiction. (?)

History is a cyclic poem written by Time upon the memories of man. *Shelley.*

History is always written *ex post facto.*

History is an impertinence and an injury, if it be anything more than a cheerful apologue or parable of my being and becoming. *Emerson.*

History is an imprisoned epic, nay, an im- 30 prisoned psalm and prophecy. *Carlyle.*

History is but a fable agreed on. *Napoleon.*

History is but the unrolled scroll of prophecy. *Garfield.*

History is indeed little more than the register of the crimes, follies, and misfortunes of mankind. *Gibbon.*

History is like sacred writing, for truth is essential to it. *Cervantes.*

History is made up of the bad actions of 35 extraordinary men. All the most noted destroyers and deceivers of our species, all the founders of arbitrary governments and false religions, have been extraordinary men, and nine-tenths of the calamities which have befallen the human race had no other origin than the union of high intelligence with low desires. *Macaulay.*

History is only a confused heap of facts. *Chesterfield.*

History is philosophy teaching by examples. *Quoted by Bolingbroke.*

History is properly nothing but a satire on mankind. *C. J. Weber.*

History is the true poetry. *Carlyle.*

History shows that the majority of the men 40 who have done anything great have passed their youth in seclusion. *Heine.*

History teems with instances of truth put down by persecution ; if not suppressed for ever, it may be thrown back for centuries. *J. S. Mill.*

Hitch your waggon to a star. *Emerson.*

Hitherto all miracles have been wrought by thought, and henceforth innumerable will be wrought ; whereof we, even in these days, witness some. *Carlyle.*

Hitherto doth love on fortune tend ; / For who not needs, shall never lack a friend ; / And who in want a hollow friend doth try, / Directly seasons him his enemy. *Ham.,* iii. 2.

Hitherto shalt thou come, but no further ; and 45 here shall thy proud waves be stayed. *Bible.*

Hizonos Dios, y maravillámonos nos—God made us, and we admire ourselves. *Sp. Pr.*

Hobbes clearly proves that every creature / Lives in a state of war by nature. *Swift.*

"Hoc age" is the great rule, whether you are serious or merry ; whether . . . learning science or duty from a folio, or floating on the Thames. Intentions must be gathered from acts. *Johnson.*

Hoc age—Mind what you are about (*lit.* do this).

Hoc erat in more majorum—This was the custom 50 of our forefathers.

Hoc erat in votis ; modus agri non ita magnus ; / Hortus ubi, et tecto vicinus jugis aquæ fons, / Et paulum silvæ super his foret—This was ever my chief prayer : a piece of ground not too large, with a garden, and a spring of never-failing water near my house, and a little woodland besides. *Hor.*

Hoc est quod palles ? cur quis non prandeat, hoc est ?—Is it for this you look so pale ? is this a reason why one should not dine ? *Pers.*

Hoc est / Vivere bis, vita posse priore frui— To be able to enjoy one's past life is to live twice. *Martial.*

Hoc fonte derivata clades, / In patriam, populumque fluxit—From this source the disaster flowed that has overwhelmed the nation and the people. *Hor.*

5 Hoc genus omne—All persons of that kind.

Hoc Herculi Iovis satu, edito' potuit fortasse contingere, nobis non item—This might perchance happen to Hercules, of the seed royal of Jove, but not to us. *Cic.*

Hoc loco—In this place.

Hoc maxime officii est, ut quisquis maxime opus indigeat, ita ei potissimum opitulari— It is our prime duty to aid him first who most stands in need of our assistance. *Cic.*

Hoc opus, hic labor est—This is a work, this is a toil. *Virg.*

10 Hoc patrium est, potius consuefacere filium / Sua sponte recte facere, quam alieno metu —It is a father's duty to accustom his son to act rightly of his own free-will rather than from fear of the consequences. *Ter.*

Hoc pretium ob stultitiam fero—This reward I gain for my folly. *Ter.*

Hoc scito, nimio celerius / Venire quod molestum est, quam id quod cupide petas—Be sure of this, that that which is disagreeable comes more speedily than that which you eagerly desire. *Plaut.*

Hoc signo vinces—By this sign (the cross) you will conquer. *M.*

Hoc virtutis opus—This is virtue's work. *M.*

15 Hoc volo, hoc jubeo ; sit pro ratione voluntas —This I wish, this I require : be my will instead of reason. *Juv.*

Hodie mihi, cras tibi—My turn to-day, yours to-morrow.

Hodie nihil, cras credo—To-morrow I will trust, not to-day. *Varro.*

Hodie vivendum amissa præteritorum cura— Let us live to-day, forgetting the cares that are past. *An Epicurean maxim.*

Hoi polloi—The multitude. *Gr.*

20 Hoist up the sail while gale doth last— / Tide and wind wait no man's pleasure ! / Seek not time when time is past— / Sober speed is wisdom's leisure ! *Southwell.*

Hold all the skirts of thy mantle extended when heaven is raining gold. *Eastern Pr.*

Hold the living dear and honour the dead. *Goethe.*

Hold their farthing candle to the sun. *Young, of critics.*

Hold thou the good ; define it well. *Tennyson.*

25 Hold up thy head ; the taper lifted high / Will brook the wind when lower tapers die. *Quarles.*

Holy fields, / Over whose acres walked those blessed feet / Which fourteen hundred years ago were nail'd, / For our advantage, on the bitter cross. 1 *Hen. IV.*, i. 1.

Holy men at their death have good inspirations. *Mer. of Ven.*, i. 2.

Hombre de barba—A man of intelligence. *Sp.*

Hombre pobre todo es trazas—A poor man is all schemes. *Sp. Pr.*

Home, in one form or another, is the great 30 object of life. *J. G. Holland.*

Home is heaven for beginners. *C. H. Parkhurst.*

Home is home, be it never so homely. *Pr.*

Home is the place of Peace ; the shelter, not only from all injury, but from all terror, doubt, and division. *Ruskin.*

Home should be an oratorio of the memory, singing to all our after life melodies and harmonies of old-remembered joy. *Ward Beecher.*

Home, the nursery of the infinite. *Channing.* 35

Home-keeping youth have ever homely wits. *Two Gent. of Ver.*, i. 1.

Homer's Epos has not ceased to be true ; yet is no longer our Epos, but shines in the distance, if clearer and clearer, yet also smaller and smaller, like a receding star. It needs a scientific telescope, it needs to be reinterpreted and artificially brought near us, before we can so much as know that 'twas a sun. . . . For all things, even celestial luminaries, much more atmospheric meteors, have their rise, their culmination, their decline. *Carlyle.*

Homine imperito nunquam quidquam injustius / Qui, nisi quod ipse fecit, nihil rectum putat— Nothing so unjust as your ignorant man, who thinks nothing right but what he himself has done. *Ter.*

Hominem non odi sed ejus vitia—I do not hate the man, but his vices. *Mart.*

Hominem pagina nostra sapit—My pages con- 40 cern man. *Mart.*

Hominem quæro—I am in quest of a man. *Phædr. after Diogenes.*

Homines ad deos nulla re propius accedunt quam salutem hominibus dando—In nothing do men so nearly approach the gods as in giving health to men. *Cic.*

Homines amplius oculis quam auribus credunt : longum iter est per præcepta, breve et efficax per exempla—Men trust their eyes rather than their ears : the road by precept is long and tedious, by example short and effectual. *Sen.*

Homines nihil agendo discunt male agere—By doing nothing men learn to do ill. *Cato.*

Homines plus in alieno negotio videre, quam 45 in suo—Men see better into other people's business than their own. *Sen.*

Homines proniores sunt ad voluptatem, quam ad virtutem—Men are more prone to pleasure than to virtue. *Cic.*

Homines, quo plura habent, eo cupiunt ampliora—The more men have, the more they want. *Justin.*

Homini necesse est mori—Man must die. *Cic.*

Homini ne fidas nisi cum quo modium salis absumpseres—Trust no man till you have eaten a peck of salt with him, *i.e.*, known him so long as you might have done so. *Pr.*

Hominibus plenum, amicis vacuum—Full of men, vacant of friends. *Sen.*

Hominis est errare, insipientis perseverare—It is the nature of man to err, of a fool to persevere in error.

Hominum sententia fallax—The opinions of men are fallible. *Ovid.*

Homme assailli à demi vaincu—A man assailed is half overpowered. *Fr.*

5 Homme chiche jamais riche—A niggardly man is always poor. *Fr. Pr.*

Homme d'affaires—A business man. *Fr.*

Homme d'esprit—A witty man. *Fr.*

Homme d'état—A statesman. *Fr.*

Homme d'honneur—A man of honour. *Fr.*

10 Homme instruit—A learned or literary man. *Fr.*

Homo ad res perspicacior Lynceo vel Argo, et oculeus totus—A man more clear-sighted for business than Lynceus or Argus, and eyes all over. *Apul.*

Homo antiqua virtute ac fide—A man of the old-fashioned virtue and loyalty. *Ter.*

Homo constat ex duabus partibus, corpore et anima, quorum una est corporea, altera ab omni materiae concretione sejuncta—Man is composed of two parts, body and soul, of which the one is corporeal, the other separated from all combination with matter. *Cic.*

Homo doctus in se semper divitias habet—A learned man has always riches in himself. *Phædr.*

15 Homo extra est corpus suum cum irascitur—A man when angry is beside himself. *Pub. Syr.*

Homo fervidus et diligens ad omnia paratur—The man who is earnest and diligent is prepared for all things. *Thomas à Kempis.*

Homo homini aut deus aut lupus—Man is to man either a god or a wolf. *Erasmus.*

Homo is a common name to all men. I *Hen. IV.*, ii. 1.

Homo multarum literarum—A man of many letters, *i.e.*, of extensive learning.

20 Homo multi consilii et optimi—A man always ready to give his advice, and that the most judicious.

Homo nullius coloris—A man of no party.

Homo qui erranti comiter monstrat viam, / Quasi lumen de suo lumine accendit, facit ; Nihilominus ipsi luceat, cum illi accenderit—He who kindly shows the way to one who has gone astray, acts as though he had lighted another's lamp from his own, which both gives light to the other and continues to shine for himself. *Cic.*

Homo solus aut deus aut demon—Man alone is either a god or a devil.

Homo sum, et nihil humani a me alienum puto—I am a man, and I reckon nothing human alien to me. *Ter.*

25 Homo toties moritur, quoties amittit suos—A man dies as often as he loses his relatives. *Pub. Syr.*

Homo trium literarum—A man of three letters, *i.e.*, FUR, "a thief." *Plaut.*

Homo unius libri—A man of one book. *Thomas Aquinas' definition of a learned man.*

Homunculi quanti sunt, cum recogito—What poor creatures we men are, when I think of it. *Plaut.*

Honest labour bears a lovely face. *T. Dekker.*

Honest men marry soon, wise men never. *Sc.* 30 *Pr.*

Honesta mors turpi vita potior—An honourable death is better than an ignominious life. *Tac.*

Honesta paupertas prior quam opes malæ—Poverty with honour is better than ill-gotten wealth. *Pr.*

Honesta quædam scelera successus facit—Success makes some species of crimes honourable. *Sen.*

Honesta quam splendida—Honourable rather than showy. *M.*

Honestum non est semper quod licet—What is 35 lawful is not always honourable. *L.*

Honestum quod vere dicimus, etiamsi a nullo landatur, laudabile est sua natura—That which we truly call honourable is praiseworthy in its own nature, even though it should be praised by no one. *Cic.*

Honesty is like an icicle; if it once melts, that is the last of it. *Amer. Pr.*

Honesty is the best policy. *Pr.*

Honesty is the poor man's pork and the rich man's pudding. *Pr.*

Honesty may be dear bought, but can ne'er be 40 an ill pennyworth. *Sc. Pr.*

Honi soit qui mal y pense—Evil be to him that evil thinks. *Royal M. Fr.*

Honnêtes gens—Upright people. *Fr.*

Honneur et patrie—Honour and country. *M.*

Honor Deo—Honour be to God. *M.*

Honor est præmium virtutis—Honour is the 45 reward of virtue. *Cic.*

Honor fidelitatis præmium—Honour is the reward of fidelity. *M.*

Honor sequitur fugientem—Honour follows him who flies from her. *M.*

Honores mutant mores — Honours change manners.

Honos alit artes, omnesque incenduntur ad studia gloria—Honours encourage the arts, for all are incited towards studies by fame. *Cic.*

Honour a physician with the honour due unto 50 him for the uses which ye may have of him, for the Lord hath created him. *Ecclus.*

Honour all men. Love the brotherhood. Fear God. Honour the king. *St. Peter.*

Honour and ease are seldom bedfellows. *Pr.*

Honour hath no skill in surgery. . . . Honour is a mere scutcheon. I *Hen. IV.*, v. 1.

Honour is nobler than gold. *Gael. Pr.*

Honour is not a virtue in itself; it is the mail 55 behind which the virtues fight more securely. *G. H. Calvert.*

Honour is unstable, and seldom the same; for she feeds upon opinion, and is as fickle as her food. *Colton.*

Honour is venerable to us because it is no ephemeris. *Emerson.*

Honour to whom honour is due. *St. Paul.*

Honour travels in a strait so narrow, / Where one but goes abreast. *Troil. and Cress.*, iii. 3.

Honour won't patch. *Gael. Pr.* 60

Honourable (*Ehrlich*) is a word of high rank, and implies much more than most people attach to it. *Arndt.*

Honours, like impressions upon coin, may give an ideal and local value to a bit of base metal; but gold and silver will pass all the world over, without any other recommendation than their own weight. *Sterne.*

Honours to one in my situation are something like ruffles to a man that wants a shirt. *Goldsmith, of himself.*

Honour's the moral conscience of the great. *D'Avenant.*

Honteux comme un renard qu'une poule aurait pris—Sheepish as a fox that has been taken in by a fowl. *La Font.*

5 Hope deferred maketh the heart sick. *Bible.*

Hope is a curtail dog in some affairs. *Merry Wives*, ii. 1.

Hope is a good anchor, but it needs something to grip. *Pr.*

Hope is a lover's staff; walk hence with that, / And manage it against despairing thoughts. *Two Gent. of Ver.*, iii. 1.

Hope is a pleasant acquaintance but an unsafe friend. He'll do on a pinch for your travelling companion, but he's not the man for your banker. *Amer. Pr.*

10 Hope is a waking man's dream. *Pr.*

Hope is itself a species of happiness, and perhaps the chief happiness which this world affords; but, like all other pleasures, its excesses must be expiated by pain; and expectations improperly indulged must end in disappointment. *Johnson.*

Hope is not the man for your banker, though he may do for your travelling companion. *Haliburton.*

Hope is the best part of our riches. *Bovee.*

Hope is the only good which is common to all men. *Thales.*

15 Hope is the ruddy morning ray of joy, recollection is its golden tinge; but the latter is wont to sink amid the dews and dusky shades of twilight, and the bright blue day which the former promises breaks indeed, but in another world and with another sun. *Jean Paul.*

Hope never comes that comes to all. *Milton.*

Hope never spread her golden wings but in unfathomable seas. *Emerson.*

Hope not wholly to reason away your troubles; but do not feed them with attention, and they will die imperceptibly away. *Johnson.*

Hope, of all ills that men endure, / The only cheap and universal cure. *Cowley.*

20 Hope springs eternal in the human breast; / Man never is, but always to be, blest. *Pope.*

Hope springs exulting on triumphant wing. *Burns.*

Hope thou not much, and fear thou not at all. *Quoted by Swinburne.*

Hope to joy is little less in joy / Than hope enjoyed. *Rich. II.*, ii. 3.

Hoping and waiting is not my way of doing things. *Goethe.*

25 Hora e sempre—Now and always. *M.*

Horæ cedunt, et dies, et menses, et anni, nec præteritum tempus unquam revertitur —Hours and days, months and years, pass away, and time once past never returns. *Cic.*

Horæ / Momento cita mors venit, aut victoria læta—In a moment of time comes sudden death or joyful victory. *Hor.*

Horas non numero nisi serenas—I mark no hours but the shining ones. *Of a dial.*

Horrea formicæ tendunt ad inania nunquam; / Nullus ad amissas ibit amicus opes—As ants never bend their way to empty barns, so no friend will visit departed wealth. *Ovid.*

Horresco referens—I shudder as I relate. *Virg.* 30

Horribile dictu—Horrible to relate.

Horror ubique animos, simul ipsa silentia terrent—Everywhere horror seizes the soul, and the very silence is dreadful. *Virg.*

Horror vacui—Abhorrence of a vacuum.

Hors de combat—Out of condition to fight. *Fr.*

Hors de propos—Not to the purpose. *Fr.* 35

Hortus siccus—A dry garden; a collection of dried plants.

Hos successus alit; possunt quia posse videntur—These are encouraged by success; they prevail because they think they can. *Virg.*

Hospice d'accouchement—A maternity hospital. *Fr.*

Hospice d'allaitement — A foundling hospital. *Fr.*

Hospitality must be for service, not for show, 40 or it pulls down the host. *Emerson.*

Hostis est uxor invita quæ ad virum nuptum datur—The wife who is given in marriage to a man against her will becomes his enemy. *Plaut.*

Hostis honori invidia—Envy is honour's foe. *M.*

Hôtel de ville—A town-hall. *Fr.*

Hôtel Dieu—The house of God; the name of an hospital. *Fr.*

Household words. *Hen. V.*, iv. 3. 45

Housekeeping without a wife is a lantern without a light. *Pr.*

Houses are built to live in, and not to look on. *Bacon.*

How are riches the means of happiness? In acquiring they create trouble, in their loss they occasion sorrow, and they are the cause of endless divisions amongst kindred! *Hitopadesa.*

How beautiful is death, seeing that we die in a world of life and of creation without end! *Jean Paul.*

How beautiful is youth! how bright it gleams, / 50 With its allusions, aspirations, dreams! / Book of beginnings, story without end, / Each maid a heroine, and each man a friend. *Longfellow.*

How beautiful to die of a broken heart on paper! Quite another thing in practice! Every window of your feeling, even of your intellect, as it were begrimmed and mudbespattered, so that no pure ray can enter; a whole drug-shop in your inwards; the foredone soul drowning slowly in a quagmire of disgust. *Carlyle.*

How bitter a thing it is to look into happiness through another man's eyes! *As You Like It*, v. 2.

How blessed might poor mortals be in the straitest circumstances, if only their wisdom and fidelity to Heaven and one another were adequately great. *Carlyle, apropos to his life at Craigenputtock.*

How blessings brighten as they take their flight! *Young.*

How blest the humble cotter's fate ! / He woos his simple dearie ; / The silly bogles, wealth, and state, / Can never make them eerie. *Burns.*

How can a man be concealed ? How can a man be concealed ? *Confucius.*

How can he be godly who is not cleanly ? *Pr.*

How can man love but what he yearns to help ? *Browning.*

5 How can we expect a harvest of thought who have not had a seed-time of character ? *Thoreau.*

How can we learn to know ourselves ? Never by reflection, but only through action. Essay to do thy duty, and thou knowest at once what is in thee. *Goethe.*

How charming is divine philosophy ! *Milton.*

How creatures of the human kind shut their eyes to the plainest facts, and by the mere inertia of oblivion and stupidity live at ease in the midst of wonders and terrors. *Carlyle.*

How difficult it is to get men to believe that any other man can or does act from disinterestedness. *B. R. Haydon.*

10 How dire is love when one is so tortured ; and yet lovers cannot exist without torturing themselves. *Goethe.*

How doth the little busy bee / Improve each shining hour, / And gather honey all the day / From every opening flower. *Watts.*

How dull it is to pause, to make an end, / To rust unburnish'd, not to shine in use, / As though to breathe were life. *Tennyson.*

How enormous appear the crimes we have not committed ! *Mme. Necker.*

How far that little candle throws his beams ! / So shines a good deed in a naughty world. *Mer. of Ven., v. 1.*

15 How fast has brother followed / From sunshine to the sunless land. *Wordsworth.*

How few think justly of the thinking few ; / How many never think, who think they do ! *Jane Taylor.*

How foolish and absurd, nay, how hurtful and destructive a vice is ambition, which, by undue pursuit of honour, robs us of true honour ! *Thomas à Kempis.*

How forcible are right words ! *Bible.*

How fortunate beyond all others is the man who, in order to adjust himself to fate, is not required to cast away his whole preceding life ! *Goethe.*

20 How full of briers is this working-day world ! *As You Like It, i. 3.*

How glorious a character appears when it is penetrated with mind and soul. *Goethe.*

How good is man's life, the mere living ! how fit to employ / All the heart, and the soul, and the senses for ever in joy ! *Browning.*

How happy could I be with either, / Were t'other dear charmer away ! *Gay.*

How happy is he born or taught / That serveth not another's will ; / Whose armour is his honest thought, / And simple truth his utmost skill. *Sir Henry Wotton.*

25 How happy is the blameless vestal's lot ! / The world forgetting, by the world forgot. *Pope.*

How happy is the prince who has counsellors near him who can guard him against the effects of his own angry passions ; their names shall be read in golden letters when the history of his reign is perused. *Scott.*

How happy should we be . . . / If we from self could rest, / And feel at heart that One above, / In perfect wisdom, perfect love, / Is working for the best ! *Anstice.*

How hard it is (for the Byron, for the Burns), whose ear is quick for celestial messages, to " take no counsel with flesh and blood," and instead of living and writing for the day that passes over them, live and write for the eternity that rests and abides over them ! *Carlyle.*

How hardly man the lesson learns, / To smile, and bless the hand that spurns : / To see the blow, to feel the pain, / And render only love again ! *Anon.*

How hardly shall they who have riches enter 30 into the kingdom of God ! *Jesus.*

How ill white hairs become a fool and a jester. *2 Hen. IV., v. 5.*

How indestructibly the good grows, and propagates itself, even among the weedy entanglements of evil ! *Carlyle.*

How is each of us so lonely in the wide bosom of the All ? *Jean Paul.*

How is it possible to expect that mankind will take advice, when they will not so much as take warning ? *Swift.*

How little do the wantonly or idly officious 35 think what mischief they do by their malicious insinuations, indirect impertinence, or thoughtless babblings ! *Burns.*

How little is the promise of the child fulfilled in the man. *Ovid.*

How long halt ye between two opinions ? *Bible.*

How long I have lived, how much lived in vain ! / How little of life's scanty span may remain ! / What aspects old Time in his progress has worn ! / What ties cruel fate in my bosom has torn ! / How foolish, or worse, till our summit is gain'd ! / And downward, how weaken'd, how darken'd, how pain'd ! *Burns.*

How many ages hence / Shall this our lofty scene be acted over / In states unborn and accents yet unknown ! *Jul. Cæs., iii. 1.*

How many causes that can plead for them- 40 selves in the courts of Westminster, and yet in the general court of the universe and free soul of man, have no word to utter ! *Carlyle.*

How many cowards, whose hearts are all as false / As stairs of sand, wear yet upon their chins / The beards of Hercules and frowning Mars ! / Who, inward searched, have livers white as milk. *Mer. of Venice, iii. 2.*

How many honest words have suffered corruption since Chaucer's days ! *Middleton.*

How many illustrious and noble heroes have lived too long by a day ! *Rousseau.*

How many men live on the reputation of the reputation they might have made ! *Holmes.*

How many people make themselves abstract 45 to appear profound ! The greatest part of abstract terms are shadows that hide a vacuum. *Joubert.*

How many things by season season'd are /
To their right praise and true perfection !
Mer. of Venice, v. 1.

How many things, just and unjust, have no
higher sanction than custom ! *Ter.*

How much a dunce that has been sent to
roam / Excels a dunce that has been kept
at home ! *Cowper.*

How much better is it to get wisdom than
gold ! and to get understanding rather to be
chosen than silver ! *Bible.*

5 How much better it is to weep at joy than to
joy at weeping ! *Much Ado*, i. 4.

How much easier it is to be generous than
just ! *Junius.*

How much lies in laughter, the cipher-key
wherewith we decipher the whole man.
Carlyle.

How much the wife is dearer than the bride !
Lyttelton.

How narrow our souls become when absorbed
in any present good or ill ! It is only the
thought of the future that makes them
great. *Jean Paul.*

10 How noble is heroic insight without words in
comparison to the adroitest flow of words
without heroic insight ! *Carlyle.*

How noiseless is thought ! No rolling of
drums, no tramp of squadrons, or immeasurable tumult of baggage-waggons, attends
its movements ; in what obscure and sequestered places may the head be meditating
which is one day to be crowned with more
than imperial authority ; for kings and emperors will be among its ministering servants ; it will rule not over, but in all heads,
and bend the world to its will. *Carlyle.*

How oft do they their silver bowers leave
To come to succour us that succour want !
Spenser.

How one is vexed with little things in this
life ! The great evils one triumphs over
bravely, but the little eat away one's heart.
Mrs. Carlyle.

How paint to the sensual eye what passes in
the holy-of-holies of man's soul ; in what
words, known to these profane times, speak
even afar-off of the unspeakable ? *Carlyle.*

15 How poor are they that have not patience ! /
What wound did ever heal but by degrees ?
Othello, ii. 3.

How poor, how rich, how abject, how august, /
How complicate, how wonderful is man !
Young.

How prone to doubt, how cautious are the
wise ! *Pope, after Homer.*

How quick to know, but how slow to put in
practice, is the human creature ! *Goethe.*

How quickly Nature falls into revolt / When
gold becomes her object ! 2 *Hen. IV.*,
iv. 4.

20 How rarely reason guides the stubborn
choice, / Rules the bold hand or prompts
the suppliant voice. *Johnson.*

How ready some people are to admire in a
great man the exception rather than the
rule of his conduct ! Such perverse worship
is like the idolatry of barbarous nations,
who can see the noonday splendour of the
sun without emotion, but who, when he is
in eclipse, come forward with hymns and
cymbals to adore him. *Canning.*

How rich a man is, all desire to know, / But
none enquire if good he be or no. *Herrick.*

How sad a path it is to climb and descend
another's stairs ! *Dante.*

How science dwindles, and how volumes
swell, / How commentators each dark pas-
age shun, / And hold their farthing candle to
the sun ! *Young.*

How shall a man escape from his ancestors, or 25
draw off from his veins the black drop which
he drew from his father's or his mother's
life ? *Emerson.*

How shall he give kindling in whose inward
man there is no live coal, but all is burnt out
to a dead grammatical cinder ? *Carlyle.*

How shall we know whether you are in earnest, if the deed does not accompany the
word ? *Schiller.*

How sharper than a serpent's tooth it is / To
have a thankless child ! *King Lear*, i. 4.

How small a part of time they share / That
are so wondrous sweet and fair ! *E. Waller.*

How small, of all that human hearts endure, / 30
That part which laws or kings can cause or
cure ! / Still to ourselves, in every place
consigned, / Our own felicity we make or
find. *Johnson.*

How should he be easy who makes other men's
cares his own ? *Thomas à Kempis.*

How should thy virtue be above the shocks
and shakings of temptation, when even the
angels kept not their first estate, and man
in Paradise so soon fell from innocence ?
Thomas à Kempis.

How silver-sweet sound lovers' tongues by
night, / Like softest music to attending ears !
Rom. and Jul., ii. 2.

How soon "not now" becomes "never !"
Luther.

How sour sweet music is, when time is broke 35
and no proportion kept ! So is it in the
music of men's lives. *Rich. II.*, v. 5.

How still the evening is, / As hushed on purpose to grace harmony ! *Much Ado*, ii. 3.

How sweet it is to hear one's own convictions
from a stranger's mouth ! *Goethe.*

How sweet the moonlight sleeps upon this
bank ! / Here will we sit and let the sounds
of music / Creep in our ears : soft stillness
and the night / Become the touches of sweet
harmony. *Mer. of Ven.*, v. 1.

How the sight of means to do ill deeds / Make
deeds ill done ! *King John*, iv. 2.

How the world wags ! *As You Like It*, ii. 7. 40

How they gleam like spirits through the
shadows of innumerable eyes from their
thrones in the boundless depths of heaven !
Carlyle, on the stars.

How use doth breed habit in a man ! *Two
Gent. of Ver.*, v. 4.

How vainly seek / The selfish for that happiness denied / To aught but virtue ! *Shelley.*

How we clutch at shadows (in this dream-
world) as if they were substances, and
sleep deepest while fancying ourselves most
awake ! *Carlyle.*

How weary, stale, flat, and unprofitable / 45
Seem to me all the uses of this world.
Ham., i. 2.

How well he's read, to reason against reading !
Love's L. Lost, i. 1.

How were friendship possible? In mutual devotedness to the good and true, otherwise impossible; except as armed neutrality or hollow commercial league. *Carlyle.*

How wonderful is Death, / Death and his brother Sleep! / One, pale as yonder waning moon, / With lips of lurid blue; / The other, rosy as the morn, / When, throned on ocean's wave, / It blushes o'er the world: / Yet both so passing wonderful. *Shelley.*

How wounding a spectacle is it to see those who were by Christ designed for fishers of men, picking up shells on the shore, and unmanly wrangling about them too! *Decay of Piety.*

How wretched is the man that hangs on by the favours of the great! *Burns.*

5 Howe'er it be, it seems to me / 'Tis only noble to be good. / Kind hearts are more than coronets, / And simple faith than Norman blood. *Tennyson.*

However, an old song, though to a proverb an instance of insignificance, is generally the only coin a poet has to pay with. *Burns.*

However brilliant an action, it should not be esteemed great unless the result of a great motive. *La Roche.*

However far a man goes, he must start from his own door. *Pr.*

However varied the forms of destiny, the same elements are always present. *Schopenhauer.*

10 Howsoever thou actest, let heaven be moved with thy purpose; let the aim of thy deeds traverse the axis of the earth. *Schiller.*

Huc propius me, / Dum doceo insanire omnes, vos ordine adite—Come near me all in order, and I will convince you that you are mad, every one. *Hor.*

Huic maxime putamus malo fuisse nimiam opinionem ingenii atque virtutis — This I think to have been the chief cause of his misfortune, an overweening estimate of his own genius and valour. *Nep., of Themistocles.*

Huic versatile ingenium sic pariter ad omnia fuit, ut natum ad id unum diceres, quodcunque ageret—This man's genius was so versatile, so equal to every pursuit, that you would pronounce him to have been born for whatever thing he was engaged on. *Livy, on the elder Cato.*

Human action is a seed of circumstances (*Verhängnissen*) scattered in the dark land of the future and hopefully left to the powers that rule human destiny. *Schiller.*

15 Human beliefs, like all other natural growths, elude the barriers of system. *George Eliot.*

Human brutes, like other beasts, find snares and poison in the provisions of life, and are allured by their appetites to their destruction. *Swift.*

Human courage should rise to the height of human calamity. *Gen. Lee.*

Human creatures will not go quite accurately together, any more than clocks will. *Carlyle.*

Human felicity is lodged in the soul, not in the flesh. *Sen.*

20 Human intellect, if you consider it well, is the exact summary of human worth. *Carlyle.*

Human judgment is finite, and it ought always to be charitable. *W. Winter.*

Human knowledge is the parent of doubt. *Greville.*

Human life is a constant want, and ought to be a constant prayer. *S. Osgood.*

Human life is everywhere a state in which much is to be endured and little to be enjoyed. *Johnson.*

Human life is more governed by fortune than 25 by reason. *Hume.*

Human nature in its fulness is necessarily human; without love, it is inhuman; without sense (*nous*), inhuman; without discipline, inhuman. *Ruskin.*

Human nature . . . / Is not a punctual presence, but a spirit / Diffused through time and space. *Wordsworth.*

Human nature (*Menschheit*) we owe to father and mother, but our humanity (*Menschlichkeit*) we owe to education. *Weber.*

Human reason is like a drunken man on horseback; set it up on one side, and it tumbles over on the other. *Luther.*

Human society is made up of partialities. 30 *Emerson.*

Humani nihil alienum—Nothing that concerns man is indifferent to me. *M.*

Humanität sei unser ewig Ziel—Be humanity evermore our goal. *Goethe.*

Humanitati qui se non accommodat, / Plerumque pœnas oppetit superbiæ—He who does not conform to courtesy generally pays the penalty of his haughtiness. *Phædr.*

Humanity is about the same all the world over. *Donn Piatt.*

Humanity is better than gold. *Goldsmith.* 35

Humanity is constitutionally lazy. *J. G. Holland.*

Humanity is great but men are small. *Börne.*

Humanity is never so beautiful as when praying for forgiveness, or else forgiving another. *Jean Paul.*

Humanity is one, and not till Lazarus is cured of his sores will Dives be safe. *Celia Burleigh.*

Humanity is the virtue of a woman, generosity 40 of a man. *Adam Smith.*

Humanum amare est, humanum autem ignoscere est—It is natural to love, and it is natural also to forgive. *Plaut.*

Humanum est errare—To err is human.

Humble wedlock is far better than proud virginity. *St. Augustine.*

Humbleness is always grace, always dignity. *Lowell.*

Humiles laborant ubi potentes dissident—The 45 humble are in danger when those in power disagree. *Phædr.*

Humility disarms envy and strikes it dead. *Collier.*

Humility is a virtue all preach, none practise, and yet everybody is content to hear. The master thinks it good doctrine for his servant, the laity for the clergy, and the clergy for the laity. *Selden.*

Humility is a virtue of so general, so exceeding good influence, that we can scarce purchase it too dear. *Thomas à Kempis.*

Humility is often a feigned submission which we employ to supplant others. *La Roche.*

Humility is the altar upon which God wishes that we should offer Him His sacrifices. *La Roche.*

Humility is the hall-mark of wisdom. *Jeremy Collier.*

Humility is the only true wisdom by which we prepare our minds for all the possible vicissitudes of life *Arliss' Lit. Col.*

Humility is the solid foundation of all the virtues. *Confucius.*

5 Humility, that low, sweet root / From which all heavenly virtues shoot. *Moore.*

Humour has justly been regarded as the finest perfection of poetic genius. He who wants it, be his other gifts what they may, has only half a mind; an eye for what is above him, not for what is about him or below him. *Carlyle.*

Humour is a sort of inverse sublimity, exalting, as it were, into our affections what is below us, while sublimity draws down into our affections what is above us. *Carlyle.*

Humour is consistent with pathos, while wit is not. *Coleridge.*

Humour is of a genial quality and is closely allied to pity. *Henry Giles.*

10 Humour is properly the exponent of low things; that which first renders them poetical to the mind. *Carlyle.*

Humour is the mistress of tears. *Thackeray.*

Humour, warm and all-embracing as the sunshine, bathes its objects in a genial and abiding light. *Whipple.*

Hundreds of people can talk for one who can think, but thousands can think for one who can see. To see clearly is poetry, prophecy, and religion all in one. *Ruskin.*

Hunger and cold betray a man to his enemy. *Pr.*

15 Hunger is a good cook. *Gael. Pr.*

Hunger is the best sauce. *Pr.*

Hunger will break through stone walls. *Pr.*

Hungry bellies have no ears. *Pr.*

Hunt half a day for a forgotten dream. *Wordsworth.*

20 Hunters generally know the most vulnerable part of the beast they pursue by the care which every animal takes to defend the side which is weakest. *Goldsmith.*

Hunting was the labour of savages in North America, but the amusement of the gentlemen of England. *Johnson.*

Hurtar el puerco, y dar los pies por Dios—To steal the pig, and give away the feet for God's sake. *Sp. Pr.*

Husbands can earn money, but only wives can save it. *Pr.*

Hyperion to a satyr; so loving to my mother, / That he might not beteem the winds of heaven / Visit her face too roughly. *Ham.*, i. 2.

25 Hypotheses non fingo—I frame no hypotheses. *Sir Isaac Newton.*

Ἁπλοῦν τὸ δίκαιον, ῥάδιον τὸ ἀληθες—Justice is simple, truth easy. *Lycurgus.*

Hypothesen sind Wiegenlieder, womit der Lehrer seine Schüler einlullt— Hypotheses are the lullabies with which the teacher lulls his scholars to sleep. *Goethe.*

Hysteron proteron—The last first, or the cart before the horse. *Gr.*

I.

I am a man / More sinned against than sinning. *King Lear*, iii. 2.

I am afraid to think what I have done; / Look 30 on't again I dare not. *Macb.*, ii. 2.

I am always afraid of a fool; one cannot be sure that he is not a knave as well. *Hazlitt.*

I am always as happy as I can be in meeting a man in whose society feelings are developed and thoughts defined. *Goethe.*

I am always ill at ease when tumults arise among the mob—people who have nothing to lose. *Goethe.*

I am amazed, methinks, and lose my way / Among the thorns and dangers of the world. *King John*, iv. 3.

I am as free as Nature first made man, / Ere 35 the base laws of servitude began, / When wild in woods the noble savage ran. *Dryden.*

I am black, but I am not the devil. *Pr.*

I am bound to find you in reasons, but not in brains. *Johnson.*

I am but a gatherer and disposer of other men's stuff. *Sir Henry Wotton.*

I am constant as the northern star, / Of whose true-fix'd and resting quality / There is no fellow in the firmament. *Jul. Cæs.*, iii. 1.

I am convinced that the Bible always becomes 40 more beautiful the better it is understood, that is, the better we see that every word which we apprehend in general and apply in particular had a proper, peculiar, and immediately individual reference to certain circumstances, certain time and space relations, *i.e.*, had a specially direct bearing on the spiritual life of the time in which it was written. *Goethe.*

I am equally an enemy to a female dunce and a female pedant. *Goldsmith.*

I am fortune's fool. *Rom. and Jul.*, iii. 1.

I am fully convinced that the soul is indestructible, and that its activity will continue through eternity. It is like the sun, which, to our eyes, seems to set in night; but it has in reality only gone to diffuse its light elsewhere. *Goethe.*

I am monarch of all I survey, / My right there is none to dispute; / From the centre all round to the sea, / I am lord of the fowl and the brute. *Cowper.*

I am more afraid of my own heart than of the 45 Pope and all his cardinals. I have within me the great pope, self. *Luther.*

I am neither so weak as to fear men, so proud as to despise them, or so unhappy as to hate them. *Marmontel.*

I am never merry when I hear sweet music. *Mer. of Ven.*, v. 1.

I am no herald to inquire of men's pedigrees; it sufficeth me if I know their virtues. *Sir P. Sidney.*

I am no orator, as Brutus is; / But, as you know me all, a plain blunt man, / That loves my friend. *Jul. Cæs.*, iii. 2.

I am not mad; I would to heaven I were! / 50 For then 'tis like I should forget myself. *King John*, iii. 4.

I am not what I am. *Twelfth Night*, iii. 1; *Othello*, i. 1.

I am nothing if not critical. *Othello*, ii. 1.

"I am searching for a man." *Diogenes, going about Athens by day with a lit lantern.*

I am Sir Oracle, / And when I ope my lips, let no dog bark. *Mer. of Ven.*, i. 1.

5 I am sorry to see how small a piece of religion will make a cloak. *Sir W. Waller.*

I am very content with knowing, if only I could know. *Emerson.*

I am very fond of the company of ladies. I like their beauty ; I like their delicacy ; I like their vivacity ; and I like their silence. *Johnson.*

I and time against any two. *Philip of Spain.*

I augur better of a youth who is wandering on a path of his own than of many who are walking aright upon paths which are not theirs. *Goethe.*

10 I awoke one morning and found myself famous. *Byron.*

I believe in great men, but not in demigods. *Bovee.*

I believe more follies are committed out of complaisance to the world than in following our own inclinations. *Lady Mary Montagu.*

I believe there are few persons who, if they please to reflect on their past lives, will not find that had they saved all those little sums which they have spent unnecessarily they might at present have been masters of a competent fortune. *Eustace Budgell.*

I beseech you, dear brethren, think it possible that you may be wrong. *Cromwell.*

15 I bide my time. *M.*

I can but trust that good shall fall / At last— far off—at last, to all. *Tennyson.*

"I can call spirits from the vasty deep." "Why, so can I, or so can any man ; but will they come when you do call for them ? " *1 Hen. IV.*, iii. 1.

I can count a stocking-top while a man 's getting 's tongue ready ; an' when he out wi' his speech at last, there 's little broth to be made on't. *George Eliot.*

I can teach you to command the devil, / And I can teach you to shame the devil, / By telling truth. *1 Hen. IV.*, ii. 1.

20 I can tell you, honest friend, what to believe : believe life ; it teaches better than book and orator. *Goethe.*

I cannot call riches better than the baggage of virtue. . . . It cannot be spared or left behind, but it hindereth the march. *Bacon.*

I cannot hide what I am ; I must be sad when I have cause, and smile at no man's jests ; eat when I have stomach, and wait for no man's leisure ; sleep when I am drowsy, and tend on no man's business ; laugh when I am merry, and claw no man in his humour. *Much Ado*, i. 3.

I cannot love thee as I ought, / For love reflects the thing beloved ; / My words are only words, and move / Upon the topmost froth of thought. *Tennyson.*

I cannot praise a fugitive and cloistered virtue, unexercised and unbreathed, that never sallies out and seeks her adversary, but slinks out of the race where that immortal garland is to be run for, not without dust and heat. *Milton.*

I cannot think of any character below the 25 flatterer, except he that envies him. *Steele.*

I can't work for nothing, and find thread. *Pr.*

I care not though the cloth of state should be / Not of rich Arras, but mean tapestry. *George Herbert.*

I charge thee, fling away ambition ; / By that sin fell the angels. *Hen. VIII.*, iii. 2.

I chatter, chatter, as I flow / To join the brimming river, / For men may come and men may go, / But I go on for ever. *Tennyson.*

I contented myself with endeavouring to make 30 your home so easy that you might not be in haste to leave it. *Lady Montagu (to her daughter).*

I could a tale unfold, whose lightest word / Would harrow up thy soul, freeze thy young blood, / Make thy two eyes, like stars, start from their spheres, / Thy knotted and combined locks to part, / And each particular hair to stand on end, / Like quills upon the fretful porcupine. *Ham.*, i. 4.

I could have better spared a better man. *1 Hen. IV.*, v. 4.

I could not but smile at a woman who makes her own misfortunes and then deplores the miseries of her situation. *Goldsmith.*

I count life just a stuff / To try the soul's strength on. *Browning.*

I cuori fanciulli non vestone a bruno—A child's 35 heart wears no weeds. *B. Zendrini.*

I danari del comune sono come l' acqua benedetta, ognun ne piglia—Public money is like holy water ; everybody helps himself to it. *It. Pr.*

I dare do all that may become a man ; / Who dares do more, is none. *Macb.*, i. 7.

I dare to be honest, and I fear no labour. *Burns.*

I, demens ! et sævas curre per Alpes, / Ut pueris placeas, et declamatio fias—Go, madman, and run over the savage Alps to please schoolboys, and become the subject of declamation. *Juv., of Hannibal.*

I desire no future that will break the ties of 40 the past. *George Eliot.*

I die by the help of too many physicians. *Alexander the Great.*

I do but sing because I must, / And pipe but as the linnets sing. *Tennyson.*

I do know of these / That therefore only are reputed wise / For saying nothing. *Mer. of Ven.*, i. 1.

I do know, / When the blood burns, how prodigal the soul / Lends the tongue vows. *Ham.*, i. 3.

I do not like "but yet," it does allay / The 45 good precedence ; fie upon "but yet :" / "But yet" is as a jailer to bring forth / Some monstrous malefactor. *Ant. and Cleop.*, ii. 5.

I do not love a man who is zealous for nothing. *Goldsmith.*

I do not love thee, Dr. Fell, / The reason why I cannot tell ; / But this alone I know full well, / I do not love thee, Dr. Fell.

I do not need philosophy at all. *Goethe.*

I do pity unlearned gentlemen on a rainy day. *Falkland.*

"I don't care," is a deadly snare. *Pr.*

I earn that I eat, get that I wear; owe no man hate, envy no man's happiness; glad of other men's good, content with my harm. *As You Like It*, iii. 2.

I esteem that wealth which is given to the worthy, and which is day by day enjoyed; the rest is a reserve for one knoweth not whom. *Hitopadesa.*

I fatti sono maschii, le parole femine—Deeds are masculine, words feminine. *It. Pr.*

5 I favoriti dei grandi oltre all' oro di regali, e l'incenso delle lodi, tocca loro anche la mirra della maldicenza—The favourites of the great, besides the gold of gifts and the incense of flattery, must also partake of the myrrh of calumny. *It. Pr.*

I fear God, and, next to God, I chiefly fear him who fears Him not. *Saadi.*

I fear thy nature; / It is too full of the milk of human kindness / To catch the nearest way. *Macb.*, i. 5.

I feel within me a peace above all earthly dignities, a still and quiet conscience. *Hen. VIII.*, iii. 2.

I find nonsense singularly refreshing. *Talleyrand.*

10 I for ever pass from hand to hand, / And each possessor thinks me his own land. / All of them think so, but they all are wrong; / To none but Fortune only I belong. *Anon., of a field.*

I found Rome brick, I left it marble. *Augustus Cæsar.*

I gaed a waefu' gate yestreen, / A gate, I fear, I'll dearly rue; / I got my death frae twa sweet een, / Twa lovely een o' bonnie blue. *Burns.*

"I go at last out of this world, where the heart must either petrify or break." *Chamfort, at his last moments.*

I go through my appointed daily stage, and I care not for the curs who bark at me along the road. *Frederick the Great.*

15 I gran dolori sono muti—Great griefs are dumb. *It. Pr.*

I grieve that grief can teach me nothing, nor carry me one step into real nature. *Emerson.*

I grudge the dollar, the dime, the cent I give to such men as do not belong to me and to whom I do not belong; (but) there is a class of persons to whom, by all spiritual affinity, I am bought and sold; for them I will go to prison if need be. *Emerson.*

I guadagni mediocri empiono la borsa—Moderate profits fill the purse. *It. Pr.*

I had as lief not be, as live to be / In awe of such a thing as I myself. *Jul. Cæs.*, i. 2.

20 I had better never see a book than be warped by its attraction clean out of my own orbit and made a satellite instead of a system. *Emerson.*

I had rather be a dog, and bay the moon, / Than such a Roman. *Jul. Cæs.*, iv. 3.

"I had rather be first here than second in Rome." *Cæsar, in an insignificant townlet.*

I had rather be Mercury, the smallest among seven (planets), revolving round the sun, than the first among five (moons) revolving round Saturn. *Goethe.*

I had rather believe all the fables in the legends, the Talmud, and the Koran, than that this universal frame is without a mind. *Bacon.*

I had rather dwell in the dim fog of supersti- 25 tion than in air rarified to nothing by the air-pump of unbelief. *Jean Paul.*

I had rather have a fool to make me merry than experience to make me sad. *As You Like It*, iv. 1.

I had rather people laugh at me while they instruct me than praise me without benefiting me. *Goethe.*

I hae a penny to spend, / There—thanks to naebody; / I hae naething to lend— / I'll borrow frae naebody. *Burns.*

I hate a style that slides along like an eel, and never rises to what one can call an inequality. *Shenstone.*

I hate bungling as I do sin, but particularly 30 bungling in politics, which leads to the misery and ruin of many thousands and millions of people. *Goethe.*

I hate ingratitude more in a man / Than lying, vainness, babbling, drunkenness, / Or any taint of vice whose strong corruption / Inhabits our frail blood. *Twelfth Night*, iii. 1.

I have a kind of alacrity in sinking. *Merry Wives*, iii. 5.

I have a very poor opinion of a man who talks to men what women should not hear. *Richardson.*

I have all I have ever enjoyed. *Bettine.*

I have always been a quarter of an hour 35 before my time, and it has made a man of me. *Nelson.*

I have always despised the whining yelp of complaint, and the cowardly, feeble resolve. *Burns.*

I have always found that the road to a woman's heart lies through her child. *Judge Haliburton.*

I have been reasoning all my life, and find that all argument will vanish before one touch of Nature. *Colman.*

I have been tempted by opportunity, and seconded by accident. *Marmontel.*

I have been too much occupied with things 40 themselves to think either of their beginning or their end. *Goethe.*

I have bought / Golden opinions from all sorts of people. *Macb.*, i. 7.

I have ever held it as a maxim never to do that through another which it was possible for me to execute myself. *Montesquieu.*

I have, God wot, a largë field to ear; / And weakë be the oxen in my plough. *Chaucer.*

I have great hope of a wicked man, slender hope of a mean one. *Ward Beecher.*

I have known some men possessed of good 45 qualities which were very serviceable to others, but useless to themselves; like a sun-dial on the front of a house, to inform the neighbours and passengers, but not the owner within. (?)

I have learned in whatsoever state I am therewith to be content. *St. Paul.*

I have little knowledge which I find not some way useful to my highest ends. *Baxter.*

I have lost the ring, but I have my finger still. *It. and Sp. Pr.*

I have never been able to conquer this ferocious wild beast (impatience). *Calvin.*

I have never seen a greater monster or miracle in the world than myself. *Montaigne.*

I have no idea of the courage that braves Heaven. *Burns.*

I have no notion of a truly great man that could not be all sorts of men. *Carlyle.*

5 I have no other but a woman's reason; / I think him so because I think him so. *Two Gent. of Ver.,* i. 2.

I have no spur / To prick the sides of my intent. *Macb.,* i. 7.

I have no words, / My voice is in my sword. *Macb.,* v. 7.

I have saved the bird in my bosom, *i.e.,* kept my secret. *Pr.*

I have seen some nations, like overloaded asses, / Kick off their burdens, meaning the higher classes. *Byron.*

10 I have seldom known any one who deserted truth in trifles that could be trusted in matters of importance. *Paley.*

I have set my life upon a cast. / And I will stand the hazard of the die. *Rich. III.,* v. 4.

I have that within which passeth show ; / These but the trappings and the suits of woe. *Ham.,* i. 2.

I have this great commission, / From that supernal judge that stirs good thoughts / In any breast of strong authority, / To look into the blots and stains of right. *King John,* ii. 1.

I have thought some of Nature's journeymen had made men, and not made them well; they imitated humanity so abominably. *Ham.,* iii. 2.

15 I hear, yet say not much, but think the more. 3 *Hen. VI.,* iv. 1.

I hold ambition of so airy and light a quality, that it is but a shadow's shadow. *Ham.,* ii. 2.

I hold every man a debtor to his profession. *Bacon.*

I hold it cowardice / To rest mistrustful where a noble heart / Hath pawn'd an open hand in sign of love. 3 *Hen. VI.*

I hold it truth, with him who sings / To one clear harp in divers tones, / That men may rise on stepping-stones / Of their dead selves to higher things. *Tennyson.*

20 I hold the world but as the world, Gratiano ; / A stage, where every man must play a part, / And mine a sad one. *Mer. of Ven.,* i. 1.

I hope I don't intrude. *Paul Pry.*

I humbly trust I should not change my opinions and practice, though it rained garters and coronets as the reward of apostasy. *Havelock.*

I jouk (duck aside) beneath misfortune's blows / As well's I may ; / Sworn foe to sorrow, care, or prose, / I rhyme away. *Burns.*

I know but of one solid objection to absolute monarchy ; the difficulty of finding any man adequate to the office. *Fielding.*

25 I know enough to hold my tongue, but not to speak. *Pr.*

I know no evil death can show, which life / Has not already shown to those who live / Embodied longest. *Byron.*

I know no evil so great as the abuse of the understanding and yet there is no one vice more common. *Steele.*

I know no judgment of the future but by the past. *Patrick Henry.*

I know nothing sublime which is not some modification of power. *Burke.*

I know only one thing sweeter than making a 30 book, and that is to project one. *Jean Paul.*

I know that dancin' 's nonsense ; but if you stick at everything because it's nonsense, you wonna go far in this life. *George Eliot.*

"I know that it is in me, and out it shall come." *Sheridan to his friends over their disappointment at the failure of his maiden speech.*

I know that my Redeemer liveth. *Job, in the Bible.*

I know that nothing is mine but the thought that flows tranquilly out of my soul, and every gracious (*günstige*) moment which a loving Providence (*Geschick*) permits me thoroughly (*von Grund aus*) to enjoy. *Goethe.*

I labour, and you get the pearl. *Talmud.* 35

I let every one follow his own bent, that I may be free to follow mine. *Goethe.*

I like a good hater. *Johnson.*

I live in the crowd of jollity, not so much to enjoy company as to shun myself. *Johnson.*

I live not in myself, but I become / Portion of that around me ; and to me / High mountains are a feeling. *Byron.*

I look upon an able statesman out of business 40 like a huge whale, that will endeavour to overturn the ship unless he has an empty cask to play with. *Steele.*

I love a hand that meets mine own with a grasp that causes some sensation. *Mrs. Osgood.*

I love everything that's old—old friends, old tunes, old manners, old books, old wine. *Goldsmith.*

I love God and little children. *Jean Paul.*

I love him not, nor fear him ; there's my creed. *Hen. VIII.,* ii. 2.

I love my friends well, but myself better. 45 *Pr.*

I love sometimes to doubt, as well as to know. *Dante.*

I love / The name of honour more than I fear death. *Jul. Cæs.,* i. 2.

I love to browse in a library. *Johnson.*

I'll make assurance doubly sure, / And take a bond of fate. *Macb.,* iv. 1.

I made all my generals out of mud. *Napoleon.* 50

I make the most of my enjoyments ; and as for my troubles, I pack them in as little compass as I can for myself, and never let them annoy others. *Southey.*

I might have my hand full of truth, and open only my little finger. *Fontenelle.*

I mourn not those who lose their vital breath ; / But those who, living, live in fear of death. *Lucillus.*

I must be cruel, only to be kind. *Ham.,* iii. 4.

"I must sleep now." *Byron's last words.* 55

I must work the work of Him that sent me while it is day ; the night cometh when no man can work. *Jesus.*

I'm never less at leisure than when at leisure, nor less alone than when alone. *Scipio Africanus.*

I'm not denyin' the women are foolish; God Almighty made 'em to match the men. *George Eliot.*

I'm not one of those who can see the cat i' the dairy an' wonder what she's come after. *George Eliot.*

I'm sure sma' pleasure it can gie, / E'en to a deil, / To skelp an' scaud (scald) puir dogs like me, / An' hear us squeel. *Burns.*

5 I never could believe that Providence had sent a few men into the world ready booted and spurred to ride, and millions ready saddled and bridled to be ridden. *Richard Rumbold.*

I never could tread a single pleasure under foot. *Browning.*

I never heard tell of any clever man that came of entirely stupid people. *Carlyle.*

I never knew a man of letters ashamed of his profession. *Thackeray.*

I never knew any man grow poor by keeping an orderly table. *Lord Burleigh.*

10 I never knew any man in my life who could not bear another's misfortunes perfectly as a Christian. *Pope.*

I never saw, heard, or read that the clergy were beloved in any nation where Christianity was the religion of the country. *Swift.*

I never whisper'd a private affair / Within the hearing of cat or mouse, / No, not to myself in the closet alone, / But I heard it shouted at once from the top of the house; / Everything came to be known. *Tennyson.*

I only look straight before me at each day as it comes, and do what is nearest me, without looking further afield. *Goethe.*

I picciol cani trovano, ma i grandi hanno la lepre—The little dogs hunt out the hare, but the big ones catch it. *It. Pr.*

15 I pick up favourite quotations and store them in my mind as ready armour, offensive or defensive, amid the struggle of this turbulent existence. Of these there is a very favourite one from Thomson: "Attach thee firmly to the virtuous deeds / And offices of life; to life itself, / With all its vain and transient joys, sit loose." *Burns.*

I pity men who occupy themselves exclusively with the transitory in things and lose themselves in the study of what is perishable, since we are here for this very end that we may make the perishable imperishable, which we can do only after we have learned how to appreciate both. *Goethe.*

I pity the man who can travel from Dan to Beersheba, and cry: 'Tis all barren. *Swift.*

I pounce on what is mine wherever I find it. *Marmontel.*

I prize the soul that slumbers in a quiet eye. *Eliza Cook.*

20 I quote others only in order the better to express myself. *Montaigne.*

I renounce the friend who eats what is mine with me, and what is his own by himself. *Port. Pr.*

I say beware of all enterprises that require new clothes, and not rather a new wearer of clothes. *Thoreau.*

I say the acknowledgment of God in Christ, / Accepted by thy reason, solves for thee / All questions on the earth and out of it. *Browning.*

I scorn the affectation of seeming modesty to cover self-conceit. *Burns.*

I secundo omine—Go, and may all good go with 25 you. *Hor.*

I see my way as birds their trackless way. *Browning.*

I see that sensible men and conscientious men all over the world are of the one religion of well-doing and daring. *Emerson.*

I see thy vanity through the holes of thy coat. *Plato, to the Cynic.*

I seek divine simplicity in him who handles things divine. *Cowper.*

I seek not to wax great by others' waning. 30 *2 Hen. VI., iv. 10.*

"I shall go to-morrow," said the king. "You shall wait for me," quoth the wind. *Gael. Pr.*

I shall light a candle of understanding in thine heart which shall not be put out. *Esdras.*

I shall perhaps tremble in my death-hour, but before shall I never. *Lessing.*

I should be glad were all the meadows on the earth left in a wild state, if that were the consequence of men's beginning to redeem themselves. *Thoreau.*

I stay there on my bond. *Mer. of Ven., iv. 1.* 35

I stout and you stout, who will carry the dirt out? *Pr.*

I take it to be a principal rule of life not to be too much addicted to any one thing. *Ter.*

I talk of chalk and you of cheese. *Pr.*

I think a lock and key a security at least equal to the bosom of any friend whatever. *Burns.*

I think it is as scandalous for a woman not 40 to know how to use a needle as for a man not to know how to use a sword. *Lady Montagu.*

I think nothing is to be hoped from you if this bit of mould under your feet is not sweeter to you than any other in this world. *Thoreau.*

I think sculpture and painting have an effect to teach us manners and abolish hurry. *Emerson.*

I think women have an instinct of dissimulation; they know by nature how to disguise their emotions far better than the most consummate male courtiers can do. *Thackeray.*

I tremble for my country when I reflect that God is just. *T. Jefferson.*

I very much fear that our little terraqueous 45 globe is the lunatic asylum of the universe. *Voltaire.*

I've had my say out, and I shall be th' easier for't all my life. *George Eliot.*

I've never any pity for conceited people, because I think they carry their comfort about with them. *George Eliot.*

I've wandered east, I've wandered west, / Through many a weary way; / But never, never can forget / The love of life's young day. *Motherwell.*

I waive the quantum o' the sin, / The hazard of concealing; / But oh! it hardens a' within, / And petrifies the feeling. *Burns.*

I want that glib and oily art, / To speak and purpose not; since what I well intend, / I'll do 't before I speak. *King Lear*, i. 1.

I was not born for courts or great affairs ; / I pay my debts, believe, and say my prayers. *Pope.*

I was well, would be better, took physic and died. *Epitaph.*

I wasted time, and now doth time waste me. *Rich. II.*, v. 5.

5 I watch the wheels of Nature's mazy plan, / And learn the future by the past of man. *Campbell.*

I were but little happy if I could say how much. *Much Ado*, ii. 1.

I will a round unvarnish'd tale deliver / Of my whole course of love. *Othello*, i. 3.

I will be as harsh as truth and as uncompromising as justice. *W. Lloyd Garrison.*

I will chide no breather in the world but myself, against whom I know most faults. *As You Like It*, iii. 2.

10 I will divide my goods ; / Call in the wretch and slave : / None shall rule but the humble, / And none but toil shall have. *Emerson.*

I will get it from his purse or get it from his skin. *Pr.*

I will give thrice as much to any well-deserving friend ; but in the way of bargain, mark me, I will cavil on the ninth part of a hair. 1 *Hen. IV.*, iii. 1.

I will lay a stone at your door, *i.e.*, never forgive you. *Pr.*

I will listen to any one's convictions, but pray keep your doubts to yourself ; I have plenty of my own. *Goethe.*

15 I will move the world. *Archimedes.*

I will speak daggers to her, but use none. *Ham.*, iii. 2.

I will wear my heart upon my sleeve / For daws to peck at. *Othello*, i. 1.

I wish there were some cure, like the lover's leap, for all heads of which some single idea has obtained an unreasonable and irregular possession. *Johnson.*

I would applaud thee to the very echo, that should applaud again. *Macb.*, v. 3.

20 I would choose to have others for my acquaintance, but Englishmen for my friends. *Goldsmith.*

I would condone many things in one-and-twenty now, that I dealt hardly with at middle age. God Himself, I think, is very willing to give one-and-twenty a second chance. *J. M. Barrie.*

I would desire for a friend the son who never resisted the tears of his mother. *Lacretelle.*

I would fain avoid men ; we can give them no help, and they hinder us from helping ourselves. *Goethe.*

I would give all my fame for a pot of ale and safety. *Hen. V.*, iii. 2.

25 I would have been glad to have lived under my woodside, to have kept a flock of sheep, rather than undertaken such a government as this. *Cromwell.*

"I" (self-love) would have the world say "I," / And all things perish so if she endure. *Sir Edwin Arnold.*

I would it were bed-time, Hal, and all well. 1 *Hen. IV.*, v. 1.

I would not enter on my list of friends . . . the man / Who needlessly sets foot upon a worm. *Cowper.*

I would not for much that I had been born richer. *Jean Paul.*

I would rather be found suffering than doing 30 what is unjust. *Phocion.*

I would rather be the author of one original thought than conqueror of a hundred battles. *W. B. Clulow.*

I would rather make my name than inherit it. *Thackeray.*

Ibi omnis / Effusus labor—By that (one negligence) all his labour was lost. *Virg.*

Ibidem—In the same place.

Ibis, redibis non morieris in bello—Thou shalt 35 go, thou shalt return, thou shalt not die in battle ; or, Thou shalt go, thou shalt not return, thou shalt die in battle. *An ambiguous oracle, due to the uncertain application of the adverb " non."*

Ibit eo quo vis, qui zonam perdidit—He who has lost his purse (*lit.* girdle) will go wherever you wish. *Hor.*

Iceland is the finest country on which the sun shines. *Iceland Pr.*

Ich bin des trocknen Tons nun satt, / Muss wieder recht den Teufel spielen—I am now weary of this prosing style, and must again play the devil properly. *Goethe, " Mephisto."*

Ich bin ein Mensch gewesen, / Und das heisst ein Kämpfer sein—I have been a man, and that is to be a fighter. *Goethe.*

Ich bin es müde, über Sklaven zu herrschen— 40 I am tired of ruling over slaves. *Frederick the Great.*

Ich bin zu alt, um nur zu spielen ; / Zu jung, um ohne Wunsch zu sein—I am too old for mere play ; too young to be without a wish. *Goethe, " Faust."*

Ich denke so : / Was nicht zusammen kann / Bestehen, ist am besten sich zu lösen – In my regard 'twere best throw that into the pot which can no longer hold itself together. *Schiller.*

Ich dien—I serve. *Ger. M.*

Ich finde nicht die Spur, / Von einem Geist, und alles ist Dressur – I find no trace of spirit here ; it is all mere training. *Goethe, " Faust."*

Ich fühl' ein ganzes Heer in meiner Brust— 45 I feel a whole host on my bosom. *Körner.*

Ich fühle Mut, mich in die Welt zu wagen / Der Erde Weh, der Erde Glück zu tragen— I feel courage enough to cast myself into the world, to bear earth's woe and weal. *Goethe.*

Ich glaube, dass alles was das Genie, als Genie thut, unbewusst geschieht—Everything that genius, as genius, does, is in my regard done unconsciously. *Goethe.*

"Ich glaube an einen Gott." Das ist ein schönes löbliches Wort ; aber Gott anerkennen, wo und wie er sich offenbare, das ist eigentlich die Seligkeit auf Erden—"I believe in a God." That is a fine praiseworthy saying ; but to acknowledge God, where and as He reveals Himself, that is properly our blessedness on this earth. *Goethe.*

Ich habe es öfters rühmen hören, / Ein Komödiant könnte einen Pfarrer lehren—I have often heard say that a player might teach a parson. *Goethe, " Faust."*

Ich habe genossen das irdische Glück; / Ich habe gelebt und geliebet—I have experienced earthly happiness; I have lived and I have loved. *Schiller.*

Ich habe gethan, was ich nicht lassen konnte —I have done what I could not get done. *Schiller.*

Ich habe hier blos ein Amt und keine Meinung —I hold here an office merely, and no opinion. *Schiller.*

Ich habe nichts als Worte, und es ziemt / Dem edlen Mann, der Frauen Wort zu achten —I have nothing but words, and it becomes the noble man to respect a woman's word. *Goethe.*

5 Ich heisse der reichste Mann in der getauften Welt: Die Sonne geht in meinem Staat nicht unter—I pass for the richest man in the baptized world; the sun never sets in my dominions. *Philip II. of Spain's boast.*

Ich möchte mich gleich dem Teufel übergeben, / Wenn ich nur selbst kein Teufel wär—I would give myself up at once to the devil if only I were not a devil myself. *Goethe, Mephistopheles in "Faust."*

Ich muss, das ist die Schrank', in welcher mich die Welt, / Von einer, die Natur von andrer Seite hält—I must—that is the barrier within which the world confines me on the one hand and Nature on the other. *Rückert.*

Ich schweige zu vielem still; denn ich mag die Menschen nicht irre machen, und bin wohl zufrieden, wenn sie sich freuen, da wo ich mich ärgere—I keep silent to a great extent, for I don't choose to lead others into error, and am well content if they are happy in matters about which I vex myself. *Goethe.*

Ich setze die Souveränität fest wie einen eisernen Felsen—I plant the royal power firm as a rock of iron. *Frederick William I. of Prussia.*

10 Ich singe, wie der Vogel singt, / Der in den Zweigen wohnet / Das Lied, das aus der Kehle dringt, / Ist Lohn, der reichlich lohnet —I sing but as the bird sings which dwells among the branches; the lay which warbles from the throat is a reward that richly recompences. *Goethe.*

Ich stehe in Gottes Hand, und ruh' in Gottes Schooss / Vor ihm fühl' ich mich klein, in ihm fühl' ich mich gross—I stand in God's hand and rest in God's bosom; before Him I feel little, in Him I feel great. *Rückert.*

Ich thue recht und scheue keinen Feind—I do the right and fear no foe. *Schiller.*

Ici l'honneur m'oblige, et j'y veux satisfaire— Here honour binds me, and I am minded to satisfy her. *Corneille.*

Id arbitror / Adprime in vitâ esse utile, ne quid nimis—This I consider to be a valuable principle in life, not to do anything in excess. *Ter.*

15 Id cinerem, aut manes credis curare sepultos? —Do you think that ashes and buried spirits of the departed care for such things? *Virg.*

Id commune malum; semel insanivimus omnes —It is a common calamity; we have all been mad once. *Mantuanus.*

Id demum est homini turpe, quod meruit pati —That only brings disgrace on a man which he has deserved to suffer. *Phæd.*

Id est—That is.

Id facere laus est quod decet, non quod licet— The man is deserving of praise who does what it becomes him to do, not what he is free to do. *Sen.*

Id genus omne—All persons of that description. 20

Id maxime quemque decet, quod est cujusque maxime suum—That best becomes a man which is most peculiarly his own. *Cic.*

Id mutavit, quoniam me immutatum videt—He has changed his mind because he sees me unchanged. *Ter.*

Id nobis maxime nocet, quod non ad rationis lumen sed ad similitudinem aliorum vivimus —This is especially ruinous to us, that we shape our lives not by the light of reason, but after the fashion of others. *Sen.*

Ideals are the world's masters. *J. G. Holland.*

Ideals can never be completely embodied in practice; and yet ideals exist, and if they be not approximated to at all, the whole matter goes to wreck. *Carlyle.*

Ideas must work through the brains and arms of good and brave men, or they are no better than dreams. *Emerson.*

Ideas often flash across our minds more complete than we could make them after much labour. *La Roche.*

Idem—The same.

Idem quod—The same as.

Idem velle et idem nolle ea demum firma 30 amicitia est—To have the same likes and the same dislikes is the sole basis of lasting friendship. *Sall.*

Idle folks lack no excuses. *Pr.*

Idle people have the least leisure. *Pr.*

Idleness and pride tax with a heavier hand than kings and parliaments. *Ben. Franklin.*

Idleness in the midst of unattempted tasks is always proud. *P. Brooks.*

Idleness is an appendix to nobility. *Burton.* 35

Idleness is many gathered miseries in one name. *Jean Paul.*

Idleness is only the refuge of weak minds and the holiday of fools. *Pr.*

Idleness is the badge of gentry, the bane of body and mind, the nurse of naughtiness, the step-mother of discipline, the chief author of mischief, one of the seven deadly sins, the cushion on which the devil chiefly reposes, and a great cause not only of melancholy, but of many other diseases. *Burton.*

Idleness is the greatest prodigality in the world. *Pr.*

Idleness is the root of all evil. *Pr.* 40

Idleness is the sepulchre of a living man. *Anselm.*

Idleness rusts the mind. *Pr.*

Idolatry is simply the substitution of an "Eidolon," phantasm, or imagination of good for that which is real and enduring, from the highest Living Good which gives life, to the lowest material good which ministers to it. *Ruskin.*

Idoneus homo—A fit man.

If a barrel-organ in a slum can but drown 45 a curse, let no Christian silence it. *Prof. Drummond.*

If a beard were all, the goat would be winner. *Dan. Pr.*

If a book come from the heart, it will contrive to reach other hearts. *Carlyle.*

If a book is worth reading, it is worth buying. *Ruskin.*

If a cause be good, the most violent attack of its enemies will not injure it so much as an injudicious defence of it by its friends. *Colton.*

If a dog has a man to back him, he will kill a baboon. *Wit and Wisdom from West Africa.*

5 If a donkey bray at you, don't bray at him. *Pr.*

If a God did not exist, it would be necessary to invent one. *Voltaire.*

If a great thing can be done at all, it can be done easily; but it is in that kind of ease with which a tree blossoms after long years of gathered strength. *Ruskin.*

If a house be divided against itself, that house cannot stand. *Jesus.*

If a man be born in a stable, that does not make him a horse. *Pr.*

10 If a man cannot be a Christian in the place where he is, he cannot be a Christian anywhere. *Ward Beecher.*

If a man could bequeath his virtues by will, and settle his sense and learning upon his heirs as certainly as he can his lands, a noble descent would then indeed be a valuable privilege. *Anon.*

If a man deceives me once, shame on him; if he deceives me twice, shame on me. *Pr.*

If a man do not erect in this age his tomb ere he dies, he will live no longer in monument than the bell rings and the widow weeps. *Much Ado*, v. 2.

If a man empties his purse into his head, no man can take it from him. *Ben. Franklin.*

15 If a man fear or reverence God, he must hate covetousness; and if he fear or reverence covetousness, he must hate God. *Ruskin.*

If a man hath too mean an opinion of himself, it will render him unserviceable both to God and man. *John Selden.*

If a man have freedom enough to live healthily and work at his craft, he has enough; and so much all can easily obtain. *Goethe.*

If a man have not a friend, he may quit the stage. *Bacon.*

If a man is not virtuous, he becomes vicious. *Bovee.*

20 If a man knows the right way, he need not trouble himself about wrong paths. *Lessing.*

If a man makes himself a worm, he must not complain when trodden on. *Kant.*

If a man makes me keep my distance, the comfort is he keeps his own at the same time. *Swift.*

If a man once fall, all will tread on him. *Pr.*

If a man read little, he had need of much cunning to seem to know that he doth not. *Bacon.*

25 If a man speaks or acts with a pure thought, happiness follows him like a shadow that never leaves him. *Buddha.*

If a man wishes to become rich, he must appear rich. *Goldsmith.*

If a man with the material of enjoyment around him and virtually within his reach walks God's earth wilfully and obstinately with a gloomy spirit, . . . making misery his worship, we feel assured he is contravening his Maker's design in endowing him with life. *W. R. Greg.*

If a man would be alone, let him look at the stars. *Emerson.*

If a man wound you with injuries, meet him with patience; hasty words rankle the wound, soft language dresses it, forgiveness cures it, and oblivion takes away the scar. *J. Beaumont.*

If a man write a book, let him set down only 30 what he knows. I have guesses enough of my own. *Goethe.*

If a man s gaun doun the brae, ilka ane gi'es him a jundie (push). *Sc. Pr.*

If a noble soul is rendered tenfold beautifuller by victory and prosperity, an ignoble one is rendered tenfold and a hundredfold uglier, pitifuller. *Carlyle.*

If a people will not believe, it must obey. *Tocqueville.*

If a pig could give his mind to anything, he wouldn't be a pig. *Dickens.*

If a word be worth one shekel, silence is worth 35 two. *Rabbi Ben Azai.*

If ae sheep loup (jump) the dike, a the lave (rest) will follow. *Sc. Pr.*

If aged and life-weary men have called to their neighbours: "Think of dying!" we younger and life-loving men may well keep encouraging and reminding one another with the cheerful words: "Think of wandering!" *Goethe.*

If all be well within, . . . the impertinent censures of busy, envious men will make no very deep impression. *Thomas à Kempis.*

If all dogs on this earth should bark, / It will not matter if you do not hark. *Saying.*

If all the misfortunes of mankind were cast 40 into a public stock in order to be equally distributed among the species, those who now think themselves the most unhappy would prefer the share they have already to that which would fall to them by such a division. *Socrates.*

If all the world were falcons, what of that? / The wonder of the eagle were the less, / But he not less the eagle. *Tennyson.*

If all the year were playing holidays, / To sport would be as tedious as to work. 1 *Hen. IV*, i. 2.

If all were rich, gold would be penniless. *Bailey.*

If an ass goes a-travelling, he'll not come home a horse. *Pr.*

If an ass kicks me, shall I strike him again? 45 *Socrates.*

If an ass looks in, you cannot expect an apostle to look out. *Lichtenberg.*

If an idiot were to tell you the same story every day for a year, you would end by believing him. *Burke.*

If any false step be made in the more momentous concerns of life, the whole scheme of ambitious designs is broken. *Addison.*

If any man minister, let him do it as of the ability which God giveth. *St. Peter.*

If any man will come after me, let him deny 50 himself, and take up his cross and follow me. *Jesus.*

If any one tells you that a man has changed his character, don't believe it. *Mahomet.*

If any speak ill of thee, fly home to thy own conscience and examine thy heart. If thou art guilty, it is a fair correction; if not guilty, it is a fair instruction. *George Herbert.*

If any would not work, neither should he eat. *St. Paul.*

If blushing makes ugly people so beautiful, ought it not to make the beautiful still more beautiful? *Lessing.*

If coals do not burn, they blacken. *Pr.*

5 If cheerfulness knocks for admission, we should open our hearts wide to receive it, for it never comes inopportunely. *Schopenhauer.*

If children grew up according to early indications, we should have nothing but geniuses. *Goethe.*

If cut (in the costume) betoken intellect and talent, so does the colour betoken temper and heart. *Carlyle.*

If destructive criticism is injurious in anything, it is in matters of religion, for here everything depends upon faith, to which we cannot return when we have once lost it. *Goethe.*

If each one does his duty as an individual, and if each one works rightly in his own vocation, it will be well with the whole. *Goethe.*

10 If ever a fool's advice is good, a prudent man must carry it out. *Lessing.*

If every fool wore a crown, we should all be kings. *Welsh Pr.*

If everybody knew what one says of the other, there would not be four friends left in the world. *Pascal.*

If evil be said of thee, and if it be true, correct thyself; if it be a lie, laugh at it. *Epictetus.*

If fame is only to come after death, I am in no hurry for it. *Martial.*

15 If folly be a pain, there would be crying in every house. *Sp. Pr.*

If fortune favour you, be not elated; if she frown, do not despond. *Ausonius.*

If fortune give thee less than she has done, / Then make less fire, and walk more in the sun. *Sir R. Baker.*

If fortune would make a man estimable, she gives him virtues; if she would have him esteemed, she gives him success. *Joubert.*

If frequent failure convince you of that mediocrity of nature which is incompatible with great actions, submit wisely and cheerfully to your lot. *Sydney Smith.*

20 If friendship is to rob me of my eyes, if it is to darken the day, I will have none of it. *Thoreau.*

If fun is good, truth is still better, and love most of all. *Thackeray.*

If happiness ha'e not her seat / And centre in the breast, / We may be wise, or rich, or great, / But never can be blest. *Burns.*

If heraldry were guided by reason, a plough in a field arable would be the most noble and ancient arms. *Cowley.*

If Hercules and Lichas play at dice / Which is the better man, the greater throw / May turn by fortune from the weaker hand; / So is Alcides beaten by his page. *Mer. of Ven.*, ii. 1.

If honour calls, where'er she points the 25 way, / The sons of honour follow and obey. *Churchill.*

If I am anything, which I much doubt, I made myself so merely by labour. *Sir Isaac Newton.*

If I am master and you are master, who shall drive the asses? *Arab. Pr.*

If I am not worth the wooing, I surely am not worth the winning. *Longfellow.*

If I am right, Thy grace impart / Still in the right to stay; / If I am wrong, O teach my heart to find the better way. *Pope.*

If I ascend up into heaven, Thou art there; if 30 I make my bed in hell, behold Thou art there; if I take the wings of the morning, and dwell in the uttermost parts of the sea, even there shall Thy hand lead me, and Thy right hand shall hold me. *Bible.*

If I be dear to some one else, / Then I should be to myself more dear. *Tennyson.*

If I call bad bad, what do I gain? But if I call good bad, I do a great deal of mischief. *Goethe.*

If I can catch him once upon the hip, / I will feed fat the ancient grudge I bear him. *Mer. of Ven.*, i. 3.

If I choose to take jest in earnest, no one shall put me to shame for doing so; and if I choose to carry on (*treiben*) earnest in jest, I shall be always myself (*immer derselbe bleiben*). *Goethe.*

If I do lose thee (life), I do lose a thing / That 35 none but fools would keep; a breath thou art, / Servile to all the skyey influences, / That do this habitation, where thou keep'st, / Hourly inflict. *Meas. for Meas.*, iii. 1.

If I for my opinion bleed, / Opinion shall be surgeon to my hurt. 1 *Hen. VI.*, ii. 4.

If I had read as much as other men, I would have been as ignorant as they are. *Hobbes.*

If I had wit enough to get out of this wood, I have said enough to serve mine own turn. *Mid. Night's Dream*, iii. 1.

If I knew the way of the Lord, truly I would be only too glad to walk in it; if I were led into the temple of truth (*in der Wahrheit Haus*), I would not, with the help of God (*bei Gott*), go out of it again. *Goethe.*

If I lose mine honour, I lose myself. *Ant. and* 40 *Cleop.*, iii. 4.

If I love thee, what is that to thee? *Goethe.*

If I'm designed yon lordling's slave, / By Nature's law designed, / Why was an independent wish / E'er planted in my mind? *Burns.*

If I must die, / I will encounter darkness as a bride / And hug it in my arms. *Meas. for Meas.*, iii. 1.

If I seek an interest of my own detached from that of others, I seek an interest which is chimerical, and can never have existence. *James Harris.*

If I should say nothing, I should say much 45 (much being included in my love); though my love be such, that if I should say much, I should yet say nothing, it being, as Cowley says, equally impossible either to conceal or to express it. *Pope.*

If I wish for a horse-hair for my compass-sight, I must go to the stable; but the hair-bird, with her sharp eyes, goes to the road. *Thoreau.*

If ill thoughts at any time enter into the mind of a good man, he doth not roll them under his tongue as a sweet morsel. *Matthew Henry.*

If in the course of our life we see that done by others for which we ourselves at one time felt a vocation, and which we were, with much else, compelled to relinquish, then the noble feeling comes in, that only humanity altogether is the true man, and that the individual can only rejoice and be happy when he has the heart (*Muth*) to feel himself in the whole. *Goethe.*

If in youth the universe is majestically unveiling, and everywhere heaven revealing itself on earth, nowhere to the young man does this heaven on earth so immediately reveal itself as in the young maiden. *Carlyle.*

"If" is the only peacemaker—much virtue in "if." *As You Like It*, v. 4.

5 If it be a bliss to enjoy the good, it is still greater happiness to discern the better; for in art the best only is good enough. *Goethe.*

If it be asked, What is the improper expectation which it is dangerous to indulge, experience will quickly answer that it is such expectation as is dictated not by reason but by desire—an expectation that requires the common course of things to be changed, and the general rules of action to be broken. *Johnson.*

If it be aught toward the general good, / Set honour in one eye, and death i' the other, / And I will look on both indifferently; / For, let the gods so speed me, as I love / The name of honour more than I fear death. *Jul. Cæs.*, i. 2.

If it be possible, as much as lieth in you, live peaceably with all men. *St. Paul.*

If it is a happiness to be nobly descended, it is not less to have so much merit that nobody inquires whether we are so or not. *La Bruyère.*

10 If it is disgraceful to be beaten, it is only a shade less disgraceful to have so much asked. *Carlyle.*

If it rains—well! If it shines—well! *Pr.*

If it were done when 'tis done, then 'twere well / It were done quickly . . . that but this blow / Might be the be all and the end all here. *Mach.*, i. 7.

If it were not for hope, the heart would break. *Pr.*

If it were not for respect to human opinions, I would not open my window to see the Bay of Naples for the first time, whilst I would go five hundred leagues to talk with a man of genius whom I had not seen. *Mme. de Staël.*

15 If Jack were better, Jill would not be so bad. *Pr.*

If ladies be but young and fair, / They have the gift to know it. *As You Like It*, ii. 7.

If life, like the olive, is a bitter fruit, then grasp both with the press and they will yield the sweetest oil. *Jean Paul.*

If man had a higher idea of himself and his destiny, he would neither call his business amusement nor amuse himself instead of transacting business. *Goethe.*

If man is not kin to God by his spirit, he is a base and ignoble creature. *Bacon.*

If men duly felt the greatness of God, they 20 would be dumb, and for very veneration unwilling to name Him. *Goethe.*

If money be not thy servant, it will be thy master. The covetous man cannot so properly be made to possess wealth as that it may be said to possess him. *Bacon.*

If money go before, all ways do lie open. *Merry Wives*, ii. 2.

If music be the food of love, play on; / Give me excess of it, that, surfeiting, / The appetite may sicken, and so die. *Twelfth Night*, i. 1.

If my person be crooked, my verses shall be straight. *Pope.*

If Nature is one and a living indivisible 25 whole, much more is mankind, the image that reflects and creates Nature, without which Nature were not. *Carlyle.*

If new-got gold is said to burn the pockets till it be cast forth into circulation, much more may new truth. *Carlyle.*

If, of all words of tongue and pen, / The saddest are, "It might have been," / More sad are these we daily see : "It is, but hadn't ought to be." *Bret Harte.*

If once you find a woman gluttonous, expect from her very little virtue ; her mind is enslaved to the lowest and grossest temptation. *Johnson.*

If one advances confidently in the direction of his dreams, and endeavours to live the life which he has imagined, he will meet with a success unexpected in common hours. *Thoreau.*

If one age believes too much, it is but a natu-30 ral reaction that another age should believe too little. *Buckle.*

If one door shuts, another will open. *Pr.*

If one sees one's fellow-creature following damnable error, by continuing in which the devil is sure to get him at last, are you to let him go towards such consummation, or are you not rather to use all means to save him? *Carlyle.*

If one were to think constantly of death, the business of life would stand still. *Johnson.*

If our era is an era of unbelief, why murmur at it? Is there not a better coming—nay, come? *Carlyle. See Matt.* v. 4.

If people did not flatter one another, there 35 would be little society. *Vauvenargues.*

If people take no care for the future, they will soon have sorrow for the present. *Chinese Pr.*

If people were constant, it would surprise me. For see, is not everything in the world subject to change? Why then should our affections continue? *Goethe.*

If people would whistle more and argue less, the world would be much happier and probably just as wise. *Book of Wisdom.*

If poverty is the mother of crimes, want of sense is the father of them. *La Bruyère.*

If poverty makes a man groan, he yawns in 40 opulence. *Rivarol.*

If reasons were as plenty as blackberries, I would give no man a reason upon compulsion. 1 *Hen. IV.*, ii. 4.

If Satan ever laughs, it must be at hypocrites ; they are the greatest dupes he has. *Colton.*

If she be not fit for me, / What care I for whom she be ? *G. Wither.*

If solid happiness we prize, / Within our breast this jewel lies, / And they are fools who roam. / The world has nothing to bestow ; / From our own selves our joys must flow, / And that dear hut, our home. *N. Cotton.*

If sorrow falls, / Take comfort still in deeming there may be / A way to peace on earth by woes of ours. *Sir Edwin Arnold.*

5 If speculation tends to a terrific unity, in which all things are absorbed, action tends directly backwards to diversity. *Emerson.*

If that God give, the deil daurna reave (bereave). *Sc. Pr.*

If that thy fame with every toy be posed, / 'Tis a thin web which poisonous fancies make ; / But the great soldier's honour was composed / Of thicker stuff, which would endure a shake. *George Herbert.*

If the Almighty waited six thousand years for a man to see what He has made, I may well wait two hundred for others to see what I have seen. *Kepler. See Isa.* xxviii. 16 (*last clause*).

If the ancients left us ideas, to our credit be it spoken that we moderns are building houses for them. *A. B. Alcott.*

10 If the beard were all, the goat might preach *Dan. Pr.*

If the blind lead the blind, both shall fall into the ditch. *Heb. Pr.*

If the cap fit, wear it. *Pr.*

If the chaff-cutter had the making of us, we should all be straw, I reckon. *George Eliot.*

If the counsel be good, no matter who gave it. *Pr.*

15 If the deil were dead, folk would do little for God's sake. *Sc. Pr.*

If the devil takes a less hateful shape to us than to our fathers, he is as busy with us as he was with them. *Lowell.*

If the doctor cures, the sun sees it ; if he kills, the earth hides it. *Sc. Pr.*

If the East loves infinity, the West delights in boundaries. *Emerson.*

If the eye were not of a sunny nature (*sonnenhaft*), how could it see the sun ? If God's own power did not exist within us, how could the godlike delight us ? *Goethe.*

20 If the farmer cannot live who drives the plough, how can he live who drives a fast-trotting mare ? *Pr.*

If the heart of a man is depressed with cares, / The mist is dispelled when a woman appears. *Gay.*

If the hungry lion (invited to a feast of chickenweed) is to feast at all, it cannot be on the chickenweed, but only on the chickens. *Carlyle.*

If the king is in the palace, nobody looks at the walls. It is when he is gone, and the house is filled with grooms and gazers, that we turn from the people to find relief in the majestic men that are suggested by the pictures and the architecture. *Emerson.*

'If the Lord tarry, yet wait for Him," for He "will surely come" and heal thee. *Thomas à Kempis.*

If the mountain will not come to Mahomet, 25 Mahomet will go to the mountain. *Mahomet.*

If the nose of Cleopatra had been a little shorter, it would have changed the history of the world. *Pascal.*

If the paternal cottage still shuts us in, its roof still screens us ; and with a father we have as yet a prophet, priest, and king, and an obedience that makes us free. *Carlyle.*

If the pills were pleasant, they would not be gilded. *Pr.*

If the poet have nothing to interpret and reveal, it is better that he remain silent. *C. Fitzhugh.*

If the poor man cannot always get meat, the 30 rich man cannot always digest it. *Henry Giles.*

If the profession you have chosen has some unexpected inconveniences, console yourself by reflecting that no profession is without them. *Johnson.*

If the single man plant himself indomitably on his instincts, and there abide, the huge world will come round to him. *Emerson.*

If the sun shines on me, what matters the moon ? *Pr.*

If the sky fall, we shall catch larks. *Pr.*

If the time don't suit you, suit yourself to the 35 time. *Turk. Pr.*

If the tongue had not been formed for articulation, man would still be a beast in the forest. *Emerson.*

If the true did not possess an objective value, human curiosity would have died out centuries ago. *Renan.*

If the weather don't happen to be good for my work to-day, it's good for some other man's, and will come round to me to-morrow. *Dickens.*

If the world were put into one scale and my mother into the other, the world would kick the beam. *Lord Langdale.*

If the young knew, if the old could, there's 40 nothing but would be done. *Pr.*

If there be / A devil in man, there is an angel too. *Tennyson.*

If there be light, then there is darkness ; if cold, heat ; if height, depth ; if solid, fluid ; if hard, soft ; if rough, smooth ; if calm, tempest ; if prosperity, adversity ; if life, death. *Pythagoras.*

If there be no enemy, no fight ; if no fight, no victory ; if no victory, no crown. *Savanar.*

If there be not a religious element in the relations of men, such relations are miserable and doomed to ruin. *Carlyle.*

If there were no clouds, we should not enjoy 45 the sun. *Pr.*

If there were no falsehood in the world, there would be no doubt ; if no doubt, no inquiry ; and if no inquiry, no wisdom, no knowledge, no genius. *Landor.*

If there were no fools, there would be no knaves. *Pr.*

If there were only one religion in the world, it would be haughtily and licentiously despotic. *Frederick the Great.*

If there's a hole in a' your coats, / I rede ye tent it : / A chiel's amang you takin' notes, / And faith he'll prent it. *Burns. of Capt. Grose.*

If they do these things in the green tree, what shall be done in the dry? *Jesus.*

If they hear not Moses and the Prophets, neither will they be persuaded though one rose from the dead. *Jesus.*

If thou art a master, be sometimes blind; if a servant, sometimes deaf. *Fuller.*

If thou art rich, thou art poor; / For, like an ass whose back with ingots bows, / Thou bear'st thy heavy riches but a journey, / And death unloads thee. *Meas. for Meas.,* iii. 1.

5 If thou art wise, thou knowest thine own ignorance; and thou art ignorant, if thou knowest not thyself. *Luther.*

If thou be a severe, sour-complexioned man, then here I disallow thee to be a competent judge. *Izaac Walton.*

If thou be master-gunner, spend not all / That thou canst speak at once, but husband it. *George Herbert.*

If thou bear the cross cheerfully, it will bear thee. *Thomas à Kempis.*

If thou canst let others alone in their matters, they likewise will not hinder thee in thine. *Thomas à Kempis.*

10 If thou cast away one cross, without doubt thou shalt find another, and that perhaps more heavy. *Thomas à Kempis.*

If thou deniest to a laborious man and a deserving, thou killest a bee; if thou givest to other than such, thou preservest a drone. *Quarles.*

If thou doest well, shalt thou not be accepted? *Bible.*

If thou faint in the day of adversity, thy strength is small. *Bible.*

If thou hast fear of those who command thee, spare those who obey thee. *Rabbi Ben Azai.*

15 If thou hast run with the footmen, and they have wearied thee; then how canst thou contend with horses? and if in the land of peace, wherein thou trustedst, they wearied thee, then how wilt thou do in the swelling of Jordan? *Bible.*

If thou love learning, thou shalt be learned. *Isocrates.*

If thou seest the oppression of the poor, . . . marvel not at the matter: for He that is higher than the highest regardeth; and there be higher than they. *Bible.*

If thou sustain injustice, console thyself; the true unhappiness is in doing it. *Democrates.*

If thou wouldst profit by thy reading, read humbly, simply, honestly, and not desiring to win a character for learning. *Thomas à Kempis.*

20 If thou wouldst reap in love, / First sow in holy fear; / So life a winter's morn may prove / To a bright endless year. *Keble.*

If thy estate be good, match near home and at leisure; if weak, far off and quickly. *Lord Burleigh.*

If thy son can make ten pound his measure, / Then all thou addest may be called his treasure. *George Herbert.*

If to do were as easy as to know what were good to do, chapels had been churches and poor men's cottages princes' palaces. *Mer. of Ven.*, i. 2.

If truth be with thy friend, be with them both. *George Herbert.*

If vain our toil, we ought to blame the culture, 25 not the soil. *Pope.*

If virtue keep court within, honour will attend without. *Pr.*

If we are not famous for goodness, we are practically infamous. *Spurgeon.*

If we are rich with the riches which we neither give nor enjoy, we are rich with the riches which are buried in the caverns of the earth. *Hitopadesa.*

If we are told a man is religious, we still ask what are his morals; but if we hear he has honest morals, we seldom think of the other question, whether he be religious. *Shaftesbury.*

If we are wise, we may thank ourselves; if we 30 are great, we must thank fortune. *Bulwer Lytton.*

If we bear what we must bear with murmuring and grudging, we do but gall our shoulders with the yoke, and render that a heavy unprofitable load which might be fruitful and glorious. *Thomas à Kempis.*

If we . . . / Cannot defend our own doors from the dog, / Let us be worried, and our nation lose / The name of hardiness and policy. *Hen. V.*, i. 2.

If we cannot help committing errors, we must build none. *Goethe.*

If we cannot live so as to be happy, let us at least live so as to deserve happiness. *Fichte.*

If we cast off one burden, we are immediately 35 pursued and oppressed by another. *Thomas à Kempis.*

If we clear the metaphysical element out of modern literature, we shall find its bulk amazingly diminished, and the claims of the remaining writers, or of those whom we have thinned by this abstraction of their straw-stuffing, much more easily adjusted. *Ruskin.*

If we could have a little patience, we should escape much mortification. Time takes away as much as it gives. *Mme. de Sévigné.*

If we could read the secret history of our enemies, we should find in each man's life sorrow and suffering enough to disarm all hostility. *Longfellow.*

If we do not find happiness in the present moment, in what shall we find it? *Goldsmith.*

If we do not now reckon a great man literally 40 divine, it is that our notions of the divine are ever rising higher; not altogether that our reverence for the divine, as manifested in our like, is getting lower. *Carlyle.*

If we do well here, we shall do well there. *J. Edwin.*

If we engage into a large acquaintance and various familiarities, we set open our gates to the invaders of most of our time. *Cowley.*

If we examine our thoughts, we shall find them always occupied with the past and the future. *Pascal.*

If we fail to conquer smaller difficulties, what will become of us when assaulted by greater? *Thomas à Kempis.*

If we hope for what we are not likely to possess, we act and think in vain, and make life a greater dream and shadow than it really is. *Addison.*

If we live truly, we shall see truly. *Emerson.*

If we love those we lose, can we altogether lose those we love? *Thackeray.*

If we reflect on the number of men we have seen and know, and consider how little we have been to them and they to us, what must our feelings be? (*wie wird uns da zu Muthe*). We meet with the man of genius (*Geistreich*) without conversing with him, with the scholar without learning from him, with the traveller without gaining information from him, the amiable man without making ourselves agreeable to him. And this, alas! happens not merely with passing acquaintances; society and families conduct themselves similarly towards their dearest members, cities towards their worthiest citizens, peoples towards their most excellent princes, and nations towards their most eminent men. *Goethe.*

5 If we saw all the things that really surround us, we should be imprisoned and unable to move. *Emerson.*

If we should all bring our misfortunes into one place, most of us would be glad to take our own home again rather than take a proportion out of the common stock. *Solon.*

If we shut Nature out at the door, she will come in at the window. *Sir R. L'Estrange.*

If we sit down sullen and inactive, in expectation that God should do all, we shall find ourselves miserably deceived. *Rogers.*

If we will disbelieve everything because we cannot certainly know all things, we shall do much as wisely as he who would not use his legs, but sit still and perish because he had no wings. *Locke.*

10 If we wish to do good to men, we must pity and not despise them. *Amiel.*

If we would amend the world, we should mend ourselves and teach our children what they should be. *Wm. Penn.*

If we would endeavour like brave men to stand in the battle, surely we should feel the assistance from Heaven. *Thomas à Kempis.*

If we would have a genuine torment, let us wish for too much time. *Goethe.*

If we would put ourselves in the place of other people, the jealousy and dislike which we often feel towards them would depart, and if we put others in our place, our pride and self-conceit would very much decrease. *Goethe.*

15 If what happens does not make us richer, we must bid it welcome if it make us wiser. *Johnson.*

If "wise memory" is ever to prevail, there is need of much "wise oblivion" first. *Carlyle.*

If within the sophisticated man there is not an unsophisticated one, then he is but one of the devil's angels. *Thoreau.*

If women were humbler, men would be honester. *Vanbrugh.*

If wrong our hearts, our heads are right in vain. *Young.*

20 If ye believe a' ye hear, ye may eat a' ye see. *Sc. Pr.*

If ye gi'e a woman a' her will, / Guid faith, she'll soon o'ergang ye. *Burns.*

If you agree to carry the calf, they'll make you carry the cow. *Pr.*

If you anticipate your inheritance, you can at last inherit nothing. *Johnson.*

If you are idle, be not solitary; if you are solitary, be not idle. *Johnson.*

If you cannot bite, never show your teeth. 25 *Pr.*

If you cannot drive the engine, you can clear the road. *Pr.*

If you cannot have the best, make the best of what you have. *Pr.*

If you cannot make a man think as you do, make him do as you think. *Amer. Pr.*

If you can't get a loaf, don't throw away a cake. *Pr.*

If you can't heal the wound, don't tear it open. 30 *Dan. Pr.*

If you can't pay for a thing, don't buy it. If you can't get paid for it, don't sell it. So you will have calm days, drowsy nights, and all the good business you have now, and none of the bad. *Ruskin.*

If you command wisely, you'll be obeyed cheerfully. *Pr.*

If you criticise a fine genius, the odds are that you are out of your reckoning, and instead of the poet, are censuring your own caricature of him. *Emerson.*

If you desire faith, then you've faith enough. *Browning.*

If you desire to enjoy my light, you must sup- 35 ply oil to my lamp. *Pr.*

If you dinna see the bottom, don't wade (*i.e.*, don't venture, if you can't see your way). *Sc. Pr.*

If you dissemble sometimes your knowledge of that you are thought to know, you shall be thought, another time, to know that you know not. *Bacon.*

If you do anything for the sake of the world, it will take good care that you shall not do it a second time. *Goethe.*

If you do not err, you do not attain to understanding. *Goethe.*

If you do not wish a man to do a thing, you 40 had better get him to talk about it; for the more men talk, the more likely they are to do nothing else. *Carlyle.*

If you don't do better to-day, you'll do worse to-morrow. *Pr.*

If you don't touch the rope, you won't ring the bell. *Pr.*

If you eat, eat a portion; do not eat all. *Wit and Wisdom from West Africa.*

If you have a good seat, keep it. *Pr.*

If you have a special weakness, do not expose 45 it by attempting to do things which will bring it out. *Spurgeon.*

If you have built castles in the air, your work need not be lost; that is where they should be. Now put the foundations under them. *Thoreau.*

If you have lived one day, you have seen all. *Montaigne.*

If you have tears, prepare to shed them now. *Jul. Cæs.*, iii. 2.

If you have time, don't wait for time. *Ben. Franklin.*

If you know how to spend less than you get, you have the philosopher's stone. *Ben. Franklin.*

If you lie upon roses when young, you will lie upon thorns when old. *Pr.*

If you listen to David's harp, you shall hear as many hearse-like airs as carols. *Bacon.*

If you live among men, the heart must either break or turn to brass. *Chamfort.*

5 If you make a law against dancing-masters imitating the fine gentleman, you should with as much reason enact, that no fine gentleman shall imitate the dancing-master. *Goldsmith.*

If you pity rogues, you are no great friend of honest men. *Pr.*

If you pull one pig by the tail, all the rest will squeak. *Dut. Pr.*

If you put a chain around the neck of a slave, the other end fastens itself around your own. *Pr.*

If you raise one ghost, you will have the churchyard in motion. *Pr.*

10 If you read the Bible with a predetermination to pick out every text you approve of, on these terms you will find it entirely intelligible and wholly delightful; but if you read it with a real purpose of trying to understand it, and obey, and so read it all through steadily, you will find it, out and out, the crabbedest and most difficult book you ever tried. *Ruskin.*

If you resolve to do right, you will soon do wisely; but resolve only to do wisely, and you will never do right. *Ruskin.*

If you run after two hares, you will catch neither. *Pr.*

If you say nothing, nobody will repeat it. *Pr.*

If you seek warmth of affection from a similar motive to that from which cats and dogs and slothful persons hug the fire, you are on the downward road. *Thoreau.*

15 If you sell the cow, you sell her milk too. *Pr.*

If you sit down a mere philosopher, you will rise almost an atheist. *Anon.*

If you tell me all you see, you'll tell what will make you feel shame. *Gael. Pr.*

If you throw all your money into the sea, yet count it before you let it go. *Old saying.*

If you trust before you try, / You may repent before you die. *Pr.*

20 If you want a pretence to whip a dog, say that he ate the frying-pan. *Pr.*

If you want learning, you must work for it. *J. G. Holland.*

If you want to gain a reputation for eccentricity and to be universally dreaded, blurt out the plain truth on all occasions. *Ano*

If you want to know a man, make a solitary journey with him. *Pr.*

If you want work done, go to the man who is already fully occupied. *Pr.*

25 If you were as eager to discover good as evil, and had the same delight in spreading the report of it; if good examples were made public as the bad ones always are, do you not think that the good would weigh down the balance? But gratitude speaks so low, and indignation so loudly, that you cannot hear but the last. *Marmontel.*

If you wish a wise answer, you must put a rational question. *Goethe.*

If you wish to astonish the whole world, tell the simple truth. *Rahel.*

If you would be a smith, begin with blowing the fire. *Pr.*

If you would be pungent, be brief, for it is with words as with sunbeams, the more they are condensed the deeper they burn. *Saxe.*

If you would be well served, you must serve 30 yourself. *Pr.*

If you would cease to dislike a man, try to get nearer his heart. *J. M. Barrie.*

If you would create something, you must be something. *Goethe.*

If you would ensure a peaceful old age, be careful of the acts of each day of your youth; for with youth the deeds thereof are not to be left behind. *Isaac Disraeli.*

If you would eschew pain, eschew pleasure. *The Cynics.*

If you would have a faithful servant and one 35 you like, serve yourself. *Ben. Franklin.*

If you would have it well done, you must do it yourself; you must not leave it to others. *Pr.*

If you would know and not be known, live in a city. *Colton.*

If you would learn to write, it is the street you must learn it in. *Emerson.*

If you would love mankind, you should not expect too much from them. *Helvetius.*

If you would make Fortune your friend; when 40 people say money is to be got here and money is to be got there, take no notice; mind your own business; stay where you are; and secure all you can get, without stirring. *Goldsmith.*

If you would rule the world quietly, you must keep it amused. *Anon.*

If you would slip into a round hole, you must make a ball of yourself. *George Eliot.*

If you would succeed, you must not be too good. *It. Pr.*

If you would understand an author, you must understand his age. *Goethe.*

If you would work any man, know his nature 45 and fashions, and so lead him. *Bacon.*

If your mind and its affections be pure, and sincere, and moderate, nothing shall have the power to enslave you. *Thomas à Kempis.*

If your wife is short, stoop to her. *Pr.*

Ignavis semper feriæ sunt—To the indolent every day is a holiday. *Pr.*

Ignavissimus quisque, et, ut res docuit, in periculo non ausurus, nimio verbis et lingua ferox—Every recreant, who, as experience has proved, will fly in the hour of danger, is the most boastful in his words and language afterwards. *Tacit.*

Ignavum fucos pecus a præsepibus arcent— 50 They (the bees) drive from their hives the drones, a lazy pack. *Virg.*

Ignem gladio scrutare modo—Only stir the fire with a sword! *Hor.*

Ignem ne gladio fodito—Do not stir the fire with a sword. *Pr.*

Ignis aurum probat, miseria fortes viros—Fire tests gold; adversity strong men. *Sen.*

Ignis 'fatuus—A deceiving light ; a "Will-o'-the-wisp."

Ignis sacer—"St. Anthony's fire." *Pliny.*

Ignobile vulgus—The base-born multitude.

Ignoramus — An ignorant person (*lit.* we are ignorant).

5 Ignorance is a heavy burden. *Gael. Pr.*

Ignorance is a prolonged infancy, only deprived of its charm. *De Boufflers.*

Ignorance is bold, and knowledge reserved. *Thucydides.*

Ignorance is the curse of God, knowledge the wing wherewith we fly to heaven. 2 *Hen. VI.*, iv. 7.

Ignorance is the dominion of absurdity. *Froude.*

10 Ignorance is the mother of devotion. *Jeremy Taylor.*

Ignorance is the mother of impudence. *Pr.*

Ignorance is the night of the mind, but a night without moon or star. *Confucius.*

Ignorance is the primary source of all misery and vice. *Cousin.*

Ignorance is preferable to error. *Jefferson.*

15 Ignorance never settles a question. *Disraeli.*

Ignorance shuts its eyes and believes it is right. *Punch.*

Ignorant of guilt, I fear not shame. *Dryden.*

Ignorantia facti excusat—Ignorance of the fact excuses. *L.*

Ignorantia legis excusat neminem—Ignorance of the law excuses nobody. *L.*

20 Ignoratio elenchi—Ignoring of the point at issue.

Ignoratione rerum bonarum et malarum, maxime hominum vita vexatur—Through ignorance of the distinction between good and bad, the life of men is greatly harassed. *Cic.*

Ignorent populi, si non in morte probaris, / An scires amicus pati—The world would not know, if you did not prove by your death, that you knew how to bear up against adverse circumstances. *Lucan, of Pompey.*

Ignoscas aliis multa, nil tibi—You should pardon many things in others, nothing in yourself. *Auson.*

Ignoti nulla cupido—There is no desire for what is unknown. *Pr.*

25 Ignotis errare locis, ignota videre / Flumina gaudebat, studio minuente laborem—He delighted to wander over unknown regions, to visit unknown rivers, the interest lessening the fatigue. *Ovid.*

Ignotum argenti pondus et auri—An untold mass of silver and gold. *Virg.*

Ignotum per ignotius — The unknown by the still more unknown.

Ihr Kinder, lernet jetzt genug, / Ihr lernt nichts mehr in alten Zeiten — Ye children, learn enough *now*, nothing more will you be able to learn ere long. *Pfeffel.*

Ihr sagt es sei nichts als Glück / Zu siegen ohne die Tacktick / Doch besser ohne Tacktick siegen / Als mit derselben unterliegen —You say it is nothing but luck to gain a victory without tactics, yet it is better to conquer without them, than therewith to be beaten. *Tyrolese Pr.*

Ihr sucht die Menschen zu benennen, und 30 glaubt am Namen sie zu kennen / Wer tiefer sieht, gesteht sich frei, / Es ist das Anonymes dabei—Ye seek to name men, and think that ye know them by name ; he who sees deeper will freely confess there is something in them which there is no name for. *Goethe.*

Il a inventé l'histoire—He has invented history. *Mme. du Deffand, of Voltaire.*

Il a la mer à boire—He has the sea to drink up, *i.e.*, has undertaken an impossible task. *Fr. Pr.*

Il a la tête près du bonnet—He is of a passionate temper (*lit.* has his head near his cap). *Fr. Pr.*

Il a le diable au corps—The deuce (*lit.* the devil) is in him. *Fr. Pr.*

Il a le verbe haut—He assumes a high tone ; he 35 has a loud voice. *Fr. Pr.*

Il a le vin mauvais—He is quarrelsome over his wine. *Fr. Pr.*

Il a les yeux à fleur de tête—He has prominent eyes. *Fr. Pr.*

Il a mangé son pain blanc le premier—He has eaten the best first. *Fr. Pr.*

Il a plus que personne l'esprit que tout le monde a—He has more than any other the mind which every one has. *Montesquieu.*

Il a travaillé pour le roi de Prusse—He has 40 worked for the King of Prussia, *i.e.*, laboured in vain. *Fr. Pr.*

Il a vu le loup—He has seen the world. *Fr. Pr.*

Il aboye à tout le monde—He barks at everybody. *Fr. Pr.*

Il arrive comme Mars en Carême—He arrives opportunely (*lit.* like March in Lent). *Fr. Pr.*

Il attend, que les alouettes lui tombent toutes rôties—He expects larks to rain down all ready roasted. *Hans Sachs.*

Il buon mercato vuota la borsa—Great bargains 45 empty the purse. *It. Pr.*

Il buono è buono, ma il meglio vince—Good is good, but better surpasses it. *It. Pr.*

Il can battuto dal bastone ha paura dell ombra—The dog that has been beaten with a stick is afraid of its shadow. *It. Pr.*

Il castigo puo differirsi ma non si toglie—Punishment may be tardy, but it is sure to overtake the guilty. *It. Pr.*

Il conduit bien sa barque — He manages his affairs well. *Fr. Pr.*

Il connaît l'univers et ne se connaît pas—He 50 knows everything and does not know himself. *La Font.*

Il coûte peu à amasser beaucoup de richesse, et beaucoup à en amasser peu—It costs little trouble to amass a great deal of wealth, but great labour to amass a little. *Fr. Pr.*

Il diavolo tenta tutti, ma l'ozioso tenta il diavolo—The devil tempts all, but the idle man tempts the devil. *It. Pr.*

Il donne des entrailles à tous les mots—He gives pathos to all his words. *Joubert, of Rousseau.*

Il en est d'un homme qui aime, comme d'un moineau, pris à la glu ; plus il se débat, plus il s'embarrasse—It is with a man in love, as with a sparrow caught in bird-lime ; the more he struggles, the more he is entangled. *Fr. Pr.*

Il en fait ses choux gras—He feathers his nest 55 with it. *Fr. Pr.*

Il est aisé d'ajouter aux inventions des autres —It is easy to add to the inventions of others. *Fr. Pr.*

Il est aisé d'aller à pied, quand on tient son cheval par la bride—It is easy to go afoot when one leads one's horse by the bridle. *Fr. Pr.*

Il est aux anges—He is supremely happy (*lit.* with the angels).

Il est avis à vieille vache qu'elle ne fût oncques veau—The old cow persuades herself that she never was a calf. *Fr. Pr.*

5 Il est bien aisé à ceux qui se portent bien de donner des avis aux malades—It is very easy for those who are well to give advice to the sick. *Fr. Pr.*

Il est bien difficile de garder un trésor dont tous les hommes ont la clef—It is very difficult to guard a treasure of which all men have the key. *Fr. Pr.*

Il est bien fou qui s'oublie—He is a great fool who forgets himself. *Fr. Pr.*

Il est bon d'être ferme par tempérament et flexible par réflexion—It is good to be firm by temperament and pliable by reflexion. *Vauvenargues.*

Il est bon d'être habile, mais non pas de le paraître—It is good to be clever, but not to show it. *Fr. Pr.*

10 Il est comme l'oiseau sur la branche—He is unsettled or wavering (*lit.* like a bird on a branch). *Fr. Pr.*

Il est peu de distance de la roche Tarpéienne au Capitole—It is but a short way from the Tarpeian rock to the Capitol. *Mirabeau.*

Il est plus aisé d'être sage pour les autres que pour soi-même—It is easier to be wise for others than for ourselves. *La Roche.*

Il est plus honteux de se défier de ses amis que d'en être trompé—It is more disgraceful to suspect our friends than to be deceived by them. *La Roche.*

Il est souvent plus court et plus utile de cadrer aux autres que de faire que les autres s'adjustent à nous—It is often more easy and more convenient to conform to others than to make others conform to us. *La Bruyère.*

15 Il est temps d'être sage quand on a la barbe au menton—It is time to be wise when you have a beard on your chin. *Fr. Pr.*

Il est tout prêché qui n'a cure de bien faire— He is past preaching to who does not care to do well. *Fr. Pr.*

Il est trop difficile de penser noblement, quand on ne pense que pour vivre—It is too difficult to think nobly when one thinks only to get a livelihood. *Rousseau.*

Il faisoit de necessité vertu—He made a virtue of necessity. *Rabelais.*

Il fallait un calculateur, ce fut un danseur qui l'obtint—A financier was wanted, a dancing-master got the post. *Beaumarchais.*

20 Il faut attendre le boiteux—We must wait for the lame. *Fr. Pr.*

Il faut avaler bien de la fumée aux lampes avant que de devenir bon orateur—A man must swallow a great deal of lamp-smoke before he can be a good orator. *Fr. Pr.*

Il faut avoir pitié des morts—One must have pity on the dead. *Victor Hugo.*

Il faut avoir une âme—It is indispensable that we should have a soul. *Tolstoi.*

Il faut de plus grandes vertus pour soutenir la bonne fortune que la mauvaise—It requires greater moral strength to bear good fortune than bad. *La Roche.*

Il faut en affrontant l'orage / Penser, vivre et 25 mourir en roi—I must in face of the storm think, live, and die as a king. *Frederick the Great.*

Il faut hurler avec les loups—You must howl if you are among wolves. *Fr. Pr.*

Il faut laver son linge sale en famille—One's filthy linen should be washed at home. *Fr. Pr.*

Il faut payer de sa vie—One must pay with his life. *Fr. Pr.*

Il faut perdre un véron pour pêcher un saumon— We must lose a minnow to catch a salmon. *Fr. Pr.*

Il faut qu'une porte soit ouverte ou fermée— 30 A door must either be open or shut. *Brueys et Palaprat.*

Il faut savoir s'ennuyer—One must accustom one's self to be bored. *Lady Bloomfield.*

Il faut sortir de la vie ainsi que d'un banquet, / Remerciant son hôte, et faisant son paquet —One must quit life as one does a banquet, thanking the host and packing up one's belongings. *Voltaire.*

Il fuoco non s'estingue con fuoco—Fire is not extinguished by fire. *It. Pr.*

Il fut historien pour rester orateur—He turned historian that he might still play the orator.

Il me faut du nouveau, n'en fût-il point au 35 monde—I must have something new, even were there none in the world. *La Fontaine.*

Il meglio è l'inimico del bene—Better is an enemy to well. *It. Pr.*

Il meurt connu de tous et ne se connaît pas— He dies known by all and does not know himself. *Vauquelin des Yvetaux.*

Il mondo è di chi ha pazienza—The world is his who has patience. *It. Pr.*

Il mondo è fatto a scale ; / Chi le scende, e chi le sale—The world is like a staircase; some are going up and some going down. *It. Pr.*

Il mondo sta con tre cose : fare, disfare, e dare 40 ad intendere—The world gets along with three things : doing, undoing, and pretending. *It. Pr.*

Il monta sur ses grands chevaux—He mounted his high horse. *Fr. Pr.*

Il nage entre deux eaux—He keeps fair with both parties (*lit.* swims between two waters). *Fr. Pr.*

Il n'a ni bouche ni éperon—He has neither wit nor go in him (*lit.* he has neither mouth nor spur). *Fr.*

Il n'a pas inventé la poudre—He was not the inventor of gunpowder. *Fr. Pr.*

Il n'a pas l'air, mais la chanson—He has not 45 the tune, but the song. *Fr. Pr.*

Il n appartient qu'aux grands hommes, d'avoir de grands défauts—It is only great men who can afford to have great defects. *La Roche.*

Il n'attache pas ses chiens avec des saucisses —He does not chain his dogs together with sausages. *Fr. Pr.*

Il n'avait pas précisément des vices, mais il était rongé d'une vermine de petits défauts, dont on ne pouvait l'épurer—He had not vices exactly, but he was the prey to a swarm of small faults of which there was no ridding him. *Fr.*

Il n'est d'heureux que qui croit l'être—Only he is happy who thinks he is. *Fr. Pr.*

Il n'est orgueil que de pauvre enrichi—There is no pride like that of a poor man who has become rich. *Fr. Pr.*

Il n'est pas d'homme nécessaire—There is no man but can be dispensed with. *Fr. Pr.*

Il n'est pas échappé qui traîne son lien—He is not escaped who still drags his chains. *Fr. Pr.*

5 Il n'est rien d'inutile aux personnes de sens—There is nothing useless to people of sense. *La Fontaine.*

Il n'est sauce que d'appétit—Hunger is the best sauce. *Fr. Pr.*

Il ne fait rien, et nuit à qui veut faire—He produces nothing, and hinders those who would. *Fr.*

Il ne faut jamais se moquer des misérables, / Car qui peut s'assurer d'être toujours heureux ?—We must never laugh at the miserable, for who can be sure of being always happy? *La Fontaine.*

Il ne faut pas nous fâcher des choses passées —We should not trouble ourselves (*Sc.* fash) about things that are past. *Napoleon.*

10 Il ne faut pas parler latin devant les Cordeliers—It doesn't do to talk Latin before the Grey Friars. *Fr. Pr.*

Il ne faut pas voler avant que d'avoir des ailes —One must not fly before he develops wings. *Fr. Pr.*

Il ne faut point parler corde dans la famille d'un pendu—Never speak of a rope in the family of one who has been hanged. *Fr. Pr.*

Il ne sait plus de quel bois faire flèche—He is put to his last shift (*lit.* knows of no wood to make his arrow). *Fr. Pr.*

Il ne sait sur quel pied danser—He knows not on which foot to dance (*i.e.* he is at his wit's end).

15 Il n'y a de nouveau que ce qui a vieilli—There is nothing new but what has become antiquated. *Fr. Pr.*

Il n'y a de nouveau que ce qui est oublié— There is nothing new but what is forgotten. *Mdlle. Bertine.*

Il n'y a de sots si incommodes que ceux qui ont de l'esprit—There are no fools so unsufferable as those who have wit. *La Roche.*

Il n'y a pas à dire—There is no use saying anything ; the thing is settled. *Fr. Pr.*

Il n'y a pas de cheval si bon qu'il ne bronche pas—There is no horse so sure-footed as never to trip. *Fr. Pr.*

20 Il n'y a pas de gens plus affairés que ceux qui n'ont rien à faire—There are no people so busy as those who have nothing to do. *Fr. Pr.*

Il n'y a pas de petit ennemi—There is no such thing as an insignificant enemy. *Fr. Pr.*

Il n'y a peut-être point de vérité qui ne soit à quelque esprit faux matière d'erreur—There is, perhaps, no truth that is not to some false minds matter of error. *Vauvenargues.*

Il n'y a plus de Pyrénées—There are no longer any Pyrenees. *Louis XIV., on the departure of the Duke of Anjou from Paris for Spain.*

Il n'y a point au monde si pénible métier que celui de se faire un grand nom. La vie s'achève que l'on a à peine ébauché son ouvrage—There is not a more laborious undertaking in the world than that of earning a great name ; life comes to a close before one has well schemed out one's course. *La Bruyère.*

Il n'y a point de chemin trop long à qui marche 25 lentement et sans se presser, il n'y a point d'avantages trop éloignés à qui s'y prépare par la patience—No road is too long for him who advances slowly and does not hurry, and no attainment is beyond his reach who equips himself with patience to achieve it. *La Bruyère.*

Il n'y a point de plus cruelle tyrannie que celle que l'on exerce à l'ombre des lois et avec les couleurs de la justice—There is no crueller tyranny than that which is perpetrated under the shield of law and in the name of justice. *Montesquieu.*

Il n'y a que la vérité qui blesse—It is only the truth that offends (*lit.* wounds). *Fr. Pr.*

Il n'y a que le matin en toutes choses—There is only the morning in all things. *Fr. Pr.*

Il n'y a que le premier pas qui coûte—It is only the first step which costs. *Fr. Pr.*

Il n'y a que les honteux qui perdent—It is only 30 the bashful who lose. *Fr. Pr.*

Il n'y a que les morts qui ne reviennent pas —It is only the dead who do not return. *Barère.*

Il n'y a rien de si puissant qu'une république où l'on observe les lois, non pas par crainte, non pas par raison, mais par passion—There is no commonwealth so powerful as one in which the laws are observed not from a principle of fear or reason, but passion. *Montesquieu.*

Il n'y a rien que la crainte et l'espérance ne persuadent aux hommes—There is nothing that fear and hope does not persuade men to do. *Vauvenargues.*

Il paraît qu'on n'apprend pas à mourir en tuant les autres—It does not appear that people learn how to die by taking away the lives of others. *Chateaubriand.*

Il passa par la gloire, il passa par le crime, et il 35 n'est arrivé qu'au malheur—He passed through glory and through crime, and has landed only in misfortune. *Said of Napoleon III.*

Il penseroso—The pensive man. *It.*

Il plaît à tout le monde et ne saurait se plaire —He pleases all the world but cannot please himself. *Boileau, of Molière.*

Il porte le deuil de sa blanchisseuse—He wears mourning for his laundress, *i.e.,* his linen is dirty. *Fr. Pr.*

Il riso fa buon sangue—Laughter makes good blood ; puts one in good humour. *It. Pr.*

Il rit bien qui rit le dernier—He laughs with 40 reason who laughs the last.

Il sabio muda conscio, il nescio no—A wise man changes his mind, a fool never. *Sp. Pr.*

Il se fait entendre, à force de se faire écouter —He makes himself understood by compelling people to listen to him. *Villemain.*

Il se faut entr'aider ; c'est la loi de nature—We must assist one another ; it is the law of Nature. *Fr. Pr.*

Il sent le fagot—He is suspected of heresy (*lit.* he smells of the faggot). *Fr.*

Il tacer non fu mai scritto—Silence was never 45 written down. *It. Pr.*

Il tempo è un galant 'uomo—Time is a fine lord (or lady). *Mazarin.*

Il tempo buono viene una volta sola—The good time comes but once. *It. Pr.*

Il tempo è una lima sorda—Time is a file that emits no noise. *It. Pr.*

Il trouverait à tondre sur un œuf—He would skin a flint (*lit.* find something to shave on an egg). *Fr. Pr.*

Il va du blanc au noir—He runs to extremes (*lit.* from white to black). *Fr. Pr.*

Il vaut mieux avoir affaire à Dieu qu'à ses saints—It is better to deal with God than with His saints. *Fr. Pr.*

Il vaut mieux être fou avec tous, que sage tout seul—Better to be mad with everybody, than wise all alone. *Fr. Pr.*

5 Il vaut mieux être marteau qu'enclume—It is better to be hammer than anvil. *Fr. Pr.*

Il vaut mieux être singe perfectionné qu'un Adam dégénéré—Better a perfect ape than a degenerate man. *Claparède.*

Il vaut mieux faire envie que pitié—It is better to be envied than pitied. *Fr. Pr.*

Il vaut mieux tâcher d'oublier ses malheurs que d'en parler—It is better to try and forget one's misfortunes than to speak of them. *Fr. Pr.*

Il vero punge, e la bugia unge—Truth stings and falsehood salves over. *It. Pr.*

10 Il villano en su tierra, y el hidalgo donde quiera—The clown in his own country, the gentleman where he pleases. *Sp. Pr.*

Il volto sciolto, i pensieri stretti—The countenance open, the thoughts reserved. *It. Pr.*

Il y a anguille sous roche—There is a snake in the grass; a mystery in the affair. *Fr. Pr.*

Il y a bien des gens qu'on estime, parce qu'on ne les connaît point—Many people are esteemed merely because they are not known. *Fr. Pr.*

Il y a dans la jalousie plus d'amour-propre que d'amour—There is more self-love than love in jealousy. *La Roche.*

15 Il y a des gens à qui la vertu sied presque aussi mal que le vice—There are some men on whom virtue sits almost as awkwardly as vice. *Bouhours.*

Il y a des gens auxquels il faut trois cent ans pour commencer voir une absurdité—There are people who take three hundred years before they begin to see an absurdity. *Fr. (?)*

Il y a des gens dégoûtants avec du mérite, et d'autres qui plaisent avec des défauts—There are people who disgust us in spite of their merits, and others who please us in spite of their faults. *La Roche.*

Il y a des gens qui ressemblent aux vaudevilles, qu'on ne chante qu'un certain temps—Some men are like the ballads that are sung only for a certain time. *La Roche.*

Il y a des reproches qui louent, et des louanges qui médisent—There are censures which are commendations, and commendations which are censures. *La Roche.*

20 Il y a des vérités qui ne sont pas pour tous les hommes et pour tous les temps—There are truths which are not for every man and for every occasion. *Fr. (?)*

Il y a encore de quoi glaner—There are still other fields to glean from; the subject is not exhausted. *Fr. Pr.*

Il y a fagots et fagots—There is a difference between one faggot and another. *Molière.*

Il y a plus de quarante ans que je dis de la prose sans que j'en susse rien—I have been speaking prose forty years without knowing it. *Molière.*

Il y a plus fous acheteurs que de fous vendeurs—There are more foolish buyers than foolish sellers. *Fr. Pr.*

Il y a quelque chose dans les malheurs de nos 25 meilleurs amis qui ne nous déplaît pas—There is something in the misfortunes of our best friends which does not displease us. *Fr. Pr.*

Il y a souvent de l'illusion, de la mode, du caprice dans le jugement des hommes—In the judgments of people there is often little more than self-deception, fashion, and whim. *Voltaire.*

Il y a une espèce de honte d'être heureux à la vue de certaines misères—It is a kind of shame to feel happy with certain miseries before our eyes. *Fr.*

Il y en a peu qui gagnent à être approfondis—Few men rise in our esteem on a closer scrutiny. *Fr. Pr.*

Il y va de la vie—Life depends on it; it is a matter of life or death.

Iliacos intra muros peccatur et extra—Sin is 30 committed as well within the walls of Troy as without, *i.e.*, both sides were to blame. *Hor.*

Ilicet infandum cuncti contra omina bellum / Contra fata deum, perverso numine poscunt—Forthwith, against the omens and against the oracles of the gods, all to a man, under an adverse influence, clamour for unholy war. *Virg.*

Ilka (every) blade o' grass keps (catches) it ain drap o' dew. *Sc. Pr.*

Ilka dog has his day. *Sc. Pr.*

Ilk happing bird, wee, helpless thing, / That, in the merry months of spring, / Delighted me to hear thee sing, / What comes o' thee? / Where wilt thou cower thy chittering wing, an' close thy e'e? *Burns, "A Winter Night."*

Ill bairns are best heard at hame. *Sc. Pr.* 35

Ill begun, ill done. *Dut. Pr.*

Ill can he rule the great that cannot reach the small. *Spenser.*

Ill comes upon war's back. *Pr.*

Ill-doers are ill thinkers. *Pr.*

Ill fares the land, to hastening ills a prey, / 40 Where wealth accumulates and men decay. *Goldsmith.*

Ill fortune never crushes that man whom good fortune deceived not. *Ben Jonson.*

Ill got, ill spent. *Pr.*

Ill-gotten wealth seldom descends to the third generation. *Pr.*

Ill habits gather by unseen degrees, / As brooks make rivers, rivers run to seas. *Dryden.*

Ill hearing mak's ill rehearsing. *Sc. Pr.* 45

Ill-humour is nothing more than an inward feeling of our own want of merit, a dissatisfaction with ourselves. *Goethe.*

Ill luck comes by pounds and goes away by ounces. *It. Pr.*

Ill news comes apace. *Pr.*

Ill weeds are not hurt by frost. *Sp. and Port. Pr.*

Ill weeds grow apace. *Pr.* 50

Illa dolet vere quæ sine teste dolet—She grieves sincerely who grieves when unseen. *Mart.*

Illa est agricolæ messis iniqua suo—That is a harvest which ill repays its husbandman. *Ovid.*

Illa laus est, magno in genere et in divitiis maximis, / Liberos hominem educare, generi monumentum et sibi—It is a merit in a man of high birth and large fortune to train up his children so as to be a credit to his family and himself. *Plaut.*

Illa placet tellus in qua res parva beatum / Me facit, et tenues luxuriantur opes—That spot of earth has special charms for me, in which a limited income produces happiness, and moderate wealth abundance. *Mart.*

Illa victoria viam ad pacem patefecit—By that victory he opened the way to peace.

Illæso lumine solem—[To gaze] on the sun with undazzled eye. *M.*

5 Illam, quicquid agit, quoquo vestigia flectit, / Componit furtim, subsequiturque decor—In whatever she does, wherever she turns, grace steals into her movements and attends her steps. *Tibull.*

Ille crucem sceleris pretium tulit, hic diadema —That one man has found a cross the reward of his guilt ; this one, a diadem. *Juv.*

Ille igitur nunquam direxit brachia contra / Torrentem ; nec civis erat qui libera posset / Verba animi proferre, et vitam impendere vero—He never exerted his arms against the torrent, nor was he a citizen who would frankly utter the sentiments of his mind, and stake his life for the truth. *Juv.*

Ille per extentum funem mihi posse videtur / Ire poeta, meum qui pectus inaniter angit / Irritat mulcet falsis terroribus implet / Ut magus : et modo me Thebis, modo ponit Athenis—That man seems to me able to do anything (*lit.* walk on the tight-rope) who, as a poet, tortures my breast with fictions, can rouse me, then soothe me, fill me with unreal terrors like a magician, set me down either at Thebes or Athens. *Hor.*

Ille potens sui / Lætusque degit, cui licet in diem / Dixisse, Vixi : cras vel atra / Nube polum pater occupato / Vel sole puro— The man lives master of himself and cheerful, who can say day after day, " I have lived ; tomorrow let the Father above overspread the sky either with cloud or with clear sunshine." *Hor.*

10 Ille sinistrorsum, hic dextrorsum, abit : unus utrique / Error, sed variis illudit partibus— One wanders to the left, another to the right ; both are equally in error, but are seduced by different delusions. *Hor.*

Ille terrarum mihi præter omnes / Angulus ridet—That nook of the world has charms for me before all else. *Hor.*

Ille vir, haud magna cum re, sed plenus fidei —He is a man, not of large fortune, but full of good faith. *Hor.*

Illi inter sese multa vi brachia tollunt / In numerum, versantque tenaci forcipe massam—They (the Cyclops), keeping time, one by one raise their arms with mighty force, and turn the iron lump with the biting tongs. *Virg.*

Illi robur et æs triplex / Circa pectus erat, qui fragilem truci / Commisit pelago ratem / Primus—That man had oak and triple brass around his breast who first intrusted his frail bark to the savage sea. *Hor.*

15 Illic apposito narrabis multa Lyæo—There, with the wine in front of you, you will tell many a story. *Ovid.*

Illud amicitiæ sanctum ac venerabile nomen, Nunc tibi pro vili sub pedibusque jacet— The sacred and venerable name of friendship is now despised and trodden under foot. *Ovid.*

Illusion on a ground of truth is the secret of the fine arts. *Joubert.*

Illustrious acts high raptures do infuse, / And every conqueror creates a muse. *Waller.*

Ils chantent, ils payeront—Let them sing ; they will have the piper to pay. *Mazarin.*

Ils n'ont rien appris, ni rien oublié—They have 20 learned nothing and forgotten nothing. *Talley-rand, of the Bourbons.*

Ils s'amusaient tristement, selon la coutume de leur pays—They (the English) are heavy-laden in their amusements, according to the custom of their country. *Froissart.*

Ils se ne servent de la pensée que pour autoriser leurs injustices, et emploient les paroles que pour déguiser leurs pensées—Men use thought only to justify their unjust acts, and employ speech only to disguise their thoughts. *Voltaire.*

Ils sont passés, ces jours de fête—They are gone, those festive days. *Grétry.*

Ils veulent être libres et ne savent pas être justes—They wish to be free and understand not how to be just. *Abbé Sieyès.*

Im Alter erstaunt und bereut man nicht mehr 25 —In old age one is astonished and repents no more. *Goethe.*

Im Becher ersaufen mehr als im Meer—More are drowned in the wine-cup than in the sea. *Ger. Pr.*

Im Ganzen, Guten, Wahren resolut zu leben —To live resolutely in the whole, the good, the true. *Goethe.*

Im Gedränge hier auf Erden / Kann nicht jeder, was er will—In the press of things on earth here, not every one can do what he would. *Goethe.*

Im Grabe ist Ruh !—In the grave is rest ! *Lang-haufen, Heine.*

Im Leben ist der Mensch zehn Jahre in Kriege 30 und zehn in der Irre, gleich dem Ulysses— Man, like Ulysses, spends ten years in war and ten in wandering. *Feuerbach.*

Im Leben ist nichts Gegenwart — In life is the present nothing, or there is no present. *Goethe.*

Im Mangel, nicht im Ueberfluss / Keimt der Genuss—Enjoyment germinates not in abundance but in want. *Herder.*

Im Schmerze wird die neue Zeit geboren—In pain is the new time born. *Chamisso.*

Im Unglück halte aus ; / Im Glücke halte ein —In bad fortune hold out ; in good, hold in. *Ger. Pr.*

Im Wasser kannst du dein Antlitz sehn, / Im 35 Wein des andern Herz erspähn—In water thou canst see thine own face, in wine thou canst see into the heart of another. *Pr.*

Imaginary evils soon become real ones by indulging our reflections on them. *Swift.*

Imagination is always the ruling and divine power, and the rest of the man is only the instrument which it sounds, or the tablet on which it writes. *Ruskin.*

Imagination is a mettled horse that will break the rider's neck when a donkey would have carried him to the end of his journey, slow but sure. *Southey.*

Imagination is but a poor matter when it has to part company with understanding. *Carlyle.*

Imagination is central; fancy, superficial. *Emerson.*

Imagination is Eternity. *Wm. Blake.*

Imagination is the eye of the soul. *Joubert.*

5 Imagination is the mightiest despot. *Auerbach.*

Imagination is too often accompanied with a somewhat irregular logic. *Disraeli.*

Imagination rules the world. *Napoleon.*

Imitation is born with us, but what we ought to imitate is not easily found. *Goethe.*

Imitation is the sincerest flattery. *Colton.*

10 Imitation is suicide. *Emerson.*

Immediate are the acts of God, more swift / Than time or motion. *Milton.*

Immer etwas Neues, selten etwas Gutes— Always something new, seldom anything good. *Ger. Pr.*

Immer Neues spriesset / Eh' ein Mensch geniesset / Mit Verstand das Alte—Not till a new thing sprouts up does a man ever enjoy intelligently that which is old. *Rückert.*

Immer wird, nie ist— Always a-being, never being. *Schiller.*

15 Immer zu! Immer zu! / Ohne Rast und Ruh! —Ever onward! ever onward! without rest and quiet. *Goethe.*

Immer zu misstrauen ist ein Irrthum wie immer zu trauen — Always to distrust is an error, as well as always to trust. *Goethe.*

Immo id, quod aiunt, auribus teneo lupum / Nam neque quomodo a me amittam, invenio : neque, uti retineam scio—It is true they say I have caught a wolf by the ears; for I know not either how to get rid of him or keep him in restraint. *Ter.*

Immodest words admit of no defence, / For want of decency is want of sense. *Roscommon.*

Immoritur studiis, et amore senescit habendi —He is killing himself with his efforts, and in his greed of gain is becoming an old man. *Hor.*

20 Immortale odium et nunquam sanabile vulnus —A deadly hatred, and a wound that can never be healed. *Juv., on the effects of religious contention between neighbours.*

Immortalia ne speres monet annus, et almum / Quæ rapit hora diem—The year in its course, and the hour that speeds the kindly day, admonishes you not to hope for immortal (*i.e.*, permanent) blessings. *Hor.*

Immortality will come to such as are fit for it ; and he who would be a great soul in future must be a great soul now. *Emerson.*

Imo pectore—From the bottom of the heart.

Impatience changeth smoke to flame. *Erasmus.*

25 Impatience dries the blood sooner than age or sorrow. *Chapin.*

Impatience is the principal cause of most of our irregularities and extravagances. *Sterne.*

Impatience waiteth on true sorrow. *3 Hen. VI., iii. 3.*

Impavidum ruinæ ferient—The wreck of things will strike him unmoved. *Hor.*

Impera parendo—Command by obeying. *M.*

Imperat aut servit collecta pecunia cuique— 30 Money amassed is either our slave or our tyrant. *Hor.*

Imperfection is in some sort essential to all that we know of life. It is the sign of life in a mortal body, that is, of a state of progress and change. *Ruskin.*

Imperfection means perfection hid, / Reserved in part to grace the after-time. *Browning.*

Imperfections cling to a man, which, if he wait till he have brushed off entirely, he will spin for ever on his axis, advancing nowhither. *Carlyle.*

Imperia dura tolle, quid virtus erit ?—Remove severe restraint, and what will become of virtue? *Sen.*

Imperious Cæsar, dead and turn'd to clay, / 35 Might stop a hole to keep the wind away. *Ham., v. 1.*

Imperium et libertas—Empire and liberty. *Cic.*

Imperium facile iis artibus retinetur, quibus initio partum est—Power is easily retained by those arts by which it was at first acquired. *Sall.*

Imperium in imperio—A government within a government.

Impertinent and lavish talking is in itself a very vicious habit. *Thomas à Kempis.*

Impetrare oportet, quia æquum postulas— 40 You ought to obtain what you ask, as you only ask what is fair. *Plaut.*

Implacabiles plerumque læsæ mulieres — Women, when offended, are generally implacable.

" Impossible " est un mot que je ne dis jamais— "Impossible" is a word which I never utter. *Collin d'Harteviilles.*

Impossible is the precept " Know thyself," till it be translated into this partially possible one, " Know what thou canst work at." *Carlyle.*

Impossible ! Ne me dites jamais ce bête de mot — Impossible ! Never name to me that blockhead of a word. *Mirabeau, to his secretary, Dumont.*

" Impossible " n'est pas français—" Impossible " 45 is not French. *Napoleon.*

"Impossible," when Truth and Mercy and the everlasting voice of Nature order, has no place in the brave man's dictionary. *Carlyle.*

"Impossible !" who talks to me of impossibilities ? *Chatham.*

Impotentia excusat legem—Inability suspends the action of law. *L.*

Impransus—One who has not dined, or who can't find a dinner.

Imprimatur—Let it be printed. 50

Imprimis—First of all.

Imprimis venerare Deos—Before all things reverence the gods. *Virg.*

Improbæ / Crescunt divitiæ, tamen / Curtæ nescio quid semper abest rei—Riches increase to an enormous extent, yet something is ever wanting to our still imperfect fortune. *Hor.*

Improbe amor, quid non mortalia pectora cogis ?—Cruel love ! what is there to which thou dost not drive mortal hearts ? *Virg.*

Improbe Neptunum accusat, qui naufragium 55 iterum facit—He who suffers shipwreck twice is unjust if he throws the blame on Neptune. *Pub. Syr.*

Improbis aliena virtus semper formidolosa est —To wicked men the virtue of others is always matter of dread. *Sall.*

Impromptu—Off-hand; without premeditation.

Improvement is Nature. *Leigh Hunt.*

Imprudent expression in conversation may be forgotten and pass away; but when we take the pen into our hand, we must remember that *litera scripta manet. Blair.*

5 Impudence is no virtue, yet able to beggar them all. *Sir T. Osborne.*

Impunitas semper ad deteriora invitat—Impunity always tempts to still worse crimes. *Coke.*

In a boundless universe / Is boundless better, boundless worse. *Tennyson.*

In a calm sea, every man is a pilot. *Pr.*

In a commercial nation impostors are abroad in all professions. *Wm. Blake.*

10 In a fair gale every fool may sail, but wise behaviour in a storm commends the wisdom of the pilot. *Quarles.*

In a free country there is much complaining but little suffering; under a despotism, much suffering but little complaining. *Giles' Proverbs.*

In a good lord there must first be a good animal, at least to the extent of yielding the incomparable advantage of animal spirits. *Emerson.*

In a great soul everything is great. *Pascal.*

In a healthy state of the organism all wounds have a tendency to heal. *Mme. Swetchine.*

15 In a lawsuit nothing is certain but the expense. *A. Butler.*

In a leopard the spots are not observed. *Herbert's Coll.*

In a lottery, where there is (at the lowest computation) ten thousand blanks to one prize, it is the most prudent choice not to venture. *Lady Montagu.*

In a man's letters his soul lies naked; his letters are only the mirror of his breast. *Johnson.*

In a matter of life and death don't trust your mother; she might mistake a black bean (used in voting) for a white one. *Alcibiades.*

20 In a narrow circle the mind grows narrow; the more a man expands, the larger his aims. *Schiller.*

In a noble race, levity without virtue is seldom found. In a mine of rubies, when shall we find pieces of glass? *Hitopadesa.*

In a poem there should be not only the poetry of images, but also the poetry of ideas. *Joubert.*

In a symbol there is concealment and yet revelation, silence and speech acting together, some embodiment and revelation of the infinite, made to blend itself with the finite, to stand visible, and, as it were, attainable there. *Carlyle.*

In a thousand pounds of law there is not an ounce of love. *Pr.*

25 In a valiant suffering for others, not in a slothful making others suffer for us, did nobleness ever lie. *Carlyle.*

In acta—In the very act.

In action, a great heart is the chief qualification; in work, a great head. *Schopenhauer.*

In æquali jure melior est conditio possidentis— Where the right is equal, the claim of the party in possession is the best. *L.*

In æternum—For ever.

In all battles, if you await the issue, each 30 fighter has prospered according to his right. His right and his might, at the close of the account, were the same. *Carlyle.*

In all faiths there is something true / . . . Something that keeps the Unseen in view, / . . . And notes His gifts with the worship due. *Dr. Walter Smith.*

In all human action, those faculties will be strong which are used. *Emerson.*

In all human narrative, it is the battle only, and not the victory, that can be dwelt on with advantage. *Carlyle.*

In all literary history there is no such figure as Dante, no such homogeneousness of life and works, such loyalty to ideas, such sublime irrecognition of the unessential. *Lowell.*

In all matters prefer the less evil to the 35 greater, and solace yourself under any ill with the reflection that it might be worse. *Spurgeon.*

In all provinces there are artists and artisans; men who labour mechanically in a department, without eye for the whole, not feeling that there is a whole; and men who inform and ennoble the humblest department with an idea of the whole, and habitually know that only in the whole is the partial to be truly discerned. *Carlyle.*

In all science error precedes the truth, and it is better it should go first than last. *Horace Walpole.*

In all situations (out of Tophet) there is a duty, and our highest blessedness lies in doing it. *Carlyle.*

In all straits the good behave themselves with meekness and patience. *Thomas à Kempis.*

In all things that live there are certain irregu-40 larities and deficiencies, which are not only signs of life, but sources of beauty. *Ruskin.*

In all things, to serve from the lowest station upwards is necessary. *Goethe.*

In all times it is only individuals that have advanced science, not the age. *Goethe.*

In all true work, were it but true hand-labour, there is something of divineness. *Carlyle.*

In all vital action the manifest purpose and effort of Nature is, that we should be unconscious of it. . . . Nature so meant it with us; it is so we are made. *Carlyle.*

In allem andern lass dich lenken / Nur nicht 45 im Fühlen und im Denken—In everything else let thyself be led, only not in feeling and in thinking. *v. Sallet.*

In alms regard thy means and others' merit. / Think Heaven a better bargain than to give / Only thy single market-money for it. *George Herbert.*

In ambiguo—In doubt.

In America you can get tea, and coffee, and meat every day. But the only true America is that country where you are at liberty to pursue such a mode of life as may enable you to do without these. *Thoreau.*

In an aristocratical institution like England, not trial by jury, but the dinner is the capital institution. It is the mode of doing honour to a stranger to invite him to eat, and has been for many a hundred years. *Emerson.*

In anima vili—On a subject of little worth.

In annulo Dei figuram ne gestato—Wear not the image of the Deity in a ring, *i.e.*, do not use the name of God on frivolous occasions, or in vain. *Pr.*

In any controversy, the instant we feel angry we have already ceased striving for truth and begun striving for ourselves. *Goethe.*

5 In aqua scribis—You are writing on water. *Pr.*

In arena ædificas — You are building on sand. *Pr.*

In arguing, be calm; for fierceness makes / Error a fault, and truth discourtesy. *George Herbert.*

In argument with men, a woman ever / Goes by the worse, whatever be her cause. *Milton.*

In art and in deeds, only that is properly achieved which, like Minerva, springs full-grown and armed from the head of the inventor. *Goethe.*

10 In art, to express the infinite one should suggest infinitely more than is expressed. *Goethe.*

In articulo mortis—At the point of death.

In audaces non est audacia tuta—Daring is not safe against daring men. *Ovid.*

In beato omnia beata—With the fortunate everything is fortunate. *Hor.*

In bocca chiusa non c' entran mosche—Flies can't enter into a mouth that is shut. *It. Pr.*

15 In books lies the soul of the whole past time; the articulate audible voice of the past, when the body and material substance of it has altogether vanished like a dream. *Carlyle.*

In breathing there are two kinds of blessings (*Gnaden*): inhaling the air and exhaling (*lit.* discharging) it; the former is oppressive, the latter refreshing; so strangely is life mingled. Thank God when He lays a burden on thee, and thank Him when He takes it off. *Goethe.*

In bunten Bildern wenig Klarheit, / Viel Irrtum und ein Fünkchen Wahrheit, / So wird der beste Trank gebraut, / Der alle Welt erquickt und auferbaut — With little clearness (light) in motley metaphors, much falsehood and a spark of truth, is the genuine draught prepared with which every one is refreshed and edified. *Goethe.*

In buying horses and taking a wife, shut your eyes and commend yourself to God. *It. Pr.*

In caducum parietem inclinare—To lean against a falling wall. *Pr.*

20 In calamitoso risus etiam injuria est—Even to smile at the unfortunate is to do them an injury. *Pub. Syr.*

In capite—In chief.

In casu extremæ necessitatis omnia sunt communia—In a case of extreme emergency all things are common. *L.*

In Catholic countries religion and liberty exclude each other; in Protestant ones they accept each other. *Amiel.*

In cauda venenum—Poison lurks in the tail; or, there is a sting in the tail. *Pr.*

In causa facili, cuivis licet esse diserto—In an 25 easy matter any man may be eloquent. *Ovid.*

In character, in manner, in style, in all things the supreme excellence is simplicity. *Longfellow.*

In cheerful souls there is no evil; wit shows a disturbance of the equipoise. *Novalis.*

In childhood be modest, in youth temperate, in manhood just, and in old age prudent. *Socrates.*

In choosing friends, we should choose those whose qualities are innate, and their virtues virtues of the temperament. *Amiel.*

In Christ the infinite itself has come down to 30 the level of the finite, and the finite has been raised to the level of the infinite, and in His single person the spirit of the universe stands revealed. *Ed.*

In civil broils the worst of men may rise to honour. *Plutarch.*

In clothes, cheap handsomeness doth bear the bell. *George Herbert.*

In clothes clean and fresh there is a kind of youth with which age should surround itself. *Joubert.*

In cœlo nunquam spectatum impune cometam—A comet is never seen in the sky without indicating disaster. *Claud.*

In cœlo quies—There is rest in heaven. 35

In cœlum jacularis — You are aiming at the heavens; your anger is bootless.

In commendam—In trust or recommendation.

In common things the law of sacrifice takes the form of positive duty. *Froude.*

In communism, inequality springs from placing mediocrity on a level with excellence. *Proudhon.*

In composing a book, the last thing that one 40 learns is to know what to put first. *Pascal.*

In constitutional states, liberty is a compensation for heaviness of taxation; in despotic ones, lightness of taxation is a compensation for liberty. *Montesquieu.*

In contemplation, if a man begin with certainties, he shall end in doubts; but if he will be content to begin with doubts, he shall end in certainties. *Bacon.*

In conversation, boldness now bears sway. *George Herbert.*

In conversation, humour is more than wit, easiness more than knowledge. *Sir Wm. Temple.*

In courtesy rather pay a penny too much than 45 too little. *Pr.*

In crucifixo gloria mea—I glory in the Crucified.

In cumulo—In a heap.

In curia—In the court.

In cute curanda plus æquo operata juventus—Youth unduly busy with pampering the outer man. *Hor.*

In days of yore nothing was holy but the 50 beautiful. *Schiller.*

In deep waters men find great pearls. *Pr.*

In deinem Glauben ist dein Himmel, / In deinem Herzen ist dein Glück—In thy faith is thy heaven, in thy heart thy happiness. *Arndt.*

In deinem Nichts hoff' ich das All zu finden—In thy nothing hope I to find the all. *Goethe.*

In delay / We waste our lights in vain, like lamps by day. *Rom. and Jul.*, i. 4.

In Deo spero—In God I hope. *M.* 55

In der jetzigen Zeit soll Niemand schweigen oder nachgeben ; man muss reden und sich rühren, nicht um zu überwinden, sondern sich auf seinem Posten zu erhalten ; ob bei der Majorität oder Minorität, ist ganz gleich-gültig—At the present time no one should yield or keep silence ; every one must speak and bestir himself, not in order to gain the upper hand, but to keep his own position—whether with the majority or the minority is quite indifferent. *Goethe.*

In der Kunst ist das Beste gut genug—In art the best is good enough. *Goethe.*

In der Noth allein / Bewähret sich der Adel grosser Seele — In difficulty alone does the nobility of great souls prove itself. *Schiller.*

In dictione—In the expression, or the form.

5 In die Hölle kommt man mit grösserer Mühe, als in den Himmel—It's harder work getting to hell than heaven. *Ger. Pr.*

In diem—To some future day.

In diem vivere—To live from hand to mouth.

In dim eclipse disastrous twilight sheds / On half the nations, and with fear of change perplexes monarchs. *Milton.*

In diving to the bottom of pleasures we bring up more gravel than pearls. *Balzac.*

10 In doubtful matters courage may do much ; in desperate, patience. *Pr.*

In dubiis—In matters of doubt.

In dubiis benigniora semper sunt præferenda —In cases of doubt we should always lean to the side of mercy. *L.*

In dulci jubilo—Now sing and be joyful. *Peter of Dresden.*

In duty prompt, at every call, / He watch'd, and wept, and felt, and prayed for all. *Gold-smith.*

15 In dyeing the spiritual nature there are two processes—first, the cleansing and wringing out, which is the baptism with water ; and then the infusing of the blue and scarlet colours, gentleness and justice, which is the baptism with fire. *Ruskin.*

In eadem re utilitas et turpitudo esse non potest—In the same thing usefulness and base-ness cannot coexist. *Cic.*

In eating, after nature is once satisfied, every additional morsel brings stupidity and dis-tempers with it. *Goldsmith.*

In eburna vagina plumbeus gladius—A leaden sword in an ivory sheath. *Diogenes, of an empty fop.*

In eloquence, the great triumphs of the art are when the orator is lifted above him-self ; when consciously he makes himself the mere tongue of the occasion and the hour, and says what cannot but be said. *Emerson.*

20 In equilibrio—In equilibrium.

In esse—In actual being.

In every age and clime we see / Two of a trade can never agree. *Gay.*

In every battle the eye is first conquered. *Tac.*

In every beginning think of the end. *Pr.*

25 In every bone there is marrow, and within every jacket there is a man. *Saadi.*

In every change there will be many that suffer real or imaginary grievances, and therefore many will be dissatisfied. *Johnson.*

In every child their lies a wonderful deep. *Schumann.*

In every country the sun rises in the morning. *Pr.*

In every creed there are two elements—the Divine substance and the human form. The form must change with the changing thoughts of men ; and even the substance may come to shine with clearer light, and to reveal unexpected glories, as God and man come nearer together. *R. W. Dale.*

In every department of life we thank God that 30 we are not like our fathers. *Froude.*

In every department one must begin as a child ; throw a passionate interest over the subject ; take pleasure in the shell till one has the happiness to arrive at the kernel. *Goethe.*

In every epoch of the world, the great event, parent of all others, is it not the arrival of a thinker in the world ? *Carlyle.*

In every fault there is folly. *Pr.*

In every great epoch there is some one idea at work which is more powerful than any other, and which shapes the events of the time and determines their ultimate issues. *Buckle.*

In every heart are sown the sparks that kindle 35 fiery war ; occasion needs but fan them, and they blaze. *Cowper.*

In every landscape the point of astonishment is the meeting of the sky and the earth, and that is seen from the first hillock as well as from the top of the Alleghanies. *Emerson.*

In every life there is an upward and a down-ward tendency (*Trieb*) ; he is to be praised who remains steadfast in the mean between. *Rückert.*

In every man there is a certain feeling that he has been what he is from all eternity, and by no means became such in time. *Schelling.*

In every parting there is an image of death. *George Eliot.*

In every phenomenon the beginning remains 40 always the most notable moment. *Carlyle.*

In every rank, or great or small, / 'Tis industry supports us all. *Gray.*

In every ship there must be a seeing pilot, not a mere hearing one. *Carlyle.*

In every the wisest soul lies a whole world of internal madness, an authentic demon-empire ; out of which, indeed, his world of wisdom has been creatively built to-gether, and now rests there, as on its dark foundation does a habitable flowery earth-rind. *Carlyle.*

In every village there will arise a miscreant to establish the most grinding tyranny by calling himself the people. *Sir R. Peel.*

In exalting the faculties of the soul we annihi- 45 late, in a great degree, the delusion of the senses. *Aimé-Martin.*

In extenso—In full.

In extremis—At the point of death.

In failing circumstances no man can be relied on to keep his integrity. *Emerson.*

In Faith and Hope the world will disagree, / But all mankind's concern is Charity. *Pope.*

In faith everything depends on "that" you be- 50 lieve ; in knowledge everything depends on "what" you know, as well as how much and how well. *Goethe.*

In fashionable circles general satire, which attacks the fault rather than the person, is unwelcome; while that which attacks the person and spares the fault is always acceptable. *Jean Paul.*

In ferrum pro libertate ruebant—They rushed upon the sword in defence of their liberty. *M.*

In flagranti delicto—In the act.

In flammam flammas, in mare fundis aquas—You add fire to fire, and water to the sea.

5 In for a penny, in for a pound. *Pr.*

In forma pauperis—As a pauper or poor man.

In foro conscientiæ—Before the tribunal of conscience.

In frosty weather a nail is worth a horse. *Sp. Pr.*

In furias ignemque ruunt; amor omnibus idem—They rush into the flames of passion; love is the same in all. *Virg.*

10 In futuro—In future; at a future time.

In general, indulgence for those we know is rarer than pity for those we know not. *Rivarol.*

In general, pride is at the bottom of all great mistakes. *Ruskin.*

In generalibus latet dolus—In general assertions some deception lurks.

In giants we must kill pride and arrogance; but our greatest foes, and whom we must chiefly combat, are within. *Cervantes.*

15 In Glück Vorsichtigkeit, in Unglück Geduld—In good fortune, prudence; in bad, patience. *Ger. Pr.*

In good bearing beginneth worship. *Hazlitt's Coll.*

In good years, corn is hay; in ill years, straw is corn. *Hazlitt's Coll.*

In granting and in refusing, in joy and in sorrow, in liking and in disliking, good men, because of their own likeness, show mercy unto all things which have life. *Hitopadesa.*

In great states, children are always trying to remain children, and the parents wanting to make men and women of them. In vile states, the children are always wanting to be men and women, and the parents to keep them children. *Ruskin.*

20 In health, to be stirring shall profit thee best; / In sickness, hate trouble, seek quiet and rest. *Thomas Tusser.*

In heaven ambition cannot dwell, / Nor avarice in the vaults of hell. *Southey.*

In heaven the angels are advancing continually to the spring-time of their youth, so that the oldest angel appears the youngest. *Swedenborg.*

In Heaven's sight the mere wish to pray is prayer. (?)

In her eyes that never weep, lightnings are laid asleep. *A. Mary F. Robinson.*

25 In her first passion, woman loves her lover, / In all the others, all she loves is love. *Byron.*

In high life every one is polished and courteous, but no one has the courage to be hearty and true. *Goethe.*

In Him we live and move and have our being. *St. Paul.*

In hoc signo spes mea—In this sign is my hope. *M.*

In hoc signo vinces—By this sign (the cross) thou shalt conquer. *M.*

In hoc statu—In this state or condition. 30

In hope to merit heaven by making earth a hell. *Byron.*

In idleness alone is there perpetual despair. *Carlyle.*

In illo viro, tantum robur corporis et animi fuit, ut quocunque loco natus esset, fortunam sibi facturus videretur—In that man there was such oaken strength of body and mind, that whatever his rank by birth might have been, he gave promise of attaining the highest place in the lists of fortune. *Livy, of Cato the elder.*

In intercourse with people of superior station, all that is required is not to be perfectly natural, but always to keep within the line of a certain conventional propriety. *Goethe.*

In jedem Menschen ist etwas von allen Men- 35 schen—In every man there is something of all men. *Lichtenberg.*

In judicando criminosa est celeritas—In pronouncing judgment, haste is criminal. *L.*

In just and equal measure all is weighed; / One scale contains the sum of human weal, / And one, the good man's heart. *Shelley.*

In King Cambyses' vein. 1 *Hen. IV.*, ii. 4.

In lapidary inscriptions a man is not upon oath. *Johnson.*

In learning anything, its first principles alone 40 should be taught by constraint. *Goethe.*

In letters, if anywhere, we look for the man, not for the author. *Blair.*

In life a friend may be often found and lost; but an old friend never can be found, and Nature has provided that he cannot easily be lost. *Johnson.*

In life, as in art, the beautiful moves in curves. *Bulwer Lytton.*

In life every situation may bring its own peculiar pleasures. *Goldsmith.*

In life there is no present. *Byron.* 45

In limine—At the threshold or outset.

In literature to-day there are plenty good masons, but few good architects. *Joubert.*

In loco parentis—In the place of a parent.

In long-drawn systole and long-drawn diastole must the period of faith alternate with the period of denial; must the vernal growth, the summer luxuriance of all opinions, spiritual representations and creations, be followed by and again follow the autumnal decay, the winter dissolution. *Carlyle.*

In love all is risk. *Goethe.* 50

In love we are all fools alike. *Gay.*

In love we never think of moral qualities, and scarcely of intellectual ones. Temperament and manner alone, with beauty, excite love. *Hazlitt.*

In loving thou dost well, in passion not, / Wherein true love consists not. *Milton.*

In magnis et voluisse sat est—In great things it is enough even to have willed. *Propertius.*

In maiden meditation, fancy-free. *Mid. N.'s 55 Dream*, ii. 1.

In manners tranquillity is the supreme power *Mme. de Maintenon.*

In marriage, as in other things, contentment excels wealth. *Molière.*

In matters of conscience, first thoughts are best; in matters of prudence, last thoughts are best. *Robert Hall.*

In mediæval art, thought is the first thing, execution the second; in modern art, execution is the first thing and thought the second. *Ruskin.*

In mediæval art, truth is first, beauty second; in modern art, beauty is first, truth second. *Ruskin.*

In medias res—Into the midst of a thing at once.

In medio tutissimus ibis—You will go safest in the middle or in a middle course. *Ovid.*

5 In medio virtus—Virtue lies in the mean. *Pr.*

In meinem Revier / Sind Gelehrten gewesen / Ausser ihrem Brevier / Konnten sie keines lesen—In my domain there have been learned men, but outside their breviary they could read nothing. *Goethe.*

In meinem Staate kann jeder nach seiner Façon selig werden—In my dominions every one may be happy in his own fashion. *Frederick the Great.*

In melle sunt sitæ linguæ vestræ atque orationes, / Corda felle sunt lita atque aceto—Your tongues and your words are steeped in honey, but your hearts in gall and vinegar. *Plaut.*

In memoriam—To the memory of.

10 In men we various ruling passions find; / In women, two almost divide the mind; / Those, only fix'd, they first or last obey, / The love of pleasure and the love of sway. *Pope.*

In mercatura facienda multæ fallaciæ et quasi præstigiæ exercentur—In commerce many deceptions, not to say juggleries, are practised.

In misfortune, in error, and when the time appointed for certain affairs is about to elapse, a servant who hath his master's welfare at heart ought to speak unasked. *Hitopadesa.*

In moderating, not in satisfying desires, lies peace. *Bp. Heber.*

In modern England the ordinary habits of life and modes of education produce great plainness of mind in middle-aged women. *Ruskin.*

15 In morals, as in art, saying is nothing, doing is all. *Renan.*

In morals good-will is everything, but in art it is ability. *Schopenhauer.*

In morals, what begins in fear usually ends in wickedness; in religion, what begins in fear usually ends in fanaticism. *Mrs. Jameson.*

In much corn is some cockle. *Pr.*

In much wisdom is much grief, and he that increaseth knowledge increaseth sorrow. *Bible.*

20 In my Father's house are many mansions. *Jesus.*

In my virtue (*Tugend*) I wrap myself and sleep. *Platen.*

In Nature there's no blemish but the mind; / None can be called deformed but the unkind. *Twelfth Night*, iii. 4.

In Nature things move violently to their places, and calmly in their place; so virtue in ambition is violent, in authority settled and calm. *Bacon.*

In Nature we never see anything isolated, but everything in connection with something else which is before it, beside it, under it, and over it. *Goethe.*

In necessariis unitas, in dubiis libertas, in 25 omnibus charitas—In essential matters, unity, in doubtful, liberty; in all, charity. *Melanthon.*

In nine cases out of ten, the evil tongue belongs to a disappointed man. *Bancroft.*

In no time or epoch can the Highest be spoken of in words—not in many words, I think, ever. *Carlyle.*

In nocte consilium—In the night is counsel; take a night to think over it; sleep upon it.

In nomine—In the name of.

In nomine Domini incipit omne malum—In the 30 name of the Lord every evil begins. *Mediæval Pr.*

In nubibus—In the clouds.

In nuce Iliad—An Iliad in a nutshell.

In obscuro—In obscurity.

In old age nothing any longer astonishes us. *Goethe.*

In old times men used their powers of painting 35 to show the objects of faith; in later times they used the objects of faith to show their powers of painting. *Ruskin.*

In omni re vincit imitationem veritas—In everything truth surpasses its imitation or copy. *Cic.*

In omnia paratus—Prepared for all emergencies. *M.*

In omnibus quidem, maxime tamen in jure, æquitas est—In all things, but particularly in law, regard is to be had to equity. *L.*

In one thing men of all ages are alike; they have believed obstinately in themselves. *Jacobi.*

In oratory the will must predominate. *Hare.* 40

In order to do great things, it is necessary to live as if one were never to die. *Vauvenargues.*

In order to love mankind, we must not expect too much of them. *Helvetius.*

In order to manage an ungovernable beast, he must be stinted in his provender. *Queen Elizabeth.*

In our age of down-pulling and disbelief, the very devil has been pulled down; you cannot so much as believe in a devil. *Carlyle.*

In our fine arts, not imitation, but creation, is 45 the aim. *Emerson.*

In our judgment of human transactions the law of optics is reversed; we see the most indistinctly the objects which are close around us. *Whately.*

In our own breast, there or nowhere flows the fountain of true pleasure. *Wieland.*

In pace leones, in prælio cervi—Brave as lions in peace, timid as deer in war.

In pain is a new time born. *Chamisso.*

In pari materia—In a similar matter. 50

In partibus infidelium—In unbelieving countries.

In peace, there's nothing so becomes a man / As modest stillness and humility; / But when the blast of war blows in our ears, / Then imitate the action of the tiger; / Stiffen the sinews, summon up the blood, / Disguise fair Nature with hard-favour'd rage, / Then lend the eye a terrible aspect; / Let it pry through the portage of the head / Like the brass cannons. *Hen. V.*, iii. 1.

In peace, who is not wise? *Hitopadesa.*

In perfect wedlock, the man, I should say, is the head, but the woman the heart, with which he cannot dispense. *Rückert.*

In perpetuam rei memoriam — In everlasting remembrance of a thing.

In pertusum ingerimus dicta dolium—We are pouring our words into a perforated cask, *i.e.*, are throwing them away. *Plaut.*

In petto—Within the breast; in reserve. *It.*

5 In pios usus—For pious uses.

In Plato's opinion, man was made for philosophy; in Bacon's opinion, philosophy was made for man. *Macaulay.*

In pleno—In full.

In politics, as in life, we must above all things wish only for the attainable. *Heine.*

In politics, merit is rewarded by the possessor being raised, like a target, to a position to be fired at. *Bovee.*

10 In politics, what begins in fear usually ends in folly. *Coleridge.*

In pontificalibus—In full canonicals.

In portu quies—Rest in port. *M.*

In posse—Possibly; in possibility.

In practical life, the wisest and soundest men avoid speculation. *Buckle.*

15 In præsenti—At present.

In pretio pretium est; dat census honores, / Census amicitias; pauper ubique jacet — Worth lies in wealth; wealth purchases honours, friendships; the poor man everywhere is neglected. *Ovid.*

In pride, in reasoning pride, our error lies; / All quit their sphere and rush into the skies. *Pope.*

In principatu commutando, civium / Nil præter domini nomen mutant pauperes—In a change of masters the poor change nothing except their master's name. *Phædr.*

In private grieve, but with a careless scorn; / In public seem to triumph, not to mourn. *Granville.*

20 In proportion as one simplifies his life, the laws of the universe will appear less complex, and solitude will not be solitude, nor poverty poverty, nor weakness weakness. *Thoreau.*

In propria persona—In person.

In prosperity caution, in adversity patience. *Dut. Pr.*

In prosperity no altars smoke. *It. Pr.*

In puris naturalibus—Stark naked.

25 In quietness and in confidence shall be your strength. *Bible.*

In quite common things much depends on choice and determination, but the highest which falls to our lot comes from no man knows whence. *Goethe.*

In radiant, all-irradiating insight, a burning interest, and the glorious, melodious, perennial veracity that results from these two, lies the soul of all worth in all speaking men. *Carlyle.*

In re—In the matter of.

In referenda gratia, debemus imitari agros fertiles qui plus multo afferunt quam acceperunt—In repaying kindness, we ought to imitate fertile lands, which give back much more than they have received. *Cic.*

In regard to a book, the main point is what it 30 brings me, what it suggests to me. *Goethe.*

In regard to virtue, each one finds certainty by consulting his own heart. *Renan.*

In religion as in friendship, they who profess most are ever the least sincere. *Sheridan.*

In religion, the sentiment is all; the ritual or ceremony indifferent. *Emerson.*

In religion / What damnéd error but some sober brow / Will bless it and approve it with a text? *Mer. of Ven.*, iii. 2.

In rerum natura—In the nature of things. 35

In resolving to do our work well, is the only sound foundation of any religion whatsoever; and by that resolution only, and what we have done, and not by our belief, Christ will judge us, as He has plainly told us He will. *Ruskin.*

In reverence is the chief joy and power of life. *Ruskin.*

In Rome the Ten Commandments consist of the ten letters, Da pecuniam, Give money. *C. J. Weber.*

In sæcula sæculorum—For ages and ages; for ever and ever.

In sanguine fœdus—A covenant ratified in blood. 40 *M.*

In saying aye or no, the very safety of our country and the sum of our well-being lies. *L'Estrange.*

In science read the newest works; in literature, the oldest. *Bulwer Lytton.*

In science the new is an advance; but in morals, as contradicting our inner ideals and historic idols, it is ever a retrogression. *Jean Paul.*

In science we have to consider two things: power and circumstance. *Emerson.*

In se magna ruunt—Great interests are apt to 45 clash with each other. *Lucan.*

In seipso totus, teres, atque rotundus—Perfect in himself, polished, and rounded. *Hor.*

In self-trust all the virtues are comprehended. *Emerson.*

In serum rem trahere—To protract the discussion, or the sitting, to a late hour. *Livy.*

In service, care or coldness / Doth ratably thy fortunes mar or make. *George Herbert.*

In situ—In its original position. 50

In small proportion we just beauties see, / And in short measures life may perfect be. *Ben Jonson.*

In so complex a thing as human nature, we must consider it hard to find rules without exceptions. *George Eliot.*

In solitude the mind gains strength and learns to lean upon itself. *Sterne.*

In solo Deo salus—Salvation in God alone. *M.*

In solo vivendi causa palato est—To gratify the 55 palate is the sole object of their existence. *Juv.*

In some men a certain mediocrity of mind helps to make them wise. *La Bruyère.*

In some men there is a malignant passion to destroy the works of genius, literature, and freedom. *Junius.*

In some sort, love is greater than God. *Jacob Böhme.*

In some things all, in all things none, are crossed. *R. Southwell.*

In spite of all his faults, there is no creature 60 worthier of affection than man. *Goethe.*

In spite of all misfortunes, there is still enough to satisfy one. *Goethe.*

In spite of all the evil that is said of the unfortunates, kings sometimes have their good qualities too. *The Miller of Sans Souci.*

In spite of seeming difference, men are all of one pattern. *Emerson.*

In statu quo—In the state in which it was.

5 In stinting wisdom, greatest wisdom lies. *Sir Richard Baker.*

In such a world as this a man who is rich in himself is like a bright, warm, happy room at Christmastide, while without are the frost and snow of a December night. *Schopenhauer.*

In taking revenge, a man is but even with his enemy ; but in passing it over, he is superior. *Not traceable.*

In tale or history your beggar is ever the first antipode to your king. *Lamb.*

In tenui labor, at tenuis non gloria—Slight is the subject of my work, but not the glory. *Virg.*

10 In terrorem—As a warning.

In that fire-whirlwind (of the burning of the world-Phœnix), creation and destruction proceed together ; ever as the ashes of the old are blown out, do organic filaments of the new mysteriously spin themselves ; and amid the rushing and waving of the whirlwind element come tones of a melodious death-song, which end not but in tones of a more melodious birth-song. *Carlyle.*

In the adversity of our best friends we always find something that does not altogether displease us. *La Roche.*

In the balance, hero dust / Is vile as vulgar clay : / Thou, mortality, art just / To all that pass away. *Byron.*

In the breast of every single man there slumbers a frightful germ (*Keim*) of madness (*Wahnsinn*). *Feuchtersleben.*

15 In the career of nations no less than of men, the error of their intellect and the hardening of their hearts may be accurately measured by their denial of spiritual power. *Ruskin.*

In the catalogue ye go for men. *Macb.*, iii. 1.

In the childhood of nations speaking was singing ; let this be repeated in the childhood of the individual. *Jean Paul.*

In the coldest flint there is hot fire. *Pr.*

In the confidence of youth man imagines that very much is under his control ; in the disappointment of old age, very little. *Draper.*

20 In the darkest spot on earth / Some love is found. *Procter.*

In the degree in which you delight in the life of any creature, you can see it ; not otherwise. *Ruskin.*

In the denial of self is the beginning of all that is truly generous and noble. *Carlyle.*

In the destitution of the wild desert does our young Ishmael acquire for himself the highest of all possessions, that of self-help. *Carlyle.*

In the divine commandment, "Thou shalt not steal," if well understood, is comprised the whole Hebrew decalogue, with Solon's and Lycurgus's constitutions, Justinian's pandects, the Code Napoleon, and all codes, catechisms, divinities, moralities whatsoever that man has devised (and enforced with altar-fire and gallows-ropes) for his social guidance. *Carlyle.*

In the division of the inheritance, friendship 25 standeth still. *Dut. Pr.*

In the dullest existence there is a sheen of inspiration or of madness (thou partly hast it in thy choice which of the two) that gleams in from the circumambient eternity, and colours with its own hues our little islet of time. *Carlyle.*

In the dusk the plainest writing is illegible. *Goethe.*

In the end / Things will mend. *Pr.*

In the end we retain from our studies only that which we practically apply. *Goethe.*

In the evening one may praise the day. *Pr.* 30

In the exact proportion in which men are bred capable of warm affection, common-sense, and self-command, and are educated to love, to think, and to endure, they become noble, live happily, die calmly, are remembered with perpetual honour by their race, and for the perpetual good of it. *Ruskin.*

In the eye of the Supreme, dispositions hold the place of actions. *Blair.*

In the face of every human being his history stands plainly written, his innermost nature steps forth to the light ; yet they are the fewest who can read and understand. *Bodenstedt.*

In the fact that hero-worship exists, has existed, and will for ever exist universally among mankind, mayest thou discern the corner-stone of living rock, whereon all politics for the remotest time may stand secure. *Carlyle.*

In the family where the house-father rules 35 secure, there dwells the peace (*Friede*) which thou wilt in vain seek for elsewhere in the wide world outside. *Goethe.*

In the field none other can supply our place, each must stand alone,—on himself must rely. *Schiller.*

In the fine arts, as in many other things, we know well only what we have not learned. *Chamfort.*

In the fog of good and evil affections, it is hard for man to walk forward in a straight line. *Emerson.*

In the godlike only has man strength and freedom. *Carlyle.*

In the good as well as in the evil of life, less 40 depends upon what befalls us than upon the way in which we take it. *Schopenhauer.*

In the great duel (of opinion), Nature herself is umpire, and does no wrong. *Carlyle.*

In the great hand of God I stand. *Macb.*, ii. 3.

In the grimmest rocky wildernesses of existence there are blessed well-springs, there is an everlasting guiding star. *Carlyle.*

In the hands of genius the driest stick becomes an Aaron's rod, and buds and blossoms out in poetry. *H. N. Hudson.*

In the husband, wisdom ; in the wife, gentle- 45 ness. *Pr.*

In the interchange of thought use no coin but gold and silver. *Joubert.*

In the land of promise a man may die of hunger. *Dut. Pr.*

In the lexicon of youth, which fate reserves for a bright manhood, there is no such word as fail. *Bulwer Lytton.*

In the meanest hut there is a romance, if you knew the hearts there. *Varnhagen von Ense.*

In the midst of life we are in death. *Burial Service.*

In the midst of the sun is the light, in the midst of the light is the truth, and in the midst of the truth is the imperishable being. *The Vedas.*

In the mind, as in a field, though some things may be sown and carefully brought up, yet what springs naturally is the most pleasing. *Tac.*

5 In the mirror we see the face; in wine, the heart. *Ger. Pr.*

In the modesty of fearful duty / I read as much as from the rattling tongue / Of saucy and audacious eloquence. *Mid. Night's Dream,* v. 1.

In the morning mountains; / In the evening fountains. *Herbert's Coll.*

In the morning of life, work ; in the mid-day, give counsel; in the evening, pray. *Gr. saying.*

In the morning sow thy seed, and in the evening withhold not thine hand: for thou knowest not whether shall prosper, either this or that, or whether they both shall be alike good. *Bible.*

10 In the multitude of words there wanteth not sin. *Bible.*

In the ordinary concerns of life, moral energy is more serviceable than brilliant parts ; while in the more important, these latter are of little weight without it, evaporating only in brief and barren flashes. *Prescott.*

In the perishable petals of the flower there resides more spirit and life than in the lumpish granite boulder that has defied the tear and wear of thousands of years. *Feuerbach.*

In the place where the tree falleth, there it shall lie. *Bible.*

In the pursuit of intellectual pleasure lies every virtue ; of sensual, every vice. *Goldsmith.*

15 In the religion of Christ, as in the philosophy of Hegel, the negative principle is the creative, or determinative, principle. Christianity begins in No, subsists in No, and survives in No, to the spirit of the world ; this it at first peremptorily spurns, and then calmly disregards as of no account. *Ed.*

In the same measure in which you wish to receive, you must give. If you wish for a whole heart, give a whole life. *Rückert.*

In the smallest cottage there is room enough for two lovers. *Schiller.*

In the spiritual world, as in the astronomical, it is the earth that turns and produces the phenomena of the heavens. *Carlyle.*

In the spiritual world there is properly no in and no out. *Jean Paul.*

20 In the state nobody can enjoy life in peace, but everybody must govern ; in art, nobody will enjoy what has been produced, but every one wants to reproduce on his own account. *Goethe.*

In the sweat of thy brow shalt thou eat thy bread. *Bible.*

In the true Utopia, man will rather harness himself with his oxen to his plough, than leave the devil to drive it. *Ruskin.*

In the unhappy man forget the foe. *Addison.*

In the utmost solitudes of Nature, the existence of hell seems to me as legibly declared by a thousand spiritual utterances as that of heaven. *Ruskin.*

In the way of righteousness is life ; and in the 25 pathway thereof there is no death. *Bible.*

In the wilderness of life there are springs and palm-trees. *S. Lover.*

In the winter, warmth stands for all virtue. *Thoreau.*

In the works of many celebrated authors men are mere personifications. We have not a jealous man, but jealousy ; not a traitor, but perfidy ; not a patriot, but patriotism. The mind of Bunyan, on the contrary, was so imaginative that personifications, when he dealt with them, became men. *Macaulay.*

In the world's opinion marriage, as in a play, winds up everything ; whereas it is, in fact, the beginning of everything. *Mme. Swetchine.*

In the world-strife now waging, the victory 30 cannot be by violence ; and every conquest under the Prince of War retards the standards of the Prince of Peace. *Ruskin.*

In the wreck of noble lives / Something immortal still survives. *Longfellow.*

In theatro ludus—Like a scene at a play.

In these days, whether we like it or not, the power is with the tongue. *Lord Salisbury.*

In these sick days, when the born of heaven first descries himself in a world such as ours, richer than usual in two things, in truths grown obsolete, and trades grown obsolete —what can the fool think but that it is all a den of lies, wherein whoso will not speak lies and act lies must stand idle and despair? *Carlyle.*

In these times we fight for ideas, and news- 35 papers are our fortresses. *Heine.*

In things pertaining to enthusiasm, no man is sane who does not know how to be insane on proper occasions. *A. B. Alcott.*

In things that may have a double sense, it is good to think the better was intended ; so shall we still both keep our friends and quietness. *Feltham.*

In this blunder still you find, / All think their little set mankind. *Hannah More.*

In this theatre of man's life, it is reserved only for God and angels to look on. *Pythagoras.*

In this wild element of a life, man has to 40 struggle onwards ; now fallen, deep-abased ; and ever, with tears, repentance, with bleeding heart, he has to rise again, struggle again, still onwards. That his struggle be a faithful, unconquerable one—that is the question of questions. *Carlyle.*

In this world, full often our joys are only the tender shadows which our sorrows cast. *Ward Beecher.*

In this world it is not what we take up, but what we give up, that makes us rich. *Ward Beecher.*

In this world there is one godlike thing, the essence from first to last of all of godlike in it—the veneration done to human worth by the hearts of men. *Carlyle.*

In thy breast are the stars of thy fate. *Schiller.*

In thy thriving still misdoubt some evil : / Lest gaining gain on thee, and make thee dim / To all things else. *George Herbert.*

In time comes he whom God sends. *Herbert's Coll.*

In time the savage bull doth bear the yoke. *Much Ado*, i. 1.

In time we hate that which we often fear. *Ant. and Cleop.*, i. 3.

In times of anarchy one may seem a despot in order to be a saviour. *Mirabeau.*

5 In times of danger it is proper to be alarmed until danger be near at hand; but when we perceive that danger is near, we should oppose it as if we were not afraid. *Hitopadesa.*

In times of misfortune men's understandings even are sullied. *Hitopadesa.*

In times of necessity the words of the wise are worthy to be observed. *Hitopadesa.*

In too much disputing truth is lost. *Fr. Pr.*

In totidem verbis—In so many words.

10 In toto—In the whole; entirely.

In toto et pars continetur—In the whole the part also is contained.

In transitu—In passing.

In treachery it is not the fraud, but the cold-heartedness, that is chiefly dreadful. *Ruskin.*

In trinitate robur—My strength lies in trinity (or triunity). *M.*

15 In true marriage lies / Nor equal, nor unequal: each fulfils / Defect in each, and always thought in thought, / Purpose in purpose, will in will, they grow, / The single pure and perfect animal, / The two-cell'd heart beating, with one full stroke, / Life. *Tennyson.*

In turbas et discordias pessimo cuique plurima vis—In seasons of tumult and discord, the worst men have the greatest power. *Tac.*

In unoquoque virorum bonorum habitat Deus —God has his dwelling within every good man. *Sen.*

In usum Delphini—For the use of the Dauphin.

In utero—In the womb.

20 In utramvis dormire aurem—To sleep on both ears, *i.e.*, soundly, as no longer needing to keep awake. *Pr.*

In utraque fortuna paratus—Prepared in any change of fortune. *M.*

In utroque fidelis—Faithful in both. *M.*

In vacuo—In empty space.

In vain do they talk of happiness who never subdued an impulse in obedience to a principle. *Horace Mann.*

25 In vain does the mill clack / If the miller his hearing lack. *Herbert's Coll.*

In veritate religionis confido—I confide in the truth of religion. *M.*

In veritate victoria—Victory lies with the truth. *M.*

In vino veritas—There is truth in wine; that is, the truth comes out under its influence.

In vitium ducit culpæ fuga—In flying from one vice we are sometimes led into another. *Hor.*

30 In water you may see your own face; in wine the heart of another. *Pr.*

In well-regulated civil society there is scarcely a more melancholy suffering to be undergone than what is forced on us by the neighbourhood of an incipient player on the flute or violin. *Goethe.*

In wenig Stunden / Hat Gott das Rechte gefunden—God takes but a short time to find out the right. *Goethe.*

In wonder all philosophy began; in wonder it ends; and admiration fills up the interspace. *Coleridge.*

In wonder the spirits fly not as in fear, but only settle. *Bacon.*

In working well, if travail you sustain, / Into 35 the wind shall lightly pass the pain, / But of the deed the glory shall remain. *Nicholas Grimwald.*

In works of labour or of skill, / I would be busy too, / For Satan finds some mischief still / For idle hands to do. *Watts.*

In writing readily, it does not follow that you write well; but in writing well, you must be able to write readily. *Quinct.*

In your own country your name, in other countries your appearance. *Heb. Pr.*

In youth and beauty wisdom is but rare. *Pope, after Homer.*

In youth it is too early, in old age it is too late 40 to marry. *Diogenes.*

In youth, one has tears without grief; in age, grief without tears. *Jean Paul.*

Inactivity cannot be led to good. *Hannah More.*

Inanis verborum torrens—An unmeaning torrent of words. *Quinct.*

Incedis per ignes / Suppositos cineri doloso— You are treading on fire overlaid by treacherous ashes. *Hor.*

Incidit in Scyllam qui vult vitare Charybdim 45 —He falls into Scylla in struggling to escape Charybdis. *Pr.*

Incendit omnem feminæ zelus domum—The jealousy of a woman sets a whole house in a flame. *Pr.*

Incense is a tribute for gods only but a poison for mortals. *Goethe.*

Inceptis gravibus plerumque et magna professis, / Purpureus, late qui splendeat, unus et alter / Adsuitur pannus—Oftentimes to lofty beginnings and such as promise great things, one or two purple patches are stitched on in order to make a brilliant display. *Hor.*

Incerta hæc si tu postules / Ratione certa facere, nihilo plus agas, / Quam si des operam ut cum ratione insanias — If you require reason to make that certain which is uncertain, you are simply attempting to go mad by the rules of reason. *Ter.*

Incerta pro nullis habetur—What is uncertain 50 is to be treated as non-extant. *L.*

Incerti sunt exitus belli—The results of war are uncertain. *Cic.*

Incertum est quo te loco mors expectet; itaque in omni loco illam expecta—It is uncertain in what place death awaits you; be ready for it therefore in every place. *Sen.*

Incessant scribbling is death to thought. *Carlyle.*

Incessu patuit Dea—By her gait the goddess stood revealed. *Virg.*

Incidents ought not to govern policy; but 55 policy, incidents. *Napoleon.*

Inclusio unius est exclusio alterius—The mention by name of the one implies the exclusion of the other. *L.*

Incoctum generoso pectus honesto—A heart imbued with generous honour. *Pers.*

Inconsiderate persons do not think till they speak; or they speak, and then think. *Judge Hale.*

Inconsistencies of opinion, arising from changes of circumstances, are often justifiable. *Daniel Webster.*

Increased means and increased leisure are the two civilisers of men. *Disraeli.*

5 Incrédules les plus crédules—The incredulous are the most credulous. *Pascal.*

Incudi reddere—To return to the anvil, *i.e.*, to improve or recast. *Hor.*

Inde datæ leges ne fortior omnia posset—Laws have been ordained to the end that the stronger may not have everything their own way. *L.*

Inde iræ et lacrimæ — Hence rage and tears. *Juv.*

Indecision and delay are the parents of failure. *Canning.*

10 Independence, in all kinds, is rebellion; if unjust rebellion, why parade it and everywhere prescribe it. *Carlyle.*

Independence, in all kinds, is rebellion. Were your superiors worthy to govern, and you worthy to obey, reverence for them were even your only possible freedom. *Carlyle.*

Independence, like honour, is a rocky island without a beach. *Napoleon.*

Independence you had better cease to talk of, for you are dependent not only on every act of people whom you never heard of, who are living round you, but on every past act of what has been dust for a thousand years. *Ruskin.*

Index expurgatorius—An expurgatory index.

15 Indica tigris agit rabida cum tigride pacem / Perpetuam : sævis inter se convenit ursis. / Ast homini ferrum letale incude nefanda / Produxisse parum est—The Indian tigers live in perpetual peace with each rabid tigress ; savage bears agree among themselves, but man without remorse beats out the deadly sword on the accursed anvil. *Juv.*

Indictum sit—Be it unsaid.

Indigestion is the devil—nay, 'tis the devil and all. It besets a man in every one of his senses. *Burns.*

Indigna digna habenda sunt hæres quæ facit —Things unbecoming are to be held becoming if the master does them. *Plaut.*

Indignant good sense is often the perfection of absurdity. *Thackeray.*

20 Indignante invidia florebit justus — The just man will prosper in spite of envy. *M.*

Indigne vivit per quem non vivit alter—He by whom another does not live does not deserve to live.

Indignor quidquam reprehendi, non quia crasse / Compositum, illepideve putetur, sed quia nuper—I feel indignant when a work is censured not as uncouth or rough, but as new.

Individuality is everywhere to be spared and respected, as the root of everything good. *Jean Paul.*

Individuality is of far more account than nationality. *Schopenhauer.*

25 Individually man is a weak being, but strong in union with others. *Herder.*

Individuals may form communities, but it is institutions alone can create a nation. *Disraeli.*

Individuals must be modest, but modesty degrades nations. *Gioberti.*

Indocilis pauperiem pati—One that cannot learn to bear poverty. *Hor.*

Indocilis privata loqui—Incapable of betraying secrets. *Lucan.*

Indocti discant, et ament meminisse periti— 30 Let the ignorant learn, and the learned take pleasure in refreshing their remembrance. *President Hénault, after Pope.*

Indolence and stupidity are first cousins. *Rivarol.*

Indolence is the paralysis of the soul. *Lavater.*

Indolence is the sleep of the mind. *Vauvenargues.*

Industria floremus—By industry we flourish. *M.*

Industriæ nil impossibile—Nothing is impossible 35 to industry.

Industry is Fortune's right hand, and Frugality her left. *Pr.*

Industry is the parent of success.

Industry is the parent of virtue.

Industry need not wish. *Ben. Franklin.*

Indutus virtute ab alto—Anointed with virtue 40 from above.

Inest et formicæ sua bilis—Even the ant has its bile.

Inest sua gratia parvis—Even little things have a grace of their own.

Inest virtus et mens interrita lethi—He has a valiant heart and a soul undaunted by death. *Ovid.*

Infancy is the perpetual Messiah, which comes into the arms of fallen men, and pleads with them to return to Paradise. *Emerson.*

Infancy presents body and spirit in unity ; the 45 body is all animated. *Coleridge.*

Infandum, regina, jubes renovare dolorem— Indescribable, O Queen, is the grief you bid me renew. *Virg.*

Infecta pace—Without effecting a peace. *Ter.*

Inferior poetry is an injury to the good, inasmuch as it takes away the freshness of rhymes, blunders upon and gives a wretched commonality to good thoughts, and, in general, adds to the weight of human weariness in a most woeful and culpable manner. *Ruskin.*

Infidelity is not always built upon doubt, for this is diffident ; nor philosophy always upon wisdom, for this is meek ; but pride is neither. *Colton.*

Infidelity, like death, admits of no degrees. 50 *Mme. de Girardin.*

Infinite is the help man can yield to man. *Carlyle.*

Infinite pity, yet also infinite rigour of law ; it is so Nature is made. *Carlyle.*

Infinite toil would not enable you to sweep away a mist ; but, by ascending a little, you may often overlook it altogether. *Helps.*

Inflatum plenumque Nerone propinquo—Puffed up and full of his relationship to Nero. *Juv.*

Inflict not on an enemy every injury in your 55 power, for he may afterwards become your friend. *Saadi.*

Influence is to be measured not by the extent of surface it covers, but by its kind. *Channing.*

Infra dignitatem—Beneath one's dignity.

Ingenii largitor venter—The belly is the bestower of genius.

Ingeniis patuit campus, certusque merenti / Stat favor : ornatur propriis industria donis —The field is open to talent and merit is sure of its reward. The gifts with which industry is crowned are her own. *Claud.*

5 Ingenio facies conciliante placet—When the disposition wins us, the features please. *Ovid.*

Ingenio non ætate adipiscitur sapientia—Wisdom is a birth of Nature, not of years.

Ingenio stat sine morte decus—The honour accorded to genius is immortal. *Propert.*

Ingeniorum cos æmulatio—Rivalry is the whetstone of talent.

Ingenium ingens / Inculto latet hoc sub corpore—A great intellect lies concealed under that uncouth exterior. *Hor.*

10 Ingenium mala sæpe movent—Misfortunes often stir up genius. *Ovid.*

Ingenium res adversæ nudare solent, celare secundæ—As a rule, adversity reveals genius, and prosperity conceals it. *Hor.*

Ingens telum necessitas—Necessity is a powerful weapon.

Ingentes animos angusto in corpore versant—They have mighty souls at work within a stinted body. *Virg.*

Ingenuas didicisse fideliter artes / Emollit mores, nec sinit esse feros—A faithful study of the liberal arts refines the manners and corrects their harshness. *Ovid.*

15 Ingrata patria, ne ossa quidem habebis—Ungrateful country, thou shalt not have even my bones. *Scipio.*

Ingratis servire nefas—To serve the ungrateful is an offence to the gods.

Ingratitude and compassion never cohabit in the same breast. *South.*

Ingratitude drieth up wells, / And time bridges fells. *Wodroephe.*

Ingratitude is a crime so shameful, that the man was never yet found who would acknowledge himself guilty of it. (?)

20 Ingratitude! thou marble-hearted fiend, / More hideous, when thou show'st thee in a child, / Than the sea-monster. *King Lear,* i. 4.

Ingratus est qui remotis testibus agit gratiam —He is an ungrateful man who is unwilling to acknowledge his obligation before others. *Sen.*

Ingratus unus miseris omnibus nocet — One ungrateful man does an injury to all needy people. *Pub. Syr.*

Inimicus et invidus vicinorum oculus — An enemy and an envious man is an eye over his neighbour. *Pr.*

Iniqua nunquam regna perpetua manent—Authority founded on injustice is never of long duration. *Sen.*

25 Iniquum est aliquem rei sui esse judicem—It is unjust that any one should be judge in his own cause. *Coke.*

Initia magistratuum nostrorum meliora ferme, et finis inclinat—The commencement of our official duties is characterised by greater vigour and alacrity, but towards the end they flag. *Tac.*

Initium est salutis, notitia peccati—The first step in a man's salvation is knowledge of his sin. *Sen.*

Injuria absque damno—Injury without loss.

Injuriæ spretæ exolescunt, si irascaris agnitæ videntur—Injuries that are slighted and unnoticed are soon forgotten ; if you are angry, they are seen to be acknowledged. *Pr.*

Injuriam qui facturus est jam facit—He who is 30 bent on doing an injury has already done it. *Sen.*

Injuriarum remedium est oblivio—Oblivion is the best remedy for injuries. *Pr.*

Injuries come only from the heart. *Sterne.*

Injusta ab justis impetrare non decet ; / Justa autem ab injustis petere, insipientia est—To ask what is unreasonable from the reasonable is not right ; to ask what is reasonable from the unreasonable is folly. *Plaut.*

Inmost things are all melodious, naturally utter themselves in song. The meaning of song goes deep. *Carlyle.*

Innocence has a friend in heaven. *Schiller.* 35

Innocence is a flower which withers when touched, and blooms not again though watered with tears. *Hooper.*

Inopem me copia fecit—Plenty has made me poor ; wealth makes wit waver. *Ovid.*

Inopi beneficium bis dat, qui dat celeriter—He confers a twofold benefit on a needy man who does so quickly. *Pub. Syr.*

Inops, potentem dum vult imitari, perit—An incapable man who attempts to imitate a capable is sure to come to grief. *Phædr.*

Inquinat egregios adjuncta superbia mores— 40 The best manners are stained by the addition of pride. *Claud.*

Inquisitiveness as seldom cures jealousy as drinking in a fever quenches the thirst. *Wycherley.*

Ins Innre der Natur / Dringt kein erschaffner Geist. / Glückselig, wem sie nur / Die äussre Schale weist—No created spirit penetrates into the inner secret of Nature. Happy he to whom she shows but the outer shell. *Haller.*

Insani sapiens nomen ferat, æquus iniqui, / Ultra quod satis est virtutem si petat ipsam —Let the wise man bear the name of fool, and the just of unjust, if he pursue Virtue herself beyond the proper bounds. *Hor.*

Insanire parat certa ratione modoque—He is preparing to act the madman with a certain degree of reason and method. *Hor.*

Insanity is often the logic of an accurate 45 mind overtasked. *Holmes.*

Insanus omnis furere credit cæteros — Every madman believes that all others are mad. *Syr.*

Insculpsit—He engraved it.

Inservi Deo et lætare—Serve God and rejoice. *M.*

Insipientis est dicere, Non putarem—It is the part of a fool to say, "I should not have thought so."

Insita hominibus natura violentiæ resistere— 50 It is natural to man to resist oppression. *Tac.*

Insita mortalibus natura, propere sequi quæ piget inchoare — People are naturally ready enough to follow in matters in which they are disinclined to take the lead. *Tac.*

Insolence is pride when her mask is pulled off. *Pr.*

Insouciance—Indifference. *Fr.*

Insperata accidunt magis sæpe quam quæ speres—What you do not expect happens more frequently than what you do. *Plaut.*

Inspicere, tanquam in speculum, in vitas omnium / Jubeo, atque ex aliis sumere exemplum sibi—I would have you to look into the lives of all, as into a mirror, and draw from others an example for yourself. *Ter.*

Inspiration must find answering inspiration. *A. B. Alcott.*

5 Inspirations that we deem our own are our divine foreshadowing and foreseeing of things beyond our reason and control. *Longfellow.*

Inspiring bold John Barleycorn! / What dangers thou canst make us scorn! *Burns.*

Instar omnium—Like all the others.

Instead of the piteous and frightful figure of Death, stepping whip in hand by the peasant's side in the field, . . . place there a radiant angel, sowing with full hands the blessed grain in the smoking furrow. *George Sand.*

Instead of watching the bird as it flies above our heads, we chase his shadow along the ground; and, finding we cannot grasp it, we conclude it to be nothing. *Hare.*

10 Instinct is a great matter; I was a coward on instinct. *1 Hen. IV.*, ii. 4.

Instinct is intelligence incapable of self-consciousness. *John Sterling.*

Instruction does much, but encouragement everything. *Goethe.*

Intaminatis fulget honoribus—He shines with unspotted honours. *M.*

Integer vitæ scelerisque purus / Non eget Mauris jaculis neque arcu—The man of upright life and free from crime has no need of Moorish javelin or bow. *Hor.*

15 Integrity gains strength by use. *Tillotson.*

Integrity is the shortest and nearest way to our end, carrying us thither in a straight line, and will hold out and last longest. *Tillotson.*

Integrity without knowledge is weak and useless, and knowledge without integrity is dangerous and dreadful. *Johnson.*

Intellect annuls fate; so far as a man thinks, he is free. *Emerson.*

Intellect is aristocratic; charity is democratic. *Amiel.*

20 Intellect is not speaking and logicising; it is seeing and ascertaining. *Carlyle.*

Intellect lies behind genius, which is intellect constructive. *Emerson.*

Intellectual fairness is often only another name for indolence and inconclusiveness of mind, just as love of truth is sometimes a fine phrase for temper. *J. Morley.*

Intellectual tasting of life will not supersede muscular activity. *Emerson.*

Intelligabilia, non intellectum, fero—I provide you with things intelligible, but not with intelligence.

25 Intemperans adolescentia effetum corpus tradet senectuti—An incontinent youth will transmit a worn-out bodily frame to old age. *Cic.*

Intemperate wits will spare neither friend nor foe, and make themselves the common enemies of mankind. *L'Estrange.*

Intense study of the Bible will keep any man from being vulgar in point of style. *Coleridge.*

Inter alia—Among other matters.

Inter amicos omnium rerum communitas—Among friends all things are common. *Cic.*

Inter arma leges silent—In the midst of arms 30 the laws are silent. *Cic.*

Inter canem et lupum—Between the dog and the wolf; at the twilight.

Inter cetera mala, hoc quoque habet stultitia proprium, semper incipit vivere—Among other evils, folly has also this special characteristic, it is always beginning to live. *Sen.*

Inter delicias semper aliquid sævi nos strangulat—In the midst of our enjoyments there is always some wrong to torture us. *Pr.*

Inter Græcos græcissimus, inter Latinos latinissimus—In Greek he is the most accomplished Grecian, and in Latin the most thorough Latinist.

Inter malleum et incudem—Between the hammer 35 and the anvil.

Inter nos—Between ourselves.

Inter nos sanctissima divitiarum / Majestas—Among us the most sacred majesty is that of riches. *Juv.*

Inter pueros senex—An old man among boys. *Pr.*

Inter spem curamque, timores inter et iras, / Omnem crede diem tibi diluxisse supremum :/ Grata superveniet quæ non sperabitur hora—In the midst of hope and care, in the midst of fears and passions, believe each day that dawns on you is your last; welcome will steal upon you the hour that is not hoped for. *Hor.*

Inter sylvas Academi quærere verum—Amid 40 the woods of Academus to seek for truth. *Hor.*

Inter utrumque tene—Keep a mid course between the two extremes. *Ovid.*

Inter vivos—Among the living.

Interdum lacrymæ pondera vocis habent—Sometimes tears have the weight of words. *Ovid.*

Interdum stultus bene loquitur—Sometimes a fool speaks reasonably.

Interdum vulgus rectum videt, est ubi peccat 45 —Sometimes the common people judge aright; at other times they err. *Hor.*

Interea gustus elementa per omnia quærunt, / Nunquam animo pretiis obstantibus ; interius si / Attendas, magis illa juvant, quæ pluris emuntur—Meantime they search for relishes through all the elements, with minds regardless of expense ; look at it closely, those things please more which cost the higher price. *Juv.*

Interest blinds some people and enlightens others. *La Roche.*

Interest is the spur of the people, but glory that of great souls. *Rousseau.*

Interest reipublicæ ut quisque re sua bene utatur—It is for the interest of the state that every one make a good use of his property.

Interest speaks all sorts of tongues, and plays 50 all sorts of parts, even the part of the disinterested. *La Roche.*

Interim fit aliquid—Something is going on meanwhile. *Ter.*

Into a mouth shut flies fly not. *Pr.*

Into contradicting / Be thou never led away ;/ When with the ignorant they strive, / The wise to folly fall away. *Goethe.*

Into each life some rain must fall, / Some days must be dark and dreary. *Longfellow.*

Intolerabilius nihil est quam fœmina dives—There is nothing more insufferable than a rich woman. *Juv.*

Intra muros—Within the walls.

Introite, nam et hic dii sunt—Enter, for here too are gods. *Heraclitus, from Arist.*

5 Intuition is the clear conception of the whole at once. It seldom belongs to man to say without presumption, "I came, I saw, I conquered." *Lavater.*

Intus et in cute novi hominem—I know the man inside and out. *Pers.*

Intus et in jecore ægro / Nascuntur domini—Masters spring up in our own breasts, and from a morbid liver. *Pers.*

Intus si recte, ne labora—If inwardly right, don't worry.

Intuta quæ indecora—What is unbecoming is unsafe. *Tac.*

10 Inveni portum, Spes et Fortuna valete, / Sat me lusistis, ludite nunc alios—I have reached the port; hope and fortune, farewell; you have made sport enough of me; make sport of others now. *Lines at the end of Le Sage's "Gil Blas."*

Invent first, and then embellish. *Johnson.*

Invention breeds invention. *Emerson.*

Invention is the talent of youth, and judgment of age. *Swift.*

Inventions have all been invented over and over fifty times. Man is the arch-machine, of which all these shifts drawn from himself are toy models. *Emerson.*

15 Invia virtuti nulla est via—No way is impassable to virtue. *Ovid.*

Invidia gloriæ comes—Envy is the attendant on glory. *Ovid.*

"Invidia," jealousy of your neighbour's good, has been, since dust was first made flesh, the curse of man; and "charitas," the desire to do your neighbour grace, the one source of all human glory, power and material blessing. *Ruskin.*

Invidia Siculi non invenere tyranni / Tormentum majus—Sicilian tyrants invented nothing that is a greater torment than envy. *Juv.*

Invidiam ferre aut fortis aut felix potest—Only the brave or the fortunate are able to endure envy. *Pub. Syr.*

20 Invidiam placare paras, virtute relicta?—Are you trying to appease envy by the abandonment of virtue?

Invidus alterius macrescit rebus opimis—The envious man grows lean at the prosperity of another. *Hor.*

Invidus, iracundus, iners, vinosus, amator, / Nemo adeo ferus est, ut non mitescere possit, / Si modo culturæ patientem commodet aurem—The envious, the passionate, the indolent, the drunken, the lewd—none is so savage that he cannot be tamed, if he only lend a patient ear to culture. *Hor.*

Invisa nunquam imperia retinentur diu—Hated governments never hold out long. *Sen.*

Invisa potentia, atque miseranda vita eorum, qui se metui quam amari malunt—The power is detested, and the life wretched, of those who would rather be feared than loved. *Corn. Nep.*

25 Invita Minerva—Without genius or the requisite inspiration; against the will of Minerva.

Invitat culpam qui peccatum præterit—He who overlooks one crime invites the commission of another. *Pub. Syr.*

Invitum qui servat idem facit occidenti—He who saves a man against his will, does the same as if he killed him. *Hor.*

Invitum sequitur honos—Honour follows him unsolicited. *M.*

I·.ward cheerfulness is an implicit praise and thanksgiving to Providence under all its dispensations. *Addison.*

Ipsæ rursum concedite sylvæ—Once again, ye 30 woods, adieu! *Virg.*

Ipse dixit—He himself (viz. Pythagoras) said it. Assertion without proof.

Ipse docet quid agam : fas est et ab hoste doceri—He himself teaches me what to do; one ought not to be above taking a lesson even from an enemy. *Ovid.*

Ipse Jupiter, neque pluens omnibus placet, neque abstinens—Even Jupiter himself cannot please all, whether he sends rain or fair weather. *Pr.*

Ipse pavet; nec qua commissas flectat habenas, / Nec scit qua sit iter ; nec, si sciat, imperet illis—Scared himself, he knows neither how to turn the reins intrusted to him, nor which way to go; nor if he did, could he control the horses. *Ovid, of Phaethon.*

Ipsissima verba—The exact words. 35

Ipso facto—By the fact itself.

Ipso jure—By the law itself.

Ir por lana, y volver trasquilado—To go for wool and come back shorn. *Sp. Pr.*

Ira furor brevis est; animum rege, qui, nisi paret, / Imperat : hunc frenis, hunc tu compesce catena—Anger is a shortlived madness; control thy temper, for unless it obeys, it commands thee; restrain it with bit and chain. *Hor.*

Ira quæ tegitur nocet ; / Professa perdunt 40 odia vindictæ locum—Resentment which is concealed is dangerous; hatred avowed loses its opportunity of revenge. *Sen.*

Irarum tantos volvis sub pectore fluctus?—Dost thou roll such billows of wrath within your breast? *Virg.*

Iratus cum ad se redit, sibi tum irascitur—When an angry man returns to himself, he is angry with himself. *Pub. Syr.*

Ire tamen restat, Numa quo devenit et Ancus—It still remains for you to go where Numa has gone, and Ancus before you. *Hor.*

Iron sharpeneth iron; so a man sharpeneth the countenance of his friend. *Bible.*

Iron with often handling is worn to nothing. 45 *Lyly's Euphues.*

Irony is an insult conveyed in the form of a compliment. *Whipple.*

Irony is jesting hidden behind gravity. *John Weiss.*

Irremeabilis unda—The river there is no recrossing ; the styx. *Hor.*

Irresolution loosens all our joints; like an ague, it shakes not this limb or that limb, but all the body is at once in a fit. The irresolute man hatches nothing, but addles all his actions. *Feltham.*

Irritabis crabrones—You will irritate the hor- 50 nets. *Plaut.*

Irritation, like friction, is likely to generate heat instead of progress. *George Eliot.*

Irrthum verlässt uns nie ; doch ziehet ein höher Bedürfniss immer den strebenden Geist leise zur Wahrheit hinan—Error never leaves us, yet a higher need always draws the striving spirit gently on to truth. *Goethe.*

Is a man one whit the better because he is grown great in other men's esteem? *Thomas à Kempis.*

Is any place so inaccessible that an ass laden with gold cannot penetrate? *Philip of Macedon to a scout who pronounced a certain territory impregnable.*

Is beauty vain because it will fade? Then are earth's green robe and heaven s light vain. *Pierpont.*

5 Is cadet ante senem, qui sapit ante diem—He will die before he is old who is prematurely wise. *Pr.*

Is common opinion the standard of merit? *Thomas à Kempis.*

Is habitus animorum fuit, ut pessimum facinus auderent pauci, plures vellent, omnes paterentur—Such was the public temper, that some few dared to perpetrate the vilest crimes, more were fain to do so, and all looked passively on. *Tac.*

Is it in destroying and pulling down that skill is displayed? The shallowest understanding, the rudest hand, is more equal to that task. *Burke.*

Is it not astonishing that the love of repose keeps us in continual agitation? *Stanislaus.*

10 Is it not strange that men should be so ready to fight for religion and so reluctant to observe its precepts? *Lichtenberg.*

Is it not the same to whoso wears a shoe as if the earth were thatched all over with leather? *Hitopadesa.*

Is it right to despair, and shall truth make us sad? *Renan.*

Is maxime divitiis utitur, qui minime divitiis indiget—He employs riches to the best purpose who least needs them. *Sen.*

Is mihi demum vivere et frui anima videtur, qui aliquo negotio intentus, praeclari facinoris aut artis bonae famam quaerit—He alone appears to me to live and to enjoy life, who, being engaged in some business, seeks reputation by some illustrious action or some useful art. *Sall.*

15 Is mihi videtur amplissimus qui sua virtute in altiorem locum pervenit—He is in my regard the most illustrious man who has risen by his own virtues. *Cic.*

Is not belief the true God-announcing miracle? *Novalis.*

Is not cant the *prima materia* of the devil, from which all falsehoods, imbecilities, abominations body themselves, from which no true thing can come? *Carlyle.*

Is not light greater than fire? It is the same element in a state of purity. *Carlyle.*

Is not marriage an open question when it is alleged, from the beginning of the world, that such as are in the institution wish to get out, and such as are out wish to get in? *Emerson.*

20 Is not shame the soil of all virtue, of all good manners and good morals? *Carlyle.*

Is ordo vitio careto, caeteris specimen esto—Let this class (viz. the nobility of Rome) be free from vice and a pattern to the rest. *The Twelve Tables.*

Is sapiens qui se ad casus accommodet omnes ; / Stultus pugnat in adversis ire natator aquis —He is a wise man who adapts himself to all contingencies ; the fool struggles like a swimmer against the stream.

Is that a wonder which happens in two hours ; and does it cease to be wonderful if happening in two millions? *Carlyle.*

Is the God present, felt in my own heart, a thing which Herr von Voltaire will dispute out of me or dispute into me? To the "worship of sorrow" (Christianity) ascribe what origin and genesis thou pleasest, has not that worship originated and been generated ; is it not here? Feel it in thy heart and then say whether it is of God! *Carlyle.*

Is the jay more precious than the lark because 25 his feathers are more beautiful? *Tam. of Shrew,* iv. 3.

Is there anything of its own nature beautiful or not beautiful? The beauty of a thing is even that by which it shineth. *Hitopadesa.*

Is there evil in a city, and the Lord hath not done it? *Bible.*

Is there for honest poverty / That hangs his head, and a' that? / The coward slave we pass him by, / We dare be poor for a' that. *Burns.*

Is there no God, then? but at best an absentee God, sitting idle, ever since the first Sabbath, at the outside of His universe, and seeing it go? *Carlyle.*

Is there no stoning save with flint and rock? 30 *Tennyson.*

Is there no way to bring home a wandering sheep but by worrying him to death? *Thomas Fuller.*

Is this a dagger which I see before me, / The handle toward my hand? Come, let me clutch thee. *Macb.,* ii. 1.

Is thy complexion sour? / Then keep such company. *Herbert.*

Is your trumpeter dead, that you are obliged to praise yourself? *Pr.*

Isaac's fond blessing may not fall on scorn, / 3b Nor Balaam's curse on love which God hath blest. *Keble.*

Island ez hinn besta haud sun solinn shinnar uppä—Iceland is the best land on which the sun shines. *Icelandic Pr.*

Isolation is the sum-total of wretchedness to a man. *Carlyle.*

Ist's Gottes Werk, so wird's besteh'n / Ist's Menschenwerk, wird's untergeh'n—If it be God's work, it will stand ; if man's, it will perish.

Ista decens facies longis vitiabitur annis ; / Rugaque in antiqua fronte senilis erit—That comely face of thine will be marred by length of years, and the wrinkle of age will one day scar thine aged brow. *Ovid.*

Istaec in me cudetur faba—I shall have to smart 40 for it (*lit.* that bean will hit me). *Ter.*

Istuc est sapere, non quod ante pedes modo est / Videre, sed etiam illa quae futura sunt / Prospicere—That is wisdom, not merely to see what is immediately before one's eyes, but to forecast what is going to happen. *Ter.*

Istuc est sapere, qui, ubicunque opus sit, animum possis flectere—You are a wise man if you can easily direct your attention to whatever may require it. *Ter.*

It (love) adds a precious seeing to the eye. *Love's L. Lost*, iv. 3.

It belongs to great men to have great defects. *Fr. Pr.*

It can do us no harm to look at what is extraordinary with our own eyes. *Goethe.*

It chanceth in an hour that cometh not in seven years. *Pr.*

5 It costs more to revenge injuries than to bear them. *Pr.*

It dawns no sooner for one's early rising. *Port. Pr.*

It exalteth a man from earthly things to love those that are heavenly. *Thomas à Kempis.*

It happens as with cages, the birds without despair to get in, and those within despair of getting out. *Montaigne.*

It happens to men of learning as to ears of corn; they shoot up and raise their heads high while they are empty; but when full and swelled with grain, they begin to flag and droop. (?)

10 It has been well said that our anxiety does not empty to-morrow of its sorrows, but only empties to-day of its strength. *Spurgeon.*

It is a bad trade that of censor; he is sure to incur the hatred of those he censures, without finding them improved by the correction. *Guy Patin.*

It is a beautiful trait in the lover's character, that he thinks no evil of the object loved. *Longfellow.*

It is a beggarly conception to judge as if poetry should always be capable of a prose rendering. *John Morley.*

It is a brave act of valour to contemn death; but when life is more terrible than death, it is then the truest valour to dare to live. *Sir T. Browne.*

15 It is a characteristic of true genius to disturb all settled ideas. *Goethe.*

It is a clear gain to sacrifice pleasure in order to avoid pain. *Schopenhauer.*

It is a common error to think that in politics legislation is everything and administration nothing. *Macaulay.*

It is a common failing of old men to attribute all wisdom to themselves. *Fielding.*

It is a common law of Nature, which no time will ever change, that superiors shall rule their inferiors. *Dionysius.*

20 It is a custom / More honoured in the breach than the observance. *Ham.*, i. 4.

It is a damnable audacity to bring forth that torturing Cross, and the Holy One who suffers on it, and to expose them to the light of the sun, which hid its face when a reckless world forced such a sight on it; to take these mysterious secrets, in which the divine depth of sorrow lies hid, and play with them, fondle them, trick them out, and rest not till the most reverend of all solemnities appears vulgar and paltry. *Goethe.*

It is a delusion (*Wahn*) to suppose that adversity (*Unglück*) makes man better. As well believe that the rust makes the knife sharp, dirt promotes purity, and mud clarifies the stream. *Bodenstedt.*

"It is a devout imagination." *The Regent Murray's answer to John Knox's proposal to conserve the property of the Church for the spiritual benefit of the lieges.*

It is a fair and holy office to be a prophet of Nature. *Novalis.*

It is a fine thing to command, though it were 25 but a herd of cattle. *Cervantes.*

It is a foul bird that dirties its own nest. *Pr.*

It is a golden rule not to judge men according to their opinions, but according to the effect these opinions have on their character. *Lichtenberg.*

It is a good divine that follows his own instructions. *Mer. of Ven.*, i. 2.

It is a good horse that never stumbles, and a good wife that never grumbles. *Pr.*

It is a good thing to stay away till one's com- 30 pany is desired, but not so good to stay after it is desired. *Johnson.*

It is a grave offence to bind a Roman citizen, a crime to flog him, almost the act of a parricide to put him to death; what shall I call crucifying him? Language worthy of such an enormity it is impossible to find. *Cic.*

It is a great ease to have one in our own shape a species below us, and who, without being enlisted in our service, is by nature of our retinue. *Steele.*

It is a great journey to life's end. *Pr.*

It is a great misfortune not to possess talent enough to speak well, or sense enough to hold one's tongue. *La Bruyère.*

It is a great mistake to think that because 35 you have read a masterpiece once or twice or ten times, therefore you have done with it. . . . You ought to live with it and make it part of your daily life. *John Morley.*

It is a great piece of folly to sacrifice the inner for the outer man. *Schopenhauer.*

It is a great pity when the man who should be the head figure is a mere figure-head. *Spurgeon.*

It is a great point of wisdom to find out one's own folly. *Pr.*

It is a great shame to a man to have a poor heart and a rich purse. *Cato.*

It is a great sin to swear unto a sin, / But a 40 greater still to keep a sinful oath. *2 Hen. VI.*, v. 1.

It is a great step in finesse to make people under-estimate your acuteness. *La Bruyère.*

It is a hard winter when one wolf eats another. *Pr.*

It is a kindly spirit which actually constitutes the human element in man. *Schiller.*

It is a long lane that has no turning. *Pr*

It is a long way from granite to the oyster; 45 farther yet to Plato, and the preaching of the immortality of the soul. *Emerson.*

It is a low benefit to give me something; it is a high benefit to enable me to do somewhat of myself. *Emerson.*

It is a lucky eel that escapes skinning. *George Eliot.*

It is a main lesson of wisdom to know your own from another's. *Emerson.*

It is a man's sincerity and depth of vision that makes him a poet. *Carlyle.*

It is a mathematical fact that the casting of a pebble from my hand alters the centre of gravity of the universe. *Carlyle.*

It is a maxim of those who are esteemed perfect, that abundance is the perverter of reason. *Hitopadesa.*

It is a mere and miserable solitude to want true friends, without which the world is but a wilderness. *Bacon.*

It is a moral impossibility that any son or daughter of Adam can stand on any ground that mortal treads, and gainsay the healthy tenure on which we hold our existence. *Dickens.*

5 It is a poor art that the artisan can't live by. *It. Pr.*

It is a poor heart that never rejoices. *Pr.*

It is a poor horse that is not worth its oats. *Dan. Pr.*

It is a poor mouse that has but one hole. *Pr.*

It is a poor sport that is not worth the candle. *George Herbert.*

10 It is a profound error to presume that everything has been discovered; it is to take the horizon which bounds the eye for the limit of the world. *Lemierre.*

It is a proof of mediocrity of intellect to be addicted to relating stories. *La Bruyère.*

It is a rare thing, except it be from a perfect and entire friend, to have counsel given us, but such as shall be bowed and crooked to some ends which he hath that giveth it. *Bacon.*

It is a reproach to be the first gentleman of one's race, but greater to be the last. *Pr.*

It is a sad house where the hen crows louder than the cock. *Pr.*

15 It is a shame for a man to desire honour because of his ancestors, and not to deserve it by his own virtue. *St. Chrysostom.*

It is a sign that your reputation is small or sinking if your own tongue must praise you. *Judge Hale.*

It is a sin against hospitality to open your doors and shut up your countenance. *Pr.*

It is a small virtue to keep silence on matters, but a grave fault to speak of what should be kept silent. *Ovid.*

It is a sorry goose that will not baste itself. *Pr.*

20 It is a strange habit of wise humanity to speak in enigmas only. *Ruskin.*

It is a universal weakness of human nature to have an inordinate faith in things unseen and unknown, and to be affected unduly by them. *Cæsar.*

It is a very good world to live in, / To lend, or to spend, or to give in ; / But to beg, or to borrow, or to get a man's own, / It is the very worst world that ever was known. *Rochester.*

It is a very risky, nay, a fatal thing, to be sociable. *Schiller.*

It is a virtue in hermits to forgive their enemies as well as their friends ; but it is a fault in princes to show clemency towards those who are guilty. *Hitopadesa.*

25 It is a wise father that knows his own child. *Mer. of Ven.*, ii. 2.

It is absurd to contend for any sense of words in opposition to usage ; for all senses are founded upon usage, and upon nothing else. *Paley.*

It is advisable that a man should know at least three things :—first, where he is ; secondly, where he is going ; thirdly, what he had best do under the circumstances. *Ruskin.*

It is all in my eye, *i.e.*, it is nowhere else. *Pr.*

It is allowed by the laws of war to deceive an enemy by feints, false colours, spies, false intelligence, or the like ; but by no means in treaties, truces, signals of capitulation or surrender. *Paley.*

It is always an ease, and sometimes a happi-30 ness, to have nothing. *Joseph Hall.*

It is always by adventurers that great deeds are done, and not by the sovereigns of great empires.

It is always good when a man has two irons in the fire. *F. Beaumont.*

It is always necessary to show some good opinion of those whose good opinion we solicit. *Johnson.*

It is always term time in the court of conscience. *Pr.*

It is always the individual, not the age, that 35 stands up for the truth. *Goethe.*

It is always vitally important to ourselves to be scrupulously true. *Spurgeon.*

It is an argument of great wisdom to do nothing rashly, nor to be obstinate and inflexible in our opinions. *Thomas à Kempis.*

It is an assured sign of a worthy and generous spirit whom honour amends ; for honour is, or should be, the place of virtue. *Bacon.*

It is an egregious error to go by the exception instead of the rule. *Pascal.*

It is an equal failing to trust everybody and 40 to trust nobody. *Pr.*

It is an honour for a man to cease from strife. *Bible.*

It is an ill sign to see a fox lick a lamb. *Pr.*

It is an ill wind that blows nobody good. *Pr.*

It is as difficult to appropriate the thoughts of others as to invent. *Emerson.*

It is as easy to be a scholar as a gamester. 45 *Haweis.*

It is as easy to deceive one's self without perceiving it, as it is difficult to deceive others without their finding it out. *La Roche.*

It is as great a point of wisdom to hide ignorance, as to discover knowledge. (?)

It is as little the part of a wise man to reflect much on the nature of beings above him as of beings beneath him. *Ruskin.*

It is as much a part of true temperance to be pleased with the little that we know and the little that we can do as with the little that we have. *Ruskin.*

It is as much intemperance to weep too much 50 as to laugh too much. *Pr.*

It is as natural for the old to be prejudiced as for the young to be presumptuous ; and in the change of centuries each generation has something to judge for itself. *Ruskin.*

It is as rare as it is pleasant to meet an old man whose opinions are not ossified. *J. F. Boyes.*

It is as sport to a fool to do mischief. *Bible.*

It is at least fatal to the philosophic pretension of a line or stanza if, when it is fairly reduced to prose, the prose discloses that it is nonsense. *John Morley.*

It is bad, having once known the right, / And the impulse of nobleness prized, / To accept the less worthy, and order the fight / For a cause that is meaner, and walk by a light / That you once had despised. *Dr. Walter Smith.*

It is beneath the dignity of a soul that has but a grain of sense to make chance, and winds, and waves the arbitrary disposers of happiness. *Lucas.*

5 It is best not to be angry ; and best, in the next place, to be quickly reconciled. *Johnson.*

It is best to rise from life as from a banquet, neither thirsty nor drunken. *Arist.*

It is best to take half in hand and the rest by and by. *Pr.*

It is best to take with thankfulness and admiration from each man what he has to give. *John Morley.*

It is better and kinder to flog a man to his work than to leave him idle till he robs and flog him afterwards. *Ruskin.*

10 It is better for a young man to blush than to turn pale. *Cato.*

It is better for the man whom God helps than for him who rises early. *Cervantes.*

It is better living on a little than outliving a great deal. *(?)*

It is better not to live at all than to live dishonoured. *Sophocles.*

It is better to be a self-made man, filled up according to God's original pattern, than to be half a man, made after some other man's pattern. *J. G. Holland.*

15 It is better to be affected with a true penitent sorrow for sin than to be able to resolve the most difficult cases about it. *Thomas à Kempis.*

It is better to be lost than to be saved all alone. *Amiel.*

It is better to be nothing than a knave. *M. Antoninus.*

It is better to be the hammer than the anvil. *Fr. Pr.*

It is better to be the head o' the commonalty than the tail o' the gentry. *Sc. Pr.*

20 It is better to be wrong by rule than to be wrong with nothing but the fitful caprice of our disposition to impel us. *Natalia in "Wilhelm Meister."*

It is better to cleanse ourselves of our sins now, than to reserve them to be cleansed at some future time. *Thomas à Kempis.*

It is better to create than to be learned. Creating is the essence of life. *Niebuhr.*

It is better to die once than live always in fear of death. *Cæsar.*

It is better to do well than to say well. *Pr.*

25 It is better to dwell in a corner of the housetop than with a brawling woman in a wide house. *Bible.*

It is better to fight for the good than to rail at the ill. *Tennyson.*

It is better to go to the house of mourning, than to go to the house of feasting. *Bible.*

It is better to have a lion at the head of an army of sheep than a sheep at the head of an army of lions. *Defoe.*

It is better to have friends in our passage through life than grateful dependants ; and as love is a more willing, so it is a more lasting tribute than extorted obligation. *Goldsmith.*

It is better to have loved and lost than never 30 to have loved at all. *Tennyson.*

It is better to have evil days when one is young than when one is old. *Carlyle.*

It is better to have to do with God than with His saints. *Fr. Pr.*

It is better to hear the rebuke of the wise than for a man to hear the song of fools. *Bible.*

It is better to live by begging one's bread than to gratify the mouth at the expense of others. *Hitopadesa.*

It is better to live in a haunted forest . . . 35 than to live amongst relations after the loss of wealth. *Hitopadesa.*

It is better to live on the crust of your own industry than on the fruits of other people's. *Cervantes.*

It is better to make friends than adversaries of a conquered race. *B. R. Haydon.*

It is better to trust the eye than the ear. *Ger. Pr.*

It is bitter fare eating one's own words. *Dan. Pr.*

It is but the outer hem of God's great mantle 40 our poor stars do gem. *Ruskin.*

It is but vain to waste honey on those that will be caught with gall. *Quarles.*

It is by attempting to reach the top by a single leap that so much misery is produced in the world. *Cobbett.*

It is by being conversant with the inventions of others that we learn to invent, as by reading the thoughts of others we learn to think. *Joshua Reynolds.*

It is by faith that poetry as well as devotion soars above this dull earth. *Henry Giles.*

It is by his personal conduct that any man of 45 ordinary power will do the greatest amount of good that is in him to do. *Ruskin.*

It is by imitation, more than by precept, that we learn anything. *Burke.*

It is by presence of mind in untried circumstances that the native metal of a man is tested. *Lowell.*

It is by study that we become contemporaries of every age and citizens of the world. *(?)*

It is certain my belief gains quite infinitely the moment I can convince another mind thereof. *Novalis.*

It is certain that either wise bearing or 50 ignorant carriage is caught as men take diseases, one of another. *2 Hen. IV., v. 1.*

It is character which builds an existence out of circumstance. Our strength is measured by our plastic power. *Carlyle.*

It is cheap enough to say, "God help you." *Pr.*

It is common to esteem most what is unknown. *Tac.*

It is commonly the imagination which is wounded first, rather than the heart ; it is so much more sensitive. *Thoreau.*

It is courage that conquers in war, and not good weapons. *Sp. Pr.*

It is cowardly to quit the post the gods elect for us before they permit us. *Pythagoras.*

It is delightful, after wandering in the thick darkness of metaphysics, to behold again the fair face of Truth. *Carlyle.*

It is delightful to transport one's self into the spirit of the past, to see how a wise man has thought before us, and to what a glorious height we have at last reached. *Goethe.*

5 It is difficult to act a part long, for where truth is not at the bottom, nature will peep out and betray itself one time or other. *South.*

It is difficult to descend with grace without seeming to fall. *Blair.*

It is difficult to do good without multiplying the sources of evil. *Ruskin.*

It is difficult to feel deep veneration and great affection for one and the same person. *La Roche.*

It is difficult to know at what moment love begins; it is less difficult to know that it has begun. *Longfellow.*

10 It is difficult to say whether irresolution renders a man the more unhappy or the more despicable; also whether it is productive of worse consequences to make a bad resolution, or none at all. *La Bruyère.*

It is difficulties that give birth to miracles. *Dr. Sharpe.*

It is dreary (*öde*) to be able to respect nothing but one's self. *Fr. Hebbel.*

It is doubt (*Zweifel*) which turns good into bad. *Goethe.*

It is downright madness to contend where we are sure to be worsted. *L'Estrange.*

15 It is easier for a wit to keep fire in his mouth, than to hold in a witty saying that he is burning to tell. *Cic.*

It is easier not to begin to go wrong than it is to turn back and do better after beginning. *President Garfield.*

It is easier to carry the world in one's thoughts than on one's shoulders. *A. B. Alcott.*

It is easier to know man in general than men in particular. *La Roche.*

It is easier to suppress the first desire than to satisfy all that follow it. *Ben. Franklin.*

20 It is easier to worship than to obey. *Jean Paul.*

It is easier to write an indifferent poem than to understand a good one. *Montaigne.*

It is easy for a man who sits idle at home, and has nobody to please but himself, to ridicule or censure the common ways of mankind. *Johnson.*

It is easy for men to write and talk like philosophers; but to act with wisdom, there's the rub. *Rivarole.*

It is easy in the world to live after the world's opinion; easy in solitude to live after our own; but the great man is he who in the midst of the crowd keeps with perfect sweetness the independence of solitude. *Emerson.*

25 It is easy to be a spendthrift with other people's property. *Platen.*

It is easy to condemn; it is better to pity. *Abbott.*

It is easy to criticise an author, but it is difficult to appreciate him. *Vauvenargues.*

It is easy to give offence, though it is hard to appease. *Grillparzer.*

It is easy to open a shop, but hard to keep it open. *Chinese Pr.*

It is easy to screw one's self up into high and 30 ever higher altitudes of Transcendentalism, and see nothing under one but the everlasting snows of Himalaya, the earth shrinking into a planet, and the indigo firmament sowing itself with daylight stars; but whither does it lead? One dreads always to inanity and mere injuring of the lungs. *Carlyle to Emerson.*

It is enough for thee to know what each day wills; and what each day wills the day itself will tell. *Goethe.*

It is exactly in the treatment of trifles that a man shows what he is. *Schopenhauer.*

It is exceedingly difficult for a man to be as narrow as he could have been had he lived a century ago. *Whipple.*

It is excellent / To have a giant's strength, but tyrannous / To use it like a giant. *Meas. for Meas.*, ii. 2.

It is falling in with their own mistaken ideas 35 that makes fools and beggars of the half of mankind. *Young.*

It is fancy, not the reason of things, that makes us so uneasy. *L'Estrange.*

It is far better to give work which is above the men than to educate the men to be above their work. *Ruskin.*

It is far easier to make a great rush than to plod steadily on through a long life. *Spurgeon.*

It is far from universally true that to get a thing you must aim at it. There are some things which can only be gained by renouncing them. *Renan.*

It is far more difficult to be simple than to be 40 complicated; far more difficult to sacrifice skill and ease exertion in the proper place, than to expend both indiscriminately. *Ruskin.*

It is folly to lay out money in the purchase of repentance. *Ben. Franklin.*

It is folly to live in Rome and strive with the Pope. *Pr.*

It is folly to pretend that one ever wholly recovers from a disappointed passion. Such wounds always leave a scar. *Longfellow.*

It is for the sake of him (the virtuous man) and of those like him that the earth exists and maintains itself in being. *Renan.*

It is for truth that God created genius. *La- 45 martine.*

It is for want of application, rather than of means, that men fail of success. *La Roche.*

It is force and right that determine everything in the world; force till right is ready. *Joubert* (?).

It is fortune, not wisdom, that rules man's life. *Cic.*

It is from books that wise men derive consolation in the troubles of life. *Victor Hugo.*

It is from the difference we feel between the 50 finitude of fact and the infinitude of fantasy that all the evils spring which torment humanity. *Rousseau.*

It is fruition, and not possession, that renders us happy. *Montaigne.*

It is generally a sign of a small mind to think differently from great minds. *Goethe.*

It is given us to live only once in the world. *Goethe.*

It is good for a man to be driven, were it by never such harsh methods, into looking at this great universe with his own eyes, for himself and not for another, and trying to adjust himself truly there. *Carlyle.*

5 It is good that we sometimes be contradicted, and that we always bear it well; for perfect peace cannot be had in this world. *Jeremy Taylor.*

It is good to do nothing bad, but better to wish nothing bad. *M. Claudius.*

It is good to fear the worst; the best can save itself. *Pr.*

It is good to lend to God and the soil; they pay good interest. *Dan. Pr.*

It is good to rub and polish our brains against that of others. *Montaigne.*

10 It is great, it is manly, to disdain disguise. *Young.*

It is great prudence to gain as many friends as we honestly can, especially when it may be done at so easy a rate as a good word. *Judge Hale.*

It is hard even to the most miserable to die. *Pr.*

It is hard for an empty sack to stand upright. *Pr.*

It is hard to be poor and honest. *Pr.*

15 It is hard to carry a full cup. *Pr.*

It is hard to kick against the pricks. *Pr.*

It is hard to maintain the truth, but much harder to be maintained by it. *South.*

It is hard to put old heads on young shoulders. *Pr.*

It is hard to suffer wrong and pay for it too. *Pr.*

20 It is harder to avoid censure than to gain applause; for this may be done by one great or wise action in an age; but to escape censure, a man must pass his whole life without saying or doing one ill or foolish thing. (?)

It is harder to marry a daughter well than to bring her up well. *Pr.*

It is harder to weave than to gather wool. *Spurgeon.*

It is harder work to resist vices and passions, than to toil in bodily labours. *Thomas à Kempis.*

It is his excess of sensibility that distinguishes man from other animals. *Schopenhauer.*

25 It is his moral sentences on mankind or the state that rank the prose writer among the sages. *John Morley.*

It is his restraint which is honourable to a man, not his liberty. *Ruskin.*

It is human nature to hate him whom you have injured. *Tac.*

It is idleness that creates impossibilities; and where men care not to do a thing, they shelter themselves under a persuasion that it cannot be done. *South.*

It is ill standing in dead men's shoes. *Pr.*

30 It is ill to take out of the flesh what is bred in the bone. *Pr.*

It is impossible completely to understand what we do not love. *Mrs. Jameson.*

It is impossible for any man to form a right judgment of his neighbour's sufferings. *Addison.*

It is impossible that an ill-natured man can have a public spirit; for how should he love ten thousand men who never loved one? *Pope.*

It is impossible that anything so natural, so necessary, and so universal as death should ever have been designed by Providence as an evil to mankind. *Swift.*

35 It is impossible to be a hero in anything unless one is first a hero in faith. *Jacobi.*

It is impossible to be just, if one is not generous. *Pascal.*

It is in great perils we see great acts of daring. *Regnard.*

It is in human nature soon to relax when not impelled by personal advantage or disadvantage. *Goethe.*

It is in the politic as in the human constitution; if the limbs grow too large for the body, their size, instead of improving, will diminish, the vigour of the whole. *Goldsmith.*

40 It is in the soul of man, when reverence, love, intelligence, magnanimity have been developed there, that the Highest can disclose itself face to face in sun-splendour, independent of all cavils and jargonings;—there, of a surety, and nowhere else. *Carlyle.*

It is in the world that a man, devout or other, has his life to lead, his work waiting to be done. *Carlyle.*

It is in trifles that the mind betrays itself. *Bulwer.*

It is in vain for a man to be born fortunate, if he be unfortunate in his marriage. *Dacier.*

It is incalculable what by arranging, commanding, and regimenting you can make of men. *Carlyle.*

45 It is inconceivable how much wit it requires to avoid being ridiculous. *Chamfort.*

It is incredible how much the mind can do to sustain the body. *Goethe.*

It is indeed all twilight in this world, a trifle more or less. *Goethe.*

It is indeed only in old age that intellectual men attain their sublime expression. *Schopenhauer.*

It is infamy to die and not be missed. *C. Wilcox.*

50 It is invariably found that the contented man is a weak man. *John Wagstaffe.*

It is joy to think the best we can of human kind. *Wordsworth.*

It is just those who grope with the mole and cling with the bat who are vainest of their sight and of their wings. *Ruskin.*

It is less difficult to bear misfortunes than to remain uncorrupted by pleasure. *Tac.*

It is madness to make fortune the mistress of events, because in herself she is nothing, but is ruled by prudence. *Dryden.*

55 It is matter of the commonest remark how a timid man who is in love will show courage, or an indolent man will show diligence. *Matthew Arnold.*

It is meet / That noble minds keep ever with their likes ; / For who so firm that cannot be seduced ? *Jul. Cæs.*, i. 2.

It is mere cowardice to take safety in negations. *George Eliot.*

It is mere Philistinism on the part of private individuals to bestow too much interest on matters that do not concern them. *Goethe.*

It is more blessed to give than to receive. *Jesus.*

5 It is more difficult, and calls for higher energies of the soul, to live a martyr than to die one. *H. Mann.*

It is more honourable to be raised to a throne than be born to one ; fortune bestows the one, merit obtains the other. *Petrarch.*

It is more important to discover a new source of happiness on earth than a new planet in the sky. (?)

It is more kindly to laugh at human life than to grin at it. *Wieland.*

It is more painful to do nothing than something. *Pr.*

10 It is more pleasing to see smoke brightening into flame than flame sinking into smoke. *Johnson.*

It is much easier to be critical than to be correct. *Disraeli.*

It is much easier to bind on a wreath than to find a head worthy to wear it. *Goethe.*

It is much easier to recognise error than to find truth ; the former lies on the surface, the latter rests in the depths. *Goethe.*

It is much more easy to inspire a passion than a faith. *Simms.*

15 It is much safer to obey than to govern. *Thomas à Kempis.*

It is natural to a man to believe what he wishes to be true, and to believe it because he wishes it. *Schopenhauer.*

It is natural to man to regard himself as the final cause of creation. *Goethe.*

It is naught, it is naught, saith the buyer ; but when he is gone his way, then he boasteth. *Bible.*

It is never permitted to any one in heaven to stand behind another and look at the back of his head : for then the influx which is from the Lord is disturbed. *Swedenborg.*

20 It is never too late to mend. *Pr.*

It is never wise to slip the bonds of discipline. *Lew. Wallace.*

It is no man's business whether he has genius or not : work he must, whatever he is, but quietly and steadily ; and the natural and unforced results of such work will always be the things that God meant him to do, and will be his best. *Ruskin.*

It is no mean happiness to be seated in the mean. *Mer. of Ven.*, i. 2.

It is no more in our power to love always than it was not to love. *La Bruyère.*

25 It is no more possible to prevent thought from reverting to an ideal than the sea from returning to the shore. *Joseph Cook.*

It is no small commendation to manage a little well. He is a good waggoner that can turn in a little room. *Bp. Hall.*

It is no such heinous matter to fall afflicted, as, being down, to lie dejected. *S. Chrysostom.*

It is no wonder man's religion has much suffering in it ; no wonder he needs a suffering God. *George Eliot.*

It is nobler to become great than to be born great. *Pr.*

It is nobler to convert souls than to conquer 30 kingdoms. *Louis le Debonnaire.*

It is not a question how much a man knows, but what use he can make of what he knows. *J. G. Holland.*

It is not advisable to reward where men have the tenderness not to punish. *L'Estrange.*

It is not always necessary that the true should embody (*verkörpere*) itself ; enough if it hovers around spiritually and produce accordance (*Uebereinstimmung*) in us ; if it hover (*wogt*) through the atmosphere in earnest friendly tones like the sound of bells. *Goethe.*

It is not an unhealthy (*kränkelnde*) moral philosophy, but a sturdy morality that is of any profit to us. *Feuchtersleben.*

It is not because of his toils that I lament for 35 the poor ; we must all toil, or steal, which is worse ; no faithful workman finds his task a pastime. . . . But what I do mourn over is that the lamp of his soul should go out ; that no ray of heavenly, or even earthly, knowledge should visit him ; but only in the haggard darkness, like two spectres, Fear and Indignation bear him company. *Carlyle.*

It is not by shirking difficulties that we can remove them or escape them. *M. R. Greg.*

It is not enough that a poet possess inspiration ; his inspiration must be that of a cultured spirit. *Schiller.*

It is not enough to aim ; you must hit. *It. Pr.*

It is not enough to know how to steal ; one must know also how to conceal. *It. Pr.*

It is not enough to know, one must also apply ; 40 it is not enough to will to do, one must also do. *Goethe.*

It is not enough to speak, but to speak true. *Mid. Night's Dream*, v. 1.

It is not enough to take steps which may some day lead to a goal ; each step must be itself a goal and a step likewise. *Goethe.*

It is not every man that can afford to wear a shabby coat. *Colton.*

It is not everybody one would set to choose a horse or a pig ; how much less a member of Parliament ? *Ruskin.*

It is not everybody who can bend the bow of 45 Ulysses, and most men only do themselves a mischief by trying to bend it. *John Morley.*

It is not fit to tell others anything but what they can take up. A man understands nothing but what is commensurate with him. *Goethe.*

It is not from masters, but from their equals, that youths learn a knowledge of the world. *Goldsmith.*

It is not from nature, but from education and habits, that our wants are chiefly derived. *Fielding.*

It is not given to the world to be contented. *Goethe.*

It is not good for man to be, especially to work, 50 alone. *Goethe.*

It is not good to have an oar in every one's boat. *Camden.*

It is not good to meddle with divine mysteries. *Goethe.*

It is not good to pass by that we dislike, even to gain that which we like; for the water of life becometh mortal when mixed with a poison. *Hitopadesa.*

It is not he who gives abuse or blows who affronts, but the view we take of these things as insulting. *Epictetus.*

It is not his own individual sins that the hero atones for, but original sin, *i.e.*, the crime of existence. *Schopenhauer.*

5 It is not history which educates the conscience; it is conscience which educates history. *Amiel.*

It is not in man that walketh to direct his steps. *Bible.*

It is not juggling that is to be blamed, but much juggling; for the world cannot be governed without it. *Selden.*

It is not lost that comes at last. *Pr.*

It is not merely by virtue of the sunlight that falls now, and the rain and dew which it brings, that we continue here, but by virtue of the sunlight of æons of past ages. *John Burroughs.*

10 It is not metre, but metre-making agreement that makes a poem, a thought so passionate and alive, that, like the spirit of a plant or an animal, it has an architect of its own, and adorns nature with a new thing. *Emerson.*

It is not poetry, but prose run mad. *Pope.*

It is not possible to buy obedience with money. *Carlyle.*

It is not proper to place confidence in one who cometh without any apparent cause. *Hitopadesa.*

It is not propositions, not new dogmas and a logical exposition of the world, that are our first need; but to watch and tenderly cherish the intellectual and moral sensibilities, those fountains of right thought, and woo them to stay and make their home with us. *Emerson.*

15 It is not quite so easy to do good as those may imagine who never try. *Rd. Sharp.*

It is not so much our neighbour's interest as our own that we love him. *Bp. Wilson.*

It is not so much the being exempt from faults, as the having overcome them, that is an advantage to us. *Swift.*

It is not strength, but art obtains the prize. *Pope.*

It is not the beard that makes the philosopher. *Pr.*

20 It is not the custom when a prince doth sneeze to say, as to other persons, " God help you," but only to make a low reverence. *Gerbier.*

It is not the face which deceives; it is we who deceive ourselves in reading in it what is not there. *Schopenhauer.*

It is not the fact that a man has riches which keeps him from the kingdom of heaven, but the fact that riches have him. *Dr. Caird.*

It is not the fraud, but the cold-heartedness which is chiefly dreadful in treachery. *Ruskin.*

It is not the greatness of a man's means that makes him independent, so much as the smallness of his wants. *Cobbett.*

It is not the insurrections of ignorance that 25 are dangerous, but the revolts of intelligence. *Lowell.*

It is not the knowledge, but the use which is made of it that is productive of real benefit. *Scott.*

It is not the loss of heritage / That makes life poor; it is that, stage by stage, / Some leave us with a lessening faith in man, / And less of love than when our life began. *Dr. Walter Smith.*

It is not the manner of noble minds to leave anything half done. *Wieland.*

It is not the number of facts he knows, but how much of a fact he is himself, that proves the man. *Bovee.*

It is not the punishment, but the crime that is 30 the disgrace. *Alfieri.*

It is not the quantity, but the quality of knowledge which determines the mind's dignity. *W. E. Channing.*

It is not the reading of many books that is necessary to make a man wise and good, but the well-reading of a few. *R. Baxter.*

It is not the stamp on the coin that gives it its value, though on the bank-note it is. *J. Burroughs.*

It is not the victory that constitutes the joy of noble souls, but the combat. *Montalembert.*

It is not thy works, which are all mortal, 35 infinitely little, . . . but only the spirit thou workest in, that can have worth or continuance. *Carlyle.*

It is not titles that reflect honour on men, but men on their titles. *Machiavelli.*

It is not to taste sweet things, but to do noble and true things, and vindicate himself under God's heaven as a God-made man, that the poorest son of Adam dimly longs. *Carlyle.*

It is not, truly speaking, the labour that is divided, but the men; divided into mere segments of men, broken into small fragments and crumbs of life; so that all the little piece of intelligence that is left in a man is not enough to make a pin or a nail, but exhausts itself in making the point of a pin or the head of a nail. *Ruskin.*

It is not want, but rather abundance that creates avarice. *Montaigne.*

It is not want of good fortune, want of happi- 40 ness, but want of wisdom that man has to dread. *Carlyle.*

It is not well to make great changes in old age. *Spurgeon.*

It is not what he has, nor even what he does, which directly expresses the worth of a man, but what he is. *Amiel.*

It is not wisdom, but ignorance which teaches men presumption. *Bulwer Lytton.*

It is not with saying, " Honey, honey," that sweetness comes into the mouth. *Turk. Pr.*

It is not work that kills men, it is worry. '5 It is not the revolution that destroys the machinery, but the friction. *Ward Beecher.*

It is of more importance to teach manners and customs than to establish laws and tribunals. *Mirabeau.*

It is of no use running; to set out betimes is the main point. *La Fontaine.*

It is of some consequence for a man to forego his own inclinations, even in matters of no great importance. *Thomas à Kempis.*

It is often because an author proceeds from the thought to the expression, and the reader from the expression to the thought, that a clear writer is obscure. *Speroni.*

It is often easier, as well as more advantageous, to conform to the opinions of others than to persuade them into ours. *La Bruyère.*

It is often even wise to reveal what cannot long remain concealed. *Schiller.*

5 It is one of the wretchednesses of the great that they have no approved friends. *Channing.*

It is one soul which animates all men. *Emerson.*

It is one thing to be tempted, another thing to fall. *Shakespeare.*

It is one thing to see that a line is crooked, and another thing to be able to draw a straight one. *Rd. Sharp.*

It is one thing to speak much, and another to speak pertinently. *Pr.*

10 It is only a part of art that can be taught; the artist needs the whole. *Goethe.*

It is only at the first encounter that a face makes its full impression upon us. *Schopenhauer.*

It is only because they are not used to taste of what is excellent that the generality of people take delight in silly and insipid things, provided they be new. *Goethe.*

It is only by labour that thought can be made healthy, and only by thought that labour can be made happy. *Ruskin.*

It is only by universals, and never by singulars, that we can think. *Dr. Hutchison Stirling.*

15 It is only God's business to make laws, and the lawyer's to read and enforce them. *Ruskin.*

It is only in society that a man's powers can have full play. *Schopenhauer.*

It is only in their misery that we recognise the hand and finger of God leading good men to good. *Goethe.*

It is only kindred griefs that draw forth our tears, and each weeps really for himself. *Heine.*

It is only men collectively that live the life of man. *Goethe.*

20 It is only necessary to grow old to become indulgent. I see no fault committed that I have not committed myself. *Goethe.*

It is only on reality that any power of action can be based. *Emerson.*

It is only people who possess firmness that can possess true gentleness. *La Roche.*

It is only reason that teaches silence. The heart teaches us to speak. *Jean Paul.*

It is only rogues who feel the restraints of law. *J. S. Holland.*

25 It is only strict precision of thought that confers facility of expression. *Schiller.*

It is only the finite that has wrought and suffered; the infinite lies stretched in smiling repose. *Emerson.*

It is only time that possesses full reality, and our existence lies in it exclusively. *Schopenhauer.*

It is only when a man is alone that he is really free. *Schopenhauer.*

It is only when it is bent that the bow shows its strength. *Grillparzer.*

It is only with renunciation that life, strictly 30 speaking, can be said to begin. *Goethe.*

It is our relation to circumstances that determines their influence over us. The same wind that carries one vessel into port may blow another off shore. *Bovee.*

It is petty expenses that empty the purse. *It. Pr.*

It is pleasant to die if there be gods, and sad to live if there be none. *Marcus Antoninus.*

It is possible to sin against charity, when we do not sin against truth. *Pr.*

It is precisely in accepting death as the end 35 of all, and in laying down, on that sorrowful condition, his life for his friends, that the hero and patriot of all time has become the glory and safety of his country. *Ruskin.*

It is profound ignorance that inspires a degenerate tone. *La Bruyère.*

It is proof of a high culture to say the greatest matters in the simplest way. *Emerson.*

It is proper and beneficial sometimes to be left to thyself. *Thomas à Kempis.*

It is prudent to be on the reserve even with your best friend, when he betrays a too eager curiosity to worm out your secret. *La Bruyère.*

It is rare indeed that there is not ample 40 occasion for grumbling. *John Wagstaffe.*

It is religion that has formed the Bible, not the Bible that has formed religion. *R. D. C. Levin.*

It is sad to have to live in a place where all our activity must simmer within ourselves. *Goethe.*

It is sad to see how an extraordinary man so often strangles himself, struggling in vain with himself, his circumstances, and his time, without once coming upon a green branch. *Goethe.*

It is said no man is a hero to his valet. The reason is that it requires a hero to recognise a hero. The valet, however, will probably know well enough how to estimate his equals. *Goethe.*

It is so much easier to do what one has done 45 before than to do a new thing, that there is a perpetual tendency to a set mode. *Emerson.*

It is St. Christopher that carries Christ, not Christ St. Christopher, *i.e.*, in this myth, it is not Christ that bears the Church, but the Church that bears Christ. *Ed.*

It is sure to be dark if you shut your eyes. *Pr.*

It is the ambiguous distracted training which they are subject to that makes men uncertain; it awakens wishes when it should quicken tendencies. *Goethe.*

It is the best sign of a great nature, that it opens a foreground, and, like the breath of morning landscapes, invites us onward. *Emerson.*

It is the best use of fate to teach a fatal cour- 50 age. *Emerson.*

It is the bright day that brings forth the adder, / And that craves wary walking. *Jul. Cæs.*, ii. 1.

It is the cause, not the death, that makes the martyr. *Napoleon.*

It is the common error of builders and parents to follow some plan they think beautiful (and perhaps is so) without considering that nothing is beautiful which is displaced. *Lady Montagu.*

It is the common wonder of all men how, among so many millions of faces, there should be none alike. *Sir Thomas Browne.*

It is the company, and not the charge that makes the feast. *Pr.*

5 It is the condition of humanity to design what never will be done, and to hope what never will be attained. *Johnson.*

It is the curse of kings to be attended / By slaves, that take their humours for a warrant. *King John.*

It is the curse of talent, that, though it works more surely and persistently than genius, it reaches no goal ; while genius, hovering for long on the summit (*Spitze*) of the ideal, looks round, smiling, far above. *Schumann.*

It is the dim haze of mystery that adds enchantment to pursuit. *Rivarole.*

It is the fate of a woman / Long to be patient and silent, to wait like a ghost that is speechless, / Till some questioning voice dissolves the spell of its silence. *Longfellow.*

10 It is the fate of the great ones of the earth to begin to be appreciated by us only after they are gone. *Old Ger. saying.*

It is the first of all problems for a man to find out what kind of work he is to do in this universe. *Carlyle.*

It is the first principle of economy to make use of available vital power first, then the inexpensive natural forces, and only at last to have recourse to artificial power. *Ruskin.*

It is the flash that murders ; the poor thunder never harm'd head. *Tennyson.*

It is the frog's own croak that betrays him. *Pr.*

15 It is the glistening and softly-spoken lie, . . . the patriotic lie of the historian, the provident lie of the politician, the zealous lie of the partisan, the merciful lie of the friend, and the careless lie of each man to himself, that cast that black mystery over humanity, through which we thank any man who pierces, as we would thank one who had dug a well in the desert. *Ruskin.*

It is the glorious doom of literature that the evil perishes and the good remains. *Bulwer Lytton.*

It is the great error of reformers and philanthropists in our time to nibble at the consequences of unjust power, instead of redressing the injustice itself. *J. S. Mill.*

It is the greatest invention man has ever made, this of marking down the unseen thought that is in him by written characters. *Carlyle.*

It is the heart that makes the critic, not the nose. *Max Muller.*

20 It is the height of folly to throw up attempting because you have failed. Failures are wonderful elements in developing the character. *Anon.*

It is the inspiration of the Almighty that giveth man understanding. *Job.*

It is the law of fate that we shall live in part by our own efforts, but in the greater part by the help of others ; and that we shall also die in part for our own faults, but in the greater part for the faults of others. *Ruskin.*

It is the life in literature that acts upon life. *J. G. Holland.*

It is the little rift within the lute / That by and by will make the music mute, / And, ever widening, slowly silence all. *Tennyson.*

It is the lot of man to suffer. *Disraeli.* 25

It is the mark of a great man to treat trifles as trifles, and important matters as important. *Lessing.*

It is the master-wheel which makes the mill go round. *Pr.*

It is the monotony of his own nature that makes solitude intolerable to a man. *Schiller.*

It is the music in the ear that finds and interprets the music of the orchestra. *C. H. Parkhurst.*

It is the nature of despair to blind us to all 30 means of safety. *Fielding.*

It is the nature of extreme self-lovers, as they will set an house on fire, an it were but to roast their eggs. *Bacon.*

It is the nature of parties to retain their original enmities far more firmly than their original principles. *Macaulay.*

It is the office of the Church to teach, not to train. *Ward Beecher.*

It is the ordinary way of the world to keep folly at the helm, and wisdom under the hatches. *Pr.*

It is the part of a good man to do great and 35 noble deeds, though he risks everything. *Plutarch.*

It is the part of a wise man to resist pleasures, but of a foolish one to be a slave to them. *Epictetus.*

It is the poet's function to keep before the minds of the people not only the underlying truths and beauties of all Nature, but the high and pure ideal of humanity which all should strive to attain. *C. Fitzhugh.*

It is the possession of a great heart or a great head, and not the mere fame of it, which is of worth and conducive to happiness. *Schopenhauer.*

It is the power of thought which gives man the mastery over Nature, the thoughts go forth into the world. *Hans Andersen.*

It is the privilege of every human work which 40 is well done, to invest the doer with a certain haughtiness. *Emerson.*

It is the privilege of genius that to it life never grows common-place, as to the rest of us. *Lowell.*

It is the property of every hero to come back to reality ; to stand upon things, not shows of things. *Carlyle.*

It is the secret of the world that all things subsist, and do not die, but only retire a little from sight, and afterwards return again. *Emerson.*

It is the setting up of a claim to happiness that ruins everything in the world. *Merck to Goethe.*

It is the strange fate of man that even in the 45 greatest evils the fear of worse continues to haunt him. *Goethe.*

It is the temper of the highest hearts, like the palm-tree, to strive most upwards when it is most burdened. *Sir P. Sidney.*

It is the thought writ down we want, / Not its effect, not likenesses of likenesses ; / And such descriptions are not, more than gloves / Instead of hands to shake, enough for us. *J. Bailey.*

It is the treating of the common-place with the feeling of the sublime that gives to art its true power. *J. F. Millet.*

It is the unseen and spiritual in man that determines the outward and actual. *Carlyle.*

5 It is the vain endeavour to make ourselves what we are not that has strewn history with so many broken purposes and lives left in the rough. *Lowell.*

It is the wise alone who are capable of discerning that impartial justice is the truest mercy. *Goldsmith.*

It is the witness still of excellency / To put a strange face on his own perfection. *Much Ado,* ii. 3.

It is the work of a philosopher to be every day subduing his passions and laying aside his prejudices. *Addison.*

It is through the feeling of wonder that men philosophise. *Arist.*

10 It is time enough to answer questions when they are asked. *Emerson.*

It is time enough to doff your hat when you see the man. *Dan. Pr.*

It is time to fear when tyrants seem to kiss. *Pericles,* i. 2.

It is to be doubted whether he will ever find the way to heaven who desires to go thither alone. *Feltham.*

It is too late to husband when all is spent. *Pr.*

15 It is too late to spare when the bottom is bare. *Pr.*

It is true greatness to have in one the frailty of a man and the security of a god. *Sen.*

It is truth that makes a man angry. *Pr.*

It is useless to attempt to reason a man out of a thing he was never reasoned into. *Swift.*

It is useless to deny with the tongue that which man gives credence to with the heart. *Johnson.*

20 It is very easy to obey a noble ruler who convinces (*überzeugt*) while he commands us. *Goethe.*

It is very good to be left alone with the truth sometimes, to hear with all its sternness what it will say to one. *Carlyle.*

It is very little that we can ever know of the ways of Providence or the laws of existence ; but that little is enough, and exactly enough. *Ruskin.*

It is war's prize to take all advantages, / And ten to one is no impeach of valour. 3 *Hen. VI.,* i. 4.

It is we that are blind, not Fortune. *Sir T. Browne.*

25 It is well that there is no one without a fault, for he would not have a friend in the world. He would seem to belong to a different species. *Hazlitt.*

It is well to go for a light to another man's fire, but by no means to tarry by it. *Plutarch.*

It is when the hour of conflict is over, that history comes to a right understanding of the strife, and is ready to exclaim: "Lo! God is here, and we knew it not." *Bancroft.*

It is wholesomer for the moral nature to be restrained, even by arbitrary power, than to be allowed to exercise arbitrary power. *J. S. Mill.*

It is wisdom alone that can recognise wisdom. *Carlyle.*

It is wise not to know a secret, and honest 30 not to reveal it. *Pr.*

It is with a fine genius as with a fine fashion ; all those are displeased at it who are not able to follow it. *Warton.*

It is with diseases of the mind as with those of the body ; we are half dead before we understand our disorders, and half cured when we do. *Colton.*

It is with history as it is with nature, as it is with everything profound, past, present, or future ; the deeper we earnestly search into them, the more difficult are the problems that arise. He who does not fear these, but boldly confronts them, will, with every step or advance, feel himself both more at his ease and more highly educated. *Goethe.*

It is with ideas as with pieces of money ; those of least value generally circulate the best. *Punch.*

It is with narrow-soul'd people as with narrow-35 neck'd bottles ; the less they have in them the more noise they make in pouring it out. *Swift.*

It is with our thoughts as with flowers. Those whose expression is simple carry their seed with them ; those that are double, by their richness and pomp charm the mind, but produce nothing. *Joubert.*

It is with words as with sunbeams ; the more they are condensed, the deeper they burn. *Southey.*

It makes a great difference to the force of any sentence whether there be a man behind it or no. In the learned journal, in the influential newspaper, I discern no form ; only some irresponsible shadow ; oftener some moneyed corporation, or some dangler, who hopes, in the mask and robes of his paragraph, to pass for somebody. *Emerson.*

It matters less to a man where he is born than where he can live. *Turk. Pr.*

It matters little whether a man be mathema- 40 tically, or philologically, or artistically cultivated, so he be cultivated. *Goethe.*

It matters not how a man dies, but how he lives. *Johnson.*

It matters not that a woman is well dressed if her manners be bad ; ill-breeding mars a fine dress more than dirt. *Plaut.*

It matters not whether our good-humour be construed by others into insensibility, or even idiotism ; it is happiness to ourselves. *Goldsmith.*

It may be we shall touch the Happy Isles, / And see the great Achilles whom we knew. *Tennyson.*

It may indeed be that man is frightfully threshed at times by public and domestic ill-fortune, but the ruthless destiny, if it smites the rich sheaves, only crumples the straw; the grains feel nothing of it, and bound merrily hither and thither on the threshing-floor, unconcerned whether they wander into the mill or the cornfield. *Goethe.*

It must be bad indeed if a book has a more demoralising effect than life itself. *Goethe.*

It needs a man to perceive a man. *A. B. Alcott.*

It ne'er was wealth, it ne'er was wealth, / That coft contentment, peace, or pleasure; / The bands and bliss o' mutual love, / O that's the chiefest warld's treasure! *Burns.*

5 It never occurs to fools that merit and good fortune are closely united. *Goethe.*

It never rains but it pours. *Pr.*

It never smokes but there's fire. *Pr.*

It offends me to the soul to hear a robustious periwig-pated fellow tear a passion to tatters, to very rags, to split the ears of the groundlings, who for the most part are capable of nothing but inexplicable dumb show and noise. *Ham.*, ii. 2.

It oft falls out to have what we would have; we speak not what we mean. *Meas. for Meas.*, ii. 4.

10 It requires a great deal of boldness and a great deal of caution to make a great fortune, and when you have got it, it requires ten times as much wit to keep it. *Emerson.*

It requires a great deal of poetry to gild the pill of poverty. *Mme. Deluzy.*

It requires a long time to know any one. *Cervantes.*

It requires more than mere genius to be an author. *La Bruyère.*

It requires much courage not to be downhearted in the world. *Goethe.*

15 It requires no preterhuman force of will in any young man or woman . . . to get at least half an hour out of a solid busy day for good and disinterested reading. *John Morley.*

It seems a law of society to despise a man who looks discontented because its requirements have compelled him to part with all he values in his life. *Goethe.*

It seems as if them as aren't wanted here are th' only ones as aren't wanted i' the other world. *George Eliot.*

It should not be suspected of a man, whose life hath been spent in noble deeds, that his reason is lost, when he is only involved in trouble. A fire may be overturned, but its flames will never descend. *Hitopadesa.*

It so falls out, / That what we have we prize not to the worth / Whiles we enjoy it; but being lack'd and lost, / Why then we rack the value. *Much Ado*, iv. 1.

20 It takes a good many spadefuls of earth to bury the truth. *Ger. Pr.*

It takes a great deal of living to get a little deal of learning. *Ruskin.*

It takes a great man to make a good listener. *Helps.*

It takes much more penetration to discover a fool than a clever man. *Cato.*

It takes ten pounds of common-sense to carry one pound of learning. *Persian Pr.*

It was a stroke / Brought the stream from the 25 flinty rock. *Dr. W. Smith.*

It was alway yet the trick of our English nation, if they have a good thing, to make it too common. *2 Hen. IV.*, i. 2.

It was always the aim of the artists as well as the wise men of antiquity, to mean much though they might say little. *Winkelmann.*

It was for beauty that the world was made. *Quoted by Emerson.*

It was the nightingale, and not the lark / That pierced the fearful hollow of thine ear. *Rom. and Jul.*, iii. 5.

It was the wisdom of the ancients to regard 30 the most useful as the most illustrious. *Sen.*

It were better to be of no church than bitter for any. *W. Penn.*

It were easier to stop Euphrates at its source than one tear of a true and tender heart. *Byron.*

It were good for a man to have some anchorage deeper than the quicksands of this world; for these drift to and fro so as to baffle all conjecture. *Carlyle.*

It were no virtue to bear calamities if we did not feel them. *Mme. Necker.*

It will be all the same a hundred years hence. 35 *Pr.*

It will be an ill web to bleach. *Pr.*

It will have blood; they say, blood will have blood; / Stones have been known to move, and trees to speak. *Macb.*, iii. 4.

It will never out of the flesh that's bred in the bone. *Ben Jonson.*

It would be better that we should not exist, than that we should guiltily disappoint the purposes of existence. *Ruskin.*

It would be some advantage to live a primitive 40 and frontier life, though in the midst of an outward civilisation, if only to learn what are the gross necessaries of life, and what methods have been taken to obtain them. *Thoreau.*

It's a gude heart that says nae ill, but a better that thinks nane. *Sc. Pr.*

It's a poor man that always counts his sheep. *Pr.*

It's a poor sport that's not worth the candle. *George Herbert.*

It's a sair field where a's slain. *Sc. Pr.*

It's a small joke sets men laughing when they 45 sit a-staring at one another wi' a pipe i' their mouths. *George Eliot.*

It's a weary warld, and naebody bides in't. *J. M. Barrie.*

It's all very well having a ready-made rich man, but it may happen he'll be a ready-made fool. *George Eliot.*

It's an ill wind that blaws naebody gude. *Sc. Pr.*

It's aye the cheapest lawyer's fee / To taste the barrel. *Burns.*

It's bad flesh that won't take salt; worse is 50 the body that won't take warning. *Gael. Pr.*

It's difficult to give sense to a fool. *Gael. Pr.*

It's dogged as does it. *Pr.*

It's good sheltering under an old hedge. *Pr.*

It's hard sailing when there is no wind. *Pr.*

It's hard to take the twist out of an oak that grew in the sapling. *Gael.*

It's hard to tell which is Old Harry when everybody's got boots on. *George Eliot.*

5 It's harder work getting to hell than to heaven. *Ger. Pr.*

It's hardly in a body's power / To keep, at times, frae being sour, / To see how things are shared. *Burns.*

It's height makes Grantham steeple stand awry. *Pr.*

It's ill livin' in a hen-roost for them as doesn't like fleas. *George Eliot.*

It's ill living where everybody knows everybody. *Pr.*

10 It's ill talking between a full man and a fasting. *Sc. Pr.*

It's ill wool that will take no dye. *Pr.*

It's lang ere the devil dee by the dyke-side. *Sc. Pr.*

It's never too late to learn. *Pr.*

It's no in titles nor in rank ; / It's no in wealth like London bank, / To purchase peace and rest : / It's no in makin' muckle mair, / It's no in books, it's no in lear, / To mak' us truly blest. *Burns.*

15 It's no tint (lost) that a friend gets. *Sc. Pr.*

It's no use filling your pocket full of money if you have got a hole in the corner. *George Eliot.*

It's no use killing nettles to grow docks. *Pr.*

It's no use pumping a dry well. *Pr.*

It's not "What has she?" but "What is she?" *Pr.*

20 It's poor eating where the flavour of the meat lies in the cruets. *George Eliot.*

It's poor friendship that needs to be constantly bought. *Gael. Pr.*

It's pride that puts this country down ; / Man, take thine old cloak about thee. *Old ballad.*

It's sin, and no poverty, that maks a man miserable. *Sc. Pr.*

It's them as take advantage that get advantage i' this world, I think ; folks have to wait long enough before it's brought to 'em. *George Eliot.*

25 It's too late to cast anchor when the ship is on the rocks. *Pr.*

It's wiser being good than bad ; / It's safer being meek than fierce ; / It's fitter being sane than mad. / My own hope is, a sun will pierce / The thickest cloud earth ever stretch'd ; / That after last returns the first, / Though a wide compass round be fetch'd ; / That what began best can't end worst, / Nor what God blessèd once prove accurst. *Browning.*

It's your dead chicks take the longest hatchin'. *George Eliot.*

Ita lex scripta—Thus the law is written.

Ivory does not come from a rat's mouth. *Chinese Pr.*

J.

J'ai bonne cause—I have good cause or reason. 30 *M.*

J'ai en toujours pour principe de ne faire jamais par autrui ce que je pouvais faire par moi-même—I have ever held it as a maxim never to do that through another which it was possible for me to do myself. *Montesquieu.*

J'ai failli attendre—I was all but kept waiting. *Louis XIV., as his carriage drove up just at the last moment.*

J'ai graissé la patte au concierge — I have tipped the door-keeper (*lit.* greased his paw). *Fr. Pr.*

J'ai ris, me voilà désarmé—I was set a-laughing, and lo ! I was at once disarmed. *Piron.*

J'ai toujours vu que, pour réussir dans le 35 monde, il fallait avoir l'air fou et être sage— I have always observed that to succeed in the world a man must seem simple but be wise. *Montesquieu.*

J'ai trouvé chaussure à mon pied—I have found a good berth (*lit.* shoes for my feet). *Fr. Pr.*

J'ai vécu—I existed through it all (the Reign of Terror). *Siéyès.*

J'ai voulu voir, j'ai vu—I wish to see, and have seen. *Racine.*

J'aime mieux ma mie—I love my lass better. *A French Old Song.*

J'appelle un chat un chat, et Rolet un fripon— 40 I call a cat a cat, and Rolet a knave. *Boileau.*

J'embrasse mon rival, mais c'est pour l'étouffer —I press my rival to my heart, but it is to smother him. *Corneille.*

J'en passe et des meilleurs—I pass by them, and better than they. *Victor Hugo.*

J'étais poète, historien, / Et maintenant je ne suis rien—I was once a poet and a historian, and now I am nothing. *Boudier, for his epitaph.*

J'étais pour Ovide à quinze ans, / Mais je suis pour Horace à trente—I was for Ovid at fifteen, but I am for Horace at thirty. *Ducerceau.*

J'évite d'être long, et je deviens obscur—In 45 avoiding to be diffuse, I become obscure. *Boileau, after Horace.*

J'y suis, et j'y reste—Here I am, and here I remain. *MacMahon in the trenches before the Malakoff.*

Ja, das Gold ist nur Chimäre—Yes, gold is but a chimæra. *Scribe-Meyerbeer.*

Ja, der Krieg verschlingt die Besten !—Yes, war swallows up the best people ! *Schiller.*

Ja, grosse Männer werden stets verfolgt, / Und kommen immer in Verlegenheiten— Yes, great men are always subject to persecution, and always getting into straits. *Schiller.*

Ja, so schätzt der Mensch das Leben, als 50 heiliges Kleinod, / Dass er jenen am meisten verehrt, der es trotzig verschmähet—Yes, man values life as a sacred jewel in such a way that he reveres him most who haughtily scorns it. *Platen.*

Jacet ecce Tibullus, / Vix manet e toto parva quod urna capit—See, here Tibullus lies ; of all that he was there hardly remains enough to fill a little urn. *Ovid.*

Jack at a pinch. *Pr.*

Jack is as good as Jill. *Pr.*

Jack-o'-both sides is, before long, trusted by nobody, and abused by both parties. *Pr.*

Jack of all trades and master of none. *Pr.*

5 Jack shall pipe and Jill shall dance. *G. Wither.*

Jack will never be a gentleman. *Pr.*

Jack's as good as his master. *Pr.*

Jacta alea est—The die is cast. *Cæsar, when he passed the Rubicon.*

Jactitatio — A boasting. *Jactitation of marriage is cognisable in the Ecclesiastical Courts. L.*

10 Jam nunc minaci murmure cornuum / Perstringis aures ; jam litui strepunt—Even now you stun our ears with the threatening murmur of horns ; already I hear the clarions sound. *Hor.*

Jam pauca aratro jugera regiæ / Moles relinquent—Soon will regal piles leave but few acres to the plough. *Hor.*

Jam portum inveni, Spes et Fortuna valete ! / Nil mihi vobiscum est, ludite nunc alios—Now I have gained the port, hope and fortune, farewell ! I have nothing more to do with you ; go now and make sport of others. *A Greek epitaph.*

Jam redit et Virgo, redeunt Saturnia regna—Now the Virgin goddess of justice returns ; now the reign of Saturn and age of gold returns. *Virg.*

Jam seges est ubi Troja fuit, resecandaque falce / Luxuriat Phrygio sanguine pinguis humus—New fields of corn wave where Troy once stood, and the ground enriched with Trojan blood is luxuriant with grain ready for the sickle. *Ovid.*

15 Jam summa procul villarum culmina fumant—Now the high tops of the far-off villas send forth their smoke. *Virg.*

Jamais abattu—Never cast down. *M.*

Jamais arrière—Never behind. *M.*

Jamais l'innocence et le mystère n'habitèrent long tems ensemble—Innocence and mystery never dwelt any length of time together. *Fr.*

Jamais la cornemuse ne dit mot si elle n'a le ventre plein—The bagpipe never utters a word till its belly is full. *Fr. Pr.*

20 Jamais long nez n'a gâté beau visage—A big nose never disfigured a handsome face, *i.e.*, it is disfigured already. *Fr. Pr.*

Jamais nous ne goûtons de parfaite allégresse ; / Nos plus heureux succès sont mêlés de tristesse—We never taste happiness in perfection ; our most fortunate successes are mixed with sadness. *Corneille.*

Jamais on ne vaincra les Romains que dans Rome—The Romans will never be conquered except in Rome. *Fr.*

Jamque opus exegi, quod nec Jovis ira, nec ignis, / Nec poterit ferrum, nec edax abolere vetustas — And now I have completed what neither the wrath of Jove, nor fire, nor the sword, nor the corroding tooth of time will be able to destroy. *Ovid.*

Januæ mentis—Inlets of knowledge (*lit.* gates of the mind).

25 Januis clausis—With closed doors.

Jardin des plantes—A botanical garden. *Fr.*

Jasper fert myrrham, thus Melchior, Balthazar aurum. / Hæc quicum secum portet tria nomina regum, / Solvitur a morbo, Domini pietate, caduco—Jasper brings myrrh, Melchior frankincense, and Balthazar gold. Whoever carries with him the names of these three kings (the three kings of Cologne, the Magi) will, by the grace of God, be exempt from the falling sickness. *A Mediæval charm.*

Je allseitiger, je individueller—The more universal a man is, the greater he is as an individual. *Mme. Varnhagen von Ense.*

Je cognois tout, fors que moy-mesme—I know everything except myself. *Old Fr.*

30 Je crains Dieu, cher Abner, et n'ai pas d'autre crainte—I fear God, Abner, and have no other fear. *Racine.*

Je crains l'homme d'un seul livre—I am afraid of the man of one book. *Thomas Aquinus.*

Je fetter der Floh, je magerer der Hund—The fatter the flee, the leaner the dog. *Ger. Pr.*

Je jouis des ouvrages qui surpassent les miens —I enjoy works which surpass my own. *La Harpe.*

Je laisse à penser la vie / Que firent ces deux amis—I leave you to imagine the festive time these two friends (the town mouse and the country mouse) had of it. *La Fontaine.*

35 Je le tiens—I hold it. *M.*

Je m'en vais chercher un grand peut-être ; tirez le rideau, la farce est jouée—I am going in quest of a great perhaps ; let the curtain drop, the farce is played out. *Rabelais, on his deathbed.*

Je m'en vais voir le soleil pour la dernière fois ! —I shall see the sun for the last time. *Rousseau's last words.*

Je m'estonne fort pourquoy / La mort osa songer a moy / Qui ne songeais jamais à elle—I wonder greatly why death should condescend to think of me, who never thought of her. *Regnier.*

Je maintiendrai le droit—I will maintain the right. *M.*

40 Je me fie en Dieu—I put my trust in God. *M.*

Je mehr der Brunnen gebraucht wird, desto mehr giebt er Wasser—The more the well is used, the more water it gives. *Ger. Pr.*

Je mehr Gesetze, je weniger Recht—The more laws, the less justice. *Ger. Pr.*

Je mehr man das Ich versteckt, je mehr Welt hat man—The more we merge our I, the larger is our world. *Hippel.*

Je mets en fait que, si tous les hommes savaient ce qu'ils disent les uns des autres, il n'y aurait pas quatre amis dans le monde —I lay it down as beyond dispute that if every one knew what every one said of another, there would not be four friends in the world. *Pascal.*

45 Je minder sich der Kluge selbst gefällt, / Um desto mehr schätzt ihn die Welt—The less the sage pleases himself, the more the world esteems him. *Gellert.*

Je n'ai fait celle-ci plus longue que parceque je n'ai pas eu le loisir de la faire plus courte —I have made this (letter) a rather long one, only because I had not the leisure to make it shorter. *Pascal.*

Je n'ai mérité / Ni cet excès d'honneur ni cette indignité — I have deserved neither so much honour nor such disgrace. *Corneille.*

Je n'ai point d'ennemis que ceux de l'état—I have no enemies whatever but those of the state. *Richelieu to his confessor on his death-bed.*

Je n'oublierai jamais—I will never forget. *M.*

Je ne change qu'en mourant — I change only when I die. *M.*

Je ne changerois pas mon répos pour tous les trésors du monde—I would not exchange my leisure hours for all the wealth in the world.

5 Je ne cherche qu'un—I seek but one. *M.*

Je ne connais que trois moyens d'exister dans la société : être ou voleur, ou mendiant, ou salarié--I know only three means of subsisting in society : by stealing, begging, or receiving a salary. *Mirabeau, to the Clergy.*

Je ne puis pas me refondre—I cannot change my opinion or purpose (*lit.* recast myself). *Fr.*

Je ne sais quoi—I know not what. *Fr.*

Je pense—I think. *M.*

10 Je pense plus—I think more. *M.*

Je plie et ne romps pas—I bend, but don't break. *La Font.*

Je prends mon bien où je le trouve—I take my own where I find it. *Molière.*

Je sais à mon pot comment les autres bouillent —I can tell by my own pot how others boil. *Fr. Pr.*

Je schöner die Wirthin, je schwerer die Zeche —The fairer the hostess the heavier the bill. *Ger. Pr.*

15 Je sens qu'il y a un Dieu, et je ne sens pas qu'il n'y en ait point ; cela me suffit—I feel there is a God, and I don't feel there is none ; that is enough for me. *La Bruyère.*

Je suis assez semblable aux girouettes, qui ne se fixent que quand elles sont rouillées—I am like enough to the weathercocks, which don't veer only when they become rusty. *Voltaire.*

Je suis oiseau, voyez mes áiles ! / Je suis souris ; vivent les rats—I am a bird, see my wing ! I am a mouse ; long live the rats. *La Fontaine.*

Je suis prêt—I am ready. *M.*

Je suis riche des biens dont je sais me passer —I am rich in the goods that I can do without. *Vigée.*

20 Je t'aime d'autant plus que je t'estime moins— I love you all the more the less I esteem you. *Collé Cocatrix.*

Je veux de bonne guerre—I am for fairplay in war. *M.*

Je veux le droit—I mean to have my right. *M.*

Je veux que, le dimanche, chaque paysan ait sa poule au pot—It is my wish that every peasant may have a fowl in his pot on Sundays. *Henry IV. of France.*

Je vis en espoir—I live in hope. *M.*

25 Je vois, je sais, je crois, je suis. désabusé— I see, I know, I believe, I am undeceived. *Corneille.*

Je voudrais voir un homme sobre, modéré, chaste, équitable prononcer qu'il n'y-a point de Dieu ; il parlerait du moins sans intérêt ; mais cet homme ne se trouve point—I should like to see a man who is sober, moderate, chaste and just assert that there is no God ; he would speak disinterestedly at least, but such a man is not to be found. *La Bruyère.*

Je vous apprendrai à vivre—I will teach you better manners (*lit.* to live). *Fr. Pr.*

Je vous ferai voir de quel bois je me chauffe— I will let you see what metal I am made of (*lit.* with what wood I heat myself). *Fr. Pr.*

Je weniger die Worte, je besser Gebet—The fewer the words, the better the prayer. *Ger. Pr.*

Jealous in honour, sudden and quick in quarrel, / 30 Seeking the bubble reputation / Even in the cannon's mouth. *As You Like It,* ii. 7.

Jealousy dislikes the world to know it. *Byron.*

Jealousy / Hath in it an alchemic force to fuse / Almost into one metal love and hate. *Tennyson.*

Jealousy is a painful passion ; yet without some share of it, the agreeable affection of love has difficulty to subsist in its full force and violence. *Hume.*

Jealousy is always born with love, but it does not always die with it. *La Roche.*

Jealousy is cruel as the grave; the coals 35 thereof are coals of fire, which hath a most vehement flame. *Bible.*

Jealousy is love's bed of burning snarl. *George Meredith.*

Jealousy is often the helpmate of sweet love. *Kingsley.*

Jealousy is the forerunner of love, and some-times its awakener. *F. Marion Crawford.*

Jealousy is the rage of a man. *Bible.*

Jealousy is the sister of love, as the devil is 40 the brother of the angel. *Weber.*

Jealousy : / It is the green-eyed monster that doth mock / The meat it feeds on. *Othello,* iii. 2.

Jealousy lives upon doubts ; it becomes mad-ness or ceases entirely as soon as we pass from doubt to certainty. *La Roche.*

Jean a étudié pour être bête—John has been to college to learn to be a fool. *Fr. Pr.*

Jean s'en alla comme il était venu—John went away as he came. *La Fontaine's epitaph, written by himself.*

Jeddart justice : First hang a man, and syne 45 (then) try him. *Sc. Pr.*

Jede grosse Zeit erfasst den ganzen Menschen —Every great epoch seizes possession of the whole man. *Mommsen.*

Jede Macht, welche wir über andere Gegen-stände ausüben, hängt von der Macht ab, die wir über uns selbst besitzen—All the power which we, in every case, exercise over other objects depends on the power we have over ourselves. *Cötvös.*

Jede That der Weltgeschichte / Zeugt auch wieder eine That—Every deed in the history of the world begets another deed in turn. *Arnold Schlönbach.*

Jede Unthat, / Trägt ihren eignen Racheengel schon, / Die böse Hoffnung unter ihrem Herzen—Every evil deed already bears its own avenging angel, the dread of evil, in the heart of it. *Schiller.*

Jedem das Seine ist nicht zu viel—To no one is 50 his own too much. *Ger. Pr.*

Jedem redlichen Bemühn / Sei Beharrlichkeit verliehn. Be perseverance vouchsafed to every honest endeavour. *Goethe.*

Jeden anderen Meister erkennt man an dem, was er ausspricht; was er weiss, ver-schweigt, zeigt mir den Meister des Styls —Every other master may be known by what he expresses ; what he wisely suppresses reveals to me the master of style. *Schiller.*

Jeder ausserordentliche Mensch hat eine gewisse Sendung, die er zu vollführen berufen ist—Every man above the ordinary has a certain mission which he is called to fulfil. *Goethe.*

Jeder freut sich seiner Stelle, / Bietet dem Verächter Trutz—Every one is proud of his office, and bids defiance to the scorner. *Schiller.*

Jeder gilt so viel als er hat—Every one is worth as much as he has. *Ger. Pr.*

Jeder ist seiner Worte bester Ausleger—Every one is the best interpreter of his own words. *Ger. Pr.*

5 Jeder Jüngling sehnt sich so zu lieben. / Jedes Mädchen so geliebt zu sein : / Ach, der heiligste von unsern Trieben / Warum quillt aus ihm die grimme Pein ?—The youth longs so to love, the maiden so to be loved ; ah ! why does there spring out of this holiest of all our instincts such agonising pain ? *Goethe.*

Jeder Krämer lobt seine Ware—Every dealer cracks up his wares. *Ger. Pr.*

Jeder Mensch muss nach seiner Weise denken : denn er findet auf seinem Wege immer ein Wahres, oder eine Art von Wahrem, die ihm durchs Leben hilft ; nur darf er sich nicht gehen lassen ; er muss sich controliren ; der blosse nackte Instinct geziemt nicht dem Menschen—Every man must think in his own way ; for on his own pathway he always finds a truth, or a measure of truth, which is helpful to him in his life ; only he must not follow his own bent without restraint ; he must control himself ; to follow mere naked instinct does not beseem a man. *Goethe.*

Jeder Morgen ruft zu, das Gehörige zu thun, und das Mögliche zu erwarten—We are summoned every morning to do what it requires of us, and to expect what it may bring. *Goethe.*

Jeder muss der Natur seine Schuld bezahlen —Every one must pay his debt to Nature. *Ger. Pr.*

10 Jeder muss ein Paar Narrenschuhe zerreissen, zerreisst er nicht mehr—Every one must wear out one pair of fool's shoes, if he wear out no more. *Ger. Pr.*

Jeder, sieht man ihn einzeln, ist leidlich klug und verständig ; / Sind sie in corpori, gleich wird euch ein Dummkopf daraus—Every man, as we see him singly, is tolerably wise and intelligent ; but see him in a corporate capacity, and you think him a born blockhead and fool. *Schiller.*

Jeder stirbt / Und sterben ist die grösste That für jedem—Every one dies, and for every one to die is his greatest act. *L. Schefer.*

Jeder Tag hat seine Plage / Und die Nacht hat ihre Lust — Every day has its torment, and the night has its pleasure. *Philina, in Goethe.*

Jeder Weg zum rechten Zwecke / Ist auch recht in jeder Strecke—Every road to the right end is also right in every stretch (step or turn) of it. *Goethe.*

15 Jeder Zustand, ja jeder Augenblick, ist von unendlichem Werth, denn er ist der Repräsentant einer ganzen Ewigkeit—Every condition, nay, every moment, is of infinite value, for it is the representative of a whole eternity. *Goethe.*

Jedes ausgesprochene Wort erregt den Eigensinn—Every uttered (*lit.* outspoken) word rouses our self-will. *Goethe.*

Jedes Weib will lieber schön als fromm sein— Every woman would rather be handsome than pious. *Ger. Pr.*

Jedes Weibes / Fehler ist des Mannes Schuld— The husband is to blame for the fault of the wife (in every case). *Herder.*

Jedwede Tugend / Ist fleckenrein bis auf den Augenblick / Der Probe—Every virtue is stainless up to the moment of trial. *Schiller.*

Jedwede Zeit hat ihre Wehen—Every time has 20 its sorrows. *Freiligrath.*

Jedweder ist des dunkeln Schicksals Knecht— Every one is dark fate's thrall. *Schillerbuch.*

Jeer not others upon any occasion. *South.*

Jeerers must be content to taste of their own broth. *Pr.*

Jejunus raro stomachus vulgaria temnit—The hungry stomach rarely scorns plain fare. *Hor.*

Jeshurun waxed fat and kicked. *Bible.* 25

Jess would have been an omnivorous reader of books had it not been her conviction that reading was idling. *George Eliot.*

Jest not with the eye, nor religion. *Pr.*

Jest so that it may not become earnest. *Sp. Pr.*

Jest with an ass, and he will flap you in the face with his tail. *Pr.*

Jest with your equals. *Dan. Pr.* 30

Jesters do oft prove prophets. *King Lear, v. 3.*

Jesting brings serious sorrows. *Pr.*

Jesting lies bring serious sorrows. *Pr.*

Jesting Pilate, asking, "What is truth ?" had not the smallest chance to ascertain it. He could not have known it had it had a god shown it to him. *Carlyle.*

Jesus Christ belonged to the true race of pro- 35 phets. He saw with open eye the mystery of the soul. Drawn by its severe harmony, ravished with its beauty, He lived in it, and had His being there. *Emerson.*

Jesus hominum salvator—Jesus the Saviour of men. *M.*

Jesus of Nazareth, and the life He lived and the death He died ;—through this, as through a miraculous window, the heaven of Martyr Heroism, the "divine depths of sorrow," of noble labour, and the unspeakable silent expanses of eternity, first in man's history disclose themselves. *Carlyle.*

Jesus of Nazareth was not poor, though He had not where to lay His head. (?)

Jesus speaks always from within, and in a degree that transcends all others. In that is the miracle. *Emerson.*

Jet d'eau—A jet of water. *Fr.* 40

Jeter le manche après la cognée—To throw the helve after the hatchet. *Fr. Pr.*

Jetzt giebt es keine Riesen mehr ; Gewalt / Ist für den Schwachen jederzeit ein Riese— There are no more any giants now ; for the weak, force is a giant at all times. *Schiller.*

Jeu d'enfant –Child's play. *Fr.*

Jeu de hazard—Game of chance. *Fr.*

Jeu de mains, jeu de vilain — Horse-play, or 45 practical joking, is vulgar. *Fr.*

Jeu de mots—Quibble ; pun. *Fr.*

Jeu de théâtre—Stage-trick ; clap-trap. *Fr.*

Jeune chirurgien, vieux médecin—A surgeon (should be) young, a physician old. *Fr. Pr.*

Jeune, et dans l'âge heureux qui méconnait la crainte—Young, and at that happy age which knows no fear. *Fr.*

Jeune, on conserve pour sa vieillesse ; vieux, on épargne pour la mort—In youth men save for old age ; in old age, they hoard for death. *La Bruyère.*

Jewels five words long, / That on the stretch'd forefinger of all time / Sparkle for ever. *Tennyson.*

Jo ædlere Blod, jo mindre Hovmod—The nobler the blood, the less the pride. *Dan. Pr.*

5 Jo argere Skalk, je bedre Lykke—The greater knave, the better luck. *Dan. Pr.*

Jo mere af Lov, jo mindre af Ret—The more by law, the less by right. *Dan. Pr.*

Joan is as good as my lady in the dark. *Pr.*

John Gilpin kiss'd his loving wife ; / O'erjoy'd was he to find / That, though on pleasure she was bent, / She had a frugal mind. *Cowper.*

Johnsons are rare ; yet, Boswells are perhaps still rarer. *Carlyle.*

10 Join hands with God to make a man to live. *George Herbert.*

Joindre les mains, c'est bien ; les ouvrir, c'est mieux—To fold the hands (in prayer) is well ; to open them (in charity) is better. *Fr. Pr.*

Joke at your leisure ; ye kenna wha may jibe yoursel'. *Sc. Pr.*

Joke with a slave, and he'll soon show his heels. *Ar. Pr.*

Jong rijs is te buigen, maar geen oude boomen —Young twigs will bend, but not old trees. *Dut. Pr.*

15 Jonge lui, domme lui ; oude lui, koude lui— Young folk, silly folk ; old folk, cold folk. *Dut. Pr.*

Jouk and let the jaw (or jaup) gae by, *i.e.*, duck and let the dash of dirty water pass over you. *Sc. Pr.*

Jour de fête—Holiday. *Fr.*

Jour de ma vie—The day of my life. *M.*

Jour gras—Flesh day. *Fr.*

20 Jour maigre—Fish day. *Fr.*

Journal pour rire—Comic journal. *Fr.*

Journalists are like little dogs ; whenever anything stirs they immediately begin to bark. *Schopenhauer.*

Journeys end in lovers' meeting, / Every wise man's son doth know. *Twelfth Night,* ii. 3.

Jove tonante cum populo agi non est fas— When Jove thunders there must be no parleying with the people. *Cic.*

25 Jovis omnia plena—All things are full of Jove, *i.e.*, of the deity. *Virg.*

Joy ? a moon by fits reflected in a swamp or watery bog. *Wordsworth.*

Joy and grief are never far apart. *Willmott.*

Joy and sorrow / Are to-day and to-morrow. *Pr.*

Joy descends gently upon us like the evening dew, and does not patter down like a hailstorm. *Jean Paul.*

30 Joy has this in common with pain, that it robs men of reason. *Platen.*

Joy, in a changeable subject, must necessarily change as the subject changeth. *S. Bern.*

Joy is a guest who generally comes uninvited. *Schopenhauer.*

Joy is a sunbeam between two clouds. *Mme. Deluzy.*

Joy is as a raiment fine, / Spun of magic threads divine ; / Which as you are in act to don, / The wearer and the robe are gone. *Sophocles.*

Joy is buyable—by forsaking all that a man 35 hath. *Ruskin.*

Joy is like the ague ; one good day between two bad ones. *Dan. Pr.*

Joy is more divine than sorrow ; for joy is bread, and sorrow is medicine. *Ward Beecher.*

Joy is the best of wine. *George Eliot.*

Joy is the mainspring in the whole round of universal Nature ; joy moves the wheels of the great timepiece of the world ; she it is that loosens flowers from their buds, suns from their firmaments, rolling spheres in distant space not seen by the glass of the astronomer. *Schiller.*

Joy is the sweet voice, joy the luminous cloud. 40 *Coleridge.*

Joy may elevate, ambition glorify, but sorrow alone can consecrate. *Horace Greely.*

Joy must have sorrow ; sorrow, joy. *Goethe.*

Joy never feasts so high as when the first course is of misery. *Suckling.*

Joy ruled the day and love the night. *Dryden.*

Joy shared is joy doubled. *Goethe.* 45

Joy surfeited turns to sorrow. *Pr.*

Joy wholly from without is false, precarious and short. Joy from within is like smelling the rose on the tree ; it is more sweet, and fair, and lasting. *Young.*

Joy's a subtle elf ; / I think man's happiest when he forgets himself. *Cyril Tourneur.*

Joys are for the gods ; / Man's common course of nature is distress ; / His joys are prodigies ; and like them too, / Portend approaching ill. The wise man starts / And trembles at the perils of a bliss. *Young.*

Joys are our wings, sorrows are our spurs. 50 *Jean Paul.*

Joys carried too far change into sorrows. *Justin Bertuch.*

Joy's recollection is no longer joy, while sorrow's memory is a sorrow still. *Byron.*

Joys shared with others are more enjoyed. *Pr.*

Joys, tender and true, / Yet all with wings. *Proctor.*

Joyful to live, yet not afraid to die. *Prior.* 55

Joyfulness (*Freudigkeit*) is the mother of all virtues. *Goethe.*

Jubilate Deo—Be joyful in the Lord.

Jucunda est memoria præteritorum malorum —The recollection of past miseries is pleasant. *Cic.*

Jucunda et idonea dicere vitæ—To describe what is pleasant and suited for life. *Hor.*

Jucunda rerum vicissitudo—A delightful change 60 of circumstances.

Jucundi acti labores—It is pleasant to think of labours that are past. *Cic.*

Jucundum et carum sterilis facit uxor amicum —A wife who has no children makes (to her husband's heirs) a dear and engaging friend. *Juv.*

Judex damnatur cum nocens absolvitur—The judge is found guilty when a criminal is acquitted. *Pub. Syr.*

Judex non potest esse testis in propria causa—A judge cannot be a witness in his own cause. *Coke.*

Judge before friendship, then confide till death, / Well for thy friend, but nobler far for thee. *Young.*

Judge me, ye powers; let fortune tempt or frown, I am prepared; my honour is my own. *Lansdowne.*

5 Judge not according to the appearance, but judge righteous judgment. *Jesus.*

Judge not of men and things at first sight. *Pr.*

Judge not, that ye be not judged. *Jesus.*

Judge not the Lord by feeble sense, / But trust Him for His grace. *Cowper.*

Judge not the play before the play is done; / Her plot has many changes; every day / Speaks a new scene; the last act crowns the play. *Quarles.*

10 Judge not the preacher. . . . Do not grudge / To pick out treasures from an earthen pot. / The worst speak something good; if all want sense, / God takes a text and preacheth patience. *George Herbert.*

Judge of the pleasure of the heart by the pleasure of the eye. *Bacon.*

Judge thou me by what I am, / So shalt thou find me fairest. *Tennyson.*

Judge thyself with a judgment of sincerity, and thou wilt judge others with a judgment of charity. *Mason.*

Judges and senates have been bought for gold; / Esteem and love were never to be sold. *Pope.*

15 Judges are but men, and are swayed, like other men, by vehement prejudices. *D. Dudley Field.*

Judges ought to be more learned than witty, more reverent than plausible, and more advised than confident. Above all things, integrity is their portion and proper virtue. *Bacon.*

Judgment for an evil thing is many times delayed some day or two, some century or two, but it is sure as life, it is sure as death. *Carlyle.*

Judgment is forced upon us by experience. *Johnson.*

Judgment is not a swift-growing plant; it requires time and culture to mature it. *H. Ballou.*

20 Judgment is turned away backward, and justice standeth afar off; for truth is fallen in the street, and equity cannot enter. *Bible.*

Judgment must sway the feelings and keep them in their right place, or harm will be done where good was intended. *Spurgeon.*

Judgments are prepared for scorners, and stripes for the back of fools. *Bible.*

Judgments that are made on the wrong side of the danger amount to no more than an affectation of skill, without either credit or effect. *L'Estrange.*

Judicandum est legibus, non exemplis—Judgment should be given according to law and not precedent. *L.*

25 Judicata res pro veritate accipitur—A matter that has been adjudged is received as true. *L.*

Judice te mercede caret, per seque petenda est / Externis virtus incomitata bonis—In your judgment virtue needs no reward, and is to be sought for her own sake, unaccompanied by external benefits. *Ovid.*

Judicia Dei sunt ita recondita ut quis illa scrutari nullatenus possit—The purposes of God are so abstruse that no one can possibly scrutinise them. *Cic.*

Judicio acri perpendere—To weigh with a keen judgment. *Lucret.*

Judicious persons will think all the less of us because of the ill-judged praises of our silly friends. *Spurgeon.*

30 Judicis est innocentiæ subvenire—It is the duty of the judge to support innocence. *Cic.*

Judicis est judicare secundum allegata et probata—It is the judge's duty to decide in accordance with what is alleged and proved. *L.*

Judicis est jus dicere non dare—It is the judge's duty to enunciate the law, not to make it. *L.*

Judicis officium est, ut res, ita tempora rerum quærere—It is the judge's duty to inquire into not only the facts, but the circumstances. *Ovid.*

Judicium a non suo judice datum nullius est momenti—Judgment given by a judge in a matter outside his jurisdiction is of no legal force. *L.*

35 Judicium Dei—The judgment of God (as by ordeal).

Judicium parium aut leges terræ—The judgment of our peers or the laws of the land. *L.*

Judicium subtile videndis artibus—A judgment nice in discriminating works of art. *Hor.*

Jugez un homme par ses questions, plutôt que par ses réponses—Judge of a man by his questions rather than his answers. *Fr.*

Jugulare mortuos—To stab the dead; to slay the slain. *Pr.*

40 Juncta juvant—Trivial things when united aid each other.

Junctæque Nymphis Gratiæ decentes — The beauteous Graces linked hand in hand with the nymphs. *Hor.*

Junge Faullenzer, alte Bettler—A young idler makes an old beggar. *Ger. Pr.*

Junger Spieler, alter Bettler—Young a gambler, old a beggar. *Ger. Pr.*

Jungere dextras—To join right hands; to shake hands. *Virg.*

45 Jungere equos Titan velocibus imperat Horis—Titan commands the swift-flying Hours to yoke the horses of the sun. *Ovid.*

Juniores ad labores — The younger men for labours, *i.e.*, the heavier burdens.

Jupiter est quodcunque vides, quocunque moveris—Whatever you see, wherever you turn, there is Jupiter (Deity). *Lucan.*

Jupiter in multos temeraria fulmina torquet, / Qui pœnam culpa non meruere pati—Jupiter hurls his reckless thunderbolts against many who have not guiltily deserved such punishment. *Ovid.*

Jupiter tonans—The thunderer Jove.

50 Jura negat sibi nata, nihil non arrogat armis—He says that laws were not framed for him; he claims everything by force of arms. *Hor.*

Jurado ha el vano de lo negro no hacer blanco—The bath has sworn not to wash the black man white. *Sp. Pr.*

Jurare in verba magistri—To swear by the words of the master.

Juravi lingua, mentem injuratam gero—I have sworn with my tongue, but I bear a mind unsworn. *Cic.*

Jure divino—By Divine right, or ordination of heaven.

Jure humano—By human law, or the will of the people.

5 Jure, non dono—By right, not by gift. *M.*

Jure repræsentationis—By right of representation. *L.*

Jurgia præcipue vino stimulata caveto—Above all, avoid quarrels excited by wine. *Ovid.*

Juris utriusque doctor—Doctor of both laws, civil and canon.

Juristen, böse Christen—Jurists are bad Christians. *Ger. Pr.*

10 Jus civile—The civil or Roman law.

Jus civile neque inflecti gratia, neque perfringi potentia, neque adulterari pecunia debet—The law ought neither to be warped by favour, nor broken through by power, nor corrupted by money. *Cic.*

Jus commune—The common or customary law.

Jus devolutum—A devolved right, specially of a presbytery in Scotland to present to a benefice, the patron having failed to do so. *L.*

Jus et norma loquendi—The law and rule of language.

15 Jus gentium—The law of nations, as the basis of their international relations.

Jus gladii—The right of the sword.

Jus in re—A real right. *L.*

Jus omnium in omnia, et consequenter bellum omnium in omnes—The right of all to everything, and therefore of all to make war on all. *Hobbes.*

Jus mariti—The right of a husband. *L.*

20 Jus postliminii—The law of recovery of forfeited rights. *L.*

Jus primogenituræ—The right of primogeniture. *L.*

Jus proprietatis—The right of property. *L.*

Jus regium—Royal right, or right of the Crown. *L.*

Jus sanguinis—The right of consanguinity, or blood. *L.*

25 Jus summum sæpe summa malitia est—Extreme law is often extreme wrong. *Ter.*

Jusqu'où les hommes ne se portent-ils point par l'intérêt de la religion, dont ils sont si peu persuadés, et qu'ils pratiquent si mal?—To what excesses are not men carried in the interest of a religion of which they have little or no faith, and which they so badly practise? *La Bruyère.*

Just a kind word and a yielding manner, and anger and complaining may be avoided. *Spurgeon.*

Just a path that is sure, / Thorny or not, / And a heart honest and pure / Keeping the path that is sure, / That be my lot. *Dr. W. Smith.*

Just and true are thy ways, thou King of saints. *Bible.*

30 Just are the ways of God, / And justifiable to men; / Unless there be who think not God at all. *Milton.*

Just as a moth gnaws a garment, so doth envy consume a man. *St. Chrysostom.*

Just as "dirt is something in its wrong place," so social evils are mainly wrong applications of right powers. *H. Willett.*

Just as gymnastic exercise is necessary to keep the body healthy, so is musical exercise necessary to keep the soul healthy; the proper nourishment of the intellect and passions can no more take place without music than the proper functions of the stomach and the blood without exercise. *Plato, interpreted by Ruskin.*

Just as the flint contains the spark, unknown to itself, which the steel alone can wake into life, so adversity often reveals to us hidden gems which prosperity or negligence would cause for ever to lie hid. *Billings.*

Just at the age 'twixt boy and youth, / When 35 thought is speech, and speech is truth. *Scott.*

Just enou', and nae mair, like Janet Howie's shearers' meat. *Sc. Pr.*

Just hatred of scoundrels, fixed, irreconcilable, inexorable enmity to the enemies of God; this, and not love of them, is the backbone of any religion whatsoever, let alone the Christian. *Carlyle.*

Just knows, and knows no more, her Bible true,/ A truth the brilliant Frenchman never knew. *Cowper.*

Just laws are no restraint upon the freedom of the good, for the good man desires nothing which a just law will interfere with. *Froude.*

Just plain duty to know, / Irksome or not, / 40 And truer and better to grow / In doing the duty I know, / That I have sought. *Dr. W. Smith.*

Justa razon engañar el engañador—It is fair to cheat the cheater. *Sp. Pr.*

Justæ causæ facilis est defensio—The defence of a just cause is easy.

Juste milieu—Right medium. *M. of the government of Louis Philippe.*

Justi ut sidera fulgent—The just shine as the stars. *M.*

Justice always is, whether we define or not. 45 Everything done, suffered, or proposed in Parliament, or out of it, is either just or unjust; either is accepted by the gods and eternal facts, or is rejected by them. *Carlyle.*

Justice and humanity have been fighting their way, like a thunderstorm, against the organised selfishness of human nature. God has given manhood but one clue to success —utter and exact justice. *Wendell Phillips.*

Justice and judgment are the habitation of God's throne. *Bible.*

Justice and reverence are the everlasting central law of this universe. *Carlyle.*

Justice and truth alone are capable of being "conserved" and preserved. *Carlyle.*

Justice and truth are two points of such ex- 50 quisite delicacy, that our coarse and blunted instruments will not touch them accurately. *Pascal.*

Justice consists in doing no injury to men; decency in giving no offence. *Cic.*

Justice consists mainly in the granting to every human being due aid in the development of such faculties as it possesses for action and enjoyment, . . . taking most pains with the best material. *Ruskin.*

Justice gives sentence many times / On one man for another's crimes. *Butler.*

Justice (such as Giotto represents her) has no bandage about her eyes, and weighs not with scales, but with her own hands ; and weighs, not merely the shares and remunerations of men, but the worth of them ; and finding them worth this or that, gives them what they deserve—death or honour. *Ruskin.*

Justice is always violent to the party offending, for every man is innocent in his own eyes. *Daniel Defoe.*

Justice is blind ; he knows nobody. *Dryden.*

5 Justice is conformity to what the Maker has seen good to make. *Carlyle.*

Justice is lame as well as blind among us. *Otway.*

Justice is love's order. *J. M. Gibbon.*

Justice is not postponed. A perfect equality adjusts its balance in all parts of life. *Emerson.*

Justice is the bread of the nation ; it is always hungry for it. *Chateaubriand.*

10 Justice is the first virtue of those who command, and stops the complaints of those who obey. *Diderot.*

Justice is the freedom of those who are equal. Injustice is the freedom of those who are unequal. *Jacobi.*

Justice is the great end of civil society. *Dudley Field.*

Justice is the keynote of the world, and all else is ever out of tune. *Theod. Parker.*

Justice is the whole secret of success in governments ; as absolutely essential to the training of an infant as to the control of a mighty nation. *Simms.*

15 Justice is truth in action. *Disraeli.*

Justice, like lightning, ever shall appear, / To few men's ruin, but to all men's fear. *Swetnam.*

Justice may be furnished out of fire, as far as her sword goes ; and courage may be all over a continual blaze. *Addison.*

Justice must and will be done. *Carlyle.*

Justice of thought and style, refinement in manners, good breeding, and politeness of every kind, can come only from the trial and experience of what is best. *Duncan.*

20 Justice pleaseth few in their own house. *Pr.*

Justice satisfies everybody, and justice alone. *Emerson.*

Justice, self-command, and true thought are our salvation. *Plato.*

Justice, the miracle-worker among men. *John Bright.*

Justice were cruel weakly to relent ; / From Mercy's self she got her sacred glaive : / Grace be to those who can and will repent ; / But penance long and dreary to the slave. *Thomson.*

25 Justice, while she winks at crimes, / Stumbles on innocence sometimes. *Butler.*

Justice without power is inefficient ; power without justice is tyranny. *Pascal.*

Justice without wisdom is impossible. *Froude.*

Justicia, mas no por mi casa—Justice by all means, but not in my own house. *Sp. Pr.*

Justissimus unus / Et servantissimus æqui—Just and observant of what is right, as no other is. *Virg.*

Justitia erga Deum religio dicitur ; erga parentes pietas—The discharge of our duty 30 towards God is called religion ; towards our parents, piety. *Cic.*

Justitia est constans et perpetua voluntas jus suum cuique tribuendi—Justice is the constant and unswerving desire to render to every man his own. *Just.*

Justitia est obtemperatio scriptis legibus—Justice is conformity to the written laws. *Cic.*

Justitia et pax—Justice and peace. *M.*

Justitia nihil expetit præmii—Justice seeks no reward. *Cic.*

Justitia non novit patrem nec matrem, solum 35 veritatem spectat—Justice knows neither father nor mother ; it regards the truth alone. *L.*

Justitia tanta vis est, ut ne illi quidem, qui maleficio et scelere pascuntur, possint sine ulla particula justitiæ vivere—There is such force in justice, that those even who live by crime and wickedness cannot live without some small portion of it among them. *Cic.*

Justitia virtutum regina—Justice is the queen of virtues. *M.*

Justitiæ partes sunt, non violare homines verecundiæ non offendere—It is the office of justice to injure no man ; of propriety, to offend none. *Cic.*

Justitiæ soror fides—Faith the sister of justice. *M.*

Justitiæ tenax—Tenacious of justice. *M.* 40

Justum bellum quibus necessarium, et pia arma quibus nulla nisi in armis relinquitur spes—War is just to those to whom it is necessary ; and to take up arms is a sacred duty with those who have no other hope left. *Livy.*

Justum et tenacem propositi virum, / Non civium ardor prava jubentium, / Non vultus instantis tyranni / Mente quatit solida—Not the rage of the citizens commanding wrongful measures, not the aspect of the threatening tyrant, can shake from his firm purpose the man who is just and resolute. *Hor.*

Justus propositi tenax—A just man steadfast to his purpose. *Hor.*

Justus ut palma florebit—The just shall flourish as a palm tree. *M.*

Juvante Deo—By the help of God. *M.* 45

Juvenile vitium regere non posse impetum—It is the failing of youth not to be able to restrain its own violence. *Sen.*

K.

Καδμεία νίκη—A Cadmæan victory, *i.e.*, one in which the conquerors suffer as much as the conquered.

Καὶ τοῦτο τοι τ᾽ ἀνδρεῖον, ἡ προμηθία—And forethought too is a manly virtue. *Euripides.*

Καιρὸν γνῶθι—Know your opportunity. *Pittachus, one of the seven sages of Greece.*

Κακὸν ἀναγκαῖον—A necessary evil. 50

Κακοῦ κόρακος κακὸν ᾠόν—From a bad crow a bad egg. *Pr.*

Kalendæ Græcæ—Never (*lit.* the Greek Kalends).

Kalte Hand, warmes Herz—A cold hand, a warm heart. *Ger. Pr.*

Kann auch der Sonne Kraft ein irrer Stern entwallen? / Wie könnte denn ein Mensch aus Gottes Liebe fallen?—Can a planet wander away even from the power of the sun? How then can man fall out of the love of God? *Rückert.*

Kann er mir mehr als seine Seele geben?— Can he give me more than his soul? *Lortzing.*

Kann ich Armeen aus der Erde stampfen? / Wächst mir ein Kornfeld in der flachen Hand?—Can I stamp armies out of the earth? Does a field of corn grow on the palm of my hand? *Schiller.*

Kannst dem Schicksal widerstehen, / Aber manchmal giebt es Schläge; / Will's nicht aus dem Wege gehen, / Ei! so geh' du aus dem Wege.—Thou canst withstand fate, but many a time it gives blows. Will it not go out of thy way, why then, go thou out of its. *Goethe.*

5 Kannst du nicht allen gefallen durch deine That und dein Kunstwerk : / Mach' es wenigen recht; vielen gefallen ist schlimm— If thou canst not by thy act or thy art please every one, be it thy endeavour to please a few ; to attempt to please many is naught. *Schiller.*

Kannst du nicht der Welt entsagen, / Winkt das Glück dir nimmer zu—If thou canst not renounce the world, the genius of happiness never salutes thee. *Prutz.*

Kannst du nicht schön empfinden, dir bleibt doch, vernünftig zu wollen, / Und als ein Geist zu thun, was du als Mensch nicht vermagst—If thou canst not have fineness of feelings, it is still open to thee to will what is reasonable, and to do as a spirit what thou canst not do as a man. *Goethe.*

Kartenspiel ist des Teufels Gebetsbuch—A pack of cards is the devil's prayer-book. *Ger. Pr.*

Κατ' ἐξοχήν — By way of excellence; pre-eminently.

10 Κατόπιν ἑορῆς—After the feast ; too late.

Κάτθανε καὶ Πάτροκλος, ὅπερ σέο πολλὸν ἀμείνων—Even Patroclus is dead, who was much better than thou. *Hom.*

Kauf bedarf hundert Augen ; Verkauf hat an einem genug—One who buys needs a hundred eyes ; one is enough for him who sells. *Ger. Pr.*

Kaufen ist wohlfeiler als Bitten — Buying is cheaper than asking. *Ger. Pr.*

Kaum ist ein Irrthum unterdrückt, so erhebt sich wieder ein anderer, den man schon in tiefe Vergessenheit begraben glaubte—No sooner is one error suppressed than another rises up again which was believed to be buried in eternal oblivion. *Oersted.*

15 Keep a gamester from dice, and a good student from his book. *Merry Wives,* iii. 1.

Keep a thing seven years, and you find a use for it. *Sc. Pr.*

Keep all thy native good, and naturalise / All foreign of that name ; but scorn their ill ; / Embrace their activeness, not vanities. *George Herbert.*

Keep always in your mind that, with due submission to Providence, a man of genius has been seldom ruined but by himself. *Johnson.*

Keep company with the humble, with the devout, and with the virtuous ; and confer with them of things that edify. *Thomas à Kempis.*

20 Keep cool, and you command everybody. *St. Just.*

Keep good company, and you shall be of the number. *Pr.*

Keep me in patience ; and, with ripened time, / Unfold the evil which is here wrapt up / In countenance. *Meas. for Meas.,* v. 1.

Keep my judgments and do them. *Bible.*

Keep not standing fix'd and rooted ; / Briskly venture, briskly roam ; / Head and hand, where'er thou foot it, / And stout heart are still at home. / In what land the sun does visit, / Brisk are we, whate'er betide ; / To give space for wandering is it / That the world was made so wide. *Goethe.*

Keep oot o' his company wha cracks o' his 25 cheatery, *i.e.*, boasts of cunning. *Sc. Pr.*

Keep some till more come. *Pr.*

Keep the bowels open, the head cool, and the feet warm, and a fig for the doctors. *Pr.*

Keep the common road and you are safe. *Pr.*

Keep the dogs near when thou suppest with the wolf. *Eastern Pr.*

Keep the doors of thy mouth from her that 30 lieth in thy bosom. *Bible.*

Keep the imagination sane ; that is one of the truest conditions of communion with heaven. *Hawthorne.*

Keep thy father's commandment, and forsake not the law of thy mother. *Bible.*

Keep thy foot when thou goest to the house of God, and be more ready to hear than to give the sacrifice of fools. *Bible.*

Keep thy heart with all diligence ; for out of it are the issues of life. *Bible.*

Keep thy mind always at its own disposal. 35 *Thomas à Kempis.*

Keep thyself perfectly still, however it may storm around thee. The more thou feelest thyself to be a man, so much the more dost thou resemble the gods. *Goethe.*

Keep to companions of your own rank. *Goldsmith.*

Keep to your subject close in all you say ; / Nor for a sounding sentence ever stray. *Dryden.*

Keep well while you are well. *Pr.*

Keep what you want, cast what you can, and 40 expect nothing back once lost or once given. *Ruskin.*

Keep you in the rear of your affection, / Out of the shot and danger of desire. *Ham.,* i. 3.

Keep your ain fish guts for your ain seamaws, *i.e.*, what you don t need yourselves for your own friends. *Sc. Pr.*

Keep your breath to cool your own crowdie (cold stirabout), *i.e.*, till you can use it to some purpose. *Sc. Pr.*

Keep your eyes wide open before marriage ; half-shut afterwards. *Amer. Pr.*

Keep your gab steeket (mouth shut) when ye 45 kenna (know not) your company. *Sc. Pr.*

Keep your hurry in your fist. *Irish Pr.*

Keep your idea while you can ; let it still circulate in your blood, and there fructify ; inarticulately inciting you to good activities ; giving to your whole spiritual life a ruddier health. And when the time comes for speaking it you will speak it all the more concisely and the more expressively ; and if such a time should never come, have you not already acted it and uttered it as no words can ? *Carlyle.*

Keep your mouth and keep your friend. *Dan. Pr.*

Keep your mouth shut and your een open. *Sc. Pr.*

Keep your shop, and your shop will keep you. *Pr.*

Keeping from falling is better than helping up. *Pr.*

5 Kein Baum fällt auf den ersten Schlag—No tree falls at the first blow. *Ger. Pr.*

Kein Bündniss ist mit dem Gezücht der Schlangen—No covenant is to be made with the serpent's brood. *Schiller.*

Kein Ding ist so schlecht, dass es nicht zu etwas nützen sollte—There's nothing so bad as not to be of service for something. *Ger. Pr.*

Kein grosser Mann muss eines natürlichen Todes sterben—No great man is ordained to die a natural death. *Goethe.*

Kein Kaiser hat dem Herzen vorzuschreiben —No emperor has power to dictate to the heart. *Schiller.*

10 Kein kluger Streiter hält den Feind gering —No prudent antagonist thinks light of his adversary. *Goethe.*

Kein Mann ist im Stande, den Werth eines Weibes zu fühlen, das nicht sich zu ehren weiss—No man is able to feel the worth of a woman who knows not how to respect herself. *Goethe.*

Kein Mensch ergründet sein Verhängniss— No man ever fathoms the mystery of his fate. *Bodenstedt.*

Kein Mensch kann so ganz Teufel sein, dass er / Des Lichtes letzten Strahl in sich ersticke —No man can be so entirely evil as to stifle the last ray of light in his soul. *Körner.*

Kein Mensch / Muss das Unmögliche erzwingen wollen—No man must seek to constrain the impossible. *Goethe.*

15 Kein Mensch muss müssen—No man is compelled to be compelled (*lit.*, must must). *Lessing.*

Kein schöner Ding ist wohl auf Erden / Als Frauenlieb, wem sie mag werden—There is no finer thing, I ween, on earth than woman's love to him who may be the object of it. *Luther.*

Kein Schurke ist so dumm, dass er nicht einen Grund für seine Niederträchtigkeit fände— No scoundrel is so stupid as not to find a reason for his vile conduct. *Körner.*

Kein Wunder, dass wir uns Alle mehr oder weniger im Mittelmässigen gefallen, weil es uns in Ruhe lässt; es giebt das behagliche Gefühl, als wenn man mit seines Gleichen umginge—No wonder we are all more or less content with the ordinary, for it leaves us undisturbed; we have the comfortable feeling of having only to deal with our like. *Goethe.*

Keine Gaukelkunst berückt / Das Flammenauge, das ins Innere blickt—By no juggler's art can you beguile the eye of fire which glances into the inner soul of things. *Goethe.*

20 Keine Kunst ist, Geister loszulassen; / Kunstgerecht sie binden, ist die Kunst—There is no art in freeing spirits; to bind them by art is art. *Rückert.*

Keine Probe ist gefährlich, zu der man Muth hat—No ordeal is hazardous which one has the courage to face. *Goethe.*

Keinen Glauben hat die Liebe / Als den Glauben an sich selber!—Love has no faith but faith in itself. *Bodenstedt.*

Keinen Reimer wird man finden, / Der sich nicht den besten hielte, / Keinen Fiedler, der nicht lieber / Eigne Melodien spielte— You will meet with no rhymer who does not think himself the best, no fiddler who does not prefer to play his own tunes. *Goethe.*

Keiner ist so klug, dass er nicht ein wenig Narrheit übrig hätte—No one is so wise as not to have a little folly to spare. *Ger. Pr.*

Ken when to spend, and when to spare, and 25 when to buy, and you'll ne'er be bare. *Sc. Pr.*

Ken yoursel', and your neebours winna mistak' you. *Sc. Pr.*

Kennst du das herrliche Gift der unbefriedigten Liebe? / Es versengt und erquickt, zehret am Mark und erneut's— Knowest thou the lordly poison of disappointed love? It withers up and quickens, consumes to the marrow and renews. *Goethe.*

Kennst du das Land, wo die Citronen blüh'n? —Know'st thou the land where the lemon-trees bloom? *Goethe.*

Keyholes are the occasions of more sin and wickedness than all the other holes in this world put together. *Sterne.*

Ki sokat markol, keveset szorit — He who 30 roves much takes firm root nowhere. *J. Arany.*

Kill, and thou shalt be killed, and they shall kill him who kills thee. *Sp. Pr.*

Kill no more than you can salt. *Dan. Pr.*

Kin or no kin, evil to him who has nothing. *It. Pr.*

Kind hearts are more than coronets, and simple faith than Norman blood. *Tennyson.*

Kind words are worth much and they cost 35 little. *Pr.*

Kind words don't wear the tongue. *Dan. Pr.*

Kind words prevent a good deal of that perverseness which rough and imperious usage often produces in generous minds. *Locke.*

Kindle not a fire that you cannot extinguish. *Pr.*

Kindliness decreases when money is in question. *Hausemann.*

Kindness by secret sympathy is tied; / For 40 noble souls in nature are allied. *Dryden.*

Kindness canna aye lie on ae side o' the hoose. *Sc. Pr.*

Kindness comes o' will; it canna be coft (bought). *Sc. Pr.*

Kindness has resistless charms; / All things else but weakly move; / Fiercest anger it disarms, / And clips the wings of flying love. *Rochester.*

Kindness, in act at least, is in our power, but fondness is not. *Johnson.*

Kindness in us is the honey that blunts the 45 sting of unkindness in another. *Landor.*

Kindness in women, not their beauteous looks, shall win my love. *Tam. the Shrew*, iv. 2.

Kindness is a good thing in itself. *Johnson.*

Kindness is lost upon an ungrateful man. *Pr.*

Kindness is the golden chain by which society is bound together. *Goethe.*

Kindness is virtue itself. *Lamartine.* 50

Kindness, nobler ever than revenge. *As You Like It*, iv. 3.

Kindness out of season destroys authority. *Saadi.*

Kindness overcomes a' dislike. *Sc. Pr.*

Kindness will creep whaur it canna gang. *Sc. Pr.*

5 Kindnesses, like grain, increase by sowing. *Pr.*

Kindnesses misplaced are nothing but a curse and a disservice. *Ennius.*

Kindred weaknesses induce friendship as often as kindred virtues. *Bovee.*

Kings alone are no more than single men. *Pr.*

Kings and bears aft worry their keepers. *Sc. Pr.*

10 Kings and their subjects, masters and slaves, find a common level in two places—at the foot of the cross and in the grave. *Colton.*

Kings are but the slaves of their position ; they dare not follow what their own hearts dictate. *Schiller.*

Kings are like stars ; they rise and set ; they have / The worship of the world, but no repose. *Shelley.*

Kings are said to have long arms ; but every man should have long arms, and should pluck his living, his instruments, his power, and his knowing from the sun, moon, and stars. *Emerson.*

Kings are willing to be aided, but not surpassed. *Grattan.*

15 Kings' caff (chaff) is better than ither folk's corn, *i.e.*, perquisites in his service are better than the wages others give. *Sc. Pr.*

Kings' cheese gangs half awa' in parings, *i.e.*, in the expense of collecting it. *Sc. Pr.*

Kings chiefly in this should imitate God ; their mercy should be above all their works. *Wm. Penn.*

Kings do with men as with pieces of money ; they give them what value they please, and we are obliged to receive them at their current, and not at their real value. *La Roche.*

Kings fight for empires, madmen for applause. *Dryden.*

20 Kings hae long lugs (ears). *Sc. Pr.*

Kings have long arms. *Pr.*

Kings may be bless'd, but Tam was glorious, / O'er a' the ills o' life victorious. *Burns.*

Kings ought to be kings in all things. *Adrian.*

Kings ought to shear, not skin their sheep. *Herrick.*

25 Kings' titles commonly begin by force, / Which time wears off, and mellows on to right. *Dryden.*

Kings who affect to be familiar with their companions make use of men as they do of oranges, which, when they have well sucked, they throw away. *Alva.*

Kings will be tyrants from policy, when subjects are rebels from principle. *Burke.*

Kings wish to be absolute, and they are sometimes told that the best way to become so is to make themselves beloved by the people ; but the maxim, unhappily, is laughed at in court. *Rousseau.*

Kiss (a) from my mother made me a painter. *Ben. West.*

Kisses are like grains of gold or silver found 30 upon the ground, of no value themselves, but precious as showing where a mine is near. *George Villiers.*

Kisses are pledges and incentives of love. *Cotton.*

Kisses are the messengers of love. *Dan. Pr.*

Kissing goes by favour. *Pr.*

Klein gewin brengt rijkdom in — Small gains bring riches in. *Dut. Pr.*

Kleine Diebe henkt man, grosse lässt man 35 laufen—We hang little thieves, but we let big ones off. *Ger. Pr.*

Kleine Diebe henkt man, vor grossen zieht man den Hut ab—We hang little thieves, and doff our hats to big ones. *Ger. Pr.*

Kleine Feinde und kleine Wunden sind nicht zu verachten—Paltry enemies and trifling wounds are not to be despised. *Ger. Pr.*

Kleine Geschenke erhalten die Freundschaft —Little gifts keep friendship green. *Montesquieu.*

Kleiner Profit und oft, ist besser wie grosser und selten—Slender profits and often are better than large ones and seldom. *Ger. Pr.*

Kluge Männer suchen wirthliche Frauen— 40 Prudent men woo thrifty women—*Ger. Pr.*

Knave ! because thou strikest as a knight ; / Being but knave, I hate thee all the more. *Tennyson.*

Knavery is supple, and can bend, but honesty is firm and upright, and yields not. *Collier.*

Knavery may serve for a turn, but honesty is best in the long-run. *Pr.*

Knavery's plain face is never seen till used. *Othello*, ii. 1.

Knaves easily believe that others are like 45 themselves ; they can hardly be deceived, and they do not deceive others for any length of time. *La Bruyère.*

Knaves starve not in the land of fools. *Churchill.*

Knaves will thrive when honest plainness knows not how to live. *Shirley.*

Kneeling ne'er spoiled silk stockings ; quit thy state ; / All equal are within the church's gate. *George Herbert.*

Know ere thou hint, and then thou may'st slack : / If thou hint ere thou know, then it is too late. *Pr.*

Know, fools only trade by the eye. *Quarles.* 50

Know from the bounteous heaven all riches flow ; / And what man gives, the gods by man bestow. *Pope.*

Know how sublime a thing it is to suffer and be strong. *Longfellow.*

Know, Nature's children all divide her care ; / The fur that warms a monarch warm'd a bear. *Pope.*

Know of a truth that only the time-shadows have perished or are perishable ; that the real being of whatever was, and whatever is, and whatever will be, is even now and for ever. *Carlyle.*

Know that nothing can so foolish be / As 55 empty boldness. *George Herbert.*

Know that the loudest roar of the million is not fame ; that the wind-bag, are ye mad enough to mount it, will burst, or be shot through with arrows, and your bones too shall act as scarecrows. *Carlyle.*

Know then this truth (enough for man to know), / Virtue alone is happiness below. *Pope.*

Know then thyself; presume not God to scan; / The proper study of mankind is man. *Pope.*

Know thy thought—believe it—front heaven and earth with it, in whatsoever words nature and art have made readiest for thee. *Carlyle.*

Know thyself, for through thyself only thou canst know God. *Ruskin.*

5 Know whom to honour, and emulate, and follow; know whom to dishonour and avoid, and coerce under hatches, as a foul rebellious thing—this is all the Law and all the Prophets. *Carlyle.*

Know ye not that the friendship of the world is enmity with God? *St. James.*

Know ye not who would be free themselves must strike the blow? / By their right arms the conquest must be wrought. *Byron.*

Know ye the land where the cypress and myrtle / Are emblems of deeds that are done in their clime; / Where the rage of the vulture, the love of the turtle, / Now melt into sorrow, now madden to crime? *Byron.*

Knowing I loved my books, he furnished me / From mine own library with volumes that / I prize above my dukedom. *Tempest, i. 2.*

10 Knowing is seeing. *Locke.*

Know'st thou yesterday, its aim and reason; / Work'st thou well to-day for worthy things; / Calmly wait the morrow's hidden season; / Need'st not fear what hap soe'er it brings. *Carlyle, after Goethe.*

Knowledge advances by steps, and not by leaps. *Macaulay.*

Knowledge always desires increase; it is like fire, which must first be kindled by some external agent, but which will afterwards propagate itself. *Johnson.*

Knowledge and timber should not be much used until they are seasoned. *Holmes.*

15 Knowledge and Wisdom, far from being one, / Have ofttimes no connection. Knowledge dwells / In heads replete with thoughts of other men; / Wisdom, in minds attentive to their own. *Cowper.*

Knowledge becomes evil if the aim be not virtuous. *Plato.*

Knowledge being to be had only of visible and certain truth, error is not a fault of our knowledge, but a mistake of our judgment, giving assent to that which is not true. *Locke.*

Knowledge by rote is no knowledge, it is only a retention of what has been intrusted to the memory. *Montaigne.*

Knowledge by suffering entereth, / And life is perfected by death. *E. B. Browning.*

20 Knowledge comes, but wisdom lingers. *Tennyson.*

Knowledge comes from experience alone. *Carlyle.*

Knowledge conquered by labour becomes a possession — a property entirely our own. *S. Smiles.*

Knowledge descries alone, wisdom applies; / That makes some fools, this maketh none but wise. *Quarles.*

Knowledge exists to be imparted. *Emerson.*

Knowledge has its penalties and pains as 25 well as its prizes. *Bulwer Lytton.*

Knowledge hath a bewildering tongue, and she will stoop and lead you to the stars, and witch you with her mysteries, till gold is a forgotten dross, and power and fame toys of an hour, and woman's careless love light as the breath that breaks it. *Willis.*

Knowledge humbleth the great man, astonisheth the common man, and puffeth up the little man. *Pr.*

Knowledge in music is in the thinking, and not in memorising. *H. E. Holt.*

Knowledge introduceth man to acquaintance; and, as the humble stream to the ocean, so doth it conduct him into the hard-acquired presence of the prince, whence fortune floweth. *Hitopadesa.*

Knowledge is a perennial spring of wealth, 30 . . . and of itself is riches. *Saadi.*

Knowledge is a retreat and shelter for us in advanced age; and if we do not plant it when young, it will give us no shade when we grow old. *Chesterfield.*

Knowledge is as food, and needs no less / Her temp'rance over appetite, to know / In measure what the mind may well contain, / Oppresses else with surfeit, and soon turns / Wisdom to folly, as nourishment to wind. *Milton.*

Knowledge is boundless; human capacity limited. *Chamfort.*

Knowledge is easy unto him that understandeth. *Bible.*

Knowledge is escape from one s self. (?) 35

Knowledge is essential to freedom. *Channing.*

Knowledge is just like the sun in the heavens, inviting us to noble deeds and lighting our path. *M. Harvey.*

Knowledge is like current coin. A man may have some right to be proud of possessing it, (only) if he has worked for the gold of it, and assayed it, and stamped it, so that it may be received of all men as true, or earned it fairly, being already assayed. *Ruskin.*

Knowledge is more than equivalent to force. *Bacon.*

Knowledge is most surely engraved on brains 40 well prepared for it. *Rousseau.*

Knowledge is no burden. *Pr.*

Knowledge is not an inert and passive principle, which comes to us whether we will or no; but it must be sought before it can be won; it is the product of great labour, and therefore of great sacrifice. *Buckle.*

Knowledge is not education, and can neither make us happy nor rich. *Ruskin.*

Knowledge is not happiness, and science but an exchange of ignorance for that which is another kind of ignorance. *Byron.*

Knowledge is of things we see; / And yet we 45 trust it comes from thee, / A beam in darkness; let it grow. *Tennyson.*

Knowledge is power. *Bacon.*

Knowledge is proud that he has learn'd so much; / Wisdom is humble that he knows no more. *Cowper.*

Knowledge is that which, next to virtue, truly and essentially raises one man above another *Addison.*

Knowledge is the consequence of time, and multitude of days are fittest to teach wisdom. *Jeremy Collier.*

Knowledge is the excellency of man, whereby he is usually differenced from the brute. *Swinnock.*

Knowledge is the knowing that we cannot know. *Emerson.*

Knowledge is the material with which genius builds her fabrics. *Bryant.*

5 Knowledge is the parent of love; wisdom, love itself. *Hare.*

Knowledge is the treasure, but judgment the treasurer, of a wise man. *Wm. Penn.*

Knowledge is the treasure of the mind, but discretion is the key to it, without which it is useless. The practical part of wisdom is the best. *Feltham.*

Knowledge is to one a goddess, to another only an excellent cow. *Schiller.*

Knowledge, love, power, constitute the complete life. *Amiel.*

10 Knowledge may not be as a courtesan for pleasure and vanity only; or as a bondwoman, to acquire and gain for her master's use; but as a spouse, for generation, fruit, and comfort. *Bacon.*

Knowledge of my way is a good part of my journey. *A. Warwick.*

Knowledge of our duties is the most useful part of philosophy. *Whately.*

Knowledge of the world is dearly bought at the price of moral purity. *E. Wigglesworth.*

Knowledge perverted is knowledge no longer. *Bulwer Lytton.*

15 Knowledge produceth humility; from humility proceedeth worthiness; from worthiness riches are acquired; from riches religion, and thence happiness. *Hitopadesa.*

Knowledge puffeth up, but charity edifieth. *St. Paul.*

Knowledge shall vanish away. *St. Paul.*

Knowledge that a thing is false is a truth. *Schopenhauer.*

Knowledge that terminates in curiosity and speculation is inferior to that which is useful, and of all useful knowledge that is the most so which consists in a due care and just notion of ourselves. *St. Bernard.*

20 Knowledge, the wing wherewith we fly to heaven. *2 Hen. VI., iv. 7.*

Knowledge to their eyes her ample page, / Rich with the spoils of time, did ne'er unroll; / Chill penury repress'd their noble rage, / And froze the genial current of the soul. *Gray.*

Knowledge, when wisdom is too weak to guide her, / Is like a headstrong horse that throws the rider. *Quarles.*

Knowledge without education is but armed injustice. *Hor.*

Knowledge without integrity is dangerous and dreadful. *Johnson.*

25 Knowledge without justice ought to be called cunning rather than wisdom. *Plato.*

Knowledge without practice is like a glass eye, all for show, and nothing for use. *Swinnock.*

Known unto God are all His works from the beginning of the world. *St. Paul.*

Komm jedem, wie er sei, mit edeln Sinn entgegen, / Vielleicht wird dann in ihm, was edel ist, sich regen—Accost whoever you may meet with noble feeling; perhaps what is noble will begin to stir in him. *J. Trojan.*

Kraft erwart' ich vom Mann, des Gesetzes Würde behaupt' er; / Aber durch Anmuth allein herrschet und herrsche das Weib—I look for power in the man; he affirms the dignity of the law; but the woman rules, and will continue to rule, through grace alone. *Schiller.*

Krankes Fleisch, kranker Geist—Sickly in body, 30 sickly in mind. *Ger. Pr.*

Krieg bis aufs Messer—War to the knife. *Ger.*

Krieg ist ewig zwischen List und Argwohn, / Nur zwischen Glauben und Vertraun ist Friede—War is unending between cunning and mistrust; only between faith and trust is there peace. *Schiller.*

Κρεῖσσον τοι σοφίη καὶ μεγαλῆς ἀρετῆς—Wisdom is better than even great valour. *Theognis.*

Κρείτων ἡ πρόνοια τῆς μεταμελείας—Thought beforehand is better than regret afterwards. *Dionysius of Hal.*

Κτῆμα ἐς ἀεί—A possession for ever. *Thucy- 35 dides.*

Κῦδος—Fame; glory. *Gr.*

Kühl bis an's Herz hinan—Cool to the very heart. *Goethe.*

Κυνὸς ὄμματ' ἔχων—Having dog's eyes. *Hom.*

Kunst ist die rechte Hand der Natur. Diese hat nur Geschöpfe, jene hat Menschen gemacht—Art is the right hand of Nature. The latter has made only creatures, the former has made men. *Schiller.*

Kurz ist der Lieb' Entzücken, doch ewig ist 40 die Pein—Short is the rapture of love, but eternal is the pain. *S. Rossini.*

Kurz ist der Schmerz, und ewig ist die Freude! —Short is the pain and eternal the joy! *Schiller.*

Kyrie eleeison—Lord, have mercy upon us.

Kythe (appear) in your ain colours, that folk may ken ye. *Sc. Pr.*

L.

L'absence est à l'amour ce qu'est au feu le vent; / Il éteint le petit, il allume le grand —Absence is to love what wind is to a fire; it quenches the small flame and quickens the large. *Bussy.*

L'adresse surmonte la force—Skill surpasses 45 strength. *Fr. Pr.*

L'adversité est sans doute un grand maître; mais ce maître se fait payer cher ses leçons, et souvent le profit qu'on en retire ne vaut pas le prix qu'elles ont coûté—Adversity is without doubt a great teacher, but this teacher makes us pay dear for his instructions, and often the profit we derive from them is not worth the price we are required to pay. *Rousseau.*

L'adversité fait l'homme, et le bonheur les monstres—Men are formed in adversity, monsters in prosperity. *Fr.*

L'affaire s'achemine—The affair is going forward. *Fr.*

L'âge d'or était l'âge où l'or ne regnait pas—The golden age was the age in which gold did not reign. *Lézay de Marnézia.*

L'âge d'or, qu'une aveugle tradition a placé jusqu'ici dans le passé, est devant nous—The golden age, which a blind tradition has hitherto placed behind us, is before us. *St. Simon.*

L'aigle d'une maison est un sot dans une autre—The eagle of one house is a fool in another. *Gresset.*

L'aimable siècle où l'homme dit à l'homme, / Soyons frères, ou je t'assomme—That loving time when one man said to another, "Let us be brothers, or I will brain you." *Le Brun, of French Revolution times.*

5 L'Allégorie habite un palais diaphane—Allegory dwells in a transparent palace. *Lemierre.*

L'Allegro—The merry Muse.

L'âme n'a pas de secret que la conduite ne révèle—The heart has no secret which our conduct does not reveal. *Fr. Pr.*

L'âme qui n'a point de but établi, elle se perd ; c'est n'être en aucun bien, qu'être par tout —The soul which has no fixed purpose in life is lost ; to be everywhere is to be nowhere. *Montaigne.*

L'ami du genre humain n'est point du tout mon fait—He who is the friend of every one has no interest for me. *Molière.*

10 L'amitié est l'amour sans ailes—Friendship is love without wings, *i.e.,* is steadfast. *Fr. Pr.*

L'amour apprend aux ânes à danser—Love teaches even asses to dance. *Fr. Pr.*

L'amour de la justice n'est, en la plus part des hommes, que la crainte de souffrir l'injustice —The love of justice is, in the majority of mankind, nothing else than the fear of suffering injustice. *La Roche.*

L'amour est le roman du cœur, / Et le plaisir en est l'histoire—Love is the heart's romance, pleasure is its history. *M. de Bièvre.*

L'amour est un vrai recommenceur—Love is a true renewer. *Bussy-Rabutin.*

15 L'amour est une passion qui vient souvent sans savoir comment, et qui s'en va aussi de même—Love is a passion which comes often we know not how, and which goes also in like manner. *Fr.*

L'amour et la fumée ne peuvent se cacher— Love and smoke cannot be concealed. *Fr. Pr.*

L'amour-propre est le plus grand de tous les flatteurs—Self-love is the greatest of all flatterers. *La Roche.*

L'amour-propre est un ballon gonflé de vent, dont il sort des tempêtes quand on lui fait une piqûre—Self-love is a balloon blown up with wind, from which tempests of passion issue as soon as it is pricked into. *Voltaire.*

L'amour-propre offensé ne pardonne jamais— Self-love offended never forgives. *Vigée.*

20 L'amour soumet la terre, assujettit les cieux, / Les rois sont à ses pieds, il gouverne les dieux—Love rules the earth, subjects the heavens ; kings are at his feet ; he controls the gods. *Corn.*

L'anglais a les préjugés de l'orgueil, et les français ceux de la vanité—The English are predisposed to pride, the French to vanity. *Rousseau.*

L'anime triste di coloro / Che visser senza infamia, e senza lodo—The sad souls of those who lived without blame and without praise. *Dante.*

L'animal delle lunghe orecchie, dopo aver beveto dà calci al secchio—The ass (*lit.* long-eared animal), after having drunk, gives a kick to the bucket. *It. Pr.*

L'apparente facilité d'apprendre est cause de la perte des enfants—The apparent facility of learning is a reason why children are lost. *Rousseau.*

L'appétit vient en mangeant—Appetite comes 25 with eating, *i.e.,* the more one has, the more one would have. *Rabelais.*

L'arbre de la liberté ne croît qu'arrosé par le sang des tyrans—The tree of liberty grows only when watered by the blood of tyrants. *Barere.*

L'arco si rompe se sta troppo teso—The bow when overstrained will break. *It. Pr.*

L'argent est un bon passe-partout—Money is a good pass-key or passport. *Fr. Pr.*

L'argent est un bon serviteur et un méchant maître—Money is a good servant, but a bad master. *Fr. Pr.*

L'art de vaincre est celui de mépriser la mort 30 —The art of conquering is that of despising death. *Mme. de Sivry.*

L'asino che ha fame mangia d'ogni strame— The ass that is hungry will eat any kind of litter. *It. Pr.*

L'aspettar del malo è mal peggiore / Forse che non parebbe il mal presente—The anticipation of evil is perhaps worse than the evil is felt to be when it comes. *Tasso.*

L'atrocité des lois en empêche l'exécution— The severity of the laws prevents the execution of them. *Montesquieu.*

L'avare est comme ces amans qu'un excès d'amour empêche de jouir—The miser is like a lover the excess of whose passion bars the enjoyment of it. *Fr.*

L'avenir—The future. *Fr.* 35

L'élévation est au merité, ce que la parure est aux belles personnes—Exalted station is to merit what the ornament of dress is to handsome persons. *Fr.*

L'éloquence a fleuri le plus à Rome lorsque les affaires ont été en plus mauvais état—Eloquence flourished most in Rome when its affairs were in the worst condition. *Montaigne.*

"L'empire, c'est la paix"—"The empire, that is peace." *Napoleon III.*

L'empire des lettres—The republic of letters. *Fr.*

L'ennui du beau, amène le goût du singulier 40 —When we tire of the beautiful it induces a taste for singularity. *Fr.*

L'ennui naquit un jour de l'uniformité—Ennui was born one day of uniformity. *Lamotte-Houdard.*

L'enseigne fait la chalandise—A good sign attracts custom. *La Fontaine.*

L'esclave n'a qu'un maître ; l'ambitieux en a autant qu'il y a de gens utiles à sa fortune— A slave has but one master ; the ambitious man has as many as there are people who help him to his fortune. *La Bruyère.*

L'espérance est le songe d'un homme éveillé— Hope is the dream of a man awake. *Fr. Pr.*

L'esprit a son ordre, qui est par principes et 45 démonstrations, le cœur en a un autre—The mind has its way of proceeding by principles and demonstrations ; the heart has a different method. *Pascal.*

L'esprit de la conversation consiste bien moins à en montrer beaucoup qu'à en faire trouver aux autres—Wit in conversation consists much less in displaying much of it than in stimulating it in others. *La Bruyère.*

L'esprit de la plupart des femmes sert plus à fortifier leur folie que leur raison—The wit of most women goes more to strengthen their folly than their reason. *La Roche.*

L'esprit de modération doit être celui du législateur—A legislator should be animated by the spirit of moderation. *Montesquieu.*

L'esprit est le dieu des instants, le génie est le dieu des âges—Wit is the god of the moments, but genius is the god of the ages. *Fr.*

5 L'esprit est toujours la dupe du cœur—The mind is always the dupe of the heart. *La Roche.*

L'esprit est une plante dont on ne sauroit arrêter la végétation sans la faire périr—Wit is a plant of which you cannot arrest the development without destroying it. *Fr. Pr.*

L'esprit qu'on veut avoir, gâte celui qu'on a—The wit which we strive to possess spoils that which we naturally possess. *Gresset.*

L'esprit ressemble aux coquettes; ceux qui courent après lui sont ceux qu'il favorise le moins—Wit is like a coquette; those who run after it are the least favoured. *Fr.*

"L'état, c'est moi"—"The state, I am the state." *Louis XIV.*

10 L'état doit avoir aussi des entrailles—The state as well as the individual ought to have a feeling heart. *Cousin.*

"L'Europe m'ennuie"—"I am tired of Europe." *Napoleon, when he took the field against Russia.*

L'exactitude est la politesse des rois—Punctuality is the politeness of kings. *Max. of Louis XVIII.*

L'excellence et la grandeur d'une âme brille et éclate d'avantage dans le mepris de richesse—The excellence and greatness of a soul are most conspicuously and strikingly displayed in the contempt of riches. *Fr.*

L'expérience de beaucoup d'opinions donne à l'esprit beaucoup de flexibilité, et l'affermit dans celles qu'il croit les meilleures—Acquaintance with a wide range of opinion imparts to the mind great flexibility, and confirms it in those which it believes to be the best. *Fr.*

15 L'imitazione del male supera sempre l'essempio; come per il contrario l'imitazione del bene è sempre inferiore—He who imitates what is bad always goes beyond his model, while he, on the contrary, who imitates what is good always comes short of it. *Guicciardini.*

L'impromptu est justement la pierre de touche de l'esprit—Impromptu is precisely the touchstone of wit. *Molière.*

L'habit ne fait point le moine—It is not the garb he wears that makes the monk. *Pascal.*

L'heure est à Dieu, l'espérance à tous—The hour appertains to God, hope to all. *Fr.*

L'histoire n'est que le tableau des crimes et des malheurs—History is but a picture of crimes and misfortunes. *Voltaire.*

20 L'homme absurde est celui qui ne change jamais—The absurd man is he who never changes. *Barthélemy.*

L'homme est de glace aux vérités, / Il est de feu pour les mensonges—Man is as ice to what is true, and as fire to falsehood. *La Fontaine.*

L'homme est sourd à ses maux tant qu'à ses intérêts quand il s'agit de ses plaisirs—Men are regardless of their misfortunes as well as their interests when either are in competition with their pleasures. *Fr.*

L'homme est toujours l'enfant, et l'enfant toujours l'homme—The man is always the child, and the child is always the man. *Fr.*

L'homme est un apprenti, la douleur est son maître; / Et nul ne se connaît, tant qu'il n'a pas souffert—Man is an apprentice, pain is his master; and none knows himself so long as he has not suffered. *A. de Musset.*

L'homme n'est jamais moins misérable que 25 quand il paraît dépourvu de tout—Man is never less miserable than when he appears destitute of everything. *Fr.*

L'homme n'est ni ange ni bête, et le malheur veut que qui veut faire l'ange fait la bête—Man is neither an angel nor a brute, but, as the evil genius will have it, he who aspires to be an angel degenerates into the brute. *Pascal.*

L'homme n'est qu'un roseau, le plus faible de la nature, mais c'est un roseau pensant—Man is only a reed, the weakest in nature, but he is a reed that thinks. *Pascal*

L'homme nécessaire—The right man. *Fr.*

L'homme propose et Dieu dispose—Man proposes and God disposes. *Fr. Pr.*

L'homme vraiment libre ne veut que ce qu'il 30 peut, et fait ce qu'il lui plaît—The man who is truly free wills only what he can, and does only what pleases him. *Rousseau.*

L'honneur acquis est caution de celui qu'on doit acquérir—Honour acquired is an earnest of that which is to follow. *La Roche.*

L'hypocrisie est un hommage que le vice rend à la vertu—Hypocrisy is the homage which vice renders to virtue. *La Roche.*

L'imagination est la folle du logis—Imagination is the madcap of the brain (*lit.* the merryandrew of the dwelling). *Malebranche.*

L'imagination galope, le jugement ne va que le pas—The imagination gallops, the judgment merely walks. *Fr.*

L'impossibilité où nous sommes de prouver 35 que Dieu n'est pas, nous découvre son existence—The impossibility which we feel of proving that there is not a God reveals to us His existence. *Fr.*

L'incrédulité est une croyance, une religion très exigeante, qui a ses dogmes, sa liturgie, ses pratiques, ses rites . . . son intolerance, ses superstitions—Incredulity is a belief, a religion highly peremptory, which has its dogmas, its liturgy, its practices, its rites, . . . its intolerance, and its superstitions. *Alphonse Karr.*

L'incroyable—The incredible; past belief.

L'industrie des hommes s'épuise à briguer les charges, il ne leur en reste plus pour en remplir les devoirs—The energies of men are so exhausted in canvassing for places, that they have none left to perform the duties which belong to them. *Fr.*

L'influence féminine devient l'auxiliaire indispensable de tout pouvoir spirituel, comme le moyen âge l'a tant montré—The influence of woman proves to be the indispensable auxiliary of all spiritual power, as the Middle Ages have so abundantly testified. *(?)*

L'ingegno, che spopola e che spalea / E l'asino d'un pubblico insolente, / Che mai lo pasce e sempre lo cavalca—The genius which devastates and destroys is the ass of the insolent public, who always mount and ride it, but never feed it. *Giuseppe Giusti.*

L'injustice à la fin produit l'indépendance—Independence in the end is the fruit of injustice. *Voltaire.*

L'institut des Jésuites est une épée, dont la poignée est à Rome et la pointe partout—The order of the Jesuits is a sword, the handle of which is at Rome and the point everywhere. *Dupin.*

L'Italia farà da se—Italy will do it by herself. *M. of the Italian Revolution of* 1849.

5 L'occasion fait le larron—Opportunity makes the thief. *Fr. Pr.*

L'on espère de vieillir et l'on craint la vieillesse ; c'est à dire l'on aime la vie et l'on fuit la mort—We hope to grow old, yet we dread old age ; that is to say, we love life and shrink from death. *La Bruyère.*

L'on ne peut aller loin dans l'amitié, si l'on n'est pas disposé se pardonner, les uns aux autres, les petits défauts—Friendship cannot go far if we are not disposed mutually to forgive each other's venial faults. *La Bruyère.*

L'on ne vaut dans ce monde que ce que l'on veut valoir—We are valued in this world at the rate at which we desire to be valued. *La Bruyère.*

L'on se repent rarement de parler peu, très souvent de trop parler : maxime usée et triviale que tout le monde sait, et que tout le monde ne pratique pas—We rarely repent of having spoken too little, very often of having spoken too much : a maxim this which is old and trivial, and which every one knows, but which every one does not practise. *La Bruyère.*

10 L'or est une chimère—Gold is but a chimæra, or fabulous monster. *S. Meyerbeer.*

L'orateur cherche par son discours un archevêché, l'apôtre fait des conversions ; il mérite de trouver ce que l'autre cherche—The preacher aims by his eloquence at an archbishopric, the apostle makes converts ; he deserves to get what the other aims at. *La Bruyère.*

L'oreille est le chemin du cœur—The ear is the road to the heart. *Voltaire.*

L'orgueil ne veut pas devoir, et l'amour-propre ne veut pas payer—Pride wishes not to owe, and self-love does not wish to pay. *La Roche.*

L'ozio é il padre di tutti i vizi—Idleness is the parent of all the vices. *It. Pr.*

15 L'ultima che si perde è la speranza—Hope is the last thing we lose. *It. Pr.*

L'une des marques de la médiocrité d'esprit est de toujours conter—One of the marks of a mediocrity of intellect is to be given to storytelling. *La Bruyère.*

L'union fait la force—Union is strength. *M.*

L'usage fréquent des finesses est toujours l'effet d'une grande incapacité, et la marque d'un petit esprit—The frequent recourse to finesse is always the effect of incapacity and the mark of a small mind. *Fr.*

La beauté de l'esprit donne de l'admiration, celle de l'âme donne de l'estime, et celle du corps de l'amour—The charms of wit excite admiration, those of the soul esteem, and those of the body love. *Fr.*

La beauté sans vertu est une fleur sans par- 20 fum—Beauty without virtue is a flower without fragrance. *Fr. Pr*

La biblioteca è l'nutrimento dell' anima—Books are nourishment to the mind. *It. Pr.*

La bonne fortune et la mauvaise sont nécessaire à l'nomme pour le rendre habile—Good fortune and bad are alike necessary to man in order to develop his capability. *Fr.*

La bride sur le cou—With loose reins ; at full speed. *Fr.*

La buena vida padre y madre olvida—Prosperity forgets father and mother. *Sp. Pr.*

La carrière des lettres est plus épineuse que 25 celle de la fortune. Si vous avez le malheur d'être médiocre, voilà des remords pour la vie ; si vous réussissiez, voilà des ennemis ; vous marchez sur le bord d'un abîme entre le mépris et la haine—A literary career is a more thorny path than that which leads to fortune. If you have the misfortune not to rise above mediocrity, you feel mortified for life ; and if you are successful, a host of enemies spring up against you. Thus you find yourself on the brink of an abyss between contempt and hatred. *Voltaire.*

La carrière ouverte aux talents—The course is open to men of talent—the tools to the man that can handle them (of which truth Napoleon has been described as the great preacher). *Fr.*

La Charte sera désormais une vérité—The Charter shall be henceforward a reality. *Louis Philippe.*

La clémence des princes n'est souvent qu'une politique pour gagner l'affection des peuples—The clemency of princes is often only a political manœuvre to gain the affections of their subjects. *La Roche.*

La colpa seguira la parte offensa / In grido, como suol—Blame, as is wont, wreaks its rage on those who suffer wrong. *Dante.*

La condition par excellence de la vie, de la 30 santé et de la force chez l'être organisé, est l'action. C'est par l'action qu'il developpe ses facultés, qu'il en augmente l'énergie, et qu'il atteint la plénitude de sa destinée—The chief condition on which depends the life, health, and vigour of an organised being is action. It is by action that it develops its faculties, that it increases its energy, and that it attains to the fulfilment of its destiny. *Proudhon.*

La confiance fournit plus à la conversation que l'esprit—Confidence contributes more to conversation than wit. *La Roche.*

La conscience est la voix de l'âme, les passions sont la voix du corps—Conscience is the voice of the soul, the passions are the voice of the body. *Rousseau.*

La constance des sages n'est que l'art de renfermer leur agitation dans leur cœur—The constancy of the wise is nothing but the art of shutting up whatever might disturb them within themselves. *La Roche.*

La corruption de chaque gouvernement commence presque toujours par celle des principes—The decay of every government almost always dates from the decay of the principles on which it is founded. *Montesquieu.*

La cour est comme un édifice bâti de marbre ; 35 je veux dire qu'elle est composée d'hommes fort durs mais fort polis—The court is like an edifice built of marble ; I mean, it is composed of men very hard but very polished. *La Bruyère.*

La cour ne rend pas content, elle empêche qu'on ne le soit ailleurs—The court does not make a man happy, and it prevents him from being so elsewhere. *La Bruyère.*

La crainte suit le crime, et c'est son châtiment —Fear haunts crime, and this is its punishment. *Voltaire.*

La crédulité est plutôt une erreur qu'une faute, et les plus de gens de bien en sont susceptibles —Credulity is rather an error than a fault, and the worthiest people are most subject to it. *Fr.*

La criaillerie ordinaire fait qu'on s'y accoutume et chacun la méprise—By continually scolding your inferiors, they at length become accustomed to it, and despise your reproof. *Fr.*

5 La critique est aisée, et l'art est difficile—Criticism is easy, and art is difficult. *Destouches.*

La décence est le teint naturel de la vertu, et le fard du vice—Decency is the natural complexion of virtue and the deceptive guise of vice. *Fr. Pr.*

La défense est un charme ; on dit qu'elle assaisonne les plaisirs, et surtout ceux que l'amour nous donne — Prohibition acts as a charm ; it is said to give a zest to pleasures, especially to those which love imparts. *La Fontaine.*

La diffidenza è la madre della sicurtà—Diffidence (caution) is the mother of safety. *It. Pr.*

La dissimulation la plus innocente n'est jamais sans inconvénient ; criminel ou non, l'artifice est toujours dangereux, et presque inévitablement nuisible — Dissimulation, even the most innocent, is always embarrassing ; whether with evil intent or not, artifice is always dangerous, and almost inevitably disgraceful. *La Bruyère.*

10 La docte antiquité est toujours vénérable, / Je ne la trouve pas cependant adorable—To the learning of antiquity I always pay due veneration, but I do not therefore adore it as sacred. *Boileau.*

La donna è mobile—Woman is inconstant. *It.*

La durée de nos passions ne dépend pas plus de nous que la durée de notre vie—The duration of our passions no more depends upon ourselves than the duration of our lives. *La Roche.*

La faiblesse de l'ennemi fait notre propre force —The weakness of the enemy forms part of our own strength. *Pr.*

La faim chasse le loup hors du bois—Hunger drives the wolf out of the wood. *Fr. Pr.*

15 La fama degli eroi spetta un quarto alla loro audacia, due quarti alla sorte e l'altro quarto ai loro delitti—Great men owe a fourth part of their fame to their daring, two-fourths to fortune, and the remaining fourth to their crimes. *U. Foscolo.*

La farina del Diavolo, va tutta in crusca—The devil's meal turns all to chaff. *Sp.*

La farine du diable s'en va moitié en son—The devil's meal goes half to bran. *Fr. Pr.*

La faveur met l'homme au-dessus de ses égaux ; et sa chute au-dessous — Favour exalts a man above his equals, and his fall or disgrace beneath them. *La Bruyère.*

La femme est l'élément le plus moral de l'humanité—Woman is the element in humanity that has the most moral nature. (?).

20 La feuille tombe à terre, ainsi tombe la beauté —The leaf falls to earth, so also does beauty.

La finesse n'est ni une trop bonne ni une très mauvaise qualité : elle flotte entre le vice et la vertu ; il n'y a point de rencontre où elle ne puisse, et peut-être où elle ne doive être suppléée par la prudence — Finesse is neither a very good nor yet a very bad quality. It hovers between vice and virtue, and there are few occasions in which it cannot be, and perhaps ought not to be superseded by common prudence. *La Bruyère.*

La fleur des pois—The tip-top of fashion. *Fr.*

La force, proprement dite, c'est-ce qui régit les actes, sans régler les volontés—Force, strictly speaking, is that which rules the actions without regulating the will. (?)

La fortune du pot—Pot-luck. *Fr.*

La fortune passe partout—The vicissitudes of 25 fortune are felt everywhere. *M.*

La fortune vend ce qu'on croit qu'elle donne— Fortune sells what we think she gives. *Fr. Pr.*

La France est une monarchie absolue, tempérée par des chansons—France is an absolute monarchy tempered by epigrams. *Quoted by Chamfort.*

La France marche à la tête de la civilisation —France leads the van in the civilisation of the world. *Guizot.*

La garde meurt et ne se rend pas—The guard dies but does not surrender. *Ascribed to Gen. Cambronne at Waterloo.*

La générosité suit la belle naissance ; / La 30 pitié l'accompagne et la reconnaissance— Generosity follows in the train of high birth ; pity and gratitude are attendants. *Corneille.*

La gola e'l sonno e l'oziose piume / Hanno del mondo ogni vertù sbandita—Lust, sleep, and idleness have banished every virtue out of the world. *Petrarch.*

La goutte de rosée à l'herbe suspendue, / y réfléchit un ciel aussi vaste, aussi pur, / Que l'immense océan dans ses plaines d'azur —The drop of dew which hangs suspended from the grass-blade reflects a heaven as vast and pure as the ocean does in its wide azure plains. *Lamartine.*

La grammaire, qui sait régenter jusqu'aux rois—Grammar, that knows how to lord it even over kings. *Molière.*

La grande nation—The great nation. *Napoleon when General Bonaparte, of France.*

La grande sagesse de l'homme consiste à 35 connaître ses folies—It is in the knowledge of his follies that man shows his superior wisdom. *Fr. Pr.*

La guerre ou l'amour—War or love. *M.*

La jeunesse devrait être une caisse d'épargne —Youth ought to be a savings' bank. *Mme. Swetchine.*

La jeunesse vit d'espérance, la vieillesse de souvenir — Youth lives on hope, old age on memory. *Fr. Pr.*

La justice de nos jugements et de nos actions n'est jamais que la rencontre heureuse de notre intérêt avec l'intérêt public—The justice of our judgment and actions is never anything but the happy coincidence of our private with the public interest. *Helvetius.*

La justice et la vérité sont deux pointes si 40 subtiles, que nos instrumens sont trop émoussés pour y toucher exactement—Justice and truth are two points so fine that our instruments are too blunt to touch them exactly. *Pascal.*

La langue des femmes est leur épée, et elles ne la laissent pas rouiller—The tongue of a woman is her sword, which she seldom suffers to rust. *Fr. Pr.*

La légalité nous tue—Legality will be the death of us. *M. Viennet.*

La libéralité consiste moins à donner beaucoup, qu'à donner à-propos—Liberality consists less in giving a great deal than in giving seasonably. *La Bruyère.*

La libertad es la juventud eterna de las naciones—Liberty is the eternal youth of the nations. *Gen. Foy.*

5 La liberté, convive aimable, / Met les deux coudes sur la table—Liberty, an amiable guest, puts both her elbows upon the table, *i.e.*, is free and at her ease. *Voltaire.*

La liberté est ancienne ; c'est le despotisme qui est nouveau—Liberty is of ancient date ; it is despotism that is new. *Fr.*

La lingua batte dove la dente duole—The tongue strikes where the tooth aches. *It. Pr.*

La loi ne saurait égaliser les hommes malgré la nature—The law cannot equalise men in spite of nature. *Vauvenargues.*

La maladie sans maladie. The disease without disease, *i.e.*, hypochondria. *Fr.*

10 La manière de former les idées est ce qui donne caractère à l'esprit humain—It is the way in which our ideas are formed that a character is imparted to our minds. *Rousseau.*

La marque d'un mérite extraordinaire est de voir que ceux qui l'envient le plus, sont contraints de le louer—The proof of superior merit is to see how those who envy it most are constrained to praise it. *Fr.*

La menzogna c'insegue anche sotterra—Falsehood follows us even into the grave. *Giuseppe Nicolini.*

La mode est un tyran dont rien nous délivre, / A son bizarre goût il faut s'accommoder—Fashion is a tyrant from which there is no deliverance ; all must conform to its whimsical taste. *Fr.*

La modération des faibles est médiocrité—The moderation of the weak is mediocrity. *Vauvenarques.*

15 La moitié du monde prend plaisir à médire, et l'autre moitié à croire les médisances—One half of the world takes delight in slander, and the other half in believing it. *Fr. Pr.*

La moltiplicità delle leggi e dei medici in un paese sono egualmente segni di malore di quello—A multiplicity of laws and a multiplicity of physicians in any country are proofs alike of its bad state. *It. Pr.*

La montagne est passée, nous irons mieux—We are over the hill ; we shall go better now. *Frederick the Great's last words.*

La moquerie est souvent indigence d'esprit—Derision is often poverty of wit. *La Bruyère.*

La morale trop austère se fait moins aimer qu'elle ne se fait craindre ; et qui veut qu'on profite de ses leçons donne envie de les entendre—Morality when too austere makes itself less loved than feared ; and he who wishes others to profit from its lessons should awaken a desire to listen to them. *Fr.*

20 La mort est plus aisée à supporter sans y penser, que la pensée de la mort sans péril—Death is more easy to bear when it comes without thought of it, than the thought of it without the risk of it. *Pascal.*

La mort ne surprend point le sage ; / Il est toujours prêt à partir, / S'étant su lui-même avertir / Du temps où l'on se doit résoudre à ce passage—Death is no surprise to the wise man ; he is always ready to depart, having learnt to anticipate the time when he must make up his mind to take his last journey. *La Fontaine.*

La musique seule est d'une noble inutilité, et c'est pour cela qu'elle nous émeut si profondément ; plus elle est loin de tout but, plus elle se rapproche de cette source intime de nos pensées que l'application à un objet quelconque reserve dans son cours—Music alone is nobly non-utilitarian, and that is why it moves us so profoundly ; the further it is removed from serving any purpose, the nearer it approaches that inner spring of our thoughts which the application to any object whatever hampers in its course. *Mme. de Staël.*

La naissance n'est rien où la vertu n'est pas—Birth is nothing where virtue is not. *Molière.*

La nation en deuil—The nation in mourning. *Montalembert on Poland.*

La nation ne fait pas corps en France ; elle 25 réside toute entière dans la personne du roy—In France the nation is not a corporate body ; it resides entirely in the person of the king. *Louis XIV.*

La nature a donné deux garants de la chastité des femmes, la pudeur et les remords ; la confession les prive de l'un, et l'absolution de l'autre—Nature has given two safeguards for female chastity, modesty and remorse, but confession deprives them of the one and absolution of the other. *Fr.*

La nature aime les croisements—Nature is partial to cross-breedings. *Fourier.*

La nature est juste envers les hommes—Nature is just to men. *Montesquieu.*

La nature s'imite—Nature imitates herself. *Pascal.*

La nuit porte conseil—The night brings good 30 counsel. *Fr. Pr.*

Là ou ailleurs—There or elsewhere. *M.*

Là où la chèvre est attachée, il faut qu'elle broute—The goat must browse where it is tethered. *Fr. Pr.*

La parfaite valeur est de faire sans témoins ce qu'on serait capable de faire devant tout le monde—Sterling worth shows itself in doing unseen what we would be capable of doing in the eye of the world. *La Roche.*

La parole a été donnée à l'homme pour déguiser sa pensée—Speech has been given to man to conceal his thought. *Voltaire.*

La passion déprave, mais elle élève aussi—Pas- 35 sion depraves, but it also elevates. *Lamartine.*

La passion fait souvent un fou du plus habile homme, et rend souvent habiles les plus sots—Love often makes a fool of the cleverest man, and often gives cleverness to the most foolish. *La Roche.*

La patience est amère, mais le fruit en est doux—Patience is bitter, but it yields sweet fruit. *Rousseau.*

La patience est l'art d'espérer—Patience is the art of hoping. *Vauvenargues.*

La patience est le remède le plus sûre contre les calomnies : le temps, tôt ou tard, découvre la vérité—Patience is the surest antidote against calumny ; time, sooner or later, will disclose the truth. *Fr.*

La patrie veut être servie, et non pas dominée —Our country requires us to serve her, and not to lord it over her. *Fr.*

La pauvreté n'est pas un péché, / Mieux vaut cependant la cacher—Poverty is not a sin; but it is better to hide it. *Fr. Pr.*

La perfection marche lentement, il lui faut la main du temps—Perfection is attained by slow degrees; she requires the hand of time. *Voltaire.*

La peur est un grand inventeur—Fear is a great inventor. *Fr. Pr.*

5 La philosophie non seulement dissipe nos inquiétudes, mais elle nous arme contre tous les coups de la fortune—Philosophy not only dissipates our anxieties, but it arms us against the buffets of fortune. *Fr.*

La philosophie qui nous promet de nous rendre heureux, trompe—Philosophy, so far as she promises us happiness, deceives us. *Fr.*

La philosophie triomphe aisément des maux passés, et des maux à venir; mais les maux présents triomphent d'elle—Philosophy triumphs easily enough over misfortunes that are past and to come, but present misfortunes triumph over her. *La Roche.*

La plupart des hommes, pour arriver à leurs fins, sont plus capables d'un grand effort que d'une longue persévérance—To attain their ends most people are more capable of a great effort than of continued perseverance. *La Bruyère.*

La plupart des peuples, ainsi que des hommes, ne sont dociles que dans leur jeunesse; ils deviennent incorrigibles en vieillisant—Most nations, as well as men, are impressible only in their youth; they become incorrigible as they grow old. *Rousseau.*

10 La plupart des troubles de ce monde sont grammairiens—The majority of the troubles in this world are the fault of the grammarians. *Montaigne.*

La plus belle victoire est de vaincre son cœur —The noblest victory is to conquer one's own heart. *La Fontaine.*

La plus courte folie est toujours la meilleure— The short folly is always the best. *Fr.*

La plus part des hommes emploient la première partie de leur vie à rendre l'autre misérable —The generality of men expend the early part of their lives in contributing to render the latter part miserable. *La Bruyère.*

La plus part des hommes n'ont pas le courage de corriger les autres, parcequ'ils n'ont pas le courage de souffrir qu'on les corrige—The generality of mankind have not the courage to correct others, because they have not themselves the courage to bear correction.

15 La poesia non muore—Poetry does not die. *B. Zendrini.*

La politesse est l'art de rendre à chacun sans effort ce que lui est socialement dû—Politeness is the art of rendering spontaneously to every one that which is his due as a member of society. *Fr.*

La popularité c'est la gloire en gros sous— Popularity is glory in penny-pieces. *Victor Hugo.*

La prière est un cri d'espérance—Prayer is a cry of hope. *A. de Musset.*

La propriété c'est le vol—Property, that is theft. *Proudhon.*

La propriété exclusive est un vol dans la 20 nature — Exclusive ownership is a theft in nature. *Fr.*

La prospérité fait peu d'amis—Prosperity makes few friends. *Vauvenargues.*

La raison du plus fort est toujours la meilleure —The argument of the strongest is always the best, *i.e.,* has most weight. *La Fontaine.*

La raison émancipée n'a pas nui à la cause de Dieu; elle l'a servie — The emancipation of reason has not injured the cause of God; it has promoted it. *V. Cousin.*

La raison seule peut faire des lois obligatoires et durables—Reason alone can render laws binding and stable. *Mirabeau.*

La recherche de la paternité est interdite— 25 Investigation of paternity is forbidden. *Code Napoléon.*

La recherche du vrai, et la pratique du bien, sont les deux objets les plus importants de la philosophie—The pursuit of what is true and the practice of what is good are the two most important objects of philosophy. *Voltaire.*

La reconnaissance est un fardeau, et tout fardeau est fait pour être secoué—Gratitude is a burden, and every burden is made to be shaken off. *Diderot.*

La réputation d'un homme est comme son ombre, qui tantôt le suit, et tantôt le précède; quelquefois elle est plus longue, et quelquefois plus courte que lui—A man's reputation is like his shadow, which sometimes follows, sometimes precedes him, and which is occasionally longer, occasionally shorter than he is. *Fr.*

La roche Tarpéienne est près du Capitole— The Tarpeian rock is near the Capitol, *i.e.,* the place of execution is near the scene of triumph. *Jouy-Spontini.*

La ruse est le talent des égoïstes, et ne peut 30 tromper que les sots que prennent la turbulence pour l'esprit, la gravité pour la prudence, effronterie pour le talent, l'orgueil pour la dignité?—Cunning is the accomplishment of the selfish, and can only impose upon silly people, who take bluster for sense, gravity for prudence, effrontery for talent, and pride for dignity. *Mirabeau.*

La sage conduite roule sur deux pivots, le passé et l'avenir—Prudent conduct turns on two pivots, the past and the future, *i.e.,* on a faithful memory and forethought. *La Bruyère.*

La sauce vaut mieux que le poisson—The sauce is better than the fish. *Fr. Pr.*

La science du gouvernement n'est qu'une science de combinaisons, d'applications et d'exceptions, selon le temps, les lieux, les circonstances—The science of government is only a science of combinations, applications, and exceptions, according to time, place, and circumstance. *Rousseau.*

La seule vertu distingue les hommes, dès qu'ils sont morts—By their virtues alone are men distinguished after they are dead. *L'Abbé de Choisy.*

La silence est la vertu de ceux qui ne sont 35 pas sages—Silence is the virtue of the foolish. *Bouhours.*

La speranza è l'ultima ch'abbandona l'infelice— Hope is the last to abandon the unhappy. *It. Pr.*

La témpérance et le travail sont les deux vrais médicins de l'homme—Temperance and labour are the two real physicians of man. *Rousseau.*

La terre est couverte de gens qui ne méritent pas qu'on leur parle—The earth swarms with people who are not worth talking to. *Voltaire.*

La verdad es hija de Dios—Truth is the daughter of God. *Sp. Pr.*

La verdad es sempre verde—Truth is always green. *Sp. Pr.*

La vérité est cachée au fond du puits—Truth is hidden at the bottom of a well. *Fr. Pr.*

5 **La vérité ne fait pas autant de bien dans le monde que ses apparences y font de mal**—Truth does not produce so much good in the world as the hypocritical profession of it does mischief. *Fr.*

La vertu a des appas qui nous portent au véritable bonheur—Virtue has attractions which lead us to true happiness. *Fr.*

La vertu dans l'indigence est comme un voyageur, que le vent et la pluie contraignent de s'envelopper de son manteau—Virtue in want is like a traveller who is compelled by the wind and rain to wrap himself up in his cloak. *Fr. Pr.*

La vertù è simile ai profume, che rendono più grato ordore quando triturati—Virtue is like certain perfumes, which yield a more agreeable odour from being rubbed. *It.*

La vertu est la seule noblesse—Virtue is the only true nobility. *M.*

10 **La vertu est partout la même; c'est qu'elle vient de Dieu, et le reste est des hommes**—Virtue is everywhere the same; the reason is it proceeds from God, and the rest is from men. *Voltaire.*

La vertu fut toujours en minorité sur la terre—Virtue has ever been in the minority on earth. *Robespierre.*

La vertu n'iroit pas si loin, si la vanité ne lui tenait compagnie—Virtue would not go so far if vanity did not bear her company. *La Roche.*

La vicinanza de' grandi sempre è pericolosa ai picoli; sono grandi come il fuoco, che brucia eziandio quei che vi gettano dell' incenso se troppo vi si approsimino—The neighbourhood of the great is always dangerous to the little. The great are to them as a fire which scorches those who approach it too nearly. *It.*

La vida es corta y la esperanza larga, / El bien huye de mi y el mal se alarga—Life is short, yet hope endures; good flies off, but evil ever lurks about. *Luis de Góngora.*

15 **La vie des héros a enrichi l'histoire, et l'histoire a embelli les actions des héros**—The lives of heroes have enriched history, and history has embellished the exploits of heroes. *La Bruyère.*

La vieillesse nous attache plus de rides en l'esprit qu'en visage—Old age contracts more wrinkles on the mind than the countenance. *Montaigne.*

La ville est le séjour de profanes humains, les dieux habitent la campagne—Towns are the dwelling-places of profane mortals; the gods inhabit rural retreats. *Rousseau.*

La violence est juste où la douceur est vaine—Force is legitimate where gentleness avails not. *Corneille.*

La volontà è tutto—The will is everything. *It. Pr.*

La vraie science et le vrai étude de l'homme, 20 **c'est l'homme**—The real science and the real study for man, is man himself. *Charron.*

Labitur et labetur in omne volubilis ævum—The stream flows, and will go on flowing for ever. *Hor.*

Labitur occulte, fallitque volubilis ætas—Time glides on stealthily, and eludes us as it steals past. *Ovid.*

Labor ipse voluptas—Labour itself is a pleasure. *M.*

Labor omnia vincit / Improbus, et duris urgens in rebus egestas—Persevering labour overcomes all difficulties, and want that urges us on in the pressure of things. *Virg.*

Laborare est orare—Work is worship (*lit.* to 25 labour is to pray). *Monkish Pr.*

Labore—By labour. *M.*

Labore et honore—By labour and honour. *M.*

Labore vinces—By labour you will conquer. *M.*

Laborum dulce lenimen—The sweet soother of my toils. *Hor. to his lyre.*

Labour bestowed on nothing is fruitless. *Hito-* 30 *padesa.*

Labour endears rest, and both together are absolutely necessary for the proper enjoyment of human existence. *Burns.*

Labour for labour's sake is against nature. *Locke.*

Labour has a bitter root but a sweet taste. *Dan. Pr.*

Labour is exercise continued to fatigue; exercise is labour used only while it produces pleasure. *Johnson.*

Labour is life. From the inmost heart of the 35 **worker rises his God-given force—the sacred celestial life-essence breathed into him by Almighty God.** *Carlyle.*

Labour is preferable to idleness, as brightness to rust. *Plato.*

Labour is the beginning, the middle, and the end of art. *Anon.*

Labour is the fabled magician's wand, the philosopher's stone, and the cap of Fortunatus. *J. Johnson.*

Labour is the instituted means for the methodical development of all our powers under the direction and control of the will. *J. G. Holland.*

Labour is the Lethe of both past and present. 40 *Jean Paul.*

Labour is the ornament of the citizen; the reward of toil is when you confer blessings on others; his high dignity confers honour on the king; be ours the glory of our hands. *Schiller.*

Labour is the talisman that has raised man from the condition of the savage. *M'Culloch.*

Labour itself is but a sorrowful song, / The protest of the weak against the strong. *Faber.*

Labour, if it were not necessary for the existence, would be indispensable for the happiness, of man. *Johnson.*

Labour, like everything else that is good, is 45 **its own reward.** *Whipple.*

Labour like this our want supplies, / And they must stoop who mean to rise. *Cowper.*

Labour of the hands, even when pursued to the verge of drudgery, is perhaps never the worst form of idleness (for the mind); it has a constant and imperishable moral. *Thoreau.*

Labour past is pleasant. *Pr.*

Labour to keep alive in your breast that little spark of celestial fire—conscience. *Washington.*

Labour, wide as the earth, has its summit in heaven. *Carlyle.*

5 Labour with what zeal we will, / Something still remains undone, / Something uncompleted still / Waits the rising of the sun. *Longfellow.*

Lachen, Weinen, Lust und Schmerz / Sind Geschwister-Kinder—Laughing and weeping, pleasure and pain, are cousins german. *Goethe.*

Lacrymæque decoræ, / Gratior et pulchro veniens in corpore virtus—His tears, that so well become him, and a merit still more pleasing that shows itself in his fair form. *Virg.*

Lactuca innatat acri / Post vinum stomacho—Lettuce after wine floats on the acrid stomach. *Hor.*

Lad's love is lassie's delight, / And if lads won't love, lassies will flite (scold). *Craven.*

10 Lad's love's a busk of broom, hot awhile and soon done. *Pr.*

Lade nicht alles in ein Schiff—Embark not your all in one venture. *Ger. Pr.*

Ladies like variegated tulips show ; / 'Tis to their changes half their charms they owe. *Pope.*

Læso et invicto militi—For our wounded but unconquered soldiery. *Inscription on the Berlin Invalidenhaus.*

Lætus in præsens animus, quod ultra est / Oderit curare, et amara lento / Temperet risu. Nihil est ab omni / Parte beatum—The mind that is cheerfully contented with the present will shrink from caring about anything beyond, and will temper the bitters of life with an easy smile. There is nothing that is blessed in every respect. *Hor.*

15 Lætus sorte tua vives sapienter—You will live wisely if you live contented with your lot. *Pr.*

Lætus sum laudari a laudato viro—I am pleased to be praised by a man who is so praised as you are. *Cic.*

Laisser dire le monde, et toujours bien faire, c'est une maxime, qui étant bien observée assure notre repos, et établit enfin notre réputation—To let the world talk, and always to act correctly, is a maxim which, if well observed, will secure our repose, and in the end establish our reputation. *Fr.*

Laissez dire les sots, le savoir a son prix—Let ignorance talk, learning has its value. *La Fontaine.*

Laissez faire, laissez passer !—Let it be ! Let it pass ! *Gournay, Quesnay.*

20 Laissez faire—the "let alone" principle, is, in all things which man has to do with, the principle of death. It is ruin to him, certain and total, if he lets his land alone—if he lets his fellow-men alone—if he lets his own soul alone. *Ruskin.*

Laissez-leur prendre un pied chez vous, / Ils en auront bientôt pris quatre—Let them take one foot in your house, and they will soon have taken four (give them an inch and they will take an ell). *La Fontaine.*

Lamenting becomes fools, and action wise folk. *Sir P. Sidney.*

Lampoons and satires, that are written with wit and spirit, are like poisoned darts, which not only inflict a wound, but make it incurable. *Addison.*

Land is the right basis of an aristocracy. No true aristocracy but must possess the land. *Carlyle.*

Land of lost gods and godlike men. *Byron of* 25 *Greece.*

Land should be given to those who can use it, and tools to those who can use them. *Ruskin.*

Land was never lost for want of an heir. *Pr.*

Lands intersected by a narrow firth / Abhor each other. Mountains interposed / Make enemies of nations, which had else, / Like kindred drops, been mingled into one. *Cowper.*

Lands mortgaged may return, and more esteemed ; / But honesty once pawned is ne'er redeemed. *Middleton.*

Lang ill, soon weel. *Sc. Pr.* 30

Lang syne, in Eden's bonny yaird, / When youthfu' lovers first were pair'd, / And all the soul of love they shared, / The raptured hour, / Sweet on the fragrant flowery swaird, / In shady bower, / Then you, ye auld sneck-drawing (latch-lifting) dog, / Ye cam' to Paradise incog, / And play'd on man a cursèd brogue, / (Black be your fa') / And gied the infant warld a shog (shake), / 'Maist ruin'd a'. *Burns to the Deil.*

Langage des halles — Language of the fish-market. *Fr.*

Lange ist nicht ewig—Long is not for ever. *Ger. Pr.*

Lange Ueberlegungen zeigen gewöhnlich, dass man den Punkt nicht im Auge hat, von dem die Rede ist ; übereilte Handlungen, dass man ihn gar nicht kennt—Long pondering on a matter usually indicates that one has not properly got his eye on the point at issue ; and too hasty action that he does not know it at all. *Goethe.*

Langes Leben heisst viele überleben—To live 35 long is to outlive many. *Goethe.*

Langeweile ist ein böses Kraut / Aber auch eine Würze, die viel verdaut—Ennui is an ill weed, but also a condiment which digests a good deal. *Goethe.*

Langh festjen is nin brae sperjen—A long fast saves no bread. *Fris. Pr.*

Langsam nur im Menschengeiste / Reift das Saatkorn der Erkenntniss, / Doch die Blumen wachsen schnell—The seed-grain of knowledge ripens but slowly in the spirit of man, yet the flowers grow fast. *Bodenstedt.*

Language at its infancy is all poetry. *Emerson.*

Language is always wise. *Emerson.* 40

Language is fossil poetry. *Trench.*

Language is not only the vehicle of thought, it is a great and efficient instrument in thinking. *Sir H. Davy.*

Language is only clear when it is sympathetic. *Ruskin.*

Language is properly the servant of thought, but not unfrequently it becomes its master. *W. B. Clulow.*

Language is the armoury of the human mind, and at once contains the trophies of its past, and the weapons of its future, conquests. *Coleridge.*

Language is the dress of thought. *Johnson.*

Language is the memory of the human race. It is a thread of nerve of life running through all the ages, connecting them into one common, prolonged, and advancing existence. *Wm. Smith.*

Language most shows a man ; speak that I may see thee. *Ben Jonson.*

5 Languages are more properly to be called vehicles of learning than learning itself. . . . True knowledge consists in knowing things, not words. *Lady Montagu.*

Languages are the barometers of national thought and character. *Hare.*

Languages are the pedigree of nations. *Johnson.*

Lapidary inscriptions should be historical rather than lyrical. *Carlyle.*

Lapis philosophorum—The philosopher's stone.

10 Lapis qui volvitur algam non generat—A rolling stone gathers no moss. *Pr.*

Lapsus memoriæ—A slip of the memory.

Lares et penates—Household gods.

Large bodies are far more likely to err than individuals. The passions are inflamed by sympathy ; the fear of punishment and the sense of shame are diminished by partition. Every day we see men do for their faction what they would die rather than do for themselves. *Macaulay.*

Large charity doth never soil, but only whiten, soft white hands. *Lowell.*

15 Large fortunes are all founded either on occupation of land, or usury, or taxation of labour. *Ruskin.*

Large fortunes cannot be made by the work of any one man's hands or head. *Ruskin.*

Large masses of mankind, in every society of our Europe, are no longer capable of living at all by the things which have been. *Carlyle.*

Largitio fundum non habet—Giving has no bottom. *Pr.*

Las manos blancas no ofenden—White hands cannot harm one. *Sp. Pr.*

20 Lasciate ogni speranza, voi ch'entrate—Abandon all hope, ye who enter here. *Dante.*

Lascivi soboles gregis—The offspring of a wanton herd. *Hor.*

Lass das Vergangne vergangen sein — Let what is past be past. *Goethe, Faust to Margaret in the end.*

Lass deine Zunge nie das Amt des Schwertes führen— Never let thy tongue do the work of the sword. (?)

Lass dich nicht verblüffen—Don't let yourself be disconcerted. *Herder.*

25 Lass die Leute reden und die Hunde bellen— Let the people talk and the dogs bark. *Ger. Pr.*

Lass die schwerste Pflicht dir die allerheiligste Pflicht sein—Let the most arduous duty be the most sacred of all to thee. *Lavater.*

Lass die Winde stürmen auf des Lebens Bahn, / Ob sie Wogen türmen gegen deinen Kahn / Schiffe ruhig weiter, wenn der Mast auch bricht, / Gott ist dein Begleiter, er vergisst dich nicht—Let winds storm on life's course, even though they swell over and threaten thy skiff. Sail quietly on, even if the mast gives way. God is thy convoy ; He forgets thee not. *Tiedge.*

Lass diesen Händedruck dir sagen / Was unaussprechlich ist—Let this pressure of the hand reveal to thee what is unutterable. *Goethe, Faust to Margarite.*

Lass ruhn, lass ruhn die Toten, / Du weckst sie mit Klagen nicht auf—Let them rest, let thy dead ones rest, thou awakest them not with thy wailing. *Chamisso.*

Lasses and glasses are brittle wares. *Sc. Pr.* 30

Lasst fahren hin das allzu Flüchtige ! / Ihr sucht bei ihm vergebens Rat ! / In dem Vergangnen lebt das Tüchtige / Verewigt sich in schöner That—Let the too transient pass by ; ye seek counsel in vain of it. Yet what will avail you lives in the past, and lies immortalised in what has been nobly done. *Goethe.*

Lasst uns hell denken, so werden wir feurig lieben — Let us think clearly, we shall love ardently. *Schiller.*

Last come, worst served.

Last in bed, best heard. *Pr.*

Last, not least. *Jul. Cæs.*, iii. 1. *Lear*, i. 1.   35

Last scene of all, . . . / Is second childishness and mere oblivion ; / Sans teeth, sans eyes, sans taste, sans everything. *As You Like It*, ii. 7.

Late children are early orphans. *Sp. Pr.*

Late fruit keeps well. *Ger. Pr.*

Lateat scintillula forsan—A small spark may perhaps lurk unseen. *M.*

Laterem laves—You may as well wash a clay 40 brick white. *Ter.*

Latet anguis in herba—There is a snake in the grass. *Virg.*

λάθε βιώσας—Remain hidden in life. *Epicurus.*

Latitat—He lurks ; a writ of summons (Law).

Latius regnes, avidum domando / Spiritum, quam si Libyam remotis / Gadibus jungas, et uterque Pœnus / Serviat uni—By subduing an avaricious spirit you will rule a wider empire than if you united Lybia to the far-off Gades, and the Carthaginian on both shores should be subject to you alone. *Hor.*

Latrante uno, latrat statim et alter canis— 45 When one dog barks, another straightway begins to bark too. *Pr.*

Latrantem curatne alta Diana canem ?—Does the high-stepping Diana care for the dog that bays her ? *Pr.*

Laudant quod non intelligunt — They praise what they don't understand.

Laudari a viro laudato maxima est laus—To be commended by a man of high repute is the greatest possible praise.

Laudat venales qui vult extrudere merces— He praises his wares who wishes to palm them off upon others. *Hor.*

Laudato ingentia rura, Exiguum colito—Praise 50 a large estate, but cultivate a small one. *Virg.*

Laudator temporis acti—The praiser of bygone times. *Hor.*

Laudatur ab his, culpatur ab illis—Some praise him, others censure him. *Hor.*

Laudatus abunde, / Non fastiditus si tibi, lector, ero—Abundantly, reader, shall I be praised if I do not cause thee disgust. *Ovid.*

Laudem virtutis necessitati damus—We give to necessity the praise of virtue. *Quinct.*

Laudibus arguitur vini vinosus—He is convicted of being a wine-bibber by his praises of wine. *Hor.*

5 Laudo Deum verum, plebem voco, congrego clerum, / Defunctos ploro, pestem fugo, festa decoro—I praise the true God, I summon the people, I call together the clergy, I bewail the dead, I put to flight the plague, I celebrate festivals. *Inscription on a church bell.*

Laudo manentem ; si celeres quatit / Pennas, resigno quæ dedit, et mea / Virtute me involvo probamque / Pauperiem sine dote quæro—I praise her (Fortune) while she stays with me ; if she flaps her swift pinions, I resign all she has given me, and wrap myself up in my own virtue and pay my addresses to honest undowered poverty. *Hor.*

Laugh and be fat. *Ben Jonson.*

Laugh at all twaddle about fate. A man's fate is what he makes it, nothing else. *Anon.*

Laugh at leisure ; ye may greet (weep) ere nicht. *Sc. Pr.*

10 Laugh not too much : the witty man laughs least : / For wit is news only to ignorance. / Less at thine own things laugh : lest in the jest / Thy person share, and the conceit advance. *George Herbert.*

Laugh where we must, be candid where we can, / But vindicate the ways of God to man. *Pope.*

Laughing cheerfulness throws the light of day on all the paths of life ; sorrow is more confusing and distracting than so-called giddiness. *Jean Paul.*

Laughter almost ever cometh of things most disproportioned to ourselves. *Sir P. Sidney.*

Laughter and tears are meant to turn the wheels of the same machinery of sensibility ; one is wind-power, and the other water-power, that is all. *Holmes.*

15 Laughter, holding both his sides. *Milton.*

Laughter is akin to weeping, and true humour is as closely allied to pity as it is abhorrent to derision. *H. Giles.*

Laughter is one of the very privileges of reason, being confined to the human species. *Leigh Hunt.*

Laughter is the cipher-key wherewith we decipher the whole man. *Carlyle.*

Laughter leaves us doubly serious shortly after. *Byron.*

20 Laughter makes good blood. *It. Pr.*

Laughter should dimple the cheek, not furrow the brow. *Feltham.*

Laus Deo—Praise be to God. *M.*

Laus est facere quod decet, non quod licet—It is doing what we ought to do, and not merely doing what we may do, that is the ground of praise.

Laus in proprio ore sordescit—Self-praise is offensive. *Pr.*

25 Laus magna natis obsequi parentibus—Great praise is the meed of children who respect the wishes of their parents. *Phaedr.*

Lavish promises lessen credit. *Hor.*

Lavishness is not generosity. *Pr.*

Law and equity are two things which God hath joined, but which man hath put asunder. *Colton.*

Law cannot persuade when it cannot punish. *Pr.*

Law has her seat in the bosom of God, her 30 voice in the harmony of the world. *Hooker.*

Law is a bottomless pit ; keep far from it. *Pr.*

Law is a lottery. *Pr.*

Law is not law if it violates the principles of eternal justice. *L. M. Child.*

Law is powerful, necessity more so. *Goethe.*

Law it is which is without name, or colour, or 35 hands, or feet ; which is smallest of the least, and largest of the large ; all, and knowing all things ; which hears without ears, sees without eyes, moves without feet, and seizes without hands. *Emerson.*

Law licks up a'. *Sc. Pr.*

Law-makers should not be law-breakers. *Pr.*

Law, man's sole guardian ever since the day when the old brazen age in sadness saw love fly the world. *Schiller.*

Law teaches us to know when we commit injury and when we suffer it. *Johnson.*

Law that shocks equity is reason's murderer. 40 *A. Hill.*

Lawless are they that make their wills their law. *Sh.*

Laws act after crimes have been committed ; prevention goes before them both. *Zimmermann.*

Laws and rights are transmitted like an inveterate hereditary disease. *Goethe.*

Laws are generally found to be nets of such texture as the little creep through, the great break through, and the middle size are alone entangled in. *Shenstone.*

Laws are intended to guard against what 45 men may do, not to trust what they will do. *Junius.*

Laws are like cobwebs, which may catch small flies, but let wasps and hornets break through. *Swift.*

Laws are like spider webs, small flies are ta'en, / While greater flies break in and out again. *Braithwaite.*

Laws are not made for particular cases, but for men in general. *Johnson.*

Laws are not made like nets—to catch, but like sea-marks—to guide. *Sir P. Sidney.*

Laws are not masters, but servants, and he 50 rules them who obeys them. *Ward Beecher.*

Laws are not our life, only the house wherein our life is led ; nay, they are but the bare walls of the house ; all whose essential furniture, the inventions and traditions and daily habits that regulate and support our existence, are the work not of Dracos and Hampdens, but of Phœnician mariners, of Italian masons, and Saxon metallurgists, of philosophers, alchymists, prophets, and the long-forgotten train of artists and artisans, who from the first have been jointly teaching us how to think and how to act, how to rule over spiritual and physical nature. *Carlyle.*

Laws are the silent assessors of God. *W. R. Alger.*

Laws are the sovereigns of sovereigns. *Louis XIV.*

Laws are the very bulwarks of liberty. They define every man's rights, and stand between and defend the individual liberties of all. *J. G. Holland.*

Laws are usually most beneficial in operation on the people who would have most strongly objected to their enactment. *Ruskin.*

Law's costly; tak' a pint and 'gree. *Sc. Pr.*

Laws exist in vain for those who have not the courage and the means to defend them. *Macaulay.*

5 Laws grind the poor, and rich men rule the law. *Goldsmith.*

Laws, like cobwebs, catch flies, but let hornets go free. *Pr.*

Laws of Nature are God's thoughts thinking themselves out in the orbs and the tides. *C. H. Parkhurst.*

Laws should be like death, which spares no one. *Montesquieu.*

Laws undertake to punish only overt acts. *Montesquieu.*

10 Laws were made for rogues. *It. Pr.*

Laws, written, if not on stone tables, yet on the azure of infinitude, in the inner heart of God's creation, certain as life, certain as death, are there, and thou shalt not disobey them. *Carlyle.*

Lawyers and painters can soon make black white. *Pr.*

Lawyers and woodpeckers have long bills. *Pr.*

Lawyers are always more ready to get a man into troubles than out of them. *Goldsmith.*

15 Lawyers are needful to keep us out of law. *Pr.*

Lawyers' houses are built of fools' heads. *Fr. Pr.*

Lawyers, of whose art the basis / Is raising feuds and splitting cases. *Butler.*

Lawyers' robes are lined with the obstinacy of litigants. *It. Pr.*

Lawyers will live as long as mine and thine does. *Ger. Pr.*

20 Lay by, like ants, a little store, / For summer lasts not evermore. *Pr.*

Lay by something for a rainy day. *Pr.*

Lay not all the load on the lame horse. *Pr.*

Lay not that flattering unction to your soul. *Ham., iii. 4.*

Lay not thine heart open to every one, but treat of thy affairs with the wise and such as fear God. *Thomas à Kempis.*

25 Lay the blame at the right door. *Pr.*

Lay the proud usurpers low! / Tyrants fall in every foe! / Liberty's in every blow! / Forward! let us die. *Burns.*

Lay thy hand upon thy halfpenny twice before thou partest with it. *Pr.*

Lay up and lay out should go together. *Pr.*

Lay up that you may lay out. *Pr.*

30 Lazarus did not go to Abraham's bosom because he was poor, or every sluggard would go there easily. *Spurgeon.*

Laziness begins with cobwebs and ends with iron chains. *Pr.*

Laziness is nothing unless you carry it out. *Pr.*

Laziness travels so slowly that poverty soon overtakes him. *Ben. Franklin.*

Lazy as Ludlam's dog, that laid his head against the wall to bark. *Pr.*

Lazy folks ask for work with their lips, but 35 their hearts pray God that they may not find it. *Creole saying.*

Lazy folk's stomachs don't get tired. *Uncle Remus.*

Lazy is the hand that ploughs not. *Gael. Pr.*

Le beau monde—The fashionable world. *Fr.*

Le bestemmie fanno come le processioni ; ritornano donde partirono — Curses are like processions, they come back to whence they set out. *It. Pr.*

Le bien ne se fait jamais mieux que lorsqu'il 40 opère lentement—Good is never more effectually done than when it is produced slowly. *Fr. Pr.*

Le bon sens vulgaire est un mauvais juge quand il s'agit des grandes choses — Good common-sense is a bad judge when it is a question of high matters. *Renan.*

Le bon temps viendra — The good time will come. *M.*

Le bonheur de l'homme en cette vie ne consiste pas à être sans passions, il consiste à en être le maître—The happiness of man in this life does not consist in being devoid of passions, but in mastering them. *Fr.*

Le bonheur des méchants comme un torrent s'écoule—The happiness of the wicked passes away like a brook. *Racine.*

Le bonheur des peuples dépend et de la félicité 45 dont ils jouissent au dedans et du respect qu'ils inspirent au dehors — The welfare of nations depends at once on the happiness which they enjoy at home and the respect which they command abroad. *Helvetius.*

Le bonheur et le malheur des hommes ne dépendent pas moins de leur humeur que de la fortune—The happiness and unhappiness of men depend as much on their dispositions as on fortune. *La Roche.*

Le bonheur n'est pas chose aisée ; il est trèsdifficile de le trouver en nous, et impossible de le trouver ailleurs—Happiness is no easy matter ; it is very hard to find it within ourselves, and impossible to find it elsewhere. *Chamfort.*

Le bonheur ne peut être / Où la vertu n'est pas—Happiness cannot exist where virtue is not. *Quinault.*

Le bonheur ou le malheur vont ordinairement à ceux qui ont le plus de l'un ou de l'autre— Good fortune or bad generally falls to those who have the greatest share of either. *La Roche.*

Le bonheur semble fait pour être partagé 50 —Happiness seems appointed to be shared. *Racine.*

Le bruit est si fort, qu'on n'entend pas Dieu tonner—The noise (of things) is so deafening that we cannot hear God when He thunders. *Fr. Pr.*

Le bruit est pour le fat, la plainte est pour le sot, / L'honnête homme trompé s'éloigne et ne dit mot—Blustering is for the fop, whimpering for the fool ; the sensible man when deceived goes off and says nothing. *Lanoue.*

Le chemin est long du projet à la close—The road is a long one from the projection of a thing to its accomplishment. *Molière.*

Le ciel me prive d'une épouse qui ni m'a jamais donné d'autre chagrin que celui de sa mort—Heaven bereaves me of a spouse who never caused me any other vexation than by her death. *Louis XIV. of his wife.*

Le citoyen peut périr, et l'homme rester—The citizen may perish and man remain. *Montesquieu.*

Le cœur a ses raisons, que la raison ne connoit pas— The heart has its reasons, which reason does not know. *Pascal.*

Le cœur de l'homme n'est jamais si inflexible que son esprit—The heart of man is never so inflexible as his intellect. *Lamartine.*

5 Le cœur d'une femme est un vrai miroir qui reçoit toutes sortes d'objets sans s'attacher à aucun—The heart of woman is a real mirror, which reflects every object without attaching itself to any. *Fr.*

Le congrès ne marche pas ; il danse—The Congress does not advance ; it dances. *The Prince de Ligne of the Vienna Congress.*

Le conquérant est craint, le sage est estimé, / Mais le bienfaiteur plait, et lui seul est aimé—The conqueror is held in awe, the sage is esteemed, but it is the benevolent man who wins our affections and is alone beloved. *Fr.*

Le conseil manque à l'âme, / Et le guide au chemin—The soul wants counsel, and the road a guide. *Fr.*

Le contraire des bruits qui courent des affaires, ou des personnes, est souvent la vérité—The converse of what is currently reported about things and people is often the truth. *La Bruyère.*

10 Le contrat du gouvernement est tellement dissous par despotisme que le despot n'est le maître qu'aussi long temps qu'il est le plus fort ; et que si tôt qu'on peut l'expulser, il n'a point à réclaimer contre la violence—The contract of government is so dissolved by despotism, that the despot is master only so long as he is the strongest, and that as soon as there is power to expel him, he has no right to protest against the violent proceeding. *Rousseau.*

Le corps politique, aussi bien que le corps de l'homme, commence à mourir dès sa naissance, et porte en lui-même les causes de sa destruction—The body politic, like the body of man, begins to die as soon as it is born, and bears within it the seeds of its own dissolution. *Rousseau.*

Le cose non sono come sono, ma come si vedono—Things are not as they are, but as they are regarded. *It. Pr.*

Le courage est souvent un effet de la peur—Courage is often an effect of fear. *Fr. Pr.*

Le coûte en ôte le goût—The cost takes away from the relish. *Fr. Pr.*

15 Le cri d'un peuple heureux est la seule éloquence qui doit parler des rois—The acclaim of a happy people is the only eloquence which ought to speak in the behalf of kings.

Le crime fait la honte, et non pas l'échafaud—It is the crime that's the disgrace, not the scaffold. *Corneille.*

Le désespoir comble non seulement notre misère, mais notre faiblesse—Despair gives the finishing blow not only to misery, but to weakness. *Vauvenargues.*

Le désespoir redouble les forces — Despair doubles our powers. *Fr. Pr.*

Le despotisme tempéré par l'assassinat, c'est notre Magna Charta—Despotism tempered by assassination is our Magna Charta. *A Russian noble to Count Münster on the murder of the Czar Paul.*

Le dessous des cartes—The lower side of the 20 cards. *Fr.*

Le devoir, c'est l'âme intérieure, c'est la vie de l'éducation—Duty is the inner soul, the life of education. *Michelet.*

Le devoir des juges est de rendre justice, leur métier est de la différer ; quelques uns savent leur devoir, et font leur métier—The duty of judges is to administer justice, but their practice is to delay it ; some of them know their duty, but adhere to the practice. *La Bruyère.*

Le diable était beau quand il était jeune—The devil was handsome when he was young. *Fr. Pr.*

Le divorce est le sacrement de l'adultère—Divorce is the sacrament of adultery.

Le doute s'introduit dans l'âme qui rêve, la foi 25 descend dans l'âme qui souffre—Doubt insinuates itself into a soul that is dreaming ; faith comes down into one that struggles and suffers.

Le droit est au plus fort en amour comme en guerre, / Et la femme qu'on aime aura toujours raison—Right is with the strongest in love as in war, / And the woman we love will always be right. *A. de Musset.*

Le feu qui semble éteint souvent dort dans la cendre—The fire which seems extinguished often slumbers in the ashes. *Corneille.*

Le génie c'est la patience — Genius is just patience. *Fr. Pr.*

Le génie n'est autre chose qu'une grand aptitude à la patience—Genius is nothing else than a sovereign capacity for patience. *Buffon.*

Le géologue est un nouveau genre d'anti- 30 quaire—The geologist is a new species of antiquarian. (?)

Le gouvernement représentatif est la justice organisée, la raison vivante, la morale armée—Representative government is justice organised, reason in living action, and morality armed. *Royer Collard.*

Le grand art de la supériorité, c'est de saiser les hommes par leur bon côté—The great art of superiority is getting hold of people by their right side. *Mirabeau.*

Le grand monarque—The grand monarch, Louis XIV.

Le grandeur et le discernement sont des choses différentes, et l'amour pour la vertu, et pour les vertueux une troisième chose—High rank and discernment are two different things, and love for virtue and for virtuous people is a third thing. *La Bruyère.*

Le hazard donne les pensées ; le hazard les 35 ôte : point d'art pour conserver ni pour acquérir—Chance suggests thoughts ; changes deprive us of them : there is no rule for preserving or acquiring them. *Pascal.*

Le hazard est un sobriquet de la Providence—Chance is a nickname for Providence. *Chamfort.*

Le jeu est le fils de l'avarice et le père du désespoir—Gambling is the son of avarice and the father of despair. *Fr. Pr.*

Le jeu n'en vaut pas la chandelle—The game is not worth the candle. *Fr. Pr.*

Le jour viendra—The day will come. *M.*

Le masque tombe, l'homme reste / Et le héros s'évanouit — The mask falls off, the man remains, and the heroic vanishes. *J. B. Rousseau.*

Le mauvais métier que celui de censeur—A bad business that of censor. *Guy Patin.*

Le méchant n'est jamais comique—A bad man is never amusing. *De Maistre.*

Le médicin Tant-pis et le médicin Tant-mieux—The pessimist and the optimist (*lit.* Doctor So-much-the-worse and Doctor So-much-the-better). *La Fontaine.*

5 Le mérité est souvent un obstacle à la fortune; c'est qu'il produit toujours deux mauvais effets, l'envie et la crainte—Merit is often an obstacle to fortune; the reason is it produces two bad effects, envy and fear. *Fr.*

Le mieux est l'ennemi du bien—Better is the enemy of well. *Fr. Pr.*

Le moindre grain de mil serait bien mieux mon affaire—The smallest grain of millet would serve my needs better. *La Fontaine, "The Cock and the Pearl."*

Le moineau en la main vaut mieux que l'oie qui vole—A sparrow in the hand is worth a goose on the wing. *Fr. Pr.*

Le monde, chère Agnès, est une étrange chose—The world, dear Agnes, is a queer concern. *Molière.*

10 Le monde est le livre des femmes—The world is the book of women. *Rousseau.*

Le monde est plein de fous, et qui n'en veut pas voir / Doit se tenir tout seul et casser son miroir—The world is full of madmen, and he who would not see one must keep himself quite alone and break his looking-glass.

Le monde paye d'ingratitude—The world pays with ingratitude. *Fr. Pr.*

Le monde savant—The learned world. *Fr.*

Le mort est le dernier trait du tableau de la vie—Death is the finishing touch in the picture of life. *Fr.*

15 Le mot de l'énigme—The key to the riddle. *Fr.*

Le moy est haïssable — Egotism is hateful. *Pascal.*

Le moyen le plus sûr de se consoler de tout ce qui peut arriver, c'est de s'attendre toujours au pire—The surest way to console one's self against whatever may happen is always to expect the worst. *Fr.*

Le nombre des élus au Parnasse est complet—The list of the elect of Parnassus is made up. (?)

Le nombre des sages sera toujours petit—The wise will always be few in number.

20 Le parjure est une vertu, / Lorsque le serment fut un crime—Perjury is a virtue when the oath was a crime. *Voltaire.*

Le pas—Precedence in place or rank. *Fr.*

Le pays du mariage a cela de particulier, que les étrangers ont envie de l'habiter, et les habitans naturels voudroient en être exilés—The land of matrimony possesses this peculiarity, that strangers to it would like to dwell in it, and the natural inhabitants wish to be exiled. *Montaigne.*

Le pédant et l'instituteur disent à peu près les mêmes choses; mais le premier les dit à tout propos; le second ne les dit que quand il sûr de leur effet—The pedant and the teacher say nearly the same things; but the former on every occasion, the latter only when he is sure of their effect. *Rousseau.*

Le petit monde—The lower orders. *Fr.*

Le peuple anglais pense être libre; il ne l'est 25 que durant l'élection des membres du parlement—The English think they are free; they are free only during the election of members of Parliament. *Rousseau.*

Le peuple est le cœur du pays—The people is the heart of a country. *Lamartine.*

Le peuple ne comprend que ce qu'il sent. Les seuls orateurs pour lui sont ceux qui l'émeuvent—The people understand only what they feel; the only orators that can affect them are those who move them. *Lamartine.*

Le plaisir le plus délicat est de faire celui d'autrui — The most exquisite pleasure consists in promoting the pleasures of others. *La Bruyère.*

Le plus âne des trois n'est pas celui qu'on pense—The greatest ass of the three is not the one who seems so. *La Fontaine, "The Miller, his Son, and his Ass."*

Le plus dangereux ridicule des vieilles per- 30 sonnes qui sont aimables, c'est d'oublier qu'elles ne le sont plus—For old people, however estimable, to forget that they are no longer old is to expose themselves to certain ridicule. *La Roche.*

Le plus lent à promettre est toujours le plus fidèle à tenir—He who is slow in promising is always the most faithful in performing. *Rousseau.*

Le plus sage est celui qui ne pense point l'être—The wisest man is he who does not think he is so. *Boileau.*

Le plus semblable aux morts meurt le plus à regret—He who most resembles the dead dies with most reluctance. *La Fontaine.*

Le plus véritable marque d'être né avec de grandes qualités, c'est d'être né sans envie—The sure mark of being born with noble qualities is being born without envy. *La Roche.*

Le premier écu est plus difficile à gagner que 35 le second million—The first five shillings are harder to win than the second million. *Fr. Pr.*

Le premier soupir de l'amour est le dernier de la sagesse—The first sigh of love is the last of wisdom. *Charron.*

Le présent est gros de l'avenir—The present is big with coming events. *Leibnitz.*

Le présent est pour ceux qui jouissent, l'avenir pour ceux qui souffrent—The present is for those who enjoy, the future for those who suffer. *Fr.*

Le public! combien faut-il de sots pour faire un public? — The public! How many fools must there be to make a public? *Chamfort.*

Le réel est étroit, le possible est immense—The 40 real is limited, the possible is unlimited. *Lamartine.*

Le refus des louanges est souvent un désir d'être loué deux fois—The refusal of praise often proceeds from a desire to have it repeated.

Le repos est une bonne chose, mais l'ennui est son frère—Repose is a good thing, but ennui is his brother. *Voltaire.*

Le reste ne vaut pas l'honneur d'être nommé—The rest don't deserve to be mentioned. *Corneille.*

Le roi est mort; vive le roi!—The king is dead; long live the king! *The form of announcing the death of a French king.*

Le roy et l'état—The king and the state. *M.* 45

Le roi le veut—The king wills it. *The formula of royal assent in France.*

Le roi régne et ne gouverne pas---The king reigns but does not govern. *Thiers at the accession of Louis Philippe.*

Le roi s'avisera—The king will consider it. *The form of a royal veto in France.*

Le sage entend à demi-mot—A hint suffices for a wise man. *Fr. Pr.*

Le sage quelquefois évite le monde de peur d'être ennuyé—The wise man sometimes shuns society from fear of being bored. *La Bruyère.*

5 Le sage songe avant que de parler à ce qu'il doit dire ; le fou parle, et ensuite songe à ce qu'il a dit—A wise man thinks before he speaks what he ought to say ; the fool speaks and thinks afterwards what he has said. *Fr. Pr.*

Le savoir faire—Knowing how to act ; ability.

Le savoir vivre—Knowing how to live ; good manners.

Le secret d'ennuyer est celui de tout dire—The secret of boring people is saying all that can be said on a subject. *Voltaire.*

Le sens commun est le génie de l'humanité—Common sense is the genius of humanity. *Goethe.*

10 Le sentiment de la liberté est plus vif, plus il y entre de malignité—The passion for liberty is the keener the greater the malignity associated with it. *Fr.*

Le silence du peuple est la leçon des rois—The silence of the people is a lesson to kings. *M. de Beauvais.*

Le silence est l'esprit des sots, / Et l'une des vertus du sage—Silence is the wit of fools, and one of the virtues of the wise man. *Bonnard.*

Le silence est la vertu de ceux qui ne sont pas sages—Silence is the virtue of those who want it. *Bouhours.*

Le silence est le parti le plus sûr pour celui qui se défie de soi-même—Silence is the safest course for the man who is diffident of himself. *La Roche.*

15 Le soleil ni la mort ne se peuvent regarder fixement—Neither the sun nor death can be looked at fixedly. *La Roche.*

Le sort fait les parents, le choix fait les amis—It is to chance we owe our relatives, to choice our friends. *Delille.*

Le style est l'homme même—The style is the man himself. *Buffon.*

Le superflu, chose très-nécessaire—The superfluous, a thing highly necessary. *Voltaire.*

Le temps est un grand maître, il régle bien les choses—Time is a great master ; it regulates things well. *Corneille.*

20 Le temps guérit les douleurs et les querelles, parcequ'on change, on n'est plus le même personne—Time heals our griefs and wranglings, because we change, and are no longer the same. *Pascal.*

Le temps n'épargne pas ce qu'on fait sans lui—Time preserves nothing that has been done without her, *i.e.*, that has taken no time to do. *Favolle.*

Le tout ensemble—The whole together. *Fr.*

Le travail du corps délivre des peines de l'esprit ; et c'est ce qui rend les pauvres heureux—Bodily labour alleviates the pains of the mind, and hence arises the happiness of the poor. *La Roche.*

Le travail éloigne de nous trois grand maux, l'ennui, le vice, et le besoin—Labour relieves us from three great evils, ennui, vice, and want. *Fr.*

Le trépas vient tout guérir ; / Mais ne bou- 25 geons d'où nous sommes : / Plutôt souffrir que mourir, / C'est la devise des hommes—Death comes to cure everything, but let us not stir from where we are. "Endure sooner than die," is the proper device for man. *La Fontaine.*

Le trident de Neptune est le sceptre du monde—The trident of Neptune is the sceptre of the world. *Lemierre.*

Le vesciche galleggiano sopre aqua, mentre le cose di peso vanno al fondo—Bladders swim on the surface of the water, while things of weight sink to the bottom. *It. Pr.*

Le vivre et le couvert, que faut-il davantage ?—Life and good fare, what more do we need ? *La Fontaine, "The Rat in Retreat."*

Le vrai mérite ne depend point du temps ni de la mode—True merit depends on neither time nor mode. *Fr. Pr.*

Le vrai moyen d'être trompé, c'est de se croire 30 plus fin que les autres—The most sure way to be imposed on is to think one's self cleverer than other people. *La Roche.*

Le vrai n'est pas toujours vraisemblable—The true is not always verisimilar. *Fr. Pr.*

Le vrai peut quelquefois n'être pas vraisemble—What is true may sometimes seem unlike truth. *Boileau.*

Lead, kindly light, amid th' encircling gloom, / Lead thou me on. *Newman.*

Lead thine own captivity captive, and be Cæsar within thyself. *Sir Thomas Browne.*

Leal heart leed never. *Sc. Pr.* 35

Lean liberty is better than fat slavery. *Pr.*

Lean not upon a broken reed, which will not only let thee fall, but pierce thy arm too. *Thomas à Kempis.*

Lean, rent, and beggared by the strumpet wind l *Mer. of Ven.*, ii. 6.

Learn a craft while you are young, that you may not have to live by craft when you are old. *Pr.*

Learn never to repine at your own misfor- 40 tunes, or to envy the happiness of another. *Addison.*

Learn of the little nautilus to sail, / Spread the thin oar and catch the driving gale. *Pope.*

Learn taciturnity ; let that be your motto. *Burns.*

Learn that nonsense is none the less nonsense because it is in rhyme ; and that rhyme without a purpose or a thought that has not been better expressed before is a public nuisance, only to be tolerated because it is good for trade. *C. Fitzhugh.*

Learn the value of a man's words and expressions, and you know him. Each man has a measure of his own for everything ; this he offers you inadvertently in his words. He who has a superlative for everything wants a measure for the great or small. *Lavater.*

Learn to be good readers, which is perhaps a 45 more difficult thing than you imagine. Learn to be discriminative in your reading ; to read faithfully, and with your best attention, all kinds of things which you have a real interest in—a real, not an imaginary—and which you find to be really fit for what you are engaged in. *Carlyle to students.*

Learn to be pleased with everything; with wealth so far as it makes us of benefit to others; with poverty, for not having much to care for; and with obscurity, for being unenvied. *Plutarch.*

Learn to creep before you leap. *Pr.*

Learn to hold thy tongue. Five words cost Zecharias forty weeks' silence. *Fuller.*

Learn to labour and to wait. *Longfellow.*

5 Learn to say before you sing. *Pr.*

Learn to say No! and it will be of more use to you than to be able to read Latin. *Spurgeon.*

Learn wisdom from the follies of others. *Pr.*

Learn you a bad habit, an' ye'll ca'd a custom. *Sc. Pr.*

Learn young, learn fair; / Learn auld, learn mair. *Sc. Pr.*

10 Learned fools are the greatest of all fools. *Ger. Pr.*

Learned Theban. *Lear*, iii. 4.

Learned without sense and venerably dull. *Churchill.*

Learning by study must be won, / 'Twas ne'er entail'd from son to son. *Gay.*

Learning hath gained most by those books by which printers have lost. *Fuller.*

15 Learning hath its infancy, when it is almost childish; then its youth, when luxurious and juvenile; then its strength of years, when solid; and lastly its old age, when dry and exhaust. *Bacon.*

Learning is a companion on a journey to a strange country. *Hitopadesa.*

Learning is a dangerous weapon, and apt to wound its master if it is wielded by a feeble hand, and by one not well acquainted with its use. *Montaigne.*

Learning is a livelihood. *Hitopadesa.*

Learning is a sceptre to some, a bauble to others. *Pr.*

20 Learning is a superior sight. *Hitopadesa.*

Learning is an addition beyond / Nobility of birth; honour of blood, / Without the ornament of knowledge, is / A glorious ignorance. *Shirley.*

Learning is better than hidden treasure. *Hitopadesa.*

Learning is better worth than house or land. *Crabbe.*

Learning is but an adjunct to ourself; / And, where we are, our learning likewise is. *Love's L. Lost*, iv. 3.

25 Learning is not to be tacked to the mind, but we must fuse and blend them together, not merely giving the mind a slight tincture, but a thorough and perfect dye. *Montaigne.*

Learning is pleasurable, but doing is the height of enjoyment. *Novalis.*

Learning is strength inexhaustible. *Hitopadesa.*

Learning is the dictionary, but sense the grammar, of science. *Sterne.*

Learning is the source of renown, and the fountain of victory in the senate. *Hitopadesa.*

30 Learning itself, received into a mind / By nature weak or viciously inclined, / Serves but to lead philosophers astray, / Where children would with ease discern the way. *Cowper.*

Learning, like money, may be of so base a coin as to be utterly devoid of use; or, if sterling, may require good management to make it serve the purpose of sense and happiness. *Shenstone.*

Learning, like the lunar beam, affords light, not heat. *Young.*

Learning makes a man a fit companion for himself. *Pr.*

Learning makes a man wise, but a fool is made all the more a fool by it. *Pr.*

Learning needs rest; sovereignty gives it. 35 Sovereignty needs counsel; learning affords it. *Ben Jonson.*

Learning once made popular is no longer learning. *Johnson.*

Learning passes for wisdom among them who want both. *Sir W. Temple.*

Learning puffeth men up; words are but wind, and learning is nothing but words; ergo, learning is nothing but wind. *Swift.*

Learning to a man is a name superior to beauty. *Hitopadesa.*

Learning to the inexperienced is a poison. 40 *Hitopadesa.*

Learning without thought is labour lost. *Pr.*

Least said is soonest mended. *Pr.*

Leave a jest when it pleases you best. *Pr.*

Leave a man to his passions, and you leave a wild beast of a savage and capricious nature. *Burke.*

Leave a welcome behind you. *Pr.* 45

Leave all piggies' ears alone rather than seize upon the wrong one. *Spurgeon.*

Leave all things to a Father's will, / And taste, before him lying still, / Even in affliction, peace. *Anstice.*

Leave all to God, / Forsaken one, and stay thy tears! *Winkworth.*

Leave Ben Lomond where it stands. *Sc. Pr.*

Leave her to heaven, / And to those thorns 50 that in her bosom lodge, / To prick and sting her. *Ham.*, i. 5.

Leave it if you cannot mend it. *Pr.*

Leave not the meat to gnaw the bones, / Nor break your teeth on worthless stones. *Pr.*

Leave off no clothes / Till you see a June rose. *Pr.*

"Leave off your fooling and come down, sir." *Oliver Cromwell.*

Leave the court ere the court leave you. 55 *Sc. Pr.*

Leave the great ones of the world to manage their own concerns, and keep your eyes and observations at home. *Thomas à Kempis.*

Leave this keen encounter of our wits, / And fall somewhat into a slower method. *Rich. III.*, i. 2.

Leave to-morrow till to-morrow. *Pr.*

Leave to the diamond its ages to grow, nor expect to accelerate the births of the eternal. *Emerson.*

Leave well alone. *Pr.* 60

Leave you your power to draw, / And I shall have no power to follow you. *Mid. Night's Dream*, ii. 2.

Leaves enough, but few grapes. *Pr.*

Leaves have their time to fall, / And flowers to wither at the north wind's breath, / And stars to set ; but all, / Thou hast all seasons for thine own, O death ! *Mrs. Hemans.*

Leaving for gleaner makes farmer no leaner. *Pr.*

Lebe, wie du, wenn du stirbst, / Wünschen wirst, gelebt zu haben—Live, as you will wish to have lived when you come to die. *Gellert.*

Leben athme die bildende Kunst, / Geist fordr' ich vom Dichter—Let painting and sculpture breathe life ; it is spirit itself I require of the poet. *Schiller.*

5 Leben heisst träumen ; weise sein heisst angenehm träumen—To live is to dream, to be wise is to dream agreeably. *Schiller.*

Leberide cæcior—Blinder than a serpent's slough. *Pr.*

Led by illusions romantic and subtle deceptions of fancy, / Pleasure disguised as duty, and love in the semblance of friendship. *Longfellow.*

Leeze me o' drink ; it gies us mair / Than either school or college ; / It kindles wit, it waukens lair (learning), / It pangs (stuffs) us fu' o' knowledge. *Burns.*

Legant prius et postea despeciant—Let them read first, and despise afterwards. *Lope de Vega.*

10 Legatus a latere—An extraordinary Papal ambassador.

Lege totum si vis scire totum—Read the whole if you wish to know the whole.

Legem brevem esse oportet quo facilius ab imperitis teneatur—A law ought to be short, that it may be the more easily understood by the unlearned. *Sen.*

Leges ad civium salutem, civitatumque incolumitatem conditæ sunt—Laws were framed for the welfare of citizens and the security of states. *Cic.*

Leges bonæ malis ex moribus procreantur—Good laws are begotten of bad morals. *Pr.*

15 Leges mori serviunt—Laws are subordinate to custom. *Plaut.*

Leges posteriores priores contrarias abrogant —Later statutes repeat prior contrary ones. *L.*

Leges sunt inventæ quæ cum omnibus semper una atque eadem voce loquerentur—Laws are so devised that they may always speak with one and the same voice to all. *Cic.*

Legimus ne legantur—We read that others may not read. *Lactantius.*

Legis constructio non facit injuriam—The construction of the law does injury to no man. *L.*

20 Legum ministri magistratus, legum interpretes judices ; legum denique idcirco omnes servi sumus, ut liberi esse possimus—The magistrates are the ministers of the laws, the judges their interpreters ; we are all, in short, servants of the laws, that we may be free men. *Cic.*

Leib und Seele schmachten in hundert Banden, die unzerreissbar sind, aber auch in hundert andern, die ein einziger Entschluss zerreisst —Body and soul languish under a hundred entanglements from which there is no deliverance, but also in hundreds of others which a single resolution can snap away. *Feuchtersleben.*

Leicht zu sättigen ist, und unersättlich, die Liebe—Love is at once easy to satisfy and insatiable. *Rückert.*

Leichter trägt, was er trägt, / Wer Geduld zur Bürde legt—He bears what he bears more lightly who adds patience to the burden. *Logan.*

Leisure and solitude are the best effect of riches, because mother of thought. Both are avoided by most rich men, who seek company and business, which are signs of their being weary of themselves. *Sir W. Temple.*

Leisure for men of business, and business for 25 men of leisure, would cure many complaints. *Mrs. Thrale.*

Leisure is seldom enjoyed with perfect satisfaction except in solitude. *Zimmermann.*

Leisure is the reward of labour. *Pr.*

Leisure is time for doing something useful ; this leisure the diligent man will obtain ; the lazy man never. *Ben. Franklin.*

Lend, hoping for nothing again. *Bible.*

Lend only what you can afford to lose. 30 *Pr.*

Length of saying makes languor of hearing. *J. Roux.*

Lenior et melior fis, accedente senecta—You become milder and better as old age advances. *Hor.*

Leniter ex merito quidquid patiare ferendum est, / Quæ venit indigne pœna dolenda venit —Whatever you suffer deservedly should be borne with resignation ; the penalty that comes upon us undeservedly comes as a matter of just complaint. *Ovid.*

Lenity is part of justice. *Joubert.*

Lenity will operate with greater force, in some 35 instances, than rigour. It is, therefore, my first wish to have my whole conduct distinguished by it. *G. Washington.*

Leonem larva terres—You frighten a lion with a mask. *Pr.*

Leonina societas—Partnership with a lion.

Leonum ora a magistris impune tractantur— The mouths of lions are with impunity handled by their keepers. *Sen.*

Leporis vitam vivit—He lives the life of a hare, *i.e.,* always full of fear. *Pr.*

Lern' entbehren, O Freund, / Beut Trotz dem 40 Schmerz und dem Tode, / Und kein Gott den Olymps fühlet sich freier, als du—Learn to dispense with things, O friend, bid defiance to pain and death, and no god on Olympus breathes more freely than thou. *Bürger.*

Lerne vom Schlimmsten Gutes, und Schlimmes nicht vom Besten—Learn good from the worst, and not bad from the best. *Lavater.*

Les affaires ? c'est bien simple : c'est l'argent des autres—Business ? That's easily defined : it is other people's money. *Dumas fils.*

Les affaires font les hommes—Business makes men. *Fr.*

Les amertumes sont en morale ce que sont les amers en médicine—Afflictions are in morals what bitters are in medicine. *Fr.*

Les âmes privilégiées rangent à l'égal des 45 souverains—Privileged souls rank on a level with princes. *Frederick the Great.*

Les amis, ces parents que l'on se fait soimême—Friends, those relations that we make ourselves.

Les amis de mes amis sont mes amis—My friends' friends are my friends. *Fr. Pr.*

Les anglais s'amusent tristement—The English have a heavy-hearted way of amusing themselves. *Sully.*

Les beaux esprits se rencontrent—Great wits draw together. *Fr. Pr.*

Les belles actions cachées sont les plus estimables—The acts that we conceal are regarded with the highest esteem. *Pascal.*

Les biens mal acquis s'en vont à vau-l'eau—Wealth ill acquired soon goes (*lit.* goes with the stream). *Fr. Pr.*

5 Les biens viennent, les biens s'en vont, / Comme la fumée, comme toute chose—Wealth comes and goes like smoke, like everything. *Bret. Pr.*

Les bras croisés—Idle (*lit.* the arms folded). *Fr.*

Les cartes sont brouillées—A fierce dissension has arisen (*lit.* the cards are mixed).

Les choses valent toujours mieux dans leur source—Things are always best at their source. *Pascal.*

Les cloches appellent à l'église, mais n'y entrent pas—The bells call to church, but they do not enter. *Fr. Pr.*

10 Les consolations indiscrètes ne font qu'aigrir les violentes afflictions—Consolation indiscreetly pressed only aggravates the poignancy of the affliction. *Rousseau.*

Les délicats sont malheureux, / Rien ne saurait les satisfaire—The fastidious are unfortunate ; nothing satisfies them. *La Fontaine.*

Les enfants sont ce qu'on les fait—Children are what we make them. *Fr. Pr.*

Les envieux mourront, mais non jamais l'envie—The envious will die, but envy never will. *Molière.*

Les esprits médiocres condamnent d'ordinaire tout ce qui passe leur portée—Men of limited intelligence generally condemn everything that is above their power of understanding. *La Roche.*

15 Les extrêmes se touchent—Extremes meet. *Mercier.*

Les femmes ont toujours quelque arrière-pensée—Women have always some mental reservation. *Destouches.*

Les femmes ont un instinct céleste pour le malheur—Women have a divine instinctive feeling for misfortune. *Fr.*

Les femmes peuvent tout, parcequ'elles gouvernent les personnes qui gouvernent tout—Women can accomplish everything, because they govern those who govern everything. *Fr. Pr.*

Les femmes sont extrêmes : elles sont meilleures ou pires que les hommes—Women indulge in extremes ; they are always either better or worse than men. *La Bruyère.*

20 Les gens qui ont peu d'affaires, sont de très grands parleurs—People who have little to do are excessive talkers. *Fr.*

Les gens sans bruit sont dangereux—Still people are dangerous. *La Fontaine.*

Les girouettes qui sont placées le plus haut, tournent le mieux—Weathercocks placed on the most elevated stations turn the most readily. *Fr. Pr.*

Les grandes âmes ne sont pas celles qui ont moins de passions et plus de vertus que les âmes communes, mais celles seulement qui ont de plus grands desseins—Great souls are not those who have fewer passions and more virtues than common souls, but those only who have greater designs. *La Roche.*

Les grands et les petits ont mêmes accidents, et mêmes fâcheries et mêmes passions, mais l'un est au haut de la roue et l'autre près du centre, et ainsi moins agité par les mêmes mouvements—Great and little are subject to the same mischances, worries, and passions, but one is on the rim of the wheel and the other near the centre, and so is less agitated by the same movements. *Pascal.*

Les grands hommes ne se bornent jamais dans 25 leurs desseins à une circonscribed sphere of action. *Bouhours.*

Les grands hommes sont non-seulement populaires : ils donnent la popularité à tout ce qu'ils touchent—Great men are not only popular themselves ; they give popularity to whatever they touch. *Fournier.*

Les grands ne sont grands que parceque nous sommes à genoux ; relevons-nous !—The great are great only because we are on our knees. Let us rise up. *Quoted by Prudhomme.*

Les grands noms abaissent, au lieu d'élever ceux qui ne les savent pas soutenir—High titles lower, instead of raising, those who know not how to support them. *La Roche.*

Les grands seigneurs ont des plaisirs, le peuple a de la joie—High people have pleasures, common people have joy. *Montesquieu.*

Les haines sont si longues et si opiniâtres, 30 que le plus grand signe de mort dans un homme malade, c'est la réconciliation—The passion of hatred is so long-lived and obstinate a malady, that the surest prognostic of death in a sick man is his desire for reconciliation. *La Bruyère.*

Les hommes extrêmement heureux et les hommes extrêmement malheureux, sont également portés à la dureté—Men extremely happy and men extremely unhappy are alike prone to become hard-hearted. *Montesquieu.*

Les hommes font les lois, les femmes font les mœurs—Men make the laws, women the manners. *Guibert.*

Les hommes fripons en détail sont en gros de très honnêtes gens—Men who are knaves severally are in the mass highly honourable people. *Montesquieu.*

Les hommes ne sont justes qu'envers ceux qu'ils aiment—Men are just only to those they love. *Fr.*

Les hommes sont cause que les femmes ne 35 s'aiment point—It is on account of the men that the women do not love each other. *La Bruyère.*

Les hommes sont rares—Men are rare. *Fr. Pr.*

Les honneurs changent les mœurs—Honours change manners. *Fr. Pr.*

Les honneurs coutent à qui veut les posséder—Honours are dearly bought by whoever wishes to possess them. *Fr. Pr.*

Les jeunes gens disent ce qu'ils font, les vieillards ce qu'ils ont fait, et les sots ce qu'ils ont envie de faire—Young people talk of what they are doing, old people of what they have done, and fools of what they have a mind to do. *Fr.*

Les jours se suivent et ne se ressemblent pas 40—The days follow, but are not like each other. *Fr. Pr.*

Les magistrates, les rois n'ont aucune autorité sur les âmes ; et pourvu qu'on soit fidèle aux lois de la société dans ce monde, ce n'est point à eux de se mêler de ce qu'on deviendra dans l'autre, où ils n'ont aucune inspection—Rulers have no authority over men's souls ; and provided we are faithful to the laws of society in this world, it is no business of theirs to concern themselves with what may become of us in the next, over which they have no supervision. *Rousseau.*

Les maladies viennent à cheval, retournent à pied—Diseases make their attack on horseback, but retire on foot. *Fr.*

Les malheureux qui ont de l'esprit trouvent des resources en eux-mêmes—Men of genius when under misfortune find resources within themselves. *Bouhours.*

Les maximes des hommes décèlent leur cœur —Men show what they are by their maxims. *Vauvenargues.*

5 Les méchants sont toujours surpris de trouver de l'habilité dans les bons—Wicked men are always surprised to discover ability in good men. *Vauvenargues.*

Les médiocrités croient égaler le génie en dépassant la raison—Men of moderate abilities think to rank as geniuses by outstripping reason. *Lamartine.*

Les mœurs du prince contribuent autant à la liberté que les lois—The manners of the prince conduce as much to liberty as the laws. *Montesquieu.*

Les mœurs se corrompent de jour en jour, et on ne saurait plus distinguer les vrais d'avec les faux amis—Our manners are daily degenerating, and we can no longer distinguish true friends from false. *Fr.*

Les moissons, pour mûrir, ont besoin de rosée, / Pour vivre et pour sentir, l'homme a besoin des pleurs—Harvests to ripen have need of dew ; man, to live and to feel, has need of tears. *A. de Musset.*

10 Les mortels sont égaux ; ce n'est point la naissance, / C'est la seule vertu qui fait la différence—All men are equal ; it is not birth, it is virtue alone that makes the difference. *Voltaire.*

Les murailles (or murs) ont des oreilles—Walls have ears. *Fr. Pr.*

Les passions personelles se lassent et s'usent ; les passions publiques jamais—Private passions tire and exhaust themselves ; public ones never. *Lamartine.*

Les passions sont les seuls orateurs qui persuadent toujours — The passions are the only orators which always convince us. *La Roche.*

Les passions sont les vents qui enflent les voiles du vaisseau ; elles le submergent quelquefois, mais sans elles il ne pourrait voguer—The passions are the winds that fill the sails of the ship ; they sometimes sink it, but without them it could not make any way. *Voltaire.*

15 Les passions sont les vents qui font aller notre vaisseau, et la raison est le pilote qui le conduit ; le vaisseau n'irait point sans les vents, et se perdrait sans le pilote—The passions are the winds which propel our vessel ; our reason is the pilot that steers her ; without winds the vessel would not move ; without pilot she would be lost. *Fr.*

Les petits chagrins rendent tendre ; les grands, dur et farouche—Slight troubles render us tender ; great ones make us hard and unfeeling. *André Chénier.*

Les peuples une fois accoutumés à des maîtres ne sont plus en état de s'en passer—People once accustomed to masters are no longer able to dispense with them. *Rousseau.*

Les plaisirs sont amers si tôt qu'on en abuse —Pleasures become bitter as soon as they are abused. *Fr. Pr.*

Les plus grands crimes ne coutent rien aux ambitieux, quand il s'agit d'une couronne— The greatest crimes cause no remorse in an ambitious man when a crown is at stake. *Fr.*

Les plus grands hommes d'une nation sont 20 ceux qu'elle met à mort—The greatest men of a nation are those whom it puts to death. *Renan.*

Les plus malheureux osent pleurer le moins— Those who are most wretched dare least give vent to their grief. *Fr.*

Les querelles ne dureraient pas longtemps, si le tort n'était que d'un côté—Quarrels would not last so long if the fault lay only on one side. *La Roche.*

Les races se féminisent—Races are becoming effeminate. *Fr.*

Les républiques finissent par le luxe ; les monarchies par la pauvreté — Luxury ruins republics ; poverty, monarchies. *Montesquieu.*

Les rivières sont des chemins qui marchent— 25 Rivers are moving roads. *Pascal.*

Les sophistes ont ébranlé l'autel, mais ce sont les prêtres qui l'ont avili—The sophists have shaken the altar, but it is the priests that have disgraced it. *Regnault de Waren.*

Les sots depuis Adam sont en majorité—Ever since Adam's time fools have been in the majority. *Delavigne.*

Les talents sont distribués par la nature, sans égard aux généalogies—Talents go by nature, not by birth. *Frederick the Great.*

Les utopies ne sont souvent que des vérités prématuriées—Utopias are often only premature truths. *Lamartine.*

Les vérités sont des fruits qui ne doivent être 30 cueillis que bien mûrs—Truths, like fruits, ought not to be gathered until they are quite ripe, *i.e.* till the time is ripe for them. *Fr. Pr.*

Les vers sont enfants de la lyre ; / Il faut les chanter, non les lire—Verses are children of the lyre ; they must be sung, not read. *Fr.*

Les vertus se perdent dans l'intérêt comme les fleuves se perdent dans la mer — Our virtues lose themselves in our interests, as the rivers lose themselves in the ocean. *La Roche.*

Les vieillards aiment à donner de bons préceptes, pour se consoler de n'être plus en état de donner de mauvais exemples—Old men like to give good precepts, to make amends for being no longer able to set bad examples. *La Roche.*

Les vieilles coutumes sont les bonnes coutumes —The old customs are the good customs. *Bret. Pr.*

Les vieux fous sont plus fous que les jeunes— 35 Old fools are more foolish than young ones. *La Roche.*

Les villes sont le gouffre de l'espèce humaine —Towns are the sink of our race. *Rousseau.*

Lèse-majesté—High-treason. *Fr.*

Leser, wie gefall' ich dir? / Leser, wie gefällst du mir?—Reader, how please I thee? Reader, how pleasest thou me? *M.*

Less in rising into lofty abstractions lies the difficulty, than in seeing well and lovingly the complexities of what is at hand. *Carlyle.*

Less of your courtesy and more of your purse. *Pr.*

5 Less of your honey and more of your honesty. *Pr.*

Lessons hard to learn are sweet to know. *Pr.*

Lessons of wisdom have never such power over us as when they are wrought into the heart through the groundwork of a story which engages the passions. *Sterne.*

Lessons of wisdom open to our view / In all life's varied scenes of gay or gloomy hue. *De Bosch.*

Let a good pot have a good lid. *Pr.*

10 Let a hoard always be made, but not too great a hoard. *Hitopadesa.*

Let a horse drink when he will, not what he will. *Pr.*

Let a man be a man, and a woman a woman. *Pr.*

Let a man be but born ten years sooner or ten years later, his whole aspect and performance shall be different. *Goethe.*

Let a man believe in God, and not in names, places, and persons. *Emerson.*

15 Let a man do his work; the fruit of it is the care of Another than he. *Carlyle.*

Let a man overcome anger by love, let him overcome evil by good; let him overcome the greedy by liberality, the liar by truth. *Buddha.*

Let a saint be ever so humble, he will have his wax taper. *Dan. Pr.*

Let a woman once give you a task, and you are hers, heart and soul; all your care and trouble lend new charms to her for whose sake they are taken. *Jean Paul.*

Let ae deil ding (beat) anither. *Sc. Pr.*

20 Let all things be done decently and in order. *St. Paul.*

Let anger's fire be slow to burn. *Pr.*

Let another do what thou wouldst do. *Pr.*

Let another man praise thee, and not thine own mouth; a stranger, and not thine own lips. *Bible.*

Let another's shipwreck be your beacon. *Pr.*

25 Let any man compare his present fortune with the past, and he will probably find himself, upon the whole, neither better nor worse than formerly. *Goldsmith.*

Let authors write for glory or reward; / Truth is well paid when she is sung and heard. *Bp. Corbet.*

Let but the mirror be clear, this is the great point; the picture must and will be genuine. *Carlyle.*

Let but the public mind once become thoroughly corrupt, and all attempts to secure property, liberty, or life by mere force of laws written on parchment will be as vain as putting up printed notices in an orchard to keep off canker-worms. *Hor. Mann.*

Let byganes be byganes, / Wha's huffed at anither, / Dinna cloot the auld days / And the new anes thegither; / Wi' the fauts and the failings / O' past years be dune, / Wi a grip o' fresh freen'ship A New-Year begin. *M. W. Wood.*

Let charity be warm if the weather be cold. 30 *Pr.*

Let dogs delight to bark and bite, / For God hath made them so. *Watts.*

Let each tailor mend his own coat. *Pr.*

Let every bird sing its own note. *Dan. Pr.*

Let every eye negotiate for itself, and trust no agent. *Much Ado*, ii. 1.

Let every fox take care of his own brush. 35 *Pr.*

Let every herring hang by its own tail. *Irish Pr.*

Let every man be fully persuaded in his own mind. *St. Paul.*

Let every man come to God in his own way. *Ward Beecher.*

Let every man do what he was made for. *Pr.*

Let every man praise the bridge he goes over. 40 *Pr.*

Let every minute be a full life to thee. *Jean Paul.*

Let every one inquire of himself what he loveth, and he shall resolve himself of whence he is a citizen. *S. Augustine.*

Let every one look to himself, and no one will be lost. *Dut. Pr.*

Let every tailor keep to his goose. *Pr.*

Let every thought too, soldier-like, be 45 stripped, / And roughly looked over. *P. J. Bailey.*

Let ev'ry man enjoy his whim; / What's he to me or I to him? *Churchill.*

Let fate do her worst; there are moments of joy, / Bright dreams of the past, which she cannot destroy; / Which come in the night-time of sorrow and care, / And bring back the features that joy used to wear. *Moore.*

Let fortune empty her whole quiver on me, / I have a soul that, like an ample shield, / Can take in all, and verge enough for more. *Dryden.*

Let fouk bode weel, and strive to do their best; / Nae mair's required; let Heaven mak' out the rest. *Allan Ramsay.*

Let gleaners glean, though crops be lean. 50 *Pr.*

Let go desire, and thou shalt lay hold on peace. *Thomas à Kempis.*

Let go quarrel and contention, nor embroil thyself in trouble and differences by being over-solicitous in thy own defence. *Thomas à Kempis.*

Let go thy hold when a great wheel runs down a hill, lest it break thy neck in following it; but the great one that goes up the hill, let him draw thee after. *Lear*, ii. 4.

Let grace our selfishness expel, / Our earthliness refine. *Gurney.*

Let her (woman) make herself her own, / To 55 give or keep, to live, and learn, and be, / All that not harms distinctive womanhood. *Tennyson.*

Let Hercules himself do what he may, / The cat will mew, and dog will have his day. *Ham.*, v. 1.

Let him be kept from paper, pen, and ink ; / So may he cease to write, and learn to think. *Prior.*

Let him count himself happy who lives remote from the gods of this world. *Goethe.*

Let him tak' his fling, and find oot his ain wecht (weight). *Sc. Pr.*

5 Let him that does not know you buy you. *Pr.*

Let him that earns eat. *Pr.*

Let him that stole steal no more ; but rather let him labour, working with his hands the thing which is good, that he may have to give to him that needeth. *St. Paul.*

Let him that thinketh he standeth take heed lest he fall. *St. Paul.*

Let him who gives say nothing, and him who receives speak. *Port. Pr.*

10 Let him who gropes painfully in darkness or uncertain light, and prays vehemently that the dawn may ripen into day, lay this precept well to heart : " Do the duty which lies nearest thee," which thou knowest to be a duty ! Thy second duty will already have become clearer. *Carlyle.*

Let him who has hold of the devil keep hold of him ; he is not likely to catch him a second time in a hurry. *Goethe.*

Let him who is reduced to beggary first try every one and then his friend. *It. Pr.*

Let him who is well off stay where he is. *Pr.*

Let him who knows not how to pray go to sea. *Pr.*

15 Let him who sleeps too much borrow the pillow of a debtor. *Sp. Pr.*

Let him who would move and convince others be first moved and convinced himself. Let a man but speak forth with genuine earnestness the thought, the emotion, the actual condition of his own heart, and other men, so strangely are we all knit together by the tie of sympathy, must and will give heed to him. *Carlyle.*

Let him who would write heroic poems make his life a heroic poem. *Milton.*

Let ilka ane soop (sweep) before his ain door. *Sc. Pr.*

Let it be your first care not to be in any man's debt. *Johnson.*

20 Let it not be grievous to thee to humble and submit thyself to the capricious humours of men with whom thou conversest in this world, but rather . . . endure patiently whatever they shall, but should not, do to thee. *Thomas à Kempis.*

Let it not be imagined that the life of a good Christian must necessarily be a life of melancholy and gloominess ; for he only resigns some pleasures, to enjoy others infinitely greater. *Pascal.*

Let John Bull beware of John Barleycorn. *Pr.*

Let justice guide your feet. *Hipparchus.*

Let knowledge grow from more to more, / But more of reverence in us dwell. *Tennyson.*

25 Let man be noble, helpful, and good, for that alone distinguishes him from every other creature we know. *Goethe.*

Let man's own sphere confine his view. *Beattie.*

Let May be oot (out) before you cast a cloot (a piece of clothing). *Sc. Pr.*

Let me be cruel, not unnatural ; / I will speak daggers to her, but use none. / My tongue and soul in this be hypocrites. *Ham.*, iii. 2.

Let me die to the sounds of the delicious music. *Last words of Mirabeau.*

Let me have men about me that are fat ; / 30 Sleek-headed men, and such as sleep o' nights ; / Yond' Cassius has a lean and hungry look ; / He thinks too much ; such men are dangerous. *Jul. Cæs.*, i. 2.

Let me have no lying ; it becomes none but tradesmen. *Winter's Tale*, iv. 3.

Let me keep from vice myself, and pity it in others. *Goldsmith.*

Let me make the ballads of a people, and I care not who makes the laws. *Quoted by Fletcher of Saltoun.*

Let me play the fool ; / With mirth and laughter let old wrinkles come, / And let my liver rather heat with wine / Than my heart cool with mortifying groans. *Mer. of Ven.*, i. 1.

Let me say amen betimes, lest the devil cross 35 my prayers. *Mer. of Ven.*, iii. 1.

Let me still take away the harms I fear, / Not fear still to be taken. *Lear*, i. 4.

Let me tell the adventurous stranger, / In our calmness lies our danger ; / Like a river's silent running, / Stillness shows our depth and cunning. *Durfey.*

Let me warn you very earnestly against scruples. *Johnson.*

Let men know that they are men, created by God, responsible to God, who work in any meanest moment of time what will last through eternity. *Carlyle's version of John Knox's gospel to the Scotch.*

Let men laugh when you sacrifice desire to 40 duty, if they will. You have time and eternity to rejoice in. *Theodore Parker.*

Let men see, let them know, a real man, who lives as he was meant to live. *M. Aurelius.*

Let never day nor night unhallow'd pass, / But still remember what the Lord hath done. *2 Hen. VI.*, ii. 1.

Let never maiden think, however fair, / She is not finer in new clothes than old. *Tennyson.*

Let no complaisance, no gentleness of temper, no weak desire of pleasing on your part, no wheedling, coaxing, nor flattery on other people's, make you recede one jot from any point that reason and prudence have bid you pursue. *Chesterfield.*

Let no man be called happy before his death. 45 *Solon.*

Let no man doubt the omnipotence of nature, doubt the majesty of man's soul ; let no lonely unfriended son of genius despair. If he have the will, the right will, then the power also has not been denied him. *Carlyle.*

Let no man measure by a scale of perfection the meagre product of reality. *Schiller.*

Let no man think he is loved by any man, when he loves no man. *Epictetus.*

Let no man trust the first false step of guilt ; it hangs upon a precipice, whose steep descent in last perdition ends. *Young.*

Let no man value at a little price a virtuous woman's counsel. *George Chapman.*

Let no mean spirit of revenge tempt you to throw off your loyalty to your country, and to prefer a vicious celebrity to obscurity crowned with piety and virtue. *Sydney Smith.*

Let no one so conceive of himself as if he were the Messiah the world was praying for. *Goethe.*

Let no one think that he can conquer the first impressions of his youth. *Goethe.*

5 Let no one who loves to be called altogether unhappy; even love unreturned has its rainbow. *J. M. Barrie.*

Let nobility and virtue keep company, for they are nearest of kin. *William Penn.*

Let none admire / That riches grow in hell; that soil may best / Deserve the precious bane. *Milton.*

Let none henceforth seek needless cause t' approve / The faith they owe; when earnestly they seek / Such proof, conclude they then begin to fail. *Milton.*

Let none presume / To wear an undeservéd dignity. *Mer. of Ven.*, ii. 9.

10 Let not him that girdeth on his harness boast himself as he that putteth it off. *Bible.*

Let not man tempt the gods, or ever desire to pry into what they graciously conceal under a veil of darkness or terror. *Schiller.*

Let not mercy and truth forsake thee. *Bible.*

Let not mirth turn to mischief. *Pr.*

Let not my bark in calm abide, / But win her cheerless way against the chafing tide. *Keble.*

15 Let not one enemy be few, nor a thousand friends many, in thy sight. *Heb. Pr.*

Let not one look of fortune cast you down; / She were not fortune if she did not frown; / Such as do braveliest bear her scorns awhile / Are those on whom at last she most will smile. *Orrery.*

Let not plenty make you dainty. *Pr.*

Let not poverty part good company. *Pr.*

Let not the emphasis of hospitality lie in bed and board; but let truth and love and honour and courtesy flow in all thy deeds. *Emerson.*

20 Let not the grass grow on the path of friendship. *American-Indian Pr.*

Let not the remembrance of thy former trials discourage thee. *Thomas à Kempis.*

Let not the sun go down upon your wrath, *i.e.*, let it set with the sun, or, as Ruskin suggests, let it never go down so long as the wrong is there. *St. Paul.*

Let not thine heart be hasty to utter anything before God: for God is in heaven, and thou upon earth; therefore let thy words be few. *Bible.*

Let not thy left hand know what thy right hand doeth. *Jesus.*

25 Let not your money become your master. *Pr.*

Let not your mouth swallow you. *Pr.*

Let not your sail be bigger than your boat. *Ben Jonson.*

Let nothing be done through strife or vainglory. *St. Paul.*

Let nothing in excess be done; with this let all comply. *Anon.*

Let observation, with extensive view, / Survey 30 mankind, from China to Peru; / Remark each anxious toil, each eager strife, / And watch the busy scenes of crowded life. *Johnson.*

Let our finger ache, and it endues / Our other healthful members ev'n to that sense / Of pain. *Othello*, iii. 4.

Let pleasure be ever so innocent, the excess is always criminal. *St. Evremond.*

Let present rapture, comfort, ease, / As heaven shall bid them, come and go; / The secret this of rest below. *Keble.*

Let pride go afore, shame will follow after. *Chapman, Jonson, and Marston.*

Let prideful priests do battle about creeds, / 35 The Church is mine that does most Christlike deeds. *Prof. Blackie.*

Let prudence number o'er each sturdy son, / Who life and wisdom at one race begun. *Burns.*

Let rumours be, when did not rumours fly? *Tennyson.*

Let sleeping dogs lie. *Sc. Pr.*

Let still the woman take / An elder than herself; so wears she to him, / So sways she level in her husband's heart; / For, boy, however we do praise ourselves, / Our fancies are more giddy and unfirm, / More longing, wavering, sooner lost and worn / Than women's are. *Twelfth Night*, ii. 4.

Let such teach others who themselves excel, / 40 And censure freely who have written well. *Pope.*

Let that which is lost be for God. *Sp. Pr.*

Let the angry person always have the quarrel to himself. *Rev. John Clark.*

Let the best horse leap the hedge first. *Pr.*

Let the cobbler stick to his last. *Pr.*

Let the dainty rose awhile / Her bashful fra- 45 grance hide; / Rend not her silken veil too soon, / But leave her, in her own soft noon, / To flourish and abide. *Keble.*

Let the dead bury their dead, *i.e.*, let the spiritually dead bury the bodily dead. *Jesus.*

Let the devil catch you by a hair, and you are his for ever. *Lessing.*

Let the devil get into the church, and he will soon be on the altar. *Ger. Pr.*

Let the foibles of the great rest in peace. *Goldsmith.*

Let the galled jade wince, our withers are un- 50 wrung. *Ham.* iii. 2.

Let the great book of the world be your principal study. *Chesterfield.*

Let the great world spin forever down the ringing grooves of change. *Tennyson.*

Let the matter be good, and let the manner befit it. *Spurgeon.*

Let the night come before we praise the day. *Pr.*

Let the path be open to talent. *Napoleon.* 55 *See La Carrière.*

Let the reader have seen before he attempts to oversee. *Carlyle.*

Let the road be rough and dreary, / And its end far out of sight, / Foot it bravely! strong or weary, / "Trust in God, and do the right." *Dr. Norman Macleod.*

Let the shoemaker stick to his last, the peasant to his plough, and let the prince understand how to rule. *Goethe.*

Let the thing we do be what it will, it is the principle upon which we do it that must recommend it. *Thomas à Kempis.*

Let the tow (rope) gang wi' the bucket. *Sc. Pr.*

Let the world slide, let the world go ; / A fig for care, and a fig for woe ! / If I can't pay, why, I can owe, / And death makes equal the high and low. *Heywood.*

Let the world wag. *Pr.*

5 Let the young people mind what the old people say, / And where there is danger keep out of the way. *Pr.*

Let them call it mischief ; / When it is past and prosper'd it will be virtue. *Ben Jonson.*

Let them obey that know not how to rule. *2 Hen. VI., v. 1.*

Let there be thistles, there are grapes ; / If old things, there are new ; / Ten thousand broken lights and shapes, / Yet glimpses of the true. *Tennyson.*

Let thine eyes look right on. *Bible.*

10 Let this be an example for the acquisition of all knowledge, virtue, and riches. By the fall of drops of water, by degrees, a pot is filled. *Hitopadesa.*

Let those have night that love the night. *Quarles.*

Let those who believe in immortality enjoy their belief in silence, and give themselves no airs about it. *Goethe.*

Let those who hope for brighter shores no more, / Not mourn, but turning inland, bravely seek / What hidden wealth redeems the shapeless shore. *Eugene Lee Hamilton.*

Let thy alms go before, and keep heaven's gate / Open for thee, or both may come too late. *George Herbert.*

15 Let thy child's first lesson be obedience, and the second will be what thou wilt. *Ben. Franklin.*

Let thy fair wisdom, not thy passion, sway. *Twelfth Night, iv. 1.*

Let thy great deeds force fate to change her mind ; / He that courts fortune boldly, makes her kind. *Dryden.*

Let thy mind still be bent, still plotting where, / And when, and how thy business may be done, / Slackness breeds worms ; but the sure traveller, / Though he alights sometimes, still goeth on. *George Herbert.*

Let thy mind's sweetness have his operation / Upon thy body, clothes, and habitation. *George Herbert.*

20 Let thy words be few. *Bible.*

Let us a little permit Nature to take her own way ; she better understands her own affairs than we. *Montaigne.*

Let us approach our friend with an audacious trust in the truth of his heart, in the breadth, impossible to be overturned, of his foundations. *Emerson.*

Let us be back'd with God, and with the seas, / Which He hath given for fence impregnable, / And with these helps only defend ourselves ; / In them, and in ourselves, our safety lies. *3 Hen. VI., iv. 1.*

Let us be content in work / To do the thing we can, and not presume / To fret because it's little. *E. B. Browning.*

Let us be men with men, and always children 25 before God. *Joubert.*

Let us be poised, and wise, and our own to-day. *Emerson.*

Let us be silent, for so are the gods. *Emerson.*

Let us beware that our rest become not the rest of stones, which, so long as they are torrent-tossed and thunder-stricken, maintain their majesty ; but when the stream is silent and the storm passed, suffer the grass to cover them and the lichen to feed upon them, and are ploughed down into dust. *Ruskin.*

Let us do the work of men while we bear the form of them. *Ruskin.*

Let us endeavour to see things as they are, 30 and then inquire whether we ought to complain. *Johnson.*

Let us enjoy the cloven flame whilst it glows on our walls. *Emerson.*

Let us fear the worst, but work with faith ; the best will always take care of itself. *Victor Hugo.*

Let us have faith that right makes might, and in that faith let us dare to do our duty as we understand it. *Lincoln.*

Let us have the crisis ; we shall either have death or the cure. *Carlyle.*

Let us know what to love, and we shall know 35 also what to reject ; what to affirm, and we shall know also what to deny ; but it is dangerous to begin with denial and fatal to end with it. *Carlyle.*

Let us learn upon earth those things that can call us to heaven. *St. Jerome.*

Let us leave the question of origins to those who busy themselves with insoluble problems, and have nothing better to do. *Goethe.*

Let us make haste to live, since every day to a wise man is a new life. *Sen.*

Let us march intrepidly wherever we are led by the course of human accidents. Wherever they lead us, on what coasts soever we are thrown by them, we shall not find ourselves absolutely strangers. *Bolingbroke.*

Let us not burden our remembrances with / 40 A heaviness that's gone. *The Tempest, v. 1.*

Let us not make imaginary evils when we have so many real ones to encounter. *Goldsmith.*

Let us not strive to rise too high, that we may not fall too low. *Schiller.*

Let us not throw away any of our days upon useless resentment, or contend who shall hold out longest in stubborn malignity. *Johnson.*

Let us th' important "now" employ, / And live as those who never die. *Burns.*

Let us, then, be up and doing, / With a heart 45 for every fate ; / Still achieving, still pursuing, / Learn to labour and to wait. *Longfellow.*

Let us, then, be what we are, and speak what we think, and in all things / Keep ourselves loyal to truth and the sacred professions of friendship. *Longfellow.*

Let us try what esteem and kindness can effect. *Johnson.*

Let vain men pursue vanity ; leave them to their own methods. *Thomas à Kempis.*

Let wealth and commerce, laws and learning die, / But leave us still our old nobility. *Lord J. Manners.*

Let wealth shelter and cherish unprotected merit, and the gratitude and celebrity of that merit will richly repay it. *Burns.*

Let whatever you are and whatever you do, grow out of a firm root of truth and a strong soil of reality. *Prof. Blackie.*

Let Whig and Tory stir their blood ; / There must be stormy weather ; / But for some true result of good, / All parties work together. *Tennyson.*

5 Let woman learn betimes to serve according to her destination, for only by serving will she at last learn to rule, and attain the influence that belongs to her in the household. *Goethe.*

Let women spin, not preach. *Pr.*

Let your daily wisdom of life be in making a good use of the opportunities given you. *Prof. Blackie.*

Let your enemies be disarmed by the gentleness of your manner, but let them feel, at the same time, the steadiness of your just resentment. *Chesterfield.*

Let your literary compositions be kept from the public eye for nine years at least. *Hor.*

10 Let your pen fall, begin to trifle with blotting-paper, look at the ceiling, bite your nails, and otherwise dally with your purpose, and you waste your time, scatter your thoughts, and repress the nervous energy necessary for your task. *G. H. Lewes.*

Let your purse be your master. *Pr.*

Let your reason with your choler question. . . . To climb steep hills / Requires slow pace at first. *Hen. VIII.*, i. 1.

Let your rule in reference to your social sentiments be simply this ; pray for the bad, pity the weak, enjoy the good, and reverence both the great and the small, as playing each his part aptly in the divine symphony of the universe. *Prof. Blackie.*

Let your speech be alway with grace, seasoned with salt, that ye may know how to answer every man. *St. Paul.*

15 Let your trouble tarry till its own day comes. *Pr.*

Let's live with that small pittance which we have ; / Who covets more is evermore a slave. *Herrick.*

Let's not unman each other—part at once ; / All farewells should be sudden when for ever, / Else they make an eternity of moments, / And clog the last sad sands of life with tears. *Byron.*

Let's take the instant by the forward top ; / For we are old, and on our quick'st decrees / Th' inaudible and noiseless foot of time / Steals ere we can effect them. *All's Well*, v. 3.

Let's teach ourselves that honourable stop, not to out-sport discretion. *Othello*, ii. 3.

20 Letters may be always made out of the books of the morning or talk of the evening. *Johnson.*

Letters of mere compliment, congratulation, or affected condolence, which have cost the authors most labour in composing, never fail of being the most disagreeable and insipid to the readers. *Blair.*

Letters that are warmly sealed are often coldly opened. *Jean Paul.*

Letters without virtue are like pearls in a dunghill. *Cervantes.*

Letting down buckets into empty wells, and growing old with drawing nothing up. *Cowper.*

Lettres de cachet—Warrants of imprisonment 25 under royal seal, liberally issued in France before the Revolution.

Leuk twice or ye loup ance, *i.e.*, look twice before you leap once. *Sc. Pr.*

Leve æs alienum debitorem facit, grave inimicum—A small debt makes a man your debtor, a large one your enemy. *Sen.*

Leve fit quod bene fertur onus—The burden which is cheerfully borne becomes light. *Ovid.*

Leve incommodum tolerandum est—A slight inconvenience must be endured. *M.*

Leve (trust) none better than thyself. *Hazlitt's* 30 *Poems.*

Level roads run out from music to every side. *Goethe.*

Leves homines futuri sunt improvidi—Light-minded men are improvident of the future. *Tac.*

Levia perpessi sumus, / Si fienda patimur—Our sufferings are light, if they are merely such as we should weep for.

Leviores sunt injuriæ, quæ repentino aliquo motu accidunt, quam eæ quæ meditate præparata inferuntur—The injuries which befall us unexpectedly are less severe than those which we are deliberately anticipating. *Cic.*

Levis est dolor qui capere consilium potest—35 Grief is light which can take advice. *Sen.*

Levis sit tibi terra—May the earth lie light on thee.

Levity is a prettiness in a child, a disgraceful defect in men, and a monstrous folly in old age. *La Roche.*

Levity is often less foolish, and gravity less wise, than each of them appears. *Colton.*

Levity of behaviour is the bane of all that is good and virtuous. *Sen.*

Levius fit patientia / Quicquid corrigere est 40 nefas—Whatever cannot be amended becomes easier to bear if we exercise patience. *Hor.*

Levius solet timere qui propius timet—A man's fears are lighter when the danger is near at hand. *Sen.*

Lex aliquando sequitur æquitatem — Law is sometimes according to equity. *L.*

Lex citius tolerare vult privatum damnum quam publicum malum—The law will sooner tolerate a private loss than a public evil. *Coke.*

Lex neminem cogit ad impossibilia—The law compels no one to do what is impossible. *L.*

Lex non scripta—The common law.   45

Lex prospicit non respicit—The law is prospective, not retrospective. *L.*

Lex scripta—The statute law.

Lex talionis—The law of retaliation.

Lex terræ—The law of the land.

Lex universa est quæ jubet nasci et mori— 50 There is a universal law which commands that we shall be born and shall die. *Pub. Syr.*

Liars act like the salt-miners ; they undermine the truth, but leave just so much standing as is necessary to support the edifice. *Jean Paul.*

Liars are always ready to take oath. *Alfieri.*

Liars are the cause of all the sins and crimes in the world. *Epictetus.*

Liars ought to have good memories. *Sidney.*

Libenter homines id, quod volunt, credunt— Men are fain to believe what they wish. *Cæsar.*

5 Libera chiesa in libero stato—A free church in a free state. *Cavour.*

Libera Fortunæ mors est : capit omnia tellus / Quæ genuit—Death is not subject to fortune ; the earth contains everything which she ever brought forth. *Luc.*

Libera me ab homine malo, a meipso—Deliver me from the evil man, from myself. *St. Augustine.*

Libera te metu mortis—Deliver thyself from the fear of death. *Sen.*

Liberality consists less in giving profusely than in giving judiciously. *La Bruyère.*

10 Liberality is not giving largely but wisely. *Pr.*

Libertas—Liberty. *M.*

Libertas est potestas faciendi id quod jure licet—Liberty consists in the power of doing what the law permits. *L.*

Libertas in legibus—Liberty under the laws. *M.*

Libertas, quæ sera, tamen respexit inertem— Liberty, which, though late, regarded me in my helpless state. *Virg.*

15 Libertas sub rege pio—Liberty under a pious king. *M.*

Libertas ultima mundi / Quo steterit ferienda loco—In the spot where liberty has made her last stand she was fated to be smitten. *Lucan.*

Liberté toute entière—Liberty perfectly entire. *M.*

Liberty, and not theology, is the enthusiasm of the nineteenth century. The very men who would once have been conspicuous saints are now conspicuous revolutionists, for while their heroism and disinterestedness are their own, the direction which these qualities take is determined by the pressure of the age. *H. W. Lecky.*

Liberty comes with Christianity, because Christianity develops and strengthens the mass of men. *Ward Beecher.*

20 Liberty exists in proportion to wholesome restraint. *Webster.*

Liberty has no actual rights which are not grafted upon justice. *Mme. Swetchine.*

Liberty has no crueller enemy than license. *Fr. Pr.*

Liberty is a principle ; its community is its security ; exclusiveness is its doom. *Kossuth.*

Liberty is a slow fruit. It is never cheap ; it is made difficult because freedom is the accomplishment and perfectness of man. *Emerson.*

25 Liberty is an old fact ; it has had its heroes and its martyrs in almost every age. *Chapin.*

Liberty is God's gift ; liberties are the devil's. *Ger. Pr.*

Liberty is not idleness ; it is an unconstrained use of time. To be free is not to be doing nothing ; it is to be one's own master as to what one ought to do or not to do. *La Bruyère.*

Liberty is of more value than any gifts ; and to receive gifts is to lose it. Be assured that men most commonly seek to oblige thee only that they may engage thee to serve them. *Saadi.*

Liberty is one of the most precious gifts that Heaven has bestowed on man, and captivity is the greatest evil that can befall him. *Cervantes.*

Liberty is quite as much a moral as a political 30 growth, the result of free individual action, energy, and independence. *S. Smiles.*

Liberty is the right of doing whatever the laws permit. *Montesquieu.*

Liberty is to the collective body what health is to every individual body. Without health no pleasure can be tasted by man ; without liberty no happiness can be enjoyed by society. *Bolingbroke.*

Liberty is to the lowest rank of every nation little more than the choice of working or starving. *Johnson.*

Liberty may be endangered by the abuse of liberty as well as by the abuse of power. *Madison.*

Liberty must be a mighty thing, for by it 35 God punishes and rewards nations. *Mme. Swetchine.*

Liberty must be limited in order to be possessed. *Burke.*

Liberty of thinking and expressing our thoughts is always fatal to priestly power, and to those pious frauds on which it is commonly founded. *Hume.*

Liberty raises us to the gods ; holiness prostrates us on the ground. *Amiel.*

Liberty, when it begins to take root, is a plant of rapid growth. *Washington.*

Liberty will not descend to a people ; a people 40 must raise themselves to liberty ; it is a blessing that must be earned before it can be enjoyed. *Colton.*

Liberty, with all its drawbacks, is everywhere vastly more attractive to a noble soul than good social order without it, than society like a flock of sheep, or a machine working like a watch. This mechanism makes of man only a product ; liberty makes him the citizen of a better world. *Schiller.*

Liberum arbitrium—Free will.

Libidinosa et intemperans adolescentia effœtum corpus tradit senectuti—A sensual and intemperate youth transmits to old age a worn-out body. *Cic.*

Libido effrenata effrenatam appetentiam efficit —Unbridled gratification produces unbridled desire. *Pr.*

Libito fè licito—What pleased her she made law. 45 *Dante.*

Libra justa justitiam servat—A just balance preserves justice.

Libraries are as the shrines where all the relics of saints full of true virtue, and that without delusion and imposture, are preserved and reposed. *Bacon.*

Libraries are the wardrobes of literature, whence men, properly informed, might bring forth something for ornament, much for curiosity, and more for use. *J. Dyer.*

License they mean when they cry liberty. *Milton.*

Liceat concedere veris—We are free to yield to 50 truth. *Hor.*

Licet superbus ambules pecunia, / Fortuna non mutat genus—Although you strut insolent in your wealth, your fortune does not change your low birth. *Hor.*

Licht und Geist, jenes im Phyischen, dieses im Sittlichen herrschend, sind die höchsten denkbaren untheilbaren Energien—Light and spirit, the one sovereign in the physical, the other in the moral, are the highest conceivable indivisible potences at work in the universe. *Goethe.*

Licuit, semperque licebit / Parcere personis, dicere de vitiis—It ever has been, and ever will be, lawful to spare the individual but to censure the vice.

Lie not in the mire, and say, "God help!" *Pr.*

Lie not, neither to thyself, nor man, nor God. Let mouth and heart be one; beat and speak together, and make both felt in action. It is for cowards to lie. *George Herbert.*

5 Liebe bleibt die goldne Leiter / Darauf das Herz zum Himmel steigt—Love is ever the golden ladder whereby the heart ascends to heaven. *Geibel.*

Liebe ist die ältest-neuste / Einz'ge Weltbegebenheit — Love is the oldest-newest sole world-event. *Rückert.*

Liebe kann nicht untergehen; / Was verwest, muss auferstehen—Love cannot perish; what decays must come to life again. *J. G. Jacobi.*

Liebe kann viel, Geld kann alles—Love cannot do much; money everything. *Ger. Pr.*

Liebe kennt der allein, der ohne Hoffnung liebt—He alone knows what love is who loves without hope. *Schiller.*

10 Liebe ohne Gegenliebe ist wie eine Frage ohne Antwort—Love unreciprocated is like a question without an answer. *Ger. Pr.*

Liebe schwärmet auf allen Wegen; / Treue wohnt für sich allein; / Liebe kommt euch rasch entgegen; / Aufgesucht will Treue sein—Love ranges about in all thoroughfares; fidelity dwells by herself alone. Love comes to meet you with quick footstep; fidelity will be sought out. *Goethe.*

Liebe ward der Welt von Gott verliehen, / Um zu Gott die Seele zu erziehen—Love was bestowed on the world by God, in order to train the soul for God. *Rückert.*

Lieber Neid denn Mitleid—Better envy than pity. *Ger. Pr.*

Lies are like nitro-glycerine—the best of judges can't tell where they are going to burst and scatter confusion. *Billings.*

15 Lies are sufficient to breed opinion, and opinion brings on substance. *Bacon.*

Lies are the ghosts of truths, the masks of faces. *J. Sterling.*

Lies have short legs. *It. and Ger. Pr.*

Lies hunt in packs. *Pr.*

Lies may be acted as well as spoken. *Pr.*

20 Lies, mere show and sham, and hollow superficiality of all kinds, which is at the best a painted lie, avoid. *Prof. Blackie to young men.*

Lies need a great deal of killing. *Pr.*

Lies that are half true are the worst of lies. *Pr.*

Life abounds in cares, in thorns, and woes; many tears flow visibly, although many more are unseen. *Antoni Malaszeski.*

Life admits not of delays. *Johnson.*

25 Life alone can rekindle life. *Amiel.*

Life, as we call it, is nothing but the edge of the boundless ocean of existence where it comes upon soundings. *Holmes.*

Life at the greatest and best is but a froward child, that must be humoured and coaxed a little till it falls asleep, and then all the care is over. *Goldsmith.*

Life belongs to the living, and he who lives must be prepared for vicissitudes. *Goethe.*

Life cannot subsist in society but by reciprocal concessions. *Johnson.*

Life every man holds dear; but the brave 30 man / Holds honour far more precious dear than life. *Troil. and Cress.*, v. 3.

Life everywhere will swallow a man, unless he rise and try vigorously to swallow it. *Carlyle.*

Life expresses. A statue has no tongue, and needs none. (?)

Life, full life, / Full-flowered, full-fruited, reared from homely earth, / Rooted in duty, . . . this is the prize / I hold most dear, more precious than the fruit / Of knowledge or of love. *Lewis Morris.*

Life has been compared to a race, but the allusion still improves, by observing that the most swift are ever the least manageable, the most apt to stray from the course. Great abilities have always been less serviceable to the possessors than moderate ones. *Goldsmith.*

Life has no memory. *Emerson.* 35

Life has no pleasure nobler than that of friendship. *Johnson.*

Life, however short, is made shorter by waste of time; and its progress towards happiness, though naturally slow, is made still slower by unnecessary labour. *Johnson.*

Life I leave, as I would leave an inn, rather than a home; nature having given it us more as a sort of hostelry to stop at, than as an abiding dwelling-place. *Cato in Cicero.*

Life in itself is neither good nor evil, but the scene of good or evil, as you make it; and if you have lived one day, you have lived all days. *Montaigne.*

Life is a campaign, not a battle, and has 40 its defeats as well as its victories. *Donn Piatt.*

Life is a casket, not precious in itself, but valuable in proportion to what fortune, or industry, or virtue has placed within it. *Landor.*

Life is a comedy to him who thinks, and a tragedy to him who feels. *Horace Walpole.*

Life is a crucible, into which we are thrown and tried. The actual weight and value of a man are expressed in the spiritual substance of the man; all else is dross. *Chapin.*

Life is a disease of the spirit; a working incited by passion. Rest is peculiar to the spirit. *Novalis.*

Life is a disease (*Krankheit*), sleep a palliative, 45 death the radical cure. *C. J. Weber.*

Life is a dream and death an awakening. *Beaumelle.*

Life is a fairy scene: almost all that deserves the name of enjoyment or pleasure is only a charming delusion; and in comes repining age, in all the gravity of hoary wisdom, and wretchedly chases away the bewitching phantom. *Burns.*

Life is a fortress which neither you nor I know anything about. Why throw obstacles in the way of its defence? Its own means are superior to all the apparatus of your laboratories. *Emerson.*

Life is a fragment, a moment between two eternities, influenced by all that has preceded, and to influence all that follows. *Channing.*

Life is a jest, and all things show it; / I thought so once, but now I know it. *Gay.*

Life is a kind of sleep; old men sleep longest, nor begin to wake until they are to die. *La Bruyère.*

5 Life is a little gleam of time between two eternities. *Carlyle.*

Life is a long lesson in humility. *J. M. Barrie.*

Life is a moment between two eternities. *Channing.*

Life is a plant that grows out of death. *Ward Beecher.*

Life is a progress from want to want, not from enjoyment to enjoyment. *Johnson.*

10 Life is a quarantine for Paradise. *C. J. Weber.*

Life is a rich strain of music suggesting a realm too fair to be. *G. W. Curtis.*

Life is a scale of degrees. Between rank and rank of our great men are wide intervals. *Emerson.*

Life is a search after power; and this is an element with which the world is so saturated—there is no chink or crevice in which it is not lodged—that no honest seeking goes unrewarded. *Emerson.*

Life is a series of surprises, and would not be worth taking or keeping if it were not. *Emerson.*

15 Life is a short day, but it is a working day. *Hannah More.*

Life is a shuttle. *The Merry Wives*, v. 1.

Life is a sincerity. In lucid intervals we say, "Let there be an entrance opened for me into realities; I have worn the fool's cap too long." *Emerson.*

Life is a sleep, love is a dream, and you have lived if you have loved. *A. de Musset.*

Life is a stream upon which drift flowers in spring and blocks of ice in winter. *Joseph Roux.*

20 Life is a succession of lessons which must be lived to be understood. All is riddle, and the key to a riddle is another riddle. *Emerson.*

Life is a voyage. *Victor Hugo.*

Life is a warfare. *Sen.*

Life is a wrestle with the devil, and only the frivolous think to throw him without taking off their coats. *J. M. Barrie.*

Life is act, and not to do is death. *Lewis Morris.*

25 Life is all a variorum; / We regard not how it goes; / Let them cant about decorum / Who have characters to lose. / A fig for those by law protected! / Liberty's a glorious feast; / Courts for cowards were erected, / Churches built to please the priest. *Burns, "Jolly Beggars."*

Life is an earnest business, and no man was ever made great or good by a diet of broad grins. *Prof. Blackie.*

Life is as tedious as a twice-told tale, / Vexing the dull ear of a drowsy man. *King John,* iii. 4.

Life is as the current spark on the miner's wheel of flints; while it spinneth there is light; stop it, all is darkness. *Tupper.*

Life is burdensome to us chiefly from the abuse of it. *Rousseau.*

Life is but a tissue of habits. *Amiel.* 30

Life is but another name for action; and he who is without opportunity exists, but does not live. *G. S. Hillard.*

Life is but thought; so think I will that youth and I are housemates still. *S. T. Coleridge.*

Life is freedom—life in the direct ratio of its amount. . . . The smallest candle fills a mile with its rays, and the pupillæ of a man run out to every star. *Emerson.*

Life is girt all round with a zodiac of sciences, the contributions of men who have perished to add their point of light to our sky. . . . These road-makers on every hand enrich us. We must extend the area of life and multiply our relations. We are as much gainers by finding a property in the old earth as by acquiring a new planet. *Emerson.*

Life is given us not to enjoy, but to overcome. 35 *Schopenhauer.*

Life is half spent before we know what life is. *Fr. Pr.*

Life is immeasurably heightened by the solemnity of death. *Alex. Smith.*

Life is kindled only by life. *Jean Paul.*

Life is like wine; he who would drink it pure must not drain it to the dregs. *Sir W. Temple.*

Life is made up, not of great sacrifices or 40 duties, but of little things, in which smiles and kindness, and small obligations given habitually, are what win the heart and secure comfort. *Sir H. Davy.*

Life is made up, not of knowledge only, but of love also. . . . The hues of sunset make life great; so the affections make some little web of cottage and fireside populous, important. *Emerson.*

Life is movement. *Arist.*

Life is no merrymaking. *Dr. W. Smith.*

Life is not as idle ore, / But iron dug from central gloom, / And heated hot with burning fears, / And dipt in baths of hissing tears, / And battered with the shocks of doom / To shape and use. *Tennyson.*

Life is not intellectual or critical, but sturdy. 45 Its chief good is for well-mixed people, who can enjoy what they find without question. *Emerson.*

Life is not long, and too much of it must not pass in idle deliberation how it shall be spent. *Johnson.*

Life is not long enough for art, not long enough for friendship. *Emerson.*

Life is not so short but there is always time enough for courtesy. *Emerson.*

Life is not the supreme good; but of all earthly ills the chief is guilt. *Schiller.*

Life is not victory, but battle. *R. D. Hitch-* 50 *cock.*

Life is poor when its old faiths are gone, / Poorest when man can trust himself alone. *Dr. Walter Smith.*

Life is probation, and this earth no goal, / But starting-point of man. *Browning.*

Life is rather a state of embryo, a preparation for life; a man is not completely born till he has passed through death. *Franklin.*

Life is ravelled almost ere we wot, / And with our vexing / To disentangle it, we make the knot / But more perplexing, / Embittering our lot. *Dr. Walter Smith.*

Life is real, life is earnest. *Longfellow.*

5 Life is sacred; but there is something more sacred still: woe to him who does not know that withal. *Carlyle.*

Life is so complicated a game, that the devices of skill are liable to be defeated at every turn by air-blown chances, incalculable as the descent of thistle-down. *George Eliot.*

Life is so healthful that it even finds nourishment in death. *Carlyle.*

Life is that which holds matter together. *Porphyry.*

Life is the art of being well deceived. *Hazlitt.*

10 Life is the best thing we can possibly make of it. *G. W. Curtis.*

Life is the jailer, death the angel sent to draw the unwilling bolts and set us free. *Lowell.*

Life is the jailer of the soul in this filthy prison, and its only deliverer is death. What we call life is a journey to death, and what we call death is a passport to life. *Colton.*

Life is the transmigration of a soul / Through various bodies, various states of being; / New manners, passions, new pursuits in each; / In nothing, save in consciousness, the same. *Montgomery.*

Life is the triumph of our mouldering clay; death of the spirit infinite, divine! *Young.*

15 Life is to be considered happy, not in warding off evil, but in the acquisition of good: and this we should seek for by employment of some kind or by reflection. *Cic.*

Life is too much for most. So much of age, so little of youth; living for the most part, in the moment, and dating existence by the memory of its burdens. *A. B. Alcott.*

Life is too short to waste / In critic peep or cynic bark, / Quarrel or reprimand; / 'Twill soon be dark. *Emerson.*

Life itself is a bubble and a scepticism, and a sleep within a sleep. *Emerson.*

Life just the stuff / To try the soul's strength on, educe the man. *Browning.*

20 Life lies before us as a huge quarry before the architect; and he deserves not the name of architect except when, out of this fortuitous mass, he can combine, with the greatest economy, fitness and durability, some form the pattern of which originated in his own soul. *Goethe.*

Life lies most open in a closed eye. *Quarles.*

Life, like a dome of many coloured glass, / Stains the white radiance of eternity. *Shelley.*

Life, like some cities, is full of blind alleys, leading nowhere; the great art is to keep out of them. *Bovee.*

Life, like the water of the seas, freshens only when it ascends towards heaven. *Jean Paul.*

Life may as properly be called an art as any 25 other, and the great incidents in it are no more to be considered as mere accidents than the severest members of a fine statue or a noble poem. *Fielding.*

Life must be lived on a higher plane. We must go up to a higher platform, to which we are always invited to ascend; there the whole aspect of things changes. *Emerson.*

Life only avails, not the having lived. *Emerson.*

Life outweighs all things, if love lies within it. *Goethe.*

Life passes through us; we do not possess it. *Amiel.*

Life protracted is protracted woe, / Time 30 hovers o'er, impatient to destroy, / And shuts up all the passages of joy. *Johnson.*

Life sues the young like a new acquaintance. . . . To us, who are declined in years, life appears like an old friend. *Goldsmith.*

Life, to be worthy of a rational being, must be always in progression: we must always purpose to do more or better than in time past. *Johnson.*

Life, upon the whole, is much more pleasurable than painful, otherwise we should not feel pain so impatiently when it comes. *Leigh Hunt.*

Life was intended to be so adjusted that the body should be the servant of the soul, and always subordinate to the soul. *J. G. Holland.*

Life was never a May-game for men; not play 35 at all, but hard work, that makes the sinews sore and the heart sore. *Carlyle.*

Life was spread as a banquet for pure, noble, unperverted natures, and may be such to them, ought to be such to them. *W. R. Greg.*

Life wastes itself while we are preparing to live. *Emerson.*

Life, whether in this world or any other, is the sum of our attainment, our experience, our character. In what other world shall we *be* more surely than we are here? *Chapin.*

Life with all it yields of joy and woe, / And hope and fear, / Is just our chance o' the prize of learning love, / How love might be, hath been indeed, and is. *Browning.*

Life without a freend is death wi' a witness. 40 *Sc. Pr.*

Life without laughing is a dreary blank. *Thackeray.*

Life would be too smooth if it had no rubs in it. *Pr.*

Life's a reckoning we cannot make twice over. *George Eliot.*

Life's a tragedy. *Raleigh.*

Life's a tumble-about thing of ups and downs. 45 *Disraeli.*

Life's but a day at most. *Burns.*

Life's but a means unto an end; that end / Beginning, mean, and end to all things— God. *Bailey.*

Life's but a walking shadow; a poor player, / That struts and frets his hour upon the stage, / And then is heard no more! It is a tale / Told by an idiot, full of sound and fury, / Signifying nothing. *Macb., v. 5.*

Life's ebbing stream on either side / Shows at each turn some mould'ring hope or joy, / The man seems following still the funeral of the boy. *Keble.*

Life's enchanted cup but sparkles near the brim. *Byron.*

Life's life ony gate (at any rate). *Scott.*

Life's no resting, but a moving ; / Let thy life be deed on deed. *Goethe.*

5 Light another's candle, but don't put out your own. *Pr.*

Light boats sail swift, though greater hulks draw deep. *Troil. and Cress.*, iii. 3.

Light burdens carried far grow heavy. *Fr. and Ger. Pr.*

Light cares (or griefs) speak ; great ones are dumb. *Sen.*

Light flashes in the gloomiest sky, / And music in the dullest plain. *Keble.*

10 Light gains make heavy purses, because they come thick, whereas the great come but now and then. *Bacon.*

Light is, as it were, a divine humidity. *Joubert.*

Light is come into the world, and men loved darkness rather than the light, because their deeds were evil. *St. John.*

Light is coming into the world ; men love not darkness ; they do love light. *Carlyle.*

Light is, in reality, more awful than darkness ; modesty more majestic than strength ; and there is truer sublimity in the sweet joy of a child, or the sweet virtue of a maiden, than in the strength of Antæus or the thunder-clouds of Ætna. *Ruskin.*

15 Light is light, though the blind man doesn't see it. *Ger. Pr.*

Light is no less favourable to merit than unfavourable to imposture. *H. Home.*

Light is, perhaps, the most wonderful of all visible things. *Leigh Hunt.*

Light is sown for the righteous, and gladness for the upright in heart. *Bible.*

Light is the burden love lays on : / Content and love brings peace and joy, / What mair hae queens upon a throne? *Burns.*

20 Light is the symbol of truth. *Lowell.*

Light not your candle at both ends. *Pr.*

Light, or, failing that, lightning—the world can take its choice. *Carlyle.*

Light seeking light doth light of light beguile. *Love's L. Lost*, i. 1.

Light suppers mak' lang life. *Sc. Pr.*

25 Light that a man receiveth by counsel from another is drier and purer than that which cometh from his own understanding and judgment, which is ever in his affections and customs. *Bacon.*

Light that makes things seen makes some things invisible. *Sir Thomas Browne.*

Light visits the hearts, as it does the eyes, of all living. *Carlyle.*

Light without life is a candle in a tomb ; / Life without love is a garden without bloom. *Pr.*

Lightly come, lightly go. *Pr.*

30 Lightning and thunder (heaven's artillery) / As harbingers before th' Almighty fly : / Those but proclaim His style, and disappear ; / The stiller sounds succeed, and God is there. *Dryden.*

Like a great poet, Nature produces the greatest results with the simplest means. There are simply a sun, flowers, water, and love. *Heine.*

Like a large heart overflowing with an impotent and vague love, the universe is ceaselessly in the agony of transformation. *Renan.*

Like a lusty winter, frosty but kindly. *Pr.*

Like a man do all things, not sneakingly. *George Herbert.*

35 Like a morning dream, life becomes more and more bright the longer we live, and the reason of everything appears more clear. *Jean Paul.*

Like a tailor's needle, say, "I go through." *Pr.*

Like an old woman at her hearth, we warm our hands at our sorrows and drop in faggots, and each thinks his own fire a sun in presence of which all other fires should go out. *J. M. Barrie.*

Like angels' visits, few and far between. *Campbell, from Blair.*

Like angels' visits, short and bright ; / Mortality's too weak to bear them long. *J. Norris.*

40 Like author. like book. *Pr.*

Like blude, like gude, like age, mak' the happy marriage. *Sc. Pr.*

Like coalesces in this world with unlike. The strong and the weak, the contemplative and the active, bind themselves together. *Fr. Robertson.*

Like cures like. *Pr.*

Like dogs in a wheel, birds in a cage, or squirrels in a chain, ambitious men still climb and climb, with great labour and incessant anxiety, but never reach the top. *Burton.*

45 Like doth quit like, and measure still for measure. *Meas. for Meas.*, v. 1.

Like draws to like, the world over. *Pr.*

Like everything else in nature, music is a becoming, and it becomes its full self when its sounds and laws are used by intelligent man for the production of harmony, and so made the vehicle of emotion and thought. *Theodore T. Munger.*

Like father, like son. *Pr.*

Like leaves on trees the race of man is found, / Now green in youth, now withering on the ground ; / Another race the following spring supplies ; / They fall successive, and successive rise. *Pope's Homer.*

50 Like master, like man. *Pr.*

Like mighty rivers, with resistless force, / The passions rage, obstructed in their course, / Swell to new heights, forbidden paths explore, / And drown those virtues which they fed before. *Pope.*

Like mistress, like maid. *Pr.*

Like mother, like daughter. *Pr.*

Like Niobe, all tears. *Ham.* i. 2.

55 Like other plants, virtue will not grow unless its root be hidden, buried from the eye of the sun. *Carlyle.*

Like our shadows / Our wishes lengthen as our sun declines. *Young.*

Like patience on a monument, / Smiling at grief. *Twelfth Night*, ii. 4.

Like priest, like people. *Pr.*

Like prince, like people. *Pr*

Like Scotsmen, aye wise ahint the hand (after the event). *Pr.*

Like talks best with like, laughs best with like, works best with like, and enjoys best with like; and it cannot help it. *J. G. Holland.*

5 Like the air, the water, and everything else in the world, the heart too rises the higher the warmer it becomes. *Cötvös.*

Like the dog in the manger, he will neither eat himself nor let the horse eat. *Pr.*

Like the hand which ends a dream, / Death, with the might of his sunbeam, / Touches the flesh and the soul awakes. *Browning.*

Like two single gentlemen rolled into one. *G. Colman.*

Likely tumbles in the fire, / When unlikely rises higher. *Pr.*

10 Limæ labor et mora—The labour and tediousness of polishing as with a file. *Hor.*

Limit your wants by your wealth. *Pr.*

Limitations refine as the soul purifies, but the ring of necessity is always perched at the top. *Emerson.*

Limiting of one's life always conduces to happiness. *Schopenhauer.*

Lingua mali loquax malæ mentis est indicium —An evil tongue is the proof of an evil mind. *Pub. Syr.*

15 Lingua mali pars pessima servi—His tongue is the worst part of a bad servant. *Juv.*

Lingua melior, sed frigida bello / Dextera— Excels in speech, but of a right hand slow to war. *Virg.*

Linguæ centum sunt, oraque centum, / Ferrea vox—It has a hundred tongues, a hundred mouths, a voice of iron. *Virg., of Rumour.*

Linguam compescere, virtus non minima est— To restrain the tongue is not the least of the virtues.

Linquenda tellus, et domus, et placens / Uxor, neque harum, quas colis, arborum, / Te, præter invisas cupressos, / Ulla brevem dominum sequetur—Your estate, your home, and your pleasing wife must be left, and of these trees which you are rearing, not one shall follow you, their short-lived owner, except the hateful cypresses. *Hor.*

20 Lions are not frightened by cats. *Pr.*

Lions' skins are not to be had cheap. *Pr.*

Lippen to (trust) me, but look to yoursel'. *Sc. Pr.*

Lips become compressed and drawn with anxious thought, and eyes the brightest are quenched of their fires by many tears. *S. Lover.*

Lips never err when wisdom keeps the door. *Delaune.*

25 Lis litem generat—Strife genders strife. *Pr.*

List geht über Gewalt—Cunning overcomes strength. *Ger. Pr.*

List his discourse of war, and you shall hear / A fearful battle render'd you in music; / Turn him to any cause of policy, / The Gordian Knot of it he will unloose, / Familiar as his garter. *Hen. V., i. 1.*

Listen at a hole, and ye'll hear news o' yoursel'. *Sc. Pr.*

Listeners never hear good of themselves. *Sp. Pr.*

Lite pendente—During the lawsuit. 30

Litem parit lis, noxa item noxam parit—Strife begets strife, and injury likewise begets injury. *Pr.*

Litera canina—The canine letter (the letter R).

Litera occidit, spiritus autem vivificat—The letter killeth, but the spirit quickeneth. *Vulgate.*

Litera scripta manet, verbum ut inane perit— Written testimony remains, but oral perishes.

Literæ Bellerophontis—A Bellerophon's letter, 35 *i.e.*, a letter requesting that the bearer should be dealt with in some summary way for an offence.

Literæ humaniores—Polite literature; arts in a university

Literary history is the great morgue where all seek the dead ones whom they love, and to whom they are related. *Heine.*

Literary men are . . . a perpetual priesthood. *Carlyle.*

Literature, as a field for glory, is an arena where a tomb may be more easily found than laurels; as a means of support, it is the very chance of chances. *H. Giles.*

Literature consists of all the books—and they 40 are not many—where moral truth and human passion are touched with a certain largeness, sanity, and attraction of form. *John Morley.*

Literature draws its sap from the deep soil of human nature's common and everlasting sympathies. *Lowell.*

Literature happens to be the only occupation in which wages are not given in proportion to the goodness of the work done. *Froude.*

Literature has her quacks no less than medicine: those who have erudition without genius, and those who have volubility without depth. *Colton.*

Literature has other aims than that of harmlessly amusing indolent, languid men. *Carlyle.*

Literature is a fragment of a fragment, and 45 of this but little is extant. *Goethe.*

Literature is a great staff, but a sorry crutch. *Scott.*

Literature is fast becoming all in all to us —our church, our senate, our whole social constitution. *Carlyle.*

Literature is representative of intellect, which is progressive; government is representative of order, which is stationary. *Buckle.*

Literature is so common a luxury that the age has grown fastidious. *Tuckerman.*

Literature is the thought of thinking souls. 50 *Carlyle.*

Literature, like virtue, is its own reward. *Chesterfield.*

Literature positively has other aims than this of amusing from hour to hour; nay, perhaps this, glorious as it may be, is not its highest or true aim. *Carlyle.*

Literature, taken in all its bearings, forms the grand line of demarcation between the human and the animal kingdoms. *W. Godwin.*

Literature, when noble, is not easy; only when ignoble. It too is a quarrel and internecine duel with the whole world of darkness that lies without one and within one;—rather a hard fight at times. *Carlyle.*

Litteræ non erubescunt — A letter does not blush. *Cic.*

Little and often fills the purse. *Pr.*

Little bantams are great at crowing. *Pr.*

Little boats must keep near shore. *Pr.*

5 Little bodies have great souls. *Pr.*

Little by little the little bird builds its nest. *Pr.*

Little children, little sorrows; big children, great sorrows. *Pr.*

Little chips light great fires. *Pr.*

Little deeds of kindness, little words of love, / Make our earth an Eden like the heaven above. *F. S. Osgood.*

10 Little dew-drops of celestial melody. *Carlyle, of Burns' songs.*

Little do men perceive what solitude is, and how far it extendeth; for a crowd is not company, and faces are but a gallery of pictures, and talk but a tinkling cymbal, where there is no love. *Bacon.*

Little drops of rain pierce the hard marble. *Lilys.*

Little drops of water, little grains of sand, / Make the mighty ocean and the pleasant land. / Thus the little minutes, humble though they be, / Make the mighty ages of eternity. *F. S. Osgood.*

Little enemies and little wounds must not be despised. *Pr.*

15 Little fishes should not spout like whales. *Pr.*

Little flower—if I could understand / What you are, root and all, and all in all, / I should know what God and man is. *Tennyson.*

Little folks like to talk about great folks. *Pr.*

Little gear, less care. *Sc. Pr.*

Little griefs are loud, great sorrows are silent. *Pr.*

20 Little is done when every man is master. *Pr.*

Little joys refresh us constantly, like house-bread, and never bring disgust; and great ones, like sugar-bread, briefly, and then with satiety. *Jean Paul.*

Little kingdom is great household, and great household little kingdom. *Bacon.*

Little-minded people's thoughts move in such small circles that five minutes' conversation gives you an arc long enough to determine their whole curve. *Holmes.*

Little minds are tamed and subdued by misfortune, but great minds rise above it. *Washington Irving.*

25 Little minds are too much wounded by little things; great minds see all, and are not even hurt. *La Roche.*

Little minds, like weak liquors, are soonest soured. *Pr.*

Little odds between a feast and a fu' wame (stomach). *Sc. Pr.*

Little of this great world can I speak, / More than pertains to feats of broil and battle; / And, therefore, little shall I grace my cause / In speaking for myself. Yet by your gracious patience, / I will a round unvarnish'd tale deliver / Of my whole course of love. *Othello*, i. 3.

Little ones are taught to be proud of their clothes before they can put them on. *Locke.*

30 Little opportunities should be improved. *Fénélon.*

Little pigeons can carry great messages. *Pr.*

Little pigs eat great potatoes. *Pr.*

Little pitchers have long ears, *i.e.*, children have. *Pr.*

Little pot, / Don't get hot / On the spot. *Pr.*

35 Little pots soon boil over. *Ger. Pr.*

Little souls on little shifts rely. *Dryden.*

Little strokes fell great oaks. *Pr.*

Little thieves have iron chains and great thieves gold ones. *Dut. Pr.*

Little things blame not: Grace may on them wait. / Cupid is little; but his godhead's great. *Anon.*

40 Little things please little minds. *Pr.*

Little troubles are great to little people. *Pr.*

Little waves with their soft white hands efface the footprints in the sands. *Longfellow.*

Little wealth, little sorrow. *Pr.*

Little wit in the head makes much work for the feet. *Pr.*

45 Little wrongs done to others are great wrongs done to ourselves. *Pr.*

Littore quot conchæ, tot sunt in amore dolores —There are as many pangs in love as shells on the sea-shore. *Ovid.*

Littus ama, altum alii teneant—Hug thou the shore, let others stand out to sea. *Virg.*

Live and learn; and indeed it takes a great deal of living to get a little deal of learning. *Ruskin.*

Live and let live. *Pr.*

50 Live as long as you may, the first twenty years are the longest half of your life. *Southey.*

Live for to-day! to-morrow's light, / To-morrow's cares shall bring to sight; / Go sleep, like closing flowers, at night, / And Heaven thy morn will bless. *Keble.*

Live in to-day, but not for to-day. *Pr.*

Live, live to-day; to-morrow never yet / On any human being rose or set. *Marsden.*

Live not for yourself alone. *Pr.*

55 Live not to eat, but eat to live. *Pr.*

Live on, brave lives, chained to the narrow round / Of Duty; live, expend yourselves, and make / The orb of Being wheel onward steadfastly / Upon its path—the Lord of Life alone / Knows to what goal of Good; work on, live on. *Lewis Morris.*

Live on what you have; live if you can on less; do not borrow either for vanity or pleasure—the vanity will end in shame, and the pleasure in regret. *Johnson.*

Live only a moment at a time. *Pr.*

Live thou! and of the grain and husk, the grape, / And ivy berry, choose; and still depart / From death to death thro' life and life, and find / Nearer and ever nearer Him, who wrought / Not Matter, nor the finite-infinite, / But this main miracle, that thou art thou, / With power on thine own act and on the world. *Tennyson.*

60 Live to learn and learn to live. *Pr.*

Live upon trust, / And pay double you must. *Pr.*

Live virtuously, and you cannot die too soon nor live too long. *Lady R. Russel.*

Live we how we can, yet die we must. *3 Hen. VI.*, v. 2.

Live with a singer if you would learn to sing. *Pr.*

Live with thy century, but be not its creature; produce for thy contemporaries, however, what they need, not what they applaud. *Schiller.*

Live with your friend as if he might become your enemy. *Pr.*

Lively feeling of situations, and power to express them, make the poet. *Goethe.*

5 Lives of great men all remind us, / We can make our lives sublime; / And departing leave behind us / Footprints on the sands of time. *Longfellow.*

Living religion grows not by the doctrines, but by the narratives of the Bible. *Jean Paul.*

Living well is the best revenge. *Pr.*

Lo ageno siempre pia por su dueño—What is another's always chirps for its master. *Sp. Pr.*

Lo, I am with you alway, even unto the end of the world. *Jesus to His disciples.*

10 Lo que hace el loco á la derreria, hace el sabio á la primeria—What the fool does at length the wise man does at the beginning. *Sp. Pr.*

Lo que no acaece en un año, acaece en un rato—A thing that may not happen in a year may happen in two minutes. *Sp. Pr.*

Lo! the poor Indian, whose untutor'd mind / Sees God in clouds, or hears Him in the wind ; / His soul proud science never taught to stray / Far as the solar walk or milky way ; / Yet simple nature to his hope has given, / Behind the cloud-topt hills, a humbler heaven. *Pope.*

Loan oft loses both itself and friend. *Ham., i. 3.*

Loans and debts make worries and frets. *Pr.*

15 Loans should come laughing home. *Pr.*

Loathsome canker lives in sweetest bud. *Shakespeare.*

Loaves put awry in the oven come out awry. *Pr.*

Loci communes—Topics.

Lock the stable before you lose the steed. *Pr.*

20 Locking the stable door when the steed is stolen. *Pr.*

Loco citato—In the place quoted.

Locum tenens—A deputy or substitute.

Locus classicus—A classical passage.

Locus est et pluribus umbris—There is room for more introductions. *Hor.*

25 Locus in quo—The place in which ; the place previously occupied.

Locus penitentiæ—Place for repentance.

Locus sigili—The place for the seal ; pointed out in documents by the letters L.S.

Locus standi—Standing in a case ; position in an argument.

Lofty mountains are full of springs; great hearts are full of tears. *Joseph Roux.*

30 Logic works ; metaphysic contemplates. *Joubert.*

Loin de la cour, loin du souci—Far from court, far from care. *Fr. Pr.*

Long customs are not easily broken ; he that attempts to change the course of his own life very often labours in vain. *Johnson.*

Long experience made him sage. *Gay.*

Long lent is not given. *Pr.*

Long talk makes short work. *Pr.* 35

Long talking begets short hearing, for people go away. *Jean Paul.*

Longa est injuria, longæ / Ambages—Long is the story of her wrongs, tedious the details. *Virg.*

Longa mora est, quantum noxæ sit ubique repertum / Enumerare : minor fuit ipsa infamia vero—It would take long to enumerate how great an amount of crime was everywhere perpetrated; even the report itself came short of the truth. *Ovid.*

Longe aberrat scopo—He is wide of the mark ; has gone quite out of his sphere.

Longe absit—Far be it from me ; God forbid. 40

Longe mea discrepat istis / Et vox et ratio—Both my language and my sentiments differ widely from theirs. *Hor.*

Longo sed proximus intervallo—Next, with a long interval between. *Virg.*

Longum iter est per præcepta, breve et efficax per exempla—The road to learning by precept is long, by example short and effectual. *Sen.*

Look above you, and then look about you. *Pr.*

Look, as I blow this feather from my face, / And 45 as the air blows it to me again / . . . Commanded always by the greater gust; / Such is the lightness of you common men. *3 Henry VI., iii. I.*

Look at home, father priest, mother priest ; your church is a hundredfold heavier responsibility than mine can be. Your priesthood is from God's own hands. *Ward Beecher.*

Look at paintings and fightings from a distance. *Pr.*

Look at the bright side of a failure as well as the dark. *Anon.*

Look at your own corn in May, / And you'll come weeping away. *Pr.*

Look before you leap. *Pr.* 50

Look before you, or you'll have to look behind you. *Pr.*

Look for squalls, but don't make them. *Pr.*

Look how the floor of heaven / Is thick inlaid with patines of bright gold; / There's not the smallest orb which thou behold'st / But in his motion like an angel sings, / Still quiring to the young-eyed cherubims. *Mer. of Ven., v. I.*

Look how we can, or sad or merrily, / Interpretation will misquote our looks. *I Hen. IV., v. 2.*

Look in the glass when you with anger glow, / 55 And you'll confess you scarce yourself would know. *Ovid.*

Look in thy heart and write. *Sir P. Sidney.*

Look not a gift horse in the mouth. *Pr.*

Look not mournfully into the past—it comes not back again ; wisely improve the present —it is thine; go forth to meet the shadowy future without fear and with a manly heart. *Longfellow.*

Look not on pleasures as they come, but go. / Defer not the least virtue ; life's poor span / Make not an ell by trifling in thy woe. / If thou do ill, the joy fades, not the pains ; / If well, the pain doth fade, the joy remains. *George Herbert.*

Look not to what is wanting in any one; consider that rather which still remains to him. *Goethe.*

Look out for a people entirely destitute of religion. If you find them at all, be assured that they are but few degrees removed from brutes. *Hume.*

Look round the habitable world, how few / Know their own good, or, knowing it, pursue. *Dryden, after Juvenal.*

Look, the morn, in russet mantle clad, / Walks o'er the dew of yon high eastern hill. *Ham.*, i. 1.

5 Look through a keyhole, and your eye will be sore. *Pr.*

Look to the players; . . . / They are the abstract and brief chroniclers of the times. *Ham.*, ii. 2.

Look to thy mouth; diseases enter there. *George Herbert.*

Look to thyself; reach not beyond humanity. *Sir P. Sidney.*

Look unto those they call unfortunate; / And, closer viewed, you'll find they are unwise. *Young.*

10 Look upon every day, O youth, as the whole of life, not merely as a section, and enjoy the present without wishing, through haste, to spring on to another. *Jean Paul.*

Look within. Within is the fountain of good, and it will ever bubble up, if thou wilt ever dig. *Marcus Aurelius.*

Lookers-on see more than the players. *Pr.*

Looking round on the noisy inanity of the world, words with little meaning, actions with little worth, one loves to reflect on the great empire of silence. The noble silent men, scattered here and there each in his department, silently thinking, silently working; whom no morning newspaper makes mention of. *Carlyle.*

Looking where others looked, and conversing with the same things, we catch the charm which lured them. *Emerson.*

15 Looks kill love, and love by looks reviveth. *Shakespeare.*

Loop'd and window'd raggedness. *Lear*, iii. 4.

Loquacity storms the ear, but modesty takes the heart. *Pr.*

Loquendum ut vulgus, sentiendum ut docti— We should speak as the populace, think as the learned. *Coke.*

Lord, help me through this warld o' care, / I'm weary sick o't late and air; / Not but I hae a richer share / Than mony ithers; / But why should ae man better fare, / And a' men brithers? *Burns.*

20 Lord, keep my memory green! *Dickens.*

Lord of himself, that heritage of woe. *Byron.*

Lord of himself, though not of lands; having nothing yet hath all. *Sir Henry Wotton* (?).

Lord of the lion heart and eagle eye, / Thy steps I follow with my bosom bare, / Nor heed the storm that howls along the sky. *Smollett.*

Lord of thy presence and no land beside. *King John*, i. 1.

25 Lord, we know what we are, but know not what we may be. *Ham.*, iv. 5.

Lorsqu'une pensée est trop faible pour porter une expression simple, c'est la marque pour la rejeter—When a thought is too weak to bear a simple expression, it is a sign that it deserves rejection. *Vauvenargues.*

Lose the habit of hard labour with its manliness, and then, / Comes the wreck of all you hope for in the wreck of noble men. *Dr. Walter Smith.*

Lose thy fun rather than thy friend. *Pr.*

Losing the bundles gathering the wisps. *Gael. Pr.*

30 Losses are comparative, only imagination makes them of any moment. *Pascal.*

Lost time is never found again. *Pr.*

Lotis manibus—With clean-washen hands.

Loud clamour is always more or less insane. *Carlyle.*

Loud laughter is the mirth of the mob, who are only pleased with silly things; for true wit or good sense never excited a laugh since the creation of the world. *Chesterfield.*

35 Loudness is a foe to melody. *Pr.*

Louer les princes des vertus qu'ils n'ont pas, c'est leur dire impunément des injures—To praise princes for virtues which they do not possess, is to insult them with impunity. *La Roche.*

Louis ne sut qu'aimer, pardonner et mourir; / Il aurait su régner s'il avait su punir—Louis (XVI.) knew only how to love, pardon, and die; had he known how to punish, he would have known how to reign. *Tilly.*

Love abounds in honey and poison. *Sp. Pr.*

Love accomplishes all things. *Petrarch.*

40 Love all, trust a few, / Do wrong to none; be able for thine enemy / Rather in power than use; and keep thy friend / Under thy own life's key; be checked for silence, / But never tax'd for speech. *All's Well*, i. 1.

Love and death are the two great hinges on which all human sympathies turn. *B. R. Haydon.*

Love and friendship exclude each other. *Du Cœur.*

Love and gratitude are seldom found in the same breast without impairing each other . . . we cannot command both together. *Goldsmith.*

Love and light winna hide. *Sc. Pr.*

45 Love and lordship like not fellowship. *Pr.*

Love and poverty are hard to hide. *Pr.*

Love and pride stock Bedlam. *Pr.*

Love and religion are both stronger than friendship. *Disraeli.*

Love and scandal are the best sweeteners of tea. *Fielding.*

50 Love and the Soul, working together, might go on producing Venuses without end, each different, and all beautiful; but divorced and separated, they may continue producing indeed, yet no longer any being, or even thing, truly godlike. *Ed.*

Love and trust are the only mother-milk of any man's soul. *Ruskin.*

Love, and you shall be loved. All love is mathematically just, as much as the two sides of an algebraic equation. *Emerson.*

Love asks faith, and faith asks firmness. *Pr.*

Love at two-and-twenty is a terribly intoxicating draft. *Ruffini.*

Love betters what is best, / Even here below, but more in heaven above. *Wordsworth.*

Love breaks in with lightning flash: friendship comes like dawning moonlight. Love will obtain and possess; friendship makes sacrifices but asks nothing. *Geibel.*

Love can do much, but duty still more. *Goethe.*

5 Love can hope where reason would despair. *Lyttleton.*

Love can neither be bought nor sold; its only price is love. *Pr.*

Love cannot clasp all it yearns for in its bosom, without first suffering for it. *Ward Beecher.*

Love concedes in a moment what we can hardly attain by effort after years of toil. *Goethe.*

Love converts the hut into a palace of gold. *Hölty.*

10 Love delights in paradoxes. Saddest when it has most reason to be gay, sighs are the signs of its deepest joy, and silence the expression of its yearning tenderness. *Bovee.*

Love delights to bring her best, / And where love is, that offering evermore is blest. *Keble.*

Love dies by satiety, and forgetfulness inters it. *Du Cœur.*

Love divine, all love excelling, / Joy of heaven to earth come down. *Toplady.*

Love does much, but money does more. *Pr.*

15 Love ends with hope: the sinking statesman's door / Pours in the morning worshipper no more. *Johnson.*

Love ever flows downward. *Quoted by Hare.*

Love, free as air, at sight of human ties, / Spreads his light wings, and in a moment flies. *Pope.*

Love, friendship, charity are subjects all / To envious and calumniating time. *Troil. and Cress.*, iii. 3.

Love furthers knowledge. *Pr.*

20 Love gives itself, and is not bought. *Longfellow.*

Love goes toward love, as schoolboys from their books; / But love from love, toward school with heavy looks. *Rom. and Jul.*, ii. 2.

Love has made its best interpreter a sigh. *Byron.*

Love has no age, as it is always renewing itself. *Pascal.*

Love has the tendency of pressing together all the lights, all the rays emitted from the beloved object, by the burning-glass of fantasy, into one focus, and making of them one radiant sun without spots. *Goethe.*

25 Love hath a large mantle. *Pr.*

Love hides ugliness. *Gael. Pr.*

Love in the heart is better than honey in the mouth. *Pr.*

Love is a bottomless pit; it is a cormorant—a harpy that devours everything. *Swift.*

Love is a boy by poets spoiled. *S. Butler.*

30 Love is a debt which inclination always pays, obligation never. *Pascal.*

Love is a familiar; love is a devil: there is no evil angel but love. Yet was Samson so tempted, and he had an excellent strength; yet was Solomon so seduced, and he had a very good wit. *Love's L. Lost*, i. 2.

Love is a personal debt. *George Herbert.*

Love is a reality which is born in the fairy region of romance. *Talleyrand.*

Love is a secondary passion in those who love most, a primary in those who love least. He who is inspired by it in a high degree is inspired by honour in a higher; it never reaches its plenitude of growth and perfection but in the most exalted minds. *Landor.*

Love is a secret no man knows / Till it within 35 his bosom glows. *Pr.*

Love is a sleep; love is a dream; and you have lived if you have loved. *Alfred De Musset.*

Love is a smoke made with the fume of sighs; / Being purged, a fire sparkling in lovers' eyes; / Being vex'd, a sea nourish'd with lovers' tears: / What is it else? A madness most discreet, / A choking gall, and a preserving sweet. *Rom. and Jul.*, i. 1.

Love is a spirit all compact of fire; / Not gross to sink, but light and will aspire. *Shakespeare.*

Love is a superstition that doth fear the idol which itself hath made. *Sir T. Overbury.*

Love is a sweet idolatry, enslaving all the soul. 40 *Tupper.*

Love is an exotic of the most delicate constitution. *Goldsmith.*

Love is an image of God, and not a lifeless image; not one painted on paper, but the living essence of the divine nature, which beams full of all goodness. *Luther.*

Love is as warm among cottars as courtiers. *Sc. Pr.*

Love is as warm in fustian as in velvet. *Pr.*

Love is blind, and lovers cannot see the pretty 45 follies that themselves commit. *Mer. of Ven.*, ii. 6.

Love is blind, and the figure of Cupid is drawn with a bandage round his eyes. Blind: yes, because he does not see what he does not like; but the sharpest-sighted hunter in the universe is Love for finding what he seeks, and only that. *Emerson.*

Love is deemed the tenderest (*zärteste*) of our affections, as even the blind and the deaf know; but I know, what few believe, that true friendship is more tender still. *Platen.*

Love is eternally awake, never tired with labour, nor oppressed with affliction, nor discouraged by fear. *Thomas à Kempis.*

Love is ever busy with his shuttle, is ever wearing into life's dull warp bright gorgeous flowers and scenes Arcadian. *Longfellow.*

Love is ever the beginning of knowledge, as 50 fire is of light; and works also more in the manner of fire. *Carlyle.*

Love is ever the gift, the sacrifice of self. *Canon Liddon.*

Love is full of unbefitting strains; / All wanton as a child, skipping and vain; / Formed by the eye, and therefore, like the eye, / Full of strange shapes, of habits, and of forms, / Varying in subjects as the eye doth roll / To every varied object in his glance. *Love's L. Lost*, v. 2.

Love is incompatible with fear. *Pub. Syr.*

Love is indestructible, / Its holy flame for ever burneth ; / From heaven it came, to heaven returneth. *Southey.*

Love is just another name for the inscrutable presence by which the soul is connected with humanity. *Simms.*

Love is kin to duty. *Lewis Morris.*

5 Love is life's end—an end, but never ending. . . . Love is life's wealth ; ne'er spent, but ever spending. . . . Love's life's reward, rewarded in rewarding. *Spenser.*

Love is like the painter, who, being to draw the picture of a friend having a blemish in one eye, would picture only the other side of his face. *South.*

Love is loveliest when embalmed in tears. *Scott.*

Love is merely a madness. *As You Like It,* iii. 2.

Love is mightier than indignation. *Ward Beecher.*

10 Love is more pleasing than marriage, because romances are more amusing than history. *Chamfort.*

Love is neither bought nor sold. *Pr.*

Love is never lasting which flames before it burns. *Feltham.*

Love is not a fire which can be confined within the breast ; everything betrays it ; and its fires imperfectly covered, only burst out the more. *Racine.*

Love is not altogether a delirium, yet has it many points in common therewith . . . I call it rather a discerning of the Infinite in the Finite, of the Idea made Real ; which discerning again may be either true or false, either seraphic or demonic, Inspiration or Insanity. *Carlyle.*

15 Love is not blind ; it is an extra eye, which shows us what is most worthy of regard. *J. M. Barrie.*

Love is not love Which alters when it alteration finds. *Shakespeare.*

Love is not to be reason'd down or lost / In high ambition or a thirst of greatness. *Addison.*

Love is old, old as eternity, but not outworn ; with each new being born or to be born. *Byron.*

Love is omnipresent in nature as motive and reward. *Emerson.*

20 Love is sparingly soluble in the words of men, therefore they speak much of it ; but one syllable of woman's speech can dissolve more of it than a man's heart can hold. *Holmes.*

Love is strong as death. Many waters cannot quench love, neither can the floods drown it. *Bible.*

Love is strongest in pursuit, friendship in possession. *Emerson.*

Love is swift, sincere, pious, pleasant, gentle, strong, patient, faithful, prudent, long-suffering, manly, and never seeking her own. *Thomas à Kempis.*

Love is the bond which never corrodes. *Dr. Parker.*

25 Love is the business of the idle, but the idleness of the busy. *Bulwer Lytton.*

Love is the eldest, noblest, and mightiest of the gods, and the chiefest author and giver of virtue in life and happiness after death. *Plato.*

Love is the greatest thing that God can give us, and it is the greatest we can give God. *Jeremy Taylor.*

Love is the joining of two souls on their way to God. *J. M. Barrie.*

Love is the master-key that opens every ward of the heart of man. *J. H. Evans.*

Love is the most easy and agreeable, and 30 gratitude the most humiliating, affection of the mind. *Goldsmith.*

Love is the mother of love. *Pr.*

Love is the occupation of an idle man, the amusement of a busy one, and the shipwreck of a sovereign. *Napoleon.*

Love is the only ink which does not fade. *Dr. Parker.*

Love is the only memory which strengthens with time. *Dr. Parker.*

Love is vanity, / Selfish in its beginning as its 35 end. *Byron.*

Love knows nothing of labour. *It. Pr.*

Love labour ; for if thou dost not want it for food, thou may'st for physic. *Wm. Penn.*

Love laughs at locksmiths. *Pr.*

Love lessens the woman's refinement and strengthens the man's. *Jean Paul.*

Love lieth deep ; Love dwells not in lip- 40 depths ; / Love laps his wings on either side the heart / . . . Absorbing all the incense of sweet thoughts, / So that they pass not to the shrine of sound. *Tennyson.*

Love lightens labour and sweetens sorrow. *Pr.*

Love like a shadow flies when substance love pursues ; / Pursuing that flies, and flying what pursues. *Merry Wives,* ii. 2.

Love, like fire, cannot subsist without continual motion, and ceases to exist as soon as it ceases to hope or fear. *La Roche.*

Love, like men, dies oftener of excess than hunger. *Jean Paul.*

Love likes not shallow mirth. *Dr. Walter* 45 *Smith.*

Love looks not with the eyes, but with the mind ; / And therefore is wing'd Cupid painted blind. *Mid. Night's Dream,* i. 1.

Love makes labour light. *J. G. Holland.*

Love makes obedience lighter than liberty. *W. R. Alger.*

Love makes time pass away, and time makes love pass away. *Fr. Pr.*

Love me little, love me long, / Is the burden of 50 my song ; / Love that is too hot and strong / Burneth soon to waste ; / Still I would not have thee cold, / Not too backward or too bold ; / Love that lasteth till 'tis old / Fadeth not in haste. *Old Ballad.*

Love me, love my dog. *Pr.*

Love mocks all sorrows but its own, and damps each joy he does not yield. *Lady Dacre.*

Love moderately ; long love doth so ; / Too swift arrives as tardy as too slow. *Rom. and Jul.,* ii. 6.

Love must be as much a light as a flame. *Thoreau.*

Love must be taken by stratagem, not by open force. *Goldsmith.*

Love never reasons, but profusely gives—gives, like a thoughtless prodigal, its all, and trembles then lest it has done too little. *Hannah More.*

Love not pleasure ; love God. This is the everlasting Yea, wherein all contradiction is solved : wherein whoso walks and works, it is well with him. *Carlyle.*

Love not sleep, lest thou come to poverty. *Bible.*

5 Love not thyself, nor give thy humours way ; / God gave them to thee under lock and key. *George Herbert.*

Love of gain never made a painter, but it has marred many. *W. Allston.*

Love of glory can only create a great hero ; contempt of it creates a great man. *Talleyrand.*

Love of men cannot be bought by cash payment ; and without love men cannot endure to be together. *Carlyle.*

Love of power, merely to make flunkeys come and go for you, is a love, I should think, which enters only into the minds of persons in a very infantine state. *Carlyle.*

10 Love of truth shows itself in being able everywhere to find and value what is good. *Goethe.*

Love on his lips and hatred in his heart : / His motto—constancy, his creed—to part. *Byron.*

Love one human being with warmth and purity, and thou wilt love the world. The heart, in that celestial sphere of love, is like the sun in its course. From the drop on the rose to the ocean, all is for him a mirror, which he fills and brightens. *Jean Paul.*

Love one time layeth burdens, another time giveth wings. *Sir P. Sidney.*

Love ought to raise a low heart and not humble a high one. *Ariosto.*

15 Love ower het (hot) soon cools. *Sc. Pr.*

Love prefers twilight to daylight. *Holmes.*

Love reckons hours for months, and days for years ; and every little absence is an age. *Dryden.*

Love requires not so much proofs as expressions of love. *Jean Paul.*

Love rules his kingdom without a sword. *Pr.*

20 Love rules the camp, the court, the grove, / And men below and saints above ; / For love is heaven, and heaven is love. *Scott.*

Love rules without a sword and binds without a cord. *Pr.*

Love rules without law. *It. Pr.*

Love sees what no eye sees ; hears what no ear hears ; and what never rose in the heart of man love prepares for its object. *Lavater.*

Love seldom haunts the breast where learning lies, / And Venus sets ere Mercury can rise. *Pope.*

25 Love should have some rest and pleasure in himself, / Not ever be too curious for a boon, / Too prurient for a proof against the grain / Of him ye say ye love. *Tennyson.*

Love should not be all on one side. *Pr.*

Love shows, even to the dullest, the possibilities of the human race. *Helps.*

Love silence rather than speech in these tragic days, when for very speaking the voice of man has fallen inarticulate to man. *Carlyle.*

Love sought is good, but given unsought is better. *Twelfth Night,* iii. 1.

Love strikes one hour—love. Those never 30 loved / Who dream that they loved once. *Elizabeth B. Browning.*

Love that can flow, and can admit increase, / Admits as well an ebb, and may grow less. *Suckling.*

Love the good and forgive the bad. *Gael. Pr.*

Love, the last relay and ultimate outpost of eternity. *D. G. Rossetti.*

Love the sense of right and wrong confounds ; / Strong love and proud ambition have no bounds. *Dryden.*

Love thinks nae ill, envy speaks nae gude. 35 *Sc. Pr.*

Love thyself, and many will hate thee. *Anon.*

Love to a yielding heart is a king, but to a resisting is a tyrant. *Sidney.*

Love to make others happy ; yes, surely at all times, so far as you can. But at bottom that is not the aim of any life. Do not think that your life means a mere searching in gutters for fallen creatures to wipe and set up. . . . In our life there is no meaning at all except the work we have done. *Carlyle.*

Love too late can never glow. *Keble.*

Love took up the harp of life, and smote on all 40 the chords with might ; / Smote the chord of Self, that, trembling, passed in music out of sight. *Tennyson.*

Love-verses, writ without any real passion, are the most nauseous of all conceits. *Shenstone.*

Love waits for love, though the sun be set, / And the stars come out, the dews are met, / And the night-winds moan. *Dr. Walter Smith.*

Love—what a volume in a word, an ocean in a tear ! *Tupper.*

Love, when founded in the heart, will show itself in a thousand unpremeditated sallies of fondness ; but every cool deliberate exhibition of the passion only argues little understanding or great insincerity. *Goldsmith.*

Love which hath ends will have an end. 45 *Dryden.*

Love, which is only an episode in the life of a man, is the entire history of a woman's life. *Mme. de Staël.*

Love, which is the essence of God, is not for levity, but for the total worth of man. *Emerson.*

Love will creep where it cannot go. *Pr.*

Love will find its way / Through paths where wolves would fear to prey. *Byron.*

Love will subsist on wonderfully little hope, 50 but not altogether without it. *Scott.*

Love with men is not a sentiment, but an idea. *Mme. de Girardin.*

Love without return is like a question without an answer. *Ger. Pr.*

Love worketh no ill to his neighbour ; therefore love is the fulfilling of the law. *St. Paul.*

Love works a different way in different minds, / The fool enlightens and the wise he blinds. *Dryden.*

Love yet lives, and patience shall find rest. *Keble.*

Love your enemies, do good to them that hate you, bless them that curse you, and pray for them which despitefully use you and persecute you. *Jesus.*

Love your neighbour, but don't tear down the fence. *Ger. Pr.*

Love yourself, and in that love / Not unconsidered leave your honour. *Hen. VIII.,* i. 2.

5 Love's fire, if it once go out, is hard to kindle. *Pr.*

Love's heralds should be thoughts, / Which ten times faster glide than the sun's beams / Driving back shadows over lowering hills. *Rom. and Jul.,* ii. 5.

Love's not love / When it is mingled with regards that stand / Aloof from the entire point. *Lear,* i. 1.

Love's of a strangely open simple kind, / And thinks none sees it 'cause itself is blind. *Cowley.*

Love's of itself too sweet; the best of all / Is when love's honey has a dash of gall. *Herrick.*

10 Love's plant must be watered with tears and tended with care. *Dan. Pr.*

Love's reasons without reason. *Cymbeline,* iv. 2.

Love's sweetest meanings are unspoken; the full heart knows no rhetoric of words, and resorts to the pantomime of sighs and glances. *Bovee.*

Love's the noblest frailty of the mind. *Dryden.*

Love's true function in the world is as the regenerator and restorer of social life, the reconciler and uniter of living men. *Ed.*

15 Love's voice doth sing as sweetly in a beggar as a king. *Decker.*

Lovely, far more lovely, the sturdy gloom of laborious indigence than the fawning simper of thriving adulation. *Goldsmith.*

Loveliness does more than destroy ugliness; it destroys matter. A mere touch of it in a room, in a street, even on a door-knocker, is a spiritual force. *Prof. Drummond.*

Loveliness / Needs not the foreign aid of ornament, / But is, when unadorn'd, adorn'd the most. *Thomson.*

Lovers and madmen have such seething brains, / Such shaping fantasies, that apprehend / More than cool reason ever comprehends. *Mid. Night's Dream,* v. 1.

20 Lovers are as punctual as the sun. *Goethe.*

Lovers are never tired of each other; they always speak of themselves. *La Roche.*

Lovers break not hours, / Unless it be to come before their time; / So much they spur their expedition. *Two Gent. of Ver.,* v. 1.

Lovers' purses are tied with cobwebs. *Pr.*

Lovers (*Verliebte*) see only each other in the world, but they forget that the world sees them. *Platen.*

25 Lovers' time runs faster than the clock. *Pr.*

Loving goes by haps; some Cupid kills with arrows, some with traps. *Much Ado,* iii. 1.

Lowliness is the base of every virtue, and he who goes the lowest builds the safest. *Bailey.*

Lowliness is young ambition's ladder, / Whereto the climber-upward turns his face; / But when he once attains the upmost round, / He then unto the ladder turns his back, / Looks in the clouds, scorning the base degrees / By which he did ascend. *Jul. Cæs.,* ii. 1.

Loyal à la mort—Loyal to death. *M.*

Loyal en tout—Loyal in all. *M.* 30

Loyal je serai durant ma vie—I will be loyal during my life. *M.*

Loyauté m'oblige—Loyalty binds me. *M.*

Loyauté n'a honte—Loyalty feels no shame. *M.*

Lubrici sunt fortunæ gressus—The footsteps of fortune are slippery.

Lubricum linguæ non facile in pœnam est 35 trahendum—A slip of the tongue ought not to be rashly punished. *L.*

Λύχνου ἀρθέντος, γυνὴ πᾶσα ἡ αὐτή—When the candle is taken away, every woman is alike. *Gr. Pr.*

Luck is ever waiting for something to turn up. Labour, with keen eyes and strong will, will turn up something. Luck relies on chance, labour on character. *Cobden.*

Luck is everything in promotion. *Cervantes.*

Luck is the idol of the idle. *Pr.*

Luck, mere luck, may make even madness 40 wisdom. *Douglas Jerrold.*

Luck seeks those who flee, and flees those who seek it. *Ger. Pr.*

Lucri bonus est odor ex re / Qualibet—The smell of gain is good, from whatever it proceeds. *Juv.*

Luctantem Icariis fluctibus Africum / Mercator metuens, otium et oppidi / Laudat rura sui: mox reficit rates / Quassas, indocilis pauperiem pati—The merchant, dreading the south-west wind wrestling with the Icarian waves, praises retirement and the rural life of his native town, but soon he repairs his shattered bark, incapable of being taught to endure poverty. *Hor.*

Ludere cum sacris—To trifle with sacred things.

Ludit in humanis divina potestas rebus, / Et 45 certam præsens vix habet hora fidem—The divine power sports with human affairs so much that we can scarcely be sure of the passing hour. *Ovid.*

Lugete o Veneres Cupidinesque—Weep, all ye Venuses and Cupids. *Cat.*

Lull'd in the countless chambers of the brain, / Our thoughts are linked by many a hidden chain; / Awake but one, and lo! what myriads rise! / Each stamps its image as the other flies. *Rogers.*

Lupo agnum eripere postulant—They insist on snatching the lamb from the wolf. *Plaut.*

Lupo ovem commisisti—You have put the sheep to the care of the wolf. *Ter.*

Lupus in fabula—It is the wolf in the story; 50 talking of him, he appeared.

Lupus non curat numerum (ovum)—The wolf is not scared by the number of the sheep. *Pr.*

Lupus pilum mutat, non mentem—The wolf changes his coat, but not his disposition. *Pr.*

Lusisti satis, edisti satis, atque bibisti; / Tempus abire tibi est—Thou hast amused thyself enough, hast eaten and drunk enough; 'tis time for thee to depart. *Hor.*

Lust—hard by fate. *Milton.*

Lust is a sharp spur to vice, which always putteth the affections into a false gallop. *St. Ambrose.*

Lust is an enemy to the purse, a canker to the mind, a corrosive to the conscience, a weakness of the wit, a besotter of the senses, and a mortal bane to all the body. *Pliny.*

Lust is, of all the frailties of our nature, / What most we ought to fear; the headstrong beast / Rushes along, impatient of the course; / Nor hears the rider's call, nor fears the rein. *Rowe.*

5 Lust of gain, in the spirit of Cain, is it better or worse / Than the heart of the citizen hissing in war on his own hearthstone? *Tennyson.*

Lust und Liebe sind die Fittiche / Zu grossen Thaten—Ambition and love are the wings to great deeds. *Goethe.*

Lust yielded to is a pleasant madness, but it is a desperate madness when opposed. *Bp. Hall.*

Lusus naturæ—A freak of nature.

Luther's shoes don't fit every country parson. *Ger. Pr.*

10 Luther's words are half battles. *Jean Paul.*

Luxuriæ desunt multa, avaritiæ omnia—Luxury is in want of many things; avarice, of everything. *Pub. Syr.*

Luxuriant animi rebus plerumque secundis; / Nec facile est æqua commoda mente pati— The feelings generally run riot in prosperity; and to bear good fortune with evenness of mind is no easy task. *Ovid.*

Luxury is a nice master, hard to be pleased. *Sir G. Mackenzie.*

Luxury is an enticing pleasure, a bastard mirth, which hath honey in her mouth, gall in her heart, and a sting in her tail. *Victor Hugo.*

15 Luxury possibly may contribute to give bread to the poor; but if there were no luxury, there would be no poor. *H. Home.*

Lydius lapis—A Lydian or test stone.

Lying and stealing live next door to each other. *Pr.*

Lying is a breach of promise; for whoever seriously addresses his discourse to another tacitly promises to speak the truth, because he knows the truth is expected. *Paley.*

Lying is a disgraceful vice, "affording testimony," as Plutarch says, "that one first despises God and then fears men." *Montaigne.*

20 Lying is the strongest acknowledgment of the force of truth. *Hazlitt.*

Lying lips are an abomination unto the Lord. *Bible.*

Lying may be pernicious in its general tendency, and therefore criminal, though it produce no particular or visible mischief to any one. *Paley.*

Lying pays no tax. *Pr.*

Lying rides on debt's back. *Pr.*

25 Lynx envers nos pareils, et taupes envers nous—Lynx-eyed to our neighbours, and mole-eyed to ourselves. *La Fontaine.*

Lyrical poetry is much the same in every age, as the songs of the nightingales in every spring-time. *Heine.*

M.

Ma vie est un combat—My life is a battle. *Voltaire.*

Macbeth does murder sleep, the innocent sleep; / Sleep, that knits up the ravell'd sleeve of care, / The death of each day's life, sore labour's bath, / Balm of hurt minds, great Nature's second course, / Chief nourisher in life's feast. *Macb.,* ii. 2.

Mach' dich nicht zu hoch, die Thür ist niedrig —Don't carry your head too high; the door is low. *Ger. Pr.*

Mach' es Wenigen recht: Vielen gefallen ist 30 schlimm—Be content to please a few; to please many is bad. *Schiller.*

Machines cannot increase the possibilities of life, only the possibilities of idleness. *Ruskin.*

Macht, was ihr wollt; nur lasst mich ungeschoren—Produce what ye like, only leave me unmolested (*lit.* unshorn). *Goethe.*

Mächtig in Werke, nicht in Worte—Mighty in deeds, not in words. *Ger. Pr.*

Macies et nova febrium / Terris incubuit cohors—A wasting disease and an unheard-of battalion of fevers have swooped down on the earth. *Hor.*

Macte nova virtute, puer, sic itur ad astra— 35 Go on in new deeds of valour, my son! That is the way to the stars. *Virg.*

Macte virtute—Persevere in virtue; go on and prosper.

Macte virtute diligentiaque esto—Persevere in virtue and diligence. *Livy.*

Maculæ quas incuria fudit—The blemishes, or errors, which carelessness has produced. *Hor.*

Mad bulls cannot be tied up with a pack-thread. *Pr.*

Mad dogs cannot live long. *Pr.* 40

Mad people think others mad. *Pr.*

Madame fut douce envers la mort, comme elle l'était envers tout le monde—She was gentle towards death, as she was towards every one. *Bossuet.*

Madness in great ones must not unwatch'd go. *Ham.,* iii. 1.

Madness is consistent, which is more than can be said for poor reason. Our passions and principles are steady in frenzy, but begin to shift and waver as we return to reason. *Sterne.*

Madness is the last stage of human debase- 45 ment. It is the abdication of humanity. Better to die a thousand times! *Napoleon.*

Madruga y verás, trabaja y habrás—Rise betimes, and you will see; labour diligently, and you will have. *Sp. Pr.*

Magalia quondam—Formerly humble huts stood here. *Virg.*

Magasins de nouveautés—Linen-draper's, or fancy goods', shop. *Fr.*

Magis gaudet quam qui senectam exuit—He rejoices more than an old man who has put off old age, *i.e.,* has become young again. *Pr.*

Magis magni clerici non sunt magis sapientes 50 —The greatest scholars are not the wisest men. *Pr.*

Magister alius casus—Misfortune is a second master. *Pliny the elder.*

Magister artis ingeniique largitor / Venter—The belly (*i.e.*, hunger or necessity) is the teacher of arts and the bestower of genius. *Pers.*

Magister dixit—The master has said so.

Magistratum legem esse loquentem, legem autem mutum magistratum—A judge is a speaking law, law a silent judge. *Cic.*

5 **Magistratus indicat virum**—Office shows the man. *M.*

Magna Charta—The Great Charter (obtained from King John in 1215).

Magna civitas, magna solitudo—A great city is a great desert. *Gr. and L. Pr.*

Magna comitante caterva — A great crowd accompanying. *Virg.*

Magna est admiratio copiose sapienterque dicentis—Great is our admiration of the orator who speaks with fluency and discretion. *Cic.*

10 **Magna est veritas et prævalebit** — Truth is mighty, and will in the end prevail.

Magna est vis consuetudinis : hæc ferre laborem, contemnere vulnus et dolorem docet—Great is the power of habit : teaching us as it does to bear fatigue and to despise wounds and pain. *Cic.*

Magna fuit quondam capitis reverentia cani, / Inque suo pretio ruga senilis erat—Great was the respect paid of old to the hoary head, and great the honour to the wrinkles of age. *Ovid.*

Magna servitus est magna fortuna—A great fortune is a great slavery. *Sen.*

Magna vis est, magnum nomen, unum et idem sentientis senatus—Great is the power, great the authority, of a senate which is unanimous in its opinions. *Cic.*

15 **Magnæ felicitates multum caliginis mentibu humanis objiciunt** — Great and sudden pro perity has a deadening (*lit.* densely darkenin) effect on the human mind. *Sen.*

Magnæ fortunæ comes adest adulatio—Adula tion is ever the attendant on great wealth.

Magnanimiter crucem sustine—Bear up bravely under the cross. *M.*

Magnanimity is the good sense of pride, and the noblest way of acquiring applause. *La Roche.*

Magnanimity owes to prudence no account of its motives. *Vauvenargues.*

20 **Magnas inter opes inops**—Poor in the midst of great wealth. *Hor.*

Magni animi est injurias despicere—It is the mark of a great mind to despise injuries. *Sen.*

Magni animi est magna contemnere, ac mediocria malle quam nimia—It is a sign of a great mind to despise greatness, and to prefer things in measure to things in excess. *Sen.*

Magni est ingenii revocare mentem a sensibus, et cogitationem a consuetudine abducere—It argues a mind of great native force to be able to emancipate itself from the thraldom of the senses, and to wean its thoughts from old habits. *Cic.*

Magni nominis umbra—The shadow of a great name. *Lucan.*

25 **Magni refert quibuscum vixeris**—It matters a great deal with whom you live. *Pr.*

Magnificat—The song of the Virgin Mary (*lit.* she magnifies). *Luke* i. 44-45.

Magnificence cannot be cheap, for what is cheap cannot be magnificent. *Johnson.*

Magnis excidit ausis—He failed in bold attempts. *Ovid.*

Magno conatu magnas nugas—By great efforts to obtain great trifles. *Ter.*

Magno cum periculo custoditur, quod multis 30 **placet**—That is guarded at great risk which is coveted by many. *Pub. Syr.*

Magno de flumine mallem / Quam ex hoc fonticulo tantundem sumere—I had rather take my glass of water from a great river like this than from this little fountain. *Hor., in reproof of those who lay by large stores and never use them.*

Magnorum haud unquam indignus avorum—Never unworthy of his illustrious ancestors. *Virg.*

Magnum est argumentum in utroque fuisse moderatum—It speaks volumes for man that, when placed in quite different situations, he displays in each the same spirit of moderation.

Magnum hoc ego duco / Quod placui tibi qui turpi secernis honestum—I account it a great honour that I have pleased a man like you, who know so well to discriminate between the base and the honourable. *Hor.*

Magnum hoc vitium vino est, / Pedes captat 35 **primum ; luctator dolosus est**—This is the great fault of wine ; it first trips up the feet : it is a cunning wrestler. *Plaut.*

Magnum pauperies opprobrium jubet / Quidvis aut facere aut pati—Poverty, that deep disgrace, bids us do or suffer anything. *Hor.*

Magnum vectigal est parsimonia—Thrift is a great revenue. *Cic.*

Magnus ab integro sæclorum nascitur ordo—The great cycle of the ages begins its round anew. *Virg.*

Magnus Alexander corpore parvus erat—The great Alexander was small in stature. *Pr.*

Magnus animus remissius loquitur et securius 40 —The talk of a great soul is at once more careless and confident than that of other men. *Sen.*

Magnus Apollo—A great oracle.

Magnus sine viribus ignis / Incassum furit —A great fire, unless you feed it, spends its rage in vain. *Virg.*

Mãi aguçosa, filha preguiçosa—A busy mother makes slothful daughters. *Port. Pr.*

Maidens' bairns and bachelors' wives are aye weel bred. *Sc. Pr.*

Maidens, like moths, are ever caught with 45 **glare, / And Mammon wins his way where seraphs might despair.** *Byron.*

Maidens should be mild and meek, / Swift to hear, and slow to speak. *Pr.*

Maids are May when they are maids, but the sky changes when they are wives. *As You Like It,* iv. 1.

Maids should be seen and not heard. *Pr.*

Maids want nothing but husbands, and when they have them they want everything. *Somerset Pr.*

Maids well summered, and warm kept, are like 50 **flies at Bartholomew-tide**—blind, though they have their eyes. *Hen. V.,* v. 2.

Maintien le droit—Maintain the right. *M.*

Mair by luck than gude guiding (management). *Sc. Pr.*

Mais au moindre revers funeste / Le masque tombe, l'homme reste / Et le héros s'évanouit —But at the least sad reverse the mask drops off, the man remains, and the hero vanishes. *J. B. Rousseau.*

Mais de quoi sont composées les affaires du monde ? Du bien d'autrui—By of what is the business of the world made up ? Of the wealth of other people. *Béroalde Verville.*

Maison d'arrêt—A jail, a prison. *Fr.*

Maison de force—A house of correction. *Fr.*

5 Maître Jacques—A handy fellow who is ready to undertake all kinds of work. *Fr.*

Majore longinquo reverentia—Respect is greater at a distance. *Tac.*

Major famæ sitis est quam / Virtutis; quis enim virtutem amplectitur ipsam, / Præmia si tollas ?—The thirst for fame is greater than that for virtue ; for, if you take away its reward, who would embrace virtue? *Juv.*

Major hereditas venit unicuique nostrum a jure et legibus, quam a parentibus—A more valuable inheritance falls to each of us in our civil and legal rights than comes to us from our fathers. *Cic.*

Major privato visus, dum privatus fuit, et omnium consensu capax imperii, nisi imperasset —He was regarded as greater than a private individual so long as he remained one, and, by the consent of all, would have been deemed worthy to rule had he never ruled. *Tac., of the Emperor Galba.*

10 Major rerum mihi nascitur ordo—A greater succession of events presents itself to my muse. *Virg.*

Major sum quam cui possit Fortuna nocere / Multaque ut eripiat, multo mihi plura relinquet. / Excessere metum mea jam bona— I am above being injured by fortune ; though she snatch away much, more will remain to me. The blessings I now enjoy transcend fear. *Ov.*

Majore tumultu / Planguntur nummi quam funera, nemo dolorem / Fingit in hoc casu / ... Ploratur lacrimis amissa pecunia veris —Money is bewailed with a greater tumult than death. No one feigns grief in this case. ... The loss of money is deplored with true tears. *Juv.*

Majoresque cadunt altis de montibus umbræ— And the shadows lengthen as they fall from the lofty mountains. *Virg.*

Majori cedo—I retire before my superior.

15 Majority is applied to number, and superiority to power. *Johnson.*

Majus et minus non variant speciem—Greater and less don't change the nature of a thing.

Make a crutch of your cross. *Pr.*

Make a virtue of necessity. *Burton.*

Make all sure, and keep all pure. *Pr.*

20 Make clean thy conscience ; hide thee there. *Quarles.*

Make clean work, and leave no tags. Allow no delays when you are at a thing ; do it and be done with it. *Prof. Blackie.*

Make doors fast upon a woman's wit, and it will out at the casement ; shut that, and 'twill out at the keyhole. *As You Like It, iv. 1.*

Make every bargain clear and plain, / That none may afterwards complain. *Pr.*

Make good cheese, if you make little. *Pr.*

Make haste slowly. *Pr.* 　25

Make hay while the sun shines. *Pr.*

Make it an invariable and obligatory law to yourself never to mention your own mental diseases. When you talk of them, it is plain that you want either praise or pity ; for praise there is no room, and pity will do you no good. *Johnson.*

Make knowledge circle with the winds ; / But let her herald, Reverence, fly / Before her to whatever sky / Bear seed of men and growth of minds. *Tennyson.*

Make no enemies ; he is insignificant indeed that can do thee no harm. *Colton.*

Make not a bosom friend of a melancholy sad 30 soul. ... He goes always heavy-loaded, and thou must bear half. *Fenélon.*

Make not another's shoes by your own foot. *Pr.*

Make not thy friend too cheap to thee, nor thyself to thy friend. *Pr.*

Make not thy sport abuses ; for the fly, / That feeds on dung, is coloured thereby. *George Herbert.*

Make not thy tail broader than thy wings. *Pr.*

Make not two sorrows of one. *Pr.* 　35

Make short the miles with talk and smiles. *Pr.*

Make temperance thy companion, so shall health sit on thy brow. *Dodsley.*

Make the most and the best of your lot, and compare yourself not with the few that are above you, but with the multitudes which are below you. *Johnson.*

Make the most of time, it flies away so fast ; yet method will teach you to win time. *Goethe.*

Make the night night, and the day day, and 40 you will have a pleasant time of it. *Port. Pr.*

Make the plaster as large as the sore. *Pr.*

Make thee my knight ? my knights are sworn to vows / Of utter hardihood, utter gentleness, / And, loving, utter faithfulness in love, / And uttermost obedience to the king. *Tennyson.*

Make thick my blood, / Stop up the access and passage to remorse, / That no compunctious visitings of Nature / Shake my fell purpose. *Macb.*, i. 5.

Make thy claim of wages for this world, and all worlds, at zero—at nothing ; thus, and thus only, hast thou the world at thy feet. *Carlyle.*

Make your educational laws strict, and your 45 criminal ones may be gentle ; but leave youth its liberty, and you will have to dig dungeons for age. *Ruskin.*

Make your hay as best you may. *Pr.*

Make your mark, but mind what your mark is. *Pr.*

Make yourself an ass, and you'll have every man's sack on your shoulders. *Dan. Pr.*

Make yourself an honest man, and then you may be sure that there is one rascal less in the world. *Carlyle.*

Make yourself necessary to the world, and 50 mankind will give you bread. *Emerson.*

Make yourselves necessary to somebody. *Emerson.*

Mal à propos—Ill-timed ; unseasonable. *Fr.*

Mala causa silenda est—'Tis best to be silent in a bad cause. *Ovid.*

Mala fides—Bad faith.

Mala gallina, malum ovum—Bad hen, bad egg. *Pr.*

Mala grammatica non vitiat chartam—Bad grammar does not vitiate a deed. *L.*

Mala mali malo mala contulit omnia mundo—The jawbone of the evil one by means of an apple brought all evils into the world.

5 Mala mens, malus animus—Bad mind, bad heart. *Ter.*

Mala merx hæc, et callida est—She's a bad bargain and a crafty one. *Plaut.*

Mala ultro adsunt—Misfortunes come unsought. *Pr.*

Maladie du pays—Home-sickness. *Fr.*

Male cuncta ministrat / Impetus—Violence (of passion) conducts everything badly. *Stat.*

10 Male imperando summum imperium amittitur —By misgovernment the supreme rule is lost. *Pub. Syr.*

Male parta male dilabuntur—Things ill gotten go ill. *Pr.*

Male partum male disperit—Property ill got is ill spent ; lightly come, lightly go. *Plaut.*

Male secum agit æger, medicum qui hæredem facit—A sick man acts foolishly for himself who makes his doctor his heir.

Male verum examinat omnis / Corruptus judex —Badly is the truth weighed by a corrupt judge. *Hor.*

15 Male vivunt qui se semper victuros putant—They live ill who think they will live for ever. *Pub. Syr.*

Malebranche saw all things in God, and M. Necker saw all things in Necker. *Mirabeau.*

Maledicus a malefico non distat nisi occasione —An evil-speaker differs from an evil-doer in nothing but want of opportunity. *Quinct.*

Malesuada fames—Hunger that tempts to evil. *Virg.*

Malheureux celui qui est en avance de son siècle—Unhappy is the man who is in advance of his time. *Fr. Pr.*

20 Mali principii malus finis—Bad beginnings have bad endings (*lit.* a bad end of a bad beginning). *Ter.*

Malice is a passion so impetuous and precipitate, that it often involves the agent and the patient. *Government of the Tongue.*

Malice sucks up the greatest part of our own venom, and poisons herself. *Montaigne.*

Malim indisertam prudentiam, quam stultitiam loquacem—I prefer sense that is faulty in expression to loquacious folly. *Cic.*

Malim inquietam libertatem quam quietum servitium—I would prefer turbulent liberty to quiet slavery.

25 Malis avibus—With a bad omen (*lit.* with bad birds). *Cic.*

Malo benefacere tantumdem est periculum / Quantum bono malefacere—To do good to the bad is a danger just as great as to do bad to the good. *Plaut.*

Malo cum Platone errare, quam cum aliis recte sentire—I had rather be wrong with Plato than think right with others. *Cic.*

Malo mihi male quam molliter esse—I prefer being ill to being idle. *Sen.*

Malo mori quam fœdari—I had rather die than be disgraced. *M.*

Malo nodo malus quærendus cuneus—For a 30 hard knot a hard tool must be sought. *Pr.*

Malorum facinorum ministri quasi exprobrantes aspiciuntur — Accomplices in evil actions are always regarded as reproaching the deed. *Tac.*

Malum consilium consultori pessimum—Bad advice is most pernicious to the adviser. *Ver. Flaccus.*

Malum est consilium quod mutari non potest—That is bad counsel which cannot be changed. *Pub. Syr.*

Malum in se—A thing evil in itself.

Malum nascens facile opprimitur ; inveteratum 35 fit robustius—An evil habit is easily subdued in the beginning, but when it becomes inveterate it gains strength. *Cic.*

Malum prohibitum—A crime because forbidden by law, such as smuggling. *L.*

Malum vas non frangitur—A worthless vessel is seldom broken. *Pr.*

Malus bonum ubi se simulat, tunc est pessimus —A bad man, when he pretends to be a good one, is worst of all. *Pub. Syr.*

Malus est enim custos diuturnitatis metus, contraque benevolentia fidelis vel ad perpetuitatem—Fear is a bad preserver of that which is intended to last ; whereas mildness and good-will ensure fidelity for ever. *Cic.*

Malus usus est enim abolendus—An evil custom should 40 be abolished. *L.*

Mammon has enriched his thousands, and has damned his ten thousands. *South.*

Mammon, the least erected spirit that fell / From heaven. *Milton.*

Mammon wins his way where seraphs might despair. *Byron.*

Man alone is born crying, lives complaining, and dies disappointed. *Sir W. Temple.*

Man always worships something ; always he 45 sees the infinite shadowed forth in some thing finite ; and indeed can and must so see it in any finite thing, once tempt him well to fix his eyes thereon. *Carlyle.*

Man am I grown, a man's work must I do. / Follow the deer? follow the Christ, the King, / Live pure, speak true, right wrong, follow the King— / Else wherefore born? *Tennyson.*

Man and man only can do the impossible ;/ . . . He to the moment endurance can lend. *Goethe.*

Man becomes greater in proportion as he learns to know himself and his faculty. Let him once become conscious of what he is, and he will soon also learn to be what he should. *Schelling.*

Man becomes man only by the intelligence, but he is man only by the heart. *Amiel.*

Man, behind his everlasting blind, which he 50 only colours differently, and makes no thinner, carries his pride with him from one step to another, and on the higher step blames only the pride of the lower. *Jean Paul.*

Man can dispense with much but not with men. *Börne.*

Man can elect the universal man, / And live in life that ends not with his breath. *R. W. Dixon.*

Man can invent nothing nobler than humanity. *Ruskin.*

Man can only learn to rise from the consideration of that which he cannot surmount. *Jean Paul.*

Man cannot be a naturalist, until he satisfies all the demands of the spirit. *Emerson.*

Man cannot choose his duties. *George Eliot.*

Man cannot live without his formulas. *Dr. Walter Smith.*

5 Man carries under his hat a private theatre, wherein a greater drama is acted than ever on the mimic stage, beginning and ending in eternity. *Carlyle.*

Man consists in truth. If he exposes truth, he exposes himself. If he betrays truth, he betrays himself. We speak not here of lies, but of acting against conviction. *Novalis.*

Man could direct his ways by plain reason, and support his life by tasteless food; but God has given us wit, and flavour, and brightness, and laughter, and perfumes, to enliven the day of man's pilgrimage, and to charm his pained steps over the burning marl. *Sydney Smith.*

Man creeps into childhood, bounds into youth, sobers into manhood, and softens into age. *H. Giles.*

Man darf nur sterben, um gelobt zu werden—One has but to die to be praised. *Ger. Pr.*

10 Man delights not me; no, nor woman neither. *Ham.*, ii. 2.

Man disputirt mehr über die Schaale, als über den Kern—People dispute more about the shell than the kernel. *Ger. Pr.*

Man does not willingly submit himself to reverence; or rather, he never so submits himself: it is a higher sense which must be communicated to his nature, which only in some peculiarly favoured individuals unfolds itself spontaneously, who on this account too have of old been looked upon as saints and gods. *Goethe.*

Man does not wish to be told the truth. *Pascal.*

Man doth what he can, and God what He will. *Pr.*

15 Man dreams of fame while woman wakes to love. *Tennyson.*

Man ever tends to reckon his own insight as final, and goes upon it as such. *Carlyle.*

Man everywhere is the born enemy of lies. *Carlyle.*

Man findet tausend Gelehrte, bis man auf einen weisen Mann stösst — We may come upon a thousand men of learning before we stumble upon a single wise man. *Klinger.*

Man for the field and woman for the hearth; / Man for the sword and for the needle she: / Man with the head and woman with the heart: / Man to command and woman to obey; / All else confusion. *Tennyson.*

20 Man, forget not death, for death certainly forgets not thee. *Turkish Pr.*

Man gives up all pretension to the infinite while he feels here that neither with thought nor without it is he equal to the finite. *Goethe.*

Man had not a hammer to begin, not a syllabled articulation; they had it all to make —and they have made it. *Carlyle.*

Man has a brief flowering season and a long fading. *Uhland.*

Man has a silent and solitary literature written by his heart upon the tables of stone in Nature; and next to God's finger, a man's heart writes the most memorable things. *Ward Beecher.*

Man has a soul as certainly as he has a body; 25 nay, much more certainly; properly it is the course of his unseen spiritual life, which informs and rules his external visible life, rather than receives rule from it, in which spiritual life the true secret of his history lies. *Carlyle.*

Man has always humour enough to make merry with what he cannot help. *Goethe.*

Man has ever been a striving, struggling, and, in spite of wide-spread calumnies to the contrary, a veracious creature. *Carlyle.*

Man has in his own soul an Eternal; can read something of the Eternal there, if he will look. *Carlyle.*

Man has not a greater enemy than himself. *Petrarch.*

Man has quite a peculiar pleasure in making 30 proselytes; in causing others to enjoy what he enjoys, in finding his own likeness represented and reflected back to him. *Goethe.*

Man has seldom an offer of kindness to make to a woman but she has a presentiment of it some moments before. *Sterne.*

Man has two and a half minutes here below —one to smile, one to sigh, and half a one to love; for in the midst of this minute he dies. *Jean Paul.*

Man, if he compare himself with all he can see, is at the zenith of his power; but if he compare himself with all he can conceive, he is at the nadir of his weakness. *Colton.*

Man is a born owl. *Carlyle.*

Man is a bundle of habits. *Pr.*   35

Man is a darkened being; he knows not whence he comes, nor whither he goes; he knows little of the world and least of himself. *Goethe.*

Man is a fallen god, who remembers heaven, his former dwelling-place. *Lamartine.*

Man is a forked radish with head fantastically carved. *Swift.*

Man is a forked straddling animal with bandy legs. *Swift.*

Man is a military animal, / Glories in gun- 40 powder and loves parade. *P. J. Bailey.*

Man is a noble animal, splendid in ashes, and pompous in the grave. *Sir T. Browne.*

Man is a poetical animal, and delights in fiction. *Hazlitt.*

Man is a spirit, and bound by invisible bonds to all men. *Carlyle.*

Man is a stream whose source is hidden. *Emerson.*

Man is a substance clad in shadows. *John 45 Sterling.*

Man is a sun; his senses are the planets. *Novalis.*

Man is a tool-using animal; . . . without tools he is nothing, with tools he is all. *Carlyle.*

Man is actually here, not to ask questions but to do work; in this time, as in all times, it must be the heaviest evil for him if his faculty of action lie dormant, and only that of sceptical inquiry exert itself. *Carlyle.*

Man is an animal that cooks his victuals. *Burke.*

Man is an animal that makes bargains; no other animal does this. *Adam Smith.*

Man is an imitative creature, and whoever is foremost leads the herd. *Schiller.*

Man is, and always was, a blockhead and dullard; much readier to feel and digest than to think and consider. *Carlyle.*

Man is, beyond dispute, the most excellent of created beings, and the vilest animal is a dog; but the sages agree that a grateful dog is better than an ungrateful man. *Saadi.*

5 Man is born not to solve the problems of the universe, but to find out where the problem begins, and then to restrain himself within the limits of the comprehensible. *Goethe.*

Man is born unto trouble, as the sparks fly upward. *Bible.*

Man is but a little thing in the midst of the objects of nature, yet, by the moral quality radiating from his countenance, he may abolish all considerations of magnitude, and, in his manners, equal the majesty of the world. *Emerson.*

Man is but a reed, the weakest thing in nature, but he is a reed that thinks. *Pascal.*

Man is created free, is free, even if he were born in chains. *Schiller.*

10 Man is created to fight; he is perhaps best of all definable as a born soldier; his life "a battle and a march" under the right generals. *Carlyle.*

Man is emphatically a proselytising creature. *Carlyle.*

Man is ever the most interesting object to man, and perhaps should be the only one to interest him. *Goethe.*

Man is explicable by nothing less than all his history. *Emerson.*

Man is fire and woman tow; the devil comes and sets them in a blaze. *Pr.*

15 Man is first a spirit, bound by invisible bonds to all men; and secondly, he wears clothes, which are the visible emblems of that fact. *Carlyle, the two main ideas emphasised in "Sartor."*

Man is for ever the born thrall of certain men, born master of certain other men, born equal of certain others, let him acknowledge the fact or not. *Carlyle.*

Man is for ever the brother of man. *Carlyle.*

Man is free as the bird is in its cage: he can move about within certain limits. *Lavater.*

Man is God's image; but a poor man is / Christ's stamp to boot: both images regard. God reckons for him, counts the favour His. *George Herbert.*

20 Man is greater than a world, than systems of worlds; there is more mystery in the union of soul with the physical than in the creation of a universe. *H. Giles.*

Man is his own star, and the soul that can / Render an honest and a perfect man, / Commands all light, all influence, all fate; / Nothing to him falls early or too late. *Beaumont and Fletcher.*

Man is intended for a limited condition; objects that are simple, near, determinate, he comprehends, and he becomes accustomed to employ such means as are at hand; but on entering a wider field he now knows neither what he would nor what he should. *Goethe.*

Man is like the worker at Gobelins, who weaves on the wrong side a tapestry of which he does not see the design. *Renan.*

Man is made great or little by his own will. *Schiller.*

Man is man by virtue of willing, not by virtue 25 of knowing and understanding; and as he is, so he sees. *Emerson.*

Man is man everywhere. *Carlyle.*

Man is man only as he makes life and nature happier to us. *Emerson.*

Man is more often injured than helped by the means he uses. *Emerson.*

Man is more than constitutions. *Whittier.*

Man is neither an angel nor a brute, and it is 30 his evil destiny if he aspires to be the former, to sink into the latter. *Pascal.*

Man is neither the vile nor the excellent being which he sometimes imagines himself to be. *Disraeli.*

Man is not a piece of clay to be moulded, but a plant to be cultivated. *Garve.*

Man is not as God, / But then most godlike, being most a man. *Tennyson.*

Man is not born to be free, and for the noble there is no fairer fortune than to serve a prince whom he honours. *Goethe.*

Man is not God, but hath God's end to serve, / 35 A master to obey, a course to take, / Somewhat to cast off, somewhat to become. *Browning.*

Man is not made to question, but adore. *Young.*

Man is not the creature of circumstances; circumstances are the creatures of men. We are free agents, and man is more powerful than matter. *Disraeli.*

Man is nothing but contradiction; the less he knows it the more dupe he is. *Amiel.*

Man is of the earth, but his thoughts are with the stars. A pigmy standing on the outward crest of this small planet, his far-reaching spirit stretches outward to the infinite, and there alone finds rest. *Carlyle.*

Man is often a wolf to man, a serpent to God, 40 and a scorpion to himself. *Spurgeon.*

Man is one, and he hath one great heart. *Bailey.*

Man is one world, and hath / Another to attend him. *George Herbert.*

Man is only truly great when he acts from his passions; never irresistible but when he appeals to the imagination. *Disraeli.*

Man is only what he becomes, but he becomes only what he is. *Amiel.*

Man is physically as well as metaphysically a 45 thing of shreds and patches, borrowed unequally from good and bad ancestors, and a misfit from the start. *Emerson.*

Man is placed in this world as a spectator; when he is tired with wondering at all the novelties about him, and not till then, does he desire to be made acquainted with the causes that create those wonders. *Goldsmith.*

Man is properly an incarnated word; the word that he speaks is the man himself. *Carlyle.*

Man is, properly speaking, based upon Hope, he has no other possession but Hope; this world of his is emphatically the Place of Hope. *Carlyle.*

Man is quite sufficiently saddened by his own passions and destiny, and need not make himself more so by the darkness of a barbaric past. He needs enlightening and cheering influences, and should therefore turn to those eras in art and literature during which remarkable men obtained perfect culture. *Goethe.*

Man is so inconsistent a creature that it is impossible to reason from his belief to his conduct, or from one part of his belief to another. *Macaulay.*

Man is so prone to occupy himself with what is most common, the soul and the senses are so easily blunted to the impressions of the beautiful and perfect, that one ought by all means to preserve the capability of feeling it. We ought every day at least to hear a little song, read a good poem, see an excellent painting, and, if possible, speak a few reasonable words. *Goethe.*

Man is that noble endogenous plant which grows, like the palm, from within outward. *Emerson.*

5 Man is the arch-machine of which all these shifts drawn from himself are toy models. He helps himself on each emergency by copying or duplicating his own structure, just so far as the need is. *Emerson.*

Man is the circled oak, woman the ivy. *Aaron Hill.*

Man is the dwarf of himself. *Emerson.*

Man is the end towards which all the animal creation has tended. *Agassiz.*

Man is the favourite (*Günstling*) of Nature, not in the sense that Nature has done everything for him, but that she has given him the power of doing everything for himself. *Zachariae.*

10 Man is the higher sense of our planet, the star which connects it with the upper world, the eye which it turns towards heaven. *Novalis.*

Man is the jewel of God, who has created this material world to keep his treasure in. *Theo. Parker.*

Man is the maker of expedients, but not of laws. In his solicitude as to his approaching lot, he has neither time nor desire to raise his eyes to the heavens to watch and record their phenomena; no leisure to look upon himself and consider what and where he is. In the imperious demand for a present support, he dare not venture on speculative attempts at ameliorating his state; he is doomed to be a helpless, isolated, spellbound savage, or, if not isolated, the companion of other savages as careworn as himself. *Draper.*

Man is the merriest species of the creation. *Addison.*

Man is the Messiah of Nature. *Novalis.*

15 Man is the meter of all things; the hand is the instrument of instruments, and the mind is the form of forms. *Arist.*

Man is the Missionary of Order; he is the servant not of the devil and chaos, but of God and the universe. *Carlyle.*

Man is the nobler growth our realms supply, / And souls are ripened in our northern sky. *Mrs. Barbauld.*

Man is the slave of beneficence. *Arab. Pr.*

Man is the sum-total of all the animals. *Oken.*

Man is the sun of the world; more than the 20 real sun. The fire of his wonderful heart is the only light and heat worth gauge or measure. Where he is, are the tropics; where he is not, the ice-world. *Ruskin.*

Man is the weeping animal born to govern all the rest. *Pliny.*

Man is the whole encyclopedia of facts. The creation of a thousand forests is in one acorn; and Egypt, Greece, Rome, Gaul, Britain, America, lie enfolded already in the first man. *Emerson.*

Man is the will and woman is the sentiment. In this ship of humanity, Will is the rudder and Sentiment the sail; when woman affects to steer, the rudder is only a masked sail. *Emerson.*

Man is to man the sorest, surest ill. . . . / Earth trembles ere her yawning jaws devour; / And smoke betrays the wide-consuming fire; / Ruin from man is most conceal'd when near, / And sends the dreadful tidings in the blow. *Young.*

Man is too near all kinds of beasts—a fawning 25 dog, a roaring lion, a thieving fox, a robbing wolf, a dissembling crocodile, a treacherous decoy, a rapacious vulture. *Cowley.*

Man ist nur eigentlich lebendig, wenn man sich des Wohlwollens Anderer freut—A man is only truly alive when he enjoys the goodwill of others. *Goethe.*

Man, it's surely a pity that thou should'st sit yonder, with nothing but the eye of Omniscience to see thee, and thou with such gift to speak. *James Carlyle to his son, when he first discovered this gift in him.*

Man kan geen loopend paard beslaan—One cannot shoe a running-horse. *Dut. Pr.*

Man kann den Menschen nicht verwehren, / Zu denken, was sie wollen—There is no hindering people from thinking what thoughts they like. *Schiller.*

Man kann ein klarer Denker ohne Gefühl, 30 aber kein starker, kühner Denker ohne dasselbe sein—Without feeling one may be a clear thinker, but not a powerful and a bold. *Klinger.*

Man kann in wahrer Freiheit leben / Und doch nicht ungebunden sein—One may enjoy true freedom, and yet be in chains. *Goethe.*

Man kann nicht stets das Fremde meiden, / Das Gute liegt uns oft so fern. / Ein echter deutscher Mann mag keinen Franzen leiden, / Doch ihre Weine trinkt er gern —We cannot always avoid what is foreign; what is good often lies so far off. A true German cannot abide the French, and yet he will drink their wines with the most genuine relish. *Goethe.*

Man kann nicht wider sein Geschick—There is no striving against one's fate. *Schiller.*

Man knows nothing but what he has learned from experience. *Wieland.*

Man kommt zu schaun, Man will am liebsten 35 sehn—People come to look; their greatest pleasure is to feast their eyes. *Goethe.*

Man lebt nur einmal in der Welt—Only once is it given us to live in the world. *Goethe.*

Man, like the gen'rous vine, supported, lives; / The strength he gains is from the embrace he gives. *Pope.*

Man little knows what calamities are beyond his patience to bear till he tries them. *Goldsmith.*

Man lives in Time, has his whole earthly being, endeavour, and destiny shaped for him by Time; only in the transitory Time-symbol is the ever-motionless eternity we stand on made manifest. *Carlyle.*

Man lives where he acts. *Renan.*

Man, living, feeling man, is the easy sport of the overmastering present. *Schiller.*

5 Man lobt den Künstler dann erst recht, wenn man über sein Werk sein Lob vergisst—We first truly praise an artist when the merit of his work is such as to make us forget himself. *Lessing.*

Man löst sich nicht allmählich von dem Leben ! —It is by no gradual process we detach ourselves from (lose our hold of) life. *Schiller.*

Man loves before he sees; his heart is open before his eyes; love must irradiate his world for him before he well knows he is in it, what it is made of, and what to make of it. *Ed.*

Man loves little and often, woman much and rarely. *Basta.*

Man, made of the dust of the world, does not forget his origin; and all that is yet inanimate will one day speak and reason. *Emerson.*

10 Man mag Amphion sein und Fels und Wald bewegen, / Deswegen kann man doch nicht Bauern widerlegen—One may be a very Amphion and be able to move trees and rocks, and yet be unable to reduce peasants to reason. *Gellert.*

Man may doubt here and there, but mankind does not doubt. *H. R. Haweis.*

Man muss die Menschen nur mit dem Krämergewicht, keinesweges mit der Goldwage wiegen—We must weigh men with merchant's scales, and by no means with the goldsmith's. *Goethe.*

Man muss handeln können, wie man will, um zu handeln, wie man soll—We must be able to act as we would in order to act as we should. *Zachariæ.*

Man muss keinem Menschen trauen, der bei seinen Versicherungen die Hand auf's Herz legt—We should trust no man who in his protestations lays his hand on his heart. *Lichtenberg.*

15 Man muss nicht reicher scheinen wollen, als man ist—We must not wish to appear richer than we are. *Lessing.*

Man muss seine Irrthümer theuer bezahlen, wenn man sie los werden will, und dann hat man noch von Glück zu sagen—Men must pay dearly for their errors, if they would be free from them, and then they may regard it a happiness to do so. *Goethe.*

Man muss, will man ein Glück geniessen, / Die Freiheit zu behaupten wissen—If we would enjoy what fortune gives us, we must know how to maintain our freedom. *Gellert.*

Man must hold fast by the belief that the incomprehensible is comprehensible, otherwise he would not search. *Goethe.*

Man must serve his time to every trade / Save censure; critics all are ready made. *Byron.*

20 Man never comprehends how anthropomorphic he is. *Goethe.*

Man, never so often deceived, still watches for the arrival of a brother who can hold him steady to a truth until he has made it his own. *Emerson.*

Man, on the dubious waves of error tost. *Cowper.*

Man only can create music, for nothing is perfect until, in some way, it touches or passes through man. *T. T. Munger.*

Man only mars kind Nature's plan, / And turns the fierce pursuit on man. *Scott.*

Man ought always to have something which 25 he prefers to life. *Seume.*

Man partly is and wholly hopes to be. *Browning.*

Man perfected by society is the best of all animals; he is the most terrible of all when he lives without law and without justice. *Arist.*

Man proposes, God disposes. *Pr.*

Man, proud man, / Dress'd in a little brief authority ; / Most ignorant of what he's most assur'd, / His glassy essence, like an angry ape, / Plays such fantastic tricks before high heaven, / As make the angels weep. *Meas. for Meas.*, ii. 2.

Man reconciles himself to almost every event, 30 however trying, if it happens in the ordinary course of nature. It is the extraordinary that he rebels against. *W. v. Humboldt.*

Man rettet gern aus trüber Gegenwart / Sich in das heitere Gebiet der Kunst, / Und für die Kränkungen der Wirklichkeit / Sucht man sich Heilung in des Dichters Träumen —We are fain to escape out of the distracted present into the untroubled sphere of art, and for the miseries of real life we seek healing in the dreams of the poet. *Uhland.*

Man schont die Alten, wie man die Kinder schont—We bear with old people as we do with children. *Goethe.*

Man shall not live by bread alone, but by every word that proceedeth out of the mouth of God. *Bible.*

Man should let alone other's prejudices and examine his own. *Locke.*

Man should not be over-anxious for a subsist- 35 ence, for it is provided by the Creator. The infant no sooner droppeth from the womb than the breasts of the mother begin to stream. *Hitopadesa.*

Man sieht sich, lernt sich kennen, / Liebt sich, muss sich trennen—We greet each other, learn to know each other, love each other, and then—we part.

Man soll die Stimmen wägen und nicht zählen—Votes ought to be weighed, not counted. *Schiller.*

Man soll kein Buch nach dem Titelblatt beurtheilen—We should not judge of a book from the title-page. *Ger. Pr.*

Man soll nicht mehr Teufel rufen, als man bannen kann—One should raise no more devils than one can lay. *Ger. Pr.*

Man spends his life in reasoning on the past, 40 complaining of the present, and trembling for the future. *Rivarol.*

Man spricht selten von der Tugend, die man hat ; aber desto öfter von der, die uns fehlt —We seldom boast (*lit.* speak) of the virtue which we have, but oftener of that which we have not. *Lessing.*

Man spricht vergebens viel, nur zu versagen, / Der and're hört von allem nur das Nein!— In vain we speak much only to refuse; the other, of all we say, hears only the " No ! " *Goethe.*

Man spricht vom vielen Trinken stets, / Doch nie vom vielen Durste—They make much of our drinking, but never think of our thirst. *Scheffel.*

Man steigt den grünen Berg des Lebens hinauf, um oben auf dem Eisberge zu sterben—We ascend the green mountain of life in order to die up there upon the glaciers. (?)

Man steigt nicht ungestraft vom Göttermahle / Herunter in den Kreis der Sterblichen—One does not descend from a banquet with the gods into a company of common mortals without suffering for it. *Grillparzer.*

5 Man supposes that he directs his life and governs his actions, when his existence is irretrievably under the control of destiny. *Goethe.*

Man, that is born of a woman, is of few days, and full of trouble. *Bible.*

Man, the aristocrat amongst the animals. *Heine.*

Man, the little god of this world, is still ever of the same stamp, and is as whimsical as on the first day. *Mephisto in Goethe.*

Man the peasant is a being of more marked national character than man the educated and refined. *Ruskin.*

10 Man thee for the high endeavour, / Shun the crowd's ignoble ease! / Fails the noble spirit never, / Wise to think and prompt to seize. *Goethe.*

Man thereby (by his fantasy as the organ of the godlike), though based to all seeming on the small visible, does nevertheless extend down into the infinite deeps of the Invisible, of which Invisible, indeed, his life is properly the bodying forth. *Carlyle.*

Man thinks he has an estate of reputation, and is glad to see one that will bring any of it home to him; it is no matter how dirty a bag it is conveyed to him in, or by how clownish a messenger, so the money is good. *Steele.*

Man! / Thou pendulum betwixt a smile and a tear. *Byron.*

Man, though, as Swift has it, " a forked straddling animal with bandy legs," yet is also a spirit, and unutterable mystery of mysteries. *Carlyle.*

15 Man unconnected is at home everywhere, unless he may be said to be at home nowhere. *Johnson.*

Man verändert sich oft und bessert sich selten —People change often enough, but seldom for the better. *Ger. Pr.*

Man wants but little here below, / Nor wants that little long. *Goldsmith.*

Man was created to work—not to speculate, or feel, or dream. *Carlyle.*

Man were better relate himself to a statue or picture than to suffer his thoughts to pass in smother. *Bacon.*

20 Man, while he loves, is never quite depraved. *Lamb.*

Man, who lives to die, dies to live well, / So if he guide his ways by blamelessness / And earnest will to hinder not, but help, / All things both great and small which suffer life. *Sir Edwin Arnold.*

Man wird nie betrogen ; man betrügt sich selbst—We are never deceived ; we deceive ourselves. *Goethe.*

Man without patience is the lamp without oil, and pride in a rage is a bad counsellor. *A. de Musset.*

Man without self-restraint is like a barrel without hoops, and tumbles to pieces. *Ward Beecher.*

Man yields to custom as he bows to fate, / 25 In all things ruled—mind, body, and estate ; / In pain, in sickness, we for cure apply / To them we know not, and we know not why. *Crabbe.*

Man's activity is all too fain to relax ; he soon gets fond of unconditional repose. *Goethe.*

Man's best candle is his understanding. *Pr.*

Man's body and his mind are exactly like a jerkin and a jerkin's lining—rumple the one, you rumple the other. *Sterne.*

Man's conviction should be strong, and so well timed that worldly advantages may seem to have no share in it. *Addison.*

Man's extremity is God's opportunity. *Pr.* 30

Man's first care should be to avoid the reproaches of his own heart; his next, to escape the censures of the world. *Addison.*

Man's grand fault is, and remains, that he has so many small ones. *Jean Paul.*

Man's grief is but his grandeur in disguise, and discontent is immortality. *Young.*

Man's gullability is not his worst blessing. *Carlyle.*

Man's heart eats all things, and is hungry 35 still. *Young.*

Man's highest merit always is as much as possible to rule external circumstances, and as little as possible to let himself be ruled by them. *Goethe.*

Man's history is little else than a narrative of designs that have failed and hopes that have been disappointed. *Johnson.*

Man's inhumanity to man makes countless thousands mourn. *Burns.*

Man's liberty ends, and it ought to end, when that liberty becomes the curse of his neighbours. *Farrar.*

Man's life and nature is as it was, and as it 40 will ever be. *Carlyle.*

Man's life is a progress, and not a station. *Emerson.*

Man's life is an appendix to his heart. *South.*

Man's life is filed by his foe. *Pr.*

Man's life is never anything but an ever-vanishing present. *Schopenhauer.*

Man's life is not an affair of mere instinct, but 45 of steady self-control. *Goethe.*

Man's life never was a sport to him; it was a stern reality—altogether a serious matter to be alive. *Carlyle.*

Man's life now, as of old, is the genuine work of God ; wherever there is a man, a God also is revealed, and all that is godlike ; a whole epitome of the Infinite, with its meanings, lies enfolded in the life of every man. *Carlyle.*

Man's love is of man's life a thing apart ; / 'Tis woman's whole existence. *Byron.*

Man's obligations do not tend toward the past. We know of nothing that binds us to what is behind : our duty lies ahead. *C. Richet.*

Man's only true happiness is to live in Hope of something to be won by him, in Reverence of something to be worshipped by him, and in Love of something to be cherished by him, and cherished—for ever. *Ruskin.*

Man's own heart must be ever given to gain that of another. *Goldsmith.*

Man's own judgment is the proper rule and measure of his actions. *Thomas à Kempis.*

5 Man's philosophies are usually the "supplement of his practice;" some ornamental logic-varnish, some outer skin of articulate intelligence, with which he strives to render his dumb instinctive doings presentable when they are done. *Carlyle.*

Man's second childhood begins when a woman gets hold of him. *J. M. Barrie.*

Man's spiritual nature is essentially one and indivisible. *Carlyle.*

Man's true, genuine estimate, / The grand criterion of his fate, / Is not—Art thou high or low? / Did thy fortune ebb or flow? *Burns.*

Man's unhappiness, as I construe, comes of his greatness; it is because there is an Infinite in him, which, with all his cunning, he cannot quite bury under the finite. *Carlyle.*

10 Man's walk, like all walking, is a series of falls. *Carlyle.*

Man's word is God in man. *Tennyson.*

Man's work lasts till set of sun; / Woman's work is never done. *Pr.*

Manche gingen nach Licht und stürzten in tiefere Nacht nur ; sicher im Dämmerschein wandelt die Kindheit dahin—Many have gone in quest of light and fallen into deeper darkness ; whereas childhood walks on secure in the twilight. *Schiller.*

Mancher wähnt sich frei, und siehet / Nicht die Bande, die ihn schnüren—Many a one thinks himself free and sees not the bands that bind him. *Rückert.*

15 Mandamus—We enjoin. A writ issuing from the Queen's Bench, commanding certain things to be done. *L.*

Manebant vestigia morientis libertatis—There still remained traces of expiring liberty. *Tac.*

Manège—Riding-house ; horsemanship. *Fr.*

Manet alta mente repostum, / Judicium Paridis spretæque injuria formæ—Deep seated in her mind remains the judgment of Paris, and the wrong done to her slighted beauty. *Virg., of Juno's vengeance.*

Mange-tout—A spendthrift (*lit.* eat-all). *Fr.*

20 Manhood begins joyfully and hopefully, not when we have made a truce with necessity, or even surrendered to it, but only when we have reconciled ourselves to it, and learned to feel that in necessity we are free. *Carlyle.*

Manhood, when verging into age, grows thoughtful, / Full of wise saws and modern instances. *As You Like It,* ii. 7.

Manibus pedibusque — With hands and feet ; with tooth and nail.

Manibus victoria dextris—Victory by my right hand. *M.*

Manifold is human strife, / Human passion, human pain ; / Yet many blessings still are rife, / And many pleasures still remain. *Goethe.*

Mankind are earthen jugs with spirits in them. 25 *Hawthorne.*

Mankind are unco' weak, / And little to be trusted ; / If self the wavering balance shake, / It's rarely right adjusted. *Burns.*

Mankind at large alway resemble frivolous children ; they are impatient of thought, and wish to be amused. *Emerson.*

"Mankind follow their several bell-wethers ; and if you hold a stick before the wether, so that he is forced to vault in his passage, the whole flock will do the like when the stick is withdrawn ; and the thousandth sheep will be seen vaulting impetuously over air, as the first did over an otherwise impassable barrier." *Carlyle, quoting Jean Paul.*

Mankind in general agree in testifying their devotion, their gratitude, their friendship, or their love, by presenting whatever they hold dearest. *Burns.*

Mankind is a science that defies definitions. 30 *Burns.*

Mankind suffer to this hour, and will for long, as is like, because they do not know what to make of the fire of Prometheus. He dared to purloin from the gods and commit into the hands of ordinary men an element (fire), which, as the result has shown, only gods and their wise-hearted offspring can with safety handle. *Ed.*

Mankind will never lack obstacles to give it trouble, and the pressure of necessity to develop its powers. *Goethe.*

Manliana—A Manlian, *i.e.,* a harsh and severe sentence, such as that of Titus Manlius, who ordered his son to be scourged and beheaded for fighting contrary to orders.

Männer richten nach Gründen ; des Weibes Urteil ist seine Liebe ; wo es nicht liebt, hat schon gerichtet das Weib—Men judge on rational grounds ; the woman's judgment is her love ; where the woman does not love, she has judged. *Schiller.*

Manners are not idle, but the fruit / Of loyal 35 nature and of noble mind. *Tennyson.*

Manners are of more importance than laws ; upon them in a great measure laws depend. *Burke.*

Manners are stronger than laws. *Pr.*

Manners are the happy ways of doing things ; each once a stroke of genius or of love, now repeated and hardened into a usage. *Emerson.*

Manners are the root, laws only the branches. *Horace Mann.*

Manners are the shadows of virtues, the 40 momentary display of those qualities which our fellow-creatures love and respect. *Sydney Smith.*

Manners carry the world for the moment, character for all time. *A. B. Alcott.*

Manners easily and rapidly mature into morals. *Horace Mann.*

Manners make laws, manners likewise repeal them. *Johnson.*

Manners make the man. *M.*

Manners must adorn knowledge, and smooth its way through the world. Like a great rough diamond, it may do very well in a closet by way of curiosity, and also for its intrinsic value. *Chesterfield.*

Männliche, tüchtige Geister werden durch Erkennen eines Irrthums erhöht und gestärkt—Sturdy manly souls are exalted and strengthened in the presence of (*lit.* by the knowledge of) an error. *Goethe.*

Μάντις δ'ἄριστος ὅστις εἰκάζει καλῶς—He is the best diviner who conjectures well. *Eurip.*

Mantua me genuit, Calabri rapuere, tenet nunc / Parthenope. Cecini pascua, rura, duces—Mantua bore me, Calabria carried me off, Naples holds me now. I sang of pastures, fields and heroes. *Virgil's epitaph.*

5 Mantua, væ l miseræ nimium vicina Cremonæ—Mantua, alas! too near the unhappy Cremona. *Quoted by Dean Swift on seeing a lady sweep a violin off a table with her dress.*

Manu forti—With a strong hand. *M.*

Manu scriptum—Written by the hand.

Manufacture is intelligible but trivial; creation is great and cannot be understood. *Carlyle.*

Manum de tabula !—Hand of the picture ! *i.e.,* leave off touching up.

10 Manum non verterim, digitum non porrexerim—I would not turn my hand or stretch out my finger. *Cic.*

Manus e nubibus—Hand from the clouds.

Manus hæc inimica tyrannis—This hand is hostile to tyrants. *M.*

Manus manum lavat—One hand washes the other.

Many a cow stands in the meadow and looks wistfully at the common. *Pr.*

15 Many a dangerous temptation comes to us in fine gay colours that are but skin-deep. *Henry.*

Many a discord betwixt man and the returning seasons soften by degrees into sweetest harmony; but that which bridges over the greatest gap is Love, whose charm unites the earth with heaven above. *Goethe.*

Many a father might say, . . . "I put in gold into the furnace, and there came out this calf." *Spurgeon.*

Many a fine dish has nothing on it. *Pr.*

Many a genius has been of slow growth. Oaks, that flourish for a thousand years, do not spring up into beauty like a reed. *G. H. Lewis.*

20 Many a good cow hath a bad calf. *Pr.*

Many a good drop of broth may come out of an old pot. *Pr.*

Many a good father hath but a bad son. *Pr.*

Many a hand moulded by Nature to give elegance of form to a kid glove is "stinted of its fair proportion" by grubbing toil. *S. Lover.*

Many a man is mad in certain instances, and goes through life without having perceived it. *Johnson.*

25 Many a man settleth more by an inch of his will than by an ell of his thrift. *Pr.*

Many a man's vices have at first been nothing worse than good qualities run wild. *Hare.*

Many a meandering discourse one hears, in which the preacher aims at nothing, and—hits it. *Whately.*

Many a one is good because he can do no mischief. *Pr.*

Many a one labours for the day he will never live to see. *Dan. Pr.*

Many a one threatens while he quakes for 30 fear. *It. and Ger. Pr.*

Many a seeming farce played on the great stage of the world is in reality a tragedy, if we could but see into the heart of it. *Anon.*

Many a true word is spoken in jest. *Pr.*

Many a young damsel has been ruined by a fine copy of verses, which she would have laughed at if she had known it had been stolen from Mr. Waller. *Lady Montagu.*

Many acquaintances, but few friends. *Johnson.*

Many acres will not make a wiseacre. *Pr.* 35

Many an honest man stands in need of help that has not the face to beg it. *Pr.*

Many an irksome noise, when a long way off, is heard as music. *Thoreau.*

Many and many a heart of woman, who has not uttered a word during her whole life, has felt more truly and intensely than the poet that has sung most sweetly. *Renan.*

Many are called but few chosen. *Jesus.*

Many are idly busy. Domitian was busy, but 40 then it was catching flies. *Jeremy Taylor.*

Many are wise in jest but fools in earnest. *Pr.*

Many arrive at second masters / Upon their first lord's neck. *Tim. of Athens, iv. 3.*

Many beat the sack, and mean the miller. *Pr.*

Many books owe their success to the good memories of their authors and the bad memories of their readers. *Colton.*

Many by-walks, many balks; many balks, 45 much stumbling. *Latimer.*

Many can argue, not many converse. *A. B. Alcott.*

Many can bear adversity, but few contempt. *Pr.*

Many can brook the weather that love not the wind. *Love's L. Lost, iv. 2.*

Many can make bricks, but cannot build. *Pr.*

Many causes that can plead well for them-50 selves in the courts of Westminster, have yet in the general court of the universe and free soul of man no word to utter. *Carlyle.*

Many children, many cares; no children, no felicity. *Bovee.*

Many commit sin and blame Satan. *Pr.*

Many cooks spoil the broth. *Pr.*

Many cut broad thongs out of other people's leather. *Pr.*

Many deceive themselves, imagining to find 55 happiness in change. *Thomas à Kempis.*

Many delight more in giving of presents than in paying their debts. *Sir P. Sidney.*

Many estates are spent in the getting, / Since women, for tea, forsook spinning and knitting, / And men, for their punch, forsook hewing and splitting. *Pr.*

Many find fault without any end, / And yet do nothing at all to mend. *Pr.*

Many flowers open to the sun, but only one follows him constantly. Heart, be thou the sunflower, not only open to receive God's blessing, but constant in looking to Him. *Jean Paul.*

Many get into a dispute well that cannot get out well. *Pr.*

Many go in quest of wool, and come back shorn. *Ger. Pr.*

Many go out for clothes, and come home stript. *Pr.*

Many good purposes lie in the churchyard. *Philip Henry.*

5 Many hands make light work. *Pr.*

Many have been harmed by speech; through thinking, few or none. *Lord Vaux.*

Many have been ruined by buying good penny-worths. *Pr.*

Many have been ruined by their fortunes; many have escaped ruin by the want of fortune. To obtain it, the great have become little, and the little great. *Zimmermann.*

Many have come to port after a great storm. *Pr.*

10 Many have genius, / But, wanting art, are for ever dumb. *Longfellow.*

Many have the talents which would make them poets if they had the genius; a few have the genius yet want the talents. *J. Sterling.*

Many have too much, but none enough. *Dan. Pr.*

Many hope that the tree may be felled who expect to gather chips by the fall. *Fuller.*

Many indifferent things which men originally did from a motive of some sort, they continue to do from habit. *J. S. Mill.*

15 Many kinds of books are permissible, but there is one kind that is not permissible, the kind that has nothing in it—*le genre ennuyeux* (the kind that bore you). *Carlyle.*

Many kiss the hand they wish cut off. *Pr.*

Many lick before they bite. *Pr.*

Many littles make a meikle. *Pr.*

Many are fain to praise what is right and do what is wrong. *Dan. Pr.*

20 Many men and women spend their lives in unsuccessful attempts to spin the flax God sends them upon a wheel they can never use. *J. G. Holland.*

Many men attain a knowledge of what is perfect, and of their own insufficiency, and go on doing things by halves to the end of their days. *Goethe.*

Many men fancy that what they experience they also understand. *Goethe.*

Many men have been capable of doing a wise thing, more a cunning thing, but very few a generous thing. *Alex. Pope.*

Many men, in all ages, have triumphed over death, and led it captive; converting its physical victory into a moral victory for themselves, into a seal and immortal consecration for all that their past life had achieved. *Carlyle.*

25 Many men involve themselves deeper in temptations by being too solicitous to decline them. *Thomas à Kempis.*

Many men know how to flatter; few men know how to praise. *Wendell Phillips.*

Many men love in themselves what they hate in others. *Benzel Sternau.*

Many men spend their lives in gazing at their own shadows, and so dwindle away into shadows thereof. *Hare.*

Many of our troubles are God dragging us, and they would end if we would stand upon our feet, and go whither He would have us. *Ward Beecher.*

Many of sounding name from Jamblicus down 30 to Aubrey have wasted their time in devising imaginary remedies for non-existing diseases. *Scott.*

Many of the supposed increasers of knowledge have only given a new name, and often a worse, to what was well known before. *Hare.*

Many old camels carry the skins of the young ones to the market. *Pr.*

Many people are sincere without being simple. They do not wish to be taken for other than they are; and they always fear lest they should be taken for what they are not. *Fénelon.*

Many people place virtue more in regretting than in amendment. *Lichtenberg.*

Many people take no care of their money till 35 they have come nearly to an end of it, and others do just the same with their time. *Goethe.*

Many people think of knowledge as of money. They would like knowledge, but cannot face the perseverance and self-denial that go to the acquisition of it. *John Morley.*

Many readers judge of the power of a book by the shock it gives their feelings. *Longfellow.*

Many rendings need many mendings. *Pr.*

Many sacrifices have been made just to enjoy the feeling of vengeance, without any intention of causing an amount of injury equivalent to what one has suffered. *Schopenhauer.*

Many see more with one eye than others with 40 two. *Ger. Pr.*

Many shall run to and fro, and knowledge shall be increased. *Bible.*

Many so spend their whole term, and in ever-new expectation, ever-new disappointment, shift from enterprise to enterprise, and from side to side, till at length, as exasperated striplings of threescore and ten, they shift into their last enterprise, that of getting buried. *Carlyle.*

Many speak the truth when they say that they despise riches and preferment; but tney mean the riches and preferment possessed by other men. *Colton.*

Many strokes, though with a little axe, / Hew down and fell the hardest timber'd oak. *3 Hen. VI.*, ii. 1.

Many talk like philosophers and live like fools 45 *Pr.*

Many that are first shall be last, and the last shall be first. *Jesus.*

Many there be that buy nothing with their money but repentance. *Pr.*

Many things are too delicate to be thought; many more to be spoken. *Novalis.*

Many things difficult to design prove easy of performance. *Johnson.*

Many things there are / That we may hope to 50 win with violence; / While others only can become our own / Through moderation and wise self-restraint. / Such is virtue; such is love. *Goethe.*

Many times death passeth with less pain than the torture of a limb ; for the most vital parts are not the quickest of sense. *Bacon.*

Many ventures make a full freight. *Pr.*

Many walk into the battle and are carried out of it. *Fielding.*

Many waters cannot quench love, neither can the floods drown it. *Bible.*

5 Many words hurt more than swords. *Pr.*

Many would be cowards if they had courage enough. *Pr.*

Many would have been worse if their estates had been better. *Pr.*

Many young persons believe themselves natural when they are really ill-mannered and coarse. *La Roche.*

Mar not what, marred, cannot be mended. *Pr.*

10 March dust is a thing / Worth ransom of a king. *Old saw.*

March winds and April showers. *Pr.*

Marchand qui perd ne peut rire—The dealer who loses is not the one to laugh. *Dandin.*

Marchandise de rencontre—Second-hand goods. *Fr.*

Marchandise qui plait est à demie vendue—Goods which please are half sold. *Fr. Pr.*

15 Mare apertum—A sea open to commerce.

Mare clausum—A sea closed to commerce.

Mare cœlo miscere — To confound sea and sky.

Mare ditat, rosa decorat—The sea enriches, the rose adorns. *M.*

Mare quidem commune certo est omnibus—The sea surely is common to all. *Plaut.*

20 Margarita e stercore—A pearl from a dunghill. *Pr.*

Maria montesque polliceri cœpit—He began to promise seas and mountains. *Sall.*

Mariage de convenance—A marriage from considerations of advantage. *Fr.*

Marie ton fils quand tu voudras, mais ta fille quand tu pourras—Marry your son when you like, your daughter when you can. *Fr. Pr.*

Mark if his birth makes any difference, if to his words it adds one grain of sense. *Dryden.*

25 Mark what another says ; for many are / Full of themselves, and answer their own notion. / Take all into thee ; then with equal care / Balance each chain of reason, like a potion. *George Herbert.*

Marmoreo Licinus tumulo jacet, at Cato parvo, / Pompeius nullo. Quis putet esse deos ? / Saxa premunt Licinum, levat altum Fama Catonem, / Pompeium tituli. Credimus esse deos—Licinus lies in a marble tomb, Cato in a humble one, Pompey in none. Who can believe that the gods exist? *Ans.*—Heavy lies the stone on Licinus ; Fame raises Cato on high ; his glories, Pompey. We believe that the gods do exist.

Marriage, by making us more contented, causes us often to be less enterprising. *Bovee.*

Marriage comes unawares, like a soot-drop. *Irish Pr.*

Marriage, indeed, may qualify the fury of his passion, but it very rarely mends a man's manners. *Congreve.*

Marriage is a desperate thing. The frogs in 30 Æsop were extremely wise ; they had a great mind to some water, but they would not leap into the well, because they could not get out again. *Selden.*

Marriage is the best state for man in general ; and every man is a worse man in proportion as he is unfit for the married state. *Johnson.*

Marriage is the bloom or blight of all men's happiness. *Byron.*

Marriage is the feast where the grace is better than the dinner. *Colton.*

Marriage is the mother of the world, and preserves kingdoms, and fills cities and churches, and heaven itself. *Jeremy Taylor.*

Marriage must be a relation either of sym- 35 pathy or of conquest. *George Eliot.*

Marriage with peace is the world's paradise ; with strife, this life's purgatory. *Pr.*

Marriages are best of dissimilar material. *Theo. Parker.*

Marriages are made in heaven. *Pr.*

Married couples resemble a pair of scissors, often moving in opposite directions, yet always punishing any one who comes between them. *Sydney Smith.*

Married in haste, we may repent at leisure. 40 *Congreve.*

Marry above your match, and you get a master. *Pr.*

Marry and grow tame. *Sp. Pr.*

Marry for love and work for siller. *Sc. Pr.*

Marry for love, but only love that which is lovely. *Pr.*

Marrying is easy, but housekeeping is hard. 45 *Pr.*

Mars gravior sub pace latet—A more serious war lies concealed under a show of peace. *Claud.*

Martem accendere cantu—To waken up the war-spirit by his note. *Virg.*

Mas vale buen amigo que pariente primo—A good friend is better than a near relation. *Sp. Pr.*

Masses are rude, lame, unmade, pernicious in their demands and influence, and need not to be flattered, but to be schooled. *Emerson.*

Mässigkeit und klarer Himmel sind Apollo 50 und die Musen—Moderation and a clear sky are Apollo and the Muses. *Goethe.*

Masters are mostly the greatest servants in the house. *Pr.*

Masters should be sometimes blind and sometimes deaf. *Pr.*

Masters two / Will not do. *Pr.*

Mastery passes often for egotism. *Goethe.*

Match-makers often burn their fingers. *Pr.* 55

Mater artium necessitas — Necessity is the mother of invention (*lit.* the arts).

Mater familias—The mother of a family.

Materia medica—Substances used in medicine ; therapeutics.

Materia prima—The primary substance or substrate.

Materialism coarsens and petrifies everything ; 60 makes everything vulgar, and every truth false. *Amiel.*

Materiem, qua sis ingeniosus, habes—You have a subject on which to show your ingenuity. *Ovid.*

Materiem superabat opus—The workmanship surpassed the material. *Ovid.*

Mathematic form is eternal in the reasoning memory; living form is eternal existence. *Wm. Blake.*

Mathematics can remove no prejudices and soften no obduracy. It has no influence in sweetening the bitter strife of parties, and in the moral world generally its action is perfectly null. *Goethe.*

μαθοῦσιν αὔδω, κοὐ μαθοῦσι λήθομαι—I speak to experts; those who are not I ignore. *Æsch.*

5 Matinée — A morning recital or performance. *Fr.*

Matrimony, the high sea for which no compass has yet been invented. *Heine.*

Matter exists only spiritually, and to represent some idea and body it forth. *Carlyle.*

Matter, were it never so despicable, is spirit, the manifestation of spirit: were it never so honourable, can it be more? *Carlyle.*

Mature fieri senem, si diu velis esse senex— You must become an old man soon if you would be an old man long. *Pr. in Cic.*

10 Maulesel treiben viel Parlaren / Dass ihre Voreltern Pferde waren—Mules boast much that their ancestors were horses. *Ger. Pr.*

Mauvaise honte—False shame. *Fr.*

Mauvaise langue—A slanderous tongue. *Fr.*

Mauvais pas—A scrape; a difficulty. *Fr.*

Mauvais sujet — A bad or worthless fellow. *Fr.*

15 Mauvais ton—Bad manners. *Fr.*

Maxim or aphorism, let us remember that this wisdom of life is the true salt of literature; that those books are most nourishing which are most richly stored with it, and that it is one of the main objects . . . which men ought to seek in the reading of books. *John Morley.*

Maxima debetur pueris reverentia—The greatest respect is due to youth (*lit.* our boys). *Juv.*

Maxima illecebra est peccandi impunitatis spes —The greatest incitement to guilt is the hope of sinning with impunity. *Cic.*

Maxima quæque domus servis est plena superbis—Every great house is full of haughty servants. *Juv.*

20 Maximas virtutes jacere omnes necesse est, voluptate dominante—Where pleasure prevails, all the greatest virtues must lie dormant. *Cic.*

Maxims are to the intellect what laws are to actions; they do not enlighten, but they guide and direct. *Joubert.*

Maximum remedium iræ dilatio est!—Deferring of anger is the best antidote to anger. *Seneca.*

Maximus in minimis—Very great in very little things.

Maximus novator tempus—Time is the greatest innovator. *Pr.*

25 "May-be" is very well, but "must" is the master. *Pr.*

May cauld ne'er catch you but a hap, / Nor hunger but in plenty's lap. *Burns.*

May never wicked fortune touzle (tease) him! / May never wicked man bamboozle him! / Until a pow as auld's Methusalem / He canty (cheerily) claw, / Then to the blessed New Jerusalem / Fleet wing awa'! *Burns.*

May the idea of pureness, extending itself even to the very morsel which I take into my mouth, become ever dearer and more luminous within me. *Goethe.*

Me judice—In my opinion or judgment.

Me justum esse gratis oportet—It is my duty 30 to show justice without recompense. *Sen.*

Μὴ κακὰ κερδαίνειν· κακὰ κέρδεα ἶσ' ἄτῃσιν —Do not make evil gains; evil gains are equal to losses. *Hesiod.*

Μὴ κίνει Καμάριναν—Don't stir Lake Camarina (otherwise pestilence).

Me miseram, quod amor non est medicabilis herbis!—Oh, unhappy me, that there should be no herbs to cure love!

Me nemo ministro / Fur erit—No one shall play the thief with my help. *Juv.*

Me non solum piget stultitiæ meæ, sed etiam 35 pudet—I am not only annoyed at my folly, I am ashamed of it. *L.*

Me, poor man, my library was dukedom large enough. *Tempest,* i. 1.

Me (they will kill) when they are mad, but you when they recover their reason. *Phocion to Demosthenes, who had threatened him with death at the hands of his fellow-citizens.*

Mea virtute me involvo—I wrap myself in my virtue. *Hor.*

Meal is finer than grain; women are finer than men. *Gael. Pr.*

Meals and matins minish never. *Pr.* 40

Mean spirits under disappointment, like small beer in a thunderstorm, always turn sour. *Randolph.*

Measure men around the heart. *Pr.*

Measure not by a scale of perfection the meagre product of reality. *Schiller.*

Measure three times before you cut once. *Pr.*

Measure your cloth ten times; you can cut 45 it but once. *Russ. Pr.*

Measures, not men, have always been my mark. *Goldsmith.*

Meat and matins hinder no man's journey. *Pr.*

Meat is devoured by the birds in the air, by the beasts in the fields, and by the fishes in the waters; so, in every situation, there is plenty. *Hitopadesa.*

Meat is more than its carving, and truth is more than oratory. *Pr.*

Mecum facile redeo in gratiam—I easily recover 50 my good-will myself. *Phædr.*

μηδὲν ἄγαν—No excess. *Anon.*

Μηδένα κακηγορείτο μηδείς—Let nobody speak mischief of anybody. *Plato.*

Medici, causa morbi inventa, curationem inventam putant—Physicians, when they have found out the cause of a disease, consider they have found out the cure. *Cic.*

Medicines are not meant to feed on. *Pr.*

Medio de fonte leporum / Surgit amari aliquid 55 quod in ipsis floribus angat—From the midst of the very fountain of delight something bitter arises to vex us even amid the flowers themselves. *Lucret.*

Medio tutissimus ibis—You will go most safely in the middle. *Ovid.*

Médiocre et rampant, et l'on arrive à tout— Be second-rate and fawning, and you may attain to anything. *Beaumarchais.*

Mediocria firma—-The middle station is the most secure. *M.*

Mediocribus esse poetis / Non Di, non homines, non concessere columnæ—Mediocrity in poets is condemned by gods and men, and booksellers too. *Hor.*

Mediocrity can talk, but it is for genius to observe. *I. Disraeli.*

Mediocrity is not allowed to poets either by gods or men. *Hor.*

5 Mediocrity of enjoyment only is allowed to man. *Blair.*

Meditation has taught all men in all ages that this world is after all but a show—a phenomenon or appearance, no real thing. *Carlyle.*

Meditation is a busy search in the storehouse of phantasy for some ideas of matters to be cast in the moulds of resolution into some forms of words and action ; in which search I find this is the best conclusion, that to meditate on the best is the best of meditations, and a resolution to make a good end is a good end of my resolutions. *A. Warwick.*

Meditation is the life of the soul; action, the soul of meditation ; honour, the reward of action. *Quarles.*

Meditation is the soul's perspective glass, whereby in her long removes she discerneth God as if he were nearer at hand. *Feltham.*

10 Medium tenuere beati ! — Happy they who steadily pursue a middle course.

Meekness is not mere white-facedness, a mere contemplative virtue ; it is maintaining peace and patience in the midst of pelting provocations. *Ward Beecher.*

Meekness is not weakness. *Pr.*

Meekness is the bridle of anger. *Saying.*

Meekness is the cherish'd bent / Of all the truly great and all the innocent. *Wordsworth.*

15 Μέγα βιβλίον μέγα κακόν—A great book is a great evil. *Callimachus.*

Meglio amici da lontano che nemici d'appresso—Better be friends at a distance than enemies near each other. *It. Pr.*

Meglio solo che mal accompagnato—Better alone than in bad company. *It. Pr.*

Meglio tardi che mai—Better late than never. *It. Pr.*

Mehr Leute beten die aufgehende, als die untergehende Sonne an — More people pay homage to the rising than to the setting sun. *Jean Paul.*

20 Mehr Licht!—More light! *Goethe's last words.* (?)

Meikle crack fills nae sack. *Sc. Pr.*

Mein einz'ger Wunsch ist meiner Wünsche Ruhe—My only wish is that my wishes should be at rest. *Rückert.*

Mein erst Gesetz ist, in der Welt / Die Frager zu vermeiden—A first rule of mine is to avoid the inquiring class of people. *Goethe.*

Mein Herz gleicht ganz dem Meere, / Hat Sturm und Ebb' und Flut, / Und manche schöne Perle / In seiner Tiefe ruht — My heart altogether resembles the sea; it has its storms, its ebbs and floods, and far down in its quiet depths rests many a shining pearl. *Heine.*

25 Mein Leben ist für Gold nicht feil—My life is not to be bartered away for gold. *Bürger.*

Mein Leipzig lob' ich mir ! / Es ist klein Paris, und bildet seine Leute—Leipzig for me ! It is quite a little Paris, and its people acquire an easy finished air (*lit.* it fashions its people). *Goethe.*

Mein Pathos brächte dich gewiss zum Lachen, / Hätt'st du dir nicht das Lachen abgewöhnt —My pathos would surely provoke you to mirth, if you had not long ago forborne to smile. *Mephisto to the Lord, in Goethe's "Faust."*

Mein Ruh' ist hin, / Mein Herz ist schwer; / Ich finde sie nimmer / Und nimmermehr— My peace is gone ; my heart is heavy; I shall find it (peace) never and nevermore. *Gretchen in Goethe's "Faust."*

Mein Sohn, nichts in der Welt ist unbedeutend. / Das erste aber und Hauptsächlichste / Bei allem ird'schen Ding ist Ort und Stunde—My son, nothing in this world is without significance, but the first and most essential matter in every earthly thing is the place where and the hour when. *Schiller.*

Mein Wille ist rein, das weitere gebe ich der 30 Vorsehung anheim!—My intention is pure ; the rest I leave in the hands of Providence. *Frederick William II. of Prussia.*

Meine Herrn, did you never hear of the man that vilified the sun because it would not light his cigar? *Carlyle's challenge to certain canting pietistic depreciators of Goethe.*

Meine Zeit in Unruhe, meine Hoffnung in Gott!—The time I live in is a time of turmoil ; my hope is in God. *Frederick William III. of Prussia.*

Meiner Idee nach ist Energie die erste und einzige Tugend des Menschen—In my regard energy is the first and only virtue of man. *W. v. Humboldt.*

Meines Lebens Wunsch ist stiller Friede— The wish of my life is a tranquil peace. *Seume.*

Mel in ore, verba lactis, / Fel in corde, fraus in 35 factis—Honey in his mouth, words of milk ; gall in his heart, deceit in his deeds.

Melancholy advanceth men's conceits more than any humour whatever. *Burton.*

Melancholy attends on the best joys of a merely ideal life. *Margaret Fuller.*

Melancholy is the pleasure of being sad. *Victor Hugo.*

Melancholy spreads itself betwixt heaven and earth, like envy between man and man, and is an everlasting mist. *Byron.*

Μελετή τὸ πᾶν—Practice is everything. *Peri-40 ander.*

Melior est conditio possidentis—The condition of the party in possession, or the defendant, is the better of the two. *L.*

Melior tutiorque est certa pax, quam sperata victoria—A certain peace is better and safer than an expected victory. *L.*

Meliora sunt ea quæ natura, quam quæ arte perfecta sunt—The things which are perfect by nature are better than those which are perfect by art. *Cic.*

Meliores priores—The better first. *L.*

Melioribus auspiciis — Under more favourable 45 auspices.

Melius est pati semel, quam cavere semper— It is better to suffer once than to be in perpetual apprehension. *Jul. Cæs.*

Melius est peccata cavere quam mortem fugere—It is better to avoid sin than to fly from death. *Thomas à Kempis.*

Melius, pejus, prosit, obsit, nil vident nisi quod libuerit—Better or worse, for good or for harm, they see nothing but what they please. *Ter.*

Mellitum venenum, blanda oratio—A flattering speech is honied poison. *Pr.*

Membra reformidant mollem quoque saucia tactum; / Vanaque sollicitis incutit umbra metum—The wounded limb shrinks from even a gentle touch, and the unsubstantial shadow strikes the timid with alarm. *Ovid.*

Même quand l'oiseau marche, on sent qu'il a des ailes—Even when a bird walks, we may see that it has wings. *Fr. Pr.*

5 Meminerunt omnia amantes—Lovers remember everything. *Ovid.*

Memini etiam quæ nolo : oblivisci non possum quæ volo—I remember what I would not, and I cannot forget what I would. *Themistocles.*

Memor et fidelis—Mindful and faithful. *M.*

Memorabilia—Things to be remembered or recorded.

Memorem immemorem facit, qui monet quod memor meminit—He who reminds a man with a good memory of what he remembers, makes him forget. *Plaut.*

10 Memoria in æterna—In eternal remembrance. *M.*

Memoria minuitur, nisi eam exerceas—Your power of recollection will wax feeble unless you exercise it. *Cic.*

Memoriter—By rote.

Memory always obeys the commands of the heart. *Rivarol.*

Memory, and thou, Forgetfulness, not yet / Your powers in happy harmony I find ; / One oft recalls what I would fain forget, / And one blots out what I would bear in mind. *Macedonius.*

15 Memory is a Muse in herself, or rather the mother of the Muses. (?)

Memory is like a purse : if it be over-full, that it cannot be shut, all will drop out of it. *Fuller.*

Memory is not so brilliant as hope, but it is more beautiful, and a thousand times more true. *G. D. Prentice.*

Memory is the cabinet of imagination, the treasury of reason, the registry of conscience, and the council-chamber of thought. *Basile.*

Memory is the conservative faculty. *Sir Wm. Hamilton.*

20 Memory is the friend of wit, but the treacherous ally of invention. *Colton.*

Memory is the golden thread linking all the mental gifts and excellencies together. *E. P. Hood.*

Memory (*Erinnerung*) is the only paradise out of which we cannot be driven. *Jean Paul.*

Memory is the primary and fundamental power, without which there could be no other intellectual operation. *Johnson.*

Memory is the scribe of the soul. *Arist.*

25 Memory, of all things good remind us still : / Forgetfulness, obliterate all that's ill. *Macedonius.*

Memory tempers prosperity, mitigates adversity, controls youth, and delights old age. *Lactantius.*

Memory, the warder of the brain. *Macb., i. 7.*

Men and communities in this world are often in the position of Arctic explorers, who are making great speed in a given direction, while the ice-floe beneath them is making greater speed in the opposite. *John Burroughs.*

Men and cucumbers are worth nothing as soon as they are ripe. *Jean Paul.*

Men and pyramids are not made to stand on 30 their head. *G. K. Pfeffel.*

Men and women who "grill" over the petty annoyances incident to existence, and inseparable from it, go to ruin like a careworn cat. *C. J. Dunphie.*

Men apt to promise are apt to forget. *Pr.*

Men are April when they woo, December when they wed. *As You Like It, iv. 1.*

Men are as the time is. *Lear, v. 3.*

Men are at best only stewards, and they are 35 very select men indeed who are elected of heaven to this honour. The most want the necessary discrimination, and are in their place only when, like Athenian maidens, "bearers of the basket." *Ed.*

Men are but children of a larger growth ; / Our appetites are apt to change as theirs, / And full as craving too, and full as vain. *Dryden.*

Men are content to be brushed like flies from the path of a great person, so that justice shall be done by him to that common nature which it is the dearest desire of all to see enlarged and glorified. *Emerson.*

Men are contented to be laughed at for their wit, but not for their folly. *Swift.*

Men are enlisted for the labour that kills ; let them be enlisted for the labour that feeds ; and let the captains of the latter be held as much gentlemen as the captains of the former. *Ruskin.*

Men are eternally divided into the two classes 40 of poet (or believer, maker, and praiser), and dunce (or unbeliever, unmaker, and dispraiser). *Ruskin.*

Men are everything, measures are comparatively nothing. *Canning.*

Men are generally more careful of the breed of their horses and dogs than of their children. *W. Penn.*

Men are happy in proportion as their range of vision, their sphere of action, and their points of contact with the world are restricted and circumscribed. *Schopenhauer.*

Men are impatient and for precipitating things ; but the Author of Nature appears deliberate throughout his operations, accomplishing his natural ends by slow successive steps. *Bishop Butler.*

Men are in general so tricky, so envious, and 45 so cruel, that when we find one who is only weak, we are too happy. *Voltaire.*

Men are led by trifles. *Napoleon.*

Men are less afraid of injuring one who awakens love than one who inspires fear. *Machiavelli.*

Men are like flies—for men are insects too, / Little in mind, howe'er our bodies run !— / We're all in sects : in sects that hate each other, / And deem it love of God to hate one's brother. *Edward Irwin.*

Men are like sheep, of which a flock is more easily driven than a single one. *Whately.*

Men are made by nature unequal: it is vain, therefore, to treat them as if they were equal. *Froude.*

Men are men; the best sometimes forget. *Othello*, ii. 3.

Men are more inclined to ask curious questions than to obtain necessary instruction. *Pasquier Quesnel.*

Men are most apt to believe what they least understand. *Pliny.*

5 Men are mostly so slow, their thoughts overrun 'em, an' they can only catch 'em by the tail. *George Eliot.*

Men are much in disposition and feelings according to the nature of the country which they inhabit. *Polybius.*

Men are much more prone (the greater is the pity) both to speak and believe ill than well of their neighbours. *Thomas à Kempis.*

Men are never so easily deceived as while they are endeavouring to deceive others. *La Roche.*

Men are never wise but returning from law. *Pr.*

10 Men are not always what they seem to be. *Lessing.*

Men are not influenced by things, but by their thoughts about things. *Epictetus.*

Men are not leaning willows, but can and must detach themselves. *Emerson.*

Men are not put into this world to be everlastingly fiddled on by the fingers of joy. *Ward Beecher.*

Men are not so ungrateful as they are said to be. If they are often complained of, it generally happens that the benefactor claims more than he has given. *Napoleon.*

15 Men are not to be measured by inches. *Pr.*

Men are often capable of greater things than they perform. They are sent into the world with bills of credit, and seldom draw to their full extent. *Walpole.*

Men are oftener treacherous through weakness than design. *La Roche.*

Men are readier to forgive calumny than admonition (*Ermahnung*). *Jean Paul.*

Men are respectable only as they respect. *Emerson.*

20 Men are seldom blessed with good fortune and good sense at the same time. *Livy.*

Men are seldom more innocently employed than when they are making money. *Johnson.*

Men are so constituted that everybody would rather undertake himself what he sees done by others, whether he has aptitude for it or not. *Goethe.*

Men are solitary among each other; no one will help his neighbour; each has even to assume a defensive attitude lest his neighbour should hinder him. *Carlyle.*

Men are tatooed with their special beliefs like so many South Sea islanders; but a real human heart, with divine love in it, beats with the same glow under all the patterns of all earth's thousand tribes. *Holmes.*

25 Men are the sport of circumstances, when the circumstances seem the sport of men. *Byron.*

Men are unwiser than children; they do not know the hand that feeds them. *Carlyle.*

Men are very generous with that which costs them nothing. *Pr.*

Men are we, and must grieve when even the shade / Of that which once was great is passed away. *Wordsworth.*

Men are what their mothers made them. *Emerson.*

Men are wiser than they know. *Emerson.*   30

Men at most differ as heaven and earth, / But women, worst and best, as heaven and hell. *Tennyson.*

Men at some time are masters of their fate. *Jul. Cæs.*, i. 2.

Men blush less for their crimes than for their weaknesses and vanities. *La Bruyère.*

Men can be estimated by those who know them not, only as they are represented by those who know them. *Johnson.*

Men / Can counsel, and speak comfort to that 35 grief / Which they themselves not feel; but, tasting it, / Their counsel turns to passion, which before / Would give preceptial medicine to rage, / Fetter strong madness in a silken thread, / Charm ache with air and agony with words. *Much Ado*, v. 1.

Men can make an idol of the Bible. *Ward Beecher.*

Men can see through a barn-door, they can. Perhaps that's the reason they can see so little o' this side on't. *George Eliot.*

Men cannot be well educated without the Bible. *Dr. Nott.*

Men cannot benefit those that are with them as they can benefit those that come after them; and of all the pulpits from which the human voice is ever sent forth, there is none from which it reaches so far as from the grave. *Ruskin.*

Men cannot live by lending money to each 40 other. *Ruskin.*

Men cannot live isolated; we are all bound together, for mutual good or else for mutual misery, as living nerves in the same body. No highest man can disunite himself from any lowest. *Carlyle.*

Men carry the head erect indeed, yet how mean and cringing are the thoughts within. *Heine.*

Men cease to interest us when we find their limitations. *Emerson.*

Men chew not when they have no bread. *Pr.*

Men commonly think according to their inclina- 45 tions, speak according to their learning and imbibed opinions, but generally act according to custom. *Bacon.*

Men complain of not finding a place of repose. They are in the wrong; they have it for seeking. What they indeed should complain of is, that the heart is an enemy to that very repose they seek. *Goldsmith.*

Men contemplate distinctions because they are stupefied with ignorance (viz., of the substantial identity of things). *Eastern saying, quoted by Emerson.*

Men deal with life as children with their play, / Who first misuse, then cast their toys away. *Cowper.*

Men deride what they do not understand, and snarl at the good and beautiful because it lies beyond their sympathies. *Goethe.*

Men descend to meet. *Emerson.*

Men do not make their homes unhappy because they have genius, but because they have not enough genius. *Wordsworth.*

Men don't and can't live by exchanging articles, but by producing them: they don't live by trade but by work. *Ruskin.*

Men dream in courtship, but in wedlock wake. *Pope.*

5 Men, elevated above all states, are now the educators of states—dead men, for instance, like Plato. *Jean Paul.*

Men err from selfishness, women because they are weak. *Mme. de Staël.*

Men fear death as children fear to go in the dark. *Bacon.*

Men fear only him who does not know them, and he who shuns them will soon misjudge them. *Goethe.*

Men feed themselves rather upon illusion than upon truth. *Amiel.*

10 Men find it more easy to flatter than to praise. *Jean Paul.*

Men have been wise in very different modes; but they have always laughed the same way. *Johnson.*

Men have but too much cause to secure themselves from men. *Goethe.*

Men have come to speak of the revelation as somewhat long ago given and done, as if God were dead. *Emerson.*

Men have many faults; / Poor women have but two; / There's nothing good they say, / And nothing right they do. *Anon.*

15 Men have their metal, as of gold and silver. *Koran.*

Men in all ways are better than they seem. *Emerson.*

Men in general experience a great joy in colour. The eye needs it as much as it does light. Let any one recall the refreshing sensation one experiences when on a gloomy day the sun shines out on a particular spot on the landscape, and makes the colours of it visible. That healing powers were ascribed to coloured precious stones may have arisen out of the deep feeling of this inexpressible pleasure. *Goethe.*

Men in great place are thrice servants—servants of the sovereign or state, servants of fame, and servants of business. *Bacon.*

Men, in spite of all their failings, best deserve our affections of all that exists. *Goethe.*

20 Men learn behaviour, as they take diseases, one of another. *Emerson.*

Men like advising the women better than doing right themselves. *Spurgeon.*

Men, like bullets, go farthest when they are smoothest. *Jean Paul.*

Men, like musical instruments, seem made to be played upon. *Bovee.*

Men, like peaches and pears, grow sweet a little while before they begin to decay. *Holmes.*

25 Men look to what people think of them; women to what they say. *Hippel.*

Men love at first, and most warmly; women love last and longest. This is natural enough, for nature makes women to be won, and men to win. *G. W. Curtis.*

Men love in haste, but they detest at leisure. *Byron.*

Men love things best; women love persons best. *Jean Paul.*

Men love to nurse their cares, and seem as uneasy without some fret, as an old friar would be without his hair-girdle. *Ward Beecher.*

Men love us, or they need our love. *Keble.* 30

Men make the best friends. *La Bruyère.*

Men may live fools, but fools they cannot die. *Young.*

Men may rise on stepping-stones / Of their dead selves to higher things. *Tennyson.*

Men might live quiet and easy enough, if they would be careful not to give themselves trouble, and forbear meddling with what other people do and say, in which they are in no way concerned. *Thomas à Kempis.*

Men more easily renounce their interests than 35 their tastes. *La Roche.*

Men must be taught as though you taught them not. *Pope.*

Men must endure / Their going hence, even as their coming hither: / Ripeness is all. *Lear, v. 2.*

Men must have righteous principles in the first place, and then they will not fail to perform virtuous actions. *Luther.*

Men must leave the ingle-nook, / And for a larger wisdom brook / Experience of a harder law, / And learn humility and awe. *Dr. Walter Smith.*

Men must work, and women must weep, / 40 Though storms be sudden, and waters deep, / And the harbour bar be moaning. *Charles Kingsley.*

Men no longer wholly believe; in this age of blindness and scientific pride, no one is any longer seen bowing before his god on both his knees. *Victor Hugo.*

Men no sooner find their appetites unanswered than they complain the times are injurious. *Raleigh.*

Men of age object too much, consult too long, adventure too little, repent too soon, and seldom drive business home to the full period, but content themselves with a mediocrity of success. *Bacon.*

Men of courage, men of sense, and men of letters are frequent; but a true gentleman is what one seldom sees. *Steele.*

Men of few words are the best men. *Henry* 45 *V., iii. 2.*

Men of genius are dull and inert in society; as the blazing meteor, when it descends to the earth, is only a stone. *Longfellow.*

Men of genius are rarely much annoyed by the company of vulgar people, because they have a power of looking at such persons as objects of amusement of another race altogether. *Coleridge.*

Men of genius do not excel in any profession because they labour in it, but they labour in it because they excel. *Hazlitt.*

Men of genius have acuter feelings than common men; they are like the wind-harp, which answers to the breath that touches it, now low and sweet, now rising into wild swell or angry scream, as the strings are swept by some passing gust. *Froude.*

Men of God have always, from time to time, walked among men, and made their commission felt in the heart and soul of the commonest hearer. *Emerson.*

Men of great gifts you will easily find, but symmetrical men never. *Emerson.*

Men of great intellect live in the world without really belonging to it. *Schiller.*

Men of great learning or genius are too full to be exact, and therefore choose to throw down their pearls in heaps before the reader, rather than be at the pains of stringing them. *Spectator.*

5 Men of great parts are often unfortunate in the management of public business, because they are apt to go out of the common road by the quickness of their imagination. *Swift.*

Men of humour are always in some degree men of genius; wits are rarely so, although a man of genius may, amongst other gifts, possess wit, as Shakespeare. *Coleridge.*

Men of most renowned virtue have sometimes by transgressing most truly kept the law. *Milton.*

Men of science should leave controversy to the little world below them. *Goldsmith.*

Men of sense esteem wealth to be the assimilation of nature to themselves, the converting of the sap and juices of the planet to the incarnation and nutriment of their design. *Emerson.*

Men of sense often learn from their enemies. *Aristophanes.*

Men of the first quality learn nothing, and become wise; men of the second rank become sensible (*klug*), and learn long; men of the third sort remain stupid, and learn words. *Rückert.*

Men of the greatest abilities are most fired with ambition, and, on the contrary, mean and narrow minds are the least actuated by it. *Addison.*

Men of true wisdom and goodness are contented to take persons and things as they are, without complaining of their imperfections or attempting to amend them. *Fielding.*

Men of uncommon abilities generally fall into eccentricities when their sphere of life is not adequate to their powers. *Goethe.*

15 Men only associate in parties by sacrificing their opinions, or by having none worth sacrificing; and the effect of party government is always to develop hostilities and hypocrisies, and to extinguish ideas. *Ruskin.*

Men only rightly know themselves as far as they have experimented on things. *Emerson.*

Men ought to find the difference between saltness and bitterness. *Bacon.*

Men possessed with an idea cannot be reasoned with. *Froude.*

Men possessing small souls are generally the authors of great evils. *Goethe.*

20 Men prize the thing ungained more than it is. *Troil. and Cress.*, i. 2.

Men rate the virtues of the heart at almost nothing, while they idolise endowments of body and intellect. *La Bruyère.*

Men rattle their chains to show that they are free. *Pr.*

Men run away to other countries because they are not good in their own, and run back to their own because they pass for nothing in the new places. *Emerson.*

Men say their pinnacles point to heaven. Why, so does every tree that buds, and every bird that rises as it sings. Men say their aisles are good for worship. Why, so is every mountain glen and rough seashore. But this they have of distinct and indisputable glory, — that their mighty walls were never raised, and never shall be, but by men who love and aid each other in their weakness. *Ruskin.*

Men seek within the short span of life to 25 satisfy a thousand desires, each of which alone is insatiable. *Goldsmith.*

Men seem to be led by their noses, but in reality it is by their ears. *Carlyle.*

Men should be prized, not for their exemption from fault, but the size of those virtues they are possessed of. *Goldsmith.*

Men should be what they seem; / Or those that be not, would they might seem none. *Othello*, iii. 3.

Men should keep their eyes wide open before marriage, and half-shut afterwards. *Mme. Scudéri.*

Men should not be told of the faults which 30 they have mended. *Johnson.*

Men show their character in nothing more clearly than by what they think laughable. *Goethe.*

Men, some to business, some to pleasure take; / But every woman is at heart a rake: / Men, some to quiet, some to public strife; / But every lady would be queen for life. *Pope.*

Men speak but little when vanity does not induce them to speak. *La Roche.*

Men spend their lives in the service of their passions instead of employing their passions in the service of their lives. *Steele.*

Men still are what they always have been, a 35 medley (*Gemisch*) of strength and weakness, often obedient to reason, and oftener to passion; so have they come down the stream of time for six thousand years, and mostly in such shape as the moment has fashioned them. *Seume.*

Men that are ruined are ruined on the side of their natural propensities. *Burke.*

Men that hazard all / Do it in hope of fair advantages. *Mer. of Ven.*, ii. 7.

Men that make / Envy and crooked malice nourishment / Dare bite the best. *Hen. VIII.*, v. 3.

Men think highly of those who rise rapidly in the world; whereas nothing rises quicker than dust, straw, and feathers. *Hare.*

Men think they are quarrelling with one 40 another, and both sides feel that they are in the wrong. *Goethe.*

Men think to mend their condition by a change of circumstances. They might as well hope to escape their shadows. *Froude, Carlyle.*

Men tire themselves in pursuit of rest. *Sterne.*

Men trust rather to their eyes than to their ears; the effect of precepts is therefore slow and tedious, whilst that of examples is summary and effectual. *Seneca.*

Men understand not what is among their hands; as calmness is the characteristic of strength, so the weightiest causes may be the most silent. *Carlyle.*

Men use, if they have an evil turn, to write it in marble, and whoso doth us a good turn we write it in dust. *Sir T. More.*

Men, who are knaves individually, are in the mass very honourable people. *Montesquieu.*

Men who begin by losing their independence will end by losing their energy. *Buckle.*

5 Men who, being always bred in affluence, see the world only on one side, are surely improper judges of human nature. *Goldsmith.*

Men who earn nothing but compliments are not likely to be very diligent in so unprofitable a service. *Spurgeon.*

Men who form their judgment upon sense often err. *Thomas à Kempis.*

Men who know the same things are not long the best company for each other. *Emerson.*

Men who make money rarely saunter; men who save money rarely swagger. *Bulwer Lytton.*

10 Men who their duties know, / But know their rights, and, knowing, dare maintain. *Sir W. Jones.*

Men will always act according to their passions. Therefore the best government is that which inspires the nobler passions and destroys the meaner. *Jacobi.*

Men will blame themselves for the purpose of being praised. *Pr.*

Men will die for an opinion as soon as for anything else. *Hazlitt.*

Men will face powder and steel, because they cannot face public opinion. *Chapin.*

15 Men will forget what we suffer, and not what we do. *Tennyson.*

Men will marry a fool that sings, sooner than one that has learned to scoff. *Dr. Walter Smith.*

Men will wrangle for religion, write for it, fight for it, die for it—anything but live for it. *Colton.*

Men work themselves into atheistical judgments by atheistical practice. *Whichcote.*

Men would be angels, angels would be gods. *Pope.*

20 Men would not live long in society, were they not the mutual dupes of each other. *La Roche.*

Men's actions are not to be judged of at first sight. *Pr.*

Men's actions are too strong for them. Show me a man who has acted, and who has not been the victim and slave of his action. *Emerson.*

Men's best successes come after their disappointments. *Ward Beecher.*

Men's evil manners live in brass; their virtues / We write in water. *Henry VIII.*, iv. 2.

25 Men's hearts ought not to be set against one another, but set with one another, and all against the evil thing only. *Carlyle.*

Men's ignorance makes the priest's pot boil. *Fr. Pr.*

Men's muscles move better when their souls are making merry music. *George Eliot.*

Men's natures wrangle with inferior things, / Though great ones are their object. *Othello*, iii. 4.

Men's prosperity is in their own hands, and no forms of government are, in themselves, of the least use. *Ruskin*

Men's souls 'twixt sorrow and love are cast. 30 *O. M. Brown.*

Men's thoughts and opinions are, in a great degree, vassals of him who invents a new phrase or reapplies an old epithet. *Lowell.*

Men's thoughts are much according to their inclinations; their discourses and speeches, according to their learning and infused opinions. *Bacon.*

Men's vows are women's traitors. *Cymbeline*, iii. 4.

Menace-moi de vivre et non pas de mourir— Threaten me with life and not with death. *Fr.*

Ménage—Housekeeping. *Fr.* 35

Mendacem memorem esse oportet — A liar ought to have a good memory. *Quinct.*

Mendaces, ebriosi, verbosi—Liars, drunkards, and wordy people.

Mendaci homini, ne verum quidem dicenti credere solemus—We give no credit to a liar, even when he speaks the truth. *Cic.*

Mendici, mimi, balatrones et hoc genus omne —Beggars, actors in farces, buffoons, and all that sort of people. *Hor.*

Mendico ne parentes quidem amici sunt—To 40 a beggar not even his own parents show affection. *Pr.*

Mendings are honourable, rags are abominable. *Pr.*

Mens æqua rebus in arduis — Equanimity in arduous enterprises. *M.*

Mens agitat molem—A mind moves or informs the mass. *Virg.*

Mens bona regnum possidet—A good mind possesses a kingdom. *Pr.*

Mens conscia recti—A mind conscious of recti- 45 tude.

Mens cujusque est quisque—The mind of the man is the man. *M.*

Mens immota manet; lachrymæ volvuntur inanes — His resolve remains unshaken; tears are shed in vain. *Virg.*

Mens interrita lethi — A mind undaunted by death. *Ovid.*

Mens invicta manet—The mind remains unsubdued.

Mens peccat, non corpus, et unde consilium 50 abfuit culpa abest—It is the mind that sins, not the body, and where there was no intention there is no criminality. *Liv.*

Mens sana in corpore sano—A sound mind in a sound body. *Juv.*

Mens sine pondere ludit—The mind is playful when unburdened.

Mensa et toro—From bed and board. *L.*

Menschenkenntniss ist Unglaube an Tugend und Redlichkeit—A knowledge of mankind tends to induce a want of faith in virtue and probity. *C. J. Weber.*

Menschlich ist es bloss zu strafen, / Aber 55 göttlich zu verzeihn—To punish is merely human, but to forgive is divine. *P. von Winter.*

Mensque pati durum sustinet ægra nihil—A mind diseased cannot bear anything harsh. *Ovid.*

Mensuraque juris / Vis erat—And might was the measure of right. *Lucan.*

Mental courage, infinitely rarer than valour, presupposes the most eminent qualities. *Diderot.*

Mental pleasures never cloy : unlike those of the body, they are increased by repetition, approved of by reflection, and strengthened by enjoyment. *Colton.*

Mental prayer (*mentale Gebet*), which includes and excludes all religions, and only in a few God-favoured men permeates the whole course of life, develops itself in most men as only a blazing, beatific feeling of the moment, immediately after the vanishing of which the man, thrown in upon himself unsatisfied and unoccupied, lapses back into the most utter and absolute weariness. *Goethe.*

5 Mentally and bodily endowed men are the most modest, while, on the other hand, all who have some peculiar mental defect think a great deal more of themselves. *Goethe.*

Mentis gratissimus error—A most delightful reverie of the mind. *Hor.*

Mentis penetralia—The inmost recesses of the mind ; the secrets of the heart.

Menu—Bill of fare. *Fr.*

Menus plaisirs—Pocket-money. *Fr.*

10 Meo sum pauper in ære—I am poor, but I am not in debt. *Hor.*

Merces virtutis laus est—Applause is the reward of virtue. *Pr.*

Mercy and truth are met together ; righteousness and peace have kissed each other. *Bible.*

Mercy but murders, pardoning those that kill. *Rom. and Jul.*, iii. 1.

Mercy is above this sceptred sway, / It is enthroned in the hearts of kings, / It is an attribute to God himself ; / And earthly power doth then show likest God's / When mercy seasons justice. *Mer. of Ven.*, iv. 1.

15 Mercy is not itself, that oft looks so ; / Pardon is still the nurse of second woe. *Meas. for Meas.*, ii. 1.

Mercy, misericordia, does not in the least mean forgiveness of sins, but pity of sorrows. *Ruskin.*

Mercy to him that shows it is the rule. *Cowper.*

Mercy turns her back to the unmerciful. *Quarles.*

Mercy's gate opens to those who knock. *Saying.*

20 Mere bashfulness without merit is awkward, and merit without modesty insolent ; but modest merit has a double claim to acceptance. *T. Hughes.*

Mere family never made a man great. Thought and deed, not pedigree, are the passports to enduring fame. *Skobeleff.*

Mere madness, to live like a wretch and die rich. *Burton.*

Mere pleasure ought not to be the prime motive of action. *Johnson.*

Mere sensibility is not true taste, but sensibility to real excellence is. *Hazlitt.*

25 Mere wishes are bony fishes. *Pr.*

Merit and good works is the end of man's motion, and conscience of the same is the accomplishment of man's rest. *Bacon.*

Merit, however inconsiderable, should be sought for and rewarded. *Napoleon.*

Merit in appearance is oftener rewarded than merit itself. *La Roche.*

Merit is never so conspicuous as when coupled with an obscure origin, just as the moon never appears so lustrous as when it emerges from a cloud. *Bovee.*

Merit lives from man to man. *Tennyson.* 30

Merry be the first, / And merry be the last, / And merry be the first of August. *Pr.*

Merry larks are ploughmen's clocks. *Love's L. Lost*, v. 2.

Merx ultronea putret—Proffered service stinks (*i.e.* is despised). *Pr.*

Mésalliance — A marriage with one of inferior rank. *Pr.*

Messe tenus propria vive—Live within your 35 means (*lit.* harvest).

Μεταβολὴ παντῶν γλυκὺ—There is always a pleasure in variety. *Euripides.*

Metaphysicians and philosophers are, on the whole, the greatest troubles the world has got to deal with. . . . Busy metaphysicians are always entangling good and active people, and weaving cobwebs among the finest wheels of the world's business, and are, as much as possible, by all prudent persons, to be brushed out of their way. *Ruskin.*

Metaphysics, with which physics cannot dispense, is that wisdom of thought which was before all physics, lives with it, and will endure after it. *Goethe.*

Μήτε δίκην δικάσῃς, πρὶν ἀμφοῖν μῦθον ἀκούσῃς — Don't pronounce sentence till you have heard the story of both parties. *Pr.*

Method is the very hinge of business. *Hannah* 40 *More.*

Method will teach you to win time. *Goethe.*

Methods are the masters of masters. *Talleyrand.*

Methought I heard a voice cry, Sleep no more ! *Macb.*, ii. 2.

Métier d'auteur, métier d'oseur—The profession of author is a daring profession. *Fr.*

Metirl se quemque suo modulo ac pede verum 45 est—It is meet that every man should measure himself by his own rule and standard. *Hor.*

Mettre les pieds dans le plat—To put one's foot in it. *Fr. Pr.*

Metuenda corolla draconis—The dragon's crest is to be feared.

Meum et tuum—Mine and thine.

Meus mihi, suus cuique est carus—Mine is dear to me, and dear is his own to every man. *Plaut.*

Mezzo termine—A middle course. *It.* 50

Micat inter omnes—It shines amongst all, *i.e.*, it outshines all. *Hor.*

Mich dräng'st den Grundtext aufzuschlagen, / Mit redlichem Gefühl einmal / Das heilige Original / In mein geliebtes Deutsch zu übertragen—I must turn up the primitive text just to translate the sacred original with honest feeling into my dear German tongue. *Faust, in Goethe.*

Mich hat mein Glaube nicht betrogen !—My faith has not betrayed me. *Schiller.*

Mich plagen keine Scrupel noch Zweifel, / Fürchte mich weder vor Hölle noch Teufel —I am troubled by no scruples or doubts ; I fear neither hell nor devil. *Faust, in Goethe.*

Mich schuf aus gröberm Stoffe die Natur, / Und zu der Erde zieht mich die Begierde—Out of coarser clay has Nature created me, and I am drawn by lust to the dust. *Schiller.*

Mid pleasures and palaces though we may roam, / Be it ever so humble, there's no place like home ; / A charm from the skies seems to hallow us there, / Which, sought through the world, is ne'er met with elsewhere. *J. H. Payne.*

Midst the crowd, the hum, the shock of men, / To hear, to see, to feel, and to possess, / And roam along, the world's tired denizen, / With none who bless us, none whom we can bless ; / . . . This is to be alone ; this, this is solitude ! *Byron.*

Mieux nourri qu' instruit—Better fed than taught. *Fr. Pr.*

5 Mieux serra—Better times are coming. *M.*

Mieux vaut glisser du pied que de la langue—Better slip with the foot than the tongue. *Fr. Pr.*

Mieux vaut perdre la laine que la brebis—Better lose the wool than the sheep. *Fr. Pr.*

Mieux vaut un bon renom, que du bien plein la maison—Better a good name than a house full of riches. *Fr. Pr.*

Mieux vaut un " Tiens " que deux "Tu l'auras"—One "Take this" is better than two " You shall have it. ' *Fr. Pr.*

10 Mieux vaut une once de fortune qu'une livre de sagesse—An ounce of fortune is better than a pound of wisdom. *Fr. Pr.*

Mieux vaut voir un chien enragé, qu'un soleil chaud en Janvier—Better see a mad dog than a hot sun in January.

Might and right do differ frightfully from hour to hour ; but give them centuries to try it in, they are found to be identical. *Carlyle.*

Mightier far / Than strength of nerve or sinew, or the sway / Of magic, potent over sun and star, / Is Love, though oft to agony distrest, / And though his favourite seat be feeble woman's breast. *Wordsworth.*

Mightiest powers by deepest calms are fed, / And sleep, how oft, on things that gentlest be. *B. M. Procter.*

15 Mighty events turn on a straw ; the crossing of a brook decides the conquest of the world. *Carlyle.*

Migravit ab aure voluptas / Omnis—All pleasure has fled from the ear, (dumb show having taken the place of dialogue on the stage). *Hor.*

Mihi est propositum in taberna mori—I purpose to end my days in an inn.

Mihi forsan, tibi quod negarit, / Porriget hora—The hour will perhaps extend to me what it has denied to you. *Hor.*

Mihi istic nec seritur nec metitur—There is neither sowing nor reaping in that affair for my benefit. *Plaut.*

20 Mihi res, non me rebus, subjungere conor—My aim is to subject circumstances to me, and not myself to them. *Hor.*

Mihi tarda fluunt ingrataque tempora — For me the time passes slowly and joyously away. *Hor.*

Mildness governs more than anger. *Pr.*

Militat omnis amans—Every lover is engaged in a war. *Ovid.*

Militiæ species amor est—Love is a kind of warfare. *Ovid.*

Mille hominum species et rerum discolor usus ; / 25 Velle suum cuique est, nec voto vivitur uno—There are a thousand kinds of men, and different hues they give to things ; each one follows his own inclination, nor do they all agree in their wishes. *Pers.*

Mille verisimili non fanno un vero—A thousand probabilities do not make one truth. *It. Pr.*

Millia frumenti tua triverit area centum, / Non tuus hinc capiet venter plus ac meus—Though your threshing-floor should yield a hundred thousand bushels of corn, will your stomach therefore hold more than mine? *Hor.*

Millions of spiritual creatures walk the earth / Unseen, both when we wake and when we sleep. *Milton.*

Minatur innocentibus qui parcit nocentibus—He threatens the innocent who spares the guilty. *Coke.*

Mind and body are intimately related ; if the 30 former is joyful, the latter feels free and well ; and many an evil flies before cheerfulness. *Goethe.*

Mind and body—that beauteous couple—exercise much and variously, but at home, at home, indoors, and about things indoors ; for God is there too. *Landor.*

Mind is stronger than matter ; mind is the creator and shaper of matter ; not brute force, but only persuasion and faith is the king of this world. *Carlyle.*

Mind is the great lever of all things ; human thought is the process by which human ends are ultimately answered. *Webster.*

Mind is the partial side of men ; the heart is everything. *Rivarol.*

Mind not high things, but condescend to men 35 of low estate. *St. Paul.*

Mind unemployed is mind unenjoyed. *Bovee.*

Mind your P's and Q's. *Pr.*

Mind your work, and God will find your wages. *Pr.*

Minds are of celestial birth ; / Make we then a heaven of earth. *Montgomery.*

Minds that have nothing to confer / Find little 40 to perceive. *Wordsworth.*

Minds that never rest are subject to many digressions. *Joubert.*

Mind the corner where life's road turns. *Pr.*

Mine honour my life is ; both grow in one ; / Take honour from me, and my life is done. *Richard II., i. 1.*

Minimæ vires frangere quassa valent—Very little avails to break a bruised thing. *Ov.*

Minima de malis—Of two evils choose the least. 45 *Pr.*

Minister flicken am Staate, / Die Richter flicken am Rate, / Die Pfarrer an dem Gewissen, / Die Aerzte an Händen und Füszen ! O Jobsen ! was flickest denn du ? / Weit besser ! Gerissene Schuh !—Ministers cobble away at the state, judges at the law, parsons at the conscience, doctors at our hands and feet ; what cobblest thou at, friend Jobson ? Far better—shoes that have been torn. *Weisse.*

Minor est quam servus, dominus qui servos timet—A master who fears his servants is lower than a servant.

Minorities lead and save the world, and the world knows them not till long afterwards. *John Burroughs.*

Minuentur atræ / Carmine curæ—Black care will be soothed by song. *Hor.*

Minuit præsentia famam — Acquaintanceship lessens fame. *Claud.*

Minus afficit sensus fatigatio quam cogitatio —Bodily fatigue affects the mind less than intense thought. *Quinct.*

Minuti / Semper et infirmi est animi exiguique voluptas / Ultio—Revenge is ever the delight of a stinted and weak and petty mind. *Juv.*

5 Minutiæ—Trifles; minute details.

Mir gäb' es keine gröss're Pein, / Wär' ich im Paradies allein — There were for me no greater torment than to be in Paradise alone. *Goethe.*

Mir wird bei meinem kritischen Bestreben / Doch oft um Kopf und Busen bang—Often during my critical studies I fear as if I would lose both head and heart. *Wagner in Goethe's "Faust."*

Mira quædam in cognoscendo suavitas et delectatio—There is a certain wonderful sweetness and delight in gaining knowledge.

Mirabile dictu !—Wonderful to be told !

10 Mirabile visu !—Wonderful to behold !

Miracles are ceased, and therefore we must needs admit the means, how things are perfected. *Hen. V.*, i. 1.

Miracles do not serve to convert, but condemn. *Pascal.*

Miramur ex intervallo fallentia—We admire at a distance things which deceive us. *Pr.*

Miremur te non tua—Let me have something to admire in yourself, not in what belongs to you. *Juv.*

15 Mirth is God's medicine. *Ward Beecher.*

Mirth is like a flash of lightning, that breaks through a gloom of clouds, and glitters for a moment; cheerfulness keeps up a kind of daylight in the mind, and fills it with a steady and perpetual serenity. *Addison.*

Mirth is short and transient, cheerfulness fixed and permanent. *Addison.*

Misce stultitiam consiliis brevem—Mix a little folly with your serious thoughts. *Hor.*

Miscellaneous reading avoid. *Prof. Blackie to young men.*

20 Mischief, thou art afoot; / Take thou what course thou wilt. *Jul. Cæs.*, iii. 2.

Mise en scène—The getting up or putting in preparation for the stage. *Fr.*

Misera contribuens plebs !—The poor tax-paying people. *Verböczy.*

Misera est magni custodia census—The custody of a large fortune is a wretched business. *Juv.*

Misera est servitus ubi jus est aut vagum aut incognitum—Obedience to the law is a hardship where the law is either unsettled or unknown. *L.*

25 Miserable beyond all names of wretchedness is that unhappy pair who are doomed to reduce beforehand to the principles of abstract reason all the details of each domestic day. *Johnson.*

Miseram pacem vel bello bene mutari—An unhappy peace may be profitably exchanged for war. *Tac.*

Misericordia Domini inter pontem et fontem— Between bridge and stream the Lord's mercy may be found. *St. Augustine.*

Miseros prudentia prima relinquit—Prudence is the first thing to forsake the wretched. *Ovid.*

Miserrima est fortuna quæ inimico caret— Most wretched is the lot of him who has not an enemy. *Pub. Syr.*

Miserum est aliorum incumbere famæ / Ne 30 collapsa ruant subductis tecta columnis—It is a wretched thing to lean for support on the reputation of others, lest the roof should fall in ruins when the pillars are withdrawn. *Juv.*

Misery acquaints a man with strange bedfellows. *Tempest*, ii. 2.

Misery and ruin to thousands are in the blast that announces the destructive demon (war). *Burns.*

Misery doth part / The flux of company. *As You Like It*, ii. 1.

Misery is like love; to speak its language truly, the author must have felt it. *Burns.*

Misery is trodden down by many, / And, being 35 low, never relieved by any. *Shakespeare.*

Misery that I miss is a new mercy. *Isaac Walton.*

Misfortune is never mournful to the soul that accepts it; for such do always see that every cloud is an angel's face. *Mrs. L. M. Child.*

Misfortune sprinkles ashes on the head of the man, but falls like dew on the head of the woman, and brings forth germs of strength of which she herself had no conscious possession. *Anna C. Mowatt.*

Misfortune, when we look upon it with our eyes, is smaller than when our imagination sinks the evil down into the recesses of the soul. *Goethe.*

Misfortunes come on wings and depart on foot. 40 *Pr.*

Misfortunes have their dignity and their redeeming power. *G. S. Hillard.*

Misfortunes never come single. *Pr.*

Misfortunes when asleep are not to be wakened. *Pr.*

Mislike me not for my complexion, / The shadow'd livery of the burnish'd sun, / To whom I am a neighbour and near bred. *Mer. of Ven.*, ii. 1.

Misreckoning is no payment. *Pr.* 45

Mist of words, / Like halos round the moon, though they enlarge / The seeming size of thoughts, make the light less / Doubly. *Bailey.*

Mistake not, man; the devil never sleeps. *Thomas à Kempis.*

Mistrust the man who finds everything good, and the man who finds everything evil, and still more the man who is indifferent to everything. *Lavater.*

Misunderstanding brings lies to town. *Pr.*

Misunderstanding goes on like a fallen stitch 50 in a stocking, which in the beginning might have been taken up with a needle. *Goethe.*

Mit deinem Meister zu irren ist dein Gewinn —To err with thy master is thy gain. *Goethe.*

Mit dem Genius steht die Natur im ewigen Bunde! / Was der eine verspricht, leistet die andre gewiss—Nature stands in eternal league with genius; what the one promises the other as surely performs *Schiller.*

Mit dem Wissen wächst der Zweifel—Doubt ever grows alongside of knowledge. *Goethe.*

Mit der Dummheit kämpfen Götter selbst vergebens—With stupidity the gods themselves fight in vain. *Schiller.*

Mit Frauen soll man sich nie unterstehn zu scherzen—One should never venture to joke with ladies. *Mephisto in Goethe's "Faust."*

Mit fremdem Gut ist leicht ein Prasser sein— It is easy to live riotously (be a rake) at another's expense. *Platen.*

Mit Kleinen thut man kleine Thaten, / Mit Grossen wird der Kleine gross—With little people we do little deeds, with great people the little one becomes great. *Goethe.*

5 Mit seltsamen Geberden / Giebt man sich viele Pein; / Kein Mensch will etwas werden, / Ein jeder will schon was sein—We are easily disconcerted by strange manners; no man is willing to become anything, every one gives himself out as already something. *Goethe.*

Mit vier Strangschlägern zu fahren ist gefährlich, aber ich werde es versuchen—It is risky to drive with four horses that kick over the traces, but I shall try. *Bismarck.*

Mit Worten lässt sich trefflich streiten / Mit Worten ein System bereiten, / An Worten lässt sich trefflich glauben, / Von einem Wort lässt sich kein Iota rauben—With words disputes may be effectively carried on; with words a system may be built up; on words one may rest religious belief; from a word must not one iota be taken. *Mephisto in Goethe's "Faust."*

Mit Worten nicht, mit Thaten lasst mich danken—Let me thank you with deeds, not with words. *Körner.*

Mitgefühl erweckt Vertrauen; / Und Vertrauen ist der Schlüssel / Der des Herzens Pforte öffnet—Sympathy awakens confidence, and confidence is the key which unlocks the doors of the heart. *Bodenstedt.*

10 Mittagsschlaf ist ein brennend Licht am Tage —Sleep at midday is a candle burning in the daytime. *Hippel.*

Mitte hanc de pectore curam—Dismiss these anxieties from your breast. *Virg.*

Mittimus—We send. A writ for transferring records from one court to another; a precept committing an accused person to prison by a justice of the peace. *L.*

Mobilis et varia est ferme natura malorum— Misfortunes generally are of a variable and changeable nature. *Juv.*

Mobilitate viget, viresque acquirit eundo—It grows by moving, and gathers strength as it speeds on. *Virg., of Fame.*

15 Mobilium turba Quiritium—A crowd of fickle citizens. *Hor.*

Mock me not with the name of free, when you have but knit up my chains into ornamental festoons. *Carlyle.*

Mockery is the fume of little hearts. *Tennyson.*

Moderari animo et orationi, cum sis iratus, non mediocris ingenii est—To be able to temper your indignation and language when you are angry is evidence of a chastened disposition. *Cic.*

Moderata durant—Things we use in moderation last long. *Sen.*

20 Moderate lamentation is the right of the dead, excessive grief the enemy to the living. *All's Well,* i. 1.

Moderate riches will carry you; if you have more, you must carry them. *Pr.*

Moderation and judgment are, for most purposes, more than the flash and the glitter even of genius. *J. Morley.*

Moderation is good, but moderation alone is no virtue (*Tugend*). *Rückert.*

Moderation is the inseparable companion of wisdom, but with genius it has not even a nodding acquaintance. *Colton.*

Moderation is the silken string running through 25 the pearl chain of all virtues. *Thomas Fuller.*

Moderation is the virtue best adapted to the dawn of prosperity. *Pitt.*

Modern education has devoted itself to the teaching of impudence, and then we complain we can no more manage our mobs. *Ruskin.*

Modern education too often covers the fingers with rings, and at the same time cuts the sinews at the wrists. *J. Sterling.*

Modern poets put a great deal of water in their ink. *Goethe.*

Modern Protestantism sees in the cross, not a 30 furca to which it is to be nailed, but a raft on which it, and all its valuable properties, are to be floated into Paradise. *Ruskin.*

Modern revolution has nothing grand about it; it is merely the resolution of society into its component atoms. *Froude.*

Modern science gives lectures on botany, to show there is no such thing as a flower; on humanity, to show there is no such thing as a man; and on theology, to show there is no such thing as a God. No such thing as a man, but only a mechanism. No such thing as a God, but only a series of forces. *Ruskin.*

Modest demeanour's the jewel of a'! *Burns.*

Modest dogs miss much meat. *Pr.*

Modest doubt is called / The beacon of the 35 wise, the tent that searches / To the bottom of the worst. *Troil. and Cres.,* ii. 2.

Modest expression is a beautiful setting to the diamond of talent and genius. *Chapin.*

Modest humility is beauty's crown, for the beautiful is a hidden thing, and shrinks from its own power. *Schiller.*

Modeste tamen et circumspecto judicio de tantis viris pronunciandum est, ne, quod plerisque accidit, damnent quæ non intelligunt —We should, however, pronounce our opinions with modesty and circumspect judgment of such men, lest, as is the case with many, we should be found condemning what we do not understand. *Quinct.*

Modesty and presumption are moral things of so spiritual a nature, that they have little to do with the body. *Goethe.*

Modesty is a quality in a lover more praised 40 by the women than liked. *Sheridan.*

Modesty is a very good thing, but a man in this country may get on very well without it. *M. on a banner in the Far West.*

Modesty is so pleased with other people's doings that she has no leisure to lament her own. *Ruskin.*

Modesty is the beauty of women. *Gael. Pr.*

Modesty is the colour of virtue. *Diogenes.*

Modesty is the sweet song-bird which no open 45 cage-door can tempt to flight. *Hafiz.*

Modesty is to merit what the shadows are to the figures on a picture; it imparts to it force and relief. *La Bruyère.*

Modesty ruins all that bring it to court. *Pr.*

Modesty seldom resides in a breast that is not enriched with nobler virtues. *Goldsmith.*

Modesty when she goes, is gone for ever. *Landor.*

5 Modo et forma—In manner and form.

Modo me Thebis, modo ponit Athenis—He sets me down now at Thebes, now at Athens, *i.e.,* the poet does so by his magic art. *Hor.*

Modo vir, modo femina—Now as a man, now as a woman. *Ovid.*

Modus operandi—The manner of operation.

Mögt ihr Stück für Stück bewitzeln, / Doch das Ganze zieht euch an—You may jeer at it bit by bit, yet the whole fascinates you. *Goethe.*

10 Moi, moi, dis je, et c'est assez—I, I, say I, and that is enough. *Corneille.*

Moins on pense plus on parle—The less people think, the more they talk. *Fr.*

Moles and misers live in their graves. *Pr.*

Molesta et importuna salutantium frequentia—A troublesome and annoying crowd of visitors.

Molle meum levibus cor est violabile telis—My tender heart is vulnerable by his (Cupid's) light arrows. *Ovid.*

15 Mollis educatio nervos omnes et mentis et corporis frangit — An effeminate education weakens all the powers both of mind and body. *Quinct.*

Mollissima corda / Humano generi dare se natura fatetur, / Quæ lachrymas dedit: hæc nostri pars optima sensus—Nature confesses that she gives the tenderest of hearts to the human race when she gave them tears. This is the best part of our sensations. *Juv.*

Mollissima tempora fandi — The most fitting moment for speaking, or addressing, one. *Hor.*

Molliter austerum studio fallente laborem—The interest in the pursuit gently beguiling the severity of the toil. *Hor.*

Molliter ossa cubent—Let his bones softly rest. *Ovid.*

20 Momento mare vertitur; / Eodem die ubi luserunt, navigia sorbentur — In a moment the sea is agitated, and on the same day ships are swallowed up where they lately sported gaily along.

Mon âme a son secret, ma vie a son mystère—My soul has a secret of its own, my life its mystery. *Arvers.*

Mon cœur aux dames, / Ma vie au roi, / A Dieu mon âme, / L'honneur pour moi—My heart to the ladies, my life to the king, and my soul to God, but my honour is my own. *On a shield in the Royal Schloss, Berlin.*

Mon Dieu est ma roche — My God is my rock. *M.*

Mon frère a mis son bonnet de travers—My brother is cross (*lit.* has put on his cap the wrong way). *Fr. Pr.*

25 Monarchy is a merchantman, which sails well, but will sometimes strike on a rock and go to the bottom; whilst a republic is a raft, which would never sink, but then your feet are always in water. *Fisher Ames.*

Monday is the key of the week. *Gael. Pr.*

Monday religion is better than Sunday profession. *Pr.*

Mone sale—Advise with salt, *i.e.,* with discretion. *M.*

Money answers everything, / Save a guilty conscience sting. *Pr.*

Money begets money. *Pr.* 30

Money borrowed is soon sorrowed. *Pr.*

Money calls, but does not stay: / It is round and rolls away. *Pr.*

Money is a bottomless sea, in which honour, conscience, and truth may be drowned. *Kazlay.*

Money is a good servant, but a dangerous master *Bouheurs.*

Money is human happiness in the abstract; 35 he, then, who is no longer capable of enjoying human happiness in the concrete, devotes his heart entirely to money. *Schopenhauer.*

Money is like an icicle, soon found at certain seasons, and soon melted under other circumstances. *Spurgeon.*

Money is not required to buy one necessity of the soul. *Thoreau.*

Money is the fruit of evil as often as the root of it. *Fielding.*

Money is the god of our time. and Rothschild is his prophet. *Heine.*

Money is the most envied, but the least en-40 joyed; health is the most enjoyed, but the least envied. *Colton.*

Money is the ruin of many. *Pr.*

Money is the sinew of love as well as of war. *Pr.*

Money, like manure, does no good till it is spread. (?)

Money makes the mare to go. *Pr.*

Money masters all things. *Pr.* 45

Money never made a man happy yet, nor will it. There is nothing in its nature to produce happiness. The more a man has, the more he wants. *Ben. Franklin.*

Money often costs too much. *Emerson.*

Money often unmakes the men who make it. *Pr.*

Money refused loses its brightness. *Pr.*

Money spent on the brain is never spent in 50 vain. *Pr.*

Moniti, meliora sequamur—Admonished, let us follow better counsels. *Virg.*

Monkeys, as soon as they have brought forth their young, keep their eyes fastened on them, and never weary of admiring their beauty; so amorous is Nature of whatever she produces. *Dryden.*

Monstro quod ipse tibi possis dare: semita certe / Tranquillæ per virtutem patet unica vitæ—I show you what you can do for yourself; the only path to a tranquil life lies through virtue. *Juv.*

Monstrum horrendum, informe, ingens, cui lumen ademptum—A monster horrible, misshapen, huge, and bereft of his one eye. *Virgil, of Polyphemus.*

Monstrum nulla virtute redemptum / A vitiis 55 —A monster whose vices are not redeemed by a single virtue. *Juv.*

Mont de piété—Pawnshop; originally store of money to lend without interest to poor people. *Fr.*

Montes auri pollicens—Promising mountains of gold. *Ter.*

Montesquieu, with his cause-and-effect philosophy, is but a clever infant spelling letters from a hieroglyphical prophetic Book, the lexicon of which lies in eternity, in Heaven. *Carlyle.*

Monuments, like men, submit to fate. *Pope.*

Monuments themselves memorials need. *Crabbe.*

5 Mony an honest man needs that hasna the face to seel: it. *Sc. Pr.*

Mony ane speirs the gate (inquires the way) they ken fu' weel. *Sc. Pr.*

Mony kinsfolk. but few freends. *Sc. Pr.*

Moonlight is sculpture. *Hawthorne.*

Moping melancholy. *Milton.*

10 Mora omnis odio est, sed facit sapientiam—All delay is hateful, but it produces wisdom. *Pub. Syr.*

Moral culture must begin with a change (*Umwandlung*) in the way of thinking, and with the founding of a character. *Kant.*

Moral education begins in making the creature to be educated clean and obedient; and it is summed up when the creature has been made to do its work with delight, and thoroughly. *Ruskin.*

Moral inability aggravates our guilt. *Scott.*

Moral prejudices are the stopgaps of virtue; and, as is the case with other stopgaps, it is often more difficult to get either out or in through them than through any other part of the fence. *Hare.*

15 Moral qualities rule the world, but at short distances the senses are despotic. *Emerson.*

Morality is a curb, not a spur. *Joubert.*

Morality is but the vestibule of religion. *Chapin*

Morality sticks faster when presented in brief sayings than when presented in long discourses. *Immerman.*

Morals are generated as the atmosphere is. 'Tis a secret the genesis of either; but the springs of justice and courage do not fail any more than salt or sulphur springs. *Emerson.*

20 Morceau—A morsel; a bit. *Fr.*

Morceau d'ensemble—Piece of music harmonised for several voices. *Fr.*

More are drowned in the beaker than in the sea. *Ger. Pr.*

More are made good by exercitation than by nature. *Democritus.*

More credit may be thrown down in a moment than can be built up in an age. *Pr.*

25 More hearts pine away in secret anguish for unkindness from those who should be their comforters than for any other calamity in life. *Young.*

More helpful than all wisdom is one draught of simple human pity that will not forsake us. *George Eliot.*

More is got from one book on which the thought settles for a definite end in knowledge, than from libraries skimmed over by a wandering eye. A cottage flower gives honey to the bee, a king's garden none to the butterfly. *Bulwer Lytton.*

More knave than fool. *Marlowe.*

More light, more life, more love. *Pr.*

More majorum—After the manner of our ancestors. 30

More matter with less art. *Ham.,* ii. 2.

More meat and less mustard. *Pr.*

More pleased we are to see a river lead / His gentle streams along a flowery mead, / Than from high banks to hear loud torrents roar, / With foamy waters on a muddy shore. *Dryden.*

More potatoes and fewer potations. *Motto for Working-men.*

More servants wait on man / Than he'll take 35 notice of. *George Herbert.*

More sinn'd against than sinning. *Lear,* iii. 2.

More springs up in the garden than the gardener sows there. *Pr.*

More suo—After his usual manner; as is his wont.

More than all things, avoid fault-finding and a habit of criticism. *Prof. Blackie to young men.*

More than kisses letters mingle souls. *Donne.* 40

More than we use is more than we want. *Pr.*

More things are wrought by prayer / Than this world dreams of. *Tennyson.*

More water glideth by the mill / Than wots the miller of. *Tit. Andron.,* ii. 1.

Mores amici noveris, non oderis—Know well, but take no offence at the manners of a friend. *Pr.*

Mores multorum vidit—He saw the manners of 45 many men. *Hor. of Ulysses.*

Morgen können wir's nicht mehr, / Darum lasst uns heute leben!—To-morrow is no longer in our power, therefore let us live to-day. *Schiller.*

Morgen, morgen, nur nicht heute! / Sprechen immer träge Leute—To-morrow, to-morrow, only not to-day, is the constant song of the idle. *C. F. Weisse.*

Morgenstunde hat Gold im Munde—The morning hour has gold in its mouth. *Gr. Pr.*

Moriamur, et in media arma ruamus—Let us die, and rush into the thick of the fight. *Virg.*

Moribus antiquis res stat Romana virisque— 50 The Roman commonwealth stands by its ancient manners and men. *Enn.*

Moribus et forma conciliandus amor—Pleasing manners and a handsome figure conciliate love. *Ovid.*

Morituri morituros salutant—The dying salute the dying.

Morose thoughts one should never send to a distance. *Goethe.*

Moroseness is the evening of turbulence. *Landor.*

Mors et fugacem persequitur virum—Death 55 pursues the man as he flees from it. *Hor.*

Mors ipsa refugit sæpe virum!—Death itself often takes flight at the presence of a man. *Lucan.*

Mors janua vitæ—Death is the gate of life.

Mors laborum ac miseriarum quies est!—Death is repose from all our toils and miseries. *Cic.*

Mors potius macula—Death rather than disgrace. *M.*

Mors sola fatetur / Quantula sint hominum 60 corpuscula—Death alone discloses how insignificant are the puny bodies of us men. *Juv.*

Mors ultima linea rerum est—Death is the farthest limit of our changing life. *Hor.*

Mortales inimicitias, sempiternas amicitias—Be our enmities for time. our friendships for eternity. *Cic.*

Mortalia acta nunquam Deos fallunt—The deeds of man never can be hid from the gods.

Mortalia facta peribunt, / Nedum sermonum stet honos et gratia vivax—All man's works must perish ; how much less shall the power and grace of language long survive ! *Hor.*

Mortality is beset on every side with crosses, and exposed to suffering every moment. *Thomas à Kempis*

5 Mortalium rerum misera beatitudo—The miserable bliss of all moral things. *Boëthius.*

Morte carent animæ, semperque priore relicta / Sede novis domibus vivunt habitantque receptæ—Souls are immortal ; and admitted, after quitting their first abode, into new homes, they live and dwell in them for ever. *Ovid.*

Mortem effugere nemo potest !—No one can escape death.

Mortuo leoni et lepores insultant—Even hares insult a dead lion. *Pr.*

Mos pro lege—Usage, or custom, for law. *L.*

10 Moses and Mahomet were not men of speculation, but men of action ; and it is the stress they laid upon the latter that has given them the power they wield over the destinies of mankind. *Renan.*

Most authors steal their works, or buy. *Pope.*

Most dangerous / Is that temptation that doth goad us on / To sin in loving virtue. *Meas. for Meas.,* ii. 2.

Most felt, least said. *Pr.*

Most joyful let the poet be ; / It is through him that all men see. *W. E. Channing.*

15 Most men and most women are merely one couple more. *Emerson.*

Most men do not know what is in them till they receive the summons from their fellows ; their hearts die within them, sleep settles upon them—the lethargy of the world's miasmata ; there is nothing for which they are so thankful as for that cry, '' Awake, thou that sleepest." *Ruskin.*

Most men forget God all day, and ask Him to remember them at night. (?)

Most men I ask little from ; I try to render them much, and to expect nothing in return, and I get very well out of the bargain. *Fénelon.*

Most men make the voyage of life as if they carried sealed orders which they were not to open till they were fairly in mid-ocean. *Lowell.*

20 Most men never reach the glorious epoch, that middle stage between despair and deification, in which the comprehensible appears to us common and insipid. *Goethe.*

Most men of action incline to fatalism, and most men of thought believe in Providence. *Balzac.*

Most men take no notice of what is plain, as if that were of no use ; but puzzle their thoughts to be themselves in those vast depths and abysses which no human understanding can fathom. *Sherlock.*

Most men think indistinctly, and therefore cannot speak with exactness. *Johnson.*

Most men will proclaim every one his own goodness : but a faithful man who can find ? *Bible.*

Most men write now as if they expected that 25 their works should live no more than a month. *Lord Orford.*

Most natures are insolvent ; cannot satisfy their own wants, have an ambition out of all proportion to their practical force, and so do lean and beg day and night continually. *Emerson.*

Most of our evils come from our vices. *Pr.*

Most of the appearing mirth in the world is not mirth, but art ; the wounded spirit is not seen, but walks under a disguise. *South.*

Most of the luxuries, and many of the so-called comforts of life, are not only not indispensable, but positive hindrances, to the elevation of mankind. *Thoreau.*

Most of the mischief in the world would never 30 happen if men would only be content to sit still in their parlours. *Pascal.*

Most people think now-a-days the only hopeful way of serving your neighbour is to make a profit out of him ; whereas, in my opinion, the hopefulest way of serving him is to let him make a profit out of me. *Ruskin.*

Most people, when they come to you for advice, come to have their own opinions strengthened, not corrected. *Billings.*

Most people who ask advice of others have already resolved to act as it pleases them. *Knigge.*

Most potent, effectual for all work whatsoever, is wise planning, firm combining and commanding among men. *Carlyle.*

Most powerful is he who has himself in his 35 power. *Seneca.*

Most religion-mongers have bated their paradises with a bit of toasted cheese. They have tempted the body with large promises of possessions in their transmortal El Dorado. *Lowell.*

Most strange that men should fear, / Seeing that death, a necessary end, / Will come when it will come. *Jul. Cæs.,* ii. 2.

Most subject is the fattest soil to weeds. *2 Hen. IV.,* iv. 4.

Most terrors are but spectral illusions. *Helps.*

Most things have two handles, and a wise 40 man takes hold of the best. *Pr.*

Most women have no characters at all. *Pope.*

Most wretched men / Are cradled into poetry by wrong ; / They learn in suffering what they teach in song. *Shelley.*

Mot à mot—Word for word.

Mot à mot on fait les gros livres—Word by word big books are made. *Fr. Pr.*

Mot d'ordre—Watchword. *Fr.* 45

Mot pour rire—A jest. *Fr.*

Mother, a maiden is a tender thing, / And best by her that bore her understood. *Tennyson.*

Mother's darlings are but milksop heroes. *Pr.*

Mother's love is the cream of love. *Pr.*

Mother's truth keeps constant youth. *Pr.* 50

Motives are better than actions. *Bovee.*

Motives are symptoms of weakness, and supplements for the deficient energy of the living principle, the law within us. *Coleridge.*

Motley's the only wear. *As You Like It,* ii. 7.

Mots d'usage—Phrases in common use. *Fr.*

Motu proprio—Of his own accord. 55

Mountains interposed / Make enemies of nations, who had else / Like kindred drops being mingled into one. *Cowper.*

Mountains never shake hands. Their roots may touch; they may keep company some way up; but at length they part company, and rise into individual, isolated peaks. So it is with great men. *Hare.*

Mourning only lasts till morning with the children of the morning. *Saying.*

Mourning tendeth to mending. *Pr.*

5 Movet cornicula risum / Furtivis nudata coloribus—The crow, stript of its stolen colours, provokes our ridicule. *Hor.*

Moving accidents by flood and field. *Othello,* i. 3.

Mrs. Chatterbox is the mother of mischief. *Pr.*

Much bruit, little fruit. *Pr.*

Much corn lies under the straw that is not seen. *Pr.*

10 Much debating goes on about the good that has been done and the harm by the free circulation of the Bible. To me this is clear: it will do harm, as it has done, if used dogmatically and fancifully; and do good, as it has done, if used didactically and feelingly. *Goethe.*

Much exists under our very noses which has no name, and can get none. *Carlyle.*

Much food is in the tillage of the poor. *Bible.*

Much in the world may be done by severity, more by love, but most of all by discernment and impartial justice. *Goethe.*

Much learning is a weariness of the flesh. *Pr.*

15 Much learning shows how little mortals know; much wealth, how little worldlings can enjoy. *Young.*

Much lies among us convulsively, nay, desperately, struggling to be born. *Carlyle.*

Much meat, much disease. *Pr.*

Much might be said on both sides. *Addison.*

Much of the good or evil that befalls persons arises from the well or ill managing of their conversation. *Judge Hale.*

20 Much of the pleasure, and all the benefit of conversation, depends upon our own opinion of the speaker's veracity. *Paley.*

Much of this world's wisdom is still acquired by necromancy—by consulting the oracular dead. *Hare.*

Much of what is great, and to all men beneficial, has been wrought by those who neither intended nor knew the good they did; and many mighty harmonies have been discoursed by instruments that had been dumb and discordant but that God knew their stops. *Ruskin.*

Much reading makes one haughty and pedantic; much observation (*Sehen*) makes one wise, sociable, and helpful. *Lichtenberg.*

Much religion, but no goodness. *Pr.*

25 Much there is that appears unequal in our life, yet the balance is soon and unexpectedly restored. In eternal alternation a weal counterbalances the woe, and swift sorrows our joys. Nothing is constant. Many an incongruity (*Missverhältniss*), as the days roll on, is gradually and imperceptibly dissolved in harmony. And ah! love knows how to reconcile the greatest discrepancy and unite earth with heaven. *Goethe.*

Mucho sabe la zorra, pero mas el que la toma —The fox is cunning, but he is more cunning who takes him. *Sp. Pr.*

Mud chokes no eels. *Pr.*

Mudar costumbre a par de muerte—To change a custom is next to death. *Sp. Pr.*

Muddy spring, muddy stream. *Pr.* 30

Mugitus labyrinthi—The bellowing of the labyrinth (a threadbare theme among weak poets). *Juv.*

Mules deliver great discourses because their ancestors were horses. *Pr.*

Mulier cupido quod dicit amanti, / In vento et rapida scribere oportet aqua—What a woman says to an ardent lover ought to be written on the winds and the swiftly flowing water. *Catull.*

Mulier profecto nata est ex ipsa mora—Woman is surely born of tardiness itself. *Plaut.*

Mulier quæ sola cogitat male cogitat—The 35 thoughts of a woman when alone tend to mischief. *Pr.*

Mulier recte olet ubi nihil olet—A woman smells sweetest when she smells not at all. *Plaut.*

Multa cadunt inter calicem supremaque labra —Many things fall between the cup and the lip. *Laber.*

Multa dies, variusque labor mutabilis ævi, / Retulit in melius—Many a thing has time and the varying sway of changeful years altered for the better. *Virg.*

Multa docet fames—Hunger (*i.e.,* necessity) teaches us many things. *Pr.*

Multa fero ut placeam genus irritabile vatum 40 —Much I endure to appease the irritable race of poets. *Hor.*

Multa ferunt anni venientes commoda secum; / Multa recedentes adimunt—The coming years bring with them many advantages; as they recede they take many away. *Hor.*

Multa gemens—Groaning deeply. *Virg.*

Multa me docuit usus, magister egregius— Necessity, that excellent master, hath taught me many things. *Pliny the younger.*

Multa novit vulpis, sed felis unum magnum— The fox knows many shifts, the cat only one great one, viz., to run up a tree. *Pr.*

Multa paucis—Much in little. 45

Multa petentibus / Desunt multa—Those who crave much want much. *Hor.*

Multa quidem scripsi; sed quæ vitiosa putavi, / Emendaturis ignibus ipse dedi—Much have I written; but what I considered faulty I myself committed to the correcting flames. *Ovid.*

Multa renascentur quæ jam cecidere, cadentque / Quæ nunc sunt in honore vocabula, si volet usus, / Quem penes arbitrium est, et jus, et norma loquendi—Many words now in disuse will revive, and many now in vogue will be forgotten, if usage wills it, in whose hands is the choice and the right to lay down the law of language. *Hor.*

Multa rogant utenda dari; data reddere nolunt —They ask many a sum on loan, but they are loath to repay. *Ovid.*

Multa senem circumveniunt incommoda—Many 50 are the discomforts that gather round old age. *Hor.*

Multa tacere loquive paratus—Ready to suppress much or speak much.

Multa tulit, fecitque puer, sudavit et alsit— Much from early years has he suffered and done, sweating and chilled. *Hor.*

Multæ manus onus levius faciunt—Many hands make light work. *Pr.*

Multæ regum aures et oculi—Kings have many ears and eyes.

Multæ terricolis linguæ, cœlestibus una—The inhabitants of earth have many tongues, those of heaven have but one.

Multarum palmarum causidicus—A pleader who has gained many causes.

5 Multas amicitias silentium diremit—Silence, or neglect, dissolves many friendships. *Pr.*

Multi adorantur in ara qui cremantur in igne —Many are worshipped at the altar who are burning in flames. *St. Augustine.*

Multi / Committunt eadem diverso crimina fato, / Ille crucem sceleris pretium tulit, hic diadema—Many commit the same crimes with a different destiny; one bears a cross as the price of his villany, another wears a crown. *Juv.*

Multi mortales, dediti ventri atque somno, indocti incultique vitam sicuti peregrinantes transiere; quibus profecto contra naturam corpus voluptati, anima oneri—Many men have passed through life like travellers in a strange land, without spiritual or moral culture, and given up to the lusts of appetite and indolence, whose bodies, contrary to their nature, were enslaved to indulgence, and their souls a burden. *Sall.*

Multi multa, nemo omnia novit—Many know many things, no one everything. *Coke.*

10 Multi nil rectum nisi quod placuit sibi ducunt —Many deem nothing right but what suits their own conceit. *Hor.*

Multi te oderint si teipsum ames—Many will detest you if you spend all love on yourself.

Multis ille bonis flebilis occidit / Nulli flebilior quam tibi—He fell lamented by many good men, by none more lamented than by thee (Virgil). *Hor., of Quinctilius.*

Multis minatur, qui uni facit injuriam—He who wrongs one threatens many. *Pub. Syr.*

Multis parasse divitias non finis miseriarium fuit, sed mutatio; non est in rebus vitium sed in animo—The acquisition of riches has been to many, not the end of their miseries, but a change in them; the fault is not in the riches, but in the disposition. *Sen.*

15 Multis terribilis caveto multos—If you are a terror to many, then beware of many. *Auson.*

Multitudinem decem faciunt—Ten constitute a crowd. *Coke.*

Multo plures satietas quam fames perdidit viros—Many more die of surfeit than of hunger.

Multos castra juvant, et lituo tubæ / Permistus sonitus, bellaque matribus / Detestata —The camp and the clang of the trumpet mingled with the clarion, and wars detested by mothers, have delights for many. *Hor.*

Multos in summa pericula misit / Venturi timor ipse mali—The mere apprehension of coming evil has driven many into positions of great peril. *Pr.*

20 Multos ingratos invenimus, plures facimus— We find many men ungrateful; we make more. *Pr.*

Multos qui conflictari adversis videantur, beatos; ac plerosque, quanquam magnas per opes, miserrimos—We may see many struggling against adversity who yet are happy; and more, although abounding in wealth, who are most wretched. *Tac.*

Multum abludit imago—The picture is outrageously unlike. *Hor.*

Multum demissus homo—A modest reserved man. *Hor.*

Multum in parvo—Much in little.

Multum, non multa—Much, not many. *Pliny.* 25

Multum sapit qui non diu desipit—He is very wise who does not long persist in folly. *Pr.*

Mundæque parvo sub lare pauperum / Cœnæ, sine aulæis et ostro, / Sollicitam explicuere frontem—A neat, simple meal under the humble roof of the poor, without hangings and purple, has smoothed the wrinkles of an anxious brow. *Hor.*

Munditiæ, et ornatus, et cultus hæc feminarum insignia sunt, his gaudent et gloriantur —Neatness, ornament, and dress, are peculiar badges of women; in these they delight and glory. *Livy.*

Munditiis capimur—We are captivated by neatness. *Ovid.*

Mundus est Dei viva statua !—The world is the 30 living image of God. *T. Campanella.*

Mundus universus exercet histrionem—All men practise the actor's art. *Petron.*

Mundus vult decipi; ergo decipiatur—The world wishes to be deceived; therefore let it be deceived.

Munera accipit frequens, remittit nunquam— He often receives presents, but never gives any. *Plaut.*

Munera, crede mihi, capiunt hominesque deosque; / Placatur donis Jupiter ipse datis !—Gifts, believe me, captivate both men and gods; Jupiter himself is won over and appeased by gifts. *Ovid.*

Munificence is not quantity, but quality. 35 *Pascal.*

Munit hæc, et altera vincit—This defends, and the other conquers. *M.*

Munus Apolline dignum—A present worthy of Apollo. *Hor.*

Munus ornare verbis—To enhance the value of a present by words. *Ter.*

Murder, though it have no tongue, will speak / With most miraculous organ. *Ham., ii. 2.*

Murder will out. *Chaucer.* 40

Murus æneus conscientia sana—A sound conscience is a wall of brass. *M.*

Mus in pice—A mouse in pitch; "a fly wading through tar."

Mus non uni fidit antro—The mouse does not trust to one hole only. *Plaut.*

Music fills up the present moment more decisively than anything else, whether it awakens thought or summons to action. *Goethe.*

Music hath charms to soothe the savage 45 breast. *Congreve.*

Music in the best sense has little need of novelty (*Neuheit*); on the contrary, the older it is, the more one is accustomed to it, the greater is the effect it produces. *Goethe.*

Music, in the works of its greatest masters, is more marvellous, more mysterious, than poetry. *H. Giles.*

Music is a kind of inarticulate unfathomable speech, which leads us to the edge of the infinite, and lets us for moments gaze into that. *Carlyle.*

Music is a language directed to the passions; but the rudest passions put on a new nature and become pleasing in harmony. *James Usher.*

Music is a prophecy of what life is to be, the rainbow of promise translated out of seeing into hearing. *Mrs. Child.*

Music is an invisible dance, as dancing is a silent music. *Jean Paul.*

Music is but wild sounds civilised into time and tune. *Fuller.*

5 Music is our fourth great material want—first food, then raiment, then shelter, then music. *Bovee.*

Music is the art of the prophets, the only art which can calm the agitations of the soul. *Luther.*

Music is the crystallisation of sound. *Thoreau.*

Music is the mediator between the spiritual and the sensual life. *Beethoven.*

Music is the most immediate means possessed by the will for the manifestation of its inner impulses. *A. R. Parsons.*

10 Music is the only one of the fine arts in which not only man, but all other animals, have a common property. *Jean Paul.*

Music is the only sensual gratification which mankind may indulge in to excess without injury to their moral and religious feelings. *Addison.*

Music is the poor man's Parnassus. *Emerson.*

Music is the true universal speech of mankind. *Weber.*

Music makes people milder and gentler, more moral and more reasonable. *Luther.*

15 Music, of all the arts, has the greatest influence over the passions, and the legislator ought to give it the greatest encouragement. *Napoleon.*

Music of the spheres. *Pericles, v. 1.*

Music oft hath such a charm / To make bad good, and good provoke to harm. *Meas. for Meas., iv. 1.*

Music, once admitted into the soul, becomes a sort of spirit, and never dies. *Bulwer Lytton.*

Music so softens and disarms the mind, / That not an arrow does resistance find. *Waller.*

20 Music stands in a much closer connection with pure sensation than any of the other arts. *Helmholtz.*

Music washes away from the soul the dust of everyday life. *Auerbach.*

Music, when healthy, is the teacher of perfect order ; and also when depraved, the teacher of perfect disorder. *Ruskin.*

Music will not cure the toothache. *Pr.*

Music wraps us in melancholy, and elevates in joy. *James Usher.*

25 Musik ist der Schlüssel vom weiblichen Herzen—Music is the key to the female heart. *Seume.*

Musik ist die wahre allgemeine Menschensprache—Music is the true universal speech of mankind. *C. J. Weber.*

Muss ist eine harte Nuss—Must is a hard nut to crack. *Ger. Pr.*

Müsset im Naturbetrachen / Immer eins wie alles achten ; / Nichts ist drinnen, nichts ist draussen, / Denn was innen, das ist aussen. / So ergreifet ohne Säumness / Heilig öffentlich Geheimniss—In the study of Nature you must ever regard one as all ; nothing is inner, nothing is outer, for what is within that is without. Without hesitation, therefore, seize ye the holy mystery thus lying open to all. *Goethe.*

Müssiggang ist aller Laster Anfang—Idleness is the beginning of all vices.

Must is a hard nut to crack, but it has a sweet 30 kernel. *Spurgeon.*

"Must" is hard, but by "must" alone can man show what his inward condition is. Any one can live unrestrainedly. *Goethe.*

Must not a great history be always an epic ? *Dr. Walter Smith.*

Mutability is the badge of infirmity. *Charron.*

Mutare vel timere sperno—I disdain either to change or to fear. *M.*

Mutatis mutandis—After making the necessary 35 changes. *L.*

Mutato nomine, de te / Fabula narratur—Change but the name, the story's told of you. *Hor.*

Mutum est pictura poema—A picture is a poem without words.

My alms-people are to be the ablest bodied I can find, the ablest minded I can make, and every day will be a duty . . . shall stand with tools at work, mattock or flail, axe or hammer. *Ruskin.*

My ancient but ignoble blood / Has crept through scoundrels ever since the Flood. (?)

My better half. *Sir Philip Sidney.* 40

My bounty is as boundless as the sea, / My love as deep ; the more I give to thee, / The more I have, for both are infinite. *Rom. and Jul., ii. 2.*

My dame fed her hens on thanks, but they laid no eggs. *Pr.*

My days are in the yellow leaf ; / The flowers and fruits of love are gone ; / The worm, the canker, and the grief / Are mine alone. *Byron.*

"My family begins with me, yours ends with you." *Iphicrates, when upbraided by a young aristocrat for his low birth.*

My fate cries out, / And makes each petty 45 artery in this body / As hardy as the Nemean lion's nerve. *Ham., i. 4.*

My first and last secret of Art is to get a thorough intelligence of the fact to be painted, represented, or, in whatever way, set forth—the fact deep as Hades, high as heaven, and written so, as to the visual face of it on this poor earth. *Carlyle.*

My grief lies onward, and my joy behind. *Lucrece.*

"My hand," said Napoleon, "is immediately connected with my head," but the sacred courage is connected with the heart. *Emerson.*

My heart leaps up when I behold / A rainbow in the sky : / So was it when my life began, / So is it now I am a man ; / So be it when I shall grow old, / Or let me die. *Wordsworth.*

My heart is true as steel. *Mid. N. Dream,* 50 *ii. 2.*

My heart resembles the ocean ; has storm, and ebb, and flow ; / And many a beautiful pearl / Lies hid in its depths below. *Heine.*

My heart's in the Highlands, my heart is not here. *Burns.*

My highest wish is to find within the God whom I find everywhere without. *Kepler.*

My house is my castle. *Pr.*

My house, my house, though thou art small, / Thou art to me the Escurial. *Pr.*

5 " My ideal of a society is one in which I would be guillotined as a Conservative." *Proudhon, to Prince Napoleon.*

My inheritance how wide and fair ! / Time is my seed-field, to Time I'm heir. *Goethe.*

My joy in friends, those sacred people, is my consolation. *Emerson.*

My joy is death ;— / Death, at whose name I oft have been afeared, / Because I wish'd this world's eternity. 2 *Hen. VI.,* ii. 4.

My mind can take no hold on the present world, nor rest in it a moment, but my whole nature rushes onward with irresistible force towards a future and better state of being. *Fichte.*

10 My mind to me a kingdom is, / Such perfect joy therein I find. *Byrd.*

My name is Norval ; on the Grampian hills my father feeds his flock. *Home.*

My notions of life are much the same as they are about travelling ; there is a good deal of amusement on the road, but, after all, one wants to be at rest. *Southey.*

My offence is rank ; it smells to heaven. *Ham.,* iii. 3.

My only books / Were woman's looks,— / And folly's all they've taught me. *Moore.*

15 My opinion, my conviction, gains infinitely in strength and sureness the moment a second mind has adopted it. *Novalis.*

My pen was never dipped in gall. *Crébillon.*

My perception of a fact is as much a fact as the sun. *Emerson.*

My pulse, as yours, doth temperately keep time, / And makes as healthful music. *Ham.,* iii. 4.

My purposes lie in the churchyard. *Philip Henry.*

20 My rigour relents : I pardon something to the spirit of liberty. *Burke.*

My son, be not now negligent, for the Lord hath chosen thee to stand before Him. *Apoc.*

My son is my son till he have got him a wife, / But my daughter's my daughter all the days of her life. *Pr.*

My soul, what's lighter than a feather? Wind. / Than wind ? The fire. And what than fire? The mind. / What's lighter than the mind? A thought. Than thought? / This bubble world. What than this bubble? Nought. *Quarles.*

My strength is as the strength of ten, because my heart is pure. *Tennyson.*

25 My way of life / Is fall'n into the sere, the yellow leaf ; / And that which should accompany old age, / As honour, love, obedience, troops of friends, / I must not look to have ; but in their stead, / Curses, not loud, but deep, mouth - honour, breath / Which the poor heart would fain deny, but dare not. *Macb.,* v. 3.

My words fly up, my thoughts remain below ; / Words, without thoughts, never to heaven go. *Ham.,* iii. 3.

My yoke is easy and my burden light. *Jesus.*

Myn leeren is spelen, myn spelen is leeren— My learning is play, and my play is learning. *Van Alphen.*

Mysteries are due to secrecy. *Bacon.*

Mysteries which must explain themselves are 30 not worth the loss of time which a conjecture about them takes up. *Sterne.*

Mysterious to all thought, / A mother's prime of bliss, / When to her eager lips is brought / Her infant's thrilling kiss. *Keble.*

Mystery magnifies danger, as a fog the sun ; the hand that warned Belshazzar derived its horrifying influence from the want of a body. *Colton.*

Mystic, deep as the world's centre, are the roots a man has struck into his native soil ; no tree that grows is rooted so. *Carlyle.*

Mysticism consists in the mistake of an accidental and individual symbol for a universal one. *Emerson.*

Mythology is not religion. It may rather be 35 regarded as the ancient substitute, the poetical counterpart, for dogmatic theology. *Hare.*

N.

N'aboyez pas à la lune—Do not cry out to no purpose (*lit.* don't bark at the moon). *Fr. Pr.*

N'est on jamais tyran qu'avec un diadème ?—Is a man never a tyrant except he wear a crown? *Chénier.*

N'importe—No matter. *Fr.*

N'oubliez—Do not forget. *M.*

Naboth was right to hold on to his home. 40 There were garnered memories that all the wealth of Ahab could not buy. *Ward Beecher.*

Nace en la huerta lo que no siembra el hortelano—More grows in the garden than the gardener ever sowed there. *Sp. Pr.*

Nach Canossa gehen wir nicht—We are not going to Canossa (where Henry IV. humbled himself before the Pope). *Bismarck.*

Nach Ehre geizt die Jugend ; / Lass dich den Ehrgeiz nicht verführen—Youth is covetous of honour ; let not this covetousness seduce thee. *Schiller.*

Nach Freiheit strebt der Mann, das Weib nach Sitte—The man strives after freedom, the woman after good manners. *Goethe.*

Nach Golde drängt, / Am Golde hängt, / Doch 45 alles. Ach, wir Armen !—Yet after gold every one presses, on gold everything hangs. Alas ! we poor ones. *Goethe.*

Nach Gottes Wesenheit ist gar nicht dein Beruf zu forschen ; forsche du nach Wesen, die er schuf—Thou art not required to search into the nature of God, but into the nature of the beings which he has created. *Rückert.*

Nacheifern ist beneiden—To emulate is to envy. *Lessing.*

Nachgeben stillt allen Krieg — Yielding stills all war. *Ger. Pr.*

Nacht muss es sein, wo Friedlands Sterne strahlen—It must be night where Friedland's stars shine. *Schiller.*

Næ amicum castigare ob meritam noxiam /
Immune est facinus—Verily, it is a thankless
office to censure a friend for a fault when he
deserves it. *Plaut.*

Nae butter 'll stick to my bread, *i.e.*, no good
fortune ever comes my way. *Sc. Pr.*

Nae freen' like the penny. *Sc. Pr.*

Nae fules like auld fules. *Sc. Pr.*

5 Nae man can be happy without a friend, nor
be sure of him till he's unhappy. *Sc. Pr.*

Nae man can live at peace unless his neighbours let him. *Sc. Pr.*

Nae man can mak' his ain hap (destiny). *Sc.
Pr.*

Nae man can tether time or tide. *Burns.*

Nae man can thrive unless his wife will let
him. *Sc. Pr.*

10 Nae man has a tack (lease) o' his life. *Sc.
Pr.*

Nae man is wise at a' times, nor wise on a'
things. *Sc. Pr.*

Nae treasures nor pleasures / Could mak' us
happy lang, / The heart aye's the part aye /
That mak's us right or wrang. *Burns.*

Nae wonder ye're auld like; ilka thing fashes
(bothers) ye. *Sc. Pr.*

Naething is a man's truly but what he cometh
by duly. *Sc. Pr.*

15 Naething is got without pains but an ill name.
Sc. Pr.

Naething is got without pains except dirt and
long nails. *Sc. Pr.*

Naething is ill said if it's no ill ta'en. *Sc. Pr.*

Nager entre deux eaux—To waver between two
parties. *Fr.*

Naiv muss jedes wahre Genie sein, oder es ist
keines—Every true genius must be natural, or
it is none. *Schiller.*

20 Naked truth is out of place before the eyes of
the profane vulgar; it can only make its
appearance thickly veiled. *Schopenhauer.*

Nakedness is uncomely, as well in mind as
body; and it addeth no small reverence to
men's manners and actions if they be not
altogether open. *Bacon.*

Nam de mille fabæ modiis dum surripis unum, /
Damnum est, non facinus mihi pacto lenius
isto—If from a thousand bushels of beans you
steal one, my loss, it is true, is in this case less,
but not your villany. *Hor.*

Nam dives qui fieri vult, / Et cito vult fieri—He
who wishes to become rich wishes to become so
quickly too. *Juv.*

Nam ego illum periisse duco, cui quidem periit
pudor—I regard that man as lost who has lost
his sense of shame. *Plaut.*

25 Nam et majorum instituta tueri, sacris ceri-
moniisque retinendis, sapientis est—For it is
the part of a wise man to protect the institutions
of his forefathers by retaining the sacred rites
and ceremonies.

Nam neque divitibus contingunt gaudia solis, /
Nec vixit male qui natus moriensque fefellit
—Joys do not fall to the rich alone; nor has he
lived ill of whose birth and death no one took
note. *Hor.*

Nam nunc mores nihil faciunt quod licet, nisi
quod lubet—Nowadays it is the fashion to make
nothing of what is proper, but only what is pleasant. *Plaut.*

Nam pro jucundis aptissima quæque dabunt
Di : / Carior est illis homo quam sibi—The
gods will give what is most suitable rather than
what is most pleasing; man is dearer to them
than he is to himself. *Juv.*

Nam quæ inscitia est adversum stimulum
calces—It is the height of folly to kick against
the pricks (*lit.* the goad). *Ter.*

Nam quum magna malæ superest audacia 30
causæ, / Creditur a multis fiducia—When
great impudence comes to the help of a bad
cause, it is taken by many for honest confidence.
Juv.

Nam scelus intra se tacitum qui cogitat ullum /
Facti crimen habet—He who secretly meditates
a crime has all the guilt of the deed. *Juv.*

Nam tua res agitur, paries cum proximus
ardet !—Your property is in peril surely if your
neighbour's house is on fire ! *Hor.*

Nam vitiis nemo sine nascitur; optimus ille est, /
Qui minimis urgetur—No man is born without
faults; he is the best who is influenced by the
fewest. *Hor.*

Namen nennen dich nicht ! Dich bilden Griffel
und Pinsel sterblicher Künstler nicht nach !
—Names do not name thee ! Graver and pencil
of mortal artist can give no idea of thee ! *Ueltzen.*

Names alter, things never alter. *Wm. Blake.* 35

Nane are so weel but they hope to be better.
Sc. Pr.

Napoleon affords us an example of the danger
of elevating one s self to the Absolute, and
sacrificing everything to the carrying out
of an idea. *Goethe.*

Napoleon, for the sake of a great name, broke
in pieces almost half a world. *Goethe.*

Narrative is linear, but Action, having breadth
and depth as well as length, is solid. *Carlyle.*

Narratur et prisci Catonis / Sæpe mero caluisse 40
virtus—It is said that the virtue even of the elder
Cato was often warmed by wine. *Hor.*

Nascentes morimur, finisque ab origine pendet
—We are born but to die (*lit.* die in being born),
and our end hangs on to our beginning. *Manilius.*

Nascimur poetæ, fimus oratores—We are born
poets, we become orators. *Cic.*

Natales grate numeras? ignoscis amicis? /
Lenior et melior fis accedente senecta?—Do
you count your birthdays thankfully? forgive
your friends? grow gentler and better with advancing age? *Hor.*

Natio comœda est—The nation is composed of
actors. *Juv.*

National character varies as it fades under in- 45
vasion or corruption; but if ever it glows
again into a new life, that life must be tempered by the earth and sky of the country
itself. *Ruskin.* (?)

National enthusiasm is the great nursery of
genius. *Tuckermann.*

National suffering is, if thou wilt understand
the words, verily a judgment of God; it has
ever been preceded by national crime. *Carlyle.*

Nations and empires flourish and decay, / By
turns command, and in their turn obey.
Dryden, after Ovid.

Nations and men are only the best when they
are the gladdest, and deserve heaven when
they enjoy it. *Jean Paul.*

Nations are only transitional forms of humanity; they must undergo obliteration, as do the transitional forms offered by the animal series. There is no more an immortality for them than there is an immobility for an embryo or any one of the manifold forms passed through in its progress of development. *Draper.*

Nations, like individuals, are born, proceed through a predestined growth, and die. One comes to its end at an early period and in an untimely way; another, not until it has gained maturity. One is cut off by feebleness in its infancy, another is destroyed by civil disease, another commits political suicide, another lingers in old age. But for every one there is an orderly way of progress to its final term, whatever that term may be. *Draper.*

Natur und Kunst, sie scheinen sich zu fliehen, / Und haben sich, eh' man es denkt, gefunden —Nature and art seem to shun each other, and have met (*lit.* found each other) ere one is aware. *Goethe.*

Natura beatis / Omnibus esse dedit, si quis cognoverit uti — Nature has granted to all to be happy, if we but knew how to use her gifts. *Claud.*

5 Natura il fece, e poi roppe la stampa—Nature fashioned him, and then broke the mould. *Ariost.*

Natura ipsa valere, et mentis viribus excitari, et quasi quodam divino spiritu afflari—To be strong by nature, to be urged on by the native powers of the mind, and to be inspired by a divine spirit, as it were. *Cic.*

Natura naturans—Nature formative.

Natura naturata—Nature passive; nature formed.

Natura nihil agit frustra—Nature does nothing in vain.

10 Natura non facit saltus — Nature makes no leaps.

Natura, quam te colimus inviti quoque — O Nature, how we bow to thee even against our will. *Sen.*

Natural abilities are like natural plants, that need pruning by study; and studies themselves do give forth directions too much at large, except they be bounded in by experience. *Bacon.*

Natural abilities can almost make up for the want of every kind of cultivation, but no cultivation for want of natural abilities. *Schopenhauer.*

Natural knowledge is come at by the continuance and progress of learning and of liberty, and by particular persons attending to, comparing, and pursuing intimations scattered up and down it, which are overlooked and disregarded by the generality of the world. *Bishop Butler.*

15 Natural objects always did and do weaken, deaden, and obliterate imagination in me. *Wm. Blake.*

Natural selection is the principle by which each slight variation, if useful, is preserved. *Darwin.*

Naturalia non sunt turpia—Natural things are without shame.

Naturam expellas furca, tamen usque recurret —Drive Nature out with a pitchfork, she will every time come rushing back. *Hor.*

Nature abhors a vacuum. *Pr.*

Nature admits no lie. *Carlyle.* 20

Nature acts towards us like an Oriental potentate with Mamelukes under him, whom he employs for some mysterious purpose, but to whom he never shows himself in person. *Renan.*

Nature alone is antique, and the oldest art a mushroom. *Carlyle.*

Nature alone is permanent. *Longfellow.*

Nature alone knows what she means. *Goethe.*

Nature always leaps to the surface, and man-25 ages to show what she is. *Boileau.*

Nature always speaks of spirit. *Emerson.*

Nature always wears the colours of the spirit. To a man labouring under calamity the heat of his own fire hath sadness in it. *Emerson.*

Nature and art are too grand to go forth in pursuit of aims; nor is it necessary that they should, for there are relations everywhere, and relations constitute life. *Goethe.*

Nature and books belong to the eyes that see them. It depends on the mood of the man whether he shall see the sunset or the fine poem. *Emerson.*

Nature and Heaven command you, at your 30 peril, to discern worth from unworth in everything, and most of all in man. *Ruskin.*

Nature and love cannot be concealed. *Ger. Pr.*

Nature and Nature's laws lay hid in night; / God said, "Let Newton be!" and all was light. *Pope.*

Nature and truth, though never so low or vulgar, are yet pleasing when openly and artlessly represented. *Pope.*

Nature builds upon a false bottom, seeks herself what she values in others, and is oftentimes deceived and disappointed. Grace reposes her whole hope and love in God, and is never mistaken, never deluded by false expectations. *Thomas à Kempis.*

Nature cannot be surprised in undress. Beauty 35 breaks in everywhere. *Emerson.*

Nature cannot but always act rightly, quite unconcerned as to what may be the consequences. *Goethe.*

Nature counts nothing that she meets with base, / But lives and loves in every place. *Tennyson.*

Nature, crescent, does not grow alone / In thews and bulk; but, as this temple waxes, / The inward service of the mind and soul / Grows wide withal. *Ham.*, i. 3.

Nature does more than supply materials; she also supplies powers. *J. S. Mill.*

Nature does not cocker us; we are children, 40 not pets; she is not fond; everything is dealt to us without fear or favour, after severe, universal laws. *Emerson.*

Nature does not like to be observed, and likes that we should be her fools and playmates. *Emerson.*

Nature does not make all great men, more than all other men, in the self-same mould. *Carlyle.*

Nature draws with greater force than seven oxen. *Ger. Pr.*

Nature ever provides for her own exigencies. *Sen.*

Nature fashions no creature without implanting in it the strength needful for its action and duration. *Carlyle.*

Nature forces on our heart a Creator ; history, a Providence. *Jean Paul.*

Nature gives healthy children much ; how much ! Wise education is a wise unfolding of this ; often it unfolds itself better of its own accord. *Goethe.*

Nature gives you the impression as if there were nothing contradictory in the world ; and yet, when you return back to the dwelling-place of man, be it lofty or low, wide or narrow, there is ever somewhat to contend with, to battle with, to smooth and put to rights. *Goethe.*

5 Nature glories in death more than in life. The month of departure is more beautiful than the month of coming. . . . Every green thing loves to die in bright colours. *Ward Beecher.*

Nature goes her own way ; and all that to us seems an exception, is really according to order. *Goethe.*

Nature had made occupation a necessity ; society makes it a duty ; habit may make it a pleasure. *Capelle.*

Nature has directly formed woman to be a mother, only indirectly to be a wife ; man, on the contrary, is rather made to be a husband than a father. *Jean Paul.*

Nature has given to each one all that as a man he needs, which it is the business of education to develop, if, as most frequently happens, it does not develop better of itself. *Goethe.*

10 Nature has lent us tears—the cry of suffering when the man at last can bear it no longer. *Goethe.*

Nature has made man's breast no windows / To publish what he does within doors, / Nor what dark secrets there inhabit, / Unless his own rash folly blab it. *Butler.*

Nature has made provision for all her children ; the meanest is not hindered in its existence even by that of the most excellent. *Goethe.*

Nature has no feeling ; the sun gives his light to good and bad alike, and moon and stars shine out for the worst of men as for the best. *Goethe.*

Nature has no moods ; they belong to man alone. *Auerbach.*

15 Nature has planted passions in the heart of man for the wisest purposes both of religion and life. *Fox.*

Nature has sometimes made a fool, but a coxcomb is always of man's own making. *Addison.*

Nature hath framed strange fellows in her time. / Some that will evermore peep through their eyes / And laugh like parrots at a bag-piper ; / And other of such vinegar aspect / That they'll not show their teeth in way of smile, / Though Nestor swear the jest be laughable. *Mer. of Venice,* i. 1.

Nature hath made nothing so base but can / Read some instruction to the wisest man. *Aleyn.*

Nature here shows art, / That through thy bosom makes me see thy heart. *Mid. N. Dream,* ii. 8.

20 Nature holds an immense uncollected debt over every man's head. *Ward Beecher.*

Nature in women is so nearly allied to art. *Goethe.*

Nature in you stands on the very verge / Of her confine. *King Lear,* ii. 4.

Nature is a friend to truth. *Young.*

Nature is a frugal mother, and never gives without measure. *Emerson.*

Nature is a mutable cloud, which is always 25 and never the same. *Emerson.*

Nature is a Sibyl, who testifies beforehand to what has been determined from all eternity, and was not to be realised till late in time. *Goethe.*

Nature is a vast trope, and all particular natures are tropes. *Emerson.*

Nature is always kind enough to give even her clouds a humorous lining. *Lowell.*

Nature is always lavish, even prodigal. *Goethe.*

Nature is always like herself. *Linnæus.* 30

Nature is always mysterious. *Ward.*

Nature is always right, and most profoundly so (*am gründlichsten*) just there where we least comprehend her. *Goethe.*

Nature is an Æolian harp, a musical instrument whose tones are the re-echo of higher strings within us. *Novalis.*

Nature is avariciously frugal ; in matter it allows no atom to elude her grasp ; in mind no thought or feeling to perish. It gathers up the fragments that nothing be lost. *Dr. Thomas.*

Nature is beyond all teaching. *Pr.* 35

Nature is but a name for an effect whose cause is God. *Cowper.*

Nature is commanded by obeying her. *Bacon.*

Nature is content with little, grace with less, but lust with nothing. *Matthew Henry.*

Nature is despotic, and will not be fooled or abated of any jot of her authority by the pertest of her sons. *Emerson.*

Nature is full of freaks, and now puts an old 40 head on young shoulders, and then a young heart beating under fourscore winters. *Emerson.*

Nature is good, but intellect is better, as the lawgiver is before the law-receiver. *Emerson.*

Nature is good, but she is not the best. *Carlyle.*

Nature is indeed adequate to Fear, but to Reverence not adequate. *Goethe.*

Nature is just towards men. It recompenses them for their sufferings ; it renders them laborious, because to the greatest toils it attaches the greatest rewards. *Montesquieu.*

Nature is no spendthrift, but takes the shortest 45 way to her ends. *Emerson.*

Nature is not an Aggregate but a Whole. *Carlyle.*

Nature is not fixed, but fluid ; spirit alters, moulds, makes it. *Emerson.*

Nature is rich ; those two eggs you ate to breakfast this morning might, if hatched, have peopled the world with poultry. *Carlyle.*

Nature is sometimes subdued, but seldom extinguished. *Bacon.*

Nature is still the grand agent in making 50 poets. *Carlyle.*

Nature is the art of God. *Sir Thomas Browne.*

Nature is the best posture-master. *Emerson.*

Nature is the immense shadow of man. *Emerson.*

Nature is the living, visible garment of God. *Goethe.*

Nature is the only book that teems with meaning on every page. *Goethe.*

Nature knows how to convert evil to good. / Nature utilises misers, fanatics, showmen, egotists to accomplish her ends; but we must not think better of the foible for that. *Emerson.*

5 Nature knows no equality; her sovereign law is subordination and dependence. *Vauvenargues.*

Nature knows no pause in progress and development, and attaches her curse on all inaction. *Goethe.*

Nature listening stood whilst Shakespeare play'd, / And wonder'd at the work herself had made. *Churchill.*

Nature made every fop to plague his brother, / Just as one beauty mortifies another. *Pope.*

Nature makes us vagabonds, the world makes us respectable. *Alexander Smith.*

10 Nature meant to make woman her masterpiece, but committed a mistake in the choice of the clay; she took it too fine. *Lessing.*

Nature must obey necessity. *Jul. Cæs.,* iv. 3.

Nature, mysterious even under the light of day, is not to be robbed of her veil; 'and what she does not choose to reveal, you will not extort from her with levers and screws. *Goethe.*

Nature needs little, fancy (*Wahn*) much. *Gr. Pr.*

Nature never did betray / The heart that loved her. *Wordsworth.*

15 Nature never hurries; atom by atom, little by little, she achieves her work. *Emerson.*

Nature never made an unkind creature; illusage and bad habits have deformed a fair and lovely creation. *Sterne.*

Nature never sends a great man into the planet without confiding the secret to another soul. *Emerson.*

Nature owns no man who is not a martyr withal. *Carlyle.*

Nature passes nurture. *Pr.*

20 Nature respects race and not hybrids. *Knox.*

Nature sent women into the world that they might be mothers and love children, to whom sacrifices must ever be offered, and from whom none can be obtained. *Jean Paul.*

Nature smiles as sweet, I ween, / To shepherds as to kings. *Burns.*

Nature stretches out her arms to embrace man; only let his thoughts be of equal greatness. *Emerson.*

Nature, study, and practice must combine to ensure proficiency in any art. *Arist.*

25 Nature suffers nothing to remain in her kingdom which cannot help itself. *Emerson.*

Nature takes as much pains in the forming of a beggar as an emperor. *Pr.*

Nature teaches beasts to know their friends. *Cor.*

Nature transcends all our moods of thought, and its secret we do not yet find. *Emerson.*

Nature trips us up when we strut. *Emerson.*

Nature understands no jesting; she is always 30 true, always serious, always severe; she is always right, and the errors and faults are always those of man. Him who is incapable of appreciating her she despises, and only to the apt, the pure, and the true, does she resign herself and reveal her secrets. *Goethe.*

"Nature veils God," but what I see of Him in nature is not veiled. *Goethe.*

Nature, which is the Time-vesture of God, and reveals Him to the wise, hides Him from the foolish. *Carlyle.*

Nature will not be Buddhist; she resents generalising, and insults the philosopher in every moment with a million of fresh particulars. *Emerson.*

Nature without discipline is of small force, and discipline without nature more feeble. *John Lily.*

Nature without learning is like a blind man; 35 learning without Nature, like a maimed one; practice without both, incomplete. *Plutarch.*

Nature works after such eternal, necessary, divine laws, that the Deity himself could alter nothing in them. *Goethe, after Spinoza.*

Nature works on the method of all for each and each for all. *Emerson.*

Nature works very hard, and only hits the white once in a million throws. In mankind, she is contented if she yields one master in a century. *Emerson.*

Nature's above art. *Lear,* iv. 6.

Nature's chief masterpiece is writing well. 40 *Duke of Buckingham.*

Nature's shadows are ever varying. *Wm. Blake.*

Nature's tears are Reason's merriment. *Rom. and Jul.,* iv. 5.

Natures that have much heat, and great and violent desires and perturbations, are not ripe for action till they have passed the meridian of their years. *Bacon.*

Natürlicher Verstand kann fast jeden Grad von Bildung ersetzen, aber keine Bildung den natürlichen Verstand — Natural intelligence may make up almost every step in culture, but no culture make up for natural intelligence. *Schopenhauer.*

Natus nemo—Not a born soul. *Plaut.* 45

Natus sum; esuriebam, quærebam; nunc repletus requiesco—I was born; I felt hungry, and sought for food; now that I am satiated, I lay me down to rest.

Naufragium in portu facere — To make shipwreck in port. *Quinct.*

Nay! evermore, / All things and thoughts, both new and old, are writ / Upon the unchanging human heart and soul. *Lewis Morris.*

Nay, let us seek at home to find / Fit harvest for the brooding mind, / And find, since thus the world grows fair, / Duty and pleasure everywhere. *Lewis Morris.*

Nay, that's past praying for. *1 Henry IV.,* 50 ii. 4.

Nay, then, farewell! / I have touch'd the highest point of all my greatness, / And, from that full meridian of my glory, / I haste now to my setting: I shall fall / Like a bright exhalation in the evening, / And no man see me more. *Wolsey, in Hen. VIII.,* iii. 2.

Ne Æsopum quidem trivit—He is a backward pupil (*lit.* he has not yet thumbed Æsop).

Ne cede malis, sed contra audentior ito—Yield not to misfortunes, but rather go more boldly to meet them. *Virg.*

Ne depugnes in alieno negotio—Do not take up the cudgels in another man's affairs. *Pr.*

Ne exeat regno—Let him not go out of the kingdom. (A writ to prevent a person leaving the country). *L.*

5 **Ne faut-il que délibérer? / La cour en conseillers foisonne : / Est-il besoin d'exécuter? /** L'on ne rencontre personne—Is a matter to be discussed? the council chamber is full of advisers. Is there something to be done? the chamber is empty. *La Font.*

Ne forçons point notre talent ; / Nous ne ferions rien avec grâce—Let us not force our faculty ; we shall in that case do nothing to good effect. *La Font.*

Ne fronti crede—Trust not to appearances.

Ne Hercules quidem contra duos—Not even Hercules could contend against two at once.

Ne Jupiter quidem omnibus placet—Not even Jupiter can please everybody. *Pr.*

10 **Ne nimium**—Not too much. *M.*

Ne obliviscaris—Do not forget. *M.*

Ne plus ultra—What cannot be surpassed ; perfection (*lit.* no more beyond).

Né pour la digestion—Born merely to consume good things. *La Bruyère.*

Ne quid detrimenti respublica capiat—See that the commonwealth suffer no detriment.

15 **Ne quid falsi dicere audeat, ne quid veri non audeat**—Let him not dare to say anything that is false, nor let him dare to say what is not true. *Cic.*

Ne quid nimis—Let there be no excess. *M.*

Ne sutor supra crepidam—Let the cobbler stick to his last. *Pliny.*

Ne te longis ambagibus ultra / Quam satis est morer—To make a long story short (*lit.* not to detain you by long digressions more than enough). *Hor.*

Ne te quæsiveris extra—Seek not thyself outside of thyself.

20 **Ne tempora perde precando**—Lose not the time that offers itself by praying. *Ovid.*

Ne tentes, aut perfice—Either attempt not, or go through with it. *M.*

Ne vile fano—Bring nothing base to the temple. *M.*

Ne vile velis—Incline to nothing vile. *M.*

Near and far do not belong to the eternal world, which is not of space and time. *Carlyle.*

25 **Near is my shirt, but nearer is my skin.** *Pr.*

Nearer the kirk the farther frae grace. *Sc. Pr.*

Nearly all our powerful men in this age of the world are unbelievers ; the best of them in doubt and misery ; the plurality in plodding hesitation, doing, as well as they can, what practical work lies ready to their hands. *Ruskin.*

Neat, not gaudy. *Charles Lamb.*

Nec aspera terrent—Not even hardships deter us. *M.*

30 **Nec caput nec pedes**—In confusion ; neither head nor tail. *Pr.*

Nec cui de te plusquam tibi credas—Do not believe any man more than yourself about yourself. *Pr.*

Nec cupias, nec metuas—Neither desire nor fear. *M.*

Nec deus intersit, nisi dignus vindice nodus—Never let a god interfere unless a difficulty arise worthy of a god's interposition. *Hor.*

Nec domo dominus, sed domino domus honestanda est—The master should not be graced by the mansion, but the mansion by the master. *Cic.*

Nec est ad astra mollis e terris via—The 35 way from the earth to the stars is no soft one. *Sen.*

Nec habeo, nec careo, nec curo—I neither have, nor want, nor care. *M.*

Nec lusisse pudet, sed non incidere ludum—There is no shame in having led a wild life, but in not breaking it off. *Hor.*

Nec male notus eques—A knight of good repute. *M.*

Nec meus audet / Rem tentare pudor, quam vires ferre recusent—My modesty does not permit me to essay a thing which my powers are not equal to accomplish. *Virg.*

Nec minor est virtus, quam quærere, parta 40 tueri ; / Casus inest illic ; hic erit artis opus—It is no less merit to keep what you have got than to gain it. In the one there is chance ; the other will be a work of art. *Ovid.*

Nec mora, nec requies—Neither delay nor cessation. *Virg.*

Nec morti esse locum—There is no room for death. *Ovid.*

Nec obolum habet unde restim emat—He hasn't a penny left to buy a halter. *Pr.*

Nec omnia, nec semper, nec ab omnibus—Neither all, nor always, nor by all.

Nec placida contentus quiete est—Nor is he 45 contented with quiet repose. *M.*

Nec pluribus impar—Not an unequal match for numbers. *M.*

Nec prece nec pretio—Neither by entreaty nor by a bribe. *M.*

Nec, quæ præteriit, iterum revocabitur unda ; / Nec, quæ præteriit, hora redire potest—Neither can the wave which has passed by be again recalled, nor can the hour which has passed ever return. *Ovid.*

Nec quærere nec spernere honorem—Neither to seek nor to despise honours. *M.*

Nec regi nec populo, sed utrique—Neither for 50 king nor for people, but for both. *M.*

Nec scire fas est omnia—It is not permitted us to know all things. *Hor.*

Nec si non obstatur propterea etiam permittitur—That an act is not prohibited, it does not follow that it is permitted. *Cic.*

Nec sibi, sed toti genitum se credere mundo—To think that he was born not for himself alone, but for the whole world. *Lucan.*

Nec soli cedit—He yields not even to the sun. *M.*

Nec temere nec timide — Neither rashly nor 55 timidly. *M.*

Nec tibi quid liceat, sed quid fecisse decebit / Occurrat—And let it not concern you what you may do, but what you ought to do. *Claud.*

Nec timeo, nec sperno—I neither fear nor despise. *M.*

Nec Veneris pharetris macer est, aut lampade fervet : / Inde faces ardent, veniunt a dote sagittæ—He is not made thin by Venus' quiver, nor does he burn with her torch ; it is from this that his fires are fed, from her dowry the arrows come. *Juv.*

Nec verbum verbo curabis reddere fidus / Interpres—Nor, as a faithful translator, should you be careful to render the original word for word. *Hor.*

Nec vidisse semel satis est, juvat usque morari, / Et conferre gradum, et veniendi discere causas—Nor is it enough to have once seen him ; they are delighted to linger near him, and to keep step with him, and to learn the reason of his coming. *Virg.*

Nec vultu destrue dicta tuo—Do not discredit your words by your looks. *Ovid.*

5 Necessary patience in seeking the Lord is better than he that leadeth his life without a guide. *Ecclus.*

Necesse est cum insanientibus furere, nisi solus relinqueris—You must be mad with the insane unless you wish to be left quite alone. *Petronius.*

Necesse est ut multos timeat, quem multi timent—He whom many fear must necessarily fear many. *Syr.*

Necessità 'l a' induce, e non diletto—Necessity, not pleasure, brings him here. *Dante.*

Necessitas non habet legem—Necessity has no law.

10 Necessity does everything well. *Emerson.*

Necessity is cruel, but it is the only test of inward strength. Every fool may live according to his own likings. *Goethe.*

Necessity is the mistress of the arts. *Pr.*

Necessity is the mother of invention. *Pr.*

Necessity is the plea for every infringement of human freedom. It is the argument of tyrants, it is the creed of slaves. *William Pitt.*

15 Necessity makes even cowards brave. *Pr.*

Necessity reforms the poor, and satiety the rich. *Tac.*

Necessity unites hearts. *Ger. Pr.*

Necessity urges desperate measures. *Cervantes.*

Necio es quien piensa que otros no piensan—He is a fool who thinks that others don't think. *Sp. Pr.*

20 Need mak's an auld wife trot. *Sc. Pr.*

Needles and pins, needles and pins ! / When a man marries his trouble begins. *Pr.*

Needs must when the devil drives. *Sc. Pr.*

Ne'er grudge and carp, / Though fortune use you hard and sharp. *Burns.*

Ne'er let your gear owergang ye, *i.e.*, never let your wealth get the better of you. *Sc. Pr.*

25 Ne'er linger, ne'er o'erhasty be, / For time moves on with measured foot. *Goethe.*

Ne'er put a sword in a wud man's (a madman's) hand. *Sc. Pr.*

Ne'er tak' a wife till ye ken what to do wi' her. *Sc. Pr.*

Ne'er the rose without the thorn. *Herrick.*

Ne'er trust muckle to an auld enemy or a new freend. *Sc. Pr.*

30 Neglecta solent incendia sumere vires—A fire, if neglected, always gathers in strength. *Hor.*

Negligence is the rust of the soul, that corrodes through all her best resolves. *Feltham.*

Negligere quid de se quisque sentiat, non solum arrogantis est, sed omnino dissoluti —To be careless of what others think of us, not only indicates an arrogant, but an utterly abandoned character. *Cic.*

Nehmt die Gottheit auf in euren Willen, / Und sie steigt von ihrem Weltenthron—Take the divine up into your will, and she descends from her world-throne. *Schiller.*

Nehmt die Stimmung wahr, / Denn sie kommt so selten—Take advantage of the right mood, for it comes so seldom. *Goethe.*

Neid zu fühlen, ist menschlich ; Schadenfreude 35 zu genissen, teuflisch—To feel envy is human ; to joy in mischief is devilish. *Schopenhauer.*

Neither a borrower nor a lender be ; / For loan oft loses both itself and friend. *Ham.,* i. 3.

Neither borrow money of a neighbour nor a friend, but of a stranger, where, paying for it, thou shalt hear no more of it. *Lord Burleigh.*

Neither crow nor croak. *Pr.*

Neither exalt your pleasures, nor aggravate your vexations, beyond their real and natural state. *Johnson.*

Neither heat, nor frost, nor thunder / Shall 40 wholly do away, I ween, / The marks of that which once hath been. *Coleridge.*

Neither hew down the whole forest, nor come home without wood. *Serv. Pr.*

Neither lead nor drive. *Pr.*

Neither our virtues nor vices are all our own. *Johnson.*

Neither painting nor fighting feed men ; nor can capital, in the form of money or machinery, feed them. *Ruskin.*

Neither praise nor blame is the object of true 45 criticism. Justly to discriminate, firmly to establish, wisely to prescribe, and honestly to award—these are the true aims and duties of criticism. *Simms.*

Neither rhyme nor reason. *Shakespeare.*

Neither seek nor shun the fight. *Gael. Pr.*

Neither sign a paper without reading it, nor drink water without seeing it. *Sp. Pr.*

Neither wise men nor fools / Can work without tools. *Pr.*

Neither woman nor man, nor any kind of crea- 50 ture in the universe, was born for the exclusive, or even the chief, purpose of falling in love or being fallen in love with. . . . Except the zoophytes and coral insects of the Pacific Ocean, I am acquainted with no creature with whom it is the one or grand object. *Carlyle.*

Neither women nor linen by candlelight. *Pr.*

Νεκρὸς οὐ δάκνει—A dead man doesn't bite. *Plutarch.*

Nem. con., abbrev. for Nemine contradicente—Nobody opposing.

Nem. diss., abbrev. for Nemine dissentiente—Same as above.

Nemesis checks, with cubit-rule and bridle, / 55 Immoderate deeds, and boastings rash and idle. *Anon.*

Nemesis is lame, but she is of colossal stature, like the gods. *George Eliot.*

Nemo allegans suam turpitudinem audiendus est—No one testifying to his own baseness ought to be heard. *L.*

Nemo dat quod non habet—Nobody can give what he does not legally possess. *L.*

Nemo debet bis puniri pro uno delicto—No man shall be twice punished for the same offence. *L.*

Nemo debet bis vexari pro una et eadem causa —No one shall be molested twice for one and the same cause. *L.*

5 Nemo debet esse judex in propria causa—No one ought to be judge in his own cause. *L.*

Nemo doctus mutationem consilii inconstantiam dixit esse—No sensible man ever charged one with inconstancy who had merely changed his opinion. ' *Cic.*

Nemo est tam senex qui se annum non putat posse vivere—There is no man so old as not to think he may live a year longer. *Cic.*

Nemo ex proprio dolo consequitur actionem— No man can sue at law upon his own fraud. *L.*

Nemo impetrare potest a papa bullam nunquam moriendi—No man can ever obtain from the Pope a dispensation from death. *Thomas à Kempis.*

10 Nemo ita pauper vivit, quam pauper natus est —No one is so poor in life as he was when he was at birth.

Nemo læditur nisi a seipso—No man is harmed but by himself. *Pr.*

Nemo malus felix, minime corruptor—No bad man is happy, least of all a seducer. *Juv.*

Nemo mathematicus genium indemnatus habebit—No astronomer will be held a genius until he is condemned. *Juv.*

Nemo me impune lacessit—No one provokes me with impunity. *M. of Scotland.*

15 Nemo mortalium omnibus horis sapit—No man is wise at all moments.

Nemo patriam in qua natus est exuere nec ligeantiæ debitum ejurare possit—No one can cast off his native country or abjure his allegiance to his sovereign. *L.*

Nemo potest mutare consilium suum in alterius injuriam—No one can change what he proposes to enact to the damage of another. *L.*

Nemo potest nudo vestimenta detrahere—You cannot strip a garment off a naked man. *Pr.*

Nemo potest personam diu ferre fictam—No one can play a feigned part long. *Sen.*

20 Nemo præsumitur alienam posteritatem suæ prætulisse—No one is presumed to have preferred another's offspring to his own. *L.*

Nemo punitur pro alieno delicto—No one must be punished for the fault of another. *L.*

Nemo quam bene vivat, sed quamdiu, curat: quum omnibus possit contingere ut bene vivat, ut diu nulli—No one concerns himself with how well he should live, only how long : while none can count upon living long, all have the chance of living well. *Sen.*

Nemo repente fuit turpissimus—No man ever became extremely wicked all at once. *Juv.*

Nemo sibi nascitur—No one is born for himself. *Pr.*

25 Nemo solus sapit—No man is wise by himself. *Plaut.*

Nemo tenetur se ipsum accusare—No one is held bound to criminate himself. *L.*

Nemo vir magnus sine aliquo afflatu divino unquam fuit—There never was a great man who had not some divine inspiration. *Cic.*

Νήποι, οὐδ' ἴσασιν ὅσῳ πλέον ἥμισυ παντός —Fools, they don't even know how much half is more than the whole. *Hesiod, from Pittacus.*

Nequaquam satis in re una consumere curam —It is by no means enough to spend all our care on a single object. *Hor.*

Neque culpa neque lauda teipsum — Neither 30 blame nor praise yourself.

Neque fœmina, amissa pudicitia, alia abnuerit —When a woman has once lost her chastity, she will shrink from nothing. *Tac.*

Neque mala vel bona quæ vulgus putet— Things are not to be judged either good or bad merely because the public think so. *Tac.*

Neque opinione sed natura constitutum est jus—Not in opinion, but in nature is law founded. *Cic.*

Neque quies gentium sine armis neque arma sine stipendiis neque stipendia sine tributis haberi queunt—The quiet of nations cannot be maintained without arms, nor can arms be maintained without pay, nor pay without taxation. *Tac.*

Neque semper arcum / Tendit Apollo—Apollo 35 does not always keep his bow bent. *Hor.*

Nequicquam sapit qui sibi non sapit—He is wise to no purpose who is not wise for himself. *Pr.*

Nervus rerum—The sinews of things.

Nescia mens hominum fati sortisque futuræ, / Et servare modum, rebus sublata secundis —Man knows not the lot appointed him, and he cannot keep within bounds when elated by prosperity. *Virg.*

Nescio qua natale solum dulcedine captos / Ducit, et immemores non sinit esse sui—I know not by what sweet charm our native soil attracts us to it, and does not suffer us ever to forget it. *Ovid.*

Nescio qua præter solitum dulcedine læti— 40 Elated beyond usual by some unaccountable delight. *Virg.*

Nescire autem quid antea quam natus sis acciderit, id est semper esse puerum. Quid enim est ætas hominis, nisi memoria rerum veterum cum superioribus contexitur?—To be unacquainted with events which took place before you were born, is to be always a child ; for where is human life if the memory fails to connect past events with others before? *Cic.*

Nescis tu quam meticulosa res sit ire ad judicem—You little know what a frightful thing it is to go to law. *Plaut.*

Nescit vox missa reverti—A word once uttered can never be recalled. *Hor.*

Nessun maggior dolore / Che ricordarsi del tempo felice / Nella miseria—There is no greater woe than the recollection in the midst of misery of happy days bygone. *Dante.*

Nessuno nasce maestro—No one is born a 45 master. *It. Pr.*

Neu Regiment bringt neue Menschen auf, / Und früheres Verdienst veraltet schnell— A new administration of affairs raises up new men, and qualifications formerly of service become soon antiquated. *Schiller.*

Neutral men are the devil's allies. *Chapin.*

Never a tear bedims the eye / That time and patience will not dry ; / Never a lip is curved in pain / That can't be kissed into smiles again. *Bret Harte.*

Never anger / Made good guard for itself. *Ant. and Cleo.*, iv. 1.

Never anything can be amiss / When simpleness and duty tender it. *Mid. N.'s Dream*, v. 1.

Never ask a favour of a man until he has had his dinner. *Punch.*

Never be afraid to doubt, if only you have the disposition to believe. *Leighton.*

5 Never bray at an ass. *Pr.*

Never burn your fingers to snuff another man's candle. *Pr.*

Never buy a pig in a poke. *Pr.*

Never by reflection, only by doing what it lies on him to do, is self-knowledge possible to any man. *Goethe.*

Never cackle till your egg is laid. *Pr.*

10 Never confuse a myth with a lie. . . . The thoughts of all the greatest and wisest men hitherto have been expressed through mythology. *Ruskin.*

Never deal in mistakes; they aye bring mischances. *Scott.*

Never deceive a friend. *Hipparchus.*

Never desire to appear clever and make a show of your talents before men. Be honest, loving, kindly, and sympathetic in all you say and do. Cleverness will flow from you naturally if you have it, and applause will come to you unsought from those who know what to applaud; but the applause of fools is to be shunned. *Prof. Blackie to young men.*

Never despise the day of small things. *Pr.*

15 Never disregard what your enemies say. *B. R. Haydon.*

Never do anything of the rectitude of which you have a doubt. *Pliny.*

Never do that by proxy which you can do yourself. *It. Pr.*

Never do things by halves. *Pr.*

Never durst poet touch a pen to write / Until his ink were temper'd with love's sighs; / O, then his lines would ravish savage ears, / And plant in tyrants mild humility. *Love's L. Lost*, iv. 3.

20 Never elated when one man's oppress'd; / Never dejected while another's bless'd. *Pope.*

Never fall out with your bread and butter. *Pr.*

Never find fault with the absent. *Pr.*

Never fish in troubled waters. *Pr.*

Never forget St. Paul's sentence, "Love is the fulfilling of the law." This is the steam of the social machine; but the steam requires regulation; it is regulated by intelligence and moderation. *Prof. Blackie to young men.*

25 Never fry a fish till it's caught. *Pr.*

Never give up the ship. *Pr.*

Never grudge a penny for a pennyworth. *Pr.*

Never grumble nor mumble. *Pr.*

Never hang a man twice for one offence. *Pr.*

30 Never have an idle hour, or an idle pound. *Pr.*

Never hold a candle to the devil. *Pr.*

Never indulge the notion that you have any absolute right to choose the sphere or the circumstances in which you are to put forth your powers of social action. *Prof. Blackie to young men.*

Never is a lang term. *Sc. Pr.*

Never is a long day. *Pr.*

Never king dropped out of the clouds. *Power.* 35

Never lean on a broken staff. *Pr.*

Never leave a certainty for an uncertainty. *Pr.*

Never leave that till to-morrow which you can do to-day. *Ben. Franklin.*

Never let any one see the bottom of your purse or your mind. *It. Pr.*

Never let Fortune be thy mistress, nor Mis- 40 fortune thy maid. *Bodenstedt.*

Never let us be discouraged with ourselves. It is not when we are conscious of our faults that we are the most wicked; on the contrary, we are less so. *Fénelon.*

Never let your zeal outrun your charity; the former is but human, the latter is divine. *Ballou.*

Never look a gift-horse in the mouth. *Pr.*

Never look for a knot in a bulrush. *Pr.*

Never look for birds of this year in the nests 45 of the last. *Cervantes.*

Never make a jest of any Scripture expressions. *Judge Hale.*

Never meet trouble half way. *Pr.*

Never mind the future: be what you ought to be; the rest is God's affair. *Amiel.*

Never mind who was your grandfather. What are you? *Pr.*

Never morning wore / To evening, but some 50 heart did break. *Tennyson.*

Never neglect small matters and expenses. *It. Pr.*

Never offer to teach fish to swim. *Pr.*

Never preach beyond your experience. *Pr.*

Never put your arm out farther than you can draw it back again. *Scott.*

Never put your hand into a wasp's nest. *Pr.* 55

Never read borrowed books. To be without books of your own is the abyss of penury. Don't endure it. And when you have to buy them, you'll think whether they're worth reading; which you had better, on all accounts. *Ruskin to a young lady.*

Never repeat old grievances. *Pr.*

Never risk a joke, even the least offensive in its nature and the most common, with a person who is not well-bred, and possessed of sense to comprehend it. *La Bruyère.*

Never say die! / Up, man, and try! *Pr.*

Never say of another what you would not have 60 him hear. *Pr.*

Never seek to tell thy love, / Love that never told can be, / For the gentle wind doth move / Silently, invisibly. *Wm. Blake.*

Never shirk the hardest work. *Pr.*

Never sigh, but send. *Pr.*

Never since Aaron's rod went out of practice, or even before it, was there such a wonder-working tool as a pen; greater than all recorded miracles have been performed by pens. *Carlyle.*

Never speak ill of those whose bread you eat. 65 *Pr.*

Never speak of love with scorn; / Such were direst treason; / Love was made for eve and morn, / And for every season. *C. Kent.*

Never spur a willing horse. *Pr.*

Never stint soap and water. *Pr.*

Never swap horses while crossing a stream. *Pr.*

Never talk half a minute without pausing and giving others an opportunity to strike in. *Sydney Smith.*

Never tell in the parlour what you heard in the kitchen. *Pr.*

5 Never tell your resolution before-hand. *Wisdom.*

Never that I could in searching find out, has man been, by time which devours much, deprived of any faculty whatsoever that he in any era was possessed of. *Carlyle.*

Never throw a hen's egg at a sparrow. *Pr.*

Never till now did young men, and almost children, take such a command in human affairs. *Carlyle.*

Never title yet so mean could prove, / But there was eke a mind which did that title love. *Shenstone.*

10 Never too old to turn; never too late to learn. *Pr.*

Never trouble yourself with trouble till trouble troubles you. *Pr.*

Never trust a wolf with the care of lambs. *Pr.*

Never try to prove what nobody doubts. *Pr.*

Never venture all in one bottom. *Pr.*

15 Never was scraper (miser) brave man. *Herbert.*

Never waste pains on bad ground; let it remain rough. Though properly looked after and cared for, it will be of best service so. *Ruskin.*

Never write anything that does not give you great pleasure; emotion is easily propagated from the writer to the reader. *Joubert.*

Never write on a subject without having first read yourself full on it; and never read on a subject till you have thought yourself hungry on it. *Richter.*

Never write what you dare not sign. *Pr.*

20 Never yet created eye / Could see across eternity. *Keble.*

Never yet has it been our fortune to fall in with any man of genius whose conclusions did not correspond better with his premises, and not worse, than those of other men; whose genius, once understood, did not manifest itself in a deeper, fuller, truer view of all things human and divine, than the clearest of your so-called laudable "practical men" had claim to. *Carlyle.*

Never yet, since the proud selfish race / Of men began to jar, did passion give, / Nor can it ever give, a right decision. *Thomson.*

Never yet / Was noble man but made ignoble talk. *Tennyson.*

New acquests are more burden than strength. *Bacon.*

25 New brooms sweep clean. *Pr.*

New, daring, and inspiring ideas are engendered only in a clear head over a glowing heart, as the richest wines grow over the volcanoes. *F. Jacobs.*

New laws, new frauds. *Pr.*

New lords, new laws. *Pr.*

New-made honour doth forget men's names; / 'Tis too respective and too sociable, / For your conversion. *King John, i. 1.*

New presbyter is but old priest writ large. 30 *Milton.*

New religion! We already, in our dim heads, know truths (of religion) by the thousand; and, yet in our dead hearts, we will not perform them by the ten, by the unit. *Carlyle.*

New scenes impress new ideas, enrich the imagination, and enlarge the power of reason. *Johnson.*

Newspapers always excite curiosity. No one ever lays one down without a feeling of disappointment. *Charles Lamb.*

Next in importance to the matter of books are their titles. *Davies.*

"Next to a lost battle, nothing is so sad as 35 a battle that has been won." *Wellington, after Waterloo.*

Next to Christmas Day the most pleasant annual epoch in existence is the advent of the New Year. *Dickens.*

Next to excellence is the appreciation of it. *Thackeray.*

Next to nae wife, a gude wife is the best. *Sc. Pr.*

Next to religion, let your care be to promote justice. *Bacon.*

Next to the assumption of power is the respon- 40 sibility of relinquishing it. *Disraeli.*

Next to the consciousness of doing a good action, that of doing a civil one is the most pleasing. *Chesterfield.*

Next to the gods, of all man's possessions his soul is the mightiest, being the most his own. *Plato.*

Next to the originator of a good sentence is the first quoter of it. *Emerson.*

Next to the satisfaction I receive in the prosperity of an honest man, I am best pleased with the confusion of a rascal. (?)

Next to theology I give to music the highest 45 place and honour; and we see how David and all the saints have wrought their godly thoughts into verse, rhyme, and song. *Luther.*

Ni l'or ni la grandeur ne nous rendent heureux —Neither wealth nor greatness render us happy. *La Font.*

Ni l'un ni l'autre—Neither the one nor the other. *Fr.*

Ni trop haut, ni trop bas; c'est le souverain style—Neither too high nor too low, that is the sovereign rule.

Nice distinctions are out of the question upon occasions like those of speech, which return every hour. *Paley, upon lying.*

Nicht alle sind Diebe, die der Hund anbellt— 50 All are not thieves whom the dog barks at. *Ger. Pr.*

Nicht alles Wünschenswerte ist erreichbar; nicht alles Erkennenswerte ist erkennbar— Not everything that is desirable is attainable, and not everything that is worth knowing is knowable. *Goethe.*

Nicht an die Güter hänge dein Herz, / Die das Leben vergänglich zieren! / Wer besitzt, der lerne verlieren; / Wer im Glück ist, der lerne den Schmerz!—Let not thy heart cling to the things which for so short a time deck out thy life. Let him who has, learn to lose, and him who is happy, familiarise himself with what may give pain. *Schiller.*

Nicht der Besitz, nur das Enthüllen, / Das leise Finden nur ist süss—Not the possession, only the unveiling and quietly finding out is sweet. *Tiedge.*

Nicht der ist auf der Welt verwaist, / Dessen Vater und Mutter gestorben, / Sondern der für Herz und Geist / Keine Lieb' und kein Wissen erworben—Not he whose father and mother is dead is orphaned in the world, but he who has won for heart and mind no love and no knowledge. *Rückert.*

Nicht die Kinder bloss speist man / Mit Märchen ab—It is not children merely that are put off with stories. *Lessing.*

Nicht draussen im Strudel verrauschender Lust / Erwarte, de Glück dir zu finden : / Die Seligkeit wohnt in der eigenen Brust, / Hier musst du sie ewig begründen !—Think not to find thy happiness out there in the whirl of riotous pleasure. Thy blessedness dwells in thy own breast ; here must thou for ever establish it. *Heine.*

5 Nicht grösseren Vortheil wüsst' ich zu nennen / Als des Feindes Verdienst erkennen—I know not a greater advantage than a due appreciation of the worth of an enemy. *Goethe.*

Nicht immer am besten erfahren ist, / Wer am ältesten an Jahren ist, / Und wer am meisten gelitten hat, / Nicht immer die besten Sitten hat !—He who is oldest in years is not always the best experienced, and he who has suffered most has not always the best morals. *Bodenstedt.*

Nicht immer macht das Kleid den Mann—Clothes do not always make the man. *Zachariæ.*

Nicht in die ferne Zeit verliere dich ! / Den Augenblick ergreife, der ist dein—Lose not thyself in a far-off time. Seize thou the moment that is thine. *Schiller.*

Nicht in kalten Marmorsteinen, / Nicht in Tempeln dumpf und tot, / In den frischen Eichenhainen / Webt und rauscht der deutsche Gott—Not in cold marble stones, not in temples damp and dead, but in fresh oak-groves weaves and rustles the German God. *Uhland.*

10 Nicht jede Besserung ist Tugend—Not every improvement is virtue. *Gellert.*

Nicht Kunst und Wissenschaft allein, / Geduld will bei dem Werke sein—Not art and science only, but patience will be required for the work. *Goethe.*

Nicht Rosen bloss, auch Dornen hat der Himmel—Heaven has not only its roses, but also its thorns. *Schiller.*

Nicht so redlich wäre redlicher—Not so honest were more honest. *Lessing.*

Nichts Abgeschmackters find' ich auf der Welt / Als einen Teufel, der verzweifelt—I know nothing more mawkish than a devil who despairs. *Goethe.*

15 Nichts Böses thun ist gut; / Nichts Böses wollen ist besser—To do nothing evil is good ; to wish nothing evil is better. *Claudius.*

Nichts führt zum Guten, was nicht natürlich ist—Nothing leads to good that is not natural. *Schiller.*

Nichts halb zu thun ist edler Geister Art—It is the manner of noble souls to do nothing by halves. *Wieland.*

Nichts ist dem Menschen so schwer zu tragen, / Als eine Reihe von guten Tagen—No burden is so heavy for a man to bear as a succession of happy days. *Müller.*

Nichts ist göttlich, als was vernünftig ist—Nothing is divine but what is agreeable to reason. *Kant.*

Nichts ist höher zu schätzen, als der Wert des 20 Tages—Nothing is to be rated higher than the value of the day. *Goethe.*

Nichts ist so elend als ein Mann, / Der alles will, und der nichts kann—Nothing is so miserable as a man who wills everything and can do nothing. *Claudius.*

Nichts stirbt, was wirklich gut und göttlich war—Nothing that was really good and godlike dies. *Arndt.*

Nichts thun lehrt Uebel thun—Doing nothing is a lesson in doing ill. *Ger. Pr.*

Nichtswürdig ist die Nation, die nicht / Ihr Alles freudig setzt an ihre Ehre—Worthless is the nation that does not gladly stake its all on its honour. *Schiller.*

Nick does not pretend to be a gentleman. 25 *Arbuthnot.*

Nicknames stick to people, and the most ridiculous are the most adhesive. *Haliburton.*

Nie kommt das Unglück ohne sein Gefolge—Misfortune never comes without his retinue. *Heine.*

Niemand ist frei, der nicht über sich selbst Herr ist—No man is free who is not lord over himself. *Claudius.*

Niemand ist mehr Sklave, als der sich für frei hält ohne es zu sein—No one is more a slave than he who considers himself free without being so. *Goethe.*

Niemand weiss, wie weit seine Kräfte gehen, 30 bis er sie versucht hat—No one knows how far his powers go till he has tried them. *Goethe.*

Niggardliness is not good husbandry. *Addison.*

Night is a good herdsman ; she brings all creatures home. *Gael. Pr.*

Night is the mither (mother) o' thoughts. *Sc. Pr.*

Night is the Sabbath of mankind, / To rest the body and the mind. *Butler.*

Night ! that great shadow and profile of the 35 day. *Jean Paul.*

Night's candles are burnt out, and jocund day / Stands tiptoe on the misty mountain-tops. *Rom. and Jul.,* iii. 5.

Night's deepest gloom is but a calm, / That soothes the wearied mind ; / The labour'd day's restoring balm, / The comfort of mankind. *Leigh Hunt.*

Nightingales will not sing in a cage. *Pr.*

Nihil a Deo vacat ; opus suum ipse implet—Nothing is void of God ; His work everywhere is full of Himself. *Sen.*

Nihil ad rem *or* versum—Not to the purpose, or 40 point.

Nihil agit qui diffidentem verbis solatur suis ; / Is est amicus qui in re dubia re juvat, ubi re est opus—He does nothing who seeks to console a desponding man with words ; a friend is one who aids with deeds at a critical time when deeds are called for. *Plaut.*

Nihil aliud necessarium ut sis miser, quam ut te miserum credas—Nothing else is necessary to make you wretched than to fancy you are so.

Nihil cum fidibus graculo — Jackdaws have nothing to do with a lute. *Gell.*

Nihil enim legit, quod non excerperet. Dicere etiam solebat, nullum esse librum tam malum, ut non aliqua parte prodesset—He read no book which he did not make extracts from. He also used to say, "No book was so bad but good of some kind might be got out of it." *Pliny the Elder.*

Nihil eripit fortuna nisi quod et dedit—Fortune takes nothing away but what she also gave. *Pub. Syr.*

Nihil est ab omni / Parte beatum—There is nothing that is blessed in every respect. *Hor.*

Nihil est annis velocius !—Nothing is swifter than our years. *Ovid.*

5 Nihil est aptius ad delectationem lectoris, quam temporum varietates, fortunæque vicissitudines—Nothing contributes more to the entertainment of a reader than the changes of times and the vicissitudes of fortune. *Cic.*

Nihil est quod credere de se / Non possit—There is nothing that it (*i.e.*, power, *potestas*) cannot believe itself capable of. *Juv.*

Nihil est quod Deus efficere non possit.—There is nothing which the Deity cannot effect. *Cic.*

Nihil est tam utile, quod in transitu prosit—Nothing is so useful as to be of profit after only a hasty study of it. *Sen.*

Nihil est tam volucre quam maledictum, nihil facilius emittitur, nihil citius excipitur, nihil latius dissipatur—Nothing is so swift as calumny, nothing more easily uttered, nothing more readily received, nothing more widely disseminated. *Cic.*

10 Nihil hic nisi carmina desunt—Nothing is wanting here except a song. *Virg.*

Nihil honestum esse potest, quod justitia vacat—Nothing can be honourable where justice is absent. *Cic.*

Nihil largiundo gloriam adeptus est—He acquired glory without bribery. *Sall.*

Nihil morosius hominum judiciis—Nothing so peevish and pedantic as men's judgments of one another. *Erasmus.*

Nihil potest rex nisi quod de jure potest—The king can do nothing but what the law allows. *L.*

15 Nihil quod est inconveniens est licitum—Nothing which is inconvenient is lawful. *L.*

Nihil scire est vita jucundissima — To know nothing at all is the happiest life. *Pr.*

Nihil scriptum miraculi causa — Nothing is written here to excite wonder, or for effect. *Tac.*

Nihil simul inventum est et perfectum—Nothing is invented and brought to perfection all at once. *Coke.*

Nihil tam absurdum dici potest ut non dicatur a philosopho—There is nothing so absurd but it may be said by a philosopher. *Cic.*

20 Nihil tam firmum est, cui periculum non sit etiam ab invalido—Nothing is so steadfast as to be free of danger from even the weakest. *Quint. Curt.*

Nihil tam munitum est, quod non expugnari pecunia possit—Nothing is so strongly fortified that it cannot be taken by money. *Cic.*

Nihil turpius est quam gravis ætate senex, qui nullum aliud habet argumentum, quo se probet diu vixisse, præter ætatem—There is nothing more despicable than an old man who has no other proof than his age to offer of his having lived long in the world. *Sen.*

Nihil unquam peccavit, nisi quod mortua est—She never once sinned but when she died. *Inscription on a wife's tomb in Rome.*

Nil actum credens, dum quid superesset agendum—He considered nothing done so long as anything remained to be done. *Lucan, of Julius Cæsar.*

"Nil admirari" is the motto which men of the 25 world always affect, thinking it vulgar to wonder or be enthusiastic. *Sir Egerton Brydges.*

Nil admirari prope est res una, Numici, / Solaque, quæ possit facere et servare beatum—To wonder at nothing, Numicius, is almost the one and only thing which can make and keep men happy. *Hor.*

Nil æquale homini fuit illi—There was no consistency in that man. *Hor.*

Nil agit exemplum litem quod lite resolvit—An illustration which solves one difficulty by involving us in another settles nothing. *Hor.*

Nil consuetudine majus—Nothing is more powerful than custom, or habit. *Ovid.*

Nil cupientium / Nudus castra peto—Naked 30 myself, I make for the camp of those who desire nothing. *Hor.*

Nil debet—He owes nothing. *L.*

Nil desperandum—There is no ground for despair.

Nil desperandum Teucro duce et auspice Teucro—Let us despair of nothing while Teucer is our leader and we under his auspices. *Hor.*

Nil dicit—He says nothing, *i.e.*, he has no defence to make. *L.*

Nil dictu fœdum visuque hæc limina tangat, / 35 Intra quæ puer est—Let nothing filthy to be said or seen touch this threshold, within which there is a boy. *Juv.*

Nil dictum quod non dictum prius—There can be nothing said now which has not been said before. *L.*

Nil ego contulerim jucundo sanus amico—As long as I have my senses, there is nothing I would prefer to an agreeable friend. *Hor.*

Nil erit ulterius quod nostris moribus addat / Posteritas ; eadem cupient facientque minores : Omne in præcipiti vitium stetit—There will be nothing left for posterity to add to our manners ; our descendants will wish for and do the same things as we do ; every vice has reached its culminating point. *Juv.*

Nil feret ad manes divitis umbra suos—The ghost of the rich man will carry nothing to the shades below. *Ovid.*

Nil fuit unquam sic impar sibi—Never was such 40 an inconsistent creature seen before. *Hor.*

Nil habet infelix paupertas durius in se, / Quam quod ridiculos homines facit—Unhappy poverty has nothing in it more galling than this, that it makes men ridiculous. *Juv.*

Nil homini certum est—There is nothing assured to mortals. *Ovid.*

Nil me officit unquam, / Ditior hic, aut est quia doctior ; est locus uni / Cuique suus—It never the least annoys me that another is richer or more learned than I ; every one has his own place assigned him. *Hor.*

Nil mortalibus arduum est—Nothing is too arduous for mortals. *Hor.*

Nil nisi cruce—No hope but in the cross. *M.* 45

Nil oriturum alias, nil ortum tale fatentes—Confessing that none like you has arisen before, none will ever arise. *Hor.*

Nil peccant oculi, si oculis animus imperet—: The eyes don't err if the mind governs them. *Pub. Syr.*

Nil proprium ducas quod mutari potest—Never deem that your own which can be changed. *Pub. Syr.*

Nil rectum nisi quod placuit sibi ducunt—They deem nothing right except what seems good to themselves. *Hor.*

Nil sine magno / Vita labore dedit mortalibus —Life has granted nothing to mankind save through great labour. *Hor.*

5 Nil sine te mei prosunt honores—The honours I obtain are nothing without thee. *Hor. to the Muse.*

Nil sole et sale utilius—Nothing so useful as the sun and salt. *Pr.*

Nil spernat auris, nec tamen credat statim— Let the ear despise nothing, nor yet be too ready to believe. *Phæd.*

Nil tam difficile est quod non solertia vincat— There is nothing so difficult but skill will surmount it. *Pr.*

Nil tam inæstimabile est quam animi multitudinis—Nothing is so contemptible as the sentiments of the mob. *Sen.*

10 Nil temere novandum — Make no rash innovations. *L.*

Nil unquam longum est, quod sine fine placet —Nothing is ever long which never ceases to please.

Nimia cura deterit magis quam emendat—Too much pains may injure rather than improve your work. *Pr.*

Nimia est voluptas, si diu abfueris a domo / Domum si redieris, si tibi nulla est ægritudo animo obviam—It is a very great pleasure if, on your return home after a long absence, you are not confronted with anything to vex you. *Plaut.*

Nimia illæc licentia / Profecto evadet in aliquod magnum malum—This extreme licentiousness will assuredly develop into some dire disaster. *Ter.*

15 Nimia subtilitas in jure reprobatur, et talis certitudo certitudinem confundit—Too much subtlety in law is condemned, and such certainty destroys certainty. *L.*

Nimirum insanus paucis videatur, eo quod / Maxima pars hominum morbo jactatur eodem—There are few, I say, to whom this fellow should appear insane, since by far the majority of people are infected with the same malady. *Hor.*

Nimis uncis / Naribus indulges—You indulge in swearing (*lit.* upturned nostrils) too much.

Nimium altercando veritas amittitur—In too eager disputation the truth is lost sight of. *Pr.*

Nimium ne crede colori—Trust not too much to appearances. *Virg.*

20 Nimius in veritate, et similitudinis quam pulchritudinis amantior — Too fastidious as regards truth, and with a greater liking for exactness than beauty. *Quinct.*

Nimm alles leicht ! das Träumen lass und Grübeln ! / So bleibst du wohlbewahrt vor tausend Uebeln—Take everything easily ; leave off dreaming and brooding ; then wilt thou be safeshielded from a thousand ills. *Uhland.*

Nimm die Welt, wie sie ist, nicht wie sie seyn sollte—Take the world as it is, not as it should be. *Ger. Pr.*

Nimm wahr die Zeit; sie eilet sich, / Und kommt nicht wieder ewiglich—Take thou good note of time ; it hurries past thee, and comes not back again for ever. *Claudius.*

Nine tailors cannot make a man. *Pr.*

Nine-tenths of existing books are nonsense, 25 and the clever books are the refutation of that nonsense. *Disraeli.*

Nine-tenths of our critics have told us little more of Shakespeare than what honest Franz Horn says his neighbours used to tell of him, "he was a great spirit, and stept majestically along." *Carlyle.*

Nine things to sight required are : / The power to see, the light, the visible thing, / Being not too small, too thin, too nigh, too far ; / Clear space, and time, the form distinct to bring. *Sir John Davies.*

Nine times out of ten it is over the Bridge of Sighs that we pass the narrow gulf from youth to manhood. That interval is usually occupied by an ill-placed or disappointed affection. We recover and we find ourselves a new being. The intellect has become hardened by the fire through which it has passed. The mind profits by the wrecks of every passion, and we may measure our road to wisdom by the sorrows we have undergone. *Bulwer Lytton.*

Nine tithes of times / Face-flatterer and backbiter are the same. *Tennyson.*

Nineteen nay-says are half a grant. *Allan* 30 *Ramsay.*

Nisi caste, saltem caute—If not chastely, at least cautiously.

Nisi Dominus, frustra—Unless the Lord be with us, all is vain. *M.*

Nisi prius—Unless before. A judicial writ.

Nisi utile est quod facias, stulta est gloria— Unless what we do is useful, our glorying is vain. *Phæd.*

Nitimur in vetitum semper, cupimusque ne-35 gata — We are ever striving after what is forbidden, and coveting what is denied us. *Ovid.*

Nitor in adversum, nec me, qui cætera vincit / Impetus, et rapido contrarius evehor orbi— I struggle against an opposing current ; the torrent which sweeps away others does not overpower me, and I make head against the on-rushing stream. *Ovid.*

"No," a monosyllable, the easiest learned by the child, but the most difficult to practise by the man, contains within it the import of a life, the weal or woe of an eternity. *Johnson.*

No accidents are so unlucky that the prudent may not draw some advantage from them. *La Roche.*

No affections and a great brain ; these are the men to command the world. *Disraeli.*

No eye ever seemed the age of Romance to 40 itself. *Carlyle.*

No age, sex, or condition is above or below the absolute necessity of modesty ; but without it one is vastly beneath the rank of man. *Barton.*

No answer is also an answer. *Pr.*

No art can be noble which is incapable of expressing thought, and no art is capable of expressing thought which does not change. *Ruskin.*

No artist-work is so high, so noble, so grand, so enduring, so important for all time, as the making of character in a child. *Charlotte Cushman.*

No ashes are lighter than those of incense, and few things burn out sooner. *Landor.*

No atheist denies a divinity, but only some name of a divinity; the God is still present there, working in that benighted heart, were it only as a god of darkness. *Carlyle.*

No author can be as moral as his works, as no preacher is as pious as his sermons. *Jean Paul.*

5 No author ever spared a brother; / Wits are gamecocks to one another. *Gay.*

No author is a man of genius to his publisher. *Heine.*

No autumn fruit without spring blossoms. *Pr.*

No beast so fierce but knows some touch of pity. *Rich. III., i. 2.*

No bees, no honey; / No work, no money. *Pr.*

10 No belief of ours will change the facts or reverse the laws of the spiritual universe; and it is our first business to discover the laws and to learn how the facts stand. *Dr. Dale.*

No belief which is contrary to truth can be really useful. *J. S. Mill.*

No bird ever flew so high but it had to come to the ground for food. *Dut. Pr.*

No blank, no trifle, Nature made or meant. *Young.*

No book is worth anything which is not worth much; nor is it serviceable until it has been read, and re-read, and loved, and loved again. *Ruskin.*

15 No book that will not improve by repeated readings deserves to be read at all. *Carlyle.*

No book was ever written down by any but itself. *Bentley.*

No ceremony that to great one 'longs, / Not the king's crown, nor the deputed sword, / The marshal's truncheon nor the judge's robe, / Become them with one half so good a grace / As mercy does. *Meas. for Meas., ii. 2.*

No chair is so much wanted (in our colleges) as that of a professor of books. *Emerson.*

No chaos can continue chaotic with a soul in it. *Carlyle.*

20 No character was ever rightly understood until it had been first regarded with a certain feeling, not of tolerance only, but of sympathy. *Carlyle.*

No cheerfulness can ever be produced by effort which is itself painful. *Goldsmith.*

No cloth is too fine for moth to devour. *Pr.*

No compound of this earthly ball / Is like another all in all. *Tennyson.*

No conflict is so severe as his who labours to subdue himself. *Thomas à Kempis.*

25 No conquest can ever become permanent which not withal show itself beneficial to the conquered as well as to the conquerors. *Carlyle.*

No corn without chaff. *Dut. Pr.*

No : creation, one would think, cannot be easy; your Jove has severe pains, and fire flames, in the head out of which an armed Pallas is struggling. *Carlyle.*

No creature smarts so little as a fool. *Pope.*

No crime is so great as daring to excel. *Churchill.*

No cross, no crown. *Quarles.* 30

No diga la lengua par do pague la cabeza— The tongue talks at the head's cost. *Sp. Pr*

No distance breaks the tie of blood : / Brothers are brothers evermore; / Nor wrong, nor wrath of deadliest mood, / That magic may o'erpower. *Keble.*

No doubt but ye are the people, and wisdom shall die with you. *Job, in Bible.*

No doubt every person is entitled to make and to think as much of himself as possible, only he ought not to worry others about this, for they have enough to do with and in themselves, if they too are to be of some account, both now and hereafter. *Goethe.*

No dynamite will ever be invented that can 35 rule; it can but dissolve and destroy Only the word of God and the heart of man can govern. *Ruskin.*

No earnest man, in any time, ever spoke what was wholly meaningless. *Carlyle.*

No earnest thinker is a plagiarist pure and simple. He will never borrow from others that which he has not already, more or less, thought out for himself. *C. Kingsley.*

No entertainment is so cheap as reading, nor any pleasure so lasting. *Lady Montagu.*

No errors are so mischievous as those of great men. *Pr.*

No evil can touch him who looks on human 40 beauty; he feels himself at one with himself and with the world. *Goethe.*

No evil dies so soon as that which has been patiently sustained. *W. Secker.*

No evil is felt till it comes, and when it comes no counsel helps. Wisdom is always too early and too late. *Rückert.*

No evil is without its compensation. *Sen.*

No evil propensity of the human heart is so powerful that it may not be subdued by discipline. *Sen.*

No experiment is dangerous the result of which 45 we have the courage to meet. *Goethe.*

No expression of politeness but has its root in the moral nature of man. *Goethe.*

No eye to watch, and no tongue to wound us, / All earth forget, and all heaven around us *Moore.*

No fact in nature but carries the whole sense of nature. *Emerson.*

No falsehood can endure / Touch of celestial temper. *Milton.*

No fathers or mothers think their own children 50 ugly. *Cervantes.*

No fishing like fishing in the sea. *Pr.*

No flattery, boy; an honest man can't live by 't; / It is a little sneaking art, which knaves / Use to cajole and soften fools withal. *Otway.*

No fool was ever so foolish, but some one thought him clever. *Pr.*

No fountain so small but that heaven may be imaged in its bosom. *Hawthorne.*

No friend a friend until he shall prove a friend. 55 *Beaumont and Fletcher.*

No frost can freeze Providence. *Pr.*

No gains without pains. *Pr.*

No ghost was ever seen by two pair of eyes. *Carlyle.*

No girl who is well bred, kind, and modest is ever offensively plain; all real deformity means want of manners or of heart. *Ruskin.*

No golden age ever called itself golden, but only expected one. *Jean Paul.*

No good book or good thing of any sort shows its best face at first; nay, the commonest quality in a true work of art, if its excellence have any depth and compass, is that at first sight it occasions a certain disappointment. *Carlyle.*

5 No good doctor ever takes physic. *It. Pr.*

No good is ever done to society by the pictorial representation of its diseases. *Ruskin.*

No good lawyer ever goes to law himself. *It. Pr.*

No good or lovely thing exists in this world without its correspondent darkness; and the universe presents itself continually to mankind under the stern aspect of warning, or of choice, the good and the evil set on the right hand and the left. *Ruskin.*

No good work whatever can be perfect; and the demand for perfection is always a sign of a misunderstanding of the ends of art. *Ruskin.*

10 No government is safe unless fortified by goodwill. *Corn. Nepos.*

No grace can save any man unless he helps himself. *Ward Beecher.*

No grain of sand / But moves a bright and million-peopled land, / And hath its Eden and its Eves, I deem. *Blanchard.*

No grand doer in this world can be a copious speaker about his doings. *Carlyle.*

No great composition was ever produced but with the same heavenly involuntariness in which a bird builds her nest. *Ruskin.*

15 No great intellectual thing was ever done by great effort. *Ruskin.*

No great man was ever other than a genuine man. *Carlyle.*

No great truth is allowed by Nature to be demonstrable to any person who, foreseeing its consequences, desires to refuse it. *Ruskin.*

No greater hell than to be a slave to fear. *Ben Jonson.*

No greater men are now than ever were. *Emerson.*

20 No greater misfortune can befall a man than to be the victim of an idea which has no hold on his life, still more which detaches him from it. *Goethe.*

No greater promisers than those who have nothing to give. *Pr.*

No hand can make the clock strike for me the hours that are past. *Byron.*

No hay dulzura sin sudor—No sweetness without sweat. *Sp. Pr.*

No hay tal razon como la del baston—There is no argument like that of a stick. *Sp. Pr.*

25 No heart opens to sympathy without letting in delicacy. *J. M. Barrie.*

No Hecuba, by aid of rouge and ceruse, is a Helen made. *Cowper.*

No herb will cure love. *Pr.*

No heroine can create a hero through love of one, but she may give birth to one. *Jean Paul.*

No honestly exerted force can be utterly lost. *Carlyle.*

No horse so blind as the blind mare. *Pr.* 30

No house without mouse; no throne without thorn. *Pr.*

No human capacity ever yet saw the whole of a thing; but we may see more and more of it the longer we look. *Ruskin.*

No human face is exactly the same in its lines on each side, no leaf perfect in its lobes, no branch in its symmetry. *Ruskin.*

No idea can succeed except at the expense of sacrifices; no one ever escapes without a stain from the struggle of life. *Renan.*

No intellectual images are without use. *Johnson.* 35

No iron chain, or outward force of any kind, can ever compel the soul of a man to believe or to disbelieve. *Carlyle.*

"No" is a surly, honest fellow—speaks his mind rough and round at once. "But" is a sneaking, evasive, half-bred, exceptuous sort of conjunction, which comes to pull away the cup just when it is at your lips. *Scott.*

No joy so great but runneth to an end; / No hap so hard but may in time amend. *Robert Southwell.*

No joy without alloy. *Pr.*

No knowledge is lost, but perfected, and 40 changed for much nobler, sweeter, greater knowledge. *Baxter.*

No labour is hard, no time is long, wherein the glory of eternity is the mark we level at. *S. Hieron.*

No law can be finally sacred to me but the law of my own nature. *Emerson.*

No leaf moves but as God wills it. *Sp. Pr.*

No legacy is so rich as honesty. *All's Well,* iii. 5.

No lie you can speak or act, but it will come, 45 after longer or shorter circulation, like a bill drawn on Nature's reality, and be presented there for payment, with the answer: "No effects." *Carlyle.*

No literature is complete until the language in which it is written is dead. *Longfellow.*

No longer pipe, no longer dance. *Pr.*

No lover should have the insolence to think of being accepted at once, nor should any girl have the cruelty to refuse at once, without severe reasons. *Ruskin.*

No lying knight or lying priest ever prospered in any age, but certainly not in the dark ones. Men prospered then only in following openly-declared purposes, and preaching candidly-beloved and trusted creeds. *Ruskin.*

No man at bottom means injustice; it is always 50 for some obscure distorted image of a right that he contends. *Carlyle.*

No man at the head of affairs always wishes to be explicit. *Macaulay.*

No man bathes twice in the same river. *Heraclitus.*

No man beholdeth prosperity who doth not encounter danger; but having encountered danger, if he surviveth, he beholdeth it. *Hitopadesa.*

No man but a blockhead ever wrote except for money. *Johnson.*

No man can antedate his experience *Emerson.* 55

No man can answer for his courage who has never been in danger. *La Roche.*

No man can be a good poet without first being a good man. *Ben Jonson.*

No man can be a poet / That is not a good cook, to know the palates / And several tastes of the time. *Ben Jonson.*

No man can be a hero in anything who is not first of all a hero in faith. *Jacobi.*

5 No man can be brave who considers pain to be the greatest evil of life ; nor temperate, who considers pleasure to be the highest good. *Cic.*

No man can be good, or great, or happy, except through inward efforts of his own. *F. W. Robertson.*

No man can be said to have the spirit who does not walk in it, or to be born of the spirit until the spirit is born of him. *Ed.*

No man can be so entirely a devil as to extinguish in himself the last ray of light. *Th. Körner.*

No man can become largely rich by his personal toil, but only by discovery of some method of taxing the labour of others. *Ruskin.*

10 No man can buy anything in the market with gentility. *Lord Burleigh.*

No man can, for a length of time, be wholly wretched, if there is not a disharmony (a folly and wickedness) within himself ; neither can the richest Crœsus, and never so eupeptic, be other than discontented, perplexed, unhappy, if he be a fool. *Carlyle.*

No man can force the harp of his own individuality into the people's heart ; but every man may play upon the chords of the people's heart, who draws his inspiration from the people's instinct. *Kossuth.*

No man can gather cherries in Kent at the season of Christmas. *Pr.*

No man can judge another, because no man knows himself ; for we censure others but as they disagree with that humour which we fancy laudable in ourselves, and commend others but for that wherein they seem to quadrate and consent with us. *Colton.*

15 No man can learn what he has not preparation for learning, however near to his eyes the object may be. *Emerson.*

No man can live half a life when he has genuinely learned that it is only half a life. The other half, the higher half, must haunt him. *Philips Brooks.*

No man can lose what he never had. *Walton.*

No man can make a good coat with bad cloth. *Pr.*

No man can produce great things who is not thoroughly sincere in dealing with himself. *Lowell.*

20 No man can quite emancipate himself from his age and country, or produce a model in which the education, the religion, the politics, the usages, and the arts of his times shall have no share. *Emerson.*

No man can read with profit that which he cannot learn to read with pleasure. *Noah Porter.*

No man can say in what degree any other person, besides himself, can be, with strict justice, called wicked. *Burns.*

No man can see over his own height. *Pr.*

No man can serve two masters. *Jesus.*

No man can thoroughly master more than one 25 art or science. *Hazlitt.*

No man can transcend his own individuality. *Schopenhauer.*

No man doth safely appear abroad but he who can abide at home. *Thomas à Kempis.*

No man doth safely rule but he that hath learned gladly to obey. *Thomas à Kempis.*

No man doth safely speak but he who is glad to hold his peace. *Thomas à Kempis.*

No man ever became, or can become, largely 30 rich merely by labour and economy. *Ruskin.*

No man ever did or ever will become truly eloquent without being a constant reader of the Bible, and an admirer of the purity and sublimity of its language. *Fisher Ames.*

No man ever prayed heartily without learning something. *Emerson.*

No man ever stated his griefs as lightly as he might. *Emerson.*

No man ever worked his passage anywhere in a dead calm. Let no man wax pale, therefore, because of opposition. *John Neale.*

No man flatters the woman he truly loves. 35 *Tuckermann.*

No man had ever a point of pride but was injurious to him. *Burke.*

No man has a claim to credit upon his own word, when better evidence, if he had it, may be easily produced. *Johnson.*

No man has a prosperity so high and firm but two or three words can dishearten it. *Emerson.*

No man has a right to say to his own generation, turning quite away from it, "Be damned." *Carlyle. to Emerson.*

No man has a worse friend than he brings 40 with him from home. *Pr.*

No man has any data for estimating, far less right of judging, the results of a life of resolute self-denial, until he has had the courage to try it himself. *Ruskin.*

No man has come to true greatness who has not felt in some degree that his life belongs to his race, and that what God gives him he gives him for mankind. *Phillips Brooks.*

No man has worked, or can work, except religiously. *Carlyle.*

No man hath a thorough taste of prosperity to whom adversity never happened. (?)

No man hath a velvet cross. *Pr.* 45

No man hath a virtue that he has not a glimpse of ; nor any man an attaint, but he carries some stain of it. *Troil. and Cress., i. 2.*

No man, having put his hand to the plough, and looking back, is fit for the kingdom of God. *Jesus.*

No man is a good physician who has never been sick. *Arab. Pr.*

No man is a hero to his valet-de-chambre. *Prince de Condé, from Plutarch.*

No man is always wise except a fool. *Pr.* 50

No man is born into this world whose work is not born with him ; there is always work, and tools to work withal, for those who will ; and blessed are the horny hands of toil. *Lowell.*

No man is born wise or learned. *Pr.*

No man is either worthy of a good home here or a heaven hereafter that is not willing to be in peril for a good cause. *Capt. John Brown.*

No man is esteemed for gay garments but by fools and women. *Sir W. Raleigh.*

No man is ever good for much who has not been carried off his feet by enthusiasm between twenty and thirty. *Froude.*

No man is ever hurt but by himself. *Diogenes.*

5 No man is ever paid for his real work, or should ever expect or demand angrily to be paid ; all work properly so called is an appeal from the seen to the unseen—a devout calling upon higher powers ; and unless they stand by us, it will not be a work, but a quackery. *Carlyle.*

No man is free who cannot command himself. *Pythagoras.*

No man is good but as he wishes the good of others. *Johnson.*

No man is justified in resisting by word or deed the authority he lives under for a light cause, be such authority what it may. *Carlyle.*

No man is nobler born than another, unless he is born with better abilities and a more amiable disposition. *Sen.*

10 No man is poor who does not think himself so. But if in a full fortune with impatience he desires more, he proclaims his wants and his beggarly condition. *Jeremy Taylor.*

No man is quite sane ; each has a slight determination of blood to the head, to make sure of holding him hard to some one point which Nature has taken to heart. *Emerson.*

No man is rich whose expenditures exceed his means ; and no one is poor whose incomings exceed his outgoings. *Haliburton.*

No man is so free as a beggar, and no man more solemnly a servant than an honest land-owner. *Ruskin.*

No man is so happy as never to give offence. *Thomas à Kempis.*

15 No man is so old but thinks he may live another day. *Pythagoras.*

No man is so sufficient as never to need assistance. *Thomas à Kempis.*

No man is so tall that he need never stretch, nor so small that he need never stoop. *Dan. Pr.*

No man is so worthy of envy as he that can be cheerful in want. *Bp. Hall.*

No man is such a conqueror as the man who has defeated himself. *Ward Beecher.*

20 No man is the wiser for his learning. . . . Wit and wisdom are born with a man. *Selden.*

No man is the worse for knowing the worst of himself. *Pr.*

No man is to be deemed free who has not perfect self-command. *Pythagoras.*

No man is wise enough or good enough to be intrusted with unlimited power. *Colton.*

No man is wise or safe but he that is honest. *Sir W. Raleigh.*

25 No man is without enemies. *Arab. Pr.*

No man is without his load of trouble. *Thomas à Kempis.*

No man lives so poor as he was born. *Pr.*

No man loves to frustrate expectations which have been formed in his favour. *Johnson.*

No man loveth his fetters, be they made of gold. *Pr.*

No man needs money so much as he who 30 despises it. *Jean Paul.*

No man needs to study history to find out what is best for his own culture. *Thoreau.*

No man or woman of the humblest sort can really be strong, gentle, pure, and good, without the world being better for it, without somebody being helped and comforted by the very existence of that goodness. *Phillips Brooks.*

No man perhaps suspects how large and important the region of unconsciousness in him is ; what a vast, unknown territory lies there back of his conscious will and purpose, and which is really the controlling power of his life. *John Burroughs.*

No man praises happiness as he would justice, but calls it blessed, as being something more divine and excellent. *Arist.*

No man regards an eruption upon the surface 35 when the noble parts are invaded, and he feels a mortification approaching to his heart. *Junius.*

"No man," said Pestalozzi, "in God's wide universe, is either willing or able to help any other man." Help must come from the bosom alone. *Emerson.*

No man sees far ; the most see no farther than their noses. *Carlyle.*

No man should be so much taken up in the search of truth, as thereby to neglect the more necessary duties of active life. *Cic.*

No man should enter into alliance with his enemy, even with the tightest bonds of union. Water made ever so hot will still quench fire. *Hitopadesa.*

No man should ever be ashamed to own he 40 has been in the wrong, which is but saying, in other words, that he is wiser to-day than he was yesterday. *Pope.*

No man should ever display his bravery who is unprepared for battle ; nor bear the marks of defiance, until he hath experienced the abilities of his enemy. *Hitopadesa.*

No man should form an acquaintance, nor enter into any amusements, with one of an evil character. A piece of charcoal, if it be hot, burneth ; and if it be cold, blackeneth the hand. *Hitopadesa.*

No man should part with his own individuality and become that of another. *Channing.*

No man should strive to precede his fellows ; for, should the work succeed, the booty is equal, and if it fail, the leader is punished. *Hitopadesa.*

No man should think so highly of himself as 45 to think he can receive but little light from books, nor so meanly as to believe he can discover nothing but what is to be learned from them. *Johnson.*

No man talks of that which he is desirous to conceal, and every man desires to conceal that of which he is ashamed. *Johnson.*

No man thoroughly understands a truth until he has contended against it. *Goethe.*

No man troubleth the beggar with questioning his religion or politics. *Lamb.*

No man was ever as rich as all men ought to be. *Old saying.*

No man was ever scolded out of his sins. 50 *Cowper.*

No man was ever so much deceived by another as by himself. *Lord Greville.*

No man was ever written out of reputation but by himself. *Monk.*

No man was more foolish when he had not a pen in his hand, or more wise when he had. *Johnson, of Goldsmith.*

No man whatever believes, or can believe, exactly what his grandfather believed. *Carlyle.*

5 No man who does not choose, enter into and walk in some narrow way of life, will ever have any moral character, any clearness of purpose, any wisdom of intelligence, or any tenderness or strength of heart. *Ed.*

No man who has once heartily and wholly laughed can be altogether irreclaimably bad. *Carlyle.*

No man who is wretched in his own heart and feeble in his own work can rightly help others. *Ruskin.*

No man who needs a monument ever ought to have one. *Hawthorne.*

No man's conscience can tell him the rights of another man. *Johnson.*

10 No man's pie is freed / From his ambitious finger. *Hen. VIII.*, i. 1.

No man's religion ever survives his morals. *South.*

No mata la carga sino la sobrecarga—Not the load, but the overload kills. *Sp. Pr.*

No matter how much faculty of idle seeing a man has, the step from knowing to doing is rarely taken. *Emerson.*

No matter what his rank or position may be, the lover of books is the richest and happiest of the children of men. *J. A. Langford.*

15 No might nor greatness in mortality / Can censure 'scape ; back-wounding calumny / The whitest virtue strikes. *Meas. for Meas.*, iii. 2.

No mill, no meal. *Pr.*

No more can you distinguish of a man / Than of his outward show ; which, God he knows, / Seldom or never jumpeth with the heart. *Rich. III.*, iii. 1.

No more dangerous snare is set by the fiends for human frailty than the belief that our enemies are also the enemies of God. *Ruskin.*

No more of your titled acquaintances boast, / And in what lordly circles you've been : / An insect is still but an insect at most, / Though it crawl on the head of a queen. *Burns.*

20 No more subtle master under heaven / Than is the maiden-passion for a maid, / Not only to keep down the base in man, / But teach high thought, and amiable words / And courtliness, and the desire of fame, / And love of truth, and all that makes a man. *Tennyson.*

No morning can restore what we have forfeited. *George Meredith.*

No mortal can both work and do good talking in Parliament or out of it ; the feat is impossible as that of serving two hostile masters. *Carlyle.*

No mortal has a right to wag his tongue, much less to wag his pen, without saying something. *Carlyle.*

No mortal's endeavour or attainment will, in the smallest, content the as unendeavouring, unattaining young gentleman ; but he could make it all infinitely better, were it worthy of him. *Carlyle.*

No mother worthy of the name ever gave herself thoroughly for her child who did not feel that, after all, she reaped what she had sown. *Beecher.* 25

No nation can be destroyed while it possesses a good home life. *J. G. Holland.*

No nation can bear wealth that is not intelligent first. *Ward Beecher.*

No nation can reform itself, as the English are now trying to do, by what their newspapers call "tremendous cheers." Reform is not joyous, but grievous ; no single man can reform himself without stern suffering and stern working ; how much less can a nation of men i Medea, when she made men young again, was wont to hew them in pieces with meat-axes ; cast them into caldrons, and boil them for a length of time. How much handier could they have but done it by "tremendous cheers" alone ! *Carlyle.*

No need to teach your grandames to suck eggs. *Pr.*

No news is good news. *Pr.* 30

No, no ! I am but shadow of myself ; / You are deceived, my substance is not here. *1 Hen. VI.*, ii. 3.

No noble task was ever easy. *Carlyle.*

No nobler feeling than this of admiration for one higher than himself, dwells in the breast of man. *Carlyle.*

No, not even faith, or hope, or any other virtue, is accepted by God without charity and grace. *Thomas à Kempis.*

No oath that binds to wrong can ever bind. 35 *Dr. Walter Smith.*

No one can bake cakes for the whole world. *Serv. Pr.*

No one can be a great thinker who does not recognise that, as a thinker, it is his first duty to follow his intellect to whatever conclusions it may lead. *J. S. Mill.*

No one can be despised by another until he has learned to despise himself. *Sen.*

No one can be in perfect accord with any one but himself. *Schopenhauer.*

No one can feel and exercise benevolence towards another who is ill at ease with himself. *Goethe.* 40

No one can find himself in himself or others ; in fact, he has himself to spin, from the centre of which he exercises his influence. *Goethe.*

No one can obtain what he does not bring with him. *Goethe.*

No one can teach religion who has it not. *Jean Paul.*

No one can teach you anything worth learning but through manual labour ; the very bread of life can only be got out of the chaff of it by rubbing it in your hands. *Ruskin.*

No one claims kindred with the poor. *Pr.* 45

No one easily arrives at the conclusion that reason and a brave will are given us that we may not only hold back from evil, but also from the extreme of good. *Goethe.*

No one eats goldfish. *Pr.*

No one ever impoverished himself by almsgiving. *It. Pr.*

No one ever possessed superior intellectual qualities without knowing them. *Bulwer.*

No one ever teaches well who wants to teach, 50 or governs well who wants to govern. *Plato.*

No one falls low unless he attempt to climb high. *Dan. Pr.*

No one gets into trouble without his own help. *Dan. Pr.*

No one has ever learned fully to know himself. *Goethe.*

No one has ever yet succeeded in deceiving the whole world, nor has the world ever combined to deceive any individual. (?)

5 No one has seen to-morrow. *Port. Pr.*

No one is a slave whose will is free. *Tyrius Maximus.*

No one is by nature noble, respected of any one, nor a wretch. His own actions conduct him either to wretchedness or to the reverse. *Hitopadesa.*

No one is free who is not master of himself. *Claudius.*

No one is more profoundly sad than he who laughs too much. *Jean Paul.*

10 No one is qualified to converse in public who is not highly contented without such conversation. *Thomas à Kempis.*

No one is qualified to entertain, or receive entertainment from others, who cannot entertain himself alone with satisfaction. *Thomas à Kempis.*

No one is rich enough to do without his neighbour. *Dan. Pr.*

No one is so hardy as to say God is in his debt, that he owed him a nobler being, for existence must be antecedent to merit. *Jeremy Collier.*

No one knows how far his powers go till he has tried. *Goethe.*

15 No one knows the weight of another's burden. *Pr.*

No one knows what he is doing while he is acting rightly, but of what is wrong we are always conscious. *Goethe.*

No one knows when he is well off. *Punch.*

No one knows where the shoe pinches but him who wears it. *Pr.*

No one knows whether death, which men in their fear apprehend to be the greatest evil, may not be the greatest good. *Plato.*

20 No one likes to bell the cat. *Pr.*

No one shall look for effectual help to another; but each shall rest content with what help he can afford himself. *Carlyle.*

No one will become anything, every one will already be something. *Goethe.*

No one would respect thee in a beggar's coat. What is the respect paid to woollen cloth, not to thee? *Jean Paul.*

No one could talk much in society if he only knew how often he misunderstands others. *Goethe.*

25 No orator can measure in effect with him who can give good nicknames. *Emerson.*

No order or profession of men is so sacred, no place so remote or solitary, but that temptations and troubles will find them out and intrude upon them. *Thomas à Kempis.*

No outward tyranny can reach the mind. *Junius.*

No padlocks, bolts, or bars can secure a maiden so well as her own reserve. *Cervantes.*

No pain, no palm; no thorns, no throne; no gall, no glory; no cross, no crown. *William Penn.*

No pains, no gains. *Pr.*   30

No passions are without their use, none without their nobleness, when seen in balanced unity with the rest of the spirit which they are charged to defend. *Ruskin.*

No patient will ever recover his health merely from the description of a medicine. *Hitopadesa.*

No pay is receivable by any true man; but power is receivable by him in the love and faith you give him. *Ruskin.*

No peace was ever won from fate by subterfuge or agreement; no peace is ever in store for any of us but that which we shall win by victory over shame or sin—victory over the sin that oppresses, as well as over that which corrupts. *Ruskin.*

No penny, no paternoster. *Pr.*   35

No people at the present day can be explained by their national religion. They do not feel responsible for it; it lies far outside of them. *Emerson.*

No person is either so happy or so unhappy as he imagines. *La Roche.*

No pillow so soft as God's promise. *Saying.*

No pin's point can you mark within the wide circle of the All where God's laws are not. *Carlyle.*

No place, no company, no age, no person is 40 temptation-free; let no man boast that he was never tempted; let him not be highminded, but fear, for he may be surprised in that very instant wherein he boasteth that he was never tempted at all. *Spencer.*

No power of genius has ever yet had the smallest success in explaining existence. *Emerson.*

No power of good can be obtained by doing nothing and by knowing nothing. *Johnson.*

No prayer, no religion, or at least only a dumb and lame one. *Carlyle.*

No principle is more noble, as there is none more holy, than that of a true obedience. *Henry Giles.*

No productiveness of the highest kind, no re- 45 markable discovery, no great thought which bears fruit and has results, is in the power of any one; such things are exalted above all earthly control. Man must consider them as an unexpected gift from above, as pure children of God, which he must receive and venerate with joyful thanks, . . . as a vessel found worthy for the reception of such divine influence. *Goethe.*

No profit canst thou gain / By self-consuming care. *Wesley.*

No profit grows where is no pleasure ta'en: / In brief, sir, study what you most affect. *Tam. the Shrew,* i. 1.

No property is eternal but God the Maker's: Whom Heaven permits to take possession, his is the right; Heaven's sanction is such permission—while it lasts. *Carlyle.*

No real happiness is found / In trailing purple o'er the ground. *Parnell.*

No really great man ever thought himself so. 50 *Hazlitt.*

No receiver, no thief. *Pr.*

No reckoning made, but sent to my account / With all my imperfections on my head. *Ham.,* i. 5.

No reports are more readily believed than those which disparage genius and soothe envy of conscious mediocrity. *Macaulay.*

No rest is worth anything except the rest that is earned. *Jean Paul.*

No revenge is more heroic than that which torments envy by doing good. (?)

No road is long with good company. *Turk. Pr.*

5 No sadder proof can be given by man of his own littleness than disbelief in great men. *Carlyle.*

No safe wading in an unknown water. *Pr.*

No sensible person ever made an apology. *Emerson.*

No si puo volar senza ale—He would fain fly, but he wants wings. *It. Pr.*

No single action creates, however it may exhibit, a man's character. *Jeremy Taylor.*

10 No slave, to lazy ease resign'd, / E'er triumphed over noble foes; / The monarch, Fortune, most is kind / To him who bravely dares oppose. *Cervantes.*

No slave's vote is other than a nuisance, whensoever, or wheresoever, or in what manner soever, it is given. *Carlyle.*

No smaller spirit can vanquish a greater. *Goethe.*

No smoke, in any sense, but can become flame and radiance. *Carlyle.*

No society can be upheld in happiness and honour without the sentiment of religion. *Laplace.*

15 No sooner is a temple built to God, but the devil builds a chapel close by. *George Herbert.*

No soul to strong endeavour yoked for ever, / Works against the tide in vain. *H. Kendall.*

No sound is dissonant which tells of life. *Coleridge.*

No speculation in those eyes / Which thou dost glare with ! *Macb.,* iii. 4.

No statesman e'er will find it worth his pains / To tax our labours and excise our brains. *Churchill.*

20 No stronger castle than a poor man's. *Serv. Pr.*

No surer does the Auldgarth bridge, that his father helped to build, carry the traveller over the turbulent water beneath it, than Carlyle's books convey the reader over chasms and confusions, where before there was no way, or only an inadequate one. *John Burroughs.*

No sword bites so fiercely as an evil tongue. *Sir P. Sydney.*

No tale so good but may be spoiled in the telling. *Pr.*

No teaching is spiritually profitable, that is of true vital avail, translateable into flesh and blood, unless with the teaching we imbibe the spirit that dictates it. *Ed.*

25 No theatre for virtue is equal to the consciousness of it. *Cic.*

No theological absurdities so glaring that they have not sometimes been embraced by men of the greatest and most cultivated understanding. No religious precepts so rigorous that they have not been adopted by the most voluptuous and most abandoned of men. *Hume.*

No thoroughly occupied man was ever yet very miserable. *Landor.*

No thought is beautiful which is not just, and no thought can be just which is not founded on truth. *Addison.*

No thought is contented. The better sort, / As thoughts of things divine, are intermixed / With scruples, and do set the word itself / Against the word. *Rich. II.,* v. 5.

No trial is dangerous which there is courage 30 to meet. *Goethe.*

No trouble, cross, or death / E'er shall silence faith and praise. *Winkworth.*

No truly great man ever founded, wilfully intended founding, a sect. *Carlyle.*

No two on earth in all things can agree; / All have some darling singularity. *Churchill.*

No two virtues, whatever relation they claim, / Nor even two different shades of the same, / Though like as was ever twin-brother to brother, / Possessing the one shall imply you've the other. *Burns.*

No useless coffin enclosed his breast, / Not in 35 sheet nor in shroud we wound him; / But he lay like a warrior taking his rest, / With his martial cloak around him. *Rev. C. Wolfe.*

No vice goes alone. *Pr.*

No victory worth having was ever won without cost. *Ruskin.*

No violent extreme endures. *Carlyle.*

No visor does become black villany / So well as soft and tender flattery. *Pericles,* iv. 4.

No weather's ill when the wind's still. *Pr.*   40

No weeping for shed milk. *Pr.*

No whip cuts so sharply as the lash of conscience. *Pr.*

No wild beast more to be dreaded than a communicative man having nothing to communicate. *Swift.*

No wild enthusiast ever yet could rest / Till half mankind were like himself possess'd. *Cowper.*

No wind is of service to him who is bound for 45 nowhere. *Fr. Pr.*

No wise combatant underrates his antagonist. *Goethe.*

No wise man can have a contempt for the prejudices of others; and he should even stand in a certain awe of his own, as if they were aged parents and monitors. They may in the end prove wiser than he. *Hazlitt.*

No wise man ever wished to be younger. (?)

No wise man should make known the loss of fortune, any malpractices in his house, his being cheated, or his having been disgraced. *Hitopadesa.*

No woman can be handsome by the force of 50 features alone, any more than she can be witty only by the help of speech. *Hughes.*

No woman is educated who is not equal to the successful management of a family. *Burnap.*

No woman is so bad but we may rejoice when her heart thrills to love, for then God has her by the hand. *J. M. Barrie.*

No woman shall succeed in Salique land. *Hen. V.,* i. 2.

No wonder is greater than any other wonder, and if once explained, it ceases to be a wonder. *Leigh Hunt.*

No wonder lasts over three days. *Pr.*   55

No wonder we are all more or less pleased with mediocrity, since it leaves us at rest, and gives the same comfortable feeling as when one associates with his equals. *Goethe.*

No word is ill spoken if it be not ill taken. *Pr.*

No words suffice the secret soul to show, / For truth denies all eloquence to woe. *Byron.*

No work, no recompense. *Pr.*

5 No working world, any more than a fighting world, can be led on without a noble chivalry of work, and laws and fixed rules which follow out of that—far nobler than any chivalry of fighting war. *Carlyle.*

No worth, known or unknown, can die even on this earth. *Carlyle.*

Nobilitatis virtus non stemma character—Virtue, not pedigree, should characterise nobility. *M.*

Nobility is a river that sets with a constant and undeviating current directly into the great Pacific Ocean of Time ; but, unlike all other rivers, it is more grand at its source than at its termination. *Colton.*

Nobility of nature consists in doing good for the good's sake. *Wm. v. Humboldt.*

10 Nobility without virtue is a fine setting without a gem. *Jane Porter.*

Nobis non licet esse tam disertis, / Qui Musas colimus severiores — We who cultivate the graver Muse are not allowed to be diffuse. *Mart.*

Noble art is nothing less than the expression of a great soul ; and great souls are not common things. *Ruskin.*

Noble housekeepers need no doors. *Pr.*

Noble spirits war not with the dead. *Byron.*

15 Nobler is a limited command, / Given by the love of all your native land, / Than a sucessive title, long and dark, / Drawn from the mouldy rolls of Noah's ark. *Dryden.*

Noblesse oblige—Rank imposes obligation. *M.*

Nobody calls himself rogue. *Pr.*

Nobody can continue easy in his own mind who does not endeavour to become least of all and servant of all. *Thomas à Kempis.*

Nobody can find work easy if much work do lie in him. *Carlyle.*

20 Nobody can live by teaching any more than by learning ; both teaching and learning are proper duties of human life, or pleasures of it, but have nothing whatever to do with the support of it. *Ruskin.*

Nobody contents himself with rough diamonds, or wears them so. When polished and set, then they give a lustre. *Locke.*

Nobody has a right to have opinions, but only knowledge. *Ruskin.*

Nobody knows who may be listening ; say nothing which you would not wish put in the daily paper. *Spurgeon.*

Nobody should be rich but those who understand it. *Goethe.*

25 Nobody will persist long in helping those who will not help themselves. *Johnson.*

Nobody will use other people's experience, nor has any of his own till it is too late to use it. *Hawthorne.*

Nobody would be afraid if he could help it. *Smollett.*

Noces de Gamache—A very sumptuous repast. *Fr.*

Nocet empta dolore voluptas—Pleasure purchased by pain is injurious. *Hor.*

Noch ist es Tag, da rühre sich der Mann, / 30 Die Nacht tritt ein, wo niemand wirken kann—It is still day, in which to be up and doing ; the night is setting in wherein no man can work. *Goethe.*

Noch lebt ein Gott, der meines Elends denkt !—A God still lives who thinks of my misery. *Chamisso.*

Noch niemand entfloh dem verhängten Geschick—No one has yet evaded the fate allotted to him. *Schiller.*

Noctemque diemque fatigat—He wears out both night and day at his work. *Virg.*

Nocturna versate manu, versate diurna—Let these be your studies by night and by day.

Nodum in scirpo quæris—You look for a knot in 35 a bulrush, *i.e.*, are too scrupulous. *Pr.*

Noisome weeds that without profit suck / The soil's fertility from wholesome flowers. *Rich. II.*, iii. 4.

Nolens volens—Whether one will or no.

Noli irritare leones—Don't irritate lions. *M.*

Noli me tangere—Touch me not.

Nolle prosequi—To be unwilling to prosecute. *L.* 40

Nolo barbam vellere mortuo leoni—I won't pluck the beard of a dead lion. *Mart.*

Nolo episcopari—I have no wish to be made a bishop. *Applied to an affected indifference to obtaining what one really desires.*

Nom de guerre—An assumed name. *Fr.*

Nom de plume—Assumed name of an author. *Fr.*

Nomen amicitia est ; nomen inane fides—Friend- 45 ship is but a name ; fidelity but an empty name. *Ovid.*

Nomen atque omen—A name and at the same time an omen. *Plaut.*

Νομίζ᾽ ἀδελφοὺς τοὺς ἀληθινοὺς φίλους—Count true friends as brothers.

Non adeo cecidi, quamvis abjectus, ut infra / Te quoque sim ; inferius quo nihil esse potest—Though cast off, I have not fallen so low as to be beneath thee, than which nothing can be lower. *Ovid.*

Non ætate verum ingenio adipiscitur sapientia—Wisdom is not attained with years, but by ability. *Plaut.*

Non agitur de vectigalibus, non de sociorum 50 injuriis ; libertas et anima nostra in dubio est—It is not a question of our revenues, nor of the wrongs of our allies ; our liberty and very lives are in peril. *Cic. in Sall.*

Non amo te, Sabidi, nec possum dicere quare ; / Hoc tantum possum dicere, non amo te—I do not love thee, Sabidius, nor can I say why ; this only I can say, I do not love thee. *Mart.*

Non Angli, sed angeli—Not Angles, but angels. *Gregory the Great, on seeing some captive British youths for sale in the slave-market at Rome.*

Non aqua, sed ruina—Not with water, but with ruin.

Non assumpsit—He did not assume. *L.*

Non bene conveniunt, nec in una sede moran- 55 tur / Majestas et amor—Majesty and love do not consort well together, nor do they dwell in the same place. *Ovid.*

Non bene imperat, nisi qui paruerit imperio—No one makes a good commander except he who has been trained to obey commands.

Non bene junctarum discordia semina rerum— The discordant seeds of things ill joined. *Ovid.*

Non c' è il peggior frutto di quello che non matura mai—There is no crop worse than fruit that never ripens. *It. Pr.*

Non ci è fumo senza fuoco—There is no smoke without fire. *It. Pr.*

Non compos mentis—Not sound in mind.

5 **Non constat**—This does not appear. *L.*

Non convivere, nec videre saltem, / Non audire licet; nec Urbe tota / Quisquam est tam prope, tam proculque nobis—I may not live with him, nor even see him or hear him; in all the city there is no one so near me and so far away. *Mart.*

Non credo tempori—I trust not to time. *M.*

Non cuicunque datum est habere nasum—Not every man is gifted with a nose, *i.e.*, has the power of keen discernment. *Mart.*

Non cuivis homini contingit adire Corinthum—It is not every man that can get to Corinth, *i.e.*, rise in the world. *Hor.*

10 **Non decipitur qui scit se decipi**—He is not deceived who is knowingly deceived. *L.*

Non deerat voluntas, sed facultas—Not the will, but the ability was wanting.

Non deficit alter—Another is not wanting. *Virg.*

Non destare il can che dorme—Do not wake a sleeping dog. *It. Pr.*

Non è in alcun luogo chi è per tutto—He is nowhere who is everywhere. *It. Pr.*

15 **Non è si tristo cane che non meni la coda**—No dog is so bad but he will wag his tail. *It. Pr.*

Non è uomo chi non sa dir di nò—He's no man who can't say "No." *It. Pr.*

Non è ver che sia la morte / Il peggior di tutti i mali ; / E un sollievo pei mortali / Che non stanchi di soffrir—Death is not, in fact, the worst of all evils ; when it comes, it is a relief to those who are worn out with suffering. *Metastasio.*

Non eadem est ætas, non mens—My age is no longer the same, nor my inclination. *Hor.*

Non eadem ratio est, sentire et demere morbos : / Sensus inest cunctis ; tollitur arte malum—To be sensible of disease and remove it is not the same thing. The sense of it exists in all ; by skill alone is disease removed. *Ovid.*

20 **Non ebur neque aureum / Mea renidet in domo lacunar**—In my dwelling no ivory gleams, nor fretted roof covered with gold. *Hor.*

Non ego avarum / Cum te veto fieri, vappam jubeo ac nebulonem—When I say, Be not a miser, I do not bid you become a worthless prodigal. *Hor.*

Non ego illam mihi dotem esse puto, quæ dos dicitur, / Sed pudicitiam, et pudorem, et sedatam cupidinem—I do not deem that a dowry which is called a dowry, but chastity, modesty, and subdued desire. *Plaut.*

Non ego mordaci distrinxi carmine quenquam ; Nec meus ullius crimina versus habet—I have not wounded any one with stinging satire, nor does my poetry contain a charge against any man. *Ovid.*

Non ego omnino lucrum omne esse utile homini existimo—I do not at all reckon that every kind of gain is serviceable to a man. *Plaut.*

25 **Non ego ventosæ venor suffragia plebis**—I do not hunt after the suffrages of the fickle multitude. *Hor.*

Non enim gazæ neque consularis / Summovet lictor miseros tumultus / Mentis et curas laqueata circum / Tecta volantes—For neither regal treasure, nor the consul's lictor, nor the cares that hover about fretted ceilings, can remove the unhappy tumults of the mind. *Hor.*

Non equidem invideo, miror magis—In sooth I feel no envy, I am surprised rather. *Virg.*

Non equidem studeo, bullatis ut mihi nugis / Pagina turgescat, dare pondus idonea fumo—I do not study to swell my page with pompous trifles, suited only to give weight to smoke. *Pers.*

Non erat his locus—This was out of place here. *Hor.*

Non esse cupidum pecunia est : non esse 30 **emacem vectigal est**—Not to be covetous is money : not to be extravagant is an estate. *Cic.*

Non est ad astra mollis a terris via—The road from the earth to the stars is not a soft one. *Sen.*

Non est bonum ludere cum Diis—It is not good to trifle with the gods. *Pr.*

Non est de pastu omnium quæstio, sed de lana—It is a matter not of feeding the sheep, but fleecing them (*lit.* of wool). *Pius II.*

Non est de sacco tanta farina tuo—So much meal cannot have come from your own sack. *Pr.*

Non est ejusdem et multa et opportuna dicere 35 —The same person will not both talk much and to the purpose. *Pr.*

Non est jocus esse malignum—There is no joking where there is spite. *Hor.*

Non est nostri ingenii—It is not within my range of ability. *Cic.*

Non est vivere, sed valere, vita—Not to live, but to be healthy is life. *Mart.*

Non exercitus, neque ~~thesauri,~~ præsidia regni sunt, verum amici—Neither armies nor treasures are the safeguards of a state, but friends. *Sall.*

Non fa buon mangiar cireggie con signori—It 40 is not good to eat cherries with great persons. *It. Pr.*

Non fumum ex fulgore, sed ex fumo dare lucem —Not to educe smoke from splendour, but light from smoke. *M.*

Non generant aquilæ columbas—Eagles do not beget doves. *M.*

Non giudicar la nave stando in terra—Don't judge of the ship from the shore. *It. Pr.*

Non hæc sine numine—These things are not without sanction of the Deity. *M.*

Non han speranza di morte—They have not 45 hope to die. *Dante.*

Non hoc ista sibi tempus spectacula poscit— The present moment is not one to indulge in spectacles of this kind. *Virg.*

Non hominis culpa, sed ista loci—It is not the fault of the man, but of the place. *Ovid.*

Non id quod magnum est pulchrum est, sed id quod pulchrum magnum—Not that which is great is noble (*lit.* beautiful), but that which is noble is great.

Non ignara mali miseris succurrere disco. See "*Haud ignara.*"

Non illa colo calathisve Minervæ / Femineas 50 **assueta manus**—Her woman's hands were not trained to the distaff or basket of (distaff-loving) Minerva. *Virg.*

Non immemor beneficii—Not unmindful of kindness. *M.*

Non in caro nidore voluptas / Summa, sed in teipso est, tu pulmentaria quære / Sudando —The pleasure (in eating) does not lie in the costly flavour, but in yourself. Seek the relish, therefore, from hard exercise. *Hor.*

Non intelligitur quando obrepit senectus—We do not perceive old age, seeing it creeps on apace. *Cic.*

Non intelligunt homines quam magnum vectigal sit parsimonia—Men do not understand what a great revenue economy is. *Cic.*

Non la philosophie, mais le philosophisme causera des maux à la France—Not the philosophy, but the philosophy of the philosophe will bring evils on France. *Voltaire in 1735.*

5 Non liquet—It is not clear. *L.*

Non magni pendis, quia contigit—You do not value it highly because it has been your lot. *Hor.*

Non me pudet fateri nescire quod nesciam—I am not ashamed to confess myself ignorant of what I do not know. *Cic.*

Non mihi sapit qui sermone, sed qui factis sapit—Not he who is wise in speech, but he who is wise in deeds is wise for me. *Greg. Agrigent.*

Non mihi si linguæ centum sint oraque centum, / Ferrea vox, omnes scelerum comprendere formas / Omnia pœnarum percurrere nomina possim—Not if I had a hundred tongues, a hundred mouths, and a voice of iron, could I retail all the types of wickedness, and run over all the names of penal woe. *Virg.*

10 Non missura cutem, nisi plena cruoris hirudo—A leech that will not leave the skin until it is gorged with blood. *Hor.*

Non multa, sed multum—Not many things, but much.

Non nobis, Domine—Not unto us, O Lord.

Non nobis solum nati sumus—We are born not for ourselves alone. *Cic.*

Non nostrum inter vos tantas componere lites —It is not for me to settle such a dispute. *Virg.*

15 Non obstante veredicto—The verdict notwithstanding. *L.*

Non olet—It has not a bad smell, *i.e.*, money. *Suetonius.*

Non omnes eadem mirantur amantque — All men do not admire and love the same objects. *Hor.*

Non omnia possumus omnes—We cannot all of us do everything. *Virg.*

Non omnibus dormio—Not for all do I sleep. *Cic.*

20 Non omnis error stultitia est dicendus—Not every error is to be called folly.

Non omnis moriar; multaque pars mei / Vitabit Libitinam—I shall not wholly die; and a great part of me shall escape the grave. *Hor.*

Non opus est magnis placido lectore poetis; / Quamlibet invitum difficilemque tenent—Great poets have no need of an indulgent reader; they hold captive every one however unwilling and hard to please he may be. *Ovid*

Non placet quem scurræ laudant, manipulares mussitant—I do not like the man whom the town gentry belaud, but of whom the people of his own class say nothing. *Plaut.*

Non posse bene geri rempublicam multorum imperiis—Under the command of many, a commonwealth cannot be well conducted. *Corn. Nep.*

Non possidentem multa vocaveris / Recte 25 beatum. Rectius occupat / Nomen beati, qui Deorum / Muneribus sapienter uti, / Duramque callet pauperiem pati, / Pejusque leto flagitium timet—You would not justly call him blessed who has great possessions; more justly does he claim the title who knows how to use wisely the gifts of the gods and to bear the hardships of poverty, and who fears disgrace worse than death. *Hor.*

Non possum ferre, Quirites, / Græcam urbem —I cannot, Romans, endure a Grecian city, *i.e.*, Greek or effeminate manners in stern old Rome. *Juv.*

Non potest severus esse in judicando, qui alios in se severos esse judices non vult—He cannot be strict in judging who does not wish others to be strict judges of himself. *Cic.*

Non progredi est regredi—Not to advance is to go back. *Pr.*

Non pronuba Juno, / Non Hymenæus adest, non illi Gratia lecto; / Eumenides stravere torum—No Juno, guardian of the marriage rites, no Hymenæus, no one of the Graces stood by that nuptial couch. *Ovid.*

Non purgat peccata qui negat—He who denies 30 his sins does not atone for them. *Pr.*

Non quam diu, sed quam bene vixeris refert—Not how long, but how well you have lived is the main thing. *Sen.*

Non qui soletur, non qui labentia tarde / Tempora narrando fallat, amicus adest—There is no friend near to console me, none to beguile the weary hours with his talk. *Ovid.*

Non ragioniam di lor; ma guarda, e passa—Talk not of them; one look, and then pass on. *Dante.*

Non revertar inultus—I will not return unavenged. *M.*

Non satis est pulchra esse poëmata; dulcia 35 sunto, / Et quocumque volent animum auditoris agunto—It is not enough that poems be beautiful; they must also be affecting and move at will the hearer's soul. *Hor.*

Non scholæ, sed vitæ discimus—We learn not at school, but in life. *Sen.*

Non scribit, cujus carmina nemo legit—That man does not write whose verses no man reads. *Mart.*

Non semper erit æstas—It will not always be summer. *Hesiod.*

Non semper erunt Saturnalia—The carnival will not last for ever.

Non sequitur—It does not follow; an unwar- 40 ranted inference.

Non si male nunc, et olim sic erit—If it is ill now, it will not also be so hereafter. *Hor.*

Non sibi sed patriæ—Not for himself, but for his country. *M.*

Non sine numine—Not without the Divine approval. *M.*

Non sum qualis eram—I am not what I once was. *Hor.*

Non tali auxilio, nec defensoribus istis / Tem- 45 pus eget—The times require other aid and other defenders than those you bring. *Virg.*

Non tu corpus eras sine pectore. Di tibi formam, / Di tibi divitias dederant, artemque fruendi—You were at no time ever a body without a soul. The gods have given you beauty, the gods have given you wealth, and the skill to enjoy it. *Horace to Tibullus.*

Non usitata, nec tenui ferar penna—I shall be borne on no common, no feeble, wing. *Hor.*

Non uti libet, sed uti licet, sic vivamus—We must live not as we like, but as we can. *Pr.*

Non v'è peggior ladro d'un cattivo libro—There is no robber worse than a bad book. *It. Pr.*

Non vixit male, qui natus moriensque fefellit—He has not lived ill whose birth and death has been unnoticed by the world. *Hor.*

5 Nonchalance—Coolness; indifference. *Fr.*

Nondum omnium dierum sol occidit—The sun of all days has not yet set. *Pr.*

None acts a friend by a deputy, or can be familiar by proxy. *South.*

None are all evil; quickening round his heart, / One softer feeling would not yet depart. *Byron.*

None are fair but who are kind. *Stanley.*

10 None are more unjust in their judgments of others than those who have a high opinion of themselves. *Spurgeon.*

None are rash when they are not seen by anybody. *Stanislaus.*

None are so desolate but something dear, / Dearer than self, possesses or possess'd / A thought, and claims the homage of a tear. *Byron.*

None are so fond of secrets as those who don't mean to keep them; such persons covet secrets as a spendthrift covets money—for the purpose of circulation. (?)

None are so hopelessly enslaved as those who falsely believe they are free. *Goethe.*

15 None are so seldom found alone, and are so soon tired of their own company, as those coxcombs who are on the best terms with themselves. *Colton.*

None are so well shod but they may slip. *Pr.*

None but a fool is always right. *Hare.*

None but a fool would measure his satisfaction by what the world thinks of it. *Goldsmith.*

None but a Goethe, at the sun of earthly happiness, can keep his Phœnix wings unsinged. *Carlyle.*

20 None but an author knows an author's cares, / Or Fancy's fondness for the child she bears. *Cowper.*

None but himself can be his parallel. *L. Theobald.*

None but men of strong passions are capable of rising to greatness. *Mirabeau.*

None but the brave deserve the fair. *Dryden.*

None can cure their harms by wailing them. *Rich. III.*, ii. 2.

25 None can pray well but he who lives well. *Pr.*

None ever saw the pillars of the firmament; yet it is supported. *Luther.*

None ever was a great poet that applied himself much to anything else. *Sir W. Temple.*

None is so deaf as he who will not hear. *Pr.*

None is so wasteful as the scraping dame; / She loseth three for one—her soul, rest, fame. *George Herbert.*

30 None is so wretched as the poor man who maintains the semblance of wealth. *Spurgeon.*

None lie that would not steal. *Gael. Pr.*

None more impatiently suffer injuries than those that are most forward in doing them. (?)

None of the affections have been noted to fascinate and bewitch but envy. *Bacon.*

None of those who own the land own the landscape; only he whose eye can integrate all the parts, that is, the poet. *Emerson.*

None of us can wrong the universe. *Emerson.* 35

None of you can tell where the shoe pinches me. *Plutarch.*

None shun the light but criminals and evil spirits. *Schiller.*

None so blind as they who will not see. *Pr.*

None so miserable as a man who wills everything and can do nothing. *Claudius.*

None so wise but the advice of others may, at 40 some time or other, be useful and necessary for him. *Thomas à Kempis.*

None think the great unhappy but the great. *Pr.*

None without hope e'er loved the brightest fair; / But love can hope where reason would despair. *Lyttelton.*

Nor are those empty-hearted whose low sound/ Reverbs no hollowness. *King Lear*, i. 1.

Nor by the wayside ruins let us mourn / Who have th' eternal towers for our appointed bourne. *Keble.*

Nor can either thy own resentment of misfor- 45 tunes within, or the violence of any calamity without, give thee sufficient grounds, from the terrible face thy present circumstances wear, to pronounce that all hope of escape and better days are past. *Thomas à Kempis.*

Nor deem the irrevocable past / As wholly wasted, wholly vain, / If, rising on its wrecks, at last / To something nobler we attain. *Longfellow.*

Nor e'en the tenderest heart, and next our own, / Knows half the reasons why we smile and sigh! *Keble.*

Nor e'er was to the bowers of bliss conveyed / A fairer spirit or more welcome shade. *T. Tickell.*

Nor Fame I slight, nor for her favours call; / She comes unlook'd for, if she comes at all. *Pope.*

Nor grieve to die when far from home; you'll 50 find / To Hades everywhere a favouring wind. *Anon.*

Nor is it possible to thought / A greater than itself to know. *Wm. Blake.*

Nor less I deem that there are powers / Which of themselves our minds impress; / That we can feel this mind of ours / In a wide passiveness. *Wordsworth.*

Nor love thy life, nor hate but what thou liv'st / Live well, how long or short permit to heaven. *Milton.*

Nor sequent centuries could hit / Orbit and sum of Shakespeare's wit. *Landor.*

Nor sink those stars in empty night; / They 55 hide themselves in heaven's own light. *Montgomery.*

Noris quam elegans formarum spectator fiem —You shall see how nice a judge of beauty I am. *Ter.*

Nos duo turba sumus—We two are a multitude (*lit.* a crowd). *Deucalion to Pyrrha after the deluge, in Ovid.*

Nos hæc novimus esse nihil—We know that these things are nothing—mere trifles. *Mart.*

Nos nostraque Deo — Both we and ours are God's. *M.*

Nos numerus sumus et fruges consumere nati We are a mere number (but ciphers), and born to consume the fruits of the earth. *Hor.*

Nos patriæ fines et dulcia linquimus arva—We leave the confines of our native country and our delightful plains. *Virg.*

Nos te, / Nos facimus, Fortuna, deam—It is we, O Fortune, we that make thee a goddess. *Juv.*

5 **Nosce tempus**—Know your time; make hay while the sun shines. *Pr.*

Noscenda est mensura sui spectandaque rebus/ In summis minimisque—A man should know his own measure, and have regard to it in the smallest matters as well as the greatest. *Juv.*

Noscitur a sociis—A man is known by the company he keeps; a word, by the context.

Nosse omnia hæc salus est adolescentulis—It is salutary for young men to know all these things. *Ter.*

Nosse volunt omnes, mercedem solvere nemo—All wish to know, but no one to pay the fee. *Juv.*

10 **Nostra nos sine comparatione delectant; nunquam erit felix quem torquebit felicior**—What we have pleases us if we do not compare it with what others have; he never will be happy to whom a happier is a torture. *Sen.*

Not a drum was heard, not a funeral note, / As his corse to the rampart we hurried : / Not a soldier discharged his farewell shot, / O'er the grave where our hero we buried. *Rev. C. Wolfe.*

Not a flower, not a flower sweet, / On my black coffin let there be strewn ; / Not a friend, not a friend greet / My poor corpse, where my bones shall be thrown ; / A thousand, thousand sighs to save, / Lay me (what you will) O where / Sad lover ne'er find my grave, / To weep there. (?)

Not a man, for being simply man, / Hath any honour, but honour for those honours / That are without him, as place, riches, favour, / Prizes of accident, as oft as merit. *Troil. and Cress.*, iii. 3.

Not a man of iron, but of live oak. *Garfield.*

15 **Not a Red Indian, hunting by Lake Winnipeg, can quarrel with his squaw, but the whole world must smart for it. Will not the price of beaver rise ?** *Carlyle.*

Not a single shaft can hit / Till the God of love sees fit. *Ryland.*

Not a vanity is given in vain. *Pope.*

Not all that heralds rake from coffin'd clay, / Nor florid prose, nor honeyed lines of rhyme, / Can blazon evil deeds or consecrate a crime. *Byron.*

Not all the water in the rough rude sea / Can wash the balm from an anointed king ; / The breath of worldly men cannot depose / The deputy elected by the Lord. *Rich. II.*, iii. 2.

20 **Not alone to know, but to act according to thy knowledge, is thy destination.** *Fichte.*

Not as a vulture, but a dove, / The Holy Ghost came from above. *Longfellow, after Fuller.*

Not body enough to cover his mind decently with ; his intellect is improperly exposed. *Sydney Smith.*

Not brute force, but only persuasion and faith is the king of this world. *Carlyle.*

Not by levity of floating, but by stubborn force of swimming, shalt thou make thy way. A grand "vis inertiæ" in thee, Mr. Bull. *Carlyle.*

Not by might, nor by power, but by my spirit, 25 saith the Lord. *Bible.*

Not by the law of force, but by the law of labour, has any man right to the possession of the land. *Ruskin.*

Not enjoyment, and not sorrow, / Is our destined end or way ; / But to act that each to-morrow / May find us farther than to-day. *Longfellow.*

Not every parish priest can wear Dr. Luther's shoes. *Pr.*

Not fame, but that which it merits, is what a man should esteem. *Schopenhauer.*

Not for fellowship in hatred, but in love am I 30 here. *Sophocles.*

Not he that commendeth himself is approved, but whom the Lord commendeth. *St. Paul.*

Not he who has many ideas, but he who has one conviction may become a great man. *Cötvös.*

Not heaven itself upon the past has power ; / But what has been, has been, and I have had my hour. *Dryden.*

Not in a man's having no business with men, but in having no unjust business with them, and in having all manner of true and just business, can either his or their blessedness be found possible, and this waste world become, for both parties, a home and peopled garden. *Carlyle.*

Not in nature, but in man is all the beauty 35 and the worth he sees. The world is very empty, and is indebted to this gilding, exalting soul for its pride. *Emerson.*

Not in pulling down, but in building up, does man find pure joy. *Goethe.*

Not in the achievement, but in the endurance, of the human soul, does it show its divine grandeur and its alliance with the infinite God. *Chapin.*

Not kings alone—the people too have their flatterers. *Mirabeau.*

Not less in God's sight is the end of the day than the beginning. *Gael. Pr.*

Not liberty, but duty, is the condition of exis- 40 tence. *George Eliot.*

Not lost, but gone before. *Sen.*

Not many words are needed to refuse ; by the refused the "no" alone is heard. *Goethe.*

Not marble, nor the gilded monuments of princes, shall outlive this powerful rhyme. *Cymbeline.* (?)

Not misgovernment, nor yet no government ; only government will now serve. *Carlyle.*

Not once or twice in our rough island-story, / 45 The path of duty was the way to glory : / He that walks it, only thirsting / For the right, and learns to deaden / Love of self, before his journey closes / He shall find the stubborn thistle bursting / Into glossy purples, which outredden / All voluptuous garden-roses. *Tennyson.*

Not one false man but does unaccountable mischief ; how much, in a generation or two, will twenty-seven millions, mostly false, manage to accumulate ? *Carlyle.*

Not one of our faculties that it is not a delight to exercise. *W. R. Greg.*

Not one of our senses that, in its healthy state, is not an avenue to enjoyment. *W. R. Greg.*

Not one word of any book is readable by you, except so far as your mind is one with its author's ; and not merely his words like your words, but his thoughts like your thoughts. *Ruskin.*

Not only all common speech, but science, poetry itself, is no other, if thou consider it, than right naming. *Carlyle.*

5 Not only has the unseen world a reality, but the only reality ; the rest being, not metaphorically, but literally and in scientific strictness, "a show." *Carlyle.*

Not our logical, mensurative faculty, but our imaginative one is king over us ; I might say, priest and prophet to lead us heavenward, or magician and wizard to lead us hellward. *Carlyle.*

Not so easily can a man tear up the roots of his old life, and transplant himself into a new soil and a foreign atmosphere. *Ed.*

Not that I loved Cæsar less, but that I loved Rome more. *Jul. Cæs.*, iii. 2.

Not the cry, but the flight of a wild duck, rouses the flock to fly and follow. *Chinese Pr.*

10 Not the glittering weapon fights the fight, but the hero's heart. *Serv. Pr.*

Not the maker of plans and promises, but rather he who offers faithful service in small matters is most welcome to one who would achieve what is good and lasting. *Goethe.*

Not this man and that man, but all men make up mankind, and their united tasks the task of mankind. *Carlyle.*

Not to attempt a gallant deed for which one has the impulse may be braver than the doing of it. *J. M. Barrie.*

Not to believe in God, but to acknowledge Him when and wheresoever He reveals Himself, is the one sole blessedness of man on earth. *Goethe.*

15 Not to desire or admire, if a man could learn it, were more / Than to walk all day like the sultan of old in a garden of spice. *Tennyson.*

Not to know me argues yourselves unknown. *Milton.*

Not to know what has been transacted in former times is to continue always a child. *Cic.*

Not to return one good office for another is inhuman ; but to return evil for good is diabolical. *Sen.*

Not to see the wood for the trees, *i.e.*, the whole for the details. *Ger. Pr.*

20 Not to speak your opinion well, but to have a good and just opinion worth speaking ; for every Parliament, as for every man, this latter is the point. *Carlyle.*

Not to talk of thy doing, and become the envy of surrounding flunkeys, but to taste of the fruit of thy doings themselves, is thine. *Carlyle.*

Not towards the impossibility, self-government of a multitude by a multitude ; but towards some possibility, government by the wisest, does bewildered Europe now struggle. *Carlyle.*

Not what I Have, but what I Do is my Kingdom. *Carlyle.*

Not what the man knows, but what he wills, determines his worth or unworth, his strength or weakness, his happiness or misery. *Lindner.*

Not what we wish, but what we want, / Oh, 25 let thy grace supply. *Merrick.*

Not when I rise above, only when I rise to, something, do I approve myself. *Jacobi.*

Not where they dash ashore and break and moan are waters deadliest. *A. Mary F. Robinson.*

Not without a shudder may a human hand clutch into the mysterious urn of destiny. *Schiller.*

Nota bene—Note well.

Notandi sunt tibi mores—The manners of men 30 are to be carefully observed. *Hor.*

Note how the falcon starts at every sight, / New from his hood, but what a quiet eye / Cometh of freedom. *Sir Edwin Arnold.*

Noth bricht Eisen—Necessity breaks iron. *Ger. Pr.*

Noth kennt kein Gebot—Necessity knows no law. *Ger. Pr.*

Noth lehrt beten—Necessity teaches to pray. *Ger. Pr.*

Nothing altogether passes away without re- 35 sult. We are here to leave that behind us which will never die. *Goethe.*

Nothing amuses more harmlessly than computation, and nothing is oftener applicable to real business or speculative inquiries. A thousand stories which the ignorant tell and believe die away at once when the computist takes them in his grip. *Johnson.*

Nothing astonishes men so much as common sense and plain dealing. *Emerson.*

Nothing at bottom is interesting to the majority of men but themselves. *Schopenhauer.*

Nothing becomes him ill that he would well. *Love's L. Lost*, ii. 1.

Nothing but a handful of dust will fill the eye 40 of man. *Arab. Pr.*

Nothing but ourselves can finally beat us. *Carlyle.*

Nothing can atone for the want of modesty, without which beauty is ungraceful and wit detestable. *Steele.*

Nothing can be beautiful which is not true. *Ruskin.*

Nothing can be done at once hastily and prudently. *Publius Syrus.*

Nothing can be hostile to religion which is 45 agreeable to justice. *Gladstone.*

Nothing can be made of nothing ; he who has laid up no material can produce no combinations. *Sir J. Reynolds.*

Nothing can be more fatal in politics than a preponderance of the philosophical, or in philosophy than a preponderance of the political, spirit. *Lecky.*

Nothing can be preserved but what is good. *Emerson.*

Nothing can be so injurious to progress as to be altogether blamed or altogether praised. *Goethe.*

Nothing can be termed mine own but what I 50 make my own by using well. *Middleton.*

Nothing can bring you peace but yourself; nothing, but the triumph of principles. *Emerson.*

Nothing can come out of a sack that is not in it. *It. Pr.*

Nothing can ferment itself to clearness in a colander. *Carlyle.*

Nothing can need a lie ; / A fault, which needs it most, grows two thereby. *Herbert.*

5 Nothing can overtake an untruth if it has a minute's start. *J. M. Barrie.*

Nothing can work me damage except myself. *St. Bernard.*

Nothing comes amiss, so money comes withal. *Tam. of the Shrew,* i. 2.

Nothing comes amiss to a hungry man. *Pr.*

Nothing contributes so much to cheerfulness as health, or so little as riches. *Schopenhauer.*

10 Nothing costs less or is cheaper than compliments of civility. *Cervantes.*

Nothing deepens and intensifies family traits like poverty and toil and suffering. It is the furnace heat that brings out the characters, the pressure that makes the strata perfect. *John Burroughs.*

Nothing destroyeth authority so much as the unequal and untimely interchange of power pressed too far and relaxed too much. *Bacon.*

Nothing dies, nothing can die. No idlest word thou speakest but is a seed cast into time, and grows through all eternity. *Carlyle.*

Nothing does so much honour to a woman as her patience, and nothing does her so little as the patience of her husband. *Joubert.*

15 Nothing done by man in the past has any deeper sense than what he is doing now. *Emerson.*

Nothing doth so fool a man as extreme passion. *Bp. Hall.*

Nothing emboldens sin so much as mercy. *Timon of Athens,* iii. 5.

Nothing endears so much a friend as sorrow for his death. The pleasure of his company has not so powerful an influence. *Hume.*

Nothing exceeds in ridicule, no doubt, / A fool in fashion, save a fool that's out ; / His passion for absurdity's so strong, / He cannot bear a rival in the throng. *Young.*

20 Nothing exposes us more to madness than distinguishing ourselves from others, and nothing more contributes to maintain our common-sense than living in community of feeling with other people. *Goethe.*

Nothing extenuate, / Nor set down aught in malice ; then must you speak / Of one, that loved not wisely, but too well. . . . of one, whose hand / Like the base Indian, threw a pearl away, / Richer than all his tribe. *Othello,* v. 2.

Nothing for nothing. *Pr.*

Nothing for nothing, and very little for a halfpenny. *Pr.*

Nothing gives such a blow to friendship as the detecting another in an untruth. It strikes at the root of our confidence ever after. *Hazlitt.*

25 Nothing good bursts forth all at once. The lightning may dart out of a black cloud ; but the day sends his bright heralds before him to prepare the world for his coming. *Hare.*

Nothing great is lightly won, nothing won is lost ; / Every good deed nobly done will repay the cost. (?)

Nothing hath got so far / But man hath caught and kept it as his prey ; / His eyes dismount the highest star ; / He is in little all the sphere. *George Herbert.*

Nothing hitherto was ever stranded, cast aside ; but all, were it only a withered leaf, works together with all ; is borne forward on the bottomless, shoreless flood of action, and lives through perpetual metamorphoses. *Carlyle.*

Nothing in haste save catching fleas. *Dut. Pr.*

Nothing in his life / Became him like the 30 leaving it ; he died / As one that had been studied in his death / To throw away the dearest thing he owed, / As 'twere a careless trifle. *Macbeth,* i. 4.

Nothing in itself deformed or incongruous can give us any real satisfaction. *Cervantes.*

Nothing in love can be premeditated ; it is as a power divine, that thinks and feels within us, unswathed by our control. *Mme. de Staël.*

Nothing in Nature, much less conscious being, / Was e'er created solely for itself. *Young.*

Nothing in the dealings of Heaven with Earth is so wonderful to me as the way in which the evil angels are allowed to spot, pervert, and bring to nothing, or to worse, the powers of the greatest men : so that Greece must be ruined, for all that Plato can say ; Geneva, for all that Calvin can say ; England, for all that Sir Thomas More and Bacon can say ; and only Gounod's "Faust" to be the visible outcome to Europe of the school of Weimar. *Ruskin.*

Nothing in the world is more haughty than a 35 man of moderate capacity when once raised to power. *Baron Wessenberg.*

Nothing is a misery, / Unless our weakness apprehend it so ; / We cannot be more faithful to ourselves / In anything that's manly, than to make / Ill-fortune as contemptible to us / As it makes us to others. *Beaumont and Fletcher.*

Nothing is at last sacred but the integrity of your own mind. Absolve yourself to yourself, and you shall have the suffrage of the world. *Emerson.*

Nothing is but what is not. *Macb.,* i. 3.

Nothing is cheap if you don't want it. *Pr.*

Nothing is constant but a virtuous mind. 40 *Shirley.*

Nothing is denied to well-directed labour ; nothing is ever to be attained without it. *Sir J. Reynolds.*

Nothing is difficult ; it is only we who are indolent. *B. R. Haydon.*

Nothing is easier than to clear debts by borrowing. *Johnson.*

Nothing is endless but inanity. *Goethe.*

Nothing is fair or good alone. *Emerson.* 45

Nothing is farther than earth from heaven, and nothing is nearer than heaven to earth. *Hare.*

Nothing is given so ungrudgingly as advice. *La Roche.*

Nothing is good for a nation but that which arises from its core and its own general wants. *Goethe.*

Nothing is good I see without respect. *Mer. of Ven.*, v. 1

Nothing is good or bad, but thinking makes it so. *Ham.*, ii. 2.

Nothing is graceful that is not our own. *Collier.*

Nothing is high because it is in a high place, and nothing low because it is in a low one. *Dickens.*

5 Nothing is impossible to the man who can will. *Emerson.*

Nothing is insipid to the wise; / To thee insipid all but what is mad; / Joy season'd high and tasting strong of guilt. *Young.*

Nothing is lasting that is feigned. *Pr.*

Nothing is less in our power than the heart, and, far from commanding it, we are forced to obey it. *Rousseau.*

Nothing is law that is not reason. *Sir Powell.*

10 Nothing is more active than thought, for it flies over the universe; nothing stronger than necessity, for all must submit to it. *Thales.*

Nothing is more binding than the friendship of companions-in-arms. *G. S. Hillard.*

Nothing is more certain than that great poets are no sudden prodigies, but slow results. *Lowell.*

Nothing is more characteristic of a man than his behaviour towards fools. *Amiel.*

Nothing is more common than mutual dislike, where mutual approbation is particularly expected. *Johnson.*

15 Nothing is more common than to express exceeding zeal in amending our neighbours, ... while at the same time we neglect the beginning at home. *Thomas à Kempis.*

Nothing is more deeply punished than the neglect of the affinities by which alone society should be formed, and the insane levity of choosing associates by others' eyes. *Emerson.*

Nothing is more disgusting than the crowing about liberty by slaves. *Emerson.*

Nothing is more easy than to clear debts by borrowing. *Johnson.*

Nothing is more free than the imagination of man. *Hume.*

20 Nothing is more hurtful to a truth than an old error. *Goethe.*

Nothing is more natural than that we should grow giddy at a great sight which comes unexpectedly before us, to make us feel at once our littleness and our greatness. But there is not in the world any truer enjoyment than at the moment when we are thus made giddy for the first time. *Goethe.*

Nothing is more ruinous for a man than when he is mighty enough in any part to right himself without right. *Jacobi.*

Nothing is more significant of the philosophy of a man than the footing on which he stands with his body. The Cynic neglects it, the Sybarite makes profit out of it, the Trappist disowns it, and the Idealist forgets it. *Lindner.*

Nothing is more surprising than the easiness with which the many are governed by the few. *Hume.*

25 Nothing is more terrible than ignorance in action. *Goethe.*

Nothing is more unjust or capricious than public opinion. *Hazlitt.*

Nothing is more vulgar than haste. *Emerson.*

Nothing is more offensive to reason (*widerwärtiger*) than an appeal to the majority; it consists of a few powerful leaders, of rogues who accommodate themselves, of weaklings who assimilate themselves, and of the mass who follow confusedly, without in the least knowing what they would be at. *Goethe.*

Nothing is new; we walk where others went; / There's no vice now but has its precedent. *Herrick.*

Nothing is of any value in books excepting the 30 transcendental and extraordinary. *Emerson.*

Nothing is old but the mind. *Emerson.*

Nothing is perfect until, in some way, it touches or passes through man. *T. T. Munger.*

Nothing is permanently helpful to any race or condition of men but the spirit that is in their own hearts, kindled by the love of their native land. *Ruskin.*

Nothing is pleasant that is not spiced with variety. *Bacon.*

Nothing is poetry which does not transport; 35 the lyre is a winged instrument. *Joubert.*

Nothing is profane that serveth to holy things. *Raleigh.*

Nothing is quite beautiful alone; nothing but is beautiful in the whole. *Emerson.*

Nothing is rarer than the use of a word in its exact meaning. *Whipple.*

Nothing is safe from fault-finders. *Pr.*

Nothing is secret that shall not be made 40 manifest; neither anything hid that shall not be known. *Jesus.*

Nothing is so atrocious as fancy without taste. *Goethe.*

Nothing is so beautiful to the eye as truth is to the mind; nothing so deformed and irreconcilable to the understanding as a lie. *Locke.*

Nothing is so perfectly amusement as a total change of ideas. *Sterne.*

Nothing is so conceivable (*begreiflich*) to the child, nothing seems to be so natural to him, as the marvellous or supernatural. *Zachariä.*

Nothing is so dangerous as an ignorant friend. 45 *La Fontaine.*

Nothing is so difficult as to help a friend in matters which do not require the aid of friendship, but only a cheap and trivial service, if your friendship wants the basis of a thorough practical acquaintance. *Thoreau.*

Nothing is so envied as genius, nothing so hopeless of attainment by labour alone. Though labour always accompanies the greatest genius, without the intellectual gift labour alone will do little. *Haydon.*

Nothing is so grand as truth, nothing so forcible, nothing so novel. *Landor.*

Nothing is so great an instance of ill-manners as flattery. If you flatter all the company, you please none; if you flatter only one or two, you affront the rest. *Swift.*

Nothing is so narrowing, contracting, harden- 50 ing, as always to be moving in the same groove, with no thought beyond what we immediately see and hear close around us. *Dean Stanley.*

Nothing is so new as what has been long forgotten. *Ger. Pr.*

Nothing is so uncertain as the minds of the multitude. *Leis.*

Nothing is superficial to a deep observer. It is in trifles that the mind betrays itself. *Bulwer Lytton.*

Nothing is there to come, and nothing past, / But an eternal now does always last. *Cowley.*

5 Nothing is thoroughly approved but mediocrity. The majority has established this, and it fixes its fangs on whatever gets beyond it either way. *Pascal.*

Nothing is thought rare / Which is not new and followed; yet we know / That what was worn some twenty years ago / Comes into grace again. *Beaumont and Fletcher.*

Nothing is to be preferred before justice. *Socrates.*

Nothing is too high for a man to reach, but he must climb with care and confidence. *Hans Andersen.*

Nothing is true but what is simple. *Goethe.*

10 Nothing is truly elegant but what unites use with beauty. *Goldsmith.*

Nothing leads to good which is not natural. *Schiller.*

Nothing lovelier can be found / In woman than to study household good, / And good works in her husband to promote. *Milton.*

Nothing makes love sweeter and tenderer than a little previous scolding and freezing, just as the grape-clusters acquire by a frost before vintage thinner skins and better flavour. *Jean Paul.*

Nothing makes the earth seem so spacious as to have friends at a distance ; they make the latitudes and longitudes. *Thoreau.*

15 Nothing marks the character of a young man more than a failure. *Anon.*

Nothing more readily pleases a vulgar mind than to find anomalies in conduct or character. *Alex. Whitelaw.*

Nothing noble or godlike in the world but has in it something of "infinite sadness." *Carlyle.*

Nothing not a reality yet got men to pay bed and board to it for long. *Carlyle.*

Nothing on earth is without difficulty. Only the inner impulse, the pleasure it gives and love enable us to surmount obstacles ; to make smooth our way, and lift ourselves out of the narrow grooves in which other people sorrowfully distress themselves. *Goethe.*

20 Nothing on earth is without significance, but the first and most essential in every matter is the place where and the hour when. *Schiller.*

Nothing, or almost nothing, is certain to me, except the Divine Infernal character of this universe I live in, worthy of horror, worthy of worship. *Carlyle.*

Nothing pleaseth but rare accidents. 1 *Hen. IV.,* i. 2.

Nothing preaches better than the ant, and she says nothing. *Ben. Franklin.*

Nothing precludes sympathy so much as a perfect indifference to it. *Haslitt.*

25 Nothing really pleasant or unpleasant subsists by nature, but all things become so by habit. *Epictetus.*

Nothing recommends a man more to the female mind than courage. *Spectator.*

Nothing remains to man, nothing is possible to him of true joy, but in the righteous love of his fellows, in the knowledge of the laws and the glory of God, and in the daily use of the faculties of soul and body with which God has endowed him. *Ruskin.*

Nothing resembles pride so much as discouragement. *Amiel.*

Nothing right can be accomplished in art without enthusiasm. *Schumann.*

Nothing seems important to me but so far as 30 it is connected with morals. *Cecil.*

Nothing so difficult as a beginning / In poesy, except perhaps the end ; / For oftentimes when Pegasus seems winning / The race, he sprains a wing, and down we tend, / Like Lucifer, when hurl'd from heaven for sinning. *Byron.*

Nothing so effectively disconcerts the schemes of sinister people as the tranquillity of great souls. *Mirabeau.*

Nothing so endures as a truly spoken word. *Carlyle.*

Nothing so lifts a man from all his mean imprisonments, were it but for moments, as true admiration. *Carlyle.*

Nothing so much contents us as that which 35 confounds us. *Goldsmith.*

Nothing so much prevents our being natural as the desire of appearing so. *La Roche.*

Nothing stands in need of lying but a lie. *Pr.*

Nothing stings so bitterly as loss of money. *Pr.*

Nothing succeeds like success. *Talleyrand.*

Nothing that has ever lived is lost ; nothing is 40 useless ; not a sigh, a joy, or a sorrow which has not served its purpose. *Mme. Gasparin.*

Nothing that is violent is permanent. *Pr.*

Nothing that lives is or can be rigidly perfect ; part of it is decaying, part nascent. The foxglove blossom—a third part bud, a third part past, a third part in full bloom—is a type of the life of this world. *Ruskin.*

Nothing truly can be made mine own but what I make mine own by using well. *Middleton.*

Nothing venture, nothing win. *Pr.*

Nothing weighs lighter than a promise. *Ger. Pr.* 45

Nothing which is unjust can hope to continue in this world. *Carlyle.*

Nothing will be mended by complaints. *Johnson.*

Nothing's more dull and negligent / Than an old lazy government, / That knows no interest of state, / But such as serves a present strait, / And, to patch up or shift, will close, / Or break alike, with friends or foes. *Butler.*

Notre défiance justifie la tromperie d'autrui—Our distrust justifies the deceit of others. *La Roche.*

Notre vie est du vent tissu—Our life is a web 50 woven of wind. (?)

Notwithstanding this great proximity of man to himself, we still remain ignorant of many things concerning ourselves. *Hale.*

Nought can be gained by a Sabbath profaned. *Saying.*

Nought else there is / But that weird beat of Time, which doth disjoin / To-day from Hellas. *Lewis Morris.*

Nought is so vile that on the earth doth live, / But to the earth some special good doth give ; / Nor aught so good, but. strain'd from that fair use, / Revolts from true birth, stumbling on abuse. *Rom. and Jul.,* ii. 3.

Nought so stockish, hard, and full of rage, / But music for the time doth change its nature. *Mer. of Venice,* v. 1.

Nought treads so silent as the foot of time. *Young.*

Nourri dans le sérail, j'en connais les détours —Brought up in the seraglio, I know all its sinuosities. *Racine.*

5 Nous avons changé tout cela—We have changed all that. *Molière.*

Nous avons tous assez de force pour supporter les maux d'autrui—We all have strength enough to bear the misfortunes of others. *La Roche.*

Nous dansons sur un volcan—We are dancing on a volcano. *M. de Salvandy, just prior to the July Revolution of* 1830.

Nous désirerions peu de choses avec ardeur, si nous connaissions parfaitement ce que nous désirons—We should desire few things with eagerness if we well knew the worth of what we are striving for. *La Roche.*

Nous maintiendrons—We will maintain. *M.*

10 Nous n'écoutons d'instincts que ceux qui sont les nôtres, / Et ne croyons le mal que quand il est venu—We listen to no instincts but such as are our own, and we believe in no misfortune till it comes. *La Fontaine.*

Nous ne savons ce que c'est que le bonheur ou le malheur absolu—We do not know what absolute good or evil is. *Rousseau.*

Nous ne sommes hommes, et nous tenons les uns aux autres, que par la parole—We are men, and associate together, solely in virtue of speech. (?)

Nous ne trouvons guère de gens de bon sens que ceux qui sont de notre avis—We seldom find any persons of good sense except those who are of our opinion *La Roche.*

Nous ne vivons jamais, mais nous esperons de vivre—We never live, but we hope to live. *Pascal.*

15 Nous sommes assemblés par la volonté nationale, nous ne sortirons que par la force—We are here by the will of the people, and nothing but the force of bayonets shall send us hence. *Mirabeau to the Marquis de Brésé.*

Nous sommes mieux seul qu'avec un sot—One had better be alone than with a fool. *Fr. Pr.*

Nous verrons, dit l'aveugle—We shall see, as the blind man said. *Fr.*

Novacula in cotem—He has met his match (*lit.* the razor against the whetstone). *Pr.*

Novels are tales of adventures which did not occur in God's creation, but only in the waste chambers (to be let unfurnished) of certain human heads, and which are part and parcel only of the sum of nothings; which, nevertheless, obtain some temporary remembrance, and lodge extensively at this epoch of the world in similar, still more unfurnished, chambers. *Carlyle.*

20 Novels are the journal or record of manners ; and the new importance of these books derives from the fact that the novelist begins to penetrate the surface, and treat this part of life more worthily. *Emerson.*

Novels for most part instil into young minds false views of life. *Schopenhauer.*

Novelty has something in it that inebriates the fancy, and not unfrequently dissipates and fumes away like other intoxication, and leaves the poor patient, as usual, with an aching heart. *Burns.*

Novelty is only in request ; and it is as dangerous to be aged in any kind of course, as it is virtuous to be constant in any undertaking. *Meas. for Meas.,* iii. 2.

Novi ego hoc sæculum, moribus quibus siet—I know this age, what its character is. *Plaut.*

Novi ingenium mulierum, / Nolunt ubi velis, 25 ubi nolis cupiunt ultro—I know the nature of women : when you will, they won't ; when you won't, they will. *Ter.*

Novos amicos dum paras, veteres cole—While you seek new friendships, take care to cultivate the old.

Novum et ad hunc diem non auditum — New, and unheard of till this day. *Cic.*

Novus homo—A new man ; a man risen from obscurity.

Now an incredible deal is demanded, and every avenue is barred. *Goethe.*

Now farewell light, thou sunshine bright, / 30 And all beneath the sky ! / May coward shame distain his name, / The wretch that dares not die. *Burns, in* " *Macpherson's Lament.*'

Now, good digestion wait on appetite, / And health on both. *Macb.,* iii. 4.

Now is now, and Yule's in winter. *Sc. Pr.*

" Now " is the watchword of the wise. *Pr.*

Now ! it is gone. Our brief hours travel post, / Each with its thought or deed, its Why or How ; / But know, each parting hour gives up a ghost / To dwell within thee—an eternal Now ! *Coleridge.*

Now join your hands, and with your hands 35 your hearts, / That no dissension hinder government. *3 Hen. VI.,* iv. 6.

Now morn her rosy steps in th' eastern clime, / Advancing, sowed the earth with orient pearl. *Milton.*

Now our fates from unmomentous things / May rise like rivers out of little springs. *Campbell.*

Now see that noble and most sovereign reason, / Like sweet bells jangled, out of tune, and harsh ; / That unmatch'd form and feature of blown youth / Blasted with ecstacy : O, woe is me, / To have seen what I have seen, what what I see. *Ham.,* iii. 2.

Now the heart is so full that a drop overfills it ; / We are happy now, because God wills it. *Lowell.*

Now 'tis the spring, and weeds are shallow-40 rooted ; / Suffer them now, and they'll o'ergrow the garden, / And choke the herbs for want of husbandry. *2 Hen. VI.,* iii. 1.

Now you have feathered your nest. *Congreve.*

Nowadays compromise and indifference rule supreme, and instead of solid grit we have putty or wax. *Spurgeon.*

Nowadays truth is news. *Sc. Pr.*

Nowhere can a man get real root-room, and spread out his branches till they touch the morning and the evening, but in his own house. *Ward Beecher.*

Nox atra cava circumvolat—Black night envelopes them with her hollow shade. *Virg.*

Noxiæ pœna par esto—Let the punishment be proportionate to the offence. *Cic.*

Nuda veritas—Undisguised truth. *Hor.*

Nudum pactum—A mere agreement. *L.*

5 Nugæ canoræ—Melodious trifles; agreeable nonsense. *Hor.*

Nugis addere pondus—To add weight to trifles. *Hor.*

Nul n'aura de l'esprit, / Hors nous et nos amis—No one shall have wit except ourselves and our friends. *Molière.*

Nul n'est content de sa fortune, ni mécontent de son esprit—No one is content with his lot or discontented with his wit. *Mme. Deshoulières.*

Nulla ætas ad perdiscendum est—There is no time of life past learning something. *St. Ambrose.*

10 Nulla dies sine linea—Let no day pass without its line. *Pr.*

Nulla falsa doctrina est, quæ non permisceat aliquid veritatis—There is no false doctrine which contains not a mixture of truth.

Nulla fere causa est, in qua non fœmina litem moverit—There's hardly a strife in which a woman has not been a prime mover. *Juv.*

Nulla fides regni sociis, omnisque potestas / Impatiens consortis erit—There is no faith among colleagues in power, and all power will be impatient of a colleague. *Lucan*

Nulla pallescere culpa—Not to grow pale at imputation of guilt. *M.*

15 Nulla placere diu, vel vivere carmina possunt / Quæ scribuntur aquæ potoribus—No poems written by water-drinkers can be long popular or live long. *Hor.*

Nulla res tantum ad discendum profuit quantum scriptio—Nothing so much assists learning, as writing down what we wish to remember.

Nulla unquam de vita hominis cunctatio longa est—No delay is too long when the life of a man is at stake. *Juv.*

Nulli jactantius mœrent, quam qui maxime lætantur—None mourn so demonstratively as those who are in reality rejoicing most. *Tac.*

Nulli secundus—Second to none.

20 Nulli te facias nimis sodalem, / Gaudebis minus et minus dolebis—Be on too intimate terms with no one; if your joy be less, so will your grief. *Mart.*

Nullius addictus jurare in verba magistri, / Quo me cunque rapit tempestas, deferor hospes—Bound to swear by the opinions of no master, I present myself a guest wherever the storm drives me. *Hor.*

Nullius boni sine socio jucunda possessio—Without a friend to share it, no good we possess is truly enjoyable. *Sen.*

Nullius in verba—At no man's dictation. *M.*

Nullum est jam dictum quod non dictum sit prius—Nothing is said now that has not been said before. *Ter.*

25 Nullum est malum majus, quam non posse ferre malum—There is no greater misfortune than not to be able to endure misfortune.

Nullum est sine nomine saxum—Not a stone but has a tale to tell. *Lucan.*

Nullum magnum ingenium sine mixtura dementiæ fuit—No great genius is ever without some tincture of madness. *Sen.*

Nullum magnum malum quod extremum est—No evil is great which is the last. *Corn. Nep.*

Nullum numen abest si sit prudentia—Where there is prudence, a protecting divinity is not far away. *Pr.*

Nullum numen habes si sit prudentia; nos te / 30 Nos facimus, Fortuna, deam cœloque locamus—Thou hast no divine power, O Fortune, where there is prudence; it is we who make a goddess of thee, and place thee in heaven. *Juv.*

Nullum quod tetigit non ornavit—There was nothing he touched that he did not adorn. *Epitaph by Johnson on Goldsmith.*

Nullum simile quatuor pedibus currit—No simile runs on all fours, *i.e.,* holds in every respect. *Pr.*

Nullum tempus occurrit regi—No lapse of time bars the rights of the crown. *L.*

Nullus argento color est, / Nisi temperato / Splendeat usu—Money has no splendour of its own, unless it shines by temperate use. *Hor.*

Nullus commodum capere potest de injuria sua 35 propria—No one can take advantage of wrong committed by himself. *L.*

Nullus dolor est quem non longinquitas temporis minuat ac molliat—There is no sorrow which length of time will not diminish and soothe. *Cic.*

Nullus est liber tam malus, ut non aliqua parte prosit—There is no book so bad that it may not be useful in some way or other. *Pliny.*

Numbers err in this: / Ten censure wrong for one who writes amiss. *Pope.*

Numerical inquiries will give you entertainment in solitude by the practice, and reputation in public by the effect. *Johnson.*

Nunc animis opus, Ænea, nunc pectore firmo 40 —Now, Æneas, you have need of courage, now a resolute heart. *Virg.*

Nunc aut nunquam—Now or never. *M.*

Nunc dimittis—Now let me depart in peace. *See Luke i. 29.*

Nunc est bibendum, nunc pede libero, / Pulsanda tellus!—Now let us drink; now let us beat the ground with merry foot. *Hor.*

Nunc patimur longæ pacis mala; sævior armis / Luxuria incubuit, victumque ulciscitur orbem—Now we suffer the evils of long peace; luxury more cruel than war broods over us and avenges a conquered world. *Juv.*

Nunc positis novus exuviis nitidusque juventa 45 —Now, all new, his slough cast off, and shining in youth. *Virg.*

Nunc vino pellite curas!—Now drive off your cares with wine. *Hor.*

Nunquam aliud natura, aliud sapientia dicit—Nature never says one thing and wisdom another. *Juv.*

Nunquam erit alienis gravis, qui suis se concinnat levem—He will never be disagreeable to others who makes himself agreeable to his own relations. *Plaut.*

Nunquam est fidelis cum potente societas—An alliance with a powerful man is never safe. *Phædr.*

Nunquam libertas gratior extat / Quam sub 50 rege pio—Liberty is never more enjoyable than under a pious king. *Claud.*

Nunquam nimis dicitur, quod nunquam satis discitur—That is never too often repeated which is never sufficiently learned. *Sen.*

Nunquam non paratus—Never unprepared. *M.*

Nunquam retrorsum—Never go back. *M.*

Nunquam se plus agere, quam nihil quum ageret; nunquam minus solum esse, quam quum solus esset—He said he never had more to do than when he had nothing to do, and never was less alone than when alone. *Cic. quoting Scipio Africanus.*

Nunquam vir æquus dives evasit cito—No just man ever became quickly rich. *Menander.*

Nuptial love maketh mankind; friendly love perfecteth it; but wanton love corrupteth and embaseth it. *Bacon.*

Nur aus vollendeter Kraft blicket die Anmuth hervor—Only out of perfected faculty does grace look forth. *Goethe.*

Nur das Gemeine / Verkennt man selten. Und das Seltene / Vergisst man schwerlich—Only what is common we rarely mistake, and what is rare we with difficulty forget. *Lessing.*

Nur das Leben hasst, der Tod versöhnt—In life alone is hatred; in death is reconciliation. *Tiedge.*

Nur das zu thun, was alle wollen, / Ist das Geheimniss jeder Macht — The secret of all power is only to do that which all would fain do. *Kinkel.*

Nur dem Fröhlichen blüht der Baum des Lebens, / Dem Unschuldigen rinnt der Born der Jugend / Auch noch im Alter—Only for the cheerful does the tree of life blossom, for the innocent the well-spring of youth keeps still flowing, even in old age. *Arndt.*

Nur dem vertrau' ich völlig, nur der imponirt nachhaltig, der über sich zu lächeln fähig ist—I trust only him perfectly, only he makes a lasting impression on me, who is capable of laughing at himself. *Feuchtersleben.*

10 Nur der Freundschaft Harmonie / Mildert die Beschwerden; / Ohne ihre Sympathie / Ist kein Glück auf Erden—Nothing but the harmony of friendship soothes our sorrows; without its sympathy there is no happiness on earth. *Mozart.*

Nur der Glaube aller stärkt den Glauben, / Wo Tausende anbeten und verehren, / Da wird die Glut zur Flamme, und beflügelt / Schwingt sich der Geist in alle Himmel auf — Only the faith of all strengthens faith; where thousands worship and reverence, there the glow becomes flame, and the spirit soar upwards on wings into all heavens. *Schiller.*

Nur der Irrthum ist das Leben, / Und das Wissen ist der Tod—Only error is life, and knowledge is death. *Schiller.*

Nur der Irrthum ist unser Teil, und Wahn ist unsre Wissenschaft—Only error is our portion, and illusion our knowledge. *Lessing.*

Nur der ist wahrhaft arm, der weder Geist noch Kraft hat—Only he is truly poor who is without soul and without faculty. *Benzel-Sternan.*

15 Nur der Starke wird das Schicksal zwingen, / Wenn der Schwächling untersinkt—Only the strong man will coerce destiny if the weakling surrenders. *Schiller.*

Nur die Hoffenden leben—Only the hoping live. *Halm.*

Nur die Lumpe sind bescheiden, / Brave freuen sich der That — Only low-born fellows are modest; men of spirit rejoice over their feats. *Goethe.*

Nur eine Mutter weiss allein, / Was lieben heisst und glücklich sein — A mother alone knows what it is to love and be happy. *Chamisso.*

Nur eine Schmach weiss ich auf dieser Erde. / Und die heisst: Unrecht thun—Only one disgrace know I in this world, and that is doing wrong. *Grillparzer.*

Nur eine Weisheit führt zum Ziele, / Doch 20 ihrer Sprüche giebt es viele—Only one wisdom leads to the goal, though the proverbs of it are many. *Bodenstedt.*

Nur Helios vermag's zu sagen, / Der alles Irdische bescheint—Only Helios (the sun-god) can tell, he sheds light on every earthly thing. *Schiller.*

Nur immer zu! wir wollen es ergründen, / In deinem Nichts hoff' ich das All zu finden—Only let us still go on! we will yet fathom it. In thy nothing hope I to find the all. *Goethe.*

Nur in der eignen Kraft ruht das Schicksal jeder Nation—Only in its own power rests the destiny of every nation. *Count v. Moltke, in 1880.*

Nur in der Schule selbst ist die eigentliche Vorschule—The true preparatory school is only the school itself. *Goethe.*

Nur in schwülen Prüfungsstunden / Sprosst 25 die Palme, die den Sieger krönt—Only in the stifling hours of trial does the palm shoot forth which decks the brow of the victor. *Salis-Seewis.*

Nur in Träumen wohnt das Glück der Erde—Only in dreams does the happiness of the earth dwell. *Rückert.*

Nur Liebe darf der Liebe Blume brechen—Only love may break the flower of love. *Schiller.*

Nur stets zu sprechen, ohne was zu sagen, / Das war von je der Redner grösste Gabe—To but speak on without saying anything has ever been the greatest gift of the orator. *Platen.*

Nur vom Edeln kann das Edle stammen—Only from the noble soul can what is noble come. *Schiller.*

Nur vom Nutzen wird die Welt regiert—It is 30 only by show of advantage that the world is governed. *Schiller.*

Nur was wir selber glauben, glaubt man uns—People give us credit only for what we ourselves believe. *Gutzkow.*

Nur wer die Last wirklich selbst trägt, kennt ihr Gewicht—Only he who really bears the burden knows its weight. *Klinger.*

Nur wer die Sehnsucht kennt / Weiss, was ich leide!—Only he who knows what yearning is knows what I suffer. *Goethe.*

Nur wer sich recht des Lebens freut, / Trägt leichter, was es Schlimmes beut—Only he who enjoys life aright finds it easier to bear the evils of it. *Bodenstedt.*

Nur wer vor Gott sich fühlet klein / Kann vor 35 den Menschen mächtig sein—He only who feels himself little in the eye of God can hope to be mighty in the eyes of men. *Arndt.*

Nur zwei Tugenden giebt's. O, wären sie immer vereinigt, / Immer die Güte auch gross, immer die Grösse auch gut!—There are only two virtues, were they but always united: goodness always also great, and greatness always also good. *Schiller.*

Nursing her wrath to keep it warm. *Burns.*

Nusquam tuta fides—There is nowhere any true honour. *Virg.*

Nutrimentum spiritus — Nourishment for the spirit! *Inscription on the Royal Library at Berlin.*

Nutritur vento, vento restinguitur ignis : / Lenis alit flammas, grandior aura necat !— Fire is fed by the wind and extinguished by the wind : a gentle current feeds it, too strong a one puts it out ! *Ovid.*

Nuts are given us, but we must crack them ourselves. *Pr.*

Nymph, in thy orisons / Be all my sins remembered. *Ham.*, iii. 1.

O.

O banish the tears of children ! Continual rains upon the blossoms are hurtful. *Jean Paul.*

5 O bitte um Leben noch ! du fühlst, mit deinen Mängeln, / Dass du noch wandeln kannst nicht unter Gottes Engeln—O still pray for life ; thou feelest that with those faults of thine thou canst not walk among the angels of God. *Rückert.*

ὁ βίος βραχὺς, ἡ δὲ τέχνη μακρή—Life is short, art is long. *Gr.*

O blicke nicht nach dem was jedem fehlt ; / Betrachte, was noch einem jeden bleibt—O look not at what each comes short in ; consider what each still retains. *Goethe.*

ὁ βούλεται, τοῦθ' ἕκαστος καὶ οἴεται—What each one wishes that he also thinks. *Demosthenes.*

O cæca nocentum / Consilia, O semper timidum scelus !—Oh, how infatuated are the counsels of the guilty ! Oh, how cowardly wickedness ever is ! *Statius.*

10 O cives, cives, quærenda pecunia primum est ; / Virtus post nummos—O citizens, citizens, you must seek for money first, for virtue after cash. *Hor.*

O Corydon, Corydon, secretum divitis ullum / Esse putas ? Servi ut taceant, jumenta loquentur, / Et canis, et postes, et marmora —O Corydon, Corydon, do you think anything a rich man does can be kept secret ? Even if his servants say nothing, his beasts of burden, and dogs, and door-posts, and marble slabs will speak. *Juv.*

O cunning enemy, that, to catch a saint, / With saints dost bait thy hook. *Meas. for Meas.*, ii. 2.

O curvæ in terris animæ et cœlestium inanes ! —Oh ye souls bent down to earth and void of everything heavenly. *Pers.*

O das Leben hat Reize, die wir nie gekannt —Oh, life has charms which we have never known. *Schiller.*

15 O das Leben ist ein langer, langer Seufzer vor dem Ausgehen des Athmens—Oh, life is a long, long sigh before emitting the breath. *Jean Paul.*

O dass die Weisheit halb so eifrig wäre / Nach Schülern und Bekehrten, als der Spott—Oh, that Wisdom were half as zealous for disciples and converts as Ridicule is. *Grillparzer.*

O dass es ewig bliebe, / Das Doppelglück der Töne wie der Liebe—Oh, that it would stay for ever, the double bliss of the tones as well as of the love. *Goethe.*

O dass sie ewig' grünen bliebe / Die schöne Zeit der jungen Liebe—Oh, that it remained for ever green, the fair season of early love. *Schiller.*

O dearest, dearest boy, my heart / For better love would seldom yearn, / Could I but teach the hundredth part / Of what from thee I learn. *Wordsworth.*

O der Magnet des Wahns zieht mächtig—Oh, 20 how powerfully the magnet of illusion attracts. *Gutzkow.*

O ein Fürst hat keinen Freund, kann keinen Freund haben—Oh, a ruler has no friend, and can have none. *Lessing.*

O faciles dare summa Deos, eademque tueri / Difficiles—How gracious the gods are in bestowing honours, how averse to ensure our tenure of them. *Lucan.*

O fallacem hominum spem—How deceitful is the hope of men. *Cic.*

O flesh, flesh, how thou art fishified. *Rom. and Jul.*, ii. 4.

O formose puer, nimium ne crede colori—Oh, 25 beauteous boy, trust not too much to the bloom on thy cheeks. *Virg.*

O fortunate adolescens, qui tuæ virtutis Homerum præconem inveneris—Oh, happy youth, to have a Homer as the publisher of thy valour. *Alexander the Great at the tomb of Achilles.*

O fortunatos nimium, sua si bona norint, / Agricolas, quibus ipsa, procul discordibus armis, / Fundit humo facilem victum justissima tellus—Oh, how happy the tillers of the ground are, if they but knew their blessings ; for whom, far from the clash of arms, the all-righteous earth pours forth from her soil an easy sustenance. *Virg.*

O foulest Circæan draught ! thou poison of popular applause ; madness is in thee, and death ; thy end is bedlam and the grave. *Carlyle.*

O glücklich ! wer noch hoffen kann, / Aus diesem Meer des Irrtums aufzutauchen. / Was man nicht weiss, das eben brauchte man, / Und was man weiss, kann man nicht brauchen—Oh, happy he who can still hope to emerge from this sea of error ! What one does not know is exactly what one should want to know, and what one knows is what one has no use for. *Faust, in Goethe.*

O God, that bread should be so dear, / And 30 flesh and blood so cheap ! *T. Hood.*

O Gott ! das Leben ist doch schön—O God ! life is nevertheless beautiful. *Schiller.*

O Gott, wie schränkt sich Welt und Himmel ein, / Wenn unser Herz in seinen Schranken banget—O God, how contracted the world and heaven becomes when our heart becomes uneasy within its barriers. *Goethe.*

O guard thy roving thoughts with jealous care, for speech is but the dial-plate of thought ; and every fool reads plainly in thy words what is the hour of thy thought. *Tennyson.*

O' guid advisement comes nae ill. *Burns.*

O Heaven ! were man / But constant, he were 35 perfect ; that one error / Fills him with faults ; makes him run through all sins. *Two Gent. of Ver.*, v. 4.

O Herz, versuch' es nur ! so leicht ist's gut zu sein : / Und es zu scheinen ist so eine schwere Pein—O heart, only try ! To be good is so easy, and to appear so is such a heavy burden. *Rückert.*

O homines ad servitutem paratos !—Oh, men, how ye prepare yourselves for slavery ! *Tac.*

O how full of briars is this working-day world. *As You Like It*, i. 3.

O how wretched / Is that poor man that hangs on princes' favours! / There is betwixt that smile he would aspire to, / That sweet aspect of princes, and their ruin, / More pangs and fears than wars or women have ; / And when he falls, he falls like Lucifer, / Never to hope again. *Henry VIII.*, iii. 2.

O hush the noise, ye men of strife, / And hear the angels sing! *Sears.*

O, if this were seen, / The happiest youth—viewing his progress through / What perils past, what crosses to ensue— / Would shut the book and sit him down and die. 2 *Hen. IV.*, iii. 1.

5 O ja, dem Herrn ist alles Kinderspiel—Oh, yes, everything is but child's play to the gentleman. *Mephisto, in Goethe.*

O judgment, thou art fled to brutish beasts, / And men have lost their reason! *Jul. Cæs.*, iii. 2.

O kaum bezwingen wir das eigne Herz ; / Wie soll die rasche Jugend sich bezähmen! —Oh, we can hardly subdue our own heart ; how shall impetuous youth restrain itself! *Schiller.*

O l'amour d'une mère! amour que nul n'oublie! / Pain merveilleux, que Dieu partage et multiplie! / Table toujours servie au paternel foyer! / Chacun en a sa part, et tous l'ont tout entier—Oh, the love of a mother, love no one forgets ; miraculous bread which God distributes and multiplies ; board always spread by the paternal hearth, whereat each has his portion, and all have it entire! *Victor Hugo.*

O Leben, wie bist du so bitter und hart—Oh, Life, how bitter and harsh thou art! *Scheffel.*

10 O let my books be then the eloquence / And dumb presagers of my speaking breast. *Browning.*

O let thy vow, / First made to heaven, first be to heaven perform'd. . . . It is religion that doth make vows kept. *King John*, iii. 1.

" O Liberty, what crimes have been committed in thy name!" *Madame Roland, as she bowed to the statue of Liberty at the place of execution.*

O Life, an age to the miserable, a moment to the happy. *Bacon.*

O life ! how pleasant is thy morning, / Young Fancy's rays the hills adorning ! / Cold-pausing Caution's lessons scorning, / We frisk away, / Like schoolboys at th' expected warning, / To joy and play. *Burns.*

15 O life ! thou art a galling load / Along a rough, a weary road, / To wretches such as I ! *Burns (Despondency).*

ὁ λόγος ἐνηνθρώπησεν, ἵνα ἡμεῖς θεοποιηθῶμεν —The Word became man, that we might become gods. *Athanasius.*

O Lord, that lend'st me life, / Lend me a heart replete with thankfulness! 2 *Hen. VI.*, i. 1.

O love, be moderate, allay thy ecstasy ; / In measure rain thy joy ; scant this excess ; / I feel too much thy blessing ! Make it less, / For fear I surfeit. *Mer. of Venice*, iii. 2.

O magna vis veritatis, quæ . . . facile se per se ipsa defendit—Oh, mighty force of truth that by itself so easily defends itself ! *Cic.*

20 O major tandem, parcas, insane, minori—Oh, thou who art a greater madman ; spare me, I pray, who am not so far gone. *Hor.*

ὁ μὴ δαρεὶς ἄνθρωπος οὐ παιδεύεται—The man who has not been scourged is not educated. *Menander.*

O mighty Cæsar ! dost thou lie so low ? / Are all thy conquests, glories, triumphs, spoils, / Shrunk to this little measure ? *Jul. Cæs.*, iii. 1.

O mihi præteritos referat si Jupiter annos ! —Oh, that Jove would but give me back the years that are past ! *Virg.*

O miseras hominum mentes ! O pectora cæca ! —Oh, how wretched are the minds of men ! oh, how blind their hearts ! *Lucret.*

O miseri quorum gaudia crimen habent !—O 25 wretched ye whose joys are tainted with guilt ! *Pseudo-Gallus.*

O most lame and impotent conclusion ! *Othello*, ii. 1.

O munera nondum / Intellecta Deum—Oh, that the gifts of the gods should not yet be understood. *Lucan.*

O my prophetic soul ! mine uncle. *Ham.*, i. 5.

O Nature ! Ha ! why do I not name thee God? Art thou not the "living garment of God ?" O Heavens ! is it, in very deed, He then that ever speaks through thee ; that lives and loves in thee, that lives and loves in me ? *Carlyle.*

O never / Shall sun that morrow see. *Macb.*, i. 5. 30

O nimium nimiumque oblite tuorum—Too, too forgetful of thy kin. *Ovid.*

O nimm der Stunde wahr, eh' sie entschlüpft. / So selten kommt der Augenblick im Leben / Der wahrhaft wichtig ist und gross—Take note of the hour ere it slips past ; so seldom does the moment come which is truly fateful and great. *Schiller.*

O noctes cœnæque deum!—Oh, nights and suppers of the gods ! *Hor.*

O passi graviora !—Oh, ye who have suffered greater misfortunes than these ! *Virg.*

ᾧ φίλοι οὐδεὶς φίλος—He who has many friends 35 has no friends. *Diogenes Laertius.*

ὁ φρόνιμος τὸ ἄλυπον διώκει οὐ τὸ ἡδύ—The aim of the wise man is not to secure pleasure, but to avoid pain. *Arist.*

O place and greatness, millions of false eyes / Are stuck upon thee ! Volumes of report / Run with these false and most contrarious quests / Upon thy doings ! thousand scapes of wit / Make thee the father of their idle dreams, / And rack thee in their fancies. *Meas. for Meas.*, iv. 1.

O pudor ! O pietas !—O modesty ! O piety ! *Mart.*

O purblind race of miserable men ! / How many among us at this very hour / Do forge a life-long trouble for ourselves, / By taking true for false, or false for true ; / Here, thro' the feeble twilight of this world / Groping, how many, until we pass and reach / That other, where we see as we are seen ! *Tennyson.*

O qualis facies et quali digna tabella !—Oh, 40 what a face and what a picture it would have been a subject for ! *Juv.*

O quanta species cerebrum non habet !—Oh, that such beauty should be devoid of brains ! *Phædr.*

O quantum in rebus inane !—Oh, what a void there is in things ! *Persius.*

O ruin'd piece of nature ! This great world / Shall so wear out to nought. *King Lear*, iv. 6.

O rus quando te aspiciam? quandoque licebit / Nunc veterum libris, nunc somno et inertibus horis / Ducere sollicitæ jucunda oblivia vitæ? —Oh, country, when shall I see thee, and when shall I be permitted to quaff a sweet oblivion of anxious life, now from the books of the ancients, now from sleep and idle hours? *Hor.*

O sancta damnatio!—Oh, holy condemnation!

O sancta simplicitas!—Oh, holy simplicity! *John Huss at the stake, on seeing an old woman hurrying up with a faggot to throw on the pile.*

O si tacuisses, philosophus mansisses—If you had only held your peace, you would have remained a philosopher. *Boëthius.*

5 O sleep, / It is a gentle thing, / Beloved from pole to pole! *Coleridge.*

O sleep, O gentle sleep, / Nature's soft nurse! how have I frighted thee, / That thou no more wilt weigh my eyelids down, / And steep my senses in forgetfulness! 2 *Hen. IV.*, iii. 1.

O sons of earth, attempt ye still to rise, / By mountains piled on mountains, to the skies? / Heav'n still with laughter the vain toil surveys, / And buries madmen in the heaps they raise. *Pope.*

O sprich mir nicht von jener bunten Menge / Bei deren Anblick uns der Geist entflieht— Oh, speak not to me of the motley mob, at the very sight of which our spirit takes flight! *Goethe.*

O süsse Stimme! Willkommener Ton / Der Muttersprach' in einem fremden Lande!— Oh, sweet voice, much-welcome sound of our mother-tongue in a foreign land! *Goethe.*

10 O tempora, O mores!—Oh, the times! oh, the manners! *Cic.*

O that estates, degrees, and offices / Were not derived corruptly, and that clear honour / Were purchased by the merit of the wearer!/ How many then would cover that stand bare ;/ How many be commanded that command ;/ How much low peasantry would then be glean'd / From the true seed of honour ; and how much honour, / Pick'd from the chaff and ruin of the times, / To be new-varnish'd. *Mer. of Ven.*, ii. 9.

O that men's ears should be / To counsel deaf, but not to flattery! *Timon of Athens*, i. 2.

O that way madness lies. *Lear*, iii. 4.

O that you could turn your eyes toward the napes of your necks, and make but an interior survey of your good selves! *Coriolanus*, ii. 1.

15 O the depth of the riches both of the wisdom and knowledge of God! How unsearchable are His judgments, and His ways past finding out! *St. Paul.*

O the wound of conscience is no scar, and Time cools it not with his wing, but merely keeps it open with his scythe. *Jean Paul.*

O these deliberate fools, when they do choose/ They have the wisdom by their wit to lose. *Mer. of Ven.*, ii. 9.

O these naughty times / Put bars between the owners and their rights. *Mer. of Ven.*, iii. 2.

O Thor, wer nicht im Augenblick den wahren Augenblick ergreift, / Wer, was er liebt, im Auge, und dennoch nach der Seite schweift— Oh, fool, he seizes not the true moment in the moment who has what he loves before his eye, and still swerves from it. *Platen.*

O Thou, / Passionless bride, divine Tranquillity, /. . . Thou carest not / How roughly men may woo thee, so they win! *Tennyson.* (?) 20

O thou who hast still a father and a mother, thank God for it in the day when thy soul is full of joyful tears, and needs a bosom wherein to shed them. *Jean Paul.*

O thoughts of men accurst! / Past and to come seem best; things present, worst. 2 *Hen. IV.*, i. 3.

O Tugend, Tugend, wie schön bist du !/ Welch' göttlich Meisterstück sind Seelen, / Die sich hinauf bis zu dir erheben—O virtue, virtue, how fair art thou! what a divine masterpiece are the souls that raise themselves up to thee! *Klopstock.*

O wad some pow'r the giftie gie us / To see oursels as ithers see us ! / It wad frae mony a blunder free us, / And foolish notion ;/ What airs in dress and gait wad lea'e us, / And e'en devotion! *Burns.*

O Wahrheit, deinen edeln Wein / Musst du 25 mit Wasser mischen; / Denn willst du ihn rein auftischen, / So nimmt er den Kopf den Gästen ein—O Truth, thy noble wine thou must mix with water, for wert thou to serve it out pure, it would get into the heads of the guests and turn them. *Rückert.*

O was im Traum die innre Stimme spricht / Das wird uns Wahrheit, wenn die Sonne leuchtet—Oh, how that which the inner voice speaks in our dreaming becomes truth to us when the sun shines! *Schillerbuch.*

O was müssen wir der Kirche Gottes halber leiden, rief der / Abt, als ihm das gebratene Huhn die Finger versengte—"What must we suffer for the Church of God's sake !" exclaimed the Abbot when the roast fowl burnt his fingers. *Ger. Pr.*

O was sind wir Grossen auf der Woge der Menschheit? Wir glauben sie zu beherrschen, und sie treibt uns auf und nieder, hin und her—Ah ! what are we great ones on the wave of humanity? We fancy we rule over it, and it sways us up and down, hither and thither. *Goethe.*

O well for him whose will is strong! / He suffers, but he will not suffer long ; / He suffers, but he cannot suffer wrong. *Tennyson.*

O wer weiss, / Was in der Zeiten Hinter- 30 grunde schlummert?— Oh, who knows what slumbers in the background of the times? *Schiller.*

O what a goodly outside falsehood hath!/ *Mer. of Ven.*, i. 3.

O what a noble mind is here o'erthrown !/ The courtier's, soldier's, scholar's eye, tongue, sword ; / The expectancy and rose of the fair state, / The glass of fashion, and the mould of form, / The observed of all observers, quite, quite down! *Ham.*, iii. 1.

O what a tangled web we weave / When first we practise to deceive. *Scott.*

O what a world is this, when what is comely / Envenoms him that bears it! *As You Like It*, ii. 3.

O what a world of vile ill-favoured faults / 35 Looks handsome in three hundred pounds a-year! *Merry Wives*, iii. 4.

O what men dare do! what men may do! / What men daily do, not knowing what they do! *Much Ado*, iv. 1.

O woman! in our hours of ease / Uncertain, coy, and hard to please, / And variable as the shade / By the light of quivering aspen made ; / When pain and anguish wring the brow, / A ministering angel thou. *Scott.*

O ye loved ones, that already sleep in the noiseless Bed of Rest, whom in life I could only weep for and never help ; and ye who, wide-scattered, still toil lonely in the monster-bearing desert, dyeing the flinty ground with your blood,—yet a little while, and we shall all meet There, and our Mother's bosom will screen us all ; and Oppression's harness, and Sorrow's fire-whip, and all the Gehenna bailiffs that patrol and inhabit ever-vexed Time, cannot thenceforth harm us any more. *Carlyle.*

O yet we trust that somehow good / Will be the final goal of ill. *Tennyson.*

Oaks fall when reeds stand. *Pr.*

5 Oars alone can ne'er prevail / To reach the distant coast ; / The breath of heav'n must swell the sail, / Or all the toil is lost. *Cowper.*

Oaths are straws, . . . and holdfast is the only dog. *Hen. V.,* ii. 3.

Ob es vom Herzen kommt, das magst du leicht verstehen : / Denn was vom Herzen kommt, muss dir zum Herzen gehen—Easily may'st thou know whether it comes from the heart ; for what comes from the heart goes straight to thine. *Körner.*

Obedience alone gives the right to command. *Emerson.*

Obedience is better than sacrifice. *Pr. from Bible.*

10 Obedience is our universal duty and destiny ; wherein whoso will not bend must break. *Carlyle.*

Obedience is the bond of rule. *Tennyson.*

Obedience is woman's duty on earth ; hard endurance is her heavy lot ; by severe service she must be purified ; but she who has served here is great up yonder. *Schiller.*

Obey something, and you will have a chance of finding out what is best to obey. But if you begin by obeying nothing, you will end by obeying Beelzebub and all his seven invited friends. *Ruskin.*

Obey thy parents ; keep thy word justly ; swear not ; set not thy sweet heart on proud array. *King Lear,* iii. 4.

15 Obiter cantare—To sing as one goes along ; to sing by the way.

Obiter dicta—Remarks by the way ; passing remarks.

Obiter dictum—A thing said in passing.

Objects close to the eye shut out much larger objects on the horizon ; and splendours born only of the earth eclipse the stars. So a man sometimes covers up the entire disc of eternity with a dollar, and quenches transcendent glories with a little shining dust. *Chapin.*

Objects imperfectly discerned take forms from the hope or fear of the beholder. *Johnson.*

20 Objects in pictures should be so arranged as by their very position to tell their own story. *Goethe.*

Oblatam occasionem tene—Seize the opportunity that is offered.

Obligation is thraldom, and thraldom is hateful. *Hobbes.*

Oblivion is the dark page whereon memory writes her light-beam characters and makes them legible ; were it all light, nothing could be read there, any more than if it were all darkness. *Carlyle.*

Oblivion is the rule, and fame the exception, of humanity. *Rivarol.*

Oblivion is the second death, which great 25 minds dread more than the first. *De Bouff-lers.*

Obreros a no ver dineros a perder—Not to watch your workmen is to lose your money. *Sp. Pr.*

Obruat illud male partum, male retentum, male gestum imperium—Let that power fall which has been wrongfully acquired, wrongfully retained, and wrongfully administered. *Cic.*

Obscuris vera involvens—Shrouding, or concealing, truth in obscurity or darkness. *Virg.*

Obscurity and affectation are the two great faults of style. *Macaulay.*

Obscurity and Innocence, twin-sisters, escape 30 temptations which would pierce their gossamer armour in contact with the world. *Chamfort.*

Obscurum per obscurius—Explaining something obscure by what is more obscure.

Obsequium amicos, veritas odium parit—Obsequiousness procures us friends ; speaking the truth, enemies. *Ter.*

Observe this short but certain aphorism, " Forsake all, and thou shalt find all." *Thomas à Kempis.*

Observe thyself as thy greatest enemy would do ; so shalt thou be thy greatest friend. *Jeremy Taylor.*

Observation is an old man's memory. *Swift.* 35

Observation may trip now and then without throwing you, for her gait is a walk ; but inference always gallops, and if she stumbles, you are gone. *Holmes.*

Observation more than books, experience rather than persons, are the prime educators. *A. B. Alcott.*

Obstinacy and heat in argument are surest proofs of folly. *Montaigne.*

Obstinacy is ever most positive when it is most in the wrong. *Mme. Necker.*

Obstinacy is the result of the will's forcing 40 itself into the place of the intellect. *Schopenhauer.*

Obstinacy is the strength of the weak. *Lavater.*

Obstupui, steteruntque comæ, et vox faucibus hæsit—I was astounded ; my hair stood on end, and my voice stuck fast in my throat. *Virg.*

Obtuseness is sometimes a virtue. *Rivarol.*

Occasio facit furem — Opportunity makes the thief. *Pr.*

Occasion reins the motions of the stirring 45 mind. *Owen Feltham.*

Occasionem cognosce—Know your opportunity.

Occasions do not make a man frail, but they show what he is. *Thomas à Kempis.*

Occidit miseros crambe repetita magistros—Cabbage repeated is the death of the wretched masters. *Juv.*

Occupation is the scythe of Time. *Napoleon.*

Occupet extremum scabies !—Murrain take the 50 hindmost ! *Hor.*

Ocean is a mighty harmonist. *Wordsworth.*

Oculi tanquam speculatores altissimum locum obtinent—The eyes, like sentinels, occupy the highest place in the body. *Cic.*

Oculis magis habenda fides quam auribus—It is better to trust to our eyes than our ears.

Oculus domini saginat equum—The master's eye makes the horse fat. *Pr.*

Oderint dum metuant—Let them show hate, provided they fear. *Cic.*

5 Oderunt hilarem tristes, tristemque jocosi, / Sedatum celeres, agilem gnavumque remissi—Sad men dislike a gay spirit, and the jocular a sad ; the quick-witted dislike the sedate, and the careless the busy and industrious. *Hor.*

Oderunt peccare boni virtutis amore — Good men shrink from wrong out of love for virtue. *Hor.*

Odi profanum vulgus et arceo — I hate the profane rabble, and keep them far from me. *Hor.*

Odi puerulos præcoci ingenio—I hate boys of precocious talent. *Cic.*

Odi, vedi, e taci, se vuoi viver in pace—Listen, see, and say nothing, if you wish to live in peace. *It. Pr.*

10 Odia qui nimium timet, regnare nescit—He who dreads hostility too much is unfit to bear rule. *Sen.*

Odimus accipitrem quia semper vivit in armis —I hate the hawk because he always lives in arms. *Ovid.*

Odium theologicum — Theological hatred ; the animosity engendered by differences of theological opinion.

Odora canum vis—The sharp scent of the hounds. *Virg.*

O'ercome thyself, and thou may'st share / With Christ His Father's throne, and wear / The world's imperial wreath. *Keble.*

15 Of a life of luxury the fruit is luxury. *Thoreau.*

Of a thoroughly crazy and defective artist we may indeed say he has everything from himself ; but of an excellent one, never. *Goethe.*

Of all actions of a man's life, his marriage does least concern other people ; yet of all actions of our life, 'tis most meddled with by other people. *John Selden.*

Of all attainable liberties, be sure first to strive for leave to be useful. *Ruskin.* (?)

Of all blinds that shut up men's vision the worst is self. (?)

20 Of all days, the one that is most wasted is that on which one has not laughed. *Chamfort.*

Of all earthly music, that which reaches the farthest into heaven is the beating of a loving heart. *Ward Beecher.*

Of all evils in story-telling, the humour of telling tales one after another in great numbers is the least supportable. *Steele.*

Of all God's gifts to the sight of man, colour is the holiest, the most divine, the most solemn. *Ruskin.*

Of all great poems Love is the absolute and the essential foundation. *C. Fitzhugh.*

25 Of all man's work of art, a cathedral is greatest. A vast and majestic tree is greater than that. *Ward Beecher.*

Of all men, a philosopher should be no swearer ; for an oath, which is the end of controversies in law, cannot determine any here, where reason only must induce. *Sir Thomas Browne.*

Of all plagues, good Heaven, thy wrath can send, / Save, save, O save me from the candid friend ! *Canning.*

Of all pleasures, the fruit of labour is the sweetest. *Vauvenargues.*

Of all points of faith the being of a God is encompassed with most difficulty, and yet borne in upon our minds with most power. *John Newman.*

Of all rights of man, the right of the ignorant 30 man to be guided by the wiser, to be gently or forcibly held in the true course by him, is the indisputablest. *Carlyle.*

Of all studies, study your present condition. *Pr*

Of all the cants which are canted in this canting world,—though the cant of hypocrisy may be the worst,—the cant of criticism is the most tormenting ! *Sterne.*

Of all the characters of cruelty, I consider that as the most odious which assumes the garb of mercy. *Fox.*

Of all the great masters, there is not one who did not paint his own present world, plainly and truly. *Ruskin.*

Of all the marvellous works of the Deity, per- 35 haps there is nothing that angels behold with such supreme astonishment as a proud man. *Colton.*

Of all the passions that possess mankind, / The love of novelty rules most the mind ; / In search of this, from realm to realm we roam, / Our fleets come fraught with every folly home. *Foote.*

Of all the possessions of a man, next to the gods, his soul is the mightiest, being the most his own. *Plato.*

Of all the pulpits from which human voice is ever sent forth, there is none from which it reaches so far as from the grave. *Ruskin.*

Of all the superstitions which infest the brains of weak mortals, the belief in prophecies, presentiments, and dreams, seems to me amongst the most pitiful and pernicious. *Goethe.*

Of all the tyrants that the world affords, / Our 40 own affections are the fiercest lords. *E. Stirling.*

Of all thieves, fools are the worst ; they rob you of time and temper. *Goethe.*

Of all things, knowledge is esteemed the most precious treasure ; because of its incapacity to be stolen, to be given away, or even to be consumed. *Hitopadesa.*

Of all those arts in which the wise excel, / Nature's chief masterpiece is writing well. *Duke of Buckingham.*

Of all wild beasts, preserve me from a tyrant ; and of all tame, a flatterer. *Ben Jonson.*

Of big words and feathers many go to the 45 pound. *Ger. Pr.*

Of error we can talk for ever, but truth demands that we should lay it to heart and apply it. *Goethe.*

Of four things every man has more than he knows—of sins, and debts, and years, and foes. *Persian Pr.*

Of God's light I was not utterly bereft, if my as yet sealed eyes, with their unspeakable longing, could nowhere see Him ; nevertheless in my heart He was present, and His heaven-written law still stood legible and sacred there. *Carlyle.*

Of great men no one should speak but one who is as great as they, so as to be able to see all round them. *Goethe.*

Of great riches there is no real use, except it be in the distribution; the rest is but conceit. *Bacon.*

Of hasty counsel take good heed, for very rarely haste is speed. *Dut. Pr.*

Of how few lives does not stated duty claim the greater part? *Johnson.*

5 Of illustrious men all the earth is the sepulchre, and it is not the inscribed column in their own land which is the record of their virtues, but the unwritten memory of them in the hearts and minds of all mankind. *Thucydides.*

Of its own unity, the soul gives unity to whatso it looks on with love. *Carlyle.*

Of making many books there is no end; and much study is a weariness of the flesh. *Bible.*

Of more than earth can earth make none possesst; / And he that least / Regards this restless world, shall in this world find rest. *Quarles.*

Of other tyrants short the strife, / But Indolence is king for life : / The despot twists, with soft control, / Eternal fetters round the soul. *Hannah More.*

10 Of pleasures, those which occur most rarely give the greatest delight. *Epictetus.*

Of real evils the number is great ; of possible evils there is no end. *Johnson.*

Of the Beautiful we are seldom capable, oftener of the Good ; and how highly should we value those who endeavour, with great sacrifices, to forward that good among their fellows ! *Goethe.*

Of the eyes that men do glare withal, so few can see. *Carlyle.*

Of the soul, the body form doth take, / For soul is form, and doth the body make. *Spenser.*

15 Of the three requisitions of genius, the first is soul ; the second, soul ; and the third, soul. *Whipple.*

Of the wealth of the world each has as much as he takes. *It. Pr.*

Of the Wrong we are always conscious, of the Right never. *Goethe.*

Of thorns men do not gather figs nor of a bramble bush gather they grapes. *Jesus.*

Of thy word unspoken thou art master; thy spoken word is master of thee. *Eastern Pr.*

20 Of two evils choose the least. *Pr.*

Of unwise admiration much may be hoped, for much good is really in it ; but unwise contempt is itself a negation ; nothing comes of it, for it is nothing. *Carlyle.*

Of what does not concern you say nothing, good or bad. *It. Pr.*

Of what significance are the things you can forget? *Thoreau.*

Of wild creatures, a tyrant; and of tame ones, a flatterer. *Bias.*

25 Off with his head ! so much for Buckingham. *Rich. III.,* iv. 3.

Offenders never pardon. *Pr.*

Offerir molto è spezie di negare—Offering extravagantly is a kind of denial. *It. Pr.*

Oft have I heard, and now believe it true, / Whom man delights in, God delights in too. *An old Minnesinger.*

Oft kommt ein nützlich Wort aus schlechtem Munde—A serviceable word often issues from worthless lips. *Schiller.*

Oft leiden kranke Seelen durch selbstgeschaff- 30 nen Wahn—Sick souls often suffer through conceits of their own creation. *G. Rossini.*

Oft schiessen trifft das Ziel—Shooting often hits the mark. *Ger. Pr.*

Oft sogar es ist weise, zu entdecken, / Was nicht verschwiegen bleiben kann—It is often wise to disclose what cannot be concealed. *Schiller.*

Oft when blind mortals think themselves secure, in height of bliss, they touch the brink of ruin. *Thomson.*

Oft zum Dichter macht die Liebe ; / Selbst ein Wunder, zeugt sie Wunder—Love often makes a poet ; herself a wonder, she works wonders. *Bodenstedt.*

Ofte er Skarlagens Hierte under reven Kaabe 35 —There is often a royal heart under a tattered coat. *Dan. Pr.*

Often a man's own angry pride / Is cap-and-bells for a fool. *Tennyson.*

Often the cock-loft is empty in those whom Nature hath built many storeys high. *Fuller.*

Oftentimes the gods send strong delusions to ensnare too credulous hearts. *Lewis Morris.*

Oftentimes, to win us to our harm, / The instruments of darkness tell us truths ; / Win us with honest trifles, to betray us / In deepest consequence. *Macb.,* i. 3.

Ofttimes nothing profits more / Than self- 40 esteem, grounded on just and right. *Milton.*

Ofttimes the pupil goes beyond his master. *Lucillius.*

Ogni cosa è d'ogni anno—Everything is of every year. *It. Pr.*

Ogni debole ha sempre il suo tiranno—Every weak man has always his tyrant. *It. Pr.*

Ogni medaglio ha il suo riverso—Every medal has its reverse. *It. Pr.*

Ogni monte ha la sua valle—Every mountain 45 has its valley. *It. Pr.*

Ogni vero non è buono a dire—Every truth is not good to be told. *It. Pr.*

Ognuno vede quel che tu pari, pochi sentono quel che tu sei—Every one sees what you seem, few know what you are. *Machiavelli.*

Oh, be he king or peasant, he is happiest / Who in his home finds peace. *Goethe.*

Oh, call my brother back to me ! / I cannot play alone ; / The summer comes with flower and bee,— / Where is my brother gone? *Mrs. Hemans.*

Oh, Death ! the poor man's dearest friend— / 50 The kindest and the best ! / Welcome the hour my aged limbs / Are laid with thee at rest ! / The great, the wealthy fear thy blow, / From pomp and pleasure torn ! / But oh ! a bless'd relief to those / That weary-laden mourn ! *Burns.*

Oh, for a lodge in some vast wilderness, / Some boundless contiguity of shade, / Where rumour of oppression and deceit, / Of unsuccessful or successful war, / May never reach me more. *Cowper.*

Oh, . . . for a man with heart, head, hand. / . . . Whatever they call him, what care I, / Aristocrat, democrat, autocrat—one / Who can rule and dare not lie ! *Tennyson.*

Oh, how sweet it is to hear our own conviction from another's lips ! *Goethe.*

Oh, it is excellent / To have a giant's strength, but it is tyrannous / To use it like a giant. *Meas. for Meas.,* ii. 2.

Oh ! Kritisieren, lieber Herr, ist federleicht, / Doch Bessermachen schwierig—Oh, criticising, good sir, is as easy as a feather is light ; 'tis making better that's the difficulty. *Platen.*

Oh, love for ever lost, / And with it faith gone out ! what is't remains / But duty, though the path be rough and trod / By bruised and bleeding feet? *Lewis Morris.*

5 Oh, Love, how perfect is thy mystic art, / Strengthening the weak, and trampling on the strong ! *Byron.*

Oh, Love ! no habitant of earth thou art— / An unseen seraph, we believe in thee. *Byron.*

Oh, no ! we never mention her ; / Her name is never heard ; / My lips are now forbid to speak / That once familiar word. *T. H. Bayly.*

Oh, nostra folle / Mente, ch'ogn aura di fortuna estolle—How our heart swells if only a breath of happiness breathe through it ! *Tasso.*

Oh, that mine adversary had written a book. *Job.*

10 Oh, that my lot might lead me in the path of holy purity of thought and deed, the path which august laws ordain—laws which in the highest heaven had their birth ; . . . The power of God is mighty in them, and doth not wax old. *Sophocles.*

Oh, that this too too solid flesh would melt, / Thaw and resolve itself into a dew ! / Or that the Everlasting had not fix'd / His canon 'gainst self-slaughter. *Ham.,* i. 2.

Oh ! the dulness and the hardness of the heart of man, which contemplates only the present, and does not rather provide for the future. *Thomas à Kempis.*

Oh, the heart is a free and a fetterless thing — / A wave of the ocean, a bird on the wing. *J. Pardoe.*

Oh, there is something in marriage like the veil of the temple of old, / That screened the Holy of Holies with blue and purple and gold ; / Something that makes a chamber where none but the one may come, / A sacredness too, and a silence, where joy that is deepest is dumb. *Dr. Walter Smith.*

15 Oh, were I seated high as my ambition, / I'd place this naked foot on necks of monarchs. *Walpole.*

Oh, what a fall was there, my countrymen ! / Then I, and you, and all of us fell down, / Whilst bloody treason flourish'd over us. *Jul. Cæs.,* iii. 2.

Oh, what damned minutes tells he o'er, / Who dotes, yet doubts ; suspects, yet soundly loves. *Othello,* iii. 3.

Oh, what is death but parting breath ? / On mony a bloody plain / I've dared his face, and in this place / I scorn him yet again. *Burns, "Macpherson's Lament."*

Oh, whistle and I'll come to ye, my lad. *Burns.*

20 Oh, woman, lovely woman ! Heaven designed you / To temper man ! We had been brutes without you. *Burns.*

Oh, worse than all ! Oh, pang all pangs above, / Is kindness counterfeiting absent love ! *Coleridge.*

Oh, would they stay aback frae courts, / And please themsels wi' country sports, / It wad for every ane be better, / The laird, the tenant, and the cottar. *Burns.*

Ohe ! jam satis est—Stay ! that is enough. *Hor.*

Ohne Begeisterung schlafen die besten Kräfte des Gemüths. Es ist ein Zunder in uns, der Funken will — Without inspiration the best powers of the mind are dormant. There is a tinder in us which needs to be quickened with sparks. *Herder.*

Ohne die Freiheit, was wärest du, Hellas ? / 25 Ohne dich, Hellas, was wäre die Welt?— Without freedom, what wert thou, Greece? Without thee, Greece, what were the world? *W. Müller.*

Ohne eine Gottheit gibt's für den Menschen weder Zweck, noch Ziel, noch Hoffnung, nur eine zitternde Zukunft, ein ewiges Bangen vor jeder Dunkelheit—Without a deity there is for man neither aim, nor goal, nor hope ; only an ever-wavering future, and eternal anxiety in every moment of darkness. *Jean Paul.*

Ohne Hast, aber ohne Rast—Unhasting, yet unresting. *Goethe's motto. Said originally of the sun.*

Ohne Haut—Without a skin.

Ohne Mehl und Wasser ist übel backen—It is ill baking without meal and water. *Ger. Pr.*

Ohne Wahl verteilt die Gaben, / Ohne Billig- 30 keit das Glück ; / Denn Patroklus liegt begraben, / Und Thersites kommt zurück— Gifts are dispensed without election, fortune without fairness ; Patroclus lies buried, and Thersites comes back. *Schiller.*

Ohne Wissen, ohne Sünde—Where there's no knowledge there's no sin. *Ger. Pr.*

οἱ ἀρούρης καρπὸν ἔδουσιν—They who eat the fruit of the field. *Hom.*

οἱ δυστυχοῦντες ἐξ ἑτέρων χείρονα πασχόντων παραμυθοῦνται—The unhappy derive comfort from the worse misfortunes of others. *Æsop.*

οἱ κύβοι Διός ἀει εὐπίπτουσι—The dice of Zeus always fall luckily. *Sophocles.*

οἱ πλείονες κακοί—The majority of mankind are 35 bad. *Bias, one of the seven sages.*

οἱ πολλοί—The multitude ; the masses.

οἵη περ φύλλων γενεή, τοιήδε καὶ ἀνδρῶν— As is the generation of leaves, such is that of men. *Hom.*

Oil, wine, and friends improve by age. *It. Pr.*

οἴμοι· τί δ'οἴμοι ; θνητὰ γὰρ πεπόνθαμεν— Alas ! but why alas ? We only suffer what other mortals do.

οἴνου δὲ μηκετ' ὄντος, οὐκ ἔστιν Κύπρις— 40 Where there is no longer any wine there is no love. *Euripides.*

ὁκόσα φάρμακα οὐκ ἰῆται σίδηρος ἰῆται, ὅσα σίδηρος οὐκ ἰῆται πῦρ ἰῆται—What medicines do not heal, the lance will ; what the lance does heal, fire will. *Hippocrates.*

Old age comes on suddenly, and not gradually, as is thought. *Rahel.*

Old age, especially an honoured old age, has so great authority, that it is of more value than all the pleasures of youth. *Cic.*

Old age is a heavy burden. *Pr.*

Old age is a tyrant, who forbids, under pain of death, the pleasures of youth. *La Roche.*

Old age is honourable. *Pr.*

Old age is not in itself matter for sorrow. It is matter for thanks if we have left our work done behind us. *Carlyle to his mother.*

Old age is sad (*trübe*), not because our joys, but because our hopes are cut short. *Jean Paul.*

5 Old age is the repose of life, the rest which precedes the rest that remains. *R. Collyer.*

Old age is wise for itself, but not wise for the community. *Bryant.*

Old age—the words are comparative, not positive. *Anon.*

Old age, though despised, is coveted by all. *Pr.*

Old age was naturally more honoured in times when people could not know much more than they had seen. *Joubert.*

10 Old birds are hard to pluck. *Pr.*

Old birds are not caught with chaff. *Pr.*

Old books, as you well know, are books of the world's youth, and new books are fruits of its age. *Holmes.*

Old-fashioned poetry, but choicely good. *Izaak Walton.*

Old friends are best. *King James I., as he slipt on his old shoes.*

15 Old friends burn dim, like lamps in noisome air ; / Love them for what they are ; nor love them less ; / Because to thee they are not what they were. *Coleridge.*

Old head and young hand. *Pr.*

Old head upon young shoulders. *Pr.*

Old heads will not suit young shoulders. *Pr.*

Old houses mended / Cost little less than new before they're ended. *C. Cibber.*

20 Old long-vexed questions, not yet solved in logical words or parliamentary laws, are fast solving themselves in facts, somewhat unblessed to behold. *Carlyle.*

Old men are twice children. *Pr.*

Old men lose one of the most precious rights of man, that of being judged by their peers. *Goethe.*

Old men should have more care to end life well than to live long. *Capt. John Brown.*

Old men's lives are lengthened shadows ; their evening sun falls coldly on the earth, but the shadows all point to the morning. *Jean Paul.*

25 Old minds are like old horses ; you must exercise them if you wish to keep them in working order. *John Adams.*

Old ovens are soon heated. *Pr.*

Old oxen have stiff horns. *Pr.*

Old shoes are easiest. *Pr.*

Old signs do not deceive. *Dan. Pr.*

30 Old wood to burn, old books to read, old wine to drink, and old friends to converse with. *Alphonso of Castile.*

Old wounds soon bleed. *Pr.*

Olet lucernam — It smells of the lamp, or midnight study.

Oleum adde camino—Add fuel to the fire. *Hor.*

Oleum et operam perdidi—I have lost both the oil and my pains. *Plaut.*

35 Olla male fervet—It does not look hopeful ; the pot boils poorly. *Pr.*

Olim meminisse juvabit—It will delight us to recall these things some day hereafter. *Virg.*

Oliver Cromwell, dead two hundred years ago, does yet speak ; nay, perhaps, now first begins to speak. *Carlyle.*

Omina sunt aliquid—There is something in omens. *Ovid.*

ὄμμα γὰρ δόμων νομίζω δεσπότου παρουσίαν —The presence of the master is, meseems, the eye of a house. *Æschylus.*

Omne actum ab agentis intentione judicandum 40 —Every act is to be judged of by the intention of the agent. *L.*

Omne ævum curæ : cunctis sua displicet ætas —Every age has its own care : each one thinks his own time of life disagreeable. *Auson.*

Omne animal seipsum diligit — Every animal loves itself. *Cic.*

Omne animi vitium tanto conspectius in se / Crimen habet, quanto major qui peccat habetur—Every vice of the mind involves a condemnation the more glaring, the higher the rank of the person who is guilty. *Juv.*

Omne capax movet urna nomen—In the capacious urn of death every name is shaken. *Hor.*

Omne corpus mutabile est ; ita efficitur ut 45 omne corpus mortale sit—Every body is subject to change ; hence it comes to pass that every body is subject to death. *Cic.*

Omne epigramma sit instar apis, aculeus illi, / Sint sua mella, sit et corporis exigui—Every epigram should be like a bee : have a sting like it, honey, and a small body. *Mart.*

Omne in præcipiti vitium stetit — Every vice ever stands on the brink of a precipice. *Juv.*

Omne malum nascens facile opprimitur : inveteratum fit plerumque robustius—Every evil is easily crushed at its birth ; when grown old, it generally becomes more obstinate. *Cic.*

Omne nimium vertitur in vitium—Every excess develops into a vice. *Pr.*

Omne scibile—Everything knowable. 50

Omne solum forti patria est—To the brave man every land is his native land. *Ovid.*

Omne tulit punctum qui miscuit utile dulci / Lectorem delectando, pariterque monendo— He gains universal applause who mingles the useful with the agreeable, at once delighting and instructing the reader. *Hor.*

Omnem crede diem tibi diluxisse supremum— Believe that each day which shines on you is your last. *Hor.*

Omnem movere lapidem—To leave no stone unturned. *Pr.*

Omnes amicos habere operosum est ; satis est 55 inimicos non habere—It is an arduous task to make all men your friends ; it is enough to have no enemies. *Sen.*

Omnes composui—I have laid them all at rest (in the grave). *Hor.*

Omnes eodem cogimur ; omnium / Versatur urna serius, ocius, / Sors exitura, et nos in æter-/ Num exsilium impositura cymbæ —We are all driven to the same ferry ; the lot of each is shaken in the urn, destined sooner or later to come forth, and place us in Charon's wherry for eternal exile. *Hor.*

Omnes homines, qui de rebus dubiis consultant, ab odio, amicitia, ira, atque misericordia vacuos esse decet—All men, who consult on doubtful matters, should be void of hatred, friendship, anger, and pity. *Sall.*

Omnes omnium caritates patria una complectitur—Our country alone comprehends all our affections for all. *Cic.*

Omnes, quibus res sunt minus secundæ, magis sunt, nescio quomodo / Suspiciosi: ad contumeliam omnia accipiunt magis; / Propter suam impotentiam se credunt negligi—All those whose affairs are unprosperous are, somehow or other, extremely suspicious; they take every hint as an affront, and think the neglect with which they are treated is due to their humble position. *Ter.*

Omnes sapientes decet conferre et fabulari—All wise people ought to confer and hold converse with each other. *Plaut.*

Omnes una manet nox, / Et calcanda semel via lethi—One night awaits us all, and the path of death must once be trodden by us. *Hor.*

5 Omni ætati mors est communis—Death is common to every age. *Cic.*

Omnia bonos viros decent—All things are becoming in good men. *Pr.*

Omnia conando docilis solertia vincit—By application a docile shrewdness surmounts every difficulty. *Manilius.*

Omnia cum amico delibera, sed de te ipso prius—Consult your friend on everything, but particularly on what affects yourself. *Sen.*

Omnia desuper—All things come from above. *M.*

10 Omnia ejusdem farinæ—All things are of the same stuff, *lit.* grain. *Pr.*

Omnia fert ætas, animum quoque—Age carries all away, and the powers of the mind too. *Virg.*

Omnia Græce! / Cum sit turpe magis nostris nescire Latine—All things must be in Greek! when it is more shameful for our Romans to be ignorant of Latin. *Juv.*

Omnia inconsulti impetus cœpta, initiis valida, spatio languescunt—All enterprises which are entered on with indiscreet zeal may be pursued with great vigour at first, but are sure to collapse in the end. *Tac.*

Omnia jam fient, fieri quæ posse negabam : / Et nihil est de quo non sit habenda fides—All things will now come to pass which I used to think impossible ; and there is nothing which we may not hope to see take place. *Ovid.*

15 Omnia mala exempla bonis principiis orta sunt—All bad precedents have had their rise in good beginnings.

Omnia mea mecum porto—All that belongs to me I carry with me. *Bias.*

Omnia mutantur, nihil interit—All things but change, nothing perishes. *Ovid.*

Omnia mutantur, nos et mutamur in illis—All things change, and we ourselves change along with them. *Borbonius.*

Omnia non pariter rerum sunt omnibus apta—All things are not alike fit for all men. *Propert.*

20 Omnia orta occident—All things that rise also set. *Sall.*

Omnia perdidimus, tantummodo vita relicta est—We have lost everything, only life is left. *Ovid.*

Omnia perversas possunt corrumpere mentes—All things tend to corrupt perverted minds. *Ovid.*

Omnia præclara rara — All excellent things are rare. *Cic.*

Omnia præsumuntur rite et solenniter esse acta—All things are presumed to have been done duly and in the usual manner. *L.*

Omnia prius experiri, quam armis, sapientem 25 decet—It becomes a wise man to try all methods before having recourse to arms. *Ter.*

Omnia profecto, cum se a cœlestibus rebus referet ad humanas, excelsius magnificentiusque et dicet et sentiet—When a man descends from heavenly things to human, he will certainly both speak and feel more loftily and nobly on every theme. *Cic.*

Omnia quæ nunc vetustissima creduntur, nova fuere . . . et quod hodie exemplis tuemur, inter exempla erit—Everything which is now regarded as very ancient was once new, and what we are defending to-day by precedent, will by and by be a precedent itself. *Tac.*

Omnia rerum principia parva sunt—All beginnings are small. *Cic.*

Omnia Romæ / Cum pretio—All things may be bought at Rome with money. *Juv.*

Omnia serviliter pro dominatione—Servile in 30 all his actions for the sake of power. *Tac., of Otho.*

Omnia subjecisti sub pedibus, oves et boves—Thou hast placed all things beneath our feet, both sheep and oxen. *Motto of the Butchers' Company.*

Omnia sunt hominum tenui pendentia filo ; / Et subito casu, quæ valuere, ruunt—All things human hang by a slender thread ; and that which seemed to stand strong of a sudden falls and sinks in ruins. *Ovid.*

Omnia tuta timens—Distrusting everything that is perfectly safe. *Virg.*

Omnia venalia Romæ—All things can be bought at Rome. *Pr.*

Omnia vincit amor, nos et cedamus amori— 35 Love conquers all the world, let us too yield to love. *Virg.*

Omnibus bonis expedit rempublicam esse salvam—It is for the interest of every good man that the commonwealth shall be safe. *Cic.*

Omnibus hoc vitium est cantoribus, inter amicos / Ut nunquam inducant animum cantare rogati, / Injussi nunquam desistant—This is a general fault of all singers, that among their friends they never make up their minds to sing, however pressed ; but when no one asks them, they will never leave off. *Hor.*

Omnibus hostes / Reddite nos populis, civile avertite bellum—Commit us to hostility with every other nation, but avert from us civil war. *Lucan.*

Omnibus in terris, quæ sunt a Gadibus usque / Auroram et Gangem, pauci dignoscere possunt / Vera bona, atque illis multum diversa, remota / Erroris nebula — In all the lands which stretch from Gades even to the region of the dawn and the Ganges, there are few who are able by removing the mist of error to distinguish between what is really good and what is widely diverse. *Juv.*

Omnibus modis, qui pauperes sunt homines, 40 miseri vivunt ; / Præsertim quibus nec quæstus est, nec didicere artem ullam—The poor live wretchedly in every way ; especially those who have no means of livelihood and have learned no craft. *Plaut.*

Omnis ars imitatio est naturæ—All art is an imitation of nature. *Sen.*

Omnis commoditas sua fert incommoda secum — Every convenience brings its own inconveniences along with it. *Pr.*

Omnis dolor aut est vehemens, aut levis; si levis, facile fertur, si vehemens, certe brevis futurus est—All pain is either severe or slight; if slight, it is easily borne; if severe, it will without doubt be brief. *Cic.*

Omnis enim res / Virtus, fama, decus, divina humanaque pulchris / Divitiis parent; quas qui construxerit, ille / Clarus erit, fortis, justus—All things divine and human, as virtue, fame, and honour, defer to fair wealth, and he who has amassed it will be illustrious, brave, and just. *Hor.*

Omnis pœna corporalis, quamvis minima, major est omni pœna pecuniaria, quamvis maxima —The slightest corporal punishment falls more heavily than the largest pecuniary penalty. *L.*

5 Omnis stulitia laborat fastidio sui—All folly is afflicted with a disdain of itself. *Sen.*

Omnium consensu capax imperii, nisi imperasset—He would have been universally deemed fit for empire, if he had never reigned. *Said of Galba by Tacitus.*

Omnium horarum homo—A man ready for whatever may chance. *Quinct.*

Omnium rerum, ex quibus aliquid acquiritur, nihil est agricultura melius, nihil uberius, nihil dulcius, nihil homine libero dignius —Of all pursuits from which profit accrues, nothing is superior to agriculture, nothing more productive, nothing more enjoyable, nothing more worthy of a free man. *Cic.*

Omnium rerum, heus, vicissitudo est — There are changes, mark ye, in all things. *Ter.*

10 On a beau prêcher à qui n'a cure de bien faire —It is no use preaching to him who has no wish to do well. *Fr. Pr.*

On a long journey even a straw is heavy. *Pr.*

On a souvent besoin d'un plus petit que soi— One has often need of one inferior to one's self. *La Fontaine.*

On a winged word hath hung the destiny of nations. *Landor.*

On affaiblit toujours tout ce qu'on exagère— We always weaken everything which we exaggerate. *La Harpe.*

15 On aime bien à deviner les autres, mais l'on aime pas à être deviné—We like well to see through other people, but we do not like to be seen through ourselves. *La Roche.*

On aime sans raison, et sans raison l'on hait— We love without reason, and without reason we hate. *Regnard.*

On apprend en faillant—One learns by failing. *Fr. Pr.*

On attrape plus de mouches avec du miel qu' vinaigre—More flies are caught with honey than vinegar. *Fr. Pr.*

On avale à pleine gorgée le mensonge qui nous flatte, et l'on boit goute à goute une vérité qui nous est amère—We swallow at one draught the lie that flatters us, and drink drop by drop the truth which is bitter to us. *Diderot.*

20 On commence par être dupe, / On finit par être fripon— People begin by being dupes, and end by being knaves. *Mme. Deshoulières, on gambling.*

On connaît les amis au besoin—Friends are known in time of need. *Fr. Pr.*

On devient innocent quand on est malheureux —We become innocent when we are unfortunate. *La Fontaine.*

On dit—They say; a flying rumour or current report. *Fr.*

On dit de gueux qu'ils ne sont jamais dans leur chemins, parce qu'ils n'ont point de demeure fixe. Il en est de même de cause qui disputent, sans avoir des notions déterminées—It is said of beggars that they are never on their way, for they have no fixed dwelling-place; it is the same with people who dispute without having definite ideas. *Fr.*

On dit, est souvent un grand menteur—" They 25 say " is often a great liar. *Fr. Pr.*

On dit, et sans horreur je ne puis le redire—It has been said, and I cannot without horror repeat it. *Racine.*

On dit que Dieu est toujours pour les gros bataillons—They say God is always with the heaviest battalions. *Voltaire.*

On doit être heureux sans trop penser à l'être —One ought to be happy without thinking too much of being so. *Fr. Pr.*

On doit des égards aux vivants; on ne doit aux morts que la vérité—Respect is due to the living; to the dead nothing but truth. *Motte.*

On donne des conseils, mais on ne donne point 30 la sagesse d'en profiter—We may give advice, but not the sense to profit by it. *La Roche.*

On eagles' wings immortal scandals fly, / While virtuous actions are but born to die. *Pope.*

On entre et on crie, / Et voilà la vie ! / On crie et on sort, / Et voilà la mort !—We come and cry, and that is life; we cry and go, and that is death. *Fr.*

On est aisément dupé par ce qu'on aime—We are easily duped by those we love. *Molière.*

On est, quand on le veut, le maître de son sort —A man, when he wishes, is the master of his fate. *Ferrier.*

On every stage the foes of peace attend. / 35 Hate dogs their flight, and insult mocks their end. *Johnson.*

On every thorn delightful wisdom grows; / In every rill a sweet instruction flows. *Young.*

On fait souvent tort à la vérité par la manière dont on se sert pour la défendre—We often injure the truth by our manner of defending it. *Fr.*

On fait toujours le loup plus gros qu'il n'est— People always make the wolf more formidable than he is. *Fr. Pr.*

On gagne peu de choses par habileté—It is little that one gains by cleverness. *(?)*

On God and godlike men we build our trust. 40 *Tennyson.*

On his own saddle one rides safest. *Pr.*

On jette enfin de la terre sur la tête, et en voilà pour jamais—Little earth is cast in the end upon the head, and there is no more of it for ever. *Pascal.*

On life's vast ocean diversely we sail, / Reason the card, but passion is the gale. *Pope.*

On Monday morning don't be looking for Saturday night. *Pr.*

On n'a jamais bon marché de mauvaise mar- 45 chandise—Bad ware is never cheap. *Fr. Pr.*

On n'a rien pour rien—Nothing can be had for nothing. *Fr. Pr.*

On n'aime plus comme on aimait jadis—People no longer love as they used to do long ago. *Fr.*

On n'auroit guère de plaisir, si l'on ne se flattoit point—A man should have little pleasure if he did not sometimes flatter himself. *Fr.*

On n'est jamais si bien servi que par soi-même—A man is never so well served as by himself. *Etienne.*

5 On n'est jamais si heureux, ni si malheureux qu'on se l'imagine—People are never either so happy or so miserable as they imagine. *La Roche.*

On n'est jamais si riche que quand on déménage—People are never so rich as when they are moving their stuff. *Fr. Pr.*

On n'est jamais si ridicule par les qualités que l'on a que par celles que l'on affecte d'avoir—We are never so ridiculous by the qualities we have as by those we affect to have. *La Roche.*

On n'est jamais trahi que par ses siens—A man is never betrayed except by his friends. *Fr.*

On n'est souvent mécontent des autres que parce qu'on l'est de soi-même—We are often dissatisfied with others because we are so with ourselves. *Fr. Pr.*

10 On ne considère pas assez les paroles comme des faits—We don't sufficiently consider that words are deeds. *Fr.*

On ne cherche point à prouver la lumière—There is no need to prove the existence of light. *Fr. Pr.*

On ne doit pas juger du mérité d'un homme par ses grandes qualités, mais par l'usage qu'il en sait faire—We should not judge of the merit of a man by his great gifts, but by the use he makes of them. *La Roche.*

On ne donne rien si libéralement que ses conseils—People are not so liberal with anything as with advice. *La Roche.*

On ne gouverne les hommes que en les servant; la règle est sans exception—Men are governed only by serving them; the rule is without exception. *V. Cousin.*

15 On ne jette des pierres qu'à l'arbre chargé de fruits—People throw stones only at the tree which is loaded with fruit. *Fr. Pr.*

On ne loue d'ordinaire que pour être loué—Praise is generally given only that it may be returned. *La Roche.*

On ne lui fait pas prendre des vessies pour des lanternes—You won't get him to take bladders for lanterns. *Fr. Pr.*

On ne méprise pas tous ceux qui ont des vices, mais on méprise tous ceux qui n'ont aucune vertu—We do not despise all those who have vices, but we despise all those who have no virtue. *La Roche.*

On ne perd les états que par timidité—It is only through timidity that states are lost. *Voltaire.*

20 On ne peut contenter tout le monde et son père—There is no pleasing everybody and one's father. *La Fontaine.*

On ne peut faire qu'en faisant—One can do only by doing. *Fr. Pr.*

On ne peut sonner les cloches et aller à la procession—One cannot ring the bells and join in the procession. *Fr. Pr.*

On ne prête qu'aux riches—People lend only to the rich. *Fr. Pr.*

On ne ramène guère un traître par l'impunité, au lieu que par la punition l'on en rend mille autres sages—No one ever reclaimed a traitor by letting him off, whereas punishment may keep thousands in the right way. (?)

On ne réussit dans ce monde qu'à la pointe de 25 l'épée, et on meurt les armes à la main—Success in life is won at the point of the sword, and we die with the weapon in our hands. (?)

On ne sait pour qui on amasse—We know not for whom we gather. *Fr. Pr.*

On ne se blame que pour être loué—Persons only blame themselves in order to obtain praise. *La Roche.*

On ne sent bien que ses propres maux—We feel only the evils that affect ourselves. *Fr. Pr.*

On ne trouve jamais l'expression d'un sentiment que l'on n'a pas; l'esprit grimace et le style aussi—It is ever impossible to express a sentiment which we do not feel; the mind grimaces, and the style too. *Lamennais.*

On ne va jamais si loin que lorsqu'on ne sait 30 pas où l'on va—One never goes so far as when he does not know where he is going. *Fr.*

On ne vaut dans ce monde que ce qu'on veut valoir—A man's worth in this world is estimated according to the value he puts upon himself. *La Bruyère.*

On ne vit dans la mémoire du monde que par des travaux pour le monde—One lives in the world's memory only by what he has done in the world's behalf. *Fr.*

ὅν οἱ θεοὶ φιλοῦσιν ἀποθνήσκει νέος—He whom the gods love dies young. *Menander.*

On pardonne aisément un tort que l'on partage—We easily pardon an offence which we had part in. *Jouy.*

On parle peu quand la vanité ne fait pas parler 35—People speak little when vanity does not prompt them. *La Roche.*

On perd tout le temps qu'on peut mieux employer—All the time is lost which might be better employed. (?)

On peut attirer les cœurs par les qualités qu'on montre, mais on ne les fixe que par celles qu'on a—People's affections may be attracted by the qualities which we affect, but they can only be won by those which we really possess. *Fr.*

On peut dire que son esprit brille aux dépens de sa mémoire—We may say his wit shines at the expense of his memory. *Le Sage.*

On peut dominer par la force, mais jamais par la seule adresse—We may lord it by force, but never by adroitness alone. *Vauvenargues.*

On peut être plus fin qu'un autre, mais non 40 pas plus fin que tous les autres—A man may be sharper than another, but not than all others. *La Roche.*

On peut mépriser le monde, mais on ne peut pas s'en passer—We may despise the world, but we cannot do without it. *Fr. Pr.*

On prend le peuple par les oreilles, comme on fait un pot par les anses—The public are to be caught by the ears, as one takes a pot by the handles. *Pr.*

On prend son bien où on le trouve—One takes what is his own wherever he finds it. *Fr. Pr.*

On prend souvent l'indolence pour la patience—Indolence is often taken for patience. *Fr. Pr.*

On Reason build Resolve! / That column of 45 true majesty in man. *Young.*

On respecte un moulin, on vole une province !
—They (obliged by law) spare a mill, but steal a
province !

On revient toujours à ses premiers amours—
We always come back to our first loves. *Etienne.*

On se heurte toujours où l'on a mal—One always knocks himself on the spot where the sore
is. *Fr. Pr.*

On se persuade mieux pour l'ordinaire par les
raisons qu'on a trouvées soi-même, que par
celles qui sont venues dans l'esprit des
autres—We are ordinarily more easily satisfied
with reasons that we have discovered ourselves,
than by those which have occurred to others.
Pascal.

5 On some men's bread butter will not stick. *Pr.*

On spécule sur tout, même sur la famine—
People speculate on everything, even on famine.
Armand Charlemagne.

On termine de longs procès / Par un peu de
guerre civile—We end protracted law-suits by
a little civil war.

On the beaten road there is tolerable travelling ; but it is sore work, and many have to
perish, fashioning a way through the impassable. *Carlyle.*

On the brink of the waters of life and truth we
are miserably dying. *Emerson.*

10 On the day of the resurrection, those who
have indulged in ridicule will be called to
the door of Paradise, and have it shut in
their faces when they reach it. *Mahomet.*

On the field of foughten battle still, / Woe
knows no limits save the victor's will. *The
Gaulliad.*

On the neck of the young man sparkles no
gem so gracious as enterprise. *Hafiz.*

On the pinnacle of fortune man does not stand
long firm. *Goethe.*

On the sea sail, on the land settle. *Pr.*

15 On the soft bed of luxury most kingdoms have
expired. *Young.*

On the stage man should stand a step higher
than in life. *Börne.*

On this account is the Bible a book of eternally
effective power, because, as long as the
world lasts, no one will step forward and
say : I comprehend it in the whole and
understand it in the particular ; but we
modestly say : In the whole it is venerable,
and in the particular practicable (*anwendar*).
Goethe.

On veut avoir ce qu'on n'a pas, / Et ce qu'on a
cesse de deplaire—We wish to have what we
have not, and what we have ceases to please.
Monvel.

On voit mourir et renaître les roses ; il n'en est
pas ainsi de nos beaux jours—We see roses die
and revive again ; it is not so with our fine days.
Charleval.

20 On wrong / Swift vengeance waits ; and art
subdues the strong. *Pope.*

Once a knave, always a knave. *Pr.*

Once a man and twice a child. *Pr.*

Once for all, beauty remains undemonstrable ;
it appears to us as in a dream, when we
behold the works of the great poets and
painters, and, in short, of all feeling artists.
Goethe.

Once is no custom. *Pr.*

25 Once is no rule. *Pr.*

Once resolved, the trouble is over. *It. Pr.*

Once sufficiently enforce the eighth commandment, the whole "rights of man" are well
cared for ; I know no better definition of the
rights of man : "Thou shalt not steal ; thou
shalt not be stolen from." What a society
were that ! Plato's Republic, More's Utopia
mere emblems of it. *Carlyle.*

Once thoroughly our own, knowledge ceases
to give us pleasure. *Ruskin.*

Once to every man and nation comes the
moment to decide, / In the strife of truth
with falsehood, for the good or evil side.
Lowell.

Once true, still more twice true, in the life of 30
the spirit is always true. *Ed.*

Ond Gierning har Vidne i Barmen—There is
a witness of the evil deed in one's own bosom.
Dan. Pr.

Ondt bliver aldrig godt för halv være kommer—Bad is never good till worse befall. *Dan.
Pr.*

One abides not long on the summit of fortune.
Pr.

One, although not possessed of a mine of gold,
may find the offspring of his own nature, that
noble ardour, which hath for its object the
accomplishment of the whole assemblage of
virtues. *Hitopadesa.*

One always has time enough if one will apply 35
it well. *Goethe.*

One and God make a majority. *Fred. Douglas.*

One anecdote is worth a volume of biography.
Channing.

One barking dog sets all the street a-barking.
Pr.

One beats the bush, and another catches the
bird. *Pr.*

One Bible I know, of whose plenary inspiration 40
doubt is not so much as possible ; nay, with
my own eyes I saw the God's hand writing
it ; whereof all other Bibles are but leaves,
say, in picture-writing, to assist the weaker
faculty. *Carlyle.*

One born on the glebe comes by habit to belong
to it ; the two grow together, and the fairest
ties are spun from the union. *Goethe.*

One can be very happy without demanding
that others should agree with one. *Goethe.*

One can bear to be rebuked, but not to be
laughed at. *Molière.*

One can live in true freedom, and yet not be
unbound. *Goethe.*

One can live on little, but not on nothing. 45
Pr.

One can never know at the first moment what
may, at a future time, separate itself from
the rough experience as true substance.
Goethe.

One cannot help doing a good office when it
comes in one's way. *Le Sage.*

One cannot say that the rational is always
beautiful ; but the beautiful is always rational, or at least ought to be so. *Goethe.*

One cannot speak the truth with false words.
Goethe.

One can't shoe a runaway horse. *Dutch Pr.* 50

One chick keeps a hen busy. *Pr.*

One cloud is enough to eclipse all the sun.
Pr.

One could not commit a greater crime against public interests than to show indulgence to those who violate them. *Richelieu.*

One could not wish any man to fall into a fault ; yet it is often precisely after a fault, or a crime even, that the morality which is in a man first unfolds itself, and what of strength he as a man possesses, now when all else is gone from him. *Goethe.*

One could take down a book from a shelf ten times more wise and witty than almost any man's conversation. *Campbell.*

One crime is everything ; two, nothing. *Mme. Deluzy.*

5 One crow never pulls out another's eyes. *Pr.*

One crowded hour of glorious life / Is worth an age without a name. *Scott.*

One does not love the heaven's lightning (seen in a great man) in the way of caresses altogether. *Carlyle.*

One dog can drive a flock of sheep. *Pr.*

One doth not know / How much an ill word may empoison liking. *Much Ado,* iii. 1.

10 One drop of hatred left in the cup of joy turns the most blissful draught into poison. *Schiller.*

One enemy is too many, and a hundred friends too few. *Pr.*

One enemy may do us more harm than a hundred friends can do us good. *Pr.*

One eye of the master does more than both his hands. *Pr.*

One eye-witness is better than ten hearsays. *Pr.*

15 One false move may lose the game. *Pr.*

One feels clearly that it is a kindly spirit which actually constitutes the human element in man. *Schiller.*

One finds human nature everywhere great and little, beautiful and ugly. . . . Go on bravely working. *Goethe.*

One fire burns out another's burning ; / One pain is lessen'd by another's anguish. *Rom. and Jul.,* i. 1.

One fool makes many. *Pr.*

20 One futile person, that maketh it his glory to tell, will do more hurt than many that know it their duty to conceal. *Bacon.*

One gets easier accustomed to a silken bed than to a sack of leaves. *Auerbach.*

One God, one law, one element, / And one far-off divine event, / To which the whole creation moves. *Tennyson.*

One good deed dying tongueless / Slaughters a thousand, waiting upon that. *Winter's Tale,* i. 2.

One good head is better than a hundred strong hands. *Pr.*

25 One good mother is worth a hundred schoolmasters. *Pr.*

One good turn deserves another. *Pr*

One good way I know of to find happiness is not by boring a hole to fit the plug. *Billings.*

One grain fills not a sack, but helps his fellows. *Pr.*

One hair of a woman draws more than a team of horses.

30 One half of the world knows not how the other half lives. *Rabelais.*

One half of the world must sweat and groan that the other half may dream. *Longfellow.*

One half the world laughs at the other. *Fr. and Ger. Pr.*

One hand full of money is more persuasive than two full of truth. *Dan. Pr.*

One hand washes another. *Pr.*

One hard word brings on another. *Pr.*   35

One head cannot hold all wisdom. *Pr.*

One hour in the execution of justice is worth seventy years of prayer. *Mahometan Pr.*

One hour's sleep before midnight is worth two after. *Pr.*

One impulse from a vernal wood / May teach you more of man, / Of moral evil and of good, / Than all the sages can. *Wordsworth.*

One is always making good use of one's time 40 when engaged with a subject that daily forces one to make advances in self-culture. *Goethe.*

One is not a whit the happier when he attains what he has wished for. *Goethe.*

One is scarcely sensible of fatigue whilst he marches to music. *Carlyle.*

One jeer seldom goeth forth but it bringeth back its equal. *Pr.*

One keep-clean is better than ten make-cleans. *Pr.*

One learns taciturnity best among those people 45 who have none, and loquacity among the taciturn. *Jean Paul.*

One lie makes many. *Pr.*

One lie needs seven lies to wait upon it. *Pr.*

One life—a little gleam of time between two eternities. *Carlyle*

One link broken, the whole chain is broken. *Pr.*

One loss brings another. *Pr.*   50

One man is born to money, and another to the purse. *Dan. Pr.*

One man makes a chair, and another man sits in it. *Pr.*

One man may lead a horse to the water, but twenty cannot make him drink. *Pr.*

One man may steal a horse more safely than another may look at him over a hedge. *Pr.*

One man receives crucifixion as the reward of 55 his villainy ; another a regal crown. *Juv.*

One man that has a higher wisdom in him is not stronger than ten men, or than ten thousand, but than all men that have it not. *Carlyle.*

One man's eyes are spectacles to another to read his heart with. *Johnson.*

One man's justice is another man's injustice ; one man's beauty another's ugliness ; one man's wisdom, another's folly ; as one beholds the same objects from a higher point. *Emerson.*

One man's meat is another man's poison. *Pr.*

One man's opinion is no man's opinion. *Pr.*   60

One may forsake a person to save a family ; one may desert a whole family for the sake of a village ; and sacrifice a village for the safety of the community ; but for one's self one may abandon the whole world. *Hitopadesa.*

One may give him a hundred instances from Holy Writ that he should not dispute ; still. it is the character of a fool to make a disturbance without a cause. *Hitopadesa.*

One may make the house a palace of sham, or he can make it a home—a refuge. *Mark Twain.*

One may often find as much thought on the reverse of a medal as in a canto of Spenser *Addison.*

One may see that with half an eye. *Pr.*

5 One may smile, and smile, and be a villain. *Ham.,* i. 5.

One may summon his philosophy when he is beaten in battle, not till then. *John Burroughs.*

One misfortune is the vigil of another. *It. Pr.*

One monster there is in this world : the idle man. *Carlyle.*

One mother is more venerable than a thousand fathers. *Manu.*

10 One murder made a villain ; / Millions, a nero. *Bp. Porteous.*

One must be careful in announcing great happiness. *Schopenhauer.*

One must be somebody in order to have an enemy. One must be a force before he can be resisted by another force. *Mme. Swetchine.*

One must be something in order to do something. *Goethe.*

One must believe in simplicity, in what is simple, in what is originally productive, if one wants to go the right way. This, however, is not granted to every one ; we are born in an artificial state, and it is far easier to make it more artificial still than to return to what is simple. *Goethe.*

15 One must have lived greatly whose record would bear the full light of day from its beginning to its close. *A. B. Alcott.*

One must not look at a gift horse in the mouth. *Pr.*

One must not swerve in one's self, not even a hair's breadth from the highest maxims of art and life ; but in empiricism, in the movement of the day, I would rather allow what is mediocre to pass than mistake the good, or even find fault with it. *Goethe.*

One must take a pleasure in the shell till one has the happiness to arrive at the kernel. *Goethe.*

One must weigh men by avoirdupois weight, and not by the jeweller's scales. *Goethe.*

20 One need only take a thing properly in hand for it to be done. *Goethe.*

One need only utter something that flatters indolence and conceit to be sure of plenty of adherents among commonplace people. *Goethe.*

One never goes farther than when he does not know whither he is going. *Goethe.*

One never needs his wit so much as when he argues with a fool. *Chinese Pr.*

One of the best rules in conversation is, never say a thing which any of the company can reasonably wish we had left unsaid. *Swift.*

25 One of the chief misfortunes of honest people is that they are cowardly. *Voltaire.*

One of the most fatal sources of the prevailing misery and crime lies in the generally accepted quiet assumption that because things have long been wrong, it is impossible they should ever be right. *Ruskin.*

One of the most singular gifts, or, if abused, most singular weaknesses, of the human mind, is its power of persuading itself to see whatever it chooses ; a great gift if directed to the discernment of the things needful and pertinent to its own work and being ; a great weakness if directed to the discovery of things profitless or discouraging. *Ruskin.*

One of the noblest qualities in our nature is that we are able so easily to dispense with greater perfection. *Vauvenargues.*

One of the old man's miseries is that he cannot easily find a companion able to partake with him of the past. *Johnson.*

One of the sublimest things in the world is 30 plain truth. *Bulwer Lytton.*

One of the worst diseases to which the human creature is liable is its disease of thinking. If it would only just look at a thing instead of thinking what it must be like, or do a thing instead of thinking it cannot be done, we should all get on far better. *Ruskin.*

One of these days is none of these days. *Pr.*

One on God's side is a majority. *Wendell Phillips.*

One ought not to praise a great man unless he is as great as he. *Goethe.*

One pair of heels is often worth two pair of 35 hands. (?)

One pirate gets nothing of another but his cask. *Pr.*

One ploughs, another sows ; / Who will reap, no one knows. *Pr.*

One power rules another, but no power can cultivate another ; in each endowment, and not elsewhere, lies the force that must complete it. *Goethe.*

One precedent creates another. They soon accumulate and constitute law. What yesterday was fact to-day is doctrine. Examples are supposed to justify the most dangerous measures ; and where they do not suit exactly, the defect is supplied by analogy. *Junius.*

One rarely sees how deeply one is in debt till 40 one comes to settle one's accounts. *Goethe.*

One really gains nothing from such interests (as occupy the newspapers). *Goethe.*

One religion after another fades away; but the religious sense, which created them all, can never become dead to humanity. *Jean Paul.*

One says more, and with more heart, in an hour than is written in years. *Goethe.*

One science only can one genius fit, / So vast is art, so narrow human wit. *Pope.*

One scream of fear from a mother may resound 45 through the whole life of her daughter. *Jean Paul.*

One sheep follows another. *Pr.*

One should abandon that country wherein there is neither respect, nor employment, nor connections, nor the advancement of science. *Hitopadesa.*

One should never ask anybody if one means to write anything. *Goethe.*

One should never risk a joke, even of the mildest and most unexceptionable character, except among people of culture and wit. *La Bruyère.*

One should never think of death. One should think of life : that is real piety. *Disraeli.*

One should not lift the rod against our enemies upon the private information of another. *Hitopadesa.*

One should not neglect from time to time to renew friendly relations by personal intercourse. *Goethe.*

One shriek of hate would jar all the hymns of heaven : / True Devils with no ear, they howl in tune / With nothing but the Devil! *Tennyson.*

5 One sickly sheep infects the flock. *Pr.*

One sin opens the door to another. *Pr.*

One single moment is decisive both of man's life and his whole future. However he may reflect, each resolution he forms is but the work of a moment; the prudent alone seize the right one. *Goethe.*

One sinner destroyeth much good. *Bible.*

One solitary philosopher may be great, virtuous, and happy in the depth of poverty, but not a whole people. *L. Iselin.*

10 One soul may have a decided influence upon another merely by means of its silent presence. *Goethe.*

One soweth and another reapeth. *Heb. Pr.*

One step above the sublime makes the ridiculous, and one step above the ridiculous makes the sublime again. *Paine.*

One stumble is enough to deface the character of an honourable life. *L Estrange.*

One sun by day, by night ten thousand shine. *Young.*

15 One swallow does not make a summer. *Pr.*

One sword keeps another in the scabbard. *Pr.*

One "Take this" is better than two "I will give you." *Sp. Pr.*

"One thing above all others," says Goethe, "I have never thought about thinking." What a thrift of thinking faculty there; thrift almost of itself equal to a fortune in these days. *Carlyle.*

One thing at a time, all things in succession. That which grows fast withers as rapidly; that which grows slowly endures. *J. G. Holland.*

20 One thing is needful. *Jesus.*

One thing there is which no child brings into the world with him ; and yet it is on this one thing that all depends for making man in every point a man ;—and that is Reverence (*Ehrfurcht*). *Goethe.*

One thorn of experience is worth a whole wilderness of warning. *Lowell.*

One thought includes all thought, in the sense that a grain of sand includes the universe. *Coleridge.*

One tires of a page of which every sentence sparkles with points, of a sentimentalist who is always pumping the tears from his eyes or your own. *Thackeray.*

25 One to another cannot be a perfect physician. *George Herbert.*

One to-day is worth two to-morrows. *Ben. Franklin.*

One tongue is sufficient for a woman. *Milton, in reference to foreign languages.*

One touch of Nature makes the whole world kin. *Troil. and Cress.*, iii. 3.

One 'ud think, an' hear some folk talk, as the men war cute enough to count the corns in a bag o' wheat wi' only smelling at it. *George Eliot.*

One who, either in conversation or in letters, 30 affects to shine and to sparkle always, will not please long. *Blair.*

One who has nothing to admire, nothing to love, except his own poor self, may be reckoned a completed character; (but) he is in the minimum state of moral perfection—no more can be made of him. *Carlyle.*

One who is master of ever so little art may be able, on a great occasion, to root up trees with as much ease as the current of a river the reeds and grass. *Hitopadesa.*

One who is out of his own country is defeated by a very trifling enemy. *Hitopadesa.*

One woe doth tread upon another's heel, / So fast they follow. *Ham.*, iv. 7.

One word with two meanings is the traitor's 35 shield and shaft. *Caucasian Pr.*

One wrong step may give you a great fall. *Pr.*

One's morning indolence is soon gone when one has once persuaded one's self to put a foot out of bed. *Goethe.*

One's piety is best displayed in his pursuits. *A. B. Alcott.*

One's too few, three's too many. *Pr.*

Oneness and otherness. It is impossible to 40 speak or think without embracing both. *Emerson.*

Only a Christ could have conceived a Christ. *Joseph Parker.*

Only a great pride, that is, a great and reverential repose in one's own being, renders possible a noble humility. *D. A. Wassou.*

Only a sweet and virtuous soul, / Like seasoned timber, never gives; / But when the whole world turns to coal, / Then chiefly lives. *George Herbert.*

Only action gives life strength; only moderation gives it a charm. *Jean Paul.*

Only an artist can interpret the meaning of 45 life. *Novalis.*

Only an inventor knows how to borrow, and every man is, or should be, an inventor. *Emerson.*

Only by joy and sorrow does a man know anything about himself and his destiny, learn what he ought to seek and what to shun. *Goethe.*

Only by pride cometh contention ; but with the well-advised is wisdom. *Bible.*

Only great men have any business with great defects. *La Roche.*

Only great souls know the grandeur there is 50 in charity. *Bossuet.*

Only he can be trusted with gifts who can present a face of bronze to expectations. *Thoreau.*

Only he deserves freedom who has day by day to fight for it. *Goethe.*

Only he helps who unites with many at the proper hour ; a single individual helps not. *Goethe.*

Only I discern / Infinite passion, and the pain / Of finite hearts that yearn. *Browning.*

Only in complicated critical cases do men find 55 out what is within them. *Goethe.*

Only in looking heavenward, take it in what sense you may, not in looking earthward, does what we call union, mutual love, society, begin to be possible. *Carlyle.*

Only in the world I fill up a place, which may be better supplied when I have made it empty. *As You Like It*, i. 2.

Only to catch happiness, for happiness is ever by you. *Goethe.*

Only lofty character is worth describing at all. *Ruskin.*

5 Only people who possess firmness can possess true gentleness. *La Roche.*

Only regard for law can give us freedom. *Goethe.*

Only so far as a man is happily married to himself is he fit for married life and family life generally. *Novalis.*

Only such persons interest us, Spartans, Romans, Saracens, English, Americans, who have stood in the jaws of need, and have by their own wit and might extricated themselves, and made man victorious. *Emerson.*

Only suffering draws / The inner heart of song, and can elicit / The perfumes of the soul. *Lewis Morris.*

10 Only that good profits which we can taste with all doors open, and which serves all men. *Emerson.*

Only that is poetry which purifies and mans me. *Emerson.*

Only the actions of the just / Smell sweet and blossom in the dust. *Shirley.*

Only the idle among the poor revolt against their state ; the brave workers die passively, and give no sign. *Ruskin.*

Only the man of worth can recognise worth in men. *Carlyle.*

15 Only the person should give advice in a matter where he himself will co-operate. *Goethe.*

Only the word of God and the heart of man can govern. *Ruskin.*

Only they who have hope live. *Halm.*

Only those books come down which deserve to last. *Emerson.*

Only those live who do good. *Tolstoi.*

20 Only those who love with the heart can animate the love of others. *Abel Stephens.*

Only to the apt, the pure, and the true does Nature resign herself and reveal her secrets. *Goethe.*

Only truth can be polished. *Ruskin.*

Only what of the past was true will come back to us ; that is the one asbestos that survives all fire. *Carlyle.*

Only when man weeps he should be alone, not because tears are weak, but they should be secret. *Bulwer Lytton.*

25 Onus probandi—The burden of proving.

Onus segni impone asello—Lay the burden on the lazy ass. *Pr.*

Open not your door when the devil knocks. *Pr.*

Open rebuke is better than secret love. *Pr.*

Opera illius mea sunt—His works are mine. *M.*

30 Operæ pretium est—'Tis worth while ; worth attending to.

Opere in longo fas est obrepere somnum—In a long work sleep must steal upon us. *Hor.*

Operosa parvus carmina fingo—I, a little one, compose laborious songs. *Hor.*

Operose nihil agunt—They toil at doing nothing. *Sen.*

Opes regum, corda subditorum—The wealth of kings is in the affections of their subjects. *M.*

ὀψὲ θεῶν ἀλέουσι μύλοι, ἀλέουσι δὲ λεπτά— 35 The mills of the gods grind slow, but they grind small.

Opiferque per orbem dicor—I am known over the world as the helper. *M.*

Opinion is a medium between knowledge and ignorance. *Plato.*

Opinion is, as it were, the queen of the world, but force is its tyrant. *Pascal.*

Opinion is the main thing which does good or harm in the world. It is our false opinions that ruin us. *Marcus Antoninus.*

Opinion is the mistress of fools. *Pr.* 40

Opinion rules the world. *Carlyle.*

Opinions concerning acts are not history ; acts themselves alone are history. *Wm. Blake.*

Opinions, like showers, are generated in high places, but they invariably descend into lower ones. *Colton.*

Opinionum enim commenta delet dies, naturæ judicia confirmat—Time effaces the fabrications of opinion, but confirms the judgments of Nature. *Cic.*

Opportunities, like eggs, come one at a time. 45 *Amer. Pr.*

Opportunities neglected are irrecoverable. *Pr.*

Opportunity has hair in front, but is bald behind ; if you meet her, seize her by the forelock, for Jove himself cannot catch her again if once let slip. *Rabelais.*

Opportunity is more powerful even than conquerors and prophets. *Disraeli.*

Opportunity makes desire. *Dut. Pr.*

Opportunity makes us known to others, but 50 more to ourselves. *La Roche.*

Oppose not rage while rage is in its force, but give it way awhile and let it waste. *Shakespeare.*

Opposition always enflames the enthusiast, never converts him. *Schiller.*

Oppress'd with grief, oppress'd with care, / A burden more than I can bear, / I sit me down and sigh ; / O Life, thou art a galling load, / Along a rough and weary road, / To wretches such as I. *Burns.*

Oppression is more easily borne than insult. *Junius.*

Opprobrium medicorum—The disgrace of physi- 55 cians. *Said of diseases that defy their skill, especially cancer.*

Optat ephippia bos piger ; optat arare caballus —The lazy ox covets the horse's trappings ; the horse would fain plough. *Hor.*

Optics sharp it needs, I ween, / To see what is not to be seen. *J. Trumbull.*

Optima quæque dies miseris mortalibus ævi / Prima fugit ; subeunt morbi tristisque senectus, / Et labor ; et duræ rapit inclementia mortis—For wretched mortals each best day of life flies first ; diseases soon steal on, and sad old age, and decay ; and the cruelty of inexorable death snatches us away. *Virg.*

Optimi consiliarii mortui—The best counsellors are the dead. *Pr.*

Optimum obsonium labor—Labour is the best sauce. *Pr.*

Opum furiata cupido—The frantic passion for wealth. *Ovid.*

Ora et labora—Pray and work. *M.*

Oracles speak. *Emerson.*

5 Oral delivery aims at persuasion, at making the listener believe he is convinced. Few persons are capable of being convinced ; the majority allow themselves to be persuaded. *Goethe.*

Orando laborando—By prayer and labour. *M.*

Orandum est ut sit mens sana in corpore sano—We should pray for a sound mind in a sound body. *Juv.*

Orate pro anima—Pray for the soul of.

Orationis summa virtus est perspicuitas—The greatest virtue of speech is perspicuity. *Quinct.*

10 Orator improbus leges subvertit—An evil-disposed orator subverts the laws.

Oratory is a warrior's eye flashing from under a philosopher's brow. *Hare.*

Oratory, like a drama, abhors lengthiness ; like the drama, it must be kept doing. *Bulwer Lytton.*

Order all thy actions, so as readily and meekly to comply with the commands of thy superiors, the desires of thy equals, the requests of thy inferiors ; so to do for all what thou lawfully mayest. *Thomas à Kempis.*

Order and quiet are good things when they can be had without the sacrifice of things that are better. *Ward Beecher.*

15 Order is a great man's need, and his true well-being. *Amiel.*

Order is heaven's first law. *Pope.*

Order is power. *Amiel.*

Order is the sanity of the mind, the health of the body, the peace of the city, the security of the state. As the beams to a house, as the bones to the microcosm of man, so is order to all things. *Southey.*

Order is truth, each thing standing on the basis that belongs to it. *Carlyle.*

20 Order, thou eye of action. *Aaron Hill.*

Ordinary people think merely of spending time ; a man with any brains, of using it. *Schopenhauer.*

Ore e sempre—Now and always. *It.*

Ore tenus—Merely from the mouth ; oral.

Organic laws can only be serviceable to, and, in general, will only be written by, a public of honourable citizens, loyal to their state and faithful to each other. *Ruskin.*

25 ὀργὴ φιλούντων ὀλίγον ἰσχύει χρόνον — The anger of lovers does not last long. *Menander.*

Originality is a thing we constantly clamour for and constantly quarrel with, as if any, observes Jean Paul, but our own could be expected to content us. *Carlyle.*

Originality is simply a fresh pair of eyes. *T. W. Higginson.*

Originality is the one thing which unoriginal minds cannot feel the use of. *J. S. Mill.*

Originality provokes originality.

30 Ornament is but the guilèd shore / To a most dangerous sea ; the beauteous scarf / Veiling an Indian beauty ; in a word, / The seeming truth which cunning times put on / To entrap the wisest. *Mer. of Ven.*, iii. 2.

Ornaments were invented by modesty. *Joubert.*

Oro è che oro vale—What is worth gold is gold. *It. Pr.*

Orthodoxy is my doxy ; heterodoxy another man's doxy. *Warburton.*

Orthodoxy is the Bourbon of the world of thought ; it learns not, neither can it forget. *Huxley.*

Os, orare, vale, communio, mensa negatur— 35 Speech, prayer. greeting, intercourse, and food are forbidden. *The sentence of excommunication.*

Ostentation is the signal flag of hypocrisy. *Chapin.*

Otez un vilain du gibet, il vous y mettra—Save a thief from the gallows, and he will cut your throat. *Fr. Pr.*

Othello's occupation's gone ! *Othello,* iii. 3.

Other exercises develop single powers and muscles, but dancing, like a corporeal poesy, embellishes, exercises, and equalises all the muscles at once. *Jean Paul.*

Other heights in other lives, God willing. 40 *Browning.*

Other men are lenses through which we read our own minds. *Emerson.*

Other men laboured, and ye are entered into their labours. *Jesus.*

Others apart sat on a hill retired, / In thoughts more elevate, and reason'd high / Of Providence, fore-knowledge, will, and fate, / Fix'd fate, free-will, fore-knowledge absolute ; / And found no end, in wand'ring mazes lost. *Milton.*

Others, more aspiring than achieving, / Achieve all in suggestion, . . . / More helpful by their infinite reaching forth / Than all completed thinking. *Dr. Walter Smith.*

Otia si tollas, periere Cupidinis arcus—Remove 45 the temptations of idleness, and Cupid's bow is useless. *Ovid.*

Otiosis nullus adsistit Deus—No deity assists the idle. *Pr.*

Otium cum dignitate—Leisure with dignity.

Otium sine literis mors est, et hominis vivi sepultura—Leisure without literature is death and burial alive. *Sen.*

οὐ χρὴ παννύχιον εὕδειν βουληφόρον ἄνδρα— It will not do for a counsellor to sleep all night. *Hom.*

Οὐ λέγειν δεινός, ἀλλὰ σιγᾶν ἀδύνατος — Not 50 formidable as a speaker, but unable to hold his tongue. *Gr.* (?)

Où peut-on être mieux qu'au sein de sa famille ? —Where can a man be better than in the bosom of his family ? *Marmontel Grétry.*

Où sont les neiges d'antan ?—Where is the snow of last year ? *F. Villons.*

οὔ τοι συνέχθειν ἀλλὰ συμφιλεῖν ἔφυν—I am here not for mutual hatred, but for mutual affection. *Soph.*

Oublier d'éclairer sa lanterne—To express one's self obscurely (*lit.* to forget to light one's lantern). *Fr.*

Oublier ne puis—I can never forget. *M.*   55

οὐδὲν γίνεται ἐκ τοῦ μὴ ὄντος—Nothing comes to be out of what is not. *Epicurus.*

οὐδὲν ῥῆμα σὺν κέρδει κακόν—No word that is profitable is bad. *Soph.*

Oui et Non sont bien courts à dire, mais avant que de les dire, il y faut penser long-temps—"Yes" and "no" are very short words to say, but we should think for some length of time before saying them.

οὐκ ἀγαθὸν πολυκοιρανίη· εἰς κοίρανος ἔστω, / Εἱς βασιλεύς—That there should be a multitude of rulers is not good ; let one be lord, one be king. *Hom.*

οὐκ αἰσχρὸν οὐδὲν τῶν ἀναγκαίων βροτοῖς— What is natural is never shameful. *Eurip.*

οὐκ ἔστιν μείζων βάσανος χρόνου οὐδενὸς ἔργου, / ὃς καὶ ὑπὸ στέρνοις ἀνδρὸς ἔδειξε νόον—There is no better test of a man's work than time, which also reveals the thought which lay hidden in his breast. *Simonides.*

5 Our acts our angels are, or good or ill, / Our fatal shadows that walk by us still. *Fletcher.*

Our admiration of the antique is not admiration of the old, but of the natural. *Emerson.*

Our affections are but tents of a night. *Emerson.*

Our affections, as well as our bodies, are in perpetual flux. *Rousseau.*

Our age is really up to nothing better than sweeping out the gutters—a scavenger age. Might it but do that well ! It is the indispensable beginning of all. *Carlyle.*

10 Our age knows nothing but reactions, and leaps from one extreme to another. *Niebuhr.*

Our ambiguous dissipating education awakens wishes when it should be animating tendencies ; instead of forwarding our real capacities, it turns our efforts towards objects which are frequently discordant with the mind that aims at them. *Goethe.*

Our ancestors are very good kind o' folks ; but they are the last people I should choose to have a visiting acquaintance with. *Sheridan.*

Our attachment to every object around us increases, in general, from the length of our acquaintance with it. *Goldsmith.*

Our best history is still poetry. *Emerson.*

15 Our best resolutions are frail when opposed to our predominant inclinations. *Scott.*

Our best thoughts come from others. *Emerson.*

Our better mind / Is as a Sunday's garment, then put on / When we have nought to do ; but at our work / We wear a worse for thrift. *Crowe.*

Our birth is but a sleep and a forgetting. *Wordsworth.*

Our books are false by being fragmentary ; the sentences are "bon mots," and not parts of natural discourse ; childish expressions of surprise or pleasure in nature—or worse. *Emerson.*

20 Our bounty, like a drop of water, disappears when diffused too widely. *Goldsmith.*

Our brains are seventy-year clocks. The angel of life winds them up once for all, then closes the case, and gives the key into the hands of the angel of the resurrection. *Holmes.*

Our charity indeed should be universal, and extend to all mankind ; but it is by no means convenient that our friendships and familiarities should do so too. *Thomas à Kempis.*

Our chief comforts often produce our greatest anxieties, and an increase of our possessions is but an inlet to new disquietudes. *Goldsmith.*

Our chief experiences have been casual. *Emerson.*

Our chief want in life is somebody who shall 25 make us do what we can. *Emerson.*

Our clock strikes when there is a change from hour to hour ; but no hammer in the Horologe of Time peals through the universe when there is a change from era to era. *Carlyle.*

Our compell'd sins / Stand more for number than accompt. *Meas. for Meas.*, ii. 4.

Our complaint is the largest tribute heaven receives, and the sincerest part of our devotion. *Swift.*

Our content / Is our best having. *Hen. VIII.*, ii. 3.

Our corn's to reap, for yet our tilth's to sow. 30 *Meas. for Meas.*, iv. 1.

Our country is wherever we are well off. *Milton.*

Our dead are never dead to us until we have forgotten them. *George Eliot.*

Our decrees / Dead to infliction, to themselves are dead ; / And liberty plucks justice by the nose, / The baby beats the nurse, and quite athwart / Goes all decorum. *Meas. for Meas.*, i. 4.

Our deeds are fetters that we forge ourselves. *George Eliot.*

Our deeds are like children born to us ; they 35 live and act apart from our own will. Children may be strangled, but deeds never. *George Eliot.*

Our deeds determine us as much as we determine our deeds. *George Eliot.*

Our delight in reason degenerates into idolatry of the herald. *Emerson.*

Our dissatisfaction with any other solution is the blazing evidence of immortality. *Emerson.*

Our domestic service is usually a foolish fracas of unreasonable demand on the one side and striking on the other. *Emerson.*

Our doubts are traitors, / And make us lose the 40 good we oft might win/By fearing to attempt. *Meas. for Meas.*, i. 5.

Our dreams drench us in sense, and sense steeps us again in dreams. *A. B. Alcott.*

Our echoes roll from soul to soul, / And grow for ever and for ever. *Tennyson.*

Our energies are actually cramped by overanxiety for success, and by straining our mental faculties beyond due bounds. *Montaigne.*

Our esteem of great powers, or amiable qualities newly discovered, may embroider a day or a week, but a friendship of twenty years is interwoven with the texture of life. *Johnson.*

Our expense is almost all for conformity. *Emer-* 45 *son.*

Our experiences of life sway and bow us either with joy or sorrow. They plant everything about us with heart-seeds. Thus a house becomes sacred. Every room has a thousand memories. *Ward Beecher.*

Our eyes see all around in gloom or glow— / Hues of their own, fresh borrowed from the heart. *Keble.*

Our fear commonly meets us at the door by which we think to run from it. *Pr.*

Our feelings are always purest and most glowing in the hour of meeting and of farewell; like the glaciers, which are transparent and rosy-hued only at sunrise and sunset. *Jean Paul.*

Our first ideas of life are generally taken from fiction rather than fact. *Schopenhauer.*

Our flatterers are our worst enemies. *Pr.*

Our friends see not our faults, or conceal them, or soften them. *Addison.*

5 Our God is a household God, as well as a heavenly one. He has an altar in every man's dwelling; let men look to it when they rend it lightly, and pour out its ashes. *Ruskin.*

Our grand business is not to see what lies dimly at a distance, but to do what lies clearly at hand. *Carlyle.*

Our greatest, being also by nature our quietest, are perhaps those that remain unknown. *Carlyle.*

Our greatest glory consists not in never falling, but in rising every time we fall. *Goldsmith.*

Our greatest misfortunes come to us from ourselves. *Rousseau.*

10 Our hand we open of our own free will, and the good flies which we can never recall. *Goethe.*

Our hap is lost, our hope but sad despair. *3 Hen., ii. 3.*

Our happiness in this world depends on the affections we are able to inspire. *Duchess de Praslin.*

Our happiness should not be laid on a too broad foundation. *Schopenhauer.*

Our hearts, frequently warmed by the contact of those whom we wish to resemble, will undoubtedly catch something of their way of thinking; and we shall receive in our own bosoms some radiation at least of their fire and splendour. *Joshua Reynolds.*

15 Our heavenward progress is something like that of the Jerusalem pilgrims of old, who for three steps forward took one backward. *Jean Paul.*

Our high respect for a well-read man is praise enough of literature. *Emerson.*

Our hoard is little, but our hearts are great. *Tennyson.*

Our hopes are but our memories reversed. *(?)*

Our human laws are but the copies, more or less imperfect, of the eternal laws, so far as we can read them. *Froude.*

20 Our humanity were a poor thing but for the divinity that stirs within us. *Bacon.*

Our ideals are our better selves. *A. B. Alcott.*

Our ideas, like pictures, are made out of lights and shadows. *Joubert.*

Our life contains a thousand springs, / And dies if one be gone; / Strange that a harp of thousand strings / Should keep in tune so long. *Watts.*

Our life is compassed round with necessity; yet is the meaning of life itself no other than freedom, than voluntary force. *Carlyle.*

25 Our life is no dream, but it may and will perhaps become one. *Novalis.*

Our life is not a mutual helpfulness; but rather, cloaked under due laws of war, named "fair competition,' and so forth, it is a mutual hostility. *Carlyle.*

Our life might be much easier and simpler than we make it. *Emerson.*

Our life should feed the springs of fame / With a perennial wave, / As ocean feeds the bubbling founts / Which find in it their grave. *Thoreau.*

Our Lord God commonly gives riches to foolish people, to whom He gives nothing else. *Luther.*

Our Lord has written the promise of the resur- 30 rection, not in books alone, but in every leaf in spring-time. *Luther.*

Our love is inwrought in our enthusiasm, as electricity is inwrought in the air, exalting its power by a subtle presence. *George Eliot.*

Our love of truth is evinced by our ability to discover and appropriate what is good wherever we come upon it. *Goethe.*

Our memories are independent of our wills. *Sheridan.*

Our minds cannot be empty; and evil will break in upon them if they are not preoccupied by good. *Johnson.*

Our minds should be habituated to the contem- 35 plation of excellence. *Joshua Reynolds.*

Our moral impressions invariably prove strongest in those moments when we are most driven back upon ourselves. *Goethe.*

Our most exalted feelings are not meant to be the common food of daily life. Contentment is more satisfying than exhilaration; and contentment means simply the sum of small and quiet pleasures. *Ward Beecher.*

Our narrow ken / Reaches too far, when all that we behold / Is but the havoc of wide-wasting Time, / Or what he soon shall spoil. *Crowe.*

Our nature is inseparable from desires, and the very word "desire" (the craving for something not possessed) implies that our present felicity is not complete. *Hobbes.*

Our natures are like oil; compound us with 40 anything, yet still we strive to swim upon the top. *Beaumont and Fletcher.*

Our notion of the perfect society embraces the family as its centre and ornament. Nor is there a paradise planted till the children appear in the foreground to animate and complete the picture. *A. B. Alcott.*

Our own heart, and not other men's opinions, forms our true honour. *Coleridge.*

Our passions and principles are steady in frenzy; but begin to shift and waver, as we return to reason. *Sterne.*

Our passions are like convulsion fits, which, though they make us stronger for the time, leave us weaker ever after. *Pope.*

Our passions are true phoenixes; when the 45 old one is burnt out, the new one rises straightway from its ashes. *Goethe.*

Our path of glory / By many a cloud is darken'd and unblest. *Keble.*

Our patience will achieve more than our force. *Burke.*

Our peasant (Burns) showed himself among us, "a soul like an Æolian harp, in whose strings the vulgar wind, as it passed through them, changed itself into articulate melody." *Carlyle.*

Our pleasures are short, and can only charm at intervals; love is a method of protracting our greatest pleasure. *Goldsmith.*

Our pleasures travel by express; our pains by parliamentary. *F. G. Trafford.*

Our poetry of the eighteenth century was prose; our prose of the seventeenth, poetry. *Hare.*

Our poets are men of talents who sing, and not the children of music. *Emerson.*

Our present time is indeed a criticising and a critical time, hovering between the wish and the inability to believe. *Jean Paul.*

5 Our purity of taste is best tested by its universality, for if we can only admire this thing or that, we may be sure that our cause for liking is of a finite and false nature. *Ruskin.*

Our purses shall be proud, our garments poor. *Tam. of the Shrew, iv. 3.*

Our ravings and complaints are but like arrows shot up into the air at no mark, and so to no purpose, but only to fall back upon our own heads and destroy ourselves. *Sir William Temple.*

Our relation to things outside of ourselves forms, and at the same time robs us of, our existence, and yet we have to do our best to adapt ourselves to circumstances; for to isolate one's self is also not advisable. *Goethe.*

Our relations are far too artificial and complicated, our nutriment and mode of life are without their proper nature, and our social intercourse is without proper love and goodwill. Every one is polished and courteous, but no one has the courage to be hearty and true. *Goethe.*

10 Our relations are ours by lot, our friends by election. *Delille.*

Our religion assumes the negative form of rejection. Out of love of the true, we repudiate the false; and the religion is an abolishing criticism. *Emerson.*

Our religion is meant to root out our vices, but it covers, nourishes, and excites them. *Montaigne.*

Our remedies oft in ourselves do lie, / Which we ascribe to heaven. *All's Well, i. 1.*

Our sacrifices are rarely of an active kind; we, as it were, abandon what we give away. It is not from resolution, but despair, that we renounce our property. *Goethe.*

15 Our self-made men are the glory of our institutions. *Wendell Phillips.*

Our senses will not admit of anything extreme: too much noise confuses us, too much light dazzles us. *Pascal.*

Our social forms are very far from truth and equity. *Emerson.*

Our sorrows are like thunder-clouds, which seem black in the distance, but grow lighter as they approach. *Jean Paul.*

Our souls much farther than our eyes can see. *Drayton.*

20 Our souls must become expanded by the contemplation of Nature's grandeur before we can fully comprehend the greatness of man. *Heine.*

Our spiritual maladies are but of opinion; we are but fettered by chains of our own forging, and which ourselves also can rend asunder. *Carlyle.*

Our spontaneous action is always the best. *Emerson.*

Our stomach for good fortune is bottomless, but the entrance to it is narrow. *Schopenhauer.*

Our strength lies in our weakness (*i.e.*, limitedness). *Hazlitt.*

Our temperaments differ in capacity of heat, 25 or we boil at different degrees. *Emerson.*

Our thinking is a pious reception. *Emerson.*

Our thoughts are often worse than we are, just as they are often better. *George Eliot.*

Our thoughts take wildest flight / Even at the moment when they should array themselves in pensive order. *Byron.*

Our time is fixed, and all our days are numbered / How long, how short, we know not: this we know, / Duty requires we calmly wait the summons, / Nor dare to stir till Heaven shall give permission. *Blair.*

Our torment is unbelief, the uncertainty as to 30 what we ought to do, the distrust of the value of what we do, and the distrust that the necessity which we all at last believe in is fair and beneficial. *Emerson.*

Our valours are our best gods. *Fletcher.*

Our vanity is the constant enemy of our dignity. *Mme. Swetchine.*

Our very hopes belied our fears, / Our fears our hopes belied; / We thought her dying when she slept, / And sleeping when she died. *T. Hood.*

Our virtues are dearer to us the more we have had to suffer for them. It is the same with our children. All profound affection admits a sacrifice. *Vauvenargues.*

Our virtues depend on our failings as their 35 root, and the latter send forth as strong and manifold branches underground as the former do in the open light. *Goethe.*

Our / Virtues lie in the interpretation of the time. *Coriolanus, iv. 7.*

Our virtues would be proud if our faults whipped them not; and our crimes would despair if they were not cherished by our virtues. *All's Well, iv. 3.*

Our whole existence is passed into words, and words, by means of tongue and ears, pass so easily into the soul. *Jean Paul.*

Our whole life is but a chamber which we are frescoing with colours, that do not appear while being laid on wet, but which will shine forth afterwards when finished and dry. *Ward Beecher.*

Our whole terrestrial being is based on Time 40 and built of Time; it is wholly a movement, a Time-impulse; Time is the author of it, the material of it. *Carlyle.*

Our wills and fates do so contrary run, / That our devices still are overthrown; / Our thoughts are ours, their ends none of our own. *Ham., iii. 2.*

Our work must be done honourably and thoroughly, because we are now men; whether we ever expect to be angels, or ever were slugs, being practically no matter. We are now human creatures, and must, at our peril, do human, that is to say, affectionate, honest, and earnest work. *Ruskin.*

Our works are presentiments of our capabilities. *Goethe.*

Our works decay and disappear, / God's frailest works abide, and look / Down on the ruins we toil to rear. *Dr. Walter Smith.*

Our worst misfortunes never happen, and most miseries lie in anticipation. *Balzac.*

Our yesterday's to-morrow now is gone, / And still a new to-morrow does come on. / We by to-morrow draw out all our store, / Till the exhausted well can yield no more. *Cowley.*

Our young men are terribly alike. *Alexander Smith.*

Ourselves are easily provided for; it is nothing but the circumstantials of human life that cost so much. *Pope.*

5 Out at sea, the universe has dwindled to a little circle of crumpled water, that journeys with you day after day, and to which you seem bound by some enchantment. *Burroughs.*

Out of debt, out of danger. *Pr.*

Out of difficulties grow miracles. *La Bruyère.*

Out of Evil comes Good; and no Good that is possible but shall one day be real. *Carlyle.*

Out of my stony griefs / Bethel I'll raise. *Adams.*

10 Out of Plato come all things that are still written and debated about among men of thought. *Emerson.*

Out of sight out of mind. *Thomas à Kempis.*

Out of the abundance of the heart the mouth speaketh. *Jesus.*

Out of the eater cometh forth meat; out of the strong cometh forth sweetness. *Samson's riddle.*

Out of the frying-pan into the fire. *Pr.*

15 Out of the suffering comes the serious mind; out of the salvation, the grateful heart; out of endurance, fortitude; out of deliverance, faith. *Ruskin.*

Out of this nettle danger we pluck this flower safety. *1 Hen. IV.*, ii. 3

Out upon the tempest of anger, the acrimonious gall of fretful impatience, the sullen frost of lowring resentment, or the corroding poison of withered envy! They eat up the immortal part of a man! ... like traitor Iscariot, betray their lord and master. *Burns.*

οὔτε τι τῶν ἀνθρωπίνων ἄξιον ὂν μεγάλης σπουδῆς—Nothing in the affairs of mankind is worth serious anxiety. *Plato.*

Outward judgment often fails, inward justice never. *Theo. Parker.*

20 Outward religion originates by society; society becomes possible by religion. *Carlyle.*

Ouvrage de longue haleine—A long-winded or tedious business. *Fr.*

Over the events of life we may have a control, but none whatever over the law of its progress. *Draper.*

Over the Time thou hast no power; solely over one man therein hast thou a quite absolute, uncontrollable power; him redeem, him make honest. *Carlyle.*

Over there it will not be otherwise than it is here. *Goethe.*

25 Overcome evil with good. *St. Paul.*

Overdone is worse than underdone. *Pr.*

Ovid finely compares a man of broken fortune to a falling column; the lower it sinks, the greater weight it is obliged to sustain. *Goldsmith.*

Owe no man anything, but to love one another; for he that loveth another hath fulfilled the law. *St. Paul.*

Oysters are not good in a month that hath not an R in it. *Pr.*

P.

Pabulum Acherontis—Food for Acheron, *i.e.*, on the verge of the grave. *Plaut.*

Pace tanti viri—If so great a man will forgive me.

Pacem hominibus habe, bellum cum vitiis—Maintain peace with men, war with their vices.

Pacta conventa—Conditions agreed upon.

Pacte de famille—A family compact. *Fr.*

Pactum non pactum est; non pactum pactum est; quod vobis lubet—A bargain is not a bargain, no bargain is a bargain, as it pleases you. *Plaut.*

Paga lo que debes, sabrás lo que tienes—Pay what you owe, and what you have you'll know. *It. Pr.*

Pagan self-assertion" is one of the elements of human worth as well as "Christian self-denial." *J. S. Mill.*

Pain has its own noble joy, when it kindles a strong consciousness of life, before stagnant and torpid. *J. Sterling.*

Pain is less subject than pleasure to capricious expression. *Johnson.*

Pain is so uneasy a sentiment that very little of it is enough to corrupt every enjoyment. *Rogers.*

Pain is the deepest thing we have in our nature, and union through pain has always seemed more real and holy than any other *Hallam.*

Pain is the positive element in life, and pleasure its negation. *Schopenhauer.*

Pain past is pleasure. *Pr.*

Pain pays the income of each precious thing. *Shakespeare.*

Painful for man is rebellious independence when it has become inevitable; only in loving companionship with his fellows does he feel safe; only in reverently bowing down before the Higher does he feel himself exalted. *Carlyle.*

Pains of love be sweeter far / Than all other pleasures are. *Dryden.*

Paint costs nothing. *Dut. Pr.*

"Paint me as I am." (?)

Painters draw their nymphs in thin and airy habits, but the weight of gold and of embroideries is reserved for queens and goddesses. *Dryden.*

Painting does not proceed so much by intelligence as by sight and feeling and invention. *Hamerton.*

Painting is silent poetry, and poetry speaking painting. *Simonides.*

Painting is the intermediate between a thought and a thing. *Coleridge.*

Palabra de boca, piedra he honda—A word from the mouth is as a stone from a sling. *Sp. Pr.*

Palabra y piedra suelta no tiene vuelta—A word and a stone once launched cannot be recalled. *Sp. Pr.*

Palam mutire plebeio piaculum est — For a common man to mutter what he thinks is a risky venture.

Palinodiam canere—To recant.

Pallida mors æquo pulsat pede pauperum tabernas, / Regumque turres — Pale Death with impartial foot knocks at the hovels of the poor and the palaces of kings. *Hor.*

5 Palma non sine pulvere—The palm, but not without a struggle. *M.*

Palma virtuti—The palm to virtue. *M.*

Palmam qui meruit ferat—Let him bear the palm that deserves it. *M.*

Panem et circenses—Bread and the games of the circus (what the Roman plebs took sole interest in). *Juv.*

Paper and leather and ink, / All are but trash / If I find not the thought / Which the writer can think. *Dr. Walter Smith.*

10 Par bene comparatum—A pair well matched.

Par droit de conquète et par droit de naissance —By right of conquest and by right of birth. *Henry IV. of France.*

Par excellence—Pre-eminently. *Fr.*

Par l'écoulement du temps—By the lapse of time. *Fr.*

Par le droit du plus fort—By the right of the strongest. *Pr.*

15 Par les mêmes voies on ne va pas toujours aux mêmes fins—The same means do not always lead to the same ends. *La Roche.*

Par ma foi ! l'âge ne sert de guère / Quand on n'a pas cela—By my faith, age serves but little if one has not that (brains). *Molière.*

Par manière d'acquit—For form's sake. *Fr.*

Par negotiis, neque supra—Equal to, and not above, his business. *Tac.*

Par nobile fratrum—A precious pair of brothers. *Hor.*

20 Par pari referto—Give him back tit for tat. *Ter.*

Par signe de mépris—In token of contempt. *Fr.*

Par ternis suppar—The two are equal to the three. *M.*

Par trop débattre la vérité se perd—The truth is sacrificed by too much disputation. *Fr. Pr.*

Par un prompt désespoir souvent on se marie, / Qu'on s'en repent après tout le temps de sa vie—We often marry in despair, so that we repent of it all our life after. *Molière.*

25 Paradise is always where love dwells. *Jean Paul.*

Paradise is for those who control their anger. *Koran.*

Paradise is under the shadow of our swords. *Mahomet.*

Parasiticam cœnam quærit—He seeks the meal of a parasite or hanger-on.

Parce, puer, stimulis et fortius utere loris— Boy, spare the goad and more firmly grasp the reins. *Ovid.*

30 Parcere personis, dicere de vitiis—To spare persons, to condemn crimes. *Mart.*

Parcere subjectis et debellare superbos—To spare the conquered, to subdue the haughty. *Virg.*

Parcite paucorum diffundere crimen in omnes —Forbear to lay the guilt of the few upon the many. *Ovid.*

Parcus Deorum cultor, et infrequens, / Insanientis dum sapientiæ / Consultus erro; nunc retrorsum / Vela dare, atque iterare cursus / Cogor relictos—A niggard and unfrequent worshipper of the gods, as long as I strayed from the way by senseless philosophy ; I am now forced to turn my sail back, and to retrace the course I had deserted. *Hor.*

Pardon is the choicest flower of victory. *Arab. Pr.*

35 Parents are commonly more careful to bestow wit on their children than virtue, the art of speaking well than of doing well ; but their manners ought to be the great concern. *Fuller.*

Parents' blessings can neither be drowned in water nor consumed in fire. *Pr.*

Parents we can have but once ; and he promises himself too much who enters life with the expectation of finding many friends. *Johnson.*

Pares cum paribus ut est in veteri proverbio facillime congregantur—As in the old proverb, " Like associates most naturally with like." *Cic.*

Parfois, élus maudits de la fureur suprême, / . . . Ces envoyés du ciel sont apparus au monde / Comme s'ils venaient de l'enfer—Sometimes these ambassadors of heaven, the accursed elect of the wrath of heaven, appear in the world as though they came from hell. *Victor Hugo.*

40 Pari passu—With equal steps or pace ; neck and neck.

Pari ratione—By parity of reason.

Paritur pax bello—Peace is produced by war. *Corn. Nep.*

Parlez du loup et vous en verrez la queue— Speak of the wolf and you will see his tail ; speak of the devil and he will appear. *Fr. Pr.*

Parlez peu et bien, si vous voulez qu'on vous regarde comme un homme de mérite—Speak little and well if you wish to be esteemed a man of merit. *Fr.*

45 Parliamentary government is government by speaking. *Macaulay.*

Pars beneficii est quod petitur si belle neges— To refuse graciously is to confer a favour. *Pub. Syr.*

Pars beneficii est quod petitur si cito neges— To refuse a favour quickly is to grant one. *Pub. Syr.*

Pars hominum vitiis gaudet constanter, et urget / Propositum : pars multa natat, modo recta capessens, / Interdum pravis obnoxia —A portion of mankind glory consistently in their vices and pursue their purpose; many more waver between doing what is right and complying with what is wrong. *Hor.*

Pars minima est ipsa puella sui—The girl herself is the least part of herself. *Ovid.*

50 Pars minima sui—The smallest part of himself or itself.

Pars sanitatis velle sanari fuit—It is a step to the cure to be willing to be cured. *Sen.*

Parsimonia est magnum vectigal—Thrift is a great revenue. *Cic.*

Parsimony is enough to make the master of the golden mines as poor as he that has nothing ; for a man may be brought to a morsel of bread by parsimony as well as profusion. *Henry Home.*

Parta tueri—Defend what you have won. *M.*

Partage de Montgomerie : tout d'un côté, rien de l'autre—A Montgomery division : everything on one side and nothing on the other. *Fr. Pr.*

Parthis mendacior—More mendacious than the Parthians. *Hor.*

Partial culture runs to the ornate ; extreme culture to simplicity. *Bovee.*

Particeps criminis—A partaker in a crime ; an accessory either before or after the fact.

5 Parties do not consider ; they only feel. *Ranke.*

Parting day / Dies like the dolphin, whom each pang imbues / With a new colour as it gasps away, / The last still loveliest, till—'tis gone, and all is gray. *Byron.*

Parting is worse than death ; it is death of love. *Dryden.*

Parting with a delusion makes one wiser than falling in with a truth. *Börne.*

Parturiunt montes, nascetur ridiculus mus—Mountains are in labour, a ridiculous mouse will be brought forth. *Hor.*

10 Party honesty is party expediency. *G. Cleveland.*

Party is the madness of many for the gain of the few. *Pope.*

Party standards are shadows in which patriotism is buried. *Bernardine de St. Pierre.*

Parva leves capiunt animos—Little minds are caught with trifles. *Ovid.*

Parva sunt hæc ; sed parva ista non contemnendo majores nostri maximam hanc rem fecerunt—These are small things ; but it was by not despising these small things that our forefathers made the commonwealth so great. *Livy.*

15 Parvis componere magna—To compare great things with small. *Virg.*

Parvula (nam exemplo est) magni formica laboris / Ore trahit quodcunque potest atque addit acervo, / Quem struit, haud ignara ac non incauta futuri—The ant, for instance, is a creature of great industry, drags with its mouth all it can, and adds to the heap it piles up, not ignorant or improvident of the future. *Hor.*

Parvula scintilla sæpe magnum suscitavit incendium—A very small spark has often kindled a great conflagration.

Parvum non parvæ amicitiæ pignus—A slight pledge of no small friendship. *M.*

Parvum parva decent—Him that is little little things become. *Hor.*

20 Pas à pas on va bien loin—Step by step one goes very far. *Fr.*

Pas un pouce de notre territoire, ni une pierre de nos forteresses !—Not an inch of our territory, not a stone of our fortresses ! *Jules Favre in 1870, to the demand of Germany.*

Pascitur in vivis livor, post fata quiescit ; / Tunc suus, ex merito, quemque tuetur honos—Envy feeds upon the living, after death it rests ; then the honour a man deserves protects him. *Ovid.*

πᾶσιν γὰρ εὖ φρονοῦσι συμμαχεῖ τύχη—Fortune always fights on the side of the prudent. *Critias.*

Pass no rash censure upon other people's words or actions. *Thomas à Kempis.*

25 Passato il pericolo gabbato il santo—When the danger is passed the saint is cheated. *It. Pr.*

Passe avant—Pass ahead. *M.*

Passe par tout—A master-key ; a pass-key.

Passez-moi la rhubarbe et je vous passerai le séné—Pass you me the rhubarb, and I will pass you the senna, *i.e.*, shut your eyes to my faults, and I will to yours. *Molière.*

Passion depraves, but also ennobles. *Lamartine.*

Passion drives the man, passions the woman ; 30 him a stream, her the winds. *Jean Paul.*

Passion is the drunkenness of the mind. *South.*

Passion is universal humanity. Without it religion, history, romance, art, would be useless. *Balzac.*

Passion looks not beyond the moment of its existence. *Bovee.*

Passion makes the best observations and the sorriest conclusions. *Jean Paul.*

Passion makes the will lord of the reason. 35 *Shakespeare.* (?)

Passion often makes a fool of the most ingenious man, and often makes the greatest blockhead ingenious. *Thomson.*

Passion, though a bad regulator, is a powerful spring. *Emerson.*

Passionate people are like men who stand upon their heads ; they see all things in the wrong way. *Plato.*

Passions are likened best to floods and streams ; / The shallow murmur, but the deep are dumb. *Sir W. Raleigh.*

Passions are the gales of life. *Pope.* 40

Passions are vices or virtues in their highest powers. *Goethe.*

Passions existed before principles ; they came into the world with us. *Mrs. Jameson.*

Passions may not unfitly be termed the mob of the man, that commits a riot upon his reason. *Wm. Penn.*

Passions spin the plot ; we are betrayed by what is false within. *George Meredith.*

Past and to come seem best, things present 45 worst. *2 Hen. IV.*, i. 2.

Pastime, like wine, is poison in the morning. *Thomas Fuller.*

Patch and long sit, / Build and soon flit. *Pr.*

Patch grief with proverbs. *Much Ado*, v. 1.

Pater familias—The father of a family.

Pater noster—Our father ; the Lord's prayer. 50

Pater patriæ—The father of his country.

παθήματα—μαθήματα—We learn from the things we suffer. *Æsop.*

Patience and perseverance overcome the greatest difficulties. *Clarissa.*

Patience, and shuffle the cards. *Cervantes.*

Patience et longueur de temps / Font plus 55 que force ni que rage—Patience and length of time accomplish more than violence and rage. *La Fontaine.*

Patience had no sooner placed herself by the mount of sorrows, but the whole heap sunk to such a degree, that it did not appear a third part so big as it was before. *Addison.*

Patience is a necessary ingredient of genius. *Disraeli.*

Patience is a plaister for all sores. *Pr.*

Patience is a remedy for every sorrow. *Pub. Syr.*

Patience is a stout horse, but it will tire at last. *Pr.*

Patience is bitter, but its fruit is sweet. *Rousseau.*

Patience is even more rarely manifested in the intellect than in the temper. *Helps.*

Patience is genius. *Buffon.*

5 Patience is good for poltroons. 3 *Hen. VI.*, i. 1.

Patience is sister to meekness, and humility is its mother. *Saying.*

Patience is the art of hoping. *Vauvenargues.*

Patience is the ballast of the soul, that will keep it from rolling and tumbling in the greatest storms. *Bp. Hopkins.*

Patience is the key of content. *Mahomet.*

10 Patience is the key of Paradise. *Turk. Pr.*

Patience is the support of weakness; impatience, the ruin of strength. *Colton.*

Patience, money, and time bring all things to pass. *Pr.*

Patience of obscurity is a duty which we owe not more to our happiness than to the quiet of the world at large. *Sydney Smith.*

Patience passe science — Patience surpasses knowledge. *M.*

15 Patience, unmoved, no marvel though she pause; / They can be meek that have no other cause. *Com. of Errors*, ii. 1.

Patience wears out stones. *Gael. Pr.*

Patience, when it is a divine thing, is active, not passive. *Lowell.*

Patience wi' poverty is a man's best remedy. *Sc. Pr.*

Patient waiters are no losers. *Pr.*

20 Patientia læsa fit furor—Patience abused becomes fury.

Patientia vinces—You will conquer by patience. *M.*

Patiently add farthing to farthing. *Goldsmith.*

Patitur qui vincit—He suffers who conquers. *M.*

Patria cara, carior libertas—Dear is my country, but liberty is dearer. *M.*

25 Patria quis exul / Se quoque fugit?—What fugitive from his country can also fly from himself? *Hor.*

Patriæ fumus igne alieno luculentior—The smoke of our own country is brighter than fire in a foreign one. *Pr.*

Patriæ infelici fidelis—Faithful to my unhappy country. *M.*

Patriæ pietatis imago—The image of his filial affection. *Virg.*

Patriæ solum omnibus carum est—The soil of their native land is dear to the hearts of all men. *Cic.*

30 Patriotism depends as much on mutual suffering as on mutual success. *Disraeli.*

Patriotism has its roots deep in the instincts and the affections. Love of country is the expansion of filial love. *D. D. Field.*

Patriotism is the last refuge of a scoundrel. *Johnson.*

Patriotism is the vital condition of national permanence. *G. W. Curtis.*

Patriotism must be founded on great principles and supported by great virtue. *Bolingbroke.*

πατρὶς γάρ ἐστι πᾶσ', ἵν' ἂν πράττῃ τις εὖ— 35 One's country is wherever things go well with him. *Aristophanes.*

Patroclus is dead, who was better by far than thou. *Hom.*

Patronage, that is, pecuniary or other economic furtherance, has been pronounced to be twice cursed, cursing him that gives and him that takes. *Carlyle.*

Pauca Catonis verba, sed a pleno venientia pectore veri—The words of Cato were few, but they came from a heart full of truth. *Lucan.*

Pauca verba—Few words.

Pauci dignoscere possunt / Vera bona, atque 40 illis multum diversa—Few men can distinguish the genuinely good from the reverse. *Juv.*

Paucis carior est fides quam pecunia—To few is good faith more valuable than money. *Sall.*, *of his own times.*

Paul Pry is on the spy. *Pr.*

Paullatim—By degrees. *M.*

Paulum sepultæ distat inertiæ / Celata virtus —Worth that is hidden differs little from buried sloth. *Hor.*

Pauper enim non est cui rerum suppetit usus. / 45 Si ventri bene, si lateri pedibusque tuis, nil / Divitiæ poterunt regales addere majus — That man is not poor who has a sufficiency for all his wants. If it is well with your stomach, your lungs, and your feet, the wealth of kings can add no more. *Hor.*

Pauper sum, fateor, patior; quod Di dant fero —I am poor, I admit; I put up with it. What the gods give I bear with. *Plaut.*

Pauper ubique jacet—Everywhere the poor man is despised. *Ovid.*

Pauperism is our social sin grown manifest. *Carlyle.*

Pauperism is the general leakage through every joint of the ship that is rotten. *Carlyle.*

Paupertas est, non quæ pauca possidet, sed 50 quæ multa non possidet—Poverty is not possessing few things, but lacking many things. *Sen.*

Paupertas fugitur, totoque arcessitur orbe— Poverty is shunned and treated as criminal throughout the world. *Lucan.*

Paupertatis pudor et fuga—The shame and the bugbear of poverty. *Hor.*

Pauperum solatio—For the solace of the poor. *M.*

Pauvres gens, je les plains; car on a pour les fous / Plus de pitié que de courroux—Poor people, I pity them; for one always entertains for fools more pity than anger. *Boileau, on disappointed authors.*

Pavore carent qui nihil commiserunt; at 55 pœnam semper ob oculos versari putant qui peccarunt—The innocent are free from fear; but the guilty have always the dread of punishment before their eyes.

Pax Cererem nutrit, pacis alumna Ceres— Peace is the nurse of Ceres; Ceres is the nursling of peace. *Ovid.*

Pax in bello—Peace in war. *M.*

Pax paritur bello—Peace is produced by war. *Corn. Nep.*

Pax vobiscum—Peace be with you.

Pay as you go is the philosopher's stone. *S.* 60 *Randolph of Roanoke.*

Pay beforehand if you would have your work ill done. *Pr*

Pay good wages, or your servants will pay themselves. *Pr.*

Pay not before thy work be done; if thou dost, it will never be well done, and thou wilt have but a pennyworth for twopence. *Franklin.*

Pay the reckoning over-night, and you won't be troubled in the morning. *Pr.*

5 Pay well when you are served well. *Pr.*

Pay what you owe, and what you're worth you'll know. *Pr.*

Pay without fail, / Down on the nail. *Pr.*

Pazza è chi non sa da che parte vien il vento— He is a senseless fellow who does not know from what quarter the wind blows. *It. Pr.*

Peace hath her victories, / No less renown'd than war. *Milton.*

10 Peace is liberty in tranquility. *Cic.*

Peace is rarely denied to the peaceful. *Schiller.*

Peace is the happy natural state of man; war his corruption, his disgrace. *Thomson.*

Peace is the masterpiece of reason. *J. Müller.*

Peace, justice, and the word of God must be given to the people, not sold. *Ruskin.*

15 Peace, of all worldly blessings, is the most valuable. *Smallridge.*

Peace with a cudgel in hand is war. *Port. Pr.*

Peacefully and reasonably to contemplate is at no time hurtful, and while we use ourselves to think of the advantages of others, our own mind comes insensibly to imitate them; and every false activity to which our fancy was alluring us is then willingly abandoned. *Goethe.*

Peccare docentes / Fallax historias movet— He deceitfully relates stories that are merely lessons in vice. *Hor.*

Peccare licet nemini—No one has leave to sin, *Cic.*

20 Peccavi—I have sinned. To cry "peccavi" is to acknowledge one's error.

Péché avoué est à moitié pardonné—A sin confessed is half forgiven. *Fr. Pr.*

Pectus est quod disertos facit—It is the heart which inspires eloquence. *Quinct.*

Pecuniam in loco negligere / Interdum maximum est lucrum—To despise money on proper occasions is sometimes a very great gain. *Ter*

Pecuniam perdidisti : fortasse illa te perderet manens—You have lost your money; perhaps, if you had kept it, it would have lost you.

25 Pedanterie setzt ganz nothwendig Leere—Pedantry quite necessarily presupposes vacancy *Rahel.*

Pedantry crams our heads with learned lumber, and takes out our brains to make room for it. *Colton.*

Pedantry is properly the overrating any kind of knowledge we pretend to. *Swift.*

Pedibus timor addidit alas—Fear gave wings to his feet.

Peevishness covers with its dark fog even the most distant horizon. *Jean Paul.*

30 Pegasus im Joche—Pegasus in harness. *Schiller.*

Peggior della morte è il turpe riposo—Worse than death is shameful repose. *Niccolo Tommaseo.*

Peine forte et dure—Heavy and severe punishment (specially that of putting heavy weights on prisoners who refused to plead).

Pelt all dogs that bark, and you will need many stones. *Pr.*

πῆμ' ἐπὶ πήματι—Evil on the top of evil.

Pence well-spent are better than pence ill-35 spared. *Pr.*

Pendente lite—While the suit is pending.

Pendre la crémaillère—To give a house-warming. *Fr.*

Penetration has an air of divination ; it pleases our vanity more than any other quality of the mind. *La Roche.*

Penitus toto divisos orbe Britannos — The Britons, quite sundered from all the world. *Virg.*

Penny goes after penny, / Till Peter hasn't 40 any. *Pr.*

Penny wise is often pound foolish. *Pr.*

Pense ce que tu veux, dis ce que tu dois— Think what you like, say what you ought. *Fr. Pr.*

Pense moult, parle peu, écris moins—Think much, speak little, write less. *Fr. Pr.*

Penser, vivre, et mourir en roi—To think, live, and die as a king. *Frederick the Great.*

Pensez à bien—Think of good. *M.* 45

People abuse freedom only where they have asserted it, not where it has been given them. *Börne.*

People are always expecting to get peace in heaven ; but you know whatever peace they get there will be ready-made. Whatever of making peace they can be blest for must be on the earth here. *Ruskin.*

People are only accustomed to revolve around themselves. *Goethe.*

People are rendered sociable by their inability to endure their own society. *Schiller.*

People are wise for the past day in the even-50 ing, but never wise enough for the coming one. *Rückert.*

People, crushed by laws, have no hopes but from power. If laws are their enemies, they will be enemies to laws ; and those who have much to hope and nothing to lose will always be dangerous, more or less. *Burke.*

People dispute a great deal about the good that is done and the harm by disseminating the Bible (*Bibelverbreitung*). To me this is clear : the Bible will do harm if, as hitherto, it is used dogmatically and interpreted fancifully, and it will do good if it is treated feelingly and applied didactically. *Goethe.*

People do not care to give alms without some security for their money ; and a wooden leg or a withered arm is a sort of draft upon heaven for those who choose to have their money placed to account there. *Mackenzie.*

People do not lack strength ; they lack will. *Victor Hugo.*

People do not mind their faults being spread 55 out before them, but they become impatient if called upon to give them up. *Goethe.*

People in adversity should preserve laudable customs. *Clarissa.*

People (in authority) are accustomed merely to forbid, to hinder, to refuse, but rarely to bid, to further, and to reward. They let things go along till some mischief happens; then they fly into a rage, and lay about them. *Goethe.*

People love to have all rash actions done in a hurry. *Goldsmith.*

People may live as much retired from the world as they like, but sooner or later they find themselves debtor or creditor to some one. *Goethe.*

People must begin before they attempt to finish or improve. *Wm. Blake.*

5 People seem to think themselves in some ways superior to heaven itself, when they complain of the sorrow and want round about them; and yet it is not the devil for certain who puts pity into their hearts. *Anne J. Thackeray.*

People should never sit talking till they don't know what to talk about. *Saying.*

People that are like-minded (*Gleichgesinnten*) can never for any length be disunited (*entzweien*); they always come together again; whereas those that are not like-minded (*Widergesinnten*) try in vain to maintain harmony; the essential discord between them will be sure to break out some day. *Goethe.*

People that have nothing to do are quickly tired of their own company. *J. Collier.*

People that make puns are like wanton boys that put coppers on the railroad tracks. They amuse themselves and other children, but their little trick may upset a freight train of conversation for the sake of a battered witticism. *Holmes.*

10 People that will crowd about bonfires may, sometimes very fairly, get their beards singed; it is the price they pay for such illumination; natural twilight is safe and free to all. *Carlyle.*

People throw stones only at trees which have fruit on them. *Pr.*

People who are always taking care of their health are like misers, who are hoarding up a treasure which they have never spirit enough to enjoy. *Sterne.*

People who are too sharp cut their own fingers. *Pr.*

People who can't be witty exert themselves to be pious and affectionate. *George Eliot.*

15 People who do not know how to laugh are always pompous and self-conceited. *Thackeray.*

People who have little to do are great talkers. The less they think the more they talk, and so women talk more than men. A nation where women determine the fashion is always talkative. *Montesquieu.*

People who honestly mean to be true really contradict themselves much more rarely than those who try to be consistent. *Holmes.*

People who live in glass houses should never throw stones. *Pr.*

People who never have any time are those who do least. *Lichtenberg.* (?)

20 People will not look forward to posterity who never look backward to their ancestors. *Burke.*

People would do well if, tarrying here for years together, they observed a while a Pythagorean silence. *Goethe.*

People would do well if they would keep piety, which is so essential and lovable in life, distinct from art, where, owing to its very simplicity and dignity, it checks their energy, allowing only the very highest mind freedom to unite with, if not actually to master, it. *Goethe.*

Per accidens—By accident, *i.e.*, not following from the nature of the thing, but from some accidental circumstance.

Per acuta belli—Through the perils of war. *M.*

Per angusta ad augusta—Through hardship to 25 triumph. *M.*

Per annum—By the year; yearly.

Per ardua liberi—Free through difficulty. *M.*

Per aspera ad astra—Over rough paths to the stars. *M.*

Per contra—On the other hand.

Per Deum et ferrum obtinui—I have obtained 30 it by God and my sword. *M.*

Per fas et nefas—By right ways and by wrong.

Per il suo contrario—By its opposite. *M.*

Per incuriam—Through carelessness.

Per mare per terram—By sea and land. *M.*

Per obitum—Through the death of. 35

Per quod servitium amisit—For loss of his or her services. *L.*

Per saltum—By a leap; by passing over the intermediate steps.

Per undas et ignes fluctuat nec mergitur—Through water and fire she goes plunging but is not submerged. *M. of Paris.*

Per varios casus, per tot discrimina rerum—Through manifold misfortunes, and so many perils. *Virg.*

Per vias rectas—By direct ways. *M.* 40

Peras imposuit Jupiter nobis duas; / Propriis repletam vitiis post tergum dedit. / Alienis ante pectus suspendit gravem—Jupiter has laid two wallets on us; he has placed one behind our backs filled with our own faults, and has hung another before, heavy with the faults of other people. *Phaedr.*

Percunctatorem fugito, nam garrulus idem est; / Nec retinent patulæ commissa fideliter aures—Avoid an inquisitive person, for he is sure to be a gossip; ears always open to hear will not keep faithfully what is intrusted to them. *Hor.*

Perdidit arma, locum virtutis deseruit, qui / Semper in augenda festinat et obruitur re—He has lost his arms and deserted the cause of virtue who is ever eager and engrossed in increasing his wealth. *Hor.*

Perdis, et in damno gratia nulla tuo—You lose, and for your loss get no thanks. *Ovid.*

Pereant amici, dum una inimici intercidant— 45 Let our friends perish, provided our enemies fall along with them. *Gr. and Lat. Pr., quoted by Cicero to condemn it.*

Pereunt et imputantur—They (hours) pass, and are placed to our account. *Mart.*

Perfect existence can only be where spirit and body are one; an embodied spirit, a spiritual body. (?)

Perfect experience must itself embrace theoretical knowledge. *Goethe.*

Perfect life is ever in one's acts to deal with innocence, which proves itself in doing wrong to no one but itself. *Goethe.*

Perfect light / Would dazzle, not illuminate, the sight; / From earth it is enough to glimpse at heaven. *Lord Houghton.*

Perfect love canna be without equality. *Sc. Pr.*

Perfect love casteth out fear. *St. John.*

Perfect love holds the secret of the world's perfect liberty. *J. G. Holland.*

5 Perfect woman, nobly planned, / To warn, to comfort, and command; / And yet a spirit still, and bright / With something of an angel light. *Wordsworth.*

Perfect works are rare, because they must be produced at the happy moment when taste and genius unite: and this rare conjunction, like that of certain planets, appears to occur only after the revolution of several cycles, and only lasts for an instant. *Chateaubriand.*

Perfecting is our destiny, but perfection is never our lot. *J. C. Weber.*

Perfection is not the affair of the scholar; it is enough if he practises. *Goethe.*

Perfer et obdura; dolor hic tibi proderit olim —Bear and endure; this sorrow will one day prove to be for your good. *Ovid.*

10 Perfer et obdura; multo graviora tulisti—Bear and endure; you have borne much heavier misfortunes than these. *Ovid.*

Perfervidum ingenium Scotorum — The very ardent temper of the Scots.

Perfida, sed quamvis perfida, cara tamen— Faithless, but, though faithless, still dear. *Tibull.*

Pergis pugnantia secum / Frontibus adversis componere—You are attempting to reconcile things which are opposite in their natures. *Hor.*

"Perhaps" hinders folks from lying. *Pr.*

15 Perhaps propriety is as near a word as any to denote the manners of the gentleman. *Hazlitt.*

Perhaps the early grave / Which men weep over may be meant to save. *Byron.*

Periculosæ plenum opus aleæ / Tractas, et incedis per ignes / Suppositos cineri doloso— The work you are treating is one full of dangerous hazard, and you are treading over fires lurking beneath treacherous ashes. *Hor.*

Periculosum est credere et non credere ; / Ergo exploranda est veritas, multum prius / Quam stulta prave judicet sententia—It is equally dangerous to believe and to disbelieve; therefore search diligently into the truth rather than suffer an erroneous impression to pervert your judgment. *Phædr.*

Periculum in mora—There is danger in delay.

20 Perierunt tempora longi / Servitii—My long period of service has led to no advancement. *Juv.*

Perimus licitis—We come to ruin by permitted things. *Pr.*

Perish discretion when it interferes with duty. *Hannah More.*

Périsse l'univers pourvu que je me venge!— Let the universe perish, provided I have my revenge! *Cyrano.*

Périssons en résistant!—Let us die resisting! *Fr.*

25 Periturae parcite chartæ—Spare the paper which is fated to perish. *Adapted from Juvenal.*

Perjuria ridet amantum Jupiter—Jupiter laughs at the perjuries of lovers. *Ovid.*

Perjurii pœna divina exitium, humana dedecus —The punishment of perjury at the hands of the gods is perdition; at the hands of man, is disgrace. *One of the laws of the Twelve Tables*

Perlen bedeuten Thränen—Pearls mean tears. *Lessing.*

Permanence is what I advocate in all human relations ; nomadism, continual change, is prohibitory of any good whatsoever. *Carlyle.*

Permanence, perseverance, persistence in spite 30 of hindrances, discouragements, and "impossibilities :" it is this that in all things distinguishes the strong soul from the weak ; the civilised burgher from the nomadic savage— the species Man from the genus Ape. *Carlyle.*

Permanence, persistence, is the first condition of all fruitfulness in the ways of men. *Carlyle.*

Permissu superiorum — By permission of the superiors.

Permitte divis cætera—Commit the rest to the gods. *Hor.*

Perpetual solitude, in a place where you see nothing to raise your spirits, at length wears them out, and conversation falls into dull and insipid. *Lady Montagu.*

Perpetuus nulli datur usus, et hæres / Hære- 35 dem alterius, velut unda supervenit undam —Perpetual possession is allowed to none, and one heir succeeds another, as wave follows wave. *Hor.*

Persecution is a tribute the great must ever pay for pre-eminence. *Goldsmith.*

Persecution is not wrong because it is cruel; it is cruel because it is wrong. *Whately.*

Persecution to persons in high rank stands them in the stead of eminent virtue. *Cardinal de Retz.*

Perseverance and audacity generally win. *Mme. Deluzy.*

Perseverance and tact are the two great 40 qualities most valuable for all men who would mount, but especially for those who have to step out of the crowd. *Disraeli.*

Perseverance, dear, my lord, / Keeps honour bright. To have done is to hang / Quite out of fashion, like a rusty mail, / In monumental mockery. *Troil. and Cres.*, iii. 3.

Perseverance is a Roman virtue that wins each godlike act, and plucks success even from the spear-proof crest of rugged danger. *Harvard.*

Perseverance performs greater works than strength. *Pr.*

Perseverance, self-reliance, energetic effort, are doubly strengthened when you rise from a failure to battle again. *Anon.*

Perseverando—By persevering. *M.* 45

Perseverantia—By perseverance. *M.*

Persevere and never fear. *Pr.*

Persevere in the fight, struggle on, do not let go, think magnanimously of man and life, for man is good and life is affluent and fruitful. *Vauvenargues.*

Persist, persevere, and you will find most things attainable that are possible. *Chesterfield.*

Personæ mutæ—Mute characters in a play. 50

Personal attachment is no fit ground for public conduct, and those who declare they will take care of the rights of the sovereign because they have received favours at his hand, betray a little mind and warrant the conclusion that if they did not receive those favours they would be less mindful of their duties, and act with less zeal for his interest. *C. Fox.*

Personal force never goes out of fashion. (?)
Personality is everything in art and poetry. *Goethe.*

Persons are love's world, and the coldest philosopher cannot recount the debt of the young soul, wandering here in nature to the power of love, without being tempted to unsay, as treasonable to nature, aught derogatory to the social instincts. *Emerson.*

Persons of fine manners make behaviour the first sign of force,—behaviour, and not performance, or talent, or, much less, wealth. *Emerson.*

5 Persons who are very plausible and excessively polite have generally some design upon you, as also religionists who call you "dear" the first time they see you. *Spurgeon.*

Perspicuity is the offset of profound thoughts. *Vauvenargues.*

Persuasion is better than force. *Pr.*

Peter's in, Paul's out. *Pr.*

Petit homme abat grand chêne—A little man fells a tall oak. *Fr. Pr.*

10 Petit maître—Fop; coxcomb. *Fr.*

Petite étincelle luit en ténèbres—A tiny spark shines in the dark. *Fr. Pr.*

Petites affiches—Advertiser. *Fr.*

Petites maisons—A madhouse. *Fr.*

Petitio principii — Begging of the question in debate.

15 Petitioners for admittance into favour must not harass the condescension of their benefactor. *Burns.*

Petits soins—Little attentions. *Fr.*

Petty laws breed great crimes. *Ouida.*

Peu d'hommes ont été admirés par leurs domestiques—Few men have been looked up to by their domestics. *Montaigne.*

Peu de bien, peu de soin—Little wealth, little care. *Fr. Pr.*

20 Peu de chose nous console, parceque peu de chose nous afflige—Little consoles us because little afflicts us. *Pascal.*

Peu de gens savent être vieux—Few people know how to be old. *La Roche.*

Peu de gens sont assez sages pour préférer le blame qui leur est utile, à la louange qui les trahit—Few people are wise enough to prefer censure which may be useful, to flattery which may betray them. *La Roche.*

Peu de moyens, beaucoup d'effet — Simple means, great results. *Fr. Pr.*

Peu de philosophie mène à mépriser l'érudition; beaucoup de philosophie mène à l'estimer—A little philosophy leads men to despise learning; a great deal leads them to esteem it. *Chamfort.*

25 Peu et bien—Little but good. *Fr.*

Peuples libres, souvenez-vous de cette maxime : on peut acquérir la liberté, mais on ne la retrouve jamais—Free people, remember this rule : you may acquire liberty, but never regain it if you once lose it. *Rousseau.*

Phaeton was his father's heir; born to attain the highest fortune without earning it; he had built no sun-chariot (could not build the simplest wheel-barrow), but could and would insist on driving one; and so broke his own stiff neck, sent gig and horses spinning through infinite space, and set the universe on fire. *Carlyle.*

φαντάσματα θεῖα, καὶ σκιαὶ τῶν ὄντων—Divine phantasms and shadows of things that are. *Gr.*

Pharmaca das ægroto, aurum tibi porrigit æger, / Tu morbum curas illius, ille tuum—You give medicine to a sick man, he hands you your fee ; you cure his complaint, he cures yours. *To a doctor.*

φείδεο τῶν κτεάνων—Husband your resources. *Gr.* 30

φήμη γε μέντοι δημόθρους μέγα σθένει—The voice of the people truly is great in power. *Æschylus.*

Philanthropy, like charity, must begin at home. *Lamb.*

"Philistine" must have originally meant, in the mind of those who invented the nickname, a strong, dogged, unenlightened opponent of the children of the light. *Heine.*

Philologists, who chase / A panting syllable through time and space, / Start it at home, and hunt it in the dark / To Gaul, to Greece, and into Noah's ark. *Cowper.*

Philosophers are only men in armour after all. 35 *Dickens.*

Philosophers call God "the great unknown." "The great misknown" would be more correct. *Joseph Roux.*

Philosophia simulari potest, eloquentia non potest—Philosophy may be feigned, eloquence cannot. *Quinct.*

Philosophy and theology are become theorem, brain-web and shadow, wherein no earnest soul can find solidity for itself. Shadow, I say; yet shadow projected from an everlasting reality within ourselves. Quit the shadow, seek the reality. *Carlyle to John Sterling.*

Philosophy can add to our happiness in no other manner but by diminishing our misery ; it should not pretend to increase our present stock, but make us economists of what we are possessed of. *Goldsmith.*

Philosophy can bake no bread; but she can 40 procure for us God, freedom, immortality. Which, then, is more practical—philosophy or economy? *Novalis.*

Philosophy does not regard pedigree; she did not receive Plato as a noble, but she made him so. *Sen.*

Philosophy dwells aloft in the Temple of Science, the divinity of its inmost shrine ; her dictates descend among men, but she herself descends not ; whoso would behold her must climb with long and laborious effort, nay, still linger in the forecourt, till manifold trial have proved him worthy of admission into the interior solemnities. *Carlyle.*

Philosophy easily triumphs over past and future ills, but present ills triumph over philosophy. *La Roche.*

Philosophy goes no further than probabilities, and in every assertion keeps a doubt in reserve. *Froude.*

Philosophy has given several plausible rules 45 for attaining peace and tranquillity, but they fall very much short of bringing men to it. *Tillotson.*

Philosophy is a bully that talks very loud when the danger is at a distance ; but the moment she is hard pressed by the enemy, she is not to be found at her post, but leaves the brunt of the battle to be borne by her humbler but steadier comrade, Religion. *Colton.*

Philosophy is a good horse in a stable, but an arrant jade on a journey. *Goldsmith.*

Philosophy is an elegant thing, if any one modestly meddles with it; but, if he is conversant with it more than is becoming, it corrupts the man. *Plato.*

Philosophy is but a continual battle against custom; an ever-renewed effort to transcend the sphere of blind custom, and so become transcendental. *Carlyle.*

Philosophy is no more than the art of making ourselves happy; that is, of seeking pleasure in regularity, and reconciling what we owe to society with what is due to ourselves. *Goldsmith.*

5 Philosophy is nothing but discretion. *Selden.*

Philosophy is properly home-sickness; the wish to be everywhere at home. *Novalis.*

Philosophy is reason with the eyes of the soul. *Simms.*

Philosophy is to poetry what old age is to youth; and the stern truths of philosophy are as fatal to the fictions of the one as the chilling testimonies of experience are to the hopes of the other. *Colton.*

Philosophy, rightly defined, is simply the love of wisdom. *Cic.*

10 Philosophy teaches us to do willingly and from conviction what others do under compulsion. *Arist.*

Philosophy, when superficially studied, excites doubt; when thoroughly explored, it dispels it. *Bacon.*

Philosophy, while it soothes the reason, damps the ambition. *Bulwer Lytton.*

Philosophy will clip an angel's wings. *Keats.*

φοβοῦ τὸ γῆρας, οὐ γὰρ ἔρχεται μονόν—Fear old age, for it does not come alone. *Gr. Pr.*

15 Phœnices primi, famæ si creditur, ausi / Mansuram rudibus vocem signare figuris—The Phœnicians, if rumour may be trusted, were the first who dared to write down the fleeting word in rude letters. *Lucan.*

Physic, for the most part, is nothing else but the substitute of exercise and temperance. *Addison.*

Physic is of little use to a temperate person, for a man's own observation on what he finds does him good or what hurts him, is the best physic to preserve health. *Bacon.*

Physical courage, which despises all danger, will make a man brave in one way; and moral courage, which defies all opinion, will make a man brave in another. *Colton.*

Physical science has taught us to associate Deity with the normal rather than with the abnormal. *Lecky.*

20 Physician, heal thyself. *Heb. Pr.*

Physicians, of all men, are most happy; whatever good success soever they have, the world proclaimeth; and what faults they commit, the earth covereth. *Pr.*

Pia fraus — A pious fraud (either for good or evil).

Pick out of mirth, like stones out of thy ground,/ Profaneness, filthiness, abusiveness. *George Herbert.*

Pickpockets and beggars are the best practical physiognomists, without having read a line of Lavater, who, it is notorious, mistook a philosopher for a highwayman. *Colton.*

Pictoribus atque poetis / Quidlibet audendi 25 semper fuit æqua potestas — The power of daring anything their fancy suggests has always been conceded to the painter and the poet. *Hor.*

Pictures and shapes are but secondary objects, and please or displease but in memory. *Bacon.*

Pie repone te—Repose in pious confidence. *M.*

Pièce de position—A heavy gun. *Fr.*

Pièce de résistance—A solid joint. *Fr.*

Pièces de théâtre—Plays. *Fr.* 30

Piety is a kind of modesty. It makes us cast down our thoughts, just as modesty makes us cast down our eyes in presence of whatever is forbidden. *Joubert.*

Piety is not a religion, although it is the soul of all religions. *Joubert.*

Piety is only a means whereby, through purest inward peace, we may attain to highest culture. *Quoted by Emerson from Goethe.*

Piety, like wisdom, consists in the discovery of the rules under which we are actually placed, and in faithfully obeying them. *Froude.*

Piety, stretched beyond a certain point, is the 35 parent of impiety. *Sydney Smith.*

Pigmæi gigantum humeris impositi plusquam ipsi gigantes vident—Dwarfs on a giant's back see more than the giant himself. *Didacus Stella.*

Pigmies are pigmies still, though perched on Alps; / And pyramids are pyramids in vales. *Young.*

Pigs grow fat where lambs would starve. *Pr.*

Pigs grunt about everything and nothing. *Pr.*

Pigs when they fly go tail first. *Pr.* 40

Pikes are caught when little fish go by. *R. Southwell.*

Pillen muss man schlingen, nicht kauen—Pills must be swallowed, not chewed. *Ger. Pr.*

Pin thy faith to no man's sleeve; hast thou not two eyes of thy own? *Carlyle.*

Pinguis venter non gignit sensum tenuem—A fat paunch does not produce fine sense. *St. Jerome, from the Greek.*

Pis-aller—A last shift. *Fr.* 45

Pitch a lucky man into the Nile and he will come up with a fish in his mouth. *Arab. Pr.*

Pitch thy behaviour low, thy projects high; / So shalt thou humble and magnanimous be. *George Herbert.*

Pith's gude at a' play but threadin' o' needles. *Sc. Pr.*

Pity and friendship are passions incompatible with each other. *Goldsmith.*

Pity and need make all flesh kin. There is no 50 caste in blood / Which runneth of one hue; nor caste in tears, which trickle salt with all. *Sir Edwin Arnold.*

Pity him who has his choice, and chooses the worse. *Gael. Pr.*

Pity is a thing often avowed, seldom felt; hatred is a thing often felt, seldom avowed. *Colton.*

Pity is imagination or fiction of future calamity to ourselves proceeding from the sense of another man's calamity. *Hobbes.*

Pity is the virtue of the law, / And none but tyrants use it cruelly. *Timon of Athens, iii. 5.*

Pity makes the world / Soft to the weak and 55 noble for the strong. *Sir Edwin Arnold.*

Pity only with new objects stays. / But with the tedious sight of woe decays. *Dryden.*

Pity shapes not into syllogisms ; / Nor can affection ape philosophy. *Lewis Morris.*

Pity, the tenderest part of love. *Yalden.*

Pity those whom Nature abuses, never those who abuse Nature. *Sheridan.*

5 Pity weakness and ignorance. bear with the dulness of understandings, or perverseness of tempers. *Law.*

Più ombra che frutto fanno gli arberi grandi— Large trees yield more shade than fruit. *It. Pr.*

Più sa il matto in casa sua che il savio in casa d'altri—The fool knows more in his own house than a wise man does in another's. *It. Pr.*

Più vale il fumo di casa mia, che il fuoco dell'-altrui—The smoke of my own house is better than the fire of another's. *It. Pr.*

Place moral heroes in the field, and heroines will follow them as brides. *Jean Paul.*

10 Placeat homini quidquid Deo placuit — That which has seemed good to God should seem good to man. *Sen.*

Plagiarists are always suspicious of being stolen from. *Coleridge.*

Plagiarists, at least, have the merit of preservation. *I. Disraeli.*

Plain dealing is dead, and died without issue. *Pr.*

Plain dealing's a jewel, but they that use it die beggars. *Pr.*

15 Plain living and high thinking. *Wordsworth.*

Plants are children of the earth; we are children of the ether. Our lungs are properly our root; we live when we breathe: we begin our life with breathing. *Novalis.*

Plaster thick, / Some will stick. *Pr.*

Plate sin with gold, / And the strong lance of justice hurtless breaks ; / Arm it in rags, a pigmy's straw does pierce it. *King Lear,* iv. 6.

Plato enim mihi unus est instar omnium—Plato alone in my regard is worth them all. *Antimachus, in Cic.*

20 Plato's scheme was impossible even in his own day, as Bacon's " New Atlantis " in his day, as Calvin's reform in his day, as Goethe's "Academe" in his. Out of the good there was in all these men, the world gathered what it could find of evil, made its useless Platonism out of Plato, its graceless Calvinism out of Calvin determined Bacon to be the meanest of mankind, and of Goethe gathered only a luscious story of seduction, and daintily singable devilry. *Ruskin.*

Plausibus ex ipsis populi, lætoque furore, / Ingenium quodvis incaluisse potest—At the applauses of the public, and at its transports of joy, every genius may grow warm. *Ovid.*

Plausus tunc arte carebat—In those days applause was unaffected. *Ovid.*

Play not for gain, but sport. *George Herbert.*

Play, that is, activity, not pleasures, will keep children cheerful. *Jean Paul.*

25 Play the man. *George Herbert.*

Pleasant tastes depend, not on the things themselves, but their agreeableness to this or that particular palate. *Locke.*

Pleasant words are as an honeycomb ; sweet to the soul, and health to the bones. *Bible.*

Pleas'd with a rattle, tickl'd with a straw. *Pope.*

Pleasure and action make the hours seem short. *Othello,* ii. 3.

Pleasure and pain, though directly opposite, 30 are yet so contrived by nature as to be constant companions. *Charron.*

Pleasure and revenge / Have ears more deaf than adders to the voice / Of any true decision. *Troil. and Cress.,* ii. 2.

Pleasure and sympathy in things is all that is real and again produces reality ; all else is empty and vain. *Goethe.*

Pleasure can be supported by illusion ; but happiness rests upon truth. *Chamfort.*

Pleasure is a wanton trout ; / An ye drink but deep ye'll find him out. *Burns.*

Pleasure is far sweeter as a recreation than a 35 business. *R. D. Hitchcock.*

Pleasure is nothing else but the intermission of pain, the enjoying of something I am in great trouble for till I get it. *John Selden.*

Pleasure is the greatest incentive to evil. *Plato.*

Pleasure is the reflex of unimpeded energy. *Sir W. Hamilton.*

Pleasure itself is painful at bottom. *Montaigne.*

Pleasure of every kind quickly satisfies. 40 *Burke.*

Pleasure preconceived and preconcerted ends in disappointment ; but disappointment, when it involves neither shame nor loss, is as good as success ; for it supplies as many images to the mind, and as many topics to the tongue. *Johnson.*

Pleasure soon exhausts us, and itself also but endeavour never does. *Jean Paul.*

Pleasure which cannot be obtained but by unreasonable and unsuitable expense, must always end in pain. *Johnson.*

Pleasure which must be enjoyed at the expense of another's pain, can never be such as a worthy mind can fully delight in. *Johnson.*

Pleasure's couch is virtue's grave. *Duganne.* 45

Pleasures are like poppies spread, / You seize the flower, its bloom is shed ; / Or, like the snowflake in the river, / A moment white, then melts for ever. *Burns.*

Pleasures lie thickest where no pleasures seem ; / There's not a leaf that falls upon the ground / But holds some joy of silence or of sound, / Some sprite begotten of a summer dream. *Blanchard.*

Pleasures waste the spirits more than pains. *Zimmermann.*

Pledges taken of faithless minds, / I hold them but as the idle winds / Heard and forgot. *Dr. W. Smith.*

Plenty, and peace, breeds cowards ; hardness 50 ever of hardiness is mother. *Cymbeline,* iii. 6.

Plenty makes dainty. *Sc. Pr.*

πλέον ἥμισυ παντός—The half (*i.e.* well used) is more than the whole (*i.e.* abused). *Hesiod.*

Plerique enim lacrimas fundunt ut ostendant ; et toties siccos oculos habent, quoties spectator definit— Many shed tears merely for show ; and have their eyes quite dry whenever there is no one to observe them. *Sen.*

Plerumque modestus / Occupat obscuri speciem, taciturnus acerbi—Usually the modest man passes for a reserved man, the silent for a sullen one. *Hor.*

Ploratur lacrymis amissa pecunia veris—The loss of money is bewailed with unaffected tears. *Juv.*

Ploravere suis non respondere favorem / Speratum meritis—They lamented that their merits did not meet with the gratitude they hoped for. *Hor.*

Plough deep while sluggards sleep. *Franklin.*

5 Plough or not plough, you must pay your rent. *Pr.*

Plunge boldly into the thick of life, and seize it where you will, it is always interesting. *Goethe.*

Plura faciunt homines e consuetudine quam e ratione—Men do more things from custom than from reason.

Plura sunt quæ nos terrent, quam quæ premunt ; et sæpius opinione quam re laboramus—There are more things to alarm than to harm us, and we suffer much oftener in apprehension than reality. *Sen.*

Plures adorant solem orientem quam occidentem—More do homage to the rising sun than the setting one. *Pr.*

10 Plures crapula quam gladius—Excess kills more than the sword. *Pr.*

Plurima mortis imago—Death in very many a form. *Virg.*

Plurima sunt quæ / Non audent homines pertusa dicere læna—There are very many things that men, when their cloaks have got holes in them, dare not say. *Juv.*

Pluris est oculatus testis unus quam auriti decem. / Qui audiunt, audita dicunt : qui vident, plane sciunt—One eye-witness is better than ten from mere hearsay. Hearers can only tell what they heard. Those who see, know exactly. *Plaut.*

Plus aloes quam mellis habet—She has more of the aloe than the honey. *Juv.*

15 Plus dolet quam necesse est, qui ante dolet quam necesse est—He who grieves before it is necessary, grieves more than is necessary.

Plus etenim fati valet hora benigni / Quam si nos Veneris commendet epistola Marti—A moment of smiling fortune is of more avail (to a soldier) than if he were recommended to Mars by an epistle from Venus. *Juv.*

Plus fait douceur que violence—Gentleness does more than violence. *La Fontaine.*

Plus impetus, majorem constantiam, penes miseros—We find greater violence and more perseverance among the wretched. *Tac.*

Plus in amicitia valet similitudo morum quam affinitas—Similarity of manners conduces more to friendship than relationship. *Corn. Nep.*

20 Plus in posse quam in actu—More in possibility than actuality.

Plus je vis l'étranger, plus j'aimai ma patrie—The more I saw of foreign countries, the more I loved my own. *De Belloy.*

Plus on approche des grands hommes, plus on trouve qu'ils sont hommes—The nearer one approaches to great persons, the more one sees that they are but men. *La Bruyère.*

Plus on lui ôte, plus il est grand—The more you take from him, the greater he is. *Quoted by Emerson.*

Plus ratio quam vis cæca valere solet—Reason can generally effect more than blind force. *Gallus.*

Plus salis quam sumptus—More taste than ex-25 pense. *Corn. Nep.*

Plus une pierre est jétée de haut, plus elle fait d'impression où elle tombe—The greater the height from which a stone is cast, the greater the impression on the spot where it falls. *Fr.* (?)

Plus vetustis nam favet / Invidia mordax, quam bonis præsentibus—Stinging envy is more merciful to good things that are old than such as are new. *Phædr.*

Plutarch warns young men that it is well to go for a light to another man's fire, but by no means to tarry by it, instead of kindling a torch of their own. *John Morley.*

Plutôt une défaite au Rhin que l'abandon du Pape !—Rather a defeat on the Rhine than abandon the Pope. *Louis Napoleon, to the proposal to buy the allegiance of Italy against Germany by the sacrifice of Rome.*

Poco dâno espanta, y mucho amansa—A little 30 loss alarms one, a great loss tames one down. *Sp. Pr.*

Poem (a) is a thought so passionate and alive, that, like the spirit of a plant or an animal, it has an architecture of its own, and adorns nature with a new thing. *Emerson.*

Poems that are great, books that are great, all of them, if you search the first foundation of their greatness, have been veridical, the truest they could get to be. *Carlyle.*

Poesie ist tiefes Schmerzen, / Und es kommt das echte Lied / Einzig aus dem Menschenherzen / Das ein tiefes Leid durchglüht—Poetry is deep pain, and the genuine song issues only from the human heart through which a deep sorrow glows. *Justin Kerner.*

Poesy is love's chosen apostle, and the very almoner of God. She is the home of the outcast, and the wealth of the needy. *Lowell.*

Poesy is of so subtle a spirit, that in pouring 35 out of one language into another it will evaporate. *Denham.*

Poeta nascitur, non fit—A poet is born, not made. *L.*

Poetica surgit / Tempestas—A storm is gathering in the poetic world. *Juv.*

Poetry comes nearer to vital truth than history. *Plato.*

Poetry creates life. *Fred. W. Robertson.*

Poetry has given me the habit of wishing to 40 discover the good and the beautiful in all that meets and surrounds me. *Coleridge.*

Poetry implies the whole truth, philosophy expresses a particle of it. *Thoreau.*

Poetry incorporates those spirits which, like angels, can never assume the body of an outward act ; and sheds the perfume of those flowers which spring up but never bear any seed. *Jean Paul.*

Poetry interprets in two ways : by expressing with magical felicity the physiognomy and movements of the outer world ; and by expressing with inward conviction the ideas and laws of the inward. *Matthew Arnold.*

Poetry is a spirit, not disembodied, but in the flesh, so as to affect the senses of living men. *Stedman.*

Poetry is always a personal interpretation of 45 life. *H. W. Mabie.*

Poetry is an art, the easiest to dabble in, and the hardest in which to reach true excellence. *Stedman.*

Poetry is an attempt man makes to render his existence harmonious. *Carlyle.*

Poetry is faith. *Emerson.*

Poetry is inestimable as a lonely faith, a lonely protest in the uproar of atheism. *Emerson.*

5 Poetry is inspiration; has in it a certain spirituality and divinity which no dissecting knife will discover; arises in the most secret and most sacred region of man's soul, as it were in our Holy of Holies; and as for external things, depends only on such as can operate in that region; among which it will be found that Acts of Parliament and the state of Smithfield Markets nowise play the chief parts. *Carlyle.*

Poetry is music in words, and music is poetry in sound; both excellent sauce, but they have lived and died poor that made them their meal. *Fuller.*

Poetry is musical thought, thought of a mind that has penetrated into the inmost heart of a thing, detected the melody that lies hidden in it, . . . the heart of Nature being everywhere music, if you can only reach it. *Carlyle.*

Poetry is only born after painful journeys into the vast regions of thought. *Balzac.*

Poetry is right royal. It puts the individual for the species, the one above the infinite many. *Hazlitt.*

10 Poetry is something to make us wiser and better by continually revealing those types of beauty and truth which God has set in all men's souls. *Lowell.*

Poetry is the art of substantiating shadows and of lending existence to nothing. *Burke.*

Poetry is the art of uniting pleasure with truth by calling imagination to the help of reason. *Johnson.*

Poetry is the breath and finer spirit of all knowledge; it is the impassioned expression which is the countenance of all science. *Wordsworth.*

Poetry is the exquisite expression of exquisite impressions. *J. Roux.*

15 Poetry is the first and last of all knowledge—it is as immortal as the heart of man. *Wordsworth.*

Poetry is the key to the hieroglyphics of nature. *Hare.*

Poetry is the language of feeling. *W. Winter.*

Poetry is the morning dream of great minds. *Lamartine.*

Poetry is the music of the soul; and, above all, of great and feeling souls. *Voltaire.*

20 Poetry is the offspring of the rarest beauty, begot by imagination upon thought, and clad by taste and fancy in habiliments of grace. *Simms.*

Poetry is the only verity, the expression of a sound mind speaking after the ideal, and not after the apparent. *Emerson.*

Poetry is the perpetual endeavour to express the spirit of the thing, to pass the brute body, and search the life and reason which cause it to exist; to see that the object is always flowing away, whilst the spirit or necessity which causes it subsists. *Emerson.*

Poetry is the record of the best and happiest moments of the happiest and best minds. *Shelley.*

Poetry is the utterance of truth,—deep, heartfelt truth. The true poet is very near the oracle. *Chapin.*

Poetry is the worst mask in the world behind 25 which folly and stupidity could attempt to hide their features. *Bryant.*

Poetry itself is strength and joy, whether it be crowned by all mankind, or left alone in its own magic hermitage. *J. Sterling.*

Poetry must first be good sense, though it is something better. *Quoted by Emerson.*

Poetry ought to go straight to the heart, because it has come from the heart; and aim at the man in the citizen, and not the citizen in the man. *Schiller.*

Poetry says more and in fewer words than prose. *Voltaire.*

Poetry should be great and unobtrusive. *Keats.* 30

Poetry should be vital, either stirring our blood by its divine movements, or snatching our breath by its divine perfection. *A. Birrell.*

Poetry uses the rainbow tints for special effects, but always keeps its essential object in the purest white light of truth. *Holmes.*

Poetry was given to us to hide the little discords of life and to make man contented with the world and his condition. *Goethe.*

Poetry, were it the rudest, so it be sincere, is the attempt which man makes to render his existence harmonious, the utmost he can do for that end; it springs therefore from his whole feelings, opinions, activity, and takes its character from these. It may be called the music of the whole inner being. *Carlyle.*

Poets and heroes are of the same race; the 35 latter do what the former conceive. *Lamartine.*

Poets and painters ha'e leave to lee. *Sc. Pr.*

Poets are all who love, who feel great truths, and tell them. *Bailey.*

Poets are liberating gods; they are free and make free. *Emerson.*

Poets are natural sayers, sent into the world for the end of expression. *Emerson.*

Poets are never young in one sense. Their 40 delicate ear hears the far-off whispers of eternity, which coarser souls must travel towards for scores of years before their dull sense is touched by them. A moment's insight is sometimes worth a life's experience. *Holmes.*

Poets are the hierophants of an unapprehended inspiration, the mirrors of the gigantic shadows which futurity casts upon the present. *Schiller.*

Poets are the unacknowledged legislators of the world. *Disraeli.*

Poets lose half the praise they should have got, / Could it be known what they discreetly blot. *Waller.*

Poets of old date, being privileged with senses, had also enjoyed external Nature; but chiefly as we enjoy the crystal cup which holds good or bad liquor for us; that is to say, in silence, or with slight incidental commentary; never, as I compute, till after the "Sorrows of Werter" was there man found who would say: Come, let us make a description: Having drunk the liquor, Come. let us eat the glass. *Carlyle.*

Poets should be lawgivers ; that is, the boldest lyric inspiration should not chide and insult, but should announce and lead the civil code, the day's work. *Emerson.*

Poets should turn philosophers in age, as Pope did. We are apt to grow chilly when we sit out our fire. *Sterne.*

Poets utter great and wise things which they do not themselves understand. *Plato.*

Point d'argent, point de Suisse—No money, no Swiss. *Fr. Pr.*

5 Policy sits above conscience. *Timon of Athens,* iii. 2.

Polished steel will not shine in the dark ; no more can reason, however refined, shine efficaciously but as it reflects the light of Divine truth shed from heaven. *John Foster.*

Politeness is benevolence in small things. (?)

Politeness is real kindness kindly expressed. *Witherspoon.*

Politeness is the flower of humanity. *Joubert.*

10 Politeness is to goodness what words are to thoughts. *Joubert.*

Politeness makes a man appear outwardly as he should be within. *La Bruyère.*

Political liberty is to be found only in moderate governments. *Montesquieu.*

Politicians think that by stopping up the chimney they can stop its smoking. They try the experiment ; they drive the smoke back, and there is more smoke than ever. *Borne.*

Politics is a deleterious profession, like some poisonous handicrafts. *Emerson.*

15 Politics is the science of exigencies. *Theodore Parker.*

πολλὰ μεταξὺ πελεῖ κύλικος καὶ χείλεος ἄκρου —Much may happen between the cup and the lip. *Gr.*

πολλὰ τὰ δεινὰ κοὐδὲν ἀνθρώπου δεινότερον πέλει—Many dread powers exist, and no one more so than man. *Sophocles.*

Pompa mortis magis terret quam mors ipsa— The solemnity associated with death awes us more than death itself.

πομφόλυξ ὁ ἄνθρωπος—Man is an air-bubble. *Gr. Pr.*

20 Ponamus nimios gemitus ; flagrantior æquo / Non debet dolor esse viri, nec vulnere major —Let us dismiss excessive laments ; a man's grief should not be immoderate, nor greater than the wound received. *Juv.*

Ponderanda sunt testimonia, non numeranda —Testimonies are to be weighed, not counted.

Pone seram, cohibe ; sed quis custodiet ipsos / Custodes ? cauta est, et ab illis incipit uxor —Fasten the bolt and restrain her ; but who is to watch over the watchers themselves ? The wife is cunning, and will begin with them. *Juv.*

Pons asinorum—The asses' bridge. *The Fifth Proposition in the First Book of Euclid.*

Ponto nox incubat atra, / Intonuere poli et crebris micat ignibus æther—Black night sits brooding on the deep ; the heavens thunder, and the ether gleams with incessant flashes. *Virg.*

25 Poor and content is rich and rich enough ; / But riches fineless is as poor as winter / To him that ever fears he shall be poor. *Othello,* iii. 3.

Poor folk hae neither ony kindred nor ony freends. *Sc. Pr.*

Poor folk seek meat for their stomachs, and rich folks stomachs for their meat. *Sc. Pr.*

Poor folks are glad of porridge. *Sc. Pr.*

Poor folks must say "Thank ye" for little. *Pr.*

Poor folk's wisdom goes for little. *Dut. Pr.* 30

Poor in abundance, famished at a feast, man's grief is but his grandeur in disguise, and discontent is immortality. *Young.*

Poor is the triumph o'er the timid hare. *Thomson.*

Poor love is lost in men's capacious minds ; / In women's it fills all the room it finds. *John Crowne.*

Poor men do penance for rich men's sins. *It. Pr.*

Poor men, when Yule is cold, / Must be content 35 to sit by little fires. *Tennyson.*

Poor men's tables are soon placed. *Pr.*

Poor naked wretches, wheresoe'er you are, / That bide the pelting of this pitiless storm, / How shall your houseless heads and unfed sides, / Your looped and windowed raggedness, defend you / From seasons such as these? O I have ta'en / Too little care of this ! *Lear,* iii. 2.

Poor tenant bodies, scant o' cash, / How they maun thole (bear) a factor's snash ; / He'll stamp and threaten, curse and swear, / He'll apprehend them, poind their gear ; / While they maun (must) stan', wi' aspect humble, / An' hear it a', and fear and tremble ! *Burns.*

Poor the raiment you may wear, / Scanty fare at best be thine ; / Let the soul within be clothed / With a majesty divine. *M. W. Wood.*

Poor though I am, despised, forgot, / Yet God, 40 my God, forgets me not ; / And he is safe, and must succeed, / For whom the Lord vouchsafes to plead. *Cowper.*

Poor, wandering, wayward man ! Art thou not tired, and beaten with stripes, even as I am? Ever, whether thou bear the royal mantle or the beggar's gaberdine, art thou so weary, so heavy-laden ; and thy bed of rest is but a grave. *Carlyle.*

Poor when I have, poor when I haven't, poor will I ever be. *Gael. Pr.*

Poortith (poverty) is better than pride. *Sc. Pr.*

Popular glory is a perfect coquette ; her lovers must toil, feel every inquietude, indulge every caprice, and perhaps at last be jilted into the bargain. *Goldsmith.*

Popular opinion is the greatest lie in the world. 45 *Carlyle.*

Popular opinions, on subjects not palpable to sense, are often true, but seldom or never the whole truth. *J. S. Mill.*

Popularity is a blaze of illumination, or alas ! of conflagration, kindled round a man ; showing what is in him ; not putting the smallest item more into him ; often abstracting much from him ; conflagrating the poor man himself into ashes and "caput mortuum." *Carlyle.*

Populus me sibilat ; at mihi plaudo / Ipse domi, simul ac nummos contemplor in arca—The people hiss me ; but I applaud myself at home as soon as I gaze upon the coins in my chest. *Hor., for the miser.*

Populus vult decipi; decipiatur—The people wish to be deceived; then let them.

Por mucho madrugar, no amanéce mas aina—Early rising does not make the day dawn sooner. *Sp. Pr.*

Porcus Epicuri—A pig of Epicurus.

Porro unum est necessarium—But one thing is needful. *M.*

5 Porte fermée, le diable s'en va—The devil goes away when he sees a shut door. *Fr. Pr.*

Portrait-painting may be to the painter what the practical knowledge of the world is to the poet, provided he considers it as a school by which he is to acquire the means of perfection in his art, and not as the object of that perfection. *Burke.*

Portraiture is the basis and the touchstone of historic painting. *Schlegel.*

Positive happiness is constitutional and incapable of increase; misery is artificial, and generally proceeds from our folly. *Goldsmith.*

Positiveness is a good quality for preachers and orators, because whoever would obtrude his thoughts and reasons upon a multitude, will convince others the more as he appears convinced himself. *Swift.*

10 Posse comitatus—The power of the county, which the sheriff has the power to raise in certain cases. *L.*

Possession is nine-tenths of the law. *Pr.*

Possession of land implies the duty of living on it, and by it, if there is enough to live on; then . . . if there is more land than enough for one's self, the duty of making it fruitful and beautiful for as many more as can live on it. *Ruskin.*

Possunt quia posse videntur—They are able because they look as if they were. *Virg.*

Post bellum auxilium—Aid after the war is over.

15 Post cineres gloria sera venit—Glory comes too late after one is reduced to ashes. *Mart.*

Post epulas stabis vel passus mille meabis—After eating, you should either stand or walk a mile. *Pr.*

Post equitem sedet atra cura—Behind the horseman sits dark care. *Hor.*

Post hoc; ergo propter hoc—After this; therefore on account of this. *A logical fallacy.*

Post mediam noctem visus quum somnia vera—He appeared to me in vision after midnight, when dreams are true. *Hor.*

20 Post nubila Phœbus—After clouds the sun. *M.*

Post prælia præmia—After battle rewards. *M.*

Post tenebras lux—After darkness light. *M.*

Post tot naufragia portum—After so many shipwrecks we reach port. *M.*

Posthumous charities are the very essence of selfishness, when bequeathed by those who, when alive, would part with nothing. *Colton.*

25 Postulata—Things admitted; postulates.

Pot ! don't call the kettle black. *Pr.*

Potatoes don't grow by the side of the pot. *Pr.*

Potentissimus est, qui se habet in potestate—He is the most powerful who has himself in his power. *Sen.*

Potter is jealous of potter, and craftsman of craftsman; and poor man has a grudge against poor man, and poet against poet. *Hesiod.*

που στῶ—Where I may stand, and plant my lever. 30 *Archimedes.*

Pound an almond, and the clear white colour will be altered into a dirty one, and the sweet taste into an oily one. *Locke.*

Pour avoir du goût, il faut avoir de l'âme—To have taste, one must have some soul. *Vauvenargues.*

Pour bien connaître un homme il faut avoir mangé un boisseau de sel avec lui—To know a man well, one must have eaten a bushel of salt with him. *Fr. Pr.*

Pour bien désirer—To desire good. *M.*

Pour bien instruire, il ne faut pas dire tout ce 35 qu'on sait, mais seulement ce qui convient à ceux qu'on instruit—To teach successfully we must not tell all we know, but only what is adapted to the pupil we are teaching. *La Harpe.*

Pour comble de bonheur—As the height of happiness. *Fr.*

Pour connaître le prix de l'argent, il faut être obligé d'en emprunter—To know the value of money, a man has only to borrow. *Fr. Pr.*

Pour connaître les autres, il faut se connaître soi-même — To know other people one must know one's self. *Fr. Pr.*

Pour couper court—To cut the matter short. *Fr.*

Pour dompter les anglais, / Il faut bâtir un 40 pont / Sur le Pas-de-Calais—To conquer the English one must build a bridge over the Straits of Dover. *A French song.*

Pour encourager les autres—To encourage the rest to go and do likewise. *Fr.*

Pour être assez bon, il faut l'être trop—To be good enough, one must be too good. *Fr. Pr.*

Pour exécuter de grandes choses il faut vivre comme si on ne devait jamais mourir—To achieve great things a man should so live as if he were never to die. *La Roche.*

Pour faire de l'esprit—To play the wit. *Fr.*

Pour faire rire—To excite laughter. *Fr.* 45

Pour faire un bon ménage il faut que l'homme soit sourd et la femme aveugle — To live happily together the husband must be deaf and the wife blind. *Fr. Pr.*

Pour forth thy fervours for a healthful mind, / Obedient passions, and a will resigned; / For love, which scarce collective man can fill; / For patience, sovereign o'er transmuted ill; / For faith, that, panting for a happier seat, / Counts death kind Nature's signal of retreat. *Johnson.*

Pour grands que soient les rois, ils sont ce que nous sommes; / Ils peuvent se tromper comme les autres hommes—However great kings may be, they are what we are; they may be deceived like other men. *Corn.*

Pour l'ordinaire la fortune nous vend bien chèrement, ce qu'on croit qu'elle nous donne—Fortune usually sells us very dear what we fancy she is giving us. *Fr.*

Pour parvenir à bonne foy—To succeed honour- 50 ably. *M.*

Pour qui ne les croit pas, il n est pas de prodiges—There are no miracles for those who have no faith in them. *Fr.*

Pour ranger le loup, il faut le marier—To tame the wolf you must get him married. *Fr. Pr.*

Pour savoir quelles étoient véritablement les opinions des hommes, je devois plutôt prendre garde à ce qu'ils pratiquoient qu'à ce qu'ils disoient — To know what men really think, I would pay regard rather to what they do than to what they say. *Descartes.*

Pour se faire valoir—To make one's self of consequence.

Pour s'établir dans le monde, on fait tout ce que l'on peut pour y paraître établi — To establish himself in the world a man must do all he can to appear already established. *La Roche.*

Pour soutenir les droits que le ciel autorise, / Abîme tout plutôt ; c'est l'esprit de l'église— To maintain your rights granted by Heaven, let everything perish rather than yield ; this is the spirit of the Church. *Boileau.*

5 Pour tromper un rival l'artifice est permis : / On peut tout employer contre ses ennemis— We may employ artifice to deceive a rival, anything against our enemies. *Richelieu.*

Pour un plaisir mille douleurs—For a single pleasure a thousand pains. *Fr. Pr.*

Pour y parvenir—To carry your point. *M.*

Povertà non ha parenti—Poor people have no relations. *It. Pr.*

Poverty and hunger have many learned disciples. *Ger. Pr.*

10 Poverty breeds strife. *Pr.*

Poverty breeds wealth, and wealth in its turn breeds poverty. The earth to form the mould is taken out of the ditch ; and whatever may be the height of the one will be the depth of the other. *Hare.*

Poverty consists in feeling poor. *Emerson.*

Poverty demoralises. *Emerson.*

Poverty ever comes at the call. *Goldsmith.*

15 Poverty has no greater foe than bashfulness. *Pr.*

Poverty, incessant drudgery, and much worse evils, it has often been the lot of poets and wise men to strive with, and their glory to conquer. *Carlyle.*

Poverty is but as the pain of piercing the ears of a maiden, and you hang jewels in the wound. *Jean Paul.*

Poverty is in want of much, avarice of everything. *Pub. Syr.*

Poverty is no crime and no credit. *Pr.*

20 Poverty is not a shame, but the being ashamed of it is. *Pr.*

Poverty is often concealed in splendour, and often in extravagance. It is the care of a great part of mankind to conceal their indigence from the rest. They support themselves by temporary expedients, and everyday is lost in contriving for to-morrow. *Johnson.*

Poverty is the mither (mother) o' a' arts. *Sc. Pr.*

Poverty is the only load which is the heavier the more loved ones there are to assist in supporting it. *Jean Paul.*

Poverty is the reward of idleness. *Dut. Pr.*

25 Poverty makes people satirical—soberly, sadly, bitterly satirical. *H. Friswell.*

Poverty of soul is irreparable. *Montesquieu.*

Poverty often deprives a man of all spirit and virtue. It is hard for an empty bag to stand upright. *Ben. Franklin.*

Poverty palls the most generous spirits ; it cows industry and casts resolution itself into despair. *Addison.*

Poverty persuades a man to do and suffer everything that he may escape from it. *Lucian.*

Poverty should engender an honest pride, that 30 it may not lead and tempt us to unworthy actions. *Dickens.*

Poverty sits by the cradle of all our great men, and rocks them up to manhood. *Heine.*

Poverty snatches the reins out of the hands of piety. *Saadi.*

Poverty takes away so many means of doing good, and produces so much inability to resist evil, both natural and moral, that it is by all virtuous means to be avoided. *Johnson.*

Poverty treads upon the heels of great and unexpected riches. *La Bruyère.*

Poverty wants some, luxury many, and avarice 35 all things. *Cowley.*

Power and permanence reside only in limitations. *Grabbe.*

Power belongeth unto God. *Bible.*

Power cannot have too gentle an expression. *Jean Paul.*

Power exercised with violence has seldom been of long duration, but temper and moderation generally produce permanence in all things. *Sen.*

Power, in its quality and degree, is the 40 measure of manhood. *J. G. Holland.*

Power is according to quality, not quantity. How much more are men than nations? *Emerson.*

Power is ever stealing from the many to the few. *Wendell Phillips.*

Power is no blessing in itself, but when it is employed to protect the innocent. *Swift.*

Power is nothing but as it is felt, and the delight of superiority is proportionate to the resistance overcome. *Johnson.*

Power is so characteristically calm, that calm-45 ness in itself has the aspect of strength. *Bulwer Lytton.*

Power, like a desolating pestilence, / Pollutes whate'er it touches ; and obedience, / Bane of all genius, virtue, freedom, truth, / Makes slaves of men, and of the human frame a mechanized automaton. *Shelley.*

Power, like the diamond, dazzles the beholder, and also the wearer ; it dignifies meanness ; it magnifies littleness ; to what is contemptible, it gives authority ; to what is low, exaltation. *Colton.*

Power to do good is the true and lawful end of aspiring. *Bacon.*

Power will intoxicate the best hearts, as wine the strongest heads. No man is wise enough, no man good enough, to be trusted with unlimited power. *Colton.*

Power's footstool is opinion, and his throne the 50 human heart. *Sir Aubrey de Vere.*

Powerful attachment will give a man spirit and confidence which he could by no means call up or command of himself ; and in this mood he can do wonders which would not be possible to him without it. *Matthew Arnold.*

Practically men have come to imagine that the laws of this universe, like the laws of constitutional countries, are decided by voting; that it is all a study of division-lists, and for the universe too depends a little on the activity of the whippers-in. *Carlyle.*

Practice aims at what is immediate; speculation at what is remote. In practical life, the wisest and soundest men avoid speculation, and ensure success, because, by limiting their range, they increase the tenacity with which they grasp events, while in speculative life the course is exactly the reverse, since in that department the greater the range the greater the command. *Buckle.*

Practice in time becomes second nature. *Anon.*

Practice is everything. *Periander.*

5 Practice makes perfect. *Pr.*

Practice must settle the habit of doing without reflecting on the rule. *Locke.*

Practise thrift, or else you'll drift. *Pr.*

Præcedentibus insta—Follow close on those who precede. *M.*

Præcepta ducunt, at exempla trahunt—Precept guides, but example draws. *Pr.*

10 Præmia virtutis honores—Honours are the rewards of virtue. *M.*

Præsis ut prosis—Be first, that you may be of service. *M.*

Præsto et persto—I press on and persevere. *M.*

Praise a fool and you may make him useful. *Dan. Pr.*

Praise a fool, and you water his folly. *Pr.*

15 Praise follows truth afar off, and only overtakes her at the grave. Plausibility clings to her skirts and holds her back till then. *Lowell.*

Praise from an enemy is the most pleasing of all commendations. *Steele.*

Praise God more, and blame neighbours less. *Pr.*

Praise is indeed the consequence and encouragement of virtue; but it is sometimes so unseasonably applied as to become its bane and corruption too. *Thomas à Kempis.*

Praise is so pleasing to the mind of man that it is the original motive of almost all our actions. *Johnson.*

20 Praise is the tribute of men, but felicity the gift of God. *Bacon.*

Praise is virtue's shadow; who courts her doth more the handmaid than the dame admire. *Heath.*

Praise, like gold and diamonds, owes its value only to its scarcity. *Johnson.*

Praise makes good men better, and bad men worse. *Pr.*

Praise Peter, but don't find fault with Paul. *Pr.*

25 Praise the bridge which carries you over. *Pr.*

Praise the hill, but keep below. *Pr.*

Praise the sea, but keep on land. *George Herbert.*

Praise undeserved is satire in disguise. *Pope.*

πρᾶος τοὺς λόγους, ὀξὺς τὰ πράγματα—Mild in speech, keen in action. *Himerius.*

30 Pray devoutly, / And hammer stoutly. *Pr.*

Pray to God, but keep the hammer going. *Pr.*

Pray to God, sailor, but pull for the shore. *Pr.*

Prayer and practice is good rhyme. *Sc. Pr.*

Prayer and provender never hinder a journey. *Pr.*

Prayer is a groan. *St. Jerome.* 35

Prayer is a powerful thing; for God has bound and tied himself thereto. *Luther.*

Prayer is a shield to the soul, a sacrifice to God, and a scourge to Satan. *Bunyan.*

Prayer is a study of truth,—a sally of the soul into the unfound infinite. *Emerson.*

Prayer is a turning of one's soul, in heroic reverence, in infinite desire and endeavour, towards the Highest, the All-excellent, Supreme. *Carlyle, in a letter to a young friend.*

Prayer is intended to increase the devotion of 40 the individual, but if the individual himself prays he requires no formulæ . . . Real inward devotion knows no prayer but that arising from the depths of its own feelings. *W. v. Humboldt.*

Prayer is the aspiration of our poor, struggling, heavy-laden soul towards its Eternal Father, and, with or without words, ought not to become impossible, nor need it ever. Loyal sons and subjects can approach the King's throne who have no "request" to make there except that they may continue loyal. *Carlyle, in a letter to a young friend.*

Prayer is the cable, at whose end appears / The anchor hope, ne'er slipp'd but in our fears. *Quarles.*

Prayer is the Christian's vital breath, / The Christian's native air. *James Montgomery.*

Prayer is the slender nerve that moves the muscles of Omnipotence. *Martin Tupper.*

Prayer is the soul's sincere desire, / Uttered 45 or unexpressed, / The motion of a hidden fire that trembles in the breast. *J. Montgomery.*

Prayer is the wing wherewith the soul flies to heaven; and meditation the eye with which we see God. *St. Ambrose.*

Prayer knocks till the door opens. *Pr.*

Prayer, like Jonathan's bow, returns not empty. *Gurnall.*

Prayer moves the hand that moves the universe. *Anon.*

Prayer must not come from the roof of the 50 mouth, but from the root of the heart. *Pr.*

Prayer purifies; it is a self-preached sermon. *Jean Paul.*

Prayer should be the key of the day and the lock of the night. *Pr.*

Prayer that craves a particular commodity, anything less than all good, is vicious. As a means to effect a private end, it is meanness and theft. *Emerson.*

Prayers are but the body of the bird; desires are its angel's wings. *Jeremy Taylor.*

Praying's the end of preaching. *George Her-* 55 *bert.*

Preaching is of much avail, but practice is far more effective. A godly life is the strongest argument that you can offer to the sceptic. *H. Ballou.*

Preaching is the expression of the moral sentiment in application to the duties of life. *Emerson.*

Précepte commence, exemple achève—Precept begins, example perfects. *Fr.*

Precepts or maxims are of great weight; and a few useful ones at hand do more toward a happy life than whole volumes that we know not where to find. *Sen.*

Preces armatæ—Armed prayers, *i.e.*, with arms to back them up.

Precious beyond price are good resolutions. Valuable beyond price are good feelings. *H. R. Haweis.*

Precious ointments are put in small boxes. *Pr.*

5 Predominant opinions are generally the opinions of the generation that is vanishing. *Disraeli.*

Prefer loss before unjust gain; for that brings grief but once, this for ever. *Chilo.*

Prejudice is a prophet which prophesies only evil. *Pr.*

Prejudice is the child of ignorance. *Hazlitt.*

Prejudice squints when it looks, and lies when it talks. *Duchess d'Abrantes.*

10 Prejudice, which he pretends to hate, is man's absolute lawgiver; mere use-and-wont everywhere leads him by the nose: thus let but a rising of the sun, let but a creation of the world happen twice, and it ceases to be marvellous, to be noteworthy or noticeable. *Carlyle.*

Prendre la clef des champs—To run away (*lit.* take the key of the fields). *Fr. Pr.*

Prendre les choses au pis—To regard matters in the most unfavourable light. *Fr.*

Prends le premier conseil d'une femme et non le second—Take a woman's first advice and not her second. *Fr. Pr.*

Prends moi tel que je suis—Take me as I am. *M.*

15 Present fears / Are less than horrible imaginings. *Macb., i. 3.*

Preserve the rights of inferior places, and think it more honour to direct in chief than to be busy in all. *Bacon.*

Pressure alone causes water to rise and directs it. *Renan.*

Presumption is our natural and original disease. *Montaigne.*

Presumptuousness, which audaciously strides over all the steps of gradual culture, affords little encouragement to hope for any masterpiece. *Goethe.*

20 Prêt d'accomplir—Ready to accomplish. *M.*

Prêt pour mon pays—Ready for my country. *M*

"Pretty Pussy" will not feed a cat. *Pr.*

Prevention is better than cure. *Pr.*

Pria Veneziani, poi Christiane—Venetian first, Christian afterwards. *Ven. Pr.*

25 Pride adds to a man's stature; vanity only puffs him out. *Chamfort.*

Pride and grace ne'er dwell in ae place. *Sc. Pr.*

Pride and poverty are ill met, yet often live together. *Pr.*

Pride feels no cold. *Pr.*

Pride flows from want of reflection and ignorance of ourselves. Knowledge and humility come upon us together. *Addison.*

30 Pride goeth before destruction, and a haughty spirit before a fall. *Bible.*

Pride hath no other glass to show itself but pride. *Troil. and Cress., iii. 3.*

Pride, ill-nature, and want of sense are the three great sources of ill-manners; without some one of these defects no man will behave himself ill for want of experience, or what, in the language of fools, is called knowing the world. *Swift.*

Pride is a flower that grows in the devil's garden. *Howell.*

Pride is lofty, calm, immovable; vanity is uncertain, capricious, and unjust. *Chamfort.*

Pride is still aiming at the blest abodes; / 35 Men would be angels, angels would be gods; / Aspiring to be gods, if angels fell, / Aspiring to be angels, men rebel. *Pope.*

Pride is the source of a thousand virtues; vanity is that of nearly all vices and all perversities. *Chamfort.*

Pride must suffer pain. *Pr.*

Pride never leaves its master till he gets a fa'. *Sc. Pr.*

Pride of origin, whether high or low, springs from the same principle in human nature; one is but the positive, the other the negative, pole of a single weakness. *Lowell.*

Pride, the never-failing vice of fools. *Pope.* 40

Pride will have a fall; for pride goeth before, and shame cometh after. *Pr.*

Pride with pride will not abide. *Pr.*

Pride would never owe, nor self-love ever pay. *La Roche.*

Pride's chickens have bonny feathers, but bony bodies. *Pr.*

Priestcraft is no better than witchcraft. *Pr.* 45

Priesthoods that do not teach, aristocracies that do not govern; the misery of that, and the misery of altering that, are written in Belshazzar fire-letters on the history of France. *Carlyle.*

Priests pray for enemies, but princes kill. *2 Hen. VI., v. 2.*

Prima et maxima peccantium est pœna peccasse—The first and greatest punishment of sinners is the conscience of sin. *Sen.*

Prima facie—At first sight or view of a case.

Primo avulso non deficit alter / aureus—The first 50 being wrenched away, another of gold succeeds. *Virg.*

Primum mobile—The primary motive power.

Primus in orbe Deos fecit timor—It was fear that first suggested the existence of the gods. *Statius.*

Primus inter pares—The first among equals.

Primus sapientiæ gradus est falsa intelligere—The first step towards wisdom is to distinguish what is false.

Princes and lords are but the breath of kings; / 55 "An honest man's the noblest work of God." *Burns.*

Princes and lords may flourish or may fade: / A breath can make them, as a breath has made. *Goldsmith.*

Principes mortales, rempublicam æternam—Princes are mortal, the republic is eternal. *Tac.*

Principi placuisse viris non ultima laus est—To have earned the goodwill of the great is not the least of merits. *Hor.*

Principiis obsta; sero medicina paratur, / Cum mala per longas convaluere moras—Resist the first beginnings; a cure is attempted too late when through long delay the malady has waxed strong. *Ovid.*

Principis est virtus maxima nosse suos—It is the greatest merit of a prince to know those his subjects. *Mart.*

Principle is a passion for truth. (?)

Principle is ever my motto, not expediency. *Disraeli.*

Prisoners of hope. *Bible.*

5 Pristinæ virtutis memores—Mindful of ancient valour. *M.*

Priusquam incipias consulto, et ubi consulueris mature facto opus est — Before you begin, consider; but having considered, use despatch. *Sall.*

Private affection bereaves us easily of a right judgment. *Thomas à Kempis.*

Private credit is· wealth; public honour is security. The feather that adorns the royal bird supports its flight; strip him of his plumage, and you fix him to the earth. *Junius.*

Private judgment with the accent on "private" is self-will; but with the accent on "judgment," it is freedom, free-will. *J. Hutchison Stirling.*

10 Private opinion is weak, but public opinion is almost omnipotent. *Ward Beecher.*

Private reproof is the best grave for private faults. *Pr.*

Private self-regard must have been wholly subordinated to, if not entirely cast out by, a higher principle of action and a purer affection before a man can become either truly moral or religious. *J. C. Sharp.*

Privatorum conventio juri publico non derogat —No bargain between individuals derogates from a law. *L.*

Privatus illis census erat brevis, / Commune magnum—Their private property was small, the public revenue great. *Hor.*

15 Privilegium est quasi privata lex—Privilege is as it were private law. *L.*

Pro aris et focis—For our altars and our hearths.

Pro bono publico—For the public good.

Pro Christo et patria—For Christ and country. *M.*

Pro confesso—As confessed or admitted.

20 Pro Deo et rege—For God and king. *M.*

Pro et con.—For and against.

Pro forma—For form's sake.

Pro hac vice—For this turn ; on this occasion.

Pro libertate patriæ — For the liberty of my country. *M.*

25 Pro patria et rege—For king and country. *M.*

Pro rata (parte)—In proportion, proportionally.

Pro re nata—For circumstances that have arisen.

Pro rege et patria—For king and country. *M.*

Pro rege, lege, et grege—For king, law, and people. *M.*

30 Pro tanto—For so much.

Pro tempore—For the time.

Pro virtute bellica—For valour in war. *M.*

Pro virtute felix temeritas—Instead of valour successful rashness. *Sen., of Alexander the Great.*

Probably imposture is of a sanative, anodyne nature, and man's gullibility not his worst blessing. *Carlyle.*

35 Probably men were never born demigods in any century, but precisely god-devils as we see ; certain of whom do become a kind of demigods. *Carlyle.*

Probatum est—It has been settled.

Probitas laudatur, et alget—Integrity is praised and is left out in the cold. *Juv.*

Probitas verus honos—Integrity is true honour. *M.*

Probitate et labore—By honesty and labour. *M.*

Probity is as rarely in accord with interest as 40 reason is with passion. *Saneal-Dubay.*

Probum non pœnitet—The upright man has no regrets. *M.*

Procellæ quanto plus habent virium tanto minus temporis—The more violent storms are, the sooner they are over. *Sen.*

Procrastination is the thief of time. *Young.*

Procul a Jove, procul a fulmine. Far from Jove, far from his thunderbolts. *Pr.*

Procul O ! procul este, profani—Away, I pray 45 you ; keep off, ye profane. *Virg.*

Prodesse quam conspici—To be of service rather than to be conspicuous. *M.*

Prodigus et stultus donat quæ spernit et odit. / Hæc seges ingratos tulit, et feret omnibus annis—The spendthrift and fool gives away what he despises and hates. This seed has ever borne, and will bear, an ungrateful brood. *Hor.*

Productions (of a certain artistic quality) are at present possible which are nought (*Null*) without being bad—nought, because there is nothing in them, and not bad, because a general form after some good model has hovered vaguely (*vorschwebt*) before the mind of the author. *Goethe.*

Profaneness is a brutal vice ; he who indulges in it is no gentleman. *Chapin.*

Professional critics are incapable of distin- 50 guishing and appreciating either diamonds in the rough state or gold in bars. They are traders, and in literature know only the coins that are current. Their critical laboratory has scales and weights, but neither crucible nor touchstone. *Joubert.*

Proffered service stinks, *i.e.*, is not appreciated. *Pr.*

Profligacy consists not in spending years of time or chests of money, but in spending them off the line of your career. *Emerson.*

Profound joy has more of severity than gaiety in it. *Montaigne.*

Progress begins with the minority. *G. W. Curtis.*

Progress is the law of life—man is not man as 55 yet. *Browning.*

Progress, man's distinctive mark alone, / Not God's and not the beasts : God is, they are ; / Man partly is, and wholly hopes to be. *Browning.*

Progress—the stride of God. *Victor Hugo.*

Prohíbetur ne quis faciat in suo, quod nocere potest in alieno—No one is allowed to do on his own premises what may injure those of a neighbour. *L.*

Prolonged endurance tames the bold. *Byron.*

Promettre c'est donner, espérer c'est jouir— 60 Promising is giving, and hoping is fruition. *Delille.*

Promise is most given when the least is said. *Chapman.*

Promises make debts, and debts make promises. *Dut. Pr.*

Promises may get friends, but it is performance that must nurse and keep them. *Owen Feltham.*

Proof of a God? A probable God! The smallest of finites struggling to prove to itself . . . and include within itself, the Highest Infinite, in which, by hypothesis, it lives and moves and has its being! Man, reduced to wander about, in stooping posture, with painfully-constructed sulphur-match, and farthing rushlight, or smoky tar-link, searching for the sun. *Carlyle.*

Prope ad summum, prope ad exitum—Near the summit, near the end. *Pr.*

Propensity to hope and joy is real riches; one to fear and sorrow, real poverty. *Hume.*

5 Proper words in proper places make the true definition of a style. *Swift.*

Properly speaking, the land belongs to these two: to the Almighty God and to all His children of men that have ever worked well on it, or shall ever work well on it. *Carlyle.*

Properly thou hast no other knowledge but what thou hast got by working. *Carlyle.*

Property has its duties as well as its rights. *Drummond.*

Property, O brother? Of my body I have but a liferent. . . . But my soul, breathed into me by God, my Me, and what capability is there, I call that mine and not thine. I will keep that, and do what work I can with it; God has given it me; the devil shall not take it away. *Carlyle.*

10 Property there is among us valuable to the auctioneer; but the accumulated manufacturing, commercial, economic skill which lies impalpably warehoused in English hands and heads, what auctioneer can estimate? *Carlyle.*

Prophecy, not poetry, is the thing wanted in these days. How can we sing and paint when we do not yet believe and see? *Carlyle.*

Prophete rechts, Prophete links / Das Weltkind in der Mitten—Prophets to right, prophets to left, the world-child between. *Goethe.*

Propositi tenax—Tenacious of my purpose. *M.*

Propriæ telluris herum natura, neque illum, / Nec me, nec quemquam statuit. Nos expulit ille: / Illum aut nequities, aut vafri inscitia juris, / Postremo expellet certe vivacior hæres—Nature has appointed neither him nor me, nor any one, lord of this land in perpetuity. That one has ejected us; either some villany or quirk at law, at any rate, an heir surviving him, will at last eject him. *Hor.*

15 Propriety of thought and propriety of diction are commonly found together. Obscurity and affectation are the two greatest faults of style. *Macaulay.*

Proprio motu—Of his own motion; spontaneously.

Proprio vigore—Of one's own strength.

Proprium humani ingenii est odisse quem læseris—It is a weakness of your human nature to hate those whom you have wronged. *Tac.*

Proque sua causa quisque disertus erat—Every one was eloquent in his own cause. *Ovid.*

20 Prose, words in their best order; poetry, the best words in the best order. *Coleridge.*

Prosperity destroys fools and endangers the wise. *Pr.*

Prosperity doth best discover vice, and adversity doth best discover virtue. *Bacon.*

Prosperity is not without many fears and distastes; and adversity is not without comforts and hopes. *Bacon.*

Prosperity is the blessing of the Old Testament; adversity is the blessing of the New, which carrieth the greater benediction and the clearer revelation of God's favour. *Bacon.*

Prosperity is the touchstone of virtue; for it 25 is less difficult to bear misfortunes than to remain uncorrupted by pleasure. *Tac.*

Prosperity seems to be scarcely safe, unless it be mixed with a little adversity. *H. Ballou.*

Prosperity tries the fortunate, adversity the great. *Pliny the Younger.*

Prosperum et felix scelus / Virtus vocatur—Crime when it succeeds is called virtue. *Sen.*

Protectio trahit subjectionem, et subjectio protectionem—Protection involves allegiance, and allegiance protection. *L.*

Protestantism is a revolt against false sove-30 reigns; the painful but indispensable first preparation for true sovereigns getting place among us. *Carlyle.*

Proud people are intolerably selfish, and the vain are gentle and giving. *Emerson.*

Prove all things; hold fast that which is good. *St. Paul.*

Proverbs are easily made in cold blood. *Joe Willet.*

Proverbs are mental gems gathered in the diamond-fields of the mind. *W. R. Alger.*

Proverbs are short sentences drawn from long 35 experience. *Cervantes.*

Proverbs are the abridgments of wisdom. *Joubert.*

Proverbs are the daughters of daily experience. *Dut. Pr.*

Proverbs are the wisdom of ages. *Ger. Pr.*

Proverbs are the wisdom of the streets. *Pr.*

Proverbs cover the whole field of man as he is, 40 and life as it is, not of either as they ought to be. *John Morley.*

Proverbs have been always dear to the true intellectual aristocracy of a nation. *Trench.*

Proverbs have, not a few of them, come down to us from remotest antiquity, borne safely upon the waters of that great stream of time which has swallowed so much beneath its waves. *Trench.*

Proverbs have pleased not one nation only, but many, so that they have made themselves a home in the most different lands. *Trench.*

Proverbs, like the sacred books of each nation, are the sanctuary of the intuitions. *Emerson.*

Proverbs please the people, and have pleased 45 them for ages. *Trench.*

Proverbs possess so vigorous a principle of life, as to have maintained their ground, ever new and ever young, through all the centuries of a nation's existence. *Trench.*

Proverbs were anterior to books, and formed the wisdom of the vulgar, and in the earliest ages were the unwritten laws of morality. *I. Disraeli.*

Provide things honest in the sight of all men. *St. Paul.*

Providence certainly does not favour individuals, but the deep wisdom of its counsels extends to the instruction and ennoblement of all. *W. v. Humboldt.*

Providence conceals itself in the details of human affairs, but becomes unveiled in the generalities of history. *Lamartine.*

Providence gives the power, of which reason teaches the use. *Johnson.*

Providence has a wild, rough, incalculable road to its end; and it is no use to try to white-wash its huge, mixed instrumentalities, to dress up that terrific benefactor in a clean shirt and white neckcloth of a student in divinity. *Emerson.*

Providence has decreed that those common acquisitions — money, gems, plate, noble mansions, and dominion—should be sometimes bestowed on the indolent and unworthy; but those things which constitute our true riches, and which are properly our own, must be procured by our own labour. *Erasmus.*

5 Providence has given to the French the empire of the land; to the English, that of the sea; to the Germans, that of—the air. *Mme. de Staël.*

Providence is but another name for natural law. *Ward Beecher.*

Providence is my next-door neighbour. *An Italian hermit.*

Providence is not counteracted by any means which Providence puts into our power. *Johnson.*

Providence may change, but the promise must stand. *Pr.*

10 Providence often puts a large potato in a little pig's way. *Pr.*

Providence provides for the provident. *Pr.*

Provision is the foundation of hospitality, and thrift the fuel of magnificence. *Sir P. Sidney.*

Provocarem ad Philippum, inquit, sed sobrium —I would appeal to Philip, she said, but to Philip sober. *Val. Max.*

Proximorum incuriosi, longinqua sectamur— Uninquisitive of things near, we pursue those which are at a distance. *Pliny.*

15 Proximus a tectis ignis defenditur ægre—A fire is difficult to ward off when next house is in flames. *Ovid.*

Proximus ardet Ucalegon—The house of your neighbour Ucalegon is on fire. *Virg.*

Proximus sum egomet mihi — I am my own nearest of kin. *Ter.*

Prudence and greatness are ever persuading us to contrary pursuits. The one instructs us to be content with our station, and to find happiness in bounding every wish : the other impels us to superiority, and calls nothing happiness but rapture. *Goldsmith.*

Prudence and love are not made for each other; as the love increases, prudence diminishes. *La Roche.*

20 Prudence is a necessary ingredient in all the virtues, without which they degenerate into folly and excess. *Jeremy Collier.*

Prudence is that virtue by which we discern what is proper to be done under the various circumstances of time and place. *Milton.*

Prudence is the virtue of the senses, the science of appearances, the outmost action of the inward life, God taking thought for oxen. *Emerson.*

Prudens futuri temporis exitum / Caliginosa nocte premit Deus ; / Ridetque, si mortalis ultra / Fas trepidat—The Deity in His wisdom veils in the darkness of night the events of the future; and smiles if a mortal is unduly solicitous about what he is not permitted to know. *Hor.*

Prudens interrogatio quasi dimidium sapientiæ —Prudent questioning is, as it were, the half of knowledge.

Prudens qui patiens—He is prudent who has 25 patience. *M.*

Prudens simplicitas—A prudent simplicity. *M.*

Prudent and active men, who know their strength and use it with limitation and circumspection, alone go far in the affairs of the world. *Goethe.*

Prudentia et constantia—By prudence and constancy. *M.*

Prudentis est mutare consilium ; stultus sicut luna mutatur—A prudent man may, on occasion, change his opinion, but a fool changes as often as the moon.

Prüft das Geschick dich, weiss es wohl warum ;/ 30 Es wünschte dich enthaltsam ! Folge stumm —Destiny is proving thee; well knows she why: she meant thee to be abstinent ! Follow thou dumb. *Goethe.*

Pshaw ! what is this little dog-cage of an earth? what art thou that sittest whining there? Thou art still nothing, nobody; true, but who then is something, somebody? *Carlyle.*

Public affairs ought to progress quickly or slowly, but the people have always too much action or too little. Sometimes with their hundred thousand arms they will over-throw everything, and sometimes with their hundred thousand feet they will crawl along like insects. *Montesquieu.*

Public feeling now is apt to side with the persecuted, and our modern martyr is full as likely to be smothered with roses as with coals. *Chapin.*

Public instruction should be the first object of government. *Napoleon.*

Public opinion is a second conscience. *W. R.* 35 *Alger.*

Public opinion is a weak tyrant compared with our own private opinion. What a man thinks of himself, that it is which determines, or rather indicates, his fate. *Thoreau.*

Public opinion is democratic. *J. G. Holland.*

Public opinion is the mixed result of the intellect of the community acting upon general feeling. *Hazlitt.*

Publicum bonum privato est præferendum— The public good must be preferred to private. *L.*

Publicum meritorum præmium—The public re- 40 ward for public services. *M.*

Pulchre ! bene ! recte !—Beautiful ! good ! correct ! *Hor.*

Pulvis et umbra sumus, fruges consumere nati —We are but dust and shadows, born merely to consume the fruits of the earth. *Hor.*

Punctuality is the soul of business. *Pr.*

Punishment follows hard upon crime. *Pr.*

Punishment is justice for the unjust. *St.* 45 *Augustine.*

Punishment is the last and the worst instrument in the hands of the legislator for the prevention of crime. *Ruskin.*

Punishment of a miser—to pay the drafts of his heir in his tomb. *Hawthorne.*

πῦρ μαχαίρᾳ μὴ σκαλεύειν—Don't stir fire with sword. *Pythagoras.*

Puras Deus non plenas adspicit manus—God looks to clean hands, not to full ones. (?)

5 Purchase the next world with this; thus shalt thou win both. *Arab. Pr.*

Pure enjoyment and true usefulness can only be reciprocal. *Goethe.*

Pure love cannot merely do all, but is all. *Jean Paul.*

Pure religion and undefiled before God and the Father is this: To visit the fatherless and widows in their affliction, and to keep himself unspotted from the world. *St. James.*

Pure truth, like pure gold, has been found unfit for circulation, because men have discovered that it is far more convenient to adulterate the truth than to refine themselves. They will not advance their minds to the standard, therefore they lower the standard to their minds. *Colton.*

10 Puridad de dos, puridad de Dios; puridad de tres, de todos es—A secret between two is God's secret; but a secret between three is all men's. *Sp. Pr.*

Purity and simplicity are the two wings with which man soars above the earth and all temporary nature. Simplicity is in the intention, purity in the affection; simplicity turns to God; purity unites with and enjoys Him. *Thomas à Kempis.*

Purity is the feminine, truth the masculine of honour. *Hare.*

Purity of mind and conduct is the first glory of a woman. *Mme. de Stäel.*

Purpose barred, it follows, / Nothing is done to purpose. *Coriolanus,* iii. 1.

15 Purpose is what gives life a meaning. *C. H. Parkhurst.*

Purposes, like eggs, unless they be hatched into action, will run into rottenness. *Samuel Smiles.*

Pursuit of knowledge under difficulties. *Lord Brougham.*

Pushing any truth out very far, you are met by a counter-truth. *Ward Beecher.*

Put a knife to thy throat, if thou be a man given to appetite. *Bible.*

20 Put a stout heart to a stey (steep) brae. *Sc. Pr.*

Put a tongue / In every wound of Cæsar that should move / The stones of Rome to rise and mutiny. *Jul. Cæs.,* iii. 2.

Put a young healthy soul full of life under the teaching of the Graces, and the soul's body and workmanship will become transparent of the soul's self. *Ed.*

Put armour on thine ears and on thine eyes. *Timon of Athens,* iv. 3.

Put money in thy purse. *Othello,* i. 3.

25 Put no trust in money; put your money in trust. *Amer. Pr.*

Put not all your crocks on one shelf. *Sc. Pr.*

Put not all your eggs in one basket. *Dut. Pr.*

Put not forth thyself in the presence of the king, and stand not in the place of great men; for better it is that it be said unto thee, Come up hither; than that thou shouldest be put lower in the presence of the prince whom thine eyes have seen. *Bible.*

Put the saddle on the right horse. *Pr.*

Put your best foot foremost. *Congreve.* 30

Put your foot down where you mean to stand. *Pr.*

Put your hand no farther than your sleeve will reach. *Pr.*

Put your hand quickly to your hat and slowly to your purse, and you'll take no harm. *Pr.*

Put your own shoulder to the wheel. *Pr.*

Put your trust in God, and keep your powder 35 dry. *Cromwell.*

Putting out the natural eye of one's mind to see better with a telescope. *Carlyle.*

Q.

Qu'est ce donc que l'aristocratie? L'aristocratie! je vais vous le dire: l'aristocratie, c'est la ligue, la coalition de ceux qui veulent consommer sans produire, vivre sans travailler occuper toutes les places sans être en état de les remplir, envahir tous les honneurs sans les avoir mérités: voilà l'aristocratie!—What, then, is the aristocracy? The aristocracy, I mean to tell you, is the league, the combination of those who are bent on consuming without producing, living without working, occupying all public posts without being able to fill them, and usurping all honours without having earned them—that is the aristocracy. *Gen. Foy.*

Qu'est-ce que le Tiers-Etat. Rien! Que veut-il être? Tout—What is the Third Estate? Nothing. What does it intend to be? Everything. *Abbé Sieyès.*

Qu'est-ce qu'un noble? Un homme qui s'est donné la peine de naître—What is a nobleman? A man who has given himself the trouble of being born. *Beaumarchais.*

Qu'heureux est le mortel qui, du monde ignoré, / 40 Vit content de soi-même en un coin retiré!—How happy the man who, unknown to the world, lives content with himself in some nook apart! *Boileau.*

Qu'il faut à chaque mois, / Du moins s'enyvre une fois—We should get drunk at least once a month. *Old Fr. Pr.*

Qu'on me donne six lignes écrites de la main de plus honnête homme, j'y trouverai de quoi le faire peudre—Give me six lines written by the most honourable man alive, and I shall find matter therein to condemn him to the gallows. *Richelieu.*

Qu'on parle bien ou mal du fameux cardinal, / Ma prose ni mes vers n'en diront jamais rien; / Il m'a fait trop de bien pour en dire du mal, / Il m'a fait trop de mal pour en dire du bien—Let the world speak well or ill of the famous cardinal, neither in my prose or verse will I mention his name; he has done me too much kindness to speak ill of him, and too much injury to speak well. *Corn. of Richelieu.*

Qu'un joueur est heureux ! sa poche est un trésor ! / Sous ses heureuses mains le cuivre devient or — How happy is a gambler ! His pocket is a treasure-store ; in his lucky hands copper turns into gold. *Regnard.*

Qu'une nuit paraît longue à la douleur qui veille !—What a long night that seems in which one is kept awake with pain. *Saurin.*

Qua vincit victos protegit ille manu—With the same hand with which he conquers he protects the conquered. *Ovid.*

Quackery has no friend like gullibility. *Pr.*

5 Quadrupedante putrem sonitu quatit ungula campum—The hoof, in its four-footed galloping, shakes the crumbling plain. *An onomatopoetic line from Virgil.*

Quæ amissa salva—Things which have been lost are safe. *M.*

Quæ e longinquo magis placent—Things please the more the farther fetched. *Pr.*

Quæ fuerant vitia mores sunt—What were once vices are now the fashion of the day. *Sen.*

Quæ fuit durum pati / Meminisse dulce est—What was hard to suffer is sweet to remember. *Sen.*

10 Quæ infra nos nihil ad nos—The things that are below us are nothing to us. *Pr.*

Quæ lucis miseris tam dira cupido ?—How is it that the wretched have such an infatuated longing for life (*lit.* the light)? *Virg.*

Quæ peccamus juvenes ea luimus senes—We pay when old for the excesses of our youth. *Pr.*

Quæ regio in terris nostri non plena laboris ?—What region of the earth is not full of the story of our calamities ? *Virg.*

Quæ sint, quæ fuerint, quæ mox ventura trahantur—What is, what has been, and what shall in time be. *Virg.*

15 Quæ supra nos nihil ad nos—Things which are above us are nothing to us. *Pr.*

Quæ sursum volo videre—I desire to see the things which are above. *M.*

Quæ te dementia cepit ?—What madness has seized you ? *Virg.*

Quæ virtus et quanta, boni, sit vivere parvo ! How great, my friends, is the virtue of living upon a little ! *Hor.*

Quæ volumus et credimus libenter, et quæ sentimus ipsi reliquos sentire putamus—What we wish we readily believe, and what we think ourselves we imagine that others think also. *Cæs.*

20 Quæque ipse miserrima vidi et quorum pars magna fui—Unhappy scenes which I myself witnessed, and in which I acted a principal part. *Virg.*

Quære verum—Seek the truth. *Pr.*

Quærenda pecunia primum, / Virtus post nummos—Money must be sought for in the first instance ; virtue after riches. *Hor.*

Quærens quem devoret—Seeking some one to devour. *M.*

Quæstio vexata—A vexed, *i.e.* much debated, question.

25 Quævis terra alit artificem—Every land supports the artisan. *Pr.*

Qualem commendes etiam atque etiam aspice, ne mox / Incutiant aliena tibi peccata pudorem—Study carefully the character of him you recommend, lest his misdeeds bring you shame. *Hor.*

Quales sunt summi civitatis viri talis est civitas — A community is as those who rule it. *Cic.*

Qualis avis, talis cantus ; qualis vir, talis oratio—As is the bird, so is its song ; as is the man, so is his manner of speech.

Qualis rex, talis grex—Like king, like people. *Pr.*

Qualis sit animus, ipse animus nescit—What 30 the soul is, the soul itself knows not. *Cic.*

Qualis vita, finis ita—As a man's life is, so is the end. *M.*

Quality is better than quantity. *Pr.*

Quam continuis et quantis longa senectus / Plena malis !—How incessant and great are the ills with which a prolonged old age is replete. *Juv.*

Quam inique comparatum est, hi qui minus habent / Ut semper aliquid addant divitioribus !—How unjust is the fate which ordains that those who have least should be always adding to the store of the more wealthy ! *Ter.*

Quam magnum vectigal sit parsimonia !—What 35 a wonderful revenue lies in thrift ! *Cic.*

Quam parva sapientia regatur—Think with how little wisdom the world is governed.

Quam propre ad crimen sine crimine !—How near to guilt a man may approach without being guilty !

Quam temere in nosmet legem sancimus iniquam !—How rashly do we sanction a rule to tell against ourselves ! *Hor.*

Quam veterrimum homini optimus est amicus—A man's oldest friend is his best. *Plaut.*

Quamvis digressu veteris confusus amici / 40 Laudo tamen—Though distressed at the departure of my old friend, yet I commend him for going. *Juv.*

Quand celui à qui l'on parle ne comprend pas et celui qui parle ne se comprend pas, c'est de la métaphysique—When he to whom a man speaks does not understand, and he who speaks does not understand himself, that is metaphysics. *Voltaire.*

Quand l'aveugle porte la bannière, mal pour ceux qui marchent derrière—When the blind man bears the standard, pity those who follow. *Fr. Pr.*

Quand le peuple est en mouvement, on ne comprend pas par où le calme peut en y rentrer ; et quand il est paisible, on ne voit pas par où le calme peut en sortir—When the people are in agitation, we do not understand how tranquility is to return ; and when they are at peace, we do not see how tranquility can depart. *La Bruyère.*

Quand les sauvages de la Louisiane veulent avoir du fruit, ils coupent l'arbre au pied et cueillent le fruit ; voilà le gouvernement despotique—When the savages of Louisiana want fruit, they cut down the tree by the root to obtain it. Such is despotic government. *Montesquieu.*

Quand les vices nous quittent, nous nous flat- 45 tons que c'est nous qui les quittons—When vices forsake us, we flatter ourselves that it is we who forsake them. *Fr.*

Quand on a tout perdu, quand on n'a plus d'espoir, / La vie est une opprobre, et la mort un devoir—When one has lost everything and has no more any hope, it is a disgrace to live and a duty to die. *Voltaire.*

Quand on est jeune, on se soigne pour plaire, et quand on est vieille, on se soigne pour ne pas déplaire—When we are young we take pains to be agreeable, and when we are old we take pains not to be disagreeable.

Quand on est mort, c'est pour longtemps—When one is dead, it is for a long while. *Fr. Pr.*

Quand on n'a pas ce que l'on aime, / Il faut aimer ce que l'on a--When we have not what we like, we must like what we have. *Fr.*

Quand on ne trouve pas son repos en soi-même, il est inutile de le chercher ailleurs—When we do not find repose in ourselves, it is in vain to look for it elsewhere. *Fr.*

5 Quand on se fait aimer, on n'est pas inutile—They are a useful people who have learnt how to please. *Ratisbonne.*

Quand on se fait entendre on parle toujours bien—We always speak well when we manage to be understood. *Molière.*

Quand on voit le style naturel, on est tout étonné et ravi ; car on s'attendait de voir un auteur, et on trouve un homme—When we see a natural style, we are astonished and charmed ; for we expected to see an author, and we find a man. *Pascal.*

Quand sur une personne on prétend se régler / C'est par les beaux côtés qu'il lui faut ressembler—When we aspire to imitate any one, it is after his fine qualities we must fashion ourselves. *Molière.*

Quand tout le monde a tort, tout le monde a raison—When all are wrong, every one is right. *Lalehaussée.*

10 Quand une fois j'ai pris ma résolution, je vais droit à mon but, et je renverse tout de ma soutane rouge—When once I have taken my resolution, I go straight to my point, and overturn everything out of my way with my red cassock. *Fr.* (?)

Quand une lecture vous élève l'esprit et qu'elle vous inspire des sentiments nobles et courageux, il est bon, et fait de main d'ouvrier—When a work has an elevating effect on the mind, and inspires you with noble and courageous thoughts, it is good and is from the hand of a master. *La Bruyère.*

Quando Dios amanece, para todos amanece—When God's light rises, it rises for all. *Sp. Pr.*

Quando el Español canta, ó rabia, ó no tiene blanca—If a Spaniard sing, he's either mad or without money. *Sp. Fr.*

Quando i furbi vanno in processione, il diabolo porta la croce—When rogues go in procession the devil carries the cross. *It. Pr.*

15 Quando non c'è, perde la chiesa—When there is nothing, the church is a loser. *It. Pr.*

Quando ullum inveniet parem ?—When shall we find his like again? *Hor.*

Quando vierás tu casa quemar llegate á escalentar—When thou seest thy house in flames, go warm thyself by it. *Sp. Pr.*

Quandoque bonus dormitat Homerus — Even the worthy Homer nods sometimes. *Hor.*

Quanta est gula, quæ sibi totos / Ponit apros, animal propter convivia natum—What a glutton is he who has whole boars served up for him, an animal created for banquets alone. *Juv.*

20 Quanti est sapere !—What a grand thing it is to be clever, or to have sense. *Ter.*

Quanto la cosa è più perfetta, / Più senta il bene e così la doglienza—The more perfect a thing is, the more susceptible of good and bad treatment. *Dante.*

Quanto piace al mondo è breve sogno—All the pleasure of the world is only a short dream. *Patrarch.*

Quanto quisque sibi plura negaverit, / A Dis plura feret — The more a man denies himself, the more will he receive from the gods. *Hor.*

Quantum — Proper quantity or allowance (*lit.* how much).

Quantum est in rebus inane !—What emptiness 25 there is in human affairs ! *Pers.*

Quantum meruit—As much as he deserved. *L.*

Quantum mutatus ab illo—How greatly changed from what he was ! *Virg.*

Quantum nobis nostrisque hace fabula de Christo profuerit notum est—Every one knows what a godsend this story about Christ has been to us and our order. *Pope Leo X.*

Quantum quisque sua nummorum servat in arca / Tantum habet et fidei—The credit of every man is in proportion to the number of coins he keeps in his chest. *Juv.*

Quantum sufficit—As much as is sufficient. 30

Quarrelling with occasion. *Mer. of Venice,* iii. 5.

Quarrels would not last long if the fault were only on one side. *La Roche.*

Qué es la vida? Un frenesi. / Qué es la vida? Una ilusion. / Una sombra, una ficcion, / Y el mayor bien es pequeño ; / Que toda la vida es sueño, / Y los sueños, sueños son !—What is life? A conceit of the fancy. What is life? An illusion, a shadow, a fiction, and the greatest earthly possession insignificant ; the whole of life nothing but a dream, and dreams are shadows. *Calderon.*

Que j'aime la hardiesse anglaise ! que j'aime les gens qui disent ce qu'ils pensent—How I like the boldness of the English ; how I like the people who say what they think ! *Voltaire.*

Que la Suisse soit libre, et que nos noms péris- 35 sent !—Let Switzerland be free and our names perish ! *Lemierre.*

Que les gens de l'esprit sont bêtes—What silly people wits are ! *Beaumarchais.*

Que mon nom soit flétri—(So be the cause triumphs) let my name be blighted. *Fr.*

Que votre âme et vos mœurs peintes dans vos ouvrages—Let your mind and manners be painted in your works. *Fr.*

Que vouliez-vous qu'il fît contre trois ?—Qu'il mourut !—What would you have him do with three against him. I would have him die. *Corn.* (?)

Quel che fa il pazzo all' ultimo, lo fa il savio 40 alla prima—The wise man does that at first which the fool must do at last. *It. Pr.*

Quelqu'éclatante que soit une action, elle ne doit passer pour grande lorsqu'elle n'est pas l'effet d'un grand dessein—An action should not be regarded as great, however brilliant it may be, if it is not the offspring of a great design. *La Roche.*

Quelque parti que je prenne je sais bien que je serai blâmé—Whatever side I take, I know well that I shall be blamed. *Louis XIV.*

Quelque soin que l'on prenne de couvrir ses passions par des apparences de piété et l'honneur, elles paraissent toujours au travers de ces voiles—Whatever care we take to conceal our passions by show of piety and honour, they always appear through these veils. *La Roche.*

Quelques crimes toujours précèdent les grands crimes—Small crimes always precede great ones. *Racine.*

Quem di diligunt, adolescens moritur, dum valet, sentit, sapit—Whom the gods love dies young, while his strength and senses and faculties are in their full vigour. *Plaut.*

Quem Jupiter vult perdere dementat prius—Him whom Jupiter wishes to ruin, he first infatuates. *Pr.*

5 Quem pœnitet peccasse pene est innocens—He who repents of having sinned is almost innocent. *Sen.*

Quem res plus nimio delectavere secundæ, / Mutatæ quatient—The man whom prosperity too much delights will be most shocked by reverses. *Hor.*

Quem te Deus esse jussit—What God bade you be. *M.*

Quemcunque miserum videris, hominem scias—Whenever you behold a fellow-creature in distress, remember that he is a man. *Sen.*

Questi non hanno speranza di morte—These have not the hope to die. *Dante.*

10 Questioning is not the mode of conversation among gentlemen. *Johnson.*

Quey (female) calfs are dear veal. *Sc. Pr.*

Qui a bruit de se lever matin peut dormir jusqu' à diner—He who has a name for rising in the morning may sleep till midday. *Fr. Pr.*

Qui a nuce nucleum esse vult, frangat nucem—He who would eat the kernel must first crack the shell. *Plaut.*

Qui a vécu un seul jour a vécu un siècle—He who has lived a single day has lived an age. *La Bruyère.*

15 Qui a vu la cour, a vu du monde, ce qu'il y a de plus, beau, le plus spécieux, et le plus orné ; qui méprise la cour après l'avoir vu méprise le monde—He who has seen the court has seen all this most beautiful, most specious, and best decorated in the world ; and he who despises the court after having seen it despises the world. *La Bruyère.*

Qui aime bien, châtie bien—Who loves well, chastises well. *Fr. Pr.*

Qui alterum incusat probri eum ipsum se intueri oportet—He who accuses another of improper conduct ought to look to himself. *Plaut.*

Qui aura esté une fois bien fol ne sera nulle autre fois bien sage—He who has once been very foolish will never be very wise. *Montaigne.*

Qui bene conjiciet, hunc vatem perhibeto optimum—Hold him the best prophet who forms the best conjectures.

20 Qui bene imperat, paruerit aliquando necesse est—He who is good at commanding must have some time been good at obeying. *Cic.*

Qui brille au second rang s'éclipse au premier—He who shines in the second rank is eclipsed in the first. *Fr. Pr.*

Qui capit ille facit—He who takes it to himself has done it. *Pr.*

Qui commence et ne parfait, sa peine perd—He who begins and does not finish loses his pains. *Fr. Pr.*

Qui conducit—He who leads. *M.*

Qui craindra la mort n'entreprendra rien sur 25 moi : qui méprisera la vie sera toujours maître de la mienne—He who fears death will never take any advantage of me ; but he who despises life will ever be master of mine. *Henry IV. of France.*

Qui craint de souffrir, souffer de crainte—He who fears to suffer suffers from fear. *Fr. Pr.*

Qui de contemnenda gloria libros scribunt, nomen suum inscribunt — Those who write books on despising fame inscribe their own name on the title-page.

Qui dedit hoc hodie, cras, si volet, auferet—He who has given to-day may, if he so please, take away to-morrow. *Hor.*

Qui est maître de sa soif est maître de sa santé—He who has the mastery of his thirst has the mastery of his health. *Fr. Pr.*

Qui est plus esclave qu'un courtisan assidu si 30 ce n'est un courtisan plus assidu ?—Who is more of a slave than an assiduous courtier, unless it be another courtier who is more assiduous still ? *La Bruyère.*

Qui facit per alium facit per se—He who does a thing by another does it himself. *Coke.*

Qui fingit sacros auro vel marmore vultus, / Non facit ille deos : qui rogat, ille facit—He does not make gods who fashions sacred images of gold or marble : he makes them such who prays to them. *Mart.*

Qui fit, Mæcenas, ut nemo, quam sibi sortem / Seu ratio dederit, seu fors objecerit, illa / Contentus vivat ; laudet diversa sequentes ? —How happens it, Mæcenas, that no one lives content with the lot which either reason has chosen for him or chance thrown in his way ; but that he praises the fortune of those who follow other pursuits? *Hor.*

Qui genus jactat suum aliena laudat—He who boasts of his descent boasts of what he owes to others. *Sen.*

Qui homo mature quæsivit pecuniam, / Nisi 35 eam mature parcit, mature esurit—He who has acquired wealth in time, unless he saves it in time, will in time come to starvation. *Plaut.*

Qui invidet minor est—He who envies another is his inferior. *M.*

Qui jacet in terra non habet unde cadat—Who lies upon the ground cannot fall. *Alain de Lille.*

Qui jeune n'apprend, vieux ne saura—He will not know when he is old who learns not when he is young.

Qui jure suo utitur, neminem lædit—He who enjoys his own right injures no man. *L.*

Qui legitis flores et humi nascentia fragra, / 40 Frigidus, O pueri fugite hinc, latet anguis in herba—Ye youths that pluck flowers and strawberries on the ground, flee hence ; a cold clammy snake lurks in the grass. *Virg.*

Qui mange du pape, en meurt—Who eats what comes from the pope dies of it.

Qui medice vivit, misere vivit—He who lives by medical prescription lives miserably. *Pr.*

Qui mentiri aut fallere insuevit patrem, / Tanto magis is audebit cæteros—He who has made it a practice to lie to or deceive his father, the more daring will he be in deceiving others. *Ter.*

Qui mores hominum multorum vidit et urbes—He who saw the manners of many men and cities. *Hor., of Ulysses.*

Qui n'a, ne peut—He who has not cannot. *Fr. Pr.*

Qui n'a pas l'esprit de son âge / De son âge a tout le malheur—He who has not the spirit of his time has all the misery of it. *Voltaire.*

Qui n'a plus qu'un moment à vivre / N'a plus rien à dissimuler—He who has only a moment to live has no more reason to dissemble. *Quinault.*

Qui n'a point d'amour n'a pas de beaux jours—He who knows not love has no happy days. *Fr.*

5 Qui n'a point de sens à trente ans n'en aura jamais—He who has not sense at thirty will never have any. *Fr. Pr.*

Qui n'a rien, ne craint rien—He who has nought fears nought. *Fr. Pr.*

Qui ne craint point la mort ne craint point les menaces—He who fears not death cares not for threats. *Corn.*

Qui ne sait obéir, ne sait commander—Who knows not how to obey knows not how to command. *Fr. Pr.*

Qui ne sait pas, trouvera à apprendre—He that does not know will find ways and means to learn. *Fr. Pr.*

10 Qui ne sait se borner, ne sut jamais écrire—He who cannot limit himself will never know how to write. *Boileau.*

Qui nescit dissimulare, nescit regnare — He who knows not how to dissemble knows not how to rule. *Louis XI.*

Qui nescit dissimulare nescit vivere—He who knows not how to dissemble, knows not how to live.

Qui nil molitur inepte—One who never makes any unsuccessful effort. *Hor.*

Qui nil potest sperare, desperet nihil—Who can hope for nothing should despair of nothing. *Sen.*

15 Qui nolet fieri desidiosus, amet—If any man wish to be idle, let him fall in love. *Ovid.*

Qui non est hodie, cras minus aptus erit—He who is not prepared to-day will be less ready to-morrow. *Ovid.*

Qui non laborat, non manducet—If any does not work, he shall not eat. *Vulgate.*

Qui non moderabitur iræ / Infectum volet esse, dolor quod suaserit et mens—He who does not restrain his anger will wish that undone which his irritation and temper prompted him to. *Hor.*

Qui non proficit, deficit—He who does not advance loses ground. *Pr.*

20 Qui non prohibet quod prohibere potest assentire videtur—He who does not prevent what he can prevent is held to consent. *L.*

Qui nunc it per iter tenebricosum, / Illuc unde negant redire quenquam—Who now is travelling along the darksome walk to the spot from which, they say, no one ever returns. *Cat.*

Qui parcit virgæ odit filium—He that spareth his rod hates the child. *M.*

Qui pardonne aisément invite à l'offenser—He who easily forgives invites offences. *Corn.*

Qui patitur vincit—He who endures conquers. *M.*

25 Qui peccat ebrius luat sobrius—He that commits an offence when drunk shall pay for it when he is sober. *L.*

Qui perd péche—He who loses sins. *Pr.*

Qui pense—He who thinks. *M.*

Qui peut ce qui lui plait, commande alors qu'il prie—He who can do what he pleases, commands when he entreats. *Corn.*

Qui porte épée porte paix—He who bears the sword bears peace. *Fr. Pr.*

Qui prête à l'ami perd au double—He who lends 30 money to a friend loses doubly. *Fr. Pr.*

Qui pro quo—Who for whom; one instead of another.

Qui proficit in literis et deficit in moribus, plus deficit quam proficit—He who is proficient in learning and deficient in morals is more deficient than proficient. *Anon.*

Qui quæ vult dicit, quod non vult audiet—He who says what he likes will hear what he does not like. *Ter.*

Qui recte vivendi prorogat horam / Rusticus expectat dum defluat amnis, at ille / Labitur et labetur in omne volubilis ævum—He who postpones the hour for living aright is as one who waits like the clown till the river flow by; but it glides and will glide on to all time. *Hor.*

Qui rit Vendredi, Dimanche pleurera—He who 35 laughs Friday will weep Sunday. *Fr. Pr.*

Qui s'excuse, s'accuse—He who excuses himself accuses himself. *Fr. Pr.*

Qui sait dissimuler, sait régner—He that knows how to dissemble knows how to reign. *Fr. Pr.*

Qui sait tout souffrir peut tout oser—He who can bear all can dare all. *Vauvenargues.*

Qui se fait brebis, loup le mange—Him who makes himself a sheep the wolf eats. *Fr. Pr.*

Qui se ressemble, s'assemble—Like associates 40 with like. *Fr. Pr.*

Qui se sent galeux se gratte—Let him who feels it resent it, or apply it (*lit.* let him scratch who feels the itch). *Fr. Pr.*

Qui se ultro morti offerant, facilius reperiuntur, quam qui dolorem patienter ferant—It is easier to find men who will volunteer to die than who will endure pain with patience. *Cæs.*

Qui semel aspexit quantum dimissa petitis / Præstant, mature redeat, repetatque relicta—Let him who has once perceived how much what he has given up is better than what he has chosen, immediately return and resume what he has relinquished. *Hor.*

Qui sert bien son pays n'a pas besoin d'aieux—He who serves his country well has no need of ancestors. *Voltaire.*

Qui sibi amicus est, scito hunc amicum omnibus 45 esse—He who is a friend to himself you may be sure he is a friend to all. *Sen.*

Qui spe aluntur, pendent, non vivunt—Those who feed on hope, hang on, they do not live. *Pr.*

Qui stultis videri eruditi volunt stulti eruditis videntur—They who wish to appear learned to fools will appear fools to learned men. *Quinct.*

Qui tacet consentire videtur—He who is silent professes consent. *L.*

Qui terret plus ipse timet—He who terrifies others is himself in continual fear. *Claud.*

Qui timide rogat, docet negare—He who asks 50 timidly courts refusal. *Sen.*

Qui trop embrasse, mal étreint—He who grasps too much grasps ill. *Fr. Pr.*

Qui uti scit, ei bona—Good to him who knows how to use it. *Ter.*

Qui veut la fin, veut les moyens—Who wills the end, wills the means. *Fr. Pr.*

Qui veut manger de noyeau, qu'il casse la noix—He that would eat the kernel must break the shell. *Fr. Pr.*

Qui veut mourir ou vaincre est vaincu rarement—He who is resolved to conquer or die is rarely conquered. *Corneille.*

Qui veut tener nette sa maison, / N'y mette ni femme, ni prêtre, ni pigeon — Let him who would keep his house clean, house in it neither woman, priest, nor pigeon. *Fr. Pr.*

Qui veut voyager loin ménage sa monture—He who has far to ride spares his horse. *Stat.*

Qui vit sans folie, n'est pas si sage qu'il croit —He who lives without folly is not as wise as he thinks. *Fr. Pr.*

5 Qui vive ?—Who goes there? *Fr.*

Qui vult decipi, decipiatur—Let him be deceived who chooses to be deceived.

Quick at meat, quick at work, *i.e.*, at that kind of work. *Sc. Pr.*

Quick removals are slow prosperings. *Pr.*

Quick resentments are often fatal. *Pr.*

10 Quick returns make rich merchants. *Pr.*

Quick sensibility is inseparable from a ready understanding. *Addison.*

Quick steps are best over miry ground. *Pr.*

Quick to borrow is always slow to pay. *Pr.*

Quick to learn and wise to know. *Burns.*

15 Quicken yourself up to duty by the remembrance of your station, who you are, and what you have obliged yourself to be. *Thomas à Kempis.*

Quicker by taking more time. *Pr.*

Quiconque a beaucoup de témoins de sa mort, meurt toujours avec courage—He who dies before many witnesses always does so with courage. *Voltaire.*

Quiconque est loup, agisse en loup—Whoever is a wolf acts as a wolf. *La Fontaine.*

Quiconque rougit est déjà coupable ; la vraie innocence n'a honte de rien—Whoever blushes confesses guilt ; true innocence feels no shame. *Rousseau.*

20 Quiconque s'imagine la pouvoir mieux écrire, ne l'entend pas—Whoso fancies he can write it (the Life of Christ) better does not understand it. (?)

Quicquid agas, prudenter agas, et respice finem—Whatever you do, do it with intelligence, and keep the end in view. *Thomas à Kempis.*

Quicquid agunt homines, votum, timor, ira, voluptas, / Gaudia, discursus, nostri est farrago libelli—Whatever men are engaged in, their wishes and fear, anger, pleasures, joys, runnings to and fro, form the medley of my book. *Juv.*

Quicquid excessit modum / Pendet instabili loco—Whatever has overstepped its due bounds is always in a state of instability. *Sen.*

Quicunque turpi fraude semel innotuit, / Etiamsi verum dicit, amittit fidem—Whoever has once been detected in a shameful fraud is not believed even if he speak the truth. *Phædr.*

25 Quid æternis minorem / Consiliis animum fatigas ?—Why harass with eternal purposes a mind too weak to grasp them? *Hor.*

Quid brevi fortes jaculamur ævo / Multa? quid terras alio calentes / Sole mutamus?—Why do we, whose life is so brief, aim at so many things? Why change we to lands warmed by another sun? *Hor.*

Quid cæco cum speculo ?—What has a blind man to do with a mirror?

Quid clarius astris ?—What is brighter than the stars? *M.*

Quid crastina volveret ætas / Scire nefas homini—It is not permitted to man to know what to-morrow may bring forth. *Stat.*

Quid datur a Divis felici optatius hora? / What 30 thing more to be wished do the gods bestow than a happy hour? *Cat.*

Quid de quoque viro, et cui dicas, sæpe caveto —Be ever on your guard what you say of any man, and to whom. *Hor.*

Quid deceat, quid non obliti—Neglectful of what is seemly and what is not. *Hor.*

Quid dem? quid non dem? renuis tu quod jubet alter—What shall I give? what withhold? you refuse what another demands. *Hor.*

Quid dignum tanto feret hic promissor hiatu ? —What will this promiser produce worthy of such boastful language? *Hor.*

Quid domini facient audent quum talia fures ? 35 —What would the masters do, when their knaves dare such things? *Virg.*

Quid enim ratione timemus / Aut cupimus ?— What do we fear or desire with reason? *Juv.*

Quid enim salvis infamia nummis ? — What matters infamy when the money is safe? *Juv.*

Quid est somnus gelidæ nisi mortis imago?— What is sleep but the image of cold death? *Ovid.*

Quid est turpius quam senex vivere incipiens ? —What is more scandalous than an old man just beginning to live ?—*Sen.*

Quid faciunt pauci contra tot millia fortes ?— 40 What can a few brave men do against so many thousand? *Ovid.*

Quid furor est census corpore ferre suo !—What madness it is to carry one's fortune on one's back ! *Ovid.*

Quid leges sine moribus / Vanæ proficiunt— What do idle laws avail without morals? *Hor.*

Quid me alta silentia cogis / Rumpere—Why force me to break the deep silence? *Virg.*

Quid non ebrietas designat ? Operta recludit ; / Spes jubet esse ratas ; in prælia trudit inertem ; / Sollicitis animis onus eximit ; addocet artes—What does not drink effect? it unlocks secrets ; bids our hopes to be realised ; urges the dastard to the fight ; lifts the load from troubled minds ; teaches accomplishments. *Hor.*

Quid non mortalia pectora cogis, / Auri sacra 45 fames ?—To what lust dost thou not drive mortal hearts, thou accursed lust for gold? *Virg.*

Quid nos dura refugimus / Ætas? Quid intactum nefasti / Liquimus?—What have we, a hardened generation, shrunk from? What have we, in our impiety, left inviolate? *Hor.*

Quid nunc—What now ; a newsmonger.

Quid obseratis auribus fundis preces ?—Why do you pour prayers into ears that are stopped? *Hor.*

Quid pro quo—Equivalent ; one thing instead of another.

Quid prodest, Pontice, longo / Sanguine cen- 50 seri, pictosque ostendere vultus / Majorum ? —What boots it, Ponticus, to be accounted of a long line, and to display the painted busts of our ancestors? *Juv.*

Quid quisque vitet, nunquam homini satis / Cautum est in horas—What he should shun from hour to hour man is never sufficiently on his guard. *Hor.*

Quid Romæ faciam? mentiri nescio—What should I do at Rome? I know not how to lie. *Juv.*

Quid si nunc cœlum ruat?—What if the sky should now fall? *Ter.*

Quid sit futurum cras fuge quærere, et / Quem sors dierum cunque dabit, lucro / Appone—Shrink from asking what is to be to-morrow, and every day that fortune shall grant you set down as gain. *Hor.*

5 Quid te exempta juvat spinis de pluribus una? —What better are you if you pluck out but one of many thorns? *Hor.*

Quid tibi cum pelago? Terra contenta fuisses—What have you to do with the sea? You should have been content with the land. *Ovid.*

Quid tristes querimoniæ / Si non supplicio culpa reciditur?—What do sad complaints avail if the offence is not cut down by punishment. *Hor.*

Quid turpius quam sapientis vitam ex insipientis sermone pendere?—What more discreditable than to estimate the life of a wise man from the talk of a fool? *Hor.*

Quid verum atque decens curo et rogo, et omnis in hoc sum—My care and study is what is true and becoming, and in this I am wholly absorbed. *Hor.*

10 Quid velit et possit rerum concordia discors—What the discordant concord of things means and can educe. *Hor.*

Quid vesper ferat, incertum est?—Who knows what the evening may bring us? *Livy.*

Quidquid erit, superanda omnis fortuna ferendo est—Our fate, whatever it be, is to be overcome by patience under it. *Virg.*

Quidquid id est, timeo Danaos et dona ferentes—Whatever it is, I fear the Greeks even when they bring gifts with them. *Virg.*

Quidquid præcipies, esto brevis, ut cito dicta / Percipiant animi dociles, teneantque fideles / Omne supervacuum pleno de pectore manat—Whatever you teach, be brief; what is quickly said, the mind readily receives and faithfully retains, everything superfluous runs over as from a full vessel. *Hor.*

15 Quien da la suyo antes de morir aparajese a bien sufrir—Who parts with his own before he dies, let him prepare for death. *Sp. Pr.*

Quien larga vida vive mucho mal vide—To live long is to see much evil. *Sp. Pr.*

Quien mas sabe mas calla—Who knows most says least. *Sp. Pr.*

Quien no va á carava, no sabe nada—He who does not mix with the crowd knows nothing. *Sp. Pr.*

Quien se muda, Dios le ayuda — God assists him who reforms himself. *Sp. Pr.*

20 Quien tiene arte, va por toda parte—Who has a trade may go anywhere. *Sp. Pr.*

Quiet continuity of life is the principle of human happiness. *Lindner.*

Quieta non movere—Don't stir things at rest.

Quietly do the next thing that has to be done, and allow one thing to follow upon the other. *Goethe.*

Quietness is best. *Sc. Pr.*

Quin corpus onustum / Hesternis vitiis animum 25 quoque prægravat una, / Atque affigit humo divinæ particulam auræ—And the body, overcharged with yesterday's excess, weighs down the soul also along with it, and fastens to the ground a particle of the divine ether. *Hor.*

Quis desiderio sit pudor aut modus / Tam cari capitis?—What shame or measure can there be to our regret for one so dear? *Hor.*

Quis enim virtutem amplectitur ipsam, / Præmia si tollas?—For who would embrace virtue herself if you took away the reward? *Juv.*

Quis fallere possit amantem?—Who can deceive a lover? *Virg.*

Quis nescit, primam esse historiæ legem, ne quid falsi dicere audeat? Deinde ne quid veri non audeat?—Who does not know that it is the first law of history not to dare to say anything that is false, and the second not to dare to say anything that is not true? *Cic.*

Quis scit an adjiciant hodiernæ crastina sum- 30 mæ / Tempora Di superi?— Who knows whether the gods above will add to-morrow's hours to the sum of to-day? *Hor.*

Quis separabit?—Who shall separate? *M.*

Quisnam igitur liber? Sapiens qui sibi imperiosus; / Quem neque pauperies neque mors neque vincula terrent; / Responsare cupidinibus, contemnere honores / Fortis, et in seipso totus teres atque rotundus—Who then is free? He who is wisely lord of himself, whom neither poverty, nor death, nor bonds terrify, who is strong to resist his appetites and despise honours, and is complete in himself, smooth and round like a globe. *Hor.*

Quisque suos patimur Manes—The ghost of each of us undergoes (in the nether world) his own special punishment or purgation.

Quit not certainty for hope. *Pr.*

Quit the world, and the world forgets you. 35 *Disraeli.*

Quit thyself manfully ; banish impatience and distrust. *Thomas à Kempis.*

Quixadas sin barbas no merecen ser honradas — Chins without beards deserve no honour. *Sp. Pr.*

Quo animo—With what intention.

Quo fata vocant—Whither the Fates call. *M.*

Quo jure—By what right. 40

Quo jure quaque injuria—Right or wrong. *Ter.*

Quo mihi fortunam, si non conceditur uti?—To what end have the gods given me fortune, if I may not use it? *Hor.*

Quo res cunque cadent, unum et commune periculum, / Una salus ambobus erit—Whatever may be the issue, we have both one common peril and one safety. *Virg.*

Quo semel est imbuta recens servabit odorem / Testa diu—The jar will long retain the odour of the liquor with which, when new, it was once saturated. *Hor.*

Quo teneam vultus mutantem Protea nodo?— 45 By what noose shall I hold this Proteus who is ever changing his shape? *Hor.*

Quoad hoc—So far (*lit.* as regards this).

Quocirca vivite fortes / Fortiaque adversis opponite pectora rebus — Wherefore live as brave men, and front adversity with stout hearts.

Quocunque aspicio, nihil est nisi mortis imago—Wherever I look I see nothing but some form of death. *Ovid.*

Quod avertat Deus !—God forbid !

Quod cito fit, cito perit—What is done quickly does not last long.

Quod commune cum alio est, desinit esse proprium—What we share with another ceases to be our own. *Quinct.*

Quod decet honestum est et quod honestum est decet—What is becoming is honourable, and what is honourable is becoming. *Cic.*

5 Quod eorum minimis mihi—As to the least of these, so to me. *M.*

Quod erat demonstrandum—Which was to be proved.

Quod erat faciendum—Which was to be done.

Quod est absurdum—Which is absurd.

Quod est ante pedes nemo spectat : cœli / Scrutantur plagas—What is at his feet no one looks at ; they scan the tracks of heaven. *Enn.*

10 Quod licet Jovi, non licet bovi—What is allowed to Jupiter is not allowed to the ox.

Quod medicorum est / Promittunt medici, tractant fabrilia fabri / Scribimus indocti doctique poemata passim—Doctors practise what belongs to doctors, workmen handle the tools they have been trained to, but all of us everywhere, trained and untrained, alike write verses. *Hor.*

Quod nimis miseri volunt, hoc facile credunt—Whatever the wretched anxiously wish for, they are ready to believe. *Sen.*

Quod non opus est, asse carum est—What you don't need is dear at a doit. *Cato.*

Quod non vetat lex, hoc vetat fieri pudor—Modesty forbids what the law does not. *Sen.*

15 Quod nunc ratio est, impetus ante fuit—What is now reason was formerly impulse or instinct. *Ovid.*

Quod potui perfeci — What I could I have done. *M.*

Quod satis est cui contingit, nihil amplius optet—Let him who for his share has enough wish for nothing more. *Hor.*

Quod scripsi, scripsi—What I have written, I have written.

Quod semper, quod ubique, et quod ab omnibus —What has been always, been everywhere, and been by all believed.

20 Quot servi, tot hostes—So many servants you maintain, so many enemies.

Quod sis esse velis, nihilque malis : / Summum nec metuas diem, nec optes—Be content to be what you are, and prefer nothing to it, neither fear nor wish for your last day. *Mart.*

Quod sursum volo videre—I wish to see that which is above. *M.*

Quod verum est, meum est—What is true belongs to me (whoever said it). *Sen.*

Quod verum tutum—What is true is safe. *M.*

25 Quod vide (or videas)—Which see.

Quondam his vicimus armis—We formerly conquered with these arms. *M.*

Quot capitum vivunt, totidem studiorum—There are as many thousands of different tastes of pursuits as there are individuals alive. *Hor.*

Quot cœlum stellas, tot habet tua Roma puellas—There are as many girls in your Rome as there are stars in the sky. *Ovid.*

Quotation confesses inferiority. *Emerson.*

30 Quotation, like much better things, has its abuses. One may quote till one compiles. *I. Disraeli.*

Quotations from profane authors, cold allusions, false pathetic, antitheses and hyperboles, are out of doors. *La Bruyère.*

Quum Romæ fueris, Romano vivite more—When you are at Rome live after the fashion at Rome. *Pr.*

Quum talis sis, utinam noster esses !—How I wish you were one of us, since I find you so worthy ! *L.*

R.

Racine passera comme le café—Racine will go out of fashion like coffee. *Mme. de Sévigné.*

35 Rage avails less than courage. *Fr. Pr.*

Rage is for little wrongs ; despair is dumb. *Hannah More.*

Rage is mental imbecility. *H. Ballou.*

Raggio d'asino non arriva al cielo—The braying of an ass does not reach heaven. *It. Pr.*

Rags, which are the reproach of poverty, are the beggar's robes and graceful insignia of his profession, his tenure, his full dress, the suit in which he is expected to show himself in public. *Lamb.*

40 Rail not in answer, but be calm, / For silence yields a rapid balm ; / Live it down ! *Dr. Henry Rink.*

Railing and praising were his usual themes ; / And both, to show his judgment, in extremes ;/ So over-violent or over-civil, / That every man with him was god or devil. *Dryden.*

Raillery is a mode of speaking in favour of one's wit against one's good nature. *Montaigne.*

Raillery is sometimes more insupportable than wrong ; because we have a right to resent injuries, but it is ridiculous to be angry at a jest. *La Roche.*

Railway travelling is not travelling at all ; it is merely being sent to a place, and very little different from becoming a parcel. *Ruskin.*

45 Rainy days will surely come ; / Take your friend's umbrella home. *Saying.*

Raise nae mair deils than ye're able to lay. *Sc. Pr.*

Raison d'état—A reason of state. *Pr.*

Raison d'être—The reason for a thing's existence.

Raisonner sur l'amour, c'est perdre la raison—To reason about love is to lose reason. *Boufters.*

50 Rake not into the bowels of unwelcome truth to save a halfpenny. *Lamb.*

Rami felicia poma ferentes—Branches bearing beauteous fruit. *Ovid.*

Rank and riches are chains of gold, but still chains. *Ruffini.*

Rank is a great beautifier. *Bulwer Lytton.*

Rank is but the guinea's stamp, / The man's the gowd for a' that. *Burns.*

55 Raphael wäre ein grosser Maler geworden, selbst wenn er ohne Hände auf die Welt gekommen wäre—Raphael would have been a great painter even if he had come into the world without hands. *Lessing.*

Rapiamus, amici, / Occasionem de die—Let us, my friends, snatch our opportunity from the passing day. *Hor.*

Rapt with zeal, pathetic, bold, and strong, / Roll'd the full tide of eloquence along. *Falconer.*

Rara avis in terris, nigroque similima cygno— A bird rarely seen on earth, and very much resembling a black swan. *Juv.*

Rara est adeo concordia formæ / Atque pudicitiæ—So rare is the union of beauty with modesty. *Juv.*

Rara fides pietasque viris qui castra sequuntur —Faith and piety are rare among the men who follow the camp. *Lucan.*

5 Rara temporum felicitate, ubi sentire quæ velis, et quæ sentias dicere licet—Such was the happiness of the times, that you might think as you chose and speak as you thought. *Tac.*

Rare benevolence, the minister of God. *Carlyle.*

Rari nantes in gurgite vasto—Swimming one here and another there in the vast abyss. *Virg.*

Rari quippe boni; numero vix sunt totidem quot / Thebarum portæ, vel divitis ostia Nili—Rare indeed are the good; in number they are scarcely as many as the gates of Thebes or the mouths of the fertile Nile. *Juv.*

Rarity imparts a charm; thus early fruits and winter roses are most prized; thus coyness sets off an extravagant mistress, while a door ever open tempts no suitor. *Mart.*

10 Rarity / Of Christian charity / Under the sun. *T. Hood.*

Raro antecedentem scelestum / Deseruit pede pœna claudo—Rarely does punishment, with halting foot, fail to overtake the criminal in his flight. *Hor.*

Raro sermo illis, et magna libido tacendi—They seldom speak, and have a great conceit of holding their tongues. *Juv.*

Rarus enim ferme sensus communis in illa / Fortuna—Common sense is generally rare in that position of life, *i.e.*, in high rank. *Juv.*

Rascals are always sociable, and the test of a man's nobility is the small pleasure he has in others' society. *Schiller.*

15 Rasch tritt der Tod den Menschen an, / Es ist ihm keine Frist gegeben, / Es stürzt ihn mitten in der Bahn, / Es reisst ihn fort vom vollen Leben. / Bereitet oder nicht; zu gehen, / Er muss vor seinen Richter stehen —Death of a sudden arrests his victim, man; there is no respite given; he falls upon him in midday, and tears him away when life is at the full. Ready to go or not, he must stand before his judge. *Schiller.*

Rashness is the faithful but unhappy parent of misfortune. *Fuller.*

Rast' ich, so rost' ich—Rest I, rust I. *Luther.*

Rast macht Rost—Rest breeds rust. *Ger. Pr.*

Rathe Niemand ungebeten—Advise no man unasked. *Ger. Pr.*

20 Rathen ist leichter denn helfen—To advise is easier than to help. *Ger. Pr.*

Rathen ist nicht zwingen—To advise is not to compel. *Ger. Pr.*

Rather an egg to-day than a hen to-morrow. *Dan. Pr.*

Rather assume thy right in silence and *de facto*, than voice it with claims and challenges. *Bacon.*

Rather bear those ills we have / Than fly to others that we know not of. *Ham.*, iii. 1.

Rather find what beauty is than anxiously in- 25 quire what it is. *Goethe.*

Rather go to bed supperless than rise in debt. *Ben. Franklin.*

Rather let my head stoop to the block than these knees bow to any save to the God of heaven. *2 Hen. VI.*, iv. 1.

Rather than be less, / Cared not to be at all. *Milton.*

Rather to do nothing than to do good is the lowest state of a degraded mind. *Johnson.*

Ratio decidendi—The reason for deciding. 30

Ratio et auctoritas, duo clarissima mundi lumina—Reason and authority, the two brightest luminaries of the world. *Coke.*

Ratio et consilium propriæ ducis artes — Thought and deliberation are the qualities proper to a general. *Tac.*

Ratio justifica—The reason which justifies.

Ratio quasi quædam lux lumenque vitæ— Reason is, as it were, the guide and light of life. *Cic.*

Ratio suasoria—The reason which persuades. 35

Rauch ist alles irdsche Wesen; / Wie des Dampfes Säule weht, / Schwinden alle Erdengrössen, / Nur die Götter bleiben stät—A vapour is all earthly existence; as a column of vapour it drifts along: vanish all earth's great ones; only the gods remain stable. *Schiller.*

Raum für alle hat die Erde—The earth is wide enough for all. *Schiller.*

Raum, ihr Herrn, dem Flügelschlag / Einer freien Seele—Room, gentlemen, for a free soul to clap its wings. *G. Herwegh.*

Raum ist in der kleinsten Hütte / Für ein glücklich liebend Paar—There is room in the smallest cottage for a happy loving pair. *Schiller.*

Ravish'd with the whistling of a name. *Pope*, 40

Rays must converge to a point in order to glow intensely. *Blair.*

Re infecta—The business being unfinished. *Cæs.*

Re ipsa repperi, / Facilitate nihil esse homini melius, neque clementia—I have learned by experience that nothing is more advantageous to a man than complaisance and clemency of temper. *Ter.*

Re opitulandum non verbis—We should assist by deeds, not in words. *Pr.*

Re secunda fortis, dubia fugax—In prosperity 45 courageous, in danger timid. *Phæd.*

Read Homer once, and you can read no more, / For all books else appear so mean, so poor, / Verse will seem prose; but still persist to read, / And Homer will be all the books you need. *Buckingham.*

Read, mark, learn, and inwardly digest. *Book of Common Prayer.*

Read my little fable : / He that runs may read. / Most can raise the flowers now, / For all have got the seed. *Tennyson.*

Read not books alone, but men, and amongst them chiefly thyself; if thou find anything questionable there, use the commentary of a severe friend rather than the gloss of a sweet-lipped flatterer; there is more profit in a distasteful truth than deceitful sweetness. *Quarles.*

Read not to contradict and confute, nor to 50 believe and take for granted, nor to find talk and discourse, but to weigh and consider. *Bacon.*

Read nothing that you do not care to remember, and remember nothing you do not mean to use. *Prof. Blackie, to young men.*

Read the book you do honestly feel a wish and curiosity to read. *Johnson.*

Reader, attend — whether thy soul / Soars fancy's flights beyond the pole, / Or darkling grubs this earthly hole / In low pursuit ; / Know, prudent, cautious self-control / Is wisdom's root. *Burns.*

Reader, if thou an oft-told tale wilt trust, / Thou'lt gladly do and suffer what thou must. *Henry Marten.*

5 Reading Chaucer is like brushing through the dewy grass at sunrise. *Lowell.*

Reading furnishes us only with the materials of knowledge ; it is thinking makes what we read ours. *Locke.*

Reading for the sense (in Shakespeare's plays) will best bring out the rhythm. *Emerson.*

Reading is thinking with another's head instead of one's own. *Schopenhauer.*

Reading makes a full man, conference a ready man, and writing an exact man. And therefore if a man write little, he had need have a great memory; if he confer little, have a present wit ; and if he read little, have much cunning to seem to know that he doth not. *Bacon.*

10 Reading without purpose is sauntering, not exercise. *Bulwer Lytton.*

Real action is in silent moments. *Emerson.*

Real friends are our greatest joy and our greatest sorrow. *Fénelon.*

Real happiness is cheap enough, yet how dearly we pay for its counterfeit ! *H. Ballou.*

Real knowledge consists not in an acquaintance with facts, which only makes a pedant, but in the use of facts, which makes a philosopher. *Buckle.*

15 Real sorrow is almost as difficult to discover as real poverty. An instinctive delicacy hides the rays of the one and the wounds of the other. *Mme. Swetchine.*

Real ugliness in either sex means always some kind of hardness of heart or vulgarity of education. *Ruskin.*

Real worth floats not with people's fancies, no more than a rock in the sea rises and falls with the tide. *Fuller.*

Real worth requires no interpreter ; its everyday deeds form its blazonry. *Chamfort.*

Reality, if rightly interpreted, is grander than fiction ; nay, it is in the right interpretation of reality and history that poetry consists. *Carlyle.*

20 Reality is, no doubt, greater and more vital to know, in so real a world and life, than any fiction ; and the thoughts of God, which the facts are, are infinitely more precious than the fancies of men about them, or even according to them ; yet is man's power of fancying, or fantasying, in harmony with the fact, the measure of his knowledge of it and vital relationship to it, and the divinely appointed means withal whereby the fact itself is brought home to our affections. *Ed.*

Reality surpasses imagination ; and we see breathing, brightening, and moving before our eyes sights dearer to our hearts than any we ever beheld in the land of dreams. *Goethe.*

Reason and experience both forbid us to expect that national morality can prevail in exclusion of religious principle. *Washington.*

Reason can never be popular. Passions and feelings may become popular ; but reason always remains the sole property of a few eminent individuals. *Goethe.*

Reason can no more influence the will and operate as a motive, than the eyes, which show a man his road, can enable him to move from place to place, or than a ship provided with a compass can sail without a wind. *Whately.*

Reason cannot show itself more reasonable 25 than to cease reasoning on things above reason. *Sir P. Sidney.*

Reason gains all men by compelling none. *Aaron Hill.*

Reason has done, what it can do, when it discovers and draws up the law ; to execute this law is reserved for him who feels the obligation of it, and has the due firmness of purpose. *Schiller.*

Reason has only to do with the becoming, the living ; but understanding with the become, the already fixed, that it may make use of it. *Goethe.*

Reason! how many eyes hast thou to see evils, and how dim—nay, blind—thou art in preventing them ! *Sir P. Sidney.*

Reason is, and exists only on what it 30 makes ; its usefulness takes the place of beauty. *Joubert.*

Reason is a historian, but the passions are the actors. *Rivarol.*

Reason is a very light rider, and easily shook off. *Swift.*

Reason is directed to the process (*das Werdende*), understanding to the product (*das Gewordene*). The former is nowise concerned about the whither, or the latter about the whence. *Goethe.*

Reason is like the sun, of which the light is constant, uniform, and lasting; fancy, a meteor of bright but transitory lustre, irregular in its motion and delusive in its direction. *Johnson.*

Reason is progressive ; instinct, stationary. 35 Five thousand years have added no improvement to the hive of the bee nor the house of the beaver. *Colton.*

Reason is the life of the law ; nay, the common law itself is nothing else but reason. *Coke.*

Reason (*Vernunft*) is the only true despot. *Rahel.*

Reason is the test of ridicule, not ridicule the test of truth. *Warburton.*

Reason itself is true and just, but the reason of every particular man is weak and wavering. *Swift.*

Reason lies between bridle and spur. *It. Pr.* 40

Reason, looking upwards, and carried to the true above, realises a delight in wisdom, unknown to the other parts of our nature. *Plato.*

Reason raise o'er instinct as you can ; / In this 'tis God directs, in that 'tis man. *Pope.*

Reason requires culture to expand it. It resembles the fire concealed in the flint, which only shows itself when struck with the steel. *Gordil.*

Reason serves when pressed, but honest instinct comes a volunteer. *Pope.*

Reason should direct, and appetite obey. *Cic.*

Reason teaches us to be silent; the heart teaches us to speak. *Jean Paul.*

Reason's a staff for age when Nature's gone ; / But youth is strong enough to walk alone. *Dryden.*

5 Reason's glimmering ray / Was lent, not to assure our doubtful way, / But guide us upward to a better day. *Dryden.*

Reason's whole pleasure, all the joys of sense, / Lie in three words,—health, peace, and competence. *Pope.*

Reasonable, or sensible, people are always the best Conversation's Lexicon. *Goethe.*

Reasoning against a prejudice is like fighting against a shadow ; it exhausts the reasoner, without visibly affecting the prejudice. Argument cannot do the work of instruction any more than blows can take the place of sunlight. *Mildmay.*

Reasoning banishes reason. *Molière.*

10 Reasons are the pillars of the fabric of a sermon, but similitudes are the windows which give the best light. *Fuller.*

Rebellentreue ist wankend — Fidelity among rebels is unsteady. *Schiller.*

Rebellion to tyrants is obedience to God. *Inscription on a cannon.*

Rebuke ought to have a grain more of salt than of sugar. *Pr.*

Rebuke with soft words and hard arguments. *Pr.*

15 Rebus angustis animosus atque / Fortis appare ; sapienter idem / Contrahes vento nimium secundo / Turgida vela—Wisely show yourself spirited and resolute when perils press you; likewise reef your sails when they swell too much by a favouring breeze. *Hor.*

Rebus in angustis facile est contemnere vitam ; / Fortiter ille facit qui miser esse potest—It is easy in misfortune to despise life ; but he does bravely who can endure misery. *Mart.*

Rebus secundis etiam egregios duces insolescere—In the hour of prosperity even the best generals are apt to be haughty and insolent. *Tac.*

Receive what cheer you may ; / The night is long that never finds the day. *Macb.,* iv. 3.

Receiving a new truth is adding a new sense. *Liebig.*

20 Recepto / Dulce mihi furere est amico—It is delightful to indulge in extravagance on the return of a friend. *Hor.*

Rechauffé—Heated again ; stale. *Fr.*

Recherché—Sought for ; much esteemed.

Recht geht vor Macht—Right goes before might. *Count v. Schwerin.*

Recht stets behält das Schicksal, denn das Herz, / In uns ist sein gebietrischer Vollzieher—Fate always carries its point, for the heart in us is its imperious executor. *Schiller.*

25 ρεχθὲν δέ τε νήπιος ἔγνω—What has happened even the fool knows. *Homer.*

Recipiunt feminæ sustentacula a nobis—Women receive supports from us. *Motto of the Pattenmakers' Company.*

Reckless youth maks ruefu' age. *Sc. Pr.*

Reckon no vice so small that you may commit it, and no virtue so small that you may overlook it. *Confucius.*

Reckon what is in a man, not what is on him, if you would know whether he is rich or poor. *Ward Beecher.*

Reckoners without their host must reckon twice. *Pr.*

Recommending secrecy where a dozen of people are acquainted with the circumstance to be concealed, is only putting the truth in masquerade, for the story will be circulated under twenty different shapes. *Scott.*

Recompense injury with justice, and recompense kindness with kindness. *Confucius.*

Recompense to no man evil for evil. *St. Paul.*

Recta actio non erit, nisi recta fuit voluntas, ab hac enim est actio. Rursus, voluntas non erit recta, nisi habitus animi rectus fuerit, ab hoc enim est voluntas—An action will not be right unless the intention is right, for from it comes the action. Again, the intention will not be right unless the state of the mind has been right, for from it proceeds the intention. *Sen.*

Recte et suaviter—Uprightly and mildly. *M.* 35

Rectius vives, Licini, neque altum / Semper urgendo, neque, dum procellas / Cautus horrescis, nimium premendo / Littus iniquum—You will live more prudently, Licinius, by neither always keeping out at sea, nor, while you warily shrink from storms, hugging too closely the treacherous shore. *Hor.*

Rectus in curia—Upright in the court, *i.e.,* having come out of it with clean hands. *L.*

Reculer pour mieux sauter—To step back in order to leap better. *Fr.*

Red as a roost-cock. *S. Devon Pr.*

Reddere personæ scit convenientia cuique— 40 He knows how to assign to each character what it is proper for him to think and say. *Hor., of a dramatic poet.*

Reddere qui voces jam scit puer, et pede certo / Signat humum, gestit paribus colludere, et iram / Colligit ac ponit temere, et mutatur in horas—The boy who just knows how to talk and treads the ground with firm foot, delights to play with his mates, is easily provoked and easily appeased, and changes every hour. *Hor.*

Rede wenig, rede wahr. Zehre wenig, zahle baar—Speak little, speak true. Spend little, pay cash down. *Ger. Pr.*

Redeat miseris, abeat fortuna superbis—May fortune revisit the wretched, and forsake the proud ! *Hor.*

Reden ist Silber und Schweigen ist Gold—Speech is silver and silence is gold. *Old Ger. Pr.*

Reden kommt von Natur, Schweigen vom 45 Verstande—Speaking comes from nature, silence from discretion. *Ger. Pr.*

Redeunt Saturnia regna—The golden age (*lit.* the reign of Saturn) is returning.

Redit agricolis labor actus in orbem, / Atque in se sua per vestigia volvitur annus—The husbandman's toil returns in a circle, and the year rolls round in its former footsteps. *Virg.*

Redlichkeit gedeiht in jedem Stande—Honesty prospers in every condition of life. *Schiller.*

Reductio ad absurdum—A reduction of an adversary's conclusion to an absurdity.

Refinement that carries us away from our fellow-men is not God's refinement. *Ward Beecher.*

Reflect that life, like every other blessing, derives its value from its use alone. *Johnson.*

Reflect upon your present blessings, of which every man has many—not on your past misfortunes, of which all men have some. *Dickens.*

Reflection dissolves reverie and burns her delicate wings. *Amiel.*

5 Reform is affirmative, conservatism negative; conservatism goes for comfort, reform for truth. *Emerson.*

Reform is not joyous but grievous; no single man can reform himself without stern suffering and stern working; how much less can a nation of men. *Carlyle.*

Reform, like charity, must begin at home. Once well at home, how will it radiate outwards, irrepressible, into all that we touch and handle, speak and work; kindling ever new light by incalculable contagion; spreading, in geometric ratio, far and wide; doing good only, wherever it spreads, and not evil. *Carlyle.*

Reformers (*Reformatorische Geister*) do not step into the arena amid a flourish of drums and trumpets; they must make their debut rather under the badge of the cross, and have been cradled at their birth in a manger; poverty and a humble pedigree is all their inheritance, and their childhood is never touched or shone upon by the glitter (*Glanze*) of the world. *K. Fischer.*

Reforms are generally most unpopular where most needed. *Martin.*

10 Refricare cicatricem—To open a wound, or an old sore, afresh.

Regard not dreams, since they are but the images of our hopes and fears. *Cato.*

Regard not much who is for thee or who against thee; but give all thy care to this, that God be with thee in everything thou doest. *Thomas à Kempis.*

Reges dicuntur multis urgere culullis, / Et torquere mero, quem perspexisse laborent, / An sit amicitia dignus—Kings are said to press with many a cup, and test with wine the man whom they desire to try whether he is worthy of their friendship. *Hor.*

Regia, crede mihi, res est, succurrere lapsis— It is a right kingly act, believe me, to succour the fallen. *Ovid.*

15 Regibus boni quam mali suspectiores sunt, semperque his aliena virtus formidolosa est —Good men are more suspected by kings than bad men; and virtue in other men is to them always a source of dread. *Sall.*

Régime—Form of government. *Fr.*

Regium donum—A royal gift.

Regnare nolo, liber ut non sim mihi—I would not be a king and forfeit my liberty. *Phædr.*

Regum æquabat opes animis; seraque revertens / Nocte domum, dapibus mensas onerabat inemptis—He equalled the wealth of kings in contentment of mind; and at night returning home, would load his board with unbought dainties. *Virg., of the husbandman.*

20 Reichen giebt man, Armen nimmt man—We give to the rich, we take from the poor. *Ger. Pr.*

Reine d'un jour—Queen for a day. *Fr.*

Reipublicæ forma laudari facilius quam evenire, et si evenit, haud diuturna esse potest—It is more easy to praise a republican form of government than to establish it; and when it is established, it cannot be of long duration. *Tac.*

Reisst den Menschen aus seinen Verhältnissen; und was er dann ist, nur das ist er— Tear man out of his outward circumstances; and what he then is, that only is he. *Seume.*

Rejecting the miracles of Christ, we still have the miracle of Christ himself. *Bovee.*

25 Rejoice in joyous things—nor overmuch / Let grief thy bosom touch / Midst evil, and still bear in mind / How changeful are the ways of humankind. *Archilochus.*

Rejoice, O young man, in thy youth, and let thy heart cheer thee in the days of thy youth, and walk in the ways of thine heart, and in the sight of thine eyes; but know thou that for all these things God will bring thee into judgment. *Bible.*

Rejoice that you have still long to live before the thought comes to you that there is nothing more in the world to see. *Goethe.*

Rejoice with them that do rejoice, and weep with them that weep. *St. Paul.*

Relata refero—I tell the story as it was told to me.

30 Relegare bona religionibus—To bequeath one's property for religious purposes. *L.*

Relever des bagatelles—To give importance to trifles.

Reliota non bene parmula—Having ingloriously left my shield behind. *Hor.*

Religentem esse oportet, religiosum nefas— A man should be religious, not superstitious. *Quoted by Aul. Gell.*

Religion and education are not a match for evil without the grace of God. *Haydon.*

35 Religion and morality, as they now stand, compose a practical code of misery and servitude. . . . How would morality, dressed up in stiff stays and finery, start from her own disgusting image, should she look into the mirror of Nature! *Shelley.*

Religion bids man prefer the endurance of a lesser evil before a greater, and nature itself does no less. *South.*

Religion, blushing, veils her sacred fires, / And unawares morality expires. *Pope.*

Religion cannot change, though we do. *Jeremy Taylor.*

Religion cannot rise above the state of the votary. Heaven always bears some proportion to earth. *Emerson.*

40 Religion contains infinite sadness. If we are to love God, he must be in distress (*lit.*, in need of help). *Novalis. See* Matt. xxvii. 46.

Religion des Kreuzes, nur du verknüpfest, in einem / Kranze der Demut und Kraft doppelte Palme zugleich—Religion of the Cross ! only thou unitest in one wreath together the twofold palm of humility and power. *Platen.*

Religion gives part of its reward in hand, the present comfort of having done our duty; and for the rest, it offers us the best security that heaven can give. *Tillotson.*

Religion, if in heavenly truths attired, / Needs only to be seen to be admired. *Cowper.*

Religion, if it be true, is central truth; and all knowledge which is not gathered round it, and quickened and illuminated by it, is hardly worth the name. *Channing.*

Religion implies revelation. *R. D. Hitchcock.*

Religion is a fire which example keeps alive, and which goes out if not communicated. *Joubert.*

Religion is a higher and supernatural life, mystical in its roots and practical in its fruits. *Amiel.*

Religion is again here, for whoever will piously struggle upward, and sacredly, sorrowfully refuse to speak lies, which indeed will mostly mean refuse to speak at all on that topic. *Carlyle.*

5 Religion is an everlasting lodestar, that beams the brighter in the heavens the darker here on earth grows the night. *Carlyle.*

Religion is as necessary to reason as reason to religion. *Washington.*

Religion is life, philosophy is thought. . . . We need both thought and life, and we need that the two shall be in harmony. *J. F. Clarke.*

Religion is neither a theology nor a theosophy, but a discipline, a law, a yoke, an indissoluble engagement. *Joubert.*

Religion is not a dogma nor an emotion, but a service. *R. D. Hitchcock.*

10 Religion is not a doubt, but a certainty,—or else a mockery and horror. *Carlyle.*

Religion is not a method, but a life. *Amiel.*

Religion is not an end, but a means. *Goethe.*

Religion is not in want of art; it rests on its own majesty. *Goethe.*

Religion is nothing if it is not everything; if existence is not filled with it. *Mme. de Staël.*

15 Religion is the basis of civil society. *Burke.*

Religion is the best armour in the world, but the worst cloak. *Bunyan.*

Religion is the eldest sister of philosophy; on whatever subjects they may differ, it is unbecoming in either to quarrel, and most so about their inheritance. *Landor.*

Religion is the highest humanity (*Humanität*) of man. *Herder.*

Religion is the most gentlemanly thing in the world. It alone will gentilise, if unmixed with cant. *Coleridge.*

20 Religion is the only metaphysic that the multitude can understand and adopt. *Joubert.*

Religion is the spice which is meant to keep life from corruption. *Bacon.*

Religion is universal, theology is exclusive; religion is humanitarian, theology is sectarian; religion unites mankind, theology divides it; religion is love—broad and all-comprising as God's love, theology preaches love and practises bigotry; religion looks to the moral worth of man, theology to his creed and denomination. *M. Lilienthal.*

Religion lies more in walk than in talk. *Pr.*

Religion, like its votaries, while it exists on earth, must have a body as well as a soul. *Colton.*

25 Religion must always be a crab fruit; it cannot be grafted and keep its wild beauty. *Emerson.*

Religion or worship is the attitude of those who see that, against all appearances, the nature of things works for truth and right for ever. *Emerson.*

Religion, poetry, is not dead; it will never die. Its dwelling and birthplace is in the soul of man, and it is eternal as the being of man. In any point of space, in any section of time, let there be a living man; and there is an infinitude above him and beneath him, and an eternity encompasses him on this hand and on that; and tones of sphere-music and tidings from loftier worlds will flit round him, if he can but listen, and visit him with holy influences, even in the thickest press of trivialities or the din of busiest life. *Carlyle.*

Religion presents few difficulties to the humble, many to the proud, innumerable ones to the vain. *Hare.*

Religion primarily means obedience; bending to something or some one. To be bound, or in bonds, as apprentice; to be bound, or in bonds, by military oath; to be bound, or in bonds, as a servant of man; to be bound, or in bonds, under the yoke of God. *Ruskin.*

Religion reveals the meaning of life, and science 30 only applies the meaning to the course of circumstances. *Tolstoi.*

Religion should be the rule of life, not a casual incident in it. *Disraeli.*

Religion without morality is a superstition and a curse; and anything like an adequate and complete morality without religion is impossible. *Mark Hopkins.*

Religion would frame a just man; Christ would make a whole man. Religion would save a man; Christ would make him worth saving. *Ward Beecher.*

Religionen sind Kinder der Unwissenheit, die ihre Mutter nicht lange überleben—Religions are the children of Ignorance, and they do not long outlive their mother. *Schopenhauer.*

Religions are not proved, are not established, 35 are not overthrown, by logic. They are, of all the mysteries of nature and the human mind, the most mysterious and inexplicable; they are of instinct, and not of reason. *Lamartine.*

Religious contention is the devil's harvest. *La Fontaine.*

Religious zeal leads to cleanliness, cleanliness to purity, purity to godliness, godliness to humility, humility to the fear of sin. *Rabbi Pinhas-Ben-Jair.*

Rèm acu tetigit—He has hit the nail on the head (*lit.* touched it with a needle-point).

Rem, facias rem, / Si possis recte, si non, quocunque modo rem—A fortune, make a fortune, honestly if you can; if not, make it by any means. *Hor.*

Rem tu strenuus auge—Labour assiduously to 40 increase your property. *Hor.*

"Remain content in the station in which Providence has placed you," is on the whole a good maxim, but it is peculiarly for home use. That your neighbour should, or should not, remain content with his position is not your business; but it is very much your business to remain content with your own. *Ruskin.*

Remark how many are better off than you are; consider how many are worse. *Sen.*

Remember Atlas was weary. *Fuller.*

Remember now thy creator in the days of thy youth. *Bible.*

Remember, now, when you meet your antagonist, to do everything in a mild agreeable manner. Let your courage be keen, but, at the same time, as polished as your sword. *Sheridan.*

Remember that all tricks are either knavish or childish. *Johnson.*

Remember that the time once yours can never be so again. *Thomas à Kempis.*

Remember that with every breath we draw, an ethereal stream of Lethe runs through our whole being, so that we have but a partial recollection of our joys, and scarcely any of our sorrows. *Goethe.*

5 Remember that you are an actor in a drama of such sort as the Author chooses. If short, then in a short one ; if long, then in a long one. If it be His pleasure that you should act a poor man, see that you act it well ; or a cripple, or a ruler, or a private citizen. For this is your business, to act well the given part ; but to choose it, belongs to another. *Epictetus.*

Remember this : that your conscience is not a law—no ; God and reason made the law, and has placed conscience within you to determine. *Sterne.*

Remember thy prerogative is to govern, and not to serve, the things of this world. *Thomas à Kempis.*

Remember your failures are the seed of your most glorious successes. Despond if you must, but don't despair. *Anon.*

Remembrance and reflection how allied! / What thin partitions sense from thought divide ! *Pope.*

10 Remembrance (*Erinnerung*) is the only Paradise from which we cannot be driven. *Jean Paul.*

Remembrance makes the poet ; 'tis the past, / Lingering within him with a keener sense / Than is upon the thoughts of common men, / Of what has been, that fills the actual world / With unreal likenesses of lovely shapes, / That were and are not. *L. E. Landon.*

Remembrance wakes with all her busy train, / Swells at my breast, and turns the past to pain. *Goldsmith.*

Remis velisque—With oars and sails ; with tooth and nail. *Pr.*

Remis ventisque—With oars and wind.

15 Remorse is as the heart in which it grows : / If that be gentle, it drops balmy dews / Of true repentance ; but if proud and gloomy, / It is the poison tree that, pierced to the inmost, / Weeps only tears of poison. *Coleridge.*

Remorse is the echo of a lost virtue. *Bulwer Lytton.*

Remorse, the fatal egg by pleasure laid. *Cowper.*

Remote from man, with God he passed his days ; / Prayer all his business, all his pleasure praise. *Parnell.*

Remove not the ancient land-mark. *Bible.*

20 Remove the cause, and the effect will cease. *Pr.*

Renascentur—They will rise again. *M.*

Render to all their dues. *St. Paul.*

Render to Cæsar the things that are Cæsar's, and to God the things that are God's. *Jesus.*

Renounce, thou must (*sollst*) renounce ! That is the song which sounds for ever in the ears of every one, which every hour sings to us hoarsely our whole life long. *Goethe in " Faust."*

Renovate animos—Renew your courage. *M.* 25

Renown is not to be sought, and all pursuit of it is vain. A person may, indeed, by skilful conduct and various artificial means, make a sort of name for himself ; but if the inner jewel is wanting, all is vanity, and will not last a day. *Goethe.*

Rente viagère—An annuity. *Fr.*

Rentes—Funds bearing interest ; stocks. *Fr.*

Rentier—A fund-holder. *Fr.*

Repartee is perfect when it effects its purpose 30 with a double edge. It is the highest order of wit, as it bespeaks the coolest yet quickest exercise of genius, at a moment when the passions are roused. *Colton.*

Repentance clothes in grass and flowers the grave in which the past is laid. *J. Sterling.*

Repentance costs very dear. *Pr.*

Repentance hath a purifying power, and every tear is of a cleansing virtue ; but these penitential clouds must be still kept dropping ; one shower will not suffice ; for repentance is not one single action, but a course. *South.*

Repentance is accepted remorse. *Mme. Swetchine.*

Repentance is good, but innocence is better. *Pr.* 35

Repentance is heart's sorrow, and a clear life ensuing. *Tempest, iii. 3.*

Repentance is nothing else but a renunciation of our will, and a controlling of our fancies, which lead us which way they please. *Montaigne.*

Repentance is the daughter of over-haste. *M. Beer.*

Repentance is the May of the virtues. *Chinese Pr.*

Repentance won't cure mischief. *Gael. Pr.* 40

Repente dives nemo factus est bonus—No good man ever became suddenly rich. *Pub. Syr.*

Reperit Deus nocentem—God finds out the guilty man.

Reply with wit to gravity, and with gravity to wit. *Colton.*

Réponse sans réplique—An answer that does not admit of reply. *Fr.*

Report makes crows blacker than they are. *Pr.* 45

Repose and cheerfulness are the badge of the gentleman—repose in energy. The Greek battle-pieces are calm ; the heroes, in whatever violent actions engaged, retain a serene aspect. *Emerson.*

Repose and happiness are what thou covetest. but these are only to be obtained by labour. *Thomas à Kempis.*

Repose is as necessary in conversation as in a picture. *Hazlitt.*

Repose is the cradle of power. *J. G. Holland.*

Repose without stagnation is the state most 50 favourable to happiness. "The great felicity of life," says Seneca, "is to be without perturbation." *Bovee.*

Reproof is a medicine like mercury or opium ; if it be improperly administered, it will do harm instead of good. *H. Mann.*

Reproof never does a wise man harm. *Pr.*

Reproof on her lips, but a smile in her eye. *S. Lover.*

Reprove thy friend privately; commend him publicly. *Solon.*

Republics end with luxury; monarchies with poverty. *Montesquieu.*

5 Reputation is an idle and false imposition, oft got without merit, and lost without deserving; you have lost no reputation at all unless you repute yourself such a loser. *Othello*, ii. 3.

Reputation is commonly measured by the acre. *Pr.*

Reputation is in itself only a farthing candle, of a wavering and uncertain flame, and easily blown out, but it is the light by which the world looks for and finds merit. *Lowell.*

Reputation is rarely proportioned to virtue. *St. Evremond.*

Reputation is what men and women think of us. Character is what God and angels know of us. *Thomas Paine.*

10 Reputation, reputation, reputation! O I have lost my reputation. I have lost the immortal part of myself, and what remains is bestial. *Othello*, ii. 3.

Reputation serves to virtue as light does to a picture. *Pr.*

Requiem æternam dona eis, Domine—Grant them eternal rest, O Lord.

Requiescat in pace—Let him rest in peace.

Rerum cognitio vera, e rebus ipsis est—The true knowledge of things is from the things themselves. *Scaliger.*

15 Res amicos invenit—Money finds friends. *Plaut.*

Res angusta domi — Straitened circumstances at home. *Juv.*

Res est blanda canor; discant cantare puellæ —Singing is a charming accomplishment: let girls learn to sing. *Ovid.*

Res est ingeniosa dare—To give requires good sense. *Ovid.*

Res est sacra miser—A man overwhelmed by misfortune is a sacred object. *Sen.*

20 Res est solliciti plena timoris amor—Love is full of anxious fears. *Ovid.*

Res gestæ—Exploits; transactions.

Res in cardine est—The affair is at a crisis (*lit.* on the hinge).

Res judicata—A case decided.

Res nolunt diu male administrari—Things refuse to be mismanaged long.

25 Res rustica—A rural affair. *Cic.*

Res severa est verum gaudium—True joy is an earnest thing.

Res sunt humanæ flebile ludibrium—Human affairs are a jest to be wept over.

Resembles ocean into tempest wrought, / To waft a feather or to drown a fly. *Young.*

Resentment gratifies him who intended an injury, and pains him unjustly who did not intend it. *Johnson.*

30 Resentment, indeed, may remain, perhaps cannot be quite extinguished in the noblest minds; but revenge never will harbour there. *Pope.*

Resentment seems to have been given us by Nature for defence, and for defence only; it is the safeguard of justice and the security of innocence. *Adam Smith.*

Reserve the master-blow. *Pr.*

Resignation is putting God between one's self and one's grief. *Mme. Swetchine.*

Resist as much as thou wilt; heaven's ways are heaven's ways. *Lessing.*

Resist not evil. *Jesus.* 35

Resist the devil, and he will flee from you. *St. James.*

Resistance ought never to be thought of but when an utter subversion of the laws of the realm threatens the whole frame of our constitution, and no redress can otherwise be hoped for. It therefore does, and ought for ever, to stand in the eye and letter of the law as the highest offence. *Walpole.*

Resolution is independent of great age, but without it one lives a hundred years in vain. *Chinese Pr.*

Resolution will sometimes relax, and diligence will sometimes be interrupted; but let no accidental surprise or deviation, whether short or long, dispose you to despondency. *Johnson.*

Resolutions are well kept when they jump 40 with inclination. *Goldsmith.*

Resolve, resolve, and to be men aspire. / Exert that noblest privilege, alone / Here to mankind indulged; control desire: / Let godlike Reason, from her sovereign throne, / Speak the commanding word "I will!" and it is done. *Thomson.*

Resolved to ruin or to rule the state. *Dryden.*

Respect a man, he will do the more. *Pr.*

Respect for one's parents is the highest of the duties of civil life. *Chinese Pr.*

Respect for others is the first condition of 45 "savoir-vivre." *Amiel.*

Respect is better procured by exacting than soliciting it. *Lord Greville.*

Respect the burden. *Napoleon.*

Respect us human, and relieve us poor. *Pope.*

Respect yourself, or no one else will respect you. *Pr.*

Respectable mediocrity offends nobody. 50 *Brougham.*

Respice finem—Look to the end.

Respicere exemplar vitæ morumque jubebo / Doctum imitatorem, et veras hinc ducere voces—I would recommend the learned imitator to study closely his model in life and manners, and thence to draw his expressions to the life. *Hor.*

Respondeat superior—Let the principal answer. *L.*

Responsibility walks hand in hand with capacity and power. *J. G. Holland.*

Rest and be thankful. *Inscription on a wayside* 55 *seat.*

Rest and success are fellows. *Pr.*

Rest and undisturbed content have now no place on earth, nor can the greatest affluence of worldly good procure them, . . . they are peculiar to the love and fruition of God alone. *Thomas à Kempis.*

Rest is for the dead. *Carlyle.*

Rest is good after the work is done. *Dan. Pr.*

Rest is the sweet sauce of labour. *Plutarch.* 60

Rest is won only by work. *Pr.*

Rest not in an ovation, but in a triumph over thy passions. *Sir Thomas Browne.*

Rest not upon scattered counsels, for they will rather distract and mislead than settle and direct. *Bacon.*

Rest! rest! Shall I not have all eternity to rest in? *Arnauld.*

Rest thy unrest in England's lawful earth. *Rich. III., iv. 4.*

Restat iter cœlo: cœlo tentabimus ire; / Da veniam cœpto, Jupiter alte, meo—There remains a way through the heavens; through the heavens we will attempt to go. High Jupiter, pardon my bold design. *Ovid, in the name of Dædalus when he escaped from the labyrinth on wings.*

5 Restore to God his due in tithe and time: / A tithe purloined cankers the whole estate. *George Herbert.*

Restraint and discipline, examples of virtue and of justice, these are what form the education of the world. *Burke.*

Restraint and obstruction (*la gêne*) constitute the principle of movement. *Renan.*

Résumé—Recapitulation; summary. *Fr.*

Resurgam—I shall rise again. *M.*

10 Retinens vestigia famæ—Retracing the footsteps of fame. *M.*

Return unto me, and I will return unto you, saith the Lord of hosts. *Bible.*

Revelation may not need the help of reason, but man does, even when in possession of revelation. Reason may be described as the candle in the man's hand, to which revelation brings the necessary flame. *Simms.*

Revelation nowhere burns more purely and more beautifully than in the New Testament. *Goethe.*

Revenge, at first though sweet, bitter erelong back on itself recoils. *Milton.*

15 Revenge barketh only at the stars, and spite spurns at that she cannot reach. *Socrates.*

Revenge commonly hurts both the offerer and the sufferer; as we see in a foolish bee, which in her anger envenometh the flesh and loseth her sting, and so lives a drone ever after. *Bp. Hall.*

Revenge converts a little right into a great wrong. *Ger. Pr.*

Revenge has no limits, for sin has none. *Fr. Hebbel.*

Revenge is a debt, in the paying of which the greatest knave is honest and sincere, and, so far as he is able, punctual. *Colton.*

20 "Revenge is a kind of wild justice." It is so, but without this wild austere stock there would be no justice in the world. *Burke.*

Revenge is a kind of wild justice, which, the more man's nature runs to, the more ought law to weed it out. *Bacon.*

Revenge is an act of passion; vengeance, of justice. *Johnson.*

Revenge is an inheritance of weak souls. *Körner.*

Revenge is barren of itself; itself is the dreadful food it feeds on; its delight is murder, and its satiety despair. *Schiller.*

25 Revenge is the abject pleasure of an abject mind. *Joubert.*

Revenge of a wrong only makes another wrong. *Spurgeon.*

Revenons à nos moutons—Let us come back to our subject (*lit.* sheep). *Pierre Blanchet.*

Reverence for human worth, earnest devout search for it, and encouragement of it, loyal furtherance and obedience to it, is the outcome and essence of all true religions, and was and ever will be. *Carlyle.*

Reverence the highest, have patience with the lowest. Let this day's performance of the meanest duty be thy religion. Are the stars too distant, pick up the pebble that lies at thy feet and from it learn the all. *Margaret Fuller.*

Reverence (*Ehrfurcht*), which no child brings 30 into the world along with him, is the one thing on which all depends for making a man in every point a man. *Goethe.*

Reverie is the Sunday of thought. *Amiel.*

Reverie, which is thought in its nebulous state, borders closely upon the land of sleep, by which it is bordered as by a natural frontier. *Victor Hugo.*

Reviewers are usually people who would have been poets, historians, biographers, if they could; they have tried their talents at one or the other, and have failed; therefore they turn critics. *Coleridge.*

Reviewers, with some rare exceptions, are a most stupid and malignant race. As a bankrupt thief turns thief-taker in despair, so an unsuccessful author turns critic. *Shelley.*

Revocate animos, mœstumque timorem / Mittite—Resume your courage, and cast off desponding fear. *Virg.*

Revolutions are like the most noxious dungheaps, which bring into life the noblest vegetables. *Napoleon.*

Revolutions are not made, they come. A revolution is as natural a growth as an oak. It comes out of the past. Its foundations are laid far back. *Wendell Phillips.*

Revolutions never go backward. *Wendell Phillips.*

Rex datur propter regnum, non regnum propter regem. Potentia non est nisi ad bonum—A king is given for the sake of the kingdom, not the kingdom for the sake of the king. His power is only for the public good. *L.*

Rex est major singulis, minor universis—The 40 king is greater than each singly, but less than all unitedly. *Bracton.*

Rex est qui metuit nihil; / Rex est qui cupit nihil—He is a king who fears nothing; he is a king who desires nothing. *Sen.*

Rex non potest fallere nec falli—The king cannot deceive or be deceived.

Rex non potest peccare—The king can do no wrong.

Rex nunquam moritur—The king never dies. *L.*

Rex regnat, sed non gubernat—The king reigns, 45 but does not govern. *Jan Zamoiski.*

Rhetoric is nothing but reason well dressed and argument put in order. *Jeremy Collier.*

Rhetoric is the art of ruling the minds of men. *Plato.*

Rhetoric is the creature of art, which he who feels least will most excel in; it is the quackery of eloquence, and deals in nostrums, not in cures. *Colton.*

Rhyme that had no inward necessity to be rhymed; it ought to have told us plainly, without any jingle, what it was aiming at. *Carlyle.*

Rich gifts wax poor when givers prove unkind. *Ham.*, iii. 1.

Rich men are indeed rather possessed by their money than possessors. *Burton.*

Rich men without wisdom and learning are but sheep with golden fleeces. *Solon.*

Rich, not gaudy. *Ham.*, i. 3.

Rich the treasure, / Sweet the pleasure ; / Sweet is pleasure after pain. *Dryden.*

Rich with the spoils of time. *Sir T. Browne.*

Richard's himself again ! *Cibber.*

Richer than rubies, / Dearer than gold, / Woman, true woman, / Glad we behold ! *Old love-song.*

Riches amassed in haste will diminish ; but those collected by hand and little by little will multiply. *Goethe.*

10 Riches and favour go before wisdom and art. *Dan. Pr.*

Riches are as a stronghold in the imagination of the rich man. *Solomon.*

Riches are for spending, and spending for honour and good actions. *Bacon.*

Riches are got wi' pain, kept wi' care, and tint (lost) wi' grief. *Sc. Pr.*

Riches are like bad servants, whose shoes are made of running leather, and will never tarry long with one master. *Brooks.*

15 Riches are of little avail in many of the calamities to which mankind are liable. *Cervantes.*

Riches are often abused, never refused. *Dan. Pr.*

Riches breed care, poverty is safe. *Dan. Pr.*

Riches bring cares. *Pr.*

Riches come better after poverty than poverty after riches. *Chinese Pr.*

20 Riches do not consist in having more gold and silver, but in having more in proportion than our neighbours. *Locke.*

Riches do not exhilarate us so much by their possession as they torment us with their loss. *Gregory.*

Riches fineless is as poor as winter / To him that ever fears he shall be poor. *Othello*, iii. 3.

Riches for the most part are hurtful to them that possess them. *Plutarch.*

Riches have made mair men covetous than covetousness has made men rich. *Sc. Pr.*

25 Riches have wings. *Pr.*

Riches profit not in the day of wrath. *Bible.*

Riches take peace from the soul, but rarely, if ever, confer it. *Petrarch.*

Riches take wings, comforts vanish, hope withers away, but love stays with us. Love is God. *Lew Wallace.*

Riches, though they may reward virtues, yet they cannot cause them ; he is much more noble who deserves a benefit than he who bestows one. *Feltham.*

30 Richt wrangs nae man. *Sc. Pr.*

Richter sollen zwei gleiche Ohren haben—Judges should have two ears, both alike. *Ger. Pr.*

Ride si sapis—Laugh, if you are wise. *Mart.*

Ridentem dicere verum / Quid vetat?—Why may a man not speak the truth in a jocular vein? *Hor.*

Ridere in stomacho—To laugh inwardly, *i.e.*, in one's sleeve.

Rides in the whirlwind and directs the storm. 35 *Addison.*

Ridet argento domus—The house is smiling with silver. *Hor.*

Ridetur chorda qui semper oberrat eadem—He is laughed at who is for ever harping away on the same string. *Hor.*

Ridicule has ever been the most powerful enemy of enthusiasm, and properly the only antagonist that can be opposed to it with success. *Goldsmith.*

Ridicule intrinsically is a small faculty ; we may say, the smallest of all faculties that other men are at the pains to repay with any esteem. It is directly opposed to thought, to knowledge, properly so called ; its nourishment and essence is denial, which hovers on the surface, while knowledge dwells far below. *Carlyle.*

Ridicule is a weak weapon when levelled at a 40 strong mind ; but common men are cowards, and dread an empty laugh. *Tupper.*

Ridicule, while it often checks what is absurd, fully as often smothers that which is noble. *Scott.*

Ridiculous modes, invented by ignorance and adopted by folly. *Smollett.*

Ridiculum acri / Fortius ac melius magnas plerumque secat res—Ridicule often settles matters of importance better and more effectually than severity. *Hor.*

Ridiculus æque nullus est, quam quando esurit —No man is so facetious as when he is hungry. *Plaut.*

Rien de plus éloquent que l'argent comptant— 45 Nothing is more eloquent than ready money. *Fr. Pr.*

Rien de plus hautain qu'un homme médiocre devenu puissant — Nothing is more haughty than a common-place man raised to power. *Fr. Pr.*

Rien n'a qui assez n'a—Who has nothing has not enough. *Fr. Pr.*

Rien n'arrive pour rien—Nothing happens for nothing. *Fr. Pr.*

Rien n'empêche tant d'être naturel que l'envie de la paraître—Nothing so much prevents one from being natural as the desire to appear so. *La Roche.*

Rien n'est beau que le vrai ; le vrai seul est 50 aimable—Nothing is beautiful but the true ; the true alone is lovely. *Boileau.*

Rien n'est plus estimable que la civilité ; mais rien de plus ridicule, et de plus à charge, que la cérémonie—Nothing is more estimable then politeness, and nothing more ridiculous or tiresome than ceremony. *Fr.*

Rien n'est plus rare que la véritable bonté ; ceux même qui croient en avoir n'ont d'ordinaire que de la complaisance ou de la faiblesse—Nothing is rarer than real goodness ; those even who think they possess it are generally only good-natured and weak. *La Roche.*

Rien n'est si dangereux qu'un indiscret ami ; / Mieux vaudroit un sage ennemi—Nothing more dangerous than an imprudent friend ; a prudent enemy would be better.

Rien ne déconcerte plus efficacement les desseins des pervers, que la tranquillité des grands cœurs—Nothing so effectively baffles the schemes of evil men so much as the calm composure of great souls. *Mirabeau.*

Rien ne m'est sûr que la chose incertaine—There is nothing certain but the uncertain. *Fr.*

Rien ne manque à sa gloire ; il manquait à la nôtre—Nothing is wanting to his glory ; he was wanting to ours. *Inscription on the bust of Molière, which was placed in the Academy in 1773.*

Rien ne pèse tant qu'un secret — Nothing presses so heavy on us as a secret. *La Fontaine.*

Rien ne peut arrêter sa vigilante audace. / L'été n'a point de feux, l'hiver n'a point de glace—Nothing can check his watchful daring. For him the summer has no heat, the winter no ice. *Boileau of Louis XIV.*

5 Rien ne ressemble plus à un honnête homme qu'un fripon—Nothing resembles an honest man more than a rogue. *Fr. Pr.*

Rien ne réussit mieux que le succès—Nothing succeeds like success.

Rien ne s'anéantit ; non, rien, et la matière, / Comme un fleuve éternel, roule toujours entière—Nothing is annihilated, no, nothing ; matter, like an ever-flowing stream, still rolls on undiminished. *Boucher.*

Rien ne s'arrête pour nous—Nothing anchors itself fast for us. *Pascal.*

Rien ne sert de courir : il faut partir à point—It's no use running ; only setting out betimes. *La Fontaine.*

10 Rien ne vaut poulain s'il ne rompt son lien—A colt is nothing worth if it does not break its halter. *Fr. Pr.*

Rien que s'entendre—Nothing but good understanding. *Said of friendship.*

Right actions for the future are the best apologies for wrong ones in the past. *T. Edwards.*

Right ethics are central, and go from the soul outward. Gift is contrary to the law of the universe. *Emerson.*

Right is more beautiful than private affection, and is compatible with universal wisdom. *Emerson.*

15 Right is right, since God is God. *Faber*

Right wrongs no man. *Pr.*

Righteousness exalteth a nation ; but sin is a reproach to any people. *Bible.*

Righteousness keepeth him that is upright in the way. *Bible.*

Rightly, poetry is organic. We cannot know things by words and writing, but only by taking a central position in the universe and living in its forms. *Emerson.*

20 Rightly to be great / Is not to stir without great argument, / But greatly to find quarrel in a straw / When honour's at the stake. *Ham.,* iv. 4.

Rigour pushed too far is sure to miss its aim, however good ; as the bow snaps that is bent too stiffly. *Schiller.*

Rinasce più gloriosa—It rises more glorious than ever. *M.*

Riñen las comadres y dicense las verdades—Gossips quarrel and tell the truth. *Sp. Pr.*

Ring out the old, ring in the new, / Ring, happy bells, across the snow ! *Tennyson.*

25 Ripening love is the stillest ; the shady flowers in this spring, as in the other, shun sunlight. *Jean Paul.*

Rira bien qui rira le dernier—He laughs well who laughs the last. *Fr. Pr.*

Rire à gorge déployée—To laugh immoderately. *Fr.*

Rire dans sa barbe—To laugh in one's sleeve.

Rise, Christopher ! thou hast found thy King, and turn / Back to the earth, for I have need of thee. / Thou hast sustained the whole world, bearing me, / The Lord of earth and heaven. *Lewis Morris.*

Rise up before the hoary head, and honour 30 the face of the old man. *Bible.*

Rising genius always shoots forth its rays from among clouds and vapours, but these will gradually roll away and disappear as it ascends to its steady and meridian lustre. *Washington Irving.*

Rising to great place is by a winding stair. *Bacon.*

Risu inepto res ineptior nulla est—Nothing is more silly than silly laughter. *Cat.*

Risum teneatis, amici ?—Can you refrain from laughter, my friends ? *Hor.*

Risus abundat in ore stultorum—Laughter is 35 common in the mouth of fools.

Rivalem patienter habe—Bear patiently with a rival. *Ovid.*

Rivers are roads which travel, and which carry us whither we wish to go. *Pascal.*

Rivers cannot fill the sea, that, drinking, thirsteth still. *Christina Rosetti.*

Rivers flow with sweet waters ; but, having joined the ocean, they become undrinkable. *Hitopadesa.*

Rivers need a spring. *Pr.* 40

Roads are many ; authentic finger-posts are few. *Carlyle.*

Roast meat at three fires ; as soon as you've basted one, another's burnin'. *George Eliot.*

Rob not the poor, because he is poor. *Bible.*

Robbing Peter to pay Paul. *Pr.*

Robespierre à pied et à cheval—Robespierre 45 on foot and on horseback, *i.e.*, Robespierre and Napoleon. *Mme. de Staël.*

Rock of ages, cleft for me, / Let me hide myself in thee. *Toplady.*

Rock'd in the cradle of the deep, / I lay me down in peace to sleep. *Emma Willard.*

Rocks whereon greatest men have oftest wreck'd. *Milton.*

Rogner les ailes à quelqu'un — To clip one's wings. *Fr.*

Rogues are always found out in some way. 50 Whoever is a wolf will act as a wolf ; that is the most certain of all things. *La Fontaine.*

Roi fainéant—A do-nothing king. *Fr.*

Roland for an Oliver, *i.e.*, one audacity capped by a greater.

Roll on, thou deep and dark blue ocean, roll ! / Ten thousand fleets sweep over thee in vain ; / Man marks the earth with ruin,—his control / Stops with the shore. *Byron.*

Roma locuta est ; causa finita est—Rome has spoken ; the case is at an end.

Romæ rus optas, absentem rusticus urbem / 55 Tollis ad astra levis—At Rome you pine unsettled for the country, in the country you laud the distant city to the skies. *Hor.*

Romæ Tibur amem, ventosus, Tibure Romam—Fickle as the wind, I love Tibur when at Rome, and Rome when at Tibur. *Hor.*

Romance and novel paint beauty in colours more charming than Nature, and describe a happiness that man never tastes. How delusive, how destructive are those pictures of consummate bliss ! *Goldsmith.*

Romance has been elegantly defined as the offspring of fiction and love. *I. Disraeli.*

Romance is the poetry of literature. *Mme. Necker.*

Romance is the truth of imagination and boyhood. Homer's horses clear the world at a bound. The child's eye needs no horizon to its prospect. . . . The palace that grew up in a night merely awakens a wish to live in it. The impossibilities of fifty years are the common-places of five. *Willmott.*

5 Romance, like a ghost, eludes touching; it is always where you are not, not where you are. The interview or conversation was prose at the time, but is poetry in memory. *G. W. Curtis.*

Romam cuncta undique atrocia aut pudenda confluunt celebranturque — All things atrocious and shameless flock from all parts to Rome. *Tac.*

Rome (room) indeed, and room enough, / When there is in it but one only man. *Jul. Cæs.*, i. 2.

Rome n'est plus dans Rome ; elle est toute où je suis—Rome is no longer in Rome; it is all where I am. *Corn.*

Rome was not built in one day. *Heywood.*

10 Root away / The noisome weeds, which without profit suck / The soil's fertility from wholesome flowers. *Rich. II.*, iii. 4.

Rore vixit more cicadæ—He lived upon dew like a grasshopper. *Pr.*

Roses fall, but the thorns remain. *Dut. Pr.*

Roses fair on thorns do grow : / And they tell me even so / Sorrows into virtues grow. *Dr. W. Smith.*

Roses grow among thorns. *Pr.*

15 Roses have thorns, and silver fountains mud ; / Clouds and eclipses stain both moon and sun. *Shakespeare.*

Rough diamonds may sometimes be mistaken for pebbles. *Sir Thomas Browne.*

Round numbers are always false. *Johnson.*

Round the world, but never in it. *Pr. of sailors.*

Rouge et noir—A game of cards (*lit.* red and black). *See Nuttall.*

20 Ruat cœlum, fiat voluntas tua—Thy will be done though the heavens should fall.

Rude am I in my speech, / And little blessed with the soft phrase of peace. *Othello*, i. 3.

Rudis indigestaque moles — A rude and unarranged mass. *Ovid.*

Ruh kommt aus Unruh, und wieder Unruh aus Ruh—Rest comes from unrest, and unrest again from rest. *Ger. Pr.*

Ruhe ist die erste Bürgerpflicht—Peace is the first duty of a citizen. *Count Schulenburg-Kehnert after the battle of Jena.*

25 Rühre die Laute nicht, wenn ringums Trommeln erschallen ; / Führen Narren das Wort, schweiget der Weisere still—Touch not the lute when drums are sounding around ; when fools have the word, the wise will be silent. *Herder.*

Ruin is most fatal when it begins from the bottom. *Goldsmith.*

Ruins are mile-stones on the road of time. *Chamfort.*

Ruins are the broken eggshell of a civilisation which time has hatched and devoured. *Julia W. Howe.*

Rule, Britannia, Britannia rules the waves ; / Britons never shall be slaves. *Thomson.*

30 Rule youth weel and age will rule itsel'. *Sc. Pr.*

Rules of society are nothing ; one's conscience is the umpire. *Mme. Dudevant.*

Rumour is a pipe / Blown by surmises, jealousies, conjectures ; / And of so easy and so plain a stop / That the blunt monster with uncounted heads, / The still-discordant wavering multitude, / Can play upon it. *2 Hen. IV.*, Induc.

Run here or there, thou wilt find no rest, but in humble subjection to the government of a superior. *Thomas à Kempis.*

Rus in urbe—Country in town. *Mart.*

35 Ruse contre ruse—Diamond cut diamond. *Fr.*

Ruse de guerre—A stratagem. *Fr.*

Rust consumes iron, and envy consumes itself. *Dan. Pr.*

Rust wastes more than use. *Fr. Pr.*

Rustica veritas—Rustic veracity.

40 Rusticus expectat dum defluat amnis ; at ille / Labitur et labetur in omne volubilis ævum —The peasant waits until the river shall cease to flow ; but still it glides on, and will glide on for all time to come. *Hor.*

S.

S'abstenir pour jouir, c'est l'épicurisme de la raison—To abstain so as to enjoy is the epicurism of reason. *Rousseau.*

'S giebt kein schöner Leben als Student-leben —There is no more beautiful life than that of the student. *Fr. Albrecht.*

S'il est vrai, il peut être—It may be, if it is true. *Fr. Pr.*

S'il fait beau, prends ton manteau ; s'il pleut, prends-le si tu veux—If the weather is fine, take your cloak ; if it rains, do as you please. *Fr. Pr.*

45 S'il y a beaucoup d'art à savoir parler à propos, il n'y en a pas moins à savoir se taire— If it requires great tact to know how to speak to the purpose, it requires no less to know when to be silent. *La Roche.*

S'il y avait un peuple de dieux, il se gouvernerait démocratiquement. Un gouvernement si parfait ne convient pas des hommes—If there were a community of gods, the government would be democratic. A government so perfect is not suitable for men. *Rousseau.*

'S ist nichts so schlimm, als man wohl denkt / Wenn man's nur recht erfasst und lenkt— There is nothing so bad as we think it if only we would apprehend and guide it aright. *Friedrich-Flotow.*

'S wird besser gehen ! 's wird besser gehen ! / Die Welt ist rund und muss sich drehen— Things will mend ! will mend ! The world is round, and must needs spin round. *Wohlbrück-Marschner.*

Saat, dich säet der Herr dem grossen. Tage der Ernte—Seed, the Lord sows thee for the great day of harvest. *Klopstock.*

Saat, von Gott gesäet, dem Tage der Garben zu reifen—Seed sown by God, to ripen against the day of the sheaf-binding. *Klopstock.*

Sabbath-days, quiet islands on the tossing sea of life. *S. W. Duffield.*

Sabbath profaned, / Whate'er may be gained, / Is sure to be followed by sorrow. *Pr.*

5 Sabbath well spent / Brings a week of content. *Pr.*

Sacco pieno rizza l'orecchio—A full sack pricks up (*lit.* erects) its ear. *It. Pr.*

Sacred courage indicates that a man loves an idea better than all things in the world ; that he is aiming neither at self nor comfort, but will venture all to put in act the invisible thought in his mind. *Emerson.*

Sacrifice is the first element of religion, and resolves itself, in theological language, into the love of God. *Froude.*

Sacrifice still exists everywhere, and everywhere the elect of each generation suffers for the salvation of the rest. *Amiel.*

10 Sacrifice, which is the passion of great souls, has never been the law of societies. *Amiel.*

Sacrificed his life to the delineating of life. *Goethe, of Schiller.*

Sacrificio dell' intelletto—Sacrifice of intellect. *Frederick the Great to D'Alembert.*

Sad natures are most tolerant of gaiety. *Amiel.*

Sad souls are slain in merry company. / Grief best is pleased with grief's society ; / True sorrow then is feelingly sufficed / When with like semblance it is sympathised. *Shakespeare.*

15 Sad wise valour is the brave complexion / That leads the van and swallows up the cities. *George Herbert.*

Sad with the whole of pleasure. *D. G. Rossetti.*

Sadness and gladness succeed each other. *Pr.*

Sae rantingly, sae wantonly, / Sae dauntingly gaed he ; / He play'd a spring, and danced it round, / Beneath the gallows-tree. *Burns.*

Säen ist nicht so beschwerlich als ernten—Sowing is not so difficult as reaping. *Goethe.*

20 Sæpe decipimur specie recti—We are often misled by the appearance of truth. *Hor.*

Sæpe est etiam sub palliolo sordido sapientia —Wisdom is often found even under a shabby coat. *Pr.*

Sæpe Faunorum voces exaud:tæ, / Sæpe visæ formæ deorum — Voices of Fauns are often heard, and shapes of gods often seen.

Sæpe in conjugiis fit noxia, cum nimia est dos —Quarrels often arise in marriages when the dowry is excessive. *Auson.*

Sæpe ingenia calamitate intercidunt—Genius often goes to waste through misfortune. *Phæd.*

25 Sæpe nihil inimicus homini quam sibi ipse— Often a man is his own worst enemy. *Cic.*

Sæpe premente Deo, fert Deus alter opem— Often when we are oppressed by one deity, another comes to our help.

Sæpe stylum vertas, iterum quæ digna legi sint / Scripturus ; neque, te ut miretur turba, labores / Contentus paucis lectoribus—You must often make erasures if you mean to write what is worthy of being read a second time ; and labour not for the admiration of the crowd, but be content with a few choice readers. *Hor.*

Sæpe summa ingenia in occulto latent—The greatest talents often lie buried out of sight. *Plaut.*

Sæpe tacens vocem verbaque vultus habet— Often a silent countenance is expressive (*lit.* has a voice and speaks). *Ovid.*

Sæpe via obliqua præstat quam tendere recta 30 —It is often better to go the circuitous way than the direct one.

Sæpius ventis·agitatur ingens / Pinus, et celsæ graviore casu / Decidunt turres, feriuntque summos / Fulmina montes—The huge pine is more frequently shaken by the winds, high towers fall with a heavier crash, and it is the mountain-tops that the thunderbolts strike. *Hor.*

Sæva paupertas, et avitus apto cum lare fundus—Stern poverty, and an ancestral piece of land with a dwelling to match. *Hor.*

Sævi inter se conveniunt ursi—Even savage bears agree among themselves. *Juv.*

Sævis tranquillus in undis—Calm in the raging waters. *M. of William I. of Orange.*

Safe bind, safe find. *Pr.*   35

Sag' eine Lüge, so hörst du die Wahrheit—Tell a lie, you will then hear the truth. *Ger. Pr.*

Sahest du nie die Schönheit im Augenblicke des Leidens, / Niemals hast du die Schönheit gesehn. / Sahest du die Freude nie in einem schönen Gesichte, / Niemals hast du die Freude gesehn—If thou hast never seen beauty in the moment of suffering, thou hast never seen beauty at all. If thou hast never seen joy in a beautiful countenance, thou hast never seen joy at all. *Schiller.*

Said will be a little ahead, but Done should follow at his heel. *Spurgeon.*

Saint cannot, if God will not. *Fr. Pr.*

Saints are sad, because they behold sin (even 40 when they speculate) from the point of view of the conscience, and not of the intellect. *Emerson.*

Sal atticum—Attic salt ; wit.

Sal sapit omnia—Salt seasons everything. *M.*

Salle-à-manger—A dining-room. *Fr.*

Salon—A drawing-room ; a picture gallery or exhibition. *Fr.*

Salt and bread make the cheeks red. *Ger. Pr.* 45

Salt is good, but if the salt have lost its savour, wherewith shall it be seasoned ? It is neither fit for the land, nor yet for the dunghill ; but men cast it out. *Jesus.*

Salt is white and pure ; there is something holy in salt. *Hawthorne.*

Salt spilt is never all gathered up. *Sp. and Port. Pr.*

Saltabat elegantius, quam necesse est probæ — She danced more daintily than a virtuous woman should. *Sall., of Sempronia.*

Salus per Christum redemptorem—Salvation 50 through Christ the Redeemer. *M.*

Salus populi suprema est lex—The well-being of the people is the supreme law. *L.*

Salute thyself : see what thy soul doth wear./ Dare to look in thy chest, for 'tis thine own,/ And tumble up and down what thou find'st there. *George Herbert.*

Salva conscientia—Without compromise of conscience.

Salva dignitate — Without compromising one's dignity.

Salva fide—Without breaking one's word.

Salve, magna parens—Hail! thou great parent! *Virg.*

Salvo jure—Saving the right.

Salvo ordine—Without dishonour to one's order.

5 Salvo pudore—With a proper regard to decency.

Sameness is the mother of disgust, variety the cure. *Petrarch.*

Sammle dich zu jeglichem Geschäfte, / Nie zersplittre deine Kräfte—Gather thyself up for every task, never dissipate (*lit.* split up) thy powers. *Bodenstedt.*

Samson was a strong man, but he could not pay money before he got it. *Ger. Pr.*

Sanan llagas, y no malas palabras—Wounds heal, but not ill words. *Sp. Pr.*

10 Sands form the mountains, moments make the year. *Young.*

Sane baro—A baron indeed. *M.*

Sang-froid—Indifference; apathy; coolness. *Fr.*

Sanno più un savio ed un matto che un savio solo—A wise man and a fool know more than a wise man alone. *It. Pr.*

Sans changer—Without changing. *Fr.*

15 Sans Dieu rien—Nothing without God. *Fr.*

Sans façon—Without ceremony. *Fr.*

Sans le goût, le génie n'est qu'une sublime folie. Ce toucher sûr par qui la lyre ne rend que le son qu'elle doit rendre, est encore plus rare que la faculté qui crée—Without taste genius is only a sublime kind of folly. That sure touch by which the lyre gives back the right note and nothing more, is even a rarer gift than the creative faculty itself. *Chateaubriand.*

Sans les femmes les deux extrémités de la vie seroient sans secours, et le milieu sans plaisir—Without woman the two extremities of life would be destitute of succour, and the middle without pleasure. *Fr.*

Sans peur et sans reproche — Fearless and blameless. *Surname of the Chevalier Bayard.*

20 Sans phrase—Without phrase; without amplification; simply. *Fr.*

Sans Souci—"No bother" here. *Name given by Frederick the Great to his country-house at Potsdam.*

Sans tache—Without stain. *M.*

Sanctio justa, jubens honesta, et prohibens contraria — A just decree, enforcing what is honourable and forbidding the contrary. *Bracton.*

Sanctum est vetus omne poema—Every old poem is sacred. *Hor.*

25 Sic vos non vobis — Thus do ye labour not for yourselves. *Virg.*

Sanctum sanctorum—Holy of holies; a study; a private room.

Sanctus haberi / Justitiæque tenax, factis dictisque mereris? / Agnosco procerem — If you deserve to be held a man without blame, and tenacious of justice both in word and deed, then I recognise in you the nobleman. *Juv.*

Sapere aude—Dare to be wise. *M.*

Sapere isthac ætate oportet, qui sunt capite candido—They who have grey heads are old enough to be wise. *Plaut.*

30 Sapiens dominabitur astris—A wise man will lord it over the stars. *Pr.*

Sapiens nihil facit invitus, nihil dolens, nihil coactus—A wise man does nothing against his will, nothing with repining or under coercion. *Cic.*

Sapiens qui prospicit—He is wise who looks ahead. *M.*

Sapientem pascere barbam — To cultivate a philosophic beard. *Hor.*

Sapienti sat—Enough for a wise man. *Plaut.*

35 Sapientissimus in septem—The wisest of the seven, viz., Thales. *Cic.*

Sapientum octavus—The eighth of the wise men. *Hor.*

Sapping a solemn creed with solemn sneer. *Byron.*

Sarcasm I now see to be, in general, the language of the devil. *Carlyle.*

Sarcasm poisons reproof. *E. Wigglesworth.*

40 Sardonicus risus—A sardonic laugh; a forced ironical laugh.

Sartor resartus—The tailor patched.

Sat cito si sat bene — Quick enough, if well enough. *Cato.*

Sat pulchra, si sat bona—Fair enough, if good enough.

Satan finds some mischief still / For idle hands to do. *Watts.*

45 Satan's friendship reaches to the prison door. *Pr.*

Satan himself is now transformed into an angel of light. *St. Paul.*

Satan now is wiser than of yore, / And tempts by making rich, not making poor. *Pope.*

Satan trembles when he sees / The weakest saint upon his knees. *Cowper.*

Satiety comes of riches, and contumaciousness of satiety. *Solon.*

50 Satire has a power of fascination that no other written thing possesses. *S. Lane-Poole.*

Satire is a sort of glass wherein beholders do generally discover everybody's face but their own. *Swift.*

Satire should, like a polished razor keen, / Wound with a touch that is scarcely seen. *Lady M. Montagu.*

Satires run faster than panegyrics. *Pr.*

Satis diu vel naturæ vel gloriæ—Long enough for the demands both of nature or of glory.

55 Satis eloquentiæ, sapientiæ parum—Fine talk enough, but little wisdom. *Sall.*

Satis est orare Jovem, quæ donat et aufert; / Det vitam, det opes, æquum mi animum ipse parabo—It is enough to pray to Jove for those things which he gives and takes away; let him grant life, let him grant wealth; I myself will provide myself with a well-poised mind. *Hor.*

Satis quod sufficit—Enough is as good as a feast (*lit.* what suffices is enough).

Satis superque est — Enough, and more than enough.

Satis superque me benignitas tua / Ditavit—Your bounty has enriched me enough, and more than enough. *Hor.*

60 Satis verborum—Enough of words.

Satis vixi; invictus enim morior—I have lived enough; I die unvanquished. *Epaminondas in Corn. Nep.*

Satisfaction consists in freedom from pain, which is the positive element of existence. *Schopenhauer.*

Satius est recurrere, quam currere male—It is better to run back than run on the wrong way. *Pr.*

Sauce for the goose is sauce for the gander. *Pr.*

Saucius ejurat pugnam gladiator, et idem / Immemor antiqui vulneris arma capit—The wounded gladiator forswears fighting, and yet, forgetful of his former wound, he takes up arms again.

Säume nicht, dich zu erdreisten, / Wenn die Menge zaudernd schweift ; / Alles kann der Edle leisten / Der versteht und rasch ergreift—If the mass of people hesitate to act, strike thou in swift with all boldness ; the noble heart that understands and seizes quick hold of opportunity can achieve everything. *Goethe.*

5 Sauter du coq à l'âne !—To change the subject abruptly ; to talk at cross purposes.

Sauve qui peut—Save himself who can.

Save a man from his friends, and leave him to struggle with his enemies. (?)

Save a thief from the gallows, and he'll cut your throat. *Pr.*

Save me, and hover o'er me with your wings, / You heavenly guards. *Ham.*, iii. 4.

10 Save something for a sore foot. *Pr.*

Savoir dissimuler est le savoir des rois—To know how to dissemble is the knowledge of kings. *Richelieu.*

Savoir-faire—Skill ; tact.

Savoir-vivre—Good breeding ; good manners. *Fr*

Savor (desire) no more than thee behoven shall, / Rede well thyself that other folks can rede, / And truth thee shalt deliver—'tis no drede. *Chaucer.*

15 Say little and say well. *Gael. Pr.*

Say nay, and take it. *Pr.*

Say no ill of the year till it be past. *Pr.*

Say not always what you know, but always know what you say. *Claudius.*

Say not, I will do so to him as he hath done to me ; I will render to the man according to his work. *Bible.*

20 Say not, / This with that lace will do well ; / But, This with my discretion will be brave. *George Herbert.*

Say not to-morrow ; the tongue's slightest slip / Nemesis watches, ere it pass the lip. *Antiphilus.*

Say not, We will suffer, for that ye must ; say rather, We will act, for that ye must not (*i.e.*, we are compelled to do the one, but not the other). *Jean Paul.*

Say nothing, and none can criticise thee. *Spurgeon.*

Say nothing good of yourself, you will be distrusted ; say nothing bad of yourself, you wilt be taken at your word. *Joseph Roux.*

25 Say, O wise man, how thou hast come by such knowledge ? Because I never was ashamed to confess my ignorance and ask others. *Herder.*

"Say well" is good, but "Do well" is better. *Pr.*

Say well or be still. *Pr.*

Say, what is taste, but the internal pow'rs / Active and strong, and feelingly alive / To each fine impulse ? *Akenside.*

Saying and doing are two different things. *Pr.*

Scald not thy lips with another man's porridge. 30 *Pr.*

Scandal breeds hatred, hatred begets divisions, division makes faction, and faction brings ruin. *Quarles.*

Scandal ever improves by opposition. *Goldsmith.*

Scandal is the sport of its authors, the dread of fools, and the contempt of the wise. *W. B. Clulow.*

Scandal, like the Nile, is fed by innumerable streams, and it is extremely difficult to trace it to its source. *Punch.*

Scandal will not rub out like dirt when it is 35 dry. *Pr.*

Scandalum magnatum—An offence against the nobility or a person in high station. *L.*

Scarcely anything is perfectly plain but what is also perfectly common. *Carlyle.*

Scarcely love's utmost may in heaven be ; / To hell it reacheth, so 'tis love at all. *Louise S. Bevington.*

Scarcely one man in a thousand is capable of tasting the happiness of others. *Fielding.*

Scarceness is what there is the biggest stock 40 of in the country. *George Eliot.*

Scarceness o' victual 'ull keep ; there's no need to be hasty wi' the cooking. *George Eliot.*

Scatter with one hand, gather with two. *Pr.*

Scelere velandum est scelus—One crime has to be concealed by another. *Sen.*

Scepticism has never founded empires, established principles, or changed the world's heart. The great doers in history have always been men of faith. *Chapin.*

Scepticism is not an end but a beginning, is as 45 the decay of old ways of believing, the preparation afar off for new, wider, and better. *Carlyle.*

Scepticism is the attitude assumed by the student in relation to the particulars which society adores ; but which he sees to be reverent only in their tendency and spirit. *Emerson.*

Scepticism is unbelief in cause and effect. *Emerson.*

Scepticism means not intellectual doubt alone, but moral doubt ; all sorts of infidelity, insincerity, and spiritual paralysis. *Carlyle.*

Scepticism, with its innumerable mischiefs, what is it but the sour fruit of a most blessed increase, that of knowledge ; a fruit, too, that will not always continue sour. (?)

Scepticism writing about belief may have great 50 gifts ; but it is really *ultra vires* there. It is blindness laying down the laws of optics. *Carlyle.*

Schadet ein Irrtum wohl ? Nicht immer ! aber das Irren / Immer schadet's. Wie sehr, sieht man am Ende des Wegs—Does an error do harm you ask ? Not always ! but going wrong always does. How far we shall certainly find out at the end of the road. *Goethe.*

Schall und Rauch umnebeln Himmels-Gluth —Sound and smoke overclouding heaven's splendour. *Goethe.*

Schäme dich deines Handwerks nicht—Think no shame of your craft. *Ger. Pr.*

Schärmerei—An enthusiasm with which one or a mass of people is infected. *Ger.*

Scheiden, ach Scheiden, Scheiden thut weh!—Parting, ah! parting; parting makes the heart ache. *Herlossohn.*

Scherze nicht mit Ernst—Jest not in earnest. *M.*

Schick dich in die Zeit—Adapt yourself to the times. *Ger. Pr.*

Schicksal und eigene Schuld—Fate and one's own deservings.

5 Schlägt die Zeit dir manche Wunde, / Manche Freude bringt ihr Lauf; / Aber eine sel'ge Stunde / Wiegt ein Jahr von Schmerzen auf—If time inflicts on thee many a wound, many a joy brings it too in its course; and one short hour of bliss outweighs a year of pains. *Geibel.*

Schlägt dir die Hoffnung fehl, nie fehle dir das Hoffen! / Ein Thor ist zugethan, doch tausend sind dir offen—Though thou art disappointed in a hope, never let hope fail thee; though one door is shut, there are thousands still open for thee. *Rückert.*

Schlagt ihn tot den Hund! Er ist Rezensent—Strike the dog dead! it's but a critic. *Goethe.*

Schlechtes sucht mit Gutem Streit—Bad keeps up a strife with good. *Bodenstedt.*

Schliesst eure Herzen sorgfältiger, als eure Thore—Be more careful to keep the doors of your heart shut than the doors of your house. *Goethe.*

10 Schmerz und Liebe ist des Menschen Teil / Der dem Weltgeschick nicht feig entwichen, / Zieht er aus dem Busen sich den Pfeil, / Ist er für die Welt und Gott verblichen—Pain and love are the portion of the man who does not like a coward shirk the world's destiny; if he plucks the arrow from his breast, he becomes as one dead for the world and God. *N. Lenau.*

Scholars are frequently to be met with who are ignorant of nothing saving their own ignorance. *Zimmermann.*

Scholarship, save by accident, is never the measure of a man's power. *J. G. Holland.*

Schön ist der Friede! Ein lieblicher Knabe / Liegt er gelagert am ruhigen Bach... / Aber der Krieg auch hat seine Ehre, / Der Beweger des Menschengeschicks—Beautiful is Peace! A lovely boy lies he reclining by a quiet rill. But war too has its honour, the promoter as it is of the destiny of man. *Schiller.*

Schön sind die Rosen eurer Jugend; / Allein die Zeit zerstöret sie. / Nur die Talente, nur die Tugend / Veralten nicht und sterben nie—Beautiful are the roses of your youth; but time destroys them; only talents, only virtue age not and never die. *Pfeffel.*

15 Schöne Blumen stehen nicht lange am Wege—Fair flowers are not left standing long by the wayside. *Ger. Pr.*

Schönheit bändigt allen Zorn—Beauty allays all angry feeling. *Goethe.*

Schrecklich blicket ein Gott, da wo Sterbliche weinen—Dreadful looks a God, where mortals weep. *Goethe.*

Schuim is geen bier—Froth is no beer. *Dut. Pr.*

Schweig, oder rede etwas, das ist besser denn Schweigen—Be silent, or say something that is better than silence. *Ger. Pr.*

20 Schweigen ist das Heiligthum der Klugheit. Es birgt nicht bloss Geheimnisse, sondern auch Fehler—Silence is the sanctuary of prudence. It conceals not merely secrets, but blemishes. *Zachariä.*

Schweigen können zeugt von Kraft, schweigen wollen von Nachsicht, schweigen müssen vom Geist der Zeit—To be able to be silent testifies of power, to will to be silent of indulgence, to be obliged to be silent of the spirit of the time. *C. J. Weber.*

Schwer ist es, aus dem Geschrei erhitzter Parteien die Stimme der Wahrheit zu unterscheiden—It is difficult to discriminate the voice of truth from amid the clamour raised by heated partisans. *Schiller.*

Science always goes abreast with the just elevation of the man, keeping step with religion and metaphysics; or, the state of science is an index of our self-knowledge. *Emerson.*

Science corrects the old creeds . . . and necessitates a faith commensurate with the grander orbits and universal laws which it discloses. *Emerson.*

Science deals exclusively with things as they 25 are in themselves. *Ruskin.*

Science dissects death. *F. W. Robertson.*

Science does not know its debt to imagination. *Emerson.*

Science falsely so called. *St. Paul.*

Science must have originated in the feeling of something being wrong. *Carlyle.*

Science has been seriously retarded by the 30 study of what is not worth knowing and of what is not knowable. *Goethe.*

Science has done much for us; but it is a poor science that would hide from us the great deep sacred infinitude of Nescience, on which all science swims as a mere superficial film. *Carlyle.*

Science has not solved difficulties, only shifted the points of difficulty. *C. H. Parkhurst.*

Science is a first-rate piece of furniture for a man's upper chamber if he has common-sense on the ground-floor. But if a man has not got plenty of good common-sense, the more science he has the worse for his patient. *Holmes.*

Science is an ocean. It is as open to the cockboat as the frigate. One man carries across it a freightage of ingots, another may fish there for herrings. *Bulwer Lytton.*

Science is busy with the hither-end of 35 things, not the thither-end. *C. H. Parkhurst.*

Science / Is but an exchange of ignorance for that / Which is another kind of ignorance. *Byron.*

Science is for those who learn, poetry for those who know. *J. Roux.*

Science is nothing but trained and organised common sense. *Huxley.*

Science is teaching man to know and reverence truth, and to believe that only so far as he knows and loves it can he live worthily on earth, and vindicate the dignity of his spirit. *Moses Harvey.*

Science is the knowledge of constant things, 40 not merely of passing events, and is properly less the knowledge of general laws than of existing facts. *Ruskin.*

Science is the systematic classification of experience. *G. H. Lewes.*

Science lives only in quiet places, and with odd people, mostly poor. *Ruskin.*

Science rests on reason and experiment, and can meet an opponent with calmness ; (but) a creed is always sensitive. *Froude.*

Science sees signs ; Poetry, the thing signified. *Hare.*

Scientia nihil aliud est quam veritatis imago—Science is but an image of the truth. *Bacon.*

Scientia popinæ—The art of cookery.

5 Scientia quæ est remota a justitia, calliditas potius quam sapientia est appellanda—Knowledge which is divorced from justice may be called cunning rather than wisdom. *Cic.*

Scientific, like spiritual truth, has ever from the beginning been descending from heaven to man. *Disraeli.*

Scientific truth is marvellous, but moral truth is divine; and whoever breathes its air and walks by its light has found the lost paradise. *Horace Mann.*

Scilicet expectes, ut tradet mater honestos / Atque alios mores, quam quos habet ?—Can you expect that the mother will teach good morals or others than her own. *Juv.*

Scinditur incertum studia in contraria vulgus —The wavering multitude is divided into opposite factions. *Virg.*

10 Scio cui credidi—I know in whom I have believed *M.*

Scio : tu coactus tua voluntate es — I know it ; you are constrained by your inclination. *Ter.*

Scire facias—Cause it to be known. *L.*

Scire potestates herbarum usumque medendi —To know the virtues of herbs and their use in healing. *Virg.*

Scire tuum nihil est, nisi te scire hoc sciat alter—It is nothing for you to know a thing unless another knows that you know it. *Pers.*

15 Scire ubi aliquid invenire possis, ea demum maxima pars eruditionis est—To know where you can find a thing is the chief part of learning.

Scire volunt omnes, mercedem solvere nemo—All would like to know, but few to pay the price. *Juv.*

Scire volunt secreta domus, atque inde timeri —They wish to know of the family secrets, and so to be feared. *Juv.*

Scit genius, natale comes qui temperet astrum —The genius, our companion, who rules our natal star, knows. *Hor.*

Scoglio immoto contro le onde sta—He stands like a rock unmoved against the waves. *M.*

20 Scorn no man's love, though of a mean degree ; / Love is a present for a mighty king,— / Much less make any one thine enemy. As guns destroy, so may a little sling. *George Herbert.*

Scorn to trample upon a worm or to sneak to be an emperor. *Saadi.*

Scorn'd, to be scorn'd by one that I scorn, / Is that a matter to make me fret ? / That a calamity hard to be borne ? *Tennyson.*

Scots, wha hae wi' Wallace bled, / Scots, wham Bruce has aften led, / Welcome to your gory bed, / Or to victory ! / Now's the day and now's the hour ; / See the front o' battle lour ; / See approach proud Edward's power, / Chains and slavery. *Burns.*

Scotsmen reckon ay frae an ill hour. *Pr.*

25 Screw not the chord too sharply lest it snap. *Pr.*

Screw your courage to the sticking-place, / And we'll not fail. *Macb., i. 7.*

Scribendi recte sapere est et principium et fons—Good sense is both the first principle and parent-source of good writing. *Hor.*

Scribere scientes—Knowing, or skilled, in writing. *M.*

Scribimus indocti doctique—All of us, unlearned and learned, alike take to writing. *Hor.*

Scripture, like Nature, lays down no defini- 30 tions. *Spinoza.*

Scruples, temptations, and fears, and cutting perplexities of heart, are frequently the lot of the most excellent persons. *Thomas à Kempis.*

Sculpture and painting have an effect to teach us manners and abolish hurry. *Emerson.*

Sculpture is not the mere cutting of the form of anything in stone ; it is the cutting of the effect of it. Very often the true form, in the marble, would not be in the least like itself. *Ruskin.*

Sculpture, the tongue on the balance of expression. *Quoted by Emerson.*

S'échauffer au dépens du bon Dieu—To warm 35 one's self in the sun (*lit.* at the expense of the good god). *M.*

Se a ciascuno l'interno affanno / Si leggesse in fronte scritto, / Quanti mai che invidia fanno / Ci farebbero pietà !—If the secret sorrows of every one could be read on his forehead, how many who now excite envy would become objects of pity ! *It.*

Se il giovane sapesse, se il vecchio potesse, e' non c' è cosa che non si facesse—If the young knew, and the old could, there is nothing which would not be done. *It. Pr.*

Se'l sol mi splende, non curo la luna—If the sun shines on me, I care not for the moon. *It. Pr.*

Se la moglie pecca, non è il marito innocente —If the wife sins, the husband is not innocent. *It. Pr.*

Se laisser prendre aux apparences—To let one's 40 self be imposed on by appearances. *Fr. Pr.*

Se moquer de la philosophie, c'est vraiment philosopher—To jest at the expense of philosophy is truly to philosophise. *Pascal.*

Se non è vero, è ben trovato—If it is not true, it is cleverly invented. *It. Pr.*

Se retirer dans un fromage de Hollande—To retire into a Dutch cheese, *i.e.*, to be contented. *La Fontaine.*

Se tu segui tua stella—Follow thou thy own star. *Dante.*

Sea Islanders ; but a real human heart, with 45 Divine love in it, beats with the same glow under all the patterns of all earth's thousand tribes. *Holmes.*

Sea things that be / On the hot sand fainting long, / Revive with the kiss of the sea. *Lewis Morris.*

Seamen have a custom when they meet a whale to fling out an empty tub by way of amusement, to divert him from laying violent hands upon the ship. *Swift.*

Search not to find what lies too deeply hid ; / Nor to know things whose knowledge is forbid. *Denham.*

Search others for their virtues, and thyself for thy vices. *Fuller.*

Searching of thy wound, I have by hard adventure found my own. *As You Like It,* ii. 4.

Second thoughts, they say, are best. *Dryden.*

Secrecy has many advantages, for when you tell a man at once and straightforward the purpose of any object, he fancies there's nothing in it. *Goethe.*

Secrecy is best taught by commencing with ourselves. *Chamfort.*

5 Secrecy is the chastity of friendship. *Jeremy Taylor.*

Secrecy is the element of all goodness; even virtue, even beauty is mysterious. *Carlyle.*

Secrecy is the soul of all great designs. *Quoted by Colton.*

Secrecy of design, when combined with rapidity of execution, like the column that guided Israel in the desert, becomes the guardian pillar of light and fire to our friends, and a cloud of overwhelming and impenetrable darkness to our enemies. *Colton.*

Secret et hardi—Secret and bold. *M.*

10 Secreta hæc murmura vulgi—Those secret whisperings of the populace. *Juv.*

Secrete amicos admone, lauda palam—Advise your friends in private, praise them openly. *Pub. Syr.*

Secrets make a dungeon of the heart and a jailer of its owner. *Amer. Pr.*

Secrets travel fast in Paris. *Napoleon.*

Sects of men are apt to be shut up in sectarian ideas of their own, and to be less open to new general ideas than the main body of men. *Matthew Arnold.*

15 Secundis dubiisque rectus—Upright, whether in prosperous or in critical circumstances. *M.*

Secundo amne defluit—He floats with the stream.

Secundum artem—According to the rules of art.

Secundum genera—According to classes.

Secundum usum—According to usage or use.

20 Security, / Is mortals' chiefest enemy. *Macbeth,* iii. 5.

Security will produce danger. *Johnson.*

Securus judicat orbis terrarum—The world's judgment is unswayed by fear. *St. Augustine.*

Sed de me ut sileam—But to say nothing of myself. *Ovid.*

Sed nisi peccassem, quid tu concedere posses? / Materiam veniæ sors tibi nostra dedit—Had I not sinned, what had there been for thee to pardon? My fate has given thee the matter for mercy. *Ovid.*

25 Sed notat hunc omnis domus et vicinia tota, / Introrsum turpem, speciosum pelle decora—But all his family and the entire neighbourhood regard him as inwardly base, and only showy outside. *Hor.*

Sed quum res hominum tanta caligine volvi / Adspicerem, lætosque diu florere nocentes, / Vexarique pios: rursus labefacta cadebat / Religio—When I beheld human affairs involved in such dense darkness, the guilty exuiting in their prosperity, and pious men suffering wrong, what religion I had began to reel backward and fall. *Claud.*

Sed tu / Ingenio verbis concipe plura meis?—But do you of your own ingenuity take up more than my words? *Ovid.*

Sed vatem egregium cui non sit publica vena, / Qui nihil expositum soleat deducere, nec qui / Communi feriat carmen triviale moneta, / Hunc qualem nequeo monstrare, et sentio tantum, / Anxietate carens animus facit—A poet of superior merit, whose vein is of no vulgar kind, who never winds off anything trite, nor coins a trivial poem at the public mint, I cannot describe, but only recognise as a man whose soul is free from all anxiety. *Juv.*

See deep enough, and you see musically; the heart of Nature being everywhere music, if you can only reach it. *Carlyle.*

See how many things there are which a man 30 cannot do himself; and then it will appear that it was a sparing speech of the ancients to say, "that a friend is another himself; for that a friend is far more than himself. *Bacon.*

See Naples, and then die. *It. Pr.*

See one promontory, one mountain, one sea, one river, and see all. *Socrates.*

See that no man put a stumbling-block, or an occasion to fall, in his brother's way. *St. Paul.*

See that you come not to woo honour, but to wed it. *All's Well,* ii. 1.

See the conquering hero comes ! / Sound the 35 trumpet, beat the drums! *Dr. Thomas Morell.*

See this last and this hammer (said the poor cobbler); that last and this hammer are the two best friends I have in this world; nobody else will be my friend, because I want a friend. *Goldsmith.*

See thou explain the infinite through the finite, and the unintelligible only through the intelligible, and not inversely. *Bodenstedt.*

See to it that each hour's feelings, and thoughts, and actions are pure and true; then will your life be such. *Ward Beecher.*

See what a scourge is laid upon your hate, / That Heaven finds means to kill your joys with love. *Rom. and Jul.,* v. 3.

See, what is good lies by thy side. *Goethe.* 40

Seein' believin', but feelin's the naked truth. *Sc. Pr.*

Seeing the root of the matter is found in me. *Bible.*

Seek, and ye shall find. *Jesus.*

Seek but provision of bread and wine, / . . . Fools to flatter, and raiment fine, / . . . And nothing of God shall e'er be thine. *Dr. W. Smith.*

Seek judgment, relieve the oppressed, judge 45 the fatherless, plead for the widow. *Bible.*

Seek not thyself without thyself to find. *Dryden.*

Seek not to know what must not be reveal'd ; / Joys only flow where fate is most conceal'd ; / Too busy man would find his sorrows more, / If future fortunes he should know before ; / For by that knowledge of his destiny / He would not live at all, but always die. *Dryden.*

Seek not to reform every one s dial by your own watch. *Pr.*

Seek one good, one end, so zealously, that nothing else may come into competition or partnership with it. *Thomas à Kempis.*

Seek the good of other men, but be not in bondage to their faces or fancies ; for that is but facility or softness, which taketh an honest mind prisoner. *Bacon.*

Seek till you find, and you'll not lose your labour. *Pr.*

Seek to be good, but aim not to be great ; / A woman's noblest station is retreat. *Lyttelton.*

Seek to make thy course regular, that men may know beforehand what they may expect. *Bacon.*

5 Seek ye the Lord while he may be found, call ye upon him while he is near. *Bible.*

Seek your salve where you got your sore. *Pr.*

Seekest thou great things? seek them not. *Jeremiah.*

Seeking for a God there, and not here ; everywhere outwardly in physical nature, and not inwardly in our own soul, where He alone is to be found by us, begins to get wearisome. *Carlyle.*

Seeking nothing, he gains all ; foregoing self, the universe grows "I." *Sir Edwin Arnold.*

10 Seeking the bubble reputation, / Even in the cannon's mouth. *As You Like It,* ii. 7.

Seele des Menschen, / Wie gleichst du dem Wasser ! / Schicksal des Menschen, / Wie gleichst du dem Wind !—Soul of man, how like art thou to water ! Lot of man, how like art thou to wind ! *Goethe.*

Seelenstärke ohne Seelengrösse bildet die bösartigen Charakters—Strength of soul without greatness of soul goes but to form evil-disposed characters. *Weber.*

Seem I not as tender to him / As any mother ? / Ay, but such a one / As all day long hath rated at her child, / And vext his day, but blesses him asleep. *Tennyson.*

Seeming triumph o'er God's saints / Lasts but a little hour. *Winkworth.*

15 Seems, madam ! nay, it is ; I know not "seems." / 'Tis not alone my inky cloak, good mother, / Nor customary suits of solemn black. / Nor windy suspiration of forced breath, / No, nor the fruitful river in the eye, / Nor the dejected 'haviour of the visage, / Together with all forms, modes, shows of grief, / That can denote truly ; these, indeed, seem, / For they are actions that a man can play : / But I have that within, which passeth show ; / These but the trappings and the suits of woe. *Ham.,* i. 2.

Seest thou a man diligent in his business? he shall stand before kings ; he shall not stand before mean men. *Bible.*

Seest thou a man that is hasty in his words? there is more hope of a fool than of him. *Bible.*

Seest thou a man wise in his own conceit ? there is more hope of a fool than of him. *Bible.*

Seest thou not, I say, what a deformed thief this fashion is? how giddily he turns about all the hot bloods between fourteen and five-and-thirty. *Much Ado,* iii. 3.

20 Segnius homines bona quam mala sentiunt— Men are not so readily sensible of benefits as of injuries.

Segnius irritant animos demissa per aurem, / Quam quæ sunt oculis subjecta fidelibus— What we learn merely through the ear makes less impression upon our minds than what is presented to the trustworthy eye. *Hor.*

Sehr leicht zerstreut der Zufall was er sammelt ;/ Ein edler Mensch zieht edle Menschen an / Und weiss sie festzuhalten — What chance gathers she very easily scatters. A noble man attracts noble men, and knows how to hold them fast. *Goethe.*

Sei gefühllos ! / Ein leichtbewegtes Herz / Ist ein elend Gut / Auf der wankenden Erde—Do not give way to feeling (*lit.* be unfeeling). A quickly sensitive heart is an unhappy possession on this shaky earth. *Goethe.*

Sei gut, und lass von dir die Menschen Böses sagen ; / Wer eigne Schuld nicht trägt, kann leichter fremde tragen—Be good, and let men say ill of thee ; he who has no sin to bear of his own can more easily bear that of others. *Goethe.*

Sei im Besitze, und du wohnst im Recht. / 25 Und heilig wird's die Menge dir bewahren —Be in possession and thou hast the right, and the many will preserve it for thee as sacred. *Schiller.*

Sei was du sein willst—Be what you would be. *Ger. Pr.*

Sein Glaube ist so gross, dass, wenn er fällt, / Glaubt er : gefallen sei die ganze Welt—His faith is so great that if it fails, he believes the whole world has fallen. *Bodenstedt.*

Sei hochbeseligt oder leide ! / Das Herz bedarf ein zweites Herz. / Geteilte Freud' ist doppelt Freude, / Geteilter Schmerz ist halber Schmerz. Be joyful or sorrowful, the heart needs a second heart. Joy shared is joy doubled ; pain shared is pain divided. *Rückert.*

Selbst erfinden ist schön ; doch glücklich von andern Gefundnes, / Fröhlich erkannt und geschätzt, nennst du das weniger dein? It is glorious to find out one's self, but call you that less yours which has been happily found out by others, and is with joy recognised and valued by you? *Goethe.*

Selbst gethan ist halb gethan—What you do 30 yourself is half done. *Ger. Pr.*

Seldom contented, often in the wrong, / Hard to be pleased at all, and never long. *Dryden.*

Seldom ever was any knowledge given to keep but to impart ; the grace of this rich jewel is lost in concealment. *Bp. Hall.*

Seldom he smiles, and smiles in such a sort, / As if he mock'd himself, and scorn'd his spirit,/ That could be moved to smile at anything. *Jul. Cæs.,* i. 2.

Seldom, in the business and transactions of ordinary life, do we find the sympathy we want. *Goethe.*

Seldom is a life wholly wrecked but the cause 35 lies in some internal mal-arrangement, some want less of good fortune than of good guidance. *Carlyle.*

Self-complacence over the concealed destroys its concealment. *Goethe.*

Self-confidence is either a petty pride in our own narrowness or a realisation of our duty and privilege as God's children. *Phillips Brooks.*

Self-confidence is the first requisite to great undertakings. *Johnson.*

Self-deception is one of the most deadly of all dangers. *Saying.*

Self-denial is indispensable to a strong char-40 acter, and the loftiest kind thereof comes only of a religious stock. *Theo. Parker.*

Self-denial is painful for a moment, but very agreeable in the end. *Jane Taylor.*

Self-distrust is the cause of most of our failures. In the assurance of strength there is strength, and they are the weakest, however strong, who have no faith in themselves or their powers. *Bovee.*

Self-interest, that leprosy of the age, attacks us from infancy, and we are startled to observe little heads calculate before knowing how to reflect. *Mme. de Girardin.*

Self-knowledge comes from knowing other men. *Goethe.*

5 Self-love exaggerates our faults as well as our virtues. *Goethe.*

Self-love is a balloon inflated with wind, from which storms burst forth when one makes a puncture in it. *Voltaire.*

Self-love is not so vile a sin / As self-neglecting. *Henry V.*, ii. 4.

Self-love is the instrument of our preservation. *Voltaire.*

Self-love may be, and as a fact often is, the first impulse that drives a man to seek to become morally and religiously better. *J. C. Sharp.*

10 Self loves itself best. *Pr.*

Self-murder ! name it not ; our island's shame ! *Blair.*

Self-respect, the corner-stone of all virtue. *Sir John Herschel.*

Self-reverence, self-knowledge, self-control, / These three alone lead life to sovereign power. / Yet not for power (power of herself / Would come uncall'd for), but to live by law, / Acting the law we live by without fear ; / And, because right is right, to follow right, / Were wisdom in the scorn of consequence. *Tennyson.*

Self-trust is the essence of heroism. *Emerson.*

15 Self-trust is the first secret of success. *Emerson.*

Self-will is so ardent and active that it will break a world to pieces to make a stool to sit on. *Cecil.*

Selfishness is that detestable vice which no one will forgive in others, and no one is without in himself. *Ward Beecher.*

Selfishness, not love, is the actuating motive of the gallant. *Mme. Roland.*

Selig der, den er im Siegesglanze findet— Happy he whom he (Death) finds in battle's splendour. *Goethe.*

20 Selig wer sich vor der Welt, / Ohne Hass verschliesst, / Einen Freund am Busen hält / Und mit dem geniesst—Happy he who without hatred shuts himself off from the world, holds a friend to his bosom, and enjoys life with him. *Goethe.*

Sell all thou hast, and give it to the poor, and follow me. *Jesus.*

Semel insanivimus omnes—We have all been at some time mad.

Semel malus, semper præsumitur esse malus— Once bad is to be presumed always bad. *L.*

Semen est sanguis Christianorum—The blood of us Christians is seed. *Tertullian.*

25 Semper ad eventum festinat—He always hastens to the goal, or issue. *M.*

Semper Augustus—Always an enlarger of the empire. *Symmachus.*

Semper avarus eget ; certum voto pete finem —The avaricious man is ever in want ; let your desire aim at a fixed limit. *Hor.*

Semper bonus homo tiro—A good man is always green. *Mart.*

Semper eadem—Always the same. *M.*

Semper eris pauper, si pauper es, Æmiliane— 30 If you are poor, Emilian, you will always be poor. *Mart.*

Semper fidelis—Always faithful. *M.*

Semper habet lites alternaque jurgia lectus, / In quo nupta jacet ; minimum dormitur in illo—The bed in which a wife lies is always the scene of quarrels and mutual recriminations ; there is very little chance of sleep there. *Juv.*

Semper honos, nomenque tuum, laudesque manebunt—Thy honour, thy renown, and thy praises shall live for ever. *Virg.*

Semper idem—Always the same. *M.*

Semper inops, quicunque cupit—He who desires 35 more is always poor. *Claud.*

Semper paratus—Always ready. *M.*

Semper tibi pendeat hamus ; / Quo minime credas gurgite, piscis erit—Have your hook always baited ; in the pool where you least think it there will be a fish. *Ovid.*

Sempre il mal non vien per nuocere — Misfortune does not always result in harm. *It. Pr.*

Send a fool to France, and he'll come a fool back. *Sc. Pr.*

Send a fool to the market, and a fool he'll 40 return. *Pr.*

Send a wise man of an errand, and say nothing to him. *Pr.*

Send your charity abroad wrapt in blankets. *Pr.*

Send your son to Ayr ; if he did weel here, he'll do weel there. *Sc. Pr.*

Senilis stultitia, quæ deliratio appellari solet, senum levium est, non omnium—The foolishness of old age, which is termed dotage, does not characterise all who are old, but only those who are frivolous. *Cic.*

Seniores priores—The elder men first. 45

Sense can support herself handsomely, in most countries, for some eighteenpence a day ; but for fantasy planets and solar systems will not suffice. *Carlyle.*

Sense hides shame. *Gael. Pr.*

Sense, shortness, and salt are the ingredients of a good proverb. *Howell.*

Sensibility would be a good portress if she had but one hand ; with her right she opens the door to pleasure, but with her left to pain. *Colton.*

Sensitive ears are good signs of health in 50 girls as in horses. *Jean Paul.*

Sensitiveness is closely allied to egotism ; and excessive sensibility is only another name for morbid self - consciousness. The cure for tender sensibilities is to make more of our objects and less of ourselves. *Bovee.*

Sensuality is the grave of the soul. *Channing.*

Sentences are like sharp nails, which force truth upon our memory. *Diderot.*

Sentiment has a kind of divine alchemy, rendering grief itself the source of tenderest thoughts and far-reaching desires, which the sufferer cherishes as sacred treasures. *Talfourd.*

Sentiment is intellectualised emotion; emotion precipitated, as it were, in pretty crystals by the fancy. *Lowell.*

Sentiment is the ripened fruit of fantasy. *Mme. Delazy.*

Sentimental literature, concerned with the analysis and description of emotion, headed by the poetry of Byron, is altogether of lower rank than the literature which merely describes what it saw. *Ruskin.*

5 Sentimentalism is that state in which a man speaks deep and true, not because he feels things strongly, but because he perceives that they are beautiful, and touching and fine to say them—things that he fain would feel, and fancies that he does feel. *F. W. Robertson.*

Senza Cerere e Bacco, Venere e di ghiaccio—Without bread and wine love is cold (*lit.* without Ceres and Bacchus, Venus is of ice). *It. Pr.*

Septem convivium, novem convitium—Seven is a banquet, nine a brawl. *Pr.*

Septem horas dormisse sat est juvenique, senique—Seven hours of sleep is enough both for old and young. *Pr.*

Sepulchri / Mitte supervacuos honores—Discard the superfluous honours at the grave. *Hor.*

10 Sequiturque patrem non passibus æquis—And he follows his father with unequal steps. *Virg.*

Sequor nec inferior—I follow, but am not inferior. *M.*

Sera in fundo parsimonia—Economy is too late when you are at the bottom of your purse. *Sen.*

Serenity, health, and affluence attend the desire of rising by labour. *Goldsmith.*

Seriatim—In order; according to rank; in due course.

15 Series implexa causarum — The complicated series of causes; fate. *Sen.*

Serit arbores quæ alteri sæculo prosint—He plants trees for the benefit of a future generation. *From Statius.*

Sermons in stones. *As You Like It,* ii. 1.

Sero clypeum post vulnera sumo—I am too late in taking my shield after being wounded. *Pr.*

Sero sapiunt Phryges—The Trojans became wise when too late. *Pr.*

20 Sero sed serio—Late, but seriously. *M.*

Sero venientibus ossa—The bones for those who come late. *Pr.*

Serpens ni edat serpentem, draco non fiet—Unless a serpent devour a serpent, it will not become a dragon, *i.e.,* unless one power absorb another, it will not become great. *Pr.*

Serpentum major concordia; parcit / Cognatis maculis similis fera. Quando leoni / Fortior eripuit vitam leo ?—There is greater concord among serpents than among men; a wild beast of a like kind spares kindred spots. When did a stronger lion deprive another of life? *Juv.*

Serum auxilium post prælium—Help comes too late when the fight is over. *Pr.*

25 Serus in cœlum redeas diuque / Lætus intersis populo—May it be long before you return to the sky, and may you long move up and down gladly among your people. *Hor. to Augustus.*

Serva jugum—Preserve the yoke. *M.*

Servabo fidem—I will keep faith. *M.*

Servant of God, well done; well hast thou fought / The better fight. *Milton.*

Servants and houses should be suited to the situation. A gem should not be placed at the feet. The same is to be understood of an able man. *Hitopadesa.*

Servata fides cineri—Faithful to the memory of 30 my ancestors. *M.*

Serve the great; stick at no humiliation; grudge no office thou canst render; be the limb of their body, the breath of their mouth; compromise thy egotism. *Emerson.*

Servetur ad imum / Qualis ab incepto processerit, et sibi constet—Let the character be kept up to the very end, just as it began, and so be consistent. *Hor.*

Service is no inheritance. *Fr. and It. Pr.*

Serviet æternum, quia parvo nescit uti—He will be always a slave, because he knows not how to live upon little. *Hor.*

Servility and abjectness of humour is implicitly 35 involved in the charge of lying. *Government of the Tongue.*

Serving one's own passions is the greatest slavery. *Pr.*

Servitude seizes on few, but many seize on servitude. *Sen.*

Ses rides sur son front ont gravé ses exploits —His furrows on his forehead testify to his exploits. *Corn.*

Sesquipedalia verba — Words a cubit long. *Hor.*

Set a beggar on horseback and he'll ride to 40 the devil. *Pr.*

Set a beggar on horseback and he will ride a gallop. *Burton.*

Set a stout heart to a stey (steep) brae. *Sc. Pr.*

Set a thief to catch a thief. *Pr.*

Set it down to thyself as well to create good precedents as to follow them. *Bacon.*

Set not your loaf in till the oven's hot. *Pr.* 45

Set out so / As all the day thou mayst hold out to go. *George Herbert.*

Set your affections on things above, not on things on the earth. *St. Paul.*

Setz' dir Perrücken auf von Millionen Locken, / Setz' deinen Fuss auf ellenhohe Socken, / Du bleibst doch immer, was du bist—Clap on thee wigs with curls without number, set thy foot in ell-high socks, thou remainest notwithstanding ever what thou art. *Goethe.*

Seven cities warred for Homer being dead, / Who living had no roof to shroud his head. *Heywood.*

Seven Grecian cities vied for Homer dead, / 50 Through which the living Homer begged his bread. *Leonidas.*

Seven hours to law, to soothing slumber seven, ten to the world allot, and all to heaven. *Sir William Jones.*

Seven times tried that judgment is / That did never choose amiss. *Mer. of Ven.,* ii. 9.

Severæ Musa tragœdiæ—The Muse of solemn tragedy. *Hor.*

Severity breedeth fear, but roughness breedeth hate. *Bacon.*

Sewing at once a double thread, / A shroud as 55 well as a shirt. *Hood.*

Sex horas somno, totidem des legibus æquis : / Quatuor orabis, des epulisque duas. / Quod superest ultra, sacris largire Camenis—Give six hours to sleep, as many to the study of law ; four hours you shall pray, and two gave to meals : what is over devote to the sacred Muses. *Coke.*

Sexu fœmina, ingenio vir—In sex a woman, in natural ability a man. *Epitaph of Maria Theresa.*

Shadow owes its birth to light. *Gay.*

Shadows fall on brightest hours. *Procter.*

5 Shadows to-night / Have struck more terror to the soul of Richard / Than can the substance of ten thousand soldiers. *Rich. III.,* v. 3.

Shake off this downy sleep, death's counterfeit, / And look on death itself. *Macb.,* ii. 3.

Shakespeare carries us to such a lofty strain of intelligent activity as to suggest a wealth that beggars his own ; and we then feel that the splendid works which he has created, and which in other hours we extol as a sort of self-existent poetry, have no stronger hold of real nature than the shadow of a passing traveller on the rock. *Emerson.*

Shakespeare does not look at a thing merely, but into it, through it, so that he constructively comprehends it, can take it asunder and put it together again ; the thing melts, as it were, into light under his eye, and anew creates itself before him. *Carlyle.*

Shakespeare is dangerous to young poets ; they cannot but reproduce him, while they imagine they are producing themselves. *Goethe.*

10 Shakespeare is no sectarian ; to all he deals with equity and mercy ; because he knows all, and his heart is wide enough for all. In his mind the world is a whole ; he figures it as Providence governs it ; and to him it is not strange that the sun should be caused to shine on the evil and the good, and the rain to fall on the just and the unjust. *Carlyle.*

Shakespeare is the greatest intellect who, in our recorded world, has left record of himself in the way of literature. I know not such power of vision, such faculty of thought in any other man, such calmness of depth ; placid joyous strength ; all things imaged in that great soul of his so true and clear, as in a tranquil unfathomable sea. A perfectly level mirror, that is to say withal, a man justly related to all things and men, a good man. *Carlyle.*

Shakespeare made his Hamlet as a bird weaves its nest. *Emerson.*

Shakespeare must have seemed a dull man at times, he was so flashingly brilliant at others. *Bovee.*

Shakespeare never permits a spirit to show itself but to men of the highest intellectual power. *Ruskin.*

15 Shakespeare says we are creatures that look before and after ; the more surprising that we do not look round a little and see what is passing under our very eyes. *Carlyle.*

Shakespeare stands alone. His want of erudition was a most happy and productive ignorance ; it forced him back upon his own resources, which were exhaustless. *Colton.*

Shakespeare, the finest human figure, as I apprehend, that Nature has hitherto seen fit to make out of our widely-diffused Teutonic clay. I find no human soul so beautiful, these fifteen hundred known years—our supreme modern European man. *Carlyle.*

Shakespeare, the sage and seer of the human heart. *H. Giles.*

Shakespeare was forbidden of heaven to have any plans. . . . Not for him the founding of institutions, the preaching of doctrines, or the repression of abuses. Neither he, nor the sun, did on any morning that they rose together, receive charge from their Maker concerning such things. They were both to shine on the evil and good ; both to behold unoffendingly all that was upon the earth, to burn unappalled upon the spears of kings, and undisdaining upon the reeds of the river. *Ruskin.*

Shakespeare (it is true) wrote perfect historical 20 plays on subjects belonging to the preceding centuries, (but) they are perfect plays just because there is no care about centuries in them, but a life which all men recognise for the human life of all time ; . . . a rogue in the fifteenth century being, at heart, what a rogue is in the nineteenth and was in the twelfth ; and an honest or a knightly man being, in like manner, very similar to other such at any other time. *Ruskin.*

Shall horses run upon the rock ? Will one plough there with oxen ? *Bible.*

Shall we receive good at the hands of the Lord, and shall we not receive evil ? *Bible.*

Shall we repine at a little misplaced charity, when an all-knowing, all-wise Being showers down every day his benefits on the unthankful and undeserving ? *Atterbury.*

Shall workmen just repeat the sin of kings and conquerors ? / As the nations cease from battle, shall the classes rouse the fray, / And scatter wanton sorrow for a shilling more a day ? *Dr. Walter Smith.*

Shallow men believe in luck, believe in circum- 25 stances. . . . Strong men believe in cause and effect. *Emerson.*

Shallow streams make most din. *Pr.*

Sallow wits censure everything that is beyond their depth. *Pr.*

"Shalls" and "wills." Never trust a Scotch man or woman who does not come to grief among them. *J. M. Barrie.*

Shame is a feeling of profanation. *Novalis.*

Shame is like the weaver's thread ; if it breaks 30 in the web, it is wholly imperfect. *Bulwer Lytton.*

Shame is worse than death. *Russ. Pr.*

Shame may restrain what law does not prohibit. *Sen.*

Shame of poverty is almost as bad as pride of wealth. *Pr.*

Shapes that come not at an earthly call / Will not depart when mortal voices bid. *Wordsworth.*

Sharpness cuts slight things best ; solid, nothing 35 cuts through but weight and strength ; the same in the use of intellectuals. *Sir W. Temple.*

She bears a duke's revenues on her back. *2 Hen. VI.,* i. 3.

She (Wisdom) is a tree of life to them that lay hold upon her : and happy is every one that retaineth her. *Bible.*

She is a wife who is the soul of her husband. *Hitopadesa.*

She is a woman, therefore may be wooed ; she is a woman, therefore may be won. *Tit. Andron.*, ii. 1.

She is a woman who can command herself. *Hitopadesa.*

5 She is not worthy to be loved that hath not some feeling of her own worthiness. *Sir P. Sidney.*

She lived unknown, and few could know / When Lucy ceased to be ; / But she is in her grave, and oh / The difference to me ! *Wordsworth.*

She looketh well to the ways of her household, and eateth not the bread of idleness. *Bible.*

She looks as if butter would not melt in her mouth. *Swift.*

She loved me for the dangers I had passed, / And I loved her that she did pity them. / This only is the witchcraft I have used. *Othello*, i. 3.

10 She never told her love, / But let concealment, like a worm i' the bud, / Feed on her damask cheek. *Twelfth Night*, ii. 4.

She (*i.e.*, Nature) only knows / How justly to proportion to the fault the punishment it merits. *Shelley.*

She pined in thought, / And with a green and yellow melancholy. / She sat like patience on a monument, / Smiling at grief. *Twelfth Night*, ii. 4.

She should be humble who would please, / And she must suffer who can love. *Prior.*

She speaks poniards, and every word stabs : if her breath were as terrible as her terminations, there were no living with her ; she would infect to the north star. *Much Ado*, ii. 1.

15 She that is ashamed to eat at table eats in private. *Pr.*

She that is born handsome is born married. *Pr.*

She that rails ye into trembling / Only shows her fine dissembling ; / But the fawner to abuse ye, / Thinks ye fools, and so will use ye. *Dufrey.*

She that takes gifts herself she sells, / And she that gives them does nothing else. *Pr.*

She that will not when she may, / When she will, she shall have nay. *Murphy.*

20 She watches him as a cat would watch a mouse. *Swift.*

She wept to feel her life so desolate, / And wept still more because the world had made it / So desolate : yet was the world her all ; / She loathed it, but she knew it was her all. *Dr. Walter Smith.*

She who makes her husband and her children happy, who reclaims the one from vice, and trains up the other to virtue, is a much greater character than ladies described in romance, whose whole occupation is to murder mankind with shafts from their quiver or their eyes. *Goldsmith.*

She's all my fancy painted her ; / She's lovely, she's divine. *William Mee.*

She's beautiful, and therefore to be woo'd ; / She's a woman, and therefore to be won. 1 *Hen. VI.*, v. 3.

Sheathe thy impatience ; throw cold water on 25 thy choler. *Merry Wives*, ii. 3.

Short allowance of victual, and plenty of nothing but Gospel ! *Longfellow.*

Short boughs, long vintage. *Pr.*

Short lived is all rule but the rule of God. *Gael. Pr.*

Short-lived wits do wither as they grow. *Loves L. Lost*, ii. 1.

Short prayers reach heaven. *Pr.* 30

Short reckonings make long friends. *Pr.*

Short swallow-flights of song, that dip / Their wings in tears and skim away. *Tennyson.*

Should auld acquaintance be forgot, / And never brought to mind? / Should auld acquaintance be forgot, / And days o' lang syne? *Burns.*

Should envious tongues some malice frame, / To soil and tarnish your good name, / Live it down. *Dr. Henry Rink.*

Should not the ruler have regard to the voice 35 of the people? *Schiller.*

Should one suffer what is intolerable? *Schiller.*

Show me one wicked man who has written poetry, and I will show you where his poetry is not poetry ; or rather, I will show you in his poetry no poetry at all. *Eliz. S. Shephard.*

Show me the man who would go to heaven alone, and I will show you one who will never be admitted. *Feltham.*

Show me the man you honour ; I know by that symptom, better than by any other, what kind of man you yourself are. For you show me there what your ideal of manhood is ; what kind of man you long inexpressibly to be, and would thank the gods, with your whole soul, for being if you could. *Carlyle.*

"Show some pity?" "I show it most of all 40 when I show justice." *Meas. for Meas.*, ii. 2.

Show the dullest clodpole, show the haughtiest featherhead, that a soul higher than himself is actually here ; were his knees stiffened into brass, he must down and worship. *Carlyle.*

Shrine of the mighty ! can it be / That this is all remains of thee? *Byron.*

Shrouded in baleful vapours, the genius of Burns was never seen in clear, azure splendour, enlightening the world ; but some beams from it did, by fits, pierce through ; and tinted those clouds with rainbow and orient colours into a glory and stern grandeur which men silently gazed on with wonder and tears. *Carlyle.*

Shun drugs and drinks which work the wit abuse ; clear minds, clean bodies, need no Sôma juice. *Sir Edwin Arnold.*

Shut not thy purse-strings always against 45 painted distress. *Lamb.*

Si ad naturam vivas, nunquam eris pauper ; si ad opinionem, nunquam dives—If you live according to the dictates of Nature, you will never be poor ; if according to the notions of men, you never will be rich. *Sen.*

Si antiquitatem spectes, est vetustissima ; si dignitatem, est honoratissima ; si jurisdictionem, est capacissima—If you consider its antiquity, it is most ancient ; if its dignity, it is most honourable ; if its jurisdiction, it is most extensive. *Coke, of the English House of Commons.*

Si bene commemini, causæ sunt quinque bibendi ; / Hospitis adventus, præsens sitis, atque futura, / Aut vini bonitas, aut quælibet altera causa—If I remember right, there are five excuses for drinking : the visit of a guest, present thirst, thirst to come, the goodness of the wine, or any other excuse you choose. *Père Sermond.*

Si cadere necesse est, occurrendum discrimini —If we must fall, let us manfully face the danger. *Tac.*

Si caput dolet omnia membra languent—If the head aches, all the members of the body become languid. *Pr.*

Si ce n'est pas là Dieu, c'est du moins son cousin-german—If that is not God, it is at least His cousin-german. *Mirabeau, of the rising sun as he lay on his death-bed.*

5 Si ce n'est toi, c'est ton frère — If you did not do it, it was your brother. *La Fontaine.*

Si claudo cohabites, subclaudicare disces— If you live with a lame man you will learn to limp. *Pr.*

Si Dieu n'existait pas, il faudrait l'inventer— If God did not exist, it would be necessary to invent him. *Voltaire.*

Si fecisti, nega ; or nega, quod fecisti—If you did it, deny it. *An old Jesuit maxim.*

Si foret in terris, rideret Democritus—If Democritus were on earth now, he would laugh. *Hor.*

10 Si fortuna juvat, caveto tolli ; / Si fortuna tonat, caveto mergi—If fortune favours you, be not lifted up ; if she fulminates, be not cast down. *Auson.*

Si fractus illabatur orbis, / Impavidum ferient ruinæ—If the world should fall in wreck about him, the ruins would crush him undaunted. *Hor. of the upright man.*

Si genus humanum, et mortalia temnitis arma ; / At sperate Deos memores fandi atque nefandi —If you despise the human race and mortal arms, yet expect that the gods will not be forgetful of right and wrong. *Virg.*

Si gravis brevis, si longus levis—If severe, short ; if long, light. *Pr.*

Si haces lo que estuviere de tu parte, / Pide al Cielo favor : ha de ayudarte—Hast thou done what was thy duty, trust Providence ; He leaves thee not. *Samaniego.*

15 Si j'avais la main pleine de vérités, je me garderais bien de l'ouvrir—If I had my hand full of truth, I would take good care how I opened it. *Fontenelle.*

Si j'avais le malheur d'être né prince — If I had had the misfortune of being born a prince. *Rousseau, in the commencement of a letter to the Duke of Würtemberg, who had asked his advice about the education of his son.*

Si je puis—If I can. *M.*

Si jeunesse savait ! si vieillesse pouvait !—If youth knew ; if age could ! *Pr.*

Si judicas, cognosce ; si regnas, jube—If you sit in judgment, investigate ; if you possess supreme power, sit in command. *Sen.*

20 Si l'adversité te trouve toujours sur tes pieds, la prospérité ne te fait pas aller plus vite—If adversity finds you always on foot, prosperity will not make you go faster. *Fr. Pr.*

Si la vie est misérable, elle est pénible à supporter ; si elle est heureuse, il est horrible de la perdre. L'un revient à l'autre—If our life is unhappy, it is painful to bear, and if it is happy, it is horrible to lose it. Thus, the one is pretty equal to the other. *La Bruyère.*

Si leonina pellis non satis est, assuenda vulpina--If the lion's skin is not enough, we must sew on the fox's. *Pr.*

Si monumentum requiris, circumspice—If you seek his monument, look around. *Inscription on St. Paul's, London, of Sir Christopher Wren.*

Si natura negat, facit indignatio versum—If nature denies the power, indignation makes verses. *Juv.*

Si non errasset, fecerat ille minus—If he had 25 not committed an error, his glory would have been less. *Mart.*

Si nous n'avions point de défauts, nous ne prendrions pas tant de plaisir à en remarquer dans les autres—If we had no faults ourselves, we should not take so much pleasure in noticing those of other people. *La Roche.*

Si nous ne nous flattions pas nous-mêmes, la flatterie des autres ne nous pourroit nuire— If we did not flatter ourselves, the flattery of others would not harm us. *Fr.*

Si parva licet componere magnis—If I may be allowed to compare small things with great. *Virg.*

Si possis suaviter, si non quocunque modo— Gently if you can ; if not, by some means or other.

Si qua voles apte nubere, nube pari—If you 30 wish to marry suitably, marry your equal. *Ovid.*

Si quid novisti rectius istis, / Candidus imperti ; si non, his utere mecum—If you know anything better than these maxims, frankly impart them to me ; if not, use these like me. *Hor.*

Si quis—If any one, *i.e.*, has objections to offer.

Si, quoties homines peccant, sua fulmina mittat / Jupiter, exiguo tempore inermis erit—If, as oft as men sin, Jove were to hurl his thunderbolts, he would soon be without weapons to hurl. *Ovid.*

Si sit prudentia—If you are but guided by prudence. *M. from Juv.*

Si tibi deficiant medici, medici tibi fiant / Hæc 35 tria ; mens hilaris, requies, moderata diæta— If you stand in need of medical advice, let these three things be your physicians : a cheerful mind, relaxation from business, and a moderate diet. *Schola Salern.*

Si tibi vis omnia subjicere, te subjice rationi— If you wish to subject everything to yourself, subject yourself first to reason. *Sen.*

Si trovano più ladri que forche—There are more thieves than gibbets. *It. Pr.*

Si veut le roi, si veut la loi—So wills the king, so wills the law. *Fr. L.*

Si vis amari, ama—If you wish to be loved, love. *Sen.*

Si vis me flere, dolendum est / Primum ipsi tibi 40 —If you wish me to weep, you must first show grief yourself. *Hor.*

Si vis pacem, para bellum—If you wish for peace, be ready for war.

Sic ait, et dicto citius tumida æquora placat— So speaks the god, and quicker than he speaks he smoothes the swelling seas. *Virg.*

Sic donec—Thus until. *M.*

Sic erat in fatis—So stood it in the decrees of fate. *Ovid.*

Sic fac omnia . . . tanquam spectet aliquis—Do everything as in the eye of another. *Sen.*

Sic itur ad astra—This is the way to the stars. *Virg.*

Sic leve, sic parvum est, animum quod laudis avarum / Subruit ac reficit—So light, so insignificant a thing is that which casts down or revives a soul that is greedy of praise. *Hor.*

5 Sic me servavit Apollo—Thus was I served by Apollo. *Hor.*

Sic omnia fatis / In pejus ruere et retro sublapsa referri—Thus all things are doomed to change for the worse and retrograde. *Virg.*

Sic præsentibus utaris voluptatibus, ut futuris non noceas—So enjoy present pleasures as not to mar those to come. *Sen.*

Sic transit gloria mundi—It is so the glory of the world passes away.

Sic utere tuo ut alienum non lædas—So use what is your own as not to injure what is another's. *L.*

10 Sic visum Veneri, cui placet impares / Formas, atque animos sub juga ahenea / Sævo mittere cum joco—Such is the will of Venus, whose pleasure it is in cruel sport to subject to her brazen yoke persons and tempers ill-matched. *Hor.*

Sich mitzutheilen ist Natur ; Mitgetheiltes aufnehmen, wie es gegeben wird, ist Bildung—It is characteristic to Nature to impart itself ; to take up what is imparted as it is given in culture. *Goethe.*

Sich selbst bekämpfen ist der allerschwerste Krieg ; / Sich selbst besiegen ist der allerschönste Sieg—To maintain a conflict with one's self is the hardest of all wars ; to overcome one's self is the noblest of all victories. *Logau.*

Sich selbst hat niemand ausgelernt—No man ever yet completed his apprenticeship. *Goethe.*

Sich über das Höherstehende alles Urtheils zu enthalten, ist eine zu edle Eigenschaft, als das häufig sein könnte—To refrain from all criticism of what ranks above us is too noble a virtue to be of every-day occurrence. *W. v. Humboldt.*

15 Sickness is catching ; Oh, were favour so, / Yours would I catch, sweet Hernia, ere I go ; / My ear would catch your voice, my eye your eye, / My tongue should catch your tongue's sweet melody. *Mid. N.'s Dream,* i. i.

Sicut ante—As before.

Sicut columba—As a dove. *M.*

Sicut lilium—As a lily. *M.*

Sie glauben mit einander zu streiten, / Und fühlen das Unrecht von beiden Seiten—They think they are quarrelling with one another, and both sides feel they are in the wrong. *Goethe.*

20 Sie scheinen mir aus einem edeln Haus, / Sie sehen stolz und zufrieden aus—They appear to me of a noble family ; they look proud and discontented. *Goethe, Frosch in the witches' cellar in " Faust."*

Sie sind voll Honig die Blumen ; / Aber die Biene nur findet die Süssigkeit aus—The flowers are full of honey, but only the bee finds out the sweetness. *Goethe.*

Sie streiten um ein Ei, und lassen die Henne fliegen—They dispute about an egg, and let the hens fly away. *Ger. Pr.*

Sigh no more, ladies, sigh no more ! / Men were deceivers ever ; / One foot in sea and one on shore, / To one thing constant never. *Percy.*

Sight before hearsay. *Dan. Pr.*

Sight must be reinforced by insight before 25 souls can be discerned as well as manners, ideas as well as objects, realities and relations as well as appearances and accidental connections. *Whipple.*

Silence and discretion are specially becoming in a woman, and to remain quietly at home. *Euripides.*

Silence at the proper season is wisdom, and better than any speech. *Plutarch.*

Silence gives (or implies) consent. *Pr.*

Silence is a friend that will never betray. *Confucius.*

Silence is a solvent that destroys personality, 30 and gives us leave to be great and universal. *Emerson.*

Silence is better than unmeaning words. *Pythagoras.*

Silence is deep as eternity ; speech is shallow as time. *Carlyle.*

Silence is more eloquent than words. *Carlyle.*

Silence is one of the great arts of conversation. *Cic.*

Silence is the best resolve for him who dis- 35 trusts himself. *La Roche.*

Silence is the chaste blossom of love. *Heine.*

Silence is the consummate eloquence of sorrow. *W. Winter.*

Silence is the element in which great things fashion themselves together ; that at length they may emerge, full-formed and majestic, into the daylight of life, which they are thenceforth to rule. *Carlyle.*

Silence is the eternal duty of man. He won't get to any real understanding of what is complex, and what is more than any other pertinent to his interests, without maintaining silence. *Carlyle.*

Silence is the mother of truth. *Disraeli.* 40

Silence is the perfectest herald of joy ; I were but little happy, if I could say how much. *Much Ado,* ii. i.

Silence is the sanctuary of discretion (*Klugheit*). It not only conceals secrets but also faults. *Zachariä.*

Silence is the sleep that nourishes wisdom. *Bacon.*

Silence is wisdom, when speaking is folly. *Pr.*

Silence often expresses more powerfully than 45 speech the verdict and judgment of society. *Disraeli.*

Silence, silence ; and be distant, ye profane, with your jargonings and superficial babblements, when a man has anything to do. *Carlyle.*

Silent leges inter arma—Laws are silent in time of war. *Cic.*

Silent men, like still waters, are deep and dangerous. *Pr.*

Silver from the living / Is gold in the giving : / Gold from the dying / Is but silver a-flying. / Gold and silver from the dead / Turn too often into lead. *Fuller.*

Simel et simul—Once and together.

Simile gaudet simili—Like loves like. *Pr.*

Similia similibus curantur—Like things are cured by like.

Simpering is but a lay-hypocrisy : / Give it a corner and the clue undoes. *George Herbert.*

5 Simple as it seems, it was a great discovery that the key of knowledge could turn both ways, that it could open, as well as lock, the door of power to the many. *Lowell.*

Simple gratitude, untinctured with love, is all the return an ingenuous mind can bestow for former benefits. Love for love is all the reward we expect or desire. *Goldsmith.*

Simplex sigillum veri—Simplicity is the seal of truth. *M. of Boerhave.*

Simplicity in character, in manners, in style : in all things the supreme excellence is simplicity. *Longfellow.*

Simplicity is in the intention, purity in the affection ; simplicity turns to God, purity unites with and enjoys him. *Thomas à Kempis.*

10 Simplicity is Nature's first step, and the last of art. *P. J. Bailey.*

Simplicity is, of all things, the hardest to be copied. *Steele.*

Simplicity is the straightforwardness of a soul which refuses to reflect on itself or its deeds. Many are sincere without being simple ; they do not wish to be taken for other than they are, but they are always afraid of being taken for what they are not. *Fénelon.*

Sin every day takes out a patent for some new invention. *Whipple.*

Sin has many tools, but a lie is the handle which fits them all. *Holmes.*

15 Sin is like the bee, with honey in its mouth but a sting in its tail. *H. Ballou.*

Sin is not a monster to be mused on, but an impotence to be got rid of. *Matthew Arnold.*

Sin is too dull to see beyond himself. *Tennyson.*

Sin seen from the thought is a diminution or loss ; seen from the conscience or will, it is a pravity or bad. *Emerson.*

Since every Jack became a gentleman, / There's many a gentle person made a Jack. *Rich. III.,* i. 3.

20 Since grief but aggravates thy loss, / Grieve not for what is past. *Percy.*

Since not only judgments have their awards, but mercies their commissions, snatch not at every favour, nor think thyself passed by if they fall upon thy neighbour. *Sir T. Browne.*

Since the invention of printing no state can now any longer be formed purely, slowly, and by degrees from itself. *Jean Paul.*

Since time is not a person we can overtake when he is past, let us honour him with mirth and cheerfulness of heart while he is passing. *Goethe.*

Since trifles make the sum of human things, / And half our misery from our foibles springs. *Hannah More.*

25 Since we have a good loaf, let us not look for cheesecakes. *Cervantes.*

Sincere wise speech (even) is but an imperfect corollary, and insignificant outer manifestation of sincere wise thought. *Carlyle.*

Sincerity, a deep, great, genuine sincerity, is the first characteristic of all men in any way heroic. *Carlyle.*

Sincerity gives wings to power. (?)

Sincerity is impossible unless it pervades the whole being ; and the pretence saps the very foundations of character. *Lowell.*

Sincerity is the face of the soul, as dissimula-30 tion is the mask. *Daniel Dubay.*

Sincerity is the indispensable ground of all conscientiousness, and by consequence of all heartfelt religion. *Kant.*

Sincerity is the way to heaven. To think how to be sincere is the way of man. *Confucius.*

Sincerity is true wisdom. *Tillotson.*

Sincerity makes the least man to be of more value than the most talented hypocrite. *Spurgeon.*

Sine amicitia vitam esse nullam—There is no 35 life without friendship. *Cic.*

Sine Cerere et Baccho, friget Venus—Without Ceres and Bacchus, Venus will starve to death, *i.e.*, without sustenance and good cheer, love can't last. *Ter.*

Sine cortica natare—To swim without bladders.

Sine cura—Without care, *i.e.*, in receipt of a salary without a care or office.

Sine die—Without appointing a day.

Sine invidia—Without envy ; from no invidious 40 feeling.

Sine ira et studio—Without aversion and without preference. *Tac.*

Sine nervis—Without force ; weak.

Sine odio—Without hatred.

Sine prole—Without offspring.

Sine qua non—An indispensable condition, *lit.* 45 without which not.

Sine virtute esse amicitia nullo pacto potest—There cannot possibly be friendship without virtue. *Sall.*

Singing should enchant. *Joubert.*

Singula de nobis anni prædantur euntes—The years as they pass bereave us first of one thing and then another. *Hor.*

Singula quid referam? nil non mortale tenemus, / Pectoris exceptis ingeniique bonis—Why go I into details? we have nothing that is not perishable, except what our hearts and our intellects endow us with. *Ovid.*

Singularity shows something wrong in the 50 mind. *Clarissa.*

Sink not in spirit: who aimeth at the sky / Shoots higher much than he that means a tree. *George Herbert.*

Sink the Bible to the bottom of the ocean, and man's obligations to God would be unchanged. He would have the same path to tread, only his lamp and his guide would be gone ; he would have the same voyage to make, only his compass and chart would be overboard. *Ward Beecher.*

Sinks to the grave with unperceived decay, / while resignation gently slopes the way. *Goldsmith.*

Sins and debts are aye mair than we think them. *Sc. Pr.*

Sint ut sunt, aut non sint—Let them be as they 55 are, or not at all.

Sir, a well-placed dash makes half the wit of our writers of modern humour. *Goldsmith.*

Sir Fine-face, Sir Fair-hands ; but see thou to it / That thine own fineness, Lancelot, some fine day / Undo thee not. *Tennyson.*

Sir, he hath fed of the dainties that are bred in a book. *Love's L. Lost,* iv. 2.

Sire, je n'avais pas besoin de cette hypothèse— Your Majesty, I had no need of that hypothesis. *Laplace's answer to Napoleon, who had asked why in his "Méchanique Céleste" he had made no mention of God.*

Sirve a señor, y sabras que es dolor—Serve a great lord, and you will know what sorrow is. *Sp. Pr.*

5 Siste, viator—Stop, traveller.

Sit in your own place, and no man can make you rise. *Pr.*

Sit mihi quod nunc est, etiam minus ; ut mihi vivam / Quod superest ævi, si quid superesse volunt Di—May I continue to possess what I have now, or even less ; so I may live the remainder of my days after my own plan, if the gods will that any should remain. *Hor.*

Sit piger ad pœnas princeps, ad præmia velox —A prince should be slow to punish, prompt to reward. *Ovid.*

Sit sine labe decus—Let my honour be without stain. *M.*

10 Sit tibi terra levis—May earth lie light upon thee.

Sit tua cura sequi ; me duce tutus eris—Be it your care to follow ; with me for your guide you will be safe. *Ovid.*

Sit venia verbis—Pardon my words.

Sive pium vis hoc, sive hoc muliebre vocari ; / Confiteor misero molle cor esse mihi— Whether you call my heart affectionate, or you call it womanish, I confess that to my misfortune it is soft. *Ovid.*

Six feet of earth make all men equal. *Pr.*

15 Six hours to sleep allot : to law be six addressed ; / Pray four : feast two : the Muses claim the rest. *On the fly-leaf of an old law-book from Coke. See* Sex horas, &c.

σκιᾶς ὄναρ ἄνθρωποι—Men are the dream of a shadow. *Pindar.*

Skilful pilots gain their reputation from storms and tempests. *Epicurus.*

Skill is stronger than strength. *Pr.*

Skill is the united force of experience, intellect and passion in their operation on manual labour. *Ruskin.*

20 Skill to do comes of doing ; knowledge comes by eyes always open, and working hands ; and there is no knowledge that is not power. *Emerson.*

Sky is the part of creation in which Nature has done more for the sake of pleasing man, more for the sole and evident purpose of talking to him and teaching him, than in any other of her works, and it is just the part in which we least attend to her. *Ruskin.*

Slackness breeds worms ; but the sure traveller, / Though he alight sometimes, still goeth on. *George Herbert.*

Slander and detraction can have no influence, can make no impression, upon the righteous Judge above. None to thy prejudice, but a sad and fatal one to their own. *Thomas à Kempis.*

Slander expires at a good woman's door. *Dan. Pr.*

Slander is a poison which extinguishes charity, 25 both in the slanderer and the person who listens to it. *St. Bernard.*

Slander lives upon succession ; / For ever housed, where it once gets possession. *Com. of Errors,* iii. 1.

Slander, / Whose edge is sharper than the sword, whose tongue / Out-venoms all the worms of Nile, whose breath / Rides on the parting winds, and doth belie / All corners of the world. *Cymbeline,* iii. 4.

Slander's mark was ever yet the fair ; / . . . A crow that flies in heaven's sweetest air. *Shakespeare.*

Slanderers do not hurt me, because they do not hit me. *Socrates.*

Slave or free is settled in heaven for a man. 30 *Carlyle.*

Slave to no sect, who takes no private road, / But looks through Nature up to Nature's God. *Pope.*

Slave to silver's but a slave to smoke. *Quarles.*

Slavery is a weed that grows on every soil. *Burke.*

Slavery is an inherent inheritance of a large portion of the human race, to whom the more you give of their own free will, the more slaves they will make themselves. *Ruskin.*

Slaves cannot breathe in England ; if their 35 lungs / Receive our air, that moment they are free ; / They touch our country, and their shackles fall. *Cowper.*

Sleep after toil, port after stormy seas, / Ease after war, death after life, doth greatly please. *Spenser.*

Sleep and death, two twins of winged race, / Of matchless swiftness, but of silent pace. *Pope's Homer.*

Sleep, gentle sleep, / Nature's soft nurse, how have I frighted thee, / That thou no more wilt weigh my eyelids down, / And steep my senses in forgetfulness ? *2 Hen. IV.,* iii. 1.

Sleep hath its own world, / A boundary between the things misnamed / Death and Existence. *Byron.*

Sleep is for the inhabitants of planets only ; in 40 another time men will sleep and wake continually at once. The great part of our body, of our humanity, yet sleeps a deep sleep. (?)

Sleep is the best cure for waking troubles. *Cervantes.*

Sleep is the sole reviver (*Labsal*) of the afflicted. *Platen.*

Sleep is to a man what winding up is to a clock. *Schopenhauer.*

Sleep lingers all our lifetime about our eyes, as night hovers all day in the boughs of the fir-tree. *Emerson.*

Sleep no more, / Macbeth does murder sleep. 45 *Macb.,* ii. 2.

Sleep seldom visits sorrow ; when it doth, / It is a comforter. *Tempest,* i. 1.

Sleep, that knits up the ravell'd sleave of care, / The death of each day's life, sore labour's bath, / Balm of hurt minds, great nature's second course, / Chief nourisher in life's feast. *Macb.,* ii. 2.

Sleep, that sometimes shuts up sorrow's eye. *Mid. N.'s Dream,* iii. 2.

Sleep, the antechamber of the grave. *Jean Paul.*

Sleep the sleep that knows not breaking, / Morn of toil, nor night of waking. *Scott.*

Slight not the smallest loss, whether it be / In love or honour; take account of all : / Shine like the sun in every corner : see / Whether thy stock of credit swell or fall. *George Herbert.*

Slippery is the flagstone at the great house door. *Gael. Pr.*

5 Sloth is the key to poverty. *Pr.*

Sloth, like rust, consumes faster than labour wears, while the used key is always bright *Ben. Franklin.*

Sloth makes all things difficult, but industry all things easy. *Ben. Franklin.*

Sloth never arrived at the attainment of a good wish. *Cervantes.*

Sloth turneth the edge of wit, study sharpeneth the mind ; a thing, be it never so easy, is hard to the idle ; a thing, be it never so hard, is easy to wit well employed. *John Lily.*

10 Slovenly (a) and negligent manner of writing is a disobliging mark of want of respect. *Blair.*

Slow and steady wins the race. *Lloyd.*

Slow fire makes sweet malt. *Pr.*

Slow-footed counsel is most sure to gain ; / Rashness still brings repentance in her train. *Lucian.*

Slow help is no help. *Pr.*

15 Slow rises worth by poverty depress'd. *Johnson.*

Slow to resolve, but in performance quick. *Dryden.*

Slowly and sadly we laid him down, / From the field of his fame fresh and gory : / We carved not a line, and we raised not a stone, / But we left him alone with his glory. *Wolfe.*

Sma' fish are better than nane. *Sc. Pr.*

Small cheer and great welcome make a merry feast. *Com. of Errors, iii. 1.*

20 Small curs are not regarded when they grin ;/ But great men tremble when the lion roars. *2 Hen. VI., iii. 1.*

Small curses upon great occasions are but so much waste of our strength and soul's health to no manner of purpose ; they are like sparrow-shot fired against a bastion. *Sterne.*

Small debts are like small shot — they are rattling on every side, and can scarcely be escaped without a wound. Great debts are like cannon of loud noise, but of little danger. *Johnson.*

Small draughts of philosophy lead to atheism, but larger bring back to God. *Bacon.*

Small faults indulged let in greater. *Pr.*

25 Small have continued plodders ever won / Save bare authority from others' books. *Love's L. Lost, i. 1.*

Small herbs have grace, great weeds do grow apace. *Rich. III., ii. 4.*

Small is it that thou canst trample the earth with its injuries under thy foot, as old Greek Zeno trained he : thou canst love the earth while it injures thee, and even because it injures thee ; for this a Greater than Zeno was needed, and he too was sent. *Carlyle.*

Small Latin and less Greek. *Ben Jonson of Shakespeare's knowledge.*

Small-pot-soon-hot style of eloquence is what our county conventions often exhibit. *Emerson.*

30 Small profits and quick returns. *Pr.*

Small rain lays great dust. *Pr.*

Small service is true service while it lasts. / Of humblest friends, bright creature ! scorn not one : / The daisy, by the shadow that it casts, / Protects the lingering dewdrop from the sun. *Wordsworth, to a child.*

Small thanks to the man for keeping his hands clean who would not touch the work but with gloves on. *Carlyle.*

Smallest of mortals, when mounted aloft by circumstances, come to seem great, smallest of phenomena connected with them are treated as important, and must be sedulously scanned, and commented on with loud emphasis. *Carlyle.*

35 Smelfungus in the grand portico of the Pantheon says, "'Tis nothing but a huge cockpit." *Sterne.*

Smile (Fortune), and we smile, the lords of many lands ; / Frown, and we smile, the lords of our own hands ; / For man is man and master of his fate. *Tennyson.*

Smiles are the language of love. *Hare.*

Smiles form the channel of a future tear. *Byron.*

Smiles from reason flow, / To brute denied, and are of love the food. *Milton.*

40 Smooth runs the water where the brook is deep ; / And in his simple show he harbours treason. / The fox barks not when he would steal the lamb. *2 Henry VI., iii. 1.*

Smooth waters run deep. *Pr.*

Smooth words make smooth ways. *Pr.*

Smuler ere og Bröd—Even crumbs are bread. *Dan. Pr.*

Snarl if you please, but you shall snarl without. *Dryden.*

45 Snatch from the ashes of your sires / The embers of their former fires ; / And he who in the strife expires / Will add to theirs a name of fear / That tyranny shall quake to hear, / And leave his sons a hope, a fame, / They too would rather die than shame. *Byron.*

So behave that the odour of your actions may enhance the general sweetness of the atmosphere. *Thoreau.*

So careful of the type she seems, / So careless of the single life. *Tennyson.*

So comes a reckoning when the banquet's o'er,— / The dreadful reckoning, and men smile no more. *Gay.*

So dawning day has brought relief— / Fareweel our night o' sorrow. *Burns.*

50 So dress and so conduct yourself that persons who have been in your company will not recollect what you had on. *Rev. John Newton.*

So far as a man thinks he is free. *Emerson.*

So far is it from being true that men are naturally equal, that no two people can be half an hour together but one shall acquire an evident superiority over the other. *Johnson.*

So full of shapes is fancy, that it alone is high-fantastical. *Twelfth Night*, i. 1.

So gieb mir auch die Zeiten wieder, / Da ich noch selbst im Werden war—Then give me back the time when I myself was still a-growing. *Goethe*.

So, here hath been dawning ! Another blue day ; / Think wilt thou let it / Slip useless away. / Out of Eternity / This new day is born ; / Into Eternity / At night doth return. / Behold it aforetime / No eye ever did : / So soon it for ever / From all eyes is hid. / Here hath been dawning, &c. *Carlyle on To-day*.

So I do my part to others, let them think of me what they will or can. . . . If I should regard such things, it were in another's power to defeat my charity, and evil should be stronger than good. But difficulties are so far from cooling Christians that they whet them. *George Herbert*.

5 So lang man lebt, sei man lebendig—So long as you live, be living. *Goethe*.

So live with men, as if God saw you ; so speak to God, as if men heard you. *Sen*.

So lonely 'twas, that God himself / Scarce seeméd there to be. *Coleridge*.

So long as a man is capable of self-renewal he is a living being. *Amiel*.

So long as any Ideal (any soul of truth) does, in never so confused a manner, exist and work within the Actual, it is a tolerable business. Not so when the Ideal has wholly departed, and the Actual owns to no soul of truth any longer. *Carlyle*.

10 So long as the "Holy Place" in their souls is left in possession of powerless opinions, men are practically without God in this world. *Froude*.

So long as you live and work, you will not escape being misunderstood ; to that you must resign yourself once for all. Be silent. *Goethe*.

So magnificent a thing is Will incarnated in a creature like fashion with ourselves, that we run to witness all manifestations thereof. *Carlyle*.

So many servants, so many enemies. *Pr*.

So many slaves, so many enemies. *Pr*.

15 So may he rest ; his faults lie gently on him. *Hen. VIII.*, iv. 2.

So much in the world depends upon getting what we want. Prosperity is to the human heart like a sunny south wall to a peach. *Holme Lee*.

So much of our time is preparation, so much is routine, and so much retrospect, that the pith of each man's genius contracts itself to a very few hours. *Emerson*.

So much to do, / So little done, such things to be. *Tennyson*.

So nigh is grandeur to our dust, / So near is God to man, / When Duty whispers low, "Thou must," / The youth replies, "I can !" *Emerson*.

20 So schaff' ich am sausenden Webstuhl der Zeit / Und wirke der Gottheit lebendiges Kleid—'Tis thus at the roaring loom of Time I ply, / And weave for God the garment thou seest him by (*lit.* the living garment of the Deity). *Goethe*.

So soon as one's heart is tender it is weak. When it is beating so warmly against the breast, and the throat is, as it were, tied tightly, and one strives to press the tears from one's eyes and feels an incomprehensible joy as they begin to flow, then we are so weak that we are fettered by chains of flowers, not because they have become strong through any magic chain, but because we tremble lest we should tear them asunder. *Goethe*.

So soon as people try honestly to see all they can of anything, they come to a point where a noble dimness begins. They see more than others ; but the consequence of their seeing more is, that they feel they cannot see at all ; and the more intense their perception, the more the crowd of things which they partly see will multiply upon them. *Ruskin*.

So soon as sacrifice becomes a duty and necessity to man, I see no limit to the horizon which opens before him. *Renan*.

So spiritual (*geistig*) is our whole daily life ; all that we do springs out of mystery, spirit, invisible force ; only like a little cloud-image, or Armida's palace, air-built, does the actual body itself forth from the great mystic deep. *Carlyle*.

So stirbt ein Held, anbetungsvoll—So dies a 25 hero to be worshipped. *Schiller*.

So study evermore is overshot ; / While it doth study to have what it would, / It doth forget to do the thing it should ; / And when it hath the thing it hunteth most, / 'Tis won as towns with fire,—so won, so lost. *Love's L. Lost*, i. 1.

So sweetly she bade me adieu, / I thought that she bade me return. *Shenstone*.

So teach us to number our days, that we may apply our hearts unto wisdom. *Bible*.

So thou be above it, make the world serve thy purpose, but do not thou serve it. *Goethe*.

So thou be good, slander doth but approve / 30 Thy worth the greater. *Shakespeare*.

So to living or dead let the solemn bell call ; / Sleeping or waking, time passes with all. *Dr. Walter Smith*.

So turns the faithful needle to the pole, / Though mountains rise between and oceans roll. *Darwin*.

So we grew together, / Like to a double cherry, seeming parted, / But yet a union in partition ; / Two lovely berries moulded on one stem. / So with two seeming bodies, but one heart. *Mid. N.'s Dream*, iii. 2.

So wise, so young, they say, do ne'er live long. *Rich. III.*, iii. 1.

So wonderful is human nature, and its varied 35 ties / Are so involved and complicate, that none / May hope to keep his inward spirit pure, / And walk without perplexity through life. *Goethe*.

So work the honey bees ; / Creatures that, by a rule in Nature, teach / The art of order to a peopled kingdom. *Henry V.*, i. 2.

Soar not too high to fall, but stoop to rise. *Fuller*.

Sobald du dir vertraust, sobald weisst du zu leben—So soon as you feel confidence in yourself, you know the art of life. *Goethe, Mephisto in* "*Faust*."

Sobriety, severity, and self-respect is the foundation of all true sociality. *Thoreau.*

Social intercourse makes us the more able to bear with ourselves and others. *Goethe.*

Social order without liberty makes of man only a product ; liberty makes him the citizen of a better world. *Schiller.*

Societatis vinculum est ratio et oratio—Reason and speech are the bond of society. *Cic.*

5 Society always consists, in greatest part, of young and foolish persons. *Emerson.*

Society cannot do without cultivated men. As soon as the first wants are satisfied, the higher wants become imperative. *Emerson.*

Society develops wit, but contemplation alone forms genius. *Mme. de Staël.*

Society does not in any age prevent a man from being what he can be. *Carlyle.*

Society does not like to have any breath of question blown on the existing order. *Emerson.*

10 Society does not love its unmaskers. *Emerson.*

Society everywhere is in conspiracy against the manhood of every one of its members. *Emerson.*

Society has always a destructive influence upon an artist :—by its sympathy with his meanest powers ; secondly, by its chilling want of understanding of his greatest ; and, thirdly, by its vain occupation of his time and thoughts. *Ruskin.*

Society has always under one or the other figure two authentic revelations, of a God and of a devil. *Carlyle.*

Society has only one law, and that is custom. *Hamerton.*

15 Society is a long series of uprising ridges, which from the first to the last offer no valley of repose. Wherever you take your stand, you are looked down upon by those above you, and reviled and pelted by those below you. *Bulwer Lytton.*

Society is a masked ball, where every one hides his real character, and reveals it by hiding. *Emerson.*

Society is a republic. When an individual endeavours to lift himself above his fellows, he is dragged down by the mass, either by ridicule or calumny. *Victor Hugo.*

Society is a troop of thinkers, and the best heads among them take the best places. *Emerson.*

Society is a wave. The wave moves onward, but the water of which it is composed does not. . . . Its unity is only phenomenal. *Emerson.*

20 Society is, and must be, based upon appearances, and not upon the deepest realities. *Hamerton.*

Society is barbarous, until every industrious man can get his living without dishonest customs. *Emerson.*

Society is composed of two great classes : those who have more dinners than appetite, and those who have more appetite than dinners. *Chamfort.*

Society is divisible into two classes : shearers and shorn. *Talleyrand.*

Society is ever under the imperious necessity of moving onward in legal forms, nor can such forms be evaded without the most serious disasters forthwith ensuing. *Draper.*

Society is founded upon cloth. *Carlyle.* 25

Society is full of infirm people, who incessantly summon others to serve them. They contrive everywhere to exhaust for their single comfort the entire means and appliances of that luxury to which our invention has yet attained. *Emerson.*

Society is infected with rude, cynical, restless, and frivolous persons, who prey upon the rest, and whom no public opinion concentrated into good manners, forms accepted by the sense of all, can reach. *Emerson.*

Society is like the echoing hills ; it gives back to the speaker his words, groan for groan, song for song. *Dr. David Thomas.*

Society is no comfort to one not sociable. *Cymbeline, iv. 2.*

Society is servile from want of will, and there- 30 fore the world wants saviours and religions. *Emerson.*

Society is the atmosphere of souls, and we necessarily imbibe from it something which is either infectious or hurtful. *Bp. Hall.*

Society is the grandmother of humanity through her daughters the inventions. *C. J. Weber.*

Society is the standing wonder of our existence ; a true region of the supernatural ; as it were, a second all-embracing life, wherein our first individual life becomes doubly and trebly alive, and whatever of infinitude was in us bodies itself forth, and becomes visible and active. *Carlyle.*

Society is well governed when the people obey the magistrates, and the magistrates obey the laws. *Solon.*

Society lives by faith, and develops by science. 35 *Amiel.*

Society rests upon conscience, not upon science. *Amiel.*

Society will pardon much to genius and special gifts ; but, being in its nature conventional, it loves what is conventional. *Emerson.*

Society wishes to be amused. I do not wish to be amused. I wish that life should not be cheap, but sacred ; the days to be as centuries, loaded, fragrant. *Emerson.*

Socius fidelis anchora tuta est—A faithful companion is a sure anchor. *M.*

Socrates quidem quum rogaretur cujatem se 40 esse diceret, Mundanum, inquit. Totius enim mundi se incolam et civem arbitrabatur—When Socrates was asked of what country he professed to be a citizen, he answered, "Of the world ;" for he considered himself an inhabitant and citizen of the whole world. *Cic.*

Soft-heartedness, in times like these, / Shows softness in the upper storey. *Lowell.*

Soft is the music that would charm for ever ; / The flower of sweetest smell is shy and lowly. *Wordsworth.*

Soft, or fair, words butter no parsnips. *Pr.*

Soft pity enters at an iron gate. *Shakespeare.*

Soft words win hard hearts. *Pr.* 45

"Softly ! softly !" caught the monkey. *Negro Pr.*

Sogno d'infermi—A sick man's dream. *Petrarch.*

Soi-disant—Self-styled. *Fr.*

Sol crescentes decedens duplicat umbras-- The setting sun doubles the increasing shadows. *Virg.*

Sol occubuit; nox nulla secuta est—The sun is set; no night has followed.

Sola Deo salus—Safety is from God alone. *M.*

Sola juvat virtus—Virtue alone assists. *M.*

Sola nobilitas virtus—Virtue is the only nobility. *M.*

5 Sola salus servire Deo—The only safety is in serving God.

Sola virtus invicta—Virtue alone is invincible. *M.*

Solamen miseris socios habuisse doloris—It is some comfort to the wretched to have others to share in their woe.

Soldats ! si les cornettes vous manquent, vous trouverez toujours mon panache blanc au chemin de l'honneur et de la gloire—Soldiers ! if you don't hear the bugle-call, you will always see my white plume in the path of honour and glory ! *Henry IV. at Ivry.*

Soldiers in peace are like chimneys in summer. *Lord Burleigh.*

10 Soldiers (there are) of the ploughshare as well as of the sword. *Ruskin.*

Soldiers ! what I have to offer you is fatigue, danger, struggle, and death ; the chill of the cold night in the free air, and heat under the burning sun ; no lodgings, no munitions, no provisions, but forced marches, dangerous watchposts, and the continual struggle with the bayonet against batteries. Those who love freedom and their country may follow me ! *Garibaldi to his Roman soldiers.* (That is the most glorious speech I ever heard in my life. *Kossuth.*)

"Solem præ jaculorum multitudine et sagittarum non videbis." "In umbra igitur pugnabimus" — "You will not see the sun for the clouds of javelins and arrows." "We shall fight in the shade then." *Cic. The Persian to Leonidas at Thermopylæ, and Leonidas' answer.*

Solem quis dicere falsum audeat ?—Who dares call the sun a liar ? *Virg.*

Soli Deo gloria—To God alone be glory. *M.*

15 Soli Deo honor et gloria—To God alone be honour and glory. *M.*

Solicitude about the future never profits ; we feel no evil till it comes ; and when we feel it, no counsel (*Rath*) helps us ; wisdom is always too early or too late. *Rückert.*

Solid pudding against empty praise. *Pope.*

Solitude can be well applied and sit righ', upon but very few persons. They must have knowledge of the world to see the follies of it, and virtue enough to despise all the vanity. *Cowley.*

Solitude cherishes great virtues and destroys little ones. *Sydney Smith.*

20 Solitude dulls the thought, too much company dissipates it. (?)

Solitude is a good school, but the world is the best theatre ; the institution is best there, but the practice here ; the wilderness hath the advantage of discipline, and society opportunities of perfection. *Jeremy Taylor.*

Solitude is as needful to the imagination as society is wholesome for the character. *Lowell.*

Solitude is impracticable, and society fatal. *Emerson.*

Solitude is not measured by the miles of space that intervene between a man and his fellows. The really diligent student in one of the crowded hives of Cambridge College is as solitary as a dervish in the desert. *Thoreau.*

Solitude is often the best society. *Pr.* 25

Solitude is the despair of fools, the torment of the wicked, and the joy of the good. (?)

Solitude is the home of the strong ; silence, their prayer. *Ravignan.*

Solitude sometimes is best society, / And short retirement urges sweet return. *Milton.*

Solitude, the safeguard of mediocrity, is to genius the stern friend, the cold, obscure shelter where moult the wings that will bear it farther than suns and stars. He who would inspire and lead his race must be defended from travelling with the souls of other men, from living, breathing, reading, and writing in the daily time-worn yoke of their opinions. *Emerson.*

Solitudinem faciunt, pacem appellant—They 30 make a solitude, and call it peace.

Sollen dich die Dohlen nicht umschrein, / Musst du nicht Knopf auf dem Kirchthurm sein—If jackdaws are not to scream around you, you must not be a ball on the church spire. *Goethe.*

Sollicitæ mentes speque metuque pavent — Minds that are ill at ease are agitated both with hope and fear. *Ovid.*

Sollicitant alii remis freta cæca, ruuntque / In ferrum : penetrant aulas, et limina regum —Some disturb unknown seas with oars, some rush upon the sword ; some push their way into courts and the portals of kings. *Virg.*

Solo cedit, quicquid solo plantatur—Whatever is planted in the soil goes with it. *L.*

Solo Deo salus — Salvation from God alone. 35 *M.*

Solo e pensoso—Alone and pensive. *Petrarch.*

Solvit ad diem—He paid to the day. *L.*

Solvitur ambulando—The problem is solved by walking, *i.e.*, the theoretical puzzle by a practical test.

Solvuntur risu tabulæ—The case is dismissed amid laughter. *Hor.*

σώματα πόλλα τρέφειν, καὶ δώματα πόλλ' 40 ἀνεγείρειν / 'Ατραπὸς εἰς πενίην ἐστὶν ἑτοιμοτάτη—To feed many mouths and build many houses is the directest road to poverty. *Gr.*

Some are atheists only in fair weather. (?)

Some are born great, some achieve greatness, and some have greatness thrust upon them. *Twelfth Night,* ii. 5.

Some are cursed with the fulness of satiety ; and how can they bear the ills of life when its very pleasures fatigue them ? *Colton.*

Some are so intent upon acquiring the superfluities of life that they sacrifice its necessaries in this foolish pursuit. *Goldsmith.*

Some books are drenched sands, on which a great soul's wealth lies in heaps, like a wrecked argosy. *Alex. Smith.*

Some books are edifices to stand as they are built ; some are hewn stones ready to form a part of future edifices ; some are quarries from which stones are to be split for shaping and after use. *Holmes.*

Some books are lees frae end to end, / And some big lees were never penn'd ; / E'en ministers they hae been kenn'd, / In holy rapture, / A rousing whid at times to vend, / And nail't wi' Scripture. *Burns.*

Some books are to be tasted, others to be swallowed, and some few to be chewed and digested. *Bacon.*

Some Cupid kills with arrows, some with traps. *Much Ado About Nothing*, iv. 1.

Some dire misfortune to portend, / No enemy can match a friend. *Swift.*

5 Some drink because they're wet, and some because they're dry. *Saying.*

Some evils are cured by contempt. *Pr.*

Some falls are means the happier to rise. *Shakespeare.*

Some faults are so nearly allied to excellence that we can scarce weed out the vice without eradicating the virtue. *Goldsmith.*

Some folk's tongues are like the clocks as run on strikin', not to tell you the time o' the day, but because there's summat wrong i' their inside. *George Eliot.*

10 Some for renown, on scraps of learning dote, / And think they grow immortal as they quote. *Young.*

Some friend is a companion at the table, and will not continue in the day of thy affliction. *Ecclus.*

Some glances of real beauty may be seen in the faces of those who dwell in true meekness. *Thoreau.*

Some grief shows much of love, / But much of grief shows still more want of wit. *Rom. and Jul.*, iii. 5.

Some hae meat that canna eat, / And some would eat that want it ; / But we hae meat and we can eat, / Sae let the Lord be thankit. *Burns.*

15 Some have been thought brave because they were afraid to run away. *Pr.*

Some men are born anvils, some are born hammers. (?)

Some men are like nails, easily drawn ; others are like rivets, not drawable at all. *John Burroughs.*

Some men are wise, and some are otherwise. *Pr.*

Some men, at the approach of a dispute, neigh like horses. Unless there be an argument going on, they think nothing is doing. *Emerson.*

20 Some men demand rough treatment everywhere. *S. C. Hall.*

Some men go through a forest and see no firewood. *Pr.*

Some men have just imagination enough to spoil their judgment. (?)

Some men, like spaniels, will only fawn the more when repulsed, but will pay little heed to a friendly caress. *Abd-el-Kader.*

Some men weave their sophistry till their own reason is entangled. *Johnson.*

25 Some men will believe nothing but what they can comprehend ; and there are but few things that such are able to comprehend. *St. Evremond.*

Some men's sins are open beforehand, going before to judgment ; and some men they follow after. *St. Paul.*

Some modern zealots appear to have no better knowledge of truth, nor better manner of judging it, than by counting noses. *Swift.*

Some must be great. *Cowper.*

Some of our weaknesses are born in us, others are the result of education ; it is a question which of the two gives us most trouble. *Goethe.*

Some of the most famous books are least 30 worth reading. Their fame was due to their doing something that needed in their day to be done. The work done, the virtue of the book expires. *John Morley.*

Some of your griefs you have cured, / And the sharpest you still have survived ; / But what torments of pain you endured / From evils that never arrived ! *Emerson, from the French.*

Some old men, by continually praising the time of their youth, would almost persuade us that there were no fools in those days ; but unluckily they are left themselves for examples. *Pope.*

Some people are all quality ; you would think they were made up of nothing but title and genealogy. The stamp of dignity defaces in them the very character of humanity, and transports them to such a degree of haughtiness that they reckon it below themselves to exercise either good-nature or good manners. *L'Estrange.*

Some people are so fond of ill-luck that they run half way to meet it. *D. Jerrold.*

Some people carry their hearts in their heads ; 35 very many carry their heads in their hearts. The difficulty is to keep them apart, yet both actively working together. *Hare.*

Some people obtain fame, and others deserve it. *Lessing.*

Some people pass through life soberly and religiously enough, without knowing why, or reasoning about it, but, from force of habit merely, go to heaven like fools. *Sterne.*

Some people will never learn anything, because they understand everything too soon. (?)

Some persons are so devotional they have not one bit of true religion in them. *B. R. Haydon.*

Some persons, instead of making a religion for 40 their God, are content to make a god of their religion. *Helps.*

Some persons take reproof good-humouredly enough, unless you are so unlucky as to hit a sore place. Then they wince and writhe, and start up and knock you down for your impertinence, or wish you good morning. *Hare.*

Some philosophers seek to exalt man by display of his greatness, others to debase him by pointing to his miseries. *Pascal.*

Some prayers, indeed, have a longer voyage than others, but then they return with richer lading at last. *Gurnall.*

Some read books only with a view to find fault, while others read only to be taught ; the former are like venomous spiders, extracting a poisonous quality, where the latter, like the bees, sip out a sweet and profitable juice. *L'Estrange.*

Some rise by sin, and some by virtue fall ; / 45 Some run from brakes of vice and answer none, / And some condemnéd for a fault alone. *Meas. for Meas.*, ii. 1.

Some slaves are scourged to their work by whips, others by restlessness and ambition. *Ruskin.*

Some straw, a room, water, and in the fourth place, gentle words. These things are never to be refused in good men's houses. *Hitopadesa.*

Some talkers excel in the precision with which they formulate their thoughts, so that you get from them somewhat to remember ; others lay criticism asleep by a charm. *Emerson.*

Some tears belong to us because we are unfortunate ; others, because we are humane ; many, because we are mortal. But most are caused by our being unwise. It is these last only that of necessity produce more. *Leigh Hunt.*

5 Some that speak no ill of any do no good to any. *Pr.*

Some there be that shadows kiss, / Such have but a shadow's bliss. *Mer. of Venice,* ii. 9.

Some to whom Heaven in wit has been profuse, / Want as much more to turn it to its use. *Pope.*

Some treasures are heavy with human tears, as an ill-stored harvest with untimely rain ; and some gold is brighter in sunshine than in substance. *Ruskin.*

Some troops pursue the bloody-minded queen / That led calm Henry. 3 *Hen. VI.,* ii. 6.

10 Some village Hampden, that with dauntless breast / The little tyrant of his fields withstood, / Some mute inglorious Milton here may rest, / Some Cromwell guiltless of his country's blood. *Gray.*

Some virtues are only seen in affliction, and some in prosperity. *Addison.*

Some wee short hours ayont the twal. *Burns.*

Some work in the morning may trimly be done, / That all the day after may hardly be won. *Tusser.*

Some would be thought to do great things who are but tools and instruments, like the fool who fancied he played upon the organ when he only blew the bellows. (?)

15 Something attempted, something done, / Has earned a night's repose. *Longfellow.*

Something between a hindrance and a help. *Wordsworth.*

Something is rotten in the state of Denmark. *Ham.,* i. 4.

Something is wanting to science until it has been humanised. *Emerson.*

Something of a person's character may be discovered by observing when and how he smiles. Some people never smile. They only grin. *Bovee.*

20 Sometimes from her eyes / I did receive fair speechless messages. *Mer. of Venice,* i. 1.

Sometimes ideas are made flesh ; they breathe upon us with warm breath ; they touch us with soft responsive hands ; they look upon us with sad, sincere eyes, and speak to us in appealing tones. *George Eliot.*

Sometimes the half is better than the whole, / And sometimes worse than none ; the dubious soul / Suspects the secret there in what is hid, / And holds the rest but trash. *Dr. Walter Smith.*

Sometimes / 'Tis well to be bereft of promised good, / That we may lift the soul, and contemplate / With lively joy the joys we cannot share. *Coleridge.*

Somnus agrestium / Lenis virorum non humiles domos / Fastidit, umbrosamque ripam— —The gentle sleep of rustic men disdains not humble dwellings and the shady bank. *Hor.*

Somnus est imago mortis—Sleep is the image of 25 death. *Cic.*

Son genre n'est pas le plus grand, mais elle est la plus grande dans son genre—Its kind is not the greatest, but it is the greatest of its kind. (?).

Sonder Falsch wie die Tauben ! und ihr beleidiget keinen ; / Aber klug wie die Schlangen und euch beleidiget keiner—Innocent as doves, you will harm no one ; but wise as serpents, no one will harm you. *Haug.*

Song is the heroic of speech. *Carlyle.*

Song is the tone of feeling. *Hare.*

Songs may exist unsung, but voices exist 30 only when they sound. *Landor.*

Soon enough, if well enough. *Pr.*

Soon hot, soon cold. *Pr.*

Soon or late the strong need the help of the weak. *Fr. Pr.*

Soon ripe, soon rotten. *Pr.*

Sooner earth / Might go round heaven, and 35 the strait girth of Time / Inswathe the fulness of Eternity, / Than language grasp the infinite of Love. *Tennyson.*

Sooner or later the truth comes to light. *Dut. Pr.*

Soothed with the sound, the king grew vain, / Fought all his battles o'er again ; / And thrice he routed all his foes, / And thrice he slew the slain. *Dryden.*

σοφὴν δὲ μισῶ· μὴ γὰρ ἐν γ᾽ἐμοῖς δόμοις / Εἴη φρονοῦσα πλεῖον ἢ γυναῖκα χρῆν—I hate a learned woman. Let no woman in my house know more than a woman should. *Eurip.*

Sordid and infamous sensuality, the most dreadful of the evils that issued from the box of Pandora, corrupts every heart and eradicates every virtue. *Fénelon.*

Sorex suo perit indicio—The mouse perishes by 40 betraying himself. *Pr.*

Sorrow breaks seasons and reposing hours, / Makes the night morning and the noontide night. *Rich. III.*

Sorrow concealed, like an oven stopped, / Doth burn the heart to cinders where it is. *Titus Andron.,* ii. 5.

Sorrow has ever produced more melody than mirth. *C. Fitzhugh.*

Sorrow has not been given us for sorrow's sake, but always as a lesson from which we are to learn somewhat, which once learned, it ceases to be sorrow. *Carlyle.*

Sorrow is always toward ourselves, not 45 heaven ; / Showing, we would not spare heaven, as we love it, / But as we stand in fear. *Meas. for Meas.,* ii. 3.

Sorrow is an enemy, but it carries a friend's message within it too. All life is as death ; and the tree Igdrasil, which reaches up to heaven, goes down to the kingdom of hell ; and God, the Everlasting Good and Just, is in it all. *Carlyle.*

Sorrow is better than laughter; for by the sadness of the countenance the heart is made better. *Bible.*

Sorrow is good for nothing but sin. *Pr.*

Sorrow is knowledge; they who know the most must mourn the deepest over the fatal truth, the tree of knowledge is not that of life. *Byron.*

Sorrow is shadow to life, moving where life doth move. *Sir Edwin Arnold.*

5 Sorrow is the mere rust of the soul. Activity will cleanse and brighten it. *Johnson.*

Sorrow, like a heavy-hanging bell, once set on ringing, with his own strength goes; then little strength rings out the doleful knell. *Shakespeare.*

Sorrow like this / Draws parted lives in one, and knits anew / The rents which time has made. *Lewis Morris.*

Sorrow of spirit (like Night among the Greeks) is the mother of gods. *Jean Paul.*

Sorrow seems sent for our instruction, as we darken the cages of birds when we would teach them to sing. *Jean Paul.*

10 Sorrow that is couched in seeming gladness / Is like that mirth fate turns to sudden sadness. *Troil. and Cress.*, i. 1.

Sorrow will pay no debt. *Pr.*

Sorrows are like thunder-clouds,—in the distance they look black, over our heads hardly gray. *Jean Paul.*

Sorrows are often evolved from good fortune. *Goethe.*

Sorrow's crown of sorrow is remembering happier things. *Tennyson.*

15 Sorrows remembered sweeten present joy. *R. Pollok.*

Sors tua mortalis; non est mortale quod optas—Thy lot is mortal, and thou wishest what no mortal may. *Ovid.*

Sort thy heart to patience; / These few days' wonder will be quickly worn. *2 Henry VI.*, ii. 4.

Sotto voce—In an undertone. *It.*

Souffrir est la première chose qu'il doit apprendre, et celle qu'il aura le plus grand besoin de savoir—To be able to endure is the first lesson which a child ought to learn, and the one which it will have the most need to know. *Rousseau.*

20 Souls made of fire, and children of the sun, with whom revenge is virtue. *Young.*

Souls must become expanded by the contemplation of Nature's grandeur before they can first comprehend the greatness of man. *Heine.*

Sound and sufficient reason falls, after all, to the share of but few men, and those few men exert their influence in silence. *Goethe.*

Sound maxims are the germs of good; strongly imprinted on the memory, they nourish the will. *Joubert.*

Sound, sound the clarion, fill the fife ! / To all the sensual world proclaim, / One crowded hour of glorious life / Is worth an age without a name. *Scott.*

25 Sound the loud timbrel o'er Egypt's dark sea ! / Jehovah has triumph'd, His people are free. *Moore.*

Sound trumpets ! — let our bloody colours wave ; / And either victory or else a grave. *3 Hen. VI.*, ii. 2.

Soupçon est d'amitié poison—Suspicion is the poison of friendship. *Fr. Pr.*

Sour woe delights in fellowship, / And needly will be rank'd with other griefs. *Rom. and Jul.*, iii. 2.

Souvent la perfidie retourne sur son auteur—Treachery often recoils on the head of its author. *Fr.*

Sow good works and you will reap gladness. *Pr.* 30

Soyez comme l'oiseau, posé pour un instant / Sur des rameaux trop frêles, / Qui sent ployer la branche et qui chante pourtant, / Sachant qu'il a des ailes—Be as the bird perched for an instant on the too frail branch which she feels bending beneath, but sings away all the same, knowing she has wings. *Victor Hugo.*

Soyez ferme—Be firm. *M.*

Soyons doux, si nous voulons être regrettés. La hauteur du génie et les qualités supérieures ne sont pleurées que des anges—Let us be gentle if we would be regretted. The pride of genius and high talents are lamented only by angels. *Chateaubriand.*

Space is the statue of God. *Joubert.*

Spare but to spend, and only spend to spare. *Pr.* 35

Spare the rod and spoil the child. *Pr.*

Sparen ist grössere Kunst als erwerben—Saving is a greater art than gaining. *Ger. Pr.*

Sparing or spending, be thy wisdom seen / In keeping ever to the golden mean. *Lucian.*

Speak every man truth with his neighbour. *St. Paul.*

Speak gently !—'tis a little thing, / Dropped 40 in the heart's deep well. *Anon.*

Speak in such a manner between two enemies, that, should they afterwards become friends, you may not be put to the blush. *Saadi.*

Speak little and to the purpose. *Pr.*

Speak little, but speak the truth. *Pr.*

Speak no evil of a man if you know it not of him for certain, and if you do know it, then ask yourself, "Why do I tell it ?" *Lavater.*

Speak not at all till you have somewhat to 45 speak ; and care simply and with undivided mind for the truth of your speaking. *Carlyle.*

Speak not peace to thyself when beset on every side with numerous and restless enemies. *Thomas à Kempis.*

Speak o' the deil and he'll appear. *Sc. Pr.*

Speak of me as I am ; nothing extenuate, / Nor set down aught in malice. Then must you speak / Of one who loved not wisely but too well. *Othello*, v. 2.

Speak that I may see thee. *Addison.*

Speak the truth, and all nature and all spirits 50 help you with unexpected furtherance ; all things alive or brute are vouchers, and the very roots of the grass underground there do seem to stir and move to bear you witness. *Emerson.*

Speak the truth and shame the devil. *Pr.*

Speak unto the children of Israel, that they go forward. *Bible.*

Speak well of the absent whenever you have a suitable opportunity. *Judge Hale.*

Speak well of your friend ; of your enemy say nothing. *Pr.*

Speak when you are spoken to, and come 55 when you are called for. *Pr.*

Speak your sincerest, think your wisest; there is still a great gulf between you and the fact. *Carlyle.*

Speaking comes by nature, silence by understanding. *Ger. Pr.*

Speaking much is a sign of vanity; for he that is lavish in words is a niggard in deed. *Sir W. Raleigh.*

Speaking without thinking is shooting without aim. *Pr.*

5 Spectatum veniunt, veniunt spectentur ut ipsæ—The ladies come to see, they come also to be seen. *Ovid.*

Spectemur agendo—Let us be tried by our actions. *M.*

Spectres exist for those only who wish to see them. *Holtei.*

Speculation should have free course and look fearlessly towards all the thirty-two points of the compass, whithersoever and howsoever it listeth. *Carlyle.*

Speech, even the commonest, has something of song in it. *Carlyle.*

10 Speech has been given to man to disguise his thought. *Talleyrand.*

Speech is a laggard and a sloth, but the eyes shoot forth an electric fluid that condenses all the elements of sentiment and passion in one single emanation. *Horace Smith.*

Speech is external thought, and thought internal speech. *Rivarol.*

Speech is like tapestry unfolded, where the imagery appears distinct; but thoughts, like tapestry in the bale, where the figures are rolled up together. *Themistocles, quoted by Bacon.*

Speech is morning to the mind; it spreads the beauteous images abroad, which else lie furled or clouded in the soul. *Nathaniel Lee.*

15 Speech is power: speech is to persuade, to convert, to compel. It is to bring another out of his bad sense into your good sense. *Emerson.*

Speech is the gift of all, but thought of few. *Cato.*

Speech is too often, not the art of concealing thought, but of quite stifling or suspending thought, so that there is none to conceal. *Carlyle.*

Speech of a man's self ought to be seldom and well chosen. *Bacon.*

Speech that leads not to action, still more that hinders it, is a nuisance on the earth. *Carlyle.*

20 Speedy execution is the mother of good fortune. *Pr.*

Spem gregis—The hope of the flock. *Virg.*

Spem pretio non emo—I do not give money for mere hopes. *Ter.*

Spend not on hopes. *George Herbert.*

Sperat infestis, metuit secundis / Alteram sortem bene præparatum / Pectus—A heart well prepared in adversity hopes for, and in prosperity fears, a change of fortune. *Hor.*

25 Sperate, et vosmet rebus servate secundis—Hope on, and reserve yourselves for prosperous times. *Virg.*

Speravi—I have hoped. *M.*

Speravimus ista / Dum fortuna fuit—I hoped that once, while fortune was favourable. *Virg.*

Spero meliora—I hope for better things. *M.*

Spes bona dat vires, animum quoque spes bona firmat; / Vivere spe vidi qui moriturus erat—Good hope gives strength, good hope also confirms resolution; him who was on the point of death, I have seen revive by hope.

Spes mea Christus—Christ is my hope. *M.*   30

Spes mea in Deo—My hope is in God. *M.*

Spes sibi quisque—Each man must hope in himself alone. *Virg.*

Spes tutissima cœlis—The safest hope is in heaven. *M.*

Spesso chi troppo fa, poco fa—Often he who does too much does little. *It. Pr.*

Spesso d'un gran male nasce un gran bene— 35 Out of a great evil there springs a great good. *It. Pr.*

Spesso i doni sono danni—Gifts are oftentimes losses. *It. Pr.*

Spesso la tardità ti toglie l'occasione et la celerità le forze—Tardiness often robs us of opportunity, and too great despatch of our force. *Machiavelli.*

Spill not the morning (the quintessence of the day) in recreation, for sleep itself is a recreation. Add not, therefore, sauce to sauce. *Fuller.*

Spinner, spin softly, you disturb me. I am praying. *Port. Prov.*

Spinoza was a God-intoxicated man (*Gott-ge-* 40 *trunkener Mensch*). *Novalis.*

Spirit is the creator. Spirit hath life in itself. And man in all ages and countries embodies it in his language as the Father. *Emerson.*

Spirit of Nature! / The pure diffusion of thy essence throbs / Alike in every human heart. / Thou aye erectest there / Thy throne of power unappealable; / Thou art the judge beneath whose nod / Man's brief and frail authority / Is powerless as the wind / That passeth idly by. / Thine the tribunal which surpasseth / The show of human justice, / As God surpasseth man. *Schelling.*

Spirit-power begins in directing animal power to other than egoistic ends. *Ruskin.*

Spirits are not finely touch'd / But to fine issues, nor Nature never lends / The smallest scruple of her excellence / But, like a thrifty goddess, she determines / Herself the glory of a creditor, / Both thanks and use. *Meas. for Meas.,* i. 1.

Spirits, when they please, / Can either sex 45 assume, or both. *Milton.*

Spiritual music can only spring from discords set in unison; but for evil there were no good, as victory is only possible by battle. *Carlyle.*

Spite of all the criticising elves, / Those who would make us feel must feel themselves. *Burke.*

Spite of cormorant devouring Time, / The endeavour of this present breath may buy / That honour which will bate his scythe's keen edge, / And make us heirs of all eternity. *Love's L.'s Lost,* i. 1.

Splendida vitia—Splendid vices. *Tertullian, of Pagan virtues.*

Splendide mendax — Nobly false or disloyal. 50 *Hor.*

Spolia opima—The richest of the spoil.

Sport is the bloom and glow of perfect health. *Emerson.*

Sprechen ist silbern, Schweigen ist golden— Speech is silvern, silence golden. *Swiss M.*

Sprich nicht von Zeit, sprich nicht von Raum, / Denn Raum und Zeit sind nur ein Traum, / Ein schwerer Traum, den nur vergisst, / Wer durch die Liebe glücklich ist—Speak not of time, speak not of space, for space and time are but a dream, a heavy dream, which he who is happy in love only forgets. *Bodenstedt.*

Sprich vom Geheimniss nicht geheimnissvoll— Speak not mysteriously of what is a mystery. *Goethe.*

5 St. Theresa right well defines the devil as an unfortunate who knows not what it is to love. *C. J. Weber.*

Stab at thee who will, / No stab the soul can kill. *Raleigh.*

Stabat mater dolorosa / Juxta crucem lacry-mosa / Qua pendebat Filius—She stood a sorrow-stricken mother, weeping by the Cross where her son hung dying.

Stabit quocunque jeceris—It will stand, which-ever way you throw it. *Legend on the three-legged crest of the Isle of Man.*

Stagnation is something more than death, it is corruption also. *Simms.*

10 Stain (blemish) not thy innocence by too deep resentment, nor take off from the brightness of thy crown by anger and impatience and eagerness to right thyself. *Thomas à Kempis.*

Stand fast! to stand or fall, / Free in thine own arbitrament it stands. *Milton.*

Stand not upon the order of your going, / But go at once. *Macb.,* iii. 4.

"Stand out of the sun." *Diogenes to Alexander the Great, and which made Alexander remark, "If I were not Alexander I would be Diogenes."*

Stand still and see the salvation of the Lord. *Bible.*

15 Stand up bravely to afflictions, and quit thy-self like a man. *Thomas à Kempis.*

Stand ye in the ways, and see, and ask for the old paths, where is the good way, and walk therein. *Bible.*

Standing on what too long we bore / With shoulders bent and downcast eyes, / We may discern—unseen before— / A path to higher destinies. *Longfellow.*

Stant cætera tigno—The rest stand on a beam. *M.*

Stare super vias antiquas—To stand upon the old ways.

20 Stark est des Menschen Arm, wenn ihn Götter stützen—Strong is the arm of man if the gods uphold it. *Schiller.*

Stars look down upon me with pity from their serene and silent places, like eyes glistening with tears over the little lot of man. Arctu-rus and Orion, Sirius and Pleiades, are still shining in their courses, clear and young, as when the shepherd first noted them in the plain of Shinar! *Carlyle.*

Stat sua cuique dies; breve et irreparabile tempus / Omnibus est vitæ; sed famam extendere factis, / Hoc virtutis opus—Each man has his appointed day; short and irreparable is the brief life of all; but to extend our fame by our deeds, this is manhood's work. *Virg.*

States are to be called happy and noble in so far as they settle rightly who is slave and who free. *Carlyle.*

Statesmen that are wise / Shape a necessity, as sculptor clay, / To their own model. *Tennyson.*

Statio bene fida carinis—A safe harbourage for 25 ships. *M.*

Status quo ante bellum—The state in which the belligerents stood before war began.

Status quo, or Statu quo, or In statu quo—The state in which a matter was.

Stay awhile to make an end the sooner. *Sir Amyas Paulet.*

Steady, durable good cannot be derived from an external cause, by reason all derived from externals must fluctuate as they fluctuate. What then remains but the cause internal; in rectitude of conduct? *James Harris.*

Steam is no stronger now than it was a hun- 30 dred years ago, but it is put to better use. *Emerson.*

Steckenpferde sind theurer als arabische Hengste — Hobby-horses are more expensive than Arab ones. *Ger. Pr.*

Steep and craggy is the path of the gods. *Porphyry.*

Steep regions cannot be surmounted except by winding paths. *Goethe.*

Stemmata quid faciunt? Quid prodest, Pon-tice, longo / Sanguine censeri?—What do pedigrees avail? Of what advantage, Ponticus, is it to be rated by the antiquity of your race? *Juv.*

Step by step one goes far. *Pr.* 35

Steps vary as much as the human face. *J. M. Barrie.*

Stern accuracy in inquiring, bold imagination in expounding and filling up, these are the two pinions on which history soars — or flutters and wabbles. *Carlyle.*

Stern daughter of the voice of God. *Words-worth, of Duty.*

Stern Ruin's ploughshare drives elate / Full on thy bloom. *Burns.*

Stet—Let it stand. 40

Stet fortuna domus—May the fortune of the house stand. *M.*

Stets ist die Sprache kecker als die That— Speech is always bolder than action. *Schiller.*

Stets liegt, wo das Banner der Wahrheit wallt, / Der Aberglaube im Hinterhalt — Where the banner of truth waves unfurled, there you will always find superstition lying in ambush. *Platen.*

Stets zu spät kommt gute Kunde, / Schlechte Kunde zu frühe—Good news comes always too late; bad, always too soon. *Bodenstedt.*

Steward or deputy may do well: but the lord 45 himself is obliged to stir in the administra-tion of justice. *Cervantes.*

Stiff (a) and laboured manner is as bad in a letter as it is in conversation. . . . Sprightli-ness and wit are graceful in letters, just as they are in conversation. *Blair.*

Stiff in opinions, always in the wrong, / Was everything by starts, and nothing long; / But in the course of one revolving moon / Was chemist, fiddler, statesman, and buf-foon. *Dryden.*

Still humanity grows dearer; / Being learned the more. *Jean Ingelow.*

Still in thy right hand carry gentle peace, / To silence envious tongues. *Henry VIII.,* iii. 2.

Still people are dangerous. *La Fontaine.*

Still raise for good the supplicating voice, / But leave to Heaven the measure and the choice. *Johnson.*

Still seems it strange that thou shouldst live for ever? Is it less strange that thou shouldst live at all? This is a miracle; and that no more. *Young.*

Still swine eat all the draff. *Pr.*

5 Still the sight of too great beauty blinds us, and we lose / The sense of earthly splendours, gaining heaven. *Lewis Morris.*

Still the skies are opened as of old / To the entrancèd gaze, ay, nearer far / And brighter than of yore. *Lewis Morris.*

Still they gazed, and still the wonder grew / That one small head could carry all he knew. *Goldsmith.*

Still to the lowly soul / He doth Himself impart, / And for His cradle and His throne / Chooseth the pure in heart. *Keble.*

Still und bewegt—Still and yet moved. *M. of Rahel.*

10 Still waters run deep. *Pr.*

Stillest streams o't water finest meadows, / And the bird that flutters least is longest on the wing. *Cowper.*

Stillness of person and steadiness of features are signal marks of good breeding. Vulgar persons can't sit still, or at least they must work their limbs or features. *Holmes.*

Stirb, Götz, du hast dich selbst überlebt—Die, Gotz; thou hast outlived thyself. *Goethe.*

Stirb und werde! / Denn so lang du das nicht hast, / Bist du nur ein trüber Gast / Auf der dunkeln Erde—Die and learn to live, for so far as thou hast not accomplished this, thou art but a darkened guest in a darkened world. *Goethe.*

15 Stirring spirits live alone: / Write on the others, "Here lies such a one." *George Herbert.*

Sto pro veritate—I stand in the defence of truth. *M.*

Stolen waters are sweet, and bread eaten in secret is pleasant. *Bible.*

Stone masons collected the dome of St. Paul's, but Wren hung it in the air. *Willmott.*

Stony limits cannot hold love out; / And what love can do, that dares love attempt. *Rom. and Jul.,* ii. 2.

20 Store of grain, O king! is the best of stores. A gem cast into the mouth will not support life. *Hitopadesa.*

Store Ord giöre sielden from Gierning—Big words seldom accompany good deeds. *Dan. Pr.*

Storms make oaks take deeper root. *Pr.*

Strait is the gate, and narrow is the way, that leadeth unto life; and few there be that find it. *Jesus.*

Strange cozenage! none would live past years again; / Yet all hope pleasure in what yet remain; / And from the dregs of life think to receive / What the first sprightly running could not give. *Dryden.*

25 Strange is the life of man, and fatal or fated are moments, / Whereupon turn, as on hinges, the gates of the wall adamantine! *Longfellow.*

Strange trade that of advocacy. Your intellect, your highest heavenly gift, hung up in the shop window like a loaded pistol for sale; will either blow out a pestilent scoundrel's brains, or the scoundrel's salutary sheriff's officer's (in a sense), as you please to choose, for your guinea. *Carlyle.*

Stranger or countryman to me / Welcome alike shall ever be. / To ask of any guest his name, / Or whose he is, or whence he came, / I hold can never be his part / Who owns a hospitable heart. *Macedonius.*

Straws show which way the wind blows. *Pr.*

Strength alone knows conflict; weakness is below even defeat, and is born vanquished. *Mme. Swetchine.*

Strength, instead of being the lusty child of 30 passions, grows by grappling with and throwing them. *J. M. Barrie.*

Strength needs support far more than weakness. A feather sustains itself long in the air. *Mme. Swetchine.*

Strength of mind is exercise, not rest. *Pope.*

Strength of mind rests in sobriety, for this keeps the reason unclouded by passion. *Pythagoras.*

Strength was the virtue of Paganism; obedience is the virtue of Christianity. *Hare.*

Strenua nos exercet inertia; navibus atque / 35 Quadrigis petimus bene vivere; quod petis hic est—Strenuous idleness gives us plenty to do; we seek to live aright by yachting and chariot-driving. What you are seeking for is here. *Hor.*

Strict laws are like steel bodices, good for growing limbs; but when the joints are knit, they are not helps, but burdens. *Sir Francis Fane.*

Strict punctuality is perhaps the cheapest virtue which can give force to an otherwise utterly insignificant character. *J. F. Boyes.*

Strictly speaking, the imagination is never governed; it is always the ruling and divine power, and the rest of the man is to it only as an instrument which it sounds, or a tablet on which it writes; clearly and sublimely if the wax be smooth and the strings true, grotesquely and wildly if they are stained and broken. *Ruskin.*

Strike, but hear me. *Themistocles to Eurybiades before battle of Salamis.*

Strike flat the thick rotundity o' the world! / 40 Crack Nature's moulds, all germens spill at once, / That make ungrateful man! *Lear,* iii. 2.

Strike those that hurt, and hurt not those that help. 1 *Hen. VI.,* iii. 3.

Strike while the iron is hot. *Pr.*

Striking manners are bad manners. *Robert Hall.*

Strip the bishop of his apron, the counsellor of his gown, and the beadle of his cocked hat, what are they? Men, mere men. Dignity, and even holiness too sometimes, are more questions of coat and waistcoat than some people imagine. *Dickens.*

Strive mightily, but eat and drink as friends. 45 *Tam. of the Shrew,* i. 2.

Strive not against the stream. *Ecclus.*

Strive to do thy duty; then shalt thou know what is in thee. *Goethe.*

Striving to better, oft we mar what's well. *Pr.*

Strong character curdles itself out of the scum into its own place and power or impotence. *Ruskin.*

Strong characters are brought out by change of situation, gentle ones by permanence. *Jean Paul.*

Strong conceit, like a new principle, carries all easily with it, when yet above common-sense. *Locke.*

5 Strong feeling must create poetry. *Moses Harvey.*

Strong folks have strong maladies. *Ger. Pr.*

Strong passions are the life of manly virtues. But they need not necessarily be evil because they are passions and because they are strong. The passions may be likened to blood horses, that need training and the curb only to enable them whom they carry to achieve the most glorious triumphs. *Simms.*

Strong reasons make strong actions. *King John,* iii. 4.

Strong Son of God, immortal Love, / Whom we that have not seen Thy face, / By faith, and faith alone, embrace, / Believing where we cannot prove. *Tennyson.*

10 Stronger than steel / Is the sword of the spirit ; / Swifter than arrows / The life of the truth is ; / Greater than anger / Is love, and subdueth. *Longfellow.*

Strongest minds / Are often those of whom the noisy world / Hears least. *Wordsworth.*

Studies perfect nature, and are perfected by experience. *Bacon.*

Studies serve for delight, for ornament, and for ability. *Bacon.*

Studiis et rebus honestis— By honourable studies and occupations. *M.*

15 Studiis florentem ignobilis oti—Indulging in the studies of inglorious leisure. *Virg.*

Studio minuente laborem — The enthusiasm lessening the fatigue. *Ovid.*

Study gives strength to the mind ; conversation, grace. *Temple.*

Study is like the heaven's glorious sun, / That will not be deep-searched with saucy looks. *Love's L. Lost,* i. 1.

Study is the bane of boyhood, the element of youth, the indulgence of manhood, and the restorative of age. *Landor.*

20 Study of the Bible will keep any man from being vulgar in style. *Coleridge.*

Study the best and highest things that are, / But of thyself an humble thought retain. *Sir J. Davis.*

Study the past if you would divine the future. *Confucius.*

Study thyself; what rank or what degree / The wise Creator hath ordained for thee. *Dryden.*

Study to be quiet; contain yourself within your own business, and let the prying, censorious, the vain and intriguing world follow their own devices. *Thomas à Kempis.*

25 Study to be what you wish to seem. *John Bate.*

Stulta maritali jam porrigit ora capistro— He is now stretching out his foolish head to the matrimonial l alter. *Juv.*

Stultus nisi quod ipse facit, nil rectum putat— The fool thinks nothing well done except what he does himself.

Stulti sunt inumerabiles — Fools are without number. *Erasmus.*

Stultitiam dissimulare non potes nisi taciturnitate— No concealing folly save by silence.

Stultitiam patiuntur opes—Riches allow one to 30 be foolish. *Hor.*

Stultitiam simulare loco, sapientia summa est —To affect folly on an occasion is consummate wisdom.

Stultorum incurata malus pudor ulcera celat— It is the false shame of fools to try to conceal uncured wounds. *Hor.*

Stultum est timere quod vitari non potest—It is foolish to distress ourselves about what cannot be avoided. *Syr.*

Stultus es, rem actam agis—You are a fool; you do what has been done already. *Plaut.*

Stultus labor est ineptiarum — The labour is 35 foolish that is bestowed on trifles. *Mart.*

Stultus, qui, patre occiso, liberos relinquat—He who kills the father and leaves the children is a fool. *Pr.*

Stultus semper incipit vivere—The fool is always beginning to live. *Pr.*

Stunden der Noth vergiss, doch was sie dich lehrten, vergiss nie—Forget the times of your distress, but never forget what they taught you. *Gesser.*

Stung by straitness of our life, made strait / On purpose to make sweet the life at large. *Browning.*

Stupid people and uneducated people do not 40 care for nice discriminations. They always have decided opinions. *William Black.*

Stupid people move like lay-figures, while every joint of an intelligent man is eloquent. *Schopenhauer.*

Stupidity has its sublime as well as genius. *Wieland.*

Stupidity is without anxiety. *Goethe.*

Sturm- und Drang-Periode — The storm-and-stress period. A literary period in Germany, the productions of which were inspired by a love of strong passion and violent action.

Style is the dress of thoughts. *Chesterfield.* 45

Style is the physiognomy of the mind. *Schopenhauer.*

Style is what gives value and currency to thought. *Amiel.*

Style may be defined, proper words in proper places. *Swift.*

Stylo inverso—With the back of the pen.

Stylum vertere—To change or correct the style. 50

Sua cuique Deus fit dira cupido—Each man makes his own dire passion a god. *Virg.*

Sua cuique quum sit animi cogitatio, / Colorque proprius—Since each man has a way of his own of thinking, and a peculiar temper. *Phæd.*

Sua cuique vita obscura est—Every man's life is dark to himself.

Sua cuique voluptas—Every man has his own liking.

Sua quisque exempla debet æquo animo pati— 55 Every one ought to bear patiently with what is after his own example. *Phæd.*

Suave, mari magno turbantibus acquora ventis/ E terra magnum alterius spěctare laborem ! —How fascinating it is when on the great sea the winds have raised its waters into billows, to witness the perils of another from the land !

Suavis est laborum præteritorum memoria—Sweet is the memory of past trouble. *Cic.*

Suaviter et fortiter—Mildly and firmly. *M.*

Suaviter in modo, fortiter in re—Gentle in manner, resolute in deed. *M.*

"Suaviter in modo, fortiter in re,"—I do not know any one rule so unexceptionably useful and necessary in every part of life. *Chesterfield.*

5 Sub cruce candida — Under the pure white cross. *M.*

Sub cruce salus — Salvation under the cross. *M.*

Sub fine—At the end.

Sub hoc signo vinces—Under this sign (the cross) thou shalt conquer. *M.*

Sub initio—At the beginning.

10 Sub Jove—In the open air.

Sub judice lis est—The question is undecided.

Sub pœna—Under a penalty. *L.*

Sub reservatione Jacobæo—With St. James's reservation ; viz., if the Lord will.

Sub rosa—Under the rose ; confidentially.

15 Sub silentio—In silence, *i.e.*, without notice being taken.

Sub specie æternitatis—In the form of eternity, *i.e.*, as a particular manifestation of a universal law.

Subdue fate, and exert human strength to the utmost of your power ; and if, when pains have been taken, success attend not, in whom is the blame ? *Hitopadesa.*

Sublata causa tollitur effectus—The cause removed, the effect is also. *L.*

Sublimer in this world know I nothing than a peasant saint, one that must toil outwardly for the lowest of man's wants, also toiling inwardly for the highest. Such a one will carry thee back to Nazareth itself. *Carlyle.*

20 Sublimi feriam sidera vertice—I shall strike the stars with my uplifted head. *Hor.*

Sublimity is Hebrew by birth. *Coleridge.*

Submitting to one wrong often brings on another. *Pr.*

Subtilis veterum judex et callidus audis—You are known as a nice and experienced judge of things old. *Hor.*

Subtlety may deceive you ; integrity never will. *Oliver Cromwell.*

25 Subverting worldly strong and worldly wise, / By simply meek. *Milton.*

Succedaneum—A substitute.

Success (by laws of competition) signifies always so much victory over your neighbour as to obtain the direction of his work and take the profits of it. This is the real source of all great riches. *Ruskin.*

Success consecrates the foulest crimes. *Sen.*

Success ? If the thing is unjust, thou hast not succeeded. *Carlyle.*

30 Success in the majority of circumstances depends on knowing how long it takes to succeed. *Montesquieu.*

Success in war, like charity in religion, covers a multitude of sins. *Sir C. Napier.*

Success is full of promise till men get it, and then it seems like a nest from which the bird has flown. *Ward Beecher.*

Success is sweet ; the sweeter if long delayed, and attained through manifold struggles and defeats. *A. B. Alcott.*

Success is the child of audacity. *Disraeli.*

Success makes men look larger, if reflection 35 does not measure them. *Joubert.*

Success makes success, as money makes money. *Chamfort.*

Success often costs more than it is worth. *E. Wigglesworth.*

Success tempts many to their ruin. *Phædr.*

Success throws a veil over the evil deeds of men. *Demosthenes.*

Success ! to thee, as to a god, men bend the 40 knee. *Æschylus.*

Successful love takes a load off our hearts and puts it on our shoulders. *Bovee.*

Such a friend as speaketh kindly to a man's face, and behind his back defeateth his designs, is like a pot of poison with a surface of milk. *Hitopadesa.*

Such a genius as philosophers must of necessity have is wont but seldom, in all its parts, to meet in one man ; but its different parts generally spring up in different persons. *Plato.*

Such a plot must have a woman in it. *Richardson.*

Such as are careless of themselves can hardly 45 be mindful of others. *Thales (?)*

Such as are in the married state wish to get out, and such as are out wish to get in. *Quoted by Emerson.*

Such as every one is inwardly, so he judgeth outwardly. *Thomas à Kempis.*

Such as we are made of, such we be. *Twelfth Night,* ii. 2.

Such hath been—shall be—beneath the sun, / That many still must labour for the one. *Byron.*

Such is hope, Heaven's own gift to struggling 50 mortals ; pervading, like some subtle essence from the skies, all things both good and bad. *Dickens.*

Such is the aspect of this shore ; / 'Tis Greece, but living Greece no more ! / So coldly sweet, so deadly fair, / We start, for soul is wanting there. *Byron.*

Such only enjoy the country as are capable of thinking when they are there ; then they are prepared for solitude, and in that case solitude is prepared for them. *Dryden.*

Such tricks hath strong imagination, / That, if it would but apprehend some joy, / It comprehends some bringer of that joy ; / Or in the night, imagining some fear, / How easy is a bush supposed a bear. *Mid. N.'s Dream,* v. 1.

Such war of white and red within her cheeks. *Tam. of the Shrew,* iv. 5.

Suche die Wissenschaft als würdest ewig du 55 hier sein, / Tugend, als hielte der Tod dich schon am sträubenden Haar—Seek knowledge, as if thou wert to be here for ever ; virtue, as if death already held thee by the bristling hair. *Herder.*

Sucht nur die Menschen zu verwirren, / Sie zu befriedigen ist schwer — Seek only to mystify men ; to satisfy them is difficult. *Goethe, the theatre-manager in " Faust."*

Sudden blaze of kindness may, by a single blast of coldness, be extinguished; but that fondness which length of time has connected with many circumstances and occasions, though it may for a while be suppressed by disgust or resentment, with or without cause, is hourly revived by accidental recollection. *Johnson.*

Sudden love is the latest cured. *La Bruyère.*

Sudden resolutions, like the sudden rise of the mercury in the barometer, indicate little else than the changeableness of the weather. *Hare.*

Sudden tumultuous popularity comes more from partial delirium on both sides than from clear insight, and is of evil omen to all concerned with it. *Carlyle.*

5 Suer sang et eau—To toil and moil (*lit.* sweat blood and water). *Fr. Phr.*

Suffer little children to come unto me, and forbid them not, for of such is the kingdom of heaven. *Jesus.*

Suffer no hour to slide by without its due improvement. *Thomas à Kempis.*

Suffer thyself to be led in everything but feeling and thinking. *Sallet.*

Sufferance is the badge of all our tribe. *Mer. of Ven.*, i. 3.

10 Suffering in human life is very widely vicarious. *Ward Beecher.*

Suffering is part of the divine idea. *Ward Beecher.*

Suffering is the mother of fools, reason of wise men. (?)

Suffering which falls to our lot in the course of nature, or by chance or fate, does not, "ceteris paribus," seem so painful as suffering which is inflicted on us by the arbitrary will of another. *Schopenhauer.*

Suffice unto thy good, though it be small, / For hoard hath hate, and climbing tickleness; (uncertainty) / Praise hath envie, and weal is blent o'er all. *Chaucer.*

15 Sufficiency is a compound of vanity and ignorance. *Temple.*

Sufficient for the day is the evil thereof. *Jesus.*

Sufficiently provided from within, he has need of little from without. *Goethe of the poet.*

Sufficit huic tumulus, cui non suffecerit orbis— A tomb now suffices for him for whom the world did not suffice. *Apropos of Alexander the Great.*

Suffundere malis hominis sanguinem, quam offundere—Seek rather to make a man blush for his guilt than to shed his blood. *Ter.*

20 Suggestio falsi—Suggestion of what is false.

Sui cuique mores fingunt fortunam — Every man's fortune is shaped for him by his own manners. *Corn. Nep.*

Sui generis—Of its own kind; of a kind of its own.

Sui juris—Of his own right. *L.*

Suis stat viribus—He stands by his own strength. *M.*

25 Suit the action to the word, the word to the action; with this special observance, that you o'erstep not the modesty of nature. *Ham.*, iii. 2.

Suivez raison—Follow reason. *M.*

Sum quod eris, fui quod es—I am what you will be, I was what you are.

Sum up at night what thou hast done by day; / And in the morning what thou hast to do. *George Herbert.*

Sume superbiam quæsitam meritis — Assume the proud place your merits have won. *Hor.*

Sumite materiam vestris, qui scribitis, æquam / 30 Viribus, et versate diu, quid ferre recusent, / Quid valeant humeri—Ye who write, choose a subject suited to your abilities, and long ponder what your powers are equal to, and what they are unable to perform. *Hor.*

Summa bona putas, aliena vivere quadra— You think it the chief good to live on another's crumbs. *Juv.*

Summa petit livor—Envy aims very high. *Ovid.*

Summa sequor fastigia rerum—I will trace the principal heads of events. *Virg.*

Summa summarum—All in all. *Plautus.*

Summæ opes inopia cupiditatum—He is richest 35 who is poorest in his desires. *Sen.*

Summam nec metuas diem, nec optes—Neither fear nor wish for your last day. *Mart.*

Summum bonum—The chief good.

Summum crede nefas animam præferre pudori, / Et propter vitam vivendi perdere causas— Consider it to be the height of impiety to prefer life to honour, and, for the sake of merely living, to sacrifice the objects of living. *Juv.*

Summum jus sæpe summa injuria est—The strictest justice is often grossest injustice. *Cic.*

σὺν δ' ἀνάγκᾳ πᾶν καλόν—Whatever is beautiful 40 is beautiful by an inner necessity. *Pindar.*

Sunbeams pour alike their glorious tide / To light up worlds or wake an insect's mirth. *Keble.*

Sunday is the core of our civilisation, dedicated to thought and reverence. *Emerson.*

Sundays observe; think when the bells do chime, / 'Tis angels' music, therefore come not late. *George Herbert.*

Sunlight is painting. *Hawthorne.*

Sunrise is often lovelier than noon. *Carlyle.* 45

Sunt bona mixta malis, sunt mala mixta bonis— Good is mixed with evil, and evil with good.

Sunt bona, sunt quædam mediocria, sunt mala plura / Quæ legis—Of those which you read, some are good, some middling, and more are bad. *Mart., of books.*

Sunt delicta tamen, quibus ignovisse velimus— There are some faults, however, which we are willing to pardon. *Hor.*

Sunt Jovis omnia plena—All things are full of the Deity. *Virg.*

Sunt lacrymæ rerum, et mentem mortalia tan- 50 gunt—Tears are due to misfortune, and mortal woes touch the heart. *Virg.*

Sunt pueri pueri, pueri puerilia tractant—Boys are boys, and boys occupy themselves with boyish things.

Sunt superis sua jura—Even the gods above are subject to law. *Ovid.*

Suo Marte—By his own prowess. *Cic.*

Super subjectam materiam—Upon the matter submitted. *L.*

Superbo è quel cavallo che non si vuol portar 55 la biada—Proud is the horse that won't carry its own oats. *It. Pr.*

Superfluity comes sooner by white hairs, but competency lives longer. *Mer. of Venice*, i. 2.

Superior powers of mind and profound study are of no use if they do not sometimes lead a person to different conclusions from those which are formed by ordinary powers of mind without study. *J. S. Mill.*

Superior strength is found in the long-run to lie with those who had the right on their side. *Froude.*

Supersedeas—You may supersede. *L.*

5 Superstition changes a man to a beast, fanaticism makes him a wild beast, and despotism a beast of burden. *La Harpe.*

Superstition is a misdirection of religious feeling. *Whately.*

Superstition is an unreasoning fear of God ; religion consists in the pious worship of the gods. *Cic.*

Superstition is but the fear of belief ; religion is the confidence. *Lady Blessington.*

Superstition is certainly not the characteristic of this age. Yet some men are bigoted in politics who are infidels in religion. *Junius.*

10 Superstition is in its death-lair ; the last agonies may endure for decades or for centuries ; but it carries the iron in its heart, and will not vex the earth any more. *Carlyle.*

Superstition is inherent in man's nature ; and when we think it is wholly eradicated, it takes refuge in the strangest holes and corners, whence it peeps out all at once, as soon as it can do so with safety. *Goethe.*

Superstition is passing away without return. Religion cannot pass away. The burning of a little straw may hide the stars in the sky ; but the stars are there, and will re-appear. *Carlyle.*

Superstition is related to this life, religion to the next ; superstition allies itself to fatality, religion to virtue ; it is by the vitality of earthly desires we become superstitious, and by the sacrifice of these desires that we become religious. *Mme. de Staël.*

Superstition is the fear of a spirit whose passions and acts are those of a man, who is present in some places, and not in others ; who makes some places holy, and not others ; who is kind to one person, and unkind to another ; who is pleased or angry according to the degree of attention you pay him, or praise you refuse him ; who is hostile generally to human pleasure, but may be bribed by sacrificing a part of that pleasure into permitting the rest. *Ruskin.*

15 Superstition is the only religion of which base souls are capable. *Joubert.*

Superstition is the poesy of life, so that it does not injure the poet to be superstitious. *Goethe.*

Superstition ! that horrid incubus which dwelt in darkness, shunning the light, with all its racks, and poison chalices, and foul sleeping draughts, is passing away without return. *Carlyle.*

Superstition without a veil is a deformed thing. *Bacon.*

Superstitions would soon die out if so many old women would not act as nurses to keep them alive. *Punch.*

20 Supple knees feed arrogance. *Pr.*

Suppose a neighbour should desire / To light a candle at your fire, / Would it deprive your flame of light / Because another profits by't. *Lloyd.*

Suppressing love is but opposing the natural dictates of the heart. *Goldsmith.*

Suppressio veri—Suppression of what is true.

Supra vires—Beyond one's powers. *Hor.*

Supremum vale—A last farewell. *Ovid.* 25

Sur esperance—In hope. *M.*

Surdo fabulam narras—You tell your story to a deaf man.

Sure as night follows day, / Death treads in pleasure's footsteps round the world, / When pleasure treads the path which reason shuns. *Young.*

Sure, he that made us with such large discourse, / Looking before and after, gave us not / That capability and godlike reason / To fust in us unused. *Ham.*, iv. 4.

Sure, of qualities demanding praise, / More go 30 to ruin fortunes, than to raise. *Pope.*

Sure those who have neither strength nor weapons to fight at least should be civil. *Goldsmith.*

Surely half the world must be blind ; they can see nothing unless it glitters. *Hare.*

Surely it is better to enclose the gulf and hinder all access, than by encouraging us to advance a little, to entice us afterwards a little further, and let us perceive our folly only by our destruction. *Johnson.*

Surely life, if it be not long, is tedious, since we are forced to call in the assistance of so many trifles to rid us of our time, of that time which can never return. *Johnson.*

Surely men of low degree are vanity, and men 35 of high degree are a lie ; to be laid in the balance they are altogether lighter than vanity. *Bible.*

Surely nobody would be a charlatan who could afford to be sincere. *Emerson.*

Surely the best way is to meet the enemy in the field, and not wait till he plunders us in our very bed-chamber. *Goldsmith.*

Surely use alone / Makes money not a contemptible stone. *George Herbert.*

Surement va qui n'a rien—He who has nothing goes securely. *Fr. Pr.*

Surfeit has killed more than hunger. *Pr.* 40

Surfeit of the sweetest things / The deepest loathing to the stomach brings. *Mid. N.'s Dream*, ii. 3.

Surfeits destroy more than the sword. *J. Fletcher.*

Surgit post nubila Phœbus—The sun rises after the clouds. *M.*

Sursum corda—Lift up your hearts. *L.*

Surtout, messieurs, pas de zèle — Above all, 45 gentlemen, no zeal. *Talleyrand.*

Sus Minervam—A pig teaching Minerva.

Susceptibility to one class of influences, the selection of what is fit for him, the rejection of what is unfit, determines for a man the character of the universe. *Emerson.*

Suspectum semper invisumque dominantibus, qui proximus destinaretur—Those in supreme power always suspect and hate their next heir. *Tac.*

Suspendens omnia naso—Sneering at everything. *Hor.*

Suspense is worse than disappointment. *Burns.*

Suspicion always haunts the guilty mind ; / The thief doth fear each bush an officer. 3 *Hen. VI.*, v. 6.

Suspicion is a heavy armour, and with its own weight impedes more than protects. *Byron.*

5 Suspicion is no less an enemy to virtue than to happiness. *Johnson.*

Suspicion is the bane of friendship. *Petrarch.*

Suspicion is very often a useless pain. *Dr. Johnson.*

Suspicion shall be all stuck full of eyes. 1 *Hen. IV.*, v. 1.

Suspicions amongst thoughts are like bats amongst birds; they ever fly by twilight; they are to be repressed, or at the least well guarded, for they cloud the mind. *Bacon.*

10 Suspicions are nothing when a man is really true, and every one should persevere in acting honestly, for all will be made right in time. *Hans Andersen.*

Süsser Wein giebt sauern Essig—Sweet wine yields sour vinegar. *Ger. Pr.*

Sustine et abstine—Bear and forbear. *M.*

Suum cuique—To every man his due. *M.*

Suum cuique decus posteritas rependunt—Posterity will pay every one his due. *Tac.*

15 Suus cuique est mos—Every one has his own way of it. *Hor.*

Suus cuique mos—Every man has his way. *Ter.*

Suum cuique tribuere, ea demum summa justitia est—To give to every man his due, that is supreme justice. *Cic.*

Swearing is invoking the witness of a spirit to an assertion you wish to make, but cursing is invoking the assistance of a spirit in a mischief you wish to inflict. *Ruskin.*

Sweep before your own door. *Pr.*

20 Sweet are the uses of adversity, / Which like the toad, ugly and venomous, / Wears yet a precious jewel in his head ; / And this our life, exempt from public haunt, / Finds tongues in trees, books in the running brooks, / Sermons in stones, and good in everything. *As You Like It.*

Sweet bird, that shunn'st the noise of folly, / Most musical, most melancholy. *Milton.*

Sweet flowers are slow, and weeds make haste. *Rich. III.*, ii. 4.

Sweet is the breath of morn, her rising sweet, / With charm of earliest birds. *Milton.*

Sweet is the lore which Nature brings ; / Our meddling intellect / Misshapes the beauteous form of things : / We murder to dissect. *Wordsworth.*

25 Sweet is true love though given in vain, / And sweet is death that puts an end to pain. *Tennyson.*

Sweet mercy is nobility's true badge. *Tit. Andron.*, i. 2.

Sweet pliability of man's spirit, that can at once surrender itself to illusions which cheat expectation and sorrow of their weary moments ! *Sterne.*

Sweet reader, do you know what a toady is ? That agreeable animal which you meet every day in civilised society. *Disraeli.*

Sweet Swan of Avon. *Ben Jonson of Shakespeare.*

Sweetest melodies are those that are by dis- 30 tance made more sweet. *Wordsworth.*

Swift kindnesses are best : a long delay / In kindness takes the kindness all away. *Anon.*

Swift to its close ebbs out life's little day. *Lyte.*

Sworn to no master, of no sect am I ; / As drives the storm, at any door I knock, / And house with Montaigne now, and now with Locke. *Pope.*

Syllables govern the world. *Coke.*

Sympathetic people are often uncommunicative 35 about themselves ; they give back reflected images which hide their own depths. *George Eliot.*

Sympathising and selfish people are alike given to tears. *Leigh Hunt.*

Sympathy can create the boldness which no other means can evoke. *Dr. Parker.*

Sympathy is the first condition of criticism ; reason and justice presuppose, at their origin, emotion. *Amiel.*

Sympathy is the first great lesson which man should learn. . . . Unless he learns to feel for things in which he has no personal interest, he can achieve nothing generous or noble. *Talfourd.*

Sympathy is the solace of the poor, but for the 40 rich there is consolation. *Disraeli.*

Sympathy is two hearts tugging at one load. *C. H. Parkhurst.*

Sympathy wanting, all is wanting ; its personal magnetism is the conductor of the sacred spark that lights our atoms, puts us in human communion, and gives us to company, conversation, and ourselves. *A. B. Alcott.*

Sympathy with Nature is a part of the good man's religion. *F. H. Hedge.*

Syne as ye brew, . . . / Keep mind that ye maun drink the yill. *Burns.*

T.

Tabesne cadavera solvat, / An rogus, haud 45 refert—It makes no difference whether corruption dissolve the carcase or the funeral pile. *Lucan.*

Tabula ex *or* in naufragio—A plank in a shipwreck ; a last shift.

Table d'hôte—A common table for guests. *Fr.*

Tableau vivant—A group in which statues or pictures are represented by living persons. *Fr.*

Tabula rasa—A smooth or blank tablet ; a blank surface.

Tacent, satis laudant—Their silence is praise 50 enough. *Ter.*

Tâche sans tache—A task, or work, without a blemish. *M.*

Tacitæ magis et occultæ inimicitiæ sunt, quam indictæ et opertæ—Enmities unavowed and concealed are more to be feared than when open and declared. *Cic.*

Tacitum vivit sub pectore vulnus—The secret wound still lives in her heart. *Virg.*

Tact is one of the first of mental virtues, the absence of which is often fatal to the best talents. It supplies the place of many talents. *Simms.*

Tadeln kann ein jeder Bauer ; besser machen wird ihm sauer—Every boor can find fault ; it would baffle him to do better. *Ger. Pr.*

Tadeln können zwar die Thoren, / Aber klüger handeln nicht—Fools can find fault indeed, but they cannot act more wisely. *Langbein.*

Tædium vitæ—Weariness of life ; disgust with existence. *Gell.*

5 Tages Arbeit, Abends Gäste, / Saure Wochen, frohe Feste, / Sei dein künftig Zauberwort —Be work by day, guests at eve, weeks of toil, festive days of joy, the magic spell for thy future. *Goethe.*

Take a bird from a clean nest. *Gael. Pr.*

Take a farthing from a thousand pounds, it will be a thousand pounds no longer. *Goldsmith.*

Take a hair of the same dog that bit you, and it will heal the wound. *Pr.*

Take a stick to a Highland laddie, and it's no him you hurt, but his ancestors. *J. M. Barrie.*

10 Take all that is given, whether wealth, / Or love, or language ; nothing comes amiss ; / A good digestion turneth all to health. *George Herbert.*

Take any subject of sorrowful regret, and see with how much pleasure it is associated. *Dickens.*

Take away desire from the heart, and you take away the air from the earth. *Bulwer Lytton.*

Take care of the pence ; the pounds will take care of themselves. *Pr.*

Take care to be an economist in prosperity ; there is no fear of your not being one in adversity. *Zimmermann.*

15 Take each man's censure, but reserve thy judgment. *Ham., i. 3.*

Take everything easy (*leicht*) ; leave off dreaming and brooding (*Grübeln*), and you will be ever well guarded from a thousand evils. *Uhland.*

Take fast hold of instruction ; let her not go : keep her, for she is thy life. *Bible.*

Take from the philosopher the pleasure of being heard, and his desire for knowledge ceases. *Rousseau.*

Take heed, and beware of covetousness ; for a man's life consisteth not in the abundance of the things which he possesseth. *Jesus.*

20 Take heed of the vinegar of sweet wine. *Pr.*

Take heed you find not that you do not seek. *Pr.*

Take-it-easy and Live-long are brothers. *Ger. Pr.*

Take my yoke upon you, and learn of me ; for I am meek and lowly in heart ; and ye shall find rest unto your souls. *Jesus.*

Take no thought for the morrow ; for the morrow shall take thought for the things of itself. *Jesus.*

25 Take no thought for your life, what ye shall eat, or what ye shall drink ; nor yet for your body, what ye shall put on. *Jesus.*

Take not His name who made thy mouth in vain : / It gets thee nothing, and has no excuse. *George Herbert.*

Take note, take note, O world, / To be direct and honest is not safe. *Othello, iii. 3.*

Take physic, pomp ; / Expose thyself to feel what wretches feel ; / That thou mayst shake the superflux to them, / And show the heavens more just. *Lear, iii. 4.*

Take the Muses' servants by the hand ; / . . . And where ye justly can commend, commend them ; / And aiblins when they winna stand the test, / Wink hard, and say the folks hae done their best. *Burns.*

Take the showers as they fall, / . . . Enough 30 if at the end of all / A little garden blossom. *Tennyson.*

Take this rule, . . . The best-bred child hath the best portion. *Pr. Herbert.*

Take thou the beam out of thine own eye ; then shalt thou see clearly to take the mote out of thy brother's. *Jesus.*

Take thought for thy body with steadfast fidelity. The soul must see through these eyes alone ; and if they are dim, the whole world is beclouded. *Goethe.*

Take time by the forelock. *Thales.*

Take time in time, ere time be tint (lost). *Sc. Pr.* 35

Take time in turning a corner. *Pr.*

Take up the torch and wave it wide, / The torch that lights Time's thickest gloom. *Bonar.*

Take your thirst to the stream, as the dog does. *Gael. Pr.*

Taking, therefore, my opinion of the English from the virtues and vices practised among the vulgar, they at once present to a stranger all their faults, and keep their virtues up only for the inquiring of a philosopher. *Goldsmith.*

Tale tuum carmen nobis, divine poeta, / Quale 40 sopor fessis—Thy song is to us, O heavenly bard, as sleep to wearied men. *Virg.*

Talent alone cannot make a writer. There must be a man behind the book. *Emerson.*

Talent for literature, thou hast such a talent ? Believe it not, be slow to believe it ! To speak or to write, Nature did not peremptorily order thee ; but to work she did. *Carlyle.*

Talent forms itself in secret ; character, in the great current of the world. *Goethe.*

Talent has almost always this advantage (*Vorsprung*) over genius—that the former endures, the latter often explodes, or runs to waste (*verpufft*). *Gutzkow.*

Talent is a cistern ; genius, a fountain. *Whipple.* 45

Talent is a gift which God has imparted in secret, and which we reveal without knowing it. *Montesquieu.*

Talent is some one faculty unusually developed ; genius commands all the faculties. *F. H. Hedge.*

Talent is something, but tact is everything. It is not a seventh sense, but is the life of all the five. It is the open eye, the quick ear, the judging taste, the keen smell, and the lively touch ; it is the interpreter of all riddles, the surmounter of all difficulties, the remover of all obstacles. *W. P. Scargill.*

Talent is that which is in a man's power ; genius is that in whose power a man is. *Lowell.*

Talent ist Form, Genie Stoff—Talent is form, 50 genius is substance. *Gutzkow.*

Talent, lying in the understanding, is often inherited ; genius, being the action of reason and imagination, rarely or never. *Coleridge.*

Talents angel-bright, if wanting worth, are shining instruments in false ambition's hand, to finish faults illustrious, and give infamy renown. *Young.*

Talents give a man a superiority far more agreeable than that which proceeds from riches, birth, or employments, which are all external. Talents constitute our very essence. *Rollin.*

Taliter qualiter—Such as it is.

5 Talk, except as the preparation for work, is worth almost nothing ; sometimes it is worth infinitely less than nothing ; and becomes, little conscious of playing such a fatal part, the general summary of pretentious nothing-nesses, and the chief of all the curses the posterity of Adam are liable to in this sublunary world. *Carlyle.*

Talk of the devil and he'll appear. *Pr.*

Talk that does not end in action is better suppressed altogether. *Carlyle.*

Talk to him of Jacob's ladder, and he would ask the number of the steps. *Douglas Jerrold.*

Talkers are no good doers. *Rich. III.*, i. 3.

10 Talking is one of the fine arts. *Holmes.*

Talking is the disease of age. *Ben Jonson.*

Talking of love is making it. *Pr.*

Talking with a host is next best to talking with one's self. . . . He is wiser than to contradict his guest in any case ; he lets him go on, he lets him travel. *Thoreau.*

Tam deest avaro quod habet, quam quod non habet—The miser is as much in want of that which he has as of that which he has not. *Pub. Syr.*

15 Tam diu discendum est, quum diu nescias, et, si proverbio credimus, quam diu vivas—You must continue learning as long as you do not know, and, if the proverb is to be believed, as long as you live. *Sen.*

Tam Marte quam Minerva—As much by Mars as by Minerva ; as much by courage as by wisdom. *Pr.*

Tam Marti quam Mercurio—As much for Mars as for Mercury ; as well qualified for war as for business.

Tam felix utinam, quam pectore candidus, essem—Oh, that I were as happy as I am clear in conscience. *Ovid.*

Tam lo'ed him like a vera brither ; / They had been fou for weeks thegither. *Burns.*

20 Tamen me / Cum magnis vixisse invita fatebitur usque / Invidia—Nevertheless, even envy, however unwilling, will have to admit that I have lived among great men. *Hor.*

Tandem fit surculus arbor—A twig in time becomes a tree. *M.*

Tandem poculum mœroris exhausit—He has exhausted at last the cup of grief. *Cic.*

τὰ νεῦρα τοῦ πολέμου—The sinews of war. *Pr.*

Tangere ulcus—To touch a sore ; to renew one's grief. *Ter.*

25 Tanquam in speculo—As in a mirror.

Tanquam nobilis—Noble by courtesy.

Tanquam ungues digitosque suos—As well as his nails and fingers : at his fingers' ends. *Pr.*

Tant de fiel entre-t-il dans l'âme des dévôts ?—Can so much gall find access in devout souls? *Boileau.*

Tant mieux—So much the better. *Fr.*

Tant pis—So much the worse. *Fr.* 30

Tant va la cruche à l'eau qu'à la fin elle se brise—The pitcher goes so often to the well that it is broken at last. *Fr.*

Tantæ molis erat Romanam condere gentem—Such a task it was to found the Roman race. *Virg.*

Tantæne animis cœlestibus iræ ?—Can heavenly minds cherish such dire resentment ? *Virg.*

Tanti eris aliis, quanti tibi fueris—You will be of as much value to others as you have been to yourself. *Cic.*

Tanto brevius omne tempus, quanto felicius— 35 The happier the moments the shorter. *Pliny.*

Tanto buon, che val niente—So good as to be good for nothing. *It. Pr.*

Tanto fortior, tanto felicior !—The more pluck, the better luck !

Tanto più di pregio reca all' opera l'umiltà dell' artista, quanto più aggiunge di valori al numero la nullità del zero—The modesty of the artist adds as much to the merit of his work as does a cipher (of no value in itself) to the number to which it is joined. *Bernini.*

Tanto vale la Messa detta quanto la cantata—A mass is as good said as sung. *It. Pr.*

Tantum quantum—Just as much as. 40

Tantum religio potuit suadere malorum—Could such cruelties have been perpetrated in the name of religion? *Lucret. in reference to the sacrifice of Iphigenia.*

Tantum series juncturaque / Tantum de medio sumptis accedit honoris—Such is the power of order and arrangement : so much grace may be imparted to subjects from common life. *Hor.*

Tantum vertice in auras / Aetherias quantum radice in Tartara tendit—Its summit stretches as far into the upper ether as its root into the nether deep.

Tantus amor laudum, tantæ est victoria curæ —Such is the love of praise, so great the anxiety for victory. *Virg.*

Tapfer ist der Löwesieger, / Tapfer ist der 45 Weltbezwinger, / Tapfer wer sich selbst bezwang—Brave is the lion-vanquisher, brave is the world-subduer, but braver he who has subdued himself. *J. G. Herder.*

Tarda sit illa dies, et nostro serior ævo—Slow may that day approach, and long after our time. *Ovid.*

Tarda solet magnis rebus inesse fides—Men are slow to repose confidence in undertakings of magnitude. *Ovid.*

Tarde, quæ credita lædunt, credimus—We are slow to believe that which, if believed, would work us harm. *Ovid.*

Tarde sed tute—Slow but sure. *M.*

Tarde venientibus ossa—To those who come late 50 the bones. *Pr.*

Tardiora sunt remedia quam mala—Remedies are slower in their operation than diseases. *Tac.*

Tasks in hours of insight willed, / In hours of gloom must be fulfilled. *Matthew Arnold.*

Taste can only be educated by contemplation, not of the tolerably good, but of the truly excellent. *Goethe.*

Taste depends upon those finer emotions which make the organisation of the soul. *Sir J. Reynolds.*

Taste, if it mean anything but a paltry connoisseurship, must mean a general susceptibility to truth and nobleness; a sense to discern and a heart to love and reverence all beauty, order, goodness, wheresoever found and in whatsoever form and accompaniment. *Carlyle.*

Taste is the very maker of judgment. *Leigh Hunt.*

Taste may change, but inclination never. *La Roche.*

5 τὰ σῦκα σῦκα, τὴν σκάφην δὲ σκάφην ὀνομάζων— Calling a fig a fig, and a spade a spade. *Plut.*

Taurum tollet qui vitulum sustulerit—He who has carried the calf will be able by and by to carry the ox. *Pr.*

Te Deum laudamus—We praise Thee, O God.

Te digna sequere—Follow what is worthy of thee. *M.*

Te, Fortuna, sequor: procul hinc jam fœdera sunto : / Credidimus fatis, utendum est judice bello—Thee, Fortune, I follow; hence far all treaties past; to fate I commit myself, and the arbitrament of war. *Lucan on the crossing of the Rubicon by Cæsar.*

10 Te hominem esse memento — Remember thou art a man.

Te sine nil altum mens inchoat—Without thee my mind originates nothing lofty. *Virg. to Mæcenas.*

Teach me to feel another's woe, / To hide the fault I see; / That mercy I to others show, / That mercy show to me. *Pope.*

Teach self-denial, and make its practice pleasurable, and you create for the world a destiny more sublime than ever issued from the brain of the wildest dreamer. *Scott.*

Teach your children poetry; it opens the mind, lends grace to wisdom, and makes the heroic virtues hereditary. *Mahomet.*

15 Teaching has not a tithe of the efficacy of training. *Horace Mann.*

Teaching is of more importance than exhortation. *Luther.*

Teaching others teacheth yourself. *Pr.*

Tearless grief bleeds inwardly. *Bovee.*

Tears are due to human misery. *Virg.*

20 Tears are often to be found where there is little sorrow, and the deepest sorrow without tears. *Johnson.*

Tears are the deluge of sin and the world's sacrifice. *Gregory Nazianzen.*

Tears are the symbol of the inability of the soul to restrain its emotion and retain its self-command. *Amiel.*

Tears, idle tears, I know not what they mean, / Tears from the depth of some divine despair / Rise in the heart and gather in the eyes, / In looking on the happy autumn fields, / And thinking of the days that are no more. *Tennyson.*

Tears of joy are the dew in which the sun of righteousness is mirrored. *Jean Paul.*

25 Tears of joy, like summer rain-drops, are pierced by sunbeams. *H. Ballou.*

Tears such as angels weep. *Milton.*

Tecum habita—Live with yourself; keep within your means.

Teeth, hair, nails, and the human species, prosper not when separated from their place. A wise man, being informed of this, should not totally forsake his native home. *Hitopadesa.*

Tel brille au second rang, qui s'éclipse au premier—Some who are eclipsed in the first rank may shine in the second. *Voltaire.*

Tel coup de langue est pire qu'un coup de 30 lance—Such a stroke with the tongue is worse than one with a lance. *Fr. Pr.*

Tel, en vous lisant, admire chaque trait, / Qui dans le fond de l'âme vous craint et vous hait—Such a one, in reading your work, admires every line, but, at the bottom of his soul, he fears and hates you. *Boileau.*

Tel excelle à rimer qui juge sottement—Some excel in rhyme who reason foolishly. *Boileau.*

Tel maître, tel valet—Like master, like man. *Fr. Pr.*

Tel père, tel fils—Like father, like son. *Fr. Pr.*

Tel vous semble applaudir, qui vous raille et 35 vous joue ; / Aimez qu'on vous conseille, et non pas qu'on vous loue—Such a one seems to applaud, while he is really ridiculing you ; attach yourself to those who advise you rather than to those who praise. *Boileau.*

Tell it not in Gath, publish it not in the streets of Askelon. *Bible.*

" Tell me how you bear so blandly the assuming ways of wild young people?" Truly they would be unbearable if I had not also been unbearable myself as well. *Goethe.*

Tell me not, in mournful numbers, / "Life is but an empty dream," / For the soul is dead that slumbers, / And things are not what they seem. *Longfellow.*

Tell me what you like, and I will tell you what you are. *Ruskin.*

Tell me where is fancy bred, / Or in the heart, 40 or in the head? / How begot, how nourished? / It is engender'd in the eyes, / With gazing fed. *Mer. of Venice, iii. 2.*

Tell me with whom you associate, and I will tell you who you are; if I know what it is with which you occupy yourself, I know what you may become. *Goethe.*

Tell the truth and shame the devil. *1 Henry IV., iii. 1.*

Telum imbelle sine ictu—A feeble dart thrown without effect. *Virg.*

Temeritas est florentis ætatis, prudentia senescentis—Rashness belongs to youth, prudence to old age. *Cic.*

Temper—a weapon that we hold by the blade. 45 *J. M. Barrie.*

Temper is so good a thing that we should never lose it. (?).

Temperament lies behind mood ; back of the caprice of will lies the fate of character ; back of both is the bias of family ; back of that, the tyranny of race ; still deeper, the power of climate, of soil, of geology, the whole physical and moral environment. Still we are free men only so far as we rise above these. *John Burroughs.*

Temperance and labour are the two best physicians of man. *Rousseau.*

Temperance is a bridle of gold. *Burton.*

Temperance is a tree which has for its root very little contentment, and for its fruit calm and peace. *Buddha.*

Temperance is the nurse of chastity. *Wycherley.*

Tempi passati !—Bygone times! *Joseph II. at sight of a picture representing a predecessor doing penance to the Pope.*

Templa quam dilecta !—How lovely are thy temples ! *M. of the Duke of Buckingham, whose family name is Temple.*

5 Tempora labuntur, tacitisque senescimus annis ; / Et fugiunt fræno non remorante dies —Time glides away, and we grow older through the noiseless years ; the days flee away, and are restrained by no rein. *Ovid.*

Tempora mutantur, nos et mutamur in illis —Times change, and we change with them. *Kaiser Lothar I.*

Tempore ducetur longo fortasse cicatrix ; / Horrent admotas vulnera cruda manus—A wound may, perhaps, through time be closed, but, when fresh, it shrinks from the touch. *Ovid.*

Tempted Fate will leave the loftiest star. *Byron.*

Tempus anima rei—Time is the soul of business.

10 Tempus edax rerum—Time, the devourer of all things. *Ovid.*

Tempus erit quo vos speculum vidisse pigebit —The time will come when it will disgust you to look in a mirror. *Ovid.*

Tempus est quædam pars æternitatis—Time is a certain fraction of eternity. *Cic.*

Tempus ferax, tempus edax rerum—Time the producer, time the devourer of kings.

Tempus fugit—Time flies.

15 Tempus in agrorum cultu consumere dulce est—It is delightful to spend one's time in the tillage of the fields. *Ovid.*

Tempus omnia revelat—Time reveals all things.

Tempus rerum imperator—Time is sovereign over all things. *M.*

Ten censure wrong for one who writes amiss. *Pope.*

τὴν δὲ μάλιστα γαμεῖν, ἥτις σέθεν ἔγγυθι ναίει—Be sure you take for wife a woman of your own neighbourhood. *Hesiod.*

20 Tenax et fidelis—Steadfast and faithful. *M.*

Tenax propositi—Tenacious of his purpose. *M.*

Tendency to sentimental whining or fierce intolerance may be ranked among the surest symptoms of little souls and inferior intellects. *Jeffrey.*

Tenderness is a virtue. *Goldsmith.*

Tenderness is the repose of passion. *Joubert.*

25 Tenebo—I will hold. *M.*

Teneros animos aliena opprobria sæpe / Absterrent vitiis—The disgrace of others often deters tender minds from vice. *Hor.*

Tenet insanabile multos / Scribendi cacoëthes—An incurable itch for writing possesses many. *Juv.*

Tenez la bride haute à votre fils—Keep a tight hand over your son (*lit.* hold the bridle high). *Fr. Pr.*

Tenir le haut du pavé—To keep the best place (*lit.* the highest side of the pavement). *Fr. Pr.*

30 Tentanda via est qua me quoque possim / Tollere humo, victorque virûm volitare per ora—I too must attempt a way by which I may raise myself above the ground, and soar triumphant through the lips of men. *Virg.*

Tenterden steeple was the cause of Goodwin Sands. *Pr.*

Ter conatus ibi collo dare brachia circum, / Ter frustra comprensa manus effugit imago —Thrice I attempted to throw my arms round her neck there, and her ghost, thrice clutched in vain, eluded my grasp. *Virg.*

Teres atque rotundum—Smooth - polished and rounded. *Hor.*

Terminus a quo—The point from which anything starts.

Terminus ad quem—The point of destination. 35

Terra antiqua, potens armis atque ubere glebæ —An ancient land, powerful in arms and in the fertility of its soil. *Virg., of Italy.*

Terra firma—Dry land, in contradistinction to sea.

Terra incognita—An unknown land or domain of things.

Terra innanzi, e terra poi—Earth originally, and earth finally. *It. Pr.*

Terra malos homines nunc educat, atque 40 pusillos—The earth now supports many bad and weak men. *Juv.*

Terræ filius — A son of the earth ; a man of obscure or low origin. *Pers.*

Terram cœlo miscent—They mingle heaven and earth.

Terrible penalty, with the ass-ears or without them, inevitable as death, written for ever in heaven, against all who, like Midas, misjudge the inner and the upper melodies, and prefer gold to goodness, desire to duty, falsehood to fact, wild nature to God, and a sensual piping Pan to a high-souled, wise-hearted, and spirit-breathing Apollo. *Ed., apropos to the fable of Midas.*

Tertium quid—A third something, produced by the union or interaction of two opposites.

Tertium sal—A third salt ; a neutral salt ; the 45 union of an acid and an alkali.

Tertius e cœlo cecidit Cato—A third Cato has come down from heaven. *Juv., in mockery.*

τῆς ἀρετῆς ἱδρῶτα θεοὶ προπάροιθεν ἔθηκαν— The gods have placed sweat in front of virtue. *Hesiod.*

Testimony is like an arrow shot from a long bow ; the force of it depends upon the strength of the hand that draws it. Argument is like an arrow from a cross-bow, which has equal force though shot by a child. *Johnson.*

Tête-à-tête—Face to face ; a private conversation. *Fr.*

Tête d'armée !—Head of the army ! *Last words* 50 *of Napoleon.*

Tête de fou ne blanchit jamais—A fool's head never grows grey. *Pr.*

Teuer ist mir der Freund, doch auch den Feind kann ich nützen ; / Zeigt mir der Freund, was ich kann, lehrt mich der Feind, was ich soll—Dear is to me the friend, yet can I make even my very foe do me a friend's part. My friend shows me what I can do ; my foe teaches me what I should do. *Schiller.*

That action is not warrantable which either blushes to beg a blessing, or, having succeeded, dares not present a thanksgiving. *Quarles.*

That but this blow / Might be the be-all and the end-all here, / But here, upon this bank and shoal of time, / We'd jump the life to come. *Macb., i. 7.*

That carries anger as the flint bears fire; / Who, much enforcèd, shows a hasty spark, / And straight is cold again. *Jul. Cæs.*, iv. 3.

That cause is strong which has not a multitude, but one strong man behind it. *Lowell.*

That circle of beings, which dependence gathers round us, is almost ever unfriendly. *Arliss.*

That civility is best which excludes all superfluous formality. (?)

5 That cutting up, and parcelling, and labelling, of the indivisible human soul into what are called "faculties," I have from of old eschewed, and even hated. *Carlyle.*

That death's unnatural that kills for loving. *Othello*, v. 2.

That elevation of mind which we see in moments of peril, if it is uncontrolled by justice, and strives only for its own advantage, becomes a crime. *Cic.*

That friendship only is, indeed, genuine when two friends, without speaking a word to each other, can, nevertheless, find happiness in being together. *Georg Ebers.*

That friendship, which is exerted in too wide a sphere, becomes totally useless. *Goldsmith.*

10 That gentleman who sells an acre of land, sells an ounce of credit. *Lord Burleigh.*

That golden key that opes the palace of eternity. *Milton.*

That government is the best which makes goverument unnecessary. *W. von Humboldt.*

That great mystery of time, were there no other; the illimitable, silent, never-resting thing called "time," rolling, rushing on, swift, silent, like an all-embracing ocean-tide, on which we and all the universe swim like exhalations, like apparitions which are and then are not—this is for ever very literally a miracle, a thing to strike us dumb; for we have no word to speak about it. *Carlyle.*

That grief is light which is capable of counsel. *Pr.*

15 That he is mad 'tis true; 'tis true, 'tis pity; / And pity 'tis 'tis true. *Ham.*, ii. 2.

That in the captain's but a choleric word, / Which in the soldier is flat blasphemy. *Meas. for Meas.*, ii. 2.

That intention which fixes upon God as its only end will keep men steady in their purposes, and deliver them from being the jest and scorn of fortune. *Thomas à Kempis.*

That is a most wretched fortune which is without an enemy. *Pub. Syr.*

That is a treacherous friend against whom you must always be on your guard. Such a friend is wine. *Bovee.*

20 That is always best which gives me to myself. *Emerson.*

That is but an empty purse that is full of other men's money. *Pr.*

That is friendship which is not feigned. *Hitopadesa.*

That is gold that is worth gold. *Pr.*

That is indeed a twofold knowledge which profits alike by the folly of the foolish and the wisdom of the wise. It is both a shield and a sword; it borrows its security from the darkness, and its confidence from the light. *Colton.*

That is not a council wherein there are no 25 sages. *Hitopadesa.*

That is not a duty in which there is not virtue. *Hitopadesa.*

That is not possible which is impossible. *Hitopadesa.*

That is not virtue from which fear approacheth us. *Hitopadesa.*

That is the best part of beauty which a picture cannot express. *Bacon.*

That is the best part of each writer which has 30 nothing private in it. *Emerson.*

That is the briefest and sagest of maxims which bids us "meddle not." *Colton.*

That is the true light which lighteth every man that cometh into the world. *St. John.*

That is the true season of love, when we believe that we alone can love, that no one could ever have loved so before us, and that no one will love in the same way after us. *Goethe.*

That is true love which is always the same, whether you give everything or deny everything to it. *Goethe.*

That is well spoken that is well taken. *Pr.* 35

That last infirmity of noble minds. *Milton.*

That learning which thou gettest by thy own observation and experience is far beyond that which thou gettest by precept; as the knowledge of a traveller exceeds that which is got by reading. *Thomas à Kempis.*

That life is long which answers life's great end. *Young.*

That low vice curiosity. *Byron.*

That man has advanced far in the study of 40 morals who has mastered the difference between pride and vanity. *Chamfort.*

That man is always happy who is in the presence of something which he cannot know to the full, which he is always going on to know. *Ruskin.*

That man is an ill husband of his honour that entereth into any action, the failing wherein may disgrace him more than the carrying of it through can honour him. *Bacon.*

That man is learned who reduceth his learning to practice. *Hitopadesa.*

That man is little to be envied whose patriotism would not gain force upon the plain of Marathon, or whose piety would not grow warmer among the ruins of Iona. *Johnson.*

That man lives twice that lives the first life 45 well. *Herrick.*

That man may last, but never lives, / Who much receives but nothing gives; / Whom none can love, whom none can thank— / Creation's blot, creation's blank. *T. Gibbons.*

That man that hath a tongue, I say, is no man, / If with his tongue he cannot win a woman. *Two Gent. of Verona*, ii. 1.

That man will never be a perfect gentleman who lives only with gentlemen. To be a man of the world we must view that world in every grade and in every perspective. *Bulwer Lytton.*

That Mirabeau understood how to act with others, and by others—this was his genius, this was his originality, this was his greatness. *Goethe.*

That must be true which all men say. *Pr.* 50

That nation is in the enjoyment of liberty which stands by its own strength, and does not depend on the will of another. *Livy.*

That net that holds no great, takes little fish. *R. Southwell.*

That one man should die ignorant who had capacity for knowledge, this I call tragedy. *Carlyle.*

That one will not, another will. *Pr.*

5 That philanthropy has surely a flaw in it which cannot sympathise with the oppressor equally as with the oppressed. *Lowell.*

That rich man is great who thinketh not himself great because he is rich ; the proud man (who is the poor man) braggeth outwardly but beggeth inwardly ; he is blown up, but not full. *S. Hieron.*

That single effort by which we stop short in the down-hill path to perdition is of itself a greater exertion of virtue than a hundred acts of justice. *Goldsmith.*

That souls which are created for one another so seldom find each other and are generally divided, that in the moments of happiest union least recognise each other—that is a sad riddle ! *Goethe.*

That State must sooner or later perish where the majority triumphs and unintelligence (*Unverstand*) decides. *Schiller.*

10 That state of life is alone suitable to a man in which and for which he was born, and he who is not led abroad by great objects is far happier at home. *Goethe.*

That strain again ! It had a dying fall : / Oh, it came o'er my ear like the sweet sound / That breathes upon a bank of violets, / Giving and stealing odour ! *Twelfth Night*, i. 1

That suit is best that best fits me. *Pr.*

That that comes of a hen will scrape. *Pr.*

That that is, is. *As You Like It*, iv. 2.

15 That the voice of the common people is the voice of God, is as full of falsehood as commonness. For who sees not that those black-mouthed hounds, upon the mere scent of opinion, as freely spend their mouths in hunting counter, or, like Actæon's dogs, in chasing an innocent man to death, as if they followed the chase of truth itself, in a fresh scent ? *A. Warwick.*

That thee is sent receive in buxomness : / The wrestling of this world asketh a fall. / Here is no home, here is but wilderness. / Forth, pilgrim, forth—on, best out of thy stall. / Look up on high, and thank the God of all. *Chaucer.*

That thought I regard as true which is fruitful to myself, which is connected with the rest of my thoughts, and at the same time helps me on. Now it is not only possible, but natural, that such a thought should not connect itself with the mind of another, nor help him on . . . consequently he will regard it as false. Once we are thoroughly convinced of this, we shall never enter upon controversies. *Goethe.*

That ugly treason of mistrust. *Mer. of Ven.*, iii. 2.

That unity which has not its origin in the multitude is tyranny. *Pascal.*

20 That very law which moulds a tear, / And bids it trickle from its source ; / That law preserves the earth a sphere, / And guides the planets in their course. *Rogers.*

That vice has often proved an emancipator of the mind is one of the most humiliating, but also one of the most unquestionable, facts in history. *Lecky.*

That virtue which requires to be ever guarded is scarcely worth the sentinel. *Goldsmith.*

That voluntary debility, which modern language is content to term indolence, will, if it is not counteracted by resolution, render in time the strongest faculties lifeless, and turn the flame to the smoke of virtue. *Johnson.*

That warrior on his strong war-horse, fire flashes through his eyes ; force dwells in his arm and heart ; but warrior and war-horse are a vision ; a revealed force, nothing more. Stately they tread the earth, as if it were firm substance. Fool ! the earth is but a film ; it cracks in twain, and warrior and war-horse sink beyond plummet's sounding. *Carlyle.*

That we devote ourselves to God is seen / In 25 living just as though no God there were. *Browning.*

That we shall die, we know ; 'tis but the time / And drawing days out, that men stand upon. *Julius Cæsar*, iii. 1.

That we should find our national existence depend on selling manufactured cotton at a farthing an ell cheaper than any other people, is a most narrow stand for a great nation to base itself on. *Carlyle.*

That we would do, / We should do when we would ; for this "would" changes, / And hath abatements and delays as many / As there are tongues, are hands, are accidents ; / And then this "should" is like a spendthrift's sigh, / That hurts by easing. *Ham.*, iv. 7.

That were but a sorry art which could be comprehended all at once ; the last point of which could be seen by one just entering its precincts. *Goethe.*

That which builds is better than that which is 30 built. *Emerson.*

That which can be done with perfect convenience and without loss, is not always the thing that most needs to be done, or which we are most imperatively required to do. *Ruskin.*

That which each man can do best, not but his Maker can teach him. *Emerson.*

That which God writes on thy forehead thou wilt come to. *The Koran.*

That which hath been is now ; and that which is to be hath already been. *Bible.*

That which I crave may everywhere be had, / 35 With me I bring the one thing needful—love. *Goethe.*

That which in mean men we entitle patience, / Is pale cold cowardice in noble breasts. *Rich. II.*, i. 2.

That which, intellectually considered, we call Reason, considered in relation to nature we call Spirit. *Emerson.*

That which is crooked cannot be made straight : and that which is wanting cannot be numbered. *Bible.*

That which is good to take is good to keep. *Pr.*

That which is in the midst of fools is made 40 known. *Bible.*

That which is not allotted the hand cannot reach, and what is allotted will find you wherever you may be. *Saadi.*

That which is past is gone and irrevocable, and wise men have enough to do with things present and to come; therefore they do but trifle with themselves that labour in past matters. *Bacon.*

That which is possible is ever possible. *Hitopadesa.*

That which is truly and indeed characteristic of the man is known only to God. *Ruskin.*

That which makes men happy is activity (*die Thätigkeit*), which, first producing what is good, soon changes evil itself into good by power working in a god-like manner. *Goethe.*

5 That which one least anticipates soonest comes to pass. *Pr.*

That which produces and maintains cheerfulness is nothing but activity. *Jean Paul.*

That which proves too much proves nothing. *Pr.*

That which seems to be wealth may in verity be only the gilded index of far-reaching ruin; a wrecker's handful of coin gleaned from the beach to which he has beguiled an argosy. *Ruskin.*

That which the droning world, chained to appearances, will not allow the realist to say in new words, it will suffer him to say in proverbs without contradiction. *Emerson.*

10 That which the sun doth not now see will be visible when the sun is out, and the stars are fallen from heaven. *Sir Thomas Browne.*

That which two will takes effect. *Pr.*

That which upholdeth him, that thee upholds—His honour. *King John,* iii. 1.

That which was bitter to endure may be sweet to remember. *Pr.*

That which we do not believe we cannot adequately say, though we may repeat the words never so often. *Emerson.*

15 That which we have we prize not to the worth; / But being lacked and lost, why then we rake its value. *Much Ado,* iv. 1.

That which we may live without we need not much covet. *Pr.*

That which will not be butter must be made into cheese. *Pr.*

That which will not be spun, let it not come between the spindle and the distaff. *Pr.*

That woman is despicable who, having children, ever feels ennui. *Jean Paul.*

20 That wretchedness which fate has rendered voiceless and tuneless is not the least wretched, but the most. *Pr.*

That's a lee wi' a lid on, / And a brass handle to tak ho'd on. *Pr.*

That's my good that does me good. *Pr.*

That's the best gown that goes up and down the house. *Pr.*

That's the humour of it. *Henry V.,* ii. 1.

25 That's what a man wants in a wife, mostly: he wants to make sure o' one fool as'll tell him he's wise. But there's some men can do wi'out that—they think so much o' themselves a'ready—an' that's how it is there's old bachelors. *George Eliot.*

The abandoning of some lower end in obedience to a higher aim is often made the very condition of securing the lower one. *J. C. Sharp.*

The abiding city and post at which we can live and die is still ahead of us, it would appear. *Carlyle.*

The absent one is an ideal person; those who are present seem to one another to be quite commonplace. It is a silly thing that the ideal is, as it were, ousted by the real; that may be the reason why to the moderns their ideal only manifests itself in longing. *Goethe.*

The absent party is still faulty. *Pr.*

The accepted and betrothed lover has lost the 30 wildest charms of his maiden in her acceptance of him. She was heaven whilst he pursued her as a star—she cannot be heaven if she stoops to such a one as he. *Emerson.*

The accusing spirit, which flew up to heaven's chancery with the oath, blushed as he gave it in; and the recording angel, as he wrote it down, dropped a tear upon the word and blotted it out for ever. *Sterne.*

The acknowledgment of our weakness is the first step towards repairing our loss. *Thomas à Kempis.*

The actual well seen is the ideal. *Carlyle.*

The advice that is wanted is commonly unwelcome; that which is not wanted is evidently impertinent. *Johnson.*

The affections of young ladies is of as rapid 35 growth as Jack's beanstalk, and reaches up to the sky in a night. *Thackeray.*

The afflictions of earth exalt the spirit and lift the soul to God. *Tiedge.*

The age made no sign when Shakespeare, its noblest son, passed away. *Willmott.*

The age of chivalry is gone. That of sophisters, economists, and calculators has succeeded; and the glory of Europe is extinguished for ever. *Burke.*

The age of curiosity, like that of chivalry, is ended, properly speaking, gone. Yet perhaps only gone to sleep. *Carlyle.*

The age of great men is going; the epoch of 40 the anthill, of life in multiplicity, is beginning. *Amiel.*

The age of miracles past! The age of miracles is for ever here. *Carlyle.*

The ages of greatest public spirit are not always eminent for private virtue. *Hume.*

The agnosticism of doubt is as far from the agnosticism of devotion as blindness for want of vision from blindness through excess of light. *James Martineau.*

The aim of all morality, truly conceived, is to furnish men with a standard of action and a motive to work by, which shall not intensify each man's selfishness, but raise him ever more and more above it. *J. C. Sharpe.*

The aim of education should be to teach us 45 rather how to think than what to think. *Beattie.*

The aim of life is work, or there is no aim at all. *Auerbach.*

The aim of the legislator should be, not truth, but expediency. *Buckle.*

The air seems nimble with the glad, / Quaint fancies of our childhood dear. *Dr. Walter Smith.*

The alchemists in their search for gold discovered other things of greater value. *Schopenhauer.*

The all in all of faith is *that* we believe; of 50 knowledge, *what* we know, as well as how much and how well. *Goethe.*

The almighty dollar. *Washington Irving.*

The alpha and omega of Socialism is the transmutation of private competing capital into united collective capital. *Schœffle.*

The amateur, however weak may be his efforts at imitation, need not be discouraged, . . . for one advances to an idea the more surely and steadily the more accurately and precisely he considers individual objects. Only it will not do to measure one's self with artists; every one must go on in his own style. *Goethe.*

The ambitious are ever followed by adulation, for such alone receive most pleasure from flattery. *Goldsmith.*

5 The amount of intellect necessary to please us is a most accurate measure of the amount of intellect we have ourselves. *Helvetius.*

The ancient Spartan custom of killing weak-bodied children is not much crueller than that of propagating weak-minded ones. *Jean Paul.*

The ancients tell us what is best; but we must learn of the moderns what is fittest. *Ben. Franklin.*

The anger of a strong man can always bide its time. *Ruskin.*

The animal is capable of enjoyment, only man is capable of serenity of mind and gladness of heart. *Jean Paul.*

10 The animals look for man's intentions right into his eyes. Even a rat, when you hunt him and bring him to bay, looks you in the eye. *H. Powers.*

The apparel oft proclaims the man. *Ham., i. 3.*

The apprehension and representation of what is individual is the very life of art. *Goethe.*

The apprehension of the good / Gives but the greater feeling to the worse. *Rich. II., i. 3.*

The arch-enemy is the arch-stupid. *Carlyle.*

15 The archer who overshoots the mark misses, as well as he that falls short of it. *Pr.*

The argument all bare is of more worth / Than when it hath my added praise beside. *Shakespeare.*

The army is a good book to open to study human life. *Alfred de Vigny.*

The army is a school in which the niggardly become generous and the generous prodigal. *Cervantes.*

The arrows of sarcasm are barbed with contempt. . . . It is the sneer in the satire or the ridicule that galls or wounds. *W. Gladden.*

20 The art of exalting lowliness and giving greatness to little things is one of the noblest functions of genius. *Palgrave.*

The art of living is like every other art; only the capacity is born with us; it must be learned and practised with incessant care. *Goethe.*

The art of pleasing is the art of deceiving. *Vauvenargues.*

The art was his to break vexations with a ready jest. *Dr. W. Smith.*

The art which is produced hastily will also perish hastily. *Ruskin.*

25 The artist belongs to his work, not the work to the artist. *Novalis.*

The artist is the son of his age; but pity for him if he is its pupil, or even its favourite. *Schiller.*

The artist must conceive with warmth (*mit Feuer*) and execute with coolness. *Winkelmann.*

The artist stands higher than the art, higher than the object: he uses art for his own purposes, and deals with the object after his own fashion. *Goethe.*

The artist's vocation is to send light into the depths of the human heart. *Schumann.*

The arts of deceit and cunning do continually 30 grow weaker, and less effectual and serviceable to them that use them. *Tillotson.*

The astonishing intellect that occupies itself in splitting hairs, and not in twisting some kind of cordage and effectual draught tackle to take the road with, is not to me the most astonishing of intellects. I want twisted cordage, steady pulling, and a peaceable-base tone of voice; not split hairs, hysterical spasmodics, and treble. *Carlyle.*

The Atlantic Ocean beat Mrs. Partington. She was excellent at a slop or a puddle, but she should not have meddled with a tempest. *Sydney Smith.*

The atmosphere of moral sentiment is a region of grandeur which reduces all material magnificence to toys, yet opens to every wretch that has reason the doors of the universe. *Emerson.*

The attainment of a truer and truer aristocracy, or government again by the Best,—all that democracy ever meant lies there. *Carlyle.*

The attempt, and not the deed, / Confounds us. 35 *Macb., ii. 2.*

The attraction of love is in an inverse proportion to the attraction of the Newtonian philosophy. *Burns.*

The author is often obscure to readers because, as has been said, he proceeds from the thought to the expression, whereas they proceed from the expression to the thought. *Chamfort.*

The awful shadow of some unseen Power / Floats, though unseen, among us. *Shelley.*

The axe of intemperance has lopped off his green boughs and left him a withered trunk. *Swift.*

The axis of the earth sticks out visibly through 40 the centre of each and every town or city. *Holmes.*

The back of one door is the face of another. *Pr.*

The back-door robs the house. *Pr.*

The backslider in heart shall be filled with his own ways. *Bible.*

The bad fortune of the good turns their faces up to heaven; and the good fortune of the bad bows their heads down to the earth. *Saadi.*

The bad (*böse*) man has not only the good, but 45 also the bad against him. *Bischer.*

The barrenest of mortals is the sentimentalist. *Carlyle.*

The basest thought about man is that he has no spiritual nature; and the foolishest, that he has, or should have, no animal nature. *Ruskin.*

The basis of good manners is self-reliance. *Emerson.*

The battle of belief against unbelief is the never-ending battle. *Carlyle.*

The beams of joy are made hotter by reflection. *Fuller.*

The bearers of the thyrsus (the symbol of the Bacchus inspiration) are many, but the Bacchants (the truly inspired) are few. *Gr. Pr.*

5 The bearing and the training of a child is woman's wisdom. *Tennyson.*

The beaten road is the safest. *Pr.*

The beautiful is a manifestation of secret laws of nature, which, but for its appearance, had been for ever concealed from us. *Goethe.*

The beautiful is higher than the good; the beautiful includes in it the good. *Goethe.*

The beautiful is like sunshine to the world; the beautiful lives for ever. *Hans Andersen.*

10 The beautiful rests on the foundation of the necessary. *Emerson.*

The beggar is never out of the fashion, or limpeth awkwardly behind it. *Lamb.*

The beggar is not expected to become bail or surety for any one. *Lamb.*

The beggar is not required to put on court mourning. *Lamb.*

The beggar is the only free man in the universe. *Lamb.*

15 The beggar is the only man in the universe who is not obliged to study appearances. *Lamb.*

The beggar weareth all colours, fearing none. *Lamb.*

The beggar's costume hath undergone less change than the Quaker's. *Lamb.*

The beginning, and very nearly the end, of bodily education for a girl, is to make sure that she can stand and sit upright; the ankle vertical, and firm as a marble shaft; the waist elastic as a reed, and as unfatiguable. *Ruskin.*

The beginning of all good law, and nearly the end of it, is that every man shall do good work for his bread, and that every man shall have good bread for his work. *Ruskin.*

20 The beginning of all temptations and wickedness is the fickleness of our own minds and want of trust in God. *Thomas à Kempis.*

The beginning of creation (in man's soul as in Nature) is light. Till the eye have vision, the whole members are in bonds. *Carlyle.*

The beginning of inquiry is disease. *Carlyle.*

The beginning of strife is as when one letteth out water: therefore leave off contention before it be meddled with. *Bible.*

The beginning of wisdom is to look fixedly on clothes (*i.e.*, symbols), till they become transparent. *Carlyle.*

25 The being whose strength exceeds its necessities is strong; the being whose necessities exceed its strength is feeble. *Rousseau.*

The bell strikes one. We take no note of time / But for its loss. *Young.*

The belly is chains to the hands and fetters to the feet. He who is a slave to his belly seldom worships God. *Saadi.*

The beloved of the Almighty are the rich who have the humility of the poor, and the poor who have the magnanimity of the rich. *Saadi.*

The benefactors of mankind are those who grumble to the best purpose. Grumbling has raised man from the condition of the gorilla to that of the judge on the bench of justice. *John Wagstaffe.*

The benevolent heart will not solicit, but com- 30 mand our reverence and applause. *Arliss.*

The benevolent person is always by preference busy on the essentially bad. *Carlyle.*

The best advice is, Follow good advice and hold old age in highest honour. *Goethe.*

The best architecture is the expression of the mind of manhood by the hands of childhood. *Ruskin.*

The best courages are but beams of the Almighty. *Mrs. Hutchinson.*

The best effect of any book is that it excites 35 the reader to self-activity. *Carlyle.*

The best fish swim near the bottom. *Pr.*

The best friends in the world may differ sometimes. *Sterne.*

The best gifts find the fewest admirers, and most men mistake the bad for the good. *Gellert.*

The best government is that which teaches us to govern ourselves. *Goethe.*

The best independence is to have something to 40 do, and something that can be done, and done most perfectly in solitude. *P. G. Hamerton.*

The best is best cheap. *Pr.*

The best is but in season best. *Allan Ramsay.*

The best is not to be explained by words. *Goethe.*

The best laid schemes o' mice an' men / Gang aft a-gley, / And lea'e us naught but grief and pain / For promised joy. *Burns.*

The best loneliness is when no human eye has 45 rested on our face for a whole day. *Auerbach.*

The best may slip, and the most cautious fall; / He's more than mortal that ne'er err'd at all. *Pomfret.*

The best mirror is an old friend. *Pr.*

The best of angels do not live in community, but by themselves. *Swedenborg.*

The best of lessons, for a good many people, would be to listen at a keyhole. It is a pity for such that the practice is dishonourable. *Mme. Swetchine.*

The best of men / That e'er wore earth about 50 him was a sufferer; / A soft, meek, patient, humble, tranquil spirit; / The first true gentleman that ever breathed. *Decker.*

The best of the sport is to do the deed and say nothing. *Pr.*

The best part of our knowledge is that which teaches us where knowledge leaves off and ignorance begins. *Holmes.*

The best path through life is the highway. *Amiel.*

The best portraits are those in which there is a slight mixture of caricature. *Macaulay.*

The best preservative to keep the mind in 55 health is the faithful admonition of a friend. *Bacon.*

The best remedy against an ill man is much ground between both. *Pr.*

The best rules to form a young man are, to talk little, to hear much, to reflect alone upon what has passed in company, to distrust one's own opinions, and value others' that deserve it. *Sir W. Temple.*

The best self-forgetfulness is to look at the things of the world with attention and love. *Auerbach.*

The best son is not enough a son. *Emerson.*

The best, the only correct actions are those which demand no explanation and no apology. *Auerbach.*

The best thing I know between France and England is the sea. *Douglas Jerrold.*

5 The best thing which we derive from history is the enthusiasm which it raises in us. *Goethe.*

The best things are worst to come by. *Walker.*

The best use of money is to pay debts. *Pr.*

The best way to come to truth is to examine things as they really are, and not to conclude they are, as we have been taught by others to imagine. *Locke.*

The best way to make the audience laugh is by first laughing yourself. *Goldsmith.*

10 The best way to please one half of the world is not to mind what the other half says. *Goldsmith.*

The best work in the world is done on the quiet. *Pr.*

The best work never was, nor ever will be, done for money at all. *Ruskin.*

The best works, and of greatest merit for the public, have proceeded from unmarried or childless men, which, both in affection and means, have married and endowed the public. *Bacon.*

The betrayer is the murderer. *Gael. Pr.*

15 The better a man is morally, the less conscious he is of his virtues. The greater the artist, the more aware he must be of his shortcomings. *Froude.*

The better day the better deed. *Walker.*

The better I know men the more I admire dogs. (?)

The better part of valour is discretion. 1 *Hen. IV.,* v. 4.

The better you understand yourself, the less cause you will find to love yourself. *Thomas à Kempis.*

20 The Bible contains many truths as yet undiscovered. *Butler.*

The Bible contains more true sublimity, more exquisite beauty, more pure morality, more important history, and finer strains of poetry and eloquence than can be collected from all other books, in whatever age or language they have been written. *Sir William Jones.*

(The Bible) contains plain teaching for men of every rank of soul and state of life, which so far as they honestly and implicitly obey, they will be happy and innocent to the utmost powers of their nature, and capable of victory over all adversities, whether of temptation or pain. *Ruskin.*

The Bible is the great family chronicle of the Jews. *Heine.*

The Bible of a nation, the practically credited God's message to a nation, is, beyond all else, the authentic biography of its heroic souls. This is the real record of the appearances of God in the history of a nation; this, which all men to the marrow of their bones can believe, and which teaches all men what the nature of this universe, when you go to work in it, really is. *Carlyle.*

The Bible tells us what Christian graces are; 25 but it is in the struggle of life that we are to find them. *Beecher.*

The biography of a nation embraces all its works. No trifle is to be neglected. A mouldering medal is a letter of twenty centuries. *Willmott.*

The bird of wisdom flies low, and seeks her food under hedges; the eagle himself would be starved if he always soared aloft and against the sun. *Landor.*

The birds without barn or storehouse are fed; / From them let us learn to trust for our bread. *Newton.*

The birth of a child is the imprisonment of a soul. *Simons.*

The birth of a golden deer is impossible. *Hito-* 30 *padesa.*

The bishop has set his foot in it, *i.e.,* the broth is singed. *Pr.* (The explanation of which, according to Grose, is: Whenever a bishop passed through a town or a village, all the inhabitants ran out to receive his blessing; this frequently caused the milk on the fire to be left till burnt.)

The biter is often bit. *Pr.*

The blanks as well as the prizes must be drawn in the cheating lottery of life. *Le Sage.*

The blast that blows loudest is soon overblown. *Smollett.*

The blaze of reputation cannot be blown out, 35 but it often dies in the socket. *Johnson.*

The blessed work of helping the world forward does not wait to be done by perfect men. *George Eliot.*

The blessing of the Lord, it maketh rich, and he addeth no sorrow with it. *Bible.*

The blind man bears the lame, and onward hies, / Made right by lending feet and borrowing eyes. *Plato the Younger.*

The block of granite, which was an obstacle in the pathway of the weak, becomes a stepping-stone in the pathway of the strong. *Carlyle.*

The blood more stirs / To rouse a lion than to 40 start a hare. *Hen. IV.,* i. 3.

The blood of man should never be shed but to redeem the blood of man. It is well shed for our family, for our friends, for our God, for our country, for our kind. The rest is vanity, the rest is crime. *Burke.*

The blood of the martyrs is the seed of the Church. *Tertullian.*

The blue-bird carries the sky on his back. *Thoreau.*

The blue of heaven is larger than the cloud. *Mrs. Browning.*

The blush is Nature's alarm at the approach of 45 sin, and her testimony to the dignity of virtue. *Fuller.*

The body of a sensualist is the coffin of a dead soul. *Bovee.*

The body of Christ is wherever human bodies are, and he who has any bitterness against his brother is always committing sacrilege. *Ward Beecher.*

The book of Nature is the book of Fate. *Emerson.*

The bookful blockhead, ignorantly read, / With loads of learned lumber in his head. *Pope.*

The books which help you most are those which make you think the most. *Theodore Parker.*

The borrower runs in his own debt. *Emerson.*

The bough that is dead shall be cut away for the sake of the tree itself. Let the Conservatism that would preserve the tree, cut it away. *Carlyle.*

The bounds of a man's knowledge are easily concealed if he has but prudence. *Goldsmith.*

5 The boy stands astonished ; his impressions guide him ; he learns sportfully ; seriousness steals on him by surprise. *Goethe.*

The boy's story is the best that is ever told. *Dickens.*

The boy's will is the wind's will, / And the thoughts of youth are long, long thoughts. *Lapland Pr.*

The brain may devise laws for the blood ; but a hot temper leaps o'er a cold decree. *Mer. of Ven.,* i. 2.

The brain-women never interest us like the heart-women ; white roses please less than red. *Holmes.*

10 The brave man thinks of himself last of all. *Schiller.*

The bravest are the tenderest, / The loving are the daring. *Bayard Taylor.*

The breach of custom / Is breach of all. *Cymbeline,* iv. 2.

The breeding of a man makes him courageous by instinct, true by instinct, loving by instinct, as a dog is ; and therefore, felicitously above, or below (whichever you like to call it), all questions of philosophy and divinity. *Ruskin.*

The British nation—and I include in it the Scottish nation—has produced a finer set of men than you will find it possible to get anywhere else in this world. *Carlyle.*

15 The bud may have a bitter taste, / But sweet will be the flower. *Cowper.*

The buke o' May-bees is very braid. *Sc. Pr.*

The burden one likes is cheerfully borne. *Pr.*

The burning of a little straw may hide the stars of the sky ; but the stars are there, and will reappear. *Carlyle.*

The burst of new light, by its suddenness, always appears inimical to the unprepared heart. *Jean Paul.*

20 The busiest of living agents are certain dead men's thoughts. *Bovee.*

The calling of a man's self to a strict account is a medicine sometimes too piercing and corrosive ; reading good books of morality is a little flat and dead . . . but the best receipt (best to work, and best to take) is the admonition of a friend. *Bacon.*

The camomile, the more it is trodden on, the faster it grows ; yet youth, the more it is wasted, the sooner it wears. 1 *Hen. IV.,* ii. 4.

The canary-bird sings the sweeter the longer it has been trained in a darkened cage. *Jean Paul.*

The cancer of jealousy on the breast can never wholly be cut out, if I am to believe great masters of the healing art. *Jean Paul.*

25 The canker galls the infants of the spring / Too oft before their buttons are disclosed, / And in the morn and liquid dew of youth / Contagious blastments are most imminent. *Ham.* i. 3.

The capacity of apprehending what is high is very rare ; and therefore, in common life a man does well to keep such things for himself, and only to give out so much as is needful to have some advantage against others. *Goethe.*

The captive bands may chain the hands, But love enslaves the man. *Burns.*

The Carlyles were men who lavished their heart and conscience upon their work ; they builded themselves, their days, their thoughts and sorrows, into their houses ; they leavened the soil with the sweat of their rugged brows. *John Burroughs.*

The casting away things profitable for the maintenance of man's life is an unthankful abuse of the fruits of God's good providence towards mankind. *Hooker.*

The castle which Conservatism is set to defend 30 is the actual state of things, good and bad. *Emerson.*

The cat shuts its eyes when stealing the cream. *Pr.*

The cause which pleased the gods has in the end to please Cato also. (?)

The centuries are all lineal children of one another ; and often, in the portrait of early grandfathers, this and the other enigmatic feature of the newest grandson will disclose itself, to mutual elucidation. *Carlyle.*

The centuries are conspirators against the sanity and authority of the soul. *Emerson.*

The certain way to be cheated is to fancy one's 35 self more cunning than others. *Charron.*

The chains of habit are generally too small to be felt till they are too strong to be broken. *Johnson.*

The champion true / Loves victory more when, dim in view, / He sees her glories gild afar / The dusky edge of stubborn war, / Than if th' untrodden bloodless field / The harvest of her laurels yield. *Keble.*

The change of a man's self is a very laborious undertaking. *Thomas à Kempis.*

The character of a nation is not to be learned from its fine folks. *Scott.*

The character of the person that commends 40 you is to be considered before you set a value on his esteem. The wise man applauds him whom he thinks most virtuous ; the rest of the world, him who is most wealthy. (?)

The character of the true philosopher is to hope all things not unreasonable. *Sir John Herschel.*

The characteristic mark of minds (*Geister*) of the first order is the directness (*Unmittelbarkeit*) of all their judgments. All that they bring forth (*vorbringen*) is the result of their own thinking. *Schopenhauer.*

The characteristic of a philosopher is that he looks to himself for all help or harm. *Epictetus.*

The characteristic of Chaucer is intensity ; of Spencer, remoteness ; of Milton, elevation : of Shakespeare, everything. *Hazlitt.*

The chariest maid is prodigal enough / If she 45 unmask her beauty to the moon. *Ham.,* i. 1.

The charitable give out at the door, and God puts in at the window. *Pr.*

The charity that thinketh no evil trusts in God and trusts in man. *J. G. Holland.*

The chaste mind, like a polished plane, may admit foul thoughts, without receiving their tincture. *Sterne.*

The cheap swearer through his open sluice / Lets his soul run for nought. *George Herbert.*

The cheapness of man is every day's tragedy. *Emerson.*

5 The chief glory of every people arises from its authors. *Johnson.*

The chief of all the curses of this unhappy age is the universal gabble of its fools, and of the flocks that follow them, rendering the quiet voices of the wise of all past time inaudible. *Ruskin.*

The chief requisites for a courtier are a flexible conscience and an inflexible politeness. *Lady Blessington.*

The chief value and virtue of money consists in its having power over human beings; a power which is attainable by other means than by money. *Ruskin.*

The child is father of the man. *Wordsworth.*

10 The child is not to be educated for the present, but for the remote future, and often in opposition to the immediate future. *Jean Paul.*

The child who desires education will be bettered by it; the child who dislikes it, only disgraced. *Ruskin.*

The child's murmuring is more and is less than words; there are no notes, and yet it is a song; there are no syllables, and yet it is language. . . . This poor stammering is a compound of what the child said when it was an angel, and of what it will say when it becomes a man. *Victor Hugo.*

The childhood shows the man / As morning shows the day. *Milton.*

The children of others we never love so much as our own; error, our own child, is so near our heart. *Goethe.*

15 The choicest thing this world has for a man is affection. *J. G. Holland.*

The Christian doctrine, that doctrine of Humility, in all senses godlike, and the parent of all godlike virtue, is not superior, or inferior, or equal to any doctrine of Socrates or Thales, being of a totally different nature; differing from these as a perfect ideal poem does from a correct computation in arithmetic. *Carlyle.*

The Christian religion having once appeared, cannot again vanish; having once assumed its divine shape, can be subject to no dissolution. *Goethe.*

The Christian religion is an inspiration and life — God's life breathed into a man and breathed through a man. *J. G. Holland.*

The Christian religion is especially remarkable, as it so decidedly lays claim to mere goodwill in man, to his essential temper, and values this independently of all culture and manifestation. It stands in opposition to science and art, and properly to enjoyment. *Novalis.*

20 The Christian religion, often enough dismembered and scattered abroad, will ever in the end again gather itself together at the foot of the cross. *Goethe.*

The Christian religion, once here, cannot again pass away; in one or the other form, it will endure through all time. As in Scripture, so also in the heart of man, it is written, "The gates of hell shall not prevail against it." *Carlyle.*

The Christianity that cannot get on without a minimum of four thousand five hundred, will give place to something better that can. *Carlyle.*

The Church is a mere organisation to help a man to fulfil his duties; it is not the source from whence those duties sprung. *Ward Beecher.*

The Church is the working recognised union of those who by wise teaching guide the souls of men. *Carlyle.*

25 The Church! Touching the earth with one small point (the event, viz., at Bethlehem of the year one); springing out of one small seed-grain, rising out therefrom, ever higher, ever broader, high as the heaven itself, broad till it overshadow the whole visible heaven and earth, and no star can be seen but through it. From such a seed-grain so has it grown; planted in the reverences and sacred opulences of the soul of mankind; fed continually by all the noblenesses of forty generations of man. The world-tree of the nations for so long! *Carlyle.*

The Churchmen fain would kill their Church, / As the Churches have killed their Christ. *Tennyson.*

The circle of noble-minded people is the most precious of all that I have won. *Goethe.*

The city does not take away, neither does the country give, solitude: solitude is within us. *Joseph Roux.*

The city is recruited from the country. *Emerson.*

30 The civil guest / Will no more talk all, than eat all the feast. *George Herbert.*

The civilised man lives not in wheeled houses. He builds stone castles, plants lands, makes life-long marriage contracts; has long-dated, hundred-fold possessions, not to be valued in the money-market; has pedigrees, libraries, law-codes; has memories and hopes, even for this earth, that reach over thousands of years. *Carlyle.*

The civilised nation consists broadly of mob, money-collecting machine, and capitalist; and when the mob wishes to spend money for any purpose, it sets its money-collecting machine to borrow the money it needs from the capitalist, who lends it on condition of taxing the mob generation after generation. *Ruskin.*

The civilised savage (*Wilde*) is the worst of all savages. *C. J. Weber.*

The Classical is healthy, the Romantic sickly. *Goethe.*

35 The clergy are at present divided into three sections: an immense body who are ignorant; a small proportion who know and are silent; and a minute minority who know and speak according to their knowledge. *Huxley.*

The cloud-capp'd towers, the gorgeous palaces, / The solemn temples, the great globe itself, / Yea, all that it inherit, shall dissolve; / And, like this insubstantial pageant faded, / Leave not a rack behind. *Tempest. iv. 1.*

The cloud incense of the altar hides / The true form of the God who there abides. *Dr. W. Smith.*

The clouds never pass against the wind. *Hitopadesa.*

The clouds that gather round the setting sun / Do take a sober colouring from an eye / That hath kept watch o'er man's mortality. *Wordsworth.*

The clouds that wrap the setting sun / . . . Why, as we watch their floating wreath, / Seem they the breath of life to breathe? / To Fancy's eye their motions prove / They mantle round the sun for love. *Keble.*

5 The clouds treat the sea as if it were a mill-pond or a spring-run, too insignificant to make any exceptions to. *John Burroughs.*

The cock, that is the trumpet of the morn, / Doth with his lofty and shrill-sounding throat / Awake the god of day. *Ham., i. 1*

The coin that is most current among mankind is flattery; the only benefit of which is that by hearing what we are not we may be instructed what we ought to be. (?)

The combined arts appear to me like a family of sisters, of whom the greater part were inclined to good company, but one was light-headed, and desirous to appropriate and squander the whole goods and chattels of the household—the theatre is this wasteful sister. *Goethe.*

The comic and the tragic lie close together, inseparable, like light and shadow. *Socrates.*

10 The command "thou shalt" is in all circumstances a hard one, unless it is softened down by the adjunct "for that which 'thou shalt' is just the same as that which rationally thou also willest." *Lindner.*

The commencement of atonement is / The sense of its necessity. *Byron.*

The common crowd but see the gloom / Of wayward deeds and fitting doom; / The close observer can espy / A noble soul and lineage high. *Byron.*

The common fluency of speech in many men and most women is owing to a scarcity of matter and a scarcity of words. *Swift.*

The common "keeping up appearances" of society is a mere selfish struggle of the vain with the vain. *Ruskin.*

15 The company of fools may at first make us smile, but at last never fails of rendering us melancholy. *Goldsmith.*

The complete poet must have a heart in his brain or a brain in his heart. *George Darley.*

The complete spiritualisation of the animal element in nature is the task of our species. *Amiel.*

The conceived is never food save to the mind that conceives. *Schiller.*

The concessions of the weak are the concessions of fear. *Burke.*

20 The condition of the great body of the people in a country is the condition of the country itself. *Carlyle.*

The condition of the most fascinated (*bezaubertsten*) enthusiast is to be preferred to him who, from sheer fear of error, dares in the end no longer to affirm or deny. *Wieland.*

The conditions necessary for the arts of men are the best for their souls and bodies. *Ruskin.*

The confidant of my vices is my master, though he were my valet. *Goethe.*

The conflict of the old, the existent, and the persistent, with development, improvement, and transfigurment is always the same. Out of every arrangement arises at last pedantry; to get rid of this latter the former is destroyed, and some time must elapse before we become aware that order must be re-established. *Goethe.*

The conscience is the inviolable asylum of the 25 liberty of man. *Napoleon.*

The conscience is the most elastic material in the world. To-day you cannot stretch it over a mole-hill, to-morrow it hides a mountain. *Bulwer Lytton.*

The conscience of the man who is given over to his passions is like the voice of the ship-wrecked mariner overwhelmed by the tempest. *Joseph Roux.*

The conscious utterance of thought by speech or action, to any end, is art. *Emerson.*

The conscious water saw its god and blushed. *Dryden, on the water into wine at Cana.*

The consolation which is derived from truth, 30 if any there be, is solid and durable; that which may be derived from error must be, like its original, fallacious and fugitive. *Johnson.*

The contagion of crime is like that of the plague. *Napoleon.*

The contingent facts of history can never become the proof of the truths of reason. *Lessing.*

The conversation of a friend is a powerful alleviator of the fatigue of walking. *Dr. Andrew Combe.*

The core will come to the surface. *Emerson.*

The cormorant Oblivion swallows up / The 35 carcases that Time has made his prey. *Crowe.*

The corpse is not the whole animal; there is still something that appertains to it, still a corner-stone, and in this case, as in every other, a very chief corner-stone—life, the spirit that makes everything beautiful. *Goethe.*

The counsel thou wouldst have another keep, first keep thyself. *Pr.*

The country where the entire people is, or even once has been, laid hold of, filled to the heart with an infinite religious idea, has "made a step from which it cannot retrograde." *Carlyle.*

The courage (*Muth*) of truth is the first condition of philosophic study. *Hegel.*

The courage that dares only die is on the 40 whole no sublime affair. . . . The courage we desire and prize is not the courage to die decently, but to live manfully. *Carlyle.*

The course of nature is the art of God. *Young.*

The course of Nature's phases, on this our little fraction of a planet, is partially known to us; but who knows what deeper courses these depend on; what infinitely larger cycle (of causes) our little epicycle revolves on? *Carlyle.*

The course of prayer who knows? *Keble.*

The course of scoundrelism, any more than that of true love, never did run smooth. *Carlyle.*

The course of true love never did run smooth. *Mid. N.'s Dream*, i. 1.

The court does not render a man contented, but it prevents his being so elsewhere. *La Bruyère.*

The court is like a palace of marble ; it is composed of people very hard and very polished. *La Bruyère.*

The court, nor cart, I like, nor loathe ; / Extremes are counted worst of all : / The golden mean betwixt them both / Doth surest sit, and fears no fall. *Old ballad.*

5 The court of the past differs from all living aristocracy in this ; it is open to labour and to merit, but to nothing else. *Ruskin.*

The covetous man heaps up riches, not to enjoy them, but to have them. *Tillotson.*

The covetous man never has money, and the prodigal will have none shortly. *Johnson.*

The coxcomb is a fool of parts, a flatterer a knave of parts. *Steele.*

The craftiest wiles are too short and ragged a cloak to cover a bad heart. *Lavater.*

10 The crafty man is always in danger ; and when he thinks he walks in the dark, all his pretences are so transparent, that he that runs may read them. *Tillotson.*

The creation of a thousand forests is in one acorn ; and Egypt, Greece, Rome, Gaul, Britain, America, lie folded already in the first man. *Emerson.*

The credit of advancing science has always been due to individuals, never to the age. *Goethe.*

The creed of the true saint is to make the best of life, and make the most of it. *Chapin.*

The crickets sing, and man's o'er-laboured sense / Repairs itself by rest. *Cymbeline*, ii. 2.

15 The cross is the invincible sanctuary of the humble. *Cass.*

The cross of Christ is the key of Paradise ; the weak man's staff ; the convert's convoy ; the upright man's perfection ; the soul and body's health ; the prevention of all evil, and the procurer of all good. *Damascen.*

The cross was the fitting close of a life of rejection, scorn, and defeat. *W. H. Thomson.*

The crow doth sing as sweetly as the lark / When neither is attended, and I think / The nightingale, if she should sing by day, / When every goose is cackling, would be thought / No better a musician than the wren. *Mer. of Venice*, v. 1.

The crowd . . . if they find / Some stain or blemish in a name of note, / Not grieving that their greatest are so small, / Inflate themselves with some insane delight, / And judge all Nature from her feet of clay, / Without the will to lift their eyes, and see / Her godlike head crown'd with spiritual fire / And touching other worlds. *Tennyson.*

20 The cruelty of the affectionate is more dreadful than that of the hardy. *Lavater.*

The cry of the God-forsaken is from the heart of God himself. *Ed.*

The cuffs and thumps with which fate, our lady-loves, our friends and foes, put us to the proof, in the mind of a good and resolute man, vanish into air. *Goethe.*

The cunning workman never doth refuse / The meanest tool that he may chance to use. *George Herbert.*

The cup of life which God offers to our lips is not always sweet ; . . . but, sweet or bitter, it is ours to drink it without murmur or demur. *W. R. Greg.*

The cups that cheer, but not inebriate. *Cowper.* 25

The cure for false theology is mother wit. *Emerson.*

The curfew tolls the knell of parting day, / The lowing herd winds slowly o'er the lea, / The ploughman homeward plods his weary way, / And leaves the world to darkness and to me. *Gray.*

The curiosity of knowing things has been given to man for a scourge. *Apocrypha.*

The curious unthrift makes his clothes too wide, / And spares himself, but would his tailor chide. *George Herbert.*

The current that with gentle murmur glides, / 30 Thou know'st, being stopp'd, impatiently doth rage. *Two Gent. of Ver.*, ii. 7.

The curtains of yesterday drop down, the curtains of to-morrow roll up ; but yesterday and to-morrow both are. Pierce into the Time-element, glance into the Eternal. *Carlyle.*

The cut (of the vesture) betokens intellect and talent, so does the colour betoken temper and heart. *Carlyle.*

The cynic is one who never sees a good quality in a man, and never fails to see a bad one. *Ward Beecher.*

The danger of dangers is illusion. *Emerson.*

The danger past and God forgotten. *Pr.* 35

The dark in soul see in the universe their own shadow ; the shattered spirit can only reflect external beauty, in form as untrue and broken as itself. *Binney.*

The darkest day, live till to-morrow, will have passed away. *Cowper.*

The darkest hour is nearest the dawn. *Pr.*

The day is longer than the brae ; we'll be at the top yet. *Gael. Pr.*

The day of days . . . is the day on which the 40 inward eye opens to the unity of things, to the omnipresence of law—sees that what is must be, and ought to be, or is the best. *Emerson.*

The day wasted on others is not wasted on one's self. *Dickens.*

The days are too short even for love, how can there ever be time for quarrelling ? *Mrs. Gatty.*

The dead do not need us ; but for ever and for evermore we need them. *Garfield.*

The dead letter of religion must own itself dead, and drop piecemeal into dust, if the living spirit of religion, freed from its charnel-house, is to arise on us, new born of Heaven, and with new healing under its wings. *Carlyle.*

The decline of literature indicates the decline 45 of the nation. The two keep pace in their downward tendency. *Goethe.*

The deeper the sorrow, the less tongue hath it. *Talmud.*

The deity works in the living, not in the dead ; in the becoming and the changing, not in the become and the fixed. *Goethe.*

The delight of the destroyer and denier is no pure delight, and must soon pass away. *Carlyle.*

The democrat is a young conservative; the conservative is an old democrat. *Emerson.*

The demonic in music stands so high that no understanding can reach it, and an influence flows from it which masters all, and for which none can account. *Goethe.*

The demonic is that which cannot be explained by reason or understanding, which is not in one's nature, yet to which it is subject. *Goethe.*

5 The dependant is timid. *Gael. Pr.*

The depth of our despair measures what capability and height of claim we have to hope. *Carlyle.*

The desire accomplished is sweet to the soul. *Bible.*

The desire of a man is his kindness : and a poor man is better than a liar. *Bible.*

The desire of perfection is the worst disease that ever afflicted the human mind. *Fontanes.*

10 The desire of power in excess caused the angels to fall; the desire of knowledge in excess caused man to fall; but in charity there is no excess, neither can man or angel come in danger by it. *Bacon.*

The desire of the moth for the star, / Of the night for the morrow, / The devotion to something afar / From the sphere of our sorrow. *Shelley.*

The desire of the slothful killeth him ; for his hands refuse to labour. *Bible.*

The destiny of any nation at any given time depends on the opinions of its young men under five-and-twenty. *Goethe.*

The destruction of the poor is their poverty. *Bible.*

15 The devil can cite Scripture for his purpose ! / An evil soul producing holy witness / Is like a villain with a smiling cheek, / A goodly apple rotten at the heart. *Mer. of Ven.,* i. 3.

The devil has a great advantage against us, inasmuch as he has a strong bastion and bulwark against us in our own flesh and blood. *Luther.*

The devil has his elect. *Carlyle.*

The devil hath power / To assume a pleasing shape. *Ham.,* ii. 2.

The devil helps his servants for a season ; but when they come once to a pinch, he leaves 'em in the lurch. *L'Estrange.*

20 The devil is a busy bishop in his own diocese. *Bishop Latimer.*

The devil is an ass. *Pr.*

The devil is an unfortunate who knows not what it is to love. *St. Theresa.*

The devil is God's ape. *Luther.*

The devil knew not what he did when he made man politic ; he crossed himself by it. *Tim. of Athens,* iii. 3.

25 The devil lurks behind the cross. *Pr.*

The devil may get in by the keyhole, but the door won't let him out. *Pr.*

The devil taketh not lightly unto his working such as he findeth occupied in good works. *St. Jerome.*

The devil tempts all other men, but idle men tempt the devil. *Arab. Pr.*

The devil tempts us not—'tis we tempt him, / Beckoning his skill with opportunity. *George Eliot.*

The devil was sick, the devil a monk would 30 be ; / The devil was well, the devil a monk was he. *Rabelais.*

The dewdrop and the star shine sisterly, / Globing together in the common work. *Sir Edwin Arnold.*

The dictum that truth always triumphs over persecution is one of those pleasant falsehoods . . . which all experience refutes. History teems with instances of truth put down by persecution. If not suppressed for ever, it may be thrown back for centuries. *J. S. Mill.*

The difference between Socrates and Jesus ? The great Conscious ; the immeasurably great Unconscious. *Carlyle.*

The difference between the great celebrities and the unknown nobodies is this, the former failed and went at it again, the latter gave up in despair. *Anon.*

The difficulty is not so great to die for a friend as 35 to find a friend worth dying for. *Henry Home.*

The difficulty is to teach the multitude that something can be both true and untrue at the same time. *Schopenhauer.*

The dignity of truth is lost with much protesting. *Ben Jonson.*

The dilettante takes the obscure for the profound, violence for vigour, the indefinite for the infinite, and the senseless for the supersensuous. *Schiller.*

The disciple is not above his master, nor the servant above his lord. *Jesus.*

The discovery of what is true, and the prac- 40 tice of that which is good, are the two most important objects of philosophy. *Voltaire.*

The discretion of a man deferreth his anger ; and it is his glory to pass over a transgression. *Bible.*

The disease of the mind leading to fatalist ruin is the concentration of man upon himself, whether his heavenly interests or his worldly interests, matters not ; it is their being his own interests which makes the regard of them mortal. *Ruskin.*

The disease which afflicts bureaucratic governments, and which they usually die of, is routine. *J. S. Mill.*

The disease with which the human mind now labours is want of faith. *Emerson.* ___

The dispute about religion and the practice of 45 it seldom go together. *Young.*

The disputes of two of equal strength and fortune are worthy of attention ; but not of two, the one great, the other humble. *Hitopadesa.*

The dissection of a sentence is as bad a way to the understanding of it, as the dissection of a beast to the biography of it. *Ruskin.*

The distances of nations are measured, not by seas, but by ignorances ; and their divisions determined, not by dialects, but by enmities. *Ruskin.*

The distant landscape draws not nigh / For all our gazing. *Keble.*

The distant sounds of music, that catch new 50 sweetness as they vibrate through the long-drawn valley, are not more pleasing to the ear than the tidings of a far-distant friend. *Goldsmith.*

The distinction between man and nature is, that man is a being becoming, and nature a being become. *Rückert.*

The distinctive character of a child is to live always in the tangible present. *Ruskin.*

The distinguishing sign of slavery is to have a price and be bought for it. *Ruskin.*

The distinguishing trait of people accustomed to good society is a calm, imperturbable quiet, which pervades all their actions and habits. *Bulwer Lytton.*

5 The Divine mind is as visible in its full energy of operation on every lowly bank and mouldering stone, as in the lifting of the pillars of heaven, and setting the foundations of the earth. *Ruskin.*

The divine power of the love, of which we cease not to sing and speak, is this, that it reproduces every moment the grand qualities of the beloved object, perfect in the smallest parts, embraced in the whole; it rests not either by day or by night, is ravished with its own work, wonders at its own stirring activity, finds the well-known always new, because it is every moment begotten anew in the sweetest of all occupations. In fact the image of the beloved one cannot become old, for every moment is the hour of its birth. *Goethe.*

The divine state, "par excellence," is silence and repose. *Amiel.*

The doctor sees all the weakness of mankind, the lawyer all the wickedness, the theologian all the stupidity. *Schopenhauer.*

The dog that fetches will carry. *Pr.*

10 The dog that starts the hare is as good as the one that catches it. *Ger. Pr.*

The dog, to gain his private ends, / Went mad, and bit the man. *Goldsmith.*

The dome of St. Peter's is great, yet is it but a foolish chip of an egg-shell compared with that star-fretted dome where Arcturus and Orion glance for ever, which latter, notwithstanding, no one looks at — because the architect was not a man. *Carlyle.*

The dome of thought, the palace of the soul. *Byron.*

The donkey means one thing and the driver another. *Pr.*

15 The doom of the old has long been pronounced and irrevocable; the old has passed away; but, alas! the new appears not in its stead; the time is still in pangs of travail with the new. Man has walked by the light of conflagrations, and amid the sound of falling cities; and now there is darkness, and long watching till it be morning. *Carlyle in 1831.*

The door must either be shut or it must be open. I must either be natural or unnatural. *Goldsmith.*

The dove found no rest for the sole of her foot. *Bible.*

The dread of censure is the death of genius. *Simms.*

The dread of something after death, / The undiscover'd country, from whose bourn / No traveller returns, puzzles the will; / And makes us rather bear those ills we have / Than fly to others that we know not of. *Ham.*, iii. 1.

The dreamer is a madman quiescent, the 20 madman is a dreamer in action. *F. H. Hedge.*

The dregs may stir themselves as they please; they fall back to the bottom by their own coarseness. *Joubert.*

The dress of words, / Like to the Roman girl's enticing garb, / Should let the play of limb be seen through it, / And the round rising form. *Bailey.*

The drunkard forfeits man, and doth divest / All worldly right, save what he hath by beast. *George Herbert.*

The dry light is ever the best. *Heraclitus.*

The drying up a single tear has more / Of 25 honest fame than shedding seas of gore. *Byron.*

The dullest John Bull cannot with perfect complacency adore himself, except under the figure of Britannia or the British Lion. *Ruskin.*

The dust of controversy is but the falsehood flying off. *Carlyle.*

The dwarf behind his steam-engine may remove mountains, but no dwarf will hew them down with the pickaxe; and he must be a Titan that hurls them abroad with his arms. *Carlyle.*

The eagle suffers little birds to sing. *Tit. Andron.*, iv. 4.

The earth hath bubbles, as the water has, / 30 And these are of them. *Macb.*, i. 3.

The earth is our workshop. We may not curse it; we are bound to sanctify it. *Mazzini.*

The earth is sown with pleasures, as the heavens are studded with stars, wherever the conditions of existence are unsophisticated. *W. R. Greg.*

The earth must supply man with the necessaries of life before he has leisure or inclination to pursue more refined enjoyments. *Goldsmith.*

The earth, that's Nature's mother, is her tomb. *Rom. and Jul.*, ii. 3.

The earthen pot must keep clear of the brass 35 kettle. *Pr.*

The ebb'd man, ne'er loved till ne'er worth love, / Comes dear'd by being lack'd. *Ant. and Cleop.*, i. 4.

The echo of the nest-life, the voice of our modest, fairer, holier soul, is audible only in a sorrow-darkened bosom, as the nightingales warble when one veils their cage. *Jean Paul.*

The effect of good music is not caused by its novelty; on the contrary, it strikes us more the more familiar we are with it. *Goethe.*

The effect of righteousness (shall be) quietness and assurance for ever. *Bible.*

The effect of violent animosities between 40 parties has always been an indifference to the general welfare and honour of the state. *Macaulay.*

The efforts of him who contendeth with one stronger than himself are as feeble as the exertions of an insect's wings. *Hitopadesa.*

The elect are whosoever will, and the non-elect whosoever won't. *Ward Beecher.*

The electric telegraph will never be a substitute for the face of a man, with his soul in it, encouraging another man to be brave and true. *Dickens.*

The element of water moistens the earth, but blood flies upwards and bedews the heavens. *John Webster.*

The elements of poetry lie in natural objects, in the vicissitudes of human life, in the emotions of the human heart, and the relations of man to man. *Bryant.*

The emphasis of facts and persons has nothing to do with time. *Emerson.*

5 The empire of woman is an empire of softness, of address, of complacency. Her commands are caresses, her menaces are tears. *Rousseau.*

The empty vessel makes the greatest sound. *Hen. V., iv. 4.*

The end crowns all, / And that old common arbitrator, Time, / Will one day end it. *Troil. and Cress., iv. 5.*

The end of all opposition is negation, and negation is nothing. *Goethe.*

The end of all right education of a woman is to make her love her home better than any other place ; that she should as seldom leave it as a queen her queendom ; nor ever feel entirely at rest but within its threshold. *Ruskin.*

10 The end of doubt is the beginning of repose. *Petrarch.*

The end of labour is to gain leisure. *Arist.*

The end of man is an action, not a thought, though it were the noblest. *Carlyle.*

The end of man is at no moment a pleasure, but a performance ; and life always and only the continual fulfilment of a worthy purpose with a will. *Ed.*

The end we aim at must be known before the way. *Jean Paul.*

15 The enemy is more easily repulsed if we never suffer him to get within us, but, upon the very first approach, draw up our forces and fight him without the gate. *Thomas à Kempis.*

"The English," says Bishop Sprat, "have too much bravery to be derided, and too much virtue and honour to mock others." *Goldsmith.*

The ennobling difference between one man and another—between one animal and another—is precisely this, that one feels more than another. *Ruskin.*

The entire grace, happiness, and virtue of (a young man's) life depend on his contentment in doing what he can dutifully, and in staying where he is peaceably. *Ruskin.*

The entire object of true education is to make people not merely do the right things, but enjoy the right things. *Ruskin.*

20 The entire system of things gets represented in every particle. *Emerson.*

The entire vitality of art depends upon its having for object either to state a true thing or adorn a serviceable one. *Ruskin.*

The envied have a brilliant fate ; / Pity is given where griefs are great. *Palladas.*

The envious man waxeth lean with the fatness of his neighbours. *Socrates.*

The envious will die, but envy never. *Molière.*

25 The errors of a great mind are more edifying than the truths of a little. *Börne.*

The errors of a wise man are literally more instructive than the truths of a fool. For the wise man travels in lofty, far-seeing regions ; the fool in low-lying, high-fenced lanes ; retracing the footsteps of the former, to discover where he deviated, whole provinces of the universe are laid open to us ; in the path of the latter, granting even that he have not deviated at all, little is laid open to us but two wheel-ruts and two hedges. *Carlyle.*

The errors of a wise man make your rule / Rather than the perfections of a fool. *Wm. Blake.*

The errors of woman spring almost always from her faith in the good or her confidence in the true. *Balzac.*

The errors of young men are the ruin of business ; but the errors of aged men amount to but this, that more might have been done, or sooner. *Bacon.*

The essence of a lie is in deception, not in 30 words. *Ruskin.*

The essence of affectation is that it be assumed ; the character is, as it were, forcibly crushed into some foreign mould, in the hope of being thereby re-shaped and beautified ; and the unhappy man persuades himself he has become a new creature of wonderful symmetry, though every movement betrays not symmetry, but dislocation. *Carlyle.*

The essence of all government among good men is this, that it is mainly occupied in the production and recognition of human worth, and in the detection and extinction of human unworthiness. *Ruskin.*

The essence of all immorality, of sin, is the making self the centre to which we subordinate all other beings and interests. *J. C. Sharp.*

The essence of all religion that was, and that will be, is to make men free. *Carlyle.*

The essence of all vulgarity lies in want of 35 sensation. *Ruskin.*

The essence of an aristocracy is to transfer the source of honour from the living to the dead, to make the merits of living men depend not so much upon their own character and actions as upon the actions and position of their ancestors. *H. Lecky.*

The essence of aphorism is the compression of a mass of thought and observation into a single saying. *John Morley.*

The essence of faith lies in this, a deep sense and conviction that in what we do, though it were single-handed, with all men standing aloof, and even saying nay to it, we have God and all his universe at our back. *Ed.*

The essence of friendship is entireness, a total magnanimity and trust. *Emerson.*

The essence of greatness is the perception 40 that virtue is enough. Poverty is its ornament. It does not need plenty, and can very well abide its loss. *Emerson.*

The essence of humour is sensibility, warm, tender, fellow-feeling with all forms of existence ; and unless seasoned and purified by humour, sensibility is apt to run wild, will readily corrupt into disease, falsehood, or, in one word, sentimentality. *Carlyle.*

The essence of justice is mercy. (?)

The essence of knowledge is, having it, to apply it ; not having it, to confess your ignorance. *Confucius.*

The essence of poetry is will and passion. *Hazlitt.*

The essence of true nobility is neglect of self. Let the thought of self pass in, and the beauty of a great action is gone, like the bloom from a soiled flower. *Froude.*

The essence of wealth consists in its authority over men; if (therefore) the apparent or nominal wealth fail in this power, it fails in essence; in fact, ceases to be wealth at all. And since the essence of wealth consists in power over men, will it not follow that the nobler and the more in number the persons are over whom it has power, the greater the wealth. *Ruskin.*

The essence or peculiarity of man is to comprehend a whole. *Emerson.*

5 The essential thing for all creatures is to be made to do right. *Ruskin.*

The Eternal is no simulacrum; God is not only there, but here or nowhere,—in that life-breath of thine, in that act and thought of thine,—and thou wert wise to look to it. *Carlyle.*

The eternal stars shine out again, as soon as it is dark enough. *Carlyle.*

The eternity, before the world and after, is without our reach; but that little spot of ground which lies betwixt those two great oceans, this we are to cultivate. *Burnet.*

The even and cheerful temper makes us pleasing to ourselves, to those with whom we converse, and to Him whom we were made to please. *Addison.*

10 The even - flow of constant cheerfulness strengthens; while great excitements, driving us with fierce speed, both wreck the ship and end often in explosions. *Ward Beecher.*

The evening brings a' hame. *Sc. Pr.*

The evil that goeth out of thy mouth flieth into thy bosom. *Pr.*

The evil that men do lives after them; / The good is oft interréd with their bones. *Jul. Cæs.*, viii. 2.

The evil wound is cured, but not the evil name. *Pr.*

15 The ewe that will not hear her lamb when it baes, will never answer a calf when it bleats. *Much Ado*, iii. 3.

The exacting a grateful acknowledgment is demanding a debt by which the creditor is not advantaged and the debtor pays with reluctance. *Goldsmith.*

The example of good men is visible philosophy. *Pr.*

The excellent is rarely found, more rarely valued. *Goethe.*

The exception proves the rule. *Pr.*

20 The excesses of our youth are draughts upon our age, payable with interest about thirty years after date. *Colton.*

The expectation of the poor shall not perish for ever. *Bible.*

The experience of each new age requires a new confession, and the world seems always waiting for its poet. *Emerson.*

The experience of suffering has been declared on the highest authority to be necessary to every poet who would touch the hearts of his fellow-creatures. *C. Fitzhugh.*

The express schoolmaster is not equal to much at present, while the unexpress, for good or for evil, is so busy with a poor little fellow. *Carlyle.*

The eye by which I see God is the same eye 25 by which he sees me. *Scheffler.*

The eye is easily daunted. *Emerson.*

The eye is not satisfied with seeing, nor the ear filled with hearing. *Bible.*

The eye is the best of artists. *Emerson.*

The eye is the mirror of the soul. *Pr.*

The eye is the only note-book of the true poet. 30 *Lowell.*

The eye is the window of the soul; even an animal looks for a man's intentions right into his eyes. *H. Powers.*

The eye—it cannot choose but see; / We cannot bid the ear be still; / Our bodies feel, where'er they be, / Against or with our will. *Wordsworth.*

The eye of a critic is often like a microscope, made so very fine and nice, that it discovers the atoms, grains, and minutest particles, without ever comprehending the whole, comparing the parts, or seeing all at once the harmony. (?)

The eye of the master will do more work than both his hands. *Ben. Franklin.*

The eye repeats every day the first eulogy on 35 things: "He saw that they were very good." *Emerson.*

The eye sees in all things what it brings with it the faculty of seeing. *Goethe.*

The eye sees not itself, / But by reflection, by some other things. *Jul. Cæs.*, i. 2.

The eye that mocketh at his father, and despiseth to obey his mother, the ravens of the valley shall pick it out, and the young eagles shall eat it. *Bible.*

The eye that sees all things else sees not itself. *Pr.*

The eyes being in the highest part, hold the 40 post of sentinels. *Cic.*

The eyes of other people are the eyes that ruin us. If all but myself were blind, I would want neither fine clothes, fine houses, nor fine furniture. *Ben. Franklin.*

The eyes of the Lord are in every place, beholding the evil and the good. *Bible.*

The face is the index of the mind. *Pr.*

The face of man gives us fuller and more interesting information than his tongue; for his face is the compendium of all he will ever say, as it is the one record of all he has thought and endeavoured. *Schopenhauer.*

The faculty for remembering is not diminished 45 in proportion to what one has learnt, just as little as the number of moulds in which you cast sand lessens its capacity for being cast in new moulds. *Schopenhauer.*

The faculty of art is to change events; the faculty of science is to foresee them. The phenomena with which we deal are controlled by art; they are predicted by science. *Buckle.*

The faculty of listening is a tender thing, and soon becomes weary and satiated. *Luther.*

The failings of good men are commonly more published in the world than their good deeds; and one fault of a deserving man shall meet with more reproaches than all his virtues praise; such is the force of ill-will and ill-nature. (?)

The faint, exquisite music of a dream. *Moore.*

The fair maid who, the first of May, / Goes to the fields at break of day, / And washes in dew from the hawthorn tree, / Will ever after handsome be. *Pr.*

The fair point of the line of beauty is the line of love. Strength and weakness stand on either side of it. Love is the point in which they unite. *Goethe.*

The fairest action of our human life is scorning to avenge an injury. *Lady E. Carew.*

5 The fairest tulip's not the sweetest flower. *Quarles.*

The faith in an Invisible, Unnameable, Godlike, present everywhere in all we see and work and suffer, is the essence of all faith whatsoever; and that once denied, or, still worse, asserted with lips only, and out of bound prayer-books only, what other thing remains credible? *Carlyle.*

The faith of a hearer must be extremely perplexed who considers the speaker, or believes that the speaker considers himself, as under no obligation to adhere to truth, but according to the particular importance of what he relates. *Paley.*

The faith that stands on authority is not faith. *Emerson.*

The faithful servant is a humble friend. *Pr.*

10 The fall from the (Christian) faith, and all the corruptions of its abortive practice, may be summed up briefly as the habitual contemplation of Christ's death instead of his life, and the substitution of his past suffering for our present duty. *Ruskin.*

The falling out of faithful friends is the renewing of love. *Pr.*

The family is the proper province for private women to shine in. *Addison.*

The family virtues are indispensable to the proper continuance of a society. *Renan.*

The fashion doth wear out more apparel than the man. *Much Ado, iii. 3.*

15 The fashion of this world passeth away. *St. Paul.*

The fatal man, is he not always the unthinking, the man who cannot think and see? *Carlyle.*

The fatal tendency of mankind to leave off thinking about a thing when it is no longer doubtful, is the cause of half their errors. A contemporary author has well spoken of "the deep slumber of a decided opinion." *J. S. Mill.*

The fatal trait (of the times) is the divorce between religion and morality. *Emerson.*

The fate of a man of feeling is, like that of a tuft of flowers, twofold; he may either mount upon the head of all, or go to decay in the wilderness. *Hitopadesa.*

20 The fate of empires depends upon the education of youth. *Arist.*

The fated will happen. *Gael. Pr.*

The fates but only spin the coarser clue; / The finest of the wool is left for you. *Dryden.*

The fathers have eaten sour grapes, and the children's teeth are set on edge. *Bible Pr.*

The faults of the superior man are like the eclipses of the sun and moon. He has his faults, and all men see them; he changes, and all men look up to him. *Confucius.*

The fear o' hell's the hangman's whip, / To 25 haud the wretch in order; / But when ye feel yer honour grip, / Let that be aye yer border. *Burns.*

The fear of the Lord is the beginning of wisdom: and the knowledge of the holy is understanding. *Bible.*

The fear of the Lord is the fountain of life. *Bible.*

The fear of the Lord is to hate evil: pride, and arrogancy, and the evil way, and the froward mouth, do I hate. *Bible.*

The fear of the Lord tendeth to life: and he that hath it shall abide satisfied. *Bible.*

The fearful unbelief is unbelief in yourself. 30 *Carlyle.*

The feast of reason and the flow of soul. *Pope.*

The feelings, like flowers and butterflies, last longer the later they are delayed. *Jean Paul.*

The female heart is just like a new india-rubber shoe; you may pull and pull at it till it stretches out a yard long; and then let go, and it will fly right back to its old shape. *Judge Haliburton.*

The fetters of the slave bind the hands only. *Grillparzer.*

The fewer our wants, the nearer we resemble 35 the gods. *Socrates.*

The fibres of all things have their tension, and are strained like the strings of a lyre. *Thoreau.*

The field cannot be well seen from within the field. The astronomer must have his diameter of the earth's orbit as a base to fix the parallax of any other star. *Emerson.*

The finding of your able man, and getting him invested with the symbols of ability, is the business, well or ill accomplished, of all social procedure whatsoever in the world. *Carlyle.*

The finer the nature, the more flaws it will show through the clearness of it; and it is a law of this universe that the best things shall be seldomest seen in their best form. *Ruskin.*

The finest composition of human nature, as 40 well as the finest china, may have a flaw in it, and this in either case is equally incurable. *Fielding.*

The finest language is chiefly made up of unimposing words. *George Eliot.*

The finest lives, in my opinion, are those who rank in the common model and with the human race, but without miracle, without extravagance. *Montaigne.*

The finest minds, like the finest metals, dissolve the easiest. *Pope.*

The finest nations in the world—the English and the American—are going all away into wind and tongue. *Carlyle.*

The finest qualities of our nature, like the 45 bloom on fruits, can be preserved only by the most delicate handling; yet we do not treat ourselves or one another thus tenderly. *Thoreau.*

The fire in the flint shows not till it's struck. *Pr.*

The fire that all things else consumeth clean / May hurt and heal. *Sir Thomas Wyatt.*

The fire that does not warm me shall never scorch me. *Pr.*

The fire which enlightens is the same fire which consumes. *Amiel.*

The first and worst of all frauds is to cheat one's self. All sin is easy after that. *Bailey.*

The first approach to riches is security from poverty. *Johnson.*

5 The first article that a young trader offers for sale is his honesty. *Pr.*

The first, as indeed the last, nobility of education is in the rule over our thoughts. *Ruskin.*

The first breath / Is the beginning of death. *Pr.*

The first business of the philosopher is to part with self-conceit. *Epictetus.*

The first condition of education is being put to wholesome and useful work. *Ruskin.*

10 The first condition of goodness is something to love; the second, something to reverence. *George Eliot.*

The first creation of God in the works of the days was the light of the sense; the last was the light of the reason; and his Sabbath-work ever since is the illumination of the spirit. *Bacon.*

The first day a man is a guest, the second a burden, the third a pest. *Laboulaye.*

The first days of spring have less grace than the growing virtue of a young man. *Vauvenargues.*

The first duty of a man is that of subduing fear; he must get rid of fear; he cannot act at all till then; his acts are slavish, not true. *Carlyle.*

15 The first duty of every man in the world is to find his true master, and, for his own good, submit to him; and to find his true inferior, and, for that inferior's good, conquer him. *Ruskin.*

The first evil those suffer who are fain to talk is that they hear nothing. *Plutarch.*

The first faults are theirs that commit them, / The second are theirs that permit them. *Pr.*

The first forty years of life furnish the text, the remaining thirty the commentary. *Schopenhauer.* (?)

The first glass for myself, the second for my friends, the third for good-humour, and the fourth for mine enemies. *Sir W. Temple.*

20 The first glass of a wine is the one which gives us its true taste. *Schopenhauer.*

The first great work / Is that yourself may to yourself be true. *Roscommon.*

The first hour of the morning is the rudder of the day. *Ward Beecher.*

The first ingredient in conversation is truth, the next good sense, the third good humour, and the fourth wit. *Sir W. Temple.*

The first lesson of life is one of vicarious suffering. *Ward Beecher.*

25 The first lesson of literature, no less than of life, is the learning how to burn one's own smoke. *Lowell.*

"The first love, which is infinite," can be followed by no second like it. *Carlyle.*

The first of the nine orders of knaves is he that tells his errand before he goes it. *Pr.*

The first period of a nation, as of an individual, is the period of unconscious strength. *Emerson.*

The first point of wisdom is to discern that which is false; the second, to know that which is true. *Lactantius.*

The first power of a nation consists in know-30 ing how to guide the plough: its second power consists in knowing how to wear the fetter. *Ruskin.*

The first principle of all human economy—individual or political—is to live with as few wants as possible, and to waste nothing of what is given us to supply them. *Ruskin.*

The first problem (in life) is to unite yourself with some one and with somewhat. *Carlyle.*

The first proof of a man's incapacity for anything is his endeavouring to fix the stigma of failure upon others. *B. R. Haydon.*

The first requisite, both in conversation and correspondence, is to attend to all the proper decorums which our own character and that of others demand. *Blair.*

The first sigh of love is the last of wisdom. 35 *Antoine Bret.*

The first sin in our universe was Lucifer's, that of self-conceit. *Carlyle.*

The first spiritual want of a barbarous man is decoration, as indeed we still see among the barbarous classes in civilised countries. *Carlyle.*

The first step towards greatness is to be honest. *Pr.*

The first test of a truly great man is his humility. I do not mean by humility, doubt of his power or hesitation in speaking his opinions; but a right understanding of the relation between what he can say and do, and the rest of the world's sayings and doings. *Ruskin.*

The first thing for acceptance of truth is to 40 unlearn human doctrines and become as a little child. *General Gordon.*

The first thing in oratory, Demosthenes used to say, was action; the second, action; and the third, action.

The first use of education is to enable us to consult with the wisest and the greatest men on all points of earnest difficulty. *Ruskin.*

The first wealth is health. Sickness is poor-spirited, and cannot serve any one; it must husband its resources to live. But health or fulness answers its own ends, and has to spare, runs over, and inundates the neighbourhoods and creeks of other men's necessities. *Emerson.*

The first year let your house to your enemy; the second to your friend; the third, live in it yourself. *Pr.*

The fittest place where man can die / Is where 45 he dies for man. *M. J. Barry.*

The flesh-bound volume is the only revelation (of God) that is, that was, or that can be. In that is the image of God painted; in that is the law of God written; in that is the promise of God revealed. *Ruskin.*

The flighty purpose never is o'ertook, / Unless the deed go with it. *Macb., iv. 1.*

The floating vapour is just as true an illustration of the law of gravity as the falling avalanche. *John Burroughs.*

The flower is the proper object of the seed, not the seed of the flower. *Ruskin.*

The flower of sweetest smell is shy and lowly. *Wordsworth.*

The flower of youth never appears more beautiful than when it bends towards the Sun of Righteousness. *Matthew Henry.*

The flute is sweet / To gods and men, but sweeter the lyre / And voice of a true singer. *Lewis Morris.*

The follies of modern Liberalism are practically summed up in the denial or neglect of the quality and intrinsic value of things. *Ruskin.*

The folly of all follies / Is to be love-sick for a shadow. *Tennyson.*

The folly of others is ever most ridiculous to those who are themselves most foolish. *Goldsmith.*

The fool doth think he is wise, but the wise man knows himself to be a fool. *As You Like It,* v. 1.

The fool is always discovered if he stayeth too long ; like the ass dressed in a tiger's skin, from his voice. *Hitopadesa.*

The fool is in himself the object of pity till he is flattered. *Steele.*

The fool needs company, the wise man solitude. *Rückert.*

The foolish and the dead alone never change their opinion. *Lowell.*

The foot of the owner is the best manure for his land. *Pr.*

The force of the guinea in your pocket depends on the default of a guinea in your neighbour's. *Ruskin.*

The form of government can never be a matter of choice ; it is almost always a matter of necessity. *Joubert.*

The formation of his character ought to be the chief aim of every man. *Goethe.*

The fortitude of a Christian consists in patience. *Dryden.*

The fortune which nobody sees makes a man happy and unenvied. *Bacon.*

The foul slime stands for the sloth and vice of man, the decay of humanity ; the fragrant flower that springs from it, for the purity and courage which are immortal. *Thoreau.*

The foundations of man are not in matter, but in spirit. *Emerson.*

The fountain which from Helicon proceeds, / That sacred stream, should never water weeds. *Wall.*

The fox puts off all with a jest. *L'Estrange.*

The fox thrives best when he is most curst. *Pr.*

The fraction of life can be increased in value not so much by increasing your numerator as by lessening your denominator. Nay, unless my algebra deceives me, unity itself divided by zero will give infinity. *Carlyle.*

The free man is he who is loyal to the laws of this universe ; who in his heart sees and knows that injustice cannot befall him here ; that, except by sloth and cowardly falsity, evil is not possible here. *Carlyle.*

The (French) Revolution was a revolt against lies, and against a betrayal of love. *Ruskin.*

The fresh air of the open country is the proper place to which we belong. It is as if the breath of God were there wafted immediately to men, and a divine power exerted its influence. *Goethe.*

The fresh gaze of a child is richer in significance than the forecasting of the most indubitable seer. *Novalis.*

The friends thou hast, and their adoption tried, / Grapple them to thy soul with hoops of steel. *Ham.,* i. 3.

The frost is God's plough, which he drives through every inch of ground, opening each clod and pulverising the whole. *Fuller.*

The fruit of friendship, in opening the understanding, is not restrained only to such friends as are able to give counsel (they indeed are best), but even without that a man learneth of himself, and bringeth his own thoughts to light, and whetteth his wits as against a stone, which itself cuts not. *Bacon.*

The fruit of life is experience, not happiness, and its fruition to accustom ourselves, and to be content, to exchange hope for insight. *Schopenhauer.*

The fruit of righteousness is sown in peace of them that make peace. *St. James.*

The fruit that's yellow / Is found not always mellow. *Quarles.*

The full moon brings fair weather. *Pr.*

The full soul loatheth a honeycomb ; but to the hungry soul every bitter thing is sweet. *Bible.*

The furiously wicked have but a short career. Bad for them, but good for the universe. *Spurgeon.*

The future comes on slowly, the present flies like an arrow, the past stands for ever still. *Schiller.*

The future destiny of the child is always the work of the mother. *Napoleon.*

The future epic of the world rests not with those near dead, but with those that are alive, and those that are coming into life. *Carlyle.*

The future hides in it / Gladness and sorrow ; / We press still thoro' ; / Nought that abides in it / Daunting us—onward ; / But solemn before us, / Veiled the dark portal, / Goal of all mortal. / Stars silent rest o'er us— / Graves under us, silent. *Goethe.*

The gain of lying is nothing else but not to be trusted of any, nor to be believed when we say the truth. *Sir Walter Raleigh.*

The game is not worth the candle. *Corn.*

The gardener's business is to tend the flowers and root out the weeds. *Bodenstedt.*

The general and perpetual voice of men is as the sentence of God himself. *Hooker.*

The general tendency of things throughout the world is to render mediocrity the ascendant power among mankind. *J. S. Mill.*

The generality never suspect the devil even when he has them by the throat. *Goethe.*

The generous, who is always just, and the just who is always generous, may, unannounced, approach the throne of Heaven. *Lavater.*

The genius of light is friendly to the noble, and, in the dark, brings them friends from afar. *Emerson.*

The genius, wit, and spirit of a nation are discovered by their proverbs. *Bacon.*

The gentle mind by gentle deeds is known. *Spenser.*

The genuine use of gunpowder I hold to be that it makes all men alike tall. *Carlyle.*

The germs of all things are in every heart. *Amiel.*

The getting of treasures by a lying tongue is a vanity tossed to and fro of them that seek death. *Bible.*

The gift blindeth the wise and perverteth the words of the righteous. *Bible.*

5 The gift of prayer is not always in our power, but in the eye of Heaven the very wish to pray is prayer. *Lessing.*

The gift which is to be given should be given gratuitously. *Hitopadesa.*

The gifted man is he who sees the essential point and leaves aside all the rest as surplusage. *Carlyle.*

The glass of fashion and the mould of form, / The observed of all observers. *Ham.,* iii. 1.

The glory dies not, and the grief is past. *Sir Egerton Brydges.*

10 The glory is not in never falling, but in rising every time you fall. *Bovee.*

The glory of a people and of an age is always the work of a small number of great men, and disappears with them. *Baron de Grimm.*

The glory of children are their fathers. *Bible.*

The glory of philosophy lies not in solving the problem, but in putting it. *Renan.*

The glory of young men is their strength : and the beauty of old men is the grey head. *Bible.*

15 The God of merely traditional believers is the great Absentee of the universe. *W. R. Alger.*

The god of this world is riches, pleasure, and pride. *Luther.*

The God who dwells in my bosom can stir my heart to its depths. *Goethe.*

The goddess Athene is armed with the Gorgon's head. *Ed.*

The gods approve the depth, and not the tumult, of the soul. *Wordsworth.*

20 The gods are just, and of our pleasant vices / Make instruments to scourge us. *King Lear,* v. 3.

The gods are long-suffering ; but the law from the beginning was, He that will not work shall perish from the earth ; and the patience of the gods has limits. *Carlyle.*

The gods are on the side of the strongest. *Emerson.*

The gods are wont to save by human means. *Goethe.*

The gods do not avenge on the son the misdeeds of the father. Each or good or bad reaps the due reward of his own actions. Parents' blessing, not their curse, is inherited. *Goethe.*

25 The gods hearken to him who hearkens to them. *Homer.*

The gods in charity oft lend their strength to man. *Schiller.*

The gods invariably make us pay dear for the great benefits they confer on us. *Corn.*

The gods of fable are the shining moments of great men. *Emerson.*

The gods sell all things at a fair price. *Ancient Pr.*

30 The gods sell to us all the goods which they give us. *Epicharmus.*

The gods, when they appear to man, are commonly unrecognised by them. *Goethe.*

The golden age hath passed away, / Only the good have power to bring it back. *Goethe.*

The golden age, that lovely prime, / Existed in the past no more than now. / And did it e'er exist, believe me, / As then it was, it now may be restored. / Still meet congenial spirits, and enhance / Each other's pleasures in this beauteous world. *Goethe.*

The golden moments in the stream of life rush past us, and we see nothing but sand ; the angels come to visit us, and we only know them when they are gone. *George Eliot.*

35 The good are always ready to be the upholders of the good in their misfortunes. Elephants even are wont to bear the burthens of elephants who have sunk in the mire. *Hitopadesa.*

The good are better made by ill, / As odours crushed are sweeter still. *Rogers.*

The good die first, / And they whose hearts are dry as summer dust / Burn to the socket. *Wordsworth.*

The good-for-nothing is he who cannot command and cannot even obey. *Goethe.*

The good is always beautiful, the beautiful is good. *Whittier.*

40 The good mother saith not, "Will you ?" but gives. *Pr.*

The good nature of the dog is not discouraged, although it often brings upon him only rebuffs ; the abusive treatment of man never offends him, because he loves man. *Renan.*

The good need little water, but the base / Free from their guilt not ocean's self can lave. *Pythian orac'e.*

The good of other times let others state ; / I think it lucky I was born so late. *Sydney Smith.*

The good old rule / Sufficeth them, the simple plan, / That they should take who have the power, / And they should keep who can. *Wordsworth.*

45 The good that passes by without returning, leaves behind it an impression that may be compared to a void, and is felt like a want. *Goethe.*

The good, the new, comes exactly from that quarter whence it is not looked for, and is always something different from what is expected. *Feuerbach.*

The good things which belong to prosperity are to be wished ; but the good things that belong to adversity are to be admired. *Bacon, from Seneca.*

The good word is an easy obligation ; but not to speak ill requires only our silence, which costs us nothing. *.(?)*

The goods of this world cannot be divided without being lessened ; but why be a niggard of that which bestows bliss on a fellow-creature, yet takes nothing from our own means of enjoyment ? *Burns.*

50 The goose that lays the golden eggs likes to lay where there are eggs already. *Spurgeon.*

The gospel is at once the assigner of our tasks and the magazine of our strength. *Decay of Piety.*

The Gothic cathedral is a blossoming in stone subdued by the insatiable demand of harmony in man. *Emerson.*

The governing class, who should be working at an ark of deliverance for themselves and us while the hours still are, do nothing but complain, "We cannot get our hands kept rightly warm," and sit obstinately burning the planks. *Carlyle.*

The government must always be a step in advance of the popular movement. *Count Arnim-Boytzenburg.*

The government of England is a government of law. *Junius.*

The gown is hers that wears it, and the world is his who enjoys it. *Pr.*

5 The graceful minuet-dance of fancy must give place to the toilsome, thorny pilgrimage of understanding. *Carlyle on the transition from the age of romance to that of science.*

The grand encourager of Delphic and other noises is the echo. *Carlyle.*

"The grapes are sour," said the fox when he could not reach them. *Pr.*

The gravest events dawn with no more noise than the morning star makes in rising. All great developments complete themselves in the world, and modestly wait in silence, praising themselves never, and announcing themselves not at all. We must be sensitive and sensible if we would see the beginnings and endings of great things. That is our part. *Ward Beecher.*

The great agent of the march of the world is pain, the unsatisfied being that craves for development and is ill at ease in the process. *Renan.*

10 The great and rich depend on those whom their power or their wealth attaches to them. *Rogers.*

The great art of ruling consists for most part in persuading the people to believe that whatever happens through us. *Cötvös.*

The great artist is the slave of his ideal. *Bovee.*

The great cause of revolutions is this : that, while nations move onward, constitutions stand still. *Macaulay.*

The great distinction between mediæval art and modern is, that the former was brought into the service of religion and the latter is not. *Ruskin.*

15 The great doers in history have always been men of faith. *Chapin.*

The great duty of life is not to give pain ; and the most acute reasoner cannot find an excuse for one who voluntarily wounds the heart of a fellow-creature. *Fredrika Bremer.*

The great error of our nature is, not to know where to stop, not to be satisfied with any reasonable acquirement, not to compound with our condition ; but to lose all we have gained by an insatiable pursuit after more. *Burke.*

The great event for the world is, now as always, the arrival in it of a new wise man. *Carlyle.*

The great facts are the near ones. *Emerson.*

20 The great felicity of life is to be without perturbation. *Sen.*

The great hope of society is individual character. *Channing.*

The great make us feel, first of all, the indifference of circumstances. *Emerson.*

The great man does, in good truth, belong to his own age ; nay, more so than any other man ; being properly the synopsis and epitome of such age with its interests and influences ; but belongs likewise to all ages, otherwise he is not great. *Carlyle.*

The great man goes ahead of his time, the prudent (*kluge*) man goes with it, the crafty man makes his own out of it, and the blockhead sets himself against it. *Bauernfeld.*

The great man has more of human nature than 25 other men organised in him. *Theodore Parker.*

The great man is he who, in the midst of the crowd, keeps with perfect sweetness the independence of solitude. *Emerson.*

The great mass of people have eyes and ears, but not much more, especially little power of judgment, and even memory. *Schopenhauer.*

The great modern recipe is to work, still to work, and always to work. *Gambetta.*

The great moments of life are but moments like the others. Your doom is spoken in a word or two. A single look from the eyes, a mere pressure of the hand, may decide it ; or of the lips, though they cannot speak. *Thackeray.*

The great point is not to pull down, but to 30 build up, and in this humanity finds pure joy. *Goethe.*

The great portion of labour is not skilled ; the millions are and must be skilless, where strength alone is wanted. *Carlyle.*

The great principle of all effort is to endeavour to do, not what is absolutely best, but what is easily within our power, and adapted to our temper and condition. *Ruskin.*

The great river-courses which have shaped the lives of men have hardly changed. *George Eliot.*

The great rule of moral conduct is, next to God, to respect time. *Lavater.*

The great school for learning is the brain itself 35 of the learner. *Carlyle.*

The great soul of the world is just. There is justice here below ; at bottom there is nothing else but justice. *Carlyle.*

The great soul that sits on the throne of the universe is not, never was, and never will be, in a hurry. *J. G. Holland.*

The great source of calamity lies in regret or anticipation ; he therefore is most wise who thinks of the present alone, regardless of the past or the future. *Goldsmith.*

The great spirits that have gone before us can survive only as disembodied voices. *Carlyle.*

The great successes of the world have been 40 affairs of a second, a third, nay, a fiftieth trial. *John Morley.*

The great thieves punish the little ones. *Pr.*

The great thing, after all, is only Forwards. *Goethe.*

The great world-revolutions send in their disturbing billows to the remotest creek, and the overthrow of thrones more slowly overturns also the households of the lowly. *Carlyle.*

The greater and more various any one's knowledge, the longer he takes to find out anything that may suddenly be asked him ; because he is like a shopkeeper who has to get the article wanted from a large and multifarious store. *Schopenhauer*

The greater height sends down the deeper fall : / And good declin'd turns bad, turns worst of all. *Quarles.*

The greater man the greater courtesy. *Tennyson.*

The greater proportion of mankind are more sensitive to contemptuous language than unjust acts ; for they can less easily bear insult than wrong. *Plutarch.*

The greatest achievements of the human mind are generally received at first with distrust. *Schopenhauer.*

5 The greatest benefit which one friend can confer upon another, is to guard, and excite, and elevate his virtues. *Johnson.*

The greatest braggards are generally the greatest cowards. *Rousseau.*

The greatest clerkes (scholars) ben not the wisest men. *Chaucer.*

The greatest difficulties lie where we are not looking for them. *Goethe.*

The greatest events of an age are its best thoughts. It is the nature of thought to find its way into action. *Bovee.*

10 The greatest expense we can be at is that of our time. *Pr.*

The greatest felicity that felicity hath is to spread. *Hooker.*

The greatest flood hath the soonest ebb ; the sorest tempest the most sudden calm ; the hottest love the coldest end ; and from the deepest desire oftentimes ensues the deadliest hate. *Socrates.*

The greatest genius is the most indebted man. *Emerson.*

The greatest happiness of the greatest number. *Priestley.*

15 The greatest hatred, like the greatest virtue and the worst dogs, is quiet. *Jean Paul.*

The greatest man in history was the poorest. *Emerson.*

The greatest man is ever a son of man (*Menschenkind*). *Goethe.*

The greatest man living may stand in need of the meanest as much as the meanest does of him. *Fuller.*

The greatest men even want much more of the sympathy which every honest fellow can give than that which the great only can impart. *Thoreau.*

20 The greatest men of a nation are those whom it puts to death. *Renan.*

The greatest men of any age, those who become its leaders when there is a great march to be begun, are separated from the average intellects of their day by a distance which is immeasurable in ordinary terms of wonder. *Ruskin.*

The greatest men, whether poets or historians, live entirely in their own age, and the greatest faults of their works are gathered out of their own age. *Ruskin.*

The greatest men will be necessarily those who possess the best capacities, cultivated with the best habits. *James Harris.*

The greatest miracle of love is to eradicate flirtation. *La Roche.*

25 The greatest misfortune of all is not to be able to bear misfortune. *Bias.*

The greatest object in the universe, says a certain philosopher, is a good man struggling with adversity ; yet there is a still greater, which is the good man that comes to relieve it. *Goldsmith.*

The greatest of all economists are the fortifying virtues, which the wisest men of all time have arranged under the general heads of Prudence, or Discretion, the spirit which discerns and adopts rightly ; Justice, the spirit which rules and divides rightly ; Fortitude, the spirit which persists and endures rightly ; and Temperance, the spirit which stops and refuses rightly. *Ruskin.*

The greatest of all injustice is that which goes under the name of law. *L'Estrange.*

The greatest of all perversities is to deny one's own nature and act contrary to its innate moral principle. *Sophocles.*

The greatest of faults, I should say, is to be 30 conscious of none. *Carlyle.*

The greatest of follies is to sacrifice health for any other advantage. *Schopenhauer.*

The greatest of heroic deeds are those which are performed within four walls and in domestic privacy. *Jean Paul.*

The greatest ornament of an illustrious life is modesty and humility, which go a great way in the character even of the most exalted princes. *Napoleon.*

The greatest part of mankind labour under one delirium or another *Fielding.*

The greatest prayer is patience. *Buddha.* 35

The greatest skill is shown in disguising our skill. *La Roche.*

The greatest scholars are not always the wisest men. *Pr.*

The greatest star is that at the little end of the telescope,—the star that is looking, not looked after, nor looked at. *Theo. Parker.*

The greatest success is confidence, or perfect understanding between sincere people. *Emerson.*

The greatest truths are commonly the sim- 40 plest. *Malesherbes.*

The greatest truths are the simplest ; and so are the greatest men. *Hare.*

The greatest vessel hath but its measure. *Pr.*

The greatest virtues of men are only splendid sins. *Augustine.* (?)

The Greeks and Romans are the only ancients who never become old. *Weber.*

The Greeks cared for man only, and for the 45 rest of the universe little or not at all ; the moderns for the universe only, and man not at all. *Ruskin.*

The Greeks were the first to exalt spirit to lordship over nature ; it was Christ who first taught us what that spirit is in itself. *Ed.*

The grey mare is the better horse. *Pr.*

The grief that does not speak / Whispers the o'er-fraught heart, and bids it break. *Macb.*, iv. 3.

The grief which all hearts share grows less for one. *Sir Edwin Arnold.*

The groundsel speaks not save what it heard 50 at the hinges. *Pr.*

The guilty mind debases the great image that it wears, and levels us with brutes. (?)

The habit and power of reading with reflection, comprehension, and memory all alert and awake, does not come at once to the natural man any more than many other sovereign virtues. *John Morley.*

The habit of looking on the best side of every event is worth more than a thousand a year. *Johnson.*

The habit of lying, when once formed, is easily extended to serve the designs of malice or interest ; like all habits, it spreads indeed of itself. *Paley.*

The habit of party in England is not to ask the alliance of a man of genius, but to follow the guidance of a man of character. *Lord John Russell.*

5 The hand of little employment hath the dantier sense. *Ham.,* v. i.

The hand that gives, gathers. *Pr.*

The Hand that hath made you fair hath made you good ; the goodness that is cheap in beauty makes beauty brief in goodness ; but grace, being the soul of your complexion, should keep the body of it ever fair. *Meas. for Meas.,* iii. i.

The happiest of men were he who, understanding his craft and working intelligently with his hands, and earning competence and freedom by the exercise of his wits, found time to live by the heart and by the brain, to understand his own work, and to love the work of God. *Mme. George Sand.*

The happiness of life is made up of minute fractions,—the little, soon-forgotten charities of a kiss, a smile, a kind look, a heartfelt compliment in the disguise of a playful raillery, and the countless other infinitesimals of pleasant thought and feeling. *Coleridge.*

10 The happiness of man depends on no creed and no book ; it depends on the dominion of truth, which is the redeemer and saviour, the Messiah and the King of glory. *Rabbi Wise.*

The happiness of the human race is one of the designs of God, but our own individual happiness must not be made our first or our direct aim. *W. R. Greg.*

The happiness we owe to ourselves is greater than that which we owe to our surroundings. *Metrodorus.*

The happy day will come when mind, heart, and hands shall be alive together, and shall work in concert ; when there shall be a harmony between God's munificence and man's delight in it. *Mme. George Sand.*

The happy have whole days, and those they choose ; / The unhappy have but hours, and those they lose. *Colley Cibber.*

15 The happy man is he who distinguishes the boundary between desires and delight, and stands firmly on the higher ground. *Landor.*

The happy think a lifetime a short stage : / One night to the unhappy seems an age. *Lucian.*

The hardest step is over the threshold. *Pr.*

The hardships or misfortunes we lie under are more easy to us than those of any other person would be, should we change conditions with him. *Hor.*

The hare leaps out of the bush where we least look for her. *Sp. Pr.*

20 The harvest truly is plenteous, but the labourers are few. *Jesus.*

The hatred which is grafted on extinguished friendship must bring forth the most deadly fruits. *Lessing.*

The head cannot understand any work of art unless it be in company with the heart. *Goethe.*

The head is a half, a fraction, until it is enlarged and inspired by the moral sentiments. *Emerson.*

The head learns new things, but the heart for evermore practises old experiences. *Ward Beecher.*

The head only reproduces what the heart 25 creates ; and so we give the mocking-bird credit when he imitates the loving murmurs of the dove. *G. J. W. Melville.*

The health of a state consists simply in this, that in it those who are wisest shall also be strongest. *Ruskin.*

The healthy know not of their health, but only the sick. *Carlyle.*

The healthy man is the compliment of the seasons, and in winter summer is in his heart. There is the south ! *Thoreau.*

The healthy understanding is not the logical argumentative, but the intuitive ; for the end of understanding is not to prove and find reasons, but to know and believe. *Carlyle.*

The heart always sees before the head can 30 see. *Carlyle.*

The heart aye's the part aye / That mak's us right or wrang. *Burns.*

The heart benevolent and kind / The most resembles God. *Burns.*

The heart can ne'er a transport know / That never feels a pain. *Lyttelton.*

The heart has eyes that the brain knows nothing of. *C. H. Parkhurst.*

The heart has its arguments with which the 35 understanding is not acquainted. (?)

The heart is a small thing, but desireth great matters. It is not sufficient for a kite's dinner, yet the whole world is not sufficient for it. *Hugo de Amma.*

The heart is deceitful above all things, and desperately wicked ; who can know it? *Bible.*

The heart is like a millstone, which gives meat if you supply it with corn, but frets itself if you don't. *C. J. Weber.*

The heart is like a musical instrument of many strings, all the chords of which require putting in harmony. *Saadi.*

The heart is like the sea, is subject to storms, 40 ebb-tide and flood, and in its depths is many a precious pearl. *Heine.*

The heart is the best logician. *Wendell Phillips.*

The heart knoweth his own bitterness ; and a stranger doth not intermeddle with his joy. *Bible.*

The heart must be beaten or bruised, and then the sweet scent will come out. *Bunyan.*

The heart must be divorced from its idols. (?)

The heart must glow before the tongue can 45 gild. *W. R. Alger.*

The heart needs not for its heaven much space, nor many stars therein, if only the star of love has arisen. *Jean Paul.*

The heart of a fool is in his mouth, but the mouth of a wise man is in his heart. *Pr.*

The heart of a wise man should resemble a mirror, which reflects every object without being sullied by any. *Confucius.*

The heart of childhood is all mirth. *Keble.*

The heart of every man lies open to the shafts of reproof if the archer can but take a proper aim. *Goldsmith.*

5 The heart of man is the place the devils dwell in. *Sir Thomas Browne.*

The heart of the righteous studieth to answer; but the mouth of the wicked poureth out evil things. *Bible.*

The heart of the wise is in the house of mourning; but the heart of fools is in the house of mirth. *Bible.*

The heart sees farther than the head. *Pr.*

The heart that is soonest awake to the flowers is always the first to be touched by the thorns. *Moore.*

10 The heart that once truly loves never forgets. *Pr.*

The heart, unlike the fancy and the imagination, is not complex, and may be reached by the same weapons of thought in the most luxurious court of Christendom as in the tent of the Arab or the wigwam of the Cherokee. *C. Fitzhugh.*

The heart which truly loves puts not its love aside . . . but grows stronger for that which seeks to thwart it. *Lewis Morris.*

The heart will break, yet brokenly live on. *Byron.*

The hearts of men are their books, events are their tutors, great actions are their eloquence. *Macaulay.*

15 The heavenly powers never go out of their road. *Emerson.*

The heavens and the earth, and all that is between them, think ye we have created them in jest? *Koran.*

The heavens and the earth are but the time-vesture of the Eternal. *Carlyle.*

The heavens declare the glory of God; and the firmament showeth his handiwork. *Bible.*

The heavenward path which a great man opens up for us and traverses generally, like the track of a ship through the water, closes behind him on his decease. *Goethe.*

20 The heaviest head of corn hangs its head lowest. *Gael. Pr.*

The heavy and the weary weight / Of all this unintelligible world. *Wordsworth.*

The Hebrew Bible, is it not, before all things, true, as no other book ever was or will be? *Carlyle.*

The height charms us, the steps to it do not; with the summit in our eye, we love to walk along the plain. *Goethe.*

The height of ability consists in a thorough knowledge of the real value of things, and of the genius of the age we live in. *La Roche.*

25 The heights by great men reached and kept / Were not attained by sudden flight, / But they, while their companions slept, / Were toiling upward in the night. *Longfellow.*

The hell of these days is the infinite terror of Not getting on, especially of Not making money. *Carlyle.*

The hen of our neighbour appears to us as a goose. *Eastern Pr.*

The herd of people dread sound understanding more than anything; they ought to dread stupidity, if they knew what was really dreadful. Understanding is unpleasant, they must have it pushed aside; stupidity is but pernicious, they can let it stay. *Goethe.*

The heroes of literary history have been no less remarkable for what they have suffered than for what they have achieved. *Johnson.*

The heroic heart, the seeing eye, of the first 30 times, still feels and sees in us of the latest. *Carlyle.*

The higher character a person supports, the more he should regard his minutest actions. *Not traceable.*

The higher enthusiasm of man's nature is for the while without exponent; yet does it continue indestructible, unweariedly active, and work blindly in the great chaotic deep. Thus sect after sect, and church after church, bodies itself forth, and melts again into new metamorphosis. *Carlyle.*

The higher the culture, the more honourable the work. *Roscher.*

The higher the wisdom, the closer its neighbourhood and kinship with mere insanity. *Carlyle.*

The higher we rise, the more isolated we 35 become, and all elevations are cold. *De Boufflers.*

The highest art is always the most religious, and the greatest artist is always a devout man. *Prof. Blackie.*

The highest elevation attainable by man is a heroic life. *Schopenhauer.*

The highest exercise of invention has nothing to do with fiction; but is an invention of new truth, what we can call a revelation. *Carlyle.*

The highest genius never flowers in satire, but culminates in sympathy with that which is best in human nature, and appeals to it. *Chapin.*

The highest gift which we receive from God 40 and Nature is Life, the revolving movement, which knows neither pause nor rest, of the self-conscious being round itself. The instinct to protect and cherish life is indestructibly innate in every one, but the peculiarity of it ever remains a mystery to us and others. *Goethe.*

The highest happiness of us mortals is to execute what we consider right and good; to be really masters of the means conducive to our aims. *Goethe.*

The highest heaven of wisdom is alike near from every point, and thou must find it, if at all, by methods native to thyself alone. *Emerson.*

The highest in God's esteem are meanest in their own. *Thomas à Kempis.*

The highest joys spring from those possessions which are common to all, which we can neither alienate ourselves nor be deprived of by others, to which kind Nature has given all an equal right—a right which she herself guards with silent omnipotence. *Goethe.*

The highest liberty is in harmony with the eternal laws. *H. Giles.*

The highest man of us is born brother to his contemporaries ; struggle as he may, there is no escaping the family likeness. *Carlyle.*

The highest melody dwells only in silence— the sphere melody, the melody of health. *Carlyle.*

The Highest not merely has, but is, reason and understanding. *Goethe.*

5 The highest political watchword is not Liberty, Equality, Fraternity, nor yet Solidarity, but Service. *A. H. Clough.*

The highest price a man can pay for a thing is to ask for it. *Pr.*

The highest problem of every art is, by means of appearances, to produce the illusion of a loftier reality. *Goethe.*

The highest problem of literature is the writing of a Bible. *Novalis.*

The highest reach of a news-writer is an empty reasoning on policy, and vain conjectures on the public management. *La Bruyère.*

10 The highest thing that art can do is to set before you the true image of the presence of a noble human being. It has never done more than this, and it might not do less. *Ruskin.*

The highest virtue of the tropics is chastity ; of colder regions, temperance. *Bovee.*

The highest wisdom is not to be always wise. *M. Opiz.*

The highway of the upright is to depart from evil. *Bible.*

The hind that would be mated by the lion / Must die for love. *All's Well,* i. 1.

15 The historian is a prophet with his face directed to the past. *Fr. v. Schlegel.*

The history of a man is his character. *Goethe.*

The history of a soldier's wound beguiles the pain of it. We lose the right of complaining sometimes by forbearing it, but we often treble the force. *Sterne.*

The history of every man should be a Bible. *Novalis.*

The history of persecution is a history of endeavours to cheat Nature, to make water run uphill, to twist a rope of sand. It makes no difference whether the actors be many or one, a tyrant or a mob. *Emerson.*

20 The history of reforms is always identical ; it is the comparison of the idea with the fact. *Emerson.*

The history of the Church is a history of the invisible as well as of the visible Church ; which latter, if disjoined from the former, is but a vacant edifice ; gilded, it may be, and overhung with old votive gifts, yet useless, nay, pestilentially unclean ; to write whose history is less important than to forward its downfall. *Carlyle.*

The history of the world is nothing but the history of successful or unsuccessful grumbling ; operating in great things as in small, . . . inculcating through all of them the great moral, that it is not good for a man to be contented with evils that he can remove. *John Wagstaffe.*

The hoary head is a crown of glory, if it be found in the way of righteousness. *Bible.*

The hollow sea-shell which for years hath stood / On dusty shelves, when held against the ear / Proclaims its stormy parent. *Eugene Lee-Hamilton.*

The Holy Supper is kept indeed / In whatso 25 we share with another's need ; / Not what we give, but what we share, / For the gift without the giver is bare. *Lowell.*

The honest heart that's free frae a' / Intended fraud or guile, / However Fortune kick the ba', / Has aye some cause to smile. *Burns.*

The honest man does that from duty which the man of honour does for the sake of character. (?)

The honest man, though e'er so poor, / Is king o' men for a' that. *Burns.*

The honourablest part of talk is to give the occasion ; and again to moderate and pass to somewhat else, for then a man leads the dance. *Bacon.*

The horse is prepared against the day of battle : 30 but safety is of the Lord. *Bible.*

The horse thinks one thing, and he that rides him another. *Pr.*

The host should be indeed a host, and a lord of the land, a self-appointed brother of his race ; called to this place, besides, by all the winds of heaven and his good genius, as truly as the preacher is called to preach. *Thoreau.*

The hottest love has the coldest end. *Socrates.*

The hour of all windbags does arrive ; every windbag is at length ripped and collapses. *Carlyle.*

The hours should be instructed by the ages, 35 and the ages explained by the hours. *Emerson.*

The hours that we pass with happy prospects in view are more pleasing than those crowned with fruition. *Goldsmith.*

The house of the childless is empty ; and so is the heart of him that hath no wife. *Hitopadesa.*

The house that is a-building looks not as the house that is built. *Pr.*

The household is the home of the man as well as of the child. *Emerson.*

The human creature needs first of all to be 40 educated, not that he may speak, but that he may have something weighty and valuable to say. *Carlyle.*

The human face is my landscape. *Sir Joshua Reynolds.*

The human heart has a sigh lonelier than the cry of the bittern. *W. R. Alger.*

The human heart is like a millstone in a mill ; when you put wheat under it, it turns, and grinds, and bruises the wheat into flour ; if you put no wheat in, it still grinds on ; but then it is itself it grinds and slowly wears away. *Luther.*

The human heart is like heaven ; the more angels the more room. *Fredrika Bremer.*

The human mind cannot go beyond the gift 45 of God. *Wm. Blake.*

The human mind, in proportion as it is deprived of external resources, sedulously labours to find within itself the means of happiness, learns to rely with confidence on its own exertions, and gains with greater certainty the power of being happy. *Zimmermann.*

The human mind is to be treated like a skein of ravelled silk, where you must cautiously secure one free end before you can make any progress in disentangling it. *Scott.*

The human mind will not be confined to any limits. *Goethe.*

The human race is in the best condition when it has the greatest degree of liberty. *Dante.*

The human soul is like a bird that is born in a cage. Nothing can deprive it of its natural longings, or obliterate the mysterious remembrance of its heritage. *Epes Sargent.*

5 The human voice has an authority and an insinuating property which writing lacks. *Joubert.*

The husbandman that laboureth must be first partaker of the fruits. *St. Paul.*

The hypocrite shows well and says well, and himself is the worst thing he hath. *Bishop Hall.*

The idea you have once spoken, if even it were an idea, is no longer yours; it is gone from you, so much life and virtue is gone, and the vital circulations of yourself and your destiny and activity are henceforth deprived of it. *Carlyle.*

The Ideal always has to grow in the Real, and to seek out its bed and board there in a very sorry way. *Carlyle.*

10 The ideal beauty is a fugitive which is never located. *Mme. Sévigné.*

The ideal of beauty is simplicity and repose; from which it follows that no youth can be a master. *Goethe.*

The ideal of friendship is to feel as one while remaining two. *Mme. Swetchine.*

The idle always have a mind to do something. *Vauvenargues.*

The ignorant classes are the dangerous classes. *Ward Beecher.*

15 The ignorant peasant without fault is greater than the philosopher with many. *Goldsmith.*

The Iliad and the Shakespeare are tame to him who hears the rude but homely incidents of the road from every traveller. *Thoreau.*

The "Iliad" of Homer is no fiction, but a ballad history, the heart of it burning with enthusiastic, ill-informed belief. *Carlyle.*

The ill that's wisely feared is half withstood, / And fear of bad is the best foil to good. *Quarles.*

The image of God cut in ebony, *i.e.*, the negro. *Fuller.*

20 The imagination, give it the least license, dives deeper and soars higher than Nature does. *Thoreau.*

The imagination is a fine faculty; yet I like not when she works on what has actually happened; the airy forms she creates are welcome as things of their own kind; but uniting with reality she produces often nothing but monsters, and seems to me, in such cases, to fly into direct variance with reason and common-sense. *Goethe.*

The imagination of man's heart is evil from his youth. *Bible.*

The imaginative power always purifies, the want of it therefore essentially defiles. *Ruskin.*

The imbecility of men is always inviting the impudence of power. *Emerson.*

The importunities and perplexities of business 25 are softness and luxury, compared with the incessant cravings of vacancy, and the unsatisfactory expedients of idleness. *Johnson.*

The impressions of our childhood abide with us, even in their minutest traces. *Goethe.*

The indignation which makes verses is, properly speaking, an inverted love; the love of some right, some worth, some goodness, belonging to ourselves or others, which has been injured, and which this tempestuous feeling issues forth to defend and revenge. *Carlyle.*

The individual and the race are always moving, and as we drift into new latitudes new lights open in the heaven more immediately over us. *Chapin.*

The individual loves and hatreds, which sum up existence and life, are the brood of Eros; for hatred is only love in some form, crossed and thwarted, and always in nature so much hostility, so much affection of some kind is there. *Ed.*

The individual soul should seek for an inti- 30 mate union with the soul of the universe. *Novalis.*

The infant / Mewling and puking in the nurse's arms. / And then the whining schoolboy, with his satchel, / And shining morning face, creeping like snail / Unwillingly to school. *As You Like It,* ii. 7.

The infinite is more sure than any other fact. The infinite of terror, of hope, of pity; did it not at any moment disclose itself to thee, indubitable, unnameable? Came it never, like the gleam of preternatural eternal oceans, like the voice of old eternities, far-sounding through thy heart of hearts? *Carlyle.*

The infinitely little have a pride infinitely great. *Voltaire.*

The influence which we exercise over other objects depends on the influence we have over ourselves. *Cötvös.*

The injuries of life, if rightly improved, will be 35 to us as the strokes of the statuary on his marble, forming us to a more beautiful shape, and making us fitter to adorn the heavenly temple. *Mather.*

The injustice done to an individual is sometimes of service to the public. *Junius.*

The ingratitude of the world can never deprive us of the conscious happiness of having acted with humanity ourselves. *Goldsmith.*

The initial virtue of the race consists in the acknowledgment of their own lowly nature, and submission to the laws of higher being. *Ruskin.*

The ink of the scholar and the blood of the martyr are of equal value in the eye of heaven. *The Koran.*

The innocent seldom find an uneasy pillow. 40 *Cowper.*

The inquiry of truth, which is the love-making or wooing of it; the knowledge of truth, which is the presence of it; and the belief of truth, which is the enjoying of it, is the sovereign good of human nature. *Bacon.*

The insolence of condescension. *Burns.*

The insolence of office. *Ham.,* iii. 1.

The inspiration of the Almighty giveth man understanding. *Bible.*

The instinctive feeling of a great people is often wiser than the wisest men. *Kossuth.*

The instruction merely clever men can give us is like baked bread, savoury and satisfying for a single day; but flour cannot be sown, and seed-corn ought not to be ground. *Goethe.*

The integrity of the upright shall guide them. *Bible.*

The intellect has only one failing: it has no conscience. *Lowell.*

5 The intellect of the wise is like glass; it admits the light of heaven and reflects it. *Hare.*

The intellectual power, through words and things / Went sounding on a dim and perilous way. *Wordsworth.*

The intelligent have a right over the ignorant; namely, the right of instructing them. *Emerson.*

The intolerant man is the real pedant. *Jean Paul.*

The invariable mark of wisdom is to see the miraculous in the common. *Emerson.*

10 The inventor of a spinning-jenny is pretty sure of his reward in his own day; but the writer of a true poem, like the apostle of a true religion, is nearly as sure of the contrary. *Carlyle.*

The invisible world is near us; or rather it is here, in us and about us; were the fleshly coil removed from our soul, the glories of the unseen were even now around us; as the ancients fabled of the spheral music. *Carlyle.*

The iron tongue of midnight hath told twelve. *Mid. N. Dream,* v. 1.

The irreligious poet is a monster. *Burns.*

The *is* of this moment is not the explanation of the *is* of the next. Except in the idea of God there is no nexus between the two. *Ed.*

15 The Israelitish people never was good for much, as its own leaders, judges, rulers, prophets have a thousand times reproachfully declared; it possesses few virtues, and most of the faults of other nations; but in cohesion, steadfastness, valour, and when all this would not serve, in obstinate toughness, it has no match. *Goethe.*

The jealous is possessed by a "fine mad devil" and a dull spirit at once. *Lavater.*

The jealous man's disease is of so malignant a nature, that it converts all it takes into its own nourishment. *Addison.*

The jest which is expected is already destroyed. *Johnson.*

The joy of a peaceful conscience is sown in tears. *Thomas à Kempis.*

20 The joys of parents are secret, and so are their griefs and fears. *Bacon.*

The judgment is like a pair of scales, and evidences like the weights; but the will holds the balance in its hand; and even a slight jerk will be sufficient, in many cases, to make the lighter scale appear the heavier. *Whately.*

The judgment of the world stands upon matter of fortune. *Sir P. Sidney.*

The judgments of the understanding are properly of force but once, and that in the strictest cases, and become inaccurate in some degree when applied to any other. *Goethe.*

The just man walketh in his integrity: his children are blessed after him. *Bible.*

The justice, / In fair round belly with good 25 capon lined, / With eyes severe and beard of formal cut, / Full of wise saws and modern instances; / And so he plays his part. *As You Like It,* ii. 7.

The keeping of bees is like the directing of sunbeams. *Thoreau.*

The key to every man is his thought. Sturdy and defying though he look, he has a helm which he obeys. *Emerson.*

The kind fool, of all kinds of fools, is worst. *Sir Richard Baker.*

The kind of speech in a man betokens the kind of action you will get from him. *Carlyle.*

The king goes as far as he may, not as far as 30 he would. *Sp. Pr.*

The king, like other people, has now and then shabby errands, and must have shabby fellows to do them. *Scott.*

The king may gang the cadger's gate, *i.e.,* may one day need his help. *Sc. Pr.*

The king protecteth the people, and they support the greatness of their sovereign. But protection is better than greatness; for the one cannot exist without the other. *Hitopadesa.*

The king's errand may come in at the cadger's gate. *Pr.*

The king's favour is toward a wise servant. 35 *Bible.*

The king's honour is that of his people. Their real honour and real interest are the same. *Junius.*

The kings of modern thought are dumb. *Matthew Arnold.*

The king's wrath is as the roaring of a lion; but his favour is as dew upon the grass. *Bible.*

The kingdom of God does not lie in elegance of speech or fineness of parts, but in innocence of life and good works. *Thomas à Kempis.*

The knowledge of man is an evening know- 40 ledge, "vesperina cognitio," but that of God is a morning knowledge, "matutina cognitio." *Emerson, from the Schoolmen.*

The knowledge of thyself will preserve thee from vanity. *Cervantes.*

The labour we delight in physics pain. *Macb.,* ii. 3.

The labourer is worthy of his hire. *Jesus.*

The lake's silver dulls with driving clouds. *Sir Edwin Arnold.*

The lamp of genius burns quicker than the 45 lamp of life. *Schiller.*

The lamp of the wicked shall be put out. *Bible.*

The land is mother of us all; nourishes, shelters, gladdens, lovingly enriches us all; in how many ways, from our first wakening to our last sleep on her blessed mother-bosom, does she, as with blessed mother's arms, enfold us all! *Carlyle.*

The land, properly speaking, belongs to these two: to the Almighty God; and to all his children of men that have ever worked well on it, or that shall ever work well on it. *Carlyle.*

The language of truth is simple. *Euripides.*

The largest soul of any country is altogether its own. *Ruskin.*

The last act crowns the play. *Quarles.*

The last, best fruit which comes to late perfection, even in the kindliest soul, is tenderness toward the hard, forbearance toward the unforbearing, warmth of heart toward the cold, philanthropy toward the misanthropic. *Jean Paul.*

The last drop makes the cup run over. *Pr.*

5 The last ounce breaks the camel's back. *Pr.*

The last pale rim or sickle of the moon, which had once been full, now sinking in the dark seas. *Carlyle by the bedside of his dying mother.*

The last perfection of our faculties is that their activity, without ceasing to be sure and earnest, become sport. *Schiller.*

The last stage of human perversion is when sympathy corrupts itself into envy ; and the indestructible interest we take in men's doings has become a joy over their faults and misfortunes. *Carlyle.*

The last thing that we discover in writing a book is to know what to put at the beginning. *Pascal.*

10 The Latin word for a flatterer (*assentator*) implies no more than a person that barely consents ; and indeed such a one, if a man were able to purchase or maintain him, cannot be bought too dear. *Steele.*

The latter part of a wise man's life is taken up in curing the follies, prejudices, and false opinions he had contracted in the former. *Swift.*

The law always limits every power which it bestows. *Hume.*

The law cannot equalise men in spite of nature. *Vauvenargues.*

The law has no eyes, the law has no hands, the law is nothing—nothing but a piece of paper, till public opinion breathes the breath of life into the dead letter. *Macaulay.*

15 The law is good if a man use it lawfully. *St. Paul.*

The law is light ; and reproofs of instruction are the way of life. *Bible.*

The law is past depth to those that, without heed, do plunge into it. *Timon of Athens,* iii. 5.

The law is the friend of the weak. *Schiller.*

The law is what we must do ; the gospel what God will give. *Luther.*

20 The law of nature is the strictest expression of necessity. *Molescholte.*

The law of perseverance is among the deepest in man ; by nature he hates change ; seldom will he quit his old house till it has actually fallen about his ears. *Carlyle.*

The law of the wise is a fountain of life. *Bible.*

The law often permits what honour prohibits. *Saurin.*

The law will never make men free ; it is men who have got to make the law free. *Thoreau.*

25 The law's made to take care o' raskils. *George Eliot.*

The laws of morality are also those of art. *Schumann.*

The laws of nature are just, but terrible. There is no weak mercy in them. *Longfellow.*

The laws of nature never vary ; in their application they never hesitate, nor are wanting. *Draper.*

The laws undertake to punish only overt acts. *Montesquieu.*

The lawyer is a gentleman who rescues your 30 estate from your enemies, and keeps it to himself. *Brougham.*

The leafy blossoming present time springs from the whole past, remembered and unrememberable. *Carlyle.*

The lean and slippered pantaloon, / With spectacles on nose and pouch on side ; / His youthful hose, well saved, a world too wide / For his shrunk shank ; and his big manly voice / Turning again towards childish treble, pipes / And whistles in his sound. *As You Like It,* ii. 7.

The learned understand the reason of the art, the unlearned feel the pleasure. *Quinct.*

The legacy of heroes—the memory of a great name and the inheritance of a great example. *Disraeli.*

The legal and proper mercy of a king of 35 England may remit the punishment, but ought not to stop the trial. *Junius.*

The lenient hand of time is daily and hourly either lightening the burden or making us insensible to the weight. *Burns.*

The less a man thinks or knows about his virtues the better we like him. *Emerson.*

The less men think the more they talk. *Montesquieu.*

The less routine the more of life. *A. B. Alcott.*

The less the wise man pleases himself, the 40 more the world esteems him. *Gellert.*

The less we deserve good fortune, the more we hope for it. *Molière.*

The less we have to do with our sins the better. *Emerson.*

The lessons of adversity are not always salutary ; sometimes they soften and amend, but as often they indurate and pervert. *Bulwer Lytton.*

The letter killeth, but the spirit giveth life. *St. Paul.*

The liberal deviseth liberal things ; and by 45 liberal things shall he stand. *Bible.*

The liberal soul shall be made fat : and he that watereth shall be watered also himself. *Bible.*

The liberty of writing letters with too careless a hand is apt to betray persons into imprudence in what they write. *Blair.*

The life is more than meat, and the body is more than raiment. *Jesus.*

The life of a fool is worse than death. *Apocrypha.*

The life of a man is tormented not by things, 50 but by opinions of things. *Immermann.*

The life of a nation is usually, like the flow of a lava stream, first bright and fierce, then languid and covered, at last advancing by the tumbling over and over of its frozen blocks. *Ruskin.*

The life of all gods figures itself to us as a sublime sadness,—earnestness of infinite battle against infinite labour. *Carlyle.*

The life of an animal, until the hour of his death, passeth away in disciplines, in elevations and depressions, in unions and separations. *Hitopadesa.*

The life of an egoist is a tissue of inconsistencies, of actions that, from his own point of view, are absurd and foolish. *Renan.*

The life of every man is a diary in which he means to write one story, and writes another. *J. M. Barrie.*

The life of every man is as the well-spring of a stream, whose small beginnings are indeed plain to all, but whose ulterior course and destination, as it winds through the expanses of infinite years, only the omniscient can discern. *Carlyle.*

5 The life of man is a journey ; a journey that must be travelled, however bad the roads or the accommodation. *Goldsmith.*

The life of the Divine Man stands in no connection with the general history of the world in his time. It was a private life ; his teaching was a teaching for individuals. *Goethe.*

The life of the lowest mortal, if faithfully recorded, would be interesting to the highest. *Quoted by Carlyle.*

The life which renews a man springs ever from within. *Goethe.*

The light by which we see in this world comes out from the soul of the observer. *Emerson.*

10 The light can be a curtain as well as the darkness. *George Eliot.*

The light of friendship is like the light of phosphorus—seen plainest when all around is dark. *Crowell.*

The light of the body is the eye ; if therefore thine eye be single, thy whole body shall be full of light. *Jesus.*

The light shineth in darkness ; and the darkness comprehended it not. *St. John.*

The light that a man receiveth by counsel from another is drier and purer than that which cometh from his own understanding and judgment, which is ever infused and drenched in his affections and customs. *Bacon.*

15 The light (which you refuse to take in) returns on you, condensed into lightning, which there is not any skin whatever too thick for taking in. *Carlyle.*

The lightning is the shorthand of the storm, / That tells of chaos. *Eric Mackay.*

The limbs of my buried ones touched cold on my soul and drove away its blots, as dead hands heal eruptions of the skin. *Jean Paul.*

The line of life is a ragged diagonal between duty and desire. *W. R. Alger.*

The lion is not so fierce as painted. *Fuller.*

20 The lips of the righteous feed many ; but fools die for want of wisdom. *Bible.*

The litigant, unlike the goose, never gets trust (trussed), although he may be roasted and dished. *John Willock.*

The little done vanishes from the sight of man who looks forward to what is still to do. *Goethe.*

The little foolery that wise men have makes a great show. *As You Like It,* i. 2.

The little man is still a man. *Goethe.*

The little mind will not by daily intercourse 25 with great minds become one inch greater ; but the noble man . . . will, by a knowledge of, and familiar intercourse with, elevated natures, every day make a visible approximation to similar greatness. *Goethe.*

The little that a just man hath is better than the riches of many wicked. *Bible.*

The lives of the best of us are spent in choosing between evils. *Junius.*

The loftier the building the deeper must the foundation be laid. *Thomas à Kempis.*

The loftiest mortal loves and seeks the same sort of things with the meanest, only from higher grounds and by higher paths. *Jean Paul.*

The loftiest of our race are those who have 30 had the profoundest grief, because they have had the profoundest sympathies. *Henry Giles.*

The longer a man's fame is likely to last, the later it will be in coming. *Schopenhauer.*

The longer life the more offence, / The more offence the greater pain, / The greater pain the less defence, / The less defence the lesser gain. *Sir T. Wyatt.*

The longer we live and the more we think, the higher value we learn to put on the friendship and tenderness of parents and of friends. *Johnson.*

The longer you read the Bible the more you will like it. *Romaine.*

The longest day soon comes to an end. *Pr.* 35

The longest life is scarcely longer than the shortest, if we think of the eternity that encircles both. *Carlyle.*

The longest wave is quickly lost in the sea. *Emerson.*

The look of a king is itself a deed. *Jean Paul.*

The loom of Fortune weaves the fine and coarsest web. *R. Southwell.*

The loom of life never stops ; and the pattern 40 which was weaving when the sun went down in the evening is weaving when it comes up to-morrow. *Ward Beecher.*

The Lord bestoweth his blessings where he findeth the vessels empty. *Thomas à Kempis.*

The Lord gave, and the Lord taketh away : blessed be the name of the Lord. *Bible.*

The Lord is a buckler to all that trust in him. *Bible.*

The Lord is a God of knowledge, and by him actions are weighed. *Bible.*

The Lord will not suffer the soul of the 45 righteous to famish : but he casteth away the substance of the wicked. *Bible.*

The loss of territory, or of a wise and virtuous servant, is a great loss, . . . for servants are not easily to be found. *Hitopadesa.*

The lot is cast into the lap ; but the whole disposing thereof is of the Lord. *Bible.*

The love of country produces good manners, and good manners also love of country. The less we satisfy our particular passions, the more we leave to our general. *Montesquieu.*

The love of gain never made a painter ; but it has marred many. *Washington Allston.*

The love of God is broader than the measure 50 of man's mind. *F. W. Faber.*

The love of letters is the forlorn hope of the man of letters. *Hazlitt.*

The love of money is the root of all evil. *St. Paul.*

The love season is the carnival of egoism, and it brings the touchstone to our natures. *George Meredith.*

The lover has more senses and finer senses than others. *Emerson.*

5 The lover, / Sighing like a furnace, with a woeful ballad / Made to his mistress' eyebrow. *As You Like It*, ii. 7.

The lower a man descends in his love, the higher he lifts his life. *W. R. Alger.*

The lower has oftentimes to be with sorrow sacrificed to the higher duties of the soul. *Ed.*

The lower nature must always be denied when you are trying to rise to a higher sphere. *Ward Beecher.*

The lunatic, the lover, and the poet, / Are of imagination all compact. *Mid. N.'s Dream*, v. 1.

10 The lust of fame is the last that a wise man shakes off. *Tac.*

The lyric poet may drink wine and live generously, but the epic poet, who shall sing of the gods and their descent unto men, must drink water out of a wooden bowl. *Emerson.*

The magic of the pen lies in the concentration of your thoughts upon one object. *G. H. Lewes.*

The magic power of love consists in its ennobling whatever its breath touches, like the sun whose golden ray transmutes even thunderclouds into gold. *Grillparzer.*

The main enterprise of the world for splendour, for extent, is the upbuilding of a man. *Emerson.*

15 The majority have no other reason for their opinions than that they are the fashion. *Johnson.*

The make-weight! The make-weight! which fate throws into the balance for us at every happiness! It requires much courage not to be down-hearted in this world. *Goethe.*

The malicious sneer is improperly called laughter. *Goldsmith.*

The man at the head of the house can mar the pleasure of the household; but he cannot make it. That must rest with the woman, and it is her greatest privilege. *Helps.*

The man comes before the citizen, and our future is greater than both. *Jean Paul.*

20 The man is only half himself, the other half is his expression. *Emerson.*

The man makes the circumstances, and is spiritually as well as economically the artificer of his own fortune, but the man's circumstances are the element he is appointed to live and work in; so that in a no less genuine sense it can be said circumstances make the man. *Carlyle.*

The man of consequence and fashion shall richly repay a deed of kindness with a nod and a smile, or a hearty shake of the hand; while a poor fellow labours under a sense of gratitude, which, like copper coin, though it loads the bearer, is yet of small account in the currency and commerce of the world. *Burns.*

The man of genius can be more easily misinstructed (*verbildet*) and driven far more violently into false courses than a man of ordinary capability. *Goethe.*

The man of genius, like a dog with a bone, sits afar and retired off the road, hangs out no sign of refreshment for man and beast, but says, by all possible hints and signs, "I wish to be alone—good-bye—farewell!" *Thoreau.*

The man of good common-sense may, if he 25 pleases, in his particular station of life, most certainly be rich. *Eustace Budgell.*

The man of intellect at the top of affairs; this is the aim of all institutions and revolutions, if they have any. *Carlyle.*

The man of intellect is lost unless he unites energy of character to intellect. When we have the lantern of Diogenes we must have his staff. *Chamfort.*

The man of wisdom is the man of years. *Young.*

The man should make the hour, not this the man. *Tennyson.*

The man that blushes is not quite a brute. 30 *Young.*

The man that hath no music in himself, / Nor is not moved with concord of sweet sounds, / Is fit for treasons, stratagems, and spoils; / The motions of his spirit are dull as night, / And his affections dark as Erebus: / Let no such man be trusted. *Mer. of Ven.*, v. 1.

The man that makes a character makes foes. *Young.*

The man that stands by himself, the universe stands also. *Emerson.*

The man that wandereth out of the way of understanding shall remain in the congregation of the dead. *Bible.*

The man to whom the universe does not reveal 35 directly what relation it has to him, whose heart does not tell him what he owes to himself and others—that man will scarcely learn it out of books; which generally do little more than give our errors names. *Goethe.*

The man truly proud thinks honours below his merit, and scorns to boast. *Swift.*

The man (Napoleon) was a divine missionary, though unconscious of it; and preached, through the cannon's throat, that great doctrine, "La carrière ouverte aux talens," "The tools to him that can handle them," which is our ultimate political evangel, wherein alone can liberty lie. *Carlyle.*

The man who can be nothing but serious or nothing but merry is but half a man. *Leigh Hunt.*

The man who can thank himself alone for the happiness he enjoys is truly blest. *Goldsmith.*

The man who cannot be a Christian in the 40 place where he is, cannot be a Christian anywhere. *Ward Beecher.*

The man who cannot blush, and who has no feelings of fear, has reached the acme of impudence. *Menander.*

The man who cannot enjoy his natural gifts in silence, and find his reward in the exercise of them, but must wait and hope for their recognition by others, must expect to reap only disappointment and vexation. *Goethe.*

The man who cannot laugh is not only fit for treasons, stratagems, and spoils; but his own whole life is already a treason and a stratagem. *Carlyle.*

The man who cannot sometimes endure his own company must have a bad heart or a deficient intellect. (?)

The man who cannot wonder, who does not habitually wonder (and worship), were he president of innumerable royal societies, and carried the whole "Méchanique Céleste" and Hegel's Philosophy, and the epitome of all laboratories and observatories with their results, in his single head, is but a pair of spectacles behind which there is no eye. *Carlyle.*

The man who does not know when to die, does not know how to live. *Ruskin.*

5 The man who does not learn to live while he is getting a living is a poorer man after his wealth is won than he was before. *J. G. Holland.*

The man who fears not death will start at no shadows. *Gr. Pr.*

The man who has imagination without learning has wings without feet. *Pr.*

The man who has no enemies has no following. *Donn Piatt.*

The man who has nothing to boast of but his illustrious ancestry is like a potato,— the only good belonging to him is underground. *Sir Thomas Overbury.*

10 The man who in this world can keep the whiteness of his soul is not likely to lose it in any other. *Alex. Smith.*

The man who in wavering times is inclined to be wavering only increases the evil, and spreads it wider and wider; but the man of firm decision fashions the universe. *Goethe.*

The man who insists upon seeing with perfect clearness before he decides, never decides. *Amiel.*

The man who invented "Ifs" and "Buts" must have first made gold out of straw choppings. *G. A. Bürger.*

The man who is always fortunate cannot easily have a great reverence for virtue. *Cic.*

15 The man who is born with a talent which he is meant to use, finds his greatest happiness in using it. *Goethe.*

The man who is in a hurry to see the full effects of his own tillage must cultivate annuals, and not forest trees. *Whately.*

The man who leaves home to mend himself and others is a philosopher; but he who goes from country to country, guided by the blind impulse of curiosity, is only a vagabond. *Goldsmith.*

The man who lives by hope will die by despair. *It. Pr.*

The man who pauses in his honesty wants little of a villain. *H. Martyn.*

20 The man who small things scorns will next, / By things still smaller be perplexed. *Goethe.*

The man who will live above his present circumstances is in great danger of living in a little time much beneath them, or, as the Italian proverb says, "The man who lives by hope will die by despair." *Addison.*

The man who works at home helps society at large with somewhat more of certainty than he who devotes himself to charities. *Emerson.*

The man who writes for fools is always sure of a large audience. *Schopenhauer.*

The man whom grown-up people love, children love still more. *Jean Paul.*

The manifestation of one's own superiority 25 may render the purchase too dear, by being bought at the terrible price of our neighbour's dislike. *Lover.*

The manners of the ill-mannered are never so odious, unbearable, exasperating, as they are to their own nearest kindred. *P. G. Hamerton.*

The many still must labour for the one! It is Nature's doom. *Byron.*

The march of intellect is proceeding at quick time; and if its progress be not accompanied by a corresponding improvement in morals and religion, the faster it proceeds, with the more violence will you be hurried down the road to ruin. *Southey.*

The march of intellect, which licks all the world into shape, has reached even the devil. *Goethe.*

The march of the human mind is slow. *Burke.* 30

The mark of the man of the world is absence of pretension. He does not make a speech; he takes a low business-tone, avoids all brag, is nobody, dresses plainly, promises not at all, performs much, speaks in monosyllables, hugs his fact. He calls his employment by its lowest name, and so takes from evil tongues their sharpest weapon. *Emerson.*

The marks of attachment, even to a fault, are an accumulation of virtues. *Hitopadesa.*

The mass of men consulted at hustings, upon any high matter whatsoever, is as ugly an exhibition of human study as the world sees. *Carlyle.*

The master of slaves has seldom the soul of a man. *Henry Mackenzie.*

The master-spirit who can rule the storm is 35 great; but he is much greater who can both raise and rule it. *E. L. Magoon.*

The mastiff is quiet while curs are yelping. *Pr.*

The material wealth of a country is the portion of its possessions which feeds and educates good men and women in it. *Ruskin.*

The May of our life blooms once, and not again. *Schiller.*

The man of true valour lies between the extremes of cowardice and rashness. *Cervantes.*

The means that Heaven yields must be em- 40 braced, / And not neglected. *Rich. II.*, iii. 2.

The measure of a master is his success in bringing all men round to his opinion twenty years later. *Emerson.*

The mechanical occupations of man, the watching any object, as it were, coming into existence by manual labour, is a very pleasant way of passing one's time, but our own activity is at the moment nil. It is almost the same as with smoking tobacco. *Goethe.*

The meditative heart / Attends the warning of each day and hour, / And practises in secret every virtue. *Goethe.*

The meek shall inherit the earth. *Jesus.*

The memory of absent friends becomes dimmed, although not effaced by time. The distractions of our life, acquaintance with fresh objects, in short, every change in our condition, works upon our hearts as dust and smoke upon a painting, making the finely drawn lines quite imperceptible, whilst one does not know how it happens. *Goethe.*

The memory of the just is blessed. *Bible.*

The men I am afraid of are the men who believe everything, subscribe to everything, and vote for everything. *Bp. Shipley.*

The merchant who was at first busy in acquiring money ceases to grow richer from the time when he makes it his business only to count it. *Johnson.*

5 The merciful shall obtain mercy. *Jesus.*

The mere existence and necessity of a philosophy is an evil. *Carlyle.*

The mere reality of life would be inconceivably poor without the charm of fancy, which brings in its bosom, no doubt, as many vain fears as idle hopes, but lends much oftener to the illusions it calls up a gay flattering hue than one which inspires terror. *W. v. Humboldt.*

The merit of originality is not novelty, it is sincerity. The believing man is the original man ; whatsoever he believes, he believes it for himself, not for another. *Carlyle.*

The meteor flag of England, / Shall yet terrific burn, / Till danger's troubled night depart, / And the star of peace return. *Campbell.*

10 The milder virtues subsist only in co-existence with the severer, and the heart which pronounces a blessing on the poor and the merciful utters with the same breath sentence of excommunication against all who are proud-spirited and cruel-hearted. *Ed.*

The mill will never grind with the water that is past. *Pr.*

The mind becomes bankrupt under too large obligations. All additional benefits lessen every hope of future returns, and bar up every avenue that leads to tenderness. *Goldsmith.*

The mind can make / Substance, and people planets of its own / With beings brighter than have been, and give / A breath to forms that can outlive all flesh. *Byron.*

The mind conceives with pain, but it brings forth with delight. *Joubert.*

15 The mind content both crown and kingdom is. *Robert Greene.*

The mind goes antagonising on, and never prospers but by fits. *Emerson.*

The mind is enlarged and elevated by mere purposes, though they end as they begin by airy contemplation. *Johnson.*

The mind is ever ingenious in making its own distress. *Goldsmith.*

The mind is its own place, and in itself / Can make a heaven of hell, a hell of heaven. *Milton.*

20 The mind must not yield to the body. *Goethe.*

The mind of a fool is empty ; and everything is empty where there is poverty. *Hitopadesa.*

The mind of a good man doth not alter, even when he is in distress ; the waters of the ocean are not to be heated by a torch of straw. *Hitopadesa.*

The mind of man is no inert receptacle of knowledge, but absorbs and incorporates into its own constitution the ideas which it receives. *H. Lecky.*

The mind of the greatest man on earth is not so independent of circumstances as not to feel inconvenienced by the merest buzzing noise about him ; it does not need the report of a cannon to disturb his thoughts. The creaking of a vane or a pulley is quite enough. Do not wonder that he reasons ill just now ; a fly is buzzing by his ear ; it is quite enough to unfit him for giving good counsel. *Pascal.*

25 The mind profits by the wrecks of every passion, and we may measure our road to wisdom by the sorrows we have undergone. *Bulwer Lytton.*

The mind that made the world is not one mind, but *the* mind. *Emerson.*

The minds of some of our statesmen, like the pupil of the human eye, contract themselves the more the stronger light there is shed upon them. *Moore.*

The mind's the standard of the man. *Watts.*

The miracles which Christ and His disciples wrought were the scaffolding, not the building. The scaffolding is removed as soon as the building is finished. *Lessing.*

30 The miser is as much in want of that which he has as of that which he has not. *Pub. Syr.*

The miser is niggardly in death ; two glances he casts on his coffin and a thousand with dismay on his anxiously-guarded treasures. *Gellert.*

The miserable have no other medicine, / But only hope. *Meas. for Meas.,* iii. 1.

The misery of man proceeds not from any single crush of overwhelming evil, but from small vexations continually repeated. *Johnson.*

The misfortune in the state is that nobody can enjoy life in peace, but that everybody must govern ; and in art, that nobody will enjoy what has been produced, but that every one wants to reproduce on his own account. *Goethe.*

35 The mixtures of spiritual chemistry refuse to be analysed. *Emerson.*

The mob has many heads, but no brains. *Pr.*

The mob is a monster, with the hands of Briareus but the head of Polyphemus,— strong to execute, but blind to perceive. *Colton.*

The mob is a sort of bear : while your ring is through its nose, it will even dance under your cudgel ; but should the ring slip and you lose your hold, the brute will turn and rend you. *Jane Porter.*

(The mob is) the scum that rises uppermost when the nation boils. *Dryden.*

40 The modest virgin, the prudent wife, or the careful matron, are much more serviceable in life than petticoated philosophers, blustering heroines, or virago queens. *Goldsmith.*

The moment an ill can be patiently borne, it is disarmed of its poison, though not of its pain. *Ward Beecher.*

The moment must be pregnant and sufficient to itself if it is to become a worthy segment of time and eternity. *Goethe.*

The moment there is a bargain over the pottage the family relation is dissolved. *Ruskin.*

The moment which is the cradle of the future is also the grave of the past. *Grillparzer.*

The moon doth not withhold the light even from the cottage of a Chandala (outcast). *Hitopadesa.*

The moon that shone in Paradise. *Hans Andersen.*

The moral difference between a man and a beast is, that the one acts primarily for use, and the other for pleasure. *Ruskin.*

5 The morality of a king is not to be measured by vulgar rules. There are faults which do him honour, and virtues that disgrace him. *Junius.*

The morality of girls is custom, not principle. *Jean Paul.*

The morality of some people is in remnants —never enough to make a coat. *Joubert.*

The more a man has in himself, the less he will want from other people—the less, indeed, other people can be to him. *Schopenhauer.*

The more a man lives, the more he suffers. *Amiel.*

10 The more angels the more room. *Swedenborg.*

The more business a man has to do, the more he is able to accomplish; for he learns to economise his time. *Judge Hale.*

The more bustling the streets become, the more quietly one moves. *Goethe.*

The more fair and crystal is the sky, / The uglier seem the clouds that in it fly. *Rich. II.,* i. I.

The more generally persons are pleasing, the less profoundly do they please. *H. Beyle.*

15 The more haste, the worse speed. *Pr.*

The more honesty a man has, the less he affects the air of a saint. *Lavater.*

The more laws you accept, the fewer penalties you will have to endure, and the fewer punishments to enforce. *Ruskin.*

The more men refine upon pleasure, the less will they indulge in excesses of any kind. *Hume.*

The more of the solid there is in a man, the less does he act the balloon. *Spurgeon.*

20 The more powerful the obstacle, the more glory we have in overcoming it; and the difficulties with which we are met are the maids of honour which set off virtue. *Molière.*

The more profound the thought, the more burdensome. *Emerson.*

The more riches a fool has, the greater fool he is. *Anon.*

The more sand has escaped from the hourglass of our life, the clearer we should see through it. *Jean Paul.*

The more sinful a man feels himself, the more Christian he is. *Novalis.*

25 The more the soul admires, the more it is exalted. *Mme. de Krudener.*

The more thou feelest thyself to be a man, so much the more dost thou resemble the gods. *Goethe.*

The more we do, the more we can do; the more busy we are, the more leisure we have. *Hazlitt.*

The more we have read, the more we have learned, the more we have meditated, the better conditioned we are to affirm that we know nothing. *Voltaire.*

The more we know, the greater our thirst for knowledge. The water-lily, in the midst of waters, opens its leaves and expands its petals at the first pattering of showers, and rejoices in the raindrops with a quicker sympathy than the parched shrub in a sandy desert. *Coleridge.*

The more we work, the more we shall be 30 trodden down. *Fr. Peasant Pr.*

The more weakness, the more falsehood; strength goes straight; every cannon-ball that has in it hollows and holes goes crooked. Weaklings must lie. *Jean Paul.*

The more you are talked about, the less powerful you are. *Disraeli.*

The morning stars sang together, and all the sons of God shouted for joy. *Bible.*

The most advanced nations are always those who navigate the most. *Emerson.*

The most brilliant flashes of wit come from a 35 clouded mind, as lightning leaps only from an obscure firmament. *Bovee.*

The most certain sign of wisdom is a continual cheerfulness. *Montaigne.*

The most civilised are as near to barbarism as the most polished steel to rust. Nations, like metals, have only a superficial brilliancy. *Rivarol.*

The most cursory observation shows that a degree of reserve adds vastly to the latent force of character. *Tuckerman.*

The most delightful letter does not possess a hundredth part of the charm of a conversation. *Goethe.*

The most difficult thing in life is to know your- 40 self. *Thales.*

The most elevated sensation of music arises from a confused perception of ideal or visionary beauty and rapture, which is sufficiently perceivable to fire the imagination, but not clear enough to become an object of knowledge. *James Usher.*

The most enthusiastic Evangelicals do not preach a gospel, but keep describing how it should and might be preached; to awaken the sacred fire of faith, as by a sacred contagion, is not their endeavour, but, at most, to describe how faith shows and acts, and scientifically distinguish true faith from false. *Carlyle in 1831.*

The most enthusiastic mystics were women. *Jean Paul.*

The most essential fact about a man is the constitution of his consciousness. *Schopenhauer.*

The most finished man of the world is he who 45 is never irresolute and never in a hurry. *Schopenhauer.*

The most gladsome thing in the world is that few of us fall very low; the saddest that, with such capabilities, we seldom rise high. *J. M. Barrie.*

The most happy man is he who knows how to bring into relation the end and the beginning of his life. *Goethe.*

The most learned are often the most narrow-minded men. *Hazlitt.*

The most important moment in man's life is certainly not the last. *Jean Paul.*

The most important part of education is right 50 training in the nursery. *Plato.*

The most important period in the life of an individual is that of his development. Later on, commences his conflict with the world, and this is of interest only so far as anything grows out of it. *Goethe.*

The most important thing is to learn to rule one's self. *Goethe.*

The most original modern authors are not so because they advance what is new, but simply because they know how to put what they have to say as if it had never been said before. *Goethe.*

The most objectionable people are the quibbling investigators and the crotchety theorists; their endeavours are petty and complicated, their hypotheses abstruse and strange. *Goethe.*

5 The most part of all the misery and mischief, of all that is denominated evil, in the world, arises from the fact that men are too remiss to get a proper knowledge of their aims, and when they do know them, to work intensely in attaining them. *Goethe.*

The most significant feature in the history of an epoch is the manner it has of welcoming a great man. *Carlyle.*

The most sorrowful occurrence often, through the hand of Providence, takes the most favourable turn for our happiness; the succession of fortune and misfortune in life is intertwined like sleep and waking, neither without the other, and one for the sake of the other. *Goethe.*

The most unhappy and frail of all creatures is man, and yet he is the proudest. *Montaigne.*

The most universal quality is diversity. *Montaigne.*

10 The most virtuous of all men is he that contents himself with being virtuous without seeking to appear so. *Plato.*

The mother-grace of all the graces is Christian good-will. *Ward Beecher.*

The mother of the useful arts is necessity; that of the fine arts is luxury. For father, the former has intellect; the latter, genius, which itself is a kind of luxury. *Schopenhauer.*

The mother's heart is always with her children. *Pr.*

The mother's yearning feels the presence of the cherished child even in the degraded man. *George Eliot.*

15 The motto of chivalry is also the motto of wisdom; to serve all and love but one. *Balzac.*

The mouth of a righteous man is a well of life: but violence covereth the mouth of the wicked. *Bible.*

The movement of sound, such as will reach the soul for the education of it in virtue, we call Music. *Plato.*

The multiplicity of facts and writings is become so great, that everything must soon be reduced to extracts. *Voltaire.*

The multiplying villanies of nature / Do swarm upon him. *Macb.,* i. 2.

20 The multitude have no habit of self-reliance or original action. *Emerson.*

The multitude is always in the wrong. *Earl of Roscommon.*

The multitude of fools is a protection to the wise. *Cicero.*

The multitude unawed is insolent; once seized with fear, contemptible and vain. *Mallet.*

The multitude which does not reduce itself to unity is confusion; the unity which does not depend upon the multitude is tyranny. *Pascal.*

The Muses (daughters of Memory) refresh us 25 in our toilsome course with sweet remembrances. *Novalis.*

The music in my heart I bore / Long after it was heard no more. *Wordsworth.*

The mustard-seed of thought is a pregnant treasury of vast results. Like the germ in the Egyptian tombs, its vitality never perishes; and its fruit will spring up after it has been buried for long ages. *Chapin.*

The mystery of a person is ever divine to him that has a sense for the godlike. *Carlyle.*

The nation is governed by all that has tongue in the nation: democracy is virtually there. *Carlyle.*

The nation is worth nothing which does not 30 joyfully stake its all on its honour. *Schiller.*

The native land of the poet's poetic powers and poetic action is the good, noble, and beautiful, which is confined to no particular province or country, and which he seizes upon and forms wherever he finds it. Therein is he like the eagle. *Goethe.*

The natural effect of sorrow over the dead is to refine and elevate the mind. *Washington Irving.*

The natural qualities pass over all others and mount upon the head. *Hitopadesa.*

The near explains the far. *Emerson.*

The nearer the church the farther from God. *Pr.* 35

The nearer we approach the goal of life, the better we begin to understand the true value of our existence, and the real weight of our opinions. *Burke.*

The necessities of my heart always give the cold philosophisings the lie. *Burns.*

The necessities of things are sterner stuff than the hopes of men. *Disraeli.*

The neck on which diamonds might have worthily sparkled will look less tempting when the biting winter has hung icicles there for gems. *S. Lover.*

The negation of will and desire is the only 40 road to deliverance. *Schopenhauer.*

The nerve that never relaxes, the eye that never blenches, the thought that never wanders—these are the masters of victory. *Burke.*

The nerves, they are the man. *Cabanis.*

The never-absent mop in one hand, and yet no effects of it visible anywhere. *Thoreau.*

The new man is always in a new time, under new conditions; his course is the fac-simile of no prior one, but is by its nature original. *Carlyle.*

The next dreadful thing to a battle lost is a 45 battle won. *Wellington.*

The night cometh, when no man can work. *Jesus.*

The night is far spent, the day is at hand: let us therefore cast off the works of darkness, and let us put on the armour of light. *St. Paul.*

The night is for the day, but the day is not for the night. *Emerson.*

The night is long that never finds the day. *Macb.,* iv. 2.

The night shows stars and women in a better light. *Byron.*

The nobility of life is work. We live in a working world. The lazy and idle man does not count in the plan of campaign. "My Father worketh hitherto, and I work." Let that text be enough. *Prof. Blackie, to young men.*

The noble character at certain moments may resign himself to his emotions; the well-bred, never. *Goethe.*

The noble ones who have lived among us have not left us; they only truly came to us when they departed, and they were then first kissed by us into immortality. *Ed.*

5 The nobler and more perfect a thing is, the slower it is in attaining maturity. *Schopenhauer.*

The nobler the virtue is, the more eager and generous resolution do thou express of attaining to it. *Thomas à Kempis.*

The noblest charms of music, though real and affecting, seem too confused and fluid to be collected into a distinct idea. Harmony is always understood by the crowd, and almost always mistaken by musicians. *James Usher.*

The noblest mind the best contentment hath. *Spenser.*

The noblest vengeance is to forgive. *Pr.*

10 The noblest works and foundations have proceeded from childless men, which have sought to express the images of their minds where those of their bodies have failed. *Bacon.*

The north wind driveth away rain: so doth an angry countenance a backbiting tongue. *Bible.*

The Now is an atom of sand, / And the Near is a perishing clod; / But Afar is as Fairy Land, / And beyond is the bosom of God. *Lord Lytton.*

The nurse's bread is sweeter than the mother's cake. *Fris. Pr.*

The oak first announces itself when, with far-sounding crash, it falls. *Carlyle.*

15 The object of all true policy and true economy is, the utmost multitude of good men on every given space of ground. *Ruskin.*

The object of art is to crystallise emotion into thought and then to fix it in form. *Delsarte.*

The object of preaching is constantly to remind mankind of what mankind are constantly forgetting; not to supply the defects of human intelligence, but to fortify the feebleness of human resolutions. *Sydney Smith.*

The object of reading is not to dip into everything that even wise men have ever written. *John Morley.*

The object of the poet is, and must be, to "instruct by pleasing," yet not by pleasing this man and that man; only by pleasing man, by speaking to the pure nature of man, can any real "instruction," in this sense, be conveyed. *Carlyle.*

20 The object of the politician is expediency, and his duty is to adapt his measures to the often crude, undeveloped, and vacillating conception of the nation. The object, on the other hand, of the philosopher is truth, and his duty is to push every principle which he believes to be true to its legitimate consequences, regardless of the results that may follow. *H. Lecky.*

The object of true religion should be to impress the principles of morality deeply in the soul. *Leibnitz.*

The obligation of veracity may be made out from the direct ill consequences of lying to social happiness. *Paley.*

The obscure is what transcends us, and what imposes itself upon us by transcending us. *Renan.*

The ocean beats against the stern dumb shore, / The stormy passion of its mighty heart. *L. C. Moulton.*

The ocean may have bounds. *Hitopadesa.* 25

The offender never pardons. *George Herbert.*

The old fox is caught at last. *Pr.*

The old gloomy cathedrals were good, but the great blue dome that hangs over all is better than any Cologne one. *Carlyle.*

The old never dies till this happen, till all the soul of good that was in it get itself transfused into the practical new. *Carlyle.*

The old order changeth, yielding place to 30 new, / And God fulfils himself in many ways, / Lest one good custom should corrupt the world. *Tennyson.*

The old prose writers wrote as if they were speaking to an audience; while among us prose is invariably written for the eye alone. *Niebuhr.*

The older we get the more we must limit ourselves, if we wish to be active. *Goethe.*

The oldest, and indeed only true, order of nobility known under the stars, is that of just men and sons of God, in opposition to unjust men and sons of Belial, which latter indeed are second oldest, and yet a very unvenerable order. *Carlyle.*

The oldest in years is not always the most experienced, and he who has suffered most has not always the best manners. *Bodenstedt.*

The one enemy we have in this universe is 35 stupidity, darkness of mind; of which darkness there are many sources, every sin a source, and probably self-conceit the chief source. *Carlyle.*

The one essential point (in regard to a wrong) is to know that it is wrong; how to get out of it you can decide afterwards at your leisure. *Ruskin.*

The one exclusive sign of a thorough knowledge is the power of teaching. *Arist.*

The one intolerable sort of slavery, over which the very gods weep, is the slavery of the strong to the weak; of the great and noble-minded to the small and mean; the slavery of wisdom to folly. *Carlyle.*

The one prudence in life is concentration. *Emerson.*

The one thing of value in the world is the 40 active soul. *Emerson.*

The one unhappiness of a man is that he cannot work, that he cannot get his destiny as a man fulfilled. *Carlyle.*

The only competition worthy a wise man is with himself. *Mrs. Jamieson.*

The only disadvantage of an honest heart is its credulity. *Sir P. Sidney.*

The only evolution of any really human interest, and worthy of any human regard, is the evolution that springs from resolution and the birth of freedom in the self-conscious soul. *Ed.*

The only failure a man ought to fear is failure in cleaving to the purpose he sees to be best. *George Eliot.*

The only faith that wears well, and holds its colour in all weathers, is that which is woven of conviction, and set with the sharp mordant of experience. *Lowell.*

The only fence against the world is a thorough knowledge of it. *Locke.*

The only freedom which deserves the name is that of pursuing our own good in our own way, so long as we do not attempt to deprive others of this, or impede their efforts to obtain it. *J. S. Mill.*

5 The only genuine Romance for grown persons is Reality. *Carlyle.*

The only gift is a portion of thyself. *Emerson.*

The only happiness a brave man ever troubled himself with asking much about was, happiness enough to get his work done. *Carlyle.*

The only liberty that is valuable is a liberty connected with order. *Burke.*

The only means of overcoming adversities is a fresh activity. *Goethe.*

10 The only medicine which does women more good than harm is dress. *Jean Paul.*

The only ornament of old age is virtue. *Amyot.*

The only poetry is history, could we tell it aright. *Carlyle.*

The only point now is what a man weighs in the scale of humanity; all the rest is nought. A coat with a star, and a chariot with six horses, at all events, imposes on the rudest multitude only, and scarcely that. *Goethe.*

The only progress which is really effective depends, not upon the bounty of Nature, but upon the energy of man. *Buckle.*

15 The only satisfaction of the will is that it encounters with no resistance. *Schopenhauer.*

The only school of genuine moral sentiment is society between equals. *J. S. Mill.*

The only serious and formidable thing in Nature is will. *Emerson.*

The only sin which we never forgive in each other is difference of opinion. *Emerson.*

The only solid instruction is that which the pupil brings from his own depths; the true instruction is not that which transmits notions wholly formed, but that which renders him capable of forming for himself good opinions. *Degerando.*

20 The only substance properly so called is the soul. *Amiel.*

The only teller of news is the poet. *Emerson.*

The only thing grief has taught me is to know how shallow it is. *Emerson.*

The only true principle for humanity is justice. *Amiel.*

The only true source of politeness is consideration. *Simms.*

25 The only victory over love is flight. *Napoleon.*

The only way to have a friend is to be one. *Emerson.*

The only way to understand the difficult parts of the Bible is first to read and obey the easy ones. *Ruskin.*

The opinions of men are as many and as different as their persons; the greatest diligence and most prudent conduct can never please them all. *Thomas à Kempis.*

The opportunity to do mischief is found a hundred times a day, and that of doing good once a year. *Voltaire.*

The ordinary man places life's happiness in 30 things external to him; his centre of gravity is not in himself. *Schopenhauer.*

The ornament of a house is the friends who frequent it. *Emerson.*

The outer passes away; the inmost is the same yesterday, to-day, and for ever. *Carlyle.*

The over-curious are not over-wise. *Massinger.*

The owl of ignorance lays the egg of pride. *Pr.*

The owl sees the sunshine and winks in its 35 nest. *Dr. Walter Smith.*

The ox lies still while the geese are hissing. *Pr.*

The pain of an unfilled wish is small in comparison with that of repentance; for the one stands in presence of the vast open future, whilst the other has the irrevocable past closed behind it. *Schopenhauer.*

The pain that any one actually feels is still of all others the worst. *Locke.*

The pain which conscience gives the man who has already done wrong is soon got over. Conscience is a coward; and those faults it has not strength enough to prevent, it seldom has justice enough to accuse. *Goldsmith.*

The pains of power are real, its pleasures are 40 imaginary. *Colton.*

The painful warrior famousèd for fight, / After a thousand victories, once foil'd, / Is from the books of honour razèd quite, / And all the rest forgot for which he toil'd. *Shakespeare.*

The painter should grind his own colours; the architect work in the mason's yard with his men; the master-manufacturer be himself a more skilful operator than any man in his mills; and the distinction between one man and another be only in experience and skill, and the authority and wealth which these must naturally and justly obtain. *Ruskin.*

The parasite courtier in the palace is the legitimate father of the tyrant. *Brougham.*

The parcel of books, if they are well chosen, . . . awakens within us the diviner mind, and rouses us to a consciousness of what is best in others and ourselves. *John Morley.*

The pardon of an offence must, as a benefit 45 conferred, put the offender under an obligation; and thus direct advantage at once accrues by heaping coals of fire on the head. *Goethe.*

The particular is the universal seen under special limitations. *Goethe.*

The passions are only exaggerated vices or virtues. *Goethe.*

The passions are the only orators who never fail to persuade. *La Roche.*

The passions, by grace of the supernal and also of the infernal powers (for both have a hand in it), can never fail us. *Carlyle.*

The passions may be likened to blood horses, 50 that need training and the curb only to enable them when they carry to achieve most glorious triumphs. *Simms.*

The passions of mankind are partly protective, partly beneficent, like the chaff and grain of the corn; but none without their use, none without nobleness when seen in balanced unity with the rest of the spirit which they are charged to defend. *Ruskin.*

The passions rise higher at domestic than at imperial tragedies. *Johnson.*

The past alone is eternal and unchangeable like death, and yet at the same time warm and joy-giving like life. *W. von Humboldt.*

The past and future are veiled; but the past wears the widow's veil, the future the virgin's. *Jean Paul.*

The past at least is secure. *Daniel Webster.*

5 The past is all holy to us; the dead are all holy; even they that were base and wicked when alive. *Carlyle.*

The past is an unfathomable depth, / Beyond the span of thought; 'tis an elapse / Which hath no mensuration, but hath been / For ever and for ever. *H. Kirke White.*

The past is to us a book sealed with seven seals, *i.e.,* which no one need hope fully to open. *Goethe.*

The path of falsehood is a perplexing maze. *Blair.*

The path of nature is indeed a narrow one, and it is only the immortals that seek it, and, when they find it, they do not find themselves cramped therein. *Lowell.*

10 The path of sorrow, and that path alone, / Leads to the land where sorrow is unknown. *Cowper.*

The path of the just is as the shining light, that shineth more and more unto the perfect day. *Bible.*

The path of things is silent. *Emerson.*

The paths of glory lead but to the grave. *Gray.*

The pathetic almost always consists in the detail of little circumstances. *Gibbon.*

15 The peace of heaven is theirs who lift their swords / In such a just and charitable war. *King John,* ii. 1.

The peacemakers shall be called the children of God. *Jesus.*

The peevish, the niggard, the dissatisfied, the passionate, the suspicious, and those who live upon others' means, are for ever unhappy. *Hitopadesa.*

The pen is mightier than the sword. *Bulwer Lytton.*

The pencil of the Holy Ghost hath laboured more in describing the afflictions of Job than the felicities of Solomon. *Bacon.*

20 The people have the right to murmur, but they have also the right to be violent, and their silence is the lesson of kings. *Jean de Beauvais.*

The people of England are the most enthusiastic in the world. *Disraeli.*

The people of this world having been once deceived, suspect deceit in truth itself. *Hitopadesa.*

The people once belonged to the kings; now the kings belong to the people. *Heine.*

The perfect flower of religion opens in the soul only when all self-seeking is abandoned. *John Burroughs.*

25 The perfection of art is to conceal art. *Quinct.*

The perfection of conversation is not to play a regular sonata, but, like the Æolian harp, to await the inspiration of the passing breeze. *Burke.*

The perfection of spiritual virtue lies in being always all there, a whole man present in every movement and moment. *Ed.*

The period of faith must alternate with the period of denial; the vernal growth, the summer luxuriance of all opinions, spiritual representations and creations must be followed by, and again follow, the autumnal decay, the winter dissolution. *Carlyle.*

The persistent aspirations of the human race are to society what the compass is to the ship. It sees not the shore, but it guides to it. *Lamartine.*

The person who in company should pretend 30 to be wiser than others, I am apt to regard as illiterate and ill-bred. *Goldsmith.*

The person who is contented to be often obliged ought not to be obliged at all. *Goldsmith.*

The person whose clothes are extremely fine I am too apt to consider as not being possessed of any superiority of fortune, but resembling those Indians who were found to wear all the gold they have in the world in a bob at the nose. *Goldsmith.*

The pest of society is egotists. There are dull and bright, sacred and profane, coarse and fine egotists. It is a disease that, like influenza, falls on all constitutions. *Emerson.*

The philosopher is he to whom the highest has descended, and the lowest has mounted up; who is the equal and kindly brother of all. *Carlyle.*

The philosopher must station himself in the 35 middle. *Goethe.*

The philosophy of grumbling is great, but not intricate . . . the proof that there is something wrong, and that a sentient human being is aware of it. *John Wagstaffe.*

The philosophy of one century is the commonsense of the next. *Ward Beecher.*

The philosophy of six thousand years has not searched the chambers and magazines of the soul. *Emerson.*

The phœnix, Hope, can wing her flight / Through the vast deserts of the skies, / And still defying fortune's spite, / Revive and from her ashes rise. *Cervantes.*

The pillow is a dumb sibyl. *Gracian.* 40

The pilot of the Galilean lake; / Two massy keys he bore, of metals twain, / The golden opes, the iron shuts amain. *Milton.*

The pious and just honouring of ourselves may be thought the radical moisture and fountain-head from whence every laudable and worthy enterprise issues forth. *Milton.*

The pious have always a more intimate connection with each other than the wicked, though externally the relationship may not always prosper as well. *Goethe.*

The pious-hearted are cared for by the gods; and by men honoured and worshipped as divinities, when once they have by death stripped off for ever their week-day garments. *Ed. after Ovid.*

The pitcher goes so often to the water that it 45 comes home broken at last. *Pr.*

The place once trodden by a good man is hallowed. After a hundred years his word and actions ring in the ears of his descendants. *Goethe.*

The plainer the dress, with greater lustre does beauty appear. *Lord Halifax.*

The plainest man that can convince a woman that he is really in love with her, has done more to make her in love with him than the handsomest man, if he can produce no such conviction. For the love of woman is a shoot, not a seed, and flourishes most vigorously only when ingrafted on that love which is rooted in the breast of another. *Colton.*

The plea of ignorance will never take away our responsibilities. *Ruskin.*

The pleasure of despising, at all times and in itself a dangerous luxury, is much safer after the toil of examining than before it. *Carlyle.*

The pleasure of talking is the inextinguishable passion of woman, coeval with the act of breathing. *Le Sage.*

5 The pleasure-seeker is not the pleasure-finder; those are the happiest men who think least about happiness. *J. C. Sharp.*

The pleasure we feel in criticising robs us of that of being deeply moved by very beautiful things. *La Bruyère.*

The pleasure we feel in music springs from the obedience which is in it, and it is full only as the obedience is entire. *Theodore T. Murger.*

The pleasure which strikes the soul must be derived from the beauty and congruity it sees or conceives in those things which the sight or imagination lay before it. *Cervantes.*

The pleasures of the world are deceitful; they promise more than they give. They trouble us in seeking them, they do not satisfy us when possessing them, and they make us despair in losing them. *Mme. de Lambert.*

10 The plenty of the poorest place is too great; the harvest cannot be gathered. *Emerson.*

The poet bestrides the clouds, the wise man looks up at them. *Arliss.*

The poet can never have far to seek for a subject; for him the ideal world is not remote from the actual, but under it and within it; and he is a poet precisely because he can discern it there. *Carlyle.*

The poet must believe in his poetry. The fault of our popular poetry is that it is not sincere. *Emerson.*

The poet must find all within himself while he is left in the lurch by all without. *Goethe.*

15 The poet must live wholly for himself, wholly in the objects that delight him. *Goethe.*

The poet should seize the particular, and he should, if there is anything sound in it, thus represent the universal. *Goethe.*

The poet's delicate ear hears the far-off whispers of eternity, which coarser souls must travel towards for scores of years before their dull sense is touched by them. *Holmes.*

The poet's eye, in a fine frenzy rolling, / Doth glance from heaven to earth, from earth to heaven, / And, as imagination bodies forth / The forms of things unknown, the poet's pen / Turns them to shapes, and gives to airy nothing / A local habitation and a name. *Mid. N.'s Dream*, v. 1.

The poet's heart is an unlighted torch, which gives no help to his footsteps till love has touched it with flame. *Lowell.*

20 The poetry of the ancients was that of possession, ours is that of aspiration; the former stands fast on the soil of the present, the latter hovers between memory and anticipation. *Schlegel.*

The point is not that men should have a great many books, but that they should have the right ones, and that they should use those that they have. *John Morley.*

The pomp of death is far more terrible than death itself. *Nathaniel Lee.*

The poor are only they who feel poor. *Emerson.*

The poor is hated even of his own neighbour. *Bible.*

The poor man's budget is full of schemes. 25 *Pr.*

The poor wren, / The most diminutive of birds, will fight, / Her young ones in her nest, against the owl. *Macb.*, iv. 2.

The poor ye have always with you, but me ye have not always. *Jesus.*

The poorer life or the rich one are but the larger or smaller (very little smaller) letters in which we write the apophthegms and golden sayings of life. *Carlyle.*

The poorest day that passes over us is the conflux of two eternities; it is made-up of currents that issue from the remotest part, and flow onwards into the remotest future. *Carlyle.*

The poorest human soul is infinite in wishes, 30 and the infinite universe was not made for one, but for all. *Carlyle.*

The poorest man may in his cottage bid defiance to all the forces of the crown. It may be frail, the wind may blow through it, the storm may enter, the rain may enter, but the king of England cannot enter! all his force dares not cross the threshold of that ruined tenement. *Chatham.*

The popular ear weighs what you are, not what you were. *Quarles.*

The popular man stands on our own level, or a hairsbreadth higher; and shows us a truth we can see without shifting our present intellectual position. The original man stands above us, and wishes to wrench us from our old fixtures, and elevate us to a higher and clearer level. *Carlyle.*

The population of the world is a conditional population; not the best, but the best that could live now. *Emerson.*

The post of honour is the post of difficulty, 35 the post of danger,—of death, if difficulty be not overcome. *Carlyle.*

The power of every great people, as of every living tree, depends on its not effacing, but confirming and concluding the labours of its ancestors. *Ruskin.*

The power of faith will often shine forth the most when the character is naturally weak. *Hare.*

The power of fortune is confessed only by the miserable, for the happy impute all their success to prudence and merit. (?)

The power of observing life is rare, that of drawing lessons from it rarer, and that of condensing the lesson in a pointed sentence is rarest of all. *John Morley.*

The power, whether of painter or poet, to de- 40 scribe rightly what he calls an ideal thing depends upon its being to him not an ideal but a real thing. No man ever did or ever will work well, but either from actual sight or sight of faith. *Ruskin.*

The practice of faith and obedience to some of our fellow-creatures is the alphabet by which we learn the higher obedience to heaven; and it is not only needful to the prosperity of all noble united action, but essential to the happiness of all noble living spirits. *Ruskin.*

The practice of submission to the authority of one whom one recognises as greater than one's self outweighs the chance of occasional mistake. *Froude.*

The praise that comes of love does not make us vain, but humble rather. *J. M. Barrie.*

The praying soul is a gainer by waiting for an answer. *Gurnall.*

5 The precepts of philosophy effect not the least benefit to one confirmed in fear. *Hitopadesa.*

The preparations of the heart in man and the answer of the tongue is from the Lord. *Bible.*

The presence of the Eternal is a presence that articulates and imparts itself in time. *Ed.*

The presence of the wretched is a burden to the happy; and alas! the happy still more so to the wretched. *Goethe.*

The present holds in it both the whole past and the whole future. *Carlyle.*

10 The present is the only reality and the only certainty. *Schopenhauer.*

The present moment is a potent divinity. *Goethe.*

The present moment is our ain, / The neist we never saw. *Burns.*

The present time is not priest-ridden, but press-ridden. *Longfellow.*

The present time, youngest born of eternity, child and heir of all the past times with their good and evil, and parent of all the future, is ever a new era to the thinking man. *Carlyle.*

15 The press beginneth to be an oppression of the land. *Fuller.*

The press is a mill which grinds all that is put into its hopper. *Bryant.*

The press is the foe of rhetoric, but the friend of reason. *Colton.*

The price of wisdom is above rubies. *Bible.*

The priest loves his flock, but the lambs more than the wethers. *Ger. Pr.*

20 The primal condition of virtue is that it shall not know of, or believe in, any blessed islands till it find them, it may be, in due time. *Ruskin.*

The primal duties shine aloft, like stars; / The charities that soothe, and heal, and bless, / Are scattered at the feet of man, like flowers. *Wordsworth.*

The primary vocation of man is a life of activity. *Goethe.*

The prince as actual ruler is always limited (*beschränkt*) by public opinion; but what is there to limit public opinion if it holds sovereign sway? *Stahl.*

The principal part of faith is patience. *George Macdonald.*

25 The principal point of greatness in any state is to have a race of military men. *Bacon.*

The prisoner is troubled that he cannot go whither he would, and he that is at large is troubled that he does not know whither to go. *L'Estrange.*

The prisoner's allowance is bread and water, but I had only the latter. *Jean Paul, in his days of poverty.*

The privilege of the country is to be alone, when we like. *Marmontel.*

The problem of life is to make the ideal real, and convert the divine at the summit of the mountain into the human at its base. *C. H. Parkhurst.*

The problem of philosophy is, for all that exists 30 conditionally, to find a ground unconditioned and absolute. *Plato.*

The prodigal robs his heir, the miser robs himself. *La Bruyère.*

The production of something, where nothing was before, is an act of greater energy than the expansion or decoration of the thing produced. *Johnson.*

The profession of riches without their possession leads to the worst form of poverty. *Spurgeon.*

The promise given was a necessity of the past; the word broken is a necessity of the present. *Macchiavelli.*

The Promised Land is the land where one is 35 not. *Amiel.*

The promises of God are yea and amen. *Hammond.*

The promises of this world are, for the most part, vain phantoms; and to confide in one's self, and become something of worth and value, is the best and safest course. *Michael Angelo.*

The promissory lies of great men are known by shouldering, hugging, squeezing, smiling, and bowing. *Arbuthnott.*

The proper confidant of a girl is her father. What she is not inclined to tell her father should be told to no one, and, in nine cases out of ten, not thought of by herself. *Ruskin.*

The proper Epic of this world is no longer 40 "Arms and the man," much less "Shirt frills and the man;" no, it is now "Tools and the man;" that, henceforth to all time is now our Epic. *Carlyle.*

The proper power of faith is to trust *without* evidence, **not** *with* evidence. *Ruskin.*

The proper reward of the good workman is to be "chosen." *Ruskin.*

The proper study of mankind is man. *Pope.*

The proper task of literature lies in the domain of belief. *Carlyle.*

The property of a man consists in (*a*) good 45 things, (*b*) goods which he has honestly got, and (*c*) goods he can skilfully use. *Ruskin.*

The prophet is the revealer of what we are to do; the poet, of what we are to love. The former too has an eye on what we are to love; how else shall he know what we are to do? *Carlyle.*

The prosperity of our neighbours in the end is our own, and the poverty of our neighbours becomes also in the end our own. *Ruskin.*

The protection of God cannot without sacrilege be invoked but in behalf of justice and right. *Kossuth.*

The proud man often is the mean. *Tennyson.*

The proudest boast of the most aspiring philo- 50 sopher is no more than that he provides his little playfellows the greatest pastime with the greatest innocence. *Goldsmith.*

The proverb says of the Genoese, that they have a sea without fish, lands without trees, and men without faith. *Addison.*

The proverbs of a nation furnish the index to its spirit and the results of its civilisation. *J. G. Holland.*

The providence of God has established such an order in the world, that of all which belongs to us, the least valuable parts can alone fall under the will of others. *Bolingbroke.*

The prudence of the best of hearts is often defeated by the tenderness of the best of hearts. *Fielding.*

5 The prudent man may direct a state, but it is the enthusiast who regenerates or ruins it. *Bulwer Lytton.*

The prudent part is to propose remedies for the present evils, and provisions against future events. (?)

The public have neither shame nor gratitude. *Hazlitt.*

The public highways ought not to be occupied by people demonstrating that motion is impossible. *Carlyle.*

The public is a personality that knows everything and can do nothing. (?)

10 The public is the majority of a society. *Johnson.*

The public sense is in advance of private practice. *Chapin.*

The public? The public is just a great baby. *Dr. Chalmers.*

The pulpit only "teaches" to be honest; the market-place "trains" to over-reaching and fraud; and teaching has not a tithe of the efficiency of training. *Horace Mann.*

The punishment of criminals should be of use; when a man is hanged he is good for nothing. *Voltaire.*

15 The punishment which the wise suffer, who refuse to take part in the government, is to live under the government of worse men. *Emerson.*

The pure in heart shall see God. *Jesus.*

The purer the golden vessel the more readily is it bent; the higher worth of women is sooner lost than that of men. *Jean Paul.*

The purest treasure mortal times afford / Is spotless reputation; that away, / Men are but gilded loam or painted clay. *Rich. II.,* i. 1.

The purse is the master-organ, soul's seat, and true pineal gland of the body social. *Carlyle.*

20 The pyramids, doting with age, have forgotten the names of their founders. *Fuller.*

The quality of mercy is not strain'd; / It droppeth as the gentle rain from heaven / Upon the place beneath. It is twice blest; / It blesseth him that gives and him that takes. / 'Tis mightiest in the mightiest; it becomes / The throned monarch better than his crown. *Mer. of Venice,* iv. 1.

The quantity of books in a library is often a cloud of witnesses of the ignorance of the owner. *Oxenstiern.*

The quantity of sorrow a man has, does it not mean withal the quantity of sympathy he has, the quantity of faculty and victory he shall have? Our sorrow is the inverted image of our nobleness. *Carlyle.*

The quarrel toucheth none but us alone, / Betwixt ourselves let us decide it then. *1 Hen. VI.,* iv. 1.

The question is not at what door of fortune's 25 palace shall we enter in, but what doors does she open to us? *Burns.*

The question is not who is the most learned, but who is the best. *Montaigne.*

The question is this : Is man an ape or angel? I, my lord, I am on the side of the angels. *Disraeli at a Church Conference in Oxford, Bp. Wilberforce in the chair.*

The question of education is for the modern world a question of life or death, a question on which depends the future. *Renan.*

The question of questions (for men and nations) is—not how far they are from heaven, but whether they are going to it. (So in art) it is not the wisdom or the barbarism that you have to estimate, not the skill or the rudeness, but the tendency. *Ruskin.*

The question of the purpose of things is com- 30 pletely unscientific. *Goethe.*

The race is not to the swift, nor the battle to the strong. *Bible.*

The race of mankind would perish did they cease to aid each other. *Scott.*

The rainbow in the morning / Is the shepherd's warning ; / The rainbow at night / Is the shepherd's delight. *Pr.*

The rank is but the guinea's stamp, / The man's the gowd for a' that. *Burns.*

The ransom of a man's life are his riches. 35 *Bible.*

The ray of light passes invisible through space, and only when it falls on an object is it seen. *Emerson.*

The readiness is all. *Ham.,* v. 2.

The real man is one who always finds excuses for others, but never excuses himself. *Ward Beecher.*

The real men of genius were resolute workers, not idle dreamers. *G. H. Lewes.*

The real Nimrod of this era, who alone does 40 any good to the era, is the rat-catcher. *Carlyle.*

The real object of education is to give children resources that will endure as long as life endures; habits that time will ameliorate, not destroy; occupation that will render sickness tolerable, solitude pleasant, age venerable, life more dignified and useful, and death less terrible. *Sydney Smith.*

The real object of the drama is the exhibition of human character. *Macaulay.*

The real science of political economy is that which teaches nations to desire and labour for the things that lead to life; and which teaches them to scorn and destroy the things that lead to destruction. *Ruskin.*

The really strong may bend, and be as strong as ever; it is the unsound that has only the seeming of strength, which breaks at last when it resists too long. *Lover.*

The reason that there is such a general out- 45 cry against flatterers is, that there are so very few good ones. *Steele.*

The reason why borrowed books are so seldom returned to their owners is, that it is much easier to retain the books than what is in them. *Montaigne.*

The reason why so few marriages are happy is because young ladies spend their time in making nets, not in making cages. *Swift.*

The reason why the character of woman is so often misunderstood, is that it is the beautiful nature of woman to veil her soul as her charms. *F. Schlegel.*

The reason why we sometimes see that men of the greatest capacities are not rich, is either because they despise wealth in comparison of something else, or, at least, are not content to be getting an estate, unless they may do it in their own way, and at the same time enjoy all the pleasures and gratifications of life. *Eustace Budgell.*

The recording angel, consider it well, is no fable, but the truest of truths; the paper tablets thou canst burn; of the "iron leaf" there is no burning. *Carlyle.*

5 The regeneration of society is the regeneration of the individual by education. *Laboulaye.*

The regions of eternal happiness are provided for those women who love their husbands the same in a wilderness as in a city; be he a saint, or be he sinner. *Hitopadesa.*

The relation of the taught to their teacher, of the loyal subject to his guiding king, is, under one shape or another, the vital element in human society. *Carlyle.*

The religion of Christ is peace and good-will, that of Christendom war and ill-will. *Landor.*

The religion of Jesus, with all its self-denials, virtues, and devotions, is very practicable. *Watts.*

10 The religion of one age is the literary entertainment of the next. *Emerson.*

The religions of the world are the ejaculations of a few imaginative men. *Emerson.*

The religions we call false were once true. They also were affirmations of the conscience correcting the evil customs of their times. *Emerson.*

The religious passion is nearly always vividest where the art is weakest; and the technical skill only reaches its deliberate splendour when the ecstasy which gave it birth has passed away for ever. *Ruskin.*

The reputation of a man is like his shadow—gigantic when it precedes him, and pigmy in its proportions when it follows. *Talleyrand.*

15 The reputation of a woman is as a crystal mirror, shining and bright, but liable to be sullied by every breath that comes near it. *Cervantes.*

The reputation of virtuous actions past, if not kept up with an access and fresh supply of new ones, is lost and soon forgotten. *Denham.*

The resentment of a poor man is like the efforts of a harmless insect to sting; it may get him crushed, but cannot defend him. *Goldsmith.*

The rest is silence. *Ham.. v. 2.*

The result (of things) is obvious, but the intention is never clear. *Rückert.*

20 The revelation of thought takes man out of servitude into freedom. *Emerson.*

The reverence of a man's self is, next religion, the chiefest bridle of all vices. *Bacon.*

The revolutionary outbreaks of the lower classes are the consequence of the injustice of the higher classes. *Goethe.*

The reward of one duty is the power to fulfil another. *George Eliot.*

The rich and poor meet together: the Lord is the maker of them all. *Bible.*

The rich are always advising the poor; but 25 the poor seldom venture to return the compliment. *Helps.*

The rich are invited to marry by that fortune which they do not want, and the poor have no inducement but that beauty which they do not feel. *Goldsmith.*

The rich becoming richer and the poor poorer, is the cry throughout the whole civilised world. *Sillar.*

The rich devour the poor, the devil the rich, and so both are devoured. *Dutch Pr.*

The rich man does not feel his wealth with any vividness. *Goethe.*

The rich man is seldom in his own halls, be- 30 cause it bores him to be there, and still he returns thither, because he is no better off outside. *Schopenhauer.*

The rich man's wealth is his strong city, and as an high wall in his own conceit. *Bible.*

The rich ruleth over the poor, and the borrower is servant to the lender. *Bible.*

The richest minds need not large libraries. *A. B. Alcott.*

The riddle of the age has for each a private solution. *Emerson.*

The ridge once gained, the path so hard of 35 late / Runs easy on, and level with the gate (to virtue). *Hesiod.*

The right divine of kings to govern wrong. *Quoted by Pope.*

The right ear, that is fill'd with dust, / Hears little of the false or just. *Tennyson.*

The right honourable gentleman is indebted to his memory for his jests, and to his imagination for his facts. *Sheridan.*

The right law of education is that you take the most pains with the best material. Never waste pains on bad ground, but spare no labour on the good, or on what has in it the capacity of good. *Ruskin.*

The right man in the right place. *A. H.* 40 *Layard in the House of Commons.*

The righteous hath hope in his death. *Bible.*

The righteous man falls oft, / Yet falls but soft; / There may be dirt to mire him, but no stones / To crush his bones. *Quarles.*

The righteousness of the upright shall deliver them. *Bible.*

The "rights" of men in any form are not worth discussing; the grand point is the "mights" of men—what portion of their "rights" they have a chance of getting sorted out and realised in this confused world. *Carlyle.*

The riotous tumult of a laugh is the mob-law 45 of the features, and propriety the magistrate who reads the Riot Act. *Holmes.*

The risings and sinkings of human affairs are like those of a ball which is thrown by the hand. *Hitopadesa.*

The river has its cataract, / And yet the waters down below / Soon gather from the foam, compact, / And, just like those above it, flow. *Dr. W. Smith.*

The river remains troubled that has not gone through a lake ; the heart is impure that has not gone through a sorrow. *Rückert.*

The road's afore you, the sky's aboon you. *Pr.*

The road to resolution lies by doubt. *Quarles.*

The road to ruin is always kept in good repair, and the travellers pay the expense of it. *Pr.*

5 The road which runs without a bend / Is that which hath a proper end. *Goethe.*

The robb'd that smiles, steals something from the thief. *Othello,* i. 3.

The romantic is the instinctive delight in, and admiration for, sublimity, beauty, and virtue, unusually manifested. *Ruskin.*

The root of almost every schism and heresy from which the Christian Church has suffered has been the effort of men to earn, rather than to receive, their salvation ; and the reason that preaching is so commonly ineffectual is, that it calls on men oftener to work for God than to behold God working for them. *Ruskin.*

The root of sanctity is sanity. A man must be healthy before he can be holy. We bathe first, and then perfume. *Mme. Swetchine.*

10 The rough material of fine writing is certainly the gift of genius ; but I as firmly believe that the workmanship is the united effort of pains, attention, and repeated trial. *Burns.*

The rough seas that spare not any man. *Pericles,* ii. 1.

The rude man requires only to see something going on. The man of more refinement must be made to feel. The man of complete refinement must be made to reflect. *Goethe.*

The rule of the footway is clear as the light, / And none can its reason withstand ; / On each side of the way you must keep to the right, / And leave those you meet the left hand. *Saying.*

The ruling passion, be it what it will, / The ruling passion, conquers reason still. *Pope.*

15 The running waves of eager life end on the motionless fixed strand of death. *Alfred Austin.*

The Sabbath was made for man, and not man for the Sabbath. *Jesus.*

The sacred wrestler, till a blessing given, / Quits not his hold, but, halting, conquers heaven. *Waller.*

The sacrifice of the wicked is abomination. *Bible.*

The saddest external condition of affairs among men, is but evidence of a still sadder internal one. *Carlyle.*

20 The safest and purest joys of human life rebuke the violence of its passions ; they are obtainable without anxiety and memorable without regret. *Ruskin.*

The safest words are always those which bring us most directly to facts. *C. H. Parkhurst.*

The safety-valves of the heart when too much pressure is laid on. *Albert Smith, on tears.*

The salve of reformation they mightily call for, but where and what the sores are which need it, as they wot full little, so they think not greatly material to search. *Hooker.*

The same motions and muscles of the face are employed both in laughing and crying. *Charron.*

The Satanic school. *Southey.* 25

"The savans and the asses in the middle." *Order of Napoleon on the eve of a cavalry charge in Egypt.*

The scholar without good-breeding is a pedant ; the philosopher, a cynic ; the soldier, a brute ; and every man disagreeable. *Chesterfield.*

The schoolboy counts the time till the return of the holidays ; the minor longs to be of age ; the lover is impatient till he is married. *Addison.*

The schoolmaster is abroad. *Brougham.*

The sea belongs to eternity, and not time, 30 and of that it sings its monotonous song for ever and ever. *Holmes.*

The sea complains upon a thousand shores. *Alex. Smith.*

The sea does not contain all the pearls, the earth does not enclose all the treasures, and the flint-stone does not enclose all the diamonds, since the head of man encloses wisdom. *Saadi.*

The sea moans over dead men's bones. *T. B. Aldrich.*

The sea that bares her bosom to the moon. *Wordsworth.*

The sea tosses and foams to find its way up to 35 the cloud and wind. *Emerson.*

The seal of truth is simplicity. *Boerhaave.*

The seat of knowledge is in the head ; of wisdom, in the heart. We are sure to judge wrong if we do not feel aright. *Hazlitt.*

The seat of law is the bosom of God ; her voice, the harmony of the world. *Hooker.*

The second fruit of friendship is healthful and sovereign for the understanding, as the first is for the affections ; for friendship maketh indeed a fair day in the affections from storm and tempests, but it maketh daylight in the understanding out of darkness and confusion of thoughts. *Bacon.*

The secret of education lies in respecting the 40 pupil. *Emerson.*

The secret of happiness is never to allow your energies to stagnate. *Adam Clarke.*

The secret of language is the secret of sympathy, and its full charm is possible only to the gentle. *Ruskin.*

The secret of making one's self tiresome is not to know when to stop. *Voltaire.*

The secret of man's being is still like the Sphinx's secret ; a riddle that he cannot rede ; and for ignorance of which he suffers death, the worst death—a spiritual. *Carlyle.*

The secret of man's nature lies in his religion, 45 in what he really believes about the world and his own place in it. *Froude.*

The secret of man's success resides in his insight into the moods of men, and his tact in dealing with them. *J. G. Holland.*

The secret of our existence is the connection between our sins and our sufferings. (?)

The secret of success in society is a certain heartiness and sympathy. *Emerson.*

The secret of success is constancy to purpose. *Disraeli.*

The secret of tiring is to say everything that can be said on the subject. *Voltaire.*

The secret things belong unto the Lord. *Bible.*

The secrets of great folk are just like the wild beasts that are shut up in cages. Keep them hard and fast snecked up, and it's a very weel or better—but ance let them out, they will turn and rend you. *Scott.*

The secrets of life are not shown except to sympathy and likeness. *Emerson.*

5 The seed of knowledge ripens but slowly in the mind, but the flowers grow quickly *Bodenstedt.*

The seeds of things are very small. *George Eliot.*

The seers are wholly a greater race than the thinkers ; (yet) a true thinker, who has a practical purpose in his thinking, and is sincere, as Plato, or Carlyle, or Helps, becomes in some sort a seer, and must be always of infinite use in his generation. *Ruskin.*

The self-same sun that shines upon his court / Hides not his visage from our cottage, but / Looks on alike. *Winter's Tale, iv. 3.*

The sense of beauty never furthered the performance of a single duty. *Ruskin.*

10 The sense of death is most in apprehension, / And the poor beetle that we tread upon / In corporal sufferance finds a pang as great / As when a giant dies. *Meas. for Meas., iii. 1.*

The sense of human dignity was the chief moral agent of antiquity, and the sense of sin of mediævalism. *H. Lecky.*

The sense of the infinite nature of Duty is the central part of all with us ; a ray as of Eternity and Immortality, immured in dusky many-coloured Time, and its births and deaths. *Carlyle.*

The senses do not deceive us, but the judgment does. *Goethe.*

The sentimental by and by will have to give place to the practical. *Carlyle.*

15 The serenity that is not felt, it can be no virtue to feign. *Johnson.*

The seven wise men of Greece, so famous for their wisdom all the world over, acquired all that fame each of them by a single sentence consisting of two or three words. *South.*

The "seventeenth" century is worthless to us except precisely in so far as it can be made the "nineteenth." *Carlyle.*

The severe and restrictive virtues are almost too costly for humanity. *Burke.*

The severity of laws impedes their execution. *Montesquieu.*

20 The shadowed livery of the burnished sun. *Mer. of Venice, ii. 1.*

The sheep slips and is up again ; the sow lies down and wallows. *Saying.*

The shepherd in Virgil grew at last acquainted with Love, and found him a native of the rocks. *Johnson.*

The ship that carries most sail is most buffeted by the winds and storms. *John Burroughs.*

The short and simple annals of the poor. *Gray.*

25 The shorter life, less count I find, / The less account the sooner made, / The account soon made, the merrier mind, / The merrier mind doth thought evade. *Sir T. Wyatt.*

The shortest and the surest way to prove a work possible is strenuously to set about it ; and no wonder if that proves it possible that for the most part makes it so. *South.*

The shortest answer is doing. *Pr.*

The shortest way to do many things is to do only one thing at once. *Samuel Smiles.*

The showy lives its little hour ; the true / To after times bears rapture ever new. *Goethe.*

The shrine is that which thou dost venerate, / 30 And not the beast that bears it on his back. *George Herbert.*

The sight of you is good for sore eyes. *Swift.*

The sign of health is unconsciousness. *Carlyle.*

The sign of the poet is that he announces what no man foretold. *Emerson.*

The significance of life is doing something. *Carlyle.*

The signs of the times. *Jesus.* 35

The silence often of pure innocence / Persuades when speaking fails. *Winter's Tale, ii. 2.*

The silence that is in the starry sky. *Wordsworth.*

The silent heavens have goings-on ; / The stars have tasks. *Wordsworth.*

The simple believeth every word. *Bible.*

The sin that practice burns into the blood, / 40 And not the one dark hour which brings remorse, / Will brand us, after, of whose fold we be. *Tennyson.*

The single snowflake—who cares for it ? But a whole day of snowflakes . . . who does not care for that ? Private opinion is weak, but public opinion is almost omnipotent. (?)

The slack sail shifts from side to side, / The boat, untrimm'd, admits the tide, / Borne down, adrift, at random tost, / The oar breaks short, the rudder's lost. *Gay.*

The sleep of a labouring man is sweet, whether he eat little or much : but the abundance of the rich will not suffer him to sleep. *Bible.*

The sleeping and the dead / Are but as pictures. *Macb., ii. 2.*

The slender vine twists around the sturdy 45 oak, for no other reason in the world but because it has not strength sufficient to support itself. *Goldsmith.*

The slight that can be conveyed in a glance, in a gracious smile, in a wave of the hand, is often the "ne plus ultra" of art. What insult is so keen, or so keenly felt, as the polite insult which it is impossible to resent? *Julia Kavanagh.*

The slow wheel turns, / The cycles round themselves and grow complete, / The world's year whitens to the harvest-tide, / And one word only am I (Psyche) sent to say . . . / To all things living, and the word is "Love." *Lewis Morris.*

The sluggard is wiser in his own conceit than seven men that can render a reason. *Bible.*

The sly shadow steals away upon the dial, and the quickest eye can discover no more but that it is gone. *Glanville.*

The small courtesies sweeten life ; the greater 50 ennoble it. *Bovee.*

The smallest annoyances disturb us most. *Montaigne.*

The smallest bird cannot light upon the greatest tree without sending a shock to its most distant fibre. *Lew Wallace.*

The smallest worm will turn, being trodden on ; / And doves will peck, in safeguard of their brood. 3 *Henry VI.*, ii. 2.

The smoke of a man's own house is better than the fire of another's. *Pr.*

The snail sees nothing but his own shell, and thinks it the grandest place in the world. *Pr.*

The social, friendly, honest man, / Whate'er he be, / 'Tis he fulfils great Nature's plan, / And none but he. *Burns.*

5 The society of women is the element of good manners. *Goethe.*

The soldier's trade, verily and essentially, is not slaying, but being slain . . . and the reason the world honours the soldier is because he holds his life at the service of the state. *Ruskin.*

The soldier's ultimate and perennial office is to punish knaves and make idle persons work ; the defence of his country against other countries, which is his office at present, will soon now be extinct. *Ruskin.*

The sole terms on which the past can become ours are its subordination to the present. *Emerson.*

The Son of man came not to be ministered unto, but to minister, and to give his life a ransom for many. */esus.*

10 The song that we hear with our ears is only the song that is sung with our hearts. *Ouida.*

The sorest tempest has the most sudden calm. *Socrates.*

The sorrow of Yesterday is as nothing ; that of To-day is bearable ; but that of To-morrow is gigantic, because indistinct. *Euripides.*

The sorrowfulest of fates is to have liberty without deserving it. *Ruskin.*

The soul is like the sun, which, to our eyes, seems to set in night ; but it has in reality only gone to diffuse its light elsewhere. *Goethe.*

15 The soul is not where it lives, but where it loves. *Pr.*

The soul knows no persons. *Emerson.*

The soul may be trusted to the end. *Emerson.*

The soul moralises the past in order not to be demoralised by it, and finds in the crucible of experience only the gold that she herself has poured into it. *Amiel.*

The soul of a man can by no agency, of men or of devils, be lost and ruined but by his own only. *Carlyle.*

20 The soul of man is a mirror of the mind of God. *Ruskin.*

The soul reveals itself in the voice only. . . . It is audible, not visible. *Longfellow.*

The soul shut up in her dark room, / Viewing so clear abroad, at home sees nothing ; / But, like a mole in earth, busy and blind, / Works all her folly up, and casts it outward / To the world's open view. *Dryden.*

The soul, / The particle of God sent down to man, / Which doth in turn reveal the world and God. *Lewis Morris.*

The soul, / Though made in time, survives for aye ; / And, though it hath beginning, sees no end. *Sir J. Davies.*

The soul's armour is never well set to the 25 heart unless a woman's hand has braced it. *Ruskin.*

The soul's dark cottage, battered and decayed,/ Lets in new light through chinks that time has made. *Waller.*

The soul's emphasis is always right. *Emerson.*

The sound of a kiss is not so loud as that of a cannon, but its echo lasts a deal longer. *Holmes.*

The sphere-harmony of a Shakespeare, of a Goethe, the cathedral music of a Milton, the humble, genuine lark-notes of a Burns. *Carlyle.*

The spider taketh hold with her hands, and is 30 in kings' palaces. *Bible.*

The spirit breatheth where it willeth, and thou hearest the voice thereof, but canst not tell whence it cometh, and whither it goeth : so is it with every one that is born of the spirit. *Jesus.*

The spirit in which we act is the highest matter. *Goethe.*

The spirit indeed is willing, but the flesh is weak. *Jesus of his disciples.*

The spirit is higher than nature. *Hegel.*

The spirit of a man will sustain his infirmity ; 35 but a wounded spirit who can bear ? *Bible.*

The spirit of moderation should be the spirit of a lawgiver. *Montesquieu.*

The spirit of poesy is the morning light, which makes the statue of Memnon sound. *Novalis.*

The spirit only can teach. *Emerson.*

The spirit was long ago liberated from the blind law of nature, and the task it is called to now is to unfold itself with freedom and clearness in the sunlight, *i.e.*, in its own light now at length conscious of itself. *Ed.*

The spiritual artist too is born blind, and does 40 not, like certain other creatures, receive sight in nine days, but far later—perhaps never. *Carlyle.*

The spiritual is ever the inner in a man becoming outer, the invisible becoming visible, the supernatural becoming natural, the infinite becoming finite, and the eternal veiling itself in the guise of time ; never an emancipation from the flesh, but ever an incarnation in flesh. *Ed.*

The spiritual is higher than the external ; the spiritual cannot be externally authenticated. *Hegel.*

The spiritual is the parent and first cause of the practical. *Carlyle.*

The spiritual man is free to rule his world, not his world to rule him. *Ed.*

The spiritual problem which Christ resolved 45 was pretty much this—the derivation of that from within man which was conceived to be above man, by the reperception of the forgotten truth that it was in His own image God made man. He first opened up the well within. *Ed.*

The spiritual universe is no more to be made out of a man's own head than the material universe or the moral universe. . . . No belief of ours will change the facts or reverse the laws of the spiritual universe. *R. W. Dale.*

The spiritual will always body itself forth in the temporal history of men ; the spiritual is the beginning of the temporal, always determines the material. *Carlyle.*

The spiritual world is not closed ; it is thy sense that is : thy heart is dead. *Goethe.*

The spring can be apprehended only while it is flowing. *Goethe.*

The springing of a serpent is from the sun ; the wisdom of the serpent, whence is that ? *Ruskin.*

5 The stars do not come to tell us it is night, but to lay beams of light through it, and give the eye a path to walk in. *Ward Beecher.*

The stars shall fade away, the sun himself / Grow dim with age, and Nature sink in years ; / But thou shalt flourish in immortal youth, / Unhurt amidst the war of elements, / The wrecks of matter and the crash of worlds. *Addison.*

The stars themselves are only bright by distance ; go close, and all is earthy ; but vapours illuminate there ; from the breath and from the countenance of God comes light on worlds higher than they. *Landor.*

The "State in danger" is a condition of things which we have witnessed a hundred times ; and as for the Church, it has seldom been out of "danger" since we can remember it. *Carlyle.*

The State must follow, and not lead, the character and progress of the citizen. *Emerson.*

10 The statesman wishes to steer, while the politician is satisfied to drift. *James Freeman Clarke.*

The steps of faith fall on the seeming void, and find the rock beneath. *Whittier.*

The still, sad music of humanity. *Wordsworth.*

The Stoic thought by slandering Happiness to woo her ; by shunning to win her ; and proudly presumed that, by fleeing her, she would turn and follow him. *Arliss.*

The Stoic was a proud man, and not a humble, and he was content if he could only have his own soul for a prey. He did not see that the salvation of one man is impossible except in the salvation of other men, and that no man can save another unless he descend into that other's case, and be, as it were, in that other's stead. *Ed.*

15 The stoical exemption which philosophy affects to give us over the pains and vexations of human life is as imaginary as the state of mystical quietism and perfection aimed at by some crazy enthusiast. *Scott.*

The stoical scheme of supplying our wants by lopping off our desires is like cutting off our feet when we want shoes. *Swift.*

The stomach has no ears. *Pr.*

The stone that lieth not in your way need not offend you. *Pr.*

The stone which the builders refused has become the head of the corner. *Bible.*

20 The storm of sad mischance will turn into something that is good, if we list to make it so. *Taylor.*

The stranger who turneth away from a house with disappointed hopes leaveth there his own offences, and departeth, taking with him all the good actions of the owner. *Hitopadesa.*

The stranger's greeting thou shouldst aye return ! *Goethe.*

The strawberry grows under the nettle, / And wholesome berries thrive and ripen best / Neighbour'd by fruit of baser quality. *Hen V., i. I.*

The stream can never rise above the spring-head. *Pr.*

The street is full of humiliations to the proud. 25 *Emerson.*

The strength and power of a country depends absolutely on the quantity of good men and women in it. *Ruskin.*

The strength of aquatic animals is the waters ; of those who dwell in towns, a castle ; of footsoldiers, their own ground ; of princes, an obedient army. *Hitopadesa.*

The string o'erstretched breaks, and the music flies ; / The string o'erslack is dumb, and music dies ; / Tune us the sitar neither low nor high. *Sir Edwin Arnold.*

The string that jars / When rudely touch d, ungrateful to the sense, / With pleasure feels the master's flying fingers, / Swells into harmony and charms the hearers. *Rowe.*

The stroke that comes transmitted through 30 a whole galaxy of elastic balls, is it less a stroke than if the last ball only had been struck and sent flying ? *Carlyle.*

The strokes of the pen need deliberation as much as those of the sword need swiftness. *Julia W. Howe.*

The strong man is the wise man ; the man with the gift of method, of faithfulness, of valour ; who has insight into what is what, into what will follow out of what, the eye to see and the hand to do. *Carlyle.*

The strong mind is nowise the mind acquainted with its strength. *Carlyle.*

The strong must build stout cabins for the weak ; / Must plan and stint ; must sow and reap and store ; / For grain takes root though all seems bare and bleak. *Eugene Lee-Hamilton.*

The strong thing is the just thing : this thou 35 wilt find throughout in our world ;—as indeed was God and Truth the maker of it, or was Satan and Falsehood ? *Carlyle.*

The strong torrents, which in their own gladness fill the hills with hollow thunder and the vales with winding light, have wet their bounden charge of field to feed and barge to bear. *Ruskin.*

The strongest arm is impotent to impart momentum to a feather. *Schopenhauer.*

The strongest castle, tower, and town, / The golden bullet beats it down. *Shakespeare.*

The strongest oaths are straw / To the fire i' the blood. *Tempest, iv. I.*

The student is to read history actively and 40 not passively ; to esteem his own life the text, and books the commentary. Thus compelled, the muse of history will utter oracles as never to those who do not respect themselves. *Emerson.*

The study of books is a languishing and feeble motion that hearts not, whereas conversation teaches and exercises at once. *Montaigne.*

The stumbler stumbles least in rugged way. *George Herbert.*

The style of an author is a faithful copy of his mind. If you would write a lucid style, let there first be light in your own mind ; and if you would write a grand style, you ought to have a grand character. *Goethe.*

The style of letters should not be too highly polished. It ought to be neat and correct, but no more. *Blair.*

The style of writing required in the great world is distinguished by a free and daring grace, a careless security, a fine and sharp polish, a delicate and perfect taste ; while that fitted for the people is characterised by a vigorous natural fulness, a profound depth of feeling, and an engaging naiveté. *Goethe.*

The sublime is in a grain of dust. *Landor.*

5 The sublime is the temple-step of religion, as the stars are of immeasurable space. When what is mighty appears in nature—a storm, thunder, the starry firmament, death—then utter the word "God" before the child. A great misfortune, a great blessing, a great crime, a noble action, are building-sites for a child's church. *Jean Paul.*

The sublime produces a beautiful calmness in the soul which, entirely possessed by it, feels as great as it ever can feel. When we compare such a feeling with that we are sensible of when we laboriously harass ourselves with some trifle, and strain every nerve to gain as much as possible for it, as it were, to patch it out, striving to furnish joy and aliment to the mind from its own creation, we then feel sensibly what a poor expedient, after all, the latter is. *Goethe.*

The sublime, when it is introduced at a seasonable moment, has often carried all before it with the rapidity of lightning, and shown at a glance the mighty power of genius. *Longinus.*

The sublimest canticle to be heard on earth is the stammering of the human soul on the lips of infancy. *Victor Hugo.*

The sublimity of wisdom is to do those things living which are to be desired when dying. *Jeremy Taylor.*

10 The substance of a diligent man is precious. *Bible.*

The substance of a man is full good when sin is not in a man's conscience. *Chaucer.*

The substantial wealth of a man consists in the earth he cultivates with its plants and animals, and in the rightly produced works of his own hands. *Ruskin.*

The success of many works is found in the relation between the mediocrity of the author's ideas and that of the ideas of the public. *Chamfort.*

The suffering man ought really "to consume his own smoke ;" there is no good in emitting smoke till you have made it into fire. *Carlyle.*

15 The sufficiency of my merit is to know that my merit is not sufficient. *St. Augustine.*

The sun can be seen by nothing but its own light. *Pr.*

The sun flings out impurities, gets balefully incrusted with spots ; but it does not quench itself, and become no sun at all, but a mass of darkness. *Carlyle.*

The sun, God's crest upon his azure shield, the heavens. *Bailey.*

The sun is God. *Turner on his deathbed.*

The sun may do its duty, though your grapes 20 are not ripe. *Pr.*

The sun passeth through pollutions, and itself remains as pure as before. *Bacon.*

The sun-steeds of time, as if goaded by invisible spirits, bear onward the light car of our destiny, and nothing remains for us but, with calm self-possession, to grasp the reins, and now right, now left, to steer the wheels, here from the precipice, and there from the rock. Whither he is hasting, who knows ? Does any one consider whence he came ? *Goethe.*

The sun's power cannot draw a wandering star from its path. How then could a human being fall out of God's love ! *Rückert.*

The sunshine of life is made up of very little beams, that are bright all the time. *Aikin.*

The superstition in which we have grown up 25 does not lose its hold over us even when we recognise it for such. Those who scoff at their fetters are not all free men. *Lessing.*

The sure way to miss success is to miss the opportunity. *Philarète Chasles.*

The surest sign of age is loneliness. *A. B. Alcott.*

The surest test of a man's critical power is his judgment of contemporaries. *La Bruyère.*

The surest way not to fail is to determine to succeed. *Sheridan.*

The surest way to have redress is to be earnest 30 in pursuit of it. *Goldsmith.*

The surgeon practises on the orphan's head. *Arab. Pr.*

The sweetest music is not in the oratorio, but in the human voice when it speaks from its instant life tones of tenderness, truth, or courage. *Emerson.*

The sweetest wine makes the sharpest vinegar. *Pr.*

The sweetness of the lips increaseth learning. *Bible.*

The sweets of love are washed with tears. 35 *George Herbert.*

The sword is but a hideous flash in the darkness ; right is an eternal ray. *Victor Hugo.*

The sympathy of sorrow is stronger than the sympathy of prosperity. *I. Disraeli.*

The system of the world is entirely one ; small things and great are alike part of one mighty whole. *Ruskin.*

The tabernacle of the upright shall flourish. *Bible.*

The tallest trees are most in the power of the 40 winds, and ambitious men of the blasts of fortune. *Wm. Penn.*

The tanager flies through the green foliage as if he would ignite the leaves. *Thoreau.*

The teaching of art is the teaching of all things. *Ruskin.*

The teachings of Heaven are given—by sad law—in so obscure, nay, often in so ironical a manner, that a blockhead necessarily reads them wrong. *Ruskin.*

The tear of joy is a pearl of the first water ; the mourning tear, only of the second. *Jean Paul.*

The tears of penitents are the wine of angels. 45 *St. Bernard.*

The tell-tale out of school is of all wits the greatest fool. *Swift.*

The temper of the pedagogue suits not with the age ; and the world, however it may be taught, will not be tutored. *Shaftesbury.*

The temperate man's pleasures are durable, because they are regular ; and all his life is calm and serene, because it is innocent. (?)

The tempest never rooteth up the grass, which is feeble, humble, and shooteth not up on high ; but exerteth its power even to distress the lofty trees ; for the great use not their might but upon the great. *Hitopadesa.*

5 The temple of our purest thoughts is—silence ! *Mrs. Hale.*

The tendency of laws should be rather to diminish the amount of evil than to produce an amount of happiness. *Goethe.*

The tendency of party-spirit has ever been to disguise and propagate and support error. *Whately.*

The tender flower that lifts it head, elate, / Helpless must fall before the blasts of fate, / Sunk on the earth, defaced its lovely form, / Unless your shelter ward th' impending storm. *Burns.*

The tender heart o' leesome luve / The gowd and siller canna buy. *Burns.*

10 The tender mercies of the wicked are cruel. *Bible.*

The term of man's life is half wasted before he has done with his mistakes and begins to profit by his lessons. *Jane Taylor.*

The test of civilisation is the estimate of woman. *G. W. Curtis.*

The test or measure of poetic genius is to read the poetry of affairs, to fuse the circumstance of to-day. *Emerson.*

The theatre has often been at variance with the pulpit ; they ought not to quarrel. How much is it to be wished that in both the celebration of nature and of God were intrusted to none but men of noble minds ! *Goethe.*

15 The There is never Here. *Schiller.*

The thin edge of the wedge is to be feared. *Pr.*

The thing a lie wants, and solicits from all men, is not a correct natural history of it, but the swiftest possible extinction of it, followed by entire silence about it. *Carlyle.*

The thing done avails, and not what is said about it. *Emerson.*

The thing men get to believe is the thing they will infallibly do. *Carlyle.*

20 The thing that hath been, it is that which shall be ; and that which is done is that which shall be done. *Bible.*

The thing that is, what can be so wonderful ? what, especially to us that are, can have such significance ? *Carlyle.*

The thing that matters most, both for happiness and for duty, is that we should strive habitually to live with wise thoughts and right feelings. *J. Morley.*

The thing to be anxious about is not to be right with man, but with mankind. *Prof. Drummond.*

The thing visible, nay, the thing imagined, the thing in any way conceived of as visible, what is it but a garment, a clothing of the higher, celestial invisible, "unimaginable, formless, dark with excess of bright" ? *Carlyle.*

The thing which is deepest rooted in Nature, 25 what we call truest, that, and not the other, will be found growing at last. *Carlyle.*

The things that destroy us are injustice, insolence, and foolish thoughts ; and the things which save us are justice, self-command, and true thought, which things dwell in the loving powers of the gods. *Plato.*

The things that threatened me, / Ne'er look'd but on my back ; when they shall see / The face of Cæsar, they are vanished. *Jul. Cæsar,* ii. 2.

The thinker requires exactly the same light as the painter, clear, without direct sunshine, or blinding reflection, and, where possible, from above. *Schlegel.*

The thinking minds of all nations call for change. There is a deep-lying struggle in the whole fabric of society ; a boundless, grinding collision of the new with the old. *Carlyle.*

The third pays for all. *Twelfth Night,* v. 1.   30

The thirst for truth still remains with us, even when we have wilfully left the fountains of it. *Ruskin.*

The thorny point / Of bare distress hath ta'en from me the show / Of smooth civility. *As You Like It,* ii. 7.

The thought is always prior to the fact ; all the facts of history pre-exist in the mind as laws. *Emerson.*

The thought is parent of the deed. *Carlyle.*

The thought of foolishness is sin. *Bible.*   35

The thoughts of the diligent tend only to plenteousness ; but of every one that is hasty only to want. *Bible.*

The thoughts of the wicked are an abomination to the Lord. *Bible.*

The thoughts of youth are long, long thoughts. *Lapland Pr.*

The thoughts we have had, the pictures we have seen, can be again called back before the mind's eye and before the imagination ; but the heart is not so obliging ; it does not reproduce its pleasing emotions. *Goethe.*

The thrall in person may be free in soul. 40 *Tennyson.*

The throne is established by righteousness. *Bible.*

The time for words has passed, and deeds alone suffice. *Whittier.*

The time has been / That when the brains were out the man should die, / And there an end. *Macb.,* iii. 4.

The time is out of joint ; O cursèd spite, / That ever I was born to set it right. *Ham.,* i. 5.

The time of breeding is the time of doing 45 children good ; and not as many who think they have done fairly if they leave them a good portion after their decease. *George Herbert.*

The time that bears no fruit deserves no name. *Young.*

The Times are the masquerade of the Eternities ; trivial to the dull, tokens of noble and majestic agents to the wise. *Emerson.*

The timid are in fear before danger, the cowardly in danger, and the courageous after danger. *Jean Paul.*

The timing of things is a main point in the dispatch of all affairs. *L'Estrange.*

The tired ocean crawls along the beach sobbing a wordless sorrow to the moon. *William Falconer.*

The toil of life alone teaches us to value the blessings of life. *Goethe.*

The tomb is the pedestal of greatness. *Landor.*

5 The tongue can no man tame ; it is an unruly evil, full of deadly poison. *St. James.*

The tongue ever turns to the aching tooth. *Pr.*

The tongue is not of steel, but it cuts. *Pr.*

The tongue is the worst part of a bad servant. *Juv.*

The tongue of the just is as choice silver. *Bible.*

10 The tongue tells the thought of one man only, whereas the face expresses a thought of nature itself ; so that every one is worth attentive observation, even though every one may not be worth talking to. *Schopenhauer.*

The tongue's aye quick at saying "Na," / Though a' the while the heart be dumb. *Gilfillan.*

The tongues of dying men / Enforce attention like deep harmony. *Rich. II.,* ii. 1.

The too good opinion man has of himself is the nursing-mother of all false opinions, both public and private. *Montaigne.*

The torments of martyrdoms are probably most keenly felt by the bystanders. *Emerson.*

15 The total loss of reason is less deplorable than the total depravation of it. *Cowley.*

The training (*Bildung*) of the thinking, of the dispositions and the morals, is the only education that deserves the name. *Herder.*

The trappings of a monarchy would set up an ordinary commonwealth. *Johnson.*

The traveller who goes round the world prepares himself to pass through all latitudes and to meet all changes. *Ward Beecher.*

The traveller without observation is a bird without wings. *Saadi.*

20 The treasures of heaven are not negations of passion but realities of intellect, from which all passions emanate, uncurbed in their eternal glory. *Wm. Blake.*

The tree doth not withdraw its shade, even from the woodcutter. *Hitopadesa.*

The tree Igdrasil, which reaches up to heaven, goes down to the kingdom of hell ; and God, the Everlasting Good and Just, is in it all. *Carlyle.*

The tree is no sooner down than every one runs for his hatchet. *Pr.*

The tree of knowledge is grafted upon the tree of life ; and that fruit which brought the fear of death into the world, budding on an immortal stock, becomes the fruit of the promise of immortality. *Sir H. Davy.*

25 The tree of knowledge is not that of life. *Byron.*

The tree of liberty only grows when watered by the blood of tyrants. *Bertrand Barère.*

The tree of silence bears the fruit of peace. *Arab. Pr.*

The tree which yieldeth both fruit and shade is highly to be esteemed ; but if Providence, perchance, may have denied it fruit, by whom is its shade refused ? *Hitopadesa.*

The trenchant blade, Toledo trusty, / For want of fighting was grown rusty, / And ate into itself, for lack / Of somebody to hew and hack. *Butler.*

The trident of Neptune is the sceptre of the 30 planet. *Lemierre.*

The triumphs of delusion are but for a day. *Macaulay.*

The trivial round, the common task, / Will furnish all we ought to ask, / Room to deny ourselves, a road / To bring us daily nearer God. *Keble.*

The true and the good will be reconciled when the two are wedded to each other in the beautiful. *Rückert.*

The true art of being agreeable is to appear well pleased with all the company, and rather to seem well entertained with them than to bring entertainment to them. *Addison.*

The true beginning is oftenest unnoticed and 35 unnoticeable. *Carlyle.*

The true "compulsory education" now needed is not catechism, but drill. *Ruskin.*

The true cross of the Redeemer is the sin and sorrow of the world. *George Eliot.*

The true end of tragedy is to purify the passions. *Arist.*

The true epic of our times is, not arms and the man, but tools and the man—an infinitely wider kind of epic. *Carlyle.*

The true eye for talent presupposes the true 40 reverence for it. *Carlyle.*

The true fire of heaven always comes from heaven direct. *Ed.*

The true function of intellect is not that of talking, but of understanding and discerning with a view to performing. *Carlyle.*

The true God's voice, voice of the Eternal, is in the heart of every man. *Carlyle.*

The true good (all of it) and glory even of this world, not to speak of any that is to come, must be bought still, as it always has been, with our toil and with our tears. That is the final doctrine, the inevitable one, not of Christianity only, but of all heroic faith and heroic being. *Ruskin.*

The true harvest of my daily life is somewhat 45 as intangible and indescribable as the tints of morning or evening. It is a little star-dust caught, a segment of the rainbow which I have clutched. *Thoreau.*

The true historical genius, to our thinking, is that which can see the nobler meaning of the events that are near him. *Lowell.*

The true labourer is worthy of his hire, but, in the beginning and first choice of industry, his heart must not be the heart of an hireling. *Ruskin.*

The true ladder of heaven has no steps. *Jean Paul.*

The true liberty of a man consists in his finding out, or being forced to find out, the right path, and to walk therein. *Carlyle.*

The true life of man is in society. *Simms.* 50

The true life of man, like God's, lies in the ungrudging imparting of himself to alike the worthy and unworthy without fear of forfeiture or claim of reward. *Ed.*

The true literary man is the light of the world ; the world's priest guiding it, like a sacred pillar of fire, in its dark pilgrimage through the waste of time. *Carlyle.*

The true mind of a nation, at any period, is always best ascertainable by examining that of its greatest men. *Ruskin.*

The true original ground of all disquiet is within. *Thomas à Kempis.*

The true philosophical act is annihilation of self; this is the real beginning of all philosophy; all requisites for being a disciple of philosophy point hither. *Novalis.*

The true poet is even more than a finder or troubadour; he is a seer, a prophet, and an interpreter between the divine and the human. *C. Fitzhugh.*

5 The true poet, who is but the inspired thinker, is still an Orpheus whose lyre tames the savage beasts, and evokes the dead rocks to fashion themselves into palaces and stately inhabited cities. *Carlyle.*

The true poetic soul needs but to be struck, and the sounds it yields will be music. *Carlyle.*

The true preacher can be known by this, that he deals out to the people his life—life passed through the fire of thought. *Emerson.*

The true scholar learns from the known to unfold the unknown, and approaches more and more to being a master. *Goethe.*

The true Shekinah is man. *St. Chrysostom.*

10 The true strength of every human soul is to be dependent on as many nobler as it can discern, and to be depended upon by as many inferior as it can reach. *Ruskin.*

The true, strong, and sound mind is the mind that can embrace equally great things and small. *Johnson.*

The True that is identical with the Divine can never be directly known by us; we behold it only in reflexion (*Abglanz*), in example, in symbol, in individual and related phenomena; we perceive it as incomprehensible life, which yet we cannot renounce the wish to comprehend. This is true of all the phenomena of the conceivable world. *Goethe.*

The true university of these days is a collection of books. *Carlyle.*

The true value of a man's book is determined by what he does not write. *Carlyle.*

15 The true veins of wealth are purple—not in rock, but in flesh—(and) the final outcome and consummation of all wealth is in producing as many as possible full-breathed, bright-eyed, and happy-hearted human creatures. *Ruskin.*

The true way of softening one's troubles is to solace those of others. *Mme. de Maintenon.*

The truly strong mind, view it as intellect or morality, or under any other aspect, is nowise the mind acquainted with its strength. *Carlyle.*

The truly sublime is always easy, and always natural. *Burke.*

The truly wise man should have no keeper of his secrets but himself. *Guizot.*

20 The truth shall make you free. *Jesus.*

The truth we need is only lightly veiled, not deeply buried by the wise hand which has designed it for us. *Gellert.*

The truth works sometimes from without as from within. *Dr. W. Smith.*

The truths of Nature are one eternal change, one infinite variety. *Ruskin.*

The two best rules for a system of rhetoric are: first, have something to say; and next, say it. *George Emmons.*

The two foes of human happiness are pain and 25 ennui. *Schopenhauer.*

The two great movers of the human mind are the desire of good and the fear of evil. *Johnson.*

The two most beautiful things in the universe are the starry heavens above us and the feeling of duty within us. *An Indian sage.*

The two most engaging powers of an author are to make new things familiar and familiar things new. *Thackeray.*

The two sources of all quack-talent are cunning and impudence. *Carlyle.*

The ultimate rule (in writing) is: Learn so far 30 as possible to be intelligible and transparent —no notice taken of your style, but solely of what you express by it. *Carlyle.*

The ultimate tendency of civilisation is towards barbarism. *Hare.*

The unconscious is the alone complete. *Goethe.*

The Understanding is indeed thy window, too clear thou canst not make it; but Fantasy is thy eye, with its colour-giving retina, healthy or diseased. *Carlyle.*

The undiscovered country, from whose bourn No traveller returns. *Ham., iii. 1.*

The unfortunate are loud and loquacious 35 in their complaints, but real happiness is content with its own silent enjoyment. *Gibbon.*

The unhappy (*malheureux*) are always wrong: wrong in being so, wrong in saying so, wrong in needing help of others, wrong in not being able to help them. *Mirabeau.*

The unimaginative person can neither be reverent nor kind. *Ruskin.*

The universe has three children, born at one time . . . called cause, operation, and effect, or, theologically, the Father, the Spirit, and the Son. These three are equal . . . and each has the power of the others latent in him. *Emerson.*

The universe is a thought of God. *Schiller.*

The universe is an infinite sphere, the centre 40 of which is everywhere, and the circumference nowhere. *Pascal after St. Augustus.*

The universe is but one vast symbol of God; nay, if thou wilt have it, what is man himself but a symbol of God; is not all that he does symbolical; a revelation to sense of the mystic god-given force that is in him; a "gospel of freedom," which he, the "Messias of Nature," preaches, as he can, by act and word? *Carlyle.*

The universe is full of love, but also of inexorable sternness and severity. *Carlyle.*

The universe is not dead and demoniacal, a charnel-house with spectres, but godlike, and my Father's. *Carlyle.*

The universe is one great city, full of beloved ones, human and divine, by nature endeared to each other. *Epictetus.*

The universe is that great egoist that decoys 45 us by the grossest bird-calls. *Renan.*

The universe is the realised thought of God. *Carlyle.*

The universe stands by him who stands by himself. *Emerson.*

The universe would not be rich enough to buy the vote of an honest man. *St. Gregory.*

The unlearned man knoweth not what it is to descend into himself and call himself to account; nor the pleasure of that most pleasant life which consists in our daily feeling ourselves become better. *Sir Walter Raleigh.*

The unlettered peasant, whose views are only directed to the narrow sphere around him, beholds Nature with a finer relish, and tastes her blessings with a keener appetite, than the philosopher whose mind attempts to grasp a universal system. *Goldsmith.*

5 The unpastured sea hungering for calm. *Shelley.*

The unworn spirit is strong; life is so healthful that it even finds nourishment in death. *Carlyle.*

The upper classes and people of wealth suffer most from ennui. *Schopenhauer.*

The Upper Crust, *i.e.*, the Upper Ten. *Amer.*

The Upper Ten, *i.e.*, the aristocracy; the upper circles (contracted from Upper Ten Thousand). *Amer.*

10 The upper current of society presents no certain criterion by which we can judge of the direction in which the under-current flows. *Macaulay.*

The upright shall dwell in the land, and the perfect shall remain in it. *Bible.*

The ups and downs of the world concern the beggar no longer. *Lamb.*

The use of knowledge in our sex, besides the amusement of solitude, is to moderate the passions, and learn to be contented with a small expense, which are the certain effects of a studious life; and it may be preferable to that fame which men have engrossed to themselves, and will not suffer us to share. *Lady Montagu.*

The use of travelling is to regulate imagination by reality, and instead of thinking how things may be, to see them as they are. *Johnson.*

15 The useful encourages itself, for the multitude produce it, and no one can dispense with it; but the beautiful must be encouraged, for few can set it forth, and many need it. *Goethe.*

The useless men are those who never change with the years. *J. M. Barrie.*

The usurer is the greatest Sabbath-breaker, because his plough goeth every Sunday. *Bacon.*

The utmost point and acme of honour is not merely in doing no evil, but in thinking none. *Ruskin.*

The uttered part of a man's life bears to the unuttered, unconscious part of it a small unknown proportion; he himself never knows it, much less do others. *Carlyle.*

20 The valiant in himself, what can he suffer? / Or what need he regard his single woes? *Thomson.*

The valour of a just man is to conquer the flesh, to contradict his own will, . . . to contemn the flatteries of prosperity, and inwardly to overcome the fears of adversity. *S. Greg.*

The valour that struggles is better than the weakness that endures. *Hegel.*

The value of a man, as of a horse, consists in your being able to bridle him, or, what is better, in his being able to bridle himself. *Ruskin.*

The value of a thing is its life-giving power. *Ruskin.*

The vanity of loving fine clothes and new 25 fashions, and valuing ourselves by them, is one of the most childish pieces of folly that can be. *Sir Matthew Hale.*

The veneration we have for many things entirely proceeds from their being carefully concealed. *Goldsmith.*

The very head and front of my offending / Hath this extent, no more. *Othello,* i. 3.

The very joy of a true man's heart is to admire, when he can; nothing so lifts him from all his mean imprisonments, were it but for moments, as true admiration. *Carlyle.*

The very meanest things are made supreme / With innate ecstasy. *Blanchard.*

The very nature of the dilettanti is that they 30 have no idea of the difficulties which lie in a subject, and always wish to undertake something for which they have no capacity. *Goethe.*

The very pain of loving is all other joys before. *Dr. Walter Smith.*

The very society of joy redoubles it, so that, whilst it lights upon my friend, it rebounds upon myself, and the brighter his candle burns the more easily will it light mine. *South.*

The vessel that will not obey her helm will have to obey the rocks. *Breton and Cornish Pr.*

The vice of our housekeeping is that it does not hold man sacred. *Emerson.*

The vices we scoff at in others laugh at us 35 within ourselves. *Sir Thomas Browne.*

The victories of character are instant, and victories for all. *Emerson.*

"The victory of Miltiades does not suffer me to sleep." *Themistocles, in reference to the battle of Marathon.*

The violets and the mayflowers are as the inscriptions or vignettes of spring. It always makes a pleasant impression on us when we open again at these pages of the book of life, its most charming chapter. *Goethe.*

The virtue of great souls is justice (*Gerechtigkeit*). *Platen.*

The virtue of justice consists in moderation, 40 as regulated by wisdom. *Arist.*

The virtue of man is, in a word, the great proof of God. *Renan.*

The virtue of prosperity is temperance; the virtue of adversity is fortitude; which in morals is the more heroical virtue. *Bacon.*

The virtue of sex is the occasion of mutual teaching; the woman preaching love in the ears of justice, and the man justice in the ears of love. *Amiel.*

The virtue of the man who lives according to the precepts of reason shows itself equally great in avoiding as in overcoming dangers. *Spinoza.*

The virtuous delight in the virtuous; but he who is destitute of the practice of virtue delighteth not in the virtuous. The bee retireth from the forest to the lotus, whilst the frog is destitute of shelter. *Hitopadesa.*

The virtuous man, from his justice and the affection he hath for mankind, is the dispeller of sorrow and pain. *Hitopadesa.*

The virtuous soul is pure and unmixed light, springing from the body as a flash of lightning darts from the cloud; the soul that is carnal and immersed in sense, like a heavy and dank vapour, can with difficulty be kindled, and caused to raise its eyes heavenward. *Heraclitus.*

The visible creation is the terminus or the circumference of the invisible world. *Emerson.*

5 The vitality of man is great. *Carlyle.*

The voice of conscience is so delicate that it is easy to stifle it; but it is also so clear that it is impossible to mistake it. *Mme. de Staël.*

The voice of prophecies is like that of whispering-places; they who are near hear nothing, those at the first extremity will know all. *Sir Thomas Browne.*

The voice of the majority is no proof of justice. *Schiller.*

The voice of the people ought always to meet with attention, though it does not always claim obedience. *Fox.*

10 The vulgar estimate themselves by what they do; the noble by what they are. *Schiller.*

The vulgar great are comprehended and adored, because they are in reality on the same moral plane with those who admire; but he who deserves the higher reverence must himself convert the worshipper. *Lord Houghton.*

The vulgar keep no account of your hits, but of your misses. *Pr.*

The wail of grief is more sympathetic than the shout of triumph. *C. Fitzhugh.*

The walking of man and all animals is a falling forward. *Emerson.*

15 The want of belief is a defect which ought to be concealed when it cannot be overcome. *Swift.*

The want of occupation is no less the plague of society than of solitude. *Rousseau.*

The want of perception is a defect which all the virtues of the heart cannot supply. *Thoreau.*

The warl'ly race may riches chase, / And riches still may flee them; / And though at last they catch them fast, / Their hearts can ne'er enjoy them. *Burns.*

The watchful mother tarries nigh, / Though sleep has clos'd her infant's eye. *Keble.*

20 The way in which we form our ideas gives character to our minds. *Rousseau.*

The way of the superior man is threefold—virtuous, he is free from anxieties; wise, he is free from perplexities; bold, he is free from fear. *Confucius.*

The way of the wicked is an abomination unto the Lord. *Bible.*

The way of the world is to make laws, but follow customs. *Montaigne.*

The way of this world is to praise dead saints and persecute living ones. *Rev. N. Howe.*

The way to avoid evil is not by maiming our 25 passions, but by compelling them to yield their vigour to our moral nature. *Ward Beecher.*

The way to avoid the imputation of impudence is not to be ashamed of what we do, but never to do what we ought to be ashamed of. *Cic.*

The way to be original is to be healthy. *Lowell.*

The way to get rid of wretchedness is to despise it; to conquer the devil is to defy him; to gain heaven is to turn your back upon it, and be as unflinching as the gods themselves. Satan may be roasted in his own flames; Tophet may be exploded with his own sulphur. *John Burroughs upon Carlyle's teaching.*

The way to heaven is set with briars and thorns; and they who arrive at the kingdom travel over craggy rocks and comfortless deserts. *Thomas à Kempis.*

The way to make thy son rich is to fill / His 30 mind with rest, before his trunk with riches. *George Herbert.*

The way to mend the bad world is to create the right world. *Emerson.*

The way to wealth is as plain as the way to market; it depends chiefly on two words—industry and frugality. *Franklin.*

The way to write quickly is to write well. *Quinct.*

The way, truth, and life have been found in Christianity, and will not now be found outside of it. *Matthew Arnold.*

The way's not easy where the prize is great. 35 *Quarles.*

The ways in which most men get their living, that is, live, are mere makeshifts, and a shirking of the real business of life; chiefly because they do not know, but partly because they do not mean better. *Thoreau.*

The weakest goes to the wall. *Rom. and Jul.,* i. 1.

The weakest spot in every man is where he thinks himself to be the wisest. *G. Emmons.*

The wealth of a country is in its good men and women, and in nothing else. *Ruskin.*

The wealth of a man is the number of things 40 which he loves and blesses, which he is loved and blessed by. *Carlyle.*

The wealth of both Indies seems in great part but an accessory to the command of the seas. *Bacon.*

The wealth of both the Indies cannot redeem one single opportunity which you have once let slip. *Thomas à Kempis.*

The wealth of the land / Comes from the forge and the smithy and mine, / From hammer and chisel, and wheel and band, / And the thinking brain and the skilful hand. *Dr. Walter Smith.*

The wealth we cannot wisely administer is an encumbrance. *Goethe.*

The weariest and most loathèd worldly life, / 45 That age, ache, penury, and imprisonment / Can lay on nature, is a paradise / To what we fear of death. *Meas. for Meas.,* iii. 1.

The wearisome is in permanence here. *Carlyle at Linlathen, in Forfarshire.*

The weary night o' care and grief / May hae a joyful morrow. *Burns.*

The web of this world is woven of necessity and contingency ; the reason of man places itself between them, and knows how to rule them both. It treats the necessary as the ground of its existence ; the contingent it knows how to direct, lead, and utilise ; and it is only while reason stands firm and steadfast that man deserves to be called the god of the earth. Woe to him who has accustomed himself from his youth to incline to find something arbitrary in what is necessary, who would fain ascribe a kind of reason to the contingent, which it were even a religion to follow ; what is that but to disown one's own understanding, and to give loose reins to one's inclinations? We imagine it piety to saunter along (*hinschlendern*) without consideration, and to allow ourselves to be determined by agreeable accidents, and finally give to the results of such a vacillating life the name of Divine guidance. *Goethe.*

The web of our life is of a mingled yarn, good and ill together ; our virtues would be proud if our faults whipped them not, and our crimes would despair if they were not cherished by our virtues. *All's Well*, iv. 3.

The wedge will rend rocks ; but its edge must be sharp and single ; if it is double, the wedge is bruised in pieces, and will rend nothing. *Carlyle.*

The wheel is always in motion, and the spoke which is uppermost will soon be under ; therefore mix trembling with all your joy. *Philip Henry.*

5 The whole art of war consists in getting at what is on the other side of the hill, or, in other words, in learning what we do not know from what we do. *Duke of Wellington.*

The whole course of things goes to teach us faith. *Emerson.*

The whole difference between a man of genius and other men . . . is that the former remains in great part a child, seeing with the large eyes of children, in perpetual wonder, not conscious of much knowledge — conscious rather of infinite ignorance, and yet infinite power. *Ruskin.*

The whole economy of nature is bent on expression. *Emerson.*

The whole interest of history lies in the fortunes of the poor. *Emerson.*

10 The whole function of the artist in the world is to be a seeing and a feeling creature ; to be an instrument of such tenderness and sensitiveness that no shadow, no hue, no line, no instantaneous and evanescent expression of the visible things around him, nor any of the emotions which they are capable of conveying to the spirit which has been given him, shall either be left unrecorded, or fade from the book of record. *Ruskin.*

The whole man to one thing at a time. *Pr.*

The whole of chivalry and of heraldry is in courtesy. *Emerson.*

The whole past is the possession of the present. *Carlyle.*

The whole spiritual universe exists only in process—what Hegel calls "Der Process des Geistes"—the process of the spirit, that is to say, not as become, but as becoming ; and if it once ceases to become, it ceases as such to be. *Ed.*

The whole universe is at all moments saying 15 "Nay" to the Spirit of God, and God's Spirit is at all moments saying "Yea" to the stolid "Nay" of the universe, which would fain be let alone ; but stubborn as the material looks and is, it has to obey, and does obey, the voice of God. *Ed.*

The whole world is, properly speaking, a tragic embarras. *Rahel.*

The whole world of truth and conscience is nothing without I. *Jean Paul.*

The wide pasture is but separate spears of grass ; the sheeted bloom of the prairies but isolated flowers. *Ward Beecher.*

The wife can carry more out of the house in her apron than the man can bring in on a harvest-waggon. *Rückert.*

The wife is the key of the house. *Pr.* 20

The wife that expects to have a good name / Is always at home as if she were lame ; / And the mind that is honest, her chiefest delight, / Is still to be doing from morning till night. *Sp. Pr.*

The will appears without its mask only in the affections and the passions. *Schopenhauer.*

The willow which bends to the tempest often escapes better than the oak which resists it. *Scott.*

The wind that has its nest in trees. *J. M. Barrie.*

The winds and the waves are always on the 25 side of the ablest navigators. *Gibbon.*

The winter of our discontent. *Rich. III.*, i. 1.

The wisdom of life is in preventing all the evil we can, and using what is inevitable to the best purpose. *Ruskin.*

The wisdom of nations lies in their proverbs, which are brief and pithy. Collect and learn them ; they are notable measures and directions for human life ; you have much in little ; they save time in speaking ; and upon occasion may be the fullest and safest answers. *William Penn.*

The wisdom of the wise and the experience of ages may be preserved by quotation. *Isaac Disraeli.*

The wise are instructed by reason, ordinary 30 minds by experience, the stupid by necessity, and brutes by instinct. *Cic.*

The wise are polite all the world over, but fools are only polite at home. *Goldsmith.*

The wise are those who travel through error to truth ; the foolish are those who persist in their error. *Rückert.*

The wise grumbler . . . is a public benefactor. *John Wagstaffe.*

The wise have all ever said the same thing, and the fools, who are always in the majority, have always done just the opposite. *Schopenhauer.*

The wise in heart shall be called prudent. 35 *Bible.*

The wise man always looks to the degree of his indulgences. *John Wagstaffe.*

The wise man can dispense with the favour of the mighty, but the mighty cannot dispense with the teaching of the wise. *Bodenstedt.*

The wise man does not grasp at what is far off in order to find what is near, and his hand does not grasp at the stars in order to kindle light. *Bodenstedt.*

The wise man, even destitute of riches. enjoyeth elevated and very honourable stations; whilst the wretch, endowed with wealth, acquireth the post of disgrace. *Hitopadesa.*

The wise man expects everything from himself; the fool looks to others. *Jean Paul.*

The wise man had rather be envied for providence than pitied for prodigality. *Socrates.*

The wise man has long ears and a short tongue. *Ger. Pr.*

5 The wise man knows his master; always some creature larger than himself, some law holier than himself. *Ruskin.*

The wise man knows that he does not know; the ignoramus thinks he knows. *Sp. Pr.*

The wise man may strive to conquer, but he should never fight; because victory, it is observed, cannot be constant to both combatants. *Hitopadesa.*

The wise man moveth with one foot, and standeth fast with the other. A man should not quit one place until he hath fixed upon another. *Hitopadesa.*

The wise man must go to the foolish, else would his wisdom go for nought, since the foolish never come to the wise. *Bodenstedt.*

10 The wise man often shuns society for fear of being bored. *La Bruyère.*

The wise man ought to despise glory, but not honour. Honour is but seldom where glory is, and glory almost more rarely still where honour is. *Seume.*

The wise man should study the acquisition of science and riches as if he were not subject to sickness and death; but to the duties of religion he should attend as if death had seized him by the hair. *Hitopadesa.*

The wise man will commit no business of importance to a proxy when he may do it himself. *L'Estrange.*

The wise men of old have sent most of their morality down the stream of time in the light skiff of apothegm or epigram. *Whipple.*

15 The wise through excess of wisdom is made a fool. *Emerson.*

The wise weigh their words in a balance for gold. *Ecclus.*

The wise will determine from the gravity of the case; the irritable, from sensibility to oppression; the high-minded, from disdain and indignation at abusive power in unworthy hands. *Burke.*

The wiser mind / Mourns less for what age takes away / Than what it leaves behind. *Wordsworth.*

The wisest at most observe only how fate leads them, and are content. *Foster.*

20 The wisest doctor is gravelled by the inquisitiveness of a child. *Emerson.*

The wisest, happiest of our kind are they / That ever walk content with Nature's way. *Wordsworth.*

The wisest is omnipresent, and reveals His secrets universally to the seeing eye and the hearing ear. The revelation in all its fullness is nowhere wanting, only the sense to discern it, and the courage to be true to it. *Ed.*

The wisest man the warl' e'er saw, / He dearly lo'ed the lasses O. *Burns.*

The wisest men are wise to the full in death. *Ruskin.*

The wisest, most melodious voice cannot in 25 these days pass for a divine one; the word "inspiration" still lingers, but only in the shape of a poetic figure, from which the once earnest, awful, and soul-subduing sense has vanished without return. *Carlyle.*

The wisest of us must, for by far the most part, judge like the simplest; estimate importance by mere magnitude, and expect that which strongly affects our own generation, will strongly affect those that are to follow. *Carlyle.*

The wisest truly is, in these times, the greatest. *Carlyle.*

The wisest woman you talk with is ignorant of something that you know, but an elegant woman never forgets her elegance. *Holmes.*

The wish was father to the thought. *2 Hen. IV.*, iv. 4.

The wished-for comes too late. *Pr.* 30

The wishing-gate opens into nothing. *Spurgeon.*

The wit of language is so miserably inferior to the wit of ideas that it is deservedly driven out of good company. *Sydney Smith.*

The wit of one man, and the wisdom of many. *Lord John Russell's definition of a proverb.*

The wit one wants spoils what one has. *Fr. Pr.*

The woman and the soldier who do not defend 35 the first pass will never defend the last. *Fielding.*

The woman that deliberates is lost. *Addison.*

The woman's cause is man's: they rise or sink / Together. *Tennyson.*

The womankind will not drill. *Carlyle, Father Andreas in "Sartor."*

The women are quick enough—they're quick enough. They know the rights of a story before they hear it, and can tell a man what his thoughts are before he knows 'em himself. *George Eliot.*

The word is always bolder than the deed. 40 *Schiller.*

The Word is very nigh unto thee, in thy mouth, and in thy heart, that thou mayest do it. *Bible.*

The word of a gentleman is as good as his bond—sometimes better. *Dickens.*

The words of a man's mouth are as deep waters, and the well-spring of wisdom as a flowing brook. *Bible.*

The words of a tale-bearer are as wounds, and they go down into the innermost parts of the belly. *Bible.*

The words of men are like the leaves of trees; 45 when they are too many they hinder the growth of the fruit. *Steiger.*

The words of the wise are as goads. *Pr.*

The words that a father speaks to his children in the privacy of home are not heard by the world, but, as in whispering-galleries, they are clearly heard at the end and by posterity. *Jean Paul.*

The work an unknown good man has done is like a vein of water flowing hidden under ground, secretly making the ground green; it flows and flows, it joins itself with other veins and veinlets; one day it will start forth as a visible perennial well. *Carlyle.*

The work of righteousness shall be peace. *Bible.*

The work of science is to substitute facts for appearances, and demonstrations for impressions. *Ruskin.*

The works of the great poets have only been read for most part as the multitude read the stars, at most, astrologically, not astronomically. *Thoreau.*

The world can never give / The bliss for which we sigh ; / 'Tis not the whole of life to live, / Nor all of death to die. *Montgomery.*

5 The world cannot be governed without juggling. *Selden.*

The world cannot do without great men, but great men are very troublesome to the world. *Goethe.*

The world considers eccentricity in great things genius : in small things, folly. *Bulwer Lytton.*

The world does not progress so quickly as a man grows old. *J. M. Barrie.*

The world exists by change, and but for that / All matter would to chaos back / To form a pillar for a sleeping god. *Anon.*

10 The world exists for the education of each man. *Emerson.*

The world exists only by the strength of its silent virtue. *Ruskin.*

The world goes up, and the world goes down, / And the sunshine follows the rain ; / And yesterday's sneer, and yesterday's frown, / Can never come over again. *C. Kingsley.*

The world grows more majestic, but man grows less. *Amiel.*

The world has no business with my life ; the world will never know my life, if it should write and read a hundred biographies of me. *Carlyle.*

15 The world has to obey him who thinks and sees in the world. *Carlyle.*

The world is a carcase, and they who gather round it are dogs. *Eastern Pr.*

The world is a comedy to those who think, a tragedy to those who feel. *Horace Walpole.*

The world is a grand book from which to become wiser. *Goethe.*

The world is a looking-glass, and gives back to every man the reflection of his own face. Frown at it, and it will in turn look sourly upon you ; laugh at it and with it, and it is a jolly kind companion. *Thackeray.*

20 The world is a prison. *Goethe.*

The world is a thing that man must learn to despise, and even to neglect, before he can learn to reverence it, and work in it and for it. *Carlyle.*

The world is a wheel, and it will all come round right. *Disraeli.*

The world is all barren to him who will not cultivate the fruit it offers. *Sterne.*

The world is always ready to receive talent with open arms. Very often it does not know what to do with genius. Talent is a docile creature. It bows its head meekly while the world slips the collar over it. It backs into the shafts like a lamb. *Holmes.*

25 The world is an excellent judge in general, but a very bad one in particular. *Lord Greville.*

The world is an old woman, that mistakes any gilt farthing for a gold coin ; whereby, being often cheated, she will henceforth trust nothing but the common copper. *Carlyle.*

The world is as you take it. *Pr.*

The world is but an allegory ; the idea is more real than the fact. *Amiel.*

The world is content with words ; few think of searching into the nature of things. *Pascal.*

The world is everywhere perfect except where 30 man comes with his pain. *Schiller.*

The world is fain to sully what is resplendent, and to drag down to the dust what is exalted. *Schiller.*

The world is for him who has patience. *It. Pr.*

The world is glorious to look at, but dreadful in reality ; it is one thing as a drama to a spectator, quite another thing to the actors in the plot, for in it the will is thwarted at every turn. *Schopenhauer.*

The world is governed much more by opinion than by laws. *Channing.*

The world is governed too much. (?) 35

The world is not our peers, so we challenge the jury. *Burns.*

The world is not thy friend, nor the world's law. *Rom. and Jul.*, v. 1.

The world is not to be despised but as it is compared with something better. Company is in itself better than solitude, and pleasure better than indolence. *Johnson.*

The world is nothing but a wheel ; in its whole periphery it is everywhere similar, but, nevertheless, it appears to us so strange, because we ourselves are carried round with it. *Goethe.*

The world is nothing ; the man is all. *Emerson.* 40

The world is only governed by self-interest. *Schiller.*

The world is so busied with selfish pursuits, ambition, vanity, interest, or pleasure, that very few think it worth their while to make any observation on what passes around them, except where that observation is a sucker, or branch of the darling plant they are rearing in their fancy. *Burns.*

The world is still deceived with ornament. / In law, what plea so tainted and corrupt, / But, being seasoned with a gracious voice, / Obscures the show of evil ? In religion, / What damned error but some sober brow / Will bless it and approve it with a text, / Hiding the grossness with fair ornament ? *Mer. of Ven.*, iii. 2.

The world is too much with us ; late and soon, / Getting and spending, we lay waste our powers ; / Little we see in Nature that is ours. *Wordsworth.*

The world is undone by looking at things at a 45 distance. *Sir Thomas More.*

The world is upheld by the veracity of good men ; they make the earth wholesome. *Emerson.*

The world is wide enough for all to live and let live, and every one has an enemy in his own talent, who gives him quite enough to do. But no ! one gifted man and one talented persecutes another . . and each seeks to make the other hateful. *Goethe.*

The world is wider than any of us think. *Carlyle.*

The world knows nothing of its greatest men. *Sir Henry Taylor.*

The world looks at ministers out of the pulpit to know what they mean when in it. *Cecil.*

The world . . . may overlook most of us ; but "reverence thyself." *Burns.*

5 The world never let a man bless it but it first fought him. *Ward Beecher.*

The world of Nature for every man is the fantasy of himself ; this world is the multiplex "image of his own dream." *Carlyle.*

The world of reality has its limits ; the world of imagination is boundless. Not being able to enlarge the one, let us contract the other ; for it is from their difference alone that all the evils arise which render us really unhappy. *Rousseau.*

The world of thought must remain apart from the world of action, for if they once coincided the problem of life would be solved, and the hope which we call heaven would be realised on earth. And therefore men " Are cradled into poetry by wrong ; / They learn in suffering what they teach in song." *Lord Houghton.*

The world owes all its onward impulses to men ill at ease. *Hawthorne.*

10 The world owes infinitely more to those who have no history than to those who have ; and the silent noble ones, who have enriched and exalted it by their mere presence, form a much grander and greater host than those who whose names stand emblazoned in written story, and are the loud boast of all. *Ed.*

The world remains ever the same. *Goethe.*

The world seldom offers us any choice between solitude on the one hand and vulgarity on the other. *Schopenhauer.*

The world-spirit is a good swimmer, and storms and waves cannot drown him. *Emerson.*

The world still wants its poet-priest, who shall not trifle with Shakespeare, the player, nor shall grope in graves with Swedenborg, the mourner ; but who shall see, speak, and act with equal inspiration. *Emerson.*

15 The world that surrounds you is the magic glass of the world within you. To know yourself you have only to set down a true statement of those that ever loved or hated you. *Lavater.*

The world throws its life into a h ro or a shepherd, and puts him where he is wanted. Dante and Columbus were Italians in their time ; they would be Russians or Americans to-day. *Emerson.*

The world truly exists only in the presence of man, acts only in the passion of man. The essence of light is in his eyes—the centre of force in his soul—the pertinence of action in his deeds. *Ruskin.*

The world, which took but six days to make, is like to take six thousand to make out. *Sir Thomas Browne.*

The world's a bubble, and the life of man less than a span. *Bacon.*

20 The world's a room of sickness, where each heart / Knows its own anguish and unrest ! / The truest wisdom there, and noblest art, / Is his who skills of comfort best. *Kebie.*

The world's a sea. *Quarles.*

The world's a wood, in which all lose their way, / Though by a different path each goes astray. *Buckingham.*

The world's battle-fields have been in the heart chiefly. More heroism has there been displayed in the household and in the closet, I think, than on the most memorable military battle-fields of history. *Ward Beecher.*

The world's great men have not commonly been great scholars, nor its great scholars great men. *Holmes.*

The world's wealth is its original men ; by 25 these and their works it is a world and not a waste ; the memory and record of what Men it loves—this is the sum of its strength, its sacred " property for ever," whereby it upholds itself and steers forward, better or worse, through the yet undiscovered deep of Time. *Carlyle.*

The worse the man, the better the soldier ; if soldiers be not corrupt, they ought to be made so. *Napoleon.*

The worse things are, the better they are. *Pr.*

The worship of beauty apart from the soul becomes an idolatry enkindling desire instead of a reverence awakening devotion. *Ed.*

The worst deluded are the self-deluded. *Bovee.*

The worst education which teaches self-denial 30 is better than the best which teaches everything else, and not that. *John Sterling.*

The worst of madmen is a saint run mad. *Pope.*

The worst of many is that their goodness is distributed rather than concentrated. They are like a sheet of water instead of being like a running stream, which can be used to turn a wheel. *Spurgeon.*

The worst superstition is to consider our own the most tolerable. *Lessing.*

The worst wheel in the waggon creaks the loudest. *Ger. Pr.*

The worst wild beast is called " Tyrant," and 35 the " Flatterer" the worst tame one. *Lessing.*

The worth of a state, in the long-run, is the worth of the individuals composing it. *J. S. Mill.*

The wrath of brothers is fierce and devilish. *Pr.*

The wrath of man worketh not the righteousness of God. *St. James.*

The wretched have no friends. *Dryden.*

The wretchedness which fate has rendered 40 voiceless and tuneless is not the least wretched, but the most. *Carlyle.*

The wrinkles of the heart are more indelible than those of the brow. *Mme. Deluzy.*

The writer of a book, is not he a preacher preaching not to this parish or that, on this day or that, but to all men in all times and places ? *Carlyle.*

The wronged side is always the safest. *Sibbes.*

The young disease, that must subdue at length, / Grows with his growth, and strengthens with his strength. *Pope.*

The young mind is naturally pliable and imita- 45 tive, but in a more advanced state it grows rigid, and must be warmed and softened before it will receive a deep impression. *Joshua Reynolds.*

The young talk generously of relieving the old of their burdens, but the anxious heart is to the old when they see a load on the back of the young. *J. M. Barrie.*

The youth gets together his materials to build a bridge to the moon, or perchance a palace on the earth; at length middle-aged, he concludes to build a woodshed with them. *Thoreau.*

The youth of the soul is everlasting, and eternity is youth. *Jean Paul.*

Their angels do always behold the face of my Father which is in heaven. *Jesus of children.*

5 Their chief pleasure is being displeased. *Whipple.*

Their only labour was to kill the time, / And labour dire it is, and weary woe. *Thomson.*

Their own will to all men, all their will to women. *Gael. Pr.*

Their strength is to sit still. *Bible.*

Theirs not to make reply, / Theirs not to reason why, / Theirs but to do or die. *Tennyson.*

10 Them as ha' never had a cushion don't miss it. *George Eliot.*

Then draw we nearer day by day, / Each to his brethren, all to God; / Let the world take us as she may, / We must not change our road. *Keble.*

Then fare-ye-weel, auld Nickie Ben, / Oh wad ye tak' a thought and men', / Ye aiblins (perhaps) might—I dinna ken, / Still hae a stake; / I'm wae to think upon yon den / E'en for your sake. *Burns.*

Then gently scan your brother man, / Still gentler sister woman; / Though they may gang a kennin' wrang, / To step aside is human. *Burns.*

Then in the strife the youth puts forth his powers, / Knows what he is, and feels himself a man. *Goethe.*

15 Then let us pray that come it may, / As come it will for a' that, / That sense an' worth, o'er a' the earth, / May bear the gree and a' that. *Burns.*

Then was I as a tree / Whose boughs did bend with fruit; but, in one night, / A storm, or robbery, call it what you will, / Shook down my mellow hangings, nay, my leaves, / And left me bare to weather. *Cymbeline, iii. 3.*

Theology is anthropology. *Feuerbach.*

Theoretical principles must sometimes be suffered to give way for the sake of practical advantages. *Pitt.*

Theories of genius are the peculiar constructions of our philosophical times; ages of genius have passed away, and they left no other record than their works. *I. Disraeli.*

20 Theories are very thin and unsubstantial; experience only is tangible. *H. Ballou.*

Theories which do not connect measures with men are not theories for this world. *Charles Fox.*

Theory and practice always act upon one another. It is possible to construe from what we do what we think, and from what we think what we will do. *Goethe.*

Theory in and by itself is of no use except in so far as it proves to us the connection (*Zusammenhang*) that subsists among the phenomena. *Goethe.*

θεὸς ἡ ἀναίδεια—Impudence is a god.

There are a thousand occasions for sorrow, 25 and a hundred for fear that day by day assail the fool; not so the wise man. *Hitopadesa.*

There are always more tricks in a town than are talked of. *Cervantes.*

There are at bottom but two possible religions —that which rises in the moral nature of man, and which takes shape in moral commandments, and that which grows out of the observance of the material energies which operate in the external universe. *Froude.*

There are attractions in modest diffidence above the force of words. A silent address is the genuine eloquence of sincerity. *Goldsmith.*

There are but three classes of men—the retrograde, the stationary, and the progressive. *Lavater.*

There are but two ways of paying debt—in-30 crease of industry in raising income; increase of thrift in laying it out. *Carlyle.*

There are cases where little can be said and much must be done. *Johnson.*

There are certain things in which mediocrity is not to be endured, such as poetry, music, painting, public speaking. *La Bruyère.*

There are certain times in our life when we find ourselves in circumstances, that not only press upon us, but seem to weigh us down altogether. They give us, however, not only the opportunity, but they impose on us the duty of elevating ourselves, and thereby fulfilling the purpose of the Divine Being in our creation. *Goethe.*

There are charms made only for distant admiration. No spectacle is nobler than a blaze. *Johnson.*

There are cloudy days for the mind as well as 35 for the world, and the man who has the most genius is twenty times a day in the clouds. *Beaumelle.*

There are depths in the soul which are deeper than hell. *Platen.*

There are enough unhappy on this earth. *Tennyson.*

There are faces so fluid with expression that we can hardly find what the mere features are. *Emerson.*

There are falsehoods which are not lies . . . which is the case in parables, fables, &c. . . . In such instances no confidence is destroyed, because none was reposed; no promise to speak the truth is violated, because none was given. *Paley.*

There are few circumstances in which it is not 40 best either to hide all or to tell all. *La Bruyère.*

There are few faces that can afford to smile. A smile is sometimes bewitching; in general vapid; often a contortion. *Disraeli.*

There are few men so obstinate in their atheism whom a pressing danger will not reduce to an acknowledgment of the Divine power. *Plato.*

There are few persons to whom truth is not a sort of insult. *Ségur.*

There are few things that are worthy of anger, and still fewer that can justify malignity. *Johnson.*

There are few thoughts likely to come across ordinary men which have not already been expressed by greater men in the best possible way ; and it is a wiser, more generous, more noble thing to remember and point out the perfect words than to invent poorer ones, wherewith to encumber temporarily the world. *Ruskin.*

There are few who, either by extraordinary endowment or favour of fortune, have enjoyed the opportunity of deciding what mode of life in especial they would wish to embrace. *Cic.*

There are few wild beasts more to be dreaded than a communicative man having nothing to communicate. *Bovee.*

There are fewer students of man than of geometry. *Pascal.*

5 There are forty men of wit for one of sense ; and he that will carry nothing about him but gold, will be every day at a loss for want of ready change. (?)

There are heads sometimes so little that there is no room for wit, sometimes so long that there is no wit for so much room. *Fuller.*

There are in man, in the beginning / And at the end, two blank book-binder's leaves— childhood and age. *Jean Paul.*

There are in the history of a man only three epochs, his birth, his life, and his death ; he is not conscious of being born ; he submits to die ; and he forgets to live. *La Bruyère.*

There are in this day, as in all days, around and in every man, voices from the gods, imperative to all, if obeyed by even none, which say audibly : Arise, thou son of Adam, son of Time, make this thing more divine, and that thing, and thyself of all things, and work, and sleep not ; for the Night cometh wherein no man can work. *Carlyle.*

10 There are in this loud stunning tide / Of human care and crime, / With whom the melodies abide / Of th' everlasting chime ; / Who carry music in their heart, / Through dusty lane and wrangling mart, / Plying their daily task with busier feet, / Because their secret souls a holy strain repeat. *Keble.*

There are interests by the sacrifice of which peace is too dearly purchased. One should never be at peace to the shame of his own soul, to the violation of his integrity or of his allegiance to God. *Chapin.*

There are many men who do not believe in evaporation. They get all they can, and keep all they get, and so are not fertilisers, but only stagnant, miasmatic pools. *Ward Beecher.*

There are many religions, but there is only one morality. *Ruskin.*

There are many troubles which you cannot cure by the Bible and the hymn-book, but which you can cure by a good perspiration and a breath of fresh air. *Ward Beecher.*

15 There are many truths of which the full meaning cannot be realised until personal experience has brought it home. *J. S. Mill.*

There are men who, by long consulting their own inclination, have forgotten that others have a claim to the same deference. (?)

There are men who dwell on the defects of their enemies. I always have regard to the merits of mine, and derive profit therefrom. *Goethe.*

There are men whose tongues are more eloquent than those of women, but no man possesses the eloquence of a woman's eye. *C. Weber.*

There are moments in life when the heart is so full of emotion, / That if by chance it be shaken, or into its depths like a pebble / Drops some careless word, it overflows ; and its secret, / Spilt on the ground like water, can never be gathered together. *Longfellow.*

There are more fools than wise men, and even 20 in the wise men more folly than wisdom. *Chamfort.*

There are more men ennobled by study than by nature. *Cic.*

There are more offences at my beck than I have thoughts to put them in, imagination to give them shape, or time to act them in. *Ham.*, iii. 1.

There are more things in heaven and earth, Horatio, / Than are dreamt of in your philosophy. *Ham.*, i. 5.

There are more ways to the wood than one. *Pr.*

There are nae fules like auld fules. *Sc. Pr.* 25

There are natures that are great by what they attain, and others by what they disdain. *H. Grimm.*

There are no better masters than poverty and want. *Dut. Pr.*

There are no chagrins so venomous as the chagrins of the idle ; no pangs so sickening as the satieties of pleasure. *Ruskin.*

There are no English lives worth reading except those of players, who by the nature of the case have bidden Respectability good-day. *Carlyle.*

There are no fixtures in Nature. The universe 30 is fluid and volatile. *Emerson.*

There are no grotesques in Nature. *Sir Thomas Browne.*

There are no laws by which we can write Iliads. *Ruskin.*

There are no obstructions more fatal to fortune than pride and resentment. *Goldsmith.*

There are no persons more solicitous about the preservation of rank than those who have no rank at all. *Shenstone.*

There are no proverbial sayings which are not 35 true. *Cervantes.*

There are no real pleasures without real needs. *Voltaire.*

There are no tricks in plain and simple faith. *Jul. Cæs.*, iv. 2.

There are no troubles which have such a wasting and disastrous effect upon the mind as those which must not be told, but which cause the mind to be continually rolling and turning over upon itself in ceaseless convolutions and unrest. *Ward Beecher.*

There are no twin souls in God's universe. *J. G. Holland.*

There are none but men of strong passions 40 capable of going to greatness ; none but such capable of meriting the public gratitude. *Mirabeau.*

There are none of the charges brought against Socialism which might not have been brought against Christianity itself. *Cötvös.*

There are omens in the air, / And voices whispering Beware !— / But never victor in the fight / Heeded the portents of fear and care. *Dr. Walter Smith.*

There are only three classes of people—those who have found God and serve him ; those who have not found God and seek him ; and those who live without either seeking or finding him—the first, rational and happy ; the second, unhappy and rational ; the third, foolish and unhappy. *Pascal.*

There are only two ways of rising in the world, either by one's own industry or by the weakness of others. *La Bruyère.*

5 There are people who will help you to get your basket on your head, because they want to see what's in it. *Negro Pr.*

There are people who would never have been in love if they had never heard love spoken of. *La Roche.*

There are proselytes from atheism, but none from superstition. *Junius.*

There are several who would, or at least pretend they would, bear much in their own business who will bear nothing at all. *Kettlewell.*

There are shades in all good pictures, but there are lights too, if we choose to contemplate them. *Dickens.*

10 There are single thoughts that contain the essence of a whole volume, single sentences that have the beauties of a large work. *Joubert.*

There are soldiers of the ploughshare as well as soldiers of the sword. *Ruskin.*

There are some cases in which human nature and its deep wrongs will be ever stronger than the world and its philosophy. *Bulwer Lytton.*

There are some faults so nearly allied to excellence that we can scarce weed out the vice without eradicating the virtue. *Goldsmith.*

There are some men who are witty when they are in a bad humour, and others only when they are sad. *Joubert.*

15 There are some people who give with the air of refusal. *Queen Christiana.*

There are some sorrows cannot be subjected / To man's construction, howsoe'er suspected. *Dr. Walter Smith.*

There are some trifles well habited, as there are some fools well clothed. *Chamfort.*

There are sorrows / Where of necessity the soul must be / Its own support. *Schiller.*

There are souls which fall from heaven like flowers ; but ere the pure and fresh buds can open, they are trodden in the dust of the earth, and lie soiled and crushed under the foul tread of some brutal hoof. *Jean Paul.*

20 There are things in this world to be laughed at, as well as things to be admired ; and his is no complete mind that cannot give to each sort his due. *Carlyle.*

There are things that should be done, not spoken ; that, till the doing of them is begun, cannot be spoken. *Carlyle.*

There are those who never reason on what they should do, but what they have done ; as if Reason had her eyes behind, and could only see backwards. *Fielding.*

There are thousands hacking at the branches of evil to one who is striking at the root. *Thoreau.*

There are three classes of authors—those who write without thinking, those who think while writing, and those who think before writing. *Schopenhauer.*

There are three difficulties in authorship—to 25 write anything worth the publishing, to find honest men to publish it, and to get sensible men to read it. *Colton.*

There are three material things, not only useful, but essential, to life—pure air, water, and earth ; and three immaterial that are equally essential — admiration, hope, and love. *Ruskin.*

There are three means of believing—by inspiration, by reason, and by custom. Christianity, which is the only rational institution, does yet admit none for its sons who do not believe by inspiration. *Pascal.*

There are three religions—the religion which depends on reverence for what is above us, denominated the ethnic ; the religion which founds itself on reverence for what is around us, denominated the philosophical ; the religion grounded on reverence for what is beneath us, which we name the Christian. *Goethe.*

There are three things in this world which deserve no quarter — hypocrisy, pharisaism, and tyranny. *F. Robertson.*

There are three things which cause perfection 30 in a man—nature, reason, use. Reason I call discipline ; use, exercise. If any one of these branches want, certainly the tree of virtue must needs wither. *John Lily.*

There are times when silence, if the preacher did but know, / Shall preach to better purpose than a sermon stale and flat. *Dr. Walter Smith.*

There are times when we are diverted out of errors, but could not be preached out of them. *Stephen Montague.*

There are truths that shield themselves behind veils, and are best spoken by implication. Even the sun veils himself in his own rays to blind the gaze of the too curious starer. *A. B. Alcott.*

There are two, and only two, forms of possible gospel or "good message"—one, that men are saved by themselves doing what is right ; and the other, that they are saved by believing that somebody also did right instead of them. The first of these gospels is eternally true and holy ; the other eternally false, damnable, and damning. *Ruskin.*

There are two kinds of genius. The first and 35 highest may be said to speak out of the eternal into the present, and must compel its age to understand it ; the second understands its age, and tells it what it wishes to be told. *Lowell.*

There are two levers for moving men—interest and fear. *Napoleon.*

There are two modes of establishing our reputation—to be praised by honest men, and to be abused by rogues. It is best, however, to secure the former, because it will be invariably accompanied by the latter. *Colton.*

There are two sides to every question. *Pr.*

There are two things that can reach the top of a pyramid, the eagle and the reptile. *D'Alembert.*

There are two ways of attaining an important end—force and perseverance; the silent power of the latter grows irresistible with time. *Mme. Swetchine.*

There are unhappy times in the world's history, when he that is the least educated will chiefly have to say that he is the least perverted; and with the multitude of false eye-glasses, convex, concave, green, even yellow, has not lost the natural use of his eyes. *Carlyle.*

5 There are very few moments in a man's existence when he experiences so much ludicrous distress, or meets with so little charitable commiseration, as when he is in pursuit of his own hat. *Dickens.*

There are very few people in this world who get any good by either writing or reading. *Ruskin.*

There are, whom heaven has blessed with store of wit, / Yet want as much again to manage it ; / For wit and judgment ever are at strife, / Tho' meant each other's aid, like man and wife. *Pope.*

There are words which are worth as much as the best actions, for they contain the germ of them all. *Mme. Swetchine.*

There be some that think their wits have been asleep, except they dart out somewhat that is piquant, and to the quick ; that is a vein which would be bridled. *Bacon.*

10 There can be no excess to love, none to knowledge, none to beauty, when these attributes are considered in the purest sense. *Emerson.*

There can be no kernel in this light nut; the soul of this man is in his clothes. *All's Well*, ii. 5.

There can be no profanity where there is no fane behind. *Thoreau.*

There can be no shame in accepting orders from those who have themselves learned to obey. *W. E. Forster.*

There can be no true aristocracy but must possess the land. *Carlyle.*

15 There can come no harm of supposing every other man better than yourself; but the supposing any man worse than yourself may be attended with very ill consequences. *Thomas à Kempis.*

There coils a fear beneath the loveliest dream. *T. Watts.*

There hath no temptation taken you but such as is common to man. *St. Paul.*

There have been in all ages children of God and of man ; the one born of the Spirit, and obeying it ; the other born of the flesh, and obeying it. *Ruskin.*

There in others' looks discover / What thy own life's course has been, / And thy deeds of years past over, / In thy fellow-men be seen. *Goethe.*

20 There is a better thing than the great man who is always speaking, and that is the great man who only speaks when he has a great word to say. *W. Winter.*

There is a black speck, say the Arabs, were it no bigger than a bean's eye, in every soul ; which, once set a-working, will overcloud the whole man into darkness and quasi-madness, and hurry him balefully into night. *Carlyle.*

There is a book, who runs may read, / Which heavenly truth imparts, / And all the love its scholars need, / Pure eyes and Christian hearts. / The works of God above, below, / Within us, and around, / Are pages in that book, to show / How God Himself is found. *Keble.*

There is a budding morrow in midnight. *Keats.*

There is a care for trifles which proceeds from love and conscience, and is most holy ; and a care for trifles which comes of idleness and frivolity, and is most base. And so, also, there is a gravity proceeding from thought, which is most noble ; and a gravity proceeding from dulness and mere incapability of enjoyment, which is most base. *Ruskin.*

There is a Cato in every man ; a severe censor 25 of his manners. And he that reverences this judge will seldom do anything he need repent of. *Burton.*

There is a certain artificial polish, a commonplace vivacity, acquired by perpetually mingling in the beau monde, which, in the commerce of the world, supplies the place of natural suavity and good-humour ; but it is purchased at the expense of all original and sterling traits of character. *Washington Irving.*

There is a certain mien and motion of the body and all its parts, both in acting and speaking, which argues a man well within. *Sterne.*

There is a certain noble pride through which merits shine brighter than through modesty. *Jean Paul.*

There is a country accent, not in speech only, but in thought, conduct, character, and manner of existing, which never forsakes a man. *La Roche.*

There is a crack in everything God has made. 30 *Emerson.*

There is a devil dwells in man as well as a divinity. *Carlyle.*

There is a different kind of knowledge good for every different creature, and the glory of the higher creatures is in ignorance of what is known to the lower. *Ruskin.*

There is a flush of the body which is full of warmth and life, and another which will pass into putrefaction. *Ruskin.*

There is a foolish corner even in the brain of the sage. *Arist.*

There is a frightful interval between the seed 35 and the timber. *Johnson.*

There is a glare about worldly success, which is very apt to dazzle men's eyes. *Hare.*

There is a God within us who breathes that divine fire by which we are animated. *Ovid.*

There is a great deal of folly in talking unnecessarily of one's private affairs. *Burns.*

There is a great difference between bearing malice, which is always ungenerous, and a resolute self-defence, which is always prudent and justifiable. *Chesterfield.*

There is a great discovery still to be made in 40 literature, that of paying literary men by the quantity they do not write. *Carlyle.*

There is a heroic innocence, as well as a heroic courage. *St. Evremond.*

There is a higher law than the constitution. *W. H. Seward.*

There is a history in all men's lives, / Figuring the nature of the times deceased; / The which observed, a man may prophesy, / With a near aim of the main chance of things / As yet not come to life: which, in their seeds / And weak beginnings, lie intreasurèd. *2 Hen. IV.*, iii. 1.

There is a kind of pride in which are included all the commandments of God, and a kind of vanity which contains the seven mortal sins. *Chamfort.*

There is a life which taketh not its hues / From earth or earthly things; and so grows pure / And higher than the petty cares of men, / And is a blessed life and glorified. *Lewis Morris.*

There is a living, literal communion of saints, wide as the world itself, and as the history of the world. *Carlyle.*

5 There is a long and wearisome step between admiration and imitation. *Jean Paul.*

There is a lust in man no charm can tame, / Of loudly publishing his neighbour's shame; / On eagle's wings immortal scandals fly, / While virtuous actions are but born and die. *Harvey.*

There is a magic in a great name. *S. Lover.*

There is a magic in the memory of schoolboy friendships; it softens the heart, and even affects the nervous system of those who have no hearts. *Disraeli.*

There is a mean in all things. Even virtue itself hath its stated limits; which not being strictly observed, it ceases to be virtue. (?)

10 There is a measure of self-regard which is right, wherein the individual self is identified with the universal self. *J. C. Sharp.*

There is a mercy that is weakness, and even treason against the common good. *George Eliot.*

There is a method in man's wickedness, / It grows by degrees. *Beaumont and Fletcher.*

There is a nobler ambition than the getting of all California, or the getting of all the suffrages that are on the planet just now. *Carlyle.*

There is a perennial nobleness, and even sacredness, in work. Were he ever so benighted, forgetful of his high calling, there is always hope in a man that actually and earnestly works. *Carlyle.*

15 There is a period of life when our backward movements are steps in advance. *Rousseau.*

There is a pleasure in poetic pains which only poets know. *Cowper.*

There is a pleasure in the pathless woods; / There is a rapture on the lonely shore; / There is society, where none intrudes, / By the deep sea, and music in its roar; / I love not the man the less, / But Nature more. *Byron.*

There is a pleasure, sure, in being mad, which none but mad men know. *Dryden.*

There is a power over and behind us, and we are the channels of its communication. *Emerson.*

20 There is a probity of manners as well as of conscience, and a true Christian will regard in a degree the conventionalities of society. *De Boufflers.*

There is a property in the horizon which no man has but he whose eye can integrate all the parts—that is, the poet. *Emerson.*

There is a rabble amongst the gentry as well as the commonalty; a sort of plebeian heads, whose fancy moves in the same wheel with the others,—men in the same level with mechanics, though their fortunes do somewhat gild their infirmities, and their purses compound for their follies. *Sir Thomas Browne.*

There is a remedy for everything but death. *Cervantes.*

There is a remedy for every wrong, and a satisfaction for every soul. *Emerson.*

There is a sacredness in tears. They are not *25* the mark of weakness, but of power. They speak more eloquently than ten thousand tongues. They are the messengers of overwhelming grief, of deep contrition, and of unspeakable love. *Washington Irving.*

There is a skeleton in every house. *Pr.*

There is a snake in the grass. *Pr.*

There is a Spanish proverb that a lapidary who would grow rich must buy of those who go to be executed, as not caring how cheap they sell; and sell to those who go to be married, as not caring how dear they buy. *Fuller.*

There is a special providence in the fall of a sparrow. *Ham.*, v. 1.

There is a spirit of resistance implanted by *30* the Deity in the breast of man, proportioned to the size of the wrongs he is destined to endure. *C. J. Fox.*

There is a Sunday conscience as well as a Sunday coat; and those who make religion a secondary concern put the coat and conscience carefully by to put on only once a week. *Dickens.*

There is a sweet little cherub that sits up aloft, to keep watch for the life of poor Jack. *Dibdin.*

There is a tendency in things to right themselves. *Emerson.*

There is a third silent party to all our bargains. The nature and soul of things takes on itself the guarantee of the fulfilment of every contract, so that honest service cannot come to loss. *Emerson.*

There is a tide in the affairs of men, / Which, *35* taken at the flood, leads on to fortune; / Omitted, all the voyage of their life / Is bound in shallows and in miseries; / On such a full sea are we now afloat; / And we must take the current when it serves, / Or lose our ventures. *Jul. Cæs.*, iv. 3.

There is a time for all things. *Pr.*

There is a time in every man's education when he arrives at the conviction that envy is ignorance. *Emerson.*

There is a time of life beyond which we cannot form a tie worth the name of friendship. *Burns.*

There is a time there for every purpose and for every work. *Bible.*

There is a time wherein one man ruleth over *40* another to his own hurt. *Bible.*

There is a true Church whenever one meets another helpfully, and that is the only holy or Mother Church which ever was or ever shall be. *Ruskin.*

There is a way which seemeth right unto a man, but the end thereof are the ways of death. *Bible.*

There is a worth in honest ignorance ; 'twere almost a pity to exchange for knowledge. *Sterne.*

There is always life for a living one. *Pr.*

There is always room for a man of force, and he makes room for many. *Emers:n.*

There is always some levity in excellent minds ; they have wings to rise and also to stray. *Joubert.*

5 There is always the possibility of beauty where there is an unsealed human eye ; of music where there is an unstopped human ear ; and of inspiration where there is a receptive human spirit, a spirit standing before. *C. H. Parkhurst.*

There is an abasement because of glory, and there is that lifteth up his head from a low estate. *Ecclus.*, xx. 11.

There is an anger that is majestic as the frown of Jehovah's brow ; it is the anger of truth and love. *Ward Beecher.*

There is an emanation from the heart in genuine hospitality which cannot be described but is immediately felt, and puts the stranger at once at his ease. *Washington Irving.*

There is a heroic innocence, as well a heroic courage. (?)

10 There is an insolence which none but those who deserve some contempt themselves can bestow, and those only who deserve no contempt can bear. *Fielding.*

There is as much difference between the counsel that a friend giveth and that a man giveth himself, as there is between the counsel of a friend and of a flatterer. *Bacon.*

There is as much ingenuity in making an felicitous application of an passage as in being the author of it. *St. Evremond.*

There is, at any given moment, a best path for every man ; the thing which, here and now, it were wisest for him to do ; whatsoever forwards him in that, were it even in the shape of blows and spurnings, is liberty ; whatsoever hinders him, were it tremendous cheers and rivers of heavy wet, is slavery. *Carlyle.*

There is but one case wherein a man may commend himself with good grace, and that is in commending virtue in another, especially if it be such a virtue whereunto himself pretendeth. *Bacon.*

15 There is but one class of men to be trembled at, and that is the stupid class, the class that cannot see ; who, alas ! are mainly they that will not see. *Carlyle.*

There is but one misfortune for a man, when some idea lays hold of him which exerts no influence upon his active life, or still more, which withdraws him from it. *Goethe.*

There is but one philosophy, and its name is Fortitude ; to bear is to conquer our fate. *Bulwer.*

There is but one solid basis of happiness, and that is the reasonable hope of a happy futurity. This may be had everywhere. *Johnson.*

There is but one temple in the world, and that is the body of man. Nothing is holier than this high form. Bending before men is a reverence done to this revelation in the flesh. We touch heaven when we lay our hand on a human body. *Novalis.*

There is but one thing without honour, smitten 20 with eternal barrenness, inability to do or to be—insincerity, unbelief. He who believes nothing, who believes only the shows of things, is not in relation with nature and fact at all. *Carlyle.*

There is certainly something of exquisite kindness and thoughtful benevolence in that rarest of gifts—fine breeding. *Bulwer Lytton.*

There is differency between a grub and a butterfly ; yet your butterfly was a grub. *Coriolanus*, v. 4.

There is enjoyment even in sadness, and the same souvenirs which have produced long regrets may also soften them. *De Boufflers.*

There is ever a certain languor attending the fulness of prosperity. When the heart has no more to wish, it yawns over its possessions, and the energy of the soul goes out, like a flame that has no more to devour. *Young.*

There is evil in every human heart, which may 25 remain latent, perhaps through the whole of life ; but circumstances may rouse it to activity. *Hawthorne.*

There is far less pleasure in doing a thing beautifully than in seeing it beautifully done. *Ruskin.*

There is for the soul a spontaneous culture, on which depends all its real progress in perfection. *Degerando.*

There is forgiveness with God and Christ for the passing sin of the hot heart, but none for the eternal and inherent sin of the cold. *Ruskin.*

There is genius of a nation, which is not to be found in the citizen, but which characterises the society. *Emerson.*

There is great force hidden in a sweet com- 30 mand. *George Herbert.*

There is in human nature an essential, though somewhat mysterious, connection of love with fear. *Henry Taylor.*

There is in human nature generally more of the fool than of the wise, and therefore those faculties by which the foolish part of men's minds is taken are most potent. *Bacon.*

There is in man a Higher than love of happiness ; he can do without happiness, and instead thereof find blessedness ! *Carlyle.*

There is in nature an accessible and an inaccessible. Be careful to discriminate between the two. Be circumspect, and proceed with reverence. . . . It is always difficult to see where the one begins and the other leaves off. He who knows it, and is wise, will confine himself to the accessible. *Goethe.*

There is in the heart of woman such a deep 35 well of love that no age can freeze it. *Bulwer Lytton.*

There is in this world infinitely more joy than pain to be shared, if you will only take your share when it is set before you. *Ruskin.*

There is little hope of equity where rebellion reigns. *Sir P. Sidney.*

There is little wisdom in knowing that every man must be up and doing, and that all mankind are made dependent on one another. *Dickens.*

There is more concern nowadays to interpret interpretations than to interpret things, and more books about books than about any other subject. We do nothing but expound one another. (?)

There is more danger in a reserved and silent friend than in a noisy babbling enemy. *L'Estrange.*

There is more pleasure in loving than in being beloved. *Pr.*

There is more serfdom in England now than at any time since the Conquest. *Disraeli.*

5 There is music in all things, if men had ears. *Byron.*

There is need, bitter need, to bring back, if we may, into men's minds, that to live is nothing unless to live be to know him by whom we live, and that He is not to be known amidst the hurry of crowds and crash of innovation, but in solitary places, and out of the glowing intelligence which he gave to men of old. *Ruskin.*

There is never a beginning, there is never an end, to the inexplicable continuity of the web of God, but always circular power returning into itself. *Emerson.*

There is never but one opportunity of a kind. *Thoreau.*

There is no better counsellor than time. *Pr.*

10 There is no better sign of a brave mind than a hard hand. *2 Hen. VI.*, iv. 2.

There is no better type of a perfectly free creature than the common house-fly. *Ruskin.*

There is no bridge from one being to another, each a self, each rests on itself, and wills only itself, knows only itself, understands only itself. *Hamerling.*

There is no brotherhood possible, at any rate stable, between man and man but a brotherhood of labour. *Ed.*

There is no cause why one man's nose is longer than another's, but because that God pleases to have it so. *Sterne.*

15 There is no class of men so difficult to be managed in a state, as those whose intentions are honest, but whose consciences are bewitched. *Napoleon.*

There is no communion possible among men who believe only in hearsays. *Carlyle.*

There is no contingency, and what to us seems only blind chance is an efflux from the depths of being. *Schiller.*

There is no courage but in innocence; no constancy but in an honest cause. *Southern.*

There is no creature so lonely as the dweller in the intellect. *W. Winter.*

20 There is no darkness but ignorance. *Twelfth Night*, iv. 2.

There is no darkness unto the conscience, which can see without light. *Sir T. Browne.*

There is no dearth of charity in the world in giving, but there is comparatively little exercised in thinking and speaking. *Sir P. Sidney.*

There is no defence against reproach but obscurity. *Addison.*

There is no den in the wide world to hide a rogue. Commit a crime, and the earth is made of glass. *Emerson.*

There is no despair so absolute as that which 25 comes with the first moments of our first great sorrow, when we have not yet known what it is to have suffered and be healed, to have despaired and have recovered hope. *George Eliot.*

There is no detraction worse than to overpraise a man. *Owen Feltham.*

There is no direr disaster in love than the death of imagination. *George Meredith.*

There is no dispute managed without passion, and yet there is scarce a dispute worth a passion. *Sherlock.*

There is no disputing against hobby-horses. *Sterne.*

There is no education like adversity. *Disraeli.* 30

There is no end in nature, but every end is a beginning. *Emerson.*

There is no end of settlements; there will never be an end; the best settlement is but a temporary partial one. *Carlyle.*

There is no event but sprung somewhere from the soul of man. (?)

There is no evil but is mingled with good. *Guicciardini.*

There is no extremity of distress which of 35 itself ought to reduce a great nation to despair. It is not the disorder, but the physician . . . which alone can make a whole people desperate. *Junius.*

There is no fatigue so wearisome as that which comes from want of work. *Spurgeon.*

There is no fear in love; but perfect love casteth out fear. *St. John.*

There is no fiercer hell than failure in a great object. *Keats.*

There is no flock, however watched and tended, / But one dead lamb is there; / There is no fireside, howsoe'er defended, / But has one vacant chair. *Longfellow.*

There is no foolishest man but knows one and 40 the other thing more clearly than any the wisest man does. *Carlyle.*

There is no gambling like politics. . . . Nothing in which the power of circumstance is more evident. *Disraeli.*

There is no genuine love for art without an ardent love for humanity. *Fr. Horn.*

There is no Gethsemane without its angel. *Rev. T. Binney.*

There is no ghost so difficult to lay as the ghost of an injury. *Alexander Smith.*

There is no God but God, the living, the self-45 subsisting. *Koran.*

There is no going to heaven in a sedan. *Pr.*

There is no good in arguing with the inevitable. *Lowell.*

There is no good in emitting smoke till you have made it into fire, which all smoke is capable of becoming. *Carlyle.*

There is no great and no small / To the soul that maketh all; / And where it cometh, all things are; / And it cometh everywhere. *Emerson.*

There is no great genius free from some tinc-50 ture of madness. *Sen.*

There is no greater evil among men than a testament framed with injustice; where caprice hath guided the boon, or dishonesty refused what was due. *Tupper.*

There is no greater fraud than a promise unfulfilled. *Gael. Pr.*

There is no greater proof of human weakness than that which betrays itself in the boast of fortune and ancestry ; these cannot ennoble us, but our conduct in life may ennoble or degrade them. *Arliss.*

There is no greater punishment than that of being abandoned to one's self. *Pasquier Quesnel.*

There is no greater wisdom than well to time the beginnings and onset of things. *Bacon.*

5 There is no grief like hate ! no pains like passions ! no deceit like sense ! Enter the path ! far hath he gone whose foot treads down one fond offence. *Sir Edwin Arnold.*

There is no grief that time will not soften. *Pr.*

There is no harm in anybody thinking that Christ is in bread. The harm is in the expectation of His presence in gunpowder. *Ruskin.*

There is no heroic poem in the world but is at bottom a biography, the life of a man ; and there is no life of a man, faithfully recorded, but is a heroic poem of its sort, rhymed or unrhymed. *Carlyle.*

There is no jesting with edge tools. *Pr.*

10 There is no joy without alloy. *Pr.*

There is no hiding of evil but not to do it. *Gael. Pr.*

There is no index of character so sure as the voice. *Disraeli.*

There is no legislation for liars and traitors ; they cannot be prevented from the pit ; the earth finally swallows them. . . . There is no law for these but gravitation. *Ruskin.*

There is no less invention in aptly applying a thought found in a book than in being the first author of the thought. *Bayle.*

15 There is no lie that many men will not believe ; there is no man who does not believe many lies ; and there is no man who believes only lies. *J. Sterling.*

There is no loss / In being small ; great bulks but swell with dross. / Man is heaven's masterpiece ; if it appear / More great, the value's less ; if less, more dear. *Quarles.*

There is no lustre (*Glanz*) without light ; that is the first rule to which every author should pay regard. *Cötvös.*

There is no man alone, because every man is a microcosm, and carries the whole world about him. *Sir Thomas Browne.*

There is no man on the streets whose biography I would not like to be acquainted with. *(?)*

20 There is no man so friendless but that he can find a friend sincere enough to tell him disagreeable truths. *Bulwer Lytton.*

There is no man so rudely punished as he that is subject to the whip of his own remorse. *Sen.*

There is no man that has not his hour, nor is there anything that has not its place. *Rabbi Ben Azai.*

There is no man that hath power over the spirit to retain the spirit ; neither hath he power in the day of death : and there is no discharge in that war. *Bible.*

There is no man that imparteth his joys to his friend, but he joyeth the more ; and no man that imparteth his griefs to his friend, but he grieveth the less. *Bacon.*

There is no man whom fortune does not visit 25 once in his life ; but when she does not find him ready to receive her, she walks in at the door, and flies out at the window. *Quoted by Montesquieu.*

There is no merit where there is no trial ; and, till experience stamps the mark of strength, cowards may pass for heroes, faith for falsehood. *Aaron Hill.*

There is no mistake ; there has been no mistake ; and there shall be no mistake. *Wellington.*

There is no more fatal blunderer than he who consumes the greater part of his life getting his living. *Thoreau.*

There is no more potent antidote to low sensuality than the adoration of beauty. *Schlegel.*

There is no more welcome gift to men than a 30 new symbol. *Emerson.*

There is no mortal extant, out of the depths of Bedlam, but lives all skinned, thatched, covered over with formulas ; and is, as it were, held in from delirium and the inane by his formulas. These are the most beneficent and indispensable of human equipments ; blessed be who has a skin and tissues, so it be a living one, and the heart-pulse everywhere discernible through it. *Carlyle.*

There is no mortal truly wise and restless at once ; wisdom is the repose of minds. *Lavater.*

There is no new thing under the sun. *Bible.*

There is no object of desire the supreme vanity of which we do not recognise and confess when once we have embraced it. *Renan.*

There is no object so foul that intense light 35 will not make beautiful. And the stimulus it affords to the sense, and a sort of infinitude which it hath like space and time, make all matter gay. *Emerson.*

There is no one the friend of another ; there is no one the enemy of another : friends, as well as enemies, are created through our transactions. *Hitopadesa.*

There is no one who does not exaggerate. *Emerson.*

There is no ordinance obliging us to fight those who are stronger than ourselves. Such fighting, as it were, with an elephant, is the same as men's fighting against rocks. *Hitopadesa.*

There is no other ghost save the ghost of our own childhood, the ghost of our own innocence, the ghost of our own airy belief. *Dickens.*

There is no other revelation than the thoughts 40 of the wise. *Schopenhauer.*

There is no outward sign of courtesy that does not rest on a deep moral foundation. *Goethe.*

There is no part of the furniture of a man's mind which he has a greater right to exult in than that which he has hewn and fashioned for himself. *Ruskin.*

There is no part of the world from whence we may not admire these planets, which roll, like ours, in different orbits round the same central sun ; . . . and whilst my soul is thus raised up to heaven, it imports me little what ground I tread upon. *Bolingbroke.*

There is no patriotic art and no patriotic science. *Goethe.*

There is no peace in ambition; it is always gloomy, and often unreasonably so. The kindness of the king, the regards of the courtiers, the attachment of my domestics, and the fidelity of a large number of friends, make me happy no longer. *Mme. de Pompadour.*

There is no permanence in doubt; it incites the mind to closer inquiry and experiment, from which, if rightly managed, certainty proceeds, and in this alone can man find thorough satisfaction. *Goethe.*

There is no permanent love but that which has duty for its eldest brother; so that if one sleeps the other watches, and honour is safe. *Stahl.*

There is no place like home. *J. H. Payne.*

5 There is no place where earth's sorrows / Are more felt than up in heaven; / There is no place where earth's failings / Have such kindly judgment given. *F. W. Faber.*

There is no policy like politeness; and a good manner is the best thing in the world, either to get a good name or to supply the want of it. *Bulwer Lytton.*

There is no pure malignity in nature. *Emerson.*

There is no qualification for government but virtue and wisdom. *Burke.*

There is no real life but cheerful life. *Addison.*

10 There is no repose for the mind except in the absolute. *Amiel.*

There is no respect for others without humility in one's self. *Amiel.*

There is no respect of persons with God. *St. Paul.*

There is no returning from a *dégout* given by satiety. *Lady Montagu.*

There is no riches above a sound body, and no joy above the joy of the heart. *Ecclus.*

15 There is no right faith in believing what is true, unless we believe it because it is true. *Whately.*

There is no road too long to the man who advances deliberately and without undue haste; there are no honours too distant to the man who prepares himself for them with patience. *La Bruyère.*

There is no royal road to geometry. *Euclid.*

There is no sanctuary of virtue like home. *E. Everett.*

There is no solemnity so deep, to a right thinking creature, as that of dawn. *Ruskin.*

20 There is no solitude in nature. *Schiller.*

There is no solitude more dreadful for a stranger, an isolated man, than a great city. So many thousands, and not one friend. *Boiste.*

There is no spirit without a body unless it be a ghost, and no body without a spirit unless it be a corpse. *German lore.*

There is no sporting with a fellow-creature's happiness or misery. *Burns.*

There is no sterner moralist than pleasure. *Byron.*

25 There is no stronger test of a man's real character than power and authority, exciting, as they do, every passion, and discovering every latent vice. *Plutarch.*

There is no such flatterer as is a man's self, and there is no such remedy against flattery of a man's self as the liberty of a friend. *Lord Bacon.*

There is no such thing as a dumb poet or a handless painter. The essence of an artist is that he should be articulate. *Stedman.*

There is no such thing as being agreeable without a thorough good-humour, a natural sweetness of temper, enlivened by cheerfulness. *Lady Montagu.*

There is no such thing as chance; and what seems to us merest accident springs from the deepest source of destiny. *Schiller.*

There is no such thing as Liberty in the uni- 30 verse: there can never be. The stars have it not; the earth has it not; the sea has it not; and we men have the mockery and semblance of it only for our heaviest punishment. *Ruskin.*

There is no sure foundation set on blood; / No certain life achieved by others' death. *King John*, iv. 2.

There is no surer argument of a weak mind than irresolution. *Tillotson.*

There is no terror, Cassius, in your threats; / For I am armed so strong in honesty / That they pass by me as the idle wind / Which I respect not. *Jul. Cæs.*, iv. 3.

There is no thought in any mind, but it quickly tends to convert itself into a power, and organises a huge instrumentality of means. *Emerson.*

There is no time so miserable, but a man may 35 be true. *Timon of Athens*, iv. 3.

There is no traitor like him whose domestic treason plants the poniard within the breast which trusted to his truth. *Byron.*

There is no true action without will. *Rousseau.*

There is no true love without jealousy. *Pr.*

There is no vague general capability in men. *Goethe.*

There is no vice or folly that requires so much 40 nicety and skill to manage as vanity. *Swift.*

There is no vice or crime that does not originate in self-love; and there is no virtue that does not grow from the love of others out of and beyond self. *Anon.*

There is no vice so simple but assumes / Some mark of virtue in his outward parts. *Mer. of Ven.*, iii. 2.

There is no venom like that of the tongue. *Pr.*

There is no wealth but life—life, including all its powers of love, of joy, and of admiration. *Ruskin.*

There is no well-doing, no godlike doing, that 45 is not patient doing. *J. G. Holland.*

There is no wisdom nor understanding nor counsel against the Lord. *Bible.*

There is no work of genius which has not been the delight of mankind, no word of genius to which the human heart and soul have not, sooner or later, responded. *Lowell.*

There is no worse fruit than that which never ripens. *It. Pr.*

There is no worse joke than a true one. *It. and Sp. Pr.*

There is none so blind as they that won't see. 50 *Swift.*

There is none so poor that he need sit on a pumpkin. That is shiftlessness. *Thoreau.*

There is not a Red Indian hunting by Lake Winnipeg can quarrel with his squaw but the whole world must smart for it; will not the price of beaver rise? *Carlyle.*

There is not any benefit so glorious in itself but it may be exceedingly sweetened and improved by the manner of conferring it. The virtue, I know, rests in the intent, but the beauty and ornament of an obligation lies in the manner of it. *Sen.*

There is not in earth a spectacle more worthy than a great man superior to his sufferings. *Addison.*

There is not in national life any real epoch, because there is nothing in reality abrupt. Events, however great or sudden, are consequences of preparations long ago made. *Draper.*

There is not one grain in the universe, either too much or too little, nothing to be added, nothing to be spared; nor so much as any one particle of it, that mankind may not be either the better or the worse for, according as it is applied. *L'Estrange.*

5 There is not so agonizing a feeling in the whole catalogue of human suffering as the first conviction that the heart of the being whom we most tenderly love is estranged from us. *Bulwer Lytton.*

There is not so much comfort in having children as there is sorrow in parting with them. *Pr.*

There is not the thickness of a sixpence between good and evil. *Pr.*

There is not yet any inventory of man's faculties. *Emerson.*

There is nothing beyond the pleasure which the study of Nature produces. Her secrets are of unfathomable depth, but it is granted to us men to look into them more and more. *Goethe.*

10 There is nothing born but has to die. *Carlyle.*

There is nothing by which I have, through life, more profited than by the just observations, the good opinion, and the sincere and gentle encouragement of amiable and sensible women. *Romilly.*

There is nothing capricious in nature. *Emerson.*

There is nothing covered that shall not be revealed; and hid, that shall not be known. *Jesus.*

There is nothing divine but what is rational. *Kant.*

15 There is nothing either good or bad, but thinking makes it so. *Ham.*, ii. 2.

There is nothing evil but what is within us; the rest is either natural or accidental. *Sir P. Sidney.*

There is nothing exasperates people more than the display of superior ability or brilliancy in conversation. They seem pleased at the time, but their envy makes them curse him at their hearts. *Johnson.*

There is nothing from without a man that entering into him can defile him; but the things which come out of him, those are they that defile the man. *Jesus.*

There is nothing good or evil save in the will. *Epictetus.*

20 There is nothing good or godlike in this world but has in it something of "infinite sadness." *Carlyle.*

There is nothing holier in this life of ours than the first consciousness of love, the first fluttering of its silken wings. *Longfellow.*

There is nothing in the world more shameful than establishing one's self on lies and fables. *Goethe.*

There is nothing in this world that will keep the devil out of one but hard labour. *Carlyle.*

There is nothing in which the power of circumstance is more evident than in politics. *Disraeli.*

There is nothing innocent or good that dies 25 and is forgotten. *Dickens.*

There is nothing insignificant, nothing! *Coleridge.*

There is nothing lighter than vain praise. *William Drummond.*

There is nothing like leather. *Pr. A cobbler's advice in an emergency.*

There is nothing like the cold dead hand of the past to take down our tumid egotism, and lead us into the solemn flow of the life of our race. *Holmes.*

There is nothing little to the truly great in 30 spirit. *Dickens.*

There is nothing more allied to the barbarous and savage character than sullenness, concealment, and reserve. *Parke Godwin.*

There is nothing more characteristic than the shakes of the hand. *Sydney Smith.*

There is nothing more charming than to see a mother with a child in her arms, and nothing more venerable than a mother among a number of her children. *Goethe.*

There is nothing more frightful than for a teacher to know only what his scholars are intended to know. *Goethe.*

There is nothing more frightful than imagina- 35 tion without taste. *Goethe.*

There is nothing more perennial in us than habit and imitation. They are the source of all working and all apprenticeship, of all practice and all learning. *Carlyle.*

There is nothing more pitiable in the world than an irresolute man, oscillating between two feelings, who would willingly unite the two, and who does not perceive that nothing can unite them. *Goethe.*

There is nothing more precious to a man than his will; there is nothing which he relinquishes with so much reluctance. *J. G. Holland.*

There is nothing more terrible to a guilty heart than the eye of a respected friend. *Sir P. Sidney.*

There is nothing new under the sun. *Bible.* 40

There is nothing of which men are so fond and so careless as life. *La Bruyère.*

There is nothing on earth divine beside humanity. *Melanchthon.*

There is nothing on earth which is not in the heavens in a heavenly form, and nothing in the heavens which is not on the earth in an earthly form. *Quoted by Emerson.*

There is nothing on earth without difficulty. Only the inner impulse, the pleasure it gives us, and love we feel, help us to overcome obstruction, to pave our way, and to raise ourselves out of the narrow circle in which others sorrowfully torture themselves. *Goethe.*

There is nothing really more monstrous in any 45 recorded savagery or absurdity of mankind than that governments should be able to get money for any folly they choose to commit, by selling to capitalists the right of taxing future generations to the end of time. *Ruskin.*

There is nothing so agonising to the fine skin of vanity as the application of a rough truth. *Bulwer Lytton.*

There is nothing so great or so goodly in creation, but it is a mean symbol of the gospel of Christ, and of the things that he has prepared for them that love him. *Ruskin.*

There is nothing so powerful as truth, and nothing so strange. *Dan. Webster.*

There is nothing so small but that we may honour God by asking his guidance of it, or insult him by taking it into our own hands. *Ruskin.*

5 There is nothing so secret but it comes to light. *Pr.*

There is nothing so sure of succeeding as not to be over brilliant, as to be entirely wrapped up in one's self, and endowed with a perseverance which, in spite of all the rebuffs it may meet with, never relaxes in the pursuit of its object. *Baron de Grimm.*

There is nothing so terrible as activity without insight. *Goethe.*

There is nothing to be found only once in the world. *Goethe.*

There is nothing to which man is not related. *Emerson.*

10 There is nothing which vanity does not desecrate. *Ward Beecher.*

There is nothing without us that is not also within us. *Goethe.*

There is often a complaint of want of parts, when the fault lies in a want of a due improvement of them. *Locke.*

There is often more true spiritual force in a proverb than in a philosophical system. *Carlyle.*

There is / One great society alone on earth ; / The noble living and the noble dead. (?)

15 There is one preacher who does preach with effect, and gradually persuade all persons ; his name is Destiny, Divine Providence, and his sermon the inflexible course of things. *Carlyle.*

There is only one cure for public distress, and that is public education, directed to make men thoughtful, merciful, and just. *Ruskin.*

There is only one mendacious being in the world, and that is man. *Schopenhauer.*

There is only one thing better than tradition, and that is the original and eternal life out of which all tradition takes its rise. *Lowell.*

There is only one true religion, but there may be many forms of belief. *Kant.*

20 There is poetry and beauty in the common lives about us, if we look at them with imaginative and sympathetic eye. *J. Morley.*

There is power over and behind us, and we are the channels of its communication. *Emerson.*

There is precious instruction to be got by finding that we are wrong. *Carlyle.*

There is properly but one slavery in the world —the slavery of wisdom to folly. *Carlyle.*

There is properly no history, only biography. *Emerson.*

25 There is, properly speaking, no misfortune in the world. Happiness and misfortune stand in continual balance. Every misfortune is, as it were, the obstruction of a stream, which, after overcoming this obstruction, bursts forth with the greater force. *Novalis.*

There is really something absurd about the Present ; all that people think of is the sight, the touch of each other, and there they rest ; but it never occurs to them to reflect upon what is to be gained from such moments. *Goethe.*

There is safety in solitude. *Saadi.*

There is scarce truth enough alive to make societies secure, but security enough to make fellowships accursed. *Meas. for Meas., iii. 2.*

There is scarcely a good critic of books born in our age, and yet every fool thinks himself justified in criticising persons. *Bulwer Lytton.*

There is sentiment in all women, and senti- 30 ment gives delicacy to thought, and tact to manner. But sentiment with men is generally acquired, an offspring of the intellectual quality, not, as with the other sex, of the moral. *Bulwer Lytton.*

There is so much of good among the worst, so much of evil in the best, such seeming partialities in providence, so many things to lessen and expand, yea, and with all man's boast, so little real freedom of his will, that to look a little lower than the surface, garb, or dialect, or fashion, thou shalt feebly pronounce for a saint, and faintly condemn for a sinner. *Tupper.*

There is so much trouble in coming into the world, and so much more, as well as meanness, in going out of it, that 'tis hardly worth while to be here at all. *Lord Bolingbroke.*

There is some soul of goodness in things evil, / Would men observingly distil it out. *Henry V., iv. 1.*

There is some use in having two attorneys in one firm. Their movements resemble those of the man and woman in a Dutch babyhouse. When it is fair weather with the client, out comes the gentleman partner to fawn like a spaniel ; when it is foul, forth bolts the operative brother to pin like a bull-dog. *Scott.*

There is something behind the throne greater 35 than the king himself. *Chatham.*

There is something in sorrow more akin to the course of human affairs than joy. *C. Fitzhugh.*

There is something irresistibly pleasing in the conversation of a fine woman ; even though her tongue be silent, the eloquence of her eyes teach wisdom. *Goldsmith.*

There is something more awful in happiness than in sorrow. *Hawthorne.*

There is something not solid in the good that is done for us. *Emerson.*

There is something of all men in every man. 40 *Lichtenberg.*

There is something so moving in the very image of weeping beauty. *Steele.*

There is something too dear in the hope of seeing again. . . . "Dear heart, be quiet ;" we say ; "you will not be long separated from those people that you love ; be quiet, dear heart!" And then we give it in the meanwhile a shadow, so that it has something, and then it is good and quiet, like a little child whose mother gives it a doll instead of the apple which it ought not to eat. *Goethe.*

There is still a real magic in the action and reaction of minds on one another. The casual deliration of a few becomes, by this mysterious reverberation, the frenzy of many; men lose the use, not only of their understandings, but of their bodily senses; while the most obdurate unbelieving hearts melt like the rest in the furnace where all are cast as victims and as fuel. *Carlyle.*

There is still enough to satisfy one in spite of all misfortunes. *Goethe.*

There is such a choice of difficulties that I am myself at a loss how to determine. *J. Wolfe to Pitt.*

There is that maketh himself rich, yet hath nothing: there is that maketh himself poor, yet hath great riches. *Bible.*

5 There is that scattereth, and yet increaseth: and there is that withholdeth more than is meet, but it tendeth to poverty. *Bible.*

There is very great necessity indeed of getting a little more silent than we are. *Carlyle.*

There is work on God's wide earth for all men that he has made with hands and hearts. *Carlyle.*

There lives more faith in honest doubt, believe me, than in half the creeds. *Tennyson.*

There may come a day when there shall be no more curse; in the meantime you must be humble and honest enough to take your share of it. *Ruskin.*

10 There may often be less vanity in following the new modes than in adhering to the old ones. It is true that the foolish invent them, but the wise may conform to, instead of contradicting, them. *Joubert.*

There must always remain something that is antagonistic to good. *Plato.*

There must be a man behind a book. *Emerson.*

There must be hearts which know the depths of our being, and swear by us, even when the whole world forsakes us. *Gutzkow.*

There must be work done by the arms, or none of us would live; and work done by the brains, or the life would not be worth having. And the same men cannot do both. *Ruskin.*

15 There must first be seducing men before seduced women. *Jean Paul.*

There needs no ghost, my lord, come from the grave / To tell us this. *Ham.*, i. 5.

There needs not a great soul to make a hero; there needs a god-created soul which will be true to its origin; that will be a great soul. *Carlyle.*

There never did and never will exist anything permanently noble and excellent in a character which was a stranger to the exercise of resolute self-denial. *Scott.*

There never was a bad man but had ability for good service. *Burke.*

20 There never was a great man unless through Divine inspiration. *Cicero.*

There never was a literary age whose dominant taste was not sickly. *Joubert.*

There never was a talent, even for real literature, but was primarily a talent for something infinitely better of the silent kind. *Carlyle.*

There never was any heart truly great and generous that was not also tender and compassionate. *South.*

There never was any party, faction, or sect in which the most ignorant was not the most violent. *Pope.*

There never was so great a thought labouring 25 in the breasts of men as now. *Emerson.*

There occur cases in human life when it is wisdom not to be too wise. *Schiller.*

There remaineth a rest to the people of God. *Bible.*

There seems to be no part of knowledge in fewer hands than that of discerning when to have done. *Swift.*

There shall no evil happen to the just. *Bible.*

There the wicked case from troubling, and 30 there the weary be at rest. *Bible.*

There was a little city, and few men within it; and there came a great king against it, and besieged it, and built bulwarks against it. Now there was found in it a poor wise man, and he by his wisdom delivered the city, yet no man remembered that same poor man. *Bible.*

There was a time when meadow, grove, and stream, / The earth and every common sight, / To me did seem / Apparelled in celestial light, / The glory and the freshness of a dream. / It is not now as it has been of yore; Turn wheresoe'er I may, / By night or day, / The things which I have seen, I now can see no more. *Wordsworth.*

There was a time when the world acted upon books. Now books act upon the world. *Joubert.*

There was but one Moses to the thousands of Israel that entered Jordan. *Ward Beecher.*

There was never a nation great until it came 35 to the knowledge that it had nowhere in the world to go for help. *C. D. Warner.*

There was never good or ill but women had to do with it. *Gaelic Pr.*

There was never yet philosopher / Who could endure the toothache patiently. *Much Ado*, v. I.

There was sense in the sentences, but the sumtotal was nonsense. *Criticism of a young preacher's discourse.*

There was speech in their dumbness, language in their very gesture. *Winter's Tale*, v. 2.

There were no ill language if it were not ill 40 taken. *Pr.*

There where thou art, there where thou remainest, accomplish what thou canst. *Goethe.*

There will always be a government of force where men are selfish. *Emerson.*

There's a brave fellow! There's a man of pluck! / A man who is not afraid to say his say, / Though a whole town's against him. *Longfellow.*

There's a courage which grows out of fear. *Byron.*

There's a divinity that shapes our ends, / 45 Rough-hew them as we will. *Ham.*, v. 2.

There's a medium in thoughtfulness and gaiety: find it out and keep to it. *Spurgeon.*

There's a special providence in the fall of a sparrow. *Ham.*, v. 2.

There's a sweeter flower than e'er / Blush'd on the rosy spray, / A brighter star, a richer bloom, / Than e'er did western heaven illume / At close of summer day— / 'Tis Love, the last best gift of Heaven. *Keble.*

There's always life for the living. *Pr.*

There's beggary in the love that can be reckoned. *Ant. and Cleop.*, i. 1.

There's folks as make bad butter, and trusten to the salt t' hide it. *George Eliot.*

There's folks 'ud stand on their heads and then say the fault was in their boots. *George Eliot.*

There's husbandry in heaven ; / Their candles are all out. *Macb.*, i. 7.

5 There's language in her eye, her cheeks, her lip, / Nay, her foot speaks. *Troil. and Cress.*, iv. 5.

There's many a good bit o' work done with a sad heart. *George Eliot.*

There's many a slip / 'Twixt the cup and the lip. *Pr.*

There's mercy in every place, / And mercy, encouraging thought, / Gives even affliction a grace, / And reconciles man to his lot. *Cowper.*

There's music in the sighing of a reed ; / There's music in the gushing of a rill ; / There's music in all things, if men had ears. *Byron.*

10 There's nae sorrow there, John, / There's neither cauld nor care, John, / The day is aye fair, / In the land o' the leal. *Lady Nairne.*

There's no armour against fate. *Shirley.*

There's no art / To find the mind's construction in the face. *Macb.*, i. 4.

There's no folk sic idiots as them that looks like geniuses. *J. M. Barrie.*

There's no glory like his who saves his country. *Tennyson.*

15 There's no grace in a benefit that sticks to the fingers. *Sen.*

There's no great banquet but some fares ill. *George Herbert.*

There's no pleasure i' living, if you're to be corked up for ever, and only dribble your mind out by the sly, like a leaky barrel. *George Eliot.*

There's no seeing one's way through tears. *Pr.*

There's no slipping up-hill again, and no standing still when once you've begun to slip down. *George Eliot.*

20 There's no work so tirin' as danglin' about an' starin', an' not rightly knowin' what you're goin' to do next ; an' keepin' your face i' smilin' order, like a grocer o' market-day. *George Eliot.*

There's not a joy the world can give like that it takes away. *Byron.*

There's not a place where Rest can say, / I'll not have Labour here ; / For Rest itself would pine away / If Labour were not near. *Hall.*

There's not a string attuned to mirth / But has its chord in melancholy. *Hood.*

There's not one wise man among twenty that will praise himself. *Much Ado*, v. 2.

25 There's not the smallest orb which thou behold'st, / But in his motion like an angel sings, / Still quiring to the young-eyed cherubims. *Mer. of Ven.*, v. 1.

There's nothing but what's bearable as long as a man can work. *George Eliot.*

There's nothing certain but uncertainty. *Pr.*

There's nothing half so sweet in life / As love's young dream. *Moore.*

There's nothing situate under heaven's eye, / But hath its bound in earth, in sea, in sky. *Comedy of Errors*, ii. 1.

There's none that can / Read God aright, un- 30 less he first spell man. *Quarles.*

There's small choice in rotten apples. *Tam. of Shrew*, i. 1.

There's something good in all weathers. If it don't happen to be good for my work to-day, it's good for some other man's to-day, and will come round to me to-morrow. *Dickens.*

There's such divinity doth hedge a king, / That treason can but peep to what it would. *Ham.*, iv. 5.

There's things it's best to put off kenning as long as we can. *J. M. Barrie.*

Thereby hangs a tale. *As You Like It*, ii. 7. 35

These / Are but the varied God. The rolling year / Is full of thee. *Thomson.*

"These are my jewels." *Cornelia, the mother of the Gracchi, when she presented her five sons to a lady who had paraded her ornaments before her.*

These cases, wherein happiness would be sinful, are just as much, but no more, the ordainments of Providence as those more common ones wherein happiness is natural and right. *W. R. Greg.*

These fair tales, which we know so beautiful, / Show only finer than our lives to-day / Because their voice was clearer, and they found / A sacred bard to sing them. *Lewis Morris.*

These limbs, whence had we them ; this 40 stormy force ; this life-blood with its burning passion ? They are dust and shadow ; a shadow-system gathered round our Me ; wherein through some moments or years, the divine essence is to be revealed in flesh. *Carlyle.*

These little things are great to little men. *Goldsmith.*

These moving things, ca'ed wife and weans, / Wad move the very heart o' stanes. *Burns.*

These violent delights have violent ends. *Rom. and Jul.*, ii. 6.

They are as sick that surfeit with too much, as they that starve with nothing. *Mer. of Venice*, i. 2.

They are but beggars that can count their 45 worth. *Rom. and Jul.*, ii. 6.

They are dead even for this life who hope for no better. *Lorenzo de Medici.*

They are never alone that are accompanied with noble thoughts. *Sir P. Sidney.*

They are not a pipe for fortune's finger, / To sound what stop she please. *Ham.*, iii. 2.

They are not all free who scorn their chains. *Lessing.*

They are not kings who sit on thrones, but 50 they who know how to govern. *Emerson.*

They are not sages who do not declare men's duty. *Hitopadesa.*

They are slaves who dare not be / In the right with two or three. *Lowell.*

They asked Lucman the fabulist, "From whom did you learn manners ?" He answered, "From the unmannerly." *Saadi.*

They can conquer who believe they can. *Virgil.*

They do most by books who could do much without them; and he that chiefly owes himself unto himself is the substantial man. *Sir T. Browne.*

They ever do pretend / To have received a wrong who wrong intend. *Daniel.*

They fool me to the top of my bent. *Ham.*, iii. 2.

They found no end, in wandering mazes lost. *Milton.*

5 They grew in beauty side by side, / They fill'd one home with glee; / Their graves are sever'd far and wide, / By mount, and stream, and sea. *Mrs. Hemans.*

They govern the world, these sweet-lipped women, because beauty is the index of a larger fact than wisdom. *Holmes.*

They had the divine right of kings to settle, these unfortunate ancestors of ours; . . . and they did, on hest of necessity, manage to settle it. *Carlyle of the Puritans.*

They have been at a great feast of languages, and stolen the scraps. *Love's L. Lost*, v. 1.

They have destroyed the beaten track to heaven; we are now compelled to make for ourselves ladders. *Joubert.*

10 They laugh that win. *Othello*, iv. 2.

They lose it (the world) that do buy it with much care. *Mer. of Ven.*, i. 1.

They love least that let men know their love. *Two Gent. of Verona*, i. 2.

They love most who are least valued. *Pr.*

They love not poison that do poison need. *Rich. II.*, v. 6.

15 They love us truly who correct us freely. *Pr.*

They most assume who know the least. *Gay.*

They must hunger in winter that will not work in summer. *Pr.*

They must often change who would be constant in happiness or wisdom. *Confucius.*

They never taste who always drink; / They always talk who never think. *Prior.*

20 They only are wise who know that they know nothing. *Carlyle.*

They only babble that practise not reflection. *Sheridan.*

They only should own who can administer. *Emerson.*

They only who build on ideas build for eternity. *Emerson.*

They pass best over the world who trip over it quickly; for it is but bog—if we stop, we sink. *Queen Elizabeth.*

25 They said that Love would die when Hope was gone, / And Love mourn'd long, and sorrow'd after Hope; / At last she sought out Memory, and they trod / The same old paths where Love had walk'd with Hope, / And Memory fed the soul of Love with tears. *Tennyson.*

They say best men are moulded out of faults, / And, for the most, become much more the better / For being a little bad. *Meas. for Meas.*, v. 1.

They say Doubt is weak, but yet, if life be in the doubt, / The living doubt is more than Faith that life did never know. *Dr. W. Smith.*

"They say so" is half a lie. *Pr.*

They, sweet soul, that most impute a crime / Are pronest to it, and impute themselves, / Wanting the mental range; or low desire / Not to feel lowest makes them level all; / Yea, they would pare the mountain to the plain, / To leave an equal baseness. *Tennyson.*

They that are above have ends in everything. 30 *Beaumont and Fletcher.*

They that are against superstition oftentimes run into it of the wrong side. If I wear all colours but black, then I am superstitious in not wearing black. *Selden.*

They that are booted are not always ready. *Pr.*

They that be whole need not a physician; but they that are sick. *Jesus.*

They that be wise shall shine as the brightness of the firmament; and they that turn many to righteousness, as the stars for ever and ever. *Bible.*

They that bear a noble mind, / Where they 35 want of riches find. *Wither.*

They that by pleading clothes / Do fortunes seek, when worth and service fail, / Would have their tale believed for their oaths, / And are like empty vessels under sail. *George Herbert.*

They that deny a God destroy man's nobility. For, certainly, man is of kin to the beasts, by his body; and if he be not of kin to God by his spirit, he is a base and ignoble creature. *Bacon.*

They that do change old love for new, / Pray gods, they change for worse. *George Peele.*

They that do nothing are in the readiest way to do that which is worse than nothing. *Zimmermann.*

They that drive away time spur a free horse. 40 *Robert Mason.*

They that govern the most make the least noise. *Selden.*

They that hold by the Divine / Clasp too the Human in their faith. *Dr. W. Smith.*

They that know one another salute afar off. *Pr.*

They that marry ancient people merely in expectation to bury them, hang themselves in hope that one will come and cut the halter. *Fuller.*

They that mean to make no use of friends will 45 be at little trouble to gain them: and to be without friendship is to be without one of the first comforts of our present state. *Johnson.*

They that observe lying vanities forsake their own mercy. *Bible.*

They that plough iniquity and sow wickedness reap the same. *Bible.*

They that stand high have many blasts to shake them; and if they fall, they dash themselves to pieces. *Richard III.*, i. 3.

They that sow in tears shall reap in joy. *Bible.*

They that sow the wind shall reap the whirl- 50 wind. *Bible.*

They that will crowd about bonfires may, sometimes very fairly, get their beards singed; it is the price they pay for such illumination; natural twilight is safe and free to all. *Carlyle.*

They told me I was everything; 'tis a lie: I am not ague-proof. *King Lear*, iv. 6.

They well deserve to have / That know the strong'st and surest way to get. *Richard II.*, iii. 3.

They went out from us, but they were not of us; for if they had been of us, they would no doubt have continued with us. *St. John.*

They who accuse and blacken thee wrongfully are much the greatest sufferers by their own malice and injustice. *Thomas à Kempis.*

They who but slowly pacèd are / By plodding on may travel far. *Wither.*

They who contract absurd habits are such as have no fear. *Johnson.*

They who crouch to those who are above them, always trample on those who are below them. *Buckle.*

5 They who do not feel the darkness will never look for the light. *Buckle.*

They who embrace the entire universe with love, for the most part love nothing but their narrow selves. *Herder.*

They who gratefully the gods adore, / Still find their joys increasing more and more. *Theocritus.*

They who have lost an infant are never, as it were, without an infant child. *Leigh Hunt.*

They who have no other trade but seeking their fortune, need never hope to find her; coquette-like, she flies from her close pursuers, and at last fixes on the plodding mechanic who stays at home and minds his business. *Goldsmith.*

10 They who lie soft and warm in a rich estate seldom come to heat themselves at the altar. *South.*

They who oppose a Ministry have always a better field for ridicule and reproof than they who defend it. *Goldsmith.*

They who place their affections on trifles at first for amusement, will find those trifles at last become their serious concern. *Goldsmith.*

They who play with the devil's rattles will be brought by degrees to wield his sword. *Fuller.*

They who pretend most to universal benevolence are either deceivers or dupes—men who desire to cover their private ill-nature by a pretended regard for all. *Goldsmith.*

15 They who resign life rather than part with liberty do only a prudent action; but those who lay it down for friends and country do a heroic one. *Steele.*

They who resist indiscriminately all improvement as innovation, may find themselves compelled at last to submit to innovations although they are not improvements. *Canning.*

They who seek only for faults see nothing else. *Pr.*

They who sustain their cross shall likewise be sustained by it in return. *Thomas à Kempis.*

They who travel in pursuit of wisdom walk only in a circle, and, after all their labour, at last return to their pristine ignorance. *Goldsmith.*

20 They who want a farthing, and have no friend that will lend them it, think farthings very good things. *Goldsmith.*

They who want money when they come to borrow, will always want money when they should come to pay. *Goldsmith.*

They who will watch Providence will never want a Providence to watch. (?)

They whom truth and wisdom lead / Can gather honey from a weed. *Cowper.*

Thick as autumnal leaves that strew the brooks / In Vallombrosa. *Milton.*

Thine ears shall hear a word behind thee, 25 saying, This is the way, walk ye in it, when ye turn to the right hand, and when ye turn to the left. *Bible.*

Thine is the right, for thine the might. *Tennyson.*

Thine own friend, and thy father's friend, forsake not; neither go into thy brother's house in the day of thy calamity: for better is a neighbour that is near than a brother far off. *Bible.*

Thine own worm be not: yet such jealousy, / As hurts not others, but may make thee better, / Is a good spur. *George Herbert.*

Things all are big with jest; nothing that's plain / But may be witty, if thou hast the vein . . . / Many affecting wit beyond their power, / Have got to be a dear fool for an hour. *George Herbert.*

Things are graceful in a friend's mouth which 30 are blushing in a man's own. *Bacon.*

Things are his property alone who knows how to use them. *Xenophon.*

Things are long-lived, and God above appoints their term; yet when the brains of a thing have been out for three centuries and odd, one does wish it would be kind enough and die. *Carlyle.*

Things are not so false always as they seem. *Carlyle.*

Things are sullen, and will be as they are, whatever we think them or wish them to be. *Cudworth.*

Things are what they are by nature, not by 35 will. *Cudworth.*

Things at the worst will cease, or else climb upward / To what they were before. *Macb., iv. 2.*

Things bad begun make strong themselves by ill. *Macb., iii. 2.*

Things base and vile, holding no quantity, / Love can transpose to form and dignity. *Mid. N.'s Dream, i. 1.*

Things fasten upon thee only according as the degree of thy own love and inclination for them gives opportunity and advantage. *Thomas à Kempis.*

Things good, great Jove, asked or unasked, 40 supply: / Thinks evil, though we ask for them, deny. *Anon.*

Things have their laws as well as men; and things refuse to be trifled with. *Emerson.*

Things ill got had ever bad success. . . . I'll leave my son my virtuous deeds behind. *3 Hen. VI., ii. 2.*

Things may serve long, but not serve ever. *All's Well, ii. 2.*

Things more excellent than every image are expressed through images. *Jamblichus.*

Things must turn when they can go no farther. 45 *Spurgeon.*

Things refuse to be mismanaged long. *Carlyle.*

Things seen are mightier than things heard. *Tennyson.*

Things will always right themselves in time, if only those who know what they want to do, and can do, persevere unremittingly in work and action. *Goethe.*

Things will never be bettered by an excess of haste. *Pr.*

Things without remedy should be without regard; what is done, is done. *Macb.*, iii. 2.

Things won are done; joy's soul lies in the doing. *Troil. and Cress.*, i. 2.

Think all you speak, but speak not all you think. *Delaune.*

5 Think and thank God. *Pr.*

Think naught a trifle, though it small appear; / Small sands the mountain, moments make the year, / And trifles life. *Young.*

Think not, dream not that thou livest, / If thy hand doth idly lie, / If thy soul for ever longing, / Yearn but for the by and bye. *M. W. Wood.*

Think not I came to send peace on the earth; I came not to send peace but a sword. *Jesus.*

Think not thy fame at every twitch will break; / By great deeds show that thou canst little do; / And do them not; that shall thy wisdom be; / And change thy temperance into bravery. *George Herbert.*

10 Think not thy own shadow longer than that of others. *Sir Thomas Browne.*

Think not your estate your own, while any man can call upon you for money which you cannot pay. *Johnson.*

Think of ease, but work on. *George Herbert.*

Think of "living!" Thy life, wert thou the "pitifullest of all the sons of earth," is no idle dream, but a solemn reality. It is thy own; it is all thou hast to front eternity with. *Carlyle.*

Think of the hosts of worlds, and of the plagues in this world-mote—death puts an end to the whole. *Carlyle.*

15 Think with awe on the slow, the quiet power of time. *Schiller.*

Think wrongly, if you please, but in all cases think for yourself. *Lessing.*

Think ye that God made the universe, and then let it run round his finger? (*am Finger laufen liesse*). *Goethe.*

Think you, 'mid all this mighty sum / Of things for ever speaking, / That nothing of itself will come, / But we must still be seeking. *Wordsworth.*

Thinkers are scarce as gold; but he whose thoughts embrace all his subject, pursues it uninterruptedly and fearless of consequences, is a diamond of enormous size. *Lavater.*

20 Think'st thou existence doth depend on time? / It doth; but actions are our epochs. *Byron.*

Thinking about sin, beyond what is indispensable for the firm effort to get rid of it, is waste of energy and waste of time. *Matthew Arnold.*

Thinking is but an idle waste of thought; / For nought is everything, and everything is nought. *Smith, "Rejected Addresses."*

Thinking is the function; living is the functionary. *Emerson.*

Thinking leads man to knowledge. He may see and hear, and read and learn, whatever he pleases, and as much as he pleases; he will never know anything of it, except that which he has thought over, that which by thinking he has made the property of his mind. *Pestalozzi.*

Thinking nurseth thinking. *Sir P. Sidney.* 25

This above all; to thine own self be true, / And it must follow as the night the day, / Thou canst not then be false to any man. *Ham.*, i. 3.

This bodes some strange eruption to our state. *Ham.*, i. 1.

This century is not ripe for my ideal; I live a citizen of those that are to come. *Schiller.*

"This comes of walking on the earth." *The Spanish swell, as he picked himself up from the ground. Sp. Pr.*

This communicating of a man's self to his 30 friend works two contrary effects, for it redoubleth joys and cutteth griefs in halves. *Bacon.*

This day / Shall change all griefs and quarrels into love. *Henry V.*, v. 2.

This day's propitious to be wise in. *Burns.*

This even-handed justice / Commends the ingredients of our poison'd chalice / To our own lips. *Macb.*, i. 7.

This ever-renewing generation of appearances rests on a reality, and a reality that is alive. *Emerson.*

This fell sergeant, death, / Is strict in his 35 arrest. *Ham.*, v. 2.

This hand, to tyrants ever sworn the foe, / For freedom only deals the deadly blow: / Then sheathes in calm repose the vengeful blade / For gentle peace in freedom's hallowed shade. *John Quincy Adams.*

This I think charity—to love God for himself, and our neighhour for God. *Sir Thomas Browne.*

This is a great—properly the greatest—moment in a man's life, when, reconciling himself to necessity, he is able with clearness of purpose to say, "Let the will of the gods be done." *Ed.*

"This is a sharp medicine, but it cures all disorders." *Raleigh of the axe of his executioner.*

This is faith; it is nothing more than obedience. 40 *Voltaire.*

This is how I define talent; it is a gift God has given us in secret, which we reveal without knowing it. *Montesquieu.*

This is not a time for purism of style; and style has little to do with the worth or unworth of a book. *Carlyle.*

This is not the liberty which we can hope, that no grievance should arise in the commonwealth, but when complaints are freely heard, deeply considered, and speedily reformed, then is the utmost bound of civil liberty attained that wise men look for. *Milton.*

This is the first condition of a living morality as well as of vital religion, that the soul shall find a true centre out from and above itself, round which it shall revolve. *J. C. Sharp.*

This is the humour of it. *Henry V.*, ii. 1. 45

This is the monstrosity in love—that the will is infinite, and the execution confined; that the desire is boundless, and the act a slave to limit. *Troil. and Cress*, iii. 2.

This is the state of man: to-day he puts forth / The tender leaves of hopes; to-morrow blossoms, / And bears his blushing honours thick upon him; / The third day comes a frost, a killing frost; / And when he thinks, good easy man, full surely / His greatness is a-ripening, nips his root, / And then he falls, as I do. *Hen. VIII.*, iii. 2.

This is the very coinage of your brain ; / This bodiless creation ecstasy / Is very cunning in. *Ham.*, iii. 4.

This is the very curse of an evil deed, that it engenders and must bring forth more evil. *Schiller.*

This is true philanthrophy, that buries not its gold in ostentatious charity, but builds its hospital in the human heart. *Harley.*

This low man seeks a little thing to do, / Sees it and does it ; / This high man, with a great thing to pursue, / Dies ere he knows it. *Browning.*

5 This man receiveth sinners, and eateth with them. *Said of Jesus by the Jews in way of reproach.*

This narrow isthmus 'twixt two boundless seas, / The past, the future—two eternities. *Moore.*

This nothing's more than matter. *Ham.*, iv. 5.

This of old is sure, / That change of toil is toil's sufficient cure. *Lewis Morris.*

This one fact the world hates—that the soul becomes. *Emerson.*

10 This present is a ruinous and ruining world. *Carlyle.*

This she knows in joys and woes, / That saints will aid if men will call ; / For the blue sky bends over all. *Coleridge.*

This so solid-seeming world is, after all, but an air-image, our Me the only reality ; and Nature, with its thousand-fold production and destruction, but the reflex of our own inward force, the " Phantasy of our Dream," or, what the earth-spirit in "Faust" names it, " the living visible garment of God." *Carlyle.*

This time, like all times, is a very good one, if we but knew what to do with it. *Emerson.*

This was a man. *Jul. Cæs.*, v. 5.

15 This was the most unkindest cut of all. *Jul. Cæs.*, iii. 2.

This will prove a brave kingdom to me, where I shall have my music for nothing. *Tempest*, iii. 2.

This world belongs to the energetic. *Emerson.*

This world is a busy scene, and man a creature destined for a progressive struggle. *Burns.*

This world is all a fleeting show, / For man's illusion given : / The smiles of joy, the tears of woe, / Deceitful shine, deceitful flow, / There's nothing true but heaven. *Moore.*

20 This world is full of fools, and he who would not wish to see one must not only shut himself up alone, but must also break his looking-glass. *Boileau.*

This world surely is wide enough to hold both thee and me ! (uncle Toby to the fly). *Sterne.*

This world, where much is to be done and little to be known. *Johnson.*

Thistles and thorns prick sore, but evil tongues prick more. *Dut. Pr.*

Tho' men may bicker with the things they love, / They would not make them laughable in all eyes, / Not while they loved them. *Tennyson.*

25 Tho' world on world in myriad myriads roll / Round us, each with different powers, / And other form of life than ours, / What know we greater than the soul? *Tennyson*

Those are not empty-hearted whose low sound / Reverbs no hollowness. *Lear*, i. 1.

Those are often raised into the greatest transports of mirth who are subject to the greatest depressions of melancholy. *Addison.*

Those deserve to be doubly laughed at that are peevish and angry for nothing to no purpose. *L'Estrange.*

Those faces which have charmed us the most escape us the soonest. *Scott.*

Those faults conscience has not strength to 30 prevent, it seldom has justice enough to accuse. *Goldsmith.*

Those friends thou hast, and their adoption tried, / Grapple them to thy soul with hoops of steel. *Ham.*, i. 3.

Those holy fields / Over whose acres walked those blesséd feet, / Which, fourteen hundred years ago were nailed, / For our advantage, on the bitter cross. 1 *Hen. IV.*, i. 1.

Those of us who are worth anything spend our manhood in unlearning the follies or expiating the mistakes of our youth. *Shelley.*

Those only are beautiful which, like the planets, have a steady, lambent light—are luminous, not sparkling. *Longfellow.*

Those only are despicable who fear to be 35 despised. *La Roche.*

Those only deserve a monument who do not need one. *Hazlitt.*

Those only obtain love, for the most part, who seek it not. *Goethe.*

Those only who know little can be said to know anything. The greater the knowledge the greater the doubt. *Goethe.*

Those people who are always improving never become great. Greatness is an eminence, the ascent to which is steep and lofty, and which a man must seize on at once by natural boldness and vigour, and not by patient, wary steps. *Hazlitt.*

Those persons who do most good are least 40 conscious of it. *Ward Beecher.*

Those tender tears that humanise the soul. *Thomson.*

Those that are the loudest in their threats are the weakest in the execution of them. *Colton.*

Those that come unsought for are commonly the most valuable, and should be secured, because they seldom return. *Bacon.*

Those that dare lose a day are dangerously prodigal ; those that dare misspend it, desperate. *Bishop Hall.*

Those that fly may fight again, / Which he can 45 never do that's slain. *Butler.*

Those that have loved longest love best. *Johnson.*

Those that think must govern those that toil. *Goldsmith.*

Those that with haste will make a mighty fire, / Begin with weak straws. *Jul. Cæs.*, i. 3.

Those who are bent to do wickedly will never want tempters to urge them on. *Tillotson.*

Those who are elevated enough in life to reason 50 and to reflect, yet low enough to keep clear of the venal contagion of a court—these are a nation's strength ! *Burns.*

Those who are quite satisfied sit still and do nothing ; those who are not quite satisfied are the sole benefactors of the world. *Landor.*

Those who attempt to level never equalise; they load the edifice of society by setting up in the air what the solidity of the structure requires to be on the ground. *Burke.*

Those who attempt to reason us out of our follies, begin at the wrong end, since the attempt naturally presupposes us capable of reason. *Goldsmith.*

Those who bring sunshine to the lives of others cannot keep it from themselves. *J. M. Barrie.*

Those who can sit at home and gloat over their thousands in silent satisfaction are generally found to do it in plain clothes. *Goldsmith.*

5 Those who carry much upon their clothes are remarked for having but little in their pockets. *Goldsmith.*

Those who do nothing generally take to shouting. *Pr.*

Those who dwell in fear dwell next door to hate; and I think it is the cowardice of women that makes them such intense haters. *Mrs. Jameson.*

Those who educate children well are more to be honoured than they who produce them; for these only gave them life, those the art of living well. *Arist.*

Those who first study fate, and say, Fate is the only cause of fortune and misfortune, terrify themselves. *Hitopadesa.*

10 Those who give the first shock to a state are naturally the first to be overwhelmed in its ruin. The fruits of public commotion are seldom enjoyed by the man who was the first to set it a-going; he only troubles the waters for another's net. *Montaigne.*

Those who have even studied good books may still be fools. *Hitopadesa.*

Those who injure one party to benefit another are quite as unjust as if they converted the property of others to their own benefit. *Cic.*

Those who make the best use of their time have none to spare. *Pr.*

Those who make the worst use of their time most complain of its shortness. *La Bruyère.*

15 Those who only run after little things will not go far. *J. M. Barrie.*

Those who profess most are ever the least sincere. *Sheridan.*

Those who regularly undertake to cultivate friendship find ingratitude generally repays their endeavours. *Arliss.*

Those who seek for something more than happiness in this world must not complain if happiness be not their portion. *Froude.*

Those who seem to doubt or deny us what is justly ours, let us either pity their prejudice or despise their judgment. *Burns.*

20 Those who set their minds to deny things, and are fond of pulling things to pieces, must be treated like deniers-of-motion; one need only keep incessantly walking up and down before them in as composed a manner as possible. *Goethe.*

Those who trust us educate us. *George Eliot.*

Those who will not be ruled by the rudder must be ruled by the rock. *Cornish Pr.*

Those who would make us feel must feel themselves. *Churchill.*

Thou art Heaven's tasker; and thy God requires / The purest of thy flour, as well as of thy fires. *Quarles.*

Thou art ignorant of what thou art, and much 25 more ignorant of what is fit for thee. *Thomas à Kempis.*

Thou art in the end what thou art. *Goethe.*

Thou art not alone if thou have faith. There is a communion of saints, unseen, yet not unreal, accompanying and brotherlike embracing thee, so thou be worthy. *Carlyle.*

Thou art the ruin of the noblest man / That ever lived in the tide of times. *Jul. Cæs., iii. 1.*

Thou art thyself to all eternity. *D. G. Rossetti.*

Thou awakest us to delight in thy praise; for 30 thou madest us for thyself, and our heart is restless until it repose in thee. *St. Augustine.*

Thou bear'st thy heavy riches but a journey. ' And death unloads thee. *Meas. for Meas., iii. 1.*

Thou canst not be entirely free till thou hast attained to such a mastery as entirely to subdue and deny thyself. *Thomas à Kempis.*

Thou dost not strive, O Sun, but, meek and still, / Thou dost the type of Jesus best fulfil, / A noiseless revelation in the sky. *F. W. Faber.*

Thou hast given me / A world of earthly blessings to my soul, / If sympathy of love unite our thoughts. *2 Hen. VI., i. 1.*

Thou hast not what others have, and others 35 have not the gift thou hast. From this imperfection springs sociability. *Gellert.*

Thou little thinkest what a little foolery governs the world. *John Selden.*

Thou mayest as well expect to grow stronger by always eating, as wiser by always reading. *Fuller.*

Thou mayest be more prodigal of praise when thou writest a letter than when thou speakest in presence. *Fuller.*

Thou must learn to break thine own will in many things if thou wilt have peace and concord with others. *Thomas à Kempis.*

Thou must live unto another if thou wilt live 40 unto thyself. *Sen.*

Thou must renounce; thou must abstain! is the eternal song which sounds in the ears of every one, which every hour is singing to us all our life long. *Goethe.*

Thou, Nature, art my goddess; to thy law / My services are bound. *King Lear, i. 2.*

Thou of an independent mind, / With soul resolved, with soul resigned; / Prepared Power's proudest frown to brave, / Who wilt not be, nor have a slave; / Virtue alone who dost revere, / Thy own reproach alone dost fear, / Approach this shrine (Independence), and worship here. *Burns.*

Thou shall hear no more complaints from me; thou shalt hear only what happens to the wanderer. *Goethe.*

"Thou shalt" is written upon life in characters 45 as legible as "Thou shalt not." *Carlyle.*

Thou shalt look outward, not inward. *Carlyle.*

Thou shalt not muzzle the ox that treadeth out the corn. *Bible.*

Thou, too curious ear, that fain / Wouldst thread the maze of Harmony, / Content thee with one simple strain, / . . . Till thou art duly trained, and taught / The concord sweet of Love divine. *Keble.*

Thou who didst the stars and sunbeams know, / Self-schooled, self-scanned, self-honoured, self-secure, / Didst walk on earth unguessed at. *M. Arnold on Shakespeare.*

Thou ! why, thou wilt quarrel with a man that hath a hair more or a hair less in his beard than thou hast. Thou wilt quarrel with a man for cracking nuts, having no other reason but because thou hast hazel eyes. . . . Thy head is full of quarrels as an egg is full of meat. *Rom. and Jul.,* iii. 1.

Thou wilt never sell thy life, or any part of thy life, in a satisfactory manner. Give it like a royal heart; let the price of it be nothing ; then hast thou in a certain sense got all for it. *Carlyle.*

Thou would'st as soon go kindle fire with snow, / As seek to quench the fire of love with words. *Two Gent. of Verona,* ii. 7.

5 Thou wouldst do little for God if the devil were dead. *Sc. Pr.*

Though a man may become learned by another's learning, he never can be wise but by his own wisdom. (?)

Though a sinner do evil an hundred times, and his days be prolonged, yet surely I know that it shall be well with them that fear God, which fear before him. *Bible.*

Though all his works abroad, / The heart benevolent and kind / The most resembles God. *Burns.*

Though ambition in itself is a vice, yet it is often the parent of virtues. *Quinct.*

10 Though an honourable title may be conveyed to posterity, yet the ennobling qualities which are the soul of greatness are a sort of incommunicable perfections, and cannot be transferred. (?)

Though gentle, yet not dull, / Strong without rage, without o'erflowing, full. *Denham.*

Though great the force of little words, / Sped in an evil hour, / As great the might, and great the good, / Of one in Wisdom's power. *M. W. Wood.*

Though He comes in many shapes, / His love is throbbing in them all, / And from His love no soul escapes, / And from His mercy none can fall. *Dr. W. Smith.*

Though he says nothing, he pays it with thinking, like the Welshman's jackdaw. *Pr.*

15 Though He slay me, I shall yet trust in Him. *Bible.*

Though I am always in haste, I am never in a hurry. *John Wesley.*

Though justice be thy plea, consider this— / That in the course of justice none of us / Should see salvation. *Mer. of Venice,* iv. 1.

Though last, not least. *Jul. Cæs.,* iii. 1.

Though little fire grows great with little wind, / Yet extreme gusts will blow out fire and all. *Tam. of Shrew,* ii. 1.

20 Though losses and crosses / Be lessons right severe, / There's wit there ye'll get there, / Ye'll find nae ither where. *Burns.*

Though lost to sight, to memory dear. *Anon.*

Though love cannot plant morals in the human breast, it cultivates them when there. *Goldsmith.*

Though much is taken, much abides. *Tennyson.*

Though old the thought and oft repress'd, / 'Tis his at last who says it best. *Lowell.*

Though peace be in every man's wishes, yet 25 the qualifications and predispositions necessary for procuring and preserving it are the care of very few. *Thomas à Kempis.*

Though scorn's malignant glances / Prove him poorest of his clan, / He's the noble—who advances / Freedom, and the cause of Man ! *C. Swain.*

Though stars in skies may disappear, / And angry tempests gather, / The happy hour may soon be near / That brings us pleasant weather. *Burns.*

Though the cat winks a while, yet sure she is not blind. *Pr.*

Though the heavens fall, the orbs of truth and justice fall not. *J. Burroughs.*

Though the world exists for thought, thought 30 is daunted in presence of the world. *Emerson.*

Though this be madness, yet there is method in't. *Ham.,* ii. 2.

Though thousands hate physic, because of the cost, / Yet thousands it helpeth, that else should be lost. *Thomas Tusser.*

Though we lose our fortune, yet we should not lose our patience. *Pr.*

Though wisdom wake, suspicion sleeps / At wisdom's gate ; and to simplicity / Resigns her charge, while goodness thinks no ill where no ill seems. *Milton.*

Though you can fret me, you cannot play upon 35 me. *Ham.,* iii. 2.

Though you had the wisdom of Newton or the wit of Swift, garrulousness would lower you in the eyes of your fellow-creatures. *Burns.*

Though you stroke the nettle ever so kindly, yet it will sting you. *Pr.*

Thought and science follow their own law of development ; they are slowly elaborated in the growth and forward pressure of humanity, in what Shakespeare calls . . . The prophetic soul / Of the wide world dreaming on things to come. *Matthew Arnold.*

Thought discovered is the more possessed. *Young.*

Thought disturbs the world, and thought of 40 God / Unsettles most of all ; for it is life, / And only life can comprehend its force, / Or guide it. *Dr. W. Smith.*

Thought expands, but lames ; action animates, but narrows. *Goethe.*

Thought is deeper than all speech ; / Feeling deeper than all thought ; / Souls to souls can never teach / What unto themselves was taught. *C. P. Cranch.*

Thought is free. *As You Like It,* i. 3.

Thought is like opium : it can intoxicate us while it leaves us broad awake. *Amiel.*

Thought is silence. *Sheridan.*   45

Thought is the property of him who can entertain it, and of him who can adequately place it. *Emerson.*

Thought is the seed of action; but action is as much its second form as thought is its first. It rises in thought, to the end that it may be uttered and acted. The more profound the thought, the more burdensome. Always in proportion to the depth of its sense does it knock importunately at the gates of the soul, to be spoken, to be done. *Emerson.*

Thought is the wind, knowledge the sail, and mankind the vessel. *Hare.*

Thought means life, since those who do not think do not live in any high or real sense. Thinking makes the man. *A. B. Alcott.*

Thought once awakened does not again slumber. *Carlyle.*

Thought takes man out of servitude into freedom. *Emerson.*

5 Thought, true labour of any kind, highest virtue itself, is it not the daughter of pain ? Born as out of the black whirlwind ; true effort in fact, as of a captive struggling to free itself—that is thought. *Carlyle.*

Thought without reverence is barren, perhaps poisonous ; at best dies, like cookery, with the day that called it forth. *Carlyle.*

Thought works in silence, so does virtue. *Carlyle.*

Thoughtlessness is precisely the chief public calamity of our day. *Ruskin.*

Thoughts are but dreams till their effects be tried. *Shakespeare.*

10 Thoughts are not always at our beck ; we must wait till they come. *Schopenhauer.*

Thoughts (are) the slaves of life, and life time's fool ; / And time, that takes survey of all the world, / Must have a stop. *1 Hen. IV., v. 4.*

Thoughts are your own ; your words are so no more. *Delaune.*

Thoughts come into our minds by avenues which we never left open, and thoughts go out of our minds through avenues which we never voluntary opened. *Emerson.*

Thoughts shut up want air, and spoil, like bales unopened to the sun. *Young.*

15 Thoughts take up no room. *Jeremy Collier.*

Thoughts that breathe and words that burn. *Gray.*

Thoughts that do often lie too deep for tears. *Wordsworth.*

Thoughts that voluntary move / Harmonious numbers. *Milton.*

Thoughts we have had and pictures we have seen can be recalled by the mind ; but the heart is not so obliging ; it does not reproduce our pleasing emotions. *Goethe.*

20 Threaten the threatener, and outface the brow / Of bragging horror ; so shall inferior eyes, / That borrow their behaviours from the great, / Grow great by your example, and put on / The dauntless spirit of resolution. *King John, v. 1.*

Threatened folks live long. *Pr.*

Three may keep a secret—if two of them are dead. *Ben. Franklin.*

Three poets in three distant ages born, / Greece, Italy, and England did adorn. / The first in loftiness of thought surpass'd ; / The next, in majesty ; in both, the last. / The force of Nature could no further go ; / To make a third, she join'd the former two. *Dryden.*

Three removes are as bad as a fire. *Ben. Franklin.*

25 Three things drive a man out of doors—smoke, a leaking roof, and a scolding wife. *Pr.*

Three things that enrich genius are contentment of mind, the cherishing of good thoughts, and the exercise of memory. *Southey.*

Three thousand miles of ocean space are less impressive than three miles bounded by rugged mountain walls. *John Burroughs.*

Three women and a goose make a market. *It., Dut., and Dan. Pr.*

Thrice happy he who without rigour saves. *Thomson.*

Thrice happy life that's from ambition free. 30 *Allan Ramsay.*

Thrice is he arm'd that hath his quarrel just ; / And he but naked, though locked up in steel, / Whose conscience with injustice is corrupted. *2 Hen. VI., iii. 2.*

Thrift must begin with little savings. *Pr.*

Thrifty be, but not covetous. *George Herbert.*

Through certain humours or passions, and from temper merely, a man may be completely miserable, let his outward circumstances be ever so fortunate. *Lord Shaftesbury.*

Through every star, through every grass 35 blade, and most through every living soul, the glory of a present God still beams. *Carlyle.*

Through steep ascents, through strait and rugged ways, / Ourselves to glory's lofty seats we raise : / In vain he hopes to reach the bless'd abode / Who leaves the narrow path for the more easy road. *Boscan.*

Through tatter'd clothes small vices do appear ; / Robes and furr'd gowns hide all. *King Lear, iv. 6.*

Through "the ruins of a falling era," not once missing his footing. *Carlyle of his father.*

Through want of enterprise and faith men are where they are, buying and selling, and spending their lives like serfs. *Thoreau.*

Through wisdom is an house builded ; and by 40 understanding it is established ; and by knowledge shall the chambers be filled with all precious and pleasant riches. *Bible.*

Throw no gift again at the giver's head ; / Better is half a loaf than no bread. *Pr.*

Throw physic to the dogs ; I'll none of it. *Macb., v. 3.*

Thu' nur das Rechte in deinen Sachen, / Das Andre wird sich von selber machen—In thy affairs do thou only what is right, the rest will follow of itself. *Goethe.*

Thursday come, and the week's gone. *Pr.*

Thus grief still treads upon the heels of plea- 45 sure ; / Married in haste, we may repent at leisure. *Congreve.*

Thus the native hue of resolution / Is sicklied o'er with the pale cast of thought. *Ham., iii. 1.*

Thus the whirligig of time brings in his revenges. *Twelfth Night, iv. 2.*

Thus we play the fools with the time ; and the spirits of the wise sit in the clouds, and mock us. *2 Hen. IV., ii. 2.*

Thus when I shun Scylla, your father, I fall into Charybdis, your mother. *Mer. of Venice, iii. 5.*

Thus with the year / Seasons return ; but not 50 to me returns / Day, or the sweet approach of even or morn, / Or sight of vernal bloom or summer's rose, / Or flocks, or herds, or human face divine ; / But cloud instead, and ever-during dark / Surrounds me. *Milton.*

Thy actions, and thy actions alone, determine thy worth. *Fichte.*

Thy friend put in thy bosom; wear his eyes / Still in thy heart, that he may see what's there. / If cause require, thou art his sacrifice. . . . / But love is lost; the way of friendship's gone. *George Herbert.*

Thy hand is never the worse for doing thy own work. *Pr.*

Thy love to me was wonderful, passing the love of women. *Bible.*

5 Thy nature / It is too full of the milk of human kindness / To catch the nearest way. *Macb.,* i. 5.

Thy people shall be willing in the day of thy power. *Bible.*

Thy praise or dispraise is to me alike, / One doth not stroke me, nor the other strike. *Ben. Jonson.*

Thy secret is thy prisoner. *Pr.*

Thy soul was like a star and dwelt apart. *Wordsworth.*

10 Thy spirit, Independence, let me share; / Lord of the lion-heart and eagle-eye! / Thy steps I follow with my bosom bare, / Nor heed the storm that howls along the sky! *Smollett.*

Thy sum of duty let two words contain; / Be humble and be just. *Prior.*

Thy true beginning and Father is in heaven, whom with the bodily eye thou shalt never behold, but only with the spiritual. *Carlyle.*

Thy wish was father, Harry, to that thought. *2 Hen. IV.,* iv. 4.

Tibi nullum periculum esse perspicio, quod quidem sejunctum sit ab omnium interitu—I can see no danger to which you are exposed, other than that which threatens the destruction of us all. *Cic.*

15 Tickle me, Bobby, and I'll tickle you. *Pr.*

Tie up thy fears. / He that forbears / To suit and serve his need, /' Deserves his load. *George Herbert.*

Tie your camel up as best you can, and then trust it to Providence. *Mahomet.*

Tief und ernstlich denkende Menschen haben gegen das Publikum einen bösen Stand— Deeply and earnestly thoughtful men stand on an unfavourable footing with the public. *Goethe.*

Tief zu denken und schön zu empfinden ist Vielen gegeben; Dichter ist nur, wer schön sagt was er dacht' und empfand—To think deeply and to feel beautifully is given to many; only he who expresses beautifully what he has thought and felt is a poet. *Geibel.*

20 Tiens à la vérité—Stick to the truth. *M.*

Tiens à ta foy—Hold to thy faith. *M.*

Tiers état—The third estate; the commons. *Fr.*

Till the hand . . . from reed or string / Draws out faint echoes of the voice Divine / That bring God nearer to a faithless world. *Lewis Morris.*

Time and chance can do nothing for those who will do nothing for themselves. Providence itself can scarcely save a people who are not prepared to make a struggle for their safety. *Canning.*

25 Time and I against any two. *Philip II.*

Time and space are not God, but creations of God; with God, as it is a universal Here, so is it an everlasting Now. *Carlyle.*

Time and thinking tame the strongest grief. *Pr.*

Time antiquates antiquities, and hath an art to make dust of all things. *Sir Thomas Browne.*

Time, as it is, cannot stay; / Nor again, as it was, can it be; / Disappearing and passing away / Are the world, and the ages, and we. *Lord Lytton.*

Time brings roses. *Pr.*

Time conquers all, and we must time obey. 30 *Pope.*

Time consecrates; and what is grey with age becomes religion. *Schiller.*

Time destroys the speculations of man, but it confirms the judgment of nature. *Cic.*

Time devours all things. *Pr.*

Time dissipates to shining ether the solid 35 angularity of facts. *Emerson.*

Time drinketh up the essence of every great and noble action which ought to be performed, and is delayed in the execution. *Hitopadesa.*

Time elaborately thrown away. *Young.*

Time gives prudence; the lord of time, inspiration; the one is a reward, the other a gift. *Börne.*

Time has a strange contracting influence on many a wide-spread fame. *Carlyle.*

Time has only a relative existence. *Carlyle.* 40

Time incessantly hasteneth on; he seeks for perfection: if thou art true, thou canst cast fetters eternal on him. *Schiller.*

Time is a continual over-dropping of moments, which fall down one upon the other and evaporate. *Jean Paul.*

Time is a strange thing. It is a whimsical tyrant, which in every century has a different face for all that one says and does. *Goethe.*

Time is a wonder-working god. In one hour many thousand grains of sand run out, so quickly do thoughts stir in the minds of men. *Schiller.*

Time is but a stream I go a-fishing in. I 45 drink at it; but while I drink I see the sandy bottom, and detect how shallow it is. Its thin current slides away, but eternity remains. I would drink deeper, fish in the sky, whose bottom is pebbly with stars. *Thoreau.*

Time is but the measure of the difficulty of a conception. Pure thought has scarcely any need of time, since it perceives the two ends of an idea almost the same moment. *Amiel.*

Time is eternity, / Pregnant with all eternity can give. *Young.*

Time is generally the best doctor. *Ovid.*

Time is incalculably long, and every day is a vessel into which very much may be poured, if one will really fill it up. *Goethe.*

Time is like a fashionable host, / That slightly 50 shakes his parting guest by the hand; / And with his arms outstretched, as he would fly, / Grasps in the comer. *Troil. and Cress.,* iii. 3.

Time is like a river, in which metals and solid substances are sunk, while chaff and straws swim upon the surface. *Bacon.*

Time is money. *Pr.*

Time is never more misspent than while we declaim against the want of it. *Zimmermann.*

Time is of more value than type, and the wear and tear of temper than an extra page of index. *R. H. Busk.*.

Time is the chrysalis of eternity. *Jean Paul.*

Time is the life of the soul. If not this, then tell me what is time? *Longfellow.*

Time is the most undefinable yet paradoxical of things ; the past is gone, the future is not come, and the present becomes the past, even while we attempt to define it, and, like the flash of the lightning, at once exists and expires. *Colton.*

5 Time is the nurse and breeder of all good. *Two Gent. of Ver.*, iii. 1.

Time is the old justice that examines all offenders. *As You Like It*, iv. 1.

Time is the stuff life is made of. *Ben. Franklin.*

Time is the wheel-track in which we roll on towards eternity. *W. v. Humboldt.*

Time is trouble and the author of destruction ; he seizeth even from afar. *Hitopadesa.*

10 Time reposes on eternity ; the truly great and transcendental has its basis and substance in eternity ; stands revealed to us as eternity in a vesture of time. *Carlyle.*

Time shall unfold what plaited cunning hides : / Who cover faults, at last shame them derides. *King Lear*, i. 1.

Time, that black and narrow isthmus between two eternities. *Colton.*

Time the shuttle drives, but you / Give to every thread its hue, / And elect your destiny. *W. H. Burleigh.*

Time trieth truth. *Pr.*

15 Time was when a Christian used to apologise for being happy. But the day has always been when he ought to apologise for being miserable. *Prof. Drummond.*

Time wasted is existence ; used, is life. *Young.*

Time, when well husbanded, is like a cultivated field, of which a few acres produce more of what is useful to life, than extensive provinces, even of the richest soil, when overrun with weeds and brambles. *Hume.*

Time, which deadens hatred, secretly strengthens love ; and in the hour of threatened separation its growth is manifested at once in radiant brightness. *Jean Paul.*

Time will discover everything to posterity ; it is a babbler, and speaks even when no question is put. *Euripides.*

20 Time works great changes. *Pr.*

Time writes no wrinkle on thine azure brow ; / Such as creation's dawn beheld, thou rollest now. *Byron.*

Time's best gift to us is serenity. *Bovee.*

Time's noblest offspring is the last. *Berkeley.*

Time's the king of men ; / He's both their parent and he is their grave, / And gives them what he will, not what they crave. *Pericles*, ii. 3.

25 Time's waters will not ebb nor stay ; / Power cannot change them, but Love may ; / What cannot be, Love counts it done. *Keble.*

Timely advised, the coming evil shun ; / Better not do the deed, than weep it done. *Prior.*

Timeo Danaos, et dona ferentes—I distrust the Greeks, even when they bring gifts. *Virg.*

Times of general calamity and confusion have ever been productive of the greatest minds. *Colton.*

Timet pudorem—He fears shame. *M.*

Timidi mater non flet—The mother of the coward 30 has no occasion to weep. *Pr.*

Timidus se vocat cautum, parcum sordidus— The coward calls himself cautious, the miser thrifty. *Pub. Syr.*

Timor Domini fons vitæ—The fear of the Lord is a fountain of life. *M.*

Tinsel reflects the sun, but warms nothing. *Prof. Drummond.*

Tired Nature's sweet restorer, balmy Sleep ! / He, like the world, his ready visit pays / Where Fortune smiles ; the wretched he forsakes : / Swift on his downy pinions flies from woe, / And lights on lids unsullied with a tear. *Young.*

Tirer le diable par la queue—To be in great 35 straits (*lit.* to pull the devil by the tail).

Tirer les marrons du feu avec la patte du chat —To make a cat's paw of any one (*lit.* to take the chestnuts from the fire with a cat's paw. *La Fontaine.*

Tirez le rideau ; la farce est jouée—Draw the curtain ; the farce is played out. *Last words of Rabelais.*

'Tis a consummation / Devoutly to be wished. *Ham.*, iii. 1.

'Tis a cruelty / To load a falling man. *Henry VIII.*, v. 2.

'Tis a folly to fret ; grief's no comfort. *Pr.* 40

'Tis a good ill that comes alone. *Pr.*

'Tis a kind of good deed to say well : / And yet words are no deeds. *Henry VIII.*, iii. 2.

'Tis a lucky day, boy, and we'll do good deeds on't. *Winter's Tale*, iii. 3.

'Tis a physic that's bitter to sweet end. *Meas. for Meas.*, iv. 6.

'Tis a question whether adversity or prosperity 45 makes the most poets. *Farquhar.*

'Tis a vile thing to die . . . / When men are unprepar'd and look not for it. *Rich. III.*, iii. 2.

'Tis all one to be a witch as to be counted one. *The Witch of Edmonton.*

'Tis always a delightful thing to see the human understanding following its imprescriptible rights in spite of all hindrances, and hurrying eagerly towards the utmost possible agreement between ideas and objects. *Goethe.*

'Tis an economy of time to read old and famed books. *Emerson.*

'Tis an old maxim in the schools / That flat- 50 tery's the food of fools ; / Yet now and then your men of wit / Will condescend to take a bit. *Swift.*

'Tis beauty that doth oft make women proud ; / 'Tis virtue that doth make them most admired ; / 'Tis government that makes them seem divine. *3 Hen. VI.*, i. 4.

'Tis better to be lowly born, / And range with humble livers in content, / Than to be perked up in a glistering grief, / And wear a golden sorrow. *Hen. VIII.*, ii. 2.

'Tis better to cry over your goods than after them. *Pr.*

'Tis better to have loved and lost / Than never to have loved at all. *Tennyson.*

'Tis but a base, ignoble mind / That mounts no higher than a bird can soar. *2 Hen. VI.,* ii. 1.

'Tis but lame kindness that does its work by halves. *Blair.*

'Tis, by comparison, an easy task / Earth to despise ; but to converse with heaven— / This is not easy. *Wordsworth.*

'Tis certainly much easier for a man to restrain himself from talking at all, than to enter into discourse without saying more than becomes him. *Thomas à Kempis.*

5 'Tis day still while the sun shines. *Pr.*

'Tis death to me to be at enmity ; / I hate it, and desire all good men's love. *Rich. III.,* ii. 1.

'Tis distance lends enchantment to the view, / And robes the mountain in its azure hue. *Campbell.*

'Tis education forms the common mind, / Just as the twig is bent, the tree's inclined. *Pope.*

'Tis ever common that men are merriest when they are from home. *Hen. V.,* i. 2.

10 'Tis expectation makes a blessing dear ; / Heaven were not heaven if we knew what it were. *Suckling.*

'Tis God / Diffused through all that doth make all one whole. *Coleridge.*

'Tis heaven alone that is given away ; / 'Tis only God may be had for the asking. *Lowell.*

'Tis impossible you should take true root, but by the fair weather that you make yourself ; it is needful that you frame the season for your own harvest. *Much Ado,* i. 3.

'Tis, in fact, utter folly to ask whether a person has anything from himself, or whether he has it from others, whether he operates by himself, or operates by means of others. The main point is to have a great will, and skill and perseverance to carry it out. All else is indifferent. *Goethe.*

15 'Tis life itself to love. *Goethe.*

'Tis life reveals to each his genuine worth. *Goethe.*

'Tis little we can do for each other. *Emerson.*

'Tis long since death had the majority. *Blair.*

'Tis mad idolatry / To make the service greater than the god. *Troil. and Cress.,* ii. 2.

20 'Tis my opinion 'tis necessary to be happy, that we think no place more agreeable than that where we are. *Lady Montagu.*

'Tis my vocation, Hal ; 'tis no sin for a man to labour in his vocation. *1 Hen. IV.,* i. 2.

'Tis not a lip, or eye, we beauty call, / But the joint force and full result of all. *Pope.*

'Tis not always necessary that truth should be embodied, it is sufficient if it hovers about in the spirit, producing harmony ; if, like the chime of bells, it vibrates through the air solemnly and kindly. *Goethe.*

'Tis not enough to keep the feeble up, / But to support them after. *Tim. of Athens,* i. 1.

25 'Tis not enough when swarming faults are writ, / That here and there are scatter'd sparks of wit. *Dryden.*

'Tis not enough your counsel still be true ; / Blunt truths more mischief than nice falsehoods do. *Pope.*

'Tis not in mortals to command success, / But we'll do more, Sempronius—we'll deserve it. *Addison.*

'Tis not prudent, 'tis not well, to meet / With purposed misconception any man, / Let him be who he may. *Goethe.*

'Tis not so above : / There is no shuffling ; there the action lies / In its true nature. *Ham.,* iii. 3.

'Tis not the drinking that is to be blamed, but 30 the excess. *Selden.*

'Tis not the whole of life to live, / Nor all of death to die. *J. Montgomery.*

'Tis not want, but rather abundance, that creates avarice. *Montaigne.*

'Tis not what man does which exalts him, but what man would do. *Browning.*

'Tis not worth while quarrelling with the world, simply to afford it some amusement. *Goethe.*

'Tis now the very witching time of night, / 35 When churchyards yawn, and hell itself breathes out / Contagion to this world. *Ham.,* iii. 2.

'Tis only humanity as a whole that perceives Nature, only men collectively that live the life of man. *Goethe.*

'Tis only in Rome one can duly prepare one's self for Rome. *Goethe.*

'Tis only in the forehead Nature plants the watchful eye ; the back, without defence, must find its shield in man's fidelity. *Schiller.*

'Tis only noble to be good ; / Kind hearts are more than coronets, / And simple faith than Norman blood. *Tennyson.*

'Tis only strict precision of thought that con- 40 fers facility of expression. *Schiller.*

'Tis only woman's womanly beauty that makes a true queen ; wherever she appears, and by her mere presence, she asserts her sovereignty. *Schiller.*

'Tis pleasant, sure, to see one's name in print ; / A book's a book, although there's nothing in't. *Byron.*

'Tis rashness to conclude affairs in a lost condition because some crosses have baulked your expectations. *Thomas à Kempis.*

'Tis said fantastic ocean doth unfold the likeness of whate'er on land is seen. *Wordsworth.*

'Tis said that virtue dwells sublime / On 45 rugged cliffs, full hard to climb ; / . . . But mortal ne'er her form may see, / Unless his restless energy / Breaks forth in sweat that gains the goal, / The perfect manhood of the soul. *Simonides.*

'Tis strange ; / And oftentimes to win us to our harm, / The instruments of darkness tell us truths ; / Win us with honest trifles, to betray 's, / In deepest consequence. *Macb.,* i. 3.

'Tis sweet to hear of heroes dead, / To know them still alive, / But sweeter if we earn their bread, / And in us they survive. *Thomson.*

'Tis the curse of service ; preferment goes by letter and affection, not by the old gradation where each second stood heir to the first. *Othello,* i. 1.

'Tis the divinity that stirs within us ; / 'Tis heaven itself that points out an hereafter, / And intimates eternity to man. *Addison.*

'Tis the fate of the noblest soul to sigh vainly 50 for a reflection of itself. *Goethe.*

'Tis the fine souls who serve us, and not what is called fine society. *Emerson.*

'Tis the fulness of man that runs over into objects, and makes his Bibles and Shakespeares and Homers so great. *Emerson.*

'Tis the good reader that makes the good book ; a good head cannot read amiss ; in every book he finds passages which seem confidences, or asides, hidden from all else and unmistakably meant for his ear. *Emerson.*

'Tis the mind that makes the body rich ; / And as the sun breaks through the darkest clouds, / So honour peereth in the meanest habit. *Tam. of Shrew,* iv. 3.

'Tis the old secret of the gods that they come in low disguises. 'Tis the vulgar great who come dizened with gold and jewels. *Emerson.*

5 'Tis the part of a poor spirit to undervalue himself and blush. *George Herbert.*

'Tis the same to him who wears a shoe as if the whole earth were thatched with leather. *Persian Pr.*

'Tis the sublime of man, / Our noontide majesty, to know ourselves / Parts and proportions of one wondrous whole ! / This fraternises man, this constitutes / Our charities and bearings. *Coleridge.*

'Tis this (religion), my friend, that streaks our morning bright. *Thomson.* (?)

'Tis too much proved that, with devotion's visage / And pious action, we do sugar o'er / The devil himself. *Ham.,* iii. 1.

10 'Tis well for once to do everything one can do, in order to have the merit of knowing one's self more intimately. *Goethe.*

'Tis well to be merry and wise, / 'Tis well to be honest and true ; / 'Tis well to be off with the old love / Before you are on with the new. (?)

'Tis when sovereigns build, carters are kept employed. *Schiller.*

'Tis with our judgments as our watches ; none / Go just alike, yet each believes his own. *Pope.*

Tit for tat is fair play. *Pr.*

15 Titles and mottoes to books are like escutcheons and dignities in the hands of a king. The wise sometimes condescend to accept of them ; but none but a fool would imagine them of any real importance. We ought to depend upon intrinsic merit, and not the slender helps of the title. *Goldsmith.*

Titles of honour add not to his worth who is himself an honour to his title. *John Ford.*

Titles of honour conferred upon such as have no personal merit are at best but the royal stamp set upon base metal. (?)

Titus, amor et deliciæ humani generis—Titus, the delight and darling of the human race. *Suetonius.*

To a child in confinement its mother's knee is · a binding-post. *Hitopadesa.*

20 To a dog the choicest thing in the world is a dog: to an ox, an ox ; to an ass, an ass ; and to a sow, a sow. *Schopenhauer.*

To a father waxing old nothing is dearer than a daughter. *Euripides.*

To a father, when his child dies, the future dies ; to a child when his parents die, the past dies. *Auerbach.*

To a new truth nothing is more mischievous than an old error. *Goethe.*

To a poet nothing can be useless. *Johnson.*

To accuse a man of lying is as much as to say 25 he is brave towards God and a coward towards man. *Montaigne.*

To achieve great things a man must so live as if he had never to die. *Vauvenargues.*

To acquire certainty in the appreciation of things exactly as they are, and to know them in their due subordination, and in their proper relation to one another—this is really the highest enjoyment to which we ought to aspire, whether in the sphere of art, of nature, or of life. *Goethe.*

To act is easy, to think is hard ; to act according to our thought is troublesome. *Goethe.*

To act with a purpose is what raises man above the brutes ; to invent with a purpose, to imitate with a purpose, is that which distinguishes genius from the petty artists who only invent to invent, and imitate to imitate. *Lessing.*

To adhere to what is set down in them, and 30 appropriate to one's self what one can for moral strengthening and culture, is the only edifying purpose to which we can turn the Gospels. *Goethe.*

To affect a quality is just to confess that you have not got it. *Schopenhauer.*

To aim at excellence, our reputation, our friends, and our all must be ventured ; by aiming only at mediocrity, we run no risk and we do little service. *Goldsmith.*

To an ill-conditioned being all pleasure is like delicate wine in a mouth embittered with gall. *Schopenhauer.*

To answer a question so as to admit of no reply, is the test of a man. *Emerson.*

To appear well-bred, a man must actually be 35 so. *Goethe.*

To appreciate the noble is a gain which can never be torn from us. *Goethe.*

To arrive at perfection, a man should have very sincere friends or inveterate enemies ; because he would be made sensible of his good or ill conduct, either by the censures of the one or the admonitions of the other. *Diogenes.*

To attack vices in the abstract without touching persons, may be safe fighting indeed, but it is fighting with shadows. *Junius.*

To banish care, scare away sorrow, and soothe pain is the business of the poet, or singer (*Sänger*). *Bodenstedt.*

To be a good poet and painter genius is re- 40 quired, and this cannot be communicated. *Goethe.*

To be a man's own fool is bad enough ; but the vain man is everybody's. *William Penn.*

To be a philosopher is but a retreat from the world, as it is man's, into the world, as it is God's. *Cowley.*

To be a philosopher is not merely to have subtle thoughts, nor even to found a school, but so to love wisdom as to live, according to its dictates, a life of simplicity, independence, magnanimity, and trust. It is to solve some of the problems of life, not only theoretically, but practically. *Thoreau.*

To be a poet is to have a soul in which knowledge passes instantaneously into feeling, and feeling flashes back as a new organ of knowledge. *George Eliot.*

To be able simply to say of a man he has character, is not only saying much of him, but extolling him; for this is a rarity which excites respect and wonder. *Goethe.*

To be able to be silent shows power; to be willing to be silent shows forbearance (*Nachsicht*); to be compelled to be silent shows the spirit of the time. *Weber.*

To be acquainted with the merit of a Ministry, we need only observe the condition of the people. *Junius.*

To be always lamenting and always complaining without raising and nerving one's self to resignation, is to lose at once both earth and heaven, and have nothing over but a watery sentimentalism. *Schopenhauer.*

5 To be always thinking about your manners is not the way to make them good; because the very perfection of manners is not to think about yourself. *Whately.*

To be an enthusiast is to be the worthiest of affection, the noblest and the best that a mortal can be. *Wieland.*

To be angry is to avenge the faults of others upon ourselves. *Pope.*

To be as good as our fathers, we must be better. Imitation is not discipleship. When some one sent a cracked plate to China to have a set made, every piece in the new set had a crack in it. *Wendell Phillips.*

To be bodily tranquil, to speak little, and to digest without effort are absolutely necessary to grandeur of mind or of presence, or to proper development of genius. *Balzac.*

10 To be born in a duck's nest in a farmyard is of no consequence to a bird if it is hatched from a swan's egg. *Hans Andersen.*

To be born with a silver spoon in the mouth. *Pr.*

To be borne seems to many ever more kingly than to bear; and a ship carried with the breeze is, in their eyes, a lordlier spectacle than when it stands against it, victoriously braving it. *Ed.*

To be disobedient through temptation is human sin; but to be disobedient for the sake of disobedience, fiendish sin. To be obedient for the sake of success in conduct is human virtue; to be obedient for the sake of obedience, angelic virtue. *Ruskin.*

To be ever beloved, one must be ever agreeable. *Lady Montagu.*

15 To be free is not to do nothing, but to be the sole arbiter of what we do and what we leave undone. *La Bruyère.*

To be good and disagreeable is high treason against the royalty of virtue. *Hannah More.*

To be great is to be misunderstood. *Emerson.*

To be great one must be positive, and gain strength through foes. *Donn Piatt.*

To be guided in the right path by those who know better than they is the first "right of man," compared with which all other rights are as nothing. *Carlyle.*

20 To be happy is not the purpose of our being, but to deserve happiness. *Fichte.*

To be happy means to be sufficient for one's self. *Arist.*

To be honest, as this world goes, is to be one man picked out of ten thousand. *Ham., ii. 2.*

To be idle and to be poor have always been reproaches; and therefore every man endeavours with his utmost care to hide his poverty from others, and his idleness from himself. *Johnson.*

To be ill thought of is sometimes for thy good, . . . if thou seek not thy own glory, but His that sent thee, the affliction will not be very grievous to be borne. *Thomas à Kempis.*

To be in too great a hurry to discharge an 25 obligation is itself a kind of ingratitude. *La Roche.*

To be introduced into a decent company, there is need of a dress cut according to the taste of the public to which one wishes to present one's self. *Goethe.*

To be magnanimous—mighty of heart, mighty of mind—is to be great in life; to become this increasingly is to "advance in life." *Ruskin.*

To be mindful of an absent friend in the hours of mirth and feasting, when his company is least wanted, shows no slight degree of sincerity. *Goldsmith.*

To be misunderstood is the cross and bitterness of life. *Amiel.*

To be obliged to wear black, and buy it into 30 the bargain, is more than my tranquillity of temper can bear. *Goldsmith.*

To be once in doubt is once to be resolved. *Othello, iii. 3.*

To be, or not to be, that is the question; / Whether 'tis nobler in the mind to suffer / The stings and arrows of outrageous fortune, / Or to take up arms against a sea of troubles, / And, by opposing, end them. *Ham., iii. 1.*

To be perfectly just, is an attribute of the divine nature; to be so to the utmost of our abilities is the glory of man. (?)

To be poor, and to seem poor, is a certain method never to rise. *Goldsmith.*

To be prepared for war is one of the most 35 effectual means of preserving peace. *Washington.*

To be provoked with every slanderous word argues a littleness of soul, a want of due regard to God. *Thomas à Kempis.*

To be rich is to have a ticket of admission to the master-works and chief men of each race. *Emerson.*

To be seventy years young is sometimes far more cheerful and hopeful than to be forty years old. *Holmes.*

To be spiritually minded is life and peace. *Paul.*

To be thus is nothing; / But to be safely thus. 40 *Macb., iii. 1.*

To be true in heart and just in act are the first qualities necessary for the elevation of humanity. *Froude.*

To be vain is rather a mark of humility than pride. *Swift.*

To be vain of one's rank or place is to disclose that one is below it. *Stanislaus.*

To be weak is miserable, / Doing or suffering. *Milton.*

To be wholly loved with the whole heart, one 45 must be suffering. *Heine.*

To be wise and love exceeds man's might. *Troil. and Cress., iii. 2.*

To be without a servant in this world is not good; but to be without a master, it appears, is a still fataller predicament for some. *Carlyle.*

To be without passion is worse than a beast; to be without reason is to be less than a man. *A. Warwick.*

To be wroth with one we love, / Doth work like madness in the brain. *Coleridge.*

To be young is to be as one of the immortals. *Hazlitt.*

5 To bear is to conquer our fate. *Campbell.*

To become properly acquainted with a truth, we must first have disbelieved it and disputed against it. *Novalis.*

To beguile the time, / Look like the time; bear welcome in your eye, / Your hand, your tongue; look like the innocent flower, / But be the serpent under 't. *Macb.*, i. 5.

To believe your own thought, to believe that what is true for you in your private heart is true for all men—that is genius. *Emerson.*

To blow is not to play the flute; you must move the fingers as well. *Goethe.*

10 To breed a fresh soul, is it not like brooding a fresh (celestial) egg, wherein as yet all is formless, powerless? Yet by degrees organic elements and fibres shoot through the watery albumen; out of vague sensation grows thought, grows fantasy and force, and we have philosophies, dynasties, nay, poetries and religions. *Carlyle.*

To bring nations to surrender themselves to new ideas is not the affair of a day. *Draper.*

To bring the generality of admirers on our side, it is sufficient to attempt pleasing a very few. *Goldsmith.*

To business that we love we rise betime, / And go to 't with delight. *Ant. and Cleop.*, iv. 4.

To call a man ungrateful is to sum up all the evil he can be guilty of. *Swift.*

15 To carry on the feelings of childhood into the powers of manhood, to combine the child's sense of wonder and novelty with the appearances which every day, for perhaps forty years, has rendered familiar; this is the character and privilege of genius, and one of the marks which distinguish genius from talent. *Coleridge.*

To cast away a virtuous friend is as bad as to cast away one's own life, which one loves best. *Sophocles.*

To catch dame Fortune's golden smile, / Assiduous wait upon her; / And gather gear by ev'ry wile / That's justified by honour; / Not for to hide it in a hedge, / Nor for a train attendant, / But for the glorious privilege / Of being independent. *Burns.*

To circumstances and custom the law must yield. *Dan. Pr.*

To climb a tree to catch a fish is talking much and doing nothing. *Chinese Pr.*

20 To climb steep hills requires slow pace at first. *Hen. VIII.*, i. 1.

To confess Christ is, first, to believe righteously, truthfully, and continently; and, then, to separate ourselves from those who are manifestly or by profession rogues, liars, and fornicators. *Ruskin.*

To conquer inclination is difficult, but if habit, taking root, gradually associates itself with it, then it is unconquerable. *Goethe.*

To conquer without danger would be to conquer without glory. *Corneille.*

To consume your own choler, as some chimneys consume their own smoke; to keep a whole Satanic school spouting, if it must spout, inaudibly, is a negative yet no slight virtue, nor one of the commonest in these times. *Carlyle.*

To corporeal beings unthought-of troubles 25 arise; so, in like manner, do blessings make their appearance. In this, I think Providence hath extended them farther than usual. *Hitopadesa.*

To dance attendance on their lordships' pleasures. *Hen. VIII.*, v. 2.

To-day comes only once, and never again returns. *Schopenhauer.*

To-day is a king in disguise. *Emerson.*

To-day is ours, we have it here, . . . / To the gods belong to-morrow. *Cowley.*

To-day must not borrow of to-morrow. *Ger. Pr.* 30

To deny is easy; nothing is sooner learned or more generally practised. As matters go, we need no man of polish to teach it; but rather, if possible, a hundred men of wisdom to show us its limits and teach us its reverse. *Carlyle.*

To depersonalise man is the dominant drift of our epoch. *Amiel.*

To despise our own species is the price we must too often pay for a knowledge of it. *Colton.*

To die for truth is not to die for one's country but to die for the world. *Jean Paul.*

To die is landing on some silent shore, / Where 35 billows never break nor tempests roar. *S. Garth.*

To die, to sleep; / No more; and by a sleep to say we end / The heartache and the thousand natural shocks / That flesh is heir to, 'tis a consummation / Devoutly to be wished. *Ham.*, iii. 1.

To die, to sleep; / No more! perchance to dream; ay, there's the rub; / For in that sleep of death what dreams may come, / When we have shuffled off this mortal coil, / Must give us pause. *Ham.*, iii. 1.

To do as much good and as little evil as we can is the brief and intelligible principle that comprehends all subordinate maxims. *R. Sharp.*

To do easily what is difficult for others is the mark of talent. *Amiel.*

To do good to the ungrateful is to throw rose- 40 water into the sea. *Pr.*

To do him any wrong was to beget / A kindness from him, for his heart was rich, / Of such fine mould, that if you sow'd therein / The seed of Hate, it blossom'd Charity. *Tennyson.*

To do justice and judgment is more acceptable to the Lord than sacrifice. *Bible.*

To do no evil is good; to intend none is better. *Claudius.*

To do nothing by halves is the way of noble minds. *Wieland.*

To do, one must be doing. *Fr. Pr.*   45

To do what is impossible for talent is the mark of genius. *Amiel.*

To doubt is to dip love in the mire. *J. M. Barrie.*

To draw a long bow, *i.e.*, exaggerate. *Pr.*

To dread no eye, and to suspect no tongue, is the greatest prerogative of innocence ; an exemption granted only to invariable virtue. *Johnson.*

To dwell alone is the fate of all great souls. *Schopenhauer.*

To each nation its believed history is its Bible. *Carlyle.*

5 To eat or drink too much, to play too much, to work too much, or to grumble too much— all these are equally pernicious. *John Wagstaffe.*

To educate the intelligence is to enlarge the horizon of its desires and wants. *Lowell.*

To educate the wise man, the State exists ; and with the appearance of the wise man, the State expires. The wise man is the State. *Emerson.*

To elevate above the spirit of the age must be regarded as the end of education. *Jean Paul.*

To endeavour all one's days to fortify our minds with learning and philosophy is to spend so much in armour that one has nothing left to defend. (?)

10 To endeavour to work upon the vulgar with fine sense is like attempting to hew blocks with a razor. *Pope.*

To endure is the first and most necessary lesson a child has to learn. *Rousseau.*

To equal a predecessor, one must have twice his worth. *Gracian.*

To err is human, to forgive divine. *Pope.*

To escape from arrangements that tortured me, my heart sought refuge in the world of ideas, when as yet I was unacquainted with the world of realities, from which iron bars excluded me. *Schiller at his training-school.*

15 To every deep there is a deeper still. *Pr.*

To everything there is a season. *Bible.*

To excite a fierce dog to capture a lame rabbit is to attack a contemptible enemy. *Chinese Pr.*

To expect an author to talk as he writes is ridiculous ; or even if he did, you would find fault with him as a pedant. *Hazlitt.*

To express the most difficult matters clearly, and everything intelligibly, is to strike coins out of pure gold. *Geibel.*

20 To fail at all is to fail utterly. *Lowell.*

To fear is easy, but grievous ; to reverence is difficult, but satisfactory. *Goethe.*

To fear the foe, since fear oppresseth strength, / Gives, in your weakness, strength unto your foe. *Rich. II.*, iii. 2.

To feel and respect a great personality, one must be something one's self. *Goethe.*

To fight and die is death destroying death ; / Where fearing dying, pays death servile breath. *Rich. II.*, iii. 2.

25 To fight with its neighbours never was, and is now less than ever, the real trade of England. *Carlyle.*

To fill the hour, that is happiness. *Emerson.*

To find out your real opinion of any one, observe the impression made upon you by the first sight of a letter from him. *Schopenhauer.*

To find recreation in amusement is not happiness. *Pascal.*

To fix a child's attention on what is present, to give him a description of a name, is the best thing we can do for him. *Goethe.*

To forget a wrong is the best revenge. *It. Pr.* 30

To forgive and forget is to throw away dearly-bought experience. *Schopenhauer.*

To forgive a man from error is to give, and not to take away. *Schopenhauer.*

To form a poet, the heart must be full to overflowing of noble feeling. *Goethe.*

To free a man from error is to give, and not to take away. *Schopenhauer.*

To gain what is fit ye're able, / If ye in faith can but excel ; / Such are the myths of fable, / If ye have observed them well. *Goethe.*

To gather riches do not hazard health ; / For, 35 truth to say, health is the wealth of wealth. *Sir Richard Baker.*

To genius irregularity is incident, and the greatest genius is often marked by eccentricity, as if it disdained to move in the vulgar orbit. *Brougham.*

To genius life never grows commonplace. *Lowell.*

To get general ideas first and make particular observations last is to invert the process of education. *Schopenhauer.*

To gild refined gold, to paint the lily, / To throw a perfume on the violet, / To smooth the ice, or add another hue / Unto the rainbow, or with taper-light / To seek the beauteous eye of heaven to garnish, / Is wasteful and ridiculous excess. *King John*, iii. 1.

To give alms is nothing unless you give 40 thought also, and therefore it is written, not "Blessed is he that feedeth the poor," but "Blessed is he that considereth the poor." *Ruskin.*

To give should be our pleasure, but to receive our shame. *Goldsmith.*

To give the world more than it gives us, to love it more than it loves us, and never to make suit for its applause, ensures a peaceful life and a happy departure. *Bodenstedt.*

To give to the human mind a direction which it shall retain for ages is the rare prerogative of a few imperial spirits. *Macaulay.*

To go back is easy, if we have missed our way on the road uphill ; it is impossible only when the road is downhill. *Froude.*

To go beyond the bounds of moderation is to 45 outrage humanity. *Pascal.*

To God belongeth the east and the west ; therefore, whithersoever ye turn yourselves to pray, there is the word of God, for God is omnipresent and omniscient. *Koran.*

To govern men, you must either excel them in their accomplishments or despise them. *Disraeli.*

To grasp, to seize, is the essence of all mastery. *Goethe.*

To great evils one must oppose great virtues ; and also to small, which is the harder task of the two. *Carlyle.*

To guard from error is not the instructor's 50 business ; but to lead the erring pupil. *Goethe.*

To guide scoundrels by love is a method that will not hold together ; hardly for the flower of men will love do ; and for the sediment and scoundrelism of them it has not even a chance to do. *Carlyle.*

To have a respect for ourselves guides our morals; and to have a deference for others governs our manners. *Sterne.*

To have all one's wants satisfied is something intolerable. *Schopenhauer.*

To have any chance of lasting, a book must satisfy, not merely some fleeting fancy of the day, but a constant longing and hunger of human nature. *Lowell.*

To have ascertained what is ascertainable, and calmly to reverence what is not, is the fairest portion that can fall to a thinking man. *Goethe.*

5 To have done anything by which you earned money merely is to have been truly idle, or worse. *Thoreau.*

To have done, is to hang / Quite out of fashion, like a rusty mail, / In monumental mockery. *Troil. and Cres.*, iii. 3.

To have gold is to be in fear, and to want it to be in sorrow. *Johnson.*

To have heard the voice / Of Godhead in the winds and in the seas, / To have known him in the circling of the suns, / And in the changeful fates and lives of men. *Lewis Morris.*

To have ideas is to gather flowers; to think is to weave them into garlands. *Mme. Swetchine.*

10 To have neither superior, nor inferior, nor equal, united manlike to you; without father, without child, without brother,—man knows no sadder destiny. *Carlyle.*

To have no assistance from other minds in resolving doubts, in appeasing scruples, in balancing deliberations, is a very wretched destitution. *Johnson.*

To have no pain, and not be bored, is the utmost happiness possible to man on earth. *Schopenhauer.*

To have read the greatest works of any great poet, to have beheld or heard the greatest works of any great painter or musician, is a possession added to the best things of life. *Swinburne.*

To have religion upon authority, and not upon conviction, is like a finger-watch, to be set forwards or backwards, as he pleases that has it in keeping. *William Penn.*

15 To have the fear of God before our eyes, and, in our mutual dealings with each other, to govern our actions by the eternal measures of right and wrong; the first of these will comprehend the duties of religion; the second, those of morality. *Sterne.*

To have the gift of life and bread to sustain it with can never suffice as a substitute for the ministry and service which the life itself is given us that we may fulfil. To find and work out this is man's only satisfaction and true reward. *Ed.*

To hear complaints is wearisome alike to the wretched and the happy. *Johnson.*

To Him no high, no low, no great, no small; / He fills, He bounds, connects and equals all. *Pope.*

To him that knoweth to do good, and doeth it not, to him it is sin. *St. James.*

20 To his (the host's) imagination all things travel save his sign-post and himself. *Thoreau.*

To hold, as 'twere, the mirror up to nature. *Ham.*, iii. 2.

To holy tears, / In lonely hours, Christ risen appears; / In social hours, who Christ would see / Must turn all tasks to charity. *Keble.*

To imitate the style of another is said to be wearing a mask. However beautiful it may be, it is through its lifelessness insipid and intolerable, so that even the most ugly living face is more engaging. *Schopenhauer.*

To improve the golden moment of opportunity, and catch the good that is within our reach, is the great art of life. *Johnson.*

To judge by the event is an error all abuse 25 and all commit; for in every instance, courage, if crowned with success, is heroism; if clouded by defeat, temerity. *Colton.*

To judge is to see clearly, to care for what is just. *Amiel.*

To keep the wolf from the door. *Pr.*

To know a man, observe how he wins his object, rather than how he loses it; for when we fail, our pride supports us,—when we succeed, it betrays us. *Colton.*

To know by rote is no knowledge; it is only to retain in the memory what is entrusted to it. *Montaigne.*

To know evil of others and not speak it, is 30 sometimes discretion; to speak evil of others and not know it, is always dishonesty. He may be evil himself who speaks good of others upon knowledge, but he can never be good himself who speaks evil of others upon suspicion. *Arthur Warwick.*

To know how to dissemble is the knowledge of kings. *Richelieu.*

To know how to grow old is the master-work of wisdom, and one of the most difficult chapters in the great art of living. *Amiel.*

To know how to suggest is the great art of teaching. *Amiel.*

To know how to wait is the great secret of success. *De Maistre.*

To know life we must detach ourselves from 35 life. *Feuerbach.*

To know my deed, 'twere best not know myself. *Macb.*, ii. 2.

To know of some one here and there with whom we accord, who is living on with us even in silence, this makes our earthly ball a peopled garden. *Goethe.*

To know one profession only, is enough for one man to know. *Goldsmith.*

To know / That which before us lies in daily life, / Is the prime wisdom. *Milton.*

To know the divine laws and inner harmonies 40 of this universe must always be the highest glory for a man; and not to know them always the highest disgrace for a man, however common it be. *Carlyle.*

To know the true opinions of men, one ought to pay more respect to their actions than their words. *Descartes.*

To know the world, a modern phrase! a modern phrase / For visits, ombre, balls, and plays. *Swift.*

To know, to esteem, to love, and then to part, / Makes up life's tale to many a feeling heart. *Coleridge.*

To know; to get into the truth of anything, is ever a mystic act, of which the best logics can only babble on the surface. *Carlyle.*

To know what is useful and what useless, and to be skilful to provide the one and wise to scorn the other, is the first need for all industrious men. *Ruskin.*

To lament the past is vain ; what remains is to look for hope in futurity. *Johnson.*

To lapse in fulness / Is sorer than to lie for need ; and falsehood / Is worse in kings than beggars. *Cymbeline*, iii. 6.

To learn obeying is the fundamental art of governing. *Carlyle.*

5 To live by one man's will became the cause of all men's misery. *Hooker.*

To live happily only means to live tolerably. *Schopenhauer.*

To live in hearts we leave behind / Is not to die. *Campbell.*

To live is not to breathe ; it is to act. *Rousseau.*

To live is to achieve a perpetual triumph. *Amiel.*

10 To live long is to outlive much. *Goethe.*

To look at things as well as we can, to inscribe them in our memory, to be observant, and let no day pass without gathering something ; then to apply one's self to those branches of knowledge which give the mind a sure direction, to apportion everything its place, to assign to everything its value (in my opinion a genuine philosophy and a fundamental mathesis), this is what we have now to do. *Goethe.*

To lose one's self in revery, one must be either very happy or very unhappy. Revery is the child of extreme. *Rivarol.*

To love and to be loved is the greatest happiness of existence. *Sydney Smith.*

To love all mankind, from the greatest to the lowest, a cheerful state of being is required ; but in order to see into mankind, into life, and still more into ourselves, suffering is requisite. *Jean Paul.*

15 To love early and marry late is to hear a lark singing at dawn, and at night to eat it roasted for supper. *Jean Paul.*

To love is to be useful to yourself ; to cause love is to be useful to others. *Béranger.*

To maintain one's self on this earth is not a hardship, but a pastime, if we would live simply and wisely. *Thoreau.*

To mak' a happy fireside clime / To weans and wife, / That's the true pathos and sublime / O' human life. *Burns.*

To make a boy despise his mother's care is the straightest way to make him also despise his Redeemer's voice ; and to make him scorn his father and his father's house, the straightest way to make him deny his God and his God's heaven. *Ruskin.*

20 To make elaborate preparations for life is one of the greatest and commonest of human follies. *Schopenhauer.*

To make proselytes is the natural ambition of every one. *Goethe.*

To make some nook of God's creation a little fruitfuller, better, more worthy of God ; to make some human hearts a little wiser, manfuller, happier, more blessed, less accursed ! It is work for a God. *Carlyle.*

To make the common marvellous, as if it were a revelation, is the test of genius. *Lowell.*

To man, in this his trial state. / The privilege is given, / When tost by tides of human fate, / To anchor fast in heaven. *Watts.*

To me more dear, congenial to my heart, / One 25 native charm, than all the gloss of art. *Goldsmith.*

To me the eternal existence of my soul is proved from my idea of activity. If I work incessantly until my death, nature will give me another form of existence when the present can no longer sustain my spirit. *Goethe.*

To me the meanest flower that blows can give / Thoughts that do often lie too deep for tears. *Wordsworth.*

To men we can give no help, and they hinder us from helping ourselves. *Jarno, in Goethe's "Wilhelm Meister."*

To misconstrue a good thing is a treble wrong —to myself, the action, and the author. *Bp. Hall.*

To-morrow, and to-morrow, and to-morrow, / 30 Creeps in this petty pace from day to day, / To the last syllable of recorded time ; / And all our yesterdays have lighted fools / To dusty death. *Macb.*, v. 5.

To-morrow is a satire on to-day, and shows its weakness. *Young.*

"To-morrow, to-morrow, only not to day," lazy people always say. *C. F. Weisse.*

To-morrow will I live, the fool does say : / To-day itself's too late ; the wise lived yesterday. *Cowley.*

To-morrow you will live, you always cry ; / In what far country does this morrow lie ? *Cowley.*

To most men experience is like the stern 35 lights of a ship, which illumine only the track it has passed. *Coleridge.*

To mourn a mischief that is past and gone, / Is the next way to draw new mischief on. *Othello*, i. 3.

To no man does Fortune throw open all the kingdoms of this world, and say : It is thine ; choose where thou wilt dwell ! To the most she opens hardly the smallest cranny or doghutch, and says, not without asperity : There, that is thine while thou canst keep it ; nestle thyself there, and bless Heaven ! *Carlyle.*

To no man, whatever his station in life, or his power to serve me, have I ever paid a compliment at the expense of truth. *Burns.*

To nurse the flowers, to root up the weeds, is the business of the gardener. *Bodenstedt.*

To obey is the best grace of woman. *Lewis* 40 *Morris.*

To one thing at one time. *Chancellor Thurlow.*

To open your windows be ever your care. *Pr.*

To overcome difficulties is to experience the full delight of existence. *Schopenhauer.*

To overcome evil with good is good, to resist evil by evil is evil. *Mahomet.*

To pass through a bustling crowd with its rest- 45 less excitement is strange but salutary. All go crossing and recrossing one another, and yet each finds his way and his object. In so great a crowd and bustle one feels himself perfectly calm and solitary. *Goethe.*

To persever / In obstinate condolement, is a course / Of impious stubbornness ; 'tis unmanly grief : / It shows a will most incorrect to heaven. *Ham.*, i. 2.

To persevere in one's duty and to be silent is the best answer to calumny. *Washington.*

To place wit before good sense is to place the superfluous before the necessary. *M. de Montlosier.*

To plough and sow, to reap and mow, my father bred me early, / For one, he said, to labour bred, was a match for fortune fairly. *Burns.*

To popular religion, the real kingdom of God is the New Jerusalem with its jaspers and emeralds ; righteousness and peace and joy are only the kingdom of God figuratively. *Matthew Arnold.*

5 To pour oil on the fire is not the way to quench it. *Pr.*

To prefer one future mode of life to another, upon just reasons, requires faculties which it has not pleased our Creator to give us. *Johnson.*

To promise is already to give ; to hope, already to enjoy. *Delille.*

To prove, as to doubt, the existence of God is to prove or doubt the existence of existence. *Jean Paul.*

To put the cart before the horse. *Pr.*

10 To raise the weaker sex in self-respect, as well as in the esteem of the stronger, is the first step from barbarism to civilisation. *Canning.*

To read without reflecting is like eating without digesting. *Burke.*

To receive a simple primitive phenomenon, to recognise it in its high significance, and to go to work with it, requires a productive spirit, which is able to take a wide survey, and is a rare gift, only to be found in very superior natures. *Goethe.*

To receive gifts is to lose liberty. *Saadi.*

To reconcile despotism with freedom is to make your despotism just. *Carlyle.*

15 To reform a world, to reform a nation, no wise man will undertake ; and all but foolish men know that the only solid, though a far slower, reformation, is what each man begins and perfects on himself. *Carlyle.*

To reign is worth ambition, though in hell ; / Better to reign in hell than serve in heav'n. *Milton.*

To rejoice in the prosperity of another is to partake of it. *William Austin.*

To remember one worthy thing, how many thousand unworthy must a man be able to forget. *Carlyle.*

To repel one's cross is to make it heavier. *Amiel.*

20 To require two things is the way to have them both undone. *Johnson.*

To rescue, to avenge, to instruct, or protect a woman is all the same as to love her. *Jean Paul.*

To revenge is no valour, but to bear. *Timon of Athens, iii. 5.*

To run away / Is but a coward's trick ; to run away / From this world's ills, that at the very worst / Will soon blow o'er. *Blair.*

To say of a man "He means well," is worth nothing except he does well. *Plaut.*

25 To say that we have a clear conscience is to utter a solecism ; had we never sinned, we would have had no conscience. *Carlyle.*

To scorn delights and live laborious days. *Milton.*

To secure and promote the feeling of cheerfulness should be the supreme aim of all our endeavours after happiness. *Schopenhauer.*

To see a world in a grain of sand / And a heaven in a wild flower, / Hold infinity in the palm of your hand, / And eternity in an hour. *Wm. Blake.*

To see and listen to the wicked is already the beginning of wickedness. *Confucius.*

30 To see clearly is poetry, prophecy, and religion—all in one. *Ruskin.*

To see her is to love her, / And love but her for ever. *Burns.*

To see some small soul pirouetting throughout life on a single text, and judging all the world because it cannot find a partner, is not a Christian sight. *Prof. Drummond.*

To see the best is to see most clearly, and it is the lover's privilege. *J. M. Barrie.*

To seek to change opinions by laws is worse than futile. *Buckle.*

35 To seem and not to be, is throwing the shuttle without weaving. *Pr.*

To seize a character, even that of one man, in its life and secret mechanism, requires a philosopher ; to delineate it with truth and impressiveness, is work for a poet. *Carlyle.*

To serve from the lowest station upwards (*von unten hinauf*) is in all things necessary. *Goethe.*

To serve God and love him is higher and better than happiness, though it be with wounded feet, and bleeding brow, and a heart loaded with sorrow. *W. R. Greg.*

To shape the whole future is not our problem ; but only to shape faithfully a small part of it, according to rules laid down. *Carlyle.*

40 To shoot wide of the mark, *i.e.*, guess foolishly when you don't know. *Pr.*

To show mercy is nothing—thy soul must be full of mercy ; to be pure in act is nothing—thou shalt be pure in heart also. *Ruskin.*

To sigh, yet feel no pain ; To weep, yet scarce know why ; / To sport an hour with beauty's charm, / Then throw it idly by. *Moore.*

To sigh, yet not recede ; to grieve, yet not repent. *Crabbe.*

To simplify complications is, in all branches of knowledge, the first essential of success. *Buckle.*

45 To sow is not so difficult as to reap. *Goethe.*

To spend much and gain little is the sure road to ruin. *Ger. Pr.*

To spend too much time in studies is sloth. *Bacon.*

To spur a free horse soon makes a jade of him. *Sterne.*

To step aside is human. *Burns.*

50 To strain at a gnat and swallow a camel. *Pr.*

To strive to get rid of an evil is to aim at something definite, but to desire a better fortune than we have is blind folly. *Goethe.*

To study nature or man, we ought to know things that are in the ordinary course, not the unaccountable things that happen out of it. *Fisher Ames.*

To succeed in the world it is much more necessary to be able to diagnose a fool than a clever man. *Cato.*

To talk without effort is, after all, the great charm of talking. *Hare.*

To taste of human flesh is less criminal in the eyes of God than to stifle human thought. *Draper.*

To tax the community for the advantage of a class is not protection; it is plunder, and I disclaim it. *Disraeli.*

To tell our own secrets is generally folly, but that folly is without guilt; to communicate those with which we are intrusted is always treachery, and treachery for the most part combined with folly. *Johnson.*

5 To the capable man this world is not dumb. *Goethe.*

To the exiled wanderer how godlike / The friendly countenance of man appears. *Goethe.*

To the Hindu the world is the dream of Brahma. *Amiel.*

To the innocent, deliverance and reparation; to the misled, compassion; and to the guilty, avenging justice. *Goethe.*

To the man of firm purpose all men and things are servile. *Goethe.*

10 To the minnow every cranny and pebble, and quality and accident, of its little native creek may have become familiar; but does the minnow understand the ocean tides and periodic currents, the trade-winds, and monsoons, and moon's eclipses; by all of which the condition of its little creek is regulated, and may (from time to time, unmiraculously enough) be quite overset and reversed? Such a minnow is man; his creek, this planet earth; his ocean, the immeasurable All; his monsoons and periodic currents, the mysterious course of Providence through æons of æons. *Carlyle.*

To the noble mind / Rich gifts wax poor when givers prove unkind. *Ham.,* iii. 1.

To the persevering mortal the blessed immortals are swift. *Zoroaster.*

To the strictly just and virtuous person everything is annexed. *Hitopadesa.*

To the understanding of anything, two conditions are equally required—intelligibility in the thing itself being no whit more indispensable than intelligence in the examiner of it. *Carlyle.*

15 To the unregenerate Prometheus Vinctus of a man, it is ever the bitterest aggravation of his wretchedness that he is conscious of virtue, that he feels himself the victim not of suffering only, but of injustice. *Carlyle.*

To the vulgar eye few things are wonderful that are not distant. It is difficult for men to believe that the man, the mere man whom they see, may perhaps painfully feel, toiling at their side through the poor jostlings of existence, can be made of finer clay than themselves. *Carlyle.*

To the wisest man, wide as is his vision, Nature remains of quite infinite depth, of quite infinite expansion; and all experience thereof limits itself to some few computed centuries and measured square miles. *Carlyle.*

To the "Worship of sorrow" (Goethe's definition of Christianity) ascribe what origin and genesis thou pleasest, has not that worship originated and been generated? Is it not here? Feel it in thy heart, and then say whether it is of God! *Carlyle.*

To think and to feel constitute the two grand divisions of men of genius—the men of reasoning and the men of imagination. *I. Disraeli.*

To think aright is the sum of human duty. 20 *Pascal.*

To think is to act. *Emerson.*

To this burden women are born; they must obey their husbands, be they never such blockheads. *Cervantes.*

To those by whom liberality is practised, the whole world is but as one family. *Hitopadesa.*

To those that have lived long together, everything heard and everything seen recalls some pleasure communicated or some benefit conferred, some petty quarrel or some slight endearment. *Johnson.*

To those to whom we owe affection, let us be 25 dumb until we are strong, though we should never be strong. *Emerson.*

To those who are fallen into misfortunes, what was a blessing becometh an evil. *Hitopadesa.*

To those whose god is honour, disgrace alone is sin. *Hare.*

To threats the stubborn sinner oft is hard, / Wrapp'd in his crimes, against the storm prepared; / But, when the milder beams of mercy play, / He melts, and throws his cumbrous cloak away. *Dryden.*

To toy with human hearts is more than human hearts will brook. *Dr. W. Smith.*

To tread upon the brink is safe, but to come a 30 step further is destruction. *Johnson.*

To try things oft, and never to give over, doth wonders. *Bacon.*

To understand one thing well is better than understanding many things by halves. *Goethe.*

To understand that the sky is blue everywhere, we need not go round the world. *Goethe.*

To understand the serious side of things requires a matured faculty; the ridiculous is caught more easily. *Froude.*

To understand things we must once have been 35 in them, and then have come out of them. *Amiel.*

To unpractised eyes, a Peak of Teneriffe, nay, a Strasburg Minster, when we stand on it, may seem higher than a Chimborazo; because the former rise abruptly, without abutement or environment; the latter rises gradually, carrying half a world along with it; and only the deeper azure of the heavens, the widened horizon, the "eternal sunshine," disclose to the geographer that the "region of change" lies far below. *Carlyle.*

To use books rightly is to go to them for help. *Ruskin.*

To use studies too much for ornament is affectation. *Bacon.*

To vice, innocence must always seem only a superior kind of chicanery. *Ouida.*

To wail friends lost / Is not by much so whole- 40 some, profitable, / As to rejoice at friends but newly found. *Love's L. Lost,* v. 2.

To wed unequally is to suffer equally. *Anon.*

To what base uses we may return, Horatio! *Ham.,* v. 1.

To what excesses men go for a religion of whose truth they are so little persuaded, and to whose precepts they pay so little regard. *La Bruyère.*

To what they know best entice all neatly ; /
For so thou dost thyself and him a pleasure.
George Herbert.

To whom is the mere glare of the fire a virtue ?
Hitopadesa.

To wilful men / The injuries that they themselves procure / Must be their schoolmasters.
King Lear, ii. 4.

To work without money, and be poor ; to work
without pleasure, and be chaste ; to work
according to orders, and be obedient. *Rules
of the Order of St. Francis.*

5 To write a good love-letter, you ought to begin without knowing what you mean to say,
and to finish without knowing what you
have written. *Rousseau.*

To write down to children's understandings is
a mistake ; set them on the scent and let
them puzzle it out. *Scott.*

To write prose, one must have something to
say, but he who has nothing to say can still
make verses. *Goethe.*

To write well is to think well, to feel well, and
to render well ; it is to possess at once
intellect, soul, and taste. *Buffon.*

To write what is worth publishing, to find
honest men to publish it, and get sensible
men to read it, are the three great difficulties in authorship. *Colton.*

10 To yield my breath, / Life's purpose unfulfilled ! this is thy sting, O Death. *Sir Noel
Paton.*

To yourself be critic most severe. *Dryden.*

Tobacco and opium have broad backs, and will
cheerfully carry the load of armies, if you
choose to make them pay high for such joy
as they give and such harm as they do.
Emerson.

Tocher's nae word in a true lover's parle.
Burns.

Todte Hunde beissen nicht—Dead dogs don't
bite. *Ger. Pr.*

15 τὸ ἦθος ἔθος ἐστὶ πολυχρόνιον—Character is
simply prolonged habit. *Plutarch.*

Toga virilis—The manly robe.

τὸ γὰρ τρέφον με, τοῦτ' ἐγὼ κρίνω θεόν—What
maintains me in life, that I regard as God. (?)

τὸ γὰρ περισσὰ πράσσειν οὐκ ἔχει νοῦν
οὐδένα—Doing more than one is able for argues
a want of intelligence. (?)

Toil is polish'd man's vocation ; / Praises are
the meed of skill ; / Kings may vaunt their
crown and station, / We will vaunt our
labour still. *Mangau.*

20 Toil on, faint not, keep watch, and pray. *Bonar.*

Toils of empires pleasures are. *Waller.*

τὸ καλόν—The beautiful.

Toleration is good for all, or it is good for
none. *Burke.*

Tolle jocos ; non est jocus esse malignum—
Away with such jokes ; there is no joking where
there is malignity.

25 Tolle periclum, / Jam vaga prosiliet frænis
natura remotis—Take away the danger, remove restraint, and vagrant nature bounds forth
free. *Hor.*

Tombs are the clothes of the dead--a grave
but a plain suit, and a rich monument one
embroidered. *Fuller.*

τὸν γὰρ οὐκ ὄντα ἅπας εἰώθεν ἐπαινεῖν—All
are wont to praise him who is no more. *Thucydides.*

τὸν τεθνηκότα μὴ κακολογεῖν—Speak not evil
of the dead. *Chilon.*

τὸ ὅλόν—The whole.

Too austere a philosophy makes few wise men ; 30
too rigorous politics, few good subjects ; and
too hard a religion, few religious persons
whose devotion is of long continuance. *St.
Evremond.*

Too early and too thoroughly we cannot be
trained to know that Would, in this world of
ours, is as mere zero to Should, and, for most
part, the smallest of fractions to Shall. *Carlyle.*

Too elevated qualities often unfit a man for
society. *Chamfort.*

Too fair to worship, too divine to love. *Milman.*

Too low they build who build beneath the stars.
Young.

Too many cooks spoil the broth. *Pr.*   35

Too many instances there are of daring men,
who by presuming to sound the deep things
of religion, have cavilled and argued themselves out of all religion. *Thomas à Kempis.*

Too much gravity argues a shallow mind.
Lavater.

Too much idleness, I have observed, fills up a
man's time much more completely, and leaves
him less his own master, than any sort of
employment whatsoever. *Burke.*

Too much is always bad ; old proverbs call /
Even too much honey nothing else than
gall. *Anon.*

Too much mercy is want of mercy. *Tennyson.* 40

Too much of a good thing. *As You Like It,*
iv. 1.

Too much of one thing is good for nothing.
Thales and Solon.

Too much painstaking speaks disease in one's
mind, as much as too little. *Carlyle.*

Too much rest is rust. *Scott.*

Too much rest itself becomes a pain. *Homer.* 45

Too much sensibility creates unhappiness ; too
much insensibility creates crime. *Talleyrand.*

Too much wit / Makes the world rotten.
Tennyson.

Too surely, every setting day, / Some lost
delight we mourn. *Keble.*

Too swift arrives as tardy as too slow. *Rom.
and Jul.,* ii. 6.

Tooth of time. *Meas. for Meas.,* v. 1.   50

Top and bottom teeth sometimes come into
awkward collision. *Ch. Pr.*

τὸ πρεπόν—That which is becoming or decorous.

Torrens dicendi copia multis / Et sua morti-
fera est facundia—To many a torrent flow of
speech and their own eloquence is fatal. *Juv.*

Toss'd on a sea of troubles, soul, my soul, /
Thyself do thou control ; / And to the weapons of advancing foes / A stubborn breast
oppose. *Archilochus.*

Tot capita, tot sensus—So many heads, so many 55
opinions. *Ter.*

Tot homines, quot sententiæ—So many men, so
many minds.

Tot rami quot arbores—So many branches, so
many trees. *M.*

Tota in minimis existit natura—The whole of nature exists in the very smallest things. *Quoted by Emerson.*

Totidem verbis—In so many words.

Toties quoties—As often, so often.

Toto cœlo—By the whole heavens ; as wide as the poles asunder.

5 Totus in toto, et totus in quafibet parte—Whole in the whole, and whole in every part. *Said of the human mind.*

Totus mundus exercet histrioniam—All the world acts the player.

τοῦ ἀριστεύειν ἕνεκα—In order to excel. *M.*

Touched by a loving heart, wakened by kindness, / Chords that were broken will vibrate once more. *Mrs. van Alstyne.*

Touching the Almighty, we cannot find him out. *Bible.*

10 Toujours—Always. *M.*

Toujours en vedette—Always on the lookout. *M. of Frederick the Great.*

Toujours perdrix—Always partridges. *Fr.*

"Toujours perdrix" is sickening *John Wagstaffe.*

Toujours prêt—Always ready.

15 Toujours propice—Always propitious. *M*

Toujours tout droit, Dieu t'aidera !—Always straightforward, and God will help you ! *M.*

Tour d'adresse—A trick of sleight of hand. *Fr.*

Tour de force—A feat of strength or skill. *Fr.*

Tourner autour du pot—To beat about the bush. *Fr.*

20 Tourner casaque—To change sides ; become a turncoat. *Pr.*

Tous frais faits—All charges paid. *Fr.*

Tous les genres sont bons hors le genre ennuyeux—All kinds are good except the kind that bores you. *Voltaire.*

Tous les hommes sont foux, et malgré tous leurs soins, / Ne diffèrent entr'eux, que du plus ou du moins—All men are fools, and notwithstanding all their care, they differ but in degree. *Boileau.*

Tous les méchants sont buveurs d'eau ; / C'est bien prouvé par le déluge—All the wicked are water-drinkers ; this the deluge proves.

25 Tout-à-fait—Quite. *Fr.*

Tout bien ou rien—All or nothing. *M.*

Tout chemin mène à Rome—Every road leads to Rome.

Tout d'en haut—All from above. *M.*

Tout doit tendre au bon sens : mais pour y parvenir / Le chemin est glissant et pénible a tenir—Everything ought to lead to good sense ; but in order to attain to it, the road is slippery and difficult to walk in. *Boileau.*

30 Tout éloge imposteur blesse une âme sincère—Praise undeservedly bestowed wounds an honest heart. *Boileau.*

Tout est contradiction chez nous : la France, à parler sérieusement, est le royaume de l'esprit et de la sottise, de l'industrie et de la paresse, de la philosophie et du fanatisme, de la gaieté et du pédantisme, des loix et des abus, de bon goût et de l'impertinence—With us all is inconsistency. France, seriously speaking, is the country of wit and folly, of industry and idleness, of philosophy and fanaticism, of gaiety and pedantry, laws and their abuses, good taste and impertinence. *Voltaire.*

Tout est perdu fors l'honneur—All is lost save our honour. *Francis I., after his defeat at Pavia.*

Tout est pour le mieux dans le meilleur des mondes possibles—All is for the best in the best possible of worlds. *Voltaire, in mockery of Leibnitz's optimism.*

Tout faiseur de journaux doit tribut au malin—Every journalist owes tribute to the evil one. *La Fontaine.*

35 Tout finit par des chansons—Everything in the end passes into song. *Beaumarchons.*

Tout flatteur vit au dépens de celui qui l'écoute—Every flatterer lives at the expense of him who listens to him. *La Fontaine.*

Tout notre mal vient de ne pouvoir être seul—All our unhappiness comes from our inability to be alone. *La Bruyère.*

Tout par raison—Everything agreeable to reason. *Richelieu.*

Tout soldat français porte dans sa giberne le bâton de maréchal de France—Every private in the French army carries a field-marshal's baton in his knapsack. *Napoleon.*

40 Tout va à qui n'a pas besoin—Everything goes to him who does not need it. *Fr. Pr.*

Tout vient à point à qui sait attendre—Everything comes in time to the man who knows how to wait. *Fr. Pr.*

Tout vient de Dieu—Everything comes from God. *M.*

Toute révélation d'un secret est la faute de celui qui l'a confié—The disclosure of a secret is always the fault of him who confided it. *Fr.*

Toutes les fois que je donne une place vacante, je fais cent mécontents, et un ingrat—Every time I appoint to a vacant post, I make a hundred discontented and one ungrateful. *Louis XIV.*

45 Towards great persons use respective boldness : / That temper gives them theirs, and yet doth take / Nothing from thine. *George Herbert.*

Towers are measured by their shadows. *Chinese Pr.*

Trade's proud empire hastes to swift decay. *Johnson.*

Traditions make up the reasonings of the simple, and serve to silence every inquiry. *Goldsmith.*

Traduttori, traditori—Translators, traitors. *It. Pr.*

50 Tragedy has the great moral defect of giving too much importance to life and death. *Chamfort.*

Tragedy warms the soul, elevates the heart, can and ought to create heroes. In this sense, perhaps, France owes a part of her great actions to Corneille. *Napoleon.*

Trahit ipse furoris / Impetus, et visum est lenti quæsisse nocentem—The very violence of their rage drags them on, and to inquire who is guilty were a waste of time. *Lucan.*

Trahit sua quemque voluptas—Each man is led by his own liking. *Virg.*

Train up a child in the way he should go : and when he is old he will not depart from it. *Bible.*

55 Tranquil pleasures last the longest. We are not fitted to bear long the burden of great joys. *Bovee.*

Tranquillity is better than jollity, and to appease pain than to invent pleasure. *Sir T. Browne.*

Transeat in exemplum—Let it stand as a precedent, or an example.

Transitory is all human work, small in itself, contemptible ; only the worker thereof and the spirit that dwelt in him is significant. *Carlyle.*

Trau keinem Freunde sonder Mängel, / Und lieb' ein Mädchen, keinen Engel—Trust no friend without faults, and love a maiden, but no angel. *Lessing.*

5 Travel gives a character of experience to our knowledge, and brings the figures upon the tablet of memory into strong relief. *Tuckerman.*

Travel in the younger sort is a part of education ; in the older, a part of experience. *Bacon.*

Travel is the frivolous part of serious lives, and the serious part of frivolous ones. *Mme. Swetchine.*

Travel teaches toleration. *Disraeli.*

Travelling is a fool's paradise. *Emerson.*

10 Travelling is like gambling ; it is ever connected with winning and losing, and generally where least expected we receive more or less than we hoped for. *Goethe.*

Tre lo sanno, tutti lo sanno—If three know it, all know it. *It. Pr.*

Tre taceranno, se due vi non sono—Three may keep counsel if two be away. *It. Pr.*

Treachery don't come natural to beaming youth : but trust and pity, love and constancy, they do. *Dickens.*

Treason doth never prosper ; what's the reason? / Why if it prosper, none dare call it treason. *Sir J. Harrington.*

15 Treason has done his worst ; nor steel, nor poison, / Malice domestic, foreign levy, nothing / Can touch him further. *Macb.*, iii. 2.

Treasures of wickedness profit nothing, but justice delivers from death. *Bible.*

Trees and fields tell me nothing ; men are my teachers. *Plato.*

Tremblez, tyrans ; vous êtes immortels — Tremble, ye tyrants ; ye cannot die. *Delille.*

Tria juncta in uno—Three joined in one. *M.*

20 Tribulation will not hurt you unless it does— what, alas ! it too often does — unless it hardens you, and makes you sour and narrow and sceptical. *Chapin.*

Tricks and treachery are the practice of fools that have not wit enough to be honest *Ben. Franklin.*

Trifles light as air / Are to the jealous confirmations strong / As proofs of holy writ. *Othello*, iii. 3.

Trifles make perfection, but perfection is no trifle. *Michael Angelo.*

Trifles make up the happiness or misery of mortal life. *Alex. Smith.*

25 Trifles themselves are elegant in him. *Pope.*

Trifles unconsciously bias us for or against a person from the very beginning. *Schopenhauer.*

Trifling precautions will often prevent great mischiefs ; as a slight turn of the wrist parries a mortal thrust. *R. Sharp.*

Trinitas in Trinitate—Trinity in Trinity. *M.*

Tristis eris, si solus eris—You will be sad if you are alone. *Ovid.*

Triumphs for nothing and lamenting toys, / 30 Is jollity for apes and grief for boys. *Cymbeline*, iv. 2.

Troops of furies march in the drunkard's triumph. *Zimmermann.*

Trop de zèle gâte tout—Too much zeal spoils all. *Fr. Pr.*

Tros Tyriusve mihi nullo discrimine agetur— Trojan or Tyrian, it shall make no difference to me. *Virg.*

Trotz alledem und alledem—For 'a that and 'a that. *F. Freiligrath.*

Trouble is a thing that will come without our 35 call ; but true joy will not spring up without ourselves. *Bp. Patrick.*

Trouble teaches men how much there is in manhood. *Ward Beecher.*

Truditur dies die, / Novæque pergunt interire lunæ—Day presses on the heels of day, and new moons hasten to their wane. *Hor.*

True art is like good company ; it constrains us in the most charming way to recognise the standard after which and up to which our innermost being is shaped by culture. *Goethe.*

True art, which requires free and healthy faculties, is opposed to pedantry, which crushes the soul under a burden. *Hamerton.*

True bravery proposes a just end, measures 40 the dangers, and, if necessary, the affront, with coldness. *Francis la None.*

True blue will never stain. *Pr.*

True comeliness, which nothing can impair, / Dwells in the mind ; all else is vanity and glare. *Thomson.*

True coral needs no painter's brush. *Pr.*

True dignity is never gained by place, and never lost when honours are withdrawn. *Massinger.*

True ease in writing comes from art, not 45 chance, / As those move easiest who have learned to dance. *Pope.*

True eloquence consists in saying all that is proper, and nothing more. *La Roche.*

True eloquence scorns eloquence. *Pascal.*

True fame is ever likened to our shade, / He sooneth misseth her, that most (haste) hath made / To overtake her ; whoso takes his wing, / Regardless of her, she'll be following ; / Her true proprietie she thus discovers, / Loves her contemners, and contemns her lovers. *Sir T. Browne.*

True fortitude I take to be the quiet possession of a man's self, and an undisturbed doing his duty, whatever evil besets him or danger lies in his way. *Locke.*

True fortitude of understanding consists in not 50 letting what we know be embarrassed by what we do not know. *Emerson.*

True friends are the whole world to one another ; and he that is a friend to himself is also a friend to mankind. Even in my studies the greatest delight I take is of imparting it to others ; for there is no relish to me in the possession of anything without a partner. *Sen.*

True friendship can afford true knowledge. It does not depend on darkness and ignorance. *Thoreau.*

True friendship is a plant of slow growth, and must undergo and withstand the shocks of adversity before it is entitled to the appelation. *Washington.*

True friendship is like sound health, the value of it is seldom known until it be lost. *Colton.*

True friendship often shows itself in refusing at the right time, and love often grants a hurtful good. *Goethe.*

True greatness is, first of all, a thing of the heart. *R. D. Hitchcock.*

True heroism consists in being superior to the ills of life, in whatever shape they may challenge him to combat. *Napoleon.*

True hope is swift, and flies with swallow's wings ; / Kings it makes gods, and meaner creatures kings. *Richard III.*, v. 2.

True humility is contentment. *Amiel.*

True humour is as closely allied to pity as it is abhorrent to derision. *Henry Giles.*

True humour is sensibility in the most catholic and deepest sense ; but it is the sport of sensibility ; wholesome and perfect therefore ; as it were, the playful teasing fondness of a mother to her child. *Carlyle.*

10 True humour springs not more from the head than from the heart ; it is not contempt, its essence is love ; it issues not in laughter, but in still smiles, which lie far deeper. It is a sort of inverse sublimity, exalting, as it were, into our affections what is below us, while sublimity draws down into our affections what is above us. *Carlyle.*

True influence is latent influence. *Renan.*

True joy is a serene and sober motion ; and they are miserably out, that take laughing for rejoicing ; the seat of it is within, and there is no cheerfulness like the resolutions of a brave mind that has fortune under its feet. *Sen.*

True joy is only hope put out of fear. *Lord Brooke.*

True knowledge is of virtues only. *Ruskin.*

15 True knowledge of any thing or any creature is only of the good of it. *Ruskin.*

True liberty is a positive force, regulated by law ; false liberty is a negative force, a release from restraint. *Philip Schaff.*

True love is still the same ; the torrid zones, / And those more rigid ones, it must not know ; / For love grown cold or hot / Is lust or friendship, not / The thing we show. *Suckling.*

True love is that which enobles the personality, fortifies the heart, and sanctifies the existence. *Amiel.*

True love is the parent of a noble humility. *Channing.*

20 True love will creep, not having strength to go. *Quarles.*

True love works never for the loved one so, / Nor spares skin-surface, smoothing truth away. *Browning.*

True love's the gift which God has given / To man alone beneath the heaven. *Scott.*

True mercy is ashamed of itself ; hides itself, and does not complain. You may know it by that. *Varnhagen von Ense.*

True modesty avoids everything that is criminal ; false modesty everything that is unfashionable. *Addison.*

True morality scorns morality ; that is, the morality of the judgment scorns the morality of the mind, which is without rules. *Pascal.* 25

True music is intended for the ear alone ; whoever sings it to me must be invisible. *Goethe.*

True nobility is derived from virtue, not birth. *Burton.*

True obedience is true liberty. *Ward Beecher.*

True poetry is truer than science, because it is synthetic, and seizes at once what the combination of all the sciences is able, at most, to attain as a final result. *Amiel.*

True quietness of heart is gotten by resisting our passions, not by obeying them. *Thomas à Kempis.* 30

True religion is always mild, propitious, and humble ; plays not the tyrant, plants no faith in blood, nor bears destruction on her chariot-wheels ; but stoops to polish, succour, and redress, and builds her grandeur on the public good. *James Miller.*

True religion is the poetry of the heart ; it has enchantments useful to our manners ; it gives us both happiness and virtue. *Joubert.*

True religion teaches us to reverence what is under us, to recognise humility and poverty, mockery and despite, wretchedness and disgrace, suffering and death, as things divine. *Goethe, of the Christian religion.*

True repentance consists in the heart being broken for sin, and broken from sin. *Thornton.*

True repentance is to cease from sin. *St. Ambose.* 35

True sense and reason reach their aim / With little help from art or rule. / Be earnest ! Then what need to seek / The words that best your meaning speak ? *Goethe.*

True, sharp, precise thought is preferable to a cloudy fancy ; and a hundred acres of solid earth are far more valuable than a million acres of cloud and vapour. *C. Fitzhugh.*

True singing is of the nature of worship ; as indeed all true working may be said to be ; whereof such singing is but the record, and fit melodious representation, to us. *Carlyle.*

True statesmanship is the art of changing a nation from what it is into what it ought to be. *W. R. Alger.*

True taste is for ever growing, learning, reading, worshipping, laying its hand upon its mouth because it is astonished, casting its shoes from off its feet because it finds all ground holy. *Ruskin.* 40

True valour lies in the middle between cowardice and rashness. *Cervantes.*

True virtue, being united to heavenly grace of faith, makes up the highest perfection. *Milton.*

True virtue's soul's always in all deeds all. *Donne.*

True wit never made us laugh. *Emerson.*

Truly great men are always simple-hearted. *Klinger.* 45

Truly great men are ever most heroic to those most intimate with them. *Ruskin.*

Truly there is a tide in the affairs of men ; but there is no gulf-stream setting for ever in one direction. *Lowell.*

Truly unhappy is the man who leaves undone what he can do, and undertakes what he does not understand; no wonder he comes to grief. *Goethe.*

Trusse up thy packe, and trudge from me, to every little boy, / And tell them thus from me, their time most happy is, / If to theyr time they reason had, to know the truth of this. *Chaucer.*

Trust as little as you can to report, and examine all you can by your own senses. *Johnson.*

Trust begets truth. *Pr.*

5 Trust, but not too much. *Pr.*

Trust dies because bad pay poisons him. *Pr.*

Trust him little who praises all, him less who censures all, and him least who is indifferent about all. *Lavater.*

Trust in that man's promise who dares to refuse that which he fears he cannot perform. *Spurgeon.*

Trust in the Lord, and do good, so shalt thou dwell in the land, and verily thou shalt be fed. *Bible.*

10 Trust in the Lord with all thine heart; and lean not unto thine own understanding. In all thy ways acknowledge him, and he shall direct thy paths. *Bible.*

Trust instinct to the end, though you can render no reason. *Emerson.*

Trust me not at all or all in all. *Tennyson.*

Trust me, that for the instructed, time will come / When they shall meet no object but may teach / Some acceptable lesson to their minds / Of human suffering or human joy. / For them shall all things speak of man. *Wordsworth.*

Trust men, and they will be true to you; treat them greatly, and they will show themselves great. *Emerson.*

15 Trust no future, howe'er pleasant; / Let the dead past bury its dead. / Act, act in the living present; / Heart within, and God o'erhead! *Longfellow.*

Trust no man who pledges you with his hand on his heart. *Lichtenberg.*

Trust not him that hath once broken faith. *3 Hen. VI., iv. 4.*

Trust not in him that seems a saint. *Fuller.*

Trust not the heart of that man for whom old clothes are not venerable. *Carlyle.*

20 Trust not this hollow world; she's empty; hark, she sounds. *Quarles.*

Trust not those cunning waters of his eyes, for villany is not without such rheum. *King John, iv. 3.*

Trust that man in nothing who has not a conscience in everything. *Sterne.*

Trust thyself; every heart vibrates to that iron string. *Emerson.*

Truth alone wounds. *Napoleon.*

25 Truth and fidelity are the pillars of the temple of the world; when these are broken, the fabric falls, and crushes all to pieces. *Feltham.*

Truth and oil are ever above. *Pr.*

Truth being weighed against a thousand Aswamedha sacrifices, was found to be of more consequence than the whole thousand offerings. *Hitopadesa.*

Truth contradicts our nature, error does not, and for a very simple reason: truth requires us to regard ourselves as limited, error flatters us to think of ourselves as in one or other way unlimited. *Goethe.*

Truth, crushed to earth, shall rise again, / The eternal years of God are hers; / But error, wounded, writhes with pain, / And dies among his worshippers. *W. C. Bryant.*

Truth does not conform itself to us, but we 30 must conform ourselves to it. *M. Claudius.*

Truth does not consist in minute accuracy of detail, but in conveying a right impression; and there are vague ways of speaking that are truer than strict facts would be. When the Psalmist said, "Rivers of water run down mine eyes, because men keep not thy law," he did not state the fact, but he stated a truth deeper than fact and truer. *Dean Alford.*

Truth does not do as much good in the world as the shows of it do of evil. *La Roche.*

Truth dwells not in the clouds; the bow that's there / Doth often aim at, never hit the sphere. *George Herbert.*

Truth for ever on the scaffold, wrong for ever on the throne. *Lowell.*

Truth from his lips prevail'd with double sway, / 35 And fools who came to scoff remain'd to pray. *Goldsmith.*

Truth has a quiet breast. *Rich. II., i. 3.*

Truth has no gradations; nothing which admits of increase can be so much what it is as truth is truth. There may be a strange thing, and a thing more strange; but if a proposition be true, there can be none more true. *Johnson.*

Truth hath always a fast bottom. *Pr.*

Truth hath better deeds than words to grace it. *Two Gent. of Verona, ii. 2.*

"Truth," I cried, "though the heavens crush 40 me for following her; no falsehood, though a whole celestial Lubberland were the price of apostasy!" *Carlyle.*

Truth in its own essence cannot be / But good. *Byron.*

Truth, in the great practical concerns of life, is so much a question of the reconciling and combining of opposites, that very few have minds sufficiently capacious and impartial to make the adjustment with an approach to correctness. *J. S. Mill.*

Truth irritates only those whom it enlightens, but does not convert. *Pasquier Quesnel.*

Truth is a good dog; but beware of barking too close to the heels of an error, lest you get your brains kicked out. *Coleridge.*

Truth is a queen who has her eternal throne 45 in heaven, and her seat of empire in the heart of God. *Bossuet.*

Truth is a stronghold, and diligence is laying siege to it; so that it must observe all the avenues and passes to it. *South.*

Truth is always consistent with itself, and needs nothing to help it out; it is always near at hand, and sits upon our lips, and is ready to drop out before we are aware. *Tillotson.*

Truth is always strange, stranger than fiction. *Byron.*

Truth is as impossible to be soiled by any outward touch as the sunbeam. *Milton.*

Truth is born with us ; and we must do violence to nature, to shake off our veracity. *St. Evermond.*

Truth is God's daughter. *Pr.*

Truth is never learned, in any department of industry, by arguing, but by working and observing. *Ruskin.*

Truth is one, for ever absolute, but opinion is truth filtered through the moods, the blood, the dispositions of the spectator. *Wendell Phillips.*

5 Truth is quite beyond the reach of satire. *Lowell.*

Truth is simple and gives little trouble, but falsehood gives occasion for the frittering away of time and strength. *Goethe.*

Truth is simple indeed, but we have generally no small trouble in learning to apply it to any practical purpose. *Goethe.*

Truth is the body of God, and light his shadow. *Plato.*

Truth is the daughter of Time. *Pr.*

10 Truth is the easiest part of all to play (*das leichteste Spiel von allen*). Present thyself as thou art (*stelle dich selber dar*), and thou runnest no risk of falling out of thy rôle. *Rückert.*

Truth is the highest thing that man may keep. *Chaucer.*

Truth is the root, but human sympathy is the flower of practical life. *Chapin.*

Truth is the shortest and nearest way to our end, carrying us thither in a straight line. *Tillotson.*

Truth is to be costly to you—of labour and patience ; and you are never to sell it, but to guard and to give. *Ruskin.*

15 Truth is to be loved purely and solely because it is true. *Carlyle.*

Truth is too simple for us ; we do not like those who unmask our illusions. *Emerson.*

Truth is tough. It will not break, like a bubble, at a touch ; nay, you may kick it about all day like a football, and it will be round and full at evening. Does not Mr. Bryant say that Truth gets well if she is run over by a locomotive, while Error dies of lockjaw if she scratches her finger ? *Holmes.*

Truth is truth to the end of reckoning. *Meas. for Meas.,* v. 1.

Truth itself shall lose its credit, if delivered by a person that has none. *South.*

20 Truth lies at the bottom of a well, the depth of which, alas ! gives but little hope of release. *Democritus.*

Truth, like gold, is not the less so for being newly brought out of the mine. *Locke.*

Truth, like roses, often blossoms upon a thorny stem. *Hafiz.*

Truth, like the juice of a poppy, in small quantities, calms men ; in larger, heats and irritates them, and is attended by fatal consequences in its excess. *Landor.*

Truth, like the sun, submits to be obscured : but, like the sun, only for a time. *Bovee.*

25 Truth, like the Venus de Medici, will pass down in thirty fragments to posterity ; but posterity will collect and recompose them into a goddess. *Richter.*

Truth loves open dealing. *Henry VIII.,* iii. 1.

Truth may be stretched, but cannot be broken, and always gets above falsehood, as oil does above water. *Cervantes.*

Truth may languish, but can never perish. *Pr.*

Truth may lie in laughter, and wisdom in a jest. *Dr. W. Smith.*

30 Truth may perhaps come to the price of a pearl, that showeth best by day, but it will not rise to the price of a diamond or carbuncle, that showeth best in varied lights. *Bacon.*

Truth, or clothed or naked let it be. *Tennyson.*

Truth provokes those whom it does not convert. *Bp. Wilson.*

Truth reaches her full action by degrees, and not at once. *Draper.*

Truth, says Horne Tooke, means simply the thing trowed, the thing believed ; and now, from this to the thing itself, what a new fatal deduction have we to suffer. *Carlyle.*

35 Truth scarce ever yet carried it by vote anywhere at its first appearance. *Locke.*

Truth seeks no corners. *Pr.*

Truth shines with its own light ; it is not by the flames of funeral piles that the minds of men are illuminated. *Belisarius.*

Truth should be strenuous and bold ; but the strongest things are not always the noisiest, as any one may see who compares scolding with logic. *Chapin.*

Truth will be uppermost one time or another like cork, though kept down in the water. *Sir W. Temple.*

40 Truth will bear / Neither rude handling, nor unfair / Evasion of its wards, and mocks / Whoever would falsely enter there. *Dr. Walter Smith.*

Truth's a dog that must to kennel. He must be whipped out, when the lady brach may stand by the fire and stink. *Lear,* i. 4.

Truths are first clouds, then rain, then harvests and food. *Ward Beecher.*

Truths that wake, / To perish never. *Wordsworth.*

Try and Trust will move mountains. *Pr.*

45 Try for yourselves what you can read in half-an-hour, ... and consider what treasures you might have laid by at the end of the year ; and what happiness, fortitude and wisdom they would have given you during all the days of your life. *John Morley.*

Try it, ye who think there is nothing in it : try what it is to speak with God behind you. *Ward Beecher.*

Try to do your duty, and you at once know what is in you. *Goethe.*

Try to forget our cares and our maladies, and contribute, as we can, to the cheerfulness of each other. *Johnson.*

Try what repentance can ; what can it not ? Yet what can it, when one cannot repent ? *Ham.,* iii. 2.

50 Tu, Domine, gloria mea—Thou, O Lord, art my glory. *M.*

Tu dors, Brutus, et Rome est dans les fers !— Sleepest thou, Brutus, and Rome in bonds ! *Voltaire.*

Tu ne cede malis, sed contra audentior ito / Quam tua te fortuna sinet—Do not yield to misfortunes, but advance more boldly to meet them, as your fortune shall permit you. *Virg.*

Tu ne quæsieris, scire nefas, quem mihi quem tibi / Finem di dederint, Leuconoë—Forbear to inquire, thou mayst not know, Leuconoë, for you may not know what the gods have appointed either for you or for me. *Hor.*

Tu nihil invita dices faciesve Minerva—You must say and do nothing against the bent of your genius, *i.e.*, in default of the necessary inspiration. *Hor.*

Tu pol si sapis, quod scis nescis—You, if you are wise, will not know what you do know. *Ter.*

Tu quamcunque Deus tibi fortunaverit horam, / Grata sume manu; nec dulcia differ in annum, / Ut quocunque loco fueris, vixisse libenter / Te dicas—Receive with a thankful hand every hour that God may have granted you, and defer not the comforts of life to another year; that in whatever place you are, you may say you have lived agreeably. *Hor.*

5 Tu quoque—You too; you're another.

Tu quoque, Brute !—You too, Brutus !

Tu recte vivis, si curas esse quod audis—You live a true life if you make it your care to be what you seem. *Hor.*

Tu si animum vicisti, potius quam animus te, est quod gaudeas—If you have conquered your inclination, rather than your inclination you, you have something to rejoice at. *Plaut.*

Tu si hic sis, aliter sentias—If you were in my place, you would think differently. *Terence.*

10 Tu vincula frange—Break thy chains. *M.*

Tua camicia non sappia il secreto—Let not your shirt know your secret. *It. Pr.*

Tua res agitur—It is a matter that concerns you.

Tuebor—I will protect. *M.*

Tui me miseret, mei piget—I pity you and vex myself. *Ennius.*

15 Tunica propior pallio est—My tunic is nearer than my cloak. *Plaut.*

Turba Remi sequitur fortunam, ut semper, et odit / Damnatos—The Roman mob follows the lead of fortune, as it always does, and hates those that are condemned. *Juv.*

Turn, Fortune, turn thy wheel with smile or frown ; / With that wild wheel we go not up or down ; / Our hoard is little, but our hearts are great. *Tennyson.*

Turn him to any cause of policy, / The Gordian knot of it he will unloose, / Familiar as his garter. *Henry V.*, i. 1.

Turpe est aliud loqui, aliud sentire; quanto turpius aliud scribere, aliud sentire !—It is base to say one thing and to think another ; how much more base to write one thing and think another ! *Sen.*

20 Turpe est in patria peregrinari, et in eis rebus quæ ad patriam pertinent hospitem esse—It is disgraceful to live as a stranger in one's country, and be an alien in those matters which affect our welfare. *Manutius.*

Turpius ejicitur quam non admittitur hospes—It is more disgraceful to turn a guest out than not to admit him. *Ovid.*

Turris fortissima est nomen Jehovah—A most strong tower is the name of Jehovah. *M.*

Tuta petant alii. Fortuna miserrima tuta est ; / Nam timor eventus deterioris abest—Let others seek security. My most wretched fortune is secure ; for there is no fear of worse to follow. *Ovid.*

Tuta scelera esse possunt, non secura—Wickedness may be safe, but not secure. *Sen.*

Tuta timens—Fearing even safety. *Virg.* 25

Tutte quanti—Et cetera. *It.*

Tuum est—It is thine. *M.*

'Twas doing nothing was his curse— / Is there a vice can plague us worse ?´ *Hannah More.*

'Twas strange, 'twas passing strange, / 'Twas pitiful ; 'twas wondrous pitiful. *Othello*, i. 3.

Twenty people can gain money for one who 30 can use it ; and the vital question for individuals and for nations, is never "how much do they make," but "to what purpose do they spend." *Ruskin.*

'Twere all as good to ease one beast of grief, / As sit and watch the sorrows of the world / In yonder caverns with the priests who pray. *Sir Edwin Arnold.*

Twist ye, twine ye ! even so, / Mingle shades of joy and woe, / Hope, and fear, and peace, and strife, / In the thread of human life. *Scott.*

Two are better than one, because they have a good reward for their labour. *Bible.*

Two dogs over one bone seldom agree. *Pr.*

Two dogs strive for a bone, and a third runs 35 away with it. *Pr.*

Two gifts are indispensable to the dramatic poet ; one is the power of forgetting himself, the other is the power of remembering his characters. *Stoddart.*

Two grand tasks have been assigned to the English people—the grand Industrial task of conquering some half, or more, of the terraqueous planet for the use of man ; then, secondly, the grand Constitutional task of sharing, in some pacific endurable manner, the fruit of said conquest, and showing all people how it might be done. *Carlyle.*

Two heads are better than one, or why do folks marry ? *Pr.*

Two in distress make sorrow less. *Pr.*

Two is company, but three is none. *Pr.* 40

Two kitchen fires burn not on one hearth. *Pr.*

Two may keep counsel, putting one away. *Pr.*

Two may talk and one may hear, but three cannot take part in a conversation of the most sincere and searching sort. *Emerson.*

Two meanings have our lightest fantasies, / One of the flesh, and of the spirit one. *Lowell.*

Two men I honour, and no third. First, the 45 toilworn craftsman that with earth-made implement laboriously conquers the earth, and makes her man's. . . . A second man I honour, and still more highly—him who is seen toiling for the spiritually indispensable ; not daily bread, but the bread of life. . . . These two in all their degrees I honour ; all else is chaff and dust, which let the wind blow whither it listeth. *Carlyle.*

Two misfortunes are twice as many at least as are needful to be talked over at one time. *Sterne.*

Two of a trade seldom agree. *Pr.*

Two orders of poets I admit, but no third ; the creative (Shakespeare, Homer, Dante), and reflective or perceptive (Wordsworth, Keats, Tennyson); and both these must be first-rate in their range. *Ruskin.*

Two pots stood by a river, one of brass, the other of clay ; the water carried them away; the earthen vessel kept aloof from the other. *L'Estrange.*

Two principles in human nature reign— / Self-love to urge, and reason to restrain. *Pope.*

Two qualities are demanded of a statesman who would direct any great movement of opinion in which he himself takes a part ; he must have a complete understanding of the movement itself, and he must be animated by the same motives as those which inspire the movement. *Lamartine.*

Two removals are as bad as a fire. *Pr.*

5 Two sorts of writers possess genius ; those who think, and those who cause others to think. *J. Roux.*

Two stars keep not their motion in one sphere. *Hen. IV., v. 4.*

Two things a man should never be angry at ; what he can help, and what he cannot. *Pr.*

Two things I abhor : the learned in his in-fidelities, and the fool in his devotions. *Mahomet.*

Two things strike me dumb: the infinite starry heavens, and the sense of right and wrong in man. *Kant.*

10 Two things, well considered, would prevent many quarrels : first, to have it well ascer-tained whether we are not disputing about terms rather than things ; and, secondly, to examine whether that on which we differ is worth contending about. *Colton.*

Type of the wise who soar, but never roam, / True to the kindred points of Heaven and Home. *Wordsworth.*

Tyran, descends du trône, et fais place à ton maître—Tyran, come down from the throne, and give place to your master ! *Corn.*

Tyranny and anarchy are never far asunder. *Bentham.*

Tyranny is irresponsible power . . . whether the power be lodged in one or many. *Canning.*

U.

15 Üb' immer Treu und Redlichkeit / Bis an dein kühles Grab — Be sure thou always practise fidelity and honesty till thou lie in thy cold grave. *L. H. Hölty.*

Über allen Gipfeln / Ist Ruh—Over all heights is rest. *Goethe.*

Über die Berge mit Ungestüm—Over the moun-tains by storm. *Kotzebue.*

Über vieles kann / Der Mensch zum Herrn sich machen, seinen Sinn / Bezwinget kaum die Not und lange Zeit—Man can make him-self master over much, hardly can necessity and length of time subdue his spirit. *Goethe.*

Überall bin ich zu Hause, / Ueberall bin ich bekannt—Everywhere am I at home, every-where am I known. *F. Hückstädt.*

20 Übereilung thut nicht gut ; / Bedachtsamkeit macht alle Dinge besser—Precipitation spoils everything ; consideration improves everything. *Schiller.*

Uberibus semper lacrymis, semperque paratis / In statione sua, atque expectantibus illam / Quo jubeat manare modo—With tears always in abundance, and always ready at their station, and awaiting her signal to flow as she bids them. *Juv., of a pettish woman.*

Uberrima fides—The fullest confidence ; implicit faith.

Überzeugung soll mir niemand rauben / Wer's besser weiss, der mag es glauben—No one shall deprive of this conviction that a man's faith in a thing is not weaker, but stronger, the better he knows it. *Goethe.*

Ubi amici, ibi opes—Where there are friends there is wealth. *Plaut.*

25 Ubi amor condimentum inerit cuivis placiturum credo—Where love enters to season a dish, I believe it will please any one. *Plaut.*

Ubi bene, ibi patria—Where it is well with me, there is my country. *Pr.*

Ubi dolor, ibi digitus—Where the pain is, there the finger will be. *Pr.*

Ubi homines sunt modi sunt—Where men are there are manners.

Ubi idem et maximus et honestissimus amor est, aliquando præstat morte jungi quam vita distrahi—Where there exists the greatest and most honourable love, it is sometimes better to be joined in death than separated in life. *Valerius Maximus.*

30 Ubi jus, ibi remedium—Where there is a right there is a remedy. *L.*

Ubi jus incertum, ibi jus nullum—Where the law is uncertain there is no law. *L.*

Ubi lapsus ? Quid feci ?—Where have I made slip ? What have I done ? *M.*

Ubi major pars est, ibi est totum—Where the greater part is, there the whole is. *L.*

Ubi mel, ibi apes—Where there is honey to be found, there will be bees. *Plaut.*

35 Ubi sæva indignatio cor ulterius lacerare nequit—Where bitter indignation cannot lacerate my heart any more. *Swift's epitaph.*

Ubi summus imperator non adest ad exer-citum, / Citius quod non facto 'st usus fit, quam quod facto 'st opus—When the com-mander-in-chief is not with the army, that is sooner done which need not to be done than that which requires to be done. *Plaut.*

Ubi supra—Where above mentioned.

Ubi timor adest, sapientia adesse nequit — Where fear is present, wisdom cannot be. *Lac-tantius.*

Ubi uber, ibi tuber—There are no roses without thorns. *Pr.*

40 Ubicunque ars ostentatur, veritas abesse vide-tur—Wherever there is a display of art, truth seems to us to be wanting.

Ubique—Everywhere. *M.*

Ubique patriam reminisci — I remember my country everywhere. *M.*

Übung macht den Meister—Practice makes per-fect (*lit.* the master). *Ger. Pr.*

Ugliest of trades have their moments of plea-sure. If I were a grave-digger, or even a hangman, there are some people I could work for with a great deal of enjoyment. *Douglas Jerrold.*

45 Ulcus tangere—To touch a sore. *Ter.*

Ulterius ne tende odiis—Press no further with your hate. *Virg.*

Ultima ratio regum—The last argument of kings. *Inscription on cannon.*

Ultima semper / Expectanda dies homini, dicique beatus / Ante obitum nemo supremaque funera debet—The last day must always be awaited by man, and no man should be pronounced happy before his death and his final obsequies. *Ovid.*

Ultima Thule—Remotest Thule. *Virg.*

Ultimatum—A final proposition or condition.

5 Ultimum moriens—The last to die or disappear.

Ultimus Romanorum—The last of the Romans.

Ultra posse nemo obligatur—Nobody can be bound to do beyond what he is able to do. *L.*

Ultra vires—Beyond the powers or rights possessed.

Um das Leben zu erkennen, muss man sich vom Leben absondern—To know life, a man must separate himself from life. *Feuerbach.*

10 Um einen Mann zu schätzen, muss man ihn / Zu prüfen wissen—In order to estimate a man, one must know how to test him. *Goethe.*

Um Gut's zu thun, braucht's keiner Ueberlegung ; / Der Zweifel ist's, der Gutes böse macht, / Bedenke nicht ! gewähre wie du's fühlst—To do good needs no consideration ; it is doubt that makes good evil. Don't reflect ; do good as you feel. *Goethe.*

Un ángulo me basta entre mis lares, / Un libro y un amigo, un sueño breve, / Que no perturben deudas ni pesares—Enough for me a nook by a hearth of my own, a good book, a friend, a short sleep, unburdened by debt and sorrow. *Rioja.*

Un bienfait reproché tint toujours lieu d'offense —To reproach a man with your kindness to him is tantamount to an affront. *Fr.*

Un bon ami vaut mieux que cent parents—A good friend is worth more than a hundred relations. *Fr. Pr.*

15 Un bon ouvrier n'est jamais trop chèrement payé—The wages of a good workman are never too high. *Fr. Pr.*

Un clou chasse l'autre—One nail drives out another. *Fr. Pr.*

Un corps débile affaiblit l'âme—A feeble body weakens the mind. *Rousseau.*

Un des plus grands malheurs des honnêtes gens c'est qu'ils sont de lâches—One of the greatest misfortunes of worthy people is that they are cowards. *Voltaire.*

Un Dieu, un roy—One God, one king. *M.*

20 Un dîner réchauffé ne valut jamais rien—A dinner warmed up again was never worth anything. *Boileau.*

Un enfant en ouvrant les yeux doit voir la patrie, et jusqu'à la mort ne voir qu'elle—A child, on first opening his eyes, ought to see his country, and till death through life see only it. *Fr.*

Un fat quelque fois ouvre un avis important— A simpleton often suggests a significant bit of advice. *Boileau.*

Un fou avise bien un sage—A wise man may learn of a fool. *Fr. Pr.*

Un frère est un ami donné par la nature—A brother is a friend provided by nature. *Legouvé père.*

25 Un gentilhomme qui vit mal est un monstre dans la nature—A nobleman who leads a degraded life is a monster in nature. *Molière*

Un homme d'esprit seroit souvent bien embarrassé sans la compagnie des sots—A man of wit would often be much embarrassed if it were not for the company of fools. *La Roche.*

Un homme toujours satisfait de lui-même, peu souvent l'est des autres ; rarement on l'est de lui—A man who is always well satisfied with himself seldom is so with others, and others rarely are with him. *La Roche.*

Un homme vous protège par ce qu'il vaut ; une femme par ce que vous valez. Voilà pourquoi de ces deux empires, l'un est si odieux, l'autre si doux—A man protects you by what he is worth ; a woman by what you are worth. That is why the empire of the one is so odious, and the other so sweet. *Fr.*

Un livre est un ami qui ne trompe jamais—A book is a friend that never deceives us. *Fr.*

Un menteur est toujours prodigue de serments 30 —A liar is always lavish of oaths. *Corn.*

Un père est un banquier donné par la nature— A father is a banker provided by nature. *Fr.*

Un peu d'encens brulé rajuste bien des choses —A little incense offered puts many things to rights.

Un peu de fiel gâte beaucoup de miel—A little gall spoils a great deal of honey. *Fr. Pr.*

Un renard n'est pas pris deux fois à un piège —A fox is not caught twice in the same trap. *Fr. Pr.*

Un sot n'a pas assez d'étoffe pour être bon—A 35 fool has not stuff in him to turn out well. *La Roche.*

Un sot savant est sot plus qu'un sot ignorant —A learned fool is more a fool than an ignorant one. *Fr. Pr.*

Un sot trouve toujours un plus sot qui l'admire —Every fool finds a greater to admire him. *Boileau.*

Un soupir, un regard, un mot de votre bouche, / Voilà l'ambition d'un cœur comme le mien— A sigh, a look, a word from your lips, that is the ambition of a heart like mine. *Racine.*

Un souvenir heureux est peut-être sur terre / Plus vrai que le bonheur—A happy recollection is perhaps in this world more real than the happiness it recalls. *Fr.* (?)

Un "tiens" vaut mieux que deux "tu l'aura" 40 —One "take this" is worth more than two "you-shall-have-it." *Fr. Pr.*

Un viaggiatore prudente non disprezza mai il suo paese—A wise traveller never depreciates his own country. *Goldoni.*

Una dies aperit, conficit una dies—In one day it opens its blossoms, in one day it decays. *Auson. of the rose.*

Una salus victis nullam sperare salutem—The only safety for the conquered is to hope for no safety. *Virg.*

Una voce—With one voice ; unanimously.

Unbedingte Thätigkeit, von welcher Art sie 45 sei, macht zuletzt bankerott—Undisciplined activity in any line whatever ends at last in failure. *Goethe.*

Unbidden guests / Are often welcomest when they are gone. *1 Hen. VI.*, ii. 2.

Unbounded courage and compassion join'd, / Tempting each other in the victor's mind, / Alternately proclaim him good and great, / And make the hero and the man complete. *Addison.*

Uncertainty and expectation are the joys of life. *Congreve.*

Uncertainty! fell demon of our fears! The human soul, that can support despair, supports not thee. *Mallet.*

Unconsciousness belongs to pure unmixed life; consciousness, to a diseased mixture and conflict of life and death; unconsciousness is the sign of creation; consciousness, at best, that of manufacture. So deep, in this existence of ours, is the significance of mystery. *Carlyle.*

Unconsciousness is one of the most important conditions of a good style in speaking or in writing. *R. S. White.*

5 Und bin ich strafbar, weil ich menschlich war? Ist Mitleid Sünde?—And am I to suffer for it because I was born a man? Is pity a sin? *Schiller.*

Und da keiner wollte leiden, / Dass der andre für ihn zahle / Zahlte keiner von den beiden—And as neither would allow the other to pay for him, neither paid at all. *Heine.*

Und der Mensch versuche die Götter nicht / Und begehre nimmer und nimmer zu schauen, / Was sie gnädig bedecken mit Nacht und Grauen—And let not man tempt the gods, and let him never, never desire to behold what they have graciously hid under a veil of night and terror. *Schiller.*

Und ob die Wolke sie verhülle, / Die Sonne bleibt am Himmelszelt! / Es waltet dort ein heiliger Wille; / Nicht blindem Zufall dient die Welt—And though the cloud veils his light, the sun is ever in the tent of heaven. There a holy will holds sway, to no blind chance is the world the servant. *Fr. Kind-Weber.*

Und scheint die Sonne noch so schön, / Am Ende muss sie untergehen—And though the sun still shines so brightly, in the end it must go down. *Heine.*

10 Und vor der Wahrheit mächt'gem Siege / Verschwindet jedes Werk der Lüge—And before the mighty triumph of the truth, every work of lies will one day vanish. *Schiller.*

Und was kein Verstand der Verständigen sieht / Das übet in Einfalt ein kindisch Gemüt—And what no intelligence of the intelligent sees, that is practised in simplicity by a childish mind. *Schiller.*

Und wenn die Welt voll Teufel wär' / Und wollt uns gar verschlingen / So fürchten wir uns nicht so sehr, / Es soll uns doch gelingen—And were this all devils o er, / And watching to devour us, / We lay it not to heart so sore, / Not they can overpower us. *Luther.*

Und wenn ich dich lieb habe, was geht es dich an?—And if I love thee, wha' is that to thee? *Goethe.*

Und wenn ihr euch nur selbst vertraut, / Vertrauen euch die andern Seelen—And if ye only trust yourselves, other souls will trust you. *Goethe.*

15 Und wer mich nicht verstehen kann, / Der lerne besser lesen—And let him who cannot understand me learn to read better. *Goethe.*

Undank ist der Welt Lohn—Ingratitude is the world's reward. *Ger. Pr.*

Unde fames homini vetitorum tanta ciborum est?—Why does man hunger so much after forbidden fruit? *Ovid.*

Unde habeas quærit nemo; sed oportet habere—Whence you have got your wealth, nobody inquires; but you must have it. *Juv.*

Unde / Ingenium par materiæ?—Where can we find talent equal to the subject? *Juv.*

Unde tibi frontem libertatemque parentis, / 20 Cum facias pejora senex?—Whence can your authority and liberty as a parent come, when you, who are old, do worse things? *Juv.*

Under a despotic government there is no such thing as patriotic feeling, and its place is supplied in other ways, by private interest, public fame, and devotion to one's chief. *La Bruyère.*

Under all sorrow there is the force of virtue; over all ruin, the restoring charity of God. To these alone we have to look; in these alone we may understand the past, and predict the future destiny of the ages. *Ruskin.*

Under all speech that is good for anything there lies a silence that is better. *Carlyle.*

Under fair words have a care of fraud. *Port. Pr.*

Under sackcloth there is something else. *Sp.* 25 *and Port. Pr.*

Under the sky is no uglier spectacle than two men with clenched teeth and hell-fire eyes hacking one another's flesh, converting precious living bodies and priceless living souls into nameless masses of putrescence, useful only for turnip-manure. *Carlyle.*

Under the weight of his knowledge, a man cannot move so lightly as in the days of his simplicity. *Ruskin.*

Under white ashes there often lurk glowing embers. *Dan. Pr.*

Underground / Precedency's a jest; vassal and lord, / Grossly familiar, side by side consume. *Blair.*

Underneath this stone doth lie / As much 30 beauty as could die; / Which in life did harbour give / To more virtue than doth live. *Jonson, on Elizabeth, Countess of Rutland.*

Understanding is a wellspring of life unto him that hath it. *Bible.*

Understanding is the most important matter in everything. *Hans Andersen.*

Understanding is the wages of a lively faith, and faith is the reward of a humble ignorance. *Quarles.*

Undertake no more than you can perform. *Pr.*

Undipped people may be as good as dipped, 35 if their hearts are clean. *Ruskin's rendering of the faith of St. Martin.*

Undique ad inferos tantundem viæ est—Descend by what way you will, you come at last to the nether world. *Anaxagoras.*

Une faute niée est deux fois commise—A fault denied is twice committed. *Fr. Pr.*

Une froideur ou une incivilité qui vient de ceux qui sont au-dessus de nous nous les fait haïr, mais un salut ou un sourire nous les réconcilie—A coldness or an incivility from such as are above us makes us hate them, but a salute or a smile quickly reconciles us to them.

Une grande âme est au-dessus de l'injustice, de la douleur, de la moquerie; et elle seroit invulnérable si elle ne souffroit par la compassion—A great soul is proof against injustice, pain, and mockery; and it would be invulnerable if it were not open to compassion.

Une nation boutiquière—A nation of shopkeepers. *B. Barrère, Napoleon, of England.*

Une once de vanité gâte un quintal de mérite— An ounce of vanity spoils a hundredweight of merit. *Fr. Pr.*

Une seule foi, une seule langue, un seul cœur —One faith, one tongue, one heart. *Fr. Pr.*

Une souris qui n'a qu'un trou est beintôt prise —A mouse that has only one hole is soon taken. *Fr. Pr.*

5 **Uneasy lies the head that wears a crown.** *2 Hen. IV., iii. 1.*

Unendlich ist das Räthsel der Natur—Endless is the riddle of Nature. *Körner.*

Unendlichkeit kann nur das Wesen ahnen / Das zur Unendlichkeit erkoren ist— Only that being can surmise the infinite who is chosen for infinity. *Liedge.*

Unequal combinations are always disadvantageous to the weaker side. *Goldsmith.*

Unequal marriages are seldom happy ones. *Pr.*

10 **Unextinguish'd laughter shakes the skies.** *Pope.*

Unfaith in aught is want of faith in all. *Tennyson.*

Unfortunate and imprudent are two words for the same thing. *Fr. Pr.*

Unfortunately friends too often weigh one another in their hypochondriacal humours, and in an over-exacting spirit. One must weigh men by avoirdupois weight, and not by the jeweller's scales. *Goethe.*

Unfortunately, it is more frequently the opinions expressed on things than the things themselves that divide men. *Goethe.*

15 **Ung je servirai**—One will I serve. *M.*

Ung roy, ung foy, ung loy—One king, one faith, one law. *M.*

Ungern entdeck' ich höheres Geheimniss—It is with reluctance I ever unveil a higher mystery. *Goethe.*

Unguibus et rostro—With nails and beak; with tooth and nail.

Unguis in ulcere—A nail in the wound. *Cic.*

20 **Unhappy is the man for whom his own mother has not made all mothers venerable.** *Jean Paul.*

Unhappy lot of man! Hardly has the mind attained maturity, when the body begins to pine away. *Montesquieu.*

Unhappy state of kings! it is well the robe of majesty is gay, or who would put it on? *Hannah More.*

Unheedful vows may heedfully be broken; / And he wants wit that wants resolvèd will, / To learn his wit to exchange the bad for better. *Two Gent. of Verona, ii. 6.*

Uniformity must tire at last, though it be uniformity of excellence. We love to expect, and when expectation is disappointed or gratified, we want to be again expecting. *Johnson.*

25 **Uni æquus virtuti, atque ejus amicis**—Friendly to virtue alone and to the friends of virtue. *Hor.*

Unica virtus necessaria—Virtue is the only thing necessary.

Union does everything when it is perfect; it satisfies desires, it simplifies needs, it foresees the wishes of the imagination; it is an aisle always open, and becomes a constant fortune. *De Senancour.*

Union (combination) is best for men, either with their own tribe or with strangers; for even a grain of rice groweth not when divided from its husk. *Hitopadesa.*

Union is strength. *Pr.*

Unitate fortior—Stronger by being united. *M.* 30

"United we stand, divided we fall," / It made and preserves us a nation. *G. P. Morris.*

Unity, agreement, is always silent or soft-voiced; it is only discord that loudly proclaims itself. *Carlyle.*

Unity and morality belong to philosophy, not to poetry. *Wm. Blake.*

Unity and simplicity are the two true sources of beauty. Supreme beauty resides in God. *Winckelmann.*

Uniforms are often masks. *Wellington.* 35

Universal love is a glove without fingers, which fits all hands alike, and none closely; but true affection is like a glove with fingers, which fits one hand only, and sits close to that one. *Jean Paul.*

Universal plodding prisons up / The nimble spirits in the arteries, / As motion and long-during action tires / The sinewy vigour of the traveller. *Love's L. Lost, iv. 3.*

Universal suffrage I will consult about the quality of New Orleans pork or the coarser kinds of Irish butter; but as to the character of men, I will if possible ask it no question. *Carlyle.*

Universus mundus exercet histrioniam— All the world practises the player's art.

Unjust acquisition is like a barbed arrow, 40 which must be drawn backward with horrible anguish, or else will be your destruction. *Jeremy Taylor.*

Unkind language is sure to produce the fruits of unkindness, that is, suffering in the bosom of others. *Bentham.*

Unkindness destroys love. *Pr.*

Unkindness has no remedy at law; let its avoidance be with you a point of honour. *Hosea Ballou.*

Unknell'd, uncoffin'd, and unknown. *Byron.*

Unlawful desires are punished after the effect 45 of enjoying; but impossible desires are punished in the desire itself. *Sir P. Sidney.*

Unlearn not what you have learned. *Antisthenes.*

Unlearned men of books assume the care, / As eunuchs are the guardians of the fair. *Young.*

Unless a man can link his written thoughts with the everlasting wants of men, so that they shall draw from them as from wells, there is no more immortality to the thoughts and feelings of the soul than to the muscles and the bones. *Ward Beecher.*

Unless a man works he cannot find out what he is able to do. *Hamerton.*

Unless a tree has borne blossoms in spring, 50 you will vainly look for fruit on it in autumn. *Hare.*

Unless above himself he can / Erect himself, how poor a thing is man! *Daniel.*

Unless music exalt and purify, virtually it is not music at all. *Ruskin.*

Unless quickened from above and from within, art has in it nothing beyond itself which is visible beauty. *Dr. John Brown.*

Unless the people can be kept in total darkness, it is the wisest way for the advocates of truth to give them full light. *Whately.*

Unless we are accustomed to them from early youth, splendid chambers and elegant furniture are for people who neither have nor can have any thoughts. *Goethe.*

Unless we can cast off the prejudices of the man and become as children, docile and unperverted, we need never hope to enter the temple of philosophy. *Sir Wm. Hamilton.*

Unless we place our religion and our treasure in the same thing, religion will always be sacrificed. *Epictetus.*

5 Unless we see our object, how shall we know how to place or prize it in our understanding, our imagination, our affections? *Carlyle.*

Unlesson'd girl, unschool'd, unpractised; / Happy in this, she is not yet so old / But she may learn. *Mer. of Venice*, iii. 2.

Unlike my subject now shall be my song; / It shall be witty, but it shan't be long. *Chesterfield.*

Unlike the sun, intellectual luminaries shine brightest after they set. *Colton.*

Unmarried men are best friends, best masters, best servants, but not always best subjects; for they are light to run away, and almost all fugitives are of that condition. *Bacon.*

10 Unmingled good cannot be expected; but as we may lawfully gather all the good within our reach, we may be allowed to lament over that which we lose. *Johnson.*

Unmingled joys to no one here befall; / Who least, hath some; who most, hath never all. *Coleridge.*

Unmöglich ist's, was Edle nicht vermögen—That is impossible which noble souls are unable to do. *Goethe.*

Unnatural deeds / Do breed unnatural troubles: infected minds / To their deaf pillows will discharge their secrets. *Macb.*, v. 1.

Unnumbered suppliants crowd preferment's gate, / Athirst for wealth, and burning to be great; / Delusive fortune hears the incessant call, / They mount, they shine, evaporate, and fall. *Johnson.*

15 Uno avulso non deficit alter—If one is torn away, another takes its place. *M.*

Uno ictu—At once (*lit.* at one blow).

Uno impetu—At once (*lit.* by one onset).

Uno levanto la caza, y otro la mata — One starts the game, and another carries it off. *Sp. Pr.*

Unproductive truth is none. But there are products which cannot be weighed in patent scales, or brought to market. *J. Sterling.*

20 Unpublished nature will have its whole secret told. *Emerson.*

Unreasonable haste is the direct road to error. *Molière.*

Unreflective minds possess thoughts only as a jug does water, by containing them. In a disciplined mind knowledge exists like vital force in the physical frame, ready to be directed to tongue, or hand, or foot, hither, thither, anywhere, and for any use desired. *Coley.*

Unseasonable mirth always turns to sorrow. *Cervantes.*

Unselfish and noble acts are the most radiant epochs in the biography of souls. When wrought in the earliest youth, they lie in the memory of age like the coral islands, green and sunny amidst the melancholy waste of ocean. *Dr. Thomas.*

Unser Gefühl für Natur gleicht der Empfin- 25 dung des Kranken für die Gesundheit—Our feeling for nature is like the sensation of an invalid for health. *Schiller.*

Unsociable tempers are contracted in solitude, which will in the end not fail of corrupting the understanding as well as the manners, and of utterly disqualifying a man for the satisfactions and duties of life. Men must be taken as they are, and we neither make them nor ourselves better by flying from or quarrelling with them. *Burke.*

Unstable as water, thou shalt not excel. *Bible.*

Unstained thoughts do seldom dream on evil; / Birds never limed no secret bushes fear. *Shakespeare.*

Unstät treiben die Gedanken / Auf dem Meer der Leidenschaft—Unsteady is the course of thought on the sea of passion. *Schiller.*

Unsterblich ist was einmal hat gelebt—What 30 has once lived is immortal. *G. Kinkel.*

Unsterblich sein, das ist der Dichtkunst Los—Immortality is the destiny of the poetic art *Feuchtersleben.*

Unter allen Völkerschaften haben die Griechen den Traum des Lebens am schönsten geträumt—Of all peoples the Greek has dreamt most enchantingly the dream of life. *Goethe.*

Unter mancherlei wunderlichen Albernheiten der Schulen kommt mir keine so vollkommen lächerlich vor, als der Streit über die Aechtheit alter Schriften, alter Werke. Ist es denn der Autor oder die Schrift die wir bewundern oder tadeln? es ist immer nur der Autor, den wir vor uns haben; was kümmern uns die Namen, wenn wir ein Geisteswerk auslegen?—Among the manifold strange follies of the schools, I know no one so utterly ridiculous and absurd as the controversy about the authenticity of old writings, old works. Is it the author or the writing we admire or censure? It is always the author we have before us. What have we to do with names, when it is a work of the spirit we are interpreting? *Goethe.*

Unthinking, idle, wild, and young, / I laughed, and danced, and talked, and sung. *Princess Amelia.*

Until men have learned industry, economy, and 35 self-control, they cannot be safely intrusted with wealth. *Gladstone.*

Until you know as much about other people's affairs as they do themselves, it is not very safe to laugh at them or to find fault with them. *W. E. Forster.*

Unto every one that hath shall be given, and he shall have abundance; but from him that hath not shall be taken away even that which he seemeth to have. *Jesus.*

Unto him who works, and feels he works, / This same grand year (the Golden Year) is ever at the doors. *Tennyson.*

Unto the pure all things are pure. *St. Paul.*

Unto the youth should be shown the worth of 40 a noble and ripened age, and unto the old man, youth; that both may rejoice in the eternal circle, and life may in life be made perfect. *Goethe.*

Untwine me from the mass / Of deeds which make up life, one deed / Power shall fall short in or exceed. *Browning.*

Unum pro multis dabitur caput—One will be sacrificed for many. *Virg.*

Unus et idem—One and the same. *M.*

Unus Pellæo juveni non sufficit orbis ; / Æstuat infelix angusto limite mundi—One world is not enough for the youth of Pella ; the unhappy man frets at the narrow limits of the world. *Juv. of Alexander the Great.*

5 Unus vir nullus vir—One man is no man. *Pr.*

Unvanquished Time, the conqueror of conquerors, and lord of desolation. *Kirke White.*

Unverhofft kommt oft—The unlooked-for often happens. *Ger. Pr.*

Unverzeihlich find' ich den Leichtsinn ; doch liegt er im Menschen—Levity I deem unpardonable, though it lies in the heart of man. *Goethe.*

Unwept, unhonour'd, and unsung. *Scott.*

10 Unwilling service earns no thanks. *Dan. Pr.*

Unwise work, if it but persist, is everywhere struggling towards correction and restoration to health ; for it is still in contact with Nature, and all Nature incessantly contradicts it, and will heal it or annihilate it ; not so with unwise talk, which addresses itself, regardless of veridical Nature, to the universal suffrages ; and can, if it be dexterous, find harbour there, till all the suffrages are bankrupt and gone to Houndsditch. *Carlyle.*

Unworthy offspring brag most of their worthy descent. *Dan. Pr.*

Uom, se' tu grande o vil ? Muori, e il saprai—Man, whether thou be great or vile, die, and it will be known. *Alfieri.*

Up and try. *Wollaston.*

15 Up from unfeeling mould, / To seraphs burning round the Almighty's throne, / Life rising still on life, in higher tone, / Perfection forms, and with perfection bliss. *Thomson.*

Up ! my friend, and quit your books, / Or surely you'll grow double. / Up ! up ! my friend, and clear your looks, / Why all this toil and trouble ? *Wordsworth.*

Upbraiding turns a benefit into an injury. *Pr.*

Upon every occasion, be sure to make a conscience of what you do or say. *Thomas à Kempis.*

Upon the common course of life must our thoughts and our conversation be generally employed. *Johnson.*

20 Upon the education of the people of this country the fate of this country depends. *Disraeli.*

Upon the heat and flame of thy distemper / Sprinkle cool patience. *Ham.*, iii. 4.

Uprightness, judgment, and sympathy with others will profit thee at every time and in every place. *Goethe.*

Urbem lateritiam invenit, marmoream reliquit —He found a city of brick, and left it one of marble. *Suet. of the Rome of Cæsar Augustus.*

Urbem quam dicunt Romam, Melibœe, putavi, / Stultus ego, huic nostræ similem—The city, Melibœus, which they call Rome, I foolishly imagined to be like this town of ours. *Virg.*

Urbem venalem et mature perituram, si emp- 25 torem invenerit—A city for sale and ripe for ruin, once it finds a purchaser. *Sall. of Rome.*

Urbes constituit ætas : hora dissolvit. Momento fit cinis, diu sylva—It takes an age to build a city, but an hour involves it in ruin. A forest is long in growing, but in a moment it may be reduced to ashes. *Sen.*

Urbi et orbi—For Rome (*lit.* the city) and the world.

Urit enim fulgore suo, qui prægravat artes / Infra se positas : exstinctus amabitur idem —He who depresses the merits of those beneath him blasts them by his very splendour ; but when his light is extinguished, he will be admired. *Hor.*

Ursprünglich eignen Sinn lass dir nicht rauben ! / Woran die Menge glaubt, ist leicht zu glauben—Let no one conjure you out of your own native sense of things ; what the multitude believe in is easy to believe. *Goethe.*

Urticæ proxima sæpe rosa est—The nettle is 30 often next to the rose. *Ovid.*

Use almost can change the stamp of nature, / And either curb the devil, or throw him out. *Ham.*, iii. 4.

Use doth breed a habit in a man. *Two Gent. of Verona*, v. 4.

Use every man after his desert, and who should 'scape whipping ? Use them after your own honour and dignity ; the less they deserve, the more merit is in your bounty. *Ham.*, ii. 2.

Use him (the frog or bait) as if you loved him. *Isaak Walton.*

Use is the judge, the law, and rule of speech. 35 *Roscommon.*

Use makes a better soldier than the most urgent considerations of duty—familiarity with danger enabling him to estimate the danger. He sees how much is the risk, and is not afflicted with imagination ; knows practically Marshal Saxe's rule, that every soldier killed costs the enemy his weight in lead. *Emerson.*

Use sin as it will use you ; spare it not, for it will not spare you ; it is your murderer, and the murderer of the whole world. Use it, therefore, as a murderer should be used ; kill it before it kills you ; and though it bring you to the grave, it shall not be able to keep you there. *Baxter.*

Use sometimes to be alone. *George Herbert.*

Use the pen ; there is no magic in it, but it keeps the mind from staggering about. (?)

Use thy youth so that thou mayest have com- 40 fort to remember it when it hath forsaken thee, and not sigh and grieve at the account thereof. Use it as the springtime which soon departeth, and wherein thou oughtest to plant and sow all provisions for a long and happy life. *Sir Walter Raleigh.*

Used with due abstinence, hope acts as a healthful tonic ; intemperately indulged, as an enervating opiate. The visions of future triumph, which at first animate exertion, if dwelt upon too intently, will usurp the place of the stern reality ; and noble objects will be contemplated, not for their own inherent worth, but on account of the day-dreams they engender. Thus hope, aided by imagination, makes one man a hero, another a somnambulist, and a third a lunatic ; while it renders them all enthusiasts. *Sir J. Stephen.*

Useful be where thou livest, that they may / Both want and wish thy pleasing presence still. / Kindness, good parts, great places, are the way / To compass this. *George Herbert.*

Usefulness comes by labour, wit by ease. *George Herbert.*

Usque ad aras—To the very altars ; to the last extremity.

Usque ad nauseam—Till one is utterly sick of it.

5 Usque adeone mori miserum est?—Is it then so very dreadful to die? *Virg.*

Usque adeone / Scire tuum nihil est, nisi te scire hoc sciat alter?—Is then your knowledge to pass for nothing unless others know of it?

Usually speaking, the worst-bred person in company is a young traveller just returned from abroad. *Swift.*

Usury is a " concessum propter duritiam cordis " (a concession on account of hardness of heart) ; for, since there must be borrowing and lending, and men are so hard of heart as they will not lend freely, usury must be permitted. *Bacon.*

Usus est tyrannus—Custom is a tyrant. *Pr.*

10 Usus promptum facit—Practice makes perfect. *Pr.*

Ut ager, quamvis fertilis, sine cultura fructuosus esse non potest, sic sine doctrina animus—As a field, however fertile, can yield no fruit without culture, so neither can the mind of man without education. *Sen.*

Ut canis e Nilo—Like the dog by the Nile, *i.e.,* drinking and running. *Pr.*

Ut desint vires, tamen est laudanda voluntas —The will is commendable, though the ability may be wanting. *Ovid.*

Ut homines sunt, ita morem geras ; / Vita quam sit brevis, simul cogita—As men are, so must you humour them. Think, at the same time, how short life is. *Plaut.*

15 Ut homo est, ita morem geras—As a man is, so must you humour him. *Ter.*

Ut infra—As mentioned below.

Ut metus ad omnes, poena ad paucos perveniret—That fear may reach all, punish but few. *L.*

Ut mos est—As the custom is. *Juv.*

Ut pictura, poësis—It fares with a poem as with a picture. *Hor.*

20 Ut placeas, debes immemor esse tui—That you may please others you must be forgetful of yourself. *Ovid.*

Ut plerique solent, naso suspendis adunco / Ignotos—As is the way with most people, you turn up your nose at men of obscure origin. *Hor.*

Ut possedis—As you now are ; as you possess.

Ut prosim—That I may benefit others. *M.*

Ut quimus, quando ut volumus non licet—As we can, when we cannot as we wish. *Ter.*

25 Ut quisque contemtissimus et ludibrio est, ita solutæ linguæ est—The more despicable and ridiculous a man is, the readier he is with his tongue. *Sen.*

Ut ridentibus arrident, ita flentibus adflent, / Humani vultus—Human countenances, as they smile on those who smile, so they weep with those that weep. *Hor.*

Ut sæpe summa ingenia in occulto latent! —How often are men of the greatest genius lost in obscurity! *Plaut.*

Ut sementem feceris, ita et metes—As you have sown so shall you also reap. *Cic.*

Ut sunt humana, nihil est perpetuum—As human affairs go, nothing is everlasting. *Plaut.*

Ut sunt molles in calamitate mortalium animi! 30 —How weak are the hearts of mortals under calamity! *Tac.*

Ut supra—As mentioned above.

Utendum est ætate ; cito pede labitur ætas — We must make use of time ; time glides past at a rapid pace. *Ovid.*

Uterque bonus belli pacisque minister—A good administrator equally in peace or in war. *Ovid.*

Utile dulci—The useful with the agreeable.

Utinam tam facile vera invenire possem, quam 35 falsa convincere!—Would that I could as easily find out the true as I can detect the false. *Cic.*

Utopia—An imaginary republic nowhere existing.

Utque alios industria, ita hunc ignavia ad famam protulerat — While other men have attained to fame by their industry, this man has by his indolence. *Tac.*

Utrum horum mavis accipe—Take which you prefer.

Utrumque vitium est, et omnibus credere et nulli—It is equally an error to confide in all and in none. *Sen.*

Uttered out of time, or concealed in its season, 40 good savoureth of evil. *Tupper.*

Uttering such dulcet and harmonious breath, / That the rude sea grew civil at her song, / And certain stars shot madly from their spheres / To hear the sea-maid's music. *Mid. N. Dream,* ii. 2.

Uxorem, Posthume, ducis? / Dic qua Tisiphone, quibus exagitare colubris—Are you marrying a wife, Posthumous? By what Fury, say, by what snakes are you driven mad? *Juv.*

Uxori nubere nolo meæ—I will not marry a wife to be my master. *Mart.*

V.

Vache ne sait ce que vaut sa queue jusqu'à-ce-qu'elle l'ait perdue — The cow doesn't know the worth of her tail until she has lost it. *Fr. Pr.*

Vacuus cantat coram latrone viator—The tra-45 veller with an empty purse sings in the face of the robber. *Juv.*

Vade in pace—Go in peace.

Vade mecum—Go with me ; a constant companion ; a manual.

Vade retro!—Avaunt!

Væ victis!—Woe (*i.e.,* extermination) to the conquered!

Vaillant et veillant—Valiant and on the watch. *M.* 50

Vain for the rude craftsman to attempt the beautiful ; only one diamond can polish another. *Goethe.*

Vain hope to make people happy by politics! *Carlyle.*

Vain is the help of man. *Bible.*

Vain man would be wise, though man be born like a wild ass's colt. *Bible.*

Vain men delight in telling what honours have been done them, what great company they have kept, and the like; by which they plainly confess that these honours were more than their due. *Swift.*

Vain people are loquacious; and proud, taciturn. *Schopenhauer.*

Vain pomp and glory of this world, I hate ye. *Hen. VIII., iii. 2.*

5 Vain to send the purblind or blind to the shore of a Pactolus never so golden : these find only gravel ; the seer and finder alone picks up golden grains there. *Carlyle.*

Vain, very vain, my weary search to find / That bliss which only centres in the mind. *Goldsmith.*

Vainglory blossoms, but never bears. *Pr.*

Val meglio piegarsi che rompersi—Better submit than be ruined. *It. Pr.*

Val più un asino vivo che un dottore morto— A living ass is better than a dead doctor. *It. Pr.*

10 Val più un' oncia di discrezione che una libra di sapere—An ounce of discretion is worth more than a pound of knowledge. *It. Pr.*

Valeant mendacia vatum — Away with the fictions of poets ! *Ovid.*

Valeat quantum valere potest—Let it pass for what it is worth.

Valeat res ludicra, si me / Palma negata macrum, donata reducit opimum—Farewell to the drama if the palm as it is granted or denied makes me happy or miserable. *Hor.*

Valet anchora virtus—Virtue is a sure anchor. *M.*

15 Valet ima summis / Mutare, et insignem attenuat Deus, / Obscura promens—The Deity has power to supplant the highest by the lowest, and he dims the lustre of the exalted by bringing forth to the light things obscure. *Hor.*

Validius est naturæ testimonium quam doctrinæ argumentum—The testimony of nature is weightier than the arguments of the learned. *St. Ambrose.*

Valour consists in the power of self-recovery. *Emerson.*

Valour in distress challenges respect, even from an enemy. *Plutarch.*

Valour is the fountain of Pity too ;—of Truth, and all that is great and good in man. *Carlyle.*

20 Valour is worth little without discretion. *Pr.*

Valour would cease to be a virtue if there were no injustice. *Agesilaus.*

Vana quoque ad veros accessit fama timores— Idle rumours were also added to well-founded apprehensions. *Lucan.*

Vanitas vanitatum, et omnia vanitas—Vanity of vanities, all is vanity. *Vulgate.*

Vanity and coarse pride give gold ; friendship and love give flowers. *Grillparzer.*

25 Vanity Fair. *Bunyan.*

Vanity, however artfully concealed or openly displayed, always counteracts its own purposes. *Arliss.*

Vanity in an old man is charming. It is a proof of an open nature. Eighty winters have not frozen him up or taught him concealments. In a young person it is simply allowable ; we do not expect him to be above it. *Bovee.*

Vanity is a blue-bottle, which buzzes in the window of the wise. *Pr.*

Vanity is of a divisive, not a uniting nature. *Carlyle.*

Vanity is rather a mark of humility than pride. 30 *Swift.*

Vanity is so anchored in the heart of man that the lowest drudge must boast and have his admirers ; and the philosophers themselves desire the same. *Pascal.*

Vanity is the food of fools. *Swift.*

Vanity is the pride of Nature. *Pr.*

Vanity is the vice of low minds ; a man of spirit is too proud to be vain. *Swift.*

Vare, Vare, redde mihi legiones meas !—Varus, give me back my legions ! *Suet. Exclamation of Augustus Cæsar on hearing of the slaughter of his troops under Varus by Arminius.*

Variæ lectiones—Various readings.

Varietas delectat—Variety is charming. *Phædrus.*

Variety alone gives joy ; / The sweetest meats the soonest cloy. *Prior.*

Variety is the condition of harmony. *J. F. Clarke.*

Variety is the mother of enjoyment. *Disraeli.* 40

Variety is the principal ingredient in beauty ; and simplicity is essential to grandeur. *Shenstone.*

Variety of mere nothings gives more pleasure than uniformity of somethings. *Jean Paul.*

Variety's the very spice of life, / That gives it all its flavour. *Cowper.*

Variorum notæ—Notes of various authors.

Varium et mutabile semper / Fœmina—Woman is ever changeable and capricious. *Virg.* 45

Vary and intermingle speech of the present occasion with arguments, tales with reasons, asking of questions with telling of opinions, and jest with earnest ; for it is a dull thing to tire, and, as we say now, to jade anything too far. *Bacon.*

Vast chain of being ! / From Nature's chain whatever link you strike / Tenth or ten thousandth breaks the chain alike. *Pope.*

Vaulting ambition, which o'erleaps itself, / And falls on the other. *Macb.,* i. 7.

Vaux mieux avoir affaire à Dieu qu'à ses saints—Better to have dealings with God than his saints. *Fr. Pr.*

Vectigalia nervi sunt reipublicæ—Taxes are the 50 sinews of the commonwealth. *Cic.*

Vedentem thus et odores—Selling frankincense and perfumes. *Hor., of worthless works fated to wrap up parcels.*

Vedi Napoli, e poi muori—See Naples and then die. *It. Pr.*

Vehemens in utramque partem, aut largitate nimia aut parsimonia—Ready to rush to either extreme of lavish liberality or niggardly parsimony. *Ter.*

Veiosque habitante Camillo, / Illic Roma fuit —When Camillus dwelt at Veii, Rome was there. *Lucan.*

Vel cæco appareat—Even a blind man could 55 perceive it. *Pr.*

Vel capillus habet umbram suam—Even a hair has its shadow. *Pub. Syr.*

Velis et remis—With sails and oars.

Vellem nescire literas !—I wish I never knew how to read or write ! *Nero on signing a death-warrant.*

Velocem tardus assequitur—The slow overtakes the swift. *Pr.*

Velocius ac citius nos / Corrumpunt vitiorum exempla domestica, magnis / Cum subeant animos auctoribus—The examples of vice at home more easily and more quickly corrupt us than others, since they steal into our minds under the highest authority. *Juv.*

Velox consilium sequitur pœnitentia—Repentance generally follows hasty counsels. *Pub. Syr.*

5 **Veluti in speculum**—As if in a mirror.

Velvet paws hide sharp claws. *Pr.*

Vendere fumos—To sell smoke, or make empty pledges.

Vendetta boccon di Dio—Revenge is a sweet morsel for a god. *It. Pr.*

Veneering oft outshines the solid wood. *Burns.*

10 **Venerable to me is the hard hand**—crooked, coarse — wherein, notwithstanding, lies a cunning virtue, indefeasibly royal, as of the sceptre of this planet. Venerable, too, is the rugged face, all weather-tanned, besoiled, with its rude intelligence ; for it is the face of a man living manlike. *Carlyle.*

Vengeance belongeth unto me ; I will recompense, saith the Lord. *Bible.*

Vengeance has no foresight. *Napoleon.*

Vengeance (*Rache*) has no limits, for sin has none. *F. Hebbel.*

Vengeance is mine ; I will repay, saith the Lord. *St. Paul.*

15 **Vengeance is wild justice.** *Pr.*

Vengeance taken will often tear the heart and torment the conscience. *Schopenhauer.*

Veni, Creator Spiritus—Come, Creator Spirit.

Veni, vidi, vici—I came, I saw, I conquered. *Julius Cæsar's despatch to a friend at Rome on his defeat of Pharnaces.*

Venia necessitati datur—Pardon is conceded to necessity. *Cic.*

20 **Venient annis / Sæcula seris, quibus Oceanus / Vincula rerum laxet, et ingens / Pateat tellus, Tiphysque novos / Detegat orbes ; nec sit terris / Ultima thule**—In later years a time will come when Ocean shall relax his bars, and a vast territory shall appear, and Tiphys shall discover new worlds, and Thule shall be no longer the remotest spot on earth. *Sen. predicting the discovery of America.*

Venire facias—Cause to come. (Writ of a sheriff to summon a jury.) *L.*

Venit summa dies et ineluctabile tempus / Dardaniæ—The last day and inevitable hour of Troy is come. *Virg.*

Vent au visage rend un homme sage—Wind in the face (*i.e.* adversity) makes a man wise. *Pr.*

Ventis secundis—With a fair wind.

25 **Ventre à terre**—At full speed ; with all one's might. *Fr.*

Ventre affamé n'a point d'oreilles—A hungry belly has no ears. *Fr. Pr.*

Ventum ad supremum est—A crisis has come ; we are at our last shift. *Virg.*

Ventum seminabant et turbinem metent—They were sowing the wind, and they shall reap the whirlwind. *Vulgate.*

Venus, if men at sea you save, / And rescue from the whirling wave, / Me too, a lover, I implore, / Save from worse shipwreck here on shore. *Anon.*

Venus is beautiful, no doubt ; but the artist 30 that created her is more beautiful still. *Ed.*

Venus will not charm so much without her attendant Graces, as they will without her. *Chesterfield.*

Ver non semper viret—The spring does not always flourish. *M.*

Vera redit facies, dissimulata perit—Our natural countenance comes back, the assumed mask falls off. *Petron.*

Verachtung ist der wahre Tod—The true death is being treated with contempt. *Schiller.*

Verba dat omnis amans—Every lover makes fair 35 speeches. *Ovid.*

Verba facit mortuo—He talks to a dead man ; he wastes words. *Plaut.*

Verba ligant homines, taurorum cornua funes—Words bind men, cords the horns of bulls.

Verba rebus aptare—To fit words to things, *i.e.*, call a spade a spade.

Verba volant, scripta manent—What is spoken flies, what is written remains.

Verbaque provisam rem non invita sequentur 40—Words will not fail when the matter is well considered. *Hor.*

Verbatim et literatim—Word for word and letter for letter.

Verbi causa, *or* **gratia**—For example ; for instance.

Verbo tenus—In name ; as far as the words go.

Verborum paupertas, imo egestas—A poverty of words, or rather an utter want of them. *Sen.*

Verbosa ac grandis epistola venit / A Capreis 45—A verbose and haughty epistle came from Capreæ (the Emperor Tiberius's palace). *Juv.*

Verbum Dei manet in æternum—The command of God endures through eternity. *M.*

Verbum Domini manet in æternum—The word of the Lord endureth for ever. *Vulgate.*

Verbum sat sapienti—A word is enough to a wise man. *Pr.*

Verbunden werden auch die Schwachen mächtig—Even the weak become strong when they are united. *Schiller.*

Vergebens dass ihr ringums wissenschaftlich 50 schweift, / Ein jeder lernt nur was er lernen kann !—In vain that ye go ranging round about in your scientific, or learned, inquiries ; each one learns only what he can. *Mephisto, to the scholar in Goethe's " Faust."*

Vergieb soviel du kannst, und gieb soviel du hast—Forgive as much as thou canst, and give as much as thou hast. *Rückert.*

Verily, verily, I say unto thee, Except a man be born of water and the spirit (of death, that is, and of life), he cannot enter the kingdom of God. *Jesus.*

Veritas, a quocunque dicitur, a Deo est—Truth, by whomsoever spoken, comes from God.

Veritas et virtus vincunt—Truth and virtue conquer. *M.*

Veritas nihil veretur nisi abscondi—Truth fears 55 nothing but concealment.

Veritas non recipit magis ac minus—Truth admits not of greater and less. *Wilkins.*

Veritas odium parit—The truth begets hatred.

Veritas temporis filia—Truth is the daughter of Time.

Veritas vel mendacio corrumpitur vel silentio —Truth is violated by falsehood or by silence. *Ammian.*

Veritas victrix—Truth the conqueror. *M.*

Veritas vincit—Truth conquers. *M.*

5 Veritas visu et mora, falsa festinatione et incertis valescunt—Truth is established by inspection and delay ; falsehood thrives by haste and uncertainty. *Tac.*

Veritatis simplex oratio est—The language of truth is simple, *i.e.,* it needs not the ornament of many words. *Sen.*

Vérité sans peur—Truth without fear. *M.*

Verletzen ist leicht, heilen schwer—To hurt is easy, to heal is hard. *Ger. Pr.*

Vermögen sucht Vermögen — Ability seeks ability. *Ger. Pr.*

10 Vernunft und Wissenschaft, Des Menschen allerhöchste Kraft !—Reason and knowledge, the highest might of man ! *Goethe.*

Versate diu, quid ferre recusent, / Quid valeant humeri—Weigh well what your shoulders can and cannot bear. *Hor.*

Verschoben ist nicht aufgehoben—To put off is not to let off. *Ger. Pr.*

Verse itself is an absurdity except as an expression of some higher movement of the mind, or as an expedient to lift other minds to the same ideal level. *Lowell.*

Verstand ist mechanischer, Witz ist chemischer, Genie organischer Geist—Understanding is a mechanically, wit a chemically, and genius an organically, acting spirit. *Fr. Schlegel.*

15 Verstellung ist der offnen Seele fremd—Dissimulation is alien to the open soul. *Schiller.*

Verstellung, sagt man, sei ein grosses Laster, / Doch von Verstellung leben wir—Dissimulation they say is very wicked, yet we live by dissimulation. *Goethe.*

Vertere seria ludo—To turn from grave to gay. *Hor.*

Vertrauen erweckt Vertrauen — Confidence awakens confidence. *Friedrich August II. von Sachsen.*

Verum ubi plura nitent in carmine, non ego paucis / Offendar maculis—But where many beauties shine in a poem, I will not be offended at a few blots. *Hor.*

20 Verus amicus est is qui est tanquam alter idem —A true friend is he who is, as it were, a second self. *Cic.*

Verwelkt, entblättert, zertreten sogar / Von rohen Schicksalsfüssen— / Mein Freund, das ist auf Erden las Los / Von allem Schönen und Süssen—To wither away, be disleaved, be trodden to dust even by the rude feet of Fate, that, friend, is the lot on earth of everything that is beautiful and sweet. *Heine.*

Very few enjoy money, because they can't get enough. *Amer. Pr.*

Very few men acquire wealth in such a manner as to receive pleasure from it. *Ward Beecher.*

Very few men, properly speaking, live at present, but are providing to live another time. *Not traceable.*

25 Very few people are good economists of their fortune, and still fewer of their time. *Chesterfield.*

Very fine pagoda if ye could get any sort of god to put in it. *Carlyle to Bunsen of Cologne Cathedral.*

Very great benefactors to the rich, or those whom they call people at their ease, are your persons of no consequence. *Steele.*

Very learned women are to be met with, just as female warriors ; but they are seldom or never inventors. *Voltaire.*

Very like a whale. *Ham.,* iii. 2.

Verzeih dir nichts und den Andern viel—For- 30 give thyself nothing, others much. *Ger. Pr.*

Verzeihn ist leicht, allein vergessen schwer— To forgive is easy, but to forget hard. *Schiller.*

Verzeiht ! Es ist ein gross Ergötzen / Sich in den Geist der Zeiten zu versetzen, / Zu schauen, wie vor uns ein weiser Mann gedacht, / Und wie wir's dann zuletzt so herrlich weit gebracht—Pardon ! It is a great pleasure to transport one's self into the spirit of the times, to see how a wise man thought before us, and to what a glorious height we have at last carried it. *Goethe, Wagner to Faust.*

Vestibulum domus ornamentum est—The hall is the ornament of a house, *i.e.,* first impressions have great weight. *Pr.*

Vestigia morientis libertatis—The footprints of expiring liberty. *Tac.*

Vestigia nulla retrorsum—There is no stepping 35 backward.

Vestigia torrent—The footprints frighten me. *Hor.*

Vestis virum facit—The garment makes the man. *Pr.*

Vetera extollimus, recentium incuriosi—We extol what is old, regardless of what is of modern date. *Tac.*

Vetustas pro lege semper habetur—Ancient custom is always held as law. *L.*

Vi et armis — By force and arms ; by main 40 force.

Via crucis, via lucis—The way of the cross is the way of light. *M.*

Via media—A middle way or course ; any middle course. *M.*

Via trita est tutissima—The beaten path is the safest. *Coke.*

Via trita, via tuta—The beaten path is the safe path. *L.*

Viam qui nescit qua deveniat ad mare, / Eum 45 oportet amnem quærere comitem sibi—He who knows not his way straight to the sea should choose the river for his guide. *Plaut.*

Viamque insiste domandi, / Dum faciles animi juvenum, dum mobilis ætas—Enter upon the way of training while the spirits in youth are still pliant, while they are at that period when the mind is docile. *Virg.*

Vice—In place of.

Vice is a monster of such frightful mien, / As to be hated needs but to be seen ; / Yet seen too often, familiar with her face, / We first endure, then pity, then embrace. *Pope.*

Vice is its own punishment. *Pr.*

Vice is learned without a schoolmaster. *Dan.* 50 *Pr.*

Vice itself lost half its evil by losing all its grossness. *Burke.*

Vice, like disease, floats in the atmosphere. *Hazlitt.*

Vice versa—The terms being reversed; in reverse order.

Vicissitudes of fortune, which spares neither man nor the proudest of his works, which buries empires and cities in a common grave. *Gibbon.*

Vicisti Galilæe!—Thou hast conquered, O Galilæan! *Julian the Apostate on his deathbed, apostrophising Christ.*

Victoria concordia crescit—Victory is increased by concord. *M.*

5 Victoriæ gloria merces—Glory is the reward of victory. *M.*

Victory belongs to the most persevering. *Napoleon.*

Victory or Westminster Abbey. *Nelson at Trafalgar.*

Victrix causa Diis placuit, sed victa Catoni—The conquering cause pleased the gods, the conquered one Cato. *Lucan.*

Victrix fortunæ sapientia—Wisdom overcomes fortune. *Juv.*

10 Vide licet—Namely; you may see.

Vide ut supra—See preceding statement.

Video meliora proboque, / Deteriora sequor—I see and approve the better course, but I follow the worse. *Ovid.*

Viel Klagen hör' ich oft erheben / Vom Hochmut, an der Grosse übt. / Der Grossen Hochmut wird sich geben, / Wenn unsre Kriecherei sich giebt—Much complaining I often hear raised against the proud bearing of the great. The pride of the great will disappear as soon as we cease our cringing. *Körner.*

Viel Rettungsmittel bietest du? Was heisst' es? / Die beste Rettung, Gegenwart des Geistes—Many a remedy offerest thou? What is the worth of it? The best remedy (the sole deliverance) is the presence of the spirit. *Goethe.*

15 Viele Freunde und wenige Nothhelfer—Many friends and few helpers in distress. *Ger. Pr.*

Vieles wünscht sich der Mensch, und doch bedarf er nur wenig; / Denn die Tage sind kurz, und beschränkt der Sterblichen Schicksal—Much wishes man for himself, and yet needs he but little; for the days are short, and limited is the fate of mortals. *Goethe.*

Vigilantibus—To those that watch. *M.*

Vigilantibus, non dormientibus, subveniunt jura—The laws assist those who watch, not those who sleep. *L.*

Vigor ætatis fluit ut flos veris—The vigour of manhood passes away like a spring flower.

20 Vile is the vengeance on the ashes cold, / And envy base to bark at sleeping fame. *Spenser.*

Vilius argentum est auro, virtutibus aurum—Silver is of less value than gold, gold than virtue. *Hor.*

Vincere scis, Hannibal, victoria uti nescis—You know how to conquer, Hannibal, but you know not how to profit by your victory. *Maherbal in Livy.*

Vincit amor patriæ—The love of our country outweighs all other considerations. *Virg.*

Vincit omnia veritas—Truth conquers all things. *M.*

25 Vincit qui se vincit—He is a conqueror who conquers himself. *M.*

Vinegar given is better than honey bought. *Arab. Pr.*

Vino dentro, senno fuora—When wine is in, wit is out. *It. Pr.*

Vino diffugiunt mordaces curæ—Corroding cares are dispelled by wine. *After Horace.*

Violence does ever justice unjustly. *Carlyle.*

Violence of sorrow is not at the first to be 30 striven withal; being, like a mighty beast, sooner tamed with following than overthrown by withstanding. *Sir P. Sidney.*

Violent combativeness for particular sects, as Evangelical, Roman Catholic, High Church, Broad Church, or the like, is merely a form of party egoism, and a defiance of Christ, not a confession of Him. *Ruskin.*

Violent delights have violent ends, / And in their triumph die, like fire and powder, / Which, as they kiss, consume. *Rom. and Jul.*, ii. 6.

Violent fires soon burn out. *Pr.*

Violent mirth is the foam, and deep sadness the subsidence, of a morbid fermentation. *Johnson.*

Violent passions are formed in solitude. In 35 the bustle of the world no object has time to make a deep impression. *Henry Home.*

Violenta nemo imperia continuit diu; / Moderata durant—No one ever held power long by violence; it lasts only when wielded with moderation. *Sen.*

Vir bonus est quis? / Qui consulta patrum, qui leges juraque servat—What man is to be called good? He who obeys the decrees of the fathers, he who respects the laws and justice. *Hor.*

Vir sapiens forti melior—A wise man is better than a strong.

Vires acquirit eundo—She acquires strength as she advances. *Virg., of Fame.*

Virescit vulnere virtus—Virtue flourishes from 40 a wound. *M.*

Viret in æternum—It flourishes for ever. *M.*

Virgilium vidi tantum—Virgil I have only seen. *Ovid.*

Viribus unitis—With united strength. *M. of Joseph I.*

Viris fortibus non opus est mœnibus—Brave men have no need of walls.

Virtue alone can procure that independence 45 which is the end of human wishes. *Petrarch.*

Virtue alone has majesty in death. *Young.*

Virtue alone is not sufficient for the exercise of government; laws alone carry themselves into practice. *Mencius.*

Virtue alone outbuilds the pyramids; / Her monuments shall last when Egypt's fall. *Young.*

Virtue and goodness tend to make men powerful in this world; but they who aim at the power have not the virtue. *Newman.*

Virtue does not consist in doing what will be 50 presently paid; it will be paid some day; but the vital condition of it, as virtue, is that it shall be content in its own deed, and desirous rather that the pay of it, if any, should be for others. *Ruskin.*

Virtue, if it could only be beheld by our eyes, would excite a marvellous love for wisdom. (?)

Virtue is an absolute Amen, uttered with reference to the obscure ends that Providence pursues through us. *Renan.*

Virtue is an angel ; but she is a blind one, and must ask of Knowledge to show her the pathway that leads to her goal. Mere knowledge, on the other hand, like a Swiss mercenary, is ready to combat either in the ranks of sin or under the banners of righteousness ; ready to forge cannon-balls or to print New Testaments ; to navigate a corsair's vessel or a missionary ship. *Horace Mann.*

Virtue is beauty ; but the beauteous-evil / Are empty trunks o'erflourished by the devil. *Twelfth Night*, iii. 4.

Virtue is bold, and goodness never fearful. *Meas. for Meas.*, iii. 1.

Virtue is choked with foul ambition. 2 *Hen. VI.*, iii. 1.

5 Virtue is free-will to choose the good, not tool-usefulness to forge at the expedient. *Carlyle.*

Virtue is its own reward, and brings with it the truest and highest pleasures ; but they who cultivate it for the pleasure's sake are selfish, not religious, and will never have the pleasure, because they never can have the virtue. *Newman.*

Virtue is like a rich stone, best plain set. *Bacon.*

Virtue is like precious odours, most fragrant where they are incensed or crushed. *Bacon.*

Virtue is necessary to a republic. *Montesquieu.*

10 Virtue is not a knowing, but a willing. *Zachariä.*

Virtue is safe only when it is inspired. *C. H. Parkhurst.*

Virtue is the adherence in action to the nature of things, and the nature of things makes it prevalent. It consists in a perpetual substitution of being for seeming, and with sublime propriety God is described as saying, I AM. *Emerson.*

Virtue is the fount whence honour springs. *Marlowe.*

Virtue is the health of the soul ; it gives a flavour to the smallest leaves of life. *Joubert.*

15 Virtue is the queen of labourers. *Pr.*

Virtue itself offends when coupled with forbidding manners. *Bp. Middleton.*

Virtue itself turns vice, being misapplied, / And vice sometime 's by action dignified. *Rom. and Jul.*, ii. 3.

Virtue, like a plant, will not grow unless its root be hidden, buried from the eye of the sun. Let the sun shine on it, nay, do but look at it privily thyself, the root withers, and no flower will glad thee. *Carlyle.*

Virtue, like a strong and hardy plant, will root when it can find an ingenuous nature and a mind not averse to labour. *Plutarch.*

20 Virtue, like health, is the harmony of the whole man. *Carlyle.*

Virtue may be stern, but never cruel, never inhuman. *Schiller.*

Virtue, not misery, is the appointed road to heaven. *W. R. Greg.*

Virtue often trips and falls on the sharp-edged rocks of poverty. *Eugene Sue.*

Virtue pardons the wicked, as the sandal-tree perfumes the axe which strikes it. *Saadi.*

25 Virtue repulsed, yet knows not to repine, / But shall with unattainted honour shine. *Swift.*

Virtue should be considered as a part of taste, and we should as much avoid deceit or sinister meanings in discourse as we would puns, bad language, or false grammar. (?)

Virtue shows quite as well in rags and patches as she does in purple and fine linen. *Dickens.*

Virtue that goes unrewarded is doubly beautiful. *Seume.*

Virtue that wavers is not virtue. *Milton.*

Virtue, though clothed in a beggar's garb, 30 commands respect. *Schiller.*

Virtue, though in rags, will keep one warm *Dryden, after Horace.*

Virtue, which breaks through all opposition / And all temptations can remove, / Most shines and most is acceptable above. *Milton.*

Virtue which is according to the precepts of reason, appears equally great in avoiding as in overcoming dangers. *Spinoza.*

Virtuous and vicious every man must be ; / Few in the extreme, but all in a degree. *Pope.*

Virtus ariete fortior—Virtue is stronger than a 35 battering-ram. *M.*

Virtus est medium vitiorum, et utrinque reductum—Virtue is the mean between two vices, and equally removed from either. *Hor.*

Virtus est militis decus—Valour is the soldier's honour. *Livy.*

Virtus est vitium fugere, et sapientia prima / Stultitia caruisse—It is virtue to shun vice, and the first step of wisdom is to be free from folly. *Hor.*

Virtus hominem jungit Deo—Virtue unites man with God. *Cic.*

Virtus in actione consistit—Virtue consists in 40 action. *M.*

Virtus in arduis—Valour in difficulties.

Virtus laudatur et alget—Virtue is praised and is left to freeze in the cold. *Juv.*

Virtus mille scuta—Virtue is as good as a thousand shields. *M.*

Virtus post nummos — After money virtue. *Hor.*

Virtus probata florebit—Approved virtue will 45 flourish. *M.*

Virtus, recludens immeritis mori / Cœlum, negata tentat iter via ; / Cœtusque vulgares, et udam / Spernit humum fugiente penna—Virtue, opening heaven to those who deserve not to die, explores her way by a path to others denied, and spurns with soaring wing the vulgar crowds and the foggy earth. *Hor.*

Virtus repulsæ nescia sordidæ / Intaminatis fulget honoribus ; / Nec sumit aut ponit secures / Arbitrio popularis auræ—Virtue, which knows no base repulse, shines with unsullied honours, neither receives nor resigns the fasces (*i.e.*, badges of office) at the will of popular caprice. *Hor.*

Virtus requiei nescia sordidæ — Virtue which knows no mean repose. *M.*

Virtus semper viridis—Virtue is always flourishing (*lit.* green). *M.*

Virtus sola nobilitat—Virtue alone confers nobi- 50 lity. *M.*

Virtus vincit invidiam—Virtue subdues envy. *M.*

Virtute et opera—By virtue and industry. *M.*

Virtute, non astutia—By virtue, not by cunning. *M.*

Virtute, non verbis—By virtue, not by words. *M.*

Virtute quies — In virtue there is tranquillity. *M.*

Virtutem doctrina paret, naturane donet? — Does training produce virtue, or does nature bestow it? *Hor.*

Virtutem incolumem odimus, / Sublatam ex oculis quærimus invidi — We in our envy hate virtue when present, but seek after her when she is removed out of our sight. *Hor.*

Virtuti nihil obstat et armis — Nothing can withstand valour and arms. *M.*

5 **Virtuti non armis fido** — I trust to virtue, not to arms. *M.*

Virtutibus obstat / Res angusta domi — Straitened domestic means obstruct the path to virtue. *Juv.*

Virtutis avorum præmium — The reward of the valour of my forefathers. *M.*

Virtutis expers verbis jactans gloriam / Ignotos fallit, notis est derisui — A fellow who brags of his prowess and is devoid of courage, imposes on strangers but is the jest of those who know him. *Phædrus.*

Virtutis fortuna comes — Fortune is the companion of valour. *M.*

10 **Vis comica** — Comic power, or a talent for comedy.

Vis consili expers mole ruit sua / Vim temperatam Di quoque provehunt / In majus ; idem odere vires / Omne nefas animo moventes — Force, without judgment, falls by its own weight ; moreover, the gods promote well-regulated force to further advantage ; but they detest force that meditates every crime. *Hor.*

Vis inertiæ — The inert property or resisting power of matter.

Vis unita fortior — Power is strengthened by union. *M.*

Vis viva — The power residing in a body in virtue of its motion.

15 **Visage fardé** — A painted, or dissembling, countenance. *Fr.*

Visible ploughmen and hammermen there have been, ever from Cain and Tubal Cain downwards ; but where does your accumulated agricultural, metallurgic, and other manufacturing skill lie warehoused ? *Carlyle.*

Vita brevis, ars longa — Life is short, art is long.

Vita dum superest, bene est — If only life remain, I am content. *Mæcenas.*

Vita hominis sine literis mors est — Life without letters is death. *M.*

20 **Vita est hominum quasi quum ludas tesseris** — The life of man is like a game with dice. *Ter.*

Vita sine proposito vaga est — A life without a purpose is a rambling one. *Sen.*

Vitæ est avidus, quisquis non vult / Mundo secum pereunte mori — He is greedy of life who is unwilling to die when the world around him is perishing. *Sen.*

Vitæ philosophia dux, virtutis indagatrix — O philosophy, thou guide of life and discoverer of virtue. *Cic.*

Vitæ post-scenia celant — They conceal the secret actions of their lives (*lit.* what goes on behind the scenes). *Lucret.*

25 **Vitæ summa brevis spem nos vetat inchoare longam** — The short span of life forbids us to spin out hope to any length. *Hor.*

Vitæ via virtus — Virtue is the way of life. *M.*

Vital truth is in its very nature self-evident ; carries its witness within itself, and needs only to be understood to be at once accepted as true. *Ed.*

Vitam impendere vero — To devote one's life to the truth. *Juv.*

Vitam regit fortuna, non sapientia — Fortune rules this life, and not wisdom. *Cic.*

Vitanda est improba Siren / Desidia — You must 30 avoid sloth, that wicked Syren. *Hor.*

Vitavi denique culpam, / Non laudem merui — I have, in brief, avoided what is censurable, not merited what is commendable. *Hor.*

Vitia nobis sub virtutum nomine obrepunt — Vices steal upon us under the name of virtues. *Sen.*

Vitia otii negotio discutienda sunt — The vice of doing nothing is only to be shaken off by doing something. *Sen.*

Vitiis nemo sine nascitur ; optimus ille / Qui minimis urgetur — No man is born without faults ; he is the best who is oppressed with fewest. *Hor.*

Vitiosum est ubique, quod nimium est — Too 35 much of anything is in every case a defect. *Sen.*

Vitium commune omnium est, / Quod nimium ad rem in senecta attenti sumus — It is a fault common to us all, that in old age we become too much attached to worldly interests. *Ter.*

Viva voce — By the living voice.

Vivat Rex *or* **Regina** — Long live the king or queen.

Vive la bagatelle ! — Success to trifling ! *Fr.*

Vive la nation ! — Long live the nation ! *Fr.* 40

Vive ut vivas — Live that you may live. *M.*

Vive, valeque — Long life to you and farewell. *M.*

Vivent les gueux ! — Long live the beggars ! *Fr.*

Vivere est cogitare — Living is thinking. *Cic.*

Vivere militare est — To live is to fight. *Sen.* 45

Vivere sat vincere — To conquer is to live enough. *M.*

Vivere si recte nescis, decede peritis — If you know not how to live aright, quit the company of those who do. *Hor.*

Vivida vis animi — The strong force of genius. *Lucret.*

Vivimus aliena fiducia — We live by trusting one another. *Pliny the elder.*

Vivit post funera virtus — Virtue survives the 50 grave. *M.*

Vivite fortes, / Fortiaque adversis opponite pectora rebus — Live as brave men, and breast adversity with stout hearts. *Hor.*

Vivitur exiguo melius : natura beatis / Omnibus esse dedit, si quis cognoverit uti — Men live best upon a little : nature has ordained all to be happy, if they would but learn how to use her gifts. *Claud.*

Vivitur parvo bene, cui paternum / Splendet in mensa tenui salinum ; / Nec leves somnos timor aut cupido / Sordidus aufert — He lives well on little on whose frugal board the paternal salt-cellar shines, and whose soft slumbers are not disturbed by fear or the sordid passion for gain. *Hor.*

Vivo et regno, simul ista reliqui, / Quæ vos ad cœlum fertis rumore secundo — I live and am a king, as soon as I have left those interests of the city, which you exalt to the skies in such laudation. *Hor.*

Vivre, c'est penser et sentir son âme—To live is to think, and feel one has a soul of his own. *Fr.*

Vivre n'est pas respirer ; c'est agir——Living is not breathing ; it is acting. *Rousseau.*

Vivunt in Venerem frondes, etiam nemus omne per altum / Felix arbor amat; nutant ad mutua palmæ / Fœdera, populeo suspirat populus ictu, / Et platani platanis, alnoque assibilat alnus—The leaves live to love, and over the whole lofty grove each happy tree loves ; palm nods to palm in mutual pledge of love ; the poplar sighs for the poplar's embrace ; plane whispers to plane, and alder to alder. *Claud., in anticipation of the sexual system of Linnæus.*

Vix a te videor posse tenere manus—I feel hardly able to keep my hands off you. *Ovid.*

5 Vix decimus quisque est, qui ipse sese noverit — Hardly one man in ten knows himself. *Plaut.*

Vix ea nostra voco—I scarcely call these things our own. *M.*

Vixere fortes ante Agamemnona / Multi ; sed omnes illacrymabiles / Urgentur, ignotique longa / Nocte, carent quia vate sacro—Many brave men lived before Agamemnon ; but all of them, unwept and unknown, are o'erwhelmed in endless night, because no sacred bard was there to sing their praises. *Hor.*

Vixi dubius, anxius morior, nescio quo vado— I have lived in doubt, I die in anxiety, and I know not whither I go. *Ascribed to a Pope of Rome.*

Voce d'uno, voce di niuno—Voice of one, voice of none. *It. Pr.*

10 Vogue la galère !—Come what may ! *Fr.*

Voilà le soleil d'Austerlitz—That is the sun of Austerlitz. *Napoleon.*

Voilà une autre chose—That's quite another matter. *Fr.*

Voilà une femme qui a des lunes—There is a woman who is full of whims (*lit.* has moons). *Fr. Pr.*

Volenti non fit injuria—An injury cannot be done to a consenting party, *i.e.*, if he consents or connives, he cannot complain. *L.*

15 Volez de vos propres ailes—Do for yourself (*lit.* fly with your own wings). *Fr. Pr.*

Voll, toll—Full, foolish. *Ger. Pr.*

Voll Weisheit sind des Schicksals Fügungen— Full of wisdom are the ordinations of Fate. *Schiller.*

Vollkommenheit ist die Norm des Himmels ; / Vollkommenes Wollen, die Norm des Menschen—Perfection is the rule of heaven ; to will the perfect, that of man. *Goethe.*

Volo non valeo—I am willing but unable. *M.*

20 Volte face—A change of front. *Fr.*

Voluntas non potest cogi—The will cannot be forced.

Voluptates commendat rarior usus—Pleasures are enhanced that are sparingly enjoyed. *Juv.*

Vom Rechte, das mit uns geboren ist, / Von dem ist, leider ! nie die Frage — Of the right that is born with us, of that unhappily there is never a question. *Goethe, Mephisto in "Faust."*

Vom Sein zum Sein geht alles Leben über— / Zum Nichtsein ist kein Schritt in der Natur —All life passes over from being to being. There is no step in Nature into non-being. *Tiedge.*

Vom sichern Port lässt sichs gemachlich 25 rathen—It is easy to give advice from a port of safety. *Schiller.*

Vom Vater hab' ich die Statur / Des Lebens ernstes Führen ; / Von Mütterchen die Frohnatur, / Und Lust zu fabulieren—From my father inherit I stature and the earnest conduct of life ; from motherkin my cheerful disposition and pleasure in fanciful invention. *Goethe, of himself.*

Von der Gewalt, die alle Wesen bindet, / Befreit der Mensch sich, der sich überwindet—From the power which constrains every creature man frees himself by overcoming himself. *Goethe.*

Von der Menschheit—du kannst von ihr nie gross genug denken ; / Wie du im Busen sie trägst, prägst du in Thaten sie aus—Of humanity thou canst never think greatly enough ; as thou bearest it in thy bosom, thou imprintest it in thy deeds. *Schiller.*

Vor dem Glauben / Gilt keine Stimme der Natur—In matters of faith the voice of nature has no standing (before the Inquisition). *Schiller.*

Vor dem Tode erschrickst du? Du wünchest 30 unsterblich zu leben ! ; Leb' im Ganzen ! Wenn du lange dahin bist, es bleibt—Art thou afraid of death? Thou wishest for immortality? Live in the whole ! When thou art long gone, it remains. *Schiller.*

Vor Leiden kann nur Gott dich wahren, / Unmuth magst du dir selber sparen—From suffering God alone can guard thee ; from ill-humour thou canst guard thyself. *Geibel.*

Vorwärts—Forward. *M. of Blücher.*

Vorwärts musst du / Denn rückwärts kannst du nun nicht mehr—Forwards must thou, for backwards canst thou now no more. *Schiller.*

Vos finesses sont cousues de fil blanc—Your arts are easily seen through (*lit.* sewed with white thread). *Fr. Pr.*

Vota vita mea—My life is devoted. *M.* 35

Vote it as you please ; there is a company of poor men that will spend all their blood before they see it settled so. *Cromwell.*

Votes should be weighed, not counted. *Schiller.*

Vouloir c'est pouvoir—Where there's a will, there's a way (*lit.* to will is to be able). *Fr. Pr.*

Vous bridez le cheval par la queue—You begin at the wrong end (*lit.* bridle the horse by the tail). *Fr. Pr.*

Vous êtes orfèvre, Monsieur Josse !—You are a 40 goldsmith, Monsieur Josse ! *i.e.*, an interested party. *Molière.*

Vous ne jouez donc pas le whist, Monsieur ? Hélas ! quelle triste vieillesse vous vous préparez !—Not play at whist, sir? Alas ! what a dreary old age you are preparing for yourself. *Talleyrand.*

Vous prenez tout ce qu'il dit au pied de la lettre—You take everything he says literally. *Fr. Pr.*

Vous voulez prendre la lune avec les dents— You attempt impossibilities (*lit.* wish to take the moon with your teeth). *Fr. Pr.*

Vows made in storms are forgotten in calms. *Pr.*

Vox audita perit, litera scripta manet—The 45 word that is heard perishes, the letter that is written remains.

Vox clamantis in deserto—The voice of one crying in the wilderness. *Vulgate.*

Vox et præterea nihil—A voice and nothing more.

Vox faucibus hæsit—His voice stuck fast in his throat.

Vox is the God of this universe. *Carlyle.*

5 **Vox populi, vox Dei**—The voice of the people is the voice of God.

Vox tantum atque ossa supersunt. / Vox manet—The voice and bones are all that's left ; the voice remains. *Ovid.*

Voyez comme il brûle le pavé—See how fast he drives (*lit.*, burns the pavement). *Fr. Pr.*

Vulgar opulence fills the street from wall to wall of the houses, and begrudges all but the gutter to everybody whose sleeve is a little worn at the elbows. *John Weiss.*

Vulgarity consists in a deadness of the heart and body, resulting from prolonged, and especially from inherited conditions of " degeneracy," or literally " unracing ; " gentle-manliness being another name for intense humanity. And vulgarity shows itself in dulness of heart, not in rage or cruelty, but in inability to feel or conceive noble character or emotion. Dulness of bodily sense and general stupidity are its material manifestations. *Ruskin.*

10 **Vulgarity in manners defiles fine garments more than mud.** *Plautus.*

Vulgus ex veritate pauca, ex opinione multa, æstimat—The masses judge of few things by the truth, of most things by opinion. *Cic.*

Vultus est index animi—The countenance is the index of the mind. *Pr.*

W.

Wachsamkeit ist die Tugend des Lasters—Vigilance is the virtue of vice. *C. J. Weber.*

Waft yourselves, yearning souls, upon the stars ; / Sow yourselves on the wandering winds of space ; / Watch patient all your days, if your eyes take / Some dim, cold ray of knowledge. The dull world / Hath need of you—the purblind, slothful world ! *Lewis Morris.*

15 **Wage du zu irren und zu träumen : / Hoher Sinn liegt oft im kind'schen Spiel**—Dare to err and to dream ; a deep meaning often lies in the play of a child. *Schiller.*

Wages are no index of well-being to the working man ; without proper wages there can be no well-being ; but with them also there may be none. *Carlyle.*

Wahres und Gutes wird sich versöhnen, / Wenn sich beide vermählen im Schönen—True and good will be reconciled when both are wedded in the beautiful. *Rückert.*

Wahrheit gegen Freund und Feind—Truth in spite of friend and foe alike. *Schiller.*

Wahrheit immer wird, nie ist—Truth always is a-being, never is. *Schiller.*

20 **Wahrheit wird wohl gedrückt, aber nicht erstickt**—Truth may be smothered, but not extinguished. *Ger. Pr.*

Wait upon him whom thou art to speak to with thine eye ; for there be many cunning men that have secret heads and transparent countenances. *Burton.*

Waiting answers sometimes as well as working. *Mrs. Gatty.*

Walk not with the world where it is walking wrong. *Carlyle.*

Walk this world with no friend in it but God and St. Edmund, and you will either fall into the ditch or learn a good many things. *Carlyle.*

Wann ? wie ? und wo ? das ist die leidige 25 Frage—When ? how ? and where ? That is the vexing question. *Goethe.*

Want is the mother of industry. *Pr.*

Want makes wit. *Pr.*

Want maketh even servitude honourable. *Hitopadesa.*

Want o' wit is waur than want o' siller. *Sc. Pr.*

Want of care does us more damage than want 30 of knowledge. *Ben. Franklin.*

Want of courage upon some occasions assumes the appearance of ignorance, and betrays us when we most want to excel. *Goldsmith.*

Want of humility or self-denial is simply the want of all religion, of all moral worth. *Carlyle.*

Want of prudence is too frequently the want of virtue ; nor is there on earth a more powerful advocate for vice than poverty. *Goldsmith.*

Want of tenderness is want of parts, and is no less a proof of stupidity than depravity. *Johnson.*

Want supplieth itself of what is next. *Bacon.* 35

Wanton jests make fools laugh and wise men frown. *Fuller.*

War disorganises, but it is to re-organise. *Emerson.*

War has its sweets, Hymen its alarms. *La Fontaine.*

War has no pity. *Schiller.*

War is a game which, were their subjects 40 wise, kings should not play at. *Cowper.*

War is a terrible trade ; but in the cause that is righteous, / Sweet is the smell of powder. *Longfellow.*

War its thousands slays, peace its ten thousands. *Beilby Porteous.*

War ought to be the only study of a prince. *Machiavelli.*

War suspends the rules of moral obligation, and what is long suspended is in danger of being totally abrogated. *Burke.*

War—the trade of barbarians, and the art of 45 bringing the greatest physical force to bear on a single point. *Napoleon.*

War, with all its evils, is better than a peace in which there is nothing to be seen but usurpation and injustice. *Pitt.*

Wäre der Geist nicht frei, dann wär' es ein grosser Gedanke, / Dass ein Gedanken-monarch über die Seele regiert—Only if the spirit of man were not free, would the thought be a great one that there is a monarch of thought who rules over our souls. *Platen.*

Warm fortunes are always sure of getting good husbands. *Goldsmith.*

Warm your body by healthful exercise, not by cowering over a stove. *Thoreau.*

Warm your spirit by performing independently noble deeds, not by ignobly seeking the sympathy of your fellows, who are no better than yourself. *Thoreau.*

Warn them that are unruly, support the weak, be patient toward all men. *St. Paul.*

Wars should be undertaken in order that we may live in peace without suffering wrong. *Cic.*

5 Was, and is, and will be, are but " is." *Tennyson.*

Was der Löwe nicht kann, das kann der Fuchs —What the lion cannot manage to do, the fox can. *Ger. Pr.*

Was der Socialismus will, ist nicht Eigenthum aufheben, sondern im Gegentheile individuelles Eigenthum, auf die Arbeit gegründetes Eigenthum erst einführen—What Socialism means is not to abolish property, but, on the contrary, to establish individual property, property founded on labour. *Lassalle.*

Was die Fürsten geigen, müssen die Unterthanen tanzen—Subjects must dance as princes fiddle to them. *Ger. Pr.*

Was die heulende Tiefe da unten verhehle, / Das erzählt keine lebende glückliche Seele —What the howling deep down there conceals, no blessed living soul can tell. *Schiller.*

10 Was die innere Stimme spricht / Das täuschet die hoffende Seele nicht—By what the inner voice speaks the trusting soul is never deceived. *Schiller.*

Was die Natur versteckt, zieht Unsinn an das Licht—What Nature hides from our gaze, want of sense and feeling drags to the light. *Lessing.*

Was die Sage erzählt / Mit Geschichte vermählt, / Mit Phantasie im Verein, / Das lass dir willkommen sein—Let what legend relates, wedded to history and in union with fantasy, be welcome to thee. (?)

Was du besitzest, kann ein Raub des Schicksals sein ; / Was du besassest, bleibt für alle Zeiten dein—What you possess is at the mercy of fortune ; what you possessed remains your own for ever. *Lorm.*

Was du denkest, sei wahr ; und wie du denkest, so rede ! / Wolle das Gute, so folgt Segen und Freude der That—Be what thou thinkest true ; and as thou thinkest, so speak. Will what is good ; then will follow blessing and joy from the deed. *C. L. Fernow.*

15 Was du ererbt von deinen Vätern hast, / Erwirb es, um es zu besitzen. / Was man nicht nützt, ist eine schwere Last ; / Nur was der Augenblick erschafft, das kann er nützen —What thou hast inherited from thy sires, acquire so as to possess it as thy own. What we use not is a heavy burden ; only what the moment produces can the moment profit by. *Goethe.*

Was einmal sein muss, wird nie zu früh gethan —What must be can never be too quickly done. *Rückert.*

Was ever woman in this humour woo'd ? / Was ever woman in this humour won ? *Rich. III.,* i. 2.

Was geboren ist auf Erden / Muss zu Erd' und Asche werden—What is born on earth must to earth and ashes return. *J. G. Jacobi.*

Was gelten soll, muss wirken und muss dienen —To be of any worth a thing must be productive and serviceable. *Goethe.*

Was glänzt ist für den Augenblick geboren ; / 20 Das Echte bleibt der Nachwelt unverloren— What dazzles is produced for the moment ; what is genuine remains unlost to posterity. *Goethe.*

Was Gott thut, das ist wohlgethan—What God does is well done. *S. Rodigast.*

Was hab' ich mehr als meine Pflicht gethan ? / Ein guter Mann wird stets das Bessre wählen — What have I done more than my duty ? A good man will always select what is better. *Schiller.*

Was Hände bauten, können Hände stürzen— What hands have built, hands can pull down. *Schiller.*

Was Hänschen nicht lernt, lernt Hans nimmermehr—What little Jack does not learn, big John never will. *Ger. Pr.*

Was hilft es mir, dass ich geniesse ? Wie 25 Träume fliehn die wärmsten Küsse, / Und alle Freude wie ein Kuss—What help is there for me in enjoyment ? As dreams vanish the warmest kisses, and as such is all joy. *Goethe.*

Was hilft laufen, wenn man nicht auf dem rechten Weg ist ?—What boots running if one is on the wrong road ? *Ger. Pr.*

Was hilft's, wenn ihr ein Ganzes dargebracht ? / Das Publikum wird es euch doch zerpflücken —What boots it to present a whole ? The public will be sure to pull it to pieces for you. *Goethe.*

Was ich besitze, mag ich gern bewahren ; der Wechsel unterhält, doch nützt er kaum— What I possess I would like to keep ; change is entertaining, but is scarcely advantageous. *Goethe.*

Was ich besitze, seh' ich wie im weiten, / Und was verschwand, wird mir zu Wirklichkeiten —What I possess I see in the distance ; and what has vanished becomes for me actuality. *Goethe.*

Was ich nicht loben kann, davon sprech' ich 30 nicht—I do not speak of what I cannot praise. *Goethe.*

Was im Leben uns verdriesst / Man im Bilde gern geniesst—What annoys us in life we enjoy in a picture. *Goethe.*

Was in dem Herzen Anderer von uns lebt, / Ist unser wahrestes und tiefstes Selbst— What of us lives in the heart of others is our truest and deepest self. *Herder.*

Was ist deine Pflicht ? Die Forderung des Tages—What is thy duty ? To accept the challenge of the passing day.

Was ist der Tod ? Nach einem Fieber / Ein sanfter Schlaf, der uns erquickt ! / Der Thor erschreckt darüber, / Der Weise ist entzückt—What is death ? A gentle sleep, which refreshes us after a fever. The fool is frightened at it ; the wise man overjoyed. *Winter.*

Was ist ein Held ohne Menschenliebe ?— 35 What is a hero without love for man ? *Lessing.*

Was ist noch schlimmer als das Uebel ? Wenn man es nicht zu ertragen weiss— "What is still worse than evil ?" Inability to bear it. *C. J. Weber.*

Was ist unser höchstes Gesetz ? Unser eigener Vortheil—What is our highest good ? Our own advantage. *Goethe.*

Was lehr' ich dich vor allen Dingen ? / Könntest mich lehren von meiner Schatte zu springen !—What before all shall I teach you ? That you could teach me to jump off my shadow ! *Goethe.*

Was man einmal ist, das muss man ganz sein—What we are at any moment we should be entirely. *Bodenstedt.*

Was man Gott opfern will, muss man nicht vom Teufel einsegnen lassen—We must not let the devil consecrate what we mean for God. *Ger. Pr.*

Was man in der Jugend wünscht, hat man im Alter die Fülle—What one wishes in youth one has to the full when old. *Goethe, by way of motto to the second part of his " Wahrheit und Dichtung."*

Was man nicht versteht, besitzt man nicht— What we don't understand we do not possess. *Goethe.*

5 Was man sein will, sei man ganz—What one will be, let him entirely be. *W. F. Flotow.*

Was man zu heftig fühlt, fühlt man nicht allzulang—Very acute suffering does not last long. *Goethe.*

Was Menschen säen, werden die Götter ernten ; / Gott spricht durch seine Welt, der Mensch durch seine That—What men sow the gods will reap. God speaks through his world, man through his deed. *Tiedge.*

Was mir ein Augenblick genommen, / Das bringt kein Frühling mir zurück—What a moment has taken from me no spring brings back to me. *Hoffmann.*

Was never evening yet / But seemed far beautifuller than its day. *Browning.*

10 Was nicht von innen keimt hervor, / Ist in der Wurzel schwach—What does not germinate forth from within is weak at its root. *Uhland.*

Was nicht zusammen kann bestehen, thut am besten sich zu lösen—What cannot exist together had better separate. *Schiller.*

Was niemals unser war, entbehrt man leicht— We easily dispense with what we never had. *Platen.*

Was nützt, ist nur ein Theil des Bedeutenden —What is useful forms but a part of the important. *Goethe.*

Was soll der fürchten, der den Tod nicht fürchtet ?—What shall he fear who does not fear death ? *Schiller.*

15 Was there ever, since the beginning of the world, a universal vote given in favour of the worthiest man or thing ? *Carlyle.*

Was there, is there, or will there be a great intellect ever heard tell of without being first a true and great heart to begin with ? Never. . . . Think it not, suspect it not. Worse blasphemy I could not readily utter. *Carlyle to John Sterling.*

Was thy life given to thee / For making pretty sentences, and play / Of dainty humour for the mirthful heart / To be more merry, or to serve thy kind, / Redressing wrong ? *Dr. W. Smith.*

Was uns alle bändigt, das Gemeine—What enthrals us all is the common. *Goethe.*

Was vergangen, kehrt nicht wieder ; / Aber ging es leuchtend nieder, / Leuchtet's lange noch zurück !—What has gone by returns not again, but if it went down shining, it reflects its light for long. *Karl Förster.*

20 Was vernünftig ist, das ist wirklich ; und was wirklich ist, das ist vernünftig—What is rational is actual ; and what is actual is rational. *Hegel.*

Was verschmerze nicht der Mensch ?—What can man not put up with ? *Schiller.*

Was wir als Schönheit hier empfunden, / Wird einst als Wahrheit uns entgegengehn — What we have felt here as beauty will one day confront us as truth. *Schiller.*

Waste not time by trampling upon thistles because they have yielded us no figs. Here are books, and we have brains to read them ; here is a whole Earth and a whole Heaven, and we have eyes to look on them. *Carlyle.*

Watch and pray, that ye enter not into temptation. *Bible.*

Watch thy tongue ; out of it are the issues of 25 life. *Carlyle.*

Watched pot never boils. *Pr.*

Watchman, what of the night ? *Bible.*

Water, air, and cleanliness are the chief articles in my pharmacopœia. *Napoleon.*

Water cannot rise above the level from which it springs ; no more can moral theories. *J. C. Sharp.*

Water, water everywhere, / And all the boards 30 did shrink, / Water, water everywhere, / Nor any drop to drink. *Coleridge.*

Waters that are deep do not babble as they flow. *Pr.*

We acquire the strength we have overcome. Without war, no soldier ; without enemies, no hero. The sun were insipid if the universe were not opaque. *Emerson.*

We all bear the misfortunes of other people with a heroic constancy. *La Roche.*

We all complain of the shortness of time, and yet have much more than we know what to do with. Our lives are spent either in doing nothing at all, or in doing nothing to the purpose, or in doing nothing that we ought to do ; we are always complaining our days are few, and acting as though there would be no end of them. *Sen.*

We all know a hundred whose coats are well 35 made, and a score who have excellent manners ; but of gentlemen how many ? Let us take a little scrap of paper and each make out his list. *Thackeray.*

We all know that the secret of breakdown and wreck is seldom so much an insufficient knowledge of the route, as imperfect discipline of the will. *John Morley.*

We all live upon the hope of pleasing somebody ; and the pleasure of pleasing ought to be greatest, and at last always will be greatest, when our endeavours are exerted in consequence of our duty. *Johnson.*

We always believe that God is like ourselves : the indulgent affirm him indulgent ; the stern, terrible. *Joubert.*

We always live prospectively, never retrospectively, and there is no abiding moment. *Jacobi.*

We always take credit for the good, and attri- 40 bute the bad to fortune. *La Fontaine.*

We are able easily to dispense with greater perfection. *Vauvenargues.*

We are all a kind of chameleons, taking our hue, the hue of our moral character, from those who are about us. *Locke.*

We are all, at times, unconscious prophets. *Spurgeon.*

We are all best affected to them who are of the same opinion as ourselves. *Thomas à Kempis.*

We are all born for love. It is the principle of existence, and its only end. *I. Disraeli.*

We are all collective beings, let us place ourselves as we may; for how little have we, and are we, that we can strictly call our own property? *Goethe.*

We are all frail; but esteem none more frail than thyself. *Thomas à Kempis.*

5 We are all richer for the measurement of a degree of latitude on the earth's surface. *Emerson.*

We are all visionaries, and what we see is our soul in things. *Amiel.*

We are always complaining our days are few, and acting as though there would be no end of them. *Addison.*

We are always looking into the future, but we see only the past. *Mme. Swetchine.*

We are ancients of the earth / And in the morning of the times. *Tennyson.*

10 We are apt to mistake our vocation by looking out of the way for occasions to exercise great and rare virtues, and by stepping over the ordinary ones that lie directly in the road before us. *Hannah More.*

We are apt to pick quarrels with the world for every little foolery. *L'Estrange.*

We are as liable to be corrupted by books as by companions. *Fielding.*

We are as much informed of a writer's genius by what he selects as by what he originates. *Emerson.*

We are as turkeys driven, with a stick and red clout, to market. *Sterne.*

15 We are awkward for want of thought. The inspiration is scanty, and does not arrive at the extremities. *Emerson.*

We are born with faculties and powers capable almost of anything, such, at least, as might carry us further than can easily be imagined; but it is only the exercise of those powers that gives us ability and skill in anything, and leads us towards perfection. *Locke.*

We are bound to be honest, but not to be rich. *Pr.*

We are but of yesterday, and know nothing, because our days upon earth are a shadow. *Bible.*

We are children for the second time at twenty-one, and again when we are grey and put all our burden on the Lord. *J. M. Barrie.*

20 We are come too late, by several thousand years, to say anything new in morality. The finest and most beautiful thoughts concerning manners have been carried away before our times, and nothing is left for us but to glean after the ancients and the more ingenious of the moderns. *La Bruyère.*

We are content with personating happiness—to feel it is an art beyond us. *Mackenzie.*

We are contented because we are happy, and not happy because we are contented. *Landor.*

We are created to seek truth; to possess it is the prerogative of a higher power. *Montaigne.*

"We are creatures that look before and after." the more surprising that we do not look round a little, and see what is passing under our eyes. *Carlyle.*

We are great philosophers to each other, but 25 not to ourselves. *Bulwer Lytton.*

We are here for the express purpose of stamping on things perishable an imperishable worth. *Goethe.*

We are in a series of which we do not know the extremes, and believe that it has none. *Emerson.*

We are in great danger; / The greater therefore should our courage be. *Hen. V.,* iv. 1.

We are inclined to believe those whom we do not know, because they have never deceived us. *Johnson.*

We are incompetent to solve the times. . . . 30 We can only obey our own polarity. *Emerson.*

We are instinctively more inclined to hope than to fear; just as our eyes turn of themselves towards light rather than darkness. *Schopenhauer.*

We are less convinced by what we hear than by what we see. *Herodotus.*

We are members of one great body. Nature planted in us a mutual love, and fitted us for a social life. We must consider that we were born for the good of the whole. *Sen.*

"We are men, my liege."—/ Ay, in the catalogue ye go for men. *Macb.,* iii. 1.

We are near awakening when we dream that 35 we dream. *Novalis.*

We are ne'er like angels till our passion dies. *Denham.*

We are never farther from what we wish than when we fancy that we have what we wished for. *Goethe.*

We are never made so ridiculous by the qualities we have as by those we affect to have. *La Roche.*

We are never more discontented with others than when we are discontented with ourselves. *Amiel.*

We are never more like God than when we 40 are doing good. *Calvin.*

We are never present with, but always beyond ourselves. Fear, desire, and hope are still pushing us on towards the future. *Montaigne.*

We are never properly ourselves till another thinks entirely as we do. *Goethe.*

We are never so happy or so unhappy as we imagine. *La Roche.*

We are not called upon to judge ourselves. / With circumspection to pursue his path, / Is the immediate duty of a man. *Goethe.*

We are not ignorant of his devices. *St. Paul* 45 *of the Evil One.*

We are not indebted to the reason of man for any of the great achievements which are the landmarks of human action and human progress. *Disraeli.*

We are not, indeed, satisfied with our own opinions, whatever we may pretend, till they are ratified and confirmed by suffrage of the rest of mankind. We dispute and wrangle for ever; we endeavour to get men to come to us when we do not go to them. *Sir Joshua Reynolds.*

We are not sent into this world to do anything into which we cannot put our hearts. We have certain work to do for our bread, and that is to be done strenuously ; other work to do for our delight, and that is to be done heartily ; neither is to be done by halves or shifts, but with a will ; and what is not worth this effort is not to be done at all. *Ruskin.*

We are not strong by our power to penetrate, but by our relatedness. *Emerson.*

We are not to be astonished that the wise walk more slowly in their road to virtue than fools in their passage to vice ; since passion drags us alone, while wisdom only points out the way. *Confucius.*

We are not to lead events, but to follow them. *Epictetus.*

5 We are not to quarrel with the water for inundations and shipwrecks. *L Estrange.*

We are not troubled by the evanescence of time, if the eternal is every moment present. *Goethe.*

We are often governed by people not only weaker than ourselves, but even by those whom we think so. *Lord Greville.*

We are often prophets to others only because we are our own historians. *Mme. Swetchine.*

We are only so far worthy of esteem as we know how to appreciate. *Goethe.*

10 We are only vulnerable and ridiculous through our pretensions. *Mme. de Girardin.*

We are ourselves / Our heaven and hell, the joy, the penalty, / The yearning, the fruition. *Lewis Morris.*

We are pent, / Who sing to-day, by all the garnered wealth / Of ages of past song. *Lewis Morris.*

We are reformers in spring and summer ; in autumn and winter we stand by the old ; reformers in the morning, conservers at night. *Emerson.*

We are rid of the Wicked One, but the wicked are still with us. *Goethe.*

15 We are ruined not by what we really want, but by what we think we do. *Colton.*

We are seldom sure that we sincerely meant what we omitted to do. *Johnson.*

We are slaves, / The greatest as the meanest —nothing rests / Upon our will . . . And when we think we lead, we are most led. *Byron.*

We are such stuff / As dreams are made on ; and our little life / Is rounded with a sleep. *Tempest, iii. 3.*

We are sure to be losers when we quarrel with ourselves ; it is a civil war, and in all such contentions, triumphs are defeats. *Colton.*

20 We are sure to judge wrong if we do not feel aright. *Hazlitt.*

We are taxed twice as much by our idleness, three times as much by our pride, and four times as much by our folly ; and from these taxes the Commissioners cannot ease or deliver us by allowing an abatement. *Ben. Franklin.*

We are the children of our own deeds. *Victor Hugo.*

We are the miracle of miracles — the great inscrutable mystery of God. We cannot understand it, we know not how to speak of it ; but we may feel and know, if we like, that it is verily so. *Carlyle.*

We are the slaves of objects round us, and appear little or important according as these contract or give us room to expand. *Goethe.*

We are to earn the joys of a higher existence, 25 not by scorning, but by using, all the gifts of God in this. *W. R. Greg.*

We are too good for pure instinct. *Goethe.*

We are very fond of some families because they can be traced beyond the Conquest, whereas indeed the farther back the race is, as being the nearer allied to a race of robbers and thieves. *De Foe.*

We are wiser than we know. *Emerson.*

We ask advice, but we mean approbation. *Colton.*

We barter life for pottage. *Keble.*   30

We boast our light ; but if we look not wisely on the sun itself, it smites us into darkness. *Milton.*

We build statues of snow, and weep to see them melt. *Scott.*

We by Fancy may assuage / The festering sore by Fancy made. *Keble.*

We can conceive or desire nothing more exquisite or perfect than what is round us every hour. *W. R. Greg.*

We can do more good by being good than in 35 any other way. *Rowland Hill.*

We can do nothing against the truth, but for the truth. *St. Paul.*

We can finish nothing in this life, but we can make a beginning, and bequeath a noble example. *Smiles.*

We can hardly be confident of the state of our own minds, but as it stands attested by some external action. *Johnson.*

We can have no dependence upon morality without religion ; so, on the other hand, there is nothing better to be expected from religion without morality. *Sterne.*

We can live without our friends, but not with- 40 out our neighbours. *Pr.*

We can more easily avenge an injury than requite a kindness ; on this account, because there is less difficulty in getting the better of the wicked than in making one's self equal with the good. *Cic.*

We can never soon enough convince ourselves how easily we can be dispensed with in the world. *Goethe.*

We can offer up much in the large, but to make sacrifices in little things is what we are seldom equal to. *Goethe.*

We can only know a little, and the question is merely whether or not we know this well. *Goethe.*

We can only possess wealth according to our 45 capacity. *Ruskin.*

We can receive anything from love, for that is a way of receiving it from ourselves ; but not from any one who assumes to bestow. *Emerson.*

We can sometimes love what we do not understand, but it is impossible completely to understand what we do not love. *Mrs. Jameson.*

We can take up no scheme, however wild and impracticable, but it will strike off some flower or fruit from the tree of knowledge. *Ward Beecher.*

We cannot abolish fate, but we can in a measure utilise it. The projectile force of the bullet does not annul or suspend gravity ; it uses it. *John Burroughs.*

We cannot all be masters, nor all masters / Cannot be truly follow'd. *King Lear*, v. 3.

We cannot all serve our country in the same way, but each may do his best, according as God has endowed him. *Goethe.*

We cannot approach beauty. Its nature is like opaline dove's-neck lustres, hovering and evanescent. Herein it resembles the most excellent things, which have all this rainbow character, defying all attempts at appropriation and use. *Emerson.*

5 We cannot be just if we are not humane. *Vauvenargues.*

We cannot be kind to each other here for an hour ; / We whisper, and hint, and chuckle, and grin at a brother's shame ; / However we brave it out, we men are a little breed. *Tennyson.*

We cannot but speak the things we have seen and heard. *St. Peter and St. John.*

We cannot conquer fate and necessity, yet we can yield to them in such a manner as to be greater than if we could. *Landor.*

We cannot fashion our children after our fancy. We must have them and love them as God has given them to us. *Goethe.*

10 We cannot fight for love, as men may do ; / We should be wooed, and were not made to woo. *Mid. N.'s Dream*, ii. 2.

We cannot make our exodus from Houndsditch (*i.e.*, the now dead religion of the past) till we have got our own (*i.e.*, out of it) along with us. *Carlyle.*

We cannot overstate our debt to the past, but the moment has the supreme claim. *Emerson.*

We cannot part with our friends. We cannot let our angels go. We do not see that they only go out that archangels may come in. We are idolators of the old. We do not believe in the richness of the soul, in its proper eternity and omnipresence. *Emerson.*

We cannot pass our guardian angel's bound, / Resign'd or sullen, he will hear our sighs. *Keble.*

15 We cannot speak a loyal word and be meanly silent ; we cannot kill and not kill at the same moment ; but a moment is room enough for the loyal and mean desire, for the outflash of a murderous thought, and the sharp backward stroke of repentance. *George Eliot.*

We cannot think too highly of our nature, nor too humbly of ourselves. *Colton.*

We conceive, I think, more nobly of the weak presence of Paul than of the fair and ruddy countenance of David. *Ruskin.*

We consecrate a great deal of nonsense, because it was allowed by great men. *Emerson.*

We could not endure solitude, were it not for the powerful companionship of hope, or of some unseen one. *Jean Paul.*

20 We crave a world unreal as the shell-heard sea. *E. L. Hamilton.*

We cultivate literature on a little oatmeal. *Sydney Smith.*

We darken the cages of birds when we would teach them to sing. *Jean Paul.*

We deceive and flatter no one by such delicate artifices as we do ourselves. *Schopenhauer.*

We deem those happy who, from their experience of life, have learned to bear its ills without descanting on the burden. *Juv.*

We derive from nature no fault that may not 25 become a virtue, no virtue that may not degenerate into a fault. Faults of the latter kind are most difficult to cure. *Goethe.*

We do everything by custom, even believe by it ; our very axioms, let us boast of our Freethinking as we may, are oftenest simply such beliefs as we have never heard questioned. *Carlyle.*

We do not believe immortality because we have proved it, but we for ever try to prove it because we believe it. *James Martineau.*

We do not commonly find men of superior sense amongst those of the highest fortune. *Juv.*

We do not correct the man we hang ; we correct others by him. *Montaigne.*

We do not count a man's years until he has 30 nothing else to count. *Emerson.*

We do not determine what we will think. . . . We have little control over our thoughts. *Emerson.*

We do not die wholly at our deaths ; we have mouldered away gradually long before. *Hazlitt.*

We do not judge men by what they are in themselves, but by what they are relatively to us. *Mme. Swetchine.*

We do not know what is really good or bad fortune. *Rousseau.*

We do not teach one another the lessons of 35 honesty and sincerity that the brutes do, or of steadiness and solitude that the rocks do. The fault is commonly mutual, for we do not habitually demand any more of each other. *Thoreau.*

We don't always care most for those flat-pattern flowers that press best in the herbarium. *Holmes.*

We draw the foam from the great river of humanity with our quills, and imagine to ourselves that we have caught floating islands at least. *Goethe.*

We eagerly lay hold of a law that serves as a weapon to our passion. *Goethe.*

We easily dispense with what was never our own. *Platen.*

We enjoy ourselves only in our work, our 40 doing ; and our best doing is our best enjoyment. *Jacobi.*

We estimate (*lit.* measure) great men by their virtue, not by their success. *Corn. Nep.*

We exaggerate misfortune and happiness alike. We are never either so wretched or so happy as we say we are. *Balzac.*

We expect a bright to-morrow ; / All will be well. / Faith can sing through days of sorrow, / All, all is well. *Peters.*

We expect everything, and are prepared for nothing. *Mme. Swetchine.*

We expect in letters to discover somewhat 45 of a person's real character. It is childish indeed to expect that we are to find the whole heart of the author unveiled. . . . Still as letters from one friend to another make the nearest approaches to conversation, we may expect to see more of a character displayed in these than in other productions which are studied for public view. *Blair*

We expect old men to be conservative, but when a nation's young men are so, its funeral-bell is already rung. *Ward Beecher.*

We fail? / But screw your courage to the sticking-place, / And we'll not fail. *Macb., i. 7.*

We fancy we suffer from ingratitude, while in reality we suffer from self-love. *Landor.*

(We) feel that life is large, and the world small, / So wait till life have passed from out the world. *Browning.*

5 We find God twice—once within, once without us; within us as an eye, without us as a light. *Jean Paul.*

We forfeit three-fourths of ourselves in order to be like other people. *Schopenhauer.*

We furnish our minds as we furnish our houses—with the fancies of others, and according to the mode and age of our country; we pick up our ideas and notions in common conversation as in schools. *Bolingbroke.*

We gain nothing by being with such as ourselves. We encourage one another in mediocrity. I am always longing to be with men more excellent than myself. *Lamb.*

We gain the strength of the temptation we resist. *Emerson.*

10 We gape, we grasp, we gripe, add store to store; / Enough requires too much; too much craves more. *Quarles.*

We gild our medicines with sweets; why not clothe truth and morals in pleasant garments as well? *Chamfort.*

We give advice, but we cannot give the wisdom to profit by it. *La Roche.*

We give advice by the bucket, but take it by the grain. *W. R. Alger.*

We go by the major vote, and if the majority are insane, the sane must go to the hospital. As Satan said, "Evil, be thou my good," so they say, "Darkness, be thou my light." *Horace Mann.*

15 We hang little thieves, and take off our hats to great ones. *Ger. Pr.*

We happiness pursue; we fly from pain; / Yet the pursuit, and yet the flight is vain. *Prior.*

We hate delay, yet it makes us wise. *Pr.*

We hate some persons because we do not know them, and we will not know them because we hate them. *Colton.*

We have a great deal more kindness than is ever spoken. Maugre all the selfishness that chills like east winds the world, the whole human family is bathed with an element of love like a fine ether. *Emerson.*

20 We have all a cure of souls, and every man is a priest. *Amiel.*

We have all a speck of the motley. *Lamb.*

We have all of us one human heart. *Wordsworth.*

We have all of us our ferries (to cross over) in this world, and must know the river and its ways, or get drowned some day. *Carlyle.*

We have all strength enough to endure the troubles of others. *La Roche.*

25 We have always considered taxes to be the sinews of the state. *Cic.*

We have, and this is an interesting fact, a plant which may serve as a symbol of the most advanced age, since, having passed the period of flowers and fruit, it still thrives cheerfully without further foundation. *Goethe.*

We have but to toil awhile, endure awhile, believe always, and never turn back. *Simms.*

We have done deeds of charity, / Made peace of enmity, fair love of hate. *Rich. III., ii. 1.*

We have just enough religion to make us hate, but not enough to make us love, one another. *Swift.*

We have less charity for those who believe the 30 half of our creed than for those who deny the whole of it. *Colton.*

We have little control over our thoughts. We are the prisoners of our ideas. *Emerson.*

We have met the enemy, and they are ours. *Oliver H. Perry.*

We have more indolence in the mind than in the body. *La Roche.*

We have more mathematics than ever, but less mathesis. Archimedes and Plato could not have read the "Méchanique Céleste;" but neither would the whole French Institute see aught in that saying, "God geometrises," but sentimental rhodomontade. *Carlyle.*

We have no more / The world to choose from, 35 who, where'er we turn, / Tread through old thoughts and fair. Yet must we sing— / We have no choice. *Lewis Morris.*

We have not only multiplied diseases, but we have made them more fatal. *Rush.*

We have not read an author till we have seen his object, whatever it may be, as he saw it. *Carlyle.*

We have not the innocence of Eden; but by God's help and Christ's example, we may have the victory of Gethsemane. *Chapin.*

We have not the love of greatness, but the love of the love of greatness. *Carlyle.*

We have not wings, we cannot soar; / But 40 we have feet to scale and climb / By slow degrees, by more and more, / The cloudy summits of our time. *Longfellow.*

We have nothing to do with what is happening in space (or possibly may happen in time); we have only to attend to what is happening here—and now. *Ruskin.*

We have raised Pain and Sorrow into heaven, and in our temples, on our altars. Grief stands symbol of our faith, and it shall last as long as man is mortal and unhappy. *Wm. Smith.*

We have scotch'd the snake, but not killed it. *Macb., iii. 2.*

We have such exorbitant eyes, that, on seeing the smallest arc, we complete the curve, and when the curtain is lifted from the diagram which it served to veil, we are vexed to find that no more was drawn than just that fragment of an arc which we first beheld. *Emerson.*

We hear constantly of what Nature is doing, 45 but we rarely hear of what man is thinking. We want ideas, and we get more facts. *Buckle.*

We hear the rain fall, but not the snow. Bitter grief is loud, calm grief is silent. *Auerbach.*

We, ignorant of ourselves, / Beg often our own harms, which the wise powers / Deny us for our good ; so find we profit / By losing of our prayers. *Ant. and Cleo.*, ii. 1.

We in turn / Shall one day be Time's ancients, and inspire / The wiser, higher race, which yet shall sing ; / Because to sing is human, and high thought / Grows rhythmic ere its close. *Lewis Morris.*

We inherit, not life only, but all the garniture and form of life ; and work, and speak, and even think and feel, as our fathers, and primeval grandfathers, from the beginning, have given it us. *Carlyle.*

We injure mysteries, which are matters of faith, by any attempt at explanation in order to make them matters of reason. Could they be explained, they would cease to be mysteries ; and it has been well said that a thing is not necessarily against reason because it happens to be above it. *Colton.*

5 We keep but what we give, / And only daily dying may we live. *Lewis Morris.* •

We know accurately only when we know little ; with knowledge doubt increases. *Goethe.*

We know better than we do. *Emerson.*

We know God easily, provided we do not constrain ourselves to define him. *Joubert.*

We know not oftentimes what we are able to do, but temptations shows us what we are. *Thomas à Kempis.*

10 We know truth when we see it, let sceptic and scoffer say what they choose. *Emerson.*

We know what we are, but we know not what we may be. *Ham.*, iv. 5.

We learn nothing from mere hearing, and he who does not take an active part in certain subjects knows them but half and superficially. *Goethe.*

We learn to know a thing best in the place where it is native. *Goethe.*

We learn to know nothing but what we love ; and the deeper we mean to penetrate into any matter with insight, the stronger and more vital must our love and passion be. *Goethe.*

15 We learn wisdom from failure much more than from success ; we often discover what will do by finding out what will not do ; and probably he who never made a mistake never made a discovery. Horne Tooke used to say of his studies in intellectual philosophy, that he had become all the better acquainted with the country through having had the good luck sometimes to lose his way. *Smiles.*

We lie down and rise up with the skeleton allotted to us for our mortal companion—the phantom of ourselves. *Dickens.*

We like only such actions as have long already had the praise of men, and do not perceive that anything any man can do may be divinely done. *Emerson.*

We like slipping, but not falling ; our real desire is to be tempted enough. *Hare.*

We like to see through others, but not that others should see through us. *La Roche.*

20 We live by admiration, hope, and love ; / And even as these are well and wisely fix'd, / In dignity of being we ascend. *Wordsworth.*

We live by our imaginations, by our admirations, by our sentiments. *Emerson.*

We live in a real, and a solid, and a truthful world. In such a world only truth, in the long run, can hope to prosper. *Prof. Blackie.*

We live in a world which is full of misery and ignorance, and the plain duty of each and all of us is to try to make the little corner he can influence somewhat less miserable and somewhat less ignorant than it was before he entered it. To do this effectually, it is necessary to be fully possessed of only two beliefs : the first, that the order of nature is ascertainable by our faculties to an extent which is practically unlimited ; the second, that our volition counts for something as a condition of the course of events. *Huxley.*

We live in deeds, not years ; in thoughts, not breaths ; / In feelings, not in figures on a dial. *Bailey.* (?)

We live in the age of systems. *Rückert.*   25

We loathe what none are left to share ; / Even bless 'twere woe alone to bear. *Byron.*

We long in vain to undo what has been done. *Schopenhauer.*

We long to use what lies beyond our scope, / Yet cannot use even what within it lies. *Goethe.*

We look before and after. / And pine for what is not ; / E'en our sincerest laughter / With some pain is fraught ; / Our sweetest songs are those which tell of saddest thought. *Shelley.*

We love a girl for very different things than 30 understanding. We love her for her beauty, her youth, her mirth, her confidingness, her character, with its faults, caprices, and God knows what other inexpressible charms ; but we do not love her for her understanding. Her mind we esteem (if it is brilliant), and it may greatly elevate her in our opinion ; nay, more, it may enchain us when we already love. But her understanding is not that which awakens and inflames our passions. *Goethe.*

We love in others what we lack ourselves, / And would be everything but what we are. *R. H. Stoddart.*

We love justice greatly, and just men but little. *Joseph Roux.*

We love peace, as we abhor pusillanimity ; but not peace at any price. There is a peace more destructive of the manhood of living man than war is destructive of his material body. Chains are worse than bayonets. *Douglas Jerrold.*

We love those who admire us, but not those whom we admire. *La Roche.*

We love to see wisdom in unpretending forms, 35 to recognise her royal features under a week-day vesture. *Carlyle.*

We make trifles of terrors, ensconcing ourselves into seeming knowledge, when we should submit ourselves to an unknown fear. *All's Well*, ii. 3.

We make way for the man who boldly pushes past us. *Bovee.*

We manufacture everything there (in our manufacturing cities) except men ; we blanch cotton, and strengthen steel, and refine sugar, and shape pottery ; but to brighten, to strengthen, to refine, or to form a single living spirit, never enters into our estimate of advantages. *Ruskin.*

We may acquire liberty, but it is never recovered if it is once lost. *Rousseau.*

We may all agree in lamenting that there are so many houses where you will not find a good atlas, a good dictionary, or a good cyclopædia of reference. What is still more lamentable, in a good many more houses where these books are, is that they are never referred to or opened. *John Morley.*

We may almost say that a new life begins when a man once sees with his own eyes all that before he has but partially read or heard of. *Goethe.*

We may be as good as we please, if we please to be good. *Barrow.*

5 We may be pretty certain that persons whom all the world treats ill deserve entirely the treatment they get. *Thackeray.*

We may build more splendid habitations, / Fill our rooms with paintings and with sculptures, / But we cannot / Buy with gold the old associations! *Longfellow.*

We may daily discover crowds acquire sufficient wealth to buy gentility, but very few that possess the virtues which ennoble human nature, and (in the best sense of the word) constitute a gentleman. *Shenstone.*

We may despise the world, but we cannot do without it. *Baron Wessenberg.*

We may fall in with a thousand learned men before we fall in with one wise. *Klinger.*

10 We may give more offence by our silence than even by impertinence. *Hazlitt.*

We may grasp virtue so hard as to convert it into a vice. *Montaigne.*

We may have a law, or we may have no law, but we cannot have half a law. *Johnson.*

We may have once been slugs, and may one day be angels, but we are men now; and we must, as men, do our work honourably and thoroughly. *Ruskin.*

We may lay in a stock of pleasures, as we would lay in a stock of wine; but if we defer the tasting of them too long, we shall find that both are soured by age. *Colton.*

15 We may, like the ships, by tempests be toss'd / On perilous deeps, but cannot be lost. *Newton.*

We may not be able to parry evil thoughts, but we may surely guard against their taking root in us and bringing forth evil deeds. *Luther.*

We may outrun / By violent swiftness that which we run at, / And lose by overrunning. *Hen. VIII.*, i. 1.

We may say of angling as Dr. Boteler said of strawberries, "Doubtless God could have made a better berry, but doubtless God never did;" and so, if I might be judge, God never did make a more calm, quiet, innocent recreation than angling. *Izaak Walton.*

We may seek God by our intellect (*Verstand*), but we can find him only with the heart. *Cötvös.*

20 We may take Fancy for a companion, but must follow Reason as our guide. *Johnson.*

We mount to heaven mostly on the ruins of our cherished schemes, finding our failures were successes. *A. B. Alcott.*

We move too much in platoons; we march by sections; we do not live in our vital individuality enough; we are slaves to fashion, in mind and in heart, if not to our passions and appetites. *Chapin.*

We must accept ourselves as we are. *Scherer.*

We must accept the post to which Heaven appoints us, and do the duty to which Heaven calls us, and think it no shame, but an honour, to hold any office, however lowly, under heaven's King. *Ed.*

We must all receive and learn both from those 25 who were before us and from those who are with us. Even the greatest genius would not go far if he tried to owe everything to his own internal self. *Goethe.*

We must all toil—or steal; no faithful workman finds his life a pastime. *Carlyle.*

We must avoid fastidiousness; neatness, when it is moderate, is a virtue; but when it is carried to an extreme, it narrows the mind. *Fénelon.*

We must be as courteous to a man as we are to a picture, which we are willing to give the advantage of a good light. *Emerson.*

We must be free or die who speak the tongue / That Shakespeare spake, the faith and morals hold / Which Milton held. *Wordsworth.*

We must be our own before we can be 30 another's. *Emerson.*

We must bear what Heaven sends us; no noble heart will bear injustice. *Schiller.*

We must carry the beautiful with us, or we find it not. *Emerson.*

We must first cross a valley before we regain a favourable and cheerful height; meanwhile, let us see how we can stroll through it with our friends pleasantly and profitably. *Goethe.*

We must first pray, and then labour; first implore the blessing of God, and use those means which he puts into our hands. *Johnson.*

We must have the real thing before we can 35 have a science of the thing. *Froude.*

We must hold by what is definite, and not split up our strength in many directions. *Hegel.*

We must, if we would husband life and not waste it, bravely resolve to dispense with the dispensable, to content ourselves with the minimum of want, to stake our reputation, if such be dear to us, upon intrinsic worth, and show once again, if we can, by our mere life and labour, what are the "roots of honour" and the "veins of wealth." *Ed.*

We must judge of a form of government by its general tendency, not by happy accidents. *Macaulay.*

We must labour unceasingly to render our piety reasonable, and our reason pious. *Mme. Swetchine.*

We must needs die, and are as water spilt on 40 the ground which cannot be gathered up again. *Bible.*

We must not arrogate to ourselves a spirit of forgiveness, until we have been touched to the quick where we are sensitive and borne it meekly. *Ward Beecher.*

We must not contradict, but instruct, him that contradicts us. *Antisthenes.*

We must not judge of despots by the temporary successes which the possession of power enabled them to achieve, but by the state in which they leave their country at their death or at their fall. *Mme. de Staël.*

We must not make a scarecrow of the law. *Meas. for Meas.*, ii. 1.

We must not only strike the iron while it is hot, but strike it till it is made hot. *Sharp.*

We must not regard what the many say of us; but what he, the one man who has understanding of just and unjust, will say, and what the truth will say. *Plato.*

We must not stand upon trifles. *Cervantes.*

5 We must not stint / Our necessary actions, in the fear / To cope malicious censurers; which ever, / As ravenous fishes, do a vessel follow / That is new trimmed, but benefit no further / Than vainly longing. *Hen. VIII.*, i. 2.

We must not suppose ourselves always to have conquered a temptation when we have fled from it. *Thomas à Kempis.*

We must not take the faults of our youth with us into our old age, for old age brings with it its own defects. *Goethe.*

We must put up with our contemporaries, since we can neither live with our ancestors nor posterity. *George Eliot.*

We must sometimes cease to adhere to our own opinion for the sake of peace. *Thomas à Kempis.*

10 We must strive to make of humanity one single family. *Mazzini.*

We must take the current when it serves, / Or lose our ventures. *Jul. Cæs.*, iv. 3.

We must take the world as we find it. *Pr.*

We need change of objects. *Emerson.*

We (in England) need examples of people who, leaving Heaven to decide whether they are to rise in the world, decide for themselves that they will be happy in it, and have resolved to seek—not greater wealth, but simpler pleasure; not higher fortune, but deeper felicity; making the first of possessions self-possession, and honouring themselves in the harmless pride and calm pursuits of peace. *Ruskin.*

15 We need greater virtues to sustain good than evil fortune. *La Roche.*

We need not die while we are living. *Ward Beecher.*

We needs must love the highest when we see it, / Not Lancelot, nor another. *Tennyson.*

We never can know the truth of sin; for its nature is to deceive alike on the one side the sinner and on the other the judge. *Ruskin.*

We never can say why we love, but only that we love. The heart is ready enough at feigning excuses for all that it does or imagines of wrong; but ask it to give a reason for any of its beautiful and divine motions, and it can only look upward and be dumb. *Lowell.*

20 We never desire ardently what we desire rationally. *La Roche.*

We never learn what people are by their coming to us; we must go to them if we wish to know what they are made of, and see how they conduct or misconduct their surroundings. *Goethe.*

We never live, but we hope to live; and as we are always arranging for being happy, it cannot be but that we never are so. *Pascal.*

We never love truly but once. It is the first time. Succeeding passions are less involuntary. *Du Cœur.*

We never reflect on the man we love without exulting in our choice; while he who has bound us to him by benefits alone rises to our idea as a person to whom we have, in some measure, forfeited our freedom. *Goldsmith.*

We never see anything isolated in Nature, 25 but everything in connection with something else which is before it, beside it, under it, and over it. *Goethe.*

We never sufficiently consider that a language is properly only symbolical, only figurative, and expresses objects never immediately, but only in reflection; yet how difficult it is not to put the sign in place of the thing, always to keep the thing as it is (*das Wesen*) before one's mind, and not annihilated by the expression (*das Wort*). *Goethe.*

We often quarrel with the unfortunate to get rid of pitying them. *Vauvenargues.*

We ought certainly to despise malice if we cannot oppose it. *Goldsmith.*

We ought not, in general, to take the opinions of others upon trust, but to reason and judge for ourselves. *Locke.*

We ought not to isolate ourselves, for we 30 cannot remain in a state of isolation. Social intercourse makes us the more able to bear with ourselves and with others. *Goethe.*

We ought not to judge men by their absolute excellence, but by the distance which they have travelled from the point at which they started. *Ward Beecher.*

We ought not to quit our post without the permission of Him who commands; the post of man is life. *Pythagoras.*

We ought not to seek too high joys. We may be bright without transfiguration. *Ward Beecher.*

We ought not to teach children the sciences, but to give them a taste for them. *Rousseau.*

We ought to attempt no more than what is in 35 the compass of our genius and according to our vein. *Dryden.*

We ought to be ashamed of our pride, but never proud of our shame. (?)

We ought to obey God rather than man. *St. Peter.*

We ought to regard our servants as friends in a lower state. *Plato.*

We our betters see bearing our woes, / We scarcely think our miseries our foes. *King Lear*, iii. 6.

We owe it to our ancestors to preserve entire 40 those rights which they have delivered to our care; we owe it to our posterity not to suffer their dearest inheritance to be destroyed. *Junius.*

We owe to man higher succours than food and fire. We owe to man, man. *Emerson.*

We own whom we love. The universe is God's because He loves. *Ward Beecher.*

We pain ourselves to please nobody. *Emerson.*

We pardon as long as we love. *La Roche.*

We part with true joy almost more lightly 45 than with a beautiful dream. *Fr. Grillparzer.*

We pass our life in deliberation, and we die upon it. *Pasquier Quesnel.*

We pity in others only those evils which we have ourselves experienced. *Rousseau.*

We play the fools with the time, and the spirits of the wise sit in the clouds and mock us. *Hen. IV., ii. 2.*

We poets in our youth begin in gladness, / But thereof come in the end despondency and madness. *Wordsworth.*

We promise according to our hopes, and perform according to our fears. *La Roche.*

We properly learn from those books only which are above our criticism, which we cannot judge. *Goethe.*

5 We read far too many things, thus losing time and gaining nothing. We should only read what we admire. *Goethe.*

We readily believe what we wish to be true. *Pr.*

We reap what we sow, but Nature has love over and above that justice, and gives us shadow and blossom and fruit that spring from no planting of ours. *George Eliot.*

We receive but little advantage from repeated protestations of gratitude, but they cost them very much from whom we exact them in return. *Goldsmith.*

We reform others unconsciously when we walk uprightly. *Mme. Swetchine.*

10 We retain from our studies only that which we practically apply. *Goethe.*

We sacrifice to dress till household joys and comforts cease. Dress drains our cellar dry and keeps our larder lean. *Cowper.*

We see but the outside of the rich man's happiness; few consider him to be like the silkworm, that, when she seems to play, is at the very same time spinning her own bowels and consuming herself. *Isaac Walton.*

We see farthest into the future—and that is not far—when we most carefully consider the facts of the present. *Dr. Jowett.*

We see so darkly into futurity, we never know when we have real cause to rejoice or lament. The worst appearances have often happy consequences, as the best lead many times into the greatest misfortunes. *Lady Montagu.*

15 We see the blossoms wither and the leaves fall, but we likewise see fruits ripen and new buds shoot forth. *Goethe.*

We seek but half the causes of our deeds, / Seeking them only in the outer life, / And heedless of the encircling spirit-world, / Which, though unseen, is felt, and sows in us / All germs of pure and world-wide purposes. *Lowell.*

We seldom give our love to what is worthiest in its object. *J. M. Barrie.*

We seldom speak of the virtue we have, but much more frequently of that which we have not. *Lessing.*

"We shall fight in the shade." *Leonidas, to the threat of the Persians that their forest of arrows would darken the sun.*

20 We shall find no fiend in hell can match the fury of a disappointed woman, — scorned, slighted, dismissed without a parting pang. *Cibber.*

We shall always keep a corner of our heads open and free, that we may make room for the opinions of our friends. *Joubert.*

We should be slower to think that the man at his worst is the real man, and certain that the better we are ourselves the less likely is he to be at his worst in our company. *J. M. Barrie.*

We should be sparing in our intimacies; because it so very often happens that the more perfectly men are understood, the less they are esteemed. *Thomas à Kempis.*

We should come home from adventures, and perils, and discoveries every day with new experience and character. *Thoreau.*

We should count time by heart-throbs. / He 25 most lives / Who thinks most, feels the noblest, / Acts the best. *Bailey.*

We should despise the wretch who has never once thought what it is he is doing (*vollbringt*). *Goethe* (?).

We should distinguish between laughter inspired by joy, and that which arises from mockery. *Goldsmith.*

We should eat to live, and not live to eat. *Pr.*

We should feel sorrow, but not sink under its oppression. *Confucius.*

We should forgive freely, but forget rarely. 30 I will not be revenged, and this I owe to my enemy; but I will remember, and this I owe to myself. *Colton.*

We should guard against a talent which we cannot hope to practise in perfection. Improve it as we may, we shall always in the end, when the merit of the master has become apparent to us, painfully lament the loss of time and strength devoted to such botching. *Goethe.*

We should have all our communications with men as in the presence of God; and with God, as in the presence of men. *Colton.*

We should hold the immutable mean that lies between insensibility and anguish; our attempts should be, not to extinguish nature, but to repress it; not to stand unmoved at distress, but endeavour to turn every disaster to our own advantage. *Confucius.*

We should labour to treat with ease of things that are difficult; with familiarity, of things that are novel; and with perspicuity, of things that are profound. *Colton.*

We should live each day as if it were the full 35 term of our life. (?)

We should manage our fortune like our constitution; enjoy it when good, have patience when bad, and never apply violent remedies but in cases of necessity. *La Roche.*

We should never risk pleasantry except with well-bred people, and people with brains. *La Bruyère.*

We should never so entirely avoid danger as to appear irresolute and cowardly; but, at the same time, we should avoid unnecessarily exposing ourselves to danger, than which nothing can be more foolish. *Cic.*

We should not be too hasty in bestowing either our praise or censure on mankind, since we shall often find such a mixture of good and evil in the same character, that it may require a very accurate judgment and a very elaborate inquiry to determine on which side the balance turns. *Fielding.*

We should not spur a willing horse. *Pr.*   40

We should not trust the heart too much. The heart speaks to us very gladly, as our mouth expresses itself. If the mouth were as much inclined to speak the feelings of the heart, it would have been the fashion long ago to put a padlock on the mouth. *Lessing.*

We should often feel ashamed of our most brilliant actions were the world to see the motives from which they sprung. *La Roche.*

We should only utter higher maxims so far as they can benefit the world. The rest we should keep within ourselves, and they will diffuse over our actions a lustre like the mild radiance of a hidden sun. *Goethe.*

We should round every day of stirring action with an evening of thought. We learn nothing of our experience except we muse upon it. *Bovee.*

We should seem ignorant that we oblige, and leave the mind at full liberty to give or refuse its affections ; for constraint may indeed leave the receiver still grateful, but it will certainly produce disgust. *Goldsmith.*

5 We should take a prudent care for the future, but so as to enjoy the present. It is no part of wisdom to be miserable to-day, because we may happen to be so to-morrow. (?)

We should, to the last moment of our lives, continue a settled intercourse with all the true examples of grandeur. *Sir Joshua Reynolds.*

We shut our eyes, and, like people in the dark, we fall foul upon the very thing we search for, without finding it. *Sen.*

We sink to rise. *Emerson.*

We smile at the satire expended upon the follies of others, but we forget to weep at our own. *Mme. Necker.*

10 We sometimes meet an original gentleman, who, if manners had not existed, would have invented them. *Emerson.*

We sometimes see a change of expression in our companion, and say, His father or his mother comes to the windows of his eyes, and sometimes a remote relative. In different hours, a man represents each of several of his ancestors, as if there were seven or eight of us rolled up in each man's skin—seven or eight ancestors at least—and they constitute the variety of notes for that new piece of music which his life is. *Emerson.*

We speak that we do know, and testify that we have seen. *Jesus.*

We still are fain, with wrath and strife, / To seek for gain, to shrink from loss, / Content to scratch our shallow cross / On the rough surface of old life. *Dr. W. Smith.*

We swallow at one gulp a lie which flatters us, but only drop by drop a truth which is bitter to us. *Diderot.*

15 We take a great deal for granted in this world, and expect that everything, as a matter of course, ought to fit into our humours, wishes, and wants ; it is often only when danger threatens that we awake to the discovery that the guiding reins are held by one whom we had well-nigh forgotten in our careless ease. *Mrs. Gatty.*

We take a pleasure in being severe upon others, but cannot endure to hear of our own faults. *Thomas à Kempis.*

We take greater pains to persuade others that we are happy than in endeavouring to think so ourselves. *Confucius.*

We take no note of time but from its loss. *Young.*

We talk little if we do not talk about ourselves. *Hazlitt.*

20 We talk on principle, but we act on interest. *Landor.*

We tell our triumphs to the crowd, but our own hearts are the sole confidants of our sorrows. *Bulwer Lytton.*

We tell the ladies that good wives make good husbands ; I believe it is a more certain position that good brothers make good sisters. *Johnson.*

We that acquaint ourselves with every zone, / And pass the tropics, and behold each pole ; / When we come home, are to ourselves unknown, / And unacquainted still with our own soul. *Davies.*

We think our civilisation near its meridian ; but we are yet only at the cock-crowing and the morning star. *Emerson.*

We tolerate everybody, because we doubt 25 everything ; or else we tolerate nobody, because we believe something. *Mrs. E. B. Browning.*

We trample grass, and prize the flowers of May ; / Yet grass is green when flowers do fade away. *R. Southwell.*

We treat God with irreverence by banishing him from our thoughts, not by referring to his will on slight occasions. *Ruskin.*

We triumph without glory when we conquer without danger. *Corn.*

We unconsciously imitate what pleases us, and insensibly approximate to the characters we most admire. In this way, a generous habit of thought and of action carries with it an incalculable influence. *Bovee.*

We underpin our houses with granite ; what 30 of our habits and our lives? *Thoreau.*

We use up in the passions the stuff that was given us for happiness. *Joubert.*

We usually lose the to-day, because there has been a yesterday, and to-morrow is coming. *Goethe.*

We very often have to do things during our lives of which we do not understand the reasons, but the more clearly we understand the work we have to do, depend upon it, the better the work will be done. *W. E. Forster.*

We wander there, we wander here, / We eye the rose upon the brier, / Unmindful that the thorn is near, / Amang the banes. *Burns.*

We want but two or three friends, but these 35 we cannot do without, and they serve us in every thought we think. *Emerson.*

We want downright facts at present more than anything else. *Ruskin.*

We want foolishly to think the creed a man professes a more significant fact than the man he is. *Thoreau.*

We want one man to be always thinking, and another to be always working, and we call the one a gentleman, and the other an operative ; whereas the workman ought often to be thinking, and the thinker often to be working, and both should be gentlemen in the best sense. *Ruskin.*

We waste our best years in distilling the sweetest flowers of life into potions which, after all, do not immortalise, but only intoxicate. *Longfellow.*

We wear a face of joy because / We have been 40 glad of yore. *Wordsworth.*

We, who name ourselves its (the world) sovereigns, we, / Half dust, half deity, alike unfit / To sink or soar. *Byron.*

We will have others severely corrected, and will not be corrected ourselves. *Thomas à Kempis.*

We will not estimate the sun by the quantity of gaslight it saves us. *Carlyle.*

We will not from the helm, to sit and weep ; / But keep our course, though the rough wind say no. (?)

We will obey the voice of the Lord our God, that it may be well with us. *Bible.*

5 We wish to be happier than other people ; and this is almost always difficult, for we believe others to be happier than they are. *Montesquieu.*

We would commend a faith that even seems audacious, like that of the sturdy Covenanter Robert Bruce, who requested, as he was dying, that his finger might be placed on one of God's strong promises, as though to challenge the Judge of all with it as he should enter his presence. *Dr. Gordon.*

We wound our modesty and make foul the clearness of our deservings when of ourselves we publish them. *All's Well,* i. 3.

We wrap ourselves up in the cloak of our own better fortune, and turn away our eyes, lest the wants and woes of our brother-mortals should disturb the selfish apathy of our souls. *Burns.*

We write from aspiration and antagonism, as well as from experience. We paint those qualities which we do not possess. *Emerson.*

10 We'd jump the life to come. But, in these cases, / We still have judgment here ; that we but teach / Bloody instructions, which, being taught, return / To plague the inventor. This even-handed justice / Commends the ingredients of our poison'd chalice / To our own lips. *Macb.,* i. 7.

We'll stand up for our properties, was the beggar's song, that lived upon the alms-basket. *L'Estrange.*

Weak eyes are precisely the fondest of glittering objects. *Carlyle.*

Weak minds sink under prosperity as well as under adversity ; strong and deep ones have two highest tides—when the moon is at the full, and when there is no moon. *Hare.*

Weak persons cannot be sincere. *La Roche.*

15 Weak Virtue that amid the shade / Lamenting lies, with future schemes amused, / While Wickedness and Folly, kindred powers, / Confound the world ! *Thomson.*

Weakness of character is the only defect which cannot be amended. *La Roche.*

Weaknesses, so called, are neither more nor less than vice in disguise. *Lavater.*

Wealth and want equally harden the human heart, as frost and fire are both alien to the human flesh. Famine and gluttony alike drive nature away from the heart of man. *Theodore Parker.*

Wealth consists of the good, and therefore useful, things in the possession of the nation ; money is only the written or coined sign of the relative quantities of wealth in each person's possession. *Ruskin.*

20 Wealth cannot purchase any great private solace or convenience. Riches are only the means of sociality. *Thoreau.*

Wealth gotten by vanity shall be diminished ; but he that gathereth by labour shall increase. *Bible.*

Wealth heaped on wealth, nor truth nor safety buys ; / The dangers gather as the treasures rise. *Johnson.*

Wealth imparts a birdlime quality to the possessor, at which the man in his native power would have revolted. *Burns.*

Wealth implies the possession of what is of intrinsic value and of a capacity to use it. *Ruskin.*

25 Wealth is a shift. The wise man angles with himself only, and with no meaner bait. *Emerson.*

Wealth is not his that has it, but his that enjoys it. *Ben. Franklin.*

Wealth is the application of mind to nature ; and the art of getting rich consists not in industry, much less in saving, but in a better order, in timeliness, in being at the right spot. *Emerson.*

Wealth is the conjuror's devil ; / Whom when he thinks he hath, the devil hath him. *Herbert.*

Wealth is the possession of useful articles which we can use, (so that) instead of depending merely on a "have," it is thus seen to depend on a "can." *Ruskin.*

30 Wealth leaves us at death ; kinsmen at the grave ; but virtues of the mind unto the heavens with us we have. *Lord Vaux.*

Wealth makes wit waver. *Sc. Pr.*

Wealth maketh many friends, but the poor is separated from his neighbour. *Bible.*

Wealth of every species necessarily flows to the hands of him who exerteth himself. *Hitopadesa.*

Wealth only by its use we know. *Anon.*

35 Wealth, power, and even the advantages of youth, have little to do with that which gives repose to the mind and firmness to the frame. *Scott.*

Wealth richer than both the Indies lies for every man, if he will endure. Not his oaks only and his fruit-trees, his very heart roots itself wherever he may abide—roots itself, draws nourishment from the deep fountains of universal being. *Carlyle.*

Wealth which breeds idleness, of which the English peerage is an example, and of which we are beginning to abound in specimens in this country (America), is only a sort of human oyster-bed, where heirs and heiresses are planted, to spend a contemptible life of slothfulness in growing plump and succulent for the grave-worm's banquet. *Horace Mann.*

Wealth without contentment climbs a hill, / To feel those tempests which fly over ditches. *George Herbert.*

Wear your learning, like your watch, in a private pocket ; and do not pull it out and strike it, merely to show that you have one. If you are asked what o'clock it is, tell it, but do not proclaim it hourly and unasked, like the watchmen. *Chesterfield.*

40 Wearers of rings and chains ! / Pray do not take the pains / To set me right. / In vain my faults ye quote ; / I write as others wrote / On Sunium's height. *Landor.*

Weariness / Can snore upon the flint, when resty sloth / Finds the down pillow hard. *Cymbeline,* iii. 6.

Weary the path that does not challenge reason. Doubt is an incentive to truth, and patient inquiry leadeth the way. *H. Ballou.*

Weave in faith and God will find thread. *Pr.*

Weder sicher noch gerathen ist, etwas wider Gewissen zu thun. Hier stehe ich, ich kann nicht anders. Gott helfe mir—It is neither safe nor prudent to do aught against conscience. Here stand I, I cannot do otherwise. God be helping me. *Luther at the Diet of Worms.*

Wedlock, indeed, hath oft compared been / To publick feasts, where meet a publick rout : / When they that are without would fain go in, / And they that are within would fain go out. *Sir J. Davis.*

Wedlock is like a besieged fortress: those who are outside wish to get in, and those who are inside wish to get out. *Arab. Pr.*

5 Wee modest crimson-tipped flower, / Thou's met me in an evil hour ; / For I maun crush amang the stour / Thy slender stem ; / To spare thee now is past my power, / Thou bonny gem. *Burns.*

Wee Willie Winkie rins through the toun, / Upstairs and dounstairs, in his nicht-goun, / Tirlin' at the window, cryin' at the lock, / "Are the weans in their bed? for it's noo ten o'clock." *William Miller.*

Weed your better judgments / Of all opinion that grows rank in them. *As You Like It, ii. 7.*

Weeds make dunghills gracious. *Tennyson.*

Weel is that weel does. *Sc. Pr.*

10 Weep no more, lady, weep no more, / For sorrow is in vain ; / For violets pluck'd, the sweetest showers / Will ne'er revive again. *Anon.*

Weeping may endure for a night, but joy cometh in the morning. *Bible.*

Weh dem Lande, wo man nicht mehr singt— Woe to the land where the voice of song has gone dumb. *Seume.*

Weigh not so much what men say, as what they prove : remembering that truth is simple and naked, and needs not invective to apparel her comeliness. *Sir P. Sidney.*

Weighty things are done in solitude, that is, without society. The means of improvement consist not in projects, or in any violent designs, for these cool, and cool very soon, but in patient practising for whole long days, by which I make the thing clear to my highest reason. *Jean Paul.*

15 Weighty work must be done with few words. *Dan. Pr.*

Weise Hut, / Behält ihr Gut—Wise care keeps what it has gained. *Ger. Pr.*

Weise sein ist nicht allzeit gut—It is not always good to be wise. *Ger. Pr.*

Weiser Mann, starker Mann—A wise man is a strong man. *Ger. Pr.*

Weisheit, du wirst Unsinn / Im Mund des Schwärmers — Wisdom, thou changest into folly in the mouth of the fanatic. *Otto Ludwig.*

20 Welch Glück geliebt zu werden : / Und lieben, Götter, welch ein Glück !—What a happiness to be loved ! and to love, ye gods, what bliss ! *Goethe.*

Welcome evermore to gods and men is the self-helping man. *Emerson.*

Welcome is the best cheer. *Pr.*

Welcome, Misfortune, if thou comest alone. *Pr.*

Well at ease are the sleepers for whom existence is a shallow dream. *Carlyle.*

Well for the drones of the social hive that there 25 are bees of an industrious turn, willing, for an infinitesimal share of the honey, to undertake the labour of its fabrication. *Hood.*

Well has Ennius said, "Kindnesses misplaced are nothing but a curse and disservice." *Cic.*

Well-married, a man is winged ; ill-matched, he is shackled. *Ward Beecher.*

Well roared, lion. *Mid. N.'s Dream, v. 1.*

Well thriveth that well suffereth. *Pr.*

Well to work and make a fire, / Doth both 30 care and skill require. *Pr.*

Well, well, is a word of malice. *Cheshire Pr.*

Well, whiles I am a beggar, I will rail, / And say, there is no sin but to be rich : / And being rich, my virtue then shall be, / To say there is no vice but beggary. *King John, ii. 2.*

Well, you may fear too far.— / Safer than trust too far. *King Lear, i. 4.*

Wem nicht zu rathen ist, dem ist auch nicht zu helfen—Who will not be advised, cannot be helped. *Ger. Pr.*

Wen die Natur zum Dichter schuf, den lehrt 35 sie auch zu paaren / Das Schöne mit dem Kräftigen, das Neue mit dem Wahren—Him whom Nature has created for a poet, she also teaches to combine the beautiful with the powerful, and the new with the true. *Platen.*

Wen Gott niederschlägt, der richtet sich selbst nicht auf—He raises not himself up again whom God smites down. *Goethe.*

Wen jemand lobt, dem stellt er sich gleich— Every one puts himself on a level with him whom he praises. *Goethe.*

Wenn alle untreu werden, / So bleib' ich dir doch treu—Though all deny thee, yet will not I ever. *Novalis.*

Wenn das Geld im Kasten klingt, / Die Seele aus dem Fegfeuer springt—As soon as the money jingles in the box, the soul leaps out of purgatory. *Sallet after Tetzel.*

Wenn das Glück anpocht, soll man ihm auf- 40 thun—When fortune knocks, open the door. *Ger. Pr.*

Wenn das Leblose lebendig ist, so kann es auch wohl Lebendiges hervorbringen—When what is lifeless has life, it can also produce what has life. *Goethe.*

Wenn der Purpur fällt, muss auch der Herzog nach—If the purple goes, the duke must follow. *Schiller.*

Wenn du eine weise Antwort verlangst, / Musst du vernünftig fragen—If thou desirest a wise answer, thou must ask a reasonable question. *Goethe.*

Wenn du nicht irrst, kommst du nicht zu Verstand—If thou dost not err, thou dost not come to understand. *Goethe.*

Wenn ein Edler gegen dich fehlt, / So thu' als 45 hättest du's nicht gezählt ; / Er wird es in sein Schuldbuch schreiben / Und dir nicht lange im Debet bleiben—If a noble man has done thee a wrong, act as though thou hadst taken no note of it ; he will write it in his ledger, and not remain long in thy debt. *Goethe.*

Wenn Gott sagt: Heute, sagt der Teufel : Morgen—When God says "To-day," the devil says "To-morrow." *Ger. Pr.*

Wenn ihr's nicht fühlt, ihr werdet's nicht erjagen—If you do not feel it, you will not get it by hunting for it. *Goethe.*

Wenn man von den Leuten Pflichten fordert und ihnen keine Rechte zugestehen will, muss man sie gut bezahlen—When we exact duties from people and acknowledge no just claims they may have on us, we ought to pay them well. *Goethe.*

Wenn man was Böses thut, erschrickt man vor dem Bösen—When people do evil, they are afraid of the Evil One. *Goethe.*

Wenn mancher Mann wüsste, / Wer mancher Mann wär', / Thät' mancher Mann manchem Mann / Manchmal mehr Ehr'—If many a man knew who many a man was, many a man would do many a time more honour to many a man. *Ger. Pr.*

Wenn Moses nicht bei Aaron ist, so macht Aaron—Kälber—If Moses is not with Aaron, then Aaron makes him—calves. *Frederick the Great.*

5 Wenn sich der Verirrte findet / Freuen alle Götter sich—When the wanderer finds his way again, all the gods rejoice. *Goethe.*

Wer allen alles traut, dem kann man wenig trauen—Him who trusts everything to every one. we can trust with little. *Lessing.*

Wer darf das Kind beim rechten Namen nennen?—Who dare name the child by his right name? *Goethe.*

Wer darf ihn nennen?—Who dare name Him? *Goethe.*

Wer den Tod fürchtet, hat das Leben verloren —He who fears death is forfeit of life. *Seume.*

10 Wer der Dichtkunst Stimme nicht vernimmt, / Ist ein Barbar, er sei auch wer er sei—He who has no ear for the voice of poesy is a barbarian, be he who he may. *Goethe.*

Wer der Vorderste ist, führt die Herde—The foremost leads the herd. *Schiller.*

Wer die Leiter hinauf will, muss bei der untersten Sprosse schon beginnen—He who would mount a ladder must begin at the lowest step. *Ger. Pr.*

Wer die Wahrheit kennet und saget sie nicht, / Der bleibt fürwahr ein erbärmlicher Wicht —Verily, he is a wretched creature who knows the truth and speaks it not. *Binzer.*

Wer dir als Freund nichts nützen kann / Kann allemal als Feind dir schaden—He who can do you no service as a friend, can always work you harm as an enemy. *Gellert.*

15 Wer edel ist, den suchet die Gefahr / Und er sucht sie, sie müssen sich treffen—Whoso is noble, danger courts him, and he courts danger ; so the two are sure to meet. *Goethe.*

Wer erst klug wird nach der That, / Braucht seine Weisheit viel zu spat—He who is wise only after the deed, uses his wisdom much too late. *Rollenhagen.*

Wer fertig ist, dem ist nichts recht zu machen ; / Ein Werdender wird immer dankbar sein—To him who is finished off, nothing you can do is right ; a growing man (a learner) will be always thankful. *Goethe.*

Wer fremde Sprachen nicht kennt, weiss nichts von seiner eignen—He who knows not foreign languages knows nothing of his own. *Goethe.*

Wer fröhlich sein will sein Lebenlang / Lasse der Welt ihren tollen Gang—He who will be happy through life must leave the world alone in its own mad career. *Rückert.*

20 Wer ist der Weiseste? Der nichts anders weiss und will, als das was begegnet—Who is the wisest man? He who neither knows nor wishes for anything else than what happens. *Goethe.*

Wer ist ein unbrauchbar Man? Der nicht befehlen und auch nicht gehorchen kann— Who is a good-for-nothing? He who can neither command nor even obey. *Goethe.*

Wer ist grösser, Schiller, Goethe? / Wie man nur so mäkeln mag! / Himmlisch ist die Morgenröte, / Himmlisch ist der helle Tag— Which is greater, Schiller or Goethe? One is, or the other is, as you judge of them. Of heaven is the red dawn of morning ; of heaven the clear light of day. *Bauernfeld.*

Wer ist mächtiger als der Tod? / Wer da kann lachen, wenn er droht—Who is mightier than death? He who can smile when death threatens. *Rückert.*

Wer kann was Dummes, wer was Kluges denken, / Das nicht die Vorwelt schon gedacht? —Who can think anything stupid or sensible that the world has not thought already? *Goethe.*

25 Wer lange bedenkt, der wählt nicht immer das Beste—He who is long in making up his mind does not always choose the best. *Goethe.*

Wer lügt, der stiehlt—He who lies, steals. *Ger. Pr.*

Wer mit sich selber eins, ist eins mit Gott— He who is one with himself is one with God. *Bodenstedt.*

Wer nicht Bitteres gekostet hat, weiss nicht was süss ist—He who has not tasted bitter does not know what sweet is. *Ger. Pr.*

Wer nicht hören will, der muss fühlen—He that will not hear must be made to feel. *Ger. Pr.*

30 Wer nicht liebt Wein, Weib und Gesang / Der bleibt ein Narr sein Lebenlang—Who loves not wine, and song, remains a fool all his life long. *Luther.* (?)

Wer nichts für andre thut, thut nichts für sich —He who does nothing for others does nothing for himself. *Goethe.*

Wer nichts fürchtet, ist nicht weniger mächtiger, als der, den alles fürchtet—He who fears nothing is not less mighty than he whom everything fears. *Schiller.*

Wer nie sein Brod mit Thränen ass, / Wer nicht die kummervollen Nächte / Auf seinem Bette weinend sass / Der kennt euch nicht, ihr himmlischen Mächte—He who never ate his bread with tears, who sat not on his bed through sorrowful nights weeping, he knows you not, ye heavenly Powers. *Goethe.*

Wer oft schiesst, trifft endlich—He who shoots often, hits the mark at last. *Ger. Pr.*

35 Wer sein eigener Lehrmeister sein will, hat einen Narren zum Schüler—He who undertakes to be his own teacher has a fool for a pupil. *Ger. Pr.*

Wer sich behaglich fühlt zu Haus, / Der rennt nicht in die Welt hinaus ; / Weltunzufriedenheit beweisen / Die vielen Weltentdeckungsreisen—He who feels at ease at home, runs not out into the world beyond. The many voyages of discovery over the world argue a world-wide discontent. *Rückert.*

Wer will, der vermag—He is able who is willing. *Ger. Pr.*

Wer will was Lebendig's erkennen und beschreiben / Sucht erst den Geist herauszutreiben, / Dann hat er die Teile in seiner Hand, / Fehlt leider, nur das geistige Band —He who would know and describe anything living, sets himself to drive out the spirit first ; he has then all the parts in his hand, only unhappily the living bond is wanting. *Goethe, Mephisto in "Faust."*

Wer wohl sitzt, der rücke nicht—Let him who is well seated not stir. *Ger. Pr.*

Were a man of pleasure to arrive at the full extent of his several wishes, he must immediately feel himself miserable. *Shenstone.*

Were defeat unknown, neither would victory be celebrated with songs of triumph. *Carlyle.*

Were I a steam-engine, wouldst thou take the trouble to tell lies of me? *Carlyle.*

5 Were I so tall to reach the pole / Or grasp the ocean with my span, / I must be measured by my soul : / The mind's the standard of the man. *Watts.*

Were it no for hope the heart wad break. *Sc. Pr.*

Were it not miraculous, could I stretch forth my hand and clutch the sun? Dost thou not see that the true inexplicable God-revealing miracle lies in this, that I can stretch forth my hand at all, that I have free force to clutch aught therewith? *Carlyle.*

Were man / But constant, he were perfect. *Two Gent. of Verona*, v. 4.

Were man not a poor hungry dastard, and even much of a blockhead withal, he would cease criticising his victuals to such extent, and criticise himself rather, what he does with his victuals. *Carlyle.*

10 Were one to preach a sermon on Health, as really were worth doing, Scott ought to be the text. *Carlyle.*

Were the eye not sun-related (*sonnenhaft*), it could never see the sun ; were there not in us divine affinities, how could the divine so ravish us? *Goethe.*

"Were there as many devils in Worms as there are roof-tiles, I would on." *Luther's answer to his friends who pled with him not to go.*

Were there but one man in the world, he would be a terror to himself ; and the highest man not less so than the lowest. *Carlyle.*

Were we as eloquent as angels, we would please some men, some women, and some children much more by listening than by talking. *Colton.*

15 Were we to take as much pains to be what we ought to be as we do to disguise what we really are, we might appear like ourselves, without being at the trouble of any disguise at all. *La Roche.*

Were wisdom given me with this reservation, that I should keep it shut up within myself and not impart it, I would spurn it. *Sen.*

Were wisdom to be sold, she would give no price ; every man is satisfied with the share he has from nature. *Henry Home.*

Westward the course of empire takes its way. *Berkeley.*

What a blessed thing it is that Nature, when she invented, manufactured, and patented her authors, contrived to make critics out of the chips that were left ! *Holmes.*

20 What a delight to have a husband beside you, were it only to salute you when you sneeze, and say "God bless you !" *Molière.*

What a dismal, debasing, and confusing element is that of a sick body on the human soul or thinking part ! *Carlyle.*

What a fool is he who locks his door to keep out spirits, who has in his own bosom a spirit he dares not meet alone ; whose voice, smothered far down, and piled over with mountains of earthliness, is yet like the fore-warning trumpet of doom ! *Mrs. Stowe.*

What a force of illusion begins life with us, and attends us to the end ! *Emerson.*

What a heavy burden is a name that has become too soon famous ! *Voltaire.*

What a hell of witchcraft lies in the small orb 25 of one particular tear ! *Shakespeare.*

What a large volume of adventures may be grasped within this little span of life by him who interests his heart in everything. *Sterne.*

What a man can do is his greatest ornament, and he always consults his dignity by doing it. *Carlyle.*

What a man does not believe can never at bottom be of any true interest to him. *Carlyle.*

What a man does, that he has. *Emerson.*

What a man does, that he is. *Hegel.* 30

What a man finds good of, and what he finds hurt of, is the best physic to preserve health. *Bacon.*

What a man is contributes much more to his happiness than what he has or how others regard him. *Schopenhauer.*

What a man is irresistibly urged to say, helps him and us. *Emerson.*

What a man wills, not what he knows, determines his worth or unworth, his power or impotence, his happiness or unhappiness. *Lindner.*

What a miserable world !—trouble if we love, 35 and trouble if we do not love. *Count de Maistre.*

What a piece of work is a man ! How noble in reason ! How infinite in faculty ! In form and moving how express and admirable ! In action how like an angel ! In apprehension how like a God ! *Ham.*, ii. 2.

What a poor creature is the woman who, inspiring desire, does not also inspire love and reverence ! *Goethe.*

What a road had human nature to traverse before it reached the point of being mild to the guilty, merciful to the injurious, and humane to the inhuman ! Doubtless they were men of godlike souls who first taught this, who spent their lives in rendering the practice of this possible, and recommending it to others. *Goethe.*

What a sense of security is in an old book which Time has criticised for us ! *Lowell.*

What a strange thing man is ! and what a 40 stranger / Is woman ! *Byron.*

What a thin film it is that divides the living from the dead ! *Carlyle.*

What a vanity is painting, which attracts admiration by the resemblance of things that in the original we do not admire ! *Pascal.*

What a view a man must have of this universe who thinks he can swallow it all, who is not doubly and trebly happy that he can keep it from swallowing him ! *Carlyle.*

What a wretched thing is all fame ! A renown of the highest sort endures, say for two thousand years. And then? Why then a fathomless eternity swallows it. *Carlyle.*

What actually constitutes the human element 45 in man is a kindly spirit. *Schiller.*

What an enormous camera obscura magnifier is Tradition! How a thing grows in the human memory, in the human imagination, when love, worship, and all that lies in the human heart is there to encourage it! *Carlyle.*

What an inaccessible stronghold that man possesses who is always in earnest with himself and the things around him! *Goethe.*

What are all our histories but God manifesting himself, that he hath shaken, and tumbled down, and trampled upon everything that he hath not planted! *Oliver Cromwell.*

What are all prayers beneath / But cries of babes, that cannot know / Half the deep thought they breathe? *Keble.*

5 What are men better than sheep or goats, / That nourish a blind life within the brain, / If, knowing God, they lift not hands of prayer / Both for themselves and those who call them friend? *Tennyson.*

What are the outward details of a life, if the inner secret of it, the remorse, temptations, true, often-baffled, never-ended struggle of it, be forgotten? Details by themselves will never teach us what it is. *Carlyle.*

What are we great ones on the wave of humanity? We think we rule it when it rules us, and drives us up and down, hither and thither, as it listeth. *Goethe.*

What are words but empty sounds, that break and scatter in the air, and make no real impression? *Thomas à Kempis.*

What are your axioms, and categories, and systems, and aphorisms? Words, words. High air-castles are cunningly built of words, the words well bedded in good logic-mortar; wherein, however, no knowledge will come to lodge. *Carlyle.*

10 What Art had Homer? what Art had Shakespeare? Patient, docile, valiant intelligence, conscious and unconscious, gathered from all winds, of these two things—their own faculty of utterance, and the audience they had to utter to; add only to which, as the soul of the whole, a blazing, radiant insight into the fact, blazing, burning interest about it, and we have the whole Art of Shakespeare and Homer. *Carlyle.*

What was to the ancient world, science is to the modern. *Disraeli.*

What avail the largest gifts of Heaven, / When drooping health and spirits go amiss? / How tasteless then whatever can be given! / Health is the vital principle of bliss, / And exercise of health. *Thomson.*

What avails a superfluity of freedom which we cannot use? *Goethe.*

What avails the dram of brandy while it swims chemically united with its barrel of wort? Let the distiller pass it and repass it through his limbecs; for it is the drops of pure alcohol we want, not the gallons of water, which may be had in every ditch. *Carlyle.*

15 What belongs to everybody belongs to nobody. *Pr.*

What better time for driving, riding, walking, moving through the air by any means, than a fresh, frosty morning, when hope runs cheerily through the veins with the brisk blood and tingles in the frame from head to foot? *Dickens.*

What bitter pills, / Compos'd of real ills, / Men swallow down to purchase one false good. *Quarles.*

What boots it at one gate to make defence, / And at another to let in the foe? *Milton.*

What boots the hero-arm without a hero-eye? *Jean Paul.*

What built St. Paul's Cathedral? Look at 20 the heart of the matter, it was that divine Hebrew Book, the word partly of the man Moses, an outlaw tending his Midianitish herds four thousand years ago in the wilderness of Sinai! *Carlyle.*

What by straight path cannot be reached, / By crooked ways is never won. *Goethe.*

What can be done, you must do for yourself. *Johnson.*

What can ennoble sots, or slaves, or cowards? / Alas! not all the blood of all the Howards. *Pope.*

What can Fate devise to vanquish Love? *Lewis Morris.*

What can they see in the longest kingly line 25 in Europe, save that it runs back to a successful soldier? *Scott.*

What can we reason, but from what we know? *Pope.*

What cannot be abused is good for nothing. *Niebuhr.*

What cannot be avoided, / 'Twere childish weakness to lament or fear. *3 Hen. VI., v. 4.*

What cannot be eschew'd must be embraced. *Merry Wives. v. 4.*

What can't be cured must be endured. *Burton.* 30

What care I for words? yet words do well / When he that speaks them pleases those that hear. *As You Like It, iii. 5.*

What cares any man for appearances except as signs of what otherwise he cannot see? *Ed.*

"What cheer? Brother, quickly tell," / "Above"—"Below." "Good-night"—"All's well." *Dibdin.*

What chiefly distinguishes great artists from feeble artists is first their sensibility and tenderness; secondly, their imagination; and thirdly, their industry. *Ruskin.*

What comes from God to us, returns from 35 us to God. (?)

What comes from the heart goes to the heart. *Pr.*

What constitutes a state? . . . Men who their duties know, / But know their rights, and knowing, dare maintain. *Sir William Jones.*

What devilry soever kings do, the Greeks must pay the piper. *Pr.*

What dire offence from amorous causes springs! / What mighty contests rise from trivial things! *Pope.*

What distinguishes Christianity from all mono- 40 theistic religions lies in nothing else than in a making-dead to the law, the removal of the Kantian imperative; instead of which Christianity requires a free inclination. *Schiller.*

What divine, what truly great thing has ever been effected by force of public opinion? *Carlyle.*

What do I gain from a man into whose eyes I cannot look when he is speaking, and the mirror of whose soul is veiled to me by a pair of glasses which dazzle me? *Goethe.*

What do you mean by composing tragedies, when Tragedy in person stalks every street? (?)

What does competency in the long-run mean? It means, to all reasonable beings, cleanliness of person, decency of dress, courtesy of manners, opportunities for education, the delights of leisure, and the bliss of giving. *Whipple.*

Wha' does the utmost that he can, / Will whyles (sometimes) do mair. *Burns.*

What doth cherish weeds, but gentle air? / And what makes robbers bold, but too much lenity? *3 Hen. VI.*, ii. 6.

5 What doth the Lord require of thee, but to do justly, and to love mercy, and to walk humbly with thy God? *Bible.*

What exile from himself can flee? *Byron.*

What fates impose, that men must needs abide; / It boots not to resist both wind and tide. *3 Hen. VI.*, iv. 3.

What! fly from love? vain hope: there's no retreat, / When he has wings and I have only feet. *Archias.*

What glitters is for the moment; the genuine is for all time. *Goethe.*

10 What God does all day is not to sit waiting in churches for people to come and worship him. *Prof. Drummond.*

What God hath joined together, let not man put asunder. *Jesus.*

What God makes he never mars. *Pr.*

What good I see humbly I seek to do, / And live obedient to the law, in trust / That what will come, and must come, shall come well. *Sir Edwin Arnold.*

What governs men is the fear of truth, except such as is useful to them. *Amiel.*

15 What great thing ever happened in this world, a world understood always to be made and governed by wisdom, without meaning somewhat? *Carlyle.*

What gunpowder did for war, the printing-press has done for the mind; and the statesman is no longer clad in the steel of special education, but every reading man is his judge. *Wendell Phillips.*

What hands build, hands can pull down. *Schiller.*

What has been, may be; and what may be, may be supposed to be. *Swift.*

What has been written, as well as what has been actually done, shrivels up and ceases to be worth anything, until it has again been taken up into life, been again felt, thought, and acted upon. *Goethe.*

20 What has never anywhere come to pass, that alone never grows old. *Schiller.*

What has posterity done for us / That we, lest they their rights should lose, / Should trust our necks to gripe of noose? *John Trumbull.*

What hath he to do with a soul who doth not keep his passions in subjection? *Hitopadesa.*

What have I to do, . . . either with your amusements or your pleasures, unless it was in my power to increase their measure? *Sterne.*

What have kings that privates have not too, / Save ceremony, save general ceremony? *Hen. V.*, iv. 1.

What have not you men to answer for who 25 talk of love to a woman when her face is all you know of her, and her passions, her aspirations, are for kissing to sleep, her very soul a plaything? *J. M. Barrie.*

What he greatly thought, he nobly dared. *Pope.*

What house more stately hath there been, / Or can be, than is Man? *George Herbert.*

What hypocrites we seem to be whenever we talk of ourselves! Our words sound so humble, while our hearts are so proud. *Hare.*

What I cannot praise I speak not of. *Goethe.*

What I for many a day wished, life has not 30 granted me, but it has instead taught me this, that my wish was a foolish one. *Geibel.*

What I gave, that I have; / What I spent, that I had; / What I left, that I lost. *Epitaph inscribed on the tomb of Robert of Doncaster.*

What I have written, I have written. *Pilate of the legend he wrote over the Cross.*

What I must do is all that concerns me, not what the people think. *Emerson.*

What I object to is, not the poetry of sadness, but the sadness of poetry. Many of the poets make out the fountain of poetry to be only a fountain of tears. *Bovee.*

What, indeed, is man's life generally but a 35 kind of beast-godhood; the god in us triumphing more and more over the beast; striving more and more to subdue it under his feet? *Carlyle.*

What is a foreign country to those who have science? *Carlyle.*

What is a handful of reasonable men against a crowd with stones in their hands? *George Eliot.*

What is a man, / If his chief good and market of his time, / Be but to sleep, and feed? A beast, no more. *Ham.*, iv. 4.

What is a man profited if he shall gain the whole world and lose his own soul? *Jesus.*

What is against Nature is against God. 40 *Hebbel.*

What is all working, what is all knowing, but a faint interpreting, and a faint showing forth of the mystery, which ever remains infinite? *Carlyle.*

What, is any one, simply by birth, to be punished or applauded? *Hitopadesa.*

What is aught but as 'tis valued? *Troil. and Cress.*, ii. 2.

What is barely necessary cannot be dispensed with. *Goldsmith.*

What is becoming is honourable, and what is 45 honourable is becoming. *Cic.*

What is beneath me floors me; what is on a level with me bores me; only what is above me supports and lifts me above myself. *Anon.*

What is bought is cheaper than a gift. *Pr.*

What is bred in the bone will never come out of the flesh. *Pr.*

What is called the spirit of the times is at bottom but the spirit of the gentlemen in which the times are mirrored. *Goethe.*

What is cheapest to you now is likely to be 50 dearest in the end. *Ruskin.*

What is chiefly needed in the England of the present day is to show the quantity of pleasure that may be obtained by a consistent, well-administered competence, modest, confessed, and laborious. *Ruskin.*

What is difficulty? Only a word indicating the degree of strength requisite for accomplishing particular objects ; a mere notice of the necessity for exertion ; a bugbear to children and fools ; only a mere stimulus to men. *Samuel Warren.*

What is distance to the indefatigable ? *Hitopadesa.*

What is done by night appears by day. *Pr.*

5 What is done for those who have not their passions in subjection, is like washing the elephant (*i.e.*, washing the blackamoor white). *Hitopadesa.*

What is done in a hurry is never done well. *Pr.*

What is done is done ; has already blended itself with the boundless, ever-living, ever-working universe, and will also work there, for good or evil, openly or secretly, through all time. *Carlyle.*

What is everybody's business is nobody's business. *Izaak Walton.*

What is excellent should never be carped at nor discussed, but enjoyed and reverentially thought over in silence. *Goethe.*

10 What is extraordinary try to look at with your own eyes. *Old maxim.*

What is false taste but want of perception to discern propriety and distinguish beauty ? *Goldsmith.*

What is generally accepted as virtue in women is very different from what is thought so in men : a very good woman would make but a paltry man. *Pope.*

What is generally considered true amounts to much the same as if it were actually true. *Cötvös.*

What is genius or courage without a heart ? *Goldsmith.*

15 What is genuine but that which is truly excellent, which stands in harmony with the purest nature or reason, and which even now ministers to our highest development ! What is spurious but the absurd and the hollow, which brings no fruit—at least, no good fruit. *Goethe.*

What is gray with age becomes religion. *Schiller.*

What is happiness? To animals in this world, health. *Hitopadesa.*

What is important is to have a soul which loves truth, and receives it wherever it finds it. *Goethe.*

What is in will out. *Emerson.*

20 What is it (thy protest against the devil) properly but an altercation with him before you begin honestly fighting with him ? *Carlyle.*

What is it that keeps men in continual discontent and agitation ? It is that they cannot make realities correspond with their conceptions, that enjoyment steals away from among their hands, that the wished-for comes too late, and nothing reached and acquired produces on the heart the effect which their longing for it at a distance led them to anticipate. *Goethe.*

What is justice but another form of the reality we love—a truth acted out ? *Carlyle.*

What is kindness? A principle in the good. *Hitopadesa.*

What is known to three is known to everybody. *Pr.*

What is learned in the cradle is carried to the 25 tomb. *Pr.*

What is life but the choice of that good which contains the least of evil ! *B. R. Haydon.*

What is life except the knitting up of incoherences into coherence? *Carlyle.*

What is man but a symbol of God, and all that he does, if not symbolical, a revelation to sense of the mystic God-given force that is in him? *Carlyle.*

What is man, / If his chief good, and market of his time, / Be but to sleep and feed? A beast, no man. *Ham.*, iv. 4.

What is mine, even to my life, is hers I love ; 30 but the secret of my friend is not mine ! *Sir P. Sidney.*

What is modesty, if it deserts from truth? *Johnson.*

What is more at ease, more abstracted from the world, than a true single-hearted honesty? *Thomas à Kempis.*

What is much desired is not believed when it comes. *Sp. Pr.*

What is my life if I am no longer to be of use to others? *Goethe.*

What is nearest is often unattainably far off. 35 *Goethe.*

What is nearest us touches us most. *Johnson.*

What is new finds better acceptance than what is good or great. *Denham.*

What is noble ?--That which places / Truth in its enfranchised will, / Leaving steps, like angel-traces, / That mankind may follow still ! *C. Swain.*

What is not allotted the hand cannot reach, and what is allotted will find you wherever you may be. *Saadi.*

What is not sung is properly no poem, but a 40 piece of prose cramped into jingling lines,— to the great injury of the grammar, to the great grief of the reader, for the most part ! *Carlyle.*

What is not to be, that is not to be ; if it be to come to pass, it cannot be otherwise. This reasoning is an antidote. Why doth not the afflicted one drink of it? *Hitopadesa.*

What is not true has this advantage that it can be eternally talked about; whereas about truth there is an urgency that cries out for its application, for otherwise it has no right to be there. *Goethe.*

What is not worth reading more than once is not worth reading at all. *C. J. Weber.*

What is now called the nature of women is an eminently artificial thing—the result of forced repression in some directions, unnatural stimulation in others. *J. S. Mill.*

What is obvious is not always known, and what 45 is known is not always present. *Johnson.*

What is of the earth has no permanence ; our hearts yearn after a better land. *H. A. Hoffmann.*

What is often termed shyness is nothing more than refined sense, and an indifference to common observations. (?)

What is our life but an endless flight of winged facts or events ? *Emerson.*

What is past is past. There is a future left to all men, who have the virtue to repent and the energy to atone. *Bulwer Lytton.*

What is philosophy ? An entire separation from the world. *Hitopadesa.*

What is reason now was passion formerly. *Ovid.*

5 What is religion ? Compassion for all things that have life. *Hitopadesa.*

What is sauce for the goose is sauce for the gander. *Pr.*

What is specially true of love is, that it is a state of extreme impressionability ; the lover has more senses and finer senses than others ; his eye and ear are telegraphs ; he reads omens in the flower and cloud and face and form and gesture, and reads them aright. *Emerson.*

What is strength without a double share / Of wisdom ? vast, unwieldy, burdensome, / Proudly secure, yet liable to fall / By weakest subtleties ; not made to rule, / But to subserve where wisdom bears command. *Milton.*

What is the adored Supreme Perfection, say ?— / What, but eternal never-resting soul, / Almighty power, and all-directing day ; / By whom each atom stirs, the planets roll ; / Who fills, surrounds, informs, and agitates the whole. *Thomson.*

10 What is the best government ? That which teaches us to govern ourselves. *Goethe.*

What is the best in the world ? Healthy blood, sinews of steel, and strong nerves. *Auerbach.*

What is the body when the head is off ? *3 Hen. VI., v. 1.*

What is the city but the people ? True, the people are the city. *Coriolanus, iii. 1.*

What is the elevation of the soul ? A prompt, delicate, certain feeling for all that is beautiful, all that is grand ; a quick resolution to do the greatest good by the smallest means ; a great benevolence joined to a great strength and great humility. *Lavater.*

15 What is the good of fear ? The whole solar system were it to fall together about our ears could kill us only once. *Carlyle.*

What is the highest secret of victory and peace ? To will what God wills, and strike a league with destiny. *W. R. Alger.*

What is the majority ? Majority is nonsense (*Unsinn*). Understanding has always been only with the minority. *Schiller.*

What is the true test of character, unless it be its progressive development in the bustle and turmoil, in the action and reaction, of daily life ? *Goethe.*

What is the use of a lamp to a blind man, although it be burning in his hand ? *Hitopadesa.*

20 What is the use of health or of life, if not to do some work therewith ? *Carlyle.*

What is the voice of song, when the world lacks the ear of taste ? *Hawthorne.*

What is there good in us if it is not the power and inclination to appropriate to ourselves the resources of the outward world, and to make them subservient to our higher ends ? *Goethe.*

What ! is there no bribing death ? *Last words of Cardinal Beaufort.*

What is this day's strong suggestion ? / "The passing moment's all we rest on !" *Burns.*

What is this life of ours ? Gone in a moment, 25 burnt up like a scroll, into the blank eternity. *Carlyle interpreting young Luther's reflexion on the sudden death by his side of his friend Alexis.*

What is too great a load for those who have strength ? *Hitopadesa.*

What is truth ? *Pilate scoffingly to Jesus.*

What is twice read is commonly better remembered than what is transcribed. *Johnson.*

What is valuable is not new, and what is new is not valuable. *D. Webster.*

"What is wanting," said Napoleon one day to 30 Madame Campan, "in order that the youth of France be well educated ?" "Good mothers," was the reply. The Emperor was most forcibly struck with this answer. "Here," said he, "is a system in one word." *Abbott.*

What is writ is writ. *Byron.*

What joy a self-sufficing fortune yields, / Such modest livelihood is dear to me. The wise old maxim, "Not too much," / Too much has power my heart to touch. *Alpheus of Mitylene.*

What life only half imparts to man, posterity shall give entirely. *Goethe.*

What love can do, that dares love attempt. *Rom. and Jul., ii. 2.*

What love hides is raised as from the dead / 35 Some day, and kills the love which covered it, / And frankest truth is more than subtle wit. *Dr. Walter Smith.*

What makes all doctrines plain and clear ? / About two hundred pounds a year. / And that which was prov'd true before / Prove false again, two hundred more. *Butler.*

What makes life dreary is the want of motive. *George Eliot.*

What makes lovers never tire of each others' society is that they talk always about themselves. *La Roche.*

What makes many so discontented with their own condition is the absurd estimate they form of the happiness of others. *Fr.* (?)

What makes old age so sad is, not that our 40 joys, but that our hopes then cease. *Jean Paul.*

What makes people discontented with their condition is the chimerical idea they conceive of the happiness of others. *Thomson.*

What makes vanity so insufferable to us is that it wounds our own. *La Roche.*

What man dare do, in circumstances of danger, an Englishman will. His virtues seem to sleep in the calm, and are called out only to combat the kindred storm. *Goldsmith.*

What man dare, I dare. *Macb., iii. 4.*

What man didst thou ever know unthrift, that 45 was beloved after his means ? *Timon of Athens, iv. 3.*

What man has done, man can do. *Emerson.*

What man wants is always that the highest in his nature be set at the top and actively reign there. *Carlyle.*

What matter though I doubt at every pore . . . / If finally I have a life to show, / The thing I did, brought out in evidence / Against the thing done to me underground / By hell and all its brood, for aught I know? *Browning.*

What matters it though the Gospels contradict each other if the Gospel does not contradict itself? *Goethe.*

What matters it whether the alphabet (by which you are to spell out the meaning of life) be in large gilt letters or in small ungilt ones, so you have an eye to read it? *Carlyle.*

5 What may be dune at ony time will be dune at nae time. *Sc. Pr.*

What men prize most is a privilege, even if it be that of chief mourner at a funeral. (?)

What men usually say of misfortunes, that they never come alone, may with equal truth be said of good fortune; nay, of other circumstances which gather round us in a harmonious way, whether it arise from a kind of fatality, or that man has the power of attracting to himself things that are mutually related. *Goethe.*

What men want is not talent; it is purpose. *Bulwer Lytton.*

What millions died that Cæsar might be great! *Campbell.*

10 What must be, shall be. *Rom. and Jul.*, iv. 1.

What Nature does not reveal to thy spirit, thou wilt not wrench from her with levers and screws. *Goethe.*

What need the bridge much broader than the flood? The fairest grant is the necessity; look, what will serve is fit. *Much Ado*, i. 1.

What need we have any friends, if we should never have need of them? *Timon of Athens*, i. 2.

What needs my Shakespeare for his honour'd bones? *Milton.*

15 What of books? Hast thou not already a Bible to write and publish in print that is eternal, namely, a Life to lead? *Carlyle.*

What once were vices are now the manners of the day. *Sen.*

What people call her (England's) history is not hers at all; but that of her kings (though the history of them is worth reading), or the tax-gatherers employed by them, which is as if people were to call Mr. Gladstone's history or Mr. Lowe's, yours or mine. *Ruskin.*

What perils on a woman's life may throng, / Sitting lonely with her thoughts, that chafe and murmur like the surf! *Dr. Walter Smith.*

What persons are by starts, they are by nature. You see them at such times off their guard. Habit may restrain vice, and virtue may be obscured by passion, but intervals best discover the man. *Sterne.*

20 What profit is it for men now to live in heaviness, and after death to look for punishment? *Apocrypha.*

What proves the hero truly great, / Is never, never to despair. *Thomson.*

What quite infinite worth lies in Truth! how all-pervading, omnipotent, in man's mind is the thing we name Belief! *Carlyle.*

What rage for fame attends both great and small! / Better be damned than mentioned not at all. *John Wolcot.*

What rein can hold licentious wickedness / When down the hill he holds his fierce career? *Hen. V.*, iii. 3.

What religion do I profess! None of all you 25 name to me. Why none? Out of respect to religion. *Schiller.*

What right have you, O passer-by-the-way, to call any flower a weed? Do you know its merits, its virtues, its healing qualities? Because a thing is common, shall you despise it? If so, you might despise the sunshine for the same reason. *Anon.*

What rights are his that dare not strike for them? *Tennyson.*

"What says Lord Warwick? Shall we after them?" "After them! Nay, before them if we can." *2 Hen. VI.*, v. 3.

What shadows we are, and what shadows we pursue! *Burke.*

What shall be, shall be—that is all; / To one 30 great Will we stand and fall, / "The Scheme hath need"—we ask not why, / And in this faith we live or die. *Lewis Morris.*

What shapest thou here at the world; 'Tis shapen long ago; / The Maker shaped it, He thought it best even so. / Thy lot is appointed, go follow its hest; / Thy journey's begun, thou must move and not rest; / For sorrow and care cannot alter thy case, / And running, not raging, will win thee the race. *Goethe.*

What signifies the life o' man / An' twerna for the lasses, O? *Burns.*

What signifies the loss of a Hercules even to the loss of an idea? *Ed.*

What signifies your gear? / A mind that's scrimpit never wants some care. *Allan Ramsay.*

What should a wise man do if he is given a 35 blow? What Cato did when some one struck him on the mouth;—not fire up or revenge the insult, or even return the blow, but simply ignore it. *Sen.*

What skills it if a bag of stones or gold / About thy neck do drown thee? Raise thy head; / Take stars for money; stars not to be told / By any art, yet to be purchased. *George Herbert.*

What stronger breastplate than a heart untainted! *2 Hen. VI.*, iii. 2.

What the eye does not admire, / The heart does not desire. *Pr.*

What the eye don't see, the heart don't grieve. *Pr.*

What the fool does in the end, the wise man 40 does at the beginning. *It. Pr.*

What the heart has once owned and had, it shall never lose. *Ward Beecher.*

What the heart or the imagination dictates always flows readily; but where there is no subject to warm or interest these, constraint appears. *Blair.*

What the light of your mind pronounces incredible, that, in God's name, leave uncredited. *Carlyle.*

What the Maker sends us remains mysteriously with us after the bearer of it is dead and gone ; and we, as we "mourn over, long for, and love distant and departed" goodness, are more embraced and possessed by it than we were when it was present with us only in the flesh, and we could look upon it and handle it. *Ed.*

What the poet has to cultivate above all things is love and truth ;—what he has to avoid, like poison, is the fleeting and the false. *Leigh Hunt.*

What the Puritans gave the world was not thought, but action. *Wendell Philips.*

What the universe was thought to be in Judea and other places, this may be very interesting to know ; what it is in England here where we live and have our work to do, that is the interesting point. *Carlyle.*

5 What thou seest is not there on its own account, strictly taken, is not there at all. *Carlyle.*

What though care killed a cat : thou hast mettle enough in thee to kill care. *Much Ado, v. i.*

What though on hamely fare we dine, / Wear hodden gray, and a' that ? / Gie fools their silk, and knaves their wine, / A man's a man for a' that. *Burns.*

Wh.t though our songs to wit have no preten·e, / The fiddlestick shall scrape them into sense. *(?)*

What though success will not attend on all ! / Who bravely dares must sometimes risk a fall. *Smollett.*

10 What though the field be lost? / All is not lost ; th' unconquerable will, / And study of revenge, immortal hate, / And courage never to submit or yield. *Milton.*

What though the foot be shackled ; the heart is free. *Goethe.*

What, though thou wert rich and of high esteem, dost thou yield to sorrow because of thy loss of fortune? *Hitopadesa.*

What tragic wastes of gloom / Curtain the soul that strives and sins below ! *R. Garnet.*

What trifling silliness is the childish fondness of the every-day children of the world ! 'Tis the unmeaning toying of the younglings of the fields and forests. *Burns.*

15 What 'twas weak to do, / 'Tis weaker to lament, once being done. *Shelley.*

What unknown seas of feeling lie in man, and will from time to time break through ! *Carlyle.*

What was my morning's thought, at night's the same ; / The poor and rich but differ in the name. / Content's the greatest bliss we can procure / Frae 'boon the lift ; without it kings are poor. *Allan Ramsay.*

What was once to me / Mere matter of the fancy, now has grown / The vast necessity of heart and life. *Tennyson.*

What we are going to, is abundantly obscure ; but what all men are going from, is very plain. *John Sterling.*

20 What we are, that only can we see. *Emerson.*

What we call conscience, in many instances, is only a wholesome fear of the constable. *Bovee.*

What we call our root-and-branch reforms of slavery, war, gambling, intemperance, is only medicating the symptoms. We must begin higher up, namely, in education. *Emerson.*

What we do determine oft we break, / Purpose is but the slave to memory. *Ham., iii. 2.*

What we do not understand we have no business to judge. *Amiel.*

What we do not use is a heavy burden. 25 *Goethe.*

What we don't know is just what we need to know ; and what we do know we can make no use of. *Goethe.*

What we foolishly call vastness is not more wonderful or not more impressive than what we insolently call littleness. *Ruskin.*

What we have been makes us what we are. *George Eliot.*

What we have in us of the image of God is the love of truth and justice. *Demosthenes.*

What we have we prize not to the worth, / 30 Whiles we enjoy it ; but being lack'd and lost, / Why then we rack the value. *Much Ado, iv. i.*

What we hope ever to do with ease we may learn first to do with diligence. *Johnson.*

What we like determines what we are, and is the sign of what we are. *Ruskin.*

What we need most is not so much to realise the ideal as to idealise the real. *F. H. Hedge.*

What we poor mortals have to do is to endure and keep ourselves upright as well as and long as we can. God disposes as he thinks best. *Goethe.*

What we pray to ourselves for is always 35 granted. *Emerson.*

What we truly and earnestly aspire to be, that in some sense we are. The mere aspiration, by changing the frame of the mind, for the moment realises itself. *Mrs. Jameson.*

What we want to be pleased with flattery, is to believe that the man is sincere who gives it us. *Steele.*

What we want to believe, what it suits our convenience, or pleasure, or prejudice to believe, one need not go to sea to learn what slender logic will incline us to believe. *Burroughs.*

What? wearied out with half a life ? / Scared with this smooth unbloody strife ? / Think where thy coward hopes had flown / Had Heaven held out the martyr's crown. *Kebel.*

What were mighty Nature's self ? / Her 40 features could they win us, / Unhelp'd by the poetic voice / That hourly speaks within us ? *Wordsworth.*

What will not woman, gentle woman, dare, / When strong affection stirs her spirit up ? *Southey.*

What will you have ? quoth God ; pay for it and take it. *Pr.*

What you can't get is just what suits you. *Fr. Pr.*

What you do not risk all to part with (*dahingeben*), thou hast not loved and possessed entirely. *J. G. Fisher.*

What you enjoy is yours ; what for your heirs / 45 You hoard, already is not yours, but theirs. *From the Greek. Anon.*

What you see is but the smallest part / And least proportion of humanity ; / . . . Were the whole frame here, / It is of such a spacious lofty pitch, / Your roof were not sufficient to contain it. *i Hen. VI., ii. 3.*

What your heart thinks great is great. The soul's emphasis is always right. *Emerson.*

What's aught but as 'tis valued? *Troil. and Cress.*, ii. 2.

What's come to perfection perishes. / Things learned on earth we shall practise in heaven ; / Works done least rapidly art most cherishes. *Browning.*

What's done cannot be undone. *Macb.*, v. 1.

5 What's done we partly may compute, / But know not what's resisted. *Burns.*

What's fitting, that is right. *Goethe.*

What's gone and what's past help / Should be past grief. *Winter's Tale*, iii. 2.

What's good for the bee is good for the hive. *Pr.*

What's Hecuba to him or he to Hecuba, / That he should weep for her? *Ham.*, ii. 2.

10 What's impossible cannot be, / And never, never comes to pass. *George Colman the younger.*

What's in a name? That which we call a rose / By any other name would smell as sweet. *Rom. and Jul.*, ii. 2.

What's more miserable than discontent? *2 Hen. VI.*, iii. 1.

What's nane o' my profit will be nane o' my peril. *Sc. Pr.*

What's not set about to-day is never finished on the morrow. *Goethe.*

15 What's the good of a sun-dial in the shade? *Pr.*

What's the good of the pipe if it's not played on? *Gael. Pr.*

What's yours is mine, and what's mine's my ain. *Sc. Pr.*

Whate'er disturbs his onward course, / Whate'er brings gloom or strife, / It must away, for e'er he sings / The poet must have life. *Goethe.*

Whate'er he did was done with so much ease, / In him alone 'twas natural to please. *Dryden.*

20 Whate'er my future years may be : / Let joy or grief my fate betide ; / Be still an Eden bright to me / My own, my own fireside ! *A. A. Watts.*

Whate'er's begun in anger ends in shame. *Ben. Franklin.*

Whatever a man has to effect must emanate from him as a second self; and how would this be possible were not his first self entirely pervaded by it ? *Goethe.*

Whatever be the cause of happiness, may be made likewise the cause of misery. The medicine which, rightly applied, has power to cure, has, when rashness or ignorance prescribes it, the same power to destroy. *Johnson.*

Whatever be the motive of insult, it is always best to overlook it ; for folly scarcely can deserve resentment, and malice is punished by neglect. *Johnson.*

25 Whatever beauty may be, it has for its basis order and for its essence unity. *Father André.*

Whatever befalls us, though it is wise to be serious, it is useless and foolish, and perhaps sinful, to be gloomy. *Johnson.*

Whatever bit of a wise man's work is honestly and benevolently done, that bit is his book or his piece of art. *Ruskin.*

Whatever comes from the brain carries the hue of the place it came from ; and whatever comes from the heart carries the heat and colour of its birthplace. *Holmes.*

Whatever comes out of despair cannot bear the title of valour, which should be lifted up to such a height that, holding all things under itself, it should be able to maintain its greatness even in the midst of miseries. *Sir P. Sidney.*

Whatever crushes individuality is despotism, 30 by whatever name it may be called. *J. S. Mill.*

Whatever disunites man from God disunites man from man. *Burke.*

Whatever does not concern us is concealed from us. *Emerson.*

Whatever does not possess a true intrinsic vitality cannot live long, and can neither be nor ever become great. *Goethe.*

Whatever expands the affections or enlarges the sphere of our sympathies, whatever makes us feel our relation to the universe, and all that it inherits, in time and in eternity, to the great and beneficent Cause of all, must unquestionably refine our nature and elevate us in the scale of being. *Channing.*

Whatever foolish people read, does them 35 harm ; and whatever they write, does other people harm. *Ruskin.*

Whatever government is not a government of law is a despotism, let it be called what it may. *D. Webster.*

Whatever has exceeded its due bounds is ever in a state of instability. *Sen.*

Whatever hath been well consulted and well resolved, whether it be to fight well or to run away well, should be carried into execution in due season, without any further examination. *Hitopadesa.*

Whatever honour we can pay to their memory, is all that is owing to the dead. Tears and sorrow are no duties to them, and make us incapable of those we owe to the living. *Lady Montagu.*

Whatever in literature, art, or religion is done 40 for money is poisonous itself, and doubly deadly in preventing the hearing or seeing of the noble literature and art which have been done for love and truth. *Ruskin.*

Whatever is beautiful is also profitable. *Willmott.*

Whatever is best is safest, lies most out of the reach of human power, can neither be given nor taken away. *Bolingbroke.*

Whatever is graceful is virtuous, and whatever is virtuous is graceful. *Cic.*

Whatever is great in human art is the expression of man's delight in God's work. *Ruskin.*

Whatever is great promotes cultivation as 45 soon as we are aware of it. *Goethe.*

Whatever is highest and holiest is tinged with melancholy. The eye of genius has always a plaintive expression, and its natural language is pathos. A prophet is sadder than other men ; and He who was greater than all prophets was "a man of sorrow and acquainted with grief." *Mrs. Child.*

Whatever is, is right. *Pope.*

Whatever is known to thyself alone has always very great value. *Emerson.*

Whatever is natural admits of variety. *Mme. de Staël.*

Whatever is new is unlooked for, and ever it mends some and impairs others ; and he that is holpen takes it for a fortune, and he that is hurt for a wrong. *Bacon.*

Whatever is not made of asbestos will have to be burnt in this world. *Carlyle.*

Whatever is pure is also simple. It does not keep the eye on itself. The observer forgets the window in the landscape it displays. A fine style gives the view of fancy—its figures, its trees, or its palaces—without a spot. *Willmott.*

5 Whatever is worth doing at all is worth doing well. *Lord Chesterfield.*

Whatever lifts a man out of the common herd always redounds to his advantage, even if it sink him into a new crowd, in the midst of which his powers of swimming and wading must be put to the test again. *Goethe.*

Whatever makes religion its second object, makes it no object. *Ruskin.*

Whatever may be the natural propensity of any one, it is very hard to overcome. If a dog were made king, would he not gnaw his shoe-straps ? *Hitopadesa.*

Whatever may happen, every kind of fortune is to be overcome by bearing it. *Virg.*

10 Whatever may happen to thee, it was prepared for thee from all eternity ; and the complication of causes was from eternity spinning the thread not only of thy being, but of that which is incident to it. *Marcus Aurelius.*

Whatever mitigates the woes or increases the happiness of others, this is my criterion of goodness ; and whatever injures society at large, or any individual in it, this is my measure of iniquity. *Burns.*

Whatever of goodness emanates from the soul, gathers its soft halo from the eyes ; and if the heart be the lurking-place of crime, the eyes are sure to betray the secret. *F. Saunders.*

Whatever our wanderings, our happiness will always be found within a narrow compass, and amidst the objects more immediately within our reach. *Bulwer Lytton.*

Whatever outward thing offers itself to the eye, is merely the garment or body of a thing which already existed invisibly within. *Carlyle.*

15 Whatever purifies the heart, fortifies it. *Blair.*

Whatever sceptic could inquire for, / For every why he had a wherefore. *Butler.*

Whatever that be which thinks, which understands, which wills, which acts, it is something celestial and divine ; and upon that account must necessarily be eternal. *Cic.*

Whatever the benefits of fortune are, they yet require a palate fit to relish and taste them ; it is fruition, and not possession, that renders us happy. *Montaigne.*

Whatever the place allotted to us by Providence, that for us is the post of honour and duty. *T. Edwards.*

20 Whatever the skill of any country may be in the sciences, it is from its excellence in polite learning alone that it must expect a character from posterity. *Goldsmith.*

Whatever theologians may choose to assert, it is certain that mankind at large has far more virtue than vice. *Buckle.*

Whatever these two men (the Carlyles, father and son) touched with their hands in honest toil became sacred to them, a page out of their own lives. A silent, inarticulate kind of religion they put into their work. *John Burroughs.*

Whatever we think out, whatever we take in hand to do, should be perfectly and finally finished, that a word, if it must alter, will only tend to spoil it ; we have then nothing to do but to unite the severed, to recollect and restore the dismembered. *Goethe.*

Whatever you are, be a man. *Pr.*

Whatever you may think now, they (the deeds 25 of each day) are only biding their time ; and when you are weak and at their mercy, when the world. you fancied you were beyond, has leisure to hear their story and scoff at you, they will come forward and tell all the bitter tale. *Disraeli to young men.*

Whatso we have done is done, and for us annihilated, and ever must we go and do anew. *Carlyle.*

Whatsoever a man ought to obey, he cannot but obey. *Carlyle.*

Whatsoever a man soweth, that shall he also reap. *St. Paul.*

Whatsoever God doeth, nothing can be put to it, nor anything taken from it. *Ecclus.*

Whatsoever sensibly exists, whatsoever re- 30 presents spirit to spirit, is properly a suit of raiment put on for a season and to be laid off. *Carlyle.*

Whatsoever thine ill, / It must be borne, and these wild starts are useless. *Byron.*

Whatsoever thou takest in hand, remember the end, and thou shalt never do amiss. *Ecclus.*

Whatsoever thy hand findeth to do, do it with thy might. *Bible.*

When a base man means to be your enemy, he always begins with being your friend. *Wm. Blake.*

When a bold man is out of countenance, he 35 makes a very wooden figure on it. *Collier.*

When a child can be brought to tears, not from fear of punishment, but from repentance for his offence, he needs no chastisement. When the tears begin to flow from grief at one's own conduct, be sure there is an angel nestling in the bosom. *Horace Mann.*

When a gentleman is cudgelling his brain to find any rhyme for sorrow besides "borrow" or "to-morrow," his woes are nearer at an end than he thinks. *Thackeray.*

When a good man has talent, he always works morally for the salvation of the world. *Goethe.*

When a great man strikes out into a sudden irregularity, he needs not question the respect of a retinue. *Collier.*

When a head and a book come into collision, 40 and one sounds empty, is it always the book ? *Lichtenberg.*

When a husband is embraced without affection, there must be some reason for it. *Hitopadesa.*

When a man becomes dear to me, I have touched the goal of fortune. *Emerson.*

When a man dies, they who survive him ask what property he has left behind. The angel who bends over the dying man asks what good deeds he has sent before him. *Koran.*

When a man gives himself up to the government of a ruling passion—or, in other words, when his hobby-horse grows headstrong—farewell cool reason and fair discretion! *Sterne.*

When a man gives proof that his heart is sound and that his life is sound, there is no divergence of opinion that should keep us from fellowship with him. *Ward Beecher.*

When a man has no occasion to borrow, he finds numbers willing to lend him. *Goldsmith.*

5 When a man has not a good reason for doing a thing, he has one good reason for letting it alone. *Scott.*

When a man has once forfeited the reputation of his integrity, he is set fast; and nothing will then serve his turn, neither truth nor falsehood. *Tillotson.*

When a man is base at the heart, he blights his virtues into weaknesses; but when he is true at the heart, he sanctifies his weaknesses into virtues. *Ruskin.*

When a man is conscious that he does no good himself, the next thing is to cause others to do some. *Pope.*

When a man is going downhill, everybody gives him a kick. *Pr.*

10 When a man is in indigence, picking herbs is his philosophy; the enjoyment of his wife his only commerce, and vassalage his food. *Hitopadesa.*

When a man is in love with one woman in a family, it is astonishing how fond he becomes of every person connected with it. *Thackeray.*

When a man is treated with solemnity, he looks upon himself as a higher being, and goes through his solemn feasts devoutly. *Jean Paul.*

When a man is wrong and won't admit it, he always gets angry. *Haliburton.*

When a man lives with God, his voice shall be as sweet as the murmur of the brook and the rustle of the corn. *Emerson.*

15 When a man mistakes his thoughts for persons and things, this is madness. *Coleridge.*

When a man smiles, and much more when he laughs, it adds something to his fragment of life. *Sterne.*

When a man versed in his subject treats any topic lovingly and thoroughly, he gives us a share in his interest, and forces us to enter into the topic. *Goethe.*

When a man's dog deserts him on account of his poverty, he can't get any lower down in this world. *Amer. Pr.*

When a man's pride is subdued, it is like the sides of Mount Ætna. It was terrible during the eruption, but when that is over and the lava is turned into soil, there are vineyards and olive-trees which grow up to the top. *Beecher.*

20 When a man's ways please the Lord, he maketh even his enemies to be at peace with him. *Bible.*

When a mean wretch cannot vie with another in virtue, out of his wretchedness he begins to slander. *Saadi.*

When a misfortune is impending, I cry, "God forbid!" but when it falls upon me, I say, "God be praised!" *Sterne.*

When a noble life has prepared old age, it is not the decline that it recalls, but the first days of immortality. *Mme. de Staël.*

When a nobleman writes a book he ought to be encouraged. *Johnson.*

When a pepin is planted on a pepin-stock, the 25 fruit growing thence is called a renate, a most delicious apple, as both by sire and dame well descended. Thus his blood must needs be well purified who is gentilely born on both sides. *Fuller.*

When a poor creature (outwardly and visibly such) comes before thee, do not stay to inquire whether the "seven small children," in whose name he implores thy assistance, have a veritable existence. *Lamb.*

When a Sark-foot wife gets on her broomstick, the dames of Allonby are ready to mount. *Pr.*

When a secret is revealed, it is the fault of the man who has intrusted it. *La Bruyère.*

When a thought is too weak to be simply expressed, it is a clear proof that it should be rejected. *Vauvenargues.*

When a thought of Plato becomes a thought 30 to me,—when a truth that fired the soul of Pindar fires mine, time is no more. *Emerson.*

When a tree is dead it will lie any way; alive, it will have its own growth. *Ward Beecher.*

When a true genius appears in the world you may know him by this sign, that the dunces are all in confederacy against him. *Swift.*

When a wife has a good husband it is easily seen in her face. *Goethe.*

When a wise man findeth an occasion, he may bear away his enemy upon his shoulder, as it were. *Hitopadesa.*

When a woman wears the breeches, she has a 35 good right to them. *Amer. Pr.*

When a work has a unity, it is as much so in a part as in the whole. *Wm. Blake.*

When a writer sets to work again after a long pause, his faculties have, as it were, to be caught in the field and brought in and harnessed. *Froude.*

When a youth is fully in love with a girl, and feels that he is wise in loving her, he should at once tell her so plainly, and take his chance bravely with other suitors. *Ruskin.*

When Adam dolve and Eve span, / Who was then the gentleman? *Pr.*

When affliction thunders over our roofs, to 40 hide our heads and run into our graves shows us no men, but makes us fortune's slaves. *Ben Jonson.*

When all else is lost, the future still remains. *Bovee.*

When all is done, the help of good counsel is that which setteth business straight. *Bacon.*

When all is said, the greatest art is to limit and isolate one's self. *Goethe.*

When all the blandishments of life are gone, / The coward sneaks to death, the brave live on. *George Sewell.*

When ambitious men find an open passage, they are rather busy than dangerous; and if well watched in their proceedings, they will catch themselves in their own snare, and prepare a way for their own destruction. *Quarles.*

When an author is too fastidious about his style, you may presume that his mind is frivolous and his matter flimsy. *Sen.*

When any fit of anxiety, or gloominess or perversion of the mind, lays hold upon you, make it a rule not to publish it by complaints, but exert your whole care to hide it; by endeavouring to hide it you will drive it away. *Johnson.*

When any man finds himself disposed to complain with how little care he is regarded, let him reflect how little he contributes to the happiness of others. *Johnson.*

5 When any one ceases to care for his home, it is one of the worst possible signs of moral sickness. *Spurgeon.*

When any one has offended me, I try to raise my soul so high that the offence cannot reach it. *Descartes.*

When at one with ourselves, we are so with others. *Goethe.*

When bad men combine, the good must associate; else they will fall one by one, an unpitied sacrifice in a contemptible struggle. *Burke.*

When bairns are young they gar their parents' heads ache; when they are auld they make their hearts break. *Sc. Pr.*

10 When baseness is exalted, do not bate / The place its honour for the person's sake. *George Herbert.*

When beggars die, there are no comets seen; / The heavens themselves blaze forth the death of princes. *Jul. Cæs.*, ii. 2.

When brothers part for manhood's race, / What gift may most endearing prove / To keep fond memory in her place, / And certify a brother's love? / . . . No fading frail memorial give / To sooth his soul when thou art gone, / But wreathes of hope for aye to live, / And thoughts of good together done. *Keble.*

When caught by a tempest, wherever it be, / If it lightens and thunders, beware of a tree. *Pr.*

When children stand quiet, they have done some harm. *Pr.*

15 When children, we are sensualists; when in love, idealists. *Goethe.*

When clouds appear like rocks and towers, / The earth's refreshed with frequent showers. *Pr.*

When clouds appear, wise men put on their cloaks; / When great leaves fall, the winter is at hand. *Rich. III.*, ii. 3.

When death comes, it is never our tenderness that we repent of, but our severity. *George Eliot.*

When desperate ills demand a speedy cure, distrust is cowardice and prudence folly. *Johnson.*

20 When did friendship take / A breed for barren metal of his friend? *Mer. of Ven.*, i. 2.

When difficulties are overcome they become blessings. *Saying.*

When each comes forth from his mother's womb, the gate of gifts closes behind him. *Emerson.*

When every one minds his own business the work is done. *Dan. Pr.*

When firmness is sufficient, rashness is unnecessary. *Napoleon.*

When fools fall out for every flaw, / They run 25 horn mad to go to law; / A hedge awry, a wrong plac'd gate, / Will serve to spend a whole estate. *Saying.*

When Fortune means to men most good, / She looks upon them with a threatening eye. *King John*, iii. 1.

When found, make a note of. *Dickens.*

When fresh sorrows have caused us to take some steps in the right way, we may not complain. We have invested in a life annuity, but the income remains. *Mme. Swetchine.*

When friends meet hearts warm. *Sc. Pr.*

When friendships are real, they are not glass 30 threads or frost-work, but the solidest things we know. *Emerson.*

When God gives light he gives it for all. *Sp. Pr.*

When God will, no wind but brings rain. *Pr.*

When God would punish a land, he deprives its rulers of wisdom. *Ger. and It. Pr.*

When Goethe says that in every human condition foes lie in wait for us, "invincible save by cheerfulness and equanimity," he does not mean that we can at all times be really cheerful, or at a moment's notice; but that the endeavour to look at the better side of things will produce the habit, and that this habit is the surest safeguard against the danger of sudden evils. *Leigh Hunt.*

When Greeks joined Greeks, then was the 35 tug of war. *Lee.*

When griping grief the heart doth wound, / And doleful dumps the mind oppress, / Then music, with her silver sound, / With speedy help doth lend redress. *Rom. and Jul.*, iv. 5.

When half-gods go, / The gods arrive. *Emerson.*

When he speaks, / The air, a charter'd libertine, is still. *Hen. V.*, i. 1.

When holy and devout religious men / Are at their beads, 'tis hard to draw them thence. *Rich. III.*, iii. 7.

When I am angry, I can pray well and preach 40 well. *Luther.*

When I consider life, 'tis all a cheat. / Yet fool'd with hope, men favour the deceit; / Trust on, and think to-morrow will repay. / To-morrow's falser than the former day; / Lies worse, and while it says we shall be blest / With some new joys, cuts off what we possest. *Dryden.*

When I have told the truth, my part with it is done; and if the world will not listen, the world will just do the other way. *Carlyle.*

When I hear music, I fear no danger. I am invulnerable. I see no foe. I am related to the earliest times and to the latest. *H. D. Thoreau.*

When I strove after wisdom I appeared foolish to fools, and wise when I lived like them. The fool only esteems himself wise. *Bodenstedt.*

When I want any good head-work done, I always choose a man, if suitable otherwise, with a long nose. *Napoleon.*

When I was happy I thought I knew men, but it was fated that I should know them in misfortune only. *Napoleon.*

When I wish to ascertain the real felicity of any rational man, I always inquire whom he has to love. If I find he has nobody, or does not love those he has, I pronounce him a being deep in adversity. *Mrs. Inchbald.*

When I'm not thanked at all, I'm thank'd enough ; / I've done my duty, and I've done no more. *Henry Fielding.*

5 When ilka ane gets his ain, the thief will get the widdie (gallows). *Sc. Pr.*

When in company, people will rather be entertained than instructed. *Knegge.*

When, in your last hour (think of this), all faculty in the broken spirit shall fade away and sink into inanity—imagination, thought, effort, enjoyment—then will the flower of belief, which blossoms even in the night, remain to refresh you with its fragrance in the last darkness. *Jean Paul.*

When industry builds upon nature, we may expect pyramids. *Sir T. Browne.*

When it goeth well with the righteous, the city rejoiceth : and when the wicked perish, there is shouting. *Bible.*

10 When it rains porridge, the beggar has no spoon. *Dan. Pr.*

When it's dark at Dover, / It is dark all the world over. *Pr.*

When labour is employed, labour can consume ; when it is not employed, it cannot consume. *Daniel Webster.*

When love begins to sicken and decay / It useth an enforced ceremony. *Jul. Cæs.*, iv. 2.

When love cools our fauts are seen. *Sc. Pr.*

15 When love speaks, the voice of all the gods / Makes heaven drowsy with the harmony. *Love's L. Lost*, iv. 3.

When lovely woman stoops to folly / And finds, too late, that men betray, / What charm can soothe her melancholy ? / What art can wash her guilt away ? *Goldsmith.*

When loving hearts are separated, not the one which is exhaled to heaven, but the survivor it is which tastes the sting of death. *Duchesse de Praslin.*

When maidens sue, / Men give like gods. *Meas. for Meas.*, i. 1.

When man arrives at his highest perfection, he will (as at the creation) be again dumb. *Hawthorne.*

20 When man seized the loadstone of science, the loadstar of superstition vanished in the clouds. *W. R. Alger.*

When matters are desperate, we must put on a desperate face. *Burns.*

When men add a new wing to their house they do not call the action virtue, but if they give to a fellow-creature for their own gratification, they demand of God a good mark for it. *J. M. Barrie.*

When men are lonely they stoop to any companionship. *Lew Wallace.*

When men are pure, laws are useless ; when men are corrupt, laws are broken. *Disraeli.*

When men grow virtuous in their old age, 25 they only make a sacrifice to God of the devil's leavings. *Pope.*

When monarch reason sleeps, this mimic wakes. *Dryden.*

When money's taken, / Freedom's forsaken. *Pr.*

When musing on companions gone, / We doubly feel ourselves alone. *Scott.*

When nations are to perish in their sins, / 'Tis in the Church the leprosy begins ; / The priest, whose office is, with zeal sincere, / To watch the fountain and preserve it clear, / Carelessly nods and sleeps upon the brink, / While others poison what the flock must drink. *Cowper.*

When Nature fills the sails, the vessel goes 30 smoothly on ; and when judgment is the pilot, the insurance need not be high. *Sir T. Browne.*

When Nature is sovereign there is no need of austerity or self-denial. *Froude.*

When Nature removes a great man, people explore the horizon for a successor ; but none comes, and none will. *Emerson.*

When need is highest, help is nighest. *Ger. Pr.*

When neither he to whom we speak nor he who speaks to us understands, that is metaphysics. *Voltaire.*

When nothing is enjoyed, can there be greater 35 waste ? *Thomson.*

When on life we're tempest driven, / A conscience but a canker, / A correspondence fixed wi' heaven / Is sure a noble anchor. *Burns.*

When once a man is determined to believe, the very absurdity of the doctrine confirms him in his faith. *Junius.*

When once infidelity can persuade men that they shall die like beasts, they will soon be brought to live like beasts also. *South.*

When once our grace we have forgot, / Nothing goes right ; we would, and we would not. *Meas. for Meas.*, iv. 4.

When once the young heart of a maiden is 40 stolen, / The maiden herself will steal after it soon. *Moore.*

When once you profess yourself a friend, endeavour to be always such. He can never have any true friends that will be often changing them. (?)

When one does nothing else but while time away, it must of necessity often be a burden. *Goethe.*

When one encourages the beautiful alone, and another encourages the useful alone, it takes them both to form a man. *Goethe.*

When one is in love, one wishes to be in fetters. *Goethe.*

When one is not received as one comes, this 45 is a nether-fire pain. *Goethe.*

When one is truly in love, one not only says it, but shows it. *Longfellow.*

When one is young, one is nothing completely. *Goethe.*

When one thinks of the real agony one has gone through in consequence of false teaching, it makes human nature angry with the teachers who have added to the bitterness of life. *General Gordon.*

When our actions do not, / Our fears do make us traitors. *Macb.*, iv. 1.

When our hatred is too keen, it places us beneath those we hate. *La Roche.*

When our names are blotted out, and our place knows us no more, the energy of each social service will remain. *J. Morley.*

When people complain of life, it is almost always because they have asked impossible things from it. *Renan.*

5 When people laugh at their own jokes, their wit is very small beer, and is lost in its own froth. *Spurgeon.*

When people once are in the wrong, / Each line they add is much too long. *Prior.*

When Peter's cock begins to crow, 'tis day. *Quarles.*

When pleasure can be had, it is fit to catch it. *Johnson.*

When pleasure is arrived, it is worthy of attention ; when trouble presenteth itself, the same. Pain and pleasures have their revolutions like a wheel. *Hitopadesa.*

10 When poverty comes in at the door, love flies out at the window. *Pr.*

When pride cometh, then cometh shame ; but with the lowly is wisdom. *Bible.*

When remedies are past, the griefs are ended / By seeing the worst, which late on hopes depended. *Othello*, i. 3.

When rich villains have need of poor ones, poor ones may make what price they will. *Much Ado*, iii. 3.

When rogues fall out, honest men get their own. *Pr.*

15 When shall we three meet again, in thunder, lightning, or in rain? *Macb.*, i. 1.

When soldiers have been baptized in the fire of a battlefield, they have all one rank in my eyes. *Napoleon.*

When soon or late they reach that coast, / O'er life's rough ocean driven, / May they rejoice, no wanderer lost, / A family in heaven. *Burns.*

When sorrows come, they come not single spies, / But in battalions. *Ham.*, iv. 5.

When speech is given to a soul holy and true, time and its dome of ages becomes as a mighty whispering-gallery, round which the imprisoned utterance runs, and reverberates forever. *James Martineau.*

20 When sun is set the little stars will shine. *R. Southwell.*

When that the poor have cried, Cæsar hath wept ; / Ambition should be made of sterner stuff. *Jul. Cæs.*, iii. 2.

When the affections are moved there is no place for the imagination. *Hume.*

When the artist forgets himself in admiration of his work, there is a fatal inversion and subversion of all art whatsoever; and for Love to worship Venus, his own creation, except as an index and light to himself, is in reality Love's apostasy, not his apotheosis. *Ed.*

When the ass is given thee, run and take him by the halter; and when good luck knocks at the door, let him in, and keep him there. *Sp. Pr.*

25 When the belly is empty, the body becomes spirit ; when it is full, the spirit becomes body. *Saadi.*

When the blind lead the blind, both shall fall into the ditch; wherefore, in such circumstances, may it not sometimes be safer if both leader and led simply sit still? *Carlyle.*

When the blood burns, how prodigal the soul / Lends the tongue vows. *Ham.*, i. 3.

When the cat's away, / The mice will play. *Pr.*

When the devil dies, he never lacks a chief mourner. *Pr.*

When the fight begins within himself, / A 30 man's worth something. *Browning.*

When the fox preaches, take care of your geese. *Pr.*

When the glede's in the blue cloud, / The laverock lies still; / When the hound's in the green wood, / The hind keeps the hill. *Old ballad.*

When the gods come among men, they are not known. *Emerson.*

When the great God lets loose a thinker on this planet, then all things are at risk. There is not a piece of science, but its flank may be turned to-morrow; there is not any literary reputation, nor the so-called eternal names of fame, that may not be revised and condemned. *Emerson.*

When the heart is afire, some sparks will fly 35 out at the mouth. *Pr.*

When the heart is heavy and low, / The beauty that on earth we find, / Or strain of music on the wind, / Shall touch it like an utter woe ! *Dr. W. Smith.*

When the heart is still agitated by the remains of a passion, we are more ready to receive a new one than when we are entirely cured. *La Roche.*

When the heart of a man is sincere and tranquil, he is fain to enjoy nothing but himself; every movement, even corporeal movement, shakes the brimming nectar cup too rudely. *Jean Paul.*

When the hungry curate licks the knife, there is not much for the clerk. *Pr.*

When the man's fire and the wife's tow, in comes 40 the deil and blaws it in a lowe (flame). *Sc. Pr.*

When the master passeth over all alike without distinction, then the endeavours of those who are capable of exertion are entirely lost. *Hitopadesa.*

When the million applaud you, seriously ask yourself what harm you have done ; when they censure you, what good. *Colton.*

When the mind's free, the body's delicate. *Lear*, iii. 4.

When the new light which we beg for shines in upon us, there be who envy and oppose, if it come not in first at their casements. *Milton.*

When the oak-tree is felled, the whole forest 45 echoes with it; but a hundred acorns are planted silently by some unnoticed breeze. *Carlyle.*

When the Phœnix is fanning her funeral pyre, will there not be sparks flying? *Carlyle.*

When the power of imparting joy / Is equal to the will, the human soul / Requires no other heaven. *Shelley.*

When the quality of bravery is near, a great man's terrors are at a distance. In the hour of misfortune such a great man overcometh bravery. *Hitopadesa.*

When the reason of old establishments is gone, it is absurd to keep nothing but the burden of them. This is superstitiously to embalm a carcase not worth an ounce of the gums that are used to embalm it. *Burke.*

When the sheep is too meek, all the lambs suck it. *Spurgeon.*

When the shore is won at last, / Who will count the billows past? *Keble.*

When the soul breathes through a man's intellect, it is genius; when it breaks through his will, it is virtue; when it flows through his affection, it is love. *Emerson.*

5 When the strong box contains no more, . . . / Both friends and flatterers shun the door. *Plutarch.*

When the sun is highest, he casts the least shadow. *Pr.*

When the tale of bricks is doubled, then comes Moses. *Heb. Pr.*

When the weather been maist fair, the dust flies highest in the air. *Sir David Lindsay.*

When the will's ready the feet's licht. *Sc. Pr.*

10 When the wind (civic tumult) arises, worship the echo (retire into the country). *Pythagoras.*

When the world has once got hold of a lie, it is astonishing how hard it is to get it out of the world. You beat it about the head, till it seems to have given up the ghost, and lo! the next day it is as healthy as ever. *Bulwer Lytton.*

When they will not give a doit to relieve a lame beggar, they will lay out ten to see a dead Indian. *Tempest*, ii. 2.

When things are at their worst, they will mend. *Pr.*

When things are once come to the execution, there is no secrecy comparable to celerity, like the motion of a bullet in the air, which flieth so swift as it outruns the eye. *Bacon.*

15 When thou dost purpose ought within thy power, / Be sure to do it, though it be but small. *George Herbert.*

When thou hast thanked thy God for every blessing sent, / What time will then remain for murmurs or lament? *French.*

When thou makest presents, let them be of such things as will last long; to the end they may be in some sort immortal, and may frequently refresh the memory of the receiver. *Fuller.*

When thou wishest to give thyself delight, think of the excellencies of those who live with thee; the energy of one, the modesty of another, the liberal kindness of a third. *Marcus Aurelius.*

When three know it, all know it. *Pr.*

20 When thy judgments are in the earth the inhabitants of the world will learn righteousness. *Bible.*

When Time, who steals our years away, / Shall steal our pleasures too, / The mem'ry of the past will stay, / And half our joys renew. *T. Moore.*

When timorous knowledge stands considering, / Audacious ignorance hath done the deed. *Daniel.*

When, to gratify a private appetite, it is once resolved upon that an innocent and a helpless creature shall be sacrificed, 'tis an easy matter to pick up sticks enough from any thicket where it has strayed to make a fire to offer it up with. *Sterne.*

When two brethren strings are set alike, / To move them both but one of them we strike. *Cowley.*

When two friends have a common purse, one 25 sings and the other weeps. *Pr.*

When two friends part, they should lock up one another's secrets and exchange their keys. *Owen Feltham.*

When two loving hearts are torn asunder, it is a shade better to be the one that is driven away into action, than the bereaved twin that petrifies at home. *Charles Reade.*

When unadorn'd, adorn'd the most. *Thomson.*

When was a god found agreeable to everybody? *Carlyle.*

When we are exalted by ideas, we do not owe 30 this to Plato, but to the idea, to which also Plato was debtor. *Emerson.*

When we build (public edifices), let us think that we build for ever. *Ruskin.*

When we cannot get at the very thing we wish, never to take up with the next best in degree to it, that's pitiful beyond description. *Sterne.*

When we can't do as we would, we must do as we can. *Pr.*

When we destroy an old prejudice, we have need of a new virtue. *Mme. de Staël.*

When we discern justice, when we discern 35 truth, we do nothing of ourselves; we allow a passage to its beams. *Emerson.*

When we have broken our god of tradition, and ceased from our god of rhetoric, then may God fire the heart with his presence. *Emerson.*

When we have not what we love, we must love what we have. *Bussy-Rabutin.*

When we meet with a natural style, we are surprised and delighted, for we expected to find an author, and we have found a man. *Pascal.*

When we our betters see bearing our woes, / We scarcely think our miseries our foes. *King Lear*, iii. 6.

When we rise in knowledge, as the prospect 40 widens, the objects of our regard become more obscure, and the unlettered peasant, whose views are only directed to the narrow sphere around him, beholds nature with a finer relish, and tastes her blessings with a keener appetite, than the philosopher whose mind attempts to grasp a universal system. *Goldsmith.*

When we take people merely as they are, we make them worse; when we treat them as if they were what they should be, we improve them as far as they can be improved. *Goethe.*

When whins are out of bloom, kissing is out of fashion. *Pr.*

When wine is in, nature comes out. *George Meredith.*

When words are scarce they're seldom spent in vain, / For they breathe truth that breathe their words in pain. *Rich. II.*, ii. 1.

When words end, music begins; when they 45 suggest, it realises. *Haweis.*

When worthy men fall out, only one of them may be faulty at the first; but if strife continue long, commonly both become guilty. *Fuller.*

When you are all agreed upon the time, quoth the vicar, I'll make it rain. *Pr.*

When you are compelled to choose between two hated evils, look both full in the face, and choose that which least hampers the spirit and fetters pious deeds. *Goethe.*

When you are down, poverty, like snow-shoes, keeps your feet fast and prevents your rising. *Amer. Pr.*

When you are in doubt abstain. *Zoroaster.*

5 When you are predetermined to take one soul's advice, act without consulting further with any soul living. *Sterne.*

When you are stung by slanderous tongues (die Lästerzunge), comfort yourself with this thought : it is not the worst fruits that are gnawed by wasps. *G. A. Bürger.*

When you cannot get dinner ready, put the clock back. *Swift.*

When you do not know what to do, it is a clear indica·:ion that you are to do nothing. *Spurgeon.*

When you find yourselves tempted, be sure to ask advice ; and when you see another so, deal with him gently. *Thomas à Kempis.*

10 When you go to Rome, do as Rome does. *St. Ambrose of Milan.*

When you grind your corn, give not the flour to the devil, and the bran to God. *It. Pr.*

When you have bought one fine thing, you must buy ten more to be all of a piece. *Ben. Franklin.*

When you have got so much true knowledge as is worth fighting for, you are bound to fight or to die for it, but not to debate about it any more. *Ruskin.*

When you have nothing to say, say nothing. *Colton.*

15 When you hear that your neighbour has picked up a purse of gold in the street, never run out into the same street, looking about you, in order to pick up such another. *Goldsmith.*

When you introduce a moral lesson, let it be brief. *Hor.*

When you know a thing, to hold that you know it ; and when you do not know a thing, to allow that you do not know it : this is knowledge. *Confucius.*

When you leave the unimpaired hereditary freehold to your children, you do but half your duty. Both liberty and property are precarious, unless the possessors have sense and spirit enough to defend them. *Junius.*

When you lie down with a short prayer, commit yourself into the hands of your faithful Creator ; and when you have done, trust Him with yourself as you must do when you are dying. *Jeremy Taylor.*

20 When you organise a strike, it is war you organise ; / But to organise our labour were the labour of the wise. *Dr. Walter Smith.*

When you see a man with a great deal of religion displayed in his shop-window, you may depend upon it he keeps a very small stock of it within. *Spurgeon.*

When you see a snake, never mind where he came from. *Pr.*

When you see a woman paint, your heart needna faint. *Sc. Pr.*

When your broth's ready-made for you, you mun swallow the thickenin', or else let the broth alone. *George Eliot.*

When your head did but ache, / I knit my 25 handkerchief about your brows, / The best I had ; a princess wrought it me ; / And I did never ask it you again. *King John,* iv. 1.

Whence ? O Heavens, whither ? Sense knows not ; faith knows not ; only that it is through mystery to mystery, from God to God. *Carlyle on the drama of life.*

Whene'er a noble deed is wrought, / Whene'er is spoken a noble thought, / Our hearts, in glad surprise, / To higher levels rise. *Longfellow.*

Whenever a man talks loudly against religion, always suspect that it is not his reason, but his passions, which have got the better of his creed. A bad life and a good belief are disagreeable and troublesome neighbours ; and when they separate, depend upon it, 'tis for no other cause but quietness' sake. *Sterne.*

Whenever a separation is made between liberty and justice, neither is, in my opinion, safe. *Burke.*

Whenever I see a new-married couple more 30 than ordinarily fond before faces, I consider them as attempting to impose upon the company or themselves ; either hating each other heartily, or consuming that stock of love in the beginning of their course which should serve them throughout their whole journey. *Goldsmith.*

Whenever the offence inspires less horror than the punishment, the rigour of penal law is obliged to give way to the common feelings of mankind. *Gibbon.*

Whenever the people flock to see a miracle, it is a hundred to one but that they see a miracle. *Goldsmith.*

Whenever you find humour, you find pathos close by its side. *Whipple.*

Whensoever a man desireth anything inordinately, he is presently disquieted in himself. *Thomas à Kempis.*

Where content is there is a feast. *Pr.* 35

Where do we find ourselves ? In a series of which we do not know the extremes, and believe that it has none. *Emerson.*

Where drink goes in, wit goes out. *Pr.*

Where else is the God's presence manifested, not to our eyes only, but to our hearts, as in our fellow-men ? *Carlyle.*

Where envying and strife is, there is confusion and every evil work. *St. James.*

Where friends are in earnest, each day brings 40 its own gain, so that at last the year, when summed up, is of incalculable advantage. Details in reality constitute the life ; results may be valuable, but they are more surprising than useful. *Goethe.*

Where God gives, envy harms not ; and where he gives not, no labour avails. *L. Pr.*

Where God has built a church, there the devil would also build a chapel. *Luther.*

Where God helps, nought harms. *Pr.*

Where have they who are running here and there in search of riches such happiness as those placid spirits enjoy who are gratified at the immortal fountain of happiness ? *Hitopadesa.*

Where I am, there every one is. *Rabbi Hillel.*

Where idolatry ends, Christianity begins ; and where idolatry begins, Christianity ends. *Jacobi.*

Where ignorance is bliss, / Tis folly to be wise. *Gray.*

Where is any author in the world / Teaches such beauty as a woman's eye? *Love's L. Lost*, iv. 3.

5 Where is the good of having a right to make both yourself and your neighbours miserable? . . . Mutual accommodation is the law of the world, or its inhabitants would all be wretched together. *Mrs. Gatty.*

Where is the man who has the power and skill / To stem the torrent of a woman's will? / For if she will, she will, you may depend on't ; / And if she won't, she won't, and there's an end on't. *Dane John Monument at Canterbury.*

Where it is weakest, the thread breaketh. *Pr.*

Where law ends, tyranny begins. *Fielding.*

Where lies are easily admitted, the father of lies will not easily be excluded. *Quarles.*

10 Where love reigns, disturbing jealousy doth call himself affection's sentinel. *Shakespeare.*

Where man is, are the tropics ; where he is not, the ice-world. *Ruskin.*

Where Nature's end of language is declined, / And men talk only to conceal the mind. (?)

Where no counsel is, the people fall : but in the multitude of counsellers there is safety. *Bible.*

Where no fault is, there needs no pardon. *Pr.*

15 Where no hope is left, is left no fear. *Milton.*

Where no oxen are, the crib is clean. *Pr.*

Where no wood is, there the fire goeth out : so where there is no tale-bearer, the strife ceaseth. *Bible.*

Where none thou canst discern, make for thyself a path. *Goethe.*

Where once Truth's flame has burnt, I doubt / If ever it go fairly out. *Hannah More.*

20 Where one is wise, two are happy. *Pr.*

Where one man shapes his life by precept and example, there are a thousand who have it shaped for them by impulse and by circumstances. *Lowell.*

Where one member suffers, all the members suffer with it. *St. Paul.*

Where peace / And rest can never dwell, hope never comes, / That comes to all. *Milton.*

Where people are tied for life, 'tis their mutual interest not to grow weary of one another. *Lady Montagu.*

25 Where power is absent we may find the robe of genius, but we miss the throne. *Landor.*

Where secrecy or mystery begins, vice or roguery is not far off. *Johnson.*

Where shame is, there is fear. *Milton.*

Where the carcase is, the ravens will gather. *Pr.*

Where the devil cannot come, he will send. *Ger. Pr.*

30 Where the devil has smoothed your road, / Keep to the right like an honest man. *Dr. W. Smith.*

Where the greater malady is fix'd, / The lesser is scarce felt. *King Lear*, iii. 4.

Where the heart goes before, like a lamp, and illumines the pathway, many things are made clear that else lie hidden in darkness. *Longfellow.*

Where the heart is, there the Muses, there the gods sojourn. *Emerson.*

Where the meekness of self-knowledge veileth the front of self-respect, there look thou for the man whose name none can know but they will honour. *Tupper.*

Where there is a mother in the home, matters 35 speed well. *A. B. Alcott.*

Where there is a splashing of dirt, it is good not to meddle and to keep far away. *Hitopadesa.*

Where there is much light there is a darker shadow. *Goethe.*

Where there is music, nothing really bad can be. *Cervantes.*

Where there is mystery, it is generally supposed that there must also be evil.

Where there is no envy in the case, our pro- 40 pensity to sympathise with joy is much stronger than our propensity to sympathise with sorrow. *Adam Smith.*

Where there is no hook, to be sure there will hang no bacon. *Sp. Pr.*

Where there is no hope, there can be no endeavour. *Johnson.*

Where there is no law, there is no transgression. *St. Paul.*

Where there is no love, all are faults. *Pr.*

Where there is no shame, there is no honour. 45 *Pr.*

Where there is no sympathy with the spirit of man, there can be no sympathy with any higher spirit. *Ruskin.*

Where there is smoke there is fire. *Pr.*

Where there is too much light, our senses don't perceive ; they are only stunned or dazzled or blinded. *Pascal.*

Where there's a will there's a way. *Pr.*

Where there's muckle courtesy there's little 50 kindness. *Sc. Pr.*

Where truth is not at the bottom, Nature will always be endeavouring to return, and will peep out and betray herself one time or other. *Tillotson.*

Where two or three are gathered together in my name, there am I in the midst of them *Jesus.*

Where vice is, vengeance follows. *Sc. Pr.*

Where virtue dwells, the gods have placed before / The dropping sweat that springs from every pore, / And ere the feet can reach her bright abode, / Long, rugged, steep the ascent, and rough the road. *Hesiod.*

Where we find echoes, we generally find 55 emptiness and hollowness ; it is the contrary with the echoes of the heart. *J. F. Boyes.*

Where wealth and freedom reign, contentment fails, / And honour sinks where commerce long prevails. *Goldsmith.*

Where wilt thou go that thou wilt not have to plough? *Sp. Pr.*

Where Wisdom steers, wind cannot make you sink. *Delaune.*

Where words are scarce, they are seldom spent in vain. *Rich. II.*, ii. 2.

Where would be what silly people call Progress if not for the grumblers? *John Wagstaffe.*

Where you see your friend, trust to yourself. *Sp. Pr.*

Where your treasure is, there will your heart be also. *Jesus.*

5 Where your will is ready, your feet are light. *Pr.*

Where's the use of a woman's having brains of her own if she's tackled to a geck as everybody's a-laughing at? *George Eliot.*

Whereas Johnson only bowed to every clergyman, I would bow to every man, were it not there is a devil dwells in man as well as a divinity, and too often the bow is but pocketed by the former. *Carlyle.*

Where'er I wander, boast of this I can, / Though banished, yet a true-born Englishman. *Rich. II.*, i. 3.

Where'er we tread, 'tis haunted, holy ground. *Byron.*

10 Wherever a man dwells he will be sure to have a thorn-bush near his door. *Pr.*

Wherever a true woman comes, home is always around her. The stars may be over her head, the glow-worms in the night-cold grass may be the fire at her feet; but home is where she is; and for a noble woman it stretches far around her, better than houses ceiled with cedar or painted with vermilion, shedding its quiet light far for those who else are homeless. *Ruskin.*

Wherever in the world I am, / In whatsoe'er estate, / I have a fellowship with hearts / To keep and cultivate. *A. L. Waring.*

Wherever nature does least, man does most. *Amer. Pr.*

Wherever snow falls, there is usually civil freedom. *Emerson.*

15 Wherever the devil makes a purchase, he never fails to set his mark. *Goldsmith.*

Wherever the health of the citizens is concerned, much more where their souls' health, and as it were their salvation, is concerned, all governments that are not chimerical make haste to interfere. *Carlyle.*

Wherever the speech is corrupted the mind is also. *Sen.*

Wherever the tree of beneficence takes root, it sends forth branches beyond the sky. *Saadi.*

Wherever there is a parliament, there must of necessity be an opposition. *John Wagstaffe.*

20 Wherever there is a sky above him and a world around him, the poet is in his place; for here too is man's existence, with its infinite longings and small acquirings; its ever-thwarted, ever-renewed endeavours; its unspeakable aspirations, its fears and hopes that wander through eternity; and all the mystery of brightness and gloom that it was ever made of, in any age or climate, since man first began to live. *Carlyle.*

Wherever there is authority, there is a natural inclination to disobedience. *Judge Halyburton.*

Wherever there is cupidity, there the blessing of the Gospel cannot rest. The actual poor, therefore, may altogether fail to be objects of that blessing, the actual rich may be the objects of it in the highest degree. *Matthew Arnold.*

Wherever there is power there is age. *Emerson.*

Wherever there is war, there must be injustice on one side or the other, or on both. *Ruskin.*

25 Wherever women are honoured, the gods are satisfied. *Manu.*

Wherever work is done, victory is obtained. *Emerson.*

Wherever you see a gaming-table, be very sure Fortune is not there. . . . She is ever seen accompanying industry, and as often trundling a wheelbarrow as lolling in a coach and six. *Goldsmith.*

Wherever your lot is cast, duty to yourself and others suggests the propriety of adapting your conduct to the circumstances in which you are placed. *Samuel Lover.*

Wherefore ever ramble on? / For the good is lying near. / Fortune learn to seize alone, / For that Fortune's ever here. *Goethe.*

30 Wherefore waste I time to counsel thee / That art a votary to fond desire? *Two Gent. of Verona*, i. 1.

Wherein does barbarism consist, unless in not appreciating what is excellent? *Goethe.*

Wheresoever a man seeketh his own, there he falleth from love. *Thomas à Kempis.*

Wheresoever the carcass is, there will the eagles be gathered together. *Jesus.*

Wheresoever the search after truth begins, there life begins; wheresoever the search ceases, there life ceases. *Ruskin.*

35 Wheresoever two or three living men are gathered together, there is society; or there it will be, with its mechanisms and structures, over-spreading this little globe, and reaching upwards to Heaven and downwards to Gehenna. *Carlyle.*

Whereto serves mercy, / But to confront the visage of offence? / And what's in prayer, but this twofold force,—to be forestalled ere we come to fall, / Or pardon'd, being down? / Then I'll look up. *Ham.*, iii. 3.

Whether a child, or an old man, or a youth, be come to thy house, he is to be treated with respect; for of all men, thy guest is the superior. *Hitopadesa.*

Whether a revolution succeeds or fails, men of great hearts will always be sacrificed to it. *Heine.*

Whether he be rich or whether he be poor, if he (a man) have a good heart, he shall at all times rejoice in a cheerful countenance; his mind shall tell him more than seven watchmen that sit above upon a tower on high. *Ecclus.*

40 Whether it be for life or death, do your own work well. *Ruskin.*

Whether one show one's self a man of genius in science or compose a song, the only point is, whether the thought, the discovery, the deed, is living and can live on. *Goethe.*

Whether religion be true or false, it must be necessarily granted to be the only wise principle and safe hypothesis for a man to live and die by. *Tillotson.*

Whether the pitcher strike the stone or the stone the pitcher, it is bad for the pitcher. *Pr.*

Whether you boil snow or pound it, you can have but water of it. *Pr.*

Which death is preferable to every other? "The unexpected." *Cæsar.*

Which highest mortal, in this inane existence, had I not found a shadow-hunter or shadow-hunted ; and, when I looked through his brave garnitures, miserable enough? *Carlyle.*

5 Which is the great secret? The open secret (open, that is, to all, seen by almost none). *Goethe.*

Which is the lightest in the scale of Fate? / That where fond Cupid still is adding weight. *Quarles.*

Which of all the philosophies think you will stand? / I know not, but philosophy itself I hope will continue with us for ever. *Schiller.*

Which of your philosophical systems is other than a dream-theorem ; a net quotient, confidently given out, where divisor and dividend are both unknown? *Carlyle.*

Which way I fly is hell ; myself am hell ; / And in the lowest deep a lower deep, / Still threat'ning to devour me, opens wide, / To which the hell I suffer seems a heaven. *Milton.*

10 Whichever you do, you will regret it. *Socrates, to one who asked him whether he should marry or not.*

While a man gēts he never can lose. *Sp. Pr.*

While conscience is our friend, all is peace ; but if once offended, farewell the tranquil mind. *Mary Wortley Montagu.*

While craving justice for ourselves, it is never wise to be unjust to others. *Lew Wallace.*

While digestion lasts, life cannot, in philosophical language, be said to be extinct. *Carlyle.*

15 While grief is fresh, every attempt to divert only irritates. You must wait till grief be digested, and then amusement will dissipate the remains of it. *Johnson.*

While manufacture is the work of hands only, art is the work of the whole spirit of man ; and as that spirit is, so is the deed of it. *Ruskin.*

While men sleep, / Sad-hearted mothers heave, that wakeful lie, / To muse upon some darling child / Roaming in youth's uncertain wild. *Keble.*

While mistakes are increasing, like population, at the rate of twelve hundred a-day, the benefit of seizing one and throttling it would be perfectly inconsiderable. *Carlyle.*

While others tippled, Sam from drinking shrunk, / Which made the rest think Sam alone was drunk. *Lucian.*

20 While the serpent sheds its old skin, the new is already formed beneath. *Carlyle.*

While there is hope left, let not the weakness of sorrow make the strength of resolution languish. *Sir P. Sidney.*

While thy shoe is on thy foot, tread upon the thorns. *Pr.*

While we are indifferent to our good qualities, we keep on deceiving ourselves in regard to our faults, until we come to look upon them as virtues. *Heine.*

While we are reasoning concerning life, life is gone. *Hume.*

While we think to revenge an injury, we many 25 times begin one, and after that repent our misconceptions. *Feltham.*

While you live, tell truth and shame the devil. *1 Hen. IV., iii. 1.*

Whilst a man confideth in Providence, he should not slacken his own exertions ; for without labour he is unworthy to obtain the oil from the seed. *Hitopadesa.*

Whilst lions war and battle for their dens, / Poor harmless lambs abide their enmity. *3 Hen. VI., ii. 5.*

Whilst we converse with what is above us, we do not grow old, but grow young. *Emerson.*

Whining lover may as well request / A scorn- 30 ful breast / To melt in gentle tears, as woo the world for rest. *Quarles.*

Whistle, and I'll come to ye, my lad. *Burns.*

Whistling aloud to bear his courage up. *Blair.*

White lies always introduce others of a darker complexion. *Paley.*

Who are wise in love, love most, say least. *Tennyson.*

Who ascends to mountain-tops, shall find / 35 The loftiest peaks most wrapt in clouds and snow. *Byron.*

Who, born for the universe, narrow'd his mind, / And to party gave up what was meant for mankind ; / Though fraught with all learning, yet straining his throat / To persuade Tommy Townshend to lend him a vote. *Goldsmith.*

Who bravely dares must sometimes risk a fall. *Smollett.*

Who breaks his own bond, forfeiteth himself. *George Herbert.*

Who breathes must suffer, and who thinks must mourn ; / And he alone is bless'd who ne'er was born. *Prior.*

Who builds a church to God and not to fame, / 40 Will never mark the marble with his name. *Pope.*

Who but the poet was it that first formed gods for us ; that exalted us to them, and brought them down to us? *Goethe.*

Who buys a minute's mirth to wail a week? / Or sells eternity to get a toy? *Shakespeare.*

Who by repentance is not satisfied / Is not of heaven, nor earth. *Two Gent. of Verona, v. 4.*

Who can be patient in extremes? · *3 Hen. VI., i. 1.*

Who can compute what the world loses in the 45 multitude of promising intellects combined with timid characters, who dare not follow out any bold, vigorous, independent train of thought, lest it should land them in something which would admit of being considered irreligious or immoral? *J. S. Mill.*

Who can direct when all pretend to know? *Goldsmith.*

Who can do nothing of sovran worth / Which men shall praise, a higher task may find, / Plodding his dull round on the common earth, / But conquering envies rising in the mind. *Dr. W. Smith.*

Who can find a virtuous woman? for her price is far above rubies. The heart of her husband doth safely trust in her, so that he shall have no need of spoil. She will do him good and not evil, all the days of her life. She looketh well to the ways of her household, and eateth not the bread of idleness. Her children arise up, and call her blessed. *Bible*.

Who can heal the woes of him to whom balm has become poison, who has imbibed hatred of mankind from the fulness of love? *Goethe*.

Who can say, I have made my heart clean, I am pure from my sin? *Bible*.

Who cannot rest till he good fellows find, / He breaks up house, turns out of doors his mind. *George Herbert*.

5 Who chatters to you, will chatter of you. *Pr*.

Who coldly lives to himself and his own will may gratify many a wish; but he who strives to guide others well must be able to dispense with much. *Goethe*.

Who combats bravely is not therefore brave, / He dreads a death-bed like the meanest slave; / Who reasons wisely is not therefore wise,— / His pride in reasoning, not in acting lies. *Pope*.

Who could pin down a shadow to the ground, / And take its measure? *Dr. W. Smith*.

Who digs a pit for others falls into it himself. *Ger. Pr*.

10 Who does not act is dead; absorpt entire / In miry sloth, no pride, no joy he hath: / O leaden-hearted men, to be in love with death! *Thomson*.

Who does not help us at the needful moment never helps; who does not counsel at the needful moment never counsels. *Goethe*.

Who does not in his friends behold the world, / Deserves not that the world should hear of him. *Goethe*.

Who does the best his circumstance allows, / Does well, does nobly; angels could no more. *Young*.

Who doth not work shall not eat. *Pr*.

15 Who ever loved that loved not at first sight? *Marlowe*.

Who fastest walks, but walks astray, / Is only farthest from his way. *Prior*.

Who fears death forfeits life. *Seume*.

Who fears to do ill sets himself a task; / Who fears to do well sure should wear a mask. *Herbert*.

Who feels injustice, who shrinks before a slight, who has a sense of wrong so acute, and so glowing a gratitude for kindness, as a generous boy? *Thackeray*.

20 Who firmly can resolve, he conquers grief. *Goethe*.

Who follows all things forfeiteth his will. *George Herbert*.

Who forces himself on others is to himself a load. Impetuous curiosity is empty and inconstant. Prying intrusion may be suspected of whatever is little. *Lavater*.

Who gets by play proves loser in the end. *Heath*.

Who gives a trifle meanly is meaner than the trifle. *Lavater*.

Who gives the lilies clothing, / Will clothe his 25 people too. *Cowper*.

Who goes a-borrowing, goes a-sorrowing. *Pr*.

Who had hoped for triumph, but who was prepared for sacrifice. *I. Disraeli*.

Who has a daring eye tells downright truths and downright lies. *Lavater*.

Who has a head will not want a hat. *It. Pr*.

Who has not felt how sadly sweet / The dream 30 of home, the dream of home, / Steals o'er the heart, too soon to fleet, / When far o'er sea or land we roam? / Sunlight more soft may o'er us fall, / To greener shores our bark may come; / But far more bright, more dear than all, / That dream of home, that dream of home. *Moore*.

Who hath a greater combat than he that laboureth to overcome himself? *Thomas à Kempis*.

Who hath not known ill fortune never knew himself or his own virtue. *Mallet*.

Who here with life would sport, / In life shall prosper never; / And he who ne'er will rule himself, / A slave shall be for ever. *Goethe*.

Who, in the midst of just provocation to anger, instantly finds the fit word which settles all around him in silence, is more than wise or just; he is, were he a beggar, of more than royal blood—he is of celestial descent. *Lavater*.

Who in want a hollow friend doth try, / 35 Directly seasons him his enemy. *Ham., iii. 2*.

Who is a stranger to those who have the habit of speaking kindly. *Hitopadesa*.

Who is sure he hath a soul, unless / It see and judge, and follow worthiness, / And by deeds praise it? He who doth not this / May lodge an inmate soul, but 'tis not his. *Donne*.

Who is sure of his own motives can with confidence advance or retreat. *Goethe*.

Who is the best captain of a ship? The grumbler and the man of discipline, who will have things as they ought to be, even though he lose every sailor serving under him by his severity. *John Wagstaffe*.

Who is the best general? The grumbler who 40 insists upon having everything in mathematical order, and who has not the smallest drop of the milk of human kindness about him, whenever it is a question of duty or efficiency. *John Wagstaffe*.

Who is the happiest man? He who is alive to the merit of others, and can rejoice in their enjoyment as if it were his own. *Goethe*.

Who is the most sensible man? He who finds what is to his own advantage in all that happens to him. *Goethe*.

Who is there almost, whose mind at some time or other, love or anger, fear or grief, has not so fastened to some clog that it could not turn itself to any other object? *Locke*.

Who is there that can clutch into the wheel-spokes of destiny, and say to the spirit of the time: Turn back, I command thee? Wiser were it that we yielded to the inevitable and inexorable, and accounted even this the best. *Carlyle*.

Who is't can say, I'm at the worst? / I'm worse than ere I was, / And worse I may be yet; the worst is not, / So long as we can say, / This is the worst. *Lear*, iv. 1.

Who judgeth well, well God them send ; / Who judgeth evil, God them amend. *Sir Thomas Wyatt.*

Who keeps no guard upon himself is slack, / And rots to nothing at the next great thaw. *George Herbert.*

Who kills a man kills a reasonable creature, but he who kills a good book kills reason itself. *Milton.*

5 Who knows art half, speaks much and is always wrong; who knows it wholly, inclines to act, and speaks seldom or late. *Goethe.*

Who knows not that truth is strong, next to the Almighty? She needs no politics, nor stratagems, nor licensings to make her victorious ; those are the shifts and the defences that error uses against her power ; give her but room and do not bind her when she sleeps. *Milton.*

Who knows the mind has the key to all things else. *A. B. Alcott.*

Who knows what Love is, may not sup / On that which is not still divine. *Dr. W. Smith.*

Who leaves all receives more. *Emerson.*

10 Who looks not before finds himself behind. *Pr.*

Who loves his own sweet shadow in the streets / Better than e'er the fairest she he meets. *Burns.*

Who loves me, loves my dog. *L. Pr.*

Who loves, raves. *Byron.*

Who made the heart, 'tis He alone / Decidedly can try us ; / He knows each chord, its various tone, / Each spring, its various bias. / Then at the balance let's be mute, / We never can adjust it ; / What's done we partly may compute, / But know not what's resisted. *Burns.*

15 Who make poor "will do" wait upon "I should;" / We own they're prudent, but who owns they're good? *Burns.*

Who marks in church-time others' symmetry, / Makes all their beauty his deformity. *George Herbert.*

Who never climbs will never fa'. *Sc. Pr.*

Who never doubted never half believed. *Bailey.*

Who overcomes / By force, hath overcome But half his foe. *Milton.*

20 Who pants for glory finds but short repose ; / A breath revives him or a breath o'erthrows. *Pope.*

Who plays for more / Than he can lose with pleasure, stakes his heart. *George Herbert.*

Who questioneth much, shall learn much, and content much. *Bacon.*

Who riseth from a feast / With that keen appetite that he sits down? / Where is the horse that doth untread again / His tedious measures with the unabated fire / That he did pace them first? All things that are / Are with more spirit chaséd than enjoy'd. *Mer. of Venice*, ii. 6.

Who say, I care not, those I give for lost ; / And to instruct them, 'twill not quit the cost. *George Herbert.*

Who seeks Him in the dark and cold, / With 25 heart that elsewhere finds no rest, / Some fringe of the skirts of God shall hold, / Though round his spirit the mists may fold, / With eerie shadows and fears untold. *Dr. W. Smith.*

Who shall be true to us, / When we are so unsecret to ourselves? *Troil. and Cress.*, iii. 2.

Who shall decide when doctors disagree, / And soundest casuists doubt, like you and me. *Pope.*

Who shall place / A limit to the giant's unchained strength, / Or curb his swiftness in the forward race? *W. C. Bryant.*

Who shall say that Fortune grieves him, / While the star of hope she leaves him? *Burns.*

Who should be trusted when one's right 30 hand / Is perjured to the bosom? *Two Gent. of Verona*, v. 4.

Who shuts love out shall be shut out from love. *Tennyson.*

Who so firm that cannot be seduced? *Jul. Cæs.*, i. 2.

Who so unworthy but may proudly deck him / With his fair-weather virtue, that exults / Glad o'er the summer main? The tempest comes, / The rough winds rage aloud; when from the helm / This virtue shrinks, and in a corner lies / Lamenting. *Thomson.*

Who soars too near the sun with golden wings melts them. *Shakespeare.*

Who speaks to the instincts speaks to the 35 deepest in man, and finds the readiest response. *A. B. Alcott.*

Who spouts his message to the wilderness, / Lightens his soul and feels one burden less ; / But to the people preach, and you will find / They'll pay you back with thanks ill to your mind. *Goethe, Prof. Blackie's translation.*

Who steals my purse steals trash ; 'tis something, nothing ; / 'Twas mine, 'tis his, and has been slave to thousands ; / But he that filches from me my good name, / Robs me of that which not enriches him, / And makes me poor indeed. *Othello*, iii. 3.

Who surpasses or subdues mankind / Must look down on the hate of those below. *Byron.*

Who the race of men doth love, / Loves also him above. *Lewis Morris.*

Who to dumb forgetfulness a prey, / This 40 pleasing anxious being e'er resign'd ; / Left the warm precincts of the cheerful day, / Nor cast one longing ling'ring look behind? *Gray.*

Who track the steps of glory to the grave. *Byron.*

Who trusts in God fears not his rod. *Goethe.*

Who values a good night's rest will not lie down with enmity in his heart if he can help it. *Sterne.*

Who values that anger which is consumed only in empty menaces? *Goldsmith.*

Who walks through fire will hardly heed the 45 smoke. *Tennyson.*

Who watches not catches not. *Dut. Pr.*

"Who will guard the guards?" says a Latin verse, — "Quis custodiet ipsos custodes?" I answer, "The enemy." It is the enemy who keeps the sentinel watchful. *Mme. Swetchine.*

Who will not mercy unto others show, / How can he mercy ever hope to have? *Spenser.*

Who would bear the whips and scorns of time, / The oppressor's wrong, the proud man's contumely, / The pangs of despised love, the law's delay, / The insolence of office and the spurns / That patient merit of the unworthy takes, / When he himself might his quietus make / With a bare bodkin? *Ham.,* iii. 1.

Who would check the happy feeling / That inspires the linnet's song? / Who would stop the swallow wheeling / On her pinions swift and strong? *Wordsworth.*

Who would fardels bear, / To grunt and sweat under a weary life, / But that the dread of something after death, / The undiscover'd country from whose bourn / No traveller returns, puzzles the will, / And makes us rather bear those ills we have / Than fly to others that we know not of? *Ham.,* iii. 1.

5 Whoever acquires knowledge but does not practise it, is as one who ploughs but does not sow. *Saadi.*

Whoever aims at doing or enjoying all and everything with his entire nature, whoever tries to link together all that is without him by such a species of enjoyment will only lose his time in efforts that can never be successful. *Goethe.*

Whoever can administer what he possesses, has enough, and to be wealthy is a burdensome affair, unless you understand it. *Goethe.*

Whoever can discern truth has received his commission from a higher source than the chiefest judge in the world, who can discern only law. *Thoreau.*

Whoever can make two ears of corn or two blades of grass grow where only one grew before, deserves better of mankind, and does more service to his country, than the whole race of politicians put together. *Swift.*

10 Whoever can turn his weeping eyes to heaven has lost nothing, for there above is everything he can wish for here below. He only is a loser who persists in looking down on the narrow plains of the present time. *Jean Paul.*

Whoever converses much among old books will be hard to please among new. *Temple.*

Whoever despises mankind will never get the best out of others or himself. *Tocqueville.*

Whoever does not respect confidence will never find happiness in his path. *Saying.*

Whoever fights, whoever falls, / Justice conquers evermore. *Emerson.*

15 Whoever gives himself to this (evil-speaking and evil-wishing), soon comes to be indifferent towards God, contemptuous towards the world, spiteful towards his equals; and the true, genuine indispensable sentiment of self-estimation corrupts into self-conceit and presumption. *Goethe.*

Whoever has lived twenty years ought to know how to order himself without physic. *Tiberius, quoted by Montaigne.*

Whoever has no fixed opinions has no constant feelings. *Joubert.*

Whoever has seen the masked at a ball dance amicably together, and take hold of hands without knowing each other, leaving the next moment to meet no more, can form an idea of the world. *Vauvenargues.*

Whoever has sixpence is sovereign over all men—to the extent of the sixpence; commands cooks to feed him, philosophers to teach him, kings to mount guard over him—to the extent of sixpence. *Carlyle.*

Whoever has so far formed his taste as to be 20 able to relish and feel the beauties of the great masters, has gone a great way in his study. *Joshua Reynolds.*

Whoever is a genuine follower of truth, keeps his eye steady upon his guide, indifferent whither he is lead, provided that she is the leader. *Burke.*

Whoever is in a hurry shows that the thing he is about is too big for him. Haste and hurry are very different things. *Chesterfield.*

Whoever is king, is also the father of his country. *Congreve.*

Whoever is out of patience is out of possession of his soul. *Bacon.*

Whoever may / Discern true ends will grow 25 pure enough / To love them, brave enough to strive for them, / And strong enough to reach them, though the road be rough. *E. B. Browning.*

Whoever perseveres will be crowned. *Herder.*

Whoever serves his country well has no need of ancestors. *Voltaire.*

Whoever sinks his vessel by overloading it, though it be with gold, and silver, and precious stones, will give his owner but an ill account of his voyage. *Locke.*

Whoever thinks a faultless piece to see, / Thinks what ne'er was, nor is, nor e'er shall be. *Pope.*

Whoever will thrust Magdalen into the pit 30 will find that he has dropped with her into the flames the key that should have opened heaven for him, and assuredly shall he remain outside until she, her purification completed, shall take pity on him and bring it thence. *Celia Burleigh.*

Whoever wishes to attain an English style, familiar but not coarse, and elegant but not ostentatious, must give his days and nights to the volumes of Addison. *Johnson.*

Whoever wishes to keep a secret must hide from us that he possesses one. *Goethe.*

Whoever would persuade men to religion both with art and efficacy, must found the persuasion of it upon this, that it interferes not with any rational pleasure, that it bids nobody quit the enjoyment of any one thing that his reason can prove to him ought to be enjoyed. *South.*

Whole, half, and quarter mistakes are very difficult and troublesome to correct and sift, and it is hard to set what is true in them in its proper place. *Goethe.*

Wholesome berries thrive and ripen best, / 35 Neighbour'd by fruit of baser quality. *Hen. V.,* i. 1.

Wholly a man of action, with speech subservient thereto. *Carlyle of his father.*

Whom God teaches not, man cannot. *Gael.*

Whom Heaven has made a slave, no parliament of men, nor power that exists on earth, can render free. *Carlyle.*

"Whom the gods love die young." was said of yore. *Byron.*

Whom the grandeur of his office elevates over other men will soon find that the first hour of his new dignity is the last of his independence. *Chancellor D'Aguesseau.*

Whom the heart of man shuts out, straightway the heart of God takes in. *Lowell.*

Whom well inspir'd the oracle pronounced / Wisest of men. *Milton, of Socrates.*

Whose faith has centre everywhere, / Nor cares to fix itself to form. *Tennyson.*

5 Whoso believes, let him begin to fulfil. *Carlyle.*

Whoso boasteth himself of a false gift is like clouds and wind without rain. *Bible.*

Whoso can look on death will start at no shadows. *Greek saying.*

Whoso can speak well is a man. *Luther.*

Whoso cannot obey cannot be free, still less bear rule ; he that is the inferior of nothing, can be the superior of nothing, the equal of nothing. *Carlyle.*

10 Whoso curseth his father or his mother, his lamp shall be put out in obscure darkness. *Bible.*

Whoso devours the substance of the poor will at length find in it a bone to choke him. *Fr. Pr.*

Whoso does not good, does evil enough. *Pr.*

Whoso findeth a wife findeth a good thing, and obtaineth favour of the Lord. *Bible.*

Whoso hath love in his heart hath spurs in his sides. *It. Pr.*

15 Whoso findeth me (Wisdom) findeth life, and shall obtain favour of the Lord. *Bible.*

Whoso hath skill in this art (music) is of a good temperament, fitted for all things. *Martin Luther.*

Whoso is not a misanthropist at forty can never have loved his kind. *Chamfort.*

Whoso keepeth the fig-tree shall eat the fruit thereof ; so he that waiteth on his master shall be honoured. *Bible.*

Whoso lives for humanity must be content to lose himself. *O. B. Frothingham.*

20 Whoso mocketh the poor reproacheth his Maker ; and he that is glad at calamities shall not be unpunished. *Bible.*

Whoso rewardeth evil for good, evil shall not depart from his house. *Bible.*

Whoso robbeth his father or his mother, and saith, It is no transgression, the same is the companion of a destroyer. *Bible.*

Whoso serves the public is a poor creature (*ein armes Thier*) ; he worries himself, and no one is grateful to him for his services. *Goethe.*

Whoso should combine the intrepid candour and decisive scientific clearness of Hume with the reverence, the love, and devout humility of Johnson, were the whole man of a new time. *Carlyle.*

25 Whoso stoppeth his ears at the cry of the poor, he also shall cry himself, but shall not be heard. *Bible.*

Whoso trusteth in the Lord, happy is he. *Bible.*

Whoso, without poetic frenzy, knocks at the doors of the Muses, presuming that his art alone will suffice to make him a poet, both he and his poetry are hopelessly thrown away. *Plato.*

Whoso would find God must bring him with him ; thou seest him in things outside of thee, only when he is within thee. *Rückert.*

Whoso would work aright must not concern himself about what is ill done, but only do well himself. *Goethe.*

Whoso would write clearly must think clearly, 30 and if he would write in a noble style, he must first possess a noble soul. *Goethe.*

Whosoever and whatsoever introduces itself and appears, in the firm earth of human business, or, as we well say, comes into existence, must proceed from the world of the supernatural ; whatsoever of a material sort deceases and disappears might be expected to go thither. *Carlyle.*

Whosoever forsaketh not all that he hath, cannot be my disciple. *Jesus.*

Whosoever has not seized the whole cannot yet speak truly (much less musically, concordantly) of any part. *Carlyle.*

Whosoever hath not patience, neither doth he possess philosophy. *Saadi.*

Whosoever hath his mind fraught with many 35 thoughts, his wits and understanding do clarify and break up, in the communicating and discoursing with another. He tosseth his thoughts more easily, he marshalleth them more orderly, he seeth how they look when they are turned into words ; finally, he waxeth wiser than himself. *Bacon.*

Whosoever, in the frame of his nature and affections, is unfit for friendship, he taketh it of the beast, and not from humanity. *Bacon.*

"Whosoever quarrels with his fate, does not understand it," says Bettine ; and among all her inspired sayings, she spoke none wiser. *Mrs. Child.*

Whosoever shall do the will of my Father which is in heaven, the same is my brother, and sister, and mother. *Jesus.*

Whosoever shall exalt himself shall be abased ; and he that humbleth himself shall be exalted. *Jesus.*

Whosoever shall not receive the kingdom of 40 God as a little child, he shall not enter therein. *Jesus.*

Whosoever will be great among you, let him be your servant. *Jesus to his disciples.*

Whosoever will save his life shall lose it ; and whosoever will lose his life for my sake shall find it. *Jesus.*

Why, all the souls that were, were forfeit once ; / And He that might the vantage best have took / Found out the remedy. How would you be / If He, which is the top of judgment, should / But judge you as you are ? *Meas. for Meas.*, ii. 2.

Why am I loth to leave this earthly scene ? / Have I so found it full of pleasing charms ? / Some drops of joy with draughts of ill between ; / Some gleams of sunshine 'mid renewing storms. *Burns.*

Why are taste (*Geschmack*) and genius so 45 seldom willing to unite ? The former is shy of power, the latter scorns restraint. *Schiller.*

Why complain of wanting light ? It is courage, energy, perseverance that I want. *Carlyle.*

Why do we discover faults so much more readily than perfections? *Mme. de Sévigné.*

Why do we pray to Heaven without setting our own shoulder to the wheel? *Carlyle.*

Why does it signify to us what they think of us after death, when our being has become only an empty sound? *Auerbach.*

Why does that hyssop grow there in the chink of the wall? Because the whole universe, sufficiently occupied otherwise, could not hitherto prevent its growing. It has the might and the right. *Carlyle.*

6 Why don't the men propose, mamma? / Why don't the men propose? *T. H. Bayly.*

Why dost thou try to find / Where charity doth flow? / Upon the waters cast thy bread, / Who eats it, who may know? *Goethe.*

Why has not man a microscopic eye? / For this plain reason—man is not a fly. *Pope.*

Why insist, ye heroes, against the will of Jupiter, in pressing a Hercules into your enterprise? Know ye not that for him there is quite other work appointed, which he must do all alone, and not another with him? *Ed.*

Why is it that Love must so often sigh in vain for an object, and Hate never? *Jean Paul.*

10 Why is it that we can better bear to part in spirit than in body, and, while we have the fortitude to act farewell, have not the nerve to say it? *Dickens.*

Why is there no man who confesses his vices? It is because he has not yet laid them aside. It is a waking man only who can tell his dreams. *Sen.*

Why, man, he doth bestride the narrow world / Like a Colossus, and we petty men / Walk under his huge legs and peep about / To find ourselves dishonourable graves. *Jul. Cæs.*, i. 2.

Why, nothing comes amiss, so money comes withal. *Tam. the Shrew*, i. 2.

Why rather, sleep, liest thou in smoky cribs, / Upon uneasy pallets stretching thee, / And hush'd with buzzing night-flies to thy slumber, / Than in the perfumed chambers of the great, / Under the canopies of costly state, / And lull'd with sounds of sweetest melody? *2 Hen. IV.*, iii. 1.

15 Why seek at once to dive into / The depth of all that meets your view? / Wait for the melting of the snow, / And then you'll see what lies below. *Prof. Blackie from Goethe.*

Why should a man, whose blood is warm within, / Sit like his grandsire cut in alabaster? *Mer. of Venice*, i. 1.

"Why should calamity be full of words?" / "Let them have scope; though what they do impart / Help not at all, yet do they ease the heart." *Rich. III.*, iv. 4.

Why should honour outlive honesty? *Othello*, v. 2.

Why should I make a shadow where God makes all so bright? *Dr. Walter Smith.*

20 Why should not conscience have vacation / As well as other courts o' th' nation? *Butler.*

Why should the Garment of Praise destroy the Spirit of Heaviness? Because an old woman cannot sing and cry at the same moment . . . one emotion destroys another. *Prof. Drummond.*

Why should the poor be flatter'd? / No, let the candied tongue lick absurd pomp, / And crook the pregnant hinges of the knee, / Where thrift may follow fawning. *Ham.*, iii. 2.

Why should thy satisfaction be placed upon a thing which makes thee not one whit the better or the worse? *Thomas à Kempis.*

Why should we crave a hallow'd spot? / An altar is in each man's cot, / A church in every grove that spreads / Its living roof above our heads. *Wordsworth.*

Why should we faint and fear to live alone, / 25 Since all alone, so Heaven has willed, we die, / Nor even the tenderest heart, and next our own, / Knows half the reasons why we smile or sigh? *Keble.*

Why should we go a-jaunting when the heart wants to repose. *Dr. Walter Smith.*

Why should we have any serious disgust at kitchens? Perhaps they are the holiest recesses of the house. There is the hearth, after all,—and the settle, and the fagots, and the kettle, and the crickets. They are the heart, the left ventricle, the very vital part of the house. *Thoreau.*

Why so large cost, having so short a lease, / Dost thou upon thy fading mansion spend? *Shakespeare.*

Why such heat (crushing superstition)? Other nonsense, quite equal to it, will be almost sure to follow. *Frederick the Great to Voltaire.*

Why tell me that a man is a fine speaker if it 30 is not the truth that he is speaking? If an eloquent speaker is not speaking the truth, is there a more horrid kind of object in creation? *Carlyle.*

Why, then, the world's mine oyster, / Which I with sword will open. *Merry Wives*, ii. 2.

Why, universal plodding prisons up / The nimble spirits in the arteries, / As motion and long-during action tires / The sinewy vigour of the traveller. *Love's L. Lost*, iv. 3.

Why, what should be the fear? / I do not set my life at a pin's fee; / And for my soul, what can it do to that, / Being a thing immortal as itself? *Ham.*, i. 4.

Wicked thoughts and worthless efforts gradually set their mark upon the face, especially the eyes. *Schopenhauer.*

Wickedness is its own punishment. *Quarles.* 35

Wickedness is voluntary frenzy, and every sinner does more extravagant things than any man that is crazed and out of his wits, only that he knows better what he does. *Tillotson.*

Wide is the gate, and broad is the way, that leadeth to destruction. *Jesus.*

Wide our world displays its worth, man's strife and strife's success, / All the good and beauty, wonder crowning wonder, / Till my heart and soul applaud perfection, nothing less. *Browning.*

Wide will wear, but tight will tear. *Pr.*

Wie alles sich zum Ganzen webt / Eins in 40 dem andern wirkt und lebt!—How everything weaves itself into the whole; one works and lives in the other. *Goethe.*

Wie bitter sind der Trennung Leiden!—How bitter are the pangs of parting! *Mozart.*

Wie das Auge, hat das Herz / Seine Sprache ohne Worte—The heart, like the eye, has its speech without words. *Bodenstedt.*

Wie das Gestirn, / Ohne Hast, / Aber ohne Rast, / Drehe sich jeder / Um die eigne Last—Like a star, without haste, yet without rest, let each one revolve round his own task. *Goethe.*

Wie der alte verbrennt, steigt der neue sogleich wieder aus der Asche hervor—(Our passions are true phœnixes ;) when the old one is burnt out, the new one rises straightway out of its ashes. *Goethe.*

Wie der Sternenhimmel still und bewegt—Like the starry heavens, still and in motion. *J. C. F. Hölderlin.*

5 Wie die Alten sungen, so zwitschern auch die Jungen—As the old birds sing, so will the young ones twitter.

Wie die Blumen die Erd', und die Sterne den Himmel / Zieren, so zieret Athen Hellas und Hellas die Welt — As the flowers adorn the earth and the stars the sky, so Athens adorns Greece, and Greece the world. *Herder.*

Wie ein Pfeil nach seinem Ziele fliegt des braven Mannes Wort—Like an arrow to its aim flies the good man's word. *Platen.*

Wie eng-gebunden des Weibes Glück !—How straitened is the lot of woman ! *Goethe.*

Wie fruchtbar ist der kleinste Kreis, / Wenn man ihn wohl zu pflegen weiss !—How fruitful the smallest space if we but knew how to cultivate it ! *Goethe.*

10 Wie gewonnen, so zerronnen—Easily gained, easily spent.

Wie ist das Menschenherz so klein ! / Und doch auch da zieht Gott herein— How small is the human heart, and yet even there God enters in. *W. Hey.*

Wie schränkt sich Welt und Himmel ein, / Wenn unser Herz in seinen Schranken banget !—How earth and heaven contract when our heart frets within its barriers ! *Goethe.*

Wie? Wann? und Wo? Die Götter bleiben stumm / Du halte dich ans Weil, und frage nicht Warum?—How? when? and where? the gods keep silence. Keep you to the "Because," and ask not "Why?" *Goethe.*

Wild ambition loves to slide, not stand ; / And Fortune's ice prefers to Virtue's land. *Dryden.*

15 Wilful waste makes woeful want. *Pr.*

Will a courser of the sun work softly in the harness of a dray-horse? His hoofs are of fire, and his path is through the heavens, bringing light to all lands ; will he lumber on mud highways, dragging ale for earthly appetites from door to door? *Carlyle on the career and sorrowful fate of Burns.*

Will all great Neptune's ocean wash this blood / Clean from my hand? No, this my hand will rather / The multitudinous seas incarnadine, / Making the green one red. *Macb.*, ii. 2.

Will is deaf, and hears no heedful friends. *Shakespeare.*

Will it, and set to work briskly. *Schiller.*

20 Will localises us ; thought universalises us. *Amiel.*

Will minus intellect constitutes vulgarity. *Schopenhauer.*

"Will-to-do," which is the spirit of the true God, is eternally incompatible with "wish-to-have," which is the proper spirit of the false. *Ed.*

Willing to wound, and yet afraid to strike, / Just hint a fault, and hesitate dislike. *Pope.*

Willows are weak, yet they bind other wood. *Pr.*

Willst du den Dichter verstehen, so lerne wie 25 Dichter empfinden—Wilt thou understand a poet, then learn to feel as a poet. *G. Keil.*

Willst du dich am Ganzen erquicken, / So musst du das Ganze im Kleinsten erblicken —Wilt thou strengthen thyself in the whole, then must thou see the whole in the least object. *Goethe.*

Willst du immer weiter schweifen? / Sieh, das Gute liegt so nah! / Lerne nur das Glück ergreifen, / Denn das Glück ist immer da— Wilt thou for ever roam? See, what is good lies so near thee! Only learn to seize the good fortune that offers, for it is ever there. *Goethe.*

Willst du in's Unendliche schreiten, / Geh' nur im Endliche nach allen Seiten—Wouldst thou step forward into the infinite, keep strictly within the limits of the finite. *Goethe.*

Willst du leben, musst du dienen ; willst du frei sein, musst du sterben—Wouldst thou love, thou must serve ; would thou be free, thou must die. *Hegel.*

Willst du mit Kinderhänden / In des Schick- 30 sals Speichen greifen? / Seines Donnerwagens Lauf / Hält kein sterblich Wesen auf— Wilt thou clutch the spokes of destiny with thy child's hands? The course of its car of thunder no mortal hand can stay. *Grillparzer.*

Willst du lustig leben, geh' mit zwei Säcken, / Einen zu geben, einen um einzustecken— Would you live a merry life, go with two wallets, one for giving out and one for putting in. *Goethe.*

Wilt thou draw near the nature of the gods? Draw near them, then, in being merciful. *Sh.*

Wilt thou know a man, above all a mankind, by stringing together beadrolls of what thou namest facts? The man is the spirit he worked in ; not what he did, but what he became. *Carlyle.*

Wilt thou know thyself, see how others do ; wilt thou understand others, look into thine own heart. *Schiller.*

"Win hearts," said Burleigh to Queen Eliza- 35 beth, "and you have all men's hearts and purses." *Smiles.*

Wine and youth are fire upon fire. *Fielding.*

Wine is a mocker, strong drink is raging : and whosoever is deceived thereby is not wise. *Bible.*

Wine is a turncoat ; first a friend and then an enemy. *Fielding.*

Wine neither keeps secrets nor fulfils promises. *Pr.*

Wine washes off the daub. *Pr.* 40

Wings have we—and as far as we can go, / We may find pleasure : wilderness and wood, / Blank ocean and mere sky, support that mood / Which with the lofty, sanctifies the low. *Wordsworth.*

Wink at small faults. *Pr.*

Wir Menschen sind ja alle Brüder—We men are for certain all brothers. *Zschokke.*

Wisdom alone is a science of other sciences and of itself. *Plato.*

Wisdom and Fortune combating together, / If that the former dare but what he can, / No chance may shake it. *Ant. and Cleo.*, iii. 11.

Wisdom and knowledge shall be the stability of thy times. *Bible.*

Wisdom becomes nonsense (*Unsinn*) in the mouth of a fanatic (*Schwärmer*). *Otto Ludwig.*

Wisdom begins at the end. *Webster.*

5 Wisdom excelleth folly, as far as light excelleth darkness. *Bible.*

Wisdom is a defence, and money is a defence : but the excellency of knowledge is, that wisdom giveth life to them that have it. *Bible.*

Wisdom is a pearl ; with most success / Sought in still water and beneath clear skies. *Cowper.*

Wisdom is intrinsically of a silent nature ; it cannot at once, or completely at all, be read off in words, and is only legible in whole when its work is done. *Carlyle.*

Wisdom is justified of her children. *Jesus.*

10 Wisdom is not found with those who dwell at their ease ; rather Nature, when she adds brain, adds difficulty. *Emerson.*

Wisdom is ofttimes nearer when we stoop than when we soar. *Wordsworth.*

Wisdom is only in truth. *Goethe.*

Wisdom is that attribute through which every action of a man receives its ideal value or import (*Gehalt*). *Schleiermacher.*

Wisdom is the principal thing ; therefore get wisdom : and with all thy getting get understanding. *Bible.*

15 Wisdom is too high for a fool. *Bible.*

Wisdom makes a slow defence against trouble, though at last a sure one. *Goldsmith.*

Wisdom may be the ultimate arbiter, but is seldom the immediate agent in human affairs. *Sir J. Stephen.*

Wisdom may sometimes wear a look austere, / But smiles and jests are oft her helpmates here. *De Bosch.*

Wisdom not only gets, but, got, retains. *Quarles.*

20 Wisdom picks friends ; civility plays the rest. / A toy shunn'd cleanly passeth with the best. *George Herbert.*

Wisdom resteth in the heart of him that hath understanding. *Bible.*

Wisdom sends us to childhood ; "unless ye become as little children." *Pascal.*

Wisdom sits with children round her knees. *Wordsworth.*

Wisdom sometimes walks in clouted shoes. *Pr.*

25 Wisdom that is hid, and treasure that is hoarded up, what profit is in them both ? *Ecclus.*

Wisdom, which represents the marriage of truth and virtue, is by no means synonymous with gravity. She is L'Allegro as well as Il Penseroso, and jests as well as preaches. *Whipple.*

Wisdom will out ; it is the one thing in this world that cannot be suppressed or annulled. *John Burroughs.*

Wisdom's a trimmer thing than shop e'er gave. *George Herbert.*

Wisdom's path is steep ; but, gained the height, / The Muse's gifts will fill you with delight. *Onestes.*

Wise above that which is written. *St. Paul.* 30

Wise, cultivated, genial conversation is the best flower of civilisation, and the best result which life has to offer us—a cup for gods, which has no repentance. Conversation is our account of ourselves. All we have, all we can, all we know is brought into play, and as the reproduction, in finer form, of all our havings. *Emerson.*

Wise is the man prepared for either end, / Who in due measure can both spare and spend. *Lucian.*

Wise kings have generally wise councillors, as he must be a wise man himself who is capable of distinguishing one. *Diogenes.*

Wise men are instructed by reason ; men of less understanding, by experience ; the most ignorant, by necessity ; and beasts, by nature. *Cic.*

Wise men are not wise at all hours, and will 35 speak five times from their taste or their humour to one from their reason. *Emerson.*

Wise men are wise but not prudent, in that they know nothing of what is for their own advantage, but know surpassing things, marvellous things, difficult things, and divine things. *Ruskin.*

Wise men argue causes, and fools decide them. *Anacharsis.*

Wise men, for the most part, are silent at present, and good men powerless ; the senseless vociferate, and the heartless govern ; while all social law and providence are dissolved by the enraged agitation of a multitude, among whom every villain has a chance of power, every simpleton of praise, and every scoundrel of fortune. *Ruskin.*

Wise men mingle mirth with their cares, as a help either to forget or overcome them ; but to resort to intoxication for the ease of one's mind is to cure melancholy by madness. *Charron.*

Wise men ne'er sit and wail their loss, / But 40 cheerly seek how to redress their harms. 3 *Hen. VI.*, v. 4.

Wise men say nothing in dangerous times. *Selden.*

Wise sayings are as saltpits ; you may extract salt out of them, and sprinkle it where you will. *Cic.*

Wise sayings are not only for ornament, but for action and business, having a point or edge, whereby knots in business are pierced and discovered. *Bacon.*

Wise sayings are the guiding oracles which man has found out for himself in that great business of ours, of learning how to be, to do, to do without, and to depart. *John Morley.*

Wise to resolve, and patient to perform. *Pope.* 45

Wise, well-calculated breeding of a young soul lies fatally over the horizon in these epochs. *Carlyle.*

Wisely and slow ; they stumble that run fast. *Rom. and Jul.*, ii. 3.

Wishing, of all employments, is the worst. *Young.*

Wissen ist leichter als thun—To know is easier than to do. *Ger. Pr.*

Wit and judgment often are at strife, / Though 50 meant each other's aid, like man and wife. *Pope.*

Wit and understanding are trifles without integrity. *Goldsmith.*

Wit and wisdom are born with a man. *Selden.*

Wit, bright, rapid, and blasting as the lightning, flashes, strikes, and vanishes in an instant ; humour, warm and all-embracing as the sunshine, bathes its object in a genial and abiding light. *Whipple.*

Wit is a dangerous weapon, even to the possessor, if he knows not how to use it discreetly. *Montaigne.*

5 Wit is a pernicious thing when it is not tempered with virtue and humanity. *Addison.*

Wit is brushwood, judgment timber ; the one gives the greatest flame, the other yields the durablest heat ; and both meeting make the best fire. *Sir Thomas Overbury.*

Wit is of the true Pierian spring, that can make anything of anything. *Chapman.*

Wit marries ideas lying wide apart, by a sudden jerk of the understanding. *Whipple.*

Wit once bought is worth twice taught. *Pr.*

10 Wit strews a single ray (of the prism) separated from the rest upon an object ; never white light, that is the province of wisdom. *Holmes.*

Wit, when neglected by the great, is generally despised by the vulgar. *Goldsmith.*

Wit without employment is a disease. *Burton.*

Wit without wisdom is salt without meat. *Horne.*

Wit-work is always play, when it is good. *Ruskin.*

15 Wit's an unruly engine, wildly striking / Sometimes a friend, sometimes the engineer : / Hast thou the knack ? pamper it not with liking ; / But if thou want it, buy it not too dear. *George Herbert.*

Witchcraft has been put a stop to by Act of Parliament, but the mysterious relations which it emblemed still continue. *Carlyle.*

With all appliances and means to boot. *2 Hen. IV.,* iii. 1.

With bag and baggage. *As You Like It,* iii. 2.

With centric and eccentric scribbled o'er, / Cycle and epicycle, orb in orb. *Milton.*

20 With consistency a great soul has simply nothing to do. He may as well concern himself with his shadow on the wall. *Emerson.*

With curious art the brain, too finely wrought, / Preys on herself, and is destroyed by thought. *Churchill.*

With devotion's visage / And pious action we do sugar over / The devil himself. *Ham.,* iii. 1.

With disadvantages enough to call him down to humility, a Scotchman is one of the proudest things alive. *Goldsmith.*

With every anguish of our earthly part the spirit's sight grows clearer ; this was meant when Jesus touched the blind man's lids with clay. *Lowell.*

25 With every breath we draw, an ethereal stream of Lethe runs through our whole being, so that we have but a partial recollection of our joys, and scarcely any of our sorrows. *Goethe.*

With faith, martyrs, otherwise weak, can cheerfully endure the shame and the cross ; and without it worldings puke up their sick existence, by suicide, in the midst of luxury. *Carlyle.*

With fingers weary and worn, / With eyelids heavy and red, / A woman sat in unwomanly rags, / Plying her needle and thread— / Stitch ! stitch ! stitch ! *Hood.*

"With it, or upon it, my son." *A Spartan mother, when she handed her son his shield as he set out to fight for his country.*

With just enough of learning to misquote. *Byron.*

With love come life and hope. *John Ster-* 30 *ling.*

With malice towards none, with charity for all, with firmness in the right, as God gives us to see the right. *John Quincy Adams.*

With mirth and laughter let old wrinkles come. *Mer. of Ven.,* i. 1.

With moral, political, religious considerations, high and dear as they may otherwise be, the philosopher, as such, has no concern. *Carlyle.*

With much we surfeit ; plenty makes us poor. *Drayton.*

With narrow-minded persons, and those in a 35 state of mental darkness, we find conceit ; while with mental clearness and high endowments we never find it. In such cases there is generally a joyful feeling of strength, but since this strength is actual, the feeling is anything else you please, only not conceit. *Goethe.*

With none who bless us, none whom we can bless— / This is to be alone ; this, this is solitude ! *Byron.*

With necessity, the tyrant's plea, excused his devilish deeds. *Milton.*

With ordinary talent and extraordinary perseverance, all things are attainable. *Sir T. F. Buxton.*

With parsimony a little is sufficient, and without it nothing is sufficient, whereas frugality makes a poor man rich. *Sen.*

With patient mind thy path of duty run ; / 40 God nothing does, nor suffers to be done, / But thou thyself wouldst do, if thou couldst see / The end of all events as well as he. (?)

With poetry, as with going to sea, we should push from the shore and reach a certain elevation before we unfurl all our sails. *Goethe.*

With poetry second-rate in quality, no one ought to be allowed to trouble mankind. *Ruskin.*

With remembrance of the greater grief to banish the less. *Howard, Earl of Surrey.*

With respect to luxuries and comforts, the wisest have ever lived a more simple and meagre life than the poor. *Thoreau.*

With some life is exactly like a sleigh-drive, 45 showy and tinkling, but affording just as little for the heart as it offers much to eyes and ears. *Goethe.*

With stupidity and sound digestion man may front much ; but what in these dull, unimaginative days are the terrors of conscience to the diseases of the liver ! *Carlyle.*

With temperance, health, cheerfulness, friends, a chosen task, one pays the cheapest fees for living, and may well dispense with other physicians. *A. B. Alcott.*

With the dead there is no rivalry. In the dead there is no change. Plato is never sullen. Cervantes is never petulant. Demosthenes never comes unseasonably. Dante never stays too long. *Macaulay.*

With the Gospels one becomes a heretic. *It. Pr.*

With the majority of men unbelief in one thing is founded on blind belief in another thing. *Lichtenberg.*

5 With the possession or certain expectation of good things our demand rises, and increases our capacity for further possession and larger expectations. *Schopenhauer.*

With thought, with the ideal, is immortal hilarity, the rose of joy. Round it all the Muses sing. *Emerson.*

With too much quickness ever to be taught ; / With too much thinking to have common thought. *Pope.*

With virtue, capacity, and good conduct, one still can be insupportable. The manners, which are neglected as small things, are often those which decide men for or against you. A slight attention to them would have prevented their ill judgments. *La Bruyère.*

With well-doing ye may put to silence foolish men. *St. Peter.*

10 With what a heavy and retarding weight does expectation load the wing of time. *William Mason.*

With what is debateable I am unconcerned ; and when I have only opinions about things . . . I do not talk about them. I attack only what cannot on any possible ground be defended ; and state only what I know to be incontrovertibly true. *Ruskin.*

With women worth the being won, / The softest lover ever best succeeds. *Aaron Hill.*

Withdraw thy foot from thy neighbour's house ; lest he be weary of thee, and so hate thee. *Bible.*

Withhold not good from them to whom it is due, when it is in the power of thine hand to do it. *Bible.*

15 Within man is the soul of the whole ; the wise silence, the universal beauty, to which every part and particle is equally related— the Eternal One. *Emerson.*

Within that awful volume lies / The mystery of mysteries. *Scott.*

Within the hollow crown / That rounds the mortal temples of a king, / Keeps Death his court. *Rich. II.*, iii. 2.

Within the most starched cravat there passes a windpipe and weasand, and under the thickliest embroidered waistcoat beats a heart. *Carlyle.*

Within us all a universe doth dwell. *Goethe.*

20 Within yourselves deliverance must be sought ; / Each man his prison makes. *Sir Edwin Arnold.*

Without a belief in personal immortality religion surely is like an arch resting on one pillar, like a bridge ending in an abyss. *Max Müller.*

Without a God there is for man neither purpose, nor goal, nor hope, only a wavering future, an eternal dread of every darkness. *Jean Paul.*

Without a rich heart wealth is an ugly beggar. *Emerson.*

Without a sign his sword the brave man draws, / And asks no omen but his country's cause. *Pope.*

Without adversity a man hardly knows 25 whether he is honest or not. *Fielding.*

Without affecting stoicism, it may be said that it is our business to exempt ourselves as much as we can from the power of external things. *Johnson.*

Without cheerfulness no man can be a poet. *Emerson.*

Without discretion learning is pedantry and wit impertinence ; virtue itself looks like weakness. The best parts only qualify a man to be more sprightly in errors, and active to his own prejudice. *Addison.*

Without earnestness there is nothing to be done in life ; yet among the people we name cultivated, little earnestness is to be found. *Goethe.*

Without economy none can be rich, and with 30 it few can be poor. *Johnson.*

Without enjoyment, the wealth of the miser is the same to him as if it were another's. But when it is said of a man "he hath so much," it is with difficulty he can be induced to part with it. *Hitopadesa.*

Without eyes thou shalt want light : profess not the knowledge therefore that thou hast not. *Ecclus.*

Without friends no one would choose to live, even if he had all other good things. *Arist.*

Without God in the world. *St. Paul.*

Without great men, great crowds of people in 35 a nation are disgusting ; like moving cheese, like hills of ants or of fleas—the more, the worse. *Emerson.*

Without great men nothing can be done. *Renan.*

Without justice society is sick, and will continue sick till it dies. *Froude.*

Without me ye can do nothing. *Jesus to his disciples.*

Without passion man is a mere latent force and possibility. *Amiel.*

Without passion there is no geniality. *Mommsen.* 40

Without philosophy we should be little above the lower animals. *Voltaire.*

Without poetry our science will appear incomplete, and most of what now passes with us for religion and philosophy will be replaced by poetry. *Matthew Arnold.*

Without real masters you cannot have servants. *Carlyle.*

Without some strong motive to the contrary, men united by the pursuit of a clearly defined common aim of irresistible attractiveness naturally coalesce ; and since they coalesce naturally, they are clearly right in coalescing and find their advantage in it. *Matthew Arnold.*

Without tact you can learn nothing. Tact 45 teaches you when to be silent. Inquirers who are always inquiring never learn anything. *I. Disraeli.*

Without the spiritual world the material world is a disheartening enigma. *Joubert.*

Without the way there is no going; without the truth, no knowing; without the life, no living. *Thomas à Kempis.*

Without were fightings, within were fears. *St. Paul.*

Without wonder there is no faith. *Jean Paul.*

5 Witticisms please as long as we keep them within bounds, but pushed to excess they cause offence. *Phædr.*

Witty, above all, O be not witty; none of us is bound to be witty, under penalties; to be wise and true we all are, under the terriblest penalties. *Carlyle.*

Wives are young men's mistresses, companions for middle age, and old men's nurses. *Bacon.*

Wo der Teufel nicht hin mag; da send er seinen Boten hin — Where the devil cannot come, he will send his messenger. *Ger. Pr.*

Wo fasse ich dich, unendliche Natur?—Where can I grasp thee, infinite Nature? *Goethe.*

10 Wo grosse Höh', ist grosse Tiefe—Where there is great height there is great depth. *Schiller.*

Wo innen Sklaverei ist, wird sie von aussen bald kommen—Where there is slavery in the heart, it will soon show itself in the outward conduct. *Seume.*

Wo man singet, lass dich ruhig nieder, / Ohne Furcht, was man am Lande glaubt; / Wo man singet wird kein Mensch beraubt; / Bösewichter haben keine Lieder — Where people sing, there quietly settle, never fearing what may be the belief of the people of the land. Where people sing, nobody will be robbed. Bad people have no songs. *Seume.*

Wo viel Freiheit, ist viel Irrthum—Where there is much freedom there is much error. *Schiller.*

Wo viel Licht ist, ist starker Schatten—The shadow is deeper where the light is strong. *Goethe.*

15 Wo viel zu wagen ist, ist viel zu wägen—Where there is much to risk, there is much to consider. *Platen.*

Woe does the heavier sit / Where it perceives it is but faintly borne. *Rich. II.,* i. 3.

Woe, that too late repents. *King Lear,* i. 4.

Woe to every sort of culture which destroys the most effectual means of all true culture, and directs us to the end, instead of rendering us happy on the way. *Goethe.*

Woe to him that is alone when he falleth; for he hath not another to help him up. *Bible.*

20 Woe to that land that's govern'd by a child. *Rich. III.,* ii. 3.

Woe unto him that is never alone, and cannot bear to be alone. *Hamerton.*

Woe unto you when all men speak well of you. *Jesus.*

Woe, woe to youth, to life, which idly boasts, / I am the End, and mine the appointed Way. *Lewis Morris.*

Wohl unglückselig ist der Mann, / Der unterlässt das, was er kann, / Und unterfängt sich, was er nicht versteht; / Kein Wunder, dass er zu Grunde geht—Unhappy indeed is the man who leaves off doing what he can do, and undertakes to do what he does not understand; no wonder he comes to no good. *Goethe.*

25 Wohlgethan überlebt den Tod—Well-done outlives death. *Ger. Pr.*

Wohlthätigkeit kennt keinen Unterschied der Nation—Charity knows no distinction of nation. *Count Moltke.*

Wollt ihr auf Menschen wirken, / Müsst ihr erst Menschen werden—Would you have an influence over men, you must first become men. *Sallet.*

Wollt ihr immer leben?—Would you live for ever? *Frederick the Great to his guards, on their complaining of what they thought exposure to unnecessary danger.*

Wolves in sheep's clothing. *Jesus, of false prophets.*

Woman alone knows true loyalty of affection. 30 *Schiller.*

Woman, divorced from home, wanders unfriended like a waif upon the wave. *Goethe.*

Woman endeavours to breed her daughter a fine lady, qualifying her for a station in which she will never appear, and at the same time incapacitating her for that retirement to which she is destined. *Lady Montagu.*

Woman, in accordance with her unbroken, clear-seeing nature, loses herself, and what she has of heart and happiness, in the object she loves. *Jean Paul.*

Woman is at once the delight and the terror of man. *Amiel.*

Woman is like the reed which bends to every 35 breeze, but breaks not in the tempest. *Whately.*

Woman is mistress of the art of completely embittering the life of the person on whom she depends. *Goethe.*

Woman is not undevelopt man, / But diverse; could we make her as the man, / Sweet love were slain: his dearest bond is this / Not like to like, but like in difference. *Tennyson.*

Woman is seldom merciful to the man who is timid. *Bulwer Lytton.*

Woman is the blood-royal of life; let there be slight degrees of precedency among them, but let them be all sacred. *Burns.*

Woman is the lesser man. *Tennyson.* 40

Woman is the salvation or the destruction of the family. *Amiel.*

Woman is too soft to hate permanently; even if a hundred men have been a grief to her, she will still love the hundred and first. *G. Kinkel.*

Woman, last at the cross and earliest at the grave. *E. S. Barret.*

Woman, once made equal to man, becometh his superior. *Soc.*

Woman sees deep; man sees far. To the man 45 the world is his heart; to the woman the heart is her world. *Grabbe.*

Woman's at best a contradiction still. *Pope.*

Woman's cause is man's; they rise or sink / Together, dwarfed or godlike, bond or free. *Tennyson.*

Woman's counsel is not worth much, yet he that despises it is no wiser than he should be. *Cervantes.*

Woman's dignity lies in her being unknown; her glory, in the esteem of her husband; and her pleasure, in the welfare of her family. *Rousseau.*

Woman's fear and love hold quantity; / In neither aught, or in extremity. *Ham.*, iii. 2.

Woman's function is a guiding, not a determining one. *Ruskin.*

Woman's grief is like a summer storm, short as it is violent. *Joanna Baillie.*

Woman's heart is just like a lithographer's stone—what is once written upon it cannot be rubbed out. *Thackeray.*

5 Woman's love, like lichens upon a rock, will still grow where even charity can find no soil to nurture itself. *Bovee.*

Woman's power is for rule, not for battle ; and her intellect is not for invention or creation, but for sweet ordering, arrangement, and decision. *Ruskin.*

Woman's power is over the affections. A beautiful dominion is hers, but she risks its forfeiture when she seeks to extend it. *Bovee.*

Woman's tongue is her sword, which she never lets rust. *Mme. Necker.*

Woman's virtue is the music of stringed instruments, which sound best in a room ; but man's that of wind instruments, which sound best in the open air. *Jean Paul.*

10 Woman's work, grave sirs, is never done. *Eusden.*

Women always show more taste in adorning others than themselves ; and the reason is, that their persons are like their hearts—they read another's better than they can their own. *Jean Paul.*

Women and clergymen have so long been in the habit of using pretty words without troubling themselves to understand them, that they now revolt from the effort, as if it were impiety. *Ruskin.*

Women and men of retiring timidity are cowardly only in dangers which affect themselves, but the first to rescue when others are endangered. *Jean Paul.*

Women are as roses, whose fair flower / Being once display'd, doth fall that very hour. *Twelfth Night*, ii. 4.

15 Women are born worshippers. *Carlyle.*

Women are confined within the narrow limits of domestic assiduity, and when they stray beyond them they move beyond their sphere, and consequently without grace. *Goldsmith.*

Women are ever in extremes ; they are either better or worse than men. *La Bruyère.*

Women are like limpets, they need something to hold on by. *Sigma.*

Women are the poetry of the world, in the same sense as the stars are the poetry of heaven. Clear, light-giving, harmonious, they are the terrestrial planets that rule the destinies of mankind. *Hargrave.*

20 Women bestow on friendship only what they borrow from love. *Chamfort.*

Women cannot see so far as men can, but what they do see they see quicker. *Buckle.*

Women exceed the generality of men in love. *La Bruyère.*

Women famed for their valour, their skill in politics or their learning, leave the duties of their own sex in order to invade the privileges of men's. *Goldsmith.*

Women forgive injuries, but never forget slights. *T. C. Haliburton.*

Women have a kind of sturdy sufferance 25 which qualifies them to endure beyond, much beyond, the common run of men, but . . . they are by no means famous for seeing remote consequences in all their real importance. *Burns.*

Women, it has been observed, are not naturally formed for great cares themselves, but to soften ours. *Goldsmith.*

Women judge women hardly ; . . . they have no shading, / No softening tints, no generous allowance / For circumstance to make the picture human, / And true because so human. *Dr. Walter Smith.*

Women know by nature how to disguise their emotions far better than the most consummate male courtiers can do. *Thackeray.*

Women, like princes, find few real friends. *Lord Lyttleton.*

Women, like the plants in woods, derive their 30 softness and tenderness from the shade. *Landor.*

Women may fall when there's no strength in men. *Rom. and Jul.*, ii. 3.

Women, priests, and poultry have never enough. *Pr.*

Women should learn betimes to serve according to station, for by serving alone she at last attains to the mastery, to the due influence which she ought to possess in the household. *Goethe.*

Women that are the least bashful are not unfrequently the most modest ; and we are never more deceived than when we would infer any laxity of principle from that freedom of demeanour which often arises from a total ignorance of vice. *Colton.*

Women, though they have the warmest hearts, 35 are no citizens of the world, scarcely citizens of a town or a village, but only of their own home. *Jean Paul.*

Women who have lost their faith / Are angels who have lost their wings. *Dr. Walter Smith.*

Women wish to be loved, not because they are pretty, or good, or well-bred, or graceful, or intelligent, but because they are themselves. *Amiel.*

Women's hearts are made of stout leather ; there's a plaguy sight of wear in them. *Judge Haliburton.*

Women's jars breed men's wars. *Pr.*

Women's rage, like shallow water, / Does 40 but show their hurtless nature ; / When the stream seems rough and frowning, / There is still least fear of drowning. *Durfey.*

Women's sins are not alone the ills they do, / But those that they provoke you to. *Dr. Walter Smith.*

Wonder is from surprise, and surprise ceases upon experience. *South.*

Wonder on till truth make all things plain. *Mid. N.'s Dream.*

"Wonder," says Aristotle, "is the first cause of philosophy." This is quite as true in the progress of the individual as in that of the concrete mind; and the constant aim of philosophy is to destroy its parent. *Bulwer Lytton.*

Wondrous indeed is the virtue of a true book. Not like a dead city of stones, yearly crumbling, yearly needing repair; more like a tilled field, but then a spiritual field; like a spiritual tree, let me rather say, it stands from year to year, and from age to age (we have books that already number some one hundred and fifty human ages); and yearly comes its new produce of leaves (commentaries, deductions, philosophical, political systems, or were it only sermons, pamphlets, journalistic essays), every one of which is talismanic and thaumaturgic, for it can persuade men. *Carlyle.*

Wondrous is the strength of cheerfulness, altogether past calculation its powers of endurance. *Carlyle.*

Woodman, spare that tree! / Touch not a single bough! / In youth it sheltered me, / And I'll protect it now. *G. P. Morris.*

Words are also actions, and actions are a kind of words. *Emerson.*

5 Words are but poor interpreters in the realms of emotion. When all words end, music begins; when they suggest, it realises; and hence the secret of its strange, ineffable power. *H. R. Haweis.*

Words are but wind, but seein's believin'. *Sc. Pr.*

Words are fools' pence. *Pr.*

Words are good, but they are not the best. The best is not to be explained by words. *Goethe.*

Words are like leaves, and when they most abound / Much fruit of sense beneath is rarely found. *Pope.*

10 Words are like sea-shells on the shore; they show / Where the mind ends, and not how far it has been. *Bailey.*

Words are men's daughters, but God's sons are things. *Izaak Walton.*

Words are rather the drowsy part of poetry; imagination the life of it. *Owen Feltham.*

Words are the motes of thought, and nothing more. *Bailey.*

Words are things, and a small drop of ink, / Falling like dew upon a thought, produces / That which makes thousands, perhaps millions, think. *Byron.*

15 Words are wise men's counters, but they are the money of fools. *Hobbes.*

Words are women, deeds are men. *George Herbert.*

Words become luminous when the finger of the poet touches them with his phosphorus. *Joubert.*

Words do sometimes fly from the tongue that the heart did neither hatch nor harbour. *Feltham.*

Words, like Nature, half reveal / And half conceal the soul within. *Tennyson.*

20 Words may be counterfeit, false coined, and current only from the tongue, without the mind; but passion is in the soul, and always speaks the heart. *Southern.*

Words of love are works of love. *W. R. Alger.*

Words pay no debts. *Troil. and Cress.,* iii. 2.

Words that are now dead were once alive. *A. Coles.*

Words, "those fickle daughters of the earth," are the creation of a being that is finite, and when applied to explain that which is infinite, they fail; for that which is made surpasses not the maker; nor can that which is immeasurable by our thoughts be measured by our tongues. *Colton.*

Words to the heat of deeds too cold breath 25 give. *Macb.,* ii. 1.

Words which flow fresh and warm from a full heart, and which are instinct with the life and breath of human feeling, pass into household memories, and partake of the immortality of the affections from which they spring. *Whipple.*

Words without thoughts never to heaven go. *Ham.,* iii. 3.

Work, according to my feeling, is as much of a necessity to man as eating and sleeping. Even those who do nothing which to a sensible man can be called work, still imagine that they are doing something. The world possesses not a man who is an idler in his own eyes. *W. v. Humboldt.*

Work alone is noble. *Carlyle.*

"Work and wait," "Work and wait," is what 30 God says to us in creation and in providence. *J. G. Holland.*

Work earnestly at anything, you will by degrees learn to work at almost all things. *Carlyle.*

Work first, you are God's servants; fee first, you are the fiend's. *Ruskin.*

Work for eternity: not the meagre rhetorical eternity of the periodical critics, but for the real eternity, wherein dwelleth the Divine. *Carlyle.*

Work for immortality if you will: then wait for it. *J. G. Holland.*

Work for some good, be it ever so slowly; / 35 Cherish some flower, be it ever so lowly; / Labour! all labour is noble and holy: / Let thy great deeds be thy prayer to thy God. *Francis S. Osgood.*

Work, go, fall, rise, speak, be silent! In this manner do the rich sport with those needy men, who are held by the grip of dependence. *Hitopadesa.*

Work is for the living. *Carlyle.*

Work is not man's punishment; it is his reward and his strength, his glory and his pleasure. *George Sand.*

Work is of a religious nature,—work is of a brave nature, which it is the aim of all religion to be. "All work of man is as the swimmer's." A waste ocean threatens to devour him; if he front it not bravely, it will keep its word. By incessant wise defiance of it, lusty rebuke and buffet of it, behold how it loyally supports him,—bears him as its conqueror along! "It is so," says Goethe, "with all things that man undertakes in this world." *Carlyle.*

Work is only done well when it is done with 40 a will. *Ruskin.*

Work is our business; its success is God's. *Ger. Pr.*

Work is the cure for all the maladies and miseries of man—honest work, which you intend getting done. *Carlyle.*

Work is the inevitable condition of human life, the true source of human welfare. *Tolstoi.*

Work is the mission of man on this planet. *Carlyle.*

Work is the only universal currency which God accepts. A nation's welfare will depend on its ability to master the world ; that, on power of work ; that, on its power of thought. *Theodore Parker.*

Work, properly so called, is an appeal from the Seen to the Unseen—a devout calling upon Higher Powers ; and unless they stand by us, it will not be a work, but a quackery. *Carlyle.*

Work till the last beam fadeth, / Fadeth to shine no more ; / Work while the night is darkening, / When man's work is o'er. *Walker.*

5 Work touches the keys of endless activity, opens the infinite, and stands awe-struck before the immensity of what there is to do. *Phillips Brooks.*

Work was made for man, and not man for work. *J. G. Holland.*

Work without hope draws nectar in a sieve, / And hope without an object cannot live. *Coleridge.*

Work, work, work, / Till the brain begins to swim ; / Work, work, work, / Till the eyes are heavy and dim ; / Seam, and gusset, and band, / Band, and gusset, and seam, / Till over the buttons I fall asleep, / And sow them on in a dream. *Hood.*

Works of true merit are seldom very popular in their own day ; for knowledge is on the march, and men of genius are the "præstola-tores" or "videttes," that are far in advance of their comrades. They are not with them, but before them ; not in the camp, but beyond it. *Colton.*

10 Worldly affairs, which my friends thought so heavy upon me, they are most of them of our own making, and fall away as soon as we know ourselves. *Law.*

Worldly riches are like nuts ; many clothes are torn in getting them, many a tooth broke in cracking them, but never a belly filled with eating them. *R. Venning.*

Worse than being fool'd / Of others, is to fool one's self. *Tennyson.*

Worse than despair, / Worse than the bitter-ness of death, is hope ; / It is the only ill which can find ease / Upon the giddy, sharp, and narrow hour / Tottering beneath us. *Shelley.*

Worship is transcendent wonder ; wonder for which there is no limit or measure. *Carlyle.*

15 Worship that is false will kill the soul as quickly as no worship. *Saying.*

Worship your heroes from afar ; contact withers them. *Mme. Necker.*

Worte sind der Seele Bild—Words are the soul's magic. *Goethe.*

Worte sind gut, wenn Werke folgen—Words are good if works follow. *Ger. Pr.*

Worth makes the man, and want of it the fellow ; / The rest is all but leather or pru-nello. *Pope.*

20 Worth many thousand is the first salute ; / Him that salutes thee, therefore, friendly greet. *Goethe.*

Worthless people live only to eat and drink ; people of worth eat and drink only to live. *Socrates.*

Would they could sell us experience, though at diamond prices, but then no one would use the article second-hand ! *Balzac.*

Would we but pledge ourselves to truth as heartily as we do to a real or imaginary mistress, and think life too short only be-cause it abridges our time of service, what a new world we should have ! *Lowell.*

Would we but quit ourselves like men, and resolutely stand our ground, we should not fail of succours from above. *Thomas à Kempis.*

Would Wisdom for herself be wooed, / And 25 wake the foolish from his dream, / She must be glad as well as good, / And must not only be, but seem. *Coventry Patmore.*

Would you have men think well of you, then do not speak well of yourself. *Pascal.*

Wouldst thou a maiden make thy prize, / Thyself alone the bribe must be. *Goethe.*

Wouldst thou both eat thy cake and have it ? *George Herbert.*

Wouldst thou know thyself, then see how others act ; wouldst thou understand others, look thou into thine own heart. *Schiller.*

Wouldst thou plant for eternity ? then plant 30 into the deep infinite faculties of man, his fantasy and heart. Wouldst thou plant for year and day ? then plant into his shallow superficial faculties, his self-love and arith-metical understanding, what will grow there. *Carlyle.*

"Wouldst thou," so the helmsman answered, / "Learn the secret of the sea ? / Only those who brave its dangers / Comprehend its mystery !" *Longfellow.*

Wouldst thou subject all things to thyself ? Subject thyself to reason. *Seneca.*

Wouldst thou the life of souls discern ? / Nor human wisdom nor divine / Helps thee by aught beside to learn ; / Love is life's only sign. *Keble.*

Wouldst thou travel the path of truth and goodness ? Never deceive either thyself or others. *Goethe.*

Wounds and hardships provoke our courage, 35 and when our fortunes are at the lowest, our wits and minds are commonly at the best. *Charron.*

Wounds cannot be cured without searching. *Bacon.*

Wrap thyself up like a woodlouse, and dream revenge. *Congreve.*

Write down the advice of him who loves you, though you like it not at present. *Pr.*

Write how you will, the critic shall show the world you could have written better. *Gold-smith.*

Write, so much given to God ; thou shalt be 40 heard. *George Herbert.*

Write thy wrongs in ashes. *Sir T. Browne.*

Writers of novels and romances in general bring a double loss on their readers—they rob them both of their time and money ; repre-senting men, manners, and things, that never have been, nor are likely to be ; either con-founding or perverting history and truth, inflating the mind, or committing violence upon the understanding. *Mary Wortley Montagu.*

Writing is not literature unless it gives to the reader a pleasure which arises not only from the things said, but from the way in which they are said ; and that pleasure is only given when the words are carefully or curiously or beautifully put together into sentences. *Stopford Brooke.*

Written all of it (Christianity) in us already in sympathetic ink. Bible awakens it, and you can read. *Dr. Chalmers to Carlyle in conversation.*

Wrong is not only different from right, but it is in strict scientific terms infinitely different. *Carlyle.*

Wrongs are often forgiven, but contempt never is, Our pride remembers it for ever. It implies a discovery of weaknesses, which we are much more careful to conceal than crimes. Many a man will confess his crimes to a common friend, but I never knew a man who would tell his silly weaknesses to his most intimate one. *Chesterfield.*

5 Würf er einen Groschen auf's Dach, fiel ihm ein Thaler herunter—If he threw a penny up, a dollar came down. *Ger. Pr.*

Y.

Ye are my friends, if ye do whatsoever I command you. *Jesus to his disciples.*

Ye are the light of the world. *Jesus to his disciples.*

Ye are the people, and wisdom shall die with you. *Job.*

Ye are the salt of the earth. *Jesus to his disciples.*

10 Ye blind guides, which strain at a gnat and swallow a camel. *Jesus.*

Ye cannot serve God and mammon. *Jesus.*

Ye fearful saints, fresh courage take ; / The clouds ye so much dread / Are big with mercy, and shall break / In blessings on your head. *Cowper.*

Ye gentlemen of England / That live at home at ease, / Ah ! little do you think upon / The dangers of the seas. *Martyn Parker.*

Ye gods, it doth amaze me / A man of such a feeble temper should / So get the start of the majestic world / And bear the palm alone. *Jul. Cæs.*, i. 2.

15 Ye good yeomen, whose limbs were made in England. *Hen. V.*, iii. 1.

Ye hae a stalk o' carl-hemp in you. *Sc. Pr.*

Ye have not chosen me, but I have chosen you. *Jesus to his disciples.*

Ye mariners of England, / That guard our native seas, / Whose flag has braved a thousand years / The battle and the breeze. *Campbell.*

Ye may darken over the blue heavens, ye vapoury masses in the sky. It matters not ! Beyond the howling of that wrath, beyond the blackness of those clouds, there shines, unaltered and serene, the moon that shone in Paradise. . . . The moon that promises a paradise restored. *Mrs. Gatty.*

Ye men of gloom and austerity, who paint the 20 face of Infinite Benevolence with an eternal frown, read in the everlasting book, wide open to your view, the lesson it would teach. Its pictures are not in black and sombre hues, but bright and glowing tints ; its music—save when ye drown it—is not in sighs and groans, but songs and cheerful sounds. Listen to the million voices in the summer air, and find one dismal as your own. *Dickens.*

Ye shall know them by their fruits. *Jesus.*

Ye stars ! which are the poetry of heaven ! . . In our aspirations to be great, / Our destinies o'erleap their mortal state, / And claim a kindred with you ; for ye are / A beauty and a mystery, and create / In us such love and reverence from afar, / That fortune, fame, power, life, have named themselves a star. *Byron.*

Ye think the rustic cackle of your bourg / The murmur of the world. *Tennyson.*

Ye'll find mankind an unco squad, / And muckle they may grieve ye. *Burns.*

Yea, let all good things await / Him who cares 25 not to be great, / But as he serves or serves the state. *Tennyson.*

Yea, surely the sea like a harper laid hand on the shore as a lyre. *Swinburne.*

Year chases year, decay pursues decay, / Still drops some joy from withering life away. *Johnson.*

Years do not make sages ; they only make old men. *Mme. Swetchine.*

Years following years steal something every day ; / At last they steal us from ourselves away. *Pope.*

Years steal / Fire from the mind as vigour 30 from the limb, / And life's enchanted cup but sparkles near the brim. *Byron.*

Yes, there are things we must dream and dare, / And execute ere thought be half aware. *Byron.*

Yes, you find people ready enough to do the good Samaritan without the oil and twopence. *Sydney Smith.*

Yet a little while, and we shall all meet there, and our Mother's bosom will screen us all ; and Oppression's harness, and Sorrow's firewhip, and all the Gehenna bailiffs that patrol and inhabit ever-vexed Time, cannot harm us any more. *Carlyle.*

Yet all that poets sing, and grief hath known, / Of hopes laid waste, knells in that word— Alone. *Bulwer Lytton.*

Yet better thus, and known to be contemn'd, / 35 Than still contemn'd and flatter'd. *King Lear*, iv. 1.

Yet do I fear thy nature ; / It is too full o' the milk o' human kindness. *Macb.*, i. 5.

Yet I doubt not through the ages one increasing purpose runs, / And the thoughts of men are widen'd by the process of the suns. *Tennyson.*

Yet I've heard say, by wise men in my day, / That none are outwitted so easy as they / Who reckon with all men as if they suspect them, / And traffic in caution, and watch to detect them. *Dr. W. Smith.*

Yet one thing secures us, whatever betide, / The Scripture assures us the Lord will provide. *Newton.*

Yet taught by Time, my heart has learned to glow / For other's good and melt at other's woe. *Pope.*

Yet there are surely times when there is nought / So needed as unsettling, just to get / Out of old ruts, and seek a nobler life. *Dr. W. Smith.*

Yet this grief / Is added to the griefs the great must bear, / That howsoever much they may desire / Silence, they cannot weep behind a cloud. *Tennyson.*

Yield not thy neck / To fortune's yoke, but let thy dauntless mind / Still ride in triumph over all mischance. 3 *Hen. VI.,* iii. 3.

5 Yield not to temptation, for yielding is sin ; / Each victory will help you some other to win. *H. M. Palmer.*

Yield to God's word and will, and you will escape many a calamity. *Spurgeon.*

Yielding is sometimes the best way of succeeding. *Pr.*

Yielding, timid weakness is always abused and insulted by the unjust and unfeeling ; but meekness, when sustained by the "fortiter in re," is always respected, commonly successful. *Chesterfield.*

You accuse woman of wavering affection. Blame her not ; she is but seeking a constant man. *Goethe.*

10 You always aspire to very little at first, but as you mount the ladder, you are sure to look down upon what you formerly looked up to as the height of happiness. *Brothers Mayhew.*

You always end ere you begin. *Two Gent. of Verona,* ii. 4.

You are always willing enough to read lives, but never willing to lead them. *Ruskin.*

You are my true and honourable wife, / As dear to me as are the ruddy drops / That visit my sad heart. *Jul. Cæs.,* ii. 1.

You are not very good if you are not better than your best friends imagine you to be. *Lavater.*

15 You are obliged to your imagination for three-fourths of your importance. *Garrick.*

You are prosperous, you are great, you are "beyond the world," as I have heard people say, meaning the power or the caprice thereof ; but you are not beyond the power of events. *Disraeli to young men.*

You are to come to your study as to the table, with a sharp appetite, whereby that which you read may the better digest. He that has no stomach to his book will very hardly thrive upon it. *Earl of Bedford.*

You are transported by calamity / Thither where more attends you. *Coriolanus,* i. 1.

You arrive at truth through poetry, and I arrive at poetry through truth. *Joubert.*

20 You beat your pate, and fancy wit will come ; / Knock as you please, there's nobody at home. *Pope.*

You begin in error when you suggest that we should regard the opinion of the many about just and unjust, good and evil, honourable and dishonourable. *Plato.*

You can easily ascertain (*verstehen*) what comes from the heart, for what comes from it in another's must go to your own. *Körner.*

You can imagine thistle-down so light that when you run after it your running motion would drive it away from you, and that the more you tried to catch it the faster it would fly from your grasp. And it should be with every man, that, when he is chased by troubles, they, chasing, shall raise him higher and higher. *Ward Beecher.*

You can never be wise unless you love reading. *Johnson.*

You can never by persistency make wrong 25 right. *Johnson.*

You can speak well, if your tongue deliver the message of your heart. *John Ford.*

You canna expect to be baith grand and comfortable. *J. M. Barrie.*

You cannot abolish slavery by Act of Parliament, but can only abolish the name of it, which is very little. *Carlyle.*

You cannot climb a ladder by pushing others down. *Pr.*

You cannot fathom your mind. There is a well 30 of thought there which has no bottom ; the more you draw from it, the more clear and fruitful it will be. *G. A. Sala.*

You cannot get anything out of Nature or from God by gambling ;—only out your neighbour. *Ruskin.*

You cannot have the ware and the money both at once ; and he who always hankers for the ware without having heart to give the money for it, is no better off than he who repents him of the purchase when the ware is in his hands. *Goethe.*

You cannot have your work well done if the work be not of a right kind. *Carlyle.*

You cannot hide any secret. *Emerson.*

You cannot lead a fighting world without 35 having it regimented, chivalried ; nor can you any more continue to lead a working world unregimented, anarchic. *Carlyle.*

You cannot love the real sun, that is to say, physical light and colour, rightly, unless you love the spiritual sun, that is to say, justice and truth, rightly. *Ruskin.*

You cannot make a silk purse out of a sow's ear. *Pr.*

You cannot push a man far up a tree. *Pr.*

You cannot put a quartern loaf into a child's head ; you must break it up, and give him the crumb in warm milk. *Spurgeon.*

You cannot rear a temple like a hut of sticks 40 and turf. *Dr. W. Smith.*

You cannot save men from death but by facing it for them, nor from sin but by resisting it for them. *Ruskin.*

You cannot secure even enjoyment in stagnation. *Mrs. Gatty.*

You can't be lost on a straight road. *Pr.*

You can't "have" your pudding unless you can "eat" it. *Ruskin.*

You can't order remembrance out of a man's 45 mind. *Thackeray.*

You can't see the wood for the trees. *Pr.*

You can't tell a nut till you crack it. *Pr.*

You complain of the difficulty of finding work for your men ; the real difficulty rather is to find men for your work. *Ruskin.*

You do not believe, you only believe that you believe. *Coleridge.*

You do not educate a man by telling him what he knew not, but by making him what he was not, and what he will remain for ever. *Ruskin.*

You don't value your peas for their roots or your carrots for their flowers. Now that's the way you should choose women. *George Eliot.*

You draw me, you hard-hearted adamant; / But yet you draw not iron, for my heart / Is true as steel; leave you your power to draw, / And I shall have no power to follow you. *Mid. N.'s Dream,* ii. 2.

You feel yourself an exile in the East; but in the West too it is exile; I know not where under the sun it is not exile. *Carlyle to a young friend.*

5 You find faut wi' your meat, and the faut's all i' your own stomach. *George Eliot.*

You find yourself refreshed by the presence of cheerful people. Why not make earnest effort to confer that pleasure on others? You will find half the battle is gained if you never allow yourself to say anything gloomy. *Mrs. L. M. Child.*

You frighten me out of my seven senses. *Swift.*

You gazed at the moon and fell in the gutter. *Pr.*

You give me nothing during your life, but you promise to provide for me at your death. If you are not a fool, you know what I wish for. *Martial.*

10 You have deserved / High commendation, true applause and love. *As You Like It,* i. 2.

You have many enemies that know not / Why they are so, but, like to village curs, / Bark when their fellows do. *Hen. VIII.,* iv. 2.

You have no business with consequences; you are to tell the truth. *Johnson.*

You have no hold on a human being whose affections are without a tap-root! *Southey.*

You have not outgrown, you cannot outgrow, the need of a great and authoritative teacher. *Joseph Anderson.*

15 You have scotched the snake, not killed him. *Macb.,* iii. 2.

You have too much respect upon the world; / They lose it that do buy it with much care. *Mer. of Ven.,* i. 1.

You knock a man into the ditch, and then you tell him to remain content in the "position in which Providence has placed him." *Ruskin.*

You know how slight a line will tow a boat when afloat on the billows, though a cable would hardly move her when pulled up on the beach. *Scott.*

You know it is not my interest to pay the principal, nor is it my principle to pay the interest. *Sheridan to a creditor of his.*

20 You know no rules of charity, / Which renders good for bad, blessings for curses. *Rich. III.,* i. 2.

You know not where a blessing may light. *Pr.*

You know that in everything women write there are always a thousand faults of grammar, but, with your permission, a harmony which is rare in the writings of men. *Mme. de Maintenon.*

You lie nearest to the river of life when you bend to it. You cannot drink but as you stoop. *J. H. Evans.*

You live one half year with deception and art; / With art and deception you live t'other part. *It. Pr.*

You make but a poor trap to catch luck if you 25 go and bait it with wickedness. *George Eliot.*

You may as soon separate weight from lead, heat from fire, moistness from water, and brightness from the sun, as misery, discontent, calamity, and danger from man. *Burton.*

You may as well ask a loom which weaves huckaback why it does not make cashmere, as expect poetry from this engineer, or a chemical discovery from that jobber. *Emerson.*

You may depend upon it, religion is, in its essence, the most gentlemanly thing in the world. It will alone gentilise, if unmixed with cant; and I know nothing else that will, alone; certainly not the army, which is thought to be the grand embellisher of manners. *Coleridge.*

You may depend upon it that he is a good man whose intimate friends are all good. *Lavater.*

(You may) dig the deep foundations of a long- 30 abiding fame, / And wist not that they undermine (your) home of love and peace. *Dr. W. C. Smith.*

You may do anything with bayonets except sit on them. *Napoleon.*

You may fail to shine, in the opinion of others, both in your conversation and actions, from being superior as well as inferior to them. *Greville.*

You may grow good corn in a little field. *Pr.*

You may have to wait a bit—some of you a shorter, some a longer time; but do wait, and everything will fit in and be perfect at last. *Mrs. Gatty.*

You may imitate, but never counterfeit. *Balzac.* 35

You may know a wise man by his election of an aim, and a sagacious by his election of the means. *Rückert.*

You may overthrow a government in the twinkling of an eye, as you can blow up a ship or upset and sink one; but you can no more create a government with a word than an iron-clad. *Ruskin.*

You may paint with a very big brush, and yet not be a great painter. *Carlyle.*

You may rest upon this as an unfailing truth, that there neither is, nor ever was, any person remarkably ungrateful who was not also insufferably proud; nor any one proud who was not equally ungrateful. *South.*

You may ride 's / With one soft kiss a thousand 40 furlongs ere / With spur we heat an acre. *Winter's Tale,* i. 2.

You may say, "I wish to send this ball so as to kill the lion crouching yonder ready to spring upon me. My wishes are all right, and I hope Providence will direct the ball." Providence won't. You must do it; and if you do not, you are a dead man. *Ward Beecher.*

You might as well ask an oyster to make progress, as the people of any country in which grumbling could by any possibility be prohibited. *John Wagstaffe.*

You must be content sometimes with rough roads. *Pr.*

"You must be in the fashion," is the utterance of weak-headed mortals. *Spurgeon.*

You must begin at a low round of the ladder if you mean to get on. *George Eliot.*

You must confine yourself within the modest limits of order. *Twelfth Night*, i. 3.

You must educate for education's sake only. *Ruskin.*

5 You must empty out the bathing-tub, but not the baby along with it. *Ger. Pr.*

You must either be directed by some that take upon them to know, or take upon yourself that which I am sure you do not know, or jump the after-inquiry on your own peril. *Cymbeline*, v. 4.

You must get your living by loving, else your life is at least half a failure. *Thoreau.*

You must live for another if you wish to live for yourself. *Sen.*

You must live the life. *Lawrence Oliphant.*

10 You must lose a fly to catch a trout. *Pr.*

You must not equivocate, nor speak anything positively for which you have no authority but report, or conjecture, or opinion. *Judge Hale.*

You must not fear death, my lads; defy him, and you drive him into the enemy's ranks. *Napoleon.*

You must not fight too often with one enemy, or you will teach him all your art of war. *Napoleon.*

You must not measure every man's corn by your own bushel. *Pr.*

15 You must not suppose that everything goes right at first even with the best of us. *Mrs. Gatty.*

You must not think / That we are made of stuff so flat and dull, / That we can let our beard be shook with danger, / And think it pastime. *Ham.*, iv. 7.

You must rouse in men a consciousness of their own prudence and strength, if you would raise their character. *Vauvenargues.*

You must seek and find God in the heart. *Jean Paul.*

You need not tell all the truth, unless to those who have a right to know it all. But let all you tell be truth. *Horace Mann.*

20 You never can elude the gods when you even devise wrong. *Thales.*

You never long the greatest man to be; / No! all you say is; "I'm as good as he." / He's the most envious man beneath the sun / Who thinks that he's as good as every one. *Goethe.*

You never will love art well till you love what she mirrors better. *Ruskin.*

You often understand the true connection of important events in your life not while they are going on, nor soon after they are past, but only a considerable time afterwards. *Schopenhauer.*

You ought to read books, as you take medicine, by advice, and not advertisement. *Ruskin.*

25 You rub the sore, when you should bring the plaster. *Tempest*, ii. 1.

You said your say; / Mine answer was my deed. *Tennyson.*

You see when they row in a barge, they that do drudgery work, slash, and puff, and sweat; but he that governs sits quietly at the stern, and scarce is seen to stir. *Selden.*

You shall never take a woman without her answer, unless you take her without her tongue. *As You Like It*, iv. 1.

You shall not shirk the hobbling Times to catch a ride on the sure-footed Eternities. "The times (as Carlyle says) are bad; very well, you are there to make them better." *John Burroughs.*

You take my house, when you do take the 30 prop / That doth sustain my house; you take my life / When you do take the means whereby I live. *Mer. of Ven.*, iv. 1.

You that choose not by the view, / Choose as fair, and choose as true. *Mer. of Ven.*, iii. 2.

You traverse the world in search of happiness, which is within the reach of every man; a contented mind confers it on all. *Hor.*

You watch figures in the fields, digging and delving with spade or pick. You see one of them from time to time straightening his loins, and wiping his face with the back of his hand. . . . It is there that for me you must seek true humanity and great poetry. *Miliet.*

You were used / To say, extremity was the trier of spirits; / That common chances common men could bear; / That when the sea was calm, all boats alike / Showed mastership in floating. *Coriolanus*, iv. 1.

You who are ashamed of your poverty, and 35 blush for your calling, are a snob; as are you who boast of your pedigree, or are proud of your wealth. *Thackeray.*

You who follow wealth and power with unremitting ardour, / The more in this you look for bliss, you leave your view the farther. *Burns.*

You who forget your friends, meanly to follow after those of a higher degree, are a snob. *Thackeray.*

You will as often find a great man above, as below, his reputation, when once you come to know him. *Goethe.*

You will catch more flies with a spoonful of honey than with a cask of vinegar. *Eastern Pr.*

You will find angling to be like the virtue of 40 humility, which has a calmness of spirit and a world of other blessings attending upon it. *Izaac Walton.*

You will find rest unto your souls when first you take on you the yoke of Christ, but joy only when you have borne it as long as He wills. *Ruskin.*

You will find that most books worth reading once are worth reading twice. *John Morley.*

You will find that silence, or very gentle words, are the most exquisite revenge for reproaches. *Judge Hall.*

You will get more profit from trying to find where beauty is, than in anxiously inquiring what it is. Once for all, it remains undemonstrable; it appears to us, as in a dream, when we behold the works of the great poets and painters; and in short, of all feeling artists; it is a hovering, shining, shadowy form, the outline of which no definition holds. *Goethe.*

You will never live to my age, without you keep yourselves in breath with exercise, and in heart with joyfulness. *Sir P. Sidney.*

You will never miss the right way if you only act according to your feelings and conscience. *Goethe.*

You will never see anything worse than yourselves. *Anon.*

You wise, / To call him shamed, who is but overthrown? *Tennyson.*

5 You wish, O woman, to be ardently loved, and for ever, even until death, be thou the mother of your children. *Jean Paul.*

You write with ease to show your breeding, / But easy writing's cursed hard reading. *Sheridan.*

You'll repent if you marry, and you'll repent if you don't. *Old saying.*

Young authors give their brains much exercise and little food. *Joubert.*

Young Christians think themselves little; growing Christians think themselves nothing; full-grown Christians think themselves less than nothing. *John Newton.*

10 Young folk, silly folk; old folk, cold folk. *Dut. Pr.*

Young hot colts, being raged, do rage the more. *Rich. II., ii. 1.*

Young men are apt to think themselves wise enough, as drunken men are to think themselves sober enough. *Chesterfield.*

Young men are fitter to invent than to judge; fitter for execution than for counsel; and fitter for new projects than for settled business. *Bacon.*

Young men soon give, and soon forget affronts; old age is slow in both. *Addison.*

15 Young men think that old men are fools; but old men know young men are fools. *Chapman.*

Young people are quick enough to observe and imitate. (?)

Your acts are detectives, keener and more unerring than ever the hand of sensational novelist depicted; they will dog you from the day you sinned till the hour your trial comes off. *Disraeli to young men.*

Your born angler is like a hound that scents no game but that which he is in pursuit of. *John Burroughs.*

Your cause belongs / To him who can avenge your wrongs. *Winkworth.*

20 Your goodness must have some edge to it, else it is none. *Emerson.*

Your hands in your own pockets in the morning, is the beginning of the last day; your hands in other people's pockets at noon, is the height of the last day. *Ruskin.*

Your "if" is the only peacemaker; much virtue in "if." *As You Like It*, v. 4.

Your labour only may be sold; your soul must not. *Ruskin.*

Your learning, like the lunar beam, affords light but not heat. *Young.*

25 Your levellers wish to level down as far as themselves; but they cannot bear levelling up to themselves. *J. Boswell.*

Your noblest natures are most credulous. *Chapman.*

Your own soul is the thing you ought to look after. *Thomas à Kempis.*

Your own words and actions are the only things you will be called to account for. *Thomas à Kempis.*

Your prime one need is to do right, under whatever compulsion, till you can do it without compulsion. And then you are a Man. *Ruskin.*

Your tongue runs before your wit. *Swift.* 30

Your rusty kettle will continue to boil your water for you if you don't try to mend it. Begin tinkering and there is an end of your kettle. *Carlyle.*

Your voiceless lips, O flowers, are living preachers,—each cup a pulpit, and each leaf a book. *Horace Smith.*

Your words are like notes of dying swans—/ Too sweet to last. *Dryden.*

You're always sure to detect / A sham in the things folks most affect. *Bret Harte.*

Yours is a pauper's soul, a rich man's pelf: / 35 Rich to your heirs, a pauper to yourself. *Lucilius.*

Youth, abundant wealth, high birth, and inexperience, are, each of them, the source of ruin. What then must be the fate of him in whom all four are combined? *Hitopadesa.*

Youth beholds happiness gleaming in the prospect. Age looks back on the happiness of youth, and, instead of hopes, seeks its enjoyment in the recollection of hope. *Coleridge.*

Youth, enthusiasm, and tenderness are like the days of spring. Instead of complaining, O my heart, of their brief duration, try to enjoy them. *Rückert.*

Youth ever thinks that good whose goodness or evil he sees not. *Sir P. Sidney.*

Youth fades; love droops; the leaves of friend- 40 ship fall; a mother's secret hope outlives them all! *Holmes.*

Youth holds no society with grief. *Euripides.*

Youth is a blunder; manhood, a struggle; old age, a regret. *Disraeli.*

Youth is ever apt to judge in haste, and lose the medium in the wild extreme. *Aaron Hill.*

Youth is ever confiding; and we can almost forgive its disinclination to follow the counsels of age, for the sake of the generous disdain with which it rejects suspicion. *W. H. Harrison.*

Youth is full of sport, age's breath is short; / 45 Youth is nimble, age is lame: / Youth is hot and bold, age is weak and cold; / Youth is wild, and age is tame. *Shakespeare.*

Youth is not rich in time; it may be, poor; part with it, as with money, sparing, pay no moment but in purchase of its worth; and what its worth ask death-beds, they can tell. *Young.*

Youth is not the age of pleasure; we then expect too much, and we are therefore exposed to daily disappointments and mortifications. When we are a little older, and have brought down our wishes to our experience, then we become calm and begin to enjoy ourselves. *Lord Liverpool.*

Youth is the season of credulity. *Chatham.*

Youth is too tumultuous for felicity; old age too insecure for happiness. The period most favourable to enjoyment, in a vigorous, fortunate, and generous life, is that between forty and sixty. Life culminates at sixty *Bovee.*

Youth may make / Even with the year; but age, if it will hit, / Shoots a bow short, and lessens still his stake, / As the day lessens, and his life with it. *George Herbert.*

Youth never yet lost its modesty where age had not lost its honour; nor did childhood ever refuse its reverence, except where age had forgotten correction. *Ruskin.*

Youth no less becomes / The light and careless livery that it wears, / Than settled age his sables and his weeds, / Importing health and graveness. *Ham.*, iv. 7.

Youth should be a savings-bank. *Mme. Swetchine.*

5 Youth to itself rebels, though none else near. *Ham.*, i. 3.

Youth would rather be stimulated than instructed. *Goethe.*

Youth, when thought is speech and speech is truth. *Scott.*

Youth will never live to age, without they keep themselves in breath with exercise, and in heart with joyfulness. Too much thinking doth consume the spirits; and oft it falls out, that while one thinks too much of doing, he leaves to do the effect of his thinking. *Sir P. Sidney.*

Youthful failing is not to be admired except in so far as one may hope that it will not be the failing of old age. *Goethe.*

Z.

10 Zahltag kommt alle Tag—Pay-day comes every day. *Ger. Pr.*

Zankt, wenn ihr sitzt beim Weine, / Nicht um Kaisers Bart—Wrangle not over your wine-cups about trifles (*lit.* about the Emperor's beard). *Geibel.*

Zeal ever follows an appearance of truth, and the assured are too apt to be warm; but it is their weak side in argument, zeal being better shown against sin than persons, or their mistakes. *William Penn.*

Zeal for uniformity attests the latent distrusts, not the firm convictions, of the zealot. In proportion to the strength of our self-reliance is our indifference to the multiplication of suffrages in favour of our own judgment. *Sir J. Stephen.*

Zeal is fit for wise men, but flourishes chiefly among fools. *Tillotson.*

15 Zeal is like fire; it needs both feeding and watching. *Pr.*

Zeal is no further commendable than as it is attended with knowledge. *T. Wilson.*

Zeal is very blind or badly regulated when it encroaches upon the rights of others. *Pasquier Quesnel.*

Zeal without knowledge is a runaway horse. *Pr.*

Zeal without knowledge is like expedition to a man in the dark. *Newton.*

20 Zeit ist's, die Unfälle zu beweinen, / Wenn sie nahen und wirklich erscheinen—It is time enough to bewail misfortunes when they come and actually happen. *Schiller.*

Zeit verdeckt und entdeckt—Time covers and uncovers everything. *Ger. Pr.*

Zeitungsschreiber: ein Mensch, der seinen Beruf verfehlt hat—A journalist, a man who has mistaken his calling. *Bismarck.*

Zerstreuung ist wie eine goldene Wolke, die den Menschen, / Wär es auch nur auf kurze Zeit, seinem Elend entrückt—Amusement is as a golden cloud, which, though but for a little, diverts man from his misery. *Goethe.*

Zerstörend ist des Lebens Lauf, / Stets frisst ein Thier das andre auf—Destructive is the course of life; ever one animal eats up another. *Bodenstedt.*

25 Zerstreutes Wesen führt uns nicht zum Ziel —A distracted existence leads us to no goal. *Goethe.*

Zeus hates busybodies and those who do too much. *Euripides.*

Zielen ist nicht genug; es gilt Treffen—To aim is not enough; you must hit. *Ger. Pr.*

Zonam perdidit—He has lost his purse (*lit.* his girdle). *Hor.*

Zu leben weiss ich, mich zu kennen weiss ich nicht—How to live I know, how to know myself I know not. *Goethe.*

30 Zu Rom bestehen die 10 Gebote aus den 10 Buchstaben; / Da pecuniam—gieb Gelder—At Rome the Ten Commandments consist of ten letters—Da pecuniam—Give money. *C. J. Weber.*

Zu schwer bezahlt man oft ein leicht Versehn —One often smarts pretty sharply for a slight mistake. *Goethe.*

Zu viel Demuth ist Hochmuth—Too much humility is pride. *Ger. Pr.*

Zu viel Glück ist Unglück—Too much good luck is ill luck. *Ger. Pr.*

Zu viel Weisheit ist Narrheit—Too much wisdom is folly. *Ger. Pr.*

35 Zu viel Wissbegierde ist ein Fehler, und aus einem Fehler können alle Laster entspringen, wenn man ihm zu sehr nachhängt—Too much curiosity is a fault; and out of one fault all vices may spring, when one indulges in it too much. *Lessing.*

Zufrieden sein, das ist mein Spruch—Contentment is my motto. *M. Claudius.*

Zum Kriegführen sind dreierlei Dinge nötig—Geld! Geld! Geld!—To carry on war three kinds of things are necessary—Money! money! money! *The German Imperial commandant, Lazarus von Schwendi, in 1584.*

Zum Leiden bin ich auserkoren—To suffer am I elected. *Schikaneder-Mozart.*

Zur Tugend der Ahnen / Ermannt sich der Held—The hero draws inspiration from the virtue of his ancestors. *Goethe.*

40 Zwar eine schöne Tugend ist die Treue, / Doch schöner ist Gerechtigkeit—Fidelity indeed is a noble virtue, yet justice is nobler still. *Platen.*

Zwar nicht wissen—aber glauben / Heisst ganz richtig—Aberglauben—Not to know, but to believe, what else is it, strictly speaking, but superstition? *Franz v. Schönthan.*

Zwar sind sie an das Beste nicht gewöhnt, / Allein sie haben schrecklich viel gelesen—It is true they (the public) are not accustomed to the best, but they have read a frightful deal (and are so knowing therefore). *Goethe, the theatre manager in "Faust."*

Zwar weiss ich viel, doch möcht' ich alles wissen—True, I know much, but I would like to know everything. *Goethe,* "*Faust.*"

Zwei Fliegen mit einer Klappe schlagen—To kill two flies with one flapper; to kill two birds with one stone. *Ger. Pr.*

Zwei gute Tage hat der Mensch auf Erden; / Den Hochzeitstag und das Begrabenwerden —Man has two gala-days on earth—his marriage-day and his funeral-day. *Ger. Pr.*

Zwei Seelen und ein Gedanke, / Zwei Herzen und ein Schlag—Two souls and one thought, two hearts and one pulse. *Halen.*

5 Zwei Seelen wohnen, ach! in meiner Brust, / Die eine will sich von der andern trennen —Two souls, alas! dwell in my breast; the one struggles to separate itself from the other. *Goethe,* "*Faust.*"

Zwei sind der Wege, auf welchen der Mensch zur Tugend emporstrebt, / Schliesst sich der eine dir zu, thut sich der andre dir auf, / Handelnd erreicht der Glückliche sie, der Leidende duldend; / Wohl ihm, den sein Geschick liebend auf beiden geführt—There are two roads on which man strives to virtue; one closes against thee, the other opens to thee; the favoured man wins his way by acting, the unfortunate by endurance; happy he whom his destiny guides lovingly on both. *Schiller.*

Zweierlei Arten giebt es, die treffende Wahrheit zu sagen; / Oeffentlich immer dem Volk, immer dem Fürsten geheim—There are two ways of telling the pertinent truth—publicly always to the people, always to the prince in private. *Goethe.*

Zwischen Amboss und Hammer—Between the anvil and the hammer. *Ger. Pr.*

Zwischen heut' und morgen sind Grüfte, zwischen Versprechen und Erfüllen Klüfte—Between to-day and to-morrow are graves, and between promising and fulfilling are chasms. *Rückert.*

Zwischen Lipp' und Kelchesrand / Schwebt 10 der dunkeln Mächte Hand — Between cup and lip hovers the hand of the dark powers. *F. Kind.*

Zwischen uns sei Wahrheit—Let there be truth between us. *Goethe.*

INDEX.

A.

Aaron, in absence of Moses, 532, 4
Abasement and elevation, 471, 6
Abbot, who burnt his fingers, 322, 27
Abiding, blessedness of, 30, 50
Abilities, natural, and culture, 290, 13 ; like natural plants, 290, 12
Ability, combined with experience, 383, 37 ; contentment with one's, 199, 49 ; dependent on activity, 443, 27 ; dependent on will, 37, 56 ; everything in art, 60, 9 ; how to know one's, 507, 49 ; superior, use of, 407 2 ; the height of, 434, 24 ; trying to surpass one's, 497, 18 ; why conjoined with poverty, 451, 3
Able man, described, 7, 19 ; importance of finding and installing, 106, 22 ; 427, 38 ; men, why not rich, 451, 3
Abode, man's, in the future, 415, 27
Above, things, nothing to us, 361, 15 ; those, have ends, 479, 30
Absent, an ideal person, 415, 28
Absenteeism, moral, 521, 41
Abstract terms, emptiness of, 161, 45
Abstractions, lofty, *versus* complexities at hand, 240, 3
Absurd man, the, 223, 20
Absurdity, no, without its champion, 89, 51 ; some slow in discerning, 181, 16
Abundance, effect of, on reason, 199, 2 ; love of, 147, 54
Abuse, as against use, 1, 4 ; 2, 31 ; no argument against use, 95, 43, 44 ; provocative of abuse, 47, 41 ; what is unsusceptible of, 534, 27
Abuses, as matter of sport, 260, 33
Accent, a pervading country, 469, 29
Accessible, discrimination of, from inaccessible, 471, 34
Accidents, behaviour under all, 243, 39 ; rare, pleasure in, 316, 22
Accommodation, mutual, law of the world, 548, 5
Accord, perfect, with whom alone possible, 305, 39
Accusing spirit, and the oath, 415, 31
Acheron, greedy, 88, 21
Achieved, the, to him who looks forward, 55, 7
Achievement, exulting in, 473, 42
Achievements, greatest, first reception of, 432, 4
Achilles, the great, see, 207, 44
Acknowledgment, exacting a grateful, 426, 16
Acquaintance, large, wasteful of time, 175, 42
Acquaintances and friends, 268, 34
Acquaintanceship, expecting happiness from, 148, 11
Acquirement, every fresh, value of, 90, 56
Acquisition, unjust, 507, 40
Acquisitions, new, a burden, 297, 24
Act, an immortal seed grain, 36, 39 ; who does not, dead, 551, 10

Acting according to thought, difficult, 489, 28
Action, a great source of, 362, 41 ; a rule of, 546, 33 ; a seed of circumstances, 163, 14 ; all vital, unconscious, 184, 44 ; an unwarrantable, 412, 53 ; and thought, the worlds of, 465, 8 ; best and only correct, 418, 3 ; civil, second to doing a good, 297, 41 ; contrasted with narrative, 289, 39 ; contrasted with thought, 61, 25 ; delayed, swallowed up by time, 486, 36 ; dependent on will, 474, 37 ; dumb, 55, 9 ; effect of, as contrasted with thought, 485, 41 ; effect of, on time, 349, 29 ; every, measure of, 89, 52 ; good, dependence of, on good cheer, 126, 35 ; good, power of, 75, 7 ; great, the effect on us of, 21, 47 ; greater than sentiment, 91, 52 ; hasty, contrasted with long pondering, 229, 34 ; healthy, 153, 38 ; how to test, 149, 47 ; in, chief qualification, 184, 27 ; involuntary, 3, 57, 58 ; not thought, end of man, 425, 12 ; our fairest, 427, 4 ; our spontaneous, 339, 22 ; power of, 224, 30 ; real, the element of, 369, 11 ; rectitude of, and intention, 370, 34 ; relation of, to thought, 58, 37 ; 484, 47 ; rule for, 114, 44 ; rule of, 274, 45 ; sole basis of, 205, 21 ; spirit of, everything, 454, 32 ; tendency of, 174, 5 ; to be with decision, 57, 45 ; true rule of, 92, 29 ; virtue in, 334, 44 ; voluntary, 38, 22 ; worth of, dependent on motive, 163, 7, 10
Actions, brilliant, often matter of shame, 529, 1 ; effect on us of our, 227, 22 ; good, effect of, 128, 49 ; good, in secret, 128, 48 ; great, crowned, 133, 6 ; great, eloquence, 434, 14 ; how measured by wise men and fools, 108, 55 ; more significant than words, 493, 41 ; not to be hastily judged, 277, 21 ; our epochs, 481, 20 ; the importance of, 486, 1 ; words, 562, 4 ; wrong, apologies for, 377, 12
Activity, a noble and courageous, security of, 93, 52 ; effect of, on the soul, 400, 5 ; life without scope for, 205, 42 ; man's, ever ready to relax, 266, 26 ; reconciling effect of, 84, 39 ; sole source of cheerfulness, 415, 6 ; transforming power of, 66, 26 ; undisciplined, hopelessness of, 505, 45 ; without insight, 476, 7
Actor, might instruct a parson, 79, 20 ; well-graced, interest in, 19, 33
Acts, great success of, due to fortune, 82, 32 ; great, great thoughts in practice, 135, 21 ; great, origin of, 133, 2 ; illustrious, inspiring, 182, 18 ; individual, not to be judged, 114, 13 ; men's, detectives, 568, 17 ; our and our angels, 337, 5
Actual, all from great mystic deep, 395, 24 ; in relation to ideal, 395, 9 ; the ideal, 415, 33
Adaptation, a sovereign rule, 387, 29
Address, value of, to boy, 122, 47
Adieu, a sweet, 395, 27
Administer, ability to, 93, 36

Admiration, and imitation, step between, 470, 5; and love, 525, 34; as a feeling, 305, 33; contrasted with love, 63, 54; elevating power of, 316, 34; 443, 25; power of true, 460, 28; the power of, 525, 20, 21; unwise, contrasted with unwise contempt, 325, 21

Admonition, not readily forgiven, 274, 18

Adore, man to, not to question, 263, 36

Adulation, attendant on wealth, 259, 16; the evil of, 104, 7; to people and to kings, 107, 24

Advance, who does not, 364, 19

Advanced. age, a symbol of, 524, 26; man, unhappy, 261, 19; thinker, self-satisfaction of, 513, 32

Advancing in life, 490, 27

Advantage, or disadvantage, as motives, 202, 38; to be taken, 209, 24; price of, 9, 5

Adverbs, significance of, 126, 46

Adventure, commended, 217, 24; for story's sake, 165, 39

Adventurers, good done by, 38, 38

Adventures, possible in life, 533, 26

Adversaries, merits of, how to treat, 85, 36

Adversities, how alone to overcome, 446, 9

Adversity, a school, 472, 30; as a test, 97, 48; as a teacher, 22, 46; behaviour in, 89, 11; brave spirit in, 2, 8; compared with prosperity, 221, 48; 358, 22, 24, 26, 27; contrary effects of, 438, 43; effect of, on a man, 512, 23; enlightening power of, 559, 25; heroic endurance of, 145, 34; man struggling with, and his deliverer, 432, 26; more bearable than prosperity, 110, 33; more tolerable than contempt, 268, 47; rule for, 189, 22; temper for, 5, 13; test of strength, 177, 53; 175, 13; use of, 408, 20; virtue of, 460, 42; what it brings to light, 215, 34

Advice, bad, 261, 32, 33; best, 417, 32; common motive in asking, 284, 32, 33; giving and taking, 524, 13; giving, and the wisdom to profit by it, 524, 12; gude, seasonable, 137, 9; medical, 300, 35; men liberal with, 330, 13; motive for asking, 522, 29; of those who are well, 98, 46; 179, 5; person to give, 335, 15; rule in giving, 368, 19; 384, 11; to be followed, if good, 172, 10; unacceptable, 161, 34; wanted and not wanted, 415, 34

Advisement, good, good, 320, 34

Adviser, to conceal his superiority, 61, 18

Advising, 368, 20, 21

Advocate, trade of, Carlyle on, 403, 20

Afar, the, 445, 12

Affairs, change of, change of men, 295, 46

Affectation, a confession, 489, 31; essence of, 425, 31; in style, 323, 29

Affection, display of, to be distrusted, 547, 30; due to man, 58, 41; effect of absence on, 2, 12; entire, characteristic of, 83, 43; great, and deep veneration, incompatible, 201, 8; private, effect of, on judgment, 357, 7; profound, characteristic of, 339, 34; selfishly sought after, 177, 14; tragic effects of wounded, 138, 36; true, described, 507, 36; value of, 420, 6

Affections, holy, the band of, 40, 40; how won, 105, 15; 330, 37; our, characteristic of, 337, 7; our greatest tyrants, 324, 40; the proper objects of, 387, 47; to be moderated, 56, 31; without a tap-root, 566, 13

Affinities, spiritual, as a bond, 166, 17

Affirmation before denial, 243, 35

Affirmatives, wanted, 71, 37

Afflicted, the, of God, helplessness of, 45, 3; 531, 36

Affliction, weakness of being daunted by, 542, 40

Agamemnon, brave men before, 517, 7

Age, and youth, characteristics of, 53, 26; a thought to present to, 508, 40; as a teacher, 21, 14; compared with youth, 568, 37, 45, 49; 469, 2; crabbed, and youth, 49, 30; distrustful, 37, 16; effect of, on our views of life, 444, 36; emancipation from one's, impossible, 303, 20; every, has its characteristics, 39, 52; glory of, 430, 11; golden, whither fled, 64, 27; in man and in woman, 124, 15; of gold, the true, 23, 31; old, bashfulness in, 25, 61; our, characterised, 337, 9, 10; present, characterised, 525, 25; surest sign of, 456, 27; the function of, 60, 23; the, riddle of, how to be solved, 451, 34; the self-satisfaction of, 186, 30; this, chief curse of, 420, 6; weakening effect of, 328, 11; without brains, 341, 16

Agencies to be economised, 117, 4

Ages, great, characteristic of, 10, 43; the, and the hours, 435, 35

Agnosticism of doubt, and that of devotion, 415, 43

Agreeable, art of being, 458, 34; condition of being, 474, 28; to be, every one's duty, 90, 13

Agreement, an indifferent, commended, 15, 38

Agriculture, advantages of, 329, 8; occupation in, 411, 15

Aid at call, 482, 11

Aim, a lower, secured by devotion to a higher, 415, 26; to, not enough, 569, 27

Alacrity in sinking, 166, 32

Alarm, who sounds, safe, 83, 29

Alchemists, discoveries of, 415, 49

Alchemy, 18, 29

Alcohol, pure, the thing wanted, 534, 14

Alexander the Great at the tomb of Achilles, 320, 26; Juvenal on, 509, 4; his tomb, 400, 18

All, co-operation with, 314, 28; for man's good, 111, 34; forsaking, finding all, 323, 33; how one whole, 488, 11; in flux, 10, 54; in nothing, 185, 53; the, incomprehensibility of, 141, 33; the law and all the prophets, 220, 5; reflex of, in every man, 92, 35; things from above, 328, 9; things, how to subject, 563, 32; things of same stuff, 328, 7; to be found in No, 319, 22

Allegiance, to fallen lord, merit of, 145, 34

Allegory, a transparent palace, 222, 5

Alliance with a powerful man, 318, 49

Alliteration, 17, 10

Allotted, the, and the non-allotted, 536, 39; what is, and what is not, 414, 41

Alms, a rule in, 184, 46; giving, but not thought, 492, 40; to go before, 243, 14

Almsgiving, 305, 48

Alms-people, Ruskin's, 287, 38

Alone, doubly, 544, 28; the word, 564, 34

Alphonso of Castile, saying of, 327, 30

Altitude to unpractised eye, 496, 36

Amateur, not to be discouraged, 416, 3

Ambassador, Wotton's definition of, 14, 18

Ambition, a dream, 73, 3; a noble, 470, 13; a shadow's shadow, 167, 16; a vain, 322, 7; and love, wings to great deeds, 258, 6; as a motive, 399, 1; danger of, 2, 33; effect on mind of, 133, 32; fling away, 107, 45; 165, 28; end of, 266, 3; for place and greatness, 321, 32; freedom from, 485, 30; great, from great character, 133, 8; height of, 326, 15; hurtful vice, 161, 17; in Cæsar, 545, 21; man's, 397, 33; minds most and least actuated by, 276, 12; Mme. de Pompadour on, 474, 1; no, in heaven, 187, 21; not to be too high-pitched, 243, 42; often vain, 87, 11; parent of virtue, 484, 9; slavery, 14, 19; toil and vanity of, 249, 44; vaulting, 511, 48; way of, 556, 14

Ambitions followed by adulation, 416, 4

Ambition's hands, washing of, 19, 9

Ambitious, man and his masters, 222, 43; men, the risk to, 543, 1; thoughts, 25, 47

Amen, let me say, 241, 35

Amendment, first impulse to, 386, 9; though civilisation should go, 163, 34

America, a forecast of, 512, 20 ; the only true, 184, 48

Americans, and English, 427, 44 ; Emerson on, 335, 8

Amiss, nothing, with simpleness and duty, 296, 2

Amusement, good of, 569, 23 ; *versus* business, 173, 18 ; wish of society, 396, 38

Anarchy, and tyranny, 504, 14 ; death, 131, 13

Ancestors, deeds of, not ours, 88, 8 ; our, 332, 12 ; our duty to, 527, 40 ; people who disrespect, 345, 20 ; who has no need of, 553, 27

Ancestry, boasting of, 145, 21 ; 271, 10 ; 473, 2 ; who has nothing but, to boast of, 150, 46

Anchor, that holds, 36, 38 ; to the soul, 544, 36

Anchorage for man, 494, 24 ; necessary in this world, 208, 33

Anchoring, no, fast, 377, 8

Ancients, and moderns, teachings of, compared, 416, 7 ; our masters in morals, 521, 20 ; that don't grow old, 432, 44 ; we, 521, 9

Anecdote, value of one, 331, 37

Angel, the recording, and the oath, 415, 31 ; the recording, no fable, 451, 4

Angel's face, her, 154, 47 ; visits, 249, 38, 39

Angel-visits, 37, 27

Angels, and accommodation for them, 443, 10 ; as created, 94, 22 ; Disraeli on side of the, 450, 27 ; men one day, 526, 13 ; Swedenborg on, 187, 22 ; the best, not in community, 417, 48 ; visits of, let pass, 430, 34

Anger, a majestic, 471, 7 ; a man who provoked to, silences it, 551, 34 ; a punishment to one's self, 490, 7 ; ability to moderate, 281, 18 ; best antidote to, 271, 22 ; best restraint upon, 142, 9 ; dissolved in menaces, 552, 44 ; end of, 540, 21 ; for nothing to no purpose, 482, 28 ; how to avoid, 215, 27 ; how to overcome, 240, 16 ; no guard to itself 296, 1 ; of a strong man, 416, 8 ; often unreasonable, 466, 44 ; restraint of, 142, 9 ; slowness to, 147, 19, 20 ; the bridle of, 272, 13 ; the end of, 62, 44 ; to burn slow, 240, 21 ; unreasonable, with others, 28, 13 ; unrestrained, evil of, 364, 18 ; with one we love, 491, 3

Angler, the born, 568, 18

Angling, Izaak Walton on, 526, 18 ; like humility, 567, 40

Angry at all, angry for nothing, 148, 47 ; man beside himself, 159, 15

Anguish, great purifying power of, 6, 64

Animal, denial of, in man, 416, 47 ; every, loves itself, 327, 42 ; life of an, 439, 1

Animals summed up in man, 264, 19

Annihilation, no such thing as, 377, 7

Annoyances, the smallest, effect of, 453, 51

Annoying others, 144, 21

Answer, a perfect, 145, 31 ; the shortest, 453, 27 ; wise, how to get a, 177, 26, 531, 43

Ant, a silent preacher, 316, 23 ; lesson of, 125, 3 ; the, example of, 342, 16

Antæus, meaning of the fable, 122, 13

Antagonist, a prudent, 213, 10 ; how to meet an, 373, 1 ; an, not to be underrated, 307, 46

Anthropomorphism in thought, 60, 32

Antiquary, memory of, characterised, 21, 42

Antique, the, our admiration of, 337, 6

Antiquity, chief moral agent of, 453, 11 ; divided from us only by age, 109, 2 ; the world's youth, 16, 13

Antony over Cæsar's body, 33, 33

Anvil and hammer, 30, 31 ; 74, 20, 30

Anxiety, effect of, 198, 10 ; misery of, 34, 41 ; Plato on, 340, 18 ; specific against, 220, 11 ; to be despised, 62, 24

Ape, perfect, *versus* degenerate man, 181, 6

Aphorism, a short but certain, 323, 33 ; essence of, 425, 37 ; true salt of literature, 271, 15

Aphorisms, only words, 534, 9 ; the value of, 65, 38

Apollo to Phaëthon, 106, 34

Apology, Christian, 487, 15 ; from want of sense, 307, 7 ; who needs no, 19, 32

Apostle and preacher, different aims of, 224, 11

Apostates never genuine believers, 479, 54

Apothegms, practical ineffectuality of, 185, 16

Apparel, and the man, 416, 11 ; proclaims the man, 48, 36 ; singularity in, 149, 1

Appearance, deceptiveness of, 23, 13 ; *minus* reality, 61, 23 ; neglect of, becoming in man, 112, 31 ; *versus* reality, 325, 47

Appearances, and reality, 481, 34 ; deceptiveness of, 7, 52 ; 18, 23 ; 305, 17 ; first, deceptive, 56, 32 ; keeping up, 421, 14 ; mere, mislead, 277, 7 ; not to be trusted, 116, 39 ; power of, 61, 22 ; science of, 102, 36 ; value of, 534, 32

Appetite, a satisfied, incredulous of hunger, 48, 13 ; a well-governed, 24, 54 ; allures to destruction, 163, 16 ; change of, with age, 72, 13 ; cruelty of, 546, 23 ; from eating, 222, 25 ; ideal of, 88, 5 ; in youth, 7, 14

Appetites, unanswered, ground of complaint, 275, 42

Applaud to the very echo, 169, 19

Applause, dependence on, 152, 13 ; gaining, and avoiding censure, 202, 20 ; popular, not fame, 219, 56 ; popular, the poison of, 320, 28 ; reward of virtue, 278, 11 ; to be regarded with suspicion, 545, 42

Application, felicitous, merit of a, 471, 12 ; importance of right, 475, 4

Appreciation and criticism, 201, 27

Apprenticeship, no man's completed, 391, 13

Approved man, the, 312, 31

Aptitudes, to be tested, 79, 7

Arc, the, that we see, all that is drawn, 524, 44

Arch-enemy, the, 416, 14

Archer, how known, 14, 22

Archimedes, and his prop, 72, 4 ; exclamation of, 89, 8

Architect, a fellow-worker, 445, 42

Architecture, attraction of, 174, 23 ; Greek, character of, 136, 9 ; the best, 417, 33

Arguing, disingenuous, 145, 25 ; rule in, 185, 7

Argument, contrasted with testimony, 412, 48 ; folly of heat in, 323, 38 ; the best, 227, 22 ; vain against nature, 166, 38 ; *versus* instruction, 370, 8

Arguments, wagers for, 108, 49

Aristocracies that do not govern, 356, 46

Aristocracy, an, the likely fate of, 13, 53 ; essence of, 425, 36 ; the, defined, 360, 37 ; the right basis of, 229, 24

Aristocrat, a young, Iphicrates to, 287, 44

Armada, Spanish, scattering of, 5, 42

Armies not to be stamped out, 217, 3

Arms, a last resort, 328, 25 ; and peace, 18, 8

Army, a school of morality, 416, 18 ; book to study life in, 416, 17 ; like a serpent, 14, 25

Arrogance, how fostered, 407, 20

Art, a great step in study of, 553, 20 ; a haven of refuge, 265, 31 ; a love for, test of, 472, 42 ; a test of, 300, 43 ; a wise man's, defined, 540, 27 ; achievement in, 155, 9 ; ancient and modern, contrasted, 14, 37, 38 ; ancient, and modern science, 534, 11 ; and Christianity, 420, 19 ; and deception, life with, 566, 24 ; and life, 516, 17 ; and morals, laws of identical, 64, 25 ; and nature, compared, 290, 28 ; and nature, perfection by, 272, 43 ; and morals, rules in, compared, 188, 15, 16 ; and religion, 372, 13 ; and the religious passion, 451, 13 ; as the spirit is, 550, 15 ; different appreciations of, 53, 29 ; without breath of life, 237, 4 ; capability everything in, 130, 26 ;

condition of perfection in, 265, 23; contrasted with criticism, 225, 5; contrasted with manufacture, 550, 16; display of, to be distrusted, 504, 40; done for money, Ruskin on, 540, 40; easily learned, 414, 29; concealment of elaboration in, 54, 28; Emerson's definition of, 421, 28; false ambition in, 191, 20; first and last secret of, 287, 46; genuine, the *raison d'être* of, 91, 5; great, the work of full manhood, 9, 12; great, Ruskin's definition of, 9, 38; highest achievement of, 435, 10; highest, characterised, 434, 36; highest problem of, 435, 7; highest subject of, 60, 19; how far teachable, 205, 10; how to attain proficiency in, 292, 24; ignoble, test of, 300, 43; imitation of nature, 328, 41; in, ability everything, 60, 9; in, the only good, 173, 5; inversion and subversion of, 545, 23; less expressive than affection, 5, 40; life of, 416, 12; measure of love of, 567, 22; mediæval and modern, 431, 14; mediæval and modern, compared, 188, 1, 2; misfortune in, 442, 34; more than strength, 204, 18; necessity in, 539, 33; noble, expression of a great soul, 308, 12; noblest, 465, 20; object of, 445, 16; of both divine and earthly inspiration, 22, 30; no patriotic, 473, 44; perfection of, 18, 28; principle and aim of, 66, 8; produced hastily, 416, 24; products, nought and not bad, 357, 48; question as regards, 450, 29; rated by gold, 48, 43; sayings about, 65, 16–18; secret of power of, 207, 3; *sine quâ non* of, 100, 1; teaching of, 456, 42; technical skill in, 451, 13; the best in, 186, 2; the chief matter in any, 35, 47; the claims of, 247, 47; the faculty of, 426, 46; the great in, defined, 540, 44; the greatest, 452, 43; the ideal in, 54, 7; the last step of, 392, 10; the laws of, 438, 26; the oldest, a mushroom, 290, 22; the theatrical, 431, 8; to learned and unlearned, respectively, 70, 27; true, characterised, 499, 38, 39; unintelligible to the head alone, 433, 22; unquickened from above and within, 507, 53; when to be called fine, 136, 10; who knows, half or wholly, 552, 5; without enthusiasm, 316, 29; worthless, apart from nature, 139, 20

Artifice, danger and disgrace of, 225, 9
Artisan at home everywhere, 361, 25
Artisans and artists, 184, 36
Artist, a bad and a good, distinguished, 323, 16; an, essence of, 474, 27; and his age, 416, 26; and his art, 205, 10; 416, 28; and his work, 416, 25; 512, 30; and society, 14, 30; at thought of mob, 65, 30; conceiving and executing, 416, 27; destructive influence of society on, 396, 12; function of, 462, 10; great, and his ideal, 431, 12; greatest, characterised, 434, 36; his function, 334, 45; his praise in his work, 55, 8; his true praise, 265, 5; measuring tools of, 14, 29; modesty in, merit of, 410, 38; necessity of sight to, 448, 40; good, mark of, 418, 15; true praise of, 14, 28; Ruskin's definition of, 14, 27; 14, 30; spiritual, born blind, 454, 40; the best, 426, 28; the greatest, as defined by Ruskin, 143, 49; vocation of, 416, 29; truth in hand of, 18, 57
Artist-work, the most important, 301, 1
Artistes, conceit of, 218, 23
Artists, ancient, aim of, 208, 27; and artisans, difference between, 184, 36; great and feeble, distinctions between, 534, 34; inventing and at work, 60, 28; no standard for amateurs, 416, 3
Arts, a family of sisters, 421, 8; all fine, related, 10, 38; and nature, 221, 39; conditions necessary for, 421, 22; great, contrasted with false, 133, 9; on what their vitality depends, 425, 21; the, fine effect of culture of, 168, 42; the fine, mother and father of. 444, 12; the fine, secret of, 182, 17; the fine, the aim in, 188, 45; the fine,
574

what we know in, 190, 37; the perfection of the, 447, 25; the principle and aim of, 66, 8; to learned and unlearned, 438, 33; useful mother and father of, 444, 12
Asbestos, fate of what is not of, 541, 3
Ashes, live in their wonted fires, 77, 28; the, of your sires, 394, 45
Asketh, he that, 93, 32
Asking; timid, 364, 50; twice better than going wrong, 28, 33; 29, 48
Aspiration, its effect on us, 539, 36; persistent, of mankind, like a compass to a ship, 447, 29
Ass, bray of, 367, 38; why offensive, 85, 25; dreams of the, 58, 16; man with a head of, 41, 23; mistaking itself for a stag, 41, 8; never more than an ass, 171, 46; rather an, that carries us, 29, 26; the hungry, 222, 31; the kick of, how to treat, 171, 45
Assertion no proof, 27, 6; without discrimination, Dante on, 40, 58
Asses know asses, 79, 6
Assistance, a universal necessity, 304, 16; mutual, a law of nature, 180, 43
Association of ideas, 257, 47
Associations, old, not to be bought, 526, 6
Assuming, the most, 479, 16
Assurance doubly sure, 167, 49
Astray, who walks, 551, 16
Atheism, moral root of, 277, 18; Plato on, 466, 42; practical, defined, 395, 10; what it amounts to, 301, 3
Atheist by night, 34, 7; no good man, 211, 26
Atheist's God, the, 301, 3
Athene, the goddess, 430, 18
Athens and Greece, 556, 6
Atonement, commencement of, 421, 11
Attachment, personal, as a ground of public conduct, 346, 51; powerful, effect of, 354, 51; the law of, 337, 13; tokens of, 133, 10
Attainment, satisfactory, 313, 26
Attempt begun to be carried through, 24, 18
Attention, evil effect of constant, 46, 54
Attorney's epitaph, 155, 15
Auctioneer, the, at a non-plus, 358, 10
Audacity, the effect of, 346, 39
Augustine's prayer for deliverance, 245, 7
Auld, acquaintance, 389, 33; Nickie Ben, Burns address to, 102, 18
Austerity superseded, 544, 31
Australia, fertility of, 75, 50
Author, and his brother authors, 301, 5; cares of an, 311, 20; compared with his works, 301, 5; enraged, 49, 35; fastidious about his style, 543, 2; genius not enough for, 208, 13; how to understand an, 177, 44; most engaging powers of, 459, 28; in the regard of publisher, 301, 6; popular, wish of, 84, 18; profession of, 278, 44; reading an, 524, 37; rule in choosing, 44; unconsciously portrays himself, 90, 2; who should not be, 150, 6; without gift of selection, 151, 6
Authority, a test of character, 474, 25; based on injustice, 194, 24; based on kindness and force, 144, 5; gentleness in, commended, 175, 14; conduct of people in, 345, 1; how founded, 330, 39; how to destroy, 219, 2; how weakened, 314, 12; not to be lightly resisted, 304, 8; of a greater, submission to, 449, 2; provocative of disobedience, 548, 21
Authors and their works, 284, 11; Horace s advice to, 406, 30; most original, 444, 3; of a people, their worth, 420, 5; three classes of, 468, 24; to be content with choice readers, 379, 27; young, error of, 568, 8
Authorship, three difficulties of, 468, 25; 497, 9
Avarice, and luxury compared, 258, 11; compared with poverty, 354, 18, 35; contrasted with pov-

erty, 62, 43; how created, 204, 39; 488, 32; in contrast with gluttony, 124, 42; no, in hell, 137, 21; subduing, profit of, 230, 44
Avaricious, the, 386, 27; the, their affectation, 50, 32
Avengement, man's part, 65, 35
Avenue, every, barred now, 317, 29
Awkwardness, cause of, 521, 15; sign of genius, 133, 22
Awoke and found myself famous, 165, 10
Axioms, only words, 534, 9
Aye or no, the power of, 189, 41

B

Bachelors, old, why there are, 415, 25
Back, defence of, 488, 38; going, when easy and when impossible, 492, 44; rather than wrong, 381, 1
Backbiter, and face-flatterer, the same, 300, 29
Backsliding fatal, 478, 19
Bacon, fruitlessness of his teachings, 314, 34; treatment of, 349, 20; unconcern about his name, 110, 26
Bad, as a doctor, 129, 35; at strife with good, 382, 8; for sake of good, 125, 42; ground, pains not to be wasted on, 297, 16; in the thinking, 315, 2; man always suspicious, 80, 32; man, his enemies, 416, 45; man, opponents of, 59, 44; man, pretending to be good, 261, 38; men, ability of, 477, 19; mistaken for good, 417, 38; nothing and no one absolutely, 218, 7, 13; nothing, if understood, 78, 40; nothing so, as we think, 378, 47; once, bad always, 386, 23; railing against, deprecated, 71, 37; the fear of, 436, 18; the sparing, 31, 33; 148, 23; thing, worthless, 1, 8; when good, 331, 32.
Bairns, young and old, and their parents, 543, 9
Ballads, more powerful than laws, 241, 33
Ballot-box, a leveller, 33, 45
Banishment, bitter bread of, 76, 17
Baptism, with water and with fire, 186, 15
Barbarian, a, 150, 38
Barbarism, defined, 549, 31; first step from, 495, 10
Barbarous, character, traits of, 475, 31; man, first spiritual want of, 428, 37
Bargain, a, and the purse, 6, 38; a good, a loss, 31, 39; to be clear, 260, 23
Bargains, confined to man, 263, 1; great, no economy, 178, 45; third party to, 470, 34
Barrel-organ in a slum, 170, 45
Barter, passion for, 77, 51
Base, and depraved training in, 70, 26; man, a, who means to be your enemy, 541, 34
Baseness, at heart, effect of, on character, 542, 7; irrespective of looks, 112, 37; provision for turning, into nobleness, 21, 23
Bashfulness, a defect, 180, 30; without merit, 278, 20
Bathing, no, twice in the same river, 302, 52
Battalions, the heaviest, God with the, 329, 27
Battle, a, won, Wellington on, 444, 45; all, misunderstanding, 9, 14; ceasing for want of combatants, 88, 22; each man alone in, 190, 36; necessary to victory, 401, 46; won, as sad as one lost, 297, 35
Battlefield, mercy on the, 331, 11
Battlefields, world's, 465, 23
Bayonets, Napoleon on, 566, 31
Be, to, not to be, 490, 31
Be-all and end-all, 412, 54

Bear and endure, 346, 9, 10
Beard, or no beard, 146, 41; pride of, 170, 46
Beast, no, without some pity, 301, 8; ungovernable, how to manage, 188, 43
Beasts, wild and tame, to be avoided, 324, 44
Beau, Fielding's definition of, 1, 13
Beaufort, Cardinal, last words of, 537, 24
Beautiful, a manifestation, 417, 7; and good, 417, 8; 430, 39; benefit of, 540, 41; capacity for, rare, 325, 12; compared with rational, 331, 48; effect of fostering, 113, 55; Emerson on, 315, 37; feeling for, to be cultivated, 264, 3; formerly holy, 185, 50; foundation of, 417, 10; how to find, 526, 32; in curves, 187, 43; like sunshine, 417, 9; nothing, by itself, 314, 45; nothing, out of place, 206, 2; only in song, 114, 25; souls, short-lived, 162, 29; the alone, 482, 34; the, and the rude craftsman, 510, 51; the, in the form, 23, 42; the, lot of, 513, 21; the, reconciliation of good and true, 518, 17; things, the two most, 459, 27; test of the, 313, 43; to be encouraged, 460, 15
Beauty, a fragile good, 112, 30; a sign of purity, 153, 37; a thing of, 21, 37; adoration of, 273, 29; aim of the world, 208, 28; all, in man, 312, 35; and folly, 26, 14; and life in the small, 189, 51; and the eternal, inseparable, 153, 52; and virtue, rarely combined, 110, 42; and worship of, Goethe on, 66, 9; as seen, undefinable, 567, 44; as truth, 520, 22; attractive power of, 1, 15; basis and essence of, 540, 25; born a, born married, 42, 6; complex, 488, 22; contrasted with grace, 131, 36–38; contrasted with grace and innocence, 66, 10; contrasted with grandeur, 132, 8; dead, chaos comes again, 109, 47; defined, 197, 26; dependence of, on expression, 97, 50; effect of contrast on, 47, 33; Elysian, 81, 4; everywhere, 290, 35; fair point of the line of, 427, 3; final aim of art, 66, 8; fleeting, 70, 15; forms of, compared, 1, 15; human, effect of sight of, 301, 40; ideal, fugitive, 436, 10; ideal of, 436, 11; in a plain dress, 447, 47; in common lives, 476, 20; in the purest sense, 469, 10; like a leaf, 225, 20; moral power of, 382, 16; mortal, 22, 27; not always blessed, 322, 34; not separable from the eternal, 153, 52; not vain, because fading, 197, 4; of a rainbow character, 523, 4; one, mortification to another, 292, 8; only seen in suffering, 379, 37; personal, power of, 129, 60; persuasive power of, 10, 10; possibility of, 471, 5; principal ingredient in, 511, 41; seat and sources of, 507, 34; seldom unconscious, 105, 3; sense of, and duty, 453, 9; sought for pleasure, 20, 36; sources of, 184, 40; subtle attraction of, 99, 42; the best part of, 413, 29; the nature of, 406, 40; too great, effect on sight of, 403, 5; unconsciousness of, rare, 105, 3; undemonstrable, 331, 23; vain, 103, 24; why snarled at, 274, 49; with modesty, rare, 368, 3; without modesty, 313, 42; without virtue, 99, 25; 224, 20; worship of mere, 465, 28
"Because" our concern, not "why," 556, 13
Becoming, the, defined, 535, 45
Bed, a silken, kindly, 332, 21; the conjugal, 386, 31
Bede's tomb, inscription on, 138, 26
Bedlam, how tenanted, 253, 47
Bee, little busy, 161, 11
Bees, keeping of, 437, 26
Beggar, and king, 190, 8; and rich, different feelings of, 531, 32; at his level, 460, 12; Lamb on, 417, 11–17; on horseback, 387, 40, 41; pains taken by Nature in forming, 292, 26
Beggar'd all description, 155, 2
Beggar's, bag, 28, 54; purse, 1, 19; robes, 367, 39; the, song, 530, 11
Begging, apt to provoke disgust, 88, 32; shame of, to be spared, 123, 2

Beginning, a bad, 1, 6; a good, 6, 39; a hot, course and end of, 15, 6; and end, contrast of, 194, 26; cheerful, 8, 59; 90, 5; contrasted with ulterior steps, 9, 15; difficult, 8, 60; implies an end, 48, 12; most notable, 186, 40; no, rather than never end, 29, 34; prior to improving or finishing, 345, 4; the true, unnoticed, 458, 35

Beginnings to be resisted, 356, 59

Begun, half done, 25, 49; 68, 30

Behaviour, contagious, 109, 21; end of education, 77, 9; in private, 58, 14; learned, as we take diseases, 275, 90; rule for, 394, 46; the first sign of force, 347, 4

Being, all, founded on reason, 9, 3; every, has its own beauty, 91, 35; resigned with regret, 112, 2, 3; the chain of, 511, 47

Beings, above us and beneath us, a wise man's attitude to, 199, 48

Belial, the sons of, 445, 33

Belief, a, easy to a man, 203, 16; and conduct, inconsistency of, 264, 2; and disbelief, dangerous, 346, 18; a miracle, 197, 16; alternations of, 173, 30; affected by custom, 523, 26; easier than judgment, 93, 38; eludes system, 163, 15; flower of, in the last darkness, 544, 7; general ground of, 9, 28; impotent to change nature, 301, 10; in absurdity, 49, 50; limiting, by comprehensibility, 148, 48; modern, 565, 49; multiform, 476, 19; now-a-days, only half-hearted, 275, 41; often unintelligent, 274, 4; one's, effect on, of another's, 200, 49; only in practice, 457, 19; or disbelief, no compelling, 302, 36; our, in others, 521, 29; power of, 538, 22; 532, 28; power of a firm, 27, 19; that is contrary to truth, 301, 11; the, we incline to, 539, 38; variations of, from generation to generation, 305, 4; *versus* debate, 12, 13; want of, to be concealed, 461, 15; what regulates our, 528, 6

Beliefs, two, necessary to fulfilling our duty, 525, 23; various as men, 274, 24

Believers, traditional, the god of, 430, 15

Believing, man, the, the original, 442, 8; three means of, 468, 27; unhasting, 145, 19; without seeing, merit of, 30, 45

Bell, church, inscription on, 231, 5

Bells, church, 64, 26

Bell-wethers, men have their, 267, 28

Belly, a slave to, 417, 27; empty, effect of, on body, 545, 25; full, effect of, on spirit, 545, 25.

Belongings, our chief, inalienable, 450, 3

Beloved, how to be, 490, 14; object, centre of a paradise, 90, 6; of the Almighty, 417, 28

Below, things, nothing to us, 361, 10

Benefactor, how we regard, 527, 24

Benefactors, how to treat, 71, 26

Beneficence, defined, 28, 3; fruitful effects of, 1, 22; tree of, well-rooted, 549, 18.

Benefit, a high, compared with a low, 198, 46; affected by manner of conferring it, 475, 1; given quickly, 194, 38; that sticks to fingers, 478, 15; to one worthy of it, 28, 1

Benefits, our sense of, 385, 20; remembered, and not, 144, 54

Benevolence, impossible to one ill at ease, 305, 40; rare, 368, 6; universal, pretenders to, 480, 14.

Benevolent, heart, our regard for, 417 30; mistaken occupation of, 417, 31

Berries, two lovely, moulded on one stem, 395, 33.

Best, a test of, 413, 20; inexplicable by words 562, 8; liable to abuse, 110, 27; man, Emerson's, 145, 31; man, moulded out of faults, 479, 26; nearest, 12, 58; safety of, 540, 42; the, in the world, 537, 11; the, inexplicable by words, 67, 18; the, a sufferer, 417, 50; things, the law regarding, 427, 39; when corrupted, 48, 27; who does his, 55, 13

576

Bestride the narrow world, 142, 26.

Betrayal, only by friends, 330, 8

Betrayer, the, defined, 418, 14

Better, and worse without limit, 184, 7; enemy of well, 179, 36; 234, 6; side of things, looking at, 543, 34; the, the greater, 34, 37

Bible, a, all have to publish, 538, 15; and the Jews, 418, 23; an idol, 274, 36; an indubitably inspired, 331, 40; and religion, 205, 41; as an educator, 274, 38; effect on style of study of, 195, 26; effect of familiarity with, 439, 34; free circulation of, Goethe on, 285, 10; from the heart of nature, 33, 10; Goethe on, 164, 40; honestly studied, a difficult book, 177, 10; how it may do harm, and how good, 344, 52; how to understand difficult parts of, 446, 27; its eternally effective power, Goethe on, 331, 17; morality, 384, 45; not a panacea, 467, 14; of a nation, 418, 24; 491, 4; Sir William Jones on, 418, 21; teaching of, 418, 22, 25; the, and the man's obligations, 392, 52; the Hebrew, 434, 22; the study of and eloquence, 303, 31; true, just knows her, 215, 38; truths still latent in, 418, 20; writing a, 435, 8; 18

Bibles, how made great, 489, 1

Biography, faithfully written, a poem, 473, 8; of souls, epochs in, 508, 24

Bigot, as regards reason, 148, 53

Bigotry, an unchristian, 495, 32; effect of, on religion, 30, 18

Bird, an example, 400, 31; an old, 15, 56; in hand, 1, 37; in the wood, 81, 14; smallest, alighting on tree, 453, 52; that flutters least, 403, 11

Birds, Burns' pity of, in winter, 181, 34; by shallow rivers' falls, 34, 15; early, 75, 32; how taught to sing, 400, 9; 523, 22; old, 327, 10, 11

Birth, beginning of death, 20, 35; high, an accident, 156, 29; low, comparative advantage of, 487, 52; meanness of, not to be concealed, 46, 1; naught without sense, 270, 24; our, Wordsworth on, 337, 18; pride of mere, 398, 33

Birth-place, insignificance of, 490, 10

Births, premature, 116, 32

Bishop of gold and wood, 89, 42

Bitter, in the memory, 415, 13

Black, but not the devil, 164, 36; obliged to wear and buy, 490, 30

Blade, the trenchant, Toledo trusty, 458, 29

Blame, on the wronged, 224, 29; not on one side only, 181, 30

Blamelessness, mark of imbecility or greatness, 114, 37

Blaming self, motive in, 330, 27

Blast, the loudest, 418, 34

Blaze, a, as a spectacle, 466, 34

Blessed, man, half part of, 143, 52; the, according to Horace, 310, 25

Blessedness, must be sought and founded within, 298, 4; not in rank or wealth, 209, 14

Blessings, as they go, 160, 54; fleeting, 183, 21; in relation to ills, 31, 17; not valued till lost, 78, 18; still rife, 267, 24; unthought-of, 491, 25

Blind, and blind leaders, Carlyle's advice to, 545, 26; leading blind, 174, 11; the, and the colour, 1, 41; the, as leader, 361, 42; the very, 27, 53

Blindest, the, 474, 50

Blindness, colour, better than total, 44, 31; our, a blessing 176, 6

Bliss, an hour of, value of, 382, 5; search for, in wealth and power, vain, 567, 36; the same in all, 46, 13

Blockhead, a, cavilling of, 1, 42; according to Wm. Blake, 153, 19; and his time, 431, 24; the bookful, 418, 49

Blood, a peculiar fluid, 31, 7; alone not ennobling, 534, 23; good, a virtue of, 31, 50; hard to tame,

419, 8 ; justification of shedding, 418, 41 ; no foundation set on, 474, 31 ; through scoundrels, 287, 39

Bloom, of youth, fading, 320, 25 ; season of, only once, 441, 38

Blossom, no, no fruit, 301, 7

Blossoms, not fruits, 30, 60

Blue-stocking, estimate of, 1, 43

Blunder, the most fatal, 473, 28 ; worse than a crime, 39, 10

Blundering, a means of learning, 34, 14

Blush, a, beauty of, 172, 3 ; a, in the face, 28, 55 ; meaning of a, 418, 45

Blushing, beautifying power of, 85, 11

Bluster, a blind for cowardice, 133, 16

Blustering, for the fop, 232, 52

Boasters, of great things, 399, 14

Boasting, before victory, 242, 10

Boats, in a calm, 567, 34

Bodies, large, likely to err, 230, 13 ; without working, 126, 5

Bodily labour, alleviating, 235, 23

Body, a handsome, needs no cloak, 48, 8 ; built by spirit, 86, 2 ; effect of soul on, 110, 32 ; feeble, effect of, on mind, 505, 17 ; how to warm, 519, 1 ; light of, 439, 12 ; of man, a temple, 471, 19 ; pent, here in the, 155, 11 ; politic, evil in, 202, 39 ; politic, the, like the human body, 233, 11 ; the, and its passions, whence, 478, 40 ; the, and raiment, 438, 48 ; to be cared for, 409, 33 ; with head off, 537, 12 ; without spirit, 474, 22

Boldly, ventured, half done, 115, 52

Boldness, commended, 26, 50 ; empty, 219, 55

Bond, who breaks his, 550, 38

Bonfires, risk of crowding round, 345, 10

Book, a, a book, 488, 42 ; a bad, 208, 2 ; a, digressions in, Swift and Sterne on, 68, 11, 12 ; a, difficulty in composing, 185, 40 ; a good, destruction of, high treason, 19, 16 ; a good, value of, 283, 27 ; a good, who kills, 552, 4 ; a great, great, 7, 9 ; a hieroglyphical, 283, 2 ; a true, the virtue of, 562, 1 ; a wise man's, defined, 540, 27 ; an effective, 171, 1 ; and head in collision, 541, 40 ; as a friend, 505, 29 ; every, written for a special public, 90, 17 ; good, Milton's definition, 6, 40 ; good, to read, 90, 16 ; great, great evil, 272, 15 ; how to render, lasting, 493, 3 ; how serviceable, 301, 14 ; how written down, 301, 16 ; injurious, author of, 150, 47 ; last thing in writing, 438, 9 ; lifetime of, 22, 25 ; love of a, 147, 49 ; main worth of, 189, 30 ; man of one, 37, 20 ; 125, 27 ; no, so bad as not to yield some good, 299, 1 ; no, useless, 318, 37 ; on what condition readable, 313, 3 ; projecting, sweeter than making, 167, 30 ; right use of, 496, 37 ; test of worth in, 301, 14, 15 ; that time has criticised, 533, 39 ; the rule in writing a, 171, 30 ; the true value of a man's, 459, 14 ; to learn wisdom from, 464, 18 ; true, the writer of, 145, 35 ; what makes a good, 489, 2 ; what must be behind a, 477, 12 ; without stomach for, 565, 17 ; worth buying, 171, 2 ; worth or unworth of, independent of style, 481, 42 ; writer of, a world-preacher, 465, 42

Bookish knowledge in heads of fools, 108, 62

Books, a lover of happiness of, 305, 14 ; a substantial world, 73, 2 ; about books, 472, 1 ; advantage of buying, 296, 56 ; and brains, as possessions, 520, 23 ; and conversation, 332, 3 and nature, both belong to the seeing eye, 290, 29 ; and the heart, 434, 14 ; and the world, 477, 33 ; as records, 10, 35 ; as superseding gossip, 139, 16 ; bad, not to be read, 29, 36 ; big, how made, 284, 44 ; borrowed, 450, 46 ; castrating, 36, 43 ; clever, 300, 25 ; comparative insignificance of, 538, 15 ; compared with observation, 323, 37 ; consoling power of, 201, 49 ; contain soul of the past, 185, 15 ;

Cowley to his, 44, 47 ; critics of, at present, 476, 29 ; demoralising, 521, 12 ; diverse motives for reading, 398, 44 ; eloquence and dumb presagers, 321, 10 ; estimates of, at different ages, 8, 53 ; evil of too many, 69, 46 ; famous, some not worth reading, 398, 30 ; good, few and chosen, 129, 6 ; great actions, 91, 14 ; have their destinies, 137, 54 ; help from, 479, 1 ; in science and literature, to read, 189, 42 ; judged by sensations, 269, 37 ; Martial on, 406, 47 ; mental food, 224, 21 ; mottoes to, worthlessness of, 489, 15 ; never referred to, 526, 2 ; never to be borrowed, 296, 56 ; nine-tenths nonsense, 300, 25 ; no end of making, 325, 7 ; not permissible, 269, 15 ; not so instructive as life, 52, 33 ; not to be underrated or overrated, 304, 45 ; of most value, 271, 16 ; old and famed, why we should read, 487, 49 ; old, compared with new, 327, 12 ; old, converse with, 553, 11 ; only thing of value in, 315, 30 ; our, characterised, 337, 19 ; parcel of well chosen, suggestiveness of, 446, 44 ; point in regard to, 448, 21 ; prized above a dukedom, 220, 9 ; professorship of, desiderated, 301, 18 ; quality required in, 1, 50 ; reading of, that benefits, 204, 32 ; reason of success of many, 268, 44 ; sayings about, 397, 45, 46 ; 398, 1, 2 ; scholars, and printers, 236, 14 ; study of, contrasted with conversation, 455, 41 ; study of, no guarantee of wisdom, 483, 11 ; success of many, accounted for, 456, 13 ; that have come down, 335, 18 ; that help most, 419, 1 ; that warp to be shunned, 166, 20 ; the best effect of, 417, 35 ; the channel of wisdom, 86, 20 ; the titles of, their importance, 297, 34 ; their use and uselessness, Goethe on, 440, 35 ; to be loved early, 151, 40 ; to be read only by advice, 567, 24 ; value of, 1, 49 ; which we learn from, 528, 4 ; without thought, 340, 9 ; worth reading, 567, 42

Bored, one must get used to being, 179, 31

Bores, all men, at times, 9, 60 ; Voltaire on, 498, 22

Boring, the secret of, 235, 8

Born, fate of everything, 475, 10 ; the gently, on both sides, blood of, 542, 25

Borrower, his creditor, 419, 2

Borrowing, caution against, 294, 36, 37 ; forbidden, 251, 57 ; rule in, 32, 6 ; the lesson of, 353, 37

Bosom in one's a host, 109, 45

Boswells rarer than Johnsons, 213, 9

Boudier's epitaph, 209, 43

Bounty, an autumn, 110, 2 ; diffused too widely, 337, 20

Bourbons, the, Talleyrand on, 182, 20

Bow, Apollo's, not always bent, 295, 35 ; overstrained, 11, 9 ; test of strength of, 205, 29

Bowers of bliss, conveyed to, 311, 48

Boy, a happy, 140, 18 ; the generous, 551, 19

Boys, the purity of, to be guarded, 299, 35 ; training, of Plato on, 71, 35 ; value to, of address and accomplishments, 122, 47

Braggards, greatest cowards, 432, 6

Brain, added, difficulty added, 557, 10 ; coinage of, 482, 1 ; overwrought, 558, 21 ; product of, its quality, 540, 28

Brains cannot be given, 164, 37 ; our, seventy year clocks, 337, 21 ; when the, are out, 457, 43 ; 480, 32

Brave, man, discourse of a, 2, 7 ; man, and his word, 90, 19 ; man, mark of, 419, 10 ; man, may not yield, 113, 2 ; man, the portion of, 382, 10 ; man, unselfish, 59, 45 ; man, yields to brave, 113, 4 ; men, favoured by fortune, 113, 20 ; men, generated by brave, 112, 48 ; spirit, in adversity, 2, 8 ; the, prodigality of, 48, 60 ; youth, training of, 90, 20

Bravery, calm, 113, 3; deeds of past, hard to appreciate, 90, 18; far off, fear at hand, 42, 21; incompatible with dread of pain, 303, 5; often, in not attempting, 313, 13; seen in perils, 38, 42; the greatest, 410, 45; true, characterised, 499, 40; unyielding, 113, 2; value of, 88, 6

Bravest, tenderest, 419, 11

Bread, a crust of, and liberty, 123, 10; cast on waters, 36, 44, 45; how to earn one's, 260, 49, 50; miraculous, 321, 8; provision of, 150, 21

Breast, human, without windows, 291, 11

Breath, a, power of, 2, 9; our first, beginning of death, 428, 7

Breathe, freely, how to, 237, 40

Breathing, as inhaling and exhaling, 185, 16

Breed, in man, importance of, 95, 7

Breeding, effect of, on a man, 419, 13; fine, merit of, 471, 21; good, marks of, 403, 12; good, value of, 409, 31; high, contrasted with good, 129, 9; more than birth, 30, 25; the time of, 457, 45; wise, nowhere, 557, 46

Brevity, danger of, 32, 33

Brighter from obscurity, 84, 7

Brilliancy, affectation of, 334, 30

Brink near destruction, 496, 30

British nation, the character of, 419, 14

Britons, the, Virgil on, 344, 39

Broken heart, dying of, 160, 51

Brother, friend, provided by nature, 505, 23

Brotherhood, the only possible, 472, 13

Brothers, effect of good, on sisters, 529, 22; ever brothers, 301, 32; wrath of, 465, 37

Brow, open, open heart, 79, 32

Browning's faith and hope, 209, 26

Brute, et tu, 88, 47

Brutes, lessons they teach, 523, 35

Bubble reputation, the, 20, 3

Bubbles, fate and tragic end of all, 9, 13

Buckets, dropping, into empty wells, 57, 1

Bud, opening, to heaven conveyed, 84, 26

Buddhist, Nature no, 292, 33

Builder, better than the building, 414, 30

Building, and its foundation, 439, 28; effect of, on purse, 41, 17; too low, 497, 34; up, man's joy, 312, 36

Bullet, every, its billet, 90, 21

Bungling, hateful, 166, 30

Bunyan, in, personifications, 191, 28; to readers of his Pilgrim, 115, 1

Burden, a, cheerfully borne, 419, 17; a man's, known only to himself, 306, 15; a willing, 36, 16; cast off, another to bear, 175, 35; known only to bearer, 319, 32; light, 244, 28; 288, 27; respect the, 374, 47; laid on by necessity, 132, 43

Burdens, laid on and lifted off by God, 185, 16

Bureaucracy, tendency of, 2, 29

Burgher, the civilized, mark of, 346, 30

Buried, the, for this world, 117, 42

Burns, ambition of, 122, 24; Carlyle on, 338, 48; 389, 43; 556, 16; Carlyle's vindication of, 131, 13; his charity, 466, 13; his preference of wi. to wealth, 122, 28; his real hardship, 161, 28, his respect for truth, 494, 38; his inspiring idea, 123, 14; on effect of sin on the heart, 168, 49; reflections of, on his life, 161, 38; songs of, 454, 29; wish of, at the plough, 89, 34

Burns', prayer for humanity, 466, 15; songs, Carlyle of, 251, 10

Burnt child dreads the fire, 4, 62

Business, and desire, every man hath, 92, 1; and economy of time, 443, 11; as a man's puppet, 140, 17; contrasted with idleness, 436, 25; defined, 237, 42; definition of, 260, 2; diligent in, 385, 16; effect of, 237, 43; how to deal with, 73, 15; minding one's own, 175, 9; now war, 112, 34; one thing, generosity another, 169, 12;

other people's, attending to, 8, 17–19, 27, 36; other's, *versus* own, 158, 45; our grand, not seeing but doing, 338, 6; inattention to, 13, 6; *versus* amusement, 173, 18; we love, 491, 13; what is everybody's, 536, 8; with men above it, 105, 23

Bust, animated, hollowness of, 35, 20

Bustle, and quiet, 443, 12

Busy, aversion of, to idle, 177, 50

"But," sneaking, evasive, &c., 302, 37; the inventor of, 60, 30

"But yet," fie upon, 165, 45

"Buts," the modifying, 9, 2

Butter, bad, salted, 478, 2

Buyer, need of, for eyes, 111, 13; requirements in, 217, 12; requires a hundred eyes, 41, 10

Buyers and sellers, 181, 24

Buying and asking, 217, 13; and selling, Spanish proverb on, 470, 28; better than borrowing, 29, 18; not begging, 81, 23; prudence in, 33, 43; the rule in, 176, 31; what one cannot pay, 41, 9

Byron, his real hardship, 161, 28; the poetry of, 387, 4

Byron's, feelings for those that love and those that hate him, 155, 20; greatest grief, 110, 39; last words, 167, 56

C

Cæsar, Augustus, on losing his legions, 511, 35

Cæsar, Julius, imperious, dead, 183, 35; mighty, so low in death, 321, 22; on Cassius, 241, 30; on crossing the Rubicon, 411, 9; when he crossed the Rubicon, 210, 8; word of, as living and as dead, 33, 40

Cake, earned by baking it, 141, 36

Cakes and ale, no more, 72, 8

Calamity, great source of, 431, 38; man under, 510, 30

Calling, a, advantage of, 146, 43

Calm, no sailing in, 303, 34; nourishment of strength, 279, 14

Calmness, sign of strength, 277, 1; 354, 45; source of, 456, 6

Calumniators, their own avengers, 480, 1

Calumny, alarm at, 101, 3; best answer to, 495, 1; eagerness to spread, 3, 42; how to escape, 565, 6; how to extinguish or to justify, 36, 23; how to overcome, 47, 10; how to silence, 559, 9; no escaping, 28, 46; 305, 15; ready acceptance and spread of, 299, 9; sure to stick, 22, 42

Calvin, fruitlessness of his teachings, 314, 34; treatment of, 349, 20

Camp, English, on the eve of battle, 116, 1; virtues rare in, 368, 4

Canary bird, in a darkened cage, 419, 23

Candour, not necessarily impartiality, 23, 17; the effect of, 35, 11

Canker, loathsome, in sweetest bud, 252, 16

Cant, defined, and its progeny, 197, 17; mind to be cleared of, 43, 58

Canticle, the sublimest, 456, 8

Canvassing, exhausting effect of, 223, 38

Capabilities, defined, 99, 26

Capability, no vague general, 90, 23; unknown till tried, 306, 14

Capacity, limited, 220, 33

Capitalist, in a civilised nation, 420, 3

Capricious man, his faith, 3, 24

Captivity, type of, 109, 24; as an evil, 245, 29

Carcass, attractive power of, 549, 33

Cards, a pack of, 217, 8

Care, a fig for, 243, 3; effect of, 51, 37, foe to

gladness, 79, 15; man's first, 266, 31; not all on one object, 295, 29; profitlessness of, 306, 46; soothed by song, 280, 1; the danger of too much, 479, 11; vanity of, 16, 57; want of, 518, 30; wise, 531, 16

Careless, past preaching to, 179, 16; people, 405, 45

Carelessness, about others' opinion, a bad sign, 294, 32

Cares, effect of, 114, 46; nursed, 275, 29; others', the burden of, 162, 31

Caricature, effect of, on Hogarth, 34, 18

Carlyle, as a thinker, 453, 7; at Linlathen, 461, 46; inspiring idea of, 123, 14; James, to his son, 264, 27; of his father, 485, 38; of his mother when dying, 438, 6; on his life, and world's relation to it, 464, 14

Carlyle's, books, John Burroughs on, 307, 21; one certainty, 316, 21; reflection on his life at Craigenputtock, 160, 53; teaching, John Burroughs on, 461, 28

Carlyles, the, John Burroughs on, 419, 28; 541, 22

Carper, a, 2, 36

Carters, employment for, 489, 12

Cash payment, impotence of, 256, 8

Cassandra and the Trojans, 57, 23

Cassius, Cæsar on, 145, 4

Castles in air, foundations to be put under, 176, 46

Castor and Pollux, 36, 42

Cat, a scalded, 19, 2; 40, 43

Categories, only words, 534, 9

Cathedral, not so majestic as a tree, 324, 25

Cathedrals, of Christendom, the glory of, 276, 24; the old, and the great blue dome, 445, 28

Catiline's flight, 1, 30

Cato, a, in every man, 469, 25; has to submit, 419, 32; the elder, Livy on, 163, 13; 187, 33

Cause, a good, injury to, 171, 3; a good, needs support, 31, 25; a noble, desertion of, 200, 3; that is strong, 413, 2; the best, needs advocacy, 56, 18; true, sure of victory, 106, 8

Causes, great, never tried on the merits, 133, 14; weightiest, most silent, 277, 1

Caution, enforced at every step, 94, 8; from experience, 37, 18; mother of safety, 225, 8

Censor, the business of, 234, 2; the trade of, 198, 11

Censure, and flattery, 347, 22; and ridicule, cheap, 201, 22; avoiding, and gaining applause, 202, 20; effect of, in contrast with glory, 124, 33; from knowledge, 84, 27; how and when to administer, 106, 19; how to treat, 409, 19; linked to fame, 101, 10; not to be too hasty, 528, 39; of a friend, without thanks, 289, 1; often wrong, 318, 38; to be received with complacency, 545, 42; to begin at home, 409, 32; unqualified, evil of, 313, 49; who should, 242, 40

Censurers, fear of, 527, 5

Censures, commendations, 181, 19

Centuries, conspirators against soul, 419, 34; lineal children of one another, 419, 33

Century, present, Schiller on, 78, 45; thy, as thy life element, 252, 2

Ceremony, absurd and tiresome, 376, 51

Ceres and peace, 343, 56

Certain, quitting, for uncertain, 143, 37; sacrificed for uncertain, 38, 27; the only thing, 478, 27

Certainty, beginning with, 185, 42; by way of doubt, 474, 2; the only, 377, 1

Chaff-cutter, as creator, 174, 13

Chain, dependent on link, 32, 39

Chains, and slavery, 180, 4; golden, heavy, 128, 44; rattling of, as show of freedom, 276, 22

Chamfort's last words, 166, 13

Chamois, caught, though high-climbing, 119, 37

Champion, the, and his love of victory, 419, 37

Champions, great, special gifts of God, 134, 42

Chance, a nickname for providence, 233, 36; a second, advantage of, 48, 38; 86, 18; as a god, 103, 22; as arbiter, 172, 24; games of, traps, 118, 31; gatherings of, 385, 22; no such thing as, 474, 29; scope for, everywhere, 36, 48; unseen providence, 10, 7

Chances, common, bearable, 45, 11

Change, a call everywhere for, 457, 29; a necessity, 527, 13; cause of uneasiness, 79, 19; everything subject to, 327, 45; fear of, 186, 8; in every, dissatisfaction, 186, 26; life of world, 464, 9; love of, 377, 55; man hates, 34, 6; necessity for, 479, 18; not therefore change for better, 5, 10; seldom for the better, 266, 16; universal, 328, 17–18; 329, 9

Chaos, is come again, 96, 16; doomed that harbours a soul, 301, 19

Character, a high, essential of, 48, 61; a man's, how to raise, 567, 17; a man's history, 435, 16; alone, stable, 76, 44; and talent, how formed respectively, 85, 20; arbiter of fortune, 157, 9; contrasted with reputation, 374, 9; defined, 2, 61; 497, 15; due to many influences, 307, 9; due to way of thinking, 226, 10; formation of, 409, 43; 429, 15 good, value of, 78, 9; his, not wholly known to a man, 92, 6; how formed, 539, 28, 32; how it reveals itself, 538, 19; how to understand, 301, 20; importance of, 161, 5; individual, power of, 431, 21; its victories, 460, 36; mark of a simple, manly, 19, 32; merit of having a, 490, 1; national, tempered by environment, 289, 45; no changing one's, 171, 51; nobility of, the condition of, 477, 18; penetrated by soul, 161, 21; power of, 200, 51; 367, 41; seizing a, and delineating, 495, 36; strong, basis of, 385, 40; strong, tendency of, to eccentricity, 76, 32; the art of moulding, 301, 1; the noble and the well-bred, contrasted, 445, 3; the only, worth describing, 335, 4; true test of, 537, 18; unaffected by change of place, 44, 17; varieties in, accounted for, 529, 11; weakness of, 530, 16; what is implied in, 64, 24

Characters, people's, how to learn, 527, 21; strong, formation of, 404, 2, 3; the most passionate, and their feelings of duty, 157, 23; truthful, credulous, 49, 53

Charitable, the, and their charity, 419, 46

Charities, posthumous, characterised, 353, 24

Charity, a dearth of, 472, 22; after death, Bacon on, 145, 47; and friendship, 337, 22; Christian, rare, 368, 10; concern of all, 186, 49; contrasted with intellect, 195, 18; definition of, 481, 37; effect of, on the press, 63, 40; essential, 305, 34; its destination not to be inquired into, 555, 6; large, and white hands, 230, 14; misplaced, repining at, 388, 23; Moltke on, 560, 26; no excess in, 423, 10; of God, the restoring, 506, 22; of great souls, 334, 50; the first order of, 20, 46; the power of, 196, 17; to unrelated people, 166, 17; towards half-believer, 524, 30; that thinketh no evil, 420, 1; virtue of the woman, 121, 50

Charlatan, a poor creature, 407, 36

Charles II. in his chamber, Rochester on, 155, 14

Charm, a native, compared with art, 494, 25

Charmer, were t'other, away, 161, 23

Charms, personal, effect of, 224, 19; God-given, 126, 2

Charter, of Louis Philippe, 224, 27

Chase, joy of the, 552, 23

Chaste mind, the, mark of, 420, 2

Chastisement, contrary effects of, 40, 38; God's, not feared, 552, 42; want of, defect in education, 321, 21

Chastity, female, two safeguards to, annulled, 226, 26; in the tropics, 435, 11; the nurse of, 412, 2

Chatterers, to be guarded against, 551, 5

Chaucer, characteristic of, 419, 44; reading, 369, 5; Spenser on, 52, 51

Cheapest, the, the dearest, 535, 50

Cheapness, of its wares, as a basis for a nation, 414, 27; of man, tragedy of, 420, 4

Cheated, how to be, 419, 35

Cheating, all wakeful against, 92, 28; and being cheated, pleasure of, 72, 25

Cheek, eloquent, 123, 18

Cheerful, the, the privilege of, 319, 8

Cheerfulness, a duty to promote, 502, 48; advantage of, 566, 6; and health, 153, 31, 34; badge of gentleman, 373, 46; benefit of, 173, 38; compared with mirth, 280, 16, 17; concomitant of, 185, 27; effect of, 231, 12; 426, 10; from activity, 415, 6; in want, 304, 18; inward, thanksgiving, 196, 29; no, by painful effort, 301, 21; peculiar to man, 15, 25; pleasing to the Muses, 2, 63; root of, 314, 9; sign of wisdom, 443, 36; strength of, 562, 2; to be promoted, 495, 27; to be welcomed, 172, 5; value of, contrasted with sadness, 15, 64

Cherub, sweet little, 470, 32

Chickens, for lion, not chickenweed, 174, 22; not to be counted before hatching, 4, 20

Child, a cupid visible, 3, 3; and its mother's blessing, 3, 4; a, our model, 186, 31; a spoiled, 82, 34; a wise, 143, 13; birth of, an imprisonment, 418, 29; death of, to father, 489, 22; destiny of, how determined, 429, 38; distinctive character of, 424, 2; education of, 420, 10, 11; first lesson for, 400, 19; 492, 11; how to feed, 565, 39; how to train, 498, 54; little, man to become, 428, 42; little, Christ's love for, 406, 6; love of, for marvellous, 315, 44; our best service to a, 492, 29; play of a, 518, 15; pleasures of a, 27, 15; simplicity of, superior to intelligence of intelligent, 506, 11; stammering of, 420, 12; thankless, a, 162, 28; the, and the man, 223, 23; the first and second lesson of, 243, 15; the fresh gaze of, significance of, 429, 27; the, in the cradle, and when grown into a man, 140, 8; training of, 417, 5; who needs not chastisement, 541, 36

Childhood, a forecast, 420, 13; and age, 569, 3; conversion into, a necessity, 96, 25; depths in, 186, 27; fancies of, 415, 48; heart of, 434, 3; impressions of our, 436, 26; light of, 267, 13; man's second, 267, 5; the promise of, 172, 6

Childishness, second, 230, 36

Children, and parents, in great states and vile, 187, 19; as we make them, 238, 12; education of, compared with begetting of, 483, 8; duty of man of high birth to his, 182, 1; false training of, 341, 35; formation of the character of, 77, 8; glory of, 430, 12; healthy, and nature, 291, 3; how to keep, cheerful, 349, 24; Jesus on, 466, 4; late, 230, 37; less cared for than animals, 273, 42; little, Christ's love for, 406, 6; love of, for marvellous, 315, 44; men thrice, 521, 19; no, now, 7, 21; of God and of man, always, 469, 18; sciences not to be taught to, 527, 34; sorrow in parting with, 475, 6; the sports of, 34, 16; weakminded, propagating, 415, 6; when to be praised, 231, 25; whom they are sure to love, 441, 24; why lost, 222, 24; writing down to, 497, 6

Child's church, building sites for, 456, 5

Child's ignorance of death, 19, 30

Chimney, a little, soon heated, 143, 5

Chivalry, age of, gone, 415, 38; in what contained, 462, 12; motto of, 444, 15; of work, need of, 308, 5; the essence of virtue, 44, 28

Choice, offered to man, 127, 32; offered us, 465, 12; the last, 65, 21

Choler, one's, consuming, a virtue, 491, 24

Christ, a foe to, 147, 14; a miracle, 371, 24; and Christendom, religions of, 451, 8; and religion, 372, 33; appearances of, 493, 22; body of, 418, 47; claim of, 147, 51; condition of following, 386, 21; condition of presence of, 548, 52; confessing, what it is, 491, 21; following, 171, 50; greater than Zeno, 394, 27; greatness of, as a conception, 334, 41; His rule of judgment, 189, 36; in bread, a harmless doctrine, 473, 7; in gunpowder, 473, 7; indispensable to His disciples, 559, 38; life of, private, 439, 6; life of, who thinks he can write, 365, 20; relatives of, 554, 38; on His Father's house, 188, 20; on His mission among men, 481, 8; on His work and working day, 167, 56; promises of, greatness of, 476, 2; teaching of, 432, 46; the finite in, 185, 30; the infinite in, 185, 30; the principle unfolded by, 454, 45; the reproach of, 482, 5; the story of, Leo X. on, 362, 28; true cross of, 458, 37

Christ's, disciples, 564, 7, 9, 17; friends, 564, 6; yoke, 409, 23

Christendom minus Christianity, 94, 10

Christian, a, here or nowhere, 171, 10; a test of a, 440, 40; 443, 24; faith, the fall from, summed up, 427, 10; fortitude, 429, 16; God's gentleman, 3, 7; religion, the, 420, 16-21

Christianity, a, that will have to go, 420, 22; character of belief in, 468, 27; characteristic of, 534, 40; here, 197, 24; innate, 182, 6; love of, irrespective of truth, 147, 47; more commended than practised, 133, 13; muscular, 156, 50; on its negative side, 191, 15; parent of liberty, 245, 19; precepts of, 241, 7; secret of, 122, 4; the discovery in, 461, 34; *versus* idolatry, 548, 2; *versus* stoicism, 394, 27; virtue of, 403, 34; whatever its genesis, here, 496, 18; witness of, within, 152, 37

Christians, the blood of, 386, 24; young, growing, and full-grown, 568, 9

Christopher, St., call to, 377, 29

Chronicle, humblest, a reflex of the age, 89, 33

Church, a, test of, 242, 35; and its enemies, 239, 26; controversy in, 69, 34; her function, 65, 10; in, all equal, 219, 48; in danger, Carlyle on, 455, 8; nearer the, 444, 35; no, better than bigotry, 208, 51; ark of safety, 97, 60; spirit of, Boileau on, 354, 4; the, 420, 23-25; the history of, 435, 21; the office of, 266, 33; the only true, 470, 41; the stomach of, 65, 9; visible, without invisible, 435, 21; who builds, to God, 550, 40

Churches, name from building, 108, 23

Churchmen and their church, 420, 26

Circuitous often better than direct, 379, 30

Circumstance, believers in, 388, 25

Circumstances, and men, 274, 25; and the man, 440, 21; creatures of men, 263, 37; depressing, that elevate, 466, 33; effect on us of, 339, 8; how to treat, 88, 27; importance of change of, 276, 41; indifference of, 431, 22; our duty in reference to, 339, 8; the influence of, 205, 31; to be ruled, 266, 36

Cities, and their best citizens, 176, 4; origin of, 70, 5

Citizen, a good, 19, 20; an unworthy, 182, 7; first duty of, 378, 24; state in relation to, 455, 9; the, and the man, 233, 2

Citizens, man-made, 26, 60; of world, how we become, 200, 48

City, a great, 259, 7; a, of what composed, 31, 51; and country, 420, 28, 29; advantage of living in, 177, 37; building and destroying, 509, 26; estimates, in presence of nature, 21, 30; great, to a stranger, 474, 21; no continuing, here, 155, 7; our abiding, still ahead, 415, 27; saved by a poor man who was forgotten, 477, 31; the first, 127, 50

Civil, power, superior to the military, 37, 29; quarrels, despatch in, 104, 49; turmoil, evil of, 185, 31

Civilisation, dependence of, on freedom, 48, 45; first step to, 495, 10; near to barbarism, 443, 37; our, Emerson on, 529, 24; the founders of, 102, 25; the problem of, 143, 53; test of, 457, 12; ultimate tendency of, 459, 31

Civilised man, the, described, 4ː0, 31

Civilisers, two, 193, 4

Civility, cheap, 314, 10; the best, 413, 4; the part of, 557, 20

Claim, who makes, has no, 151, 42

Clamour, loud, insane, 253, 33

Clan, a sacrifice for its chief, 118, 5

Class, to be trembled at, 471, 15

Classes, the dangerous, 436, 14; the higher, kicked off as burdens, 167, 9; the upper, 460, 7

Classical, and romantic, 420, 34

Clay, damp, easily wrought, 17, 55

Clean, keep, better than make, 332, 44

Cleanliness next godliness, 161, 3

Cleopatra, nose of, 174, 26

Clergy, and their wranglings, 163, 3; three sections of, 420, 35; where Christianity is the established religion, 168, 11

Clergyman and their use of words, 561, 12

Clerks, the greatest, 432, 7

Clever, people, Goethe on, 121, 53; people, never from stupid, 168, 7

Cleverness, a commendable, 179, 9; little gain by, 329, 39

Cliff, tall, type of a great man, 20, 34

Climbing, possible, though soaring not, 524, 40

Cloak, take thine old, 209, 22

Cloth, bad, 37, 4; the foundation of society, 396, 25

Clothes, and the man, 61, 23; 513, 37; Carlyle's doctrine of, 541, 30; do not always make the man, 298, 7; early pride of, 251, 29; respect paid merely to, 306, 23; revealing and concealing effect of, 485, 37; rule of fashion in, 185, 32; soul in, 469, 11; superfine, 447, 32; under, a man, 186, 25; with or without the man, Carlyle on, 123, 40

Clothing, gay, whom it attracts, 304, 2

Cloud, every, not storm-pregnant, 90, 25; one, darkening power of, 331, 52; that veileth love, 90, 26; the brightness behind, 2, 3

Cloud-capt towers, 420, 36

Clouds, and the sea, 421, 5; round the setting sun, 421, 3, 4; the, regarding, 148, 5; a set-off to the sun, 174, 45

Clown, sphere of, 81, 3

Coat, a smart, 19, 59

Cobbler, to his last, 242, 44, 58; 293, 17; 386, 36

Cobblers, all, 279, 46

Cock, on its own dunghill, 118, 26; on its own midden, 3, 15; trumpet of the morn, 421, 6; when he crows, 60, 10

Coin, intellectual, in exchange of thought, 190, 46

Colander, fermentation in, 314, 3

College, education at, 71, 24; 74, 2; learning, Burns on, 74, 1

Cologne, Cathedral, Carlyle on, 513, 26; three kings of, virtue in names of, 210, 27

Colour, all good, pensive, 9, 32; as a gift of God, 324, 23; impression of, 91, 34; men's joy in, 275, 17

Colt, test of its worth, 377,. 10

Colts, young hot, how to treat, 55, 32

Columbus a world-child, 465, 16

Combat, not victory, the joy, 204, 34; the greatest, 551, 31

Combatant, a brave, 551, 7

Combinations, unequal, 507, 8

Comeliness, true, in the mind, 499, 42

Comet, a sign of disaster, 185, 34

Comfort, those who enjoy, 480, 10

Comforts, many, harmful, 284, 29; our, anxieties, 337, 23

Comic and tragic side by side, 421, 9

Command, sweet, force in, 471, 30; the right to 323, 8; to, a fine thing, 198, 25; with conviction, power of, 207, 20

Commander-in-chief, risk in his absence, 504, 36

Commanding, from obeying, 308, 56; one good at, 363, 20

Commandment, the eighth, comprehensiveness of, 190, 24; 331, 27

Commandments, the ten, in Rome, 189, 38; 569, 30

Commands, imperative upon all, 467, 9; not to be debated, 84, 22

Commendation, how to administer, 374, 3

Commendations, censures, 181, 19; to be weighed, 419, 40

Commentators, weakness of, 162, 24

Commerce, an evil effect of, 184, 9; effect of, 548, 56; effect of, on nations, 81, 39; practices in, 188, 11

Common, good, merit of serving, 142, 25; good, neglect of, a crime, 59, 50; men, endurance of, 567, 34; men, lightness of, 252, 45; men, the dread of, 367, 41; opinion, as a standard, 197, 6; seeing miraculous in the, 437, 9; the, enslaving power of, 520, 18; the, rarely mistaken, 319, 5; things, our power in, 189, 23

Commonplace, success of, 26, 52

Commons, House of, Coke on, 389, 47

Common-sense, exceptional, 315, 37; as judge in high matters, 232, 41; genius of humanity, 235, 9; in high rank, rare, 368, 13; how maintained, 314, 20; the advantage of, 440, 25

Commonwealth, strongest, based on passion, 180, 32; the condition of its welfare, 172, 9; under so many heads, 310, 24

Communications with God and man, 528, 32

Communicative man, to be dreaded, 467, 3

Communism, injustice in, 185, 39

Communities like Arctic explorers, 273, 28

Community, constituents of, 361, 27

Companion, a faithful, 396, 39; pleasant, value of, 44, 49

Companions, to chose, 217, 37

Companionship, loving, value of, 340, 45; on a journey, 119, 25; test of a man, 411, 41; wise, value of, 148, 44

Company, as marking a man, 7, 46; decent, condition of introduction into, 490, 26; descent from high, to low, 266, 4; effect of too much, 397, 20; for entertainment, 544, 6; good, effect of, on virtue, 129, 15; good, on the road, 129, 16; good, restlessness for, 551, 4; the, to keep, 217, 19, 21; *versus* solitude, 464, 38; we should seek, 524, 8

Comparison no proof,, 45, 34

Compass, susceptibility of, to error, 18, 53

Compassion, and courage joined, 505, 47; and ingratitude incompatible, 194, 17

Compelled, he who can be, 44, 20

Compensation, in nature, 90, 46; law of, 109, 35; universal, 94, 14

Competency, meaning of, 535, 2

Competition, death, 131, 13; the only worthy, 445, 42

Complaining, Burns' contempt for, 106, 46; how to avoid, 215, 27; misery of always, 490, 4; our, a reflection on heaven, 345, 5; our, Swift on, 337, 28; uselessness of, 316, 47

Complains, who, gets little compassion, 151, 43

Complaint, matter of just, 237, 33; whining, despicable, 166, 36

Complaints, cure for many, 237, 25 ; not, only events, a fit subject, 483, 44 ; our, aimlessness of, 339, 7 ; to hear, 493, 17
Completeness, attainable by all, 60, 3
Complexion, a sour, how to get rid of, 197, 33
Complies against his will, 145, 44
Compliment, the most elegant, 57, 3
Compliments, mere, no tempting bait, 277, 6
Composition, a great, how produced, 302, 14 ; literary, Horace on, 50, 44
Comprehensibility, standard of belief, 398, 25
Comprehensible, common and insipid, 284, 20
Compromise, the supreme rule now, 317, 42
Compulsion, a, that is good for a man, 202, 4 ; no reason upon, 173, 41
Computation, a touchstone, 313, 37
Concealment, contrasted with saying nothing, 8, 51 ; how to frustrate, 385, 36 ; Johnson on, 304, 46 ; like a worm in the bud, 389, 10
Conceit, minds with and without, 558, 35 ; not to be pitied, 168, 47 ; of one's own creation, effect of, 325, 30 ; strong, the power of, 404, 4 ; wise in his own, 385, 18
Conceited people as judges, 311, 10
Concentration, commended, 71, 41 ; the one prudence, 445, 39
Conceptions, our, anthropomorphic, 60, 32
Concern, our sole proper, 535, 33
Conciseness, desirableness of, 87, 1 ; in speech commended, 92, 26
Concord, among men, a contrast, 387, 23 ; and discord contrasted, 507, 32 ; and discord, relative effects of, 46, 7 ; effects of, contrasted with discord, 64, 10
Condemnation less curative than compassion, 45, 39
Condescension, insolence, 436, 42
Condition, determined by conduct, 306, 7 ; external, sign of internal, 452, 19
Conditions already laid, 63, 36
Condolement, to persevere in, 494, 46
Conduct, a rule for, 404, 24 ; as showing the man, 222, 7 ; developed in society, 104, 42 ; effect of, 473, 2 ; in our own power, 43, 27 ; Kant's rule of, 3, 45 ; not communicable, 97, 34 ; personal, power of, 200, 45 ; proper rule of, 385, 4 ; prudent, its two pivots, 227, 31 ; rules for, 394, 50 ; 395, 6 ; 323, 14 ; rule of, 70, 19–21 ; significance of, 354, 1 ; sovereign guides in, 241, 44 ; steadfastness in, 147, 29 ; to be according to circumstances, 549, 28
Conference, the advantage of, 369, 9
Confession, a new, wanted, 426, 22 ; an open, 15, 60 ; healing power of, 107, 5
Confidant of a man's vices, his master, 421, 23
Confidence, broken, lost, 149, 34 ; effect of, 105, 52 ; how won, 105, 15 ; in all or in none, 510, 39 ; lost, all lost, 150, 34 ; power of, 281, 9
Confinement, effect of, on fierceness, 88, 13
Conflict, known only to strength, 403, 29
Conforming easier than making conform, 179, 14
Conformity, easier than persuasion, 205, 3 ; what we lose by, 524, 6
Confusion, the, to be shunned, 103, 46
Confutation often mere heedless re-assertion, 119, 28
Congregation, a happy, 140, 14
Conquer, those who can, 111, 26 ; 478, 54
Conquered, man rarely, 365, 1 ; race, how to treat, 200, 39 ; the, their only safety, 505, 43
Conquering, the art of, 222, 30
Conqueror, every, has his Muse, 182, 18 ; how regarded, 233, 7 ; the greatest, 143, 50 ; 304, 19 ; the true, 514, 25
Conquest, of self, in the moment of victory, 30, 34 ; the condition of permanency of, 301, 25 ; without danger, 491, 23
582

Conquests by violence and by moderation, 269, 50
Conscience, a clear, 3, 14 ; 495, 25 ; a clear, happiness of, 140, 11 ; a coward, 446, 39 ; a good, virtue of, 171, 38 ; a guilty, 7, 16 ; a sacrifice of, 64, 30 ; a sound, invincible, 286, 41 ; a Sunday, 470, 31 ; a weak, 482, 30 ; a, without darkness, 472, 21 ; acting contrary to, 432, 29 ; and history, 204, 5 ; contrasted with passions, 224, 32 ; friendship of, advantage of, 550, 12 ; good, result of, 137, 33 ; guilty, effect of, 137, 29 ; in matters of, the rule, 187, 58 ; in man as acting or reflecting, 60, 11 ; large, none, 109, 5 ; limit of its authority, 305, 9 ; loss of, 147, 46 ; not our law, 373, 6 ; of many, 539, 21 ; pain of, 446, 39 ; peaceful, joy of, 437, 19 ; sayings about the, 421, 25–27 ; still and quiet, value of, 166, 8 ; terror of, *versus* diseases of the liver, 558, 46 ; the basis of society, 396, 36 ; the judge, 378, 31 ; the lash of, 307, 42 ; to be always consulted, 509, 18 ; voice of, 461, 6 ; without God, 3, 23 ; wound of, an open one, 322, 16
Conscientiousness, the ground of, 392, 31
Conscious and unconscious, 460, 19
Consciousness, always of the wrong, 325, 17 ; and unconsciousness contrasted, 506, 3
Conservatism, contrasted with reform, 371, 5 ; what it has to defend, 419, 30
Conservative, the, consideration for, 313, 48 ; the, defined, 423, 2 ; the, the true, duty of, 419, 3
Consider, before acting, 32, 16 ; before venturing, 85, 15
Consideration, always room for, 22, 35 ; before action, 16, 7 ; benefit of, 504, 20 ; contrasted with thought, 6, 31 ; first, and then despatch, 357, 6 ; when necessary, 560, 15
Consistency, no concern of great soul, 558, 20 ; not imperative, 71, 38
Consistent man, his faith, 3, 24
Consolation, rule in administering, 238, 10 ; the surest, 234, 17
Constancy, man's one want, 533, 8 ; not a virtue of the world, 139, 28 ; not to be expected, 173, 37 ; virtue of, 25, 63 ; only in honesty, 472, 18
Constant as the northern star, 33, 13
Constitution, the, how to preserve, 419, 3 ; the, not supreme, 469, 42 ; less than man, 263, 29
Contemplation, advantage of, 344, 17 ; for, formed, 109, 25
Contemporaries, to be borne with, 527, 8
Contempt, evil of, 141, 12 ; 149, 50 ; hard to bear, 268, 47 ; harder to bear than wrong, 432, 3 ; never forgiven, 564, 4 ; rather than castigation, 47, 6 ; unwise, contrasted with unwise admiration, 325, 21
Content, a ground of, 27, 4 ; bliss of, 539, 17 ; dependent upon God, 374, 57 ; in whatsoever state, 166, 46
Contented, man, free from anxiety, 62, 7 ; man, weak, 202, 50
Contention, from pride, 34, 12 ; how engendered, 334, 48 ; with certainty of defeat, 201, 14 ; religious, effect of, 183, 20 ; to be avoided, 240, 52 ; with words, 47, 35
Contentment, 20, 27 ; a cause of, 521, 22 ; better than riches, 82, 63 ; commended, 236, 1 ; 367, 21 ; defined, 338, 37 ; in retirement, 360, 40 ; maxim on, for home use, 372, 41 ; not portion of world, 203, 49 ; of mind, 442, 15 ; our, 337, 29 ; power of, 182, 9 ; profit of, 69, 2 ; source of, 116, 12 ; St. Paul on, 141, 45 ; state of, 505, 12 ; *versus* ambition, 141, 4 ; with little, gain in, 175, 22 ; with the present, 229, 14 ; with what we can, 243, 24 ; wisdom of, 229, 15
Contingency, no, 472, 17
Contradicting, to be avoided, 195, 52
Contradiction, a downright, 4, 45 ; a flat, 80, 1 ; a teacher, 150, 44 ; being able to stand, 140, 28 ;

good and to be borne, 202, 5 ; how to treat, 526, 42 ; the meaning of, 47, 36

Contradictions, aggregate of all, 2, 21

Contraries everywhere in nature, 95, 15

Controversy, anger in, 185, 4 ; the dust of, 424, 27

Contumaciousness, root of, 380, 49

Convenience, every, has its inconvenience, 329, 1

Conversation, a rule in, 333, 24 ; alleviating effect of, 421, 33 ; and discourse, effects of, on one's thoughts, 554, 35 ; among gentlemen, 363, 10 ; boldness in, 185, 43 ; brilliancy in, effect on people of, 475, 17 ; contrasted with reading, 455, 41 ; discretion in, 285, 19 ; due more to confidence than wit, 224, 31 ; effect of, on mind, 404, 17 ; Emerson on, 557, 31 ; essentials of, 185, 44 ; first requisite in, 428, 34 ; our pleasure in, 285, 20 ; perfection of, 447, 26 ; rare, 268, 46 ; relish for, increased with age, 138, 1 ; rule in, 11, 55 ; 511, 46 ; the charm of, 443, 39 ; the ingredients of, 428, 23 ; the worst form of, 17, 56 ; *versus* debate, 56, 17

Conversation's Lexicon, the best, 370, 7

Converse, ability to, condition of, 306, 11

Conversing with what is above us, benefit of, 550, 29

Conversion, known only to God, 20, 58 ; that is imperative, 96, 25

Converting greater than conquering, 203, 30

Conviction, one's, from another's lips, 326, 1 ; one's, infinitely strengthened by another's, 288, 15 ; openness to, rare, 104, 57 ; personal, sacredness of, 240, 37 ; power of, 312, 32 ; rare, 336, 5 ; should be strong, 266, 29

Convictions, Goethe's respect for, 169, 14 ; kicking against, 289, 29 ; one's, from a stranger, 162, 37

Cooking confined to man, 262, 49

Cooks, the father of, 127, 43

Coolness, the value of, 217, 20

Co-operation a law of life, 131, 13

Copy to be followed, 108, 11

Core not finally hidden, 421, 34

Corn, good, in small fields, 83, 17 ; who can make two ears of, grow instead of one, 553, 9

Cornelia of her sons, 478, 37

Corpse, fate of, indifferent, 408, 45 ; not the whole animal, 421, 36

Correction, failure in, from want of courage, 227, 14

Correggio before a Raphael, 14, 35

Correspondence, the first requisite in, 428, 34

Costume, cut and colour in, 172, 7

Cottage, every equipment for, 90, 29 ; smallest, large enough for love, 368, 39

Cotter, humble, Burns on, 161, 1

Council, a, sages indispensable to, 413, 25

Counsel, given rather than taken, 274, 35 ; good, how regarded, 93, 25 ; good, if not taken, 129, 17 ; good, over-night, 137, 36 ; good, rejected, 129, 18 ; good, to fools, 129, 20 ; good, value of, 542, 42 ; good, without good fortune, 129, 21 ; hasty, 325, 3 ; no counsel, 150, 7 ; no, no help, 148, 59 ; no, till asked, 123, 20 ; not at needful moment, 551, 11 ; of a friend, 471, 11 ; slow-footed, advantage, 394, 13 ; the value of, 548, 13 ; thrown away, 549, 30 ; unselfish, rare, 199, 12

Counsellor, to be without, 493, 11

Counsellors, good, lack not clients, 120, 22 ; good, value of, to prince, 161, 26 ; the best, 335, 59

Counsels, hasty, effect of, 512, 4 ; scattered, not to rest on, 375, 1

Countenance, an index, 518, 12 ; more in sorrow, 3, 29

Counting, by nose, 334, 29 ; correct, effect of, on friendships, 48, 19

Countries, the richest, now and formerly, 112, 33

Country, a great, mark of a, 133, 15 ; a, strength and power of, 445, 26 ; duty to our, 227, 1 ; effect of, on men, 274, 6 ; largest soul of a, 438, 1 ; life-long affection for, importance of, 505, 21 ; longing for the, 322, 1 ; love of, 56, 33 ; 559, 24 ; love of, and good manners, 439, 48 ; love of, comprehensiveness of, 328, 1 ; love of, sweet, 73, 55 ; merit of serving one's, 364, 44 ; one's, defined, 337, 31 ; 343, 35 ; 504, 26 ; sacrifice for, sweet, 73, 50 ; served in various ways, 523, 3 ; test of a, condition, 421, 20 ; the, privilege of, 449, 28 ; the undiscovered, 424, 19 ; 459, 34 ; to be abandoned, 333, 47 ; want of interest in one's, 502, 20 ; wealth of a, 461, 39, 43 ; who enjoy, 405, 52

Courage, a, from fear, 477, 44 ; and compassion joined, 505, 47 ; and fear, with reference to danger, 103, 32, 41 ; compared with justice, 216, 17 ; connected with heart, 287, 48 ; enough, 169, 46 ; from duty, 166, 14 ; in a bad affair, 31, 58 ; in confronting evil, 86, 4 ; mental, rarer than valour, 278, 2 ; more than rage, 367, 35 ; necessity for, 521, 28 ; often from fear, 233, 13 ; only in innocence, 472, 18 ; physical and moral, 348, 18 ; pitch it should rise to, 63, 17 ; sacred, what it evidences, 379, 7 ; shown in death, 178, 22 ; that braves heaven, 167, 3 ; that we admire, 421, 40 ; to endure, 3, 30 ; want of, 518, 31 ; with success or defeat, 493, 25

Courages, the best, 417, 34

Course, our, forward, 524, 27

Courses, bad, issue of, 33, 3

Court, does not make happy, 225, 1 ; like a marble edifice, 224, 35 ; sayings about, 422, 2–5 ; selfishness at, 82, 60 ; the, La Bruyère on, 363, 15

Courteous man, a, 147, 2

Courtesies, small and great, effect of, 453, 50

Courtesy, dependent on morality, 473, 41 ; excess of, suspicious, 548, 50 ; import of, 462, 12 ; of the heart, 85, 29 ; room for, 247, 48 ; rule in, 185, 45 ; rule of, 432, 2 ; 526, 28 ; want of, 163, 33

Courtier, an assiduous, a slave, 363, 30 ; father of the tyrant, 446, 43 ; the requisites of, 420, 7

Courtship, a dream, 275, 4

Covet all, lose all, 42, 34

Covetous, man, and his wealth, 173, 21 ; riches of, 422, 6

Covetousness, and modesty, as regards wealth, 86, 44 ; cause of, 96, 32 ; contrasted with charity, 40, 27 ; folly of, 131, 30 ; inconsistent with godliness, 171, 15 ; its object, 300, 35 ; penalty of, 13, 48 ; slavery, 244, 16

Cow, the, and the piper, 122, 25

Cowardice, pain of, in fear, 103, 41

Coward, brave, under bad fortune, 542, 44 ; the rights of, 538, 27

Cowards, boastful, 177, 49 ; not visited by God, 127, 54 ; sayings about, 487, 30, 31 ; should be allowed to desert, 109, 26 ; with hearts false as stairs of sand, 161, 41

Cowl makes not monk, 50, 39

Cowper, inspiring idea of, 123, 14

Coxcomb, a, man's own making, 291, 16 ; and the flatterer, 422, 8 ; once, one always, 109, 1

Cradle, what is learned in, 536, 25

Crack, a, in everything, 469, 30

Craft, a, advantage of having, 366, 20 ; a, to be learned when young, 235, 39 ; power of, 331, 20

Crafty, man, always in danger, 422, 10 ; man and his time, 431, 24

Creating something, the condition of, 177, 32

Creation, a thought of God, 127, 34 ; and destruction simultaneous, 190, 11 ; not to be understood, 268, 8 ; beginning of, 417, 21 ; better than learning, 200, 22 ; end of, 264, 8 ; God's manner of,

128, 16; harmony of, 332, 22; motive of, 434, 16; not easy, 301, 27; visible and invisible, 461, 4
Creation's blot, creation's blank, 413, 46
Creator, an inference from nature, 291, 2
Creature, how to understand any, 190, 21; of God, one, 128, 4; the true, of God, 128, 4
Creatures, all provided for, 142, 11
Credit, easily lost, 283, 24; given only to belief, 319, 31; private, worth of, 357, 8
Credulity, its nature, and subjects of it, 225, 3
Creed, a, always sensitive, 383, 1; a steadfast, foundation of, 34, 50; not so significant as the man, 529, 37; of the true saint, 422, 13; outworn, a pagan suckled in a, 133, 31; two elements in every, 186, 29
Creeds, effect of science on, 382, 24
Creeping in the way and running out of it, 142, 35
Cricket on the hearth, 102, 8
Crime, an equaliser, 50, 9; eschewed from disgrace it brings, 8, 20; every, avenged at the moment, 90, 33; evil of overlooking a, 196, 26; fatal prevailing source of, 333, 26; indulgence to, 332, 1; its natural punishment, 225, 2; meditated, committed, 289, 31; no consecrating, 312, 18; no hiding of, 45, 8; 472, 24; sharer in, 50, 52; that most impute a, 479, 29; the contagion of, 421, 31; the disgrace, 39, 3; 69, 17; 233, 16; when successful, 358, 28; who hinders not, 146, 56
Crimes, causes of, 173, 39; consecrated, 405, 28; great, the foreshadows of, 363, 2; not cured by cruelty, 50, 34; others', our estimate of, 161, 13; when a crown is at stake, 239, 19
Criminal laws to be gentle, 260, 44
Criminality, condition of, 277, 50
Criminals, and the light, 311, 37; different fates of, of same type, 45, 9
Cringe, effect of ceasing to, 514, 13; people who, 480, 4
Crisis, a, for both men and nations, 331, 29; significance of, 94, 58; the, to be prayed for, 243, 34
Critic, attribute of a good, 25, 2; but a, 382, 7; eye of, 426, 33; true and false, function of, 3, 37; temper required in, 30, 38; the, on style, 563, 39; what makes a, 206, 19
Critical, easier than correct, 203, 11; nothing if not, 110, 5; 165, 2; powers, the test of, 456, 28; study, distracting, 280, 7
Criticising, contrasted with making better, 326, 3; disadvantage of, 448, 6
Criticism, and appreciation, 201, 27; brightest gem of, 35, 12; contrasted with art, 225, 5; destructive, in matters of faith, 172, 8; enemy's, value of, 122, 11; first condition of, 408, 38; how to dodge, 381, 23; just, rule for, 109, 9; of self, 497, 11; of what is above us, abstaining from, rare, 391, 14; the cant of, Sterne on, 324, 32; true, the object of, 294, 45
Critics, how created, 533, 19; professional, incapacity of, 357, 50; ready made, 265, 19; Young on, 158, 23
Cromwell, Boswell's father on, 127, 46
Cromwell's judges, the Scotch on, 16, 20
Crooked cannot be straightened, 414, 38
Cross, a, and bitterness in life, 490, 29; attractive power of, 420, 20; bearing, cheerfully, 175, 8; bearing, longest, 149, 11; behind the devil, 61, 19; essential to Christianity, 43, 7; every, has its crown, 90, 22; false doctrine of, 281, 30; fitting close of the life, 422, 17; of Christ, the power of, 422, 16; one's own, hardest, 4, 38; one's, to repel, 495, 19; risk of rejecting one's, 175, 10; sanctuary of the humble, 422, 15; the, irreverence towards, 158, 21; to every one, 39, 33; the, religion of, 371, 41; the, sustaining,
584

480, 18; touchstone of faith, 105, 44; the true, of Christ, 458, 37; the, way of, 513, 41
Crosses, overrated, 488, 43
Crowd, according to Coke, 286, 16; bustling, passing through, 494, 45; not company, 3, 38
Crowded hour of glorious life, 332, 6
Crowds without great men, 559, 35
Crown, a noble, one of thorns, 93, 2; golden, 3, 39; and headache, 3, 40; noble, crown of thorns, 111, 23; not always his who has earned it, 152, 7
Crucified, the, irreverence towards, 198, 21
Cruel only to be kind, 167, 54
Cruelty, of the affectionate, 422, 20; under garb of mercy, 324, 33; weakness, 9, 18
Crumbs, bread, 394, 43
Crusaders, war-cry of, 63, 9
Cucumbers, sunbeams out of, 142, 37
Cultivated men, importance of, 396, 6
Cultivation, generally essential to usefulness, 54, 52; without ability, 290, 13
Culture, a false, defined and denounced, 560, 18; affair of inner man, 333, 38; effects of, 98, 11; for a noble soul, 15, 53; Goethe on, 207, 40; high, a proof of, 205, 37; human, our indifference to, 525, 38; moral, the root of, 283, 11; partial and extreme, 342, 3; rule in regard to, 434, 33; spontaneous, value of, 471, 27; universality of, 22, 29; the business of, 391, 11; without intelligence, 292, 44
Cunning, art of, 416, 30; dismasked, 20, 8; men, Burton of, 518, 21; on whom it imposes, 227, 30; outwitted, 89, 24; self-defeated, 82, 40; stronger than strength, 250, 26
Cup, inordinate, unblessed, 91, 36
Cupid, a rogue, 13, 58; methods of killing, 398, 2; though small, great, 251, 39
Cupidity antagonistic to the Gospel, 549, 22
Cupid's bow, how rendered useless, 336, 45; weapons, 257, 26
Curiosity, a low vice, 413, 39; a scourge, 422, 28; age of, gone, 415, 39; evil of, 218, 29; too much, 569, 35
Curse, a, 27, 21; dinna, 68, 32; to be shared by all, 477, 9
Cured, willingness to be, 34, 51
Curses, like processions, 232, 39; small, on great occasions, 394, 21
Cursing contrasted with swearing, 408, 18
Custom, a breach of, 419, 12; a, falsely so called, 236, 8; an evil, 261, 40; ancient, 513, 39; changing a, 285, 29; force of, 46, 60; 47, 1, 2; honoured in the breach, 3, 61; man's lord, 266, 25; more potent than reason, 350, 7; needs no excuse, 43, 21; often the only sanction, 162, 2; power of, 48, 37; 510, 10; power of, on belief, 523, 26; the empire of, 132, 51; the law of society, 396, 14; the power of, 299, 29
Customs, local, 82, 14; long, hard to shake off, 252, 32; meaning in old, 4, 7; observed more than laws, 461, 23; of country to be followed, 108, 12; old, 239, 34
Cyclops, the, at work, 182, 13
Cynic, a, described, 422, 33; and his body, 315, 23
Cynicism deprecated, 71, 37

D

Daggers, I will speak, 241, 28
Dainties, bred in a book, 393, 2
Daintiness of stomach, 102, 42, 45
Daisy, the, Burns to, 531, 5
Daisy's fate. man's, 89, 37
Dalliance, not too much rein to, 71, 28

Dame, the scraping, wasteful, 311, 29

Dan, from, to Beersheba, all barren, 163, 17

Dancing, a corporeal poesy, 336, 39 ; as a sign of happiness, 39, 32 ; silent music, 287, 3

Dandies, remark upon, 483, 5

Dandy, in Shakespeare, 114, 43 ; not without a heart. 559, 18

Danger, a common, 486, 14 ; common, tends to concord, 45, 25 ; despised, 43, 36 ; foreseen, 3, 64 ; how to oppose, 192, 5 ; how to treat, 528, 38 ; imminency of, 2, 42 ; no, with due courage, 301, 45 ; nothing free from, 299, 20 ; effect of, on us, 529, 15 ; on guard against, 36, 13 ; the most deadly, 385, 39

Dante, as world-child, 465, 16 ; as a figure in literary history, 184, 34 ; rank as poet, 503, 48

Daring, a defence, 22, 41 ; against daring men, 185, 12 ; all that may become a man, 165, 37 ; conceals fear, 22, 47 ; defect of, 142, 30 ; necessary for distinction, 22, 46

Dark, hours, man in, 86, 12 ; running in, 148, 15 ; the, in soul and their universe, 422, 36

Darkness, as co-factor with heat, 153, 51 ; encountered as a bride, 172, 43 ; of mind, our one enemy, 445, 35 ; prince of, his greatest enemy, 21, 39 ; powers of, how they seduce us, 488, 46 ; rather than light, 249, 12, 13 ; spiritual, how to disperse, 241, 10 ; the only, 472, 20 ; those insensible to, 480, 5

Dashes and modern humour, 392, 56

Daughter, marrying and bringing up, 202, 21 ; too much cared for, 77, 26

Daughters, fragile ware, 70, 24 ; love for, 38, 29 ; slovenly, when wives, 55, 23

David's harp, 177, 3

Dawn, its solemnity, 474, 19

Day, a, losing or misspending, 482, 44 ; a, what may bring forth, 3, 71 ; and night, how to spend, 241, 42 ; appointed, each man has his, 402, 22 ; bright, requires caution, 205, 51 ; each, how to live, 528, 35 ; each new, how to regard, 9, 17 ; end of night, 444, 48 ; end of, regarded by God, 312, 39 ; every, a Doomsday, 90, 36 ; every, a leaf n life's history, 90, 35 ; every, a rampart breach, 78, 41 ; every, how to spend, 90, 37 ; every, sets in night, 36, 17 ; every, whole of life, 253, 10 ; every, worth of, 243, 38 ; fair, sign of, 15, 1 ; of days, 422, 40 ; offices of the, 191, 8 ; parting, described, 342, 6 ; poorest passing, the conflux of eternities, 448, 29 ; still, but night setting in, 308, 30 ; the claims of the, 201, 31 ; the darkest, transient, 422, 37 ; the most wasted, 32, 20 ; the, owning, 144, 52 ; the, value of, 298, 20 ; Titus on loss of a, 13, 27 ; when to praise, 22, 12

Days, calm, how to have, 176, 31 ; fine, not as roses, 331, 29 ; my, in the yellow leaf, 287, 43 ; succeeding, unlike, 238, 40

Dazzles, a thing which, temporary nature of, 519, 20

Dead, as riders, 66, 27 ; distinguished by their virtues alone, 227, 34 ; happy, 3, 10 ; no speaking ill of, 497, 27, 28 ; of, nothing unfavourable, 58, 30 ; selves, stepping-stones, 275, 33 ; state of, 559, 2 ; the, all holy, 447, 5 ; the, and our concerns, 170, 15 ; the, Carlyle's apostrophe to, 323, 2 ; the, our need of, 422, 43 ; the, our sole duty to, 540, 39 ; the, purifying power of, 439, 17 ; the, respect due to, 329, 29 ; to bury their dead, 242, 46

Dealing, fair, blessed effect of, 312, 34 ; plain, 349, 13, 14

Dear to another, dear to self, 172, 31

Dearest, the, 54, 19

Death, a deliverer, 248, 11, 12 ; a happy, 140, 15 ; a joy, 288, 8 ; a matter of time, 414, 26 ; a man mightier than, 532, 23 ; a necessity, 10, 33 ; a new birth, 116, 2 ; a radical cure, 246, 46 ; a reconciler, 79, 24 ; a release, 61, 28 ; a sleep, 519, 34 ; a swift rider, 43, 31 ; a universal interest, 253, 41 ; an awakening, 246, 46 ; an awakening as from nightmare, 250, 7 ; and his brother sleep, 163, 2 ; and sleep, 393, 37 ; and sun not to be looked at, 235, 15 ; and the puny body, 283, 59 ; and the thought of, contrasted, 226, 20 ; beautiful, 160, 49 ; but parting breath, 326, 18 ; common to all ages, 328, 5 ; often comparatively painless, 270, 1 ; effect of, on life, 247, 37 ; end of all, 481, 14 ; everywhere, 366, 48 ; fear of, lamentable, 167, 53 ; fear of, 275, 7 ; fear of, most strange, 284, 37 ; finishing touch, 234, 14 ; gate of life, 283, 56 ; gloried in by Nature, 291, 5 ; gradual, 523, 32 ; fearlessness of him who does not fear, 520, 14 ; happy, a, 124, 37 ; honour in, 159, 31 ; how to escape or invite, 77, 38 ; how to overcome, 517, 30 ; if gods or no gods, 205, 33 ; impartiality of, 341, 4 ; implied in birth, 289, 41 ; in battle, 386, 19 ; in nature, birth, 9, 19 ; mystery of, 25, 31 ; necessary to life, 403, 14 ; no discharge from, 473, 24 ; no evil, 202, 10 ; no remedy against, 47, 31 ; no surprise to the wise, 226, 21 ; no worse than life, 167, 26 ; not feared beforehand, 168, 33 ; not subject to fortune, 245, 6 ; not the worst of evils, 309, 17 ; not to be feared, in battle, 567, 12 ; not to be forgotten, 262, 20 ; not to be thought of, 334, 1 ; of no season, 237, 1 ; only in meaner parts, 116, 16 ; ordained law of, 206, 22 ; our farthest limit, 283, 60 ; path of, to be trodden by all, 328, 4 ; patiently submitted to, 72, 38 ; peace to be made with, 74, 36 ; Plato on, 306, 19 ; pomp of, 448, 22 ; principle of, received at birth, 19, 57 ; reconciling, 319, 6 ; Regnier on, 210, 38 ; repose from all toils, 283, 57 ; river of, to be crossed by all, 327, 57 ; sayings on, 491, 35-37 ; sense of, in apprehension, 453, 10 ; sting of, 497, 10 ; sting of, felt by survivor, 544, 17 ; sudden, 368, 15 ; that puts an end to pain, 408, 25 ; the fear of, 200, 23 ; the fearless of, 364, 7 ; the fell sergeant, 481, 35 ; the most desirable, 559, 3 ; the poor man's dearest friend, 325, 50 ; the sole, 110, 7 ; the solemnity associated with, effect of, 352, 18 ; the true, 512, 34 ; the thought of, 19, 14 ; 173, 33 ; triumphed over and led captive of, 269, 24 ; 250, 19 ; way to open, 311, 50 ; who fears, 532, 9 ; 551, 17 ; who fears not, 150, 19 ; 441, 6 ; whoso can look on, 554, 7

Death-bed of a man, two queries over the, 542, 1

Debt, avoidance of, a first duty, 241, 19 ; effects of, 5, 21 ; evil of, 11, 65 ; freedom from, 86, 43 ; known when accounts come in, 333, 40 ; two ways of paying, 466, 30 ; not lessened by care, 38, 6, 7 ; to be avoided, 368, 26 ; without supper rather than in, 29, 24

Debts, all paid, 145, 50 ; and sins, their number, 392, 54 ; as legacy, 66, 11 ; cleared by borrowing, 315, 18 ; great and small, 394, 22 ; small and heavy, effect of, 244, 27

Decay, contrasted with growth, 48, 9

Deceit, deceptiveness of, 7, 28 ; effect of experience in, 447, 22 ; art of, 416, 30

Deceived, twice, a disgrace, 171, 12

Deceiving, a deception, 274, 8 ; the deceiver, pleasure of, 38, 43

Decency, connected with virtue and vice, 225, 6 ; indispensability of, 105, 51 ; want of, 183, 18

Deception, always of self, 266, 22 ; and self-deception, 199, 46 ; limited, 39, 31 ; of appearances, 56, 36 ; universal, 28, 52, 53

Decision, haste in, 4, 48

Decoration, the first spiritual want, 428, 37

Deed, committed, 27, 20 ; good, in naughty world, 161, 14 ; noble, effect on us of, 547, 27¶

versus fame of it, 155, 31; one good, dying tongueless, 332, 23; only avails, 457, 18
Deeds, causes of, spiritual, 528, 16; compared with words, 562, 16; contrasted with words, 166, 4; evil, cannot be blazoned, 312, 18; evil, vengeance in heart of, 211, 49; foul, will rise, 113, 52; good, value of, 129, 24; great, immortal, 133, 18, 19; great, power of, 243, 17; men children of their, 522, 22; more urgent than knowledge, 25, 24; name of, from issue, 159, 42; not always to be acknowledged in words, 6, 65; not forgotten, 277, 15; not words, 99, 11; of man, known to the Gods, 284, 2; one's, the aim of, 163, 10; our, sayings about, 337, 34–36; pain of, lost in the glory, 192, 35; past, compared with deeds now, 314, 15; power of, 64, 11; productive power of, 211, 48; rather than words, 281, 8; time for, 457, 42; to be reciprocated, 1, 9; unnatural, 508, 13; when properly achieved, 185, 9
Deep, the howling, and its contents, 519, 9; the riches in, 185, 51
Defeat, from self alone, 313, 41; in a foreign land, 334, 33
Defection, a, to be reprobated, 200, 3
Defects, as parts of character, 38, 28; great, who have any business with, 334, 49; moral, attributed to nature, 476, 12; allowed only to great men, 179, 46; without number, 414, 38
Defence, an insufficient, 534, 18
Deference, effect of, on manners, 493, 1
Deficiencies, as signs, 184, 40
Defilement, moral source of, 475, 18
Definite, a, to be aimed at, 526, 36
Definition, importance of, 145, 31; value of power of, 145, 9
Deformed, the, displeasing, 314, 31
Deformity, the only, 188, 22
Degeneracy from man, 94, 33
Degree, a professional, necessary, 79, 36
Deil, the, Burns to, 229, 31
Deity, omniscience of, 78, 26; the, as raising up and casting down, 511, 15
Dejection, extreme ignorance, 60, 18; great, after enthusiasm, 133, 20
Delay, danger of, 162, 34; effect of, 104, 48; effect of, on temper, 101, 30; hateful, but profitable, 283, 10; that is good, 129, 40; waste, 185, 54
Delays, dangerous, 57, 4
Deliberation, evil of too long, 532. 25; life wasted in, 527, 46; long, contrasted with hasty action, 229, 34; necessity of, 57, 43
Delicacy, admired by men, 67, 8; in thought and speech, 269, 48; sympathy inlet to, 302, 25
Delight, but a sip, 19, 45; how to foster, 546, 18; to, as an aim, 89, 4
Delights, to scorn, 495, 26; violent, their end, 514, 32; purchased with pain, 9, 21
Delirium, as a common failing, 432, 34
Deliverance, only road to, 444, 40; solely from within, 559, 20
Deliverer, the hour of his coming, 546, 7
Deluded, the worst, 465, 29
Delusion, gain in shaking off a, 79, 1; triumphs of, 458, 31
Delusions often sent as a snare, 327, 38
Demigods, incredible, 165, 11
Democracy, a, the likely fate of, 13, 53; from Christianity, 43, 2; its presence, 444, 29; meaning of, 416, 34; not our goal, 313, 22; Ruskin's definition of, 4, 8; test of, Lycurgus', 125, 8
Democrat, the, defined, 423, 2
Demon world, the, and its influence, 186, 43
Demonic, the, defined, 423, 4
Denial alternation of periods of, with faith, 187,
586

49; danger of, 243, 35; the practice and regulation of, 491, 31
Denier, the, and his delight, 423, 1
Deniers, how to treat, 483, 20
Departed, the, we love, still with us, 539, 1
Departure, our point of, clear, 539, 19
Dependence, man's, 193, 13; the evil of, 413, 3; voluntary, noble, 114, 38
Depth, the, not to be dived into, 555, 15
Deputies, God's, 125, 53
Derision, often poverty of wit, 226, 18
Descent, boasting of, 363, 34
Descriptions, practical worthlessness of, 306, 32
Desert, good or ill, as treated by God, 28, 4; what one may learn in the, 190, 23
Deserts, publishing one's, 530, 7
Designing often harder than doing, 269, 49
Desirable not always attainable, 297, 51
Desire, a viper in the bosom, 90, 40; accomplished, 423, 7; as part of our nature, 338, 39; darkening power of, 98, 27; from admiration, 538, 38; impatient of delay, 88, 12; inordinate, effect of, 547, 34; its gratification, its death, 90, 39; no satisfying, 276, 25; objects of, everywhere, 414, 35; out of the shot and danger of, 217, 41; short of, more than desert, 150, 33; suppressing, easier than satisfying, 201, 19; the breath of life, 409, 12; to be limited, 46, 56; 386, 27; to be sacrificed to duty, 241, 40; unsatisfactory fruit of, 473, 34; unsatisfied, the evil of, 386, 35; when rational, 527, 20
Desires, how to regulate, 188, 13; unlawful and impossible, 507, 45
Despair, contrasted with rage, 367, 36; effect of, on our powers, 233, 18; finishing blow to misery, 233, 17; outcome of, 540, 29; the evil of, 206, 30; the measure of hope, 423, 6
Despatch, evil of too great, 401, 37; quick, virtue of, 546, 14
Desperation, rule in, 186, 10
Despicable, the alone, 482, 35
Despising, after reading, 237, 9; only after examining, 448, 3
Despot, and his despotism, 233, 10; in times of anarchy, 192, 4; the only true, 369, 37
Despotism, defined, 540, 30, 36; defied by despair, 62, 17; effect of, on a man, 407, 5; effect on, of unsuccessful revolts against, 22, 10; fatal to patriotism, 506, 21; in Russia, 233, 19; life under a, 184, 11; modern, 226, 6
Despots, how to judge of, 526, 43; poor as others, 35, 5; sway of, 35, 5
Destination of man, 312, 20
Destinies, founding of, 30, 17; higher, a path to, 402, 17
Destiny, a preacher, 476, 15; and man, 359, 30; coerced by the strong, 319, 15; great, if not known, 86, 14; in substance always the same, 163, 9; man's, in his own hands, 92, 38; not to be arrested by us, 556, 30; our limit, 82, 61; over our horizon, 144, 37; power of, 266, 5; riddle of, how to resolve, 96, 21; saddening, 264, 1; the car of one's, how to manage, 456, 22; the saddest, 493, 10; urn of, clutching into, 313, 28; wheel of, not to be checked, 551, 44
Destroyer, of thousands, helpless to embrace two, 154, 45; the, and his delight, 423, 1
Destroyers, how to treat, 483, 20
Destroying, skill in, 197, 8
Destruction, and creation, simultaneous, 190, 11; the genius of, 224, 1; the way to, 555, 36; things that tend to our, 457, 26; violent, but new creation, 9, 22
Details, significance of, 547, 40
Detraction, in heaven's sight, 393, 23; malice of, 30, 36

Development, no pause in, 292, 6

Devil, a good defence against, 99, 5 ; a, in man, 469, 31 ; a mere protest against, not enough, 536, 20 ; a necessity, 396, 13 ; as servant of God, 79, 35 ; a temptation of, 531, 46 ; and his own temptations, 170, 6 ; as busy as ever, 174, 16 ; Burns on the occupation of, 168, 4 ; Burns' pity for, 466, 12 ; chained by telling truth, 165, 19 ; comes uncalled, 34, 49 ; difficulty of laying, 7, 61 ; driven by, 144, 36 ; familiarity with, and yet in fear of, 30, 33 ; give, his due, 123, 27 ; Goethe's, character of, 128, 24 ; handsome when young, 233, 23 ; how to deal with, 29, 28 ; how to exclude, 115, 54 ; how to keep, out, 475, 23 ; hard to scare, 144, 35 ; how to understand, 26, 53 ; knowledge of, 80, 19 ; may look a gentleman, 154, 37 ; never sleeps, 280, 47 ; not to be let go when caught, 241, 11 ; persuasive power of, 484, 5 ; playing, properly, 169, 38 ; power of, generally unsuspected, 429, 46 ; servant of, sure to go to, 108, 13 ; shiftiness of, 560, 8 ; the subtle power of, 242, 47, 48 ; sugar over, 558, 22 ; that despairs, 298, 14 ; the, abolished, 188, 44 ; the, defined, 402, 5 ; the, no outwitting, 105, 7 ; the, power of, over a man, 137, 43 ; the, sayings about, 423, 15–30 ; to be resisted, 374, 36 ; under march of intellect, 441, 29 ; use of a, 174, 15

Devil's, angel, a, 176, 17 ; chapel, ever beside God's temple, 307, 15 ; meal, 225, 16, 17 ; rattles, playing with, 480, 13 ; valet, 39, 7

Devils, easier to rouse than lay, 265, 39 ; Luther's defiance of, 506, 12

Devotion, elevating power of, 200, 44 ; not to be disturbed by work, 401, 37 ; to God, test of, 414, 25 ; too much, for religion, 398, 39 ; affectation in, 489, 9

Dew, heaven in a drop of, 225, 32

Dewdrop and the star, like sisters, 423, 31

Diamond with a flaw, 28, 57

Diamonds, rough, may be mistaken, 378, 16 ; rough, no one content with, 308, 21

Die, the, is cast, 210, 8 ; the fittest place for man to, 33, 35

Diet, moderate, benefit of, 2, 47

Difference, identity of, 102, 15

Difficulties, a choice of, 477, 3 ; greatest, where met, 432, 8 ; nearer the goal, 66, 12 ; our greatest, 64, 32 ; overcome, 543, 21 ; overcoming, 494, 43 ; that we meet, 443, 20 ; there, to be overcome, 203, 36 ; to be stormed, 504, 17 ; to Christians, 395, 4 ; who never sinks under, 153, 11

Difficulty, defined, 536, 2 ; from within, 314, 42 ; how we overcome, 475, 44 ; strength to confront, 99, 63 ; what enables us to surmount, 316, 19

Diffidence, modest, attractions of, 466, 28 ; safety of, 225, 8

Digestion, good, power of, 409, 10 ; good, wait on appetite, 317, 31

Dignity, attribute of nobleman, 80, 22 ; difficulty of attaining to, 98, 49 ; official, Dickens on, 403, 44 ; true, characteristic of, 499, 44

Dilettante, nature of, 460, 30 ; the, mistakes of, 423, 38

Diligence, and skill, power of, 105, 21 ; indispensability of, 105, 51 ; the one virtue, 68, 26 ; value of, 539, 31 ; without luck, 70, 33

Dining-out, the risk to Rousseau of, 34, 2

Dinner, a, warmed-up, 505, 20 ; the English institution, 185, 1

Diogenes, quest of, 158, 41 ; 165, 3 ; to Alexander the Great, 402, 13

Dirt, Lord Palmerston's definition of, 68, 43 ; splashing of, to be shunned, 548, 36

Dirty water, empty out, but not baby, 567, 5

Disagreeable comes more speedily than desired, 158, 12

Disagreeableness better than insipidity, 29, 12

Disaster, common, consolatory, 45, 24

Disasters, ready belief in, 4, 3

Disbelief, folly of, 176, 9

Discerning when to have done, rare gift, 105, 4

Discernment, and high rank, not synonymous, 233, 34 ; not common, 309, 8 ; spirit of, rare, 6, 17

Disciple and his master, 423, 39

Discipleship, Christian, condition of, 554, 32

Discipline, effect of, 70, 30 ; not to be slackened, 203, 21 ; power of, 301, 44 ; 375, 6 ; without nature, 292, 34

Discontent, a cause of, 38, 10 ; a world-wide, 532, 36 ; at its height, 521, 39 ; in the body politic, 19, 10 ; man's, 266, 33 ; misery of, 540, 12 ; the root of, 536, 21

Discontented, man, the, 147, 3 ; man, who is despised, 208, 16

Discontentment, a cause of, 537, 39, 41 ; common cause of, 50, 50

Discord, all, harmony, 10, 2

Discouragement, pride, 316, 28

Discourse, good, effect of, on virtue, 129, 15 ; good, qualities of, 129, 25

Discourses, meandering, Whately on, 268, 27

Discoveries, all great, from presentiment, 9, 39 ; great, from above, 306, 45

Discovery, chemical, from a jobber, 566, 27 ; joy of, 385, 29 ; limited, 199, 10

Discretion, better than wit, 15, 65 ; commended, 26, 54 ; defined, 432, 27 ; key to knowledge, 221, 7 ; out-sport not, 244, 19 ; the sanctuary of, 391, 43 ; the value of, 511, 10 ; virtue of, 381, 20 ; which interferes with duty, 346, 22

Discrimination, virtue of, 145, 32

Discussion, equipment for, 147, 13 ; false estimate of, 398, 19

Disease, removed only by skill, 309, 19 ; young, growth of, 465, 44 ; when cause known, 271, 53

Diseases, coming and going, 239, 2 ; desperate, 62, 23 ; effect of physic on, 110, 19 ; how they enter, 253, 7 ; inherited, 106, 10 ; mental, like bodily, 207, 32 ; modern, 524, 36 ; of mind, root of, 10, 40 ; representations of, demoralising, 302, 6

Disesteem, not to be regarded, 395, 4

Disgrace, in, with a sovereign, 151, 10 ; of others, as a warning, 412, 26 ; the only, 170, 17 ; 319, 19 ; to whom a sin, 496, 27

Disguise, unmanly, 202, 10

Disguising what we are, trouble in, 533, 15

Disgust, the mother of, 380, 6

Dishonour worse than death, 11, 60 ; 12, 18

Disinterestedness, incredible, 161, 9

Dislike, how to overcome, 177, 31

Disobedience, two kinds of, 490, 13

Disorder, public, origin of, 10, 21

Dispatch, and hurry, in business, 32, 61

Dispensable, no need to covet, 415, 16 ; the easily, 520, 12

Dispensation from death, no, 295, 9

Display, vanity of, 4, 49

Disposition, in the eye of God, 190, 32

Disputation, effect of, 9, 23 ; evil of too much, 300, 18 ; 341, 23 ; origin of all, 59, 25 ; without definite ideas, 329, 24

Disputes, about shell, not kernel, 262, 11 ; worthy of attention, 423, 46

Disputing, effect of, on truth, 192, 8 ; sayings about, 472, 28, 29

Disquiet, source of, 459, 2

Disraeli's mark of great man, 6, 69

Dissatisfaction, cause of, with others, 330, 9

Dissection, not biography, 423, 47

Dissension, civil, a gnawing worm, 43, 37 ; easy to sow, 267, 35

Dissimulation, a mask, 392, 30; a necessity in life, 42, 15; a royal art, 381, 11; embarrassing, 225, 9; hatefulness of, 76, 38; Schiller and Goethe on, 513, 15, 16; the power of, 364, 11, 12, 37

Distance, effect of, on view, 488, 7; kept, a comfort, 171, 22; lends enchantment, 94, 1

Distinction, reward solely of merit, 153, 17

Distinctions, illusory, 274, 47

Distinguished, being, pleasure of, 21, 55

Distress, common, a uniting power, 45, 12; effect of, 457, 32; God in, 125, 21; lesson of, not to be forgotten, 404, 38; national, no ground of despair, 472, 35; public, the one sole cure for, 476, 16

Distrust, excessive, hurtfulness of, 96, 34

Diversity, universality of, 444, 9

Divine, a good, 198, 28; affinities, proof ot, in man, 533, 11; always agreeable to reason 298, 19; grace, the law of, 375, 11; love, power of, 424, 6; mind, manifold energies of, 424, 5; modern ideas of, 175, 40; protection, not extended to injustice and wrong, 449, 48; state, *par excellence*, 424, 7; the, faith in, its range, 479, 42; the, narrow view of, 525, 17; the, not directly visible, 459, 12; the only thing, on earth, 475, 42; things, how to handle, 168, 29

Diviner, the best, 268, 3

Divinity, and philosophy, 70, 12; that doth hedge a king, 478, 33; that shapes our ends, 477, 45

Division, effect of, 381, 31

Divorce, defined, 233, 24

Doctor, dispensed with, 149, 30; experience of, 424, 8; his curing and killing, 174, 17; man his own, 553, 16; the, and his fee, 68, 38; the best, 486, 48

Doctors, a fig for the, 217, 27; cobblers, 279, 46; when, disagree, 552, 12

Doctrine, no false, without some truth, 318, 11

Document, as a witness, 40, 34

Doer, a great, always reticent, 302, 13

Doers, great, in history, 431, 15

Dog, a barking, 331, 38; a good, 31, 23; a well-bred, 24, 51; attachment to a well-bred, 58, 20; bad, 1, 7; good, and its reward, 1, 46; I'd rather be a, and bay the moon, 47, 4; 166, 21; ilka, his day, 181, 33; living, better than dead lion, 111, 29; that barks, 35, 3, 4; the, an example, 409, 38; the fawning of, 31, 13; the good nature of, 430, 41; the, in the manger, 250, 6; when an old, barks, 27, 38; will have his day, 241, 1; with a man at his back, 171, 4; with bone, 77, 29

Dogmas not our first need, 204, 14

Dogs, coward, 49, 23; that bark, 35, 3, 4, 13, 14, 34

Doing, a thing without a good reason, 542, 5; all one can, effect of, 41, 22; and saying, 7, 39; fructification of, main thing, 313, 21; ill or well, effect of, 252, 58; joy's soul in, 481, 3; leaving off, what one can, 560, 24; measure of, 142, 24; nothing, a curse, 503, 28; nothing, a lesson in ill-, 298, 23; nothing, evil of, 158, 44; nothing for others, 150, 12; nothing, hard work, 142, 43; rather than seeing done, 274, 22; rather than thinking, 333, 31; right, importance of, 426, 5; rule in regard to, 541, 5; many things, shortest way of, 453, 28; to precede speaking, 468, 21; through another what one's self can, 209, 31; well, profit of, 175, 12; without understanding, 560, 24

Doings, a man's, significance of, 533, 29, 30

Dome, azure, and that of St. Peter's, different interest in, 424, 12

Done, how to get a thing, 333, 20; not to be undone, 99, 22; 525, 27; the, annihilated for us, 541, 26; the, done, 3, 54; the little, and what is to do, 439, 22; things, done, 481, 2; the, still

588

active, 536, 7; to have, 493, 6; what is, is done, 23, 11; when to have, hard to discern, 105, 4; worthless so long as dead, 535, 19

"Don't care," a snare, 166, 1

Door, open, a temptation, 15, 61; the, to be stooped to, 258, 29

Double sense, how to treat what has, 191, 37

Doubt, as guide in conduct, 296, 16; a living, 479, 27; alongside of knowledge, 280, 53; all, yields to will, 241, 46; and faith contrasted as to their origin, 233, 25; and knowledge, 482, 38; beginning with, 185, 42; effect of knowledge on, 525, 6; effect of, on faith, 552, 18; effect of, on good, 505, 11; enfeebling effect of, 150, 22; from knowledge, 42, 7, 22; 163, 22; honest faith in, 477, 8; in, lean to mercy, 186, 12; in philosophy and in religion, 35, 24; modest, beacon of the wise, 281, 35; no, no inquiry, 174, 46; no permanence in, 474, 2; no risk in, with disposition to believe, 296, 4; parent of certainty, 474, 2; rule when in, 547, 4, 8; service of, 530, 42; the effect of, 201, 13; the end of, 425, 10; the evil of, 23, 18; the value of, 452, 3; to be once in, 490, 31

Doubtful matter, rule in, 186, 10

Doubting, as necessary as knowing, 167, 46; condition of knowing, 142, 27

Doubts, Faust on his, 278, 54; Goethe's impatience with, 169, 14; our, traitors, 337, 40; resolved by interest, 111, 43; to be affirmed or denied, 12, 28

Down, he that is, 147, 5, 6; down in the world, 3, 5; in the world, quite, 542, 18

Downhill, a man going, 542, 9

Dowries, evil of excessive, 379, 23

Dowry, a great, 71, 55; a true, 309, 22

Drama, real object of, 450, 42

Dramas on earth, composed in heaven, 127, 2

Drawing, Ruskin's caution in regard to, 142, 29

Dreadful thing, between acting and first motion of, a, 29, 60

Dream, love's young, 33, 28; the loveliest, and fear, 469, 16

Dreamer, a sort of madman, 424, 20

Dreaming, not man's end, 266, 18; of dreaming 521, 35

Dreams, children of night, 41, 52; fear underlying, 27, 50; not to be regarded, 371, 11; into realities, 92, 30; and sense, 337, 41

Dregs, always sink to bottom, 424, 21

Dress, deceptive, 233, 1; expensiveness of, 528, 11; medicine for women, 446, 10; rule for, 394, 50; standard of, 76, 19; vanity of loving, 460, 25

Drill, not catechism, now needed, 458, 36

Drink, guid, effect of, on speech, 99, 35; the effects of, 365, 44

Drinking, always, effect of, 479, 19; five excuses for, 390, 1; more deadly than thirst, 87, 30; motives for, 398, 5; the evil in, 488, 30

Drinks, to be shunned, 389, 44

Drop, power of a falling, 137, 40, 41; the last, 438, 4

Drugs, to be shunned, 389, 44

Drunkard, and his rights, 424, 23; and the attendant furies, 499, 31

Drunkenness and gluttony, evil effects of, 124, 39

Dryasdust, affecting to teach, 162, 26

Dualism, universal, 10, 50

Dulness, gentle, and its joke, 124, 24

Dumb, Kant's two things that strike, 504, 9

Dunce, a travelled and untravelled, 162, 3; as representing a class of men, 273, 40; female, offensive, 164, 41

Duped, fear of being, 151, 22; sure way to be, 235, 30

Dupes at first, knaves at last, 329, 20

Dust, a handful, power of, 313, 41; power of a little, 155, 44

Duties, first, of a man, 428, 14, 15, 25 ; holy, the band of, 40, 40 ; knowledge of, best part of philosophy, 221, 12 ; not self-elected, 262, 3 ; the primal, and charities, 449, 21

Duty, a, laid on all, 539, 34 ; a man's sphere of, 477, 41 ; a path open to all, 110, 12 ; a plain, for all, 525, 23 ; a spur to, 365, 15 ; ahead, 267, 1 ; akin to love, 255, 4 ; and pleasure, everywhere, 292, 49 ; at all hazards, 99, 54 ; before even search for truth, 304, 38 ; better known than practised, 93, 24 ; defined by Wordsworth, 402, 38 ; doing, blessedness of, 184, 38 ; doing, lesson learned by, 403, 47 ; doing one's utmost, 146, 3 ; doing what lies nearest, 168, 13 ; effect of trying to do, 502, 47 ; immediate, of man, 521, 44 ; importance of doing one's, 172, 9 ; in, prompt, 186, 14 ; its reward, 451, 23 ; knowing and doing, everything, 215, 40 ; life of education, 233, 21 ; main thing for, 457, 22 ; more potent than love, 254, 4 ; most arduous, most sacred, 230, 26 ; not speculation, supreme business of man, 140, 23 ; our aversion to, 54, 2 ; our rule, 47, 3 ; our sole concern, 296, 48 ; our, the king's, 94, 12 ; path of, way to glory, 312, 45 ; perplexities regarding, 87, 33 ; point of, 519, 33 ; present, 186, 1 ; reward of following, 146, 11 ; rule of, 366, 23 ; sense of, central, 453, 12 ; sole survivor of faith and love, 326, 4 ; stated, the large claim of, 325, 4 ; sum of, 240, 49 ; 486, 11 ; that lies nearest, to be done, 72, 10, 11 ; the assigned, to be done, 72, 9, 12 ; the condition of existence, 312, 40 ; the law of life, 251, 56 ; the sum of, 496, 20 ; the whisper of, and the response, 395, 20 ; the whole of, 103, 33 ; time for every, 127, 26 ; to others, 1, 9 ; troublesome, 93, 29 ; virtue essential to, 413, 26 ; we are now called to, 494, 11 ; weight of, when fulfilled, 84, 31 ; without God, 110, 11

Dwarf, at work without his machinery, 424, 28 ; on giant's shoulders, 4, 75

Dwarfs, on giant's back, 348, 36

Dying, a man's greatest act, 212, 12 ; before witnesses, 365, 17 ; daily, benefit of, 525, 5 ; the, and the world, 7, 23 ; twice over, 30, 28 ; without being missed, 202, 49

Dynamite, only destructive, 301, 35

E

Eagle, mew'd, a pity, 16, 36 ; as oracle, 72, 14

Eagles contrasted with gnats, 124, 44

Ear, popular, estimate of, 448, 32 ; quicker, in the dark, 53, 22 ; road to heart, 224, 12 ; the right, filled with dust, 451, 37

Early rising not equal to grace of God, 200, 11

Earnestness, advantage of, 159, 16 ; importance of, 559, 29 ; power of, 534, 2 ; test of, 162, 27

Ears, deaf to counsel, but not flattery, 322, 12 ; lead men, 276, 26 ; sensitive, sign of health, 81, 36 ; 386, 50 ; who hath, 146, 47

Earth, a great entail, 126, 3 ; but a film, 414, 24 ; despising, as a task, 488, 3 ; for the virtuous man, 201, 44 ; gifts of the, 325, 8 ; how made free, or great, 64, 11 ; made of glass, 45, 8 ; no goal, 248, 1, 2 ; population of, 228, 1 ; the all-nourishing, 114, 52 ; the, sayings about, 424, 31–34 ; the axis of, its position, 416, 40 ; the, with its injuries, trampled on or loved, 394, 27

Earthly, and heavenly, counterparts, 475, 43 ; objects and interests, obscuring power of, 323, 18

Ease of mind, the condition of, 308, 18

East and West, thought of, contrasted, 174, 18

Eating, effect of excess in, 366, 25 ; that requires sauce, 209, 20

Eccentricity, how to gain a character for, 177, 22 ; in beauty, 89, 22 ; in eyes of world, 464, 7 ; in men of ability, 276, 14

Echo, power of, 431, 6

Echoes, mostly hollow, 548, 55 ; our, 337, 42

Economist, the best, 145, 13

Economists, few good, 513, 25 ; greatest, 432, 27

Economy, as a revenue, 310, 3 ; first principle of, 206, 12 ; human, the first principle of, 428, 31 ; importance of, 559, 30 ; in prosperity, 409, 14 ; object of all, true, 445, 15 ; too late, 387, 12

Ecstasy, power of, 460, 29

Eden, innocence of, lost, 524, 38

Edicts, less potent than king, 45, 47

Edifices, great, work of ages, 133, 21 ; public, how to build, 546, 31

Education, a mistake in, 201, 37 ; aim of, 415, 45 ; 435, 40 ; an inversion of, 492, 38 ; as facilitating government, 79, 38 ; chief nobility of, 428, 6 ; effect of an effeminate, 282, 15 ; entire object of, 425, 19 ; first condition of, 428, 9 ; first step in, 158, 10 ; for heaven, St. Jerome on, 243, 36 ; importance of, 427, 20 ; 451, 5 ; 509, 20 ; 539, 22 ; in defeat, 56, 60 ; inner soul of, 233, 21 ; meaning of, 566, 1 ; modern, evil effects of, 281, 27, 28 ; moral, nature and sum of, 283, 12 ; more than knowledge, 220, 43 ; most important part of, 443, 50 ; motive of, 567, 4 ; no, better than bad, 29, 54 ; of individual, aim of the world, 464, 10 ; of most miseducation, 34, 4 ; of woman, the end of, 425, 9 ; only, that deserves the name, 458, 16 ; our ambiguous, evil of, 205, 48 ; our, dissipating, 337, 11 ; Plato on, 71, 35 ; power of, 488, 8 ; question of its importance, 450, 28 ; real object of, 450, 41 ; right law of, 451, 39 ; secret of, 452, 40 ; the best, 472, 30 ; the business of, 291, 9 ; the compulsory, needed, 458, 36 ; the end of, 492, 8 ; the first use of, 428, 42 ; the, of the world, 375, 6 ; the only real, 51, 18 ; the, wanted, 476, 16 ; whole of, 72, 48 ; wise, 291, 3 ; without capacity, 35, 35 ; without God's grace, 371, 34 ; without spirit, 169, 44 ; wrong, times of, 469, 4

Educational laws to be strict, 260, 44

Educators, our, 275, 5

Effect involved in cause, 37, 12

Effort, every healthy, character of, 91, 21 ; free, blessedness in, 89, 47 ; 95, 35 ; great principle of, 431, 32 ; unrestrained, evil of, 553, 6

Efforts, condition of success of, 10, 14 ; limit to, 527, 35 ; worthless, impress of, 555, 34

Eggs, the two, eaten at breakfast, 291, 48

Ego, merging one's, 210, 43 ; the central, 462, 17

Egoism, importance of getting rid of, 152, 1

Egoist, life of an, 439, 2

Egotism, hateful, 234, 16 ; how to bring down our, 475, 29

Egotists, a social pest, 447, 33

Elect, the, and the non-elect, 424, 42

Election, unconditional, 398, 16

Elections, advice regarding, 2, 23

Elevates, what, an advantage, 541, 6

Elevation, our, what contributes to, 540, 34

Elevations, temperature of, 434, 35

Elizabeth, Queen, Essex on, 135, 32

Elizabeth's, Queen, last words, 10, 6

Eloquence, and study of Bible, 303, 31 ; at county conventions, 394, 29 ; compared with discretion, 69, 10 ; compared with insight, 162, 10 ; continued, a bore, 49, 29 ; dependent on heart, 433, 45 ; described, 368, 1 ; high-tide of, in Rome, 222, 37 ; no feigning, 347, 32 ; the source of, 344, 22 ; triumphs of, 186, 19 ; true, characterised, 499, 46, 47

Eloquent man, the, Cicero on, 143, 19

Elsewhere as here, 87, 34

Emancipation, no art, 218, 20 ; not masterlessness, 155, 30 ; without self-government, 94, 50

Eminence, effects of, on character, 16, 49 ; the price of, 38, 4

Emotion, moments full of, 467, 19 ; presupposed in reason and justice, 408, 38 ; propagation of, from writer to reader, 297, 17 ; the outlet of, 3, 49

Emotions contrasted with thoughts, 457, 39 ; pleasing, not to be recalled, 485, 19

Emperor to die at his post, 56, 32

Empire, course of, 533, 18 ; extended, cost of, 97, 56 ; extension of, 387, 22

Empires, the fall of, 89, 9

Employment, a necessity, 15, 35 ; dependence of mental, on bodily, 106, 18 ; parent of cheerfulness, 40, 49

Empty boxes, 1, 18

Emulation, effect of, 5, 8 ; envy, 288, 47 ; hath a thousand sons, 109, 29

Encouragement, better than correction, 48, 20 ; the power of, 195, 12 ; the voice of, amid contradiction, blessed, 30, 54

End, important, two ways to attain, 469, 3 ; man's destined, and way, 372, 27 ; pre-existent in the means, 37, 12 ; sanctifies means, 50, 46 ; the, crowns all, 425, 7 ; the, crowns us, 46, 31 ; to be always considered, 83, 47 ; to be always kept in view, 541, 32 ; to be known before way, 425, 14 ; to be thought of from the beginning, 186, 24

Endeavour, honest, to be encouraged, 211, 51 ; and pleasure, effects of, 349, 42

Endeavours, too high, vanity of, 142, 23

Ending, better than beginning, well, 130, 22

Endowments, first signs of, 133, 22 ; personal, idolatry of, 276, 21

Ends, to be aimed at, 27, 25 ; true, discernment of, 553, 25

Endurance, a source of strength, 125, 43 ; commended, 539, 34 ; from habit, 138, 10 ; grandeur of, 312, 37 ; patient, commended, 241, 20 ; prolonged, effect of, 357, 59 ; the first lesson to learn, 400, 19 ; the power of, 364, 24, 38 ; value of, 88, 6

Endure sooner than die, 235, 25

Enemies, belief that our, are also God's, 305, 18 ; gaining, greater than vanquishing, 136, 44 ; how to disarm, 244, 8 ; how to regard one's, 467, 17 ; how to treat, 400, 41 ; if known, to be pitied, 175, 38 ; make no, 260, 29 ; men, by imitation, 566, 11 ; none without, 304, 51 ; secret, contrasted with open, 408, 52 ; smallest, to be most dreaded, 83, 52 ; who can love his, 552, 38

Enemy, a fleeing, a bridge of gold for, 14, 55 ; appreciating the worth of, 298, 5 ; deceiving, permissible, 199, 29 ; man his own worst, 93, 19 ; no action against, on private information, 334, 2 ; no alliance with an, 304, 39 ; no defiance of untried, 304, 41 ; no, insignificant, 180, 21 ; not to be despised, 62, 27 ; not to be injuriously treated, 193, 55 ; one, too many, 150, 28 ; 332, 11, 12 ; opinion of, not to be despised, 296, 15 ; our one, 445, 35 ; the, to be met on the field, 407, 37 ; to be fought outside the gate, 425, 15 ; to have no, wretched, 280, 29 ; way of flying, to be smoothed, 8, 2 ; weakness of, our strength, 225, 13 ; what it is to be an, 333, 12

Energies, how cramped, 337, 43

Energy, as possession, 142, 2 ; basis of health, 153, 35 ; dependence of, on misfortune, 136, 33 ; first and only virtue, 272, 33 ; in social service, not lost, 545, 3 ; of which no heed is taken, 20, 21 ; power of, 482, 17 ; proper organ of the highest, 80, 41 ; without knowledge, 12, 54

England, and France, the best thing between, 418, 4 ; as one's country, 26, 55 ; chief need of, 536, 1 ; false trade of, 492, 25 ; history of, a mis-

nomer, 538, 17 ; middle-aged women in, 188, 14 ; our standpoint, 539, 4 ; people of, enthusiastic, 447, 21 ; people wanted in, 527, 14 ; secure, if true to herself, 44, 50

England's safety, 243, 23

English, amusing themselves, 238, 1 ; and Americans, 427, 44 ; and French contrasted, 222, 21 ; at their amusements, 182, 21 ; Emerson on, 335, 8 ; Mme. de Staël on, 359, 5 ; nation, a trick of, 208, 26 ; style, how to attain, 553, 31 ; the, bravery and freedom of, 425, 16 ; the, Goldsmith on, 409, 39 ; the, Napoleon of, 507, 1 ; the, their two grand tasks, 503, 37 ; the, Voltaire on, 362, 34 ; when free, 234, 25 ; well of, undefiled, 52, 51

Englishman, a true-born, 549, 8 ; pluck of, 537, 43

Englishmen, for friends, 169, 20 ; freedom a necessity for, 526, 29

Enigmas, wise men's partiality for, 199, 20

Enjoying and hoarding, 539, 45

Enjoyment, and Christianity, 420, 19 ; and endurance, rules for, 120, 7 ; and usefulness, 360, 6 ; highest, dependent on education, 77, 5 ; how secured, 81, 43 ; in want, 182, 32 ; no help in, 519, 25 ; our best, 523, 40 ; rule for, 82, 57 ; unrestrained, evil of, 553, 6

Enlistment for labour commended, 273, 39

Enmities, for time, 284, 1

Enmity, death, 488, 6 ; man's, 193, 15 ; not to be provoked, 383, 20

Ennui, a good condiment, 229, 36 ; born of uniformity, 222, 41 ; mark of manhood, 28, 45 ; the brother of repose, 234, 42 ; the effect of, 407, 34 ; those who suffer from, 460, 7

Enough, and too much, 20, 22 ; 524, 10 ; better than too much, 11, 10 ; evil in more than, 92, 47 ; excels a sackful, 121, 41 ; misfortunes notwithstanding, 190, 1 ; more than, an anxiety, 146, 31 ; never a small quantity, 38, 14 ; where there is, 20, 32 ; who has, 553, 7

Enslavement, how to escape, 177, 46

Enterprise, in the young, 331, 12 ; man of, aim of, 24, 26

Enterprises, great, wrecked by trifles, 78, 21 ; how to carry on, 36, 28 ; indiscreetly urged, 328, 13

Entertainment, ability to give or receive, 306, 11

Enthusiasm, as test of a man, 490, 6 ; higher, of man not extinct, 434, 32 ; how generated, 21, 47 ; our love in our, 338, 31 ; political effects of, 450, 5 ; the enemy of, 376, 38 ; vulgar, 299, 25

Enthusiast, better than timid thinker, 421, 21 ; effect of opposition on, 335, 52 ; the wild, zeal of, 307, 44

Envied, the, 425, 22 ; the, rather to be pitied, 283, 36 ; the, when dead, 97, 58

Envious man, the, 425, 23

Environment, enslaving power of, 522, 24 ; importance of, 75, 1 ; the tyranny of, 11, 57

Envy, a kind of praise, 108, 57 ; a step from, to love, 141, 19 ; a gnawing moth, 215, 31 ; Burns on, 340, 17 ; characteristic of, 34, 32 ; distinct from emulation, 81, 50 ; honour's foe, 160, 42 ; human, 294, 35 ; ignorance, 470, 37 ; its malevolence, 25, 57 ; passive disgust, 141, 19 ; rather than pity, 181, 6 ; 246, 13 ; sayings about, 196, 16–22 ; singularity of, 311, 33 ; the aims of, 406, 32 ; the envious contrasted with, 238, 13 ; the last stage of perversion, 438, 8 ; the life-time of, 342, 22 ; to be lived down, 389, 34 ; tooth of, against the solid, 114, 6 ; when harmless, 59, 5

Epic, future, of world, on whom it depends, 429, 39 ; our, now and henceforth, 449, 40 ; true, of our times, 458, 39

Epicurean maxim, 158, 18

Epicurism of reason, 378, 41

Epigram, should be like a bee, 327, 46 ; the power of, 14, 57

Epoch, a glorious, which few reach, 284, 20; an, most significant feature of, 444, 6; great determining element in, 186, 34; great, mark of, 211, 46; our, dominant drift of, 491, 32; the present, 331, 9

Equality, as bond of love, 124, 9; among men, a figment, 274, 1; condition of, 554, 9; establishment of, by law, 226, 8; holy law of humanity, 124, 10; not true, 394, 52; the condition of, 147, 23; unknown to nature, 292, 5

Equanimity, happiness of, 140, 20

Equity, sundered from law, 231, 28; to be respected, 188, 38

Equivocation and evasion, 89, 13

Era, a new, advent of, unannounced, 337, 26; the present, 521, 9

Eras worthy of study, 264, 1

Err, to, human, 163, 42

Erring, Cicero on kindness to, 159, 22

Error, a mistake of judgment, 220, 17; a way back from, 23, 47; an old and new, 315, 20; an old, mischief of, 489, 23; and ignorance, 178, 14; confessing, no disgrace, 58, 36; 304, 40; consolation from, 421, 30; containing some truth, dangerous, 14, 59; contrary forms of, 182, 10; dependence of glory on, 390, 25; easier to recognise than truth, 203, 13; freeing from, 492, 33; from selfishness, 275, 6; happiness of hoping to escape from, 320, 29; human, misery of, Tennyson on, 321, 39; in youth and in age, 60, 21; insignificance of throttling one, 217, 14; 550, 19; matter of endless talk, 324, 46; natural to us, 501, 28; not always harmful, 381, 51; not every, folly, 310, 20; of opinion, 85, 6; old, evil effect of, 79, 3; our great, 431, 17; our love for, 420, 14; our portion, 319, 13; perennial, 197, 1; perseverance in, folly, 51, 1; prior to truth, 184, 37; protestation against, its importance, 12, 40; so long as one strives, 85, 40; strengthening power of an, 268, 2; the fate of, 501, 27; the only, 319, 12; to persevere in, folly, 159, 2; treatment of, as sign of wise or fool, 54, 30; utility of, 531, 44; where freedom, 560, 13; with a master, 280, 51

Errors, deliverance from, hard, 265, 16; effect of diversion on, 468, 32; ever renewed, 75, 11; not to be built, 175, 33; of a great mind, 425, 25; of a wise man, 425, 26, 27; our, dear to us, 114, 39

Errs, who, in tens, errs in thousands, 41, 19; who never, 417, 46

Eruptions, superficial, when the heart is threatened, 304, 35

Establish one's self, how to, 354, 3

Establishments, old, when to abolish, 546,

Estate, one's, while in debt, 481, 11; the third, 360, 38

Estates, how often spent, 268, 57

Esteem, and love, never sold, 214, 14; commended, 243, 47; often from ignorance, 181, 13; our desert of, 522, 9; without love, 19, 52

Eternal, in man's soul, 262, 28; no hastening births of, 236, 59; presence of, in time, 449, 7; the, no simulacrum, 426, 6

Eternities, masquerade of the, 457, 47

Eternity, and time, 486, 47; 487, 2, 10; depending on time, 126, 10; effect of hope of, 302, 41; feeling in man of, 186, 38; in time, 495, 28; looking through time, 55, 44; manifest in time, 265, 2; the spot in, ours, 426, 8; unsurveyable, 297, 20; vision of, indispensable, 150, 41; youth, 466, 3

Ethics, right, the nature of, 377, 13

Ethiopian, the, and his skin, 35, 25

Eulogy, the assumption in, 12, 39

Euphemy contrasted with blasphemy, 30, 41

Europe, bewildered, the goal of, 313, 22; fifty years of, 29, 22; the glory of, gone, 415, 38

Evangel, our ultimate political, 440, 37

Evangelicals, Carlyle on, 443, 42

Evening, and its day, 520, 9; as an emblem, 89, 26; hushed to grace harmony, 162, 36

Event, great, for world, 431, 18; out of our power, 34, 20; to be mastered at the time, 90, 44

Events, all, of importance, 94, 46; all part of a divine plan, 94, 45; coming, foreshadowed, 44, 56; fitfulness of, 252, 11; gravest, noiselessness of, 431, 8; greatest, of an age, 432, 9; in life, their connection not understood at first, 569, 23; mighty, turn on a straw, 279, 15; no being beyond power of, 565, 16; our relation to, 522, 4; source of, 472, 32; tutors, 434, 14

Everything, importance of attempting, 489, 10

Everywhere, nowhere, 222, 8

Evidence, one's own, not enough, 303, 37; to be weighed, 352, 21

Evidences like weights, 437, 21

Evil, a source of good, 401, 35; absolute, unknown to us, 317, 11; all, as a nightmare, 9, 25; all, at bottom good, 10, 7; all, within, 475, 16; anticipation of, 222, 32; as well as good from God, 388, 22; at its strongest, 26, 61; better in youth, 200, 31; beginning of every, 188, 30; by thinking of it, 6, 4; deed, curse of, 482, 2; defined, 95, 35; doing, for good, 150, 3; effect of concealment on, 8, 50; from God, 197, 27; from thoughtlessness, 33, 6; greatest, for a man, 35, 44; he that doeth, 93, 33; how to avoid, 461, 25; how to overcome, 33, 47; 240, 16; how to scare away, 24, 47; inability to bear, 519, 36; knowing and speaking, 493, 30; latent in heart, 471, 25; most common source of, 444, 5; none all, 311, 8; necessary for good, 401, 46; no absolute, 472, 34; no, felt till it comes, 301, 42; no, without compensation, 301, 43; not constant, 86, 13; not doing, and not intending, 491, 43; not struck at the root, 468, 23; not to be traced, but extinguished, 547, 22; how to overcome, 113, 6; of the day, enough, 406, 16; one, St. Paul of, 521, 45; only hiding of, 473, 11; overcoming, two ways of, 494, 44; patiently borne, 301, 41; reaction of, on self, 80, 33; report, how to treat, 172, 13; resisted, a benefit, 90, 45; sense of filthiness of, a foil, 152, 15; speaking, defence against, 171, 38; 172, 1; that goeth out of one, 426, 12; that men do, 426, 13; the beginning of, 69, 29; the root of, 170, 40; theories of, helpless against evil, 62, 41; thing, judgment of, often delayed, 214, 17; things, goodness in, 476, 33; to be overcome, 28, 14; to be simply borne, 541, 31; to come, better unknown, 38, 30; wishing no, merit of, 298, 15

Evils, easily crushed at the birth, 327, 48; extreme, alike, 9, 26; great and little, effect on one of, 133, 24; great and small, how to oppose, 492, 49; great, impotence to overcome, 175, 15, 44; guards against, 409, 16; how to shield one's self from, 300, 21; imaginary, 96, 23; imaginary, how made real, 182, 36; imaginary *versus* real, 243, 41; man's fear of, 206, 45; neglect of small, 111, 38; not imaginary, 10, 13; origin of, 261, 4; our, source of all, 201, 50; real and possible, compared, 325, 11; shunned, fallen into, 104, 40; silently bearing, 523, 24; which of two, to choose, 547, 2; which we feel, 330, 28

Evil-disposed, the, 482, 49

Evil-doer and the light, 146, 5

Evil-doers, fear of, 532, 2

Evil-speaker compared with evil-doer, 261, 17

Evil-speaking, evil of, 553, 15

Evil-wishing, evil of, 553, 15

Evolution, only worthy of regard, 445, 44

Exaggeration, common, 473, 37; weakening effect of, 329, 14

Exalted, station, ornament to merit, 222, 36; who shall be, 146, 57

Example, and precept, 252, 43; force of, 171, 36; noble, force of, 78, 44; potency of, 96, 49; the effect of, 276, 43; the power of, 375, 6; value of, 158, 43

Examples, good, power of, 129, 27, 28; perfect, evil effect of, 89, 28

Excel, daring to, 301, 29

Excellence, source of, 92, 23; the appreciation of, value of, 297, 37; to be studied, 338, 35; uniformity of, tiresome, 507, 24; what we must risk to attain, 489, 32; world's treatment of, 464, 31

Excellences, deep hidden, 40, 33

Excellency, witness of, 207, 7

Excellent, persons, tortures of, 383, 31; the, difficult, 39, 37; the, how to treat, 536, 9; the, rare and rarely valued, 426, 18; the, unfathomable, 55, 2; things, rare, 328, 23

Exception, and rule, 96, 26; going by the, 199, 39

Exceptions, according to order, 291, 6

Excess, a tendency of Nature, 94, 41; every, a vice in end, 327, 49; no, 170, 14; 271, 51; nothing in, 242, 29; of good, dangerous, 153, 38; the evil of, 350, 10; unstable, 94, 43

Exchange, as a means of life, 275, 3

Excitement contrasted with enthusiasm, 83, 38

Excitements, great, effect of, 426, 10

Exercise, benefit of, 90, 48; bodily, St. Paul's estimate of, 31, 10; defined by Johnson, 228, 34; rules for, 6, 14

Exigencies, the science of, 97, 24

Exile, everywhere, 566, 4; friendly face to, 496, 6; no exile from self, 535, 6

Existence, a distracted, waste of, 569, 25; a mystery to the greatest genius, 306, 41; all earthly, a vapour, 368, 36; contrasted with life, 487, 16; disappointed, worse than none, 208, 39; first delight of, 494, 43; laws of, our knowledge of, 207, 22; man's secret of, 452, 47; our, passed into words, 339, 38; our, purpose of, 521, 26; perfection of, 345, 47; principle and end of, 521, 2; source and destiny of all, 554, 31; the healthy tenure of, 199 4; the only explanation of, 437, 14

Existent, the, its importance, 457, 21

Expectation, a retarding weight, 559, 10; and uncertainty, as joys, 506, 1; as regulated by desire, 173, 6; effect of, on a blessing, 488, 10; of good, effect on us of, 559, 5

Expectations, and non-preparedness, 523, 44; extravagant, vain, 176, 1

Expecting nothing, blessedness of, 30, 51

Expense, our, the root of, 337, 45

Expenses, petty, effect of, on purse, 205, 32

Expensiveness, our, 340, 4

Experience, a light to truth, 467, 15; a teacher, 78, 34; and ability, possible effect of, 383, 37; as a teacher, 220, 21; as an educator, 323, 37; as inducing fear, 97, 46; authority of, 84, 30; bitter, 34, 19; bitter, advantage of, 532, 28; by indulgence in passion, 144, 20; contrasted with theory, 466, 20; incommunicable, 63, 26; its limited extent, 496, 17; knowledge of, 114, 34; like stern-lights of ship, 494, 35; man's only school, 264, 34; no antedating, 302, 55; not equal to understanding, 269, 22; one's own, and others', 75, 15; others', no demand for, 308, 26; our, of life, 337, 46; painful, as a teacher, 81, 48; perfect, 345, 48; second-hand, 563, 22; the fruit of life, 429, 31; thrift in, 34, 5; value of, 334, 22; without thought, 529, 3

Experiences, common, instructive, 72, 45; our chief, 337, 24

Experiments, subject of, 105, 26

Exposition of one another order of the day, 472, 1

Expression, clear, of difficult matters, 492, 19; correct, the source of, 43, 56; dependence of, on distinct thought, 284, 23; how to attain facility of, 488, 40; modest, virtue of, 281, 36; purpose of nature, 462, 8; test of thought, 253, 26; varieties of, accounted for, 529, 11

Expressiveness, all, 478, 5

Exquisite, the, coy, 94, 47

External things, emancipation from power of, 559, 26

Extracts, necessity for, 444, 18

Extraordinary, the, how to treat, 536, 10; only the, rebelled against, 265, 30; to be looked at, 198, 3

Extremes, violent, temporary, 307, 38

Extremity, trier of spirits, 567, 34

Eye, a commanding, 15, 5; a daring, 551, 28; a steady good, 79, 9; as an interpreter, 538, 4; as an organ of speech, 534, 42; by which one sees God, 426, 25; first overcome, 186, 23; importance of vision in, 417, 21; interpreter of heart, 214, 11; man's, not microscopic, 555, 7; one, better than two, 269, 40; only in forehead, 488, 38; seeing, of the first times, 434, 30; single, to be venerated, 18, 48; soul in the, 416, 10; the power of, 57, 26; the, sayings about, 426, 26-42; the, under distraction, 43, 16; to be single, 439, 12; to negotiate for itself, 240, 34; *versus* ear, as vehicle of knowledge, 385, 21; where love, 72, 34

Eyes, affected by our heart, 337, 47; and the belly, 63, 52; and ears, as witnesses, 63, 51; and what they indicate, 7, 13; effect of shutting, 205, 47; homes of silent prayer, 154, 48; how guarded from error, 300, 1; importance of using, 202, 4; more trusted than ears, 276, 43; more trustworthy than ears, 324, 2; never satisfied, 154, 36; one man's, spectacles to another, 332, 57; our, exorbitant, 524, 44; our, misuse of, 521, 24; posted as sentinels, 324, 1; rather than ears, 158, 43; speaking and betraying power of, 541, 12; the feast of, 264, 35; to be cared for, 409, 33; to see withal, 520, 23; to look right on, 243, 9; weak, weakness of, 530, 12; weakness of most, 325, 13; without looking, 126, 5

Eye-witness, and hearsay, 350, 13; one, value of, 332, 14

F

Fable, Love's world, 64, 13

Face, a handsome, 112, 36; and the mind, 426, 43, 44; as revealing the heart, 190, 33; expression of, contrasted with tongue, 458, 10; full impression of, 205, 11; God hath given you one, 126, 11; like a benediction, 142, 36; not deceptive, 204, 21; the index of age, 98, 42; the, of labour, Carlyle on, 512, 10; two sides of, 302, 33

Faces, expressive, 466, 38; that most charm us, 482, 29; variety in, 206, 3

Facility, how to acquire, 539, 31

Fact, and speech, gulf between, 401, 1; goodman, plain-spoken, 130, 39; not law, 5, 27; significance of a, 5, 25, 26; 287, 46; stranger than fiction, 99, 9; the question for jury, 4, 50; the importance of, 457, 21

Faction, effect of, 381, 31

Factor, rule of, and minister compared, 140, 31

Facts, all enfolded in first man, 264, 22; and the truth of reason, 421, 32; beadrolls of, insignificance of, 556, 33; dissipated by time, 486, 35; downright, our need of, 529, 36; modelled by the man, 51, 48; plainest, men blind to, 161, 8; stubborn things, 33, 7; the emphasis of, 425, 4; the great, 431, 19

Faculties, a delight to exercise, 313, 1; man's, no inventory of, 475, 8; our, and their exercise, 521, 16; our, their last perfection, 438, 7; the soul's, a misnomer, 413, 5

Faculty, indispensability of, 105, 51; not to be forced, 293, 6; the logical, 313, 6; the imaginative, 313, 6

Fail, no such word as, to youth, 190, 48

Failing at all, 492, 20

Failings, how regarded by heaven, 474, 5; lean'd to virtue's side, 156, 51

Failure, a chief cause of, 105, 22; as a teacher, 525, 15; bright side of, 252, 48; fruit of, 104, 14; in a great object, 472, 38; sure road to, 456, 29; the only, to fear, 446, 1; the parents of, 193, 9

Failures, a cause of, 386, 2; a lesson to us, 329, 17; how to regard, 373, 8; no, where no efforts, 144, 50; not to daunt us, 206, 20; often successes, 526, 21

Fair day's wages, a, Carlyle on, 5, 28

Faith, a great, 285, 27; a lively, wages of, 506, 33; all in all of, 415, 50; alternation of periods of, with denial, 187, 49; 447, 28; an audacious, 530, 6; and doubt contrasted as to their origin, 233, 25; and hope, differences about, 186, 49; and knowledge, difference between, 186, 50; approved, reward of, 105, 58; as fashion, 149, 29; commended, 243, 32, 33; demand of love, 353, 53; desire of, faith enough, 176, 34; disowned when questioned, 242, 8; essence of, 425, 38; essence of all, 427, 6; fanatic, and falsehood, 99, 62; in an omnipresent God, denial or mere lip-assertion of, 427, 6; in days of sorrow, 523, 43; in whom alone, 104, 3; knowledge in, 383, 10; lesson of, 462, 6; loss of, 146, 33; narrow, power of, 14, 26; necessary to faithful doing, 152, 41; once lost irreparable, 172, 8; only, that wears well, 446, 2; orthodox, defined, 60, 4; our slavery from want of, 485, 39; plain and simple, 467, 37; power of, 111, 26; 114, 3; 185, 52; 279, 32; 448, 37; 492, 34; 558, 26; principal part of, 449, 24; proper power of, 449, 41; resting on authority, 427, 8; right, if life right, 110, 23; right, defined, 474, 15; sister of justice, 216, 39; steps of, 455, 12; strengthened by knowledge, 504, 23; the great trial to, 384, 26; the one thing needful, 110, 17; the only sure foundation, 9, 1; the power of, 200, 44; 312, 23; 319, 11; the proper object of, 240, 14; the root of, 340, 15; want of, 110, 17; 507, 11; 558, 26; want, at present, 423, 44; wilful, confirmed by absurdity, 544, 37; with centre everywhere, 554, 4; wonder essential to, 560, 4; Voltaire's definition of, 481, 40

Faithful, in little, 147, 8; sure of reward, 105, 46

Faithfulness, commended, 28, 48

Faithless among the faithful, 100, 27

Faiths, in all, something true, 184, 31

Fallen, the, succouring, 371, 14

Falls, some, means to rise, 398, 7

False, in one thing, 101, 2; knowledge of, a truth, 221, 18; men, mischief done by, 312, 46; the, evil influence of, 2, 49

Falsehood, a salve, 181, 9; after falsehood, 100, 30; adhesiveness of, 226, 12; as weakness, 443, 31; at touch of celestial temper, 301, 49; evil of, 502, 6; goodly outside of, 322, 31; how regarded, 223, 21; in kings, 494, 3; man fire to, 92, 30; obstacle to happiness, 56, 27; path of, 447, 8; soothing, 181, 9; the success of, 512, 5; to be renounced, 501, 40

Falsehoods, that are not lies, 466, 39

Falsities, all, to be alike treated, 71, 34

Falsity of things, more seeming than real, 480, 33

Fame, a thin web, 174, 7; common, rarely wrong, 45, 13; complacency in, 312, 29; course of, 514, 39; exceptional, 323, 24; how one earns, 330, 32; in no hurry for, 172, 14; insignificance of, 155, 31; 533, 44; lessened by acquaintanceship, 280, 2; law of, 439, 31; lust of, and wise men, 440, 10; modestly enjoyed, 28, 20; obtained and deserved, 398, 36; Pope on, 311, 49; posthumous, a vain desire, 555, 3; rage for, 538, 23; the price of, 443, 32; the struggle for, 97, 48; thirst for, 260, 7; true, like our shade, 499, 48

Familiar, by proxy, 311, 7

Familiarity, lowering effect of, 181, 28

Families, and their best members, 176, 4; only two, 72, 3

Family, a happy, 140, 14; bargaining in, over the pottage, 442, 43; home of peace, 190, 35; heroism in the, 432, 32; in the bosom of one's, 336, 51; Burns' prayer for a, 545, 17; virtue, importance of, 427, 13

Famine, effect of, on heart, 530, 18; evil of, 101, 31

Fanaticism, contempt of, 90, (; defined, 90, 9; effect of, on a man, 407, 5

Fancy, charm of, 442, 7; compared with reason, 369, 34; 526, 20; contrasted with imagination, 183, 2; exacting, 292, 13; fantastical, 395, 1; giving way to understanding, 431, 5; how bred, 411, 40; over reason, what, 10, 19; sugar of life, 69, 9; the tyranny of, 201, 36; turned necessity, 539, 18; *versus* fancy, 522, 33; without taste, 315, 41

Fancying in harmony with the fact, 369, 20

Fantasies, lightest, two meanings of, 503, 44

Fantasy, compared with understanding, 459, 33; exorbitant demands of, 386, 46; function of, 66, 5; the age of, gone, 53, 25; the power of, 266, 11; the ripened fruit of, 387, 3

Far-away things, attractiveness of, 76, 11

Farces, seeming, tragedies, 268, 31

Farewell, hard to say, 555, 10; Macpherson's, 317, 30

Farewells should be sudden, 244, 17

Farthing, a good, 31, 28

Farthings, valued, 480, 20

Fashion, a bad rule, 170, 23; a maxim of, 88, 31; a tyrant, 226, 13; dominancy of, 526, 22; effect of, 427, 14; fool in, and one out of, 314, 19; glass of, 322, 32; imperious, 567, 1; old and new, how regarded, 91, 1; out of the, 19, 15; power of 385, 19; 440, 15; tyranny of, 21, 16

Fashions, change of, a tax, 39, 45; following the, 477, 10; invented by fools, 108, 53

Fastidious, the, unfortunate, 238, 11

Fastidiousness to be avoided, 526, 27

Fatalism, faith of men of action in, 284, 10

Fate, all thralls of, 212, 21; a mystery, 218, 12; action of, on willing and unwilling, 73, 41; and dreams of the past, 240, 47; and the heart, 370, 24; and the willing, 102, 47; 103, 3; and the unwilling, 102, 47; 103, 3; a pedagogue, 54, 25; a, to be evaded, 217, 4; best use of, 205, 50; Cæsar's belief in, 34, 34; certainty of, 111, 46; cuffs of, on good and resolute man, 422, 22; how to conquer, 491, 5; in drawing of heart, 62, 3; irresistible, 478, 11; master of his, cannot complain, 60, 25; most wretched, 415, 20; not to be interrogated, 503, 1; no evading, 308, 32; no striving against, 264, 33; our, what we make it, 231, 8; ordinations of, 517, 17; our, how to overcome, 366, 12; overloading of, 440, 16; quarrelling with one's, 554, 37; responsibility of, 33, 34; scale of, lightest in, 550, 6; shunned, embraced, 74, 8; stars of, in the breast, 191, 44; the book of, hidden all but a page, 154, 2; the sorrowfulest, 454, 17; to be submitted to, 535, 7; under temptation, 412, 8; undue respect to, 483, 9; what we may make of, 523, 18

Fated, the, and the feared, 54, 37

Fates, our, like rivers in their rise, 33, 19; the, work of, 427, 22

Father, banker provided by nature, 505, 31; a, deceiving, 363, 43; affection of, for daughter, 38, 29; a, function of, in a family, 174, 27; and his house, scorning, 494, 19; and son, respect of, mutual, 148, 50; and mother, indebtedness to, 65, 34; 66, 1; a priest, 252, 46; duty of, in training son, 158, 10; when old and daughter, 489, 21; words of, to his children, 463, 47

Fatherland, before life, 86, 6

Fathers, our, objects of pity, 186, 30; our, to be as good as, 490, 8

Fatigue, most wearisome, 472, 36; the best night-cap, 138, 10

Fault, a, denied, 506, 37; a, virtue out of, 332, 2; avoiding one, and rushing into another, 117, 8; condemned ere committed, 46, 10; every, at first monstrous, 93, 13; excusing of a, 14, 49; in every, folly, 186, 33; man's grand, 266, 32; which needs a lie, 314, 4

Fault-finders, nothing safe from, 315, 39

Fault-finding, not always safe, 508, 36; of fools, 409, 2, 3; our, 521, 11; to be avoided, 283, 38; without mending, 268, 58

Faultless, nothing, 553, 29

Faults, advantage from, 204, 17; allied to excellences, 468, 13; as taints of liberty, 32, 26; committing and permitting, 428, 17; confessed, half mended, 46, 16; deception as regards our, 550, 23; difficult to weed out, 398, 8; effect of a call to give up, 344, 55; Goethe on, 205, 20; greatest of, 432, 30; hard to cure, 523, 25; how corrected, 34, 9; in honest and dishonest, 69, 21; lie gently on him, 395, 15; men moulded out of, 28, 36; mended, not to be referred to, 276, 30; nature of, 9, 27; none exempt from, 92, 2; of bad and of good men, 25, 43; of others and our own, 8, 21, 22; of others, instructiveness of, 98, 16; often corrected by chance, 39, 38; of the player and the man, 10, 41; one's own, best known, 169, 9; one's own, easily pardoned, 101, 32; others' zeal in amending, 315, 15; our, not to discourage, 296, 41; our own, and our neighbour's, 91, 53; our relation to, as our own or others', 529, 16; pleasure in others', 390, 26; seeing only others' 50, 12; seeking only for, 480, 17; that kill us, 206, 22; that look handsome, 322, 35; to be thankful for, 92, 10

Faust, in a dilemma, 169, 41; Goethe's, without fruit, 314, 34

Favour, a, against one's will, 28, 2; a, what it consists in, 5, 32; a, when to ask, 296, 3; asking for, 149, 31; how to confer a, 529, 4

Favours, injudiciously conferred, 27, 56, 57; from the great, 116, 5; refusing, 341, 46, 47

Fear, a bad preserver, 261, 39; a, daily surmounting, value of, 142, 45; an inventor, 227, 4; and reverence contrasted, 492, 21; desponding, effect of, 62, 30; early and provident, 75, 31; effect of, 121, 55; 492, 22; effect of, on speech, 81, 46; getting rid of, a first duty, 428, 14; how bred, 387, 54; incompatible with love, 255, 1; incompatible with wisdom, 504, 38; inconsistent with love, 146, 13; of the Lord, 427, 26–29; perpetual, evil of, 272, 46; persuasive power of, 180, 33; sign of low birth, 57, 15; slavery to, 302, 18; stages of, 457, 48; cold, that freezes, 102, 20; those who dwell in, 483, 7; to be suppressed, 160, 22; unknown to Germans 14, 21; unlimited, 70, 47; unreasonableness of, 537, 15; who has no, 264, 6

Feared by many, fearing many, 294, 7

Fearless man, a, 532, 32; the, 150, 19

Fears, our, effects of, 545, 1

594

Feast, constituents of a, 394, 19; what constitutes, 206, 4

Feasts, by whom made and by whom eaten, 108, 56

Feather, incapable of momentum, 455, 37

Feeble, in work unhelpful, 305, 7; the, to be supported, 488, 24

Feeling, an unpleasant, a warning, 95, 5; and thought, 484, 42; as opposed to thinking, 8, 58; by whom induced, 33, 26; compared with seeing, 384, 41; delicacy of, 11, 8; how to awaken, 483, 23; 401, 47; importance of, 119, 26; in reality keener than in song, 268, 38; man of, fate of, 427, 19; not attained by hunting for it, 531, 47; not man's end, 266, 18; one's, to be trusted, 184, 45; power of, 264, 30; strong, tendency of, 404, 5; the analogy of, 44, 30

Feelings, at meeting and farewell, 338, 1; by which we live, 525, 20, 21; duration of, 427, 32; fine, without vigour of reason, 106, 27; fineness of, not given to every one, 217, 7; great, like instincts, 135, 20; our most exalted, 338, 37; the, hid in man, 539, 16

Feet, her, beneath her petticoat, 155, 1

Feigned, the, never lasting, 315, 7

Felicity, from self alone, 162, 30; greatest, 432, 11; or infelicity, a man's, how to know, 544, 3; in the soul, 163, 19

Fell, Dr., I do not love thee, 165, 47

Fellow, a lucky, 36, 40

Fellow-feeling, effect of, 5, 33

Fellowship, a, to cultivate, 542, 3; founded on truth, 150, 24; the end of existence, 312, 30

Fetters, a burden, 304, 29; when one wishes to be in, 544, 44

Feud, an old, easily renewed, 47, 27

Fibres, tension of all, 427, 36

Fiction, compared with truth, 501, 48; contrasted with fact, 369, 19, 20; inferior to fact, 99, 12; more potent than fact, 338, 2

Fictions, to resemble truth, 105, 31

Fiddlestick, the power of, 539, 8

Fidelity, among rebels, 370, 11; but a name, 308, 45; compared with justice, 569, 40; contrasted with love, 246, 11; gone, 67, 5; importance of, 501, 25; in small things, 3, 25; to be practised, 504, 15

Field, a large, to ear, 166, 43

Fields, and cities, 70, 5; holy, over whose acres, 158, 26; where joy for ever dwells, 102, 21

Fiends, absolute, 2, 18

Fight, no, no victory, 174, 43; to, and die, 492, 24; to, with stronger, no obligation to, 473, 38

Fighting, an affair of the heart, 313, 10; and being beaten, compared, 173, 10; does not feed men, 294, 44

Fights, that, and runs away, 109, 51; 146, 14

Figure, a pleasing, value of, 16, 40

Finding, not the possession, sweet, 298, 1

Fine Art, as defined by Ruskin, 106, 23

Fine, characteristic of everything, 427, 39, 40; thing, expense of buying, 547, 12

Finesse, a great step in, 198, 41; hovers between virtue and vice, 225, 21; recourse to, mark of incapacity, 227, 18

Finger-posts, authentic, few, 377, 41

Finished-off, man, no satisfying, 531, 17; *versus* becoming, 281, 5

Finite, and infinite, respective conditions of, 205, 26; let alone infinite, too much for man, 262, 21; shadows forth infinite, 261, 45

Fire, a mighty, to quickly kindle, 482, 48; a neglected, 294, 30; a slow, 19, 53; and wind, 484, 19; its power, 27, 12; little, to be trodden out, 8, 42; matter for the, 541, 3; no extinguisher, 179, 33; sayings about, 427, 46, 47; 428, 1, 2; slumbering in ashes, 233, 27; the only, worth gauge or measure, 264, 20 ; who walks through, 552, 45 ; wind-fed and wind-extinguished, 320, 1

Fires, violent, 157, 10

Fireside, my own, an Eden, 540, 20

Firm, legal, advantage of two attorneys in, 476, 34

Firmament, unseen support of, 311, 26

Firmness, and rashness, 543, 24 ; with pliability, 179, 8

Fitting, the, right, 540, 6

Flame and smoke as passing into each other, 203, 10

Flash, not the thunder, 206, 13

Flatterer, and tyrant, compared, 465, 35 ; at whose expense he lives, 498, 36 ; Latin word for, 438, 10 ; Steele on, 165, 25 ; the greatest, 474, 26 ; to be avoided, 324, 44

Flatterers, why so obnoxious, 450, 45

Flattery, a visor to villany, 307, 39 ; and censure, 347, 22 ; attractive, 23, 10 ; benefit of, 421, 7 ; easier than praise, 275, 10 ; how harmful, 390, 27 ; ill-manners, 315, 49 ; inconsistent with love, 303, 35 ; to cajole fools, 301, 52 ; to fools and wise men, 487, 50 ; what is wanting to be pleased with, 539, 37

Flaws, where they abound, 427, 39, 40

Flesh to be sacrificed to spirit, 440, 8

Flock, no, without one dead lamb, 472, 39

Flogging before better than afterwards, 200, 9

Flower, a, despising, as a weed, 538, 26 ; and seed, relation of, 428, 49 ; born to blush unseen, 117, 23 ; of humanity, and the slime it springs from, 429, 18 ; of sweetest smell, 429, 1 ; petal of, and granite boulder, 191, 12 ; mystery included in a, 251, 16 ; tender, with head elate, 457, 8 ; thoughts from a, 494, 27

Flowers, as symbols of nature, 44, 33 ; as preachers, 568, 32 ; contrasted with weeds, 408, 22 ; fair, by the wayside, 382, 15 ; the sweetest, our treatment of, 529, 39 ; Wordsworth on, 127, 18

Fluency, often scarcity, 421, 13 ; secret of, 538, 42

Flunkeyism, 271, 19

Flush of health and of death, 469, 33

Flute, a beginner on, 192, 31 ; and lyre, with voice compared, 429, 3 ; blowing on, not playing, 30, 40

Fly, not without spleen, 89, 15 ; those that, 482, 45 ; Uncle Toby to the, 125, 1 ; 482, 21

Foe, no, no friend, 144, 27 ; service of, 412, 52

Foes, our greatest, within, 187, 14 ; what they teach, 115, 13

Folk, old and young, compared, 213, 15

Folks that stand on their heads, 478, 3

Follies, in relation to wisdom, 92, 39 ; committed out of complaisance, 165, 12 ; greatest of, 432, 31 ; our own and others', differently regarded, 529, 9 ; reasoning us out of our, 483, 2

Folly, a characteristic of, 87, 25 ; 195, 31 ; compared with wisdom, 557, 5 ; disdainful of itself, 329, 5 ; greatest and commonest, 494, 20 ; how alone to conceal, 404, 29 ; in every one, 212, 10 ; learned at college, 211, 43 ; sayings about, 429, 5, 6 ; shoot, as it flies, 98, 20 ; the short, best, 227, 12 ; universal, 172, 15 ; without remedy, 80, 34

Fondness, fostered by time, &c., sure, 406, 1

Fontaine, La, epitaph of, 211, 44

Food, though given, to be wrought for, 125, 39

Fool, a great, 179, 7 ; a, how to win, 45, 1 ; a learned, 505, 36 ; a, mark of, 404, 34 ; a, when silent, 89, 16 ; a witty, and a foolish wit, 29, 7 ; a thorough, 144, 34 ; according to Wm. Blake, 153, 19 ; and his hobby, 2, 60 ; and his opinions, 359, 29 ; and learning, 236, 34 ; and wise, 10, 39 ; and wise contrasted, 252, 10 ; and wise, diverse conduct of, 538, 40 ; as he grows their, 443, 22 ; as regards reason, 148, 53 ; at forty, 30, 2 ; conscious of his folly, 151, 4 ; effect of praising, 355, 13, 14 ; familiarity with

a, 32, 59 ; getting rid of a, 31, 45 ; hard arguing with, 333, 23 ; hard to discover, 208, 23 ; his sorrows and fears, 466, 25 ; in his devotions, 504, 8 ; in his own house, knowledge of, 349, 7 ; kind, the worst, 437, 28 ; let me play the, 241, 34 ; mark of, 333, 1 ; may be knave, 164, 31 ; never changes his mind, 180, 41 ; no, without admirer, 505, 37 ; of virtue, be, not of vice, 108, 36 ; old and young, 239, 35 ; once a, always, 363, 18 ; rather than saddening experience, 166, 26 ; the conceit of, 404, 27 ; the, sayings about, 429, 7-11 ; to self worse than being fooled, 563, 12 ; truths of a, 425, 26 ; without the stuff of success, 505, 35

Foolish, man, aversion of, to the wise, 108, 38 ; ever, never wise, 151, 48 ; once very, never wise, 150, 30

Foolishest man, no, without a knowledge all his own, 472, 40

Foolishness, the thought of, 457, 35

Fools, all, 9, 62 ; 482, 20 ; 498, 23 ; behaviour to, characteristic of a man, 315, 13 ; deliberate, the wisdom of, 322, 17 ; favoured by fortune, 113, 19 ; favourites of women and fortune, 124, 36 ; gabble of, evil of, 420, 6 ; dependence of knaves on, 174, 47 ; in majority, 89, 49 ; 239, 27 ; indispensable to wise men, 118, 14 ; intelligible only to God, 66, 48 ; learn by experience, 89, 40 ; learned, 236, 10 ; many, 404, 28 ; necessary to wise men, 127, 38 ; old, 398, 32 ; our feelings towards, 343, 54 ; rush in where angels fear to tread, 109, 39 ; safety in number of, 444, 23 ; sayings about, 5, 54–68 ; 6, 1, 2 ; 90, 50–52 ; talk of, 238, 39 ; taught by experience, 97, 34 ; that boast, 399, 14 ; their company saddening, 421, 15 ; to be first won, 11, 41 ; trade by the eye, 219, 50 ; unpitied by heaven, 154, 14 ; with wit insufferable, 108, 17

Foot, had music in't, 157, 17 ; slip of, and of tongue, 81, 18

Footway, rule of, 452, 13

Fop, described, 6, 2 ; Diogenes on a, 186, 18 ; one, plague to another, 292, 8

Forbidden, the, man's hunger for, 506, 17 ; the, striven after, 300, 35

Force, affects action, not will, 225, 23 ; and right, power of, 201, 47 ; brute, as social bond, 32, 49 ; contrasted with opinion, 335, 38 ; even in a righteous cause, 89, 25 ; giant for weak, 212, 42 ; man of virtue, in, 471, 3 ; no honestly exerted, lost, 302, 29 ; personal, 347, 1 ; when legitimate, 228, 18 ; with and without judgment, 516, 11

Forebodings of evil, 114, 36

Foreign, rule insecure, 8, 25 ; the, not to be shunned, 264, 32

Foresight of what is to come paralysing, 421, 4

Forest, planting and uprooting, 509, 26

Forethought, value of, 221, 34 ; favours brave, 113, 39 ; manly, 216, 48

Forfeited, the, irrecoverable, 305, 21

Forgetfulness contrasted with memory, 273, 14, 25

Forgetting, expediency of, 88, 16

Forgiven, the, duty of, 5, 18

Forgiveness, a source of weakness and strength, 94, 57 ; natural, 163, 41 ; rule of, 513, 30 ; too ready, 364, 23 ; with God and Christ, 428, 4

Forgiving, and forgetting, Schopenhauer on, 492, 31 ; Schiller on, 513, 31

Forgotten things insignificant, 325, 23

Form, mathematical, *versus* living, 271, 2

Forms, our social, 339, 17 ; their tendency to corrupt, 21, 17

Formulas, essential, 262, 4 ; value to man of, 473, 31

Forsaking all, the profit of, 552, 9

Fortitude, as a virtue, 460, 42 ; commended, 122, 45 ; defined, 432, 27 ; the root of, 340, 15 ; true, defined, 499, 49 ; value of, 471, 17

Fortunate, better than wise, 81, 13; the always, 441, 14

Fortune, a better, to desire, 495, 51; a broken, man of, 340, 27; a fickle jade, 257, 45; a goddess, man-made, 312, 4; 318, 30; a great, 259, 13; a great, making and keeping, 208, 10; alternation of, with misfortune, 444, 7; a man's best, 54, 5; a man's, on his forehead, 414, 33; a match for, 495, 3; an expensive mistress, 353, 49; and her gifts, 225, 26; and her arrows, Dryden on, 240, 48; and ruin, 269, 8; and the prudent, 342, 23; and wisdom, 557, 1; a self-sufficing, 537, 32; an unsuitable, 50, 49; bad, may be changed to good, 455, 20; bad, virtue for, 187, 15; boast of, 473, 2; choice of, 494, 37; companion of valour, 516, 9; dependent on the character, 39, 46; diminished, how to behave under, 172, 17; does not change nature, 245, 51; effect of good and bad, 416, 44; everywhere, 549, 29; fatal lures of, 22, 34; fatal obstructions to, 467, 33; favoured of, at home, everywhere, 113, 32; favourite of, 22, 48; footsteps of, 257, 34; frowns of, not to daunt, 242, 16; frustrating power of, 38, 8; Goethe on effect on him of good and bad, 154, 26; good, 564, 5; good, a cloak, 530, 8; good, accompanied by good, 538, 7; good and bad, a necessity, 224, 22; good and bad, as elements of virtue, 136, 45; good and bad, how to act in, 182, 34; good, and good sense, 523, 28; good, folly of not embracing, 143, 6; good, from our endeavours, 129, 29; good, hard to sustain, 527, 15; good, mother of, 401, 20; good or bad, to whom it falls, 232, 49; good or bad, ill to determine, 523, 34; good or bad, to what we ascribe, 520, 40; good, our stomach for, 339, 23; good, preferred to wisdom, 137, 42; good, to the soldier, 350, 16; good, to be seized, 158, 21; good, virtue for, 187, 15; her aim in her gifts, 172, 18; how to behave under change of, 172, 16; how to manage, 528, 36; how to make, a friend, 177, 40; how to overcome, 541, 9; indifference to, 503, 17; inequalities of, Burns' lament over, 253, 19; large, misery of keeping, 280, 23; loom of, and the webs, 439, 39; making, mistress, 202, 54; maligned, 207, 24; man maker of his, 92, 17; neither to elate nor depress, 390, 10; not to be mistress, 296, 40; not to be yielded to, 565, 4; one's, in one's self, 75, 13; one's, no fleeing from, 107, 37; ounce of, value of, 279, 10; ever with industry, 549, 27; partiality of, 53, 42; power of, 163, 25; power of, by whom alone confessed, 448, 38; power of, limited, 299, 2; present and past compared, 240, 25; question about, 450, 25; reverse of, Horace in, 231, 6; ruler of life, 201, 48; smiling or frowning, 394, 36; surest passports to, 115, 3; the arbiter of, 157, 9; the favoured of, 68, 29; 307, 10; the goal of, attained, 541, 42; unstable, 331, 13, 33; vanity of seeking, 480, 9; vicissitudes of, 225, 25; 514, 2; visit of, 473, 25; the, which nobody sees, 429, 17; what the benefits of, require, 541, 18; when she means most wanted, 543, 26; with the fortunate, 185, 13; without an enemy, 413, 18; without fairness, 326, 30; without prudence, 318, 30. See Fortuna.

Fortune's fool, 164, 42

Fortunes, and husbands, 518, 48; how made formerly and now, 112, 34; large, sayings about, 230, 15, 16

Forwards, the great thing, 431, 41; the word, 517, 33

Fought all his battles o'er again, 399, 37

Fountain, smallest, heaven in, 301, 54

Fowls, far-off, Burns on, 102, 14

Fox, and hedgehog, tricks of, 18, 31; and his captor, 285, 27; and his knavery, 59, 55; and
596

lion compared, 519, 6; cunning of, 30, 14; once caught, 505, 34; one, more than enough, 79, 8; sayings about, 429, 21, 22; skin of, sewed to the lion's, 52, 14; taken in by a fowl, 160, 4

France, in, nation not corporate, 226, 25; in the van, 225, 28; inconsistences in, 498, 31; indebtedness of, to Corneille, 498, 51; monarchy in, 225, 27

Francis I. after his defeat at Pavia, 498, 32

Franklin, motto on bust of, 84, 36

Frankness, entire, permitted only to a few, 105, 10

Fraud, defined, 70, 48; detected in a, distrusted, 365, 24; first and worst, 428, 3; in generalities, 70, 52; to conceal, 114, 15

Frederick the Great, a king, 179, 25; his indifference to criticism, 166, 14; last words of, 226, 17; social ideal of, 188, 7; tired of ruling slaves, 169, 40; two sides of his character, 5, 48

Frederick William I. of Prussia's boast, 170, 9; in reference to his son, 156, 27

Free, country, life in, 184, 11; creature, a perfectly, 472, 11; man, according to Klopstock, 152, 29; man, the, defined, 429, 24; man, the only, 143, 48; no man, not lord of himself, 298, 28; not all, who mock their chains, 86, 35; settled in heaven, 393, 30; the, man, 366, 32; to be, what it is, 490, 15; who thinks himself, without being free, 298, 29; who to be deemed, 304, 22; who would be, 155, 21; 220, 7

Freedom, 265, 17; abroad *versus* slavery at home, 28, 29; absolute, 2, 19; and cultivation, 48, 45; and peace, 481, 36; but a name, 281, 6; civil, home of, 549, 14; conceded, 167, 36; condition of, 554, 9; 556, 29; dependence of, on knowledge, 220, 36; dependent on law, 53, 38; enough, 171, 17; essential to existence, 114, 35; from woman's bonds, 84, 34; her quiet eye, 313, 31; human, 61, 1, 2, 5; in chains, 264, 31; in bonds, 331, 44; native to man, 172, 42; no barriers to, 154, 30; no, without justice, 182, 24; often imaginary, 267, 14; only in obedience, 96, 22; on the mountains, 23, 9; perfect, the condition of, 483, 32; popular, Mephisto on, 54, 38; real, condition of, 205, 28; sayings about, 64, 16, 17; spiritual, attainable by all, 245, 50; the basis of, 335, 6; the condition of, 267, 20; 306, 8; the height of, 304, 13; the measure of, 394, 51; the only possible, 193, 11; the only, worth the name, 446, 4; the seat of, 67, 12; the secret of, 190, 39; true, in self-command, 90, 54; when abused, 344, 46; which we cannot use, 534, 13; who deserves, 334, 52; who has sufficient, 15, 16; with despotism, 495, 14; without self-command, 304, 6; 306, 8

Freedom's battle once begun, 109, 41

Freemen, corrupted, 48, 25

Free-will, necessity of, 265, 13; source of slavery, 393, 34; the function of, 95, 35

French, and English, contrasted, 222, 21; Mme. de Staël on, 359, 5; Revolution, first watchword of, 114, 12

Frenzy, effect of, compared with reason, 258, 44

Fretting, vanity of, 69, 2

Friend, a constant, 3, 26; a, defined, 298, 41; a desirable, 169, 22; a faithful, Napoleon on, 5, 30; a far-off, effect of tidings of, 423, 50; a good, 6, 41; a good, value of, 270, 48; 505, 16; a, love for, 30, 29; a necessity for a man, 171, 18; a reconciled, 17, 43; a reserved, danger of, 472, 2; a stranger, not an estranged, 29, 2; a, to all, 146, 61; a true, 513, 20; a, value of, 384, 30; a virtuous, casting off, 491, 16; a, with world shut out, 386, 20; an agreeable, Horace's preference for, 299, 37; an imprudent, dangerous, 376, 53; an old, not really lost, 187, 42; and his faults, 13, 29; as nettle, not echo, 29, 10; admonition of, value of, 419, 21; difficulty of helping, in trivial matters, 315, 46; essential to happiness, 289, 5; everybody's, nobody's, 222, 9; faithful and just to me, 149, 24; from enemy, 97, 8; great service of, 432, 5; having no need of, 143, 2; how to approach, 243, 22; how to keep a new, 70, 18; how to live with, 252, 3; how to treat, 486, 2; ignorant, danger from, 315, 45; man to spurn as, 169, 28; mindfulness of, when happy, 490, 28; mistaken zeal for, 145, 51; no, without fault, 207, 25; only way to have, 446, 26; only if proved, 301, 55; only, self, 78, 6; rule for choice of, 57, 50; 80, 26; rule in choosing a, 62, 4; the candid, Canning's aversion to, 123, 17; the service of a, 412, 52; the, to trust, 499, 4; the wounds of, 100, 26; to be steadfast, 544, 41; true, value of, 81, 21; turned enemy, 398, 4; want of true, misery of, 109, 3; what most endears a, 314, 18; who does not befriend, 149, 39; who cannot bear foes, 149, 38; who flatters and detracts, 405, 42; who not needs, 157, 44; without, no good enjoyable, 318, 22; worth dying for hard to find, 423, 35; wronging, penalty of, 149, 10; Zeno's definition of, 10, 12

Friendly relations, how to keep up, 334, 3

Friends, after wine-casks drained, 68, 4; a hundred, not too many, 79, 8; a necessity, 529, 35; 538, 13; a thousand, not too many, 150, 28; absent, in the memory, 442, 1; among, or enemies, 381, 7; and enemies, 242, 15; and foes, space for, 14, 53; and their characteristics, 6, 5–12, 44; and their purses, 124, 12; being without, 42, 29; better than grateful dependants, 200, 29; but a name, 308, 45; by choice, 235, 16; choice and change of, 28, 25; community among, 45, 26; created by transactions, 473, 36; dead, a magnet to next world, 75, 6; Emerson on his, 288, 7; essential to enjoyment, 318, 22; failings of, how to treat, 85, 36; faithful, falling out of, 427, 11; false, 100, 41, 42; 398, 11; feeling at misfortune of, 53, 7; good, man good, 566, 29; grapple, to thy soul, 429, 28; hard task to make, of all, 327, 55; having many, 321, 35; how to choose, 185, 29; in adversity, 13, 28; 39, 1; in distress, 514, 15; in need, having, 143, 2; indispensability of, 559, 33; lightly cast off, 142, 15; like fiddle-strings, 114, 30; misfortunes of, not displeasing, 181, 25; 190, 12; mutual property, 12, 60; no true, his who fears to make a foe, 153, 14; not four, in world, 210, 44; not to be suspected, 179, 13; old, 327, 14, 15; 361, 39; old, best, 77, 47; our, and our faults, 338, 4; our estimate for, 96, 57; preferable to wealth, 37, 54; prudence of gaining, 202, 11; real, the value of, 369, 12; reticence with, 71, 33; sayings about, 237, 46, 47; test of, 329, 21; thou hast, 482, 31; three good, 148, 46; true, hard to distinguish, 239, 8; true, to one another, 499, 51; wealth, 504, 24; when wealth sees, 160, 29; with change of fortune, 71, 15

Friendship, a selfish, 104, 45; compared with love, 114, 49; a, that is binding, 315, 11; a useless, 413, 9; after love, 141, 11; and little gifts, 219, 38; and love, 254, 3, 18; and love, incompatible, 253, 42; and passion, contrasted, 6, 11; and pity, incompatible, 348, 49; as a pleasure, 246, 36; attractive power of, 90, 57; attributes of, 13, 30–37; basis of, 350, 19; being without, 479, 45; belated, 470, 38; by proxy, 311, 7; chastity of, 384, 5; comfort of, in adversity, 25, 16; compared with hatred, 141, 21; contrasted with love, 255, 22; defined, 222, 10; 377, 11; despised, 182, 16; double effect of, 481, 30; effect of distance and absence in, 69, 39; essence of, 425, 39; experience of those who cultivate, 483, 17; fate of, 568, 40; faults notwithstanding, 11, 47; female, growth of, 104, 30; forgiving, 224, 7; fruit of, 452, 39; genuine, a test of, 413, 8; gifts of,

511, 24; grass on path of, 242, 20; greatest blow to, 314, 24; how kept green, 7, 20; ideal of, 436, 12; imperilled through money, 27, 17; imperilled by pecuniary favours, 103, 25; in dividing inheritance, 190, 25; judgment before, 214, 3; lasting, basis of, 170, 30; light of, 439, 11; no, without virtue, 392, 46; not at too heavy a cost, 172, 20; not based on feasting, 103, 59; not to be cheap, 260, 32; often due to weakness, 219, 7; our, and charity, 337, 22; that has to be constantly bought, 209, 21; the claims of, 247, 47; the first law in, 138, 49; to be mutual, 168, 21; tried in need, 128, 37; true, 413, 22; 499, 52; 500, 1–3; true, a feature of, 88, 29; true, how possible, 163, 1; true, indissoluble, 145, 39; true, without ceremony, 38, 24; unfitness for, 554, 36; value of, 392, 35; without weakness of, without strength of, 150, 45

Friendships, broken, no repairing, 32, 46; dissolved by silence or neglect, 286, 5; for eternity, 284, 1; new, not at expense of old, 317, 26; not founded on affinities, 315, 16; of years, the depth of, 337, 44; schoolboy, 470, 8; when real, 543, 30

Frog, a, if it had teeth, 89, 17

Frost, God's plough, 429, 29

Froth, not beer, 382, 18

Frugality, a small, often no economy, 12, 35; an estate, 309, 30; and fortune, 193, 35; and parsimony, 558, 39; with contentment, 70, 13

Fruit, forbidden, 112, 9; from labour, 324, 28; late, keeps well, 230, 38; present in the seed, 37, 12; test of a tree, 116, 42; the latest, ripens 55, 24; the worst, 474, 48

Fruits, the test, 564, 21

Fulness, all, here, 155, 6; lapsing in, 494, 3

Function defined, 3, 52

Fury of a woman scorned, 154, 3

Future, a form of, 519, 5; a happy, predicted by George Sand, 433, 13; a, open to all, 537, 2; always to be provided for, 173, 36; and past compared, 447, 3; anxiety about, 71, 30; concern for, bootless, 66, 20; construed from past, 1, 5; duty with regard to, 495, 39; for whom, 234, 38; greatness of, 440, 19; how to face, without fear, 220, 11; how to see farthest into, 528, 13; how to treat, 501, 15; ignorance of, 253, 25; improvidence in regard to, 326, 12; in the porch of, 429, 40; judged of by past, 167, 28; learned from past, 169, 5; not our concern, 296, 48; not to be desired, 165, 40; not to be feared, 103, 47; solicitude about, 399, 16; state, effect of uncertainty regarding, 69, 20, 50; thought of, elevating, 94, 49; veiled by God, 359, 23; what it hides, 67, 21; wisely hidden, 384, 47

Futurity, uncertainty regarding, 528, 14

G

Gaiety, a medium in, 477, 46

Gain, at expense of credit, 52, 47; effect of greed of, 183, 19; lust of, 258, 5; scent of, good, 257, 42; unjust, 356, 6; unjustly distributed, 77, 53; worldly, and loss, 20, 52

Gains, evil, losses, 271, 31; light, profit of, 249, 10; not all gains, 309, 24; small, profit of, 219, 34; unjust, instances of, 399, 8

Galba, the emperor, Tacitus on, 260, 9

Galileo and his "Yet it moves," 84, 12

Gall, a little, effect of, 505, 33

Gallant, the motive of, 386, 18

Gambler, a young, 214, 43

Gambling, and travelling, compared, 499, 10; gain

by, a loss, 551, 23 ; nature of, 565, 31 ; pedigree and progeny of, 233, 37
Gamester, keep, from dice, 217, 15
Gaming-table and fortune, 549, 27
Garb, makes not the monk, 223, 17
Garden, the first, 127, 50
Gardener, business of, 494, 39 ; grand old, and his wife, 116, 35
Garibaldi to his soldiers, 397, 11
Garrulousness, disesteem of, 484, 36
Gatherer and disposer of other men's stuff, 164, 38
Gay, the, disliked by the sad, 324, 5
Gear, gathering, for independence, 491, 17
Geese for swans, 9, 53
Gem, why so small, 19, 49
Gems, valueless as food, 403, 20
General, a, in prosperity, 370, 17 ; a, the qualities of, 368, 32 ; influence of good, on his men, 31, 61 ; the best, 551, 40
Generalising resented by Nature, 292, 33
Generality, how to win over the, 491, 12
Generalship in good fortune and bad, 73, 37
Generation, cursing one's 303, 39 ; each, a duty laid on, 199, 51
Generosity, after justice, 27, 26 ; and justice combined, power of, 429, 47 ; charm of, 129, 31 ; easier than justice, 162, 6 ; in train of high birth, 225, 30 ; rare, 269, 23 ; *versus* business, 169, 12 ; virtue of a man, 163, 40 ; with what is another's, 98, 45
Geniality defined, 133, 28
Genius, a characteristic of, 198, 15 ; a common fate of, 510, 27 ; ages of, superseded by theories of, 466, 19 ; a fine, criticism of, generally false, 176, 33 ; after the philosophic ideal, 405, 43 ; always melancholy, 540, 46 ; a mark of, 491, 8, 15, 46 ; a necessity for triumph of, 48, 65 ; and education, 77, 11 ; and wit, functions respectively of, 53, 36 ; and fortune's favours, 113, 40 ; and taste, why seldom together, 554, 45 ; and the world, 464, 24 ; as such, unconscious, 169, 47 ; at its rising, 377, 31 ; a true, natural, 289, 19 ; a truly great, mark of, 22, 6 ; by outstripping reason, 239, 6 ; capacity for patience, 233, 28, 29 ; characteristics of, 492, 36 ; connection of, with childhood, 90, 24 ; contrasted with mediocrity, 272, 3 ; contrasted with talent, 409, 44, 45, 47, 49, 50 ; 410, 1 ; contrasted with wit, 223, 4 ; dependent on attention, 22, 13 ; defined, 195, 20 ; 513, 14 ; 546, 4 ; distinctive mark of, 489, 29 ; development of, condition of, 490, 9 ; effect of adversity on, 194, 10, 11 ; effect of prosperity on, 194, 11 ; endowments peculiar to, 6, 25 ; every great, and his vocation, 91, 15 ; every work of, characteristic of, 93, 53 ; fine, envy of, 207, 31 ; great, how formed, 6, 66 ; greatest, most indebted, 432, 13 ; greatest works of, acquaintance with, 493, 13 ; honour done to, 194, 7 ; how often dumb, 269, 10 ; human, its limitations, 333, 44 ; idleness the blight of, 5, 20 ; in what its greatest power, 91, 3 ; its indebtedness, 526, 25 ; often without talent, 269, 11 ; lamp of, 37, 45 ; man of, how ruined, 217, 18 ; man of, one consideration for every, 549, 41 ; men of, all workers, 450, 39 ; men of, as men of business, 276, 5 ; men of, generosity of, 276, 4 ; men of, in advance, 563, 9 ; men of (see Men of Genius) ; men of, two divisions of, 496, 19 ; men of, unregarded, 176, 4 ; mistake and regret of, 71, 41 ; nature in league with, 280, 52 ; no great, quite sane, 318, 27 ; no lonely son of, to despair, 241, 46 ; no, without madness, 472, 50 ; noblest function of, 416, 20 ; not attainable by labour alone, 315, 47 ; not to be constrained and urged, 12, 45 ; of light, 429, 48 ; often hid under rude exterior, 21, 48 ; often of slow growth, 268, 19 ; often without talent, 269, 11 ; on the summit of

the ideal, 206, 7 ; pith of, contracted, 395, 17 ; privilege of, 206, 41 ; selection a test of, 521, 13 ; self-defended, 91, 4 ; subject to gloom, 466, 35 ; superior to intellect, 137, 38 ; test of, 494, 23 ; the bestower of, 494, 3 ; the death of, 424, 18 ; the first qualification of, 53, 33 ; the great nursery of, 289, 46 ; the highest, characterised, 434, 39 ; the patrons of, 28, 22 ; the power of, 190, 44 ; the pride of, 400, 33 ; the purpose of, 201, 45 ; the school of, 47, 42 ; the stern friend of, 397, 29 ; the three requisitions of, 325, 15 ; three things that enrich, 485, 26 ; tendency of, to eccentricity, 76, 32, 33 ; true, sign of, 22, 4 ; 542, 32 ; two kinds of, 468, 35 ; unconsciously developed, 92, 31 ; under misfortune, 379, 24 ; vain sigh of, 488, 50 ; *versus* talent, 54, 32 ; warped by education, 77, 21 ; what forms, 396, 7 ; without a heart, 536, 14 ; without moderation, 281, 24 ; without power, 548, 25 ; without taste, 380, 17 ; without training, 78, 7 ; works and words of, 474, 47 ; work of, a child of solitude, 3, 35
Geniuses, great, biographies of, 133, 29 ; those that look like, 478, 13
Genoese, proverb about, 450, 1
Gentil man, according to Chaucer, 143, 25
Gentility and vulgarity, 102, 34
Gentle, world gentle to, 121, 38 ; yet not dull 484, 11
Gentleman, a, characteristics of, 6, 27, 28 ; a, outfit of, 137, 11 ; a true, rare, 275, 44 ; a questionable, 6, 29 ; an original, 529, 10 ; best dressed, 143, 46 ; by nature, 149, 37 ; contrasted with clown, 181, 10 ; Horace's characteristics of, 86, 42 ; how formed, 77, 7 ; manners of, defined, 346, 15 ; mark of, 49, 4 ; sphere of, 81, 3 ; the badge of a, 373, 46 ; the best, 143, 47 ; the first and the last, 199, 13 ; the word of, 463, 42
Gentlemen, rare, 520, 35
Gentleness, antidote for cruelty, 22, 2 ; commended, 400, 33 ; connection of, with firmness, 205, 22 ; more pleasing than strength, 283, 33
Gentry, rabble amongst, 470, 22
Genuine, hard to eliminate, 331, 46 ; the, and the spurious, 536, 15 ; the durability of, 519, 20
Geologist, an antiquarian, 233, 30
Geometry, road to, 474, 17
German God, the, the temple of, 298, 9
Gethsemane, victory of, attainable, 524, 38
Getting, and getting by renouncing, 201, 39 ; easier than keeping, 122, 14 ; no, what we don't bring, 305, 42
Ghost, a, never visible to two, 63, 15 ; 302, 1 ; raising one, effect of, 177, 9
Ghosts, the only genuine, 473, 39 ; whom they visit, 122, 1
Giant, on the shoulders of, 37, 55 ; strength of, tyrannous to use, 201, 34
Giant's strength, how excellent, 326, 2
Gift, a, dearer than a purchase, 535, 47 ; a, in each for all, 57, 17 ; a rare, 495, 12 ; a, we can receive, 522, 46 ; an acceptable, 145, 1 ; better than a prayer, 79, 31 ; every good, from God, 91, 8, 9 ; smallest, how made great, 91, 6 ; that destroys liberty, 53, 6 ; the only, 446, 6
Gifted man, the, defined, 430, 7
Gifts, against Nature's law, 377, 13 ; an enemy's, 76, 39 ; effect of, on freedom, 544, 27 ; evil effects of, 430, 4 ; gate of, closed at birth, 543, 22 ; God's, 125, 38, 39, 42, 44, 45, 46, 48, 54 ; 126, 1, 2, 4, 10 ; of God, how to treat, 522, 25 ; of God to man, 262, 7 ; often losses, 401, 36 ; power of, 52, 30 ; receiving, a loss, 245, 28 ; the best, least admired, 417, 38 ; to receive, 495, 13 ; when givers prove unkind, 496, 11 ; who can be trusted with, 334, 51 ; winning power of, 286, 34 ; without election, 326, 30

Girl, education of, Ruskin on, 417, 18; proper confidant of, 449, 39; qualities we love in a, 525, 30
Girls, beauty and deformity in, Ruskin on, 302, 2; morality of, 443, 6
Giver, a cheerful, 127, 12; and receiver, rules for, 241, 9; love of, not gift of lover, 151, 41
Giving, an honour, 80, 18; and receiving, 191, 16; Bismarck's maxim on, 72, 29; business of rich, 119, 11; contrasted with receiving, 492, 41; effect of, 525, 5; for one's gratification, deemed a merit, 544, 22; hand, a, 6, 33; not receiving, our gain, 95, 11; prompt, 30, 26; to poor, Diderot on, 71, 21; without bottom, 230, 18
Gladiator, the wounded, 381, 3
Gladness, alternates with sadness, 379, 17; peculiar to man, 416, 9; sown for the upright, 249, 18
Gladsome thing, the most, 443, 46
Glance, a, significance of, 150, 15
Glances, progeny of, 109, 42
Glass, first to fourth, 428, 19
Glasses, cracked, easily broken, 118, 50
Glib and oily art, 169, 1
Glitter, not gold, 10, 29; the fascination of mere, 407, 32
Glitters, what, temporary, 535, 9
Gloaming, wooing in, 64, 3
Globe, the mad-house of universe, 168, 45
Gloomy temper, foolish or worse, 540, 26
Glory, a spur, 195, 47; after death, 43, 19; ambition for, 552, 20; bewitching power of, 117, 20; false, 100, 43; inveteracy of desire of, 88, 18; in rising after a fall, 430, 11; love of, Talleyrand on, 256, 7; mixt with humbleness, 132, 3; no, without danger, 88, 48; our greatest, 338, 8; paths of, 447, 13; popular, a coquette, 352, 44; rejection greater than conquest of, 78, 39; shadow of virtue, 124, 19; that is unreal, 124, 18; the custody of, as a task, 155, 36; the path to, 22, 40; the torch of, 103, 27, 28; to him who despises it, 124, 21
Gluttony, effect of, on heart, 530, 18; effect of, on mind, 186, 17
Goal, how to attain, 118, 52; our, a riddle, 539, 19; our political, 313, 22; steps to, 203, 42
God, a, all mercy, 6, 35; a blank tablet, 130, 49; a conception of, 497, 17; a, over and behind us, 470, 19; a, the hypothesis of, Laplace on the, 393, 3; acknowledging, 169, 48; acts of, 183, 11; alive to misery, 308, 31; all-avenging, 38, 26; all-pervading, 87, 17; all things full of, 57, 30; 213, 25; 214, 47; 406, 49; an absentee, 197, 29; and existence, 437, 14; and heaven, as gifts, 488, 12; and His laws, 292, 36; and His word, Koran on, 492, 46; and Mammon, service of, incompatible, 564, 11; and soil, as creditors, 202, 8; and St. Edmund, for sole friends, 518, 24; and the right, 192, 32; as builder, 91, 27; as His worshipper, 19, 44; as the only just, 84, 25; as working and suffering, or reposing, 205, 26; barred by our idolatries, 546, 36; before or in, state of feeling, 170, 11; being of, encompassed with difficulty, 324, 29; believing and acknowledging, different, 169, 48; better deal with, than saints, 200, 32; cannot be recompensed, 131, 6; cause of, and emancipation of reason, 227, 23; condition of knowing, 525, 8; denying, evil effect of, 479, 37; effect of living with, 542, 14; eternity, His vindication, 123, 7; existence of, absurdity of proving the, 82, 17; existence of a personal, 87, 24; existence of, proving or doubting, 495, 8; fear of, effect of, 484, 7; folly of proving existence of, 358, 2; for all, 93, 15; forgotten and prayed to, 284, 17; found twice, 524, 5; geometrises, quoted, 524, 34; gifts of, all good, 9, 49; give
to, his due, 375, 5; glory of, present in all things, 485, 35; good and just in all life, 399, 46; goodness of, infinite, 9, 34; helpful to the helpless, 130, 47; here or nowhere, 426, 6; His dwelling-place, 192, 17; His omnipresence and omniscience, 492, 46; how best discerned, 153, 54; how He is to be found, 526, 19; how to attain knowledge of, 220, 4; how to honour or insult, 476, 4; how to lose, 384, 44; image of, in man, 539, 29; in Christ, rational acknowledgment, Browning on, 168, 23; in history, 150, 23; in nature and man, 321, 29; in relation to universe, 481, 17; in the bosom, 430, 17; in the breast, 6, 36; in the breast, limited power of, 60, 5; in the depth of the soul, 130, 48; in the heart, 131, 2; 556, 11; in the heart of him who longs for Him, 324, 48; in the living and becoming, 422, 47; in the mouths of philosophers, 347, 36; in the whirlwind, 376, 35; in the will, His condescension, 294, 33; inscrutable, 498, 9; irreverence towards, 529, 27; kindness of, 99, 23; kingdom of, how to enter, 512, 52; kingdom of, popularly and figuratively, 495, 4; knowledge of, 437, 40; knowledge of, identified with justice, 144, 7; living to, alone, 144, 23; love of, test of, 147, 52; man needs, 203, 28; man, the key to, 478, 30; men of, have always been, 276, 1; misplaced trust in, 176, 8; name of, not to be taken in vain, 185, 3; nature of, not to be searched into, 288, 46; near to man, 395, 19; necessary to invent, 390, 7; no, agreeable to every one, 546, 29; no repose out of, 483, 30; not found in soul, not found anywhere, 152, 33; not waiting in churches, 535, 10; of this world, 430, 16; of traditional believers, 430, 15; omnipresence of, 130, 50; 131, 8; 172, 30; only to be left for a better master, 112, 40; original and end, 116, 25; our, a household God, 338, 5; our being in, 187, 27; our conception of, 520, 38; power of contrasted with man's, 262, 14; presence-chamber of, 202, 40; promises of, 449, 36; purposes of abstruse, 214, 27; record of appearances of, 418, 24; secondary, no God, 151, 50; seeking, outside the soul, 385, 8; sense of a, 211, 15; Son of, embraced by faith, 404, 9; sovereign, 89, 39; supreme, 174, 6; supreme over stars, 21, 1; the art of, 421, 41; the great proof of, 460, 41; the greatness of, 173, 20; the impossibility of proving non-existence of, 223, 35; the, of the Koran, 472, 45; the living garment of, 292, 2; the love of, 484, 13; the love of, breadth of, 439, 50; the, of our time, 282, 39; the portion of those that love, 98, 19; the power of, 299, 7; the provider, 63, 12; the soul of all, 9, 6; the true physician, 130, 52; the true, spirit of, 556, 22; the, within, 87, 3, 4; 469, 37; thy convoy in storm, 230, 27; to be acknowledged, 313, 14; to be obeyed, rather than man, 527, 37; true honouring of, 142, 54; true love of, 147, 48; trust in, 105, 25; trust in, and do right, 242, 57; trust in, commended, 547, 19; trust in, Cromwell's, 360, 35; universal conception of, 141, 38; unlimited and all containing, 493, 18; unlimited by space and time, 486, 26; unnamable, 532, 8; veiled and unveiled, 292, 31, 32; ways of, just, 215, 29, 30; web of, without beginning or end, 472, 7; what alienates from, 540, 31; what comes from, destiny of, 534, 35; what is meant for, sacred, 520, 2; where and how to know, 472, 6; where men weep, 382, 17; where to seek and find, 567, 18; who seeks, in the dark and cold, 552, 25; who would find, must bring, 554, 28; wisdom and judgments of, 322, 15; with us, everything, 371, 12; without, nothing but darkness, 326, 26; without to be sought for within, 288, 2; word of, 520, 7; word of, near, 463, 41; work of, character of, 519, 21; work of, first and last, 428, 11; works

of, a book, 469, 22 ; works of, still glorious, 66, 43 ; worshipped, if known, 63, 5

God-forsaken, cry of the, 422, 21

Godlike, the, sadness of, 475, 20 ; thing, one, in world, 191, 43

God-protected people, 66, 34

God's council chamber, no key to, 137, 16 ; delight, 325, 28 ; elect, called to be sad, 127, 51 ; gifts to man, 306, 45 ; goodness, implied in His being, 130, 40 ; help, helpless without, 156, 35 ; laws, omnipresence of, 306, 39 ; life, in man, 420, 18 ; light for all, 543, 31 ; love, no falling out of, 456, 23 ; mills, 131, 9 ; name not to be taken in vain, 409, 26 ; operations contrasted with man's, 273, 44 ; plan unfathomable, 141, 33 ; presence, the real, 547, 38 ; promise, a pillow, 306, 38 ; Sabbath work, 428, 11 ; voice, the true, 458, 43 ; work and man's contrasted, 197, 38 ; work, full of Himself, 298, 39 ; work, perfect, 127, 15, 27 ; 541, 29

Gods, avenging, feet of, 68, 17 ; effect of adoring, 480, 7 ; fate of favourites of, 330, 33 ; gifts of, misintelligence of, 321, 27 ; ground of faith in, 270, 26 ; how to draw near, 556, 32 ; how to resemble, 217, 36 ; 427, 35 ; joy of the, 532, 5 ; mills of, 335, 35 ; not to be tempted, 61, 11 ; 242, 11 ; rural, familiarity with, 113, 33 ; sayings about, 430, 20-31 ; secrets of, no prying into, 242, 11 ; tempting the, 506, 7 ; the, among men, 545, 33 ; the, and their gifts, 68, 13 ; the existence of, how suggested, 356, 52 ; the, the lavishness and stinginess of, 320, 22 ; the, the man dear to, 289, 28 ; the, the mother of, 400, 8 ; the patience of, 430, 21 ; the, the path of, 402, 32 ; the, to be reverenced, 183, 52 ; the, under law, 406, 51 ; the, voices from, 467, 9 ; their life sad, 438, 52 ; their silence, 556, 13 ; their avatars, 489, 4 ; unjustly blamed, 183, 55 ; when they arrive, 543, 37 ; whom they love, fate of, 363, 3

Goethe, and Schiller, compared, 532, 22 ; Carlyle's defence of, 272, 31 ; greatness of, Carlyle on, 311, 19 ; how he is to be read, 506, 15 ; inspiring idea of, 123, 14 ; of his inherited nature, 517, 26 ; on his studies, 166, 40 ; sphere-harmony of, 454, 29 ; treatment of, 349, 20

Goethe's, devotion to truth, 172, 39 ; greatest gain, 420, 27 ; motto, 326, 27 ; refuge from world, 114, 32

Going, and sending, difference between, 42, 37 ; back rather than going wrong, 29, 23 ; slowly, going safely, 42, 36

Gold, a chimæra, 209, 47 ; 224, 10 ; and dirt, 128, 38 ; and silver, self-commended, 160, 1 ; carrying only, 148, 49 ; evil effect of, 162, 19 ; lust of, evil of, 365, 45 ; object of ambition, 109, 43 ; power of, 9, 55 ; power of, limited, 131, 28 ; the power of, 13, 26 ; 288, 45 ; to gild refined, 492, 39 ; to have and to want, 493, 7

Golden, age, before us, 222, 2 ; age, never such to itself, 203, 3 ; age, not of gold, 222, 1 ; age, the, Goethe on, 430, 32, 33 ; key, that, 413, 11

Goldsmith, Johnson on, 305, 3 ; 318, 31 ; inspiring idea of, 123, 14

Good, ability of doing, good, 25, 41 ; absolute, unknown to us, 317, 11 ; action, one, condoning power of, 111, 22 ; alone capable of conservation, 313, 48 ; and better, fate of, 30, 16 ; all, basis of, 94, 19 ; all, from heaven, 11, 56 ; all, save God's, limited, 9, 34 ; all things for, 174, 36 ; and evil, difference between, 475, 7 ; and evil, mixed, 406, 46 ; and evil, only opposed, 95, 22 ; and evil, unexpected, 137, 39 ; and great, 94, 21 ; and ill, how to treat, 200, 26 ; angel, warning of, 29, 74 ; antagonism to, a constant necessity, 477, 11 ; association with the, 20, 32 ; at last to all, 165, 16 ; balance of, 67, 22 ; beauty of, to be regarded, 71, 37 ; bought with toil

and tears, 458, 44 ; calling, bad, 172, 32 ; compared with evil, 228, 14 ; deed, ennobling, 150, 2 ; deeds, man's wealth hereafter, 91, 7 ; deeds, noiselessness of, 30, 19 ; do, a universal rule, 98, 29 ; doing, sayings on, 70, 35-37, 40 ; doing, teaching good, 150, 4 ; doing, to the bad, 261, 26 ; doing, without occasion of evil, difficulty, 201, 7 ; done slowly, 232, 40 ; due to exercitation, 283, 23 ; easier to be, than to seem, 320, 36 ; easy to be, with no hindrance, 86, 31 ; ever near, 556, 27 ; everywhere, 549, 29 ; extreme of, to be avoided, 305, 46 ; faith, importance of, 117, 36 ; for evil, 340, 8 ; for one, not for another, 31, 18 ; fortune and good sense, rare, 274, 20 ; fortune hard to bear, 179, 24 ; fountain of, within, 253, 11 ; from bad, discrimination of, rare, 328, 39 ; from freely opened hand, 338, 10 ; from God, 94, 33 ; from seeming evil, 116, 19 ; from within, 52, 20 ; greatest, by whom wrought, 285, 22 ; growth of, amidst evil, 161, 32 ; habitual enjoyment of, 31, 19 ; how to do most, 522, 35 ; humour, a happiness, 207, 43 ; impossible to wicked, 126, 22 ; in the thinking, 315, 2 ; in the vilest, 110, 27 ; knowing, and not doing, 493, 19 ; known or pursued, 253, 3 ; lament over lost, 508, 10 ; man, a, defined, 37, 50 ; 514, 37 ; man, a, of talent, character of his work, 541, 38 ; man always a tiro, 31, 62 ; man, needs room, 60, 9 ; man, rule of a, 1, 27 ; man, satisfied from himself, 6, 48 ; man, striving in the dark right, 6, 47 ; man, the death of, 55, 44 ; man, the loyal heart of, 66, 28 ; man, the mark of, 206, 35 ; man, unenvious, 151, 9 ; man, unknown, work of, 463, 48 ; men, all things becoming in, 328, 6 ; men, duty of, when bad combine, 543, 8 ; men, helplessness of, at present, 557, 38 ; men, need of, 64, 28 ; men, treatment of failings of, 426, 48 ; men, value of, 464, 46 ; misconstruing, a treble wrong, 494, 29 ; name, carelessness of, 152, 44 ; name, once tainted, 118, 50 ; native and foreign, how to treat, 217, 17 ; news, bringer of, 144, 10 ; no, from what is not natural, 298, 16 ; no pure, in man's offer, 302, 8 ; not to be mistaken or censured, 333, 17 ; nothing, by itself, 314, 45 ; 315, 1 ; nothing so, as not to suffer from abuse, 317, 1 ; of others, securing, 152, 47 ; of others to be sought, 385, 1 ; old rule, the, 430, 44 ; on the highway, 94, 20 ; only from self, 80, 10 ; or evil as we take it, 190, 40 ; our highest, 519, 37 ; out of season, evil, 510, 40 ; people, far apart, 149, 37 ; promised, gain in being bereft of, 399, 23 ; public and private, 359, 39 ; qualities, unserviceable to one's self, 166, 45 ; rarity of, 183, 12 ; report not so easily spread as ill, 177, 25 ; sense and expression, 87, 29 ; sense and good nature, 129, 56 ; sense, how we estimate, 317, 13 ; sense, indignant, 193, 19 ; sense, road to, 498, 29 ; slow in developing, 314, 25 ; source of, 126, 34 ; thing, a disappointment at first, 302, 4 ; that is done for us, 476, 39 ; that is possible, 340, 8 ; the, behaviour of, 184, 39 ; the, easy to rule, 98, 43 ; the end of all, 10, 54 ; the genuinely, hard to know, 343, 40 ; the goal of ill, 323, 3 ; the internal source of all, 402, 29 ; the, in man, 537, 22 ; the only, that profits, 335, 10 ; the public, to be sacrificed to, 124, 20 ; the really, for ever, 298, 22 ; the really, hard to attain, 67, 32 ; the, sayings about, 430, 35-37, 39, 42, 45-47 ; the sovereign, according to Bacon, 436, 41 ; the, those who forward, to be honoured, 325, 12 ; thing out of Nazareth, 35, 26 ; things illusory, 154, 31 ; things in threes, 9, 36 ; those who do most, 482, 40 ; though small, sufficient, 406, 14 ; to be defined and held fast, 158, 24 ; to be, and disagreeable, 490, 16 ; to be done unconsciously, 242, 24 ; to be left to heaven's disposal, 403, 2 ; to be sought for, 99, 37 ; to be willed, 519, 14; to circulate, 29, 71; to him who serves the state, 564, 25; to men, condition of doing, 176, 10; to whom good, 364, 52; turn, a, merit of, 1, 14; undying, 475, 25; when it thrives best, 94, 18; while asleep, 1, 3; who best knows, 144, 11

Good-breeding, how attained, 216, 19; never affectation, 489, 35; power of, 130, 7; want of, 452, 27

Good-fellowship, ground of, 73, 45

Good-for-nothing, a, 532, 21; the, Goethe on, 430, 38

Goodness, a benefit to all, 304, 32; a characteristic of, 515, 3; and beauty, 433, 7; an end, 135, 35; a test of, 304, 7; better than wealth, 31, 55; Burns' criterion of, 541, 11; departed, mourned over a possession, 539, 1; first and second condition of, 428, 10; God's, and His providence, 128, 6; in one's friend's esteem, 565, 14; in the eye of law, 97, 3; love of, 151, 39; not famous for, infamous, 175, 27; often mere harmlessness, 268, 28; pride of, 567, 21; real, rare, 376, 52; rewarded, 19, 64; self-evolved, 303, 6; tendency of, 514, 49; test of, 276, 13; the sin-bearing power of, 385, 24; thoughts of, 484, 34; timid shyness of, 105, 18; unconcentrated, 465, 32; united with greatness, 319, 36; why snarled at, 274, 49; without edge to it, 568, 20

Goods, common, none, 119, 36

Good-will, best gift, 279, 44; everything in morals, 60, 9

Goose, a, that lays golden eggs, 91, 54; that lays the golden egg, 430, 50

Gospel, contrasted with law, 438, 19; in nature, as in Bible, 128, 2; of Christ, all great and goodly things symbols of, 476, 2; the, value of, 430, 51

Gospels, only edifying use of, 489, 30; only two possible, 468, 34; the, contradictions in, 538, 3;

Gossip, a vice, 183, 39; effect of, if circulated, 172, 12; superseded by books, 139, 16; the town's, insignificance of, 564, 23

Gossips, quarrelling of, 377, 23

Gothic cathedral, Emerson on, 430, 52

Gotten easily, gone easily, 38, 15

Govern, men, how to, 492, 47; they that, the most, 479, 41

Governing, class, conduct at present of, 431, 1; fundamental art of, 494, 4; men, Danton on, 29, 11; powers, the only, 335, 16; man's prerogative, 373, 7

Government, a, how to judge of, 526, 38; a lazy, Butler on, 316, 48; a merely business and bread-protecting, 6, 60; as a science, Rousseau on, 227, 33; best, defined, 277, 11; by wisest our goal, 313, 22; contract of, dissolved by despotism, 233, 10; democratic, among whom possible and impossible, 378, 46; despotic, 361, 44; difficulty in, 550, 46; essence of, among good men, 425, 32; forms of, futility of, 277, 29; forms of, how determined, 429, 14; good, beginning of, 9, 33; good, condition of, 396, 34; in what it resides, 301, 35; never originative, 90, 10; no dissension to hinder, 317, 35; not to waver, 6, 61; of England, 431, 3; of men, only by serving them, 330, 14; of world, 464, 5, 35, 41; officers of, 131, 19; overthrowing and creating, two different things, 566, 37; parliamentary, defined, 341, 45; qualification for, 474, 8; real, our need, 312, 44; representative, defined, 233, 31; representative of order, 250, 48; republican, Tacitus on, 371, 22; the miracle in, 315, 24; the best, 65, 7; 109, 40; 417, 39; the burden of, Cromwell on, 169, 25; the first object of, 359, 34; the only safe, 302, 10; to be in advance, 431, 2; where men are selfish, 477, 42; wisdom that suffices for, 15 47; without self-government, 2, 24

Governments, a duty of all, 549, 16; all, a compact with devil, 9, 37; bureaucratic, the fatal disease of, 423, 43; cause of decay of, 224, 34; free, tyrannies of, 114, 28; how far good, 9, 31; monstrous absurdity in modern, 475, 45; secret of success in, 216, 14

Governors, our, 522, 7; the life of all, 72, 17

Grace, a day of, 4, 1; contrasted with nature, 290, 34; 291, 38; divine, power of, 145, 5; essential, 305, 34; fascination of, 63, 48; given, as needed, 60, 15; helpless by itself, 301, 11; in contrast with gifts, 122, 36; in movement, 182, 5; melancholy, 81, 4; power of, 66, 10; purpose of, 240, 54; source of, 319, 4; stronger than nature, 132, 17; the soul of complexion, 433, 7; to be seized at once, 60, 15; to whom given, 366, 19

Graceful, the, defined, 540, 43

Gracefulness, from one's self, 315, 3

Graces, effect of teaching of, 360, 22; the, and Venus, 512, 31

Grain, value of one, 332, 28

Grammar, above kings, 225, 33; lordship claimed over, 78, 12

Grammarians, and troubles of world, 227, 10; not subject to Cæsar, 34, 35

Grandeur, a mark of, 511, 41; and comfort, incompatible, 565, 27; to be kept ever before us, 529, 6; to be shunned, 117, 10

Granite, block of, as an obstacle and stepping-stone, 418, 39; from, to immortality of the soul, 198, 45

Grapes, where sweetest, 66, 22

Grasp, a hearty, good, 167, 41

Grasping, at too much, 42, 33; 364, 51

Grass, and flowers, 529, 26; ilka blade of, 181, 37

Gratification, unbridled, evil of, 245, 44

Gratitude, a burden, 227, 27; and love incompatible, 253, 43; commended, 122, 15; less potent than fear, 103, 36; of small commercial value, 440, 22; protestations of, 528, 8; the root of, 340, 15

Grave, an early, 346, 16; a lonely, sigh for, 312, 12; as bed of rest, Carlyle in view of the, 323, 2; from, to gay, 139, 35; the, honours at, 387, 9; the, our meeting-place of rest, 564, 33; voices from the, 274, 39; wicked and weary in, 477, 30

Graves of the hamlet, 27, 52

Gravity, from thought and from dulness, 469, 24; less wise than it looks, 244, 38; too much, shallowness of, 497, 37

Gray hairs, Jean Paul on, 133, 3

Great, and good, 94, 21; and little, on Fortune's wheel, 238, 24; becoming, and being born, 203, 29; deeds, by whom done, 199, 31; folk, secrets of, like wild beasts in cages, 453, 3; from smallest, 23, 39; master, how great, 7, 2; mind, character of labours of, 91, 17; name, hard to earn, 180, 24; no, or small, to the soul, 472, 49; sacrifices to make one, 538, 9; thing, always done easily, 171, 7; thing, how and by whom done, 7, 8; thing, no, without meaning, 535, 15; wax, by others waning, 168, 30; what is, effect of, on cultivation, 540, 45; why such, 238, 27

Great man, a, and his reputation, 567, 38; ability to perceive, 208, 3; a, in midst of the crowd, 201, 24; according to Emerson, 143, 126; and his age, 431, 23, 24; and his descent, 87, 42; and his talk, 7, 9; and human nature, 431, 25; a subject only for one as great, 325, 1; characteristic of, 302, 16; 307, 32; first test of, 428, 39; heavenward path of, 434, 19; his love of justice, 151, 3; house of, flagstone at, 394, 4; Landor's test of, 6, 60; living for high ends, 6, 70; mark of, 206, 26; no, dies a natural death, 217, 8; no, without inspiration, 295, 27; quotes bravely, 7, 1; secret of, anticipated, 292, 17; speaking always or rarely, 469, 20; the faults of, 427, 24; unique,

91, 16; vacancy he leaves behind, 544, 32; who entitled to praise, 333, 34

Great men, age of, gone, 415, 40; and little, difference between, 423, 34; and world, 464, 6; 465, 2, 5; characteristics of, 108, 2; 306, 50; 431, 26; devotion to, 387, 31; difficulty of believing in, 496, 16; effect of evil fortune on, 208, 1; errors of, 301, 39; fame of, to what due, 225, 15; great mountains, 285, 2; how linked to their age, 64, 31; how we estimate, 523, 41; importance of, 559, 36; late appreciation of, 206, 10; men of faith, 381, 44; mission of, 212, 1; mutual isolation of, 63, 14; necessary, 398, 28; never limit themselves, 238, 25; of different moulds, 290, 42; perverse worship of, 162, 21; popular, 238, 26; seldom scholars, 465, 24; tender-heartedness of, 15, 42; treatment of, and fate, 209, 49; unbelief in, as a sign, 307, 5; unconscious, 285, 22; when the lion roars, 394, 20

Great souls, effect of gold on, 128, 39; effect of tranquillity of, 316, 32; in collision, 73, 36; not common, 308, 12; sign of, 205, 49; still exist, 67, 20; talk of, 259, 40; the composure of, disconcerting, 376, 54; the fate of, 492, 3; virtue of, 460, 39

Great, the, an unhappiness of, 205, 5; connection between, and the little, 281, 4; dependence of, 431, 10; dependence on, 163, 4; favourites of, 166, 5; friendship with, 74, 1; hard to win, 314, 26; intimacy with, without servility, 149, 37; neighbourhood of, dangerous, 228, 13; only, 144, 51; 153, 27; on the wave of humanity, 534, 7; pride of, how to humble, 514, 13; ruled rather than ruling, 322, 28; truly, according to à Kempis, 143, 56

Great things, all from above, 306, 45; by whom alone producible, 303, 19; by whom done, 38, 38; how to achieve, 353, 43; made up of littles, 251, 13, 14; not to be sought, 385, 7; the element of all, 391, 39

Greatest, in these times, 463, 27; man, according to Ward Beecher, 143, 51; man, the, 144, 51; men, world's treatment of its, 314, 34; the, the briefest, 432, 12; unknown, 338, 7

Greatness, aggregate of minuteness, 135, 38; and prudence, contrary counsels of, 359, 18; an essential attribute of, 303, 42; Christian, condition of, 554, 41; condition of attaining, 467, 40; despised, mark of greatness, 259, 22; essence of, 425, 40; first step to, 428, 38; growth and decay of, 102, 19; how attained, 434, 25; 482, 39; in need of defence, 22, 27; in one's self commended, 28, 39; insecurity of, 23, 12; man's proof of, 9, 57; men capable of, 311, 22; no, without inspiration, 477, 20; not to be aimed at, 385, 3; of man, how to comprehend, 200, 21; cur relation to, 524, 39; penalty of, 490, 17; potentiality of, 167, 4; qualifications for, 490, 18; root of, 278, 21; self-evolved, 303, 6; solitary, 75, 29; tendency of, to calm, 14, 34; the condition of all, 152, 39; true, mark of, 207, 16; 500, 4; various ways to, 397, 42; whom to thank for, 175, 30

Greece, and the world, 556, 6; Byron of, 229, 25; but living Greece, no more, 405, 51; her conquest, 131, 47; nothing without freedom, 326, 25; seven wise men of, ground of their fame, 453, 16

Greed, craving of, 83, 12; how to overcome, 240, 16; insatiableness of, 122, 33

Greeks, and Romans, the only ancients that continue young, 63, 47; sayings about, 432, 44-46; their dream of life, 508, 32

Green spot, our final inheritance, 41, 53

Greeting, the stranger's, to be returned, 455, 22; to be with noble feeling, 221, 28

Gregory VII. on his death-bed, 68, 23

Grief, and excess of it, 398, 13; after gladness, 98, 1; and its shadows, 75, 24; a symbol of Christianity, 524, 42; bitter and calm, 524, 46; capable of counsel, 413, 14; effect of time on, 66, 7; effect of imparting, 473, 24; expression of, 97, 57; great, effect on mind of, 133, 32; how to conquer, 142, 17; hard to master a, 93, 9; limited, 70, 47; limit of, 540, 7; love *plus* grief, 109, 46; man's, 266, 33; moderate and immoderate, 281, 20; pleasure of, 379, 14; sayings about, 432, 48, 49; shallow, 446, 22; softened with time, 473, 6; tamed with time and thinking, 486, 27; that can be advised, 244, 35; to be private, 189, 19; unedifying, 166, 16; unseen, sincere, 181, 51; wail of, 461, 13

Griefs, ended with remedies, 545, 12; from evils that have not happened, 398, 31; great, dumb, 166, 15; great, effect of, on less, 133, 33; never stated too lightly, 303, 33; when fresh, not to be dispelled, 550, 15

Grievances, old, not to be repeated, 296, 57

Grin, power of a merry, 36, 14

Groove, moving in the same, 315, 50

Grose, Captain, Burns on, 174, 49

Grotesques, no, in nature, 467, 31

Grow, ceasing to, 149, 41

Growth, contrasted with decay, 48, 9; fast and slow, 334, 19

Growths, natural, pleasing, 191, 4

Grub and butterfly, 471, 22

Grumbler, wise, a benefactor, 462, 33

Grumblers, benefactors, 417, 29

Grumbling, elevating power of, 417, 29; essential to progress, 566, 42; evil effect of, 144, 41; philosophy of, 447, 36; room for, 205, 40; too much, 492, 5

Guard, who keeps no, on himself, 552, 3

Guesses, Goethe on, 171, 30

Guest, a, rank of, 549, 37; a welcome, 146, 54

Guests, how viewed, 428, 12; unbidden, 505, 46

Guide, a true, 145, 36

Guiding-star everywhere, 190, 43

Guilt, chief earthly ill, 247, 49; communion in, levelling, 99, 3; confession of, 103, 6; conviction of, better than severity of punishment, 406, 19; counsels of, infatuated, 320, 9; danger of first step in, 241, 49; dependent on station, 327, 43; diversely rewarded, 182, 6; greatest incitement to, 271, 18; hard not to betray, 155, 35; indelible, 10, 46; misery of, 321, 25; sure to be punished, 178, 48; yoked to misery, 126, 13

Guilty, evil of sparing, 279, 29; heart, greatest terror to, 475, 39; the, what is due to, 496, 8

Guinea, power of, 429, 13

Gullibility, and quackery, 361, 4; man's, not his worst blessing, 357, 34

Gunpowder, genuine use of, 430, 1

H

Habit, bad, when to overcome, 261, 35; effect of, 366, 44; force of, 46, 59, 60; importance of, in youth, 4, 10; only motive, 269, 14; power of, 111, 33; 259, 11; 475, 36; the chains of, 419, 36; use doth breed, 162, 42

Habits, bad, effect of, 292, 16; how formed, 1, 24; ill, grow apace, 181, 44; rule in formation of, 82, 18

Hades, the descent to, easy, 98, 48

Haggis, a, charging downhill, 89, 18; Burns to a, 99, 36

Hair, a, casts a shadow, 89, 19

Hair-splitting, 142, 18

Half and whole compared, 309, 22

Half-man, a, 145, 7
Hallow'd spot, a, why crave, 555, 24
Halves, all things, 75, 25
Hame, best, 76, 10
Hamlet, Shakespeare's, how composed, 388, 12
Hammer, better, than anvil, 181, 5
Hand, a cold, 216, 53; a hard, 472, 10; and its own work, 486, 3; disfigured by toil, 268, 23; from, to mouth, 116, 6; Napoleon's, connected with his head, 287, 48; shakes of, characteristic, 475, 32; the instrument of instruments, 264, 15; the, of toil, Carlyle on, 512, 10; the touch of a vanished, 33, 20; to be educated, 95, 20
Handicraft, good, foundation of, 128, 22
Hands, before knives, 106, 35; clean, with gloves on, 394, 33; folding and opening, 213, 11; power of, 535, 17; work of the, 519, 23
Handsome figure, effect of, 283, 50
Hanging, as a correction, 523, 29
Hannibal, Maherbal to, 514, 22
Happiest, man, the, 150, 42; 443, 47; 551, 41; man, according to Goethe, 143, 27; men, the, 448, 5; of men, George Sand on, 433, 8
Happiness, a, better than, 495, 38; a condition of, 12, 6; 61, 17; 488, 20; a rare, 368, 5; always exaggerated, 330, 5; and attainment of a wish, 332, 41; and misery, kinship of, at the root, 540, 23; and misery, contrasted, 353, 8; Aristotle on, 304, 34; as a proportionate quantity, 273, 43; a, that never leaves us, 171, 25; at present, or nowhere, 175, 39; Burns' ideal of, 271, 27; but one solid basis of, 471, 18; centered in heart, 172, 22; claim to, mischief of, 206, 44; condition of, 81, 44; confined to no spot, 107, 13; constancy in, 479, 18; contrasted with sorrow, 476, 38; determining element of, 313, 24; dependent on renouncing the world, 217, 6; dependent on restraint, 250, 13; destroyed by envious fortune, 22, 34; discovery of a new, 203, 7; domestic, 70, 54, 55; earthly, experience of, 170, 1; earthly, in dreams, 319, 26; essence of, 541, 18; ever near, 335, 3; from change, illusory, 268, 55; from moderation, 23, 48; greatest, in existence, 494, 13; health, 536, 17; how to obtain, 373, 47; how to weigh, 53, 41; how we lose, 527, 22; imaginary, 521, 43; in anticipation, 93, 46; independent of prosperity and adversity, 286, 21; independent of wealth and greatness, 297, 46; in feeling one with the whole, 173, 2; in sufficiency for self, 77, 34; in the heart, 185, 52; in what to be sought, 12, 25; love of, higher in man than, 471, 33; made dependent on chance, 200, 4; main thing for, 457, 22; matrimonial, condition of, 353, 46; matter of feeling, 180, 1; meaning of, 490, 21; negatively defined, 492, 28; never perfect, 86, 29; 210, 27; no, without a friend, 289, 5; no, without love, 364, 4; not dependent on congruity of opinion, 331, 42; not promoted by argument, 173, 38; not the purpose of life, 490, 20; not to be boasted of, 333, 11; of others, hard to taste, 381, 39; offered to all, 290, 4; one good way to, 332, 28; one's, not to be thought of, 329, 28; only personated, 521, 21; or unhappiness, what determines, 533, 34; our desire for, 530, 5; power of, to swell heart, 326, 8; purpose of nature, 516, 52; pursuit of, 524, 16; rather than full purse, 81, 15; real, cheap enough, 369, 13; real, defined, 459, 35; Ruskin's definition of true, 267, 2; sayings about, 232, 43–50; 433, 9–12; seat of, 154, 7; secret of, 452, 41; seekers for more than, 483, 18; seen through another's eyes, 160, 52; sinful and natural, 478, 38; solid, in the heart, 174, 3; source of, 202, 1; the basis of, 338, 12, 13; 249, 33; the highest, 434, 41; the one condition of, 87, 12; the only, worth while, 446, 7; the principle of, 366, 21; to be deserved, 175, 34; to be found at home, 567, 32; to fill the hour, 492, 26; to attain, 532, 19; true, 87, 2; two foes of, 459, 25; unexpected, 132, 18; untasted, 60, 13; utmost possible, 493, 12; what it consists in, 12, 62; what most contributes to, 533, 32; within narrow bounds, 541, 13; without self-control, 192, 24
Happy, apology for being, 487, 15; day, a, foretold, 433, 14; days, a succession of, hard to bear, 298, 18; days bygone, misery of recalling, 295, 44; man, insensible to lapse of time, 58, 17; man, the, 433, 14, 15; man, the only, 142, 3; presence of, to wretched, 449, 8
Hard times not rare, 35, 2
Hardened, the, with time, 124, 38
Hard-heartedness, who prone to, 238, 31
Hardships, our own and others', 433, 18; stimulating effect of, 563, 35
Harm, no, but from one's self, 295, 11; 314, 6
Harmony, as accepted by the crowd and the musician, 445, 7; hard to restore, 67, 35; in which things are reconciled, Gœthe on, 285, 26; inner, everything, 151, 16; the condition of, 511, 39
Harness, die with, on back, 31, 3; necessary for a man, 12, 44
Harper, a, on one string, 376, 37
Haste, and prudence incompatible, 313, 44; but not hurry, 484, 16; evil of, 133, 34; evil of an excess of, 481, 1; raw, 75, 37; unreasonable, evil of, 508, 21; vulgar, 315, 27
Hat, man in pursuit of his, 469, 5
Hate, a grief, 473, 5; deadliest, from deepest desire, 116, 24; drop of, in cup of joy, 79, 37; effect of one shriek of, 344, 4; that blossomed into charity, 491, 41
Hater, a good, 167, 37
Hatred, a form of love, 436, 29; alien to a true man, 22, 5; avowed, 196, 40; contrasted with pity, 348, 52; deprecated, 71, 44; effect of, 381, 31; effect of, on worth of a man, 141, 3; effect of one drop of, 332, 10; effect of time on, 487, 18; grafted on extinct friendship, 433, 21; greatest, characterised, 432, 15; how provoked, 105, 15; how to overcome, 117, 14; in life alone, 319, 6; our, reason and effect of, 524, 18; poisoning power of, 332, 10; the bitterest, 2, 53; too keen, effect of, 545, 2; unproductive of good, 30, 5
Haughtiness from birth, 398, 33; from work, 206, 40
Havelock's fidelity to principle, 167, 22
Having, dependent on using, 122, 9
Hazard, motive for, 276, 37; of the die, 167, 11
Head, a great, the function of, 184, 27; a witless, 25, 4; and heart, difficult to unite, 398, 35; big, witless, 1, 28; contrasted with heart, 433, 24; empty, conceited, 58, 39; figure, mere figure-head, 198, 37; hoary, to be honoured, 377, 30; inferior to heart, 433, 25, 30; one good, value of, 332, 24; stupid, with good heart, 87, 40; that wears a crown, 140, 22; the hoary, 435, 23; to be held up, 158, 25; without moral sentiments, 433, 23
Headache, effect of a, 390, 3
Heads, grey, 380, 29; in hearts, 398, 35; little and long, 467, 6; may differ when hearts don't, 153, 48
Healing, in health, 184, 14; by medicine, lance, or fire, 326, 41
Health, a recipe for, 217, 27; a sign of, 453, 32; and exercise of, 534, 12; and sickness, rules for, 187, 20; before holiness, 452, 9; better in Nature's hand than doctor's, 29, 50; chief condition of, 224, 30; compared with money, 282, 40; dependence of, on cheerfulness, 40, 48; from labour, 387, 13; from temperance, 260, 36; good, wealth, 41, 30; how to promote, 81, 42; importance of, 245, 32; life, 309, 38; necessary for holiness, 12, 22; of citizen, bodily and spiritual,

concern of all governments, 549, 16; sacrifice of, 432, 31; secret of, 2, 47; sign of, 433, 27; source of, 116, 12; text for a sermon on, 533, 10; the flower of, 40, 51; the best preservative of, 417, 55; the sphere melody, 435, 3; the use of, 537, 20; the value of, 123, 13; 428, 43; true wealth, 492, 35

Healthy, man, and the seasons, 433, 28; the, sweet-tempered, 9, 42

Hear, who will not, 532, 29

Hearing, and obeying God's word, merit of, 30, 46; and seeing, 521, 32; before speaking, 83, 42; man, compared with the speaking, 140, 19; mere, and learning, 525, 12; not always believing, 64, 1; no, without understanding, 85, 39; not followed by faith, 32, 15; rather than sacrifice, 217, 33; value of, 116, 7

Hearsay, as a basis of communion, 472, 16

Heart, a bleeding, only healer of, 125, 11; a child's, without sorrow, 165, 35; a great, qualities of, 477, 23; a heavy, effect of beauty or music on, 545, 36; a man's, his honour, 54, 4; a merry, 147, 15; a noble, an open hand, 167, 18; a noble, immovable, 48, 6; a poor, and a rich purse, 198, 39; a product of, test of, 565, 22; a pure, to be prayed for, 135, 18; a saddened, inconsolable by words, 54, 27; a, untainted, 538, 37; an empty, 435, 37; an oracle of fate, 62, 3; an ungrateful, no melting, 107, 46; and its divine motions, 527, 19; and mind, methods of, different, 22, 45; and the Muses and gods, 548, 33; as an oracle, 64, 29; as sound as a bell, 142, 50; carrying, on tongue, 149, 40; compared to ocean, 287, 51; contracting power of, 556, 12; contrasted with head, 433, 24; doors of, shut, 382, 9; effect of fire in, 106, 40; effect of purification of, 541, 15; endowments of, 392, 49; everything, 279, 34; female, like new indiarubber shoe, 427, 33; fountain of life, 217, 34; free and fetterless, 326, 13; germs of all things in, 430, 2; gifts of, 125, 39; glowing, power of, 297, 26; God's voice in, 458, 43; good, value of, 549, 39; great, the function of, 184, 27; hardening of, measure of, 190, 15; higher, the warmer, 250, 5; human, a tablet on which all things are writ, 292, 48; honest, free frae guile, 435, 26; human, sayings about, 435, 42–44; in prosperity and adversity, 401, 24; its history, 222, 13; its place of rest, 103, 62; its romance, 222, 13; its yearnings, 536, 46; known only to God, 154, 21; light, vitality of, 8, 31; less inflexible than head, 233, 4; life of, 75, 26; like a millstone, 54, 3; like the sea, 272, 24; literature of the, 262, 24; loving, willing, 103, 43; makes us right or wrong, 289, 12; man's, insatiable, 266, 35; meditative, 441, 43; must have an object to rest on, 123, 12; my, leaps up, 287, 49; native soil of thoughts, 54, 36; noble, noblest task of, 122, 32; no traitor, 80, 17; not to be controlled, 315, 8; not to be dictated to, 218, 9; not to be too much trusted, 528, 41; not to cling too much to things, 297, 52; open not, to every one, 232, 24; place of, 549, 4; product of, its quality, 540, 28; pure, strength of, 288, 24; reflective of world, 75, 8; sayings about the, 433, 30–46; 434, 1–13; secrets of, how revealed, 222, 7; sensitive, an unhappy possession, 385, 23; simplicity of, healing and cementing, 121, 44; stout in, never God-forsaken, 131, 5; sincere and tranquil, characteristic of, 545, 38; sovereign over head, 433, 25; standard of worth, 271, 42; sunny spots in, without light, 126, 6; teaching of, compared with reason, 370, 3; thankful, prayer for, 321, 17; the, allurements that draw, 68, 3; that has gone through no sorrow, 452, 1; the great in, 144, 51; the, has its own religion, 91, 3; the, impulse of, 267, 3; the,

that is most like God, 484, 8; the, speech of, 556, 1; the true sun-flower, 268, 59; true as steel, 566, 3; true greatness of, 500, 30; to keep up, difficult, 208, 14; uneasy, effect of, on our view of things, 320, 32; unpurified by woe, 59, 52; virtues of, underrated, 276, 21; wear my, upon my sleeve, 169, 17; what comes from the, test of, 323, 7; what goes to, 534, 36; when at peace, 53, 27; when it leads the way, 548, 32; who has most, 150, 37; who touches our, as with a live coal, 142, 48; with Divine love in it, 383, 45; without error rare, 106, 17; wrinkles of, 465, 41; wrong, effect of, on head, 176, 19

Hearth, a, of one's own, value of, 54, 31; 77, 45

Heart's bitterness, control, 30, 5

Hearts, bad, effect of gold on, 128, 39; everywhere the same, 274, 24; fellowship with, to be cultivated, 549, 12; few, rightly affected to heaven, 154, 4; full of grief, masked, 117, 24; great, like great mountains, 252, 29; hard, how to win, 396, 45; highest, temper of, 207, 1; how to win, 70, 25; in heads, 398, 35; kind, value of, 163, 5; kind, more than coronets, 218, 34; loving, parted, sorrows of, 546, 27; muffled drums, 18, 35; not to be alienated, but united, 277, 25; of different moulds, 92, 19; property of, inalienable, 538, 41; reasons of, 233, 3; toying with, 496, 29

Heaven, a plain road to, 35, 32; ascent to, 485, 36; at once far and near, 314, 46; blue of, and the cloud, 418, 44; communion with, condition of, 217, 31; compensation from, 60, 16; conversing with, as a task, 488, 3; demand of, 483, 24; door of, lowly, 154, 19, 23; everywhere overhead, 473, 43; face to face in, 203, 19; fire of, source of, 458, 41; gates of, battered by prayers, 25, 64; going to, alone, 207, 13; going to, by force of habit, 398, 37; help of, 176, 12; has its thorns, 298, 12; how to purchase, 360, 5; how to respond to, 123, 6; impenetrable to prayer, 118, 10; in a dewdrop, 225, 32; in earth, 76, 6; in proportion to earth, 371, 39; life of, from soil of earth, 109, 37; near us, 154, 40; nearness of, 116, 3; nothing true but, 482, 19; old and new road to, 479, 9; once in, better than often at the door, 28, 44; only in the eye, 27, 13; road to, 515, 22; still open, as of old, 403, 6; teachings of, 456, 43; the ladder of, 458, 48; the miles to, 99, 32; the, of the soul, 545, 47; the question as regards, 450, 29; the way to, 392, 32; treasures of, 458, 20; unthinkable, 33, 39; way to, 461, 29; when deaf, 103, 49; who excluded from, 304, 1; worth much, 184, 46

Heavenly, and earthly counterparts, 475, 43; powers, sovereign ways of, 434, 15; powers, who knows not, 532, 33; things, love of, 198, 7

Heaven's, appointments to be accepted, 526, 24; judgment, just, 488, 29

Heavens, a way through, remains, 375, 4; not to be scaled, 127, 28; sayings about the, 434, 16–18; the silent, 453, 38

Heavenward progress, our, 338, 15

Heaviness that's gone to be forgotten, 243, 40

Hector, fame of, and the fall of Troy, 154, 27; love of, 154, 28; sad look of, 154, 38

Hegel on Christianity, 42, 54

Height, and depth, correlative, 560, 10; how to attain a, 526, 33; the, and the steps to it, 434, 23

Heights, other, ahead, 336, 40

Heir, an, weeping of, 139, 5

Helicon, rills from, 116, 8; the fountain of, 429, 20

Hell, a fierce, 472, 38; better to reign in, 29, 51; feeling, 27, 13; for the inquisitive, 51, 41; getting to, hard work, 186, 5; proof of existence of, 191, 24; scroll over gate of, 230, 20; the fear o', 427, 25; the, of these days, 434, 26; which way I fly, 550, 9

Hellas made strange by time, 316, 53
Help, before preaching, 144, 31; man's, to man, 494, 28; mutual, importance of, 450, 32; no effectual, from another, 306, 21; no help, 150, 7; not at needful moment, 551, 11; only in union, 15, 39; only source of, 304, 36; our power of, small, 488, 17; slow, 394, 14; spontaneous, in need, 30, 27; the rule of, 158, 8; the, to be given, 368, 44; who alone gives, 334, 53; worthlessness of. Goethe on, 169, 23
Helper, a willing, does not wait, 83, 59
Helpers in distress, 514, 15
Helpful, the only permanently, 315, 33
Helpfulness, man's, 193, 50
Helps, as a thinker, 453, 7
Henry IV. of France, wish of, 211, 23; to his soldiers at Ivry, 397, 8
Heraldic arms, the noblest, 172, 23
Heraldry, in what contained, 461, 12
Hercules and his work, 555, 8
Here, and now, as interests, 524, 41; or nowhere, our aim, 155, 48
Hereafter, witness to a, 488, 49
Heredity, in families, 419, 33; no escape from law of, 162, 25
Heresies, in Church, root of, 452, 8
Hermits, a virtue in, 199, 24
Hero, a bore at last, 91, 23; all that is necessary to make, 477, 17; and his valet, 205, 44; death of, 395, 25; desire of, to meet hero, 86, 11; dust in the balance, 190, 13; every, property of, 206, 42; faith essential to, 202, 35; glory of, 205, 35; merit of biographer of a, 142, 48; mock, under misfortune, 260, 1; no, without enemies, 520, 32; no, without humanity, 519, 35; none a, to his valet, 303, 49; proof of a, 538, 21; source of his inspiration, 569, 39; such only in heroic world, 134, 22; the first characteristic of, 392, 27
Hero-arm without hero-eye, 534, 19
Heroes, and poets, akin, 351, 35; as dead and as alive, 488, 47; effect of history on, 228, 15; legacy of, 438, 34; literary, Johnson on, 434, 29; many, too long lived, 44, 36; moral, in the field, and heroines, 349, 9; without poet, 517, 7
Heroic, act, a triumph at last, 91, 24; deeds, the greatest, 432, 32; heart, of the first times, 434, 30; when mask drops, 234, 1
Heroine, and hero, 302, 28
Heroism, in domestic life, 465, 23; the essence of, 386, 14; true, 500, 5
Hero-worship, defect in our, accounted for, 175, 40; our, effect on us of, 338, 14; the corner-stone of society, 190, 34
Hid, what cannot be, disclosing, 325, 32
Hierograms, sacred, 99, 17
High, and low, independent of place, 315, 4; and low, pleasures of, contrasted, 238, 29; apprehension of the, rare, 419, 26; looks and mean thoughts, 274, 42; man, the, a failure, 482, 4; place, men in, thrice servants, 275, 18; rank not same as discernment, 233, 34; station, effect of, 238, 22; the, low origin of, 23, 46; things, effect of converse with, 328, 26; things, exposure of, to danger, 379, 31; things, mind not, 279, 35
Higher, an acknowledgment of, necessary to man, 61, 10; reverence for a, 340, 45
Highest, attainable by the lowest, 116, 27; not to be spoken of in words, 188, 27; the, exemplar of each, 28, 12; the, in God's esteem, 434, 43; the, to be loved, 527, 17; the, to be reverenced, 375, 29; things, above control, 189, 26
Highway, not to be deserted, 71, 46; sowing in, 148, 21
Highways, public, to be kept clear, 450, 8
Hill, going down, 171, 31
Hills, seen far off .. ; steep, climbing, 244, 12

Hindus, the, vow of, 64, 34
Hint, enough for the wise, 235, 3
Hip, catch one upon, 172, 33
Historian, a, a species of prophet, 435, 15
Historical genius, the true, 458, 46
History, a great, an epical, 287, 32; a satire on humanity, 121, 54; all, a Bible, 9, 44; always a pleasure, 157, 20; and biography, identical, 476, 24; and conscience, 204, 5; effect on, of heroes, 228, 15; God in, 150, 23; how to read, 455, 40; interest of, 462, 9; laws of, Cicero's, 366, 29; man's, summarised, 266, 37; of every man, 435, 18; our best, 337, 14; our, Cromwell on, 534, 3; problems of, confronted, 207, 33; study of, profitlessness of, for self-culture, 304, 31; temporal, meaning of, 455, 1; the best benefit from, 53, 30; the facts of, 457, 33; the only poetry, 446, 12; the only true, 30, 22; the two pinions of, 402, 37; the verdict of, when possible, 207, 27; Voltaire's view of, 223, 19; what constitutes, 335, 42
Hoard, and heart, 338, 17; to be moderate, 340, 10
Hoarding, and enjoying, 539, 45; forfeiting life, 144, 53
Hobbes' thesis, 157, 47
Hobby-horses, expensiveness of, 402, 31
Holdfast, the only dog, 110, 29
Hole, a, in a' your coats, 174, 49
Holiness, different effects of, and liberty, 245, 38; no, without health, 12, 22
Holy, give not, to dogs, 123, 21; prior to unholy, 94, 22
Holy Land, the, 482, 32
Home, a golden milestone, 75, 16; a good, man unworthy of, 304, 1; a man's starting-point, 163, 8; a necessity, 105, 5; a palace, 36, 32; a source of joy, 174, 3; being far from, 102, 9; good of, 12, 4; happy at, advice to, 71, 1; how made attractive, 165, 30; how regarded in England, 82, 44; no longer cared for, a bad sign, 543, 5; no place like, 279, 2; not here, 414, 16; of one's own, and a good wife, value of, 78, 48; place of peace, 325, 48; returning under good omens, 300, 13; sacredness of, 474, 18; safest refuge, 71, 11; staying at, commended, 533, 1; the dream of, 551, 30; value of, enhanced by travel, 95, 1; where a true woman is, 549, 11
Home-life, backbone of a nation, 305, 26
Homer, art of, 534, 10; Carlyle on Iliad of, 158, 37; 436, 17; dead, rivalry for, 387, 49, 50; ground of our interest in, 70, 32; nods, 8, 38; rank as poet, 503, 48; the praise of, 368, 46
Homers, how made great, 489, 1
Homes, how, thrive, 45, 29; why unhappy, 275, 2
Honest, heart, disadvantage of, 445, 43; I dare to be, 165, 38; man, an, 15, 17; man, Burns on, 16, 65; man, the, 435, 29; man, unaffected, 443, 16; people, chief misfortune of, 333, 25; to be as this world goes, 490, 22
Honesty, a powerful fetter, 21, 44; a true, singlehearted, 536, 32; as a legacy, 302, 44; as policy, 35, 9; before riches, 521, 17; cheaper than hypocrisy, 533, 15; contrasted with knavery, 219, 42, 43, 47; if pawned, never redeemed, 229, 29; indispensableness of, 304, 24; lasts longest, 78, 25; not safe, 409, 27; often goaded to ruin, 4, 47; out of world of knaves, how, 123, 41; rare, 25, 38; recommends itself, 106, 31; strong in, 474, 33; the importance of, 428, 38; the value of, 370, 48; to be practised, 504, 15; who pauses in, 441, 19
Honey, a waste of, 200, 41; who would gather, 152, 52
Honey-bees, so work the, 395, 36
Honour, acme of, 460, 18; and duty, the post of, 541, 19; and glory, 463, 11; an earnest of more, 223, 31; an upholding power, 415, 12; as reward, 159, 46, 47; before fear of death, 173, 7; before

life, 406, 38 ; bound by, 170, 13 ; call of, to be followed, 172, 25 ; effect of, on arts, 159, 49 ; I love the name of, 167, 47 ; in the meanest habit, 20, 53 ; in what it. lies, 3, 59 ; incompatible with ease, 76, 8 ; loss of, 78, 22 ; 172, 40 ; lost, all lost, 105, 55 ; 106, 1 ; man worthy of, sure destiny of, 68, 10 ; mine, my life, 279, 43 ; more precious than life, 246, 30 ; new-made, doth forget men's names, 297, 29 ; not merely to be wooed, 384, 34 ; once lost, 7, 29 ; our true, the seat of, 338, 42 ; post of, Carlyle on, 448, 35 ; public, effect of, 357, 8 ; reward of action, 272, 8 ; stintedness in, 532, 3 ; the place of virtue, 199, 38 ; the post of, 47, 25 ; titles of, 489, 16, 17 ; to only two sets of men, 503, 45 ; to whom due, effect of, 322, 11 ; true and false, 199, 15 ; undeserved, delight in, 101, 3

Honourable, nothing, without justice, 299, 11 ; praiseworthy, 159, 36 ; the, defined, 535, 45

Honours, and manners, 238, 37 ; dearly bought, 238, 38 ; effect of, on manners, 159, 48 ; great, great burdens, 133, 35 ; hereditary, value of, 155, 22 ; how to render remote, near, 474, 16 ; men's, 312, 13

Hood, a page of, Lowell on, 130, 23

Hoof, a clattering, 155, 29

Hook, to be always baited, 386, 37

Hope, a helmet, 118, 22 ; a long, 79, 22 ; a too dear, 476, 42 ; a waking dream, 110, 4 ; 222, 44 ; against fortune, 552, 29 ; air-castles of, still in the air, 140, 24 ; all men's, 223, 18 ; all-pervasive, 405, 50 ; cherisher of life, 49, 52 ; deceitful, 320, 23 ; enjoyment, 495, 7 ; evil of want of, 548, 42 ; fed by fancy, 119, 9 ; good, the effect of, 401, 29 ; he who lives by, 441, 18 ; indulgence in, 509, 41 ; last stay to give way, 227, 36 ; living in, 147, 43 ; man's great, 265, 21 ; man's greatest happiness, 110, 41 ; man's only possession, 263, 48 ; never comes, 548, 23 ; never lose, 382, 6 ; no extinguishing of, 311, 45 ; no, no fear, 548, 15 ; often illusory, 3, 9 ; persistency of, 224, 15 ; persuasive power of, 180, 33 ; power of, 173, 13 ; 525, 20 ; prayed for, as a blessing, 37, 27 ; sayings about, 400, 31–33 ; our inclination to, 521, 31 ; term of, 5, 4 ; the phœnix, 447, 39 ; the power of, 319, 16 ; to be cherished, 112, 42 ; true, 500, 6 ; vain, gain in loss of, 20, 25 ; worse than despair, 563, 13

Hopes, a bad investment, 401, 22, 23 ; as causes of ruin, 102, 11 ; high, 82, 41 ; our, defined, 338, 18 ; vain spending on, 78, 10

Horace, his aim in life, 279, 20 ; on his muse, 63, 31

Horace's, prayer, 158, 1 ; thanksgiving to the gods, 63, 30

Horizon, a property in the, 470, 21

Horse, a willing, 32, 58 ; and his rider, 117, 7 ; bridled, ear of, 84, 20 ; even a, will stumble, 89, 20 ; grown fat, 37, 19 ; sayings about the, 435, 30, 31 ; what makes a good, 36, 1

Horses, buying, 185, 18 ; in England and Italy, 82, 45 ; to be fed, not pampered, 84, 16

Hospitable heart, who owns, 403, 27

Hospitality, a, not to be refused, 399, 2 ; genuine, effect of, 471, 8 ; not impoverishing, 168, 9 ; what it consists of, 242, 19

Host, the, characterised, 435, 32

Houndsditch, the exodus from, when possible, 523, 11

Hour, darkest, 422, 38 ; past, never returns, 292, 48 ; that brings pleasant weather, 484, 27 ; the call of, 71, 31 ; the, God's, 223, 18 ; the morning, 283, 47 ; the transient, to be seized, 36, 53

Hours, all, to be improved, 406, 7 ; happy, 435, 36

House, an empty, 435, 37 ; divided against itself, 171, 8 ; full of guests, 36, 31 ; one's own, one's real root-room, 317, 44 ; ornament of a, 446, 31 ; the, what it may be made, 333, 2

606

Household as home, 435, 39

Households, kingdoms, 251, 22

House-keeping, hard, 270, 45 ; vice of our, 460, 34

House-mother, a good, 389, 7

Houses, high, sunt storey of, 156, 31 ; repairing old, cost of, 327, 19

How, question of, 518, 25

Human, affairs, their risings and sinkings, 451, 46 ; countenances, sympathetic, 510, 26 ; element in man, 533, 45 ; face, Sir J. Reynolds on, 435, 41 ; kindness, full o' the milk o', 564, 36 ; mind, the disease of, at present, 423, 44 ; mind, saying of, 498, 5 ; nature, everywhere the same, 332, 17 ; nature, how to distort, 152, 40 ; nature, its derivation, 65, 34 ; nature, rules applicable to, 189, 52 ; nature, strength of, under wrong, 468, 12 ; nature, the peculiarity of, 3, 65 ; nature, two ruling principles in, 504, 2 ; race, character of, 100, 36 ; race, daring of, 22, 45 ; race, the, its best condition, 436, 3 ; race, the, task of, 421, 17 ; strength, to be exerted against fate, 404, 17 ; things, frail support of, 328, 32 ; worth, reverence for, the essence of all religions, 375, 28

Humanism contrasted with Christianity, 42, 56

Humanity, a common property, 524, 22 ; and education, 65, 34 ; as an invention, 261, 53 ; as a whole, the only true man, 173, 2 ; divinity of, 475, 42 ; due to education, 163, 28 ; grandmother and daughters of, 396, 32 ; grows dearer, 402, 48 ; how to elevate, 490, 41 ; imitated, so abominably, 167, 14 ; in deeds, 517, 28 ; its designs and hopes, 206, 5 ; joy of, 431, 30 ; mistrust of, evil of, 151, 46 ; only true principle of, 446, 23 ; our goal, 163, 32 ; our limit, 253, 8 ; the battle of, 215, 46 ; the essence of, 198, 43 ; the sacred law of, 84, 14 ; to be esteemed, 517, 28 ; true, in the fields, 567, 33 ; what to seek for, 527, 10 ; who lives for, 554, 19 ; without God, 338, 20

Humble, only, to rule, 169, 10 ; sanctuary of, 422, 17

Hume and Johnson, if combined, 554, 24

Humility, a noble, how possible, 334, 42 ; and knowledge, 356, 29 ; as an ornament, 432, 33 ; before God, effect of, 319, 35 ; idea of, 428, 39 ; modest, beauty's crown, 281, 37 ; the Christian doctrine of, 420, 16 ; too much, 569, 32 ; want of, 518, 32

Humour, and pathos conjoined, 547, 33 ; contrasted with wit, 558, 3 ; essence of, 425, 41 ; enough of a kind, 262, 26 ; good, effect of, on weak spirits, 118, 18 ; men of, men of genius, 276, 6 ; true, 231, 16 ; true, defined, 500, 8–10

Hunger, a teacher, 259, 2 ; 285, 39 ; best sauce, 180, 6 ; effect of, on temper, 101, 30

Hurry, effect of, 104, 48, 50 ; evil of, 536, 6 ; man in a, Whately's advice to, 441, 16 ; sign of incompetency, 553, 22

Hurting and healing, 513, 8

Husband, and wife, qualities of, 190, 45 ; and wife, as economists, 492, 19 ; the hen-pecked, and the tyrant wife, Burns' anathema on, 52, 1

Husbandman, and his labours, 436, 6 ; happiness of, 320, 27 ; unselfish labour of, 17, 29 ; Virgil of, 371, 19

Husbandry, good, good divinity, 129, 34

Huss, John, at the stake, 322, 3

Hymen contrasted with war, 518, 38

Hymn-book not a panacea, 467, 14

Hypocrisy, homage to virtue, 223, 32 ; intolerable, 468, 29 ; in managing another, 93, 47 ; where it begins, 91, 44

Hypocrite, Bishop Hall on, 436, 7 ; Burns' aversion to, 127, 10 ; worse than open sinner, 29, 47

Hypocrites, Satan's dupes, 174, 1

Hypotheses, lullabies, 164, 27 ; repudiated by Newton, 164, 25

Hypothesis, power of a good stout, 122, 5

Hyssop in chink of wall, *raison d'être* of, 555, 4

I

Icicle, image of chastity, 40, 37, 39

Idea, a single, devotion to, 168, 37 ; a single, possession by, deprecated, 169, 18 ; an idle or distracting, evil of, 110, 18 ; an infinite religious, power of, 421, 38 ; and fact compared, 464, 28 ; devotion to an, 379, 7 ; fixed, danger of, 5, 47 ; manifestation of, as beautiful, fleeting, 65, 28 ; men possessed with an, 276, 18 ; new, hard to instil, 491, 11 ; power of an, 186, 34 ; risk of sacrificing all to, 289, 37 ; superior worth of, 538, 33 ; the, and its manifestations, 65, 5 ; the, that is once spoken no longer ours, 436, 8 ; to be acted on, if it cannot be uttered, 217, 47

Ideal, accompaniments of, 559, 6 ; better than actual, 91, 55 ; 92, 9 ; attained, a low one, 149, 45; describable only when conceived as real, 448, 40 ; every one has his, 26, 58 ; from duty, 116, 31 ; in actual, 415, 33 ; now insisted on, not natural, 112, 32 ; ousted by the real, 415, 28 ; pursuing one's own, 173, 29 ; the, an illusory vision, 72, 40 ; the, for every one, and how to realise it, 124, 7 ; to grow in the real, 436, 9

Idealist, the, and his body, 315, 23

Ideals, extinct, 65, 4 ; our, defined, 338, 21

Ideas, ancient, entertainment by moderns of, 174, 9 ; change of, pleasure in, 315, 43 ; confining, controlling power of, 524, 31 ; delusive, prevalence of, 58, 10 ; hard to discern, 391, 26 ; having, and thinking, compared, 493, 9 ; how realisable, 302, 34 ; like pieces of money, 207, 34 ; made flesh, 399, 21 ; mistaken, the stupefying and pauperising effect of, 201, 35 ; new, daring and inspiring, genesis of, 297, 26 ; not measure of a man, 312, 32 ; our, like pictures, 338, 22 ; our want, not facts, 524, 45 ; power of, 546, 30 ; the shells of, 89, 38 ; those who build on, 479, 23 ; to assume a visible form, 91, 30 ; world of, of a refuge, 492, 14

Idioms, in language, 91, 11

Idiots, only, twice cozened, 116, 22 ; the greatest, 478, 13

Idle, always busiest, 180, 20 ; always dodge work, 108, 7 ; chagrins of, 467, 28 ; man, character of, 333, 8 ; man, according to Socrates, 143, 41 ; people, and their ennui, 345, 8 ; the, and the devil, 423, 28 ; the, characteristic of, 238, 20 ; their intentions, 436, 13

Idleness, a reproach, 490, 23 ; a tempting of the devil, 178, 52 ; better than a bad trade, 29, 13 ; busy, 268, 40 ; evil of, 15, 19 ; 34, 3 ; 287, 29 ; 306, 42 ; evil of encouraging, 175, 11 ; fly, 108, 1 ; harder work than industry, 97, 20 ; in youth, penalty of, 25, 37 ; its hopelessness, 187, 32 ; mischief of, 224, 14 ; strenuous, the toil of, 403, 35 ; the blight of genius, 5, 20 ; the evil of, 12, 48 ; the toil of, 153, 17 ; too much, effect of, 497, 38

Idler, a young, 214, 42 ; like a handless watch, 15, 20

Idlers, great talkers, 345, 16

Idolater, the true, 363, 32

Idolatry, a mad, 488, 19 ; the, that is condemnable, 46, 9

"If," comprehensiveness of, 24, 37 ; the inventor of, 60, 30 ; virtue in, 568, 22

Igdrasil, the tree, 399, 46

Ignorance, a modest confession of, 13, 51 ; and unconsciousness of it, 147, 36 ; as support of priestcraft, 277, 26 ; audacious, *versus* timorous knowledge, 546, 22 ; comfort of, 116, 10 ; contrasted with error, 84, 50 ; 85, 4 ; 85, 10 ; evil of, 306, 42 ; 436, 14 ; happiness, 83, 45 ; honest, 471, 1 ; human, Goethe on, 320, 29 ; in action, 315, 25 ; life-long, a tragedy, 414, 3 ; man's, 483, 25 ; of

good from bad, effect of, 178, 21 ; of self, 175, 5 ; our, fatal, 539, 26 ; rather than falsehood, 28, 56 ; sense of, from greater knowledge, 443, 28 ; sense of, mark of wisdom, 175, 5 ; that marks a superior nature, 469, 32 ; the only darkness, 472, 20 ; true, 146, 2 ; unconsciousness of, 147, 37 ; voluntary, blameworthiness of, 148, 41

Ignorant, man, an, according to the Hitopadesa, 151, 14 ; the, most violent, 477, 24

Iliad, and wayside incidents, 436, 16 ; Homer's, Carlyle on, 158, 37 ; 436, 17

Iliads, no formulæ for making, 467, 32

Ilium, sacred, fate of, 86, 33

Ill, a solace under, 184, 35 ; patiently borne, 442, 41 ; reports, credit given to, 274, 7 ; saying and thinking no, 208, 41 ; to do, who fears, 551, 18

Ill-bred man, mark of, 447, 30

Ill-done, the, no concern of ours, 554, 29

Ill-fortune, the, inexperienced in, 551, 32 ; without power on him whom good fortune deceives not, 181, 41

Ill-humour, protection from, 517, 31

Illiterate man, mark of, 447, 30

Ill-luck, fascination of, 398, 34 ; how to avert, 31, 27

Ill-mannered, manners of, to whom odious, 441, 26

Ill-manners, three sources of, 356, 32

Ill-natured man, and public spirit, 202, 33

Ills, imaginary, Burns on, 33, 11 ; in relation to blessings, 31, 17 ; the, we have to be borne, 424, 19 ; why ills, 139, 17

Ill-thought of, to be, sometimes a good, 490, 24

Ill-tidings, let, tell themselves, 123, 31

Ill-usage, effect of, 292, 16

Illusion, and after remorse, 61, 32 ; its extent, 482, 19 ; men's fondness for, 275, 9 ; no end to, 72, 50 ; power of, 349, 33 ; that gladdens contrasted with truth that saddens, 80, 2 ; the attractive power of, 320, 20 ; the danger of, 422, 34 ; which pervades life, 533, 23

Illusions, unmasking of, disliked, 502, 16

Illustrious, men, the sepulchre and the memorial of, 325, 5 ; the most, 197, 15

Ill-will, the force of, 426, 48

Images, things expressed through, 480, 44

Imagination, a need of, 397, 22 ; and reality, the worlds of, 465, 7 ; appeals to, 263, 43 ; as wings of ostrich, 157, 32 ; contrasted with judgment, 223, 34 ; death of, in love, 472, 27 ; free, as nothing else, 315, 19 ; in the poet, 448, 18 ; madcap of the brain, 223, 33 ; man's ruling and divine power, 403, 38 ; more sensitive than heart, 200, 54 ; Napoleon on the power of, 39, 8 ; necessary to recognition of truth, 105, 12 ; no imagination, 150, 8; power of, 525, 21 ; sayings about, 436, 20–23 ; science indebted to, 382, 27 ; strong, tricks of, 405, 53 ; subject only to art, 78, 37 ; surpassed by reality, 369, 21 ; the element of, 397, 22 ; to be kept sane, 217, 32 ; under the affections, 545, 22 ; want of, a grave defect, 16, 14 ; without learning, 150, 32 ; without taste, 78, 37 ; without truth, 105, 33

Imbecility, man's, effect of, 436, 24

Imitation, a source of all apprenticeship, 138, 9 ; easy, 34, 19 ; long step to, 470, 5 ; more potent than precept, 200, 46 ; not discipleship, 490, 8 ; of another's style, 493, 23 ; of evil contrasted with that of good, 223, 15 ; of good and of bad, 223, 15 ; power of, 475, 36 ; rule in, 362, 8 ; 529, 29

Immaterial things essential to life, 468, 26

Immortality, balked of, 144, 42 ; effect of disbelief in, 544, 38 ; essence of, 425, 33 ; faith in, to be enjoyed in silence, 243, 12 ; Horace's assurance of his, 310, 21 ; how we forfeit, 529, 39 ; our faith in, 523, 27 ; the blazing evidence of, 337, 38 ; the interest in, 66, 46

Impatience, Burns on, 340, 17 ; difficult to con-

quer, 167, 1 ; the evil of, 343, 11 ; to right one's self to be curbed, 402, 10
Imperial spirits, rare prerogative of, 492, 43
Imperfections, our, the secret of, 306, 22
Impious to be feared, 166, 6
Importance, airs of, deceptive, 7, 38 ; effect of imagination on, 565, 15 ; in matters of, trust unsafe, 184, 19
Impossibilities, created by idleness, 202, 28 ; faith laughs at, 100, 21
Impossible, everything at first, 92, 11 ; no binding to the, 8, 34 ; possible only to man, 261, 47 ; proof of certainty, 38, 32 ; the, 540, 10
Imposture, evils of, 9, 46 ; probably for good, 357, 34
Impression, moral, when strongest, 338, 36
Impromptu test of wit, 223, 16
Improvement, means of, 531, 14 ; not every, virtue, 298, 70 ; secondary to invention, 98, 44
Improvements, resistance to, as innovations, 480, 16
Improvidence of life, 550, 42
Impudence, a god, 466, 24 ; how to avoid imputation of, 461, 26 ; mistaken for confidence, 289, 30 ; the acme of, 440, 41
Impulse, the inner, power of, 475, 44
Impunity, evil effect of, 184, 6
In and out, in spiritual world, 191, 19
Inability, moral, and guilt, 283, 13 ; suspends law, 183, 48
Inaction, accursed, 292, .
Inanimate, the, to speak and reason, 265, 9
Inanity, alone endless, 314, 44
Incapable aping capable, 194, 39
Incapacity, the first proof of, 428, 33
Incense, a little, effect of, 505, 32 ; ashes, and burning of, 301, 2 ; on altar, obscuring effect, 421, 1
Incivility, from a superior, 506, 38
Inclination, and will, in the matter of virtue, 6, 42 ; conquering, benefit of, 503, 8 ; determining power of, 480, 39 ; natural, to be controlled, 212, 7 ; undue regard for one's own, 467, 16 ; with habit, impossible to conquer, 491, 22
Incomprehensible, comprehensible, 61, 9
Incongruous, the displeasing, 314, 31
Inconstancy man's one fault, 320, 35
Increase, the end of, 94, 40
Incredible, how to treat, 538, 43
Incredulity, a religion like the others, 223, 36
Independence, apostrophe to, 486, 10 ; commended, 11, 28 ; evil of loss of, 277, 4 ; fruit of injustice, 224, 2 ; rebellious, painful, 340, 45 ; the best, 417, 40 ; the glorious privilege of, 491, 17 ; the secret of, 204, 24
Independent mind, Burns to, 483, 43
Index, an, a saving, 487, 1
Indian, the poor, faith of, 252, 12
Indies, wealth of the, 461, 41, 42
Indifference, prevalence of, now, 317, 42 ; two kinds of, 131, 10
Indigence, man in, 542, 10
Indigestion, cause of dreams, 41, 52
Indignation, source of inspiration, 390, 24 ; that makes verses, Carlyle on, 436, 27 ; weaker than love, 255, 9
Individual, always moving, 436, 28 ; as a private door to the divine, 125, 35 ; first period of, 428, 28 ; most important period in life of, 444, 1 ; no, for his own sake, 91, 45 ; no bridge between one and another, 472, 12 ; the measure of an, 210, 28 ; the, in society, 396, 17
Individualism, absolute, 2, 20 ; adverse to welfare of the whole, 95, 14 ; preservative of power, 75, 18
Individuality, at a discount, 526, 22 ; one's, his limit, 303, 26 ; one's, sacred, 304, 43 ; planted in instinct, power of, 174, 32

Individuals, easily dispensed with, 522, 42 ; singly and corporately, 212, 11
Indolence, a perpetual holiday, 177, 48 ; an end of, 334, 37 ; king for life, 325, 9 ; mistaken for patience, 330, 44 ; our mental, 524, 33 ; that voluntary debility, evil of, 414, 23
Indolent man, in love, 202, 55
Indulgence, how we learn, 205, 20 ; rarer than pity, 187, 11
Industrious, first need of, 494, 1
Industry, as a defence, 99, 5 ; building upon Nature, 544, 8 ; condition of God's gifts, 125, 38 ; dependence on one's own, 200, 36 ; gifts that crown, 194, 4 ; its support, 186, 41 ; mistress of, 549, 27 ; mother of, 518, 26 ; the power of, 394, 7 ; unfortunate condition of, 396, 21
Inevitable, arguing with, 472, 47 ; folly of fearing or lamenting, 534, 28 ; the, folly of distress about, 404, 33 ; the, hard to bear, 54, 35 ; to be yielded to, 551, 44
Infant, crying in the night, 15, 41 ; those who have lost an, 480, 8
Infant's faith, sacredness of, 151, 47
Inference compared with observation, 323, 36
Inferior, finding one's, a first duty, 428, 15 ; the, of nothing, worthlessness of, 147, 23
Infidelity, associated with bigotry, 407, 9 ; general, as soil for religious ideas, 119, 39
Infinite, an epitome of, in every man, 266, 47 ; how to attain to, 556, 28 ; how to express, in art, 185, 10 ; in finite, 495, 28 ; nearness of, 116, 3 ; seen in finite, 261, 45 ; surest of facts, 436, 32 ; the, how to read, 384, 37
Infinity, the chosen for, 507, 7
Infirmity, the badge of, 287, 33 ; that last, of noble minds, 101, 23
Influence, defined, 9, 50 ; over men, how to attain, 560, 27 ; secret of, 436, 34 ; true, 500, 11
Influences, man needs, 264, 1
Infortune, worst kind of, 110, 31
Ingratitude, a curse on, 403, 40 ; evil of, 491, 14 ; hatefulness of, 166, 31 ; man's, 31, 2 ; our suffering from, 524, 3 ; the worst of vices, 132, 35
Ingle-nook, men must leave, 275, 39
Inheritance, as citizens, value of, 260, 8 ; anticipated, 176, 23 ; from our sires, 525, 3 ; man's, 288, 6
Inherited, the, how to profit by, 519, 15
Inhumanity, man's, 266, 38
Iniquity, Burns' measure of, 541, 11 ; sowing, penalty of, 148, 22
Injuries, benefit of, 436, 35 ; best remedy for, 194, 31 ; disregard of, mark of a great mind, 259, 21 ; effect of slighting or being angry at, 194, 29 ; not to be avenged, 154, 42 ; our sense of, 385, 20 ; revenging, costly, 198, 5 ; to be expected, 97, 23 ; to wilful men, 497, 3 ; unexpected, 244, 34
Injuring to benefit, 483, 12
Injurious under injury, 311, 32
Injury, a galling, 155, 37 ; avenging, easy, 522, 41 ; better receive than do, 2, 48 ; by a noble man, how to treat, 531, 45 ; ghost of an, 472, 44 ; how to meet an, 171, 29 ; how to recompense, 370, 32, 33 ; meditated, done, 194, 30 ; mistake in avenging, 550, 25 ; scorning to avenge, 427, 4
Injustice, committed, *versus* injustice suffered, 149, 46 ; effect of, on its perpetrator, 485, 31 ; effect of sight of, on temper, 209, 6 ; greatest, 432, 28 ; height of, 158, 38 ; Jacobi's definition of, 216, 11 ; no man means an, 302, 50 ' no success, 405, 29 ; not to be borne, 85, 16 ; rather suffer than do, 169, 30 ; to individual, 436, 36 ; unbearable, 526, 31
Inmost things melodious, 194, 34
Inner, and outer, 446, 32 ; sacrifice of, to outer, 198, 36
Innocence, a heroic, 469, 41 ; silent, persuasiveness

of, 453, 36; and obscurity, advantages of, 323, 30; and mystery, incompatibility of, 210, 18; badge of, 87, 38; coerced, like a caged lark, 44, 18; eloquence of, 15, 43; friend of, 66, 45; from misfortune, 329, 22; greatest prerogative of, 492, 2; how regarded by guilty, 151, 5; in whom alone, 104, 3; power of, 66, 10; prior to guilt, 94, 22; to be protected at any cost, 29, 44; to eye of vice, 496, 39; true, mark of, 365, 19; within, good armour, 153, 23; youth-preserving power of, 319, 8

Innocent, as doves, 399, 27; sleep of the, 436, 40; the, what is due to, 496, 8

Innovations, crude at first, 20, 45

Inquirers, Goethe's dislike to, 272, 23

Inquiries, numerical, 218, 39; scientific and learned, Mephisto on, 512, 50

Inquiry, before judgment, 27, 47; beginning of, 417, 22; default of, 174, 47; fundamental, 174, 46; the proper subject of, 288, 46

Inquisitive person to be shunned, 345, 42

Inquisitiveness, penalty of, 147, 28; implying ill-will, 51, 47

Insanity, a certain, necessary, 304, 11; common, 300, 16; contrasted with inspiration, 255, 14

Inscriptions, lapidary, 187, 39; 230, 8

Insect, an, an insect on a queen, 305, 19

Insensibility, and anguish, the mean between, 528, 33; too much, 497, 46

Insight, before eloquence, 162, 10; clear, its compass, 164, 13; deep, tendency of, 56, 51; effect of, 525, 14; indispensableness of, 391, 26; reckoned final, 262, 16; worth a life's experience, 13, 52

Insincerity, Carlyle on, 471, 20

Insinuations, Devil's rhetoric, 73, 38

Insolence from contemptible people, 471, 10

Inspiration, contrasted with insanity, 255, 14; from above time, 486, 38; from indignation, 99, 4; in the dullest, 190, 26; necessity for, 326, 24; of the Almighty, 206, 21; possibility of, 471, 5; the word, 463, 25; to be enjoyed while it lasts, 243, 31; to be waited for, 503, 2

Inspired, the truly, 417, 4

Instability, cause of, 540, 37; of things, 19, 35

Instant, the, to be taken by forward top, 244, 18

Instinct, as substitute for reason, 111, 11; contrasted with reason, 369, 35, 42; mere, no guide for a man, 212, 7; our, most sacred, 54, 2; to be trusted, 501, 11

Instincts, who speaks to the, 553, 35

Institutions, aim of all, 440, 26; ancestral, to be respected, 289, 25

Instructed, the, a time coming for, 501, 13; the half and the wholly, Goethe on, 151, 17

Instruction, divers agents of, 557, 34; effect of, 70, 30; even from an enemy, 102, 27; methods of, 462, 30; of merely clever men, 437, 2; the only solid, 446, 19; valuable as life, 409, 17

Instrument mistaken for agent, 73, 43

Instruments that boast, 399, 14

Insult, harder to bear than wrong, 432, 3; how to treat, 538, 35; 540, 24; polite, its keenness, 453, 46

Insurrection, how to foment, 90, 1

Insurrections, dangerous, 204, 25

Integrity, Cromwell on, 405, 24; reputation for, forfeited, 542, 6; sayings about, 357, 37, 38

Intellect, a large, mark of, 14, 23; a man's, measure of his worth, 163, 20; all, moral, 10, 27; and experience as lights, 94, 32; and heart, connection of, 520, 16; better than Nature, 291, 41; different forms of, and their relation to the ridiculous, 61, 30; dweller in, lonely, 472, 19; endowments of, 392, 49; error of, measure of, 190, 15; function of, 458, 42; heroism of, 100, 17; inflexible, 233, 4; life of, 75, 26; man of, his proper place in affairs, 440, 26; man of, lost

without energy, 440, 27; men of great, not of the world, 276, 3; occupied in splitting hairs, 416, 31; our ideal of, 416, 5; sayings about the, 437, 4-6; superior, always self-conscious, 305, 49; march of, 441, 28, 29; timid, loss to world from, 550, 45; without energy, 12, 32

Intellectual men, when at their best, 202, 48

Intelligence, a man of large, 37, 52; as a social bond, 32, 49; characteristic of, 1, 31; clear, the great point, 240, 27; dependence of, on misfortune, 136, 33; educating, 492, 6; men of limited, censure of, 238, 14; movements of, characterised, 404, 41; natural, power of, 292, 44; self-conscious, illusory, 162, 44; without energy, 31, 1

Intelligent, the, right of, 437, 7

Intemperance in feeling, 199, 50

Intent, secret, betrayed by outward act, 3, 44

Intention, a pure, 272, 30; evil, guilt of, 140, 41; fixed upon God as end, 413, 17; of things never clear, 451, 19

Intercourse, our social, 339, 9; social, good effect of, 396, 2

Interest, as a teacher, 64, 30; lessening fatigue, 178, 25; limit of, in people, 274, 43; *minus* self-interest, 94, 15; power of, in settling doubts, 111, 43; private, no such thing as, 172, 44

Interests, great, apt to clash, 189, 45; man's, an augury of him, 411, 41; renounced, not tastes, 275, 35

Intimacies, to be sparing in, 520, 23

Intolerable things, three, 468, 29

Intolerance, fierce, as a symptom, 412, 22

Intolerant man, the, 437, 8

Intoxication, habitual, criminality of, 138, 23

Intrepidity, commended, 243, 39

Introspection, no, 483, 46

Intrusion, prying, 551, 22

Invent, how to learn to, 200, 43

Invention after truth, 105, 33; and memory, 273, 20; highest, characterised, 434, 38; the difficult achievement, 98, 44

Inventions, adding to, 179, 1; and society, 396, 32; daughters of humanity, 121, 56; perfection of, slow, 299, 18

Inventor, a borrower, 334, 46

Investigators, quibbling, 444, 4

Invisible, embodied in visible, 266, 11; the garment of, 457, 24; world, in and about us, 437, 11

Iron, hand, in velvet glove, 15, 44; striking the, 527, 2

Irregularities as signs, 184, 40

Irremediable, not to be lamented over, 37, 28

Irresolute man, pitiable, 475, 37

Irresolution, a proof of weakness, 474, 32; effect of, 201, 10; rebuked, 161, 37

Irretrievable, the, how to treat, 114, 44

Isolation, no such thing as, 188, 24; of man from man, impossible, 274, 41; to be avoided, 527, 30

Italy, seasons in, 156, 17

J

Jack and gentleman, 392, 19

Jackdaw, the Welshman's, 484, 14

Jackdaws, how to escape the scream of, 397, 31

Jargon, dogmatic, 70, 34

Jealous, with what possessed, 437, 16

Jealousy, cancer of, 419, 24; how to get rid of, 176, 14; ineradicable, 49, 19; its malignant nature, 437, 17; love of self, 181, 14: that may make better, 480, 28; the fruit of, 78, 28; the green-eyed monster, 29, 63

Jean Paul of his early poverty, 449, 27

Jehovah, Jove, or Lord, 103, 7
Jeer, effect of one, 332, 43
Jericho, go to, 125, 2
Jest, a, expected, 437, 18; and earnest, treatment of, 172, 34; rather lose, than friend, 29, 31; preferring, to friend, 148, 51; sundering, from earnest, 151, 26; the prosperity of a, 7, 40, 41
Jester, little short of fool, 146, 45; to be shunned, 108, 3
Jesting, danger of, with the great, 98, 28; not understood by nature, 292, 30
Jests, he, at scars, 144, 6; made and repeated, 108, 56; wanton, 518, 36
Jesuit order described, 224, 3
Jesus, always with His own, 252, 9; and Socrates, difference between, 423, 33; His own sole witness, 1, 52; of Himself as Son of man, 454, 9; religion of, 451, 9; the heart of, unpenetrated, 42, 50; the teaching of, 529, 12
Jew, hath not a, eyes, 141, 16
Jewels, God's, how polished, 126, 12; hid, lost, 156, 21; merely to look at, 115, 2
Jews, the, Goethe on, 437, 15
Job, afflictions of, the record of, 447, ·9
Job's faith, 169, 33
John Bull, advice to, 241, 22; the *vis inertiæ* of, 312, 24; the pride of, 424, 26
Johnny Pigeon's epitaph, 155, 12
Joke, a, love of, 124, 24; among whom to risk a, 333, 49; the worst, 474, 49
Jokes, laughter at one's own, 545, 5; risk incurred by, 109, 34
Joking, incompatible with malignity, 497, 24; rule in, 4, 16; with ladies, 281, 2
Jollity and tranquillity, 499, 1
Journal, the learned, Emerson on, 207, 38
Journalist, Bismarck's definition of, 569, 22; to whom he owes tribute, 498, 34
Jove, prayer to, 380, 56
Joy, amid misfortune, 22, 24; and grief, in measure, 371, 25; and pain, relative amount of, 471, 36; and sorrow, 114, 48; and weeping at, 162, 5; as a teacher, 334, 47; concealment of, 145, 30; deep, awe in, 9, 20; each present, absorbing, 75, 22; effect of, as compared with that of grief, 136, 34, 35; effect of excessive, on reason, 54, 1; effect of imparting, 473, 24; effect of, on mind, 133, 32; effect of reflection on, 417, 3; fellowship in, 460, 32; great, after great change, 133, 45; great, how earned, 133, 36; how to find, 567, 41; how we part with, 527, 45; in Heaven, 532, 5; man's, only in building up, 312, 36; meaning of, 91, 37; not in joys, 64, 18; our face of, 529, 40; profound, 357, 53; seen only in a beautiful face, 379, 37; shared, 20, 7; 92, 22; shared, joy doubled, 122, 12; 385, 28; sympathy with, 548, 40; the greatest, 474, 14; three parts pain, 28, 18; true, 500, 12, 13; true, a character of, 374, 26; true, its origin, 499, 35; unfelt, hard to feign, 154, 32; vanishing, 519, 25
Joyousness, essential to all useful effort, 77, 37; mother of virtues, 64, 19
Joys, concealment of, 149, 36; connection of, with sorrows, 191, 41; each condition its own, 82, 55; highest, source of, 434, 44; killed with love, 154, 1; little and great, 251, 21; not unmingled, 508, 11; participation in another's, 152, 2; purest, how obtained, 452, 20; too high, not to be sought, 527, 33; unfelt, hard to feign, 154, 32
Judas, equal to Jesus at the ballot-box, 33, 45; even a, among the apostles, 89, 21
Judge, a lax, 310, 27; a good and faithful, 31, 60; an incompetent, 175, 6; and jury, their functions, 4, 50; and law, compared, 259, 4; appeal to the heart of, 125, 4; duties of, 214, 30-33; duty of, 390, 19; not, and reason why, 112, 6; of others,

how to, 527, 31; others, how we, 523, 33; our, he who made the heart, 552, 14; who acquits a criminal, 214, 1; who cannot punish, 7, 43; whom no king can corrupt, 154, 5
Judges, cobblers, 279, 46; function of, 237, 20; good, rare, 129, 41; should have two ears, 376, 31; the duty and practice of, 233, 22; virtue required in, 327, 58
Judging by the event, 493, 25; defined, 493, 26; men, golden rule of, 198, 27; others, 41, 4; well or evil, 551, 2
Judgment, a, well tried, 387, 52; and wit, 557, 50; 558, 6; and knowledge, 221, 6, 7; as a mark of genius, 281, 22; as the inner man, 405, 47; at the helm, 544, 30; contrasted with imagination, 223, 34; contrasted with invention, 196, 13; deceptive, 453, 13; dependent upon feeling, 522, 20; divine, 125, 22, 32, 33; 127, 47; fled to brutish beasts, 321, 6; haste in, 187, 36; how to form, 27, 47; lack of, danger of, 94, 17; last, necessary, 7, 62, 63; last, responsibility at, 568, 28; like a pair of scales, 437, 21; limit of, 539, 24; of others, 93, 20; of posterity and contemporaries, contrasted, 47, 7; of the wisest, 463, 26; one's own, as standard, 267, 4; of man and woman, 267, 34; private, Dr. Stirling on, 357, 9; private, no standard of right, 286, 10; right, rule for, 109, 9; self-satisfaction with, 93, 10; spoiled by imagination, 398, 22; the world's, 384, 22; to be according to law, 214, 24; to be charitable, 163, 21; trade on, 57, 41; vulgar, of a great man, 422, 19; weakness of, 66, 16; which we have here, 530, 10; word of, above man, 114, 13
Judgments, estimate of our, 489, 13; to be weeded of opinion, 531, 7; worthlessness of people's, 181, 26
Juggling, as governing world, 204, 7
Julian, his apostrophe to Christ, 514, 3
Juliet, love of, for Romeo, 123, 15
Jupiter, leniency of, 390, 33
Jurists bad Christians, 215, 9
Jury, function of, 4, 50
Just, cause, defence of, 215, 42; condition of being, 523, 5; for unjust, 17, 38; man may need help, 89, 32; man, rising again of, 109, 4; path of, 447, 11; perfectly, or according to ability, 490, 33; the actions of, 335, 12; the, the little of, 439, 26; the only, stern, 151, 18; the, without law, 117, 43; thing, the strong, 455, 35
Justice, a safe shield, 93, 49; a source of wrong, 9, 24; administrator of, qualities of, 152, 28; ally of religion, 313, 45; all-pervading, 431, 36; and generosity combined, power of, 429, 47; and just men, our love for, 525, 32; and liberty, effect of separating, 547, 29; as administered, 54, 23; as bandaged, 22, 28; at all risks, 105, 26, 27; compared with severity and love, 285, 13; defined, 113, 12; 408, 17; 432, 27; 536, 22; defined and described, 216, 32, 34-38; discernment of, a revelation, 546, 35; divine, instant, 125, 31; enforced in Bible, 384, 45; essence of, 425, 42; exact, mercifulness of, 95, 45; extreme, evil, 98, 3; first, 27, 25; foundation of temple of charity, 40, 29; God's, unfailing, 128, 9; guide, 241, 23; how preserved, 245, 46; how to be loved, 151, 3; impartial, truest mercy, 207, 6; in judgment and action, defined, 225, 39; in the eyes of God, 491, 42; lawyer's, *versus* God's, 161, 40; love of, 222, 12; no, without generosity, 202, 36; not to be sold, 344, 14; one hour in the execution of, 332, 37; orbs of, steadfast, 484, 29; respect for the gods, 68, 53; second to religion, 297, 39; secure, 553, 14; simple, 164, 26; springs of, 283, 19; subtlety of, 225, 40; the administration of, 402, 45; the chamber of, 46, 36; the foundation of,

117, 36 ; the, in fair round belly, 437, 25 ; the only fountain of, 63, 46 ; the reward of, 496, 13 ; those who doubt or deny, 483, 19 ; to man, desire of all, 273, 37 ; uncompromising, 169, 8 ; unfailing, 340, 19 ; virtue of, 460, 39, 40 ; virtue of great souls, 66, 30 ; virtue of the man, 121, 50 ; Westminster, and God's, different, 268, 50 ; when too severe, 406, 39 ; with the gods, 390, 12 ; without recompense, 271, 30

Juvenal on his book, 365, 22

K

Keats', epitaph, 155, 13 ; rank as poet, 503, 48
Keeping, and giving, rule in, 217, 40 ; as a merit, 293, 40
Kepler's highest wish, 288, 2
Kernel, who would eat, 364, 54
Kettle, rusty, not to be tinkered, 568, 31
Key, a gold, power of, 6, 37
Kin, a little more than, 8, 46
Kind, only the, fair, 311, 9 ; words, healing power of, 15, 27
Kindly spirit, a, the human element, 332, 16
Kindness, according to the Hitopadesa, 143, 31 ; a sudden blaze of. 406, 1 ; breaks no bones, 137, 35 ; commended, 243, 47 ; deeds of, how repaid, 440, 22 ; defined, 536, 23 ; exemplar in repairing, 189, 29 ; how to recompense, 370, 32 ; little deeds of, effect of, 251, 9 ; prevalency of, 524, 19 ; requiting, hard, 522, 41 ; soon forgotten, 50, 51 ; the joy of doing, 106, 21 ; to grateful and to ungrateful, 132, 40 ; to the good, not wasted, 31, 35
Kindnesses, misplaced, 531, 26 ; the best, 408, 31
Kindred, love of, 107, 38
King, a clown at heart, 33, 46 ; a good, 6, 44 ; a, the look of, 430, 38 ; attribute of a, 553, 23 ; an anointed, no deposing, 312, 19 ; and kingdom, relation between, 375, 39 ; contrast between, and a father, 86, 10 ; every inch a, 25, 34 ; 179, 25 ; fitness of the name, 89, 48 ; good, value of, 127, 11 ; his limits, 80, 55 ; morality of a, 443, 5 ; not a creature of chance, 296, 35 ; of England, legal mercy of, 438, 35 ; Popinjay, 35, 15 ; sayings about the, 375, 40-45 ; 437, 31-38 ; the (see **Rex**); what most becomes, 301, 17
Kingdom, a man's, 313, 23 ; of God, condition of entering, 554, 40 ; of God, in what it consists, 437, 39
Kings, a world of, 172, 11 ; and people, 534, 38 ; and people, relation of, 447, 23 ; anger of, 132, 50 ; bands of, 15, 46 ; contrasted with shepherds, 123, 43 ; courts of, composition of, 22, 1 ; divine right of, 451, 36 ; divine right of, settled, 479, 7 ; eyes and ears of, 286, 2 ; heaven-chosen for us, 35, 15 ; knowledge of, 493, 31 ; last argument of, 505, 1 ; not without good qualities, 38, 36 ; not without their virtues, 190, 2 ; only eloquence in behalf of, 233, 15 ; only privates *plus* ceremony, 535, 24 ; powerlessness of, to kill or cure, 162, 30 ; the art of, 381, 11 ; the curse of, 206, 6 ; the, of modern thought, 437, 37 ; the politeness of, 223, 12 ; the true, 478, 50 ; the wealth of, 335. 34 ; their misdeeds and the penalty, 57, 53 ; wise, and their councillors, 557, 33
Kinship, spiritual, test of, 73, 44
Kiss, echo of the sound of a, 454, 28
Kissing, full of sanctity, 157, 1
Kitchen, fundamental institution, 45, 22 ; vital part of the house, 555, 27
Kite, a carrion, 2, 37
Knave, a crafty, 3, 32 ; a, how to win, 45, 1 ; an old, 15, 57 ; and fool, 5, 58 ; found out, 81, 5 ; one

thoroughly, 91, 38 ; once, 331, 21 ; wit needed by, 109, 11
Knavery, and folly, excuse for, 102, 29 ; baseness of, 200, 17 ; defined and developed from cunning, 51, 28 ; no, if no fools, 174, 47
Knaves, first of nine order of, 428, 27 ; honourable in the mass, 238, 33
Knight, lying, in dark ages, 302, 49 ; scarce a, 145, 7
Knights of chivalry, 42, 35 ; 260, 41
Know, seeking to, 40, 59 ; three things to, 199, 27 ; to, as an act, 493, 44
"Know thyself," as a precept, 76, 42 ; 183, 43
Knowing, and doing, 525, 7 ; compared with doing, 557, 49 ; condition of, 525, 14 ; difficult, 165, 6 ; easier than doing, 175, 23 ; meaning of all, 535, 41 ; people, 99, 6 ; the step from, to doing, 305, 13 ; worth, not always knowable, 297, 51
Knowledge, a forbidden, 383, 48 ; 384, 47 ; a burden, 506, 27 ; a question of use, 203, 31 ; a rare; 477, 28 ; a steep, 110, 12 ; all in all of, 415, 50 ; all, useful, 166, 47 ; and doubt, 482, 38 ; and knowing it, 147, 34 ; and thought, 485, 1 ; as a helpmate to virtue, 515, 1 ; as a test, 147, 31 ; as a treasure, 324, 42 ; benefit of, in use, 204, 26 ; by rote, 493, 29 ; by travelling and by reading, 413, 37 ; Comte's stages of, 39, 53 ; contentment in regard to, 199, 49 ; contrasted with ignorance, 178, 7, 8 ; crediting, to others, 62, 1 ; death, 319, 12 ; definition of, 547, 17 ; diffused, 68, 5 ; dissembling, not safe, 176, 37 ; divorced from justice, 383, 5 ; effect of, on faith, 504, 23 ; essence of, 425, 43 ; excellency of, 557, 6 ; exclusively one's own, its value, 540, 48 ; for imparting, 385, 32 ; from enterprise, 269, 41 ; from others' folly and wisdom, 413, 24 ; gaining, a delight, 280, 8 ; grades in, 469, 32 ; great, an effect of, 431, 44 ; great, without vanity, effect of, 133, 46 ; growing in, happiness of, 413, 41 ; highest, 493, 40 ; how to acquire, 243, 10 ; 381, 25 ; how to seek, 405, 55 ; human, Goethe on, 320, 29 ; in a disciplined mind, 508, 22 ; in the purest sense, 469, 10 ; increased, sorrow increased, 146, 59 ; intimacy better than extent of, 102, 6 ; irreverent, 15, 45 ; its flowers and seed, 453, 5 ; its price the drawback, 312, 9 ; its quality main thing, 204, 31 ; little, who has, 42, 25 ; man of, mark of, 146, 49 ; natural, how attained, 290, 14 ; no, lost, 302, 40 ; no, without thinking, 481, 24 ; not enough, 203, 40 ; obstacle to, 383, 17 ; of causes, happiness in, 104, 24 ; of wise and ignorant contrasted, 30, 13 ; origin of, 73, 22 ; our, at best, 521, 18 ; our highest enjoyment, 489, 27 ; our, often worthless, 539, 26 ; our, an illusion, 319, 13 ; possession of, a right, 308, 22 ; question in regard to, 522, 44 ; real, the nature of, 369, 14 ; ripening and flowering of, 229, 38 ; rising in, effect of, 546, 40 ; sayings about, 493, 28-44 ; 494, 1 ; seat of, 452, 37 ; source of, 393, 20 ; strength, 147, 35 ; that is worth, 142, 4 ; that suffices, 201, 31 ; the beginning and end of, 100, 11 ; the beginning of, 254, 50 ; the best part of, 417, 52 ; the condition of acquiring, 12, 24 ; the desire of, an effect of, 423, 10 ; the key of, 392, 5 ; the only, we possess, 358, 7 ; the pearl of the faith-sea, 23, 8 ; the tree of, 136, 36 ; 458, 24 ; thirst for, 443, 29 ; thorough, test of, 445, 37 ; three stages of, 90, 38 ; to be heralded by reverence, 260, 28 ; to be reverenced, 241, 24 ; to many too costly, 269, 36 ; true, 500, 14, 15 ; true, defined, 374, 14 ; true, for life, not debate, 547, 13 ; vain pursuit of, 145, 43 ; *versus* practice, 162, 18 ; we need not travel to acquire, 496, 33 ; when alone accurate, 525, 6 ; when no longer a pleasure, 331, 28 ; with limits of satisfaction in, 93, 58 ; without energy, 12, 54 ; without God, 110, 11 ; without integrity, 195, 16 ; without knowing it, 147, 33 ; without practice,

553, 5 ; without religion, 371, 44 ; without sense, 43. 17 ; without virtue, 515, 1 ; worth of, though others know it not, 510, 6
Know'st thou the land, 218, 28
Knox, John, Earl of Morton on, 144, 19 ; gospel of, to the Scotch, 241, 39

L

Labour, a physician, 227, 37 ; and health, 153, 36 ; and rest, 478, 22 ; as a teacher, 220, 22 ; associated with pleasure, 125, 52 ; but not soul, saleable, 568, 23 ; captains of, to be honoured, 273, 39 ; clamorous at gate of morning, 43, 44 ; contrasted with luck, 257, 37 ; cultivated, effect, 51, 6 ; daughter of pain, 485, 5 ; division of, division of men, 204, 38 ; employed or unemployed, 544, 12 ; endurable only in youth, 74, 21 ; everlasting law of, 405, 49 ; evil of, not regarding, 175, 11 ; for other men, 167, 35 ; habit of, lost, man lost, 253, 27 ; hard, virtue of, 475, 23 ; honest, face of, 159, 29 ; how made happy, 205, 13 ; how made light, 12, 65 ; law of, 441, 27 ; mostly skilless, 431, 31 ; no disgrace, 84, 29 ; no living without, 174, 20 ; omnipotence and indispensability of, 314, 41 ; prescribed by Christianity, 241, 7 ; problem, the real, 565, 48 ; relieving power of, 235, 24 ; results of rising by, 387, 13 ; sayings about, 228, 23, 24 ; teachings of, 62, 13 ; the end of, 425, 12 ; to be loved, 255, 37 ; to organise work for the wise, 547, 20 ; vain, 96, 24 ; virtue in, 17, 23 ; we delight in, 437, 42 ; when unavailing, 59, 5
Labourer, Jesus on rights of, 437, 43 ; the true, and his hire, 458, 47
Labours, lingering, 129, 36 ; past, recollection of, 213, 61
Ladder, how to climb, 152, 51 ; 532, 12 ; 567, 2 ; mounting the, effect of, 565, 10
Ladders to heaven, 50, 26
Ladies, Johnson's liking for, 165, 7 ; presence of at the play, 64, 2 ; young, affections of, 415, 35
Lady, characteristic of, 6, 27 ; every, queen for life, 276, 32 ; mark of, 49, 4
Ladyism, fine, 560, 32
Lairds, Burns' advice to the, 326, 22
Laissez-faire, effect of, on masses, 123, 33
Lamb, a pet, 16, 33 ; shorn, God's care for, 66, 42
Lambs, poor harmless, 550, 28
Lame, to be waited for, 179, 20
Lamenting, misery of always, 490, 4 ; weakness of, 539, 15
Land, a, how God punishes, 543, 33 ; a, where there is no singing, 531, 12 ; at the disposal of fortune, 166, 10 ; buying, 41, 11 ; possession of, sole right to, 312, 26 ; possessors of, duty of, 353, 12 ; the, our mother, Carlyle on, 437, 47 ; the owners of, 437, 48 ; the, the proprietors of, 358, 14 ; to hastening ills a prey, 181, 40 ; where the cypress and myrtle, 220, 8
Landowner, honest, a servant, 304, 13
Landscape, charms of, 89, 44 ; point of astonishment in, 186, 36 ; property in a, 311, 34
Language, English, 82, 47 ; merit in, 104, 21 ; one, enough for a woman, 334, 27 ; only symbolical, 527, 26 ; secret of, 452, 42 ; the finest, 427, 41 ; unkind, evil of, 507, 41
Languages, a feast of, 479, 8 ; foreign, ignorance of, 532, 18
Lapse, effect of one, 334, 13
Larks caught if heavens fall, 34, 13
Lasses, brittle ware, 124, 2 ; noblest work of Nature, 23, 25

Last day, beginning and height of, 568, 21 ; day to every man, 60, 35
Laugh, a good, 6, 45 ; who knows not how to, 345, 15
Laughing, at *versus* grinning at, 86, 3 ; and weeping, cousins german, 229, 6 ; disarming, 209, 34 ; not subject to mode, 275, 11
Laughs, he who, not a bad man, 151, 30
Laughter, as a sign of worth, 305, 6 ; compared with sorrow, 400, 1 ; effect of, 180, 39 ; excessive, a sign of sadness, 306, 9 ; ill-timed, 119, 35 ; loud, vulgarity of, 253, 34 ; matter for, now, 390, 9 ; men can bear, 273, 38 ; of the cottage and court contrasted, 105, 54 ; often deceptive, 38, 1 ; our sincerest, 525, 29 ; riotous, Holmes on, 451, 45 ; significance of, 162, 7 ; 441, 1 ; two kinds, to be distinguished, 528, 27 ; unextinguished, 507, 10 ; unmannerly, 114, 42 ; virtue in, 94, 56 ; with reason, 180, 40
Law, a shield to tyranny, 180, 26 ; and equity, distinct, 84, 17, 18 ; asleep at times, 71, 53 ; combined with justice, 4, 5 ; contrasted with necessity, 121, 57 ; Cicero's definition of, 87, 7 ; evasion invented with, 103, 13 ; extreme, wrong 215, 25 ; felt as a restraint, 205, 24 ; foul chimneys of, hard to sweep clean, 67, 36 ; function of, 53, 37 ; going to, 295, 42 ; good, beginning and end of, 417, 19 ; ignorance of, no excuse, 178, 19 ; impeded by severity, 453, 19 ; love in, 184, 24 ; must be reason, 315, 9 ; no, no sin, 548, 43 ; no, without a hole in it, 85, 33 ; not to be a scarecrow, 527, 1 ; obedience to, when a hardship, 280, 24 ; of one's nature, sacredness of, 302, 42 ; one certainty in, 184, 15 ; oppression by, 344, 51 ; pleadings in, 464, 43 ; possession by, 213, 6 ; requisite in a, 237, 12, 17 ; rule of nature, 94, 25 ; sacred, 215, 11 ; sanctioned by consent, 46, 46 ; sayings about, 244, 42-46 ; 438, 12-29 ; seat of, 452, 38 ; source of, 125, 44 ; stronger than man, 113, 1 ; subtlety in, condemned, 300, 15 ; teaching of, 220, 5 ; the foundation of, 295, 33 ; the life of, 369, 36 ; to yield to circumstance and custom, 491, 18 ; virtue of, 110, 38 ; voice of, 452, 38 ; who has to execute, 369, 27 ; with public morals corrupt, 240, 28
Lawful and honourable, 159, 35
Lawgiver, man's absolute, 358, 10 ; the spirit of, 454, 36
Laws, good and bad, defined, 6, 46 ; and manners, 267, 36-38, 43 ; authors of, 238, 32 ; during war, 391, 48 ; good, from bad manners, 97, 14 ; 129, 42 ; God's and lawyers' connection with, 205, 15 ; good, origin of, 237, 14 ; good, out of bad manners, 31, 15 ; how rendered binding and stable, 227, 24 ; human, copies, 338, 19 ; in a corrupted state, 48, 28 ; just, to the good, 215, 39 ; many, a bad sign, 226, 16 ; many, evil of, 210, 42 ; ministers and interpreters of, 237, 20 ; no, for the just, 117, 43 ; oppression of, 19, 11 ; organic, Ruskin on, 336, 24 ; path of, and power of, 326, 11 ; permanence of, 85, 26 ; power of, 514, 47 ; powerlessness of, to kill or cure, 162, 30 ; proper tendency of, 457, 6 ; relation of, to penalties, 443, 17 ; Ruskin's advice as to reform of, 28, 40 ; strict, value of, 403, 36 ; the object of, 237, 13 ; the purpose of, 193, 7 ; too severe, worthless, 222, 33 ; when useless and when broken, 544, 24 ; without morals, 365, 42
Lawsuit, agreement better than, 28, 28
Lawsuits, issue of, protracted, 331, 7 ; why avoid, 118, 13
Lawyer, Brougham's definition of, 438, 30 ; profession of, 107, 11
Lawyer's, business, 205, 15 ; fee, the cheapest, 208, 49
Lawyers, by whom enriched, 108, 40 ; experience of, 424, 8

Laziness in individual and in mass, 7, 65
Lazy man, the, 1, 21
Leader, should know the way, 86, 5
Leaf, the two lobes of, 302, 33
Leal, in the land o' the, 478, 10
Learned, in his infidelities, 504, 8 ; man. a truly, 413, 43 ; man, Aquinas' definition of, 158, 27 ; man, rich, 159, 14 ; men, Goethe on, 188, 6 ; men, more numerous than wise, 526, 9 ; men not always liberal, 443, 48 ; soon, learned long, 38, 16 ; the business of, as compared with the ignorant, 193, 30
Learner, advice to, 318, 16 ; his gratitude, 532, 17
Learning, a little, dangerous, 8, 44 ; a little, hard to gain, 208, 21 ; according to quality of man, 276, 11 ; and play, 288, 28 ; by observation and experience, 413, 37 ; by seeking and blundering, 34, 14 ; chief part of, 383, 15 ; doting on scraps of, 398, 10 ; earthly, end of, 540, 3 ; ever, and never knowing, 89, 45 ; evil of its apparent facility, 222, 24 ; from living, 251, 48 ; great school for, 431, 35 ; has its value, 229, 18 ; how to advance, 187, 40 ; inferior to creating, 200, 22 ; limitation of, 79, 18 ; living by, 308, 20 ; loving, 175, 16 ; man who does not use his, 151, 32 ; matter of quality, 450, 26 ; men of great, generosity of, 276, 4 ; men of, like ears of corn, 198, 9 ; mere, 148, 45 ; much, a weariness, 285, 14 ; much, much ignorance, 285, 15 ; no, without labour, 177, 21 ; not wisdom, 304, 20 ; of antiquity, venerable, 225, 10 ; only to forget, 118, 52 ; philosophy as regulating regard for, 347, 24 ; possible, every day, 318, 10 ; rule in, 237, 41 ; rule of, 141, 37 ; sayings about, 525, 12–15 ; Solon on his, 121, 49 ; the condition of, 303, 15 ; the source of all, 138, 9 ; to be used like a watch, 530, 39 ; to last with life, 410, 15 ; vanity of fortifying one's self with, 492, 9 ; without common-sense, 208, 24 ; without discretion, 559, 28 ; without morals, 364, 32 ; without nature like a maimed man, 292, 35 ; without sense, 148, 45 ; worth anything, how to acquire, 305, 44
Leaven, power of a little, 8, 45
Legality, risk of, 226, 2
Legend, wedded to history and fancy, 519, 12
Legislation, ancient, wisdom of, 117, 17 ; and administration, mistake about, 198, 17 ; foolish, a rope of sand, 108, 37
Legislator, aim of the, 415, 47 ; should be moderate, 223, 43
Leibnitz's optimism, Voltaire's version of, 498, 33
Leisure, and solitude, Scipio Africanus on his, 168, 1 ; dependent on business, 443, 27 ; value of, 211, 4 ; without literature, 336, 48
Lending, caution against, 294, 30 ; rule of, 141, 37
Leniency at times a crime, 107, 8
Lenity, evil effect of too much, 535, 4
Leonidas at Thermopylæ, 397, 12
Leopard, spots of, not seen, 184, 16
Lesson, first, to be learned, 444, 2 ; the best, for many, 417, 49
Lethe, a stream of, in every breath, 558, 25
Letter, a, does not blush, 251, 1 ; and spirit, opposite effects of, 250, 33 ; long, reason for a, 210, 46 ; what we look for in a, 187, 41
Letters, as memorials, 32, 41 ; devotion to, a regret, 117, 26 ; mirror of a man's breast, 184, 18 ; not to be carelessly written, 438, 47 ; qualities, good and bad, in, 402, 46 ; style of, 456, 2 ; the invention of, 206, 18 ; the love of, 440, 1
Levellers, their aim, 568, 25 ; their failure, 483, 1 ; two, 219, 10
Lever, power of, Archimedes on, 169, 15
Levers that move men, 468, 36
Levity, unpardonable, 509, 8
Liar, a swearer, 8, 9 ; and his oaths, 505, 30 ; needs good memory, 8, 10

Liars, how to be treated, 71, 44 ; no legislation for, 473, 13 ; to have good memories, 277, 36
Libel, a, in a frown, 47, 51
Liberal, the, sayings about, 438, 45, 46
Liberalism, modern, the follies of, 429, 4
Liberality, defined, 226, 3 ; grounds of, to be weighed, 28, 11
Liberties, from the devil, 245, 26 ; the basis of all, 153, 35
Liberty, a form of true, 35, 46 ; and justice, effect of separating, 547, 29 ; as desired by Milton, 123, 19 ; child of the north, 56, 52 ; civil, defined, 245, 12 ; civil, utmost bound of, 481, 47 ; crowing about, by slaves, 315, 17 ; dearer than country, 343, 24 ; destroyed by gifts, 53, 6 ; effect of, on man, 396, 3 ; free and at her ease, 226, 5 ; growth of tree of, 222,26 ; headstrong, 153, 30 ; how to forfeit, 27, 60 ; how to preserve, 68, 37 ; in harmony with law, 435, 1 ; in nations, 226, 4 ; in relation to taxation, 185, 41 ; inspiring power of, 112, 46 ; lean, and fat slavery, 235, 36 ; limit of, 266, 39 ; Mme. Roland at statue of, 321, 12 ; no such thing as, 474, 30 ; of ancient date, 226, 6 ; opening of, 27, 10 ; passion for, 235, 10 ; political, where only found, 352, 12 ; possibility of, 440, 37 ; safeguard of, 77, 12 ; spirit of, Burke's deference to, 288, 20 ; the first to strive for, 324, 18 ; the only valuable, 446, 8 ; the true, of a man, 458, 49 ; tree of, how it grows, 458, 26 ; true and false, 500, 16 ; defined, 471, 13 ; turbulent, *versus* quiet slavery, 261, 24 ; under a pious king, 100, 34 ; value of, 436, 3 ; when once lost, 526, 1 ; without deserving it, 454, 13
Libraries, large, by whom not needed, 451, 33
Library, a witness against its owner, 450, 22 ; browsing in, 167, 48 ; circulating, 3, 12 ; enough, 271, 36 ; luxury of revelling in, 148, 13
Licence, an enemy to liberty, 245, 22
Licentiousness, after reformation, 6, 67
Lie, a double-distilled, 35, 28 ; a flattering, contrasted with a bitter truth, 529, 14 ; a half true, 8, 16, 29 ; a, like a snowball, 8, 14 ; a, sure to be unmasked, 27, 49 ; a, to be crushed, 8, 28 ; a, uncalled for, 53, 18 ; deformity of, 315, 42 ; essence of, 425, 30 ; inexcusable, 314, 4 ; one, in the heart, evil of, 28, 56 ; task involved in telling, 152, 26 ; what it wants, 457, 17
Lies, abhorrent to nature, 290, 20 ; all, will be dishonoured some day, 302, 45 ; and the belief of them, 473, 15 ; destroyer of, our gratitude to, 506, 15 ; doomed to vanish, 506, 10 ; establishing one's self on, 475, 22 ; great, great as great truths, 133, 47 ; how to overcome, 240, 16 ; man born enemy of, 262, 17 ; respect implied in telling, of one, 533, 4 ; scorned by the upright, 46, 32 ; self-productive, 332, 46, 47 ; that ruin humanity, Ruskin on, 206, 15 ; tolerance of, effect of, 548, 9 ; white, lead to black, 509, 33
Life, a bark against the tide, 242, 14 ; a battle and a march, 263, 10 ; a becoming, 462, 14 ; a blessed, 470, 3 ; a blossoming and a withering, 62, 16 ; a chamber being frescoed with colours, 339, 39 ; a conscious half, impossible, 303, 16 ; a constant want, 163, 23 ; a faint link between us and our hereafter, 29, 62 ; a galling load, 321, 15 ; a good, time enough for, 32, 30 ; a greeting and a parting, 265, 36 ; a happy and an unhappy, equalised, 390, 21 ; a heroic, 434, 37 ; a higher, how to earn, 522, 25 ; a law of, 443, 9 ; as led, a riddle, 538, 20 ; a little gleam of time, 332, 48 ; a loathed, compared with death, 461, 45 ; a long sigh, 320, 15 ; a long, the secret of, 568, 1 ; a merry, how to live, 556, 31 ; a mistake about, 409, 19 ; a mystery, 547, 26 ; a new, beginning of, 526, 3 ; a new, with every budding bosom, 109, 32 ; a, not worth living, 166, 19 ; a peaceful, how to ensure, 492, 42 : a progress, 266, 41 ; a pure and

true, how to attain, 384, 38 ; a quiet, specific for, 275, 34 ; a reality, and all one has, 481, 13 ; a really long, 413, 38 ; a rule in, 212, 7 ; 311, 2 ; a satisfied, 380, 61 ; a school, 310, 36 ; a sign of, 183, 31 ; a simple, benefit of, 286, 27 ; a state of endurance, 163, 24 ; a steady self-control, 266, 45 ; a stern reality, 266, 46 ; a short, advantage of, 453, 25 ; a useless, 23, 45 ; a voyage under sealed orders, 284, 19 ; a well-written, rare, 24, 55 ; a wise, 516, 53 ; according to nature or opinion, 389, 46 ; ascent of green mountain of, 266, 3 ; advancing in, 144, 48 ; aim of, 415, 46 ; all a cheat, 543, 41 ; all, as death, 399, 46 ; always a hope, 527, 22 ; amid doubt, 538, 2 ; among men, 16, 53 ; among men, breaking or hardening, 177, 4 ; an abortive, Young on the course of, 22, 15 ; an ever-vanishing present, 266, 44 ; an obscure, 311, 4 ; and art, difference of, 84, 41 ; and death, 464, 4 ; and death, a contrast, 329, 32 ; and death according to law, 94, 42 ; and death, not complete, 488, 31 ; and time, 485, 11 ; apart from world, 144, 30 ; as a study, interesting, 350, 6 ; at all, a miracle, 403, 3 ; at beginning and end, 467, 7 ; at different ages, 22, 16 ; awful and wonderful, 55, 47 ; bartered away, 522, 30 ; based on time, 339, 40 ; best and safest course of, 449, 37 ; between duty and desire, 439, 18 ; bodying forth of the invisible, 266, 11 ; Bolingbroke on, 476, 32 ; book of, interpreter of, 538, 4 ; brevity of, 262, 32 ; brighter the longer, 249, 35 ; Burns' apostrophe to, 335, 53 ; by medical prescription, 363, 42 ; Calderon on, 362, 33 ; charms of, that we never knew, 320, 14 ; cheap, and bread dear, 320. 30 ; Christian, Pascal on, 241, 21 ; compared with hope, 228, 14 ; complaints of, unjust, 545, 4 ; complete from the first, 26, 57 ; condensing lesson of, in pointed sentence, 448, 39 ; condition of art of, 395, 38 ; corner-stone of body, 421, 36 ; daily, harvest of, 458, 45 ; daily, instructiveness of, 52, 33 ; defined, 434, 40 ; 536, 26, 27 ; dependent upon "No," 300, 37 ; dependent upon death, 403, 14 ; described, 537, 1 ; detachment from, gradual, 265, 6 ; drama of, spectators of, 191, 39 ; dreary, its cause, 537, 37 ; each man's, dark to him, 404, 53 ; elaborate preparation for, folly of. 494, 20 ; epitome of many a man's, 292, 46 ; essential furniture of, whence imported, 231, 51 ; elements of a complete, 221. 9 ; evanescence of, 537, 25 ; every condition in, value of, 212, 15 ; every period, its prejudices and temptations, 93, 44, 45 ; every time of, has its care and burden, 327, 41 ; everywhere romantic, 90, 55 ; experience of, Burns', 554, 44 ; farewell of a Greek to. 210, 12 ; fateful stages in, 147. 12 ; first lesson of, 428, 24, 25 ; first, lived well. 413, 45 ; folly of wasting, 154, 16 ; fondness and carelessness of, 475, 41 ; for action, 3, 51 ; for a single day, 363, 14 ; fraction of, how to increase. 429, 23 ; fresh only from the soul, 84, 42 ; full of stumbling-blocks, 64, 21 ; gift and ministry of, contrasted, 493, 16 ; glorious, crowded hour of, 400, 24 ; God's highest gift, 434, 40 ; golden moments in, lost, 430, 34 ; great art of, 493, 24 ; great moments of, but moments, 431, 29 ; greatest ornament of an illustrious, 432, 33 ; greed of, 516, 22 ; half wasted, 457, 11 ; hampered by itself, 3, 8 ; high, people in, 187, 26 ; highest maxims of, to be respected, 333, 17 ; his, was gentle, 157, 5 ; how man spends, 265, 40 ; here only once, 264, 36 ; how rendered miserable, 227, 13 ; how rounded off, 522, 18 ; how ruled, 201, 48 ; how shaped, 548, 21 ; how to achieve, 567, 8, 9 ; how to extend, 14, 7 ; how to husband and not waste, 526, 37 ; how to know, 493, 35 ; how to make sweet, 173, 17 ; how to quit, 179, 32 ; how to take a, 567, 30 ; how to write a worthy, 8, 30 ; how we take, main point, 125, 14 ; ignorance of,

441, 4 ; in, no present, 187. 45 ; in the morning of youth, 321, 14 ; in the present, a secret, 20, 54 ; in the straitest circumstances, if wise and loyal-hearted, 160, 53 in the world, and beyond, 524, 5 ; inevitable condition of, 562, 43 ; inner genial, effect of kindling, 68, 3 ; instinct to protect and cherish, 434, 40 ; its autumn and spring, 528, 15 ; its healthfulness, 460, 6 ; its joys and sorrows, Browning on, 141, 41 ; known to few, 79, 17 ; laughing at and grinning at, 203, 8 ; learning from, 448, 39 ; length of, effect of, 439, 32, 33 ; like travelling, 288, 12 ; long, desire of, 91, 51 ; long, together, suggestiveness of, 496, 24 ; longer than misfortune. 32, 34 ; longest, shortness of, 439, 36 ; loom of, and patterns it weaves, 439, 40 ; lost in getting a living, 473, 28 ; lost, irretrievable, 80, 6 ; lottery of, 418, 33 ; made strait on purpose, 404, 39 ; made up of deception and art, 45, 56 ; main thing regarding, 310, 31 ; man's, a kind of beast-godhood, 535, 35 ; memory of a well-spent, 32, 32 ; mode of, seldom our own choosing, 467, 2 ; moments of, fatal or fated, 403, 25 ; more significant than words, 85, 21 ; more than breathing, 161, 12 ; more than meat, 438, 48 ; more than meat and clothing, 409, 25 ; mostly from hand to mouth, 105, 11 ; never stainless, 302, 33 ; no dream, 338, 25 ; no fraction of, to be sold, 484, 3 ; no longer on old lines, 230, 17 ; no pastime, 526, 26 ; no, without perplexity, 395, 35 ; not to be bartered, 272, 25 ; not judged, before death, 214, 9 ; not to be trifled with, 57, 5 ; nobility of, 445, 2 ; noble, eternal in its action, 93, 3 ; nothing that has, perfect, 316, 42 ; obscure, not therefore worthless, 289, 26 ; of man, collective, 205, 19 ; of poor and rich, small difference between, 448, 28 ; on moderate means, 182, 2 ; one's own, sacred, 75, 19 ; only a hope, 317, 14 ; ordained law of, 206, 22 ; our, a thousand-stringed harp, 338, 23 ; our chief want in, 337, 25 ; our, control over, limited, 340, 22 ; our first ideas of, 338, 2 ; our, a mutual hostility, 338, 26 ; our mode of, characterised, 339, 9 ; our, not what it might be, 338, 27, 28 ; our true, 64, 16 ; our waste of, 529, 39 ; our whole daily, of spirit birth, 395, 24 ; out of the ruins of life, 53, 24 ; outward details of, insignificance of, 534, 6 ; past, and help that lies in it, 230, 31 ; pathos and sublime of, 494, 18 ; peaceable, commended, 173, 8 ; perfect, attribute of, 345, 49 ; perfected in death, 220, 19 ; postponing, 364, 34 ; power of fortune over, 163, 25 ; primitive and frontier, advantage of, 208, 40 ; problem of, 449, 29 ; prospective, 520, 39 ; purpose of, 521, 26 ; query regarding purpose of, 520, 17 ; quiet continuity of, 366, 21 ; ragged line of, 439, 18 ; reality of, without fancy, 442, 7 ; resignation of, motive for, 480, 15 ; rising on life, 509, 15 ; river of, and its ferries, 524, 23 ; river of, how to drink out of, 566, 23 ; rule of, 182, 27 ; 237, 3 ; 519, 14 ; ruled by fortune, 516, 29 ; saved, by losing it, 554, 42 ; sacrificed to reasoning about it, 550, 24 ; sayings about, 54, 12-18 ; 517, 1, 2 ; scorn of, revered, 209, 50 ; secrets of, how revealed, 453, 4 ; servile to skyey influences, 172, 35 ; severe condition of knowing, 505, 9 ; shadow-hunting or shadow-hunted, 550, 4 ; Shakespearean rules of, 253, 40 ; significance of, 453, 34 ; signs of, 184, 40 ; simple, happiness of, 26, 10 ; simplicity of, gain in, 189, 20 ; sincere, required, 100. 13 ; sojourn in an inn. 98, 15 ; source of its value, 371, 2 ; sporting with, 551, 33 ; state of, alone suitable for a man, 414, 10 ; still beautiful, 320, 31 ; struggle of, question of, 191, 40 ; stuff to try soul's strength, 165, 34 ; subordinate to something higher, 265, 25 ; sunshine of, 456, 24 ; tediousness of, 407, 34 ; text and commentary, 428. 18 ; that is merely breathing, 153, 8 ; that we praise, 43, 22 ; the chief condition of, 224, 30 ; the clearer, the longer, 443, 23 ; the course of, destructive, 569, 24 ; the cup of, to be drunk, 422, 24 ; the dark spot in, 11, 39 ; the end of a man's, 52, 32 ; the end of, Sophocles on, 336, 53 ; the essence of, 200, 22 ; the first problem in, 428, 32 ; the fluctuations of, 94, 42 ; the fountain of, 217, 34 ; the fruition of, 429, 31 ; the fullest, 528, 25 ; the gate and way to, 403, 23 ; the great felicity in, 431, 20 ; the happiest, 83, 45 ; the interpreter of, 334, 45 ; the lot of, 94, 42 ; the longest half of, 251, 50 ; the meaning of, 338, 34 ; the noblest. 144, 32 ; the observation of, 448, 39 ; the one meaning of, 256, 38 ; the only sign of, 563, 33 ; the only wealth, 474, 44 ; the price of, life, 179, 28 ; the stuff of, 487, 7 ; the sure way to, 215, 28 ; the true, of man, 458, 51 ; the true question in, 95, 11 ; the use of, 537, 20 ; the way of, its secrets, 64, 21 ; the web of, 462, 2 ; the, which renews a man 439 8 ; things essential to, 468, 26 ; three epochs in, 467, 8 ; time's fool, 33, 29 ; to be believed before book, 165, 20 ; to be enjoyed as it passes, 503, 4 ; to be in the whole, 18, 51 ; to be still prayed for, 320, 5 ; to genius, 492, 37 ; to happy and unhappy, 433, 16 ; to miserable and to happy, 321, 13, 15 ; transitions of, 517, 24 ; tree of, ever green, 132, 42 ; true be-ginning of, 205, 30 ; true enjoyment of, 197, 14 ; true, how to live a, 503, 7 ; time of, to be wise, 179, 15 ; two ways out of, 23, 40 ; uncertainty in, source of, 205, 48   under a poor roof, 117, 10 ; up and down tendencies of, 186, 37 ; use we may make of, 522, 37 ; waste of, 365, 26 ; wasted, 269, 20 ; waves of, and strand of death, 452, 15 ; way of, 516, 26 ; way of, in sere yellow leaf, 288, 25 ; web of, heaven-woven, 79, 13 ; what has, power of, 531, 41 ; what it consists of, 525, 24 ; what makes, poor, 204, 27 ; what sur-vives wreck of, 191, 31 ; while digestion lasts, 550, 14 ; who would love, 148, 52 ; wilderness of, springs in, 191, 26 ; wisdom of, 244, 7 ; 462, 27 ; with art and deception, 566, 24 ; with its enmities, to be faced, 60, 31 ; with some, like a sleigh-drive, 558, 45 ; without a purpose, 516, 21 ; without God, 559, 22 ; without hope, 335, 17 ; without labour, 300, 4 ; without learning, 516, 20 ; without love, 249, 28 ; without self-denial, 133, 39 ; without superior, inferior, or equal, 493, 10 ; without use to others, 536, 34 ; without women, 33, 9 ; 538, 32 ; woven of old and new, 10, 3 ; woven of wind, 316, 50 ; wrecked, cause of, 385, 35

Life's, blessings, how taught to value, 458, 3 ; end, 255, 5 ; rewards, 255, 5 ; wealth, 255, 5 ; young day, love of, 168, 48

Light, a curtain, 439, 10 ; a ray of, when seen, 450, 36 ; and fire, 197, 18 ; and shadow, 560, 14 ; by which we see, 439, 9 ; by whom shunned, 311, 37 ; dry, 439, 14 ; dry. best, 73, 26 ; for the million, 508, 1 ; in a clear breast, 146, 32 ; in darkness, 439, 13 ; in nature and man, 417, 21 ; indispensability of, 105, 51 ; intense, beautifying effect of, 473, 35 ; loving, hating, 146, 5, 6 ; new, burst of a, to the unprepared heart, 419, 19 ; new, distrusted, 545, 44 ; new, dread of, 89, 54 ; new. elevating power of, 89, 54 ; new, spiritual, effect on soul of, 70, 8 ; no, without eyes, 559, 32 ; our boast of, 522, 31 ; perfect, how to attain, 439, 12 ; perfect, too dazzling, 346, 1 ; self-evident, 330, 11 ; shadow of God, 502, 8 ; sovereign in the physical world, 246, 1 ; spiritual, and its source, 116, 33 ; spiritual, never entirely extinguishable, 303, 8 ; the true, defined, 413, 32 ; too much, effect of, 548, 48 ; which we reject, 439, 15

Light, and heavy, different fortunes of, 235, 27 ; things compared. 288, 23

Light-minded men, improvident. 244, 32

Lightning, and thunder, God's harbingers, 249, 30 ; as an alternative, 249, 22 ; heaven's (in a man), not to be caressed, 332, 7 ; in the collied night, 32, 40 ; spiritual, 439, 15, 16 ; to godlike and godless men, 128, 18

Lights, broken, and shapes, 243, 8

Like, not look upon his, again, 149, 21 ; to like, 9, 30 ; 19, 39 ; 39, 28 ; 124. 8 ; 489, 20

Like-minded and of unlike-minded, the fortunes of, 345, 7

Likeness, family, 101, 35 ; in nature more than difference, 75, 3

Liking, power of, 498, 53

Likings, a man's, a test of him, 411, 39 ; signifi-cance of our, 539, 32

Lilies, the, consider, 46, 50

Limbs, too large, a weakness, 202, 39

Limit, the real definition of a thing, 21, 35 ; to progress, 87, 26

Limits, every man has, 304, 17

Line. a straight, in morals, 20, 61 ; crooked and straight, 205, 8

Linen, dirty, to be washed at home, 179, 27

Link, importance of a, 332, 49

Linnæus, the sexual system of, 517, 3

Linnet's song, feeling that inspires, 553, 3

Lion, not asleep, though silent, 52, 28 ; or sheep, as commander, 200, 28

Lion's share, 78, 8

Lions with stag for leader, 112, 35

Lips, that give a right answer, 92, 26 ; to be guarded as palace doors, 131, 12

Listener, a good, rare, 208, 22 ; a good, worth listening to, 89, 7

Listening, at keyhole, 85, 23 ; the faculty of, 426, 47 ; to some more pleasant than talking, 533, 14

Literary, ages, taste of all, 477, 21 ; career, a thorny path, 224, 25 ; composition to be kept nine years, 244, 9 ; man, the true, 458, 52 ; men of the present, 187, 47 ; work, characteristic of, 530, 9

Literature, a discovery to be made in, 469, 40 ; a noble profession, 168, 8 ; a silent, 262, 24 ; a talent for, a snare, 409, 42 ; a, when classical, 302, 46 ; and humanity, 523, 37 ; compared with the conversa-tion of a grandly simple soul, 47, 48 ; decline of, as a sign, 422, 45 ; done for money, 339, 8 ; false, 564, 1 ; first lesson of, 428, 25 ; glorious doom of, 206, 16 ; highest problem of, 435, 8 ; how concocted, 185, 17 ; its, test of a nation, 541, 20 ; life in, 206, 23 ; modern, *minus* its meta-physics, 175, 36 ; modern, temporary nature of, 284, 25 ; on oatmeal, 523, 21 ; our esteem for, 338, 16 ; proper task of, 449, 44 ; sentimental, inferio-rity of, 387, 4 ; what one wants in, 207, 2

Litigant unlike the goose, 439, 21

Litigation, misery of long, 117, 21

Little, beings, aspirations of, 91, 40 ; managing a, merit in, 203, 26 ; minds, and the faith of great ones. 99, 57 ; the infinitely, pride of, 436, 33 ; the, to be done well, 72, 15 ; things, power of, 317, 37 ; things, running after, 483, 15 ; treatment of, a spiritual sign, 54, 11 ; who cannot live upon, 387, 34

Littleness, as wonderful as vastness, 539, 27

Live, happily, how men. 190, 31 ; knowing how to, enough, 20. 30 ; let us. to-day, 158, 18 ; to, how, alone, 472, 6 ; to, to dream, 237, 5

Lived, what has, immortality of, 508, 30

Livelihood, struggle for mere, debasing, 179, 17

Lives, English, worth reading, 467, 29 ; lost in change of purpose, 269, 42 ; of the best, 439, 27 ; our, how we spend, 520, 34 ; reading, but not leading, 565, 12 ; the finest, 427, 42 ; wrecked, cause of, 207, 5

Lives, one who, for others, 551, 6 ; one who, for self, 551, 6

Living, a thing deferred, 513, 24 ; above one's means, 441, 21 ; after one's own opinion or the world's, 201, 24 ; alone, no reason to fear, 555, 25 ; and dead, how to treat, 158, 22 ; and dead, the partition between, 533, 41 ; and living dishonoured, 200, 13 ; and out-living, 200, 12 ; and thinking, contrasted, 40, 12 ; art of, like every other, 416, 21 ; as angels, 48, 40 ; being, mistake in professed study of, 532, 38 ; cheap, 559, 1 ; corked up for ever, 478, 17 ; defined, 516, 44, 45 ; earning a, without living, 441, 5 ; for eternity, hard, 161, 28 ; for others contrasted with living for self, 151, 35 ; for self or for others, 149, 43 ; greatly, test of, 333, 15 ; happily, defined, 494, 6 ; how to get a, 567, 7 ; long, sorrow in, 229, 35 ; man, test of a, 395, 8 ; mere, good, 161, 22 ; once, never lost, 316, 40 ; one day, insignificance of, 176, 47 ; right of, 60, 29 ; rule of, 113, 22 ; rules of, Dr. Johnson's, 353, 47 ; sayings about, 494, 5–10 ; secret of, 453, 1 ; so long as life, 395, 5 ; the, compared with the dead, 10, 36 ; the respect due to, 329, 29 ; to no purpose, 151, 36 ; twice, 109, 50 ; 158, 3 ; ways of getting a, 461, 36 ; well, 28, 8 ; well, our main duty, 311, 53 ; well, no man's concern, 295, 22

Loan, a double loss, 110, 14

Lochaber no more, 102, 23

Lock and key, a security, 168, 39

Lodge, oh, for a, in some vast wilderness, 325, 51

Loftiest of the race, the, characteristic of 439, 30 ; mortal, and his desires, 439, 29

Logic as compared with ethics, 88, 10

Logician, the best, 433, 41

Loneliness, extreme of, 395, 7 ; man's, inexplicable, 161, 33 ; the best, 417, 45

Longevity a sign of purity, 153, 37

Longing, vain, 525, 27–29, 31

Longwindedness, evil of, 237, 31

Look on't again I dare not, 164, 30

Looking, at the best side, habit of, 433, 2 ; not therefore seeing, 2, 38 ; not thinking, 333, 31

Looks, others', significance of, 469, 19

Loquacity, where to learn, 332, 45

Lord, good, good animal, 184, 12 ; great, service under, 393, 4 ; sayings about the, 439, 42–45 ; the, eyes of, 426, 42 ; the, fear of, 487, 32 ; the, no counsel against, 474, 46 ; the, sure to come, 174, 24 ; what He requires of us, 535, 5 ; when to seek, 385, 5

Lord's, blessings, on whom bestowed, 439, 41 ; Prayer, Napoleon on, 72, 46

Lordship, conquest, 155, 31 ; jealous of fellowship, 253, 45

Loss, first step to repair, 415, 32 ; sometimes better than gain, 87, 10 ; the smallest, not to be slighted, 394, 3

Losses, accustomed, 52, 41 ; and crosses, lessons from, 484, 20 ; comparative, 128, 23 ; 137, 34 ; great and little, effect of, 350, 30 ; relative value of, 151, 38

Lost, all is not, 539, 10 ; sought in every cranny but the right, 111, 27 ; the, valued, 110, 8

Lot, one's, matter of discontent, 218, 8 ; our, how to estimate, 260, 37 ; our, to be followed, 538, 31 ; the, its disposal, 439, 47

Louis XIV., Boileau of, 377, 4 ; kept waiting for his carriage, 209, 33 ; of his wife, 233, 1

Louis XVI., Tilly on, 253, 37

Lovable, the, and the ridiculous, congruity of, 105, 8

Love, a contrast, 172, 21 ; a cruel tyrant, 102, 1 ; a dream, 247, 18 ; a falling from, 549, 32 ; as fulfilling the law, Professor Blackie on, 295, 24 ; as our one debt, 340, 28 ; a power divine, 314, 32 ; as reconciler of things, 285, 26 ; a rule of, 546, 37 ; as seasoning, 504, 25 ; a standard, 19, 63 ; a warfare, 279, 24 ; a wonderful, 486, 4 ; accom-

paniment of, 27, 24 ; all-comprehensiveness of, 256, 12 ; all-hallowing, 74, 37 ; always at first sight, 551, 15 ; an impulse to help, 161, 4 ; and admiration, 525, 34 ; and ambition, wings, 258, 6 ; and bickering, 482, 24 ; and duty, inseparable, 474, 3 ; and esteem, never sold, 214, 14 ; and fear, connected, 471, 31 ; and God, 189, 58 ; and jealousy, 211, 33, 34, 36, 37, 40 ; 548, 10 ; and labour, effect of, 127, 16 ; and prudence, ill-matched pair, 359, 19 ; and wisdom incompatible, 13, 8 ; and reverence, objects respectively of, 110, 21 ; as a bond, 124, 9 ; as an educator, 492, 51 ; as a gift of heaven, 477, 48 ; as a present, 383, 20 ; as a teacher, 320, 19 ; as obligation, 506, 13 ; ascetic, 120, 27 ; at moment of parting, 487, 18 ; at sight, 33, 30 ; attended by memory, 479, 25 ; attraction of, its law, 146, 36 ; based on equality, 84, 13 ; before rejection, 243, 35 ; blessedness of unbroken, 104, 17 ; blind, 25, 9 ; burden of, 249, 19 ; Christian, 257, 2 ; common as light, 45, 10 ; compared with admiration, 4, 33 ; compared with friendship, 114, 49 ; compared with hatred, 141, 21 ; compared with passion, 65, 21 ; compared with severity and justice, 285, 13 ; composition of, 130, 12 ; condition of, 556, 29 ; contrasted with admiration, 63, 54 ; cooling, effect of, 544, 13, 14 ; courage in, 104, 25 ; course of true, 109, 19 ; credulous, 49, 51 ; cruel power of, 183, 54 ; daring of, 537, 34 ; deep as the sea, 287, 41 ; defined, 546, 4 ; delight of, in tormenting, 17, 36 ; described, 11, 44 ; determining power of, 480, 39 ; different kinds of, 34, 43 ; direst disaster in, 476, 27 ; disappointed, poison of, 218, 27 ; discovery of estranged, 475, 5 ; divine, described, 70, 70 ; divine power of, 424, 6 ; doubt of, 72, 20, 27 ; early, yearning after, 320, 18 ; educative power of, 222, 11, 14 ; effect of, on man, 11, 51 ; effect of absence on, 221, 44 ; effect of different kinds of, 319, 3 ; effect of, on life, 85, 14 ; effect of looks on, 253, 15 ; effect of, on a man's thinking, 543, 15 ; effect of, on broken hearts, 498, 8 ; effect of, on temper, 74, 15 ; effect of time on, 487, 18 ; effect on partisanship, 141, 13 ; end of existence, 312, 30 ; endures no tie, 108, 34 ; enjoyed, 122, 23 ; ennobling power of, 25, 59 ; enslaving, 419, 27 ; entire, a worship, 83, 44 ; essential to intelligence, 202, 31 ; everywhere, 190, 20 ; evil of want of, 548, 44 ; excess of, deprecated, 321, 18 ; excessive, to be avoided, 15, 48 ; excitement of, 187, 52 ; expanding power of, 542, 11 ; fate of, 568, 40 ; first, alone infinite, 75, 9 ; first consciousness of, 475, 21 ; first, recurrence to, 331, 2 ; first sigh of, 234, 36 ; following or fleeing, 108, 10 ; forced, 101, 53 ; forced, not lasting, 112, 7 ; genesis of, hard to date, 201, 9 ; gifts of, 511, 24 ; God's training of, 125, 45 ; greatest miracle of, 432, 24 ; happiness in, 242, 5 ; heaven-revealing power of, 173, 3 ; honoured, and why, 9, 65 ; hope in, spite of reason, 311, 42 ; hottest, 432, 12 ; how kept out, 135, 10 ; how to be won, 73, 53 ; how to reap in, 175, 20 ; idleness, 364, 15 ; ignorant of, 144, 15 ; impossible to conceal or express, 172, 45 ; impossible to Mephistopheles, 86, 38 ; indefinable by language, 399, 35 ; indefinable to a true lover, 144, 26 ; in man and in woman, 352, 33 ; in the heart, a spur, 41, 27 ; in the purest sense, 469, 10 ; incompatible with dignity, 68, 6 ; intelligence of, 116, 23 ; invincible, 534, 24 ; its coming and going, 222, 15 ; killing joy, 384, 39 ; lad's, saying about, 229, 9 ; life, 488, 15 ; magic power of, 440, 13 ; master of all arts, 69, 53 ; might of, 279, 13 ; miraculous power of, 325, 34 ; moderation in, commended, 31, 58 ; money powerless to buy, 457, 9 ; mystic art of, 326, 5 ; no cure for, 271, 33 ; no explaining, 527, 19 ; no fear in, 472, 37 ; no habitant of earth, 326, 6; no, lost, 19, 12; no, no true pain, 144, 43; no reason for, 508, 51; no retreat from, 537, 8; no struggling against, 178, 54; no, without love, 241, 48; not binding lover, 172, 41; not perfect in, 146, 13; not the sole, or even chief object of any, 294, 50; not to be scorned, 383, 20; not to be spoken of with scorn, 296, 66; of a father, 103, 8; of God, no falling out of, 217, 1; old and new, 489, 11; old, changing, for new, 479, 38; old-fashioned, dead, 330, 2; one thing needful, 414, 35; one's first, 88, 23; only known to mother, 319, 18; only victory over, 446, 25; our first, 527, 23; our, to others, 525, 31; pain of, a mystery, 212, 5; pain from, 72, 32; pains of, 340, 46; pangs in, many, 251, 46; partiality of, 269, 27; passion of, effect of, on the tongue, 545, 27; perfect, sayings about, 346, 2–4; power of, 64, 11; 319, 27; 325, 34; 457, 25; 525, 20; 558, 30; power of, on fools and clever people, 226, 36; power of, over hatred, 141, 17; power of, over sorrow, 86, 34; power of, over the gods, 544, 15; power of, in poet, 296, 19; prevalency of, 524, 19; principle of, 521, 2; pure, might of, 360, 7; rapture and pain of, 221, 40; reconciling power of, 268, 16; reflects thing beloved, 165, 23; relieving power of, 27, 29; risk of forswearing, 382, 10; room enough everywhere for, 368, 39; satisfying, 237, 22; sayings about, 13, 56–67; 14, 3; 65, 22–25; 187, 50–53; 246, 5–12; 494, 13–16; season, the, 440, 3; separated in life, 504, 29; sigh of, 555, 9; sorrowing after hope, 479, 25; specific against, 37, 31; strength of, 403, 19; 404, 10; successful, 405, 41; sudden, 406, 2; suppressing, 407, 22; sympathy of, blessing in, 483, 34; test of, 539, 44; test of citizenship, 240, 42; test of power of, 66, 25; that can be reckoned, 478, 1; that descends, 440, 6; that lets itself be known, 479, 12; the best, 482, 46; the centre of, 78, 13; the chaste blossom of, 391, 37; the deceptive power of, 329, 33; the double bliss in, 320, 17; the faith of, 218, 22; the fire of, not quenchable by words, 484, 4; the first, 428, 26; the first sigh of, 428, 35; the heart's romance, 222, 13; the hottest, 435, 33; the key to vision, 265, 7; the monstrosity in, 481, 46; the offer or refusal of, 302, 48; the only equaliser, 119, 27; the point of, 427, 3; the range of, 381, 38; the rights of, 527, 42; the true season of, 413, 33; the truth about, 537, 7; the universal sway of, 222, 20; those who can animate, 335, 20; thy, seek not to tell, 296, 61; to be paid in love, 128, 28; to be yielded to, 328, 35; to doubt, 491, 47; to God, condition of, 371, 40; to project itself as an arrow, 47, 52; to reason about, 367, 49; transposing power of, 480, 38; true, 413, 34; 500, 17–22; true, unconcealable, 80, 14; true, course of, 422, 1; true, ever the same, 54, 8; true, not to be hid, 544, 46; true, sweet, 408, 25; typified by colour, 44, 32; unconcealable, 290, 31; universal, described, 507, 36; unquenchable, 270, 4; unquenchable by words, 63, 43; unwisely directed, 528, 17; *versus* wealth, 208, 4; waywardness of, 106, 4; who shuts out, 552, 31; when deep, 83, 57; when ripening, 377, 25; when satisfied, 7, 58; who alone obtain, 482, 37; who hath, in his heart, 554, 14; who knows, 552, 8; wise in, advice to, 550, 34; without esteem, 19, 52

Love's young dream, 478, 28
Love-letter, how to write good, 497, 5
Loved, and lost, to have, 487, 54; how to be wholly, 490, 45; not lost, 176, 3; not wisely, but too well, 400, 48
Lover, a, for everything, 75, 21; accepted and betrothed, 415, 30; engaged in war, 279, 23; fine trait in character of, 198, 12; loved, 9, 56; no

deceiving, 366, 28; senses of, 537, 7; the desire of, 452, 28; unconscious of space and time, 402, 3; sayings about, 440, 4, 5
Lover's, doubts and suspicions, misery of a, 33, 21; the, privilege, 495, 33
Lovers, easily entertained, 85, 19; never tire of each other, 537, 35; self-tormentors, 161, 10; the perjuries of, and Jupiter, 346, 26; two, a spectacle for gods, 79, 34
Lovers', eyes, sharpness of, 110, 16; memories, 273, 5; quarrels, 13, 5; tongues, silver sweet, 162, 33
Loving, a heaven-soaring wing, 41, 6; and being loved, 531, 20; and hating, alike without reason, 329, 16; and losing, 200, 30; believing, 41, 5; daring, 419, 11; fearing, 41, 7; or not loving, effect of both alike, 533, 35; pain of, 460, 31; pleasure in, 472, 3; too much, 39, 14
Low man, the, a success, 482, 4
Lowest, from, a path to highest, 116, 27; the, to be borne with, 375, 29
Lowly soul, blessed, 403, 8
Loyalty to country sacred, 242, 2
Lucifer, the sin of, 428, 36
Luck, believers in, 388, 25; good, 129, 44–46; good, applied energy, 17, 12; good, too much, 569, 33; inspires pluck, 124, 35; the power of, 55, 21
Lucky, a, man, 348, 47
Ludlam's dog, 232, 34
Luminaries, intellectual, at their brightest, 508, 8
Lust, contrasted with nature, 291, 38; degrading power of, Sallust on, 286, 8
Lustre, no, without light, 473, 17
Lute, little rift in, 206, 24
Luther, at the Diet of Worms, 156, 26; 531, 2; on his way to Worms, 533, 12
Luxuries, most, harmful, 284, 29
Luxury, and avarice, compared, 258, 11; compared with poverty, 354, 35; fatal to kingdoms, 331, 15; peril of, 104, 26
Lying, accusation of, 489, 25; as vice, 31, 50; cowardly, 246, 4; habit of, 433, 3; its beginning and end, 84, 19; only for tradesmen, 241, 31; the meanness of, 387, 35; the price of, 429, 41
Lyre, a welcome, at banquet, 56, 16; the, winged, 315, 35; with voice and flute, compared, 429, 3
Lyrics, to be sung, 239, 31

M

Machine, the model, 264, 5
Machinery, does not feed men, 294, 44; indispensability of, 140, 40; ruinous effect of, 11, 43
Macpherson under the gallows, 379, 18
Mad, all, once, 386, 22; with all rather than alone, 29, 22
Madam, and moon, light of, borrowed, 114, 16
Madding crowd's ignoble strife, far from, 102, 10
Madman, a, according to Schiller, 143, 6; a sort of dreamer, 424, 20; belief of every, 194, 46; in the eye of law, 117, 44, 45
Madmen, all, 234, 16; worst of, 465, 31
Madness, a germ of, in all, 190, 14; common calamity, 170, 16; defined, 542, 15; fine, of the poet, 111, 10; how induced 314, 20; in the dullest, 190, 26; method in, 484, 21; pleasure in, 470, 18; tendency to, even in wisest, 186, 43; the element of, 81, 34
Magdalen, thrusting, into the pit, 553, 30
Magistracy, bought, justice by, 145, 23
Magistrates, function of, 237, 20
Magnanimity, meaning of, 490, 27

Mahomet, and the mountain, 174, 25 ; compared with Moses, 284, 10

Maid, love for a, moral power of, 305, 20

Maiden, a, how to win, 563, 27 ; a tender thing, 248, 47 ; in new clothes, 241, 43 ; qualities we love in, 525, 30 ; simple, in her flower, 19, 31 ; the, to love, 499, 4 ; when her heart is stolen, 544, 40

Maiden's reserve, her security, 306, 28

Maidens to be praised, 114, 14

Majesty, attribute of kings, 80, 22 ; incompatible with love, 308, 55

Majority, a clear, 333, 33 ; appeal to, against reason, 315, 28 ; going by, 524, 14 ; the, opinions of, 440, 15 ; the, what, 537, 17 ; two that make a, 331, 36 ; 333, 33 ; voice of, no proof, 461, 8 ; voice of, on any high matter, 441, 33

Maladies, cure for all, 562, 42 ; desperate, remedies for, 24, 28 ; our spiritual, source of, 339, 21

Malcontent, political, described, 12, 11

Male appointed to rule, 73, 39

Malice, to be despised, 527, 28

Malignity, no pure, 474, 7 ; unjustifiable, 466, 44

Mammon, great, 133, 49 ; power of, 259, 45

Man, a, a man, 539, 7 ; a, and his faults, 516, 24 ; a, assailed, 159, 4 ; a, at his worst, how to judge of, 528, 22 ; a bad, no association with, 304, 42 ; a bad, never amusing, 334, 3 ; a born worshipper, 261, 45 ; a communicative, Swift's dread of, 307, 43 ; a, composition of, 187, 35 ; a, counterfeit of, 143, 24 ; a, described, 143, 7 ; a, distinguishing mark of, 28, 9 ; a, dread power, 352, 17 ; a drowning, 42, 27 ; a fighter, 169, 39 ; a great and good, 142, 58 ; a happy, 140, 21 ; 166, 2 ; a hard, 143, 3 ; a, his nature, 12, 10 ; a, how he finds himself, 305, 41 ; a, how interpreted, 556, 33 ; a, knowing, difficult, 208, 12 ; a microcosm, 473, 18 ; a minnow, in the All, 496, 10 ; a moving temple of God, 90, 7 ; a mystery, 522, 23 ; a, no concealing, 161, 2 ; a, not wretched, 34, 48 ; a, one with his native soil, 331, 41 ; a, stimulating effect of sight of, 22, 14 ; a real, 241, 45 ; a reed that thinks, 223, 27 ; a, rich in himself, 190, 6 ; a, sad, 143, 3 ; a social animal, 16, 3 ; a stately edifice, 535, 27 ; a strong, 12, 9 ; 143, 10 ; a subject of study, 467, 4 ; a symbol of God, 459, 41 ; 536, 28 ; a, to meet, 164, 32 ; a, touchstone of, 34, 42 ; a well-bred, 24, 52 ; a, what best becomes, 170, 21 ; a whole number, 11, 61 ; a wilful, 24, 57 ; a wise, according to Epictetus, 143, 14 ; a wise, according to the Hitopadesa, 143, 15 ; a wise, according to Xenophon, 143, 16 ; a, worth of, 204, 42 ; ability of, 537, 46 ; affected by time, 240, 13 ; after God's or another's pattern, 200, 14 ; aim of, compared with woman's, 288, 44 ; akin to God in spirit, 173, 19 ; all a prey to, 314, 27 ; all-relatedness of, 476, 9 ; all the sphere, 314, 27 ; an actor in a drama, 373, 5 ; an exception, 464, 30 ; an individual, mature fruit of time, 15, 40 ; an interest to man, 473, 19 ; an inventor, 334, 46 ; and animal, contrast between, 416, 9 ; and ape, distinction between, 346, 30 ; and beast, moral difference of, 443, 4 ; and citizen, 440, 19 ; and his age, inseparable, 11, 49 ; and his circumstances, 440, 21 ; and his defects, how to regard, 253, 1 ; and his expression, 440, 20 ; and his God, 96, 50 ; and his inseparable attendants, 566, 26 ; and misery, twins, 109, 36 ; and nature, distinction between, 424, 1 ; and other animals, the distinction between, 202, 24 ; and world, 464, 40 ; angel as well as devil in, 174, 41 ; apprentice to pain, 223, 24 ; as a piece of work, 533, 36 ; as great or small, 473, 16 ; as his works, perishable, 35, 31 ; as regards knowledge and practice, 162, 18 ; as subject of art, 60, 19 ; as weary and heavy laden, Carlyle's apostrophe to, 352, 41 ; aspiring to be an angel, 223, 26 ; assurance of a, 3, 19 ; at

the best, 550, 4 ; attitude of, to truth and falsehood, 223, 21 ; bad, the fair words of, 137, 53 ; basest thought about, 416, 47 ; below himself, 143, 21 ; best served, 143, 22 ; bachelor, betrothed, wedded, 25, 39 ; by nature and art, 18, 45 ; call no, happy before death, 241, 45 ; central part in, 453, 12 ; centre of all beauty and worth, 312, 35 ; characteristic function of, 241, 25 ; characteristic of, known only to God, 415, 3 ; chief fault of, 60, 14 ; child of nature, 26, 60 ; compared to a clock, 44, 4 ; contrasted with woman, 560, 45 ; dear to man, 58, 22 ; dear to the gods, 36, 18 ; defined, 352, 19 ; despised by world, 465, 4 ; distinctive mark of, 489, 29 ; distinguishing qualities of, 76, 54 ; effect of favour and a fall on, 225, 18 ; either god or devil, 159, 23 ; either god or wolf, 159, 17 ; end of, 425, 12, 13 ; ever in need of man, 154, 17 ; ever wrestler rather than believer, 84, 47 ; either born king or fool, 24, 23 ; every, a potential madman, 91, 49 ; every, a quotation, 92, 12 ; every, a reflex of the All, 92, 35 ; every, a special vocation, 91, 28 ; every, a suggestion, 92, 16 ; every, at birth, 150, 29 ; every, dupe to himself, 92, 15 ; every, exceptional, 92, 14 ; every, his own valuator, 92, 27 ; every, knowledge of, special, 92, 20 ; every, in a sense alone, 92, 19 ; every, rule for, 240, 39 ; every, to follow his own star, 212, 7 ; every, when sick, 92, 13 ; extraordinary, without root in life, 205, 43 ; feeling one's self a, 217, 36 ; final destiny of, 91, 29 ; folly in, 471, 32 ; folly of, in having and not using faculties, 126, 5 ; foolishest thought about, 416, 47 ; formed to be a husband, 291, 8 ; free at first, 164, 35 ; God in, 174, 19 ; God in, a birth of faith, 100, 16 ; god or devil, 367, 41 ; God's creature, 93, 18 ; God's proper treasure, 128, 34 ; good, sign of a, 418, 15 ; great, by conviction, 312, 32 ; greatest, a son of man, 60, 6 ; greatest crime of, 111, 17 ; hard to persuade, 265, 10 ; has a good and a bad angel, 92, 8 ; has still all the faculties he ever had, 297, 6 ; highest, brother to his contemporaries, 435, 2 ; highest glory and highest disgrace of, 493, 40 ; his body and soul, 159, 13 ; his destiny, 482, 18 ; his nature the rule for, 81, 27 ; his own enemy, 91, 48 ; his own portion, 12, 26 ; his vitality, 461, 5 ; how to estimate a, 370, 29 ; 505, 10 ; how to know a, 177, 23 ; 493, 28 ; how he knows himself, 334, 47 ; how to influence a, 177, 45 ; how to study, 495, 52 ; human element in, 533, 45 ; hungry, to be alone, 87, 32 ; if alone, a terror to himself, 533, 13 ; ignorant of himself, 316, 51 ; ill to advise, 161, 34 ; in a series, 521, 27 ; immensity of his possibilities, 26, 62 ; in contrast with nature, 291, 4 ; in God's image, 125, 24 ; in himself, 522, 11 ; in his deed a precedent to man, 9, 68 ; in his self-delusion, 119, 22 ; in presence of Nature, 292, 23 ; in prosperity, 90, 32 ; in relation to his defects and talents, 12, 27 ; in relation to instinct, 522, 26 ; is what he is, 387, 48 ; interest in, 163, 31 ; is sincere, when alone, 91, 44 ; just and resolute, Horace on, 216, 42 ; key to every, 437, 27 ; knowing, and men, different, 201, 18 ; knowledge of, 437, 40 ; known by his company, 312, 7 ; known by what he honours, 389, 39 ; left to his passions, 236, 44 ; life of, a diary, 439, 3 ; life of, how led, 488, 36 ; life of, its course, 439, 4 ; like Ulysses, 182, 30 ; limit of evil in, 218, 13 ; lord of himself, and his resources, rare, 151, 11 ; lovable through his errors, 65, 6 ; lowest, life of, 439, 7 ; Luther's definition of a, 554, 8 ; made for society, 521, 33 ; master of his fate, 329, 34 ; measured by his own standard, 278, 45 ; most essential fact about, 443, 44 ; nearest God, 143, 35 ; new always in a new time, 444, 44 ; no bad, happy, 295, 12 ; no, born for himself,

295, 24 ; no, born without faults, 289, 33 ; no, but has his time, 473, 22 ; no, compelled to be compelled, 218, 15 ; no, entirely a devil, 303, 8 ; no, extraordinary, without a mission, 212, 1 ; no, friendless, 473, 20 ; no longer a temple, 95, 10 ; no, the man prayed for, 242, 3 ; no, the one waited for, 58, 38 ; no, wise at all moments, 295, 15 ; no, wise by himself, 295, 25 ; noble, attractive power of, 78, 43 ; not easy to transplant, 313, 7 ; not hindered by society, 396, 8 ; not his own guide, 204, 6 ; not men, God-made, 128, 4 ; of celestial descent, 551, 34 ; of decision, 441, 11 ; of action, the chief concern of, 58, 32 ; of genius and other men, difference between, 462, 7 ; of genius, his view of things, 297, 21 ; of genius, sayings about, 440, 23, 24 ; of noble deeds, in trouble, misjudged, 208, 18 ; of pluck, 477, 43 ; of sound brain and his knowledge, 92, 20 ; of the world, how to be, 413, 48 ; oh for a, with heart, head, hand, 325, 52 ; on the confines of two hostile empires, 95, 13 ; one, with a higher wisdom, worth of, 332, 56 ; of only one subject, 66, 44 ; only point in regard to, 446, 13 ; original, and the world, 464, 13 ; 465, 17 ; our obligations to, 527, 41 ; only sleeping and feeding, 535, 38 ; overwhelmed with misfortune, 374, 19 ; part of a whole, 489, 7 ; peculiarity of, 426, 4 ; piped to by fortune, 20, 23 ; Plato's definition of, 15, 24 ; poor, if not raised above self, 507, 51 ; power looked for in, 221, 29 ; preacher to woman, 460, 43 ; presence and passion of, 465, 17 ; presence or absence of, a difference, 548, 11 ; presumption of, rebuked, 125, 7 ; proof of a, 204, 29 ; proper study of man, 220, 2 ; pure, in this world, 441, 10 ; qualities to possess to make, 488, 14 ; real science and study of man, 228, 20 ; regarded as end of creation, 203, 17 ; religiously viewed, 91, 46 ; sayings about, 60, 32–38 ; 61, 1–13 ; 91, 44–55 ; 92, 1–44 ; science of, obscure, 267, 30 ; self-ruined, 127, 15 ; separated from his circumstances, 371, 23 ; small, surveying great, 19, 54 ; something in, as yet unnamed, 178, 30 ; something of all in every, 476, 40 ; soul of the whole, 559, 15 ; spirit of, indomitable, 504, 18 ; strange contradictions in, 162, 16 ; subject to his power, 12, 12 ; summary history of, 261, 44 ; substantiality in a, 443, 19 ; taught only by himself, 146, 30 ; test of, 489, 34 ; that hath no music in him, 440, 31 ; that stands by himself, 440, 33 ; the, and the how, 440, 29 ; the arch-machine, 196, 14 ; the beauty of, 65, 1 ; the best, 289, 33 ; the façade of a temple, 12, 11 ; the fatal, 427, 16 ; the first, significance of, 422, 11 ; the foundations of, 429, 19 ; the greatness of, how to comprehend, 339, 20 ; the highest might of, 513, 10 ; the knowledge of, price of, 491, 33 ; the life of, 465, 19 ; the life of, a journey, 439, 5 ; the little, 439, 24 ; the lot of, 52, 40 ; the merely merry, 440, 38 ; the merely serious, 440, 38 ; the more universal, the greater, 210, 28 ; the noble, with nobler, 439, 25 ; the noblest function of, 53, 45 ; the noblest, that ever lived, 483, 28 ; the of, character, 440, 32 ; the ordinary, happiness of, 446, 30 ; the real, 450, 38 ; the riddle of the world, 49, 40 ; the shadow of, 292, 1 ; the state of, 481, 47 ; the state of Wolsey on the, 102, 19 ; the substantial, 479, 1 ; the terrible, 117, 38 ; the, that blushes, 440, 30 ; the want of, 554, 46 ; the wealth of a, 461, 40 ; the, who cannot wonder, 441, 3 ; the whole, of this new time, 554, 24 ; the wisest, 14, 44 ; the, without sense of his relation to things, 440, 35 ; this was a, 157, 5 ; threefold property of a, 449, 45 ; to be obeyed, 464, 15 ; to be saved from damnable error, 173, 32 ; to free oppressed, 126, 9 ; to what appointed, 33, 17 ; treating a, with solemnity, effect of, 542, 12 ; truly blest, 440, 39 ; truly free, will and

action of, 223, 30 ; two things necessary to make a man, 544, 43 ; weakness ^, 267, 25 ; well-ordered, independence of, 147, 27 ; what exalts, 488, 33 ; when God visits him, 127, 33 ; when most God-like, 12, 8 ; when one is a, 568, 29 ; when quite destitute, 223, 25 ; when reformer and when conservative, 522, 13 ; when true, 173, 2 ; when truly alive, 264, 26 ; while living, necessary, 19, 50 ; who always wins, 142, 6 ; who bears rule, 153, 12 ; who can call to-day his own, 140, 26 ; who can define, 145, 9 ; who cannot blush, 440, 41 ; who cannot endure his own company, 441, 2 ; who cannot laugh, 441, 1 ; who cannot win a woman, 413, 47 ; who depends on public recognition, 440, 42 ; who does not fear death, 441, 6 ; who does not think what he is doing, 528, 26 ; who has no enemies, 441, 8 ; who has only ancestry to boast of, 441, 9 ; who is not passion's slave, 123, 16 ; who knows not how to live, 441, 4 ; who never decides, 441, 12 ; who never loved his kind, 554, 17 ; who owes his bread solely to heaven, 140, 27 ; who runs away, 14, 58 ; who wavers in wavering times, 441, 11 ; whom kings have most to fear, 153, 10 ; whose mother has not inspired him with veneration, 507, 20 ; whose soul is veiled by pair of glasses, 534, 42 ; why no, can judge another, 303, 14 ; within man, 92, 9 ; without a purpose, 109, 15 ; without bread, 42, 51 ; without enthusiasm, 165, 46 ; without passion, 559, 39, 40 ; without philosophy, 559, 41 ; without prayer, 534, 5 ; without shame lost, 289, 44 ; without the Bible, 392, 52 ; word of, 520, 7 ; Wordsworth's lament over, 14, 48 ; worthiest, according to Burns, 454, 4 ; worthiest of affection, 189, 60

Man's, arm, if upheld by the gods, 402, 20 ; being, secret of, the sphinx's, 452, 44 ; chief want, 538, 1 ; discontent, 352, 31 ; doings symbolic, 10, 34 ; faculty, feet not wings, 524, 41 ; finest qualities, how to preserve, 427, 45 ; first great work, 428, 21 ; gifts, 219, 51 ; greatest ornament and dignity, 533, 27 ; grief his grandeur, 352, 31 ; life, sphere of, 202, 41 ; lot, like wind, 385, 11 ; nature, secret of, 452, 45 ; needs and wishes, 514, 16 ; only true joy, 316, 27 ; origin and end, 412, 39 ; soul, majestic, 241, 46 ; true ambition, 204, 37 ; true beginning and father, 486, 12 ; true elevation, 340, 45 ; true safety, 340, 45 ; true want, 538, 8 ; two gala-days, 570, 3 ; work, a, 261, 46

Management, good, economy of, 129, 47

Manfulness, in sin as well as faith, commended by Luther, 26, 6

Manhood, a, how built up, 92, 43 ; a period of unlearning, 482, 33 ; a struggle, 568, 42 ; passing away of, 514, 19 ; possible here, 156, 22 ; sense of, elevating power of, 443, 26 ; measure of, 354, 40

Manhood's work, 402, 22

Mankind, an unco' squad, 564, 24 ; and his task, of what composed, 313, 12 ; contractedness of, 140, 9 ; contrary estimate of, 398, 42 ; does not doubt, 265, 11 ; ever in progress, 106, 20 ; evil of despising, 553, 12 ; generally bad, 326, 35 ; how interpreted, 556, 33 ; how to love, 177, 39 ; how to maintain love for, 188, 42 ; knowledge of, damaging effect of, 277, 54 ; Machiavelli on, 57, 16 ; one and a whole, 173, 25 ; proper study of, 449, 43 ; to love, and to see into, 494, 14 ; wish of, collectively, 89, 50

Manliness, commended, 366, 36

Mannerism, how produced, 139, 20

Manners, a probity in, 470, 20 ; artificial, effect of assuming, 469, 26 ; authors of, 238, 32 ; cannot be imparted, 137, 37 ; caught as diseases, 200, 50 ; composing, more than composing books, 141, 42 ; defended by ceremony, 38, 20 ; effect of pride on, 194, 40 ; effect on, of liberal arts, 194, 14 ; everywhere to be respected, 76, 14 ; fine, inventor of.

120, 26; fine, mantle of fair minds, 106, 28; fine, support of, 106. 29; good, 129, 48–51; good, and love of country, 439, 48; good, to attain to, 490, 5; good, not communicated, 128, 52; good, the basis of, 417, 1; good, the element of, 454, 5; how learned, 478, 83; importance of, 181, 17; 204. 46; 559, 8; men's evil, 277, 24; once vices, 538, 16; people of, distinguishing trait of, 424, 4; pleasing, effect of, 283, 50; refinement of, how attained, 216, 19; regulated by the king, 45, 47; root of defect in, 56, 61; striking, bad, 403, 43; strange, disconcerting, 281, 5; that speak well of the man, 469, 27; the power of, 406, 21; the supreme power in, 187, 56; to be studied, 313, 31

Manual labour, the value of, 305, 44
Manufacture, contrasted with art, 550, 16
Manufactures, our, 525, 38
Many, men, many minds, 332, 58; the, no pleasing, 123, 24; 258, 30
Maria Theresa's epitaph, 388, 2
Mark, missing the, 416, 15
Market-place, training of, 450, 13
Marksman, a good, 6, 49
Marriage, a happy, 249, 41; a query prior to, 58, 33; a way to repentance, 118, 30; a suitable, 390, 30; according to luck, 93, 31; advice regarding, 175, 21; an open question, 197, 19; an unhappy, 280, 25; as birds in cages, 198, 8; before and after, 217, 44; 262, 29; before, evil, 147, 56; concern of others in one's, 324, 17; contentment in, 187, 57; early, advantage of, 117, 2; extremes in, 64, 7; fascination of, 118, 36; for money, 148, 1; in despair, 341, 24; in opinion and reality, 191, 29; inducements to, 451, 26; kills or cures, 80, 20; may mar, 23, 22; rule in, 82, 63; 270, 23; saying on, 568, 7; significance of, 326, 14; Socrates on, 550, 10; the happiest, 124, 6; true, union in, 192, 15; unfortunate, evil of, 202, 43; well-matched and ill-matched, 531, 27; with an old person, in hope of his death, 479, 44
Marriages, unequal, 496, 41; 507, 9; why few happy, 451, 1
Married, in haste, 485, 45; life, who fit for, 335, 7; people, their mutual interest, 548, 24
Marry, times not to, 192, 40
Marrying, anticipated and experienced, 36, 34
Martyr, a, to live harder, than to die, 203, 5; blood of the, 436, 39; what makes a, 206, 1
Martyrdom, ennobled by Christianity, 42, 54; to bystanders, 458, 14
Martyrdoms as seen at the time, 9, 58
Martyrs, accepted by nature, 292, 18; the blood of, 418, 42; the modern, 359, 33
Masses, effect of giving power to, 123, 33; judgment of the, 518, 11
Master, a fellow worker, 446, 42; a good, 152, 17; and his affairs, 71, 6; and servant, unhappy relation of, 395, 14; being without a, 491, 1; careless, 2, 35; early, 75, 34; effect of presence of, 80, 53; every one finds his, 85, 27; eye of, 426, 34; finding, a first duty, 428, 15; measure of, 441, 41; minds, rare, 292, 38; no one born, 295, 45; of whole world, 150, 13; presence of, eye of house, 327, 39; qualification for, 175, 3; spirits, 56, 54; the, and the mansion, 293, 34; true, 145, 36; who fears his servants, 279, 47; who will not serve one, 42, 17
Master's eye, worth of, 53, 28
Masterhood, and servanthood, correlative, 107, 7; restriction necessary to, 152, 39
Masters, accustomed, not easily dispensed with, 239, 17; and their domestics, 105, 9; change of, to the poor, 189, 18; no serving two, 303, 24; 305, 22; not all, 523, 2; real, importance of, 559,

43; serving two, 41, 15; the great, the subject of all, 324, 34
Mastership and servantship, value of, 96, 19
Mastery, empty claim of, over others, 10, 1; essence of, 492, 48; of a subject, how to attain, 117, 32; how to attain to, 390, 36; mistaken for egoism, 65, 29; thorough, how possible, 303, 25; 305, 22
Material things essential to life, 468, 26
Mathematics, our, 524, 34
Mathesis, a fundamental, 494, 11
Matrimony, the state of, 234, 22; 405, 46
Matter, spirit-informed, 277, 43; subject to mind, 279, 32
Maturity, law of, 445, 5
Maxim, the grand modern, 38, 45; the, of maxims, 491, 38
Maxims, by themselves, 12, 33; good, value of, 129, 52; sound, the value of, 400, 23; their helpfulness, 356, 1; their, show men, 239, 4; too high, to be reserved, 529, 2
Mazes, in wandering, lost, 336, 43
Me, our, the only reality, 482, 12
Mean, a, in all things, 87, 14; deed, debasing, 150, 2; the proper course, 98, 5
Meaning well, 495, 24
Meanness, debasing, 16, 16; more hopeless than wickedness, 166, 44
Means, and end, 5, 50; I'll husband, 110, 25; must be at hand, 3, 32; to do ill deeds, 162, 39
Measures, nothing to men, 273, 41
Meat, and stomach for it, matter of thanks, 398, 14; one man's, not another's, 5, 7; where mouths, 127, 30, 42
Medal, and its reverse, 40, 3; reverse of, thought on, 333, 3
"Meddle not," as a maxim, 413, 31
Medea, her method of reform, 305, 28
Mediævalism, chief moral agent of, 453, 11
Medical skill, profession of, universal, 106, 36
Medicine, contrary effects of, 84, 35; Mephisto on the study of, 59, 58
Mediocrity, aiming at, 489, 32; helpful to make wise, 189, 56; in power, 314, 35; 376, 46; naturally pleasing to us, 308, 1; respectable, inoffensive, 374, 50; the ascendency of, a sign of the times, 429, 45; to be cheerfully accepted, 172, 19; when unendurable, 466, 32
Meekness, power of, 405, 25; true, faces of, 398, 12
Melancholy, and mirth, correlated, 482, 27; charm in, 125, 9; contrasted with cheerfulness, 40, 46; how to prevent, 81, 41
Melanchthon's rule, 188, 25
Melodies of the everlasting chime, 467, 10; the sweetest, 408, 30
Melody, in the heart of everything, 9, 47; sphere, 435, 3
Member, suffering in one, 110, 13
Memorial, more durable than brass, 96, 47
Memorials, enduring, 99, 20
Memory, and judgment compared, 21, 3; dependent on forgetfulness, 495, 18; dependent on oblivion, 176, 16; independent of will, 338, 33; necessity of exercising, 273, 11; not to be dragooned, 455; pleasures of, 546, 21; Themistocles on his, 273, 6; the dark background of, 323, 23; the faculty of, 426, 45; wise, the condition of, 176, 16; with little judgment, 26, 11
Men, a little breed, 523, 6; a thousand kinds of, 275, 25; after modern or ancient model, 124, 13; all conditioned by circumstance, 138, 29; all, play-actors, 286, 31; ambitious, like tallest trees, 456, 40; and the law, 438, 24; and their vices, how to treat, 340, 32; and women of right sort, 35, 2; angels or slugs, practically no matter, 339, 42; anvil as well as hammer, 92, 32; argumentative

398, 19 ; as individuals, and their belongings, 521, 3 ; as measured of God, 125, 29 ; as the generation of leaves, 326, 37 ; as they are born, 398, 16 ; at birth and death, 9, 60 ; at their best, 289, 49 ; blindness of, 65, 33 ; born for others, 310, 13 ; born too soon, 116, 32 ; bubbles on stream of time, 111, 40 ; but three classes of, 466, 29 ; by what standard to weigh, 333, 19 ; childless, progeny of, 445, 10 ; collective beings, 521, 3 ; collectively, respect for, despised individually, 16, 1 ; common, apologies for men, 45, 15 ; compared with plants, 349, 16 ; dangerous, 149, 13 ; differences among, 110, 20 ; dream of a shadow, 393, 16 ; driven as turkeys, 521, 14 ; effect of ignorance of, 65, 32 ; evil, characteristic of, 95, 32 ; evil of shunning, 65, 31 ; false estimate of, 162, 22 ; far-observant, often unknown to themselves, 529, 23 ; for certain brothers, 556, 41 ; glorious, Bacon on, 124, 23 ; god-devils, 357, 35 ; God's *versus* devil's, 128, 10 ; good, value of, 129, 53 ; good, mercy in, 187, 18 ; graded from birth, 21, 15 ; great (see **Great men**) ; greatest, sayings about, 432, 16–23 ; greatest, simplest, 432, 41 ; happy, full of present, 140, 23 ; how misknown, 65, 31 ; how ruined, 9, 69 ; how to be weighed, 507, 13 ; how to govern, 492, 47 ; how to make true or great, 501, 14 ; how to treat, 510, 14, 15 ; how treated by the gods, 68, 36 ; hypocrites when talking of themselves, 535, 28 ; in love, philosophy of, 542, 15 ; in one respect all alike, 188, 39 ; in the eye of God, 127, 23 ; inconstancy of, 391, 24 ; inequality among, 239, 10 ; known when in misfortune, 544, 2 ; knowledge of, advantage of, 60, 34 ; lenses, 336, 41 ; like chameleons, 520, 42 ; like fishes in sea, 107, 3 ; like nails and like rivets, 398, 17 ; like spaniels, 398, 23 ; Marmontel's feelings towards, 164, 46 ; may come and go, 165, 29 ; members of one body, 521, 33 ; most, insolvent, 284, 26 ; never present with themselves, 521, 41 ; no class of, dispensable, 86, 19 ; no greater now than have been, 302, 19 ; not common, 115, 6 ; not helpers, but hinderers, 494, 28 ; not helpful or to be helped, 169, 23 ; of ability, now often unbelievers, 293, 27 ; of genius, under misfortune, 238, 3 ; of low and of high degree, vanity, 497, 35 ; of one pattern, 190, 3 ; of retiring timidity, 561, 13 ; of unbridled passions, helping, 536, 5 ; old, lives of, 327, 24 ; old, what should be the care of, 327, 23 ; old, without judgment of their peers, 337, 22 ; on earth as soldiers fighting in a foreign land, 155, 16 ; only distinction among, 446, 42 ; only performers, not composers, 127, 2 ; only players, not authors, 127, 1 ; ordinary, aspiring to be geniuses, 239, 6 ; put off with stories, 298, 3 ; races of, compared to leaves, 249, 49 ; seat of logic of, 64, 15 ; seducing, 477, 15 ; self-made, respect for, 90, 11 ; shadows, and shadow-hunted, 538, 29 ; soldiers, 10, 60 ; some, demi-gods, 357, 35 ; some, women, 88, 20 ; symmetrical, 276, 2 ; that are ill to manage, 472, 15 ; to act as men, 28, 37 ; to act as men now, 526, 13 ; to be afraid of, 442, 3 ; to be both men and children, 243, 25 ; to be mystified, not satisfied, 405, 56 ; to be shunned, 169, 23 ; to be weighed with merchant's scales, 265, 12 ; truly great, characteristic of, 500, 45, 46 ; two, alone worthy of honour, 503, 45 ; two levers to move, 468, 36 ; unmarried, in social relations, 508, 9 ; virtue and vice of, 541, 21 ; want of concord among, 163, 18 ; what is required of, 243, 29 ; when angels, 521, 36 ; when children, philosophy of, 542, 15 ; when just, 238, 34 ; when likest gods, 158, 42 ; when maidens sue, 544, 18 ; when more divine, 52, 29 ; when most godlike, 521, 40 ; when properly themselves, 521, 42 ; who

hope for no better life, 478, 46 ; wise, full of present, 140, 23 ; with some, personifications, 191, 28. See Les hommes, 238, 31

Men's, judgments of one another, 299, 13 ; lives, a prophecy in, 470, 1

Men-children, children only, 32, 44

Mendacious being, the one, 476, 17

Mental, disease the fatalist, 423, 42 ; diseases not to be spoken of, 260, 27

Mephistopheles' account of himself, 79, 35

Mephistopheles, character of, 128, 24 ; like cat with mouse, 117, 41 ; spirit of, 60, 1

Merchandise, a, curs'd, 52, 3

Merchant, making and counting his money, 442, 4 ; profession of, 107, 11 ; the temptation of, 13, 21 ; true-bred, as a gentleman, 22, 3

Mercury, a, not made out of any log, 97, 53

Mercy, a, to be condemned, 470, 11 ; as dealt by God, 125, 25 ; attractive power of, 28, 6 ; divine sovereignty of, 33, 18 ; effect of, on sin, 314, 17 ; God's, near, 280, 27 ; God's, universal, 128, 5 ; in a king, 301, 17 ; in every place, 478, 8 ; nobility's badge, 408, 26 ; power of, on sinner, 496, 28 ; quality of, 450, 21 ; the, required, 495. 41 ; too much, 497, 40 ; true, 500, 23 ; whereto serves, 549, 36 ; who will not show, 553, 1 ; woman's virtue, 65, 35

Merit, and good fortune united, 208, 5 ; better than descent, 173, 9 ; from use of gifts, 330, 12 ; independent of time and mode, 235, 29 ; man's highest, 266, 36 ; modest, 278, 20 ; not prior to existence, 306, 13 ; often a drawback, 234, 5 ; power of, 26, 15 ; power of, in contrast with charms, 40, 32 ; proof of superior, 226, 11 ; sufficiency of one's, 456, 15 ; the test of, 473, 26 ; unprotected, to be cherished by wealth, 244, 2 ; without fame, 101, 28 ; without modesty, 278. 20

Merriest, when men are, 488, 9

Messiah, the perpetual, 193, 43

Messias of Nature, 459, 41

Metal, native, test of a man's, 200, 47

Metamorphoses, universal, 314, 28

Metaphor, a glowing, power of, 46, 11

Metaphysic, contrasted with logic, 252, 30 ; the only intelligible, 372, 20

Metaphysics, defined, 544, 34 ; in modern literature, 175, 36 ; obscurative of truth, 201, 3 ; the utmost of, 144, 9

Method, an individual matter, 75, 17 ; economy from, 260, 38

Microcosm, each, a macrocosm, 75, 20

Microscopes, and eyes, 98, 21

Middle course, safest, 188, 4 ; 271, 56 ; 272, 1, 10

Midas *versus* Apollo, 412, 43

Midnight, morrow in, 469, 23

Might, and right, the same, 184, 30 ; measure of right, 278, 1 ; stronger than right, 78, 47 ; the. the right, 480, 26 ; without right, 112, 15

Mights, of men, the main question, 451, 44

Mighty, dependent on wise, 61, 35 ; 462, 37

Migrate, why men, 276, 23

Mildness, power of, 261, 39

Military life, fascination of, 286, 18

Milk of human kindness, 166, 7

Mills, God's, grind slow, 128, 11, 12

Millstone, a, collects no moss, 79, 29

Milton, characteristic of, 419, 44 ; music of, 445, 29 ; on his blindness, 485, 50 ; some mute inglorious, 399, 10

Mind, a degraded, lowest state of, 368, 29 ; a diseased, tender, 277, 56 ; a kingdom, 288, 10 ; a moodiness of, how to treat, 543, 3 ; a small, sign of, 202, 2 ; a vacant, 2, 13 ; a well-cultivated, 24, 53 ; a willing, 24, 58 ; alone old, 315, 31 ; an incomplete, 468, 20 ; and body, intimate connection of, 266, 28 ; and heart, methods of, different,

222, 45 ; as related to body, 122, 42 ; base, mark cf. 488, 1 ; change of, mark of wisdom, 180, 41 ; character of. to what due. 461, 20 ; celestial and divine, 541, 17 ; collision of. with mind. good, 202, 9 ; conceiving and bringing forth, 442, 14 ; creative power of, 442, 13 ; dark depths in, 1, 26 ; diseased, not to be ministered to. 35, 21 ; dormant without inspiration, 326, 24 ; dupe of heart, 223, 5 ; effect of, on the body, 488, 3 ; elation of, to be restrained, 80, 15 ; elevation of mind, without justice, 413, 7 ; fastened to a clog, 551, 43 ; fields of. to be cultivated, 51, 7 ; good, wealth of, 277, 44 ; grandeur of, condition of, 490, 9 ; greatness of, proofs of, 259, 23 ; guilty, effect of, 432, 51 ; human, march of, 441, 30 ; human, sayings about, 435, 46 ; 436, 1, 2 ; in suspense, easily swayed, 74, 9 ; little, always, 25, 26 ; little, conversing with great, 439, 25 ; lofty, good, 79, 9 ; made-up, not to be advised, 47, 55 ; makes the body rich, 111, 28 ; maturity of, and bodily decay, 507, 21 ; must be stimulated, 44, 19 ; noble, contrasted with vulgar, 79, 30 ; noblest, character of, 445, 8 ; our better, 337, 17 ; power of, on body, 202, 46 ; presence of, test of a man, 200, 47 ; sayings about the, 442, 15–28 ; strong, unconscious, 455, 33 ; the form of forms, 264, 15 ; the gentle, mark of, 429, 50 ; the great, 144, 51 ; the, in the face, 478. 12 ; the, its power of persuading itself to see what it chooses, 333, 27 ; the man, 277, 46 ; 533, 5 ; the true and sound, 459, 11 ; the truly strong, unconscious, 459, 17 ; to be kept bent, 243, 18 ; to be kept in hand, 217, 35 ; under too large obligations, 442, 12 ; without education, 510. 11 ; without, of one's own, 150, 39 ; who knows the, 552, 7 ; young and advanced, 465, 45

Minds, different pursuits of different, 67, 23 ; excellent, levity in, 471, 4 ; fearless, success of, 103, 58 ; great, characteristic of, 419, 42 ; great contrasted with little, 251, 24–26 ; great, (see **Great minds**); greatest, when they generally appear, 487, 28 ; ill at ease, 397, 32 ; little, how caught, 342, 13 ; magic of action and reaction of, 477, 1 ; occupied with small matters, 39, 24 ; old, to be kept in exercise, 327, 25 ; our, how we furnish, 524, 7 ; our, when unoccupied, 338, 34 ; strongest, unknown, 404, 11 ; the finest, 427, 43 ; thoughtful, love colour, 9, 32 ; weak, weakness of, 530, 13, 14

Minister, defined in the Hitopadesa, 143, 8 ; to live by ministering, 148, 19

Ministers, how judged, 465, 3

Ministry, a, advantage of opponents of, 480, 11 ; test of a, 490, 3

Minnow, an emblem of man, 496, 10

Minor, the desire of, 452, 28

Minorities, rights of, to protection, 131, 26

Minute, every, how to fill, 293, 4

Minuteness, reverence for, in estimate of greatness, 135, 38

Mirabeau, last words of, 241, 29 ; the greatness of, 413, 49 ; to the Marquis de Brézé, 317, 15

Miracle, a, in quest of, 547, 32 ; man the, of miracles, 522, 23 ; pet child of faith, 55, 10 ; the great indestructible, 53, 44 ; the true, 533, 7

Miracles, age of, 415, 41 ; all, how achieved, 157, 43 ; cause of, 201, 11 ; faith required for, 353, 51 ; futility of, without spiritual sense, 175, 2 ; how wrought still, 32, 3 ; no longer, 3, 11 ; of Christ, 442, 29 ; the source of, 340, 7

Mirror, objects in a, 86, 37 ; the best, 417, 47

Mirth, and melancholy, correlated, 482, 27 ; hard to feign, in sorrow, 67, 30 ; most, only apparent, 284, 28 ; power of, 114, 9 ; string attuned to, 478, 23 ; unfelt, hard to feign, 154. 32 ; unreasonable, 508, 23 ; violent, 514. 34

Misanthropist at forty, 554, 17

Mischief, joy in, 294, 35 ; not to be spoken, 271, 52 ; origin of all, 10, 4 ; past and prosper'd, 243, 6 ; past, mourning, 494, 36

Misconception, purposed, evil of, 488, 28

Miser, and his losses, 13, 44 ; Dryden to the, 124, 48 ; his only right act, 24, 36 ; mind of, 538, 34 ; passion of, joyless, 222, 34 ; sayings about the, 442, 30, 31 ; the, his wants, 410, 14 ; who dies rich, 13, 23

Miserable, apology for being, 487, 15 ; only medicine of, 442, 32

Miseries, cure for all, 562, 42 ; happiness at others', 181, 27 ; our greatest, 340, 1 ; past, recollection of, 213, 58

Misers, compared with moles. 282, 12 ; greedy, rail at sordid, 136, 8 ; that gloat over their money, 483, 4

Misery, a cause of, 200, 42 ; a man's, from within, 485, 34 ; a widespread cause of, 284, 30 ; always exaggerated, 330, 5 ; another's, no matter of sport, 474, 23 ; cause of all, 494, 5 ; enduring, 370, 16 ; fatal prevailing source of, 333, 26 ; in, God's help seen, 205, 17 ; inconsistent with occupation, 307, 27 ; not to be laughed at, 180, 8 ; of man, the source of, 442, 33 ; our own making, 314, 36 ; plaint of, to be listened to, 116, 28 ; sacred even to gods, 111, 4 ; to-morrow's, not to be forestalled, 529, 5

Misfortune, a second master, 259, 1 ; and wisdom, 54, 33 ; as a school, 68, 45 ; badge of innocence, 87, 38 ; blessed, 27, 54 ; Burns under blows of, 167, 23 ; but one, for man, 110, 18 ; effect of, on understanding, 192, 6 ; greatest, 432, 25 ; how to face, 293, 2 ; indispensable to man, 136, 33 ; never alone. 298, 27 ; not to be thy maid, 296, 40 ; one, vigil of another, 333, 7 ; one's own, and others', 171, 40 ; others', admonitory, 31, 57 ; scene of a, avoided, 88, 26 ; self-caused, 41, 16 ; suggestion of, in joy, 522, 2 ; sure to come some day, 36, 47 ; talked of not disagreeable, 59, 32 ; temptation of, 186, 48 ; the greatest, 318, 25 ; the one, for a man, 471, 16 ; the parent of, 368, 16 ; a misnomer, 476, 29

Misfortunes. another's, easily borne, 168, 10 ; as a source of talk, 7, 33 ; best to forget, 181, 8 ; how lightened, 17, 20 ; in spite of, enough, 477, 2 ; not always evil, 386, 38 ; not believed in, till they come, 317, 10 ; not to be repined over, 112, 41 ; of others, easy to bear, 317, 6 ; our greatest, source of, 338, 9 ; our own and other's, 433, 18 ; our own, not the heaviest, 176, 6 ; our worst, 340, 1 ; to be boldly faced, 502, 52 ; variable, 281, 13 ; when to bewail, 569, 20 ; women's, self-made, 165, 33

Misgovernment, evil of, 261, 10 ; sophistical, dilemma on which it rests, 139, 18

Misled, the, what is due to, 496, 8

Mismanagement, doomed, 374, 24 ; not for ever, 480, 41, 46

Mist, how to escape a, 193, 52

Mistake, a general, 417, 38 ; throttling of one, inconsiderable, 550, 18 ; Wellington's protestation against, 473, 27

Mistakes, and discovery, 525, 15 ; every one makes, 180, 19 ; hard to correct and sift, 553, 34 ; root of all great, 187, 12 ; to be eschewed, 296, 11

Mistrust, treason. 414, 18

Misunderstanding, inevitable, 395, 11

Misunderstood, to be, a bitterness, 490, 29

Mob, described, 27, 46 ; Emerson's definition of, 13, 50 ; in a civilised nation, 420, 32 ; sentiments of, 300, 9 ; suffrages of. Horace on, 309, 25 ; the, a scare to poet, 322, 8 ; the fickle, 67, 7 ; the, sayings about, 442. 36–39

Mob-tumults, Goethe's uneasiness at, 164, 33

Mode, set, tendency to, 205, 45 ; the origin and character of, 65, 36

Moderation, an impregnable fortress, 112, 54 ; exceeding, 492, 45 ; in living, 334, 44 ; the good in, 23, 48 ; with a clear sky, 279, 50

Modern society *versus* Christianity, 43, 5

Moderns, and ancients, teachings compared, 416, 7 ; the, contrasted with Greeks, 432, 45

Modes, ridiculous, 376, 42

Modesty, a virtue of the low-born, 319, 17 ; as a virtue, 48, 55 ; as an ornament, 432, 33 ; as covering self-conceit, 168, 24 ; commended, 27, 48 ; contrast with loquacity, 253, 17 ; dead, 7, 34 ; divorced from truth, 536, 31 ; false, 100, 44, 45 ; in youth, 4, 41 ; misconstrued, 350, 1 ; more majestic than strength, 249, 14 ; necessity of, 300, 41 ; not promoted, 114, 50 ; of nature not to be overstepped, 406, 25 ; ornament, but drawback, 28, 21 ; the prohibitions of, 367, 14 ; true and false, 500, 24 ; Virgil's, 293, 39 ; want of, 313, 42

Mole, as oracle, 72, 14

Molière, Boileau of, 180, 37 ; inscription on his bust, 397, 2

Moment, a, capacity of, 523, 15 ; birth of a, 160, 27 ; both a cradle and a grave, 443, 1 ; claim of, 523, 12 ; divine, in a man's life, 70, 8 ; each, nearer death, 40, 2 ; event of a, 2, 40 ; every, instructive, 92, 40 ; every, of infinite value, 92, 45 ; last, exaggerated, 443, 49 ; passing, to be noted well, 321, 32 ; power of a, 19, 35 ; present, to be seized, 136, 12 ; 208, 8 ; that may become eternal, 442, 42 ; the, difficult to square with, 86, 8 ; the greatest, in life, 481, 38 ; the passing, value of, 537, 24 ; the present, 449, 11, 12 ; value of, 519, 15 ; value of every, 212, 15

Moments, decisive power of, 334, 7

Monarch, great, a mark of, 88, 37 ; of all I survey, 164, 44 ; sacredness of, 21, 8

Monarchies, how ruined, 239, 24 ; the fate of, 374, 4

Monarchs, fear of change perplexes, 103, 50

Monarchy, a, the likely fate of, 13, 53 ; absolute, one objection to, 167, 24 ; expensiveness of its trappings, 458, 17 ; Schopenhauer on, 65, 37

Money, a blessing and bane, 104, 33 ; a passport, 222, 28 ; alienating effect of, 27, 17 ; all it breeds, 52, 49 ; as servant and master, 222, 29 ; best use of, 418, 7 ; blood and life, 88, 42 ; by whom most needed, 304, 30 ; chief value and virtue of, 420, 8 ; collecting means, in a civilised nation, 420, 32 ; definition of, 530, 19 ; despising, 344, 23 ; does not feed men, 294, 44 ; effect of being with or without, 46, 12 ; either slave or tyrant, 183, 30 ; enjoyed by few, 513, 22 ; given in alms on good security, 344, 53 ; indispensable, 2, 42 ; lending, as a means of living, 274, 40 ; lending, risk in, 364, 30 ; loss of, bitter, 316, 38 ; loss of, lament over, 260, 12 ; loss of, misery from, 350, 2 ; love of, 49, 57 ; making, innocence of, 274, 21 ; man with, or without, 46, 12 ; master, if not servant, 173, 21 ; more powerful than love, 14, 3 ; 254, 14 ; breeds only money, 44, 13 ; no respect without, 127, 40 ; not to be covetous of, 309, 30 ; persuasiveness of, 332, 33 ; persuasive power of, 28, 6 ; power of, 14, 47 ; 19, 29 ; 23, 31 ; 23, 36 ; 88, 7, 9 ; 119, 30–32 ; 173, 22 ; 246, 8 ; 299, 21 ; 314, 8 ; 537, 36 ; 555, 13 ; public, like holy water, 165, 36 ; ready, eloquence of, 376, 45 ; ready, value of, 17, 53 ; Ruskin's definition of, 10, 5 ; sayings about, 119, 30–32 ; splendour in use, 318, 34 ; terror of not making, 434, 26 ; the love of, 440, 2 ; the question in regard to, 503, 30 ; want of, brings care, 14, 56 ; who want to borrow, 480, 21

Money-bag with holes, 209, 16

Moneyed man, attendant of, 28, 6

Moneyless man, 19, 28

Money-makers and money-spenders, 277, 9

Monk, danger of offending a, 27, 27

Monomania, often unperceived, 268, 24

Monument, who deserve a, 482, 36 ; who should have no, 305, 8

Mood, the right, to be seized, 294, 34

Moods belong to man alone, 291, 14

Moon, and its light for all, 443, 2 ; dispensable, 174, 33 ; the, that shine in Paradise, 564, 19 ; when the sun is there, 383, 38

Moonlight sleeps upon this bank, 162, 38

Moral, a, to be brief, 547, 16 ; achievement of man, 533, 38 ; conduct, second great rule of, 431, 34 ; energy, contrasted with brilliant parts, 191, 11 ; perfection, minimum state of, 334, 31 ; qualities, not enough, 105, 51 ; sentiment, only school of, 446, 16 ; sentiment, the atmosphere of, 416, 33

Morality, a too austere, 226, 19 ; aim of all, 415, 44 ; and civilisation, 43, 39 ; and religion, 371, 37 ; 372, 32 ; as it now is, Shelley on, 371, 35 ; contrasted with religions, 467, 13 ; department of philosophy, 507, 33 ; dependence of, on faith, 100, 12 ; implies religion, 175, 29 ; independent of the religion, 121, 42 ; national, no, without religion, 369, 22 ; not moral philosophy, our want, 203, 34 ; of some, in remnants, 443, 7 ; sum of, 493, 15 ; the laws of, 438, 26 ; true, 500, 25 ; true, the condition of, 357, 12 ; vital, first condition of, 481, 44 ; without religion, 522, 39

Morals, and art, rules in, compared, 188, 15, 16 ; cultivated by love, 484, 22 ; genesis of, 267, 42 ; good-will everything in, 60, 9 ; in youth, moulding, 97, 1 ; our teacher in, 521, 20 ; rooted in fear, 188, 17 ; straight in, alone right, 534, 21 ; the new, 189, 43 ; to be made attractive, 523, 11

More, Sir T., fruitlessness of his teachings, 314, 34

More's "Utopia," 331, 27

Morn, advancing, with rosy steps, 317, 36 ; in russet mantle, 253, 4 ; the breath of, 408, 23

Morning, a fresh, frosty, exercise in, 534, 16 ; how to use the, 401, 38 ; only a, in all things, 180, 28 ; summons of every, 212, 8 ; the first hour of, 428, 22 ; the value of, 191, 8, 9

Mortality never taken home by us, 9, 70

Mortals, fate of, Virgil on, 335, 58

Moses compared with Galen and Justinian, 55, 15

Moth, the, desire of, for the star, 423, 11

Mother, a priestess, 252, 46 ; among children Goethe on, 475, 33 ; as teacher limited, 383, 8 ; busy, and daughter, 259, 43 ; devotion of a, not thrown away, 305, 25 ; effect of scream of, on child, 333, 45 ; fondness of, 3, 4 ; in the home, effect of, 548, 35 ; Lord Langdale on his, 174, 39 ; love of a, 321, 8 ; one good, value of, 332, 25 ; the good, 430, 40 ; the power of, 429, 38 ; venerableness of a, 333, 9 ; who feels ennui, 415, 19

Mother's, care, despising, 494, 19 ; heart, 444, 13, 14 ; kiss, power of a, 219, 29 ; secret hope, 568, 40

Mother-grace, the, 444, 11

Mothers, good, value of, 537, 30 ; knowledge peculiar to, 319, 18 ; sad-hearted, while we sleep, 550, 17

Mother-tongue in a foreign land, 322, 9

Mother-wit, and false theology, 422, 26 ; better than learning, 15, 66

Motive, everything, 163, 7 ; the principal thing, 243, 1

Motives, essential to man, 127, 14 ; human, the two great, 129, 2 ; man sure of his, 551, 38

Motley, the, in every one, 524, 21

Mountain, a, in labour, 342, 9 ; beyond every, 27, 11 ; every, has its valley, 325, 45 ; scenery, impressiveness of, 485, 27

Mountains, high, a feeling, 167, 39 ; never meet, 115, 9

Mourning, the most demonstrative, 318, 18

Mouth shut, but eyes open, 43, 50

Move, one false, effect of, 332, 15

Movement, the principle of, 375, 7

Movements, all great, enthusiastic, 91, 12 ; backward, advance, 470, 15

Multitude, difficulty in teaching, 423, 36 ; faith of the, 509, 29 ; not to be followed, 108, 16 ; sayings about the, 444, 20, 23, 24

Murder, one, *versus* millions, 333, 10 ; punishment of, a necessity, 95, 6 ; sacrilegious, 46, 27 ; will speak, 110, 24

Muses, the, power of, 444, 25

Mushrooms, lowly, cared for, 146, 55

Music, a becoming, and vehicle of emotion, 249, 47 ; a characteristic of, 507, 52 ; all-relatedness of, 244, 31 ; compared with poetry, 351, 6 ; dependent on tone, 39, 6 ; effect of, 543, 43 ; effect of words on, 546, 45 ; elevated sensation of, 443, 41 ; everywhere in nature, 384, 29 ; good, effect of, 424, 38 ; hard to collect into a distinct idea, 445, 7 ; health to soul, 215, 33 ; human, 265, 23 ; in all things, 478, 9 ; in orchestra, interpreter of, 206, 29 ; in the heart, 444, 26 ; key to female heart, 287, 25 ; like softest, to attending ears, 162, 33 ; Luther's esteem for, 297, 45 ; Luther on skill in, 554, 16 ; marching to, 332, 42 ; mediocre, 466, 32 ; moral effect of, 548, 38 ; of men's lives, 162, 35 ; Plato's definition of, 444, 17 ; pleasure we feel in, 448, 7 ; possibility of, 471, 5 ; power of, 543, 36 ; power of, to change nature, 317, 2 ; quickening power of, 277, 27 ; spiritual, how produced, 401, 46 ; sweet, effect of, 164, 47 ; the demonic in, 423, 3 ; the food of love, 173, 23 ; the most heaven-affecting, 324, 21 ; the sphere of, 81, 33 ; the sweetest, 456, 32 ; the true universal speech, 287, 26 ; true, 500, 26 ; nobly non-utilitarian, 226, 22

" **Must**," God's, youth's answer to, 395, 19

Must, hard nut to crack, 287, 27

Mysteries, Divine, not to be meddled with, 204, 1 ; made matters of reason, 525, 4

Mystery, a higher, wise man unwilling to unveil, 507, 17 ; a, not to be spoken of mysteriously, 402, 4 ; abode of faith, 100, 24 ; and vice or roguery, 548, 26 ; fascination of, 284, 22 ; for whose benefit, 53, 35 ; significance of, 506, 3 ; supposed a sign of evil, 548, 39

Mystics, enthusiastic, 443, 43

Myth, a, not a lie, 296, 10

Mythology, significance of, 296, 10

Myths of fables, the, 492, 34

N

Nae luck aboot the hoose, 111, 20

Nail, worth of a, 187, 8

Name, a, better make, than inherit, 169, 32 ; a good, 6, 50 ; a good, security of, 44, 12 ; a good, worth of, 31, 46 ; a great, magic in, 470, 7 ; a, too soon famous, 533, 24 ; ambition for a, 14, 20 ; but sound and smoke, 119, 26 ; good, in man and woman, 129, 55 ; good, loss of, 105, 56 ; ill, easily got, 289, 15 ; my good, he that filches, 146, 15 ; virtuous, prized, 24, 44 ; what's in a, 540, 11

Namelessness of many things, 284, 11

Names, and virtues, different sources of, 116, 15 ; great, what they stand for, 134, 38

Naming, difficulty of, 532, 7

Naples, Bay of, Mme. de Staël on, 173, 14

Napoleon, Carlyle on, 440, 37 ; of his generals, 167, 50 ; tired of Europe, 223, 11

Napoleon III., career of, 180, 35

Narrow, circle, effect of, on mind, 184, 20 ; way, to be chosen, 305, 5 ; world, bestriding like a Colossus, 555, 12

Narrowing, a necessity for both God and man, 127, 24

Narrowness, a, not possible now, 201, 53

Narrow-souled people, like narrow-necked bottles, 207, 35

Nation, a rich and happy, 14, 32 ; a, strength of, 482, 50 ; a talkative, 345, 16 ; a truly free, 414, 1 ; and its honour, 444, 30 ; Bible of a, 492, 4 ; biography of, 418, 26 ; character of, not in its fine folks, 419, 39 ; civilised, constituents of a, 420, 32 ; composed of actors, 289, 44 ; first period of, 428, 28 ; genius of, 471, 29 ; history of, a Bible, 418, 24 ; how governed, 444, 29 ; life of, Ruskin on, 438, 51 ; narrow stand for a great, 414, 27 ; no reforming, by " tremendous cheers," 305, 28 ; proverbs of a, 450, 2 ; a, secret of destiny of, 319, 23 ; that can't defend itself deserving of being destroyed, 175, 32 ; that does not stake its all on its honour, 298, 24 ; that is indestructible, 305, 26 ; that cannot retrograde, 421, 38 ; the first and second power of a, 428, 30 ; treatment by, of its greatest men, 239, 20 ; true mind of, how to know, 459, 1 ; wealth without intelligence ruin to, 305, 27 ; what creates a, 193, 26 ; what determines destiny of, 423, 13 ; whence the good of a, 117, 40

National, character found among the peasantry, 266, 9 ; good, self-derived, 314, 48 ; greatness condition of, 477, 35 ; life without epoch, 475, 3

Nationality, characteristics of, 7, 35 ; compared with individuality, 193, 24

Nations, and their most eminent men, 176, 4 ; basis of, character of, with posterity, 541, 20 ; cause of hostility of, 229, 28 ; distances and divisions of, how to measure, 423, 48 ; effect of modesty on, 193, 27 ; glory of, 443, 37 ; great, characteristic of, 133, 18 ; in, head before heart, 13, 54 ; law of welfare of, 232, 45 ; leprosy in, Church source of, 544, 29 ; that navigate most, 443, 34 ; to ingraft new ideas on, 491, 11 ; vicissitudes of, 81, 37 ; wisdom of, 462, 28

Native, land, a man's connection with, 288, 33 ; land, its fascinating power, 295, 39 ; land, love for, 32, 25 ; land, want of for, 168, 41 ; soil, dear, 343, 29

Natural, as source of good, 298, 16 ; effect of desiring to appear, 316, 36 ; graceful, 92, 50 ; never shameful, 337, 3 ; symbolic, 92, 51 ; the, a mark of, 541, 1 ; things, without shame, 290, 17

Naturalist, requirements in, 262, 2

Nature, a great, development of, 142, 55 ; a whole, 173, 25 ; against, against God, 535, 40 ; all, unknown art, 10, 7 ; an enigma, till solved in and by man, 94, 27 ; and art at one, 290, 3 ; and her secrets, 508, 20 ; and man, 549, 13 ; and man, distinction between, 424, 1 ; and necessity barriers, 170, 7 ; and wisdom at one, 318, 47 ; as a judge, 389, 11 ; as felt by experience, 94, 32 ; as regards God, 66, 2 ; aims of, 66, 3 ; as seen by intellect, 94, 32 ; at bottom, 482, 12 ; at heart, music, 384, 29 ; be, your teacher, 44, 44 ; cheerful lesson of, 564, 20 ; circular power in, 472, 7, 31 ; cruelty in, 20, 44 ; cursed, as breeding ingratitude, 403, 40 ; diseased, oftentimes breaks forth, 69, 13 ; effect of contact with, in our city estimates, 21, 30 ; errorless, 18, 44 ; everything in, of one stuff, 94, 24 ; fashioned him, then broke the mould, 290, 5 ; filling the sails, 544, 30 ; full of milk of human kindness, 486, 5 ; gave sign of woe, 75, 46 ; gift of, to man, 264, 9 ; God's body, 9, 6 ; her carefulness and her carelessness, 394, 47 ; her gifts out of love, 528, 7 ; her means, 249, 31 ; how perfected, 404, 12 ; how to regard our, 523, 16 ; im-

partial, 5, 16 ; in smallest things, 498, 1 ; in the smallest, untameable, 5, 49 ; inanimate, way from, to spirit, 198, 45 ; inferior to grace, 131, 34 ; inferior to spirit, 454, 35 ; infinite vastness of, to the wisest, 496, 17 ; inner secret of, impenetrable, 194, 42 ; inexpugnable, 176, 7 ; judgment of, effect of time on, 486, 33 ; just, 226, 28 ; laws of, God's thoughts, 232, 7 ; life of, defined, 53, 34 ; lore of, our treatment of, 408, 24 ; love of, for her children, 219, 53 ; made up of negative and positive, 94, 26 ; makes no leaps, 290, 10 ; more potent than will, 480, 35 ; my goddess, 483, 42 ; never without a purpose, 290, 9 ; no beating back, 40, 36 ; no blank or trifle in, 301, 13 ; no caprices in, 475, 12 ; no coercing, 73, 14 ; no driving out, 290, 18 ; no fixtures in, 467, 30 ; no solitude in, 474, 20 ; not affected by greater or less, 260, 16 ; not to be baulked, 72, 41 ; not to be coerced, 538, 11 ; not to be extinguished, only repressed, 528, 33 ; not to be grasped, 560, 9 ; nothing seen isolated in, 527, 25 ; office of prophet of, 198, 24 ; omnipotent, 241, 46 ; one throughout, 287, 28 ; one touch of, 334, 28 ; one whole, 199, 1 ; one's, denying, 432, 29 ; our feeling for, 508, 25 ; outer shell of, showing, 194, 42 ; partial to cross-breedings, 226, 27 ; path of, narrowness of, 447, 9 ; perception of, 488, 36 ; pity and rigour of, 193, 51 ; pleasure of study of, 475, 9 ; pleasures of, 470, 17 ; secret of our mastery over, 206, 39 ; secrets of, not to be forced, 119, 29 ; self-imitative, 226, 29 ; self-imparting, 391, 11 ; surpasses art, 104, 51 ; teaching of, 332, 39 ; testimony of, *versus* learned arguments, 511, 16 ; the aims of, 66, 3 ; the book of, 418, 48 ; the course of, 421, 41 ; the course of, only partially known, 421, 42 ; the favourite of, 264, 9 ; the first step of, 392, 10 ; the law of, 438, 20, 27, 28 ; the living garment of God, 321, 29 ; the masterpiece of, 6, 9 ; the riddle of, 507, 6 ; the spirit of, 401, 42 ; the truths of, 459, 23 ; those to whom she reveals herself, 335, 21 ; through, up to Nature's God, 393, 31 ; to be humoured, 243, 21 ; too noble for world, 157, 6 ; unchallengeable, 2, 51 ; unhinged by gold, 162, 19 ; unwillingly dragged to light, 519, 11 ; whole sense of, where found, 301, 48 ; without danger or restraint, 497, 25 ; without the poet, 539, 40 ; wonders of, at hand, 186, 36 ; world of, mirrored in man, 465, 6
Natures, finest, flaws in, 427, 40 ; good by disdaining as well as attaining, 85, 37 ; great, two kinds of, 467, 26 ; our, like oil, 338, 40 ; sad, tolerance of, 379, 13
Navigators, ablest, fortunate, 462, 25
Nay, a woman's, worth of, 141, 43
Near, key to far, 444, 34 ; not sought in far off, 462, 38 ; the, 445, 12 ; the, neglected, 367, 9
Nearest, the, often far off, 54, 20
Neatness a virtue, 526, 27
Necessary, the barely, indispensable, 535, 44
Necessities sterner than hopes, 444, 38
Necessity, a teacher, 285, 39, 43 ; all-powerful, 14, 33 ; and fancy, 101, 46 ; and free will hostile, 95, 13 ; and law, power of, 121, 57 ; and Nature barriers, 170, 7 ; as a weapon, 194, 12 ; basis of all, 10, 56 ; earnest aspect of, 84, 40 ; from habit, 138, 11 ; hard to wield, 74, 35 ; her allotments, 5, 12 ; owns no holiday, 104, 39 ; how to anticipate, 152, 19 ; how to more than conquer, 523, 8 ; in relation to strength, 417, 25 ; its pressure beneficial, 267, 32 ; its strength, 315, 10 ; law for all but man, 8, 55 ; man in relation to, 12, 64 ; mother of invention, 276, 56 ; ground of existence, 94, 44 ; our master, 58, 18 ; power of, 313, 32-34 ; 231, 34 ; praised as virtue, 231, 3 ; rebel of all laws, 103, 42 ; ring of, always at the top, 250, 12 ; ring of, ring of duty, 140, 10 ;

superior to Nature, 292, 11 ; yoke of, to be borne, 175, 31
Need, a bitter, at present, 472, 6 ; and wish, 105, 2 ; man's first, 204, 14 ; our prime one, 568, 29
Needle, to pole, 395, 32
Negation, mere, unfruitful, 116, 18 ; the end of opposition, 425, 8 ; opposed to activity, 94, 5
Negations, taking safety under, 203, 2
Negative principle, the importance of, 191, 15
Negatives, deprecated, 71, 37
Neglect, a little, dangerous, 8, 42, 47, 49
Negligence, one, fatal, 169, 33
Negro, Fuller on, 436, 19
Neighbour's, our, prosperity and poverty, 449, 47
Neighbours, their value to us, 522, 40
Nelson's signal at Trafalgar, 82, 43
Nemesis on the alert, 381, 21
Neptune's trident, 235, 26
Nero, on signing a death-warrant, 512, 1
Nerves, the man, 444, 42
Nescience greater than science, 382, 31
Nest, one's own, beautiful, 4, 37
Nest-life, echo of, audible only in sorrow, 424, 37
Net, while fisher sleeps, 89, 5
Nets, useless where no fish, 82, 28
Nettle, how to handle, 121, 40 ; stroking a, 484, 37
Never, a long while, 38, 5
New, a precedent some day, 328, 27 ; age, a, want of, 426, 22 ; and old, discretion in regard to, 28, 16 ; and old, the conflict of, characterised, 421, 24 ; its appearance and effects of, 541, 2 ; foil, to old, 183, 13 ; in science and morals, 189, 43 ; nothing, in life, 315, 29 ; reproduction of old, or forgotten, 180, 15, 16 ; seldom good, 183, 12 ; the, and the valuable, 537, 29 ; the, how to employ, 243, 44 ; the, still but in birth pangs, 424, 15 ; unexpected quarter it comes from, 430, 46 ; year's, a, greeting, 240, 29
News, good and bad, 402, 44 ; only teller of, 446, 21
Newspaper, literature, Goethe on, 333, 41 ; the influential, Emerson on, 207, 38
Newspapers, Napoleon's dread of, 114, 1 ; our fortresses, 191, 35
News-writer, highest reach of, 435, 9
New Testament, revelation in, 375, 13
Newton, on his own worth, 172, 26
Nicknames, good, effect of, 306, 25
Niggard, always poor, 159, 5 ; contrasted with generous, 24, 7
Night, a long, 370, 18 ; and morning, rule for, 406, 28 ; cause of, to man, 76, 4 ; counsel by, 226, 30 ; deeds of, 536, 4 ; last in the train of, 99, 53 ; sayings on the, 444, 45-49 ; 445, 1 ; sober-suited matron, 44, 39 ; the darkest, followed by day, 55, 24
Nightingale, the, Milton on, 408, 21
Nights, drowsy, how to have, 176, 31
Nimbleness, contrasted with haste, 141, 5
Nimrod, the, of this era, 450, 40
Nineteenth century, the enthusiasm of, 245, 18
Nirvana, 313, 15 ; road to, 444, 40
"No," a surly, honest fellow, 302, 37 ; from merely saying, no good, 116, 18 ; power of saying, as a sign, 309, 16 ; to be deliberate, 337, 1
No, man indispensable, 180, 3 ; one called happy before death, 63, 34 ; the way to yea, 319, 22 ; value of learning to say, 236, 6
Noah's ark, mouldy rolls of, 308, 15
Nobility, a man's, a test of, 368, 14 ; a sure mark of, 234, 34 ; and virtue, of kin, 242, 6 ; appendix to, 170, 35 ; at its origin, 10, 8 ; source of, 308, 7 ; in mind, 76, 53 ; mark of true, 425, 17 ; of race, mark of, 184, 21 ; of soul, and of birth, 55, 28 ; our old, to be preserved, 244, 1 ; oldest and only true, 445, 33 ; the beginning of, 190, 22 ; the

only, 488, 39 ; true, essence of, 426, 2 ; true, its origin, 500, 27

Noble, and vulgar, self-estimates of, 461, 10 ; birth, proof of, 391, 21 ; blood, humble, 213, 4 ; descent, value of, 171, 11 ; heart, attractive power of, 385, 22 ; how men become, 190, 31 ; man, and danger, 532, 15 ; man, defined, 60, 22 ; mind, mark of, 491, 44 ; only, to be good, 163, 5 ; people, loyalty of, 15, 52 ; qualities, non-transferable, 484, 10 ; silent ones, of world, 465, 10 ; soul, proved in difficulty, 186, 3 ; souls, power of, 508, 112 ; the, appreciation of, 53, 31 ; 489, 36 ; the, defined, 484, 26 ; 53^, 38 ; the, great, 309, 48 ; the, in death, 445, ? to keep with noble, 203, 1 ; words for shield of, 116, 36

Nobleman, a definition of, 360, 39 ; a degenerate, 50^, 25 ; defined, 143, 38 ; qualities of a, 380, 27

Nobleness, attribute of all, 10, 32 ; its derivation, 319, 29 ; refining power of, 16, 16 ; test of, 76, 52 ; the idea of, 184, 25

Nobles, born, 304, 9

Nod *versus* rod, 15, 55

Noise, music in distance, 268, 37 ; not might, 14, 31 ; of things deafening, 232, 51

Noises, encourager of, 431, 6

Nomadism, evil of, 346, 29

Non-being, no step in nature to, 517, 24

Non-existent rather than ignoble, 29, 35

Nonsense, consecration of, 523, 18 ; daring, 53, 19 ; in rhyme, 235, 43 ; no objection in, 167, 31 ; refreshing, 166, 9

No-progress men to be debarred public highways, 450, 8

Northern star, constant as, 164, 39

Nose, big, and handsome face, 210, 20

Noses, counting, to ascertain truth, 398, 27 ; long, Napoleon's partiality for, 544, 1 ; the length of, 472, 14

Nothing, absolute, 2, 21 ; blessed in every respect, 299, 3 ; extenuate, 400, 48 ; for ever, 510, 29 ; for nothing, 330, 1 ; from nothing, 58, 34 ; 97, 16 ; of nothing, 24, 3 ; only once in the world, 476, 8 ; perishes, 328, 17 ; they that do, 479, 39

Novel, every, debtor to Homer, 93, 5

Novels, their unreality, 378, 1 ; writers of, and double wrong they do, 563, 42

Novelty, charm of, 87, 28 ; desire for, 179, 35 ; love of, a ruling passion, 324, 36 ; man's itch for, 87, 16 ; people's delight in, 205, 12 ; undue charm of, 536, 37

Now, the, 445, 12

Numbers, I lisp'd in, 21, 18 ; round, 378, 17

Nurse, influence of, 3, 13

Nursery, training in, 443, 50

O

Oak, felled by blows of little axe, 269, 44 ; when it falls, 445, 14

Oak-tree, when it falls and when it is planted, 545, 45

Oarsmen and steersman, 567, 27

Oath, powerless in domain of reason, 324, 26 ; that does not bind, 305, 35

Oaths, but straws, 110, 29 ; oracles, 157, 19 ; straw to passion, 455, 39

Obedience, blind, 55, 9 ; for those who can't rule, 243, 7 ; imperative, 541, 27 ; must be free, 204, 12 ; not sacrifice, 45, 48 ; Shelley on, 354, 46 ; source of all virtues, 116, 14 ; that is easy, 207, 20 ; the key to freedom, 96, 22 ; the virtue in, 364, 8 ; to heaven, how learned, 449, 1 ; true, 500, 28 ; true, virtue of, 306, 44 ; two kinds of,

490, 13 ; value of, 10, 42 ; virtue of Christianity, 403, 34 ; when to be enforced, 171, 33

Obeisance, time for, 207, 11

Obeyed, how to be cheerfully, 176, 32

Obeying and governing, 203, 15

Obeys, who, and who commands, 151, 49

Object, and expression, 527, 26 ; greatest in universe and a greater, 432, 26

Objects, all, windows into the infinite, 10, 9

Obligation, haste in discharging, 490, 25 ; limit to, 505, 7

Oblivion, the condition of memory, 176, 16 ; the cormorant, 421, 35

Obscure, the, defined, 445, 23

Obscurity, cause of, 209, 45 ; cause of, in writer, 205, 2 ; contentment with, commended, 236, 1 ; in an author, relative, 149, 8 ; patience of, a duty, 343, 13

Obsequiousness, advantage of, 323, 32

Observation, Burns on lack of, 464, 42 ; much, effect of, 285, 23 ; to precede judgment, 27, 47 ; vigilant, effect of, 92, 31 ; want of, 109, 49 ; 143, 23 ; width of, commended, 242, 30

Observed of all observers, 322, 32

Observer, a fine, characteristic of, 541, 4 ; an acute, 144, 49 ; great, a, 7, 3

Obsolete to the pot, 169, 42

Obstacles, glory in overcoming, 443, 20 ; also stepping-stones, 418, 39

Obstinacy, 1, 12 ; slavery, 15, 54

Obvious, the, ignorance of, 536, 45

Occasions, great, source of, 133, 7

Occupation, absence of, 2, 13 ; blessing of, 307, 27 ; constant, moral effect of, 46, 57 ; necessity, duty, and pleasure, 291, 7 ; sharpening effect of, 90, 3 ; want of, a plague, 461, 16

Occupa'ions, mechanical, 441, 42

Ocean, beating of, 445, 24

Offence, an, which we pardon, 330, 34 ; and punishment, disproportionate effect of, 547, 31 ; every, at first, 93, 6 ; giving and appeasing, 201, 28 ; inclination to give, 124, 16 ; none free from, 304, 14 ; not soon forgotten, 50, 51 ; pardon of, bringing under obligation, 446, 45 ; rising above, 543, 6 ; taking, 21, 27

Offences, at my beck, 467, 22

Offender, and offended, as regards memory of offence, 42, 19 ; never forgives, 146, 4 ; the, unforgiving, 42, 18–32

Offers, extravagant, denials, 325, 27

Office, a kind, natural to one, 331, 47 ; effect of, on character, 259, 5 ; high, slavery of, 554, 1 ; just pride of, 212, 2 ; testing power of, 17, 32 ; unfitness for, 179, 19 without pay, a temptation, 14, 10

Official, duty of, 170, 3

Officious, the, mischievous, 161, 35

Offspring, unworthy, boast of, 509, 12

Old, and new, discretion in regard to, 28, 16 ; and new, the conflict of, characterised, 421, 24 ; few know how to be, 105, 17 ; harness, better die in, 29, 21 ; how first appreciated, 183, 13 ; I love everything that's, 167, 42 ; idolatry of the, 523, 13 ; maid's tongues, 64, 5 ; man, an, just beginning to live, 365, 39 ; man in a house, 15, 58 ; man, one misery of, an, 333, 29 ; man, only old despicable, 299, 22 ; man, sayings of, 118, 35 ; men, and their good advice, 239, 33 ; men, beauty of, 430, 14 ; men, errors of, 425, 29 ; men, failing of, 198, 18 ; oak, twist out of, 209, 3 ; people, borne with, 265, 32 ; people, talk of, 238, 39 ; people, who forget their age, 234, 30 ; superseded by new, 445, 30 ; the, death of, 445, 29 ; the, extolled, 513, 38 ; the, once new, 328, 27 ; the, passed away, 424, 15 ; to know how to grow, 493, 32 ; what never grows, 535, 20

Old age, a burden, 132, 46 ; a peaceful, how to

attain, 177, 33; a regret, 568, 42; a time of folly, 83, 58; a weakness of, 199, 51, 52; a worn out, cause of, 245, 43; advance of, 74, 21; an anxiety of, 466, 1; and faults of youth, 527, 7; and its wrinkles, 228, 16; and memory, 225, 38; approach of, unfelt, 310, 2; benefit of knowledge to, 220, 31; beyond astonishment, 188, 34; chief characteristic of, 69, 24; desire of, 147, 42; discomforts of, 285, 50; folly and jesting unseemly in, 161, 31; Goethe on, 6, 22; grief in, 192, 41; hard to bear, 78, 31; hoarding, 213, 2; hoped for, yet dreaded, 224, 6; its sadness, 537, 40; only ornament of, 446, 11; prepared by a noble life, 542, 23; respect formerly for, 259, 12; Seneca on, 16, 8; the disappointment of, 190, 19; the dotage of, 386, 44; the ills of, 361 33; the temper of, 362, 1; those who grow virtuous in, 544, 25; time of astonishment, 182, 25; to limit itself, 445, 32; undesired, 91, 51; weakness of, 516, 36; weaknesses of, 275, 43

Oldest, not always best experienced, 298, 6
Once, better than never, 81, 20; no custom, 77, 31
One, power of, to infect all, 136, 13; see, see all, 384, 32; thing, engrossment with, 168, 37
One's, own, how a thing is made, 313, 50; own, negatively defined, 121, 45; own, right to, 330, 43; self, to be sought within, 293, 19; self, fighting with and conquering, 391, 12
Onward, ever, 183, 15
Openness of mind, indispensable in discussion, 147, 13
Opinion, advantage of wide range of, 223, 14; and force in government, 112, 16; as a guide, 34, 50; change of, not inconstancy, 295, 6; common, ignorance of, 200, 53; compared with truth, 502, 4; duel of, nature umpire in, 190, 41; effect of similarity of, 521, 1; effect of time on, 335, 44; every new, suffrages for, at first, 93, 1; inconsistencies of, often justifiable, 193, 3; inferior to heart, 54, 4; matter of indifference, 136, 1; nothing but, 94, 34; of another, test of one's, 492, 27; of us, to respect, 527, 3; of the many, worthlessness of, 565, 21; one man's, no man's, 332, 60; popular, 352, 45, 46; power of, 277, 13; 464, 34; private, 359, 36; private and public, 357, 10; public, 315, 26; 359, 35-38; public, impotence of, 534, 41; public *versus* private, 453, 41; reaction of, on one's self, 93, 39; surgeon to my hurt, 172, 36; test of worthlessness of, 157, 8; what is wanted in, 313, 20
Opinions, changing, by law, 495, 34; divisive effect of, 507, 14; false, source of, 458, 13; golden, from all, 166, 41; how to express, 281, 38; men's, fallible, 159, 3; master of all, no bigot, 151, 21; no right to have, 308, 22; of friends, room to be left for, 528, 21; of others, how to construe, 493, 41; of stupid and ignorant people, 404, 40; of things, effect on us of, 438, 50; our, condition of satisfaction with, 521, 47; our wrangling for, 521, 47; predominant, 356, 5; to be treated, 527, 29; variety of, 446, 28; want of fixed, 552, 17
Opium, carrying power of, 497, 12
Opportunities, little, to be improved, 251, 30; of evil and good compared, 446, 29; to be embraced, 441, 40; value of, 244, 7
Opportunity, a lost, 461, 42; but one, of a kind, 472, 8; folly of losing, 322, 19; how often lost, 57, 42; importance of, 247, 31; makes thief, 80, 13; power of seeing and seizing, 381, 4; temptation of, 166, 39; tempting power of, 84, 10; to be noted, 216, 49; to be seized swiftly, 381, 4; to be waited for, 12, 29
Opposition, how to face, 28, 35; parliamentary, a necessity, 549, 19; the virtue of, 303, 34
Oppression, unbearable, 194, 50; under one deity, occasion for another, 379, 26

Optics, spiritual, 464, 39; the law of, in human transactions, 188, 46
Opulence, and poverty, states of, contrasted, 173, 46; vulgar, its insolence, 518, 8
Oracle, an ambiguous, 169, 35; I am Sir, 165, 4
Oracles, heaven's, be preserved, 108, 4
Orator, a fully equipped, 150, 48; all admire, 259, 9; delivering everything for an, 109, 12; desire of, 85, 18; greatest gift of, 319, 28; qualities of, 2, 52; secret of success of, 61, 31
Orators, great, and their words, 135, 30; no, born, 289, 42; resource of, that want depth, 38, 12; that always convince, 239, 13
Oratory, first and last thing in, 428, 41; how to train for, 179, 21; mediocre, 466, 32; the aim of, 336, 5; the main point in, 313, 20; the seat of, 188, 40
Orb, the smallest, thou behold'st, 478, 25
Ordeal, that may be faced, 218, 21
Order, gain of time, 119, 14; good, importance of, 61, 33; man's law, 264, 16; our limit, 567, 3; social, without liberty, 396, 3; the power of, 410, 42; the teacher, 287, 22
Orders, no shame in obeying, 469, 13
Organ, inscription on, 156, 48
Organisation, closing of individual, 27, 10; military, foundation of, 58, 28
Origin, pride of, 356, 39
Original, how to be, 461, 27; man, and popular, contrasted, 448, 33; the, still here, 130, 52
Originality, in authors, 444, 3; merit of, 442, 8
Origins, the question of, insoluble, and for idle people, 243, 37
Orphaned, the truly, 298, **2**
Orpheus, represented in poet, 459, 5
Others, bondage to, 385, 1; often a burden to us, 8, 56; trust not to, what one's self can do, 166, 42
"Ought," God in the word, 126, 42
Ounce, the last, 438, 5
Our own, before another's, 526, 30
Oursels, to see, as others see us, 322, 24
Ourselves, to be accepted as we are, 526, 23, 24
Outer and inner, 446, 32
Outward, the, a garment of invisible within, 541, 14
Outwitted, the easily, 564. 38
Over-consideration, vanity of, 149, 48
Over-curious, the, 446, 33
Overfeeding, mortality from, 57, 19
Over-happiness no happiness, 140, 12
Overpraise, evil of, 472, 26
Ovid, on his muse, 63, 33; on his rhymes, 36, 22; on his works, 210, 23; to his muse, 132, 21
Own, one's, devotion to, 166, 17; one's, right to, 168, 18
Owner, foot of, 429, 12
Ownership, conquest, 155, 31; exclusive, theft, 227, 20
Ox, a strange, 32, 10; a tired, 32, 14; an old, steady, 32, 55; that works, not to be muzzled, 483, 47
Oyster, the first to eat an, 149, 20

P

Pactolus river, the blind and the seer at, 511, 5
Paganism, virtue of, 403, 34
Page, a, sparkling with points, 334, 24
Pain, a nether-fire, 544, 45; and joy, relative amount of, 471, 36; and pleasure, companions. 349, 30; and pleasures, revolutions of, 545, 9; as urging to labour, 95, 35; avoidance of, the aim of wise man, 321, 36; birth of higher natures,

23, 46; compensation in, 328, 2; consecrated in Christ, 524, 42; felt, the worst, 446, 38; flying, 524, 16; from happiness, 2, 62; great agent in march of world, 431, 9; how to beguile, 435, 17; how to eschew, 177, 34; ill to bear, 364, 42; man's master, 223, 24; not imaginary, 10, 13; not to be given, 431, 16; one, lessened by another, 332, 18; positive, 380, 62; risk of shirking, 382, 10; seductive power of, 88, 15; shared, divided, 385, 28; sympathetic, 242, 31; three parts in joy, 28, 18; which we give ourselves for others, 527, 43

Pains, forgotten after gains, 112, 29; too much, bad, 300, 12

Painstaking, too much, a disease, 497, 43

Painter, effect of love of gain on, 439, 49; genius necessary to, 489, 40; his own colour-grinder, 446, 42; what a, should paint, 93, 41; licence conceded to, 348, 25

Painters and poets, common licence to, 351, 36

Painting, before, blackening behind, 41, 14; does not feed men, 294, 44; in old and in later times, 188, 35; mediocre, 466, 32; moral effect of, 383, 32; that attracts by mere verisimilitude, 533, 42; with a big brush, 566, 38

Pallas, the birth of, 301, 27

Pantaloon, lean and slippered, 438, 32

Paradise, a moment in, cheap at the price of death, 78, 36; in, alone, 280, 6

Parasite, nothing without its, 75, 21

Pardon, never and always, 127, 29; nothing in yourself, 178, 23; term of, 527, 44

Pardoning, sometimes an evil, 278, 13, 15

Parent, authority of, how forfeited, 506, 20

Parents, and children, in great states and vile, 187, 19; and children, as regards mutual support, 79, 40; and children, how they regard each other, 41, 54; death of, to child, 489, 22; respect for, as a duty, 374, 43; their joys, griefs, and fears, 437, 20

Parliament, member of, difficult to choose, 203, 44

Parnassus, the elect of, 234, 18; the poor man's, 287, 12

Parsimony and frugality, 558, 39

Pars magna, 88, 36

Parsons, cobblers, 279, 46

Part, acting a, long, difficult, 201, 5; inexplicable, if whole is so, 554, 33

Particles, significance of, 425, 20

Particular, in art, to represent universal, 448, 16; the, the universal limited, 446, 46

Parties, all work together, 244, 4; how formed, 276, 15; the weakness of, 206, 32

Parting, an image of death, 186, 39; ordained of God, 85, 42; the pain of, 382, 1; the pangs of, 555, 41

Partington, Mrs., and the Atlantic, 416, 32

Partisanship, effect of, on truth, 382, 22

Parts, men of great, 276, 5

Party, a sacrifice to, 550, 36; animosities, effect of, 424, 40; best service to, 145, 8; government, evil effect of, 276, 15; in England, habit of, 433, 4; leader, his difficulties, 145, 17; man, no convincing, 144, 17; spirit, evil of, 457, 7

Passion, a disappointed, the wound of, 201, 43; a god, 404, 51; a malignant, 189, 57; being without, 491, 2; easier to inspire than faith, 203, 14; employment of, apart from reason, 144, 47; extreme, folly of, 314, 16; fit of, an exposure, 145, 14; function of, 329, 43; in the soul, 562, 20; infinite, everywhere, 334, 54; latent in every heart, 186, 35; long-cherished, 67, 26; moral power of, 226, 35; never decides aright, 297, 22; no, can be hid, 93, 42; not to be bought, 32, 21; ruling, the power of a, 542, 2; susceptibility to, 545, 37; the power of, 559, 39, 40; unsteadiness of, 34, 51; *versus* reason, 20, 20; volatile, 65, 20

Passionless, man, as regards evil, 143, 28

Passions, and feelings, contrasted with reason, 369, 23, 31; as orators, 239, 13; contrasted with conscience, 224, 32; effect of absence on, 2, 11; exaggerations, 10, 15; 65, 19; general and particular, 439, 48; gentle, fruits of, 121, 28; great, incurable diseases, 136, 47; hard to conceal, 363, 1; how to treat our, 461, 25; like rivers in their course, 249, 51; man great by his, 263, 43; man without, worthlessness of, 92, 36; man's, saddening, 264, 1; our, abuse of our, 529, 31; our, in frenzy and under reason, 338, 43; our, like convulsion fits, 338, 44; our, masters rather servants, 276, 34; our, the true phœnixes, 338, 45; 556, 3; power of the, 38, 37; private and public, 239, 12; Rousseau on his, 39, 2; sayings about, 446, 47–51; 447, 1; strong, life of manly virtues, 404, 7; subduing, a work, 207, 8; their duration, 225, 12; their use and nobleness, 306, 31; transmuted by music, 287, 1; violent, how formed, 514, 35; voice of the body, 46, 39; why implanted, 291, 15; winds of the vessel, 239, 15; without, without principle and motive, 150, 40. See **Les passions**.

Past, a form of present, 519, 5; and future, our relation to, 521, 8; cold dead hand of, curative of egotism, 475, 29; court of the, 422, 5; events, to be ignorant of, 295, 41; great spirits of, 431, 39; grief over, natural, 274, 28; how to appropriate, 454, 8; how to treat, 501, 15; key to future, 404, 22; lamenting, vain, 494, 2; no concern to us, 180, 9; no erasing the, 294, 40; not to be lamented, 103, 47; not to be undone, 23, 11; not wasted if we rise on its ruins, 311, 46; our yearning after, 15, 37; present, and future, compared, 429, 37; present, and future, how to regard, 252, 58; the barbaric, study of, 264, 1; the hours of the, 302, 22; the sayings about, 447, 2–7; the soul of, in books, 185, 15; unalterable, 312, 33

Pastime, the dearest, 65, 8

Pastor, profession of, 107, 11

Pastors, ungracious, conduct of, 71, 25

Pastures, good, 130, 3

Patch rather than a hole, 28, 27

Paternity in law, 87, 23

Pates, lean, fat paunches make, 102, 45

Path, a best, for every man, 471, 13; the beaten, safe, 513, 43, 44; the best, through life, 417, 53; the direct, 61, 33; sure and honest heart, all, 215, 28

Pathetic, the, its elements, 447, 14

Pathway, a, to be made where none visible, 548, 18

Patience, a lesson in, 75, 12; a prayer, 432, 35; abused, 343, 20; against fortune, 484, 33; an alleviator, 174, 34; and faith, 449, 24; and its fruit, 226, 37; and perseverance, power of, 180, 25; as a passion, 82, 24; as a remedy, 15, 32; as an antidote, 226, 39; attained no small feat, 124, 3; being out of, 553, 24; better than learning, 119, 19; commended, 558, 40; 566, 34; cowardice in noble hearts, 414, 36; defined, 226, 38; exhortation to, 509, 21; in man and wife, 314, 14; in seeking the Lord, 294, 5; like, on a monument, 389, 12; more than brains, 77, 32; nobler than beauty, 82, 23; Kepler's, of faith, 174, 8; oil of the lamp, 266, 23; power of, 175, 37; 179, 38; 237, 23; 295, 48; 338, 47; 342, 55; 464, 32; prayed for, 217, 22; preached by all, 9, 63; rampart of courage, 112, 53; sort thy heart to, 400, 17; *versus* haste, 54, 21; want of, 162, 15; want of, want of philosophy, 554, 34; when outraged often, 117, 47; worth the pains, 146, 20

Patient man, fury of, 29, 72

Patriot, glory of, 205, 35; the, who saves his country, 478, 14

Patriotism, as an affection, 36, 19; unfelt at Marathon, 413, 44; its substitutes under despotism, 506, 21; power of, in the heart, 315, 33
Patriots, great, excellent as men, 133, 41
Patron, Johnson's description of, 16, 22
Patronage, begging, 162, 23; two kinds of, 505, 28
Paul and David, our opinions of, 523, 17
Paunch, a fat, without fine sense, 348, 44
Pay, a true man's, 306, 33
Pay-day, its recurrence, 569, 10
Peace, a certain, safer than an expected victory, 272, 42; and anger, contrasted, 35, 6; and concord, the price of, 483, 39; and joy from content and love, 249, 19; and plenty, the brood of, 349, 50; and war, effects of, compared, 518, 42, 46; beautiful, 382, 13; becoming in men, 35, 6; dependence of, on neighbours, 289, 6; few qualified for, 484, 25; first duty of citizen, 378, 24; how alone attainable, 306, 34; how to live in, 324, 9; how to preserve, 490, 35; how to secure, 240, 51; 390, 41; in heaven and on earth, 344, 47; life in, 149, 4; man in, 188, 52, 53; no, apart from ideal, 26, 58; no, perfect, 202, 5; no, without arms, 295, 34; only ground of, 314, 1; our love for, 525, 33; sacrifices for, 467, 11; secret of, 537, 16; the foes of, 329, 35; tranquil, a wish, 272, 34
Peaceful, the, peace-making, 106, 53
Peacemakers, the, 447, 16
Peaks, loftiest, in clouds, 550, 35
Pearls, give not, to swine, 123, 21; in the deep, 185, 51; tears, 346, 28; to be dived for, 85, 7
Peasant, contrasted with philosopher, 460, 4; with fowl in pot, 211, 23
Peasantry, a brave, value of, 33, 1
Pebble, casting, from hand, effect of, 199, 1
Pedagogue, the, and the age, 457, 2
Pedant, a, defined, 16, 25; 152, 48; a female, offensive, 164, 41; and teacher contrasted, 234, 23; the real, 437, 8
Pedantry, defined, 54, 11; origin and evil of, 421, 24; vacancy, 344, 25
Pedigree, kingly, traced backwards, 534, 25; mere, of no avail, 402, 34; pride of, 522, 27
Peerage, the English, 530, 37
Pen, magic of, 440, 12; mightier than sword, 447, 18; most wonderful of tools, 296, 64; steadying power of, 509, 39; strokes of, to be deliberate, 455, 31
Penalty, according to offence, 4, 59; paid by innocent, 77, 49
Penitence, better than casuistry, 200, 15
Penny, a bad, 32, 12; to spend, I hae a, 166, 28
Penury, abyss of, 296, 56
People, a great, condition of continued power of, 448, 36; a great, instinctive feeling of, 437, 1; a, without religion, 253, 2; chief glory of a, 420, 5; choice of, measure of, 123, 42; common-place, how to win, 333, 21; effect of treating as they are or should be, 546, 41; glory of, 430, 11; great, special gifts of God, 134, 42; heart of a country, 234, 26; high-class, rule of intercourse with, 187, 34; how to move the heart of, 303, 12; how to understand, 556, 34; mass of, characterised, 431, 27; most objectionable, 444, 4; only three classes of, 468, 3; silence of, a lesson to kings, 235, 11; sympathetic, 408, 35; that sing, safe to live among, 560, 12; the, and kings, 447, 20, 23; the, and their orators, 234, 27; the miscreant calling himself, 186, 44; the, open to flattery, 312, 38; the, supreme law of, 379, 51; the, voice of, 347, 31; the, voice of, to be regarded, 389, 35; the, their fondness for deception, 353, 1; voice of, how to regard, 461, 9; with no annals, 140, 28; without laws, 79, 42
Peoples, great, conservative, 9, 40

Perception, of a fact, a fact, 288, 17; want of, fatal, 461, 17
Perdition catch my soul, 96, 16
Perfect, nothing, till humanised, 315, 32; the, around us, 522, 34; thing, treatment of, 362, 21
Perfection, by nature and by art, 272, 43; claim of, 145, 40; desire of, a disease, 423, 9; dumb, 544, 19; easily dispensed with, 333, 28; end of, 540, 3; from trifles, 499, 23; greater, dispensable, 520, 41; how to arrive at, 489, 37; in art, demand for, 302, 9; in heaven's regard and man's, 517, 18; in one's self to be aimed at, 28, 12; law of, 227, 3; sought in another, 75, 4; supreme, 537, 9; the three sources of, 468, 30
Perfumed, like a milliner, 114, 43
Perhaps, a great, in quest of, 210, 36
Perishable, to be made imperishable, 521, 26
Perjuries, lovers', 72, 6
Perjury, the punishment of, 346, 27; when a virtue, 234, 20
Permanence, the condition of, 354, 36
Perplexity, moral, 1, 39
Persecution, better than being shunned, 29, 15; history of, 435, 19
Perseverance, effect of, 496, 31; gain of, 34, 10; law of, 438, 21; power of, 80, 54; 96, 54; 135, 29; rarer than effort, 227, 8; reward of, 496, 12; 553, 26; virtue of, 56, 38; 346, 30; want of, 142, 34
Persistence, merit of, 346, 30, 31
Persistency, attracts confidence, 89, 27
Person, a third, annoyance to two, 82, 4; a worthy, respected by the good, 143, 17; mystery of a, 444, 28
Personality, great, how to respect, 492, 23
Persons, and things to be taken as they are, 276, 13; criticising of, 476, 29; great, behaviour towards, 498, 45; interesting, the only, 335, 8; the emphasis of, 425, 4; universally treated ill, 526, 5; who please us, 443, 14
Persuasion, and faith, power of, 279, 32; law of, 241, 16; power of, 104, 57; 312, 23; susceptibility to, the rule, 336, 5
Perversion, last stage of, 438, 8
Perversities, greatest of all, 432, 29
Pervert, no, fit for kingdom of God, 303, 47
Perverted minds, effect of things on, 328, 22
Pestilence, evil of, 101, 31
Peter more feared than respected, 117, 29
Petition to God, a precept, 93, 48
Petticoat government, 32, 47
Phaëton, epitaph on, 156, 14
Phariseeism intolerable, 468, 29
Pharmacopœia, Napoleon's, 520, 28
Philanthropic, the, mistaken occupation of, 417, 31
Philanthropy, a vain, 536, 5; mere, not the aim of life, 256, 38; true, 482, 3; with a flaw, 414, 5
Philina on her days and nights, 212, 13
Philip II. of Spain's boast, 170, 5
Philistinism, instance of, 203, 3
Philosopher, and the toothache, 477, 37; and trifles, 150, 17; characteristics of, 489, 42, 43; content with being, 177, 16; contrasted with peasant, 436, 15; 460, 4; defined, 447, 34, 35; dejection unseemly in, 56, 45; his first business, 428, 8; most aspiring, his proudest boast, 449, 50; object and duty of, 445, 20; should not swear, 324, 26; the, and practical interests, 558, 33; the, characteristic of, 419, 43; true, character of, 419, 41; without good-breeding, 452, 27; work for a, 495, 36
Philosopher's, stone, a, 21, 23; stone, the, 343, 60; stone, the true, 47, 18, 23; 177, 1
Philosophers, a trouble to the world, 278, 37; in talk, fools in art, 269, 45; Rousseau on, 409, 18; their opposite views of man, 398, 42

Philosophic study, the condition of, 421, 39

Philosophical, act, the true, 459, 3 ; systems, worthlessness of, 550, 8

Philosophies, man's, supplements of his practice, 267, 5

Philosophising, true, 383, 41

Philosophisings, cold, in presence of heart, 444, 37

Philosophism, fruit of, in France, 310, 4

Philosophy, a deliverer and a defender, 227, 5 ; a genuine, 494, 11 ; a test of a man's, 315, 23 ; according to Plato and to Bacon, 189, 6 ; after defeat, 333, 6 ; and adversity, 4, 71 ; and Christianity, 42, 52 ; and divinity, 70, 12 ; and misfortune, 227, 7 ; as deceptive, 227, 6 ; beginning of all, 459, 3 ; best part of, 221, 12 ; compared with poetry, 350, 41 ; compared with religion, 372, 7, 17 ; defined, 537, 3 ; divine, 161, 7 ; effects of little, and of depth in, 8, 48 ; effect of, on one in fear, 449, 5 ; existence and necessity of, 442, 6 ; first qualification for, 61, 14 ; function of, 516, 23 ; glory of, 430, 13 ; importance of, 81, 40 ; 559, 41 ; misapplied, 521, 25 ; motive to, 207, 9 ; not enough, 26, 2 ; permanent, 550, 7 ; politics harmful to, 313, 47 ; power of, 70, 9 ; problem of, 449, 30 ; sayings about, 447, 37, 38 ; small draughts of, and large, 394, 23 ; temple of, qualification for entering, 508, 3 ; the beginning and end of, 192, 33 ; the one, 471, 17 ; the first cause of, 561, 44 ; the sign of a ripened, 13, 51 ; the two objects of, 423, 40 ; too austere, 497, 30 ; vanity of fortifying one's self with, 492, 9 ; visible, 426, 17

Phocion to Demosthenes, 271, 37

Phœnix, a symbol of progress, 106, 20 ; the, burning of, 190, 11

Phœnix-bird in the fire, 545, 46

Physic, hated, yet helpful, 484, 32 ; the best, 533, 31 ; to the dogs, 485, 42

Physician, a, to be old, 212, 48 ; dispensed with, 559, 1 ; must be humane, 78, 35 ; no perfect, 334, 25 ; profession of, 107, 11 ; those who need, 479, 33 ; to be honoured, 159, 50 ; who has never been sick, 303, 48 ; wise, usefulness of, 25, 1

Physicians, I die by the help of too many, 165, 41 ; many, bad sign of a state, 226, 16 ; the two best, 411, 48 ; two real, 227, 37

Physiognomists, the best, 348, 24

Physique, effect of, on estimate of self, 278, 5

Picture, good, a sermon, 91, 10 ; poem without words, 287, 37 ; to ensure a genuine, 240, 27

Pictures, attraction of, 174, 23 ; by nature, 72, 7 ; good, shades and lights in, 488, 9 ; importance of arrangement in, 323, 20 ; pleasure in, 519, 31

Piece, a, how to compose, 119, 15

Piety, among the ruins of Iona, 413, 44 ; and reason to be combined, 526, 39 ; ascetic, 120, 27 ; but a means, 116, 38 ; defined by Cicero, 216, 30 ; how best displayed, 334, 38 ; real, 334, 1 ; the, of a reformed man, 24, 56 ; to be kept distinct from art, 345, 22

Pig, every, scrubbing, 152, 12

Pigeons, no, ready roasted, 119, 12, 13

Pilate, jesting, without eye for truth, 212, 34

Pilgrimages, profitlessness of, 148, 6

Pilgrims, few, saints, 105, 19

Pillow, a sibyl, 447, 40

Pills, sugared, 16, 56 ; to be swallowed, 348, 42

Pilot, of Galilean Lake, 447, 41 ; vigilance required in, 39, 41

Pilotage, in calm, 184, 8 ; in storm, 184, 10

Pilots, skilful, reputation of, how gained, 393, 17

Pindar, passion of, mine, 542, 30

Pious, honoured by gods and men, 51, 38 ; 447, 44

Pipe, that is not played on, 540, 16

Pity, akin to humour, 164, 9 ; ere charity, 36, 7 ; how to show, 389, 40 ; human, power of, 283, 26 ; no, without rigour, 12, 46 ; not hatred, 71,

630

44 ; object of, 425, 22 ; often more becoming than envy, 383, 36 ; our, measure of, 527, 47 ; rather than envy, 29, 27 ; through severity, 396, 44 ; virtue of law, 110, 38

Pitying better than condemning, 201, 26

Place, a consecrated, 46, 43 ; a man below his, 152, 30 ; dignified by deed, 116, 13 ; preparation for a, 488, 37 ; trodden by a good man, 447, 46

Places and place-holders, 63, 45

Plagiarism, Kingsley on, 301, 37

Plagiarists, honest, 10, 45

Plain, blunt man, a, 164, 49 ; the perfectly, 381, 37

Plain-dealing, exceptional, 313, 37 ; in disfavour, 107, 30

Plain-spokenness, an eccentricity, 177, 22

Plan, the divine, no need to understand, 155, 16

Planet, rather than moon, 166, 23 ; sceptre of the, 458, 30

Plant, often removed, 16, 39

Plate, enjoyed as earthenware, 133, 37

Plato, as a thinker, 453, 7 ; father of thought, 340, 10 ; fruitlessness of his teachings, 314, 34 ; the greatness of, 349, 19 ; thought of, mine, 542, 30 ; treatment of, 349, 20 ; wrong with, rather than right with others, 84, 45

Plato's "Republic," 331, 27

Plausibility and truth, 355, 15

Player, and the times, 253, 6 ; might teach parson, 169, 49

Playfulness after exertion, 151, 26

Playing, too much, 492, 5

Pleasant, mingled with bitter, 271, 55 ; and unpleasant, matter of habit, 316, 25

Pleasantry, must be spontaneous, 101, 43 ; with whom to risk, 528, 37

Please, others, how to, 510, 20 ; to, as a wish, 89, 4

Pleasing, art of, 416, 22 ; every one pleasing none, 151, 20 ; many a vain attempt, 217, 5 ; no, every one, 117, 6 ; pleasure of, 520, 37

Pleasure, a man of, 12, 34 ; after pain, 376, 5 ; and fear of the penalty, 65, 26 ; and pain, 32, 35 ; 340, 42 ; and pain, cousins german, 229, 6 ; as a moralist, 474, 24 ; at expense of pain, 308, 29 ; blinding power of, 223, 22 ; cost of, 10, 16 ; diving for, 186, 9 ; effect of indulgence in, 271, 20 ; effect of, on sense of time, 349, 29 ; effect of refinement upon, 443, 18 ; evil only when enslaving, 82, 51 ; excess of, criminal, 242, 32 ; from activity, 93, 50 ; illusory, hope of, 403, 24 ; intellectual and sensual, 191, 14 ; lawful, 84, 38 ; looked forward to, 79, 41 ; men's proneness to, 158, 46 ; mere, as motive of action, 278, 23 ; no compensation for pain, 31, 17 ; not to be despised, 168, 6 ; of the world, a dream, 362, 22 ; precursor of grief, 136, 37 ; pursuit of, demoralising, 147, 26 ; sacrifice of, a gain, 198, 16 ; sacrificing, to duty, 149, 35 ; satieties of, 467, 28 ; sequel to, 485, 45 ; that strikes the soul, 448, 8 ; the most exquisite, 234, 28 ; the sweetest, 324, 28 ; to an ill-conditioned being, 489, 33 ; true, the fountain of, 188, 47 ; without reason, result of, 407, 28 ; without self-flattery, 330, 3

Pleasure-seeker, the, 448, 5

Pleasures, bitter when abused, 239, 18 ; Burns on evanescence of, 33, 22 ; great, rarer than great pains, 134, 43 ; how enhanced, 517, 22 ; how to look at, 252, 58 ; like wine, 526, 14 ; mental, never cloy, 278, 3 ; not to be exalted, 294, 39 ; of the world, the, 448, 9 ; our, and pains, 339, 1 ; our, how protracted, 338, 49 ; temperate man's, 457, 3 ; the sweetest, 325, 10 ; tranquil, 498, 55

Plenty, everywhere, 271, 48

Pliability, and firmness, 179, 8 ; man's, characterised, 408, 27

Plodders, continued, gain of, from other's books, 394, 25

Plodding, effect of, 480, 2 ; not easy, 201, 38 ; universal, evil of, 555, 32

Ploughman's clocks, 278, 32

Ploughshare, soldiers of, 397, 10

Poem, a great suggestive, 91, 18 ; a heroic, at bottom, 473. 8 ; a, what makes, 204, 10 ; an indifferent, writing, and understanding a good, 201, 21 ; as image of life, 16, 43 ; heroic, qualification for composing, 153, 2 ; qualities of a true, 110, 40 ; 310, 35 ; true, writer of, his reward, 437, 10 ; which i' not sung, 536, 40

Poems, all great, foundation of, 324, 24 ; by mere water-drinkers, 318, 15 ; for the day and for all time, 138, 41 ; heroic, how to produce, 241, 17 ; old, sacred, 380, 24 ; painted window-panes, 119, 18

Poesy, difficulties in, 316, 31 ; immortal, 227, 15 ; spirit of, 454, 37

Poet, a, defined, 486, 19 ; a, for everything, 75, 21 ; a, how to understand, 556, 25 ; a necessary qualification for, 559, 27 ; a, of superior merit, not to be described, 384, 28 ; a, on canvas, same as in song, 16, 47 ; a word for, 409, 29 ; akin to madman, 24, 17 ; always waited for, 426, 22 ; and his inspiration, 203, 37 ; as representing a class of men, 273, 40 ; as revealer of beauty, 150, 50 ; business of, 489, 39 ; by birth, 350, 36 ; coin of a, 163, 6 ; delight of, in wandering, 80, 3 ; distinguished from prophet, 449, 46 ; dramatic, Horace on, 370, 40 ; dramatic, two qualifications of, 503, 36 ; everywhere in his place, 549, 20 ; eyes to other men, 284, 14 ; function of, 64, 21 ; 206, 37 ; genius necessary to, 489, 40 ; God the perfect, 127, 5 ; great, limitedness of, 311, 27 ; high watch-tower of, 59, 48 ; his resources, 406, 17 ; how formed, 492, 32 ; licence conceded to, 348, 25 ; like the eagle, 444, 31 ; lyric and epic, beverages of, 440, 11 ; native land of, 444, 31 ; Nature's teaching to, 531, 35 ; nothing useless to a, 489, 24 ; object of, 445, 19 ; of to-day, and the wealth he inherits, 522, 12 ; often child of love, 325, 34 ; pen of, tempered with love's sighs, 296, 19 ; qualification of, 252, 4 ; qualifications for, 303, 2, 3 ; satirical, a check, 18, 60 ; sayings about, 448, 11–19 ; scared by the mob, 322, 8 ; sign of the, 453, 33 ; spirit required of, 237, 4 ; suffering necessary to, 426, 23 ; the, advice to, 558, 41 ; the, and troubles of life, 540, 18 ; the, attributes of, 16, 44–46 ; the business of, 14, 16 ; the complete, his outfit, 421, 16 ; the eye of, 470, 21 ; the high priesthood of, 550, 41 ; the irreligious, 437, 13 ; the note-book of, 426, 30 ; the only teller of news, 446, 21 ; the struggle of the, 93, 51 ; the true, 459, 4–6 ; to be, one must be a poem, 152, 54 ; to sing to himself and the Muses, 34, 59 ; what he has to cultivate and shun, 539, 2 ; what it is to be a, 489, 44 ; what makes a, 198, 49 ; what makes the, 373, 11 ; with nothing to interpret and reveal, 174, 29 ; without poetic frenzy, 554, 27 ; who entitled to be called, 50, 48 ; work for a, 495, 36

Poet's gift, Horace's admiration of, 182, 8

Poetasters, conceit of, 218, 23

Poetic, art, destiny of, 508. 31 ; genius, the test of, 457, 13 ; pains, a pleasure in, 470, 16

Poet-priest still waited for, 465, 14

Poetry, ancient and modern, contrasted, 448, 20 ; and prose, defined, 358, 20 ; and words, 562, 12 ; as an educator of children, 411, 14 ; at bottom, 313, 4 ; attractive power of, 24, 39 ; averse to reasoning, 71, 32 ; born of pain or sorrow, 350, 33 ; by a bad man, 389, 37 ; compared with painting, 340, 51 ; contrasted with science, 382, 37 ; 383, 2 ; elements or subjects of, 425, 3 ; essence of, 426, 1 ; from an engineer, 566, 27 ; good, personification of, 130, 5 ; how to understand, 565, 19 ; if nonsense, when reduced to

prose, 200, 2 ; in common lives, 476, 20 ; inferior, denounced, 193, 47 ; its dwelling-place, 372, 27 ; its relation to philosophy, 345, 8 ; its sadness objected to, 535, 34 ; lyric, 258, 26 ; mediocre, 466, 32 ; mistaken test of, 198, 13 ; must be of ideas, 184, 22 ; not dead, 372, 27 ; not the thing now wanted, 358, 11 ; nursed by wrong, 284, 42 ; of eighteenth century, 339, 2 ; old-fashioned, character of, 327. 13 ; organic, 377, 19 ; popular, fault of, 448, 13 ; secondrate, condemned, 558, 42 ; surpassed by music, 286, 47 ; the elevating power of, 200, 44 ; the essence of, 369, 19 ; the kingdom of, 54, 24 ; the life of, 562, 12 ; the only, 335, 11 ; 446, 12 ; transporting, 315, 35 ; true, in the fields, 567, 33 ; true, truer than science, 500, 29 ; value and dignity of, 559, 42 ; value of, 565, 19 ; who has no ear for, 532, 10 ; without taste for, 150, 38

Poets, at first and at last, 528, 2 ; a question about, 487, 45 ; and poverty, 354, 16 ; but two orders of, 503, 48 ; contrasted with orators, 289, 42 ; good, inspired interpreters, 130, 6 ; great, and their readers, 310, 22 ; great, best qualities in, 10, 30 ; great, how their works have been read, 464, 3 ; great, of slow growth, 315, 12 ; great (see **Great Poets**) ; make witty, 157, 22 ; mediocrity in, 272, 2 ; modern, Goethe on, 281, 29 ; nature-made, 291, 50 ; our, Emerson on, 339, 3 ; sensitive, 121, 48 ; their wish, 24, 21 ; three, of Greece, Italy, and England, 485, 23 ; to be fed. not pampered, 84, 16

Poison, slow, dangerous, 16, 48 ; 79, 12 ; those that need, 479, 14

Polarity, our own, our law, 521, 30

Policy, and incidents, 192, 55 ; object of all true, 445, 15 ; the best, 35, 9

Polish, what is alone susceptible of, 335, 22

Polite people, excessively, designing, 347, 5

Politeness, benefit of, 28, 19 ; defined, 227, 16 ; estimable, 376, 51 ; morally rooted, 301, 46 ; of wise and fools, 462, 31 ; only source of, 446, 24 ; true, 38, 19 ; value of, 474, 6 ; wise and foolish, 21. 61

Political, economy, real science of, 450, 43 ; watchword, highest, 435, 5

Politician, object and duty of, 445, 20

Politicians and statesmen, contrasted, 455, 10

Politics, as gambling, 472, 41 ; bungling in, hateful, 166, 30 ; philosophy harmful to, 313, 47 ; sayings about, 189. 8–10 ; subject to circumstances, 475, 24 ; too rigorous, 497, 30

Polonius, advice of, to Laërtes, 123, 30

Pomp, insignificance of, 123, 13

Poniards, she speaks, 389, 14

Poor, and rich, 126, 15, 16 ; and sins of rich, 59, 29 ; compared with rich, 451, 24–27, 32 ; considering, 30, 49 ; fate of devourer of the, 37, 54 ; giving to, 123, 46 ; 146, 21 ; ignorance of, Carlyle on, 203, 35 ; in purse, 18, 17 ; man, a, 137. 46 ; 141, 23 ; 147, 53 ; man, a, and a liar, 423, 8 ; man, a really, 441, 5 ; man, according to Emerson, 143, 53 ; man, despised, 343. 47 ; man, how, may become rich, 34, 1 ; man, put to shifts, 158, 29 ; man who is, 304, 12 ; mercy to, blessed, 146, 50 ; not to be robbed, 377, 43 ; once, poor always, 386, 30 ; man, become rich, pride of, 180, 2 ; spectres that accompany, 203, 35 ; spirit, mark of, 489, 5 ; the alone truly, 319, 14 ; the, obsequious to rich, 63, 50 ; the, pity for, in a storm, 352, 37 ; the poverty of, 423, 14 ; the, sayings about, 448. 23–27 ; the tillage of, 285, 12 ; the uncomplaining, 59, 28 ; the wretchedness of, 328, 40 ; who think themselves so, 304, 10

Poorest, in his cottage, safety of, 448, 31 ; place, plenty of, 448, 10

Pope, not born for high life, 169, 2 ; of his religion, 408, 33 ; on his verses, 173, 24

Pope's prayer for charity, 411, 12

Populace, the, insolence of, 129, 2

Popular, man and original contrasted, 448, 33 ; the, characterises the people, 94, 48

Popularity, defined, 227, 17 ; evanescence of, 124, 28 ; fleeting, 181, 18 ; sudden, 406, 4 ; to be shunned, 51, 31

Portion, the best, 409, 31

Portraits, ancestral, in a mirror, 13, 43 ; the best, 417, 54

Position, contentment with one's, commended, 566, 17 ; filling of, main thing, 125, 36

Positive, as legible as negative, 483, 45 ; and negative, universal in nature, 94, 26 ; and negative universal, 174, 42, 43

Possess, how to, 39, 12 ; who deserve to, 479, 53

Possessing and possessed, 519, 13

Possession, a permanent, 166, 34 ; an acknowledged title, 385, 25 ; as justifying right, 27, 22 ; by right, 79, 33 ; condition of true, 316, 43 ; not mere fame, 206, 38 ; of good things, effect on us of, 559, 5 ; the only real, 167, 34 ; thorough, a test of, 539, 44 ; true, condition of, 520, 4

Possessions, a blessing or a curse, 138, 48 ; of which one has more than he knows, 324, 47 ; our, and wishes, 331, 18 ; inherited, to be employed, 82, 56

Possible, ever possible, 415, 2

Post, a vacant, effect of filling, 498, 44 ; our, not to be deserted, 527, 32

Posterity, our duty to, 527, 40 ; our obligations to, 535, 21 ; the judgment of, 47, 7

Posture-maker, the best, 291, 52

Pot, a little, 77, 30 ; of ale, fame for, 169, 24

Poultry, world peopled with, 291, 48

Poverty, a calamity, 18, 17 ; a drawback in life, 490, 34 ; a hindrance to virtue, 1, 34 ; a master, 467, 27 ; and love, incompatible, 544, 10 ; and reproach, 490, 23 ; and vice, 518, 33 ; a teacher, 150, 44 ; better than cowardice, 197, 28 ; better than vice, 29, 16 ; chill air of, 3, 5 ; condition of, without freedom, 88, 38 ; contentment with, commended, 236, 1 ; contrasted with avarice, 62, 43 ; craft of, 18, 18 ; cramping effect of, 141, 25 ; direct road to, 397, 40 ; discredit of, 24, 42 ; disgrace of, 259, 36 ; effect of, 394, 15 ; effect of, on native character, 314, 11 ; from sloth, 103, 14 ; hard to bear, 78, 31 ; hard to gild, 208, 11 ; honest, 159, 32 ; how so galling, 299, 41 ; key to, 394, 5 ; measure of, 148, 3 ; national, incompatible with national prosperity, 334, 9 ; no evil to a genuine man, 109, 3 ; of spirit, God's delight, 18, 15 ; real, 17, 4 ; 358, 4 ; sayings about, 343, 50-52 ; security of, 149, 17 ; shame of, 388, 33 ; standard of, 93, 21 ; stronger than wealth, 26, 5 ; the evil of, 530, 32 ; the sixth sense, 18, 16 ; the worst kind of, 55, 23 ; to be hidden, 227, 2 ; when one is down, 547, 3 ; which oppresses a nation, evil of, 132, 44

Power, a, over and behind us, 470, 19 ; a test of character, 474, 25 ; always jealous, 318, 13 ; an unseen, shadow of, 416, 38 ; and fate, 102, 48 ; and impotence, what determines, 533, 34 ; arbitrary, how established, 17, 27 ; constraining, how to be free from, 517, 27 ; earthly, when likest God's, 14, 41 ; everywhere, 247, 13 ; excessive, end of, 19, 8 ; how retained, 183, 37 ; innate lust for, 88, 35 ; lawless, weakness of, 121, 57 ; love of, a childish passion, 256, 9 ; our absolute, limited to ourselves, 340, 28 ; over others, condition of, 211, 47 ; pains and pleasures of, 446, 40 ; persuasiveness of, 122, 13 ; possessor of, 60, 12 ; responsibility in relinquishing, 297, 40 ; royal, firm as a rock of iron, 170, 9 ; sovereign,

the secret of, 386, 13 ; the arrogance of, 299, 6 ; the basis of all, 10, 18 ; the desire of, an effect of, 423, 10 ; the impression of, due to mass, 4, 56 ; the secret of, 319, 7 ; true, silent, 11, 33 ; unjust, to be let fall, 323, 27 ; unlimited, a risk, 304, 23 ; when apparent, 10, 17 ; wielded with violence or moderation, 514, 36 ; with age, 549, 23 ; without justice, 216, 26

Powerful, the most, 353, 28

Powers, one's, not to be dissipated, 380, 7 ; unseen, Wordsworth's faith in, 311, 52

Practice, and preaching, 355, 56 ; and theory, 466, 22 ; better than preaching, 15, 67 ; effect of, 94, 39 ; 504, 43 ; everything, 272, 40 ; power of, 96, 53 ; without Nature and learning, 292, 35

Prairies, the, 462, 18

Praise, and dispraise, alike, 486, 7 ; assumption of him who praises another, 531, 37 ; but not of one's self, 240, 23 ; by letter, 483, 38 ; from love, effect of, 449, 3 ; generally for praise, 330, 16 ; greed of, mark of weakness, 391, 4 ; ground of, 231, 23 ; more difficult than flattery, 269, 26 ; not to be too hasty, 528, 39 ; received, our estimate of, 92, 34 ; rule in, 384, 11 ; the refusal of, 234, 41 ; undeserved, effect of, on an honest heart, 498, 30 ; unqualified, evil of, 313, 49 ; vain, 475, 27 ; when deserved, 170, 19

Praising everybody, praising nobody, 152, 5

Prayer, a perfect, 19, 34 ; a short, 211, 29 ; an impotent, 62, 9 ; answered, as offered, 125, 13 ; as a wish, 430, 5 ; as teaching, 303, 32 ; before labour, 526, 34 ; condition of answer to, 153, 39 ; course of, unknown, 421, 43 ; defined, 227, 18 ; efficacy of, 19, 46 ; for grace or guidance, 172, 29 ; in heaven's sight, 187, 23 ; mental (see **Mental prayer**) ; no, no prospering, 149, 42 ; no, no religion, 306, 43 ; power of, 23, 38 ; proper matter of, 313, 26 ; the greatest, 432, 35 ; the greeting of the day, 107, 2 ; to ourselves, efficacy of, 539, 35 ; unknown power of, 283, 41 ; *versus* practice, 503, 31 ; what's in, 549, 36 ; when angry, 543, 40

Prayerless men, 534, 5

Prayers, denied, a benefit, 525, 1 ; forced, not good, 112, 14 ; only cries of babes, 534, 4 ; short, 389, 30 ; that journey far, 398, 43

Praying, best, 144, 56 ; dependent on living, 311, 25 ; disturbed by working, 105, 24 ; idle, 555, 2 ; soul, waiting of, 449, 4 ; striving, 28, 7 ; that is vain, 293, 20

Preacher, and apostle, different aims of, 224, 11 ; compared with his sermons, 301, 4 ; not to be judged, 214, 10 ; the best, 144, 57 ; the true, 459, 7 ; under the gallows, 93, 17 ; who preaches with effect, 476, 15

Preaching, effective, 30, 11 ; in wilderness or highway, 552, 36 ; object of, 445, 17 ; to the unwilling, 329, 10 ; when angry, 543, 40 ; with a full belly, 76, 26

Precedent, origin of, 333, 39

Precedents, bad, from good beginnings, 328, 15 ; creating, 387, 44

Precept and example, effects of, 355, 9, 58

Precepts, effect of, 276, 43 ; rigorous religious, endorsed by abandoned men, 307, 26

Precipitancy often instructive, 79, 11

Precipitation, evil of, 504, 20

Precocity, evil of, 398, 38 ; fate of, 11, 48

Predecessor, to equal, 492, 12

Predestination, M. Aurelius on, 541, 10

Preferment, affected scorn of, 269, 43 ; chances of, 149, 6

Prejudice, an old, need created by destroying, 546, 34 ; reasoning against, 370, 8

Prejudices, how to treat, 307, 47 ; laying aside, a work, 207, 8 ; moral, stop-gaps of virtue, 283, 14 ; one's own, to be cast out, 265, 34

Presbyter, new, old priest, 297, 30

Presence, a good, value of, 6, 51 ; effect of a, silent, 334, 10

Present, a potent divinity, 64, 20 ; absurd feeling about the, 476, 26 ; alone ours, 82, 54 ; and future, Fichte's view of, 288, 9 ; and the future, 234, 37, 38 ; complacence in comparing, with past, 201, 4 ; for whom, 234, 38 ; how to treat, 501, 15 ; importance of, 449, 10 ; in life, 182, 31 ; its comprehensiveness, 449, 9, 14 ; man's business solely with, 415, 1 ; man's tyrant, 265, 4 ; never in our thoughts, 175, 43 ; sufficiency of, 140, 23 ; sum of past and future, 414, 34 ; the, ignored, 521, 24 ; the, importance of seizing, 79, 18 ; the possession of, 462, 13 ; the, underrated, 322, 22 ; those commonplace, 415, 28 ; time, characterised, 339, 4 ; time, in labour, 477, 25 ; time, Ruskin on, 557, 38 ; time, the, 272, 32 ; 438, 31 ; time, the, in birth pangs, 285, 16 ; to be employed, 36, 27 ; to be enjoyed, 71, 12 ; 529, 5 ; value of, 92, 40

Presents, giving, rather than paying debts, 268, 56 ; the most acceptable, 2, 44 ; the quality in, 546, 17

Press, daily, Goethe on, 10, 59 ; sayings about, 449, 15–17

Presumption, of a spiritual nature, 281, 31 ; the source of, 204, 43

Pretensions, folly of our, 522, 10

Prevention, before both law and crime, 231, 42

Price, nothing without, 539, 42

Pride, a, commended, 470, 2 ; a noble, 469, 28 ; a passing flower, 75, 51 ; a shameless liar, 391, 19 ; abhorrent to gods, 86, 16 ; always injurious, 303, 36 ; and debt, 224, 13 ; and ingratitude, combined, 566, 39 ; angry, folly of, 325, 36 ; as a tax, 170, 33, 34 ; characteristics of, 147, 16 ; commended, 27, 48 ; debasing power of, 209, 22 ; effect of subdued, 542, 19 ; enraged, as a counsellor, 266, 23 ; extreme, ignorance, 60, 18 ; followed by shame, 242, 34 ; from ignorance, 446, 34 ; gifts of, 511, 24 ; Highland, 409, 9 ; how to lessen one's, 176, 14 ; in man, 261, 50 ; less, nobler the blood, 213, 4 ; matter of shame, 527, 36 ; misery of, 444, 8 ; reasoning, evil of, 189, 17 ; the food of, 107, 28 ; with the mask off, 194, 52

Priest, a Christian, Chaucer's idea of, 33, 4 ; lying, in dark ages, 302, 49 ; his love for his flock, 61, 16 ; 449, 19 ; the world's, 458, 52

Priestcraft, the support of, 277, 26

Priesthood, all men's vocation, 524, 20 ; of father and mother, 252, 46

Priests, effect of their conduct on church, 239, 26 ; false, St. Augustine on, 286, 6 ; real and sham, 18, 59

Prime Minister, no, explicit, 302, 51

Primrose, by river's brim, 16, 64

Prince, born a, a misfortune, 390, 16 ; first servant of state, 59, 56 ; greatest merit of, 357, 1 ; how to forfeit favour of, 150, 16 ; manners of, effect of, 239, 7 ; qualities of a, 393, 8

Princes, and their subjects, 519, 8 ; and wise men, 61, 35 ; false praise of, insult, 253, 36 ; hands and ears of, 118, 7 ; fault in, 199, 24 ; the clemency of, a lure, 224, 28

Princes' favours, wretchedness of depending on, 321, 2

Principle, a new, value of, 15, 4 ; steadfastness to, 167, 22

Principles, developed apart from men, 104, 42 ; our, in frenzy and under reason, 338, 43 ; right, knowledge of, *versus* love of, 151, 28 ; righteous, principal thing, 275, 38 ; steadfastness of, 104, 12 ; where no, whims, 151, 7

Printing-press, power of, 535, 16

Prisoner and free man contrasted, 449, 26

Private, affairs, talking of, 469, 38 ; soldier in France, 498, 39

Privilege, defined, 357, 15 ; our pride in, 538, 6

Probabilities, a thousand, short of one truth, 279, 26

Problem, a palpably hopeless, 123, 41 ; our first, 206, 11

Problems, soluble and insoluble, 263, 5

Procrastination, danger of, 162, 34 ; evil of, 540, 14

Prodigal compared with miser, 449, 31

Prodigals, as regards money, 49, 14

Production, greater than expansion or decoration, 449, 32 ; law of, 252, 2

Profane, negatively defined, 315, 36

Profanity, no, where no fane, 469, 12

Profession, a man's, his master, 167, 17 ; no, without its troubles, 174, 31 ; one, enough for a man, 493, 38

Professions, five great intellectual, 107, 11

Professors, great, 483, 16

Profit, contrary views of, 284, 31 ; late, better than none, 58, 45 ; no, except through pleasure, 306, 47

Profitable things, the casting away of, 419, 29

Profits, moderate, 166, 18 ; slender, but often, 219, 39

Profundity to be avoided, 11, 29

Progress, delight in sense of, 513, 32 ; dependent on man's energy, 446, 14 ; due to grumblers, 549, 2 ; human, great steps in, not due to reason, 521, 46 ; no pause in, 292, 6 ; no, retrogression, 150, 5 ; no, with half a will, 12, 53 ; no, without grumbling, 566, 42 ; often backward, 72, 43 ; often illusory, 273, 28 ; or retrogression, 10, 31 ; social, a degeneracy, 17, 2 ; symbolised by burning of Phœnix, 106, 20 ; the secret of, 312, 24 ; steps of, 94, 9 ; when we make most, 330, 30 ; 333, 22

Prohibition, as a charm, 225, 7

Projecting to accomplishing, a long road, 232, 53

Prometheus, fire of, dangerous to handle, 267, 3 ; rather than Epimetheus, 221, 34

Prometheus Vinctus, the unregenerate, the misery of, 496, 15

Promise, a debt, 17, 3 ; 152, 6 ; a gift, 495, 7 ; a, unfulfilled, 473, 1 ; a, we may trust, 501, 8 ; and performance, 10, 20 ; disappointment of, 161, 36 ; given and broken, 449, 34 ; *versus* performance, 14, 15

Promised Land, the, 449, 35

Promises, extravagant, 148, 10 ; lavish, evil of, 231, 26

Promising, and fulfilling, between, 570, 9 ; and hoping, 357, 60 ; and performing, rule in, 528, 3 ; at death, 566, 9 ; slow in, faithful in performing, 151, 12

Propensities, evil, subduable, 301, 44

Propensity, natural, stubborn, 541, 8

Proper and honourable, inseparable, 56, 41

Property, bequest of, 547, 18 ; defined by Proudhon, 227, 19 ; got dishonestly, fate of, 58, 13 ; ill got, 261, 11, 12 ; in others, right of, 527, 42 ; our own, small, 521, 3 ; parting with, before death, 152, 3 ; pleasure in, how spoiled, 312, 10 ; right of, 289, 14 ; right to, and the sanction, 306, 48 ; right to, Xenophon on, 480, 31 ; who should hold, 479, 22

Prophecies, belief in, most pernicious of superstitions, 324, 39

Prophecy, our gift of, whence, 522, 8 ; voice of, 461, 7 ; wisely denied us, 122, 35

Prophet, a, not less a man, 127, 56 ; among every people, 93, 43 ; distinguished from poet, 449, 46 ; not honoured at home, 17, 5 ; to every people, 125, 54

Prophets, armed and unarmed, 10, 37 ; false, 29, 68 ; 560, 29 ; the art of, 287, 6 ; the teaching of all, 220, 5 ; unconscious, all, 520. 43

Propriety sacrificed to pleasure, 289, 27
Prose, and verse, difference between writing, 497, 7 ; of seventeenth century, 339, 2 ; speaking, without knowing it, 99, 50 ; 181, 23 ; writer, ranked as sage, 202, 25 ; writing, ancient and modern, 445, 31
Proselytes, man's pleasure in making, 262, 30
Proselytising, a natural ambition, 494, 21
Prosperity, a comparison, 395, 16 ; and friendship, 227, 21 ; behaviour in, 89, 11 ; condition of beholding, 302, 53 ; continuous, hard to bear, 94, 28 ; different effects of, 171, 32 ; effect of, on temper, 104, 18 ; effect of sudden, 259, 15 ; forgetful, 224, 24 ; in our own hands, 277, 29 ; its attendant languor, 471, 24 ; man's, the secret of, 302, 49 ; moral effect of, 258, 12 ; national, incompatible with national poverty, 334, 9 ; no, above discouragement, 303, 38 ; no, by falsehood, 302, 49 ; no, enjoyable without adversity, 303, 44 ; of another, to rejoice in, 495, 17 ; past, memory of, 110, 31 ; road to, 140, 34 ; temper in, 5, 13 ; the rule for, 189, 22 ; to one unaffected by adversity, 390, 20 ; unhinging, 295, 38 ; virtue of, 460, 42
Protestantism, effect of, on the character, 37, 1 ; modern, and the cross, 281, 30
Protestation, to be distrusted, 265, 14
Protesting, evil of, 423, 37
Proud, man, in authority, 33, 15 ; man, in the eye of angels, 324, 35 ; inwardly a beggar, 414, 6 ; man, often mean, 449, 49 ; the, appeal to, 409, 28 ; the, compared with the vain, 511, 3 ; the, their affectation, 50, 32 ; the, their humiliation, 455, 25 ; the truly, 440, 36 ; thought for the, 111, 41
Proudhon's ideal of society, 288, 5
Proverb, defined, 17, 8 ; described, 17, 9 ; good, ingredients of, 386, 48 ; Lord J. Russell's definition of, 463, 33 ; the spiritual force of, 476, 13
Proverbial sayings, 467, 35
Proverbs, convincing power of, 415, 9 ; of the wise to be studied, 62, 26 ; significance of, 429, 49 ; William Penn on, 462, 28
Providence, a frowning, 27, 8 ; an inference from history, 291, 2 ; and an inert people, 486, 24 ; and one's wish, 566, 41 ; and things as they are, 168, 5 ; faith in, not to slacken effort, 550, 27 ; faith of men of thought, 284, 12 ; God's, the measure of, 128, 6 ; no freezing, 301, 56 ; those who watch, 480, 22 ; to be trusted 390, 14 ; trust in, Mahomet on, 486, 17 ; watching, 148, 57 ; ways of, our knowledge of, 207, 22 ; with the intelligent, 128, 13
Prudence, a guardian angel, 318, 29, 30 ; a virtue of old age, 411, 44 ; and fortune, 202, 54 ; as guide, 65, 12 ; contrasted with genius, 120, 9 ; defeated by tenderness, 450, 4 ; defined, 113, 12 ; 432, 27 ; from time, 486, 38 ; in matters of the rule, 187, 58 ; the first to forsake the wretched, 280, 28 ; the one, 445, 39 ; the part of, 450, 5 ; the sanctuary of, 382, 20 ; want of, 518, 33
Prudent, favoured by chance, 39, 39 ; man and his time, 431, 24 ; people, how they profit, 37, 17
Psyche's one word, 453, 47
Public, as judges, 569, 42 ; as master, 152, 18 ; as patrons of genius, characterised, 139, 10 ; calamity, the chief, 485, 8 ; composition of, 234, 39 ; how caught, 330, 42 ; men, wise character of, 359, 27 ; opinion, hard to defy, 277, 14 ; opinion without a sovereign, 449, 23 ; servant to, poor animals, 151, 19 ; spirit, ages of, 415, 42 ; the, described, 54, 22 ; the judgment of, 295, 32 ; the sayings about, 450, 7–12 ; the servant of, 42, 26 ; who serves, 554, 23
Pudding, cold and love, 44, 27
Pulpit, teaching of, and training of the market-

place, 450, 13 ; whose voice reaches farthest, 324, 38
Punctuality, and kings, 223, 12 ; important, 80, 4 ; Nelson's, 166, 35 ; strict, the virtue of, 403, 37
Punishment, and crime, 51, 5 (see **Crime**) ; benefit of, 330, 24 ; by the laws, 438, 29 ; contrasted with forgiveness, 277, 55 ; corporeal and pecuniary, 329, 4 ; dreaded and deserved, 126, 52 ; for one's own actions, 430, 24 ; injustice in, compensated, 138, 6 ; rule in, 318, 2 ; sayings about, 450, 14, 15 ; the greatest, 356, 48 ; 473, 3 ; the rudest, 473, 21 ; unfailing, 368, 11
Punsters, Holmes on, 345, 9
Pupil often outstrips master, 325, 41
Purchase, the time to, 76, 29
Pure, the, a characteristic of, 541, 4 ; heart, God's throne, 403, 8
Pureness, Goethe's prayer for, 271, 28
Purgation, now rather than hereafter, 200, 21
Puritans, the, and their work, 479, 7 ; their legacy to the world, 539, 3
Purity, and simplicity, 392, 9 ; of aim, attainment of, 154, 34 ; only from purity, 5, 52 ; the, required, 495, 41
Purpose, fixed, necessity of, 222, 8 ; increasing, through the ages, 564, 37 ; of things, question unscientific, 450, 30 ; one, at a time, 177, 12 ; prosecution of, 112, 51 ; single, value of, 462, 3 ; steadfastness of, 530, 3 ; to be followed by deed, 428, 47 ; when in one's power, to be carried out, 546, 15
Purposes, effect of, on the mind, 442, 17 ; good, in churchyard, 269, 4 ; how often broken, 539, 23 ; wrecked, cause of, 207, 5
Purse, a beggar's, 1, 19 ; a common, effect of having, 546, 25 ; as a friend, 63, 53 ; full of other men's money, 413, 21 ; in the head, 171, 14 ; man who has lost, 169, 36 ; the, its importance, 450, 19 ; who steals my, 552, 37
Purses among friends, 124, 12
Pursuit, enchantment of, 206, 8 ; the pleasure of, 10, 57
Pushing man, deference to, 525, 37
Pyramid, two that reach the top of, 469, 2
Pyramids, antiquity of, 73, 46 ; the, 450, 20
Pyrenees, no longer any, 180, 23

Q

Quack talent, the two sources of, 459, 29
Qualities, bad, akin to good, 88, 24 ; natural, superiority of, 444, 33 ; that ruin, rather than raise, 407, 30 ; too high, inconvenience of, 497, 32
Quarrel, pretext for, easily found, 177, 20 ; proneness to, 484, 2
Quarrelling, and both feeling in the wrong, 276, 40 ; blame of, 52, 22 ; no time for, 422, 42 ; with ourselves, 522, 19
Quarrels, entrance to, 29, 67 ; how to prevent, 504, 10 ; others', meddling with, 148, 2 ; 145, 20 ; why prolonged, 239, 22
Question, test of a man in answering, 489, 34 ; the vexing, 518, 25
Questioning, much, effect of, 552, 22 ; prudent, value of, 359, 24 ; the value of, 148, 12
Questionings, curious, 274, 3
Questions, old vexed, now sorrowfully solving themselves, 327, 20 ; test of a man, 214, 38 ; when to answer, 207, 10
Quickness, evil of too much, 559, 7
Quotation, a fine, 5, 46 ; classical, 43, 48 ; justified, 168, 20 ; the value of, 462, 29
Quotations, Burns' fancy for, 168, 15

R

Rabble, the supreme powers, 109, 14
Rabelais' last words, 210, 36
Race, a humble, how ennobled, 131, 3; always moving, 436, 28; not hybrids, respected by Nature, 292, 20
Races, growing effeminacy of, 239, 23
Rage, how to treat, 335, 51; of love turned to hatred, 154, 3
Rags, disgraceful, 277, 41
Railway travelling, Ruskin's estimate of, 128, 25
Rain, continual effect of, on blossoms, 320, 4
Rainbow as a sign, 450, 33
Rainy day, for unlearned, 165, 49
Rake at another's expense, 281, 3
Rank, but the guinea's stamp, 109, 16; concern about, 467, 34; high, a burden, 132, 45; not happiness, 209, 14; vanity of, 490, 43
Raphael, Lessing on, 367, 55
Rare, the, seldom forgotten, 319, 5
Rascal, putting, to confusion, 297, 44
Rascals, how to diminish, 260, 48
Rash, none, when not seen, 311, 11
Rashness, a fault of youth, 411, 44; discouraged, 4, 68; effect of, 394, 13; effect of, on business, 141, 5
Rational, and real, 520, 20; compared with beautiful, 331, 48
Raven, brought up, still a raven, 80, 25
Read, how to, with profit, 303, 21; things to, 368, 49
Read, not, not written, 310, 37; who has, little, 174, 24
Reader, a good, 489, 2; and author, 240, 2; and the book he reads, 93, 55; good, rare, 6, 52; how to interest a, 299, 5
Readers, busy, 32, 62
Reading, a benefit to few, 469, 6; a rule for, 297, 18; advice in regard to, 208, 15; advices on, 369, 1, 2; as an entertainment, 301, 38; counsels for, 235, 45; experiment in, 502, 45; harmful to fools, 540, 55; how to profit from, 175, 19; idling, 212, 26; importance of, 565, 24; John Morley on, 433, 1; miscellaneous, to be avoided, 280, 19; mistake about, 483, 37; much, effect of, 285, 23; much, Hobbes on, 172, 37; much, the moral effect of, compared with seeing, 12, 50; object of, 445, 18; frequent, not enough, 198, 35; rule for, 528, 5 the most pleasant and profitable, 30, 21; the object of, 368, 50; to doubt or scorn, 14, 39; 139, 34; twice, the benefit of, 537, 28; value of, 77, 7; what is not worth, twice, 536, 43; without reflecting, 495, 11; worst kind of, 17, 56
Real, and Ideal far apart, 115, 33; as contrasted with possible, 234, 40; man, a, defined by Mencius, 153, 9; rational, 520, 20; the, for ever, 219, 54; the, how to measure, 271, 43; the, to be idealised, 539, 33
Realities, hard to discern, 391, 26
Reality, always nobler than fancy, 90, 49; and fancy, the provinces of, 101, 48; and imagination, the worlds of, 465, 7; behind appearances, 481, 34; better than imagination, 14, 14; importance of, 205, 21; *minus* appearance, 61, 23; only, supportable, 316, 18; the only, 482, 12; the product of, how to regard, 241, 47; truth of, why unrecognised, 105, 12
Reaping, more difficult than sowing, 495, 45; the rule in, 510, 28
Reason, a misuse of, 207, 18; a rare guide, 162, 20; against a crowd with stones, 535, 37; agreeableness to, as a test, 298, 19; and contingency, 462, 1; and knowledge, 513, 10; and necessity, 462, 1; and instinct contrasted, 172, 46: and

piety, to be combined, 526, 39; and prudence, in conduct, 241, 44; and religion, 372, 6; and spirit, two aspects of one thing, 414, 37; and understanding, objects of, 67, 2; being without, 491, 2; compared with fancy, 526, 20; elevating power of, 68, 20; every man's, his oracle, 92, 42, 44; functions of, 329, 43; 504, 2; its rank, 435, 4; like drunk man on horseback, 163, 29; like sweet bells jangled, 317, 38; loss compared with deprivation of, 458, 15; misapplied, 468, 22; no, upon compulsion, 123, 38; not to rust unused, 407, 29; once passion, 537, 4; origin of, 102, 3; our chart, 46, 35; our delight in, abuse of, 337, 37; relation of, to revelation, 375, 12; sacredness of, 148, 33; service under, advantage of, 152, 19; sound and sufficient, the lot of few, 400, 22; sovereign with the noble, 15, 52; the function of, Cicero on, 368, 34; the pilot, 239, 15; the use of, 53, 39; those who have no, 127, 6; true, its power, 500, 36; truths of, not dependent on facts, 421, 32; *versus* blind force, 350, 24; *versus* faith, 20, 20; without the light of divine truth, 352, 6; worse appear better, 157, 15; 16
Reasonable, or unreasonable, asking what is, 194, 33; the, open to every one, 217, 7
Reasoner, a wise, 551, 7
Reasoning mule, obstinacy of, 17, 41
Reasons, nothing to the chaff, 133, 5; our own, our satisfaction in, 331, 4; strong, effect of, 404, 8
Rebellion, no equity under, 471, 37
Rebels, treatment of, 47, 38
Reckoning, when banquet's o'er, 394, 48; without host, 41, 21
Reckonings, short, 389, 31
Recollection, a happy, 505, 39; inferior to pertinency, 139, 14
Recompense, 381, 19; Fénelon on his, 284, 18; rule of, 21, 19
Reconciliation, desire for, as a prognostic, 238, 30
Recreation, necessity of, 111, 12
Redress, the surest way to, 456, 30
Refined man, characteristic of, 452, 12
Refinement, what contributes to, 540, 34
Reflection, commentary on experience, 97, 28; noble, 34, 19; they who practise not, 479, 21; value of, 77, 7
Reform, evil of unsuccessful attempts at, 22, 10; not joyous, but grievous, 305, 28
Reformation, attended by a great licentiousness, 6, 67; salve of, in ignorance of the sore, 452, 23; the, egg of, 84, 24; the only solid, 495, 15; unconscious, 528, 9
Reformers, error of our, 206, 17
Reforming a world or a nation. 495, 15
Reforms, great, negative as well as positive, 91, 19; history of, 435, 20; how far effective, 9, 59; necessary, how helped, 127, 8; our, not radical, 539, 22
Refusal, a friendly, 28, 30; less than nothing, 17, 46
Refusing, in, the "no" only heard, 266, 1
Regard, how to win, 42, 13
Regeneration accompanied with travail, 12, 7
Regimenting men, importance of, 202, 44
Regret, no, no amendment, 147, 38
Reign, to, worth ambition, 495, 16
Rejected of man, accepted of God, 112, 1
Relations, hard to discern, 391, 26; hatred among, 2, 53; our, character of, 339, 9; our, and our friends', how chosen, 339, 10
Relationships, one's, requirement in, 10, 28
Relatives, by chance, 235, 16
Religion, a bigotry, 524, 29; a cloak, 165, 5; a fruit of time, 486, 32; a God, 398, 40; a necessity to great minds, 76, 27; a new, not the thing wanted, 297, 31; and liberty in Catholic and Protestant countries, 185, 23; and love, strength of, 253, 48; and morality, divorce between, 427, 18; and wise

men, 11, 5; anything but living for, 277, 17; characteristic of, 64, 8; Cicero's definition of, 216, 30; contrasted with beliefs, 85, 38; contrasted with morality, 467, 13; contrasted with superstition, 407, 6, 7, 12, 13; dead letter of, fate of, 422, 44; defined, 537, 5; definition and power of, 452, 45; dependence of, on prayer, 306, 43; display of, 547, 21; disputing about and practising, 423, 45; done for money, Ruskin on, 540, 40; essential to education, 77, 4; effect of, 489, 8; effect of first sense of, 2, 56; effect of too deep study of, 497, 36; errors in, 464, 43; errors in, sanction of, 189, 24; essence of all, 425, 34; every established, once a heresy, 99, 43; fancy in, 101, 51; felt as a slavery, 12, 47; first object, whole object, 151, 44; first element in, 379, 8; flower of, when perfect, 447, 24; Frederick the Great on, 174, 48; from habit, 398, 37; fruit of age, 536, 16; gentilising power of, 566, 28; heartfelt, the source of all, 392, 31; how to persuade men to, 553, 33; in relation to art, 18, 50; inconsistency of our zeal for, 197, 10; indispensable to society, 307, 14; living, root of, 252, 6; made secondary, 541, 7; matter of feeling, 121, 43; Monday, 282, 27; mongers, and their dupes, 284, 36; much, no goodness, 285, 24; much profession in, 189, 32; murdered by bigotry, 30, 18; national, now no test of a people, 306, 36; no living, till dead own itself dead, 106, 54; no teaching, without having, 305, 43; no, without humanity, 142, 44; not credited, recesses for, 496, 43; not professed, 538, 25; of all sensible people, 168, 27; of one age in the next, 451, 10; of present time, 114, 22; only guide of life, 549, 42; only one true, 476, 19; origin of, in society, 340, 20; our abuse of, 339, 13; our, and treasure to be one, 508, 4; our, Emerson on, 339, 12; power of, 174, 44; rooted in fear, 188, 17; soul of, 100, 18; sum of, 493, 15; sympathy with Nature, 408, 43; talk against, suspicious, 547, 28; temple-step of, 456, 5; the all in, 189, 33; the only foundation of, 189, 36; the performance of duty, 375, 29; though undefined, no chimæra, 138, 34; to be one's own, 240, 37, 38; too hard, 497, 30; true, 500, 31-33; true, object of, 445, 21; upon mere authority, 493, 14; vestibule of, 283, 17; vital, first condition of, 481, 44; with suffering, no wonder, 203, 28; without morality, 305, 11; 522, 39; without personal immortality, 559, 21

Religions, all once true, 451, 12; Goethe's three, 468, 28; of world, 451, 11; only two possible, 466, 27; the essence of all true, 375, 28; the genesis of, 372, 34; transient, but not religious sense, 333, 42

Religious, a, not less a man, 7, 26; enthusiasm, hollowness of, 215, 26; men at their beads, 543, 39; passion, the, and art, 451, 13; principles, Hume on, 96, 1; revival, the ground on which to hope for, 422, 44

Religiousness, true, condition of, 357, 12

Relish in one's self, 310, 1

Remedies, extreme, for extreme evils, 98, 9; imaginary, for imaginary diseases, 269, 30; our, in ourselves, 339, 13; sayings about, 470, 23; slower than diseases, 410, 51

Remedy, of remedies, 514, 14; where sure, 504, 30; worse than disease, 5, 2

Remembrance our inalienable paradise, 64, 13

Reminding may cause forgetting, 273, 9

Remorse, as punishment, 473, 21; not imaginary, 10, 13

Removals, quick, 365, 8

Renounce, who needs not, 161, 19

Rent, to pay, plough or not, 17, 50

Renunciation, a life-long demand, 483, 41; effect of, 237, 40; essential to happiness, 217, 6; importance of, 205, 30

Repentance, a deathbed, 4, 6; 55, 37; a vain, 142, 52; act of, the virtue in, 414, 7; daughter of the skies, 44, 43; man not satisfied with, 559, 43; man's virtue, 66, 40; our glory, 338, 8; pain of, 446, 37; true, 500, 34, 35; with amendment rare, 117, 28

Repetition, the effect of, 171, 47

Reports, evil, belief in, 307, 1

Repose, a well-earned, 399, 15; agitating effect of our love of, 197, 9; not finding, complaint of, 274, 46; of mind, a specific for, 229, 17; shameful, evil of, 344, 31; the beginning of, 425, 10; through equipoise, 103, 46

Reproach, only defence against, 472, 23

Reproaches, best revenge of, 567, 43

Reproof, effect of, that hits a sore place, 398, 41; how to administer, 374, 3; of kings, 107, 26

Republic, contrasted with monarchy, 282, 25; necessity for, 515, 10; the want of a, 109, 13; Ruskin's definition of, 17, 49

Republics, how ruined, 239, 24

Reputation, a, dies at every word, 21, 40; a great, Napoleon on, 7, 4; a high, responsibility of, 434, 31; a sinking, sign of, 199, 16; blaze of, 418, 35; different from esteem, 87, 6; life on, prospective, 161, 44; like a man's shadow, 227, 28; loss of, 101, 7, 8; 305, 2; man's esteem for, 266, 12; of others, as a support, 280, 30; sayings about, 451, 14-16; spotless, its value, 450, 18; the bubble, 211, 30

Resentment, Burns on, 340, 17; concealed, 196, 40; not to stain innocence, 402, 10; of a poor man, 451, 17; to be restrained, 243, 43

Resentments, quick, 365, 9

Reserve, commended, 205, 39; effect of, on character, 443, 38

Resetter as bad as thief, 24, 9

Resignation, difficult, 161, 29; under unjust suffering, 237, 33

Resistance, spirit of, innate, 470, 30

Resisted, what it is to be, 333, 12

Resolution, acting with, 362, 10; bad, effect of, 201, 10; dauntless spirit of, 28, 35; ebbing, 109, 28; fate of authors of, 483, 10; help in need, 97, 39; native hue of, 485, 46; one's, to be kept secret, 297, 5; power of, 15, 34; 237, 21; road to, 452, 3; steadfast, effect of, 92, 3

Resolutions, first, most honest, 107, 1; good, 356, 3; hasty, 141, 10; our, frail, 337, 15; sudden, 406, 3

Resolve, built on reason, 330, 45; the feeble, despicable, 166, 36

Respect, at a distance, 260, 6; for others, condition of, 474, 11; lost only with loss of self-respect, 305, 38; the alone worthy of, 142, 4; to all and sundry, a risk, 549, 7

Respectability, how earned, 274, 19

Responsibility, for acts, 34, 29; not affected by ignorance, 448, 2

Respectable people, world-made, 292, 9

Rest, a man's, 278, 26; a, that remaineth, 477, 27; after all difficulty, 504, 16; and unrest, 378, 23; condition of, 378, 33; effect of, 368, 17, 18; how found in this world, 325, 8; how to find, 567, 41; in grave, 182, 29; our, not to be the rest of stones, 243, 28; peculiar to the spirit, 246, 44; perfect, not to be found, 155, 18; the secret of, 242, 33; the only, worth anything, 307, 2; too much, effect of, 497, 44, 45

Restlessness, as a motive, 399, 1; man's, accounted for, 536, 21; no wisdom where, 473, 32

Restraint, a necessity, 212, 7; by arbitrary power, 207, 28; *versus* liberty, 202, 26

Results, contrasted with details, 547, 40; great, of slow achievement, 135, 1

Resurrection, the, promise of, 338, 30

Reticence, value of, 145. 37
Retirement, good for the soul, 59, 27; love of, an extra sense, 153, 3
Retribution, divine, 125, 23. 30
Retrogression, no, 116, 2
Retrospect, pleasing, 27, 9
Revelation, and religion, 372, 1; and sense to see it, 463, 22; defined, 434, 38; independent of our seeking, 481, 18; mistake about, 275, 13; of God, the only, 428, 46; only steady guide, 34, 50; the only, 85, 32; the sole medium of divine grace, 538, 11
Revelations, two, necessary to society, 396, 13
Revenge, and pleasure, their ears, 349, 31; best, 252, 7; 492, 30; most heroic, 307, 3; sense of, 512, 8; sign of weak mind, 280, 4; study of, folly, 148, 32; taking and passing over, 190, 7; to the rude man, 22, 19
Reverence, a central law, 215, 48; a supernatural sense, 262, 12; and fear contrasted, 492, 21; and love, objects respectively of, 110, 21; as an element in thought, 484, 6; compared with fear, 291, 43; due to gods, 58, 41; not innate, and its importance, 334, 21; the first object, 21, 29; to herald knowledge, 260, 28; value of, 189, 37; with knowledge, 241, 24
Reverie, losing one's self in, 494, 12; under reflection, 371, 4
Revolt, the promoters of, 335, 13
Revolution, and its martyrs, 549, 38; by whose fault it arises, 7, 5; dangerous classes in a, 344, 51; French, meaning of, 429, 25; French, described, 122, 4; modern, merely dissolution, 281, 31
Revolutions, aim of all, 440, 26; cause of, 451, 22; fear herald of, 103, 39; great, as movements, 135, 2; great, cause of, 431, 13
Rewarding, rule in, 203, 32
Rhetoric, for, he could not ope, 111, 1; god of, ceased from, 546, 36; spiritual, the law of, 241, 16; two rules of, 459, 24; use of rules of, 109, 6
Rhyme, excellence in, a defect often in, 411, 32; the powerful, enduring power of, 312, 43; rudder of verses, 111, 2; without purpose or thought, 235, 43
Rhythm, enchanting power of, 38, 13
Rich, art of getting, 530, 27; business of, 119, 11; dependence of, 431, 10; ghost of the, and his wealth, 299, 39; hastening to be, 147, 55; how to become, 136, 43; 171, 26; making, or poor, 477, 4; man, a, 211, 19; man, a, that is great, 414, 6; man, according to Emerson, 143, 53, 54; man, ready made, 208, 47; man, the only, 144, 52; man who is, 304, 12; man's happiness, 528, 12; men, weary of themselves, 237, 24; mistake to seem, 265, 15; none, by himself, 306, 12; none so, as he should be, 304, 49; not to be flattered, 107, 19; partnership of poor with, risky, 99, 1; secrets of, can't be kept, 320, 11; that shall come to want, 148, 7; the, benefactors to, 513, 27; the, discontent of, 110, 35; the right to be, 308, 24; the, sayings about, 70, 1-3; 451, 24-32; the truly, 19, 21; what it is to be, 490, 37; what makes us, 191, 42; who would grow, 41, 29
Richard's himself again, 154, 46
Richelieu, Corneille, on, 360, 43; on his deathbed, 211, 1
Riches, a bar to felicity, 161, 30; a burden unloaded by death, 175, 4; a test of a man, 14, 46; accessible to man of common sense, 440, 25; acquisition of, no end to misery, 286, 14; affected despite of, 269, 43; all, from heaven, 219, 51; as a good, 18, 17; as excluding from heaven, 204, 22; baggage, 165, 21; best effect of, 237, 24; cause of ennui, 173, 40; chains, 307, 52; dependent on poverty, 171, 43; fascination of, 74, 13; fatal to happiness, 160, 48; first approach to, 428, 4; great, only by

taxing labour of others, 303, 9; great, sole use of, 325, 2; great, source of all, 405, 27; grow in hell, 242, 7; how dispensed, 338, 29; how to acquire, 243, 10; how to increase, 140, 3; incentives to evil, 77, 36; Jean Paul's contempt for, 169, 24; mistakes about, 128, 27; motive in coveting, 97, 47; never enough increased, 183, 53; no guarantee for digestion, 174, 30; passion for, restlessness of, 257, 43; power of, 70, 14; 530, 20; profession without possession of, 449, 33; real, 17, 4; 358, 4; the greatest, 474, 14; true, how procured, 359, 4; unenjoyed, 175, 28; we can and cannot carry, 281, 21; who delights in accumulating, 151, 2; who has enough, 20, 24
Richest, man, the, 143, 45; 406, 35
Rider, a good, on good horse, 6, 53
Ridicule, if instructive, bearable, 166, 27; settling power of, 378, 43; that benefits, 29, 45; the test of, 369, 38; unbearable, 331, 43
Ridiculous, appreciation of, test of a man, 34, 8; being, hard to avoid, 202, 45; easy to recognise, 496, 34; from affectation, 330, 7; how we become most, 521, 38; sense of, dependent on intellect, 61, 30; sense of, test of character, 276, 31; side, our, 522, 10; step from, to sublime, 334, 12
Right, and might identical, 279, 12; 184, 30; and wrong, Goethe's test of, 306, 16; as founded on possession, 27, 22; assertion of, 211, 12; at whatever cost, 71, 51; before might, 370, 23; champions for, 92, 32; consciousness of, 150, 22; divine, divine might, 70, 10; following, as right, 386, 13; Hobbes on, 215, 18; how to assume one's, 368, 23; keep to the, 548, 30; knowledge of, enough, 171, 20; man, the, 59, 47; of man, first, 490, 19; of man, most indisputable, 324, 30; of slow attainment, 567, 15; power of, 12, 1; sometimes in abeyance, 71, 52; sure to win, 111, 3; that is born with us, 517, 23; the, and no fear, 170, 12; the one thing to be done, 485, 43; the, to be anxious about, 457, 23; to look into blots of, 167, 13; way, how never to miss, 58, 46; with the strongest, 233, 26
Right-about-face, a brave word, 32, 54
Right-doing, the key to, 177, 11
Righteous man, mercy of, 18, 1
Righteousness, effect of, 424, 39; fruit of, 429, 32; overmuch condemned, 28, 15
Righting, of things in time, 480, 48; one's self without right, 315, 22
Rights, how forfeited, 96, 44; of men not worth discussing, 451, 44; permanence of, 85, 26; transmitted, 231, 43
Rigour often less effective than lenity, 237, 35
Ring gone, but not finger, 166, 48
Rings, uses of, 61, 20
Ripe moment, the, to be seized, 4, 1
Ripeness, all, 275, 37
Rising, in the world, rapid, how to esteem, 276, 39; sun, homage paid to, 272, 19
Risk, the charm of, 94, 36; to be run to save all, 9, 4
Rivalry, effect of, on talent, 194, 8; foiled, effect of, 542, 21
River, a, a guide, 513, 45; brink of that mighty, 103, 45; every, leads to the sea, 108, 14
River-courses, the great, 431, 33
Rivers, roads, 239, 25
Road, a long, 48, 22; any, a world-highway, 16, 18; common, safe, 217, 28; good, and wise traveller, different, 6, 54; how to make long, short, 474, 16; every, leads to an inn, 108, 15; right in the end, 212, 14; the, who knows, 42, 24
Robb'd, yet not robb'd, 147, 17
Robert of Doncaster's epitaph, 535, 31
Rocks, lessons they teach, 523, 35

Rod, the, sparing, 148, 24
Rogue, a, defined, 18, 20; resemblance of, to honest man, 377, 5
Rogues, not always punished, 85, 35; not to be pitied, 177, 6
Roman citizen, Cicero on punishing, 198, 31
Romance, age of, transition into that of science, 431, 5; ages of, 300, 40; everywhere, 90, 55; 191, 1; the only, for grown-up persons, 446, 5
Romances compared with history, 255, 10
Romans, Emerson on, 335, 8
Romantic, the, contrasted with the classical, 43, 49; the, defined, 452, 7
Rome, Augustus Cæsar's boast in regard to, 509, 23; better first elsewhere than second in, 166, 22
Rooks, how to get rid of, 68, 31
Room, ample, and verge enough, 122, 51; the, required, 368, 38
Root, condition of taking, 488, 13
Rose, brief life of, 505, 42; scent of, enough, 61, 21
Rosebuds, gather, while ye may, 118, 56
Roses, contrasted, 33, 5; who would gather, 152, 53
Roughness, effect of, 387, 54
Rousseau, Joubert on pathos of, 178, 53
Rousseau's last words, 210, 37
Routine, cramping to life, 437, 39; fatal effect of, 423, 43
Roving, profitlessness of, 218, 30
Rude, breast, not without inspiration, 22, 32; man, the, characteristic of, 452, 12
Rudder, or rock, 152, 43; 460, 33
Ruin, going to, 128, 26; how the gods bring about, 363, 4; how we come to, 346, 21; of everything, source of, 206, 44; of men, 276, 36; source of our, 522, 15; sources of, 568, 36; the broad road to, 69, 29; the road to, 452, 4; what underlies all, 506, 22
Ruins, grey, beams of day on, 111, 16; no cause to mourn over, 311, 44
Rule, how to, 364, 11; the desire to, 51, 34; the sovereign, 297, 48; what can and cannot, 301, 35
Ruler, a, friendless, 320, 21; a good, test of, 305, 50; as such, 17, 35; duty of, 390, 19; positive and negative qualifications of, 153, 1; qualification of, 148, 14; quality in a, 324, 10; test of a, 181, 37; to regard his people's voice, 389, 35
Rulers, limit of their authority, 239, 1; many, not good, 337, 2
Ruling, art of, 431, 11; men, and amusing them different, 8, 8; passion, power of, 452, 14; safe, the condition of, 303, 28; the art of arts, 218, 20
Rumour, growth of, 101, 5; often converse of truth, 233, 9; spread of, 281, 14
Running, the, not enough, 39, 10; vain, if on wrong road, 519, 26
Ruskin on his teachings, 559, 11
Rust, foul cankering, 113, 56
Rutland, Countess of, epitaph of, 506, 30

S

Sabbath, Christ's saying on, 452, 16; ordainer of, pity in, 151, 51; profaned, no gain, 316, 52
Sack, bad, 37, 5; empty, 79, 23
Sackcloth, what underlies, 506, 25
Sacrament, received, a benefit, 152, 8
Sacrifice, a duty, 185, 38; a sick man's, 19, 24; a sorrowful, 440, 7; as duty and necessity, effect of, 395, 23; in the eyes of God, 491, 42; necessary to realisation of idea, 302, 34; of less for greater, 332, 61
Sacrifices, in little things, hard, 522, 43; our, passive, 339, 14

Sad, man, not friend, 260, 30; the, disliked by gay, 324, 5; when has cause, 165, 22
Saddest thing, the, 443, 46
Sadness, a mark of goodness, 475, 20; deep, 514, 34; enjoyment in, 471, 23; soul's poison, 118, 17
Safety, the only, 397, 5; the parent of, 37, 15
Sagacious man contrasted with a wise, 566, 36
Sage, a, defined, 18, 54; a true, a world-pupil, 143, 11; how regarded, 233, 7; test of a, 478, 51; why esteemed by world, 210, 45
Sages ancient, aim of, 208, 27
Sailing without wind, 209, 2
Sailor, a disgrace to, 35, 10; first, daring of, 182, 14; heart of, 34, 17
Saint, peasant, toiling for bread and light, 405, 19; run mad, 111, 36; seeming, not to be trusted, 501, 18
Sainthood, questionable, 476, 31
Saints, a communion of, for all who have faith, 483, 27; a living communion of, 470, 4; God's, triumph over, 385, 14; living and dead, different treatment of, 461, 24
Salvation, a dubious, offering, 73, 31; according to Plato, 216, 22; all alone, misery, 200, 16; by human means, 430, 23; first step in, 194, 27; no, in the course of justice, 484, 17; only road to, 444, 40; things that tend to our, 457, 26
Samaritan, the good, doing, 564, 32
Same, the, everywhere, 39, 9
Samson's riddle, 340, 13
Sanctity, the root of, 452, 9
Sanctuary, shall we raze, 141, 49
Sand, no grain of, unpeopled, 302, 12
Sanity, a test of, 191, 36; how preserved, 314, 20; perfect, exceptional, 304, 11
Saracens, Emerson on, 335, 8
Sarcasm, the sting in, 416, 19
"Sartor Resartus," two main ideas of, 263, 15
Satan, finds mischief, 192, 36
Satiety, as reformer, 294, 16; fulness of, a curse, 397, 43
Satire, and poverty, 354, 25; general and personal, 187, 1; hard to suppress, 67, 29; truthful, effect of, 20, 12
Satires and lampoons, written with wit and spirit, 229, 23
Satirical vein, danger of, 146, 42
Satisfaction, effect of, 93, 57
Satisfied, and dissatisfied, different conduct of, 482, 51; well, 144, 1
Sauce, the best, 336, 1
Savage, civilised, worst, 59, 46; noble, 164, 35
Saved once, saved for ever, 79, 25
Saving, a great art, 400, 37; a man against his will, 196, 27; having, 114, 5; necessity of, as well as gaining, 363, 35
Saviour, a, vocation of, 58, 2
"Savoir-vivre," the first condition of, 374, 45
Say, having one's, 168, 46
Saying, and doing, 70, 43; 379, 38; and doing, difference between, 29, 59; before singing, 236, 5; from, to doing, a long stride, 52, 36; insincere, 503, 19; well and doing well, different effects of, 30, 7
Sayings, wise, 557, 42–44
Scaffold, not the disgrace, 39, 4
Scandal, and a lie, 8, 15; and tea, 253, 49; and the great, 109, 45; circulation of, 101, 6; lust of, 470, 6; waits on state, 135, 33
Scandals, dead, use of, 55, 30; fly, 329, 31
Scapegoat always needed, 3, 62
Scattering and increasing, 477, 5
Scenes, new, power of, 297, 32; prying behind, 152, 55
Scepticism, the misery of, 262, 48

Sceptre, snatched from tyrants, 84, 36; weight of, when known, 144, 46
Schemes, sinister, how defeated, 316, 32; our, not favoured by Zeus, 10, 11; the best laid, 417, 44
Schiller, and Goethe, compared, 532, 22; and his ideal, 481, 28; Goethe of, 379, 11; on his education, 492, 14
Schiller's, ideal, premature, 54, 9; scorn for worldly possessions, 63, 41
Schisms in Church, root of, 452, 8
Scholar, a good and ripe, 116, 9; great, common defect of, 7, 6; self-denial required in, 19, 6; the affair of, 346, 8; the ink of, its merits, 436, 39; the true, procedure of, 459, 8; without good-breeding, 452, 27
Scholars, greatest, 432, 37; greatest, not wisest men, 258, 50; seldom great men, 465, 24; unregarded, 176, 4
School, true preparatory, 319, 24
Schoolboy, the desire of, 452, 28
Schooling, good, missed, 150, 44; our, a preparation for slavery, 320, 37
Schoolmasters, express and unexpress, 426, 24; our, 526, 25
Science, a true man of, defined, 143, 40; advance in, due to individuals, 184, 42; an exchange of ignorances, 220, 44; and Christianity, 420, 19; and the theologians, 97, 59; and thought, law of, 484, 38; as truth, 500, 29; at bottom, 313, 4; children not to be taught, 527, 34; compared with conscience, 46, 40; condition of any, 526, 35; contrasted with religion, 372, 30; defined, 383, 3; dictionary and grammar of, 236, 28; falsely so called, 532, 38; its value to the race, 521, 5; men of, controversy unworthy of, 276, 8; modern, Ruskin on, 281, 32; no, patriotic, 473, 44; not in bulk, 162, 24; physical, a lesson of, 348, 19; pride of, an evil, 275, 41; prosecuted for its own sake, 81, 40; the faculty of, 426, 46; the fathers of, 247, 34; the home-making power of, 535, 36; the new in, 189, 43; the want in, 399, 18; two things to consider in, 189, 44; without poetry, 559, 42; work of, 464, 2
Sciences, advantages of study in, 157, 22; functions of the several, 131, 48; history of, a fugue, 64, 23
Scipio, Africanus, saying of, 319, 1
Scoffer, fate of, at the resurrection, Mahomet on, 331, 10
Scolding, folly of continual, 225, 4; vanity of, 304, 50
Scorning, futility of, 145, 43
Scotch, drink, Burns on, 108, 30; drink, Burns on the power of, 237, 8; the, temper of, 346, 11
Scotchman, the, Goldsmith on, 558, 23
Scoundrel, no, without his apology, 218, 17
Scoundrelism, course of, 421, 44
Scoundrels, guiding, by love, 432, 51; just hatred of, backbone of religion, 215, 37
Scribbling, incessant, evil of, 192, 53
Scripture, demand for, 22, 36; how to interpret, 93, 60; no jesting with, 296, 46
Scruples, to be guarded against, 241, 38
Scylla shunned, 485, 49
Sea, sayings about, 452, 30–35; secret of, how to learn, 563, 31; the, a harper, 564, 26; treacherous, 23, 19
Searchable and unsearchable, wise treatment of, 54, 26
Searching commended, 22, 11
Season, things in, 162, 1
Secrecy, and vice, 548, 26; once whispered, 168, 12; recommended by Burns, 25, 32; recommending, 370, 31; to be kept, 141, 48
Secret, a, hard to keep, 485, 22; a, imparted, 17, 13; between two or three, 360, 10; blame of disclosing, 498, 43; how to keep a, 177, 13; how to

lose command of, 150, 25; keeping and disclosing, 199, 18; kept and revealed, 19, 5; knowing and revealing, 207, 30; of a friend, his, not mine, 536, 30; power of a, 486, 8; the great, 550, 5; trusting, to a servant, 152, 35; weight of a, 377, 3; who would wish to keep, 553, 32; woman cannot keep, 25, 7
Secrets, all, to be laid open, 315, 40; keeping of, 11, 53; revealing, 496, 4; why coveted, 311, 13
Sectarian bigotry, Ruskin on, 514, 31
Sectary, the, mistake of, 191, 38
Sects, founders of, 307, 32; the, and reason, 93, 61
Security, insecure, 144, 45; often near ruin, 325, 33
Seducer, no, happy, 295, 12
See, they that won't, 148, 20; to, but not be seen through, our wish, 525, 19
Seed, and flower, relation of, 428, 49; and tree, interval between, 469, 35; sown by God, 379, 1, 2
Seed-corn not to be ground, 107, 48
Seed-field, man's, 288, 6
Seeing, an object, necessity of, 508, 5; and looking, different, 2, 38; before overseeing, 242, 56; believing, 41, 12; culminating in dimness of vision, 395, 22; followed by contemplation, 20, 37; for one's self, a great moment, 15, 3; in part, 539, 46; musically, 384, 29; rarer than thinking, 164, 13; thing beautifully done, pleasure of, 471, 26; through, but not being seen through, 329, 15; through, preventing seeing, 274, 37; truly, condition of, 176, 2
Seeking, compared with finding, 125, 18; or not and finding, or not, 152, 10
Seemly, the, permitted, 84, 38
Seen, compared with heard, 480, 47
Seer, a, beguiling, 218, 19; and seen, alike punished, 127, 55
Seers and thinkers compared, 453, 7
Selection, natural, defined, 290, 15; saved, trouble saved, 85, 12; the art of, importance to author 151, 6
Self, admiration of, 127, 19; admirer or lover of only, 334, 31; alone interesting, 313, 38; an eternal entity, 483, 29; as a mirror of truth, 10, 2; as one's enemy, 79, 16; concentration on, fruits of, 10, 40; conquest of, 146, 48; estimation of, 79, 14; valuation of, to be rigorous, 79, 14; harmony with, 543, 7; how best to shun, 167, 38; how to know, 465, 15; 556, 34; how to live to, 483, 40; how to regard, 323, 34; 523, 16; ignorance of, 175, 5; instance of love of, 88, 33; left to, good at times, 205, 38; Luther's fear of, 164, 45; man's, his worst blind, 324, 19; oneness with, oneness with God, 532, 27; one's, as a miracle and monster, 167, 2; one's truest and deepest, 519, 32; our estimate of, 93, 26; pious and just honouring of, 447, 42; respect only for, 201, 12; saying good or bad of, 381, 24; thinking modestly of, 150, 11; to be overcome, 324, 14; trust of, and distrust of, 105, 36; unbelief in, 427, 30; undervaluing, and others, 148, 40; where to be sought and found, 384, 46; worship of, dreary, 86, 7; dead, a stepping-stone, 167, 19
Self-abasement, effect of, 83, 11
Self-assertion and self-denial, 340, 37
Self-censure, a fishing for praise, 9, 17
Self-commendation, a legitimate, 471, 14
Self-conceit, a source of darkness, 445, 35; cause of ruin, 163, 12; how to lessen, 176, 14; not to be obtrusive, 301, 34; the first sin, 428, 36
Self-concentration, man's, his fatalest disease, 423, 42
Self-confidence, its attestation, 522, 38; the power of, 395, 38
Self-confident, the, to beware, 241, 8
Self-conquest, victory, 227, 11
Self-control, man without, 551, 33

Self-culture and study of history, 304, 31
Self-deception, 523, 23 ; the greatest, 305, 1
Self-denial, greatness of, 133, 39 ; how judge a life of, 303, 41 ; importance of teaching, 465, 30 ; Scott on the power of, 411, 13 ; superseded, 544, 31 ; the benefit of, 362, 23 ; the gain of, 385, 9 ; want of, 513, 32
Self-dependence, 8, 40 ; happiness of, 161, 24
Self-endeavour, the key to success, 34, 11
Self-esteem, due, a necessity, 171, 16, 21 ; grounded on just and right, 325, 40
Self-forgetfulness, the best, 418, 1
Self-help alone owned by nature, 292, 25 ; as an acquisition, 190, 23 ; Heaven's help, 7, 32
Self-helping man, welcome, 531, 21
Self-knowledge, a necessity 212, 6 ; a, not bad, 304, 21 ; an effect of, 418, 19 , difficult, 178, 51 ; how attained, 161, 6 ; 304, 55 ; index of, 382, 23 ; limited, 525, 11 ; never perfect, 306, 3 ; rare, 517, 5 ; source of, 276, 16 ; sum of wisdom, 117, 31 ; Thales on, 443, 40 ; the condition of, 296, 8 ; value of, 151, 25 ; 218, 26
Self-love, a balloon, 222, 18 ; and debt, 224, 13 ; blinding, 78, 29 ; excess of, 552, 11 ; function of, 504, 2 ; greatest flatterer, 222, 17 ; offended, 222, 19 ; to be cut out, 52, 17
Self-lovers, the nature of, 206, 31
Self-made men, our, 339, 15
Self-maintenance, no hardship, 434, 17
Self-neglecting, a sin, 386, 7
Self-praise offensive, 231, 24
Self-reformation, a contribution to national, 152, 9 ; a labour, 419, 38
Self-regard a right, 470, 10
Self-reliance, after failure, 346, 44 ; the virtue in, 417, 1
Self-respect, effect of, on morals, 493, 1 ; importance of, 24, 10
Self-restraint, necessity of, 305, 5 ; the virtue of, 266, 24
Self-reverence, 2, 2 ; as a virtue, 451, 21
Self-satisfied man, the, 505, 27
Self-subdual as a conflict, 301, 24
Self-sufficiency, law of, 443, 8
Self-taught, a merely, man, 532, 35
Self-trust, its comprehensiveness, 189, 47 ; the value of, 506, 14
Self-will to be subdued, 142, 4
Selfish, like sympathetic, 408, 36 ; no happiness to, 162, 43
Selfishness always a failure, 90, 47
Selling, the rule in, 176, 13
Semblance *versus* substance, regard for, 150, 14
Sense, as deceptive, 473, 5 ; and dreams, 337, 41 ; and thought, their partitions, 373, 9 ; better than loquacity, 261, 23 ; common, contrasted with fine, 106, 30 ; compared with learning, 236, 28 ; good, relation between, and good taste, 83, 51 ; higher, ennobling power of, 131, 3 ; in confronting evil, 86, 4 ; men of, and wit, 467, 5 ; native, to be respected, 509, 29 ; objects of, not there, 529, 5 ; strength, 146, 53 ; true, its power, 500, 36 ; want of, 3, 20 ; want of, and crime, 173, 39
Senses, and faith, 99, 56 ; avenues to enjoyment, 313, 2 ; delusion of, how to annihilate, 186, 45 ; man owes to experience, 37, 6 ; not deceptive, 453, 13 ; origin of, 102, 2 ; our, and impressions, 339, 16 ; our, planets, 262, 46 ; their truthfulness, 66, 16
Sensibilities, our, to be cherished, 204, 14
Sensibility, effect of, on circumstances, 46, 14 ; excessive, 386, 51 ; quick, mark of intelligence, 365, 11 ; that is true taste, 278, 24 ; too much, 497, 46 ; without humour, 425, 41
Sensible, man, a merely, his value, 7, 44 ; man, a,

640

when deceived, 232, 52 ; man, most, 551, 42 ; the, no novelty, 532, 24
Sensual indulgence, effects of, 156, 45
Sensualist, body of a, 418, 46
Sensuality, always a failure, 90, 47 ; an offence to reason, 151, 1 ; debasing, 16, 16 ; life of, how atoned for, 79, 39 ; most potent antidote to, 473, 29 ; the evil of, 399, 39
Sentence, good, the first quoter of, 297, 43 ; understanding *versus* dissecting, 423, 47 ; what gives force to, 207, 38
Sentences, our, characterised, 337, 19 ; pregnant, 468, 10
Sentiment, in women and men, 476, 30 ; no expression of, we don't feel, 330, 29 ; the sail, 264, 23 ; *versus* action, 91, 52
Sentimental, doomed, 453, 14
Sentimentalism, a watery, 490, 4
Sentimentalist, barren, 416, 47 ; the, assiduous, tiresome, 334, 24
Sentiments, social, rule for, 244, 13
Separation, rule of, 520, 11
Sequence, essential to value, 94, 23
Serenity, a gift of time, 487, 22 ; attainment of, 154, 34 ; feigning, 453, 16 ; peculiar to man, 416, 9
Serfdom in England at present, 472, 4
Serious, difficult to master, 496, 34
Seriousness, the root of, 340, 15
Sermon, criticism of a, 477, 38 ; qualities required in, 242, 53
Sermons, flowers in, 107, 54 ; in stones, 408, 20
Serpent, shedding its skin, 550, 20 ; wisdom of, whence? 455, 4
Serpent's brood, no covenant with, 218, 6
Servant, a, by nature, advantage of, 198, 32 ; a wise, the loss of, 439, 46 ; bad, worst part of, 458, 8 ; being without a, 491, 1 ; how to secure faithful, 177, 35 ; negligent, how made, 2, 35 ; never, never master, 150, 43 ; qualification for, 175, 3 ; the duty of, in misfortune, 188, 12
Servants, a necessity, 172, 27 ; ambition of, 116, 20 ; evil of many, 66, 49 ; greatest, in a house, 270, 51 ; how to regard our, 527, 38 ; many, little service, 42, 39 ; no, without real masters, 559, 45 ; of the great, airs of, 136, 49 ; that wait on man, 283, 35 ; the most abject, 70, 16
Serve, what will, fit, 538, 12
Served, how to be well, 177, 30, 35, 36 ; the best, 37, 51
Service, a, that is no slavery, 100, 34 ; care or coldness in, 189, 49 ; from below upwards, a necessity, 495, 37 ; greater than the god, 488, 19 ; measure of, 171, 49 ; of self, best, 330, 4 ; our domestic, 337, 39 ; our highest, a watchword, 435, 5 ; pride of, a merit, 150, 43 ; proffered, 278, 33 ; reciprocal, 1, 14 ; remuneration for, 532, 1 ; small, true, 394, 32 ; the curse of, 488, 48 ; the law of, 184, 41 ; value of faithful, 313, 11 ; who can do no, as a friend, 532, 14 ; with noble ease, 153, 18
Serving others, two ways of, 284, 31
Servitude, a noble, 263, 34
Set, one's own, mistake about, 149, 15
Settlements, all, temporary, 472, 31
Seventeenth century, how far of worth, 453, 17
Severity, compared with love and justice, 285, 13 ; our, thought of, at death, 543, 18
Sex, either, imperfect, 80, 8 ; virtue of, 460, 43
Shackies, the, not therefore a slave, 539, 11
Shade, we shall fight in, 397, 12
Shadow, a, no measuring, 551, 8 ; and the sun, 93, 62 ; catch not at, 36, 52 ; gazing on one's, 269, 28 ; dependent on light, 548, 37 ; on dial, 453, 49 ; failing to grasp a, 195, 9
Shadows, clutched at for substances, 162, 44 ; kissing, 399, 6 ; Nature's, 292, 41

Shakespeare, a wonder to nature, 292, 7 ; and wayside incidents, 436, 16 ; art of, 534, 10 ; Ben Jonson on, 149, 25 ; characteristic of, 419, 44 ; death of, without sign, 415, 37 ; harmony of, 454, 29 ; how made great, 489, 1 ; M. Arnold on, 484, 1 ; magic of, 33, 23 ; Milton on, 55, 35 ; 538, 14 ; rank among poets, 503, 48 ; the player, 465, 14

Shakespeare's, critics, Carlyle on, 300, 26 ; knowledge, 394, 28 ; wit, 311, 54

" Shall," same as " can," 35, 1

" Shalt," legibility of, 483, 45

" Shalt, thou," as a command, how softened, 421, 10

Shame, a barrier, 140, 24 ; false, 100, 46 ; soil of virtue, 197, 20 ; the moral virtue of, 289, 24

Sharpness, a matter of degree, 330, 40

Shekinah, the true, 459, 9

Shell, delight in the, 186, 31 ; lure to kernel, 333, 18

Shelter, the only storm-proof, at present, 66, 28 ; though given, to be wrought for, 125, 40 ; under an old hedge, 209, 1

Shepherd, a good, duty of, 31, 31

Shepherds, contrasted with kings, 123, 43

Sheridan, a witticism of, 451, 38 ; to a creditor, 566, 19

Sheridan's self-confidence, 167, 32

Shiftlessness, poverty of, 474, 51

Shine, how one may fail to, 566, 32

Ship, the best captain of a, 551, 39 ; with most sail, 453, 23

Shoe, benefit of wearing, 197, 11

Shoes, old, till new ones, 71, 48

Shooting, often, effect of, 325, 31

Shop, opening and keeping open, 201, 29

Short-cuts, circuitous, 45, 40

Shortcomings to be overlooked, 320, 7

Shot, a good, 144, 33

" Should " and " would " contrasted, 414, 28

Showy, the, and the true, 453, 29

Shrew, how to chastise, 145, 48

Shrewdness, power of, 328, 7

Shyness, meaning of so-called, 536, 47

Sibyl, impersonation of the prophetic in nature, 291, 26

Sick with too much, 109, 18

Sickness, amendment after, rare, 105, 19 ; mental, how relieved, 65, 15 ; poor-spirited, 428, 43

Sighing, plague of, 16, 38 ; vanity of, 72, 31

Sighs, the Bridge of, 300, 28

Sight, effect on, of bodily anguish, 558, 24 ; great, first impression of, 315, 21 ; partial, better than none, 26, 9 ; people vainest of their, 202, 52 ; point of, not within, 427, 37 ; requisites of, 300, 27 ; the sense of, 2, 54

Significant, and insignificant, diverse estimate of, 55, 5

Silence, a, commended, 547, 14 ; a necessity, 477, 6 ; a preacher, 468, 31 ; a Pythagorean, benefit of, 345, 21 ; a temple, 457, 5 ; a test of sagacity, 20, 26, 30 ; a, to be imitated, 243, 27 ; to maintain, ability, will, and obligation, 382, 21 ; and speech, prompters of, 205, 23 ; better than irrelevancy, 29, 40 ; better than discourse, 129, 4 ; better than propagating error, 170, 8 ; confession, 42, 31 ; compared with speech, 401, 2 ; 402, 2 ; contrasted with unrestrained talk, 488, 4 ; essential for peace, 23, 6 ; expressive, 74, 19 ; great empire of, fascination of, 253, 13 ; in these days preferable to speech, 256, 28 ; incapacity for, a misfortune, 39, 17 ; its significance, as induced, 490, 2 ; misconstrued, 350, 1 ; never recorded, 180, 45 ; of fools and wise, 235, 12 ; often safe course, 235, 14 ; or saying better, 28, 24 ; power of, 382, 20 ; reaping, 152, 20 ; rebuke for, 26, 51 ; safety of, 19, 27 ; sometimes offensive, 526, 10 ; tact required for, 378, 45 ; the significance of,

144, 8, 13, 14 ; the wish of the strong, 397, 27 ; tree of, fruit of, 458, 27 ; value of, 171, 35 ; 185, 14 ; virtue of, 367, 40 ; virtue of the foolish, 227, 35 ; virtue there is in, 26, 56 ; when a duty, 535, 29

Silent, men, and objects to be guarded against, 29, 64, 65 ; the noble, 253, 13

Siller, want of, 3, 20

Silver, love of, 147, 54

Similes, always imperfect, 318, 32

Simple, more difficult than the complex, 201, 40 ; reasonings of, 498, 48

Simpleton, a, advice of, 505, 22

Simplicity, advantage of faith in, 333, 14 ; and beauty, 507, 34 ; as a grace, Ben Jonson on, 123, 11 ; excellence of, 185, 26 ; power of, 360, 11 ; rare, 5, 24 ; seal of truth, 54, 29 ; 392, 7

Sin, a, confessed, 344, 21 ; and misery, 209, 23 ; and repentance, experience of, 93, 14 ; sundry attitudes to, Fuller on, 146, 12 ; burnt into the blood by practice, 453, 40 ; each, God-annihilating, 75, 23 ; essence of, 425, 33 ; evil of, 272, 47 ; forsaking all, 148, 39 ; found out, 28, 41 ; guilt of, dependent on knowledge, 326, 31 ; how to avoid, 149, 32 ; how to save men from, 565, 41 ; how to treat, 509, 37 ; natural to man, 13, 9 ; of hot heart and of cold, 471, 28 ; source of all, 116, 14 ; that hero atones for, 204, 4 ; the unpardonable, 446, 18 ; thinking about, waste, 481, 21 ; truth of, not to be known, 527, 18 ; without limits, 375, 18

Sincerity, as a virtue, 100, 28 ; how to constrain, 55, 33 ; simple, commended, 87, 20, 21 ; the happiness of, 171, 25 ; without simplicity, 269, 33 ; years of, 215, 35

Sing, how learn to, 252, 1 ; I, because I must, 165, 42

Singer, the business of, 66, 19

Singers, business of, 489, 39 ; the general fault of, 328, 37

Singing, according to gift, 93, 31 ; as an accomplishment, 374, 17 ; at work, Carlyle on, 123, 36 ; true, worship, 500, 38

Singularity, and fashion, 102, 30 ; none without, 307, 33 ; sign of genius, 133, 22 ; taste for, how induced, 222, 40

Sinned, more, against than sinning, 164, 29

Sinner, a worn out, most denunciatory, 25, 25 ; repentance of, joy of gods over, 532, 5

Sinners, faintly condemned, 476, 3 ; mercy of heaven to, but not fools, 154, 14

Sinning, and bearing with the sin different, 105, 6 ; occasion for pardon, 384, 24

Sins, denied, 310, 30 ; Emerson's advice in regard to, 438, 42 ; the root of all, 68, 22

Situation, to every, its own pleasures, 187, 44

Sixpence, virtue in, 553, 19

Skeleton, the, our mortal companion, 525, 16

Skies, attempt to scale, vain, 322, 7

Skill, and exertion, economy of, difficult, 201, 40 ; and labour, value of, 94, 35 ; compared with strength, 221, 45 ; mead of, 497, 19 ; not an estimable quantity, 358, 10 ; not visible, 516, 16 ; power of, 300, 8 ; the greatest, 432, 36

Skin, a living, blessedness of having, 473, 31 ; a, natural to all living, 9, 54

Sky, who aims at the, 392, 51

Slackness breeds worms, 243, 18

Slain, the, thrice he slew, 399, 37

Slander, comfort under, 547, 6 ; lives upon succession, 111, 6 ; not to be believed, 27, 31 ; provocation under, 490, 36 ; to good man, 395, 30 ; world's delight in, 226, 15

Slave, a, defined, 150, 39 ; a freedom allowed, 62, 2 ; a heaven-made, irredeemable, 553, 38 ; as regards reason, 148, 53 ; at heart, not free, 180, 4 ; born to be, 25, 58 ; fetters of, 427, 34 ; if I'm designed yon lordling's, 172, 42 ; none, with will free, 306, 6

Slave-driving, two kinds of, 399, 1

Slave-holding, effect of, 51, 52 ; enslaving, 177, 8

Slaves, all, 522, 17 ; master of, 441, 34 ; men who are, 478, 52 ; the greatest, 311, 14 ; virtue of, 103, 43

Slavery, act of will, 114, 17 ; bitter, 69, 19 ; but one, 476, 23 ; defined, 471, 13 ; in the heart, 560, 11 ; not abolishable by Parliament, 565, 28 ; only deliverance from, 96, 19 ; our, self-imposed, 339, 21 ; spiritual, 8, 26 ; the distinguishing sign of, 424, 3 ; the greatest, 387, 36 ; the one intolerable, 445, 38

Sleep, a gentle thing, 322, 5, 6 ; a palliative, 246, 45 ; and his brother Death, 163, 2 ; at midday, 281, 10 ; death's counterfeit, 388, 6 ; gift of God to His beloved, 142, 33 ; in smoky cribs, 555, 14 ; inventor of, blessed, 30, 47 ; no, where care, 36, 4 ; of rustic men, 399, 24 ; of the labouring man, 453, 43 ; our, when deepest, 162, 44 ; rule for, 387, 8 ; Shakespeare on, 258, 28 ; tired Nature's sweet restorer, 487, 34 ; when I am drowsy, 165, 22

Sleepers, and awake, alike watched over, 125, 41 ; the, to whom life is a dream, 531, 24

Sleeping, the, and the dead, 453, 44

Slippery places, standing on, 148, 28

Sloth, a thrall to, 147, 24 ; and poverty, 103, 14 ; evil of, 107, 36 ; misery entailed by, 117, 22

Slothful and waster, 142, 5

Sluggard in his own conceit, 453, 48

Sluggishness and stupidity, 103, 15

Slugs, men once, 526, 13

Small, connected with great, importance of, 394, 34 ; people, the talk of, 65, 11 ; things, man who scorns, 441, 20 ; things, not to be despised, 342, 14

Smallest space, fruitful, 556, 9

Smile, a, a test of character, 399, 19 ; a broad, after a frown, 19, 61, 62 ; from a superior, 566, 38 ; or laugh, effect of, on a man, 542, 16 ; the virtue in a, 94, 56

Smiles, characters of, 466, 41

Smiling in self-mockery, 385, 33

Smith, a poor, 143, 9

Smoke, and flame, interchangeable, 203, 10 ; consuming one's, a first lesson, 491, 24 ; convertible power of, 307, 13 ; to be emitted only as fire, 472, 48 ; when to consume and when to emit, 456, 14 ; where fire, 107, 18

Snail, the, in its shell, 454, 3

Sneer, malicious, 440, 17

Snob, Thackeray's definition of a, 567, 35, 37

Snow, statues of, 522, 32

Soaring, no, without wings, 180, 11

Sobriety, how secured, 81, 42 ; the virtue of, 403, 33

Sociability, how produced, 344, 49 ; risky, 199, 23 ; source of, 483, 35

Social, evils, nature of, 215, 32 ; hive, drones and busy bees of, 531, 25 ; intercourse, advantage of, 527, 30 ; procedure, all, dependent on finding and installing the able man, 106, 22 ; ties that warp from truth, 51, 50

Socialism, alpha and omega of, 416, 2 ; charges against, 468, 1 ; defined, 519, 7

Sociality, the foundation of, 396, 1

Societies, insecure, 467, 28

Society, a church, in one of three predicaments, 90, 28 ; advantage of, 397, 21, 22 ; based on religion, 340, 20 ; bases of, 427, 13 ; collectively representing culture, 20, 2 ; composition of, 163, 30 ; condition of, 549, 35 ; contingent on mutual dupery, 277, 20 ; conversation in, 47, 43 ; dependence of, on religion, 307, 14 ; effect of, 397, 23 ; family ideal of, 338, 41 ; fatal, 397, 23 ; fine, no help in, 488, 51 ; good, advantage of, 77, 7 ;

great hope of, 431, 21 ; how possible, 335, 1 ; importance of, to a man, 205, 16 ; in birth-pangs, 457, 29 ; no, without flattery, 173, 35 ; only one great, 476, 14 ; relation of, to humanity, 121, 56 ; rules of, nothing, 378, 31 ; the basis of, 105, 38 ; 372, 15 ; the best, 397, 25, 28 ; the bonds of, 396, 4 ; the upper and under currents of, 460, 10 ; the vital element in, 451, 7 ; whence its regeneration, 451, 5 ; without justice, 559, 37

Socrates, and Christ, 420, 16 ; and Christ, difference between, 423, 33 ; equanimity of, 63, 42 ; Milton of, 554, 3 ; of himself, 396, 40

Soil, weed-producing, value of, 21, 4

Soldier, brave, the aim of, 24, 33 ; effect of use on, 509, 36 ; his ultimate and perennial office, 454, 7 ; inspiring effect of courage of, 48, 66 ; no, without war, 520, 32 ; profession of, 107, 11 ; trade of, its nature and honourableness, 454, 6 ; without good-breeding, 452, 27

Soldier's, honour, 515, 37 ; prize and wealth, 109, 43

Soldiers, baptized in fire, Napoleon on, 545, 16 ; Napoleon on, 465, 26 ; two kinds of, 468, 11

Solidarity, instance of, 453, 52 ; of life, 474, 52

Solitude, at times best society, 111, 7 ; defined, 558, 36 ; how we endure, 523, 19 ; its safety, 476, 27 ; its unknown nature and extent, 251, 11 ; life of, in a crowd, 201, 24 ; love or dislike of, 12, 51 ; necessary for all great work, 3, 35 ; or solitariness not good for man, 203, 50 ; or vulgarity, our choice, 465, 12 ; painful, 64, 9 ; perpetual, effect of, 346, 34 ; power of, on mind, 189, 53 ; risk of, 30, 43 ; the incapable of, 560, 21 ; the virtue in, 531, 14 ; true, Byron on, 279, 3 ; unnatural, to be abandoned, 81, 24 ; who prepared for, 405, 52 ; why intolerable, 206, 28 ; within, 420, 28

Solomon, felicities of, the record of, 447, 19

Something *versus* nothing, 89, 3

Son, a, how to enrich, 461, 30 ; a, legacy to, 22, 17 ; love for, 38, 29 ; the best, 418, 2

Song, an old, 163, 6 ; ascensive forces of, 99, 58 ; effect of, contrasted with eloquence, 80, 50 ; gift of, 125, 46 ; great, sincere, 9, 41 ; its own reward, 170, 10 ; sacred, love of, 109, 27 ; the end of everything, 498, 35 ; the meaning of, 194, 34 ; the power of, 20, 5 ; 36, 24, 25 ; 37, 30 ; when great, 133, 40 ; without ear of taste, 537, 21

Songs, our sweetest, 525, 29

Sophistry, entangling power of, 398, 24

Sophists, effect of their teaching on Church, 239, 26

Sorrow, a sign of nobleness, 450, 23 ; a teacher, 159, 44 ; akin to course of things, 476, 36 ; and fear, associated with melancholy, 103, 31 ; and joy, 213, 27, 28, 37, 41, 42, 46, 50, 51, 52 ; as a teacher, 334, 47 ; consecrated in Christ, 524, 42 ; contrasted with happiness, 139, 42 ; disappearance of, under love, 86, 34 ; each present, absorbing, 75, 22 ; effect of time on, 318, 36 ; effect of, worse than giddiness, 231, 12 ; ennobled by Christianity, 42, 53 ; 43, 3 ; for loss of fortune, 539, 12 ; give, words, 123, 26 ; gnarling, mocked at, 124, 43 ; how to treat, 528, 29 ; involves joy, 114, 48 ; knowledge, 136, 36 ; over the dead, effect of, 444, 32 ; path of, 447, 10 ; real, hard to detect, 369, 15 ; self-incurred, 153, 28 ; shared, 20, 7 ; sign of deep, 422, 46 ; sympathy of, 456, 37 ; tears of, fruit of, 94, 13 ; the eloquence of, 391, 38 ; the first great, 472, 25 ; the triumph of, 42, 53, 56 ; vanity of, 531, 10 ; violence of, how to tame, 511, 30 ; what underlies all, 506, 22 ; while there is hope, 550, 21

Sorrow's, crown of sorrow, 20, 6 ; fell, tooth, 104, 27

Sorrows, a fire at which we warm our hands, 249, 37 ; all, healed by heaven, 75, 48 ; associated with pleasure, 409, 11 ; desperate, 100, 35 ; each condition its own, 82, 55 ; how they come, 545, 18 ; lighter than cares, 36, 9 ; little and great, 251, 19 ;

never wanting, 212, 20 ; not to be complained of, 543, 28 ; of earth, in eye of heaven, 474, 5 ; of yesterday, to-day, and to-morrow compared, 454, 11 ; our, like thunder-clouds, 339, 18 ; part of the divine plan, 89, 23 ; small and great, effect of, 19, 55 ; soothed by friendship, 319, 10 ; source of, 11, 13 ; true easing of, 503, 31 ; vanished, soul-quickening, 48, 59 ; we must bear, 468, 18

Soul, a fresh, breeding, 491, 10 ; a great, 184, 13 ; a man's, his mightiest possession, 297, 42 ; a noble, to the vulgar, 421, 12 ; a precious, 168, 19 ; a reality, 262, 25 ; a strong, mark of, 346, 30 ; a strong, to be prayed for, 112, 47 ; a strong, works of, 307, 16 ; a sweet and virtuous, never gives, 334, 43 ; a true, first trial questions of, 141, 34 ; a, with unsubdued passions, 535, 22 ; active, the one thing of value, 445, 40 ; an enigma to itself, 361, 30 ; an inmate, 551, 37 ; and body mutually helpful, 9, 35 ; and love, co-operating or disjoined, 253, 50 ; as God, unchangeable, 75, 45 ; beautiful, finding, a gain, 79, 5 ; black speck in every, 469, 21 ; cannot be killed, 402, 6 ; independent of counsel, 62, 37 ; depth of, approved, 430, 19 ; depths in, 466, 30 ; effect on, of chastening, 48, 5 ; elevation of, 537, 14 ; excellence and greatness of, in what seen, 223, 13 ; fiery, effect of, on body, 5, 44 ; frequent contrast of body and, 8, 41 ; gives form to body, 325, 14 ; immortality of, Goethe's faith in, 164, 43 ; great, invulnerable but for compassion, 506, 39 ; greatness of, a mark of, 81, 2 ; greatness of revelations of, 26, 63 ; his, entrusted to each man, 127, 52 ; how it regards all it loves, 325, 6 ; how rendered great, 162, 9 ; human, a bird born in a cage, 436, 4 ; immortality of, proof of, 494, 26 ; in sick body, 533, 21 ; indispensable, 179, 23 ; individual, union it should seek, 436, 30 ; indolence of, evil of, 107, 30 ; its greatness, 482, 25 ; its integrity, sacred, 314, 37 ; its palace, 6, 63 ; its spiritual position, 95, 13 ; largest, of a country, 438, 1 ; life of, 75, 26 ; 487, 3 ; like a star apart, 486, 9 ; man's, an unspeakable subject, 162, 14 ; man's, like water, 385, 11 ; man's mightiest possession, 324, 37 ; mystery in connection with, 263, 20 ; no kindling of, without soul, 162, 26 ; noble and ignoble, in prosperity contrasted, 171, 32 ; noble, fairest fortune to, 61, 5 ; of man, presence-chamber of Highest, 202, 40 ; one's anxiety about, 13, 46 ; one's own, 94, 12 ; our, our own, 94, 12 ; poorest, wishes of, 448, 30 ; sad, in merry company, 379, 14 ; salvation of, sole motive of religion, 152, 31 ; sayings about, 454, 14–27 ; secret of, inexpressible by words, 308, 3 ; sick, its physician, 65, 14 ; sickness of, common cause of, 325, 30 ; so situated that it may emancipate itself, 126, 8 ; sanctuary of, 18, 36 ; source of events, 472, 33 ; strength of, true to its high trust, 133, 42 ; strength without greatness of, 385, 12 ; strenuous, and success, 21, 2 ; that strives and sins, misery of, 539, 13 ; the, no coercing, 33, 36 ; the, everything, 352, 39 ; the, great and plain, 133, 41 ; the, indivisible, 413, 5 ; the, mirror of, 426, 29 ; the sole reality, 446, 20 ; the window of, 426, 31 ; the true strength of, 459, 10 ; thrift of having, 2, 55 ; unbelief in the richness of, 523, 13 ; virtuous and sensuous, 461, 3 ; want of the, 233, 8 ; without fixed purpose, 222, 13 ; without reflection, 20, 9 ; youth of, 466, 3

Soul's, grandeur, in what revealed, 312, 32 ; the, emphasis right, 540, 1

Souls, all, forfeit once, 554, 43 ; at work in stinted body, 194, 13 ; the, Cicero on, 284, 6 ; common, contrasted with nobler, 45, 21 ; dear to God, 33, 25 ; feeble, how they fail, 104, 4 ; fine, *versus* fine society, 488, 51 ; generous, weakness of, 120, 6 ; godlike, forbidden fleshly gratification, 128, 21 ; great, characterised, 238, 23 ; great, endurance of,

136, 48 ; great (see **Great souls**) ; hard to discern, 391, 26 ; lessons taught to, incommunicable, 484, 42 ; little, shifty, 251, 36 ; men's, the poles of 277, 30 ; noble, do nothing by halves, 298, 17 ; our chief concern, 568, 27 ; our, far-seeing, 339, 19 ; privileged, Frederick the Great on, 237, 45 ; pure, crushed to earth, 468, 19 ; related, division among, a sad riddle, 414, 8 ; sad, Dante's, 222, 22 ; small, authors of great evils, 276, 19 ; strong, related, 10, 25 ; to be saved, and souls not, 154, 15 ; to whom God manifests Himself, 127, 20 ; twin, 467, 39 ; yearning, appeal to, 518, 14

Sovereigns, a weakness of, 407, 48
Sovereignty and learning, 236, 35
Sowing, and reaping, 8, 32 ; compared with reaping, 379, 19 ; necessary to reaping, 149, 5.
Space, and time, a dream, 402, 3 ; and time, as interests, 424, 41 ; and time, but creations of God, 486, 26 ; and time, do not belong to the eternal world, 293, 24
Spared, better, a better man, 165, 32
Sparing and spending, in due measure, 557, 32
Spark, neglected, 20, 10
Sparks, and the light they give, 14, 12
Sparrow, providence in fall of, 477, 47
Spartan mother to her son, 87, 35
Spartans, the, Emerson on, 335, 8
Speak, injunction to, 523, 7 ; well, advantage of ability to, 198, 34 ; well, how to, 565, 26
Speaker, fine, who does not speak the truth, 555, 30
Speaking, a master of, 93, 56 ; a rule of, 567, 11 ; condition of, 305, 23 ; evil from, 116, 7 ; good, condition of, 506, 4 ; in childhood, 190, 17 ; man, contrasted with silent, 42, 20 ; men, soul of all worth in, 189, 27 ; much and to the point, 205, 9 ; much or seldom, significance of, 151, 17 ; rule in, 381, 18 ; rule of, 141, 37 ; 274, 45 ; sowing, 152, 20 ; well, 362, 6 ; what is implied in, 334, 40 ; what is wanted in, 313, 20 ; what one likes, 152, 11 ; without thinking, 138, 24
Spécialité, a, desirable, 141, 32
Species, Cuvier's definition of, 20, 11
Speck, black, in every soul, 469, 21
Spectacles, behind which is no eye, 441, 3 ; ugliest of, 506, 26
Speculation, among practical men, 189, 14 ; contrasted with practice, 355, 2 ; Goethe on the man of, 5, 34 ; limit of, a wise man's, 199, 48 ; no, in those eyes, 307, 18 ; not man's end, 266, 18 ; our proneness to, 331, 6 ; tendency of, 174, 5
Speculations, effect of time on, 486, 33
Speech, a knavish, by whom entertained, 7, 47 ; and fact, gulf between, 401, 1 ; and silence, 370, 44, 45 ; and thought, 484, 42 ; as a sign, 437, 29 ; combined with action, 10, 22 ; compared with action, 402, 42 ; contrasted with silence, 391, 28, 33 ; corruption in, bad sign, 549, 17 ; discretion of, 69, 10 ; disguise of thought, 182, 22 ; effect of, to a soul holy and true, 545, 19 ; fair, 1, 9 ; flattering, 273, 2 ; freedom of, risky, 341, 2 ; Goethe's rule in regard to, 519, 30 ; good, what underlies all, 506, 23 ; hour of, 253, 18 ; indiscreet, 148, 25 ; kind, power of, 150, 13 ; like a tangled chain, 157, 12 ; modern, theme of, 38, 17 ; motive of most, 330, 35 ; not safe, when one would be silent, 303, 29 ; often matter of regret, 224, 9 ; pungency of, how to attain, 177, 29 ; rarer than song, 79, 2 ; right naming, 313, 4 ; rule of, 308, 23 ; 519, 14 ; rule for, 244, 14 ; 382, 19 ; 481, 4 ; rules for, 400, 39–45, 50, 51, 55 ; 401, 1 ; subservient to action, 553, 36 ; the best, contrasted with thought, 392, 26 ; the bond of society, 317, 12 ; the dial-plate of thought, 320, 33 ; the greatest virtue of, 336, 9 ; to be sparing, and good, 100, 29 ; to be weighed, 42, 45 ; to conceal thought, 226, 34 ; to purpose, tact required for, 378, 45

Speeches, fine, of knaves or fools, 106, 31 ; long, a bore, 92, 26

Spenser, characteristic of, 419, 44

Spending, before earning, 148, 27 ; economy in, 165, 13 ; more difficult than earning, 76, 45 ; much, and gaining little, 495, 46 ; the use of, 376, 12

Spendthrift, the, 357, 47 ; with others' property, 201, 25

Sphere, chosen for one, 295, 32 ; limit of one's view, 241, 26

Sphinx-riddle, of the day, to whom insoluble, 150, 14

Spinoza, Novalis on, 131, 4

Spirit, a drop of, not water, the thing wanted, 534, 14 ; a man of, 511, 34 ; a soaring, 2, 63 ; a worthy and generous, sign of, 199, 38 ; and nature, 454, 34 ; and reason, two aspects of one thing, 414, 37 ; architect of body, 86, 2 ; confining power of, 94, 7 ; constructive power of, 94, 6 ; debauchery of, 85, 30 ; defined, 54, 16 ; hard to keep, pure, 395, 35 ; he that ruleth his, 147, 19 ; how to warm one's, 519, 2 ; in which we act, highest matter, 59, 57 ; indigenous, 60, 2 ; instance of elevation of, 54, 11 ; listening to voices of the, 144, 42 ; men of, characteristic of, 319, 17 ; oppressed by matter, 58, 19 ; power of, over nature, 290, 27 ; 291, 47 ; presence of, as remedy, 514, 14 ; small, impotent against a greater, 307, 12 ; sovereign in moral world, 246, 1 ; swifter than body, 3, 11 ; task of, 454, 39 ; the alone born of, 303, 7 ; the genuine, characterised, 59, 49 ; the interpreter of action, 3, 47 ; the mysterious ways of, 454, 31 ; the only possession of, 303, 7 ; the organ of revelation, 538, 11 ; the, sayings about, 454, 31–35 ; the striving, drawn to truth, 197, 1 ; the sword of, 404, 10 ; the, within, 533, 22 ; the work of, idle questioning about, 508, 33 ; to be under rule, 15, 31 ; *versus* flesh, 454, 34 ; *versus* letter, 438, 44 ; we love, ever mysteriously with us, 539, 1 ; who hath no rule over his, 146, 51 ; wilful gloominess of, 171, 27 ; without body, 474, 22 ; witnessed to by nature, 290, 26

Spirits, art in binding, 218, 20 ; dangerous to fraternise with, 119, 24 ; evil, and the light, 311, 37 ; from the vasty deep, 165, 17 ; great and little, their errors, 7, 7 ; great, power of, over love, 135, 10 ; how tried, 98, 10 ; locking out, 533, 22 ; no art in freeing, 218, 20 ; noble, and the dead, 308, 14 ; stirring, 403, 15 ; to be tried, 27, 32 ; victory, source of, 23, 38

Spiritual, and sensual, mediator between, 287, 8 ; chemistry, mixtures of, 442, 35 ; death, in this epoch, 331, 9 ; denial of, in man, 416, 47 ; in man determining power, 207, 4 ; leaders of the race, 533, 38 ; man judge and not judged, 147, 21 ; man, mysterious ways of, 454, 31 ; man, the, and his world, 454, 44 ; heavens, the phenomena of, how produced, 191, 18 ; nature of man, one and indivisible, 267, 7 ; opportunity thrown away, 176, 4 ; problem resolved by Christ, 454, 45 ; sovereignty of, 262, 25 ; power, denial of a test, 190, 15 ; the, sayings about, 454, 41–43 ; 456, 1, 2 ; universe, in what it exists, 462, 14 ; universe, the laws of, 454, 46 ; virtue, perfection of, 447, 27 ; word, influence of, 79, 10

Spiritually-minded, to be, 490, 39

Spirit-world, not shut, 64, 22

Splendour unseen, 145, 10

Spontaneity, destroyed by analysis, 14, 17

Sport, perfection of faculty, 438, 7 ; tedious, 171, 42

Spring, days of, 568, 38 ; the, when apprehensible, 455, 4

Spur, a, in head, 20, 19 ; no, to prick the sides of my intent, 167, 6

St. Christopher and Christ, 205, 46

St. Francis, the order of, rules of, 497, 4

St. Martin, faith of, 506, 35

St. Paul's, its builders and architect, 403, 18 ; the builder of, 534, 20

Stage, man on the, 331, 16

Stagnation, enjoyment impossible in, 565, 42

Stags with lion for leader, 112, 35

Standing, high, the risk of, 479, 48 ; still, no, 116, 2

Stanzas, ill-polished, advice as to, 88, 25

Star, a, a good steed, 81, 26 ; guiding, takes an astronomer to catch a, 81, 26 ; one's, to be followed, 383, 44 ; the greatest, 432, 38 ; without haste, without rest, 556, 2

Stars, as gems on God's mantle, 200, 40 ; but hid to reappear, 419, 18 ; Byron's apostrophe to, 564, 22 ; companions of solitude, 171, 28 ; for money, 538, 36 ; hid by heaven's own light, 311, 55 ; hide heads diminished, 22, 20 ; road to, not easy, 309, 31 ; sayings about, 455, 5–7 ; the, Carlyle on, 162, 41 ; the eternal, there, 426, 7 ; two, different spheres of, 504, 6 ; way to the, 258, 35

Start, early, 75, 35

State, a, at its greatest, 20, 41 ; a, the fate of, guided by unintelligence, 414, 9 ; a, worth in, 465, 36 ; affairs of, the question in, 53, 11 ; cloth of, may be mean, 165, 27 ; construction and destruction of, 21, 43 ; effects of prudence and enthusiasm on, 450, 5 ; element of greatness of, 449, 25 ; health of a, condition of, 433, 26 ; in danger, Carlyle on, 455, 8 ; its relation to citizen, 455, 9 ; life of a, like a stream, 54, 13 ; misfortune in, 442, 34 ; no, now purely self-derived, 392, 22 ; quality of heart of, 223, 10 ; the, false ambition in, 191, 20 ; the, Louis XIV.'s definition of, 223, 9 ; the, purpose of, 492, 7 ; the safeguards of a, 309, 39 ; what constitutes a, 534, 37

States, how lost, 330, 19 ; in, unborn and accents unknown, 161, 39

Statesman, a, out of harness, 167, 40 ; and politician contrasted, 455, 10 ; proper study of, 20, 43 ; two qualities of, 504, 3

Statesmanship, true, 500, 39

Statesmen, cobblers, 279, 46 ; minds of some, 442, 27

Station, a freak of fortune, 96, 61 ; high, a low-bred man in, 20, 13 ; high, when appreciated, 156, 33

Stations of eminence, 81, 28, 29

Statue, a, without tongue, 246, 32 ; the light on, no anxiety, 71, 36

"Steal, thou shalt not," comprehensiveness of, 331, 27

Stealing, akin to lying, 258, 17 ; sayings about, 148, 29, 30 ; 152, 23

Steel, true as, 287, 50

Step, a false, effect of, 171, 48 ; a man's greatest, in life, 60, 7 ; first difficult, 38, 2 ; first expensive, 180, 29 ; one wrong, 334, 36 ; the hardest, 432, 17

Stepping-stones, rising on, of dead selves, 167, 19

Stewards, heaven-elected, 273, 35

Still, people dangerous, 238, 21 ; waters, danger of, 241, 37

Stoic, sayings about, 455, 13, 14

Stoicism, sayings about, 455, 15, 16

Stomach, a hungry, not fastidious, 212, 24

Stone, a rolling, 18, 21 ; a white, 7, 67 ; refused by builders, 455, 18

Stones thrown only at fruit-loaded trees, 330, 15

Stoning, different kinds of, 197, 30

Stoop to rise, 395, 37

Stores, best of, 403, 20

Stories, gulling power of, 298, 3

Storm and a master-spirit, 441, 35

Story-telling, mark of mediocrity, 224, 16 ; the habit of, 199, 11 ; the least supportable, 324, 22

Straightforward, hard to walk, 190, 38

Straightforwardness, effect of, 498, 16
Strain, it had a dying fall, 414, 11
Stranded, nothing ever, 314, 28
Strange better than troublesome, 29, 33
Straws, knotting, rather than nothing, 29, 30
Stream, prudence before crossing, 42, 16
Streams, shallow, run dimpling, 88, 2
Strength, admired by women, 67, 8 ; assurance of, 386, 2 ; cause of loss of, 56, 62 ; course of, 443, 31 ; innate, 10, 23 ; not equal to desire, 65, 13 ; not to be divided, 526, 36 ; one's, ignorance of, 11, 31 ; our, measure of, 200, 51 ; our, secret of, 339, 24 ; 522, 2 ; popular estimate of, 55, 1 ; property in the, we have overcome, 520, 32 ; superior, with right, 407, 3 ; the secret of, 46, 4 ; 190, 39 ; the determining element of, 313, 24 ; varieties of, sources of, 455, 27 ; without wisdom, 537, 8
Strife, anti-Christian, 242, 28 ; genders strife, 250, 31 ; more interest in, than victory, 184, 33 ; to be left off, 417, 23
Stringed instruments, sayings about, 455, 28, 29
Striving, and forgetting, 111, 42 ; eager, from ignorance, 317, 8 ; praying, 28, 7
Stroke, a transmitted, still a stroke, 455, 30
Strokes, power of repeated, 155, 5
Strong, and unsound contrasted, 450, 44 ; for the weak, 455, 34 ; men, the faith of, 388, 25 ; not independent of help, 399, 33 ; the, love life, 10, 24
Stronger, contending with, 424, 41
Strongest, right with, 61, 26
Stubbornness, how to meet, 18, 52 ; how to treat, 4, 65
Student, brooding, Wordsworth to, 509, 16 ; diligent, solitary, 397, 24 ; the life of a, 378, 42 ; the one virtue of a, 68, 27
Students, ill-behaved, as preachers, 63, 49
Studies, for ornament, 496, 38 ; how regarded by different classes, 49, 33 ; learned, the value of, 139, 1 ; what of our, we retain, 528, 10
Study, ennobling, 467, 21 ; evermore overshot, 395, 26 ; how to enter on a, 186, 31 ; importance of, 200, 48 ; much, a weariness, 327, 7 ; the effect of, 394, 9 ; the use of, 407, 2 ; what should be our chief, 324, 31 ; without genius, 78, 7
Stuff, we are made of, 522, 18
Stumbling-block, man must have a, 111, 37 ; not to be laid, 384, 33
Stupid, class, the, 471, 15 ; the, no novelty, 532, 24
Stupidity, and indolence, 193, 31 ; and sluggishness, 103, 15 ; deadening effect of, 161, 8 ; dreadful, 434, 28 ; invincible to the gods, 281, 1 ; our one enemy, 445, 35 ; penalty of, 412, 43 ; with sound digestion, power of, 558, 46
Style, a fine, characteristic of, 541, 4 ; a natural, our pleasure in, 362, 7 ; a noble, condition of, 554, 30 ; a rugged, 166, 29 ; after a model, 94, 11 ; copy of mind, 119, 43 ; dependent on mind, 456, 1 ; every man has his, 92, 4 ; fastidiousness about, 543, 2 ; how to write a grand, 119, 43 ; how to write a lucid, 119, 43 ; master of, mark of, 211, 52 ; Swift's definition of, 358, 5 ; the man, 235, 17 ; two great faults of, 358, 15
Subject, adherence to, 217, 38 ; the power of the, 33, 32 ; will of, wanton restraint of, 95, 9
Subjects, difficult, novel and profound, how to treat, 528, 34
Sublime, an instance of, 72, 46 ; from, to ridiculous, 74, 40 ; moment in man's life, 12, 31 ; nature of, 167, 29 ; of man, the, 489, 7 ; sayings about, 456, 4–9 ; step from, to ridiculous, 334, 12 ; the truly, 459, 18
Sublimest spectacle, the, in the world, 405, 19
Sublimity, contrasted with humour, 164, 7 ; in child and maiden, 249, 14
Subordinates, need of, 329, 11

Subsistence, man's sure, 265, 35 ; Mirabeau on three means of, 211, 6
Substance, discriminated from accident, 2, 45 ; for shadow, 36, 53 ; my, is not here, 305, 31 ; the only real, 446, 20
Substitute in absence of the king, 21, 9
Succeeding, best way of, 565, 7
Success, a condition of, 5, 39 ; 209, 35 ; a diagnosis required for, 495, 53 ; a dream, 72, 49 ; a result, 159, 33 ; a secret of, 271, 57 ; by failure, 99, 27 ; condition of, 12, 36 ; conditions of, 149, 7 ; Danton on the secret of, 38, 11 ; desert of, thing to aim at, 488, 27 ; encouragement from, 160, 37 ; ever tinged with sadness, 210, 21 ; failure of, reason of, 201, 46 ; first essential of, 495, 44 ; first secret of, 386, 15 ; great secret of, 493, 34 ; honoured, 89, 10 ; how missed, 456, 26 ; how to attain, 177, 43 ; how won, 330, 25 ; in need of consolation, 89, 30 ; nothing succeeds like, 316, 39 ; secret of, 452, 46, 48, 49 ; 476, 6 ; the effect of, on our judgment, 138, 32 ; the greatest, 432, 39 ; the parent of, 193, 36 ; two ways to, 468, 3 ; worldly, glare of, 469, 36 ; worldly, Queen Elizabeth on, 479, 24
Successes often disappointments, 277, 23
Succour, angelic, 162, 12 ; from above, when sure, 563, 24
Suddenness, the shock from, 88, 14
Suffer, to, and be strong, sublime, 219, 52
Sufferance, badge of Jew, 111, 8
Sufferer, the greatest, not always best, 298, 6
Suffering, acute, of short duration, 520, 6 ; compulsory, 381, 22 ; contrasted with happiness, 139, 40 ; effect of, on native character, 314, 11 ; general, a sign of general immorality, 119, 40 ; human, cause of, 267, 31 ; human, root of, 134, 39 ; law of, 443, 9 ; necessary to being, 489, 45 ; nothing singular in, 326, 39 ; often in apprehension, 350, 8 ; our lot, 206, 25 ; protection from, 517, 31 ; remembrance of, 361, 9 ; sole remedy for, 111, 9 ; the effect of, 335, 9 ; vicarious, 428, 24
Sufferings, another's, judging of, 202, 32 ; light, test of, 244, 33 ; our, tutors, 342, 52 ; superiority to, 475, 2
Sufficiency, a moderate, 27, 55
Suffrage, universal, questionableness of, 507, 38
Sullenness, an attribute of things, 480, 34
Summit, of power, man at, 116, 30 ; the, reached by climbing, 34, 11
Summons, the, that arouses a man, 284, 16
Sun, a type of Jesus, 483, 33 ; and shadow it casts, 546, 6 ; beautifying power of, 26, 21 ; -clear, the, no arguing against, 4, 72 ; down, while yet day, 155, 3 ; extinction of, effect of, 415, 10 ; looks on all alike, 453, 8 ; never sets on my dominions, 170, 5 ; not to be economically viewed, 530, 2 ; on evil and good, 144, 28 ; real or spiritual, condition of love for, 565, 36 ; spots, vulgar judgment of, 422, 19 ; splendour of brief, 89, 29 ; the rising, Mirabeau to, 390, 4 ; the, no liar, 397, 13 ; the power of, 319, 21 ; the real and the spiritual, defined, 565, 36 ; the, sayings about, 456, 16–21 ; there, though concealed, 89, 35 ; things that love, 10, 58 ; who soars too near, 552, 34
Sunbeam, incorruptible purity of, 21, 11
Sunlight, our dependence on, 204, 9
Sun-setting, a bright, 520, 19 ; effect of, 396, 49
Suns that shine at night, 334, 14
Sunshine, from, to sunless land, 161, 15 ; those who bring us, 483, 3
Superfluities, folly of pursuit of, 397, 44
Superfluous, necessary, 235, 18
Superior, and inferior, law of, 198, 19 ; man, way of, 461, 21 ; without subjection to, no rest, 125, 6
Superiority, condition of, 554, 9 ; contrasted with majority, 260, 15 ; manifestation of, price of, 441,

25 ; the art of attaining, 233, 32 ; the condition of, 147, 23

Supernatural, Horace on introduction of, into composition, 293, 33 ; the, the source and goal of all things. 554, 31 ; the, to a child, 315, 44 ; true region of, 396, 33

Superstition, effect of, contrasted with atheism, 21, 32 ; compared with fanaticism, 101, 40 ; defined, 569, 41 ; effect of science on, 544, 20 ; Frederick the Great on Voltaire's raid against, 555, 29 ; its power over us, 456, 25 ; obstinacy of, 468, 7 ; rather than unbelief, 166, 25 ; the basis of, 53, 3 ; the worst, 465, 33 ; those opposed to. 479, 31 ; weakness of, 11, 20 ; where sure to be found, 402, 43

Supper, Holy, observance of, 435, 25

Suppliants at preferment's gate, 508, 14

Surfeit, mortality from, 286, 17 ; suffering from, 19, 58 ; they that, with too much, 478, 44

Surgeon, good, qualifications of, 6, 56 ; young, 212, 48

Suspicion, a life of, 147, 40 ; the evil of, 400, 27

Suspicious man, a, 41, 31

Swallow, the, wheeling, 553, 3

Swallow-flights, short, of song, 389, 32

Swan of Avon, sweet, 149, 25

Swearer, the cheap, 420, 3

Swedenborg, the mourner, 465, 14

Sweet, and bitter, common source of, 116, 29 ; no, without sweat, 302, 23 ; the fate of everything, 513, 21

Sweetness, fleeting, 88, 41 ; *versus* asperity, 4, 55

Swift's epitaph, 504, 35

Sword, and pen compared, 27, 51 ; and the right, 456, 36 ; good, in poor scabbard, 130, 13 ; leaden, in ivory scabbard, 7, 72 ; striking with, 148, 31

Swordsman, a good, 31, 28

Sworn foe to sorrow, care, or prose, 167, 23

Sybarite, the, and his body, 315, 23

Symbol, new, a welcome gift, 473, 30 ; the idea of a, 184, 23

Symbolic, everything, 10, 55

Symbols, who works merely with, defined, 152, 48

Sympathy, and pleasure, effects of, 349, 32 ; flower of life, 502, 12 ; in ordinary life, rare, 385, 34 ; indifference to, 316, 24 ; power of, 281, 9 ; 319, 11 ; 390, 40 ; secret of, 253, 14 ; with lowest, power of, 153, 10 ; with spirit of man, significance of, 548, 46

Systems, only words, 534, 9

T

Taciturnity, commended, by Burns, 235, 42 ; where to learn, 332, 45

Tact, and perseverance, value of, 346, 40 ; contrasted with talent, 409, 48 ; importance of, 559, 45

Taking out and never putting in, 4, 43

Tale, a round, unvarnished, 251, 28 ; an oft-told, 369, 4 ; he cometh with a, 142, 16 ; I could a, unfold, 165, 31 ; plainly told, 15, 18 ; spoiled in telling, 307, 23

Tale-bearer, words of, 463, 44

Talent, a, to be guarded against, 528, 31 ; all, moral, 10, 27 ; and character, how formed respectively, 85, 20 ; and the world, 464, 24 ; as determining and determined, 2, 57 ; as man's enemy, 464, 47 ; compared with wealth, 136, 42 ; contrasted with genius, 120, 18, 50 ; 121, 3 ; definition of, 481, 41 ; eye for, what is involved in, 458, 40 ; field open to, 194, 4 ; for literature, a, 477, 22 ; guide to vocation, 75, 14 ; great, happiness of, 17, 40 ; happiness of using, 441, 15 ; mark of, 491, 39 ;

ordinary, with perseverance, power of, 558, 38 ; the curse of, 206, 7 ; *versus* genius, 54, 32 ; a, which we cannot perfect, 29, 66

Talents, by nature, 239, 28 ; characteristic of, 382, 14 ; distinguished, not therefore discreet, 69, 44 ; great, often hid, 379, 28 ; great (see **Great talents**) ; high, the pride of, 400, 33 ; often without genius, 269, 11

Talisman, a, acknowledged by nature, 21, 23

Talk, filthy, 166, 33 ; honourablest part of, 435, 29 ; measure of, 529, 19 ; the ineffectuality of, 176, 40 ; unwise, harmfulness of, 509, 11

Talkers, a consideration for, 306, 24 ; an evil they suffer, 428, 16 ; compared with thinkers, 33, 8 ; great, 39, 23 ; two sets of, 399, 3 ; weaknesses of, 19, 13

Talking, always, effect of, 479, 19 ; and acting, motives of, 529, 20 ; caution in regard to, 345, 6 ; good, and good work, conjointly impossible, 305, 22 ; great charm of, 496, 1 ; and doing nothing, 491, 19 ; in morals and art, 53, 8 ; long, effect of, 252, 36 ; much, 148, 35, 36 ; not to be monopolised, 297, 3 ; passion of women, 448, 4 ; the rule in, 34, 28

Tall men often empty-headed, 325, 37

Tardiness, the evil of, 401, 37

Tarpeian Rock, the, 227, 29

Task, a noble, never easy, 305, 32 ; one's, how to be done, 541, 33

Taskmaster, the great, 19, 7

Taste, defined, 381, 28 ; effect of delicacy of, 57, 48 ; false, defined, 536, 11 ; good (see **Good taste**) ; purity of, test of, 339, 5 ; sense of, its exquisiteness, 137, 32 ; true, development of, 500, 40

Tastes, pleasant, 349, 26

Tattler, characterised, 21, 25

Taxation, a reason for, 295, 34 ; for benefit of a class, 496, 3 ; in relation to liberty, 185, 41 ; of posterity, for folly, 475, 45 ; on mere labour and brains, 307, 19

Taxes, self-imposed, 522, 21 ; sinews of the state, 524, 25 ; the heaviest, 170, 33 ; to the commonwealth, 511, 50

Teach, who should, 242, 40

Teachable mind, mark of, 21, 26

Teacher, a good, test of, 305, 50 ; a wise, 144, 3 ; an authoritative, ever a necessity, 566, 14 ; and pedant contrasted, 234, 23 ; business of, 492, 50 ; man's best, 414, 32 ; qualification of, 77, 22 ; 151, 45 ; the only, 454, 38 ; with imperfect knowledge, 475, 34

Teachers, our real, 231, 51 ; who have boobies to deal with, Burns' pity for, 126, 18

Teaching, a, before all, 519, 38 ; false, Gen. Gordon on, 544, 48 ; great art of, 493, 33 ; no living by, 308, 20 ; no, without inspiration, 162, 26 ; rule in, 366, 14 ; to be commensurate with intelligence in pupil, 203, 46 ; to be successful, 353, 35 ; when spiritually profitable, 307, 24

Tear, a, for pity, 142, 51 ; law that moulds, 414, 20 ; merit of drying, 424, 25 ; of joy, the, 456, 44 ; of tender heart, no stemming, 208, 32 ; the mourning, 456, 44 ; witchcraft in a, 533, 25

Tears, a debt, 406, 50 ; a necessity for man, 239, 9 ; causes of, 399, 4 ; expression of tenderness, 282, 16 ; expressiveness of, 195, 42 ; joyful, oh for a bosom in which to shed, 322, 21 ; lent by nature, 291, 10 ; motive powers, 231, 14 ; Nature's, 292, 42 ; obscuring power of, 478, 18 ; of penitents, 456, 45 ; often a bad sign, 151, 13 ; sacredness in, 470, 25 ; safety-valves, 452, 22 ; sometimes for show, 399, 53 ; soothing power of, 87, 27 ; sowing in, 479, 49 ; tender, power of, 482, 41 ; the cause of, 205, 18 ; the channels of, 394, 38 ; to be secret, 335, 24

Teeth without bread, and bread without teeth, 41, 25

Telegraph, electric, no substitute for face of a man, 425, 1

Teleology, question of, 450, 30

Telescope *versus* eye, 360, 36

Telescopes and eyes, 98, 21

Tell-tale, harm one, does, 332, 20; out of school, 457, 1

Temper, an even and cheerful, benefit of, 426, 9; and circumstance, accord between, 143, 29; fate, 12, 59; the, how to treat, 198, 39

Temperaments, our, diversity in, 339, 25

Temperance, a physician, 227, 37; and health, 153, 32, 37; 260, 36; as a virtue, 460, 42; defined, 113, 12; 432, 27; in cold latitudes, 435, 11; incompatible with love of pleasure, 303, 5; true, a part of, 199, 49

Tempers, unsociable, 508, 26

Tempest, sorest, issue of, 454, 10; the objects it attacks, 457, 4

Temple, but one, in world, 471, 19; no, easily reared, 565, 40; reared on ruins of churches, 125, 19

Temptation, a, merely fled from, 527, 6; anxiety to avoid, a snare, 269, 25; common, 469, 17; effect on us of resisting, 524, 9; enduring, blessed, 30, 53; flight from, 117, 11; no guard against, 306, 26, 40; object of, 106, 43; our desire, 525, 18; power of victory over, 565, 5; resisted, not known, 540, 5; resisting, serving God, 126, 33; to sin in loving virtue, 284, 12; virtue unequal to overcome, 162, 32; when under, 547, 9

Temptations, and trials, our own, thought hardest, 91, 50; beginning of all, 417, 20; only skin deep, 268, 15; teaching of, 525, 9

Tenants, poor, in the factor's hands, Burns on, 352, 38

Tendency, present, of things, 429, 45

Tenderness, defeating prudence, 450, 4; thought of, at death, 543, 18; throne of, 75, 49; want of, 518, 34; weakness of, 395, 21

Tennyson, rank as poet, 503, 48

Term of things, God-appointed, 480, 32

Territory, loss of, 439, 46

Terror, a life-long, horror of, 27, 46

Terrors, men amidst, 161, 8; most, illusory, 284, 39

Testament, framed with injustice, 472, 51

Testimony, written, value of, 250, 34

Teufelsdröckh, as a rejected man, at the centre of indifference, 111, 14

Thanks, at all enough, 544, 4; exchequer of poor, 89, 46; fed on, 287, 42

Thanksgiving, God-glorifying, 126, 35

Theatre, and pulpit, 457, 14; private, of great account, 262, 5

Theft, contrasted with carelessness, 36, 6; proscribed by Christianity, 241, 7

Theme, a common, hard to treat freshly, 67, 28

Theologian, experience of, 424, 8

Theologians slain by science, 97, 59

Theological absurdities embraced by the greatest men, 307, 26

Theology, and philosophy, Carlyle on, 347, 38; compared with religion, 372, 22; false, the cure for, 422, 26

Theorists, crotchety, 444, 4

Theory, all, gray, 132, 42; how to test a, 397, 38

There, never here, 457, 15

Thief, and anvil, 8, 60; and opportunity, 77, 27; saving a, 381, 8; the greatest, 324, 41

Thieves, and their chains, 251, 38; little and great, how treated, 219, 35, 36; more, than are hanged, 52, 23

Thing, a, how defined, 21, 35; that most needs to be done not easy, 414, 31

Things, all, co-operative, 11, 3; all, only halves, 75, 25; are as regarded, 233, 12; best at their

sources, 238, 8; how to know, 377, 19; more, in heaven and earth, 467, 23; often misconstrued, 33, 16; the path of, 447, 12; to be done decently and in order, 240, 20; with more spirit chased, 552, 23

Think, how to learn to, 200, 43

Thinker, accurate, compared with accurate observer, 110, 34; arrival of, an epoch, 186, 32; earnest, no plagiarist, 301, 37; fairest fortune to a, 54, 26; great, test of, 305, 37; peril to things caused by advent of, 545, 35; the, and the public, 486, 18; the light he requires, 457, 28; the, want of, 529, 38; to be guarded against, 29, 73

Thinkers, and seers compared, 453, 7; relation of, to workers, 482, 47

Thinking, a disease, 333, 31; abortiveness of always, 42, 8; acting, 496, 21; and having ideas compared, 493, 9; and living, contrasted, 40, 12; and saying, 344, 42, 43; any, rather than none, 266, 19; as wishing, 320, 8; before writing, 241, 2; clear, and ardent loving, 230, 32; contrasted with doing, 50, 42; defined, 339, 26; effect of, 475, 15; evil of too much, 559, 7; faculty, Goethe's thrift of, 334, 18; free-, a vain boast, 523, 26; how alone possible, 205, 14; leaving off, evil of, 427, 17; less harm from, than speech, 269, 6; man a terror to the devil, 21, 39; man, fairest portion of, 493, 4; man, not appreciated, 161, 16; no, no wisdom, 148, 4; often no thinking, 161, 16; power of, 485, 2; powerful and bold, 264, 30; rare, 164, 13; rule of, 274, 45; that is none, 149, 15; the rule of, 481, 16; the value of, 369, 6; too much, 152, 32; too much, effect of, 569, 8; what is implied in, 334, 40

Thirty, without sense at, 364, 5

Thomson, Littleton on the muse of, 110, 3

Thongs, from others' leather, 32, 45

Thorn, but a changed bud, 21, 41; near the rose, 529, 34

Thorns, when to trample on, 550, 22

Thought, a good, a boon, 6, 56; a good, power of, 75, 7; a great, news of, 145, 1; a monarch of, the thought of, 518, 47; a noble, effect on us of, 547, 27; a single, significance of, 20, 15; a sudden, 21, 10; a true, mark of, 414, 17; accompaniments of, 559, 6; and action, the worlds of, 465, 8; and diction, propriety of, conjoined, 358, 15; and its relation to world, 484, 30; application of, merit in, 473, 14; as expressed in action, 3, 48; compared with speech, 110, 10, 12, 13, 16, 17; constant, unconscious overflow of, 46, 58; contrasted with action, 61, 25; contrasted with will, 556, 20; dependence of, on character, 161, 5; every, once a poem, 94, 54; good, dependence of, on good cheer, 126, 35; grandeur of, 162, 11; greatness of, 311, 51; he, as a sage, 149, 14; high, rhythmic, 525, 2; how made healthy, 205, 13; how to test, 149, 47; intense, fatiguing, 280, 3; its activity, 315, 10; justice of, how attained, 216, 19; less, more talk, 282, 11; moment to seize a, 90, 44; mustard-seed of, its vitality, 444, 27; nature of, 432, 9; no, contented, 307, 29; no curbing, 264, 29; norm of, 253, 18; of ages, crystallised in a moment, 89, 38; on the sea of passion, 508, 29; one, inclusive of all, 334, 23; one's own, to be entirely credited, 220, 3; one's, to be trusted, 184, 45; original, preciousness of an, 169, 31; parent of deed, 457, 34; power in, 474, 34; power of, 94, 55; 206, 39; prior to fact, 457, 33; profound, 443, 21; property in, 484, 24; pure, independent of time, 486, 46; relation of, to action, 58, 37; revelation of its power, 451, 20; sin of stifling, 496, 2; slave of life, 432, 9; tendency of, 203, 25; that cannot be simply expressed, 542, 29; the aim of every, at its origin, 94, 53; the atmosphere of, 81, 32; the analogue of, 44, 30; the generous,

125, 17 ; the, to him who cannot think, 421, 18 ; the well of, effect of drawing from, 565, 30 ; the world-process, 279, 33 ; true and precise, superior to cloudy fancy, 500, 37 ; undying, 26, 16 ; want of, effect of. 521, 15 ; when beautiful or just, 307, 28 ; wicked, impress of, 555, 34 ; withering, hid in smiles, 117, 24

Thoughtfulness, a medium in, 477, 46

Thoughtlessness, cause of evil, 33, 5

Thoughts, appropriation and invention of, 199, 44 ; audacity of human, 44, 21 ; best expression of, to be respected, 467, 1 ; bitter, to be suppressed, 33, 12 ; dead men's, as agents, 419, 20 ; divine revelations, 96, 2 ; evil, our power over, 526, 16 ; evil, to a good man, 173, 1 ; free, but not hell-free, 119, 16 ; good, how they come, 10, 48 ; good, unexecuted, 130, 21 ; great, from above, 306, 45 ; great (see **Great thoughts**); heard in heaven, 137, 8 ; how to treat our, 428, 6 ; in the heart of, courtesy, 156, 30 ; like flowers, 207, 36 ; love's heralds, 257, 6 ; man's, with the stars, 263, 39 ; men's (see **Men's thoughts**); native soil of, 54, 36 ; no rule for preserving or acquiring, 233, 35 ; noble, the companionship of, 478, 47 ; of little-minded people, easy to gauge, 251, 23 ; of preternatural suggestion, 33, 24 ; of things, influence of, 274, 11 ; of unreflective minds, 508, 22 ; our, and ourselves, 339, 27 ; our best, 337, 16 ; our fugitive, 339, 28 ; our relation to our, 523, 31 ; outrun us, 274, 5 ; pass muster, 240, 45 ; pregnant, 468, 10 ; prostitution of, 182, 22 ; religious, mixed with scruples, 307, 29 ; roving, to be guarded, 320, 33 ; sayings about, 457, 35, 39 ; that look through words, 157, 13 ; the only immortal, 507. 48 ; thy, give no tongue, 123, 30 ; unstained and evil, 508, 28

Thraldom. a, unpitied, 147, 24 ; hateful, 323, 22

Thrall, in person, may be free, 457, 40

Threateners, not fighters, 73, 6 ; often cowards, 268, 30

Threatening. loud, 482, 42

Threats, hardening effect of, 496, 28 ; naught, 150, 19

Threshold. expectant, 90, 5

Thrift, and magnificence, 359, 12 ; as a revenue, 259, 37 ; secret of, 218, 25

Thriving, distrust of, 191, 45

Throne, a, raised to, and being born to, 203, 6 ; by what established, 457, 41 ; something behind, 476, 35

Thunder, nothing but, 48, 39

Thunderbolts on innocent, 214, 48

Thyrsus, the, bearers of, 417, 4

Tibullus, Ovid on remains of, 209, 51

Tide, but no gulf-stream, in affairs, 500, 47 ; in the affairs of men, 470, 35 ; the, to be seized, 527, 11

Time, a new, birth of, in pain, 182, 33 ; a proper, for everything, 104, 48 ; a test and a revealer, 337. 4 ; a waste of, 520, 23 ; advices in regard to, 409; 34, 35 ; ameliorating effect of, 285, 38 ; an innovator, 271, 24 ; and eternity, 88, 4 ; and I against any two, 165, 8 ; and our complaint of its shortness, 520, 34 ; and the hour, 44, 52 ; as a cure, 81, 1 ; as counsellor, 472, 9 ; as preacher, 59, 43 ; beyond our power, 340, 23 ; connection of, with eternity, 150, 41 ; dependence of things on, 481, 20 ; different relationships of men to the, 431, 24 ; driving away, 479, 40 ; earth-spirit at loom of, 395, 20 ; effect of, on a man, 240, 13 ; economised, too late, 269, 35 ; enough, if well applied, 331, 35 ; eternity made manifest, 265, 2 ; expenditure of, 97, 25 ; fleetness and tyranny of, 78, 20 ; flight of, irreparable, 117, 13 ; God's, and ours, 62, 48 ; how it is annihilated, 542, 30 ; how to baffle, 401, 48 ; how to beguile, 491, 7 ; how
648

to count, 528, 25 ; how to win, 260, 38 ; how we get rid of, 407, 34 ; ill employed, lost, 330, 36 ; in relation to eternity, 482, 6 ; in relation to life, 339, 40 ; its evanescence, compensated, 522, 6 ; its stealthy flow, 228, 22 ; its unnoticed lapse, 453, 49 ; killing, a labour, 466, 6 ; lenient hand of, 437, 36 ; man the child of, 265, 2 ; man's angel, 62, 15 ; man's inheritance and seed-field, 288, 6 ; mystery of, on, 413, 13 ; no, for saying all things, 87, 31 ; of day, known only to wise, 108, 46 ; one's distribution of, 63, 20 ; 387, 51 ; 388, 1 ; 393, 15 ; one's own, benefiting, 150, 31 ; our complaint and conduct in regard to, 521, 7 ; our, fixed, 339, 29 ; passing of, common to all, 395, 31 ; rightly seized, 63, 20 ; sayings about, 235, 19–21 ; 412, 9–17 ; 486, 24–53 ; 487, 1–25 ; silence of, 317, 3 ; take good note of, 300, 23 ; that bears no fruit, 457, 46 ; the accepted, 27, 14 ; the flight of, 412, 5 ; the havoc of, our exclusive contemplation of, 338, 38 ; the magic of, 569, 21 ; the, our treatment of, 528, 1 ; the present, Emerson on, 482, 13 ; the present, sayings about, 449, 13, 14 ; the reality of, 205, 27 ; the sun-steeds of, 456, 22 ; the thought of, 481, 15 ; the, to be studied, 174, 35 ; the weird images of, 316, 53 ; the, who wants the spirit of, 364, 2 ; things done in, 192, 1–3 ; to be economised, 81, 45 ; to be honoured in passing, 392, 23 ; to be occupied, 510, 32 ; to be seized, 176, 49 ; to be taken by the forelock, 158, 20 ; to be valued, 85, 41 ; two different attitudes to, 336, 21 ; value of, 72, 5 ; waste of, 432, 10 ; wasted on others, 4, 2 ; wasted, 269, 30 ; wasted and wasting, 169, 4 ; well or ill used, 483, 13, 14 ; well used, 332, 40 ; whiled away, a burden, 544, 42 ; who have no, 345, 19 ; wishing for too much, 176, 13. See **Il Tempo.**

Times, as representing the eternities, 457, 47 ; bad, but compensations, 67, 20 ; now babbly, now dumb, 58, 42 ; past, a seven-sealed book, 67, 19 ; spirit of the, 67, 19 ; spirit of the, defined, 535, 49 ; the, a fatal trait of, 427, 18 ; the, a tendency of, 429, 45 ; the, always mean and hard, 35, 2 ; the, and our duty to them, 567, 29 ; the background of, dark, 322, 30 ; the, unjust complaint of, 275, 42 ; the, insoluble by us, 521, 30 ; these naughty, 322, 18

Time-shadows, only, perishable, 219 54

Timid, man, in love, 202, 55

Timing of things, 458, 1

Tiresome, secret of being, 452, 43

Tit for tat, 1, 45

Title-page, as index of book, 265, 38

Titles, and men, 204, 36 ; high, effect on weak minds, 238, 28 ; noble, alone transferable, 484, 10

Titus, saying of, 65, 39

Toady, a, defined by Disraeli, 408, 28

To-day, and to-morrow, 155, 42, 43 ; 283, 45, 46 ; Carlyle on, 395, 3 ; happiness of owning, 140, 26 ; sayings about, 491, 27–30 ; value of, 107, 12 ; value of insight into, 123, 14 ; why we lose, 529, 32 ; worth of, compared with to-morrow, 334, 26

Toe, light fantastic, 44, 38

Toil, a necessity, 526, 26 ; effect of change of, 482, 8 ; effect of, on native character, 314, 11 ; sons of, Carlyle's apostrophe to, 323, 2 ; vain, without heaven's grace, 323, 5

Toiler, only, to have, 169, 10

Toleration, our, 529, 25 ; rule and limit in, 395, 9

Tomb, before death, or none, 171, 13

To-morrow, gone and coming, 340, 2 ; not to be cared for, 409, 24 ; pupil of to-day, 68, 52

Tongue, a killing and a quiet sword, 142, 41 ; and its issues, 520, 25 ; an evil persuasive, 33, 2 ; as a traveller's outfit, 41, 28 ; 42, 5 ; compared with fire and sword, 106, 38 ; cowards with the, 45, 14 ; evil, an evil mind, 250, 14 ; evil, bite of, 307, 22 ; evil, its owner, 188, 26 ; holiday to, 123, 39 ; instrument of good and evil, 153, 41 ; readiness with the, 510, 25 ; restraining, as a virtue, 250, 18 ; sayings about, 258, 5-11 ; to be confined, 46, 25 ; power of, 55, 36 ; 191, 33 ; 174, 36 ; venom of, 474, 43 ; want of eloquent, a misfortune, 39, 17 ; worst part of bad servant, 250, 15

Tongues, compared to clocks that run on striking, 398, 9 ; evil, pain of, 482, 23 ; in trees, 408, 20

Too much, a defect, 516, 35

Tools, a necessity for all, 294, 49 ; all man's invention, 262, 22 ; and the man, our modern epic, 449, 40 ; to him that can handle them, 224, 26 ; use of, confined to man, 262, 47

Top, attempt to reach, at a leap, 200, 42

Topic, lovingly and thoroughly treated, effect on us of, 542, 17

Torrents, strong, their charge, 455, 36

Touch, a sure, a rare gift, 380, 17

Towers, lofty, and their fall, 37, 49

Town and country, 127, 17

Towns, contrasted with rural retreats, 228, 17 ; great, a sort of prison, 135, 22 ; immorality of, 239, 36

Trade, a, an estate, 146, 43 ; a useful, value of, 23, 44 ; as a means of life, 275, 3 ; no, without its enjoyments, 504, 44 ; two of a, 186, 22

Trader, what he first barters, 428, 5

Tradition, magnifying power of, 534, 1 ; only one thing better than, 476, 18 ; the god of, broken, 546, 36 ; the source of all, 476, 18

Tragedies, why compose, 535, 1

Tragedy, true end of, 458, 38

Tragic and comic side by side, 421, 9

Train, the lackeyed, for others' pleasure, 110, 37

Training, mere, *versus* spirit, 169, 44 ; superior to teaching, 411, 15 ; the best, 77, 20 ; time for, 513, 46

Traitor, the greatest, 474, 36

Traitor's, a, weapons, 334, 35

Traitors, no legislation for, 473, 13

Traits, family, how deepened and intensified, 314, 11

Tranquillity, condition of, 282, 53 ; divine, 322, 20 ; incompatible with idleness, 67, 34 ; virtue in, 187, 56

Transcendental, the, a a book, 315, 30

Transcendentalism, Carlyle on, 201, 30

Transition, every, a crisis, 94, 58

Transitory, the, but an allegory, 8, 63 ; study of, as such, 168, 16

Translation, need not be verbal, 294, 2

Translators, traitors, 498, 49

Trappist, and his body, 315, 23

Traveller, a wise, and his country, 505, 41 ; who is a philosopher, 441, 17 ; who is only a vagabond, 441, 17 ; wise, and a good road, 6, 54 ; with an empty purse, 510, 45 ; without observation, 458, 19

Travellers, licence to, 21, 60 ; unregarded, 176, 4

Travelling, alone or with another, 150, 26 ; railway, Ruskin on, 367, 44 ; safe and not unpleasant, 149, 17 ; that profits not, 152, 34 ; use of, 460, 14 ; without effect on nature, 171, 44

Treachery, deliberate, penalty of, 57, 44 ; due to weakness, 274, 17 ; evil in, 204, 23 ; the price of, 400, 29 ; what is dreadful in, 192, 13

Treasure, a, hard to guard, 179, 6 ; coveted, hard to guard, 259, 30

Treasures, accumulated, purpose of, 123, 45 ; by a lying tongue, 430, 3 ; heavy with tears, 399, 8

Treatment according to desert, 509, 33

Tree, bearing bad fruit, 95, 2 ; with both fruit and shade, 458, 28 ; without blossoms, 507, 50

Trees, ability to root up, 334, 32 ; harm of transplanting, 32, 5 ; large, give more shade than fruit, 124, 11 ; old, hard to bend, 213, 14 ; short of the sky, 36, 3

Trencherman, a very valiant, 143, 12

Trial, a, that is not dangerous, 307, 30 ; the glorifying effect of, 319, 25

Trials, past, not to discourage, 242, 21

Trifles, as felt, or not felt, 12, 23 ; different estimates of, 150, 17 ; holy and a base care for, 469, 24 ; how to treat, 527, 4 ; making an amusement of, 480, 12 ; not to be despised, 481, 6 ; significance of, 202, 42 ; significance of treatment of, 201, 32 ; well habited, 468, 17

Trinity, the, according to Emerson, 459, 38

Triumph, after victory, 16, 10 ; without glory, 529, 28

Triumphs and sorrows, our, 529, 21

Tropes, everywhere, 291, 27

Trouble, best remedy for, 15, 32 ; eased by talking of it, 86, 40 ; past, memory of, 405, 1

Troubles, being chased by, 565, 23 ; cure for, 393, 41 ; due to God dragging us, 269, 29 ; effect of slight and great, 239, 16 ; how to face, 497, 54 ; light and deep, contrasted, 51, 36 ; little, worry of, 162, 13 ; no guard against, 306, 26 ; none without, 304, 26 ; of others easily borne, 524, 24 ; one's, how to soften, 459, 16 ; one's, how to treat, 167, 51 ; one's own, heaviest, 2, 58 ; that must not be told, 467, 38

Troy, no more, 117, 16, 18 ; site of, 210, 14

True, and false, price of, when paid, 111, 24 ; and good, how reconciled, 518, 17 ; being, always possible, 474, 35 ; not always verisimilar, 235, 31, 32 ; once, true always, 331, 30 ; the, alone beautiful, 376, 50 ; the, as a spirit in the atmosphere, 203, 33 ; the, harder to find than false, 510, 35 ; what is considered, same as true, 536, 13 ; what is not, advantage of, 536, 42

Trust, and distrust an error, 183, 16 ; and distrust, foresight necessary for, 112, 18 ; and distrust, Goethe on, 11, 40 ; and love, soul's nourishment, 253, 51 ; and trust not, 105, 37 ; effect of, 483, 21 ; experience before, 26, 64 ; founded on love, 27, 24 ; objects to, 329, 40 ; power of, 502, 44

Trusting every one, 149, 33

Truth, a distasteful, profitable, 368, 49 ; a genuine follower of, 553, 21 ; a new, receiving, 370, 19 ; a new, the effect on us, 21, 47 ; a, pushing, too far, 360, 18 ; a test of, 90, 12 ; 487, 14 ; abstract, importance of, 119, 38 ; an insult to many, 466, 43 ; an offence, 180, 27 ; and error, 85, 2, 3, 5, 8, 9 ; and goodness, how to travel the path of, 563, 34 ; and its expression, 331, 49 ; and purity, 360, 12 ; and reality, the tap-root of life, 244, 3 ; and the imitation of it, 188, 36 ; and the utterance of, a necessity for man, 9, 67 ; arguing deceitfully for, 148, 34 ; at any cost, 29, 43 ; at heart, effect of, on character, 542, 7 ; awful, of things, 47, 50 ; beauty of, 315, 42 ; being alone with, 207, 21 ; beholding, after being lost in metaphysics, 201, 3 ; belief of, 436, 41 ; best way to, 418, 8 ; better than consistency, 345, 17 ; better than wit, 537, 35 ; by count of noses, 398, 27 ; by doubting, 73, 30 ; by poetry, 565, 19 ; characteristic of, 531, 13 ; commended, 243, 46 ; consolation from, 421, 30 ; dearer than a friend, 13, 39 ; discernment of, 553, 8 ; discernment of, a revelation, 546, 35 ; devotion to, effect of, 563, 23 ; duty towards, done when told, 543, 42 ; duty with regard to, 67, 4 ; easy, 164, 26 ; effect of mere, 23, 42 ; enough, if in the air, 488, 23 ; every, not to be told, 325, 46 ; power of fear of, over men, 535, 14 ; firmness for, 153, 20 ; first condition of accepting, 428, 40 ; general, seldom applied, 119, 41 : good and harm of telling,

67, 6; great, against whom barred, 302, 17; harsh, 169, 8; he that is of, 93, 34; how regarded, 223, 21; how to draw out, 379, 36; how to know a. thoroughly, 491,6; how to understand, thoroughly, 304, 47; impotent without enthusiasm, 83, 39; in dreams, 322, 26; in fashion of the day, 22, 7; in head and in hand, 18, 57; in light, 191, 3; in possession of a child, 41, 37; indifference to, in trifles, 167, 10; injured by defence of it, 329, 37; inquiry of, 436, 41; irritating, 58, 11; its defender, 199, 35; its power and strangeness, 476, 3; knowledge of, 436, 41; language of, 437, 49; lost in disputation, 300, 18; love of, importance of, 536, 18; love of, test of, 256, 10; maintaining and being maintained by, 202, 17; man cold to, 92, 30; man's relation to, 521, 23; might of, 133, 43; 259, 10; more than oratory, 271, 49; mother of, 391, 41; naked, an offence, 289, 20; need not be all told, 390, 15; new, damaged by old error, 79, 3; new, seeks circulation, 173, 26; new, the challenge of, 92, 52; no, not error to some, 180, 22; not all to be told, 567, 19; not consistency, 71, 38; not easy to bury, 208, 20; not relished by man, 262, 13; not to be all disclosed, 167, 52; not to be served out pure, 322, 25; not to be thwarted, 522, 36; objective value of, 174, 37; of the essence of man, 262, 6; often in jest, 268, 32; only to be spoken, 400, 39; open to sight, 525, 10; opposed by the age, 199, 35; orbs of, steadfast, 484, 29; our concern not consequences, 566, 12; our love of, evidence of, 338, 32; permanency of, 457, 25; persecution of, J. S. Mill on, 423, 32; plain, sublimity of, 333, 30; power of, 514, 24; precious and divine, 111, 32; products of, that cannot be weighed, 508, 19; pure, adulteration of, 360, 9; qualities of, 315, 48; quickened by God into deeds, 125, 17; rejected, a sword, 22, 8; reserved, 10, 61; reveals itself like God, 55, 3; risk of speaking, 148, 26; 323, 32; sacrificed for shadows, 38, 23; satisfying recompense of, 240, 26; sayings about, 228, 2–5; 512, 53–57; 513, 1–6; 518, 18–20; scientific, of old date, 383, 6; search for, secondary to duty, 304, 38; seal of, 54, 29; seeking or not seeking, a sign, 549, 34; self-defensive power of, 321, 19; simplicity, a test of, 316, 9; stings, 181, 9; strong, almost as God, 552, 6; subtlety of, 225, 40; that has to be reserved, 419, 26; the knowing and not speaking, 532, 13; the life of the, 404, 10; the only asbestos, 335, 23; the, sayings about, 459, 20–22; the, two ways of telling, 570, 7; the urgency of, 536, 42; the vouchers for the, 400, 50; the, will out, 548, 51; thirst for, abiding, 457, 31; those who follow, 480, 23; Time's daughter, 63, 23; to be bought, but not sold, 33, 42; to be made attractive, 524, 11; to be veiled, 289, 20; to die for, 491, 34; to whom to confess, 3, 22; unpalatable, 107, 23; vanishing, 67, 5; *versus* charity, 205, 34; violation of, social effect of, 95, 8; vital, by our very side, 33, 31; what it demands of us, 324, 46; when seen, loved, 111, 31; uncertain who has found, 92, 23; why derided, 274, 49; with friend to be both loved, 175, 24; worth of, 538, 22. See **Falsehood** and **Justice**.

Truth-doer, and the light, 146, 6

Truthfulness, the importance of, 199, 36

Truth-seeker, a, a citizen of the world, 152, 14

Truths, blunt, effect of, 488, 26; like fruits, 239, 30; often employed to deceive, 325, 39; new, only old with a new name, 269, 31; select, 181, 20; shielded by veils, 468, 33; spiritual or vital, nature of, 516, 27; the greatest, 432, 40

Tub, every, on its own bottom, 95, 4; to a whale, 383, 47

Tumult, seasons of, evil in, 192, 16

Tumults, civic, to be shunned, 546, 10; of mind, not easily allayed, 309, 26

Turner on his death-bed, 456, 19

Twa lovely een, Burns on seductiveness of, 166, 12

Twigs, young, 213, 14

Twilight, disastrous, 186, 8; lot of man, 52, 40; natural, safety of, 479, 51; world's light, 202, 47

Two, souls in one breast, 570, 5; things, to require, 495, 20

Type, less valuable than time, 487, 1; Nature's carefulness of, 394, 47

Tyranny, and law, 548, 8; intolerable, 468, 29; limited, 306, 27; law and justice under disguise of, 180, 26; worst sort of, 25, 42

Tyrant, always in fear, 152, 24; and serf, not God-made, 168, 5; his fear, 364, 49; kiss of, admonitory, 207, 12

Tyrants, plea of, 558, 37; Burns against, 232, 26; not for ever, 103, 45; who wear no crown, 288, 37

U

Ugliness, the root of, 369, 16

Ulysses, bow of, bending, 203, 45

Unanimity in a council, 259, 14

Unascertainable, the, how to regard, 492, 4

Unbaptized, the, with clean hearts, 506, 35

Unbelief, Carlyle on, 471, 20; contrasted with belief, 27, 30; effect of, 415, 14; foundation of, 27, 16; founded on blind belief, 559, 4; in man, 84, 47; our age of, not without hope, 173, 34; prevalent among men of ability, 293, 27; the battle against, 417, 2; the fearful, 427, 30; the, that torments us, 339, 30

Unborn, rather be, than untaught, 29, 17; the blessed, 550, 39

Uncertain, the, how to treat, 192, 49, 50

Uncle Toby, ways of Sterne's, 121, 39

Unconquerable man, an, 153, 5

Unconscious, the, region of, 304, 33; the, value of, 459, 32

Unconsciousness, commended by Christ, 242, 24; sign of health, 453, 32

Unction, flattering, 110, 15

Understanding, and expression, 87, 29; and reason, objects of, 67, 2; and wit, 558, 1; candle of, in heart, 168, 32; compared with fantasy, 459, 33; contrasted with reason, 369, 28, 33; defined, 513, 14; dulness of, how to treat, 349, 5; end of, 433, 29; error essential to, 176, 39; evil of abuse of, 167, 27; forgiving, 45, 52; fortitude of, 499, 50; healthy, defined, 433, 29; high source of, 436, 44; its rank, 435, 4; judgments of, Goethe on, 437, 23; man's best candle, 266, 27; no, without love, 522, 47; of people better than censure, 29, 53; one thing well, 496, 32; perfect, value of, 432, 39; power of, 485, 40; sound, the dread of, 434, 28; source of, 206, 21; the condition of hearing, 11, 62; the condition of, 12, 38; the modern god, 431, 5; the, pursuing its rightful course, 486, 48; things, condition of, 496, 35; two conditions of, 496, 14; value of, 153, 11; 162, 4; way for, 100, 22; without, without purpose, 79, 28

Undertaking too much, 66, 24

Undertakings, great, distrusted, 410, 47; great, the requisite to, 385, 38

Undiscovered, the, country, 553, 4

Uneasiness, the cause of our, 201, 36

Unemployed, the, a burden, 82, 56

Unexpected, the, happens, 195, 2

Unfortunate, blessing an evil to, 496, 26; man, an, according to Goethe, 143, 20; the, unwise, 253, 9

Ungrateful, man, an, 194, 21; men, different kinds of, 143, 57; service to, 194, 16; to do good to, 491, 40

Unhappiness, cause of, 521, 22 ; cause of all our, 498, 37 ; imaginary, 521, 43 ; man's, cause of, 267, 9 ; source of, 303, 11 ; the one, for a man, 445, 41 ; the true, 175, 18

Unhappy, the, 447, 17 ; the, a comfort of, 326, 33 ; the always wrong, 459, 36 ; the, and their time, 433, 14 ; the, cared for by God, 125, 51 ; the, on earth, 466, 37

Unhelpful, the, 305, 7

Unimaginative, the, defects of, 459, 37

Uninquisitiveness, man's, 359, 14

Unintelligible, how to interpret, 384, 37

Union, power of, 11, 50 ; 15, 39 ; 89, 41 ; motive for, and the power of it, 559, 44 ; strength, 224, 17

Unity, in a work, test of, 542, 36 ; not uniformity, 103, 46

Universe, a, in each man, 559, 19 ; a man's, how determined, 407, 47 ; a thought of God, 54, 34 ; and particles that compose it, 475, 4 ; as seen from England, contrasted from that as seen from Judea, 539, 4 ; divine-infernal, 316, 21 ; each man to adjust himself in, 202, 4 ; ever in transformation, 249, 32 ; great soul of, 431, 37 ; how bound together, 21, 5 ; laws of, mistake regarding, 355, 1 ; nature of, 467, 30 ; the, no wronging, 311, 35 ; the, sayings about, 459, 38-46 ; 460, 1, 2 ; the, out at sea, 340, 5 ; those who love the whole, 480, 6 ; to him who thinks he can swallow it all, 533, 43 ; under government, 92, 49 ; *versus* the spirit of God, 462, 15

University, the true modern, 459, 13 ; years, importance of, 2, 32

Unjust, in little, 147, 8 ; thing, doomed, 316, 46

Unkindness, not of nature, 292, 16 : pining effect of, 283, 25 ; small, 19, 56

Unlearn, who needs not, 161, 19

Unlearned man, the ignorance of, 460, 3

Unlearning, a slow business, 56, 48 ; not right, 141, 24

Unlooked-for, the, 509, 7

Unnatural, imperfect, 94, 51

Unnecessary, the, dear, 81, 6

Unprosperous, the, suspicious, 328, 2

Unpunctuality, loss in, 139, 15

Unreality, never patronised long, 316, 18

Unseen and unknown, power over us of, 199, 21

Unsettling, times of, needed, 565, 2

Unsophisticated man, the, 176, 17

Unsought, those that come, 482, 43

Unthinking persons, their speech, 193, 2

Untruth, an, that has the start, 314, 5

Unused, the, a burden, 519, 15

Up and doing, 243, 45

Upholstery, for whom, 508, 2

Upright, highway of, 435, 13 ; subject to hatred and envy, 141, 3

Uprightness, a sure card, 148, 43 ; commended, 539, 34

Urn, storied, hollowness of, 35, 20

Use, constant, effect of, 104, 42 ; effect of, on strength, 184, 32 ; essential to possession, 316, 43 ; power of, 111, 33 ; what we do not, 539, 26

Useful, but part of important, 520, 13 ; encourages itself, 460, 15 ; only to be gloried in, 300, 34 ; with agreeable, mingling of, 327, 52 ; regard of the ancients for, 208, 30

Usefulness, condition of, 144, 38 ; incompatible with baseness, 186, 16

Useless, nothing, to sensible people, 180, 5 ; people, 460, 16 ; to self, useless to others, 151, 15

Usurer and his plough, 460, 17

Utmost, the, who does, 535, 3

Utopia, Emerson's, 169, 10 ; the true, life in, 191, 22

Utopias, premature truths, 239, 29

Uttered, the, and unuttered, part of life, 460, 19

V

Vagabonds, nature-made, 292, 9

Vain, man, folly of, 489, 41 ; men, how to treat 243, 48

Vainglory, anti-Christian, 242, 28

Vale of life, cool, sequestered, 102, 10

Valetudinarians like misers, 345, 12

Valiant, and his sufferings, 460, 20 ; as compared with cowards, 49, 26 ; the most truly, 153, 26 ; valour of, 3, 17

Valour, against adversity, 4, 69 ; contrasted with endurance, 460, 22 ; definition of, 103, 53 ; in distress, 69, 48 ; mean of, 441, 39 ; of just man, 460, 21 ; power of, 540, 29 ; sad, wise, 379, 15 ; the better part of, 418, 18 ; the truest, 198, 14 ; true, defined, 500, 41

Valours, our, our best gods, 339, 31

Value, in men and things, 460, 23, 24 ; the one thing of, 445, 40

Vanity, a mark of humility, 490, 42 ; a preservative against, 437, 41 ; a source of, 40, 33 ; a, which is deadly, 470, 2 ; application to, of truth, 476, 1 ; as lack of understanding, 92, 7 ; as regards fashions, 477, 10 ; compared with pride, 356, 34, 36 ; corrupting power of, 507, 2 ; desecrating power of, 476, 10 ; difficult to manage, 474, 40 ; in rags, 168, 28 ; inherent in mankind, 92, 48 ; masterpiece of, 100, 44 ; our, *versus* dignity, 339, 32 ; why insufferable, 537, 42

Vanquished, he could argue still, 89, 36

Vapour, floating, subject to gravity, 428, 48

Variety, source of pleasure, 278, 36 ; the zest in, 315, 34

Vase, a bungled, 14, 6

Veil, a, of the gods, not to be lifted, 242, 11 ; 506, 7

Veils, the moral value of, 289, 21

Venerate, the untrained to, 507, 20

Veneration, deep and great affection, incompatible, 201, 8 ; secret of, 460, 26 ; that is god-like, 191, 43

Vengeance, deep, begotten of deep silence, 56, 55 ; gods of, their action, 66, 6 ; nature of, 375, 22 ; noblest, 445, 9 ; sacrifices from, 269, 39

Venturing, warrant for, 176, 36

Venus, the cruel pleasure of, 391, 10

Veracity as a duty, 445, 22

Verse that wounds, curst by Pope, 52, 2

Verses, writing, no special craft, 367, 11

Vesture, colour of, 422, 32 ; cut of, 422, 32

Vexations not to be aggravated, 294, 39

Vice, all, under a guise of virtue, 474, 42 ; an emancipator of the mind, 414, 21 ; and virtue, methods of, contrasted, 45, 41 ; dignified by action, 515, 18 ; every, brink of a precipice, 327, 47 ; evil of, 66, 31 ; eradicable with time, 75, 27 forsaking, 361, 45 ; in the form of example, 512, 3 ; only antidote for, 171, 19 ; Roman, Juvenal on, 299, 38 ; under disguise of virtue, 100, 33

Vices, attacking, in the abstract, 489, 38 ; how regarded, 50, 11 ; insinuating power of, 516, 22 , not all our own, 294, 43 ; often from good qualities, 268, 26 ; that have banished virtue, 225, 31

Vicissitude, advantage in, 12, 43

Vicissitude, a Cadmæan, 216, 47 ; by force, 552, 19 ; celebrated in song, 533, 3 ; different effects of, 171, 32 ; greatest, 391, 12 ; main thing, 178, 29 ; masters of, 444, 41 ; no, without cost, 307, 37 ; noblest, 227, 11 ; not by violence, 191, 30 ; reward of, 514, 5 ; secret of, 537, 10 ; without bloodshed, 132, 14

Victuals, one's, criticising, 533, 9

Vigilance as a virtue, 518, 13

Vile, nothing so, as to yield no good, 317, 1

Villains, rich and poor, in league, 545, 13
Villainy, diverse rewards of, 332, 55
Vine round the oak, and the reason, 453, 45
Vinegar, the sharpest, 456, 33
Violence, as a manager, 261, 9; short-lived, 20, 42
Violent, the, short-lived, 316, 41
Violin, a beginner on, 192, 31
Virgil's, ambition, 412, 30; epitaph, 268, 4
Virtue, a defence, 5, 1; 36, 35; a soul raised to, a masterpiece, 322, 23; attainment of, 445, 6; according to reason, 460, 44; and vice, how to treat, 370, 28; alone happiness, 220, 1; as a covering, 188, 21; as an anchor, 511, 14; attribute of, 382, 14; base of every, 257, 27; best plain set, 120, 8; certainty in, where to find, 189, 31; cheap without trial, 154, 20; child of freedom, 67, 12; complacent fair-weather, 552, 33; condition of its growth, 249, 55; consciousness of, 91, 2; cornerstone of, 386, 12; decease of, Cicero on, 128, 46; defined, 546, 4; dependence of, on misfortune, 136, 33; divine path to, 412, 47; element of, 485, 5, 7; end of life, 111, 35; enduring, 70, 15; for its own sake, 214, 26; force of, 506, 22; foundation of all, 164, 4; her sublime elevation, 488, 45 Hesiod's path to, 451, 35; how to acquire, 243, 10; how to see her form, 488, 45; how to seek, 405, 55; in a beautiful form, 132, 24; in ambition and in authority, 188, 23; in regretting, 269, 34; initial, of the race, 436, 38; its brother, 307, 34; its own reward, 11, 1; joy of, in being put to test, 119, 6; least, not to be deferred, 67, 25; less in favour than vice, 149, 44; love for, 233, 34; made a vice, 526, 11; manifestation of, measure of, 19, 64; measure of a man's, 13, 1; must be dignified, 156, 34; never cruel, 140, 38; no, quite unconscious, 303, 46; no tax on, good of, 89, 53; not valued by fortunate, 67, 27; obstructions to, 23, 46; only want of, despised, 330, 18; ostentation in, 149, 3; parent of, 193, 37; pathway to, 548, 54; primal condition of, 449, 20; produced by collision, 44, 28; proper theatre of, 307, 25; pure, till tried, 212, 19; pursuit of, beyond bounds, 194, 43; sayings about, 66, 29–33; 228, 6–12; 397, 3, 4, 6; 515, 35–54; 516, 1–9; silent, arm of world, 464, 11; sometimes awkwardly set, 181, 15; that can't be bought, rare, 105, 13; that requires to be guarded, 414, 22; the only necessity, 507, 26; the sentinel, 46, 38; to be exercised, 165, 24; to her votaries, 48, 7; true, 500, 42, 43; two roads to, 570, 6; under calumny, 34, 54; under oppression, 50, 2; *versus* pedigree, 164, 48; we boast of, 265, 41; weak, 530, 14; within, honour without, 175, 26; without discretion, 559, 28; without its reward, 260, 7; without restraint, 183, 34; zeal for, value of, 331, 34
Virtues, acknowledged by Christianity, 43, 6; and faults, interchangeable, 523, 25; at different ages, 185, 28; fortifying, 432, 27; gentlemanly, rare, 526, 7; godlike, parent of all, 420, 16; greatest, Augustine on, 432, 43; late in maturing, 438, 3; lost in interests, 239, 32; milder, correlated to severer, 442, 10; not all our own, 294, 43; one's thinking of, 438, 37; our, sayings about, 339, 34–37; permanency of our, 530, 30; severe and restrictive, 453, 18; to profit one, 509, 22; two chief, 319, 36; two kinds of, 399, 11; we speak of, 528, 18
Virtuous, deeds and their reward, 109, 22; most, of men, 444, 10; sayings about the, 461, 1–3, 21; the, defined, 540, 43
Visible, garment of invisible, 457, 24
Vision, clearness of its comprehensiveness, 495, 30; consequence of intensified, 395, 22; imperfect, effect of, 323, 19; limit of, for most, 304, 37; measure of our, 539, 20; now, through a glass darkly, 110, 28; the, of visions for a man, 422, 40

Visionaries, all, 521, 6
Visions, the, we see, 521, 6
Vitality, fate of what has no, 540, 33
Vocation, a peculiar, to every one, 75, 14; apt to mistake our, 521, 10; chosen for one, 296, 32; of man, primary, 449, 22
Voice, as index of character, 473, 12; human, power of, 436, 5; is in my sword, 167, 7; inner, to be trusted, 519, 10; of man, general and perpetual, 429, 44; soft, gentle, and low, 155, 4; wisest, no longer divine, 463, 25
Void, in things, 321, 42
Voltaire, impotency of his logic, 197, 24; in relation to his time, 82, 34; on his life, 258, 27
Volubility different from pertinency, 42, 49
Volume, flesh-bound, the only revelation of God, 428, 46
Vote, of a slave, a nuisance, 307, 11
Votes, should be weighed, 265, 37; worthlessness of decisions by, 520, 15
Voting, decision by, Cromwell's protest against, 517, 36
Vow to heaven to be first paid, 321, 11
Vows, unheedful, 507, 23
Vox populi, vox dei, falsehood of, 414, 15
Vulgar, incapable of pure truth, 289, 20; people, mark of, 403, 12; respect of, for wealth, 136, 42; sayings about, 461, 10–12; working on, with fine sense, 492, 10
Vulgarity, and fashion, 102, 30, 34; condemned, 64, 9; essence of, 425, 35; marks of, 69, 30; or solitude, 465, 12
Vulnerable, point, our, 522, 10; point, the, 164, 20

W

Wages, God's business, 279, 38; never to be angrily demanded, 304, 5; our claim of, 260, 43
Waggons, creaking, 49, 39
Wailing, no remedy, 311, 24; over the dead, ineffectual, 230, 29
Waiting, advantage of, 94, 16; in vain, 20, 14; not Goethe's way, 160, 24
Walking, a falling forward, 461, 14; a series of falls, 13, 2
Wallets, our two, 345, 41
Wanderers o'er eternity, 33, 27
Wandering, think of, 171, 37
Want, caused by haste, 141, 7; effect of, on heart, 530, 18; full satisfaction of, 493, 2; prayer of, to be listened to, 116, 28; that man has to dread, 204, 40
Wants, four material, 287, 5; knowledge and effort necessary for supply of, 152, 38; man's, 266, 17; source of our, 203, 48; which we are insensible of, 12, 30
War, a game which subjects might veto, 33, 32; an iron cure, 60, 27; and peace, Schiller on, 221, 32; art of, Napoleon on, 567, 13; art of, Wellington on, 462, 5; begun, hell let loose, 137, 19; conquest by cruelty in, 50, 33; conquest in, 201, 1; epithets of, 27, 33, 41, 44, 45; evil, 181, 38; evil of, 101, 31; 191, 30; for war, 155, 8; final aim of, 59, 54; glorious, pride, pomp, and circumstance of, 102, 22; hell enlarged, 122, 31; honour of, 382, 13; horror of, 506, 26; how to look on, 27, 43; how to still, 288, 48; legitimate object of, 27, 42; man in time of, 188, 52; mistakes in, inevitable, 150, 36; murder, 98, 28; no second blunder in, 30, 30; once business, 112, 34; right form of, 106, 6; ruin to thousands, 280, 32; sacrifices in, 209, 48; sign of injustice, 549, 24; sources of, 116, 11; success in, 405, 31;

success in, right earned by, 150, 1 ; three things required in, 569, 37 ; when just, 216, 41

Ware, bad, never cheap, 329, 45 ; no, without the money, 565, 32

Warfare, the greatest, 391, 12 ; the spiritual, of these days, 191, 35

Warlike people, vices of all, 119, 42

Warmth, great, at outset, an evil sign, 135, 23 ; in winter, 191, 27

Warning, comparative worthlessness of, 334, 22 ; word, not heeded, 23, 10

Warnings, earth full of, 75, 47

Warrior, an old, 15, 59 ; and war-horse, but a vision, 414, 24

Warriors, great, why remembered, 135, 24

Wars and mothers, 27, 35

Waste, caused by haste, 141, 7 ; where no enjoyment, 544, 35

Waster, after an earner, 77, 40

Watching, vain, 96, 24

Water, afar, and fire, 3, 32 ; and blood, different destinations of, 425, 2 ; and wine as mirrors, 192, 30 ; as servant and master, 106, 39 ; drinking, 73, 8 ; not to be quarrelled with, 522, 5 ; pure, to be sought at the fountain, 42, 38 ; smooth, to be guarded against, 57, 34 ; spilt upon the ground, 21, 13 ; that has passed the mill, 45, 54 ; where the brook is deep, 394, 40

Waters, still, deadliest, 313, 27

Wattle, Captain, 63, 44

Wave, the longest, 439, 37

Waves, tainted with death, 103, 45

Way, a, fashioning, through the impassable, 331, 8 ; best, to be chosen, however rough, 42, 43 ; good, to be inquired after, 402, 16 ; how to make, 312, 24 ; noiseless tenor of their, 102, 10 ; seeing one's, 168, 26 ; that seemeth right, 470, 42 ; truth and life, importance of the, 560, 2 ; wrong in one's own, rather than right in another, 45, 2

Ways to end, many, 10, 44

Wayside, building by, 145, 22

Weak, man, every, under a tyrant, 325, 43 ; the, concessions of, 421, 19 ; the, moderation of, 226, 14 ; the, strength of, 323, 41 ; when united, 512, 49

Weakest, the, 386, 2 ; spot, the, in every one, 461, 38

Weaklings must lie, 443, 31

Weakness, and ignorance, how to treat, 349, 5 ; born vanquished, 403, 29 ; every man his, 92, 5 ; how not to expose a, 176, 45 ; innate and acquired, 398, 29 ; man's, God's respect for, 125, 28 ; mischief of, 58, 7 ; misery of, 490, 44 ; not so dependent as strength, 403, 30

Weaknesses, concealment of our, 564, 4

Weal, every, has its woe, 90, 34 ; human, the sum of, 187, 37

Wealth, a burden, unless understood, 553, 7 ; a dubious gain, 415, 8 ; a form of, 357, 8 ; a man's, the measure of, 533, 29 ; a spring of, 220, 30 ; accompaniments of, 49, 56 ; amassing, 178, 51 ; and freedom, effect of, 548, 56 ; and place, get, 122, 6 ; and poverty, 354, 11 ; and poverty, connection of, with moral qualities, 152, 21 ; Butler's definition of, 111, 39 ; by mere labour and economy, 303, 30 ; condition of possessing, 522, 45 ; deference to, 329, 3 ; effect of, 194, 37 ; essence of, 426, 3 ; evanescence of, 238, 5 ; first, 428, 43 ; for sake of independence, 118, 55 ; gaining, *versus* guiding, 119, 10 ; gathering, 118, 57 ; powerless to give happiness, 35, 30 ; gotten before wit, 146, 19 ; hidden, here, 243, 13 ; how to save men from, 565, 41 ; ill-acquired, 238, 4 ; ill-gotten, not lasting, 181, 43 ; in relation to man and woman, 124, 14 ; instability of, 77, 44 ; its destination nowadays, 53, 14 ; limit to want, 250, 11 ; loss of, misery of, 200, 35 ; lust of, evil of, 345, 43 ;

man's best, 6, 58 ; man's true, 91, 7 ; material, of a country defined, 441, 37 ; moral condition of the power of, 508, 35 ; much, little enjoyment, 285, 15 ; natural, according to Socrates, 47, 21 ; not a source of pleasure, 513, 23 ; not quickly won, 132, 5 ; not happiness, 209, 14 ; of Indies, who would bring home, 152, 50 ; or want, children of, common fate of, 41, 53 ; people of, 216, 7 ; poor, keeping up appearance of, 311, 30 ; poor man's, 41, 45 ; parted with before death, 41, 13 ; power of, 189, 16 ; rapidly accumulated, 319, 2 ; ruinous to a nation without intelligence, 305, 27 ; sayings about, 461, 39-44 ; source of, no question, 506, 18 ; the only, 474, 44 ; the substantial, of a man, 456, 12 ; the world's, 465, 25 ; to men of sense, 276, 9 ; true veins of, 459, 15 ; unjust, fate of, 145, 27 ; *versus* men, 181, 40 ; way to, 461, 32 ; without enjoyment, 559, 31 ; which is wealth, 166, 3 ; without rich heart, 559, 23

Weapon, murderous, dangerous to carry, 119, 23

Weapons of war, Luther's estimate, 35, 19

Wearing out, compared with rusting, 105, 14

Weary, stale, flat, and unprofitable, 162, 45

Weathercock, like a, 211, 16

Weathers, something good in all, 478, 32

Web, a tangled, 322, 33 ; begun, sure of thread, 109, 20

Wedded people, most, one couple more, 284, 15

Wedge, to be effectual, 462, 3

Wedlock, an awakening, 275, 14 ; humble, 163, 43 ; perfect, man and woman in, 189, 1 ; state of sorrow, 78, 19

Weeds, as a sign of the soil, 13, 49 ; native to fattest soil, 284, 38 ; noisome, 308, 36 ; showiness of, 23, 43 ; to be weeded out in time, 317, 40

Weep, women appointed to, 33, 17

Weeping, as king, and not weeping as father, 86, 10 ; beauty, the image of, 476, 41 ; eyes turned to heaven, 553, 10 ; in children rather than men, 29, 8

Weights, greatest, how God hangs, 125, 49

Weighty, willing to be weighed, 151, 23

Welfare, human, source of, 562, 43 ; 563, 2 ; national, condition of, 144, 7 ; of the whole, importance of, 86, 1

Well, a bad, 32, 11

Well, or ill, matter of feeling, 93, 22 ; to do, who fears, 551, 18

Well-being, essential to being, 27, 21

Well-considered, the, and well-resolved, to be done, 540, 38

Well-doing, here or nowhere, 175, 41 ; patient doing, 474, 45

Well-done, the value of, 560, 25 ; twice done, 48, 31

Well-read man, respect for, 338, 16

Well-springs everywhere, 190, 43

Wellington, saying of, at Waterloo, 140, 32

Wheat, a corn of, must die, 96, 18

Wheel of fortune, the, and its spokes, 462, 4

Wheels, great, uphill and downhill, 240, 53

When, question of, 518, 25

Whence, the question of, vain, 488, 14

Where, and when, significance of, 272, 29 ; question of, and how, 518, 25

Wherefore, the, dark to us, 55, 4

Whetstone, office of, 117, 37

Whim, every man his, 240, 46

Whimpering for the fool, 232, 52

Whining, sentimental, as a symptom, 412, 22

Whips and scorns of time, 553, 2

Whirligig of time, the, 485, 47

Whisky Burns on, 195, 6

Whisperings, cut-throat, 52, 15, 18

Whist, Talleyrand on, 517, 41

Whistled for want of thought, 149, 18

Whole, a, never seen, 302, 32 ; a, thrown away on public, 519, 27 ; everything woven into the, 555, 40 ; the, connection with, to be aimed at, 11, 38 ; the, how to benefit by, 556, 26

Wholeness, not halfness, the rule, 520, 1, 5

Wholesome and poisonous, how man learns what is, 37, 6

Wicked, and wicked one, 522, 14 ; as judged by the deluge, 498, 24 ; career of, 429, 36 ; compared with indiscreet, 109, 44 ; fellow become pious, 24, 56 ; listening to, 495, 29 ; men, their disbelief in good, 239, 5 ; not to be envied, 114, 45 ; perfidy of, a blessing, 44, 37 ; sacrifice of, 452, 18 ; still with us, 58, 33 ; tender mercies of, 457, 10 ; uneasy in presence of good, 184, 1

Wickedness, a method in, 470, 12 ; beginning of, 417, 20 ; cowardly, 320, 9 ; extreme, never of sudden growth, 295, 23 ; its own reward, 11, 1 ; licentious, its career, 538, 24 ; treasures of, 499, 16

Widows, easy-crying, 76, 12

Wife, a childless, a dear friend, 213, 62 ; a, marrying, 510, 42, 43 ; a, to a man, 13, 3 ; and a fortune, 29, 1 ; and children, hostages to fortune, 146, 44 ; and weans, Burns on, 478, 42 ; as a trial, 93, 16 ; as husband, 20, 49 ; choice of, 277, 16 ; 412, 19 ; choosing, 185, 18 ; dearer than bride, 162, 8 ; described, 389, 2 ; dowry of, 72, 1 ; fault of, due to husband, 212, 18 ; good, value of, 17, 16 ; 54, 31 ; husband answerable for, 383, 39 ; love for, 38, 29 ; my true and honourable, 565, 13 ; rule in choosing a, 62, 4 ; sayings about a, 462, 19–21 ; secret of her influence, 36, 36 ; what a man wants in a, 415, 25 ; who findeth a, 554, 13 ; whom to choose for, 42, 42, 46 ; with a good husband, how known, 542, 33

Wilderness, life and light in, 190, 43

Wiles, the craftiest, a bad cloak, 422, 9

Will, a divided, evil of, 152, 46 ; a divine, faith in, 538, 30 ; a holy, lives, 79, 13 ; alone formidable, 446, 17 ; an independent, 62, 37 ; analogue of, 44, 30 ; and inclination in relation to virtue, 6, 43 ; and judgment, 437, 21 ; and way, 532, 37 ; as law, 231, 41 ; authoritative, 89, 43 ; centre of good and evil, 475, 19 ; everything, 228, 19 ; firm, power of a, 151, 8 ; government of, better than knowledge, 131, 23 ; in affections and passions, 462, 22 ; incarnated, our interest in manifestations of, 395, 12 ; its nature, 517, 21 ; its only satisfaction, 446, 15 ; man's determining force, 313, 24 ; man's want, 344, 54 ; no compelling, 5, 6 ; no, no wit, 149, 19 ; obstructed, 182, 28 ; omnipotence of, 315, 5 ; peculiar to man, 8, 55 ; power of, 17, 19 ; 517, 38 ; power of right, 241, 46 ; power of, with skill and perseverance, 488, 14 ; preciousness to a man of his, 475, 38 ; ready, the power of, 546, 9 ; sovereign in the world, 94, 29 ; the great of, 144, 51 ; the, of God, 125, 44 ; the rudder, 264, 23 ; the soul of deed, 6, 36 ; thwarted in world, 464, 33 ; usurping the place of intellect, 323, 40 ; virtue of a strong, 322, 29 ; who forfeits his, 551, 21

"Will do," making, wait upon " I should," 552, 15

Willing, all, effecting nothing, 152, 46 ; everything and doing nothing, 298, 21 ; the virtue of, 263, 25

Willingness not enough, 203, 40

Willow and oak, 462, 23

Wills, our, and fates, contrary, 339, 41

Wind, sowing, 479, 50 ; the, observing, 148, 5 ; the, with and against, 490, 12

Windbags, their doom, 435, 34

Windows, prying into, 148, 9

Winds of heaven to visit, 164, 24

Wine, a blessing and bane, 104, 33, 36 ; effect of, on nature, 546, 43 ; eloquence from, 104, 2 ; great fault of, 259, 35 ; good (see **Good wine**) ; no, if drunk like water, 142, 22 ; no, no love, 326, 40 ; power of, 16, 29 ; 514, 28 ; revealing power of, 182, 35 ; sweet, vinegar from, 112, 44 ; sweet, when sour, 408, 11 ; tasting of, 428, 20 ; treacherous friend, 413, 19 ; women, and song, who loves not, 532, 30

Wine-cup more fatal than the sea, 182, 26

Wings, brave, gift of, 125, 37 ; people vainest of their, 202, 52 ; without feet, 150, 32

Winking with the eye, 148, 58

Winter in lap of May, 33, 37

Wisdom, a mark of, 391, 28 ; a point of, 199, 47 ; aim of, not happiness, 81, 22 ; and gray hairs, 136, 15 ; and her charge, 484, 34 ; and misfortune, 54, 33 ; and wit, 558, 2, 13 ; and wit, natural gifts, 304, 20 ; appeals of, disregarded, 112, 4 ; at another's expense, 104, 19 ; before gold, 29, 49 ; beginning of, 417, 24 ; better than valour, 221, 33 ; bird of, her flight, 418, 27 ; condition of, 153, 34 ; constancy in, 479, 18 ; contrasted with knowledge, 220, 15, 20, 23, 47 ; 221, 5 ; dependent of, on courage, 139, 13 ; discernment of, 557, 33 ; divine, effect of belief in, 161, 27 ; effect of, 548, 20 ; essential to justice, 216, 27 ; fair, to rule, 243, 16 ; first and second point of, 428, 29 ; first order of, 20, 46 ; first step of, 515, 38 ; first step towards, 356, 54 ; forms in which we love, 525, 35 ; from ability, 308, 49 ; function of, 197, 41 ; great, a mark of, 199, 37 ; great point of, 198, 38 ; greatest, 473, 4 ; hallmark of, 164, 2 ; high, allied to insanity, 434, 34 ; high value of, 133, 44 ; highest, 435, 12 ; highest heaven of, near, 434, 42 ; how gained, 12, 21 ; how recognisable, 207, 29 ; how to learn, 236, 7 ; how we learn, 525, 15 ; human, honour due to, 123, 34 ; in deeds, 310, 8 ; in keeping golden mean, 400, 38 ; in mouth of fanatic, 531, 19 ; infused into everything, 92, 46 ; invariable mark of, 437, 9 ; knowledge involved in practice of, 150, 18 ; Lavater's definition of, 473, 32 ; learning rules of, without conforming to them, 151, 33 ; lesson in, to be welcomed, 176, 15 ; lessons of, 240, 7, 8 ; main lesson of, 198, 48 ; man of, 440, 28 ; master-work of, 493, 32 ; matter of years, 55, 27 ; men's, 522, 28 ; mile-stones on road to, 300, 28 ; not always wise, 65, 2 ; not self-derived, 295, 25 ; not to be too wise, 86, 15 ; 477, 26 ; of the wise, 462, 38 ; only one, avails, 319, 20 ; oracles of, 285, 21 ; power of, 485, 40 ; 514, 9 ; price of, 449, 18 ; profession *versus* practice of, 93, 37 ; road to, how measured, 442, 25 ; seat of, 452, 37 ; shown in sense of follies, 225, 35 ; simple, our love for, 144, 3 ; source of, 194, 6 ; striving after, in the eyes of fools, 543, 44 ; sublimity of, 456, 9 ; superiority of, 548, 58 ; talking and acting, two things, 201, 23 ; taught by age, 21, 14 ; taught by Nature, 329, 36 ; test of, 276, 13 ; that is too late, 532, 16 ; that would win men, 563, 25 ; the greatest, 190, 5 ; the prime, 493, 39 ; those who follow, 480, 23 ; three paths to, 34, 19 ; throughout life rare, 242, 36 ; to be husbanded, 175, 7 ; to them that hold her, 389, 1 ; too early or too late, 66, 20 ; too late, 344, 50 ; too much, 569, 34 ; travelling in quest of, 480, 19 ; truest, 465, 20 ; unmarketable if for sale, 533, 17 ; value of, 162, 4 ; *versus* fortune, 141, 15 ; *versus* learning, 484, 6 ; wellspring of, 463, 43 ; which one is forbidden to impart, 533, 16 ; who findeth, 554, 15 ; whom to thank for, 175, 30 ; wish to be alone in, 39, 16 ; without self-respect, 295, 36 ; world's treatment of, 206, 34 ; worth of, 332, 56

Wisdom's root, 369, 3

Wise, always few, 234, 19 ; and fool, as regards speech, 235, 5 ; and foolish, contrasted, 80, 58 ; 197, 22 ; 462, 32, 34 ; 463, 2, 9 ; and foolish, difference between, 10, 39 ; and their defect of zeal for converts, 320, 16 ; and their words, 67,

10; as serpents, 30, 4; 399, 27; be, to-day, 30, 1; be, with speed, 30, 2; cautious, 162, 17; ears and tongues of, 61, 34; everything, already thought, 8, 62; few to be followed, 108, 16; for saying nothing, 165, 43; in time, 153, 29; learn from their enemies, 16, 51; life of, compared with that of poor, 558, 44; man, a mark of, 478, 24; man, a, reticencies of, 307, 49; man, a very, 286, 26; man and fool, 362, 40; man and poet, 448, 11; man and the state, 492, 7; man and the world, 151, 37; man, as distinct from learned, 8, 1; man, characteristic of, 151, 26; 197, 42; man, contrasted with sagacious, 566, 36; man, his rule in action, 380, 31; man, latter part of his life, 438, 11; man looks ahead, 380, 32; man, lordship of, 380, 30; man, mouth of, 434, 1; man, progress of, compared with that of fool, 522, 3; man, strong, 531, 18; man, that is esteemed by world, 438, 40; man, the keeper of his secrets, 459, 19; man, the reflections of, wisely limited, 199, 48; man, the strong, 455, 32; men and fools, 5, 54, 57, 60, 61, 62, 64, 65; 108, 54; men and poverty, 354, 16; men, folly in, 467, 20; men, indispensable to God, 126, 21; men rarer than learned, 526, 9; men, the little foolery of, 439, 23; not independent of advice, 311, 40; nothing insipid to, 315, 6; prone to doubt, 162, 17; saws and modern instances, full of, 267, 21; sayings about, 462, 30-38; 463, 1-17; the, blessedness of, 479, 34; the constancy of, defined, 224, 33; the, folly in, 469, 34; the, guide of, 65, 12; the, law of, 438, 22; the, should confer together, 328, 3; the only, 479, 20; the only, sad, 151, 18; the only wretched, 116, 10; their aversion to society, 235, 4; thoughts of, how expressed, 296, 10; thoughts of, value of, 85, 32; to be, and to love, impossible, 490, 46; when compelled into silence, 378, 25; who to be called, 34; 45, wise to himself, 144, 2; words of, 463, 46; words of, in troublous times, 192, 7

Wisely worldly, be, not worldly wise, 29, 75

Wisest, content with destiny, 67, 11; man, the, 68, 47; 532, 20; man, often not wise at all, 143, 44; sayings about, 463, 19-28; who thinks not himself so, 234, 32

Wish, an unfulfilled, pain of, 446, 37; effect of, gratification of every, 533, 2; father to thought, 104, 38; one's, when in love, 544, 44; an ungranted, lesson in, 535, 30

Wishes, and powers, chasm between, 140, 13; God's, *versus* man's, 62, 11; how our, lengthen with years, 249, 56; youthful, 520, 3

Wishing, and possessing, 521, 37; to be despised, 62, 24

Wishing-gate, the, 463, 31

Wit, affectation of, 480, 29; and folly, balanced, 109, 33; and judgment, at strife, 469, 7; and sense, 467, 5; and wisdom, natural gifts, 304, 20; at a nonplus without folly, 12, 37; at the expense of memory, 330, 38; best, 32, 17; contrasted with genius, 223, 4; contrasted with humour, 164, 8; defined, 513, 14; disturbance of equipoise, 185, 27; given in vain, 199, 7; how developed, 396, 7; how it comes, 510, 2; how spoiled, 223, 7; how to reply to, 373, 43; in conversation, 223, 1; its most brilliant flashes, 443, 35; kind of, to be bridled, 469, 9; like a coquette, 223, 8; little, weary feet, 251, 44; men of, fools necessary to, 505, 26; men of, two classes of, 468, 14; must be spontaneous, 101, 43; never at home, 157, 18; news only to ignorance, 231, 10; not confined to one, 10, 49; not to be arrested, 223, 6; not to be importuned, 565, 20; not to be too refined, 71. 45; one's, matter of self-complacency, 318, 8; of language and of ideas, contrasted, 463, 32; preferring, to good sense, 495, 2; relation of, to talent, 83, 50; sparks of, not enough, 488, 25; the body and soul of, 32, 36, 37;

the highest order of, 373, 30; thrown away, 10, 50; too much, evil effect of, 497, 47; touchstone of, 223, 16; true, 500, 44; true, characteristic of, 253, 34; unsparing, 31, 52; value of one's own, 15, 63; without modesty, 313, 42

Wit's pedlar, 144, 4

Witch, a, being, and being reckoned, 487, 47

Within, what is not from, weak at root, 520, 10

Without, within, 476, 11

Wits, and dunces, 25, 5; effect of dainty living on, 102, 45; great, allied to madness, 135, 26, 27; intemperate, 195, 25; never puzzled, 150, 10; rarely men of genius, 276, 6; shallow, their censure, 388, 27; short-lived, 389, 29; silly people, 362, 36; without thinking, 126, 5

Witticism, holding in, difficult, 201, 15

Witty, who can't be, 345, 14

Wives, choice of, 105, 20; economy, virtue of, 164, 23; ill, 1, 1

Woe, sour, delight of, in fellowship, 400, 28; that heritage of, 253, 21; trappings and suits of, 385, 15; trappings of, 167, 12; trifling with, evil of, 252, 58

Woes, a way to peace, 174, 4; mortal, the pathos of, 406, 50; that cannot be healed, 551, 2

Wolf, caught by ears, 183, 17; changes coat, not character, 257, 52

Wolsey, on his fall, 292, 51; reflection of, on his fall, 138, 31

Woman, a, at the window, 71, 17; a, four storeys high, 27, 36; a gluttonous, 173, 28; a, in every strife, 318, 12; a learned, Euripides on, 399, 38; a loving, a priestess, 91, 43; a, mode of showing love to, 495, 25; how, openly bad, 16, 31; a perfect, 16, 28; a restriction upon, 21, 49; a spiritual auxiliary, 223, 39; a, to be praised, 103, 24; a true, home always around, 549, 11; admiration of, for courage, 316, 26; aim of, 288, 44; always extreme, 24, 5; and her passion for love, 187, 25; as protector, 505, 28; as taskmaster, 240, 18; a truly educated, 307, 51; born of tardiness, 285, 34; case of, betrayed, 544, 16; changeable, 71, 18; character of, 511, 45; circling ivy, 264, 6; counsel of virtuous, 242, 1; courage of, under strong affection, 539, 41; daring of, 22, 44; defined, 389, 4 (see **She**); delight and terror of man, 35, 34; beautiful, Fontenelle's description of, 1, 17; difference between the "yes" and "no" of, 29, 58; disappointed, fury of, 528, 20; disgrace for a, 168, 40; divination in, 70, 6; empire of, characterised, 425, 5; end of education of, 425, 9; errors of, source of, 425, 28; every, alike in the dark, 257, 36; every, at heart a rake, 276, 32; fine, conversation of, 476, 37; first glory of, 360, 13; formed to be a mother, 291, 8; functions of, contrasted with man's, 262, 19; grace of, 494, 40; good, compared with a man, 24, 41; handsomeness in, 307, 50; heart of, 233, 5; heart of pious, 75, 49; her laughing and weeping, 104, 36; her prison and kingdom of heaven, 65, 25; honoured, God pleased, 549, 25; how she can make sure of love, 568, 5; in argument with men, 185, 8; in unwomanly rags, 558, 28; in humanity, 225, 19; in love, 307, 52; inconstant, 225, 11; influence of, on a man's career, 48, 41; jealousy of, 192, 46; life without, 380, 18; like a mill, 11, 12; lost, 295, 31; lot of, 556, 8; love for, in ignorance of her, 535, 25; love in, 471, 35; love of, contrasted with man's, 265, 8; man's indebtedness to, 33, 9; manners of, everything, 207, 42; men without, 326, 20; ministering angel, 323, 1; mission of, 292, 21; mistake in creating, 292, 10; moved by jewels, 74, 6; Nature's masterpiece, 292, 10; noblest station of, 385, 3; not to have her own way, 176, 21; offended, 183, 41; one language enough for, 334, 27 ; only admirable, 30, 3 ; our ruler, 69, 18 ; patience in, 314, 14 ; perfect, 346, 5 ; perfected, 76, 7 ; power of mere love on, 448, 1 ; power of one hair of, 332, 29 ; power of, to dispel cares, 174, 21 ; preacher to man, 460, 43 ; privilege in the household of, 440, 18 ; queen through her grace, 221, 29 ; ready with her answer, 567, 28 ; reputation of, 451, 15 ; rich, insufferable, 196, 2 ; road to the heart of, 166, 37 ; rule of, by serving, 244, 5 ; sentiment, 264, 23 ; sayings about, 463, 35-39 ; sharpness of vision of, 85, 31 ; smiles of, 27, 34 ; stranger than man, 533, 40 ; the pettish, 504, 21 ; thoughts of, alone, 285, 35 ; to be her own, 240, 55 ; to wed an older than herself, 242, 39 ; tongue of, 226, 1 ; tow, 263, 14 ; true, value of, 376, 8 ; unjustly accused, 565, 9 ; virtues becoming in, 391, 27 ; virtuous, described, 551, 1 ; vision and world of, as contrasted with man's, 55, 6 ; wakes to love, 262, 15 ; what makes a, queen, 488, 41 ; what the word contains, 59, 51 ; who does not inspire love and reverence, 533, 37 ; who wears the breeches, 542, 35 ; why misunderstood, 451, 2 ; wise and foolish, 95, 17 ; wisest and elegant, contrasted, 463, 28 ; wish of every, 212, 17 ; wit in, 307, 50 ; with brains tackled to a geck, 549, 6 ; with dowry enough, 74, 12 ; word of a, in love, 285, 33 ; word of, to be respected, 170, 4 ; worth in, 218, 11 ; worth wooing, lover who wins, 559, 12 ; worthy of love, 389, 5. See **Mulier.**

Woman's, a, reason, 167, 5 ; advice, how to treat, 356, 13 ; eye, eloquent, 467, 18 ; 111, 44 ; judgment, 267, 34 ; life, 538, 18 ; looks, books, 288, 14 ; lot, Schiller on, 323, 12 ; love, 266, 48 ; love, preciousness of, 218, 16 ; will, 548, 6 ; will, the power of, 38, 9 ; wisdom, 417, 5 ; wit, not to be confined, 260, 22 ; work, 267, 12

Womanhood, genius in, 120, 23

Women, a blessing and bane, 104, 33 ; and others' opinions of them, 275, 25 ; as haters, 483, 8 ; as mystics, 443, 43 ; as talkers, 345, 16 ; best medicine for, 446, 10 ; brain-, compared with heart-women, 419, 9 ; burden they are born to, 496, 22 ; business of, 244, 6 ; characteristic of, 238, 17, 19 ; cause of their errors, 275, 6 ; dependence on, of honesty in men, 176, 18 ; differences among, 110, 20 ; 274, 31 ; discreet, characteristic of, 69, 5 ; education of, not to be committed to men, 71, 23 ; effect of beauty on, 487, 51 ; effect of government on, 487, 51 ; effect of virtue on, 487, 51 ; fair, know it, 173, 16 ; fate of, 206, 9 ; finer than men, 27, 39 ; foolish, 168, 2 ; given to dissimulation, 168, 43 ; good, power of, 78, 42 ; good, Romilly's obligations to, 475, 11 ; good, the only grudges of, 130, 32 ; grace in, better than beauty, 131, 33 ; great, characteristics of, 135, 28 ; higher worth of, its risk, 450, 17 ; how to choose, 566, 2 ; in England and in Italy, 82, 45 ; inextinguishable passion of, 448, 4 ; influence of, on manners, 61, 29 ; invention among, 513, 28 ; love of, 275, 26, 28 ; middle-aged in England, 188, 14 ; most, without character, 284, 41 ; nature in, allied to art, 291, 21 ; nature of, Terence on, 317, 25 ; parts they play, 477, 36 ; peculiar badges of, 286, 28 ; power of, 238, 18 ; power of kindness in, 218, 46 ; proper province for, 427, 12 ; pursuits of, and men's, 10, 47 ; sayings about, 64, 14, 15 ; 67, 8, 9 ; seduced, 477, 15 ; services of, 78, 23, 24 ; so-called nature of, 536, 44 ; society of, value of, 454, 5 ; sole precious good for, 24, 44 ; that are serviceable, 442, 40 ; that inspire the greatest passion, 37, 57 ; the book of, 234, 10 ; their power to govern, 479, 6 ; to be praised, 114, 14 ; to what appointed, 33, 17 ; two faults of, 275, 14 ; two passions in, 188, 10 ; use of knowledge to, 460, 13 ; virtue in, contrasted with that of men, 536, 12 ;

who grill, fate of, 273, 31 ; who love their husbands, their reward, 451, 6 ; why they dislike one another, 238, 35 ; wit in, 223, 2 ; worth of, 11, 6 ; writings of, 566, 22

Women's, eyes, books, arts, academies, 116, 34 ; fancies less giddy than men's, 242, 39 ; tongues, 59, 53

Won, the, never lost, 314, 26

Wonder, and fear, effect on the spirits of, 192, 34 ; deemed vulgar, 299, 25 ; inevitable, 35, 23 ; refraining from, 299, 26 ; significance of, 441, 3

Wonderful, not affected by time, 197, 23

Wonders, all alike, 307, 54 ; man amidst, 161, 8

Wood, not seen for the trees, 142, 14

Woods and fields, senses of, 31, 12

Wooed, women should be, 523, 10

Wooing, and winning, 172, 28 ; of prudent men, 219, 40 ; Scotch, 30, 35 ; time, favourite, 64, 3

Wool, gathering and weaving, 202, 22

Word, a living, value of, 29, 38 ; a man's, distrust by the pedant of, 22, 36 ; a profitable, 336, 57 ; an immortal seedgrain, 36, 39 ; enough to wise, 63, 39 ; every idle, to be accounted for, 91, 31 ; fit, prosperity of, 125, 17 ; free, 55, 9 ; from the Lord, effect of, 533, 33 ; God's, man's true bread, 265, 33 ; idlest, a seed, 314, 13 ; ill, effect of, on liking, 332, 9 ; in a twisted ear, 53, 43 ; in season, pregnancy of, 25, 19, 20 ; incarnated, 263, 47 ; its abiding meaning, 11, 34 ; known by context, 312, 7 ; man's, weight of, 267, 11 ; of an hour, significance of, 333, 43 ; of God, its obscurity, 456, 43 ; of God, not to be sold, 344, 14 ; once vulgarised, 25, 17 ; power of a, 80, 5 ; saddest, 110, 30 ; significance of a, 110, 36 ; single often a poem, 19, 36 ; spoken and written, 517, 45 ; the, he that spake it, 149, 28 ; to wise man, 512, 48 ; truly spoken, lasting, 316, 33 ; unspoken, contrasted with spoken, 325, 19 ; uttered, effect of, on self-will, 212, 16 ; uttered, irreclaimable, 88, 43 ; 295, 43 ; when it flows free, 65, 27 ; why the, became man, 321, 16 ; winged, power of, 329, 13 ; with two meanings, serviceableness of, 334, 35

Words, a man's, significance of, 235, 44 ; a mist of, 280, 46 ; air-castles of, 156, 28 ; and secrets of the soul, 308, 3 ; and the soul, 563, 17 ; at hand, with something to say, 87, 29 ; big, not associated with good deeds, 403, 21 ; bonds, 157, 19 ; cheerful, from the living to the living, 171, 37 ; choice of, 85, 22 ; comparative insignificance of, 85, 21 ; compared with thoughts, 485, 12, 16 ; contentment with, 464, 29 ; contrasted with deeds, 166, 4 ; corruption of, 161, 42 ; deeds, 330, 10 ; deeds rather than, 281, 8 ; definition of, called for, 57, 9 ; dress of, 424, 22 ; empty sound, 534, 8 ; fine, and fit, 107, 10 ; fine, without deeds, 106, 32 ; gentle and quiet, effectiveness of, 121, 29 ; good (see **Good words**); hasty in, 385, 17 ; immodest, unjustifiable, 183, 18 ; impotency of, in sorrow, 54, 27 ; in pain, 546, 44 ; inadequacy of, 417, 43 ; kind (see **Kind words**); less expressive than actions, 3, 50 ; like leaves, 463, 45 ; like sunbeams, 207, 37 ; magic wrought by, 281, 7 ; many, involving lies, 87, 5 ; men of few, 275, 45 ; of breath, 28, 47 ; of earnest men, 301, 36 ; of great men, weight of, 133, 23 ; of others to be weighed, 270, 25 ; only words, 165, 23 ; perfect, to be respected, 466, 1 ; persuasive power of, 122, 16 ; power of, 33, 38 ; 77, 8 ; 512, 37 ; 534, 9 ; power of, over us, 339, 38 ; readiness of, condition of, 512, 40 ; right, value of, 161, 18 ; saddest and sadder, 173, 27 ; safest, 452, 21 ; sense of, dependent on usage, 199, 26 ; their shortcoming, 67, 18 ; taking, for things, 100, 31 ; that are thunderbolts, 51, 2 ; that live for ever, 213, 3 ; that please, 534, 31 ; to be few, 242, 23 ; usage in, 285, 48 ; vagueness in use of, 315, 38 ; valuable, 469, 8 ; waste of, 2,

39 ; when good, 563, 18 ; when ideas fail, 76, 28 ; when scarce, effective, 549, 1 ; without thoughts, never to heaven go, 288, 26

Wordsworth, inspiring idea of, 123, 14 ; lament of, when old, 477, 32 ; prayer of, 123, 35 ; rank as poet, 503, 48

Work, a, how proved possible, 453, 26 ; advice in regard to, 260, 21 ; all, an appeal to the unseen, 304, 5 ; all, religious, 303, 43 ; all, to be well done, 549, 40 ; all true, divine, 184, 43 ; and worker, proper relation between, 201, 37 ; aright, whoso would, 554, 29 ; as his, a man's measure, 19, 43 ; best, how done, 418, 11 ; best, never done for money, 418, 12 ; by arms and brains necessary, 477, 14 ; diligence in, reward of, 443, 30 ; effect of intelligence on, 529, 33 ; every man's, born with him, 303, 51 ; every noble, impossible at first, 93, 4 ; for a God, 494, 22 ; for all, 477, 7 ; for eternity, or only for day, condition of, 563, 30 ; for mere money, 493, 5 ; for which one is unfit, 501, 1 ; good, and good talk, conjointly impossible, 305, 22 ; good, condition of, 565, 33 ; good, test of, 362, 11 ; great intellectual, without effort, 302, 15 ; half done, 269, 20 ; how it may be done, 543, 23 ; how to attain expertness in, 68, 28 ; how to get, done, 177, 24 ; ill done, the, not our concern, 152, 45 ; important factors in all, 284, 34 ; in, the chief qualification, 184, 27 ; and its instruments, 79, 26 ; man appointed to, 33, 17 ; man's best, 12, 52 ; man's end, 266, 18 ; man's necessity, 203, 22 ; mission of man, 262, 48 ; 266, 18 ; necessities for, 105, 51 ; need of a chivalry of, as that of fighting, 308, 5 ; no great, easy, 308, 19 ; not left half done, 204, 28 ; not under taskmaster's eye, 9, 66 ; of a man, true, a second self, 540, 22 ; of a strong soul, 307, 16 ; of genius, test of every true, 549, 41 ; of merit acknowledged at last, 25, 21 ; only honoured when finished, 8, 5 ; our destiny, and how it should be done, 522, 1 ; our, not fruit of it, our concern, 240, 15 ; our, to be worst of men, 339, 42 ; paid beforehand, 42, 40 ; real, never paid, 304, 5 ; resumption of, after a long pause, 542, 37 ; solid bit of, 6, 55 ; standard of, 125, 15 ; tiring, 478, 20 ; to be thoroughly finished, 541, 23 ; transitoriness of, 499, 3 ; unwise, hopefulness of, 509, 11 ; *versus* charity, 441, 22 ; victory, 549, 26 ; weighty, how to do, 531, 15 ; well done, effect of on worker, 206, 40 ; who will not, 172, 2 ; willing to, unwilling to wait, 151, 24 ; with a sad heart, 478, 6 ; worship, 228, 25

Worker, happiness of, 508, 38 ; high and wise, Emerson on, 110, 1 ; the, want of, 529, 38

Workers, and their spirit, superior to the work, 499, 3 ; brave, fate of, 335, 13

Working, meaning of all, 535, 41 ; too much, 492, 5 ; true, worship, 500, 38

Working-day world, full of briars, 321, 1

Workman, a cunning, and his tools, 422, 23 ; good, his wages, 505, 15 ; good, proper reward of, 449, 42 ; test of, 11, 16

Workmen, how made, 98, 31 ; not superintending, effect of, 41, 24 ; on the war-path, 388, 24

Works, cherished by art, 540, 3 ; good, necessary for salvation, 130, 37 ; good, the fruit of faith, 99, 61 ; 100, 12, 23 ; great, due to perseverance, 135, 29 ; man's, as his mind, 111, 18 ; noblest, authors of, 444, 10 ; our, sayings about, 339, 43, 44 ; perfect, rare, and why, 346, 6 ; the best, authors of, 418, 13 ; worth of, in the spirit, 204, 35

World, a believing, Carlyle's faith in, and hope of, 25, 22 ; a book to study, 242, 51 ; a queer concern, 234, 9 ; a stage, 10, 52 ; 167, 20 ; a working, this, 445, 2 ; all the, players, 498, 6 ; all's right with, 128, 8 ; an air-image, 482, 12 ; and thought, 484, 30 ; as good and as bad, 199,

22 ; as it is, best, 538, 31 ; as known to us, limited, 149, 16 ; bad paymaster, 234, 12 ; best theatre, 397, 21 ; blindness of, 407, 32 ; burden of, 395, 18 ; but a show, 272, 6 ; carrying, in thought and in fact, 201, 17 ; children of, silliness of, 539, 14 ; conditional, 125, 5 ; different views of the, 117, 39 ; down in the, 171, 23 ; effect of kindness to, 176, 38 ; Emerson's good-bye to, 129, 14 ; envy of, 86, 17 ; everything in, tangled and fleeting, 94, 30 ; fact hated by, 482, 9 ; fashion of, 111, 15 ; first illuminated by love, 265, 7 ; folly in government of, 483, 36 ; for all, 92, 21 ; forgetfulness of, 366, 35 ; forgetting, by the world forgot, 161, 25 ; friendship of, price of, 220, 6 ; God of, 44, 54 ; God of, always the same, 60, 26 ; God's statue, 286, 30 ; governed by a holy will, 506, 8 ; great soul of, characterised, 431, 36 ; great success of the, 431, 40 ; half, and other half, 5, 5 ; hampering action of, 114, 32 ; heartlessness of, Chamfort on, 166, 13 ; his, who can wait, 179, 38 ; history, its import, 67, 13 ; history of, 435, 22 ; hope for the, 378, 48 ; hospital, 48, 44 ; hostility of, 104, 15 ; how governed, 46, 30 ; 139, 33 ; how it gets along, 179, 40 ; how it is governed, 319, 30 ; how it may become a home and peopled garden, 312, 34 ; 493, 37 ; how to amend, 176, 11 ; how to astonish, 177, 27 ; how to enlarge one's, 210, 43 ; how to learn to reverence, 464, 21 ; how to mend, 461, 31 ; how to please, 418, 10 ; how to rule quietly, 177, 41 ; how to subdue, 260, 43 ; how to take, 527, 12 ; how to treat, if not renounced, 52, 31 ; how ruled, 112, 10 ; humouring, follies from, 165, 12 ; idea of, how obtained, 553, 18 ; in the hand, 25, 23 ; in these days, 191, 34 ; insupportable, if not of God, 138, 33 ; interest in a man's conflict with, 444, 1 ; its two luminaries, 368, 31 ; judgment of, 67, 13 ; 437, 22 ; in one's old age, 484, 8 ; knowledge of, dearly bought, 221, 13 ; law of, 118, 5 ; let great, spin for ever, 113, 53 ; lighter than thought, 288, 23 ; lights of, only temporarily obscured, 419, 81 ; like a staircase, 179, 39 ; literally a show, 313, 5 ; madhouse, to the philosopher, 58, 10 ; main enterprise of, 440, 14 ; man of the mark of, 441, 31 ; master of, 143, 55 ; material without the spiritual, 560, 1 ; men born to command, 300, 39 ; men debtor or creditor to, 345, 3 ; mistake of the young soul about, 191, 34 ; most finished man of, 443, 44 ; necessity of knowing, 151, 27 ; new, with every dawn, 109, 32 ; no better seen, 64, 4 ; no conformity to, when wrong, 518, 23 ; " no " to the, significance of, 70, 17 ; noi·y inanity of, 253, 13 ; not dumb to the capable, 496, 5 ; not meant only for the few, 168, 5 ; not ruled by blind chance, 89, 35 ; not to be tutored, 457, 2 ; not to be wooed for rest, 550, 30 ; nothing without Greece, 326, 25 ; one half, and the other, 78, 46 ; 332, 30, 31 ; only fence against, 446, 3 ; our dependence on, 330, 41 ; population of 448, 34 ; promises of, 449, 37 ; quarrelling with, to amuse it, 488, 34 ; quicksands of, 208, 33 ; rational, how to regard, 67, 1 ; real sun of, 264, 20 ; rhythmic order of, 115, 23 ; sayings about, 67, 14–17 ; 464, 4–47 ; 465, 1–25 ; 482, 17–22 ; scorn of, how to treat, 241, 40 ; secret of, 206, 43 ; selfishness of, 104, 15 ; servant to him above it, 395, 29 ; slave of, 143, 55 ; solidarity of, instance of, 312, 15 ; spiritual, not closed, 455, 2 ; sign of, as still young, 111, 45 ; suffrages of, how to gain, 314, 37 ; system of, one, 456, 38 ; the, dispensing with, 526, 8 ; the forsaken of, but seemingly so, 477, 13 ; the only habitable, 95, 12 ; the, want of, 396, 30 ; this, no home for a man, 156, 24 ; this present, Carlyle on, 482, 10 ; this unintelligible, 434, 21 ; this working-day, 161, 20 ; thorns and dangers of, 164, 34 ; to a resolute man, 496, 9 ; to be taken as it

is, 300, 22 ; to be understood, not judged, 29, 53 ;
to every man as to the first man, 150, 29 ; to know,
493, 43 ; to the child and to the grown man, 140,
8 ; to the Hindu, 496, 7 ; to the liberal, 496, 23 ;
to the wise man in retreat, 151, 37 ; too much respect to, 566, 16 ; tragic *embarras*, 462, 16 ; two
ways of rising in, 468, 4 ; under power of a lie, 546,
11 ; unseen, alone real, 313, 5 ; wags, 162, 40 ; wax,
to a firm will, 151, 8 ; we live in, 525, 22, 23 ;
weary, 208, 46 ; web of, 53, 39 ; 462, 1 ; who
looks, in the face, 144, 24 ; whole, not deceived
or deceiving, 306, 4 ; wide, for wandering in, 217,
24 ; wishes to be deceived, 286, 32 ; without and
within. relation of, 75, 8 ; working, necessity
of being regimented, 565, 35 ; worshipped or
despised, 147, 32 ; would be deceived, 63, 25
World's, ills, to run away from, 495, 23 ; joy, 478,
21 ; masters, 170; 24 ; reward, the, 506, 16 ;
sovereigns, Byron on, 529, 41 ; the, mine oyster,
555, 31 ; work, by whom forwarded, 418, 36
World-epoch, great event in, 186. 32
World-revolutions, great, far-reaching effects of,
431, 43
World-spirit, the, 465, 13
World-traveller, a, 458, 18
Worldly people and their riches, 461, 18
Worlds, imagined new, 75, 2
Worm, no god dare wrong, 103, 48
Worries, who has no, makes worries, 42, 11
Worry, not work, killing, 204, 45
Worse, appear the better reason, 33, 2
Worship, easier than obedience, 201, 20 ; its
beginning, 187, 16 ; no true, now-a-days. 275, 41 ;
significance of, 441, 3
Worst, the, we can see, 568, 3 ; things at the,
546, 12 ; when not at the, 552, 1
Worth, a thing's, measure of, 21, 36 ; all, in man,
312, 35 ; definition of, 94, 38 ; determining element in, 313, 24 ; felt by loss, 30, 10 ; 42, 48 ;
hidden, worthless, 343, 44 ; how determined, 486,
1 ; irrespective of looks, 112, 37 ; known after
loss, 539, 30 ; man's, how rated, 330, 31 ; man's,
measure of, 533, 30 ; man's reverence for, 389,
41 ; man's, test of, 545, 30 ; measure of, 212, 3 ;
of thing, test of, 519, 19 ; or unworth, what determines, 533, 34 ; real, 369, 17, 18 ; revealed by
life, 488, 16 ; sterling, mark of, 226, 33 ; substantial, before ornament, 106, 47 ; test of, 482,
26 ; the achievement of, 17, 39 ; to be distinguished from unworth, 290, 30 ; undying,
308, 6 ; who can recognise, 335, 14
Worthless, always worthless, 25, 26 ; man, a,
defined, 59, 1
Worthy, men, at odds, the blame, 546, 46 ; people,
a misfortune of, 505, 18
Would and shall compared, 497, 31 ; and should,
compared, 497, 31 ; must yield to can, 42, 14
" Would " and " should " contrasted, 414, 28
Wound always leaves a scar, 25, 28 ; 88, 17
Wrath, as dealt by God, 125, 25 ; nursing her,
118, 58 ; sun not to set upon, 242, 22
Wreath easier to find than find wearer, 79, 21
Wreck, a beacon, 25, 29 ; of life, secret of,
520, 36
Wren, the poor, pluck of, 448, 26
Wren's monument, 390, 23
Wrestling, strength from, 149, 9
Wretch, concentred all in self, 62, 28
Wretched, comfort to, 73, 49 ; 397, 7 ; in heart,
unhelpful, 305, 7 ; learned to succour, 141, 27 ;
presence of, to happy, 449, 8 ; regard for, a duty,
87, 9 ; the most, 239, 21 ; weakness of the, 87, 13
Wretchedness, from fancy, 298, 42 ; intentional,
impious, 143, 30 ; *must* complain, 25, 30 ; source
of, 303, 11 ; that is voiceless, 415, 20 ; to be
pitied by man, 30, 32

Write, how to, 364, 10 ; rule for one who intends
to, 333, 48 ; where to learn to, 177, 38
Writer, best part of, 413, 30 ; book for a, 252, 56 ;
good, mark of, 91, 11 ; good, rare, 6, 52 ; great,
mark of, 7, 10 ; original, and the taste to appreciate
him, 91, 13 ; sure of many readers, 441, 23 ; wise,
25, 2
Writers, all great, writers of history, 91, 20 ; all
immortal, source of inspiration of, 9, 45 ; clear
and turbid, 43, 57 ; great, and their words, 135,
30 ; who have genius, 504, 5
Writing, advantage of, 369, 9 ; art of, secret
of, 53, 9 ; benefit to few, 469, 6 ; clear, condition of, 554, 30 ; condition of, 305, 23 ; ease
in, how acquired, 499, 45 ; easy, Sheridan on,
568, 6 ; fine, the root of, 452, 10 ; for eternity,
hard, 161, 28 ; for money, 302, 54 ; friends, delay
in, 21, 28 ; good, allegorical, 130, 38 ; good, condition of, 506, 4 ; good, source of, 383, 27 ;
insincere, 503, 19 ; itch for, 412, 27 ; master of,
93, 56 ; men, soul of all worth in, 189, 27 ; of fools,
harmful, 540, 35 ; passion for, 383, 29 ; plainest,
in dusk, 190, 27 ; rule in, to the public, 11, 55 ;
rules for, 297, 17–19 ; slovenly, uncourteous, 394,
10 ; styles of, 456, 3 ; ultimate rule in, 459, 30 ;
well, and writing readily, 192, 37 ; well, merit
of, 324, 43 ; well, requisites for, 497, 8 ; without
purpose, 244, 10
Writings, ancient, folly of controversy about,
508, 33
Written, what is, remains, 184, 4 ; worthless, so
long as dead, 535, 19
Wrong, and God, 3, 55 ; and the law, 3, 56 ; as
regards right, 6, 3 ; avengement of, 331, 20 ; by
rule and by caprice, 200, 20 ; difficult to avoid,
86, 9 ; doing, a disgrace, 319, 19 ; forgetting of,
a revenge, 112, 22 ; going, always harmful, 381,
51 ; going, and turning back, 201, 16 ; going, result of, 545, 6 ; in the place of truth, 501, 34 ; instruction from finding we are, 476, 22 ; knowledge
of, dispensable, 171, 20 ; matter of consciousness
never right, 325, 17 ; possible to be, 165, 14 ;
suffering and paying for, 202, 19 ; to know, the
first essential thing, 445, 36 ; to one threatening
to many, 286, 13 ; with many, 29, 57
Wrongs, little, 251, 45
Wrong-doer never pardons, 112, 27
Wrong-doing punished on earth, 8, 61

Y

Yea, the everlasting, 256, 3
Years, a man's, counting, 523, 30
" Yes " to be deliberate, 337, 1
Yesterday and to-morrow, both are, 422, 31
Yielding commended, 37, 32, 34
Yoke, an easy, 288, 27
Young, idea, to teach, 57, 51 ; in age, advantage
of being, 490, 38 ; in youth happy, 124, 38 ; man,
best rules for, 417, 57 ; man, growing virtue of,
428, 13 ; man's life, happiness and virtue of, 425,
18 ; men, and their command in affairs, 297, 8 ;
men, conservativeness in, a bad sign, 524, 1 ;
men, errors of, 425, 29 ; men, glory of, 430, 14 ;
men, love for, 122, 46 ; men, our, 340, 3 ; men,
Professor Blackie to, 295, 13 ; men, task of, 214,
46 ; men, the conceit of, 305, 24 ; talk of, 238, 39 ;
the, Goethe's tolerance with, 411, 37 ; to be
dealt gently with, 169, 21 ; what it is to be, 491, 4
Younger, the wish to be, 307, 48
Youth, a lesson to teach, 508, 40 ; ambitious
schemes of, at mid-age, 466, 2 ; and age, respective liveries of, 112, 5 ; and hope, 225, 38 ;

and its knowledge of world, 203, 47 ; and old age, as regards impressibility, 227, 9 ; and wine, 556, 36 ; as evil time, rather than age, 200, 31 ; beautiful, 160, 50 ; bridge from, to manhood, 300, 28 ; characteristics of, 22, 33 ; conceit in, misery of, 560, 23 ; conceit of, 93, 7 ; confidence of, 190, 19 ; contractedness of, 140, 9 ; dalliance, evil of, 177, 2 ; education of, 95, 20 ; eternal, how attained, 95, 39 ; excesses of, 426, 20 ; failing of, 216, 46 ; first impressions of, indelible, 242, 4 ; flower of, when most beautiful, 429, 2 ; follies of, to be unlearned in manhood, 482, 33 ; foolhardiness in, 48, 62 ; grief in, 192, 41 ; hard to restrain, 321, 7 ; heedfulness in, commended, 243, 5 ; home-keeping, 158, 36 ; importance of training, 378, 30 ; in love, Ruskin's advice to, 542, 38 ; incomplete, 544, 47 ; incontinence in, effect of, 195, 24 ; inspiration of, 23, 41 ; learning to be a man, 466, 14 ; not necessarily inexperienced, 12, 42 ; penalty of, liberty to, 260, 44 ; perils of, 419, 25 ; pliability and obstinacy of, 38, 25 ; profession of, naturalness in, 270, 8 ; reckless, 370, 27 ; responsibility of, 423, 13 ; roses of, 382, 14 ; temper of, 362, 1 ; the guide of, 60, 23 the more it is wasted, 419, 22 ; thoughts of, 419, 7 ; 457, 38 ; thrift in, 213, 2 ; time to learn, 178, 28 ; to be modest, 4, 41 ; 56, 34 ; to be respected, 271, 17 ; to be saving, 225, 37 ; to be used as a spring-time, 509, 40 ; too covetous of honour, 288 43 ; virtuous, happy season of, 140, 24 ; wandering in his own way, 165, 9 ; weakness of, 199, 51 ; what he strives for, 60, 24 ; wisdom and beauty in, rare, 192, 39 ; without enthusiasm, 304, 3 ; yearning for, 395, 2

Youthful impressions, Goethe on, 460, 38

Z

Zeal, a, commended, 384, 49 ; blind, 30, 57, 59, not to outrun charity, 296, 42 ; religious, effects of, 372, 37

Zeus, dice of, 326, 34

SUPPLEMENT

A

A babe in a house is a well-spring of pleasure, a messenger of peace and love. *Tupper.*

A boy's will is the wind's will, / And the thoughts of youth are long, long thoughts. *Longfellow.*

A brave man, were he seven times king, / Is but a brave man's peer. *Swinburne.*

A castle girt about and bound / With sorrow, like a spell. *Swinburne.*

5 "A clear fire, a clean hearth, and the rigour of the game." This was the celebrated wish of old Sarah Battle (now with God), who, next to her devotions, loved a good game of whist. *Lamb.*

A crown and justice? Night and day / Shall first be yoked together. *Swinburne.*

A daughter of the gods, divinely tall, / And most divinely fair. *Tennyson.*

A dem'd damp, moist, unpleasant body. *Dickens (Mr. Mantalini, in " Nicholas Nickleby ").*

A finished gentleman from top to toe. *Byron.*

10 A full-celled honeycomb of eloquence / Stored from all flowers. Poet-like he spoke. *Tennyson.*

A great devotee of the Gospel of Getting On. *G. Bernard Shaw.*

A heart at leisure from itself, / To soothe and sympathise. *Anna L. Waring.*

A land of settled government, / A land of just and old renown, / Where Freedom slowly broadens down / From precedent to precedent. *Tennyson.*

A lie travels round the world while Truth is putting on her boots. *C. H. Spurgeon.*

15 A little faith all undisproved. *E. B. Browning.*

A little group of wise hearts is better than a wilderness of fools. *Ruskin.*

A little sorrow, a little pleasure, / Fate metes us from the dusty measure / That holds the date of all of us ; / We are born with travail and strong crying, / And from the birth-day to the dying / The likeness of our life is thus. *Swinburne.*

A little while she strove, and much repented, / And whispering " I will ne'er consent "—consented. *Byron.*

A loving little life of sweet small works. *Swinburne.*

20 A maid whom there were none to praise, / And very few to love. *Wordsworth.*

A man can have but one life, and one death, / One heaven, one hell. *Robert Browning.*

A man he seems of cheerful yesterdays / And confident to-morrows. *Wordsworth.*

A man that studieth revenge keeps his own wounds green. *Bacon.*

A moth-eaten rag on a worm-eaten pole, / It doesn't look likely to stir a man's soul ; / 'Tis the deeds that were done 'neath the moth-eaten rag, / When the pole was a staff and the rag was a flag. *Gen. Sir E. Bruce Hamley.*

25 A name to be washed out with all men's tears. *Swinburne.*

A needless Alexandrine ends the song, / That, like a wounded snake, drags its slow length along. *Pope.*

A noble aim, / Faithfully kept, is as a noble deed. *Wordsworth.*

A noise like of a hidden brook / In the leafy month of June, / That to the sleeping woods all night / Singeth a quiet tune. *Coleridge.*

A patriot is a fool in every age. *Pope.*

A precedent embalms a principle. *Disraeli.*   30

A progeny of learning. *Sheridan (Mrs. Malaprop, in " The Rivals ").*

A quality / Which music sometimes has, being the Art / Which is most nigh to tears and memory. *Wilde.*

A rosebud set with little wilful thorns, / And sweet as English air could make her, she. *Tennyson.*

A savage spot as holy and enchanted / As e'er beneath a waning moon was haunted / By woman wailing for her demon lover. *Coleridge.*

A sinful soul possessed of many gifts, / A spacious 35 garden full of flowering weeds. *Tennyson.*

A smattering of everything, and a knowledge of nothing. *Dickens.*

A soul that pity touched, but never shook. *Campbell.*

A thousand wants / Gnaw at the heels of men. *Tennyson.*

A torturer of phrases into sonnets. *Scott.*

A true man, pure as faith's own vow, / Whose honour 40 knows not rust. *Swinburne.*

A wound, though cured, yet leaves behind a scar. *Oldham.*

Across the margent of the world I fled, / And troubled the gold gateways of the stars, / Smiting for shelter on their clangéd bars ; / Fretted to dulcet jars / And silvern chatter the pale ports o' the moon. *Francis Thompson.*

Across the walnuts and the wine. *Tennyson.*

Ah, but a man's reach should exceed his grasp, / Or what's heaven for? *Robert Browning.*

Ah, did you once see Shelley plain, / And did he stop 45 and speak to you, / And did you speak to him again ? / How strange it seems, and new ! *Robert Browning.*

Ah ! don't say that you agree with me. When people agree with me I always feel that I must be wrong. *Wilde.*

Ah Love ! could you and I with Fate conspire / To grasp this sorry Scheme of Things entire, / Would not we shatter it to bits—and then / Re-mould it nearer to the Heart's Desire ! *Fitzgerald (" Omar Khayyám ").*

Ah, ye knights of the pen ! May honour be your shield, and truth tip your lances ! Be gentle to all gentle people. Be modest to women. Be tender to children. And as for the Ogre Humbug, out sword, and have at him. *Thackeray.*

Ah ! when shall all men's good / Be each man's rule, and universal Peace / Lie like a staff of light across the land, / And like a lane of beams athwart the sea ? *Tennyson.*

Alas ! how easily things go wrong ! / A sigh too deep, or a kiss too long, / And then comes a mist and a weeping rain, / And life is never the same again. *Geo. Macdonald.*

All are architects of Fate, / Working in these walls of Time. *Longfellow.*

All colours will agree in the dark. *Bacon.*

5 All good moral philosophy, as was said, is but a hand-maid to religion. *Bacon.*

All other goods by Fortune's hand are given ; / A wife is the peculiar gift of heaven. *Pope.*

All our past proclaims our future : Shakespeare's voice and Nelson's hand, / Milton's faith and Wordsworth's trust in this our chosen and chainless land, / Bear us witness : come the world against her, England yet shall stand. *Swinburne.*

All seems infected that the infected spy, / As all looks yellow to the jaundiced eye. *Pope.*

All service ranks the same with God—/ With God, whose puppets, best and worst, / Are we : there is no last nor first. *Robert Browning.*

10 All speech, written or spoken, is a dead language, until it finds a willing and prepared hearer. *Stevenson.*

All that are lovers of virtue, and dare trust in His providence, and be quiet, and go a-angling. *Izaak Walton.*

All that is, at all, / Lasts ever, past recall : / Earth changes, but thy soul and God stand sure. *Robert Browning.*

All that we see or seem / Is but a dream within a dream. *Poe.*

All that's the matter with me is the affliction called a multiplying eye. *Hardy.*

15 All we have of freedom—all we use or know—/ This our fathers bought for us, long and long ago. *Kipling.*

All who joy would win / Must share it—Happiness was born a twin. *Byron.*

Always verify your references. *Dr. Routh.*

Amazing pomp ! / redouble this amaze ; / Ten thousand add ; add twice ten thousand more ; / Then weigh the whole ; one soul outweighs them all. *Young.*

Ambition first sprung from your blest abodes ; / The glorious fault of angels and of gods. *Pope.*

20 Among the sea of upturned faces. *Scott.*

Among the smaller duties of life I hardly know any one more important than that of not praising where praise is not due. *Sydney Smith.*

An excuse is a lie guarded. *Swift.*

An illogical opinion only requires rope enough to hang itself. *A. Birrell.*

An oyster may be crossed in love. *Sheridan.*

25 An unforgiving eye, and a damned disinheriting countenance. *Sheridan (" School for Scandal ").*

An' you've gut to git up airly / Ef you want to take in God. *Lowell.*

And a bird overhead sang *Follow,* / And a bird to the right sang *Here* ; / And the arch of the leaves was hollow, / And the meaning of May was clear. *Swinburne.*

And a proverb haunts my mind, / As a spell is cast ; / " The mill cannot grind / With the water that is past." *Sarah Doudney.*

And all Arabia breathes from yonder box. *Pope.*

And all my mother came into mine eyes, / And gave 30 me up to tears. *Henry V, iv, 6.*

And all your fortune lies beneath your hat. *Oldham.*

And, best beloved of best men, liberty, / Free lives and lips, free hands of men free-born. *Swinburne.*

And blessings on the falling out / That all the more endears, / When we fall out with those we love, / And kiss again with tears. *Tennyson.*

And broad-based under all / Is planted England's oaken-hearted mood, / As rich in fortitude / As e'er went worldward from the island-wall. *Bayard Taylor.*

And darest thou, then, / To beard the lion in his 35 den, / The Douglas in his hall ? *Scott.*

And dye conjecture with a darker hue. *Byron.*

And even the ranks of Tuscany / Could scarce forbear to cheer. *Macaulay.*

And from the discontent of man / The world's best progress springs. *Ella Wheeler Wilcox.*

And grasps the skirts of happy chance, / And breasts the blows of circumstance. *Tennyson.*

And hated, with the gall of gentle souls. *E. B.* 40 *Browning.*

And he who gives a child a treat / Makes joy-bells ring in Heaven's street, / And he who gives a child a home / Builds palaces in Kingdom come. *John Masefield.*

And if thou wilt, remember, / And if thou wilt, forget. *Christina Rossetti.*

And in thy joyous Errand reach the Spot / Where I made one — turn down an empty Glass ! *Fitzgerald (" Omar Khayyám ").*

And lightly was her slender nose / Tip-tilted like the petal of a flower. *Tennyson.*

And many a thought did I build up on thought, / As 45 the wild bee hangs cell to cell. *Robert Browning.*

And musing on the little lives of men, / And how they mar this little by their feuds. *Tennyson.*

" And now, sir," said Dr. Johnson, " we will take a walk down Fleet Street." (Ascribed to Dr. Johnson, but invented by G. A. Sala for the title-page of " Temple Bar Magazine.")

And one man is as good as another—and a great dale betther, as the Irish philosopher said. *Thackeray.*

And round thee with the breeze of song / To stir a little dust of praise. *Tennyson.*

And so, as Tiny Tim observed, God bless Us, Every 50 One ! *Dickens.*

And, spite of pride, in erring reason's spite, / One truth is clear, whatever is, is right. *Pope.*

And still to-morrow's wiser than to-day. / We think our fathers fools, so wise we grow ; / Our wiser sons, no doubt, will think us so. *Pope.*

And sweet red splendid kissing mouth. *Swinburne.*

And the best and the worst of this is / That neither is most to blame, / If you've forgotten my kisses, / And I've forgotten your name. *Swinburne.*

And the night shall be filled with music, / And the 55 cares that infest the day / Shall fold their tents, like the Arabs, / And as silently steal away. *Longfellow.*

And then and then came Spring, and Rose-in-hand / My thread-bare Penitence apieces tore. *Fitzgerald (" Omar Khayyám ").*

And then in the fulness of joy and hope, / Seemed washing his hands with invisible soap, / In imperceptible water. *Hood.*

And this was all the Harvest that I reap'd—/ " I came like Water, and like Wind I go." *Fitzgerald* (" *Omar Khayyám* ").

And Thought leapt out to wed with Thought / Ere Thought could wed itself with Speech. *Tennyson.*

And thus he bore without abuse / The grand old name of gentleman, / Defamed by every charlatan, / And soiled with all ignoble use. *Tennyson.*

5 And 'tis remarkable, that they / Talk most who have the least to say. *Prior.*

And what is so rare as a day in June ? / Then, if ever, come perfect days. / Then heaven tries earth if it be in tune, / And over it softly her warm ear lays. *Lowell.*

And what so tedious as a twice-told tale ? *Pope.*

And when his frown of hatred darkly fell, / Hope withering fled—and Mercy sighed farewell. *Byron.*

And yet the fate of all extremes is such, / Men may be read, as well as books, too much. / To observations which ourselves we make, / We grow more partial, for the observer's sake. *Pope.*

10 Anger makes dull men witty, but it keeps them poor. *Bacon.*

As for the women, though we scorn and flout 'em, / We may live with, but cannot live without 'em. *F. Reynolds.*

As headstrong as an allegory on the banks of the Nile. *Sheridan (" The Rivals ").*

As learned commentators view / In Homer more than Homer knew. *Swift.*

As nothing can confound / A wise man more than laughter from a dunce. *Byron.*

15 As rich and purposeless as is the rose, / Thy simple doom is to be beautiful. *Stephen Phillips.*

As some sea-gipsy that hath lost his star. *Anon.*

As soon / Seek roses in December—ice in June ; / Hope constancy in wind, or corn in chaff ; / Believe a woman or an epitaph, / Or any other thing that's false, before / You trust in critics, who themselves are sore. *Byron.*

As the French say, there are three sexes—men, women, and clergymen. *Sydney Smith.*

As unto the bow the cord is, / So unto the man is woman ; / Though she bends him, she obeys him, / Though she draws him, yet she follows ; / Useless each without the other ! *Longfellow.*

20 At the door of life, by the gate of breath, / There are worse things waiting for men than death. *Swinburne.*

Authority forgets a dying king. *Tennyson.*

B

Barkis is willin'. *Dickens (" David Copperfield ").*

Be good, sweet maid, and let who will be clever : / Do lovely things, not dream them, all day long ; / And so make Life, and Death, and that For Ever, / One grand sweet song. *Kingsley.*

Be silent always when you doubt your sense. *Pope.*

25 Be wise to-day ; 'tis madness to defer. *Young.*

" Beauty is truth, truth beauty,"—that is all / Ye know on earth, and all ye need to know. *Keats.*

Beauty's silken bond, / The weakness that subdues the strong, and bows Wisdom alike and folly. *Robert Browning.*

Belt upon belt, the wooded, dim / Blue goodness of the Weald. *Kipling.*

Better be courted and jilted, / Than never be courted at all. *Campbell.*

Better heresy of doctrine, than heresy of heart. 30 *Whittier.*

Better not do the deed than weep it done. *Prior.*

Blindness is the firstborn of success. *Byron.*

Blow, bugle, blow, set the wild echoes flying. *Tennyson.*

Blow out, you bugles, over the rich Dead ! / There's none of these so lonely and poor of old, / But, dying, has made us rarer gifts than gold. / These laid the world away ; poured out the red / Sweet wine of youth . . . and those that would have been, / Their sons, they gave, their immortality. *Rupert Brooke.*

Blunt truths more mischief than nice falsehoods do. 35 *Pope.*

Books are men of higher stature, / And the only men that speak aloud for future times to hear. *E. B. Browning.*

Books, like proverbs, receive their chief value from the stamp and esteem of ages through which they have passed. *Sir W. Temple.*

Books which are no books . . . things in books' clothing. *Lamb.*

" Bother Mrs. Harris ! " said Betsy Prig. " I don't believe there's no sich a person ! " *Dickens (" Martin Chuzzlewit ").*

Bravery never goes out of fashion. *Thackeray* 40

Bright names will hallow song. *Byron.*

Bright with names that men remember, loud with names that men forget. *Swinburne.*

Britannia needs no bulwark, / No towers along the steep, / Her march is o'er the mountain waves, / Her home is on the deep. *Campbell.*

Broad-based upon her people's will, / And compassed by the inviolate sea. *Tennyson.*

Burrow awhile and build, broad on the roots of 45 things. *Robert Browning.*

But a bird's weight can break the infant tree / Which after holds an aery in its arms. *Robert Browning.*

But every woman is at heart a rake. *Pope.*

But from sharp words and wits men pluck no fruit, / And gathering thorns they shake the tree at root ; / For words divide and rend ; / But silence is most noble till the end. *Swinburne.*

But God has a few of us whom He whispers in the ear; / The rest may reason and welcome : 'tis we musicians know. *Robert Browning.*

But I, being poor, have only my dreams. / I have 50 spread my dreams under your feet ; / Tread softly, because you tread on my dreams. *W. B. Yeats.*

But of all the lunar things that change, / The one that shows most fickle and strange, / And takes the most eccentric range, / Is the moon—so called—of honey ! *Hood.*

But—Oh ! ye lords of ladies intellectual, / Inform us truly, have they not henpecked you all ? *Byron.*

But on and up, where Nature's heart / Beats strong amid the hills. *Lord Houghton.*

But still the Vine her ancient Ruby yields, / And still a Garden by the Water blows. *Fitzgerald (" Omar Khayyám ").*

But sweet as the rind was the core is ; / We are fain 55 of thee still, we are fain, / O sanguine and subtle Dolores, / Our Lady of Pain. *Swinburne.*

But the Devil whoops, as he whooped of old : " It's clever, but is it Art ? " *Kipling.*

But the jingling of the guinea helps the hurt that Honour feels. *Tennyson.*

But the tender grace of a day that is dead / Will never come back to me. *Tennyson.*

But there is neither East nor West, Border, nor Breed, nor Birth, / When two strong men stand face to face, though they come from the ends of the earth. *Kipling.*

5 But this thing is God, / To be man with thy might, / To grow straight in the strength of thy spirit, and live out thy life as the light. *Swinburne.*

But thought and faith are mightier things than time / Can wrong, / Made splendid once with speech, or made sublime / With song. *Swinburne.*

But thousands die, without or this or that, / Die, and endow a college, or a cat. *Pope.*

But till we are built like angels, with hammer and chisel and pen, / We will work for ourself and a woman, for ever and ever, Amen. *Kipling.*

But trust that those we call the dead / Are breathers of an ampler day / For ever nobler ends. *Tennyson.*

10 But Truth inspired the Bards of old, / When of an iron age they told, / Which to unequal laws gave birth / And drove Astræa from the earth. *Wordsworth.*

But when to mischief mortals bend their will, / How soon they find fit instruments of ill. *Pope.*

But with the morning cool repentance came. *Scott.*

By all ye will or whisper, / By all ye have or do, / The silent, sullen peoples / Shall weigh your God and you. *Kipling.*

By mutual confidence and mutual aid / Great deeds are done, and great discoveries made. *Pope.*

15 By pains men come to greater pains ; and by indignities men come to dignities. *Bacon.*

C

Can hardly tell how to cry bo to a goose. *Swift.*

Ce qu'il nous faut pour vaincre, c'est de l'audace, encore de l'audace, toujours de l'audace ! What we require in order to conquer is audacity, yet more audacity, and always audacity. *Danton.*

Chains or conquest, liberty or death. *Addison.*

Change lays not her hand upon truth. *Swinburne.*

20 Children know, / Instinctive taught, the friend and foe. *Scott.*

Clothed in white samite, mystic, wonderful. *Tennyson.*

Codlin's the friend, not Short. *Dickens.*

Come away ! Poverty's catching. *Aphra Behn.*

Come, fill the Cup, and in the Fire of Spring / The Winter Garment of Repentance fling. *Fitzgerald ("Omar Khayyám").*

25 Come into the garden, Maud, / For the black bat, night, hath flown. *Tennyson.*

Comes the blind Fury with the abhorred shears / And slits the thin-spun life. *Milton.*

Congenial spirits part to meet again. *Campbell.*

Conscience has no more to do with gallantry than it has with politics. *Sheridan.*

Cool, and quite English, imperturbable. *Byron.*

30 Creed and test / Vanish before the unreserved embrace of catholic humanity. *Wordsworth.*

Crosses and troubles a-many have proved me. / One or two women (God bless them !) have loved me. *Henley.*

Curled minion, dancer, coiner of sweet words. *Matthew Arnold.*

Curse on that man who business first designed, / And by 't enthralled a freeborn lover's mind. *Oldham.*

Custom, that unwritten law, / By which the people keep even kings in awe. *Davenant.*

D

Dangers breed fears, and fears more dangers bring. 35 *Baxter.*

Dear as remembered kisses after death. *Tennyson.*

Death aims with fouler spite / At fairer marks. *Quarles.*

Death but entombs the body ; life the soul. *Young.*

Death gives us more than was in Eden lost. / This king of terrors is the prince of peace. *Young.*

Death had he seen by sudden blow, / By wasting 40 plague, by tortures slow, / By mine or breach, by steel or ball, / Knew all his shapes, and scorned them all. *Scott.*

Death loves a shining mark, a signal blow. *Young.*

Debt is the prolific mother of folly and of crime. *Disraeli.*

Deceit and treachery skulk with hatred, but an honest spirit flieth with anger. *Tupper.*

Despair, the twin-born of devotion. *Swinburne.*

Do not all charms fly / At the mere touch of cold 45 philosophy ? *Keats.*

Do the work that's nearest, / Though it's dull at whiles, / Helping, when we meet them, / Lame dogs over stiles. *Kingsley.*

Do you hear the children weeping, O my brothers, / Ere the sorrow comes with years ? *E. B. Browning.*

Do you know what a pessimist is ?—A man who thinks everybody as nasty as himself, and hates them for it. *G. Bernard Shaw.*

Down to Gehenna or up to the Throne / He travels the fastest who travels alone. *Kipling.*

Dreamer of dreams, born out of my due time, / Why 50 should I strive to set the crooked straight ? *William Morris.*

Dust into Dust, and under Dust, to lie, / Sans Wine, sans Song, sans Singer, and—sans End ! *Fitzgerald ("Omar Khayyám").*

E

Each day brings its petty dust / Our soon-choked souls to fill, / And we forget because we must, / And not because we will. *Matthew Arnold.*

Each has his own tree of ancestors, but at the top of all sits Probably Arboreal. *Stevenson.*

Each night we die, / Each morn are born anew : each day, a life ! *Young.*

England was merry England, when / Old Christmas 55 brought his sports again.s / 'Twa Christmas broached the mightiest ale, / 'Twas Christmas told the merriest tale ; / A Christmas gambol oft could cheer / The poor man's heart through half the year. *Scott.*

Entire and sure the monarch's rule must prove, / Who founds her greatness on her subjects' love. *Prior.*

Envy, to which the ignoble mind's a slave, / Is emulation in the learn'd or brave. *Pope.*

Envy's a coal comes hissing hot from Hell. *P. J. Bailey.*

Error is a hardy plant; it flourisheth in every soil. *Tupper.*

Even bees, the little almsmen of spring-bowers, / Know there is richest juice in poison-flowers. *Keats.*

Even copious Dryden wanted, or forgot, / The last and greatest art, the art to blot. *Pope.*

Every door is barred with gold, and opens but to golden keys. *Tennyson.*

5 Every word man's lips have uttered / Echoes in God's skies. *A. A. Procter.*

Examples draw when precept fails, / And sermons are less read than tales. *Prior.*

Experience, the name men give to their mistakes. *Wilde.*

F

False things may be imagined, and false things composed; but only truth can be invented. *Ruskin.*

Falsehood and fraud shoot up on every soil, / The product of all climes. *Addison.*

10 Falsehood flies and truth comes limping after it, so that when men come to be undeceived it is too late. *Swift.*

Falsehoods which we spurn to-day / Were the truths of long ago. *Whittier.*

Fame, impatient of extremes, decays / Not more by envy than excess of praise. *Pope.*

Fame is at best an unperforming cheat; / But 'tis substantial happiness to eat. *Pope.*

Fame is like a river, that beareth up things light and swoln, and drowns things weighty and solid. *Bacon.*

15 Farewell! / For in that word—that fatal word—howe'er / We promise—hope—believe—there breathes despair. *Byron.*

Fashion, the arbiter and rule of right. *Steele.*

Faultless to a fault. *Robert Browning.*

Fear hath a hundred eyes, that all agree / To plague her beating heart. *Wordsworth.*

Fellowship is heaven, and lack of fellowship is hell; fellowship is life, and lack of fellowship is death; and the deeds that ye do upon the earth, it is for fellowship's sake that ye do them. *William Morris*

20 Few are qualified to shine in company, but it is in most men's power to be agreeable. *Swift.*

Few, but full of understanding, are the books of the library of God. *Tupper.*

Few things are harder to put up with than the annoyance of a good example. *Mark Twain.*

Fill the can and fill the cup : / All the windy ways of men / Are but dust that rises up, / And is lightly laid again. *Tennyson.*

First, then, a woman will, or won't, depend on't : / If she will do't, she will ; and there's an end on't. *Aaron Hill.*

25 Fixed as a habit or some darling sin. *Oldham.*

Flatterers make cream cheese of chalk. *Hood.*

Flower in the crannied wall, / I pluck you out of the crannies, / I hold you here, root and all, in my hand, / Little flower—but *if* I could understand / What you are, root and all, and all in all, / I should know what God and man is. *Tennyson.*

Flowers are lovely; Love is flower-like; / Friendship is a sheltering tree; / O! the joys, that came down shower-like, / Of Friendship, Love, and Liberty, / Ere I was old. *Coleridge.*

For courtesy wins woman all as well / As valour. *Tennyson.*

For fools admire, but men of sense approve. *Pope.* 30

For good ye are and bad, and like to coins, / Some true, some light, but every one of you / Stamped with the image of the king. *Tennyson.*

For he / Must serve who fain would sway—and soothe—and sue— / And watch all time—and pry into all place— / And be a living lie—who would become / A mighty thing amongst the mean. *Byron.*

For hope is but the dream of those that wake. *Prior.*

For hope shall brighten days to come, / And memory gild the past. *Moore.*

For I was of Christ's choosing, I, God's knight, / No 35 blinkard heathen stumbling for scant light. *Swinburne.*

For I, who hold sage Homer's rule the best, / Welcome the coming, speed the going, guest. *Pope.*

For if we live, we die not, / And if we die, we live. *Swinburne.*

For it is said by man expert / That the eye is traitor of the heart. *Sir Thomas Wyatt.*

For it was in the golden prime / Of good Haroun Alraschid. *Tennyson.*

For man is man, and master of his fate. *Tennyson.* 40

For manners are not idle, but the fruit / Of loyal nature, and of noble mind. *Tennyson.*

For many a time / I have been half in love with easeful Death. *Keats.*

For the man's love once gone never returns. *Tennyson.*

For the sire lives in his sons, and they pay their father's debt, / And the lion has left a whelp wherever his claw was set. *Henley.*

For the sword outwears its sheath, / And the soul 45 wears out the breast. *Byron.*

For thou, if ever god-like foot there trod / These fields of ours, wert surely like a god. *Swinburne.*

For, trust me, they who never melt / With pity, never melt with love. *Moore.*

For what are the voices of birds, / Ay, and of beasts—but words, our words, / Only so much more sweet? *Robert Browning.*

For who's a prince or beggar in the grave? *Otway.*

For words, like Nature, half reveal / And half conceal 50 the Soul within. *Tennyson.*

Fools! For I also had my hour; / One far fierce hour and sweet : / There was a shout about my ears, / And palms before my feet. *G. K. Chesterton*, of the donkey.

Forget that I remember, / And dream that I forget. *Swinburne.*

Fortunes come tumbling into some men's laps. *Bacon.*

"Frank and explicit"—that is the right line to take when you wish to conceal your own mind and to confuse the minds of others. *Disraeli.*

Freedom hallows with her tread / The silent cities 55 of the dead. *Byron.*

Freedom, hand in hand with labour, / Walketh strong and brave. *Whittier.*

From the death of the old the new proceeds, / And the life of truth from the rot of creeds. *Whittier.*

From too much love of living, / From hope and fear set free, / We thank with brief thanksgiving / Whatever gods may be / That no life lives for ever; / That dead men rise up never; / That even the weariest river / Winds somewhere safe to sea. *Swinburne.*

G

Genius has somewhat of the infantine : / But of the childish not a touch or taint. *Robert Browning.*

Get place and wealth, if possible, with grace ; / If not, by any means get wealth and place. *Pope.*

Give fools their gold, and knaves their power ; / Let fortune's bubbles rise and fall ; / Who sows a field, or trains a flower, / Or plants a tree, is more than all. *Whittier.*

Go where glory waits thee, / But while fame elates thee, / Oh ! still remember me. *Moore.*

5 God Almighty first planted a garden : and indeed it is the purest of human pleasures. *Bacon.*

God be thanked, the meanest of His creatures / Boasts two soul-sides,—one to face the world with, / One to show a woman when he loves her. *Robert Browning.*

"God bless all our gains," say we ; / But "May God bless all our losses," / Better suits with our degree. *E. B. Browning.*

God for His service needeth not proud work of human skill ; / They please Him best who labour most in peace to do His will. *Wordsworth.*

God himself is the best Poet, / And the Real is His Song. *E. B. Browning.*

10 God's gifts put man's best dreams to shame. *E. B. Browning.*

God's true priest is always free ; / Free, the needed truth to speak, / Right the wronged, and raise the weak. *Whittier.*

Gold ! Gold ! Gold ! Gold ! / Bright and yellow, hard and cold. / . . . How widely its agencies vary— / To save—to ruin—to curse—to bless ; / As even its minted coins express, / Now stamped with the image of good Queen Bess, / And now of a Bloody Mary. *Hood.*

Good-breeding is the blossom of good-sense. *Young.*

Gorgonised from head to foot / With a stony British stare. *Tennyson.*

15 Grace is given of God, but knowledge is bought in the market. *A. H. Clough.*

Grant me but health, thou great Bestower of it, and give me but this fair goddess as my companion, and shower down thy mitres, if it seem good unto Thy Divine Providence, upon those heads which are aching for them. *Sterne.*

Great in the council, glorious in the field. *Pope.*

Great is their love who love in sin and fear. *Byron.*

Green-dense and dim-delicious, bred o' the sun. *Robert Browning.*

H

20 Habit is habit, and not to be flung out of the window by any man, but coaxed downstairs a step at a time. *Mark Twain.*

Habit rules the unreflecting herd. *Wordsworth.*

Half our daylight faith's a fable ; / Sleep disports with shadows too. *Campbell.*

Happy must be the State / Whose ruler heedeth more / The murmurs of the poor / Than flatteries of the great. *Whittier.*

Hated by fools, and fools to hate, / Be that my motto and my fate. *Swift.*

25 Have drown'd my Honour in a shallow Cup, / And sold my Reputation for a Song. *Fitzgerald* ("Omar Khayyám").

He added a new terror to death. *Dr. Arbuthnot* (18 cent.), in reference to Curll, an unscrupulous publisher of letters.

He fixed thee, 'mid this dance / Of plastic circumstance. *Robert Browning.*

He gave it for his opinion, "That whoever could make two ears of corn, or two blades of grass, to grow upon a spot of ground where only one grew before, would deserve better of mankind, and do more essential service to his country, than the whole race of politicians put together." *Swift.*

He gives nothing but worthless gold / Who gives from a sense of duty. *Lowell.*

He had but one eye, and the popular prejudice runs 30 in favour of two. *Dickens* (of Mr. Squeers, in "Nicholas Nickleby").

He had used the word in its Pickwickian sense. *Dickens* ("Pickwick Papers").

He is all fault who hath no fault at all : / For who loves me must have a touch of earth. *Tennyson.*

He is master and lord of his brothers / Who is worthier and wiser than they. *Swinburne.*

He is the fountain of honour. *Bacon.*

He knew the precise psychological moment when to 35 say nothing. *Wilde.*

He knows not how to wink at human frailty, / Or pardon weakness that he never felt. *Addison.*

He left a Corsair's name to other times, / Linked with one virtue and a thousand crimes. *Byron.*

He mouths a sentence as curs mouth a bone. *Rev. Charles Churchill.*

He never mocks, / For mockery is the fume of little hearts. *Tennyson.*

He owned with a grin / That his favourite sin / Is 40 pride that apes humility. *Southey.*

He's half absolved, who has confessed. *Prior.*

He's true to God who's true to man ; wherever wrong is done / To the humblest and the weakest 'neath the all-beholding sun. *Lowell.*

He smarteth most who hides his smart, / And sues for no compassion. *Sir W. Raleigh.*

He seems so near and yet so far. *Tennyson.*

He that can draw a charm / From rocks, or woods, 45 or weeds, or things that seem / All mute, and does it—is wise. *B. W. Procter* (Barry Cornwall).

He that loves but half of Earth / Loves but half enough for me. *Quiller-Couch.*

He that only rules by terror / Doeth grievous wrong. *Tennyson.*

He that roars for liberty / Faster binds a tyrant's power, / And the tyrant's cruel glee / Forces on the freer hour. *Tennyson.*

He that will not live by toil / Has no right on English soil ! *Kingsley.*

He, their sire, / Butchered to make a Roman holiday. 50 *Byron.*

He thinks posterity a packhorse, always ready to be loaded. *Disraeli.*

He was the mildest mannered man / That ever scuttled ship or cut a throat. *Byron.*

He went like one that hath been stunned / And is of a sense forlorn : / A sadder and a wiser man, He rose the morrow morn. *Coleridge.*

He who has the truth at his heart need never fear the want of persuasion on his tongue. *Ruskin.*

He who hath not a dram of folly in his mixture, 55 hath pounds of much worse matter in his composition. *Lamb.*

He who loves not his country, can love nothing. *Byron.*

He will hold thee, when his passion shall have spent its novel force, / Something better than his dog, a little dearer than his horse. *Tennyson.*

He wreathed the rod of criticism with roses. *Isaac D'Israeli.*

Heard melodies are sweet, but those unheard are sweeter. *Keats.*

Heard the heavens fill with shouting, and there rained a ghastly dew / From the nations' airy navies grappling in the central blue. *Tennyson.*

5 Heart on her lips and soul within her eyes, / Soft as her clime and sunny as her skies. *Byron.*

Here and here did England help me : how can I help England ?—say, / Whoso turns as I, this evening, turn to God to praise and pray, / While Jove's planet rises yonder, silent over Africa. *Robert Browning.*

Here with a Loaf of Bread beneath the Bough, / A Flask of Wine, a Book of Verse—and Thou / Beside me singing in the Wilderness— / And Wilderness is Paradise enow. *Fitzgerald (" Omar Khayyám ").*

Him / That was a god, and is a lawyer's clerk, / The rentroll Cupid of our rainy isles. *Tennyson.*

His cogitative faculties immersed / In cogibundity of cogitation. *Henry Carey.*

10 His face, / The tablet of unutterable thoughts. *Byron.*

His heart was one of those which most enamour us, / Wax to receive, and marble to retain. *Byron.*

His honour rooted in dishonour stood, / And faith unfaithful kept him falsely true. *Tennyson.*

His life is a watch or a vision / Between a sleep and a sleep. *Swinburne.*

His square-turned joints, and strength of limb, / Showed him no carpet knight so trim. *Scott.*

15 History is a pageant and not a philosophy. *A. Birrell.*

Honest men / Are the soft easy cushions on which knaves / Repose and fatten. *Otway.*

Honour and shame from no condition rise ; / Act well your part ; there all the honour lies. *Pope.*

Honour has come back, as a king, to earth, / And paid his subjects with a royal wage ; / And Nobleness walks in our ways again ; / And we have come into our heritage. *Rupert Brooke.*

Honour is a baby's rattle. *Randolph.*

20 Hope, for a season, bade the world farewell, / And Freedom shrieked—as Kosciusko fell ! *Campbell.*

Hope is a good breakfast, but it is a bad supper. *Bacon.*

Hope knows not if fear speak truth, nor fear whether hope be not blind as she : / But the sun is in heaven that beholds her immortal, and girdled with life by the sea. *Swinburne.*

Hope tells a flattering tale, / Delusive, vain, and hollow. *Miss Wrother.*

Hope, the paramount duty that Heaven lays, / For its own honour, on man's suffering heart. *Wordsworth.*

25 How little do we know that which we are ! / How less what we may be ! The eternal surge / Of time and tide rolls on and bears afar / Our bubbles. *Byron.*

How little we may come to know Romance by the cloak she wears, and how humble must be he who would surprise the heart of her ! *David Grayson.*

How many a thing which we cast to the ground / When others pick it up becomes a gem. *George Meredith.*

How sad and bad and mad it was— / But then, how it was sweet ! *Robert Browning.*

How soon we come to distinguish the books of the mere writers from the books of real men ! For true literature, like happiness, is ever a by-product ; it is the half-conscious expression of a man greatly engaged in some other undertaking ; it is the song of one working. There is something inevitable, unrestrainable about the great books ; they seemed to come despite the author. " I could not sleep," says the poet Horace, " for the pressure of unwritten poetry." *David Grayson.*

However we brave it out, we men are a little breed. 30 *Tennyson.*

Humanity always becomes a conqueror. *Sheridan (" Pizarro ").*

Humble because of knowledge ; mighty by sacrifice. *Kipling.*

Humour is odd, grotesque, and wild, / Only by affectation spoiled ; / 'Tis never by invention got ; / Men have it when they know it not. *Swift.*

I

I always know when Lady Slattern has been before me. She has a most observing thumb. *Sheridan (" The Rivals ").*

I am, in plainer words, a bundle of prejudices—made 35 up of likings and dislikings. *Lamb.*

I am the master of my fate : / I am the captain of my soul. *Henley.*

I am the very slave of circumstance / And impulse—borne away with every breath ! *Byron.*

I do not blame such women, though, for love, / They pick much oakum ; earth's fanatics make / Too frequently heaven's saints. *E. B. Browning.*

I do not know what I was playing, / Or what I was dreaming then, / But I struck one chord of music, / Like the sound of a great Amen. *A. A. Procter.*

I expect to pass through this world but once. Any 40 good, therefore, that I can do, or any kindness that I can show to any fellow-creature, let me do it now. Let me not defer or neglect it, for I shall not pass this way again. Attributed to *Stephen Crellett (U.S.A.).*

I fear to love thee, Sweet, because / Love's the ambassador of loss. *Francis Thompson.*

I fled Him, down the nights and down the days ; / I fled Him, down the arches of the years ; / I fled Him, down the labyrinthine ways / Of my own mind ; and in the mist of tears / I hid from Him, and under running laughter. *Francis Thompson.*

I hate cynicism a great deal worse than I do the devil ; unless, perhaps, the two were the same thing ? *Stevenson.*

I have always thought that every woman should marry, and no man. *Disraeli.*

I have had playmates, I have had companions, / In 45 my days of childhood, in my joyful schooldays, / All, all are gone, the old familiar faces. *Lamb.*

I have no remedy for fear ; there grows / No herb of help to heal a coward's heart. *Swinburne.*

I heard the trailing garments of the night / Sweep through her marble halls ! *Longfellow.*

I know not if I know what true love is, / But if I know, then, if I love not him, / I know there is none other I can love. *Tennyson.*

I love thee, I love thee, / 'Tis all that I can say ; / It is my vision in the night, / My dreaming in the day. *Hood.*

I love to lose myself in other men's minds. *Lamb.* 50

I mean your borrowers of books—those mutilators of collections, spoilers of the symmetry of shelves, and creators of odd volumes. *Lamb.*

I ne'er could any lustre see / In eyes that would not look on me ; / I ne'er saw nectar on a lip / But where my own did hope to sip. *Sheridan.*

I never found the companion that was so companionable as solitude. *H. D. Thoreau.*

I only ask for information. *Dickens* (*Rosa Dartle, in* "*David Copperfield*").

5 I own the soft impeachment. *Sheridan* (*Mrs. Malaprop, in* "*The Rivals*").

I reckon there's more things told than are true, / And more things true than are told. *Kipling.*

I remember, I remember, / How my childhood fleeted by, / The mirth of its December, / And the warmth of its July. *Praed.*

I remember, I remember, / The fir trees dark and high ; / I used to think their slender tops / Were close against the sky ; / It was a childish ignorance, / But now 'tis little joy / To know I'm further off from Heaven / Than when I was a boy. *Hood.*

I shall never be friends with roses ; / I shall loathe sweet pines, where a note grown strong / Relents and recoils, and climbs and closes. *Swinburne.*

10 I slept, and dreamed that life was Beauty ; / I woke, and found that life was Duty. *Ellen Hooper.*

I sometimes think that never blows so red / The Rose as where some buried Cæsar bled ; / That every Hyacinth the Garden wears / Dropt in its lap from some once lovely Head. *Fitzgerald* ("*Omar Khayyám*").

I the heir of all the ages, in the foremost files of time. *Tennyson.*

I think it was Jekyll who used to say that the further he went west, the more convinced he felt that the wise men came from the east. *Sydney Smith.*

"I thought *Love* had been a joyous thing," quoth my Uncle Toby.—"'Tis the most serious thing, an' please your Honour (sometimes), that is in the world." *Sterne.*

15 I was ever a fighter, so—one fight more, / The best and the last ! / I would hate that death bandaged my eyes and forbore, / And bade me creep past. *Robert Browning.*

I weigh the man, not his title ; 'tis not the king's stamp can make the metal heavier or better. *Wycherley.*

I will go back to the great sweet mother, / Mother and lover of men, the sea. *Swinburne.*

I will pluck it from my bosom, though my heart be at the root. *Tennyson.*

If blood be the price of admiralty, / Lord God, we ha' paid in full ! *Kipling.*

20 If from society we learn to live, / 'Tis solitude should teach us how to die. *Byron.*

If I should die think only this of me : / That there's some corner of a foreign field / That is for ever England. *Rupert Brooke.*

If the world were filled with music, / O how our hearts would long / For one sweet strain of silence / To end the ceaseless song. *Anon.*

If thou hast never been a fool, be sure thou wilt never be a wise man. *Thackeray.*

If thou wouldst view fair Melrose aright, / Go visit it by the pale moonlight. *Scott.*

25 It to her share some female errors fall, / Look on her face, and you'll forget them all. *Pope.*

If you get simple beauty, and nought else, / You get about the best thing God invents. *Robert Browning.*

If you have genius, industry will improve it ; if you have none, industry will supply its place. *Sir Joshua Reynolds.*

Ignobly vain and impotently great. *Pope.*

Ill fares it with the flock / If shepherds wrangle when the wolf is nigh. *Scott.*

Imagination droops her pinion. *Byron.* 30

Imagination wanders far afield. *Young.*

Impassioned logic, which outran / The hearer in its fiery course. *Tennyson.*

In came Mrs. Fezziwig, one vast substantial smile. *Dickens* ("*A Christmas Carol*").

"In case anything turned up," which was his favourite expression. *Dickens* (*of Mr. Micawber, in* "*David Copperfield*").

In every heart some viewless founts are fed / From 35 far-off hillsides where the dews were shed ; / On the worn features of the weariest face / Some youthful memory leaves its hidden trace. *O. W. Holmes.*

In Flanders Fields the poppies blow / Between the crosses, row on row, / That mark our place, and in the sky / The larks, still bravely singing, fly, / Scarce heard amidst the guns below. / We are the dead. / Short days ago / We lived, felt dawn, saw sunset glow, / Loved and were loved ; and now we lie / In Flanders Fields. *Lieut.-Col. John McCrae (reprinted by permission of the Proprietors of "Punch").*

In folly's cup still laughs the bubble joy. *Pope.*

In hawthorn-time the heart grows light. *Swinburne.*

In linden-time the heart is high, / For pride of summer passing by / With lordly laughter in her eye. *Swinburne.*

In man's most dark extremity / Oft succour dawns 40 from Heaven. *Scott.*

In me there dwells / No greatness, save it be some far-off touch / Of greatness to know well I am not great. *Tennyson.*

In poetry there is always fallacy, and sometimes fiction. *Scott.*

In records that defy the tooth of time. *Young.*

In that fierce light which beats upon a throne. *Tennyson.*

In the Parliament of man, the Federation of the 45 world. *Tennyson.*

In the Spring a livelier iris changes on the burnish'd dove ; / In the Spring a young man's fancy lightly turns to thoughts of love. *Tennyson.*

In this dim world of clouding cares, / We rarely know, till 'wildered eyes / See white wings lessening up the skies, / The angels with us unawares. *Massey.*

Indifference and hypocrisy between them keep orthodoxy alive. *I. Zangwill.*

Inebriated with the exuberance of his own verbosity. *Disraeli.*

Inscribe all human effort with one word, / Artistry's 50 haunting curse, the Incomplete. *Robert Browning.*

Insects / Have made the lion mad ere now ; a shaft / I' the heel o'erthrew the bravest of the brave. *Byron.*

Intellect obscures more than it illumines. *I. Zangwill.*

Is it, in heaven, a crime to love too well ? *Pope.*

Is it so small a thing / To have enjoyed the sun, / To have lived light in the Spring, / To have loved, to have thought, to have done ? *Matthew Arnold.*

Is not compromise of old a god among you? *Swinburne.*

Is not Precedent indeed a King of men ? *Swinburne.*

"Is this," I cried, / "The end of prayer and preaching ? / Then, down with pulpit, down with priest, / And give us Nature's teaching." *Whittier.*

Is this that haughty, gallant, gay Lothario ? *Rowe.*

5 It is a melancholy truth, that even great men have their poor relations. *Dickens* ("*Bleak House*").

It [charm] is a sort of bloom on a woman. If you have it, you don't need to have anything else ; if you don't have it, it doesn't much matter what else you have. *Barrie.*

It is easy to find fault, if one has that disposition. There was once a man who, not being able to find any other fault with his coal, complained that there were too many prehistoric toads in it. *Mark Twain.*

It is not the lie that passeth through the mind, but the lie that sinketh in, and settleth in it, that doth the hurt. *Bacon.*

It is the characteristic of a certain blunderer called genius to see things too far in advance. *Charles Reade.*

10 It is the fault of dreamers to fear fate. *Stephen Phillips.*

It is worse than a crime—it is a blunder. *Joseph Fouché (Minister of Police under Napoleon).*

It must be so,—Plato, thou reasonest well !—/ Else whence this pleasing hope, this fond desire, / This longing after immortality ? *Addison.*

It requires a surgical operation to get a joke well into a Scotch understanding. *Sydney Smith.*

It takes two to speak the truth—one to speak, and another to hear. *H. D. Thoreau.*

15 It was prettily devised of Æsop ; the fly sat upon the axle-tree of the chariot-wheel, and said, What a dust do I raise ! *Bacon.*

It was roses, roses, all the way. *Robert Browning.*

Italia ! oh, Italia ! thou who hast / The fatal gift of beauty. *Byron.*

Itch of vulgar praise. *Pope.*

J

Just for a scrap of paper [a treaty], Great Britain was going to make war on a kindred nation. *Von Bethmann-Hollweg (German Chancellor, 1914),* quoted by Sir Edward Goschen, British Ambassador at Berlin.

K

20 Kindness is very indigestible. It disagrees with very proud stomachs. *Thackeray.*

Kindnesses are easily forgotten ; but injuries ?— what worthy man does not keep *those* in mind ? *Thackeray.*

Knowledge is a steep which few may climb, / While Duty is a path which all may tread. *Sir Lewis Morris.*

L

Language is but a poor bull's-eye lantern wherewith to show off the vast cathedral of the world. *Stevenson.*

Laugh, and the world laughs with you, / Weep, and you weep alone ; / For sad old earth must borrow its mirth, / But has trouble enough of its own. *Ella Wheeler Wilcox.*

25 Lend, lend your wings ! I mount ! I fly ! / O grave ! where is thy victory ? O death, where_is thy sting ? *Pope.*

Let life burn down, and dream it is not death. *Swinburne.*

Let Love clasp Grief, lest both be drowned. *Tennyson.*

Let not the conceit of intellect hinder thee from worshipping mystery. *Tupper.*

Let such forego the poet's sacred name, / Who rack their brains for lucre, not for fame. *Byron.*

Let us have no meandering. *Dickens* ("*David* 30 *Copperfield*").

Liberty and Union, now and for ever, one and inseparable. *Daniel Webster.*

Life is at best but a froward child, which must be coaxed and played with until the end comes. *Sir W. Temple.*

Life is like a cup of tea ; the more heartily we drink, the sooner we reach the dregs. *Barrie.*

Life is mostly froth and bubble, / Two things stand like stone— / Kindness in another's trouble, / Courage in your own. *A. L. Gordon.*

Life is love, and heart on heart, / We press 3 5 too close in church and mart, / To keep a dream or grave apart. *E. B. Browning.*

Light quirks of music, broken and uneven, / Make the soul dance upon a jig to heaven. *Pope.*

Light is the dance, and doubly sweet the days, / When, for the dear delight, another pays. *Pope.*

Like a dog, he hunts in dreams. *Tennyson.*

Like a pale martyr in his shirt of fire. *Alex. Smith.*

Like our shadows, / Our wishes lengthen, as our 40 sun declines. *Young.*

Like that strange song I heard Apollo sing, / While Ilion like a mist rose into towers. *Tennyson.*

Live pure, speak true, right wrong, follow the King— / Else, wherefore born ? *Tennyson.*

Lives obscurely great. *Sir Henry Newbolt.*

Lo ! as the wind is, so is mortal life, / A moan, a sigh, a sob, a storm, a strife. *Sir E. Arnold.*

Lo ! some we loved, the loveliest and the best / That 45 Time and Fate of all their Vintage prest, / Have drunk their Cup a Round or two before, / And one by one crept silently to Rest. *Fitzgerald* ("*Omar Khayyám*").

London is a modern Babylon. *Disraeli.*

Look at thy heart, and when its depths are known, / Then try thy brother's, judging by thine own. *O. W. Holmes.*

Look for me in the nurseries of Heaven. *Francis Thompson.*

Look next on greatness ; say where greatness lies : / "Where, but among the heroes and the wise ? " *Pope.*

Look to your health ; and if you have it, praise God, 50 and value it next to a good conscience ; for health is the second blessing that we mortals are capable of : a blessing that money cannot buy. *Izaak Walton.*

Lord of myself, accountable to none ; / But to my conscience, and my God alone. *Oldham.*

Love ceases to be a pleasure when it ceases to be a secret. *Aphra Behn.*

Love finds an altar for forbidden fires. *Pope.*

Love hangs like light about your name / As music round the shell. *Swinburne.*

Love is the marrow of friendship, and letters are the 55 Elixir of love. *Howell.*

Love scarce is love that never knows / The sweetness of forgiving. *Whittier.*

M

Macaulay is like a book in breeches . . . He has occasional flashes of silence that make his conversation perfectly delightful. *Sydney Smith.*

Magic casements, opening on the foam / Of perilous seas, in fairy lands forlorn. *Keats.*

Man is a creature who lives not upon bread alone. but principally by catch-words. *Stevenson.*

Man is man's A.B.C. There is none can / Read God aright, unless he first spell man. *Quarles.*

5 Man is the hunter; woman is his game. *Tennyson.*

Man's rich with little, were his judgment true; / Nature is frugal, and her wants are few. *Young.*

Manners with fortunes, humours turn with climes, / Tenets with books, and principles with times. *Pope.*

Many books belong to sunshine, and should be read out of doors. Clover, violets, and roses breathe from their leaves; they are most lovable in cool lanes, along fieldpaths, or upon stiles overhung by hawthorn; while the blackbird pipes, and the nightingale bathes its brown feathers in the twilight copse. *Robert Aris Willmott.*

Men are more eloquent than women made; / But women are more powerful to persuade. *Randolph.*

10 Men / May bear the blazon wrought of centuries, hold / Their armouries higher than arms imperial; Yet / Know that the least their countryman, whose hand / Hath done his country service, lives their peer, / And peer of all their fathers. *Swinburne.*

Men may live fools, but fools they cannot die. *Young.*

Men, my brothers, men the workers, ever reaping something new : / That which they have done but earnest of the things that they shall do. *Tennyson.*

Men touch them, and change in a trice / The lilies and languors of virtue / For the raptures and roses of vice. *Swinburne.*

Mercy's indeed the attribute of heaven. *Otway.*

15 Mid-May's eldest child, / The coming musk-rose, full of dewy wine, / The murmurous haunt of flies on summer eves. *Keats.*

Might there not be / Some power in gentleness we dream not of? *Stephen Phillips.*

Milton! Thou should'st be living at this hour : / England hath need of thee; she is a fen / Of stagnant waters. *Wordsworth.*

Minds, / By nature great, are conscious of their greatness, / And hold it mean to borrow aught from flattery. *Rowe.*

Minority is no disproof : / Wisdom is not so strong and fleet / As never to have known defeat. *L. Housman.*

20 Moments like to these / Rend men's lives into immortalities. *Byron.*

Mont Blanc is the monarch of mountains; / They crowned him long ago / On a throne of rocks, in a robe of clouds, / With a diadem of snow. *Byron.*

Mony a little maks a meikle (Many a small thing makes a big thing). *Scots pr.*, often misquoted as "Every mickle maks a muckle."

Morality was made for man, not man for morality. *I. Zangwill.*

Most can raise the flowers now, / For all have got the seed. *Tennyson.*

25 Most of his faults brought their excuses with them. *Prior.*

Most writers steal a good thing when they can. *B. W. Procter (Barry Cornwall).*

Move upward, working out the beast, / And let the ape and tiger die. *Tennyson.*

Mr. Weller's knowledge of London was extensive and peculiar. *Dickens (" Pickwick Papers ").*

Music can soften pain to ease. *Pope.*

Music that gentlier on the spirit lies / Than tir'd 30 eyelids upon tir'd eyes. *Tennyson.*

My foot is on my native heath, and my name is MacGregor. *Scott.*

My good name, which was as white as a tulip. *Wycherley.*

My little dears, who learn to read, / Pray early learn to shun / That very foolish thing indeed / The people call a Pun. *Hook.*

"My other piece of advice, Copperfield," said Mr. Micawber, " you know. Annual income twenty pounds, annual expenditure nineteen nineteen six, result happiness. Annual income twenty pounds, annual expenditure twenty pounds ought and six, result misery. The blossom is blighted, the leaf is withered, the God of Day goes down upon the dreary scene, and—and, in short, you are for ever floored ! " *Dickens (" David Copperfield ").*

My poverty, but not my will, consents. *Romeo* 35 *and Juliet, v, 1.*

N

Necessity, thou tyrant conscience of the great! *Swift.*

Never ascribe to an opponent motives meaner than your own. *Barrie.*

Never the lotos closes, never the wild-fowl wake, / But a soul goes out on the East Wind that died for England's sake. *Kipling.*

Never the time and the place / And the loved one all together. *Robert Browning.*

Never was isle so little, never was sea so lone, / But 40 over the scud and the palm-trees an English flag was flown. *Kipling.*

No is no negative in a woman's mouth. *Sir Philip Sidney.*

No man doth well but God hath part in him. *Swinburne.*

No man ever spake as he that bade our England be but true, / Keep but faith with England fast and firm, and none should bid her rue; / None may speak as he : but all may know the sign that Shakespeare knew. *Swinburne.*

No man was ever yet a great poet without being at the same time a profound philosopher. *Coleridge.*

No one minds what Jeffrey says—it is not more than 45 a week ago that I heard him speak disrespectfully of the equator. *Sydney Smith.*

No pleasure is comparable to the standing upon the vantage ground of truth. *Bacon.*

No rock so hard but that a little wave / May beat admission in a thousand years. *Tennyson.*

No scandal about Queen Elizabeth, I hope. *Sheridan (" The Critic ").*

None judge so wrong as those who think amiss. *Pope.*

Nor can any noble thing be wealth except to a noble 50 person. *Ruskin.*

Nor can belief touch, kindle, smite, reprieve / His heart who has not heart to disbelieve. *Swinburne.*

Not a kindlier life or sweeter / Time, that lights and quenches men, / Now may quench or light again. *Swinburne.*

Not like the piebald miscellany, man. *Tennyson.*

Not only around our infancy / Doth heaven with all its splendours lie ; / Daily, with souls that cringe and plot, / We Sinais climb and know it not. *Lowell.*

Not till earth be sunless, not till death strike blind the skies, / May the deathless love that waits on deathless deeds be dead. *Swinburne.*

Not to put too fine a point upon it. *Dickens ("Bleak House").*

5 Not what we give, but what we share,— / For the gift without the giver is bare ; / Who gives himself with his alms feeds three, — / Himself, his hungering neighbour, and me. *Lowell.*

Not with dreams, but with blood and with iron / Shall a nation be moulded at last. *Swin urn.*

Nothing can satisfy, but what confounds / Nothing. but what astonishes, is true. *Young.*

Nothing except a battle lost can be half so melancholy as a battle won. *Wellington.*

Nothing is achieved before it be thoroughly attempted. *Sir Philip Sidney.*

10 Nothing is ever done beautifully which is done in rivalship, nor nobly which is done in pride. *Ruskin.*

Nothing is fixed, that mortals see or know, / Unless perhaps some stars be so. *Swift.*

Nothing is so impudent as Success—unless it be those she favours. *Planché.*

Nothing so needs reforming as other people's habits. *Mark Twain.*

Nurture your mind with great thoughts. To believe in the heroic makes heroes. *Disraeli.*

O

15 O Caledonia ! stern and wild, / Meet nurse for a poetic child ! / . . . Land of the mountain and the flood, / Land of my sires ! *Scott.*

O fall'n at length that tower of strength / Which stood four-square to all the winds that blew. *Tennyson.*

O, for a beaker full of the warm South, / Full of the true, the blushful Hippocrene, / With beaded bubbles winking at the brim, / And purple-stained mouth. *Keats.*

O for a blast of that dread horn On Fontarabian echoes borne ! *Scott.*

O Love, O fire ! once he drew / With one long kiss my whole soul through / My lips, as sunlight drinketh dew. *Tennyson.*

20 O lyric Love, half angel and half bird, / And all a wonder and a wild desire ! *Robert Browning.*

O ! many a shaft, at random sent, / Finds mark the archer little meant ! / And many a word, at random spoken, / May soothe or wound a heart that's broken. *Scott.*

O miracle of noble womanhood ! *Tennyson.*

O, rank is good, and gold is fair, / And high and low mate ill ; / But love has never known a law / Beyond its own sweet will. *Whittier.*

O selfless man and stainless gentleman. *Tennyson.*

25 O that I now, I too were / By deep wells and water-floods, / Streams of ancient hills, and where / All the wan green places bear / Blossoms cleaving to the sod, / Fruitless fruit, and grasses fair, / Or such darkest ivy-buds / As divide thy yellow hair, / Bacchus, and their leaves that nod, / Round thy fawnskin brush the bare / Snow-soft shoulder of a god. *Swinburne.*

O, to feel the beat of the rain, and the homely smell of the earth, / Is a tune for the blood to jig to, a joy past power of words. *John Masefield.*

O what a crocodilian world is this ! *Quarles.*

O woman, lovely woman, nature made thee / To temper man ; we had been brutes without you, / Angels are painted fair to look like you. *Otway.*

" Odious ! in woollen ! 'twould a saint provoke ! " / Were the last words that poor Narcissa spoke. *Pope.*

O'er all there hung a shadow and a fear ; / A sense 30 of mystery the spirit daunted, / And said as plain as whisper to the ear, / The place is Haunted. *Hood.*

Of all the griefs that mortals share, / The one that seems the hardest to bear / Is the grief without community. *Hood.*

Of all the horrid, hideous sounds of woe, / Sadder than owl-songs or the midnight blast, / Is that portentous phrase, " I told you so." *Byron.*

Of happy men that have the power to die, / And grassy barrows of the happier dead. *Tennyson.*

Often change doth please a woman's mind. *Sir Thomas Wyatt.*

Oh, Amos Cottle ! Phœbus ! What a name, / To 35 fill the speaking trump of future fame ! *Byron.*

Oh, bed ! Oh, bed ! delicious bed ! / That heaven upon earth to the weary head. *Hood.*

" Oh ! darkly, deeply, beautifully blue," / As some-one, somewhere sings about the sky. *Byron.*

Oh ! ever thus from childhood's hour, / I've seen my fondest hopes decay ; / I never loved a tree or flower, / But 'twas the first to fade away. / I never nursed a dear gazelle, / To glad me with its soft black eye, / But when it came to know me well, / And love me, it was sure to die ! *Moore.*

Oh, God ! it is a fearful thing / To see the human soul take wing / In any shape, in any mood— / I've seen it rushing forth in blood, / I've seen it on the breaking ocean / Strive with a swoln, convulsive motion. *Byron.*

Oh ! that we two were Maying. *Kingsley.* 40

Oh, the little more, and how much it is ! And the little less, and what worlds away ! *Robert Browning.*

Oh, to be in England now that April's there ! *Robert Browning.*

Old customs, habits, superstitions, fears, / All that lies buried under fifty years. *Whittier.*

Old songs, the precious music of the heart ! / A few strong instincts and a few plain rules. *Wordsworth.*

Old thanks, old thoughts, old aspirations, / Outlive 45 men's lives and lives of nations. *Swinburne.*

Om mani padme hum, the Sunrise comes ! / The Dewdrop slips into the shining Sea. *Sir E. Arnold.*

On the earth the broken arcs ; / in the heaven, a perfect round. *Robert Browning.*

Once did she hold the gorgeous East in fee, / And was the safeguard of the West. *Wordsworth, of Venice.*

One Cæsar lives ; a thousand are forgot. *Young.*

One crowded hour of glorious life / Is worth an age 50 without a name. *Major Mordaunt* (1791), quoted without acknowledgment by *Scott* in " *Old Mortality.*"

One half will never be believed, / The other never read. *Pope.*

One hates an author that's *all author,* fellows / In foolscap uniform turned up with ink. *Byron.*

One hopeless dark idolater of Chance. *Campbell.*

One may quote till one compiles. *Isaac D'Israeli.*

One moment may with bliss repay/ Unnumbered hours of pain. *Campbell.*

One of the most striking differences between a cat and a lie is that a cat has only nine lives. *Mark Twain.*

5 One pulse of passion—youth's first fiery glow,—/ Are worth the hoarded proverbs of the sage : / Vex not thy soul with dead philosophy ; / Have we not lips to kiss with, hearts to love, and eyes to see ? *Wilde.*

One simile, that solitary shines / In the dry desert of a thousand lines. *Pope.*

One thing is certain, that Life flies ; / One thing is certain, and the Rest is Lies ; / The Flower that once has blown for ever dies. *Fitzgerald* ("*Omar Khayyám*").

One who never turned his back, but marched breast forward, / Never doubted clouds would break, / Never dreamed, though right were worsted, wrong would triumph, / Held we fall to rise, are baffled to fight better / Sleep to wake. *Robert Browning.*

One who, to all the heights of learning bred, / Read books and men, and practised what he read. *Geo. Stepney.*

10 One wild Shakespeare, following Nature's lights, / Is worth whole planets filled with Stagyrites. *Moore.*

Or ever the silver cord be loosed, or the golden bowl be broken, or the pitcher be broken at the fountain, or the wheel broken at the cistern. *Bible.*

Or hear old Triton blow his wreathéd horn. *Wordsworth.*

Or lend fresh interest to a twice-told tale. *Byron.*

Or that eternal want of pence, / Which vexes public men. *Tennyson.*

15 Our charity begins at home, / And mostly ends where it begins. *Horace Smith.*

Our country ! In her intercourse with foreign nations may she always be in the right ; but our country, right or wrong ! *Decatur.*

Our disputants put me in mind of the scuttle-fish, that when he is unable to extricate himself, blackens the water about him till he becomes invisible. *Addison.*

Our little systems have their day ; / They have their day and cease to be. *Tennyson.*

Our pride misleads, our timid likings kill. *Wordsworth.*

20 Out of the world's way, out of the light, / Out of the ages of worldly weather, / Forgotten of all men altogether. *Swinburne.*

P

Peace more sweet / Than music, light more soft than shadow. *Swinburne.*

Pens are most dangerous tools, more sharp by odds / Than swords, and cut more keen than whips or rods. *John Taylor.*

Perpetual emptiness ! unceasing change ! / No single volume paramount, no code, / No master spirit, no determined road : / But equally a want of books and men. *Wordsworth.*

Persuasion hung upon his lips. *Sterne.*

25 Perverts the Prophets, and purloins the Psalms. *Byron.*

Philosophy ! the lumber of the schools. *Swift.*

Planets of the pale populace of heaven. *Robert Browning.*

Plain dealing is the best when all is done. *Prynne.*

Pleasure's a sin, and sometimes sin's a pleasure. *Byron.*

Poets and painters, as all artists know, / May shoot 30 a little with a lengthened bow. *Byron.*

Possession means to sit astride of the world, / Instead of having it astride of you. *Kingsley.*

Poured thick and fast the burning words which tyrants quake to hear. *Macaulay.*

Poverty is no disgrace to a man, but it is confoundedly inconvenient. *Sydney Smith.*

Power laid his rod and rule aside, / And Ceremony doffed her pride. *Scott.*

Praise is rebuke to the man whose conscience alloweth 35 it not. *Tupper.*

Prince of sweet songs made out of tears and fire ; / A harlot was thy nurse, a God thy sire ; / Shame soiled thy song, and song assoiled thy shame. / But from thy feet now death hath washed the mire, / Love reads out first, at head of all our choir, / Villon, our sad bad glad mad brother's name. *Swinburne.*

Procrastination is the thief of time. *Young.*

"Pro-di-gi-ous ! " exclaimed Dominie Sampson. *Scott* ("*Guy Mannering*").

Public wrongs are but popular rights in embryo. *Sir Chas. Darling.*

Puffing is of various sorts ; the principal are, the 40 puff direct, the puff preliminary, the puff collateral, the puff collusive, and the puff oblique, or puff by implication. *Sheridan* ("*The Critic*").

Pygmies are pygmies still, though perched on Alps ; / And pyramids are pyramids in vales. / Each man makes his own stature, builds himself : / Virtue alone outbuilds the pyramids : / Her monuments shall last, when Egypt's fall. *Young.*

R

Rapt Cecilia, seraph-haunted queen / Of harmony. *Wordsworth.*

Reading is to the mind what exercise is to the body. *Steele.*

Read rascal in the hollow of his back, / And scoundrel in the supple-sliding knee. *Tennyson.*

Reading Milton is like dining off gold plate in a 45 company of kings ; very splendid, very ceremonious, and not a little appalling. *Alexander Smith.*

Reforms are less to be dreaded than revolutions, for they cause less reaction. *Sir Chas. Darling.*

Renown's all hit or miss ; / There's fortune even in fame, we must allow. *Byron.*

Respect was mingled with surprise, / And the stern joy which warriors feel / In foemen worthy of their steel. *Scott.*

Rest springs from strife, and dissonant chords beget / Divinest harmonies. *Sir Lewis Morris.*

Ring out the darkness of the land, / Ring in the 50 Christ that is to be. *Tennyson.*

Ring out the feud of rich and poor. *Tennyson.*

Ring out the thousand wars of old, / Ring in the thous- and years of peace. *Tennyson.*

Ring out, wild bells, to the wild sky. *Tennyson.*

Rough to common men, / But honeying at the whisper of a lord. *Tennyson.*

S

Saint Augustine! well hast thou said, / That of our vices we can frame / A ladder, if we will but tread / Beneath our feet each deed of shame. *Longfellow.*

Say-all-you-know shall go with clouted head, / Say-nought-at-all is beaten. *William Morris.*

Scarce of earth nor all divine. *Tennyson.*

Science is a first-rate piece of furniture for a man's upper-chamber, if he has common-sense on the ground floor. *O. W. Holmes.*

5 Science moves, but slowly, slowly, creeping on from point to point. *Tennyson.*

Scorn not the Sonnet; Critic, you have frowned, / Mindless of just honours; with this key / Shakespeare unlocked his heart. *Wordsworth.*

Scratch the Christian and you find the pagan—spoiled. *I. Zangwill.*

Self-defence is a virtue, / Sole bulwark of all right. *Byron.*

Selfishness is the only real atheism; aspiration, unselfishness, the only real religion. *I. Zangwill.*

10 Sense is our helmet, wit is but the plume. *Young.*

Shame, that stings sharpest of the worms in hell. *Swinburne.*

She may still exist in undiminished vigour, when some traveller from New Zealand shall, in the midst of a vast solitude, take his stand on a broken arch of London Bridge to sketch the ruins of St. Paul's. *Macaulay,* of the Roman Catholic Church.

She moves a goddess, and she looks a queen. *Pope.*

She sang the tears into his eyes, / The heart out of his breast. *Christina Rossetti.*

15 She walks—the lady of my delight— / A shepherdess of sheep. / Her flocks are thoughts; She keeps them white; / She guards them from the steep. *Alice Meynell.*

She walks the waters like a thing of life, / And seems to dare the elements to strife. *Byron.*

Ships that pass in the night, and speak each other in passing; / Only a signal shown, and a distant voice in the darkness; / So on the ocean of life, we pass and speak one another; / Only a look and a voice, then darkness again and silence. *Longfellow.*

Sidney's sister, Pembroke's mother, / Death, ere thou hast slain another / Learn'd and fair and good as she, / Time shall throw a dart at thee. *William Browne* (often wrongly attributed to Ben Jonson).

Silence in love bewrays more woe / Than words, though ne'er so witty; / A beggar that is dumb, you know, / May challenge double pity. *Sir W. Raleigh.*

20 Silence is the gratitude of true affection. *Sheridan* ("Pizarro").

Silence is the mother of Truth. *Disraeli.*

Silence, the great Empire of Silence: higher than the stars; deeper than the Kingdoms of Death! It alone is great; all else is small.—I hope we English will long maintain our *grand talent pour le silence.* *Carlyle.*

Silence, uttering love that all things understand. *Swinburne.*

Similes are like songs in love: / They much describe; they nothing prove. *Prior.*

25 Sir Plume, of amber snuff-box justly vain, / And the nice conduct of a clouded cane. *Pope.*

Sleep; and if life was bitter to thee, pardon; / It sweet, give thanks; thou hast no more to live: / And to give thanks is good, and to forgive. *Swinburne.*

Small will I be among the small, and great among the great. *Pindar.* A variant of proverb: Do, at Rome as Rome does.

So live, that when thy summons comes to join / The innumerable caravan, which moves / To that mysterious realm, where each shall take / His chamber in the silent halls of death, / Thou go not, like the quarry-slave at night, / Scourged to his dungeon; but, sustained and soothed / By an unfaltering trust, approach thy grave, / Like one who wraps the drapery of his couch / About him, and lies down to pleasant dreams. *Bryant.*

So, naturalists observe, a flea / Hath smaller fleas that on him prey; / And these have smaller still to bite 'em, / And so proceed *ad infinitum*; / Thus every poet in his kind / Is bit by him that comes behind. *Swift.*

So sorrow is cheered by being poured / From one 30 vessel into another. *Hood.*

So sweetly mawkish, and so smoothly dull; / Heady, not strong; o'erflowing, though not full. *Pope.*

So the struck eagle, stretched upon the plain, / No more through rolling clouds to soar again, / Viewed his own feather on the fatal dart, / And winged the shaft that quivered in his heart. *Byron.*

Society is now one polished horde, / Formed of two mighty tribes, the Bores and Bored. *Byron.*

Solitude is the best nurse of wisdom. *Sterne.*

Some circumstantial evidence is very strong—as 35 when you find a trout in the milk. *H. D. Thoreau.*

Some dead lute-player / That in dead years had done delicious things. *Swinburne.*

Some feelings are to mortals given, / With less of earth in them than heaven. *Scott.*

Some lie beneath the churchyard stone, / And some before the Speaker. *Praed.*

Some praise at morning what they blame at night, But always think the last opinion right. *Pope.*

Soon as the evening shades prevail, / The moon 40 takes up the wondrous tale, / And nightly to the listening earth / Repeats the story of her birth. *Addison.*

Spake full well, in language quaint and olden, / One who dwelleth by the castled Rhine, / When he called the flowers, so blue and golden, / Stars, that in earth's firmament do shine. *Longfellow.*

Speaking truth is like writing fair, and only comes by practice. *Ruskin.*

Speech is silver, silence is golden. *Pr.*

Speed the soft intercourse from soul to soul, / And waft a sigh from Indus to the Pole. *Pope.*

Standing, with reluctant feet, / Where the brook 45 and river meet, / Womanhood and childhood fleet. *Longfellow.*

Stolen glances, sweeter for the theft. *Byron.*

Stood for his country's glory fast, / And nailed her colours to the mast. *Scott.*

Storehouse of the mind, garner of facts and fancies. *Tupper.*

Strait-laced, but all-too-full in bud / For Puritanic stays. *Tennyson.*

Stung by the splendour of a sudden thought. *Robert* 50 *Browning.*

Sublime tobacco! which from east to west / Cheers the tar's labour or the Turkman's rest. *Byron.*

Such is; what is to be ? / The pulp so bitter, how shall taste the rind ? *Francis Thompson.*

Summer has set in with his usual severity. *Coleridge.*

Sunset and evening star, / And one clear call for me ! / And may there be no moaning of the bar / When I put out to sea. *Tennyson.*

Surprise is so essential an ingredient of art that no wit will bear repetition. *Sydney Smith.*

5 Suspicion's but at best a coward's virtue. *Otway.*

Swift shuttles of an Empire's loom that weave us, main to main, / The Coastwise Lights of England give you welcome back again. *Kipling.*

T

Take care of the sense, and the sounds will take care of themselves. *C. L. Dodgson (" Lewis Carroll ").*

Take 'old o' the Wings of the Mornin', / An' flop round the earth till you're dead ; / But you won't get away from the tune that they play / To the bloomin' old rag over'ead. *Kipling.*

Take up the White Man's burden—/ Send forth the best ye breed— / Go, bind your sons to exile / To serve your captives' need. *Kipling.*

10 Tell the truth or trump—but get the trick. *Mark Twain.*

Tell you what I like the best— / Long about knee-deep in June, / 'Bout the time strawberries melts / On the vines—some afternoon / Like to jes' git out and rest, / And not work at nothin' else. *J. Whitcomb Riley.*

That all-softening, overpowering knell, / The tocsin of the soul—the dinner bell. *Byron.*

That fatal sergeant, Death, spares no degree. *Earl of Stirling.*

That life is long which answers life's great end. *Young.*

15 That man greatly lives, / Whate'er his fate, or fame, who greatly dies. *Young.*

That mighty truth—how happy are the good ! *Campbell.*

That not a worm is cloven in vain, / That not a moth with vain desire / Is shrivelled in a fruitless fire, / Or but subserves another's gain. *Tennyson.*

That thou, light-wingèd Dryad of the trees, / In some melodious plot / Of beechen green, and shadows numberless, / Singest of summer in full-throated ease. *Keats.*

That womankind had but one rosy mouth, / To kiss them all at once from north to south. *Byron.*

20 That worst of tyrants, an usurping crowd. *Pope.*

That's the wise thrush ; he sings each song twice over / Lest you should think he never could recapture / The first fine careless rapture. *Robert Browning.*

The aim, if reached or not, makes great the life ; / Try to be Shakespeare, leave the rest to fate. *Robert Browning.*

The Assyrian came down like a wolf on the fold, / And his cohorts were gleaming in purple and gold. *Byron.*

The atrocious crime of being a young man . . . I shall neither attempt to palliate nor deny. *Pitt,* in a speech as reported and coloured by Dr. Johnson.

25 The awful beauty of self-sacrifice. *Whittier.*

The Ball no Question makes of Ayes and Noes, / But Right or Left as strikes the Player goes ; / And He that toss'd Thee down into the Field, / He knows about it all—He knows—HE knows ! *Fitzgerald (" Omar Khayyám ").*⁋

The bards sublime, / Whose distant footsteps echo / Through the corridors of Time. *Longfellow.*

The bearing and the training of a child is woman's wisdom. *Tennyson.*

The bearings of this observation lays in the application on it. *Dickens.*

The blind wild beast of force. *Tennyson.*   30

The blunders of youth are preferable to the triumphs of manhood, or the success of old age. *Disraeli.*

The children born of thee are sword and fire, / Red ruin, and the breaking up of laws. *Tennyson.*

The Christless code, / That must have life for a blow. *Tennyson.*

The clothing of our minds certainly ought to be regarded before that of our bodies. *Steele.*

The cowslip is a country wench, / The violet is a nun ; 35 / But I will woo the dainty rose, / The queen of every one. *Hood.*

The cruellest lies are often told in silence. *Stevenson.*

The dangerous bar in the harbour's mouth is only grains of sand. *Tupper.*

The defects of great men are the consolation of dunces. *Isaac D'Israeli.*

The delight that consumes the desire, / The desire that outruns the delight. *Swinburne.*

The desire of knowledge, like the thirst of riches, 40 increases ever with the acquisition of it. *Sterne.*

The devil hath not in all his quiver's choice / An arrow for the heart like a sweet voice. *Byron.*

The dew that on the violet lies / Mocks the dark lustre of thine eyes. *Scott.*

The dirty nurse, Experience, in her kind / Hath fouled me. *Tennyson.*

The end is come of pleasant places, / The end of tender words and faces, / The end of all, the poppied sleep. *Swinburne.*

The end must justify the means. *Prior.*   45

The enormous faith of many made for one. *Pope.*

The feast is good, until the reck'ning come. *Quarles.*

The feather, whence the pen / Was shaped that traced the lives of these good men, / Dropped from an angel's wing. *Wordsworth.*

The female of the species is more deadly than the male. *Kipling.*

The first Almighty Cause / Acts not by partial, but 50 by general, laws. *Pope.*

The fretful stir / Unprofitable, and the fever of the world. *Wordsworth.*

The fruit of my tree of knowledge is plucked, and it is this, " Adventures are to the Adventurous." *Disraeli.*

The great beacon-light God sets in all, / The conscience of each bosom. *Robert Browning.*

The great street paved with water, filled with shipping, / And all the world's flags flying, and seagulls dipping. *John Masefield.*

The golden mean, and quiet flow / Of truths that 55 soften hatred, temper strife. *Wordsworth.*

The " good old times "—all times when old are good. *Byron.*

The happy only are the truly great. *Young.*

The hare-brained chatter of irresponsible frivolity. *Disraeli.*

The harmonious spheres / Make music, though unheard their pealing / By mortal ears. *Campbell.*

The harvest of a quiet eye / That broods and sleeps 60 on his own heart. *Wordsworth.*

The health of the people is really the foundation upon which all their happiness and all their powers as a State depend. *Disraeli.*

The insupportable labour of doing nothing. *Steele.*

The isles of Greece, the isles of Greece! / Where burning Sappho loved and sung, / Where grew the arts of war and peace— / Where Delos rose, and Phœbus sprung! / Eternal summer gilds them yet, / But all, except their sun, is set. *Byron.*

The itch of disputing will prove the scab of churches· *Sir H. Wootton.*

5 The keenest pangs the wretched find / Are rapture to the dreary void, / The leafless desert of the mind, / The waste of feelings unemployed. *Byron.*

The last was Fear, that is akin to Death; / He is Shame's friend, and always as Shame saith, / Fear answers him again. *Swinburne.*

The light that lies / In woman's eyes, / Has been my heart's undoing. *Moore.*

The light that never was on sea or land, / The consecration, and the poet's dream. *Wordsworth.*

The magic of first love is our ignorance that it can ever end. *Disraeli.*

10 The malice of a good thing is the barb that makes it sting. *Sheridan ("School for Scandal").*

The man that lays his hand upon a woman, / Save in the way of kindness, is a wretch, / Whom 'twere gross flattery to name a coward. *John Tobin.*

The many make the household / But only one the home. *Lowell.*

The moan of doves in immemorial elms, / And murmuring of innumerable bees. *Tennyson.*

The mob of gentlemen who wrote with ease. *Pope.*

15 The mountains look on Marathon, / And Marathon looks on the sea. *Byron.*

The Moving Finger writes; and, having writ, / Moves on : nor all thy Piety nor Wit / Shall lure it back to cancel half a Line, / Nor all thy Tears wash out a Word of it. *Fitzgerald ("Omar Khayyám").*

The noble lord is the Rupert of debate. *Disraeli· of Lord Stanley.*

The noble temptation to see too much in everything. *G. K. Chesterton.*

The noblest answer, unto such, / Is kindly silence when they bawl. *Tennyson.*

20 The only way to get rid of a temptation is to yield to it. *Wilde.*

The outworn rite, the old abuse, / The pious fraud transparent grown. *Whittier.*

The path of a good woman is indeed strewn with flowers; but they rise behind her steps, not before them. "Her feet have touched the meadows, and left the daisies rosy." *Ruskin.*

The patriot's blood's the seed of Freedom's tree. *Campbell.*

The pleasing way is not the right : / He that would conquer Heaven must fight. *Quarles.*

25 The poetry of earth is never dead. *Keats.*

The poets, who on earth have made us heirs / Of truth and pure delight by heavenly lays. *Wordsworth.*

The power of thought—the magic of the Mind. *Byron.*

The proper process of unsinning sin / Is to begin well doing. *Robert Browning.*

The purest and most thoughtful minds are those which love colour the most. *Ruskin.*

The question was, would it bring a blush into the 30 cheek of the young person? *Dickens, of Mr. Podsnap ("Our Mutual Friend").*

The reading which has pleased, will please when repeated ten times. *Horace.*

The remedy is worse than the disease. *Bacon.*

The resolution to avoid an evil is seldom framed till the evil is so far advanced as to make avoidance impossible. *Hardy.*

The rose is fairest when 'tis budding new, / And hope is brightest when it dawns from fears ; / The rose is sweetest washed with morning dew, / And love is loveliest when embalmed in tears. *Scott.*

The sacred rust of twice ten hundred years. *Pope.* 35

The Scripture, in time of disputes, is like an open town in time of war, which serves indifferently the occasions of both parties. *Swift.*

The sea ! The sea ! The open sea ! / The blue, the fresh, the ever free. *B. W. Procter (Barry Cornwall).*

The secret of success in life is known only to those who have not succeeded. *J. Churton Collins.*

The shadow cloaked from head to foot, / Who keeps the keys of all the creeds. *Tennyson.*

The Shadow stayed not, but the splendour stays, / 40 Our brother, till the last of English days. *Swinburne.*

The spacious times of great Elizabeth. *Tennyson.*

The spirit walks of every day deceased ; / And smiles an angel, or a fury frowns. *Young.*

The spot where love's first links were wound, / That ne'er are riven, / Is hallowed down to earth's profound, / And up to Heaven! *Campbell.*

The still sweet fall of music far away. *Campbell.*

The story always old, and always new. *Robert* 45 *Browning.*

The stream is brightest at its spring, / And blood is not like wine. *Whittier.*

The sweet wise death of old men honourable. *Swinburne.*

The sweetest name [Mary] that mortals bear / Were best befitting thee ; / And she to whom it once was given, / Was half of earth and half of heaven. *O. W. Holmes.*

"The time has come," the Walrus said, / "To talk of many things : / Of shoes—and ships—and sealing-wax— / Of cabbages—and kings— / And why the sea is boiling hot— / And whether pigs have wings." *C. L. Dodgson ("Lewis Carroll").*

The true old times are dead, / When every morning 50 brought a noble chance, / And every chance brought out a noble knight. *Tennyson.*

The tumult and the shouting dies, / The captains and the kings depart ; / Still stands thine ancient sacrifice, / A humble and a contrite heart. / Lord God of Hosts, be with us yet, / Lest we forget, lest we forget. *Kipling.*

The unimaginable touch of time. *Wordsworth.*

The vile are only vain ; the great are proud. *Byron.*

The virtue lies / In the struggle, not the prize. *Lord Houghton.*

The vow that binds too strictly snaps itself. *Tennyson.* 55

The wicked are wicked, no doubt, and they go astray and they fall, and they come by their deserts ; but who can tell the mischief which the very virtuous do? *Thackeray.*

The victim o' connubiality. *Dickens ("Pickwick").*

The will to do, the soul to dare. *Scott.*

The woman that cries hush bids kiss : I learnt / So much of her that taught me kissing. *Swinburne.*

The word Papa gives a pretty form to the lips. Papa, potatoes, poultry, prunes and prism are all very good words for the lips ; especially prunes and prism. *Dickens.*

The words she spoke of Mrs. Harris, lambs could not forgive, nor worms forget. *Dickens (Mrs. Gamp).*

The world has no such flower in any land, / And no such pearl in any gulf the sea, / As any babe on any mother's knee. *Swinburne.*

5 The world is a bundle of hay, / Mankind are the asses who pull ; / Each tugs it a different way, / And the greatest of all is John Bull. *Byron.*

The world is so full of a number of things, / I'm sure we should all be as happy as kings. *Stevenson.*

The Youth of a Nation are the trustees of Posterity. *Disraeli.*

The zeal of fools offends at any time, / But, most of all, the zeal of fools in rhyme. *Pope.*

Then felt I like some watcher of the skies / When a new planet swims into his ken ; / Or like stout Cortez when, with eagle eyes, / He stared at the Pacific—and all his men / Looked at each other with a wild surmise— / Silent, upon a peak in Darien. *Keats.*

10 Then love was the pearl of his oyster, / And Venus rose red out of wine. *Swinburne.*

Then none was for a party ; / Then all were for the state ; / Then the great man helped the poor, / And the poor man loved the great. *Macaulay.*

Then to side with Truth is noble when we share her wretched crust, / Ere her cause bring fame and profit, and 'tis prosperous to be just ; / Then it is the brave man chooses, while the coward turns aside, / Doubting in his abject spirit, till his Lord is crucified. *Lowell.*

Then ye returned to your trinkets ; then ye contented your souls / With the flannelled fools at the wicket, or the muddied oafs at the goals. *Kipling.*

There are not many things cheaper than supposing and laughing. *Swift.*

15 There are some meannesses which are too mean even for man—woman, lovely woman alone, can venture to commit them. *Thackeray.*

There are strings in the human heart that had better not be vibrated. *Dickens (Simon Tappertit, in " Barnaby Rudge ").*

There are very few who would not rather be hated than laughed at. *Sydney Smith.*

There, but for the grace of God, goes, etc. Ascribed to *Richard Baxter* (1615-91).

There is a garden in her face, / Where roses and white lilies grow. *Thos. Campion.*

20 There is but one task for all— / For each one life to give. / Who stands if freedom fall ? / Who dies if England live ? *Kipling.*

There is no future pang / Can deal that justice on the self-condemned / He deals on his own soul. *Byron.*

There is no joy comparable to the making of a friend, and the more resistant the material the greater the triumph. Baxter, the carpenter, says that when he works for enjoyment he chooses curly maple. *David Grayson.*

There is no man but speaketh more honestly than he can do or think. *Bacon.*

There is no pleasure like the pain / Of being loved· and loving. *Praed.*

There is no truer truth obtainable / By man, than 25 comes of music. *Robert Browning.*

There is no trusting to appearances. *Sheridan (" School for Scandal ").*

There is nothing in this world constant but inconstancy. *Swift.*

There is nothing makes a man suspect much, more than to know little. *Bacon.*

There is nothing truly valuable which can be purchased without pains and labour. *Addison.*

There is only one religion, though there are a hundred 30 versions of it. *G. Bernard Shaw.*

There is only one way of seeing things rightly, and that is, seeing the whole of them. *Ruskin.*

There may be heaven ; there must be hell ; / Meantime, there is our earth here—well ! *Robert Browning.*

There never yet was human power / Which could evade, if unforgiven, / The patient search and vigil long / Of him who treasures up a wrong. *Byron.*

There shall never be one lost good ! What was shall live as before. *Robert Browning.*

There was a laughing devil in his sneer. *Byron.* 35

There was an Ape in the days that were earlier ; / Centuries passed and his hair became curlier ; / Centuries more gave a thumb to his wrist,—/ Then he was Man,—and a Positivist. *Mortimer Collins.*

There was room in the long free lines of the van to fight for it side by side— / There was beating-room for the heart of a man, in the days when the world was wide. *Henry Lawson.*

There's a further good conceivable / Beyond the utmost earth can realise. *Robert Browning.*

There's life alone in duty done, / And rest alone in striving. *Whittier.*

There's mile-stones on the Dover road. *Dickens.* 40

There's night and day, brother, both sweet things ; sun, moon, and stars, brother, all sweet things ; there's likewise a wind on the heath. Life is very sweet, brother ; who would wish to die ? *Geo. Borrow.*

They enslave their children's children who make compromise with sin. *Lowell.*

They never fail who die / In a great cause. *Byron.*

" They order," said I, " this matter better in France." *Sterne.*

They take the rustic murmur of their bourg / For 45 the great wave that echoes round the world. *Tennyson.*

Think, in this batter'd Caravanserai / Whose Doorways are alternate Night and Day, / How Sultàn after Sultàn with his Pomp Abode his Hour or two, and went his way. *Fitzgerald ("Omar Khayyám").*

Thinking the deed, and not the creed, / Would help us in our utmost need. *Longfellow.*

This / I ever held worse than all certitude, / To know not what the worst ahead might be. *Swinburne.*

This is a London particular . . . a fog, miss. *Dickens (" Bleak House ").*

This is the English, not the Turkish court ; / Not 50 Amurath an Amurath succeeds, / But Harry, Harry. *Henry IV, v. 2.*

This is truth the poet sings, / That a sorrow's crown of sorrow is remembering happier things. *Tennyson.*

This life is all chequered with pleasures and woes. *Moore.*

This proverb flashes through his head, / The many fail : the one succeeds. *Tennyson.*

This the just right of poets ever was, / And will be still, to coin what words they please. *Oldham.*

These oft are stratagems which errors seem, / Nor is it Homer nods, but we that dream. *Pope.*

Those best can bear reproof who merit praise. *Pope.*

5 Those two amusements for all fools of eminence. Politics or Poetry. *Steele.*

Those veiléd nuns, meek violets. *Hood.*

Thou add'st but fuel to my hate. *Scott.*

Thou art long, and lank, and brown, / As is the ribbed sea-sand. *Wordsworth.*

Thou hast conquered, O pale Galilean. *Swinburne.*

10 Thou wert my guide, philosopher, and friend. *Pope.*

Though our works / Find righteous or unrighteous judgment, this / At least is ours, to make them righteous. *Swinburne.*

Though the mills of God grind slowly, yet they grind exceeding small ; / Though with patience He stands waiting, with exactness grinds He all. *Longfellow.*

Though we called your friend from his bed this night, he could not speak for you, / For the race is run by one and one and never by two and two. *Kipling.*

Thought is often bolder than speech. *Disraeli.*

15 Thought is the soul of act. *Robert Browning.*

Thoughts from the tongue that slowly part, / Glance quick as lightning through the heart. *Scott.*

Through all the faultful Past. *Tennyson.*

Time *goes*, you say ? Ah, no ! / Alas, Time stays ; we go. *Austin Dobson.*

Time, the avenger ! *Byron.*

20 'Tis an old lesson ; Time approves it true, / And those who know it best, deplore it most ; / When all is won that all desire to woo, / The paltry prize is hardly worth the cost. *Byron.*

'Tis from high life high characters are drawn ; / A saint in crape is twice a saint in lawn. *Pope.*

'Tis hard to say if greater want of skill / Appear in writing or in judging ill. *Pope.*

'Tis held that sorrow makes us wise. *Tennyson.*

'Tis nothing but a Magic Shadow-show, / Play'd in a Box whose Candle is the Sun, / Round which we Phantom Figures come and go. *Fitzgerald* ("*Omar Khayyám*").

25 'Tis sweet to hear the honest watch-dog's bark / Bay deep-mouthed welcome, as we draw near home ; / 'Tis sweet to know there is an eye will mark / Our coming, and look brighter when we come. *Byron.*

'Tis the last rose of summer / Left blooming alone ; / All her lovely companions / Are faded and gone. *Moore.*

'Tis the pest / Of love that fairest joys give most unrest. *Keats.*

'Tis the taught already that profits by teaching. *Robert Browning.*

To all swift things for swiftness did I sue ; / Clung to the whistling mane of every wind. *Francis Thompson.*

30 To avenge a private, not a public, wrong. *Pope.*

To be conscious that you are ignorant is a great step to knowledge. *Disraeli.*

To be intelligible is to be found out. *Wilde.*

To Cerberus they give a sop, / His triple barking mouth to stop. *Swift.*

To die would be an awfully big adventure ! *Barrie.*

To doubt her fairness were to want an eye, / To 35 doubt her pureness were to want a heart. *Tennyson.*

To every man upon this earth / Death cometh soon or late ; / And how can man die better / Than facing fearful odds, / For the ashes of his fathers, / And the temples of his Gods ? *Macaulay.*

To follow virtue even for virtue's sake. *Pope.*

To love her was a liberal education. *Steele.*

To love one maiden only, cleave to her, / And worship her by years of noble deeds, / Until they won her. *Tennyson.*

To loyal hearts the value of all gifts / Must vary as 40 the giver. *Tennyson.*

To nurse a blind ideal like a girl. *Tennyson.*

To pile up honey upon sugar, and sugar upon honey, to an interminable tedious sweetness. *Lamb.*

To rest, the cushion and soft dean invite, / Who never mentions hell to ears polite. *Pope.*

To reverence the King, as if he were / Their conscience, and their conscience as their King, / To break the heathen, and uphold the Christ, / To ride abroad redressing human wrongs, / To speak no slander, no, nor listen to it, / To honour his own word as if his God's. *Tennyson.*

To set the Cause above renown, / To love the game 45 beyond the prize, / To honour, while you strike him down, / The foe that comes with fearless eyes. *Sir Henry Newbolt.*

To sport with Amaryllis in the shade, / Or with the tangles of Neæra's hair ? *Milton.*

To stretch the octave 'twixt the dream and deed, / Ah, that's the thrill ! *R. le Gallienne.*

To the glory that was Greece, / And the grandeur that was Rome. *Poe.*

To those who walk beside them, great men seem / Mere common earth ; but distance makes them stars. *Massey.*

To win the secret of a weed's plain heart / Reveals 50 some clue to spiritual things. *Lowell.*

Tobacco is the tomb of love. *Disraeli.*

Tradition wears a snowy beard, romance is always young. *Whittier.*

Training is everything. The peach was once a bitter almond ; cauliflower is nothing but cabbage with a college education. *Mark Twain.*

Trust not yourself ; but your defects to know, / Make use of every friend—and every foe. *Pope.*

True friendship's laws are by this rule expressed, / 55 Welcome the coming, speed the parting guest. *Pope.*

True humility, / The highest virtue, mother of them all. *Tennyson.*

True patriots we ; for be it understood, / We left our country for your country's good, / No private views disgraced our generous zeal, / What urged our travels was our country's weal. *George Barrington.*

True wit is nature to advantage dressed, / What oft was thought, but ne'er so well expressed. *Pope.*

Truth ever lovely—since the world began, / The foe of tyrants, and the friend of man. *Campbell.*

Truth is armed / And can defend itself. It must out, 60 madam. *Philip Massinger.*

Truth is eternal, and the son of heaven. *Swift.*

Truth is within ourselves : it takes no rise / From outward things, whate'er you may believe. / There is an inmost centre in us all, / Where truth abides in fulness. *Robert Browning.*

Truth never was indebted to a lie. *Young.*

Truth sits upon the lips of dying men. *Matthew Arnold.*

Truths turn into dogmas the moment they are disputed. *G. K. Chesterton.*

5 Turning, for them who pass, the common dust / Of servile opportunity to gold. *Wordsworth.*

'Twas honest metal and honest wood, in the days of the Outward Bound, / When men were gallant and ships were good—roaming the wide world round. / The gods could envy a leader then when ' Follow me, lads ! ' he cried—/ They faced each other and fought like men in the days when the world was wide. *Henry Lawson.*

Two human loves make one divine. *E. B. Browning.*

Two Voices are there ; one is of the sea, / One of the mountains ; each a mighty Voice, / In both from age to age thou didst rejoice, / They were thy chosen music, Liberty ! *Wordsworth.*

Twy-natured is no nature. *Tennyson.*

U

10 Unto the man of yearning, thought / And aspiration to do aught / Is in itself almost an act. *D. G. Rossetti.*

Upon the great world's altar stairs / That slope through darkness up to God. *Tennyson.*

V

Vex not thou the poet's mind / With thy shallow wit ; / Vex not thou the poet's mind, / For thou can'st not fathom it, / Clear and bright it should be ever, / Flowing like a crystal river, / Bright as light and clear as wind. *Tennyson.*

Vich is your partickler wanity ? Vich wanity do you like the flavour on best ? *Dickens (" Pickwick ").*

Vital spark of heavenly flame ! / Quit, oh, quit this mortal frame. *Pope.*

W

15 War, war is still the cry, " War even to the knife ! " *Byron.*

War's a brain-spattering, windpipe-splitting art, / Unless her cause by right be sanctified. *Byron.*

Was it a vision, or a waking dream ? / Fled is that music :—Do I wake or sleep ? *Keats.*

We all of us live too much in a circle. *Disraeli.*

We are always doing, says he, something for Posterity, but I would fain see Posterity do something for us. *Steele.*

20 We are none of us infallible, not even the youngest. *W. H. Thompson.*

We call it only pretty Fanny's way. *Thos. Parnell.*

We find great things are made of little things, / And little things go lessening, till at last / Comes God behind them. *Robert Browning.*

We must consult Brother Jonathan. *George Washington,* in reference to his secretary, Colonel Jonathan Trumbull.

We shift and bedeck and bedrape us, / Thou art noble and nude and antique ; / Libitina, thy mother, Priapus / Thy father, a Tuscan and Greek. *Swinburne.*

We were the first that ever burst / Into that silent 25 sea. *Coleridge.*

Wealth I ask not, hope nor love, / Nor a friend to know me ; / All I ask, the heaven above, / And the road below me. *Stevenson.*

Wearing all that weight / Of learning lightly like a flower. *Tennyson.*

Wearing the white flower of a blameless life. *Tennyson.*

Well-timed silence hath more eloquence than speech. *Tupper.*

Were death denied, to live would not be life ; / Were 30 death denied, e'en fools would wish to die. *Young.*

What a world of gammon and spinnage it is, though, ain't it ? *Dickens (" David Copperfield ").*

What ardently we wish, we soon believe. *Young.*

What can alone ennoble fight ? / A noble cause. *Campbell.*

What deep wounds ever closed without a scar ? *Byron.*

What does the world, told truth, but lie the more ? 35 *Robert Browning.*

What is a cynic ?—A man who knows the price of everything, and the value of nothing. *Wilde.*

What is prudery ? 'Tis a beldam, / Seen with wit and beauty seldom. *Pope.*

What is the life of man ? Is it not to shift from side to side, from sorrow to sorrow ?—to button up one cause of vexation and unbutton another ? *Sterne.*

What is truth ? said jesting Pilate ; and would not stay for an answer. *Bacon.*

What most we wish, with ease we fancy near. 40 *Young.*

What Reason weaves, by Passion is undone. *Pope.*

What should they know of England who only England know ? *Kipling.*

What, then, is man ? The smallest part of nothing, / Day buries day, month month, and year the year / Our life is but a chain of many deaths. *Young.*

What thin partitions sense from thought divide. *Pope.*

What things have we seen / Done at the Mermaid ! 45 heard words that have been / So nimble, and so full of subtile flame, / As if that everyone from whence they came / Had meant to put his whole wit in a jest, / And had resolved to live a fool the rest / Of his dull life. *Beaumont.*

What woman, however old, has not the bridal-favours and raiment stowed away, and packed in lavender, in the inmost cupboards of her heart ? *Thackeray.*

What youth deemed crystal, age finds out was dew. *Robert Browning.*

What's the earth / With all its art, verse, music, worth—/ Compared with love, found, gained, and kept ? *Robert Browning.*

What's the odds so long as the fire of souls is kindled at the taper o' conwiviality, and the wing of friendship never moults a feather ? *Dickens (Dick Swiveller, in " The Old Curiosity Shop").*

What's time ? Leave Now for dogs and apes ! / Man 50 has Forever. *Robert Browning.*

Whatever creed be taught or land be trod, / Man's conscience is the oracle of God. *Byron.*

Whatever day / Makes man a slave, takes half his worth away. *Pope.*

When a man fell into his anecdotage it was a sign for him to retire from the world. *Disraeli.*

When a man's busy, why leisure / Strikes him as wonderful pleasure ; / 'Faith, and at leisure once is he ? / Straightway he wants to be busy. *Robert Browning.*

When all of Genius which can perish dies. *Byron.*

5 When ingratitude barbs the dart of injury, the wound has double danger in it. *Sheridan* (" *School for Scandal* ").

When late I attempted your pity to move, / Why seemed you so deaf to my prayers ? / Perhaps It was right to dissemble your love, / But—why did you kick me downstairs ? *J. P. Kemble.*

When most the world applauds you, most beware ; / 'Tis often less a blessing, than a snare. / Distrust mankind ; with your own heart confer ; / And dread even there to find a flatterer. *Young.*

When she had passed, it seemed like the ceasing of exquisite music. *Longfellow.*

When the hounds of spring are on winter's traces, / The mother of months in meadow or plain / Fills the shadows and windy places / With lisp of leaves and ripple of rain. *Swinburne.*

10 When the stars pitch the golden tents / Of their high campment on the plains of night. *Francis Thompson.*

Whenever a child says " I don't believe in fairies," there's a little fairy somewhere that falls right down dead. *Barrie.*

Where children are not, heaven is not. *Swinburne.*

Where lives the man that has not tried, / How mirth can into folly glide, / And folly into sin ? *Scott.*

Where London's column, pointing at the skies, / Like a tall bully, lifts the head, and lies. *Pope.*

15 Where the Rudyards cease from Kipling, / And the Haggards ride no more. *J. K. Stephen.*

Where, where was Roderick then ? / One blast upon his bugle horn / Were worth a thousand men. *Scott.*

Where's the coward that would not dare / To fight for such a land ? *Scott.*

Whether the charmer sinner it or saint it ; If folly grow romantic, I must paint it. *Pope.*

Whether the one True Light, / Kindle to Love, or Wrath consume me quite, / One Glimpse of It within the Tavern caught / Better than in the Temple lost outright. *Fitzgerald* (" *Omar Khayyám*").

20 While stands the Coliseum, Rome shall stand ; / When falls the Coliseum, Rome shall fall ; / And when Rome falls—the World. *Byron.*

Who battled for the True, the Just. *Tennyson.*

Who breaks a butterfly upon a wheel ? *Pope.*

Who drives fat oxen should himself be fat. *Dr. Johnson.*

Who first invented work, and bound the free / And holiday-rejoicing spirit down ? *Lamb.*

25 Who hath not owned, with rapture-smitten frame, / The power of grace, the magic of a name ? *Campbell.*

Who hears music, feels his solitude / Peopled at once. *Robert Browning.*

Who is the happy Warrior ? Who is he / That every man in arms should wish to be ? / It is the generous spirit, who, when brought / Among the tasks of real life, hath wrought / Upon the plan that pleased his childish thought : / Whose high endeavours are an inward light / That makes the path before him always bright. *Wordsworth.*

Who keeps one end in view makes all things serve. *Robert Browning.*

Who knows most, doubts not ; entertaining hope / Means recognising fear. *Robert Browning.*

Who last a century can have no flaw ; / I hold that 30 wit a classic, good in law. *Pope.*

Who love too much, hate in the like extreme. *Pope.*

Who makes by force his merit known, / And lives to clutch the golden keys, / To mould a mighty state's decrees, / And shape the whisper of the throne. *Tennyson.*

Who reasons wisely is not therefore wise, / His pride in reasoning, not in acting, lies. *Pope.*

Who saw life steadily, and saw it whole. *Matthew Arnold.*

Who sees with equal eye, as God of all, / A hero 35 perish, or a sparrow fall, / Atoms or systems into ruins hurled, / And now a bubble burst, and now a world. *Pope.*

Who shoots at the midday sun, though he be sure he shall never hit the mark, yet as sure he is he shall shoot higher than he who aims at a bush. *Sir Philip Sidney.*

Who speaks the truth stabs Falsehood to the heart, / And his mere word makes despots tremble more / Than ever Brutus with his dagger could. *Lowell.*

Who swerves from innocence, who makes divorce / Of that serene companion—a good name, / Recovers not his loss ; but walks with shame, / With doubt, with fear, and haply with remorse. *Wordsworth.*

Whose life was like the violet sweet, / As climbing jasmine pure. *Wordsworth.*

Whose yesterdays look backward with a smile. 40 *Young.*

Why so pale and wan, fond lover ? / Prithee, why so pale ? *Suckling.*

Wide and sweet and glorious as compassion. *Swinburne.*

Wines that, Heaven knows when, / Had sucked the fire of some forgotten sun, / And kept it through a hundred years of gloom. *Tennyson.*

Wise men may think, what hardly fools would say. *Swinburne.*

Wit talks most, when least she has to say. *Young.* 45

Wit that can creep, and pride that licks the dust. *Pope.*

Wit's whetstone, Want, there made us quickly learn. *John Taylor.*

With a little hoard of maxims preaching down a daughter's heart. *Tennyson.*

With a smile on her lips and a tear in her eye. *Scott.*

With affection beaming in one eye, and calculation 50 out of the other. *Dickens.*

With love that scorns the lapse of time, / And ties that stretch beyond the deep. *Campbell.*

With prudes for proctors, dowagers for deans, / And sweet girl-graduates in their golden hair. *Tennyson.*

With this for motto, Rather use than fame
Tennyson.

With women the heart argues, not the mind. *Matthew Arnold.*

Without the smile from partial beauty won, / Oh ! what were man ?—a world without a sun. *Campbell.*

Woe to the Crown that doth the Cowl obey. *Wordsworth.*

5 Words are, of course, the most powerful drug used by mankind. *Kipling* (in a speech).

Words are the tokens current and accepted for conceits, as moneys are for values. *Bacon.*

Would you have your songs endure ? / Build on the human heart. *Robert Browning.*

Write me as one that loves his fellow men. *Leigh Hunt.*

Wrong and right / Are twain for ever : nor, though night kiss day, / Shall right kiss wrong and die not. *Swinburne.*

Y

10 Ye are better than all the ballads / That ever were sung or said ; / For ye are living poems, / And all the rest are dead. *Longfellow*, of children.

Yet holds the eel of science by the tail. *Pope.*

Yet what is all that fires a hero's scorn / Of death ? —the hope to live in hearts unborn. *Campbell.*

Yet what is / Death, so it be glorious ? 'Tis a sunset. *Byron.*

You are as welcome as the flowers in May. *Charles Macklin.*

You are not like Cerberus, three gentlemen at once, 15 are you ? *Sheridan* (" *The Rivals* ").

You find people ready enough to do the Samaritan, without the oil and the twopence. *Sydney Smith.*

You have hit the nail on the head. *Rabelais.*

You may break, you may shatter the vase if you will, / But the scent of the roses will hang round it still. *Moore.*

You may either win your peace or buy it : win it, by resistance to evil ; buy it, by compromise with evil. *Ruskin.*

" You must not tell us what the soldier, or any other 20 man, said, sir," interposed the judge ; " it's not evidence." *Dickens* (" *Pickwick Papers* ").

You shall see them on a beautiful quarto page, where a neat rivulet of text shall meander through a meadow of margin. *Sheridan.*

You tell me Doubt is devil-born. *Tennyson.*

Your new-caught, sullen peoples, / Half devil and half child. *Kipling.*

You're my friend— / What a thing friendship is, world without end ! *Robert Browning.*

Youth once gone is gone : / Deeds, let escape, are 25 never to be done. *Robert Browning..*

INDEX

** *The first number refers to the page, the second to the number of the quotation on the page*

A

Absolved, half, who has confessed, 6, 41
Admiralty, if blood be the price of, 8, 19
Adventures, to the adventurous, 14, 52
Africa, while Jove's planet rises over, 7, 6
Age, iron, 4, 10 ; without a name, 11, 50
Ages, heir of all che, 8, 12 ; of worldly weather, 12, 20
Agreeable, in most men's power to be, 5, 20
Agreement, danger of, 1, 46
Aim, a noble, 1, 27 ; makes great the life, 14 22
Alexandrine, a needless, 1, 26
Allegory, headstrong as an, 3, 12
Altar stairs, great world's, 18, 11
Amaryllis, to sport with, 17, 46
Ambition, from blest abodes, 2, 19
Amen, like the sound of a great, 7, 39
Amurath, an Amurath succeeds, 16, 50
Ancestors, each his own tree of, 4, 53
Anecdotage, when a man fell into, 19, 2
Angels, with us unawares, 8, 47
Anger, makes dull men witty, 3, 10 ; honest spirit flieth with, 4, 43
Angling, for lovers of virtue, 2, 11
Answer, the noblest, 15, 19
Ape, and tiger die, 10, 27 ; in the days that were earlier, 16, 36
Apollo, strange song, 9, 41
Appearances, no trusting to, 16, 26
Arabia, breathing from box, 2, 29
Arabs, tents folded like, 2, 55
Arboreal, probably, 4, 53
Art, " Clever, but is it ? " 4, 1 ; to blot, 5, 3 ; surprise an essential ingredient of, 14, 4
Artistry, haunting curse of, 8, 50
Astræa, driven from earth, 4, 10
Audacity, what we require is, 4, 17
Authority, and dying king, 3, 21
Authors, fellows in foolscap uniform, 11, 52

B

Babe, a, in a house, 1, 1 ; on any mother's knee, 16, 4
Babylon, London a modern, 9, 46
Back, one who never turned his, 12, 8 ; rascal in hollow of, 12, 44
Bar, only grains of sand, 14, 37
Bards, sublime, 14, 27
Barkis is willin', 3, 22
Ball, no Question makes, 14, 26
Battle, won, more melancholy, 11, 8
Beaker, full of the warm South, 11, 17
Beast, working out the, 10, 27
Beauty, truth, 3, 26 ; silken bond of, 3, 27 ; life was, 8, 10 ; if you get simple, 8, 26 ; fatal gift of, 9, 17 ; smile won from, 20, 3
Bed, heaven upon earth, 11, 36
Bees, little almsmen of spring-bowers, 5, 2
Beggar, in the grave, 5, 49 ; that is dumb, 13, 19
Bell, dinner, tocsin of the soul, 14, 12
Bells, ring out, wild, 12, 53
Betsy Prig and Mrs. Harris, 3, 39

Beware, when most the world applauds, 19, 7
Bird, weight can break infant tree, 3, 46
Birds, what are the voices of, 5, 48
Blindness, firstborn of success, 3, 32
Blood, price of admiralty, 8, 19 ; patriot's, 15, 23; not like wine, 15, 46
Blot, the art to, 5, 3
Blue, grappling in the central, 7, 4
Blunder, worse than a crime, 9, 11
Blush, into the cheek of the young person, 15, 30
Body, a dem'd damp, 1, 8
Books, men of higher stature, 3, 36 ; receive their chief value, 3, 37 ; things in books' clothing, 3, 38 ; of the library of God, 5, 21 ; of real men, 7, 29 ; I mean your borrowers of, 8, 1 ; belong to sunshine, 10, 8 ; a want of, 12, 23
Bores and Bored, two mighty tribes, 13, 33
Bourg, rustic murmur of their, 16, 45
Bow, as cord is to, 3, 19
Boy's will, a, 1, 2
Brave man, a, seven times king, 1, 3
Bravery, never out of fashion, 3, 40
Bread, Loaf of, beneath the Bough, 7, 7
Britannia, needs no bulwark, 3, 43
Broad-based, upon people's will, 3, 44
Brother Jonathan, we must consult, 18, 23
Bubbles, beaded, winking at the brim, 11, 17
Bugle, set the wild echoes flying, 3, 33 ; blow out, over the rich Dead, 3, 34
Burden, the White Man's, 14, 9
Butchered, to make a Roman holiday, 6, 50
Butterfly, break upon a wheel, 19, 22
Business, curse him who first designed, 4, 33
Busy, when a man's, 19, 3

C

Cabbages, and kings, 15, 49
Cæsar, one, lives, 11, 49
Caledonia, stern and wild, 11, 15
Cane, nice conduct of a clouded, 13, 25
Caravan, the innumerable, 13, 28
Caravanserai, in this batter'd, 16, 46
Cares, infesting day, 2, 55
Casements, magic, 10, 2
Castle, a, girt with sorrow, 1, 4
Catch-words, man lives by, 10, 3
Catholic humanity, and creed and test, 4, 30
Cauliflower, cabbage with a college education, 17, 53
Cause, the first Almighty, 14, 50 ; never fail who die in a great, 16, 43 ; above renown, 17, 45 ; noble, ennobles fight, 18, 33
Century, no flaw who last a, 19, 30
Cerberus, give a sop to, 17, 33 ; three gentlemen at once, 20, 15
Ceremony, doffed her pride, 12, 34
Chains, or conquest, 4, 18
Chance, skirts of happy, 2, 39 ; dark idolater of, 12, 1
Change, lays not hand on truth, 4, 19 ; pleases a woman's mind, 11, 34

Charity, begins at home. 12, 15
Charm, he that can draw a, 6, 45 ; in a woman, 8, 6
Charmer, whether sinner it or saint it, 19, 18
Charms, fly at mere touch of cold philosophy, 4, 45
Child, given a treat or home, 2, 41
Children, know friend and foe, 4, 20 ; do you hear the, weeping ? 4, 47 ; born of thee, 14, 32 ; enslave their children's, 16, 42 ; where not, heaven is not, 19, 12 ; living poems, 20, 10
Choosing, I was of Christ's, 5, 35
Christ, ring in the, 12, 50
Christian, scratch the, 13, 7
Christmas, broached mightiest ale, 4, 55
Circle, live too much in a, 18, 18
Circumstance, blows of, 2, 39 ; dance of plastic, 6, 27 ; the very slave of, 7, 37
Circumstantial evidence, 13, 35
Cities, silent, of the dead, 5, 55
Clergymen, one of three sexes, 3, 18
Clime, soft as her, 7, 5
Coal, and prehistoric toads, 9, 7
Code, the Christless, 14, 33
Codlin, the friend, 4, 22
Cogitation, in cogibundity of, 7, 9
Coins, good and bad, like to, 5, 31 ; stamped with the image of the king, 5, 31
Colour, purest minds those which love, 15, 29
Colours, agreeing in dark, 2, 4 ; nailed to the mast, 13, 47
Company, few qualified to shine in, 5, 20
Compassion, sues for no, 6, 43 ; wide and sweet and glorious as, 19, 42
Compromise, a god of old, 9, 1
Confessed, half absolved who has, 6, 41
Conjecture, dye a darker hue, 2, 36
Connubiality, victim o', 15, 57
Conscience, apart from gallantry and politics, 4, 28 ; accountable to, 9, 51 ; of each bosom, 14, 53 ; the oracle of God, 18, 51
Conversation, flashes of silence in, 10, 1
Cool, and quite English, 4, 29
Cord, silver, be loosed, 12, 11
Corn, whoever could make two ears to grow, 6, 23
Corsair's, name, left a, 6, 37
Cortez, like stout, 16, 9
Council, great in the, 6, 17
Countenance, damned disinheriting, 2, 25
Country, he who loves not his, 6, 56 ; our, right or wrong, 12, 16 ; for your country's good, 17, 57
Courage, in trouble, 9, 34
Courted, and jilted, 3, 29
Courtesy, wins woman as well as valour, 5, 29
Cowl, crown and, 20, 4
Creed, vanishes before catholic humanity, 4, 30 ; deed, not the, 16, 47
Creeds, life of truth proceeds from the rot of, 5, 57 ; keys of all the, 15, 39
Crime, debt mother of, 4, 42 ; worse than a, 9, 11 ; of being a young man, 14, 24
Crimes, linked with a thousand, 6, 37
Criticism, rod of, wreathed with roses, 7, 2
Critics, trust in, 3, 17
Crooked, strive to set straight, 4, 50
Crosses, a-many have proved me, 4, 31
Crowd, an usurping, 14, 20
Crown, a, and justice, 1, 6 ; that obeys the Cowl, 20, 4
Crystal, what youth deemed, 18, 47
Cup, fill the, 4, 24 ; drowned Honour in a shallow, 6, 25 ; have drunk their, 9, 45
Cupid, rentroll, of our rainy isles, 7, 8
Curled, minion, 4, 32
Custom, that unwritten law, 4, 34
Cynic, what is a, 18, 36
Cynicism, worse than the devil, 7, 43

D

Dance, of plastic circumstance, 6, 27 ; light is the, 9, 37
Dangers, breed fears, 4, 35
Dark, colours agree in, 2, 4
Daughter, a, of the gods, 1, 7
Day, tender grace of dead, 4. 3 ; brings its petty dust, 4, 52 ; each, a life ; 4, 54 ; spirit walks of every, 15, 42

Dead, the rich, 3, 34 ; breathes of an ampler day, 4, 9 silent cities of the, 5, 55 ; men rise up never, 5, 58 ; grassy barrows of the happier, 11, 33
Death, but one, 1, 21 ; worse things waiting than, 3 3, 20 ; kisses remembered after, 4, 36 ; aims at fairer marks, 4, 37 ; but entombs the body, 4, 38 ; king of terrors, 4, 39 ; knew all his shapes, 4, 40 ; loves a shining mark, 4, 41 ; half in love with easeful, 5, 42 ; added a new terror to, 6, 26 ; where is thy sting ? 9, 25 ; ere thou has slain another, 13, 18 ; silent halls of, 13, 28 ; that fatal sergeant, 14, 13 ; of old men honourable, 15, 47 ; cometh soon or late, 17, 36 ; denied, fools would wish to die, 18, 30 ; hero's scorn of, 20, 12 ; 'tis a sunset, 20, 13
Debt, prolific mother of folly and crime, 4, 42
Deceit, skulking with hatred, 4, 43
December, roses in, 3, 17
Deed, better undone than regretted, 3, 31 ; thinking the, 16, 47 ; octave 'twixt dream and, 17, 47
Deeds, done by mutual confidence and aid, 4, 14 ; done for fellowship's sake, 5, 19 ; deathless, 11, 3 ; let escape, never to be done, 20, 25
Delight, that consumes desire, 14, 39
Despair, twin-born of devotion, 4, 44 ; breathes in farewell, 5, 15
Devil, whoops as of old, 4, 1 ; half, half child, 20, 23
Devotion, despair twin-born of, 4, 44
Dew, rained a ghastly, 7, 4
Die, without or this or that, 4, 7 ; we live, if we, 5, 37 ; if I should, 8, 21 ; an awfully big adventure, 17, 34
Dies, greatly lives who greatly, 14, 15
Disbelief, and belief, 10, 51
Disputing, itch of, 15, 4
Dog, something better than his, 7, 1 ; hunts in dreams, 9, 38
Dogs, lame, helping over stiles, 4, 46
Dolores, O sanguine and subtle, 3, 55
Door, barred with gold, 5, 4
Doubt, is devil-born, 20, 22
Dream, a, within a dream, 2, 13 ; doing, not dreaming, 3, 23 ; that I forget, 5, 52
Dreamers, fault of, 9, 10
Dreams, I have only my, 3, 50 ; dreamer of, 4, 50 ; like a dog, he hunts in, 9, 38 ; with blood and iron, not with, 11, 6
Dryden, copious, 5, 3
Dunce, confounding the wise, 3, 14
Dust, into dust, 4, 51 ; each day brings its petty, 4, 52 ; that rises up, 5, 23
Duty, gold worthless when given from sense of, 6, 29 ; found that life was, 8, 10 ; a path all may tread, 9, 22

E

Earth, in tune, 3, 6 ; ends of the, 4, 4 ; he that loves but half of, 6, 46 ; homely smell of, 11, 26 ; broken arcs on the, 11, 47 ; scarce of, 13, 3 ; the listening, 13, 40 ; poetry of, 15, 25 ; half of, 15, 48 ; what, compared with love, 18, 48
Ease, in full-throated, 14, 18 ; gentlemen who wrote with, 15, 14
East, wise men came from the, 8, 13 ; a soul goes out on the East wind, 10, 38 ; the gorgeous, 11, 48
Elizabeth, no scandal about Queen, 10, 48 ; spacious times of great, 15, 41
Elms, immemorial, 15, 13
Eloquence, a full-celled honeycomb of, 1, 10
Emulation, in the learned or brave, 4, 57
End, justifies the means, 14, 45 ; one, in view, 19, 28
Endow, a college or a cat, 4, 7
England, stand against the world, 2, 7 ; oaken-hearted mood, 2, 34 ; merry England, 4, 55 ; here and here did England help me, 7, 6 ; that is for ever, 8, 21 ; a fen of stagnant waters, 10, 17 ; keep but faith with, 10, 43 ; now that April's there ! 11, 42 ; Coastwise Lights of, 14, 6 ; who dies if England live ? 16, 20 ; what should they know of, 18, 42
English, cool and quite, 4, 29 ; flag was flown, 10, 40
Envy, ignoble mind a slave to, 4, 57 ; a coal hissing hot from Hell, 4, 58
Epitaph, believe an, 3, 17
Equator, speak disrespectfully of the, 10, 45

Error, a hardy plant, 5, 1
Evidence, what the soldier said not, 20, 20
Evil, resolution to avoid an, 15, 33
Example, annoyance of a good, 5, 22
Examples, draw when precept fails, 5, 6
Excuse, a lie guarded, 2, 22
Experience, name given to mistakes, 5, 7 ; the dirty
　　nurse, 14, 43
Eye, a multiplying, 2, 14 ; unforgiving, 2, 25 ; traitor
　　of the heart, 5, 38 ; he had but one, 6, 30 ; harvest
　　of a quiet, 14, 60 ; will mark our coming, 17, 25 ;
　　sees, as God, with equal, 19, 35 ; affection beaming
　　in one, 19, 50
Eyes, my mother came into my, 2, 30 ; popular
　　prejudice runs in favour of two, 6, 30 ; that would
　　not look on me, 8, 2 ; tired eyelids upon tired,
　　10, 30 ; sang tears into his, 13, 14 ; dark lustre of
　　thine, 14, 42 ; light in woman's, 15, 7

F

Face, tablet of unutterable thoughts, 7, 10 ; look on
　　her, 8, 25 ; trace of youthful memory, 8, 35 ; a garden
　　in her, 16, 19
Faces, sea of upturned, 2, 20 ; the old familiar, 7, 45
Fail, who die in a great cause never, 16, 43 ; many,
　　17, 1
Fairness, to doubt her, 17, 35
Fairies, I don't believe in, 19, 11
Fairy lands forlorn, 10, 2
Faith, undisproved, 1, 15 ; mightier than time, 4, 6 ;
　　half our daylight, a fable, 6, 22 ; unfaithful, 7, 12 ;
　　of many made for one, 14, 46
Falling out, blessings on, 2, 33
False, things may be imagined, 5, 8
Falsehood, shoots up on every soil, 5, 9 ; flies, and
　　truth comes limping after it, 5, 10
Falsehoods, blunt truths more mischievous, 3, 35 ;
　　truths of long ago, 5, 11
Fame, impatient of extremes, decays, 5, 12 ; sub-
　　stantial happiness to each, 5, 13 ; like a river, 5, 14 ;
　　fortune even in, 12, 47
Fanatics, earth's, make heaven's saints, 7, 38
Far, so near and yet so, 6, 44
Farewell, that fatal word, 5, 15
Fashion, arbiter and rule of right, 5, 16
Fate, and Love, 1, 47 ; architects of, 2, 3, man,
　　master of his, 5, 40 ; master of my, 7, 36
Fathers, considered fools, 2, 52 ; ashes of his, 17, 36
Fault, faultless to a, 5, 17 ; who hath no fault is all,
　　6, 32 ; it is easy to find, 9, 7
Faultless, to a fault, 5, 17
Faults, brought their excuses with them, 10, 25
Fear, hath a hundred eyes, 5, 18 ; no remedy for,
　　7, 46 ; a shadow and a, 11, 30 : Shame's friend,
　　15, 6
Fears, more dangers bring, 4, 35
Feast, good until reckoning, 14, 47
Feather, dropped from an angel's wing, 14, 48
Feelings, less of earth than heaven, 13, 37
Fellowship, is heaven, 5, 19
Female, of species more deadly, 14, 49
Feud, of rich and poor, 12, 51
Feuds, marring lives, 2, 46
Field, who sows a, 6, 3 ; glorious in the, 6, 17　toss'd
　　Thee down into the, 14, 26
Fighter, I was ever a, 8, 15
Fill, the can and cup, 5, 23
Finger, Moving, writes, 15, 16
Fires, forbidden, 9, 53
Fixed, nothing that mortals see or know, 11, 11
Flag, a moth-eaten rag, 1, 24 ; English, was flown,
　　10, 40
Flanders fields, in, 8, 36
Flattery, cream cheese of chalk, 5, 26
Flea, hath smaller fleas, 13, 29
Fleet Street ;Dr. Johnson and, 2, 47
Flower, tip-tilted like petal of, 2, 44 ; in the crannied
　　wall, 5, 27 ; who trains a, 6 ,3 ; that once has blown,
　　12, 7 ; white, of a blameless life, 18, 28
Flowers, are lovely, 5, 28 ; most can raise the, 10, 24 ;
　　stars in earth's firmament, 13, 41 ; as in May,
　　20, 14
Fly, on the chariot wheel, 9, 15
Foemen, worthy of their steel, 12, 48

Fog, a London particular, 16, 49
Folly, debt mother of, 4, 42 ; he who does not possess
　　a dram of, 6, 55 ; bubble joy in cup of, 8, 37
　　mirth glide into, 19, 13 ; if, grow romantic, 19, 18
Fool, before becoming wise, 8, 23
Fools, admire, men of sense approve, 5, 30 ; I also
　　had my hour, 5, 51 ; give their gold, 6, 3 ; hated
　　by, 6, 24 ; men may live, 10, 11 ; zeal of, 16, 8 ;
　　flannelled, 16, 13 ; and wise men, 19, 44
Force, blind wild beast of, 14, 30
Forget, because we must, 4, 52 ; that I remember,
　　5, 52 ; lest we, 15, 51
Forgiving, sweetness of, 9, 56
Fortune, beneath one's hat, 2, 31 ; bubbles of, 6, 3 ;
　　even in fame, 12, 47
Fortunes, tumbling into men's laps, 5, 53
Four-square, to all the winds that blew, 11, 16
Frailty, knows not how to wink at, 6, 36
France, they order this matter better in, 16, 44
Frank, and explicit, the right line to take, 5, 54
Fraud, and falsehood, product of all climes, 5, 9 ;
　　pious, 15, 21
Freedom, broadening down, 1, 13 ; bought by our
　　fathers, 2, 15 ; hallows with her tread, 5, 55 ; hand
　　in hand with labour, 5, 56 ; shrieked—as Kosciusko
　　fell ! 7, 20 ; who stands if it fall ? 16, 20
Friend, making of a, 16, 22 ; guide, philosopher and,
　　17, 10 ; make use of every, 17, 54
Friendship, is a sheltering tree, 5, 28 ; making of,
　　16, 22 ; true laws of, 17, 55 ; wing of, 18, 49 ; what
　　a thing it is, 20, 24
Frivolity, chatter of irresponsible, 14, 58
Fury, the blind, 4, 26

G

Galilean, O pale, 17, 9
Game, beyond the prize, 17, 45
Gammon and spinnage, what a world of, 18, 31
Garden, spacious but weedy, 1, 35 ; by the Water
　　blows, 3, 54 ; God Almighty first planted a, 6, 5
Gazelle, I never nursed a dear, 11, 38
Gehenna, down to, 4, 49
Gem, many a thing cast to the ground becomes a, 7, 27,
Genius, somewhat of the infantine, 6, 1 ; and industry,
　　8, 27 ; a certain blunderer called, 9, 9 ; when all
　　that can perish, 19, 4
Gentleman, a, finished, 1, 9 ; grand old name of,
　　3, 4 ; stainless, 11, 24
Gentleness, some power in, 10, 16
Getting on, the Gospel of, 1, 11
Gift, bare without the giver, 11, 5
Gifts, value must vary as the giver, 17, 40
Give, not what we, 11, 5
Girl-graduates, sweet, 19, 52
Glances, stolen, 13, 46
Glass, turn down empty, 2, 43
Glory, where, awaits thee, 6, 4
God, puppets of, 2, 9 ; to take in, 2, 26 ; bless us,
　　2, 50 ; whispers in the ear, 3, 49 ; this thing is,
　　4, 5 ; books of the library of, 5, 21 ; God's knight,
　　5, 35 ; first planted a garden, 6, 5 ; bless all our
　　gains, 6, 7 ; needeth not proud work of human
　　skill, 6, 8 ; the best Poet, 6, 9 ; His gifts put man's
　　best dreams to shame, 6, 10 ; true priest of,
　　always free, 6, 11 ; grace given of, 6, 15 ; true to,
　　as to man, 6, 42 ; whoso turns, as I, to, 7, 6 ; account-
　　able alone to, 9, 51 ; there, but for the grace of,
　　16, 18 ; mills of, 17, 12 ; comes behind them,
　　18. 22 ; conscience, the oracle of, 18, 51
God-like, foot there trod, 5, 46
Goddess, moves a, 13, 13
Gods, temples of his, 17, 36
Gold, every door barred with, 5, 4 ; bright and yellow,
　　hard and cold, 6, 12 ; worthless when given from
　　sense of duty, 6, 29
Golden prime of good Haroun Alraschid, 5, 39
Good, all men's, 2, 1 ; how happy are the, 14, 16 ;
　　shall never be one lost, 16, 34 ; a further, con-
　　ceivable, 16, 38
Good-breeding, blossom of good-sense, 6, 13
Goose, cry bo to a, 4, 16
Gorgonised, with a stony British stare, 6, 14
Grace, given of God, 6, 15 ; power of, 19, 25
Grass, whoever could make two blades to grow, 6, 28

Grave, who's a prince or beggar in the, 5, 49 ; where is thy victory ? 9, 25
Great, necessity, tyrant conscience of, 10, 36 ; among the, 13, 27 ; men, distance makes them stars, 17, 49 ; things made of little things, 18, 22
Greatness, some far-off touch of, 8, 41 ; where it lies, 9, 49 ; minds conscious of, 10, 18
Greece, isles of, 15, 3 ; glory that was, 17, 48
Grief, without community, 11, 31
Guest, welcome the coming, 5, 36 ; 17, 55
Guide, philosopher and friend, 17, 10
Guinea, jingling of the, 4, 2

H

Habit, fixed as a, 5, 25 ; not to be flung out, but coaxed, 6, 20 ; rules the unreflecting herd, 6, 21
Habits, other people's, 11, 13
Haggards, ride no more, 19, 15
Half, one, never believed, 11, 51
Hands, washing with invisible soap, 3, 1
Happiness, born a twin, 2, 16
Happy, truly great only, 14, 57
Harmonies, dissonant chords beget divinest, 12, 49
Harmony, queen of, 12, 42
Haroun Alraschid, golden prime of good, 5, 39
Hate, with gall of gentle souls, 2, 40 ; fools to, 6, 24 ; preferable to laughter, 16, 17 ; add'st but fuel to my, 17, 7
Hated, rather be, than laughed at, 16, 17
Hatred, frown of, 3, 8 ; deceit and treachery skulk with, 4, 43
Haunted, beneath a waning moon, 1, 34 ; the place is, 11, 30
Health, grant me but, 6, 16 ; as a fair goddess, 6, 16 ; a blessing money cannot buy, 9, 50 ; of the people, 15, 1
Heart, a, at leisure, 1, 12 ; Nature's, beats strong, 3, 53 ; eye traitor of the, 5, 38 ; on her lips, 7, 1 ; wax to receive, 7, 11 ; no herb to heal a coward's, 7, 46 ; though at the root, 8, 18 ; viewless founts are fed, 8, 35 ; in hawthorn time, 8, 38 ; in linden time, 8, 39 ; treads on heart, 9, 35 ; judging by thine own, 9, 47 ; nor can belief touch his, 10, 51 ; previous music of the, 11, 44 ; strings in the human, 16, 16 ; inmost cupboards of, 18, 46
Hearts, a group of wise, 1, 16 ; mockery the fume of little, 6, 39
Heath, my foot is on my native, 10, 31
Heathen, no blinkard, 5, 35
Heaven, one, 1, 21 ; in the nurseries of, 9, 48 ; mercy the attribute of, 10, 14 ; doth with all its splendours lie, 11, 2 ; perfect round in the, 11, 47 ; pale populace of, 12, 27 ; he that would conquer, 15, 24 ; half of, 15, 48 ; there may be, 16, 32 ; above, 18, 26
Heavens, filled with shouting, 7, 4
Hell, one, 1, 21 ; there must be, 16, 32 ; never mentions to ears polite, 17, 43
Henpecked, lords of ladies intellectual, 3, 52
Herd, habit rules the unreflecting, 6, 21
Heresy, of doctrine, 3, 30
Heroes, belief in heroic makes, 11, 14
History, a pageant, not a philosophy, 7, 15
Homer, viewed by learned commentators, 3, 13 his rule the best, 5, 36 ; nods, 17, 3
Honest spirit flieth with anger, 4, 43
Honey, pile up, upon sugar, 17, 42
Honour, with no rust, 1, 40 ; hurt that honour feels, 4, 2 ; drowned in a shallow Cup, 6, 25 ; the fountain of, 6, 34 ; rooted in dishonour stood, 7, 12 ; rising from no condition, 7, 17 ; come back as a king, 7, 18 ; a baby's rattle, 7, 19
Hope, fled withering, 3, 8 ; the dream of those that wake, 5, 33 ; shall brighten days to come, 5, 34 ; a good breakfast, 7, 21 ; and fear, 7, 22 ; brightest, 15, 34 ; to live in hearts unborn, 20, 12
Horn, that dread, 11, 18 ; wreathéd, 12, 12 ; one blast upon, 19, 16
Horse, a little dearer than his, 7, 1
Hour, I also had my, 5, 51 ; from childhood's, 11, 38 ; one crowded, 11, 50 ; abode his Hour or two, 16, 46
Humbug, the Ogre, 1, 48
Humility, true, highest virtue, 17, 56

24

Humour, spoiled by affectation, 7, 33
Hyacinth, the Garden wears, 8, 11

Ideal, nurse a blind, 17, 41
Ignorance, consciousness of, great step to knowledge, 17, 31
Ilion, like a mist rose into towers, 9, 41
Immortality, longing after, 9, 12
Impeachment, I own the soft, 8, 5
Incomplete, curse of artistry, 8, 50
Inconstancy, nothing constant but, 16, 27
Infallible, none of us, 18, 20
Infection, seen by the infected, 2, 8
Information, I only ask for, 8, 4
Ingratitude, barbs the dart of injury, 19, 5
Injuries, kept in mind, 9, 21
Intelligible, to be, to be found out, 17, 32

J

Jilted, courted and, 3, 29
John Bull, greatest of all is, 16, 5
Johnson, Dr., a walk down Fleet Street, 2, 47
Joke, a surgical operation, 9, 13
Joy, to win, 2, 16
Joys, that came down shower-like, 5, 28
June, leafy month of, 1, 28 ; a day in, 3, 6 ; ice in 3, 17 ; knee-deep in, 14, 11

K

Keys, to clutch the golden, 19, 12
Kick me downstairs, 19, 6
Kindness, disagrees with proud stomachs, 9, 20 ; easily forgotten, 9, 21 ; in another's trouble, 9, 34
King, follow the, 9, 42 ; to reverence the, 17, 44
Kings, kept in awe by custom, 4, 34 ; of cabbages and, 15, 49 ; captains and the, 15, 51
Kiss, a, too long, 2, 2 ; with tears, 2, 33 ; forgotten kisses, 2, 54 ; with one long, 11, 19
Kisses, remembered after death, 4, 36
Knife, war to the, 18, 15
Knight, no carpet, 7, 14
Knowledge, bought in the market, 6, 15 ; humble because of, 7, 32 ; a steep few may climb, 9, 27 ; extensive and peculiar, 10, 28 ; desire of, 14, 40 ; and doubt, 19, 29

L

Labour, Freedom, hand in hand with, 5, 56
Ladies, intellectual, 3, 52
Lady, of Pain, 3, 55 ; of my delight, 13, 15
Land, a, of settled government, 1, 13 ; would not dare to fight for, 19, 17
Last, no, nor first, 2, 9
Laughing, not many things cheaper, 16, 14
Learning, a progeny of, 1, 31 ; wearing that weight of, 18, 27
Letters, elixir of love, 9, 55
Liberty, best beloved of men, 2, 32 ; or death, 4, 18 ; he that roars for, 6, 48 ; and Union, inseparable, 9, 31 ; thy chosen music, 18, 8
Libitina, thy mother, 18, 24
Lie, a fast traveller, 1, 14 ; a living, 5, 32 ; that sinketh in, 9, 8 ; difference between cat and, 12, 4 before the Speaker, 13, 38
Lies, the cruellest, 14, 36
Life, likeness of, 1, 17 ; of sweet small works, 1, 19 ; but one, 1, 21 ; never the same again, 2, 2 ; one grand sweet song, 3, 23 ; thin-spun, 4, 26 ; entombs the soul, 4, 38 ; no, lives for ever, 5, 58 ; a watch or a vision, 7, 13 ; was Beauty, 8, 10
Life, but a froward child, 9, 32 ; like a cup of tea, 9, 33 ; mostly froth and bubble, 9, 34 ; treads on life, 9, 35 ; as the wind is, so is mortal, 9, 44 ; not a kindlier or sweeter, 10, 52 ; crowded hour of glorious, 11, 50 ; flies, 12, 7 ; which answers life's great end, 14, 14 ; secret of succession, 15, 38 ; one, to give, 16, 20 ; alone in duty done, 16, 39 ; all chequered with pleasures and woes, 16, 52 ; of man, 18, 38 ; a chain of many deaths, 18, 43 ; saw it steadily, 19, 34 ; like the violet, 19, 39

Light, stumbling for scant, 5, 35 ; which beats upon a throne, 8, 44 ; in woman's eyes, 15, 7 ; never was on sea or land, 15, 8

Linked, with one virtue and a thousand crimes, 6, 37

Lion, beard in his den, 2, 35 ; has left a whelp, 5, 44

Lip, I ne'er saw nectar on a, 8, 2

Lips, persuasion hung upon his, 12, 24 ; papa gives a pretty form to the, 16, 2 ; a smile on her, 19, 49

Little, more and how much it is ! 11, 41 ; to know, makes a man suspect much, 16, 28

Live, we die not, if we, 5, 37

Lives, free, and lips, 2, 32 ; men's little, 2, 46 ; that man greatly, 14, 15

Living, too much love of, 5, 58

Loaf of Bread beneath the Bough, 7, 7

Logic, impassioned, 8, 32

London, a modern Babylon, 9, 46 ; Mr. Weller's knowledge of, 10, 28 ; course of, 19, 14

Loom, swift shuttles of an Empire's, 14, 6

Lord, honeying at whisper of a, 12, 54

Losses, may God bless all our, 6, 7

Lothario, gallant, gay, 9, 4

Lotos, never closes, 10, 38

Love, and Fate, 1, 47 ; founded on subjects', 4, 56 ; is flower-like, 5, 28 ; once gone, never returns, 5, 43 ; never melt with, 5, 47 ; great when in sin and fear, 6, 18 ; a touch of earth, 6, 32 ; loves but half of earth, 6, 46 ; ambassador of loss, 7, 41 ; I know not what is true, 7, 48 ; vision in the night, 7, 49 ; most serious thing in the world, 8, 14 ; a young man's fancy turns to, 8, 46 ; a crime to love too well, 8, 53 ; and Grief, 9, 27 ; no pleasure when no secret, 9, 52 ; about your name, 9, 54 ; marrow of friendship, 9, 55 ; deathless, 11, 3 ; O, Love, O fire ! 11, 19 ; half angel and half bird, 11, 20 ; has never known a law, 11, 23 ; silence in, 13, 19 ; magic of first, 15, 9 ; is loveliest, 15, 34 ; where first links were wound, 15, 43 ; the pearl of his oyster, 16, 10 ; the pest of, 17, 27 ; her, a liberal education, 17, 38 ; one maiden only, 17, 39 ; what's the earth, compared with, 18, 48 ; dissemble your, 19, 6 ; too much, 19, 31 ; that scorns the lapse of time, 19, 51

Loved, no pleasure like pain of being, 16, 24

Lover, demon, 1, 34 ; a freeborn mind, 4, 33 ; so pale and wan, 19, 41

Loves, two human, 18, 7

Lute-player, some dead, 13, 36

M

Maid, a, none to praise, 1, 20 ; be good, sweet, 3, 23

Malice, of a good thing, 15, 10

Man, of yesterdays and to-morrows, 1, 22 ; a true, 1, 40 ; reach and grasp, 1, 44 ; discontent of, 2, 38 ; as good as another, 2, 48 ; with thy might, 4, 5 ; master of his fate, 5, 40 ; that ever scuttled ship, 6, 52 ; a sadder and a wiser, 6, 53 ; weigh the, 8, 16 ; Parliament of, 8, 45 ; man's A.B.C., 10, 4 ; the hunter, 10, 5 ; morality made for, 10, 23 ; the piebald miscellany, 11, 1 ; O selfless, 11, 24 ; crime of being a young, 14, 24 ; that lays his hand on a woman, 15, 11 ; but speaketh more honestly, 16, 23 ; and a Positivist, 16, 36 ; what, then, is, 18, 43 ; has Forever, 18, 50 ; a world without a sun, 20, 3

Mankind, the asses who pull, 16, 5 ; distrust, 19, 7

Manners, fruit of loyal nature, 15, 41

Many, make the household, 15, 12 ; fail, one succeeds, 17, 1

Mark, Death loves a shining, 4, 41

Market, knowledge bought in the, 6, 15

Martyr, in his shirt of fire, 9, 39

Mawkish, so sweetly, 13, 31

Maxims, little hoard of, 19, 48

May, meaning of, 2, 27

Maying, that we two were, 11, 40

Mean, a mighty thing amongst the, 5, 32

Meandering, let us have no, 9, 30

Meannesses, woman alone can commit, 16, 15

Melodies, unheard, are sweeter, 7, 3

Melrose, if thou wouldst view fair, 8, 24

Memory, gild the past, 5, 34

Men, read, as books, too much, 3, 9 ; when two strong, 4, 4 ; windy ways of, 5, 23 ; honest, soft easy cushions for knaves, 7, 16 ; are a little breed, 7, 30 ; the workers, 10, 12 ; read books and, 12, 9 ; a want of books and, 12, 23 ; defects of great, 14, 38 ; loves his fellow, 20, 8

Mercy, sighed farewell, 3, 8

Merit, makes known by force, 19, 32

Mermaid, what things have we seen done at the, 18, 45

Micawber, advice to David Copperfield, 10, 34

Mile-stones, on the Dover road, 16, 40

Mill, cannot grind with water past, 2, 28

Milton, thou shouldst be living, 10, 17 ; reading, 12, 45

Mind, when you wish to conceal your own, 5, 54 ; labyrinthine ways of my own, 7, 42 ; nurture with great thoughts, 11, 14 ; reading to the, 12, 43 ; storehouse of the, 13, 48 ; leafless desert of the, 15, 5 ; magic of the, 15, 27

Minds, lose oneself in other men's, 7, 50 ; clothing of our, 14, 34

Minion, curled, 4, 32

Mirth, can into folly glide, 19, 13

Mischief, when mortals bend their will to, 4, 11

Mockery, the fume of little hearts, 6, 39

Moment, the precise psychological, 6, 35 ; repay unnumbered hours of pain, 12, 3

Monarch, rule entire and sure, 4, 56

Moon, a waning, 1, 34 ; pale ports o' the, 1, 42 ; of honey, 3, 51

Morn, born anew each, 4, 54

Mother, came into my eyes, 2, 30

Mountains, monarch of, 10, 21 ; look on Marathon, 15, 15

Mouth, sweet red splendid kissing, 2, 53 ; purple-stained, 11, 17

Mouths a sentence, 6, 38

Mrs. Harris, and Betsy Prig, 3, 39 ; 16, 3

Music, the Art nearest to tears, 1, 32 ; night filled with, 2, 55 ; 'tis we musicians know, 3, 49 ; I struck one chord of, 7, 39 ; if the world were filled with, 8, 22 ; light quirks of, 9, 36 ; peace more sweet than, 12, 21 ; still sweet fall of, 15, 44 ; no truer truth obtainable, 16, 25 ; fled is that, 18, 17 ; ceasing of exquisite, 19, 8 ; and solitude, 19, 26

Musk-rose, full of dewy wine, 10, 15

Mystery, worshipping, 9, 28

N

Nail, hit on the head, 20, 17

Name, washed out with tears, 1, 25 ; forgotten, 2, 54 ; left a Corsair's, 6, 37 ; as white as a tulip, 10, 32 ; Phœbus ! what a, 11, 35 ; our sad bad glad mad brother's, 12, 36 ; sweetest that mortals bear, 15, 48 ; magic of a, 19, 25 ; makes divorce of a good, 19, 38

Names, hallow song, 3, 41 ; that men remember, 3, 42

Nature, heart beats strong amid hills, 3, 53 ; teaching of, 9, 3 ; is frugal, 10, 6 ; twy-natured is no, 18, 9

Navies, the nations' airy, 7, 4

Near, and yet so far, 6, 44

New, proceeds from death of old, 5, 57

Night, the black bat, 4, 25 ; we die each, 4, 54 ; trailing garments of the, 7, 47 ; ships that pass in the, 13, 17

Nightly, to the listening earth, 13, 40

Noble, thing wealth to a noble person, 10, 50 ; and nude and antique, 18, 24

Nobleness, walks in our ways again, 7, 18

Nobly, nothing done, in pride, 11, 10

Nose, slender and tip-tilted, 2, 44

Nothing, precise psychological moment when to say, 6, 35 ; insupportable labour of doing, 15, 2

Now, leave, for dogs and apes, 18, 50

O

Oafs, muddied, at the goals, 16, 13

Observation, bearings of this, 14, 29

Observations, we ourselves make, 3, 9

Old, new proceeds from death of, 5, 57

Opinion, an illogical, 2, 23 ; last one right, 13, 39

Opportunity, dust of servile, to gold, 18, 5

Orthodoxy, kept alive by indifference and hypocrisy, 8, 48

P

Outward Bound, days of the, 18, 6
Oxen, who drives fat, 19, 23
Oyster, crossed in love, 2, 24

Pains, men come to greater, 4, 15 ; nothing truly valuable without, 16, 29
Painters, shoot with lengthened bow, 12, 30
Palms, before my feet, 5, 51
Paper, a scrap of, 9, 19
Party, none was for a, 16, 11
Passion, shall have spent its novel force, 7, 1 ; one pulse of, 12, 5
Past, proclaiming future, 2, 7 ; the faultful, 17, 17
Patriot, a, as a fool, 1, 29 ; blood of, 15, 23
Patriots, true, 17, 57
Pays, when another, 9, 37
Peace, universal, 2, 1 ; death, the prince of, 4, 39 ; thousand years of, 12, 52 ; win or buy it, 20, 19
Peach, once a bitter almond, 17, 53
Pen, knights of the, 1, 48
Pence, eternal want of, 12, 14
Penitence, thread-bare, 2, 56
Peoples, silent, sullen, 4, 13
Persuasion, truth at heart makes up for want of, 6, 54
Pessimist, definition of a, 4, 48
Philosophy, moral, handmaid to religion, 2, 5 ; charms fly at mere touch of, 4, 45 ; lumber of the schools, 12, 26
Phrase, that portentous, 11, 32
Phrases, tortured into sonnets, 1, 39
Pickwickian, used in that sense, 6, 31
Pity, they who never melt with, 5, 47
Place, get wealth and, 6, 2
Plato, thou reasonest well, 9, 12
Pleasures, a garden the purest of human, 6, 5
Poet, God the best, 6, 9 ; sacred name, 9, 29 ; and a profound philosopher, 10, 44 ; lengthened bow, 12, 30 ; bit by him that comes behind, 13, 29 ; vex not mind of, 18, 12
Poetry, pressure of unwritten, 7, 29 ; always fallacy in, 8, 42 ; amusement for fools, 17, 5
Poets, who have made us heirs, 15, 26 ; just right of, 17, 2
Point, not to put too fine a, 11, 4
Poison-flowers, richest juice in, 5, 2
Politicians, more essential service than that of whole race of, 6, 28
Politics, or poetry, amusement for fools, 17, 5
Poppies, blow in Flanders Fields, 8, 36
Positivist, Man—and a, 16, 36
Posterity, as a packhorse, 6, 51 ; always doing something for, 18, 19
Poverty, catching, 4, 23 ; not my will, consents, 10, 35 ; no disgrace, 12, 33
Praise, not praising where not due, 2, 21 ; little dust of, 2, 49 ; fame decays by excess of, 5, 12 ; itch of vulgar, 9, 18 ; a rebuke, 12, 35 ; at morning what they blame at night, 13, 39
Precedent, from, to precedent, 1, 13 ; and principle, 1, 30 ; a Kaffir of men, 9, 2
Precept, examples drawn for, 5, 6
Prejudices, a bundle of, 7, 35
Pretty Fanny's way, 18, 21
Priapus, thy father, 18, 24
Pride, that apes humility, 6, 40 ; nothing done nobly in, 11, 10 ; misleads, 12, 19 ; that licks the dust, 19, 46
Priest, true, of God always free, 6, 11
Prince, in the grave, 5, 49 ; of sweet songs, 12, 36
Progeny, a, of learning, 1, 31
Progress, world's best, 2, 38
Prophets, perverts the, 12, 25
Prudery, what is, 18, 37
Prudes, for proctors, 19, 52
Prunes, and prism, 16, 2
Psalms, purloins the, 12, 25
Pulp, how shall taste the rind ? 14, 1
Pun, that very foolish thing, 10, 33
Pureness, to doubt her, 17, 35
Pyramids, in vales, 12, 41

Q

Queen Bess, stamped with the image of good, 6, 12
Queen Elizabeth, no scandal about, 10, 48
Quote, till one compiles, 12, 2

R

Race, run by one and one, 17, 13
Rag, a moth-eaten, 1, 24 ; the bloomin' old, 14, 8
Rain, to feel the beat of, 11, 26
Rapture, first fine careless, 14, 21
Rascal, in hollow of back, 12, 44
Reading, which has pleased, 15, 31
Reason, weaves, by Passion undone, 18, 41 ; not always wisdom, 19, 33
References, verify your, 2, 17
Relations, great men have their poor, 8, 5
Religion, the only real, 13, 9 ; only one, 16, 30
Remedy, worse than the disease, 15, 32
Remember, or forget, 2, 42 ; forget that I, 5, 52 ;
Repentance, cool with morning, 4, 12 ; Winter Garment of, 4, 24
Reproof, best can bear, who merit praise, 17, 4
Reputation, sold for a Song, 6, 25
Rest, alone in striving, 16, 39
Revenge, a man that studieth, 1, 23
Revolutions, reforms less to be dreaded, 12, 46
Right, Fashion arbiter and rule of, 5, 16 ; and wrong, 20, 9
Righteous works, 17, 11
Rivalship, nothing done beautifully in, 11, 10
River, weariest, winds somewhere safe to sea, 5, 58
Rivulet, of text, 20, 21
Road, below me, 18, 26
Rock, not proof against a wave, 10, 47
Roman, a, holiday, 6, 50
Roman Catholic Church, Macaulay on the, 13, 12
Romance, how little we may come to know, 7, 26 ; always young, 17, 52
Rome, grandeur that was, 17, 48 ; when falls—the World, 19, 20
Rose, rich and purposeless, 3, 15 ; never blows so red, 8, 11 ; queen of every one, 14, 35 ; fairest when budding new, 15, 34 ; last, of summer, 17, 26
Rosebud, a, set with thorns, 1, 33
Roses, rod of criticism wreathed with, 7, 2 ; I shall never be friends with, 8, 9 ; all the way, 9, 16 ; scent of the, 20, 18
Rudyards, cease from Kipling, 19, 15
Rule, by terror wrong, 6, 47
Rupert of debate, 15, 17
Rust, sacred, 15, 35

S

Sacrifice, mighty by, 7, 32 ; thine ancient, 15, 51
Saint, 'twould provoke, 11, 29 ; in crape, 17, 21
Samaritan, ready enough to do the, 20, 16
Samite, clothed in white, 4, 21
Science, eel of, 20, 11
Scotch, and a joke, 9, 13
Scoundrel, in supple-sliding knee, 12, 44
Scripture, in time of disputes, 15, 36
Scuttle-fish, disputants like the, 12, 17
Sea, inviolate, 3, 44 ; mother and lover of men, 8, 17 ; never so ione, 10, 40 ; Dewdrop slips into shining, 11, 46 ; when I put out to, 14, 3 ; the open, 15, 37 ; into that silent, 18, 25
Sea-gipsy, and lost star, 3, 16
Sea-sand, as is the ribbed, 17, 8
Seeing, things rightly, only one way, 16, 31
Self-condemned, justice on his own soul, 16, 21
Self-sacrifice, awful beauty of, 14, 25
Sense, of a, forlorn, 6, 53 ; of mystery, 11, 30 ; take care of the, 14, 7 ; thin partitions divide from thought, 18, 44
Sentence, mouths a, 6, 38
Sermons, less read than tales, 5, 6
Serve, who fain would sway must, 5, 32
Service, ranking with God, 2, 9
Sexes, three, according to French, 3, 18
Shadow, light more soft than, 12, 21 ; cloaked from head to foot, 15, 39 ; stayed not, 15, 40

Shadow-show, nothing but a Magic, 17, 24
Shaft, at random sent, 11, 21 ; that quivered in his heart, 13, 32
Shakespeare, none may speak as he, 10, 43 ; one wild, 12, 10 ; unlocked his heart, 13, 6 ; try to be, 14, 22
Share, but what we, 11, 5
Sheep, a shepherdess of, 13, 15
Shelley, 1, 45
Shepherds, wrangling when wolf nigh, 8, 29
Ship, mildest-mannered man that ever scuttled, 6, 52
Shoes, and ships and sealing-wax, 15, 49
Silence, when doubting one's sense, 3, 24 ; most noble till the end, 3, 48 ; one sweet strain of, 8, 22 ; in love, 13, 19 ; gratitude of true affection, 13, 20 ; mother of truth, 13, 21 ; great Empire of, 13, 22 ; is golden, 13, 43 ; well-timed, 18, 29
Simile, that solitary shines, 12, 6
Sin, some darling, 5, 25 ; his favourite, 6, 40 ; pleasure's a, 12, 29 ; process of unsinning, 15, 28
Sinais, climb and know it not, 11, 2
Sire, lives in his sons, 5, 44 ; butchered to make a Roman holiday, 6, 50
Skies, sunny as her, 7, 5 ; like some watcher of the, 16, 9
Sky, as someone sings about the, 11, 37
Slave, whatever day makes man a, 19, 1
Sleep, disporting with shadows, 6, 22 ; poppied, 14, 44
Small, among the small, 13, 27
Smart, smarteth most who hides his, 6, 43
Smattering, a, of everything, 1, 36
Smile, one vast substantial, 8, 33
Sneer, a laughing devil in his, 16, 35
Soap, invisible, 3, 1
Solitude, no companion so companionable as, 8, 3 ; should teach us how to die, 8, 20 ; best nurse of wisdom, 13, 34 ; peopled by music, 19, 26
Song, breeze of, 2, 49 ; made sublime with, 4, 6 ; the Real, God's, 6, 9
Songs, to endure, 20, 7
Sonnet, scorn not the, 13, 6
Sorrow, cheered by being poured, 13, 30 ; sorrow's crown of, 16, 51 ; makes us wise, 17, 23
Soul, a sinful, and gifts, 1, 35 ; touched by pity, 1, 37 ; standing sure, 2, 12 ; one, outweighing all, 2, 18 ; soon-choked, 4, 52 ; wears out the breast, 5, 45 ; meanest of His creatures boasts two soul-sides, 6, 6 ; within her eyes, 7, 5 ; captain of my, 7, 36 ; through my lips, 11, 19 ; take wing, 11, 39 ; vex not with dead philosophy, 12, 5 ; soft intercourse from soul to, 13, 44 ; tocsin of the, 14, 12 ; to dare, 15, 58
Sounds, will take care of themselves, 14, 7
Spark, vital, 18, 14
Speech, a dead language, 2, 10 ; made splendid once with, 4, 6 ; thought bolder than, 17, 14
Speed the going guest, 5, 36
Spheres, harmonious, 14, 59
Spirits, congenial, meet again, 4, 27
Spot, savage, holy and enchanted, 1, 34 ; where love's first links were wound, 15, 43
Spring, and Rose-in-hand, 2, 56 ; the Fire of, 4, 24 ; and love, 8, 46 ; to have lived light in the, 8, 54 ; hounds of, 19, 9
St. Paul's, sketch the ruins of, 13, 12
Stare, gorgonised with a stony British, 6, 14
Stars, gold gateways of the, 1, 42 ; nothing fixed except some, 11, 11 ; pitch the golden tents, 19, 10
State, happy, whose ruler heeds the murmurs of the poor, 6, 23 ; all were for the, 16, 11
Stays, Puritanic, 13, 49
Steel, foemen worthy of their, 12, 48
Stiles, helping lame dogs over, 4, 46
Story, always old and always new, 15, 45
Stream, brightest at its spring, 15, 46
Strife, rest springs from, 12, 49
Success, blindness firstborn of, 3, 32 ; nothing so impudent as, 11, 12 ; in life, 15, 38
Succour, dawns from Heaven, 8, 40
Sultàn, after Sultàn, with his Pomp, 16, 46
Sun, green-dense and dim-delicious, bred o' the, 6, 19 ; 'neath the all-beholding, 6, 42 ; shoots at the mid-day, 19, 36
Sweet, how it was, 7, 28
Sweetness, an interminable tedious, 17, 42

Sword, outwears its sheath, 5, 45
Systems, have their day, 12, 18

T

Tale, twice-told, 3, 7 ; 12, 13
Tales, sermons less read than, 5, 6
Talk, most when least to say, 3, 5
Tall, divinely, and fair, 1, 7
Taught, profits by teaching, 17, 28
Tavern, one Glimpse of it within, 19, 19
Temptation, only way to get rid of, 15, 20
Tents, folded like Arabs, 2, 55
Terror, he that only rules by, 6, 47
Text, rivulet of, 20, 21
Things, broad on roots of, 3, 45
Thought, built on thought, 2, 45 ; wedding with thought, 3, 3 ; mightier than time, 4, 6 ; splendour of a sudden, 13, 50 ; bolder than speech, 17, 14 ; soul of act, 17, 15 ; almost an act, 18, 10
Thoughts, from the tongue slowly part, 17, 16
Throat, mildest-mannered man that ever cut a, 6, 52
Throne, fierce light which beats upon, 8, 44 ; shape the whisper of the, 19, 32
Thumb, a most observing, 7, 34
Time, eternal surge of, 7, 25 ; the tooth of, 8, 43 ; thief of, 12, 37 ; corridors of, 14, 27 ; unimaginable touch of, 15, 52 ; *goes*, you say ? 17, 18 ; the avenger, 17, 19 ; what's ? 18, 50
Times, good old, 14, 56 ; spacious, 15, 41 ; true old, 15, 50
Tiny Tim—" God bless Us, Every One ! " 2, 50
To-morrows, confident, 1, 22 ; wiser than to-day, 2, 52
Tobacco, sublime, 13, 51 ; tomb of love, 17, 51
Toil, he that will not live by, 6, 49
Tools, pens most dangerous, 12, 22
Toujours de l'audace, 4, 17
Tower, of strength, fallen, 11, 16
Travels, the fastest, alone, 4, 49
Treachery, skulking with hatred, 4, 43
Tread, on my dreams, 3, 50
Tree, who plants a, 6, 3
Trees, light-winged Dryad of the, 14, 18
Trout, in the milk, circumstantial evidence, 13, 35
True, more things told than are, 8, 6 ; nothing, but what astonishes, 11, 7 ; Light, the one, 19, 19 ; who battled for the, 19, 21
Truth, one clear, 2, 51 ; beauty, 3, 26 ; inspired Bards of old, 4, 10 ; only can be invented, 5, 8 ; comes limping after falsehood, 5, 10 ; life of, from the rot of creeds, 5, 57 ; at heart makes up for want of persuasion, 6, 54 ; takes two to speak the, 9, 14 ; standing on vantage ground of, 10, 46 ; speaking, like writing fair, 13, 42 ; tell, or trump, 14, 10 ; that mighty, 14, 16 ; noble to side with, 16, 12 ; foe of tyrants, 17, 59 ; must out, 17, 60 ; son of heaven, 17, 61 ; within ourselves, 18, 1 ; never indebted to a lie, 18, 2 ; on lips of dying men, 18, 3 ; what is, 18, 39 ; who speaks the 19, 37
Truths, blunt, more mischief than falsehoods, 3, 35 ; of long ago, 5, 11, that soften hatred, 14, 55 ; turn into dogmas, 18, 4
Tuscany, ranks of, 2, 37
Tyrant, power bound faster, 6, 48 ; cruel glee, 6, 48
Tyrants, quake to hear, 12, 32 ; that worst of, 14, 20

U

Understanding, books, few but full of, 5, 21
Use, rather than fame, 20, 1

V

Vain, ignobly, 8, 28 ; vile only, 15, 53
Valour, courtesy wins woman as well as, 5, 29
Verbosity, exuberance of his own 8, 49
Verify your references, 2, 17
Verse, a Book of, and Thou, 7, 7
Vice, raptures and roses of, 10, 13
Vices, frame a ladder of, 13, 1
Villon, sad bad glad mad brother's name, 12, 36
Vine, her ancient Ruby yields, 3, 54
Violets, veilèd nuns, 17, 6

Virtue, linked with one, 6, 37 ; lilies and languors of, 10, 13 ; suspicion a coward's, 14, 5 ; lies in the struggle, 15, 54 ; follow, for virtue's sake, 17, 37
Virtuous, mischief they do, 15, 56
Vision, was it a ? 18, 17
Voice, an arrow for the heart, 14, 41 ; each a mighty, 18, 8
Volumes, creators of odd, 8, 1
Vow, that binds too strictly, 15, 55

W

Wanity, vich is your partickler ? 18, 13
Want, wit's whetstone, 19, 47
Wants, gnawing at the heel, 1, 38
War, to the knife ! 18, 15 ; a brain-spattering, wind-pipe-slitting art, 18, 16
Warrior, the happy, 19, 27
Watch-dog's honest bark, 17, 25
Water, imperceptible, 3, 1 ; came like, 3, 2 ; Garden by the, 3, 54 ; great street paved with, 14, 54
Waters, she walks the, 13, 16
Weakness, pardon, that was never felt, 6, 36
Weald, blue goodness of, 3, 28
Wealth, get place and, 6, 2
Weed's plain heart, secret of a, 17, 50
Weep, and you weep alone, 9, 24
Welcome, as flowers in May, 20, 14
Wells, by deep, and water floods, 11, 25
West, neither East nor, 4, 4
Whatever, is, is right, 2, 51
Whist, Sarah Battle on, 1, 5
White man's burden, 14, 9
Wife, a, gift of heaven, 2, 6
Wilderness, is Paradise enow, 7, 7
Will, to do, 15, 58
Wind, going like, 3, 2 ; constancy in, 3, 17 ; on the heath, 16, 41 ; whistling mane of, 17, 29
Wine, and walnuts, 1, 43 ; sans, 4, 51 ; a Flask of, 7, 7 ; Venus rose red out of, 16, 10
Wines, sucked the fire of some forgotten sun, 19, 43
Wisdom, known defeat, 10, 19 ; of woman, 14, 28
Wise, confounded by dunce's laughter, 3, 14 ; madness to defer, 3, 25 ; master and lord of his brothers, 6, 33 ; who draws a charm from rocks or woods or weeds, 6, 45 ; must be a fool first, 8, 23
Wish, what we, we soon believe, 18, 32 ; what most we, 18, 40
Wishes, lengthen as our sun declines, 9, 40
Wit, but the plume, 13, 10 ; will not bear repetition, 14, 4 ; true, 17, 58 ; talks most, when least to say, 19, 45 ; that can creep, 19, 46 ; Want, whetstone of, 19, 47
Wolf, shepherds wrangle when nigh, 8, 29 ; came down like a, 14, 23

Woman, and consent, 1, 18 ; and demon lover, 1, 34 ; cannot live without, 3, 11 ; believe a, 3, 17 ; to man, as cord to bow, 3, 19 ; at heart a rake, 3, 47 ; work for ourself and a, 4, 8 ; will or won't, depend on't, 5, 24 ; courtesy wins, 5, 29 ; should marry, 7, 44 ; man's game, 10, 5 ; nature made thee, 11, 28 ; wisdom of, 14, 28 ; path of a good, 15, 22 ; that cries hush bids kiss, 16, 1 ; and meannesses, 16, 15 ; bridal-favours and raiment, 18, 46
Womanhood, miracle of noble, 11, 22 ; and childhood, 13, 45
Womankind, but one rosy mouth, 14, 19
Women, one or two have loved me, 4, 31 ; more powerful to persuade, 10, 9 ; heart, not mind, argues, 20, 2
Woo, when all is won all desire to, 17, 20
Woollen, Odious ! in, 11, 29
Word, echoes in God's skies, 5, 5 ; farewell, that fatal, 5, 15 ; used in its Pickwickian sense, 6, 31 ; at random spoken, 11, 21 ; makes despots tremble, 19, 37.
Words, men pluck no fruit from sharp, 3, 48 ; divide and rend, 3, 48 ; coiner of sweet, 4, 32 ; what are the voices of birds but, 5, 48 ; like Nature, half reveal, 5, 50 ; tyrants quake to hear, 12, 32 ; most powerful drug, 20, 5 ; tokens current and accepted, 206,
Work, do the nearest, 4, 46 ; who first invented, 19, 24
World, great wave that echoes round the, 16, 45 ; of gammon and spinnage, 18, 31 ; when most it applauds, 19, 7
World, pass through it but once, 7, 40 ; Federation of the, 8, 45 ; vast cathedral of the, 9, 23 ; what a crocodilian, 11, 27 ; to sit astride the, 12, 31 ; fever of the, 14, 51 ; a bundle of hay, 16, 5 ; so full of a number of things, 16, 6 ; when the world was wide, 16, 37 ; 18, 6
Worm, not cloven in vain, 14, 17
Worst, ahead might be, 16, 48
Worthier, and wiser, master and lord of his brothers, 6, 33
Wound, leaving a scar, 1, 41
Wounds, ever closed without a scar ? 18, 34
Writers, steal a good thing, 10, 26
Writing, greater want of skill in, 17, 22
Wrong, how easily things go, 2, 2 ; wherever done 6, 42 ; who treasures up a, 16, 33 ; a private, not a public, 17, 30 ; and right, 20, 9

Y

Years, all that lies buried under fifty, 11, 43
Yesterdays, of cheerful, 1, 22 ; look backward with a smile, 19, 40
Youngest, not infallible, 18, 20
Youth, the thoughts of, 1, 2 ; red sweet wine of, 3, 34 ; first fiery glow of, 12, 5 ; blunders of, 14, 31 ; trustee of Posterity, 16, 7 ; once gone, is gone, 20, 25